KU-237-895

THE COMMON LAW LIBRARY

# McGregor on Damages

**VOLUMES IN THE COMMON LAW LIBRARY**

Arlidge, Eady & Smith on Contempt
Benjamin's Sale of Goods
Bowstead & Reynolds on Agency
Bullen & Leake & Jacob's Precedents of Pleadings
Charlesworth and Percy on Negligence
Chitty on Contracts
Clerk & Lindsell on Torts
Gatley on Libel and Slander
Goff & Jones, The Law of Restitution
Jackson & Powell on Professional Negligence
McGregor on Damages
Phipson on Evidence

The Common Law Library

# McGREGOR ON DAMAGES

Twentieth Edition

By

JAMES EDELMAN
**A Justice of the High Court of Australia**

Chapter on Procedure revised by

SIMON COLTON QC, **Barrister, One Essex Court, London**

Chapter on the Human Rights Act revised by

DR JASON N.E. VARUHAS, **Associate Professor Melbourne Law School, The University of Melbourne**

SWEET & MAXWELL

Published in 2018 by Thomson Reuters (Professional) UK Limited,
trading as Sweet & Maxwell.
Thomson Reuters is registered in England & Wales,
Company number 1679046.
Registered office and address for Service:
5 Canada Square, Canary Wharf, London, E14 5AQ.

For further information on our products and services, visit *http://www.sweetandmaxwell.co.uk*.

Computerset by Sweet & Maxwell.
Printed and bound by CPI Group (UK) Ltd, Croydon, CR0 4YY.
No natural forests were destroyed to make this product: only farmed timber was used and replanted.
A CIP catalogue record for this book is available from the British Library.

ISBN: 978-0-414-06415-7

# Previous Editions

| | |
|---|---|
| First edition by John D. Mayne | 1856 |
| Second edition by Lumley Smith | 1872 |
| Third edition by John D. Mayne and Lumley Smith | 1877 |
| Fourth edition by John D. Mayne and Lumley Smith | 1884 |
| Fifth edition by John D. Mayne and Lumley Smith | 1894 |
| Sixth edition by John D. Mayne and Lumley Smith | 1899 |
| Seventh edition by John D. Mayne and Lumley Smith | 1903 |
| Eighth edition by Lumley Smith, K.C. | 1909 |
| Ninth edition by Coleman Phillipson | 1920 |
| Tenth edition by Frank Gahan | 1927 |
| Eleventh edition by His Honour Judge Earengey, K.C. | 1946 |
| Twelfth edition by Harvey McGregor | 1961 |
| Thirteenth edition by Harvey McGregor | 1972 |
| Fourteenth edition by Harvey McGregor, Q.C. | 1980 |
| Fifteenth edition by Harvey McGregor, Q.C. | 1988 |
| Sixteenth edition by Harvey McGregor, Q.C. | 1997 |
| Seventeenth edition by Harvey McGregor, Q.C. | 2003 |
| Eighteenth edition by Harvey McGregor, Q.C. | 2009 |
| Nineteenth edition by Harvey McGregor, C.B.E., Q.C. | 2014 |
| Twentieth edition by His Honour Justice James Edelman | 2018 |

*To*
*Dinah and Ray*

# FOREWORD

This volume claims to trace its descent from *A Treatise on the Law of Damages* published in 1854, by John Dawson Mayne (1828–1917), a young Irishman fresh from Trinity College who was seeking to make his name at the English Bar. After a couple of years he gave it up and went to make his legal career in India, where he became Advocate General of Madras and, in 1908, retired and in crotchety old age, wrote *The Triumph of Socialism and How it Succeeded*, a satirical history foretelling the disasters that would overtake Great Britain if it elected a socialist government.

The claim to Victorian ancestry is however as doubtful as Mayne's own claims to Norman descent (he was an avid and imaginative genealogist) because when Harvey McGregor, another young man seeking to make his name at the English Bar, took over the book in 1960, he entirely rewrote it. By his own account, he was looking for an area of law in which there was little competition. Subjects like sale of goods, bills of lading and charter parties were already served by canonical works. But damages had only Mayne. Of the previous edition published in 1946, a reviewer had written: "To describe Mayne as an old friend would be the purest affectation. It has always—at any rate in living memory—had the reputation of being a horrible book." The subject of damages was, in American real estate terms, a tear-down, a potential vacant site on which a new structure could be erected. Harvey's first (12th) edition went out under the name "Mayne and McGregor" but thereafter it was *McGregor on Damages* and Harvey insisted he was not an editor but *the author*.

Harvey McGregor ("both my names are associated with rabbits", he used to say) was as Scottish as could be, son of an engineer at the Aberdeenshire railway town of Inverurie and grandson of a local station master. But for reasons I never quite discovered, he finished his schooling in Scarborough and thereby qualified for one of the scholarships at The Queen's College, Oxford which were reserved for Yorkshire schools. There he was taught by Tony Honoré, a privilege which I also enjoyed two or three years later. He did well at the Bar and took silk in 1978, but his real love was the law rather than advocacy. The main expression of this love was of course "The Book", which went through eight editions in his hands, but he was a prodigious worker and also did drafting for the Law Commission on a contract code and for the Cayman Island government on trust law.

Like many Oxford-educated barristers with academic inclinations, Harvey did some teaching at week-ends for one of the colleges – first Wadham and then New College. New College made him a Fellow and then in 1985 elected him Warden. I think it is fair to say that his time as Warden was the high point of his life. The Warden's Lodgings of New College, as I remember them before his election, were, like most of the Lodgings of heads of houses in the older colleges, rather like a somewhat decayed country house: very miscellaneous brown furniture, good but worn carpets, old curtains and walls in need of redecoration. Harvey moved in with his partner John Davy and Pippa Irwin, a still beautiful 67-year-old wartime film actress whom he described as his housekeeper but who acted as a glamorous hostess. A more unusual *ménage à trois* could not have occupied the Lodgings in the six hundred year history of the college. Soon one heard breathless reports from fellows about the redecorations: walls painted orange, bright carpets, modern pictures.

But the greatest change was in the entertainment which the new Warden offered. Harvey was an enthusiastic amateur pianist and was never happier than when he was putting on a concert for his friends and colleagues. It must be admitted that these events tended to resemble those put on at Toad Hall by Mr Toad. There would be a piano sonata, played by Harvey, or possibly a piano duet with a student or another head of house (the Wardens of All Souls and Wadham, Patrick Neill and Klaus Moser, were also good amateur pianists and Harvey once organised a concert for all three of them billed as Wardens in Concert). Then there would be a recital of Barbar the Elephant, in French, with expression, by Harvey, accompanied by Harvey on the piano, followed by Noel Coward songs sung by Harvey to his own piano accompaniment. And so on. At his memorial service in the college, the Warden truly said 'Harvey was the impresario of his own life.'

There were other resemblances to Mr Toad; the rapid alternations between contrition (when a delegation of fellows went to tell him he had grossly overspent the budget on redecorating the lodgings) and reversion to boastfulness ("the college is lucky to have me") as well as warmth and generosity, to students and in particular young musicians. And then there were the parties. Harvey delighted in giving parties. Almost any excuse would do. His departure from New College was marked by a dinner for friends and colleagues which filled the hall, followed (as the invitation promised) by dancing. When he had a stroke in 2015, his partner had to write round to cancel the party he was about to give to celebrate – I forget exactly what, but I think it was an anniversary of his moving into his flat in Gray's Inn. If he had survived some seven months longer till his ninetieth birthday, the party would have been quite something. However, and despite having The Book placed on the table next to his bed in hospital in Edinburgh ("so that the medical staff can see I know about suing for negligence"), he died there peacefully some three weeks later.

The Book is universally acknowledged to have been a great achievement. In his preface his last edition, Harvey wrote:

> "I have noted that judges and others not in the know tend to refer not to the author but to the editors, or occasionally the editor, of the book. The reference to editors no doubt comes from the fact that a book on a subject of this size and complexity is today likely to command a whole series of editors…; the reference to editor probably comes from the expectation that at my great age I have given up the writing or from the assumption that I am dead. But I remain alive and I remain the author."

Now The Book passes into the hands, not of a team, but of a single editor, chosen by Harvey himself. But I cannot imagine a better choice for this onerous task and expect there to be many years for which it remains the canonical authority on the subject.

Lennie Hoffman — Brick Court Chambers

August 2017.

# PREFACE

On 27 June 2015, Harvey McGregor passed away. My acquaintance with him, and with his late, and dear, partner, John Davy, was too brief. It was only in December 2014, several years after an initial request, that I agreed to continue the work on his book. Our plan, sadly accelerated due to Harvey's death, was that the succession would take place in 2020 when I would take an accrued sabbatical from judicial duties. On a number of occasions, Harvey told me that his greatest joy in passing on his life's work was that it would remain as a single person's work rather than becoming the product of a team. For him, and for me, coherence in the law is a paramount value. The value of coherence is one of the core principles that I aim to maintain as the editor of what was, and will remain for many years, *his* book. The book is Harvey's greatest academic legacy. Partly due to its goal of coherence, partly due to its astonishingly comprehensive coverage, and partly due to its incisive commentary, for more than a century it has been the first port of call, and often also the last, for any academic, practitioner, or judge who encounters a problem on damages. It is also one of the few works that contains historical background so that the evolution of doctrine can be understood. It is an immense repository of learning.

Although *McGregor on Damages* has a strong claim to be the greatest work on damages ever written, no work is ever complete. The development of the book is not merely a matter of updating and adding new cases. It requires two major changes which will be implemented over several editions. The first area of change is a long process of rationalisation. This rationalisation is needed for the readership of judges, practitioners, and academics. Although historical discussion is important in many areas, a balance needs to be struck between clarity (including simplicity) and a record of history. The second area of change is to remove some inconsistencies that have developed between some chapters in the book. The existence of inconsistencies in a 2,000 page book which incorporates all developments in a large area of law is inevitable. As Harvey said to me, the prospect of inconsistencies is reduced by having the responsibility for the book concentrated primarily in a single person.

In this 20th edition, the developments in these two areas of change have been incremental. In some areas the book has grown rather than shrunk. There are two new chapters (disgorgement damages and damages for breach of an undertaking). But, overall, the process of rationalisation with a focus upon principle has begun. This will be a slow process. Although I produced much of the first, and all of the second, supplement to the 19th edition, I only obtained the manuscript to begin preparation of the 20th edition during September 2016. Nevertheless, this edition has set the scene for rationalisation of, and coherence in, the book by incorporating one very significant structural change. That change is to focus upon developing and applying an underlying meaning and purpose of damages throughout the book. As chapter 1 now explains in detail, an award of damages is simply a money award for wrongdoing. The purpose of damages is to eradicate, as far as reasonable, the consequences of a wrong which fall within the scope of the duty breached by the wrongdoer. That meaning and purpose is applied in explaining the operation of damages in the various areas considered throughout the book.

Over the final years of his work, Harvey had been moving the book towards this definition and purpose of damages. Earlier editions of *McGregor on Damages* written by Harvey since 1961 had developed a definition of damages based around the principle that damages must be awarded to compensate, and must be for common law wrongdoing. Added to this were restrictions that damages must be an unconditional lump sum, and awarded in sterling. But Harvey came to accept that none of the four restrictions on his definition of damages represented the law. Periodic payments in personal injury actions disproved the assertion that damages are unconditional, lump sum payments, and, since *Miliangos v George Frank (Textiles)* [1976] A.C. 443, damages could be awarded in currencies other than sterling. Most fundamentally, Harvey abandoned the two dogmata he introduced in 1961: that damages must be compensatory for loss and that they must be for common law wrongdoing.

The first of these dogmata, that damages must be compensatory for loss, is inconsistent with the existence of nominal damages, exemplary damages, and damages based upon a wrongdoer's gain. The earliest English usage of "damages" included cases where a money award was three times the loss suffered by the defendant; an award which was plainly not a compensatory award (*Act 8 Hen. VI*, c. 9 (1430) "Le pleyntif recovera ses damages au treble vers le defendant"). In earlier editions of this book, Harvey doubted the utility of nominal damages, sought to abolish exemplary damages and restitutionary damages, and considered that disgorgement following an account of profits fell outside the scope of a textbook on damages. But, over time, he came to accept that each of these long-standing awards of damages was legitimate. The consequence was a broader definition of damages. This broader definition revealed types of damages that had previously been concealed. The most significant of these are restitutionary damages to reverse the receipt of value and disgorgement damages to strip a wrongdoer of profit. These are both very significant awards in the claimant's armory. But they are commonly neglected.

The second dogma, that damages are concerned only with common law wrongdoing, would mean that actions for infringement of equitable rights cannot be described as damages. That dogma had deep roots. The first edition of Sir Arthur Underhill's *A Concise Guide to Modern Equity* (1885) did not even acknowledge a power to award damages in equity. The first edition of Edmund Snell's *The Principles of Equity* (1868) (at p. 475) and the first English edition of Joseph Story's classic American work on equity (W Grigsby (ed), *Commentaries on Equity Jurisprudence* by Mr Justice Story (1884) at pp. 534-535) said that it was 'settled' that there can be no relief where only damages are sought in equity. But there were notable exceptions. When a bill was sought for compensation for deceit in equity in *Peek v Gurney* (1873) L.R. 6 HL 377, Lord Chelmsford said that loss suffered as a result of fraudulent misrepresentations could be recovered by a suit in chancery. The Lord Chancellor observed that the proceeding in equity "is precisely analogous to the common law action for deceit" and "is a suit instituted to recover damages" (at 393). Slowly courts and commentators recognised that compensation for breach of equitable duties and damages is a "distinction without a difference": *Acquaculture Corporation v New Zealand Green Mussel Co Ltd* [1990] 3 N.Z.L.R. 299 at 301, per Cooke P; *Base Metal Trading Ltd v Shamurin* [2004] EWCA Civ 1316 at [19], per Tuckey LJ. But tradition dies hard. Sir Peter Millett remarked extrajudicially in 1998 that, "Woe betide a Chancery Junior who spoke of 'damages for breach of trust' or 'damages for breach of fiduciary duty'... Nowadays these misleading expressions are in common use. It is time that the usage was stamped out": 'Equity's Place in the Law of Commerce' (1998) 114 L.Q.R. 214 at 227.

The task of removing the traces of these two dogmata from the book is a significant undertaking. The recognition that damages are not confined to compensation for loss has meant that the chapter on restitutionary damages has been substantially rewritten and a new chapter has been added to explain the operation of the award of an account of profits, which is really better described as disgorgement damages. However, this edition has only just begun the slow process of integrating within damages awards the money awards given for equitable wrongdoing. For the time being, the reader will need to read this book together with specialised works on equity.

Although the broad definition of damages permits a coherent understanding of damages, it is also important that each type of money award for wrongdoing be justified and its aims understood. Money awards should not be made for wrongdoing unless they purport to eradicate some reasonable consequence within the scope of the duty breached, even if that consequence requires only an award of nominal damages to address the lack of acknowledgement of wrongdoing. Sometimes the consequence is "normal" or common to others in the same circumstance. On other occasions the consequential damages are particular to the claimant. The coherence of damages with this goal of eradicating consequences was, however, threatened by the growth of "vindicatory damages". These were substantial damages awards which were made independently of any consequence of the wrongdoing. Such damages awards cannot be justified. The decision of the Supreme Court in *R. (on the application of Lumba (Congo)) v Secretary of State for the Home Department* [2012] 1 A.C. 245 put these awards to rest. This has been recognised in the chapter on vindicatory damages. However, the continued use of "vindication" in relation to damages for defamation and invasion of privacy has the potential to confuse. The awards of damages in these areas need to find new nomenclature that reflects, more accurately, their nature.

As Harvey had done in previous editions, I have continued the practice of having the chapters on procedure and human rights written by specialist editors. The outstanding procedure chapters, parts which have been substantially rewritten, were the fine product of the encyclopaedic knowledge of Simon Colton QC of One Essex Court. And the excellent chapter on human rights is now written by Associate Professor Jason Varuhas, of the University of Melbourne, who is one of the world's leading authors in this area. Despite my goal of ultimately reducing and simplifying the content of this book, that chapter has grown very substantially. The reason for this is the importance for English law, in the likely period of transition that it faces, to isolate, identify, and resolve the significant uncertainties concerning damages under the Human Rights Act, which are in some respects novel.

I am very grateful to a number of other people who assisted with the revision of this book and with its production. Lord Hoffmann's typically beautiful prose about his friend is the perfect opening to the first edition of this Book (capitalised, as Harvey would have described it) which, for the first time in more than half a century, does not bear Harvey's name as author. I also owe a significant debt to my associate, Jordan English, for his research and assistance and to the team from Thomson Reuters for the production of the book. The Thomson team was as follows: Lindsay Emerson and, her replacement in 2017, Sohini Banerjee; Lorna Pearce who provided invaluable research assistance in relation to legislation updates; and Katherine Brewer.

Finally, an apology. This book has not traditionally been written in gender neutral language, although all revisions and re-written parts have been. The style of centuries past will be reduced or removed in future editions as the book is modernised and rationalised further.

JJE 8 September 2017.

# TABLE OF CONTENTS

## PART 5 HUMAN RIGHTS



## PART 6 PROCEDURE

# TABLE OF CASES

Herbert Clayton & Jack Waller Ltd v Oliver [1930] A.C. 209; [1930] All E.R. Rep. 414 HL. . . . . . . . . . . . . . . . . . . . . . . . . . . . . . . . . . . . . . . . . . . . . . . . . . . . . . 10-035, 24-008, 33-028

King (Deceased), Re; sub nom Robinson v Gray; King, Re [1963] Ch. 459; [1963] 2 W.L.R. 629; [1963] 1 All E.R. 781; [1963] R.V.R. 245; (1963) 107 S.J. 134 CA . . . . 4-017, 28-047, 28-054

# TABLE OF STATUTES

# TABLE OF STATUTORY INSTRUMENTS

# TABLE OF CIVIL PROCEDURE RULES AND RULES OF THE SUPREME COURT

CHAPTER 1

# INTRODUCTORY

TABLE OF CONTENTS



## 1. A DEFINITION OF DAMAGES

Damages are an award in money for a civil wrong. This definition has undergone considerable evolution over the twenty editions of this book. This definition of damages has evolved to a recognition now that there are only three requirements for a damages award: (1) an award in money; (2) for a wrong; (3) which is a civil wrong. The aim of damages, as a money award for a civil wrong, is to eradicate the consequences that fall within the scope of the duty breached. **1-001**

When the previous author of this book, Dr Harvey McGregor, first rewrote it in 1961 the key elements in his definition concerned the substance of the award—pecuniary compensation, for a tort or breach of contract. The remaining elements concerned the form of the award—the immediate, unconditional lump sum and its currency. All of the elements in the subsidiary, procedural part of the definition have disappeared over the years. With the introduction in the extensive area of personal injury litigation of interim payments in 1970[1] of provisional damages in 1982 and of periodical payments where the parties consent in 1996,[2] the need for an immediate, unconditional lump sum was removed. And with the 1976 House of Lords decision in *Miliangos*,[3] the need for the award in a case with a foreign element to be in sterling also evaporated. **1-002**

More needs to be said about the elements in the principal, substantive part of the 1961 definition. Despite the adoption of the 1961 definition by Lord Hailsham LC in *Broome v Cassell & Co*,[4] it is now recognised that the 1961 definition of damages was too narrow. In the current definition the references to compensation and to tort and contract are omitted. The reasons for this radical change are explained below. In the revised definition the required wrong is referred to as a civil wrong. This is done *ex abundante cautela* to ensure that wrongs which are crimes are excluded. Formerly, this was not required since in the 1961 definition the wrong had to be a tort or breach of contract. **1-003**

---

1 Extended to all actions for damages in 1980.

2 For details of all these see paras 40-004 and following.

3 [1976] A.C. 443; see paras 20-024 and following.

4 [1972] A.C. 1027 at 1070E.

## (1) The requirement of a wrong

**1-004** The requirement of a wrong is entirely necessary; it is an essential feature of damages. There is thus excluded from damages three common types of case giving pecuniary satisfaction by success in an action because they are not dependent on wrongdoing. These are actions for money payable by the terms of a contract, actions for restitution based on unjust enrichment, and actions under statutes where the right to recover is independent of any wrong.

**1-005** (1) Actions claiming money due and payable under the terms of a contract are for money which the contracting party has promised to pay. They are based not on a wrong done but on a promise made. They are in a sense a form of specific performance, ensuring that a contractual obligation is carried out. Illustrations are provided by actions for the price of goods sold and delivered, actions for salary or wages for services rendered, actions for rent, actions for freight and actions to recover moneys payable under insurance policies.[5] In traditional terminology the contrast is between actions of debt and actions for damages.[6] Actions of debt are to be distinguished from actions for damages for breach of a contract and do not require consideration here.[7]

**1-006** (2) Actions claiming monetary restitution in the law of unjust enrichment (actions introduced centuries ago described as quasi-contract, and then implied contract) did not depend upon a wrong done to the claimant. Often there was no wrong available upon which the claimant might sue. Illustrations are provided by actions for money paid under a mistake of fact, actions for money paid under a contract which is in some way vitiated, and actions to recover money paid to a third party for which the defendant is primarily liable.[8] Such claims seek payment not of a loss suffered by the claimant but of a benefit received by the defendant. When restitution is awarded for a wrong then this award can be described as (restitution-

---

5 Curiously, by resort to a fiction, English law does see an action claiming money under a contract of indemnity insurance as an action for damages, with all the unfortunate results to which this leads: see *The Fanti* [1991] 2 A.C. 1 at 35G, per Lord Goff, *The Italia Express* [1992] 2 Lloyd's Rep. 281 and, in particular, *Sprung v Royal Insurance (UK) Ltd* [1999] 1 Lloyd's Rep. I.R. 111 CA. The Law Commission and the Scottish Law Commission produced a Joint Paper (Issue Paper 6) for consultation, entitled *Insurance Contract Law: Damages for Late Payment and the Insurer's Duty of Good Faith*, in which the reversal of *Sprung* was put forward as a solution and the isolation in this matter of England from Scotland and the rest of the common law world documented. Responses to the Joint Paper showed strong support for reform and a full Consultation Paper (No.201) covering more ground, entitled *Insurance Contract Law: Post Contract Duties and Other Issues*, followed at the end of 2011 setting out proposals for reform with responses required within three months. No Law Commission Report on the matter has yet appeared. And see too in relation to insurance *Bedfordshire Police Authority v David Constable* [2009] Lloyd's Rep. I.R. 39 where the term damages was held not to have an established legal meaning in the context of an insurance policy's coverage of police liability under the Riot (Damage) Act 1886.

6 *Bartoline Ltd v Royal & Sun Alliance Insurance Plc* [2007] 1 All E.R. (Comm) 1043, with its detailed discussion, again in an insurance context, of the meaning of damages (paras 77 and following), is a useful illustration of a liability to pay a debt under statute being held not to be a liability to pay damages.

7 A reference to some such actions is retained at the beginning of a number of chapters or sections so as to make the position entirely clear. Otherwise they do not make an appearance.

8 See generally Goff and Jones, *The Law of Unjust Enrichment*, 8th edn (London: Sweet & Maxwell 2011).

ary) damages. These do fall for consideration here; they will be reached in due course.[9]

(3) Actions claiming money under statutes, where the claim is made independently of a wrong, are not actions for damages.[10] Actions in respect of benefits under the Social Security Acts provide an excellent illustration; further examples are provided in the sphere of employment by claims for redundancy payments and, most probably,[11] by claims for unfair dismissal, both of which are now provided for under the Employment Rights Act 1996.[12] On the other hand, actions claiming money which are based upon statutes which have created a tort are actions for damages and are within the definition adopted here. The statutory tort may be one the existence of which is spelt out by the courts from the general duty imposed by the statute,[13] or the statute may create the tort expressly, as do what is now the Fatal Accidents Act 1976 in favour of a deceased's dependants for loss of dependency[14] and what is now s.90 of the Financial Services and Markets Act 2000 in favour of persons incurring loss through reliance on untrue statements in security listing particulars and company prospectuses[15]; somewhat similar is the liability in damages imposed by s.2(1) of the Misrepresentation Act 1967 for negligent misrepresentation inducing a contract.[16] Further illustrations appeared in the three statutes directed to allowing actions on account of sex, race and disability discrimination, each of the three stating that acts of discrimination could be made the subject of civil proceedings in like manner "as any other claim in tort ... for breach of statutory duty".[17] These statutory torts have now been brought under the umbrella of the Equality Act 2010 which, in repealing all three of the earlier statutes and taking over in their stead, unfortunately does not repeat this clear statement.[18] A statute allowing actions for damages which has survived the repeals of the Equality Act 2010 is the Harassment Act 1997.[19] Earlier, in the Housing Act 1988, there was introduced a new tortious liability in damages against a landlord unlawfully depriving the residential occupier of his occupation.[20] **1-007**

---

9 For the whole range of restitutionary damages see Ch.14, below.

10 *Bartoline Ltd v Royal & Sun Alliance Insurance Plc* [2007] 1 All E.R. (Comm) 1043, with its detailed discussion, in an insurance context, of the meaning of damages (paras 77 and following), is a useful illustration of a liability to pay a statutory debt being held not to be a liability to pay damages.

11 See para.33-002, below.

12 Pt X for unfair dismissal, Pt XI for redundancy payments.

13 See the treatment of breach of statutory obligation in the standard books on tort.

14 See paras 41-003 and following, below.

15 Before 1986 this provision had appeared in the Companies Act of the day; for the details see para.49-009, below. Although speaking of compensation, this has been held not to be, either as to the amount recoverable or as to the mode of measuring it, something different from damages and its measure is precisely the same as in an action of deceit. It is believed that in legislation going back to mid-Victorian times a tort is created despite the use of the word compensation rather than the word damages.

16 See the subsection at para.49-049, below.

17 Sex Discrimination Act 1975 s.66(1), Race Relations Act 1976 s.57(1) and Disability Discrimination Act 1995 s.25(1).

18 All that we have is a statement in the very lengthy Explanatory Note to the Act that the Act is designed to replicate earlier legislation.

19 A case in point is *Jones v Ruth* [2012] 1 W.L.R. 1495 CA where the need for foreseeability of damage was in issue; facts at para.39-022, below.

20 Sections 27 and 28. See paras 39-069 and following, below.

### (2) The omission of the reference to pecuniary compensation

**1-008** It seemed at the time of the 1961 edition that there was very little in the way of damages that was not compensatory, not based on providing compensation for loss to a person to whom a wrong had been done. There were nominal damages which are of little importance in the damages world. As they do not offer real damages at all, they are not much of a departure from the compensatory principle. There were also liquidated damages which are not the equivalent of compensation but form an agreed alternative to compensation usually based on a bona fide estimate of the amount of loss to which the contemplated breach of contract will give rise, an amount which in the event is most likely to differ from the actual loss on breach. As their aim is directed to compensation, they cannot be said to form a radical departure from the compensation principle. That left only exemplary damages which clearly were not concerned with compensation but with deterrence and, therefore, punishment. Yet in the 1961 edition there was put forward the suggestion that the great bulk of the cases where the award appeared to be of an exemplary nature could be explained on the basis that these awards constituted aggravated damages for injury to feelings. There was, it was said, a double rationale. And indeed only two or three years later the distinction was built on by Lord Devlin in *Rookes v Barnard*,[21] to introduce severe limitations on the availability of exemplary damages. Of course all three types of damages—nominal, liquidated and exemplary—were, then as now, fully treated in this book, but it is understandable that they were then seen as exceptions to the true compensatory role of damages.

**1-009** Over fifty years have passed since then and things have changed. While himself regarding exemplary damages as anomalous in a compensatory world, Lord Devlin in *Rookes* felt that he could not rid the law of them entirely and retained two common law categories both of which are alive and well today, and doing good business in the punishment of two categories of defendant.[22] Much more newly recognised on the scene are restitutionary damages and disgorgement damages which come into play when the defendant's wrong, whether a tort or a breach of contract or an equitable wrong, has (respectively) given him a benefit or caused a profit greater than the loss, if any, suffered by the claimant. Such awards are the antithesis of compensation. There was another, controversial, type of damages which is unconcerned with loss. That is vindicatory damages. In Ch.17 of this book, the decline and ultimate rejection of vindicatory damages as a general phenomenon will be explained. Although the label "vindication" continues to have some life in limited pockets of the law such as defamation and invasion of privacy, it should not be seen as a different measure of damages from the usual compensatory measure. Vindicatory damages, properly described, are intended not to compensate for loss, of which there may be little or none, but simply as a sum of money to affirm the existence of a right that has been breached. Since the decline of vindicatory dam-

---

21 [1964] A.C. 1129. See para.13-004, below.

22 See paras 13-017 to 13-027, below. Lord Hoffmann's comments in *The Gleaner Co Ltd v Abrahams* [2004] 1 A.C. 628 PC at [41] that compensatory damages may be considered as fulfilling the dual function of compensation and of punishment, deterrence or example, and that this is an entirely orthodox view of such damages, are to be treated with caution. There is no doubt that the size of the award against an intentional tortfeasor may deter, and be an example to others, but this is not the aim of the award. An award will punish only if it has the aims of punishment.

ages, awards that are now described as vindicatory must be either illegitimate or re-explained.

1-010 With now numerous categories of case in which the courts will be looking to make damages awards not following the compensatory principle, it is right to recognise these as additional types of damages rather than as exceptional. Hence we start with compensatory damages, which of course take the great bulk of the learning,[23] and follow on with non-compensatory damages.[24]

### (3) The omission of the reference to tort and breach of contract

1-011 Two things were clear at the time of the 1961 edition. One was that statute had not created any monetary causes of actions based on a wrong which were independent of torts and contracts. The other was that monetary compensatory claims under equity's exclusive jurisdiction, as for breach of fiduciary duty or breach of trust, were few and far between, and in any event were categorised not as equitable damages but as equitable compensation. For damages, common law wrongs by way of tort and breach of contract ruled the day. Again, things have changed over the years on both statutory and equitable fronts. A statute has at last appeared under which damages may be awarded independently of a tort or breach of contract, and claims for equitable compensation for breach of fiduciary duty in lieu of a claim for damages for negligence, tortious or contractual, have since the 1990s become fashionable and taken a leap forward; partly consequent upon the collapse of the property market and in the context of solicitors' professional negligence, such actions being brought in the hope of achieving a greater recovery than would appear to have been available at law.

1-012 **(a) Damages under the Human Rights Act and other statutes** A whole new area of damages was introduced by the passing of the Human Rights Act 1998. The Act provides a right to damages for breach of Convention rights where there is neither a tort nor a breach of contract. Section 7 gives a claim against public authorities which have acted, or proposed to act, in a way which is incompatible with a right under the European Convention of Human Rights. Section 8 provides that the remedies which may be granted include damages and further provides that, in determining when and how much to award, the courts take into account the principles applied at Strasbourg. Damages awarded may not follow the principles laid down for common law damages.[25] While the cause of action created by s.7 is similar to an action in tort for breach of domestic statutory duty, it cannot be classified as a tort but is sui generis.[26] Thus we now have an action for damages cre-

---

[23] Chapter 4 to 11.

[24] Chapters 12 to 17.

[25] Thus in *Marcic v Thames Water Utilities Ltd (No.2)* [2002] Q.B. 1003 at first instance it was held that damages could be awarded in respect of future wrongs under the Act even if they could not be at common law. The Court of Appeal on the appeal on liability ([2002] Q.B. 929 CA) did not comment on this nor, on the appeal from the Court of Appeal, did the House of Lords [2004] 2 A.C. 42. See the case at para.39-023, below.

[26] With this the House of Lords agreed in the leading authority on the award of damages under the Human Rights Act, *R. (on the application of Greenfield) v Secretary of State for the Home Department* [2005] 1 W.L.R. 673, HL, Lord Bingham, speaking for the court, saying concisely (at [19]): "The 1998 Act is not a tort statute, its objects are different and broader". See further at paras 50-086 and following, below.

ated by statute that is not linked to the commission of a tort or the breach of a contract. A separate chapter outside the treatment of contract and tort is devoted to this cause of action.[27]

1-013 Apart from the major area of claims concerning damages for breaches of the Human Rights Act, there are many other statutes which confer rights to damages. This book does not deal with all of those statutes. This is because the principles to be applied in each case can be heavily dependent upon statutory text, context and purpose rather than upon underlying common law norms. For instance, in *The Mayor's Office for Policing and Crime v Mitsui Sumitomo Insurance Co (Europe) Ltd*,[28] the Supreme Court considered the meaning of the words "sustained loss by such injury, stealing, or destruction" in s.2 of the Riot (Damages) Act 1886. The court held that the word "loss" did not include consequential losses. Instead, the court said that the statute was "a self-contained statutory scheme which did not mirror the common law of tort".[29]

1-014 **(b) Damages in equity** Far wider in scope than Human Rights Act damages are claims made under equity's exclusive jurisdiction. And then there is the category of damages in equity's concurrent or auxiliary jurisdiction stemming from Lord Cairns' Act. To these we turn first.

1-015 *(i) Damages in equity's concurrent or auxiliary jurisdiction* The Chancery Amendment Act 1858, commonly called Lord Cairns' Act, gave statutory jurisdiction for a court of equity to award damages in addition to or in substitution for granting either an injunction or specific performance; this power is now contained in s.50 of the Senior Courts Act 1981, though the courts to this day continue to refer to the repealed Lord Cairns' Act rather than to the replacement s.50. In very many cases in which an injunction or specific performance could be granted in equity, there will be a tort or breach of contract upon which damages could equally well be awarded at common law, and in all such cases there is a change only in method and not in substance[30]; suggestions that a claimant might fare better in equity, on the ground that equity alone has the facility to give damages calculated upon values at the time of the court's judgment as opposed to the time of the wrong,[31] have proved groundless.[32] But the power to award damages has been interpreted as not confined to cases in which the claimant could recover damages at common law, and in two respects the equitable jurisdiction is wider[33]: damages can be awarded for breach

---

27 See Ch.50, below.

28 [2016] A.C. 1488.

29 [2016] A.C. 1488 at [34].

30 See Lord Wilberforce in *Johnson v Agnew* [1980] A.C. 367 at 400C and G, saying authoritatively that Lord Cairns' Act "does not provide for the assessment of damages on any new basis" and gives "no warrant for the court awarding damages differently from common law damages". Thus the possibility of aggravated damages in equity under Lord Cairns' Act is canvassed in *Cardwell v Walker* [2004] 2 P. & C.R. 9, p.122, at paras 66 and following.

31 See *Wroth v Tyler* [1974] Ch.30 at para.27-009, below.

32 See *Radford v De Froberville* [1977] 1 W.L.R. 1262 at para.27-049, below; *Malhotra v Choudhury* [1980] Ch. 52 CA, at para.25-009, below; *Johnson v Agnew* [1980] A.C. 367 at para.27-040, below; and cf. the full analysis of McMullin J in *Souster v Epsom Plumbing Co* [1974] 2 N.Z.L.R. 515.

33 A possible third respect, suggested by the decisions of *Capital and Suburban Properties v Swycher* [1976] Ch. 319 CA, and *Biggin v Minton* [1977] 1 W.L.R. 701, has been properly scotched by the House of Lords in *Johnson v Agnew* [1980] A.C. 367: see para.27-035, below. Equity may go procedurally beyond the common law under Lord Cairns' Act, as in *Oakacre v Claire Cleaners*

of a purely equitable right,[34] and damages can be awarded for prospective loss once and for all in respect of certain wrongs where the common law is confined to giving damages by successive actions as more damage appears,[35] with the equitable jurisdiction interpreted as allowing an award of damages even if such a wrong is only threatened or apprehended.[36]

*(ii) Damages in equity's exclusive jurisdiction* Historically, the principal tool in equity for awarding money was the action for an account. This was not historically seen as an action for damages. Indeed, on one view, the action for an account of administration in common form had more in common with a claim asserting a right rather than a complaint of a wrong.[37] In contrast, an action against a trustee for an account based upon wilful default was said to be "not readily distinguishable from damages except with the aid of a powerful legal microscope".[38] To that can be added the claims for losses suffered as a result of a breach of fiduciary duty. Other money claims in equity are even more obviously akin to claims for damages at common law. One example is a claim for deceit. In *Peek v Gurney*,[39] Lord Chelmsford said that the loss suffered as a result of fraudulent misrepresentations could be recovered by a suit in Chancery which was "precisely analogous to the common law action for deceit" and "is a suit instituted to recover damages".[40] Another example is a breach of confidence where information is confidential which has been regarded as an equitable wrong. History and tradition have usually seen these remedies described as claims for equitable compensation rather than for damages, and this way of looking at the law has been accepted in earlier editions as providing the route to exclude these awards from a book on damages. The traditional approach has been deep set at the Chancery Bar.[41] But the traditional view has far less traction today. It is commonly recognised that it is more coherent to treat, and understand, common law and equity together as in the vast majority of cases both are concerned with compensation.[42] This more open view is to be **1-016**

*(Holdings)* [1982] Ch. 197. In relation to a contract of sale of land a writ was, as was conceded, properly and not prematurely issued claiming specific performance with damages in addition or in lieu. The specific performance claim became otiose because the land was later conveyed to the purchaser. It was held that the court could continue to consider the damages claim although it could not have done so at law where the writ was premature on account of having been issued before the contractual completion date.

34 See *Eastwood v Lever* (1863) 4 De G.J. & S. 114 (breach of covenant running with the land only in equity); *Brightlingsea Haven Ltd v Morris* [2009] EWHC 3061 (QB) (denial of the equitable right of occupation of lodges on a caravan park).

35 See *Hooper v Rogers* [1975] Ch. 43 CA (nuisance by withdrawal of support likely to cause future physical damage).

36 See *Leeds Industrial Co-operative Society v Slack* [1924] A.C. 851.

37 *Partington v Reynolds* (1858) Drew. 253 at 255–256; 62 E.R. 98 at 99 (Kindersley VC); relied upon more recently in *Agricultural Land Management Ltd v Jackson (No.2)* [2014] W.A.S.C. 102; (2014) 48 W.A.R. 1, 67 at [349].

38 *Bartlett v Barclays Bank Trust Co Ltd (No.2)* [1980] Ch. 515 at 545.

39 *Peek v Gurney* (1873) L.R. 6 H.L. 377.

40 (1873) L.R. 6 H.L. 377 at 390, 393.

41 See the extra-judicial comment of Millett LJ at 114 L.Q.R. (1998) 225: "Woe betide a Chancery Junior who spoke of 'damages for breach of trust' or 'damages for breach of fiduciary duty'".

42 See Millett LJ again, this time judicially, in *Bristol and West Building Society v Mothew* [1998] Ch. 1 CA at 17G: "Although the remedy which equity makes available … is equitable compensation rather than damages, this is merely the product of history and … in my opinion is a distinction without a difference".

preferred. We should not allow in any corner of our legal system a characterisation of substance to be ruled by historic jurisdictional divides.

**1-017** While not siding with the traditionalists, this book does not yet cover all money awards of civil wrongs in equity. This is a significant omission because they also fall easily within the revised definition of damages. In an ideal, integrated world compensation by way of common law damages and by way of equitable damages would be dealt with together. However, the general rules where the compensation is in equity are not well known or understood and are still developing. For instance, it does not yet appear to be settled whether the common law rules as to causation and remoteness, which are so central to common law damages for tort and breach of contract, apply in equity; thus Lord Browne-Wilkinson in the important case of *Target Holdings Ltd v Redferns*,[43] thought that they did not apply to breach of trust.[44] The same may apply to contributory negligence. Few cases in equity have considered recovery of non-pecuniary loss and the possibility of awarding exemplary damages has been raised but only in theory. It follows that an integrated approach is not yet possible. It would be necessary, after covering the huge volume of material on common law damages, to deal separately with the limited amount of learning on equitable damages. This would add substantially to the length of a book which needs further containment rather than expansion. The law as it stands covering equitable damages can be found, well addressed, in other texts, and the reader is directed to the standard works on equity and trusts.[45]

**1-018** It must, however, be acknowledged that this position is becoming increasingly difficult to maintain. The observations of Lord Browne-Wilkinson in *Target Holdings v Redferns*, quoted in the paragraph above, if applied as an absolute proposition would not be consistent with those of Lord Toulson in *AIB Group (UK) Plc v Mark Redler & Co Solicitors*,[46] who observed that in *Bank of New Zealand v New Zealand Guardian Trust Co Ltd*,[47] Tipping J had

> "rightly observed that while historically the law has tended to place emphasis on the legal characterisation of the relationship between the parties in delineating the remedies available for breach of an obligation, the nature of the duty which has been breached can often be more important, when considering issues of causation and remoteness, than the classification or historical source of the obligation".

**1-019** The consequence is that the existence of equitable damages is recognised in the new definition of damages but much coverage has previously been left to other texts. This approach will disappear eventually over subsequent editions of this book. Already, breach of confidence or confidential information is fully covered.[48] One reason for these equitable wrongs being covered before the others is that the dam-

---

43 [1996] A.C. 421.

44 "Even if the immediate cause of the loss is the dishonesty or failure of a third party, the trustee is liable to make good the loss to the trust estate if, but for the breach, such loss would not have occurred... Thus the common law rules of remoteness and causation do not apply": [1996] A.C. 421 at 434E–F.

45 *Snell's Equity*, 33rd edn (London: Sweet & Maxwell, 2015), Underhill and Hayton, *Law of Trusts and Trustees*, 19th edn (LexisNexis, 2016), *Lewin on Trusts*, 19th edn (London: Sweet & Maxwell, 2015).

46 [2014] 3 W.L.R. 1367 at [59]. Compare Lord Reed SPJ at [136]–[137]. See also *Daniel v Tee* [2016] EWHC 1538 (Ch).

47 [1999] 1 N.Z.L.R. 664.

48 At paras 48-026 to 48-033, below.

ages appear to be the same whether looked at through common law or equitable eyes but also because courts have often attached the common law label "tort" to this wrong.[49] Another development in this edition of the book is a new chapter on disgorgement damages,[50] which refers to the disgorgement of profits following an account of profits taken as a result of a common law or equitable wrong.

## 2. THE COVERAGE OF DAMAGES

As has been said above, before damages can be recovered in an action there must be a wrong committed. Even if a loss has been incurred, no damages can be awarded in the absence of a wrong: it is *damnum sine iniuria.*[51] Therefore the preliminary question to be answered, before any issue of damages can arise, is whether a wrong has been committed. The consideration of this question cannot be entered into here: to do so would entail writing into the book practically the whole of the law of torts, breach of contract and equitable wrongs. A text on the law of damages should not and cannot deal with the question of the existence of a liability. It must accept that the reader is satisfied, from knowledge or from other commentaries, that a liability exists: the assistance a book on damages properly gives is on how to decide the extent and the measurement of a liability once established. It is true that it is sometimes difficult to disentangle the two questions of existence of a liability and the extent of a liability, particularly in the tort of negligence. But this is no good reason for reciting most of the law of torts, breach of contract, or other wrongs and, as the difficulties of distinction are very much localised to the tort of negligence, they can be dealt with adequately in the treatment of the general problem of the limits of liability[52] and the particular problem of remoteness of damage.[53] **1-020**

At the other end of the scale from *damnum sine iniuria* is *iniuria sine damno.* In earlier editions of this book it was suggested that if no loss has been incurred only nominal damages could be awarded if a wrong has been committed.[54] But this requires that the damages response to wrongdoing must be tied to one consequence: loss. This is demonstrably incorrect. Damages respond to numerous consequences other than loss. They respond to consequences which give rise to a need for specific or general deterrence (exemplary damages), gains that the defendant receives from the claimant (restitutionary damages), and gains which are net profits made by the wrong (disgorgement damages). **1-021**

---

49 See the cases discussed at para.48-026, below.

50 See Ch.15.

51 See *Bourhill v Young* [1943] A.C. 92 at 106, per Lord Wright: "Damage due to the legitimate exercise of a right is not actionable, even if the actor contemplates the damage. It is *damnum absque injuria.* The damage must be attributable to the breach by the defendant of some duty owing to the plaintiff." *Mogul Steamship Co v McGregor, Gow & Co* [1892] A.C. 25 and *Bradford Corp v Pickles* [1895] A.C. 587 are among the most celebrated examples of *damnum sine injuria.*

52 See Ch.6, below.

53 See Ch.8, below.

54 Nominal damages are dealt with in Ch.12, below.

# PART 1A: COMPENSATORY DAMAGES: OBJECT AND TERMINOLOGY

## Chapter 2

# THE OBJECT OF AN AWARD OF COMPENSATORY DAMAGES

Table of Contents



### (1) The principle of compensation

**2-001** Compensatory damages are, far and away, the most common type of damages. The object of an award of compensatory damages is to give the claimant compensation for the loss or injury[1] he has suffered within the scope of the defendant's duty.[2] The heads or elements of damage recognised as such by the law are divisible into two main groups: pecuniary and non-pecuniary loss. The former comprises all financial and material loss incurred, such as loss of business profits or expenses of medical treatment. The latter comprises all losses which do not represent an inroad upon a person's financial or material assets, such as physical pain or injury to feelings. The former, being a money loss, is capable of being arithmetically calculated in money, even though the calculation must sometimes be a rough one where there are difficulties of proof. The latter, however, is not so calculable. Money is not awarded as a replacement for other money, but as a substitute for that which is generally more important than money: it is the best that a court can do.[3]

**2-002** The statement of the general rule as to the measure of compensatory damages, a rule equally applicable to tort and contract, has its origin in the speech of Lord

---

1 Sometimes the word "damage" is used as a synonym for loss. As explained in Ch.1, this terminology is best avoided. The law of "damages" is concerned with money awards for all remediable consequences of a wrong, not merely losses which have been suffered. The use of one or more of "damage", "loss", or "injury" can be construed as confined to physical damage, loss or injury or as extending to cover the purely financial or economic has arisen in the context of clauses introducing exemptions from liability. While the wider construction prevailed in *Nippon Yusen Kaisha v Acme Shipping Corp* [1972] 1 W.L.R. 74 CA, the narrower was upheld in *Louis Dreyfus & Cie v Parnaso Cia Naviera* [1959] 1 Q.B. 408. In the particular context of whether a time limit for lodging claims under the Warsaw Convention on international air carriage applied, "damage" to baggage was held in *Fothergill v Monarch Airlines* [1981] A.C. 251 to include loss of contents of baggage.

2 The proposition that the basic criterion is what the claimant has lost and not what the defendant ought fairly and reasonably to pay finds a valuable illustration in *General Tire & Rubber Co v Firestone Tyre & Rubber Co* [1975] 1 W.L.R. 819 HL; see the case at para.48-041, below.

3 Compare *The Mediana* [1900] A.C. 113 at 116, per Lord Halsbury LC: "How is anybody to measure pain and suffering in moneys counted? Nobody can suggest that you can by arithmetical calculation establish what is the exact sum of money which would represent such a thing as the pain and suffering which a person has undergone by reason of an accident. But nevertheless the law recognises that as a topic upon which damages may be given." See similarly *Fletcher v Autocar and Transporters* [1968] 2 Q.B. 322 CA at 339, per Diplock LJ; *Parry v Cleaver* [1970] A.C. 1 at 22, per Lord Morris.

Blackburn in *Livingstone v Rawyards Coal Co.*[4] He there defined the measure of damages as:

> "that sum of money which will put the party who has been injured, or who has suffered, in the same position as he would have been in if he had not sustained the wrong for which he is now getting his compensation or reparation."

This statement has been consistently referred to or cited with approval,[5] or restated in similar language.[6] It is thus a statement which has stood the test of time and is not to be regarded as in any way compromised by Lord Hoffmann's well-known speech in *Banque Bruxelles Lambert v Eagle Star Insurance Co* (commonly referred to as *SAAMCO*).[7] He there disagreed with the description of Lord Blackburn's principle by the Court of Appeal in *SAAMCO* as "the necessary point of departure" in arriving at the correct measure of damages, and said:

> "I think that this was the wrong place to begin. Before one can consider the principle on which one should calculate the damages to which a plaintiff is entitled as compensation for loss, it is necessary to decide for what kind of loss he is entitled to compensation."[8]

What Lord Hoffmann is concerned with here is the ascertainment of the scope of the defendant's duty as an exercise preliminary to the ascertainment of the damages to which the breach of the duty gives rise. This point was reiterated by the Supreme Court in *BPE Solicitors & Anor v Hughes-Holland*.[9] As will be seen in a moment,[10] there are many limits to be placed on Lord Blackburn's formulation—causation, remoteness, mitigation and certainty are the principal ones—and *SAAMCO* should be looked at as presenting us, as do other cases, with what may be the first of these limitations. There is no doubt that Lord Hoffmann would be in full agreement with Lord Blackburn's statement as to what, subject to limitations, damages seek to do, but if one started with Lord Hoffmann one would never get to Lord Blackburn. Yet the ground rule is Lord Blackburn's although one does not stop with it. With this analysis Jackson LJ has agreed in *Grange v Quinn*,[11] saying that Lord Hoffmann's comments in *SAAMCO* "do not detract from the fact that Lord Blackburn's principle is the point from which one starts".[12]

---

4 (1880) 5 App. Cas. 25 at 39.

5 As in *Banco de Portugal v Waterlow* [1932] A.C. 452 at 474, per Viscount Sankey LC; in *Monarch S.S. Co v Karlshamns Oljefabriker* [1949] A.C. 196 at 221, per Lord Wright; in *British Transport Commission v Gourley* [1956] A.C. 185 at 197, per Earl Jowitt; in *The Heron II* [1969] 1 A.C. 350 at 420C, per Lord Upjohn; in *General Tire & Rubber Co v Firestone Tyre & Rubber Co* [1975] 1 W.L.R. 819 HL at 824C, per Lord Wilberforce; in *Swingcastle v Gibson* [1991] 2 A.C. 223 at 232D, per Lord Lowry; in *Alfred McAlpine Construction Ltd v Panatown Ltd* [2001] 1 A.C. 518 at 562G, per Lord Jauncey; in *Rees v Darlington Memorial Hospital NHS Trust* [2004] 1 A.C. 309 at [129], per Lord Scott; in *Golden Strait Corp v Nippon Yusen Kubishika Kaisha (The Golden Victory)* [2007] 2 A.C 353 at [80], per Lord Brown.

6 As in *Victoria Laundry v Newman* [1949] 2 K.B. 528 CA at 539, per Asquith LJ ("in the same position, so far as money can do so, as if his rights had been observed"); in *The Albazero* [1977] A.C. 774 at 841C, per Lord Diplock ("to put the person whose right has been invaded in the same position as if it had been respected so far as the award of a sum of money can do so").

7 [1997] A.C. 191.

8 [1997] A.C. 191 at 211A.

9 [2017] UKSC 21 at [31]–[33].

10 See para.2-004, below.

11 [2013] EWCA Civ 24 CA.

12 [2013] EWCA Civ 24 CA at [76].

2-003 While Lord Blackburn's statement does good service as a rule covering compensatory damages for both tort and contract, there lurks a dangerous ambiguity in it where contract is concerned. In respect of tort the rule as stated by him refers to putting the claimant into the position he would have been in had the tort not been committed; in respect of contract it refers to putting him into the position he would have been in had the contract not been broken. But in the case of contract the rule might, on a surface analysis, be taken to refer to putting the claimant into the position he would have been in had the contract never been made, and that there is such a perhaps unrealised ambiguity[13] is brought out by the fact that Earl Jowitt in *British Transport Commission v Gourley*,[14] immediately followed up his reference to Lord Blackburn's statement with the remark that "the principle is sometimes referred to as the principle of restitutio in integrum", a principle which encompasses only the tort meaning, being used mainly in cases of damage to or destruction of ships.[15] And Bowen LJ in *The Argentino*,[16] said that the principle of restitutio in integrum applies to both tort and contract, a statement which is only confusing. In practice the potential ambiguity is most apparent in actions of deceit and for breach of warranty of authority.[17] It is better, therefore, for contract itself to take an alternative way of framing the general rule. First clearly stated by Parke B in *Robinson v Harman*,[18] and also consistently cited with approval[19] or restated in similar language,[20] the rule is that the claimant is entitled to be placed, so far as money can do it, in the same position as he would have been in had the contract been performed.[21]

## (2) Compensation less than loss

2-004 The general rule is, however, only a starting point, for upon it a number of important limits are engrafted which may result in the claimant recovering less than the amount which would put him in the position he would have been in had the tort

---

13 Compare Oliver Wendell Holmes's fallacious but persuasive doctrine of "commit a tort, commit a contract".

14 [1956] A.C. 185 at 197.

15 It is used in such a case, *The Columbus* (1849) 3 W. Rob. (Adm.) 158 at 162, by Dr Lushington, defining it as "the principle of replacing the party who has received the damage in the same position in which he would have been, provided the collision had not occurred"; cited by Lord Esher MR dissenting in *The Argentino* (1888) 13 P.D. 191 CA at 196.

16 (1888) 13 P.D. 191 CA at 200.

17 See, respectively, paras 49-002 and 36-002, below.

18 (1848) 1 Ex. 850 at 855.

19 As in *Lock v Furze* (1866) L.R. 1 C.P. 441 at 450 to 451, per Martin B; in *Watts v Mitsui* [1917] A.C. 277 at 241, per Lord Dunedin; in *The Heron II* [1969] 1 A.C. 350 at 414B and 420D, per Lord Pearce and Lord Upjohn respectively; in *Alfred McAlpine Construction Ltd v Panatown Ltd* [2001] 1 A.C. 518 at 562F, per Lord Jauncey; in *Golden Strait Corp v Nippon Yusen Kubishika Kaisha (The Golden Victory)* [2007] 2 A.C. 353 at [29], per Lord Scott.

20 As in *Lock v Furze* (1866) L.R. 1 C.P. 441 at 453, per Blackburn J; in *Wertheim v Chicoutimi Pulp Co* [1911] A.C. 301 PC at 307, per Lord Atkinson (practically the same wording as Parke B, and frequently referred to); in *British Westinghouse Co v Underground Ry* [1912] A.C. 673 at 689, per Viscount Haldane LC; in *Hill v Showell* (1918) 87 L.J.K.B. 1106 at 1108 and 1114, per Viscount Haldane and Lord Parmoor respectively; in *Monarch S.S. Co v Karlshamns Oljefabriker* [1949] A.C. 196 at 220, per Lord Wright; in *The Heron II* [1969] 1 A.C. 350 at 400F, per Lord Morris; in *The Albazero* [1977] A.C. 774 at 841D, per Lord Diplock; in *Transfield Shipping Inc v Mercator Shipping Inc (The Achilleas)* [2009] 1 A.C. 61 at [14], per Lord Hoffmann.

21 The Court of Appeal in *Howard-Jones v Tate* [2012] 2 All E.R. 369 CA corrected the trial judge who had awarded damages based on the pre-contractual position: see the case at para.27-031, below.

or breach of contract never been committed. Rigorously to insist upon such full compensation would be too harsh upon defendants.[22] The loss for which the claimant will be compensated is cut down by a variety of factors: thus he cannot recover damages for that part of the loss due to his contributory negligence,[23] nor for such loss of which the defendant's conduct is not the cause, nor for such loss which is not within the scope of the protection of the particular tort or contract,[24] nor for loss which he should have avoided,[25] nor for loss which is too uncertain,[26] nor for some past and prospective losses.[27] These factors are all given extended consideration[28]: many of them are frequently grouped under the compendious term "remoteness of damage". The width of meaning commonly given to this term can easily lead to muddled and telescoped thinking by grouping diverse factors under the same name, and separate analysis is therefore important.[29] At the same time this umbrella use of "remoteness of damage" can serve to point to the common denominator of these various factors: they all delimit the consequences and losses for which the claimant can recover compensation. In this way the term "remoteness of damage" can be distinguished from the term "measure of damages", the former referring to the consequences and losses for which the claimant can recover compensation, and the latter referring to the method of calculating the compensation for the particular consequence or loss.

### (3) Compensation greater than loss

At the other end of the scale there are certain circumstances in which the claimant will recover more than his loss as defined by Lord Blackburn's general rule. Here we are concerned with excess of loss which is by way of compensation; the categories of damages where more than a claimant's loss may be recovered by him because loss is not the basis of recovery have yet to be dealt with.[30] The circumstances in which there is compensation beyond loss occur infrequently and are of far less general importance than the circumstances leading to a diminished recovery. There are three varieties[31] of compensation beyond loss. **2-005**

The first variety is bound up with the issue of mitigation and concerns those cases where the claimant is allowed to recover the normal measure of damages that the **2-006**

---

22 *Compare Victoria Laundry v Newman* [1949] 2 K.B. 528 CA at 539, per Asquith LJ: "This purpose, if relentlessly pursued, would provide him [the claimant] with a complete indemnity for all loss de facto resulting from a particular breach, however improbable, however unpredictable."

23 Chapter 7, below.

24 Chapter 8, below.

25 Chapter 9, below.

26 Chapter 10, below.

27 Chapter 11, below.

28 Book I, Pt III, below. The difficult distinctions between some of these factors are considered in Chs 7 to 11, below.

29 See, especially, Ch.6, below.

30 See Book 2, Chs 12 to 17 below.

31 There are also the cases in which the wrong committed by the defendant has involved an interference with the claimant's property, of whatever form, whereby the defendant has gained some use of the property, and the courts award the claimant a sum representing the value of the user even where it is clear that the claimant would not have used the property himself, so that he had not suffered a pecuniary loss by being deprived of it. While the courts have tended to press such recoveries into the compensatory damages mould, the cases are properly regarded as affording claimants non-compensatory damages, today recognised in the true role of restitutionary damages. These are fully dealt with in Ch.14, below.

law awards in such circumstances, although this normal loss has been diminished for the claimant by other events. The principal illustrations of this situation are where a person physically injured collects money on his accident insurance policy,[32] or pension money,[33] or is given gratuitous assistance from a charitable fund[34]; and where a lessor of land, which is delivered to him at the end of the term in disrepair, nevertheless has succeeded in reletting to a new lessee who has covenanted to repair.[35] The rationale of these decisions is that the law regards such events as collateral and therefore not to be taken into account in deciding what is the claimant's loss. The difficulty is in finding a clear yardstick to distinguish what is and what is not collateral.[36] Thus it was for long thought, following a decision of 1920, that where a buyer of goods, which fall short of warranty, has succeeded in reselling them at a price higher than their value in their defective state, the resale is collateral and not to be taken into account in reduction of the buyer's damages[37]; however, in a decision of 1996, the opposite solution was reached.[38] This whole thorny problem is best considered when dealing with mitigation of damage. Within the first variety is also the situation where a normal loss suffered is not one which is peculiar to the claimant. For instance, a seller might breach a contract for the sale of goods by the delivery of defective goods. If the buyer suffers, and will suffer, no loss on resale but nevertheless still recovers the normal loss then the buyer will be compensated for a loss which was not suffered. Again, as we will see in Ch.25, these are questions bound up with mitigation.[39]

**2-007** The second variety stems from the frequent impossibility of repairing damaged property without putting it into a better condition than it was before the damage had been inflicted, since repairing with old and worn materials is not a practical possibility. In these circumstances the question arises whether there should be a deduction from the cost of repair of the amount by which the property, after repair, is more valuable than beforehand. The very first cases tended to hold that there should indeed be such a deduction,[40] this solution appearing both in cases where land was tortiously damaged[41] and in cases where lessees were in breach of covenants to repair.[42] But, at a comparatively early date, the cases concerning damage to ships rejected the argument that there must be a deduction on account of "new for old"[43] since, as was well expressed by Dr Lushington, if the claimant:

---

32 *Bradburn v G. W. Ry* (1874) L.R. 10 Ex. 1.

33 *Parry v Cleaver* [1970] A.C. 1.

34 *Redpath v Belfast and County Down Ry* [1947] N.I. 167.

35 *Haviland v Long* [1952] 2 Q.B. 80 CA. Formerly, the lessor could recover the cost of repairs even where they were not to be done at all, not to be completely done, or to be done at a third party's expense; s.18(1) of the Landlord and Tenant Act 1927 was designed to alter this situation. For details see paras 28-055 and following, below.

36 Contrast the different approaches of the three members of the court in *London Building Society v Stone* [1983] 1 W.L.R. 1242 CA.

37 *Slater v Hoyle & Smith* [1920] 2 K.B. 11 CA.

38 *Bence Graphics International v Fasson UK* [1998] Q.B. 87 CA.

39 See para.25-070 below.

40 "Otherwise the plaintiff would be a gainer by the accident": *Lukin v Godsall* (1795) Peake Add. Cas. 15 at 16, per Lord Kenyon.

41 *Lukin v Godsall* (1795) Peake Add. Cas. 15; *Hide v Thornborough* (1846) 2 C. & K. 250; and compare *Dodd v Holme* (1834) 1 A. & E. 493.

42 *Soward v Leggatt* (1836) 7 C. & P. 613 (see especially at 617); *Yates v Dunster* (1855) 11 Ex. 15.

43 *The Gazelle* (1844) 2 W. Rob. (Adm.) 279; *The Pactolus* (1856) Swab. 173.

"derives incidentally a greater benefit than mere indemnification, it arises only from the impossibility of otherwise effecting such indemnification without exposing him to some loss or burden, which the law will not place on him."[44]

This approach has been adopted in modern times in relation to damage to land, whether caused tortiously[45] or through breach of contract,[46] and has been applied to chattels other than ships.[47] Thus where a contractual breach resulted in the destruction of a factory, the Court of Appeal refused to allow any deduction from the damages, which were based on the costs of rebuilding, on account of what was described as "betterment", for, as Widgery LJ pointed out,

"to do so would be the equivalent of forcing the plaintiffs to invest their money in the modernising of their plant which might be highly inconvenient for them".[48]

Lord Denning MR pointed out that, when their factory was destroyed, the claimants had no choice but to replace it as soon as they could, not only to keep their business going but also to mitigate their loss of profit.[49] On the other hand, where the necessity of the case does not demand reinstatement, claimants may find themselves limited to claiming for the diminution of the value of the property in question. This is so, for instance, where a house has been purchased in reliance on a negligent surveyor's report, the cost of putting the property into the condition described in the report not being required to put the purchaser into the position he would have been in had the surveying contract been properly fulfilled.[50]

---

44 *The Gazelle* (1844) 2 W. Rob. (Adm.) 279 at 281. The analogy of the marine insurance rule of deducting one-third new for old, which Dr Lushington had to reject and on which Lord Kenyon had earlier relied in *Lukin v Godsall* (1795) Peake Add. Cas. 15, is no longer of concern since modern policies either exclude the rule or subject it to important exceptions: see *British Shipping Laws*, Vol.4, 11th edn (1961), para.529. This does not appear in the latest edition of the equivalent volume of *British Shipping Laws, Marsden on Collisions*, 13th edn (London: Sweet & Maxwell, 2003), para.15-41, which simply states that "no deduction is made from the damages in respect of unavoidable betterment".

45 *Hollebone v Midhurst and Fernhurst Builders* [1968] 1 Lloyd's Rep. 38; *Haysman v MRS Films Ltd* [2008] EWHC 2494 (QB).

46 *Harbutt's "Plasticine" v Wayne Tank & Pump Co* [1970] 1 Q.B. 447 CA. But claimants must not go further than they need: *Scott Wilson Kirkpatrick & Partners v Ministry of Defence* [2001] 73 Con. L.R. 52 CA.

47 *Bacon v Cooper (Metals)* [1982] 1 All E.R. 397 (rotor for machine for fragmenting steel; breach of contract). And compare at para.37-021, below, *Lagden v O'Connor* [2004] 1 A.C. 1067 where hiring a car from a hire car company brought additional benefits for which the claimant did not have to account: see especially Lord Hope at [30]–[35].

48 *Harbutt's "Plasticine" v Wayne Tank & Pump Co* [1970] 1 Q.B. 447 CA at 473. See similarly at 468 and 476, per Lord Denning MR and Cross LJ respectively.

49 [1970] 1 Q.B. 447 CA at 468. He distinguished the destruction of a chattel, saying that "if a secondhand car is destroyed, the owner only gets its value; because he can go into the market and get another secondhand car to replace it": at 468. But this may not be possible with all chattels: see *Bacon v Cooper (Metals)* [1982] 1 All E.R. 397, above ("rotors, unlike motor cars, are not bought and sold secondhand": at 399d); even as to cars see *Moore v D.E.R.* [1971] 1 W.L.R. 1476 CA at para.37-069, below. It was on the ground that the rule of no deduction of "new for old" applies only to damaged property repaired and not to destroyed property replaced that Colman J in *Voaden v Champion, The Baltic Surveyor* [2001] 1 Lloyd's Rep. 739 refused the cost of a replacement ship of greater value than the ship sunk. Such a rigid distinction between the two categories does not appear to accord with principle.

50 *Philips v Ward* [1956] 1 W.L.R. 471 CA, *Perry v Sidney Phillips & Son* [1982] 1 W.L.R. 1297 CA, *Watts v Morrow* [1991] 1 W.L.R. 1421 CA and *Smith and Smith v Peter North* [2002] Lloyd's Rep. P.N. 111 CA, are the principal cases. Where the cost of putting the property into the condition as

**2-008** The third variety where, at first glance, it appears that compensation is awarded beyond loss is where the claimant recovers an award commonly, but misleadingly, described as "transferred loss". In *Lowick Rose LLP v Swynson Ltd*,[51] Lord Sumption, delivering the decision of four members of the Supreme Court, said that the principles applies where the

> "known object of a transaction is to benefit a third party or a class of persons to which a third party belongs, and the anticipated effect of a breach of duty will be to cause loss to that third party".

For instance, in cases of carriage of goods by sea even if title and risk to the goods has passed to the consignee, the shipper can still sue the shipowner for negligence causing loss or damage to the cargo.[52] The rationale was given by Lord Diplock as being that, unless the terms provide otherwise, the shipper enters the contract with the shipowner for the benefit of all persons who may acquire an interest in the goods.[53] But expressed only in these terms, this principle of "transferred loss" is an anomaly because it is contrary to rules of privity of contract. As applied to owners of property it became known as the "narrow ground". However, the principle was extended to commercial contracts generally in *Linden Gardens Trust v Lenesta Sludge Disposals Ltd*,[54] where Lord Griffiths re-explained it on a "broad ground" and reconciled it with privity of contract by explaining that the loss was genuinely suffered by the claimant because of the claimant's interest in providing the third party the intended benefit. However, as Lord Sumption emphasised in *Lowick Rose LLP v Swynson Ltd*, the principle can only be applied where (i) there would be a "black hole" because the third parties cannot recover themselves; and (ii) the claimant enters the contract with the manifested object of benefitting the third party.[55]

### (4) COMPENSATION IS NOT DISCRETIONARY

**2-009** It follows from the previous discussion that an award of compensatory damages is made as a matter of right. It is not a matter of discretion. Even when a right to compensatory damages is created by statute, the use of permissive words like "may award damages" is unlikely to be understood as creating the radical change of making compensatory damages a matter of judicial discretion. This issue was decided as a preliminary issue in *Energy Solutions EU Ltd v Nuclear Decommissioning Authority*.[56] In that case, the primary judge was concerned with a claim for damages under Regulation 47J(2)(c) of the Public Contracts Regulations 2006[57] which provides that a court "may award damages to an economic operator which

---

described has been allowed, as in *Freeman v Marshall* (1966) 200 E.G. 777, this is only on the basis that this cost does not exceed the amount by which the value of the property as it stands falls below its value as described—or, more accurately, below the price paid. For details see paras 34-050 to 34-060, below.

51 [2017] UKSC 32; [2017] 2 W.L.R. 1161.

52 *Dunlop v Lambert* (1839) 2 Cl. & F. 626.

53 *The Albazero* [1977] A.C. 774 at 847.

54 *Linden Gardens Trust v Lenesta Sludge Disposals Ltd* [1994] 1 A.C. 85. See also *Alfred McAlpine Construction Ltd v Panatown Ltd* [2001] 1 A.C. 518 at 547–548, per Lord Goff, 568, per Lord Jauncey, 577–578, per Lord Browne-Wilkinson, 582–583, per Lord Millett.

55 [2017] UKSC 32 at [15]–[16].

56 [2015] EWCA Civ 1262.

57 Now reg.98(2)(c) of the Public Contracts Regulations 2015 (SI 2015/102).

has suffered loss or damage as a consequence of the breach". Edwards-Stuart J held[58] that much clearer wording than the mere use of "may" was needed before the Regulations would be held to introduce the novel concept of discretionary damages.

[58] Public Contracts Regulations 2015 (SI 2015/102), reg.98(2)(c), para.93.

CHAPTER 3

# TERMINOLOGY USED IN COMPENSATORY DAMAGES AWARDS AND EXCLUSION CLAUSES

TABLE OF CONTENTS



## (1) GENERAL AND SPECIAL DAMAGE

**3-001** In the cases, damage or damages are often said to be "general" or "special", and these two terms are usually contrasted with each other. Yet the terms are used in a variety of different meanings, and if these meanings are not kept separate the indiscriminate use of the terms only spells confusion. Such a separation is not seen very often,[1] and it is therefore wise to elucidate these terms at the very start.

**3-002** The first meaning of general and special damage concerns liability: it relates principally to contract, coinciding with the distinction between the well-known first and second rules in *Hadley v Baxendale*[2] which are dealt with later.[3] It is best expressed by Lord Wright in *Monarch S.S. Co v Karlshamns Oljefabriker*,[4] where he said:

> "The distinction there drawn [in *Hadley v Baxendale*] is between damages arising naturally (which means in the normal course of things) and cases where there were special and extraordinary circumstances beyond the reasonable prevision of the parties. In the latter event it is laid down that the special facts must be communicated by and between the parties. The distinction between these types is usually described in English law as that between general and special damages."

In *Kpohraror v Woolwich Building Society*,[5] where the action was for breach of contract in wrongfully dishonouring a cheque, the general law, which both parties accepted as governing the claim, was stated to be that "the plaintiff may recover general damages under the first head of the rule in *Hadley v Baxendale* and special damages under the second head of the rule when the necessary facts are proved".[6] And Lord Macnaghten said in *Ströms Bruks Aktie Bolag v Hutchison*[7]: "in cases of contract special or exceptional damages cannot be claimed unless such damages

---

1 About the only good attempt at clarification is that of Bowen LJ in *Ratcliffe v Evans* [1892] 2 Q.B. 524 CA at 528 to 529. The various meanings are set out by Stuart-Smith J in *Arroyo v Equion Energin Ltd* [2013] EWHC 3150 (TCC) at [13], referring to this text.

2 (1854) 9 Ex. 341.

3 See paras 8-160 and following, below.

4 [1949] A.C. 196 at 221.

5 [1996] 4 All E.R. 119 CA.

6 [1996] 4 All E.R. 119 CA at 122e.

7 [1905] A.C. 515 at 526.

were within the contemplation of both parties at the time of the contract." If this distinction were applied to tort, all tort damages would count as general.

The second meaning of general and special damage concerns proof: it has more connection with tort, but the clearest statement comes in a contract case, *Prehn v Royal Bank of Liverpool*,[8] where Martin B put the distinction thus: **3-003**

> "General damages … are such as the jury may give when the judge cannot point out any measure by which they are to be assessed, except the opinion and judgment of a reasonable man. Special damages are given in respect of any consequences reasonably and probably arising from the breach complained of."[9]

This type of general damage is usually concerned with non-pecuniary losses, which are difficult to estimate, the principal examples being the injury to reputation in defamation[10] and the pain and suffering in cases of personal injury. Pecuniary loss is also to be found as general damage within this meaning, both in contract and in tort. In tort there is the loss of business profits caused by the defendant's inducement of breach of contract or passing off[11] or the defendant's libelling of the claimant.[12] So too in the event of a person's goods being tortiously damaged, whereas a claim for the cost of replacement goods hired during the goods' repair requires proof of special damage, in the absence of a hiring of replacement goods, or of a liability for such, a claimed loss of use has to be proved as general damage.[13] In contract there is the injury to credit and reputation caused by the defendant's failure to pay the claimant's cheques or honour his drafts. These are pecuniary losses which it is difficult to estimate at all accurately.[14]

This distinction is closely connected with that between torts actionable per se and torts actionable only on proof of damage, but the resemblance does not justify either the conclusion that when a tort is actionable per se the law necessarily presumes some substantial damage, or the conclusion that when a tort is actionable only on proof of some damage it necessarily follows that all damage is special damage. The first is disproved by a case like *Constantine v Imperial Hotels*,[15] where the defendants refused to accommodate the claimant in their hotel and this refusal was held to give the claimant an action in tort, in which, however, he was awarded only nominal damages. The second is disproved by the simple case of an action for personal injury resulting from negligence, the tort of negligence requiring damage as one of its essential ingredients. **3-004**

---

8 (1870) L.R. 5 Ex. 92.

9 (1870) L.R. 5 Ex. 92 at 99–100.

10 See *Tripp v Thomas* (1824) 3 B. & C. 427.

11 *Goldsoll v Goldman* [1914] 2 Ch. 603 and *Draper v Trist* [1939] 3 All E.R. 513 CA, respectively.

12 *Cambridge v Makin* [2011] EWHC 12 (QB).

13 *Bee v Jenson (No.2)* [2008] R.T.R. 7 CA at para.37-054, below (in a footnote); and see *The Mediana* [1900] A.C. 113 at 117–118, per Lord Halsbury, quoted at para.34-049, below.

14 See *Rolin v Steward* (1854) 14 C.B. 595; *Prehn v Royal Bank of Liverpool* (1870) L.R. 5 Ex. 92; *Wilson v United Counties Bank* [1920] A.C. 102; *Kpohraror v Woolwich Building Society* [1996] 4 All E.R. 119 CA and *Nicholson v Knox Ukiwa & Co* [2008] P.N.L.R. 33 at 782. So too, general damages can be awarded under cross-undertakings in respect of loss occasioned by search and freezing orders where the orders have been wrongly obtained: *Al Rawas v Pegasus Energy Ltd (No.2)* [2008] EWHC 617 (QB); see at [31] and following, especially at [35] where the trial judge said he considered there to be "a close analogy between the stopping of a cheque by a bank and the obtaining of a freezing order". This follows the similar case of *Columbia Picture Industries v Robinson* [1987] Ch. 38 where, however, the damages awarded were not stated to be general damages.

15 [1944] K.B. 693.

**3-005** The third meaning of general and special damage concerns pleading. The distinction here is put thus by Lord Dunedin in *The Susquehanna*[16]:

> "If there be any special damage which is attributable to the wrongful act that special damage must be averred and proved, and, if proved, will be awarded. If the damage be general, then it must be averred that such damage has been suffered, but the quantification is a jury question."

And in *Ströms Bruks Aktie Bolag v Hutchison*[17] Lord Macnaghten, after stating that he thought the division into general and special damages was more appropriate to tort than contract, said:

> "General damages' ... are such as the law will presume to be the direct natural or probable consequence of the action complained of. 'Special damages,' on the other hand, are such as the law will not infer from the nature of the act. They do not follow in ordinary course. They are exceptional in their character and, therefore, they must be claimed specially and proved strictly."[18]

Here, in pleading, general damage is wider than its second meaning, for it includes losses the amount of which the law will not presume since this is capable of calculation, and therefore evidence to assist the court in doing the calculation must be given if the claimant wishes to obtain substantial damages on the general head. Thus, in a personal injury case, loss of future earning capacity and future expenses are general damage in pleading[19] but the claimant must clearly give evidence of amount. On the other hand, general damage in pleading tends to be narrower than its first meaning.[20] Thus, in a personal injury case again, the loss of earnings and the expenses incurred between injury and trial must be pleaded as special damage; yet they are ordinary foreseeable consequences. The present distinction is set out in regard to personal injury cases by Lord Goddard in *British Transport Commission v Gourley*[21] where he said:

> "In an action for personal injuries the damages are always divided into two main parts. First, there is what is referred to as special damage, which has to be specially pleaded and proved. This consists of out-of-pocket expenses and loss of earnings incurred down to the date of trial, and is generally capable of substantially exact calculation. Secondly, there is general damage which the law implies and is not specially pleaded. This includes compensation for pain and suffering and the like, and, if the injuries suffered are such as to lead to continuing or permanent disability, compensation for loss of earning power in the future."

A contract example of special damage in pleading, which is clearly not within the

---

16 [1926] A.C. 655 at 661.

17 [1905] A.C. 515.

18 [1905] A.C. 515 at 525 to 526.

19 Thus in *Potter v Metropolitan Ry* (1873) 28 L.T. 735 it was held that the amount the claimant would have earned if the accident had not occurred need not be alleged as it did not represent special damage. But a particular loss of future earnings not arising in the ordinary way has to be pleaded as special damage: see *Domsalla v Barr* [1969] 1 W.L.R. 630 CA, at para.51-024, below.

20 Occasionally it may in certain respects be wider: see especially *Ward v Smith* (1822) 11 Price 19 at para.51-018, below, where, in relation to pleading, the interrelation of these various meanings is further considered.

21 [1956] A.C. 185 at 206. And applied to wrongful death cases in *Cookson v Knowles* [1979] A.C. 556: see para.41-042, below.

second rule in *Hadley v Baxendale* and hence the first meaning, is to be found in actions for wrongful dismissal, where the claim for the wages the claimant would have earned but for the breach, less any substitute salary he has earned since his dismissal, is treated invariably as special damage. The point was assumed in *Monk v Redwing Aircraft Co*,[22] where the only issue was as to the particularity of the special damage, but in *Hayward v Pullinger*[23] Devlin J thought that the earlier Court of Appeal case decided the matter. He held, accordingly, that where the claimant claimed in his statement of claim "damages for wrongful dismissal" without more, and the damage for which he wished to recover was the loss of salary and commission he would have earned during the period of notice to which he was contractually entitled, this was special damage, and, as it had not been specifically pleaded, the statement of claim was defective.[24] The reason why these various items of damage have been held to be special for the purpose of pleading, although general for the purpose of liability, would seem to be that where damage has become crystallised and concrete since the wrong, the defendant could be surprised at the trial by the detail of its amount, although it is of a type which he could expect as a consequence of the wrong. As Lord Donovan said in *Perestrello v United Paint Co*,[25] the obligation to particularise arises:

> "not because the nature of the loss is necessarily unusual, but because a plaintiff who has the advantage of being able to base his claim upon a precise calculation must give the defendant access to the facts which make such calculation possible."[26]

Accordingly, where in *Whalley v PF Developments*[27] the district judge refused to award damages for damage which technically should have been pleaded, the Court of Appeal reversed since by the time of trial the parties knew exactly what case they were making and meeting and there was no prejudice. And in *Arroyo v Equion Energin Ltd*[28] Stuart-Smith J, while doubting the usefulness of resorting to the terms general damages and special damages when considering whether a pleading amendment was required,[29] took the line that the level of precision required in pleading a particular head of damage should be determined by the need to provide a fair and sufficient indication of the case that was being brought and that the opposing party had to meet.[30]

The fourth meaning is a meaning of special damage only. To the rule that when a tort is actionable only upon proof of damage not all damage is special damage,[31] **3-006**
there are two clear exceptions[32]: the case of most slanders and the case of public nuisance. Since no action lies in respect of general damage to reputation in the first case, all damage is called special; and since in the second case no action is avail-

22 [1942] 1 K.B. 182 CA. Applied in *Phipps v Orthodox Unit Trusts* [1958] 1 Q.B. 314 CA.
23 [1950] 1 All E.R. 581.
24 For an illustration from sale of goods, see *Anglo-Cyprian Trade Agencies v Paphos Wine Industries* [1951] 1 All E.R. 873.
25 [1969] 1 W.L.R. 570 CA.
26 [1969] 1 W.L.R. 570 CA at 579.
27 [2013] EWCA Civ 306 CA.
28 [2013] EWHC 3150 (TCC).
29 [2013] EWHC 3150 (TCC) at [13].
30 [2013] EWHC 3150 (TCC) at [14].
31 See para.3-004, above.
32 Injurious falsehood (other than passing off) may provide a third exception. For more details, see para.51-025, below.

able to an individual for damage which is to the public generally, all damage, again, is called special. This last meaning touches upon both liability and pleading: liability depends upon the existence of the special damage, and the action will fail if the special damage is not pleaded.

### (2) NORMAL AND CONSEQUENTIAL LOSSES

**3-007** Since there is so much ambiguity in the use of the terms general and special damage, they are not relied upon to any extent in this work.[33] Only in the more particular meaning of special damage in relation to slander, and of special damage in relation to pleadings, is use made of this terminology.[34]

**3-008** Instead, another scheme of analysis is adopted. In the law of torts, where non-pecuniary losses tend to predominate, the pattern generally used is simply to consider separately the various heads of damage. But in contract, where pecuniary losses are nearly ubiquitous, and in torts concerning property which in this respect are similar to contract, another distinction is taken and built upon. This is the useful and important division between normal and particular consequential losses. In shorthand these are described as "normal" losses and "consequential" losses although, in matter of fact, both are concerned with consequences of a wrong. The normal loss is that loss which every claimant in a like situation will be expected to suffer; the "particular consequential loss" is that loss which is related to the circumstances of the particular claimant. In contract the normal loss can generally be stated as the market value of the property, money or services that the claimant should have received under the contract, less either the market value of what he does receive or the market value of what he would have transferred but for the breach. Consequential losses particular to the claimant include anything beyond this normal measure and are recoverable if not too remote. Such losses also contain a useful and important division: this is the division into the negative loss of gains that the claimant would have made had the wrong not been committed and the positive expenses to which he is put by reason of the commission of the wrong. The former is best illustrated by the claimant's loss of profits, through user or sale, from being deprived of goods through their non-delivery in breach of contract or through their tortious destruction or conversion. The latter finds a good example in the compensation a claimant buyer has to pay to his sub-buyer when the defendant seller fails to deliver the goods, delivers them late or delivers them in a defective condition. This distinction, though not frequently made use of in English law,[35] can boast Roman antiquity.[36]

**3-009** The distinction between normal measure and particular consequential losses is well brought out in the previsions as to damages in the Sale of Goods Act 1979,

---

[33] Compare Bowen LJ in *Ratcliffe v Evans* [1892] 2 Q.B. 524 CA at 529, who preferred to avoid the term "special damage" since the term, although "intelligible enough in particular contexts, tends, when successively employed in more than one context and with regard to different subject-matter, to encourage confusion in thought".

[34] See Chs 44 and 49, respectively.

[35] Compare *Chandris v Union of India* [1956] 1 W.L.R. 147 CA, where a provision in a charterparty that the charterers would pay "any expense incurred by the shipowners" was held to cover out-of-pocket expenses but not loss of time or loss of profits. This provides an illustration of the practical importance of the distinction.

[36] The Romans framed the distinction in terms of *lucrum cessans* and *damnum emergens*. See *Digest 9.2 passim* and Lawson, *Negligence in the Civil Law* (1950), pp.59 to 60.

replacing its classic forbear the Sale of Goods Act 1893 famously drafted by Chalmers in a successful endeavour to reproduce the existing common law. The second subsection of ss.50 and 51 of the Act dealing, respectively, with damages for non-acceptance and for non-delivery of goods sold each state the general measure of damages as the loss directly and naturally resulting in the ordinary course of events from the particular breach: this clearly includes all losses, both normal and consequential. The third subsection of each section states the prima facie measure of damages to be the difference between contract price and market price: this is the normal loss. Thus the normal measure of damages is, in the case of a buyer claimant, the market value of the goods that should have been received under the contract less the price that would have been transferred but for the breach and, in the case of a seller claimant, the price that should have been received less the market value of the goods that would have been transferred but for the breach. The second subsection of s.53 of the Act dealing with damages for breach of warranty is in similar terms to that of ss.50 and 51, thus including all losses, while the third subsection states the prima facie measure of damages, and therefore the normal loss, to be the difference between the market value of the goods as warranted and their value as they are. Thus the normal measure of damages here is the value of goods that the buyer should have received under the contract less the value of the goods that are received.

**(a) Scope of what is normal loss** Much of the above two paragraphs as appeared in an earlier edition of this work was successfully cited by the claimants in *Van der Garde v Force India Formula One Team Ltd*,[37] in support of the proposition that the normal measure of damages is represented by the value of the promised performance denied to the claimant[38] so as to apply beyond contracts of sale of goods to contracts for services. Contracts between the claimants, a motor racing driver and his company, and the defendant, a company which owned and operated a Formula One motor racing team, provided for the defendant, in return for a payment of $3 million which the claimants made, to permit the claimant driver to drive a Formula One racing car in testing, practising and racing for a minimum of 6,000 kilometres. In breach of contract, the defendant permitted the claimant driver to drive for only 2,004 kilometres. The claimants claimed damages on three fronts, each in the alternative, the primary claim[39] being for damages based upon the value of that part of the defendant company's promised performance which, although paid for, had been denied to the claimant racing driver. Stadlen J agreed that this represented the normal measure of damages in contracts for services as well as in contracts for the sale of goods, and upheld the claim. The effect of the decision was that damages were awarded which did not represent the particular financial loss or psychological harm suffered by the claimant. 3-010

As a matter of principle the result in this case is correct. It requires an appreciation that a normal loss is any adverse consequence experienced by anyone in a claimant's position, even if the adverse consequence might not have an effect on the claimant's financial situation or the claimant's psychological well being. A consequence of the breach of contract in *Van der Garde* was that the claimant did 3-011

37 [2010] EWHC 2373 Q.B.

38 [2010] EWHC 2373 Q.B at [414].

39 For the other two see paras 10-093 and 14-046, below. The claimants' earlier claim in restitution had failed for want of a total failure of consideration.

not receive a valuable service. That service could be valued. The result aligns neatly with the circumstance of a claimant who did not receive a promised good. However, only strands of authority were available to Stadlen J in coming to his decision. There were a few employment cases[40] in which it was accepted that, where an employee fails to carry out his duties, the employer is entitled to damages based on the value to him of the services which have not been provided, and also dicta of Sir Thomas Bingham in *White Arrow Express Ltd v Lamey's Distribution Ltd*,[41] to the effect that in the ordinary way a party who has contracted for a superior service and received an inferior one has obviously suffered a loss[42] and that the one who has been short-changed should be entitled to damages based not on the contract price but on the value of the services that he has not received. In other words, it is the market value of what is not received that is relevant and not a slice of the contract price.[43] While *Van der Garde* is not of the rendering of inferior services but of a short delivery of services, the same principles must apply. Stadlen J came to a valuation of the missing services at the high figure of $1,865,000,[44] which he awarded.[45]

3-012 **(b) The division between normal measure and (particular) consequential losses** The meaning attributed to consequential loss as all loss beyond the normal loss[46] receives substantial support in the authorities on contract, going back as far as Parke B in *Mondel v Steel*,[47] where he said that in an action for damages for the defective performance of a contract for goods sold or for services rendered, "as well the difference between the price contracted for and the real value of the articles or of the work done, as any consequential damage, might have been recovered",[48] and appearing much later at House of Lords level in *Kaye v Hosier & Dickinson*.[49] As for the field of tort, it is clear that there is an acceptance of the same meaning as between normal measure and consequential loss in torts causing damage to property[50] and in the tort of deceit[51] also.[52]

---

40 *National Coal Board v Galley* [1958] 1 W.L.R. 16 CA is the most important.

41 (1995) 15 Tr.L.R 69 CA.

42 He illustrated this by positing the case of the person who hires a luxury car and receives a small car, the person who orders an excellent meal and receives a run-of-the-mill meal, the person who contracts for violin lessons from a renowned violinist and receives violin lessons from a nonentity.

43 A point emphasised by Stadlen J at [2010] EWHC 2373 (QB) at [487].

44 Contrast the alternative award of $100,000 for the driver's loss of opportunity to advance his career, at para.10-093, below.

45 That the defendant was refused leave to appeal not only by Stadlen J but also by the Court of Appeal may be some indication that it was in agreement with Stadlen J's holding unless it was simply focusing on the merits which clearly lay with the claimants. While the decision is thought undoubtedly to be correct, conforming with the rule of being placed in the position as if the contract had been performed, it is suspected that further consideration will be given to the issue in the future.

46 See para.3-008, above.

47 (1841) 8 M. & W. 858.

48 (1841) 8 M. & W. 858 at 870.

49 [1972] 1 All E.R. 121 HL; see at 128e, 131d and especially Lord Diplock at 139c to j and 142j to 143a. See, too, *George Cohen v Dock & Inland Waterways Executive* (1950) 84 Lloyd's Rep. 97 CA, (normal loss for breach of a lessee's repairing covenant was cost of reinstatement and court spoke of "consequential damages over and above the cost of rebuilding the wall": (1950) 84 Lloyd's Rep. 97 CA at 133, col.2) and *Davis & Co v Afa-Minerva* [1974] 2 Lloyd's Rep. 27 (normal loss for failure to install adequate burglar alarm system would be the amount by which the value of an adequate system would be greater and the court said that the cost of repairing the damage done and the value of what was stolen "is consequential loss and claimable": at 32, col.2).

50 See *Workington Harbour and Dock Board v Towerfield* [1951] A.C. 112 (especially at 161); *A.M.F. International v Magnet Bowling* [1968] 1 W.L.R. 1028 (especially at 1049 to 1050); and *The*

By contrast, in the context of contractual exclusions of liability for consequential loss or damage, the courts have consistently seen the distinction between normal loss and consequential loss differently, as that between losses falling within the first and the second rules in *Hadley v Baxendale*,[53] respectively. There is today a vast array of authorities, mainly in the Court of Appeal, which hold an exclusion clause to be inapplicable because the damage or loss does not fall within the second rule in *Hadley v Baxendale*. The present law therefore being entirely clear on this, it seems no longer necessary to set out the cases in any detail and simply naming them in the footnotes should suffice.[54] The authorities start with two Court of Appeal cases of some time ago,[55] are followed by a series of four cases at the turn of the century,[56] and continue up to the present.[57] In addition, there are a number of first instance decisions covering the same period.[58] All these cases support giving to the term consequential loss the meaning which confines it to loss or damage within the second rule in *Hadley v Baxendale*. **3-013**

This whole approach, it is believed, is to be deprecated. The starting point, as in every case of construction of contracts, is the terms of the contract itself. Where those terms are expressed in general words, excluding "consequential losses" then it is very difficult to see why the consequential loss to which reference is made is not that which the law has recognised to be the losses which are particular to that individual claimant's circumstances. There is no need, with the Unfair Contract Terms Act 1977 and Consumer Rights Act 2015 on the statute book, to abandon for the protection of contracting parties the division between the normal and the consequential which has long been accepted by the general law. As for businessmen, to the extent that they are not protected by the Act, it can surely be said that they are able to look after themselves, know what they are doing when they enter contracts, and have no intention of departing from the natural meaning of consequential loss in favour of the forced and unrealistic meaning espoused by the **3-014**

---

*Eschersheim* [1975] 1 W.L.R. 83 (especially at 91) and [1976] 1 W.L.R. 339 CA (especially at 350 and 361).

51 See *Doyle v Olby* [1969] 2 Q.B. 158 CA, especially at 167A per Lord Denning MR referring to Collins MR in *McConnell v Wright* [1903] 1 Ch. 546 CA, and Lord Atkin in *Clark v Urquhart* [1930] A.C. 28, similarly, at 67–68.

52 The Victorian Court of Appeal was in full agreement in *Environmental Systems Pty Ltd v Peerless Holdings Pty Ltd* [2008] VSCA 26 with the above analysis which was cited in large part from the then current edition by Nettle JA [2008] VSCA 26 at [87]. See this Australian case further at para.3-015, below.

53 (1854) 9 Ex. 341. See paras 8-160 and following, below.

54 Facts and findings can be found at para.1-137 of the 18th edition of this book.

55 *Millar's Machinery Co v David Way & Son* (1935) 40 Com. Cas. 204 CA and *Croudace Construction v Cawoods Concrete Products* [1978] 2 Lloyd's Rep. 55 CA.

56 *British Sugar Plc v NEI Power Projects* (1998) 87 B.L.R. 42 CA; *Deepak Fertilisers and Petrochemicals Corp v ICI Chemicals & Polymers* [1999] 1 Lloyd's Rep. 387 CA; *Hotel Services Ltd v Hilton International Hotels (UK) Ltd* [2000] 1 A.E.R. (Comm) 750 CA; *Watford Electronics Ltd v Sanderson CFL Ltd* [2001] B.L.R. 143 CA.

57 *GB Gas Holdings Ltd v Accenture (UK) Ltd* [2010] EWCA Civ 912 CA; see Longmore LJ at [66].

58 *Saint Line v Richardsons* [1940] 2 K.B. 99; *Pegler Ltd v Wang (UK) Ltd* [2000] B.L.R. 218; *Addax Ltd v Arcadia Petroleum Ltd* [2000] 1 Lloyd's Rep. 493; *Choil Trading SA v Sahara Energy Resources Ltd* [2010] EWHC 374 (Comm). Yet in *Exportadora Valle de Collina SA v AP Moller-Maersk A/S* [2010] EWHC 3224 (Comm) Flaux J had no difficulty in declaring summarily, without a mention of any of the authorities, that the clause excluding liability for consequential loss in the contract before him precluded recovery for losses which, while pleaded as consequential loss, did not appear to fall within the second rule in *Hadley v Baxendale*. It may be of course that he so held because of the claimant's manner of pleading.

authorities. The abandonment of the division in contract does not sit well with its retention in tort.[59] It is also illogical and fails to make practical sense to confine consequential loss in contract to loss falling within the second rule in *Hadley v Baxendale*, being contradictory for one contracting party to communicate special circumstances to the other so as to fix him with a liability for loss to which he would not otherwise be subject and at the same time to accept an exclusion of liability in respect of the selfsame loss.[60]

**3-015** Despite the weight of authority the issue of the interpretation of the general legal term "consequential loss" for exclusion clause purposes should not be regarded as foreclosed. It has not yet reached the Supreme Court and it is significant that Lord Hoffmann, whose views carry the utmost weight, has in *Caledonian North Sea Ltd v British Telecommunications Plc*,[61] expressed a "wish to reserve the question of whether, in the context of the contracts in the *Hotel Services* and similar cases,[62] the construction adopted by the Court of Appeal was correct".[63] And there are earlier decisions at House of Lords level dealing with exclusion clauses which appear to accept the natural meaning of the division between normal measure and consequential loss.[64] Also, Australia has, as so often, seen the light. In *Environmental Systems Pty Ltd v Peerless Holdings Pty Ltd*[65] the Court of Appeal of the Supreme Court of Victoria forcefully rejected the English thinking. Citing practically all of the argument appearing in the then current edition of this work,[66] Nettle JA (now of the High Court of Australia), with whose judgment the other judges agreed, was persuaded that the analysis made in this work was right and that, as he put it, "in point of principle … the English authority appears to be flawed".[67] In consequence the court, reversing on this the judge below, held that various expenses incurred by the claimant, which constituted losses which went beyond the normal measure but were still in the ordinary course of things within the first rule in *Hadley v Baxendale*, were caught by the clause in the contract excluding liability for consequential loss.[68] This decision has since been accepted and also followed in other Australian states although, as two leading Western Australian judges have observed, the approach of Nettle JA did not prescribe a fixed and inflexible rule.[69] In South Australia Bleby J in *Alstrom Ltd v Yogowawa Australia Pty Ltd*[70] has endorsed Nettle JA, reviewing the English cases, which were not followed, and commenting that to limit the mean-

---

59 For tort, see para.3-012, above.

60 Sedley LJ said in *Hotel Services Ltd v Hilton International Hotels (UK) Ltd* [2000] 1 All ER (Comm) 750 CA at [10] that he found this argument somewhat difficult to accept but his objection to it is not thought to be convincing.

61 [2002] 1 Lloyd's Rep. 553 HL.

62 Being the major ones of the cases cited at para.3-013, above.

63 [2002] 1 Lloyd's Rep. 553 HL at [100].

64 See *Pollock & Co v Macrae*, 1922 S.C. (HL) 192 (especially as interpreted in *Mechans v Highland Marine Charters*, 1964 S.C. 48 at 64); *Gloucestershire County Council v Richardson* [1969] 1 A.C. 480 (see, especially, per Lord Wilberforce at 507A).

65 [2008] VSCA 26.

66 [2008] VSCA 26 at [90].

67 [2008] VSCA 26 at [87], referring to the four Court of Appeal decisions set out by him ([2008] VSCA 26 at [89]) which are cited in para.3-013, above.

68 [2008] VSCA 26 at [94].

69 *Patersons Securities Ltd v Financial Ombudsman Service Ltd* [2015] WASC 321 at [126], per Mitchell J; *Regional Power Corporation v Pacific Hydro Group Two Pty Ltd (No.2)* (2013) 46 W.A.R. 281 at [91]–[92], per Kenneth Martin J.

70 [2012] SASC 49.

ing of consequential losses to losses arising under the second rule in *Hadley v Baxendale* was unduly restrictive and failed to do justice to the language used.[71] The Supreme Court of New South Wales has also indicated acceptance of Nettle JA's approach,[72] as seems also to be the case with the Supreme Court of Queensland.[73]

Thus it is hoped that the day will arrive when English law finds itself able, in the words of Sedley LJ giving the judgment of the court in *Hotel Services Ltd v Hilton International Hotels (UK) Ltd*,[74] **3-016**

> "to restore to the word 'consequential' the natural meaning of which commercial and legal usage in exclusion clauses has long since robbed it".[75]

The pathway to this approach has been paved in *Transocean Drilling (UK) Ltd v Providence Resources Plc*.[76] Transocean contracted with Providence for Transocean to provide its semi-submersible drilling rig for use by Providence. Transocean breached its contract by failing to supply the rig in good working condition. Providence suffered losses from additional overheads as a result of the delay (wasted costs of personnel, equipment, and third party services). The short issue on the appeal was whether these overhead costs were "consequential losses" which had been excluded by cl.20 of the contract. There were two limbs of cl.20. The first was concerned with "any indirect or consequential loss or damages under English law". The critical words of the second limb of cl.20 applied to exclude the following to the extent that the first limb did not apply:

> "... loss of use (including, without limitation, loss of use or the cost of use of property, equipment, materials and services including without limitation, those provided by contractors or subcontractors of every tier or by third parties), loss of business and business interruption".

It was conceded that the first limb did not apply. The Court of Appeal held that the loss fell within the meaning of the second limb. Moore-Bick LJ delivered the decision with which the other Lord Justices agreed. He explained the difficulties that the expression "consequential loss" had caused in English law and questioned whether the modern English decisions described above would be decided in the same way today once it is accepted that the meaning of expressions like "consequential loss" depends upon particular context. So much can be immediately accepted. However, the particular context of cl.20 was unusually rich with detail. But this is not common. A mere reference to "consequential loss" should still permit the starting point of the courts to be that the losses which have been excluded are all those losses which are not the "normal loss" that would be suffered by any claimant in that position.

---

71 [2012] SASC 49 at [281].

72 See *Waterbrook at Yowie Bay Pty Ltd v Allianz Insurance Pty Ltd* [2008] NSWSC 1451 at [77].

73 See *MGC Properties Pty Ltd v Tang* [2009] QSC 322, at [21]–[25] where, while the earlier case was distinguished on the facts, the court appeared to agree with Nettle JA's reasoning.

74 [2000] 1 A.E.R. (Comm) 750 CA.

75 [2000] 1 A.E.R. (Comm) 750 CA at [11].

76 [2016] EWCA Civ 372.

# PART 1B: THE HEADS OF COMPENSATORY DAMAGES

CHAPTER 4

# PECUNIARY LOSSES

TABLE OF CONTENTS



**4-001** Pecuniary losses can arise from any injury, whether physical injury or not. For they refer to the type of damage and not the manner in which the damage was inflicted. Many, if not most, of the losses caused through physical injury to the claimant or his property are pecuniary ones, such as loss of earnings, loss of profits, expenses of medical treatment, costs of repair or replacement. It is as well to stress this point, since there exists, in addition to the distinction between pecuniary and non-pecuniary loss, which is the important one in damages,[1] a distinction between physical and pecuniary injury which is relevant in the totally different context of establishing a duty of care in tort.[2]

## I. CONTRACT

### 1. BASIC PECUNIARY LOSSES: THE NORMAL MEASURE OF DAMAGES

**4-002** Contracts are concerned with the mutual rendering of benefits. If one party makes default in performing his side of the contract, then the basic loss to the other party

---

1 See para.2-001, above.

2 See *Hedley Byrne & Co v Heller & Partners* [1964] A.C. 465 and subsequent cases at para.6-004, below.

is the market value of the benefit of which he has been deprived through the breach. Put shortly, the claimant is entitled to compensation for the loss of his bargain. This is what may best be called the normal measure of damages in contract.

Benefits can be classified into three principal types: **4-003**

(1) property;
(2) money;
(3) services.

Breaches of contract can similarly be classified into three basic forms[3] comprising:

(1) non-performance;
(2) delayed performance;
(3) defective performance.

Such breaches may be committed either by the transferor or by the transferee of the benefit. Since most contracts are based upon a money consideration[4] it is assumed that it is the transferee that pays money as the price of the transfer, the term "transfer" referring here not only to the transferring of property, but to the provision of money by way of loan and to the rendering of services.

### (a) Breach by transferor

*(i) Non-performance* Where the breach of contract consists in a failure to transfer property, the basic loss is the market value of the property, always deducting the contract price if it has not already been paid to the person in breach. The prime example of this is in sales of goods[5]; it will also apply to hire of goods and hire-purchase of goods,[6] to sales of stocks and shares,[7] and today[8] to all sales and leases of land. **4-004**

Where the breach of contract consists in a failure to lend money, the basic loss is the difference between the terms upon which the borrower had made the loan and the terms upon which he can go into the market and effect a substitute loan for himself.[9] **4-005**

Where the breach of contract consists in a failure to render services, the basic loss is the price the claimant would have to pay in the market in order to obtain such services, always deducting the contract price if that has not yet been paid. The best example is the contract of carriage, whether of goods or of persons. If the carrier fails to carry, the basic measure of damages is the market rate less the contract rate.[10] Also, in building and construction contracts, the measure against the defaulting builder is what it will cost the claimant to have the work done less the contract **4-006**

---

3 This is to be regarded as a basic pattern and not necessarily exhaustive.

4 It is not, however, difficult to apply the general principles dealt with in the text to the very much rarer contracts of exchange of property and/or services for property and/or services.

5 Sale of Goods Act 1979 s.51(3); compare *Barrow v Arnaud* (1846) 8 Q.B. 595 at 609 to 610.

6 There are no clear cases.

7 *Shaw v Holland* (1846) 15 M. & W. 136.

8 Since abolition in 1989 of the restrictive rule in *Bain v Fothergill* (1874) L.R. 7 H.L. 158; for details of the rule and its demise see the footnotes to para.27-005, below.

9 Compare *South African Territories v Wallington* [1897] 1 Q.B. 692 CA at 696–697, per Chitty LJ.

10 *Monarch SS Co v Karlshamns Oljefabriker* [1949] A.C. 196 (carriage of goods: failure to carry to the right place); *Hinde v Liddell* (1875) L.R. 10 Q.B. 265 at 268, per Blackburn J in argument (carriage of persons).

price.[11] Similarly, where an employer sues an employee for failure to carry out his contract of employment, the measure is the market price of similar services less the contract price.[12]

4-007 It should be noticed that in all these cases the claimant may not have performed his side of the contract or may have performed it only in part, and in these events account is taken, in making the assessment of damages, of the expense which the claimant has been saved by being relieved of the necessity of performance. The object to keep constantly in mind in contract cases is that the claimant is to be put in the position he would have been in had the contract been performed.

4-008 *(ii) Delayed performance* Where the breach consists in a delayed transfer of property, the basic loss is the market value at the date of due delivery less the market value at the date of actual delivery. The prime example is once again the sale of goods,[13] and again will apply to hire and hire-purchase of goods, to sale of stocks and shares, and today[14] to all sales and leases of land.

4-009 In assessing a delay in lending money the same type of basic loss can be worked out; there are very few authorities.

4-010 Where the breach consists in a late rendering of services, the basic loss is the value to the claimant of the services if rendered at the due date less their value at the time actually rendered. In the case of a contract of carriage of goods, the basic loss is generally their market value at the date of due delivery less their market value at the date of actual delivery.[15] Similar principles will apply in the case of building contracts and contracts of service; again there are no clear authorities.

4-011 *(iii) Defective performance* Where the breach is a transfer of property which is either defective or is not of the quality promised, the basic loss is the value of the property as represented less its market value in fact. This is well established for sales of goods[16]; it will apply mutatis mutandis to hire and hire-purchase,[17] and to sales of stocks and shares.[18] It also applies to the sale and lease of land,[19] but the cases on leases where the lessor is in breach of repair covenants indicate that the basic loss may be taken either as the diminution in the value of the claimant's interest in the property or the cost of repairs.[20]

4-012 Where the breach of contract is in the rendering of defective services the posi-

---

11 *Mertens v Home Freeholds Co* [1921] 2 K.B. 526 CA.

12 *Richards v Hayward* (1841) 2 M. & G. 574; *National Coal Board v Galley* [1958] 1 W.L.R. 16 CA.

13 Compare *Elbinger Aktiengesellschaft v Armstrong* (1874) L.R. 9 Q.B. 473 at 477, per Blackburn J citing Willes J in *Borries v Hutchinson* (1865) 18 C.B. N.S. 445 at 465. But see *Croudace Construction v Cawood Concrete Products* [1978] 2 Lloyd's Rep. 55 at para.25-040, below.

14 Since abolition in 1989 of the restrictive rule in *Bain v Fothergill* (1874) L.R. 7 H.L. 158: for details of the rule and its demise see the footnotes to para.27-005, below.

15 *Collard v S.E. Ry* (1861) 7 H. & N. 79. *The Parana* (1877) 2 P.D. 118 CA, in so far as it attempted to impose a restrictive rule not unlike the *Bain v Fothergill* rule where the carriage is by sea, was overthrown by the House of Lords in *The Heron II* [1969] 1 A.C. 350.

16 Sale of Goods Act 1979 s.53(3); *Dingle v Hare* (1859) 29 L.J.C.P. 143.

17 *Brown v Sheen and Richmond Car Sales* [1950] 1 All E.R. 1102.

18 *Lion Nathan v CC Bottlers* [1996] 1 W.L.R. 1438 HL at 1441G.

19 Sale cases are *Jenkins v Jones* (1882) 9 Q.B.D. 128 CA; *Bunny v Hopkinson* (1859) 27 Beav. 565 (both total eviction); *Eastwood v Ashton* [1913] 2 Ch. 39 (partial eviction); *Turner v Moon* [1901] 2 Ch. 825 (no good right to convey). Lease cases are *Williams v Burrell* (1845) 1 C.B. 402; *Lock v Furze* (1866) L.R. 1 C.P. 441 (both total eviction); *Rolph v Crouch* (1867) L.R. 3 Ex. 44 (partial eviction). The restrictive rule in *Bain v Fothergill* (1874) L.R. 7 H.L. 158 never applied here.

20 *Hewitt v Rowlands* (1924) 93 L.J.K.B. 1080 CA; *McCoy & Co v Clark* (1982) 13 H.L.R. 87 CA; *Calabar Properties v Stitcher* [1984] 1 W.L.R. 287 CA; *Bradley v Chorley Borough Council* (1985)

tions are more diverse. If property is affected adversely, as where there is defective performance of a building contract or where a carrier damages the goods in transit, the basic loss is the diminution in the value of the property. In the case of an ordinary service contract, however, there is no clear basic loss: perhaps most loss will be consequential.[21] And in the case of a carrier who loses the goods, the basic loss is their value less the contract price of carriage if not yet paid.[22]

Whether, in all these cases of defective performance affecting property, the claimant is entitled to measure his basic loss of the diminution in the property's value only by the diminution in market price or may, alternatively, claim the cost of putting the property into proper condition, is a question to which no clear-cut answer is possible. Each case must be looked at separately to see what is reasonable.[23] **4-013**

**(b) Breach by transferee** In all the situations up to now the claimant has been the person at the receiving end of the property, loan or services. Conversely, it may be the transferee of the property, loan or services who is in default.[24] The division into breaches by non-performance, delayed performance and defective performance does not have the same clear application here, although the cases can be worked out on this pattern. **4-014**

Non-performance is easily the most important: it will consist of failure to pay for the property, loan or services. The basic loss is worked out as the converse of the basic loss which arises on the transferor's non-performance; in other words, it is the contract price less the market price. This is so where goods sold,[25] hired[26] or hire-purchased[27] are not accepted, where shares sold are not accepted,[28] and in the case of sale[29] and lease[30] of land.[31] Similar rules apply where services are not accepted. Thus in contracts of carriage the normal measure of damages for failure to supply cargo is the contract rate of freight less the market rate, although this measure crystallised in this conventional form only slowly.[32] Wrongful dismissal of an employee also gives the normal measure in somewhat unconventional form as the contract wage subject to a deduction of any substitute wage the claimant earns or should earn in mitigation of damage.[33] And with a wrongfully dismissed agent the normal measure of damages is the amount that he would have earned under the **4-015**

---

17 H.L.R. 305 CA.

21 Compare *Lister v Romford Ice Co* [1957] A.C. 555.

22 *Rodocanachi v Milburn* (1886) 18 Q.B.D. 67 CA.

23 Compare, e.g. in relation to building contracts, *East Ham Corp v Bernard Sunley* [1966] A.C. 406 with *Applegate v Moss* [1971] 1 Q.B. 406 CA, and see *Ruxley Electronics v Forsyth* [1996] A.C. 344 at para.31-014, below. Compare *Yeoman Credit Co v Apps* [1962] 2 Q.B. 508 CA (hire-purchase) at para.26-006, below.

24 This assumes contracts in which the consideration moving from at least one party is money as opposed to the very much rarer exchange contracts.

25 Sale of Goods Act 1979 s.50(3); *Compare Barrow v Arnaud* (1846) 8 Q.B. 595 at 610.

26 See *National Cash Register v Stanley* [1921] 3 K.B. 292, *Interoffice Telephones v Freeman* [1958] 1 Q.B. 190 CA and *Robophone Facilities v Blank* [1966] 1 W.L.R. 1428 CA.

27 The authorities on hire-purchase, however, are somewhat confused: see paras 26-018 and following, below.

28 *Jamal v Moolla Dawood* [1916] 1 A.C. 175 PC.

29 *Laird v Pim* (1841) 7 M. & W. 474.

30 *Marshall v Mackintosh* (1898) 78 L.T. 750.

31 The restrictive rule in *Bain v Fothergill* (1874) L.R. 7 H.L. 158 never applied here.

32 See *Hunter v Fry* (1819) 2 B. & Ald. 421; *Smith v McGuire* (1858) 3 H. & N. 554; *Aitken Lilburn v Ernsthausen* [1894] 1 Q.B. 773 CA.

33 Since *Beckham v Drake* (1849) 2 H.L.C. 579; see at 607–608, per Erle J advising their Lordships.

contract[34]; there will be no deduction of the market value of the agent's services where, as is general, the agent will not have given his time exclusively to the principal.

4-016 Delay in payment is generally of no great importance as far as actions for damages are concerned, but they should be worked out on converse lines to the cases of delay by the transferor.

4-017 Defective performance only appears where the property transferred is intended by the contract to be returned eventually to the transferor. This is the case in leases where the lessee is in breach of his covenants, particularly the covenant to repair where the measure is the diminution in the value of the reversion in an action during the tenancy,[35] and is the cost of repairs not exceeding the diminution in the reversion's value in an action at the end of the term.[36]

## 2. Consequential Pecuniary Losses

### (1) Gains prevented by the breach

4-018 **(a) Loss of use, loss of profits, interest** Where the breach of contract consists in a failure to deliver property on time or at all, the claimant may suffer pecuniary loss by being deprived of the use of the property during the period of delay or, in the case of complete failure to deliver, until such time as he is able to procure a substitute. Similarly, where the breach of contract consists in a delivery of defective property, the claimant may be deprived of its use while the defect is being remedied or while a substitute is being acquired. This loss of use is most likely to result in a head of claim in damages when it results in loss of business profits to the claimant.[37] Such loss of business profits may be by reason of a loss of the user required to make the profits, loss of a specific sale to a third party, or loss of general custom.[38] If no such losses have been incurred or if the court refuses their recovery on the ground of remoteness, then a sum calculated by way of interest upon the property, during the period the claimant is deprived of it or before he has acquired a substitute, may be allowed.[39]

4-019 Most of the illustrations arise in contracts for the sale or for the carriage of

---

34 *Inchbald v Western Neilgherry Coffee Co* (1864) 17 C.B. N.S. 733; *Trollope v Martyn* [1934] 2 K.B. 436 CA.

35 *Doe d. Worcester School Trustees v Rowlands* (1841) 9 C. & P. 734 at 739, per Coleridge J; *Ebbetts v Conquest* [1895] 2 Ch. 377 CA at 384, 386, per Lopes and Rigby LJJ respectively; *Re King* [1962] 1 W.L.R. 632 (reversed at [1963] Ch. 459 CA but on grounds not touching the issue of damages).

36 *Morgan v Hardy* (1886) 17 Q.B.D. 770; *Joyner v Weeks* [1891] 2 Q.B. 31 CA; as limited by s.18(1) of the Landlord and Tenant Act 1927. Compare *Tito v Waddell (No.2)* [1977] Ch. 106 at para.28-055, below.

37 Where a business continues after the breach of contract, the claim must be for loss of profits and not for the value of the business as diminished by the breach: *MMP GmbH v Antal International Network Ltd* [2011] EWHC 1120 (Comm) (franchise agreement wrongly terminated). Only where the business has entirely ceased or been abandoned as a result of the breach of contract can the claim be for the value of the business. Compare *UYB. v British Railways Board* (2001) 81 P. & C.R. DG 19 CA (breach by lessor of land) at para.28-011, below

38 In *JP Morgan Chase Bank v Springwell Navigation Corp* [2006] P.N.L.R. 28 at 528 (contract for financial advice) loss of profits was held to be recoverable in addition to loss of the portfolio which would have generated the profits.

39 In *Earl's Terrace Properties Ltd v Nilsson Design Ltd* [2004] B.L.R. 273 at [63] this paragraph in the then current edition was cited and applied. But to have allowed recovery for the claimed loss of use would have gone too far in *Bella Casa Ltd v Vinestone Ltd* [2006] B.L.R. 72: see the case at para.31-019, below.

goods,[40] and where the court refuses such damages it is not because they do not form a recognised head of damage but because the damage is too remote. For reasons that are considered elsewhere[41] such damage is more likely to be held to be too remote in cases of carriage of goods than in cases of sale of goods. Nevertheless, successful claims have been made not only in sales contracts, both for loss of user profits[42] and loss of resale profits,[43] but also in carriage contracts, and again in respect of both lost user[44] and lost sale[45] profits. On the other hand, recovery for loss of custom is generally refused both in sale[46] and carriage,[47] but again this is on the ground of remoteness and not because this is an impermissible head of damage; indeed recovery has been allowed in sale.[48] In the absence of any such positive recoveries, general loss of use of property has been sometimes compensated by an award of interest as damages.[49]

**(b) Loss of future reputation, of publicity, of credit** Loss of reputation generally makes for a non-pecuniary loss but it may also involve a pecuniary one for which damages may be awarded in contract. As Hallett J said in *Foaminol Laboratories v British Artid Plastics*[50]: 4-020

> "A claim for mere loss of reputation is the proper subject of an action for defamation, and cannot ordinarily be sustained by means of any other form of action … [but] if pecuniary loss can be established, the mere fact that the pecuniary loss is brought about by the loss of reputation caused by a breach of contract is not sufficient to preclude the plaintiffs from recovering in respect of that pecuniary loss."

It is thus established that a claimant can recover for such a pecuniary loss in three particular types of case:

(1) where the wrongful dismissal of an actor[51] causes him loss of publicity[52];

---

40 *Cottrill v Steyning & Littlehampton Building Society* [1966] 1 W.L.R. 753 provides an illustration of recovery for loss of profits where the sale was of land and there was a failure to complete. For recovery for loss of use of hire-purchased goods during repair, see *Smith v Spurling Motor Bodies* (1961) 105 S.J. 967 CA and *Charterhouse Credit Co v Tolly* [1963] 2 Q.B. 683 CA at 712.

41 See para.8-214, below.

42 Important cases are: *Cory v Thames Ironworks Co* (1868) L.R. 3 Q.B. 181; *Re Trent and Humber Co Ex p. Cambrian Steam Packet Co* (1868) L.R. 4 Ch. App. 112; *Victoria Laundry v Newman* [1949] 2 K.B. 528 CA; all are delayed delivery cases. See also *Steam Herring Fleet v Richards* (1901) 17 T.L.R. 731.

43 Important cases are: *Hydraulic Engineering Co v McHaffie* (1878) 4 Q.B.D. 670 CA; *Patrick v Russo-British Export Co* [1927] 2 K.B. 535; *Hall v Pim* (1928) 33 Com. Cas. 324 HL. See also *Lyon v Fuchs* (1920) 2 Ll. L. Rep. 333; *Frank Mott v Muller* (1922) 13 Ll. L. Rep. 492; and, for a lost profits claim by seller rather than buyer, *North Sea Energy Holdings v Petroleum Authority of Thailand* [1997] 2 Lloyd's Rep. 418.

44 *Montevideo Gas Co v Clan Line* (1921) 37 T.L.R. 866 CA.

45 *Simpson v L.N.W. Ry* (1876) 1 Q.B.D. 274; *The Pegase* [1981] 1 Lloyd's Rep. 175; *Panalpina International Transport v Densil Underwear* [1981] 1 Lloyd's Rep. 187.

46 *Doe v Bowater* [1916] W.N. 185.

47 *Mann v General Steam Navigation Co* (1856) 26 L.T. O.S. 247; *The Pegase* [1981] 1 Lloyd's Rep. 175.

48 *G.K.N. Centrax Gears v Matbro* [1976] 2 Lloyd's Rep. 555 CA.

49 *British Columbia Saw Mill Co v Nettleship* (1868) L.R. 3 C.P. 499; *Heskell v Continental Express* [1950] 1 All E.R. 1033.

50 [1941] 2 All E.R. 393 at 399–400.

51 And similar persons, such as the author of a screenplay: *Tolnay v Criterion Films* [1936] 2 All E.R. 1625; compare a theatrical production company's claim for loss of publicity through not receiving

(2) where there has been a failure or a mismanagement of the advertising of the claimant's business[53]; and
(3) where the defendant fails to honour the claimant's drafts thereby causing him loss of credit,[54] or otherwise fails in breach of contract to sustain the claimant's financial credit.[55]

This head of damage may be recoverable in other types of case[56]; that these are likely to be few is suggested by the fact that in the three established types of case the loss was particularly contemplated by the parties to the contract. There is, however, one important development. For long it was accepted—erroneously, it had previously been submitted in this work—that the House of Lords in *Addis v Gramophone Co*,[57] had laid down that there could be no recovery for financial loss through loss of reputation arising from an employee's wrongful dismissal. Now in *Mahmud v Bank of Credit and Commerce International SA*,[58] the House has held that in principle damages may be awarded for such loss caused by breach of a contract of employment where the breach is of the implied term of trust and confidence.[59]

4-021 **(c) Loss of services of relatives** Very seldom will loss of the services of spouse, child or other relative ground recovery in contract, but that it is a possible head of damage is shown by the antiquated case of *Jackson v Watson*.[60] The claimant bought tinned salmon which his wife ate. On her death through food poisoning, he successfully sued the seller for damages in respect of the pecuniary loss of his wife's services, being now required to employ extra servants in the house.[61] In Farwell LJ's opinion the damages should be assessed "on the basis of the probable duration of their joint lives and the loss to the husband during that period".[62]

---

programme credits for a highly successful play: *Brighton v Jones* [2004] E.M.L.R. 26 at 507, [89] and following. Also, a dismissed apprentice can recover for his loss of training: *Dunk v George Waller & Son* [1970] 2 Q.B. 163 CA.

52 *Marbé v George Edwardes* [1928] 1 K.B. 269 CA; approved and applied in *Clayton v Oliver* [1930] A.C. 209. *Withers v General Theatre Corp* [1933] 2 K.B. 536 CA, which had limited recovery to loss of future publicity and refused damages for injury to existing reputation, was overruled in *Mahmud v Bank of Credit and Commerce International SA* [1998] A.C. 20.

53 *Marcus v Myers* (1895) 11 T.L.R. 327; *Aerial Advertising Co v Batchelors Peas* [1938] 2 All E.R. 788; but damages for the particular loss of the co-operation of magazine editresses denied: *Foaminol Laboratories v British Artid Plastics* [1941] 2 All E.R. 393.

54 *Rolin v Steward* (1854) 14 C.B. 595; *Kpohraror v Woolwich Building Society* [1996] 4 All E.R. 119 CA; *Nicholson v Knox Ukiwa & Co* [2008] P.N.L.R. 33 at 782.

55 *Wilson v United Counties Bank* [1920] A.C. 102.

56 See, e.g. *Anglo-Continental Holidays v Typaldos* [1967] 2 Lloyd's Rep. 61 CA, where travel agents were awarded damages for loss of goodwill when the shipowners with whom they had arranged a cruise substituted a smaller and less attractive ship with a less attractive timetable of stopovers at ports en route; and *Barrow v Chappell & Co* [1976] R.P.C. 355 where the award in respect of the defendant's delay in publishing a musical work composed by the claimant may be attributable to this head of damage.

57 [1909] A.C. 488.

58 [1998] A.C. 20.

59 For the details see paras 33-031 and 33-032, below. But not yet where the breach is wrongful dismissal: see *Johnson v Unisys Ltd* [2003] 1 A.C. 518 at para.33-026, below.

60 [1909] 2 K.B. 193 CA.

61 The claim for medical and funeral expenses succeeded without being contested both here and in the similar earlier case of *Frost v Aylesbury Dairy Co* [1905] 1 K.B. 608 CA.

62 [1909] 2 K.B. 193 CA at 204.

## (2) Expenses caused by the breach

Many types of expenses may be incurred by the claimant as a result of the breach which will constitute a recoverable loss. Reasonable expenditure by the claimant in inquiring and searching for goods, the delivery of which has been delayed by the defendant carrier, has been allowed[63]; the same would apply in the case of goods lost by a carrier, or where their non-delivery or delayed delivery is under a contract of sale. And where goods sold are delivered late so as to dislocate the buyer's business arrangements and thus involve him in further expense, this expenditure is often recovered as damages. Examples in the cases are of extra freight and insurance incurred by the claimant in forwarding the goods to his sub-buyer at a costlier season of the year[64]; the increased cost of building barges through the delay in the arrival of steel plates[65]; and the extra labour costs incurred in the claimant's timber-yard by reason of the late delivery of cranes.[66] Similar principles will apply where the goods sold are never delivered, and where the contract is one of carriage with non-delivery or delayed delivery.[67] Conversely, where goods sold are not accepted, recovery has been allowed for storage charges until such time as another purchaser is found.[68] Again, where defective goods have been delivered to the claimant under a contract of sale he may recover various expenditures made necessary by the defect, such as the cost of pulling down and rebuilding a wall which he had constructed with defective mortar,[69] the cost of rebuilding a factory burnt down,[70] the cost of repairing a machine broken up in processing a defective supply of steel,[71] management expenses and management and staff time taken up,[72] or medical expenses which may result where the claimant is physically injured by the defect in the goods.[73] Indeed, physical injury to the claimant will in contract generally constitute a consequential loss, and expenses of cure therefore fall within this category. So too, where there is expense incurred, in acquiring a substitute for what the defendant has failed to provide, in excess of the cost of the substitute, recovery has been allowed for such outlay, as where an evicted lessee incurs expenses in moving to, and setting up in, new premises[74]; similarly, the cost of alternative ac- **4-022**

---

63 *Hales v L.N.W. Ry* (1863) 4 B. & S. 66; *Giachetti v Speeding* (1899) 15 T.L.R. 401; *Heskell v Continental Express* [1950] 1 All E.R. 1033, see especially at 1046; and see *Woodger v G.W. Ry* (1867) L.R. 2 C.P. 318 at 321.

64 *Borries v Hutchinson* (1865) 18 C.B. N.S. 445.

65 *Watson v Gray* (1900) 16 T.L.R. 308.

66 *Henderson v Meyer* (1941) 46 Com. Cas. 209.

67 In *S.S. Ardennes (Cargo Owners) v S.S. Ardennes (Owners)* [1951] 1 K.B. 55 increased import duty charged to the claimant resulting from delayed carriage was allowed; it appears to have been admitted.

68 *Harlow & Jones v Panex International* [1967] 2 Lloyd's Rep. 509.

69 *Smith v Johnson* (1899) 15 T.L.R. 179.

70 *Harbutt's "Plasticine" v Wayne Tank & Pump Co* [1970] 1 Q.B. 447 CA.

71 *Bacon v Cooper (Metals)* [1982] 1 All E.R. 397.

72 *The Salvage Association v CAP Financial Services Ltd* (1995) 22 F.S.R. 654 at 685; *Borealis AB v Geogas Trading SA* [2011] 1 Lloyd's Rep.482; *Azzurri Communications Ltd v International Telecommunications Equipment Ltd* [2013] EWPCC 17.

73 Compare *Square v Model Dairies* [1939] 2 K.B. 365 CA (milk); *Wilson v Rickett Cockerell* [1954] 1 Q.B. 598 CA (coal).

74 *Grosvenor Hotel v Hamilton* [1894] 2 Q.B. 836 CA.

commodation may be recovered where a lessee is forced to move while his lessor's failure to repair is being remedied.[75]

**4-023** One of the most interesting and probably one of the most frequent types of recoverable expenditure involves money paid by the claimant in proceedings with a third party which have been brought about by the defendant's breach of contract.[76] Thus compensation paid to a third party, whether under a court judgment or by way of settlement, has been recovered as damages against the defendant, as where the third party is a sub-buyer of goods sold by the defendant to the claimant,[77] a person physically injured by such goods,[78] or a buyer from the claimant of goods carried by the defendant for the claimant.[79] Similarly, fines paid by the claimant under a prosecution in respect of dangerous goods sold to him by the defendant have been held recoverable as damages.[80] And there are even more cases allowing the recovery as damages of legal costs incurred by the claimant in defending such actions and prosecutions, sometimes successfully[81] but usually unsuccessfully.[82] Conversely, costs incurred by the claimant in bringing an action as a result of the defendant's breach have been recovered as damages, again whether the action has been brought successfully[83] or unsuccessfully.[84]

## 3. AN ALTERNATIVE MEASURE: RECOVERY FOR EXPENSES RENDERED FUTILE BY THE BREACH

**4-024** In all the above cases where the claimant is suing for loss of bargain it is important to keep in mind that not only must the defendant be credited with the amount the claimant has saved by no longer having to perform his side of the bargain,[85] but the claimant cannot also recover, in addition to the loss which is intended to represent the loss of his bargain, any expenses he has incurred in preparation or in part performance. Such expenses represent part of the price that the claimant has to incur to secure his bargain. If he recovers for the loss of his bargain, it would be inconsistent that he should in addition recover for expenses which were necessarily laid out by him for its attainment.[86] Thus where, as in *Re*

---

75 See *Calabar Properties v Stitcher* [1984] 1 W.L.R. 287 CA.

76 This whole subject is treated in Ch.21, below, and only a few cases are given here.

77 *Grébert-Borgnis v Nugent* (1885) 15 Q.B.D. 85 CA (non-delivery); *Elbinger Aktiengesellschaft v Armstrong* (1874) L.R. 9 Q.B. 473 (delayed delivery); *Biggin v Permanite* [1951] 2 K.B. 314 CA (breach of warranty); *Hardwick Game Farm v Suffolk Agricultural Poultry Producers Association* [1969] 2 A.C. 31 (breach of warranty); *Contigroup Companies Inc v Glencore AG* [2005] 1 Lloyd's Rep. 241 (delayed delivery).

78 *Mowbray v Merryweather* [1895] 2 Q.B. 640 CA.

79 *The Ocean Dynamic* [1982] 1 Lloyd's Rep. 88.

80 *Crage v Fry* (1903) 67 J.P. 240; *Cointat v Myham* [1913] 2 K.B. 220. But not if mens rea can be attributed to the claimant.

81 *Agius v Great Western Colliery* [1899] 1 Q.B. 413 CA. But a new regime on the recovery of costs as damages is in the air: see at paras 21-003 and following, below.

82 *Hammond v Bussey* (1888) 20 Q.B.D. 79 CA, is the leading case.

83 *Henderson v Squire* (1869) L.R. 4 Q.B. 170. But a new regime on the recovery of costs as damages is in the air: see at paras 21-003 and following, below.

84 *Randell v Trimen* (1856) 18 C.B. 786; *Bowmaker (Commercial) v Day* [1965] 1 W.L.R. 1396.

85 And credited also with any gains made possible for the claimant by the breach of contract. Thus in *Associated British Ports v Ferryways NV* [2008] 2 Lloyd's Rep. 353 (contract to provide goods handling services at a port) both such savings and such gains had to be credited: see [2008] 2 Lloyd's Rep. 353 at [55].

86 Compare *Cullinane v British "Rema" Manufacturing Co* [1954] 1 Q.B. 292 CA at 308, per Jenkins

*Daniel*,[87] buyers of land recovered for their loss of bargain upon the seller's failure to convey, they could not also recover the expenses of investigating title.[88] There are also early cases of claims for delayed delivery against carriers of goods where the claimant's expenses of hiring staff rendered fruitless by the late delivery have been disallowed.[89] The need to go this way in the assessment of bargain damages may sometimes have been lost sight of, and a double recovery involving an inconsistency of compensation allowed. This may have happened in *Hydraulic Engineering Co v McHaffie*,[90] where, on the defendant's failure to deliver on time a particular part of a machine that was designed to be used by the claimant in making the whole machine for a third party, the claimant recovered both the expense incurred in making the machine and the profits which he lost when the third party refused to take the machine because of its not being ready on time. Only if the profits claimed were net of the expense incurred would there be no double recovery, but whether the judgments are referring to gross or net profits cannot be culled from the report. So too, some of the expenditure for which recovery was allowed in *Bridge UK.Com Ltd v Abbey Pynford Plc*,[91] appears to have been expenditure which would have been incurred in order to make the profits, and should therefore not have been allowed as profits were also successfully claimed.

### (1) The alternative measure: the general rule

The law has, however, developed along the lines of allowing the claiming of wasted expenses and out-of pocket loss not in addition to, but as an alternative to, claiming for loss of bargain. In other words, a claimant is claiming not to be put into the position he would have been in had the contract been performed, but to be put into the position he would have been in had it never been made, which is a measure of damages akin to that in tort. Here it is said that it is the protection of the claimant's reliance interest rather than of his expectation interest which is achieved. In such cases expenses incurred in preparation or in part performance will be properly recoverable and will not involve an inconsistency of compensation. For a long time it was not firmly established that this alternative measure existed and was available, at his choice, to a claimant. While the awards in the several cases found could be regarded, on analysis, as applications of this alternative measure of damages, little, if anything, is said in them about wasted expenditure or expenses rendered futile and nothing on the availability to a claimant of an election between **4-025**

---

LJ who dealt with the point very clearly in relation to a claim for loss of profits.

87 [1917] 2 Ch. 405.

88 "If they had had the property conveyed to them, of course they would have had to incur all the expense of investigating the title": [1917] 2 Ch. 405 at 412, per Sargant J. Similarly, in the days when breach of promise of marriage was actionable before legislation intervened in 1970, a claimant could not recover for expenses incurred or gains forgone in anticipation of marriage in addition to obtaining damages for the loss of the benefit of the marriage: *Compare Finlay v Chirney* (1888) 20 Q.B.D. 494 CA (purchase of wedding clothes); *Riley v Brown* (1929) 98 L.J.K.B. 739 (purchase of house); *Quirk v Thomas* [1916] 1 K.B. 516 CA (giving up a business).

89 *Gee v Lancashire and Yorkshire Ry* (1860) 6 H. & N. 211; *Le Peintur v S.E. Ry* (1860) 2 L.T. 170; *Wilson v Lancashire and Yorkshire Ry* (1861) 9 C.B. N.S. 632; *Woodger v G.W. Ry* (1867) L.R. 2 C.P. 318; *Candy v Midland Ry* (1878) 38 L.T. 226. Yet where the delayed delivery has been by a seller of goods, similar losses in hiring staff have, it would seem mistakenly, been recovered or been said to be recoverable: *Waters v Towers* (1853) 8 Ex. 401; *Steam Herring Fleet v Richards* (1901) 17 T.L.R. 731; *Saint Line v Richardsons* [1940] 2 K.B. 99 at 105, per Atkinson J.

90 (1878) 4 Q.B.D. 670 CA.

91 [2007] EWHC 728 TCC.

measures. It is thought therefore that these cases can now be put on one side[92] and concentration focussed on what has followed.

4-026 *Anglia Television Ltd v Reed*,[93] can be said to be the decision that marks the turning point. Lord Denning MR with whom his brethren simply agreed, there said, in a refreshingly short judgment, that in such a case as that before the court the claimant has an election to claim for loss of profits or for his wasted expenditure[94] so that, if he cannot prove what his profits would have been, he can claim in the alternative for the expenditure which has been thrown away,[95] as the claimant in Anglia Television successfully did.

### (2) The availability of the alternative measure to a claimant

4-027 Circumstances which compel a claimant to take this route and proceed in this way are the difficulty and uncertainty in proving the amount of the benefit that would have accrued to him from the bargain.[96] This is as Lord Denning MR said in *Anglia Television v Reed*,[97] and is well illustrated by that case. The claimant television company employed the defendant actor to play the leading role in a film which the claimant had decided to make for television. When later the defendant repudiated the contract and refused to perform, the claimant was unable to find a suitable substitute for the defendant, and the film was abandoned. Being unable to prove what profit would have been obtained had the film been made with the defendant in it, a virtually impossible task for a television company unable to show a film, the claimant company claimed to recover its expenditure which had been wasted by the defendant's breach. The issue in the case was whether the claimant company could recover the expenditure which it had already incurred in employing other personnel for the projected film before entering into the contract with the defendant, and it was held that it could recover for such pre-contractual expenditure as well as for its post-contractual expenditure since it was reasonably within the

---

92 The cases are: *Molling v Dean* (1902) 18 T.L.R. 535 (buyer of defective goods rejected by sub-buyer recovered cost of their carriage to and from sub-buyer, but only on basis that not too remote); *Wallington v Townsend* [1939] 1 Ch. 588 (buyer of unconveyed land recovered conveyancing expenses); *Lloyd v Stanbury* [1971] 1 W.L.R. 535 (buyer of unconveyed land recovered not only conveyancing expenses but a host of other expenditures); *Collins v Howard* [1949] 1 All E.R. 507 (recovery of loss on repurchase of shares sold to provide funds for a project not proceeded with in breach of contract (argument only concerned remoteness, on which reversed: [1949] 2 All E.R.324 CA)). There are also some early cases against agents for breach of warranty of authority allowing recovery of expenses rendered futile by the agent's lack of authority: *Collen v Wright* (1857) 7 E. & B. 301 (affirmed (1858) 8 E. & B. 647); *Pow v Davis* (1861) 1 B. & S. 220; *Spedding v Nevell* (1869) L.R. 4 C.P. 212. For more detail in this connection on any of these cases see earlier editions of this work at Ch.2.

93 [1972] 1 Q.B. 60 CA.

94 While the Court of Appeal in the somewhat earlier *Cullinane v British "Rema" Manufacturing Co* [1954] 1 Q.B. 292 CA had already spoken in terms of such an election, this was said in a rather special situation and did not feature, as it did directly in *Anglia Television*, in the decision. This difficult and controversial case, where the claim was split into two parts, is dealt with at paras 4-044 to 4-049, below.

95 [1972] 1 Q.B. 60 CA at 64H–65A.

96 Formerly, claims for wasted expenditure were made where proceeding for loss of profits was debarred by law as well as where debarred by difficulty of proof. This arose where under the exceptional rule in *Bain v Fothergill*, (1874) L.R. 7 H.L. 158, legislatively removed in 1989, the claimant as a purchaser or lessee of land was disentitled to loss of profits and confined to recovery of the expenses thrown away, represented by the deposit paid and the cost of investigating title. For details of the rule and its demise see the footnotes to para.27-005, below.

97 See preceding paragraph.

contemplation of the parties that all the expenditure would be wasted if the contract was broken by the defendant. While this does more than put a claimant in his pre-contractual position, and therefore goes somewhat beyond the strict protection of the reliance interest, the decision is to be regarded as based on the assumption that a contracting party expects to cover his expenses by the profit he makes and as therefore giving him his potential loss of profit to the limit of his expenditure, whether pre-contractual or post-contractual. Beyond this, it is thought that a claimant should be entitled to claim wasted expenditure in circumstances where no profit was anticipated because the claimant was a non-profit-making body. Indeed the damages which are given for the loss of use of non-profit-earning chattels, in particular ships,[98] tend to be based upon the expenditure which has been laid out on their acquisition and upkeep.[99]

### (3) The limitations on claiming the alternative measure

While in *Anglia Television v Reed*,[100] Lord Denning MR stated that a claimant claiming damages for breach of contract had an election to claim for loss of profits or for wasted expenditure rendered futile, and in *C.C.C. Films (London) v Impact Quadrant Films*,[101] Hutchison J held that a claimant had an unfettered choice to claim one measure or the other,[102] there are undoubted limitations upon the entitlement to claim on the basis of reliance as distinct from the basis of expectation. In effect, the reliance measure is not a measure separate from, and independent of, the expectation measure but is a measure governed by the principle upon which the expectation measure is based, the principle, as stated famously by Baron Parke in *Robinson v Harman* in 1848,[103] that the claimant is entitled to be put in the same position as if the contract had been performed. Reliance damages cannot go beyond what would be recoverable on the expectation basis. By far the principal reason for a claimant's being unable to claim the alternative measure is where he has made a bad bargain but other situations in which the alternative measure is not available because taking the claimant beyond expectation interest damages have appeared. 4-028

**(a) Where the claimant has made a bad bargain** There is no entitlement to recover damages based on reliance expenditure where the claimant has made a bad bargain; he cannot put himself in a better position than if the contract had been properly performed. This was for long an unconsidered issue but, a decade after *Anglia Television* had established the availability of the election between the two measures of damages,[104] the issue came before the Court of Appeal in *C&P Haul-* 4-029

98 See paras 37-056 and following, below

99 The unusual Australian case of *McRae v Commonwealth Disposals Commission* (1951) 84 C.L.R. 377 is particularly instructive in the context of wasted expenditure and difficulty in proving profit loss. The claimant bought from the defendants an oil tanker together with its contents which the defendants had advertised as lying off a named reef and as containing oil. The claimant went to considerable expense to reach and salvage the tanker but it turned out that neither tanker nor reef existed. The claimant successfully claimed as damages the expenses he had incurred to no avail. This case is best known on the issue of when a contract is void for common mistake; yet it is thought that the consideration of what damages were claimed and awarded is relevant here.

100 [1972] 1 Q.B. 60 CA.

101 [1985] Q.B. 16.

102 [1985] Q.B. 16 at 32A–D. See the case at para.4-030, below.

103 Cited at para.2-003, above.

104 See para.4-026, above.

*age v Middleton.*[105] In a contract for the licence of premises for use in the licensee's vehicle repair business, it was provided that any fixtures put in should remain. The licensee executed extensive works to make the premises suitable for his purposes. When he was unlawfully and summarily ejected, a sympathetic local council agreed, despite their earlier objection, to his carrying on the business in the garage at his house, which was at no rent. Also, his ejection came only 10 weeks before the licensors, as was held, would have lawfully terminated the licence. The breach of contract had thus caused the licensee no damage. On his claim to recover for the expenditure he had incurred on the premises, he was awarded only nominal damages, as damages for breach of contract did not include compensating an injured party for entering into the contract or a sum to place him in a better financial position than if the contract had been properly performed. Ackner LJ cited extensively from the judgment of Berger J in the equivalent British Columbian case of *Bowlay Logging v Domtar*,[106] a case cited in this connection in the then current edition of this work[107]; in that judgment Berger J said:

> "If the law of contract were to move from compensating for the consequences of breach to compensating for the consequences of entering into contracts, the law would run contrary to the normal expectations of the world of commerce. The burden of risk would be shifted from the plaintiff to the defendant. The defendant would become the insurer of the plaintiff's enterprise. Moreover, the amount of the damages would increase not in relation to the gravity or consequences of the breach but in relation to the inefficiency with which the plaintiff carried out the contract."[108]

**4-030** The placing of the onus of proof of a bad bargain becomes crucial since whether the claimant's receipts would have exceeded his outlay or whether he might even have gone on to make a net profit, is a question to which it will often be difficult, if not impossible, for either claimant or defendant to offer a resolution. In *CCC Films (London) v Impact Quadrant Films*[109] Hutchison J arrived at the sensible conclusion that the onus lay on the defendant to prove that the bargain was a bad one. A licence to exploit, distribute and exhibit in various countries three films was granted to the claimants by the defendants for a consideration of US $12,000. The consideration was paid but the taped recordings of the films were, in breach of contract, sent uninsured and by ordinary post by the defendants and never arrived at their destination. Without these tapes the claimants were unable to make effective use of the licence. They claimed as damages for breach of the contract the US $12,000 expended by them in acquiring the licence. Neither the claimants nor the defendants adduced any evidence on whether the claimants would have lost profits or but for the breach of contract would have recouped their expenditure. Hutchison J held that, while damages for wasted expenditure were unavailable if the expenditure would not have been recouped had the contract been properly performed, the burden was on the defendant to show this was so and thereby to displace the claimant's prima facie right to claim for his wasted expenditure.[110] Accordingly, as the defendants had failed to discharge this burden the claimants were

---

105 [1983] 1 W.L.R. 1461 CA.

106 [1978] 4 W.W.R. 105.

107 14th edn (London: Sweet & Maxwell, 1980).

108 [1978] 4 W.W.R. 105 at 117; quoted at [1983] 1 W.L.R. 1461 CA, 1467F–G.

109 [1985] Q.B. 16.

110 A claimant should therefore use care in his choice. Required by the court in *Anglo Group Plc v Winther Browne & Co* (2001) 72 Con. L.J. 118 to choose between wasted expenditure and lost

entitled to recover the US $12,000 by way of damages. Hutchison J recognised that *Anglia Television v Reed*,[111] was a decision consistent with his own holding[112] but relied principally on the express holdings in, once again, the *Canadian Bowlay Logging v Domtar*,[113] and in two American cases, one of which, *L. Albert & Son v Armstrong Rubber Co*,[114] has long been an important authority in the United States of America.[115] While stating that, even without the assistance of such authorities, he would have held on principle that the onus was on the defendant,[116] he expressly adopted the reasoning of Learned Hand CJ in *Albert & Son v Armstrong Rubber Co*,[117] the key sentence of which deserves quoting, namely:

> "It is often very hard to learn what the value of the performance would have been; and it is a common expedient, and a just one, in such situations to put the peril of the answer upon that party who by his wrong has made the issue relevant to the rights of the other."[118]

Hutchison J's decision has undoubtedly assisted claimants over the years. A contemporary illustration of this is found in *Yam Seng Pte v International Trade Corporation Ltd*.[119] The defendant company being in breach of a contract granting the claimant company the right to distribute fragrances, the claimant was entitled to recover its wasted expenditure as the defendant had not attempted to discharge the burden of showing the financial return the claimant would have made had there been no breach.[120] **4-031**

**(b) Situations other than that of the bad bargain** The true basis of the reliance measure allowing recovery of wasted expenditure was examined and considered at length by Teare J in a penetrating judgment in *Omak Maritime Ltd v Mamola Challenger Shipping Co*.[121] The question as to true basis arose in the context of a long-term time charterparty terminated as a result of the owners' acceptance of the charterers' repudiation in unusual circumstances. The charterers had repudiated because of their inability to enter into an intended sub-charter, and repudiation came at a time when the market rate of hire was higher than the charterparty rate of hire. The owners were therefore able to trade their ship at the higher market rate unrestricted by the lower contract rate. They nevertheless claimed as damages the expenses they had incurred in preparing to perform the charterparty, the charterparty requiring them to make substantial modifications to the ship prior to its delivery, and arbitrators decided in their favour. **4-032**

After a thorough review of the authorities considered in the above paragraphs, Teare J came to the sensible conclusion that both the expectation claim and the reli- **4-033**

profits, the claimant chose lost profits and then failed to prove any. Had he opted for wasted expenditure, he would have passed the onus of proof on lost profits to the defendant.

111 [1972] 1 Q.B. 60 CA; see the case at para.4-027, above.

112 [1985] Q.B. 16 at 38E to F.

113 [1978] 4 W.W.R. 105; see para.4-029, above.

114 178 F. (2d) 182 (1949).

115 The other case was *Dade County v Palmer & Baker Engineers Inc* 339 F. (2d) 208 (1965).

116 [1985] Q.B. 16 at 38E to F.

117 178 F. (2d) 182 (1949).

118 178 F. (2d) 182 (1949) at 189; quoted at [1985] Q.B. 16 at 39F.

119 [2013] EWHC 111 (QB).

120 [2013] EWHC 111 (QB) at [186] and following.

121 [2011] 1 Lloyd's Rep. 47.

ance claim are governed by Baron Parke's principle,[122] which requires the court to make a comparison between the claimant's present position and what it would have been had the contract been performed.[123] Accordingly, since the owners, by trading their ship at the higher market rate had more than recuperated the wasted expenditure, they were not entitled to damages. The appeal was allowed and the arbitrators' award set aside.[124]

4-034 *Omak* was followed in *Ampurius Nu Homes Holdings Ltd v Telford Homes (Creekside) Ltd*.[125] A claim for wasted expenditure which had been incurred in a property development contract failed not because the claimant was seeking to escape from a bad bargain as it genuinely believed the contract to be for its advantage but because the defendant had established that the claimant would not have made a profit from the contract such as would have absorbed the expenditure claimed.[126] And a further situation, the bad bargain apart, where a claimant may not be entitled to sue for wasted reliance expenditure because it would put him in a better position than if the contract had been properly performed, can arise in the somewhat peculiar contract of warranty of authority where the authority warranted is the authority of a solicitor agent to conduct litigation on behalf of a principal.[127]

4-035 **(c) Where there is also a claim for loss of bargain** Implicit in what has been said above lies an entirely different form of limitation. While a claimant can elect for the alternative reliance measure based on wasted expenditure, he cannot claim it and the expectation measure in the alternative. For this reason the claim for wasted expenditure received short shrift from the Court of Appeal in *Filobake Ltd v Rondo Ltd*,[128] since it was attempted to be made as well as a claim for lost profits. The defendant had supplied the claimant with equipment for use in its business as a manufacturer of pastry products. Following installation and payment the claimant came to view the equipment as unable to produce pastry in accordance with its requirements and therefore as not fit for its purpose. Its claim for damages was first and foremost for loss of profits but this claim failed miserably on the altar of proof. Fearing such failure the claimant very late in the day had advanced in the alternative the claim for wasted expenditure, seeking leave to amend particulars of claim and grounds of appeal accordingly. Leave was refused. The Court of Appeal pointed out that, while a claimant may always have a choice between lost profits and wasted expenditure, it was not permissible to run the two claims in the alternative.[129] Indeed since the authorities indicated that the claim for wasted expenditure was available

---

122 See para.4-028, above.

123 [2011] 1 Lloyd's Rep. 47 at [65].

124 The same result could have been achieved in *Omak* by the application of mitigation principles, in particular by resort to Viscount Haldane's famous exposition in *British Westinghouse Co v Underground Railway* in 1912 of the rule that, when a contracting party has taken action arising out of the transaction which has diminished his loss, the effect in diminution of the loss by that action is to be taken into account. Here there can be no doubt that the owners' trading of their ship at the higher rate was such an action. Indeed in his conclusion Teare J added in the mitigation point to his basic ground. But there was no need to resort to the principles of mitigation by way of avoided, as distinct from avoidable, loss. The correct solution came without them.

125 [2012] EWHC 1820 Ch.

126 See [2012] EWHC 1820 Ch. at paras [131] and following and [149].

127 See the discussion and cases at paras 36-020 to 36-022, below, especially the references to Eve J's judgment in *Fernée v Gorlitz* [1915] 1 Ch. 177.

128 [2005] EWCA Civ 563 CA.

129 [2005] EWCA Civ 563 CA at [64].

only where it was difficult or impossible for the claimant to prove what profit had been lost, such a claim could hardly be available to a claimant who was attempting, even if unsuccessfully, to recover for loss of profits.[130] The Court of Appeal also rightly considered it a serious objection to running the two claims together that the burden of proof under a lost profits claim lay with the claimant but under a wasted expenditure claim, as we have seen, lay with the defendant.[131]

### (4) Expectation, reliance and restitution

So far we have been concerned with only two interests of the victim of a breach of contract, that represented by his expectation from the contract and that represented by his reliance on the contract. Yet the common law now recognises a third and fourth interest: restitution and disgorgement. Restitution looks to the removal and reversal of benefits acquired under the contract by the contract breaker. It might arise as an action for unjust enrichment or it could be based upon a breach of contract. Disgorgement looks to the stripping of causally related profits from the contract breaker. Although the quantum of an award based on any interest might, in some circumstances, equal another, this does not mean that any interest is a "back door" version of the other. Each is motivated by different concerns. Hence, in *Baturina v Chistyakov*[132] counsel was right to refuse an invitation to submit that the reliance interest was an illegitimate attempt to seek restitution by the "back door". The wasted expenditure for which recovery was allowed was different in character as between *Anglia Television Ltd v Reed*[133] and *CCC Films (London) v Impact Quadrant Films*.[134] In *Anglia* it was the television company's expenditure in employing personnel other than the defendant for its projected film, an expenditure which in no way benefited the defendant; in *Quadrant* it was the expenditure of US $12,000 representing the consideration for the acquisition of the licence, an expenditure which was of direct benefit to the defendant. Thus only the reliance interest could be in issue in the one, but both the reliance and restitution interests were present in the other.[135] **4-036**

Three interests were in play in the Court of Appeal decision in *Grange v Quinn*,[136] where the three members of the court were in sharp disagreement with one another as to the right approach to the facts of the case, only a majority decision emerging. The claimant had taken a six year lease of property together with the business, a sandwich shop, which was run on the property, paying a premium of £10,000. After six months she was wrongfully evicted by the defendant. She initially brought a claim for loss of profits but difficulties of proof caused her to switch to claiming the premium as damages. The Recorder decided that, had the lease continued, she would never have been able to generate sufficient profits to recover the premium she had paid, and dismissed her claim. In the Court of Appeal Arden LJ accepted the Recorder's analysis and, on the basis that here was a bad bargain where the reli- **4-037**

130 [2005] EWCA Civ 563 CA at [65].

131 [2005] EWCA Civ 563 CA at [64].

132 [2017] EWHC 1049 (Comm) at [230].

133 [1972] 1 Q.B. 60 CA.

134 [1985] Q.B. 16.

135 The *locus classicus* distinguishing three interests, although conflating restitution and disgorgement and not recognising that the source of restitution could be the breach of contract or a separate claim for unjust enrichment, is the celebrated article by Fuller and Perdue appearing in two parts in the *Yale Law Journal* of 1936-37: The Reliance Interest in Contract Damages, 46 Yale L. J. 52 and 373.

136 [2013] EWCA Civ 24 CA.

ance expenditure would never have been recouped, would have dismissed the claimant's appeal. In contrast was Gloster J, as she then was, who thought that the Recorder had got it all wrong and, re-analysing the evidence, was satisfied that the defendant had not shown that the claimant had made a bad bargain. On this basis the appeal was allowed. In her analysis she drew attention to the important point that the authorities show that to succeed the defendant must show that it is from the gross returns, rather than the net, that the claimant would not have recouped the expenditure.[137] The premium was recoverable subject to a credit being given for the benefit to the claimant of her six months' occupation before eviction. Jackson LJ abandoned the wasted expenditure approach entirely, being of the view that a lessee evicted early in the course of the lease was entitled to the normal measure of damages of the price paid for the lease plus, where appropriate, any incidental expenses.[138] There was no need to embark upon detailed calculations to see whether the claimant had paid too much for the lease. He cited and relied on the similar case of a lessee's eviction in *Sampson v Flood*[139]where the Court of Appeal held correct the trial judge's award of the amount paid for the lease together with the conveyancing fees, being, as Sir George Waller noted, the amount the lessee was out of pocket. Accordingly, Jackson LJ too was prepared to allow the appeal, agreeing with Gloster J that recovery of the premium be subject to a credit for the short occupation, and leaving us with somewhat of a difficulty in formulating the true ratio decidendi of the decision.

**4-038** The approach of Arden LJ and Gloster J is orthodox and acceptable, even if they come to different conclusions on the facts, but Jackson LJ's way of finding the claimant entitled to repayment of the premium must be challenged.[140] The normal measure of damages for a lessee's eviction is not to be measured by the price paid but by the value of the unexpired term of the lease, as is recognised by Gloster J in her well crafted and reasoned judgment.[141] In other words the normal measure reflects, as it should, the expectation interest and not the reliance interest. This then means that, without knowing it, he was taking the wasted expenditure route in awarding, in effect, reliance damages. So too *Sampson v Flood* is, on analysis, an application of the alternative measure allowing recovery of wasted expenditure, as is also recognised by Gloster J.[142]

**4-039** Moving next to the restitution interest, the difficult question is, as pointed out in previous editions of this work, whether the extent of restitution is controlled by the contract where the claimant has made a bad bargain so that he is debarred from claiming his wasted expenditure by way of his reliance interest. Although Jackson LJ was treating the matter before him as one of damages, he clearly did not think the extent of restitution was controlled by the contract as he adopted the suggestion, from a previous edition of this work, that the purchase price fell into a different category from other heads of wasted expenditure, saying that, to a claim by the purchaser of an asset for return of the price paid by him where the seller through breach has the asset in his hands, it is hardly a good defence that the asset was worth

---

137 [2013] EWCA Civ 24 CA at [102] and [103].

138 [2013] EWCA Civ 24 CA at [82] and [83].

139 [1989] 2 E.G.L.R. 49 CA.

140 Although grateful for his various approving references to this work.

141 [2013] EWCA Civ 24 CA at [98], referring to the normal measure as stated in a previous edition of this work.

142 [2013] EWCA Civ 24 CA at [97].

much less than had been paid for it.[143] And he added that it would be manifestly unjust if in such circumstances the seller could retain the asset and still keep the purchase price.[144] Gloster J commented that the simplicity, and indeed the fairness, of this approach had considerable attraction but indicated that, without argument directed to the point, and in particular to the relationship between damages and restitution in this context, a decision on the matter was for another day.[145] The matter needs then to be addressed here.

No English case has to date squarely faced the question of whether one who has **4-040** purchased at an over-value, and paid for, an asset may recover the price from a seller who in breach of contract has not delivered the asset. We need to look elsewhere in the common law for the answer and we find that in the United States of America a right of recovery has long been recognised, exemplified by the early *Bush v Canfield*.[146] The plaintiff bought from the defendant 2,000 barrels of wheat flour at a price of US $7 a barrel, paying US $5,000 in advance with the residue to be paid by instalments after delivery. At the time of due delivery the price of flour stood at US $5.50 a barrel. The defendant never delivered. The plaintiff brought suit for damages and recovered his US $5,000, the court rejecting the defendant's argument that the damages should be limited to the value of the flour.[147] This is in effect a restitutionary claim for unjust enrichment, allowed by being regarded as existing independently of the contract. In other words, whereas, as we have seen, the reliance interest is controlled by the expectation interest, the restitution interest, where based on unjust enrichment, is not. It should be noted, however, that in the United States this solution may not be afforded where the claimant has rendered services, rather than paid money, to the defendant under a losing contract and the defendant in breach of contract does not pay the claimant for the services. Here there has been a long-running debate over whether the restitutionary measure should be subject to the contractual ceiling. There are cases going either way.[148] One well-known and controversial case where the contractual ceiling was ignored is *Boomer v Muir*,[149] the claimant being awarded on a quantum meruit an amount greatly in excess of the contract price. The reason for imposing the contract price as a ceiling on recovery appears to be that it may not be easy to ascertain precisely what the services rendered are worth to the defendant, and from the restitutionary angle it is his benefit that matters. We may ask, however, in terminology coming from an early era, whether there should be a difference between a claim for money had and received and a quantum meruit for services.

With money paid by the claimant the above analysis is all very well where the **4-041** claimant has received nothing from the defendant in part performance of his obligations under the contract, but where the defendant has part performed we in England

---

143 [2013] EWCA Civ 24 CA at [84].

144 [2013] EWCA Civ 24 CA at [85].

145 [2013] EWCA Civ 24 CA at [108].

146 2 Conn. 485 (1818).

147 Chief Justice Swift put the position well. "The defendant has violated his contract; and it is not for him to say, that if he had fulfilled it, the plaintiffs would have sustained a great loss, and that this ought to be deducted from the money advanced. … The plaintiffs have been disappointed in their arrangements; the defendant has neglected his duty; and retains in his hands five thousand dollars of the money of the plaintiffs, without consideration. Nothing can be more just than that he should refund it".

148 See the long lists of cases going the one way in fn.90 and of cases going the other way in fn.91 of s.68.14 of the many volumed *Williston on Contracts*, 4th edn (USA: Thomson Reuters, 2003).

149 24 P.2d 570 (Cal.App.1933).

have to contend with the rule, unsatisfactory but still with us, that a total failure of consideration is required before the claim in restitution, by way of an action for money had and received, emerges. Thus in the important *Quadrant* case[150] Hutchison J noted that counsel for the defendants had contended that the claimants could not maintain a claim for restitution,[151] and this was presumably on the ground that they would be unable to show a total failure of consideration. In the recent case of *Khan v Malik*[152] the trial judge, having taken the mistaken view that wasted expenditure did not include the payment of money so as to be recoverable under the reliance measure in the absence of a bad bargain[153] and that therefore the payment of money was recoverable only in unjust enrichment, being by an action for money had and received on a total failure of consideration, took the further view that it would undermine the requirement that there be a total failure of consideration before the victim of the breach of contract could recover his moneyas restitution of unjust enrichment if the same result could be achieved simply by claiming the money by way of damages.[154] Yet to go along these lines puts paid to Jackson LJ's approach in *Grange v Quinn* where, ignoring damages by way of wasted expenditure, he was prepared to award as damages the £10,000 premium paid by the claimant but only after crediting, as proposed by Gloster J, the value of the six months' occupation that the defendant had allowed her.[155] At the same time Jackson LJ's approach is attractive because it leads to a fair result and, as Gloster J saw, would be required where the wasted expenditure route could not be taken in the presence of a bad bargain. And it is thought that this fair result can be achieved.

**4-042** For today not only do we have restitution in play for unjust enrichment in the contractual context but also we have restitutionary damages and in the new world of restitutionary damages a favourable outcome lies. Restitutionary damages for a wrong such as breach of contract, as we will see in Ch.14 of this book, are the counterpart to restitution for unjust enrichment. The measure of restitution should be identical in each case, subject to the possibility of different defences. The defendant's gain by way of purchase money less his partial performance is greater than the claimant's loss by virtue of his having made a bad bargain, and that gain should be restored to the claimant. From what Jackson LJ and Gloster J said in *Grange v Quinn*,[156] it would seem that they would agree.

**4-043** The final interest is disgorgement of profits or, the label which is preferred in Ch.15, disgorgement damages. These are a money award for a wrong (hence, "damages") which strip a defendant of profits made as a result of the wrong. They are particularly attractive when the profit gained by the contract breaker is greater than the loss suffered by the victim of the breach. As Lord Mance, when in the Court of Appeal in *Experience Hendrix v PPX Enterprise Inc*,[157] put it, the decision in *Attorney General v Blake*,[158] leaves future courts with the task of hammering out on

---

150 At para.4-030, above.

151 [1985] Q.B. 16 at 29A.

152 [2011] EWHC 1319 Ch.

153 Mistaken because clearly inconsistent with the decision in the *Quadrant* case and the reasoning in *Grange v Quinn*, both of which were concerned with payments of money made in reliance on the contract.

154 [2011] EWHC 1319 Ch at [130].

155 See the analysis of the case at para.4-037, above.

156 See their comments at para.4-039, above.

157 [2003] EWCA Civ 323 CA at [16].

158 [2001] 1 A.C. 268.

the anvil of decided cases[159] when and how far disgorgement damages should be available. It is therefore suggested that we have here a further category where justice requires that disgorgement damages be allowed.

### (5) The significance of the Cullinane decision

*Cullinane v British "Rema" Manufacturing Co*,[160] is a controversial decision of a majority of the Court of Appeal in this area of the law dating from the middle of the last century. For long it was cited just for its clear statement, probably the first one, that a claimant may choose between expectation damages and reliance damages but cannot have both. Now in the 21st century it has taken on a mystique of its own, which takes it beyond this to the general statement that a claimant cannot claim both capital outlay and income profits. We find Chadwick LJ, delivering the judgment of the Court of Appeal in *Filobake Ltd v Rondo Ltd*,[161] making reference to "the *Cullinane* principle",[162] to claimant's counsel's speaking of what he had to establish to come "within the *Cullinane* rule"[163] and to defendant's counsel's arguing "in the context of the *Cullinane* jurisprudence".[164] Yet no one seems to be quite sure what the case stands for, Chadwick LJ also referring to "the [then] 51 years for which whatever *Cullinane* does decide has been the law".[165] The case must therefore now be examined with great care. **4-044**

The claimant bought a clay pulverising plant from the defendants who warranted that the plant would be able to pulverise the claimant's clay at a specified rate. This it failed to do. The claimant claimed damages in respect of the capital expended in buying and assembling the plant, allowance being made for its residual value and an outstanding amount of the purchase price. In addition he claimed damages for loss of profits, stated in the pleadings to be for the first year after delivery of the plant "and continuing". The estimated useful life of the plant was 10 years and in the course of the proceedings the defendants asked the plaintiff to specify what was meant by "and continuing". The answer received gave rise, in the view of Evershed MR, to the whole difficulty in the case.[166] "And continuing" was stated to refer to the period up to the date of the trial which was, as it happened, to the very day three years after delivery of the plant to the claimant. It was accepted that the claimant could not claim both for loss of capital and for loss of profit if he had not placed this limitation on the profit. Did then placing this limitation make a difference? To examine this it is necessary to look separately at the position in the first three years and in the remaining seven years. **4-045**

A claim for loss of profits can be set out in one of two ways. On the facts of *Cullinane* the claimant could simply claim the estimated amount of the profits he would have made by use of the plant or, producing the same result, he could claim recoupment of his capital outlay on the plant and in addition the excess of the estimated profits over the amount of the capital outlay. From the particulars of damage in the **4-046**

---

159 The phrase of Lord Steyn in the appeal in *Blake* [2001] 1 A.C. 268.
160 [1954] 1 Q.B. 292 CA.
161 [2005] EWCA Civ 563 CA.
162 [2005] EWCA Civ 563 CA at [60].
163 [2005] EWCA Civ 563 CA at [61].
164 [2005] EWCA Civ 563 CA at [66].
165 [2005] EWCA Civ 563 CA at [68].
166 [1954] 1 Q.B. 292 CA at 304.

claimant's pleadings, which are fully set out at the beginning of the case report,[167] it would seem that he had attempted to employ the second of these methods in calculating his loss of profits for the first three years of plant usage. Thus there first appears the detail of his capital outlay[168] which is followed by a loss of profits calculation,[169] being the receipts generated by the plant in three years after deduction of the original capital outlay attributable to three years, confusingly referred to as depreciation. This was sufficient to satisfy Morris LJ, who dissented, that the award below of what he called the net loss of profits together with the capital outlay should be upheld. By contrast, Evershed MR and Jenkins LJ considered, rather surprisingly, that the amount deducted was insufficient to leave only the excess of profits over expended capital and they therefore allowed the appeal, holding the claimant entitled to his loss of profits figure only. Both said specifically that by the award below the claimant was being given his damages "twice over".[170] Chadwick LJ was therefore right in saying in *Filobake Ltd v Rondo Ltd*,[171] at least in respect of the claim for the first three years of the plant's operation, that the holding on the Cullinane facts that the overlap between the loss of profits and the installation expenses meant that, to allow both, would grant double compensation was as far as *Cullinane* went. To this extent there is nothing new as it has always been acknowledged that the alternative measure based on capital outlay is alternative to, and in no way cumulative with, the conventional measure based on loss of profits.

**4-047** Turning to the position with the remaining seven years that the plant could have operated, the majority of the court considered that a claim for loss of profits based on capital outlay together, presumably, with the excess of receipts over such outlay was possible but, as the claimant had chosen not to claim profits for the remaining seven years, no award fell to be made.[172] However, Morris LJ in dissent was prepared to award the capital outlay over the remaining seven years of the plant's useful life, and it is thought that this should be acceptable because, although in one sense it could be regarded as a claim for potential loss of profit up to the limit of the claimant's capital expenditure—and loss of profit was not being claimed for the remaining seven years—it could equally be regarded as a claim based on the alternative measure. This possibility led to the thought, expressed in earlier editions of this work, that it might be possible to divide or split one's claim so as to sue as to part for loss of profits and as to part for expenditure rendered futile by the breach, called again, in the terminology now appearing, wasted expenditure.[173] However, this possibility cannot be said to form part of the conclusion of *Cullinane* being only part of the thinking prompted by Morris LJ's dissent and, in addition, it is dependent upon claimants limiting their loss of profits claim in time, as

---

167 [1954] 1 Q.B. 292 CA at 293 to 294.

168 In paras A, B and C of the particulars of damage.

169 In para.E of the particulars of damage.

170 [1954] 1 Q.B. 292 CA at 307 and 312 respectively.

171 [2005] EWCA Civ 563 CA at [60].

172 See Evershed MR at [1954] 1 Q.B. 292 CA at 306–307.

173 In the earlier *Foaminol Laboratories v British Artid Plastics* [1941] 2 All E.R. 393 the claimant intended to put on the market a summer cream for which the defendant was supplying the containers. The defendant failed to deliver them in time and the market was lost to the claimant, who recovered damages for advertising and other expenses incurred in preparation for the intended sales, and for loss of profits on the initial sales. Hallett J pointed out, at p.395, that this was not giving the advertising expenditure twice over "because this advertising expenditure was not intended merely to promote and produce these initial sales" but also future sales. While this was not a double recovery, it did involve a split claim.

was done in *Cullinane*, a situation which seems unlikely to arise.[174] Certainly, no cases similar to Cullinane have made their appearance in the 60 years since that decision.

That a claim for loss of capital outlay may feature in a computation of lost profit **4-048** is brought out in the judgment of the High Court of Australia in *T C Industrial Plant Pty v Robert's Queensland Pty*,[175] where the court examined the *Cullinane* decision in great detail, coming to much the same conclusions on it as set out above with the result that the High Court was prepared to hold that the buyer of a stone-crushing machine was entitled to claim not only the outlay incurred by him but also the profits lost to him because the machine was not up to warranty. This was on the basis that the lost profits claimed were limited to the excess of the estimated profits over the amount of the capital outlay.[176] At first instance the official referee had awarded a sum for capital outlay together with a sum for lost profits and it was only because it was not clear to the High Court how he had arrived at his figure for lost profits and whether it was limited to the excess over capital outlay that the matter was sent back for further consideration.[177]

The result of all this is that there can be said to be no special *Cullinane* rule, *Cullinane* principle or *Cullinane* jurisprudence. All that *Cullinane* does is to confirm, **4-049** in a very unusual situation, that reliance claims for wasted capital expenditure and expectation claims for lost income profits stand separately and that therefore, should there be an overlap between the two, this is unacceptable. That the claims stand separately was already implicitly accepted by the time of *Cullinane* and is much more clearly illustrated by the *Anglia Television* case.[178] *Cullinane* in this century has bedevilled the courts, being used to support the argument that capital and income claims always lie in the alternative whereas the decision is only applicable in the context of alternative claims for expectation damages and reliance damages. So in *Browning v Brachers*,[179] where the claimants ran a business of rearing goats on their farm and were claiming against the defendant for selling them a diseased goatherd,[180] *Cullinane* was wrongly invoked to argue that they could not claim both for the resultant diminution in the capital value of the farm and for the resultant loss of profits. The argument was rejected both at trial and by the Court of Appeal. Such a claim did not involve double counting as the claimants had two distinct assets, the business and the farm, so that a combination of compensation for the revenue loss of profits and the capital loss in the value of the farm was appropriate.[181] *Cul-*

---

174 Allowing a split or divided claim is open to the objection that the burden of proof on one part of the claim would be on the claimant and on the other part on the defendant, an objection which is pointed to by the Court of Appeal in *Filobake Ltd v Rondo Ltd* [2005] EWCA Civ 563 CA at para.4-035, above.

175 (1964) 37 A.L.J.R. 289.

176 This is well put at (1964) 37 A.L.J.R. 289, 293 col.2. Canada has also had problems with *Cullinane* see *Sunnyside Greenhouses v Golden West Seeds* (1972) 27 D.L.R. (3d) 434 (Alberta Sup.Ct., App. Div.) affirmed by the Supreme Court (1973) 33 D.L.R. (3d) 384.

177 See (1964) 37 A.L.J.R. 289 at 294 col.1. This decision has been accepted in Australia ever since as *North Sydney Leagues' Club Ltd v Synergy Protection Agency Pty Ltd* [2010] NSWSC 256 shows where it was held to govern the outcome in that case: see [2010] NSWSC 256 at [18].

178 See at para.4-026, above.

179 [2005] EWCA Civ 753 CA. The report at [2005] P.N.L.R. 44 at 901 is just a one page note; it does not set out the lengthy judgments on the appeal.

180 See the facts further at para.10-096, below.

181 [2005] EWCA Civ 753 CA at [140] and [253].

*linane* was again wrongly invoked in *4 Eng Ltd v Harper*,[182] where the claimant, deceived into buying share capital in a worthless company, would but for the deceit have bought the share capital in a different company.[183] It was held that there was no inconsistency in claiming for the loss of the income profits he would have made from the other company and the capital profit that would have been realised by its acquisition. In neither *Browning* nor *4 Eng* was the claim being made for wasted expenditure and for the alternative measure; so *Cullinane* could have no application whatsoever.[184] Counsel should not be bemused by *Cullinane* into thinking that claims for loss of income profits and loss of capital profits must be alternative and not cumulative. Indeed it would be best if in future *Cullinane* could be put one side for it serves only to confuse.

## II. TORT

**4-050** Pecuniary losses do not feature as commonly in tort as in contract. This is because contract is almost exclusively concerned with the protection of the claimant's commercial interests, while tort protects also such interests of the claimant as his personal safety and his good reputation. One more commonly talks of basic pecuniary losses in relation to torts concerning property.

### 1. BASIC PECUNIARY LOSSES: THE NORMAL MEASURE OF DAMAGES

**4-051** Where the claimant's goods have been damaged, the basic pecuniary loss is the diminution in their value which is normally measured by the reasonable cost of repair,[185] and generally without making any deduction from the damages on account of the fact that after repair the goods are in better condition than they were before the tort.[186] On the other hand, the basic pecuniary loss is the market value of the goods where they have been destroyed[187] or misappropriated.[188] Where it is land that has been damaged, the basic pecuniary loss is again the diminution in value[189] and this may, if the circumstances warrant, be measured by the cost of replacement or repair,[190] sometimes allowing only a partial or limited reinstate-

---

182 [2009] Ch. 91.

183 See the facts further at para.49-025, below.

184 This was well appreciated by David Richards J in *4 Eng* from his cogent reasoning, at [2009] Ch. 91 at [49], as to why *Cullinane* was not applicable to the facts of *4 Eng*.

185 *Darbishire v Warran* [1963] 1 W.L.R. 1067 CA at 1071, per Harman LJ. But not if it is unreasonable to effect the repair: [1963] 1 W.L.R. 1067 CA at 1071.

186 Compare *the Gazelle* (1844) 2 W. Rob. (Adm.) 279 at 281: "The right against the wrongdoer is for a restitutio in integrum, and this restitution he is bound to make without calling upon the party injured to assist him in any way whatsoever." Most of the cases on goods concern damage to ships. See para.2-007, above.

187 *The Clyde* (1856) Swab. 23 at 24; compare *Liesbosch Dredger v S.S. Edison* [1933] A.C. 449.

188 Compare *Caxton Publishing Co v Sutherland Publishing Co* [1939] A.C. 178 at 190: "The principle on which damages for conversion should be awarded ... is well settled." The parties agreed that the proper measure of damages was the value of the property at the time of conversion. See also *BBMM Finance (Hong Kong) v Eda Holdings* [1990] 1 W.L.R. 409 PC.

189 *Jones v Gooday* (1841) 8 M. & W. 146.

190 *Hollebone v Midhurst & Fernhurst Builders* [1968] 1 Lloyd's Rep. 38; *Dodd Properties v Canterbury City Council* [1980] 1 W.L.R. 433 CA. The circumstances did not warrant in *Hole & Son (Sayers Common) v Harrisons of Thurnscoe* [1973] 1 Lloyd's Rep. 345 or in *Taylor (Wholesale) v Hepworths* [1977] 1 W.L.R. 659.

ment,[191] sometimes deducting the amount by which the land as repaired is more valuable than it was in its condition before the tort,[192] but sometimes not.[193] Destruction of land is hardly likely, and as to its misappropriation by occupation and user the claimant will generally reclaim it *in specie*, thus making the basic loss the reasonable rental value for the period of wrongful occupation, technically known as mesne profits, although restitutionary damages is now a conceptually more satisfying way of understanding these awards.[194]

Somewhat similar is the case of personal injuries: the basic pecuniary loss may be said to be the claimant's loss of earnings or, more strictly, a sum representing his loss of future earning capacity.[195] **4-052**

Finally, where the tort is one interfering with business relations the basic loss tends to become the loss of business profits, although loss of profits is generally a consequential loss: for convenience the matter is treated with the other loss of profits cases.[196] **4-053**

## 2. Consequential Pecuniary Losses

### (1) Gains prevented by the tort

**(a) Loss of use, loss of profits, interest** Where the claimant's goods have been damaged he may be allowed damages for loss of profits,[197] or, where no specific loss of profit can be shown, he may be awarded damages for general loss of use,[198] or, in default of either of the preceding, an award of interest may be given.[199] Similarly, where goods have been destroyed, successful claims have ranged from damages for loss of profits[200] to awards of interest.[201] Misappropriation of goods also may give rise to awards of damages for loss of profits[202] or for loss of use,[203] and again interest should be allowed in default of either.[204] In the analogous situations concerning land, damage to the land should lead to the same heads of claim[205]; destruction does not present a practical possibility, while misappropriation by occupation and **4-054**

---

191 Compare *Lodge Holes Colliery Co v Wednesbury Corp* [1908] A.C. 323 and *Dodd Properties v Canterbury City Council* [1980] 1 W.L.R. 433 at 439H–441H.

192 See *Lukin v Godsall* (1795) Peake Add. Cas. 15.

193 *Hollebone v Midhurst & Fernhurst Builders* [1968] 1 Lloyd's Rep. 38. See para.2-007 above.

194 Compare *Whitwham v Westminster Brymbo Coal Co* [1896] 2 Ch. 538 CA; *Penarth Dock Engineering Co v Pounds* [1963] 1 Lloyd's Rep. 359; *Swordheath Properties v Tabet* [1979] 1 W.L.R. 285 CA; *Inverugie Investments v Hackett* [1995] 1 W.L.R. 713 PC.

195 *Phillips v L.S.W. Ry* (1879) 4 Q.B.D. 406; (1879) 5 Q.B.D. 78 CA; (1879) 5 C.P.D. 280 CA, and countless subsequent cases. Occasionally the loss of earnings is better classified as a consequential loss, as in *Kralj v McGrath* [1986] 1 All E.R. 54.

196 See para.4-056, below.

197 *The Risoluto* (1883) 8 P.D. 109; *The Argentino* (1889) 14 App. Cas. 519; *The Soya* [1956] 1 W.L.R. 714 CA; *The World Beauty* [1970] P. 144 CA; *Dixons (Scholar Green) v J L Cooper* (1970) 114 S.J. 319 CA; *The Naxos* [1972] 1 Lloyd's Rep. 149.

198 *The Gazelle* (1844) 2 W. Rob. (Adm.) 279.

199 Compare *The Hebe* (1847) 2 W. Rob. (Adm.) 530; *The Norseman* [1957] P. 224.

200 *The Kate* [1899] P. 165; *The Racine* [1906] P. 273 CA; *The Empress of Britain* (1913) 29 T.L.R. 423; *Liesbosch Dredger v S.S. Edison* [1933] A.C. 449.

201 *The Amalia* (1864) 5 New Rep. 164n.; *The Northumbria* (1869) L.R. 3 A. & E. 6; *Liesbosch Dredger v S.S. Edison* [1933] A.C. 449; *The Berwickshire* [1950] P. 204.

202 *Bodley v Reynolds* (1846) 8 Q.B. 779.

203 *Bodley v Reynolds* (1846) 8 Q.B. 779.

204 There are no clear cases.

205 *Rust v Victoria Graving Dock Co* (1887) 36 Ch. D. 113 CA.

user is generally temporary as the claimant will sue for recovery of the land and damages for loss of use will represent the normal measure.[206] Damages for loss of profits are also recoverable in actions of deceit.[207]

**4-055** Even where the tort is one whereby the law seeks to protect the claimant's person rather than his property, damages in respect of lost business profits may be awarded. This is so in the case of false imprisonment[208] and in the case of malicious prosecution.[209] Such awards have also been made in libel,[210] in slanders actionable per se[211] and in slanders actionable only on proof of special damage.[212]

**4-056** Where the tort is one interfering with business relations, loss of profits tends to become the basic loss. Indeed, in the tort of inducement of breach of contract this type of loss is frequently inferred.[213] And loss of profits has been awarded in the tort of injurious falsehood generally,[214] in its particular common law variety of passing off,[215] in the analogous actions for infringement of rights in statutorily protected property by way of trade marks,[216] patents[217] and copyright,[218] and in actions arising out of the improper use of confidential information.[219]

**4-057** **(b) Loss of services of relatives** The recovery of damages for the loss of the services of a relative has been confined almost completely to tort, because such interests as these are generally only protected by the law of tort.[220] At one time, loss of services grounded recovery where the defendant had tortiously injured the claimant's wife or child and, earlier, seduction and enticement and also adultery had given rise to liability, but statute has abolished all these claims,[221] which are now past history. What remains, and here not at common law but through statute,[222] is that, where a person is killed in circumstances in which, had he or she only been injured, he would have had an action against the defendant in respect of the injury,

---

[206] Compare *Whitwham v Westminster Brymbo Coal Co* [1896] 2 Ch. 538 CA; *Penarth Dock Engineering Co v Pounds* [1963] 1 Lloyd's Rep. 359; *Swordheath Properties v Tabet* [1979] 1 W.L.R. 285 CA; *Inverugie Investments v Hackett* [1995] 1 W.L.R. 713 PC.

[207] *Parabola Investments Ltd v Browallia Cal Ltd* [2011] Q.B. 477 CA.

[208] *Childs v Lewis* (1924) 40 T.L.R. 870.

[209] Compare to *Childs v Lewis* (1924) 40 T.L.R. 870.

[210] *Harrison v Pearce* (1859) 32 L.T. O.S. 298.

[211] *Evans v Harries* (1856) 1 H. & N. 251; *McManus v Beckham* [2002] 1 W.L.R. 2982 CA.

[212] *Storey v Challands* (1837) 8 C. & P. 234.

[213] *Exchange Telegraph Co v Gregory* [1896] 1 Q.B. 147 CA; *Goldsoll v Goldman* [1914] 2 Ch. 603; *Brents Brewery Co v Luke Hogan* [1945] 2 All E.R. 570.

[214] *Riding v Smith* (1876) 1 Ex. D. 91; *Ratcliffe v Evans* [1892] 2 Q.B. 524 CA.

[215] *Spalding v Gamage* (1918) 35 R.P.C. 101 CA; *Draper v Trist* [1939] 3 All E.R. 513 CA.

[216] *Alexander v Henry* (1895) 12 R.P.C. 360.

[217] *Watson, Laidlaw & Co v Pott Cassells & Williamson* (1914) 31 R.P.C. 104 HL; *American Braided Wire Co v Thomson* (1888) 44 Ch. D. 274 CA.

[218] *Birn v Keene* [1918] 2 Ch. 281.

[219] *Seager v Copydex (No.2)* [1969] 1 W.L.R. 809 CA. With tort as with breach of contract the claim will be for loss of future business profits only where the business continues after the tort. If the business ceases or is abandoned because of the tort, a claim for the value of the business at cessation or abandonment takes the place of a claim for future business profits. For contract see *MMP GmbH v Antal International Network Ltd* [2011] EWHC 1120 (Comm) in the first footnote to para.4-018, above.

[220] *Jackson v Watson* [1909] 2 K.B. 193 CA, provides the clearest contractual case.

[221] First, adultery, seduction and enticement by the Law Reform (Miscellaneous Provisions) Act 1970 ss.4 and 5, and the *actio per quod consortium et servitium amisit* by the Administration of Justice Act 1982 s.2, which latter also abolished all of the equivalent actions in the context of master and servant.

[222] Now Fatal Accidents Act 1976, as amended.

the husband, wife, civil partner, child and other specified relatives of the deceased may recover for the loss of the pecuniary benefit arising from the relationship which would have been derived by them from the continuance of the life.[223]

In such cases the claimant's complaint was of an act of the defendant directed at the relative to the claimant's injury. Conversely, the act may be directed at the claimant to the detriment of his or her domestic relationships, as where a husband leaves his claimant wife as a result of her being slandered[224] or physically disfigured[225] by the defendant, or a wife leaves both her children and her claimant husband,[226] or a wife divorces her claimant husband,[227] where physical injury at the hands of the defendant has brought about a change of personality. **4-058**

## (2) Expenses caused by the tort

The claimant may incur many types of expenses as a result of the tort. Often the expenditure is made in order to keep the damage within reasonable bounds. This is so where money is laid out in acquiring or hiring a substitute where the claimant's property is damaged, destroyed or misappropriated[228]; where medical expenses are incurred to ameliorate the claimant's physical injury caused by the defendant[229]; or where there is expenditure upon advertisements to counteract the effect of the defendant's infringement of the claimant's trade mark,[230] or upon extensive inquiries to detect the extent of the defendant's unlawful machinations whether in deceit[231] or in inducing breaches of contract and in conspiracy,[232] or upon managerial or staff time to deal with remedial work or to counter the damage done.[233] **4-059**

These various expenses may be considered as examples of steps taken in mitigation of damage, but some of them are so common, such as medical expenses in personal injury cases, that they do not tend to be thought of specifically from this angle. **4-060**

Other expenses are completely removed from the sphere of mitigation. A good illustration is afforded by the recovery of funeral expenses which statute has allowed in claims surviving or deriving from a death.[234] An interesting group of cases here involves the recovery as damages of legal costs incurred in bringing or defend- **4-061**

---

223 This basic rule was originally laid down in *Franklin v S.E. Ry* (1858) 3 H. & N. 211 at 214.

224 See *Lynch v Knight* (1861) 9 H.L.C. 577.

225 *Lampert v Eastern National Omnibus Co* [1954] 1 W.L.R. 1047.

226 *Oakley v Walker* (1977) 121 S.J. 619. Compare *Huxley v Berg* (1815) 1 Stark. 98, where the claimant's wife died through terror at the defendant's violent trespass into the claimant's house; specific recovery for this was denied.

227 *Jones v Jones* [1985] Q.B. 704 CA; but see *Pritchard v J. H. Cobden* [1988] Fam. 22 CA.

228 *Davis v Oswell* (1837) 7 C. & P. 804 (conversion); but the substitute must be a commensurate one: contrast *Watson Norie v Shaw* (1967) 111 S.J. 117 CA with *H. L. Motorworks v Alwahbi* [1977] R.T.R. 276 CA and *Brain v Yorkshire Rider Ltd* [2007] Lloyd's Rep. I.R. 564.

229 *Lim Poh Choo v Camden and Islington AHA* [1980] A.C. 174; and countless other cases.

230 *Spalding v Gamage* (1918) 35 R.P.C. 101 CA.

231 *4 Eng Ltd v Harper* [2009] Ch. 91.

232 *British Motor Trade Association v Salvadori* [1949] Ch. 556; *Admiral Management Services Ltd v Para-Protect Europe Ltd* [2002] 1 W.L.R. 2722; *R-V Versicherung AG v Risk Insurance and Reinsurance Solutions SA* [2006] EWHC 42 (Comm).

233 *Tate & Lyle Food and Distribution v Greater London Council* [1982] 1 W.L.R. 149; *Carisbrooke Shipping CV5 v Bird Port Ltd* [2005] 2 Lloyd's Rep. 626; *Aerospace Publishing Ltd v Thames Water Utilities Ltd* (2007) 110 Con. L.R. 1 CA; *Bridge UK.Com Ltd v Abbey Pynford Plc* [2007] EWHC 728 TCC. *Nationwide Building Society v Dunlop Haywards (DHL) Ltd* [2010] 1 W.L.R. 258.

234 Law Reform (Miscellaneous Provisions) Act 1934 s.1(2)(c) and Fatal Accidents Act 1976 (as amended) s.3(5) respectively.

ing earlier legal proceedings. However, the successful tort cases, unlike the contract cases,[235] do not generally concern earlier proceedings between the now claimant and a third party—although there is no reason in principle why they should not, and one or two illustrations of successful claimants can indeed be found[236]—but deal with earlier proceedings in which the now defendant was directly or obliquely involved. Thus claimants have recovered as damages in the later action the legal costs incurred in the successful defence of a malicious prosecution[237] and in gaining release from a false imprisonment.[238]

## (3) Expenses rendered futile by the tort

**4-062** Expenses rendered futile by the wrong do not have the same importance in tort as they have in contract for the reason that the claimant is not in tort taking action in reliance upon the defendant's promise. There are, however, some cases where they appear, particularly where a chattel has to undergo repairs necessitated by damage caused by the defendant. In such circumstances the claimant may recover the wages of a ship's officers and crew who are properly retained during the repair period,[239] or a sum for overhead charges generally.[240] Such expenses are mentioned here only to complete the analysis, and to stress the fact that they necessarily form an alternative, and not an additional, head of damage to that of loss of profits.

---

235 See para.4-023, above.

236 *The Solway Prince* (1914) 31 T.L.R. 56; *Morton-Norwich Products v Intercen (No.2)* [1981] F.S.R. 337. In both cases the now claimant had also been claimant, and a successful one, in the prior action. But a new regime on the recovery of costs as damages is in the air: see at paras 21-003 and following below.

237 *Saville v Roberts* (1699) 1 Ld. Raym. 374; *Berry v British Transport Commission* [1962] 1 Q.B. 306 CA.

238 *Pritchet v Boevey* (1833) 1 Cr. & M. 775.

239 *The Inflexible* (1857) Swab. 200.

240 *London Transport Executive v Foy Morgan* [1955] C.L.Y. 743; contrast *London Transport Executive v Court* [1954] C.L.Y. 888. But there could be no recovery in *Batt v Highgate Private Hospital* [2005] P.I.Q.R. Q1 at l for the expense of an operation rendered futile because it led to the death of the patient: see [2005] P.I.Q.R. Q1 at [8] to [15], and further on the case in the footnote at the end of para.41-130, below.

CHAPTER 5

# NON-PECUNIARY LOSSES

TABLE OF CONTENTS



The pattern of non-pecuniary losses shows a much greater difference between tort and breach of contract: in tort they are the rule, in contract the exception. **5-001**

## I. TORT

In the law of torts, non-pecuniary losses flourish, since a large part of the protection given by the law of torts is to such interests as personal safety and personal reputation, which are interests not immediately connected with monetary considerations. The law of torts indeed bestraddles all the recognised heads of non-pecuniary loss. **5-002**

Five heads of non-pecuniary loss were set out in the 1961 edition of this work, the first written by Dr McGregor, and were considered there in relation both to tort and to contract. They comprised (1) pain and suffering and loss of amenity; (2) physical inconvenience and discomfort; (3) mental distress; (4) social discredit; and (5) loss of society of spouse or child. Apart from the fifth and last of these heads of loss, which had a very limited range and became only of historical interest after the abolition of the various torts infringing family relationships,[1] the first four have stood the test of time. So much is this so that when in 2012 the Court of Appeal ruled in its further hearing of *Simmons v Castle*,[2] that damages for all types of non-pecuniary loss in all types of civil claim[3] were to be increased by 10 per cent,[4] Lord **5-003**

---

[1] For details see Ch.3 in earlier editions. Bereavement damages are now available for spouses and parents on a death but their entitlement to such damages is statutory: see para.41-019, below.

[2] [2013] 1W.L.R. 1239 CA; further hearing from p.1243.

[3] In the first hearing ([2013] 1W.L.R. 1239 CA at 1240) only certain torts and certain types of non-pecuniary loss had been included.

[4] For the procedural history and reasons for this development, stemming from the package of reforms appearing in the *Jackson Report on Civil Litigation Costs*, see para.51-044, below. Since these procedural reasons are irrelevant to cases heard in the Employment Tribunal, His Honour Judge

Judge CJ, when asked as to what types of loss were covered by the ruling, said that the court believed that the best guidance was to be found in this chapter, and set out word for word the above heads,[5] giving them in the court's formal recommendation as five rather than four by sub-dividing pain and suffering and loss of amenity,[6] as the heads of loss to which the 10 per cent increase was to apply.

### (1) PAIN AND SUFFERING AND LOSS OF AMENITIES

**5-004** Where a tort results in physical injury to the claimant, one of the basic heads of damage is in respect of the pain and suffering incurred. "Pain and suffering" is now a term of art, so constantly has it been used by the courts, and there appears to be no exact difference between pain on the one hand and suffering on the other. It has been suggested that "pain" is the immediately felt effect on the nerves and brain of some lesion or injury to a part of the body, while "suffering" is distress which is not felt as being directly connected with any bodily condition. On this analysis "pain" needs no further elucidation; suffering would include fright at the time of the injury, fear of future incapacity, either as to health or possible death, to sanity or to the ability to make a living, and humiliation, sadness and embarrassment caused by disfigurement.[7] Although this work treats mental distress (below at heading (4)) as a separate head of non-pecuniary loss, there can sometimes be a fine line between an award for suffering and an award for mental distress. In *ABC v WH*,[8] the third party defendant was found liable for assault and intentional infliction of emotional harm due to his direct physical sexual abuse of the claimant as well as his emotional manipulation of her and encouragement of her to send him indecent images. The claimant suffered serious distress, including making more than one attempt on her life and injuring herself. The trial judge awarded damages of £25,000, for "pain, suffering and loss of amenity" but it is clear that these damages also included a component for mental distress.

**5-005** Furthermore, if the injury so disables the claimant as to lessen more negatively his enjoyment of life by impeding or preventing the pursuit of his former activities, he may recover damages for what is termed "loss of amenities". This element could probably have been subsumed under "suffering", but the courts since about the middle of the last century have erected it into a separate head of damage,[9] although in practice it turns out to be little more than a verbal distinction whenever, as is normal, a single assessment is made to cover both matters.[10]

---

Serota held *in De Souza v Vinci Construction UK Ltd* March 2015 EAT, not following two earlier decisions by which he was not bound, that the *Simmons v Castle* 10 per cent uplift has no application in the Employment Tribunal.

5 [2013] 1W.L.R. 1239 CA at [48] of the further hearing.

6 [2013] 1W.L.R. 1239 CA at [50] of the further hearing.

7 This analysis was initially derived from McCormick, *Damages* (Minnesota, 1935), p.88.

8 [2015] EWHC 2687 (QB).

9 The clearest statement is that of Birkett LJ in *Manley v Rugby Portland Cement* (1951) CA No.286 (quoted at para.40-258, below). For other statements introducing the term "loss of amenities" at about the same time, see Asquith LJ in *Shearman v Folland* [1950] 2 K.B. 43 CA at 51 and 52; *Haygarth v Grayson Rollo* [1951] 1 Lloyd's Rep. 49 CA at 51; and *British Transport Commission v Gourley* [1956] A.C. 185 at 197 and 216, per Earl Jowitt and Lord Keith respectively.

10 Awards today can be high. Quadriplegia and the severest brain damage today both command up to £354,260 according to the Judicial College's *Guidelines for the Assessment of General Damages in Personal Injury Cases*, 14th edn (2017), Ch.2 and Ch.3; and see further para.40-281, below. These maxima will continue to require adjustment for inflation; the 10% increase introduced by *Simmons*

Formerly, if the injury so disabled the claimant as to cut down his expectation of life, he might recover damages for this loss. This head of damage was established in *Flint v Lovell*,[11] then applied[12] to a survival action where the victim had died from the injury, and finally interpreted[13] as being based, for the purposes of assessment of damages, not so much upon loss of expectation of life as upon loss of expectation of happiness. The right to damages for loss of expectation of life has been abolished by statute[14] in order to prevent recovery in survival actions, but with the specific exception that in actions by living victims the court, in assessing damages for pain and suffering, shall take into account any suffering caused or likely to be caused by awareness of the reduction in life expectation.[15] It is now, as it had been before *Flint v Lovell*, part of the damages for pain and suffering. **5-006**

Where the tort has resulted in some interference with the claimant's physical person short of impact, the claimant again has recovered for pain and suffering, and, if relevant, loss of amenities and expectation of life. This will arise much less frequently. Injury to health by nervous or emotional shock[16]—now referred to as psychiatric illness or damage[17]—though at one time it did not ground recovery,[18] today provides a clear illustration.[19] In false imprisonment, it has long[20] been recognised that injury to health by reason of the confinement forms a recoverable **5-007**

---

*v Castle* [2013] 1 W.L.R. 1239 CA (see para.5-003, above) has already been incorporated in the Guidelines figures.

11 [1935] 1 K.B. 354 CA.

12 In *Rose v Ford* [1937] A.C. 826.

13 In *Benham v Gambling* [1941] A.C. 157.

14 Administration of Justice Act 1982 s.1(1)(a).

15 Administration of Justice Act 1982 s.1(1)(b).

16 . See *Behrens v Bertram Mills Circus* [1957] 2 Q.B. 1 at 28, per Devlin J: "When the word 'shock' is used in them [i.e. the cases], it is not in the sense of mental reaction but in a medical sense as the equivalent of nervous shock."

17 In *Attia v British Gas* [1988] Q.B. 304 CA at 317 Bingham LJ considered nervous shock to be a misleading and inaccurate term, preferring psychiatric damage, and the Law Commission's Report (Law Com. No.249 (1998)) on this type of damage is entitled *Liability for Psychiatric Illness*. This expression, or psychiatric loss, has now taken over.

18 *Victorian Railway Commrs v Coultas* (1888) 13 App. Cas. 222 PC.

19 *Wilkinson v Downton* [1897] 2 Q.B. 57; *Dulieu v White* [1901] 2 K.B. 669; *Chadwick v British Railways Board* [1967] 1 W.L.R. 912; *Hinz v Berry* [1970] 2 Q.B. 40 CA; *McLoughlin v O'Brian* [1983] 1 A.C. 410; *Hale v London Underground* [1993] P.I.Q.R. Q30; *Page v Smith* [1996] A.C. 155. *Frost v Chief Constable of the South Yorkshire Police* [1998] Q.B. 254 CA (reversed on liability, sub nom. *White v Chief Constable of the South Yorkshire Police* [1999] 2 A.C. 455); *W v Essex County Council* [2001] 2 A.C. 592; *Greatorex v Greatorex* [2000] 1 W.L.R. 1970 (but no duty of care). Yet there was no recovery for psychiatric illness where the tort was constituted by negligent failure to design adequate foundations for a house: *Storey v Charles Church Developments Plc* (2001) 73 Con. L.R. 1 (where there was a concurrent claim in contract). The House of Lords in *Wainwright v The Home Office* [2004] 2 A.C. 406 made it clear that *Wilkinson v Downton* (above in this note), the earliest of the successful cases of what was then called nervous shock, is to be understood as covering only psychiatric illness and not mental distress short thereof. And the Supreme Court *O (A Child) v Rhodes* [2016] A.C. 219, reversing the Court of Appeal, held that *Wilkinson v Downton* did not apply in relation to the publication of an autobiographical book by a father which might lead to his child's psychiatric illness. The controversial *Hambrook v Stokes* [1925] 1 K.B. 141 CA was a claim under the Fatal Accidents Act, where non-pecuniary loss was then not recoverable.

20 *Lowden v Goodrick* (1791) Peake 64; *Pettit v Addington* (1791) Peake 87.

loss.[21] And in cases of nuisance, by noise, fumes and the like, there can be no doubt that the claimant could recover for resultant injury to health.[22]

**5-008** As to illness resulting from a tort which is designed to protect primarily not the claimant's physical person but his reputation or his freedom from abusive legal process, there is little authority. No recovery was allowed in the difficult slander case of *Allsop v Allsop*.[23] This case is at once doubtful and special,[24] and it in no way debars the courts from holding that loss through ill health is recoverable in torts other than slander, such as malicious prosecution.

**5-009** At the foot of the scale come torts against property. These are hardly likely to result in illness to the owner. Possibly they might do so when conducted with violence, but in such a case the damages are more likely to be increased by another route, that of an award for injury to feelings.[25] However, it would seem that in such an award there could properly be included damages for injury to health.

### (2) Physical inconvenience and discomfort

**5-010** Where the claimant is physically injured he may also suffer from inconvenience, but such a loss will generally be included in the damages for pain and suffering and loss of amenities of life.[26] But where the tort has resulted in some interference with the claimant's person short of physical injury yet has caused him physical inconvenience, the latter must necessarily appear as a separate head of damage. Although the expression "damages for inconvenience" is not generally to be found in tort,[27] damages have been expressly awarded under this head in deceit[28] and there are other torts where damages are in effect awarded under this head. One is false imprisonment, where the claimant recovers for the loss of his liberty, though involving injury neither to health nor to pocket. Another is nuisance, where one of the principal complaints of a claimant is that he has been inconvenienced and annoyed by noise, smell, interference with easements and the like.[29] And even where the action is in negligence there has been recovery for the discomfort of living in damaged property[30] and for the inconvenience to a car owner of being without his car where he has not hired a substitute for the time taken to repair the damage to it.[31]

---

21 *Hsu v Commissioner of Police of the Metropolis* [1998] Q.B. 498 CA (at para.42-022, below) is a modern illustration.

22 See *Alcoa Minerals of Jamaica Plc v Broderick* [2002] 1 A.C. 371 at para.39-020, below.

23 (1860) 5 H. & N. 534.

24 See the full discussion at para.8-084, below.

25 See para.5-013, below, especially *Owen and Smith v Reo Motors* (1934) 151 L.T. 274 CA.

26 Thus in *Shearman v Folland* [1950] 2 K.B. 43 CA at 50 Asquith LJ said that for the difference between life in a hospital and life in an hotel the claimant fell to be compensated under the head of general damages for pain and suffering and for loss of amenities.

27 Compare contract where it is found: see para.5-017, below.

28 *Mafo v Adams* [1970] 1 Q.B. 548 CA; *Saunders v Edwards* [1987] 1 W.L.R. 1116 CA.

29 See *Halsey v Esso Petroleum Co* [1961] 1 W.L.R. 683; *Bone v Seale* [1975] 1 W.L.R. 797 CA; *Bunclark v Hertfordshire C.C.* (1977) 243 E.G. 381 and 455; *Barr v Biffa Waste Services Ltd* [2011] 4 All E.R. 1065: all at para.39-020, below.

30 *Ward v Cannock Chase District Council* [1986] Ch. 546. See *Storey v Charles Church Developments Plc* (2001) 73 Con. L.R. 1 (negligence and contract) with claimants living in faultily designed house: "anxiety and distress resulting from the physical discomfort and inconvenience caused by the property damage and by remedial works are to be compensated for in damages": at 15.

31 *Beechwood Birmingham Ltd v Hoyer Group UK Ltd* [2011] Q.B. 357 CA; see the case at para.37-062, below.

### (3) SOCIAL DISCREDIT

The tort of defamation exists to protect reputations; any such non-pecuniary loss by social discredit is recoverable essentially as mental distress, actual or anticipated.[32] However, recovery may also be made for injury to reputation in malicious prosecution[33]; and it can also add to the damages given in false imprisonment.[34] These, however, may be the only torts where such damages run.[35] Certainly they are available neither in conspiracy[36] nor in injurious falsehood[37] and they may not be available in torts affecting goods.[38] 5-011

### (4) MENTAL DISTRESS

Mental distress is not by itself sufficient damage to ground an action. As Devlin J said in *Behrens v Bertram Mills Circus*[39]: 5-012

> "The general principle embedded in the common law [is] that mental suffering caused by grief, fear, anguish and the like is not assessable."[40]

Hence it was held by the House of Lords in *Rothwell v Chemical & Insulating Co Ltd*,[41] that, pleural plaques resulting from exposure to asbestos not constituting physical injury so as to found a cause of action[42], the mental anxiety over future disease, even when aggregated with physiological change and risk, could not give rise to a legal claim.[43]

On the other hand, once liability has been established, then in certain torts compensation for injury to feelings may be included in the damages, and indeed in torts infringing family relationships the injury to feelings represented the principal loss. These torts, however, have all been abolished by statute,[44] so that what were once the most important illustrations of this head of non-pecuniary loss have been removed from the scene, and there are left at common law only those torts in which 5-013

32 Hence such loss is not recoverable in slanders not actionable per se.

33 "There are three sorts of damage any of which would be sufficient ground to support this action. (1) The damage to a man's fame, as if the matter whereof he is accused be scandalous ...": per Lord Holt in *Saville v Roberts* (1699) 1 Ld. Raym. 374 at 378, the leading case.

34 See Lawrence LJ in *Walter v Alltools* (1944) 61 T.L.R. 39 CA at 40: "A false imprisonment does not merely affect a man's liberty; it also affects his reputation. The damage continues until it is caused to cease by an avowal that the imprisonment was false."

35 See *Lonrho v Fayed (No.5)* [1993] 1 W.L.R. 1489 CA at 1504E, per Stuart-Smith LJ, distinguishing false imprisonment and malicious prosecution, and implicitly defamation, from other torts.

36 *Lonrho v Fayed (No.5)* [1993] 1 W.L.R. 1489 CA.

37 See *Joyce v Sengupta* [1993] 1 W.L.R. 337 CA, at para.48-013, below.

38 See the discussion at paras 8-128 to 8-130, below.

39 [1957] 2 Q.B. 1 at 28.

40 See *Lynch v Knight* (1861) 9 H.L.C. 577 at 598, per Lord Wensleydale: "Mental pain or anxiety the law cannot value, and does not pretend to redress, when the unlawful act complained of causes that alone."

41 [2008] A.C. 281.

42 *Rothwell* has been statutorily reversed in both Scotland and Northern Ireland, each enacting that asbestos-related pleural plaques shall constitute an actionable personal injury: see, respectively, Damages (Asbestos related Conditions) (Scotland) Act 2009 and Damages (Asbestos-related Conditions) Act (Northern Ireland) 2011. *McCauley v Harland & Wolff Plc* [2014] NIQB 91 is a Northern Ireland damages case following upon the statutory reversal.

43 See the case further at para.40-008, below.

44 Law Reform (Miscellaneous Provisions) Act 1970 ss.4 and 5.

injury to feelings generally forms a subsidiary element in the damages. Thus injury to feelings would seem to be allowable in torts which primarily protect reputation, certainly in libel and in slanders actionable per se[45] and most probably in malicious prosecution. The same is true of assault[46] and has been recognised as being true of deceit.[47] Invasion of privacy, stemming from breach of confidence in its personal as distinct from its commercial form, has from the beginning of the century begun to attract damages for injured feelings.[48] Increasingly in trespass to property or nuisance there has been an award for mental distress or anxiety[49]; on the other hand, it has been held that this head of non-pecuniary loss cannot be claimed in the tort of conspiracy[50] while the position with injurious falsehood is not yet settled.[51] Negligence resulting in economic loss[52] is unlikely to lead to damages for mental distress.[53] Statutory torts involving discrimination which formerly appeared in separate statutes[54] have now been brought under the umbrella of the Equality Act 2010 where it is provided, as it had been before, that an award of damages in respect

---

45 *Goslin v Corry* (1844) 7 M. & G. 342 at 346 (damages "for the mental suffering arising from the apprehension of the consequences of the publication"); *Ley v Hamilton* (1935) 153 L.T. 384 HL at 386 (damages for "the insult offered or the pain of a false accusation"); *McCarey v Associated Newspapers* [1965] 2 Q.B. 86 CA at 104 (damages "may also include the natural injury to the feelings"); *Fielding v Variety Inc* [1967] 2 Q.B. 841 CA at 855 ("entitled to be compensated … for the anxiety and annoyance"); *John v MGN* [1997] Q.B. 586 CA at 607F (the sum awarded "must … take account of the distress, hurt and humiliation which the defamatory publication has caused").

46 See *Lane v Holloway* [1968] 1 Q.B. 379 CA.

47 *Doyle v Olby (Ironmongers)* [1969] 2 Q.B. 158 CA at 170 (may be appropriate to consider "worry, strain, anxiety and unhappiness"); *Mafo v Adams* [1970] 1 Q.B. 548 CA at 558 (damages may be increased where there are "circumstances which aggravate the suffering and injury"); *Shelley v Paddock* [1978] Q.B. 120; *Saunders v Edwards* [1987] 1 W.L.R. 1116 CA; *East v Maurer* [1991] 1 W.L.R. 461 CA; *A v B* [2007] EWHC 1246 (QB); *Kinch v Rosling* [2009] EWHC 286 (QB).

48 *Cornelius v de Taranto* [2001] E.M.L.R. 12 at 329 (damages not in issue in CA); *Campbell v MGN Ltd* [2002] E.M.L.R. 30, at 617 (damages not in issue in CA or HL); *Archer v Williams* [2003] E.M.L.R. 38 at 869; *Douglas v Hello! Ltd* [2004] E.M.L.R. 2 at 13 (these damages not in issue in CA); *McKennitt v Ash* [2006] E.M.L.R. 10 at 178 (damages not addressed in CA); *Mosley v News Group Newspapers Ltd* [2008] E.M.L.R. 20 at 679. These first instance cases are considered at paras 47-005 to 47-007, below.

49 *Owen and Smith v Reo Motors* (1934) 151 L.T. 274 CA (explained on these lines by Lord Devlin in *Rookes v Barnard* [1964] A.C. 1129 at 1229); *Drane v Evangelou* [1978] 1 W.L.R. 455 CA; *Millington v Duffy* (1984) 17 H.L.R. 232 CA; and the other cases at para.39-073, below. Also *Scutt v Lomax* (2000) 79 P. & C.R. D31 CA; *Bryant v Macklin* [2005] EWHC Civ 762; *Anslow v Norton Aluminium Ltd* [2012] EWHC 2610 (QB) and compare *Barr v Biffa Waste Services Ltd* [2011] 4 All E.R. 1065: all at para.39-020, below.

50 *Lonrho v Fayed (No.5)* [1993] 1 W.L.R. 1489 CA.

51 Against: *Fielding v Variety Inc* [1967] 2 Q.B. 841 CA at 850 ("the claimants … can only recover damages for their probable money loss, and not for their injured feelings"); in favour: *Joyce v Sengupta* [1993] 1 W.L.R. 337 CA at 348E ("instinctively recoil from the notion that in no circumstances can an injured claimant obtain recompense … for understandable distress").

52 The damages recoverable for non-economic loss by a car owner deprived of his car through negligence would seem to be for inconvenience rather than distress: see *Beechwood Birmingham Ltd v Hoyer Group UK Ltd* at para.5-010, above.

53 *Verderame v Commercial Union Insurance Co Plc* [2000] Lloyd's Rep. P.N. 557 CA, a case of professional negligence, held that where the duty of care arises in respect of economic loss there will be no recovery of damages for mental distress any more than there would be if the professional negligence claim were brought, as is commoner, in contract. For mental distress in contract where professional negligence can occasionally lead to an award see paras 5-023 and following, below.

54 Notably Sex Discrimination Act 1975, Race Relations Act 1976 and Disability Discrimination Act 1995. All three and the Regulations that go with them are repealed by the provisions, in force and prospective, of the Equality Act 2010.

of discrimination "may include compensation for injured feelings".[55] The statutory tort involving harassment[56] allows for damages "for any anxiety caused by the harassment".[57] Another example is the tort of intentional infliction of emotional harm. In *ABC v WH*,[58] damages for the tort of intentional infliction of emotional harm were awarded for "pain, suffering and loss of amenity" including a component for mental distress.

Two particular points should be made on recovery for mental distress. First, with all the intentional torts the damages may be aggravated where the mental distress of the claimant has been exacerbated by the unpleasant nature of the defendant's conduct; consideration of the levels of awards will appear in the chapters devoted to particular torts. Secondly, it is thought that damages for mental distress, whether aggravated or not, should be restricted to individuals and be unavailable to corporate claimants since corporations have no feelings to injure. Such authority as there is, was, for some time, conflicting but moving in the right direction.[59] Fortunately, however, the Court of Appeal in the appeal from the last of the cases here footnoted, has declared in *Eaton Mansions (Westminster) Ltd v Stinger Compania de Inversion SA*,[60] after a review of the authorities, that damages for mental distress are not recoverable by a company.[61] **5-014**

---

55 Section 119(4); adding, as before, "(whether or not it includes compensation on any other basis)". By contrast, in *R. v Secretary of State for Transport, Ex p. Factortame Ltd (No.7)* [2001] 1 W.L.R. 942 TCC, one of the *Factortame* cases involving discrimination by the United Kingdom against the owners of foreign fishing vessels, it was held that Art.52 of the European Communities Treaty, which gives the right to nationals of one Member State to establish themselves in another Member State, was concerned only with economic loss.

56 Protection from Harassment Act 1997, which has survived the arrival of the Equality Act 2010.

57 Section 3(2). Awards were made on this basis in *S&D Property Investments Ltd v Nisbet* [2009] EWHC 1726 (Ch) (where it was rightly said that anxiety need not amount to mental illness: [2009] EWHC 1726 (Ch) at [72] and following), in *Rayment v Ministry of Defence* [2010] EWHC 218 (QB) (£5,500 for bullying, humiliating and insulting an employee) and *Roberts v Bank of Scotland* [2013] EWCA Civ 882 CA (£7,500 for bombardment of phone calls to customer by bank).

58 [2015] EWHC 2687 (QB).

59 The holding in *Messenger Newspapers Group v National Graphical Association* [1984] I.R.L.R. 397 that aggravated damages may be awarded not only to an individual but to a company or other inanimate body is considered to be wrong; to the contrary is *Columbia Picture Industries v Robinson* [1987] Ch. 38 where, under a cross-undertaking for losses occasioned by a search order, the damages were divided in the proportion of three to one between the individual and corporate claimants as such a split "recognises that contumely and affront affect individuals, not inanimate corporations": at 88H. In *Collins Stewart Ltd v Financial Times Ltd (No.2)* [2006] E.M.L.R. 5 at 100, a defamation case, it has again been rightly held that aggravated damages were not to be awarded to a corporate claimant with no feelings to injure: [2006] E.M.L.R. 5 at [30] and [31]. Rather than saying that *Messenger* was wrong, Gray J unconvincingly distinguished it on the ground that it concerned exemplary damages: [2006] E.M.L.R. 5 at [32]. So too in *McKennitt v Ash* [2006] E.M.L.R. 10 at 178, a claim for breach of confidence and invasion of privacy, damages for hurt feelings and distress were awarded to the individual claimant but not to the company she controlled: *McKennitt v Ash* [2006] E.M.L.R. 10 at [162]. Tugendhat J in *Hays Plc v Hartley* [2010] EWHC 1068 (QB) at [24] stated categorically that "a corporation is not entitled to damages for injury to feelings". He said much the same in *Metropolitan International Schools Ltd v Designtechnica Corp* [2010] EWHC 2411 (QB) at [14] and in *Cooper v Turrell* [2011] EWHC 3269 (QB), with the result that in the latter he awarded more to the individual claimant than to the corporate claimant. And in *Eaton Mansions (Westminster) Ltd v Stinger Compania de Inversion SA* [2012] EWHC 3354 Ch on the basis of the above authorities Edward Bartley Jones QC, sitting as a Deputy High Court Judge, held a corporate claimant disentitled to aggravated damages: [2012] EWHC 3354 Ch at [70] to [74].

60 [2013] EWCA Civ 1308 CA.

61 [2013] EWCA Civ 1308 CA at [30]. Patten LJ, giving the only reasoned judgment, talks throughout of aggravated damages but it is mental distress damages that he has in mind, as what he says at

## II. Contract

5-015 Contract is primarily concerned with commercial matters and therefore the protection afforded by the law of contract is primarily directed to commercial losses. Indeed it was once said that "in an action founded on breach of contract the only kind of loss … which is a subject for compensation is a financial loss".[62] But this is today no longer an accurate statement, as will appear as the various heads of non-pecuniary loss are considered.

5-016 The same five heads of non-pecuniary loss considered above in relation to tort are considered below in relation to contract. As was said when dealing with tort,[63] when in 2012 the Court of Appeal ruled in its further hearing of *Simmons v Castle*,[64] that damages for all types of non-pecuniary loss in all types of civil claim[65] were to be increased by 10 per cent[66]—with contract specifically included in addition to tort[67]—and was asked about what types of loss were covered, Lord Judge CJ said that the court believed that the best guidance was to be found in this chapter, and set out word for word the same heads as here,[68] giving them in the court's formal recommendation as five rather than four by sub-dividing pain and suffering and loss of amenity[69] as the heads of loss to which the 10 per cent increase was to apply.

### (1) Physical inconvenience and discomfort

5-017 Substantial physical inconvenience and discomfort caused by a breach of contract will entitle a claimant to damages. This was early established in *Burton v Pinkerton*,[70] where a seaman was set down at a foreign port in breach of his contract of employment and recovered damages for inconvenience and discomfort[71]; and in *Hobbs v L.S.W. Ry*,[72] where a man and his family were set down by the defendant railway company at the wrong station so late on a wet night that they had to walk several miles home in the rain in the absence of available conveyance or hotel, and damages for the physical inconvenience were recovered. Mellor J in the latter case

---

[2013] EWCA Civ 1308 CA at [27] clearly shows.

62 *Sunley v Cunard White Star* [1939] 2 K.B. 791 at 799, per Hallett J.

63 See at para.5-003, above.

64 [2013] 1W.L.R. 1239 CA; further hearing from 1243.

65 In the first hearing ([2013] 1W.L.R. 1239 CA; from 1240) only certain torts and certain types of non-pecuniary loss had been included.

66 For the procedural history and reasons for this development, stemming from the package of reforms appearing in the *Jackson Report on Civil Litigation Costs*, see para.51-044, below. Since these procedural reasons are irrelevant to cases heard in the Employment Tribunal, His Honour Judge Serota held in *De Souza v Vinci Construction UK Ltd* March 2015 EAT, not following two earlier decisions by which he was not bound, that the *Simmons v Castle* 10 per cent uplift has no application in the Employment Tribunal.

67 [2013] 1W.L.R. 1239 CA at [46] of the further hearing.

68 [2013] 1W.L.R. 1239 CA at [48] of the further hearing.

69 [2013] 1W.L.R. 1239 CA at [50] of the further hearing. In previous editions of this work the further head of loss of society of relatives had been added at the end of the chapter. This was done only to make clear that, as in the only known case of *Jackson v Watson* [1909] 2 K.B. 193 CA (facts at para.4-021, above), recovery is confined to loss of services of relatives, which is a pecuniary loss.

70 (1867) L.R. 2 Ex. 340.

71 He failed to recover in respect of his imprisonment by the authorities in the port, but this was because it was too remote. Damages in respect of imprisonment of a tenant, by reason of the landlord not paying the rates in breach of contract, were allowed in *Atkins v Hutton* (1910) 103 L.T. 514 CA, although the words inconvenience and discomfort did not appear.

72 (1875) L.R. 10 Q.B. 111.

was careful to indicate what he meant by inconvenience, limiting it to "real physical inconvenience" to the exclusion of "the mere inconvenience" of anger and disappointment.[73]

Modern authorities have followed and applied these two cases. In *Bailey v Bullock*[74] the claimant instructed the defendant solicitor to press urgently for possession of a house, which the claimant had let to a third party. The defendant's clerk, who knew that the claimant, with his wife and child, had no other living accommodation, failed to start proceedings, but deceived the claimant for nearly two years into believing that he had. On discovering the deception, the claimant instructed other solicitors and obtained possession of the house, but during all this time he, with his wife and child, had lived in discomfort in a small house with his wife's parents. He recovered, inter alia, damages for this inconvenience and discomfort, the court holding that the two earlier cases clearly established this head of damage in a proper case.[75] Similarly, in *Buckley v Lane Herdman & Co*,[76] damages for physical inconvenience were awarded against solicitors who had negligently exchanged contracts for the sale of the claimants' old home before exchanging contracts for their new one in breach of an express term that the two transactions be simultaneous to protect the claimants not only financially but from homelessness.[77] In *Stedman v Swan's Tours*[78] the principle was applied to inconvenience and discomfort caused by the reservation of very inferior hotel rooms for the claimants at their holiday destination by the defendant travel agency, so that, alternative accommodation being impossible to find, their whole holiday was spoiled.[79] In *Rawlings v Rentokil Laboratories*,[80] where a damp-proof system was inadequately installed in the claimant's house, he recovered damages for the discomfort and inconvenience in being in the house in its defective state. The Court of Appeal has endorsed, as in *Calabar Properties v Stitcher*,[81] and *Elmcroft Developments v Tankersley-Sawyer*,[82] the recovery of damages for the discomfort and loss of enjoyment, even ill health, which living with a lack of repair has engendered and in *Watts v Morrow*[83] also endorsed the trial judge's award of damages for physical inconvenience and discomfort[84] where the claimant husband and wife had had to live effectively on a building site while the house they had 5-018

73 (1875) L.R. 10 Q.B. 111 at 122. This limitation to physical inconvenience has now to a substantial extent gone: see paras 5-023 and following, below.
74 [1950] 2 All E.R. 1167.
75 [1950] 2 All E.R. 1167 at 1171; a slight pecuniary flavour is nevertheless introduced by the comment that "it would, indeed, be curious if ... because the plaintiff suffered the inconvenience rather than incur expense to avoid it, he should be deprived of any remedy": [1950] 2 All E.R. 1167 at 1171. A somewhat similar case is *Collard v Saunders* [1971] C.L.Y. 11161.
76 [1977] C.L.Y. 3143.
77 For further details, see paras 34-017 and 34-047, below.
78 (1951) 95 S.J. 727 CA.
79 Further, but ill-reported, decisions followed, allowing damages for physical inconvenience in like circumstances, but all of these have been largely overtaken by the current preparedness to give damages for the disappointment of a spoiled holiday even in the absence of physical inconvenience: see para.5-025, below.
80 [1972] E.G.D. 744.
81 [1984] 1 W.L.R. 287 CA.
82 (1984) 15 H.L.R. 63 CA.
83 [1991] 1 W.L.R. 1421 CA.
84 But not the amount; the trial judge's £4,000 for each claimant was reduced to £750 for each.

purchased was repaired around them. Bingham LJ went so far as to say in *Watts*[85] that damages were in his view "recoverable for physical inconvenience and discomfort caused by the breach and mental suffering directly related to that inconvenience and discomfort". *Patel v Hooper & Jackson*,[86] is a further award of damages for the relative discomfort of living in less salubrious premises and *Holder v Countrywide Surveyors*,[87] a further award for inconvenience and related distress where defects in a house made living in it impossible.[88] In *Farley v Skinner*[89] the House of Lords held, reversing the majority decision of the Court of Appeal, that being troubled at one's house by excessive aircraft noise constitutes physical inconvenience and discomfort grounding recovery.[90] If the various matters in the cases in the text above have been held to constitute physical inconvenience and discomfort, surely suffering severe noise from aircraft must also.[91]

**5-019** Even inconvenience that is not strictly physical may prove to be an element in the damages. This is suggested by *Piper v Daybell Court-Cooper & Co*,[92] where the defendant solicitor failed to reveal to the claimant a right of way existing over the premises which he was contemplating buying as a home, and damages were awarded to him for the inconvenience of having his neighbour crossing and re-crossing in front of his windows.

## (2) PAIN AND SUFFERING AND LOSS OF AMENITIES

**5-020** There would seem to be no doubt that damages recoverable for personal injury caused by breach of contract would include the normal non-pecuniary losses in such cases of pain and suffering and loss of amenities.[93] It is true that in many cases of such contractual liability there is a concurrent liability in tort, of which the stock example is a railway company's negligence causing injury to a passenger. But this concurrence need not exist. It might not exist where a purchaser of goods is injured in using or consuming by reason of a breach of warranty. And it did not exist in *Summers v Salford Corporation*.[94] A tenant was cleaning a window when the sash cord broke, the window fell, and her hands were both badly injured. She successfully sued the landlord for breach of the covenant, implied by statute, of fitness for habitation, and there is nothing to suggest that the award of damages was not based on the normal assessment for personal injury. Similar are the cases where a tenant has sued successfully in respect of personal injury caused by the landlord's breach of his covenant to repair, as in *Griffin v Pillett*,[95] and *Porter v Jones*.[96] Again, a

[85] [1991] 1 W.L.R. 1421 CA at 1445H.
[86] [1999] 1 W.L.R. 1792 CA; facts at para.9-085, below.
[87] [2003] P.N.L.R. 3 at 29.
[88] See too *Storey v Charles Church Developments Plc* (2001) 73 Con. L.R. 1 at para.5-010, above.
[89] [2002] 2 A.C. 732.
[90] [2002] 2 A.C. 732 at [30], [57]–[60], and [108].
[91] Note Lord Scott's useful consideration at [85] of what is physical for these purposes. See the case further at paras 5-029, 5-030 and 34-062, below, particularly at para.5-030 for a questionable qualification made by Lord Scott now departed from.
[92] [1969] E.G.D. 535.
[93] See paras 5-004 to 5-006, above.
[94] [1943] A.C. 283.
[95] [1926] 1 K.B. 17.
[96] (1943) 112 L.J.K.B. 173 CA. See too *Kimber v Willett* [1947] K.B. 570 CA (contract to remove and clean carpet; claimant caught her foot in hall carpet left loose).

concurrent liability in tort did not exist in *Hobbs v L.S.W. Ry*,[97] where damages were claimed in respect of a cold caught by the wife through walking home in the rain, and while it is true that this part of the claim failed, it was only on the ground of remoteness.[98] Also, in *Cox v Philips Industries*,[99] an employee, suing his employers for breach of contract, recovered for illness due to relegation to a position of less responsibility than that to which he was entitled.[100]

Beyond this, the courts have shown a preparedness to award damages against solicitors for the deterioration of a client's physical and nervous condition during the period of delay, attributable to the solicitor's negligence, in hearing his action for personal injury, it being now medically recognised that the health of a person physically injured may be impaired by so-called compensation neurosis until such time as his claim for damages is settled. Such recovery was allowed in both *Wales v Wales*,[101] and *Malyon v Lawrence Messer & Co*.[102] On the other hand, in *Cook v Swinfen*,[103] where the solicitor's negligent defence of the divorce proceedings in which the now claimant was respondent resulted in her being adjudicated the guilty party and obtaining maintenance neither for herself nor for her son, damages were refused in respect of the ensuing breakdown in her health since this was not a reasonably foreseeable result of her failure in the litigation and was, accordingly, too remote.[104] **5-021**

Damages for loss of amenities may appear where there is no physical injury to the person. This was so in *Newman v Framewood Manor Management Co Ltd*,[105] where the lessor of an apartment in a block of flats was in breach of covenant in the provision of leisure facilities by way of swimming pool, jacuzzi and gym. The Court of Appeal allowed the claimant damages, though of a modest amount, for her loss of amenity in the use of the premises.[106] **5-022**

### (3) MENTAL DISTRESS[107]

It was once the law that no damages could be recovered in contract for injury to the feelings. This proposition, heralded in *Hamlin v G.N. Ry*,[108] where the claimant was set down by the defendant railway company at the wrong town and, there being no further conveyance that evening, spent the night there, was accepted in **5-023**

---

97 (1875) L.R. 10 Q.B. 111: facts at para.5-017, above.

98 And even the remoteness point has been doubted in *McMahon v Field* (1881) 7 Q.B.D. 591 CA.

99 [1976] 1 W.L.R. 638.

100 This aspect of the decision would not seem to be affected by its overruling in connection with mental distress: see para.5-027, below.

101 (1967) 111 S.J. 946.

102 (1968) 112 S.J. 623. And see *Collard v Saunders* [1971] C.L.Y. 11161 (recovery for nervous breakdown due to acquisition of defective premises).

103 [1967] 1 W.L.R. 457 CA.

104 But Lord Denning MR said in *Heywood v Wellers* [1976] Q.B. 446 CA at 459C, in the context of a successful claim for damages for mental distress (see para.5-025, below), that *Cook v Swinfen* "may have to be reconsidered".

105 [2012] EWCA Civ 159 CA.

106 [2012] EWCA Civ 159 CA at [42] and following.

107 As with tort, damages for mental distress are now available only to individuals and not to companies. For the position in tort see para.5-014, above.

108 (1856) 1 H. & N. 408; no damages can be given "for the disappointment of mind occasioned by the breach of contract": at 411, per Pollock CB.

*Hobbs v L.S.W. Ry*,[109] where not even a hotel was available,[110] and established by the House of Lords in *Addis v Gramophone Co*,[111] where it was held that damages for the wrongful dismissal of a servant could not include compensation for his injured feelings, even if he had been dismissed in a harsh and humiliating manner. Such damages have also been refused in *Groom v Crocker*,[112] where a solicitor was in breach of contract by wrongly admitting negligence on the part of the claimant, his client, in an action brought against the latter in respect of a car collision; and in *Bailey v Bullock*,[113] of which the facts have already been given,[114] it was held to be clear that the claimant could not recover for "the annoyance or mental distress" in being his father-in-law's lodger and not an independent householder.[115]

**5-024** It was, however, respectfully suggested in the 1961 edition of this work, the first written by Dr McGregor, that there is no reason why there could not be exceptions in proper cases to this sound general rule. The reason for the general rule is that contracts normally concern commercial matters and that mental suffering on breach is not in the contemplation of the parties as part of the business risk of the transaction. If, however, the contract is not primarily a commercial one, in the sense that it affects not the claimant's business interests but his personal, social and family interests, the door should not be closed to awarding damages for mental suffering if the court thinks that in the particular circumstances the parties to the contract had such damage in their contemplation.[116]

**5-025** Support for this approach came in some abundance in the 1970s. The new view was heralded by a Scots case, *Diesen v Samson*,[117] where a bride was awarded damages for distress and disappointment by reason of having no pictorial record of her wedding as the defender photographer in breach of contract failed to appear there,[118] and that damages for mental distress may be recovered in contract became firmly established through two important decisions of the Court of Appeal, *Jarvis v Swan's Tours*,[119] and *Heywood v Wellers*,[120] the former of which was followed and applied to similar facts by that court in *Jackson v Horizon Holidays*.[121] *Jarvis*,[122] and *Jackson*,[123] both involved spoiled holidays. The claimant in *Jarvis* had booked a

---

[109] (1875) L.R. 10 Q.B. 111; "for the mere inconvenience, such as annoyance and loss of temper, or vexation, or for being disappointed in a particular thing which you have set your mind upon, … you cannot recover damages": at 122, per Mellor J.

[110] However, the fact that damages for physical inconvenience were awarded shows that the line between this head and that of physical inconvenience (para.5-017, above) can be fine.

[111] [1909] A.C. 488; "in proceedings which have cast a long shadow over the common law": per Lord Nicholls in *Eastwood v Magnox Electric Plc* [2005] 1 A.C. 503 at [1]. See Addis at paras 5-031 to 5-034, below.

[112] [1939] 1 K.B. 194 CA.

[113] [1950] 2 All E.R. 1167.

[114] See para.5-018, above.

[115] [1950] 2 All E.R. 1167 at 1170.

[116] See Lord Scott in a House of Lords decision in this area, *Farley v Skinner* [2002] 2 A.C. 732 at [75]: "In my opinion, the issue can and should be resolved by applying the well-known principles in *Hadley v Baxendale* (1854) 9 Ex. 341."

[117] 1971 S.L.T. (Sh. Ct.) 49.

[118] The passage in the 1961 edition, arguing that damages for mental distress should be recoverable in appropriate cases of contract, was expressly adopted by the judge.

[119] [1973] Q.B. 233 CA.

[120] [1976] Q.B. 446 CA.

[121] [1975] 1 W.L.R. 1468 CA.

[122] [1973] Q.B. 233 CA.

[123] [1975] 1 W.L.R. 1468 CA.

winter sports holiday in Switzerland in reliance on what Edmund Davies LJ called the defendant travel agents' "lavishly illustrated brochure with its ecstatic text",[124] only to discover that the "great time"[125] which had been promised did not materialise and the many facilities which he had been led to expect were simply not there. The holiday proved a great disappointment, and the Court of Appeal gave the claimant damages for the disappointment, distress, annoyance and frustration caused by the breach of contract, regarding as espousing limitations which were no longer acceptable the early statements in *Hamlin* and in *Hobbs*,[126] that damages in contract are not available to a claimant for inconvenience stopping short of physical inconvenience. In a proper case damages for mental distress can be recovered in contract, and a contract for a holiday was a proper case.[127] Then came *Heywood*,[128] which presented a very different fact situation. Solicitors instructed by the claimant to bring proceedings to restrain a man from molesting her so bungled the proceedings that the molestation continued, and the Court of Appeal allowed her damages for her resulting mental distress and upset.

After these cases there was a period when it seemed that damages for mental distress in contract were destined, with general Court of Appeal endorsement, to take giant strides. *Perry v Sidney Phillips & Son*,[129] seemed to allow for damages for distress in a contract for the survey of a house, *Buckley v Lane Herdman & Co*,[130] in a contract with solicitors in relation to a house, and *Cox v Philips Industries*,[131] at first instance, even in a contract of employment on, admittedly, somewhat special facts, the employee complaining not of dismissal but of having been relegated to a position of less responsibility. In a contract of lease of land, Lord Denning MR suggested in *McCall v Abelesz*,[132] that damages for mental distress would be recoverable where there was a breach of the covenant of quiet enjoyment resulting in disturbance and harassment by a landlord of a tenant,[133] a view which was adopted, even after a general change of heart had appeared,[134] in *Sampson v Floyd*,[135] and in *Calabar Properties v Stitcher*,[136] breach of the lessor's covenant to repair was held to lead to such damages. The law stood thus when a further edition of this work was being finalised in 1987,[137] but a more limiting attitude was on its way and retraction just round the corner. 5-026

---

[124] [1973] Q.B. 233 CA at 239B.

[125] [1973] Q.B. 233 CA at 239B.

[126] See para.5-023, above.

[127] Recovery for a spoilt holiday was allowed in *Jackson v Chrysler Acceptances* [1978] R.T.R. 474 CA, (see the case at para.26-013, below) and was again addressed, as to the correct measure of damages, in *Milner v Carnival Plc* [2010] 3 All E.R. 701 CA (an important case: details at para.34-095, below). A contract for air transport, en route for a holiday, is not within this category so as to allow recovery for distress: See *Cowden v British Airways Plc* [2009] 2 Lloyd's Rep. 653.

[128] [1976] Q.B. 446 CA.

[129] [1982] 1 W.L.R. 1297 CA.

[130] [1977] C.L.Y. 3143.

[131] [1976] 1 W.L.R. 638.

[132] [1976] Q.B. 585 CA.

[133] Lord Denning MR went as far as to say that "it is now settled that the court can give damages for the mental upset and distress caused by the defendant's conduct in breach of contract": [1976] Q.B. 585 CA at 594.

[134] See para.5-027, below.

[135] [1989] 2 E.G.L.R. 49 CA.

[136] [1984] 1 W.L.R. 287 CA; and *Elmcroft Developments v Tankersley-Sawyer* (1984) 15 H.L.R. 63 CA.

[137] The cases up to this time are all to be found there: 15th edn (London: Sweet & Maxwell, 1988), paras 99 and 100.

**5-027** The downturn started with *Bliss v South East Thames Regional Health Authority*[138] holding that damages for mental distress were not recoverable by an employee suing not for wrongful dismissal but for breach of the implied term of trust and confidence; *Cox v Philips Industries*[139] was overruled. Dillon LJ echoed in more detail the sentiment already expressed in *Heywood v Wellers*,[140] but until *Bliss* virtually ignored in the intervening cases, that in effect the appropriate context for damages for mental distress was where the predominant object of the contract was the provision of some mental satisfaction, whether by the giving of pleasure or the removal of distress[141]; a contract of employment was not such a contract. Then in rapid succession came a series of cases in the Court of Appeal refusing damages for mental distress, and for the same reasons, in the other types of contract in which they had formerly been allowed.[142] In *Hayes v James & Charles Dodd*,[143] the defendant solicitor had wrongly advised the claimants that there was essential rear access to the larger business premises they were purchasing so that, without that access, the business had to be closed down and the premises eventually disposed of, but no recovery was allowed to the claimants for their anguish and vexation caused by all this; the contract was a commercial one. In *Watts v Morrow*[144] the defendant surveyor had wrongly pronounced the house the claimants were purchasing to be in good condition but their distress at having to live effectively on a building site while extensive repairs were carried out did not sound in damages; again the contract was a commercial one. In *Branchett v Beaney*,[145] the defendant landlords constructed an access way to a new house which it was proposed to build across the front garden of the claimant, an old lady who was their tenant, but it was held that breach of the covenant for quiet enjoyment in the lease did not give rise to damages for the claimant's injured feelings and mental distress; the term enjoyment in the covenant did not refer to the derivation of pleasure but simply to the exercise, use and benefit of the right. Somewhat later came *Alexander v Rolls Royce Motors*,[146] where no damages for distress and disappointment were awarded against the seller and repairer of a prestigious car. The earlier cases[147] which had apparently produced different results were interpreted as being limited to the distress caused by physical discomfort,[148] which had for long been accorded recovery,[149] or were doubted.[150]

---

138 [1987] I.C.R. 700 CA.

139 [1976] 1 W.L.R. 638. *Bliss* had already been heralded by *Shove v Downs Surgical* [1984] 1 All E.R. 7 but it was a case of wrongful dismissal.

140 [1976] Q.B. 446 CA at 463H to 464A, per Bridge LJ: "a clear distinction … between mental distress which is an incidental consequence … of the misconduct of litigation … and mental distress … which is the direct and inevitable consequence of the … failure to obtain the very relief which it was the sole purpose of the litigation to secure."

141 [1987] I.C.R. 700 CA at 718; his precise formulation was "a contract to provide peace of mind or freedom from distress".

142 The curious *W v Egdell* [1990] Ch. 359, where the claimant murderer unsuccessfully claimed damages for his distress at the disclosure of a medical report on him by the defendant doctor, was the first case in which *Bliss* was applied but it was not grounded in contract.

143 [1990] 2 All E.R. 815 CA.

144 [1991] 1 W.L.R. 1421 CA.

145 [1992] 3 All E.R. 910 CA.

146 [1996] R.T.R. 95 CA.

147 Those at para.5-026, above.

148 In particular, *Perry v Sidney Phillips & Son* [1982] 1 W.L.R. 1297 CA.

149 See paras 5-017 to 5-019, above. *Holder v Countrywide Surveyors* [2003] P.N.L.R. 3 at 29 again il-

In *Watts v Morrow*,[151] Bingham LJ summed up the position which had developed, thus: **5-028**

"A contract-breaker is not in general liable for any distress, frustration, anxiety, displeasure, vexation, tension or aggravation which his breach of contract may cause to the innocent party. This rule is not, I think, founded on the assumption that such reactions are not foreseeable, which they surely are or may be, but on considerations of policy.[152] But the rule is not absolute. Where the very object of a contract is to provide pleasure, relaxation, peace of mind or freedom from molestation, damages will be awarded if the fruit of the contract is not provided or if the contrary result is procured instead."[153]

Thus the House of Lords rightly refused damages for mental distress in *Johnson v Gore Wood & Co*,[154] where the claimant property developer had engaged the defendant solicitor to advise him in connection with an acquisition for development of land over which he had an option to purchase and the solicitor's mishandling of the matter led to anxiety as a result of the protracted litigation process to which the developer was subjected, extra financial embarrassment for him and his family, and deterioration in the family relationships. The contract was a purely commercial one. The Court of Appeal refused damages for disappointment and distress on account of a solicitor's poor preparation for divorce proceedings in *Channon v Lindley Johnstone*,[155] and arising from the Official Solicitor's bad handling of litigation in *Howell-Smith v Official Solicitor*.[156] Disappointment at not receiving publicity by way of credits in programmes for a highly successful play did not sound in damages in *Brighton v Jones*,[157] and no damages for distress were given in *Wiseman v Virgin Atlantic Airways Plc*,[158] where airline staff ridiculed the claimant and refused to let him board a plane.

The House of Lords departed somewhat from Bingham LJ's approach in the context of a somewhat special contract for a survey in *Farley v Skinner*.[159] The defendant surveyor, retained by the claimant to survey a house and asked specifically to state whether the property was affected by aircraft noise, which the claimant particularly wished to avoid, negligently failed to discover that the house was so affected. The House of Lords, rightly reversing the majority decision of the Court of Appeal, held that the claimant was not precluded from recovery for the distress caused to him by the excessive aircraft noise over the house since the contract came **5-029**

---

lustrates the appropriateness of recovery for distress accompanying physical inconvenience; see the case at para.5-018, above.

150 As was *Sampson v Floyd* [1989] 2 E.G.L.R. 49 CA.

151 [1991] 1 W.L.R. 1421 CA.

152 Though foreseeable, the mental distress could still be said not to have been in the contemplation of the parties as something for which the defendant would be liable: see further on this at para.8-209, below.

153 [1991] 1 W.L.R. 1421 CA.

154 [2002] 2 A.C. 1.

155 [2002] P.N.L.R. 41 CA at 884.

156 [2006] P.N.L.R. 21 CA at 394. The earlier solicitor case of *Dickinson v Jones Alexander & Co* [1993] 2 F.L.R. 321 would today probably be regarded as wrong in allowing damages for mental distress to a wife against solicitors who, while aware of her fragile mental health, had handled her divorce proceedings badly so as to leave her with inadequate financial provision. None of the cases of the previous few years which had brought the law into its present position (see para.5-027, above) appears to have been cited.

157 [2004] E.M.L.R. 26 at 507; see [87] and [88].

158 [2006] EWHC 1566 (QB).

159 [2002] 2 A.C. 732.

within the exceptional category mapped out by Bingham LJ in *Watts*. It sufficed for recovery that the provision of peace of mind or the avoidance of distress was a principal object of the contract without being its sole or entire object or purpose; the contrary argument accepted by the Court of Appeal is convincingly demolished by Lord Steyn in *Farley*.[160] What was said in *Farley v Skinner* was adopted by the Court of Appeal in *Yearworth v North Bristol NHS Trust*[161] to hold that claimants might recover for mental distress suffered on learning that sperm of theirs which had been banked with a fertility unit for later use had been damaged and lost to them.[162]

**5-030** In this context it is also important to consider the influence of the decision of the House of Lords in *Ruxley Electronics v Forsyth*.[163] A house owner contracted to have a swimming pool built in his garden and it was not built according to the specifications as to depth but the shortfall was found neither to be dangerous nor to diminish the value of the pool. The House of Lords, having held that the cost of reinstatement could not be claimed as damages because it would be unreasonable to reinstate, further held that where, as in the case before the court, there has been a breach of performance resulting in loss of expectation of performance or satisfaction of a personal preference, damages may be awarded at a modest level for non-pecuniary loss. Here then is a recovery for non-pecuniary loss in a contract of a commercial nature where it would be difficult to say that a principal object of the contract was the provision of some mental satisfaction. The decision may not have a very wide range; it could be limited to cases of the *Ruxley* type where reinstatement is not allowed and, without an award for non-pecuniary loss, the claimant is going to be confined to nominal damages against a defendant who has failed to fulfil his contractual promise. In not applying *Ruxley* the Court of Appeal in *Farley v Skinner (No.2)*,[164] distinguished it on the ground that the contract there called for an end result whereas that in *Farley* was a contract for professional services negligently performed. This is a distinction without a difference in the context of recovery for mental distress and the House of Lords, in reversing in *Farley*,[165] had no difficulty in rejecting it.[166] *Farley* is, of course, similar to *Ruxley* in that the only redress that the claimant could have was for his non-financial loss, there being no available claim for financial loss because the claimant had chosen to retain the

---

160 [2002] 2 A.C. 732 at [23] and [24]. *Knott v Bolton* (1995) 11 Con. L.J. 375 CA, where damages for disappointment had been refused against an architect who had designed a house lacking the impressive staircase stipulated, was overruled. Where in *Haysman v MRS Films Ltd* [2008] EWHC 2494 (QB) the claimant had contracted with the defendant film company for the use of his home as the location for a film and the defendant in making the film had caused extensive damage to the property, damages for mental distress were achieved by the trial judge regarding provision of peace of mind as an important object of the contract; but it is thought that this goes too far. As for the non-pecuniary award in *Demarco v Perkins* [2006] P.N.L.R. 27 CA at 512 to a claimant suffering from the stigma of a bankruptcy which could have been revoked but for the defendant accountancy firm's negligent handling of its retainer, it was agreed by the parties that "a material element in a retainer is the provision of peace of mind and the avoidance of distress": [2006] P.N.L.R. 27 CA at [55]. For more on *Farley* see para.5-018, above and paras 5-030 and 34-062, below.

161 [2010] Q.B. 1 CA.

162 Here was breach of a bailment rather than breach of a contract but the Court of Appeal amalgamated the two in its analysis of what damages should be available.

163 [1996] A.C. 344.

164 [2000] P.N.L.R. 441 CA.

165 [2002] 2 A.C. 732.

166 The matter is well put by Lord Steyn at [2002] 2 A.C. 732 at [25].

house and put up with the aircraft noise and because the trial judge had held that the presence of the aircraft noise did not diminish the value of the house on the market.[167] However, Lord Scott's comment,[168] that if there had been a reduction in market value as a result of the aircraft noise the claimant could not have recovered both the difference in value and damages for discomfort, seems dubious. Allowing both would surely not be double recovery as he suggests; pecuniary loss and non-pecuniary loss lead to two separate and distinct recoveries. Lord Scott might be right in a *Ruxley* situation where the non-pecuniary award may be considered to be dependent upon the non-existence of a pecuniary one but in *Farley* the discomfort and distress caused by the excessive noise was completely independent of its effect upon the market value of the property. Lord Scott's dictum has now been firmly disapproved by Newey J in *Herrmann v Withers LLP*.[169] Citing with approval what is said above in this paragraph, he held the claimant purchasers of a residential property entitled to damages for the disappointment and the loss of amenity in being unable to use a communal garden in addition to the damages awarded representing the diminution in value of the property from the lack of garden use.[170]

These developments had not directly touched on the House of Lords decision which had laid the foundation for the rule of no damages for mental distress in contract, *Addis v Gramophone Co*,[171] with its refusal of such damages to a wrongfully dismissed employee. *Addis* had not been addressed by their Lordships over the whole of the last century; then at the beginning of this, it has suddenly fallen for consideration by them on two occasions, first in *Johnson v Gore Wood & Co*,[172] and next in *Johnson v Unisys Ltd*.[173] Although in neither was recovery for mental distress in the context of employment contracts in issue—the former was a claim for mental distress but arising out of a contract with a professional[174] while the latter was a claim arising out of an employment contract but a claim for pecuniary loss only[175]—what was said in those cases about recovery for mental distress may suggest that the continued existence of *Addis*, which Lord Woolf MR in the Court of Appeal in *Unysis*[176] described as "a cornerstone of the law of" employer and employee,[177] may be at risk. **5-031**

Thus in *Gore Wood*,[178] Lord Cooke was at pains to distance himself from any approval of *Addis*.[179] He pointed out that, in severely confining damages for wrongful dismissal, their Lordships' House of those days had seen the relationship of employer and employee as no more than an ordinary commercial one which was "a world away from the concept now". He pointed out that *Addis* had not been applied, so as to refuse damages for mental distress in all employment circumstances, **5-032**

---

167 See the facts of the case at para.5-029, above.
168 [2002] 2 A.C. 732 at [109].
169 [2012] EWHC 1492 Ch.
170 [2012] EWHC 1492 Ch at [125]–[128]. Full facts at para.9-107, below.
171 [1909] A.C. 488.
172 [2002] 2 A.C. 1.
173 [2003] 1 A.C. 518.
174 Facts at para.5-028, above.
175 Facts at para.33-026, below.
176 [1999] 1 All E.R. 854 CA.
177 [1999] 1 All E.R. 854 CA at 858e.
178 [2002] 2 A.C. 1.
179 [2002] 2 A.C. 1 at 50B to F.

in either Canada[180] or New Zealand,[181] and concluded: "I take leave to doubt the permanence of *Addis* in English law."[182]

**5-033** The position in *Unisys*,[183] was more complicated. In *Mahmud v Bank of Credit and Commerce International SA*,[184] the House had already decided that where the employee's claim was not simply for damages for wrongful dismissal but for breach of some other term of the contract, in that case of the so-called trust and confidence term, *Addis* did not stand in the way of recovery of pecuniary loss; non-pecuniary loss was not an issue. In *Unisys*, again only pecuniary loss was in issue but their Lordships, other than perhaps Lord Steyn, were unable to find breach of the trust and confidence term or any other term. Nor were they prepared to find for a term which dealt with wrongful dismissal because any extension of the law in relation to wrongful dismissal had been precluded by the legislation giving employees a remedy for unfair dismissal. Accordingly, the claim for pecuniary loss failed and a claim for non-pecuniary loss must equally have failed, indeed a fortiori. However, had there been a breach of a term of the employment contract independent of dismissal *tout court*, there are indications that at least some of their Lordships would have been prepared to contemplate recovery for mental distress. Thus Lord Hoffmann referred to the preparedness of a Canadian judge to award damages for mental distress and loss of reputation and prestige where there was breach of an implied obligation on an employer to be honest and to refrain from insensitive and unfair conduct, and added:

> "Such an approach would in this country have to circumvent or overcome the obstacle of *Addis* … Speaking for myself, I think that, if this task was one which I felt called upon to perform, I would be able to do so."[185]

Lord Millett agreed that

> "the general rule [namely, of no recovery for non-pecuniary loss whether to feelings or to reputation] would seem to be a sound one, at least in relation to ordinary commercial contracts entered into by both parties with a view of profit".[186]

However, while

> "in *Addis*'s case the House of Lords treated a contract of employment as an ordinary commercial contract terminable at will … contracts of employment are no longer regarded as purely commercial contracts entered into between free and equal agents".[187]

Two further cases in this area have followed in the House of Lords, *Dunnachie v Kingston upon Hull City Council*,[188] and *Eastwood v Magnox Electric Plc*,[189] but neither adds to or advances the issue. *Eastwood* was concerned with matters other

---

[180] Citing *Brown v Waterloo Regional Board of Commissioners of Police* 136 D.L.R. (3d) 49 (1982).
[181] Citing *Whelan v Wanitaki Meats Ltd* [1991] 2 N.Z.L.R. 74.
[182] [2002] 2 A.C. 1 at 50F.
[183] [2003] 1 A.C. 518.
[184] [1998] A.C. 20.
[185] [2003] 1 A.C. 518 at [44].
[186] [2003] 1 A.C. 518 at [70].
[187] [2003] 1 A.C. 518 at [71] and [77]. Lord Bingham, without delivering a separate speech, said that he agreed with those of Lords Hoffmann and Millett.
[188] [2005] 1 A.C. 226.
[189] [2005] 1 A.C. 503.

than mental distress and non-financial loss[190] and *Dunnachie* was limiting its outlawing of recovery for non-financial loss to unfair dismissal claims.[191] Nor does *Edwards v Chesterfield Royal Hospital NHS Foundation Trust*,[192] take the matter further as the Supreme Court was disallowing a claim for financial loss, but it would follow that there could a fortiori be no recovery for mental distress.

The above views appearing in cases at the highest level, admittedly of an obiter nature, suggest that the general rule in *Addis* may soon be abandoned and that, in addition, one should not adhere too closely to the somewhat limiting test, for recovery of damages for mental distress, of whether a principal object of the contract is to promote enjoyment or avoid distress but simply to apply the wider, more principled test of whether recovery for the particular loss is within the contemplation of the contracting parties. This is how it was put by Lord Millett: "In such cases [namely, cases of ordinary commercial contracts]", he said in *Unisys*, "non-pecuniary loss such as mental suffering consequent on breach is not within the contemplation of the parties and is accordingly too remote."[193] While the current position is that there can be no recovery for mental distress arising from the employer's breach of the implied term of trust and confidence, this having been held by the Court of Appeal in *Bliss v South East Thames Regional Health Authority*,[194] and in *French v Barclays Bank*,[195] and accepted as the law in *Gogay v Hertfordshire County Council*,[196] this may not remain the position for much longer. **5-034**

## (4) SOCIAL DISCREDIT

That no damages are recoverable for injury to the reputation is a proposition closely connected with, and established by the same authorities as, the proposition, now to a very large degree eroded, that no damages are recoverable for injury to the feelings.[197] The cornerstone for this further proposition was once again *Addis v Gramophone Co*,[198] which made clear, in the context of wrongful dismissal, that any non-pecuniary loss through loss of reputation is not to be compensated. Even if by wrongful dismissal the servant's reputation suffers so as to cause him a pecuniary loss, *Addis* suggests, and the courts have so far accepted, that this does not lead to damages[199]; this must be a fortiori true of non-pecuniary loss. In *Groom v Crocker*,[200] and in *Bailey v Bullock*,[201] the refusal of damages for mental suffering was linked with their refusal for "social discredit" in the one case and "loss of prestige" in the other. However, the consideration now given to *Addis* by the House of Lords in *Johnson v Gore Wood & Co*,[202] and *Johnson v Unisys Ltd*,[203] has put the **5-035**

---

190 See the case at para.33-031, below.
191 See the case at para.33-003, below.
192 [2012] 2 A.C. 22. See the case at para.33-027, below.
193 [2003] 1 A.C. 518 at [70]. And see similarly Lord Scott in *Farley v Skinner*, cited at para.5-024, above.
194 [1987] I.C.R. 700 CA; see the case at para.5-027, above.
195 [1998] I.R.L.R 646 CA.
196 [2000] I.R.L.R. 703 CA.
197 See paras 5-023 to 5-028, above.
198 [1909] A.C. 488.
199 This is dealt with at para.4-020, above.
200 [1939] 1 K.B. 194 CA; facts at para.5-023, above.
201 [1950] 2 All E.R. 1167; facts at para.5-018, above.
202 [2002] 2 A.C. 1.
203 [2003] 1 A.C. 518.

law here into somewhat of a state of flux. For, as we have seen,[204] while that consideration was primarily in relation to mental distress, and indeed pecuniary loss, the thrust of the discussion embraced injury to reputation as well as injury to feelings. Thus, as has already been pointed out but deserves repetition here, Lord Cooke said quite generally in *Gore Wood* that he took leave "to doubt the permanence of *Addis* in English law"[205] while Lord Hoffmann said in *Unisys* that, to overcome *Addis*, he felt prepared to award damages for mental distress and "loss of reputation and prestige".[206] Whether we shall see the limited retreat from the refusal of contract damages mapped out for mental distress followed by any comparable retreat in the field of contract damages for tarnished reputations is unsure. It may turn out that the new thinking will find application only to the contract of employment as the likeliest contract to affect reputation in its breach.

204 See the extended treatment at paras 5-031 to 5-034, above.
205 [2002] 2 A.C. 1, 50F; at para.5-032, above.
206 [2003] 1 A.C. 518 at [43]; at para.5-033, above.

# PART 1C: THE LIMITS OF COMPENSATORY DAMAGES

Chapter 6

# THE GENERAL PROBLEM OF LIMITS

Table of Contents



6-001 To award damages so as to put the claimant, as far as money can do, in the position he would have been in had the tort or breach of contract never occurred, would place too great a burden upon defendants. Some limits must be imposed upon this starting figure, and the defining and refining of these limits by the courts over the years have produced the most difficult, and hence the most interesting, problems in the whole field of damages.[1] The principal difficulties may be said to arise from two general issues: first, the distinction between the existence of a liability and the limits or extent of a liability the existence of which has been established, and, secondly, the distinctions between the various limits which have been imposed upon an existing liability.

## 1. Interrelation of Existence and Extent of Liability

6-002 In considering the general problem of the limits of compensatory damages there arises first a difficulty which is never very far away in problems of damages but which is at this point at its most acute. This is the difficulty of distinguishing the question of the existence of a liability to pay damages from the question of the extent of a liability to pay damages. Strictly the first does not concern damages at all, but in dealing with the second it is very difficult to disentangle the two questions. This is the case far more in tort than in contract, and *par excellence* in the tort of negligence. The difficulties are increased by the fact that there is an overlapping of concepts, and the same problem may sometimes be dealt with as a question of existence of liability, based on duty and scope of duty, and sometimes as one of extent, based on remoteness and causation. Thus, to take an illustration of this, in *Conarken Group Ltd v Network Rail Infrastructure Ltd*,[2] where road drivers had inflicted damage to railway tracks causing disruption of rail services, duty, scope of duty and remoteness, together with foreseeability, causation and

1 More learned writing covers this section of the book than any other. Particularly is this true of remoteness. Other matters here, especially mitigation, have had less treatment than their importance and intricacy deserve.

2 [2011] EWCA Civ 644 CA.

reasonableness, were all under discussion in the claim by the railway authorities against the road drivers.[3]

### (1) Duty and remoteness

In the tort of negligence, it is not always easy to separate the question of whether there has been a breach of the duty of care owed to the claimant from the question of whether, such a breach having been established, a particular item of damage is recoverable. In more familiar, but less exact, terms: is the problem one of duty of care or one of remoteness of damage?[4] "No duty" or "no duty broken" is the situation in which the conduct of the defendant is held not to constitute a wrong vis-à-vis the claimant; "damage being too remote" is the situation in which, although the defendant's conduct may constitute a wrong to the claimant, the damage in question is not closely enough related to the wrong. Similar fact patterns can give rise to cases in either category, as is well illustrated by *Perl (Exporters) v Camden London Borough Council*[5] in the first category and *Lamb v Camden London Borough Council*,[6] in the second, both of which were concerned with the impact of the acts of an independent third party which were intended to inflict on the claimant the damage in issue.[7] **6-003**

In earlier editions the development of the law on the duty of care was laid out, primarily through cases in the House of Lords, in order to show when the solution lay within the ambit of the first question without recourse to the second. There was the lack of a general duty of care to avoid economic loss until *Hedley Byrne & Co v Heller & Partners*,[8] came along, a decision which went further in *Anns v Merton London Borough Council*,[9] itself retracted in *Murphy v Brentwood District Council*,[10] but accompanied by a surge forward in such cases beginning with *Caparo Industries v Dickman*.[11] There were the decisions denying a duty of care to the physically injured where only physical injury to a third party could have been foreseen, our classic illustration of the unforeseeable plaintiff[12]—now the unforeseeable claimant—being *Bourhill v Young*.[13] Then there was the decision in *The Wagon Mound*,[14] departing from *Re Polemis*,[15] and imposing a liability not for direct consequences but for foreseeable consequences only, with the result that duty and remoteness stood on the same footing with no practical need to distinguish between them. All these results are encompassed in a consideration of the ambit of the duty of care, fully dealt with in other texts.[16] **6-004**

---

3 [2011] EWCA Civ 644 CA at [29]. See the case at para.39-029, below.
4 *Bourhill v Young* [1943] A.C. 92 is the leading case pointing this distinction in these terms.
5 [1984] Q.B. 342 CA.
6 [1981] Q.B. 625 CA.
7 See both cases at para.8-059, below.
8 [1964] A.C. 465.
9 [1978] A.C. 728.
10 [1991] 1 A.C. 398.
11 [1990] 2 A.C. 605.
12 A term appearing more commonly in American usage and perhaps best illustrated by the well-known American case of *Palsgraf v Long Island R.R. Co*, 248 N.Y. 339; 162 N.E. 99 (1928).
13 [1943] A.C. 92.
14 [1961] A.C. 338; see paras 8-032 and 8-088, below.
15 [1921] 3 K.B. 560 CA; see paras 8-031 and 8-088, below.
16 See the standard works on tort.

**6-005** *The Wagon Mound*,[17] however, leaves us with a single area of difference between the existence and the extent of liability. It drew a distinction, which later cases have built upon, between damage different in degree and damage different in type, so that, provided the type of damage inflicted was foreseeable and the duty of care thereby satisfied, the tortfeasor may be liable in damages for a more extensive degree of damage of that type than he could have anticipated.[18]

### (2) Volenti non fit injuria, remoteness and contributory negligence

**6-006** These three limits of recovery need to be considered together here for this reason. The first, volenti non fit injuria, goes to the existence of a liability while the other two, remoteness and contributory negligence, go to its extent.

**6-007** A person cannot claim damages for injury to himself or damage to his property where he has consented to the infliction of the harm or taken on himself the risk of such harm, a proposition enshrined in the maxim volenti non fit injuria. Thus although it has been held, in *R. v Donovan*,[19] where a girl consented to a beating for sexual gratification, that her consent afforded her chastiser no defence when criminally prosecuted for assault, it is clear that it would have been a complete defence had the girl sued him in tort for assault. Where, at the other end of the scale, liability rather than being based on intentional acts is strict, as it is under s.2 of the Animals Act 1971 for injuries caused by animals but with the volenti defence introduced by s.5(2), that defence succeeded in *Goldsmith v Patchcott*,[20] in barring a claim by a horse rider for injuries from her fall from the horse. However, it is in negligence cases that the maxim is most often prayed in aid by defendants. While here the confines of its operation are hard to state with any precision,[21] it is seldom indeed that the defence succeeds. Thus even a suicide was held not to allow a successful plea of volenti in either *Reeves v Commissioner of Police of the Metropolis*,[22] or *Corr v IBC Vehicles Ltd*.[23] Details of the cases would be out of place here since the maxim, if applied, removes any liability at all.

**6-008** Nevertheless it is important to realise that a particular set of facts may involve an overlapping of volenti and remoteness as competing solutions to the problem. *Cutler v United Dairies*,[24] is a good illustration of this. The claimant had attempted to hold a restive horse in a field and was injured when the horse suddenly reared. His action for damages failed, and for this both volenti and remoteness were invoked by the Court of Appeal. So too in *Reeves v Commissioner of Police of the Metropolis*,[25] and in *Corr v IBC Vehicles Ltd*,[26] each of which involved a suicide, volenti and remoteness, by way of novus actus, were both in play[27] but neither was

---

17 [1961] A.C. 338; see paras 8-032 and 8-088, below.

18 See paras 8-092 to 8-096, below.

19 [1934] 2 K.B. 498 CA.

20 [2012] EWCA Civ 183 CA.

21 See, e.g. the difficulties involved in *Dann v Hamilton* [1939] 1 K.B. 509.

22 [2000] 1 A.C. 360; facts at para.8-065, below.

23 [2008] A.C. 884; facts at para.8-065, below.

24 [1933] 2 K.B. 297 CA. As to the decision itself, it must now be read in the light of *Haynes v Harwood* [1935] 1 K.B. 146 CA.

25 [2000] 1 A.C. 360.

26 [2008] A.C. 884.

27 Together with contributory negligence; see para.6-009, below.

held to be applicable.[28] In these three cases the same result would have been reached by either route, but it is important not to telescope the two concepts in the consideration of any problem, as somewhat different criteria may govern their application. Thus the courts are slow to decide against a claimant on the ground of volenti in a negligence action; there is less hesitancy in holding damage too remote.

For similar reasons volenti and contributory negligence may overlap, contributory negligence being the situation in which the claimant's failure to take reasonable care for his own safety has contributed to the damage. Here it is of far greater practical importance to keep the two separate, as the defence of volenti bars the action while contributory negligence, since 1945, will only reduce the damages.[29] In *Reeves v Commissioner of Police of the Metropolis*,[30] and again in *Corr v IBC Vehicles Ltd*,[31] both volenti and contributory negligence were in play[32]; only contributory negligence was held to be applicable in *Reeves* while neither was applied in *Corr*.[33] **6-009**

## 2. INTERRELATION OF VARIOUS FACETS OF THE EXTENT OF LIABILITY

Even when past the hurdle of establishing the existence of a liability, further difficulties arise in distinguishing among themselves the various limits set by the courts upon the recovery of damages. **6-010**

### (1) Contributory negligence, remoteness and mitigation

A claimant may have his damages cut down because his own conduct has constituted contributory negligence, has rendered some of the damage too remote, or has constituted a failure to mitigate the damage, which may be defined as a failure on the part of the claimant to take reasonable steps either to reduce the original loss or to avert further loss. This covers the whole ground of contributory negligence and mitigation, but damage may be too remote from causes other than the claimant's conduct, whether acts of third parties or natural events: this factor does, of course, distinguish remoteness from the other two, but since the difficulties to be discussed arise only with cases of remoteness stemming from the claimant's conduct, cases of remoteness beyond these are not included in the present context. **6-011**

A person crosses the street without due care for his own safety and is run down by a negligent motorist. A person, temporarily crippled by being run down one day by a negligent motorist, hobbles across the street the following day and is run down by a careful motorist whom he would have been able to avoid but for the prior injury. A person, run down by a negligent motorist, unreasonably fails or refuses to enter hospital for treatment. In all of these illustrations one could conceivably use any of the three concepts and say that the damages are to be reduced on the ground of contributory negligence, or of remoteness, or of failure to mitigate. In practice the first is likely to be categorised only as contributory negligence and the **6-012**

---

28 The facts of the two cases are at para.8-065, below.
29 See Ch.7, below.
30 [2000] 1 A.C. 360.
31 [2008] A.C. 884.
32 Together with remoteness: see para.6-008, above.
33 For the facts of the two cases see para.8-065, below.

second as contributory negligence or remoteness, while the third could be considered as contributory negligence, remoteness or failure to mitigate. Where then do the differences lie?

6-013 Contributory negligence, remoteness, mitigation—it is submitted that this is the order in which they fall to be considered, so that if the case is one of contributory negligence the other two will generally not come into play, while if the matter is solved at the stage of remoteness then mitigation will never be in issue. The distinctions between these three limits on damages need to be examined, the important practical distinction being that a finding of contributory negligence reduces the damages whereas a finding of remoteness or mitigation can eliminate them.

6-014 **(a) Contributory negligence and remoteness** Generally speaking, contributory negligence arises at the time of or before the defendant's wrong: this puts the first illustration above[34] into this category, and certainly a defendant would have little or no hope of arguing successfully for an application of the remoteness doctrine to eliminate rather than cut down his liability in such circumstances. But this leaves out the other two illustrations from this category, despite the fact that ordinary linguistic usage would allow the term contributory negligence to be applied to them. Before 1945[35] matters following upon a wrong were never considered to bar an action for the initial injury on the ground of later contributory negligence, and today a defendant should be no more entitled to invoke s.1 of the Law Reform (Contributory Negligence) Act of that year to cut down his liability for the initial injury.[36] But beyond this, a claimant should, generally speaking, not be in a position to argue that he is entitled to reduced damages for any increased injury to which his later negligence has contributed, instead of being entitled to no damages at all, on account of remoteness, for injury flowing from his subsequent act.[37]

6-015 However, there may occasionally be cases in which it is proper for the court to refuse to apply the remoteness doctrine to cut out recovery altogether in respect of injury subsequent to a wrong and yet to apply the contributory negligence doctrine to reduce the recoverable damages in respect of it. Such a case was *Sayers v Harlow U.D.C.*[38] The claimant, locked in a public lavatory owing to the defendants' negligence, attempted to climb over the door but slipped and injured herself. The Court of Appeal held first that the damage was not too remote, but then proceeded to reduce the damages on account of the claimant's contributory negligence. Here, of course, the injury subsequent to the wrong was the only injury suffered by the claimant; the more interesting, and more important situation, is where the subsequent injury is additional to injury inflicted at the time of the wrong for which the defendant is undoubtedly liable. In *The Calliope*,[39] a ship of that name sustained damage in a collision with another ship, the Carlsholm, attributable to the fault of both. In view of the damage and the time lost, the master of the Calliope decided

---

34 In the preceding paragraph but one.

35 Contributory negligence has concerned extent and not merely existence of liability only since 1945; see para.7-001, below.

36 This was fully accepted in *The Calliope* [1970] P. 172, dealt with in the next paragraph.

37 Thus *Environment Agency v Ellis* [2009] P.I.Q.R. P5 CA at 85 (facts at para.10-018, below) shows that, where the intervening act of the claimant was a further accident by falling off a ladder, this will either eliminate the damages or have no effect on them. No question of apportionment or of reduction of the damages could arise: see at [2009] P.I.Q.R. P5 CA at [37] and [38].

38 [1958] 1 W.L.R. 623 CA.

39 [1970] P. 172.

to proceed to a point up river and lie there over the ebb tide. Next day, while executing a turning manoeuvre in the river, the Calliope sustained further damage. Brandon J took the view that he was not required to choose between holding the Carlsholm liable for all the further damage or for none of it; instead it was open to him to find as a matter of law, and he did find on the facts, that the further damage was caused partly by the original collision and partly by the intervening negligence of the Calliope, thereby allowing the court to give partial recovery to the owners of the Calliope for the further damage to their ship.[40]

Brandon J, however, rightly recognised that in a great many cases the chain of causation will be broken by the intervention of the claimant's negligence between the original casualty and the subsequent damage, and that **6-016**

> "cases where it would be right to find that such damage was caused both by such intervening negligence and by the original negligence which resulted in the casualty may well be comparatively rare".[41]

Thus there are illustrations among the ship collision cases themselves where all recovery for subsequent damage has been refused on the ground of remoteness,[42] and in *McKew v Holland and Hannen and Cubitts*,[43] which was decided nearly contemporaneously with *The Calliope*,[44] the House of Lords did not seek to give the claimant reduced damages for injury caused by falling downstairs when his leg was still affected by the injury for which the defendant was liable, but refused all recovery for the subsequent injury.[45] Then there is the unusual and interesting result in *Barings Plc v Coopers & Lybrand*,[46] where, in relation to events following upon the commission of the wrong, contributory negligence and remoteness had an effect on the damages in combination. The defendant auditors had negligently failed to uncover unauthorised trading by an employee which had resulted over time in huge losses to the claimant employer companies, but mismanagement of the companies was such that for long the unauthorised trading, and hence the losses, went undetected by them. The trial judge concluded[47] that there had been increasing contributory negligence, starting at 50 and finishing at 80 per cent, until eventu-

---

40 Since the Calliope had been contributorily negligent in the initial collision, thereby leading to an apportionment of liability for the initial damage, it was necessary to make a sub-apportionment of liability in respect of the further damage, but Brandon J made it clear that had the Calliope been blameless in the initial collision he would have applied the same principles and made an apportionment, as opposed to a sub-apportionment, of liability for the further damage: [1970] P. 172 at 178. The Calliope was held to be 55 per cent responsible for the initial damage and 50 per cent responsible for the subsequent damage, so that the owners were entitled to recover 22.5 per cent of the subsequent damage: see [1970] P. 172 at 186.

41 [1970] P. 172 at 184.

42 See *Grant v S.S. Egyptian* [1910] A.C. 400; *The Glendinning* (1943) 76 Ll. L. Rep. 86; *The Fritz Thyssen* [1968] P. 255; all at para.8-078, below.

43 [1969] 3 All E.R. 1621 HL; facts at para.8-074, below. Compare the contract case of *Quinn v Burch Bros (Builders)* [1966] 2 Q.B. 370 CA, where the decision for the defendant was affirmed on the ground that the damage was too remote without touching upon the contributory negligence issue which was raised below; see the case at paras 7-011 and 8-151, below.

44 [1970] P. 17.

45 See para.8-074, below.

46 [2003] Lloyd's Rep. I.R. 566.

47 After a very lengthy and thorough analysis. See [2003] Lloyd's Rep. I.R. 566 at [893]–[910], [945]–[964] and [1058]–[1068].

ally the chain of causation had been broken.[48] Thus for a time only contributory negligence was in issue; then remoteness took over.[49]

6-017 The danger of too easy an adoption of the solution charted by *The Calliope*,[50] is that it could lead to imposing new liabilities on defendants which were not there before. Thus it is generally accepted that if the claimant, on his way to hospital from a street accident in which the defendant has tortiously injured him, is injured further by a falling tree or by a motorist, whether negligently or not, the defendant is not liable for the further injury.[51] It therefore should not be in any way arguable that the defendant could become subject to a partial liability for such further injury if the claimant himself, by proceeding negligently to the hospital, has contributed to its occurrence.

6-018 **(b) Contributory negligence and mitigation** Distinguishing between the application of contributory negligence and that of mitigation is comparatively easy. In this context contributory negligence comes in only before the commission of the wrong, mitigation necessarily after its commission. Thus where a claimant, run down by a negligent defendant, has unreasonably failed or refused to enter hospital for treatment, this is invariably seen not as contributory negligence but as a failure to mitigate, leading to no recovery for the loss that would have been avoided by the medical treatment.[52] It has never been suggested that the courts should make an apportionment as between claimant and defendant in respect of this loss so as to allow the claimant a partial recovery in respect of it.

6-019 **(c) Remoteness and mitigation** Distinguishing between remoteness and mitigation can also be difficult. One reason for this is that there are cases which fall within both categories by reason of each issue forming a separate ratio decidendi, as in *Banco de Portugal v Waterlow*,[53] and *Simon v Pawsons & Leafs*,[54] while in *Owners of the Ship "Front Ace" v Owners of "Vicky 1"*,[55] the claimant's acts in not getting its damaged ship repaired in time to avoid the loss of a future fixture were examined from both the angle of causation and the angle of mitigation. Sometimes indeed the line between remoteness and mitigation is blurred by the court itself, as in *Compania Naviera Maropan v Bowaters*.[56]

6-020 It is suggested that damage in this context may be too remote if the conduct of the claimant subsequent to the wrong separately increases the original damage as

---

48 [2003] Lloyd's Rep. I.R. 566 at [1069].

49 [2003] Lloyd's Rep. I.R. 566 at [892].

50 [1970] P. 17.

51 See para.8-080, below.

52 As illustrations see *Marcroft v Scruttons* [1954] 1 Lloyd's Rep. 395 CA and *McAuley v London Transport Executive* [1957] 2 Lloyd's Rep. 500 CA at para.9-066, below.

53 [1932] A.C. 452: facts at para.9-095, below. The two matters are clearly taken separately only in Viscount Sankey LC's speech of the majority speeches: see at 473 to 476 for remoteness and at 468 to 472 for mitigation. The minority speeches also have a suggestion of taking the two issues separately: see Lord Warrington of Clyffe at 481 to 482 and 485 and Lord Russell of Killowen at 503.

54 (1933) 38 Com. Cas. 151 CA: facts at para.9-049, below. The two issues are confused in the Commercial Cases report; the headnote says that the claimant failed because the damage was too remote but this was the holding only of Scrutton and Slesser LJJ, while Greer LJ, and Slesser LJ again, held that the damage could have been mitigated.

55 [2008] 2 All E.R. (Comm) 42 CA.

56 [1955] 2 Q.B. 68 CA.

opposed to failing to reduce the future loss which would flow from the original damage: this puts the second of the above illustrations into this category but leaves out the third,[57] again despite the fact that ordinary linguistic usage would allow the term remoteness to be applied to it. The substantial number of cases dealing with the refusal of an injured person to undergo an operation to improve his physical condition, and decided by the application of mitigation principles, cases from *Marcroft v Scruttons*,[58] to *Geest Plc v Lansiquot*,[59] lend support to this distinction. The important practical point in placing acts or omissions failing to reduce the future loss which would flow from the original damage under the rubric of mitigation is that on the issue of mitigation, in contrast to the issue of remoteness, the onus of proof is on the defendant.[60]

## (2) Remoteness and certainty

Even where the claimant has satisfactorily shown that the damage in question is not too remote, he may still fail to recover in respect of that damage if he is unable to prove it with certainty. The law requires a reasonable degree of persuasiveness in proof of the fact of damage and the amount of damage. Thus a claimant claiming for the loss of profits on a sale of a chattel wrongfully damaged, destroyed or not delivered by the defendant may fail to recover for such a loss on the ground of remoteness, both in contract[61] and in tort.[62] But a claimant claiming for the loss of the chance of gaining a prize, by entering in a competition a chattel which has been wrongfully damaged, destroyed or not delivered by the defendant, has still to satisfy the court, even if he has crossed the hurdle of remoteness, that there exists a sufficient certainty that such a loss might have accrued to him.[63] In very early days the two different issues tended to become merged, with a tendency to subsume the question of certainty under the then vague umbrella term of remoteness, a tendency encouraged by the fact that a particular set of circumstances might give rise to a consideration of both issues as was well illustrated by the cases dealing with the loss of profits of fishing.[64] Today, with the doctrine of remoteness no longer in its forma- **6-021**

---

57 For these illustrations see para.6-012, above.

58 [1954] 1 Lloyd's Rep. 395 CA.

59 [2002] 1 W.L.R. 3111 PC. These cases are all dealt with at paras 9-020, 9-066 and 9-088, below.

60 *Roper v Johnson* (1873) L.R. 8 C.P. 167; *Garnac Grain Co v Faure & Fairclough* [1968] A.C. 1130. Another practical difference used to be that, while it was laid down in *Liesbosch Dredger v S.S. Edison* [1933] A.C. 449 that damage caused by the claimant's impecuniosity is in tort too remote, where the loss is within the range of the prima facie recoverable damage the defendant cannot claim that the claimant's damages must be reduced because he could have mitigated them had he had the financial resources, a view based on a dictum of Lord Collins in *Clippens Oil Co v Edinburgh and District Water Trustees* [1907] A.C. 291 at 303 (dictum cited at para.9-097, below).The *Liesbosch* rule has now been abandoned (see paras 8-110 and following) so that Lord Collins's dictum has taken over for both remoteness and mitigation, though it is true to say that Lord Collins's dictum has always been difficult to reconcile with the rule in *The Liesbosch*, Lord Hope in *Lagden v O'Connor* [2004] 1 A.C. 1067 rightly saying that it made a distinction without a difference: [2004] 1 A.C. 1067 at [51].

61 See *Williams v Reynolds* (1865) 6 B. & S. 495, an early sale of goods case.

62 See *Saleslease Ltd v Davis* [1999] 1 W.L.R. 1664 CA, a case of conversion.

63 This is implicit in the loss of a chance cases stemming from *Chaplin v Hicks* [1911] 2 K.B. 786 CA.

64 See *The Columbus* (1849) 3 W. Rob. (Adm.) 158, *The City of Rome* (1887) 8 Asp. M.L.C. 542n and *The Anselma de Larrinaga* (1913) 29 T.L.R. 587, all at para.10-036, below. Illustrative also is the frequently posed problem of whether a claimant who is tortiously injured en route for an interview for a highly lucrative post, resulting in missing the interview and loss of the chance of the post, can recover in respect of that loss.

tive stages but highly elaborated and refined, it can be said that the issue of certainty has been extracted from the coils of remoteness and erected it into a separate concept in its own right.[65] It is so treated in this book.[66]

65 The breakaway took place in the USA in the late 19th century, where much progressive thought on the issue of certainty appeared at an early date: see McCormick, *Damages* (Minnesota, 1935), Ch.4; Sedgwick, *Damages*, 9th edn (1913), Vol.1, Ch.9.
66 See Ch.12, below.

## Chapter 7

# REDUCTION OF DAMAGES FOR CONTRIBUTORY NEGLIGENCE

Table of Contents



The Law Reform (Contributory Negligence) Act 1945, by allowing apportionment of damages for the first time at common law in cases of contributory negligence,[1] brought such cases from the category concerning existence of liability into that concerning extent, and hence brought them within the ambit of a text on damages. The operation of apportionment need not detain us long but requires a separate chapter in order to bring out clearly the whole analytic pattern outlined in the previous chapter. **7-001**

Section 1(1) enacted that: **7-002**

> "Where any person suffers damage as the result partly of his own fault and partly of the fault of any other person or persons, a claim in respect of that damage shall not be defeated by reason of the fault of the person suffering the damage, but the damages recoverable in respect thereof shall be reduced to such extent as the court thinks just and equitable having regard to the claimant's share in the responsibility for the damage."[2]

Section 4, apart from providing that damage includes loss of life and personal injury, contains a definition of fault which is important in ascertaining the scope of contributory negligence. It runs:

> ""Fault" means negligence, breach of statutory duty or other act or omission which gives rise to a liability in tort or would, apart from this Act, give rise to the defence of contributory negligence."

This definition may be regarded as being divisible into two parts. The first part is applicable to defendants, for whom fault means

---

1 It was anticipated in Admiralty by the Maritime Conventions Act 1911.

2 In *Sowden v Lodge* [2005] 1 W.L.R. 2129 CA where, in deciding whether the claimant's accommodation and care should be by a private arrangement or a residential arrangement (facts at para.40-190, below), the Court of Appeal rightly held that it should not take into account that the claimant might be unable to afford a private arrangement for life because, on account of her contributory negligence, she would recover only half of the damages for full liability. The damages were to be assessed applying ordinary principles and it was the sum so assessed which was to be reduced for contributory negligence.

"negligence, breach of statutory duty or other act or omission which gives rise to a liability in tort"

and the second part is applicable to claimants, for whom fault means

"[any] act or omission which … would, apart from this Act, give rise to the defence of contributory negligence".

This division has now twice been endorsed at House of Lords level, in *Reeves v Commissioner of Police of the Metropolis*[3] and in *Standard Chartered Bank v Pakistan National Shipping Corporation*.[4]

## 1. Liability in Tort

### (1) Scope

7-003 The 1945 Act was of course passed with tort rather than contract in mind and its prime concern within tort was with the ubiquitous tort of negligence, for it was here—with the everyday case of the personal injury for which both sides were to blame—that the shortcomings of the all or nothing rule of the common law had been so evident. The question arises as to whether the Act applies where there is other than negligence on the part of the defendant or the claimant or both.

7-004 Where the tort is one of strict liability, as with certain breaches of statutory duty and with liability under the rule in *Rylands v Fletcher*,[5] it is presumably the case that contributory negligence may be invoked to reduce the damages; there is no authority. On the other hand, where the tort committed is an intentional one, with deliberate rather than negligent conduct on the part of the defendant, it is thought inappropriate to reduce the claimant's damages on account of his contributory negligence and for this result there is a good deal of authority. It has been so held at first instance in *Corporacion Nacional del Cobre del Chile v Sogemin Metals*,[6] a claim for conspiracy to bribe, and in *Nationwide Building Society v Thimbleby*,[7] a claim in deceit. In addition, the Act has been interpreted by the House of Lords in *Standard Chartered Bank v Pakistan National Shipping Corporation*,[8] as not allowing deceitful conduct—contributory intention rather than contributory negligence—to be raised as a defence in the tort of deceit. It was held that such conduct would not have given rise to a defence of contributory negligence at common law and therefore, applying the second limb of the definition of fault applicable to claimants,[9] did not do so under the Act. The Court of Appeal in *Co-operative Group (CWS) Ltd v Pritchard*,[10] has followed this in a case of assault and battery, thereby taking the rule to intentional torts causing physical damage,[11] the earlier cases having been concerned with torts leading to economic loss.[12]

---

3 [2000] 1 A.C. 360, per Lord Hope at 382D to E.
4 [2003] 1 A.C. 959, per Lord Hoffmann at [11].
5 (1868) L.R. 3 H.L. 330.
6 [1997] 1 W.L.R. 1396.
7 [1999] P.N.L.R. 733.
8 [2003] 1 A.C. 959.
9 See para.7-002, above.
10 [2012] Q.B. 320 CA.
11 Lord Denning MR's suggestion in *Murphy v Cullane* [1977] Q.B. 94 CA, where both parties had been involved in a criminal affray (see the case at para.42-010, below), that the damages could be

By contrast, the Act can apply, and apportionment be allowed, where the intentional and deliberate misconduct is that of the claimant and such conduct is meeting only negligent, and not intentional, conduct on the part of the defendant. It was so held by the House of Lords in *Reeves v Commissioner of Police of the Metropolis*,[13] where a prisoner's committing suicide was held to constitute contributory negligence for the purposes of the Act. Yet in the exceptional circumstances of the claimant's suicide in *Corr v IBC Vehicles Ltd*,[14] no deduction was made in the House of Lords for contributory negligence. Two members of the House held that there was no contributory negligence and, while the remaining three thought otherwise, two of them considered it inappropriate to determine the proper apportionment as the question of contributory negligence had hardly been touched upon in the courts below. So too in the similar exceptional circumstances of the claimant's committing manslaughter rather than suicide, the Court of Appeal in *Gray v Thames Trains Ltd*,[15] returned the question of contributory negligence to the court below.[16] **7-005**

## (2) Apportionment

Whether there has been contributory negligence in a particular case so as to bring the 1945 Act into play remains a question of liability and falls still outside the ambit of this book. It is only apportionment itself which is relevant to damages once the Act's applicability has been established. Yet here little of utility can be said as figures, amounts and percentages are so much a matter of impression for the trial judge[17] depending on the particular circumstances.[18] Moreover, s.1(1) gives the court a discretion to apportion on the lines of what it thinks "just and equitable".[19] **7-006**

---

reduced for contributory negligence is inconsistent with the view that contributory negligence has never been a defence open to a defendant who had intended to harm a claimant. Not surprisingly, Lord Rodger in *Standard Chartered Bank v Pakistan National Shipping Corp* [2003] 1 A.C. 959 at [45], questioned whether Lord Denning's observation was sound.

12 Yet, somewhat curiously, the court thought the position was by no means certain, Aikens LJ after a lengthy and very thorough survey of the law ([2003] 1 A.C. 959 at [28]–[60]) basing his eventual conclusion ([2003] 1 A.C. 959 at [61] and [62]) on the clear statements of principle in the House of Lords in *Reeves* and the *Standard Chartered Bank* case, while Smith LJ expressed regret that the law as it stood required her not to allow apportionment ([2003] 1 A.C. 959 at [85]). For a further aspect of the case see para.42-011, below, where the possibility of reducing the damages on the ground not of contributory negligence but of provocation is examined.

13 [2000] 1 A.C. 360.

14 [2008] A.C. 884.

15 [2009] A.C. 1339 (CA).

16 Later reversed by the House of Lords, [2009] A.C. 1339 by application of the ex turpi causa maxim. See the case further at para.8-065, below.

17 The provision of s.1(6) that, where there is a jury trial, it is the jury's function to apportion is of little, if any, relevance today.

18 Where there is failure to wear a car seat belt specific apportionments have been accepted as appropriate ever since *Froom v Butcher* [1976] Q.B. 286 CA, laid down that damages be reduced by 25 per cent where the injury would have been prevented and by 1 per cent where it would have been less severe. The appropriate percentage reduction was again considered, together with that for driving with a driver known to have been drinking heavily, in *Best v Smyth* [2010] EWHC 1541 (QB) at [12] and [13]. If in cases of very serious injury it can be shown, exceptionally, from medical or other evidence that the wearing of a seat belt was likely to have made no difference, the trial judge will be justified in making no reduction in the damages for contributory negligence. This was accepted by the Court of Appeal in a valuable review in *Stanton v Collinson* [2010] EWCA Civ 81 CA of seat belt contributory negligence. The attempt in *Gawler v Raettig* [2007] EWHC 373 (QB) to obtain a

**7-007** That the decision on apportionment is so much a matter of impression is dramatically illustrated by *Jackson v Murray*,[20] a case from Scotland of a child running into the path of an oncoming vehicle, a not unfamiliar story in the annals of contributory negligence. Not only was the trial judge's reduction of the 13-year-old girl's damages by 90 per cent changed down by the Scots appeal court to 70 per cent and further changed down by the Supreme Court to 50 per cent but also the reduction by the Supreme Court was only by a bare majority, the minority agreeing with the Scots appeal court's 70 per cent. Reference was made to the potentially dangerous nature of driving a car, which could do much more damage to a person than a person was likely to do to a car. And it was agreed that an appeal court could only interfere with an apportionment made if it could be said that it lay outside the generous ambit within which reasonable disagreement was possible. Clearly, however, different views were taken as to whether here this generous ambit had or had not been crossed. The majority speech and the minority one are both worth perusal.

**7-008** This guidance of the Supreme Court Justices in *Jackson* on the correct approach of an appellate court to apportionment in contributory negligence has since been adopted by the Court of Appeal in *McCracken v Smith*,[21] where there had been a collision between a minibus and a trial bike being recklessly and illegally driven. It was again held, though here unanimously, that the generous ambit within which reasonable disagreement was possible had been crossed, and the court increased, rather than reduced, the trial judge's 30 per cent attributed to the claimant, the bike's pillion rider, to 50 per cent (together with an agreed 15 per cent on account of the claimant's not wearing a crash helmet).

**7-009** Apportionment is to be assessed upon the degree of blame or blameworthiness of the claimant and not solely on a test of causation, although fault not causally contributing to the damage cannot be taken into account in the first place.[22] That blame is the basis is shown primarily by the use of the word "responsibility" in s.1(1), and also by the use there of the term "just and equitable". Denning LJ put it thus in *Davies v Swan Motor Co*[23]:

> "Whilst causation is the decisive factor in determining whether there should be a reduced amount payable to the plaintiff, nevertheless, the amount of the reduction does not depend solely on the degree of causation. The amount of the reduction is such an amount as may be found by the court to be 'just and equitable', having regard to the claimant's 'share in the responsibility' for the damage. This involves a consideration, not only of the causative potency of a particular factor, but also of its blameworthiness."[24]

---

substantial increase in the conventional reduction rightly failed.

19 See para.7-002, above.

20 [2015] UKSC 5; [2015] 2 All E.R. 805.

21 [2015] EWCA Civ 380.

22 Fault not causally contributing to the damage and therefore not to be taken into account in the damages is illustrated by *Scullion v Bank of Scotland Plc* [2011] P.N.L.R. 5 at 68 (facts at para.49-067, below): see [2011] P.N.L.R. 5 at [81] to [86]. The Court of Appeal reversed on liability ([2011] 1 W.L.R. 3212 CA) but did not touch on this point.

23 [1949] 2 K.B. 291 CA at 326.

24 This point may seem simple. Yet under the analogous statutory provisions for apportionment between tortfeasors, Hilbery J in *Smith v Bray* (1939) 56 T.L.R. 200 held the basis of apportionment to be causation, although later judges have subsequently disagreed with this view. Thus in *Brian Warwicker Partnership Ltd v Hok International Ltd* [2006] P.N.L.R. 5 CA at 79 which also concerned apportionment in a contribution claim between joint tortfeasors, it was said to be established that in deciding on apportionment the court may have regard to both the causative potency of the claimant's fault and the claimant's blameworthiness: [2006] P.N.L.R. 5 CA at [37],

One particular issue concerning the operation of apportionment troubled the courts in the wake of the landmark decision in *Banque Bruxelles Lambert v Eagle Star Insurance Co*,[25] commonly called SAAMCO, that a claimant lender suing for professional negligence cannot claim for his real loss, however foreseeable, but is restricted to the loss, when less, which is attributable to the breach of duty for which the defendant alone is liable.[26] If, as in so many of these cases, the claimant's negligent lending practices have contributed to its loss,[27] is the apportionment to be made on the real loss or on the lesser attributable loss? The House of Lords decided for the first of these alternatives, and thereby in the claimant's favour, in *Platform Homes Loans Ltd v Oyston Shipways Ltd*,[28] reversing the Court of Appeal and resolving a conflict of many earlier first instance decisions. **7-010**

## 2. Liability in Contract

### (1) Scope

The law was for long in a state of uncertainty as to whether or not the 1945 Act applied to contract at all; the natural reading of that part of the definition of fault which is taken to refer to the defendant's conduct—"negligence, breach of statutory duty or other act or omission which gives rise to a liability in tort"[29]—would appear to leave contract out. Cases on the question moved in either direction.[30] Uncertainty was eventually resolved, but not until 1989, by the Court of Appeal in **7-011**

---

per Arden LJ. In *Sahib Foods Ltd v Paskin Kyriakides Sands* [2004] P.N.L.R. 22 CA at 403, where questions arose of how far the causing and the spreading of a fire was the fault of the defendant and how far the fault of the claimant, causation and blameworthiness, and even duty, required lengthy analysis by the Court of Appeal. In *Rehill v Rider Holdings Ltd* [2012] EWCA Civ 628 CA, a typical road accident personal injury claim, Richards LJ said that he found it difficult to draw a clear distinction between considerations of causation and of fault ([2012] EWCA Civ 628 CA at [30]) while in *Starks v Chief Constable of Hertfordshire* [2013] EWCA Civ 782 CA, again a road traffic accident personal injury claim, Underhill LJ said that it was not a case where the distinction could be made ( [2013] EWCA Civ 782 CA at [17]). In *Blackmore v Department of Communities and Local Government* Unreported 23 October 2014 County Court, where the cause of an employee's injury and subsequent death was by the combined effect of his smoking and his exposure to asbestos by his employers, the trial judge held that he need not base the deduction for contributory negligence on a mathematical calculation of relative contribution to risk. Instead he considered that the employers should bear the lion's share of responsibility on account of their prolonged breaches of statutory duty and, while the risk from the employee's smoking was probably twice or thrice the risk from the employers' asbestos, he assessed the contributory negligence at 30 per cent.

25 [1997] A.C. 191.

26 See para.34-073, below.

27 See the cases at para.7-018, below.

28 [2000] 2 A.C. 190. On the particular facts and figures in the case, applying the 20 per cent contributory negligence to the real loss of some £600,000 brought the figure to £480,000 and therefore within the £500,000 overvaluations by the defendants for which alone they were liable and therefore that amount was fully recoverable. Had application of the 20 per cent reduction not taken the claimant's loss within the overvaluation, then the overvaluation figure would have applied to fix the amount recoverable. In either situation no reduction of the overvaluation figure comes into play.

29 See para.7-002, above.

30 *Quinn v Burch Bros (Builders)* [1966] 2 Q.B. 370 CA and *De Meza & Stuart v Apple Van Straten Shena & Stone* [1975] 1 Lloyd's Rep. 498 CA at first instance favoured the application of the Act to contract and the later first instance decisions in *Basildon District Council v J. E. Lesser (Properties)* [1985] Q.B. 839 and *A.B. Marintrans v Comet Shipping Co* [1985] 1 W.L.R. 1270 held the contrary.

*Forsikringaktieselskapet Vesta v Butcher*,[31] the relevant facts of which were these. The defendant brokers negligently failed to take action on instructions given to them by the claimant insurance company with the result that the claimants' reinsurers, defendants against whom the claimants also claimed, might have been enabled to repudiate liability to the claimants when a loss occurred eight months later. In the event, the defendant reinsurers were held not entitled to repudiate and were therefore liable to the claimants so that the issue of the damages payable by the defendant brokers did not arise. Nonetheless the liability of the defendant brokers was considered by the court—it would become relevant should the defendant reinsurers' appeal succeed[32]—and it was held that, because the claimants had had ample opportunity in the eight months to put the brokers' failure to take action right, they had been contributorily negligent, and that this contributory negligence entitled the court to make an apportionment and thereby award to the claimants less than their whole loss. It was accepted that the claimants were entitled to formulate the claim made against the brokers in either contract or tort, either for breach of their contractual obligations or for breach of their tortious duty of care.

**7-012** The Court of Appeal adopted Hobhouse J below[33] in his identification of three categories of case in which the question of the applicability of the Act can arise, no clear separation between these categories having been made or having appeared in the earlier cases. The categories as stated by Hobhouse J were these:

> "(1) Where the defendant's liability arises from some contractual provision which does not depend on negligence on the part of the defendant.
>
> (2) Where the defendant's liability arises from a contractual obligation which is expressed in terms of taking care (or its equivalent) but does not correspond to a common law duty to take care which would exist in the given case independently of contract.
>
> (3) Where the defendant's liability in contract is the same as his liability in the tort of negligence independently of the existence of any contract."[34]

Here the case clearly fell within category (3) and the Court of Appeal decided that to this category the Act applied.[35] O'Connor LJ was fortified, as was Hobhouse J, in this conclusion by the earlier Court of Appeal decision in *Sayers v Harlow UDC*,[36] by which he considered the court bound, where without any discussion of the present issue damages were reduced for a physically injured claimant entitled to claim concurrently in contract and in tort. In a passage quoted with approval by O'Connor LJ, Hobhouse J had said further:

> "The category (3) question has arisen in very many different types of case and the answer is treated as so obvious that it passes without any comment. It is commonplace that actions are brought by persons who have suffered personal injuries as the result of the negligence of the person sued and that there is a contractual as well as tortious relationship.

---

31 [1989] A.C. 852 CA.

32 The contributory negligence issue did not go to the House of Lords, their Lordships being concerned only with the defendant insurers' appeal against liability.

33 [1986] 2 All E.R. 488.

34 [1986] 2 All E.R. 488 at 508f to g; in the CA at [1989] A.C. 852 at 860F to G.

35 By contrast, the High Court of Australia has not taken this approach and has held in *Astley v Austrust Ltd* [1999] Lloyd's Rep. P.N. 758 HCA that in no case of contract liability can contributory negligence be introduced to reduce damages.

36 [1958] 1 W.L.R. 623 CA.

In such cases apportionment of blame is invariably adopted by the court notwithstanding that the plaintiff could sue in contract as well as in tort."[37]

At the same time the Court of Appeal made it clear that the Act would not and did not apply either to category (1) or—more interestingly because more likely to be in dispute—to category (2).[38] There must be a liability in tort before the liability in contract, which co-exists, will attract the application of the Act. O'Connor LJ adopted the construction of Pritchard J in the New Zealand case of *Rowe v Turner Hopkins & Partners*,[39] that **7-013**

"the Contributory Negligence Act cannot apply unless the cause of action is founded on some act or omission on the part of the defendant which gives rise to liability in tort".[40]

This indeed fits with the natural reading of the first part of the definition of fault referred to above[41] and the law has remained settled along these lines ever since. Thus in *Barclays Bank Plc v Fairclough Ltd*,[42] where the defendant's breach of its strict contractual obligation to clean to the specified standard the roof of the claimant's warehouse, causing contamination with asbestos which required expensive remedial work, the Court of Appeal held that contributory negligence did not apply to reduce the damages; it was a category (1) case.[43] In *Raflatac Ltd v Eade*,[44] where the defendant head contractor was contractually but not tortiously liable for the negligence of its sub-contractor causing damage to the claimant's property, contributory negligence was held to be inapplicable; it was a category (2) case. And in *UCB Bank Plc v Hepherd Winstanley & Pugh*,[45] where the defendant solicitors' negligence in respect of loans which the claimant bank had made sounded in tort as well as in contract, the damages were reduced by 25 per cent on account of the bank's contributory negligence; it was a category (3) case.[46]

While the law appears settled, its wisdom may still be questioned. In particular, it might be thought sensible to bring category (2) within the ambit of the applicability of contributory negligence. Why should it matter that the defendant's breach has been of a contractual duty of care rather than of a tortious duty of care? Such an extension was indeed recommended by the Law Commission in its Report on *Contributory Negligence as a Defence in Contract*[47]; it also receives some support from New Zealand. For while in *Forsikringaktieselskapet Vesta v Butcher*,[48] O'Connor LJ had relied on Pritchard J in the New Zealand case of *Rowe v Turner* **7-014**

---

[37] [1986] 2 All E.R. 488 at 509d to 509e; in the CA at [1989] A.C. 852 at 860H to 861A.

[38] The Court of Appeal considered *Basildon District Council v J.E. Lesser (Properties)* [1985] Q.B. 839 (at para.7-011, above) to be a category (1) case and therefore accepted the result there, but *A.B. Maritrans v Comet Shipping Co* [1985] 1 W.L.R. 1270 (at para.7-011, above) to be a category (3) case so that it was not followed.

[39] [1980] 2 N.Z.L.R. 550.

[40] [1989] A.C. 852 CA at 866C.

[41] See para.7-002, above.

[42] [1995] Q.B. 214.

[43] *Fairclough* was followed and applied in *Mortgage Express v Iqbal Hafeez Solicitors* [2011] EWHC 3037 Ch and in *Harrison v Technical Sign Company Ltd* unreported 25 September 2012.

[44] [1999] 1 Lloyd's Rep. 50.

[45] [1999] Lloyd's Rep. P.N. 963 CA.

[46] There are many such cases as the citations in para.7-018, below, show. Both category (1) and category (3) were in issue in *Mueller Europe Ltd v Central Roofing (South Wales) Ltd* [2013] EWHC 237 (TCC); see at [114]–[119].

[47] Law Com. 219 (1993).

[48] [1989] A.C. 852 CA.

*Hopkins & Partners*,[49] for a construction limited to the inclusion of category (3) cases,[50] it was pointed out by Cooke P in the later New Zealand case of *Mouat v Clark Boyce*,[51] that in the appeal in *Rowe* the court had drawn attention to the opposing view that the Act can apply wherever negligence is an essential ingredient of the claimant's cause of action whatever the source of the duty.[52] On this interpretation, said Cooke P in endorsing it in *Mouat*, the Act applies to category (2) as well as to category (3) cases,

> "both to cases of a purely contractual duty of care and to cases of a duty of care arising from contract and tort concurrently".[53]

The proper way to approach the definition of fault in the 1945 Act would then be, in the words of Cooke P, to construe the reference there to negligence as covering carelessness in any context. However, ever since the House of Lords endorsement in *Henderson v Merrett Syndicates Ltd*,[54] of a general concurrence of liability in contract and tort, there will be hardly any cases falling within category (2) that do not fall also within category (3).[55]

**7-015** Far more important would be a move to make contributory negligence available in category (1) cases. The Law Commission in its Consultation Paper on Contributory Negligence as a Defence in Contract,[56] which had preceded its Report on the subject, had provisionally recommended that contributory negligence should apply to all of the three categories. It then excluded category (1), against the views of the majority of its distinguished consultees, in its final Report,[57] principally on the ground that allowing category (1) would result in uncertainty, turning contract claims of no great complexity into battles over comparative fault. It is thought that this fear is exaggerated; certainly the UNIDROIT Principles of International Commercial Contracts allow contributory negligence, though not so-called, to be introduced across the board.[58] Moreover, where there appears to be contributory negligence on the part of the claimant, there is the danger for him that the court may hold for the defendant on grounds of volenti, absence of cause or failure to mitigate. It seems unfortunate that the court must choose the all or nothing route and be debarred from choosing apportionment. However, a move to include category (1) would require the 1945 Act to be amended; no interpretation of the statutory definition of fault could embrace the case of strict liability in contract.

## (2) Apportionment

**7-016** With contract as with tort, apportionment should be based not upon causation but upon degrees of blameworthiness[59] and the Platform Homes ruling of the House of Lords will equally apply; what has been said under tort on these matters should be

---

49 [1980] 2 N.Z.L.R. 550.
50 See para.7-013, above.
51 [1992] 2 N.Z.L.R. 559 CA at 564.
52 See [1982] 1 N.Z.L.R. 178 CA at 181.
53 [1992] 2 N.Z.L.R. 559 CA at 565.
54 [1995] 2 A.C. 145.
55 *Raflatac Ltd v Eade* [1999] 1 Lloyd's Rep. 506 is such a case: see para.7-013, above.
56 Law Commission, *Contributory Negligence as a Defence in Contract* (HMSO, 1990), Law Com. No.114.
57 See para.7-014, above.
58 Art.7.4.7. The latest version of these is dated 2010.
59 But see the footnote at the end of para.7-009, above.

referred to.[60] There remains the question of the degree of reduction of the damages about which little was said.[61]

There is perhaps no real need to examine the amounts and percentages by which damages have been reduced in contract any more than this has had to be considered in tort. However, while initially there was a paucity of cases dealing with contributory negligence in a contractual context, the situation was totally changed with the celebrated spate of litigation arising out of the collapse of the property market and generated by building societies and other lenders suing surveyors, valuers and solicitors for misleading them as to the value of the property taken by them as security,[62] and it may be useful to look at the approach to apportionment of such cases where reduction of damages for contributory negligence is today a common feature. Also in some ways it may be less easy in contract than in tort to get a feel of what level of reduction is appropriate. **7-017**

The amount of the reduction in damages on account of the imprudence in lending practices can be quite striking. In the 12 mortgage lending claims decided under the rubric of *Nationwide Building Society v Balmer Radmore*,[63] one claim merited a reduction of 90 per cent,[64] one of 75 per cent[65] and three of two-thirds.[66] There are also cases in which the reduction on account of contributory negligence is small, as in *The Mortgage Corporation v Halifax (SW) Ltd*,[67] where the reduction was by 20 per cent.[68] And the willingness to invoke contributory negligence in this field has encouraged the courts to apply the 1945 Act where it is contributory negligence other than of lenders in their lending practices that is in issue and to reduce damages by significant amounts.[69] However, in endorsing, in *The Housing Loan Corporation v Brown*,[70] the 75 per cent reduction of the damages that the trial judge would have made had the lending claimant's claim for damages not failed, the Court of Appeal said that the amount of reduction of the damages on account of contribu- **7-018**

---

60 See paras 7-009 and 7-010, above.

61 See para.7-006, above.

62 See paras 34-064 and following, below.

63 [1999] Lloyd's Rep. P.N. 241.

64 *Nationwide Building Society v Archdeacons* [1999] Lloyd's Rep. P.N. 549.

65 *Nationwide Building Society v Balmer Radmore* [1999] Lloyd's Rep. P.N. 558.

66 See also the reduction of the lender's damages in *Birmingham Midshires Mortgage Services v Phillips* [1998] P.N.L.R. 468 by 60 per cent, in *Nationwide Building Society v Littlestone & Cowan* [1999] Lloyd's Rep. P.N. 625 by 66 per cent, in *Omega Trust Co Ltd v Wright Son & Pepper (No.2)* [1998] P.N.L.R. 337 by 70 per cent, in *Nationwide Building Society v Dunlop Haywards (DHL) Ltd* [2010] 1 W.L.R. 258 by 50 per cent, in *Webb Resolutions Ltd v E Surv Ltd* [2012] EWHC 3653 (TCC) by 50 per cent, in *First National Commercial Bank v Andrew S. Taylor Commercial Ltd* [1997] P.N.L.R. 37, had the defendant surveyors and valuers been found negligent, by 75 per cent and in *Paratus AMC Ltd v Countryside Surveyors Ltd* [2011] EWHC 3307 Ch by 60 per cent.

67 [1999] Lloyd's Rep. P.N. 159.

68 In *Nationwide Building Society v Abdullah* [1999] Lloyd's Rep. P.N. 616 the reduction was not by a percentage but by the amount of the loss attributable to an additional advance, while in *Skipton Building Society v Lea Hough & Co* [2000] P.N.L.R. 545 the lender's contributory negligence resulted in the claim failing entirely because without that negligence there would have been no loss.

69 e.g. *UCB Bank Plc v Hepherd Winstanley & Pugh* [1999] Lloyd's Rep. P.N. 963 CA: 25 percent reduction; *Lloyds Bank Plc v Parker Bullen* [2000] Lloyd's Rep. P.N. 51: 50 per cent reduction; *Barings Plc v Coopers Lybrand* [2003] Lloyd's Rep. I.R. 566: 50 per cent reduction, escalating to 60 per cent and then to 80 per cent; *Slattery v Moore Stephens* [2004] P.N.L.R. 14, p.241: 50 per cent reduction (on part of the damages).

70 [1999] Lloyd's Rep. P.N. 185 CA.

tory negligence in these cases is "unamenable to standardisation and is, and remains, essentially a matter for the trial judge".[71]

## 3. LIABILITY UNDER THE MISREPRESENTATION ACT

**7-019** That the 1945 Act applies to claims for damages under s.2(1) of the Misrepresentation Act 1967,[72] where available,[73] follows from the existence of the concurrent tortious liability at common law for negligent misrepresentation. Sir Donald Nicholls VC so decided in *Gran Gelato v Richcliff (Group)*,[74] following the Court of Appeal's reasoning in *Forsikrings Vesta*.[75] By contrast, the 1945 Act should not apply to a claim under s.2(2), which deals with innocent misrepresentation,[76] as there will not be a concurrent liability in tort for misrepresentation that is not negligent.

---

71 [1999] Lloyd's Rep. P.N. 185 CA at 200, col.1.

72 See s.2(1) at paras 49-049 and following, below.

73 See the exclusion in s.2(4) of the Misrepresentation Act 1967 where claims exist under Pt 4A of the Consumer Protection from Unfair Trading Regulations 2008 (SI 2008/1277).

74 [1992] Ch. 560. In the event no reduction in the claimant's damages was made by him on the ground that one induced to act upon a representation should be entitled to rely upon its truth without the representor, who intended the representee to act on it, being able to say that its correctness could have been checked by him. This may explain the enigmatic statement of the trial judge in *Peekay lntermark Ltd v Australian and New Zealand Banking Group Ltd* [2005] P.N.L.R. 42 at 853, [98], where damages were awarded under s.2(1) of the 1967 Act (see the case, reversed by the Court of Appeal on liability, at para.49-060, below), that in the absence of a plea of contributory negligence he did not have to consider whether contributory negligence would in principle be applicable to the case in the light of *Gran Gelato*.

75 [1989] A.C. 852 CA; see this at para.7-012, above.

76 See s.2(2) at paras 49-070 and following.

CHAPTER 8

# REMOTENESS OF DAMAGE

TABLE OF CONTENTS

**8-001** Much learned writing has appeared upon the difficult and interesting question of remoteness of damage, particularly in tort. It is not possible or desirable in a textbook on damages to give the detailed theoretical discussion that this topic merits; all that is attempted is a statement of the existing law. On a question which has given rise to so much controversy, it is difficult to organise the material in a manner which will give general satisfaction. What is aimed at is a clear, rather than an invulnerable, analysis.

**8-002** A basic distinction is that the term "remoteness" has more than one meaning, referring both to a limit upon causation and to scope of the protection afforded by the law. The first question is whether the defendant in the eyes of the law caused the particular damage to the claimant; the second, which on a strict analysis arises only if the first has been answered in the claimant's favour, is whether the law protects the claimant from the particular damage he has suffered. Upon this distinction the whole structure of this chapter is built.

**8-003** A preliminary point concerns the question of the onus of proof. Conflicting dicta appear on this issue. It has been said, particularly by Lord Sumner in *S.S. Singleton Abbey v S.S. Paludina*,[1] that the claimant must show that a particular item of damage is not too remote before he can recover for it; it has also been said, particularly by Lord Haldane and Lord Dunedin in *The Metagama*,[2] that the defendant must show that a particular item of damage is too remote if he is not to be held liable for it. These various dicta were considered by Lord Merriman P in *The Guildford*,[3] and, without attempting to resolve the divergence of opinion in the House of Lords, he favoured the view that it was the claimant's onus. In the case before him he held

---

1 [1927] A.C. 16 at 25–26. Similar statements appear in the Court of Appeal, reported sub nom. *The Paludina* [1925] P. 40 CA at 43, 48 and 49–50, per Bankes, Scrutton and Atkin LJJ respectively. In *The Oropesa* [1942] P. 140 at 144, Langton J treated the onus as being on the claimant, and Lord Wright in the Court of Appeal agreed entirely with his judgment on this: [1943] P. 32 CA at 40.

2 (1927) 29 Ll. L. Rep. 253 HL at 254 and 256 respectively; Lord Dunedin's was a dissenting judgment. The case is also reported sub nom. *Canadian Pacific Ry v Kelvin Shipping Co* (1927) 138 L.T. 369 HL. These dicta were repeated in *The Genua* [1936] 2 All E.R. 798 at 802, and in *The Bharatkhand* [1952] 1 Lloyd's Rep. 470 at 480, where the same view was put forward (at 479). See, similarly, *Philco Radio v Spurling* [1949] 2 All E.R. 882 CA at 886, per Singleton LJ.

3 [1956] P. 364; see, especially, at 370.

that, where the master of the claimant's ship had refused, after collision, an offer of towage and the ship had sunk before other means of rescue could bring her to safety, it was for the claimant to prove that his master's refusal of the offer was reasonable and not for the defendant to prove it unreasonable, an onus which the claimant successfully discharged.[4] Since a claimant must prove his case, it seems undoubtedly correct that he must prove for which items of damage he may properly recover. Although these cases only deal with tort, with causation, and with consequences following upon a new intervening act which is generally that of the claimant,[5] there is no reason why the rule that the onus of proof is on the claimant should not apply to all issues of remoteness.

## I. Tort

In relation to tort, remoteness in its causation aspect has generally been taken as the primary concern: the question is whether in law the defendant's tort caused the claimant's damage, whether in law the claimant's damage resulted from the defendant's tort. In the past less attention has been paid, although unjustifiably, to remoteness in so far as it concerns the scope of protection given by the particular tort; today it gets more attention. **8-004**

### (A) *Causation*

### 1. Cause in Fact and Cause in Law

While the seemingly endless debates upon the question of cause have centred upon the question of causation in law, the anterior question is always present, the question whether a defendant's act or omission is a cause in fact of the injury to a claimant. It might be thought that it goes without saying that there must be a factual causal connection between defendant's act and claimant's damage and this is indeed true for the vast multitude of claims and cases. It is nevertheless important to identify this question, and particularly important today because there has been a resurgence of reference in the cases to the so-called "but for" test[6] as the generally accepted test for cause in fact, without the court being clear, or making it clear, that the test is relevant for cause in fact and not at all for cause in law. References to "but for" have now become prominent. **8-005**

### (1) Cause in fact

For the determination of whether a defendant's wrongful conduct is a cause in fact of the damage to a claimant the test, which has almost universal acceptance, is the so-called "but for" test. The defendant's wrongful conduct is a cause of the claimant's harm if such harm would not have occurred without it; "but for" it. This is the threshold which claimants must cross if their claim for damages is going to get anywhere. Satisfying the cause in fact test is in the vast multitude of cases a **8-006**

---

4 Yet there remains a tendency in ship collision cases to place the onus on the defendant to prove that the further damage to the ship was as a result of a new act following the collision, particularly where the act is that of the claimant; see, e.g. *The Fritz Thyssen* [1968] P. 255, especially at 259, and *The Lucile Bloomfield* [1967] 2 Lloyd's Rep. 308, especially at 313.

5 All but *Philco Radio v Spurling* [1949] 2 All E.R. 882 CA deal with ship collisions.

6 Defined below at para.8-006.

necessary condition of the imposition of liability; it is by no means a sufficient condition because the all important cause in law tests, as we shall see, must be satisfied as well.

8-007 The importance of the cause in fact test lies not in its everyday observance but in its very occasional breach. For, as we shall see, there are situations where the test proves inadequate to the task, situations where fairness and reasonableness require that there be a relaxation in the standard of factual causation required. These will be examined in due course.[7] A departure from the "but for" test thus serves to extend the scope of a defendant's liability; this is in marked contrast to the tests for legal causation which are designed to limit liability. To these we now turn.

## (2) Cause in law

8-008 Causation in law takes us into an entirely different field. It is never enough simply to satisfy the "but for" test in order to establish "legal cause" which is shorthand for legal limits on causation. To take an extreme example: a mother gives birth to a son who, when he grows up, commits a murder. Yet "but for" the mother's decision to have a child the murder would never have happened; on the "but for" test she is a cause in fact of the murder. In simple, if mundane, terms this shows what lies behind the grander, frequently cited maxim of Bacon that "it were infinite for the law to judge the causes of causes and their impression one of another".[8] While, of course, it is true that the mother will bear no responsibility for the murder on account of lack of negligent or other tortious activity on her part, it is the law that removes her from being a cause of the murder through the mechanism of legal cause.

8-009 **(a) Terminology and analysis of legal causation** Causation in law, unlike causation in fact, is a knotty problem, and the reports are full of expressions such as direct cause, proximate cause, effective cause, breaking the chain of causation, and supervening cause. These familiar terms are in many ways more of a hindrance than a help because their very familiarity has blunted any precision of meaning they may have once had.[9] It is tempting to avoid them completely: but to do so leads to the equal disadvantage of wrenching the decisions out of any pattern that they already have. It is therefore proposed to divide the authorities into two groups with familiar terminology, and define what is meant here by the terminology. The first group will deal with direct consequences, the second with consequences following upon a novus actus interveniens or a nova causa interveniens. To avoid the constant use of the double Latin phrase resort is had to the term "new intervening force"; this today has the further merit of showing a little respect for the ruling that Latin is no longer to be used in the law, being user-unfriendly. The meaning attached to these two groups is this. In all the difficult cases on causation it will be found that there is a third factor in the situation beyond the claimant's damage and the defendant's act: direct consequences are defined as those where this third factor preceded the defendant's act; consequences following upon a new intervening

---

7 See paras 8-016 and following, below.

8 Bacon, *Maxims of the Law*, Reg.I.

9 "As these different epithets and formulae are used almost indiscriminately, something more must be done than to choose an epithet which has been used in a decided case": *Weld-Blundell v Stephens* [1920] A.C. 956 at 984, per Lord Sumner.

force are defined as those where the third factor follows the defendant's act. The total formulation, therefore, of what falls to be decided in these questions of causation is whether, given a third factor, the claimant's damage results from the defendant's act, a formulation which has the great merit of a common sense approach.[10]

This formulation may appear to leave out or ignore what are sometimes known as concurrent causes. Exact synchronisation between the timing of the defendant's act and the third factor indeed produces a third category, but it does not call for separate treatment since in the nature of things it happens infrequently and since the result is clear: both defendant's act and third factor are causes of the damage. More difficult are cases without such exact synchronisation; in these it is said that either the defendant's act or the third factor forms a continuing cause and therefore is not to be regarded as preceding the other in time. However, it is submitted that the concept of continuing cause can be more confusing than helpful since there is no clear test of when a cause continues to operate and when a cause ceases to operate. Furthermore, the cases of concurrent causes fall without difficulty into the pattern adopted here. If the defendant's act is the second in time, then the damage will be a direct consequence, as defined here, of his act, and his act will be held to be a cause of it: this is best illustrated by *Hill v New River Co.*[11] If the defendant's act is the first in time, then the defendant will still be held to be a cause of the damage if the intervening factor is of the type which does not relieve the prior actor of liability: this is best illustrated by *Burrows v March Gas Co.*[12] In all cases on causation the sole issue being considered is whether the defendant is liable: whether the third factor is an act which is culpable and which may also impose liability on some other party is immaterial. If it is a third party's culpable act, then the claimant may be in a position to sue two parties or to elect between them; if the third factor is the claimant's culpable act, then his damages may be reduced on the grounds of his contributory negligence. But as far as the present investigation is concerned the situation is well stated by Devlin J in *Heskell v Continental Express*[13] where he said: **8-010**

> "Where the wrong is a tort, it is clearly settled that the wrongdoer cannot excuse himself by pointing to another cause. It is enough that the tort should be a cause and it is unnecessary to evaluate competing causes and ascertain which of them is dominant."

**(b) Legal causation and The Wagon Mound** Various strictures were passed on the causation test by their Lordships in *Overseas Tankship (UK) v Morts Dock and Engineering Co (The Wagon Mound)*[14] and, although these have tended to fade into history and be referred to no longer, it remains important to deal with them as they are still in the books. *The Wagon Mound* is, of course, the landmark decision in which the Judicial Committee of the Privy Council, in declaring overruled[15] the **8-011**

---

[10] This formulation and common sense approach is taken from Hart and Honoré, *Causation in the Law*, 2nd edn (Oxford: OUP, 1985); see, especially, Ch.6.

[11] (1868) 9 B. & S. 303: facts at para.8-119, below.

[12] (1872) L.R. 7 Ex. 96: facts at para.8-056, below. Similar are *Sharp v Avery* [1938] 4 All E.R. 85 CA, and *Smith v Harris* [1939] 3 All E.R. 960 CA, also at para.8-056, below.

[13] [1950] 1 All E.R. 1033 at 1047.

[14] [1961] A.C. 388 PC; facts at para.8-032, below.

[15] At this first reference in this chapter to *The Wagon Mound* it may still be worth recording, on a historical note, that, while technically the law of England was not changed by a decision on the law of New South Wales, from where the appeal to the Judicial Committee originated (a point of great

Court of Appeal decision in *Re Polemis*,[16] purported to reinstate foreseeability and to oust causation as the test of the extent of liability in an action of negligence. Speaking there of the test of direct consequence, Viscount Simonds considered that it led "to nowhere but the never-ending and insoluble problems of causation".[17] Furthermore, the impression he gained from the scores of cases in which liability for negligence had been discussed was that the courts had at times been "in grave danger of being led astray by scholastic theories of causation and their ugly and barely intelligible jargon".[18] From all this it might seem that the test of causation was no longer an appropriate one for the problems of remoteness, and that foreseeability had taken over as the new criterion.

**8-012** But causation cannot be so easily superseded. This becomes particularly clear when one looks beyond the tort of negligence itself. For in many torts where liability is strict and independent of negligence, foreseeability cannot *ex hypothesi* be the test of the extent of liability. Thus causation must remain the test of the extent to which a defendant is liable under the rule in *Rylands v Fletcher*[19]: indeed, some of the so-called "defences" to that particular tort, such as that based upon the act of a stranger, may perhaps be said to stem from the fact that the damage is causally too remote. Cattle trespass[20] is another tort in point. If the defendant's trespassing animals should infect the claimant's animals with disease, it is submitted that the defendant should be liable for this damage although he could not reasonably have foreseen that his animals were suffering from an infectious disease at the time of the trespass.[21] And it is also significant that in *The Wagon Mound*,[22] where the claimants had claimed both in negligence and in nuisance, the Judicial Committee remitted the case on the issue of nuisance.[23] Furthermore, in the tort of negligence itself, as indeed in all other torts, it must be shown that the defendant's breach of duty of care has, as a matter of fact, caused the damage to the claimant,[24] and in certain cases the defendant will not be liable for foreseeable damage because he cannot be shown to have caused it in fact.[25]

**8-013** The boundary between causation and foreseeability is interestingly illustrated by *Essa v Laing Ltd*.[26] The Court of Appeal there held, by a majority, that in the case before it, a statutory tort claim under the Race Relations Act 1976, the test for

---

importance for the 1961 edition of this text), the decision was immediately accepted here, being applied soon after at appellate level, both by the Court of Appeal in *Doughty v Turner* [1964] Q.B. 518 CA (facts at para.8-115, below), and by the House of Lords, in an appeal from Scotland, in *Hughes v Lord Advocate* [1963] A.C. 837 (facts at para.8-117, below).

16 [1921] 3 K.B. 560 CA; facts at para.8-031, below.

17 [1961] A.C. 388 PC at 423.

18 [1961] A.C. 388 PC at 419.

19 (1868) L.R. 3 H.L. 330. Their Lordships in *The Wagon Mound* [1961] A.C. 388 PC expressly stated that they had not found it necessary to consider this rule and that nothing they said was intended to reflect upon it: at 426 to 427.

20 Now replaced by a statutory liability for trespassing livestock which covers much the same ground: see para.39-034, below.

21 See *Theyer v Purnell* [1918] 2 K.B. 333, where, however the court tended to go on foreseeability: see para.39-035, below.

22 [1961] A.C. 388 PC.

23 See [1961] A.C. 388 PC at 427. It was indeed eventually decided in *Overseas Tankship (UK) v Miller S.S. Co (The Wagon Mound (No.2))* [1967] 1 A.C. 617 PC, that liability in nuisance was not independent of negligence.

24 See para.8-006, above.

25 See the cases at para.8-015, below.

26 [2004] I.C.R. 746 CA.

recoverable loss was causation without the superimposition of a test of reasonable foreseeability. A racial taunt by his foreman at work caused the claimant immense distress which led to his leaving his job and to severe depression amounting to psychiatric illness. The defendant employers' argument, which had been accepted by the employment tribunal, that they were not liable for the illness because only the distress was foreseeable, was rejected on two separate grounds. The first ground for rejection[27] was that, in the circumstances of direct discrimination by racial abuse in the face of the victim, the victim should be compensated for loss which arises naturally and directly from the wrong, whether or not that loss was foreseeable.[28] Clarke LJ examined the policy behind the statute and concluded that, since it had been introduced to remedy a very great evil, it should be sufficient for the claimant to show that his injury was caused by the act of discrimination.[29] Pill LJ, pointing out that the facts of the case were akin to the torts of assault and battery—where it is known that reasonable foreseeability is not a requirement—in that there was deliberate conduct towards and in the presence of the victim though the abuse was verbal and not physical, added that the position might be otherwise where the discrimination took other forms.[30] "Different considerations may apply within the confines of a single tort".[31] Rix LJ, dissenting, wished to retain here the requirement of reasonable foreseeability. He could find nothing in the statute which required a conclusion that the rule of remoteness for this statutory tort should be one of pure causation[32] and he expressed himself as reluctant to promote a test which varied with the nature of the discrimination.[33]

The overall effect of the decision in *The Wagon Mound*[34] may be said to be this. **8-014**
In the tort of negligence causation has now taken a back place to foreseeability, which must be shown as to all damage for which recovery is sought; outside negligence where foreseeability has little importance as a policy requirement,[35] the causation test is unaffected, although in the case of consequences following upon a new intervening force cause will continue to be frequently based on

27 The second is dealt with at para.8-100, below.

28 See Pill LJ at [2004] I.C.R. 746 CA at [39].

29 [2004] I.C.R. 746 CA at [49].

30 [2004] I.C.R. 746 CA at [39].

31 [2004] I.C.R. 746 CA at [34]. In so saying he was adverting to Lord Nicholls's analysis in *Kuwait Airways Corp v Iraqi Airways Co* [2002] 2 A.C. 883, which was given detailed consideration in all three judgments, where in the context of conversion Lord Nicholls drew a distinction in relation to conversion between the converter who was dishonest and the converter who was not: see para.38-070, below.

32 [2002] 2 A.C. 883 at [105].

33 [2002] 2 A.C. 883 at [106]. *Essa v Laing* was applied, so as not to require a foreseeability test to be satisfied, in *Unifi v Massey* [2008] I.C.R. 62 CA where the claimant complained of injured feelings and a stroke through breach of her statutory right not to be unjustifiably disciplined by her trade union: [2008] I.C.R. 62 CA at [28]–[30].

34 [1961] A.C. 388 PC.

35 Thus with an intentional tort a defendant should be liable for consequences which, though technically unforeseeable, were intended (see paras 8-050 and 8-062, below) and also for consequences which were both unforeseeable and unintended. As to the latter see, for deceit, Lord Denning MR in *Doyle v Olby (Ironmongers)* [1969] 2 Q.B. 158 CA at 167B to C, cited with apparent approval by Lord Hoffmann in *Banque Bruxelles Lambert v Eagle Star Insurance Co* [1997] A.C. 191 at 215F; and, for battery, the Canadian case of *Allan v New Mount Sinai Hospital*, 109 D.L.R. (3d) 634 (1980) (reversed on other grounds), especially at 643, per Linden J.

foreseeability.[36] But in all cases the causation requirement must still be satisfied despite the fact that it may not often be an issue.

## 2. CAUSE IN FACT: THE NORM AND THE EXCEPTIONS

### (1) The norm

8-015 The basic proposition that a defendant cannot be liable for an injury where it is not shown that his acts or omissions are a cause in fact of that injury is variously illustrated. In *Barnett v Chelsea and Kensington Hospital Management Committee*,[37] a night watchman presented himself to the defendants' hospital casualty department, complaining of prolonged vomiting after drinking tea, and was instructed by the medical officer on duty to go home to bed and call in his own doctor. Five hours later the night-watchman was dead as a result of arsenic poisoning from the tea. An action by his widow claiming that death had resulted from the medical officer's negligence in not diagnosing or treating her husband's condition was unsuccessful: as her husband would have died of the poisoning even if he had been admitted to the wards five hours before his death and treated with all care, the claimant had failed to establish on the balance of probabilities that the defendants' negligence had caused the death.[38] In *Carslogie S.S. Co v Royal Norwegian Government*,[39] the claimant's ship was negligently damaged by the defendant, and one item of foreseeable loss was the loss of profit that might be incurred by reason of the ship's detention for repair. In the event, the claimant had temporary repairs effected which rendered the ship seaworthy, and proceeded to New York for the completion of permanent repairs. However, the ship was rendered unseaworthy by heavy weather en route, thus requiring immediate repair. At New York, both sets of repairs were effected concurrently, and the period taken would have been no less had only the heavy weather repairs been carried out. In these circumstances the House of Lords held that the claimant was not entitled to any damages for loss of profit in respect of the 10 days which would have been required to repair separately the damage to the ship done by the defendant, since the detention for this repair was not the cause of any loss of profit.[40]

---

36 See paras 8-035 and following, below.

37 [1969] 1 Q.B. 428.

38 Similar are *Ward v The Leeds Teaching Hospitals NHS Trust* [2004] Lloyd's Rep. Med. 530 where a mother's psychiatric illness was caused by the death of her child and not by events surrounding the death ([2004] Lloyd's Rep. Med. 530 at [23] and [24]) and *John Mowlem Construction Plc v Neil F Jones & Co Solicitors* [2004] P.N.L.R. 45 CA at 925, with causation negatived where solicitor's advice to notify insurers of a potential claim would have been ignored had it been given. Somewhat similar too are the cases where a defendant escapes liability because the person injured or the goods damaged are already in an injured or damaged condition so that the operation undergone or the repairs carried out would have been necessary without the defendant's intervention (*Cutler v Vauxhall Motors* [1971] 1 Q.B. 418 CA: person injured; *Performance Cars v Abraham* [1962] 1 Q.B. 33 CA: car damaged) or simply that the injured or damaged condition would have been the same without the defendant's intervention (*Steel v Joy* [2004] 1 W.L.R. 3002 CA: person injured).

39 [1952] A.C. 292.

40 Whether the heavy weather damage had preceded or followed the defendant's act was immaterial. "If the fact is that one of two casualties made the vessel unseaworthy and the other did not, the problem of liability is solved and the time sequence is irrelevant": [1952] A.C. 292 at 311, per Lord Normand. See further on this case at para.37-042, below.

## (2) The exceptions

The exceptions that have appeared to the rule that the "but for" test must be satisfied concentrate upon the tort of negligence. Only the tort of conversion has also fallen for consideration. However, in principle the exceptions are applicable, whatever the tort or breach of contract. **8-016**

**(a) Negligence** The typical situation where an extension of liability may prove necessary in the interests of fairness and reasonableness, with a consequent departure from the "but for" test, is where two or more acts or events or agencies are involved and the wronged claimant is unable to prove which act, event or agency has caused the harm. The classic case of this nature is where two members of a shooting party fire to the injury of the claimant who is unable to prove which of the two shots has hit him. Half a century ago such a situation led to decisions in both the USA and Canada, and in *Summers v Tice*,[41] and *Cook v Lewis*,[42] respectively the claimant succeeded against both marksmen. Indeed two millennia ago Roman jurists were coming to the same conclusion where several persons attacked and killed a slave and it could not be shown who had administered the fatal blow; this is detailed by Lord Rodger in *Fairchild v Glenhaven Funeral Services Ltd*.[43] There are as yet no authorities here but it is possible that, should such a case arise, the same result would follow. **8-017**

It was the cases of the last half century involving industrial disease, particularly disease of the lung by way of silicosis, asbestosis, pneumoconiosis or mesothelioma, which brought up the issue in England, and even more so in Scotland.[44] The starting point was *Bonnington Castings Ltd v Wardlaw*,[45] closely followed by *Nicholson v Atlas Steel Foundry and Engineering Co Ltd*.[46] In *Bonnington* the claimant workman had been exposed to siliceous dust from a pneumatic hammer without breach of duty and from certain swing grinders in breach of duty. It was held sufficient for liability that the dust from the swing grinders had materially contributed to the claimant's injury. As explained below, for some time this was erroneously thought to be an exception to "but for" liability. As Lord Rodger said of *Bonnington* in *Fairchild*[47]: **8-018**

> "since it is enough that the defendant's wrongful act materially contributed to the claimant's injury, the law is not applying the *causa sine qua non* or 'but for' test of causation".

In *Nicholson* also, it was later, erroneously, said to be sufficient that the wrongful act had materially contributed to the injury; the claimant workman had again been exposed to siliceous dust from a pneumatic hammer without breach of duty but the dust remained longer in the atmosphere because the ventilation, in breach

41 33 Cal. 2d 80; 199 P. 2d 1 (1948).

42 [1952] 1 D.L.R. 1; [1951] S.C.R. 830.

43 [2003] 1 A.C. 32 at [157]–[160]. He then goes on to consider "slightly more recent authorities" [161] of the latter part of the 20th century.

44 Most of the House of Lords cases (cited in the text below) were appeals from Scotland. See the large number of Scottish cases cited by Lord Rodger in his very valuable speech in *Fairchild v Glenhaven Funeral Services Ltd* [2003] 1 A.C. 32.

45 [1956] A.C. 613.

46 [1957] 1 W.L.R. 613 HL (Sc).

47 [2003] 1 A.C. 32 at [129].

of duty, was inadequate. The matter rested there until *McGhee v National Coal Board*,[48] produced more confusion for the courts. There the claimant workman was unable to prove whether the dermatitis he had contracted came from brick dust to which he had been exposed during work without breach of duty by the defendant employer or from brick dust which was still on his body as he cycled home but which would have been removed by the showers that the defendant had in breach of duty failed to provide. Whereas in *Bonnington* and in *Nicholson* the progress of the disease was essentially cumulative, in *McGhee* the dermatitis might have started from a single abrasion which could have occurred during the innocent exposure at the kiln or during the guilty exposure on the cycle ride home. Nevertheless the House of Lords held for the claimant on the basis that it was sufficient that the defendant's wrongful conduct had materially contributed to the risk of injury. This undoubted development and expansion of the law of factual causation was adopted and advanced further by the House in *Fairchild* by deciding that, where the claimant workman had contracted mesothelioma from the inhalation of asbestos dust in the course of a series of employments but was unable to prove that the damage arose in and during one of the employments rather than in and during any other since, similarly to *McGhee*, the mesothelioma might have started from a single fibre inhaled when working for a particular employer, the employers were liable as having materially contributed to the risk of contracting the disease.[49]

**8-019** The House of Lords took *Fairchild* further in *Barker v Corus (UK) Plc*,[50] by holding in favour of a claimant whose husband had died from mesothelioma, having been exposed to asbestos not only when working for the defendant but when self-employed. Lord Hoffmann said[51]:

> "The purpose of the *Fairchild* exception is to provide a cause of action against a defendant who has materially increased the risk that the claimant will suffer damage and may have caused that damage, but cannot be proved to have done so because it is impossible to show, on a balance of probability, that some other exposure to the same risk may not have caused it instead. For this purpose, it should be irrelevant whether the other exposure was tortious or non-tortious, by natural causes or human agency or by the claimant himself."

Lord Scott was of the same view[52] but the other members of the court, Lord Rodger, Lord Walker and Lady Hale, based themselves[53] on the further decision in the case that liability could be apportioned between defendants as they were severally

---

48 [1973] 1 W.L.R. 1 HL (Sc).

49 That the defendant's activities need not be shown to be the dominant cause, in the context of concurrent events, is neatly illustrated by *Loftus-Brigham v London Borough of Ealing* (2006) 103 Con. L.R. 102 CA where the claim was in nuisance as well as negligence, the rules of causation being the same in both: (2006) 103 Con. L.R. 102 CA at [14]–[16]. Two causes of damage to a house by subsidence were in play, the roots of the defendant local authority's trees lining the claimants' property and the claimants' climbing plants on the walls and roof of their house. The Court of Appeal held that the trial judge was wrong to have dismissed the householders' claim because they had not shown the tree roots to be what he called the dominant cause of the damage. The test he should have applied was whether the tree roots had materially contributed to the damage. See too on the test of material contribution in the context of building contracts *Great Eastern Hotel v John Laing Construction* (2005) 99 Con. L.R. 45 at para.31-011, below.

50 [2006] 2 A.C. 572.

51 [2006] 2 A.C. 572 at [17].

52 [2006] 2 A.C. 572 at [59].

53 See at, respectively, [2006] 2 A.C. 572 at [101], [117] and [128].

liable.[54] Given then that a defendant was liable only to the extent of his own contribution, the balance of fairness was to apply the *Fairchild* exception in favour of an employee who was himself responsible for a material exposure.[55]

In *Wilsher v Essex Area Health Authority*,[56] in the field of clinical negligence the House of Lords, reversing the Court of Appeal, had held, where there were several possible causes of a premature baby's developing retrolental fibroplasia, resulting in blindness, other than the defendant's negligent administration of excess oxygen, that the defendant health authority was not liable to the claimant for his injury even though the defendant's conduct had enhanced the risk of injury. This decision was approved by the House of Lords in *Fairchild*.[57] To have held for the claimant in *Wilsher* would have been a dilution too far of the "but for" test. In *McGhee*, and again in *Fairchild* there was only one possible cause, one possible agent, which was dust, brick dust or asbestos dust. To come within the *Fairchild* principle the claimant must show that his injury was caused by the eventuation of the kind of risk created by the defendant's wrongdoing—it is insufficient that only one of a number of causes is the eventuation of the risk so created—and this will require proving that the injury was caused by the same agency as that which was involved in the defendant's wrongdoing, or at least by an agency operating in much the same way as in the case, suggested by Lord Rodger and supported by Lord Hoffmann, of the workman suffering injury **8-020**

> "from exposure to dusts coming from two sources, the dusts being particles of different substances each of which, however, could have caused his injury in the same way".[58]

*Fairchild* marks the high point in English law of the departure from the requirement that cause in fact must be shown before damages can be awarded. How far *Fairchild* has wider implications is uncertain. Yet it is not thought, important as the decision is, that it will lead to a vast extension of liability—although it gets much citation from claimants[59]—for one can conceive of only a very limited number of situations falling within its scope.[60] There are undoubtedly cases beyond those **8-021**

---

54 The issue of joint and several liability is dealt with at paras 10-021 to 10-024, below. There were three appeals to the Lords, by three workmen, all of which involved the issue of apportionment but only this one concerned the current issue, the others falling squarely within Fairchild itself since all the particular claimant's exposures to asbestos had been attributable to the negligence of employers or of occupiers of premises.

55 It was held in *Heneghan v Manchester Dry Docks Ltd* [2014] EWHC 4190 (QB) that Fairchild, together with the related *Barker v Corus*, applied as much to the contraction of lung cancer as to the contraction of mesothelioma. See the case at para.10-021, the footnote at the end of the passage, below.

56 [1988] A.C. 1074.

57 See [2003] 1 A.C. 32 at [22], [70] and [149]. Only a faulty interpretation of *McGhee* by Lord Bridge in *Wilsher* was disapproved: see [22] in fin, [70] and [150].

58 [2003] 1 A.C. 32 at [170]; Lord Hoffmann at [72]. Also the two cars in *Fitzgerald v Lane* [1987] 1 Q.B. 781 CA: see at para.8-021, below.

59 Thus Fairchild was unsuccessfully prayed in aid by the claimants in both *Sanderson v Hull* [2009] P.I.Q.R. P7 CA at 114 and *Wootton v J.Docter Ltd* [2009] L.S. Law Med. 63 CA. This led in *Sanderson* to a very full analysis of the speeches in *Fairchild*. Neither case involved mesothelioma.

60 The invocation of Fairchild by counsel in the Court of Appeal in *Gregg v Scott* [2003] Lloyd's Rep. Med. 105 CA, attempting to harness the material contribution approach to the case of diminished chance of recovery through delayed medical diagnosis, got nowhere: see especially Mance LJ at paras [51]–[59], together with Simon Brown LJ at paras [98]–[100]. Mance LJ further said at [61]: "Fairchild may, academically, invite the question whether there are less extreme circumstances where difficulties of proof may lead to a widening of the field for recovery of damages for loss of prospects,

concerning dangerous shooting parties and creeping industrial disease. Even before *Fairchild* an illustration in the context of road, rather than shooting, accidents was provided by *Fitzgerald v Lane*,[61] where the negligent driving of two cars combined to injure a pedestrian in circumstances in which it was impossible to unravel the contribution of each car to the injury.[62] And the discussion of principle by the Court of Appeal in *Hatton v Sutherland*,[63] again before *Fairchild*, suggests that occupational stress-related illness, rather than industrial disease, is another candidate for the *Fairchild* treatment. There are also analogous American cases allowing recovery despite the inability to satisfy the "but for" test, such as the interesting *Sindell v Abbott Laboratories*,[64] where women taking injurious drugs were unable to identify the particular manufacturer and damages were awarded against the manufacturers in an imaginative manner by basing them upon market share.[65] But while *Wilsher*,[66] still stands as good law, the cases are not likely to be many. One significant pointer, and a pointer to a limited application, is that every one of the myriad of worldwide cases cited in the speeches in the House of Lords in *Fairchild* was a case of personal injury or wrongful death.[67]

**8-022** The very exceptional nature of the causation test in *Fairchild* was confirmed in *International Energy Group Ltd v Zurich Insurance Plc UK*.[68] The claimant employer exposed an employee to asbestos dust over 27 years of employment. The

---

but the speeches do not themselves either identify or encourage this prospect". The material contribution approach does not appear to have been pursued by the claimant in the Lords: [2005] 2 A.C. 176. See the case at para.10-052, below.

61 [1987] 1 Q.B. 781 CA.

62 All three judgments refer fairly extensively to *McGhee* and *Wilsher*.

63 [2002] 2 All E.R. 1 CA at [35] and following. Nothing said at this point in *Hatton* is affected by *Barber v Somerset CC* [2004] 1 W.L.R. 1089 HL where the House of Lords allowed the further appeal of one of the appellants in four conjoined appeals which had been heard earlier in the Court of Appeal under the title *Hatton v Sutherland*. The discussion of principle in *Hatton*, headed "Apportionment and quantification", deals not only with the above cases before Fairchild but also with some of the further ones considered, in relation to certainty of damage, at paras 10-014 and following, below.

64 26 Cal. 3d 588; 607 P. 2d 924 (1980).

65 Unlike this Californian case the House of Lords cases of industrial disease did not for long concern themselves with apportionment, the issue always being the all or nothing one: liability or no liability. Cases of apportionment appeared at Court of Appeal level, such as *Thompson v Smiths Shiprepairers (North Shields)* [1984] Q.B. 405 and *Holtby v Brigham & Cowan (Hull) Ltd* [2000] 3 All E.R. 421 CA, and eventually in the House of Lords in *Barker v Corus (UK) Plc* [2006] 2 A.C. 572. These cases are considered in the context of certainty of damage at paras 10-015 and following below.

66 [1988] A.C. 1074.

67 The Court of Appeal rightly refused in *Clough v First Choice Holidays and Flights Ltd* [2006] P.I.Q.R. P22 CA at 325 to extend the principles appearing in *Fairchild* and the related authorities to a case of personal injury which arose out of a single incident and which was in no way exceptional. At a swimming pool the claimant, walking with wet feet along the top of a wall which had not been painted by the defendants in charge of the pool with non-slip paint, slipped off the wall to his serious injury. Here the ordinary rule of causation had to apply so that the claimant had to satisfy the court, which he had failed to do, that on the balance of probabilities it was the absence of non-slip paint that caused or materially contributed to his slip and subsequent fall. To show that there was a risk was not enough. The risk of a slip by someone walking along the wall top with wet feet was inevitable and the fact that the claimant slipped did not of itself demonstrate that the slip resulted from the absence of non-slip paint. *Environment Agency v Ellis* [2009] P.I.Q.R. P5 CA at 85 (facts at para.10-018, below), where *Clough* is considered, is a further personal injury case involving a single incident where again Fairchild could have no application: see [2009] P.I.Q.R. P5 CA at [21] to [25].

68 [2016] A.C. 509.

employee contracted mesothelioma. The employee compromised his claim with his employer and the employer sought an indemnity from its insurer. The insurer had provided cover for six of the 27 years of employment for injuries or disease "caused during any period of insurance and arising out of … his employment". As the claim was governed by the laws of Guernsey the Compensation Act 2006 did not apply. Much of the decision turned upon principles concerning contribution between the insurer and the employer and other insurers who were liable for other years of the 27 year period. However, the importance of the decision for the purpose of causation is in relation to the regrets expressed by their Lordships at having departed from the "but for" test for causation and the manner in which the *Fairchild* exception would be confined. In the majority, Lord Mance (with whom Lords Clarke, Carnwath and Hodge agreed) spoke of the rule in *Fairchild* as an "exceptional basis of a weak or broad causal link consisting of exposure to a risk".[69] Lord Hodge, in a concurring judgment, said that the case was an example of how the courts have continued to grapple with the consequences of departing from the "but for" test of causation.[70] In the minority, Lord Sumption (with whom Lord Neuberger and Lord Reed agreed) also expressed some regret about the decision in *Fairchild*. His Lordship referred to the post-retirement lament of Lord Hoffmann that the House of Lords in *Fairchild* did not perform its ordinary function of changing the common law to modify some principle that is found to be unsatisfactory. Instead, a special exception was created

> "which could not be justified by reference to any general principle and depended on a distinction which had no rational factual or legal justification".[71]

Although the rule cannot rationally be confined only to mesothelioma, the causal principle described by their Lordships as the "*Fairchild* enclave" is likely to be confined, as Lords Neuberger and Reed said, to a "disease which has the unusual features of mesothelioma"".[72]

**8-023** The contours of the *Fairchild* enclave were considered in *Reaney v University Hospital of North Staffordshire NHS Trust*.[73] In that case, the Court of Appeal confirmed that although no distinction could be drawn between cases of medical negligence and others, the but for test for causation was only to be displaced in cases where there is a material contribution, and there are gaps in medical science. The Master of the Rolls, Lord Dyson, with whom Tomlinson and Lewison LJJ agreed,[74] approved the statement from *Bailey v Ministry of Defence*[75]:

> "In my view one cannot draw a distinction between medical negligence cases and others. I would summarise the position in relation to cumulative cause cases as follows. If the evidence demonstrates on a balance of probabilities that the injury would have occurred as a result of the non-tortious cause or causes in any event, the claimant will have failed to establish that the tortious cause contributed. Hotson's case exemplifies such a situation. If the evidence demonstrates that 'but for' the contribution of the tortious cause the injury would probably not have occurred, the claimant will (obviously) have discharged the

69 [2016] A.C. 509 at [39].
70 [2016] A.C. 509 at [98].
71 [2016] A.C. 509 at [128].
72 [2016] A.C. 509 at [191].
73 [2015] EWCA Civ 1119.
74 [2015] EWCA Civ 1119 at [35].
75 [2009] 1 W.L.R. 1052 at [46].

> burden. In a case where medical science cannot establish the probability that "but for" an act of negligence the injury would not have happened but can establish that the contribution of the negligent cause was more than negligible, the 'but for' test is modified, and the claimant will succeed."

This statement suggests that cases of "material contribution" are an exception to the "but for" test where the negligence was not necessary for the loss but merely contributed to loss that would have occurred anyway. As we saw above, a similar statement was made by Lord Rodger in *Fairchild*.[76]

The suggestion in *Bailey* that "material contribution" should be given a meaning which creates an alternative test for causation was rejected by the Privy Council in *Williams v The Bermuda Hospitals Board (Bermuda)*.[77] Mr Williams had acute appendicitis but the hospital he attended delayed his treatment and appendectomy. He suffered loss because he was seriously unwell for several weeks with complications including sepsis. The sepsis had already begun to develop but the hospital's delay exacerbated the development of it. One question was whether the culpable delay had caused the loss suffered. Lord Toulson, giving the advice of the Privy Council, held that the delay had caused the complications. The central argument concerned the meaning of the decision in *Bonnington*. The Privy Council[78] emphasised that the House of Lords in *Bonnington* had assumed that the pneumoconiosis was a cumulative injury not a divisible injury. Hence the "guilty dust" had increased the severity of the injury. Further, *Bonnington* was concerned with liability, not quantum. There was no submission that the quantum should be limited to the amount by which the injury had been increased by the guilty dust. In other words, the "material contribution" of the guilty dust in *Bonnington* was still a "but for" cause of the loss because the loss, in its totality would not have occurred without the guilty dust. For this reason, the Privy Council[79] held that the Court of Appeal in *Bailey* was incorrect to suggest that the material contribution test in *Bonnington*, "involved a departure from the "but-for" test". The Privy Council in *Williams* also rejected the submission that the material contribution approach in *Bonnington* was confined to cases where the sources of the loss were simultaneous (the guilty dust and the innocent dust). However, the Privy Council said that the sequence of events might still be relevant to determine whether an earlier event had been so overtaken by later events that it was not a material contribution to the outcome.[80]

Unfortunately, without reference to *Williams*, in *Heneghan v Manchester Dry Docks Ltd*,[81] the Court of Appeal returned to the erroneous understanding of "material contribution". In that case, Mr Heneghan died of lung cancer caused by his exposure to asbestos fibres whilst he was employed successively by each of the six defendants. His son could not prove by biological evidence which exposure had led to the cell changes that caused the disease. However, counsel argued that statistical evidence could prove how much each defendant had increased the risk of the disease. The Court of Appeal applied the *Fairchild* exception, as developed in

---

76 [2003] 1 A.C. 32 at [129].
77 [2016] UKPC 4.
78 At [32].
79 At [47].
80 [2016] UKPC 4 at [39].
81 [2016] EWCA Civ 86.

*Barker v Corus UK Ltd.*[82] There was a compelling case to do so, especially since the Court of Appeal held that the circumstances were not materially different from *Fairchild*. However, the Master of the Rolls, with whom Tomlinson and Sales LJJ agreed, said that there are three ways of proving causation in disease cases[83]: (1) by showing that "but for" the defendant's negligence, the claimant would not have suffered the disease; (2) by showing that the disease is caused by the cumulative effect of an agency, part of which is attributable to breach of duty on the part of the defendant which made a "material contribution" to the injury; and (3) by showing that the disease is indivisible (such as mesothelioma) and the defendant materially increased the risk of the victim contracting the disease: the *Fairchild* exception. Mr Heneghan succeeded only on category (3) for the increased risk of injury and hence he could not recover the full amount of damages for a material contribution to an injury (category (2)). Nevertheless, category (2) has the potential to confuse by suggesting, contrary to the decision in *Williams*, that material contribution is an alternative to "but for" causation.

The two decisions in *Williams* and *Heneghan* were confronted by Picken J in *John v Central Manchester and Manchester Children's University Hospitals NHS Foundation Trust.*[84] That case involved the defendant hospital's negligence in delaying a CT scan of Dr John's brain after an accident. Dr John suffered a brain injury from his accident which was exacerbated by a post-operative infection. However, a further factor was the hospital's delay. If Dr John's CT scan had not been delayed by an hour, he would have been operated upon an hour earlier and he would have avoided a period of raised intra-cranial pressure for an hour. The primary judge considered the three categories from *Heneghan*, as he was required to do, and held that since Dr John's case was not an industrial disease case, it was not concerned with contribution to risk (category (3)). He treated it as concerned with material contribution to injury or damage (category (2)). He concluded that since the material contribution test applied to multi-factor cases as well as single factor cases, full damages should be recovered, without apportionment for the extent to which any other cause contributed to the injury. In other words, Dr John recovered not merely for the amount by which the delay increased his injury. He recovered for the whole of the injury. The primary judge held[85] that if the "material contribution" test is satisfied, then causation is made out and the entirety of the loss can be recovered if it is not possible to attribute particular damage to a specific cause. The difficulty with this conclusion is that it conflates two different concepts. The material contribution is to the injury but the loss which has been caused is the increase or exacerbation of the injury. In other words, the brain injury would have occurred even without the hospital's negligence but the increase in the injury from the material contribution would not. Unless causation is confined in this way, the material contribution test would genuinely be a new test for causation separate from the "but for" test.

In addition to the cases where, with two or more acts or events or agencies, the wronged claimant is unable to prove which act, event or agency has caused the harm, there are certain cases, starting well before *Fairchild* in which an initial injury has, as it were, become subsumed in a later one so that the "but for" test is not satisfied because the later injury would have been suffered in any event. The leading **8-024**

82 [2006] 2 A.C. 572.
83 [2006] 2 A.C. 572 at [23].
84 [2016] EWHC 407 (QB).
85 [2016] EWHC 407 (QB) at [98].

case on this is *Baker v Willoughby*.[86] The claimant's leg had been severely injured in a car accident caused by the defendant's negligence but, before his claim in respect of this injury had been heard, he was involved in an armed robbery in which his injured leg was shot and as a result had to be amputated. The House of Lords refused to accept that the fact of the second injury should lead to a substantial decrease in the claimant's damages on the ground that the defendant could not properly be regarded as having caused an injury which would have occurred without his participation. "The later injuries", said Lord Reid, "merely become a concurrent cause of the disabilities caused by the injury inflicted by the defendant"[87]; the defendant is in effect to be held to have caused the damage if his participation would have been necessary to bring it about in the absence of other factors sufficient to do so. Thus cause was here very much an issue, and particularly as the House was reversing the decision of the Court of Appeal that the loss following the amputation was not attributable to the defendant.[88]

**8-025** The causal success of the claimant in *Baker v Willoughby*[89] was not repeated in *Jobling v Associated Dairies*[90] where the claimant suffered an injury to his back which partially disabled him and then succumbed to an illness, myelopathy, which totally incapacitated him; it was held by the House of Lords that the supervening illness was to be taken into account and that therefore there could be no recovery for loss of earnings from the date of total incapacity to the date of trial and for the future from the date of trial.[91] However, none of their Lordships was prepared to impugn, though some expressed their doubts as to, the correctness of *Baker v Willoughby* itself—Lord Keith took the view that the decision was correct[92] and if it survives, as it is thought that it should,[93] then the causation basis must survive with it because the claimant's recovery for the total injury must be dependent upon a favourable outcome for him on the causal issue; *Jobling* is then to be regarded as a decision which brings in policy, entirely correctly, in the context of a non-tortious supervening event, to limit the wide scope of recovery based on causation alone. If, however, *Baker* should eventually go—and there is always this possibility in the light of their Lordships' comments on it in *Jobling*—the law on the effect of successive causes will necessarily change.

**8-026** Cases involving two consecutive injuries have continued to appear. In *Rahman v Arearose Ltd*[94] an employer was negligent in not protecting his employee from becoming the victim of an assault at work injuring his right eye, which was then so negligently treated by the hospital that the eye was lost. The Court of Appeal did not interfere with the separate awards of general damages but found more difficult the single figure that had been awarded for the pecuniary loss. The court agreed that this fell to be apportioned but without every head of damage falling within the apportionment, so that the loss of earnings preceding the hospital's negligence was

---

86 [1970] A.C. 467.
87 [1970] A.C. 467 at 494.
88 Also reported at [1970] A.C. 467.
89 [1970] A.C. 467.
90 [1982] A.C. 794.
91 See *Unifi v Massey* [2008] I.C.R. 62 CA (in the footnote at the end of para.8-013, above) where acceleration of a stroke was to be taken into account in the conventional way by discounting and not, as held below, by apportionment: [2008] I.C.R. 62 CA at [38]–[51].
92 [2008] I.C.R. 62 CA at 815H.
93 The implications of the two cases are further considered at paras 40-039 to 40-043, below.
94 [2001] Q.B. 351 CA.

to be attributed to the employer as he was solely responsible for their loss. The most serious damage to the claimant, the psychological injury, fell to be apportioned, but because its sequelae had a synergistic effect, with the two causes reacting with each other,[95] the case became much more complex than either *Baker* or *Jobling*.[96] In *Wright v Cambridge Medical Group*[97] there were two consecutive wrongs which, similarly, were said by Lord Neuberger MR to have had a synergistic interaction.[98] There was a doctor's delay for just over two days in referring a very young child to a hospital for treatment and there was the hospital's delay for nearly three days in carrying out the treatment, by the end of which time permanent damage to the hip was inevitable. Only the doctor was sued[99] and was held liable notwithstanding the later default of the hospital. This constituted a reversal of the trial judge but only by a majority, Dame Janet Smith regarding the case as very close to the line[100] and Elias LJ dissenting.[101] Then there is *Steel v Joy*.[102] The claimant was the victim of an accident involving the first defendant and later of another involving the second. The symptoms of his congenital spinal condition were accelerated by a good number of years by the first accident; the second accident would have had the same effect as the first if the first had not already occurred. The Court of Appeal held the second defendant not responsible for the consequences of the first injury even though but for the first accident the second one would have caused similar injury. Since the claimant had already suffered the damage at the hands of the first defendant, the second defendant had not caused it. Neither *Rahman* nor *Baker* was said to be in point. Instead, *Performance Cars v Abraham*,[103] a similar case but in a different context,[104] was followed.[105]

A further question to which *Baker v Willoughby*,[106] gives rise is as to whether it can be prayed in aid so as to entitle a claimant to contend that, in assessing his damages for an initial tortious injury, there should be disregarded a later tortious injury which was hypothetical rather than actual. This question appeared in *Heil v Rankin*.[107] A police officer's duties had led him into dangerous situations which had affected him psychologically, first a serious and very frightening criminal incident involving shooting and then an incident with a car and its drunken driver; it was the latter that was the subject of the proceedings, the defendant being the driver. Further such incidents, again involving the commission of a tort, might occur at work in the future and have the effect of foreshortening the claimant's career in the **8-027**

---

95 [2001] Q.B. 351 CA at 368C.

96 Both of these cases were commented on rather inconclusively by the court: [2001] Q.B. 351 CA at 367C to G.

97 [2013] Q.B. 312 CA.

98 [2013] Q.B. 312 CA at [36].

99 Curiously, the hospital had not been brought into the litigation. This was commented upon adversely by the Court of Appeal as it seemed the obvious thing to have done.

100 [2013] Q.B. 312 CA at [132].

101 The reasoning in the judgments is detailed, close and complex.

102 [2004] 1 W.L.R. 3002 CA.

103 [1962] 1 Q.B. 33 CA.

104 See para.37-010, below.

105 Steel is reported together with a prior case, *Halsey*, primarily on an issue of costs. The causation issue, arising only in *Steel*, is at [55]–[70].

106 [1970] A.C. 467.

107 [2001] P.I.Q.R. Q3 CA at 16. The issue in the appeal dealt with here is other than the issue of uplift in general damages for which the case, as lead case, is generally known: see [2001] Q.B. 272 CA at paras 40-278 and following, below.

police force. It was rightly held that this eventuality must be taken into account in reduction of damages; to do so was simply an application of the rule requiring a discount for the contingencies of life.[108] That rule could not be applied in *Baker v Willoughby* without resulting in the claimant not recovering from the two tortfeasors full compensation for his injuries[109] because of the further rule, upon which the second tortfeasor could rely, that he is entitled to take the claimant as he finds him.[110] The danger to be avoided in *Baker* was under-compensation and this required the second actual tort to be disregarded. Here the danger to be avoided was over-compensation and this required the second hypothetical tort to be taken into account.[111]

**8-028** *Chester v Afshar*,[112] can also be seen as involving something of a departure from the cause in fact test. The defendant neurosurgeon, in advising the claimant who had an aversion to surgery to undergo elective surgery on her spine, negligently failed to warn her of the very small risk of suffering nerve damage through developing what was known as *cauda equina* syndrome. The surgery was performed without negligence but the claimant was unfortunate enough to develop the syndrome. The claimant established that, had the risk been brought to her attention, she would not have undergone the surgery at that time but would have sought advice on alternatives to surgery. She could not prove, however, that she would not have undergone the surgical procedure in the future and suffered the same injury. A majority of the House of Lords held for the claimant, thereby affirming the decision of the Court of Appeal. The majority accepted that the defendant's failure to warn neither affected the risk nor was the effective cause of the injury so that the claimant could not satisfy the conventional tests of causation. However, the majority further considered that the issue of causation was to be addressed by reference to the scope of the doctor's duty to advise his patients of the risks of treatment, a duty which was closely connected with the need for the patient's consent and was central to her right to make an informed choice. In the light of these considerations justice required a narrow modification of traditional causation principles to vindicate the claimant's right of choice and to provide a remedy for the breach. Thus the majority was prepared to make a further limited modification—that is, further to the *Fairchild* modification[113]—of conventional causation principles.

**8-029** It is thought that this controversial decision—there were two dissents in the House of Lords—has a very limited application and is unlikely to step outside its own context, the context of the duty to warn of the dangers and risks of medical treatment.[114] The correlative right of the patient is one of great significance,[115] the

---

[108] For these, see paras 40-128 and following, below.

[109] On this, see the case at para.40-040, below.

[110] See per Otton LJ at [2001] P.I.Q.R. Q3 CA at 16, [16]–[18].

[111] Somewhat analogous to the various negligence cases in the text is *Vision Golf v Weightmans* [2005] EWHC 1675 Ch, where there had been a protracted failure by the defendant solicitors to comply with the claimant company's instructions to apply for relief from forfeiture of its lease, and it was held no answer to the company's claim for loss arising from the forfeiture, which happened, that there had been a further failure to apply for relief from forfeiture by other solicitors subsequently instructed (the subsequent report, [2007] P.N.L.R. 8at 229, deals with the damages, being the value of the lost lease). Much of Lord Nicholls's causation analysis in the conversion case of *Kuwait Airways Corp v Iraqi Airways Co* [2002] 2 A.C. 883 (at para.8-030, below) was cited.

[112] [2005] 1 A.C. 134.

[113] See paras 8-020 and 8-021, above.

[114] The decision made an appearance in *Birch v University College Hospital NHS Foundation Trust* [2008] EWHC 2237 (QB).

duty in the absence of imposing liability is deprived of its force and emptied of its content, and it is difficult to think of other rights and duties which adhere to a similar pattern. Of course the decision was bound to encourage claimants to try to have it applied to professional negligence, other than clinical negligence, where very commonly there is a failure to warn or to advise. Such attempts, however, were rapidly struck down by the Court of Appeal on two occasions. This happened in *White v Paul Davidson & Taylor*,[116] where a solicitor had failed to advise his client that the effect of a notice to quit was to terminate a tenancy and this failure deprived the client of the opportunity to decide whether or not to take the course of resisting possession proceedings even to appeal. It happened again in *Beary v Pall Mall Investments*,[117] where a financial adviser had failed to advise his client that a risk-free annuity would have been an alternative investment to the high-risk one that he was proposing. Most recently, the exceptional nature of the decision was highlighted in *Crossman v St George's Healthcare NHS Trust*,[118] by Judge Peter Hughes QC who said

> "it is important to keep in mind the exceptional and limited nature of the extension to conventional causation principles that the majority in the House of Lords intended to make".[119]

In obiter dicta[120] he considered whether a patient who, due to a mistake of the hospital, had an operation earlier than would have otherwise been the case, would be entitled to recover under *Chester*. It was suggested that this scenario fell into a lesser and different category—the claimant was

> "duly warned of the risks of surgery and the surgery was carried out by the surgeon he had consulted".[121]

**(b) Conversion** The question arose in *Kuwait Airways Corporation v Iraq Airways Co*,[122] as to whether in the strict liability tort of conversion the "but for" test—would the injury have happened but for the wrongful act?—must be satisfied and accordingly cause in fact shown. Six aircraft of the claimant Kuwait airline were converted by the defendant Iraqi airline by incorporation in the latter's fleet but it was found by Aikens J that they would have been flown to Iran by the Iraqi government, and so converted, even if they had not been incorporated in the defendant's fleet. At first instance Aikens J had held that he was bound to apply the "but for" test but the Court of Appeal disagreed[123] as did the House of Lords.[124] Lord Nicholls in the leading speech said: **8-030**

> "Each person in a series of conversions wrongfully excludes the owner from the possession of the goods. This is the basis on which each is liable to the owner. This is the nature

115 See e.g. *Chester v Afshar* [2005] 1 A.C. 134 at [56].

116 [2005] P.N.L.R. 15 CA at 245.

117 [2005] P.N.L.R. 35 CA at 674.

118 [2016] EWHC 2878 (QB).

119 *Crossman v St George's Healthcare NHS Trust* [2016] EWHC 2878 (QB) at [53].

120 His Honour having found in the Claimant's favour on conventional causation principles.

121 *Crossman v St George's Healthcare NHS Trust* [2016] EWHC 2878 (QB) at [54].

122 [2002] 2 A.C. 883 CA at 896, HL at 1075; facts at para.38-071, below.

123 See [2002] 2 A.C. 883 at CA at [519]–[522] of a long passage in a much longer (673 paras) judgment.

124 See the lengthy, though not always clear, analysis of Lord Nicholls at [2002] 2 A.C. 883 HL at [59]–[85].

of the tort of conversion. The wrongful acts of a previous possessor do not therefore diminish the plaintiff's claim in respect of the wrongful acts of a later possessor. Nor … is it anything to the point that, absent the defendant's conversion, someone else would wrongfully have converted the goods. The likelihood that, had the defendant not wronged the plaintiff, somebody would have done so is no reason for diminishing the defendant's liability and responsibility for the loss he brought upon the plaintiff."[125]

## 3. CAUSE IN LAW: DIRECT CONSEQUENCES

**8-031** In *Re Polemis*,[126] leakage from cases of petrol contained in a ship's general cargo had produced a considerable amount of petrol vapour in one of the holds. Stevedores employed by the defendant charterers to shift cargo placed heavy planks across a hatchway, and the negligent use of a sling precipitated one of these planks into the hold. It struck some substance, caused a spark, a rush of flames from the hold instantaneously followed, and eventually the fire totally destroyed the ship. In a dispute between the charterers and the shipowners,[127] arbitrators found that the destruction of the ship could not reasonably have been foreseen from the falling of the plank, though some damage to the ship was reasonably foreseeable. The charterers sought to limit their liability to the foreseeable damage; and alternatively contended that, although they might be liable for the unexpected extent of damage which was reasonably foreseeable, they were not liable for a type of damage which could not reasonably have been foreseen. The Court of Appeal held that the charterers were liable for all the damage.

**8-032** In *The Wagon Mound*,[128] a large quantity of furnace oil was discharged through negligence from the defendants' ship, moored alongside a wharf at Morts Bay. The oil spread over much of the bay, particularly along the foreshore near a wharf belonging to the claimant shipbuilders and repairers, who were engaged in refitting a ship there and using for this purpose electric and oxy-acetylene welding equipment. The claimants, believing furnace oil in the open to be uninflammable, continued their operations. The following day, however, molten metal falling from the claimants' wharf caused the oil under or near the wharf to become ignited, and a fire, fed initially by the oil, spread rapidly and severely damaged both the wharf and the equipment on it. For this damage the claimants sued. It was found by the judge at first instance that apart from damage by fire the claimants had suffered some slight damage because the oil had got upon their slipways and interfered with their use of the slips; this damage was presumably foreseeable by the defendants but, the damage being slight, no claim for compensation was made in respect of it. It was further found that the defendants neither knew nor could reasonably have known that furnace oil was capable of being set on fire when spread on water. On these findings, the Judicial Committee of the Privy Council held that the claimants were not entitled to recover for the unforeseeable damage by fire, and dismissed

125 [2002] 2 A.C. 883 HL at [82].

126 [1921] 3 K.B. 560 CA.

127 There was a contractual relationship between the parties but the case was decided in tort.

128 [1961] A.C. 388 PC. The full title is *Overseas Tankship (UK) v Morts Dock and Engineering Co (The Wagon Mound)* but this important decision has come to be known, for ease of reference, by the name of the ship which formed its centrepiece. In earlier editions of this book Dr McGregor explained that he was largely responsible for this naming of *The Wagon Mound* which was decided in the same year as his first edition of this work appeared.

their action in so far as it related to negligence.[129] In so doing, their Lordships declared overruled the earlier decision in *Re Polemis*.

In holding the charterers liable in *Re Polemis* for the unforeseeable damage, the Court of Appeal had to decide two points in the claimant's favour: first, that the defendant's act caused the damage, and secondly, that the tort of negligence protected the claimant from damage which the defendant could not reasonably have foreseen. These two ingredients in the case are not generally separated, but a proper analysis of this central decision demands such a separation. Of these two points it is that concerning policy in which the radical nature of the decision lies, and it is at this level, it is submitted, that its disapproval in *The Wagon Mound* operates.[130] Therefore these two decisions, and all related cases, are dealt with later under the policy aspect of remoteness.[131] Nonetheless it is important to stake out here the claims of these cases on the issue of causation, which has at least the distinction of being the antecedent issue of the two. The general rule is, it is submitted, that where the third factor in the situation, be it act, event or state of affairs, has already occurred at the time of the wrongful act, the law will hold the wrongful act to be the cause of the damage in the absence of subsequent intervening factors, even although the third factor be improbable, abnormal, and unforeseeable. Whether, where the third factor is improbable, abnormal and unforeseeable, the defendant may escape liability turns on the issue of policy. **8-033**

The only decision in the defendant's favour which has tended to stress causation rather than policy is *Liesbosch Dredger v S.S. Edison*,[132] but the House of Lords there was really evading the policy issue, as the Judicial Committee pointed out in *The Wagon Mound*.[133] In any event whether looked at from the viewpoint of causation or of policy, that aspect of *The Liesbosch* is no longer with us.[134] Another decision where causation and policy appear to have got confused is *Total Transport Corporation v Arcadia Petroleum, The Eurus*.[135] It too should be dealt with under policy but because of Staughton LJ's foray into the realm of cause—he was the only member of the court so to venture—the case is best touched upon at this point.[136] Charterers, wishing to obtain a February rather than a January bill of lading so that they would have to pay their suppliers substantially less for the oil they were shipping, instructed the master that loading should be completed in February, the vessel not being due to arrive and give notice of readiness to load until 31 January. The owners duly completed loading in the early hours of 1 February, both parties being unaware of the so-called "8 o'clock rule" prevailing in Nigeria that any oil shipment which was completed before 8 o'clock in the morning of the first day of the month was treated as though it had been completed on the last day of the preceding month. Was then the relevant cause of the charterers having to pay out more money to their suppliers the master's failure to obey orders or the 8 o'clock rule? Based on the general rule here proposed it clearly could not be the 8 o'clock rule **8-034**

[129] An alternative claim in nuisance was remitted to the lower court.

[130] See further as to the bearing of *The Wagon Mound* on causation, paras 8-088 to 8-121, below.

[131] See paras 8-088 to 8-121, below.

[132] [1933] A.C. 449.

[133] [1961] A.C. 388 PC at 424.

[134] See paras 8-110 to 8-113, below.

[135] [1998] 1 Lloyd's Rep. 351 CA.

[136] Also the case was contract. But cause does not differ as between tort and contract and, since cause has far more impact in tort than in contract and since Staughton LJ concentrated upon the tort rather than the contract statement of principle (see next note), the issue is considered here.

since it represented a state of affairs existing before the wrongfully timed loading. But Staughton LJ thought the 8 o'clock rule was a serious causal candidate, cited our general rule from the previous paragraph[137] and expressed his disagreement with it.[138] He was no doubt concerned that the owners should not become liable because of the peculiar Nigerian rule but, since the court was holding for the owners on other grounds, his concern was unnecessary and his comments accordingly obiter. The important point, which Staughton LJ would appear not to have appreciated, is that policy would have seen to it that liability would not have followed upon the elimination of the 8 o'clock rule as a relevant cause. For it is stated in the above text after the general rule for causation[139] that whether the defendant will escape liability where the third factor is improbable, abnormal and unforeseeable turns on policy, and policy since *The Wagon Mound*,[140] as we shall see,[141] has favoured no liability in respect of the improbable, abnormal and unforeseeable. The 8 o'clock rule would have satisfied all three epithets.

### 4. CAUSE IN LAW: CONSEQUENCES FOLLOWING UPON A NEW INTERVENING FORCE[142]

**8-035** Very different considerations apply where the third factor intervenes between the act of the defendant and the damage to the claimant because of the strong tendency to introduce foreseeability as the test of cause into such cases. This can lead to confusion in so far as it suggests that, if the damage which the claimant incurs was foreseeable, the defendant will necessarily be liable, and that, if it was not foreseeable, he can in no circumstances be liable. Though this is generally true it is not always so. As to the first limb of the proposition there are certain exceptional cases in which the defendant will not be liable for foreseeable damage because he cannot be shown to have caused it. This is illustrated by a decision such as *Harnett v Bond*.[143] More important is the second limb of the proposition. In the more common case of an act, as opposed to an event, as the new intervening force, the question is not so much whether the defendant could have reasonably foreseen that the act would occur in the sense that it was probable that the third party should act as he did: the question is rather whether it was in accordance with human nature that he acted as he did. This formulation explains much more easily such cases as the so-called "rescue" cases,[144] decisions where the third party has acted negligently,[145] and such particular authorities as *HMS London*,[146] than does a rationale which at-

---

137 And, since the case was contract, its contractual equivalent now at para.8-142, below. Also cited was an equivalent sentence from Hart and Honoré, *Causation in the Law*, 2nd edn (Oxford: OUP, 1985).

138 [1998] 1 Lloyd's Rep. 351 CA at 361, col.2.

139 See para.8-033, above.

140 [1961] A.C. 388 PC.

141 See paras 8-088 and following below.

142 This phrase is used to cover both novus actus interveniens and nova causa interveniens.

143 [1925] A.C. 669: facts at para.8-047, below. See, too, *Carslogie S.S. Co v Royal Norwegian Government* [1952] A.C. 292 and *Barnett v Chelsea and Kensington Hospital Management Committee* [1969] 1 Q.B. 428 at para.8-015, above, and *Ward v Weeks* (1830) 7 Bing. 211 at para.8-061, below. See *McKew v Holland and Hannen and Cubitts* [1969] 3 All E.R. 1621 HL, at para.8-074, below.

144 See paras 8-070 to 8-073, below.

145 See from a contract case, Lord Wright in *Smith Hogg v Black Sea Insurance Co* [1940] A.C. 997 at 1005: "A negligent act is as much a co-operating cause, if it is a cause at all, as an act which is not negligent."

146 [1914] P. 72; facts at para.8-046, below.

tempts to press them within the test of reasonable foreseeability. And in the case of an event as the new intervening force, there is no question of reasonable foreseeability where the event is dependent upon the defendant's act in the sense that it would not have happened but for the defendant's act: this is best illustrated by a situation involving a mechanical freak.[147] Where the event is independent of the defendant's act in the sense that it would have happened in any case, then foreseeability is more likely to make an appearance, but the question should still be whether it is or is not in accordance with the ordinary course of physical nature: the criterion is still cause. However, in view of the Judicial Committee's decision in *The Wagon Mound*[148] limiting recovery in the tort of negligence to foreseeable damage, it would now seem to be necessary in negligence cases to adopt a rationale which will bring the cases as far as possible within the reasonable foreseeability test.[149]

The classification of new intervening forces which do not relieve the defendant of liability is a difficult task, for it is the type of problem for which everyone has his own classification. Here division is made first between intervening acts and intervening events. Then, intervening acts are themselves divided in two different ways. First, they are divisible between acts of third parties and acts of the claimant himself; the former more generally present a clear issue of remoteness, as the latter may involve the related problems of contributory negligence and mitigation. Secondly, intervening acts are also usefully divisible, it is suggested, between those acts where the actor is not a completely free chooser because he acts under a disability or in order to safeguard his own or another's interests, and where, therefore, his acts are not generally legally or otherwise culpable, and those acts where there is no such justification for his conduct. **8-036**

## (1) Intervening acts of a third party[150]

### (a) Acts where the third party is not a completely free chooser

*(i) Acts by parties[151] not fully responsible: adults, children and animals* The intervening act of a person who is not fully responsible for his actions will not generally relieve the defendant of liability. A well-known statement of the law in this respect is that of Hamilton LJ, later Lord Sumner, in *Latham v Johnson*[152]: **8-037**

> "Children acting in the wantonness of infancy and adults acting on the impulse of personal peril may be and often are only links in a chain of causation extending from such initial negligence to the subsequent injury. No doubt each intervener is a *causa sine qua non*, but unless the intervention is a fresh, independent cause, the person guilty of the original negligence will still be the effective cause, if he ought reasonably to have anticipated such interventions and to have foreseen that if they occurred the result would be that his negligence would lead to mischief."

Intervening acts of animals, however, seem to present rather different problems.

---

147 For the definition of mechanical freak, see fn. at the end of para.8-079, below.
148 [1961] A.C. 388 PC; see para.8-088, below.
149 See paras 8-120 and 8-121 and also paras 8-092 and 8-093, below.
150 "Party" includes animals in this context.
151 See preceding note.
152 [1913] 1 K.B. 398 CA at 413.

**8-038** The case of an adult acting on the impulse of personal peril finds ideal illustration in the famous old case of *Scott v Shepherd*,[153] where the defendant threw a squib into a crowd, of whom one after the other in self-defence threw it off themselves until, exploding, it put out the claimant's eye. The defendant was held liable for this damage. This doctrine of "alternative danger", as it is frequently called, is not limited to acts done "in the agony of the moment" as opposed to action taken after reflection, nor it is limited to circumstances where the danger is to the actor's person as opposed to his property.[154] Since, however, such cases do not depend upon acting on impulse, they are dealt with later when considering acts done by the third party to safeguard his own interests.[155] The two sets of cases are analogous, and the division, which is essentially a matter of analytical style, is adopted in order to bring out the factor of absence of responsibility in the present section and thus keep the cases of adults here in line with those concerning children and animals.

**8-039** Intervening acts of children are not likely to form a new cause so as to relieve the defendant of liability.[156] The cases have unanimously discounted the intervening act of a child, and indeed the arguments leading to judgment for the claimant have in most of them been on other points; it was apparently accepted that the defendant could not shelter behind the child's intervening act as such.[157] Perhaps the cases which most nearly represent the present issue are *Martin v Stanborough*,[158] where a child moved a wood block from under the wheel of the defendant's car which he had left unattended on a hill with only the block of wood to keep it stationary; and *Shiffman v Order of St John*,[159] where a child played upon the guy-ropes of a flagpole, which ropes were its only support.[160]

**8-040** Intervening acts of animals present problems of their own. The position is best summed up in the Court of Appeal judgments in *Aldham v United Dairies*.[161] Lord Greene MR said there:

> "If a man negligently relaxes his hold on an animal it does not necessarily follow that he is liable for the damage caused by the animal in its state of freedom, for that damage may

---

153 (1773) 2 Wm. Bl. 892.

154 Lord Sumner had wished in *S.S. Singleton Abbey v S.S. Paludina* [1927] A.C. 16 at 28 not to extend the doctrine to danger to property, but, as will be seen, the contrary view of Lord Phillimore in the same case (at 33) has prevailed.

155 See paras 8-041 and 8-042, below.

156 This, of course, is always on the assumption, in cases of negligence, that the defendant was negligent in the first place. It may well be that the defendant was not negligent at all as he could not reasonably have foreseen any injury or damage; this was the position in *McDowall v G.W. Ry* [1903] 2 K.B. 331.

157 Such cases are *Dixon v Bell* (1816) 5 M. & S. 198; *Bebee v Sales* (1916) 32 T.L.R. 413; and *Burfit v Kille* [1939] 2 K.B. 743, in all of which the child fired a gun; *Haynes v Harwood* [1935] 1 K.B. 146 CA, where the child threw a stone at a horse, causing it to bolt; *Coates v Rawtenshall BC* (1937) 157 L.T. 415 CA, where the child placed a chain across a chute; and *Wells v Metropolitan Water Board* (1937) 54 T.L.R. 104, where the child opened a lid in the roadway. In *Lynch v Nurdin* (1841) 1 Q.B. 29, where the child claimant climbed on to an unattended horse and cart, another child made the horse move on, and the claimant fell, the accent in the decision was only upon the claimant's act: see para.8-066, below.

158 (1924) 41 T.L.R. 1.

159 [1936] 1 All E.R. 557.

160 See, too, *Engelhart v Farrant* [1897] 1 Q.B. 240 CA, of which, however, Lord Sumner was somewhat critical in *Weld-Blundell v Stephens* [1920] A.C. 956 at 989.

161 [1940] 1 K.B. 507 CA.

be due to a spontaneous act of the animal for which the want of care gives the opportunity, but of which it is not the cause."[162]

And du Parcq LJ stated more generally, and as an established rule, that:

"even if a defendant's omission to control or secure his horse is negligent, an act on the part of the horse which is contrary to its ordinary nature cannot be regarded, in the absence of special circumstances, as being directly caused by such negligence."[163]

These statements were dicta in so far as the court held the defendant liable for injury done by a restive pony which he had negligently left unattended in the highway, since he knew the pony to be restive and the claimant's injury resulted from its restiveness. Yet these dicta bear out the similar earlier dicta of Erle CJ in *Cox v Burbidge*[164] where the issue of the effect of the animal's intervening act was removed at source by the holding that the defendant was not negligent in the first place.[165] In actions of cattle trespass the same approach is found, again by way of dicta in *Manton v Brocklebank*[166] and in *Buckle v Holmes*,[167] where Warrington and Atkin LJJ respectively put forward the view that a person is only liable for damage done by his trespassing animal in so far as the damage results from acts of the animal which are in accordance with its ordinary nature. On the other hand, in *Wormald v Cole*,[168] where a claimant recovered for physical injuries inflicted by a trespassing heifer, Lord Goddard CJ inclined to the view that the claimant would have succeeded in her action even if the animal had directly attacked her, although he, with the rest of the court, left the point open.[169] From the point of view of causation, the proposition that an animal's act may be sufficiently spontaneous so as to relieve the defendant of liability must apply equally whether the action lies in negligence or in cattle trespass: if the courts wish to establish any divergence between them it must be on grounds of policy.[170]

*(ii) Acts by persons safeguarding their own interests* Where a wrongful act of 8-041
the defendant interferes with the rights of a third party who, in the exercise or defence of his own rights, acts in such a way that the claimant suffers injury, the defendant will be liable for his injury. This is established by *Clark v Chambers*.[171] The defendant wrongfully obstructed a roadway by placing on it a *cheval de frise*. A third party, wishing to pass along the road, removed the obstruction and placed it on the footpath with the result that the claimant collided with it and was injured. He recovered damages for this injury.[172]

---

162 [1940] 1 K.B. 507 CA at 511.

163 [1940] 1 K.B. 507 CA at 514. He repeated this view, as Lord du Parcq, in *Searle v Wallbank* [1947] A.C. 341 at 360.

164 (1863) 13 C.B. N.S. 430 at 436–437.

165 As with cases involving children, the court often decides for the defendant on the ground that he was not initially negligent, e.g. *Lathall v Joyce* [1939] 3 All E.R. 854.

166 [1923] 2 K.B. 212 CA at 227, per Warrington LJ.

167 [1926] 2 K.B. 125 CA at 130, per Atkin LJ.

168 [1954] 1 Q.B. 614 CA.

169 [1954] 1 Q.B. 614 CA at 625.

170 See paras 8-082 and following, below. Thus the statutory liability for trespassing livestock, which has now superseded cattle trespass, draws the line at recovery for personal injury: see para.39-034, below.

171 (1878) 3 Q.B.D. 327.

172 Lord Sumner nevertheless expressed doubt about the correctness of this decision in *Weld-Blundell*

**8-042** The principle illustrated by *Clark v Chambers*,[173] is akin to that of the doctrine of "alternative danger" already referred to[174]; indeed Cockburn CJ said[175] that the case was "within the principle of *Scott v Shepherd*".[176] As has been pointed out[177] the doctrine of "alternative danger" is not limited to impulsive acts due to imminent personal peril. The refinements of the doctrine beyond this stage are really cases of action taken to safeguard the actor's interests. They have arisen mainly in cases concerning ship collisions, and are more copiously illustrated by cases in which it is the claimant[178] who is the intervening actor; these, though strictly analogous, are dealt with separately below.[179] *The Oropesa*,[180] presents a half-way house. In that case two ships came into collision due to the negligence of both. The master of the first ship decided to go by lifeboat to the second ship to confer upon the best measures to be taken to preserve his crew and his ship, which was helpless in a high sea. The lifeboat capsized en route, drowning some of the men in it, and the personal representatives of one of them successfully sued the owners of the ship for damages. There were two intervening acts here: that of the master in deciding to launch the lifeboat and that of the deceased in getting into it. There was thus an intervening act both by a third party and by the deceased, but it was the former that was stressed by the court. In holding that these intervening acts did not relieve the defendant of liability, Lord Wright in the leading speech laid down this test:

> "If the master and the deceased in the present case had done something which was outside the exigencies of the emergency, whether from miscalculation or from error, the plaintiffs would be debarred from saying that a new cause had not intervened. … To break the chain of causation it must be shown that there is something which I will call ultroneous, something unwarrantable, a new cause which disturbs the sequence of events, something which can be described as either unreasonable or extraneous or extrinsic."[181]

The most important example of such an intervention of a new cause after such a collision is the House of Lords decision in *S.S. Singleton Abbey v S.S. Paludina*.[182] This result classes the third party as a free agent, and such cases are collected later when dealing with actors who are free choosers[183]: they should, however, be compared and contrasted with the present cases.

---

*v Stephens* [1920] A.C. 956 at 989, but this was in the context of a case of remoteness connected with defamation, which has exceptional aspects: see para.8-061, below.

173 (1878) 3 Q.B.D. 327.

174 See para.8-038, above.

175 (1878) 3 Q.B.D. 327 at 338.

176 (1773) 2 Wm. Bl. 892: facts at para.8-038, above.

177 See para.8-038, above.

178 Or the claimant's servant, which amounts to the same thing in this connection; see the cases in para.8-068, below.

179 See paras 8-067 to 8-069, below.

180 [1943] P. 32 CA.

181 [1943] P. 32 CA at 39. In the report in [1943] 1 All E.R. 211 CA at 215, he spoke of the ship being "in the grip of the casualty". His graphic way of expressing what may break the chain of causation, which is well-known, was prayed in aid in *Owners of the Ship "Front Ace" v Owners of "Vicky 1"* [2008] 2 All E.R. (Comm) 42 CA, another ship collision case, to assist in holding there to be no break.

182 [1927] A.C. 16: facts at para.8-052, below.

183 See paras 8-045 and following, below.

*(iii) Acts by persons safeguarding the interests of others* It is established that where a claimant intervenes to rescue the person or property of a third party from the results of the defendant's tort and is himself injured, his act of rescue is not a new cause which will prevent him from recovering damages from the defendant.[184] Analogously, if the claimant is injured in the course of a third party's attempt to rescue him or another in such circumstances, the defendant ought to be liable for that injury. **8-043**

A somewhat similar situation has arisen in slander cases. Thus it was laid down in *Speight v Gosnay*,[185] that the utterer of a slander is liable for damage caused by its repetition if there was a moral duty on the person to whom it was uttered to repeat it. This proposition had earlier found an application in *Derry v Handley*,[186] where the third party repeated the slander to his wife, being under a moral duty to do so since she was employing the claimant, and the claimant recovered for the damage caused by the wife's dismissal of him. A fortiori the damage is not too remote where the third party's duty is a legal one, as in *Kendillon v Maltby*,[187] where the claimant constable had been dismissed by the police commissioners as a result of an inspector of police reporting to them, in pursuance of his legal duty, a slander uttered by the defendant magistrate in trying a case. **8-044**

**(b) Acts where the third party is a free chooser** Where there is full and free choice in the intervening act, the defendant is much less likely to be held liable. The basic reason for this is that where a completely free intervening act is a lawful one damage does not generally result, and where it is a wrongful one it will be held to form a new cause. This is, however, only the general position: there are exceptional cases and there are difficult cases.[188] **8-045**

*(i) Lawful acts* The situation of the lawful intervening act resulting in damage is infrequent[189]; the few cases where it has occurred are divided in their results, which suggests that no general rule can be laid down. Again reasonable foreseeability, although generally the test of causation, is not exclusively the test. Thus in *HMS London*,[190] the claimant's ship was taken into dry dock for repairs of damage inflicted by the defendant, and a dockworkers' strike, which was presumed to be legal in the absence of any evidence to the contrary, delayed the repairs. The claimant recovered damages for the loss of the use of his ship during the additional period of the strike. *Casey v Morane Ltd*,[191] may also be seen as an illustration of a lawful act not breaking the causal link where reasonable foreseeability was not considered. A disciplinary hearing was held in consequence of an accident at work as a result of which the injured employee was demoted, thereby suffering a loss in earnings. **8-046**

---

184 See paras 8-070 to 8-073, below.

185 (1890) 60 L.J.Q.B. 231 CA.

186 (1867) 16 L.T. 263.

187 (1842) Car. & M. 402.

188 For the resolution (moot on account of no liability) of a somewhat unusual question of remoteness involving third party acts in the area of economic torts see *Douglas v Hello! Ltd* [2006] Q.B. 125 CA at [238]–[242].

189 Free choice is, of course, assumed throughout. Lawful intervening acts without free choice have already been dealt with: see paras 8-035 to 8-044, above.

190 [1914] P. 72. This case, being an action of negligence, may now have to be based on foreseeability if it is to survive: see para.8-035, above.

191 [2001] I.C.R. 316 CA.

In his claim for damages, liability was apportioned by consent, 85 per cent to the employer and 15 per cent to the employee. At the subsequent assessment of damages hearing the employee was awarded his lost income, subject to his agreed 15 per cent deduction, and this award was upheld by the Court of Appeal who rejected the employer's contention that the employee's loss of income was a result of the demotion rather than of the accident itself. It was said that normally where an employee's conduct leading to an accident was objectively reviewed resulting in demotion and a consequent loss of income, it was likely that the relevant cause of that loss would be that conduct alone even where the employer's breach of duty had been a contributory factor to the accident. However, here the disciplinary hearing against the employee was inconsistent with the finding of the employer's high level of responsibility for the accident; had that been appreciated at the time, the disciplinary hearing would not have taken place. The relevant cause of the employee's loss of income was therefore the accident itself and his loss of pay accordingly flowed from the accident.[192]

**8-047** The most instructive comparison is between two decisions which arose out of the same facts. The facts were these. A doctor negligently gave a certificate that one Harnett, who at all material times was sane and fit to be at large, was in his opinion of unsound mind. Acting upon this certificate a justice of the peace made an order for the reception and detention of Harnett in a licensed house as a lunatic, and this order was carried into effect. Harnett was then granted leave of absence from the licensed house on trial, with power in the manager of the house to take him back at any time during the trial period should his mental condition require it. During the trial period Harnett went to see a Commissioner in Lunacy who, after seeing him, informed the manager by telephone that he was not in a fit state of mind to be at large, and detained him for a few hours while the manager sent attendants to take him back to the licensed house. For nearly nine years Harnett was detained in various institutions, after which time he escaped and brought first an action of false imprisonment against the Commissioner in Lunacy and later an action for negligent certification against the doctor.[193] In the first action, *Harnett v Bond*,[194] the House of Lords held that the Commissioner in Lunacy was only liable for the detention until the arrival of the attendants, and that the subsequent detention of the claimant at the various institutions was due to the reassumption of control over the claimant by the manager of the licensed house. In the second action, *Harnett v Fisher*,[195] it was held at first instance by Horridge J that the doctor's certificate was "a direct cause of the reception order and detention",[196] so that the doctor would have been liable in damages for the whole detention of nearly nine years had the judge not also held that the action was out of time and statute-barred. This judgment for the

---

[192] See, too, *Robinson v Post Office* [1974] 1 W.L.R. 1176 CA, especially at 1189C to G (doctor's decision to administer anti-tetanus injection held not to be negligent and therefore not a novus actus interveniens). And see *The Sivand* [1998] 2 Lloyd's Rep. 97 CA (facts at para.8-116, below), where the works carried out by the third party contractors in repairing the claimants' damaged property turned out to be much more expensive than could have been foreseen: see at 108, col.1, per Hobhouse LJ.

[193] There was also an action against the manager which failed, and is of no relevance here. The other person in this series of events, the justice of the peace, was immune from suit.

[194] [1925] A.C. 669.

[195] [1927] A.C. 573.

[196] [1927] 1 K.B. 402 at 410.

defendant was affirmed by both the Court of Appeal[197] and the House of Lords upon the latter point alone; on the point of remoteness there was no adjudication nor were any very clear views expressed.[198] An earlier case on the same type of facts, *Everett v Griffiths*,[199] had followed a similar pattern. Lord Reading CJ had decided at first instance the opposite way from Horridge J on the remoteness point; the Court of Appeal and House of Lords had then affirmed on the different ground that there was no negligence. However, in the higher courts more firm views had been expressed upon the issue of cause. In the Court of Appeal Scrutton LJ took the view that the damage was too remote,[200] while ranged on the other side were Atkin LJ[201] and, in the House of Lords, Lord Finlay,[202] who said:

> "It is impossible to exclude from consideration as an element of damage flowing from such a certificate of lunacy, if negligently given, the fact that the order followed. Not only is the medical certificate a condition precedent to the making of the order, but it may also have a most important effect in leading the justice to the conclusion that the person is a lunatic."

The result of this extensive disagreement was that when a third case arose with similar facts, *De Freville v Dill*,[203] McCardie J felt that the balance of authority required him to hold that the doctor defendant was liable for the claimant's detention, although he would probably have decided the other way had he been unfettered by precedent.[204]

The dividing line between these two types of case, that of the Commissioner sued for false imprisonment and that of the doctor sued for negligent certification, is a thin and precarious one. Atkin LJ in *Everett v Griffiths*[205] thought the distinction a sound one, apparently on the ground that, whereas the subsequent decision by court or manager to detain the claimant would be influenced by the doctor's certificate, it would not be influenced by the fact of the false imprisonment as such. He compared the case of a doctor's certificate with that of a libel addressed to a claimant's employer accusing the claimant of dishonesty whereby he was dismissed; in such a case Atkin LJ imagined that: **8-048**

> "it would be no answer to rely upon the employer's 'independent volition,' even though the defendant desired to leave the matter for the employer's consideration, and did not intend the plaintiff's dismissal."[206]

Defamation is indeed a good analogy. In *Longdon-Griffiths v Smith*[207] it was held that, where the claimant's employment had been lawfully determined by his employer in accordance with the terms of the claimant's contract of service in **8-049**

---

197 [1927] 1 K.B. 402 CA.

198 Lord Sumner and Lord Atkinson seemed to favour the view that the damage was too remote, while Lord Blanesburgh probably tended to Horridge J's view: [1927] A.C. 573 at 584, 594 to 595 and 599–600, respectively.

199 [1920] 3 K.B. 163 CA; affirmed [1921] A.C. 631.

200 [1920] 3 K.B. 163 CA at 196 to 197.

201 [1920] 3 K.B. 163 CA at 219.

202 [1921] 1 A.C. 631 at 667 to 668.

203 (1927) 138 L.T. 83; see especially at 88 to 98.

204 (1927) 138 L.T. 83 at 89.

205 [1920] 3 K.B. 163 CA at 219.

206 [1920] 3 K.B. 163 CA at 219.

207 [1950] 2 All E.R. 662; the present issue is not dealt with in the report at [1950] 2 K.B. 295.

consequence of a slander uttered to him by the defendant, this damage was not too remote.[208] If, however, the third party's action in refusing to have or continue association with the claimant was not a normal human reaction to the defamatory statement, then such damage will indeed be too remote. This was so in *Speake v Hughes*,[209] where the claimant had been dismissed as a result of a slander addressed to his employers by the defendant that he had removed from the defendant's house with his rent unpaid. That his employers might remonstrate with him and exert some pressure on him to pay the rent was all that they might be expected to do. Somewhat similar is *Chamberlain v Boyd*,[210] where the claimant failed to obtain election to a club, since the defendant had slandered him with a view to retaining the existing club election rules and so securing the claimant's exclusion. As Lord Coleridge said:

> "A club could not be influenced as to its mode of election by considerations favourable or unfavourable to the character of one or two persons who might hereafter become candidates for election."[211]

**8-050** This leads on to the question of whether the defendant is to be held liable for consequences which, although following upon the intervention of a third party's act, the defendant intended to happen. It is generally stated that intended consequences can never be too remote[212]: to support this is cited Lord Lindley's dictum in *Quinn v Leathem*,[213] that "the intention to injure the plaintiff … disposes of any question as to remoteness of damage". This proposition, when taken to its logical conclusion, is too extreme.[214] For one thing the defendant must have acted in some way: wishful thinking of harm is not enough. Lord Dunedin's words in *Harnett v Bond*[215] are instructive in this connection. He said:

> "Bond had no power to say that *Harnett* should be detained at [the licensed house], and nothing that Bond thought or intended could make any difference as to [the manager's] power to put an end to his liberty on probation or his responsibility for taking that step."

Perhaps all that can be said is that the courts will be less likely in an uncertain case to hold the defendant free from liability for damage following upon the intervening act where it is clear that he intended that damage, especially if his intention was malicious.[216]

**8-051** Finally, it should be noted that there may be occasions when the defendant will be held not to have caused the loss but only to have provided the occasion for the loss by making the intervening act possible. This was the position in *Saddington v*

---

208 Much earlier cases had come to the same conclusion without any argument on the issue of remoteness; they are listed at para.44-013 (in a footnote), below.

209 [1904] 1 K.B. 138 CA.

210 (1883) 11 Q.B.D. 407 CA.

211 (1883) 11 Q.B.D. 407 CA at 412. The holding that the loss of friends and society was too remote in *Weldon v De Bathe* (1885) 54 L.J.Q.B. 113 CA, seems dubious.

212 Most of the standard texts state this maxim.

213 [1901] A.C. 495 at 537.

214 This is ably discussed in Hart and Honoré, *Causation in the Law*, 2nd edn (Oxford: OUP, 1985), pp.170 to 172.

215 [1925] A.C. 669 at 686–687: facts at para.8-047, above.

216 The problem of intended consequences arises more frequently when the intervening act is wrongful; this is considered at para.8-062, below.

*Colleys Professional Services*,[217] and again in *Moore v Zerfah*.[218] Loans on mortgage were made to wives and their husbands, and the money lent was lost by the husband or by the husband's company. Actions were brought by the wives against valuers and brokers respectively on the basis that the wives would not have agreed to the loans but for negligence on the part of the defendant professionals. Both claims failed. The defendants' breach of duty did not cause the loss of the money but merely gave the opportunity for the loss to occur through the intervening act of the husband or the husband's company.[219]

*(ii) Wrongful acts*[220] Nor can any hard and fast rule be laid down as to wrongful intervening acts. The tendency has been to hold the defendant not liable for the further damage.[221] This was the result reached by a bare majority of the House of Lords in *S.S. Singleton Abbey v S.S. Paludina*,[222] the most important example of the intervention of a new cause in a ship collision case. Three ships, one belonging to the defendant, one to the claimant and one to a third party, were moored to a harbour quay. The defendant's ship through negligence dragged her anchors and fell upon and damaged the claimant's ship, causing it to fall in turn upon the third party's ship. The claimant's and the third party's ships then manoeuvred under their own steam in the harbour to keep away from the shore, and some 20 minutes later, when the defendant's ship was well clear of both, collided again, sinking the third party's ship and further damaging that of the claimant. The majority held that the claimant could not recover for this further damage from the defendant because the third party's ship was not free from blame in relation to the second collision with the claimant's ship, and therefore this intervening act of the third party relieved the defendant of liability for the further damage.[223] The third party was no longer in the grip of the casualty,[224] but was acting as a free agent. In *Ruoff v Long*[225] the third parties acted irresponsibly. The defendant had left his lorry stationary and unattended on the highway. Two soldiers got into it and managed with some difficulty to start it up, and it ran backwards into the claimant's shop. It was held that in the circumstances the defendant was not negligent as the lorry had been left in a safe condition, but it was said further that, even if he had been negligent, he would not have been liable by reason of the intervening act of the soldiers. And where a workman, injured by the defendant, underwent medical treatment which increased his injury due to **8-052**

217 [1999] 1 Lloyd's Rep. P.N. 140 CA.

218 [1999] 1 Lloyd's Rep. P.N. 144 CA.

219 *Galoo v Bright Grahame Murray* [1994] 1 W.L.R. 1360 CA, an equivalent case in contract (at para.8-153, below), was followed and applied. It was further said that the same result would be achieved by holding that loss of the money was not damage of a kind that was foreseeable—this in *Saddington*—or in respect of which the defendants owed a duty to protect the claimants—this in *Moore*.

220 Wrongful act of a third party does not of course include the wrongful act of the defendant tortfeasor, so that in an employee's claim for disability discrimination the unfair dismissal by the employer cannot constitute an intervening act breaking the chain of causation: *HM Prison Service v Beart (No.2)* [2005] I.R.L.R. 568 CA.

221 The important *Banque Keyser Ullmann v Skandia (UK) Insurance Co* [1991] 2 A.C. 249, which involved contract as well as tort, could be referred to here but it is thought not really to be a case on damages.

222 [1927] A.C. 16.

223 Lord Sumner also held that the claimant's conduct in relation to the second collision was a new intervening cause. This aspect of the case is dealt with at para.8-078, below.

224 This graphic phrase is that of Lord Wright in *The Oropesa*, as reported at [1943] 1 All E.R. 211 CA at 215.

225 [1916] 1 K.B. 148.

the surgeon's negligence, the defendant was held not liable for the further injury by the House of Lords in *Hogan v Bentinck Collieries*,[226] upholding and following the similar decision of the Court of Appeal in *Rothwell v Caverswall Co*,[227] Lord Normand said:

> "I start from the proposition which seems to me to be axiomatic, that if a surgeon, by lack of skill or failure in reasonable care, causes additional injury or aggravates an existing injury and so renders himself liable in damages, the reasonable conclusion must be that his intervention is a new cause, and that the additional injury or the aggravation of the existing injury should be attributed to it and not to the original accident. On the other hand, an operation prudently advised and carefully carried out should not be treated as a new cause, whatever its consequences may be."[228]

**8-053** All this, however, is only one side of the picture and the law has moved on. It was significant that there was a dissent both in *Hogan v Bentinck Collieries*,[229] and in *Rothwell v Caverswall Co*,[230] by Lord MacDermott and Scott LJ respectively.[231] Lord MacDermott's view merits quotation. He said:

> "When, in order to rid himself of his incapacity for work, a workman reasonably submits himself to surgical treatment at the hands of a qualified practitioner, why should the risk of some error of judgment or some lack of efficiency on the part of the latter in the course of the treatment fall on the workman so as to rob him of his right to compensation?"[232]

And Lord Simonds, as one of the majority, was at pains to stress

> "the fact which, to my mind, lies at the root of the controversy, that it is, first and last, a question of fact for the arbitrator to determine from what a present incapacity results".[233]

This suggested that circumstances could exist where a court would be entitled to hold a defendant liable for increased injury due to negligent treatment by a doctor.[234] Thus when the issue arose again in *Rahman v Arearose Ltd*,[235] where the Court of Appeal, after citing *Hogan* and saying that English law was "somewhat equivocal

---

226 [1949] 1 All E.R. 588 HL. This case and *Rothwell v Caverswall Co* [1944] 2 All E.R. 350 CA, which it upheld, were both under the Workmen's Compensation Acts, but this does not affect their relevance to the present issue.

227 [1944] 2 All E.R. 350 CA.

228 [1949] 1 All E.R. 588 HL at 596. Thus the doctor's negligence in not following accepted procedure for administering an anti-tetanus injection did not amount to a novus actus interveniens in *Robinson v Post Office* [1974] 1 W.L.R. 1176 CA, since it had no causative effect whatsoever.

229 [1949] 1 All E.R. 588 HL.

230 [1944] 2 All E.R. 350 CA.

231 Scott LJ thought that several workmen's compensation cases refusing a claimant compensation for injury as increased by negligent medical treatment were inconsistent with another line of cases represented by *Dunham v Clare* [1902] 2 K.B. 292 CA; Lord Macdermott thought the two lines were strictly reconcilable but conflicted in their underlying principles.

232 [1949] 1 All E.R. 588 HL at 600–601.

233 [1949] 1 All E.R. 588 at 592.

234 The injured party can be in a dilemma. He may find on the one hand that he cannot recover for further injury caused by negligent treatment and on the other that he cannot recover for injury that could have been prevented but for his refusal to undergo medical treatment: see the cases at para.8-078, below. Lord Simonds in *Hogan v Bentinck Collieries* [1949] 1 All E.R. 588 HL at 594 recognised this potential hardship but felt that such a possibility could not outweigh the broad considerations which led him to decide for the defendant in that case.

235 [2001] Q.B. 351 CA.

on the question",[236] was quite clear that the subsequent negligence of a doctor was not a novus actus breaking the chain of causation and thereby absolving the original tortfeasor from further liability. "It does not seem to be established as a rule of law", said Laws LJ, "that later negligence always extinguishes the causative potency of an earlier tort".[237] The Court of Appeal has also held in *Webb v Barclays Bank Plc*,[238] in the context of contribution proceedings between an injured claimant's employer and her medical adviser, that negligence in the administration of treatment by the medical adviser did not relieve the employer, the tortfeasor earlier in time, of liability for the claimant's subsequent condition. The chain of causation would only be broken if the medical treatment were grossly negligent. This is a sensible decision but, curiously, no reference was made by the court in *Webb* to either *Hogan* or *Rothwell*; from the comment in the single judgment that "unsurprisingly, there is no general rule on this question",[239] these cases would appear not to have been drawn to the court's attention.

Somewhat analogous to these cases of subsequent medical negligence is *HMS London*.[240] There the claimant's ship was taken into dry dock for repairs of damage inflicted by the defendant, and the repairs were delayed owing to a strike of dockworkers. It was held that damages for loss of use during the additional period of the strike were recoverable. Evans P pointed out that no evidence had been given that the strike was illegal, but he stated further that it was "in the ordinary course of business [that] industrial disputes may and do occur, and strikes ensue"[241]; this could well include, in later days, illegal strikes. **8-054**

Further and stronger support is given to the proposition that a defendant may remain liable, even after a wrongful intervening act, by two Court of Appeal decisions of the same year as *Hogan v Bentinck Collieries*.[242] In *Philco Radio v Spurling*,[243] five packing cases containing dangerously inflammable material were delivered in error by the defendant to the claimant's premises: this act was held to be negligent. A typist approached the cases while holding a lighted cigarette and caused an explosion; whether she intended to cause a fire was not clear. The Court of Appeal held that the defendant was liable for the damage caused by the explosion, but two different grounds appear. Singleton and Jenkins LJJ decided on the ground that the typist had caused the conflagration accidentally, and that it if had been established that she had intended to cause a fire they would have decided otherwise.[244] However, Tucker LJ went further and decided upon the ground that, although there was evidence that the conflagration was not merely accidental, there was none that the typist knew and appreciated the fact that the scrap was highly inflammable.[245] In *Davies v Liverpool Corporation*,[246] a bus conductor, a servant of the defendants, failed to come down from the top deck to the platform at a bus stop **8-055**

---

236 [2001] Q.B. 351 CA at 366D.

237 [2001] Q.B. 351 CA at 366G. At the same time the later tortfeasor would continue to participate in the liability: see the facts and the case further at para.8-026, above.

238 [2001] Lloyd's Rep. Med. 500 CA.

239 [2001] Lloyd's Rep. Med. 500 CA at 510, col.2.

240 [1914] P. 72.

241 [1914] P. 72 at 80.

242 [1949] 1 All E.R. 588 HL. And see *West v Hughes of Beaconsfield* [1971] R.T.R. 298.

243 [1949] 1 All E.R. 882 CA.

244 [1949] 1 All E.R. 882 CA at 887 and 888–889, respectively.

245 [1949] 1 All E.R. 882 CA at 886.

246 [1949] 2 All E.R. 175 CA.

with the result that the passenger rang the bell for the driver to start, and the claimant, who at that moment was getting on to the bus, fell and was injured as the bus moved off. The defendants were held liable for this injury.

8-056 *Philco Radio v Spurling*,[247] is similar to the older case of *Burrows v March Gas Co*,[248] which is frequently dealt with as a case of concurrent causes.[249] The defendant gas company supplied the claimant with a defective gas pipe from which gas leaked, a gasfitter negligently approached the leak with a naked light and an explosion followed. The defendant company was held liable for the resulting damage to the claimant, Kelly CB speaking of a "concurrent act of negligence" on the gasfitter's part. Other cases in which the court has used the concept of a continuing negligence on the defendant's part are *Sharp v Avery*,[250] and *Smith v Harris*.[251] In both cases the defendant was the leader of two motorcyclists who negligently led the other driver into a dangerous situation, and the latter's act in following resulted in injury to his pillion rider. The pillion rider successfully sued the defendant in each case.

8-057 *Davies v Liverpool Corporation*,[252] basically illustrates the situation where the negligence consists in the failure to guard against the very act that happened. The judgments of Tucker and Denning LJJ are complementary in that, while the latter talked of reasonable foreseeability,[253] the former called the intervening act "one of the things against the happening of which the conductor is required to be on the platform".[254] A somewhat different example of the defendant's duty being to guard against the particular intervening act is provided by *Northwestern Utilities v London Guarantee Co*.[255] The defendants were carrying natural gas at high pressure and a third party, constructing a storm sewer beneath the defendants' main, caused a break in it, which led to an escape of gas, which resulted in the destruction of the claimant's hotel by fire. The defendants were held liable for this damage as they had failed in their duty to guard against the risk of damage through the third party's operations, since these were conspicuous and since the defendants were engaged on a dangerous operation themselves.

8-058 In none of the cases so far has the third party intended to inflict the damage upon the claimant. Generally such a wrongful intention on the part of the third party will relieve the defendant of liability.[256] That this is not always so can again be illustrated by cases of negligence consisting in a failure to guard against the very act that happened.[257] In *Petrovitch v Callinghams*,[258] the defendants, who had been engaged by the claimant's husband to carry out decorations on his London house, were held liable for the theft of the claimant's jewellery by a thief who had entered the house through the street door left ajar by one of the defendants' painters dur-

[247] [1949] 1 All E.R. 822 CA.
[248] (1872) L.R. 7 Ex. 96; affirming (1870) L.R. 5 Ex. 67.
[249] See para.8-010, above, as to the treatment of concurrent and continuing causes in this chapter.
[250] [1938] 4 All E.R. 85 CA.
[251] [1939] 3 All E.R. 960 CA.
[252] [1949] 2 All E.R. 175 CA.
[253] [1949] 2 All E.R. 175 CA at 177.
[254] [1949] 2 All E.R. 175 CA at 176.
[255] [1936] A.C. 108 PC.
[256] As in *Darren Joseph Horton v Taplin Contracts Ltd* [2003] B.L.R. 74 CA: fellow workman deliberately pushed over scaffold tower with limited guardrails and no stabilisers on which claimant was working, causing him to fall.
[257] See the similar situation in contract cases at para.8-145, below.
[258] [1969] 2 Lloyd's Rep. 386.

ing a tea break.[259] And in *Dorset Yacht Co v Home Office*,[260] the House of Lords held, on a preliminary point of law, that the defendants could be liable for the damage caused to the claimants' yacht by Borstal boys in an attempt to escape from the island on which they were working, an attempt made possible by the failure of the defendants' officers, in whose charge the boys were, to exercise any effective control or supervision over them. The boys had first boarded and set in motion another yacht in which they collided with and damaged the claimant's yacht, which they then boarded, cast adrift, and did further damage to by their subsequent conduct. All of the boys had criminal records, including convictions for breaking and entering premises, for larceny and for taking away vehicles without consent. Lord Reid said that, where intervening human action is likely to happen, it did not matter whether that action was innocent, tortious or criminal. He said:

> "Unfortunately, tortious or criminal action by a third party is often the 'very kind of thing' which is likely to happen as a result of the wrongful or careless act of the defendant.... I think that the taking of a boat by the escaping trainees and their unskilled navigation leading to damage to another vessel was the very kind of thing that these Borstal officers ought to have seen to be likely."[261]

In *Al-Kandari v Brown and Co*,[262] the failure was to guard not against the specific act that happened but against the sort of act that might be anticipated. The defendants, who were the solicitors of a Kuwaiti national, failed in their duty of care to the claimant, the Kuwaiti's wife, not to allow out of their possession her husband's passport, which included their two children, by releasing it to the Kuwaiti embassy. The embassy was persuaded by the husband's deceit in turn to release it to him, whereupon he kidnapped the claimant and abducted the children using the passport to get them out of the country and back to Kuwait. The claimant successfully claimed for her injuries suffered during the kidnapping, which the Court of Appeal held, reversing the trial judge, to have been the natural and probable consequence of the defendants' negligence.[263] So too where in *Bullimore v Pothecary Witham Weld*[264] the former employer of the claimant solicitor gave to her prospective employer an adverse reference which was discriminatory and the prospective employer retracted, also in a discriminatory manner, its offer of employment, both employers being considered as thereby having committed the statutory tort of sexual discrimination, the Employment Appeal Tribunal held that the former employer was liable for the resultant loss of earnings of the claimant despite the tortious act of the prospective employer. As was said,[265] withdrawal of the offer was,

---

259 The claimant's damages were, however, reduced on account of contributory negligence in leaving her jewellery unlocked.

260 [1970] A.C. 1004.

261 [1970] A.C. 1004 at 1030. Although the bulk of the damage to the yacht may have been caused by the boys' inability to handle boats and not by wanton conduct on their part, this was not a controlling factor. See, e.g. Lord Morris at 1034 saying that the officers must have appreciated that the boys might interfere with one of the yachts "either in an escape attempt or by reason of some other prompting", and his reference to deliberate damage at 1035.

262 [1989] Q.B. 665 CA.

263 See the same result in *Hamilton-Jones v David & Snape* [2004] 1 W.L.R. 924 at para.8-145, below. The facts (at para.34-048 below) were "strikingly similar" (per Neuberger J, [2004] 1 W.L.R. 924 at [64]) but the claim was in contract.

264 [2011] I.R.L.R. 18.

265 [2011] I.R.L.R. 18 at [20].

in the words of Lord Reid in *Dorset Yacht*, the very kind of thing that was likely to happen on receipt of a damaging reference.

**8-059** Intervening acts of trespassers damaging and stealing property, which featured in four further cases later than Petrovitch and Dorset Yacht above, did not lead the courts concerned to the same result in each. In *Lamb v Camden London Borough Council*,[266] the bursting of a water main, for which the defendant council was responsible, in the road outside the claimant's Hampstead house caused it to become unsafe and to be vacated for several months while the claimant arranged for repairs to be carried out. During this period squatters entered and did considerable damage for which the claimant was, however, refused recovery. Lord Denning MR was critical of what Lord Reid had said in *Dorset Yacht Co v Home Office*[267] but Oliver LJ said that:

> "I concur with Lord Denning MR … in regarding the straight test of foreseeability, at least in cases where the acts of independent third parties are concerned, as one which can, unless subjected to some further limitation, produce results which extend the ambit of liability beyond all reason…. I still regard Lord Reid's test as a workable and sensible one, subject only to this; that I think that he may perhaps have understated the degree of likelihood required before the law can or should attribute the free act of a responsible third person to the tortfeasor."[268]

He thought that the likelihood test was a somewhat uncertain touchstone and that some more stringent standard might be required.[269] In the event he concluded that it would not have reasonably been foreseen that by breaking a water main in the road the claimant's house would be invaded by squatters. In *Perl (Exporters) v Camden London Borough Council*,[270] the defendant council's premises, which adjoined those of the claimant, were unoccupied and insecure, allowing thieves to enter who, by knocking a hole in the party wall, gained access to the claimant's premises from which they stole. The claimant was denied recovery for his losses but the case was argued and decided more on duty of care than on remoteness.[271] Next appeared *Ward v Cannock Chase District Council*,[272] where the claimant owned two of the cottages in a terrace belonging to the defendant council, the policy of which, since the area was zoned for industrial development, was to board up the cottages it owned as they became vacant with the result that they fell into disrepair and were being damaged by vandals. Here the court allowed recovery for such damage as was considered to be sufficiently foreseeable; only the loss in respect of the chattels on the premises was disallowed because the claimant could have taken steps to secure the chattels, as opposed to the premises themselves, against the depredations of vandals. In the view of Scott J the case differed in two important respects from *Lamb v Camden London Borough Council*[273]: first, the likelihood of unoccupied property in the claimant's vicinity receiving the attention of vandals was very much higher than in Hampstead; secondly, whereas in the earlier case the council

266 [1981] Q.B. 625 CA.

267 [1970] A.C. 1004; see para.8-058, above.

268 [1981] Q.B. 625 at 644A to B.

269 [1981] Q.B. 625 at 644C. Watkins LJ's instinctive feeling was that the damage was too remote even though reasonably foreseeable: 647C to D.

270 [1984] Q.B. 342 CA.

271 See para.6-003, above.

272 [1986] Ch. 546.

273 [1981] Q.B. 625 CA.

was responsible only for the burst water main in the road, in the later one it was at fault not only in omitting to keep the terraced cottages in a safe condition but also in its continued failure to repair the damage to the two belonging to the claimant.[274] Much more recently there is *Chubb Fire Ltd v The Vicar of Spalding*.[275] Boy vandals entered an open and unattended medieval church and set off the fire extinguishers in the church, thereby covering the fabric, fittings and organ with a fine dust which had to be expensively cleaned. The church's claim for the cleaning costs from the fire extinguisher suppliers, on the basis that the church should have been warned that discharge of the type of extinguisher installed could cause damage, foundered in the Court of Appeal. This was on the ground that that any such warning would have not been acted upon by the church. However, Aikens LJ in his leading judgment[276] would have decided that the church's claim must fail also on the ground that the fire extinguisher suppliers could not be held liable for the vandalism which constituted a new intervening act, an act which indeed had occurred seven years after the extinguishers had been installed. On this issue the other members of the court preferred not to express a view.[277]

Also in conversion, recovery for deliberate damage to property by a third party has been given. This the Court of Appeal allowed in *Kuwait Airways Corporation v Iraq Airways Co*.[278] At the same time, however, the court said that it thought that in conversion there was little or no room for the concept of a new intervening act breaking the chain of causation[279] and the House of Lords there[280] appeared to be prepared to take the same view. This would seem to follow from the rule laid down that it is no answer for a converter to say that, had he not converted the goods, they would have been subsequently converted by another.[281] **8-060**

Defamation cases also go to show that the defendant is not necessarily absolved by reason of the fact that the claimant's damage has been intentionally inflicted by the third party. Particularly relevant are cases of slanders which are actionable only upon proof of pecuniary loss, because such loss is in the nature of things caused through third parties refraining or ceasing from dealing or associating with the claimant.[282] Also, the slander is often spread to the ears of the person so refraining or ceasing from dealing with the claimant by its repetition by another. There is thus scope for two types of intervening acts which may both appear in the same case,[283] but each requires separate consideration here. (1) Where the intervening act is the third party's wrongful refusal to, or to continue to, deal or associate with the claimant, which wrongful refusal will be by way of breach of contract[284] and is generally by wrongful dismissal from employment, it was formerly held in *Vicars v Wilcocks*,[285] that such damage was too remote. This was, however, based upon the **8-061**

---

[274] [1986] Ch. 546 at 570C to F. The case is considered in more detail at para.39-009, below.

[275] [2010] EWCA Civ 981 CA.

[276] [2010] EWCA Civ 981 CA at [50]–[73].

[277] [2010] EWCA Civ 981 CA at [83] and [85].

[278] [2002] 2 A.C. 883 CA; facts at para.38-071, below.

[279] See [2002] 2 A.C. 883 CA at [546].

[280] [2002] 2 A.C. 883 HL.

[281] See para.8-030, above.

[282] Cases where the third party has lawfully severed relations with the defamed claimant have already been dealt with: see para.8-049, above.

[283] See, e.g. in *Vicars v Wilcocks* (1806) 8 East 1: see para.46-010, below.

[284] Including the marriage contract: compare *Lynch v Knight* (1861) 9 H.L.C. 577.

[285] (1806) 8 East 1.

since discredited doctrine that, where a wrongful act of the defendant caused a wrongful act of another for which the claimant would have a right to sue the latter, he could not have a right of action against the original wrongdoer also.[286] Today it may well be that a different result would be reached, at least if the third party's dismissal of the claimant would not have been wrongful had the slander been true.[287] If, of course, the refusal to continue association with the claimant would not be the natural reaction even assuming the slander to be true, then the defendant should be relieved of liability. This was the position in *Lynch v Knight*,[288] where a husband turned out his wife as a result of a slander that she had almost been seduced before her marriage. Such conduct on the part of the husband in these circumstances was held to stem from his particular idiosyncrasy of temperament, and the damage was held too remote. (2) Where the intervening act is the third party's repetition of the slander, it was decided in *Ward v Weeks*,[289] that the damage suffered by the refusal of the person to whom the slander had been repeated to sell the claimant goods on credit was too remote,

> "such a spontaneous and unauthorised communication cannot be considered as the necessary consequence of the original uttering of the words."[290]

The decision was followed throughout the 19th century,[291] but it underwent some criticism, especially by Kelly CB in *Riding v Smith*,[292] on the ground that, human nature being what it is, nothing was more likely than that the slander would be repeated. Nonetheless *Ward v Weeks*,[293] was approved by a bare majority of the House of Lords in *Weld-Blundell v Stephens*,[294] and, although that case was for damages for breach of contract, it was generally taken as settling the law also for tort. Lord Sumner recognised the probability that the intervening act would take place, "for more than half of human kind are tale-bearers by nature",[295] and for this reason the rule in *Ward v Weeks*,[296] has frequently been regarded as an exception to the general rule that a defendant is not relieved of liability by a foreseeable intervening act, or, to use what it is submitted is a preferable formulation, by an intervening act which is in accordance with human nature. The rule in *Ward v Weeks*,[297] has now been somewhat modified by two decisions of the Court of Appeal, *Slipper v British Broadcasting Corporation*,[298] and *McManus v Beckham*,[299] in both of which it was held that there could be liability for the extended damage due to repetition by the reviewing in the national press of a defamatory film in *Slipper* and by the reporting in the national press of defamatory statements about a shopkeeper's

---

[286] The doctrine has not been law since *Lumley v Gye* (1853) 2 E. & B. 216.
[287] A dictum of Atkin LJ in *Everett v Griffiths* [1920] 3 K.B. 163 CA at 219 lends support to this view. It is cited at para.8-048, above.
[288] (1861) 9 H.L.C. 577.
[289] (1830) 7 Bing. 211.
[290] (1830) 7 Bing. 211 at 215.
[291] The authorities are listed in full at para.46-015 (in a footnote), below.
[292] (1876) 1 Ex D. 91 at 94.
[293] (1830) 7 Bing. 211.
[294] [1920] A.C. 956; facts at para.8-146, below.
[295] [1920] A.C. 956 at 991.
[296] (1830) 7 Bing. 211.
[297] (1830) 7 Bing. 211.
[298] [1991] 1 Q.B. 283 CA.
[299] [2002] 1 W.L.R. 2982 CA.

merchandise in *McManus*. However, the court in *McManus* indicated that it wished to impose a stricter test than that of foreseeability, and this may have been designed still to exclude liability where the repetition is by a tale-bearer. Thus even the rule as modified[300] may perhaps still be seen as an exception to the general rule.[301]

This again[302] leads on to the question of whether the defendant is to be held liable for consequences which, although following upon the intervention of a third party's act, the defendant himself intended to happen. Again the answer was formerly in the negative by reason of the once current doctrine that, where the wrongful act of the defendant caused a wrongful act of another for which the claimant would have a right to sue the latter, he could not have a right of action against the original wrongdoer.[303] The famous decision of *Lumley v Gye*,[304] which finally overthrew this doctrine, and at the same time established the new tort of inducement of breach of contract, was in fact a case in which the defendant intended the consequences which took place, namely that the third party, an opera singer, should break her contract with the claimant theatre manager. Indeed, practically all cases of inducement of breach of contract form illustrations of intended consequences that are not too remote.[305] It was in this type of context that Lord Lindley delivered his often cited dictum in *Quinn v Leathem*,[306] that "the intention to injure the plaintiff ... disposes of any question as to remoteness of damage". But, as already pointed out,[307] this maxim is too sweeping if taken literally: for one thing the defendant must have acted as well as just thought. However, there is a tendency for the courts to hold the defendant liable for intended consequences where there would be no liability in the absence of such intention. This is so in the case of slanders reported by a third party. The rule in *Ward v Weeks*,[308] does not apply, according to the exceptions laid down in *Speight v Gosnay*,[309] where the defendant authorised or intended the repetition. **8-062**

## (2) Intervening acts of the claimant

Where the intervening act is that of the claimant himself, the problem may find solution by way of the doctrines of contributory negligence or of mitigation of damage which here compete with that of remoteness. The difficulties in separating these three doctrines when it comes to a particular set of facts have already been considered.[310] **8-063**

---

300 There are various exceptions to the rule in *Ward v Weeks* listed in *Speight v Gosnay* (1890) 60 L.J.Q.B. 231 CA; they are dealt with at para.46-016, below.

301 These two cases and their impact are fully considered at paras 46-017 to 46-019, below.

302 See para.8-050, dealing with lawful acts.

303 The doctrine rested upon the decision in *Vicars v Wilcocks* (1806) 8 East 1 and a dictum of Lord Eldon in *Morris v Langdale* (1800) 2 B. & P. 284. For more details see para.46-012, below.

304 (1853) 2 E. & B. 216.

305 The old cases of *Ashley v Harrison* (1793) 1 Esp. 48, where the defendant libelled a concert singer who consequently refused to sing at the oratorio for fear of being badly received, and *Taylor v Neri* (1795) 1 Esp. 386, where the defendant by beating an actor prevented him from performing for the claimant, in both of which the resultant damage to the claimant was held too remote, cannot be considered as sound law after *Lumley v Gye* (1853) 2 E. & B. 216.

306 [1901] A.C. 495 at 537.

307 See para.8-050, above.

308 (1830) 7 Bing. 211; see para.8-061, above.

309 (1890) 60 L.J.Q.B. 231 CA.

310 See paras 6-011 to 6-020, above.

8-064 **(a) Acts where the claimant is not a completely free chooser** The cases of third parties acting under a disability, or in order to safeguard their own interests or the interests of others, have their exact counterpart in the cases where the claimant so acts. Indeed there are more authorities covering this situation than that involving a third party.

8-065 *(i) Acts by claimants not fully responsible: adults and children* The classic illustration of an adult claimant acting on an impulse of personal peril is *Jones v Boyce*.[311] There the horses of the defendant's stage coach ran away and "in the agony of the moment" the claimant jumped off the coach and was injured. Had he stayed where he was he would have been uninjured as the coach did not overturn. Nevertheless the defendant was held liable for his injury. This doctrine of "alternative danger", as has been explained when dealing with acts of third parties, covers cases beyond those of impulsive action due to personal peril, but such cases are dealt with when considering acts done by the claimant to safeguard his own interests.[312] A rather different example of an adult's act for which he was not fully responsible was first provided by *Pigney v Pointers Transport Services*.[313] The defendant injured a man who, as a result of neurosis induced by the injury, took his own life, and it was held that his widow could recover[314] in respect of his death: the damage she suffered was not too remote.[315] In *Reeves v Commissioner of Police of the Metropolis*,[316] where a man who was a known suicide risk killed himself while in police custody, the police were held liable to his estate for their failure to take care to prevent him from committing suicide. His act of self-destruction did not constitute a novus actus since it was the precise outcome against which the police were under a duty to guard. To hold the suicide to be a novus actus would be to deprive that duty of all meaningful content. And the House of Lords in *Corr v IBC Vehicles Ltd*,[317] went further in allowing recovery than it did in *Reeves*, for in *Corr* the defendant was not custodian but employer, so that it could not be said that the suicide was a consequence from which there was a duty to protect the employee. A horrific accident at work resulting in terrible head injuries led not only to appalling physical consequences but to a deep depressive illness which drove the victim after several years to kill himself. It was held that his suicide had been a direct result of the depressive illness at a time when his capacity to make reasoned judgments about his future was impaired and that therefore the chain of causal consequences for which the defendant was liable had not been broken by the suicide as a novus actus interveniens.[318] Subsequently, in *Gray v Thames Trains Ltd*,[319] where the claimant, after being injured in a train crash which affected him psychologically, had killed a stranger leading to hospitalisation for manslaughter, the Court of Appeal, relying on the reasoning of the House of Lords in *Corr*,[320] considered that it

[311] (1816) 1 Stark. 493.
[312] See para.8-067, below. The reasons behind this treatment are given at para.8-038, above.
[313] [1957] 1 W.L.R. 1121.
[314] Strictly in this case, and the cases that follow in the text, the claimant was not the intervening actor but these cases bear a closer analogy to claimant's than to third party's intervening act.
[315] But see *Pigney* further in the footnote at the end of this paragraph.
[316] [2000] 1 A.C. 360.
[317] [2008] A.C. 884.
[318] On novus actus see in particular the speech of Lord Bingham at [2008] A.C. 884 at [14]–[16].
[319] [2009] A.C. 1339 CA.
[320] [2009] A.C. 1339 CA at [36]–[44].

was strongly arguable that the claimant should not be disentitled from recovering for loss of earnings during his hospitalisation, as killing another should no more than killing oneself be regarded in the particular circumstances as a novus actus breaking the chain of causation.[321] The decision of the court was, however, that the clamant was not debarred from claiming by the ex turpi causa rule, disagreeing with the trial judge on this, and all the issues of remoteness, which had hardly featured in the court below, were sent back for further consideration.[322]

Children too young to be responsible may also bring injury upon themselves by an intervening act which will not relieve the defendant of liability. In *Lynch v Nurdin*,[323] the defendant negligently left his horse and cart unattended in the street, and the claimant, aged seven, climbed into it, while another boy made the horse move on and so caused the claimant to fall out and suffer injury. It was held that the defendant was liable despite the claimant's intervening act. Lord Denman CJ said of the defendant: **8-066**

> "The most blameable carelessness of his servant having tempted the child, he ought not to reproach the child with yielding to that temptation. He has been the real and only cause of the mischief. He has been deficient in ordinary care; the child, acting without prudence or thought, has, however, shown these qualities in as great a degree as he could be expected to possess them."[324]

Similarly, in *Yachuk v Oliver Blais Co*,[325] where a child aged nine years prevailed on the defendant's servant to sell him a small quantity of petrol by falsely stating that he wanted it for his mother's car and then burned himself badly by using it in a children's game and causing it to catch fire, the Judicial Committee of the Privy Council, approving the principles stated by Lord Denman CJ, held the defendant liable for the injury. And even when a child's age brings with it a degree of responsibility, the defendant's liability is not eliminated but only cut down because the child is old enough to be regarded as contributing to the accident. Thus in *Evans v Souls Garages Ltd*,[326] where a 13-year-old injured himself by sniffing petrol which the defendant had negligently sold him, the chain of causation was held not broken but there was a finding of one-third contributory negligence, doubtless because of the age of the child.[327]

---

321 [2009] A.C. 1339 CA at [45].

322 And the issue of contributory negligence was also sent back: see para.7-005, above. However, the Court of Appeal was reversed by the House of Lords, [2009] A.C. 1339, holding that the ex turpi causa maxim did apply: thereby again removing the need to consider remoteness issues. The Court of Appeal in *Corr v IBC Vehicles Ltd* [2007] Q.B. 46 CA held *Pigney* (in text above) to have been correctly decided—there is no reference to the case in the House of Lords—but on a ground which is no longer acceptable (see [2007] Q.B. 46 CA at [101], per Wilson LJ). For another ground, now otiose, of the decision in *Pigney* see para.41-011, below. As for the limits of the ex turpi causa rule as expounded by the House of Lords in *Gray v Thames Trains Ltd* [2009] 1 A.C. 1339, see *Griffin v UHY Hacker Young & Partners* [2010] EWHC 146 Ch. *McCracken v Smith* [2015] EWCA Civ.380 (at para.7-007, above) is a further case where ex turpi causa and contributory negligence are intertwined.

323 (1841) 1 Q.B. 29.

324 (1841) 1 Q.B. 29 at 38–39.

325 [1949] A.C. 386 PC.

326 [2001] T.L.R. 50.

327 In *Gough v Upshire Primary School* [2002] E.L.R. 169 the judge was prepared to say that an eight-year-old playing on a swing could be held contributorily negligent to a substantial degree: see [2002] E.L.R. 169 at [25].

8-067 *(ii) Acts by claimants safeguarding their own interests* Where the defendant's wrongful act causes the claimant to act in such a way, in the exercise or defence of his rights, that he suffers damage, he can recover for this damage from the defendant. *Dee Conservancy Board v McConnell*[328] illustrates this. A ketch belonging to the defendants sank owing to their negligence and obstructed the navigation of the river of which the claimants were conservators. The defendants abandoned the wreck and the claimants paid to have this wreck removed. It was held that they could recover the amount paid from the defendants as damages. In *Sayers v Harlow UDC*,[329] where the claimant, locked in a public lavatory owing to the negligence of the defendants, attempted to climb over the door but slipped and injured herself, the damage was held to be not too remote.[330] And in *Vinmar International Ltd v Theresa Navigation SA*[331] the claimant cargo owner's decision to continue loading cargo although there was a serious risk of its being contaminated by the cargo already loaded was seen by the court, approaching the issue in terms both of remoteness and of mitigation, as an intervening act of the claimant which did not break the chain of causation.[332]

8-068 As has been pointed out,[333] the refinements of the doctrine of "alternative danger" beyond impulsive acts due to imminent peril really involve cases of action taken to safeguard the actor's interests. Illustrations have appeared principally in ship collision cases. The leading case in this connection is a House of Lords decision reported variously as *The Metagama*,[334] and as *Canadian Pacific Ry v Kelvin Shipping Co*.[335] The claimant's ship, after being damaged by collision with the defendant's, was beached, but in such a way that she slipped off the bank into the fairway of the river, thus increasing the cost of salvage. The claimant recovered in respect of this increased cost as those in charge of his ship had not shown carelessness in the way they beached her. Lord Haldane said:

> "What those in charge of the injured ship do to save it may be mistaken, but if they do whatever they do reasonably, although unsuccessfully, their mistaken judgment may be a natural consequence for which the offending ship is responsible, just as much as is any physical occurrence. Reasonable human conduct is part of the ordinary course of things, which extends to the reasonable conduct of those who have sustained the damage and who are seeking to save further loss."[336]

Similarly, in *The Genua*,[337] the damaged ship was beached, and at a spot where the damaged parts were unsupported, thereby greatly aggravating the damage. The claimant recovered for the whole damage as there was no lack of ordinary nautical skill in the beaching. In *The City of Lincoln*,[338] one of the earliest cases of this

---

328 [1928] 2 K.B. 159 CA.
329 [1958] 1 W.L.R. 623 CA.
330 The damages were, however, reduced on account of the claimant's contributory negligence. See *The Calliope* [1970] P. 172 at para.8-069, below.
331 [2001] 2 Lloyd's Rep. 1.
332 [2001] 2 Lloyd's Rep. 1 at 15. For the mitigation aspect see para.9-106, below.
333 See para.8-065, above.
334 (1927) 29 Ll. L.R. 253 HL.
335 (1927) 138 L.T. 369 HL.
336 (1927) 138 L.T. 369 HL at 370.
337 [1936] 2 All E.R. 798.
338 (1890) 15 P.D. 15 CA.

type,[339] the claimant's ship had lost her steering compass, log and charts in the collision and, in making for a port of safety, grounded because of the loss of the means of safe navigation. The damage by grounding was held not too remote. In *The Guildford*,[340] the master of the damaged ship refused an offer of towage from the ship responsible for the collision, preferring to wait for a tug. The tug arrived five hours later and started the towage, but the ship sank within a mile of safety. It was contended that safety would have been reached in time had the original offer of towage been accepted and that therefore the damage by sinking was too remote. Recovery in respect of the sinking was, however, allowed as it had been satisfactorily proved that the master's refusal of the offer was "a reasonable and seamanlike decision".[341] Similarly, in *The Lucile Bloomfield*,[342] the sinking of the ship following upon a collision was held to be not too remote because, although with hindsight some of the decisions taken by those in charge might be criticised, an omission to take such precautions as good seamanship required had not been shown.[343]

The complementary situation is of course where the master of the claimant's ship **8-069**
acts in such a way as to class him as a free agent: here the defendant is relieved of liability for any further damage following on the intervening act. These cases are collected later at a more convenient point,[344] but should be compared and contrasted with those just dealt with. *S.S. Singleton Abbey v S.S. Paludina*,[345] is the leading case on damage to a ship which was held to be too remote owing to an intervening act, though an act of a third party in that case; *The Metagama*,[346] is the leading case on damage to a ship which was held to be not too remote despite an intervening act; and the difference between such cases, as Lord Wright pointed out in *The Oropesa*,[347] is basically a question of fact. It should also be borne in mind that a third and intermediate solution has been put forward by Brandon J in *The Calliope*,[348] where he held that further damage to a ship was not too remote despite an intervening act, but that the damages must be reduced because of the contributory negligence inherent in the intervening act.[349]

---

339 For earlier cases see *The Mellona* (1847) 3 Wm. Rob. 7 and *The Pensher* (1857) Swab. 211.

340 [1956] P. 364.

341 [1956] P. 364 at 373. These cases also deal with the divergent opinions on burden of proof in remoteness; this is dealt with at para.8-003, above.

342 [1967] 2 Lloyd's Rep. 308.

343 [1967] 2 Lloyd's Rep. 308 at 313. Further decisions following the same pattern are *The Hendrik* [1964] 1 Lloyd's Rep. 371 and *The Bharatkhand* [1952] 1 Lloyd's Rep. 470; see, too, *The Magnolia* [1955] 1 Lloyd's Rep. 417 where, in a Fatal Accidents Act claim for the death by drowning of the skipper of a trawler sunk by the defendants' negligence, the court rejected the defendants' argument that they were not liable because the skipper had lost his life by remaining too long on board the sinking trawler. A good many of these cases also deal with the divergent opinions on burden of proof in remoteness; this is dealt with at para.8-003, above.

344 See para.8-078, below.

345 [1927] A.C. 16: facts at para.8-052, above.

346 (1927) 29 Ll. L. Rep. 253 HL.

347 As reported at [1943] 1 All E.R. 211 CA at 213: "I am confirmed in my view that the problem here is a question of fact by the curious difference of opinion which seems to have occurred in the two leading cases."

348 [1970] P. 172.

349 See para.6-015, above, for a detailed consideration of this decision. The Metagama at para.8-069, above and the other shipping cases at para.8-078, below were referred to the court in *Morris v Richards* [2004] P.I.Q.R. Q3 CA at 30 in the context of holding that a physically injured claimant taking new employment and then losing it was not thereby disqualified from recovering damages

**8-070** *(iii) Acts by claimants safeguarding the interests of others: rescue cases* In the important case of *Haynes v Harwood*,[350] the defendant's servant negligently left a horse and van unattended in a busy street at a time when there were many children about. The horse ran away, and the claimant, a police constable, eventually managed to stop it but was injured in so doing. In resisting his claim for damages the defendant contended that the damage was too remote[351]; but the Court of Appeal held that the defendant ought to have contemplated that someone might try to stop the horse in order to prevent injury to life and limb, and that, as the police were under a general duty to protect life and property, the act of the claimant and the injuries sustained by him were the natural and probable consequences of the defendant's negligence.[352]

**8-071** The principle clearly enunciated here had already been partially applied where there had not been an out and out "rescue" in *Brandon v Osborne Garrett*,[353] a decision approved by the Court of Appeal in *Haynes v Harwood*,[354] itself. Owing to the defendant's negligence some broken glass fell upon the husband of the claimant, who, herself standing in a place of safety, had tried to pull him from the spot and in so doing was injured. It was held that she had acted as a reasonable person would have done and could recover for her injury.[355] The principle of *Haynes v Harwood*,[356] was extended in *Morgan v Aylen*,[357] to cover rescue by a claimant under not a legal but only a moral duty to come to the aid of the person in danger, a point left open in the root case.[358] There the claimant attempted to save a child whom she was seeing home; recovery has also been allowed in *Baker v Hopkins*,[359] where the rescuer was a doctor summoned to the aid of two parties trapped in a gas-filled well,[360] and in *Chadwick v British Railways Board*,[361] where a householder near the scene of a serious train accident suffered psychiatric damage after helping all night in rescue activities.[362] However, rescuers who suffer psychiatric damage have been held not to be in a special category and are, therefore, secondary victims subject to the limitations imposed on such.[363] This was decided by the House of Lords, by a

---

for loss of earnings in respect of the period following the loss of her new position.

350 [1935] 1 K.B. 146 CA.

351 It was also contended, and also unsuccessfully, that the doctrine of volenti non fit injuria operated as a defence.

352 Applied in *The Gusty* [1940] P. 159 to a rescue at sea.

353 [1924] 1 K.B. 548.

354 [1935] 1 K.B. 146 CA.

355 Though also not exactly a rescue case see, too, *McGovern v British Steel Corp* [1986] I.C.R. 608 CA (claimant attempted to remove obstruction in gangway).

356 [1935] 1 K.B. 146 CA.

357 [1942] 1 All E.R. 489.

358 See [1935] 1 K.B. 146 CA at 164, per Maugham LJ.

359 [1959] 1 W.L.R. 966 CA. The defendant's contention that the rescuer had been "unreasonably" brave was rejected.

360 Moreover, Barry J's view, expressed obiter at first instance, that the principle would also apply where it was the defendant himself who was rescued from danger to which he had exposed himself by his own carelessness (see [1958] 1 W.L.R. 993 at 1004) is now confirmed: see text of the following paragraph.

361 [1967] 1 W.L.R. 912.

362 The fact that the risk run by the rescuer was not of the same kind as that run by the rescued was held to be immaterial: [1967] 1 W.L.R. 912 at 921 to 922. Contrast with these various cases *Cutler v United Dairies* [1933] 2 K.B. 297 CA at para.8-077, below.

363 For secondary victims and the limitations placed upon them see para.8-097, below.

bare majority, in *White v Chief Constable of the South Yorkshire Police*,[364] refusing recovery to police officers at the Hillsborough football stadium disaster, police officers whose duty to rescue would have been legal rather than moral. *Chadwick v British Railways Board*,[365] was approved by the majority but on the basis that the rescuer there was in personal physical danger as he might have been injured by a wrecked carriage collapsing on him as he helped in the rescue activities; accordingly, he would have been a primary victim.[366]

The principle enunciated in *Haynes v Harwood*,[367] has also been extended in **8-072**
*Hyett v G.W. Ry*,[368] to cover rescue not of persons but of property in danger; there the claimant, working on his employer's property, attempted to put out a fire which was a danger to the property, but not to life and limb. Tucker LJ said:

> "It is no doubt material to consider in every case whether or not it is life or property which is in danger. It is material to consider the relationship of the plaintiff who intervenes in the matter to the person in peril. It is reasonable to consider the degree of danger and risk and so forth."[369]

*Videan v British Transport Commission*[370] established that the same principles apply even where the defendant is under no duty of care to the person rescued, in that case a child trespasser, and *Harrison v British Railways Board*,[371] that they also apply, following Commonwealth authority,[372] where the person being rescued is himself the person creating the dangerous situation and is therefore himself the defendant.[373]

Yet, in this context of rescue, the natural and probable consequences of a **8-073**
defendant's negligence do not extend beyond

> "injury and damage from accidents of a kind or class which might normally be foreseen or contemplated"

though it is immaterial that "the particular accidents could not be expected". Stephenson LJ so concluded after a review of the earlier rescue cases in *Knightley v Johns*.[374] In that case the defendant had driven his car negligently so as to overturn it near to the exit of a road tunnel carrying one-way traffic. There followed what was described by the trial judge as a series of acts of ineptitude on the part of the police; in particular, a police inspector forgot to close the tunnel immediately to traffic as required by police regulations and instructed the claimant, a police constable, to ride his motorcycle the wrong way down the tunnel in order to do so. The defend-

---

364 [1999] 2 A.C. 455, reversing the decision of the Court of Appeal, also by a majority, in the name of *Frost v Chief Constable of the South Yorkshire Police* [1998] Q.B. 254 CA.

365 [1967] 1 W.L.R. 912.

366 See [1999] 2 A.C. 455 at 499D and 509E to F, per Lord Steyn and Lord Hoffmann respectively. For primary victims and the wider liability towards them, see para.8-097, below.

367 [1935] 1 K.B. 146 CA.

368 [1948] 1 K.B. 345 CA.

369 [1935] 1 K.B. 146 CA at 347 to 348.

370 [1963] 2 Q.B. 650 CA.

371 [1981] 3 All E.R. 679.

372 *Horsley v MacLaren, The Ogopogo* in the Supreme Court of Canada, reported at [1971] 2 Lloyd's Rep. 410.

373 Firemen as "rescuers" are in no different category: see *Salmon v Seafarers Restaurants* [1982] 1 W.L.R. 1264, especially at 1272G to H.

374 [1982] 1 W.L.R. 349 CA at 360H to 361A.

ant was held not liable for the injury suffered by the claimant when he came into collision with an approaching car; the chain of causation had been broken. As Stephenson LJ put it:

> "The ordinary course of things took an extraordinary course. The length and irregularities of the line leading from the first accident to the second have no parallel in the reported rescue cases, in all of which the plaintiff succeeded in establishing the original wrongdoer's liability."[375]

Somewhat less convincing is the decision in *Crossley v Rawlinson*,[376] where recovery was denied to an AA patrol man who was injured when his foot went into a hole on a roadside path down which he was running to assist in putting out a fire negligently started by the defendant on his lorry.

**8-074** *(iv) Acts by claimants when subject to a disability imposed by the tort* Where physical injury caused by the defendant's wrongful act limits the claimant's facility of movement and action, the defendant may be liable for further injury arising from this lack of facility. In *Wieland v Cyril Lord Carpets*,[377] the claimant, soon after leaving the hospital where she had had a collar fitted to her neck which had been injured two days previously in an accident due to the defendants' negligence, fell as she was descending some stairs with her son, thereby sustaining injury to her ankles. Apart from being in a rather nervous condition at the time due to a combination of her visit to the doctor and the shake-up from the accident, the constriction of the movement of her head caused by the collar deprived the claimant of her usual ability to adjust herself automatically to the bifocal glasses which she had worn for many years, and these factors together produced some unsteadiness. Eveleigh J held the claimant entitled to recover for the injury to her ankles because he regarded this further injury as attributable to the original negligence of the defendants. Not only, he said, has it

> "long been recognised that injury sustained in one accident may be the cause of a subsequent injury"[378]

but also

> "it can be said that it is foreseeable that one injury may affect a person's ability to cope with the vicissitudes of life and thereby be a cause of another injury".[379]

With this case should be contrasted *McKew v Holland and Hannen and Cubitts*,[380] where the House of Lords held against the claimant in his claim in respect of a further and severe injury caused by falling down a staircase when his left leg unexpectedly gave way beneath him, which it had a tendency to do on occasions as a result of a minor injury for which the defendants were admittedly liable. The circumstances giving rise to the fall were, however, markedly different from those in the earlier case, occurring nearly a month after the original accident when the claimant, holding his child by the hand, made to descend a steep staircase without

---

375 [1982] 1 W.L.R. 349 CA at 367G to H.
376 [1982] 1 W.L.R. 369.
377 [1969] 3 All E.R. 1006.
378 [1969] 3 All E.R. 1006 at 1009.
379 [1969] 3 All E.R. 1006 at 1010.
380 [1969] 3 All E.R. 1621 HL.

a handrail and without the available assistance of his wife and brother-in-law. This act was sufficiently unreasonable to break the chain of causation so that the further injury fell to be regarded as caused by the claimant's own conduct. Lord Reid, with whom Lords Hodson and Dilhorne expressly concurred,[381] thought that this result followed even if the claimant's conduct was foreseeable. He said:

> "It is often easy to foresee unreasonable conduct or some other novus actus interveniens as being quite likely. But that does not mean that the defender must pay for damage caused by the novus actus. It only leads to trouble that if one tries to graft on to the concept of foreseeability some rule of law to the effect that a wrongdoer is not bound to foresee something which in fact he could readily foresee as quite likely to happen. For it is not at all unlikely or unforeseeable that an active man who has suffered such a disability will take some quite unreasonable risk. But if he does he cannot hold the defender liable for the consequences."[382]

Here then the defendant is taken not to have caused an injury which was foreseeable, and, while this result is a perfectly proper one in exceptional cases,[383] it would be unwise to reach too readily the conclusion that a defendant ceases to be liable for foreseeable consequences merely because they have arisen out of unreasonable conduct on the part of the claimant. It might even be asked whether it would not have been better for the House to have held the defendant liable but to have made a very substantial reduction from the claimant's damages on account of his contributory negligence, thereby adopting the approach taken practically contemporaneously, in the context of a ship collision, by Brandon J in *The Calliope*.[384]

**(b) Acts where the claimant is a free chooser** An intervening act done with full and free choice by the claimant differs from such an act of a third party in that the claimant's act is not likely to be technically wrongful. Failure to act for his own safety, for instance, will constitute carelessness but will not by itself constitute a breach of duty to another.[385] Therefore no division between lawful and wrongful acts is required or even appropriate here.[386] **8-075**

Where the claimant is a free chooser the defendant is much more likely to be relieved of liability for increased damage resulting from the claimant's act. It is at this point that the distinction between contributory negligence, remoteness and mitigation becomes most acute. Since it is here that it becomes most likely that the claimant may fail in his action in respect of the increased damage, it is of great practical importance whether the axe falls by way of contributory negligence, where **8-076**

---

381 Lord Upjohn merely concurred; Lord Guest, in a separate speech, took the view that the claimant had behaved unreasonably in attempting to save himself by leaping forward down the stairs, and therefore had two reasons for holding against him: [1969] 3 All E.R. 1621 HL at 1625 to 1626.

382 [1969] 3 All E.R. 1621 HL at 1623.

383 See para.8-035, above.

384 [1970] P. 172 at para.6-015, above. See too *Environment Agency v Ellis* [2009] P.I.Q.R. P5 CA at 85 in the footnote at the end of para.6-014, above; facts at para.10-018, below.

385 In *Barings Plc v Coopers & Lybrand* [2003] Lloyd's Rep. I. R. 566 where the claimants, three companies in the Barings group which collapsed on account of the unauthorised trading of a fraudulent employee, sued their auditor for negligence in its audit, leading to a failure to uncover the unauthorised trading and to consequent mounting losses, there was explored in massive detail ([2003] Lloyd's Rep. I. R. 566 at [781] to [879]) whether the acts and omissions of the claimants in serious mismanagement broke the chain of causation and, if so, at what point in time.

386 Such a division is used for third party acts: see para.8-045, above.

the claimant can at least recover an apportioned part of his increased damage; by way of remoteness, where the onus is on the claimant to prove the defendant liable for the increased damage; or by way of mitigation, where the onus is on the defendant to show himself not liable for the increased damage. The difficulties of these distinctions need not be analysed again,[387] but it is important to keep them in mind when considering the following cases; the decision in *The Calliope*,[388] applying the contributory negligence doctrine in preference to the remoteness doctrine so as to allow a limited recovery in a ship collision case, is of particular significance.[389]

**8-077** Most of the cases here form the complement to those where the claimant has succeeded because his intervening act has been reasonably taken for the safeguarding of his own or another's interests.[390] Here the claimant fails because his act is unreasonable although similarly motivated.[391] Thus in *Adams v Lancashire and Yorkshire Ry*,[392] where a passenger fell out of a train in trying to shut a door which flew open, although there was room in the carriage for him to sit away from the door and the train would have stopped at a station in a few minutes, it was held that he could not recover for his injury. In *Cutler v United Dairies*,[393] the claimant similarly failed where his injury was sustained in effecting an unreasonable "rescue" of a runaway horse. In *Arkin v Borchard Lines Ltd*,[394] where the claimant and the defendant were fierce competitors in the provision of liner operating services, the claimant, suing for heavy trading losses it had suffered in consequence of the defendant's breach of the Treaty of Rome, had continued in the market, in which the defendant had achieved a dominant position, and as a result had incurred these losses. Since it was held that no reasonable liner operator would have remained in the market, the decision to remain and the decision to reduce rates to suicide levels were so irrational that they could not be justified, and therefore the predominant cause of the claimant's continuing losses was held to be its failure to withdraw from the market.

**8-078** Two groups of cases stand out in this connection: further ship collision cases, and cases of injured claimants failing to undergo medical treatment. (1) In some of the ship collision cases the court has held that the claimant, when acting in such a way as to inflict further damage on his ship, was no longer in the grip of the casualty,[395] but was acting as a free agent.[396] In *S.S. Singleton Abbey v S.S. Paludina*,[397] which

---

387 They are fully analysed at paras 6-011 and following, above.

388 [1970] P. 172.

389 See para.6-015, above, for a detailed consideration of this decision. And see also in this connection *Barings Plc v Coopers & Lybrand* [2003] Lloyd's Rep. I.R. 566 at para.6-016, above and *Owners of the Ship "Front Ace" v Owners of "Vicky 1"* [2008] 2 All E.R. (Comm) 42 CA at para.6-019, above.

390 See paras 8-067 to 8-073, above.

391 Not all the cases, however, are of this type. See, e.g. *Glover v L.S.W. Ry* (1867) L.R. 3 Q.B. 25, where a passenger was unjustifiably removed from a railway carriage by the defendant railway company and the defendant was held not liable for the passenger's loss of a pair of race-glasses which he had negligently left behind in the carriage.

392 (1869) L.R. 4 C.P. 739.

393 [1933] 2 K.B. 297 CA.

394 [2003] 2 Lloyd's Rep. 225.

395 This is the graphic phrase of Lord Wright in *The Oropesa as reported at* [1943] 1 All E.R. 211 CA at 215.

396 As contrasted to the claimant in each of the ship collision cases at para.8-068, above. In *The Calliope* [1970] P. 172 Brandon J pointed out that, of the 13 cases collected by him of ship collisions

has already been considered as an example of a third party's wrongful act relieving the defendant of liability for further damage, Lord Sumner also gave the claimant's intervening act as a reason for holding for the defendant. In *The Flying Fish*,[398] and again in *The Glendinning*,[399] no recovery was allowed for further damage to the claimant's ship by reason of her mismanagement after a collision for which the defendant was liable in tort. Similarly, in *The Fritz Thyssen*,[400] no recovery was allowed for the sinking of a ship where the master had repeatedly refused all assistance after a collision which had severely damaged her, since on the facts his refusal was unreasonable and amounted to an omission to take the vital precautions required by good seamanship which in all probability would have averted a total loss.[401] Again, in *Grant v S.S. Egyptian*,[402] where the claimant failed to examine the damage when his ship foundered from a collision, so that the ship sank, the defendant was held liable for the foundering but not for the sinking.[403] Even where the claimant's act is in no way culpable the damage he incurs may be too remote. This was the position in *The San Onofre*.[404] After the defendant's ship had negligently collided with the claimant's ship, the latter attempted to save the former, which was badly damaged, by lashing her alongside and towing her inshore. While so towing, the claimant's ship grounded in a fog sustaining further damage, but the claimant failed to recover for this damage on the ground of remoteness. Scrutton LJ said:

> "The question whether damage is sufficiently direct consequence of negligence to be recoverable, or is too remote, is rather a question of first impression. I am clear that if a negligent driver on the road injures himself in a collision with another vehicle, whose driver and a stranger thereupon take the injured man to hospital and meet with an accident in so doing, neither of them can recover damages for the accident from the negligent driver as consequences of his original negligence. The present case seems to me exactly similar."[405]

(2) In a number of cases it has been held that whether a claimant's refusal to undergo an operation after being physically injured by the defendant debars him from recovery for damage that would not otherwise have been suffered, turns on the reasonableness or the unreasonableness of the refusal. In two workmen's

---

followed by further damage, in only three had the court found causative intervening negligence by the claimant breaking the chain of causation: at 178.

[397] [1927] A.C. 16; facts at para.8-052, above.

[398] (1865) 34 L.J. Adm. 113 PC.

[399] (1943) 76 Ll. L. Rep. 86.

[400] [1968] P. 255.

[401] Cairns J said *The Fogo* [1967] 2 Lloyd's Rep. 208 at 223–224 that he would there have followed *The Fritz Thyssen* if he had not held for the defendants on the ground that the claimants were entirely to blame for the initial collision.

[402] [1910] A.C. 400.

[403] This case is moving out of the realm of remoteness into that of mitigation.

[404] [1922] P. 243 CA.

[405] [1922] P. 243 CA at 253. Similar is Bankes LJ at 248 to 249; but see Atkin LJ at 254 to 255, who expressed the view that if, in a collision negligently caused by the defendant, the defendant was injured so that his life was in danger while the claimant's car was damaged, and the claimant rushed the defendant to hospital in his damaged car as the only reasonable means of conveyance, resulting in further damage to the claimant's car or injury to himself en route, "such injuries might well be the direct result of the original collision".

compensation claims, the House of Lords held in *Steele v Robert George*,[406] and *Richardson v Redpath*,[407] that on the facts of both the refusal was reasonable and did not prevent the claimant from recovering for his full loss; the conclusion of the Judicial Committee of the Privy Council has been the same in two damages claims, *Selvanayagam v University of the West Indies*,[408] and *Geest Plc v Lansiquot*.[409] A contrary result was reached by the Court of Appeal in *Marcroft v Scruttons*,[410] on the ground that the claimant's refusal was unreasonable. It is submitted elsewhere, however, that these cases are more properly based upon the mitigation doctrine than upon that of remoteness.[411]

## (3) Intervening events

**8-079** Little falls to be said about intervening events. Where the event is dependent upon the defendant's act in the sense that it would not have occurred had the defendant not acted as he did, then the defendant will be liable for all the damage. This is the situation where a physical force is set in motion by the defendant's act which engenders certain reactions which are mechanical freaks.[412]

**8-080** On the other hand, where the event is independent of the defendant's act in the sense that it would have happened whether the defendant had acted or not, then the defendant will not be liable for further damage following upon the happening of the event if the event can be regarded as a coincidence. A classic illustration is of the claimant who, on his way to hospital from a street accident in which the defendant has tortiously injured him, is hit by a falling tree and thus injured further.[413] The important decision in *Carslogie S.S. Co v Royal Norwegian Government*,[414] also

---

406 [1942] A.C. 497.

407 [1944] A.C. 62.

408 [1983] 1 W.L.R. 585 PC.

409 [2002] 1 W.L.R. 3111 PC. These two cases, however, differed on where the onus of proof lay: see para.9-020, below.

410 [1954] 1 Lloyd's Rep. 395 CA.

411 See para.6-020, above. Better treated under mitigation is also, it is submitted, *Emeh v Kensington Area Health Authority* [1985] Q.B. 1012 CA, where the claimant's decision not to have an abortion was held not to be a novus actus relieving the defendants from liability for their negligent failure to sterilise the claimant: see the case at para.9-089, below.

412 There are no cases of mechanical freaks in English law. An illustration is provided by the American case of *Bunting v Hogsett*, 139 Pa. 363; 21 A. 31 (1891), the facts of which are given in Hart and Honoré, *Causation in the Law*, 2nd edn (Oxford: OUP, 1985), pp.176 to177, thus: "Defendant ran an engine over a track which crossed a railway at two places. His engineer drove negligently at the approach to one crossing and collided with a train. Just before the collision he shut off steam. The jar of the collision reopened the throttle and the engine ran backwards and struck the train a second time at the other crossing, injuring plaintiff." The authors add: "Here the reversal of the engine, being itself the consequence of the defendant's servant's act, though a 'freak', did not prevent claimant's injury being the consequence of the original negligence, although but for its connection with defendant's act the freak reversal of the engine might have been regarded as an extraordinary intervening event and so as negativing causal connection between the defendant's negligence and the plaintiff's injury." *Sneesby v Lancashire and Yorkshire Ry* (1875) 1 Q.B.D. 42, where a train frightened some cows which then ran amok and injured themselves, is perhaps the nearest one can get to an English illustration of this type of case.

413 See *Hogan v Bentinck Collieries* [1949] 1 All E.R. 588 HL at 601, per Lord MacDermott: "If he [the person tortiously injured] gets burned because the hospital he has entered goes on fire, or if he is maimed because the ambulance taking him, say, from hospital to a convalescent home is involved in a street accident, I would not link the resulting incapacity with the original injury."

414 [1952] A.C. 292.

falls within this category. The claimant's ship, negligently damaged by the defendant's, had temporary repairs effected to render her seaworthy, and subsequently proceeded to New York to carry out permanent repairs. En route she was rendered unseaworthy by heavy weather, thus requiring immediate repair. At New York both sets of repairs were effected concurrently, and the period taken would have been no less had only the heavy weather repairs been carried out. It was held by the House of Lords, reversing the Court of Appeal, that the claimant was not entitled to any damages for loss of use or demurrage for the 10 days which would have been required to repair the tort damage separately.

Where, however, the intervening event, although independent of the defendant's act, is one which is in no way abnormal but in the ordinary course of things, then the defendant will remain liable for the further damage. This is best illustrated by *Monarch S.S. Co v Karlshamns Oljefabriker*,[415] which is an action for breach of contract and is therefore considered later, but the principle of which would apply equally to tort. Also considered under contract is the decision of the Court of Appeal in the claimant's favour in *Rubenstein v HSBC Bank Plc*,[416] where the solicitor defendant was liable for negligent investment advice in tort as well as contract, the intervening event being the general collapse of the market.[417] **8-081**

### (B) SCOPE OF PROTECTION: THE LIMITS OF POLICY

Causation in law is only one of the limits on causation. Even after it has been resolved that the defendant's act is the cause in law of the claimant's injury, the claimant may yet be unable to recover damages for that injury if it is an injury to an interest which is not protected by the particular tort. This, after duty and after causation, is the third limb of the basic question concisely stated by Denning LJ in *Roe v Minister of Health*[418]: "Is the consequence within the risk?" Outside the particular case of unforeseeable damage caused by a negligent act,[419] this problem was for long little explored so that the strands of authority were few. Now one aspect of the problem has been propelled into the limelight by the decisions of the House of Lords and Supreme Court in *Banque Bruxelles Lambert v Eagle Star Insurance Co*,[420] and *BPE Solicitors & Anor v Hughes-Holland*[421] respectively.[422] **8-082**

#### 1. DAMAGE WHERE NO SEPARATE LIABILITY HAS BEEN ESTABLISHED

The problem is seen at its simplest in those torts which are actionable only upon proof of special damage and the requisite special damage is confined to particular types of loss. These are, principally, malicious prosecution and most slanders. In the case of malicious prosecution it was decided in *Quartz Hill Gold Mining Co v* **8-083**

415 [1949] A.C. 196; facts at para.8-156, below.
416 [2012] EWCA Civ 1184 CA. See para.8-157, below.
417 Where an architect's defective design of a rainwater drainage system had led to a flood damaging the claimant's property, an earlier flood, of which the claimant was unaware, did not break the chain of causation between the architect's negligence and the claimant's damage: *Pearson Education Ltd v The Charter Partnership Ltd* [2007] B.L.R. 324 CA.
418 [1954] 2 Q.B. 66 CA at 85.
419 See paras 8-086 and following, below.
420 [1997] A.C. 191.
421 [2017] UKSC 21.
422 For this aspect see paras 8-132 and following, below.

*Eyre*,[423] that the costs incurred by the now claimant in defending himself in the prior civil proceedings which were over and above the assessed costs for which he had obtained judgment, did not constitute such damage as would ground the action,[424] although such extra costs have formed a recognised head of damage in appropriate cases.[425] Similarly, in the case of most slanders, injury to reputation and the allied injury to feelings do not constitute such damage as will ground the action when they fall short of pecuniary loss: this well-established proposition is illustrated in the authorities by *Roberts v Roberts*,[426] and *Weldon v De Bathe*.[427]

**8-084** A more complex illustration in relation to slanders is found in the difficult and interesting case of *Allsop v Allsop*.[428] A married woman's illness resulting from her being slandered was there held to constitute damage that was too remote to be recoverable. There are a number of very different reasons which may have urged the court to this conclusion. In the first place, the decision came at a time when the principles with regard to psychiatric injury as opposed to physical injury by impact had not been worked out. The same error was perpetrated in the now discredited case of *Victorian Ry Commissioners v Coultas*,[429] and for the same reason, i.e. that the damage was too remote.[430] In so far as the decision in *Allsop v Allsop*,[431] rests upon this ground it can no longer be accepted today.[432] In the second place, the court expressed the view that the damage was too remote because it depended upon the peculiarities and temperament of the particular individual.[433] In so far as the decision rests upon this ground it is submitted that it again cannot be accepted today, since any physical abnormality of the claimant would not appear to prevent recovery in negligence,[434] and therefore should not, a fortiori, in slander. But, thirdly, *Allsop v Allsop*,[435] may be supported from another direction, on the ground that loss through ill health was not within the scope of the protection of the particular tort, even though it did result in a pecuniary loss.[436] Martin B's remark that "the law is jealous as to actions for mere words"[437] is significant: so too is the fact that Bramwell B did not feel there was any distinction between injury to feelings and injury to health. What was at the back of the court's mind seems to have been the

---

423 (1883) 11 Q.B.D. 674 CA. Considered as well established in *Wiffen v Bailey and Romford UDC* [1915] 1 K.B. 600 CA, but criticised in *Berry v British Transport Commission* [1962] 1 Q.B. 306 CA. See para.44-011, below.

424 Aliter with costs in defending criminal proceedings: see *Berry v British Transport Commission* [1962] 1 Q.B. 306 CA at para.44-008, below.

425 But unfortunately doubt has now been cast on this: see paras 21-003 and following, below.

426 (1864) 5 B. & S. 384.

427 (1885) 54 L.J.Q.B. 113 CA. The law is fully discussed at para.46-003, below.

428 (1860) 5 H. & N. 534.

429 (1888) 13 App. Cas. 222 PC.

430 And in the first English case allowing recovery for psychiatric injury, *Wilkinson v Downton* [1897] 2 Q.B. 57, the defendant unsuccessfully relied on *Allsop v Allsop* (1860) 5 H. & N. 534.

431 (1860) 5 H. & N. 534.

432 The modern law was established with the decisions in *Wilkinson v Downton* [1897] 2 Q.B. 57 and *Dulieu v White* [1901] 2 K.B. 669.

433 (1860) 5 H. & N. 534 at 538 and 539, per Pollock CB and Martin B, respectively.

434 Under the rule in *Re Polemis* [1921] 3 K.B. 560 CA, whether the illness was foreseeable or unforeseeable, under the rule in *The Wagon Mound* [1961] A.C. 388 PC, because the illness would probably be regarded as foreseeable. See paras 8-092 and 8-093, below.

435 (1860) 5 H. & N. 534.

436 It was the pecuniary loss arising from the sickness and not the non-pecuniary loss that was being claimed.

437 (1860) 5 H. & N. 534 at 539.

need to confine such slander actions within strictly defined limits, so that resulting ill health did not ground recovery because it was not an interest protected by the tort. Whether this conclusion was sound, in view of the fact that the loss was a pecuniary one, may be doubted; but it is basically a matter of policy, and this remains the one ground upon which *Allsop v Allsop*[438] could be supported today.

Somewhat similar considerations apply in another important case of slander not actionable per se, *Lynch v Knight*.[439] Again the slander was of a married woman, but this time she lost not her health but her husband. The decision in favour of the defendant went on the ground that the damage was too remote in that the husband's conduct in turning out the wife was not a reasonable or natural consequence of the slander, but was due to his idiosyncrasies of temperament; yet beyond this, conflicting views were expressed as to whether the wife's loss of her husband's consortium was damage for which she could in any event recover.[440] The answer lies once again in deciding what is the scope of the protection which the tort affords.[441] **8-085**

## 2. Foreseeable Damage Caused in an Unforeseeable Manner or to an Unforeseeable Degree Where a Breach of a Duty to the Claimant to Take Care Has Been Established

The question of scope of protection can become even more involved where the claimant has succeeded in establishing some tortious liability on the part of the defendant. Here the general problem is whether the claimant can recover for damage to a secondary interest where a separate liability in respect of a primary interest has been established. However, there falls first for consideration one particular intermediate situation[442] which has attracted much attention, namely where there is an element of unforeseeability in the damage caused by the negligent act. The situation is intermediate in that foreseeable damage which, by virtue of being foreseeable, has made the act negligent in the first place may itself have been inflicted in addition to damage with an unforeseeable element, so that there is clearly a separate tortious liability in respect of it, or damage with an unforeseeable element alone may have been inflicted, so that the situation is nearer to that where no separate liability has been established. **8-086**

This situation reintroduces both direct consequences and consequences following upon a new intervening force,[443] but whereas in relation to causation the accent is on the latter, in relation to policy it is on the former.[444] **8-087**

---

438 (1860) 5 H. & N. 534.

439 (1861) 9 H.L.C. 577.

440 Lord Campbell thought that it was ((1861) 9 H.L.C. 577 at 589) and Lord Cranworth was strongly inclined to agree ((1861) 9 H.L.C. 577 at 595). Lord Brougham and Lord Wensleydale thought it was not, but the latter's view was purely on the ground that he regarded the wife as having suffered no pecuniary or material loss: see para.46-003, below.

441 It is important to appreciate that their Lordships' disagreement only goes to the question of whether a wife's loss of her husband's consortium is an actionable head of damage in slanders not actionable per se. Whatever conclusion is come to on this does not answer the question whether it is an actionable head of damage in cases of personal injury (*Lampert v Eastern National Omnibus Co* [1954] 1 W.L.R. 1047) or whether it could ground other causes of action. See *Best v Fox* [1952] A.C. 716 at 732, per Lord Goddard CJ.

442 For treatment of the general problem, see paras 8-122 and following, below.

443 For the definition of these, see para.8-009, above.

444 For the reasons for this, see para.8-120, below.

## (1) Direct consequences

**8-088** In *The Wagon Mound*,[445] the facts of which have been given in treating causation,[446] the Judicial Committee of the Privy Council laid down that the test of the extent of liability in the tort of negligence should be the same as the test of its existence, namely reasonable foreseeability. Lord Sumner's dictum in *Weld-Blundell v Stephens*,[447] that

> "what the defendant ought to have anticipated as a reasonable man ... goes to culpability not to compensation" was declared to be "fundamentally false",[448]

and the decision in *Re Polemis*,[449] holding that a defendant could be liable in negligence for unforeseeable damage "so long as the damage is in fact directly traceable to the negligent act",[450] was disapproved and declared overruled.

**8-089** The reasons of policy behind this new view were stated by Viscount Simonds thus:

> "It does not seem consonant with current ideas of justice or morality that for an act of negligence, however slight or venial ... the actor should be liable for all consequences, however unforeseeable and however grave, so long as they can be said to be 'direct.' It is a principle of civil liability, subject to qualifications which have no present relevance, that a man must be considered to be responsible for the probable consequences of his act. To demand more of him is too harsh a rule, to demand less is to ignore that civilised order requires the observance of a minimum standard of behaviour."[451]

More specifically, legal reasoning followed in dealing with Lord Sumner's proposition in *Weld-Blundell v Stephens*.[452] Viscount Simonds first considered the situation where the foreseeable damage had merely remained in the realm of prevision. He said:

> "There can be no liability until the damage has been done. It is not the act but the consequences on which tortious liability is founded. Just as (as it has been said) there is no such thing as negligence in the air, so there is no such thing as liability in the air. Suppose an action brought by A for damage caused by the carelessness (a neutral word) of B, for example, a fire caused by the careless spillage of oil. It may, of course, become relevant to know what duty B owed to A, but the only liability that is in question is the liability for damage by fire. It is vain to isolate the liability from its context and to say that B is or is not liable, and then to ask for what damage he is liable. For his liability is in respect of that damage and no other. If, as admittedly it is, B's liability (culpability) depends on the reasonable foreseeability of the consequent damage, how is that to be determined except by the foreseeability of the damage which in fact happened—the dam-

---

[445] [1961] A.C. 388 PC. The full title is *Overseas Tankship (UK) v Morts Dock and Engineering Co (The Wagon Mound)* but this important decision has come to be known, for ease of reference, by the name of the ship which formed its centrepiece. In earlier editions of this book Dr McGregor explained that he was largely responsible for this naming of *The Wagon Mound* which was decided in the same year as his first edition of this work appeared.

[446] See para.8-032, above.

[447] [1920] A.C. 956 at 984.

[448] [1961] A.C. 388 PC at 425.

[449] [1921] 3 K.B. 560 CA; facts at para.8-031, above.

[450] [1921] 3 K.B. 560 CA at 577, per Scrutton LJ.

[451] [1961] A.C. 388 PC at 422 to 423.

[452] [1920] A.C. 956 at 984.

age in suit? And, if that damage is unforeseeable so as to displace liability at large, how can the liability be restored so as to make compensation payable?"[453]

Viscount Simonds then considered the situation where the foreseeable damage has itself been translated into fact, since it was argued that this gave rise to a different position. He said:

"To hold B liable for consequences however unforeseeable of a careless act, if, but only if, he is at the same time liable for some other damage however trivial, appears to be neither logical nor just. This becomes more clear if it is supposed that similar unforeseeable damage is suffered by A and C but other foreseeable damage, for which B is liable, by A only. A system of law which would hold B liable to A but not to C for the similar damage suffered by each of them could not easily be defended.

Fortunately, the attempt is not necessary. For the same fallacy is at the root of the proposition. It is irrelevant to the question whether B is liable for unforeseeable damage that he is liable for foreseeable damage, as irrelevant as would the fact that he had trespassed on Whiteacre be to the question whether he has trespassed on Blackacre. Again, suppose a claim by A for damage by fire by the careless act of B. Of what relevance is it to that claim that he has another claim arising out of the same careless act? It would surely not prejudice his claim if that other claim failed: it cannot assist it if it succeeds. Each of them rests on its own bottom, and will fail if it can be established that the damage could not reasonably be foreseen."[454]

The decision in *The Wagon Mound*[455] thus lays down a rule which, in providing **8-090** a single test for the existence and extent of liability in negligence, is at once neat and relatively simple,[456] and may seem to make it unnecessary to deal further with the problem of unforeseeable damage raised by the decision in *Re Polemis*.[457] Certainly, it is by now unnecessary to deal with this problem on account of the technical argument that the law of England is not changed by a decision on the law of New South Wales whence the appeal to the Judicial Committee originated. For, heralded by a statement of Lord Parker CJ within a year of *The Wagon Mound*[458] in *Smith v Leech Brain*[459] that he would be prepared, as trial judge, to follow the decision, the House of Lords itself, within two years, accepted its authority in *Hughes v Lord Advocate*,[460] an appeal from Scotland.[461] There remains, however, a substantive reason for still dealing with the problem of unforeseeable damage, namely that *The Wagon Mound*,[462] in the terms of Viscount Simonds's speech, seeks only to bar recovery for unforeseeable types of damage: if the damage is of a type that is foreseeable, then recovery is still available even if the degree of damage is

---

453 [1961] A.C. 388 PC at 425.

454 [1961] A.C. 388 PC at 425–426.

455 [1961] A.C. 388 PC.

456 It cannot, however, be said to be any more or any less logical than the rule in *Re Polemis* [1921] 3 K.B. 560 CA, despite Viscount Simonds' cogent legal reasoning quoted in the text. For the matter is one of pure policy and is therefore open to criticism only at the policy level. The new rule indeed represents one facet of the modern trend, appearing in other areas of tort, away from strict liability and back to liability based upon fault.

457 [1921] 3 K.B. 560 CA.

458 [1961] A.C. 388 PC.

459 [1962] 2 Q.B. 405 at 415.

460 [1963] A.C. 837.

461 As did the Court of Appeal in *Doughty v Turner Manufacturing Co* [1964] 1 Q.B. 518 CA; see especially at 525 and 532.

462 [1961] A.C. 388 PC.

unforeseeable or if the precise manner in which the damage occurs is unforeseeable. This is supported as to degree from *Smith v Leech Brain*,[463] onwards[464] and as to manner from *Hughes v Lord Advocate*,[465] to *Page v Smith*,[466] and indicates that various cases and dicta which have formerly been able to shelter under the rule in *Re Polemis*,[467]—in particular those preceding that decision,[468] which in some ways marked an extension rather than a complete change of the law—are unaffected by the new view ushered in by *The Wagon Mound*.[469] It is submitted that the general position, as it has developed since *The Wagon Mound*,[470] was decided, is that, where the improbable, abnormal and unforeseeable factor in the situation, be it act, event or state of affairs, has already occurred at the time of the wrongful act, the law will not hold the defendant liable for damage which, though caused by him, is of a type which he could not reasonably have foreseen, but may nevertheless hold him liable, in the absence of subsequent factors,[471] for damage occurring to an unforeseeable extent or arising in an unforeseeable manner, provided it is of a type which he could reasonably have foreseen.

**8-091** An event preceding the wrongful act may be said to form a circumstance, or to give rise to a state of affairs, existing at the time of the wrongful act: such events are therefore categorised as "existing states of affairs". On the other hand, an act preceding the wrongful act calls for no special nomenclature.

**8-092** **(a) Existing states of affairs: physical abnormalities of the claimant or of his property** It has never been seriously disputed that an admitted or established wrongdoer is liable for any increased injury to his victim by reason of an abnormal physical susceptibility. Kennedy J's statement of this principle in *Dulieu v White*,[472] is well known:

> "If a man is negligently run over or otherwise negligently injured in his body it is no answer to the sufferer's claim for damages that he would have suffered less injury, or no injury at all, if he had not had an unusually thin skull or an unusually weak heart."

Or in the more concise words of Lord Wright in *Bourhill v Young*[473]: "If the wrong is established the wrongdoer must take the victim as he finds him." The absence of decisions in the reports on this point is only proof of the universal acceptance of the principle,[474] which should apply equally to damage to a chattel with an abnormal

---

463 [1962] 2 Q.B. 405; facts at para.8-094, below.

464 Facts of succeeding cases at para.8-094, below.

465 [1963] A.C. 837; facts at para.8-117, below.

466 [1996] A.C. 155; facts at para.8-097, below.

467 [1921] 3 K.B. 560 CA.

468 See Kennedy J's dictum in *Dulieu v White* [1901] 2 K.B. 669 at 679 on abnormal physical susceptibilities at para.8-092, below and the cases allowing lost charterparty profits at para.8-105, below.

469 [1961] A.C. 388 PC.

470 [1961] A.C. 388 PC.

471 Subsequent intervening factors may prevent the defendant's act from being the cause of the damage to the claimant: see paras 8-035 and following, above.

472 [1901] 2 K.B. 669 at 679.

473 [1943] A.C. 92 at 109 to 110.

474 *Fowler v Hawksley* (1951) 95 S.J. 788 CA, and *Love v Port of London Authority* [1959] 2 Lloyd's Rep. 541 are pre-Wagon Mound examples where earlier disabilities were taken into account as increasing the loss of future earning capacity. See, too, *Marcroft v Scruttons* [1954] 1 Lloyd's Rep. 395 CA, especially at 401, per Denning LJ.

physical susceptibility, such as a fragile vase.[475]

No doubt was cast upon the correctness of this principle by their Lordships in *The Wagon Mound*.[476] Their only attack was on the rule in *Re Polemis*,[477] itself, and the present principle was extant long before *Re Polemis*,[478] had been decided. However, there would now seem to be a change of emphasis in framing the rationale of such cases: whereas, while *Re Polemis*,[479] held sway, they tended to be used as the simplest and least controversial illustrations of liability for unforeseeable damage, under the rule in *The Wagon Mound*,[480] they are to be regarded as cases of liability for an unforeseeable degree of damage of a foreseeable type.[481] For their Lordships regarded as an important distinction that between damage different in degree and damage different in type, so that, if some damage of one type is foreseeable, it may be that more extensive damage of that type is not too remote.[482] Thus Viscount Simonds said that, in an action by A for fire damage caused by B's careless spillage of oil, "the only liability that is in question is the liability for damage by fire"[483]; and, in commenting on *Smith v London & S.W. Ry*,[484] observed that 8-093

> "the point to which the court directed its mind was not unforeseeable damage of a different kind from that which was foreseen, but more extensive damage of the same kind".[485]

This interpretation of *The Wagon Mound*[486] was adopted by Lord Parker CJ in *Smith v Leech Brain*.[487] In that case the claimant's husband was struck by a piece of molten metal and suffered a small burn on his lip. Subsequently, cancer developed from which he died. The court found that the burn was the promoting agency of cancer in tissues which already had a pre-malignant condition, and that the burn caused in whole or in part the cancer and the death, because, but for the burn, cancer would not necessarily ever have developed. The defendant was held liable for the death although he could not reasonably have foreseen that the burn would cause cancer and death. Lord Parker CJ said: 8-094

---

475 This principle, however, does not go so far as to allow a physically injured claimant to claim the cost of running a fully-equipped house together with nursing staff merely because his difficult personality would prevent him from fitting well into a home for the disabled: *Cunningham v Harrison* [1973] Q.B. 942 CA. Nor does the principle run so far as to protect tortfeasors rather than vulnerable claimants. Thus where there are successive personal injuries to a claimant negligently inflicted, the first actor cannot avoid or reduce his liability by arguing that the second actor's liability falls to be increased because he must take his victim as he finds him, namely, already injured by the first actor: *Rahman v Arearose Ltd* [2001] Q.B. 351 CA (facts at para.8-026, above); see [2001] Q.B. 351 CA at 365H to 366A together with 367A to B.

476 [1961] A.C. 388 PC.

477 [1921] 3 K.B. 560 CA.

478 [1921] 3 K.B. 560 CA.

479 [1921] 3 K.B. 560 CA.

480 [1961] A.C. 388 PC.

481 See paras 8-182 to 8-184, below, the similar submission in relation to contract.

482 This must be taken as suggesting an approach rather than positing a cast-iron rule. In other circumstances damage different only in degree may not be recoverable: see paras 8-106 and 8-107, below.

483 [1961] A.C. 388 PC at 426.

484 (1870) L.R. 6 C.P. 14; See the fn. at the end of para.8-114, below as to this case.

485 [1961] A.C. 388 PC at 416.

486 [1961] A.C. 388 PC.

487 [1962] 2 Q.B. 405.

"I am quite satisfied that the Judicial Committee in the case did not have what I may call, loosely, *Wagon Mound* case did not have what I may call, loosely, the thin skull cases in mind. It has always been the law of this country that a tortfeasor takes his victim as he finds him. … The work of the courts for years and years has gone on on that basis. There is not a day that goes by where some trial judge does not adopt that principle, that the tortfeasor takes his victim as he finds him. If the Judicial Committee had any intention of making an inroad into the doctrine, I am quite satisfied that they would have said so."[488]

**8-095** Lord Parker CJ went on to adopt the distinction, also taken in the text, between damage different in degree and damage different in type. He referred to Lord Simonds's comment on *Smith v London & S.W. Ry*,[489] and on the basis of this concluded:

"The Judicial Committee were, I think, disagreeing with the decision in the *Re Polemis* case that a man is no longer liable for the type of damage which he could not reasonably anticipate. The Judicial Committee were not, I think, saying that a man is only liable for the extent of damage which he could anticipate, always assuming the type of injury could have been anticipated."[490]

He then proceeded to apply this to the circumstances before him. He said:

"In those circumstances, it seems to me that this is plainly a case which comes within the old principle. The test is not whether these employers could reasonably have foreseen that a burn would cause cancer and that he would die. The question is whether these employers could reasonably foresee the type of injury he suffered, namely, the burn. What, in the particular case, is the amount of damage which he suffers as a result of that burn, depends upon the characteristics and constitution of the victim."[491]

**8-096** Similar decisions to that of Lord Parker CJ were soon after reached a number of times at first instance: in *Warren v Scruttons*,[492] where damage to the claimant's finger caused an ulcer in his eye and he recovered for the total injury although only that to the finger was reasonably foreseeable; in *Lines v Harland and Wolff*,[493] and *Boom v Thomas Hubback & Son*,[494] in each of which the claimant recovered for a bad back caused by a combination of the accident for which the defendant was responsible and, in the one case, a pre-existing spinal condition and, in the other, pre-existing osteoarthritis; in *Jason v Batten (1930)*,[495] where the claimant recovered for a coronary thrombosis caused by a combination of the injury by the defendant and a pre-existing arterial disease[496]; and in *Vacwell Engineering Co v B.D.H. Chemicals*,[497] where recovery was allowed for serious damage to the claimants' property caused by a lethal explosion although the defendants, who were negligent

---

488 [1962] 2 Q.B. 405 at 414.

489 (1870) L.R. 6 C.P. 14; see para.8-093, above.

490 [1962] 2 Q.B. 405 at 415.

491 [1962] 2 Q.B. 405.

492 [1962] 1 Lloyd's Rep. 497.

493 [1966] 2 Lloyd's Rep. 400.

494 [1967] 1 Lloyd's Rep. 491.

495 [1969] 1 Lloyd's Rep. 281.

496 But in the last two of these cases the damages were substantially discounted as the accident only precipitated an illness to which the claimant would eventually have succumbed. *Malcolm v Broadhurst* [1970] 3 All E.R. 508 equates emotional abnormalities with physical abnormalities; on the other hand, *McLaren v Bradstreet* (1969) 113 S.J. 471 CA, indicates that the tortfeasor does not have to take the emotional abnormalities of the family of the injured claimant as he finds them.

497 [1971] 1 Q.B. 88. For the concurrent claim in contract which also succeeded, see para.8-188, below.

in having supplied the claimants with a chemical, boron tribromide, without warning them of the danger of explosion, could only reasonably have foreseen a minor explosion causing minor damage.[498] To add to these first instance cases is the further Court of Appeal decision in *Robinson v Post Office*.[499] There the claimant, after suffering a minor wound to his chin, was given an injection of anti-tetanus serum, or ATS, from which he developed encephalitis, and the defendants were held liable for the ensuing serious disabilities although the onset of encephalitis was not reasonably foreseeable, the claimant being peculiarly susceptible to the serum by reason of having been given it on a previous occasion. "The case is governed," said Orr LJ, delivering the judgment of the court,

> "by the principle that the Post Office had to take their victim as they found him, in this case with an allergy to a second dose of ATS".[500]

Where, however, the damage in dispute is different in type from that which is admittedly foreseeable, then it is clear that the disputed damage must be regarded as too remote as unforeseeable. This is, of course, primarily illustrated by *Re Polemis*,[501] itself, where both the damage in dispute and the admittedly foreseeable damage were to property. However, with injury to the person the House of Lords has held, it is thought rightly, in *Page v Smith*,[502] though by a bare majority and reversing the Court of Appeal, that all personal injuries are to be regarded as of the same type and that there is no scope for the argument that physical injury by impact is different in kind from psychiatric injury. In that case the claimant was in a collision which left him physically unhurt, with no external injury of any kind, but suffering from psychiatric damage, the accident causing the onset of myalgic encephalomyelitis, otherwise abbreviated to ME, from which he had suffered for 20 years but which was then in remission. Their Lordships distinguished between primary victims and secondary victims of an accident—the former being those who might anticipate physical injury to themselves by virtue of being within the range of such foreseeable injury, the latter being those who suffer from what they see or hear of physical injury caused to others[503]—and held that in the case of a claimant who was a primary victim the test was whether the defendant could reasonably **8-097**

[498] See, especially, [1971] 1 Q.B. 88 at 109 to 110 where Rees J relied on Lord Parker CJ's judgment in *Smith v Leech Brain* [1962] 2 Q.B. 405. An appeal was settled, after argument before the Court of Appeal, on the basis that judgment should be entered for the claimants by consent but limited to 80 per cent of the damages: [1971] 1 Q.B. 111 CA. Lord Denning MR is reported, at [1970] 3 All E.R. 553 CA, as saying that this result was very likely almost the same as the court itself would have arrived at, from which it may be inferred that the Court of Appeal too would have regarded the damage as not too remote. The 80 per cent limit can be explained as reflecting a reduction for contributory negligence.

[499] [1974] 1 W.L.R. 1176 CA.

[500] [1974] 1 W.L.R. 1176 CA at 1191G.

[501] [1921] 3 K.B. 560 CA.

[502] [1996] A.C. 155.

[503] Where psychiatric injury to a claimant wrongly convicted and imprisoned through the negligence of his solicitor was in issue in *McLoughlin v Jones* [2002] Q.B. 1312 CA, Hale LJ was prepared to consider whether a loss of liberty was as much an interference with bodily integrity as loss of a limb so as to make the claimant a primary rather than a secondary victim: see [2002] Q.B. 1312 CA at [57]–[59]. Claims for damages under s.76 of the Civil Aviation Act 1982 were held to attract the normal common law rules with their distinction between primary and secondary victims in *Glen v Korean Airlines Co Ltd* [2003] Q.B. 1386. The distinction between primary and secondary victims of psychiatric illness is further considered in *Hunter v British Coal Corp* [1999] Q.B. 140 CA.

foresee that his conduct would expose the claimant to the risk of personal injury, whether physical or psychiatric.[504] Thus such a claimant did not have to prove that psychiatric injury was reasonably foreseeable; the defendant must take his victim as he found him, with an eggshell personality as much as with an egghell skull. Lord Lloyd, who gave the leading majority speech, said:

> "In an age when medical knowledge is expanding fast, and psychiatric knowledge with it, it would not be sensible to commit the law to a distinction between physical and psychiatric injury, which may already seem somewhat artificial, and may soon be altogether outmoded. Nothing will be gained by treating them as different 'kinds' of personal injury so as to require the application of different tests in law."[505]

He added:

> "It could not be right that a negligent defendant should escape liability for psychiatric injury just because, though serious physical injury was foreseeable, it did not in fact transpire. Such a result in the case of a primary victim is neither necessary, logical nor just."[506]

Accordingly, Denning LJ's celebrated dictum in *King v Phillips*[507]—from the days when psychiatric illness was known as nervous shock—that "the test of liability for shock is foreseeability of injury by shock", a much cited dictum[508] which had been endorsed by the Judicial Committee in *The Wagon Mound*,[509] was disapproved as incorrect. Its proper application is limited to secondary victims of accidents.[510]

---

504 Psychiatric illness arising from stress at work did not lead to liability on the employer in *Pratley v Surrey CC* [2004] I.C.R. 159 CA as neither physical nor psychiatric injury was held to be reasonably foreseeable.

505 [1996] A.C. 155 at 188E. For how far, for the purposes of art.17 of the Warsaw Convention 1929 scheduled to the Carriage by Air Act 1961, the term "bodily injury" or "lésion corporelle" covers psychiatric illness, see *Morris v KLM Royal Dutch Airlines and King v Bristow Helicopters Ltd* [2002] 2 A.C. 628.

506 [1996] A.C. 155 at 189A. In *Simmons v British Steel Plc* [2004] I.C.R. 585 HL where there was immediate physical injury, recovery was allowed for subsequent psychiatric injury which, it was alleged, sprang not from the accident itself but from the claimant's anger at the happening of the accident. Not only was there no reason to draw a distinction on this basis but it was doubted if such a distinction could be realistically drawn at all. See the valuable analysis of the authorities by Lord Rodger at [2004] I.C.R. 585 HL at [53]–[67]. *Page v Smith* was also applied in *Donachie v Chief Constable of Greater Manchester* [2004] EWCA Civ 405 CA, here by the Court of Appeal, where physical injury to a police officer was foreseeable but psychiatric injury resulted.

507 [1953] 1 Q.B. 429 CA at 441.

508 Indeed relied upon in editions of this work before *Page v Smith* was decided.

509 [1961] A.C. 388 PC at 426.

510 Though a necessary condition, reasonable foreseeability is not a sufficient condition in secondary victim cases. In *Alcock v Chief Constable of the South Yorkshire Police* [1992] 1 A.C. 310, from Lord Oliver's speech in which the classification of primary and secondary victims apparently derives, the House of Lords required that there be not only reasonable foreseeability but also proximity to the event in time and space and proximity of relationship between primary and secondary victims. The Alcock limitations were extended to rescuers and employees, who are put into the position of secondary victims, by the further House of Lords decision in *White v Chief Constable of the South Yorkshire Police* [1999] 2 A.C. 455, reversing *Frost v Chief Constable of the South Yorkshire Police* [1998] Q.B. 254 CA (see the case further at para.8-071, above). The *Alcock* limitations are regarded as control mechanisms, intended to keep cases of this nature within acceptable bounds and in formulating them in *Alcock*, in the words of Lord Hoffmann in *White* (otherwise *Frost*), at [1999] 2 A.C. 455. 511B, the search for principle had been called off. The latest decision is that of the Court of Appeal in *Taylor v A. Novo (UK) Ltd* [2014] Q.B. 150 CA where a daughter was denied recovery for a psychiatric illness induced by witnessing her mother's collapse and death from an injury at work

*Page v Smith* may appear to have been taken further in *Corr v IBC Vehicles Ltd*,[511] where the House of Lords held that the claimant, the widow of an employee whose horrific injury at work had eventually driven him to suicide, did not need to establish that at the time of the accident her husband's suicide had been reasonably foreseeable by his employers, the defendants. Suicide was not a kind of damage which was separate from psychiatric and physical injury and therefore did not need to be separately foreseeable. However, Lord Neuberger said that the widow's claim would succeed whatever the position with *Page v Smith* because the deceased's deep depression was a foreseeable consequence of the horrific injury and the suicide was then a direct consequence of that depression.[512] **8-098**

The decision in *Schneider v Eisovitch*,[513] where a claim in respect of psychiatric injury was based upon foreseeability of injury by physical impact, gathers strength from their Lordships' decision in *Page v Smith*.[514] The claimant was injured and her husband killed in a car accident; later, in hospital, she suffered psychiatric illness on being told of her husband's death. She recovered both for the injury by impact and the psychiatric injury, although the authorities of the day supported the view that in such circumstances the incidence of psychiatric injury would not be reasonably foreseeable by the defendant because the claimant did not see, but was only subsequently told of, her husband's death. Paull J said: **8-099**

> "The plaintiff, having a cause of action for the negligence of the defendant, may add the consequences of shock caused by hearing of her husband's death when estimating the amount recoverable on her cause of action."[515]

At one time this was regarded as a straightforward application of the rule in *Re Polemis*,[516] and, therefore, as falling together with *Re Polemis* itself. Now it can be seen, after *Page v Smith*,[517] that the psychiatric injury is not to be considered as of a different kind from the injury by physical impact and is therefore recoverable.

Somewhat similar is *Essa v Laing Ltd*,[518] where injury to feelings arising from racial abuse was reasonably foreseeable but psychiatric illness, which occurred, was not. It was held, by a majority, that the lack of reasonable foreseeability did not matter as the two injuries were of the same type and not of a different kind.[519] Praying in aid the reasoning of the House of Lords in *Page v Smith*,[520] that physical injury and psychiatric injury are of the same type, Clarke LJ said that he did not see why injury to feelings and psychiatric injury should not also be so treated[521]; indeed he **8-100**

---

three weeks earlier caused by her employers' negligence. The Master of the Rolls in the only reasoned judgment meticulously examined a whole series of cases in the field, leading and other, to conclude that to allow recovery where the death was witnessed but the accident itself was not would be taking a step too far: [2014] Q.B. 150 CA at [29] and following.

511 [2008] A.C. 884.

512 [2008] A.C. 884 at [54] and [55]. Lord Mance agreed with Lord Neuberger on this: [2008] A.C. 884 at [46]. On remoteness issues see the case also at para.8-065, above.

513 [1960] 2 Q.B. 430.

514 [1996] A.C. 155.

515 [1960] 2 Q.B. 430 at 442.

516 [1921] 3 K.B. 560 CA.

517 [1996] A.C. 155.

518 [2004] I.C.R. 746 CA.

519 This was the second ground for the decision for the claimant. The first ground concerned causation and foreseeability and is at para.8-013, above.

520 [1996] A.C. 155.

521 [2004] I.R.C. 746 CA at [55].

said that in his opinion it would be very odd, in the light of Page, if foreseeability of injury to feelings were not sufficient to obviate the need to show foreseeability of psychiatric injury.[522] Pill LJ pointed out that injury to feelings and psychiatric injury can show a substantial degree of overlap and that this did not support a conclusion that the injuries are of a different kind.[523] For the dissenting Rix LJ, on the other hand, they were indeed of a different kind, injury to feelings being a common-day experience and something distinct from illness.[524]

**8-101** It should, however, be kept in mind that the wisdom of the decision in *Page v Smith* has been doubted. For its departure from the rule that liability for psychiatric injury requires foreseeability of psychiatric injury and its distinction in this connection between primary and secondary victims, the decision received lengthy and trenchant criticism from Lord Goff in *White v Chief Constable of the South Yorkshire Police*,[525] and attacks by academics, though not by practitioners, on the decision have been rife.[526] While in the House of Lords in *Corr v IBC Vehicles Ltd*[527] the decision was questioned by neither side, their Lordships were well aware that it might be challenged before them in the future. A successful challenge would then restore Denning LJ's celebrated dictum[528] to its pinnacle.

**8-102** Where the admittedly foreseeable damage is to the claimant's property and the damage in dispute is to the claimant's person, or vice versa, recovery will be refused under the rule in *The Wagon Mound*.[529] How far, however, this marks a change in the practical result is uncertain, as it had not been firmly established that this situation fell within the rule in *Re Polemis*.[530] The nearest case was *Thurogood v Van den Berghs*.[531] The defendant was held liable in negligence[532] where the claimant's hand was caught and injured in a revolving fan in circumstances in which

> "it was reasonably foreseeable that some damage might result; for instance, a necktie or clothing might well get caught in the revolving blades and some corporeal injury ensue".[533]

This was not strictly injury to the person where only injury could be foreseen to property, because it seems from this that it could be foreseen that the injury to the person might result from the injury to the property, in this case the claimant's clothing. Nevertheless Asquith LJ said further:

---

522 [2004] I.R.C. 746 CA at [65].

523 [2004] I.R.C. 746 CA at [42].

524 [2004] I.R.C. 746 CA at [117]. In *Unifi v Massey* [2008] I.C.R. 62 CA where injury to feelings arising from unjustifiable discipline by a trade union was reasonably foreseeable but a stroke, which occurred, was not, *Essa v Laing* was followed: [2008] I.C.R. 62 CA [31] and [32].

525 [1999] 2 A.C. 455 at 473D to 480F. The case report in the CA has the claimant as Frost rather than White.

526 Many of the articles by academicians are listed by Lord Goff [1999] 2 A.C. 455 at 474H to 475A, where he also refers to the Law Commission having recorded the very favourable view of practitioners to the decision.

527 [2008] A.C. 884.

528 At para.8-097, above.

529 [1961] A.C. 388 PC.

530 [1921] 3 K.B. 560 CA.

531 [1951] 2 K.B. 537 CA.

532 The claimant's claim under the Factories Acts also succeeded.

533 [1951] 2 K.B. 537 CA at 551, per Asquith LJ whose judgment on this issue was concurred in by the other two members of the court.

> "Directness of causation is the sole criterion of recoverability. The actual damage may be wholly different in character, magnitude or in the detailed manner of its incidence, from anything which could reasonably have been anticipated."[534]

On the other hand, in *Bourhill v Young*[535] Lord Wright had earlier stated that the rule in *Re Polemis*,[536]

> "must be understood to be limited, however, to 'direct' consequences to the particular interest of the plaintiff which is affected."

It is submitted that Asquith LJ's approach represented the proper application of *Re Polemis* to this situation, for it is difficult to see why policy should dictate a limitation upon the rule merely because the foreseeable damage is to property and the unforeseeable is to the person, or vice versa.[537] This would mean that here *The Wagon Mound*[538] has effected a practical change.

**(b) Existing states of affairs: pecuniary abnormalities of the claimant or of his property** So far all the abnormalities considered have been physical. They may, however, be pecuniary, in the sense that the injured person or property may be financially more valuable or more frail than the defendant could have reasonably anticipated. Whereas with physical abnormality only weakness is relevant, both strength and weakness can have important effects in the pecuniary field. **8-103**

*(i) Strength* A well-known dictum of Scrutton LJ in *The Arpad*[539] puts the legal position concisely and memorably: **8-104**

> "You negligently run down a shabby-looking man in the street, and he turns out to be a millionaire engaged in a very profitable business which the accident disables him from carrying on; or you negligently and ignorantly injure the favourite for the Derby whereby he cannot run. You have to pay damages resulting from the circumstances of which you have no notice. You have to pay the actual loss to the man or his goods at the time of the tort."

No doubt was cast on the correctness of this principle by the Judicial Committee in *The Wagon Mound*,[540] and it is submitted that the approach in such cases should follow the same lines as that in the corresponding cases of liability for increased damage to person or property because of an abnormal physical weakness, namely that recovery was allowed because under *Re Polemis*,[541] it was immaterial whether the damage was classed as foreseeable or unforeseeable and because now under *The Wagon Mound*,[542] ruling it is possible to regard the damage as foreseeable in type

---

534 [1951] 2 K.B. 537 CA at 552.

535 [1943] A.C. 92 at 110.

536 [1921] 3 K.B. 560 CA.

537 Whether, where there is injury to the person and also to the property of the claimant, there are or are not two separate causes of action (*Brunsden v Humphrey* (1884) 14 Q.B.D. 141 CA, which said that there were, has now come under some suspicion: see paras 11-004 to 11-006, below) is irrelevant for this issue.

538 [1961] A.C. 388 PC.

539 [1934] P. 189 CA at 202 to 203; a dissenting judgment but not affecting this point.

540 [1961] A.C. 388 PC.

541 [1921] 3 K.B. 560 CA.

542 [1961] A.C. 388 PC.

even if not in degree.[543] Lord Wright's dictum in *Bourhill v Young*,[544] that "if the wrong is established the wrongdoer must take the victim as he finds him" applies equally here.

8-105 Does the same apply where the peculiarly high value is not intrinsic—the market value of the man, the horse, or the chattel, as it were—but depends on the special use to which the property is being put or upon the specially remunerative contracts on which the person is engaged? Under *Re Polemis* the position in an action of negligence was unclear. In a good number of cases the loss of profits upon a charterparty has been held recoverable where the claimant's ship has been damaged, as in *The Star of India*,[545] and in *The Argentino*,[546] or totally destroyed as in *The Kate*,[547] *The Racine*,[548] and *The Empress of Britain*.[549] Similarly in *Liesbosch Dredger v S.S. Edison*,[550] the claimants recovered for profits lost on a contract for the performance of which they required the dredger negligently sunk by the defendants.[551] No limitation upon the damages is suggested in these cases upon the ground that the charterparties in question might have been unusually profitable. It is true that Lord Herschell spoke in *The Argentino*[552] of "an ordinary maritime adventure" and "the loss of the fair and ordinary earnings of such a vessel on such an adventure", but this is equivocal. Also equivocal is the denial of recovery for particularly high lost profits in *The Soya*,[553] and in *The Naxos*,[554] since these claims were concerned with the issue of recovery of lost profits not on the particular charterparty to which the ship was proceeding at the time of the collision but on charterparties further into the future.[555] The distinction taken in *The Star of India*,[556] between an action in contract where foreseeability was necessary and one against a tortfeasor where it was not, is more important; so too is Lord Wright's formulation of the measure of damages in *Liesbosch Dredger v S.S. Edison*.[557] He said:

> "The true rule seems to be that the measure of damages in such cases is the value of the ship to her owner as a going concern at the time and place of the loss. In assessing that

---

543 See paras 8-092 to 8-096, above.
544 [1943] A.C. 92 at 109 to 110.
545 (1876) 1 P.D. 466. Followed in *The Consett* (1880) 5 P.D. 229.
546 (1889) 14 App. Cas. 519.
547 [1899] P. 165.
548 [1906] P. 273 CA.
549 (1913) 29 T.L.R. 423.
550 [1933] A.C. 449.
551 All these cases are considered in detail at paras 37-033, 37-072 and 37-073, below; the facts are therefore not repeated here.
552 (1889) 14 App. Cas. 519 at 523.
553 [1956] 1 W.L.R. 714 CA.
554 [1972] 1 Lloyd's Rep. 149.
555 See paras 37-034 and 37-035, below. See also Lord Porter in *Morrison S.S. Co v Greystoke Castle* [1947] A.C. 265 at 295 to 296, where, although he cited most of the cases in the text as showing that damages may take into consideration the loss of a contract and that the rule in *Re Polemis* had effected no change in this principle, he appears to regard *Re Polemis* as removing the necessity of reasonable foreseeability only in cases of physical consequences, so that in the case before him there might have been an argument on remoteness "if the special contract contained any unusual terms" (at 296), which it did not. The case, however, was a rather special one, in that there was held to be liability in negligence despite the absence of any physical damage to the claimant, and the decision goes rather to existence than to extent of liability.
556 (1876) 1 P.D. 466 at 472, citing, significantly, *France v Gaudet* (1871) L.R. 6 Q.B. 199 at para.8-108, below.
557 [1933] A.C. 449 at 463 to 464.

> value regard must naturally be had to her pending engagements, either profitable or the reverse."

It is somewhat ironic to find that this famous decision supports in this respect a wide recovery independent of foreseeability, when its main claim to fame is, or was, in the other direction.[558]

Whether the application of the rule in *The Wagon Mound*,[559] to claims for loss of profits on charterparties and the like will now rule out recovery of exceptional profits on the ground that the defendant could not have reasonably foreseen such a loss is not yet clear. Since the difference between the loss of a contract with an average profit margin and the loss of an exceptionally lucrative contract is only one of degree, it can be forcefully argued that, by analogy with the cases involving physical abnormalities of the claimant or his property,[560] the damage is not too remote. On the other hand, it may be said that even such damage is to be regarded as too remote and unforeseeable where it relates not to the normal loss which every claimant in a like situation will suffer—where his property is damaged the diminution in its market price, and where he himself is injured his loss of earning capacity—but relates to a consequential loss which is special to the circumstances of the particular claimant—the loss of a charterparty, or the loss of a post through missing an interview.[561] That there can be recovery for loss of profits where this kind of loss is foreseeable but its substantial extent and the manner of its coming about are not is well supported by the Court of Appeal's decision in *Network Rail Infrastructure Ltd v Conarken Group Ltd*,[562] where the defendants' negligent damage to the claimant's railway tracks caused severe disruption of rail services; this remoteness aspect of the case is later analysed in the context of tortious damage to land.[563] **8-106**

The charterparty cases, in so far as they can be said to stand for a recovery of exceptional profits, may not only be inconsistent with the decision in *The Wagon Mound*,[564] itself, but were already out of line with the majority decision in *The Arpad*,[565] where, however, the action was for misappropriation by conversion and not for damage or destruction by negligence. The loss of his goods by the conversion deprived the claimant of the exceptionally high profits upon a contract he had made to sell them, and the Court of Appeal held by a majority that he could not recover the loss of profit, taking the view that in this respect the measure of damages was to be calculated upon the same principles in tort as in contract.[566] At the time, in view of *Re Polemis*,[567] and even today, in view of *The Heron II*,[568] the argu- **8-107**

---

558 See paras 8-110 to 8-113, below.

559 [1961] A.C. 388 PC.

560 See paras 8-092 to 8-096, above.

561 For the distinction between normal and consequential losses see paras 3-007 to 3-012, above. Another factor here is that loss of personal earning capacity tends to be included within normal loss but generally not loss of the earning potential of property. Basically this reflects the tendency of the law to give more protection against personal injury than against property damage.

562 [2011] EWCA Civ 644 CA.

563 See the case at para.39-029, below where the full facts are set out.

564 [1961] A.C. 388 PC.

565 [1934] P. 189 CA. The dissent, a strong one, was by Scrutton LJ.

566 There was also a claim for breach of contract, that the court's holding upon the measure in contract was correct is clear; on this Scrutton LJ. agreed with his brethren.

567 [1921] 3 K.B. 560 CA.

568 [1969] 1 A.C. 350: see para.24-007, below.

ment from contract was hardly a sound one, for in contract the damages are restricted by the contemplation of the parties, a factor which has no relevance in tort. However, *The Arpad* was followed and applied in a further conversion case, *Saleslease Ltd v Davis*.[569]

8-108 *The Arpad*,[570] and with it *Saleslease*,[571] of course in one sense gain weight from the decision in *The Wagon Mound*,[572] but in another sense they are untouched by the Judicial Committee's decision which was concerned only with the tort of negligence. Because liability in conversion is strict and not based on fault so that the test of foreseeability has not the central relevance that it has in negligence, it was suggested in earlier editions that, if the matter came to be tested in the House of Lords, their Lordships might well consider the strong dissenting judgment of Scrutton LJ in *The Arpad* to be more consistent with principle, with the earlier conversion case of *France v Gaudet*,[573] and with the main cases of recovery for lost charterparties decided before the introduction of the rule in *The Wagon Mound*.[574] To an extent this suggestion has come to fruition with the further conversion case, this time in the House of Lords, of *Kuwait Airways Corporation v Iraq Airways Co*.[575] While the Court of Appeal there[576] accepted that it was bound by *The Arpad* and *Saleslease* to require foreseeability for recovery, in the House of Lords Lord Nicholls, in the leading speech, was able to be more bold. He drew a distinction between the converter who is knowing and dishonest and the converter who is not, and expressed the view that, while the remoteness test for the latter should be that of foreseeability, the test for the former should be the wider one of whether the loss arose directly and naturally.[577] This received support from other members of the House; Lord Hope said that he wished to associate himself with Lord Nicholls's approach on the issue[578] while Lord Hoffmann expressed agreement with his speech in general.[579] While, as Lord Nicholls himself said, all this was obiter[580] since he considered the damage to be foreseeable and therefore on either approach recoverable, it seems likely that this sensible, if compromise, view will now prevail.[581]

8-109 There remains the case of the person engaged on specially remunerative contracts. This is generally posed as the problem of the man who by a tortious injury is disabled from performing a contract of an unusual and exceptionally remunerative character. Whether he can recover for such a loss was expressly left open in *The Arpad*[582] by Greer LJ[583] It is submitted that the principles considered in rela-

---

569 [1999] 1 W.L.R. 1664 CA. Again there was a dissent but this was only on the issue of whether or not the damage was foreseeable. See the case further at para.38-070, below.

570 [1934] P. 189 CA.

571 [1999] 1 W.L.R. 1664 CA.

572 [1961] A.C. 388 PC.

573 (1871) L.R. 6 Q.B. 199.

574 [1961] A.C. 388 PC.

575 [2002] 2 A.C. 883.

576 Court of Appeal also reported at [2002] 2 A.C. 883.

577 [2002] 2 A.C. 883 at [100]–[114].

578 [2002] 2 A.C. 883 at [169].

579 [2002] 2 A.C. 883 at [125].

580 [2002] 2 A.C. 883 at [99].

581 These cases are further considered at paras 38-070 to 38-072, below, together with *Sandeman Coprimar SA v Transitos y Transportes Integrales SL* [2003] Q.B. 1270 CA where the Court of Appeal simply accepted that in a negligent conversion the test was reasonable foreseeability: see [2003] Q.B. 1270 CA at [25]–[31].

582 [1934] P. 189 CA at 221.

tion to the loss of exceptionally profitable contracts through tortious interference with the claimant's property[584] should apply equally where the tort is one affecting his person.

*(ii) Weakness* With financial weakness, it is only that of the claimant himself which can increase the damages. The fact that his property is of little or no value, such as a poor racehorse or a profitless charterparty, clearly cannot. The law in this situation was explored by the House of Lords in *Liesbosch Dredger v S.S. Edison*,[585] where Lord Wright famously ruled that a claimant's financial weakness could not be allowed to increase the damages. His so-called impecuniosity rule, after a long controversial life of 70 years, has at last been departed from by the House of Lords in *Lagden v O'Connor*,[586] but it is thought sensible to retain a statement of the rule in its original context so as to be able to make sense of all the case law which has had to wrestle with it over time and so as to be clear and sure of what the departure from it entails. **8-110**

The defendants negligently sank the claimants' dredger which was engaged in operations under contract in the normal course of the claimants' business as civil engineers. Other comparable dredgers were available for purchase, but the claimants had invested all their funds in the Liesbosch and were therefore unable to buy one. Had they bought, the delay in resuming the operation would have been comparatively short. As it was, much additional time was lost, and considerable further expenses in wages and maintenance were incurred before the claimants succeeded in finding a dredger which they could take on hire; and this dredger was more expensive to work. The House of Lords held that the claimants could not claim for the expenses, loss and damage incurred over and above that which would have been incurred had they bought another dredger. Lord Wright, in whose speech all the other members of the House concurred, said: **8-111**

> "The appellants' actual loss in so far as it was due to their own impecuniosity arose from that impecuniosity as a separate and concurrent cause, extraneous to and distinct in character from the tort; the impecuniosity was not traceable to the respondents' acts, and in my opinion was outside the legal purview of the consequences of these acts."[587]

On this rule as thus stated two matters need to be addressed. First, Lord Wright's causation argument has been shown to be misplaced. *Re Polemis*,[588] which then ruled the day on remoteness of damage in tortious negligence,[589] was distinguished by him on the ground that it **8-112**

583 In *Hoey v Felton* (1861) 11 C.B. N.S. 142 loss of a situation, which the claimant alleged he would have obtained had he not missed an appointment through illness caused by a false imprisonment, was held to be too remote.

584 See paras 8-105 to 8-108, above.

585 [1933] A.C. 449.

586 [2004] 1 A.C. 1067. Lord Hope, who together with Lord Walker considered the status of *The Liesbosch* rule, ended his speech with: "I would hold that this rule should now be departed from": [2004] 1 A.C. 1067 at [62]. More on this case is at paras 8-113 and 37-021, below.

587 [2004] 1 A.C. 1067 at 460.

588 [1921] 3 K.B. 560 CA.

589 See para.8-031, above.

"was concerned with the immediate physical consequences of the negligent act, and not with the co-operation of an extraneous matter such as the plaintiff's want of means"[590]

but, as Viscount Simonds pointed out in *The Wagon Mound*,[591] causally the claimant's financial weakness is no more extraneous than his physical weakness or his financial strength. It follows that the limitation imposed by *The Liesbosch*,[592] is really a matter of policy rather than a matter of causation. Secondly, when it became realised that the question was one of policy rather than of cause, it became far easier to depart from Lord Wright, and this was done to such an extent that it could be said that, before reaching its quietus, this aspect of *The Liesbosch* had already been distinguished nearly out of existence. The arguments in cases distinguishing it which were discussed at this point in an earlier edition can now be forgotten; the particular cases themselves are dealt with at appropriate points later in the text.[593]

**8-113** The ground of policy having now been stripped away, what precisely has taken its place? For this we must turn to *Lagden v O'Connor*.[594] An impecunious claimant was held entitled to recover hire car company charges that a claimant who was not impecunious could not have recovered, and Lord Hope, after an extensive review of the authorities on the impecuniosity issue, said[595]:

"It is clear that the law has moved on, and that the correct test of remoteness today is whether the loss was reasonably foreseeable. The wrongdoer must take his victim as he finds him.[596] … This rule applies to the economic state of the victim in the same way as it applies to his physical and mental vulnerability."[597]

It is to be noted that Lord Hope links his test of reasonable foreseeability to the familiar rule that a wrongdoer must take his victim as he finds him. This is important because it avoids the argument, which might well be advanced, that in the circumstances of a particular case the claimant's impecuniosity could not have been reasonably foreseen. We have noted when dealing with physical abnormalities that what must be reasonably foreseeable is the type or kind, and not the degree, of damage or loss and that this is entirely consistent with the introduction in *The Wagon Mound*,[598] of a reasonable foreseeability test for liability in tort.[599] After *Lagden v O'Connor* what has formerly applied to the claimant with the egg-shell skull is to apply equally to the claimant with the egg-shell bank balance.

---

590 [1933] A.C. 449 at 461.

591 [1961] A.C. 388 PC at 424.

592 [1933] A.C. 449.

593 See *Dodd Properties v Canterbury City Council* [1980] 1 W.L.R. 433 CA at para.39-018, below; *Perry v Sidney Phillips & Son* [1982] 1 W.L.R. 1297 CA at para.34-063, below; *Alcoa Minerals of Jamaica Plc v Broderick* [2002] 1 A.C. 371 PC at para.39-019, below.

594 [2004] 1 A.C. 1067.

595 [2004] 1 A.C. 1067 at [61].

596 For this he cited a dictum of Lord Collins in *Clippens Oil Co v Edinburgh and District Water Trustees* [1907] A.C. 291 at 303. However, this dictum, as Lord Wright himself had pointed out, concerns mitigation of damage rather than remoteness, though it has been nigh impossible to find the line of separation between Lord Collins and Lord Wright. See Lord Collins's dictum, and the discussion, at paras 9-097 to 9-099, below.

597 Only a majority favoured allowing the claimant recovery on account of impecuniosity in the particular circumstances (for these see para.37-021, below) but the House was unanimous that the time had come to bury the rule in *The Liesbosch*.

598 [1961] A.C. 388 PC.

599 See the extended discussion at paras 8-093 and following, above.

**(c) Other existing states of affairs** The existing abnormalities may not exist in the person injured or the property damaged. This was so on the facts of *The Wagon Mound*,[600] itself. Once again, the decision will have affected previous cases in which the claimant's recovery has been based squarely upon the rule in *Re Polemis*.[601] Such a case was *Kilgollan v Cooke*.[602] There the defendants' machine was not sufficiently guarded within the requirements of the Factories Acts. The defendants could have foreseen a trivial accident, of which there had been many, by reason of people being struck by broken or flailing wire, but they could not reasonably have foreseen that the claimant would be blinded in the eye. It was held that the defendants could not escape liability for a serious injury like this if such an injury would not have occurred but for the defendants' want of care in guarding against the trivial injuries which they knew did occur. The decision clearly cannot survive the re-introduction of the foreseeability test by *The Wagon Mound*,[603] since the injury inflicted was of a different type from the foreseeable injury.[604] **8-114**

Conversely, *Sharp v Powell*,[605] is a pre-*Polemis*[606] decision which after 40 years in the wilderness has been expressly reinstated by their Lordships in *The Wagon Mound*.[607] The defendant washed a van in a street and allowed the water to run down the gutter to a nearby grating from which it would ordinarily have drained away into the sewer. However, a hard frost had obstructed the grating with ice and the water flowed over the paving and froze, causing the claimant's horse to slip and break its leg. This damage was held to be too remote as the defendant could not reasonably have known that the grating was obstructed; it would equally be held to be too remote today. As for an illustration, falling within this category of other existing states of affairs, of damage held to be too remote in the cases following upon *The Wagon Mound*,[608] decision, this is provided by *Doughty v Turner Manufacturing Co*.[609] The asbestos cement cover of a cauldron containing molten liquid was inadvertently knocked into the cauldron by one of the defendants' employees and slid beneath the molten liquid causing it to erupt a minute or two later and injure the claimant. In the then state of knowledge it was not reasonably foreseeable that the immersion of the cover would result in an explosion of the molten liquid; all that was reasonably foreseeable was that knocking the cover into the cauldron might cause the molten liquid to splash over the edge. The defendants were held not liable for the claimant's injury resulting from the explosion because it was damage of a kind altogether different from a foreseeable splash of the liquid in the cauldron. **8-115**

However, if the damage which occurs is of a type which is foreseeable, then here as elsewhere *The Wagon Mound*[610] does not operate to cut down the defendant's **8-116**

---

600 [1961] A.C. 388 PC.

601 [1921] 3 K.B. 560 CA.

602 [1956] 2 All E.R. 294 CA.

603 [1961] A.C. 388 PC.

604 For the relevance of this distinction see paras 8-090 and following, above. As for another much canvassed pre-*Polemis* decision that also falls into this category, *Smith v L.S.W. Ry* (1870) L.R. 6 C.P. 14, the generally held view today is that it was decided in the claimant's favour because there was evidence that the defendant could have foreseen the consequences that actually followed.

605 (1872) L.R. 7 C.P. 253.

606 [1921] 3 K.B. 560 CA.

607 [1961] A.C. 388 PC at 418.

608 [1961] A.C. 388 PC.

609 [1964] 1 Q.B. 518 CA. See, too, *Tremain v Pike* [1969] 1 W.L.R. 1556 (exposure to rats causing Weil's disease).

610 [1961] A.C. 388 PC.

liability. This was so in *The Sivand*,[611] where the existing abnormality was that of the seabed. The defendants' vessel negligently damaged the claimants' harbour installations and the repairing of these cost much more than originally anticipated because the contractors encountered unforeseen conditions in the soil strata of the seabed which caused their equipment to be damaged and their work consequently disrupted, delayed and extended in amount, for all of which they were entitled under their contract with the claimants to charge more.[612]

**8-117** But whereas in relation to abnormalities of the claimant or his property the rule is evidenced by cases, like *The Sivand*[613] above, of damage unforeseeable in extent,[614] in the present context the principal illustrations are cases where the unforeseeability lay in the manner of the occurrence of the damage. First, in *Hughes v Lord Advocate*,[615] the House of Lords held that, where the damage caused to the claimant was of the same kind as that which was foreseeable, in this case injury by burning, the defendant was not absolved from liability because the exact manner in which the accident happened could not have been anticipated. The defendant's workmen had negligently left unguarded in a public street a manhole which was covered by a tent and surrounded by burning paraffin lamps. The claimant, an eight-year-old boy, entered the tent with another boy, bringing in one of the lamps with a view to descending into the manhole. The accident happened when the claimant tripped over the lamp and knocked it into the manhole, when a violent explosion occurred and the claimant fell into the manhole sustaining severe injuries from burns. It was reasonably foreseeable that children might suffer injury by burning if they were allowed into the tent with the lamp, particularly if the lamp fell or broke. What could not have been reasonably foreseen was that the burns would be caused by an immediate combustion of paraffin vapour setting off an explosion. The House of Lords rejected the argument that because the explosion was the agent which caused the burning and was unforeseeable, therefore the accident was not reasonably foreseeable. The damage foreseeable and the damage occurring were both damage by fire coming from a known source of danger, the lamp; that the lamp behaved in an unpredictable way was immaterial.[616]

**8-118** *Jolley v Sutton London Borough Council*,[617] is a similar case reaching the House of Lords of liability for injury where, once again, there was the combination of a young boy playing and an object, here an abandoned boat, which was an attraction to children. The boat was rotten though appearing sound, so that the defendant council to whom it belonged could reasonably foresee that children might play

---

611 [1998] 2 Lloyd's Rep. 97 CA.

612 See [1998] 2 Lloyd's Rep. 97 CA at 106, col.2, per Evans LJ. Other aspects of this case are considered in the footnote at the end of para.8-046, above and in para.9-106, below.

613 [1998] 2 Lloyd's Rep. 97 CA.

614 See paras 8-093 to 8-096, above.

615 [1963] A.C. 837.

616 The House of Lords applied its decision in *Hughes v Lord Advocate* to the situation in *Corr v IBC Vehicles Ltd* [2008] A.C. 884 where the victim of a horrific accident at work had eventually succumbed to deep depression and committed suicide. Many arguments were unsuccessfully advanced to defeat his widow's claim (see at paras 6-007 to 6-009 above, with the facts at para.8-065, above), one of which was that the suicide was not reasonably foreseeable. It was held that it was unnecessary for this to be shown; as in *Hughes* the manner of the occurrence of the damage, here by suicide, did not have to be foreseeable. See too *Bradford v Robinson Rentals* [1967] 1 W.L.R. 337 also applying *Hughes v Lord Advocate*: some injury from exposure to severe weather foreseeable, frostbite caused.

617 [2000] 1 W.L.R. 1082 HL.

on the boat and be injured. The claimant and another boy decided to prop up the boat in order to repair it, thereby rendering it unstable. The boat fell on the claimant, crushing him. While the Court of Appeal had held the defendants not liable since the accident was of a different type and kind from anything that the defendants could reasonably have foreseen,[618] the House of Lords reversed, taking the view that the accident and injury which occurred were within the description which could be said to have been reasonably foreseeable. This difference in result shows how difficult it is to predict how courts will move in deciding whether the damage occurring and the damage foreseeable are of the same or of a different type or kind.[619]

**(d) Preceding acts of the claimant or of a third party** All prior cases have concerned abnormal characteristics of the claimant or his property or some other abnormal state of affairs. The third factor may also be a preceding act of the claimant or of a third party: generally this has not relieved the defendant of liability, and the rule in *The Wagon Mound*,[620] is not likely to lead to different results in this situation. If the act is that of the claimant and involves failure to take care for his own safety, the defendant will generally remain liable but the claimant's damages are likely to be reduced under the related doctrine of contributory negligence.[621] If the act is that of a third party which involves negligence, this will generally result in giving the claimant the right to sue the third party as well, without preventing him from suing the defendant. This is best illustrated by *Hill v New River Co.*[622] The defendant negligently left unguarded a stream of water spouting up in the middle of the highway. The claimant's horses, frightened by the water, bolted and fell into an unfenced excavation made by a third party at the side of the highway. The defendant was held liable for the injury to the horses. 8-119

### (2) Consequences following upon a new intervening force

The issue of policy has hardly operated in relation to liability for consequences following upon a new intervening force because of the tendency in such cases to introduce foreseeability as the test of cause.[623] This has meant that if the claimant has satisfied the court on the issue of cause he has generally also satisfied the court that the defendant could reasonably have foreseen the damage which occurred. For such damage a defendant can by no resort to policy evade his clear liability. All the problems have accordingly been concentrated at the causation level.[624] 8-120

The Privy Council's decision in *The Wagon Mound*,[625] can therefore have little effect upon the existing body of law dealing with consequences following upon a 8-121

[618] [1998] 1 W.L.R. 1546 CA.

[619] In *Sandeman Coprimar SA v Transitos y Transportes Integrales SL* [2003] Q.B. 1270 CA it was held that loss through payment of duty on importation of goods was not of the same type as loss through payment on a guarantee in respect of such duty and that therefore liability could not be imposed: see [2003] Q.B. 1270 CA at [28] and [39]. The case, dealt with at para.8-215, below, was in negligence as well as conversion.

[620] [1961] A.C. 388 PC.

[621] *Sigurdson v British Columbia Electric Ry* [1953] A.C. 291 PC, shows, however, that the defendant's act can occasionally be held to be the sole cause of the damage, so that no reduction is made for contributory negligence.

[622] (1868) 9 B. & S. 303.

[623] See paras 8-035 and following, above.

[624] See paras 8-035 and following, above

[625] [1961] A.C. 388 PC; see paras 8-088 and following, above.

new intervening force.[626] However, if exceptionally, a situation should arise where cause and foreseeability diverge, it is clear that here also, in their Lordships' view, foreseeability takes precedence over causation as the test of liability. Thus Viscount Simonds said:

> "If it would be wrong that a man should be held liable for damage unpredictable by a reasonable man because it was 'direct' or 'natural,' equally it would be wrong that he should escape liability, however 'indirect' the damage, if he foresaw he could reasonably foresee the intervening events which led to its being done .... Thus foreseeability becomes the effective test."[627]

Three comments, stemming from points already discussed, may be made on this. First, it may be necessary, in order to keep in line with *The Wagon Mound*,[628] to explain certain negligence cases, which were not squarely based upon foreseeability, on the footing that the damage could have been said to have been reasonably foreseeable.[629] Secondly, it is submitted that even foreseeability is not enough to impose liability in negligence for damage which has not been caused by the defendant's act: *Carslogie v Royal Norwegian Government*,[630] is the best illustration of this. Thirdly, outside the tort of negligence the test of foreseeability may have little relevance.[631]

### 3. Damage to a Secondary Interest where a Separate Liability in Respect of a Primary Interest has been Established

**8-122** Torts designed to protect one interest of the claimant, who in the event suffers damage to another interest, reach to the core of the whole problem of scope of protection. The situation envisaged is this. A particular tort exists to protect primarily a certain interest of the claimant, whether it be the safety of his person or of his property, the inviolability of his reputation or his economic relationships. As a result of the commission of the tort, the claimant suffers damage to an interest other than that which the tort is designed to protect primarily. Can the claimant recover in respect of this damage? If he can, it is sometimes graphically said that such damages are parasitic damages.[632] This expression, though in some ways useful, is, it is submitted, a misnomer. The fact that the rationale of a tort's existence is the protection of one particular interest primarily does not exclude it from protecting some other interest secondarily, once the primary interest has been infringed. This is a matter of policy, not of being parasitic. No one has suggested, for instance, that the rule in *Re Polemis*,[633] in its heyday, had introduced a parasitic element in damages, but the same argument would apply there although at another level. Lord Denning MR was therefore quite right in *Spartan Steel and Alloys v Martin & Co*,[634]

---

626 See paras 8-035 and following, above.
627 [1961] A.C. 388 PC at 426.
628 [1961] A.C. 388 PC.
629 See para.8-035.
630 [1952] A.C. 292 at para.8-015, above. And see, outside negligence, *Harnett v Bond* [1925] A.C. 669 at para.8-047, above, and *Ward v Weeks* (1830) 7 Bing. 211 at para.8-059, above.
631 See para.8-012, above.
632 See Street, *Foundations of Legal Liability* (New York, 1906), Vol.1, pp.461 and following. His may be the earliest use of the term.
633 [1921] 3 K.B. 560 CA.
634 [1973] Q.B. 27 CA.

to take issue with the term parasitic damages. He said:

> "The phrase … conveys to my mind the idea of damages which ought not in justice to be awarded, but which somehow or other have been allowed to get through by hanging on to others. If such be the concept underlying the doctrine, then the sooner it is got rid of the better."[635]

But in castigating the terminology he has, perhaps understandably, fallen into the error of misstating the doctrine, and certainly getting rid of the terminology does not allow one to get rid of all claims to recover in respect of secondary interests. The question of recovery or no recovery remains one of policy; fortunately, Lawton LJ clearly recognised that this was so.[636]

It remains to be seen when policy will allow damages to a secondary interest to be recoverable. Some dicta would suggest that all damage is recoverable once liability has been established. Thus in *Horton v Colwyn Bay Urban Council*,[637] Buckley LJ said: **8-123**

> "If an actionable wrong has been done to the claimant he is entitled to recover all the damage resulting from that wrong, and nonetheless because he would have had no right of action for some part of the damage if the wrong had not also created a damage which was actionable."[638]

This is an over-simplification, and there is no necessity in principle to adopt such a sweeping statement. Each tort is different and, since the matter is one of policy, each can be decided in a different way from the next one.[639] The few authorities also support a more piecemeal approach: they deal with a heterogeneity of situations.

The simplest case is where the further damage is of exactly the same type as that protected by the tort, and its best illustration is found in infringements of an easement of light. If the ancient lights of a building are wrongfully obstructed together with other windows in the building which are not legally protected, damages may be awarded for the total obstruction.[640] Again, in the now abolished tort of maintenance, the claimant could recover not only for the costs that the court had awarded him against the maintained party, and which the maintained party had been unable to pay, but also costs that he had incurred over and above this sum.[641] **8-124**

A step further is taken where the extra damage is of the same type as one only of the types of loss against the infliction of which the tort primarily affords protection, and this similar type of primary loss may or may not have been incurred in the particular case. This is exemplified by malicious prosecution. Costs incurred by the now claimant in defending himself in a civil suit over and above the assessed costs for which he has obtained judgment do not constitute damage to ground the action, but it may be that such costs could be added where there is other damage **8-125**

---

635 [1973] Q.B. 27 CA at 35F.

636 [1973] Q.B. 27 CA at 49G to H.

637 [1908] 1 K.B. 327 CA at 341.

638 Damage in this sense must be confined to the elements of legal damage already discussed (see Chs 4 and 5, above) but, as pointed out, there seems to be no head of damage that is not legal damage in respect of at least some torts or breaches of contracts.

639 These last two sentences were cited from the 12th edition of this work by Lawton LJ in *Spartan Steel and Alloys v Martin & Co* [1973] Q.B. 27 CA, as "correctly and neatly sum[ming] up the position": at 49G.

640 *Griffith v Richard Clay & Sons* [1912] 2 Ch. 291 CA.

641 *Bradlaugh v Newdegate* (1883) 11 Q.B.D. 1. But see paras 21-003 and following, below.

sufficient to ground the action,[642] whether the other damage be some other variety of pecuniary loss or not.[643] The matter is undecided and purely one of policy.

8-126 More complex still is the position where the further damage is of a totally different type from the types of primary loss. In slanders not actionable per se it is clear that the one thing which does not constitute special damage sufficient to ground that action is the non-pecuniary injury to the claimant's reputation itself, or to his feelings.[644] Whether, where pecuniary damage exists which grounds the action, damages for the injury to reputation or to feelings are recoverable is again undecided and is again a matter of policy. There are dicta either way. Against recovery is Williams J in *Brown v Smith*[645]; in favour are Martin B in *Dixon v Smith*,[646] and the interesting dictum of Lord Wensleydale in *Lynch v Knight*[647]:

> "Mental pain or anxiety the law cannot value, and does not pretend to redress, when the unlawful act complained of causes that alone; though where a material damage occurs, and is connected with it, it is impossible a jury, in estimating it, should altogether overlook the feelings of the party interested."[648]

The same issue has made its appearance with the torts of inducement of breach of contract, conspiracy and injurious falsehood, in all three of which it is again necessary to show pecuniary loss to ground an action. Once pecuniary loss has been shown, may non-pecuniary loss by way of injury to feelings be added to the damages? *Pratt v British Medical Association*,[649] is authority for this in the tort of inducement of breach of contract,[650] *Quinn v Leathem*,[651] provided authority for the tort of conspiracy[652] but this has now been departed from in *Lonhro v Fayed (No.5)*.[653] *Joyce v Sengupta*,[654] declined to decide the point for injurious falsehood,[655] but authority has now been provided in *Khodaparast v Shad*,[656] allowing damages for injured feelings in an injurious falsehood claim. By contrast, where the non-pecuniary loss is by way of injury not to feelings but to reputation, in none of these three torts are damages allowed for this secondary loss. This was decided, also in *Lonhro*,[657] for conspiracy; *Joyce*,[658] regarded it as the true position for injurious falsehood.[659] And in a very different area of tort law the Court of Appeal in *Spartan Steel and Alloys v Martin & Co*,[660] rightly refused to accept that, where foreseeable financial loss in respect of certain property did not, standing alone, give rise

---

642 See para.8-083, above. But see paras 21-003 and following, below.
643 The three heads of damage sufficient to ground the action are set out by Lord Holt in *Savile v Roberts* (1699) 1 Ld. Raym. 374 at 378. See para.44-002, below.
644 See para.8-083, above.
645 (1855) 13 C.B. 596 at 600.
646 (1860) 5 H. & N. 450 at 453.
647 (1861) 9 H.L.C. 577.
648 (1861) 9 H.L.C. 577 at 598. The other dicta are set out at para.46-022, below.
649 [1919] 1 K.B. 244.
650 See [1919] 1 K.B. 244 at 281 to 282, quoted at para.48-008, below.
651 [1901] A.C. 495.
652 See [1901] A.C. 495 at 498, quoted at para.48-024, below.
653 [1993] 1 W.L.R. 1489 CA.
654 [1993] 1 W.L.R. 337 CA.
655 See the two cases at, respectively, paras 48-024 and 48-013, below.
656 [2000] 1 W.L.R. 618 CA, at para.48-013, below.
657 [1993] 1 W.L.R. 1489 CA.
658 [1993] 1 W.L.R. 337 CA.
659 See the cases at, respectively, para.48-025 and para.48-014, below.
660 [1973] Q.B. 27 CA.

to a liability in negligence, recovery for such loss might nevertheless be allowed once physical damage to other property, albeit indirect but for which an action in negligence did lie, had been shown.[661] For if the law, in the sphere of negligent physical acts, gives no protection from foreseeable financial loss to a person in the absence of physical damage, direct or indirect, to his property, it must surely be wrong to regard, as within the scope of protection afforded by the tort of negligence, foreseeable financial loss which extends beyond such property as happens to be physically damaged.[662]

**8-127** In some torts, however, the cases make it clear that, in addition to the type of primary loss, recovery is possible for a totally different type of damage, which has therefore been accepted as falling within the scope of the protection of the tort. Cattle trespass illustrates this. Originally recovery in such cases was confined to damage to the land itself and to crops,[663] but it became established that liability in cattle trespass could include damages in respect of injury to other animals,[664] injury to goods[665] and injury to the person.[666] Now cattle trespass has been replaced by a statutory liability for trespassing livestock excluding, on policy grounds, personal injury from its ambit.[667] In other torts, the courts fluctuate between acceptance and rejection of secondary types of loss. This is particularly so in trespass to land. A number of rather old cases hold or state that the claimant, in an action for trespass to land, could recover as a separate head of damage in respect of his daughter's seduction,[668] his cattle's infection,[669] or the removal of his goods,[670] but not in respect of injury through his wife's illness and death,[671] or to his own reputation through slander.[672] These cases are hardly reconcilable, but it is interesting that in the cases in which the secondary loss was refused as a separate head of damage[673] it was allowed to be used in aggravation of the damages awarded for the primary loss. This suggests that the secondary loss here is slowly being accepted as within the scope of the protection afforded by the tort of trespass to land. Indeed, where in these cases aggravation of the damages has been on account of non-pecuniary loss, the second-

---

661 Edmund-Davies LJ did not have to decide the point as, dissenting, he was prepared to allow the claimants recovery of such foreseeable financial loss even in the absence of any physical damage to their property.

662 But it would seem right that a physically injured wife should be entitled to claim in negligence for the loss of consortium of her husband through his desertion consequent on her injury: see *Lampert v Eastern Omnibus Co* [1954] 1 W.L.R. 1047 at para.40-064, below, regarded as a case of so-called parasitic damages by Lawton LJ in *Spartan Steel and Alloys v Martin & Co* [1973] Q.B. 27 CA at 49D; and that, even though the action *per quod* has been abolished by statute, a physically injured husband should have a similar entitlement and also an entitlement to recover for increased expenditure if his wife is lost to him: see *Oakley v Walker* (1977) 121 S.J. 619 and *Jones v Jones* [1985] Q.B. 704 CA, but see *Pritchard v J. H. Cobden* [1988] Fam. 22 CA, all at paras 40-064 and 40-198, below.

663 *Wormald v Cole* [1954] 1 Q.B. 614 CA at 621, per Lord Goddard CJ.

664 *Lee v Riley* (1865) 18 C.B. N.S. 722; *Ellis v Loftus Iron Co* (1874) L.R. 10 C.P. 10; *Theyer v Purnell* [1918] 2 K.B. 333.

665 *Cooper v Ry Executive* [1953] 1 W.L.R. 223.

666 *Wormald v Cole* [1954] 1 Q.B. 614 CA.

667 See, for more detail, paras 39-034 and 39-035, below.

668 *Bennett v Alcott* (1787) 2 T.R. 166.

669 *Anderson v Buckton* (1719) 1 Strange 192.

670 See *Pritchard v Long* (1842) 9 M. & W. 666.

671 See *Huxley v Berg* (1815) 1 Stark. 98.

672 *Bracegirdle v Orford* (1813) 2 M. & S. 77. See the authorities at paras 8-128 to 8-130, below for their effect on this case which was concerned with reputation.

673 Including *Davis v Bromley UDC* (1903) 67 J.P. 275 CA.

ary loss has to be a separate head of damage in addition to the primary pecuniary loss since aggravated damages may be awarded only in respect of non-pecuniary loss.[674]

**8-128** Damages for injury to reputation have also been claimed in torts to goods. Thus in *Thurston v Charles*,[675] the defendant, a member of a town corporation, wrongfully communicated to the other members a letter written to the claimant by a third party which contained statements defamatory of the claimant. The claimant brought suit both for defamation and for trespass or conversion. The count on defamation failed because the communication was held privileged, but the other succeeded with damages being given in effect for the injury to the claimant's reputation. On the other hand, in *Dixon v Calcraft*,[676] an action not in tort but upon a statute, the damage alleged was that, by seizing the claimant's ship on a suspicion of her being unsafe, an imputation was cast on the claimant's character as a shipowner. Lord Esher MR said:

> "No such claim for damages was ever yet sustained in an action for seizing a chattel. If compensation were given for such an injury, it would be a kind of compensation unknown to the English law. It seems to me clear that this damage could not be recovered in an action for such a detention of a chattel, if wrongful. It could not be given by way of aggravation of damages in respect of wounded feelings. Such a thing was never heard of. Nor could it be given for injury to character, because that would really be giving damages as for libel or slander, though the matter complained of is not anything written or spoken."[677]

**8-129** In *Lonrho v Fayed (No.5)*,[678] a case of conspiracy far removed from the field of torts to goods, the Court of Appeal held that *Thurston v Charles*,[679] is unsound and cannot stand; the view stated in *Dixon v Calcraft*,[680] is to be preferred. Yet it may be questioned how far this essentially obiter pronouncement affects torts to goods generally. *Thurston v Charles* was said to be inconsistent with a cache of cases in 1993 which declined to allow claims to be made for injury to the reputation other than in defamation; for such damages suit could not be brought in injurious falsehood,[681] in negligence[682] or in conspiracy.[683] However, it should be noted that in all these cases, including *Thurston v Charles*, the claimant's complaint centred upon the making of statements for which, for one reason or another, he could not, or did not wish to, sue in defamation and the courts' concern has been that defendants are not denied the familiar defences of justification, privilege and fair comment by allowing claimants to proceed by a different cause of action. Where, however, a statement is not involved and these defences are of no relevance, then the rationale for overturning *Thurston v Charles* itself has nothing upon which to operate.

---

674 This point was made by Sir Donald Nicholls VC in *Joyce v Sengupta* [1993] 1 W.L.R. 337 at 348H to 349A, and correctly made despite Sir Michael Kerr's contrary approach which he there developed with the aid of some of the cases cited above in this paragraph.

675 (1905) 21 T.L.R. 659.

676 [1892] 1 Q.B. 458 CA.

677 [1892] 1 Q.B. 458 CA at 464; see, too, at 466, per Lopes LJ.

678 [1993] 1 W.L.R. 1489 CA.

679 (1905) 21 T.L.R. 659.

680 [1892] 1 Q.B. 458 CA.

681 *Joyce v Sengupta* [1993] 1 W.L.R. 337 CA.

682 *Spring v Guardian Assurance* [1993] I.C.R. 412 CA. But *Spring* was later reversed: [1995] 2 A.C. 296; the Lords were unimpressed by the argument that a claim in negligence should not be allowed to overtake an action in defamation.

683 *Lonrho v Fayed (No.5)* [1993] 1 W.L.R. 1489 CA, itself.

Further cases of torts to goods may be examined with this point in mind. In *Brewer v Dew*,[684] an action for seizing goods under an unfounded claim for a debt, damages were given for the annoyance and disturbance to the claimant in carrying on his business and for the injury to his credit caused by his being believed insolvent so that his lodgers left him. It seems that these damages are to be regarded as having been awarded as compensatory rather than exemplary: similar damages were certainly given as compensatory in *Smith v Enright*,[685] a case of replevin, and although the award in *Owen & Smith v Reo Motors*,[686] may appear to have been on an exemplary basis, it has now been interpreted as in fact compensatory by Lord Devlin in *Rookes v Barnard*.[687] If the analysis propounded above[688] has merit these cases may not be brought down in the fall of *Thurston v Charles*.[689] Or, alternatively, these cases may have escaped the strictures of the court in *Lonrho v Fayed (No.5)*,[690] which was primarily concerned with injury to reputation in its non-pecuniary aspect, and may then survive if they are interpreted as limiting their recovery to injury to feelings and to the pecuniary consequences of the injury to reputation. Indeed it was submitted in the 15th edition of this work, and in the following words,[691] that, since these torts involve the right to use the goods, the damages may properly contain an element of insult but should stop short of giving compensation for defamation, at least where it is for the general non-pecuniary loss of reputation that the claim is made as opposed to resultant pecuniary loss of trade. **8-130**

Indeed, it may be that where the secondary loss is a pecuniary one it is much more likely to be protected than if it were non-pecuniary. *Campbell v Paddington Corporation*,[692] is such a case. The defendants wrongfully erected a stand in a highway obstructing the view of the claimant, who occupied premises adjoining the highway, and so prevented her from profitably using her premises for viewing Edward VII's funeral procession. She recovered damages for this loss of profit and the defendants' argument that no damages were recoverable for loss of a view was rejected. Lush J said: **8-131**

> "The meaning of the proposition is that if a person by an act not otherwise unlawful interferes with the view or prospect from a house, the owner or occupier of the house has no right of action … [but here] the defendants begin with an act wrongful in itself; if such an act is the source and origin of loss to the plaintiff, then, provided the loss is sufficiently closely connected with the wrongful act, it is a loss for which the plaintiff is entitled to redress. There are many cases of wrongful acts causing the loss of the enjoyment of a benefit which could not be enforced, where nevertheless it has been held that damages are recoverable."[693]

As illustrations he cited the loss of hospitality or of voluntary contributions in cases of slander.[694]

---

684 (1843) 11 M. & W. 625.
685 (1893) 63 L.J.Q.B. 220.
686 (1934) 151 L.T. 274 CA.
687 [1964] A.C. 1129 at 1229; see the fn. at the end of para.13-004 and para.38-088, below.
688 See para.8-129, above.
689 (1905) 21 T.L.R. 659.
690 [1993] 1 W.L.R. 1489 CA.
691 See 15th edn (1988), para.219.
692 [1911] 1 K.B. 869.
693 [1911] 1 K.B. 869 at 878 to 879.
694 It was said in earlier editions that even pecuniary losses would seem to be outside the scope of protec-

## 4. Damage Outside the Scope of the Duty

**8-132** The idea that the damage to the claimant must fall within the scope of the duty owed to him has always been embedded in the law—it is implicit in Denning LJ's question with which this discussion of scope of protection opened, the question of whether the consequence is within the risk[695]—but the idea was given a great boost by Lord Hoffmann's speech in *Banque Bruxelles Lambert v Eagle Star Insurance Co*,[696] commonly called *SAAMCO*, the gist of which was reiterated by the Supreme Court in *BPE Solicitors v Hughes-Holland*.[697] Consideration of scope of duty may be seen as coming before the issue of causation, but it may also be conveniently considered at this point.

**8-133** In *SAAMCO* mortgagees had suffered severe losses after lending on the strength of a negligent over-valuation of the property mortgaged.[698] These losses were incurred in part by reason of the valuers' over-valuation but largely on account of the collapse of the property market. It was held by the House of Lords, overturning the Court of Appeal, that the valuers were liable only for the loss resulting from the over-valuation; the loss arising from the collapse of the market was not within the scope of the duty owed by them. "The real question in this case", said Lord Hoffmann, "is the kind of loss in respect of which the duty is owed".[699]

**8-134** Hard and distinct rules on scope of duty cannot be laid down. Each particular case must be taken as it comes. However, as the Supreme Court decision in *BPE Solicitors v Hughes-Holland*,[700] shows, there is an important guiding principle. That guiding principle is whether the loss flows from the feature which made the conduct wrongful.[701] Where the case is one in which a defendant assumes responsibility to a claimant for the performance of a task, it is necessary to ask whether the assumption of responsibility concerns the risks of the whole transaction or just a part of it. The fall in the market was not within the scope of the duty assumed in *SAAMCO*. Similarly, in *BPE Solicitors*, the risks of a development project were not within the scope of the duty of a conveyancer who had been instructed to draw up a facility agreement.

**8-135** Some cases, indeed most cases, are easy. Thus in *Darby v National Trust*,[702] where the duty to warn against swimming in a pond was directed to the danger of catching Weil's disease, there could be no liability for death by drowning as this fell outside the scope of the duty to warn against swimming.[703] Also reasonably straightforward is Lord Hoffmann's "over-simplified"[704] illustration in *SAAMCO*,[705]

---

tion of tort when the loss would not have occurred but for the claimant's prior wrong or but for the claimant's own financial instability, this being the result, respectively, of *Neville v London Express Newspaper* [1919] A.C. 368 and *Liesbosch Dredger v S.S. Edison* [1933] A.C. 449. In this connection, however, both decisions have been consigned to history, the one by the abolition of the tort of maintenance and the other by the abandonment, in *Lagden v O'Connor* [2004] 1 A.C. 1067, of the impecuniosity rule.

695 See para.8-082, above.

696 [1997] A.C. 191.

697 [2017] UKSC 21.

698 Facts at para.34-073, below.

699 [1997] A.C. 191 at 212C.

700 [2017] UKSC 21.

701 [2017] UKSC 21 at [38].

702 [2002] P.I.Q.R. P27 CA at 372.

703 See [2002] P.I.Q.R. P27 CA at 377–378.

704 *BPE Solicitors v Hughes-Holland* [2017] UKSC 21 at [1].

now cited, it seems, upon every conceivable occasion, of the man who would not have gone mountaineering had he been properly advised by his doctor of a weak knee.[706] It is not going to be part of the duty of the doctor to protect the man from accidents unrelated to the condition of his knee. If, on the other hand, the accident, or any other accident, is attributable to the knee and happens in the course of an activity in which the man would not have engaged but for the doctor's advice, this would fall within the scope of the duty. But cases can be difficult to resolve as to the scope of the duty, as is shown by the opposing views often taken of a case by the House of Lords, the Court of Appeal and the court of first instance. Contrasts abound. Thus whereas in *SAAMCO* the valuers were held liable only for the loss resulting from the over-valuation and not for the much greater loss from the property market collapse, in *Aneco Reinsurance Underwriting v Johnson & Higgins*,[707] where brokers had failed to effect valid insurance, they were held liable not just for the loss resulting from their failure properly to insure but for the much greater loss resulting from their client having no reinsurance at all. Again, should the duty of a doctor carrying out a failed sterilisation encompass paying for the upbringing of the unwanted child?[708] For nearly two decades from *Emeh v Kensington and Chelsea and Westminster Area Health Authority*,[709] the Court of Appeal thought that it did, but the House of Lords in *McFarlane v Tayside Health Board*,[710] has ruled otherwise.

Scope of duty also featured in the Court of Appeal's treatment of damages in **8-136**
*Thomson v Christie Manson & Woods Ltd*.[711] The defendant auctioneers had described in their sale catalogue a lot comprising two vases as Louis XV and the trial judge held that they were negligent in not warning the claimant purchaser that there could be some doubt about the vases' provenance; in short, the catalogue should have described them as probably Louis XV. On damages the trial judge then held that the auctioneers' liability was constituted by the difference between the price paid by the claimant and the actual value of the vases taking into account the uncertainties about them which were now known. While reversing on liability the Court of Appeal nevertheless passed on the issue of damages, disagreeing with the trial judge and holding the correct measure to be the difference between the price the claimant had paid and the value the vases would have had at the time of the auction if they had been correctly described, viz., as probably Louis XV, or if she had been properly advised, viz., that they were probably Louis XV. On this basis she would not have suffered the loss that a sale by her would now bring about but this

705 [1997] A.C. 191.

706 [1997] A.C. 191 at 213D.

707 [2002] 1 Lloyd's Rep. 157 HL.

708 *Aneco* was distinguished and *SAAMCO* applied in *Capita Alternative Fund Services (Guernsey) Ltd v Drivers Jonas* [2011] EWHC 2336 (Comm). Surveyors had negligently advised the purchasers of a shopping centre development as to its value and commercial prospects. The damages were limited to the difference between what the purchasers had paid and what they should have paid on the basis of correct advice. They did not extend to all the business losses that followed purchase: see [2011] EWHC 2336 (Comm) at [298] to [309]. The case went to the Court of Appeal but the application of *SAAMCO* was not there challenged: [2012] EWCA Civ 1417 CA at [20].

709 [1985] Q.B. 1012 CA.

710 [2002] 2 A.C. 59.

711 [2005] P.N.L.R. 38 CA at 713.

was not a factor to be taken into account any more than was the fall in the market in *SAAMCO*.[712]

**8-137** The scope of the duty is often clearer where it is a duty arising from statute rather than from the common law. This is because the purpose behind the statute can generally be ascertained without difficulty. The old case of *Gorris v Scott*,[713] provides a well-known illustration. The purpose of a statutory requirement to provide pens for sheep aboard a ship was the prevention of the spreading of contagious disease among them. A failure to provide adequate pens in breach of the statutory duty did not therefore lead to liability for the death of sheep swept overboard in a storm. A modern illustration appears in *Algrete Shipping Co Inc v International Oil Pollution Compensation Fund, The Sea Empress*.[714] As a result of a spillage of oil into the sea from a tanker off the Cornish coast, local fishermen were prevented by the contamination from supplying whelks under contract to the claimant. This led to inability to process whelks, far from the scene of the spillage disaster, with consequent loss of profits. The claim for this loss failed, the court describing it as of a secondary nature and as

> "a form of economic loss which is outside the intended scope of a statute closely focused on physical contamination and its consequences".[715]

The case is thus a scope of duty one. From exposure to platinum salts in their employment, the five claimants in *Greenway v Johnson Matthey Plc*[716] developed sensitivity to platinum. While this sensitisation did not produce physical or physiological harm to them, it prevented their continuing in their work involving contact with platinum. It was held, applying SAAMCO, that the scope of the employer's statutory duty lay in the safeguarding of its employees from the risk of personal harm and the claimants were therefore debarred from suing for their economic loss: see *Greenway v Johnson Matthey Plc*.[717]

**8-138** The interaction between causation and scope of duty is of importance. Though primarily put in contract, *Galoo v Bright Grahame Murray*,[718] was a case also in tort, as is generally so with the professional negligence claims which today take much of the time of the courts.[719] The negligent failure of auditors to discover and report upon inaccuracies in the audited accounts of the claimant companies, which would have shown the companies to be insolvent, led the companies to continue to trade and so incur further losses. The auditors were held not liable for these further losses on the ground that they had not caused them but had only provided the opportunity for them to be incurred.[720] There is much to be said for moving the rationalisation of this result away from cause to scope of duty. Certainly in

---

712 For an illustration in the field of copyright of loss falling outside the scope of duty see *USP Plc v London General Holdings Ltd* [2006] F.S.R. 6 CA at 65 at para.48-054 (in first footnote), below.

713 (1874) L.R. 9 Ex. 125.

714 [2003] 1 Lloyd's Rep. 327 CA.

715 [2003] 1 Lloyd's Rep. 327 CA at 336, col.2.

716 [2014] EWHC 3957 (QB).

717 At [34].

718 [1994] 1 W.L.R. 1360 CA.

719 Exceptionally, the obligation of care will arise only in contract as with the solicitor's negligence in *Haugesund Kommune v Depfa ACS Bank* [2011] 3 All E.R. 655 CA, where Norwegian law applied: facts at para.34-010, below.

720 See the case at para.8-153, below.

*Equitable Life Assurance Society v Ernst & Young*,[721] a not dissimilar case, Langley J confessed to finding it easier to analyse *Galoo* in terms of scope of duty than of causation,[722] and Lord Hoffmann has himself said so extra-judicially.[723]

## II. CONTRACT

The distinction between the two meanings of "remoteness"—that limiting causation and that relating to scope of protection—applies as much to contract as to tort. The importance of the two meanings tends, however, to be reversed. In contract remoteness in its causation aspect is subsidiary. Often it is ignored or confused with the other aspect[724]; that it exists separately is made particularly clear by *Monarch S.S. Co v Karlshamns Oljefabriker*,[725] where both aspects of remoteness were in issue.[726] The really important aspect here is that of the scope of the protection afforded by the contract. The scope of the protection is in contract marked out by what is in the contemplation of the parties, a principle embodied in the famous rule in *Hadley v Baxendale*.[727] Causation is, however, the first to be considered. **8-139**

### *(A) CAUSATION*

Problems of limiting causation do not bedevil damages in contract nearly as much as they do in tort. The principal reason for this is that the difficult cases on causation are mostly concerned with physical injury or damage, which is much more germane to tort than to contract.[728] Difficult cases do appear, however, for solution. In *Galoo v Bright Grahame Murray*,[729] the Court of Appeal indicated that the question of how the court decided whether or not the breach of contract was the cause of the claimant's loss fell to be answered "by the application of the court's common sense".[730] While in a way this has always been so—to a submission that the "modern doctrine of causation" was to be found in *Galoo*, Staughton LJ wisely retorted that there was "nothing particularly modern about it"[731]—it does not particularly assist with an analysis of the authorities. **8-140**

---

721 [2003] Lloyd's Rep. P.N. 88.

722 [2003] Lloyd's Rep. P.N. 88 at [85]. The decision itself was reversed in part: [2004] P.N.L.R. 16 CA at 269.

723 In a talk, *Causation and Common Sense*, to the Chancery Bar Association, 15 June 1999. There are, however, cases in which cause necessarily predominates over scope of duty, as appears to have been the case on one of the issues in *Green v Alexander Johnson* [2005] EWCA Civ 775 CA, an appeal on the computation of damages arising out of a barrister's negligence: see the discussion at [2005] EWCA Civ 775 CA at [23] and following.

724 See, e.g. *Haynes v Harwood* [1935] 1 K.B. 146 CA at 156 and *Sayers v Harlow UDC* [1958] 1 W.L.R. 623 at 625, where problems of causation were considered as falling under the rule in *Hadley v Baxendale* (1854) 9 Ex. 341.

725 [1949] A.C. 196.

726 See, especially, Lord Wright, who, after dealing with the conventional aspect of remoteness in contract as epitomised in the rule in *Hadley v Baxendale* (1854) 9 Ex. 341, said: "But a question of remoteness in another connection and in another sense has been raised. That is in reference to remoteness in the sense of causal connection": at 225.

727 (1854) 9 Ex. 341.

728 For a claim involving causation between employee and employer, which could be regarded as being in contract as much as in tort, see *Casey v Morane Ltd* [2001] I.C.R. 316 CA, at para.8-046, above.

729 [1994] 1 W.L.R. 1360 CA.

730 [1994] 1 W.L.R. 1360 CA at 1375A, per Glidewell LJ. See the case at para.8-153, below.

731 Referred to in *British Racing Drivers' Club v Hextall Erskine & Co* [1996] P.N.L.R. 523 at 541C.

8-141 It is proposed to group the few cases in contract in the same twofold way as were the many in tort.[732] This helps to give coherence to the available authorities.

### 1. DIRECT CONSEQUENCES

8-142 One does not generally hear of "direct" consequences of the *Re Polemis*[733] type in contract. If, however, a breach of contract caused physical injury or damage in circumstances where there was no concurrent tort, it is thought that the same principles would apply, including, if the situation required it, those applied in *Re Polemis*,[734] for the principles of causation cannot alter with the boundaries of contract and tort.[735] As with tort, it seems that a state of affairs existing at the time of the breach of contract will not negative causal connection.[736] Indeed what has been said on direct consequences in tort damages[737] should be applicable mutatis mutandis in contract.[738] Whether the claimant can recover for damage directly caused is another question, and is considered later.

### 2. CONSEQUENCES FOLLOWING UPON A NEW INTERVENING FORCE

8-143 With consequences following upon a new intervening force there is, again, much less authority in contract, as the problems which arise with intervening acts and events are primarily tort ones. Should any such problem arise in contract which is not already covered by existing authority, there seems no reason why the bulk of the equivalent law on tort damages[739] should not apply mutatis mutandis.[740]

#### (1) Intervening acts of a third party

8-144 Generally, the authorities on intervening acts of a third party in contract are slight[741] and therefore reliance must be placed upon the analogous cases in tort.[742]

---

732 For the grouping in tort, see para.8-009, above. As with tort, concurrent and continuing causes are included in the two-fold grouping: see para.8-010, above.

733 [1921] 3 K.B. 560 CA. It has already been submitted that, in relation to causation, the principle of *Re Polemis* is unaffected by the decision in *The Wagon Mound* [1961] A.C. 388 PC: see para.8-033, above.

734 [1921] 3 K.B. 560 CA.

735 In *Re Polemis* [1921] 3 K.B. 560 CA, there was a contractual relationship between the parties but the case was decided in tort.

736 See Blackburn J in *Horne v Midland Ry* (1873) L.R. 8 C.P. 131 at 140: "If a man contracts to carry a chattel and loses it, he must pay the value though he may discover that it was more valuable than he had supposed."

737 See paras 8-031 to 8-034, above.

738 Indeed the contract case of *Total Transport Corp v Arcadia Petoleum, The Eurus* [1998] 1 Lloyd's Rep. 351 CA, has been considered under tort, together with Staughton LJ's disagreement, at 361, col.2, with the rule stated in the text that pre-existing states of affairs do not affect causation, a disagreement which is challenged both here and there: see para.8-034, above.

739 See paras 8-035 to 8-081, above.

740 The Court of Appeal in *Beoco v Alfa Laval Co* [1995] Q.B. 137 CA, agreed with this and proceeded to apply the equivalent tort law: see the case at para.8-152, below. So, too, in *Galoo v Bright Grahame Murray* [1994] 1 W.L.R. 1360 CA, it was accepted that the principles applicable to liability in the difficult area of causation were the same in contract and in tort: see at 1369H.

741 *Wiseman v Virgin Atlantic Airways Plc* [2006] EWHC 1566 (QB) is such a case, the loss, which was clearly too remote, arising from the claimant's being robbed during his unwilling stay in a country forced on him by the defendant airline's refusal in breach of contract to transport him home.

742 See paras 8-037 and following, above.

To this there is one important exception, where indeed the authorities are more profuse in contract then in tort itself. This is the situation where an intervening voluntary act of a third party, intended by him to cause the damage, is perpetrated in circumstances where the defendant's contractual duty to the claimant is to take care that such an act does not happen. It is only because the defendant's duty is to guard against the very harm which results that the law holds him liable. There is a variety of illustrations of this situation. The leading example is *London Joint Stock Bank v Macmillan*.[743] A customer of the claimant bank, in breach of his duty to the bank not to draw cheques so as to facilitate fraud, signed for a trusted clerk a cheque for £2 drawn in such a way as to enable the clerk readily to alter the amount to £120; this sum he obtained from the bank and absconded. The House of Lords held that the customer was liable to the bank for the forged increase. Lord Finlay LC said: **8-145**

> "The fact that a crime was necessary to bring about the loss does not prevent its being the natural consequence of the carelessness."[744]

In *De la Bere v Pearson*,[745] the defendants, who published a newspaper, undertook to give advice to their readers and were asked by the claimant to recommend a good stockbroker. Without sufficient inquiries they recommended a broker who was not a member of the Stock Exchange and was an undischarged bankrupt, and who immediately misappropriated to his own use the money sent to him by the claimant. The defendants were held liable for the loss. In *Stansbie v Troman*,[746] the defendant, who was carrying out decorations in the claimant's house under contract with him and had been left alone there by the claimant's wife, failed to lock the house when he left it to obtain some wallpapers. During his absence thieves broke in and stole property of the claimant for the loss of which the defendant was held liable. The Court of Appeal approved the statement of the judge below that

> "the act of negligence itself consisted in the failure to take reasonable care to guard against the very thing that in fact happened".[747]

In *Marshall v Rubypoint*,[748] because the defendant landlords, in breach of their repairing covenant, had allowed the front door of the premises in which the claimant was a tenant to fall into serious disrepair, burglars were able to enter on three occasions, inflicting personal injury on the claimant and stealing and damaging his property. He was held entitled to recover for all these items of loss; none of the burglaries constituted a novus actus. In these cases the intervening act was a crime: a fortiori the damage would not have been too remote if the intervening act had been a tort or even not actionable. This was the position in *Hamilton-Jones v David & Snape*,[749] where the negligence of the claimant's solicitor gave the opportunity to the Tunisian father of her children improperly to remove them out of the country to Tunisia.

This principle must not, however, be carried too far. On the other side of the line **8-146**

---

743 [1918] A.C. 777.
744 [1918] A.C. 777 at 794.
745 [1908] 1 K.B. 280 CA.
746 [1948] 2 K.B. 48 CA.
747 [1948] 2 K.B. 48 CA at 52. On this ground Lord Sumner's famous dictum in *Weld-Blundell v Stephens* [1920] A.C. 956 at 986 (cited in the next paragraph) was distinguished.
748 [1997] 1 E.G.L.R. 69 CA.
749 [2004] 1 WL.R. 924; facts at para.32-048, below.

fall cases like *Cobb v G.W. Ry*,[750] and the well-known, difficult and bare majority decision in *Weld-Blundell v Stephens*.[751] In the former it was held that the defendant railway company, which had negligently allowed its carriages to be overcrowded, was not liable to the claimant passenger for the loss he incurred by being robbed while travelling. This was not the specific act against the happening of which it was the defendant's duty to guard.[752] In the latter the claimant, when employing the defendant chartered accountant to investigate the affairs of a company, libelled certain officials of the company in his letter of instructions to the defendant. As a result of the defendant's negligence in leaving the letter at the company's office it was read by a third party, who communicated its contents to the officials, who in turn sued the now claimant for libel and recovered damages. These damages the claimant sought to recover in an action for breach of contract against the defendant, together with the costs he had had to pay and had himself incurred in the prior action. The House of Lords by a bare majority held that he could recover only nominal damages upon two grounds, the better known of which[753] is summed up in the proposition from Lord Sumner's speech, frequently quoted since, that:

> "in general … even though A is in fault, he is not responsible for injury to C which B, a stranger to him, deliberately chooses to do. Though A may have given the occasion for B's mischievous activity, B then becomes a new and independent cause."[754]

This majority holding presents two difficulties which are not easy to surmount. First, the intervening act was probably foreseeable since, as Lord Sumner admitted, "more than half of human kind are tale-bearers by nature"[755]; secondly, in the words of the dissenting Viscount Finlay, "the very thing happened which it was his [the defendant's] duty to guard against".[756] The second difficulty is the one in immediate issue here, but the concurrence of the two tends to show that a situation involving libel is for some not very clear reason to be regarded as exceptional.[757] Otherwise it is difficult to see when a situation should fall within the principles of *Weld-Blundell v Stephens*,[758] rather than within those of *London Joint Bank v Macmillan*,[759] and the other authorities in the last paragraph.[760]

**8-147** There is also the occasional case where the act of the third party was in no way

---

[750] [1894] A.C. 419.

[751] [1920] A.C. 956.

[752] Similar is *Pounder v N.E. Ry* [1892] 1 Q.B. 385, where the facts and result were similar except that the claimant was not robbed but assaulted. In *Cobb v G.W. Ry* [1894] A.C. 419, Earl Selborne was dubious about this decision but only on the ground that in the particular circumstances the defendant should have known that an assault was probable; the rest of the court reserved their opinions on this point.

[753] The other ground is dealt with at para.8-210, below.

[754] [1920] A.C. 956 at 986.

[755] [1920] A.C. 956 at 991. And again, at 987: "Taking men as we find them, few things are more certain than the repetition of a calumny confidentially communicated, even on an honourable understanding of secrecy."

[756] [1920] A.C. 956 at 974.

[757] As to the first difficulty being exceptional see para.8-061, above.

[758] [1920] A.C. 956.

[759] [1918] A.C. 777.

[760] See *Re Polemis* [1921] 3 K.B. 560 CA at 577, per Scrutton LJ: "Perhaps the House of Lords will some day explain why, if a cheque is negligently filled up, it is a direct effect of the negligence that someone finding the cheque should commit forgery; while if someone negligently leaves a libellous letter about it is not a direct effect of the negligence that the finder should show the letter to the person libelled."

intended to cause the loss or damage, being negligent or even innocent. *Lepla v Rogers*,[761] provides a good 19th century illustration[762] and being in the field of breach of covenants in a lease it is set out in that context,[763] while *British Racing Drivers' Club v Hextall Erskine & Co*,[764] is a modern illustration. The failure of the defendant solicitors to advise the claimants, a company limited by guarantee and its wholly-owned subsidiary, that a proposed investment required the approval of the members of the company permitted the directors to proceed with a bad investment without the knowledge of the members. The contention that the loss of the shares was caused by the directors adopting, as a matter of commercial judgment, a transaction which was misconceived and not by the defective legal advice was rejected. Carnwarth J said:

> "In cases of solicitor's negligence, it is unlikely that the conduct of the solicitor will itself be the direct cause of the damage which is suffered. More usually the basis of the claim is the solicitor's failure to protect the client against some other effective cause. The question therefore is whether the particular loss was within the reasonable scope of the dangers against which it was the solicitor's duty to provide protection."[765]

That question was answered in the affirmative. What the directors did in investing was precisely what they would have been prevented from doing had the proper legal advice been forthcoming.

## (2) Intervening acts of the claimant

Where it is the claimant who is the intervening actor, the issue of remoteness may be complicated by the possible appearance of the connected doctrines of contributory negligence and of mitigation of damage.[766] It was some time before the former was heard of in contract[767]; the latter has appeared fairly frequently in the cases together with, or even overlapping, the plea of remoteness.[768] **8-148**

Again, the principles applied in the corresponding tort cases should apply[769]: this is on the whole borne out by the existing cases. As with tort there is a preponderance of intervening acts of masters of ships leading to physical damage to their vessels. In *Compania Naviera Maropan v Bowaters*,[770] the defendant charterers **8-149**

---

761 [1893] 1 Q.B. 31.

762 See, too, *Halestrap v Gregory* [1895] 1 Q.B. 561.

763 Facts at para.28-096, below.

764 [1996] P.N.L.R. 523.

765 [1996] P.N.L.R. 523 at 539F.

766 See paras 6-011 to 6-020, above. See *County Ltd v Girozentrale* [1996] 3 All E.R. 834 CA at 858d to f, per Hobhouse LJ: "The related principles of remoteness of damage, contributory negligence, and mitigation of damage are all legal principles which … directly concern the evaluation of the responsibility of the relevant party for his own conduct and for the losses or other consequences that are the subject-matter of the litigation.… Contributory negligence was irrelevant and no question of mitigation of loss arose until the breach was discovered and it is not in dispute that at that time the plaintiffs took the appropriate steps." Facts of this case, which concerns intervening acts of the claimant, are at para.8-150, below.

767 The question of contributory negligence in contract is considered at paras 7-011 and following, above.

768 See, e.g. *Compania Naviera Maropan v Bowaters* [1955] 2 Q.B. 68 CA.

769 See paras 8-063 and following, above. The Court of Appeal in *Beoco v Alfa Laval Co* [1995] Q.B. 137 CA, agreed with this and proceeded to apply the principles as worked out in tort: see the case at para.8-152, below.

770 [1955] 2 Q.B. 68 CA.

nominated an unsafe loading place for the claimants' ship, and the master, placed on the horns of a dilemma, obeyed the defendants' nominating order, placing reliance on an assurance of safety given by the defendants' pilot, with the result that the ship was physically damaged. Hodson LJ said:

> "The question is one of causation. If the master, by acting as he did, either caused the damage by acting unreasonably in the circumstances in which he was placed, or failed to mitigate the damage, the charterers would be relieved, accordingly, from the liability which would otherwise have fallen upon them."[771]

It was held, however, that the master had acted reasonably and the claimants could therefore recover for the damage. In *Wilson v Newport Dock Co*,[772] the defendants had contracted to receive the claimant's ship at a specified time, but when she duly arrived she could not be admitted owing to the breaking of one of the chains of the dock gates. Although the day was stormy the captain anchored her opposite the dock, and at the turn of the tide she grounded on a sandbank and broke her back. The court was unable to decide whether the defendants were liable for this damage in the absence of a finding by the jury as to whether or not it was possible to have taken the ship to a place of safety, although they had found that neither captain nor pilot was negligent. A new trial was therefore ordered. Martin B alone thought that these findings sufficed to make the defendants liable, basing his conclusions upon the rule in *Jones v Boyce*,[773] and indeed the case should be regarded in the light of the many tort cases on ship collisions which have since clarified the law and which may suggest that today the court would endorse Martin B's view.[774]

**8-150** There are cases outside those concerning ships where the claimant's intervening acts and omissions have been held not to break the chain of causation. *County Ltd v Girozentrale Securities*,[775] is a case of some complexity. Brokers handling the underwriting by bankers of a share issue in a publicly quoted company, in order to obtain indicative commitments to subscribe, represented to certain potential investors, contrary to the terms of their letter of engagement and therefore outside their authority, that the issue would not go ahead unless it was fully placed. This allowed these investors the chance to reconsider confirmed commitments. The bankers went ahead with the issue as if they had indicative commitments for the entirety of the placement when they should have known that that was not the case; in particular they accepted the doubtful quality of indicative commitments from the chairman of the company without making proper inquiries. In the event the bankers, as underwriters, were left with a substantial number of shares which were not taken up and on which they made a loss. The Court of Appeal, deciding in favour of the bankers and reversing the judge below,[776] held that the brokers' breach of contract was an effective cause of the loss and that it remained effective

---

771 [1955] 2 Q.B. 68 CA at 98–99; similarly Morris LJ said that if the damages could not be recovered it would be "for the reason that they would not be the result of the breach of contract, but of the deliberate and unnecessary act of those in control of the ship": at 104.

772 (1866) L.R. 1 Ex. 177.

773 (1816) 1 Stark. 493: facts at para.8-065, above.

774 For an important case on an insurance policy where there was an intervening act of a ship's master, see *Smith Hogg v Black Sea Insurance Co* [1940] A.C. 997.

775 [1996] 3 All E.R. 834 CA.

776 The judge had particularly relied upon Scott LJ's judgment, of which the Court of Appeal was somewhat critical, in *Schering Agrochemicals v Resibel* [1992] CA. Transcript 1298; the facts are set out in the judgments of the Court of Appeal here.

notwithstanding that the bankers, in making their own inquiries, had not done so with sufficient care. Hobhouse LJ said:

> "The plaintiffs' conduct was not voluntary in the sense of being undertaken with a knowledge of its significance. Conduct which is undertaken without an appreciation of the existence of the earlier causal factor will normally only suffice to break the causal relationship if the conduct was reckless. It is the character of reckless conduct that it makes the actual state of knowledge of that party immaterial."[777]

*Borealis AB v Geogas Trading SA*,[778] also is factually and legally complex. The defendant supplied goods to the claimant, being butane feedstock which was heavily contaminated with fluorides. This caused extensive physical damage to the claimant's plant and equipment, with consequent disruption of business and loss of profits. The defendant argued that the chain of causation had been broken by the claimant's failure to react appropriately to the triggering of an alarm, which had sounded soon after the discharge of the goods had commenced at the claimant's plant, by taking no action in response. The alarm was not intended to deal with matters other than contaminants; the claimant was wholly unaware that there had been a breach of contract by the supply of contaminated goods and therefore wholly unaware of any impending danger. The claimant's response to the alarm, although well short of best practice, was held not to be unreasonable and, even if unreasonable, certainly not reckless, so that the chain of causation was not broken.[779]

On the other hand, in *Quinn v Burch Bros (Builders)*,[780] where the defendant building contractors' breach of contract consisted of a failure to supply a step-ladder to the claimant, to whom they had sub-contracted plastering and other ancillary building work, and the claimant's damage consisted of injuries suffered when he fell from an unfooted trestle which he had made use of in the absence of a step-ladder, the Court of Appeal held the defendants not liable. Here the breach of contract did not cause the accident but merely gave the claimant the opportunity to injure himself by the use of unsuitable equipment. A person contracting to supply a chattel and failing to do so, or to do so on time, cannot generally be held liable if the other contracting party then proceeds to injure himself by using a defective chattel in substitution. It was not, said Sellers LJ,[781] as if the defendants' obligation to supply a ladder to the claimant had arisen by virtue of a master and servant relationship, or as if the defendants had provided a faulty step-ladder which, he thought, would perhaps be comparable in principle to *Compania Naviera Maropan v Bowaters*,[782] with its nomination of an unsafe port.[783] **8-151**

This was taken further in *Beoco v Alfa Laval Co*[784] where it was held by the Court **8-152**

---

[777] [1996] 3 All E.R. 834 CA at 857c to d.

[778] [2011] 1 Lloyd's Rep. 482.

[779] The Court of Appeal in *Stacey v Autosleeper Group Ltd* [2014] EWCA Civ. 1551 relied on both the *Girocentrale* and the *Borealis* cases to hold that the buyer of a motor home was entitled to damages for breach of warranty for his loss, by way of costs of litigation with his sub-buyer, as his failure to notice the inconsistency between the gross weight stamped on the chassis plate and the greater gross weight warranted was not reckless.

[780] [1966] 2 Q.B. 370 CA.

[781] [1966] 2 Q.B. 370 CA at 390–391.

[782] [1955] 2 Q.B. 68 CA; see para.8-149, above.

[783] See *Vacwell Engineering Co v B.D.H. Chemicals* [1971] 1 Q.B. 88 where the claimants' method of handling a dangerous chemical supplied by the defendants did not prevent recovery.

[784] [1995] Q.B. 137 CA.

of Appeal that the claimant was not entitled to recover damages from the defendant which he would not have incurred by way of loss of profit on lost production during the period necessary to repair the defect in goods or materials supplied by the defendant and caused by his breach of contract where, because of some supervening act or event, these repairs are not carried out or are subsumed in other more expensive repairs. A defective heat exchanger installed at the claimant's works by the first defendant, and inadequately repaired by the second defendant on discovery of the defect, subsequently exploded, causing damage to the claimant's plant and loss of production. The supervening act or event was the negligence of the claimant's engineers in putting the heat exchanger back into service without making proper tests to see that the repair had been properly carried out in circumstances when they knew of the risk of explosion if it was not. In deciding the case against the claimant the Court of Appeal relied heavily upon the cases in tort, and particularly upon the many cases dealing with the expenses of repair and the loss of profits where ships have been tortiously damaged.[785]

**8-153** The important *Galoo v Bright Grahame Murray*,[786] may also be considered as a case involving intervening acts of the claimant breaking the causal link. The claimant companies claimed against the defendant auditors for negligently failing to discover and report upon inaccuracies in the audited accounts which would have revealed the insolvency of the companies so that they would have ceased to trade immediately and subsequent losses would have been avoided. The Court of Appeal held the defendants not liable for these trading losses because their breach of contract was not the dominant and effective cause of the claimants' loss but had merely given the opportunity for that loss to be sustained. Somewhat similar is *Cossey v Lonnkvist*,[787] where an accountant, retained by the claimants to obtain bank finance for a business they were buying, misinformed the bank of the business's turnover and the claimants, having gone ahead with the purchase, suffered loss as a result. They were held entitled to nominal damages only as their loss was not caused by the accountant's breach of contract, there being no causative link between the accountant's soliciting of finance and the claimants' decision to purchase the business.

**8-154** In contrast to the result in *Galoo* is the recovery for trading losses in *Tom Hoskins Plc v EMW Law*.[788] The claimant company instructed the defendant solicitor to sell its pub businesses since it was suffering financial difficulties, which the solicitor knew, and was trading at a loss, which the solicitor did not know but might have suspected. The solicitor's negligent handling of the sale meant that the company was only able to complete the sale late. There was no option of ceasing to trade as the sale was of the businesses as going concerns so that the company could not stem its trading losses, which therefore went on. This intervening act of continuing to trade was held not to stand in the way of the company claiming for these trading losses.[789] Also to be contrasted with *Galoo* is *MacMahon v Hamilton*,[790] from Northern Ireland where the defendant's breach of duty was held to be the cause of, and not merely the occasion for, the claimant's losses on an overdraft and

---

785 These are fully dealt with at paras 37-031 to 37-044, below.
786 [1994] 1 W.L.R. 1360 CA.
787 [2000] Lloyd's Rep. P.N. 885 CA.
788 [2010] EWHC 479 Ch.
789 See, distinguishing *Galoo*, at [142] to [157] of the judgment.
790 [2002] Lloyd's Rep. P.N. 93.

remortgage. The defendant solicitor, instructed by the claimant to issue proceedings against a third party, had assured the claimant that this had been done, that judgment for £20,000 had been entered and that enforcement proceedings had been put in hand. This was entirely false information on the strength of which the claimant ran up a large overdraft which required the re-mortgaging of his family home. Upon the claim against the third party becoming statute-barred, the claimant sued the solicitor and at first instance recovered for the loss connected with the overdraft and remortgage. While the Court of Appeal allowed the solicitor's appeal,[791] his appeal was only in relation to the award on account of the capital element of the remortgage, the court holding that the incurring of an obligation to repay a capital sum could not amount to a loss. But the claimant's entitlement to the rest of the damages awarded was not put in doubt.[792]

### (3) Intervening events

As with tort, an intervening event will not relieve the defendant of liability if it is dependent or if, although independent, it could reasonably be expected to happen.[793] Authority on dependent events is lacking, but there are some interesting examples of independent events connected with delay in the departure and arrival of chartered ships. **8-155**

Of these easily the most important is the House of Lords decision in *Monarch S.S. Co v Karlshamns Oljefabriker*.[794] By reason of the defendant's failure to provide a seaworthy ship for the carriage of the claimant's cargo, the voyage was delayed so that the ship could not reach her Swedish destination before the outbreak of the Second World War, and was ordered by the Admiralty to Glasgow. **8-156**

The cost of transhipping the cargo was held to be a consequence of the breach of contract, since the outbreak of war was such a possibility that the claimant could have anticipated it. The matter was put clearly by Lord Porter, distinguishing the case of a ship struck by lightning or running into a typhoon, which would have been avoided but for the delay.

> "Either may happen as much at one place or time as another. whereas delay, at a time when war is likely to occur, gives more opportunity for its incidence than a speedy and proper dispatch would give. Where, however, the basis of liability is delay, it is, as I think, the reasonable anticipation which matters."[795]

A similar result had been reached in *The Wilhelm*,[796] where the master had delayed the departure of the ship with the result that, when winter came, she was frozen in the port till spring. The defendant was held liable for the whole delay since the possibility of being frozen in was apparent. The House of Lords in *Monarch S.S. Co v Karlshamns Oljefabriker*,[797] approved this decision and at the same time

---

[791] See sub nom *MacMahon v James Doran & Co* [2002] P.N.L.R. 33 CA (NI) at 755.

[792] *Barings Plc v Coopers & Lybrand* [2003] Lloyd's Rep. I.R. 566 where the negligent failure in detection of the defendant auditors was held to be causative for a time and then to cease to be causative (facts at para.6-016, above) is a case of intervening omissions rather than intervening acts of the claimant.

[793] These terms are fully explained in dealing with tort at paras 8-079 to 8-081, above.

[794] [1949] A.C. 196.

[795] [1949] A.C. 196 at 215.

[796] (1866) 14 L.T. 636.

[797] [1949] A.C. 196.

distinguished *Associated Portland Cement v Houlder*,[798] where the defendant's ship had not arrived in port to load the claimant's goods by the due date and the following day, while still en route, was sunk by a submarine. The defendant was held liable in damages only in respect of the one day. Here the intervening event was in no way to be anticipated.[799]

8-157 Outside the cases involving ships, there are authorities from the professional negligence field. *Pearson v Sanders Witherspoon*,[800] is a useful illustration of an independent event and of the importance of whether it could reasonably have been expected to happen. The liability of a solicitor, whose negligence lay in not pursuing his client's claim against a company timeously, was held not to reach to loss arising from the client's inability to enforce an eventual judgment by reason of the intervening event of the company's insolvency. Liability would not arise until such time as the solicitor had received information showing the likelihood of the company's going into receivership.[801] The claimant in *Andrews v Barnett Waddingham*,[802] took out a with-profits annuity relying upon the negligent advice of his actuary as to the statutory protection he would obtain were the life assurance company issuing the annuity to become insolvent. In the event, the life assurance company struck bad times and it was this that led to the claimant's loss and not any lack of statutory protection, no insolvency being anticipated. In these circumstances the Court of Appeal set aside the trial judge's award of damages to the claimant, pointing out that the fact that the claimant would not have taken out the with-profits annuity had he been properly advised did not entitle him to recover the loss he had in fact sustained in consequence of his acquiring the annuity.[803] By contrast is the Court of Appeal's decision in *Rubenstein v HSBC Bank Plc*.[804] The claimant had told the defendant bank that he wished to invest, without risk, money coming from the sale of his home and to have easy access to his money for the purchase of another home. The bank advised him to invest in a form of bond which was subject to market losses while telling him that the investment was the same as a cash deposit. When the risk materialised on the collapse of the market, the bank was held liable for the claimant's losses.

### (B) SCOPE OF PROTECTION: CONTEMPLATION OF THE PARTIES

8-158 The starting point in resolving a problem as to the measure of damages for breach of contract is the rule that the claimant is entitled to be placed, so far as money can do it, in the same position as he would have been in had the contract been performed.[805] This rule is limited first, but not substantially, by the principles as to causation just dealt with; the second and much more far-reaching limit is that the scope of protection is marked out by what was in the contemplation of the parties.

---

798 (1917) 86 L.J.K.B. 1495.

799 See actions on insurance policies and the like, which are, of course, not for damages, claiming in respect of loss of a ship resulting from being on a wartime operation followed by bad weather conditions: *Leyland Shipping Co v Norwich Fire Insurance Co* [1918] A.C. 350; *Yorkshire Dale S.S. Co v Minister of War Transport* [1942] A.C. 691.

800 [2000] P.N.L.R. 110 CA.

801 See [2000] P.N.L.R. 110 CA at 125A–B.

802 [2006] P.N.L.R. 24 CA at 432.

803 See in particular Richards LJ at [2006] P.N.L.R. 24 CA at [41] to [45].

804 [2012] EWCA Civ 1184 CA.

805 See para.2-003, above.

When damage is said to be too remote in contract it is generally this latter factor that is in issue. When in 1848 Parke B first clearly stated in *Robinson v Harman*,[806] the starting rule for the assessment of an award of contract damages, no general rules as to whether damage might be too remote had been formulated, and, as Asquith LJ put it in *Victoria Laundry v Newman*[807]:

> "this purpose, if relentlessly pursued, would provide him [the claimant] with a complete indemnity for all loss de facto resulting from a particular breach, however improbable, however unpredictable."[808]

It was necessary that some limitation should be introduced,[809] and this task was achieved in *Hadley v Baxendale*,[810] in 1854, the most celebrated case in the field of contract damages.

Before turning to the rule in *Hadley v Baxendale* it is for consideration whether the new emphasis, stemming from *SAAMCO*,[811] on scope of duty needs to be addressed in contract as it has been in tort.[812] It may be that the scope of duty issue can be contained within the scope of protection afforded by the test of contemplation of the parties. In other words, the parties will be taken to contemplate that which the court regards as falling within the scope of the duty. Otherwise, it will be necessary to expand the coverage of scope of protection, here being considered, to take in scope of duty as well as contemplation of the parties. It was said, when dealing under tort with *Galoo v Bright Grahame Murray*,[813] which is also and primarily a contract case, that it may be easier to explain that decision on the basis of scope of duty rather than on the basis of a limit on causation, which was the approach of the Court of Appeal.[814] If then the losses through continued trading in ignorance of an insolvent condition were not within the scope of the auditors' duty, would it not be equally reasonable to say that such losses were not within the parties' contemplation?[815] Lord Hoffmann has now in *The Achilleas*,[816] tried to bring **8-159**

806 (1848) 1 Ex. 850 at 855.

807 [1949] 2 K.B. 528 CA at 539.

808 Thus cases of that time were very generous to claimants, especially *Black v Baxendale* (1847) 1 Ex. 410 and *Waters v Towers* (1853) 8 Ex. 401. Today, as with all cases decided before *Hadley v Baxendale* (1854) 9 Ex. 341 on questions of remoteness in contract, they cannot be regarded as very compelling authorities.

809 There were a few scattered limitations already existing, in matters where the type of contract had frequently been before the court. The limitation of importance, which is no longer law today, was the restrictive rule laid down in *Flureau v Thornhill* (1776) 2 Wm. Bl. 1078 in connection with sales and leases of land.

810 (1854) 9 Ex. 341.

811 Otherwise *Banque Bruxelles Lambert v Eagle Star Insurance Co* [1997] A.C. 191.

812 See paras 8-132 to 8-138, above.

813 [1994] 1 W.L.R. 1360 CA.

814 See the case at para.8-153, above. The liability of the employer in 8-156 *Greenway v Johnson Matthey Plc* [2014] EWHC 3957 (QB), considered at para.8-137, above, was in breach of contract as well as in tort for breach of statutory duty. The result was the same. The employer's duty, operating through an implied term imposed by the law, was to maintain a safe place of work and to care for the physical safety of employees; thus the implied term was exactly co-extensive with the tortious obligation. So in contract as in tort the scope of the duty did not go beyond physical injury to reach economic loss: see [2014] EWHC 3957 (QB) at [43]–[47].

815 In *Demarco v Perkins* [2006] P.N.L.R. 27 CA at 512, where the defendant accountants had failed through negligence to advance the annulment of the claimant's bankruptcy by a particular route, the defendants were held not liable for the consequences of failure to obtain annulment by another route which in truth could never have been achieved, a correct result which may be arrived at by invok-

*SAAMCO* and scope of duty into the contact damages field but, it is thought, did not there succeed.[817] In the scope of duty case of *Haugesund Kommune v Depfa ACS Bank*,[818] where the duty of care of solicitors arose only in contract as Norwegian law applied, it was common ground that it was appropriate to consider the scope of that contractual duty in the terms laid down in *SAAMCO* and the cases following it.[819] This, however, was not introducing *SAAMCO* and scope of duty in the same way that Lord Hoffmann, as we shall see, was attempting to do in *The Achilleas*.

## 1. The Rule in Hadley v Baxendale

**8-160** In *Hadley v Baxendale*,[820] the claimants' millshaft was broken and they gave it to the defendant carriers to take to the makers as a model for a new one. On making the contract, the defendants' clerk was informed that the article to be carried was the broken shaft of a mill and that the claimants were owners of the mill.[821] The defendants delayed the millshaft's delivery, and the claimants claimed to recover for the loss of profits while the mill, as a result of the delay, remained idle. The court rejected the claim on the ground that the facts which the defendants were held to know were not sufficient to

> "show reasonably that the profits of the mill must be stopped by an unreasonable delay in the delivery of the broken shaft by the carriers to the third person".[822]

The general rule upon which this was based was enunciated by Alderson B delivering the court's judgment, and its great importance and the constant reference made to it in later cases require the relevant passage to be quoted in full. It runs thus:

> "We think the proper rule in such a case as the present is this: where two parties have made a contract which one of them has broken, the damages which the other party ought to receive in respect of such breach of contract should be such as may fairly and reasonably be considered either arising naturally, i.e. according to the usual course of things, from such breach of contract itself, or such as may reasonably be supposed to have been in the contemplation of both parties, at the time they made the contract, as the probable result of the breach of it. Now, if the special circumstances under which the contract was actually made were communicated by the claimants to the defendants and thus known to both parties, the damages resulting from the breach of such a contract, which they would reasonably contemplate, would be the amount of injury which would ordinarily follow from a breach of contract under these special circumstances so known and communicated.

---

ing causation, scope of duty or contemplation of the parties.

816 [2009] 1 A.C. 61.

817 See the analysis of the case at paras 8-168 and following, below.

818 [2011] 3 All E.R. 655 CA. Fully considered at para.34-010, below.

819 [2011] 3 All E.R. 655 CA at [73].

820 (1854) 9 Ex. 341.

821 In *Victoria Laundry v Newman* [1949] 2 K.B. 528 CA at 537 to 538 Asquith LJ pointed out that the headnote in *Hadley v Baxendale* (1854) 9 Ex. 341 and the statement of facts at 344 are misleading in so far as they say that the defendants' clerk was told that the mill was stopped and the shaft must be sent immediately. One can only assume that the claimants gave evidence to this effect and it was not accepted by the court. For if it had been accepted, the court must surely, said Asquith LJ ([1949] 2 K.B. 528 at 537), have decided for the claimants under the rule as stated in relation to special circumstances.

822 (1854) 9 Ex. 341 at 355.

> But, on the other hand, if these special circumstances were wholly unknown to the party breaking the contract, he, at the most, would only be supposed to have had in his contemplation the amount of injury which would arise generally, and in the great multitude of cases not affected by any special circumstances, from such a breach of contract. For, had the special circumstances been known, the parties might have specially provided for the breach of contract by special terms as to the damages in that case; and of this advantage it would be very unjust to deprive them. Now the above principles are those by which we think the jury ought to be guided in estimating the damages arising out of any breach of contract."[823]

The phraseology of the judgment has been criticised on many occasions, particularly the expressions "arising naturally" and "probable consequences".[824] The term "direct consequences" achieved a certain vogue in contract[825] at about the same time as it was making its name in tort,[826] but this term is only properly applicable to remoteness as a limit on causation.[827] Indeed many of the suggested alternatives have themselves been criticised. Also there was a tendency first to regard the rule established by the judgment as three rules,[828] and then as two rules, the first dealing with the ordinary case and the second dealing with the case where there were known special circumstances. These two factors, namely the abundance of phraseology and the breakdown of the rule into parts, led to confusion, and a restatement of the rule for modern conditions became a real need. This restatement came with the Court of Appeal decision in 1949 in *Victoria Laundry v Newman*,[829] so that today the intervening discussions of phraseology and classifications of the rule are only a matter of history and need no detailing here. **8-161**

## 2. The Rule Restated in Victoria Laundry v Newman in 1949

In *Victoria Laundry v Newman*,[830] the claimants, launderers and dyers, claimed successfully for loss of general business profits arising from the defendant's delay in delivering a boiler he had sold to them, the defendant being aware of the nature of the claimants' business and that they intended to put the boiler into use in the shortest possible time. In granting these damages the Court of Appeal restated the principles as laid down in *Hadley v Baxendale*,[831] and the relevant passage from the judgment of the court, delivered by Asquith LJ, puts the matter so clearly that it deserves full quotation. In the view of the court the propositions which emerged from the authorities as a whole were these: **8-162**

> "(1) It is well settled that the governing purpose of damages is to put the party whose rights have been violated in the same position, so far as money can do so, as if his rights had been observed. This purpose, if relentlessly pursued, would provide him with a complete indemnity for all loss de facto resulting from a particular breach,

---

823 (1854) 9 Ex. 341 at 354 to 355.

824 See, especially, Lord Sumner in *Weld-Blundell v Stephens* [1920] A.C. 956 at 983.

825 See, e.g. *Weld-Blundell v Stephens* [1920] A.C. 956 at 983, per Lord Sumner; *Elliott Steam Tug Co v Shipping Controller* [1922] 1 K.B. 127 CA at 140 per Scrutton LJ; *Admiralty Commissioners v S.S. Susquehanna* [1926] A.C. 655 at 661, per Lord Dunedin.

826 For example in *Re Polemis* [1921] 3 K.B. 560 CA.

827 See paras 8-140 and following, above.

828 They were dealt with as three up to and including the 10th edition (1927) of *Mayne on Damages*.

829 [1949] 2 K.B. 528 CA.

830 [1949] 2 K.B. 528 CA.

831 (1854) 9 Ex. 341.

however improbable, however unpredictable. This, in contract at least, is recognised as too harsh a rule. Hence,

(2) In cases of breach of contract the aggrieved party is only entitled to recover such part of the loss actually resulting as was at the time of the contract reasonably foreseeable as liable to result from the breach.

(3) What was at that time reasonably so foreseeable depends on the knowledge then possessed by the parties, or, at all events, by the party who later commits the breach.

(4) For this purpose, knowledge 'possessed' is of two kinds; one imputed, the other actual. Everyone, as a reasonable person, is taken to know the 'ordinary course of things' and consequently what loss is liable to result from a breach of contract in that ordinary course. This is the subject matter of the 'first rule' in *Hadley v Baxendale*. But to this knowledge, which a contract-breaker is assumed to possess whether he actually possesses it or not, there may have to be added in a particular case knowledge which he actually possesses, of special circumstances outside the 'ordinary course of things,' of such a kind that a breach in those special circumstances would be liable to cause more loss. Such a case attracts the operation of the 'second rule' so as to make additional loss also recoverable.

(5) In order to make the contract-breaker liable under either rule it is not necessary that he should actually have asked himself what loss is liable to result from a breach. As has often been pointed out, parties at the time of contracting contemplate not the breach of the contract, but its performance. It suffices that, if he had considered the question, he would as a reasonable man have concluded that the loss in question was liable to result.

(6) Nor, finally, to make a particular loss recoverable, need it be proved that upon a given state of knowledge the defendant could, as a reasonable man, foresee that a breach must necessarily result in that loss. It is enough … if he could foresee it was likely so to result. It is indeed enough if the loss (or some factor without which it would not have occurred) is a 'serious possibility' or a 'real danger.' For short, we have used the word 'liable' to result. Possibly the colloquialism 'on the cards' indicates the shade of meaning with some approach to accuracy."[832]

**8-163** There are two factors in this lucid restatement of principle which stand out. The first is that the test of the extent of liability is reasonable foreseeability, as stated in the second proposition and further defined in the fifth and sixth propositions. The second is that what is reasonably foreseeable depends upon knowledge, actual or imputed, as stated in the third proposition and further defined in the fourth proposition.[833] However, it is necessary next to look at the important qualifications introduced on the first of these tests by the House of Lords in *Czarnikow v Koufos, The Heron II*.[834]

## 3. THE RESTATED RULE AS QUALIFIED IN THE HERON II IN 1967

**8-164** In *The Heron II*,[835] where the House of Lords upheld the claim of charterers to recover for the shipowner's late delivery of a consignment of sugar the difference between the market prices of sugar at due delivery and at actual delivery, their Lordships subjected to a thorough examination Asquith LJ's restatement of principle in

[832] [1949] 2 K.B. 528 CA at 539 to 540.

[833] The first proposition merely states the undoubted starting rule. This has already been considered: see para.2-002, above

[834] [1969] 1 A.C. 350.

[835] [1969] 1 A.C. 350. The full title is *Czarnikow v Koufos, The Heron II* but this important decision has come to be known, for ease of reference, by the name of the ship which formed its centrepiece.

*Victoria Laundry v Newman*,[836] expressing "varying degrees of enthusiasm" for it.[837] Lord Reid was particularly critical. His main attack was on Asquith LJ's use of the test of reasonable foreseeability. "To bring in reasonable foreseeability", he said,

> "appears to me to be confusing measure of damages in contract with measure of damages in tort".[838]

While in tort

> "the defendant will be liable for any type of damage which is reasonably foreseeable as liable to happen even in the most unusual case, unless the risk is so small that a reasonable man would in the whole circumstances feel justified in neglecting it".[839]

Lord Reid was satisfied that for contract the court in *Hadley v Baxendale*:

> "did not intend that every type of damage which was reasonably foreseeable by the parties when the contract was made should either be considered as arising naturally, i.e. in the usual course of things, or be supposed to have been in the contemplation of the parties. Indeed the decision makes it clear that a type of damage which was plainly foreseeable as a real possibility but which would only occur in a small minority of cases cannot be regarded as arising in the usual course of things or be supposed to have been in the contemplation of the parties: the parties are not supposed to contemplate as grounds for the recovery of damage any type of loss or damage which on the knowledge available to the defendant would appear to him as only likely to occur in a small minority of cases."[840]

Accordingly, in Lord Reid's opinion, the proper test is whether the loss in question is:

> "of a kind which the defendant, when he made the contract, ought to have realised was not unlikely to result from the breach ... the words 'not unlikely' ... denoting a degree of probability considerably less than an even chance but nevertheless not very unusual and easily foreseeable."[841]

Having formulated the test in this way, Lord Reid then proceeded to jettison all of the related phrases which Asquith LJ had introduced in his restatement. He took exception to "liable to result" because he thought that

> "one would usually say that when a person foresees a very improbable result he foresees that it is liable to happen"[842];

he considered that:

> "in the ordinary use of language there is a wide gulf between saying that some event is not unlikely or quite likely to happen and saying merely that it is a serious possibility, a real danger, or on the cards."[843]

While far less sweeping in their condemnation of Asquith LJ's terminology, the **8-165**

---

836 [1949] 2 K.B. 528 CA.
837 The expression is Donaldson J's in *Aruna Mills v Dhanrajmal Gobindram* [1968] 1 Q.B. 655 at 668.
838 [1969] 1 A.C. 350 at 389.
839 [1969] 1 A.C. 350 at 385–386.
840 [1969] 1 A.C. 350 at 385.
841 [1969] 1 A.C. 350 at 382 to 383; and similarly at 388.
842 [1969] 1 A.C. 350 at 389.
843 [1969] 1 A.C. 350 at 390. The issue of remoteness and contemplation of the parties again reached the House of Lords in a Scottish appeal, *Balfour Beatty Construction (Scotland) Ltd v Scottish Power* 1994 S.C. (H.L.) 20; see the case the fn. at the end of para.8-191 and paras 8-199 to 8-201, below.

rest of their lordships basically agreed with Lord Reid's analysis. Thus Lord Upjohn specifically agreed that the terminology of reasonable foreseeability was to be avoided, for the assessment of damages as between contracting parties

> "should depend on their assumed common knowledge and contemplation and not on a foreseeable but most unlikely consequence"[844];

the others in effect accepted that the kinds of loss for which recovery is to be allowed are those which are not unlikely to result from breach,[845] much reliance being placed on the House's earlier decision in *Hall v Pim*,[846] which, as Lord Reid rightly said:

> "must be taken to have established that damages are not to be regarded as too remote merely because, on the knowledge available to the defendant when the contract was made, the chance of the occurrence of the event which caused the damage would have appeared to him to be rather less than an even chance."[847]

At the same time, while their Lordships were unanimous in rejecting the colloquialism "on the cards" as far too imprecise and even "capable of denoting a most improbable and unlikely event",[848] the expressions "a serious possibility" and "a real danger" commended themselves to the majority of the House as correctly giving the required shade of meaning.[849] "Liable to result" was generally regarded as a convenient, innocuous phrase which did not really advance the matter further.[850]

**8-166** Yet it is fair to say that, taken as a whole, Asquith LJ's careful restatement in *Victoria Laundry v Newman*,[851] has survived the various strictures appearing in their Lordships' speeches. For Lord Morris, Asquith LJ's "illuminating judgment" was "a most valuable analysis" of the *Hadley v Baxendale* rule[852]; for Lord Pearce, it was

> "a justifiable and valuable clarification of the principles which *Hadley v Baxendale* was intending to express."[853]

Donaldson J in *Aruna Mills v Dhanrajmal Gobindram*,[854] expressed the opinion that, subject to two qualifications introduced by their Lordships, namely the minor one of the rejection of the colloquialism "on the cards" and the major one that the references to losses as being reasonably foreseeable should now be read as referring to losses as having been in the parties' contemplation as likely to result, *Victoria*

---

844 [1969] 1 A.C. 350 at 422.

845 See [1969] 1 A.C. 350 at 406, 410–411 and 416–417, per Lords Morris, Hodson and Pearce respectively.

846 (1928) 33 Com. Cas. 324 HL. The decision is treated at some length in each of the speeches: see [1969] 1 A.C. 350 at 387–388, 405–406, 410, 414–415 and 424.

847 [1969] 1 A.C. 350 at 388.

848 [1969] 1 A.C. 350 at 425, per Lord Upjohn; see also at 390, 399 and 415.

849 [1969] 1 A.C. 350 at 399, 415 and 425, per Lords Morris, Pearce and Upjohn respectively.

850 Lord Pearce thought the words "ambiguous" but "useful as shorthand for a collection of definable ideas": [1969] 1 A.C. 350 at 415; Lord Hodson thought the expression "colourless" but one on which he did "not find it possible to improve": [1969] 1 A.C. 350 at 410–411.

851 [1949] 2 K.B. 528 CA.

852 [1969] 1 A.C. 350 at 399.

853 [1969] 1 A.C. 350 at 417; and similarly at 414.

854 [1968] 1 Q.B. 655.

*Laundry v Newman*[855] "remained unimpaired as the classic authority on the topic" of remoteness in contract.[856] Certainly, no doubts were cast upon Asquith LJ's second criterion, that liability depends upon actual or imputed knowledge, and even the objection to his first criterion of reasonable foreseeability was really that it was liable to be misunderstood rather than that it was necessarily wrong, for Lord Reid admitted that, in using the phrase "reasonably foreseeable", Asquith LJ may well have meant foreseeable as a likely result.[857]

Asquith LJ's two criteria as modified and explained by the House of Lords, that concerning likelihood and that concerning knowledge, need to be considered in more detail, but first there must be looked at a further House of Lords decision in which are put forward suggestions that meeting these criteria may yet not suffice to impose liability. **8-167**

## 4. THE IMPACT OF THE DECISION IN THE ACHILLEAS IN 2008

### (1) The decision

*The Achilleas*[858] was a claim by shipowners for the late redelivery by charterers of a ship let to them under a time charter. The ship had embarked on a final voyage which was legitimate in the sense that it was reasonably anticipated that it would be completed before the due date for redelivery had arrived. Unfortunately, the ship had encountered delays during the voyage which had led to a redelivery that had overrun the due date by nine days. A subsequent charter fixture which the shipowners had made could therefore not be fulfilled on time. Because the shipowners were unable to deliver at the contractual date and because the always volatile conditions in the shipping market were at the time extremely volatile, the new charterers were in a position to renegotiate very substantially downwards the daily rate. The shipowners' claim was for the difference between the original daily rate and the revised daily rate over the period of the new charter. **8-168**

A majority of experienced arbitrators and judges of great commercial experience at first instance and in the Court of Appeal[859] held for the shipowners. The House of Lords unanimously reversed. In doing so, the House took the opportunity, in the words of Lord Walker, **8-169**

> "to revisit some important general issues [which] are all aspects of how the rule in *Hadley v Baxendale* has been developed or modified by 150 years of case law".[860]

The five speeches indicate that on two of these general issues all were agreed. They were agreed that the extent of liability in damages depended upon what was in the contemplation of the contracting parties at the time the contract was entered into, and they were agreed that, in line with Lord Reid's analysis in *The Heron II*,

---

[855] [1949] 2 K.B. 528 CA.

[856] [1968] 1 Q.B. 655 at 668.

[857] [1969] 1 A.C. 350 at 389.

[858] [2009] 1 A.C. 61. The full title is *Transfield Shipping Inc v Mercator Shipping Inc, The Achilleas* but, as is now common, this important decision has come to be known, for ease of reference, by the name of the ship which formed its centrepiece. This had already happened with the other two key decisions of the House of Lords on remoteness of damage, *Overseas Tankship (UK) v Morts Dock and Engineering Co (The Wagon Mound)* [1961] A.C. 388 and *Czarnikow v Koufos, The Heron II* [1969] 1 A.C. 350.

[859] The arbitrators and the judges were so described by Lord Walker: at [65].

[860] [2009] 1 A.C. 61 at [66].

liability did not extend beyond results which were not unlikely and therefore did not reach that which was only reasonably foreseeable. But beyond this there was stark disagreement, with two entirely different approaches being taken to the question of recoverability.

**8-170** Lord Rodger's approach was straightforward and traditional, entirely consistent with what had gone before on the issue of remoteness of damage in contract. "Amid a cascade of different expressions", he said,[861]

> "it is important not to lose sight of the basic point that, in the absence of special knowledge, a party entering into a contract can only be supposed to contemplate the losses which are *likely* to result from the breach in question—in other words, those losses which will generally happen in the ordinary course if the breach occurs."

While he referred to losses likely to result—the italicisation of the word likely is his—rather than to losses not unlikely to result, which was Lord Reid's formulation, this must surely come to the same thing. So the question for Lord Rodger was whether the owners' loss of the particular fixture was a likely result of the breach of contract and the answer he gave was that it was not. With this approach Lady Hale was in full agreement. She said that if the appeal were to be allowed, as to which she had doubts, she would wish it to be on what she referred to as the ground identified by Lord Rodger.[862]

**8-171** Lord Hoffmann and Lord Hope approached the question to be resolved from an entirely different, and novel, direction. For them it was necessary to show that the contracting party had assumed responsibility for the particular loss which had occurred. The essence of this approach, and its difference from the traditional approach, are most clearly put by Lady Hale. In her words, one is required to ask not only whether the parties are to be taken to have had the loss within their contemplation at the time of contracting but also whether they are to be taken to have had liability for the loss within their contemplation at that time.[863] This approach did not appeal to Lady Hale. She said:

> "It seems to me that it adds an interesting but novel dimension to the way in which the question of remoteness of damage in contract is to be answered, a dimension which does not clearly emerge from the classic authorities. There is scarcely a hint of it in *The Heron II*."[864]

**8-172** This novel dimension may be seen as an attempt on the part of Lord Hoffmann to impose upon contract law damages the concept of scope of duty which he had introduced into the law of tort in the so-called *SAAMCO* decision[865]; indeed he argues from *SAAMCO* in some detail in his speech.[866] The thinking seems to be this: those consequences for which responsibility is assumed lie within the scope of the

---

861 [2009] 1 A.C. 61 at [52].

862 [2009] 1 A.C. 61 at [93]. In the hearings below the majority of the arbitrators, the trial judge and Court of Appeal had all held the loss of the particular fixture to be a not unlikely result of the breach of contract. The question of why Lord Rodger and, somewhat reluctantly, Lady Hale came to the opposite conclusion is addressed when we come to consider what likelihood of a result must be shown: see paras 8-192 and 8-193, below.

863 [2009] 1 A.C. 61 at [92]. Lady Hale refers not simply to loss and liability for loss but to, and italicises, "type of loss" and "liability for … type of loss". The significance and importance of this is considered later: see para.8-192, below.

864 [2009] 1 A.C. 61 at [93].

865 *South Australia Asset Management Corp v York Montague Ltd* [1997] A.C. 191.

866 [2009] 1 A.C. 61 at [14]–[17].

duty. Neither assumption of responsibility nor scope of duty is taken up by Lord Rodger and Lady Hale. Lord Rodger said that he had not found it necessary to explore the issues concerning *SAAMCO* and assumption of responsibility[867] while Lady Hale, having indicated that she saw the assumption of responsibility argument as novel,[868] added that she was not immediately attracted to the idea of introducing into the law of contract the scope of duty concept.[869]

It was said in a previous edition of this work that what Lord Hoffmann and Lord Hope propose is full of difficulty, uncertainty and impracticality. How are we to tell what the contracting parties are taken to be thinking about assumption of responsibility? When contracting, assumption of responsibility must be determined objectively, indeed, for it is well known that parties entering a contract are thinking of its performance rather than of its breach. Lord Hoffmann accepted that it would only be in unusual circumstances that departure from the ordinary foreseeability rule and resort to the assumption of responsibility test would be called for.[870] What then is an unusual case, a very special case, an extraordinary case, an exceptional case—word it as you will—in which the damages will depart from the norm? Two reasons were given by Lord Hoffmann in *The Achilleas* for placing that case into the extraordinary category. The one was that the loss claimed would have been completely unquantifiable at the time of contracting, the other that the general understanding of the shipping market was that the claimed loss was not a recoverable loss.[871] This, however, is all that we have to answer the question. **8-173**

Also in a previous edition of this work it was suggested that the view of Lord Hoffmann and Lord Hope did not command a clear majority so as to make it into the ratio decidendi of *The Achilleas*. This was said with some confidence as the speech of the fifth member of the court, Lord Walker, was quite ambiguous on this issue, particularly when he concluded by saying that the appeal should be allowed not only for the reasons he had given but also for the further reasons given not only by Lord Hoffmann and Lord Hope but also by Lord Rodger.[872] Hamblen J in *Sylvia Shipping Co Ltd v Progress Bulk Carriers Ltd*[873] recognised that there is confusion about the ratio on account of Lord Walker having agreed with both sides, but he came to the conclusion,[874] that, because Lord Walker agreed with Lords Hoffmann and Hope, the rationale of assumption of responsibility has the support of the majority.[875] However, as Hamblen J recognised, if one says that there was a majority for the broader approach it must equally be the case that there was a majority for the orthodox approach because Lord Walker also agreed with Lord Rodger, and given this duality the strict rules of precedent lend support to preferring the older over the newer approach. **8-174**

Yet the strict rules of precedent apart, the assumption of responsibility test ap- **8-175**

867 [2009] 1 A.C. 61 at [63].
868 See the previous paragraph.
869 [2009] 1 A.C. 61 at [93].
870 [2009] 1 A.C. 61 at [11].
871 Hamblen J usefully sets out these reasons of Lord Hoffmann in *Sylvia Shipping* [2010] 2 Lloyd's Rep. 81 at [33].
872 [2010] 2 Lloyd's Rep. 81 at [87].
873 [2010] 2 Lloyd's Rep. 81.
874 After citing the argument in this work and the contrary one in *Chitty on Contract*.
875 See his judgment at [36]–[39]. By contrast Flaux J in *ASM Shipping Ltd of India v TTMI Ltd of England, The Amer Energy* [2009] 1 Lloyd's Rep. 293 would appear to regard those favouring the orthodox approach as forming the majority, and thus providing the *ratio*: see at [17] and [18].

pears to be here to stay with us, at least for the time being,[876] because in the five years that have passed since *The Achilleas* was decided this new test has been examined and adhered to not only in a number of first instance cases[877] but also in the Court of Appeal.[878] We therefore turn to consider these developments.[879]

## (2) The aftermath of the decision

8-176 As predicted in previous editions of this work, Lord Hoffmann's and Lord Hope's speeches in *The Achilleas* were bound to bring forward defendants, and particularly shipping defendants, who would argue that the law of remoteness had been radically changed by the decision so that they could not now be liable for foreseeable losses as they had not assumed responsibility for them in the sense of agreeing to pay for them should they happen. Three cases of this nature soon appeared, the first two involving the chartering of ships and the third the leasing of aircraft, in order *ASM Shipping Ltd of India v TTMI Ltd of England, The Amer Energy*,[880] *Sylvia Shipping Co Ltd v Progress Bulk Carriers Ltd*,[881] and *Pindell Ltd v Airasia Berhad (Pindell)*.[882] The two shipping cases, which were appeals from arbitration awards by defendants in reliance on the new test put forward in *The Achilleas* and which concerned charterparties—a voyage charterparty for a single voyage in *The Amer Energy* and a time charterparty in *Sylvia Shipping*—dealt with breach of contract by the shipowner rather than by the charterer, with a breach which resulted in a loss of profit through the cancellation of charters, breach by providing the charterer with the ship late in *The Amer Energy* and breach by failure to maintain the ship, leading to delay in readiness to load, in *Sylvia Shipping*. *Pindell* is similar for aircraft and their leasing. The claimant had contracted to sell aircraft to a third party on their return by the defendant lessee at the end of the lease. On the defendant's failure to return the aircraft on time, the sale fell through.

8-177 In all three cases the judge was satisfied that the House of Lords in *The Achilleas* had no intention of laying down a completely new test for the recoverability of damages for breach of contract. For Flaux J in *The Amer Energy* the rule in

---

[876] It will be recalled that Lord Rodger in *The Achilleas* was not prepared to take a view on the propriety of an assumption of responsibility test while Baroness Hale was very much against it: see paras 8-171 and 8-169, above.

[877] *ASM Shipping Ltd of India v TTMI Ltd of England, The Amer Energy* [2009] 1 Lloyd's Rep. 293; *Sylvia Shipping Co Ltd v Progress Bulk Carriers Ltd* [2010] 2 Lloyd's Rep. 81; *Pindell Ltd v Airasia Berhad (Pindell)* [2010] EWHC 2516 (Comm).

[878] *Siemens Building Technologies FE Ltd v Supershield Ltd* [2010] 1 Lloyd's Rep. 349 CA; *John Grimes Partnership Ltd v Gubbins* [2013] EWCA Civ 37 CA.

[879] It is, however, worth setting out why the strict rules of precedent, which even in this day and age should not be disregarded, indicate that the old approach must prevail over the new. There is the rule adopted by the distinguished Lord Greene MR in *Gold v Essex County Council* [1942] 2 K.B. 293, 298 CA, when the Court of Appeal was considering the binding force on it of *Hillyer v St Bartholomew's Hospital* [1909] 2 K.B. 820 CA aid that "in a case when two members of the court base their judgments, the one on a narrow ground confined to the necessities of the decision and the other on wide propositions which go far beyond those necessities, and the third member of the court expresses his concurrence in the reasoning of both, I think it right to treat the narrow ground as the real ratio decidendi." There is also 19th and early 20th century support for the proposition that, where the House of Lords is equally divided, it is the decision appealed from that stands. For these rules of precedent, see s.9 of Ch.II of the definitive work on the subject, Cross and Harris, *Precedent in English Law*, 4th edn (Oxford: Clarendon Press, 1991).

[880] [2009] 1 Lloyd's Rep. 293.

[881] [2010] 2 Lloyd's Rep. 81.

[882] [2010] EWHC 2516 (Comm).

*Hadley v Baxendale*, as refined in subsequent cases, still ruled the day.[883] With this Hamblen J in *Sylvia Shipping* agreed, stressing the importance of its being made clear, so as to discourage *Achilleas*-based defences, that there is no new generally applicable test,[884] while Tomlinson J in *Pindell* also agreed, saying that *The Achilleas* had not effected a major change to the approach to the recoverability of contract damages.[885] In all three cases, as in *The Achilleas*, the claim was for loss of profits through loss of fixtures. In all three it was held that the case displayed no unusual or exceptional quality so that the orthodox test could not be ousted by the new thinking. The lost profit was awarded in *The Amer Energy* and in *Sylvia Shipping*; in *Pindell* it was not but only because, applying the orthodox approach, Tomlinson J found that it was a loss not likely to result.

In these shipping cases the essential difference lies in the fact that in *The Achilleas* the fixture lost was that of the shipowner and in *The Amer Energy* and *Sylvia Shipping* it was that of the charterer. Thus, while there was a general market understanding that damages for a charterer's delay in returning the ship to the shipowner are limited to the difference between charter rates and market rates, there was no similar market understanding where there is a shipowner's delay in making the ship available to the charterer Also there is the difference that, while a follow-on fixture made by a shipowner at the end of a charter can be made for any period of time however long, so that there is an unpredictable and unquantifiable element making the liability disproportionate, a fixture by way of sub-charter during the currency of a charter cannot be for longer than the period of the charter, so that the potential loss falls within fixed confines.[886] These differences are in line with Lord Hoffmann's two reasons for application of his assumption of responsibility test,[887] **8-178**

A very different type of case, where again the defence relied on the assumption of responsibility test to reduce the liability for damages, eventually surfaced in the Court of Appeal. In *John Grimes Partnership Ltd v Gubbins*,[888] the question before the court was whether a developer of land, whose development had been delayed by the failure of a consulting engineer to perform tasks which he had contracted to perform by an agreed date, could recover damages for the loss he suffered from a diminution in the market value of the development during the period that its completion was thereby delayed. The claimant was a farmer with planning permission to develop for affordable houses a field adjacent to a busy highway, with a road to be built within the site to serve the houses. It was the farmer's intention to have the road adopted by the highway authority so that it could be maintained at the public expense, and this required the authority's agreement and approval of the design of the road. The farmer employed the defendant consulting engineer to design the road by an agreed date, the defendant being well aware that this work formed an essential part of the permitted residential development. The engineer's failure to meet the agreed date delayed the development to a time when the market value of the development had fallen and the farmer successfully claimed damages for the resulting loss to him. The engineer sought to escape liability by reliance on his not having assumed responsibility for this loss but failed, the trial judge hold- **8-179**

883 [2009] 1 Lloyd's Rep. 293 at [17].
884 [2010] 2 Lloyd's Rep. 81 at [49].
885 [2010] EWHC 2516 (Comm) at [84].
886 This is how Hamblen J in *Sylvia Shipping* argues the distinction: [2010] 2 Lloyd's Rep. 81 at [73].
887 At para.8-173, above.
888 [2013] EWCA Civ 37 CA.

ing that losses arising from movements in the property market were reasonably foreseeable and that the case was not one of those unusual ones which fell outside the *Hadley v Baxendale* approach. The Court of Appeal upheld this decision, thereby confirming the propriety of using the traditional approach and with Sir David Keene, who gave the leading judgment, pointing out that it was undisputed that no evidence had been put before the trial judge to show that there was some general understanding or expectation in the property world that a person in the engineer's position would not have been taken to have assumed responsibility for losses arising from movements in the property market where there had been delay in breach of contract.[889] Here again in coming to a decision there is resort to this criterion of Lord Hoffmann for estimating the unusual or exceptional nature of a contract requiring the application of his assumption of liability test. So far there seems to have been no resort to his other criterion of unquantifiability of loss.[890] Indeed it is thought that, should the claimed loss be unquantifiable, unpredictable, uncontrollable or disproportionate,[891] in all likelihood the damages would be held to be too remote simply by application of the rule in *Hadley v Baxendale*.[892]

**8-180** Thus in the years since *The Achilleas* was decided there appear to have been no cases, either at first instance or at Court of Appeal level, in which damages have been cut down, or cut out, by the application of the assumption of responsibility test.[893] In the light of this, it is to be hoped that the time of the courts will no longer be taken up, indeed wasted, by defendants bringing forward the new test in unsuitable cases.

**8-181** It but remains to address the Court of Appeal's interesting decision in *Siemens Building Technologies FE Ltd v Supershield Ltd*,[894] where the assumption of responsibility test was applied not so as to disallow recovery for a loss likely to result but to allow recovery for a loss unlikely to result from the breach of contract. A connection on a float valve in the water tank supplying a sprinkler system in a new office building failed and water from the tank overflowed, causing extensive damage to equipment. Though the water had overflowed there were drains capable of carrying away escaping water, but the drains had become blocked. The claimant, at the end of the line of the many sub-contractors involved with the installation of the sprinkler system, had settled the claims of the parties up the contractual chain and sought to recover the amount paid in settlement from the defendant with whom the claimant had contracted to do the supply and installation work. The defendant resisted this claim on the ground that the claimant's settlement was unreasonable since there was available to the claimant the defence of remoteness of damage on the basis that a failure of the float valve was unlikely to result in a flood as the probability was that the water would escape through the drains. The distinctive feature of the case was that the float valve and the drains were both

---

889 [2013] EWCA Civ 37 CA at [25].

890 For these criteria of his see para.8-170, above.

891 The words used by Hamblen J's words in *Sylvia Shipping*: [2010] 2 Lloyd's Rep. 81 at [40].

892 Compare the irrecoverability of the profits from the exceptionally lucrative dyeing contracts in the familiar case of *Victoria Laundry v Newman*: para.8-183, below.

893 A further case in which *The Achilleas* and the assumption of responsibility test was held to have no application is *Saipol SA v Inerco Trade SA* [2014] EWHC 2211 (Comm) where there was a sale of sunflower seed oil contaminated in the shipping of it: see [2014] EWHC 2211 (Comm) at [15]–[18]. Also in *SC Confectia SA v Miss Mania Wholesale Ltd* [2014] EWCA Civ. 1484, where there was a sale of defective garments, the Court of Appeal held *The Achilleas* to have no possible application: see [2014] EWCA Civ. 1484 at [15], and [24]–[26].

894 [2010] 1 Lloyd's Rep. 349 CA.

designed to control the flow of water involved in the operation of the sprinkler system, and in the annals of remoteness in contract this feature of simultaneous failure of separate protective measures was novel. Toulson LJ, in the only reasoned judgment, regarded *Hadley v Baxendale*, as have all the other judges propelled into considering this somewhat esoteric area of contract damages,[895] as remaining the standard rule, a rule which, as he said, has been rationalised on the basis that it reflects the expectation to be imputed to the parties in the ordinary case, imposing a liability in damages only if, at the time of contracting, a reasonable person would have had damages of the kind suffered in mind as not unlikely to result from a breach. Invoking the authority of *The Achilleas* and *SAAMCO*, he reasoned that there may be cases where the court, on examining the contract and the commercial background, decides that the standard approach would not reflect the parties' reasonable expectation. Therefore even if failure of the proper operation of the float valve was unlikely to result in a flood because the probability was that the water would escape through the drains, this did not make the loss resulting from the flood too remote. The defendant was responsible for installing the sprinkler system in such a way that the water used for it was properly contained. It therefore assumed a contractual responsibility to prevent its escape, so that the flood resulting from the water escape, even if it was unlikely, was within the scope of the defendant's contractual duty to prevent.[896] It followed therefore that the settlement up the contractual chain made by the claimant was entirely reasonable. Toulson LJ accepted that in *The Achilleas*, and in *SAAMCO*, the effect of departure from the standard approach was exclusionary by relieving the contract breaker from liability for loss that was not unlikely to occur, but correctly concluded that logically the effect can be inclusionary.[897] This would mean that the assumption of liability test can operate as an alternative rather than an addition to the *Hadley v Baxenale* test.

## 5. The Degree of Likelihood Required

What is sufficiently likely within the criterion advanced by their Lordships in *The Heron II*,[898] is clearly something that will vary with the circumstances of each case.[899] In these circumstances it is proposed first to examine a few of the decided cases to show what has and what has not been held to be likely to result or, as it is generally put, not unlikely to result, and then to consider further cases in which the difficult distinction between type of loss and degree of loss is addressed. **8-182**

### (1) In general

Leaving the difficult decision in *The Achilleas* on one side for the moment, it is useful to see what degree of likelihood to result has been required by the authorities generally in order to impose liability on a contracting party. We may start with the three cases, before *The Achilleas*, which have been most intimately concerned in the modern development of the current criteria. On the facts of *Victoria Laundry* **8-183**

---

[895] See paras 8-177 and 8-178, above.
[896] [2010] 1 Lloyd's Rep. 349 CA at [45].
[897] [2010] 1 Lloyd's Rep. 349 CA at [43].
[898] [1969] 1 A.C. 350.
[899] Some of the more important types of case are considered at paras 8-211 to 8-215, below.

*v Newman*,[900] it could be said that the defendants as an engineering company should have realised "without any express intimation"[901] that it was not unlikely that launderers and dyers, buying new plant, would lose profits by a five-month delay. The claimants were held not entitled to recover for the specific loss on certain exceptionally lucrative dyeing contracts but this did not preclude them from recovering:

> "some general (and perhaps conjectural) sum for loss of business in respect of dyeing contracts to be reasonably expected, any more than in respect of laundering contracts to be reasonably expected."[902]

On the facts of *Monarch S.S. Co v Karlshamns Oljefabriker*,[903]—the case in which the expressions "serious possibility" and "real danger" were first propounded by Lord du Parcq,[904] to be later adopted by Asquith LJ in *Victoria Laundry v Newman*,[905]—it could be said that the defendants should have realised that it was not unlikely that war would break out, that embargoes would then be imposed, and that transhipment of the cargo, with its consequent expense, would thereby become necessary.[906] On the facts of *The Heron II*,[907] it could be said that the defendants should have realised that it was not unlikely that the claimants would lose a favourable market for sale if the goods were delivered late. Of the conclusions drawn in these three cases this indeed was the easiest of all to draw, for what was in issue was not the recovery of damages for a consequential loss but merely the establishment of a normal measure of damages which, in the context of delayed delivery of goods carried by sea, had been too long checked by the persistent influence of the decision in *The Parana*.[908]

**8-184** *East Ham Corporation v Bernard Sunley*,[909] decided in the House of Lords before *The Heron II*, affords a good illustration of a claimant's recovery in respect of consequences which the defendant should have realised were not unlikely to result from the breach of contract.[910] In that case defects in a building faultily constructed by the defendant had only appeared some years after its completion. When the architect had issued his final certificate the defects were not at that time discoverable on reasonable examination, but an examination at some earlier stage of the building operations would have disclosed them. Having held on liability that the claimants were only precluded from complaining of defects reasonably discoverable at the time of the final certificate, the court then held on damages that it must have been in the contemplation of the parties that the architects might fail to notice defects during the process of the work, and accordingly that the proper measure was

---

900 [1949] 2 K.B. 528 CA; facts at para.8-162, above.
901 [1949] 2 K.B. 528 CA at 543.
902 [1949] 2 K.B. 528 CA at 543.
903 [1949] A.C. 196; facts at para.8-156, above.
904 [1949] A.C. 196 at 233 and 234.
905 [1949] 2 K.B. 528 CA.
906 Where, as here, consequences following upon a new intervening force are in issue, the test of causation must also be satisfied: see paras 8-143 to 8-157, above.
907 [1969] 1 A.C. 350; facts at para.8-164, above.
908 (1877) 2 P.D. 118 CA; see paras 32-029 to 32-031, below.
909 [1966] A.C. 406.
910 See also *The Subro Valour* [1995] 1 Lloyd's Rep. 509, in the fn. at the end of para.32-042, below.

not the cost of reinstatement at the time the architect ought to have discovered the defects but the higher cost at the time the defects were in fact discovered.[911]

A further case in the House of Lords allowing recovery for damage held not too remote is *Jackson v Royal Bank of Scotland*.[912] The defendant bank had negligently sent not to the claimants, who were importers of goods for sale to customers, but to the claimants' principal customer documents which revealed the claimants' substantial profit margin on their sales to the customer causing the customer in future to buy direct from the claimants' supplier. The House of Lords rejected, as had the courts below, the defendant bank's argument that it could not have contemplated or foreseen that its disclosure would lead to the termination of the claimants' trading relationship with their customer so that the claimants' loss of profits consequent on the termination was too remote.[913] At the same time the House of Lords held that the Court of Appeal had gone wrong in limiting the bank's liability for loss of these profits to a period of one year from termination on the ground of remoteness. By limiting the recovery to one year's loss of profits the Court of Appeal would appear, said Lord Hope giving the leading speech, to have "misunderstood the effect of the rules that were identified in *Hadley v Baxendale*".[914] Accordingly, the House restored the judge's award of lost profits over a number of years, though on a decreasing basis as the likelihood that the customer would in any event have terminated the trading relationship increased, going only to the time when an award for a further year would have been too speculative.[915] **8-185**

An illustration on the other side of the line is provided by *Bates v Barrow*.[916] The defendant brokers were held to be in breach of their contractual duty to the claimants, who were Lloyd's Names, in placing cover for the claimants under policies with a Finnish insurance company which proved to be void for illegality and unenforceable against that company as it was not authorised to carry out insurance business in the United Kingdom. It was nevertheless held by Gatehouse J that the loss which would accrue to the claimants if they were unable to be indemnified by the insurers was too remote because the Finnish company was regarded on the London market as entirely respectable and solid security; that it would, in the then insurance market climate, plead its own default and refuse to honour the policies not only was not a real danger or a serious possibility—Gatehouse J used the terms interchangeably—but was "virtually unthinkable".[917] Clearly then, it was not likely to result. **8-186**

---

911 While both Lord Upjohn and Lord Pearson, adopting Asquith LJ's now discredited phrase, said that failure by the architect to notice the defective work was "on the cards" ([1966] A.C. 406 at 445 and 451 respectively), it would seem from the tenor of their speeches that they would equally have regarded such a failure as not unlikely to result.

912 [2005] 1 W.L.R. 377 HL.

913 See [2005] 1 W.L.R. 377 HL at [27]–[29].

914 [2005] 1 W.L.R. 377 HL at [25].

915 See on all this [2005] 1 W.L.R. 377 HL at [35] to [38].

916 [1995] 1 Lloyd's Rep. 680.

917 [1995] 1 Lloyd's Rep. 680 at 691, col.2.

## (2) Type of loss and degree of loss

8-187 **(a) Physical damage** The insistence of the House of Lords in *The Heron II*,[918] an insistence endorsed by the House in *The Achilleas*,[919] that for contract damages the test of reasonable foreseeability be abandoned or, at the least, be interpreted more narrowly than in tort may cause some difficulty when consideration is given to the case of physical injury to a claimant with an abnormal susceptibility, whether of the "egg-shell skull" or the "shabby millionaire" variety, or of physical damage to his property which has a similar susceptibility. For is it possible to say that such physical injury or physical damage was not unlikely to occur? Even before *The Heron II* the matter had never been clearly tested in contract because of the very frequent concurrence of a liability in tort,[920] but it is thought that, just as recovery in such cases in tort has survived *The Wagon Mound*[921] with its narrowing of the range of liability in negligence to reasonably foreseeable consequences,[922] so too recovery in such cases in contract will survive the somewhat constricting influence of *The Heron II*.[923] It is significant that in that case the House was not concerned with damage of a greater degree than could have been anticipated but with whether the type of damage, namely loss of market, was within the contemplation of the parties; this difference is indeed underlined by Lord Pearce in a revealing passage in his speech. He said:

> "I do not think that Alderson B [in *Hadley v Baxendale*] was directing his mind to whether something resulting in the natural course of events was an odds-on chance or not. A thing may be a natural (or even an obvious) result even though the odds are against it. Suppose a contractor was employed to repair the ceiling of one of the Law Courts and did it so negligently that it collapsed on the heads of those in court. I should be inclined to think that any tribunal (including the learned baron himself) would have found as a fact that the damage arose 'naturally, i.e. according to the usual course of things.' Yet if one takes into account the nights, week-ends, and vacations, when the ceiling might have collapsed, the odds against it collapsing on top of anybody's head are nearly ten to one. I do not believe that this aspect of the matter was fully considered and worked out in the judgment. He was thinking of causation and type of consequence rather than of odds."[924]

It is submitted that, in contract as in tort, it should suffice that, if physical injury or damage is within the contemplation of the parties, recovery is not to be limited because the degree of physical injury or damage could not have been anticipated.

8-188 Such cases as there are appear to point to this conclusion. In *Vaile v Hobson*,[925] an action was brought for breach of a contract to repair the carburettor of the claimant's motor lorry whereby the lorry was damaged. The defendants contended that the claimant had failed to connect the engine switch of the lorry when driving it, that under the rule in *Hadley v Baxendale*,[926] the defendants had never contemplated at the time of the contract that the carburettor would be used in a lorry

---

918 [1969] 1 A.C. 350.
919 [2009] 1 A.C. 61.
920 For cases where there is only a contractual liability for physical injury, see *Summers v Salford Corp* [1943] A.C. 283 and the other cases considered at para.5-020, above.
921 [1961] A.C. 388.
922 See paras 8-092 to 8-096, above.
923 [1969] 1 A.C. 350.
924 [1969] 1 A.C. 350 at 416–417.
925 (1933) 149 L.T. 283.
926 (1854) 9 Ex. 341.

with a disconnected engine switch, and that therefore they were not liable for damage which would not have occurred had the carburettor been used in a properly equipped lorry. Talbot J rejected this contention and held for the claimant on the ground that the damage fell within the first rule in *Hadley v Baxendale*[927]; interestingly, he used the term "direct result of the breach of contract."[928] In *Great Lakes S.S. Co v Maple Leaf Milling Co*,[929] the claimants' ship was chartered by the defendants for a voyage at the termination of which she was to proceed to the defendants' elevator to lighter. The ship was kept waiting for lightering, and while she was so waiting the water fell and she grounded on an anchor which, unknown to the parties, was in the harbour. The Privy Council upheld the claimants' claim in contract for the resulting damage to the ship. Lord Carson said:

> "It was the breach of contract in not lightering the vessel which was the immediate cause of the damage, and the fact that such damage might not have occurred if the anchor had not been sunk can make no difference. If grounding takes place in breach of contract, the precise nature of the damage incurred by grounding is immaterial."[930]

In *Vacwell Engineering Co v B.D.H. Chemicals Ltd*,[931] where, in supplying a chemical called boron tribromide to the claimants, the defendants had failed in breach of contract to warn them of the danger of explosion if the chemical came into contact with water, and a lethal explosion occurred causing serious damage to the claimants' property, this damage was held not too remote although only a minor explosion involving minor damage was reasonably foreseeable.[932] Again it was said, here by Rees J, that the damage was "the direct result of the supply of boron tribromide without an adequate warning label".[933] Significantly, this decision came after *The Heron II*.[934] Rees J indeed referred to the case and quoted the headnote to the report in the House of Lords, but he did not appear to regard anything their Lordships had said there as precluding him from coming to a decision in the claimants' favour.[935]

The strongest support to the conclusion that physical injury or damage within the **8-189**
contemplation of the parties is recoverable even if occurring to an unanticipated degree comes in the important *Parsons (Livestock) v Uttley Ingham & Co*[936] where Scarman LJ adopted the statement of that conclusion in the 13th edition of this work. The claimants ordered from the defendants, to whom their requirements were known, a hopper in which to store nuts in bulk for feeding to their top grade pig herd. Because the defendants failed to ensure that a ventilator on the hopper was open, they were in breach of the implied term in the contract that the hopper would be reasonably fit for storing nuts in a condition suitable for feeding to the pigs. The

---

927 (1854) 9 Ex. 341.

928 (1933) 149 L.T. 283 at 284.

929 (1924) 41 T.L.R. 21 PC.

930 (1924) 41 T.L.R. 21 PC at 23.

931 [1971] 1 Q.B. 88.

932 The claimants' concurrent claim in tort for negligence also succeeded; See the fn. at the end of this paragraph.

933 [1971] 1 Q.B. 88 at 106.

934 [1969] 1 A.C. 350.

935 [1971] 1 Q.B. 88 at 107. An appeal was settled, after argument before the Court of Appeal, on the basis that judgment should be entered for the claimants by consent on the concurrent claim in negligence but limited to 80 per cent of the damages: at 111 CA. Lord Denning MR is reported, at [1970] 2 All E.R. 553 CA, as saying that this result was very likely almost the same as the court itself would have arrived at, but no inference can be drawn from this that the claimants would have failed before the Court of Appeal in their claim in contract.

936 [1978] Q.B. 791 CA.

lack of ventilation caused the nuts dispensed by the hopper to be mouldy, and this condition of the nuts in its turn caused an outbreak of an intestinal infection, known as *E. coli*, which produced injury and death throughout the herd. The claimants claimed damages in respect of the death of 254 pigs, loss of profits, and expenses incurred in combating and mastering the outbreak of infection; the defendants contended that they were liable for none of these items of loss. The trial judge's finding that at the time of the contract the parties could not have contemplated that there would be a serious possibility that the feeding of mouldy pignuts would cause illness to the pigs that ate them would seem at first sight to favour the defendants' contention. Scarman LJ, however, pointed out that it was "necessary to note the essence—and the limits—of the finding"[937] of the judge, and that it was

> "not a finding that [the defendants] could not reasonably have had in contemplation that a hopper unfit for its purpose of storing food in a condition suitable for feeding to the pigs might well lead to illness".[938]

The judge had held that the assumption to be made was "of the parties asking themselves not what is likely to happen if the nuts are mouldy but what is likely to happen to the pigs if the hopper is unfit for storing the nuts suitable to be fed to them",[939] and Scarman LJ, having stated that he considered that the judge was right to make this assumption,[940] concluded:

> "It does not matter, in my judgment, if [the defendants] thought that the chance of physical injury … was slight, or that the odds were against it, provided they contemplated as a serious possibility the type of consequence, not necessarily the specific consequence, that ensued on breach. Making the assumption as to breach that the judge did, no more than common sense was needed for them to appreciate that food affected by bad storage conditions might well cause illness in the pigs fed upon it."[941]

Orr LJ agreed with the reasoning of Scarman LJ.

8-190 **(b) Economic loss** Lord Denning MR reached the same conclusion in *Parsons v Uttley Ingham*[942] as Scarman LJ but by a different route. He drew a distinction between physical injury and damage on the one hand and economic loss by way of loss of profit without such injury or damage on the other, and held that, while in the latter case there must be contemplation of the consequences as a serious possibility, in the former case it should suffice that the consequences were foreseen as a slight possibility.[943] Accordingly, since there was a slight, though not a serious, possibility that pigs might become ill if fed with mouldy pignuts, he agreed that the defendants were liable for the loss incurred through the death of the pigs and expenses incurred thereby.[944] While the two different approaches led to a common solution in the instant case, the route taken by Lord Denning MR to arrive at it is unsatisfactory. Translating the serious possibility that he posits into the now generally used test of result that is not unlikely, this leaves his slight possibility back at

937 [1978] Q.B. 791 CA at 811C.
938 [1978] Q.B. 791 CA at 811D.
939 [1978] Q.B. 791 CA at 812G.
940 [1978] Q.B. 791 CA at 812H.
941 [1978] Q.B. 791 CA at 813D to E.
942 [1978] Q.B. 791 CA.
943 [1978] Q.B. 791 CA at 802G to H and 803B to C.
944 [1978] Q.B. 791 CA at 804E to F.

the tort test, rejected for contract, of reasonable foreseeability. Yet rather than drawing uneasy distinctions between slight possibilities and serious possibilities depending upon whether the consequence in question is physical injury or damage on the one hand or economic loss on the other, surely it is better to accept the distinction between type of loss and degree of loss and apply it to physical injury or damage and economic loss alike.

Moreover, there are to be found cases which show that the distinction between type of loss and degree of loss has run over into the economic sphere. Thus *Wroth v Tyler*,[945] shows that, if there is a contemplation of a particular type of economic loss, the fact that its quantum may be much greater than could have been anticipated will not prevent recovery for the whole loss. The buyers of a house were claiming damages from the seller for his failure to complete and were held entitled[946] to claim as damages the market price of a similar house at the time of the judgment in the action, less the contract price, although the rise in house prices over the relevant period had been of an unprecedented magnitude.[947] This approach is confirmed by the Court of Appeal in *Brown v K.M.R. Services*,[948] another of the claims by Lloyd's Names against their underwriting agents. The defendants argued unsuccessfully that the catastrophic losses suffered by the claimants as a result of becoming members of high risk syndicates were too remote on the basis that the scale and magnitude of the financial disasters which struck were unprecedented and therefore unforeseeable. Since it must always have been foreseeable, and a not unlikely result, that the claimants might suffer some financial loss from their excessive exposure, it was immaterial to their liability that the degree of that loss was unforeseeable.[949] **8-191**

So finally we come back to *The Achilleas*.[950] Now there is no doubt that their Lordships accepted that the distinction between type of loss and degree of loss applied in the economic sphere in which the case before them lay. Lord Rodger addresses the contracting parties' contemplation of "the kind of loss" for which they can claim damages,[951] Lady Hale contrasts the two approaches in the case to remoteness of damage in terms of "this type of loss" and "liability for this type of loss",[952] and Lord Hoffmann specifically states that it is accepted that a contracting party can be liable for loss of "the type or kind" envisaged even if the loss is unforeseeably large.[953] In practice, however, more difficulty will arise in the categorisation of loss into types or kinds where the damage in issue is purely economic than where physical injury or damage is concerned, and it is therefore believed that the basis of the disagreement between their Lordships and all those who went before is simply that majority arbitrators, trial judge and Court of Appeal regarded the loss of the fixture as the same type of loss as the normal loss of the difference between charter and market rates and the Lords did not. **8-192**

---

945 [1974] Ch. 30.

946 See, especially, [1974] Ch. 30 at 60G to 62E.

947 The case is dealt with further at para.27-009, below.

948 [1995] 2 Lloyd's Rep. 513 CA.

949 There may also be noted the Scots case of *Balfour Beatty Construction (Scotland) Ltd v Scottish Power*, 1994 S.C. (H.L.) 20 where the claim was in respect of expenditure incurred and the Inner House of the Court of Session decided in favour of the pursuers on the ground that the loss which occurred differed only in degree and not in kind from the loss that the contracting parties must have contemplated. The House of Lords reversed, but on an anterior ground: see at paras 8-199 to 8-201, below.

950 [2009] 1 A.C. 61; considered at paras 8-168 and following, above.

951 [2009] 1 A.C. 61 at 60.

952 [2009] 1 A.C. 61 at 92.

953 [2009] 1 A.C. 61 at 21.

**8-193** What then accounts for these different views? The difference would seem to stem from whether concentration was on the market generally, leading to a finding of the same type of loss, or was on the particular contract, producing a finding of a different type of loss. When Lord Rodger expressed the view that:

> "neither party would reasonably have contemplated that an overrun of nine days would 'in the ordinary course of things' cause the owners the kind of loss for which they claim damages"[954]

he clearly had the particular fixture that had been concluded in mind. Moreover, there is support for their Lordships' view in the formative case of *Victoria Laundry v Newman*,[955] itself—a case which is indeed referred to in this connection by Lord Hoffmann—[956] where it was held, as is well known, that the contracting parties' contemplation of loss of profits in general as a serious possibility did not allow a claim for a particular loss of exceptional profits to succeed.[957] This is because such a claim is to be regarded as for a different kind or type of loss, as Stuart-Smith LJ made clear in rejecting the defendant counsel's contrary contention in his unsuccessful attempt to avoid liability for an unanticipated degree of loss in *Brown v K.M.R. Services*.[958] He said that he did not see

> "any difficulty in holding that loss of ordinary business profits are different in kind from those flowing from a particular contract which gives rise to very high profits."[959]

On the other hand, where the loss can be regarded as a general loss and not one tied to a particular contract, as for instance where the breach of contract causes to be unavailable assets which would clearly have been used for general investment, *Wroth v Tyler* and *Brown v KMR Services*,[960] should be followed and recovery allowed even if the degree of investment loss is unusual or exceptional.[961]

---

954 [2009] 1 A.C. 61 at 60.

955 [1949] 2 K.B. 528 CA. See para.8-162, above.

956 [2009] 1 A.C. 61 at [22].

957 See para.8-183, above.

958 [1995] 2 Lloyd's Rep. 513 CA. See the case at para.8-191, above.

959 [1995] 2 Lloyd's Rep. 513 CA at 542, col.1. The position is the same where the claim for lost profits on a particular contract has been by the seller of goods rather than the familiar such claim by the buyer. Thus at first instance in *North Sea Energy Holdings v Petroleum Authority of Thailand* [1997] 2 Lloyd's Rep. 418 sellers of oil failed to recover for their anticipated profit which was huge, being the difference between the price at which they were selling to their buyers and the far lower price at which they were acquiring the oil from their suppliers, because the particular contract with the suppliers was an unusual and extraordinary bargain of which the buyers had no cognisance. The Court of Appeal affirmed on an anterior point at [1999] 1 Lloyd's Rep. 483 CA. See the case further at para.25-129, below.

960 These two cases are at para.8-191, above.

961 Counsel's argument on remoteness in *Borealis AB v Geogas Trading SA* [2011] 1 Lloyd's Rep. 482 (facts at para.8-150, above) that loss of profits occurring almost a year after the incidence of the breach of contract was not the type or kind of loss for which there could be recovery ([2011] 1 Lloyd's Rep. 482 at [121(i)]) got nowhere. Remoteness is at [2011] 1 Lloyd's Rep. 482 at 48 and 120–126.

## 6. THE DEGREE OF KNOWLEDGE REQUIRED

### (1) Actual and imputed knowledge

It is often very difficult to tell, when reading a particular case, whether the court is deciding the issue under the "first rule" or the "second rule" in *Hadley v Baxendale*,[962] especially when the decision is in the claimant's favour.[963] The reason for this is that actual knowledge and imputed knowledge so easily shade into one another. That the defendant knew a particular fact may bring the second rule into play; on the other hand, knowledge of that same fact might have been imputed to him even if he had not known it, so that he would in any event have been liable under the first rule.[964] It is suggested that actual knowledge is only relevant if without that knowledge there would not have been a liability. In many cases the knowledge would have been imputed in any event because it was within "the ordinary course of things"; for instance knowledge might well be imputed in a particular case that the claimant was a launderer or a furniture dealer, or that he ran a business. Or put another way, the defendant will be taken to have known that the claimant might have been, say a furniture dealer, when he purchases a large quantity of furniture, and might therefore lose business profits by a failure or delay in delivery if no market existed in which he could repurchase.[965] Such damage is of the type ordinarily resulting from the breach of like contracts; if in fact the damage does not occur and there is no loss of business profits because the claimant is buying to furnish his own home, the defendant can just count himself fortunate. These considerations go to show that there can be no rigid division between the "first rule" and the "second rule", and that the modern re-statement of the rule as a totality is a salutary trend. A present-day manifestation of this approach appears in *Kpohraror v Woolwich Building Society*,[966] where, in an action for the wrongful dishonour by a banker of a customer's cheque, general damages under the first rule were awarded for injury to the customer's credit but special damages under the second rule were refused for trading losses which the banker could not have anticipated. Evans LJ in a judgment concurred in by his brethren said: 8-194

> "The contentions for both parties were presented as if in a straitjacket imposed by the strict application of the rule in *Hadley v Baxendale* so as to require the separate consideration of each of the two limbs. … I would prefer to hold that the starting point for any application of *Hadley v Baxendale* is the extent of the shared knowledge of both parties when the contract was made. … When that is established, it may often be the case that the first

---

962 (1854) 9 Ex. 341.

963 Thus in *Borries v Hutchinson* (1865) 18 C.B. N.S. 445 the decision appears to be under the first rule, but Brett MR's explanation of it in *Grébert-Borgnis v Nugent* (1885) 15 Q.B.D. 85 CA at 90–91 would put it under the second. In the latter case liability for loss of sub-sale profits was admitted, but whereas Brett MR would have placed these damages under the first rule (at 89), Bowen LJ seemed to favour the second (at 93). See, too, Blackburn J in *Elbinger Aktiengesellschaft v Armstrong* (1874) L. R. 9 (QB) 473 who started off rather on the basis of the first rule (at 477) but then decided on the second (at 479).

964 See Lord Pearce in *The Heron II* [1969] 1 A.C. 350 at 416: "According to whether one categorises a fact as basic knowledge or special knowledge the case may come under the first part of the rule or the second. For that reason there is sometimes difference of opinion as to which is the part which governs a particular case and it may be that both parts govern it."

965 The existence or non-existence of a market is a vital factor, as Devlin J pointed out in *Kwei Tek Chao v British Traders & Shippers* [1954] 2 Q.B. 459 at 489.

966 [1996] 4 All E.R. 119 CA.

and second parts of the rule overlap, or at least that it is unnecessary to draw a clear line of demarcation between them."[967]

Indeed Devlin J in *Biggin v Permanite*,[968] said that the division of *Hadley v Baxendale*,[969] into two rules "has sometimes proved misleading"; since the restatement in *Victoria Laundry v Newman*,[970] there is "only one area of indemnity to be explored".[971] And the common ground between the two rules, or the two limbs of the rule, is again emphasised by the House of Lords in *Jackson v Royal Bank of Scotland*.[972]

**8-195** One reason why the division of the rule can lead to confusion is pointed out by Devlin J in *Biggin v Permanite*,[973] a case which concerned a sale of goods which the claimant buyer intended, to the defendant seller's knowledge, to resell. It is that damages under the second rule in *Hadley v Baxendale*,[974] are sometimes referred to as if the rule embodied a specially beneficial measure to a claimant who would fulfil the necessary conditions. No doubt it is true that the second rule generally operates in the claimant's favour, but Devlin J thought it was capable of operating in either direction.[975] He used the sub-sale by way of illustration. A profitable sub-sale which fails through the breach is often not allowed to augment the damages because it is not within the contemplation of the parties, while conversely an unprofitable sub-sale which is carried through despite the breach cannot, if outside the parties' contemplation, reduce the damages measured by a notional loss in market value.

"If, however, a sub-sale is within the contemplation of the parties, I think that the damages must be assessed by reference to it, whether the plaintiff likes it or not. … If it is the plaintiff's liability to the ultimate user that is contemplated as the measure of damages and

---

967 [1996] 4 All E.R. 119 CA at 127g to 128a. See also, e.g. *Hall v Meyrick* [1957] 2 Q.B. 455 CA, where Ashworth J held the claim to be "one which may be said to be within both parts of the rule": at 471 (this was reversed on other grounds by the Court of Appeal); and Singleton LJ in *Compania Naviera Maropan v Bowaters* [1955] 2 Q.B. 68 CA at 93: "The damages sustained in this case fall under one, or under both, of the limbs of the rule." See *Hall v Pim* (1928) 33 Com. Cas. 324 HL at 335, where Lord Shaw criticised the "ultra-analysis" of dividing the rule in *Hadley v Baxendale* (1854) 9 Ex. 341 into two parts, and *The Heron II* [1969] 1 A.C. 350 at 385, where Lord Reid said he did "not think that it was intended that there were to be two rules or that two different standards or tests were to be applied"; see at 421, per Lord Upjohn.

968 [1951] 1 K.B. 422 at 436; reversed by the Court of Appeal [1951] 2 K.B. 314 CA, on grounds not affecting these remarks.

969 (1854) 9 Ex. 341.

970 [1949] 2 K.B. 528 CA.

971 It can indeed be said to be largely an academic question whether recovery for a contractual loss falls under the first or the second rule in *Hadley v Baxendale* except, formerly, in one case, namely in relation to the recovery of interest for the non-payment of money where the law developed in a curious way. Interest was held to be recoverable as damages as of right if falling within the second rule (*Wadsworth v Lydall* [1981] 1 W.L.R. 598 CA) but not if within the first (*The President of India v La Pintada Compania Navigacion* [1985] A.C. 104). The House of Lords in *Sempra Metals Ltd v Inland Revenue Commissioners* [2008] A.C. 561 has now held such a distinction to be an error: see para.19-065, below.

972 [2005] 1 W.L.R. 377 HL (facts at para.8-185, above): see in particular the speech of Lord Walker at [46]–[49].

973 [1951] 1 K.B. 422.

974 (1854) 9 Ex. 341.

975 [1951] 1 K.B. 422 at 436.

it is in fact used without injurious results so that no such liability arises, the plaintiff could not claim the difference in market value, and say that the sub-sale must be disregarded."[976]

And the same point was made in *The Heron II*[977] by Lord Pearce where he said:

"Of course the extension of the horizon need not always increase the damage; it might introduce a knowledge of particular circumstances, e.g. a sub-contract, which show that the plaintiff would in fact suffer less damage than a more limited view of the circumstances might lead one to expect."[978]

*Louis Dreyfus Trading Ltd v Reliance Trading Ltd*,[979] illustrates precisely the operation of the rule that damages must be assessed by reference to a sub-sale in the contemplation of the parties even if this does not suit the claimant. Since the parties to the sale of a cargo of sugar had in their contemplation a sub-sale by the buyer already made and on which the buyer might eventually have made a profit, the sub-sale, it was held, could be brought into account against the buyer.[980] *Duncan Investments Ltd v Underwood*[981] also is illustrative of the situation where what was within the contemplation of the parties led to a reduction rather than an increase in the damages. A portfolio of properties had been bought by the claimant on the negligent advice of estate agents as to the prices which the individual properties would realise. The properties, if sold individually, would realise much more than if sold all together. Since the estate agents had advised on individual prices and knew that the claimant's intention was to sell the properties individually, the individual prices were the proper prices to take for the damages assessment. In the particular circumstances this factor led, on appeal, to a lower award, being based on the amount paid by the claimant for the properties less their individual resale values and not, as was held below, less their resale value as a single portfolio. **8-196**

## (2) Extent to which knowledge will be imputed

Knowledge will be imputed, according to the test in *Victoria Laundry v Newman*,[982] if it is in "the ordinary course of things", and it would seem that somewhat similar criteria will apply in deciding what the defendant should have known as apply to deciding what he should have realised would be not unlikely to result.[983] Each case, however, must be taken on its own facts in deciding what knowledge is to be **8-197**

---

976 [1951] 1 K.B. 422 at 436.

977 [1969] 1 A.C. 350.

978 [1969] 1 A.C. 350 at 416; his italics. See similarly *Trans Trust S.P.R.L. v Danubian Trading Co* [1952] 2 Q.B. 297 CA at 306, per Denning LJ: "The buyer knew that the sellers could not obtain the goods at all unless the credit was provided. The foreseeable loss was the loss of profits, no matter whether the market price of the goods went up or down. It is, therefore, the proper measure of damages."

979 [2004] 2 Lloyd's Rep. 243.

980 However, it was for the defendant seller to demonstrate on the evidence that the impact of the sub-sale was such that the prima facie measure of damages was inappropriate, and the matter was sent back to the arbitral tribunal initially deciding the case to give the defendant a chance to prove this, the arbitrators having applied the prima facie measure without considering the possibility that it might be displaced. See the case further at para.25-110, below.

981 [1998] P.N.L.R. 754 CA.

982 [1949] 2 K.B. 528 CA.

983 Buckley J's comments to the contrary in *Diamond v Campbell-Jones* [1961] Ch. 22 at 26, have lost much of their force since the disapproval of Asquith LJ's expression "on the cards" in *The Heron II* [1969] 1 A.C. 350.

imputed to the defendant: all that can be pointed to three factors which are relevant in arriving at a decision.

8-198 (1) The business or profession of the parties, and particularly of the claimant, may throw light upon what knowledge can be imputed. Thus the authorities show a trend towards giving damages for loss of business or resale profits against a seller of goods but not against a carrier of goods.[984] As Lord Upjohn pointed out in *The Heron II*,[985]

> "a carrier of goods ... is not carrying on the same trade as the consignor of goods and his knowledge of the practices and exigencies of the other's trade may be limited and less than between buyer and seller of goods who probably know far more about one another's business".[986]

And it seems that a seller of land also is less likely to be held liable for loss of such profits than is a seller of goods. In *Diamond v Campbell-Jones*,[987] the buyer of a leasehold house in Mayfair, who was in business as a dealer in real estate and had bought and converted a number of central London town houses, claimed as damages, in an action against the repudiating seller, the profit he would have made upon the conversion of the house into flats and offices. Buckley J, in rejecting this claim and awarding only the normal measure of contract price less market price, said:

> "I cannot believe that Lord Wright, in ... the *Monarch Steamship Co* case,[988] meant that anyone entering into a contract must be treated as having constructive notice of the nature of the other party's business, or of its probable bearing on the loss which that other party might suffer in consequence of a breach of contract. In some cases the nature or the subject-matter of a contract or of its terms may be such as to make it clear that one of the parties is entering into the contract for the purpose of a particular business, and the circumstances may be such that the court will infer that the other party must have appreciated that this was so. It seems to me, however, that this can rarely be the case where the contract is for the sale of land. The vendor of a shop equipped for use as a butcher's shop would not, in my judgment, be justified by that circumstance alone in assuming, and ought not to be treated as knowing, that the purchaser would intend to use it for the business of a butcher rather than that of a baker or candlestick-maker, at any rate in the absence of covenants or other forms of restriction confining its use to butcher's business. Special circumstances are necessary to justify imputing to a vendor of land a knowledge that the purchaser intends to use it in any particular manner."[989]

8-199 Two short passages from Lord Wright in the *Monarch Steamship Co* case[990] had been read by Buckley J in *Diamond v Campbell-Jones*,[991] first,

> "the court will ... assume that the parties as business men have all reasonable acquaintance with the ordinary course of business"

and secondly,

---

984 See the cases at paras 8-212 to 8-214, below.

985 [1969] 1 A.C. 350.

986 [1969] 1 A.C. 350 at 424, echoing a very similar comment of Asquith LJ in *Victoria Laundry v Newman* [1949] 2 K.B. 528 CA at 537. For carriage of goods cases in the context of remoteness see paras 8-214 and 8-215, below.

987 [1961] Ch. 22.

988 At para.8-156, above.

989 [1961] Ch. 22 at 35–36.

990 At para.8-156, above.

991 [1961] Ch. 22 at 34.

"as reasonable business men each must be taken to understand the ordinary practices and exigencies of the other's trade or business".

These two passages were reintroduced in *Balfour Beatty Construction (Scotland) Ltd v Scottish Power*,[992] an appeal from Scotland, in support of the pursuers' claim for damages. Since after *The Heron II*,[993] in the late 1960s the issue of remoteness of damage in contract had not reached the House of Lords again until *Balfour Beatty*, and since the House reversed the Inner House of the Court of Session which in turn had reversed the Lord Ordinary, the case is one of some significance.

The pursuers were engaged in constructing in concrete a roadway together with **8-200** an aqueduct. The defenders provided under contract to the pursuers a supply of electricity to run the pursuers' plant for the mixing of the concrete. When the first stage of the aqueduct was nearing completion the plant ceased to operate because of a failure of the electricity supply and the construction work had to be halted. As the operation required a continuous pour to avoid the rapid hardening of the concrete, the interruption of the pour and the consequent hardening of the concrete led to a condemnation of the whole operation, so that all that had been done for the first stage had to be demolished and work had to start again. The pursuers raised an action against the defenders claiming damages for breach of contract which for all practical purposes comprised the cost of the demolition and reconstruction. The Lord Ordinary held for the defenders on the ground that the pursuers' loss went beyond what the defenders might reasonably have contemplated. The Inner House of the Court of Session reversed on the ground that it must have been in the contemplation of the parties that the interruption of the electricity supply would call for some remedial measures and that the measures required differed only in degree and not in kind from those contemplated.[994] The House of Lords in turn reversed, restoring the Lord Ordinary and effectively adopting his reasoning, that it was not in the contemplation of the parties that the interruption of the electricity supply would lead to the necessity of remedial works as distinct from an interruption of production. For the House of Lords everything turned on what the defenders were to be taken to know about the operation of the pursuers' business.

Lord Jauncey, who gave the only speech concurred in by his brethren, said that **8-201** he did not understand Lord Wright in the *Monarch Steamship Co* case,[995] to be laying down a general rule

"that in all circumstances contracting parties are presumed to have reasonable knowledge of the course of business conducted by each other".[996]

He continued:

"It must always be a question of circumstances what one contracting party is presumed to know about the business activities of the other. No doubt the simpler the activity of the one, the more readily can it be inferred that the other would have reasonable knowledge thereof. However, when the activity of A involves complicated construction or manufacturing techniques, I see no reason why B who supplies a commodity which A intends to use in the course of those techniques should be assumed, merely because of the order for the commodity, to be aware of the details of all the techniques undertaken by A

---

992 1994 S.C. (H.L.) 20.
993 [1969] 1 A.C. 350.
994 For this aspect of the case see the footnote at the end of para.8-191, above.
995 See at para.8-199, above.
996 1994 S.C. (H.L.) 20 at 31G.

and the effect thereupon of any failure of or deficiency in that commodity. Even if the Lord Ordinary had made a positive finding that continuous pouring was a required part of industrial practice it would not follow that in the absence of any other evidence suppliers of electricity ... should have been aware of that practice."[997]

**8-202** (2) Where the defendant defaults in supplying a self-contained profit-earning whole, the knowledge imputed may be greater than where his default is in supplying part of that whole, being, as Asquith LJ said in *Victoria Laundry v Newman*,[998] "significant in so far as it bears on the capacity of the supplier to foresee the consequences of non-delivery". But he also stated that in the court's view:

> "there is no intrinsic magic in this connection, in the whole as against a part. ... If it is clear from the nature of the part (or the supplier of it is informed) that its non-delivery will have the same effect as non-delivery of the whole, his liability will be the same as if he had defaulted in delivering the whole."

And in the particular case, damages for loss of business profits were awarded where the non-delivery had been of a part only.

**8-203** (3) Where the defendant defaults in supplying or accepting goods he will be taken, by the weight of authority, to have contemplated that changes might arise in the state of the market. As Parker LJ said in *Interoffice Telephones v Freeman*,[999] where the hirer of an office telephone installation had repudiated the contract:

> "Whether it be a hiring agreement or a contract for the sale of goods, where the purchaser has failed to take delivery, the defaulting party must contemplate that damages will vary according to the state of the market, including questions of supply and demand."

On the other hand in *Robophone Facilities v Blank*,[1000] where the facts were basically similar, Lord Denning MR expressed doubts as to the correctness of Parker LJ's statement, taking the view that the defaulting hirer need only contemplate that his suppliers' stock would be such as to meet current demand.[1001] However, the view of Lord Denning MR is at odds not only with the decision in *Interoffice Telephones v Freeman*,[1002] itself but with the sale of goods cases of *Re Vic Mill*,[1003] and *Thompson v Robinson*[1004]; moreover, where the default is in the supply rather than in the acceptance of goods, it is clear that the supplier is taken to contemplate that there may not be an available market in which the other contracting party can acquire substitute goods. Indeed it would seem that Lord Denning MR's view was in all likelihood coloured by his well-evidenced concern for the protection of hirers and hire-purchasers.[1005]

---

997 1994 S.C. (H.L.) 20 at 31 to 32B. See, too, at para.28-027, below, *City and Metropolitan Properties v Greycroft* [1987] 1 W.L.R. 1085, especially at 1089B to H (knowledge by lessor of lessee's use).

998 [1949] 2 K.B. 528 CA at 543–544.

999 [1958] 1 Q.B. 190 CA at 202.

1000 [1966] 1 W.L.R. 1428 CA.

1001 [1966] 1 W.L.R. 1428 CA at 1437.

1002 [1958] 1 Q.B. 190 CA; facts at para.26-015, below. The majority in *Robophone Facilities v Blank* [1966] 1 W.L.R. 1428 CA, were able to bypass the issue by upholding, Lord Denning MR dissenting, the contracting parties' provision for liquidated damages: see para.16-096, below, and further at para.26-016, below.

1003 [1913] 1 Ch. 465 CA; facts at para.25-130, below.

1004 [1955] Ch. 177; facts at para.25-130, below.

1005 See paras 26-014 to 26-022, below.

### (3) Effect of actual knowledge

Where actual knowledge is required to impose liability upon the defendant for particular losses, he must have that knowledge at the time of entering into the contract; knowledge after this time, although before breach, is not enough. This is clear from Asquith LJ's propositions in *Victoria Laundry v Newman*[1006] and is obviously correct.[1007] Bramwell B in *Gee v Lancashire & Yorkshire Ry*,[1008] suggested that in the course of the performance of a contract one party might give notice to the other of any particular consequence which would result from the breaking of the contract, and then have a right to say: **8-204**

> "If you, after that notice, persist in breaking the contract, I shall claim the damages which will result from the breach."

This view is wrong.[1009]

A more difficult question is whether the revelation of facts by the claimant to the defendant, in order to show him that an extraordinary loss will occur if the defendant is in breach of his contract, will per se involve the defendant in liability for such loss. This matter was considered in a number of cases following soon after *Hadley v Baxendale*.[1010] First, Willes J in *British Columbia Saw Mill Co v Nettleship*,[1011] said: **8-205**

> "The mere fact of knowledge cannot increase the liability. The knowledge must be brought home to the party sought to be charged, under such circumstances that he must know that the person he contracts with reasonably believes that he accepts the contract with the special condition attached to it… Knowledge on the part of the carrier is only important if it forms part of the contract. It may be that the knowledge is acquired casually from a stranger, the person to whom the goods belong not knowing or caring whether he had such knowledge or not. Knowledge, in effect, can only be evidence of fraud, or of an understanding by both parties that the contract is based upon the circumstances which are communicated."

In *Horne v Midland Ry*,[1012] similar views were expressed, both in the lower court by Keating J[1013] and on appeal by Martin and Lush BB,[1014] although Blackburn J

---

1006 [1949] 2 K.B. 528 CA.

1007 Similarly, *Hydraulic Engineering Co v McHaffie* (1878) 4 Q.B.D. 670 CA at 676, per Brett LJ. In the absence of any English decisions on the point, the Australian case of *Kollman v Watts* [1963] V.L.R. 396 provides a neat illustration of the rule that the defendant's liability cannot be increased through the acquisition of knowledge between time of contracting and time of breach.

1008 (1860) 6 H. & N. 211 at 218.

1009 In *Jackson v Royal Bank of Scotland* [2005] 1 W.L.R. 377 HL (facts at para.8-185, above) the House of Lords corrected the Court of Appeal's "error of principle" (at [36]) and confirmed that the time for assessing what is within the parties' reasonable contemplation—to which their knowledge would be relevant—is the time of the making of the contract and not, as the Court of Appeal had held, the time of its breach. Lord Hope, making the leading speech, pointed out that this clear rule gave the parties the opportunity to limit their liability in damages when they are making their contract: see [2005] 1 W.L.R. 377 HL at [35] and [36].

1010 (1854) 9 Ex. 341.

1011 (1868) L.R. 3 C.P. 499 at 509.

1012 (1873) L.R. 8 C.P. 131, affirming (1872) L.R. 7 C.P. 583.

1013 (1872) L.R. 7 C.P. 583 at 591 to 592: "I think, giving the fullest effect to *Hadley v Baxendale*, and the rule there laid down, but which ought not to be extended, we cannot hold the defendants liable in respect of a loss resulting from an exceptional state of things which was not communicated to them at the time. There must, if it be sought to charge the carrier with consequences so onerous, be distinct

and Cleasby B reserved their opinion.[1015] The same view was again put forward by the court in *Elbinger Aktiengesellschaft v Armstrong*.[1016]

**8-206** These dicta, however, have long been suspect, and in *The Heron II*,[1017] Lord Upjohn expressed his disagreement with them and his view that they should not be followed.[1018] He said:

> "If parties enter into the contract with knowledge of some special circumstances, and it is reasonable to infer a particular loss as a result of those circumstances that is something which both must contemplate as a result of a breach. It is quite unnecessary that it should be a term of the contract."[1019]

In *The Pegase*[1020] Robert Goff J considered that "the decided cases appear to support the opinion so expressed".[1021] Moreover, in no case has a defendant with actual notice of special circumstances been held not liable for damage, which was not unlikely to result on the basis of that notice, on the ground that the notice had not been made part of the contract. In *British Columbia Saw Mill Co v Nettleship*,[1022] and *Horne v Midland Ry*,[1023] the defendant succeeded on the ground that no adequate actual notice had been given to him; in *Elbinger Aktiengesellschaft v Armstrong*,[1024] the claimant was able to succeed even in the absence of actual notice of the special circumstances. It is submitted, in agreement with Lord Upjohn, that it goes too far to require that the defendant's assent to take the risk of the extra liability must be made a term of the contract, for it is then approaching the status of a warranty, and comes dangerously near to destroying the whole doctrine of notice. Thus what would be the effect of an oral notice upon a written contract, and particularly upon a written contract which the law required to be in writing for its enforceability?[1025] The doctrine of notice can stand without being rigidly confined in this way. No doubt the idea behind making the assent of the parties a term of the contract is to safeguard the defendant who had the knowledge but did not wish to accept the risk. If the knowledge comes casually from someone other than the claimant, then on any view the defendant would not be liable. If, on the other hand, the knowledge does come from the claimant, either with or without the express statement that he will hold the defendant liable for the consequences—and the difficult case is where there is no such express statement—then the defendant is always entitled to reply that he is not prepared to accept the risk. If he fails to take any such action the law must hold him liable. The fact that there are no cases in which the defendant has been made liable when he clearly had no intention of accepting the risk attached to the special circumstances goes to show that no general practical

---

evidence that he had notice of the facts, and assented to accept the contract upon those terms." Willes J said (at 591) that he adhered to his earlier remarks (quoted in text) in *British Columbia Saw Mill Co v Nettleship* (1868) L.R. 3 C.P. 499.

1014 (1873) L.R. 8 C.P. 131 at 139 and 145 respectively.

1015 (1873) L.R. 8 C.P. 131 at 141 and 146–147 respectively.

1016 (1874) L.R. 9 Q.B. 473 at 478.

1017 [1969] 1 A.C. 350.

1018 [1969] 1 A.C. 350 at 421 to 422.

1019 [1969] 1 A.C. 350 at 422.

1020 [1981] 1 Lloyd's Rep. 175.

1021 [1981] 1 Lloyd's Rep. 175 at 182, col.2.

1022 (1868) L.R. 3 C.P. 499.

1023 (1873) L.R. 8 C.P. 131.

1024 (1874) L.R. 9 Q.B. 473.

1025 In *Hydraulic Engineering Co v McHaffie* (1878) 4 Q.B.D. 670 CA the contract was written but an oral notice was held sufficient to attract damages under the second rule.

hardship results. One reason for this may be that defendants, particularly carriers and the like, have in the past often imposed an express limitation of liability.

However, a defendant will still only be liable for damage resulting from special circumstances when those special circumstances have been brought home to him in such a way as to show that he has accepted, or is taken to have accepted, the risk. Not only must the parties contemplate that the damage resulting from the special circumstances may occur, but they must further contemplate that the defendant is taking the risk of being liable for such consequences should they occur.[1026] Normally the two run together, but not necessarily. Thus in *Muhammad v Ali*,[1027] in *Trans Trust S.P.R.L. v Danubian Trading Co*,[1028] and in *Wadsworth v Lydall*,[1029] damages have been properly awarded in contract in respect of loss arising from the claimant's impecuniosity because his impecuniosity was in the contemplation of the parties[1030]; by the same token the circumstances might dictate a refusal of such damages because, although the fact of the claimant's impecuniosity was known to both parties, liability for loss arising therefrom was not in their contemplation.[1031] **8-207**

## 7. THE OVERALL REQUIREMENTS OF PUBLIC POLICY

Over and above the contemplation of the parties there is the overall public policy of the law: this has sometimes, although very occasionally, prevented recovery even for damage that could be said to have been in the parties' contemplation. Two very different sets of such cases appear in this connection.[1032] **8-208**

---

[1026] *Mulvenna v Royal Bank of Scotland Plc* [2003] EWCA Civ 1112 CA is a case where, in holding against the claimant, the court relied on the need to show that the defendant accepted the risk to which the special circumstances gave rise. See especially at [2003] EWCA Civ 1112 CA at [26]; the passage from the text above was cited at [2003] EWCA Civ 1112 CA at [25]. See *Robophone Facilities v Blank* [1966] 1 W.L.R. 1428 CA at 1448, per Diplock LJ.

[1027] [1947] A.C. 414 PC.

[1028] [1952] 2 Q.B. 297 CA.

[1029] [1981] 1 W.L.R. 598 CA.

[1030] See *Aruna Mills v Dhanrajmal Gobindram* [1968] 1 Q.B. 655 (facts at para.25-056 below), where the claimant recovered for loss arising from devaluation of the Indian rupee because, although at that time damage from fluctuations in currency values was ordinarily too remote, this devaluation was in the circumstances in the contemplation of the parties.

[1031] Conversely, though exceptionally, it would seem that a defendant can be liable for special loss even where he has no knowledge of the special circumstances which have made such loss likely to result from his breach. This would be so, according to Diplock LJ in *Robophone Facilities v Blank* [1966] 1 W.L.R. 1428 CA at 1448, if the defendant had expressly undertaken, as a term of the contract, to be responsible for all actual loss to the claimant occasioned by his breach, whatever that loss might turn out to be. In particular he thought that a stipulated sum to be paid on breach would be liquidated damages, as opposed to a penalty, if it was a genuine pre-estimate of the loss which was in fact likely to result even though it might not be in line with the loss which the defendant could have anticipated as likely to result in the ordinary course of things: at 1448. Compare the possibility of taking irrecoverable losses into account to support a claim for specific relief, at para.16-023, below (in a footnote).

[1032] A third set of cases which featured in earlier editions up to 1988, namely cases where the claimant was debarred by the rule in *Bain v Fothergill* (1874) L.R. 7 H.L. 158 from claiming for his loss of bargain, has been eliminated. This is because that rule has been abolished: for details of the rule and its demise see the footnotes to para.27-005, below.

## (1) Where the claimant sues in respect of non-pecuniary injury to feelings or reputation

8-209 In much earlier editions of this textbook this category of case was included.[1033] Then damages in contract for mental distress made their appearance with the decisions in *Jarvis v Swan Tours*,[1034] and *Jackson v Horizon Holidays*,[1035] and such were the great strides that this new liability began to make that such damages seemed to have become a securely established feature of English contract law. The category was therefore discarded from the editions which followed.[1036] But then came a downturn in the cases allowing damages for mental distress in contract and because such damages, though not gone from the law, became restricted to a particular type of contract the category was reinstated in recent editions[1037] and is retained in this. The details of these oscillations appear elsewhere.[1038] Bingham LJ stated the general rule, which he accepted was not absolute, in this way in *Watts v Morrow*[1039]:

> "A contract-breaker is not in general liable for any distress, frustration, anxiety, displeasure, vexation, tension or aggravation which his breach of contract may cause to the innocent party. This rule is not, I think, founded on the assumption that such reactions are not foreseeable, which they surely are or may be, but on considerations of policy."[1040]

Nor, again as a matter of policy, may injury to reputation be recovered in contract; on this *Addis v Gramophone Co*,[1041] is the classic authority. However, the validity of *Addis*, both in relation to injury to feelings and to non-pecuniary injury to reputation, is coming under a certain amount of scrutiny at the highest appellate level.[1042]

## (2) Where but for the claimant's prior wrong he would have suffered no damage from the defendant's breach of contract

8-210 At the time of the defendant's breach of contract there may already be in existence a wrongful act of the claimant which is a contributory cause of the damage. From the point of view of causation it is the defendant's act which causes the damage, operating as it does upon a state of affairs already affected by the claimant's act. It should only be the wrongfulness of the claimant's act which leads the courts to deny him recovery as a matter of policy. The leading case is *Weld-Blundell v Stephens*,[1043] the facts of which have already been given but which are of sufficient importance to justify setting them out again in the present connection. The claimant, when employing the defendant chartered accountant to investigate the affairs of a company, libelled certain officials of the company in his letter of instructions to the defendant. This letter came to the officials' knowledge as a result of the defendant's negligence in leaving it at the company's office, and in a libel action

---

[1033] The editions of 1961 and 1972.
[1034] [1973] Q.B. 233 CA.
[1035] [1975] 1 W.L.R. 1468 CA.
[1036] The editions of 1980 and 1988.
[1037] The editions of 1997 and 2003.
[1038] See paras 5-023 and following, above.
[1039] [1991] 1 W.L.R. 1421 CA.
[1040] [1991] 1 W.L.R. 1421 CA at 1445F.
[1041] [1909] A.C. 488.
[1042] See paras 5-031 to 5-035, above.
[1043] [1920] A.C. 956.

against the now claimant the officials recovered heavy damages. These damages the claimant sought to recover in an action for breach of contract against the defendant, together with the costs he had had to pay and had himself incurred in the prior action. The House of Lords, by a bare majority, held that he could recover only nominal damages upon two grounds. The ground which is the relevant one here, and the one for which the case is less well known,[1044] is variously framed in the majority speeches in terms of cause and in terms of policy. Lord Sumner based his decision upon cause, regarding the claimant's letter as the *causa causans* of his damage, and the defendant's failure to exercise care with the letter as the *causa sine qua non*.[1045] Lord Dunedin on the other hand based his decision upon policy, upon the rule that

> "a man cannot recover damages because he has had to make reparation for a wrongful act committed by himself".[1046]

Lord Wrenbury, however, is found to support both views, but with more accent on that of cause.[1047] In this uncertainty of ratio decidendi, it is submitted that the policy ground is preferable for the reasons given above. Nevertheless, in the two cases following and applying their Lordships' decision, *Bradstreets v Mitchell*,[1048] and *Howard v Odhams Press*,[1049] the court has picked out and relied upon the causal ground.[1050] Both cases again concerned breach of contractual obligation not to disclose information which revealed that the claimant had committed a wrong: in the former, as in the parent case, the revelation was that the claimant had libelled a third party who thereupon successfully sued him, while in the latter the revelation was that the claimant had committed a fraud which resulted in expulsion from his trade union and inability to obtain further employment. In both cases only nominal damages were recovered.[1051]

## 8. Types of Contract in Which the Rule in Hadley v Baxendale Has Been Developed

It is not possible to detail every type of case in which the rule in *Hadley v Baxendale*,[1052] has been applied, but there are two types of contract in which it has had a greater reception than in others and to which it owes much for its development. These merit some consideration.[1053] **8-211**

---

1044 The other ground is dealt with at para.8-146, above.
1045 [1920] A.C. 956 at 981.
1046 [1920] A.C. 956 at 976.
1047 [1920] A.C. 956 at 998.
1048 [1933] Ch. 190.
1049 [1938] 1 K.B. 1 CA.
1050 See, especially, *Howard v Odhams Press* [1938] 1 K.B. 1 CA at 48, per Greene LJ.
1051 A case formerly important in tort and analogous to these is *Neville v London Express Newspaper* [1919] A.C. 368 where the result was properly framed in terms of policy and cause was not relied on: see the footnote at the end of para.8-131, above.
1052 (1854) 9 Ex. 341.
1053 Cases outside these two types of contract on the issue of remoteness will be found in the later chapters dealing with particular contracts. See, e.g. *Pilkington v Wood* [1953] Ch. 770, at para.34-013, below (claim by client against solicitor for negligence); *Silvey v Pendragon* [2001] I.R.L.R 685 CA, at para.33-006, below in the penultimate footnote (claim by employee against employer for wrongful dismissal).

## (1) Breach of contract by seller of goods

8-212 Many cases have dealt with the situation of a seller of goods making default by non-delivery, delayed delivery, or breach of warranty, with the result that the buyer has been put in breach of a resale contract that he has made with a third party. The buyer has then claimed successfully or unsuccessfully loss of profit on the resale,[1054] sometimes in addition the compensation he had been obliged to pay his sub-buyer,[1055] and sometimes, even further, the costs he had incurred in the defence of an action brought against him for damages by the sub-buyer.[1056] Whether the claim has succeeded or not has turned upon whether the seller knew at the time of the contract that the buyer would resell. All of these cases are considered in detail when dealing with the contract of sale of goods[1057]; here it is only the general view that matters. It is significant that it is in the earlier cases that recovery is denied, and also that the second rule in *Hadley v Baxendale*,[1058] is squarely invoked to allow recovery less frequently as the cases progress in time. The high-water mark of recovery where there was a probability of resale without any definite knowledge on the part of the seller comes with the 1927 cases of *Hall v Pim*,[1059] in the House of Lords and of *Patrick v Russo-British Grain Export Co*.[1060]

8-213 Fewer claims for loss of profits by user, as opposed to resale, appear in the books and those which do have generally been successful. The leading authority is *Victoria Laundry v Newman*,[1061] which makes clear that such profits may be recovered under the first rule in *Hadley v Baxendale*.[1062] Earlier successful claims were approved and applied.[1063]

---

1054 Successful claims were made for delayed delivery in *Hydraulic Engineering Co v McHaffie* (1878) 4 Q.B.D. 670 CA; and for non-delivery in *Lyon v Fuchs* (1920) 2 Ll. L. Rep. 333; *Frank Mott v Muller* (1922) 13 Ll. L. Rep. 492; *Patrick v Russo-British Grain Export Co* [1927] 2 K.B. 535; *Hall v Pim* (1928) 33 Com. Cas. 324 HL. Unsuccessful claims were made for non-delivery in *Williams v Reynolds* (1865) 6 B. & S. 495; *Thol v Henderson* (1882) 8 Q.B.D. 457.

1055 Successful claims were made for non-delivery in *Grébert-Borgnis v Nugent* (1885) 15 Q.B.D. 85 CA; for delayed delivery in *Elbinger Aktiengesellschaft v Armstrong* (1874) L.R. 9 Q.B. 473 and *Contigroup Companies Inc v Glencore AG* [2005] 1 Lloyd's Rep. 241; and for breach of warranty in *Pinnock v Lewis* [1923] 1 K.B. 690; *Dobell v Barber* [1931] 1 K.B. 219 CA; *Biggin v Permanite* [1951] 2 K.B. 314 CA and *Hardwick Game Farm v Suffolk Agricultural Poultry Producers Association* [1969] 2 A.C. 31. Unsuccessful claims were made for non-delivery in *Borries v Hutchinson* (1865) 18 C.B. N.S. 445; for delayed delivery in *Portman v Middleton* (1858) 4 C.B. N.S. 322; and for breach of warranty in *Bostock v Nicholson* [1904] 1 K.B. 725.

1056 Successful claims were made for delayed delivery in *Agius v Great Western Colliery* [1899] 1 Q.B. 413; and for breach of warranty in *Hammond v Bussey* (1888) 20 Q.B.D. 79 CA; *Pinnock v Lewis* [1923] 1 K.B. 690; *Bennett v Kreeger* (1925) 41 T.L.R. 609; *Kasler v Slavouski* [1928] 1 K.B. 78. Unsuccessful claims do not appear.

1057 See Ch.25, below.

1058 (1854) 9 Ex. 341.

1059 (1928) 33 Com. Cas. 324 HL, a case, however, which has now been favourably commented upon by the House of Lords in *The Heron II* [1969] 1 A.C. 350.

1060 [1927] 2 K.B. 535. For an unsuccessful claim by not a buyer but a seller of goods for a loss of exceptional profits, see *North Sea Energy Holdings v Petroleum Authority of Thailand* [1997] 2 Lloyd's Rep. 418 (affirmed on other grounds: [1999] 1 Lloyd's Rep. 483 CA).

1061 [1949] 2 K.B. 528 CA.

1062 (1854) 9 Ex. 341.

1063 *Cory v Thames Ironworks Co* (1868) L.R. 3 Q.B. 181; *Re Trent & Humber Co Ex p. Cambrian Steam Packet Co* (1868) L.R. 4 Ch. App. 112. These cases are of delayed delivery but the same will clearly apply to non-delivery. Later successful claims involve breach of warranty: *Cullinane v British "Rema" Manufacturing Co* [1954] 1 Q.B. 292 CA; *Bacon v Cooper (Metals)* [1982] 1 All E.R. 397.

## (2) Breach of contract by carrier of goods

While claims against sellers for loss of profits on resale or in user have on the whole succeeded, similar claims against carriers who have failed to deliver goods, delayed their delivery, or delivered them in bad condition, have in the past practically always failed. These include the three important early cases of *Hadley v Baxendale*,[1064] itself and *British Columbia Saw Mill Co v Nettleship*,[1065] as to user profits, and *Horne v Midland Ry*,[1066] as to sale profits[1067] and also the later, equally unsuccessful claims for user profits in *Heskell v Continental Express*,[1068] and for sale profits in *The Arpad*.[1069] The reason for the more rigid application of the contemplation of the parties doctrine to carriers than to sellers follows as **8-214**

> "a natural result of the fact that a carrier is supposed to know less about the commodity he carries and to undertake less responsibility in connection with it".

So said Roche J in *Montevideo Gas Co v Clan Line*,[1070] one of the successful claims made for loss of profits against carriers, where the carrier knew the coal carried was urgently required by the claimant to make gas and that another supply or an adequate substitute would not be quickly obtainable. This view was endorsed in two of the leading modern cases on remoteness of damage in contract. In *Victoria Laundry v Newman*[1071] Asquith LJ, pointing to the fact that the courts had been slow to allow loss of profits against a carrier, said:

> "This was not, it would seem, because a different principle applies in such cases, but because the application of the same principle leads to different results. A carrier knows less than a seller about the purposes for which the buyer or consignee needs the goods, or about other 'special circumstances' which may cause exceptional loss if due delivery is withheld."[1072]

And in *The Heron II*[1073] Lord Upjohn said that, while each of the contracting parties

> "must be taken to understand the ordinary practices and exigencies of the other's trade ... it must be remembered when dealing with the case of a carrier of goods by land, sea or air, he is not carrying on the same trade as the consignor of the goods and his knowledge of the practices and exigencies of the other's trade may be limited and less than between buyer and seller of goods who probably know far more about one another's business."[1074]

---

1064 (1854) 9 Ex. 341.
1065 (1868) L.R. 3 C.P. 499.
1066 (1873) L.R. 8 C.P. 131.
1067 Other early unsuccessful claims, of no great importance, are *Le Peintur v S.E. Ry* (1860) 2 L.T. 170; *Simmons v S.E. Ry* (1861) 7 Jur. 849; *Hales v L.N.W. Ry* (1863) 4 B. & S. 66; *G.W. Ry v Redmayne* (1866) L.R. 1 C.P. 329. All are cases of delayed delivery.
1068 [1950] 1 All E.R. 1033.
1069 [1934] P. 189 CA.
1070 (1921) 37 T.L.R. 544 at 545; affirmed, at 866 CA.
1071 [1949] 2 K.B. 528 CA.
1072 [1949] 2 K.B. 528 CA at 537.
1073 [1969] 1 A.C. 350.
1074 [1969] 1 A.C. 350 at 424. This distinction is not affected by the wider liability that has been imposed upon carriers by the decision in *The Heron II* itself: see paras 32-029 to 32-031, below.

Yet, in *The Pegase*,[1075] Robert Goff J said that he could

> "find in the cases no rule of policy either excluding, or imposing special criteria in respect of, the recovery of damages for loss of profits, whether the relevant contract be a contract of sale or a contract of carriage, whether the breach be non-delivery or delayed delivery, and whether the profits claimed to have been lost are resale profits or profits from loss of use."[1076]

"In truth", as Roche J put it in *Montevideo Gas Co v Clan Line*,[1077] where loss of user profits on a non-delivery was awarded,

> "distinctions between the liability of a carrier and a seller depend on matters of fact and not of law".[1078]

Thus damages for loss of profits on a sale are found to have been allowed in *The Pegase*,[1079] where carriage of a cargo by sea was delayed, in the early *Simpson v L.N.W. Ry*,[1080] and *Jameson v Midland Ry Co*,[1081] where parcels carried by rail were delayed, and in *Panalpina International Transport v Densil Underwear*,[1082] where there was a delayed consignment of goods by air.

**8-215** Claims other than for the loss of sale or user profits have been made against carriers. On the issue of remoteness two cases may be contrasted.[1083] In the one case, *Papera Traders Co Ltd v Hyundai Merchant Marine Co Ltd, The Eurasian Dream (No.2)*,[1084] damage was held to be too remote as not within the contemplation of a carrier of goods by sea, damage represented by the contingency fee the owners of the goods had to pay, through their insurer, to a recovery agent handling their claims against the carrier.[1085] The other case is *Sandeman Coprimar SA v Transitos y Transportes Integrales SL* at first instance.[1086] The claimants, exporters of whisky to Spain, acquired from the Spanish tax authorities tax seals of nominal value for use in sealing their whisky bottles to indicate that Spanish excise duty had been duly paid by them. They contracted with the defendant carrier for the carriage by road from Spain to Scotland of cartons containing these tax seals. The cargo was lost in the course of carriage and the claimants were required to pay to the Spanish tax authorities under a guarantee an amount equivalent to the excise duty which would have been recovered on the bottles to which the seals should have been attached. The claimants claimed this amount from the carrier by way of common law damages[1087] and the trial judge[1088] held against the carrier as it was aware of the nature of the seals and the consequences that would attend their loss.[1089]

---

1075 [1981] 1 Lloyd's Rep. 175; facts at para.32-039, below.
1076 [1981] 1 Lloyd's Rep. 175 at 183, col.1.
1077 (1921) 37 T.L.R. 544.
1078 (1921) 37 T.L.R. 544 at 545.
1079 [1981] 1 Lloyd's Rep. 175.
1080 (1876) 1 Q.B.D. 274.
1081 (1884) 50 L.T. 426.
1082 [1981] 1 Lloyd's Rep. 187.
1083 Where, as in Jack L. *Israel v Ocean Dynamic Lines SA, The Ocean Dynamic* [1982] 2 Lloyd's Rep. 88, the complaint is of damage to the goods in transit no question of remoteness is likely to arise.
1084 [2002] 2 Lloyd's Rep. 692.
1085 The trial judge wished to categorise the claim as one for costs rather than damages.
1086 *Sandeman Coprimar SA v Transitos y Transportes Integrales SL* unreported 6 July 2001.
1087 There were also complex claims under the Convention scheduled to the Carriage of Goods by Road Act 1965 not relevant here.

1088 There was an appeal, at [2003] Q.B. 1270 CA, but it involved not the claim in contract against the carrier, by then insolvent, but claims in negligence and conversion against other defendants to whom the carriage had been sub-contracted. The appeal is dealt with elsewhere; see in particular para.38-072, below.

1089 This knowledge of the carrier appears in the appeal judgment: [2003] Q.B. 1270 CA at [21].

Chapter 9

# MITIGATION OF DAMAGE

Table of Contents

## I. Various Meanings of the Term "Mitigation"

The expression "mitigation of damage" is an umbrella term applied, in the books and in the cases, to a number of matters, some of which are related and some of which are completely unconnected. Surprisingly, in view of the importance of the subject, these differences have not been fully analysed in English law; yet it is vital to an understanding of the issues to separate the various meanings of the term.[1] **9-001**

### 1. Principal Meaning: The Three Rules as to the Avoiding of the Consequences of a Wrong

The principal, and proper, meaning of the term "mitigation", adopted in this chapter, concerns avoiding of the consequences of a wrong, whether tort or breach of contract. This forms probably the only exact use of the term. Even if the subsidiary or residual meanings enumerated below cannot strictly be called incorrect, the use of the term "mitigation" in connection with them needs to be qualified, if not completely discarded, as matters are only confused by employing one term to describe disparate concepts. **9-002**

The principal meaning comprises three different, although closely interrelated, rules. This analysis into three rules, although clearly implicit in the cases, is one which had not, at the time this book was first rewritten by Dr McGregor in the late 1950s, been given explicit statement in English law. It is submitted that such a division lends clarity to a difficult topic. The three rules are these. **9-003**

(1) The first and most important rule is that the claimant must take all reasonable steps to mitigate his or her loss consequent upon the defendant's wrong and cannot recover damages for any such loss which he or she failed, through unreasonable action or inaction, to avoid. Put shortly, the claimant cannot recover for reasonably avoidable loss. **9-004**

(2) The second rule is the corollary of the first. It is that where the claimant does take reasonable steps to mitigate the loss to him consequent upon the defendant's wrong he or she can recover for loss incurred in so doing; this is so even though the resulting damage is in the event greater than it would have been had the mitigating steps not been taken. Put shortly, the claimant can recover for loss incurred in reasonable attempts to avoid loss. **9-005**

(3) The third rule is that where the claimant does take reasonably necessary steps to mitigate the loss to him or her consequent upon the defendant's wrong, and where these steps are successful, the defendant is entitled to the benefit accruing from the claimant's action and is liable only for the loss as lessened; this is so even though the claimant would not have been debarred under the first rule from recovering the whole loss, which would have accrued in the absence of his successful mitigating steps, by reason of these steps not being ones which were required of him under the first rule. In addition, where the loss has been mitigated by other reasonably foreseeable means, the claimant can again recover only for the loss as lessened. Put shortly, the claimant cannot generally recover for avoided loss. **9-006**

---

1 It is the loss that has to be avoided and not the wrong itself. The curious suggestion of an avoidable wrong appeared in the patent case of *Alan Nuttall Ltd v Fri-Jado UK Ltd* [2010] EWHC 1966 (Pat) at [37] and following.

**9-007** These three rules were endorsed in *Thai Airways International Public Co Ltd v KI Holdings Co Ltd*.[2] In that case, Thai Airways claimed damages from KI Holdings for breaches of contract in relation to the supply of economy class aircraft seats. Some seats were delivered late and others were not delivered. Thai Airways was prevented from using five of its aircraft for 18 months pending the delivery of the seats from another supplier. The issue at trial was whether Thai Airways had mitigated its loss. Leggatt J endorsed these three different rules for mitigation,[3] although suggesting that the three rules had an underlying unity based on causation. There is some underlying unity in the notion of "factual" causation but "factual" causation is not sufficient. As Leggatt J recognised[4] the unity also lies in a rule that damages are assessed as if the claimant acted reasonably, if in fact it did not act reasonably. The discussion in this chapter is consistent with the concept of acting reasonably as deconstructed into various norms including the dominant norm that it is reasonable for a claimant to enter an available market as soon as possible to obtain a substitute for a defendant's performance.

## 2. The Two Subsidiary or Residual Meanings

**9-008** There are also two subsidiary or residual meanings of the term "mitigation". These have no connection with the three rules comprised in the principal meaning, because they are not concerned with the avoiding of the consequences of the defendant's wrong but come into play at an earlier stage in the matter. The first appears in cases where the conduct, character and circumstances of the claimant and the defendant affect the assessment of the damages; the second appears in cases where both the claimant and the defendant are in breach of contract.

**9-009** (1) In certain torts, particularly those of defamation, false imprisonment and malicious prosecution, the measure of damages may be affected by the conduct, character and circumstances of both claimant and defendant. These factors are said to go in aggravation or in mitigation of the damage. Thus the damage is most commonly aggravated, and the damages correspondingly increased,[5] by the defendant's bad motives or wilfulness; the prime illustration of this is in defamation where one of the principal elements in estimating the damages is the malice of the defendant.[6] The use of the term "aggravated damage" also avoids confusing statements such

---

2 [2015] EWHC 1250 Comm.

3 [2015] EWHC 1250 Comm at [32].

4 [2015] EWHC 1250 Comm at [33], quoting Dyson and Kramer (2014) 130 L.Q.R. 259 at 263.

5 Frequently the expression used is aggravation and/or mitigation of "damages" and not of "damage". There is justification for both, since both the damage and the damages are made more or made less. Nevertheless it is submitted that it is preferable to adhere to the singular word "damage" for two reasons. First, this is the logical order, as the damage must be aggravated or mitigated before the damages can be aggravated or mitigated. Secondly, in relation to aggravation, this helps to keep separate damages awarded as compensation to the claimant and damages awarded as punishment of the defendant, a distinction which, as explained by Lord Devlin in *Rookes v Barnard* [1964] A.C. 1129 at 1221, has in the past been too frequently blurred (see para.13-004, below). "Aggravated damage" indicates that the loss to the claimant is increased and can therefore only have reference, or lead on, to compensatory damages; but "aggravated damages" is ambiguous in this respect and could refer equally to compensatory damages and to exemplary damages.

6 See paras 46-047 to 46-051, below. Increased damages on account of aggravation of damage must always be refused where intentional misconduct is not a feature of the tort, as in *Johnson v Gore Wood & Co* [2002] 2 A.C. 1 where the claim lay in negligence. Nor were such damages appropriate for the concurrent claim there for breach of contract.

as that aggravated damages "are only to be awarded where the compensation element is not in itself sufficient to properly compensate".[7] The damage may also be aggravated by reason of the good character and reputation of the claimant, but there is less authority on this because generally no evidence can be introduced to show the good character of the claimant unless his character is attacked in evidence by the defendant. Conversely, the damage may be mitigated, and the damages correspondingly reduced, either by the defendant's bona fides or by the bad character and reputation of the claimant. The commonest illustration is again defamation where evidence to disprove the defendant's malice is allowed in mitigation to reduce the damages as is also an apology by the defendant,[8] while evidence as to the claimant's bad reputation also makes a frequent appearance.[9] And while nothing is said about aggravation of damages in ss.27 and 28 of the Housing Act 1988, which sections give an action for damages to tenants unlawfully evicted by their landlords, there is a specific provision empowering the court to mitigate the damages on account of the conduct of the tenant or of anyone living with him, a provision which has been brought into play after a near decade of disuse.[10]

This meaning of the term "mitigation" simply deals with particular items which go to show that the injury is not as great as would prima facie appear: no question of subsequently lessening the loss arises. Indeed in all cases it is important to look and see what the actual injury is, quite apart from subsequent steps taken by the claimant, and if it is shown to be less than normal the measure of damages will be less than the normal measure in that particular kind of case; there is no need to say that the damages are mitigated by the amount by which they are less than the normal measure. The particular cases, both as to mitigation and as to aggravation, are therefore best dealt with when dealing with the particular torts which give rise to them.[11] **9-010**

(2) Where the claimant, suing the defendant in respect of his failure to perform a contract, is also himself in breach of contract, the loss thereby accruing to the defendant may in certain cases go in mitigation or reduction of the amount which the claimant can recover in his action. Such cases tend to arise when the claimant's action is not for damages for breach of contract, but is for money payable by the terms of a contract,[12] such as the price or value of goods sold,[13] of services rendered,[14] or of a combination of the two.[15] **9-011**

This meaning of the term "mitigation" deals with the manner in which damages resulting from a breach of contract by the claimant can be deducted from the claim made by the claimant in respect of that contract. It is analogous to cases of contributory negligence[16] in that both parties are at fault and a subtraction is made: nevertheless a reduction of damages on the ground of contributory negligence is not referred **9-012**

---

7 *C v WH* [2015] EWHC 2687 (QB) at [104].

8 See paras 46-052 to 46-059 below.

9 See paras 46-060 to 46-067 and following, below.

10 See para.39-081, below.

11 See especially Chs 42 to 47, below.

12 This distinction is dealt with at para.1-005, above.

13 See, e.g. *Parson v Sexton* (1847) 4 C.B. 899 (contract to sell an engine; breach of warranty as to its power).

14 See, e.g. *Chapel v Hickes* (1833) 2 Cr. & M. 214 (contract to erect buildings; defective erection).

15 See, e.g. *Allen v Cameron* (1833) 1 Cr. & M. 832 (contract to sell, plant and tend trees; failure to tend properly).

16 See Ch.7, above.

to as "mitigation". Indeed the cases, which are all very old,[17] refer only to reduction of the damages so that in this context the term "mitigation" does not surface. In any event the only question that arises in these contract cases is a matter of procedure and of pleading, namely whether the defendant can claim the damages for the claimant's breach, in full or in part, with or without pleading the matter as set-off or counterclaim. This question is not germane to a book on damages and does not call for treatment. Whether, where such a reduction is allowed,[18] the measure of reduction will represent the measure of damages that the defendant could have recovered in a separate action against the claimant, is similarly outside this book.

**9-013** Thus, while the second subsidiary or residual meaning of the term "mitigation" is excluded from the book altogether, both such meanings are excluded from this chapter.

## II. THE RULE AS TO AVOIDABLE LOSS: NO RECOVERY FOR LOSS WHICH THE CLAIMANT OUGHT REASONABLY TO HAVE AVOIDED

**9-014** The extent of the damage resulting from a wrongful act, whether tort or breach of contract, can often be considerably lessened by well-advised action on the part of the person wronged. In such circumstances the law requires him to take all reasonable steps to mitigate the loss consequent on the defendant's wrong, and refuses to allow him damages in respect of any part of the loss which is due to his neglect to take such steps. Even persons against whom wrongs have been committed are not entitled to sit back and suffer loss which could be avoided by reasonable efforts or to continue an activity unreasonably so as to increase the loss. This well-established rule finds its most authoritative expression in the speech of Viscount Haldane LC in the leading case of *British Westinghouse Co v Underground Ry*,[19] where he said:

> "The fundamental basis is thus compensation for pecuniary loss naturally flowing from the breach; but this first principle is qualified by a second, which imposes on a claimant the duty of taking all reasonable steps to mitigate the loss consequent on the breach, and debars him from claiming any part of the damage which is due to his neglect to take such steps."[20]

---

[17] See para.9-011, above.

[18] See, e.g. by s.53(1)(a) of the Sale of Goods Act 1979. For an illustration allowing set-off in equity, see *British Anzani v International Marine Management* [1980] Q.B. 637.

[19] [1912] A.C. 673 at 689. The decision concerned avoided loss, and the facts are therefore stated at para.9-121, below.

[20] Other authoritative statements of the rule are to be found in *Dunkirk Colliery Co v Lever* (1878) 9 Ch. D. 20 CA at 25, per James LJ, cited with approval by Viscount Haldane LC in *British Westinghouse Co v Underground Ry* [1912] A.C. 673 at 689: "What the plaintiffs are entitled to is the full amount of the damage which they have really sustained by a breach of the contract; the person who has broken the contract not being exposed to additional cost by reason of the plaintiffs not doing what they ought to have done as reasonable men, and the plaintiffs not being under any obligation to do anything otherwise than in the ordinary course of business": and also in *Jamal v Moolla Dawood* [1916] 1 A.C. 175 PC at 179, per Lord Wrenbury: "It is undoubted law that a plaintiff who sues for damages owes the duty of taking all reasonable steps to mitigate the loss consequent upon the breach and cannot claim as damages any sum that is due to his own neglect. But the loss to be ascertained is the loss at the date of the breach. If at that date the plaintiff could do something or did something which mitigated the damage, the defendant is entitled to the benefit of it."

There are various general points about this important doctrine which may conveniently be collected at this early stage.

## 1. VARIOUS ASPECTS OF THE RULE

**(a) Application to contract and tort** Lord Haldane referred only to pecuniary loss but presumably because he was dealing with a breach of contract and not a tort. Most cases do indeed stem from contract and concern the mitigation of pecuniary loss; but the principle applies equally to non-pecuniary loss and to tort, as in the case of a claimant who, having been physically injured, fails to take reasonable steps to obtain medical aid and thereby fails to cut down the pain and suffering resulting from the injury.[21] Lord Sumner in *Admiralty Commissioners v S.S. Chekiang*,[22] and again in *Admiralty Commissioners v S.S. Susquehanna*,[23] clearly recognised the application of the mitigation doctrine to tort and in *The Liverpool (No.2)*,[24] Lord Merriman P said similarly: "The classic statement [namely of Lord Haldane], although made in an action arising out of a breach of contract, applies equally, mutatis mutandis, to tort." **9-015**

**(b) A question of fact not a question of law** In *Payzu v Saunders*,[25] both Bankes and Scrutton LJJ said that the question of mitigation of damage is a question of fact[26]; in *The Solholt*[27] Sir John Donaldson MR said[28] that **9-016**

> "whether a loss is avoidable by reasonable action on the part of the claimant is a question of fact not law" and that "this was decided in *Payzu v Saunders*".[29]

It has never been doubted since; today it tends to be regarded as trite law. Two significant consequences of mitigating being a matter of fact and not law can be highlighted. The first is that once a court of first instance has decided that there has been, or has not been, a failure to mitigate, it is difficult to persuade an appellate court to come to a different view. Mitigation being a question of fact, "it is therefore rarely appropriate", said Potter LJ in *Standard Chartered Bank v Pakistan National Shipping Corporation*,[30] "to interfere with the conclusions of the trial judge based as they are on the evidence (or lack of satisfactory evidence) before him". The *Solholt*,[31] and *Standard Chartered Bank v Pakistan National Shipping Corporation*,[32] themselves both provide good illustrations of this as does *Uzinterimpex J.S.C. v Standard Bank Plc*,[33] the Court of Appeal upholding the trial judges' findings of failure to mitigate in the first case[34] and of no failure to mitigate in the other two.[35]

---

21 See the cases at para.9-066, below.
22 [1926] A.C. 637 at 646.
23 [1926] A.C. 637 at 663.
24 [1963] P. 64 at 77 to 78.
25 [1919] 2 K.B. 581 CA.
26 [1919] 2 K.B. 581 CA at 588 and 589 respectively.
27 [1983] 1 Lloyd's Rep. 605 CA.
28 [1983] 1 Lloyd's Rep. 605 CA at 608, col.1.
29 [1919] 2 K.B. 581 CA.
30 [2001] 1 All E.R. Comm. 822 CA at [47].
31 [1983] 1 Lloyd's Rep. 605 CA.
32 [2001] 1 All E.R. Comm. CA 822.
33 [2008] 2 Lloyd's Rep. 456 CA; see at [50].
34 See the case at para.9-053, below.

**9-017** A second consequence of mitigation being a matter of fact is that factors concerning whether there has been compliance with the duty to mitigate cannot be elevated to decisive legal requirements. In *Secretary of State for Health v Servier Laboratories Ltd*,[36] Henderson J rejected a submission that a duty to mitigate can only arise where a claimant has knowledge (actual or constructive) of the wrongdoing and/or the loss suffered in consequence of it.[37] Although the claimant's knowledge was highly relevant, "its relevance is to the question of fact whether the claimant acted reasonably in all the circumstances".[38] Of course what was being referred to in all these cases in relation to both consequences was whether a claimant, required to take all reasonable steps to mitigate his loss if he is to recover for that loss, has or has not failed to do so; whether there is in the particular circumstances a need to mitigate in the first place will be a question of law.[39]

**9-018** (c) **The question of duty** Lord Haldane spoke of the claimant as having a duty to mitigate, and this is the common and convenient way of stating the rule. The expression is, however, a somewhat loose one since there is no "duty" which is actionable or which is owed to anyone by the claimant. He cannot owe a duty to himself; the position is similar to that of a claimant whose damages are reduced because of his contributory negligence. Pearson LJ in *Darbishire v Warran*,[40] gave the proper analysis when he said:

> "It is important to appreciate the true nature of the so-called 'duty to mitigate the loss' or 'duty to minimise the damage'. The claimant is not under any contractual obligation to adopt the cheaper method: if he wishes to adopt the more expensive method, he is at liberty to do so and by doing so he commits no wrong against the defendant or anyone else. The true meaning is that the claimant is not entitled to charge the defendant by way of damages with any greater sum than that which he reasonably needs to expend for the purpose of making good the loss. In short, he is fully entitled to be as extravagant as he pleases but not at the expense of the defendant."[41]

This has been re-emphasised by Sir John Donaldson MR, delivering the judgment of the court in *The Solholt*,[42] where he said:

> "A plaintiff is under no duty to mitigate his loss, despite the habitual use by the lawyers of the phrase 'duty to mitigate'. He is completely free to act as he judges to be in his best interests. On the other hand, a defendant is not liable for all loss suffered by the plaintiff in consequence of his so acting. A defendant is only liable for such part of the plaintiff's loss as is properly caused by the defendant's breach of duty."[43]

The point was again reiterated by Lord Toulson (with whom Lord Neuberger, Lord Mance and Lord Clarke agreed) in *Bunge SA v Nidera BV*[44] saying that

---

35 See the cases at, respectively, para.9-074 and para.9-078, below.

36 [2016] EWHC 2381 Ch.

37 *Secretary of State for Health v Servier Laboratories Ltd* [2016] EWHC 2381 Ch at [37].

38 *Secretary of State for Health v Servier Laboratories Ltd* [2016] EWHC 2381 Ch at [47].

39 For circumstances in which the need to mitigate may not arise, see paras 9-021 and following, below.

40 [1963] 1 W.L.R. 1067 CA.

41 [1963] 1 W.L.R. 1067 CA at 1075. See similarly *Wallems Rederij v Muller* [1927] 2 K.B. 99 at 104–105, per Mackinnon J.

42 [1983] 1 Lloyd's Rep. 605 CA.

43 [1983] 1 Lloyd's Rep. 605 CA at 608, col.1.

44 [2015] UKSC 43 at [81].

"the so-called duty to mitigate is not a duty in the sense that the innocent party owes an obligation to the guilty party to do so."

**(d) The question of causation** In *Koch Marine Inc v D'Amica Società di Navigatione, The Elenad'Amico*,[45] Robert Goff J quoted the three rules relating to mitigation initially put forward in this text[46] and then said: 9-019

"Now, in my judgment, these three aspects of mitigation are all really aspects of a wider principle which is that, subject to the rules of remoteness, the plaintiff can recover, but can only recover, in respect of damage suffered by him which has been caused by the defendant's legal wrong. In other words, they are aspects of the principle of causation."[47]

It is thought that this embracing of the principle of causation is unhelpful—even confusing—in relation to all three rules but particularly in relation to the first of the three, the one now under consideration.[48] In *Standard Chartered Bank v Pakistan National Shipping Corporation*,[49] which was concerned with the first rule[50] whereas The Elena d'Amico had been concerned with the third,[51] Potter LJ, giving the only reasoned judgment in the Court of Appeal, referred without disapproval to the trial judge's adoption of these principles of mitigation of damage set out by Robert Goff J which he, the trial judge, had summarised thus:

"The orthodox view is that the rule as to avoidable loss is merely an aspect of the fundamental principle of causation that a plaintiff can recover only in respect of damage caused by the defendant's wrong. The rule is ... that the plaintiff ... cannot recover for a loss avoidable by reasonable action on his own part, because, if he could reasonably have avoided it, it would not be regarded as caused by the wrongdoer."[52]

Now the matter can no doubt be put in this way in terms of causation but it does not tell us very much.[53] What must be ascertained is whether the claimant has acted, or failed to act, reasonably. This, as we have seen,[54] is a question of fact and one that is capable of resolution by an examination of the circumstances of the particular case. Adding causation into the mix gives no assistance. There is indeed a danger here, as elsewhere, of using causation as a disguise for the real ground of a decision.[55] It is significant that the cases on the avoidable loss aspect of mitigation are not full of references to causation.

---

45 [1980] 1 Lloyd's Rep. 75.

46 The passage quoted is now at paras 9-004 to 9-006, above.

47 [1980] 1 Lloyd's Rep. 75 at 88, col.2. See also *Bunge SA v Nidera BV* [2015] UKSC 43 at [81] per Lord Toulson.

48 Causation in relation to the second and third rules is considered later: see paras 9-102 and 9-112, below.

49 [2001] 1 All E.R. Comm. 822 CA.

50 See the case at para.9-074, below.

51 See the case at para.9-139, below.

52 At [1999] 1 Lloyd's Rep. 747 at 758.

53 Or as Moore-Bick LJ said in *Uzinterimpex J.S.C. v Standard Bank Plc* [2008] 2 Lloyd's Rep. 456 CA at [56]: "I am not sure that to [view mitigation in terms of causation] adds greatly to one's understanding of the principles."

54 See para.9-016, above.

55 Thus Moore-Bick LJ in *Uzinterimpex J.S.C. v Standard Bank Plc* [2008] 2 Lloyd's Rep. 456 CA identified, and avoided, such a danger, and a serious one, for that case at [2008] 2 Lloyd's Rep. 456 CA at [56]–[58].

9-020 **(e) The question of onus** The onus of proof on the issue of mitigation is on the defendant. If he fails to show that the claimant ought reasonably to have taken certain mitigating steps, then the normal measure will apply.[56] This has been long settled, ever since the decision in *Roper v Johnson*,[57] and was confirmed by the House of Lords in *Garnac Grain Co v Faure & Fairclough*.[58] Yet in *Selvanayagam v University of the West Indies*[59] the Judicial Committee of the Privy Council held that, where a physically injured claimant had refused to undergo medical treatment to alleviate his injury, the burden was on him to prove that he had acted reasonably, a burden which he was found to have discharged. Any suggestion that personal injury may differ from the commercial context which gave the rule as to onus its genesis comes up against the two authoritative decisions of the House of Lords in which it was laid down that the burden of proof remains with the defendant in the particular case of the refusal of medical treatment, namely *Steele v Robert George & Co*,[60] and *Richardson v Redpath, Brown & Co*.[61] It was concluded, in the two editions of this text following on *Selvanayagam*, that the decision of the Privy Council, being against the entire weight of authority, was arrived at per incuriam, but it was nevertheless inconvenient to have a decision at this high level still on the books. Fortunately, the matter has finally been laid to rest by the Judicial Committee of the Privy Council itself in *Geest Plc v Lansiquot*,[62] a further case of the unpreparedness to undergo a medical operation being held not to be a failure to mitigate, though again a decision that would have been in the claimant's favour wherever the onus lay.[63] Indeed such had been the criticism of *Selvanayagam*,[64] that in the Privy Council in *Geest* counsel accepted that it was wrong, and with this the court agreed.[65] The Privy Council there also made it clear that a defendant proposing to argue for a claimant's failure to mitigate must give notice well before the hearing, by the pleadings or otherwise, to enable the claimant to prepare to meet the argument.[66] At the same time, the cases of claims for the cost of hiring a replacement car while a tortiously damaged car is being repaired show that the claimant

---

56 That onus can sometimes have great practical importance is usefully illustrated by *Saunders v Williams* [2003] B.L.R. 125 CA. The defendant had damaged a party wall and the claimant had failed to have it repaired for three years, partly because of shortage of money. The Court of Appeal decided to reassess the damages rather than order a new trial but, because of a lack of findings by the trial judge, did not have the material to decide whether or not the claimant had acted reasonably in not repairing. In these circumstances the court held, Chadwick LJ citing the rule on onus from this text, that, because the defendant had not proved the claimant had acted unreasonably, she was entitled to full damages.

57 (1873) L.R. 8 C.P. 167. The defendant had repudiated the contract before the time of due performance; see further at para.9-021, below.

58 [1968] A.C. 1130 at 1140; also a repudiation case. The onus is the same for avoided loss: See para.9-115, below.

59 [1983] 1 W.L.R. 585 PC.

60 [1942] A.C. 497; see at 501, 502, 506 and 508.

61 [1944] A.C. 62; see at 72, 73 and 75.

62 [2002] 1 W.L.R. 3111 PC.

63 See the case further at paras 9-066 and 9-088, below.

64 [1983] 1 W.L.R. 585 PC.

65 [2002] 1 W.L.R. 3111 PC at [14]. Thus showing how the Privy Council's reasoning and use of the authorities in *Selvanayagam* was faulty, as was done in some earlier editions, is no longer necessary.

66 [2002] 1 W.L.R. 3111 PC at [16]. *Calix v Attorney General of Trinidad and Tobago* [2013] UKPC 15 is a curious case on onus in mitigation where the issue before the Privy Council concerned the failure to apply for bail by a claimant suing for malicious prosecution because of his prosecution on a charge of rape after his acquittal on a related charge of robbery: see [2002] 1 W.L.R. 3111 PC at [18]–[22].

must establish that he has a need for a replacement car and cannot require the defendant to prove the contrary.[67] Here one has not arrived at the issue of mitigation and defendant's onus.

**(f) Whether need to mitigate before contractual breach** A claimant need take no steps in mitigation until a wrong has been committed against him.[68] Thus the attempt, which is often made, to use the "duty" to mitigate damage to force upon a party to a contract an acceptance of a repudiation of the contract by the defendant, is misconceived. Where a party to a contract repudiates it, the other party has an option to accept or not to accept the repudiation. If he does not accept it there is still no breach of contract, and the contract subsists for the benefit of both parties and no need to mitigate arises. On the other hand, if the repudiation is accepted this results in an anticipatory breach of contract in respect of which suit can be brought at once for damages, and, although the measure of damages is still prima facie assessed as from the date when the defendant ought to have performed the contract, this amount is subject to being cut down if the claimant fails to mitigate after his acceptance of the repudiation. 9-021

These principles have from an early day found illustration in sale of goods cases, especially in actions for non-delivery against a repudiating seller, and also, although there are fewer cases, in actions for non-acceptance against a repudiating buyer. Thus on a seller's repudiation when the market was rising, it was held in *Brown v Muller*,[69] that a buyer who had not accepted the repudiation was entitled to claim the normal measure of damages based on the market price at the time of due delivery, there being no need for him to take mitigating steps; in *Roper v Johnson*,[70] and again much later in *Garnac Grain Co v Faure & Fairclough*,[71] that a buyer who had accepted the repudiation was still entitled to claim the normal measure based on the market price at the time of due delivery, because, although now required to mitigate, it was not shown that he had failed to do so; but in *Melachrino v Nickoll*,[72] it was said that a buyer who had accepted the repudiation was limited to the lower price at which it was shown that he could have bought equivalent goods in the market before the date of due delivery.[73] The same principles apply mutatis mutandis where it is the buyer who has repudiated.[74] 9-022

Employment contracts also provide illustrations. Thus in *Shindler v Northern Raincoat Co*,[75] the defendant company, in the course of the claimant's employment by them under a 10-year agreement, wrongfully repudiated the contract by informing the claimant that they would not continue to require his services as from 9-023

---

67 Initially so held in *Park Lane BMW v Whipp* unreported 20 May 2009 (at [16] and [17]), approved on this by the Court of Appeal in *Beechwood Birmingham Ltd v Hoyer Group UK Ltd* [2011] Q.B. 357 CA and applied in *Singh v Yaqubi* [2013] EWCA Civ 23 CA. See these cases at para.9-070 below.

68 *Secretary of State for Health v Servier Laboratories Ltd* [2016] EWHC 2381 (Ch) at [25].

69 (1872) L.R. 7 Ex. 319. *Leigh v Paterson* (1818) 8 Taunt. 540 is similar.

70 (1873) L.R. 8 C.P. 167.

71 [1968] A.C. 1130; see especially at 1140.

72 [1920] 1 K.B. 693.

73 In fact the price had fallen between accepted repudiation and due delivery so that the failure to buy in did not in the event constitute a failure to mitigate. See, too, *Kaines v Österreichische Warenhandelsgesellschaft* [1993] 2 Lloyd's Rep. 1 CA.

74 All the cases, both on non-delivery and on non-acceptance, are dealt with in Ch.25, below at paras 25-018 and 25-124, respectively.

75 [1960] 1 W.L.R. 1038.

an apparently unspecified later date, but only removed him from office at an extraordinary general meeting of the company some months after this repudiation. It was held that the claimant was not required to mitigate by accepting alternative offers of employment between the defendants' wrongful repudiation and their removal of him from office because during this period there had been no breach: the claimant had not accepted the repudiation and the "defendants had a locus poenitentiae".[76] Somewhat similarly in *Abrahams v Performing Right Society*,[77] where the contract provided for two years' notice or for payment in lieu of notice, the summary dismissal of the employee was held not to constitute a breach of contract so that the employee was entitled to the payment in lieu without any need to mitigate by taking alternative employment during the two years. By summarily dismissing the claimant the defendant was not breaking the contract but electing between two modes of performance, namely serving notice or paying money. His election of the latter meant that the money was due as a debt under the contract and no question of mitigation arose. However, the Court of Appeal in *Cerberus Software v Rowley*,[78] by a majority and reversing both tribunals below, took a different view where the employer neither gave notice nor made the payment in lieu. There was therefore, it was said, a breach of contract giving rise to a requirement to mitigate, which led to a very small award as the employee had found better paid employment almost immediately. This is an important decision in view of the frequent appearance today in employment contracts of payment in lieu of notice clauses. *Abrahams* was distinguishable because there the payment in lieu was held to be a contractual right whereas in *Cerberus* the provision for payment was in permissive terms, giving the employer the right to elect whether to pay in lieu of notice. It was concluded from this that the summary dismissal constituted a breach of contract giving rise to the requirement to mitigate. The decision is an unfortunate one in that it advantages the employer who deliberately makes no payment over the employer who does pay. Indeed such an employer will be able to reduce the damages not only against an employee who has found alternative remunerative employment but also against one who has not, yet reasonably should have. It may be that a fairer solution could have been found by regarding the sum to be paid in lieu as liquidated damages, a liquidated damages provision always ousting any requirement to mitigate.[79]

9-024 **(g) Whether need to mitigate by discontinuing contractual performance** Nor, it seems, need a claimant take steps to mitigate loss, even after the defendant's performance of the contract which he has repudiated falls due, by accepting the repudiation and suing for damages. He may instead, where he can do so without the defendant's assistance, perform his side of the contract and claim in debt for the contract price. Even if this involves incurring expense in the performance of the contract which, in face of the defendant's repudiation, is rendered useless, the claimant is not required to minimise the loss by accepting the repudiation and suing for damages. This conclusion was reached in *White and Carter v McGregor*.[80] The claimants, advertising agents, contracted with the sales

---

76 [1960] 1 W.L.R. 1038 at 1048.
77 [1995] I.C.R. 1028 CA.
78 [2001] I.C.R. 376 CA.
79 See para.16-022, below.
80 [1962] A.C. 413.

manager of the defendant garage proprietor to display on litter bins advertisements for the defendant's garage for three years. The defendant, on hearing of the contract, wrote at once to the claimants to cancel it but the claimants refused, displayed the advertisements in accordance with the agreement, and sued for the contract price. The House of Lords, by a majority, held that the claimants were entitled to carry out the contract and claim in debt for the price, and were not obliged to accept the repudiation and sue for damages.

This decision was soon after followed in *Anglo-African Shipping Co v Mortner*.[81] The claimants in New York agreed with the defendants in London to act as a confirming house in respect of an order for the purchase of goods by the defendants from American suppliers, and as the defendants' shipping agents in procuring shipment of the goods to the defendants in London. It was further agreed that the defendants, in addition to paying a commission, would reimburse the claimants the price of the goods paid by them under their confirmation of the order and all expenses incurred by them as the defendants' agents. After the claimants had contracted personally with the suppliers to pay them the purchase price of the goods the defendants cancelled their order and then refused to pay the claimants. The suppliers having delivered the goods to the claimants for shipment, the claimants proceeded to ship them to the defendants in London and successfully sued the defendants for the price, expenses and commission. It was held that the claimants were under no duty to mitigate by not shipping the goods once the defendants had said that they did not propose to accept them. 9-025

How absolute is the claimant's right to ignore a repudiation and carry on with performance has still, nearly 50 years on, to be fully worked out by the courts. Lord Reid in *White and Carter v McGregor*,[82] said: 9-026

> "It may well be that, if it can be shown that a person has no legitimate interest, financial or otherwise, in performing the contract rather than claiming damages, he ought not to be allowed to saddle the other party with an additional burden with no benefit to himself. If a party has no interest to enforce a stipulation, he cannot in general enforce it: so it might be said that, if a party has no interest to insist on a particular remedy, he ought not to be allowed to insist on it. And, just as a party is not allowed to enforce a penalty, so he ought not to be allowed to penalise the other party by taking one course when another is equally advantageous to him."[83]

In the case itself the defendant had not attempted to prove that the claimant had had no legitimate interest in completing performance, and it was improbable, added Lord Reid, that any such case could have been made out. In *Anglo-African Shipping Co v Mortner*,[84] the judge said that the facts of the case before him tended "to show the practical justice" of *White and Carter v McGregor*[85]; for if the claimants had been required to sell the goods in New York and not ship them to London there would have been

---

[81] [1962] 1 Lloyd's Rep. 81.
[82] [1962] A.C. 413.
[83] [1962] A.C. 413 at 431.
[84] [1962] 1 Lloyd's Rep. 81.
[85] [1962] A.C. 413.

> "no doubt, all kinds of arguments thereafter as to whether the plaintiffs had in fact sold them at the best possible price or as to whether they could have sold them in some other market".[86]

And, further, the claimant might have various sub-contracts for the purpose of performance, e.g. taking shipping space, and if there is a duty to mitigate by accepting repudiation

> "he would have to cancel those sub-contracts in a way which might be extremely damaging commercially to himself".[87]

**9-027** A limitation from another direction on the entitlement to continue performance in the face of a breach was also adverted to by Lord Reid in *White and Carter v McGregor*,[88] a limitation to the effect that a contracting party may not be able to perform his side of the contract without some degree of intervention on the part of the other contracting party.[89] This limitation found application in *Hounslow London Borough Council v Twickenham Garden Developments*[90] where Megarry J, on the assumption that the borough council there had wrongfully repudiated a contract for the construction of certain buildings, considered that the building contractors were not entitled to continue construction against the borough council's wishes. While he recognised[91] Lord Reid's qualification in *White and Carter v McGregor*[92] that a contracting party may not be entitled to perform his side of the contract where he has no legitimate interest in doing so,[93] he relied for his decision upon this further qualification introduced by Lord Reid and held that *White and Carter v McGregor*[94] had no application to the case before him

> "first, because a considerable degree of active co-operation under the contract by the borough is requisite, and second, because the work is being done to property of the borough".[95]

This can go a long way to restricting the operation of *White and Carter v McGregor* for, as Lord Reid there recognised,

> "in most cases the circumstances are such that an innocent party is unable to complete the contract and earn the contract price without the assent or co-operation of the other party".[96]

**9-028** The most common situation giving rise to the problem in the authorities has been where there has been a repudiatory breach of a charterparty by the charterer, and the owner of the vessel, declining to accept the repudiation, has awaited the end of the charterparty, with the vessel remaining available to the charterer throughout, and claimed the charter hire. Three cases of this nature, all subsequent to those already considered, have gone in different directions. The first, and the most complex

---

86 [1962] 1 Lloyd's Rep. 81 at 94.
87 [1962] 1 Lloyd's Rep. 81 at 94.
88 [1962] A.C. 413.
89 [1962] A.C. 413 at 429.
90 [1971] Ch. 233.
91 [1971] Ch. 233 at 253B.
92 [1962] A.C. 413.
93 See para.9-026, above.
94 [1962] A.C. 413.
95 [1971] Ch. 233 at 254A to B.
96 [1962] A.C. 413 at 430.

because repair obligations clouded the straightforward issue, was *Attica Sea Carriers Corporation v Ferrostaal Poseidon Bulk Reederei, The Puerto Buitrago*.[97] There the Court of Appeal, on the assumption that in a charterparty by demise the charterers' obligation to repair the vessel was a condition precedent to their right to redeliver her to the owners, considered that the owners were not entitled to claim the contract hire until such time as the charterers repaired or redelivered, and reversed the judgment of the court below. Orr LJ relied on both of Lord Reid's qualifications,[98] and in this Browne LJ agreed with him,[99] but gave little indication of why no legitimate interest in performance existed or of why the owners' contractual performance required co-operation from the charterers. Lord Denning MR, true to form, was more forthright. Basing himself solely on the qualification as to legitimate interest he considered that *White and Carter v McGregor*,[100]

> "has no application whatever in a case where the plaintiff ought, in all reason, to accept the repudiation and sue for damages—provided that damages would provide an adequate remedy for any loss suffered by him. The reason is because, in suing for the money, the plaintiff is seeking to enforce specific performance of the contract—and he should not be allowed to do so when damages would be an adequate remedy."[101]

That the claimants ought, in all reason, to sue for damages was undoubtedly so in the case before the Court of Appeal because, in Lord Denning MR's words, "it would be economic nonsense to go to the expense of repairing" the vessel[102]; not only would the repairs have cost twice as much as the ship would be worth when repaired but after repair the shipowners were likely to be able to sell her only as scrap.

Much simpler circumstances were presented by the next two cases though they arrived at different results. In both *Gator Shipping Corporation v Trans-Asiatic Oil Ltd, The Odenfeld*,[103] and *Clea Shipping Corporation v Bulk Oil International Ltd, The Alaskan Trader*,[104] time charterers repudiated but the shipowners refused to accept the repudiation, kept the vessel ready at the charterers' disposal and claimed the charter hire.[105] Kerr J in *The Odenfeld*,[106] without using the terminology of legitimate interest, found the owners entitled so to claim, while Lloyd J in *The Alaskan Trader*,[107] specifically basing himself on the absence of legitimate interest, found the owners not so entitled. Although Lloyd J attempted to distinguish Kerr J's decision on the facts, it is a little difficult to see where the difference between the two cases lies.[108] Also their views differed upon whether Lord Reid's other limitation[109] would apply to a time charterparty. Lloyd J said he thought that **9-029**

97 [1976] 1 Lloyd's Rep. 250 CA.
98 [1976] 1 Lloyd's Rep. 250 CA at 255 to 256.
99 [1976] 1 Lloyd's Rep. 250 CA at 256.
100 [1962] A.C. 413.
101 [1976] 1 Lloyd's Rep. 250 CA at 255.
102 [1976] 1 Lloyd's Rep. 250 CA at 254.
103 [1978] 2 Lloyd's Rep. 357.
104 [1984] 1 All E.R. 129.
105 There was this difference, that in the latter case, rather than the owners suing for the hire, the charterers had paid and were suing for its repayment, but that in no way affected the principle.
106 [1978] 2 Lloyd's Rep. 357.
107 [1984] 1 All E.R. 129.
108 Lloyd J in *The Alaskan Trader* [1984] 1 All E.R. 129 at 137h gives the difficulty of calculating damages as one ground relied upon by Kerr J for allowing the charter hire to be claimed.
109 See para.9-027, above.

there was much to be said for the charterers' argument that the owners did not earn their hire simply by holding the vessel and the services of their master and crew at the charterers' disposal and that a time charter was a contract for services, to be performed by the owners through the master and crew and through the use of their vessel,[110] but added that he was not going to commit himself to this view since Kerr J had found a similar argument unimpressive.[111] It was, however, conceded in *The Alaskan Trader* that, where an employee has been wrongfully dismissed, he cannot earn remuneration by holding himself at the disposal of the employer but is confined to his damages remedy.[112]

**9-030** No more was heard of the present problem for some 20 years after *The Alaskan Trader*.[113] The question of whether owners were bound to accept repudiation by charterers and sue for damages then made an appearance in *Ocean Marine Navigation Ltd v Koch Carbon Inc, The Dynamic*,[114] and the issue arose four-square, in the context of leases rather than charterparties, with the termination of a tenancy in *Reichman v Beveridge*.[115] The defendant solicitors leased premises from the claimants for a five-year term. After three years the solicitors ceased practice and upon so doing ceased paying rent. A year later the claimants, not having forfeited the lease or instructed agents to market the premises, sued successfully for the rent, now in arrears. The Court of Appeal held that to resist the claim the defendants would have to show that it was wholly unreasonable for the claimants to elect to keep the contract alive and that damages would be an adequate remedy, or that the claimants had no legitimate reason for making such an election. The defendants had not so shown; the court's reasons for this conclusion are well set out in the concluding section of Lloyd LJ's single judgment.[116] One unusual, and clearly important, factor in the case was the rather odd uncertainty, in the absence of decisions, whether lessors could recover damages for the loss of future rent if they terminated.

**9-031** *Isabella Shipowner SA v Shagang Shipping Co Ltd*,[117] returns us to charterparties and to a holding, by Cooke J, that the shipowners' refusal to accept redelivery by the charterers under a long term time charter was in order so as to entitle the owners to keep the contract on foot and claim the hire that would fall due. Cooke J considered, it is thought rightly, that a time charter is subject to the rule in *White and Carter v McGregor*,[118] as its performance by the owners did not need the charterers' co-operation and assistance; if the charterer failed to give any orders, Cooke J said, the vessel would simply stay where it was, awaiting orders but earning hire.[119] Then for a finding that the owners had no legitimate interest in continu-

[110] *The Alaskan Trader* [1984] 1 All E.R. 129 at 138g to j.

[111] [1984] 1 All E.R. 129 at 139b. Kerr J's view has now been adopted: see para.9-031, below.

[112] [1984] 1 All E.R. 129 at 138j to139a. A dismissal of the holder of a public office which is null and void bears no analogy with wrongful dismissal, and the office holder is entitled to the remuneration attaching to the office while he remains ready, willing and able to render service: *McLaughlin v Governor of the Cayman Islands, The Times,* 27 July 2007 PC.

[113] [1984] 1 All E.R. 129.

[114] [2003] 2 Lloyd's Rep. 693. Since it was unclear whether the arbitrator had correctly applied the relevant principles, the matter was remitted in order to examine this: see [2003] 2 Lloyd's Rep. 693 at [19]–[ 26].

[115] [2007] 1 P. & C.R. 20 CA, p.358.

[116] See [2007] 1 P. & C.R. 20 CA at [39]–[42].

[117] [2012] 2 Lloyd's Rep. 61.

[118] Differing views on this had earlier been expressed in *The Odenfeld* [1978] 2 Lloyd's Rep.357 and *The Alaskan Trader* [1984] 1 All E.R. 129 : see para.9-029, above.

[119] [1984] 1 All E.R. 129 at [37].

ing with the charter, it had to be shown, and by the charterers, that it was wholly unreasonable for the owners to continue.[120] The charterers wished to compel the shipowners in mitigation of loss to trade in a difficult spot market where substitute time charters were impossible—something which with their right to sub-let the charterers could take the risk of doing themselves—and to argue about the quantum of damages at a much later date. Far safer from the owners' point of view to be entitled to the payment of hire up front, semi-monthly in advance, and on any default to bring suit for it.[121] Damages would thus be an inadequate remedy and the owners could not be faulted for their maintaining of the charter.

Leggatt J examined the legitimate interest principle in the wider context of the need for good faith in contractual dealings, a requirement he considered was now coming to be recognised in the common law. He came to the conclusion that there was no legitimate interest to decline to accept the repudiatory breach since after a certain date the carrier was suffering no loss and was keeping the contract alive merely in order to claim demurrage indefinitely.

*White and Carter v McGregor*,[122] made a further appearance, being applied in **9-032** *MSC Mediterranean Shipping Co SA v Cottonex Anstalt*.[123] The Swiss seller of a large consignment of raw cotton to a purchaser in Bangladesh contracted to have it shipped by a carrier in 35 of the carrier's sea containers. The contract of carriage provided that for 14 days after the discharge of the cargo in the containers the shipper was entitled to retain the containers without charge. After expiry of those 14 days the shipper was required to pay container demurrage at a specified daily rate until the containers were returned. The provision was completely open-ended so that it appeared that payment of demurrage could continue indefinitely.

The market for raw cotton collapsed shortly after the conclusion of the contract **9-033** of sale. So the purchaser sought to escape from the contract and did not collect the cotton. A dispute ensued but the purchaser eventually agreed to pay. On 27 September 2011, the shipper informed the carrier that it no longer had title to the containers. On 2 February 2012, the carrier offered to sell the containers to the shipper but no agreement could be reached. In commercial terms the containers had then been lost. The cotton remained in the containers until the time of the trial.

The Court of Appeal held that the carrier did not have a legitimate interest to **9-034** refuse to accept the breach after 2 February 2012. The decision of the primary judge, Leggatt J, had been that the legitimate interest ceased on 27 September 2011. The Court of Appeal disagreed, finding that the commercial purpose of the agreement only failed on 2 February 2012 so that the *White and Carter* principle did not apply from that date. After that date the carrier was suffering no loss and was keeping the contract alive merely in order to claim demurrage indefinitely. Referring to *Geys v Société Générale*,[124] Moore-Bick LJ (with whom Tomlinson LJ and Keehan J agreed) said[125] that the true explanation of the legitimate interest restriction may be that in an appropriate case the court in the exercise of its general equitable jurisdiction will decline to grant the innocent party the remedy to which he or she would normally be entitled.

---

[120] See the points made at [1984] 1 All E.R. 129 at [42] to [44].

[121] See the points made at [1984] 1 All E.R. 129 at [47] and [48].

[122] [1962] A.C. 413.

[123] [2016] EWCA Civ 789.

[124] [2013] 1 A.C. 523.

[125] [2016] EWCA Civ 789 at [40].

**9-035** The paucity of authority shows the situation to be uncommon and perhaps shows an unwillingness of contracting parties who have suffered a repudiatory breach to embark upon this line of argument. In any event the widest interpretation of Lord Reid's two limitations on the operation of *White and Carter v McGregor*,[126] is to be commended. On the legitimate interest limitation it is thought that only if damages are shown to be inadequate—as could be said to have been the case in *Anglo-African Shipping Co v Mortner*,[127]—or to be uncertain—as was the case in *Reichman v Beveridge*[128]—or to be both—as was the case in *Isabella Shipowner SA v Shagang Shipping Co Ltd*[129]—without which inadequacy or uncertainty a decree of specific performance would never be allowed, should the innocent party be entitled to claim in debt. It is but economic waste to allow a contracting party, when it is of no benefit to him, to carry through a performance unwanted by the other contracting party.[130] It is salutary to look at the long held position in the United States where, as Lloyd J said in *The Alaskan Trader*,[131]

> "the courts take the uncomplicated view that whether the repudiation is accepted or not, the innocent party is *always* obliged to mitigate his damages".[132]

**9-036** It should be appreciated that the problems presented by *White and Carter v McGregor*,[133] do not, strictly speaking, concern damages at all: here the claimant's claim is in debt rather than for damages, for money payable under the terms of the contract rather than for compensation payable by reason of its breach. These cases of debt have been included here because they give rise to issues which are so very analogous to those appertaining to mitigation in its proper context of damages that it is important at once to be aware that the one situation is, though similar, separate and distinct from the other and to guard against any assumption that conclusions arrived at in relation to the one necessarily apply to the other. Thus, for instance, *Anglo-African Shipping Co v Mortner*,[134] suggests that, while a claimant suing in debt need not act so as to prejudice his commercial reputation any more than a claimant suing for damages,[135] it may be that he need act with only his own interests in mind, whereas with mitigation proper the claimant must act with the defendant's interests in mind as well as his own.[136]

**9-037** **(h) Application of mitigation to the actual loss or the recoverable loss** Under the principles laid down in *Banque Bruxelles Lambert v Eagle Star Insurance Co*,[137] commonly called SAAMCO, a claimant claiming for professional negligence can-

---

126 [1962] A.C. 413.

127 [1962] 1 Lloyd's Rep. 81; see the case at para.9-026, above.

128 [2007] 1 P. & C.R. 20 CA at 358; see the case at para.9-030, above.

129 [2012] 2 Lloyd's Rep. 61; see the case at para.9-031, above.

130 See the question posed in *White and Carter v McGregor* [1962] A.C. 413 of whether one who has contracted to go to Hong Kong at his own expense to make a report for a large fee should be entitled, when informed before he has incurred any expenses that the other contracting party no longer wants the report, to set off for Hong Kong and produce the report in order to claim the fee.

131 [1984] 1 All E.R. 129.

132 [1984] 1 All E.R. 129 at 137e; italics his. This was established in the United States very early in the leading case of *Clark v Marsiglia*, 1 Denio 317 (N.Y. 1845).

133 [1962] A.C. 413.

134 [1962] 1 Lloyd's Rep. 81.

135 See para.9-096, below.

136 See para.9-081, below.

137 [1997] A.C. 191.

not claim for his real loss, however foreseeable, but is restricted to the loss, when less, which is attributable to the breach of duty for which alone the defendant is liable.[138] It is thought that mitigation should attach, in the claimant's favour, to the real loss and not to the lesser attributable loss; the alternative smacks of a double deduction. The preferred solution is in line with that arrived at on contributory negligence by the House of Lords in *Platform Homes Loans Ltd v Oyston Shipways Ltd*.[139] Indeed the trial judge, on account of a failure to mitigate, had made a reduction from the actual loss before applying the SAAMCO limitation, and this approach was rehearsed without criticism in the speeches in the House of Lords. But in neither court was the point argued.[140]

**(i) Mitigation applies even to consequences intended by a tortfeasor** The issue of whether a plea of failure to mitigate can be raised in respect of consequences intended by the tortfeasor arose in *Secretary of State for Health v Servier Laboratories Ltd*.[141] It was alleged in that case that the defendant had wrongfully perpetuated a monopoly, permitting the supply of a particular drug at a higher price than would otherwise have been the case in a competitive market. The claims were brought under arts 101 and 102 of the Treaty on the Functioning of the European Union and for the economic tort of interference with the claimants' economic interests. The defendants sought to amend to allege that the claimants had failed take reasonable steps to mitigate their losses. The claimants submitted that mitigation was not required in respect of consequences intended by a tortfeasor. At this pleading stage, the primary judge, Henderson J, rejected the claimants' submission that **9-038**

> "[t]he same policy that rules out the defence of contributory negligence as regards an intended consequence rules out the duty to mitigate damages also".[142]

The primary judge rightly rejected this submission because the exclusion of intended damage would in many cases make the doctrine impossible to operate with any certainty. Claimants will rarely know, when the doctrine of mitigation comes into play, whether the loss was intended by the defendant.[143]

## 2. The Rule and its Relationship to the Normal Measure of Damages

There are not many decisions which illustrate the rule that loss which should have been mitigated is not recoverable. The reason for this is that either the court has held that the claimant has not failed to mitigate the loss so that he recovers in respect of the whole damage,[144] or, probably more commonly, the issue has never reached the point of litigation because the claimant has in his own interests taken the necessary steps to mitigate. Indeed, so clear is the way of mitigation in many cases that **9-039**

---

138 For details, see para.34-073, below.

139 [2000] 2 A.C. 190. See para.7-010, above.

140 For a somewhat similar calculation, also rightly in the claimant's favour, see *Ministry of Defence v Wheeler* [1998] 1 W.L.R. 537 CA, at para.10-105, below.

141 [2016] EWHC 2381 Ch.

142 [2016] EWHC 2381 Ch at [57], relying upon Glanville William's, *Joint Torts and Contributory Negligence*, (Stevens & Sons,1951).

143 *Secretary of State for Health v Servier Laboratories Ltd* [2016] EWHC 2381 (Ch) at [60].

144 That the onus of proof is on the defendant (see para.9-020, above) does of course favour the claimant in this connection.

it often tends to become incorporated into the normal measure of damages. When this happens it loses its identity and does not expressly appear as a separate issue.[145]

9-040 Such a situation arises particularly in cases of sale of goods. Thus, if a seller fails to deliver the goods contracted for, the buyer cannot sit back on a rising market or wait until his sub-sale to a third party has fallen through, but must go into the market with all reasonable speed and buy equivalent goods there. This mitigating step is incorporated into the normal measure of damages by s.51(3) of the Sale of Goods Act 1979, which provides that in an action for non-delivery the measure of damages, where there is an available market for the goods in question, is prima facie to be ascertained by the difference between the contract price and the market price at the time the goods ought to have been delivered. Conversely, if a buyer of goods fails to accept them, the seller must take steps to resell them to another and not sit back on a falling market.[146] This, similarly, is incorporated into the normal measure of damages by s.50(3) of the Sale of Goods Act 1979, which provides that in an action for non-acceptance the measure of damages, where there is an available market for the goods in question, is prima facie to be ascertained by the difference between the contract price and the market price at the time the goods ought to have been accepted.

9-041 Yet in contracts involving the rendering of services and the non-acceptance of these services as the breach, as where an employee's services are dispensed with or a carrier's services are not taken up, although it is clear that the claimant must try to sell his services elsewhere, this mitigating step may not yet have become fully incorporated into the normal measure of damages. For wrongful dismissal the fullest statement of the normal measure of damages is still the early statement of Erle CJ in *Beckham v Drake*.[147] He said:

> "The measure of damages for the breach of promise now in question is obtained by considering what is the usual rate of wages for the employment here contracted for, and what time would be lost before a similar employment could be obtained. The law considers that employment in any ordinary branch of industry can be obtained by a person competent for the place, and that the usual rate of wages for such employment can be proved, and that it is the duty of the servant to use diligence to find another employment."

Thus the salary obtained from alternative employment upon wrongful dismissal was being regarded specifically as mitigation rather than as built into the normal measure, and this was still the approach taken as late as *Ministry of Defence v Wheeler*.[148] In that case this may have been because the amount the employees would have earned under their contracts was subject to the loss of a chance doctrine

[145] See *Compania Financiera "Soleada" v Hamoor Tanker Corp, The Borag* [1981] 1 W.L.R. 274 CA, where the Court of Appeal said that expenditure incurred in obtaining the release of a ship arrested in breach of contract was to be regarded simply as expenditure for which recovery would be allowed if not too remote and not, as the judge had held below, as expenditure by way of mitigation of a wrongful act. The acquisition of alternative computer systems to replace the one purchased under the negligent advice of the defendant consultant, which gave rise to the main damages issue in *Stephenson Blake (Holdings) Ltd v Streets Heaver Ltd* [2001] Lloyd's Rep. P.N. 44, should not have been looked at as a matter of mitigation ([2001] Lloyd's Rep. P.N. 44 at [72]–[82], [158]–[202]) rather than as one of normal measure.

[146] *Dunkirk Colliery Co v Lever* (1878) 9 Ch. D. 20 CA at 25, where James LJ stated the general rule as to mitigation cited in the last footnote in para.9-014, above, was a case of non-acceptance of goods sold.

[147] (1849) 2 H.L.C. 579 at 607 to 608.

[148] [1998] 1 W.L.R. 637 CA.

but adoption of the built-in approach would have made it easier for the Court of Appeal to reach the difficult but correct conclusion that it did reach.[149] So, too, for failure to supply cargo for carriage the normal measure was stated by Kay LJ in *Aitken Lilburn v Ernsthausen*[150] thus:

> "The general rule is, that when such a breach by non-delivery of [i.e. failure to supply] cargo occurs the owners are entitled to damages to the amount of the freight thereby lost. But if they fill up the ship on their own account, the amount of freight so earned goes in reduction of such damages."

For A. L. Smith LJ in the same case, on the other hand, the normal measure of damages was

> "the difference between the charterparty freight and the net freight actually earned, after deducting expenses".[151]

The correct trend in these cases of employment contracts and contracts of carriage, it is submitted, must be towards the incorporation of the normal mitigating step into the normal measure of damages.[152] The practical importance of defining the normal measure in this way lies in the burden of proof.[153]

However, it is important to be certain of what the normal measure of damages is, before deciding what form of mitigation is properly incorporated within it. Particularly instructive is a comparison of the normal measure of damages where goods sold are not delivered in breach of contract and of the normal measure where goods are tortiously misappropriated. In the case of sale of goods the buyer must go into the market for a replacement, or at least cannot sit back on a rising market and then claim damages on the basis of the increased price: but no such step towards replacement need be taken by the victim of a misappropriation. **9-042**

This is made particularly clear by the Court of Appeal decision in *Rosenthal v Alderton*.[154] This established that a claimant suing in the former[155] detinue was entitled to claim, in the absence of a return of the property, the market price at the time of the judgment; thus any rise in the market price between detention and judgment was at the risk of the defendant. Only if the claimant unduly delayed his ac- **9-043**

---

149 See the case at para.10-105, below. For a somewhat similar calculation involving mitigation, again rightly in the claimant's favour, see at para.9-037, above.

150 [1894] 1 Q.B. 773 CA at 777.

151 [1894] 1 Q.B. 773 CA at 777 at 781.

152 In this connection the authorities on carriage are considered in some detail at paras 32-063 to 32-067, below. *London Building Society v Stone* [1983] 1 W.L.R. 1242 CA, provides an interesting diversity of view on whether moneys which might be available to a claimant should come into the computation of damages as part of the normal measure or by way of mitigation, or indeed at all. The claimants had lent money on mortgage on the strength of the defendant's valuation of a worthless property, so that the money was lost to the claimants subject to their extraction of money from their borrower. To O'Connor LJ the question was whether recovery by the claimants from the mortgagor could come in at all to reduce their damages against the defendant valuer (at 1257A to B), to Stephenson LJ it was whether the claimants had failed to mitigate by not attempting to obtain any recovery from the mortgagor (at 1262D to E), while to Sir Denys Buckley "it does not depend upon mitigation by the plaintiff of his primary loss, but upon a reduction in the amount of that primary loss, by the expected performance by the covenantor of his covenant" (at 1259F). See the case at para.34-080, below.

153 See para.9-020, above, and, in the context of contracts of carriage, para.32-067, below.

154 [1946] K.B. 374 CA.

155 See paras 38-002 to 38-004, below.

tion on a rising market would the damages be less than the market price at the time of judgment,[156] as the failure to sue within a reasonable time was a failure to mitigate. Now detinue has been abolished and superseded by conversion,[157] but the result is the same in conversion though admittedly reached by a different route. The normal measure is taken to be not the value of the goods at the time of judgment but their value at the time of conversion, and to this there is added as consequential loss any market increase in value between then and the earliest time that the action could have been brought to trial. This proposition appears to be established for conversion by the Court of Appeal decision in *Sachs v Miklos*,[158] which permitted a claimant to recover at the end of the Second World War the market value of goods converted near the beginning of the war, this value being greatly increased during the war years, provided that he neither knew nor ought to have known of the conversion during this period and provided also that there was not undue delay in his bringing an action after knowledge.[159] However, although neither in detinue did, nor in conversion does, the claimant fail at his peril to replace on a rising market,[160] he must accept redelivery of the goods if offered by the defendant at trial, provided the goods are still in the same condition. This followed naturally in the case of detinue which was primarily an action claiming redelivery rather than damages, but it was also established for conversion from the time of *Fisher v Prince*,[161] decided in 1762. This power of the court to stay the proceedings where the goods are brought into court and the claimant refuses to accept them does not indeed result in a smaller recovery for him: he merely is compelled to take specific restitution in lieu of damages.[162]

**9-044** The reason for basing the damages for failure to deliver goods in breach of contract, but not the damages for tortious misappropriation of goods, upon the assumption of replacement may be that in the case of contract the claimant will generally still have available for purchasing a replacement in the market the money with which he had intended to pay the price, a factor which has no application in the cases of tort. From this reasoning it would follow that even in contract a claimant should not be restricted in his damages by reason of an assumption of replacement of the goods if he has already paid the contract price for them to the defendant. Indirect support for this view is given in a number of old but, it is thought, still relevant and useful cases. Thus in *Gainsford v Carroll*,[163] the claimant's contention that the damages for non-delivery of goods sold should be the market price at the time of trial was rejected on the ground that he still had the money on breach

---

[156] See para.38-021, below.

[157] See the preceding fn. but one.

[158] [1948] 2 K.B. 23 CA. The dictum of Greer LJ in *Hall v Barclay* [1937] 3 All E.R. 620 CA at 623, that "where you are dealing with goods which can be readily bought in the market, a man whose rights have been interfered with is never entitled to more than what he would have to pay to buy a similar article in the market", should be read in the light of this decision; the "never" would seem to be too strong a word.

[159] For the solution the courts have reached where the market price falls between the time of wrong and the time of trial, and for a full consideration of the general problems involved in this field, see paras 38-011 and following, below.

[160] See paras 39-017 to 39-018, below, the cases which entitle a claimant who has suffered damage to his land and buildings to defer reinstatement from the date of tort to the date of judgment, thereby increasing the award to be made.

[161] (1762) 3 Burr. 1363.

[162] The rule in *Fisher v Prince* and the relevant authorities are considered at para.38-081, below.

[163] (1824) 2 B. & C. 624.

with which he had intended to pay the purchase price. In *Shaw v Holland*,[164] an equivalent case of non-delivery of shares sold, the court rejected the time of trial as the time that the market price should be taken, as "the plaintiff had his money in his own possession, and might have gone into the market and bought other shares as soon as the contract was broken".[165] In *Barrow v Arnaud*,[166] a tort action on the case similar to detinue, where the defendant collector of customs was being sued by the claimant for refusing to sign a bill of entry for his corn under a claim of customs duty, the claimant recovered for the loss he suffered by reason of a fall in the market, the court pointing out that he might not have had any money to pay the defendant the customs duty demanded. These cases generally make reference to actions for not replacing stock, where similarly it has been held, as in *Shepherd v Johnson*,[167] that the claimant is entitled to recover the market value to which the stock has risen between the time of the wrong and the time of the trial, because the defendant here holds the claimant's money and thus prevents him from using it.[168] Yet when it came to the test in a sale of goods case in which the purchase price had been partially prepaid, it was held in *Startup v Cortazzi*[169] that the claimant still should have replaced. Whether this is basically consistent with the dicta in and rationale of the above sale of goods and shares cases, and with the decisions in actions for not replacing stock, may be doubted. It is, indeed, encouraging to see that the door is not closed to rejection of the view embodied in *Startup v Cortazzi*,[170] for Atkin LJ in *Aronson v Mologa Holzindustrie*[171] treated the matter as an open point.[172]

At the other end of the scale from the problem that mitigating steps cannot be incorporated into the normal measure till it is known what the normal measure is, **9-045**
is the problem, which arises once the normal measure with built-in mitigating step has been established, of whether this step has indeed cut down the loss, since there are certain cases in which such cutting down is only apparent and not real. This is especially so in cases where the defendant has in breach of contract failed to accept goods which the claimant has sold him as in *Thompson v Robinson*,[173] or has manufactured and supplied to him as in *Re Vic Mill*,[174] or has hired to him as in *Interoffice Telephones v Freeman*.[175] In all these cases the claimant had indeed suc-

---

164 (1846) 15 M. & W. 136.

165 (1846) 15 M. & W. 136 at 146.

166 (1846) 8 Q.B. 595.

167 (1802) 2 East 211.

168 A more complex situation is presented when the market has both risen and fallen between the time of wrong and the time of trial. Stocks and shares are particularly prone to such a fluctuation, but the principles involved apply equally to goods. Here the award of the highest intermediate market value commands some support, though more in principle than in authority. However, there are several types of case in which this issue can arise, and they require separate treatment. They are principally (1) actions for breach of contract in not replacing stock: see para.29-014, below; (2) actions for conversion and in the former detinue: see para.38-022, below; (3) actions for failure to carry stock on margin, which may be either breach of contract or conversion; see paras 34-089 to 34-091, below.

169 (1835) 2 C.M. & R. 165.

170 (1835) 2 C.M. & R. 165.

171 (1927) 32 Com. Cas. 276 CA at 289 to 291.

172 The proposition that, provided the circumstances are appropriate, immediate replacement by a contracting party may not be called for has gathered weighty support in the context of sale of land: see the cases at para.27-009, below.

173 [1955] Ch. 177.

174 [1913] 1 Ch. 465 CA.

175 [1958] 1 Q.B. 190 CA. It can also be so, as *Sony Computer Entertainment Ltd v Cinram Logistics*

ceeded in selling, supplying or hiring the goods in question to a third party at a similar profit to that which he would have made under his contract with the claimant, and in each case it was contended by the defendant that he had thereby avoided any loss and was, therefore, not entitled to more than nominal damages. This contention, however, ignored the fact that the state of the market was such that the claimant would have been able to make such a contract with a third party even if the defendant had carried out his. In the words of Hamilton LJ in *Re Vic Mill*,[176]

> "the fallacy … is in supposing that the second customer was a substituted customer, that, had all gone well, the makers would not have had both customers, both orders, and both profits".[177]

If, on the other hand, the state of the market or the state of the defendant's manufacturing facilities was such that demand exceeded supply, the contract made with the third party would be a substituted contract, the loss would be avoided and the damages would therefore be nominal: this was the position in *Charter v Sullivan*,[178] which represents, in relation to the sale of cars, the converse of *Thompson v Robinson*.[179]

**9-046** The situation with non-acceptance of goods arises again in cases of non-acceptance by the defendant of the claimant's services. The fact that the claimant has made a similar service contract does not necessarily entail that he has avoided the loss. He will not have done so if he would have been capable of carrying out both contracts simultaneously, as will very frequently be the case where the claimant, especially if a company, would perform the contract by employing others to do the actual work. If, on the other hand, the defendant has bargained for the claimant's exclusive services, any other service contract made by the claimant on the defendant's breach will be a substituted contract, and the benefit derived from it will be taken into account in assessing damages against the defendant.

### 3. ILLUSTRATIONS OF CIRCUMSTANCES RAISING THE ISSUE OF WHETHER LOSS SHOULD HAVE BEEN AVOIDED

**9-047** Here it is useful to distinguish between situations where the door to mitigation is not opened by the defaulting party and situations where it is. Where tort is concerned, cases in the former category are infinitely more common than those in the latter, whereas cases in the latter category predominate over those in the former where contract is in issue.[180]

---

*UK Ltd* [2008] EWCA Civ 955 CA shows, where a seller fails to achieve his sale because the goods are stolen in transit to the purchaser. Sony saw the question squarely as one of mitigation. See the case at para.32-020, below.

176 [1913] 1 Ch. 465 CA at 473.

177 Whether changes in the state of the market are to be taken to be within the contemplation of the defendant is a separate issue of remoteness dealt with at para.8-203, above.

178 [1957] 2 Q.B. 117 CA.

179 [1955] Ch. 177. The principle of this decision does not apply to secondhand cars: see *Lazenby Garages v Wright* [1976] 1 W.L.R. 459 CA at para.25-130, below.

180 Neither contract nor tort was involved in *Al-Rawas v Pegasus Energy Ltd* [2007] EWHC 2427 (QB). It was an enquiry into damages on cross-undertakings for losses occasioned by the imposition of freezing orders later set aside. A loan was obtained in order to pay money into court to avoid freezing order restrictions and, in the claim for the difference between the interest on the money lent and the money in court, there was held to be no failure to mitigate in not having pursued other methods

## (1) Contract

**(a) In general: where the door to mitigation is not opened by the party in breach** Illustrations here straddle a variety of contracts, from sale of goods to lease of land and reaching to contracts for the professional services of surveyors, valuers and solicitors.[181] **9-048**

*(i) Sale of goods* In *Simon v Pawsons & Leafs*,[182] the claimant ordered certain material from the defendant which the defendant promised to stock for her but failed to do so. The result of the claimant's not obtaining the material from the defendant was that she lost an appointment as maker of school clothes to a school. The Court of Appeal refused damages to her for her loss of this appointment because, inter alia, she had had ample opportunity, after she learnt of the defendant's breach in failing to stock material for her, to buy equivalent material elsewhere but had made no attempt to do so.[183] In *Toepfer v Warinco AG*,[184] the omission of buyers of meal to protest that the wrong kind of meal was being delivered by the sellers, which allowed such wrong delivery to continue, was held to constitute a failure to mitigate. By contrast, in *Browning v Brachers*,[185] the Court of Appeal took the view, contrary to that of the trial judge, that the claimants, who were complaining that the defendant had sold them an infected goatherd,[186] were not required, in mitigation, to have taken particular steps suggested by experts in the case to control the infection.[187] **9-049**

*(ii) Lease of land* In *Tucker v Linger*,[188] where a landlord in breach of covenant failed to supply materials to the tenant with which to repair the premises, the tenant failed to recover for damage caused to his crops in his barn by bad weather because the barn was out of repair, since he ought to have provided himself with the necessary materials and done the repair, and charged the landlord with the price of the materials.[189] Where a tenant failed to give notice to his landlord of disrepair, **9-050**

---

of finance.

181 Building contracts make a brief appearance in *Tomlinson v Wilson* unreported 11 May 2007 (QB) (TCC), where the owner of a defectively built house extension was required in mitigation to repair rather than demolish and rebuild.

182 (1933) 38 Com. Cas. 151 CA.

183 *Greer and Slesser* LJJ decided on this ground: see (1933) 38 Com. Cas. 151 CA at 163 and 165 respectively. Slesser LJ also decided, as did Scrutton LJ, on the ground that the damage was too remote.

184 [1978] 2 Lloyd's Rep. 569.

185 [2005] EWCA Civ 753 CA. The report at [2005] P.N.L.R.44 at 901 is just a one page note; it does not set out the lengthy judgments on the appeal.

186 See the facts at para.10-096, below.

187 See [2005] EWCA Civ 753 CA at [138], [162] and following and [228] to [236]. Various failures of the claimant in the wake of the delivery of defective goods in *Borealis AB v Geogas Trading SA* [2011] 1 Lloyd's Rep. 482 (facts at para.8-150, above) were argued by the defendant, unsuccessfully, to be failures to mitigate: see [2011] 1 Lloyd's Rep. 482 at [127] and following. In *SC Confectia SA v Miss Mania Wholesale Ltd* [2014] EWCA Civ 1484 there was a sale of defective garments which the buyer sold on and, on discovery of the defects, wished to retrieve the garments from its sub-buyer but could not do so as the sub-buyer had gone into liquidation. The Court of Appeal held that there was no failure to mitigate, but the one reasoned judgement is not thought to be too clear either on mitigation or, for the purpose of damages, on the correct valuation of the garments.

188 (1882) 21 Ch. D. 18.

189 It is true that Kay J relied on the tenant's duty to repair under his independent covenant to repair: *Tucker v Linger* (1882) 21 Ch. D. 18 at 30. But it would seem the tenant should not recover even in the absence of such a duty upon him.

so that the landlord took no action and the disrepair, and with it the discomfort and inconvenience to the tenant, were allowed to continue, this failure was held to be a failure to mitigate in *Minchburn v Peck*.[190] It was thus the damages for non-pecuniary loss that were reduced; the trial judge's view, causing him to make no reduction in his award, that the doctrine of mitigation was confined to commercial contracts and did not apply as between landlord and tenant, was rejected without difficulty by the Court of Appeal. Similar is *Shine v English Churches Housing Group*,[191] where the lessee, even under a series of court orders, for long refused to vacate the premises, making it impossible for the lessor to effect the repairs until the lessee's eventual vacation, with the result that they took a good deal longer than they otherwise would have done. The Court of Appeal reduced the award to the lessee because his conduct was held to constitute a failure to mitigate.[192]

**9-051** *(iii) Contracts for professional services: surveyors, valuers and solicitors* While formerly the general rule refusing recovery for mitigable loss was sparsely illustrated in contract, the spate of litigation at the end of the last century by mortgage lenders, caught out by a collapsing market, against their professional advisers, where borrower and security have proved inadequate, gave a boost to the law on contractual mitigation. Various types of failure to act in mitigation have appeared in claims by mortgage lenders, and also house purchasers, against their surveyors, valuers and solicitors who have negligently advised on the property being mortgaged, or purchased. A failure to enforce the borrower's security appeared in *Western Trust & Savings Ltd v Travers & Co*,[193] a claim by mortgage lenders against their solicitors for a negligent report on title to the mortgaged property. The lenders' failure first to bring an action for possession of the property was held to be a failure to mitigate since this was the normal, and not difficult, method of enforcing the security; as a result the damages were reduced to a nominal amount. By contrast, in *The Mortgage Corporation v Halifax (SW) Ltd*,[194] the defendants failed to satisfy the court that the claimant lenders had been unreasonably tardy in obtaining possession from the mortgagor borrower; the fact that the claimants were at the time unaware that they were victims of the defendants' negligence was an important fact in assessing whether there had been a failure to mitigate.[195] Another type of failure to mitigate is a failure to effect an earlier sale of the security when market prices were more favourable. This appeared in three of the eight cases decided under the umbrella of *Bristol and West Building Society v Fancy & Jackson*.[196] Also, although the speeches in the House of Lords in *Platform Homes Loans Ltd v Oyston Shipways Ltd*,[197] do not elucidate why the trial judge there saw fit to reduce the damages on account of a failure to mitigate, the decision at first instance being unreported, it was probably on account of a late and less advantageous sale. A somewhat different case of a failure to mitigate by not selling the property earlier is *Patel v Hooper & Jackson*.[198] The claimants were not mortgage lenders but

190 (1988) 20 H.L.R. 392 CA.
191 [2004] H.LR. 42 CA at 727.
192 See [2004] H.L.R. 42 at [111]–[113].
193 [1997] P.N.L.R. 295 CA.
194 [1999] Lloyd's Rep. P.N. 159.
195 See [1999] Lloyd's Rep. P.N. 159 at 183–184.
196 [1997] 4 All E.R. 582. See at 623 to 624 where the mitigation issue is dealt with rather briefly.
197 [2000] 2 A.C. 190.
198 [1999] 1 W.L.R. 1792 CA.

purchasers of a house on the strength of a negligent report and valuation by the defendant surveyors. The house proved to be uninhabitable unless restored at a cost that the claimants could not afford. Their claim for the cost of temporary alternative accommodation for the seven years up to the time of trial was allowed for the first five years only, since it was held that by then they should have offered the house for sale and sold it.[199]

Negligent advice causing losses can also lead to a reduction in liability if the client fails to mitigate the loss. *LSREF III Wight Ltd v Gateley LLP*,[200] involved negligence by a firm of solicitors who had been retained by a bank to provide advice in relation to property being offered as security for a loan. The negligence was a failure to advise about an insolvency forfeiture clause in a lease over the property. The security was worth £240,000 less than it would have been if the clause had not been present. Prior to the trial, the lessor offered to remove the clause for £150,000. The solicitors offered to pay this. But the bank (by its assignee) refused this offer. The solicitors alleged that the bank (or its assignee) had failed to mitigate its loss. The Court of Appeal accepted this submission. The Court of Appeal held that the loss was suffered at the time of entry into the transaction. Simply because the security had not been realised did not prevent the loss being suffered, as measured by the difference in value between the security with the clause and the security without the clause. Realisation of the security would simply crystallise that loss. The bank had unreasonably failed to mitigate that loss by failing to accept the lessor's offer to vary the lease.

**(b) In particular: where the door to mitigation is opened by the party in breach** The most abundant authority on contractual mitigation appears in cases where the opportunity of mitigating has arisen through the possibility of further negotiation with, and in particular through an offer made by, the party in breach himself. In *Payzu v Saunders*,[201] which remains the leading case on non-recoverable mitigable loss in this contractual context, Scrutton LJ stated that counsel's contention that 9-052

> "in considering what steps should be taken to mitigate the damage all contractual relations with the party in default must be excluded"

was contrary to his experience.[202] This is confirmed by the authorities which deal primarily with two types of contract, contracts of sale and contracts of employment; contracts of carriage also feature and contracts for hire of goods.

*(i) Contracts of sale* In *Payzu v Saunders*,[203] the defendant, a dealer in silk, sold 400 pieces of crêpe de chine to the claimant which were to be delivered in nine monthly instalments and which were to be paid for within one month of each delivery less 2.5 per cent discount. The claimant failed to make punctual payment 9-053

---

199 See, too, *Skipton Building Society v Lea Hough & Co* [2000] P.N.L.R. 545 where the action failed because the lender had disposed of the mortgage debt to a third party for a price that was far too low. The judge said that the claimant's action, apart from being negligent, could be expressed as a failure to take reasonable steps to mitigate: at 555C.

200 [2016] EWCA Civ 359 CA.

201 [1919] 2 K.B. 581 CA.

202 [1919] 2 K.B. 581 CA at 589.

203 [1919] 2 K.B. 581 CA.

on the first instalment and the defendant, in the bona fide but erroneous belief that the non-payment was due to the claimant's insolvency, refused in breach of contract to deliver any further instalments on the arranged credit. He offered to deliver to the claimant at the contract price against cash, an offer refused, on a rising market, by the claimant. It was held that the claimant should have mitigated his loss by accepting this offer and that, therefore, his damages were limited to what he would have suffered had he accepted it, which would have been only the loss of the useful period of credit. In *The Solholt*,[204] where delivery a day late by the sellers of a ship gave the buyers a right of cancellation which they exercised although the market value of the ship at the time had appreciated by $500,000 over the contract price, the court refused to award this amount, which represented the normal measure of damages,[205] or indeed any amount to the buyers because they had failed to mitigate their loss by negotiating a further contract for the purchase of the ship at the original contract price, the judge below having found that such an offer, if made to the sellers, would have been accepted by them. This goes somewhat further than *Payzu*[206]—some may think too far—in the defendant's favour in that it requires the claimant not merely to consider a further offer by the defendant but to seek out the defendant with a further proposal himself. On the other hand, it was held in *Strutt v Whitnell*,[207] that a buyer of a house, suing his seller after conveyance because he was unable to obtain vacant possession on account of a tenant refusing to leave, was not required, in mitigation of damage, to accept the offer of the seller to repurchase the house at the contract price.

**9-054** In *The Solholt*,[208] the Court of Appeal was bound both by the decision in *Payzu v Saunders*,[209] and that in *Strutt v Whitnell*,[210] but was sceptical about the latter, reconciling it with the former only "by treating it as a decision turning on reasonableness and its own special facts".[211] The defendants, in breach of contract by being unable to give the claimant vacant possession of the house they had sold to him because of the presence of a sitting tenant, offered to buy it back. The claimant refused to do so and successfully sued for the difference between the value of the house with, and its value without, vacant possession, which came out at £1,900. The defendants argued that the claimant should have mitigated by repurchasing and was entitled to nominal damages only. Sir John Donaldson MR in *The Solholt* commented on *Strutt v Whitnell* thus:

> "If the House of Lords ever had to consider the decision, it might well hold that the judgments totally confuse the proposition that in deciding whether to rescind or affirm a contract the innocent party need have no regard to considerations of mitigation of loss with the proposition that, having made such an election, he will be able to recover such loss as was unavoidable following that election and that in some, perhaps exceptional, circumstances it may be reasonable at a stage after the decision to rescind or affirm the contract to adopt a course of action which will nullify the effect of that decision."[212]

---

204 [1983] 1 Lloyd's Rep. 605 CA.

205 See para.25-004, below.

206 [1919] 2 K.B. 581 CA.

207 [1975] 1 W.L.R. 870 CA.

208 [1983] 1 Lloyd's Rep. 605 CA.

209 [1919] 2 K.B. 581 CA.

210 [1975] 1 W.L.R. 870 CA.

211 [1983] 1 Lloyd's Rep. 605 CA at 609.

212 [1983] 1 Lloyd's Rep. 605 CA at 609.

However, it is not right to say that there was any such confusion in the *Strutt v Whitnell*[213] judgments. For the position in that case was very different from that in the other two. It was not concerned with a performance of the contract of sale by taking delivery of the property but with an offer to undo the contract by taking back the property. Submitting to the undoing of the contract and giving up the remedy in damages entirely was said not to be called for. As Cairns LJ said of the claimant[214]:

> "He must have had some commercial reason in his mind and one would imagine that it must have been in the hope of the house improving in value and possibly in the hope that eventually he would be able to get the sitting tenant out and get a better price for it."

Indeed the defendant's offer to repurchase was seen as simply equivalent to an offer to pay damages, but in kind rather than in money. For Cairns LJ also said that, if the contentions of the defendants' counsel were right,

> "it would logically follow that if the offer that had been made by the defendants had been not 'We will take the house back' but 'We will pay you £1,900 damages' and the plaintiff had then, for some reason, refused that offer and had brought an action for damages it could be said that he ought to have accepted the offer and thereby mitigated his damages and therefore he was entitled to nothing at all. That cannot be."[215]

Yet while the result in *Strutt v Whitnell* is to be supported, there may be **9-055**
circumstances when it would be appropriate for the buyer to accept an offer by the seller to repurchase the goods sold to him, as indeed was held in *Houndsditch Warehouse Co v Waltex*,[216] an earlier first instance decision which in the light of *Strutt v Whitnell* may have to be reconsidered or, preferably, distinguished. The seller of some 300 dozen men's braces, who was in breach of warranty of quality, offered to take back at a reasonable price the whole stock of braces that the buyer had been unable, because of defects in the braces, to sell on to his retailers. It was held that the buyer should have accepted this offer to mitigate his loss and that the damages must be reduced accordingly. Here the buyer had no use for the remaining braces which were held to be valueless in his hands and he was therefore claiming as damages the contract price he had paid for the remaining stock, without the normal deduction for residual value, together with the profit that he would have made on the stock's resale. It clearly was reasonable for him, and to his immediate advantage, to accept the price offered to take the stock off his hands rather than persist with a claim for the full contract price of that stock. The trial judge therefore made a broad brush reduction to that part of the buyer's claim while holding him still entitled to the profit that he had failed to make on that stock as a result of the breach. In a sense the seller's offer was again an offer to pay damages, though here only part of the damages, but the case is very different from *Strutt v Whitnell* where the undoing of the whole contract was being proposed.[217]

---

213 [1975] 1 W.L.R. 870 CA.

214 [1975] 1 W.L.R. 870 CA at 874A.

215 [1975] 1 W.L.R. 870 CA at 873C. The Court of Appeal, citing this passage from Cairns LJ's judgment, followed *Strutt v Whitnell*, though in a very different context, in *Copley v Lawn* [2009] EWCA Civ 580 CA (at para.9-077, below), clearly regarding *Strutt* as a perfectly correct decision.

216 [1944] K.B. 579.

217 *Strutt v Whitnell* was applied in *Velmore Estates v Roseberry Homes Ltd* [2006] 2 P. & C.R. 10 at 230 to allow the seller of land the normal measure of damages for the buyer's failure to complete

**9-056** It is important to note, in dealing with these somewhat difficult cases, that a curious feature of *Payzu v Saunders*,[218] and *The Solholt*,[219] is that the result in both gave an uncovenanted and undeserved profit to the party in breach. In each case the market had risen by the time of the seller's breach, the buyer without the silk in the one case and the ship in the other was unable to profit from this rise and, the buyer being refused the damages which would have made up for it, the profit from the market rise was made available to the defaulting seller. It is unclear why the buyer in these two cases refused to take the silk or ship when it was clearly to his advantage to do so and, while it might be thought to be fairer to have the seller pay the damages and not make the profit, it can equally be said that the buyer had only himself to blame for losing out. It has been suggested that the cases cannot be explained in terms of mitigation of loss as the loss only comes into being if the damages are refused,[220] so that one has a somewhat circular position, but it can be said that the loss arises when the silk or ship is not delivered and that this loss can be eliminated by a later acceptance of silk or ship by the buyer. And though in *Houndsditch Warehouse Co v Waltex*,[221] the seller did not make a profit out of its breach, it can again be said that the buyer had only himself to blame for losing out. Had he accepted the seller's offer of payment for the stock to be returned he would not have found his damages for the valueless stock in his hands reduced. Also there is no difficulty in explaining the decision in terms of mitigation; the loss related to the fact that the remaining stock was valueless in the buyer's hands and he could and should have mitigated this loss by accepting the seller's offer to pay him for taking it off his hands.

**9-057** Where the seller's initial breach is in delivering defective goods rather than not delivering the goods at all and the seller's offer is to put the goods right rather than to take them back, the position is simpler and there is much less likelihood that a refusal of goods put right will constitute a failure to mitigate. Thus in *Heaven & Kesterton v Etablissements François Albiac*,[222] it was held, where a buyer under a c.i.f. contract had rightly rejected the goods on the ground of defective quality, that he was not required to accept them if afterwards offered in mitigation. In *Truk (UK) Ltd v Tokmakidis GmbH*,[223] the buyer of a defective vehicle, who was held properly to have rejected it, was also held in all the circumstances not to have failed to mitigate by refusing to accept a repaired vehicle from the seller.[224]

**9-058** *(ii) Contracts of carriage* Where there is a breach by failure to carry persons or goods followed by a further offer to carry, or, conversely, there is a failure to provide

---

of contract price less market price, there being no requirement for the seller to mitigate by accepting offers by the buyer after breach to go ahead with the purchase at the original price. In *Activa DPS Europe SARL v Pressure Seal Solutions Ltd* [2012] EWCA Civ 943 CA the decision was again applied. The seller of machines to a buyer who failed to pay for them was held not to have failed to mitigate by refusing the offer to return the machines that the buyer had not resold since, while the victim of a breach of contract has to take the available steps to reduce the loss, there is no call to act so as to reverse the transaction: see Patten LJ, giving the only reasoned judgment, at [2012] EWCA Civ 943 CA at [33]–[36].

[218] [1919] 2 K.B. 581 CA.
[219] [1983] 1 Lloyd's Rep. 605 CA.
[220] See Bridge, (1989) 105 L.Q.R. 398 criticising *Payzu v Saunders* and, in particular, *The Solholt*.
[221] [1944] K.B. 579.
[222] [1956] 2 Lloyd's Rep. 316.
[223] [2000] 1 Lloyd's Rep. 543.
[224] [2000] 1 Lloyd's Rep. 543 at 552, col.2.

persons or goods for carriage followed by a further offer to make such provision, the question arises as to whether there is a failure to mitigate by not taking up the further offer. Two cases provide here a useful contrast; the one is old, concerns carriage of persons and the carrier in breach, the other is modern, concerns carriage of goods and the carrier the victim of the breach. In *Ansett v Marshall*,[225] the defendant in breach of contract had refused to carry the claimant on a ship to Australia under the belief that he had not paid his entire fare, but upon immediately afterwards finding out the error had offered the claimant an alternative passage on another ship sailing a week later, an offer refused by the claimant who stayed on in England to sue the defendant. The case concerned a question of costs, but Crompton J said to the defendant's counsel in argument:

> "He could not recover as damages in this action the expense of more than a few days' delay, for you show that you offered him another passage to Australia almost immediately."[226]

By contrast in *UBC Chartering Ltd v Liepaya Shipping Co, The Liepaya*,[227] shipowners were held not to have failed to mitigate on account of not having accepted additional employment for the vessel from the charterers who were in breach of the time charterparty by redelivering the vessel prematurely. The owners were entitled to require that any deal should be without prejudice to their claim but the charterers saw their offer as being in satisfaction of any possible claim. This apart, the parties could not agree on rates. However, the owners being entitled to have their negotiations judged against the background of the existing market, the court was unable to say that the owners' rate expectations were unreasonable so that the charterers had failed to prove that the owners' unpreparedness to accept the rates offered was unreasonable.

*(iii) Contracts of hire of goods* For use in the warehouses of the claimant's cheese business, the defendant in *Manton Hire and Sales Ltd v Ash Manor Cheese Company Ltd*,[228] had supplied the claimant with a fork lift truck which turned out to be of unsuitable dimensions due to the faulty measurements made by the defendant. The transaction had been effected with the assistance of a financing arrangement whereby the defendant had sold the truck to a finance company which had hired it to the claimant for a five year term; so we are talking about hire of goods rather than sale of goods. On being informed that the truck was effectively unusable by the claimant, the defendant made an offer to effect modifications that would make the truck suitable for the claimant's purposes. This offer was rejected and the claimant proceeded to claim damages against the defendant by way of an indemnity for the moneys owed and paid to the finance company.[229] There was held to be no failure to mitigate by non-acceptance of the modification offer as it was vague, unparticularised and unconvincing, nor was there a failure to mitigate by not inviting another offer from the defendant or permitting the defendant to make a **9-059**

225 (1853) 22 L.J.Q.B. 118.
226 (1853) 22 L.J.Q.B. 118 at 119.
227 [1999] 1 Lloyd's Rep. 649.
228 [2013] EWCA Civ 548 CA.
229 The claim, while in contract, will have been on the collateral contract that has been held to arise where purchases are financed in this way.

further offer. *The Solholt*,[230] where not being prepared to enter into further negotiations had been held to be a failure to mitigate,[231]did not compel a like result in a contract between a local cheese company and a local forklift truck company as in a contract between a buyer and a seller in the sophisticated shipping market.[232]

9-060 *(iv) Contracts of employment* Because of the personal nature of the contract of employment offers of the party in default in such contracts are far less likely to be refused at the claimant's peril. As Bankes LJ said in *Payzu v Saunders*[233]:

> "There may be cases where as matter of fact it would be unreasonable to expect a plaintiff to consider any offer made in view of the treatment he has received from the defendant. If he had been rendering personal services and had been dismissed after being accused in presence of others of being a thief, and if after that his employer had offered to take him back into his service, most persons would think he was justified in refusing the offer, and that it would be unreasonable to ask him in this way to mitigate the damages in an action of wrongful dismissal."[234]

And Scrutton LJ pointed to a contrast between service contracts and commercial contracts, saying:

> "In certain cases of personal service it may be unreasonable to expect a plaintiff to consider an offer from the other party who has grossly injured him; but in commercial contracts it is generally reasonable to accept an offer from the party in default."[235]

A further consideration which can avoid a dismissed employee's refusal of an offer of re-employment being construed as a failure to mitigate is where the offer is of employment which is not of an equal seniority or status as formerly.

9-061 These principles are illustrated by *Shindler v Northern Raincoat Co*,[236] and by *Yetton v Eastwoods Froy*.[237] In the former the claimant, suing for wrongful dismissal, was held not to have acted unreasonably in refusing other offers of employment from the defendant company,[238] primarily because[239] these offers, if accepted, would have entailed his acting under the direction of persons with whom he had quarrelled in the course of the dispute over his dismissal; moreover, one of the offers had been made on the terms that the claimant should not act on his legal

---

230 [1983] 1 Lloyd's Rep. 605 CA.

231 See the case at para.9-053, above.

232 See the cogent reasoning of Tomlinson LJ, who gave the only reasoned judgment, at [2013] EWCA Civ 548 CA at [39] to [41].

233 [1919] 2 K.B. 581 CA.

234 [1919] 2 K.B. 581 CA at 588 to 589.

235 [1919] 2 K.B. 581 CA at 589. See, too, McCardie J at first instance: "I feel no inclination to allow in a mercantile dispute an unhappy indulgence in far-fetched resentment or an undue sensitiveness to slights or unfortunately worded letters. Business often gives rise to certain asperities. But I agree that the plaintiffs in deciding whether to accept the defendant's offer were fully entitled to consider the terms in which the offer was made, its bona fides or otherwise, its relation to their own business methods and financial position, and all the circumstances of the case; and it must be remembered that an acceptance of the offer would not preclude an action for damages for the actual loss sustained": at 586.

236 [1960] 1 W.L.R. 1038.

237 [1967] 1 W.L.R. 104.

238 Strictly the offers were made by a company which had owned the share capital of the defendant company but had sold it to a third company which did not wish to retain the claimant's services. The case is therefore in substance one in which the means of mitigation came through the party in breach.

239 This was the main consideration; there were other, minor ones: see [1960] 1 W.L.R. 1038 at 1049.

rights against the defendant company for damages for breach of contract.[240] In the latter the claimant, dismissed as managing director of the defendant company, was held not to have acted unreasonably in refusing the defendant's offer of employment as assistant managing director, partly because this would have marked a significant step down in status and partly because the dismissal had taken place in an arbitrary and high-handed fashion.[241] Somewhat similarly, in *Clayton-Greene v de Courville*,[242] an actor with a contractual right to an important part in a play was held not to have acted unreasonably in refusing a minor part at the same salary, in *Edwards v Society of Graphical &Allied Trades*,[243] a skilled worker in the printing business was held not to have acted unreasonably in refusing the defendants' offer of work as a general labourer[244] and in *Basnett v J. & A. Jackson*,[245] a works manager was held not to have acted unreasonably in declining the employers' offer of a position as works clerk.

These various cases should be contrasted with *Brace v Calder*.[246] Two persons out of a partnership of four employing the claimant resigned from the partnership, this operating as a technical dismissal of the claimant.[247] The remaining two, however, offered to keep him on in his employment, but he refused this offer. It was held that he should have accepted it in mitigation and he was awarded only nominal damages. In *Barnes v Port of London Authority*,[248] where the claimant workman, not wrongfully dismissed but negligently injured by the defendant employer, had refused an offer by him of suitable alternative work, he was held entitled to special damages for loss of wages only up to the time of such offer. And in *Wilding v British Telecommunications Plc*,[249] all three courts that heard the case concluded that the employee's refusal of an offer of re-employment was a failure to mitigate; the case was one of unfair dismissal rather than wrongful dismissal but the same principles of mitigation apply. At the same time it was said that it was not enough for the employer to show that it would have been reasonable for the employee to take the mitigating step; the employer must go further and show that it would have been unreasonable for the employee not to do so.[250] **9-062**

*Bowes v Press*,[251] provides an old illustration in the converse case of employees refusing to work and subsequently offering to do so. It was there held that the employer's damages were not to be reduced on account of his refusal of the offer, for its acceptance would virtually have involved allowing the defendants to work under other than the contractual conditions. **9-063**

---

240 See [1960] 1 W.L.R. 1038 at 1049. The court also endorsed the claimant's refusal of this offer, which was the first in time, on another ground: the offer had been made before the defendant's repudiation had ripened into a breach, and therefore at a time when the claimant was not required to accept any offer, however reasonable. This is dealt with at para.9-021, above.

241 See [1967] 1 W.L.R. 104 at 118 to 119, where the judge set out the various factors which he took into account.

242 (1920) 36 T.L.R. 790.

243 [1971] Ch. 354 CA.

244 Breach was not of contract of service but of contract with a trade union.

245 [1976] I.C.R. 63.

246 [1895] 2 Q.B. 253 CA.

247 It was called a "technical dismissal" by McCardie J in *Payzu v Saunders* [1919] 2 K.B. 581.

248 [1957] 1 Lloyd's Rep. 486.

249 [2002] I.C.R. 1079 CA.

250 See especially Sedley LJ at paras [53]–[55].

251 [1894] 1 Q.B. 202 CA.

## (2) Tort

9-064 **(a) In general: where the door to mitigation is not opened by the party in default** In earlier days cases of mitigation involving tort appeared only from time to time. Today they are quite common and cover a wide field. Illustrations are to be found stretching from personal injury to car damage, from fraudulent misrepresentation[252] to public nuisance.

9-065 *(i) Personal injury* The commonest mitigating step for a claimant whose injuries prevent him from continuing in his former job is of course to seek such other employment of which he is capable. In so doing, a claimant is only required to act reasonably. Thus in *Conner v Bradman & Co*,[253] where the injured claimant could no longer work as a mechanic and decided to train as a less well remunerated taxi-driver, this did not constitute a failure to mitigate. He was not obliged to seek alternative employment to which he would not be suited and for which he had no obvious aptitude and experience; he was simply obliged to find alternative employment which he could reasonably do. The loss of a new job which the injured person has taken will not necessarily be regarded as a failure to mitigate, as *Morris v Richards*[254] shows.

9-066 Where there is physical injury the victim may be required to mitigate the damage by taking steps to put himself in good medical hands. Thus in *McAuley v London Transport Executive*,[255] it was held that the injured claimant's refusal to undergo an operation was unreasonable, so that the defendant was only liable for loss of wages up to the time when he would have returned to work had he had the operation.[256] And in *Marcroft v Scruttons*,[257] there was also held, on the same type of facts, to be a failure to mitigate, even though in that case the injury had made the claimant frightened of hospitals.[258] On the other hand, in *Savage v Wallis*,[259] where the medical evidence was evenly balanced as to whether a slight operation would have cleared up the claimant's headaches, he was held not to have acted unreasonably in refusing to have the operation. Similarly in *Geest Plc v Lansi-*

---

252 While the great majority of cases in tort dealing with mitigation concern the tort of negligence, it was pointed out in *Standard Chartered Bank v Pakistan National Shipping Corp* [1999] 1 Lloyd's Rep. 747 that the same principles of mitigation apply to intentional torts.

253 [2007] EWHC 2789 (QB).

254 [2004] P.I.Q.R. Q3 CA at 30.

255 [1957] 2 Lloyd's Rep. 500 CA.

256 See, too, the Australian case of *Xenos v Curnow* (1975) 12 S.A.S.R. 301 where there were two agreed alternative surgical operations available to deal with the claimant's hip injury, one giving immediate restoration of earning capacity but leaving restricted movement and the other giving unrestricted movement but, by having to be deferred, leaving earning capacity for a time impaired. Damages were assessed on the assumption that the claimant adopt that course which would minimise his loss in terms of money: see especially at 315.

257 [1954] 1 Lloyd's Rep. 395 CA.

258 See, too, *Morgan v T. Wallis* [1974] 1 Lloyd's Rep. 165. The House of Lords in *Steele v Robert George* [1942] A.C. 497 and again in *Richardson v Redpath* [1944] A.C. 62, both of which were workmen's compensation claims, had previously recognised the rule in such circumstances but in both had held on the facts that it had not been shown that the claimant's refusal to undergo a surgical operation was unreasonable. In the context of damages claims *Selvanayagam v University of the West Indies* [1983] 1 W.L.R. 585 PC (at para.9-020, above) is similar, and also in the Privy Council there is *Eaton v Johnston* [2008] UKPC 1 (no failure to mitigate by not acting on surgeon's advice).

259 [1966] 1 Lloyd's Rep. 357 CA.

*quot*,[260] where there was very little evidence on the medical prognosis and on how the operation would affect the claimant's back pain, her decision not to undergo an operation was held to be reasonable.[261]

The victim of a physical injury may also be required to mitigate the damage by taking steps to prosecute his action with all reasonable speed where he has been advised that he is suffering from compensation neurosis. Thus in *James v Woodall Duckham Construction Co*,[262] the claimant was medically advised about a year after the injury that the psychosomatic pain which was incapacitating him from work would cease only after his claim against the defendants had been settled or determined by the court. Nevertheless he did not issue a writ for another year, a further two-and-a-half years passed before a statement of claim was delivered, and the case was not heard until six-and-a-quarter years had elapsed from the time of injury. In these circumstances it was held that, since the claimant had unnecessarily prolonged the period of his incapacity for work, he could not recover for loss of earnings for the period in respect of which he had delayed his return to work, and accordingly loss of earnings for only three of the six-and-a-quarter years should be allowed.[263] **9-067**

*(ii) Goods: damage and destruction* Where goods have been damaged and their owner seeks to recover his expenditure in repairing them, the cost of repair is generally categorised as an expense incurred in order to mitigate loss. Whether the cost is recoverable turns therefore upon the reasonableness or otherwise of effecting the repairs. This is well illustrated by two contrasting cases concerning the repair of cars, *Darbishire v Warran*[264] and *O'Grady v Westminster Scaffolding*,[265] in both of which the claimant had had his damaged car repaired at a cost in excess of its market value instead of trying to replace it. These are fully considered when dealing specifically with damage to goods.[266] And a similar test of reasonableness for the purposes of mitigation is applied where the claimant's claim is for the cost of hiring a substitute while the damaged article is being repaired. Again the cases involve cars. A series of cases from *Watson Norie v Shaw*,[267] to *Opoku v Tintas*,[268] considers the question of whether hiring a prestige car, or hiring a car for a prolonged period, indicates a failure to mitigate. These cases too are fully considered when dealing specifically with damage to, and destruction of, goods.[269] **9-068**

---

260 [2002] 1 W.L.R. 3111 PC.

261 Nor is a personally injured claimant required to mitigate by using a mobility allowance to obtain less costly transport under a motability scheme: *Eagle v Chambers (No.2)* [2004] 1 W.L.R. 3081 CA. See also *Sarti v Nederlandsche Houtimport Maatschappij* [1968] 2 Lloyd's Rep. 135 where the claimant was held not to have acted unreasonably in not going back to work earlier than he did and in then engaging in light work only; the test, it was said, was not whether he could have resumed work earlier. But in *Butler v Thompson* [2005] EWCA Civ 864 CA the claimant was held not to be making the most of her reduced earning capacity, and she could, and should, do somewhat more.

262 [1969] 1 W.L.R. 903 CA.

263 Similar is *Lines v Harland & Wolff* [1966] 2 Lloyd's Rep. 400 where the court limited the claimant's recovery to two of the three-and-three-quarter years between injury and trial.

264 [1963] 1 W.L.R. 1067 CA.

265 [1962] 2 Lloyd's Rep. 238.

266 See para.37-005, below.

267 [1967] 1 Lloyd's Rep. 515 CA.

268 *Opoku v Tintas* unreported 5 July 2013 CA.

269 See paras 37-015, 37-016 and 37-069, below.

**9-069** *Dimond v Lovell*,[270] where the substitute car was hired from a credit car hire company, is a curious case which requires separate consideration on mitigation.[271] Credit car hire companies levy a higher charge than do ordinary car hire companies because, among other things, they do not charge the hirer until after the hirer's damages claim has been concluded. The House of Lords, by a bare majority, held that the claimant was entitled to recover only the lower charges that an ordinary car company would have levied. Lord Hoffmann, delivering the leading majority speech, based this conclusion on the rule, dealt with below,[272] that additional benefits obtained as a result of taking mitigating steps must be brought into account. It is thought, however, that the rule as to avoided loss assumes the claimant to be better off than before the wrong, which was not the case in *Dimond*, and that therefore the decision can only be explained, and justified, on the present ground, which may be difficult to do as it was agreed that hiring from an accident hire company with its higher charges was a reasonable thing to do.[273] In other words, the case can only properly be explained as a case of avoidable loss rather than one of avoided loss.[274]

**9-070** The claimant in *Beechwood Birmingham Ltd v Hoyer UK Group Ltd*[275] was a substantial company of motor dealers. Whenever one of its cars suffered an accident necessitating a period off the road for repairs, it was the claimant's practice to provide a replacement during the repair period from its available pool of cars which was large enough to avoid the necessity to hire in from outside. Nevertheless the claimant's service manager, to whom the tortiously damaged car had been allocated, rather than simply reallocating to himself a similar car from the claimant's stock, this being the claimant's usual practice, hired an equivalent substitute vehicle, the hiring in fact being from a credit car hire company. The claimant claimed the hire charges as special damages but in this was unsuccessful. The trial judge found the hiring to constitute a failure to mitigate and the Court of Appeal saw no reason to disturb this finding. The claimant had not acted reasonably in hiring a replacement vehicle when one was easily available from the claimant's stock, and the need for a replacement vehicle had not been shown.[276] Similarly, the Court of Appeal in *Singh v Yaqubi*,[277] affirmed the trial judge who had held that the claimant had failed to show the need for him to hire an expensive Rolls Royce car while the damaged Rolls Royce car was being repaired, he being a member of a two man partnership who had at his disposal six other cars of equally prestigious make.

---

[270] [2002] 1 A.C. 384.

[271] Ch.37 has a detailed analysis of the decision, at paras 37-019 and 37-020, below.

[272] See paras 9-108 and following, below.

[273] See para.9-081, below.

[274] *Dimond v Lovell* [2002] 1 A.C. 384 was distinguished in *Lagden v O'Connor* [2004] 1 A.C. 1067 where recovery of the higher charges was allowed, the claimant being impecunious: see the case at para.37-021, below. Only the spot rate and not the credit hire rate was allowed in *Heap-Hammond v TNT UK* unreported 15 June 2007 CC District Judge, on the basis of a failure to mitigate.

[275] [2011] Q.B. 357 CA.

[276] See [2011] Q.B. 357 CA at [25] to [32]. Cited with approval (at [28]) was *Park Lane BMW v Whipp* unreported 20 May 2009 Oxford County Court, where hire charges for a substitute car were not allowed as special damages to a car dealership claimant as there was no need for a substitute car at all. The question as to what damages the claimant in *Beechwood* was entitled in lieu is dealt with elsewhere, at paras 37-054 and 37-062, below.

[277] [2013] EWCA Civ 23 CA.

*(iii) Wrongful interference with goods* It has already been pointed out[278] that a claimant whose goods have been wrongfully misappropriated is not required to replace the goods before trial even though the market is rising. Yet the failure to sue within a reasonable time after discovery of the misappropriation is a failure to mitigate where the market is rising. This follows, although somewhat obliquely, from the Court of Appeal decisions in *Rosenthal v Alderton*,[279] and *Sachs v Miklos*,[280] as to the former[281] detinue and as to conversion respectively. In *Rosenthal* the court held that the measure of damages in detinue was based on the market value of the goods at the time of judgment, but with the important qualification that the election to sue in detinue despite an earlier conversion was available to the claimant "at any rate where he was not aware of the conversion at the time".[282] Another way of putting this practical result, and analytically a sounder one, was to allow detinue to be brought in any event, but to hold a failure to sue with reasonable speed after knowledge to be a failure to mitigate. In *Sachs* the court held that the rise in value of the goods converted, between the time the claimant knew or ought to have known of the conversion, and should have brought suit, and the time, much later, when the conversion action was brought by the claimant, "is not damage which he can recover as flowing from the wrongful act".[283] This in effect gave the same result in conversion as in detinue; today it must be achieved by the conversion route alone.[284] **9-071**

While the important *Rosenthal v Alderton*[285] and *Sachs v Miklos*[286] are not generally thought of as dealing with mitigation as such, it has always been implicitly accepted that the need to avoid or minimise loss arises where goods are converted in the same way as with all other torts. Only today has this been challenged in *Uzinterimpex J.S.C. v Standard Bank Plc*,[287] the argument praying in aid, among other things, the proprietary overtones of conversion. Soundly rejected though the argument was by the Court of Appeal, Moore-Bick LJ nonetheless devoted a large part of his careful judgment, with which his brethren agreed, to countering it.[288] **9-072**

*(iv) Wrongful interference with land* A failure to mitigate in the context of public nuisance appeared in *Wandsworth London Borough Council v Railtrack Plc*.[289] Pigeon droppings from the defendants' railway bridge caused considerable inconvenience to pedestrians passing below. Though the claimants were held entitled to the cost of abatement, they were not allowed their full outlay because they should have mitigated the damage by pigeon-proofing the bridge at an early stage rather than incurring escalating costs in cleaning up later. The damages were basically affirmed on appeal.[290] **9-073**

---

278 See paras 9-042 and 9-043, above.
279 [1946] 1 K.B. 374 CA.
280 [1948] 2 K.B. 23 CA.
281 See paras 38-002 to 38-004, below.
282 [1946] 1 K.B. 374 CA at 379.
283 [1948] 2 K.B. 23 CA at 40.
284 See the preceding note but two.
285 [1946] 1 K.B. 374 CA.
286 [1948] 2 K.B. 23 CA.
287 [2008] 2 Lloyd's Rep. 456 CA. Facts at para.9-078, below.
288 [2008] 2 Lloyd's Rep. 456 CA at [54]–[69]. Once again *Strutt v Whitnell* [1975] 1 W.L.R. 870 CA was produced in support of the argument; see para.9-053, above.
289 [2001] 1 W.L.R. 368.
290 [2002] Q.B. 756 CA at [27]. Underpinning the foundations of a building to counteract a nuisance

9-074 *(v) Deceit* Even the tort of deceit has proved illustrative of the issue of mitigation. In *Standard Chartered Bank v Pakistan National Shipping Corporation*[291] the claimant bank had been deceived by the defendant's falsely dated bills of lading into making payment to the seller of a cargo. Following upon the results of this deception the bank was entitled to sell the cargo and claim as damages the difference between the amount paid over to the seller and the amount that the cargo had realised. The defendant contended that the claimant had failed to mitigate in not realising the cargo at a better price. This contention failed.[292]

9-075 **(b) In particular: where the door to mitigation is opened by the party in default** Situations where the door to mitigation is opened by the tortfeasor, which are very familiar in the contractual context,[293] have been virtually unknown in tort, at least in the cases. But suddenly cases have started to appear.

9-076 The first appearance in tort was with two appeals in the County Court in cases of a familiar variety—claims for the cost of hire of a car while the claimant's own damaged car is being repaired—but arriving at different results. In both cases, *Evans v TNT Logistics Ltd*[294]and *Steadman v TNT Express Ltd*,[295] the defendant had offered the claimant a suitable replacement car at no cost to him during the period of repair—now commonly referred to as a courtesy car—but the claimant did not take up the defendant's offer[296] and instead hired a car from a credit car hire company. In *Evans*, the earlier case, His Honour Judge Wynn Rees, having not surprisingly, by the application of mitigation principles, declined to award the amount charged by the credit hire company in the presence of the free replacement offer, nevertheless rejected the defendant's argument that there should be no damages at all and awarded the cost to the defendant of providing the car, which was substantially below the credit hire company's charge, by viewing the defendant's offer as an offer of damages in kind rather than in money. However, His Honour Judge Oliver-Jones in *Steadman* would have none of this. He took the view that, since acceptance of the defendant's offer would have eliminated the claimant's loss under this head of damage, that was an end of the matter, the cost of the car to the defendant being entirely immaterial to the issue of the measure of the claimant's damages.[297] With this His Honour Judge Langan in two cases heard together, *Copley v Lawn*

caused by the advance of tree roots, instead of seeking less expensive remedies, was not a failure to mitigate: *L.E. Jones Ltd v Portsmouth City Council* [2003] 1 W.L.R. 427 CA; see at [26].

291 [1999] 1 Lloyd's Rep. 747; affirmed [2001] 1 All E.R. Comm. 822 CA.

292 See the case further at para.49-040, below.

293 See paras 9-052 to 9-063, above.

294 [2007] Lloyd's Rep. I.R. 708, CC Circuit Judge.

295 *Steadman v TNT Express Ltd* unreported 19 June 2008 CC Circuit Judge.

296 In *Evans* the claimant was unaware of the defendant's offer, having passed the letter containing it to her insurance company without reading it, but nothing turned on this.

297 *Steadman* at [15]. The contract cases of *Payzu v Saunders* [1919] 2 K.B. 581 CA and *The Solholt* [1983] 1 Lloyd's Rep. 605 CA, where a buyer's refusal to accept the contractual goods at the originally agreed price led to nominal damages (see para.9-053, above), together with the further contract case of *Strutt v Whitnell* [1975] 1 W.L.R. 870 CA, where a buyer's refusal to accept the seller's offer to buy back the contractual property at the originally agreed price did not affect the damages, were said by both judges to be distinguishable and of no relevance. Nevertheless it is thought that the result reached in *Evans* is entirely consistent with the decision in *Strutt v Whitnell* (see the analysis of this case at para.9-054, above), and this was eventually confirmed by the Court of Appeal in the *Copley* appeal: see the paragraph below.

and *Maden v Haller*,[298] agreed, and accordingly followed *Steadman* in preference to *Evans*, allowing no damages for their hire costs to either of the claimants. At first sight the result arrived at in *Steadman*, *Copley* and *Maden* looks to be the right one on the basis that the claimant would have eliminated his loss by accepting the defendant's offer. But this fails to take into account that this result leaves the defendant paying no damages at all in respect of the car hire claim although, had the claimant acted reasonably and accepted his offer, he would have had to bear the cost to him of the substitute car. Accepting the view that the cost of the car to the defendant is immaterial means that, where its cost to him equalled or was even greater than the cost of hire that the claimant could prima facie claim, the defendant would still be exempted from liability in damages if his offer of the car free was turned down. Of course it might be said that here the refusal of the offer does not constitute a failure to mitigate as its acceptance in no way improves the claimant's position. However, it surely cannot be right that, if defendants' insurers were in a position to hire cars to offer to claimants at marginally below the basic hire rate, or spot rate, that claimants would be claiming, they would have to pay no hire damages to claimants not accepting their offer. If this were so, they would effectively be acting in terrorem of claimants. When this was the judicial state of play, it was considered right to endorse Judge Wynn Rees's careful judgment in *Evans*, recognising as it does that the aim of the mitigation doctrine is to protect defendants from having to pay too much in damages. As Lord Wrenbury put it in his authoritative statement of the mitigation rule in *Jamal v Moolla Dawood*[299]:

> "If … the plaintiff could do something … which mitigated the damage, the defendant is entitled to the benefit of it."

This controversial issue has since gone to the Court of Appeal in an appeal from Judge Langan's decisions in the *Copley* and *Maden* cases.[300] The issue was unresolved by the court's holding that in the particular circumstances of each of the two cases neither claimant had acted unreasonably in failing to take up the defendant's offer of a car. The court was therefore asked to resolve the stark conflict which had appeared in the lower court authorities and, following *Strutt v Whitnell*,[301] concluded that if a claimant does unreasonably reject or ignore a defendant's offer he does not forfeit his damages claim altogether but is entitled to recover at least the cost that the defendant can show he would reasonably have incurred.[302] Thus the Court of Appeal fortunately agreed with the *Evans* case and with the result advanced in this work. Then in a further case of a free or courtesy car being offered to and refused by the claimant while her own car was being repaired, *Sayce v TNT (UK) Ltd*,[303] where the trial judge had refused to follow *Copley*, the Court of Appeal allowed the appeal upon the ground of procedural irregularity. Nevertheless Moore-Bick LJ, who gave the leading judgment, said that he was unhappy with the reasoning in *Copley* while recognising that it had received support in this work[304]; the other Lord Justices did not address the matter.[305] **9-077**

---

298 *Maden v Haller* unreported 4 November 2008.
299 [1916] 1 A.C. 175 PC at 179.
300 *Copley v Lawn*; *Maden v Haller* [2009] EWCA Civ 580 CA.
301 [1975] 1 W.L.R. 870 CA (at paras 9-053 and 9-054, above).
302 See the argument at [2009] Lloyd's Rep. I.R. 496 CA at [25]–[30].
303 [2012] 1 W.L.R. 1261 CA.
304 [2012] 1 W.L.R. 1261 CA at [27] to [29].

9-078 The fact situation in the next case is far removed from that of car hire by owners of damaged cars. *Uzinterimpex J.S.C. v Standard Bank Plc*,[306] is a very complex case arising out of a contract for the sale of cotton. It involved a dispute between the claimant seller of the cotton and the defendant bank financing the purchase on behalf of a buyer now in insolvent liquidation. The judge having held that the bank, by refusing to release the documents of title to the cotton, had converted the cotton, the bank proposed to the seller that the cotton be realised, and the proceeds placed in a blocked account, so as to preserve its value, against deterioration, fall in market value and continuing storage charges, for the benefit of whichever party should ultimately prove to be entitled to the cotton. The seller's unpreparedness to agree to this was held to be a failure on its part to mitigate loss. It had been found by the trial judge that the seller's attitude to the bank had not unreasonably been coloured by a lack of faith and confidence, the bank having behaved badly in a number of ways, but this did not suffice to justify the seller's refusal to agree to the sale of the cotton. The whole transaction was a commercial one where it was more appropriate for commercial men to consider profit and loss than to stand on principle.[307]

## 4. Standard of Conduct which the Claimant must Attain when Assessing what Steps should have been Taken by Him

### (1) The criterion of reasonableness and the standard of reasonableness

9-079 In mitigating his loss the claimant victim of a wrong is only required to act reasonably and the standard of reasonableness is not high in view of the fact that the defendant is an admitted wrongdoer. Lord Macmillan put this point well for contract in *Banco de Portugal v Waterlow*[308]; his remarks apply equally to tort. He said:

> "Where the sufferer from a breach of contract finds himself in consequence of that breach placed in a position of embarrassment the measures which he may be driven to adopt in order to extricate himself ought not to be weighed in nice scales at the instance of the party whose breach of contract has occasioned the difficulty. It is often easy after an emergency has passed to criticise the steps which have been taken to meet it, but such criticism does not come well from those who have themselves created the emergency. The law is satisfied if the party placed in a difficult situation by reason of the breach of a duty owed to him has acted reasonably in the adoption of remedial measures and he will not be held disentitled to recover the cost of such measures merely because the party in breach can suggest that other measures less burdensome to him might have been taken."[309]

---

[305] In *Copley* leave to appeal was refused by the Supreme Court and, partly because of this, the Court of Appeal in *Sayce* refused leave to appeal, although with Moore-Bick LJ saying that it would be beneficial for the issue to be considered by the Supreme Court as soon as a suitable opportunity arose: .[2012] 1 W.L.R. 1261 CA at [30].

[306] [2008] EWCA Civ 819 CA.

[307] [2008] EWCA Civ 819 CA at [51]–[53]. Compare, in the context of contract, the remarks of McCardie J in *Payzu v Saunders* [1919] 2 K.B. 581, 586 at para.9-060, above.

[308] [1932] A.C. 452 at 506.

[309] Words adopted and applied in *Bacon v Cooper (Metals)* [1982] 1 All E.R. 397 (facts at para.25-083, below) and in *Al Rawas v Pegasus Energy Ltd* [2007] EWHC 2427 (QB) (claimant subject to search and freezing orders had not been shown to have acted unreasonably in taking out a loan so

Whether the claimant has acted reasonably is in every case a question of fact, not of law.[310]

9-080 Moreover, the standard of reasonableness is the same whatever the cause of action; it is not a lower one where the defendant is an intentional tortfeasor. Toulson J rightly so decided in *Standard Chartered Bank v Pakistan National Shipping Corporation*,[311] an assessment of damages for deceit and conspiracy in relation to bills of lading.[312] After a careful analysis of the authorities he

> "conclude[d] that once a plaintiff discovers that he is a victim of a fraud, the same rule about avoidable loss applies for the purpose of assessing damages in an action of deceit or conspiracy as would apply in any action for tort or breach of contract".[313]

9-081 At the same time, in assessing reasonableness, while it has been said that the claimant is "not bound to nurse the interests" of the defendant,[314] it has also, and for long, been said that the claimant must act with the defendant's as well as his own interests in mind.[315] This is well illustrated by two cases concerning tortious damage to the claimant's motorcar. In *Darbishire v Warran*,[316] the claimant was unable to recover the cost of repairing his shooting brake because, although the vehicle was reliable and suited his needs, to repair it was uneconomic. The Court of Appeal pointed out that, while the claimant may have acted reasonably as far as he was concerned,

> "the true question was whether the plaintiff acted reasonably as between himself and the defendant and in view of his duty to mitigate the damages".[317]

In *Dimond v Lovell*,[318] while her damaged car was being repaired, Mrs Dimond hired a substitute car from an accident hire company which had higher charges than an ordinary car hire company because of allowing her credit on the charges until the conclusion of her damages claim. The House of Lords, reversing the courts below, held that the higher charges could not be recovered although it was accepted by all that Mrs Dimond had acted reasonably in going to an accident hire

---

as to be able to pay a very large sum into court). See the similar remarks of Roskill J in *Harlow and Jones v Panex (International)* [1967] 2 Lloyd's Rep. 509 at 530, rejecting the argument that the claimants, suing for non-acceptance of goods sold, acted unreasonably, in the light of their liability for storage charges, in not accepting any offer they could get for the goods. See also *Hayes v James & Charles Dodd* [1990] 2 All E.R. 815 CA at 820e, where the claimants might have surrendered the lease of premises at a much earlier date so as to avoid continuing accrual of rent (facts at para.34-016, below), per Staughton LJ: "but they were placed in a difficult situation through the fault of the defendants, and I would not criticise them for failing to adopt that course."

310 See para.9-016, above. For a whole series of ways in which the defendant argued unsuccessfully that the claimant should have acted to mitigate his loss see, at great length, *BSkyB Ltd v HP Enterprise Services UK Ltd* [2010] EWHC 86 (TCC) at [1712]–[1800].

311 [1999] 1 Lloyd's Rep. 747.

312 Facts at para.49-040, below.

313 [1999] 1 Lloyd's Rep. 747 at 760, col.1. The Court of Appeal, [2001] 1 All E.R. Comm. 822, implicitly confirmed that this was the right approach by its silence on the issue. Mitigation was not an issue in the Lords: [2003] 1 A.C. 959.

314 *Harlow and Jones v Panex (International)* [1967] 2 Lloyd's Rep. 509 at 530, per Roskill J.

315 *Smailes v Hans Dessen* (1906) 94 L.T. 492 at 493, col.2, per Channell J.

316 [1963] 1 W.L.R. 1067 CA.

317 [1963] 1 W.L.R. 1067 CA at 1072, per Harman LJ; see, too, [1963] 1 W.L.R. 1067 CA at 1076, per Pearson LJ; see the case at para.37-005, below, for more detail.

318 [2002] 1 A.C. 384.

company.[319] That recovery of the higher hire charges should not be allowed was the majority view only.[320]

9-082 The criterion for reasonableness, stated concisely in the words of James LJ in *Dunkirk Colliery Co v Lever*,[321] which were cited with approval by Viscount Haldane in *British Westinghouse Co v Underground Ry*,[322] is that the claimant is not "under any obligation to do anything other than in the ordinary course of business". This terminology, with its reference to business, is geared more to contract than to tort, and, although most of the cases are contract cases, it is better, in order to include tort, to speak simply of the ordinary course or of the ordinary course of events.[323] Even more precisely, it might be best simply to speak of things done which are reasonably necessary, with the requirement of reasonableness directing attention to the nature of the claimant's actions, which will generally be reasonable where they are ordinary.

## (2) Illustrative decisions

9-083 On the whole the illustrative decisions go to show what the claimant need *not* do in order to come up to the required standard; this in itself suggests that the standard is not a demanding one. Various rules are formulated below. However, decisions are now appearing which go to show what the claimant *does* have to do to come up to the required standard. These will be examined first.

9-084 **(a) Illustrations of what is required of the claimant in mitigation** Illustrations of conduct which the need to mitigate requires of a claimant have appeared particularly in the now common claims by mortgage lenders against their professional advisers when borrower and security have proved inadequate. Two particular types of failure to act in mitigation have surfaced in this type of claim. The first type, a failure to enforce the borrower's security, appeared in *Western Trust & Savings Ltd v Travers & Co*.[324] In a claim by mortgage lenders against their solicitors for a negligent report on title to the mortgaged property, the lenders' failure first to bring an action for possession of the property was held to be a failure to mitigate as this was the normal, and not difficult, method of enforcing the security. As a result the damages were reduced to a nominal amount.[325] The second type, a failure to effect

[319] A sale by a claimant may be in the interest of both parties even if a later sale, as advocated by the defendant, would have produced a better price: *Metelmann & Co v N.B.R. (London)* [1984] 1 Lloyd's Rep. 614 CA, especially at 633, col.2 to 634, col.1, per Browne-Wilkinson LJ (facts at para.9-105, below). The need to take into account the interest of both parties was also touched upon in *Koch Marine Inc v D'Amica Società di Navigazione, The Elena d'Amico* [1980] 1 Lloyd's Rep. 75; see at 85, col.2, per Robert Goff J.

[320] See the case, and the subsequent *Lagden v O'Connor* [2004] 1 A.C. 1067, at paras 37-020 and 37-021, below for further detail. The decision was arrived at on the basis of a loss avoided (for avoided loss see paras 9-108 and following, below) but it is thought only to be justifiable as a case of avoidable loss (see para.9-069, above).

[321] (1878) 9 Ch. D. 20 CA at 25.

[322] [1912] A.C. 673 at 689.

[323] The principles and rules discussed in the above paragraphs were applied in *Conner v Bradman & Co Ltd* [2007] EWHC 2789 (QB) to find that there had been no failure to mitigate; facts at para.9-065, above.

[324] [1997] P.N.L.R. 295 CA.

[325] Contrast *The Mortgage Corp v Halifax (SW) Ltd* [1999] Lloyd's Rep. P.N. 159 where the defendants failed to satisfy the court that the claimants had been unreasonably tardy in obtaining posses-

an earlier sale of the security when market prices were more favourable, appeared in the various cases decided under the umbrella of *Bristol and West Building Society v Fancy & Jackson*.[326] In three of the eight this was held to constitute a failure to mitigate, thereby reducing the damages.[327] And although the speeches in the House of Lords in *Platform Homes Loans Ltd v Oyston Shipways Ltd*,[328] do not elucidate why the trial judge there saw fit to reduce the damages on account of a failure to mitigate—the decision at first instance is unreported—it was probably also on account of a late and less advantageous sale.[329]

A somewhat different case of a failure to mitigate by not first bringing a claim other than against the defendant is *Walker v Medlicott & Son*.[330] A disappointed beneficiary under a will, by not pursuing a claim for rectification of the will before suing his solicitor for negligence in its drafting, was held to have failed to mitigate; the claimant would have no greater difficulty in establishing a right to rectification than in establishing liability against the solicitor. And a failure to mitigate by not selling property earlier again finds illustration in *Patel v Hooper & Jackson*.[331] The claimants were not mortgage lenders but purchasers of a house on the strength of a negligent report and valuation by the defendant surveyors. The house proved to be uninhabitable unless restored at a cost that the claimants could not afford. Their claim for the cost of temporary alternative accommodation for the seven years up to the time of trial was allowed for the first five years only, since it was held that by then they should have offered the house for sale and sold it.[332] **9-085**

**(b) Illustrations of what is not required of the claimant in mitigation** Ten rules on what a claimant need not do to attain the required standard can be extracted from the cases.[333] **9-086**

*(i) A claimant need not risk his money too far* In *Lesters Leather and Skin Co v Home and Overseas Brokers*,[334] the claimant bought snakeskins from the defendant to be delivered at a United Kingdom port, and properly rejected them on their **9-087**

---

sion from the mortgagor borrower. The fact that the claimants were at the time unaware that they were victims of the defendants' negligence was an important fact in assessing whether there had been a failure to mitigate: see at 183 to 184.

326 [1997] 4 All E.R. 582.

327 [1997] 4 All E.R. 582 at 623 to 624 where the mitigation issue is dealt with rather briefly.

328 [2000] 2 A.C. 190.

329 For another case involving a lender claimant see *Skipton Building Society v Lea Hough & Co* [2000] P.N.L.R. 545 where the action failed because the lender had disposed of the mortgage debt to a third party for a price that was far too low.

330 [1999] 1 W.L.R. 727 CA.

331 [1999] 1 W.L.R. 1792 CA. It will be seen that this case and the preceding ones illustrating the standard of conduct required of a claimant in mitigation have also been set out at para.9-051, above, in illustrating some of the circumstances which give rise to issues of mitigation. This is in order to present the decisions from different angles and avoid extensive cross-referencing.

332 House owners not giving their builders the opportunity to remedy defects, which the builders could have done with no cost to themselves or the house owners, was held to be a failure to mitigate in *Woodlands Oak Ltd v Conwell* [2011] EWCA Civ 254 CA; see at [18] and following.

333 The rule that a claimant, tortiously deprived of goods, need not seek a replacement in the market, is incorporated into the normal measure of damages: see paras 9-042 and 9-043, above. It does not therefore fall to be included here. Furthermore, certain illustrations of what is not required of a claimant to satisfy the standard relate to the special situation where the defendant himself has offered the opportunity to mitigate. These are more conveniently dealt with at paras 9-052 to 9-063 and 9-075 to 9-078, above.

334 (1948) 64 T.L.R. 569 CA.

arrival as being not merchantable. The Court of Appeal awarded the claimant damages for his loss of profit, rejecting the defendant's argument that the claimant should have mitigated by buying skins available in India on the ground that this was a risk which he was not bound to take. Singleton LJ quoted Sellers J's remark at first instance that

> "it is one thing to enter into a contract. It would be another thing to have got the goods actually here".[335]

And Lord Goddard CJ said:

> "I cannot say that the buyers are bound to go hunting the globe to find out where they can get skins."[336]

Similarly, in *Jewelowski v Propp*,[337] where the claimant was induced by the defendant's fraudulent mispresentation to advance money on a debenture to a company which later went into liquidation, it was said that he could not be required to buy the company's assets so that, by reselling them afterwards at a higher amount than he paid for them, he would reduce his loss.[338] Lewis J said that a claimant "cannot be called on to spend money[339] to enable him to minimise the damages"; this would be "going far beyond the rule".

**9-088** *(ii) A claimant need not risk his person too far in the hands of surgeons* In *Steele v Robert George*,[340] and again in *Richardson v Redpath*,[341] both workmen's compensation claims, the House of Lords, and in *Selvanayagam v University of the West Indies*,[342] a damages claim, the Judicial Committee of the Privy Council, held on the facts before them that the refusal of a physically injured claimant to undergo a dangerous and risky surgical operation did not constitute a failure to mitigate. The same was held of the refusal in *Savage v Wallis*,[343] of a slight operation where medical evidence was evenly balanced on the prospects of its success, and of the refusal of a back operation in *Geest Plc v Lansiquot*,[344] where no doctor had advised on the chances of success of the operation, on the relief the claimant could reasonably have hoped for from the operation, or on the risk, however small, that the operation would lead to a worsening of the claimant's condition.[345] On the other hand, where the operation would not be regarded by reasonable men as a risky one, then a refusal to allow it will be a failure to mitigate on the part of the claimant; such a result was

---

335 (1948) 64 T.L.R. 569 CA at 570.

336 (1948) 64 T.L.R. 569 CA at 569.

337 [1944] K.B. 510.

338 The fact that he did resell the assets at a higher amount brings into operation another principle: see paras 9-108 and following, below. Lewis J considered the case on the footing of avoidable loss whereas it was one of avoided loss.

339 "Risk money" would be a truer term; a claimant may have to spend money in mitigation, as in repairs (see *Tucker v Linger* (1882) 21 Ch. D. 18 at para.9-050, above) or upon a surgical operation (see *McAuley v London Transport Executive* [1957] 2 Lloyd's Rep. 500 CA, at para.9-066, above.

340 [1942] A.C. 497.

341 [1944] A.C. 62.

342 [1983] 1 W.L.R. 585 PC.

343 [1966] 1 Lloyd's Rep. 357 CA.

344 [2002] 1 W.L.R. 3111 CA.

345 See [2002] 1 W.L.R. 3111 CA at [15].

reached by the Court of Appeal in *Marcroft v Scruttons*,[346] and again in *McAuley v London Transport Executive*.[347]

*(iii) A claimant need not have an abortion to end an unwanted pregnancy* Thus in *Emeh v Kensington Area Health Authority*,[348] where the defendants had negligently performed a sterilisation operation on the claimant, a mother of three children, with the result that she later found herself once again pregnant, she was held entitled to recover inter alia for her own loss of future earnings and for maintenance of the child, and the court would have none of the defendants' argument that these losses were the claimant's responsibility as they stemmed from her own decision not to have an abortion. Slade LJ said that **9-089**

> "save in the most exceptional circumstances, I cannot think it right that the court should ever declare it unreasonable for a woman to decline to have an abortion in a case where there is no evidence that there were any medical or psychiatric grounds for terminating the particular pregnancy."[349]

This is somewhat akin to the cases under the second rule above, and indeed Slade LJ pointed to the fact that the operation to terminate the claimant's pregnancy

> "would not have been entirely without risk, and no doubt would have involved her in considerable pain and discomfort".[350]

After *Emeh* claims arising out of failed sterilisations became quite common until the House of Lords in *McFarlane v Tayside Health Board*,[351] put paid to this whole development,[352] and in the 15-year period during which such claims thrived it was accepted, in all the cases working out the measure of damages in relation to bringing up the child, that the decision to have the child rather than undergo an abortion was not a failure to mitigate.[353]

*(iv) A claimant need not take the risk of starting an uncertain litigation against a third party* Thus in *Pilkington v Wood*,[354] the claimant bought freehold land from a seller who purported to convey the property as beneficial owner, the defendant acting as the claimant's solicitor in the transaction. When the claimant later tried to sell the property he found the title was defective, since the seller was a trustee of the property and had committed a breach of trust in buying it himself. In the **9-090**

---

346 [1954] 1 Lloyd's Rep. 395 CA.

347 [1957] 2 Lloyd's Rep. 500 CA; and at first instance in *Morgan v T. Wallis* [1974] 1 Lloyd's Rep. 165. See too the *Australian Xenos v Curnow* (1975) 12 S.A.S.R. 301 in the second footnote to para.9-066, above.

348 [1985] Q.B. 1012 CA.

349 [1985] Q.B. 1012 CA at 1024H. And Purchas LJ restated in this context the general rule that "it would be intolerable if a defendant, … having … placed the plaintiff in a position in which a choice or decision had to be made, was able closely to analyse that decision so as to show that it might not have been the right choice and thereby escape his liability": at [1027D].

350 [1985] Q.B. 1012 CA at 1024D. There was, however, a tendency for the court to see the problem as one of remoteness as much as one of mitigation: see paras 6-019 and 8-078, above.

351 [2000] 2 A.C. 59.

352 See para.40-288, below.

353 See, e.g. *Allen v Bloomsbury Health Authority* [1993] 1 All E.R. 651 at 653d: "the defendants … did not try to contend that [the plaintiff] had acted unreasonably in deciding not to have a termination".

354 [1953] Ch. 770.

claimant's action against the defendant solicitor for negligence, the latter contended that before suing him the claimant ought to have mitigated his damage by suing the seller on an implied covenant of title. This contention was rejected by Harman J because, even conceding that the defendant had offered an adequate indemnity against costs in an action against the seller and that the seller was solvent and therefore worth suing, it was not clear that the claimant had a good prima facie right of action against the seller. The judge stated that he was of the opinion that

> "the so-called duty to mitigate does not go so far as to oblige the injured party, even under an indemnity, to embark on a complicated and difficult piece of litigation against a third party".[355]

**9-091** Cases that take the *Pilkington v Wood*[356] line continue to appear. In *Horsfall v Haywards*,[357] the intended beneficiaries under a negligently drafted will were held not to have failed to mitigate in not issuing rectification proceedings because, in the particular circumstances, there was no prospect that rectification would have resulted in any material recovery of the funds, already distributed, to compensate the claimants for the loss of their interest under the will. In *Pozzolanic Lytag v Bryan Hobson Associates*,[358] since any claim against the third party would be fraught with uncertainty, the claimant was even more clearly not required to embark on what was at best speculative litigation in mitigation. In *Dean v Allin & Watts*,[359] there was held to be no failure by the claimant to mitigate where the complex and uncertain litigation involved would have been not in bringing a claim against a third party but in defending a claim brought by a third party.[360] To embark on expensive legal action in the United States was not required of the claimant in mitigation in *Center Optical (Hong Kong) Ltd v Jardine Transport Services (China) Ltd*,[361] and in *British Racing Drivers' Club v Hextall Erskine & Co*,[362] the argument that the damages should be reduced because the claimants should have settled litigation against a third party more favourably was rejected.[363] In *Williams v Glyn Owen &Co*,[364] the buyer of a farm was held not to have failed to mitigate by not bringing an action against his vendor before bringing his action against his negligent solicitor. It was said by Jonathan Parker LJ[365] that it could not be assumed that a claim for damages against the vendor would have been a straightforward affair, but in what way it would not have been straightforward is not revealed. Where in *Olafsson v Foreign & Commonwealth Office*,[366] a default judgment obtained in Iceland on a damages claim of the claimant had been set aside on account of defective service for which the defendant government department was responsible, the claimant

---

355 [1953] Ch. 770 at 777. It was contended alternatively that the claimant should have taken out a policy of insurance against the consequences of the defect in title. This contention failed as well since there was no evidence that such a policy could be obtained: [1953] Ch. 770 at [777] and [778]. The case is also important in relation to remoteness of damage.

356 [1953] Ch. 770.

357 [1999] Lloyd's Rep. P.N. 332 CA.

358 (1999) 63 Con. L.R. 81.

359 [2000] Lloyd's Rep. P.N. 469.

360 [2000] Lloyd's Rep. P.N. 469 at 495 to 496.

361 [2001] 2 Lloyd's Rep. 678 (Hong Kong); see at 689, [63].

362 [1996] P.N.L.R. 523.

363 See [1996] P.N.L.R. 523 at 542–543.

364 [2004] P.N.L.R. 20 CA at 367; facts at para.10-073, below.

365 [2004] P.N.L.R. 20 CA at [69].

366 [2009] EWHC 2608 (QB).

sought to recover from the defendant the loss of the default judgment and attendant wasted costs. It was held that the claimant was not required to mitigate by seeking a second default judgment as the outcome of it was undoubtedly uncertain, the suit might well fail, the costs would be substantial and probably greater than on the first claim.[367]

By contrast, there is the preparedness, appearing in professional negligence cases, for the courts to see a failure to make a straightforward claim against a third party before suing the professional himself as a failure to mitigate. This was already seen in *Western Trust & Savings Ltd v Travers & Co*,[368] and in *Walker v Medlicott & Son*.[369] In effect, the classic *Pilkington v Wood*,[370] and the cases in the previous paragraph taking the same line are interpreted as being concerned with there being no need to embark on complex, difficult and uncertain litigation. **9-092**

*(v) A claimant need not destroy or sacrifice rights or property of his own*[371] This point was put with characteristic clarity by Scrutton LJ in *Elliott Steam Tug Co v Shipping Controller*.[372] The claimants chartered a tug from the owners entitling them to the tug's services until they should give 14 days' notice determining the charterparty. In the course of this contract the tug was requisitioned by the Admiralty, from whom the claimants proceeded to claim statutory compensation under two heads, namely for the amount of hire for which they continued to be liable under the charterparty, and for loss of profits. The tribunal, allowing compensation for only 30 days under each head, said that the claimants should have minimised their loss by determining the charterparty and gave them the 30 days in which to have done so. Unfortunately there was no appeal to the Court of Appeal on the first head, but Scrutton LJ stated his disagreement with the tribunal on it. "At common law", he said: **9-093**

> "the owner of a ship while under a duty to act reasonably to reduce damages is under no obligation to destroy his own property to reduce the damages payable by the wrongdoer. The leasehold tenant of a house would not be bound to stop paying rent to his superior landlord during the period during which a wrongdoer prevented him using the house, because by so doing he would reduce the damages the wrongdoer had to pay if by so doing he lost the tenancy of the house after the wrong of the tortfeasor was repaired, or finished in its effects. It is common practice at common law to recover, (1) net profits lost; (2) standing charges which have reasonably to be incurred and which are not made up by profits by reason of the wrongdoer's action. In other words in a case of temporary loss of a chattel, gross profits lost are recovered so far as expenses of earning them reasonably continue; and the reasonableness is from the point of view of the owner of the chattel. If the expenses cease their amount is set off against the gross profit otherwise lost."[373]

---

367 See especially [2009] EWHC 2608 (QB) at [33].

368 [1997] P.N.L.R. 295 CA, at para.9-084, above.

369 [1999] 1 W.L.R. 727 CA, at para.9-085 above.

370 [1953] Ch. 770.

371 This does not mean that the claimant may not be obliged to spend money: see para.9-087, last fn., above. Within this category may perhaps be placed *Gregory v Shepherds* [2000] Lloyd's Rep. P.N. 724 CA, where the Court of Appeal, disagreeing with the judge below, held that the claimants, unable for nine years to sell their holiday apartment abroad because of a defect in title which the defendant solicitor had overlooked, had not failed to mitigate by not renting out the apartment during the period of delay in sale.

372 [1922] 1 K.B. 127 CA.

373 [1922] 1 K.B. 127 CA at 140 and 141.

But the situation was different in *Weir v Dobell*,[374] where the defendant sub-chartered a ship from the claimant for a particular voyage at a rate higher than the claimant had to pay under the head charterparty, which was for the same voyage and which, in the events that happened, the claimant had a right to cancel. In these circumstances it was held, when the defendant refused to load, that the claimant was under an obligation to exercise his right to cancel the head charterparty in mitigation of damage. Here the vital factors were that the two charterparties were co-extensive and that there was no residue of the head charterparty following on the termination of the sub-charterparty to preserve.[375]

9-094 *(vi) A claimant need not take steps to recover compensation for his loss from parties who, in addition to the defendant, are liable to him for the same loss*[376] This is an undoubted principle and it is a principle which, strictly speaking, stands on its own feet independently of mitigation. It is mentioned here largely because it quite often becomes associated with mitigation in the minds of both judges and commentators.[377] On this matter *The Liverpool (No.2)* is the central case. It was in this case that Harman LJ made the first clear statement of the principle, pointing out that otherwise it would have been unnecessary for the legislature to make provision for contribution and indemnity between joint and several tortfeasors.[378] Indeed *The Liverpool (No.2)* goes as far as to show that, even if the third party offers payment of the amount for which he is liable, the claimant is not required to accept it in mitigation. In that case the defendants' ship through negligence came into collision in port with another ship which sank. The claimant harbour board sued the defendants, whose liability was limited,[379] for expense incurred and damage sustained in clearing the port of the wreck. However, the claimants had also taken steps to enforce their statutory right against the owners of the wreck to recover from them any expenses outstanding after raising and selling the wreck, and not only had this amount been established but the money had been tendered, refused by the

374 [1916] 1 K.B. 722.

375 These two vital factors were not present in *Glory Wealth Shipping PTE Ltd v North China Shipping Ltd* [2010] EWHC 1692 (Comm), a further case of breach by a sub-charterer giving rise to the question of mitigation on the part of the head charterer. In holding against the sub-charterer on mitigation, David Steel J rightly saw the case as different on account of there being no right to cancel the head charterparty and the two charterparties not being co-terminous: [2010] EWHC 1692 (Comm) at [13]. Yet there is also the more important difference between the cases that the head charterer had in *Glory Wealth*, and had not in *Weir v Dobell*, returned the ship to the owner. *Glory Wealth* is therefore not about whether mitigation principles required the return of the ship in order to reduce loss but about whether the ship's actual return had in fact reduced loss. The one case is about whether loss has been avoided, the other about whether loss should have been avoided; we have moved from avoidable loss to avoided loss, and *Glory Wealth* is considered at para.9-141, below.

376 That it is for the same loss distinguishes this rule from the cases considered under rule (iv) at paras 9-090 to 9-092, above.

377 As a judicial instance, in *Cottingham v Attey Bower & Jones* [2000]. P.N.L.R. 557 at [29] the trial judge said of the claimants that he did "not consider that they were required first to endeavour to mitigate their loss by suing" another party who was perhaps the more obvious defendant. As for commentators, in *Haugesund Kommune v Depfa ACS Bank* [2010] 2 Lloyd's Rep. 323 at first instance the formulation of the issue in the present paragraph of this text was preferred to the different formulation in *Halsbury's Laws*, where it was said that not pursuing another potential defendant might constitute a failure to mitigate: see [2010] 2 Lloyd's Rep. 323 at [20] and [21].

378 [1963] P. 64 CA at 83; unnecessary if, as he put it, "any tortfeasor could oblige the creditor to sue the other debtors in order to alleviate his burden".

379 Under the then Merchant Shipping Act 1894, as amended.

claimants, and then put on deposit by the owners of the wreck.[380] In such circumstances the Court of Appeal held that the claimants were under no duty to satisfy part of their damages by accepting the money already on deposit. Harman LJ, delivering the court's judgment, pointed to the analogy that

> "it has never been the law that a creditor having a security against a third party for his debt must give credit for that when proving in the bankruptcy".[381]

*(vii) A claimant need not act so as to injure innocent persons* On the notorious facts of *Banco de Portugal v Waterlow*,[382] where there had been a large issue of forged bank notes printed by the defendant, it was held by the House of Lords that the claimant bank was entitled to give genuine notes in exchange for forged ones. The bank was entitled to do so in protection of innocent holders of forged notes[383] and to claim from the defendant as damages for breach of contract the market value of the genuine notes given in exchange and the cost of printing the genuine notes withdrawn from circulation.[384] **9-095**

*(viii) A claimant need not prejudice his commercial reputation* In *Finlay v Kwik Hoo Tong*[385] the claimants had bought goods for August shipment to them by the defendants and had resold them on different terms, the contract of resale, unlike the contract of sale, providing that the date of the bill of lading should be conclusive evidence of the date of shipment. The goods were not shipped by the defendants until September, but the bills of lading bore an August date. The claimants could have wiped out their loss by forcing the goods on their sub-buyers, but to enforce their legal rights in the circumstances would have injured their commercial reputation, and they refused to do so. It was held that their refusal was reasonable and not a failure to mitigate. Similar, but in the context of the chartering and sub-chartering of a ship by the claimants, is *The Lily Prima*.[386] In *Banco de Portugal v Waterlow*,[387] the bank was held entitled to give genuine notes for forged ones also to protect its own credit and the national currency,[388] and recover the value of the **9-096**

---

380 The purpose behind the claimants' refusal to accept the money was to enable them to prove for a larger share against the limited fund available for the satisfaction of those damaged by the defendants' negligence. The situation was also complicated by the fact that the owners of the wreck were also suing the defendants: this raised the issue of whether there was a double proof.

381 [1963] P. 64 CA at 84. That, 50 years on, *The Liverpool (No.2)* remains good law has been accepted on more than one occasion by the Court of Appeal. In *Peters v East Midlands Strategic Health Authority* [2010] Q.B. 48 CA that court said that *The Liverpool (No.2)* can stand on its own feet without resort to the mitigation principle by reliance on the rule that a person has an unfettered discretion to claim for his full loss against any of the persons liable to him for that loss, in *Peters* for the cost of care against a tortfeasor and a local authority (see the case at para.40-191, below). Again, the Court of Appeal in *Haugesund Kommune v Depfa ACS Bank* [2011] 3 All E.R. 655 CA discussed the principle in *The Liverpool (No.2)* and reached the conclusion that it was not in doubt (at [34] to [40]), though it was considered to be there inapplicable as it was concerned with established loss and the question before the court was whether the loss was established (at [41], [84] and [85]; see the case at paras 34-010, below).

382 [1932] A.C. 452.

383 And in protection of itself: see para.9-096, below.

384 See [1932] A.C. 452 at 471, per Viscount Sankey.

385 [1929] 1 K.B. 400 CA.

386 [1976] 2 Lloyd's Rep. 487, especially at 503 where this paragraph as it appeared in the 13th edition (1972) was cited. The mitigation point was not referred to in the CA.

387 [1932] A.C. 452; facts at para.9-095, above.

388 And in protection of third parties: see para.9-095, above.

new notes issued and the cost of printing the old ones withdrawn.[389] In *A Nelson & Co Ltd v Guna SpA*,[390] where there was breach of a distribution agreement, there was held to be no failure to mitigate where the claimant on the breach had found itself in an uncertain and complex situation and was not called upon to take risks outside the normal course of business.[391]

9-097 *(ix) A claimant will not be prejudiced by his financial inability to take steps in mitigation* This rule stems from what Lord Collins said in *Clippens Oil Co v Edinburgh and District Water Trustees*[392]:

> "In my opinion the wrongdoer must take his victim *talem qualem*, and if the position of the latter is aggravated because he is without the means of mitigating it, so much the worse for the wrongdoer, who has got to be answerable for the consequences flowing from his tortious act."

Over the years Lord Collins's dictum has been applied variously. It was applied in *Robbins of Putney v Meek*,[393] a claim for non-acceptance of goods sold, where the price at which the claimant resold the goods was used in the calculation of his damages despite the fact that impecuniosity had forced him to dispose of the goods by what in normal circumstances would have been a premature sale. Also in *Bunclark v Hertfordshire CC*,[394] impecuniosity was held to justify the claimant's delay in carrying out repairs to his flat, again by an application of Lord Collins's dictum.[395] So too in *Dodd Properties v Canterbury City Council*,[396] the Court of Appeal awarded to the claimants the higher cost of repair of their building, damaged by the defendants, at the time of action since they had been financially unable to effect repairs at the time the damage had been done, Megaw LJ turning to Lord Collins's dictum in arriving at this conclusion.[397]

9-098 The same result has been reached in other cases without any reference to the *Clippens* case. Thus in *Martindale v Duncan*,[398] impecuniosity was held to justify the claimant's delay in carrying out repairs to his car,[399] but in contrast to *Bunclark v Hertfordshire C.C.*[400] this holding did not depend on invoking Lord Collins's dictum. So too there was no mention of *Clippens* in either *Mattocks v Mann*,[401]

---

389 See, especially, [1932] A.C. 452 at 471, per Viscount Sankey, citing *Finlay v Kwik Hoo Tong* [1929] 1 K.B. 400 CA, with approval.

390 [2011] EWHC 1202 (Comm).

391 See generally [2011] EWHC 1202 (Comm) at [41] to [47]. In *Deutsche Bank AG v Total Global Steel Ltd* [2012] EWHC 1201 (Comm), where the claimant had bought in a specialised market carbon emission units, the mitigating steps proposed by the defendant were not required as they would have prejudiced the claimant's reputation. In *H.L. Motorworks v Alwahbi* [1977] R.T.R. 276 CA, where a Rolls Royce was damaged in the hands, as bailees, of the claimant repairers who reimbursed the owner for the full cost of hiring a substitute Rolls Royce, it was held that they were justified in so doing with a view to preserving the owner's goodwill, without suggesting to him that he should have hired a less grand car.

392 [1907] A.C. 291 at 303.

393 [1971] R.T.R. 345.

394 (1977) 234 E.G. 381 at 455.

395 (1977) 234 E.G. 381 at 461. Facts at para.39-017, below.

396 [1980] 1 W.L.R. 433 CA.

397 [1980] 1 W.L.R. 433 CA at 453D.

398 [1973] 1 W.L.R. 574 CA.

399 Facts at para.37-017, below.

400 In the preceding paragraph.

401 [1993] R.T.R. 13 CA.

which concerned the length of time a car was hired,[402] or in *Perry v Sidney Phillips & Son*,[403] or even by the Judicial Committee of the Privy Council in *Alcoa Minerals of Jamaica Plc v Broderick*,[404] both of which cases dealt with the repair of an impecunious claimant's house.[405] What these decisions were more concerned with, in order to allow recovery, was distinguishing *Liesbosch Dredger v S.S. Edison*,[406] where Lord Wright had famously laid down that damage suffered by a claimant on account of his impecuniosity was too remote.[407] Now Lord Wright had himself cited the dictum of Lord Collins and concluded that it was not in point since it was

> "dealing not with the measure of damage, but with the victim's duty to minimise damage, which is quite a different matter".[408]

The difficulty however, which has never been properly resolved, is in ascertaining the point at which *Clippens* takes over from *The Liesbosch*, the point at which mitigation takes over from remoteness.

Fortunately, this problem has now evaporated since at last the House of Lords in *Lagden v O'Connor*,[409] has departed from Lord Wright's long controversial ruling in *The Liesbosch*.[410] From now on therefore it matters not by which route the impecunious claimant is protected, the cross-over point need no longer be investigated and our rule based on Lord Collins's dictum need no longer be concerned that it may be displaced by arguments on remoteness. **9-099**

*(x) A claimant need not be prejudiced by paying money in performance of a contract which is unenforceable against him* This rule is suggested by *W v Veolia Environmental Services*,[411] another of the many credit car hire cases that are today appearing in the courts. The payment under a contract that was unenforceable against the hirer, so that there was no legal obligation for him to pay, of credit hire charges for a car needed by him while his car, damaged by the defendant, was being repaired did not constitute a failure to mitigate.[412] **9-100**

## III. THE COROLLARY: RECOVERY FOR LOSS INCURRED IN ATTEMPTS TO MITIGATE THE DAMAGE

The claimant, during his efforts to mitigate the damage, may incur further loss, which will often be a loss which is not in addition to, but in place of and less than, the loss which he is attempting to mitigate. This is particularly so in the case of **9-101**

---

402 Facts at para.37-017, below.

403 [1982] 1 W.L.R. 1297 CA.

404 [2002] 1 A.C. 371 PC.

405 Facts at paras 34-063 and 39-019, below, respectively. *Alcoa Minerals* was applied in *Smith and Smith v South Gloucester Council* [2002] 3 E.G.L.R. 1 CA to inability not to repair a house but to buy another house.

406 [1933] A.C. 449.

407 See para.8-111, above.

408 [1933] A.C. 449 at 461. He cast no doubt on the correctness of what Lord Collins had said despite what the headnote to *The Liesbosch* misleadingly states, as Cantley J pointed out in *Dodd Properties v Canterbury City Council* [1980] 1 W.L.R. 433 at 443B.

409 [2004] 1 A.C. 1067.

410 See paras 8-110 to 8-113, above.

411 [2011] EWHC 2020 (QB).

412 See the case further at para.37-019, below.

expenses. The expenses incurred by the claimant as the result of the tort or breach of contract for which recovery is allowed in the cases are generally expenses incurred to avoid or minimise a loss. This is so where money is laid out in acquiring or hiring a substitute where the claimant's property is damaged, destroyed or misappropriated[413]; where medical expenses are incurred to ameliorate the claimant's physical injury caused by the defendant[414]; where there is expenditure upon advertisements to counteract the effect of the defendant's infringement of the claimant's trade mark,[415] upon extensive inquiries to detect the extent of the defendant's unlawful machinations in inducing breaches of contract and in conspiracy,[416] or upon the foundations of a building to counteract the effects of a nuisance.[417] These various examples may be considered as examples of steps taken in mitigation of damage, but some of them are so common, such as medical expenses in personal injury cases, that they tend not to be thought of specifically from this angle.[418] Whether regarded specifically as mitigation or not, the rule allowing recovery for such expenses is at base the corollary of the rule refusing recovery for loss that could reasonably have been mitigated.

**9-102** Moreover, the corollary goes further and allows recovery for losses and expenses reasonably incurred in mitigation even though the resulting damage is in the event greater than it would have been had the mitigating steps not been taken.[419] This general principle may be said to be akin to, and even a part of, the rule, met with in remoteness of damage, that a claimant's intervening act reasonably taken to safeguard his interests, whether taken in the "agony of the moment"[420] or not,[421] does not relieve the defendant of liability for the resulting loss.[422] This further dimension of the corollary indeed represents the second of the three rules of mitigation as put forward in this text.[423] It should be noted that in applying to the rules, which he quoted, his analysis of mitigation in terms of causation Robert Goff J in *Koch Marine Inc v D'Amica Società di Navigatione, The Elena d'Amico*,[424] ap-

---

413 *The Yorkshireman* (1826) 2 Hagg. Adm. 30n. and compare *Dimond v Lovell* [2002] 1 A.C. 384 (damage): see paras 37-015 to 37-028, below; *Tradebe Solvent Recycling Ltd v Coussens of Bexhill Ltd* [2013] EWHC 3786 (QB): see at [79]; *Moore v D.E.R.* [1971] 1 W.L.R. 1476 CA (destruction): see para.37-069, below; *Davies v Oswell* (1837) 7 C. & P. 804 (misappropriation): see para.38-067, below.

414 Usually costs of care, as in *S v Distillers Co (Biochemicals)* [1970] 1 W.L.R. 114 and countless other cases.

415 *Spalding v Gamage* (1918) 35 R.P.C. 101 CA: see the case in the footnote at the end of para.48-017, below.

416 *British Motor Trade Association v Salvadori* [1949] Ch. 556; *R-V Versicherung AG v Risk Insurance and Reinsurance Solutions SA* [2006] EWHC 42 (Comm).

417 *Delaware Mansions Ltd v Westminster City Council* [2002] 1 A.C. 321; *L.E. Jones v Portsmouth City Council* [2003] 1 W.L.R. 427 CA.

418 And see *Compagnia Financiera "Soleada" v Hamoor Tanker Corp, The Borag* [1981] 1 W.L.R. 274 CA in the fn. at the end of para.9-039, above.

419 Of course the unsuccessful steps taken must have been reasonably taken. Thus as the claimant in *Riyad Bank v Ahli United Bank (UK) Plc* [2005] 2 Lloyd's Rep. 409 was held not to have shown that it was reasonable to incur the expenses of buying out shareholders, which increased the loss, the claim for such expenses could not have succeeded: see [2005] 2 Lloyd's Rep. 409 at [168]–[172].

420 As in *Jones v Boyce* (1816) 1 Stark. 493.

421 As in *The Metagama* (1927) 29 Ll. L. Rep. 253 HL, otherwise reported as *Canadian Pacific Co v Kelvin Shipping Co* (1927) 138 L.T. 369 HL.

422 See paras 8-065 to 8-069, above.

423 See paras 9-003 to 9-006, above.

424 [1980] 1 Lloyd's Rep. 75 at 88, col.2

plied the analysis to the second rule as much as to the other two, and it is considered that this is of no greater use here than it was found to be in relation to the central first rule. The test for recovery is not causation but simply whether the act or omission which gave rise to the increased loss was a reasonable step for the claimant to take.[425]

9-103 At the date of this book's initial compilation and publication in 1961, this principle boasted no clear illustration in English law. The only support found for the principle came in one comment and one decision, both of which are still germane. The comment was that of Lord Atkinson in *Wilson v United Counties Bank*.[426] He there said:

> "If one man inflicts an injury upon another the resort by the sufferer to reasonable expedients for the bona fide purpose of counteracting, curing or lessening the evil effects of the injury done him, does not necessarily absolve the wrongdoer, even though the sufferer's efforts should, in the result, undesignedly aggravate the result of the injury."

The decision, which was the first to get near to being an example of this situation, was *Jones v Watney, Combe, Reid & Co*.[427] It was an action for personal injury in which the defendant contended that he was not liable in damages for the aggravation of the injury to the claimant's foot by reason of her walking on the foot too soon after the accident. Lush J directed the jury to

> "look at all the circumstances of the case, the medical advice received, the need for action, the usual or extraordinary character of what is actually done, and the precautions taken during the doing of it. The injured person need not act with perfect knowledge and ideal wisdom, but upon the other hand cannot claim damages for such injuries as are really due to wanton, needless, or careless conduct on his own part. If what is done reasonably and carefully augments the injuries, that may be regarded as a natural consequence of the accident."[428]

The jury held the defendant liable for the total injury.

9-104 Then soon after the promulgation in this text of the principle of recovery for increased loss through unsuccessful mitigating action, the principle started to come into its own. The statement of it was first quoted from the 1961 edition and applied in *Lloyds and Scottish Finance v Modern Cars and Caravans (Kingston)*.[429] The defendants there had sold to the claimants a caravan which was not their property and which was subsequently seized by the sheriff who, upon the defendants protesting, instituted interpleader proceedings against them. At the defendants' suggestion the claimants claimed the caravan, but this claim was withdrawn after legal advice that it was not maintainable, and the claimants paid the costs of the interpleader proceedings. It was held that these costs could be included within the damages for breach of warranty. Edmund Davies J considered that where steps intended to be by way of mitigation were

---

425 See the discussion in relation to the first rule at para.9-019, above.
426 [1920] A.C. 102 at 125.
427 (1912) 28 T.L.R. 399.
428 (1912) 28 T.L.R. 399 at 400.
429 [1966] 1 Q.B. 764.

"taken at the instigation of the defendants, I do not think it is open to them to assert that such steps were not reasonable".[430]

Next came *Esso Petroleum Co v Mardon*.[431] There the defendant had taken a three-year tenancy agreement of a filling station on the strength of the claimant oil company's estimate of the station's potential throughput of petrol, an estimate which proved disastrously optimistic. When the truth came out the defendant gave the claimants notice, but the claimants, eager to keep the station open and controlled by a good tenant, offered to the defendant, who accepted, a new tenancy agreement on more favourable terms. The losses in the business continued however, and accordingly the overall loss to the defendant was exacerbated rather than reduced. In the defendant's successful counterclaim for breach of warranty and negligent misrepresentation when sued by the claimants for, inter alia, possession of the premises, the Court of Appeal refused to accept that the effect of the statement constituting both the warranty and the misrepresentation was spent by the date on which the defendant entered into the new tenancy agreement, reversing on this the judge below who had taken such date as the cut-off point for the damages. In entering into the second tenancy agreement the defendant was acting reasonably in an effort to mitigate the loss to himself and the claimants so that the loss sustained after that date was attributable to the original statement and was recoverable as damages from the claimants.[432]

**9-105** These cases, however, only provided illustrations of recovery for loss due to unsuccessful mitigating action which was instigated by the defendant. A wider acceptance was needed. This was heralded by the comment, on a more general plane, of Winn LJ.in *The World Beauty*[433] where he said that he was not aware of any express statement in the cases

"but it is implicit in the principle, that if mitigating steps are reasonably taken and additional loss or damage results notwithstanding the reasonable decision to take those steps, then that will be in addition to the recoverable damage and not a set-off against the amount of it."

By the 1980s, decisions allowing recovery of increased losses triggered by reasonable, but unsuccessful, conduct began to appear. The sale of 2,000 tonnes of sugar in *Metelmann & Co v N.B.R. (London)*,[434] provided the scene for perhaps the first clear illustration, although an illustration in the peculiar context of anticipatory breach of contract with its own special rules as to mitigation.[435] In sale of goods these rules are to the effect that, on repudiation by the buyer before the time fixed for his acceptance, the damages are still prima facie calculated at that time but become subject to a duty to mitigate on the part of the seller once he has accepted the repudiation. In *Metelmann* the seller, immediately upon acceptance of the buyer's repudiation, made a sale in a reasonable attempt at mitigation but, as events turned out, on the date fixed for acceptance the market price was higher. The seller was nevertheless held entitled to have the damages based upon the lower price at

430 [1966] 1 Q.B. 764 at 782 and 783.
431 [1976] Q.B. 801 CA.
432 [1976] Q.B. 801 CA at 812C to E, 829B to F and 833B to G. This case is further dealt with at para.49-062, below.
433 [1970] P. 144 CA at 156.
434 [1984] 1 Lloyd's Rep. 614 CA.
435 See para.9-021, above.

which the sale had been made. As Browne-Wilkinson LJ put it:

> "In addition to the basic damages … Metelmann is entitled to be compensated for the additional damage flowing from the attempt to mitigate."[436]

The principle is now fully accepted. Evidence of this is to be found in a series of modern shipping cases. In *Nigerian National Shipping Lines v Mutual Ltd, The Windfall*,[437] it was held that the claim for the loss of the sale of a vessel wrongfully arrested would still succeed even if the loss of the sale turned out to be because of the claimant's chartering and reflagging of the vessel, a reasonable act of mitigation made in an effort to obtain the vessel's release; here the attempt at mitigation would have caused the whole loss claimed.[438] In *The Sivand*,[439] where the claimant's harbour installations had been damaged by the defendant's vessel and the act of mitigation was the common one of repairing the damage done, it was held to be no good reason for not allowing the full outlay that the repair had cost much more than had been foreseen.[440] In *Vinmar International Ltd v Theresa Navigation SA*,[441] the claimant cargo owner's decision to continue loading cargo although there was a serious risk of its being contaminated by the cargo already loaded was seen by the court as a reasonable but unsuccessful attempt at mitigation.[442] Outside shipping cases there is the sale of goods case of *Choil Trading SA v Sahara Energy Resources Ltd*.[443] The claimant buyer's sub-buyer had, on account of defects, rejected the cargo of naphtha sold to it, thus leaving the claimant with the cargo on his hands. The claimant decided to hedge against its open position, this being normal practice in a volatile market and constituting a reasonable attempt at mitigation. Because the market then rose the claimant was able to sell the cargo elsewhere for more than it had bought it, but the market rise meant that a loss was necessarily suffered on the hedge, which loss, as it turned out, was greater than the eventual profit made on the cargo sold to the claimant by the defendant. For this net loss the claimant was held entitled to recover.[444] **9-106**

*Herrmann v Withers LLP*[445] is an important case in the present context because of the peculiar feature that the expense successfully claimed had not in fact been incurred by the claimants. The defendant solicitors wrongly advised the claimant **9-107**

---

436 [1984] 1 Lloyd's Rep. 614 at 634, col.2. The facts of the case are at para.25-124, below.

437 [1998] 2 Lloyd's Rep. 664.

438 Nor did it matter that the act of mitigation, if reasonable, put the claimant in breach of contract with another: see [1998] 2 Lloyd's Rep. 664 at 671, col.2–672, col.1.

439 [1998] 2 Lloyd's Rep. 97 CA.

440 See [1998] 2 Lloyd's Rep. 97 CA at 108, col.1, per Hobhouse LJ. The facts of the case are at para.8-116, above.

441 [2001] 2 Lloyd's Rep. 1.

442 [2001] 2 Lloyd's Rep. 1 at 15. The issue was approached in terms both of mitigation and of remoteness; for the remoteness aspect, see para.8-067, above.

443 [2010] EWHC 374 (Comm). Facts at para.25-065, below.

444 See the complex computation at [2010] EWHC 374 (Comm) at [156] to [161]. In his discussion of the process of hedging, Christopher Clarke J pointed out that the defendant was well aware of the likelihood that the claimant would hedge (at [156]) which may suggest that in the absence of such knowledge he would have considered that, or would have had to consider whether, the damage was too remote. But remoteness does not come into the picture and has no application where acts taken in mitigation are concerned. The claimant has suffered damage, damage which is in no way too remote, and he is simply seeking by action to mitigate that damage. All that matters, to allow recovery, is that the action taken by the claimant is reasonable. For more on this see para.9-019, above.

445 [2012] EWHC 1492 Ch.

purchasers of a residential property in a London Borough that the property enjoyed a statutory right of access to a communal garden. Negotiations with the Borough after completion of the purchase brought an offer from the Borough of a licence to use the garden for a fee of £25,000. The non-acceptance of this offer was held by Newey J to constitute a failure to mitigate as the grant of the licence offered would have alleviated to a great extent the disadvantage of not having the statutory right of access to the garden.[446] Accordingly, the damages in respect of the diminution in the value of the residential property were limited to the difference between its value with the statutory right of access to the garden and its value with only a licence to use the garden, but the claimants were held entitled in addition to damages represented by the £25,000 cost of the licence together with the costs that would have been incurred in negotiating and agreeing it. Thus the claimants' recovery of this amount was not in respect of expenditure incurred in the taking of mitigating action but in respect of expenditure which was not incurred by reason of the failure to mitigate. It is thought that *Herrmann* is the first decision where damages have been claimed and allowed for expenditure which has not been incurred at all. One can see the logic and sense of this result. Had the claimants incurred the expenditure required by the mitigating action, they would have recovered for this expenditure in lieu of recovering for the greater loss that would have incurred had they not mitigated. If they fail to mitigate and so cannot recover for the loss that could and should have been avoided, they should still be entitled to recover for the loss that would have remained after they had mitigated, viz., for the expenditure not in fact incurred. In short, the claimants should be able to recover not only for the loss remaining after mitigation but also for what would have been the remaining loss had they mitigated.[447]

## IV. The Rule as to Avoided Loss: No Recovery Generally for Loss Which the Claimant has Avoided by Reasonably Necessary Means

**9-108** There remains the third of the three rules of mitigation as put forward in this text.[448] This third rule is primarily directed at this situation. Frequently a claimant will have taken the required reasonable steps of mitigation and thereby have avoided such part of the loss as was avoidable. No difficulty arises in such circumstances. But the claimant may have gone further and by sound action have avoided more consequences than the dictates of the law required of him. In such circumstances the position has been definitively stated by Viscount Haldane LC in the leading case of *British Westinghouse Co v Underground Ry*.[449] He put the rule thus:

> "When in the course of his business he [the plaintiff] has taken action arising out of the transaction, which action has diminished his loss, the effect in actual diminution of the loss he has suffered may be taken into account even though there was no duty on him to act."[450]

---

446 His very detailed reasons for holding that the claimants ought reasonably to have pursued the offer of a licence appear at [2012] EWHC 1492 Ch at [82].

447 See Newey J at [2012] EWHC 1492 Ch at [90] to [94].

448 The three rules are at paras 9-003 to 9-006, above.

449 [1912] A.C. 673.

450 [1912] A.C. 673 at 689.

Later in his speech he said similarly:

> "Provided the course taken to protect himself by the plaintiff in such an action was one which a reasonable and prudent person might in the ordinary conduct of business properly have taken, and in fact did take whether bound to or not, a jury or an arbitrator may properly look at the whole of the facts and ascertain the result in estimating the quantum of damage."[451]

He emphasised, however, that

> "the subsequent transaction, if to be taken into account, must be one arising out of the consequences of the breach and in the ordinary course of business".[452]

Where steps are taken by the claimant after the wrong which cut down his loss, the important practical question is therefore to ascertain which, if any, of the steps taken come within and satisfy Viscount Haldane's formulation, what subsequent transactions of the claimant are to be regarded as arising out of the consequences of the wrong and also, in the case of contract, as arising in the ordinary course of business. This question, which might be more neatly stated as whether the claimant's conduct was reasonably necessary, will be considered in due course[453]; it represents the core of the problem of mitigation by way of avoided loss.[454] **9-109**

## 1. The Three Subdivisions of the Rule

Losses may, however, be mitigated in ways other than through actions taken by the claimant after he has suffered the wrong, be it breach of contract or tort. There are two such ways. First, and in particular, actions by third parties may relieve the claimant of loss which he would otherwise have incurred. Secondly, actions taken by claimants themselves before they have suffered the wrong may have a similar effect.[455] Thus there can be said to be three sub-divisions of the third rule. **9-110**

It is common to describe actions by third parties and actions before the wrong by claimants as giving rise to mitigation of loss[456] but it is clear that Viscount Haldane's formulation, which concerns steps taken by the claimant after suffering the wrong, is of no relevance in this context. Resort must therefore be had to a wider formulation, and one which more readily includes tort, a formulation which is that matter completely collateral and merely *res inter alios acta* cannot be used in **9-111**

---

451 [1912] A.C. 673 at 690.

452 [1912] A.C. 673 at 690. See, too, at 691: "arise out of the transactions the subject-matter of the contract."

453 See paras 9-117 and following, below.

454 For a somewhat curious and dubious application in tort of the mitigation principle enunciated in the British Westinghouse case, see *Dimond v Lovell* [2002] 1 A.C. 384. It is thought that the *British Westinghouse* principle is concerned with avoided loss and, being directed to ensuring that the claimant is not in a better position than before the wrong, can have no proper application to the aspect of the House of Lords decision in *Dimond* dealt with at para.37-020, below. By contrast, the Court of Appeal in the somewhat similar *Burdis v Livsey* [2003] Q.B. 36 CA, was rightly unprepared to hold that there had been a mitigation of the damage: see the case at para.37-008, below. .

455 Sometimes the loss may be lessened by a combination of third-party and claimant actions.

456 "Compensating advantages" is the term used by Burrows in his valuable *Remedies for Torts and Breach of Contract*, 3rd edn (Oxford: OUP, 2004), which he applies to all cases of avoided loss, but he does recognise, at p.156, "as it is sometimes alternatively expressed, that losses mitigated would not be compensated".

mitigation of damage.[457] This has the great merit of stating the rule not only concisely but also completely since it includes the situations which fall within Viscount Haldane's formulation as well as the two others. Its demerit is that it gives no indication of how the rule operates and of what solutions would be reached when applying it to particular circumstances. Indeed, as will be seen, the line between those avoided consequences which are collateral and those which are not is an exceedingly difficult one to draw and its drawing is not assisted by the fact that the relevant decided cases are widely dispersed over many fields.

**9-112** Nor is understanding of the third rule of mitigation[458] assisted by climbing the slippery slopes of causation. In his analysis of mitigation in terms of causation in *Koch Marine Inc v D'Amica Società di Navigatione, The Elena d'Amico*,[459] Robert Goff J applied the analysis to the third rule as much as to the other two, and it is considered that it is of no greater use here than it was found to be in relation to the central first rule or to the second rule.[460] The test in relation to the third rule, as we shall see, is variously constituted and described. It may be said to turn upon whether the benefit comes from an act taken in consequence of the wrong, whether the benefit arises out of the act of mitigation itself, whether the act giving rise to the benefit forms part of a continuous transaction starting with the wrong. The test is again not causation.

## 2. VARIOUS ASPECTS OF THE RULE

**9-113** Of the various aspects of the rule on avoidable loss considered,[461] a few fall for consideration similarly in relation to avoided loss. Most are clearly irrelevant; thus no question of duty to mitigate can arise nor any question of the need to take steps before breach or to discontinue performance. There is, however, an additional issue which does not make an appearance in relation to avoidable loss; this arises out of the need to distinguish between the mitigation of loss and the existence of no loss at all.

**9-114** **(a) Application to contract and tort** While Viscount Haldane's formulation of this rule, with its reference to steps taken in the ordinary course of business, is understandably geared to contract rather than to tort, *British Westinghouse Co v*

---

457 This passage was cited with approval, and applied, by Butler-Sloss LJ in *Salih v Enfield Health Authority* [1991] 3 All E.R. 400 CA at 405d: see the case at para.9-127, below. Lord Reid had said in *British Transport Commission v Gourley* [1956] A.C. 185 at 214 that he could find no better words than "matters completely collateral", taken from the then edition of *Mayne on Damages*, for a general description of what is too remote and therefore not to be taken into consideration in the assessment of the damages. It should, however, be noted that *Gourley*, which was dealing with the deductibility of income tax (see Ch.17, below), has nothing to do with mitigation, as Lord Reid himself pointed out in *Parry v Cleaver* [1970] A.C. 1. On the deductibility of pensions from the lost earnings of a physically injured claimant (dealt with in the context of mitigation at para.9-166, first footnote, below) he said: "Two questions can arise. First, what … are the sums which he would have received but for the accident but which by reason of the accident he can no longer get? And secondly, what are the sums which he did in fact receive as a result of the accident but which he would not have received if there had been no accident? …*Gourley*'s case had nothing whatever to do with the second question": at 13C and E.

458 See paras 9-003 to 9-006, above.

459 [1980] 1 Lloyd's Rep. 75 at 88 col.2

460 See the discussion in relation to the first rule at para.9-019, above.

461 See paras 9-015 to 9-037, above.

*Underground Ry*,[462] being a case of breach of contract, the rule applies also to tort. Not only is this shown by the cases[463] but also finds expression in the judgment of Lord Merriman P in *The Liverpool (No.2)*.[464] He there said that Viscount Haldane's

> "classic statement, although arising out of a breach of contract, applies equally, mutatis mutandis, to tort",

citing there[465] both the opening part of the statement on avoidable loss[466] and the following part on avoided loss.[467] The mutatis mutandis allows the reference to the ordinary course of business to be disregarded when it comes to tort, and also permits substitution of consequences of the tort for consequences of the breach of contract.

**(b) The question of onus** Where it appears that steps have been taken by the claimant to avoid loss which are to be taken into account in assessing the damages, the onus is on the defendant to prove that, and also how far, loss has thereby been avoided. Thus in *The World Beauty*,[468] where the claimants' ship had been damaged in a collision while engaged on a charter and the claimants had attempted to mitigate their loss by advancing the commencement of a later charter, it was held in their claim for loss of profits that it was for the defendant to prove the value of the advancement.[469] **9-115**

**(c) The preliminary issue of mitigation of loss or no loss** It is very important, however, first to ascertain whether any loss has in fact been incurred; cases of no loss are to be excluded from consideration. For it may be that the benefit provided by the act of the third party prevents the loss from arising in the first place rather than reduces or eliminates a loss already incurred.[470] The commission of the wrong does not produce an immediate loss but a potential future loss. A familiar illustration of this is found in the everyday case of personal injury requiring medical attention. As Lord Bridge put it in *Hunt v Severs*[471]: **9-116**

> "If an injured plaintiff … receives free treatment under the National Health Service, his need has been met without cost to him and he cannot claim the cost of the treatment from the tortfeasor."

This is in effect potential future damage from the tort which in the event was never suffered. Other cases are to be explained similarly along these lines. In *Kennedy v Van Emden*,[472] the negligent advice of the claimants' solicitors resulted in their taking leases on payment of illegal premiums. Their claims against the solici-

---

462 [1912] A.C. 673.

463 See paras 9-125 to 9-127 and 9-143 to 9-152, below.

464 [1963] P. 63.

465 [1963] P. 63 at 77 to 78.

466 At para.9-014, above.

467 At para.9-108, above.

468 [1970] P. 144 CA. For the full facts see paras 9-125 and 37-036, below.

469 [1970] P. 144 CA at 154 and 158, per Lord Denning MR and Fenton Atkinson LJ respectively. The onus is the same for avoidable loss: see para.9-020, above.

470 The confusing *R&M Stansfield Enterprises Ltd v Axa Insurance UK Plc* [2006] EWCA Civ 881 CA may perhaps be thus explained, the value of assets released by the defendant eliminating in part the loss of profits claimed: see [2006] EWCA Civ 881 CA at [46]–[48].

471 [1994] 2 A.C. 350 at 361F.

472 [1996] P.N.L.R. 409 CA.

tors, however, were not for the loss of the premium moneys. Their potential loss was that they would have been unable themselves to charge a premium on disposal of their leases but by the time of the trial this was no longer so as subsequent legislation had made premiums lawful. Accordingly, the potential future loss never materialised and there could be no recovery in respect of it; no mention is made in the judgments of mitigation of loss.[473] In *McKinnon v e.surv Ltd*,[474] property, purchased by the claimant on the strength of the defendant's negligent report and which had been subject to movement, was so no longer and had not been since the time of the purchase; however, it would not have been possible to establish this until after the date of purchase. In these circumstances the claimant was held entitled in damages to the purchase price less the value not subject to movement and not to the purchase price less the value if subject to that movement. The fact that the purchase price was over the true value was due to the claimant having paid too high a price for the property or to defects, other than a tendency to movement, negligently undiscovered by the defendant. For the result in the case to be right it must have been the latter; if the former, the claimant should have been entitled to no damages at all. In *Murfin v Campbell*,[475] the claimant, in reliance on what he maintained was the defendant's negligent advice, gave a warranty which obliged him to pay over the amount by which the losses of a company exceeded a specified sum but the obligation to pay would only arise when a series of loan notes became redeemable. As things turned out the loan notes never did become redeemable so that no payment had to be made by the claimant. Nevertheless, he sought to recover the amount of the payment as damages on the basis that it represented his loss at the time of the wrong but he rightly failed because in the event he had suffered no loss.[476] And the proper explanation of the important House of Lords decision in *Dimond v Lovell*,[477] is to be found here. While her car, which had been damaged by the defendant's negligence, was being repaired the claimant hired another car under a hiring agreement which, being improperly executed, was unenforceable against her. The House of Lords held that she was not entitled to claim the cost of hiring the substitute car.[478] The potential future loss had not materialised so that there was no loss rather than a loss mitigated. Again there was no discussion in the speeches of mitigation of loss upon this issue.[479]

## 3. ACTIONS TAKEN AFTER THE WRONG BY THE CLAIMANT

**9-117** Actions taken after the breach of duty by the claimant himself are directly within the principles laid down in *British Westinghouse Co v Underground Ry*,[480] and, as already said,[481] it is here that is found the core of the problem. When this text was

---

473 Or even of loss avoided by the changed legislation. All the case turned on was the point in time at which the loss fell to be assessed, the time of wrong or the time of trial.

474 [2003] 2 E.G.L.R. 57.

475 [2011] EWHC 1475 Ch.

476 Many of the cases scattered throughout this work were cited in support of his claim but none was really in point other than *Kennedy v Van Emden* (in the text, above) and it was against him.

477 [2002] 1 A.C. 384.

478 Contrast *Burdis v Livsey* [2003] Q.B. 36 CA, at para.37-008, below.

479 There was a mitigation issue but it was on a different point: see the case at paras 9-081 and 9-109, above and para.37-020, below.

480 [1912] A.C. 673.

481 At para.9-109, above.

initially compiled in the late 1950s the matter was not well worked out in the authorities and all that could be done was to sketch what the law probably was. Over the intervening years a formidable body of case law has gradually appeared and today hardly a year goes by without a difficult decision on this issue facing the courts. While the decisions have been incorporated in the text of succeeding editions, by the start of the 21st century the time had come to seek out a fuller, more exact and more exacting analysis to get the cases into line. This has been done to assist in the task of arriving at appropriate conclusions in future fact situations.

Before turning to these cases, it should be said that some applications of the rule are admittedly simple and are so straightforward as generally to be taken for granted. Thus where the claimant has recovered damages from a third party who is also liable, as by being a joint tortfeasor for instance, he cannot recover damages over again from the defendant for the same loss.[482] Again, where a claimant has accepted the return of his goods which the defendant had converted, he cannot sue the defendant for their value.[483] **9-118**

It transpired that all of the cases in the 20th century which were extant at the date of the book's initial compilation concerned sale, generally of goods.[484] They were cases where on the defendant's default the claimant takes steps to remedy his situation either by acquiring substitutes or by disposing of the goods to a third party. It was found that benefits gained by a buyer through acquisition of substitutes, or by a seller through profitable use of the item sold, were taken into account in claims for lost profits while benefits gained through disposition to third parties, in claims whether by buyer or seller for the normal measure of damages, were ignored. While the cases now go well beyond sale and have moved into many other fields, both contractual and tortious, it is thought both possible and sensible to build upon the distinction between these two groups of cases for an analysis of the totality of the authorities. **9-119**

In any event, it is suggested that the basic rule is that the benefit to the claimant, if it is to be taken into account in mitigation of damage, must arise out of the act of mitigation itself; this approach has been adopted by the courts in quite a number of cases. It may be regarded as simply another way of expressing Viscount Haldane's requirement that the transaction giving rise to the benefit "must be one arising out of the consequences of the breach". As we have seen, a matter which "arises out of" the consequences of the breach has been described as one arising **9-120**

---

482 See, e.g. *Burn v Morris* (1834) 2 Cr. & M. 579.

483 See, e.g. *Moon v Raphael* (1835) 2 Bing. N.C. 310. And in *Evans Marshall & Co v Bertola SA and Independent Sherry Importers* [1976] 2 Lloyd's Rep. 17 HL, where the claimants were claiming damages on account of the defendants' wrongful termination of the claimants' sole distributorship in the UK of the defendants' sherry, it was not questioned that any profits made from another distributorship which the claimants had acquired in place of the broken distributorship had to be taken into account in mitigation of the claimants' loss, the argument ranging round the factual questions of what profits had been made and what profits would have been made.

484 Three old cases outside sale had appeared between 1830 and 1875, all well before the general rule had been enunciated in *British Westinghouse Co v Underground Ry* [1912] A.C. 673 (see para.9-108, above). It is therefore not surprising that the first two, *Staniforth v Lyall* (1830) 7 Bing. 169 and *Oldershaw v Holt* (1840) 12 A.& E. 590, did not properly address the issue while the third, *Jebsen v East and West India Dock Co* (1875) L.R. 10 C.P. 300, may be a mistaken application of the rule in the light of modern authority. The first two cases are considered at para.9-134, below and the third at para.9-153, below.

from the "ordinary course of business"[485] although a better expression would be whether the claimant's action is reasonably necessary.[486]

### (1) Situations where the benefit is generally taken into account

9-121 **(a) Sale** Where a seller fails to deliver goods, or delivers defective goods, and the buyer wishes to claim damages for the loss of profit he would have made from the goods, he must show that he has taken reasonable steps in mitigation by attempting to acquire a substitute. If, then, in acquiring such a substitute the claimant gains some benefit, this must be taken into account in assessing the damages. This was the situation in the leading case of *British Westinghouse Co v Underground Ry*.[487] Turbines supplied under contract to the claimant railway company were deficient in power and in economy of working and not in accordance with the contract. The claimant used them for a time, but ultimately replaced them by others of a different make and design which were more powerful and which brought in greater profit than the original machines would have, even had they been up to standard. The claimant claimed to recover as damages the cost of the substitute, a consequential loss,[488] but this loss was held not recoverable since the consequential gain in profits and saved expenses was to be taken into account, and on balance no net loss showed on the purchase of the substitute.

9-122 The converse situation, where the breach of contract was not by the seller and supplier of the goods but by the buyer to whom they were supplied, arose in *Hill v Showell*.[489] The claimants had agreed to manufacture and supply cartridge clips for the defendants to be made from steel supplied by the defendants which they failed to supply, thereby preventing the claimants from carrying out the contract. The claimants sued for their profit calculated at the price they would have received under the contract less the cost to them of manufacturing and producing the clips, but it was held by the House of Lords that evidence was admissible to show that the claimants were enabled, because of the breach, to execute other profitable orders as this was relevant in assessing the damages in their claim for loss of profits. Viscount Haldane said:

> "If, in the course of his business, he [the plaintiff] has taken action which has actually arisen out of the situation in which his machinery was rendered free by reason of the breach, and by taking on new contracts occasioned by this situation has diminished his loss, he must give credit for the diminution, even though he may have gone somewhat out of his way to make fresh efforts because of the position in which he found himself with unemployed machinery."[490]

---

[485] *Bacciottini v Gotelee & Goldsmith (A Firm)* [2016] EWCA Civ 170 CA at [49], per Davis LJ; *Fulton Shipping Inc of Panama v Globalia Business Travel SAU ("The New Flamenco")* [2015] EWCA Civ 1299 at [23], per Longmore LJ

[486] *Globalia Business Travel SAU v Fulton Shipping Inc of Panama* [2017] UKSC 43 at [32].

[487] [1912] A.C. 673.

[488] For the meaning attached to consequential loss, see paras 3-008 and following, above. No question arose in this case as to the loss incurred during the years of use of the turbines by reason of their not being up to standard.

[489] (1918) 87 L.J.K.B. 1106 HL, Lord Dunedin dissenting.

[490] (1918) 87 L.J.K.B. 1106 HL at 1108; see, too, at 1114, per Lord Parmoor. Contrast *Re Vic Mill* [1913] 1 Ch. 465 CA, which was cited in *Hill*, where, as explained at para.9-045 above, the manufacture and supply of the *same* goods to other customers did not cut down the loss because of the state of the market.

Even before the House of Lords decided *British Westinghouse*,[491] the Judicial Committee of the Privy Council had addressed the same issue in *Erie County Natural Gas Co v Carroll*,[492] where the sale was with a reservation and there had been a failure to supply back to the original transferor. The claimant had transferred gas leases to the defendant, reserving the use of such gas as would be sufficient to supply certain plant operated by him in his business. When the defendant wrongfully cut off the gas supply due under the reservation clause, the claimant procured the gas required for his plant by the acquisition of other gas leases from independent sources and by the construction of works to produce gas. When subsequently the claimant sold his business, he sold for more than they cost him the substituted gas leases and the works constructed by him. The Judicial Committee of the Privy Council, reversing the Ontario Court of Appeal, held the claimant entitled to only nominal damages in his action against the defendant for breach of contract on the ground that the measure of damages was the cost to the claimant of procuring the substitute gas. Lord Atkinson said: **9-123**

> "It would have been competent for the plaintiffs to have abstained from procuring gas in substitution for that which the defendants should have supplied to them, and have sued the defendants for damages for breach of their contract. They did not take that course. They chose to perform on behalf of the defendants, in a reasonable way, that contract for them and to obtain from an independent source a sufficient quantity of gas similar as near as might be in character and quality to that which they were entitled to receive. In such cases it is well established that the measure of damages is the cost of procuring the substituted article, not at all the price at which the substituted article when procured could have been sold by the person who has procured it."[493]

A hundred years on from these three key decisions *Glencore Energy UK Ltd v Transworld Oil Ltd*,[494] provides a somewhat different case of a buyer's loss reduced by action taken in mitigation. On the seller's repudiation of its sale of oil, the buyer, having accepted the repudiation, proceeded to reduce its loss by closing out its hedges, as to allow them to run on would have been to speculate in the movement of the price of oil, it being accepted that hedging was an integral part of the seller's business. Blair J took this reduction of loss into account in assessing the damages though his analysis somewhat confuses avoided loss and avoidable loss.[495] Another contemporary sale of goods case where it is thought that this rule as to avoided loss should have been applied is *M&J Marine Engineering Services Co Ltd v Shipshore Ltd*,[496] but, as we shall see, Field J arrived at the proper result by a somewhat different route.[497] **9-124**

## (b) Other situations

*(i) Tort* The issue of whether account must be taken of loss avoided by the claimant's action in response to the wrong inflicted made its *début* in the field of **9-125**

[491] [1912] A.C. 673.
[492] [1911] A.C. 105 PC.
[493] [1911] A.C. 105 PC at 116 to 117.
[494] [2010] EWHC 141 (Comm).
[495] See [2010] EWHC 141 (Comm) at [78].
[496] [2009] EWHC 2031 (Comm).
[497] The case is dealt with under sale of goods at para.25-031, below.

tort in *The World Beauty*,[498] a claim arising out of a ship collision. Once again, there was the acquisition of a substitute, here for the damaged ship, and in addition there was the earlier profitable use of that ship on the completion of repairs. Accordingly, the benefit did arise out of the act, or in this case acts, of mitigation and had therefore to be brought into account. At a time when freight rates were low the claimants' tanker suffered serious damage in a collision while operating under a charterparty negotiated at a time when, following upon the closure of the Suez Canal towards the end of 1956, freight rates were very high. The claimants chartered another ship at the low rates then prevailing, employing her as a substitute ship to perform the charter, and on completion of the necessary repairs to the damaged ship advanced by some 100 days her employment under a second charter, which had also been negotiated when freight rates had been very high and which was a seven-year time charter. The Court of Appeal held that against the losses due to the collision must be set both the profit made by the substitute ship under the remainder of the first charter and the gain attributable to the making of the profit on 100 days of the second charter seven years earlier than it would otherwise have accrued.[499] Credit had not to be given, however, for the whole of the high 100-day profit under the second charter because the earning of that profit did not flow from a step taken in consequence of the collision but from the negotiation of the second charter months previously.

**9-126** After *The World Beauty*[500] came *Bellingham v Dhillon*.[501] Here it was a personal injury which triggered the acquisition by the claimant of a substitute producing the benefit and the case neatly illustrates the basic rule that benefit is taken into account where it arises out of the act of mitigation itself.[502] Because of injuries received in a car accident for which the defendant was liable, the claimant, who owned and ran a driving school, lost the opportunity of buying on hire-purchase an expensive driving simulator, which enabled driving tuition to be given in a lecture room rather than in a car on the road. Some three-and-a-half years later, however, he was able to buy the same equipment as liquidated stock for a fraction of the original price. In his claim for the three-and-a-half year loss of profits which he would have made had he had the original simulator, it was held that there must be brought into account the profits in fact earned by the substitute simulator. In the result the claimant was unable to show any loss on the simulator venture.

**9-127** *Salih v Enfield Health Authority*[503] presented a more unusual illustration. Parents of a child born suffering from congenital rubella syndrome sued the health authority for failure to diagnose and warn of this danger with the result that no steps were taken to terminate the pregnancy. The parents had planned to have further children but decided not to do so because of the difficulty and strain involved in bringing up a handicapped child. In these circumstances their claim for the cost of maintenance of the handicapped child was held by the Court of Appeal, reversing the judge below, to be limited to the extra cost of caring for the child's special needs

---

498 [1970] P. 144 CA.

499 The court was divided on how precisely this latter gain should be calculated.; see para.37-036, below.

500 [1970] P. 144 CA.

501 [1973] Q.B. 304.

502 See para.9-120, above. The whole of para.246 of the 13th edition (1972), which formed the substance of what are now paras 9-117 to 9-120, above, was cited, particular emphasis being placed on the concluding sentence stating the basic rule: [1973] Q.B. 304 at 307B to D.

503 [1991] 3 All E.R. 400 CA.

and did not include the basic cost of maintenance. Citing Viscount Haldane's formulation of the rule for contract in *British Westinghouse Co v Underground Ry*,[504] together with the wider formulation embracing tort from the then current edition of this work,[505] Butler-Sloss LJ, giving the leading judgment, went on to say:

> "The contemplated cost … would be spent on an identical purpose, in pari materia with the costs of [the handicapped child] and cannot be said to be merely collateral. The decision of the parents not to have another child and the consequential saving of likely future expenditure is, in my judgment, a relevant consideration upon which the defendants were entitled to rely."[506]

In *Bacciottini v Gotelee and Goldsmith (A Firm)*[507] the appellants purchased a property for development. They would not have purchased the property but for negligent advice from their solicitors who failed to inform them that the property was subject to a planning restriction. The appellants subsequently had the restriction removed. They sought damages for the negligence of their solicitors of £100,000 as the difference in value due to the presence of the planning restriction although the restriction had been removed. The Court of Appeal affirmed the decision of the primary judge for damages of only £250, representing the cost of the application to the local authority to remove the planning restriction. The Court of Appeal held that, irrespective of whether the appellants should have mitigated their losses, the reality was that they took the step of applying to remove the restriction, and avoided their putative loss. **9-128**

*(ii) Other contracts* Contracts other than those of sale have produced illustrations of benefits of which account had to be taken in the computation of the damages. In sale, as has been seen, the benefit has generally come through the acquisition of a substitute. The nearest equivalent in the authorities outside sale is provided by *Lavarack v Woods of Colchester*,[508] the substitute there being for the salary of which the claimant employee had been deprived through wrongful dismissal by the defendant company. The dismissal released the employee from a provision in his contract not, without the defendant's consent, to become interested in any other businesses. He took employment with another company at a modest salary and acquired half of the shares in it, which shares increased in value so that he made a profit out of their purchase. It was held that his damages fell to be cut down by the profit made by him on the shares as the profit arose from his loss-avoiding action. At the same time he acquired shares in a company other than the one now employing him, which shares also increased in value, but he was not required to bring this profit into account in the damages. Although he was able to acquire these shares only because released from his obligation not to buy into other businesses, their acquisition was not an action taken to avoid the consequences of the breach of contract. Little is said of mitigation—indeed the only mention of it is by Diplock LJ at the start of his judgment where he expressed general agree- **9-129**

---

504 [1912] A.C. 673. See para.9-108, above.

505 Now at para.9-111, above.

506 [1991] 3 All E.R. 400 CA at 405d to e. The earlier tort case of *Jewelowski v Propp* [1944] K.B. 510 involving fraudulent misrepresentation was decided under principles of avoidable loss rather than avoided loss (facts at para.9-087, above) but looked at as a case of avoided loss, which it was, it is thought to be dubious in the light of these later authorities in the text.

507 [2016] EWCA Civ 170 CA.

508 [1967] 1 Q.B. 278 CA.

ment with what Lord Denning MR had there decided on "loss and the mitigation of that loss"[509]—but it is clearly a case of mitigation by way of avoided loss.

9-130 A decade later came *Nadreph v Willmet & Co.*[510] The claimants, who held the leasehold reversion on certain premises, wished, on the expiry of the tenancy to which their holding was subject, to retain for their own use the part of the premises which their tenants had themselves sub-let while being willing to grant the tenants a new tenancy of the part of which they were in occupation. The defendants, the claimants' solicitors, served notice on the tenants, as instructed, terminating their tenancy but stating, contrary to instructions, that the claimants would oppose a grant of a new tenancy of any part of the premises, with the result that, by virtue of the provisions of the Landlord and Tenant Act 1954, the tenants became entitled to claim compensation of £133,276 from the claimants. The defendants successfully argued that they were entitled to set off against the damages arising from the liability to pay compensation any greater benefit that the vacation by the tenants of that part of the premises which they occupied would bring to the claimants, by way of securing another tenant or for use for their own business, than would have resulted from the continuance of the tenants' occupation of the premises. This benefit would arise out of the act of mitigation itself, whether the act of occupying and using the premises or the act of letting to another tenant, and it was no answer to rely upon the assertion, as the claimants did, that

> "there is no authority which establishes that a benefit secured in mitigation of damage of one kind can be set off against damage of a wholly different kind".[511]

9-131 Beyond these important illustrations in *Lavarack* and *Nadreph* of benefits taken into account in a contractual context, a growing miscellany of similar cases is to be found, from the 1990s on, in each of which the act giving rise to the benefit would appear to have arisen out of the consequences of the breach, the benefit out of the act of mitigation itself.[512] *Floods of Queensferry Ltd v Shand Construction Ltd*,[513] moves into the field of building contracts where the claimant sub-contractor company was claiming against the main contractor company for the cost of plant and management services, the sub-contractor company being in turn indebted to its own supplier, a related company, which had provided the plant and management services. In order to avoid its own liquidation, the claimant sub-contractor had secured a very large reduction in its indebtedness to its supplier by negotiating credit notes which the supplier did not intend to take up, thereby writing off the debts. The claimant sub-contractor was held to have mitigated its loss by this negotiation. In *Port of Sheerness v Brachers*,[514] account was taken of the substantial savings that the claimant employers made in their wages bill as a result of settling unfair dismissal claims of their employees, for which financial loss by the settlements the

---

509 [1967] 1 Q.B. 278 CA at 291G.

510 [1978] 1 W.L.R. 1537.

511 [1978] 1 W.L.R. 1537 at 1540E. While the headnote here is not very clear, the headnote in the report at [1978] 1 All E.R. 746 is positively confusing and mistaken in its repeated reference to the "sub-let premises" as it is the benefit accruing in relation to the part of the premises which had not been sub-let that is relevant: see the judgment of Whitford J, at [1978] 1 W.L.R. 1537 at 1539H and [1978] 1 All E.R. 746 at 749f to g.

512 One exception there is, in *The Timawra* [1996] 2 Lloyd's Rep. 166, at para.9-132, below.

513 [1999] B.L.R. 319; a later claim under the same name is in the notes at paras 49-079 and 49-080, below.

514 [1997] I.R.L.R. 214.

negligently advising defendant solicitors were liable. In *Linklaters Business Services v Sir Robert McAlpine Ltd*,[515] tenants who had successfully claimed against contractors for the cost of replacing defective pipework,[516] and who had entered into an agreement with their landlords that for future rent reviews the defects would be regarded as remedied provided the landlords contributed £200,000 towards the replacement cost, were required to give credit for this sum in their damages claim.[517] Although nothing was said in this sensible decision of Viscount Haldane's test that for a subsequent transaction to be taken into account in mitigation it must arise out of the consequences of the breach,[518] clearly this test was abundantly satisfied.[519]

The miscellany includes a number of charterparty cases. In *The Kriti Rex*,[520] a claim by the charterers for a failure by the owners to provide a seaworthy vessel, credit had to be given for losses avoided by the charterers in not completing the voyage on which the vessel was at the time engaged but not for losses saved thereafter. Where in *Zodiac Maritime Agencies Ltd v Fortescue Metals Group Ltd*,[521] the claim was by the shipowner against the charterer for repudiation of the charterparty during its course[522] and the shipowner succeeded in nominating the ship for an earlier charter by negotiating for its substitution, it was held that the earnings from that charter were to be taken into account in assessing the shipowner's loss since employing the ship under the earlier charter was part of a continuous dealing with the situation, the cause of the renegotiation of the one charter being the termination of the other.[523] In *Dalwood Marine Co v Nordana Line SA*,[524] there was a wrongful repudiation of a charterparty by the charterer which prima facie entitled the shipowner to the contractual rate of hire up until the contractual date of redelivery less the hire that could be earned from alternative employment during that period.[525] By contrast, in *The Timawra*,[526] a claim by charterers for damages arising out of the contractual failure of the owners to dry dock the chartered vessel in January, it was held that credit for the later dry docking in July did not have to be given; the benefit would not have arisen out of the act of mitigation itself.[527] **9-132**

515 [2010] EWHC 2931 (TCC).

516 Facts at para.31-012, below.

517 See [2010] EWHC 2931 (TCC) at [156] to [163].

518 See paras 7-009 and following above.

519 Where in *Red River UK Ltd v Sheikh* [2010] EWHC 1100 Ch the defendants in breach of contract had sabotaged certain refinancing so that the claimants had to abandon their planned development of a property site and merely sold the property, Henderson J said that he saw considerable force in the argument that, had he held the claimants entitled to the profit that would have been made on the development, any profit on the sale of the property would have had to be taken into account against the development profit because the sale represented an alternative way of realising the development potential of the property and therefore formed part of a single commercial enterprise by the claimants: see at [165] and [168].

520 [1996] 2 Lloyd's Rep. 171.

521 [2011] 2 Lloyd's Rep. 360.

522 See para.32-068, below.

523 See [2011] 2 Lloyd's Rep. 360 at [68]–[72].

524 [2010] 2 Lloyd's Rep. 315.

525 See the case further at para.32-068, below, showing that the owners made a profit from the alternative employment of the ship and were therefore entitled to no damages.

526 [1996] 2 Lloyd's Rep. 166.

527 In the context of charterparties and benefits to be taken into account, see the interesting and important *Omak Maritime Ltd v Mamola Challenger Shipping Co* [2011] 1 Lloyd's Rep. 47 at paras 4-032 and 4-033, above.

### (2) Situations where the benefit is generally ignored

9-133 **(a) Sale** Where a seller fails to deliver goods, delivers them late, or delivers defective goods, and the buyer claims only the normal measure of damages with no claim for lost profits or other consequential losses, there is no necessity for the buyer, in the interests of mitigation, to buy other goods in the market in the case of failure to deliver, or to sell the goods on delivery in the case of delay or defects. It should follow therefore, if the claimant in the one case buys later when the market has fallen, or in the other case sells later when the market has risen, that this gain to the claimant should redound to his advantage and not be brought in so as to reduce his damages. A clear illustration of this proposition is provided[528] by an early case, *Jones v Just*,[529] where the claimant bought first quality hemp and second quality hemp was delivered. The market price of hemp then rose, enabling the claimant to resell the delivered hemp at substantially above the market price at which the first quality hemp had stood at the time of delivery. Nevertheless the normal measure of damages under s.53(3) of the Sale of Goods Act 1893 was held to apply.

9-134 In the converse situation where a buyer of goods fails to accept them and the seller subsequently resells them on a rising market, a corresponding result is reached. The principal case is *Jamal v Moolla Dawood*.[530] A buyer of shares refused to accept them, the market rose and the seller resold; this gain to the seller was ignored in assessing the seller's damages. In *Campbell Mostyn v Barnett*,[531] this was applied to a sale of goods.[532]

9-135 The reason for these results, in contrast to the results in *British Westinghouse* and

---

[528] All the other cases of profitable resales successfully carried out concern resales made before breach. They are, principally, *Wertheim v Chicoutimi Pulp Co* [1911] A.C. 301 PC; *Williams v Agius* [1914] A.C. 510 and *Slater v Hoyle & Smith* [1920] 2 K.B. 11 CA: see paras 9-174 to 9-176, below.

[529] (1868) L.R. 3 Q.B. 197.

[530] [1916] 1 A.C. 175 PC.

[531] [1954] 1 Lloyd's Rep. 65 CA.

[532] Although involving lease and carriage contracts rather than sale, it is thought best at this early stage to note, historically, two cases from the first half of the 19th century in which subsequent profitable contracts were taken into account but, in the light of the sale contracts in the text, would not be today. In *Oldershaw v Holt* (1840) 12 A. & E. 590 the claimant lessor, having forfeited the defendant's lease for breach of a covenant to build, relet the premises at an increased rent; this was taken into account in assessing the damages, which as a result were only nominal. There is no suggestion in the case that this increased rent was any greater than the market rent at the time of the defendant's breach, and the decision cannot be relied upon for more than the proposition that a resale price may be evidence of the market price (a proposition which is the most fully illustrated in the sale of goods cases: see Ch.25, passim, below). For any proposition beyond this, the decision could not stand with the cases in the text where the point was fully considered. The same must also be said for *Staniforth v Lyall* (1830) 7 Bing. 169, where the defendant charterer failed to supply a cargo for the claimant's ship and the claimant succeeded in obtaining as a substitute a far more remunerative cargo than the defendant was bound to supply; this was taken into account in assessing the damages, which again were nominal. It is submitted here too that the case can only be sound authority if the rate at which the substitute cargo was carried represented the market rate of freight at the time of breach. It should be remembered that at the time of *Staniforth v Lyall* the normal measure of damages in contracts of carriage where the breach was a failure to supply cargo had not crystallised. There was for a long time a tendency to regard the normal measure not as the contract rate of freight less the market rate, which would follow general principles of contract damages, but as the contract rate of freight in full which would then be subject to the rules of mitigation; this is fully considered at paras 32-063 to 32-067, below. Indeed, it may be said generally that, if principles of remoteness were not worked out by the courts before *Hadley v Baxendale* in 1854 (see paras 8-158 and following, above), principles of mitigation a fortiori could not have been.

the other sale cases dealt with above,[533] is this. A sale by the seller of unaccepted goods to a third party on a rising market or a purchase by the buyer of other available goods from a third party on a falling market[534] is to be regarded as an independent transaction and not one taken into account in mitigation of loss. As is pointed out in the cases, if the claimant seller, with the goods on his hands,[535] chooses not to sell them and the market falls, he would not be able to claim against the buyer for the fall in price. Conversely, if the claimant buyer, without the goods, chooses not to buy in others, he cannot claim to recover in respect of the rise in price. It can be said, in both cases, that his loss crystallises at the date of breach.

In a valuable judgment in *Koch Marine Inc v D'Amica Società di Navigatione, The Elena d'Amico*[536] Robert Goff J so explained the position. Citing the cases of *Jamal v Moolla Dawood* and *Campbell Mostyn v Barnett*,[537] he posited the question of why, as a matter of principle, a buyer buying in on a market falling after the breach cannot be compelled to bring the saving into account on the thinking that his purchase is nothing more nor less than a step taken in mitigation of his damage[538] and answers the question by saying that the buyer's decision to buy in or not to buy in immediately upon breach **9-136**

> "is an independent decision, independent of the breach, made by the buyer on his assessment of the market".[539]

The rather special situation, involving favourable purchase, which arose in *Pagnan & Fratelli v Corbisa Industrial Agropacuaria*,[540] led to a different result. There the claimants, after non-delivery, subsequently bought the self-same goods from their own seller at a renegotiated and substantially reduced price. This purchase was found by the court not to be an independent or disconnected transaction but to be part of a course of continuous dealing between the parties themselves and it was held, applying the principles laid down in *British Westinghouse Co v Underground Ry*,[541] that this later purchase must be taken into account so as to oust the normal measure of damages under s.51(3) of the Sale of Goods Act 1979 and to debar the claimants from any recovery.[542] This explanation of the decision—that buying the same goods from the same seller, rather than substitute goods, was not an independent transaction—and the decision itself have been invariably accepted in later cases.[543] **9-137**

A somewhat different benefit to a claimant, one not arising out of a favourable **9-138**

---

533 See paras 9-121 to 9-123, above.

534 Or indeed a sale by the buyer of delayed or defective goods on a rising market: see *Jones v Just* (1868) L.R. 3 Q.B. 197 at para.9-133, above.

535 Or indeed the buyer with goods on his hands: see previous note.

536 [1980] 1 Lloyd's Rep. 75.

537 At para.9-134, above.

538 [1980] 1 Lloyd's Rep. 75, at 87, col.2–88, col.1.

539 [1980] 1 Lloyd's Rep. 75 at 89, col.1.

540 [1970] 1 W.L.R. 1306 CA.

541 [1912] A.C. 673, citing Viscount Haldane's criterion for deduction (at 692) that the claimants' course of action formed "part of a continuous dealing with the situation ... and was not an independent or disconnected transaction".

542 *Jamal v Moolla Dawood* [1916] 1 A.C. 175 PC and *Campbell Mostyn v Barnett* [1954] 1 Lloyd's Rep. 65 CA, dealt with at para.9-134, above, were distinguished.

543 As in *Koch Marine Inc v D'Amici Società di Navigazione, The Elena d'Amico* [1980] 1 Lloyd's Rep. 75; *Hussey v Eels* [1990] 2 Q.B. 227 CA; *Gardner v Marsh & Parsons* [1997] 1 W.L.R. 489 CA; *Mobil North Sea Ltd v British Railways Board* [2001] 2 All E.R. (Comm) 289 CA.

sale or purchase by him, fell not to be taken into account in *Mobil North Sea Ltd v British Railways Board*,[544] as again the benefit was held not to arise out of an act of mitigation. Defective valves had been sold and supplied by the defendants to the claimants to be used for a building project on which the claimants were sub-contractors. The existence of the defects required the valves' replacement by the claimants and also put the claimants in breach of their contract with the main contractor on the project, who was making parallel claims against the claimants and against the defendants. Over a year after the valves had been replaced, allowing the performance of the project to continue, the sub-contractors settled the main contractor's claim against them. The Court of Appeal held that any benefit to the claimants from this settlement was to be ignored. Rix LJ, giving the leading judgment, regarded the replacement of the valves by the claimant sub-contractors as their only act of mitigation; he saw their settlement with the main contractor, the details of which do not appear, as rather constituting a reformulation of their relations and a reorganisation of the terms upon which they would continue to conduct litigation against the defendants.[545]

### (b) Other situations

9-139 *(i) Other contracts* The principles enunciated in the cases of sale where at a time after the breach of contract buyer or seller makes an advantageous purchase or sale[546] apply to other contracts involving any form of property where there is a need to consider disposal of the property or acquisition of alternative property after breach. Contracts of carriage by way of charterparty provide the commonest useful example. Dealing with such a case in *Koch Marine Inc v D'Amica Società di Navigatione, The Elena d'Amico*,[547] Robert Goff J, after considering these sale principles, said:

> "In my judgment the same principles are applicable in the assessment of the damages to be awarded where there has been a repudiation by a shipowner of a time charter. If, at the date of breach, there is an available market, the normal measure of damages will be the difference between the contract rate and the market rate for chartering a substitute ship for the balance of the charter period. If however the time charterer decides not to take advantage of that market then, generally speaking, that will be his own business decision independent of the wrong; and the consequences of that decision are his. If he judges the market correctly, he reaps the benefit; if he judges it incorrectly, then the extra cost falls upon him."[548]

The case was one in which, because chartering rates were about to rise, the charterers had judged the market incorrectly in failing immediately upon breach to hire a substitute vessel; they were held disentitled to claim the profits that they would have made had they taken on a substitute vessel. But it is implicit in the decision that had rates fallen after the breach and the charterers, judging the market correctly, had waited before hiring a substitute vessel, the benefit arising from this wise move would not have been taken into account in the damages assessment; the charterers

---

544 [2001] 2 All E.R. (Comm) 289 CA.

545 [2001] 2 All E.R. (Comm) 289 CA at [32].

546 See paras 9-133 to 9-134, above. Compare the two defunct cases, involving lease and carriage, in the fn. at the end of para.9-134, above.

547 [1980] 1 Lloyd's Rep. 75.

548 [1980] 1 Lloyd's Rep. 75 at 89, col.2.

would still have been entitled to the normal measure of damages.

*Dampskibselskabet "Norden" A/S v Andres & Cie SA*[549] provides a variation on *The Elena d'Amico*,[550] but essentially arrives at the same result, confirming that a failure to make a substitute contract which would have proved profitable did not entitle the claimant to more than it would cost to enter a substitute contract, this latter representing the normal measure of damages. *Norden* involved a somewhat unusual form of contract, a forward freight swap agreement which is a bet upon whether the market freight rate will over a certain period of time, or for a certain type of voyage, move higher or lower than the price agreed by the parties as the basis of the bet. The defendant, who had entered into such an agreement for the year 2001 with the claimant, in breach of contract discontinued performance in March and the claimant claimed the profit that it would have made had the defendant carried through the contract to its end. The defendant argued instead for the damages to be based upon what it would have cost the claimant to have entered into a substitute contract in March, which the claimant had not done although, as was held, there was an available market.[551] Toulson J agreed. Here the claimant's unsuccessful claim was not based upon the profit that it would have made on a substitute contract, as had been unsuccessfully argued for in *The Elena d'Amico*,[552] but upon the profit it would have made on the broken contract had it been carried through. This, however, in the particular circumstances amounted to the same thing; with the way market freight rates turned out, the profit that would have been made on a substitute contract would, after allowing for the higher price payable for that contract reflected in the damages awarded, have matched the profit that would have been made on the original contract. Once again the speculation which way the market, here the market freight rate, would go was the speculation of the claimant.[553] **9-140**

Further charterparty cases of today illustrative of Lord Goff's *Elena d'Amico* principle[554] are *Glory Wealth Shipping PTE Ltd v North China Shipping Ltd*,[555] and *Zodiac Maritime Agencies Ltd v Fortescue Metals Group Ltd*.[556] In *Glory Wealth* the charterer under a time charter had sub-chartered the ship also by time charter. There was an accepted repudiation by the sub-charterer with the ship redelivered to the charterer some six months before contract would have allowed it. The charterer continued sub-chartering for a time but before the six months were up redelivered the ship to the shipowner without being, apparently, in breach of contract. The normal measure of the difference between the sub-charter rate and the market rate throughout the whole of the six-month period was held to apply and **9-141**

---

549 [2003] 1 Lloyd's Rep. 287.

550 [1980] 1 Lloyd's Rep. 75.

551 Whether there was an available market was the first issue in the case: see the fn. at the end of para.25-120, below.

552 See para.9-139, above.

553 Little or nothing was indeed said in *Norden* of mitigation. This can be ascribed to the fact that, as explained elsewhere, the normal measure has the mitigating step built into it: see paras 9-039 and 9-040, above.

554 Outside charterparties, a contract case where the benefit was not taken into account is *Earl's Terrace Properties Ltd v Nilsson Design Ltd* [2004] B.L.R. 273. The claimant company, suing its architect for delay in completion of a housing project, did not have to take into account in the damages claimed any increase in profit from the delayed sale of the houses on a rising market. The sales at higher prices were unconnected with the breach of contract which had brought about the delay: see [2004] B.L.R. 273 at [99]–[108] and the case details at para.29-011, below.

555 [2010] EWHC 1692 (Comm).

556 [2011] 2 Lloyd's Rep. 360.

what the claimant had saved in having no further hire payments to make up the line under the head charter was not to be brought into account in the computation of the damages. David Steel J said[557]:

> "The early redelivery … should be treated as an independent speculation not caused by the repudiation of the sub-charter".

The position had crystallised at the time of the acceptance of the repudiation and the result follows precisely the reasoning in *The Elena d'Amico*. In *Zodiac Maritime* the charterer had repudiated a five-year voyage charter about a year after its commencement. There being held to be no available market at the time of the charterer's breach so that the normal measure of the difference between market rate and charter rate could not be applied, it was further held that the later appearance of an available market before the charter period would have expired was of no significance. A line had been drawn under the transaction after the occurrence of the breach, thereby removing subsequent market movements from the equation.[558] Here, unusually, it was the charterer rather than the shipowner who was contending for the application of the normal measure of damages.[559]

**9-142** The same principle can be seen in *Globalia Business Travel SAU v Fulton Shipping Inc of Panama*.[560] In that case, charterers repudiated a charterparty. The owners accepted the repudiation but had difficulty in obtaining a new charter. So, in October 2007, they sold the ship for US $23,765,000 and claimed from the charterers in breach the loss of profits from the charter, amounting to around €7,500,000. By the time of hearing in November 2009, the value of the ship had fallen to $7,000,000. The charterers claimed that the owners were required to bring into account the large benefit from early sale of the ship. This would have meant that the owners reaped a large profit and suffered no loss caused by the breach. It had been found as a "clear" fact by the arbitrator that but for the breach the owners would not have sold the vessel.[561] In other words, the profit made was caused by the breach. Nevertheless, in the decision of the Supreme Court, given by Lord Clarke, it was held that the profit on the sale did not need to be brought into account by the owners. Lord Clarke described the result in the language of "legal" causation.[562] By this, he meant that the decision to sell the vessel was an independent commercial decision taken by the owners at their own risk.[563] It was not a reasonably necessary response to the breach.[564] So the owners could not have claimed from the charterers for capital losses suffered if the market had risen rather than fallen.

**9-143** *(ii) Tort* The action taken by the claimants in *Hussey v Eels*,[565] was held not to cut down their loss. A negligent misrepresentation was made by the defendants that

---

557 [2010] EWHC 1692 (Comm) at [15].

558 [2011] 2 Lloyd's Rep. 360 at [62]–[66].

559 On the principle that the determination of loss should be at the breach date see Briggs J in *Anthracite Rated Investments (Jersey) Ltd v Lehman Brothers Finance SA* [2011] 2 Lloyd's Rep. 538 at [117] and [118].

560 [2017] UKSC 43.

561 Quoted by the Court of Appeal in *Fulton Shipping Inc of Panama v Globalia Business Travel SAU ("The New Flamenco")* [2015] EWCA Civ 1299 at [11].

562 [2017] UKSC 43 at [33].

563 [2017] UKSC 43 at [32]. And see above at 9-136.

564 [2017] UKSC 43 at [32].

565 [1990] 2 Q.B. 227 CA.

the bungalow that they were selling to the claimants for £53,250 had not been subject to subsidence. Because repairs would be very costly the claimants decided that the best course was to demolish the bungalow and to apply for planning permission to erect two others in its place. They then sold the property with the benefit of the planning permission, which they had obtained, to a developer for £78,500. In their claim for damages they were held entitled to the normal measure represented by the contract price less the value of the bungalow in its unsound condition at the date of the sale; the defendants' argument that the claimants' loss had been eliminated by their sale to the developer was rejected. A profit on the resale of a defective property, the purchase of which has been induced by a negligent misrepresentation, was not to be taken into account in the assessment of damages for the misrepresentation if the resale was not part of a continuous transaction commencing with the original purchase of the property. Since the claimants had purchased the house to live in and had indeed lived in it for a considerable period, it was held to follow that when they unlocked the property's development potential they did so for their own benefit and were not required to bring it into account in mitigation of damages.[566]

Yet in *Hussey*,[567] it could surely be said, since the acts of applying for planning permission and then selling upon obtaining it were designed to deal with the difficulties raised by the subsidence affecting the property, that those acts arose from the consequences of the wrong and the benefit from acts taken in mitigation. No reference is made to these central tests stemming from Viscount Haldane in *British Westinghouse*[568]; instead the Court of Appeal relies upon the need for a continuous transaction if a benefit is to be taken into account. It is true that this approach can also be culled from British Westinghouse where Viscount Haldane viewed the arbitrator as having decided that the purchase by the claimants of the new machines **9-144**

> "formed part of a continuous dealing with the situation in which they found themselves, and was not an independent or disconnected transaction".[569]

But this statement is made only when Viscount Haldane is dealing with the particular facts and not when laying down the definitive general principle. And, more importantly, the statement makes clear that for a dealing or transaction not to be continuous it must be independent and disconnected, which it would be difficult to say that the application for planning permission and sale were in *Hussey*. Indeed the situation in *Hussey* was not very different in essence, despite being different in context, from that in the key case which established the principle of avoided loss, *British Westinghouse v Underground Ry*. Defective turbines are replaced by turbines which are more effective; a defective bungalow is to be replaced by two satisfactory ones.[570]

---

566 *Hussey* was followed and applied in *Hodge v Clifford Cowling & Co* [1990] 2 E.G.L.R. 89 CA, but it is not clear that the purchase for the claimants' business of the particular property which brought in the benefit avoided the loss from the business property depreciated by the defendant's negligence—the claimant had had to settle for an onerous lease because his right to apply for a favourable one had been lost—as that further property might have been purchased in any event.

567 [1990] 2 Q.B. 227 CA.

568 [1912] A.C. 673. See at para.9-108 and para.9-122, above.

569 [1912] A.C. 673 at 692.

570 *Dominion Mosaics and Tile Co v Trafalgar Trucking Co* [1990] 2 All E.R. 246 CA, decided shortly before *Hussey v Eels*, does not take the matter much further as there is no argument on mitigation, none of the familiar mitigation cases appearing in any of the judgments. The buildings in which the

9-145 *Hussey* has been described as "an exceptional case turning on its own facts".[571] However, the Court of Appeal in *Quilter v Hodson Developments*,[572] was of the view that the case is not "as exceptional as all that".[573] Lord Justice Floyd, delivering the judgment of the Court said:

> "Many people buying property with a defect will not want to move for a while and, if any subsequent sale is not undertaken as part of their obligation to mitigate their loss, should be able to recover loss calculated on the traditional basis of the difference in value between the value of the property as represented and the property's true value at the date of purchase."[574]

In that case, the plaintiff had purchased an apartment for £240,000 from a vendor developer who had made misrepresentations about the existences of disputes with other residents. The Court of Appeal upheld an award of £15,000, being the difference between the market value of the apartment as represented and its value having regard to the defects. The award was made although the plaintiff had sold the property two years later for £275,000. Although the defendant had not argued that the plaintiff had any obligation to mitigate by reselling, the Court of Appeal cast doubt on whether such a submission would have succeeded, saying that the sale was

> "in the ordinary course of her domestic life rather than being due to the defects in the heating system which were in the course of being repaired".[575]

9-146 The decision in *Quilter v Hodson Developments Ltd* should be supported on the basis of the disconnect between the defect and the later sale. This still leaves *Hussey* as an anomalous result. Other cases also contrast with *Hussey* in the reasoning given for why a benefit should not be taken into account as accruing to the claimant. In *Blue Circle Industries v Ministry of Defence*,[576] the defendant's breach of statutory duty not to damage property through nuclear activity resulted in the claimant's estate becoming contaminated with radioactive material in 1989, making it virtually unsaleable until the necessary remedial work, carried out by the defendant, had been completed several years later, during a period of falling prices, in 1994. The claimant, who had lost the chance of a profitable sale in the interim,[577] was held entitled to damages represented by the diminution in the value and saleability of the estate. The market having turned, the value of the estate had increased over its value at the time that it had again become saleable in 1994, and in calculating the damages the trial judge, while accepting that the award should reflect the fall in the market value while the estate remained unsaleable, decided that account should also be taken of the increase in market value thereafter. With this the Court of Appeal

---

claimants carried on their business were so damaged by a fire negligently caused that they acquired new premises in which to continue and the main issue was their entitlement to claim the acquisition cost: see at paras 39-009 and 39-010, below. Subsequently they sold the new premises at a profit, having taken a lease of still further premises, and the defendants' argument that this benefit be taken into account was very briefly rejected: see [1990] 2 All E.R. 246 CA at 252f and 256e. This is probably correct; the claimants' loss would have crystallised when they bought the new premises.

571 *Gardner v Marsh and Parsons* [1997] 1 W.L.R. 489 at 510, per Peter Gibson LJ (dissenting).

572 [2016] EWCA Civ 1125.

573 [2016] EWCA Civ 1125 at [36].

574 [2016] EWCA Civ 1125 at [36].

575 [2016] EWCA Civ 1125 at [38].

576 [1999] Ch. 289 CA.

577 This aspect of the case is dealt with elsewhere: para.10-093, below.

disagreed and held that the claimant was entitled to have its damages assessed by reference to the value at 1994. The loss to the claimant had crystallised, and, as was said, the causative effect of the damage had ended, at the time when the estate could have been sold, with the result that the risk of a downturn in the market then passed to the claimant and with it the benefit of an increase should the market move up.

A similar result was reached in the difficult *Primavera v Allied Dunbar Assurance Plc*,[578] which needs close analysis. In 1987 the claimant raised a loan of £500,000 to fund the acquisition through his company of a restaurant and linked the loan to a pension scheme designed to produce a tax-free lump sum of £500,000 for the repayment of the loan in seven years' time. For the scheme to produce this sum it was necessary for the claimant to receive very substantial annual earnings by way of salary from his company for three consecutive years during the plan's proposed seven-year operation. This could easily have been achieved through the claimant's successful company. However, his financial adviser, the defendant, being fearful of losing commission, deliberately withheld this information from the claimant, so that for the succeeding years the claimant paid himself a much smaller salary from his company, taking instead large dividends from it. When in 1995 the claimant decided to take the lump sum which he supposed to be available, he discovered that on the basis of the earnings he had been paid only some £125,000 was available by way of lump sum. At this point the defendant negligently and mistakenly informed the claimant that Revenue rules meant that in any event the lump sum that the claimant could take was capped at £150,000, which was also far less than was required for repayment of the loan, so that, even if the necessary salary payments had been made to him, it would have been impossible to receive a £500,000 lump sum. As a result of this it appeared in 1995 that the scheme had entirely failed. He took no steps in 1995 to receive any sum from the pension scheme but chose to keep in place the pension fund, and with it the loan, to the full extent. Then in 1997 it was discovered that the Revenue rules did not apply to the scheme, so that there never had been a £150,000 cap on the lump sum. With this knowledge the claimant proceeded to award himself the necessary salary over the next three years so that by 2000 the £500,000 lump sum finally became available. However, he still did not cash in, but retained, his policy which by 2000 had grown very substantially in value. **9-147**

The defendant argued that the increased value of the policy by 2000 must be taken into account in assessing the claimant's damages. The Court of Appeal, while finding the defendant's argument most persuasive, finally did not agree. The court took the view that the claimant's loss had crystallised in 1995 and that any decision that he made after that as to what steps to take in relation to his pension fund, which might be profitable or otherwise, was a matter for him. Had the value of the pension fund decreased rather than increased between 1995 and 2000, it was thought that the defendant would not have been liable for the downturn. In the words of Simon Brown LJ giving the leading judgment: **9-148**

> "The various steps taken by the [claimant] after 1995 were not properly to be regarded as steps taken reasonably in mitigation of his loss. Rather (as in *Blue Circle* in 1994 and in *Downs v Chappell* in the spring of 1990) the choice of how to deal with his situation

[578] [2003] P.N.L.R. 12 at 276 CA.

which confronted him in 1995 as a result of the [defendant's] negligence was his and the speculation from that point on was on his own account."[579]

*Downs v Chappell*,[580] to which Simon Brown LJ refers, produced a crystallisation of loss which went against the claimant.[581] All three decisions are based on the premise that the loss crystallised at a particular time after which changes in value in either direction were for the claimant. This feature of the cases is reminiscent of the well established authorities in the field of sale and carriage contracts where values are taken at the time of breach and later market changes ignored.[582]

**9-149** It should be noted, however, that the claimant's position would in the view of Mance LJ have looked very different had there been no intervening misrepresentation in 1995 as to the existence of the £150,000 cap. The claimant would have thought not that the scheme had failed because of the cap but that it could be resurrected by his paying himself the necessary salary over the next three years so as to make a £500,000 lump sum available to him by 1998. "Assuming that he had done so," said Mance LJ,

> "... there would have been a strong case for determining whether he had suffered any loss by a comparison of the positions"[583]

in 1995 and 1998. No crystallisation of the loss would have occurred in 1995. However, this was here a hypothetical situation.

**9-150** Then there is the decision in *Barings Plc v Coopers & Lybrand*,[584] the result in which is difficult to support in the light of the decisions so far considered, decisions to which the judge, Evans-Lombe J, does not appear to have been directed. The defendant auditors had negligently failed to uncover an employee's unauthorised trading which had resulted over time in huge losses to the claimant employer companies, losses which had been subject to very substantial fluctuations both before and after the time that it was held the unauthorised trading, and hence the losses, should have been detected by the claimants themselves. Evans-Lombe J, referring to this time as the cut-off date for the calculation of losses, being the time when the chain of causation was broken, held that, while the claimants could not increase their damages by claiming the highest amount to which the losses had climbed after the cut-off date, the defendants were nevertheless entitled to argue for the lowest amount to which the losses had fallen on the ground that the reduction in losses constituted a benefit to be taken into account.

**9-151** Yet surely the correct analysis, in line with the authorities, is that the loss to the claimants had crystallised at the cut-off date when the causative effect of the damage was held to have ended. From that date the claimants are to be regarded as being solely responsible for the losses. They are now considered to be fully in charge of the business and what they do with it is a matter for their business judgment; it is, as Robert Goff J put it in *The Elena d'Amico*,[585] "[their] own business decision

---

579 [2003] P.N.L.R. 276 CA at [29].

580 [1997] 1 W.L.R. 426 CA.

581 *Downs* did not concern itself with mitigation—not a single one of the familiar mitigation cases is cited in Hobhouse LJ's sole judgment—yet it is considered that mitigation principles could and should have prevented the crystallisation of loss there. See the case at para.49-030, below.

582 See paras 9-133 to 9-136 and 9-139, above.

583 [2003] P.N.L.R. 276 CA at [44].

584 [2003] Lloyd's Rep. I.R. 566.

585 [1980] 1 Lloyd's Rep.75. The passage from his judgment is set out at para.9-139, above.

independent of the wrong". The risk of an increase in losses therefore passed to the claimants and with it the benefit of a decrease. The fact that they may still not have known at the cut-off date of the unauthorised trading, and consequently of the defendants' breach of contract, may distinguish the case from the other authorities where at the time of crystallisation of loss the claimant knew of the loss and of the defendant's wrong; but this should not make a difference. Once the court has held that the chain of causation is broken, what is done in the future lies in the hands of the claimants. To hold otherwise would make a nonsense of the decision on causation, for if it were still possible to look to the extent of the losses at future dates, it would mean that cause was still operating against the defendants. Indeed logically it would allow increases in the losses to be taken into account, which Evans-Lombe J was properly not prepared to allow, as well as decreases.

Evans-Lombe J's reasoning had gone along the following lines. He posited two hypothetical cut-off dates falling after the cut-off date he had himself chosen; the first fell at the time when the losses were at their highest, standing at some £84 million, the second fell two and a half months later when the losses had reduced to some £44 million. He then argued from these two positions that it would be odd if the defendants were required to pay less when it took the claimants longer to find out what their fraudulent employee had been doing. But this misses the point. A decision on the cut-off date is a decision on when the claimants ought fully to have known the position; there is no question of the claimants being more at fault the later they are taken to acquire the relevant knowledge. It is purely fortuitous whether the losses are at their low ebb or have reached their ceiling, or are somewhere in between, at the moment of cut-off.[586] **9-152**

### (3) Situations where the position is unclear

In *Jebsen v East and West Indian Dock Co*,[587] the defendant, in breach of a contract to discharge the claimant's ship, was late in completing her discharge with the result that the claimant lost the fares of the passengers who were due to sail on the ship for America. In consequence, another two ships, also owned by the claimant,[588] gained these passengers, but it was held that this factor could not be allowed to reduce the claimant's damages. Here the benefit which the defendant wished to offset arose from the emergence of the opportunity to put other property of his, which happened to be available, to immediate profitable use in substitution, accordingly did not arise out of any act of mitigation, and therefore was properly disregarded. In *Platt v London Underground*,[589] the claimant had leased two kiosks at the defendant's underground station under two separate leases and doing different businesses. In derogation from its grant the defendant restricted access of the public to the one, thereby increasing the trade of the other. The increased profits had to be taken into account in assessing the damages for the lost profits of the restricted **9-153**

---

586 As it happened, the level of losses at the time that the chain of causation was held to be broken was very near to the lowest to which the losses subsequently fell—some £27 million as opposed to some £25 million—so that, by holding that the defendants' liability was to be calculated by reference to the £25 million, no great harm was done.

587 (1875) L.R. 10 C.P. 300.

588 Only some of the claimants were also owners of the other two ships, but the court said the result would have been the same if there had only been one claimant who was the owner of both ships: (1875) L.R. 10 C.P. 300 at 305.

589 [2001] 2 E.G.L.R. 121.

kiosk. These two decisions, separated by well over a century, would appear to be inconsistent with each other and could suggest that the law has moved on and is now taking a new view.

## 4. Actions Taken After the Wrong by Third Parties

9-154 In the nature of things, actions taken after breach by third parties cannot be within the principles laid down in *British Westinghouse Co v Underground Ry*,[590] as what is envisaged are steps taken by the claimant himself. Cases where the action which confers the benefit is that of a third party are not well documented or indeed analysed.

9-155 The most common outcome is that actions taken after breach by third parties which reduce the loss suffered are taken into account in reduction of damages. An example is *Lowick Rose LLP v Swynson Ltd*.[591] In that case, a firm of accountants negligently failed to exercise care in a due diligence report into a prospective borrower. The lending company lent money in 2006 and 2007 to the borrower in reliance upon this report. The owner of the lending company lent money to the borrower in 2008. When the borrower was in severe financial distress, the owner of the lending company personally repaid the 2006 and 2007 loans discharging the debt owed by the borrower. The owner of the lending company did this for various commercial reasons. The Supreme Court held that the accountants were not liable for the 2006 and 2007 loans because these were losses that had not been suffered; the loans had been repaid. The owner of the lending company "discharged the very liability whose existence represented [the lending company's] loss".[592] Lord Sumption, with whom Lords Neuberger, Clarke and Hodge agreed, explained the general rule that loss which has been avoided is not recoverable as damages although acknowledging that it is difficult to identify a single principle underlying every case of collateral payments which do not reduce the loss.[593]

### (1) The particular case of gratuitous assistance afforded

9-156 In cases of personal injury it has been long established, and never doubted, that where a third party has gratuitously come to the injured person's financial rescue by payment of medical or living expenses, or continued payment of wages, or by way of a general sum not in relation to a particular head of loss, the benefits so conferred upon the injured person do not go in mitigation of his damages. In *Liffen v Watson*,[594] the claimant's father provided her with free board and lodging during the period when she was unable to continue in her employment as a domestic servant, her employer having remunerated her not only by wages but by board and lodging. In *Dennis v L.P.T.B.*[595] the claimant's employer and the Ministry of Pensions paid the claimant, in sick pay and in pension, amounts which together equalled his wages. In *Cunningham v Harrison*,[596] ex gratia payments had again been made

---

590 [1912] A.C. 673.
591 [2017] UKSC 32.
592 [2017] UKSC 32 at [13].
593 [2017] UKSC 32 at [11].
594 [1940] 1 K.B. 556 CA.
595 [1948] 1 All E.R. 779.
596 [1973] Q.B. 942 CA.

by a sympathetic employer. In *Redpath v Belfast and County Down Ry*,[597] a charitable fund, voluntarily subscribed to by the public, was set up to aid victims of a railway disaster, and the claimant, one of the victims, received a sum from this fund. No deduction was made in any of these cases from the damages on account of such payment or other assistance.[598]

This rule of no deduction from the damages was applied where the claim was other than for personal injury in *Hamilton-Jones v David & Snape*.[599] The claimant, suing her solicitor for negligence in allowing her children to be removed to Tunisia by their Tunisian father, was awarded, inter alia, the substantial travel costs of visiting her children in Tunisia from time to time although these costs had been paid by her mother. Neuberger J, generalising the principle, said[600] that he could "see no reason, in logic or policy, as to why the principle should be limited", as was being contended, to personal injury claims. Rather it seemed to him that in essence **9-157**

> "the principle can be said to be based on the proposition that the gratuitous payment of money by third parties to the claimant is *res inter alios acta*, as between the claimants and the defendants".

He added:

> "There is no reason why payments made to the claimant by third parties, particularly when those payments are made out of natural love and affection for the claimant, should be credited to the benefit of the person whose negligence has harmed the claimant, and to the disadvantage of the claimant. Indeed, it would seem almost absurd if that were the law."

## (2) The particular case of converted or distrained goods applied to pay debts

One category of case of action by a third party going in reduction of damages stands out as rather special and as having existed for a very long time. This is where the defendant has converted the claimant's goods and the goods are then applied to paying off a debt owed by the claimant to a third party.[601] If this application is one that is authorised by law and which the defendant is powerless to prevent, as where the claimant's landlord distrains the goods for the claimant's arrears of rent, then the amount of the debt thus satisfied will go in reduction of the normal measure of damages in conversion, i.e. the market value of the goods. In *Plevin v Henshall*,[602] such a reduction was allowed even after judgment, the distress itself taking place after judgment. And even where the application of the goods or their proceeds to the payment of the claimant's debts is not one which the defendant was powerless **9-158**

---

597 [1947] N.I. 167.

598 The cases are dealt with in more detail at paras 40-159, 40-160 and 40-224, below. It may be that the benefit thus accruing to the injured person may not remain with him, as he may be under an obligation to pay back to the third party if he should recover damages from the defendant (see, in particular, *Dennis v L.P.T.B.* [1948] 1 All. E.R. 779 and *Hunt v Severs* [1994] 2 A.C. 350 at paras 40-160 and 40-228, below), but this does not affect the damages that the defendant must pay.

599 [2004] 1 W.L.R. 924.

600 [2004] 1 W.L.R. 924 at [74].

601 Similar principles would presumably have applied where the action was in the former detinue.

602 (1833) 10 Bing. 24.

to prevent, and indeed is an application which the defendant himself may have effected, this factor may go in reduction of the damages. The authority for this proposition lies in the Court of Appeal judgments in *Underwood v Bank of Liverpool*,[603] where the defendant bank had converted cheques of the claimant company by crediting them to the company's sole director. Although the question of damages was not up for decision, Scrutton LJ took the view, with which Atkin LJ agreed, that the fact that the sole director had used some of the proceeds of the cheques in discharging the claimant company's liabilities might go in mitigation of damages, and an inquiry as to the exact facts in this regard was directed. He referred to the dictum of Byles J. in *Edmondson v Nuttall*,[604] that

> "you could not mitigate damages for conversion of a bag of money by showing that the defendant had out of the bag of money converted paid the debt of the claimant",[605]

and added that he was:

> "not sure that the learned judge had in his mind the equitable doctrines under which a person who had in fact paid the debts of another without authority was allowed the advantage of his payments."[606]

**9-159** The reference to equity and to equitable doctrines[607] suggests that the court is moving away from strict common law conceptions of damages altogether, and tends to highlight the somewhat exceptional nature of this type of case. The exceptional quality is also emphasised both by the strict limits placed upon allowing the amount of a claimant's paid debts to go in reduction of the damages awarded him and by the fact that the rationale of these limits is not very clearly defined. Thus it was held in *Edmondson v Nuttall*[608] that, where the application of the goods to the payment of the debt was authorised by law but the legal process was in favour of the defendant himself as the claimant's creditor, no reduction of the normal measure of damages fell to be made. And in *Lloyds Bank v Chartered Bank*,[609] where the claimant was suing for conversion of cheques by the defendant bank in paying them to the claimant's accountant, the Court of Appeal held that the damages were not to be reduced by reason of the fact that the accountant had used some of the cheques to pay not the claimant's debts but his own debts to the claimant.

**9-160** In some other cases, however, notably in actions for wrongful distress for rent, deduction of the amount of the debt paid from the value of the goods has been made in order to arrive at what the loss is and at the normal measure, no resort to doctrines of mitigation being required. Thus the normal measure of damages has been the value of the goods wrongfully distrained less the rent due in actions for ir-

---

603 [1924] 1 K.B. 775 CA.

604 (1864) 17 C.B. N.S. 280.

605 [1924] 1 K.B. 775 CA at 794.

606 [1924] 1 K.B. 775 CA at 794.

607 The equitable doctrine to which Scrutton LJ was referring comes into operation where an agent has borrowed money on his principal's behalf but without his authority and has used it to pay off the liabilities of the principal. In these circumstances the lender, who cannot sue the principal on the contract of loan, is subrogated to the rights of the principal's creditors who have been paid with the money lent, and to this extent the lender can recover: see, inter alia, *Reid v Rigby* [1894] 2 Q.B. 40; *Bannatyne v MacIver* [1906] 1 K.B. 103 CA; *Reversion Fund and Insurance Co v Maison Cosway* [1913] 1 K.B. 364 CA.

608 (1864) 17 C.B. N.S. 280.

609 [1929] 1 K.B. 40 CA.

regular[610] and for excessive,[611] but not for illegal,[612] distress. However, the common law right to distress for rent has been abolished, as from 6 April 2014, by the Tribunals, Courts and Enforcement Act 2007, setting up in its place an elaborate procedure under which it is not yet known how damages payable, with or without mitigation, will be assessed.[613]

## (3) Miscellaneous situations

There remains for consideration a series of cases, all very modern, in which the benefit has effectively been provided by a third party but has not been taken into account in the damages. Once again, the cases cannot be within the *British Westinghouse*,[614] principles because of the involvement of the third party and, in order to fashion a test which would prove suitable for cases of loss avoided by the intervention of third parties, the courts have been moving towards the test of whether act and benefit can be seen as all part of a continuous transaction starting with the breach of duty. This approach, as we have seen, does make an appearance in *British Westinghouse* but was not specifically relied upon in the context of claimant, as opposed to third party, action avoiding loss until much later in *Hussey v Eels*,[615] a case of some difficulty.[616] **9-161**

In *Gardner v Marsh and Parsons*,[617] where the claimants purchased a leasehold maisonette with a serious structural defect which their defendant surveyor had failed to detect, they were held by a majority of the Court of Appeal to be entitled to the normal measure of damages based on the value of the property in its defective state at the time of purchase[618] although the defects had been rectified at the claimants' landlord's expense two years after the discovery of the defect and some five years after the purchase. The landlord's action in repairing the property had been at the claimants' insistence in performance of a contractual obligation and it would appear to be because of this that the court dealt with the case as one in the conventional category of loss avoided by act of the claimant himself. It is thought, however, to be more realistic to treat the case as involving a benefit provided by a third party, although the result should be the same in whichever of the two ways the case is approached. In any event the repairs were said by Hirst LJ, in the majority, to be "*res inter alios acta* and therefore collateral", which is, of course, familiar terminology but tells us little, and also to be "not part of a continuous transaction **9-162**

610 See *Biggins v Goode* (1832) 2 Cr. & J. 364 and subsequent cases.

611 See *Wells v Moody* (1835) 7 C. & P. 59 and subsequent cases.

612 Where the normal measure has been the value of the goods without allowing any deduction for the rent properly due.

613 For details see para.38-089, below.

614 [1912] A.C. 673.

615 [1990] 2 Q.B. 227 CA. Other than in *Pagnan & Fratelli v Corbisa Industrial Agropacuaria* [1970] 1 W.L.R. 1306 CA: at para.9-137, above.

616 On all this see para.9-144, above.

617 [1997] 1 W.L.R. 489 CA.

618 The measure awarded, with which the Court of Appeal did not express disagreement, was the value of the property in its defective condition deducted from its value without the defects rather than deducted from the price paid by the claimants. This value and the price may well not have differed—and the point decided in the case is unaffected by this issue—but it is unfortunate that the measure is improperly stated, especially as the authorities cited in its favour, *Philips v Ward* [1956] 1 W.L.R. 471 CA and *Perry v Sidney Phillips & Son* [1982] 1 W.L.R. 1297 CA, do not support it.

of which the purchase … was the inception",[619] which may be questioned in the light of the fact that, in Viscount Haldane's book, for a transaction to be regarded as not continuous it must also be independent and disconnected.[620] Although clearly dealing with action of the claimant and not of a third party, *Hussey v Eels*[621] was, not surprisingly, relied upon but the difficulties with that decision have already been canvassed.[622] Hirst LJ held the repairs eventually executed to be not part of a continuing transaction "having regard to the intervening events and to the long interval of time"[623] but the passage of years between duty broken and loss avoided should not control the result. It is thought that Peter Gibson LJ's well reasoned dissenting judgment is to be preferred. He concluded it by saying:

> "Once the property had been put in repair at no cost to the plaintiffs, in my judgment they cannot be allowed double recovery by an award of damages against the defendants … To allow the plaintiff's claim would be contrary to justice, common sense and the *British Westinghouse* principle."[624]

**9-163** A similar result was arrived at by the trial judge in *Devine v Jefferys*.[625] The claimants, who in 1988 had purchased a house with the aid of a building society mortgage in reliance on the defendant surveyor's negligent valuation report, were awarded the normal measure of damages represented by the amount by which the property had been overvalued, although in the event this loss had been averted by reason of the building society's agreeing in 1999, in consequence of the claimants' falling far behind with their mortgage repayments, to release the entire mortgage debt, the release being in exchange for a transfer of the house to the society and the grant of a seven-year tenancy of it to the claimants. As in *Gardner v Marsh and Parsons*,[626] the trial judge dealt with the case as one in the conventional category of loss avoided by act of the claimant himself, but again it is thought that, while it should not affect the result, it is more realistic to regard the case as one of a benefit provided by a third party. In line with *Hussey v Eels*,[627] and *Gardner*,[628] both of which were relied upon, the trial judge held that the release of the mortgage debt could not be said to arise out of the consequences of the wrong or to be part of a continuous transaction commencing with the purchase of the house 11 years earlier.[629] Again, this result is not to be commended. Though the time gap was even longer than in *Gardner*, the releasing of the mortgage debt need not have been seen as a transaction independent of and disconnected from—the words of Viscount Haldane himself[630]—the surveyor's overvaluation of the property. The trial judge regarded the damages that precedent required him to award as a windfall for the

---

619 [1997] 1 W.L.R. 489 CA at 503H.
620 See para.9-144, above.
621 [1990] 2 Q.B. 227 CA.
622 See para.9-144, above.
623 [1990] 2 Q.B. 227 CA at 503H.
624 [1990] 2 Q.B. 227 CA at 511C to D. Contrast *Kennedy v Van Emden* [1996] P.N.L.R. 409 CA, where, in a claim against solicitors, subsequent legislation which eliminated the damage was taken into account. For an explanation of *Kennedy* on the basis of there being no loss, as opposed to no mitigation of loss, see para.9-116, above.
625 [2001] Lloyd's Rep. P.N. 301.
626 [1997] 1 W.L.R. 489 CA.
627 [1990] 2 Q.B. 227 CA.
628 [1997] 1 W.L.R. 489 CA.
629 [2001] Lloyd's Rep. P.N. 301 at 306, col.2.
630 See para.9-144, above.

claimants and, although he thought that with their difficulties they might deserve it more than most, commented succinctly that "it does represent a loss which has never actually hit their pockets".[631]

*Needler Financial Services v Taber*,[632] again raised the issue of the deductibility of a benefit received from a third party but a receipt in no way instigated by the claimant himself. The defendant was an individual pension holder who had become a victim of pensions mis-selling, having been persuaded in 1990 by the claimant financial services company to transfer the benefits under his existing pension into a personal pension plan with Norwich Union which, as he discovered on retirement in 1998, afforded him a smaller pension than would have been the pension which he had given up. The loss sustained by the defendant was calculated by the Pensions Ombudsman by taking the difference in value between the pensions, which difference in capital terms amounted to over £20,000. On demutualisation in 1997 the defendant had been allotted shares in Norwich Union in respect of his personal pension plan which shares he had sold, also in 1997, for a little short of £8,000. The issue arose as to whether, in arriving at the amount of the compensation due to the defendant for his loss, the claimant was entitled to take this into account as a credit. Sir Andrew Morritt VC held that the claimant was not so entitled as **9-164**

> "the benefit was not caused by and did not flow, as part of a continuous transaction, from the negligence".[633]

This result of some importance—it was said that it would affect 126,000 claims—is to be regretted. The simpler, and it is thought correct, approach is to compare everything which the defendant had acquired by virtue of the personal pension plan with everything he would have received under the abandoned pension. The ongoing personal pension plan can surely be regarded as a continuous transaction, the test which the authorities appear to be applying here. As for the point on causation, it has already been submitted that causation is of little assistance for deciding issues of mitigation; an examination of the authorities which concern themselves with the knotty problem of dividing what is collateral from what is not collateral shows that they do not rely on causation for the solution.[634] By fortunate contrast to *Needler*, deduction of a benefit coming from a third party was held to be allowable in *Rubenstein v HSBC Bank Plc*.[635] In a claim for loss in respect of a bond unsuitably recommended by a bank,[636] the Court of Appeal agreed with the trial judge that there should be deducted from the damages the amount of an ex gratia payment made by the issuers of the bond to bondholders on account of a monetary recovery they had made on certain bond connected assets, since the pay-

---

631 [2001] Lloyd's Rep. P.N. 301 at 307, col.2. *Linklaters Business Services v Sir Robert McAlpine Ltd* [2010] EWHC 2931 (TCC) is also a case which could be regarded as not falling within the conventional category of loss avoided by act of the claimant himself but as loss avoided by a third party's act but, whichever way one goes, the result, allowing deduction, is right. The case is at para.9-131, above.

632 [2002] Lloyd's Rep. P.N. 32.

633 [2002] Lloyd's Rep. P.N. 32 at [26].

634 See paras 9-019 and 9-112, above.

635 [2012] EWCA Civ 1184 CA.

636 The main issue in *Rubenstein* turned on causation and remoteness and on this is considered, with the facts, at para.8-157, above.

ment, to which the claimant had no contractual entitlement, arose directly in consequence of investment in the bond.[637]

## 5. Actions Taken Before the Wrong by The Claimant

9-165 In the nature of things, actions taken before the breach of duty cannot be within the principles laid down in *British Westinghouse Co v Underground Ry*,[638] since these require the action to arise out of the consequences of that breach, the benefit to arise out of the act of mitigation. Illustrations of the impact of actions taken before the wrong has been suffered come from two very different directions, and there is no clear test for whether benefit arising is or is not to be taken into account. There are the cases (1) where financial precautions by way of insurance are taken before injury against the eventuality of injury and (2) where sub-contracts made before breach are carried out despite breach.

### (1) Insurance taken out before injury against the eventuality of injury

9-166 Where the claimant has taken precautions against injury by way of insurance[639] and is then physically injured by the wrong of the defendant, the damages recoverable will not be diminished by the amount of insurance paid. This was settled as long ago as *Bradburn v G.W.R.*,[640] where it was held that a sum received by the claimant on a policy of accident insurance was not to be taken into account in an action by him for damages in respect of the injury for which he had been paid the insurance moneys. It remains undoubted law today. It forms one of the two exceptions to the rule of deductibility of collateral benefits in personal injury cases[641] endorsed by the House of Lords on a number of occasions[642] and is justified on the basis that the fruits of the claimant's thrift and foresight should in fairness enure to his advantage and not to that of the defendant.[643]

9-167 Insurance moneys paid to a deceased's dependants claiming under the Fatal Accidents Act are similarly not deducted from the damages they receive. This, however, is because statute so provides, today's Fatal Accidents Act stipulating the non-deduction of all collateral benefits.[644] The Law Commission has recommended statutory reform so as to have a consistent approach to collateral benefits

---

637 [2012] EWCA Civ 1184 CA at [133]– [136].

638 [1912] A.C. 673.

639 In editions of this work up to 1997 pensions had been included together with insurance in this section, basing this inclusion on Lord Reid's analogising pensions to insurance in *Parry v Cleaver* [1970] A.C. 1, asking rhetorically of the claimant: "why should it make any difference that he insured by arrangement with his employer rather than with an insurance company?": at 14. But on further thought it is considered more appropriate to deal with pensions together with all the other collateral benefits in personal injury claims, analogising in particular to sick pay: see at paras 40-149 and following, below.

640 (1874) L.R. 10 Ex. 1.

641 The other is charitable payments and the like; at para.40-159, below.

642 See para.40-150, below.

643 While the claimant's damages entitlement to car hire paid by an insurance company was said in *Bee v Jenson* [2007] 4 All E.R. 791 CA at [24], to be the logical result of the classic *Bradburn* case, the decision has more in common with the cases at paras 9-168 and 9-169, below, since the damages were held for the insurance company. See the case at paras 37-023 and 37-052, below.

644 See the current version of s.4 of the Fatal Accidents Act 1976 at para.41-111, below.

as between personal injury claims, where collateral benefits are generally deducted, and wrongful death claims,[645] but reform would not affect the non-deduction of insurance moneys; indeed insurance moneys had formed the first category of benefit for which statute decreed no deduction.[646]

Outside accident insurance in personal injury claims and claims for wrongful death, again no deduction of insurance moneys is made from the damages where insurance has been taken out in advance to cover the eventuality of loss, but this is for a very different reason and one unrelated to mitigation. This situation is to be found particularly in the now familiar claims of mortgage lenders against negligent solicitors, as in *BPE Solicitors v Hughes-Holland*,[647] or against negligent valuers, as in *Banque Bruxelles Lambert v Eagle Star Insurance Co Ltd*,[648] and also in the now equally familiar claims by Lloyd's Names against negligent members or managing agents, as in *Brown v KMR Services Ltd*.[649] Here there has been no double recovery because the insurance contract is one of indemnity so that the claimant is obliged to repay the insurer. *Arab Bank Plc v John D. Wood Commercial Ltd*,[650] confirms the position. Moneys paid or payable under a mortgage indemnity policy did not fall to be deducted from the damages claimed by the lender against his negligent professional adviser because the policy, which in this case had been taken out for the benefit of the lending bank by the borrower as a requirement of the loan, was an indemnity insurance. On payment under the policy the insurers acquired subrogated rights to pursue the negligent adviser and there was no question of double recovery by the bank. **9-168**

In *FNCB Ltd v Barnet Devanney (Harrow) Ltd*,[651] the proceeds of a contingency policy were not to be brought into account in the assessment of damages as, once again, there could be no double recovery. The contingency insurers, if they had paid, were subrogated to the claimant's rights and, if they had not paid, the recovery of damages went in diminution of the contingency claim. Had there been no subrogation Morritt LJ, with whose judgment Lindsay LJ agreed, would nonetheless have reached the same result. This was on the basis that the matter **9-169**

> "would come within the exception [to deductibility] established in *Parry v Cleaver* for the proceeds of insurance effected by the plaintiff for his own benefit".[652]

It is thought, however, that Sedley LJ's reservations about assimilation to the cases of personal accident insurance

> "rather than to the principle that however many premiums an insured has paid on however many policies, he may recover a loss once only"[653]

are compelling.

---

645 See the last fn. in para.41-115, below.

646 As early as 1908: see para.41-110, below. Even when, before this date, insurance moneys had been deducted, the precautionary insurance will generally have been taken out by the deceased rather than by the claimant dependants themselves.

647 [2017] UKSC 21.

648 [1995] 2 All E.R. 769; at first instance.

649 [1994] 4 All E.R. 385; at first instance.

650 [2000] 1 W.L.R. 857 CA.

651 [2000] P.N.L.R. 248 CA.

652 [2000] P.N.L.R. 248 CA at 264G. *Parry v Cleaver* [1970] A.C. 1 in fact dealt with pensions, not insurance.

653 [2000] P.N.L.R. 248 CA at 265D.

### (2) Sub-contracts already made before breach

9-170 Buyers of goods or shares and lessors of land have on occasion entered into a sub-sale or sub-lease made before breach which, if taken into account in the assessment of damages, would result in a nominal award or at least an award falling below the normal measure. For example, if a buyer of defective goods has been able to carry through a sub-sale without his buyer complaining of the defects, can it be said that the loss has thereby disappeared? The cases dealing with sale have wrestled with this issue up to the present day; the cases dealing with leases are much fewer, and generally older, and may require some re-thinking in the light of the direction in which the sale cases seem to be moving.

9-171 **(a) Sale** In returning in the context of avoided loss to contracts of sale we come to them from a different angle. Whereas, when earlier considering avoided loss in contracts for the sale of goods or shares where there is a resale of the goods or shares, or a repurchase of substitute goods or shares, after the breach of contract has occurred,[654] both breach by seller and breach by buyer were relevant, here we are concerned with sub-sales, which can only be made by the buyer, and we are therefore concerned only with breach by the seller.

9-172 The three major forms of seller's breach, viz., by non-delivery, by delayed delivery and by defective delivery, again fall to be considered. The situation envisaged is that the buyer has sub-sold the goods, or shares, contracted for before the seller's breach has occurred, or even before the contract has been made, at a price which is lower than the value that would be taken for assessment of the normal measure of damages, viz., the value at the date when delivery was due in the case of non-delivery and delayed delivery, and the value as warranted in the case of defective delivery.[655] It is further envisaged that where the defendant has delivered defective goods or delivered goods late the claimant buyer nevertheless carries through the sub-sale and his sub-buyer pays the full contractual price, either waiving objections to the defect or delay or because the defect was not sufficiently large or the delay sufficiently long to affect the sub-contract. And it is also envisaged that where the defendant has not delivered at all, so that the claimant cannot carry through his sub-sale, the claimant neither goes into the market to acquire a substitute nor is sued for damages for his non-delivery by his sub-buyer. Moreover, the equivalent situations can occur, mutatis mutandis, in contracts of carriage of goods, viz., by their loss in transit, their arrival late or their arrival in a damaged condition.[656] In none of these situations, in carriage contracts as much as in sale contracts, can it be said that the claimant's action arose out of the consequences of the breach, the further contract being by that time already made, so that the solution, whatever it turns out to be, is not reached as a matter of mitigation in the strict sense.[657]

9-173 *(i) The three early leading authorities* The legal position was, for not far short of a century, dominated by three decisions on sale of goods, one in each of the three categories of breach with which we are concerned. A decision of the Privy Council

---

654 See paras 9-121 to 9-124 and 9-133 to 9-139, above.
655 See Ch.25 below, passim.
656 See Ch.32 below, passim.
657 See paras 9-003 and following, above.

in a case of delayed delivery was followed by one of the House of Lords on non-delivery, with a Court of Appeal decision on defective delivery bringing up the rear.

With breach by non-delivery the leading case is *Williams v Agius*,[658] decided in 1914. Having bought a cargo of coal from Agius, Williams resold before the time fixed for delivery a cargo of similar amount and description to one Ghiron at a price higher than the contract price but lower than what turned out to be the market price at the time when Agius failed in breach of contract to deliver. The House of Lords held that the normal measure of damages applied and that the sub-sale price to Ghiron was irrelevant to reduce Williams's damages. In so doing their Lordships strongly approved the Court of Appeal's decision in *Rodocanachi v Milburn*,[659] where the contract that was breached was not one of sale but of carriage of goods, the non-delivery resulting from the goods being lost at sea in the course of carriage. The price at which the charterer had sold the goods in advance of the breach of contract, a price lower than that at the time of due delivery, was not allowed to reduce the damages.[660] 9-174

A few years before *Williams v Agius* the Privy Council had reached a contrary result in *Wertheim v Chicoutimi Pulp Co*,[661] a case which featured delayed delivery rather than non-delivery. The defendant had contracted to sell and deliver to the claimant many tons of wood pulp but had delivered late, and the market price of wood pulp at the port of delivery had dropped considerably between the time specified for delivery and the time of actual delivery. The claimant had resold the wood pulp under a number of sub-contracts, in some cases entered into before the contract with the defendant and in other cases before its breach,[662] and all at a price substantially higher than the market price at the port of delivery at the time of actual delivery, although lower than the market price there at the time of due delivery. All these sub-contracts appear to have been successfully performed; presumably this was either because the delivery dates under them were sufficiently in advance as not to be prejudiced by the defendant's delay or because the sub-buyers waived their right to object to a delay in the claimant's performance to them. The Privy Council held that the measure of damages was limited to the market price at the port of delivery at the time specified for delivery less the price on the resale, Lord Atkinson saying of the claimant that 9-175

> "the real value of the goods to him is proved by the very fact of this sale to be more than market value, and the loss he sustains must be measured by that price, unless he is, against all justice, to be permitted to make a profit by the breach of contract."[663]

---

658 [1914] A.C. 510.

659 (1886) 18 Q.B.D. 67 (CA).

660 The question whether these sub-contracts are material to increase, as opposed to reduce, the damages involves quite different considerations, depending upon the application of the rule in *Hadley v Baxendale* (1854) 9 Ex. 341, and in particular upon the defendant's actual or imputed knowledge with regard to the sub-contract. The question is totally one of remoteness, and cases of this type (see para.8-212 and Ch.25, passim) do not assist in dealing with the present problem. Thus the perplexity that is sometimes found at the difficulty of reconciling cases which fall within the different groups is misplaced; see for instance, at para.25-029, below, the Court of Appeal's perplexity in *Finlay v Kwik Hoo Tong* [1929] 1 K.B. 400 CA at the difficulty of reconciling *Williams v Agius* [1914] A.C. 510 and *Hall v Pim* (1928) 33 Com. Cas. 324 HL. Similarly, Evershed J's comments in *Brading v McNeill* [1946] Ch. 145 at 152 fail to take into account this important distinction.

661 [1911] A.C. 301 PC.

662 [1911] A.C. 301 PC at 306.

663 [1911] A.C. 301 PC at 307 to 308.

**9-176** Next in time came the Court of Appeal's *Slater v Hoyle & Smith*,[664] a decision which has received much attention over the years. This case concerned defective delivery amounting to breach of warranty and it was held that the sub-contract was on principle immaterial to reduce the damages. The claimant bought cotton from the defendant in order to fulfil a contract of sale of cotton cloth already made by him with a third party. The cloth delivered by the defendant was of inferior quality, and the claimant claimed from him the normal measure of damages, namely the market price at delivery of the cloth as warranted less the market price at delivery of the inferior cloth. The claimant had used the inferior quality cloth to fulfil his sub-contract and had received the full contract price from his sub-buyer, the latter not taking any legal proceedings against him. The price paid by the sub-buyer was greater than the market price at delivery of the inferior cloth, though less than the market price of the cloth as warranted. In these circumstances the defendant contended, not only that the measure of damages should be the market price at delivery of the cloth as warranted less the resale price, but that the claimant had suffered no damage whatsoever since, had the other cloth been as warranted, he would still have obtained the same price for it from the third party in fulfilment of the sub-contract. The Court of Appeal rejected this contention and awarded the claimant the damages he claimed. Scrutton LJ was unprepared to extend the principle of *Wertheim*,[665] a decision of which he was somewhat critical, from the case of delayed delivery, which *Wertheim* was, to the case of delivery of defective goods, preferring to take the analogy of the case of non-delivery of goods, which *Agius*[666] was.

**9-177** *(ii) The position today* How have these decisions fared over the years and how are they regarded today as we approach their centenary? It can be said that for long none of them had been seriously challenged but of late questions have surfaced.

**9-178** Questions first arose over the last of the decisions in time, *Slater v Hoyle & Smith*.[667] This was in *Bence Graphics International v Fasson UK*,[668] which like *Slater* reached the Court of Appeal. Vinyl film used to make identification decals for bulk containers had been supplied by the defendants to the claimants who printed words or numbers on the film and cut it to size so that it could be applied to the containers. By reason of defects in its manufacture, the film supplied tended to degrade so that the decals became illegible and the buyers, to whom the claimants had sold the decals made by them with the vinyl film, registered complaints about the poor labelling. A claim by one buyer was settled; the claimants' major buyer gave intimation of a claim but this had not so far been pursued. The Court of Appeal had therefore to decide whether the damages should be the prima facie measure, namely the value of the goods as they should have been less their value as they were, or measured by the actual loss suffered, which appeared to be less. The majority favoured the latter measure, Auld LJ being of the view that, in the context of a breach of warranty claim by a buyer who had successfully sold the goods on, whether in original or modified form, *Slater v Hoyle & Smith* was due for reconsideration.

---

664 [1920] K.B. 11 CA.
665 [1911] A.C. 301 PC; at para.9-175, above.
666 [1914] A.C. 510; at para.9-174, above.
667 [1920] K.B. 11 CA.
668 [1998] Q.B. 87 CA.

*Bence Graphics* itself was not a case in which the claimant buyer had entered into a sub-sale before the contract with, or before the breach of contract by, the seller of the goods. Indeed it is unlikely that the further sale could have been made in advance of the sale to the claimants since that sale was of the decal which had to be made by the claimants using the vinyl film. The issue which *Bence Graphics* was addressing was whether the contemplation of contracting parties could operate so as to justify an award of damages below the normal measure, and the decision, in line with earlier authority,[669] was that, where the contracting parties contemplated that the buyer would incorporate the goods sold in a further product to be sold on, the damages must be related to that sale even if thereby the buyer would achieve a lower award than if the usual damages, based on value of the goods as warranted and their value as is, were awarded. Mitigation, in any sense of that term, was not under consideration. However, it is clear that, if presented with the factual situation appearing in *Slater*, the majority would wish not to follow that decision. It is thought that this approach is certainly to be preferred. Paraphrasing Lord Atkinson in *Wertheim*,[670] to ignore the sub-sale permits the claimant to make a profit from the breach of contract. The proper analogy for defective delivery where the sub-sale is carried through must be with delayed delivery where the sub-sale is carried through and not with non-delivery where ex hypothesi the sub-sale cannot be carried through. In other words, despite what Scrutton LJ may have said in *Slater*,[671] the proper analogy here must be with Wertheim rather than with Agius. **9-179**

Moreover, the taking of the sub-sale into account in the delayed delivery case of *Wertheim v Chicoutimi Pulp Co*,[672] has not been similarly criticised. The only problem with it is that the Privy Council when paying attention to the sub-sale price did not go far enough. For the result attained by the Privy Council is a somewhat hybrid one, neither ignoring the sub-contracts completely nor taking them into account entirely; had the court done the latter, which would appear to be preferable, the damages would have been nominal since the claimant would have obtained the same amount as he did from his sub-buyers even if there had been no delay.[673] But subject to this error, the taking account of the sub-sale at the lower price is to be commended since it is what mitigation principles demand—and it is interesting to see that the decision has now received a degree of endorsement in *The Golden Victory*,[674] by a House of Lords divided on a different issue, both by Lord Scott[675] in the majority and by Lord Bingham[676] in the minority. **9-180**

Turning, finally, to non-delivery of goods or shares, we find that over the many intervening years since *Williams v Agius*,[677] and *Rodocanachi v Milburn*,[678] neither decision has been questioned so that as late as *Bear Stearns Bank Plc v Forum Equity Ltd*,[679] in 2007, the price at which the buyers of shares had sold to a third party below the market price at due delivery was held to be irrelevant and not to **9-181**

669 See para.8-195, above.
670 See at para.9-175, above.
671 See at para.9-176, above.
672 [1911] A.C. 301 PC.
673 See the defendant's contention in *Slater v Hoyle & Smith* [1920] 2 K.B. 11 CA, at para.9-176 above.
674 [2007] 2 A.C. 353. See this case at paras 10-117 to 10-121, below.
675 [2007] 2 A.C. 353 at [30].
676 [2007] 2 A.C. 353 at [13].
677 [1914] A.C. 510.
678 (1886) 18 Q.B.D. 67 CA.
679 [2007] EWHC 1576 (Comm).

be preferred, in the assessment of damages, to that market price.[680] Of course with non-delivery, differing from both delayed and defective delivery, the sub-sale by the buyer, or the sale by the charterer, cannot be carried through so that taking that sale into account would not result in nominal damages but would simply lead to damages based on that sale price less the contract price. And a further, and vital, difference which follows from the inability to carry through that sale is that sub-seller or charterer may buy in the market in order to deliver to their buyer and, should they not do so, may be subject to a claim for damages by their buyer for non-delivery. In either of these circumstances—and these possibilities can arise also with delayed and defective delivery—it would clearly be wrong to bring into the damages assessment the price at which the buyer or charterer has sold. But where they do not go into the market and are not subject to a damages claim, not to base the damages on their sale price must surely overcompensate them and shows a failure to apply principles of mitigation. And this was precisely the position in both *Agius* and *Rodocanachi*.[681] *Agius* was a very curious case in that Williams's sub-purchaser, Ghiron, had sold the cargo he had bought from Williams back to Agius so that one had a circular position with no question of Williams going into the market or being sued for damages by Ghiron. And on this *Rodocanachi* is even clearer. The cargo consigned for carriage by the defendant's ship had been sold by the charterers at the lower price on a "to arrive" basis so that non-delivery by the defendant shipper relieved them of all liability to their buyer without any need to go into the market to repurchase.[682]

**9-182** In various cases, which may not have involved a sub-sale made before the breach of the main contract but simply a sub-sale which has followed on the breach, indications of concern or doubt over the propriety of the results in *Agius* and *Rodocanachi* have now started to appear. First, in *Altonpride v Canbright Ltd*,[683] where sulphur not delivered by the seller was resold by the buyer at $72 per metric ton, we find Alliott J saying that, while without the benefit of authority he would have considered the appropriate damages to be the buyer's loss of profit,

> "authority of some antiquity [viz. *Agius* and *Rodocanachi*] demonstrates that such an approach would be wrong".

He accordingly awarded damages based on the market price at due delivery of $78 per metric ton. Then in *Sony Computer Entertainment UK Ltd v Cinram Logistics UK Ltd*,[684] a case of carriage rather than sale of goods where the claimant was only claiming the price at which he was selling the goods, a price which was discounted below the market price, Rix LJ commented that, even if the claimant was content not to claim the market price, it "might (or might not) have been obliged to limit itself to the profit on the sales".[685] This hardly squares with regarding Agius and Rodocanachi as of unquestionable authority. More outspoken,

680 Facts at para.29-004, below.

681 And appears to have been the position in *Bear Stearns*.

682 Of course one would assume that, whenever the defendant, whether seller or carrier, is arguing that the claimant's sale price should be taken for the damages rather than market value, the claimant's immediate rejoinder will be, where it is the case, that he has had to enter the market for a substitute or is having to meet a claim for damages from his buyer.

683 *Altonpride v Canbright Ltd* unreported 31 July 1998 (QB).

684 [2008] EWCA Civ 955 CA.

685 [2008] EWCA Civ 955 CA at [50].

however, has been Langley J in *Oxus Gold Plc v Templeton Insurance Ltd*,[686] where there was a sale of shares which, had they been delivered, the buyer would have sold on below the price at which the market stood at due delivery. Holding that what he called "the dictates of the highest authority" required him to award the market price, Langley J confessed to

> "the irrelevant and presumptuous thought that there is not much to be said for a law of damages as absolutist as"

that carved out by *Agius* and *Rodocanachi*.[687]

In summary, it is suggested that, in this uncertain and fluid state of the authorities in this small but important corner of the mitigation issue, the best solution may be this. Whatever the breach, whether it be by non-delivery, delayed delivery or defective delivery, the presumption should be that the buyer is entitled to have his sub-sale ignored but the seller is also entitled to rebut this presumption if he can show positively that the buyer neither has bought substitute goods after the breach nor is subject to a damages claim from his sub-buyer. And this solution should apply equally, mutatis mutandis, to contracts of carriage of goods. It is a solution that is in accordance with the rule that the burden of proof on the issue of mitigation is on the party in breach.[688] **9-183**

**(b) Lease** The other illustration of the effect on damages of sub-contracts successfully carried through is provided by leases of land. The situation appears at first glance to be rather different from that in the sale cases. A defendant lessee, in breach of his covenant to repair, delivers up the property at the end of the term in disrepair, but the claimant lessor has already granted a new lease to a third party to run from the expiration of the defendant's lease under which the third party has covenanted to repair, so that the performance of the defendant's covenant to repair is a matter of pecuniary indifference to the claimant. In such circumstances, once again, it cannot be said that the claimant's action arose out of the consequences of the breach, the sub-contract being by that time already made, so that once again the situation does not give rise to an issue of mitigation proper.[689] **9-184**

The principal authority here is *Joyner v Weeks*,[690] where the result reached, both at first instance and in the Court of Appeal, was that the sub-contract should be immaterial to reduce the damages; the normal measure of damages at common law being the cost of the repairs, that was the amount awarded. Now it is true that s.18(1) of the Landlord and Tenant Act 1927 set a statutory ceiling on the old common law normal measure of the cost of repairs by enacting that the damages should be limited to the amount by which the value of the reversion had diminished, and by specifically laying down that no damages are recoverable for breach of a covenant to repair if it appears that the repairs would not be carried out because the premises are to be pulled down or structurally altered. But the decision of the Court **9-185**

[686] [2007] EWHC 770 (Comm).

[687] [2007] EWHC 770 (Comm) at [80]. He so confessed with "some very limited encouragement from *The Golden Victory*"; this important decision of the House of Lords is dealt with at paras 10-117 to 10-121 and 32-074, below.

[688] On the onus of proof for avoided loss see para.9-115, above.

[689] See paras 9-108 and following, above.

[690] [1891] 2 Q.B. 31 CA.

of Appeal in *Haviland v Long*,[691] indicates that this subsection has not affected the measure of damages where the covenanted repairs are to be carried out in full under a sub-contract though not by the lessor himself. In that case there was again a new lease made by the claimant lessor with a third party who covenanted to do the repairs, and, although the claimant had arranged to pay over to the third party any sum that he obtained from the defendant on account of the defendant's failure to repair, it would seem from the reasoning of all three members of the court that the cost of repairs would still have been recoverable even if the claimant lessor had stood to benefit by dint of an advantageous bargain with the third party. Denning LJ in particular was quite categorical, saying:

> "The fact that the landlord has an undertaking from a new tenant to do the repairs does not go in diminution of damages. It is *res inter alios acta*."[692]

On this footing, therefore, *Joyner v Weeks*,[693] stands as good law today.[694]

9-186 *Joyner*,[695] and *Haviland*,[696] are still cited today as illustrations of awards of damages which properly go beyond the claimant's loss[697] but there is a tension between these cases and the modern climate of stressing that a claimant's damages should not go beyond compensation for loss.[698] There is also tension with the doubts appearing about similar awards in the cases of sale, in particular the doubts expressed in *Bence Graphics International v Fasson UK*,[699] over the result in the analogous case of defective delivery of goods sold.[700] It may be that cases like *Joyner* and *Haviland* should be understood as a special form of money award which is not really damages at all but akin to monetised specific performance.

---

691 [1952] 2 Q.B. 80 CA.

692 [1952] 2 Q.B. 80 CA at 84.

693 [1891] 2 Q.B. 31 CA.

694 Curiously Denning J himself had said earlier in *Westminster v Swinton* [1948] 1 K.B. 524 at 534 that "it was in order to remedy *Joyner v Weeks* that s.18 of the Landlord and Tenant Act 1927 was passed". Cases which are clearly rendered no longer law by s.18(1) are *Rawlings v Morgan* (1865) 18 C.B. N.S. 776 and *Inderwick v Leech* (1885) 1 T.L.R. 484, where the repairs were not to be done at all because the premises were to be pulled down, in the first case by a third party and in the second by the claimant himself. This had been held in both not to go in reduction of the damages; now s.18(1) specifically requires that it shall.

695 [1891] 2 Q.B. 31 CA.

696 [1952] 2 Q.B. 80 CA.

697 As in *Burdis v Livsey* [2003] Q.B. 36 CA; see at [91].

698 Notably by Lord Bridge in *Hunt v Severs* [1994] 2 A.C. 350.

699 [1998] Q.B. 87 CA.

700 See paras 9-171 to 9-179, above.

# CHAPTER 10

# CERTAINTY OF DAMAGE AND LOSS OF CHANCE

TABLE OF CONTENTS



## I. THE PROBLEM OF CERTAINTY

A claimant claiming damages must prove his or her case. To justify an award of substantial damages where loss is asserted the claimant must satisfy the court both as to (i) the fact of damage, that is an adverse consequence; and (ii) as to its amount.[1] If the claimant satisfies the court on neither, the action will fail, or at the most the claimant will be awarded nominal damages where a right has been infringed.[2] If the fact of damage is shown but no evidence is given as to its amount so that it is virtually impossible to assess damages, this will generally permit only **10-001**

[1] *Senate Electrical Wholesalers Ltd v Alcatel Submarine Networks Ltd* [1999] 2 Lloyd's Rep. 423 CA, illustrates, in a very complex case, the failure of a claimant to prove the relevance of the quantum of damages for which it was contending, namely, that the true value of the business sold was to be calculated by applying a profits/earnings ratio to the difference between warranted and actual profit: see at 430 to 431.

[2] For nominal damages of this variety see paras 12-001 to 12-003, below.

an award of nominal damages; this situation is illustrated by the old cases of *Dixon v Deveridge*,[3] and *Twyman v Knowles*.[4]

**10-002** On the other hand, where it is clear that some substantial loss has been incurred, the fact that an assessment is difficult because of the nature of the damage is no reason for awarding no damages or merely nominal damages. As Vaughan Williams LJ put it in *Chaplin v Hicks*,[5] the leading case on the issue of certainty:

> "The fact that damages cannot be assessed with certainty does not relieve the wrongdoer of the necessity of paying damages."[6]

Indeed if absolute certainty were required as to the precise amount of loss that the claimant had suffered, no damages would be recovered at all in the great number of cases. This is particularly true since so much of damages claimed are in respect of prospective, and therefore necessarily contingent, loss. Of course, as Devlin J said in *Biggin v Permanite*[7]:

> "Where precise evidence is obtainable, the court naturally expects to have it, [but] where it is not, the court must do the best it can."

Generally, therefore, although it remains true to say that "difficulty of proof does not dispense with the necessity of proof",[8] the standard demanded can seldom be that of certainty. Even if it is said that the damage must be proved with reasonable certainty, the word "reasonable" is really the controlling one, and the standard of proof only demands evidence from which the existence of damage can be reasonably inferred and which provides adequate data[9] for calculating its amount. The clearest statement of the position is that of Bowen LJ in *Ratcliffe v Evans*,[10] where he said:

> "In all actions accordingly on the case where the damage actually done is the gist of the action, the character of the acts themselves which produce the damage, and the circumstances under which these acts are done, must regulate the degree of certainty and particularity with which the damage done ought to be stated and proved. As much certainty and particularity must be insisted on, both in pleading and proof of damage, as is reasonable, having regard to the circumstances and to the nature of the acts themselves by which the damage is done. To insist upon less would be to relax old and intelligible principles. To insist upon more would be the vainest pedantry."

**10-003** In *Zabihi v Janzemini*,[11] where the valuation of missing converted jewellery was in issue, the essence of the opening two paragraphs of this chapter in an earlier edition but one, as set out by the Court of Appeal,[12] were relied upon by Blackburne J below and distilled by him in the statement, also set out by the Court of Appeal,[13]

---

3 (1825) 2 C. & P. 109; facts at para.12-005, below.

4 (1853) 13 C.B. 222: facts at para.12-005, below.

5 [1911] 2 K.B. 786 CA: facts at para.10-040, below.

6 [1911] 2 K.B. 786 CA at 792. The statement was restricted to contract, but it applies equally to tort.

7 [1951] 1 K.B. 422 at 438.

8 *Aerial Advertising Co v Batchelors Peas* [1938] 2 All E.R. 788 at 796, per Atkinson J.

9 *Ashcroft v Curtin* [1971] 1 W.L.R. 1731 CA, is, however, an illustration of a claimant's failure to provide adequate data: facts in a footnote to para.40-082, below.

10 [1892] 2 Q.B. 524 CA at 532 to 533.

11 [2009] EWCA Civ 851 CA; facts at para.38-049, below.

12 At [2009] EWCA Civ 851 CA at [27].

13 At [2009] EWCA Civ 851 CA at [29].

that

> "the court must do its best on such evidence as it feels able to accept to place some kind of value on [the] jewellery ... even if its precise identity cannot be established and therefore its value must be in doubt."

The Court of Appeal agreed that Blackburne J was right to do his best to come to a valuation figure provided that he was entitled to accept the evidence on which he relied as sufficient evidence of value. By a majority it was held that he had had adequate data to support the award which he had made.

The issue of valuation and proof of value arose in a different context in *Experience Hendrix LLC v Times Newspapers Ltd*,[14] with Blackburne J, now Sir William Blackburne, again as trial judge. A newspaper publisher had infringed the claimant companies' rights in the performance and recording of a concert by issuing a free CD of the concert to purchasers of its newspaper. The claimant companies claimed damages to compensate them for their resultant loss, the infringement having delayed the launch of their own project which related to a film of the concert. The judge found it impossible to forecast, so as to provide a reliable basis for computing losses, what the box office takings were likely to be for a film which had yet to be released, which at the time of the trial had not even been completed and which none of the independent experts had seen in any shape or form and, if they had, would not have had the relevant expertise to comment on. This great uncertainty, however, did not mean that the judge should award no damages on the basis that the claimant companies had not proved their loss; since they clearly had suffered loss, to award no damages would have been a most unsatisfactory outcome.[15] Fortunately, two figures emerged to which it was possible, as Sir William Blackburne put it, to anchor an assessment of the claimant companies' losses from the delay.[16] The first came from a distribution agreement with another company and the second from a rival offer made for some of the performance rights.[17] **10-004**

In *IRT Oil and Gas Ltd v Fiber Optic Systems Technology (Canada) Inc*,[18] the claimant company was the exclusive sales agent for Africa under a five-year contract with the defendant which entitled the claimant to a percentage of the purchase price of all sales in Africa that it negotiated. Some time into the contract the defendant wrongfully terminated the contract. In the claim for damages Tugendhat J recognised that there was no way that he could make reliable findings as to what the prospective sales would have been over the remaining years of the contract but he did have evidence that sales had been made in other parts of the world and he was satisfied that the agency had some value. He agreed with the claimant's counsel that he must do the best that he could and arrived at an amount of damages by, as he put it, putting a figure on the chance that the claimant would have made a profit.[19] **10-005**

Further cases presenting this difficulty of showing the amount of profitable sales that would have been made by the claimant had there been no tort or breach of **10-006**

---

[14] [2010] EWHC 1986 (Ch).

[15] [2010] EWHC 1986 (Ch) at [204].

[16] [2010] EWHC 1986 (Ch) at [205].

[17] See the case further at para.48-055, below.

[18] [2009] EWHC 3041 (QB).

[19] On all this see [2009] EWHC 3041 (QB) at [94] and following.

contract by the defendant have indicated that the claimant is assisted by the principle in the very old case of *Armory v Delamirie*,[20] which has today received a new lease of life, the principle being that the court is required to resolve uncertainties by making assumptions generous to the claimant where it is the defendant's wrongdoing which has created those uncertainties. These cases are *Fearns v Anglo-Dutch Paint & Chemical Co Ltd*,[21] and *Double Communications Ltd v News Corporation International Ltd*.[22] What the courts in both cases fail to notice is that the authorities bringing *Armory v Delamirie* into the modern world are concerned with proof of the loss of a chance in the strict sense, that is to say with situations where the chance is seen as an identifiable loss in itself, in particular where the chance relates to success in a damages action eliminated by a solicitor's negligence.[23] The authorities do not go beyond this situation. In this connection the sensible comments of Moore-Bick LJ in *Zabihi v Janzemoni*,[24] are worth noting, while the subsequent refusal of Hamblen J to apply the *Armory v Delamirie* principle to the facts in *Porton Capital Technology Funds v 3M UK Holdings Ltd*,[25] is to be commended. In 2007 the defendants in *Porton* agreed to buy the entire shareholding of a company from the shareholder claimants. The consideration for the purchase was a cash sum together with what was referred to as an earn out payment based on net sales for the year 2009, the defendants being required to continue the business. The earn out payment was the principal return to be made by the claimants from the sale. The defendants in breach of contract closed down the business so that there were no sales in 2009. The claimants, relying on *Armory v Delamirie*, argued that, since the very actions of the defendants in breaching the contract had made the quantification of damages more difficult, the court should resolve any uncertainties in the claimants' favour. Hamblen J did not accept the argument. The claim was for lost profits for breach of contract where there were evidence and documentation relating to the claim; the evidential playing field was a level one. The *Armory v Delamirie* principle should not be extended further than necessary.

On one view, the *Armory* principle was expanded by the Court of Appeal in *Representative Claimants (Gulati) v MGN Ltd*,[26] where the Court of Appeal upheld sizeable awards for phone hacking despite the absence in some cases of any records detailing the hacking and other wrongful activities. In the judgment with which the other judges agreed, Arden LJ said that the award of damages was

> "an example of the ability of the law to prevent a person responsible for wrongdoing from escaping liability to his victim, without disturbing the general rule as to the conditions of liability".

On an expansive view, Arden LJ might be read as suggesting that a claim can be brought for loss caused by hacking against a proved hacker without proving any of the instances of hacking. This cannot be what Arden LJ meant. Her Ladyship's remarks are better understood as suggesting that in all of the circumstances of that

---

20 At para.38-049, below.

21 [2010] EWHC 1708 Ch at [70].

22 [2011] EWHC 961 (QB) at [4] and [5].

23 See para.10-095, below and the discussion at para.10-047, below.

24 [2009] EWCA Civ 851 CA. Comments set out at para.38-049, below

25 [2011] EWHC 2895 (Comm).

26 [2015] EWCA Civ 1291 at [107].

case, inferences can be drawn of the nature and extent of the hacking which occurred based on the extent of the related wrongdoing by MGN.

It is important to consider in some detail the question of what the courts will accept as reasonable certainty that an alleged loss has occurred or will occur. Cases in which absolute certainty is possible, and in which precise evidence is therefore expected by the court, do not need treatment here. These are cases such as where the claimant claims for loss of earnings or expenses already incurred, i.e. between the time of accrual of the action and the time of trial,[27] or where the claim is for the difference between the contract price and a clear and undoubted market price. What does require consideration are the principal categories of case where substantial damages may be awarded although the nature of the damage prevents absolute certainty of proof. **10-007**

## II Circumstances in Which Damages May be Awarded although the Nature of the Damage Prevents Absolute Certainty of Proof

### 1. Where Damage is Presumed

In certain cases general damages may be awarded in the sense of damages **10-008**

> "such as the jury may give when the judge cannot point out any measure by which they are to be assessed, except the opinion and judgment of a reasonable man".[28]

The damages are said to be at large.

Tort provides most of the illustrations and the home ground of such cases is to be found in torts which involve interference with the claimant's relationships with other people generally. This would seem to be because damages are particularly difficult to assess where loss is caused by reason of other people refusing to enter into or ceasing from relationships, whether of a business or social nature, with the claimant. The tort of defamation is perhaps the most important in this respect. Thus in *Tripp v Thomas*,[29] where the defendant suffered judgment by default, the claimant gave no evidence and the jury awarded £40, it was held that this award should stand as the jury were not bound in such circumstances to give nominal damages only. Another illustration is found in conspiracy. Thus in *Quinn v Leathem*[30] the following passage appears from the trial judge's notes of the evidence: **10-009**

> "I told the jury that pecuniary loss, directly caused by the conduct of the defendants, must be proved in order to establish a cause of action, and I advised them to require to be satisfied that such a loss to a substantial amount had been proved by the plaintiff. I declined to tell them that if actual and substantial pecuniary loss was proved to have been directly caused to the plaintiff by the wrongful acts of the defendants they were bound to limit the amount of damages to the precise sum so proved."

Contract, on the other hand, having less concern with matters involving interference with the claimant's relationships with other people generally, provides few situations in which the court is ready to presume damage. The one clear case is that **10-010**

---

27 However, even such past loss may occasionally fall foul of the requirement of certainty, as in *Ashcroft v Curtin* [1971] 1 W.L.R. 1731 CA: facts in a footnote to para.40-082, below.

28 *Prehn v Royal Bank of Liverpool* (1870) 5 Ex. 92 at 99–100, per Martin B.

29 (1824) 3 B. & C. 427.

30 [1901] A.C. 495 at 498.

damages may be given for the general pecuniary loss by injury to credit and reputation caused by the defendant's failure to pay the claimant's cheques or honour his drafts,[31] a pecuniary loss which it is difficult to estimate at all accurately. Established as long ago as *Rolin v Steward*,[32] confirmed in *Kpohraror v Woolwich Building Society*,[33] and still applied as in *Nicholson v Knox Ukiwa & Co*,[34] the clearest explanation of the rule appears in Lord Birkenhead's speech in *Wilson v United Counties Bank*,[35] where he said that

> "the ratio decidendi in such cases is that the refusal to meet the cheque, under such circumstances, is so obviously injurious to the credit of a trader[36] that the latter can recover, without allegation of special damage, reasonable compensation for the injury done to his credit".

## 2. WHERE THE LOSS IS NON-PECUNIARY

**10-011** Even where it is clear that a loss has been incurred without damage being presumed, it cannot be calculated in money with mathematical precision where it is one of the many non-pecuniary losses for which recovery is given, particularly in tort.[37] This is no good reason for refusing damages altogether. Money in such cases is not awarded as replacement for other money, but as a substitute for that which is generally more important than money: it is the best that a court can do. Lord Halsbury LC put the matter well in *The Mediana*[38]:

> "How is anybody to measure pain and suffering in moneys counted? Nobody can suggest that you can by arithmetical calculation establish what is the exact sum of money which would represent such a thing as the pain and suffering which a person has undergone by reason of an accident. But nevertheless the law recognises that as a topic upon which damages may be given."

Similar statements have continued over the years to appear in the reports.[39]

## 3. WHERE IT IS UNCERTAIN HOW A PECUNIARY LOSS IS TO BE MEASURED

**10-012** A pecuniary loss may itself occasionally be difficult to assess although it is clear that it has been incurred.[40] Thus in *Biggin v Permanite*,[41] where in an action against a seller for delivering defective goods Devlin J held that the claimant was entitled to claim damages in respect of the diminution in the market value of the goods, he

---

31 For details see paras 34-085 to 34-087, below.

32 (1854) 14 C.B. 595.

33 [1996] 4 All E.R. 119 CA.

34 [2008] P.N.L.R. 33 at 782.

35 [1920] A.C. 102 at 112.

36 No longer limited to a trader: see *Kpohraror v Woolwich Building Society* [1996] 4 All E.R. 119 CA at para.34-085, below.

37 See Ch.5, above.

38 [1900] A.C. 113 at 116.

39 Illustrative are *Fletcher v Autocar and Transporters* [1968] 2 Q.B. 322 CA at 339, per Diplock LJ, and *Parry v Cleaver* [1970] A.C. 1 at 22, per Lord Morris.

40 In assessing the uncertain loss of profits arising from a supplier's breach of an exclusive supply agreement in *Globe Motors Inc v TRW Lucas Varity Electric Steering Ltd* [2015] EWHC 553 (Comm), the judge had little alternative, after very lengthy submissions by both sides on the calculation of the damages, to taking a broad brush approach.

41 [1951] 1 K.B. 422; the decision was reversed, but on other grounds: [1951] 2 K.B. 314 CA.

further held that it was no bar to awarding substantial damages to the claimant that it was impossible to measure precisely the amount of the market diminution. The judge said:

> "It seems to me that one can very rarely arrive at an accurate figure of unsound value. Where the breach is non-delivery, there is often a market price which can be quoted, or evidence can be given of the price at which at the relevant date similar goods were changing hands, but there is rarely any market price for damaged goods since their value depends on the extent of the damage. If the actual damaged goods are sold with all faults, good evidence can be obtained of the difference in value, but such a sale is not always possible, and a claim for substantial damages cannot be limited to goods which have been sold."[42]

A different case of uncertainty of loss appeared in *Gerber Garment Technology Inc v Lectra Systems Ltd*,[43] where the claimant holding company was unable to prove that the loss of profits of its wholly-owned subsidiaries was a loss to itself. By contrast, the claimant, again a holding company, was held to have overcome this hurdle in *George Fischer (Great Britain) Ltd v Multi Construction Ltd*,[44] and recovered pound for pound the loss of its subsidiary.[45] Also in the context of nuisance it was recognised in *Jan de Nul (UK) v NV Royale Belge*,[46] where silt had been deposited in an estuary, that damages could be awarded although it was impossible to assess the effects of the nuisance with any degree of monetary precision. **10-013**

## 4. Where it is Uncertain How Much of the Loss, Pecuniary or Non-pecuniary, is Attributable to the Defendant's Breach of Duty

In the last half century cases involving industrial disease, particularly asbestos related disease, have frequently claimed the attention of the courts, on many occasions reaching the House of Lords. Serious difficulties have arisen because of the fact that these diseases can take very many years to manifest themselves, taking a **10-014**

---

42 [1951] 1 K.B. 422 at 438. See, similarly, *Chaplin v Hicks* [1911] 2 K.B. 786 CA at 792, per Vaughan Williams LJ: "No one has ever suggested that, because there is no market, there are no damages. In such a case the jury must do the best they can, and it may be that the amount of their verdict will really be a matter of guesswork." For an interesting case where there was uncertainty about how a pecuniary loss was to be measured see *Zabihi v Janzemini* [2009] EWCA Civ 851 CA at para.10-003, above. Difficulty in valuing a pecuniary loss was also faced in *Experience Hendrix LLC v Times Newspapers Ltd* [2010] EWHC 1986 Ch, and in *IRT Oil and Gas Ltd v Fiber Optic Systems Technology (Canada) Inc* [2009] EWHC 3041 (QB), considered at paras 10-004 and 10-005, above, respectively.

43 [1997] R.P.C. 443 CA.

44 [1995] 1 B.C.L.C. 260 CA.

45 There is also in this area the uncertainty over shareholders' losses where the direct loss is to the company; such losses being termed reflective losses. While the general rule is that the shareholder cannot sue where the company has an action, the no reflective loss principle is not to be over-indulged and does not always stand in the way of the shareholder claiming damages, as *Shaker v Al-Bedrawi* [2003] Ch. 350 CA; *Giles v Rhind* [2003] Ch. 618 CA (the damages assessment follows at [2004] 1 B.C.L.C. 385) and *Pearce v European Reinsurance Consultants and Run-Off Ltd* [2006] P.N.L.R. 8 at 142 show. *Webster v Sandersons Solicitors* [2009] P.N.L.R. 37 at 773, CA is another case involving, inter alia, shareholders' reflective losses. The application of the reflective loss principle in relation to damages is further discussed in the factual context of *Malhotra v Malhotra* [2014] EWHC 113 (Comm) at [53]–[63], *Energenics Holdings Pte Ltd v Ronendra Nath Hazarika* [2014] EWHC 1845 Ch at [60]–[70], and *Barnett v Creggy* [2014] EWHC 3080 Ch at [92]–[99].

46 [2000] 2 Lloyd's Rep. 700.

long period to establish themselves and a further period of latency before symptoms appear. In the claims brought by employees who have contracted the particular disease, the employers have generally been held to be at fault not in exposing their employees to the dangerous substance or process but in failing to take adequate and appropriate steps to protect them from such exposure.

**10-015** Very often it has taken industry a long time to appreciate the existence of the danger so that employers have not been at fault until such time as knowledge of the danger has made their continuing failure to take steps to counter it a breach of their duty to their employees. What then is the situation of the employee who has suffered detrimental exposure on both sides of this dividing line? An early case presenting this situation is *Crookall v Vickers Armstrong Ltd.*[47] From 1930 to 1951 the claimant, employed by the defendant, was engaged in work which involved a risk of contracting the serious disease of silicosis. Not until the year 1942 was the risk generally recognised and appreciated, and therefore not until that date did the defendant's failure to take all reasonable steps to ensure that the claimant wore a mask during his work constitute actionable negligence. In 1951 the claimant was certified to be suffering from silicosis, which had started to develop in about 1939 as a result of his having inhaled silica particles during the period of his employment. In his action for damages it was held that to the extent that the claimant's present condition was attributable to the period before the defendant's breach of duty, and therefore before the accrual of a cause of action, no damages could be awarded; the damages must be limited to so much of the total injury as was suffered after the defendant's breach of duty, or, in other words, to the extent to which the claimant's condition had been aggravated by the defendant's breach of duty.[48] The same situation arose again in a different context in *Thompson v Smiths Shiprepairers (North Shields)*,[49] where the matter was examined more fully by Mustill J. The claimants were workmen in shipyards who claimed damages against the defendants, their employers, for loss of hearing caused by exposure to excessive noise in the course of the many years of their work, the oldest having been employed from 1928 and the youngest from 1944. It was held that 1963 marked the dividing line between a reasonable policy of following the general practice of inaction by acceptance of the view that the risk of deafness was an inescapable feature of the industry and a failure to take reasonable precautions against the risk of deafness by the provision of ear protectors. In issue therefore was the extent, if any, to which the claimants were entitled to recover for their, principally non-pecuniary, loss,[50] it indeed being argued that the defendants should be liable for the totality of the loss.[51] This, however, was held to be unacceptable. Mustill J said:

> "If we know, and we do know, for by the end of the case it was no longer seriously in dispute, that a substantial part of the impairment took place before the defendants were in breach, why in fairness should they be made to pay for it? The fact that precise

---

47 [1955] 1 W.L.R. 659.

48 Contrast *Clarkson v Modern Foundries* [1957] 1 W.L.R. 1210 at paras 11-022 and 11-023, below, a decision of the era before the passing of the Limitation Act 1963.

49 [1984] Q.B. 405.

50 The claimant's claim for handicap in the labour market (for which see para.40-096, below) failed.

51 Praying in aid in particular *McGhee v National Coal Board* [1973] 1 W.L.R. 1 HL, for which see in this context para.10-019, below. However, *McGhee* was distinguished on the ground that it dealt with an evidential gap in the causal connection between negligence and injury and here such causal connection was a proved fact: see [1984] Q.B. 405 at 441G to 443B.

quantification is impossible should not alter the position. The whole exercise of assessing damages is shot through with imprecision. I see no reason why the present impossibility of making a precise apportionment of impairment and disability in terms of time, should in justice lead to the result that the defendants are adjudged liable to pay in full, when it is known that only part of the damage was their fault. What justice does demand, to my mind, is that the court should make the best estimate which it can, in the light of the evidence, making the fullest allowances in favour of the plaintiffs for the uncertainties known to be involved in any apportionment."[52]

A more complex situation arises where it is not a question of what has been termed innocent exposure and guilty exposure; instead all the exposure is guilty but the guilt is shared between a number of employers. Given the great length of time usually required for an asbestos related disease to take hold, which is up to 40 years, this situation is far from being uncommon. No decision appeared favouring an apportionment of the damages between the various employers in these circumstances until the decision of the Court of Appeal in *Holtby v Brigham & Cowan (Hull) Ltd*.[53] The claimant had suffered injury by exposure to asbestos dust during his work as a marine fitter with a series of employers over some 24 years and brought a claim against the defendant for whom he had worked for about half that time. It was held, applying *Thompson*, that the defendant was liable only to the extent that it had contributed towards the disability. The majority also held that the onus of proving causation remained on the claimant but said that such cases should not be decided upon onus of proof. In the words of Stuart-Smith LJ: **10-016**

"The question should be whether at the end of the day and on consideration of all the evidence, the claimant has proved that the defendants are responsible for the whole or a quantifiable part of his disability. The question of quantification may be difficult and the court only has to do the best it can using its common sense ... to achieve justice, not only to the claimant but the defendant, and among defendants."[54]

The Court of Appeal took the same approach in *Allen v British Rail Engineering Ltd*,[55] where the issue arose in the context of exposure between a level of exposure which was innocent and a guilty excess. The claimant suffered from a condition called vibration white finger caused by the use of hand-held vibrating tools while working for the defendant and the damages attributable to the period of this employment were reduced by half because compliance with the defendant's duty would only have required reduction of the claimant's exposure by half.[56] Again it was said, as the fourth of five propositions which were enunciated, that "the court must do the best it can on the evidence to make the apportionment"[57] and the judg- **10-017**

---

52 [1984] Q.B. 405 at 443D to 444A. The latter part of this passage was cited in *Rahman v Arearose Ltd* [2001] Q.B. 351 CA, where, in a case of successive tortious injuries by two defendants (facts at para.8-026, above), it was held to be plainly unjust to proceed on the footing that a defendant was responsible for the whole of the claimant's damage when he demonstrably was not since, on the evidence, the defendants' respective torts were the causes of distinct aspects of the claimant's overall injury.

53 [2000] 3 All E.R. 421 CA.

54 [2000] 3 All E.R. 421 CA at [20].

55 [2001] I.C.R. 942 CA.

56 There were further apportionments in respect of an earlier period when the exposure was innocent and a later period when the claimant had moved to another employer (with whom he had settled); neither of these apportionments was contested.

57 [2001] I.C.R. 942 CA at [20].

ment concluded with:

> "We accept that there are difficulties but it is important to recognise that the judge was faced with a choice between awarding nothing … doing her best to make an attribution … or holding [the defendants] liable for the consequences of [their] non-negligent actions. The first and last of these courses certainly involved substantial injustice to one party or the other. The middle course which she took involved a risk to both parties of a minor injustice. We consider she was right to choose the middle course."[58]

This reflects the view of Glyn Jones J as long ago as 1955 in the earliest of the above cases, *Crookall v Vickers-Armstrong Ltd*.[59] Positing a case of a claimant's employment shared between two employers each of whom had been in breach, he said:

> "It would be unjust, I think, to make the first employer pay for damage done after the plaintiff left his employment, and equally unjust to make the second employer liable for damage done by the first."[60]

Apportionment was again allowed in *Rugby Joinery (UK) Ltd v Whitfield*,[61] the condition being, as in *Allen*, vibration white finger and the exposure being, as in *Crookall* and *Thompson*, between innocent and guilty on a time basis under a single employer. It was accepted that there should be apportionment, the issue being how apportionment should be worked out; straight line on a time basis was rejected as, in the circumstances, unfair to the claimant.

**10-018** In other cases there has been full liability with no apportionment, this being on the ground that there had been no proof that the damage was in part innocently, rather than tortiously, caused. In *Brookes v South Yorkshire Passenger Transport Executive*,[62] another vibration white finger case, full recovery was allowed with no apportionment since it was not shown that the innocent exposure had caused any damage to the claimant.[63] Similarly, in *Hartman v South Essex Mental Health & Community Care NHS Trust*,[64] where there was psychiatric injury to one of the claimants from stress at work, apportionment was held inappropriate as it had not been shown by the employer, upon whom the burden lay, that the employee's illness was attributable in part to non-negligent stress.[65] And the Court of Appeal again recognised in *Harris v BRB (Residuary) Ltd*,[66] a case like *Thompson* of excessive noise at work causing deafness, that there could be apportionment of damages in appropriate circumstances, but none such had been either pleaded or proved by the employer defendant.[67] Moreover, apart from these cases of no apportionment on account of the lack of proof of causation, *Environment Agency v Ellis*,[68] shows that there are other reasons for denying apportionment. An injury to the claimant's back from an accident at work for which his employers were liable was exacerbated by

---

58 [2001] I.C.R. 942 CA at [31].

59 [1955] 1 W.L.R. 659; see the case at para.10-015, above.

60 [1955] 1 W.L.R. 659 at 668.

61 [2006] P.I.Q.R. Q2 CA at 40 (reported again at Q6, at 81).

62 [2005] EWCA Civ 452 CA.

63 [2005] EWCA Civ 452 CA at [24]–[27].

64 [2005] I.C.R. 782 CA.

65 [2005] I.C.R. 782 CA at [119]–[124].

66 [2005] I.C.R. 1680 CA.

67 [2005] I.C.R. 1680 CA at [84] to [87].

68 [2009] P.I.Q.R. P5 CA at 85.

his later fall from a ladder and his still later and more serious fall down stairs. Apportionment of the damages in respect of these two falls, which the trial judge had allowed, was held by the Court of Appeal to be inappropriate as what were referred to as "the *Holtby/Allen* principles" did not apply to single accident cases as distinct from cases of injury arising from successive exposures to harm.[69]

There have already been considered in the remoteness chapter in the context of causation a series of House of Lords decisions, all of which have concerned asbestos related disease and in all of which defendant employers were held liable for the total injury to their employee because material contribution was held to amount to causation.[70] In the first three, *Bonnington Castings Ltd v Wardlaw*,[71] *Nicholson v Atlas Steel Foundry and Engineering Co Ltd*,[72] and *McGhee v National Coal Board*,[73] there was a single employer and an exposure to the asbestos dust not between innocent and guilty on a time basis, as was the case in both *Crookall* and *Thompson*,[74] and again in *Rugby Joinery*,[75] but between a level of exposure which was innocent and a guilty excess, as in *Allen*.[76] In the fourth decision, *Fairchild v Glenhaven Funeral Services Ltd*,[77] there was, as in *Holtby*,[78] exposure taking place over a series of employments. It may then be asked why there was no talk of apportionment in any of these cases. The answer is simple. In none of them was there a claim for apportionment; all the defendants were arguing, though unsuccessfully, that they were not liable at all. And as Stuart-Smith LJ said in *Holtby*[79]: **10-019**

> "[A claimant] will be entitled to succeed if he can prove that the defendant's tortious conduct made a material contribution to his disability. But strictly speaking the defendant is liable only to the extent of that contribution. However, if the point is never raised or argued by the defendant, the claimant will succeed in full as in the *Bonnington* case and *McGhee*'s case."[80]

Could there now be apportionment in these cases in which full liability was imposed if the defendant employers argued for it? Here a vital distinction falls to be drawn between *Bonnington* and *Nicholson* on the one hand, in both of which the industrial disease was silicosis, and *McGhee* and *Fairchild* on the other, where the claimant contracted dermatitis in the first and mesothelioma in the second. Silicosis is a cumulative disease which becomes progressively more severe but, as explained earlier,[81] the dermatitis in *McGhee* might have come from a single abrasion and the mesothelioma in *Fairchild* from the inhalation of a single fibre, so that the disease is not progressive but may have taken hold at a particular point in time. Here we **10-020**

---

69 [2009] P.I.Q.R. P5 CA at [39].
70 See paras 8-017 and following, above, especially para.8-018.
71 [1956] A.C. 613.
72 [1957] 1 W.L.R. 613 HL.
73 [1973] 1 W.L.R. 1 HL.
74 At para.10-015, above.
75 At para.10-017, above.
76 At para.10-017, above.
77 [2003] 1 A.C. 32.
78 At para.10-016, above.
79 [2000] 3 All E.R. 421 CA at [20].
80 Lord Bingham and Lord Rodger in *Fairchild* simply noted that no argument on apportionment was addressed to the House or advanced without commenting upon how such an argument would have fared: [2003] 1 A.C. 32 at [34] and [125] respectively.
81 See para.8-018, above.

are presented with an indivisible injury[82] where it is difficult to argue for apportionment; whether there be one defendant or several, he or they will be taken to have caused the total injury.[83]

**10-021** The question of apportionment between several defendants in a mesothelioma case eventually had to be addressed by the House of Lords. In three appeals sub nom *Barker v Corus (UK) Plc*[84] from the Court of Appeal's rejection of apportionment[85] their Lordships held instead, with Lord Rodger dissenting, that defendants should not be liable, jointly and severally, for all the damage consequent upon the contraction of mesothelioma by the claimant but should be liable, severally, each for an aliquot share, apportioned according to the share of the risk created by the particular defendant's negligence. Their Lordships did not consider how the apportionment was to be worked out, as this would be a question of fact in each case, but indicated various factors upon which the assessment could depend; clearly relevant is the duration of the exposure for which a defendant was responsible but the intensity of the exposure could also play a part.[86]

**10-022** The difficulty that their Lordships faced in holding in favour of the apportionment result was that, if *Fairchild* and the crucial earlier *McGhee*, properly interpreted, had decided that materially increasing the risk of injury was no different from making a material contribution to the injury so that either was equivalent to causing it, then joint and several liability for the total injury would be the consequence. An analysis of the speeches in the two cases shows that there is much to be said for this interpretation and it was an interpretation for which the dissenting Lord Rodger strongly argued, thereby placing him on the side of joint and several liability. Nevertheless the rest of their Lordships were prepared to hold that the defendant's making a material increase in the risk of causing the injury did not

---

82 For indivisible injuries, see para.8-017, above.

83 And see the general discussion of all these issues, in the context not of industrial disease but of psychiatric, or physical, illness related to occupational stress, in *Hatton v Sutherland* [2002] 2 All E.R. 1 CA at [35] and following. Nothing said in this connection in *Hatton* is affected by *Barber v Somerset CC* [2004] 1 W.L.R. 1089 HL where the House of Lords allowed the further appeal of one of the appellants in the four conjoined appeals which had been heard earlier in the Court of Appeal under the *Hatton v Sutherland* title.

84 [2006] 2 A.C. 572.

85 Facts relating to the leading appeal at para.8-019, above.

86 *Heneghan v Manchester Dry Docks Ltd* [2014] EWHC 4190 (QB) was a claim brought on account of the death from lung cancer of a smoker who had been exposed to asbestos during his working life. The defendants were six of his employers over a period of some 10 years; earlier employers were not sued. It was agreed between the parties that the share of the deceased's exposure to asbestos attributable to the six employers sued was some 35 per cent; also agreed was the distribution of the exposures between the six. It was agreed by the medical experts that on the balance of probabilities it was the exposure to asbestos and not the smoking that caused the death. The issue to be decided was whether the defendants were each liable for the whole of the damage caused or for only the 35 per cent. In a long complex judgment, Jay J decided for the 35 per cent, applying the *Fairchild* principle together with the apportionment ruling in *Barker v Corus*. In contrast, Jay J refused to award damages in *Saunderson v Sonae Industria (UK) Ltd* [2015] EWHC 2264 (QB). In that case, group litigation was brought by thousands of claimants for personal injuries arising from negligence and public nuisance when fire broke out at the defendant's chemical plant in Kirkby. The plant was near the claimants' homes or workplaces. The claimants failed to establish liability. At [186], Jay J explained that the *Fairchild* principle meant that it was incumbent on the claimants to prove on the balance of probabilities that they were within the relevant envelope of material risk as that concept is properly understood. It is insufficient that there was a risk in the sense that the claimants had *some* exposure such as a minuscule exposure, measurable only in arts per trillion. The exposure must be at a level that was capable of causing personal injury.

constitute the causing of it so that, the basis of liability thereby becoming the creation of the risk, rather than the creation of the injury, the damage which the defendant was to be regarded as causing was only the creation of that risk, an interpretation which Lord Rodger considered to be fatally flawed. As Lord Hoffmann put it:

> "If that is the right way to characterise the damage [viz., the creation of the risk], then it does not matter that the disease as such would be indivisible damage. Chances are infinitely divisible and different people can be separately responsible to a greater or lesser degree for the chances of an event happening."[87]

This opened the door to making each defendant severally liable for a share of the damages rather than liable *in solidum* for the whole of the damages. It should be noted that it also opened the door, perhaps the side or back door, to loss of a chance[88] in personal injury cases, allowing it in for industrial disease while having in *Gregg v Scott*,[89] denied it entry for clinical injury.[90]

The decision in *Barker v Corus* was thus a substantial victory for defendants. It placed the risk of the insolvency of tortfeasors or their insurers not on the other tortfeasors or their insurers but upon the claimant himself. The victory has, however, proved to be short-lived as legislation reversing *Barker v Corus* for mesothelioma victims was speedily introduced, effectively upholding the position taken by the dissenting Lord Rodger in *Barker v Corus*. The relevant provision is to be found in the Compensation Act 2006. By an elaborate s.3 it is provided that any person liable in tort for exposing another to asbestos resulting in mesothelioma shall be liable for the whole damage and not just an aliquot part. This liability, subs.(2) makes clear, is irrespective of whether other exposure to asbestos was, to put it simply, guilty or innocent. It is then enacted, by subs.(3), that this does not prevent claims for contribution or findings of contributory negligence. The section continues, in subs.(4), to provide that between several defendants the court should base apportionment on the duration of the exposure for which each defendant is liable unless it thinks that another basis for determining contribution is more appropriate or the defendants have agreed the apportionment as between themselves. **10-023**

Two features of this legislation, of which it can be said one is more of principle and the other more of practice, call for attention. As to principle, the only industrial disease which is covered is mesothelioma. This means that for any other industrial disease which results in an indivisible injury—and it seems that the dermatitis in *McGhee* was so regarded in that case[91]—the House of Lords decision in *Barker v Corus* still stands, while apportionment continues to be possible for the far more common divisible injury because the disease is progressive, such as the vibration white finger in *Allen* and *Rugby Joinery*, the deafness in *Thompson*, the asbestos related disease in *Holtby*, the silicosis in *Crookhall*,[92] and now also the silicosis, **10-024**

---

87 [2006] 2 A.C. 572 at [35].

88 See Lord Walker's reference in *Barker v Corus* to "an analysis based on 'increase in risk' (or its mirror image 'loss of a chance')": at [114].

89 [2005] 2 A.C. 176.

90 Nevertheless Lord Walker in *Barker v Corus* said, after a reference to *Gregg v Scott*, that in his view the loss of chance principle in personal injury cases must be restricted to mesothelioma "and other conditions having the same distinctive aetiology and prognosis (such as the dermatitis caused by brick dust in *McGhee*)": [2006] 2 A.C. 572 at [114].

91 See the case at para.8-018, above; and see the previous note.

92 See all these cases at paras 10-015 to 10-017, above.

where no apportionment was claimed at the time, in *Bonnington* and *Nicholson*.[93] As to practice, s.3 of the Compensation Act 2006 continues with somewhat of an olive branch by stating that regulations may be made to provide compensation to defendants and their insurers where they are unable to obtain contribution from another defendant or that defendant's insurer, and regulations were speedily made.[94] It will be seen that this only assists a defendant where other defendants also liable are in the frame; where in a mesothelioma case the damage not attributable to a defendant is from an innocent source, or is for an innocent period, his liability for the whole damage remains unabated.

**10-025** In *Sienkiewicz v Greif (UK) Ltd*[95] the question was eventually raised of whether the *Fairchild* exception—as the rule is referred to by the Supreme Court in *Sienkiewicz*—applied where there is only one defendant responsible for exposure to asbestos, with the victim having been also at risk of developing mesothelioma from low level exposure to asbestos in the general atmosphere, referred to as environmental exposure. The Supreme Court sitting as a court of seven unanimously answered the question in the affirmative. As Lord Dyson put it:

> "In view of the present state of medical knowledge, a single exposure claim would founder on the same rock of uncertainty [a term taken from Lord Bingham in *Fairchild* and adopted throughout the speeches in *Sienkiewicz*] as a multiple exposure claim. The [*Fairchild*] exception was devised as a matter of policy to overcome the injustice that claimants would suffer if they were prevented by the rock of uncertainty from establishing causation in mesothelioma cases .... There is no reason in policy or principle why the exception should not apply to a single exposure claim just as it does to a multiple exposure claim."[96]

In Lord Brown's opinion there was simply no logical stopping place between the case of successive negligent employers and the case before the court.[97]

**10-026** The Court of Appeal[98] had taken the view that the test of causation to be applied was not whether the defendant's participation had materially increased the risk of contracting mesothelioma but whether the defendant's participation had at least doubled that risk. The court will have compared the low level environmental exposure to asbestos with the also light exposure by the single defendant of the office worker victim at its factory,[99] concluding it to be unfair to expose to liability a defendant whose contribution to the contracting of the disease could have been less

---

93 See these cases at paras 10-019 and 10-020, above.

94 By SI 2006/3259. Five whole subsections of s.3, subss.(7) to (11), are devoted to explaining how the regulations are to work. The regulations that have been made provide for the compensation to be paid by the scheme manager under the Financial Services Compensation Scheme established by Pt XV of the Financial Services and Markets Act 2000. How this scheme for compensation is working in practice is not known.

95 [2011] 2 A.C. 229.

96 [2011] 2 A.C. 229 at [212].

97 [2011] 2 A.C. 229 at [184]. The Court of Appeal had arrived at the same result in a curious way by construing s.3 of the Compensation Act 2006 (at para.10-023, above) as laying down that a person is liable in tort in all cases where he has materially increased the risk of contracting mesothelioma, an interpretation which was rightly regarded as wrong by the Supreme Court: see Lord Phillips and Lord Rodger at [2011] 2 A.C. 229 at [70] and [130]–[132] respectively.

98 [2010] Q.B. 370 CA.

99 The exposure was even lighter in *Willmore v Knowsley Metropolitan Borough Council*, the cojoined appeal, where the victim had been exposed to asbestos as a girl in the single defendant's school.

than that of the environment to which the whole world is exposed. The Supreme Court would have none of this. Lord Rodger insisted that a claimant need prove nothing more than material increase of the risk and that the doubling of the risk was irrelevant, adding that the Court of Appeal's purported guidance to the courts should not be followed.[100] At the same time the draconian consequences for an employer who has been responsible for only a small proportion of the overall exposure of a claimant to asbestos dust, or for his insurers, were recognised by Lord Phillips.[101] Lord Brown went further and doubted whether the special treatment given to mesothelioma cases was justified when it necessarily went so far as to apply, logically, to one negligent employer or negligent occupier unable to get any contribution from fellow tortfeasors,[102] concluding his speech by saying that he had difficulty in accepting that the courts should now

> "be thinking of creating any other special rules regarding the principles governing compensation for personal injury".

The rule that was adopted in *Reaney v University Hospital of North Staffordshire NHS Trust*,[103] is that the "but for" test for causation is displaced only in cases where there is a material contribution and there are gaps in medical science. **10-027**

## 5. Where it is Uncertain whether a Particular Pecuniary Loss will be or would have been Incurred

A pecuniary loss may also be difficult to assess because, like so much of loss for which damages are recoverable, it relates to the future, and is therefore necessarily contingent upon other factors. This covers a wide field, ranging from gains prevented by the defendant's wrong to expenses made necessary by the defendant's wrong.[104] There is generally less uncertainty about the latter: they are therefore dealt with first. **10-028**

### (1) Prospective expenses

Prospective expenses may reach so far into the future that they are difficult to assess, as in the case of medical treatment and nursing attendance where the claimant is severely disabled or disabled for life. In such circumstances the court will do its best to reach a fair assessment. Thus assessments in respect of medical care and treatment covering the rest of the claimant's life have frequently to be made.[105] **10-029**

If a particular expense has already been incurred but not yet paid by the claimant, the amount thereof may be included in the damages where the claimant is under a legal liability to pay the third party. Thus in *Mason v Barker*,[106] where a penalty had been paid in order to bring about the release of the claimant from a false **10-030**

---

100 [2011] 2 A.C. 229 at [161].

101 [2011] 2 A.C. 229 at [58].

102 [2011] 2 A.C. 229 at [184].

103 [2015] EWCA Civ 1119 at [35]. But see para.8-023, above.

104 This useful division is considered in detail in Ch.4, above.

105 As in, e.g. *Roach v Yates* [1938] 1 K.B. 256 CA; *Lim Poh Choo v Camden and Islington Area Health Authority* [1980] A.C. 174; *Thomas v Wignall* [1987] Q.B. 1098 CA; *Hunt v Severs* [1994] 2 A.C. 350; and a thousand more cases.

106 (1843) 1 C. & K. 200.

imprisonment, it was held that the claimant could recover as damages the amount so paid whether it had been paid by himself or by some third party whom he was liable to reimburse. In *Randall v Raper*,[107] where the claimant buyer had been sued by his sub-buyer for damages, he recovered this amount from his seller although he had not paid the sub-buyer.[108] A further and modern illustration of a sale and sub-sale of goods, here of a cargo of gasoline in defective condition, is provided by *Total Liban SA v Vitol Energy SA*.[109] Should, however, it be clear and certain that the liability will never be discharged, and the expense never paid, by the claimant, recovery will be denied him so as to avoid his reaping a windfall; it was so held in *Biffa Waste Services Ltd v Maschinenfabrik Ernst Hese GmbH*.[110]

**10-031** Where the claimant had incurred not a legal but only a moral liability to pay the particular expense, it was at first held, in *Dixon v Bell*,[111] that the amount thereof could not be included in the damages. The expense in question was a medical one, that of a physician's fees, payment of which could not at that time be legally enforced by the physician. In *Allen v Waters*,[112] the claimant had incurred but had not paid hospital fees, and, while the majority of the Court of Appeal included the amount of these in the damages because they held that the claimant was legally liable to pay them, Goddard LJ similarly included them although he held that the hospital's claim against the claimant for the fees was barred by lapse of time. In *Donnelly v Joyce*,[113] the Court of Appeal expressed some difficulty in discovering the true ratio decidendi of this decision,[114] but made it clear that, however an injured claimant's medical expenses were financed, he was entitled to recovery in respect of them, and whether he had any liability, legal or simply moral, to repay anyone in respect of them was immaterial. In *Dennis v L.P.T.B.*,[115] where lost earnings rather than medical expenses were in issue, and where the moral obligation to pay the third party arose only if, and not until, the lost earnings were awarded in the claimant's damages, Denning J utilised the power, which he considered that the court had, to direct that the amount, when received by the claimant, be held by him under an obligation to pay it over to the third party. However, the law has moved on since these decisions so that it would seem that the issues need no longer concern us; certainly since *Browning v War Office*,[116] wages paid and payable are deductible from the claimant's damages[117] and *Hunt v Severs*,[118] has decided that damages

---

107 (1858) E.B. & E. 84.

108 A similar result was reached about the same time in *Smith v Howell* (1851) 6 Exch. 730 where, however, the action was not for damages but was an action on an indemnity. The claimant lessee assigned his lease to the defendant, taking an indemnity against all "costs, damages, and expenses which he might incur" from breaches by the assignee of the covenants in the lease. The assignee did commit breaches, for which the claimant was sued by his lessor and judgment recovered against him by default. It was held that he might recover the amount of the damages and the costs of the judgment by default, in an action on the indemnity, though he had not yet paid them himself.

109 [1999] 2 Lloyd's Rep. 700.

110 [2009] P.N.L.R.1 at 1.

111 (1816) 1 Stark. 287.

112 [1935] 1 K.B. 200 CA.

113 [1974] Q.B. 454 CA.

114 [1974] Q.B. 454 CA at 466H to 467B.

115 [1948] 1 All E.R. 779.

116 [1963] 1 Q.B. 750 CA.

117 See para.40-152, below.

118 [1994] 2 A.C. 350.

awarded to the claimant for his gratuitous care are to be held in trust for the carer.[119] The possible appearance of moral obligations to pay has thus evaporated, with the claimant either unentitled initially to receive the benefit by way of damages or required to pass the benefit on to its provider.

If a particular expense may or may not be incurred in the future, different techniques have been adopted to deal with the situation where the expense consists of damages that a buyer or seller might have to pay to his own buyer or seller. In *Household Machines v Cosmos Exporters*,[120] the claimant was held entitled to a declaration of indemnity limited to such damages as in law were due from the defendant to the claimant in respect of damages which the claimant might be held liable to pay and/or might reasonably pay in respect of the discharge of his legal liability to his sub-buyer. But in *Trans Trust S.P.R.L. v Danubian Trading Co*,[121] the Court of Appeal did not approve the awarding of a declaration in the converse situation where a claimant seller was claiming from his buyer the amount by which he might be liable over to his own seller. This view, however, was obiter, since the court held that in the circumstances the damage was too remote. Denning LJ said: **10-032**

> "If the liability of the sellers to a third party were within the contemplation of the parties, but had not yet been assessed, then the proper course for the judge was to reserve that head of damages. Judgment could be entered for the damages already ascertained, leaving the rest to be ascertained later by the same or another judge."[122]

And Somervell LJ, after pointing out that difficult questions might arise in quantifying the damage, depending, for example, on variation of the terms between contract and sub-contract and on the question of whether the sub-contractee had mitigated, said:

> "No declarations ought to prejudice or preclude a proper determination of these issues, on which the defendants should be entitled to be heard. It might be more satisfactory if there were liberty to apply for directions as to the determination of these issues, if any, and quantification of damages under this head as between plaintiffs and defendants, should disputes arise. Some order in this form, at any rate in some cases, might be more satisfactory than a declaration in the form ordered."[123]

In *Deeny v Gooda Walker*[124] Phillips J adopted the view of the Court of Appeal in the *Trans Trust*[125] case and expressly applied it so as to defer dealing with the claimants' future losses until the extent of these had been determined.[126] Today a somewhat greater preparedness generally to postpone the adjudication on issues of damages is appearing. This was done in *A v National Blood Authority*,[127] where it was anticipated, in a case of hepatitis infection, that further medical treatment would be required, but it is important to know that the judge had taken the course of

---

119 However, it is not thought that family carers are paying much attention to their apparent trust entitlement. See paras 40-228 and 40-229, below for details.

120 [1947] 1 K.B. 217.

121 [1952] 2 Q.B. 297 CA: facts at para.25-133, below.

122 [1952] 2 Q.B. 297 CA at 307.

123 [1952] 2 Q.B. 297 CA at 303.

124 [1995] 1 W.L.R. 1206.

125 [1952] 2 Q.B. 297 CA: facts at para.25-133, below.

126 See para.10-039, below.

127 [2002] Lloyd's Rep. Med. 487.

postponing assessment at the invitation of the parties.[128] In *Browning v Brachers*,[129] where the damages included costs assessed some years earlier against the claimants in another action,[130] costs that the claimants might never be required to pay as there had been no attempt at their enforcement to date, the court considered that the best course was to order the defendant to indemnify the claimants should the costs be pursued and payment of them by the claimants follow.[131] In *Adan v Securicor Custodial Services Ltd*,[132] the court would not agree to postponing the adjudication of damages where there was a largely speculative chance that the injured claimant might cease to be mentally impaired and in the care of and at the expense of the State, and be returned to the community in need of extensive care and accommodation. Here the uncertainty was not as to the quantification of the expenses as an established head of loss but as to whether the loss would come about at all.[133] By contrast, in *Cook v Cook*,[134] the same judge as in *Adan*, because the long-term outcome for the child claimant, injured from birth, was so uncertain and speculative, postponed the adjudication of future loss until she reached the age of 16 when the court would be in a far better position to assess her needs in adult life.[135] In *Markel International Insurance Co Ltd v Surety Guarantee Consultants Ltd*,[136] where, arising out of a claim for conspiracy to defraud, claimants had been exposed to liabilities on surety bonds, it was not disputed that they were entitled to an indemnity in respect of future claims by beneficiaries of the bonds.[137] Thus the law in this area appears to be developing with the lines not yet settled. All these comparatively recent cases, indeed all the cases since *Trans Trust* in the middle of the last century, have been decisions at first instance on this issue, and a ruling from the Court of Appeal is overdue.

## (2) Prospective earnings

**10-033** Claims for loss of prospective earnings arise every day in personal injury cases, and two factors militate against any exactness in the assessment of the loss, namely the uncertainty as to the precise length of time that the claimant's disability will last, and the uncertainty as to the precise pattern that the claimant's future earnings would, but for the injury, have taken. Neither of these uncertainties prevents the court from making an assessment of the probable loss. Similar difficulties are also surmounted daily in claims for loss of support in fatal injury cases, since the calculation of lost support is based upon what the deceased would have earned over the years if he had lived. How precisely the courts make their calculation in these two types of claim is dealt with later.[138]

---

[128] On this see the case in more detail at para.52-045, below together with CPR r.3.1(2) cited there.
[129] [2004] P.N.L.R. 28 at 517.
[130] Facts at para.10-096, below.
[131] This holding was not challenged in the appeal: see [2005] EWCA Civ 753 CA at [149].
[132] [2005] P.I.Q.R. P6 at 79.
[133] See at [2005] P.I.Q.R. P6 at [23].
[134] [2011] EWHC 1638 (QB).
[135] For a criticism of the result in *Cook v Cook*, see para.52-045, below.
[136] [2008] EWHC 3087 (Comm).
[137] [2008] EWHC 3087 (Comm) at [8].
[138] In relation to loss of a chance, the assessment of prospective earnings in personal injury cases is given extended consideration at paras 10-082 and following, below. For personal injury claims generally, see paras 40-066 and following, below, for fatal injury claims, paras 41-038 and following, below.

### (3) Loss of general business and professional profits

*Ratcliffe v Evans*,[139] is the leading case which deals with the question of the degree of certainty that must be shown where loss of general business or professional profits is alleged. The Court of Appeal, speaking of slander, recognised that substantial damages might be awarded in those cases **10-034**

> "where a general loss of custom is the natural and direct result of the slander and where it is not possible to specify particular instances of the loss".[140]

The case itself was one of injurious falsehood, and the court directed its conclusions to all actions on the case where damage is the gist of the action[141]; indeed these conclusions apply with equal force to all cases of loss of profits.

An interesting example is loss of profits through loss of the publicity which the defendant has contracted to afford the claimant. This has been adjudicated upon in two situations. (1) It has been held that an actor,[142] wrongfully dismissed, may recover damages for the loss of the opportunity of enhancing or maintaining his reputation[143]: what the court is calculating is the amount of professional profits lost by being deprived of "the opportunity to play in public some part which will attract attention".[144] (2) Where the defendant has failed to advertise the claimant's business, the contract being one to advertise, the claimant may recover the amount of business profits lost although the estimate must necessarily be approximate. The authority for this is *Marcus v Myers*.[145] The claimant, a ladies' tailor, contracted with the defendants, the proprietors and publishers of a weekly newspaper called the *Jewish Chronicle*, for 52 successive insertions over a year on the front page of the newspaper. The claimant, having no means of window display, had to rely on advertising as the only way of attracting customers. The contract to advertise was made in consequence of the great success of a previous contract for 13 successive insertions in the paper, the claimant being the only ladies' tailor who advertised therein and the paper being the special journal of the prosperous Jewish world. The defendants, in breach of contract, discontinued the advertisement in the course of the year, and from then the claimant's business fell off and he did not gain a single new Jewish customer. It was held that the evidence of the loss of business, which was not accounted for in any other way, was proper for the consideration of the jury in estimating damages. **10-035**

Recovery for loss of profits of fishing, where the defendant has tortiously destroyed the claimant's fishing vessel, has been refused in three cases, *The Columbus*,[146] *The City of Rome*,[147] and *The Anselma de Larrinaga*.[148] The first two **10-036**

---

139 [1892] 2 Q.B. 524 CA.

140 [1892] 2 Q.B. 524 CA at 531.

141 See the quotation from the case at para.10-002, above.

142 Also the author of a screen play entitled to a screen credit: *Tolnay v Criterion Films* [1936] 2 All E.R. 1625.

143 *Marbé v George Edwardes* [1928] 1 K.B. 269 CA; *Clayton v Oliver* [1930] A.C. 209; See *Withers v General Theatre Corp* [1933] 2 K.B. 536 CA. The cases are fully considered at para.33-028, below; see too, at para.33-030, below, apprentice's loss of future prospects through loss of training.

144 The phrase is Greer LJ's in *Withers v General Theatre Corp* [1933] 2 K.B. 536 CA at 554. The *Withers* limitation to damage to an already existing reputation was abandoned in *Mahmud v Bank of Credit and Commerce International SA* [1998] A.C. 20: see para.33-028, below.

145 (1895) 11 T.L.R. 327.

146 (1849) 3 W. Rob. (Adm.) 158.

were decided at a time when it was thought that no loss of profits was recoverable upon the tortious destruction of a ship; the third distinguished the authorities allowing loss of profits from charterparties on the ground of

> "there being a contract for an ascertainable amount—a very different thing from the speculative question of the possibility of catching fish".[149]

It is submitted elsewhere[150] that after *Liesbosch Dredger v S.S. Edison*,[151] with its calculation of the value of the ship to her owner as a going concern, these decisions are dubious. On the particular issue of whether the loss of fishing is too speculative and uncertain, the principles considered here show that this is an argument which has little merit when it is directed to a refusal to give any damages at all for loss of profits. However, in *Bailey & Co v Balholm Securities*,[152] Kerr J thought that the cases showed recovery by a trader only where he had lost the opportunity of being better off without being exposed to the risk of being worse off, and that a person who had been prevented from speculating in commodity futures, as the claimant there alleged he had been, may have lost the chance of making money or may have been saved from losing money. The loss of a general opportunity to trade was, in his view, much too speculative to allow a money value to be placed on it.[153]

**10-037** A very different result to that in *Bailey v Balholm* was arrived at in *Parabola Investments Ltd v Browallia Cal Ltd*.[154] An individual trader through a company, the claimant, which had been set up by him for trading in stocks, shares and derivatives had for more than 10 years consistently made profits from his trading, profits sometimes of a spectacular nature, until for a period of about seven months he was defrauded by a broker employed by the defendant financial institution. The fraud took the form of misrepresenting that the trader was trading profitably and misrepresenting the size of the trading fund. Over the seven months the fund was depleted by several million pounds. The claimant company maintained that it was entitled to the substantial profits that would have been made had the amount by which the fund had been depleted been available for trading, both during the months while the fraud continued and during the much longer period from discovery of the fraud to trial. The defendant maintained that it should not be liable for more than the restoration of the trading fund plus interest, on the ground that the profits claimed were speculative. Flaux J had decided in the claimant's favour, pointing out that the defendant's submissions that the claimant needed to prove that a specific amount of profits would have been earned was flawed since precise calculation was impossible.[155] Beyond this he took the entirely proper view that the trader's past success had been a matter not of luck but of astuteness and the Court of Appeal saw no reason to interfere with his quantification of the claimant's loss of profits.[156]

**10-038** Recovery for loss of business profits again successfully featured in *Vasiliou v*

[147] (1887) 8 Asp. M.L.C. 542n.
[148] (1913) 29 T.L.R. 587.
[149] (1913) 29 T.L.R. 587.
[150] See paras 37-071 to 37-076, below.
[151] [1933] A.C. 449.
[152] [1973] 2 Lloyd's Rep. 404.
[153] [1973] 2 Lloyd's Rep. 404 at 416.
[154] [2011] Q.B. 477 CA.
[155] [2011] Q.B. 477 CA at [20] to [22].
[156] [2011] Q.B. 477 CA at [25].

*Hajigeorgiou*.[157] The claimant had leased premises from the defendant for use as a restaurant and breaches by the defendant of the covenant of quiet enjoyment had made it impossible for the claimant to trade for two periods of time. The trial judge found the claimant to be an accomplished restaurateur whose restaurant would be successful and assessed his loss of profits on that basis, arriving, with the assistance of expert evidence, at an assessment of expected turnover, gross and net profit, and rate of growth. In upholding the award, the Court of Appeal confirmed that the judge had been right not to apply a discount, for which the defendant had contended, to recognise the chance that the restaurant might not have been successful. To do so would have been inconsistent with the judge's finding that the restaurant would be a success.[158]

As with prospective expenses[159] it may be possible, though exceptional, to postpone a decision on the loss of prospective business and professional profits. This was done in *Deeny v Gooda Walker*.[160] The claimants were Lloyd's Names suing in respect of their liability on insurance claims which adversely affected their profits. The defendants' application to have postponed that proportion of the damages which represented future claims was granted, Phillips J considering that the special features of the Lloyd's litigation, which included the difficulty of assessment, favoured awarding damages in respect of the claimants' underwriting losses only when they were sustained.[161] **10-039**

## (4) Loss of a chance

**(a) The development of the law** It is the famous decision in *Chaplin v Hicks*,[162] which is generally regarded as having introduced the loss of a chance doctrine into the law of England. A well-known actor and theatrical manager of the day, Seymour Hicks, devised a competition, which he advertised in a newspaper, offering engagements as actresses to the 12 contestants selected by the votes of readers of the newspaper. Readers were invited to select those whom they considered the most beautiful from the contestants' photographs which were to be published in the paper. Because the response was so great, with some 6,000 applications, the conditions had to be changed. Seymour Hicks was to select 300 from the 6,000, the newspaper readers were then to vote on the 300 from their photographs, and from the 50 who got the most votes Mr Hicks was to interview and choose the 12 winners. Miss Chaplin succeeded in becoming one of the 50 finalists but, in breach of contract, she was not given adequate notice of the interviews and the 12 winners were chosen in her absence. The jury awarded £100, the equivalent of some £8,000 today, and the Court of Appeal upheld the award. Vaughan Williams LJ said that he was unable to agree with the contention that in a case which involved so many contingencies it was impossible to say what was the claimant's pecuniary loss. He agreed that **10-040**

> "the presence of all the contingencies upon which the gaining of the prize might depend makes the calculation not only difficult but incapable of being carried out with certainty or precision"

---

157 [2010] EWCA Civ 1475 CA.

158 See in particular Patten LJ.s excellent analysis at paras 15 and following.

159 See para.10-032, above.

160 [1995] 1 W.L.R. 1206.

161 See the case further at para.52-044, below and CPR r.3.1(2) cited at para.52-045, below.

162 [1911] 2 K.B. 786 CA.

but wished

> "to deny with emphasis that, because precision cannot be arrived at, the jury has no function in the assessment of damages".[163]

**10-041** It has been well said[164] that the theatre impresario when he launched his competition for aspiring actresses can have had no idea that he was opening a legal Pandora's box. For the cases show that, since the opening salvo in *Chaplin v Hicks*, loss of a chance has moved in all directions, backwards and forwards. Just as Burroughs J famously said in *Richardson v Mellish*,[165] of public policy that

> "it is a very unruly horse and when you get astride it you never know where it will carry you",[166]

the same could well be said of loss of a chance. It is therefore worth summarising, in advance of going to the detail of the cases, the century of development of the loss of a chance idea that we have seen.

**10-042** For some decades after *Chaplin v Hicks* loss of a chance remained quiescent; no evil spirit flew out of Pandora's box. Then in the 1950s a number of cases pushed the idea forward, each of which concerned the all too common negligent solicitor and the most important of which was *Kitchen v Royal Air Force Association*,[167] in the Court of Appeal, the first of the cases of personal injury or wrongful death claims becoming statute-barred because of a solicitor's failure to issue a writ in time. Loss of a chance moved quietly on till it took a setback with the refusal of the House of Lords to apply it to personal injury in *Hotson v East Berkshire Area Health Authority*,[168] where but for negligent delay in diagnosis of a schoolboy's hip injury there would have been a 25 per cent chance of averting a disability made inevitable by the late diagnosis. Soon after, loss of a chance in its original domain appeared to take a giant leap forward by its being allowed by *Allied Maples v Simmons & Simmons*,[169] another key case, to range over the whole territory of dependency on the acts of third parties. Next a favourable appearance was made in the context of loss of earnings claims by the physically injured, with claimants being held entitled to damages for the loss of the chance, in *Doyle v Wallace*,[170] of becoming a drama teacher and in *Langford v Hebran*,[171] of all sorts of careers other than that of professional boxer now denied by the injury.[172] However, the House of Lords was again unprepared to allow recovery for loss of a chance in personal injury in *Gregg v Scott*,[173] where there was delay in the diagnosis of a malignant lymphoma which reduced the chance of cure by 17 per cent. In interesting contrast there is the

163 [1911] 2 K.B. 786 CA at 791 to 792.
164 By Lord Neuberger in an address to the Professional Negligence Bar Association on Loss of a Chance in 2005.
165 (1824) 2 Bing. 229.
166 (1824) 2 Bing. 229 at 252.
167 [1958] 1 W.L.R. 563 CA.
168 [1987] A.C. 750.
169 [1995] 1 W.L.R. 1602 CA.
170 [1998] P.I.Q.R. Q146 CA.
171 [2001] P.I.Q.R. Q13 CA at 160.
172 In *Clarke v Maltby* [2010] EWHC 1201 (QB) it was the loss of the chance of progressing up the solicitor ladder that was in issue.
173 [2005] 2 A.C. 176.

later House of Lords decision in *Barker v Corus (UK) Ltd*,[174] where employers who had negligently exposed a workman to asbestos dust leading to mesothelioma were held severally, and not jointly, liable which meant that each was being held liable for making a material increase in the risk of injury; the personal injury damages awarded were therefore effectively for loss of a chance.

**(b) The range of the loss of a chance doctrine: general principles** Before turning to the authorities which in modern times have cascaded over the law reports, it is important to address the question, which has much troubled the courts, of how wide ranging is the loss of a chance doctrine. In short, when does a claimant have to prove on a balance of probabilities that a particular result would have come about and when need he prove only that a chance, which may be less than a probability, of achieving that particular result has been lost. The distinction is of immense importance, separating as it does the cases where the claimant will be awarded all or nothing and the cases where a percentage of loss will come his way. **10-043**

*(i) The distinction between past events and future events* The first distinction to which one must have regard appears most clearly in an important passage of Lord Reid's speech in *Davies v Taylor*,[175] where he said: **10-044**

> "When the question is whether a certain thing is or is not true—whether a certain event did or did not happen—then the court must decide one way or the other. There is no question of chance or probability. Either it did or it did not happen. But the standard of civil proof is a balance of probabilities. If the evidence shows a balance in favour of it having happened, then it is proved that it did in fact happen."[176]

He continued:

> "You can prove that a past event happened, but you cannot prove that a future event will happen and I do not think that the law is so foolish as to suppose that you can. All that you can do is to evaluate the chance. Sometimes it is virtually 100 per cent: sometimes virtually nil. But often it is somewhere in between. And if it somewhere in between I do not see much difference between a probability of 51 per cent and a probability of 49 per cent."[177]

Also important is the similar passage from the speech of Lord Diplock a few years earlier in *Mallett v McMonagle*.[178] He there said:

> "The role of the court in making an assessment of damages which depends on its view as to what will be and what would have been is to be contrasted with its ordinary function in civil actions of determining what was. In determining what did happen in the past a court decides on the balance of probabilities. Anything that is more probable than not it treats as certain. But in assessing damages which depend on its view as to what will happen in the future or would have happened in the future if something had not happened in the past, the court must make an estimate as to what are the chances that a particular thing

174 [2006] 2 A.C. 572.
175 [1974] A.C. 207.
176 [1974] A.C. 207 at 213.
177 [1974] A.C. 207 at 213.
178 [1970] A.C. 166.

will or would have happened and reflect those chances, whether they are more or less than even, in the amount of damages it awards."[179]

10-045 With matters past, therefore, the court has to determine on the balance of probabilities whether the defendant's act caused the claimant's loss, and if the answer is in the affirmative there is full recovery, while if in the negative there is none. It is this that explains the decision of the House of Lords against the claimant schoolboy in *Hotson v East Berkshire Area Health Authority*.[180] A hip injury which he incurred in a school accident was through negligence not diagnosed by the defendant hospital authority until five days had elapsed. Had the correct diagnosis been made immediately, with consequent appropriate treatment, there remained a 75 per cent risk of the claimant schoolboy's disability developing, but the defendants' breach of duty had turned that risk into an inevitability. The defendants contended that damages for loss of the 25 per cent chance of avoiding the disability were not claimable since the claimant had not shown that on the balance of probabilities the negligence had caused the disability. The House of Lords upheld this contention, exonerating the defendants entirely from liability for the claimant's disability on the basis that its sole cause had been the original accident so that no loss of a chance was caused to the claimant by the defendants' subsequent negligence. Lord Mackay said:

> "The fundamental question of fact to be answered in this case related to a point in time before the negligent failure to treat began. It must, therefore, be a matter of past fact. It did not raise any question of what might have been the situation in a hypothetical state of facts."[181]

Later in his speech he said:

> "The judge's findings in fact mean that the sole cause of the plaintiff's avascular necrosis was the injury he sustained in the original fall, and that implies … that when he arrived at the hospital for the first time he had no chance of avoiding it. Accordingly, the subsequent negligence of the authority did not cause him the loss of such a chance."[182]

10-046 *(ii) The distinction between causation of loss and quantification of loss* This second, equally important, distinction is related to the first, that between past and future events. When we are looking at past events we are necessarily in the realm of causation; the test is balance of probabilities and chances just do not matter. But when we are looking to the future we are concerned with the quantification of loss and here chances are all-important; an assessment of damages is entitled, indeed is required, to take into account all manner of risks and possibilities. The passages from Lord Reid and Lord Diplock already quoted[183] bring this out clearly. It is therefore the case that a loss of a chance, and its assessment, is frequently involved in the quantification process, and this has always been so and long before *Chaplin v Hicks* was decided.

---

179 [1970] A.C. 166 at 176E to G. There are similar, more recent comments to the same effect and again at the highest level but they add nothing to these classic statements of Lords Reid and Diplock.

180 [1987] A.C. 750.

181 [1987] A.C. 750 at 785D.

182 [1987] A.C. 750 at 789M.

183 At para.10-044, above.

It is submitted that losses of a chance appearing in the process of quantification do not fall within the loss of a chance doctrine. Loss of a chance proper, as it may be termed, has a more limited field. It comes in before we get to quantification; indeed it comes in at the causation stage. How is this? It is because there are situations where the law has recognised, and has treated, the loss of a chance as a form of loss, an identifiable head of loss in itself. To take Lord Hoffmann's way of putting it in *Barker v Corus (UK) Ltd*,[184] **10-047**

> "the law treats the loss of a chance of a favourable outcome as compensatable damage in itself".[185]

Causation is then established by showing that the claimant has lost the chance and showing this on the balance of probabilities. This then makes for three stages in the enquiry: first, it must be ascertained whether loss of a chance is recognised as a head of damage or loss in itself; secondly, it must be shown that on the balance of probabilities the claimant has lost the particular chance; thirdly, the lost chance must be quantified by resort to percentages and proportions.[186]

The circumstances in which the law is prepared to recognise the loss of a chance as itself an identifiable head of loss, as itself constituting compensatable damage, are when the provision of the chance is the object of the duty that has been breached. This comes out clearly in *Chaplin v Hicks* itself where Fletcher Moulton LJ emphasised that **10-048**

> "the very object and scope of the contract were to give the plaintiff the chance of being selected a prize-winner".[187]

An alternative formulation is that it can be said that the essence of the breach of duty is that it deprives the claimant of the chance or opportunity of securing a favourable outcome. All this can be tested against the cases. Miss Chaplin was deprived of the opportunity of winning the competition. In *Hall v Meyrick*,[188] the first case after *Chaplin* properly involving loss of a chance, the solicitor's failure to warn his client that her marriage to the man who had made a will in her favour would revoke it lost her the opportunity to take corrective action by securing a new will. In *Kitchen v Royal Air Force Association*,[189] the widow was deprived of the chance of succeeding in her Fatal Accidents Act claim which was within the object of the solicitor's retainer. In *Spring v Guardian Assurance Plc*,[190] where a bad refer-

---

184 [2006] 2 A.C. 572. This difficult case is considered at paras 10-021 and 10-022, above and para.10-056, below

185 [2006] 2 A.C. 572 at [36].

186 What Toulson LJ convincingly says at [23] of his judgment in *Parabola Investments Ltd v Browallia Cal Ltd* [2011] Q.B. 477 CA. (facts at para.10-037, above) and what Patten LJ equally convincingly says at [25] of his judgment in *Vasiliou v Hajigeorgiou* [2010] EWCA Civ 1475 CA (facts at para.10-038, above) fully support the analysis set out here. The term "loss of a chance proper" is there used; while Patten LJ has "loss of chance as such". See too, in *AerCap Partners Ltd v Avia Asset Management AB* [2010] EWHC 2431 (Comm), Gross LJ's exploration of the distinction between all or nothing causation and percentage loss of a chance in relation to an issue where there was no hope of loss of a chance applying: [2010] EWHC 2431 (Comm) at [70]–[77], especially the detailed [76].

187 [1911] 2 K.B. 786 CA at 795.

188 [1957] 2 Q.B. 455.

189 [1958] 1 W.L.R. 563 CA.

190 [1995] 2 A.C. 296.

ence had been negligently given to a potential employer by the employee's former employer and it was said—by way of dictum[191] as their Lordships were dealing with duty of care—that the employee need only show that he had lost a reasonable chance of employment and not that he *would* have been employed; the object of the duty breached was to give the employee the chance of being employed by the person receiving the reference. As for *Allied Maples v Simmons & Simmons*,[192] a key decision in this area yet to be considered,[193] where the solicitor, advising on the purchase of certain properties, failed to secure the purchaser from certain onerous liabilities, the essence of the breach of duty was that it deprived the purchaser of the chance of avoiding a liability, rather than of securing a benefit, and it was within the object of the solicitor's retainer to ensure that his client had that chance.[194] Indeed the result of negligence by a solicitor will, perhaps invariably, be to deprive his client of the chance or opportunity of securing a favourable outcome in the matter with which the solicitor is dealing, making this the archetypal illustration of loss of a chance in its proper sphere. And in a case well before professional negligence claims became frequent, *Domine v Grimsdall*,[195] we have another illustration of loss of a chance proper. The claimant issued execution against a judgment debtor and the defendant bailiff seized some of the debtor's furniture for an execution sale but improperly did not remove it from the debtor's premises. For this default of the defendant the claimant recovered for the loss of the chance that the debtor might have made a payment on account of the debt to prevent the removal of the furniture. The very object of the defendant's duty was the protection of the claimant's security.

**10-049** Contingencies and chances have to be taken into account as much in quantification cases as in pure loss of a chance cases, but cases where the consideration of lost chances and lost opportunities comes in only at the quantification level and which therefore have nothing to do with causation are not cases of loss of a chance proper. Yet the Court of Appeal appears to have started to look at them as such in the personal injury field, and at a time when the House of Lords decision in *Hotson* outlawing loss of a chance proper from personal injury undoubtedly ruled the day.[196] It started with *Doyle v Wallace*,[197] where the young claimant had aimed to qualify and be employed as a drama teacher, failing which she would have had to settle for less remunerative clerical or administrative work. It continued with the much more complicated *Langford v Hebran*,[198] the complications being due to the fact that, whereas in *Doyle* there were only two potential careers envisaged, in *Langford* there was a whole series of career options put forward for consideration for a young, highly successful professional boxer.[199] Although loss of a chance was utilised in both cases in assessing the loss of earning capacity, this was pure quantification of damages. To the extent that there has to be a discounting when a chance is lost, the chance here is generally assessed by resort to the familiar discount for the

---

191 [1995] 2 A.C. 296 at 327F to G, per Lord Lowry.
192 [1995] 1 W.L.R. 1602 CA.
193 See paras 10-058 to 10-060, below.
194 Stuart Smith LJ in his definitive judgment said, at [[1995] 1 W.L.R. 1602 CA at 1613E, that he agreed with Lord Lowry's dictum in Spring.
195 [1937] 2 All E.R. 119.
196 *Hotson* is at para.10-045, above.
197 [1998] P.I.Q.R. Q146 CA.
198 [2001] P.I.Q.R. Q13 CA at 160.
199 And see too *Clarke v Maltby* [2010] EWHC 1201 (QB) where a career in only one field had to be considered.

contingencies of life, and *Doyle* and *Langford* can be regarded simply as cases of contingencies writ large. They are not cases of loss of a chance proper. How far indeed it is necessary or appropriate to resort to the use of loss of a chance percentages in the quantification process in personal injury will be considered in some detail when we turn to particular types of cases involving losses of a chance.[200]

Cases in other fields can be found that should be regarded as quantification cases and not cases of loss of a chance proper.[201] *Blue Circle Industries v Ministry of Defence*,[202] is a good illustration. Property was damaged through nuclear activity, rendering it unsalable until remedial work was carried out. The recovery by the owner for the loss of the opportunity to make a profitable sale lay well within the principles of quantification. The damage was to the property and the result of this damage was the inability to sell it; as Chadwick LJ said, the "loss of opportunity was the direct result of the contamination".[203] The early case of *Richardson v Mellish*,[204] is also a quantification case.[205] The defendant employed the claimant to command a ship which was chartered by the defendant to the East India Company for two voyages. In an action for failing to implement the contract, the defendant argued that he was liable in damages for what the claimant would have earned on the first voyage only, because it was in the discretion of the East India Company not to allow the claimant to command the ship on the second voyage, but the argument was unsuccessful because the company generally permitted the renewal of such appointments. Here it was the loss of the captaincy which had to be quantified.[206] **10-050**

200 See paras 10-069 and following below.

201 The damages in *IRT Oil and Gas Ltd v Fiber Optic Systems Technology (Canada) Inc* [2009] EWHC 3041 (QB) undoubtedly fell into the quantification category: see the case at para.10-005, above. As for *Amalgamated Metal Corp Plc v Wragge & Co* [2011] EWHC 887 (Comm), where solicitors were sued for settling without authority at too low a figure their client's claim against the tax authorities in respect of advance corporation tax which should not have been paid to them, assessment of damages on a loss of a chance basis was out of the question: see [2011] EWHC 887 (Comm) at [119] and following.

202 [1999] Ch. 289 CA.

203 [1999] Ch. 289 CA at 315F.

204 (1824) 2 Bing. 229.

205 While *Richardson v Mellish* was cited in *Chaplin v Hicks* [1911] 2 K.B. 786 CA, this was simply in support of the proposition that "the existence of a contingency, which is dependent on the volition of a third person, is not enough to justify us in saying that the damages are incapable of assessment" ([1911] 2 K.B. 786 CA at 799, per Farwell LJ), the case of Richardson being "obviously in the teeth of" the contrary proposition ([1911] 2 K.B. 786 CA at 794, per Fletcher-Moulton LJ).

206 Three other early cases should be kept in mind for their dicta indicating that there can be no recovery for lost chances, dicta which must now be regarded as wrong. They seem to be all quantification of loss cases rather than causation of loss cases. The first is *Watson v Ambergate Ry* (1851) 15 Jur. 448. A prize had been offered for the best model of a machine for loading barges and the claimant sent one by the defendant's railway. It arrived too late and the claimant lost his chance of the prize. Clearly this loss was too remote under the rule in *Hadley v Baxendale*, then undecided, but Erle J's "great doubts whether that chance was not too contingent and remote to be the subject of damages" (at 450) can no longer be indorsed so far as the issue of certainty goes. In *Sapwell v Bass* [1910] 2 K.B. 486, the defendant contracted that his stallion should serve one of the brood mares of the claimant, a breeder of racehorses, during the following season. Before this time arrived the defendant disabled himself from performance by selling the stallion to a third party. The claimant claimed for the loss of the chance of acquiring a valuable foal, but Jelf J held such damage was too contingent and uncertain, agreeing with Erle J's view in *Watson v Ambergate Ry*. He added that, had he been at liberty to speculate on the chances, he might still have come to the same result on the facts; in other words the chance lost may not have been worth more than the amount the claimant had contracted to pay for it. The Court of Appeal in *Chaplin v Hicks* [1911] 2 K.B. 786 said that the decision could only be supported on this latter interpretation, and the real ratio decidendi was disapproved: see

Even a case that tends to be thought of as a loss of a chance case, *Davies v Taylor*,[207] the case where a wife who had left her husband shortly before his death and was claiming that there would have been a reconciliation, should be regarded as a quantification case. The claimant widow's loss, if it existed, was a loss of dependency but she was unable to prove it, the chance of reconciliation being speculative only.[208] *The Law Debenture Trust Corporation Plc v Electrim SA*,[209] is a further quantification case. The amount of damages payable to bondholders for a breach of condition in the bonds issued to them turned upon the valuation of certain company assets which was to be carried out by investment bankers. It was held that, however difficult it might be to arrive at a value, the court must attempt an estimate and there was rejected the defendant's argument that, as the valuation depended upon the hypothetical actions of third party investment bankers, it was appropriate to assess the damages on the basis of the loss of the chance of the notional bankers arriving at a particular valuation.[210] The court did not consider the case to be a loss of a chance case at all and Arden LJ, delivering the judgment of the court, pointed to

> "the dangers of extending it [i.e. the loss of a chance doctrine] to commercial cases, especially valuation cases where permutations may be infinite".[211]

**10-051** *(iii) A loss of chance requires a real and substantial chance* There are two simple and basic points to bear in mind when considering proof of loss of chance. The first is that loss of chance is a broad brush assessment. It does not involve anything resembling a hypothetical trial to determine what recovery would actually have occurred. As Gloster LJ has explained, there are sound reasons of public policy for this approach. One of them is the scarcity of judicial resources.[212] Another reason, to which Gloster LJ referred, is the absurdity of well-resourced defendants being permitted effectively to put a claimant to proof of every aspect of the hypothetical scenario.[213] The second point is that a loss of chance claim requires a real chance. A chance which is negligible will not permit recovery. The difficult question then is what is a negligible chance? In *Harding Homes (East Street) Ltd & Ors v Bircham Dyson Bell (a firm)*,[214] the defendant solicitors were negligent by including an all monies clause in a guarantee given by the claimant builders to a bank in relation to a property development. The guarantee should have been limited to interest shortfall and cost overruns. The claimants alleged that they lost the op-

---

especially at 797, and also at 800 to 801. And in *Chamberlain v Boyd* (1883) 11 Q.B.D. 407 CA, where the claimant through slander had lost a chance of re-election to membership of a club, the court considered this too uncertain a loss for assessment. "The 'chance' of an advantage", said Bowen LJ, "is not the same as the advantage": at 416. To this extent the case is no longer correct, although the decision can still stand as the damage was held too remote for other reasons; also it was a case of slander where pecuniary loss had to be shown, a requirement which the courts do not easily find to be satisfied; see paras 46-002 and following, below.

207 [1974] A.C. 207.

208 *Checkprice (UK) Ltd v Revenue and Customs Commissioners* [2010] EWHC 682 (Admin) is a further illustration of a lost chance that was so speculative that it had to be evaluated at nil, thereby allowing no compensatory damages: see the case at para.38-009, below.

209 [2010] EWCA Civ 1142 CA.

210 See [2010] EWCA Civ 1142 CA at [40] to [49].

211 [2010] EWCA Civ 1142 CA at [48]. See the case further at para.10-086, below.

212 *Perry v Raleys Solicitors* [2017] EWCA Civ 314 at [36].

213 *Perry v Raleys Solicitors* [2017] EWCA Civ 314 at [36].

214 [2015] EWHC 3329 Ch.

portunity for a more profitable result arising from negotiations about the development with the bank. The trial judge, Proudman J, considered whether the loss of opportunity was of something of value, that is something that had a real and substantial rather than a merely negligible prospect of success. In concluding that prospects of success were negligible, the trial judge,[215] followed *Thomas v Albutt*,[216] where Morgan J said that if "the prospects were 10 per cent or less, then I should regard them as negligible". It is difficult to justify such mathematical precision in relation to a broadly expressed approach to "negligible" prospects of success. But even if this point were to be expressed in mathematical terms, the better approach is that a "negligible" prospect should be assessed in light of the circumstances. For instance, a 10 per cent prospect of succeeding in relation to a transaction worth billions of pounds might not be negligible for the same company compared with one which is worth thousands.

*(iv) The distinctions as they apply to personal injury cases* In the light of these vital distinctions—the distinction between past and future events and the distinction between causation of loss and quantification of loss—and the implications and consequences of them, we turn to another key House of Lords decision in this area, a decision in which both aspects of these distinctions featured, not only causation and the past but quantification and the future. *Gregg v Scott*,[217] is similar to *Hotson* in being a case of a negligent delay in medical diagnosis. The claimant consulted his doctor about a lump under his arm which the doctor wrongly diagnosed as a benign lipoma instead of the malignant lymphoma which it was. The doctor negligently failed, as the judge found, to refer the claimant for a specialist opinion with the result that his treatment was delayed by nine months and his chances of cure, in the sense of a period of remission for at least 10 years, were thereby reduced, as was also found by the judge, from 42 per cent to 25 per cent. In these circumstances the trial judge held against the claimant, considering himself bound by *Hotson* to do so. The Court of Appeal by a majority upheld the judge, and the House of Lords in turn affirmed by a bare majority. **10-052**

The claimant attempted to succeed first by avoiding the causation hurdle and having the case seen as a quantification case, where of course chances and contingencies are invariably taken into account. The argument, which had been used in the Court of Appeal by the dissenting Latham LJ in order to find for the claimant, ran thus. Since the nine-month delay in treatment had allowed the cancer to spread and the tumour to enlarge, this amounted to physical injury, and recovery for what was referred to by Latham LJ as "the reduced prospects of successful treatment"[218] could be allowed as consequential loss flowing from this established injury. That there was no certainty about this consequential loss did not matter as, in quantifying loss, possibilities as well as probabilities can be taken into account. But, as Lord Hoffmann pointed out in his analysis of the quantification argument,[219] for loss to be recoverable it must be shown that the damage in question was attributable to the defendant's wrongful act. Thus where the claimant's hip is tortiously injured there can be recovery for the possibility that it will develop arthritis since the injury to **10-053**

215 [2015] EWHC 3329 Ch at [167].
216 [2015] EWHCA 2817 Ch at [461].
217 [2005] 2 A.C. 176.
218 [2003] Lloyd's Rep. Med. 105 CA at [41].
219 [2005] 2 A.C. 176 at [67]–[71].

the hip is attributable to, and caused by, the wrongful act; similarly, there was recovery in *Doyle v Wallace*,[220] as we have just seen[221] and will see further,[222] for the possibility that the claimant would have had higher earnings had she qualified as a drama teacher since her loss of earnings was attributable to, and caused by, the defendant who injured her. In the instant case, however, it was necessary to show that the loss of life expectation claimed for was attributable to, and caused by, the defendant's negligence which had allowed the cancer to spread. This was not known and had not, as the trial judge had held, been proved. The case was a causation case and not a quantification case. The controlling distinction is most concisely formulated in a sentence of a Canadian judge, Master J,[223] cited approvingly by Lord Hoffmann in *Gregg v Scott*[224]:

> "The rule against recovery of uncertain damages is directed against uncertainty as to cause rather than as to extent or measure".

The quantification argument therefore did not avail the claimant, and Lord Hope's introduction of *Doyle* and the related *Langford v Hebran*,[225] in support of his minority holding for the claimant[226] is misconceived.[227]

**10-054** The claimant then turned to loss of a chance proper. In essence the majority of their Lordships held that the loss of a chance doctrine had no application to cases of clinical negligence or indeed to personal injuries generally. Loss of a chance as established in the economic sphere was not to be extended to the physical sphere. The existing loss of a chance cases are dependent upon human activity and human decisions which are in their very nature uncertain, and where such uncertainties come into the assessment of damages, the loss of a chance approach makes sense. By contrast, with physical injury there is no inherent uncertainty as to cause but only a lack of knowledge, and lack of knowledge is dealt with in the law by the burden of proof, so that it is appropriate to apply the balance of probabilities rule to the situation, an approach which will favour sometimes the defendant and, also, sometimes the claimant. It may of course be said that this distinction has only legal principle and legal consistency, and not fairness and justice, on its side, and that whether such a difference should be reflected in the law of damages, so as to cause loss of a chance not to be moved into the personal injury and fatal accident sphere, may be open to question and will be doubted by some. However, Baroness Hale was concerned from a different angle about any departure from the status quo; she saw

---

220 [1998] P.I.Q.R. Q146 CA; see at para.10-083, below.

221 At para.10-049, above.

222 At para.10-083, below.

223 In *Kranz v McCutcheon* 18 Ont. W.N. 395 (1920).

224 And earlier in Scotland in *Kenyon v Bell* 1953 S.C. 125 at 128.

225 These two cases are at para.10-042, above together with paras 10-083 and 10-084, below.

226 [2005] 2 A.C. 176 at [119].

227 The claimant employee in *Smithurst v Sealant Construction Services Ltd* [2011] EWCA Civ 1277 CA sustained a disc prolapse as a result of his employer's negligence and could no longer work. At the time he was at risk of suffering a similar disc prolapse which was likely to occur within the next two years. On the basis of causation of loss the trial judge considered that the claimant should have full damages for two years and none thereafter. The Court of Appeal disagreed with this reasoning, pointing out that the case was one of quantification of loss rather than of causation of loss, but regarded the result as acceptable. The result represented an adoption of the acceleration approach in place of the more usual assessment of risk approach: for all this see [2011] EWCA Civ 1277 CA at [9], [16] and [22]. In endorsing the acceleration approach the Court of Appeal followed its earlier decision in *Kenth v Heimdale Hotel Investments Ltd* [2001] EWCA Civ 1283 CA.

it as playing havoc with the rules on proof. She thought, if loss of a chance was taken further in the personal injury field, that a claimant would be able to argue that where he could show a percentage chance of proving his case he should be entitled to that percentage of the damages and, if this were to be allowed, a claimant able to satisfy the balance of probabilities test could be restricted to the percentage of loss he was able causatively to prove.[228] The Court of Appeal agreed in *Wright v Cambridge Medical Group*,[229] that the loss of a chance approach cannot be taken in claims for personal injury and particularly in claims for clinical negligence. By the defendant doctor's negligent delay in referring the child claimant to a hospital for treatment, the claimant lost the chance of receiving prompt medical treatment which would have avoided permanent injury but which had not in fact been forthcoming. Though not strictly determinative of the case, the House of Lords' decision in *Gregg v Scott* was relied upon.[230]

As for the view of the minority that a failure to hold for the claimant would constitute a wrong without a remedy—as stated by Lord Nicholls[231] and Lord Hope[232]—this gets us nowhere for it begs the question. They assume that a wrong has been done, which is the very question that it is for the court to decide. Yet the minority Lords have better strings to their bow. The delays in the clinical negligence cases of *Hotson* and *Gregg v Scott* increased the risk of an unfavourable outcome and diminished the chance of a favourable outcome; it can be put either way, as it was by Lord Walker in *Barker v Corus (UK) Ltd*,[233] considered below, where he spoke of "an analysis based on 'increase in risk' (or its mirror image 'loss of a chance')".[234] These cases were therefore perfectly crafted for the introduction of loss of a chance.[235] And it may be said that Baroness Hale need not be concerned that the whole question of proof of personal injury would be jeopardised as only a tiny number of personal injury cases would be affected. **10-055**

The House of Lords has now allowed loss of a chance to creep into the personal injury field in *Barker v Corus (UK) Ltd*,[236] another case of claimant workers contracting mesothelioma from the inhalation of asbestos dust in the course of a series of employments. So as to allow apportionment of the damages between the various employers by holding them severally rather than jointly liable, their Lordships were prepared to see the basis of liability as being not in causing the injury but in increasing the risk of causing the injury.[237] Here then was a damages award based only on the chance that the negligence caused the injury, with no clear basis given for not allowing the extension of such awards to all areas of personal injury damages. This was not lost on Lord Rodger who in his vigorous, if solitary, dissent in *Barker v Corus* pointed out that by its decision the House was creating difficulties for itself on the loss of a chance front in personal injury.[238] Lord Walker, **10-056**

---

228 [2005] 2 A.C. 176 at [222]–[225].

229 [2011] EWCA Civ 669 CA.

230 [2011] EWCA Civ 669 CA at [82] to [84] and [93].

231 [2005] 2 A.C. 176 at [2] and [25].

232 [2005] 2 A.C. 176 at [106].

233 [2006] 2 A.C. 572.

234 [2006] 2 A.C. 572 at [114].

235 See the formulations proposed for the application of the loss of a chance doctrine at paras 10-047 and 10-048, above.

236 [2006] 2 A.C. 572.

237 See the full explanation of the decision at paras 10-021 and 10-022, above.

238 [2006] 2 A.C. 572 at [85].

on the other hand, was confident that the loss of chance principle in personal injury cases is restricted to mesothelioma and conditions with the same aetiology and prognosis.[239] This is undoubtedly true as the law now stands, but it cannot be denied that *Hotson* and *Gregg* are now in some danger. And the danger can be seen to be not insubstantial when it is remembered that *Hotson* is a decision which some have found unattractive—the House was there reversing both the Court of Appeal and the trial judge—that there are those who would be happy to see both *Hotson* and *Gregg* go, and that it is noticeable that, whereas the unpreparedness to let loss of a chance into personal injury was unanimous in *Hotson*, it only had the support of a bare majority in the much more recent *Gregg v Scott*.

**10-057** *(v) The distinction between acts of the claimant and acts of third parties* It will be seen that only a passing reference has been made above to the important *Allied Maples v Simmons & Simmons*,[240] today the most cited decision on loss of a chance because of Stuart Smith LJ's valuable elaboration there of what falls within the realm of loss of a chance and what requires proof on the balance of probabilities, an elaboration which is generally understood to represent the current law on the subject. The reason for *Allied Maples* not having featured so far in the discussion, which has been general, is that it is concerned with the situation, which is specific, where the chance lost is dependent upon how a third party might have acted or have failed to act. The typical such case is where negligent advice is given by a professional, most commonly a solicitor. Not all loss of chance cases, however, as is sometimes thought, are of this nature. Thus in the common case of a solicitor's negligence causing the loss of a client's claim where the value of the claim which has to be estimated lies in the hands of the court or, in the case of settlement, in the hands of bilateral negotiation—these were the words of Rix LJ in *Dixon v Clement Jones Solicitors*[241]—it is somewhat difficult to see as a third party, other than tangentially, either the court or the other party to the lost litigation. Where, in the context of personal injury, loss of a chance has been introduced for mesothelioma victims in *Barker v Corus*,[242] no third party action at all is brought into the damages calculation. So too in the cases, admittedly not of loss of a chance proper, where in the quantification of personal injury damages the unfolding careers of the claimants have been spoken of in terms of loss of a chance, as in *Doyle v Wallace*,[243] *Langford v Hebran*,[244] and *Clarke v Maltby*,[245] no action of specific third parties is involved. Cases of all these types being already covered, it now falls to address situations where the chance lost has been dependent upon third party action or inaction.

**10-058** *Allied Maples* concerned negligent advice by a solicitor, the archetypal case of a lost chance dependent on third party action. The claimants were advised by the defendant solicitors in their purchase of certain business and shop properties. The solicitors had allowed the sale to the claimants to proceed with the deletion of a warranty by the sellers that no contingent liabilities existed whereas there was a li-

---

239 [2006] 2 A.C. 572 at [114].
240 [1995] 1 W.L.R. 1602 CA.
241 [2005] P.N.L.R. 6 at 93, [42]. See the case at para.10-064, below.
242 [2006] 2 A.C. 572. See the case at para.10-056, above.
243 [1998] P.I.Q.R. Q146 CA. See the case at para.10-049, above.
244 [2001] P.I.Q.R. Q13 CA at 160. See the case at para.10-049, above.
245 [2010] EWHC 1201 (QB). See the case at para.10-085, below.

ability on a lease which in due course materialised. Two questions arose in relation to causation and damages. The first question was whether, if the defendants had properly advised the claimants of the effect of deleting the warranty, the claimants would have taken steps to obtain from the sellers some protection, by way of warranty or otherwise, against this liability. The second question was whether the sellers would have been prepared to accede to such a request by the claimants.

In his definitive judgment Stuart-Smith LJ distinguished between three types of situation or categories.[246] In his first category fall cases in which the defendant's negligence consists in some positive act or misfeasance and the question of causation is one of historical fact. This is of course the situation to which, as we have seen,[247] Lord Reid in *Davies v Taylor*,[248] and Lord Diplock in *Mallett v McMonagle*,[249] were referring. Proof on the balance of probabilities prevails here. In the second category fall cases in which the defendant's negligence consists of an omission where causation depends not upon a question of historical fact but upon the answer to the hypothetical question what would the claimant have done if there had been no negligence. How the claimant would have reacted is again subject to proof on the balance of probabilities. In the third category fall cases in which the claimant's loss depends upon the hypothetical action of a third party, whether in addition to action by the claimant or independently of it. Here the claimant need only show that he had a substantial chance of the third party acting in such a way as to benefit him. In the case before the court, therefore, the claimants had to show on the balance of probabilities, before any recovery was possible, that they would have sought a degree of protection against the contingent liability; it was held that in this they succeeded. However, they needed to show only that there was a significant chance, which could be less than likely, that the third party would have been prepared to afford them this protection; the majority, Millett LJ dissenting, held that the loss of such a chance had been made out and it was assessed at 50 per cent. Stuart-Smith LJ's analysis thus entirely explains why *Sykes v Midland Bank Executor and Trustee Co*,[250] a decision which some have thought to be difficult, is not a loss of chance case. There the defendant solicitors, in advising the claimant firm of architects and surveyors in relation to an underlease of part of a building in central London which the claimants were proposing to take for the expansion of their business from Hull, negligently failed to explain to the claimants that, while under the provisions of the underlease their lessor could not arbitrarily withhold consent to their assigning or subletting, the superior lessors could. The defendant solicitors were also aware that the claimants might wish to assign or sublet in the future. In the event, the superior lessors did refuse consent to a later proposed subletting, but the claimants were awarded only nominal damages in their action against their solicitors, not indeed because the Court of Appeal was unprepared to award damages for loss of the opportunity to sublet but because the claimants had failed to establish that, had they been properly advised, they would probably not have entered into the underlease or at least not on the terms on which they did. This then was a case within Stuart-Smith LJ's second category. 10-059

246 See [1995] 1 W.L.R. 1602 CA at 1604 to 1611.
247 At para.10-044, above.
248 [1974] A.C. 207.
249 [1970] A.C. 166.
250 [1971] 1 Q.B. 113 CA.

**10-060** The only respect in which one might cavil with Stuart-Smith LJ's valuable analysis is with his method of division of his first two categories, namely the division between acts and omissions of the defendant generating liability. It is thought that the essence of the second category is not liability based upon omission but the need to ascertain how the claimant will react; the first category does not concern itself with actions after the occurrence of the wrong, whether of claimant or third party, and seems equally relevant for acts and omissions. A defendant may be liable for an omission which does not involve subsequent acts of the claimant; thus occupiers' liability is frequently based upon omissions causing physical injury. Conversely, an act as well as an omission may result in action or inaction by the claimant; thus specific wrong advice, which can hardly be classified just as a failure to give the right advice, will generally require an investigation into the reaction thereto of the claimant. It is, however, thought that over the years since the decision the first and second categories have been interpreted as each covering both acts and omissions, with the controlling distinction between them turning on whether past historical fact or future possible conduct is in issue.

**10-061** The central distinction which Stuart Smith LJ drew in *Allied Maples* was of course between a claimant needing only to show that he had a substantial chance of a third party acting in such a way as to benefit him and having to prove on the balance of probabilities what he himself would or would not have done. It is considered that this has always been the law as far as third parties' actions are concerned; what is thought to be newer, or perhaps just more clearly revealed, is Stuart Smith LJ's requirement that the claimant must establish upon the balance of probabilities what his own actions would have been. Yet the distinction drawn has not been heralded by all as a wise one. In the criticism of the loss of a chance doctrine as thus expounded, the critics invariably point to Lord Hoffmann's referring in *Gregg v Scott*,[251] to the distinction as an apparently arbitrary one, though generally ignoring that he added that it "obviously rests on grounds of policy", the policy reasons being unspecified.[252] But it is submitted that the criticism is misplaced.

**10-062** While at first glance it may seem somewhat strange to have different tests applicable to hypothetical acts of the claimant and hypothetical acts of third parties, it can be seen to make sense, with nothing at all arbitrary about it and with no need to bring in public policy to justify it. For a claimant can hardly claim for the loss of the chance that he himself *might* have acted in a particular way; he must show that he *would* have; it cannot surely be enough for a claimant to say that there was a *chance* that he would have so acted. The onus is on a claimant to prove his case and he therefore must be able to show how he would *in fact* have behaved. There is no such onus on third parties. The claimant's position in this is well illustrated by *McWilliams v Arrol*,[253] a House of Lords case from Scotland, where a widow, suing for the death of her husband because of his employers' failure to provide him with a safety belt, failed in her action because she could not show that he would have used the safety belt had it been provided; it was not enough to show that he *might* have used it. Would not Miss Chaplin have had to show on the balance of

---

[251] [2005] 2 A.C. 176.
[252] [2005] 2 A.C. 176 at [83].
[253] [1962] 1 W.L.R. 295 HL.

probabilities that, if she had been given adequate notice of the interviews by Seymour Hicks, she would have attended?[254]

This approach is supported by taking into account the position of defendants who like claimants are subject to the balance of probabilities rule; the parties to an action are not entitled to fall back on chance when it comes to ascertaining what they would or would not have done. It is true that nothing is said in *Allied Maples* about the defendant's position but this is probably because the defendant's conduct has little to do with loss of a chance; one is not really concerned with what the defendant would or would not have done in the aftermath of the commission of a wrong. Still, loss of a chance apart, a defendant's actions must pass the balance of probability test, as is shown by *Bolitho v City and Hackney Health Authority*,[255] where the House of Lords was quite clear that the doctor at fault in not attending a child patient had to show, to avoid liability, that she would not have intubated had she attended, not merely that there was a chance that she would not have done so. **10-063**

Some difficulty is encountered with the decision in *Dixon v Clement Jones Solicitors*,[256] which, while looking like a run of the mill case of solicitors' negligence in conducting litigation, yet appears to mark a departure from the application to claimants of the balance of probability rule. Mrs Dixon's action against her accountant had been struck out for her solicitor's failure to serve a statement of claim. The accountant had negligently failed to advise her of the financial dangers of entering a business transaction which was likely to be, and in the event proved to be, a losing one, but the trial judge found that, on the balance of probabilities, she would have ignored her accountant's advice and gone ahead with the transaction in any event. This, however, did not cause her action against her solicitor to fail. The Court of Appeal reasoned thus. While her action against her accountant would have failed if she could not prove that, given the correct advice, she would not have gone ahead with the transaction, it was the *chance* of whether she would have gone ahead that was relevant in her action against the solicitor, being simply one issue within all the other issues that had to be assessed for their prospects.[257] The trial judge had therefore been entitled to award her damages on the basis that she had a 30 per cent chance of succeeding against her solicitor. For the court to have decided otherwise would have been virtually to commit it to conducting a trial within a trial which the courts have said they do not, and must not, do.[258] The claim against the accountants can perhaps be regarded as an asset lost which must be valued and the settlement value of the claim may be taken as an appropriate yardstick for this, but it is the case that we are here into very fine distinctions. It is true that *Dixon* does not drive a coach and horses through the rule for claimants, having a limited range in applying only to claims for negligent conduct of litigation resulting in the litigation being lost to the claimant. Rix LJ in *Dixon* contrasted such claims with claims against solicitors and other professionals that arise out of transactions in which **10-064**

---

254 Facts of *Chaplin v Hicks* at para.10-040, above. In *Floyd v John Fairhurst & Co* [2004] P.N.L.R. 41 CA at 795 (facts at para.10-078, below) it was accepted on all sides that the claimant had to establish on the balance of probabilities what his own actions would have been.

255 [1998] A.C. 232.

256 [2005] P.N.L.R. 6 CA at 93.

257 [2005] P.N.L.R. 6 CA at [42], per Rix LJ.

258 "It is the prospects and not the hypothetical decision in the lost trial that have to be investigated": [2005] P.N.L.R. 6 CA at 27, per Rix LJ. See too para.10-096, below.

solicitors or other professionals have negligently advised, to which the rules set out in *Allied Maples*, which he cited, continue to apply.[259]

**10-065** It has so far been assumed that the critics of the distinction made by Stuart Smith LJ in *Allied Maples* would wish to remove the anomaly, as they see it, by putting claimants, and also defendants, under the wing of third parties, in other words, by subjecting hypothetical acts of claimants, defendants and third parties alike to the chance test rather than the probability test. But His Honour Judge Hodge in *Stone Heritage Developments Ltd v Davis Blank Furniss*,[260] boldly went in the other direction, applying the balance of probabilities test to third party actions because the third parties had been before the court,[261] and since he held that the balance of probabilities test was not satisfied,[262] the claimants in that case could not succeed. There was in fact no need for Judge Hodge so to decide as he had already held against the claimants on other grounds, and the Court of Appeal was able to by-pass the issue by dismissing the appeal on the ground that the defendant had not been negligent, ending its single judgment by simply saying that

> "the proper test by which to assess the likelihood or otherwise of a third party … acting in any particular manner should be considered in a wider context than that which this appeal affords".[263]

In *4 Eng Ltd v Harper*,[264] where whether the claimant would have been able to acquire a company from third parties was in issue,[265] it was again argued that balance of probabilities should be applied because the third parties were before the court. Because there was insufficient evidence from the third parties to come to a view, David Richards J considered that he had no option but to apply the approach established in *Allied Maples*.[266] Similarly, with little evidence of whether a third party would have completed a contract with the claimant, Floyd J had no hesitation in taking the loss of a chance approach to the damages in *Tom Hoskins Plc v EMW Law*.[267] While David Richards J preferred to express no view on whether, with sufficient evidence from the third parties, the balance of probabilities would have been the right test to apply,[268] Floyd J appeared to be against allowing third party evidence to move the law from loss of a chance to balance of probabilities.[269] With this idea being very much in the air, its merits and demerits need to be addressed.

**10-066** In *Stone Heritage* his Honour Judge Hodge considered that the rationale for the distinction between claimants and third parties is that claimants can give evidence upon which a view can be taken but third parties are generally not before the court. This is a rationale which does not appear in any of the authorities. Judge Hodge appeared to think that this was the rationale based on public policy that Lord Hoffmann was propounding in *Gregg v Scott* but, as has been pointed out,[270] Lord

---

259 See [2005] P.N.L.R. 6 CA at [31] and following.

260 *Stone Heritage Developments Ltd v Davis Blank Furniss* unreported 1 June 2006.

261 See at [330] to [334] of his extremely long judgment.

262 See *Stone Heritage Developments Ltd v Davis Blank Furniss* unreported 1 June 2006 at [335].

263 [2007] EWCA Civ 765 CA at [47].

264 [2009] Ch. 91.

265 Facts at para.49-025, below.

266 [2009] Ch. 91 at [57] and [58].

267 [2010] EWHC 479 Ch; see [125] to [128].

268 See [2009] Ch. 91 at [58].

269 See [2010] EWHC 479 Ch at [126].

270 At para.10-061, above.

Hoffmann does not provide us with the public policy ground that he may have had in mind. In any event Judge Hodge's rationale is considered to be misconceived. In this whole area we are dealing with loss of a chance and this is so whether the chance lost is or is not dependent on the actions of a third party.[271] There should be no difference between the various cases. No doubt where a third party's acts are in issue and the third party is called upon to give evidence, this will assist the court in determining the strength, or the weakness, of the chance, which might lead to total recovery or a nil recovery,[272] but there is no need for the court to apply the balance of probabilities test so as to have to decree a total, or else a nil, recovery where uncertain, despite the third party's evidence, of how he would have acted. Moreover, it would be unfortunate if decisions should turn on the availability or otherwise of witnesses which would generally be fortuitous and could be tactically arranged.

It is also of concern that, if a balance of probabilities test were to be adopted where a third party had given evidence, there could be a danger of this approach spilling over into other areas with disastrous effects. Thus a compelling argument for taking the chance route is that if you take the balance of probabilities route you have to end up, if the test is satisfied, by giving full recovery and not proportionate damages. Taking a typical case of a solicitor failing to issue a writ in time where the client's underlying action, now lost to him, would have had somewhat over a 50 per cent chance of succeeding—which has been true in many of the decided cases—you have to award that client the full damages that he would have obtained in the underlying action. And going back to the *fons et origo* of it all, *Chaplin v Hicks*, if balance of probabilities had been applied and the jury, now the judge, charmed by Miss Chaplin, had come to the view that she would probably end up as one of the chosen 12, the damages awarded would have to have been on the basis that she would have been a winner. And at the other end of the scale, adoption of Judge Hodge's rationale might mean, in a case where the claimant was not before the court because he was already dead, that the balance of probabilities test for claimants would have to be abandoned. In *McWilliams v Arrol*[273] the husband not using the safety belt was dead but this did not alter the position on proof on the balance of probabilities, Lord Reid specifically saying that he did not agree with the proposition that if a man is dead you can never prove what he would have done.[274] **10-067**

The principle that hypothetical actions of third parties are assessed on the basis of a need to prove a "substantial chance" but that a claimant's hypothetical actions must be proved on the balance of probabilities was confirmed in *Wellesley Partners LLP v Withers LLP*.[275] In that case, Floyd LJ, in the leading judgment on this issue, set out his basic understanding of the position before undertaking a comprehensive examination of the authorities to confirm that it was correct. His Lordship said that the claimant head-hunters (WP) needed to prove their actions on the balance of probabilities but only a real and substantial chance of benefit from the actions of the third party (Nomura). His Lordship said:

> "I would have thought that, applying those principles to the present case, it would be plain that, whilst WP would need to show on the balance of probabilities that, but for the

[271] See on this para.10-057, above.
[272] As in the cases set out at para.10-094, below.
[273] [1962] 1 W.L.R. 295 HL; at para.10-062, above.
[274] [1962] 1 W.L.R. 295 HL at 306.
[275] [2015] EWCA Civ 1146.

negligence complained of, they would have opened a US office (a question of causation dependent on what the claimant would have done in the absence of a breach of duty), the actual loss which they claimed to have been caused by the defendant was dependent on the hypothetical actions of a third party, namely Nomura. Accordingly, in line with well-established principle, the chances of Nomura deciding to award the mandates to WP would have to be reflected in the award of damages."[276]

**10-068** *(v) Situations in which loss of a chance has no part to play* The range of loss of a chance having now been fully explored, it remains only to point to a variety of cases where there is displayed today's unfortunate tendency to argue loss of a chance in situations where it can have no conceivable application. The temptation is of course great; if total success cannot be achieved, aiming for a percentage success is attractive. Thus in *Rushmer v Countrywide Surveyors (1994) Ltd*,[277] where surveyors had failed to report serious structural defects in a property, it was contended that the correct measure of damages was based upon the loss of the chance to renegotiate the purchase price. This argument rightly received short shrift. *Fyffes Group Ltd v Templeman*,[278] introduced a complex situation involving contract, tort and secret commissions, where the attempt to raise the loss of a chance argument to displace the requirement of balance of probabilities failed.[279] The same attempt also failed in *A v National Blood Authority*,[280] where claimants were affected by a virus arising from the supply of a defective product.[281] And the court in *Janciuk v Winerite*,[282] boldly and wisely said, in rejecting the employee's claim to be compensated for the loss of the chance that he might not have been dismissed if a contractual disciplinary procedure had been operated, that they regarded his "attempt to introduce the loss of a chance into the calculation of the damages as a heresy".[283] Sometimes it is the defendant who, heading for a fall, grasps at loss of a chance in a desperate attempt to lessen his liability. Thus in *Owners of the Ship "Front Ace" v Owners of "Vicky 1"*,[284] where a ship collision was held to have caused the loss of a fixture finalised by the claimant shipowner before the collision, the defendant shipowner's argument that a discount of 20 per cent should be made to reflect the chance that the claimant's ship would not have been profitably employed, while accepted by the Registrar hearing the case, was shown by the Court of Appeal to be undoubtedly misconceived.[285] In *Wellesley Partners LLP v Withers LLP*[286] a head-hunting firm claimed damages for the loss of a chance of obtaining a profitable contract with an investment bank. The Court of Appeal separated two different enquiries: (i) on the balance of probabilities would the headhunters have obtained the contract? (ii) Did they lose a chance of making profit? Consistently with the approach to deny the reduction of damages in cases like *Front Ace* considered in the previous paragraph, the Court of Appeal held that the loss of chance quantification applies only to the latter question.

---

276 [2015] EWCA Civ 1146 at [100].
277 [2000] P.N.L.R. 529.
278 [2000] 2 Lloyd's Rep. 643.
279 [2000] 2 Lloyd's Rep. 643 at 667, col.1 to 668, col.1.
280 [2002] Lloyd's Rep. Med. 487.
281 [2002] Lloyd's Rep. Med. 487 at 252, col.1 to 254, col.1.
282 [1998] I.R.L.R. 63.
283 [1998] I.R.L.R. 63 at 64.
284 [2008] 2 All E.R. (Comm) 42 CA.
285 [2008] 2 All E.R. (Comm) 42 CA at [68] and following.
286 [2015] EWCA Civ 1146.

**(c) The range of the loss of a chance doctrine: particular cases** While it is important to distinguish loss of a chance proper as a matter of causation from loss of a chance as a matter of quantification,[287] both are given consideration when dealing with particular types of case. This is because both have an impact on the issue of certainty. Whether a particular case falls within the one or the other category can generally be ascertained by looking back to the earlier discussion. Occasionally, also, where a quantification loss of a chance is involved, it is indicated that this is so. **10-069**

*(i) Claims against solicitors* It is claims against solicitors for professional negligence which have featured the most extensively in the cases where the issue has been of damages for loss of a chance and generally of loss of a chance proper. *Allied Maples v Simmons & Simmons*,[288] itself was such a claim. The great mass of case law is probably about equally divided between cases of negligent advice[289] and cases of negligent handling of litigation. **10-070**

The cases concerning non-contentious matters in which clients have been given negligent advice start with, and are well illustrated by, *Hall v Meyrick*.[290] The defendant failed to warn the claimant that her marriage would revoke a will made in her favour by her intended husband. The marriage took place and two years later the husband died intestate. The claimant claimed damages on the ground that, owing to the absence of warning by the defendant, she failed to take steps to obtain a new will from her husband after their marriage, and thus lost "the chance or opportunity to secure [the] benefits of such a will".[291] Four contingencies appeared: (1) that the claimant would have remembered the warning if given; (2) that her husband would have been willing to execute a new will; (3) that the new will would have been wholly in her favour; (4) that he would not later have revoked it. It was held at first instance[292] that she was entitled to recover for loss of the chance, but, on account of the various contingencies, not to the full difference between the value of her interest under a will leaving her everything and the value of her interest in intestacy. As Ashworth J said: **10-071**

> "The more the contingencies, the lower the value of the chance or opportunity of which the plaintiff was deprived."[293]

---

287 For a full analysis of this distinction see paras 10-049 to 10-050, above.

288 [1995] 1 W.L.R. 1602 CA.

289 There are also cases of negligent failure to follow instructions rather than of negligent advice, such as *Talisman Property Co Ltd v Norton Rose* [2006] 3 E.G.L.R. 59 CA where solicitors, instructed to serve an unopposed notice to the renewal of a tenancy, served an opposed one with disastrous consequences. The chance lost, in a complicated case, turned on whether counsel's advice would or would not have been taken to establish the rightful tenant of the premises in question; for computation of the lost chance see para.10-103, below. Or there may be negligence in the manner of performance, as in *Stovold v Barlows* [1996] P.N.L.R. 91 CA. where the defendant solicitor delayed sending the deeds of a house, which the claimant wished to sell, to his potential purchaser who proceeded to buy another house. The Court of Appeal held that the claimant lost the chance that the intending purchaser would have bought the claimant's house had the deeds arrived in time, and assessed that chance at 50 per cent.

290 [1957] 2 Q.B. 455.

291 [1957] 2 Q.B. 455 at 471.

292 The Court of Appeal (also reported at [1957] 2 Q.B. 455) reversed the decision on other grounds and declined to comment on the issue of damages.

293 [1957] 2 Q.B. 455 at 471.

With the hindsight of the decision in *Allied Maples v Simmons & Simmons*,[294] only the last three of these contingencies are relevant for loss of a chance; as the first involved the claimant, she would have to show on a balance of probabilities that she would have remembered the solicitor's warning.

**10-072** About the same time *Otter v Church, Adams, Tatham & Co*[295] was decided. A solicitor misinformed a client as to the latter's interest in certain property, thus depriving him of the opportunity of increasing his estate by making the property, which was settled property, his own absolutely. The error was discovered only after his death, when it was too late for him to effect a remedy, and his personal representatives successfully claimed damages against the defendants, the measure being calculated as the loss to the estate occasioned by the passing of the settled property to the next tenant in tail, due allowance being made for the possibility that the deceased on being properly advised might not have disentailed.[296] This decision was, however, rightly criticised in *Allied Maples v Simmons & Simmons*[297] by Stuart-Smith LJ, who pointed out that it was not a case involving action by a third party since the deceased and his estate have to be regarded as the same[298]; there should have been full recovery with no discount once the judge had decided that it was highly probable that the deceased would have disentailed had he been properly advised. Indeed this correct criticism of *Otter*[299] had already been voiced by Salmon LJ in *Sykes v Midland Bank Executor and Trustee Co.*[300]

**10-073** Since *Allied Maples*, cases of loss of a chance consequent on negligent advice have proliferated. The chance to be evaluated in *Hartle v Laceys*,[301] where there was a sale of property to a third party, was the chance, in the absence of the defendant solicitor's negligence in relation to the registration of a restrictive covenant, of the third party being prepared to buy from the claimant; the chance was assessed at 60 per cent. The chance to be evaluated in *Motor Crown Petroleum Ltd v S. J. Berwin & Co*,[302] where solicitors were negligent in not advising their client to challenge the local planning authority's plan, a challenge which it was held would have been successful, was the chance, given that successful challenge, of the planning inspector allowing the appeal against the refusal of the application for planning permission; the chance was assessed at 40 per cent. The chance to be evaluated in *Perkin v Lupton Fawcett*,[303] where the solicitor had negligently allowed the wrong clause into a contract, was the chance of negotiating a variation of the clause, a chance assessed at only 20 per cent. What had to be assessed in *Maden v Clifford Coppock & Carter*,[304] where the solicitor negligently advised on the costs consequences of litigation with a third party, was the chance that the third party might not have agreed to a settlement.[305] The discount that the Court of Appeal decided upon for this was a comparatively small 20 per cent. The claim against the solicitor in *Wil-*

294 [1995] 1 W.L.R. 1602 CA.
295 [1953] 1 Ch. 280.
296 See especially at 290.
297 [1995] 1 W.L.R. 1602 CA.
298 [1995] 1 W.L.R. 1602 CA at 1612.
299 [1953] 1 Ch. 280.
300 [1971] 1 Q.B. 113 CA at 130B to D.
301 [1999] Lloyd's Rep. P.N. 315 CA.
302 [2000] Lloyd's Rep. P.N. 438 CA.
303 [2008] P.N.L.R. 30 at 736.
304 [2005] P.N.L.R. 7 CA at 112.
305 See the facts at para.34-035, below.

*liams v Glyn Owen & Co*[306] was for failing to advise the claimant, buying a farm for its immediate stocking with breeding ewes, to serve a completion notice upon the vendor when it became apparent that the vendor would not be able to give vacant possession on the date fixed for completion and therefore not in time to allow stocking before the market for breeding ewes had disappeared. Although completion could not have taken place in time to catch the market even if a completion notice had been served, account had to be taken of the chance that, had a notice been served, the vendor would have agreed a date for completion which would have provided the claimant with sufficient assurance to enable him to purchase breeding stock. That chance being assessed by the Court of Appeal at 40 per cent, the claimant was held entitled to that percentage of the profit he would have made had he bought in time. In *Berry v Laytons*,[307] a solicitor had negligently advised his client as to his rights, so that he settled under his contract of employment and did not pursue his employer under the EU legislation which would have given him more. The trial judge took the view that the claimant would have settled with his employer and arrived at a settlement figure, which was awarded, calculated at 60 per cent of the amount that the claimant would have claimed against his employer. And the claim in *Wellesley Partners LLP v Withers LLP*,[308] involved negligence by solicitors which deprived the claimant head-hunting firm of the opportunity of a profitable contract, assessed as a 60 per cent chance. Further successful loss of a chance cases involving solicitors' negligent advice are set out later when dealing with contracts for professional services.

Other cases have concerned the negligent handling of litigation by solicitors. One of the earliest cases is *Cook v Swinfen*,[309] where divorce proceedings in which the claimant was respondent were negligently conducted by the defendant solicitor with the result that the claimant was adjudicated the guilty party and no application was made for maintenance either for herself or for her son. Damages were awarded for the loss of her chance of obtaining a more favourable outcome of the divorce suit, since she might also have obtained a decree, and for the loss of her chance of obtaining maintenance for herself and her son. In *Acton v Graham Pearce & Co*,[310] the solicitor's negligence lay in mishandling the defence of his client to a criminal prosecution, resulting in the client's conviction. The award of only 50 per cent of the client claimant's total loss seems somewhat niggardly in light of the fact that his conviction had been set aside on appeal. In *Pearson v Sanders Witherspoon*,[311] the solicitor's negligence lay in not pursuing his client's claim against a company timeously so that judgment, once obtained, could not be enforced because the company had gone into receivership. An amount equal to only 50 per cent of this judgment was awarded as damages for reasons dealt with later.[312] In *Hickman v Blake Lapthorn*,[313] the claimant's personal injury claim had been settled at a gross undervalue but the value of the claim fell to be discounted by 50 per cent to reflect the claimant's chance of losing on liability. In *Hanif v Middleweeks*,[314] the solicitor's **10-074**

306 [2004] P.N.L.R. 20 CA at 367.
307 [2009] EWHC 1591 (QB).
308 [2015] EWCA Civ 1146.
309 [1967] 1 W.L.R. 457 CA.
310 [1997] 3 All E.R. 909.
311 [2000] P.N.L.R. 110 CA.
312 See para.10-097, below.
313 [2006] P.N.L.R. 20 at 371.
314 [2000] Lloyd's Rep. P.N. 920 CA.

negligence again consisted of a failure to pursue expeditiously his clients' claim, here against their insurers, so that the claim had been dismissed for want of prosecution. The claimants were held to have had a 20 per cent chance of succeeding against their insurers. *Feakins v Burstow*,[315] was a complex case where the solicitor's negligence lay in his conducting of proceedings, in particular in his failure to assemble evidence, whereby the claimant sheep exporter, sued by the authorities for the return of certain premium payments, was unable to show that, because of an exemption of his sheep, payment was not due from him. The court held that there was a 60 per cent chance that the outcome of the proceedings would have been in the claimant's favour had it not been for his solicitor's negligence. In some cases no discount has been made, as in *Dickinson v Jones Alexander & Co*,[316] where the claim against the solicitor was for settling a wife's claim in divorce proceedings for far too inadequate financial provision. It was held that, since there had been only a negligible risk of the wife obtaining less than the proper award in the divorce proceedings, the damages would be based on that assumption. In another case, the Court of Appeal rejected the conclusion of the trial judge that the claimant had only a negligible prospect of success, explaining that the trial judge's conclusion had been based upon an approach which effectively descended into a hypothetical trial by asking what the principal issue in the claim would have been.[317]

**10-075** In *Martin Boston & Co v Roberts*,[318] where solicitors, acting for a client in an action brought against him, compromised an application by them for security for costs by taking a personal guarantee from a third party without seeking a charge, as they should have done, on the third party's house, the client's claim against the solicitors for his irrecoverable costs succeeded in full. Simon Brown LJ would have nothing of the argument that, had the charge been sought, the third party might not have been prepared to give it. "In my judgment", he said,[319]

> "this was plainly a *Sykes v Midland Bank Executor and Trustee Co*[320] situation [and] was a far cry from a *Kitchen v Royal Air Force Association*[321] type of case".

This may or may not be right. If the application for security for costs would not have been compromised had a charge been sought but proved unattainable, then it is right, though calling it a *Sykes* situation may not be correct; if the compromise would have gone ahead even if the third party, though requested to give a charge, had declined to do so, then it is wrong, as the case is now a loss of a chance case.

**10-076** One of the commonest illustrations of mishandled litigation is that which involves a claim in respect of personal injury or wrongful death becoming statute-barred due to the negligence of the claimant's solicitor. In these circumstances the Court of Appeal in *Kitchen v Royal Air Force Association*,[322] the earliest and perhaps the leading case on this issue, awarded £2,000 to a claimant widow, it being agreed that £3,000 was the highest she would have been awarded had her Fatal

---

315 [2006] P.N.L.R. 6 at 94.

316 [1993] 2 F.L.R. 321. And see *White v Jones* [1995] 2 A.C. 207 CA, in the footnote at the end of para.10-073, above, where again no discount was made in a claim against the solicitor.

317 *Perry v Raleys Solicitors* [2017] EWCA Civ 314 at [35].

318 [1996] P.N.L.R. 45 CA. See also *Harding Homes (East Street) Ltd & Ors v Bircham Dyson Bell (a firm)* [2015] EWHC 3329 (Ch)

319 [1996] P.N.L.R. 45 CA at 55.

320 See para.10-059, above.

321 See para.10-076, below.

322 [1958] 1 W.L.R. 563 CA.

Accidents Act claim in respect of her husband's death been brought to trial. Soon after, in *Yardley v Coombes*,[323] £1,000 was awarded on the basis that the claimant's claim for personal injuries against his employers would have had a fair chance of success and, had it succeeded, would have resulted in an award for some £3,000. Much more recently the Privy Council had to deal in *Phillips & Co v Whatley*,[324] with a claim against a solicitor where there was not only the question of whether the statute-barred personal injury action would have been successful but also the question of whether damages awarded would have been paid by the insurer. There was therefore a double loss of a chance.[325]

*(ii) Claims against insurance brokers* Loss of a chance has appeared in actions against insurance brokers by their clients for inadequately insuring them. These claims have from time to time been met with the argument that no action lay because the clients would not have been able to claim on the policy which should have eventuated on the ground that some fault on the client's part would in law have allowed the insurance company to repudiate the policy. The courts, however, have seen the issue rather as one of the degree of chance that the insurance company would in practice have repudiated on account of the insured's fault. In the result they have in some cases held that in practice there would have been no repudiation and have allowed full recovery, as in *Fraser v B.N. Forman (Productions)*,[326] and *Dunbar v A. & B. Painters*,[327] while in others the full claim has been discounted, by one third in *Everett v Hogg Robinson*,[328] and by 70 per cent in *O. & R. Jewellers v Terry and Jardine Insurance Brokers*.[329] It was necessary in this last case to assess the chance not only of whether the insurance company would have taken the defence on the policy available to it but also of whether, had the broker's duty been performed, the claimant would have had any policy at all. It was the assessment of the loss of this double chance which led to the very substantial discount there. As for the much earlier decision in favour of the defendant broker in *Cheshire v Vaughan*,[330] it is believed to be wrong in the light of these later authorities.[331] **10-077**

*(iii) Claims against accountants* In *University of Keele v Price Waterhouse*,[332] a university, which wished to set up a tax-efficient profit-related pay scheme for its employees, was wrongly advised by the defendant accountants as to the number of participating employees required for the scheme to be valid, with the result that the scheme failed and the university had to pay substantial amounts in tax to the Inland Revenue, amounts which it sought to recover as damages from the defendants. It was held that the proper approach to the damages was to consider the chance that the university would have had, if it had been properly advised, to achieve the **10-078**

---

[323] (1963) 107 S.J. 575.

[324] [2008] Lloyd's Rep. I.R. 111 PC.

[325] This aspect of the case is dealt with at para.10-103, below.

[326] [1967] 1 W.L.R. 898 CA.

[327] [1986] 2 Lloyd's Rep. 38 CA. *Fraser* and *Dunbar* were applied in *Arbory Group Ltd v West Craven Insurance Services* [2007] Lloyd's Rep. I.R. 491.

[328] [1973] 2 Lloyd's Rep. 217 CA.

[329] [1999] L.R.L.R. 436.

[330] [1920] 3 K.B. 240 CA; the case is dealt with at para.35-007, below.

[331] See, too, *Bollom & Co Ltd v Byas Mosley & Co* [2000] Lloyd's Rep. I.R. 136 where the nature of the claim, by insured against insurance broker, was said to be for damages for the lost chance of recovering more from the insurer than the insured had done.

[332] [2004] P.N.L.R. 8 at 112.

required number of employee participants. The court assessed the chances of success at 80 per cent, thereby entitling the university to recover 80 per cent of the moneys it had paid over in tax.[333] *Floyd v John Fairhurst & Co*,[334] also involved a negligent accountant and tax adviser. When advising the claimant in relation to a compulsory purchase of his land, the tax adviser failed to inform the claimant of the availability of so-called roll-over relief against capital gains tax if he reinvested his compensation in replacement qualifying assets. Since it was accepted that the claimant had to show not simply that he had lost the chance of taking advantage of roll-over relief but that on the balance of probabilities he would have done so[335] and since the trial judge and the Court of Appeal both held that he had failed in this, his claim necessarily failed. Nonetheless both courts considered the damages to which the claimant would have been entitled had he satisfied them that he would have utilised the roll-over relief.[336]

**10-079** In *First Interstate Bank of California v Cohen Arnold*,[337] the claimant bank had advanced moneys to finance a development secured by a mortgage over certain properties and by a personal guarantee, the defendant accountants wrongly and negligently having assured the claimants that the guarantor was a man of great wealth. The properties were eventually sold by the claimant bank at a considerable loss with no recourse against the guarantor. The case brings in, as did *Allied Maples v Simmons & Simmons*,[338] questions both of hypothetical actions by the claimant and of hypothetical actions by third parties. The right approach, said the Court of Appeal, was first to decide whether on the balance of probabilities the claimants would have taken immediate steps to market the mortgaged properties had they not received the assurance from the defendants, then to decide what the chances of such a successful sale would have been and discount accordingly the amount at which the properties would have been expected to sell on an immediate marketing.

**10-080** *(iv) Claims against surveyors* In *Francis v Barclays Bank Plc*,[339] a bank's sale of land to a company provided that, if the company sold the land with planning permission for residential development within 10 years, the bank would be entitled to half of the price at which the company sold. About a year after the sale by the bank the company offered it an immediate £25,000 if it would limit its future entitlement to £75,000. The bank would only agree to this if it regarded it as unlikely that the planning status of the land would change and be brought within the boundary for permitting residential development. The bank consulted the surveyor as to the prospects of such re-designation and the surveyor negligently advised that the prospects were slim. Accordingly the bank accepted the company's offer, the land was duly re-designated, planning permission was obtained and the company sold for over £2 million. The surveyor argued that his negligence had caused the bank no loss as the company would have deferred sale with planning permission until the 10-year period had elapsed, thereby entitling the bank to no part of the company's

---

333 No damages issue appears in the appeal: [2004] P.N.L.R. 43 CA at 888.
334 [2004] P.N.L.R. 41 CA at 795.
335 [2004] P.N.L.R. 41 CA at [10].
336 The various heads are considered very fully and fairly in Arden LJ's leading judgment but of course they no longer required to be estimated as loss of a chance damages.
337 [1996] P.N.L.R. 17 CA.
338 [1995] 1 W.L.R. 1602 CA.
339 [2005] P.N.L.R. 18 at 297.

selling price. The trial judge held, however, that it was twice as likely that the company would have gone ahead with the sale, as it did, and not have awaited the expiry of the 10 years; this represented the lost chance. *Dennard v PricewaterhouseCoopers LLP*,[340] on the other hand involved a sale to, rather than by, a bank. The defendant valuer had negligently undervalued certain private finance initiative projects, the interests of the claimants in which they were selling to a bank. The award of damages for the loss of the chance of increasing the purchase price was 75 per cent of the amount by which the trial judge estimated that the bank, on a proper valuation, would have been prepared to go higher.[341] In *Malmesbury v Strutt & Parker*,[342] chartered surveyors, advising clients on the grant by them of a lease, were negligent in not seeking a turnover rent from the lessee. The first issue in *Malmesbury*,[343] was to evaluate the lost chance of the lessee agreeing to a turnover rent and to what percentage of the turnover rent would come to the lessors.[344]

*(v) Claims against other professional advisers* In *Gascoine v Ian Sheridan & Co and Latham*,[345] where the claimant's medical negligence claim had been struck out seven years after service of writ for want of prosecution, action was brought against the barrister in addition to the solicitor. Negligence in the conduct of the litigation was admitted by both and the only issue was the assessment of the chance of success of the medical negligence claim. The barrister was included as defendant with the solicitor also in *Luke v Wansbroughs*,[346] and *Hickman v Blake Lapthorn*,[347] by claimants alleging that the negligence of their professional advisers had lost them the chance of doing better in litigation.[348] In *John D Wood & Co (Residential and Agricultural) v Knatchbull*,[349] an estate agent's negligent failure to inform his client properly on prices rendered him liable in damages for the client's loss of a chance of selling his property at a higher figure.[350] **10-081**

*(vi) Personal injury claims* One may start a consideration of personal injury claims and loss of a chance by turning to the frequently-posed problem of whether a claimant, who is tortiously injured en route for an interview for a highly lucrative post resulting in loss of interview and loss of the chance of the post, can recover in respect of the loss of the post. The anterior, and more difficult, problem is whether **10-082**

---

340 [2010] EWHC 812 Ch.

341 See [2010] EWHC 812 Ch at [200] to [207].

342 [2007] P.N.L.R. 29 at 571.

343 Facts, and second issue, at para.34-082, below.

344 In assessing this chance, however, Jack J may not have realised its full impact as a comparison of [149] with [163] of his judgment indicates.

345 (1994) 5 Med. L.R. 437.

346 [2005] P.N.L.R. 2 at 15; the claim against both failed, but the case is useful because of the neat juxtaposition of loss of the chance of winning the action, which the defendants had settled at an undervalue and which was for malicious falsehood causing the ruin of an army career, and loss of earnings in that career. The former was calculated along loss of a chance lines, the latter in traditional fashion by discounting for contingencies: see the section from the judgment on quantum at [121]–[126]. Compare personal injury claims at paras 10-082 and following, below.

347 [2006] P.N.L.R. 20 at 371; see the case at para.10-074, above.

348 *Gosfield School Ltd v Birkett Long* [2006] P.N.L.R 19 at 342 is a further example of a claim, albeit unsuccessful, where both solicitor and barrister were sued.

349 [2003] 1 E.G.L.R. 33.

350 Facts at para.34-092, below.

this damage is too remote[351]; but if this is resolved in the claimant's favour, there seems no reason why the claimant should be debarred from all recovery on the grounds of uncertainty. And there is support in the case of *Mulvaine v Joseph*,[352] for allowing recovery for the loss of the chance of obtaining work or employment. An American club professional golfer, while on a European tour, had his hand injured as a result of a taxi-driver's negligence and he was awarded damages

> "for loss of opportunity of competing in tournaments, the ensuing loss of experience and prestige which might have resulted in him becoming a tournament professional in America and loss of a chance of winning prize money".[353]

But in the quantification of loss the personal injury cases have now gone much further down the loss of a chance road.

**10-083** In *Doyle v Wallace*,[354] the claimant, injured at 19, maintained that she would have qualified and been employed as a drama teacher, failing which she would have obtained clerical or administrative work, which was less remunerative. The defendant argued that this was not a loss of a chance case and that "the judge should have decided what probably would have happened",[355] contending that it was not probable that the claimant would have become a drama teacher. The trial judge thought differently and for his award for loss of earnings he took the midpoint between a drama teacher's salary and the lower clerical or administrative salary. In this he was upheld by the Court of Appeal who considered he had been correct to apply a percentage as a means of quantification. Being therefore a quantification of loss case and not a loss of chance case proper, it was unnecessary, and probably wrong, for the Court of Appeal to hold that "the loss of a chance to become a dance teacher fell within Stuart Smith LJ's third category"[356] in *Allied Maples*. This category, concerning the action of a third party, is directed to the action of a specific third party, or occasionally specific third parties, and not to third parties in general. There is a world of difference between the specific potential employer about to interview the claimant for a position and employers in general who might take the claimant on as a drama teacher.[357]

**10-084** Much more complicated than *Doyle* was *Langford v Hebran*.[358] The complications were due to the fact that, whereas in *Doyle* there were only two potential careers envisaged, in *Langford* there was a whole series of career options put forward for consideration for a young, highly successful professional boxer struck down in a car collision. Because he would have retired from fighting at a comparatively early age and then worked at something else, it was necessary to think in terms of a two-stage career. Not only were various possibilities canvassed

---

351 Considered at para.8-109, above. It was on this ground that the claimant failed in *Hoey v Felton* (1861) 11 C.B. N.S. 142, and on this it is now questionable.

352 (1968) 112 S.J. 927.

353 (1968) 112 S.J. 927; including damages "for disappointment felt by the plaintiff through the frustration of his plans". Contrast the refusal of recovery in *McGee v Francis Shaw & Co* [1973] R.T.R. 409, where the chance of going abroad on remunerative employment would never have materialised because of a work strike.

354 [1998] P.I.Q.R. Q146 CA.

355 [1998] P.I.Q.R. Q146 CA at 148.

356 [1998] P.I.Q.R. Q146 CA at 150.

357 See para.10-057, above where it is argued that loss of chance matters extend beyond the third party actions of *Allied Maples*.

358 [2001] P.I.Q.R. Q13 CA at 160.

for the second stage but his fighting career was divided into various degrees of sporting success. Permutations abounded, everything carefully orchestrated in a report by a forensic accountant. Percentages were allocated to what were called the various scenarios, these percentages being worked out by using what was termed the stand alone method at first instance and by using what was termed the additional value method on appeal. For the welter of detail the judgments must be studied. Again, it was a quantification of loss calculation and not at all a loss of a chance situation in the true sense.

*Langford v Hebran* came under consideration in *Clarke v Maltby*,[359] where a career in only one field was under scrutiny. The career prospects of a badly injured solicitor were at the heart of her claim for loss of earnings. Three scenarios were advanced before the trial judge. Stated in summary, the claimant's progression was to be from a partnership in a regional law firm to one in a medium-sized city firm to one in a large city firm, and the chances of achieving this progression were held to be 100 per cent, 85 per cent and 30 percent respectively.[360] Thus the method adopted in *Langford v Hebran* was followed.[361] Even more clearly the case is one of quantification and not of loss of a chance proper. **10-085**

That there is generally no need to go down the loss of a chance route, not even when the court is presented with a young claimant at, or before, the start of his or her career, is very lucidly explained by Potter LJ in the sole reasoned judgment in *Herring v Ministry of Defence*,[362] where the claimant was a young man who, at the time of his serious injury in a parachuting accident while in the army air service, was contemplating an eventual career with the police. Potter LJ pointed out that, while the assessment of future loss is in a broad sense the assessment of a series of chances as to the likely future progress of the claimant in employment, such assessment has not traditionally been regarded as necessitating application of the technique of percentage assessment for loss of a chance based on the likely actions of third parties as articulated in *Allied Maples*.[363] Thus where a young claimant is just starting out in working life, the court may be able to select a career model appropriate to be used for the multiplicand in calculating earnings loss—in *Herring* it was a career in the police force—and the chance that the claimant will not in the event embark on that career or, having done so, may leave it will not be significant if the likelihood is, as it was in *Herring*, that he will move to similarly remunerated employment. In such a case it is neither necessary nor appropriate to adopt the percentage chance approach. That approach was only called for where the change in career was one that would significantly alter earning potential, which had been the position in both *Doyle* and *Langford*.[364] But "those decisions", said Potter LJ, **10-086**

> "have not purported to replace the traditional method of adjusting the multiplier or multiplicand within the career model appropriate to the particular claimant so as to reflect (a) the likelihood of an increase in earnings at some point in the claimant's career and (b)

359 [2010] EWHC 1201 (QB).

360 See [2010] EWHC 1201 (QB) at [84] to [94] together with the elaborate calculations appearing in an appendix to the judgment.

361 Also in *Tait v Gloucestershire Hospitals NHS Foundation Trust* [2015] EWHC 848 (QB) the *Langford* method is adopted: see at [88].

362 [2004] 1 All E.R. 44 CA.

363 [2004] 1 All E.R. 44 CA at [25].

364 At paras 10-083 and 10-084, above, respectively.

those contingencies/vicissitudes in respect of which a discount appears to be appropriate."[365]

Consequently, there was no need in *Herring* to consider loss of chances, the conventional method of assessment could be used, and the issue remaining was as to the proper discount to make for so-called contingencies.[366] So too the Court of Appeal agreed in *The Law Debenture Trust Corporation Plc v Electrim SA*,[367] that in assessing loss of earnings in personal injury cases the loss of a chance approach ought not to replace the traditional approach of adjusting the multiplier and the multiplicand.[368]

**10-087** The Court of Appeal adopted and applied its analysis in *Brown v Ministry of Defence*,[369] where the claimant's army career had been brought to an abrupt end through an accident right at its start during her basic training course. In respect of her lost earnings it was the case that not only would she have been likely to move to a career with a similar level of earnings but by the time of the trial she had already done so. Accordingly, loss of earnings did not represent a large part of her claim, but what is important here is that, as Moore-Bick LJ delivering the valuable judgment of the court indicated, the assessment could be done in the conventional way by route of contingencies and adjustments to the multiplicand without embarking on loss of a chance territory.[370] What the dispute in *Brown* centred around was the claimant's pension rights. If the claimant had continued for her full service term of 22 years, she would have qualified for an immediate pension whereas, if she retired earlier from service, the pension would not be payable until she attained 60. Thus completion of a full term had a significant effect on the value of her pension rights. The judges below—there had been two hearings—had reached the conclusion that on the balance of probabilities the claimant would have served a full term and awarded her damages based on a loss of full pension rights. The Court of Appeal disagreed; there should be separate assessments of the pension rights based on various periods during which the claimant might have remained in service as this would considerably reduce the award.[371] Therefore for the award for loss of pension rights, as opposed to the award for loss of earnings, it was appropriate to take the percentage approach and consider what were the chances that she would have retired at particular dates along the way.[372]

**10-088** In the light of *Herring* and *Brown*, cases have been able to avoid the loss of a chance route. Whereas in *Langford v Hebran* the career-ending injury was to a young professional boxer, it was to a young professional footballer in *Appleton v El Safty*,[373] and in *Collett v Smith*.[374] In *Appleton*, where the claimant's career in football had to be given up after negligent treatment of a comparatively minor injury, Christopher Clarke J's careful and elaborate computation of the damages,

---

365 [2004] 1 All E.R. 44 CA at [25].

366 This aspect of the case is dealt with at para.40-141, below.

367 [2010] EWCA Civ 1142 CA; with reference to this paragraph as it appeared in an earlier edition of this work.

368 [2010] EWCA Civ 1142 CA at [48].

369 [2006] P.I.Q.R. Q9 CA at 109.

370 See the judgment at [2006] P.I.Q.R. Q9 CA at [26].

371 See at [2006] P.I.Q.R. Q9 CA at [34] and [35].

372 Worked out with detailed care by the Court of Appeal: see [2006] P.I.Q.R. Q9 at [28]–[30].

373 [2007] EWHC 631 (QB).

374 [2008] EWHC 1962 (QB).

which took various chances about how the football career would have progressed into account, was successfully achieved without even mention of *Doyle* and *Langford*, or indeed of a single case. In *Collett*, where the negligent injury had been on the football field, Swift J, after referring briefly to several cases on loss of a chance including *Doyle* and *Langford*,[375] then proceeded to a careful and elaborate computation of the damages which equally took into account chances about the football career's likely progress, but without mentioning *Doyle* and *Langford* further. In the appeal[376] the trial judge's award was analysed in detail by Smith LJ in her leading judgment without resort to any authority and the trial judge was upheld, a principal issue being whether her discount of 15 per cent on the loss of future earnings had been too generous to the footballer claimant. While loss of a chance was naturally spoken of, the tenor of the judgment is in quantification terms. In *Leesmith v Evans*,[377] the injury was to a young motorcyclist whose career was to be in the entertainment lighting industry. Cooke J held that the possible steps in the progress of the claimant's career, which was only just beginning at the time of the accident, could be taken into account in the usual way in the assessment of the appropriate multiplier and multiplicand. He specifically said that he had no need to adopt the *Doyle* and *Langford* approach and could follow the more conventional course as indicated by the Court of Appeal in *Herring* and *Brown*.[378] The distinction between this conventional course and the route by way of a loss of a chance calculation is well brought out in *Heil v Rankin*,[379] a decision after *Doyle* but before *Herring*. The trial judge had assessed the claimant's loss of earnings in the police force on the basis of the loss of the chance of remaining in police service in the same capacity until retirement age, a chance expressed by the judge in percentage terms and assessed by him at 25 per cent. In varying this percentage, which the Court of Appeal thought over-pessimistic, to 50 per cent[380] Otton LJ, delivering the court's judgment, pointed out that, in discounting the loss of earnings to retirement age by a percentage, "the judge did no more than apply what has become known as the 'vicissitudes' principle",[381] the vicissitudes discount being more commonly known as the discount for the contingencies of life.[382]

The uncertainties as to the future were even greater and more extensive than ever in *XYZ v Portsmouth Hospitals NHS Trust*.[383] The claimant had reached the top in the employed sector of the pharmaceutical industry and had already at the time of his severe injury resigned from his very senior post in order to set up his own pharmaceutical business where the rewards would be far greater. It thus fell to the court to consider whether the new business would have started at all, how quickly it would have succeeded, what level of turnover it would have reached and when, and finally the amount for which the business would have sold at the end of the day. In an elaborate, careful judgment Spencer J arrived at a whole series of percentage **10-089**

375 [2008] EWHC 1962 (QB) at [93] to [96].
376 [2009] EWCA Civ 583 CA.
377 [2008] EWHC 134 (QB).
378 [2008] EWHC 134 (QB) at [102].
379 [2001] P.I.Q.R. Q3 CA at 16: facts at para.8-027, above.
380 [2001] P.I.Q.R. Q3 CA at [32] and [33].
381 [2001] P.I.Q.R. Q3 CA at [12].
382 See paras 40-128 and following, below. And see, outside personal injury, *Luke v Wansbroughs* [2005] P.N.L.R. 2 at 15 at para.10-081, above.
383 [2011] EWHC 243 (QB).

chances.[384] Once again, the case is one of quantification and not of loss of a chance proper.

**10-090** There are also several cases of negligence in medical treatment or medical diagnosis where what was in issue was loss of a chance in the proper sense of that term. In *Pearman v North Essex Health Authority*[385] it was held that the claimant had to prove that the correct treatment by the hospital would probably have made a difference and he could not recover damages simply for the loss of a chance of making a complete or better recovery. In analogous fact situations *Hardaker v Newcastle Health Authority*,[386] came to the same conclusion by applying *Hotson*,[387] but *Smith v National Health Service Litigation Authority*,[388] allowed recovery for loss of the chance by distinguishing *Hotson* and holding that *Allied Maples*,[389] applied. As the law currently stands, with *Gregg v Scott*[390] now backing up *Hotson*,[391] *Smith* surely was wrong. Certainly Stanley Burnton J in *Hardaker* had no doubt that it was.[392]

**10-091** *(vii) Wrongful death claims* Claims under the Fatal Accidents Act for loss of dependency generally involve persons undoubtedly dependent on the deceased, but a case may take on the attributes of a claim for loss of a chance when the likelihood that the deceased would have provided support for the claimant is slim. This arose in *Davies v Taylor*,[393] itself, where there was only a speculative chance that a reconciliation between the claimant widow and her deceased husband would have come about,[394] and again in *Barnett v Cohen*,[395] where the claim of parents for eventual support by their deceased infant child was "pressed to extinction by the weight of multiplied contingencies".[396] No award for loss of a chance was awarded in either case; both are quantification of loss cases

**10-092** *(viii) Claims arising in connection with contracts of employment* In *Spring v Guardian Assurance*,[397] the claimant's ex-employer, Guardian Assurance, negligently gave a bad reference for him to Scottish Amicable Assurance, a potential employer of the claimant. The House of Lords, having held that Guardian Assurance owed a duty of care to the claimant in the giving of references, remitted the case for the ascertainment of whether the breach of duty had caused the claimant

---

384 See his summary of each at [2011] EWHC 243 (QB) at [260].

385 [2000] Lloyd's Rep. Med. 174.

386 [2001] Lloyd's Rep. Med. 512.

387 [1987] A.C. 750; at para.10-045, above.

388 [2001] Lloyd's Rep. Med. 90.

389 [1995] 1 W.L.R. 1602 CA; at para.10-058, above.

390 [2005] 2 A.C. 176.

391 For the analysis of *Gregg v Scott* see paras 10-052 and following, above.

392 [2001] Lloyd's Rep. Med. 512 at [70]. In *Rust-Andrews v First-tier Tribunal* [2011] EWCA Civ 1548 CA, a personal injury claim for compensation under the Criminal Injuries Compensation Scheme, deciding on the correctness of limiting the damages for loss of future earnings to a number of years brought in balance of probabilities and loss of a chance before the Court of Appeal.

393 [1974] A.C. 207.

394 See the case at para.41-030, below, where *Hayes v South East Coast Ambulance Service NHS Foundation Trust* [2015] EWHC 18 (QB) is cited as a case in which the chance of reconciliation was very high.

395 [1921] 2 K.B. 461.

396 [1921] 2 K.B. 461 at 472. See the case at para.41-099, below.

397 [1995] 2 A.C. 296.

loss and for the assessment of damages. In this connection Lord Lowry in his speech said:

> "Once the duty of care is held to exist and the defendants' negligence is proved, the plaintiff only has to show that by reason of that negligence he has lost a reasonable chance of employment (which would have to be evaluated) and has thereby sustained loss ... He does not have to prove that, but for the negligent reference, Scottish Amicable *would* have employed him."[398]

But it is thought that the loss of a chance doctrine had no proper application to the many employee claims in *Bank of Credit and Commerce International v Ali*[399] for so-called stigma compensation by reason of being put at a disadvantage in the labour market by the spectacular collapse in a welter of fraud of the bank employing them. The trial judge's statement in that case that *Allied Maples*

> "clearly lays down that in the case of applications for jobs to be made in the future after the date of the trial, the court must adopt the 'loss of a chance' approach and decide whether stigma will deprive them of a real chance of success on future applications for employment"[400]

must be wrong.[401]

*(ix) Miscellaneous types of claim* Damages on the basis of loss of the chance of **10-093**
a profitable sale of property in a claim for breach of statutory duty not to damage property through nuclear activity were awarded in *Blue Circle Industries v Ministry of Defence*.[402] The claimant's estate having becoming contaminated with radioactive material, it was virtually unsaleable until the completion of remedial work carried out during a period of falling prices. *Albion Water Ltd v Dwr Cymru Cyfyngedig*,[403] heard in the Competition Appeal Tribunal, involved the issuing of an anti-competitive, unlawfully high price for water which resulted in the loss to the claimant of the opportunity to conclude a profitable contract for the supply of water in bulk.[404] In *4 Eng Ltd v Harper*,[405] the loss of a chance principle was held to apply to an action of deceit as much as to a claim in negligence. Here the claimant company claimed damages for, among other things, loss of profits from the

398 [1995] 2 A.C. 296 at 327F to G. In *Allied Maples v Simmons & Simmons* [1995] 1 W.L.R. 1602 CA, Stuart-Smith LJ said he agreed with Lord Lowry's statement.

399 [1999] 4 All E.R. 83.

400 [1999] 4 All E.R. 83 at 110d.

401 See the case in a footnote to para.33-031, below and compare *Janciuk v Winerite* [1998] I.R.L.R. 63 at para.10-068, above: employee's unsuccessful claim for loss of chance of non-dismissal. *Harper v Virgin Net Ltd* [2004] I.R.L.R. 390 CA establishes that an employee suing for damages for summary wrongful dismissal without the contractual notice to which she was entitled cannot claim for the loss of a chance of recovering compensation for unfair dismissal on the basis that by the end of the contractual notice, but not by the end of the statutory notice to which entitled under the unfair dismissal provisions, she would have had the necessary qualifying service to support a claim for unfair dismissal. Properly analysed, there was no loss of a chance. The employee did not lose her right to claim for unfair dismissal as she never had such a right; she fell short of the length of continuous service prescribed by the legislature as the gateway to such a right: See especially Chadwick LJ's judgment at [25] and [26]. *Harper* was applied in *Wise Group v Mitchell* [2005] I.C.R. 896 EAT.

402 [1999] Ch. 289 CA.

403 [2013] C.A.T. 6.

404 The loss of a chance aspect of the case is at [190]–[223].

405 [2009] Ch. 91.

particular company that it would have sought to purchase instead of what turned out to be the worthless company fraudulently sold to it by the defendants.[406] A high percentage recovery was allowed since David Richards J was satisfied not only that the claimant had established on the balance of probabilities that it would have been able and willing to purchase the company on certain specified terms[407] but also that there was an 80 per cent chance that the owners of that company would have been prepared to sell it to the claimant.[408] *S.B.J. Stephenson Ltd v Mandy*,[409] illustrates the operation of loss of a chance in the field of breach of confidential information. The claimant was awarded damages for the loss of the chance of retaining eight clients who had left because of solicitation by the defendant through his possession of the confidential information. So too in *Take Ltd v BSM Marketing*,[410] there was misuse of information obtained in confidence, which required calculating the loss of the chance that the claimant would have continued to receive orders from a particular client. Commercial contracts of sale, too, have made their appearance on the loss of a chance front. The situation in *North Sea Energy Holdings v Petroleum Authority of Thailand*,[411] was complex, and actions of the claimant, of the third party and also of the defendant—the seller of the oil, the seller's seller and the buyer respectively—all fell to be considered cumulatively in order to ascertain whether the claimant would have been able to deliver the oil. Only nominal damages were awarded to the claimant since it was held that there was no chance or no real chance of the third party producing the oil for the claimant to sell on to the defendant. The claimant's actions were therefore of less significance but to these the balance of probabilities test was applied, while the standard for the defendant's actions was not properly passed upon.[412] Even where in *Les Laboratoires Servier v Apotex Inc*,[413] the claim was for compensation brought on a cross-undertaking as to damages on account of being restrained by injunction from infringing a patent later held to be invalid, loss of a chance was invoked by the court,[414] being the loss of the chance, or opportunity, to enter a new market barred on account of the injunction. The claimants in *Nicholas Prestige Homes v Neal*[415] were estate agents and the defendant was a house owner who sold her house through another estate agent in breach of her sole agency agreement with the claimants. The claimants were held entitled to damages for the loss of the chance of themselves selling the house and earning their commission. In *Van der Garde v Force India Formula One Team Ltd*,[416] damages of $100,000 were held to be awardable for the claimant motor racing driver's loss of opportunity of enhancing his experience and reputation in the field of mo-

---

406 Full facts at para.49-025, below.
407 [2009] Ch. 91 at [80].
408 [2009] Ch. 91 at [92].
409 [2000] F.S.R. 286.
410 [2007] EWHC 3513 (QB).
411 [1999] 1 Lloyd's Rep. 483 CA; facts at para.25-129, below.
412 See especially Waller LJ, delivering the court's judgment, [1999] 1 Lloyd's Rep. 483 CA at 493–496.
413 [2009] F.S.R. 3 at 220.
414 The judge, at [2009] F.S.R. 3 at 220, [5(d)], even cited Vaughan Williams LJ in *Chaplin v Hicks* (see para.10-040, above) as bearing on the resolution of the matter of compensation before him.
415 [2010] EWCA Civ 1552 CA.
416 [2010] EWHC 2373 (QB); facts at para.3-010, above.

tor racing and thereby his ability to participate in remunerative Formula One testing and racing competitions.[417]

**(d) Assessment of the value of the lost chance** Sometimes the court has an easy ride and can satisfy itself without difficulty that no chance has been lost, or that the chance lost was at most wholly speculative. Thus in *Halifax Building Society v Urquart-Dykes and Lord*,[418] that the negligent advice of a trade mark agent had prevented his principal from reaching a better deal with a competitor than was achieved was considered purely speculative so that there was no loss of a valuable chance[419]; in *Casey v Hugh James Jones & Jenkins*,[420] there was held to have been no real or substantial, but only a speculative, chance that the claimant's personal injury claim would have succeeded; in *Gosfield School Ltd v Birkett Long*,[421] the chance lost was held to be too speculative to have a money value put on it.[422] Conversely, the court may find itself satisfied that realisation of the chance was a virtual certainty so that it becomes appropriate to award what would have been awarded against the original defendant. Thus in the Irish *McGrath v Kiely and Powell*,[423] the claimant was awarded against her solicitor and her doctor the whole of the extra damages she would have obtained in her successful personal injury claim had the full extent of her injuries been revealed to the court. Full recovery was also allowed by the Court of Appeal in *White v Jones*,[424] and in *Nicholson v Knox Ukiwa & Co*,[425] there was held to be no chance that the claimant's action against his bank would have failed.[426] So too in *Nicholas Prestige Homes v Neal*,[427] there was no chance that the estate agents would not have succeeded in selling the defendant's property[428] so that, as Ward LJ said, no discount had to be made for imponderables.[429] **10-094**

*(i) Where the chance relates to success in a damages claim* The Court of Appeal held in *Mount v Barker Austin*,[430] that, while the claimant client had the legal burden of proving that he had a real and substantial, as opposed to a negligible or speculative, chance of success in the original claim to which he was a party, the evidential burden of proof of the contrary shifted to the solicitor defendant. In **10-095**

---

417 All at [2010] EWHC 2373 (QB) at [376]–[412]. This was only the residual claim in *Van der Garde*, much larger sums being held to be awardable on either of two other grounds dealt with at para.3-010, above and para.14-046, below.

418 [1997] R.P.C. 55.

419 [1997] R.P.C. 55 at 87, line 18.

420 [1999] Lloyd's Rep. P.N. 115.

421 [2006] P.N.L.R 19 at 342.

422 [2006] P.N.L.R 19 at [125] to [131]; the claim, against solicitor and barrister, would have failed on earlier issues of breach of duty and causation. For other cases of chances too speculative to permit any recovery see the wrongful death cases at para.10-091, above, Cancer Research Campaign v Ernest Brown & Co [1998] P.N.L.R. 592 and *Veitch v Avery* (2007) 115 Con. L.R. 70 at para.10-073, above (in a fn.), and *Checkprice (UK) Ltd v Revenue and Customs Commissioners* [2010] EWHC 682 (Admin) at para.38-009, below.

423 [1965] I.R. 497.

424 [1995] 2 A.C. 207 CA. See the case at para.10-073(in a footnote), above.

425 [2008] P.N.L.R. 33 at 782; facts at para.34-086, below.

426 [2008] P.N.L.R. 33 at 98 and following.

427 [2010] EWCA Civ 1552 CA.

428 Facts at para.10-093, above.

429 [2010] EWCA Civ 1552 CA at [33].

430 [1998] P.N.L.R. 493 CA.

*Mount* itself the defendant solicitor was held to have discharged what was described as the heavy burden of demonstrating that the claimant client would have been bound to fail in the original claim. *Mount* also laid down further propositions[431] adverse to defendant solicitors. First, it was said that, if the court now has greater difficulty in discerning the strength of the claimant's original claim, or defence, than it would have had at the time of the original action, such difficulty should not count against him but rather against his negligent solicitor. Secondly, it was said that generally speaking, when evaluating the claimant's chances of success, one would expect the court to tend towards a generous assessment given that it was the defendant's negligence which lost the claimant the opportunity of succeeding in full or fuller measure. And further emphasis on the advantageous position of a claimant in a loss of a chance case is made in *Browning v Brachers*,[432] by bringing in, as have earlier cases there cited, the well-known and, though very old, still important decision in *Armory v Delamirie*.[433] Jonathan Parker LJ, giving the only reasoned judgment with which the others agreed, there said that the principle in that case

> "raises an evidential (i.e. rebuttable) presumption in favour of the claimant which gives him the benefit of any relevant doubt. The practical effect of that is to give the claimant a fair wind in establishing the value of what he has lost."[434]

**10-096** Moreover, as was also emphasised by the Court of Appeal in *Browning v Brachers*, and earlier in *Dixon v Clement Jones Solicitors*,[435] it is not the task of the court to attempt to conduct a trial of the lost action but simply to assess its prospects of success. Nevertheless it is instructive to see that, while this is the aim, it did not prevent somewhat different results being arrived at in *Browning* by the trial judge[436] and by the Court of Appeal.[437] The case concerned the sale of a goat-farming business where the seller had brought an action against the buyers alleging that part of the price had not been paid and the buyers counterclaimed for lost profits alleging that the goatherd sold to them had infected their own herd. The buyers' side of the litigation was handled so badly by their solicitor that the counterclaim was dismissed with costs; at about the same time the seller's claim was settled. In the buyers' successful action against their solicitor for professional negligence the trial judge applied what he called a broad brush approach without attempting to retry the putative action itself. He made estimates of what the buyers would have been awarded for loss of profits and of what the seller would have been awarded for unpaid price had their respective claims succeeded and then applied discounts of 30 per cent and 25 per cent respectively to take account of the chance of failure. In the Court of Appeal, while there was no dispute about the 30 per cent liability discount[438] the buyers' damages were substantially increased because the judge's

---

431 All are in the judgment of Simon Brown LJ: [1998] P.N.L.R. 493 CA at 510.

432 [2005] EWCA Civ 753 CA. The report at [2005] P.N.L.R. 44 at 901 is just a one page note; it does not set out the lengthy judgments on the appeal.

433 (1722) 1 Strange 505. For the *Armory v Delamirie* principle see para.38-049, below where it is raised in a somewhat different context.

434 [2005] EWCA Civ 753 CA at [210]. He considered the impact of *Armory v Delamirie* generally at [2005] EWCA Civ 753 CA at [204] to [213]. Facts in the next paragraph.

435 [2005] P.N.L.R. 6 CA at 93; for this case see para.10-064, above.

436 [2004] P.N.L.R. 28 at 517.

437 [2005] EWCA Civ 753 CA. The report at [2005] P.N.L.R. 44 at 901 is just a one page note; it does not set out the lengthy judgments on the appeal.

438 Indeed there was no appeal about it: see [2005] EWCA Civ 753 CA at [24].

estimates of their potential loss of profits had been ungenerous and faulty.[439] As for the 25 per cent discount which had brought the seller's very small claim for unpaid price down from the £8,000s to the £6,000s,[440] this went out of the window as the Court of Appeal held that the proper figure to take was the £5,000 at which the seller's claim had been earlier settled.[441]

In the early *Kitchen v Royal Air Force Association*,[442] Parker LJ had simply said that **10-097**

> "if the plaintiff can satisfy the court that she would have had some prospect of success then it would be for the court to evaluate those prospect,"[443]

but in the later *Yeoman's Executrix v Ferries*,[444] a Scots case, the Court of Session pointed out that it did not follow that the claimant should be denied substantial damages against the defendant solicitors merely because the court was itself of the view that on the evidence the claimant would have lost in the now statute-barred claim against his employer. The judge must consider the position as at the date the action would have been raised against the employer, taking into account not only the fact that the jury, which in a Scots case would have heard the claim, might have been more sympathetically inclined towards the claimant but also the fact that the action might have been settled. Later still in *Harrison v Bloom Camillin*,[445] Neuberger J in a careful and elaborate judgment explored many issues involving computation of the loss of the chance to bring now statute-barred legal proceedings: the propriety of taking into account the possibility that the action might be settled, the application of different discounts to different claims and different heads of damage, the greater readiness of a court to determine the likelihood of success or failure where the issue was one of law rather than of fact or opinion. And in *Pearson v Sanders Witherspoon*,[446] where the solicitor's negligence lay in not pursuing his client's claim against a company timeously so that judgment, once obtained, could not be enforced because the company had gone into receivership, the court did not simply award the amount of that judgment but arrived at a much smaller figure for the value of the lost chance, after a careful scrutiny and detailed analysis of the merits of the claim with its various heads of loss, the company not having appeared at the hearing. The court arrived at a 50 per cent reduction since a judgment, even if obtained timeously, might still not have been enforceable or not enforceable in its entirety.

---

439 See the issues in the appeal set out at [2005] EWCA Civ 753 CA at [154] and the Court of Appeal's conclusions on all these matters at [2005] EWCA Civ 753 CA at [214] to [236].

440 See [2005] EWCA Civ 753 CA at [10] and [143].

441 [2005] EWCA Civ 753 CA at [237] and [259]. In addition, the trial judge held the buyers entitled to damages in respect of the costs payable by them to the seller in respect of the unsuccessful counterclaim; a discount of 25 per cent was applied here to cater for the fact that, even if the buyers had been successful, some part of the costs of their counterclaim could well have been disallowed (see [2004] P.N.L.R. 28 at 517, [96]). This aspect of the case, upon which there was no appeal (see [2005] EWCA Civ 753 CA at [149]), may or may not be regarded as concerning the loss of a chance.

442 [1958] 1 W.L.R. 563 CA.

443 [1958] 1 W.L.R. 563 CA at 576.

444 1967 S.L.T. 332.

445 [2000] Lloyd's Rep. P.N. 89.

446 [2000] P.N.L.R. 110 CA.

**10-098** The logically correct proposition is that the damages that would have been awarded in the original action fall to be assessed at the time when the original action would have been heard,[447] or in some cases settled, as opposed to the frequently much later time that the claim against the solicitor is heard. For it is the chance of this outcome to the litigation that has been lost; certainly it would seem wrong for the solicitor to have to pay in damages more than the claimant would have recovered in the original action. The issue has now come before the Court of Appeal three times. On the first occasion, in 2000, what is considered to be the right solution, where taking subsequent events into account would increase the damages, came to grief, despite its firm support in earlier Australian and Canadian cases.[448] This was in *Charles v Hugh James Jones & Jenkins*.[449] The Court of Appeal there held, where the claimant's original action was for personal injury, that the deterioration in his physical condition could be taken into account although the deterioration was subsequent to the time at which the original action would have been heard. Yet there was an important qualification made in Swinton Thomas LJ's leading judgment; the court reserved its position on what would be the effect of the appearance after the notional trial date of an entirely new worsening condition.[450]

**10-099** The Court of Appeal returned to the problem in *Dudarec v Andrews*,[451] where once again the defendant solicitor had failed properly to pursue the claimant's personal injury claim, the action having been struck out for want of prosecution. The main issue in that action would have been whether, the claimant having been diagnosed as having a false aneurysm which seriously affected his ability to work, his refusal to have surgery to correct it, surgery which was slightly risky, constituted a failure to mitigate. However, by the time the action against the solicitor came on, which was eight years after the personal injury claim would have been heard, it had transpired that there had not been a false aneurysm after all. The claimant's ability to work had in truth never been affected.[452] But there is not a clear holding that subsequent events can be taken into account because the view was taken that, had the personal injury claim been heard in 1996, in preparing for trial the non-existence of the false aneurysm would have been discovered.

**10-100** The Court of Appeal returned to the problem again in *Whitehead v Hibbert Pownall & Newton*,[453] where at last it was presented with a radical change of circumstances which had come about, and which could not have been discovered,

---

[447] And also at the place where it would have been heard; See *Malyon v Lawrence Messer & Co* (1968) 112 S.J. 623, where damages were assessed on the basis of the fruits of the claimant's action had it been tried in West Germany, where the accident causing the physical injury happened, and also in 1962, when the case would have been heard but for the defendant solicitor's negligence.

[448] *Johnson v Perez* (1988) 82 A.L.R. 587 HC of Australia (increase through inflation in tariff for pain and suffering not to be taken into account); *Nikolaou v Papasavas Phillips & Co* (1988) 82 A.L.R. 617 HC of Australia (deterioration in claimant's injured leg to be ignored); *Rose v Mitton* (1994) 111 D.L.R. (4th) 217 CA of Nova Scotia (increase in claimant's loss of earning capacity to be ignored). This solution also later received strong support in the Scots courts in *Campbell v Inray* (reported at [2004] P.N.L.R. 1 at 1) from Lord Emslie, cogently criticising, and indicating the anomalies of, the English approach (at [49]).

[449] [2000] 1 W.L.R. 1278 CA.

[450] [2000] 1 W.L.R. 1278 CA at 1290G.

[451] [2006] 1 W.L.R. 3002 CA.

[452] While the three judgments of the court do not follow the same pattern, in all three there is to be found a preference for Swinton Thomas LJ's approach in *Charles* over the Scots Lord Emslie's in *Campbell* (referred to in a fn. to para.10-098, above).

[453] [2008] P.N.L.R. 25 at 625.

before the time when the claim upon which the defendant solicitors had been instructed would have been heard but for their negligent handling of it. For the claimant in that claim had died, having committed suicide. The case, unlike the earlier ones, was not one of straightforward personal injury through negligence. Rather the negligence consisted in the failure of a hospital authority's clinicians to diagnose spina bifida in the child that the claimant had been carrying, thereby depriving her of the opportunity of a termination.[454] The claim against the solicitors, which was brought by the administrators of the mother's estate she having died intestate, sought damages for the costs of the child's care uncurtailed by the death, damages which it was taken that the mother would have been able to claim had she lived on. The judgments, which cover a substantial number of issues, are elaborate but the decision at the heart of the case can be expressed shortly: the claim for the costs of the child's care from the time of the mother's suicide until the time her death would have occurred in the normal course failed. The court was not prepared to ignore the suicide and to act as if it had never happened.

In *Charles*,[455] the taking into account of developments after the notional trial date served to increase the damages. By contrast, in *Dudarec* and again in *Whitehead* this caused the damages to be significantly smaller, if not eliminated. In a previous edition of this text the question was asked whether, if after the notional trial date for the original action a newly discovered miracle cure were to restore the claimant to his pre-accident condition or he were to meet an unexpected death, a court would be happy with the logic of awarding a whole normal lifetime of sizeable earnings and onerous medical expenses. Clearly, as *Whitehead* shows, a court would not be, and rightly so. And in the previous edition it was also suggested that the best route to the resolution of the dilemma posed by logic and sense here pulling in different directions was to invoke the mitigation rule that there can be no recovery not only for avoidable loss but also for loss which has in fact been avoided unless the matter is collateral.[456] Of course this has no application to cases where taking subsequent events into account increases the damages, and it is significant that Laws LJ ended his judgment in *Whitehead*[457] with this: **10-101**

> "There may be cases where a supervening event, happening after the notional trial date, would if taken into account in the later action swell the damages rather than diminish them. Different considerations might then arise. Nothing I have said is intended to express a view about such a case."

In both *Dudarec* and *Whitehead* the court sought to justify its conclusion by another route, and one which could be applied equally to the cases where the damages would be increased, as in *Charles*, rather than diminished. This was by reliance on the broad general principle that, in Harman LJ's words in *Curwen v James*,[458] "the court should never speculate where it knows", a principle based on Lord Macnaghten's speech in *Bwllfa and Merthyr Dare Steam Collieries v Pontypridd Waterworks Co*.[459] Yet praying in aid this perfectly acceptable, and **10-102**

---

454 Such a case may yet be regarded as one of personal injury, important for limitation purposes; the matter is uncertain. See para.40-282, below.

455 And in the Australian and Canadian cases, and also the Scots case, cited at para.10-098, above.

456 See this rule at paras 9-108 and following above.

457 [2008] P.N.L.R. 25 at 625, [29].

458 [1963] 1 W.L.R. 748 CA; see para.40-053, below.

459 [1903] A.C. 426 at 431. Cited and relied on by Sedley LJ in *Dudarec* [2006] 1 W.L.R. 3002 CA at

universally accepted, principle is entirely inappropriate in this context where the very question is what was known when judgment should have been given in the mishandled claim and not what was known when the claim against the solicitor was eventually heard.

10-103 *(ii) Method of computation where there is more than one factor in the loss of a chance* Starting at the turn of the century quite a few cases have appeared in which more than one chance has been lost, requiring the court to arrive at the proper method of computation. These cases have practically all been against solicitors[460] on account of their negligent pursuit of their clients' claims, by failure to initiate proceedings in time or in other ways. The computation issue first surfaced in *Harrison v Bloom Camillin (No.2)*.[461] In the suit against solicitors for the late service of a writ against the claimants' accountants, Neuberger J applied a discount of 35 per cent on account of the uncertainty of proving the accountants' negligence and, to the 35 per cent reached, applied a further discount of 20 per cent for the uncertainty of proving causation against the accountants, ending up with an overall discount of 48 per cent.[462] Later cases fortunately have expressed the position more clearly by looking at the positive side and at the percentage chance of success in relation to each contingency, as this makes the calculation arithmetically simpler. The Privy Council took this line in *Phillips & Co v Whatley*.[463] In addition to the chance of proving negligence in the claimant's personal injury claim, there was the chance of whether the defendant's insurer, being in the position of not having to pay the damages awarded, would have paid them. The 70 per cent holding for the success of the first chance fell to be multiplied by the 40 per cent holding for the success of the second, giving an overall 28 per cent loss of a chance.[464] Similar computations were carried out in two Court of Appeal cases. In *Sharpe v Addison*,[465] a 40 per cent chance of proving negligence in a personal injury claim was amalgamated with a 25 per cent chance in respect of contributory negligence to give an expected overall recovery of 10 per cent.[466] In *Talisman Property Co Ltd v Norton Rose*,[467] the 50 per cent chance of consulting counsel was amalgamated with the 70 per cent chance of following counsel's advice to give an overall 35 per cent loss of chance.[468] *Haithwaite v Thomson Snell & Passmore*,[469] at first instance returns us, in a personal injury context, to the chances appearing in the opening case of *Harrison* of proving negligence and proving causation. Here 40 per cent was multiplied by 75 per cent to give a 30 per cent loss of chance award.[470]

---

[56] and by Laws LJ in *Whitehead* [2008] P.N.L.R. 25 CA at 625, [25], where it was also relied on by Rimer LJ at [80].

460 The exception is *Joyce v Bowman Law Ltd* [2010] P.N.L.R. 22 at 413.

461 [2000] Lloyd's Rep. P.N. 404.

462 The rather complex arithmetic is 35 per cent, plus 100 less 35 per cent of 20 per cent

463 [2008] Lloyd's Rep. I.R. 111 PC.

464 [2008] Lloyd's Rep. I.R. 111 PC at [47]. As counsel in the case I can say that it was not even argued that this might not be the correct method for the computation.

465 [2004] P.N.L.R. 23 CA at 426.

466 See the analysis by Rix LJ at [2004] P.N.L.R. 23 CA at [30] to [35].

467 [2006] 3 E.G.L.R. 59 CA.

468 See at [2006] 3 E.G.L.R. 59 CA at [57] and [58].

469 [2010] Lloyd's Rep. P.N. 98.

470 The method, sometimes advanced, of adding the two percentage discounts together is clearly misconceived. This could eliminate the lost chance entirely, or even give it a negative value.

So far there have been only two lost chances to be amalgamated. Then came *Joyce v Bowman Law Ltd*,[471] where the negligence of a firm of conveyancers had resulted in its client's failure to obtain a buyer's option over land that he would have developed. The trial judge, while prepared to award the development profit, took as many as four lost chances into account to pare down his award to the client to only 28.9 per cent of that profit—the chance of the client obtaining the buyer's option, the chance of his exercising it, the chance of his obtaining planning permission and the chance of his obtaining funding for the development. Yet in further cases where there has been a good number of contingencies to be considered, trial judges have not gone through the exercise of allocating separate percentages to each and thereby substantially lowering the damages to be awarded. They have simply produced a global percentage figure. Thus in *Tom Hoskins Plc v EMW Law*,[472] where the question as to whether a particular deal would have gone through involved multiple contingencies—agreement to the terms, attempts to renegotiate or extend completion, and others—Floyd J sensibly considered that it would be wrong for him to apply percentage upon percentage, and thereby reduce the damages to be awarded dramatically, because the contingencies were not independent of each other.[473] In *Di Matteo v Marcus Lee & Co*,[474] Slade J also arrived at an overall percentage figure for the lost chances identified by her. These were whether a husband, suing his divorce solicitors for their failure to inform him of an offer made by his wife in settlement, would, if so informed, himself have made a counter offer of a specific but lower amount, whether the wife would have accepted that offer if made, whether he would have pursued his claim against his divorce solicitors and whether that claim would have succeeded. Slade J simply put the overall value of the loss of chance at 25 per cent. This, however, does not sit well with her putting only a 20 per cent value on the chance of the wife accepting the offer if made.[475] **10-104**

*(iii) Need to discount on both sides of the equation* Where the claimant claims in respect of a chance to make a particular gain from his property or his services, it is frequently the case that there falls to be deducted, whether in the normal course or on account of mitigation, the lesser gain that he eventually makes or will make from disposal of that property or rendering of those services. In these circumstances in *Hartle v Laceys*,[476] where the claimant through the defendant's negligence lost the chance of an advantageous sale of his land but subsequently was able to sell the land at a lower price, it was rightly held that the proper approach was to take the lost gain less the actual gain and apply to this net figure the percentage chance, which was 60 per cent, of making the gain that was lost. *Hartle* was applied in the later, though earlier reported, decision of *Ministry of Defence v Wheeler*,[477] where servicewomen claimants, wrongfully dismissed on account of pregnancy, lost the chance of continuing to earn in the armed forces after maternity leave but obtained alternative employment at lower rates of pay. The alternative approach, unsuccess- **10-105**

---

471 [2010] EWHC 251 Ch.
472 [2010] EWHC 479 Ch.
473 [2010] EWHC 479 Ch at [133].
474 [2010] EWHC 312 (QB).
475 For all this see [2010] EWHC 312 (QB) at [9], [10], [61] and [67].
476 [1999] Lloyd's Rep. P.N. 315 CA.
477 [1998] 1 W.L.R. 637 CA.

fully contended for by the defendants in these cases, was to apply the percentage chance to the lost gain and deduct from the resulting figure the whole of the actual gain. This method of computation would lead to unfair results and could well eliminate the damages entirely even though the chance of achieving the lost gain stood at a high percentage.

### (5) Where certainty of loss is dependent upon the defendant's actions

10-106 **(a) Damages to be based upon defendant's least onerous obligation** Where the person upon whose will a contingency depends is not a third party, bringing in the loss of a chance principle already fully discussed,[478] but is the defendant himself in breach of contract, then a very different principle comes into play. That principle is that where the defendant has the option of performing a contract in a variety of ways, damages for breach by him must be assessed on the assumption that he will perform it in the way most beneficial to himself and not in that most beneficial to the claimant. This was well settled in the 19th century,[479] but finds its main applications later. The simplest illustration is that of the defendant who has promised to do one of two things and fails to do either. Here the damages will be assessed on the basis of the alternative less burdensome to the defendant.[480] The cases, however, do not reveal any such simple situation; the alternatives are more muted. One would say that there is more than one way, rather than that there are alternative ways, for the defendant to perform his contractual obligations. Thus in an action for non-delivery of 200 tonnes, 5 per cent more or less, of goods sold, the sellers were held liable only up to 190 tonnes in *Re Thornett & Fehr*.[481] Similarly, from the damages of market price less contract price for non-delivery of silver sold there was deducted in *Johnson Matthey Banking v The State Trading Corporation of India*,[482] a tolerance of 1.5 per cent since the sellers might lawfully have made use of that tolerance in performing their contract.[483] In an action by an actor for wrongful dismissal, *Withers v General Theatre Corporation*,[484] he recovered no damages for

---

[478] See paras 10-057 and following, above.

[479] See especially *Cockburn v Alexander* (1848) 6 C.B. 791 at 814, per Maule J cited in *Deverill v Burnell* (1873) L.R. 8 C.P. 475 at 481 by Bovill CJ (dissenting, but on the particular contract's interpretation); and *Robinson v Robinson* (1851) 1 De G.M. & G. 247 at 257 to 258, per Lord Cranworth. All these early, and other early, cases are dealt with by Toulson LJ in the important *Durham Tees Valley Airport Ltd v bmibaby Ltd* [2011] 1 Lloyd's Rep. 68 CA, considered at para.10-110, below.

[480] This is to be distinguished from the case of the contract which requires the defendant, if he has not done one thing, to do another. This category of case does not fall within this area and has nothing to do with a defendant's entitlement to take the least burdensome path for him; if he has not done the one thing, he must do the other, and damages will be based on his failure to do the other, however burdensome that may be for him. Cases in this category are found uncommonly but are illustrated by the early case of *Deverill v Burnell* (1873) L.R. 8 C.P. 475 and is also used by Toulson LJ as an illustration of this category at [111] of *Durham Tees Valley Airport Ltd v bmibaby Ltd* [2011] 1 Lloyd's Rep. 68 CA, for which important decision see para.10-110, below.

[481] [1921] 1 K.B. 219.

[482] [1984] 1 Lloyd's Rep. 427.

[483] See similarly *Kyprianou v Pim & Co* [1977] 2 Lloyd's Rep. 570, where, conversely, the action was for non-acceptance and the option of 10per cent more or less was the buyer's. And see *Kaines v Österreichische Warrenhandelsgesellschaft* [1993] 1 Lloyd's Rep. 1 at 8, col.2, per Steyn J.

[484] [1933] 2 K.B. 536 CA. This was the second ratio decidendi in the case, taken only by the majority. Only the first was overruled in *Mahmud v Bank of Credit and Commerce International SA* [1998]

the loss of the opportunity to appear at a famous theatre as the defendant had an option as to the theatres at which the claimant should appear. In *Horkulak v Cantor Fitzgerald International*,[485] a case of wrongful dismissal involving breach of the implied term of trust and confidence, the claimant employee's contract provided that, if the financial results of the defendant employing company should follow a particular pattern, the company was entitled to reduce the employee's salary by up to 25 per cent. The financial results being such as to entitle the company to make the reduction, it was held at first instance that the damages must be calculated on the basis of a salary reduced by the whole 25 per cent.[486]

A common context for cases of defendant's choice or option has been carriage of goods by sea. In an action for failure to provide cargo to a carrier, the damages were assessed in *Kaye Steam Navigating Co v Barnett*,[487] on the assumption that the cargo owner would have opted for discharge at that port where discharge would have cost the carrier the most. This decision was applied in *Spiliada Maritime Corporation v Louis Dreyfus Corporation*,[488] where damages were assessed against charterers for their wrongful repudiation of a charterparty on the assumption that they would have used all the laytime available to them so as to produce, since the freight was fixed, the least profitable result for the owners. *The World Navigator*,[489] concerned sellers of 30,000 tonnes of maize to be delivered free on board a particular vessel and an express provision in the contract with the buyers that the sellers should load at a minimum average rate of 500 tonnes a day. The sellers were in breach of an implied term as to facilitating the entry of the vessel into a loading berth, with the result that her arrival for loading was delayed by many days and the buyers claimed damages by way of demurrage. However, the sellers loaded with speed and completed the loading well within the time which it would have taken had the vessel arrived on time for loading and loading had proceeded at the average rate of 500 tonnes a day, which was permitted to the sellers. The buyers were refused damages by the Court of Appeal. 10-107

The rule that a defendant in breach of contract is entitled to act in the manner least burdensome to him goes beyond contracts where alternative ways of performing are available to him. It has made a not infrequent appearance in employment contracts where the question has been whether an employer in breach, generally by wrongful dismissal of an employee, need go beyond his contractual obligations and confer on the employee a benefit of which the employee has a reasonable expectation but no contractual entitlement. Here two pairs of cases are to be contrasted, *Lavarack v Woods of Colchester*,[490] with *Horkulak v Cantor Fitzgerald International*,[491] in the Court of Appeal and, earlier, *Beach v Reed Corrugated Cases*,[492] and *Bold v Brough, Nicholson & Hall*,[493] at first instance. In *Lavarack* where increased salaries had 10-108

A.C. 20.

485 [2003] I.C.R. 697.

486 See [2003] I.C.R. 697 at [87]. On the appeal ([2005] I.C.R. 402 CA) this result was not challenged. For the further aspect of the damages relating to certainty of loss with which the appeal was alone concerned see para.10-108, below.

487 (1932) 48 T.L.R. 440.

488 [1983] Com. L.R. 268.

489 [1991] 2 Lloyd's Rep. 23 CA.

490 [1967] 1 Q.B. 278 CA.

491 [2005] I.C.R. 402 CA.

492 [1956] 1 W.L.R. 807.

493 [1964] 1 W.L.R. 201.

replaced the employers' bonus scheme discontinued after the employee's wrongful dismissal, he was held by a majority, Lord Denning MR dissenting, not to be entitled to damages based on the increase in salary that could have come to him had he continued in the employment. By contrast, in *Horkulak* it was held that a reasonable and bona fide performance of a contractual obligation to pay to an employee a discretionary bonus required that the bonus be paid. In *Beach* the claim of a director for the loss under his company's retirement benefit scheme failed as the company had the right to discontinue the whole scheme or any participant's assurance under it at any time.[494] By contrast, in *Bold* the employee was held entitled to claim under his employers' pension scheme because, while there was again a right to discontinue the scheme as a whole, there was no discretion to withhold pension contributions as long as the scheme continued. These four cases are given detailed consideration later when dealing specifically with contracts of employment.[495]

10-109 **(b) Where there is a discretion as to the manner of contractual performance** The choice that the person in breach of contract has, however, must always be one that he may lawfully exercise within the four walls of the contract and still be performing it. This rule has found its application in cases where the defendant has had contractual obligations as to purchase, sale or publication but with a discretion as to the quantity to be bought, sold or published of the items in question. The first case presenting this situation is *Abrahams v Reiach*,[496] where publishers undertook to republish in book form the claimant's magazine articles, paying a royalty on each copy sold, and then refused to publish the book. They were not allowed to rely on the fact that the form, price, date of publication and number of copies to be printed were left to their discretion so as to limit the damages to the agreed royalty on the smallest number of copies that could be described as a publication of the book. The Court of Appeal did reduce the damages because the defendants had a certain amount of leeway and permissible option, but the damages could not fall below the basis of a sufficient publication to constitute a performance of the contract by the defendants. Somewhat later came *Paula Lee v Robert Zehil & Co*.[497] The defendants, appointed sole distributors for the sale of the claimant dress manufacturers' range of garments, had undertaken to purchase not less than 16,000 garments each season but wrongfully repudiated the agreement when it had still two seasons to run. The defendants' contention that they were entitled to choose the cheapest garments, in effect a one-garment range, was not accepted by Mustill J since, while the damages were to be assessed by the defendants' making choices of garments which were the least financially unfavourable to them, the choices had to be such as could be regarded as reasonable. Accordingly, Mustill J held in favour of damages based on a reasonable selection but still such reasonable selection as would yield the lowest price.

10-110 The decision of the Court of Appeal in *Durham Tees Valley Airport Ltd v bmibaby Ltd*,[498] has cast a new light on how to deal with cases where there is a discretion as to the manner in which the contractual obligation is to be performed, and has radically departed from the approach taken by Mustill J in *Paula Lee*. In *Durham Tees*

---

[494] [1956] 1 W.L.R. 807; see especially at 816 and 817.
[495] See paras 33-009 to 33-012, below.
[496] [1922] 1 K.B. 477.
[497] [1983] 2 All E.R. 390.
[498] [2011] 1 Lloyd's Rep. 68 CA.

the defendant airline had contracted to base and fly two aircraft from the claimant's airport over a 10-year period but the contract failed to specify criteria as to the manner of performance in terms of flight or passenger numbers. In these circumstances the defendant airline argued that damages had to be based on the minimum number of flights that it was contractually bound to operate and, since that was impossible to elicit from the contract, the award must be nil. Unsurprisingly, this argument did not appeal to the court.

In the forefront of the authorities considered in the closely reasoned judgments of Patten and Toulson LJJ, with whom Mummery LJ simply agreed, was *Abrahams v Reiach* as it was a case of a similar nature and also a decision of a very strong Court of Appeal. The two Lord Justices were of the view that Atkin LJ in that case had effectively held that the court must attempt to make an estimate of how the contract would have worked out in practice, how it would have been performed by the defendant. Toulson LJ saw Bankes LJ's judgment as saying much the same while Patten LJ spoke of Atkin LJ and Bankes LJ as forming a majority.[499] They therefore disagreed with the solution put forward and applied by Mustill J in *Paula Lee* which they considered to be based on his misinterpretation of Atkin LJ's reasoning in *Abrahams v Reiach*.[500] **10-111**

Patten LJ put the conclusion reached in this way.[501] The court must carry out a factual enquiry as to how the contract would have been performed had it not been repudiated. The court must look at the relevant economic and other surrounding circumstances to decide on the level of performance that the defendant would have adopted. It has to be assumed that the defendant would have performed the contract in his own interests having regard to the relevant factors at the time but not to assume that he would act uncommercially merely to spite the claimant.[502] Toulson LJ explicitly agreed with all this,[503] adding that, given the uncertainty of any prediction about the long-term future of the economy in general and the aircraft industry in particular, caution would be needed at trial in arriving at the assessment of the damages. Thus it can be said that the least onerous obligation rule has now no proper application to cases where there is a discretion as to the manner of the performance of a contractual obligation.[504] **10-112**

---

499 So the rather narrow view, as it was called, of the third member of the strong court, Scrutton LJ, need not be gone into.

500 See Patten LJ at [2011] 1 Lloyd's Rep. 68 CA at [75] and [76] and Toulson LJ at [135] and [136]. In *And So to Bed v Dixon* [2001] F.S.R. 935, where the defendants wrongfully terminated a franchise agreement under which they were to buy bedroom furnishings from the claimants and to pay royalties upon the amount sold, the damages were equated to the royalties on the trading to be expected from a reasonable and bona fide performance of the defendants' minimum contractual obligations. This is another case which is clearly affected adversely by the decision in *Durham Tees*; it was not referred to by the Court of Appeal.

501 [2011] 1 Lloyd's Rep. 68 CA at [79].

502 This passage from Patten LJ's judgment was cited and applied in *Jet2.com Ltd v SC Compania Nationala de Transporturi Aeriene Romane Tarom SA* [2012] EWHC 622 (QB) to a breach of contract for aircraft maintenance (at [71]) but with the decision on quantum coming later at [2012] EWHC 2752 (QB) (at [1]).

503 [2011] 1 Lloyd's Rep. 68 CA at [147].

504 In *Jones v Ricoh UK Ltd* [2010] EWHC 1743 Ch, Roth J fully considered *Durham Tees* and also considered the earlier Court of Appeal decision in *Mulvenna v Royal Bank of Scotland Plc* [2003] EWCA Civ 1112 CA. Neither case is reported on any issue of damages, although many citations from this part of this work appear in Waller LJ's leading judgment in *Mulvenna*; indeed neither *Ricoh* nor *Mulvenna* was a decision on the quantum of damages, both being defendants' applications for summary judgment. It is hardly necessary therefore to set out the facts of the cases but it can be said that,

10-113 **(c) Where there is no choice as to the manner of contractual performance** For the least onerous obligation rule to apply, there must be a choice available to the contracting party on how to perform. For there may be only one way in which he is entitled to render performance, as in *Lion Nathan v CC Bottlers*.[505] The defendant seller of the share capital of a company was in breach of a warranty to make a proper forecast of the company's profits and it was held that the damages were to be based on the share value a proper forecast would have produced and not on the highest figure in the range of reasonable forecasts. There was no question of the defendant being entitled to perform by choosing within that range; what there had to be was a bona fide estimate of the profits made without regard to how it affected the sale price, up or down. And in *Chaplin v Hicks*,[506] where Seymour Hicks himself was the person who was to judge the beauty contest, he could hardly have argued successfully that in the circumstances he would have "opted" not to choose Miss Chaplin as one of the 12 winners.[507]

## (6) Where certainty as to the loss suffered is dependent on future events

10-114 The situation can arise where, despite having committed a breach of contract producing a liability in damages, the party in breach would have become entitled at a later date to bring the contract to an end and thereby reduce the damages payable, even to nominal. Certainty of damage is therefore dependent on events occurring after the breach of contract and the question is whether such later events may be taken into account in the assessment of the recoverable damages.

10-115 The important authorities in this area lie in the field of charterers' rights to cancel charterparties. The leading case is *The Mihalis Angelos*.[508] Charterers, who were entitled to cancel the charterparty should the ship fail to arrive at the loading port before 20 July, purported to cancel on 17 July. On the basis that this was an anticipatory breach which, being accepted, entitled the shipowners to damages,[509] it was held that the damages were nominal because the charterers would certainly have exercised their option to cancel when the ship failed, as was already inevitable, to arrive at the loading port by July 20. Megaw LJ said of the claimant:

> "If the contractual rights which he has lost were capable by the terms of the contract of being rendered either less valuable or valueless in certain events, and if it can be shown that those events were, at the date of acceptance of the repudiation, predestined to hap-

---

if it came to damages, both would seem to fall within the category of case, exemplified by the contract of employment decisions at para.10-108, above, where there is reasonable expectation of, but no contractual entitlement to, a benefit.

505 [1996] 1 W.L.R. 1438 HL.

506 [1911] 2 K.B. 786 CA.

507 See the facts at para.10-040, above. Cases appearing in this section on certainty of loss dependent on the defendant's actions—*Lavarack*, *Horkulak* and *Durham Tees*—come under consideration in *IBM United Kingdom Holdings Ltd v Dalgleish* [2015] EWHC 389 Ch. See the case at para.33-031 fn.186, below.

508 [1971] 1 Q.B. 164 CA.

509 It should be remembered that, while a contracting party after acceptance of an anticipatory breach is relieved of his obligation to perform his side of the bargain, his ability or inability to perform remains crucial to the damages recoverable, as *North Sea Energy Holdings v Petroleum Authority of Thailand* [1997] 2 Lloyd's Rep. 418 (at para.25-129, below) shows (point not considered on appeal).

pen, then in my view the damages which he can recover are not more than the true value, if any, of the rights which he has lost, having regard to those predestined events."[510]

*The Mihalis Angelos* has been followed and applied where the charterer in breach has not become entitled to terminate at a date after the breach but the charterparty would after the breach simply and inevitably have come to an end earlier than its due date. This was the position in *The Seaflower*.[511] Here it was the charterer's purported termination which constituted the breach but as the charterers would have been entitled to end the charterparty soon after because certain approvals contractually required had not been obtained, the shipowners were entitled to damages only up to that time. This case shows that the principle in *The Mihalis Angelos* is not confined to anticipatory breaches[512] or to predestined events. **10-116**

Where the charterers' right to cancel is neither predestined to happen, as in *The Mihalis Angelos*, nor anticipated in certain events, as in *The Seaflower*, but at the time of breach lies in the mists of the future and yet by the time of trial events have come about which would have given the charterers the right to cancel, the question arises as to whether the court, in assessing the shipowners' damages, is entitled to take into account that the charterers could and would eventually have rightfully cancelled. This issue arose in *The Golden Victory*[513] where there was a repudiatory, though not anticipatory, breach of a charterparty by the charterers. The charter was a time charter for a seven-year period and at repudiation had nearly four more years to run. The owners claimed the normal measure of damages based upon the difference between the charter rate and the lower market rate for the four years but, because the contract would have entitled the charterers to cancel on the outbreak of the Second Gulf War between the UK and Iraq some 14 months after the repudiation, it was held by a bare majority of the House of Lords, affirming the unanimous courts below, that the owners' claim for damages ran only for this shorter period. It was said that the point at issue had never been considered by the House and remained open for decision,[514] there being no definitive previous authority.[515] **10-117**

Two well-established and related principles underlay, and justified, the decision of the majority. The first is what is coming to be known as the *Bwllfa* principle, taken from Lord Macnaghten's exposition of it in the case of that name,[516] to the effect that where the court assessing damages has knowledge of what has actually happened it should not speculate about what might have happened but base itself on what is now known to have happened; in the words of Lord Robertson in *Bwllfa*, "estimate and conjecture are superseded by facts".[517] Therefore that the charterers would have cancelled on the outbreak of the Second Gulf War has to be taken into **10-118**

---

510 [1971] 1 Q.B. 164 CA at 210. See too *Northern Foods Plc v Focal Foods Ltd* [2003] 2 Lloyd's Rep. 728 where *The Mihalis Angelos* with its predestined events was invoked in support of limiting the claimant buyers to nominal damages: see at [10.1]–[10.6.]

511 [2000] 2 Lloyd's Rep. 37.

512 Had the issue arisen in *Walkinshaw v Diniz* [2001] 1 Lloyd's Rep. 632 in relation to one of the breaches of contract alleged, but not established, against a racing car driver well into the performance of his racing contract, the breach would have been a repudiatory breach which was in no way anticipatory: see at [77] where *The Mihalis Angelos* is cited. The Court of Appeal in affirming, [2002] 2 Lloyd's Rep. 165 CA, agreed that there would be no damages upon termination: see at [26].

513 [2007] 2 A.C. 353.

514 [2007] 2 A.C. 353 at [63].

515 [2007] 2 A.C. 353 at [48].

516 Its compendious title is set out in full at para.10-102, above.

517 [1903] A.C. 426 at 432.

account. The second principle is the fundamental one, Lord Blackburn's statement of which in the *Livingstone* case[518] is universally cited, that the object of damages is to restore the injured party to the position he would have been in but for the breach. Therefore such a cancellation by the charterers had to be taken into account for, if ignored, the owners' position would not have been restored but substantially improved.

**10-119** In the light of these persuasive principles it becomes of significance to see how the minority, constituted by Lord Bingham and Lord Walker, was able to come to a different view. The emphasis here was on the need for certainty and finality in charter transactions. Lord Bingham cited several cases which had applied the *Bwllfa* principle and concluded that none of the cases involved repudiation of a commercial contract where there was an available market.[519] If there was an available market there was no good reason, the argument went, not to apply the general rule that damages for breach of contract fell to be assessed at the date of breach when the shipowners could enter the market and make a substitute contract, bringing in the normal measure of the difference between contract rate and market rate for the remaining charter period; to this situation the *Bwllfa* principle had no application. As for Lord Blackburn's paramount principle that damages are about compensation for loss, Lord Bingham accepted it but, the argument ran here, where there was an available market at the time of breach this crystallises the loss so that there can be no question of the loss being diminished, or increased, by what happens subsequently. Both arguments lead to the demands of certainty and finality being met.

**10-120** It will be seen that it is the existence of an available market—which there was in *The Golden Victory*—that is the crucial factor in this thinking. Yet what has become known as the available market rule properly applies only to the ascertainment of the market rate. Thus on the occurrence of the repudiation the injured party has the opportunity to mitigate the loss by going into the market and if he decides not to re-enter the market he does so at his own risk; the loss has become crystallised on breach and subsequent events are to be ignored. This was made clear many years ago in the valuable decision of Robert Goff J, as he then was, in *The Elena d'Amico*.[520] Different considerations apply to the determination of the duration of a contract. All this is well brought out in the majority speeches of Lord Carswell and Lord Brown in *The Golden Victory*, the latter's conclusion being that the owners' argument sought "to extend the effect of the available market rule well beyond its proper scope".[521] In effect, in the words of Lord Carswell[522]

> "considerations of certainty and finality have in this case to yield to the greater importance of achieving an accurate assessment of the damages based on the loss actually incurred".[523]

---

518 At para 2-002, above.

519 [2007] 2 A.C. 353 at [12].

520 See this case at paras 9-136 and 9-139, above.

521 [2007] 2 A.C. 353 at [83].

522 [2007] 2 A.C. 353 at [63]; following upon those of Lord Mance in the Court of Appeal, which he cited and with which he expressed agreement: at [56].

523 While not dealing with the future exercise of a defendant's option, and therefore not of direct relevance here, the somewhat curious *Falmouth Docks and Engineering Co v Fowey Harbour Commissioners* [1975] 1 Lloyd's Rep. 319 CA, is instructive in this area. Charterers contracted to use plant for dredging during the summer months of 1969 and 1970 for two roughly equal periods totalling not less than 12 weeks, and then used the plant for 17 weeks in the summer of 1969 and not at

The consequences arising from the principles in the decision in *The Golden Victory*,[524] have taken some time to develop. Numerous disputes arose after that decision concerning its application. Some cases concerned breach of warranty where shares in a company had been sold; in all of the cases the argument *that The Golden Victory* should be applied was unsuccessful. The issue received consideration by Popplewell J in the earliest case, *Ageas (UK) Ltd v Kwik-Fit (GB) Ltd*.[525] The breach of warranty resulted from an overstatement in the company accounts of revenue and assets by reason of the bad debts of the company at the time of contracting being understated. By the time of trial four years later the bad debts had become much less. The level of bad debt was the future uncertain contingency, which later became certain, upon which the party in breach relied to reduce, if not eliminate, the damages. Popplewell J rightly held that *The Golden Victory* was not in point. The measure of damages fell to be assessed in the usual way at the time that the contract was made which was also the time of breach. The risk of what would happen to the bad debt position was effectively transferred to the buyer who was entitled to the benefit if the company business did well and be subject to the loss if it did badly. The compensatory principle was unoffended and there was no windfall to the buyer.[526] Similar is *Hut Group Ltd v Nobahar-Cookson*.[527] Neither the assets and li- **10-121**

all in 1970. Damages were held to be nominal because, the minimum period having been exceeded, no loss arose from the failure to divide the use nearly equally between the two years. In *Multiplex Construction (UK) Ltd v Cleveland Bridge UK Ltd* [2008] EWHC 2220 TCC where a contractor in a construction contract had wrongfully repudiated at a time when the employer had resolved to remove certain of the contractor's obligations and had already engaged another contractor to perform them, it was held that, in assessing the damages payable by the contractor, the court should disregard the contractor's failure to perform these particular obligations: see [2008] EWHC 2220 TCC at [1543]. (The appeal, on various grounds, does not touch on this point: [2010] EWCA Civ 139 CA.) This is no doubt correct but it difficult to see how it is an application, as the judge maintained, of the principles in *The Mihalis Angelos* and *The Golden Victory* that post-repudiation events can be taken into account to reduce the damages for the repudiation. Again no *future* events appear to have been in issue. So too in *Leofelis SA v Lonsdale Sports Ltd* [2012] EWHC 485 Ch, while *The Mihalis Angelos* and *The Golden Victory* were extensively cited, they did not contribute to the decision of Roth J. The licensee of a series of trade marks for sports clothing and leisure goods claimed damages against the licensor proprietor of the trade marks for breach of an exclusive licence agreement. The benefit to the licensee derived from royalties obtained by sub-licensing others to manufacture or sell goods bearing the trade marks. Part way through the licence period the licensee sought to terminate the agreement on account of an alleged repudiatory breach by the licensor, claiming damages for its lost royalty income to the end of the licence period several years later. The ground on which the licensee relied to repudiate the agreement was found not to be a repudiatory breach but the licensee subsequently discovered other breaches which would have allowed repudiation, and it has been accepted since *Boston Deep Sea Fishing and Ice Co v Ansell* (1888) 36 Ch. D. 339 CA that a party can retrospectively justify termination of a contract by reference to a repudiatory breach of which the party was unaware at the time of termination. Nevertheless Roth J held that, because the licensee when terminating the agreement did not know of the breach entitling it to repudiate, the termination was not on account of a breach which allowed repudiation and therefore could not give an entitlement to claim damages based on loss of royalty income to the time that the licence would have ended: see his reasoning at [65] and [66]. Reliance had again been placed on *The Mihalis Angelos*, but Roth J said that he found the decision of no assistance, pointing out that it concerned not a claim against, but a claim by, the party alleging repudiation: at [63] and [64]. The matter then went twice to the Court of Appeal as *The Trademark Licensing Co Ltd v Leofelis SA* [2012] EWCA Civ 985 and 1366 CA. At the first hearing the Court of Appeal declared that Roth J on the facts before him had come to the right decision ([2012] EWCA Civ 985 CA at [21] and [33]), repeating this at the second hearing ([2012] EWCA Civ 1366 CA at [22]).

524 [2007] 2 A.C. 353.

525 [2014] EWHC 2178 (QB).

526 [2014] EWHC 2178 (QB) at [29].

abilities nor the profit and loss of the company had been fairly presented and the question was, once again and with *The Golden Victory* again in mind, the extent to which matters following the breach of warranty could be taken into account in the assessment of the damages. Blair J, who not unreasonably was unclear as to what the future uncertain contingency here comprised, held that such matters were not to be taken into account as, again, the outcome of all contingencies were risks transferred to the buyer which reaped the benefit or suffered the loss depending on how the business did.[528] As for the curious case of *Bir Holdings Ltd v Mehta*,[529] where the claim was by the seller of shares on account of its breach of warranty entitling the buyer to retain a substantial part of the purchase price and where *The Golden Victory* was again brought into play, matters following upon the breach were not taken into account in the assessment of damages, although it appears that the case did not involve future uncertain contingencies.[530]

**10-122** The first major case to reach the Supreme Court after *The Golden Victory* was *Bunge SA v Nidera BV*.[531] That case concerned a contract for the sale of goods with delivery in a single tranche rather than over a specified period of time and also with an available market. Here it could be said that, on the seller's repudiatory breach accepted by the buyer, the loss to the buyer crystallised so that subsequent events became irrelevant. The seller in the case had breached, by repudiation, a contract for the sale of Russian wheat to be delivered free on board a particular ship where a temporary ban imposed by the Russian government on the export of wheat continued in force at the time for due delivery of the wheat. The sellers argued that it was necessary to take account of events occurring after the breach which showed that the same loss would have been suffered even without the repudiation. The buyers' first argument was that the majority view in *The Golden Victory* should not apply to a single cargo. The second argument for the buyers was that *The Golden Victory* was wrongly decided. The third argument was that the agreed damages clause had excluded the compensatory principle enunciated in *The Golden Victory*.

**10-123** As to the first argument, Lord Sumption (with whom Lords Neuberger, Mance and Clarke agreed) said that the dicta from Lord Scott of Foscote in *The Golden Victory* should not be understood as confining the principle to cases involving situations involving successive performances. The principle also applied to a single instance of performance. Cases involving a single instance of performance might be factually different but the compensatory principle applies to them in the same way. Lord Toulson, who also agreed with Lord Sumption, said that there was "no logical foundation" for a distinction between a single instance of performance and successive performances.[532]

**10-124** As to the second argument, Lord Sumption held that the decision in *The Golden Victory* was neither new nor heterodox. His Lordship rejected the clarion call for certainty on the basis that, although important, "it can rarely be thought to justify an award of substantial damages to someone who has not suffered any".[533] Lord

527 [2014] EWHC 3842 (QB).
528 [2014] EWHC 3842 (QB) at [212]–[219].
529 [2014] EWHC 3903 Ch.
530 See the discussion from [2014] EWHC 3903 Ch at [66] to [81].
531 [2015] UKSC 43.
532 [2015] UKSC 43 at [87].
533 [2015] UKSC 43 at [23].

Toulson, who also agreed with Lord Sumption, also expressed the view that *The Golden Victory* was correctly decided and consistent with previous case law.[534]

As to the third argument, Lord Sumption held that agreed damages clauses were not necessarily to be regarded as a code, and further that there was no presumption that an agreed damages clause was intended to exclude the common law. However, such a damages clause may be assumed, in the absence of clear words, not to have been intended to operate arbitrarily. An arbitrary operation would include one which produced a result unrelated to anything which, by the compensatory principle, the parties could reasonably have expected to approximate to the true loss. In this case, the agreed damages clause was not a complete code and the provision was consistent with the application of the compensatory principle. Lord Sumption said: **10-125**

> "The real difference between the majority and the minority turned on the question what was being valued for the purpose of assessing damages. The majority were valuing the chartered service that would actually have been performed if the charterparty had not been wrongfully brought to a premature end. On that footing, the notional substitute contract, whenever it was made and at whatever market rate, would have made no difference because it would have been subject to the same war clause as the original contract ... The minority on the other hand considered that one should value not the chartered service which would actually have been performed, but the charterparty itself, assessed at the time that it was terminated, by reference to the terms of a notional substitute concluded as soon as possible after the termination of the original. That would vary, not according to the actual outcome, but according to the outcomes which were perceived as possible or probable at the time that the notional substitute contract was made. The possibility or probability of war would then be factored into the price agreed in the substitute contract."[535]

[534] [2015] UKSC 43 at [87].
[535] [2015] UKSC 43 at [21]. See also at [88], per Lord Toulson.

Chapter 11

# PAST AND PROSPECTIVE DAMAGE

Table of Contents



**11-001** The final limit placed upon the amount of damages which may be awarded as compensation is of a different character to those already considered: it is a temporal limit. A wrong, whether tort or breach of contract, is committed, a writ claiming damages is issued, and an action is tried by the court. When the court comes to assess the damages, how far can damages be awarded for loss accruing before the commission of the wrong, for loss accruing before the commencement of the action by issue of the writ, and for loss which accrues or will accrue after the issue of the writ or after the judgment of the court? In short, how far can a claimant recover for past[1] and prospective damage?

**11-002** A complication is introduced into the situation because in certain circumstances the same facts may give rise to more than one cause of action. How this affects questions of recovery for past and prospective damage is dealt with in due course; but it is necessary to clear the ground by considering the four types of case where

[1] This of course is a particular meaning of "past".

more than one cause of action arises. The first two of these are concerned with problems of liability rather than damages: only the latter two directly affect the issue of damages. It is thought, however, that the general pattern is made clearer, and a piecemeal view avoided, if all are briefly dealt with.

## I. Introductory: Circumstances in Which the Same Set of Facts Gives Rise to More than One Cause of Action

### 1. Where there are Two Separate Acts Resulting in Two Separate Wrongs

Where there are two separate acts resulting in two separate wrongs two causes of action arise. This is a fairly simple situation in tort, but in contract it is more complex since, although, as Talbot J said in *Conquer v Boot*,[2] **11-003**

> "there may, of course, be many promises in one contract, the breach of which is a separate cause of action",

the view that

> "the breach of every promise express or implied in a contract gives rise to a different cause of action [is] putting the matter too high"

according to Pilcher J in *Daniels v Carmel Exporters*.[3] As an instance of separate breaches of the same contract giving rise to different causes of action, he cited the case of successive breaches of an instalment contract.[4]

### 2. Where a Single Act Violates Two Separate Interests Protected by the Law

Where a single act violates two separate interests protected by the law two causes of action arise. There is no complete catalogue of what is and what is not a separate interest. The leading case is *Brunsden v Humphrey*,[5] in the Court of Appeal, which involved a road collision injuring the claimant and damaging the vehicle he was driving, and which established that the physical safety of one's person and the physical safety of one's property are separate interests so as to give rise to two causes of action. Similarly, in *The Oropesa*,[6] there were held to be separate causes of action available to the personal representatives of a deceased sailor in respect of the loss of the sailor's personal effects and in respect of his loss of expectation of life. And where the damage is only to property it was decided by *Gibbs v Cruikshank*,[7] in which the defendant had trespassed on the claimant's land and seized goods there for distress, that interference with one's goods and interference with one's land give rise to two separate causes of action since this represents **11-004**

---

2 [1928] 2 K.B. 336 at 344.

3 [1953] 2 Q.B. 242 at 252.

4 [1953] 2 Q.B. 242 at 252.

5 (1884) 14 Q.B.D. 141 CA. Finlay LJ in *Derrick v Williams* [1939] 2 All E.R. 559 CA at 566A, said it was "a case which has always been regarded as a case of much authority"; but see now at para.11-005, below.

6 [1943] P. 32 CA; see especially at 35.

7 (1873) L.R. 8 C.P. 454.

interference with two separate protected interests. Similarly, in *Ash v Hutchinson*,[8] it was held that two separate causes of action arose from infringement of copyright by authorising the reproduction of a literary work and from infringement of copyright by actually reproducing it.

**11-005** However, precisely a hundred years on from *Brunsden v Humphrey*,[9] the Court of Appeal started, in *Buckland v Palmer*,[10] to express reservations about the correctness of what was only a majority decision, with Lord Coleridge CJ dissenting, a decision which reversed the court below and of the result of which even Bowen LJ. of the majority was dubious. Griffiths LJ confessed that he had always had difficulty in following the reasoning of the majority[11] and a decade later in *Talbot v Berkshire County Council*,[12] Stuart-Smith and Mann LJJ treated the decision with some scepticism.[13] The Supreme Court of Canada in *Cahoon v Franks*,[14] refused to follow the English rule, a refusal which also reflects the dominant practice in the USA. What concerned the judges in *Talbot v Berkshire County Council*,[15] was not so much the issue of one or two causes of action but rather that allowing a second action to proceed fell foul of the well accepted rule in *Henderson v Henderson*,[16] a case which, had it been cited in *Brunsden v Humphrey*,[17] might, in the view of Stuart-Smith and Mann LJJ, have led to a different result there.[18] The rule in *Henderson v Henderson*,[19] is that a claimant is barred by cause of action estoppel from pursuing a claim which could have been litigated at the same time as a claim previously brought. "It is contrary to public policy and abusive of process", said Mann LJ in *Talbot v Berkshire County Council*,[20]

> "that matters which could have been litigated in earlier proceedings should thereafter be allowed to proceed. This is the true basis of the doctrine".

It would seem, therefore, that the days of *Brunsden v Humphrey*,[21] and also of the cases which arrive at the same result even in different contexts,[22] are numbered.

**11-006** Yet estoppel and the principle of interest reipublicae ut sit finis litium can apply only to prevent a claimant, and not a defendant, from invoking *Brunsden v Humphrey*.[23] While the rule of that case normally operates, and in all the English cases has operated,[24] in the claimant's favour, this is not necessarily so, as the *Canadian Cahoon v Franks*,[25] illustrates. There the question was whether the claimant who had sued for damage to his car should be allowed after the short limita-

---

8 [1936] Ch. 489 CA.
9 (1884) 14 Q.B.D. 141 CA.
10 [1984] 1 W.L.R. 1109 CA.
11 [1984] 1 W.L.R. 1109 CA at 1116A.
12 [1994] Q.B. 290 CA.
13 [1994] Q.B. 290 CA at 296F to G and 301A.
14 (1968) 63 D.L.R. (2d) 274.
15 [1994] Q.B. 290 CA.
16 (1843) 3 Hare 100.
17 (1884) 14 Q.B.D. 141 CA.
18 [1994] Q.B. 290 CA at 296F to G and 301A.
19 (1843) 3 Hare 100.
20 [1994] Q.B. 290 at 301B CA.
21 (1884) 14 Q.B.D. 141 CA.
22 Namely, the cases cited at para.11-004, above.
23 (1884) 14 Q.B.D. 141 CA.
24 Namely, the cases cited at para.11-004, above.
25 (1968) 63 D.L.R. (2d) 274.

tion period of a year had expired, to amend his claim so as to include damage to his person. Only by not following *Brunsden v Humphrey*,[26] was the Supreme Court of Canada able to allow the claimant his amendment. Whether the English courts will be prepared to take their indicated disapproval of *Brunsden v Humphrey* to hold for the claimant rather than for the defendant in such circumstances remains to be seen. If they do, and it is thought likely that they will, they would be deciding that, estoppel apart, there was indeed only one cause of action despite the violation of two separate interests that these cases postulate.

No similar difficulty arises within these various interests where there is undoubtedly only one cause of action. Thus, in the case of the interest in personal safety, there were not separate causes of action in respect of pain and suffering and in respect of loss of expectation of life,[27] whether suit was brought by the victim himself or, as in *Derrick v Williams*,[28] by his personal representatives[29]; these were merely different heads of damage within the same cause of action. Similarly, as Sankey LJ said in *Conquer v Boot*,[30] an injured claimant cannot claim that he has two causes of action, one for loss of a leg and one for loss of a finger and injury to his head.[31] In *Walkin v South Manchester Health Authority*,[32] a failed sterilisation case, both parties accepted that there were not two causes of action, one for the personal injury to the claimant in the form of an unwanted pregnancy and the other for the financial burden of parenthood and bringing up a child.[33] And in relation to property rather than to the person, where in *Buckland v Palmer*,[34] a car was damaged in a collision and there was a claim by the owner for her uninsured loss of £50 followed by a claim by her insurance company for the insured remainder of the loss, Griffiths LJ said that it would in his view be **11-007**

> "quite impossible to contend that there are separate causes of action in respect of different parts of the damaged property".[35]

It should, however, be noted that, while a second action may not be brought, the courts have power to remove any stay that there should be on the first action and to allow any amendment of that claim; this was recognised in *Derrick v Williams*,[36] as possible if there were good grounds and was granted in *Buckland v Palmer*.[37]

---

26 (1884) 14 Q.B.D. 141 CA.

27 The claim for damages for loss of expectation of life has since been abolished by the Administration of Justice Act 1982 s.1.

28 [1939] 2 All E.R. 559 CA.

29 The entitlement of the personal representatives to claim for the deceased's loss of expectation of life was only established between the time of the first and second actions.

30 [1928] 2 K.B. 336 at 340.

31 And see *Higgins v Arfon B.C.* [1975] 1 W.L.R. 524 at para.11-020, below.

32 [1995] 1 W.L.R. 1543 CA.

33 Since the question was whether, for limitation purposes, the claimant could ignore the former damage and bring suit only for the latter (see the case at para.40-282, below), the reasoning in *Brundsden v Humphrey* (at para.11-004, above) was, as Auld LJ remarked ([1995] 1 W.L.R. 1543 CA at 1548B), very much at the heart of the claimant's argument. Claims for the latter damage are now largely outlawed by the House of Lords decision in *McFarlane v Tayside Health Board* [2000] 2 A.C. 59: see paras 40-288 and following, below.

34 [1984] 1 W.L.R. 1109 CA.

35 [1984] 1 W.L.R. 1109 CA at 1116B.

36 [1939] 2 All E.R. 559 CA.

37 [1984] 1 W.L.R. 1109 CA.

**11-008** The next situation to consider is where two people are injured and one not only has a claim on account of the physical injury to himself but also has an action stemming from the physical injury to the other person. Here he has two causes of action. This was once so where a husband and wife were injured, giving the husband a cause of action for his own physical injury and also an action *per quod* for the loss of his wife's services and consortium if the injury to the wife was also a tort against her.[38] Also where the husband is injured and the wife killed, or vice versa, the injured party has an action for his or her own injury and also a separate action under the Fatal Accidents Act in respect of loss of dependency caused him or her by the death of the spouse. That there are separate causes of action in such circumstances, allowing separate actions at different times without the one barring the other, was decided by *Marginson v Blackburn*.[39] And indeed there is one situation where only one person has been physically injured, which gives rise to two causes of action vested in another person. This is where an injury is fatal and the same person has the surviving action as personal representative and the dependant's action as a relative. If the action which gives the lesser damages is pursued first, the other action can be brought later for the residue. Nevertheless all that has been said must now be viewed in the context of the modern disapproval of *Brunsden v Humphrey*,[40] on account of the rule that a claimant is barred by cause of action estoppel from pursuing a claim which could have been litigated at the same time as a claim previously brought.[41] Indeed in *Talbot v Berkshire County Council*,[42] the Court of Appeal appears to have been of the view that, had this point been taken in *Marginson v Blackburn County Council*,[43] the case might have been decided differently.[44]

**11-009** Finally, where the same interest is protected by a number of torts there would seem to be only one cause of action. Thus in *Gibbs v Cruikshank*,[45] it was held that only one action lay in respect of trespass to goods and replevin of the same goods. It should follow that only one cause of action arises for personal injury although caused by a number of torts, such as trespass, negligence and nuisance.

### 3. WHERE A SINGLE ACT CONSTITUTES A CONTINUING WRONG

**11-010** Where a single act constitutes a continuing wrong it is said to give rise to a continuing cause of action. Lindley LJ said in *Hole v Chard Union*,[46] that

> "speaking accurately, there is no such thing; but what is called a continuing cause of action is a cause of action which arises from the repetition of acts or omissions of the same kind as that for which the action was brought."

In such a case a fresh cause of action arises with every minute.

**11-011** It is important therefore to ascertain what constitutes a continuing wrong. The

---

38 The action per quod was abolished by the Administration of Justice Act 1982 s.2.

39 [1939] 2 K.B. 426 CA.

40 (1884) 14 Q.B.D. 141 CA.

41 See para.11-005, above.

42 [1994] Q.B. 290 CA.

43 [1939] 2 K.B. 426 CA.

44 See the analysis of the case by Stuart-Smith and Mann LJJ: [1994] Q.B. 290 at 297D and 300G respectively.

45 (1873) L.R. 8 C.P. 454.

46 [1894] 1 Ch. 293 CA at 295 to 296.

Court of Appeal said in *National Coal Board v Galley*,[47] that a continuing cause of action, and therefore a continuing wrong, is not

> "constituted by repeated breaches of recurring obligations nor by intermittent breaches of a continuing obligation. There must be a quality of continuance both in the breach and in the obligation".[48]

This suggests a somewhat strict interpretation of the concept of continuing wrong and continuing cause of action. In considering the dividing line, it is convenient to treat tort and contract separately.

### (1) Tort

The problem arises primarily in tort, and the home ground for continuing torts is trespass and nuisance. In *National Coal Board v Galley*,[49] it was accepted that "the general proposition that persistence in tortious conduct of particular kinds such as trespass or nuisance constitutes a continuing cause of action must be regarded as established".[50] **11-012**

Thus a trespass by placing and leaving some object on another's land is a trespass which continues as long as that object remains there. It is a continuing tort. This is well illustrated by *Holmes v Wilson*,[51] where the defendant built buttresses on the claimant's land and continued the erection over the line.[52] On the other hand, a trespass by making a hole in another's land is a trespass which is over and done the moment the hole is made. This is well illustrated by *Clegg v Dearden*,[53] where the defendant made an aperture in the claimant's mine through which water began and continued to flow; this was nevertheless not a continuing trespass. Nuisance is similar. A person who commits a nuisance is under a constant legal obligation to abate it, and for as long as he fails to do so he is every moment committing a fresh nuisance. This is well illustrated by *Shadwell v Hutchinson*,[54] which was an action for the continued obstruction of ancient lights. On the other hand, there is not the same scope for non-continuing nuisances which give only one cause of action: it would require that the very fact of causing the damage brought the nuisance to an end.[55]

### (2) Contract

In *National Coal Board v Galley*[56] the Court of Appeal said that whether a breach of contract amounted to a continuing one: **11-013**

---

47 [1958] 1 W.L.R. 16 CA.
48 [1958] 1 W.L.R. 16 CA at 27.
49 [1958] 1 W.L.R. 16 CA.
50 [1958] 1 W.L.R. 16 CA at 26.
51 (1839) 10 A. & E. 503.
52 See, too, *Bowyer v Cooke* (1847) 4 C.B. 236 with similar facts, but the case dealt with costs. Counsel said that *Holmes v Wilson* could not now be disputed: *Bowyer v Cooke* (1847) 4 C.B. 236 at 242.
53 (1848) 12 Q.B. 576.
54 (1831) 4 C. & P. 333. See, too, *Rosewell v Prior* (1702) 2 Salk. 460.
55 See, e.g. *Wringe v Cohen* [1940] 1 K.B. 229 CA.
56 [1958] 1 W.L.R. 16 CA.

"must depend on the nature of the particular obligation broken. For example, a contract of service for a specified term might contain a stipulation that the employee should not during the period of his service carry on or be concerned in any other business of the same kind as the employer's business. If the employee, in breach of such a stipulation, did proceed to carry out some other business of the kind in question, the breach would, we think, clearly be a continuing one, in that the employee would *de die in diem* be continuously in breach of the stipulation so long as the prohibited business was carried on. But where a contract requires payments to be made on stated dates (for example, a contract to pay an annuity of £1,000 p.a. in equal monthly instalments on the first day of each calendar month) failure to pay the instalment due on 1 February is not, we should have thought, a continuance of the cause of action constituted by failure to pay the instalment due on 1 January, but a distinct cause of action arising for the first time on 1 February and at no earlier date."[57]

For these reasons the Court of Appeal held that, where in breach of contract an employee failed to work Saturday shifts at a colliery, there was no continuing cause of action but only repeated breaches of a recurring obligation.

### 4. WHERE A SINGLE ACT NOT ACTIONABLE PER SE CAUSES SEPARATE DAMAGE ON TWO SEPARATE OCCASIONS

**11-014** Where a single act not actionable per se causes separate damage on two separate occasions, it seems that two causes of action accrue. The authority for this proposition is the leading and difficult House of Lords decision in *Darley Main Colliery Co v Mitchell*.[58] There an excavation on the defendant's land had caused a subsidence on the claimant's land for which action was brought and damages were recovered, and then the same excavation caused a new subsidence. It had already been decided by the House of Lords in *Backhouse v Bonomi*,[59] that an excavation without damage gave no cause of action so that for the purpose of the Statute of Limitations the cause of action did not accrue till the damage. This meant that the cause of action consisted of the non-continuous act plus the later resulting damage. The new damage combined with the original wrongful act gave a new cause of action. This, it is submitted, is the proper explanation of *Darley Main Colliery Co v Mitchell*.[60] It would appear to be impossible to say that there was a continuing tort after the decision in *Backhouse v Bonomi*[61]; indeed, Lord Blackburn in his dissent said that, if he could have taken the view that the tort was a continuing one, he would have agreed with his brethren in the result. Also the later decisions in *Greenwell v Low Beechburn Co*,[62] and *Hall v Norfolk*,[63] that a defendant getting title after commission of the act is not liable, cannot stand with the view that there is a continuing tort here. It seems, therefore, that the somewhat ambiguous speeches of

---

57 [1958] 1 W.L.R. 16 CA at 26.

58 (1886) 11 App. Cas. 127. *Darley Main* was successfully prayed in aid in the unusual case of *Phonographic Performance Ltd v Department of Trade and Industry* [2004] 1 W.L.R. 2893 involving breach of statutory duty in the field of copyright (see [2004] 1 W.L.R. 2893 at [17] and following ) but not in the further curious case of *Iqbal v Legal Services Commission* [2005] EWCA Civ 623 CA involving alleged breach of statutory duty and misfeasance in public office in withholding legal aid board funds from the claimant (see [2005] EWCA Civ 623 CA at [19] and following).

59 (1861) 9 H.L.C. 503.

60 (1886) 11 App. Cas. 127.

61 (1861) 9 H.L.C. 503.

62 [1897] 2 Q.B. 165.

63 [1900] 2 Ch. 493.

Lord Fitzgerald and Lord Halsbury, which go partly on the basis of continuing tort and partly on the basis of wrongful act not actionable till damage, must be interpreted on the latter basis.[64]

## II. Past Loss: Damage Before Accrual of the Cause of Action

No damages can be given on account of any loss before the cause of action arose. **11-015** This is so clear that it is hardly controverted. An old case of 1697, *Prince v Moulton*,[65] shows that the principle was established very early. Judgment was arrested there, as the declaration stated that the defendant on 3 August caused the claimant's meadow to be overflowed whereby he lost all the use and profit of it from 2 July. A modern case of 1955, *Crookall v Vickers-Armstrong*,[66] neatly illustrates the practical operation of the rule. From 1930 to 1951 the claimant, employed by the defendant, was engaged in work which involved a risk of contracting the serious disease of silicosis. Not until the year 1942 was the risk generally recognised and appreciated, and therefore not until that date did the defendant's failure to take all reasonable steps to ensure that the claimant wore a mask during his work constitute actionable negligence. In 1951 the claimant was certified to be suffering from silicosis, which had started to develop in about 1939 as a result of his having inhaled silica particles during the period of his employment. In his action for damages it was held that to the extent that the claimant's present condition was attributable to the period before the defendant's breach of duty, and therefore before the accrual of a cause of action, no damages could be awarded; the damages must be limited to so much of the total injury as was suffered after the defendant's breach of duty, or, in other words, to the extent to which the claimant's condition had been aggravated by the defendant's breach of duty.

*Crookall*, though a modern authority, was the first in the series of damages cases **11-016** involving industrial diseases with which the courts have had to deal, cases of diseases which take a long period to establish themselves and where the employer's negligence is in failure to give adequate protection from exposure to the dangerous substance or process. The spotlight has fallen, after *Crookall* and frequently at House of Lords level, on cases not of an innocent period of exposure followed by a guilty period—which is required for the purpose of examination of the question of recovery for past loss—but on cases where either there has been an innocent level of exposure and a guilty level[67] or there have been periods of guilty exposure by different employers.[68] For long, in the cases which have reached the Lords the

64 Lord Bramwell based his judgment on the concept of a further category of acts which are rightful in themselves and which only become wrongful on proof of damage. It is submitted that one cannot distinguish between an act wrongful from the start but only actionable on damage and an act rightful in itself and only actionable on damage. As Lord Blackburn pointed out in his dissent, there is no such thing as an act which is "rightful" until damage results and then by the fact of damage alone thereupon becomes "wrongful". But Lord Bramwell's judgment rejected the continuing tort notion for the particular facts of the case, and is therefore nearer to the view which is regarded here as the proper interpretation of the case.

65 (1697) 1 Ld. Raym. 248.

66 [1955] 1 W.L.R. 659.

67 *Bonnington Castings v Wardlaw* [1956] A.C. 613; *Nicholson v Atlas Steel Foundry and Engineering Co Ltd* [1957] 1 W.L.R. 613 HL; *McGhee v National Coal Board* [1973] 1 W.L.R. 1 HL; *Allen v British Rail Engineering Ltd* [2001] I.C.R. 942 CA.

68 *Holtby v Brigham & Cowan (Hull) Ltd* [2000] 3 All E.R. 421 CA; *Fairchild v Glenhaven Funeral Services Ltd* [2003] A.C. 32; *Barker v Corus (UK) Plc* [2006] 2 A.C. 572.

defendants have been held liable for the whole injury without any such apportionment as is found in *Crookall*, but this can be said to be because apportionment was not argued and the contest was between no liability and full liability. Now, however, apportionment is becoming the order of the day. Moreover, directly relevant to *Crookall* and to the recovery for past loss before accrual of action are two cases which did involve innocent exposure followed in time by guilty exposure but not involving the ubiquitous lung disease. In *Thompson v Smiths Shiprepairers (North Shields)*,[69] where the claimant workmen were complaining of deafness, apportionment was decreed, while in *Rugby Joinery (UK) Ltd v Whitfield*,[70] where the complaint was of vibration white finger, apportionment was accepted as appropriate.[71] It seems clear then that *Crookall* would be decided the same way today.[72]

**11-017** One situation where it is important to keep this obvious rule in mind is where a party repudiates a contract before the time fixed for his performance. Unless and until such a repudiation is accepted by the other party it is a mere nullity and there is no breach of contract. If, subsequently, the repudiation is accepted or there is a failure to perform, either of which will produce a breach, the damages will fall to be assessed as from that breach, and none can be awarded in respect of loss arising solely between the unaccepted repudiation and the later breach.[73]

## III. PAST LOSS: DAMAGE BEFORE COMMENCEMENT OF THE ACTION

**11-018** Since, in the nature of things, some time must elapse between the moment that an action accrues to a claimant and the moment that he takes steps to seek a remedy by issuing a writ claiming damages, it is everyday practice to award damages in respect of the period between the accrual of a cause of action and the commencement of an action by issue of a writ. On the other hand, the victim of a wrong is not allowed to wait indefinitely before seeking redress, and if he waits too long he may find that the defendant can set up the Statute of Limitations[74] as a bar to his action completely.

**11-019** Even where the damage may not accrue till some long time after the accrual of the cause of action—which is possible where damage is, as in contract and in certain torts, not the gist of the action—the Statute of Limitations[75] will still run from the time the cause of action arose. This was said, in several earlier editions of this book, to be illustrated by the two cases of *Short v McCarthy*,[76] and *Howell v Young*,[77] which concerned breaches of contract by solicitors. It is true that the modern cases of *Midland Bank Trust Co v Hett, Stubbs & Kemp*,[78] and *Forster v Outred & Co*,[79]

---

69 [1984] Q.B. 405.

70 [2006] P.I.Q.R. Q2 CA at 40 (reported again at Q6 at 81).

71 See the discussion of all these cases in the context of certainty of damage at paras 10-014 and following, above.

72 For the position where part of the exposure has occurred outside the limitation period, see *Clarkson v Modern Foundries* [1957] 1 W.L.R. 1210 at para.11-022, below.

73 See *Avery v Bowden* (1856) 6 E. & B. 953 and the standard texts on contract.

74 The law relating to limitation of actions was formerly contained in a series of statutes collectively referred to as the Statute (or Statutes) of Limitations. These were replaced by the Limitation Act 1939, now itself replaced by the Limitation Act 1980, as amended.

75 See previous note.

76 (1820) 3 B. & Ald. 626.

77 (1826) 5 B. & C. 259.

78 [1979] Ch. 384.

which have been prepared to hold solicitors liable to their clients in the tort of negligence, as an alternative to their contractual liability, have since interpreted *Howell v Young*,[80] as being as much an action on the case, where damage is an essential element, as an action for breach of contract, with the damage accruing at the same moment as the breach of duty,[81] but the two early cases still support the proposition initially advanced. "In an action of assumpsit", said Bayley J in *Howell v Young*,[82]

> "the Statute of Limitations begins to run not from the time the damage results from the breach of the promise, but the time when the breach of promise takes place. The case of *Short v McCarthy*[83] is an authority in point."

And Holroyd J Started his judgment with:

> "I am of opinion that the Statute of Limitations is a complete bar to this action. The cause of action is the misconduct or negligence of the attorney."[84]

Of course now that the solicitor can be sued in the tort of negligence the point becomes academic in this context, but it could turn out to have relevance elsewhere.

In those cases of tort in which damage is indeed the gist of the action but where the damage, though accrued, is not known to have accrued until much later, the same result was reached, first in the case of injury to the person, and then in the case of damage to buildings, caused by tortious negligence where the effects of the injury or damage did not become apparent for many years. This was established by the House of Lords in *Cartledge v Jopling & Sons*,[85] for personal injury and in *Pirelli General Cable Works v Oscar Faber & Partners*,[86] for property damage. However, statute intervened to amend the law in 1963 in the case of personal injury and in 1986 in the case of damage to property. The current position is that under the provisions of s.11 of the Limitation Act 1980 the limitation period expires in personal injury claims three years—which is the normal limitation period for such claims—from the accrual of the cause of action or, if later, three years from the date of the claimant's knowledge, as defined,[87] and that under the provisions of s.14A, as inserted by s.1 of the Latent Damage Act 1986, the limitation period in actions for negligence[88] in respect of latent damage not concerning personal injury[89] expires 11-020

79 [1982] 1 W.L.R. 86 CA.

80 (1826) 5 B. & C. 259.

81 See [1979] Ch. 384 at 406C to 407E and [1982] 1 W.L.R. 86 CA at 95C to H. The point was not raised in the speeches in *Henderson v Merrett Syndicates* [1995] 2 A.C. 145 which confirmed the *Midland Bank* case.

82 (1826) 5 B. & C. 259 at 265.

83 (1820) 3 B. & Ald. 626.

84 (1826) 5 B. & C. 259 at 266.

85 [1963] A.C. 758.

86 [1983] 2 A.C. 1.

87 See s.11(4).Where action is brought by the personal representatives on the injured party's death, it is the knowledge of the personal representatives that counts: s.11(5). Similar provision is made by s.12(2) for actions arising under the Fatal Accidents Acts, where for the purpose of ascertaining the date of knowledge each dependant is taken separately: s.13(1)). The court also has a wide discretion to allow an action for personal injury or wrongful death to proceed even if the time-limit, in its new form, has expired. See generally the standard texts on tort.

88 Construed as actions for the tort of negligence and so as not including actions for breach of contract founded on negligent conduct: *Iron Trades Mutual Insurance Co v Buckenham* [1990] 1 All E.R. 808; *Societé Commerciale de Réassurance v ERAS* [1992] 2 All E.R. 82 CA. Contrast the wording

six years—which is the normal limitation period for negligence actions generally—from the accrual of the cause of action or, if later, three years from the date of the claimant's knowledge, as defined.[90] This latter statutory change can assist not only property owners suing for damage to their buildings but also clients claiming for economic loss against their professional advisers where, as in *Forster v Outred & Co*,[91] the loss is held to have occurred, long before the client was aware of it, at the time when he acted on the advice.[92] A novel feature of the Latent Damage Act 1986 is that it provides, by way of the insertion of a new s.14B in the Limitation Act 1980, that an action for negligence which is not in respect of personal injury[93] will be barred after 15 years from the negligent act or omission even though there has by then been neither accrual of the cause of action—by virtue of the occurrence of damage—nor knowledge, as defined, of the claimant. The general questions of when an action accrues and of when the Statute of Limitations applies are, of course, matters going to the existence of liability and therefore not germane to the subject of damages, but it can be said that, as a rule, either recovery may be had for all damage arising between the cause of action's accrual and the action's commencement, or the action will be totally barred by the Statute of Limitations. This latter was the position in *Higgins v Arfon Borough Council*,[94] where counsel for the claimant, debarred from total recovery, argued in the alternative, but unsuccessfully,[95] for a partial recovery.[96]

**11-021** There is, however, one intermediate situation. This arises where there is more than one cause of action either because there is a continuing wrong or because a single act not actionable per se has caused separate damage on two separate occasions.[97] With regard to a continuing wrong this gives rise to a fresh cause of action every moment for as long as the wrongful state of affairs exists, so that even though the first commission of the wrong may have occurred outside the limitation period the action is not barred so far as it relates to the continuance of the tort within the period. Thus, in the old case of *Coventry v Apsley*,[98] the claimant claimed damages successfully in respect of that part of a false imprisonment which was inside the limitation period and unsuccessfully as to the part which was outside. With regard to a single act not actionable per se causing separate damage on two separate occasions, the intermediate situation to which this gives rise is illustrated by *Crumbie v Wallsend Local Board*.[99] There the defendant made an excavation under a street which caused a subsidence of the claimant's land that began at a

of s.11 dealing with personal injury claims.

89 Or death; see last fn. but one.

90 Actions in respect of defective products attract special provisions: see the Limitation Act 1980 s.11A, inserted by the Consumer Protection Act 1987.

91 [1982] 1 W.L.R. 86 CA.

92 Although there had been a tendency to distinguish this decision in later cases.

93 Or death: see last fn.87.

94 [1975] 1 W.L.R. 524.

95 See [1975] 1 W.L.R. 524 at 533E to 534B.

96 That the decision was soon overruled by *Sparham-Souter v Town and Country Developments (Essex)* [1976] Q.B. 858 CA in so far as it refused total recovery (though in effect later reinstated by *Pirelli General Cable Works v Oscar Faber & Partners* [1983] 2 A.C. 1) did not affect the point on partial recovery.

97 Circumstances giving rise to more than one cause of action are considered at paras 11-003 to 11-014, above.

98 (1691) 2 Salk. 240.

99 [1891] 1 Q.B. 503 CA.

period outside the relevant Statute of Limitations and went on down to the commencement of the action. It was held[100] that the further subsidence taking place within the limitation period constituted a distinct cause of action for which the claimant could claim, despite the fact that he was debarred from claiming for the earlier subsidence.

But where it is impossible in this intermediate situation to discover which part of the damage occurred inside the limitation period and which part outside, the claimant was held entitled to recover for the total injury in *Clarkson v Modern Foundries*.[101] The claimant contracted pneumoconiosis as a result of exposure to pathogenic dust during the period of his employment by the defendant from 1940 to 1951; this constituted a continuing negligence on the part of the defendant. The claimant, however, did not issue a writ claiming damages until 1955, so that with the relevant six-year limitation period he could not recover for damage which had been incurred prior to 1949. Nevertheless, since the claimant had established that the years 1949 to 1951 had made a material contribution to his illness, he was held entitled to recover for his whole injury as the defendants were unable to show which part was attributable to the period before 1949 and which to the period after 1949. **11-022**

The practical force of this decision has of course been dissipated for personal injury cases by the provisions introduced by the Limitation Act of 1963,[102] but the principle it embodies still holds and it is always possible, though unlikely, that it might prove applicable elsewhere. In coming to his decision Donovan J considered himself bound by *Bonnington Castings v Wardlaw*,[103] to hold that, since there was a material contribution to the injury within the limitation period, the claimant could recover for the full injury. However, *Bonnington* can now be regarded as past history as cases are mounting in which, where material contribution suffices, the court has shown itself prepared to make a reasonable estimate of the part of the damage for which the defendant is liable and the part for which he is not.[104] It could therefore be said that today an apportionment would be appropriate in a case like *Clarkson*.[105] Yet there may be a persuasive argument for not making an apportionment here even where a reasonable estimate of that part of the damage which occurred within the limitation period is possible because, as Donovan J said in distinguishing the earliest apportionment case of *Crookall v Vickers-Armstrong Ltd*,[106] **11-023**

> "the defendants were in breach of … duty before [and not after] the plaintiff contracted pneumonoconiosis … [and] the question is simply whether the plaintiff is too late to recover for the whole injury".[107]

In short, there may be a difference between past loss before accrual of a cause of action and past loss before commencement of an action. Perhaps it is only a dif-

---

100 On the authority of *Darley Main Colliery Co v Mitchell* (1886) 11 App. Cas. 127: facts at para.11-014, above. The damage had been continuous and had not occurred on two occasions clearly separated in time, but this was nevertheless held to fall within the rule established by *Darley Main Colliery Co v Mitchell*.

101 [1957] 1 W.L.R. 1210.

102 See para.11-020, above.

103 [1956] A.C. 613.

104 See the full discussion of the authorities at paras 10-014 and following, above and also the discussion at para.11-016, above.

105 [1957] 1 W.L.R. 1210.

106 [1955] 1 W.L.R. 659; see the case at para.11-015, above.

107 [1957] 1 W.L.R. 1210.

ference as to burden of proof: the claimant must prove that the damage occurred after the cause of action accrued, but, once he has succeeded in doing this, it is for the defendant to show that part or all of that damage occurred outside the limitation period.[108]

## IV. Prospective Loss: Damage After Commencement of the Action

### 1. The Rule

#### (1) Where there is a single cause of action

11-024 The rule is that damages for loss resulting from a single cause of action will include compensation not only for damage accruing between the time the cause of action arose and the time the action was commenced, but also for the future or prospective damage reasonably anticipated as the result of the defendant's wrong, whether such future damage is certain or contingent. Perhaps the commonest illustration of the rule is an action for personal injuries where every day damages are awarded which take into account prospective pain and suffering, prospective loss of amenities of life, prospective medical expenses and prospective loss of earnings.[109]

11-025 Indeed, the matter is so taken for granted that it is hard to find any direct authority dealing with the question. *Hodsoll v Stallebrass*,[110] however, provides an illustration. A master brought an action *per quod servitium amisit* against the defendant who had injured his servant, and recovered damages for the loss of his services after the time of action brought, down to the time when the disability might be expected to cease in the future. The reason why this apparently obvious result was controverted by the defendant in this case is to be found in the different result reached in a number of other cases dealing with the loss of the services of an apprentice by reason not of his injury but of his leaving work. These cases are all rather special because a contract of apprenticeship remains in force even though the apprentice has absented himself from the service, at least where the apprenticeship is by deed.[111] Thus in *Lewis v Peachey*,[112] where an apprentice had unlawfully quit his master's service, it was held that the master, in an action against the apprentice's father who was the other party to the contract, could only recover for loss to the time of action brought and not for prospective loss to the time when the term would end. A similar result had been reached much earlier in the old case of *Horn v Chandler*,[113] where the apprentice himself was sued in covenant by the master for leaving. It is suggested that the rationale of these cases is that, since the absence of the minor apprentice cannot of itself avoid the contract, there can be no total breach of the contract but only a continuing breach from moment to moment for as long as the apprentice stays away. This gives a continuing wrong with a continu-

[108] Donovan J in *Clarkson* considered the onus there to be on the defendant: [1957] 1 W.L.R. 1210 at 1213.

[109] The question of how certain the prospect must be to allow such damages to be awarded is another matter and is considered at paras 10-028 and following, above.

[110] (1840) 11 A. & E. 301.

[111] See *Lewis v Peachey* (1862) 1 H. & C. 518 at 520, per Pollock CB and Wilde B.

[112] (1862) 1 H. & C. 518. Similar decisions are *Berri v Howard* (1861) 2 F. & F. 403 and *Russell v Shinn* (1861) 2 F. & F. 395.

[113] (1670) 1 Mod. 271.

ing cause of action and, therefore, falls within the special rule applying to such: this is dealt with below.[114] On the other hand, it is submitted that the other old case of *Hambleton v Veere*,[115] where the action against the defendant was in tort for procuring the claimant's apprentice to depart from his service, is to be explained on rather different lines. Again, it was held that damages could not properly be assessed down to the end of the apprenticeship term because the apprentice might return and the claimant might by law compel him to do so. It could hardly be said here that there was a continuing wrong on the defendant's part, and the only valid reason for refusing an assessment of damages down to the end of the term could be that the damage was too contingent or uncertain in view of the possibility of the apprentice's return.[116]

### (2) Where there is more than one cause of action; the exceptional case of the continuing wrong

Where there is more than one cause of action recovery for prospective loss can **11-026** only be given in respect of the particular cause of action that is the subject of the claim. Of course, where the plurality of causes of action arises from the fact that there are two separate acts causing two separate wrongs, or that there is a single act violating two separate protected interests, then the two available actions can be brought together, thus achieving recovery for all prospective loss. But where there is a continuing wrong, and to a lesser extent where there is a single act causing separate damage on two separate occasions,[117] the further causes of action lie still in the future and, therefore, it is impossible to bring an action to recover for prospective loss even if it is foreseeable. The rule here is that where a single act constitutes a continuing wrong, damages at common law can only be awarded in respect of loss accruing before the commencement of the action by issue of the writ. The authority for this proposition is to be found in *Battishill v Reed*.[118] In that case a continuing nuisance had been committed by the defendant by erecting a building the eaves and gutter of which overhung the claimant's wall, and it was held that evidence of the diminution in the value of the claimant's premises was rightly rejected as not giving the true measure of damages; only the loss up to the commencement of the action could be awarded. However, this inconvenient result for a claimant is mitigated in a number of ways.

First, by a long-standing rule of court, which started life as RSC Ord.36 r.58,[119] **11-027** the common law was modified so as to allow damages in the case of a continuing cause of action "to be assessed down to the time of the assessment".[120] The only

---

114 See para.11-026, below. See also *Hodsoll v Stallebrass* (1840) 11 A. & E. 301 at 304, where Littledale J said, in argument, of *Horn v Chandler*: "There a fresh cause of action arose every day."

115 (1669) 2 Wms. Saund. 169.

116 Questions of how certain the prospective loss must be to warrant the award of damages in respect of it are dealt with at paras 10-028 and following, above.

117 Circumstances giving rise to more than one cause of action are considered at paras 11-003 to 11-014, above.

118 (1856) 18 C.B. 696.

119 Later it became RSC Ord.36B r.7 and, finally, RSC Ord.37 r.6.

120 This provision was, of course, of no use to the claimant if he could not show that there was a continuing cause of action, as he could not in *N.C.B. v Galley* [1958] 1 W.L.R. 16 CA: facts at para.11-013, above.

clear case in which this rule has been applied is *Hole v Chard Union*.[121] There the action was for nuisance in polluting the claimant's stream with sewage. The claimant obtained judgment for a perpetual injunction and for an inquiry as to damages. Three years later the damages were assessed, and were assessed down to the time of assessment, the defendant in the interim having continued to pollute the stream.[122] However, nothing to the same effect as the old rule of court makes an appearance in the Civil Procedure Rules. This apparent lacuna suggests that there is no longer provision for assessment of damages down to the date of trial, which would be an unfortunate, and presumably unintended, result. It would be particularly unfortunate in nuisance cases. In *Hole v Chard* itself the Court of Appeal seems to have considered that the jurisdiction to award damages down to the time of assessment was derived from the then RSC Ord.36 r.58 and, if this is so, logic would suggest that, providing that one of the Civil Procedure Rules can be found to be broad enough to encompass the power previously contained in Ord.36 r.58 and its successors, the sensible and highly convenient jurisdiction to award damages to the date of assessment may be taken to have been preserved. The obvious candidate is CPR r.1.1. This states in its sub-rule (1) that

> "these rules are a new procedure code with the overriding objective of enabling the court to deal with cases justly".[123]

Since the rationale for Ord.36 r.58, as expressed by the Court of Appeal in *Hole v Chard*, was the commendably pragmatic concern to avoid the need for a claimant to commence a second action merely to recover damages accruing from the issue of the writ until judgment,[124] the overriding objective of dealing with cases justly would surely be served by continuing to award damages in the old way. It may be, of course, that the compilers of the CPR, in not troubling to replace the former rule of court, were relying on the fact that in practice an assessment of damages to trial will be agreed to between the parties to the litigation, as it can be in the interest of neither that, otherwise, fresh actions would have to be brought in a continuum, with all today's high cost implications of such a procedure.

**11-028** Even if still available, assessment down to trial only provides a partial amelioration for the claimant, and a second weapon, made available to a claimant by the common law itself, gave him a more radical, though more oblique, assistance. This consists in suing twice, relying on an award of large damages in the second action. This result was endorsed by Jervis CJ in *Battishill v Reed*,[125] where he said:

> "I think the jury did right to give, as they generally do, nominal damages only in the first action; and if the defendant persists in continuing the nuisance, then they may give such damages as may compel him to abate it."[126]

The disadvantage to a claimant of taking this course is that it requires him to

---

[121] [1894] 1 Ch. 294 CA.

[122] In *De Soysa v De Pless Pol* [1912] A.C. 194 PC, a contract for a lease contained a condition precedent that the intending lessors should complete by a fixed date certain specified works. This they failed to do, and in an action for damages the assessment was carried down to the date of judgment. However, there was little or no argument on the point.

[123] To which "and at proportionate cost" was added in 2013.

[124] See [1894] 1 Ch. 294 CA at 296, per Lindley LJ.

[125] (1856) 18 C.B. 696.

[126] (1856) 18 C.B. 696 at 714; see, too, at 717, per Williams J.

bring two separate actions and it is in equity that a claimant will find his third, and most satisfactory, method of redress.

Apart from any question of damages, equity has power to award an injunction, or in the case of contract specific performance, where there is a continuing wrong, thus dealing with the matter of the future. Beyond this, equity has been empowered since 1858,[127] in cases where it has had jurisdiction to grant an injunction or specific performance, to award damages in addition or in substitution. This power has been interpreted as not confined to cases in which the claimant could recover damages at common law,[128] and in particular in the present connection the equitable jurisdiction allows awards as to the future, giving compensation for permanent injury once and for all. A modern illustration is *Hooper v Rogers*,[129] where the claim was for a nuisance which was occasioned by withdrawal of support and which was likely to cause physical damage in the future. What the court is doing, where such damages are awarded in lieu of an injunction, is making the defendant pay for a licence to commit the wrong by in effect legalising his act. And indeed, in *Leeds Industrial Co-operative Society v Slack*,[130] equity went further still than the common law ever could by awarding damages in the case of a wrong not yet committed but only threatened or intended,[131] since there was jurisdiction to award an injunction in such a case.[132] **11-029**

## 2. The Corollary

### (1) Where there is a single cause of action

The corollary of the proposition that damages for prospective loss resulting from a single cause of action may be recovered in one action is the proposition that such damages must be recovered in one action once and for all. If the claimant fails to secure recovery for all his damage in one action he cannot bring another action to repair the omission. This principle applies equally to cases where the damage is or ought to be evident to the claimant before trial of the first action, where there is no real hardship in refusing a second action, and to cases where the damage does not become evident until after trial of the first action and is sufficiently unanticipated as not to be claimed as prospective damage, in which case refusal of a second action will cause hardship where the unanticipated loss was great. **11-030**

The first category is illustrated by a variety of cases. In *Rowntree v Allen*,[133] a firm had assigned its business to the claimants as a going concern, including the benefit of all the firm's current contracts. One of these contracts was for the supply by the defendant of caustic soda. The soda supplied was of inferior quality and the use of it by the firm resulted in a loss of business before the assignment to the claimants. After the assignment the claimants, not knowing the cause of the loss, continued **11-031**

---

127 By the Chancery Amendment Act 1858, commonly called Lord Cairns' Act s.2. The powers given by s.2 are now contained in the Senior Courts Act 1981 s.50.

128 See para.1-015, above.

129 [1975] Ch. 43 CA.

130 [1924] A.C. 851.

131 Damages for future wrongs may also now be available under the Human Rights Act 1998: see at first instance *Marcic v Thames Water Utilities Ltd (No.2)* [2002] Q.B. 1003.

132 For the principles governing the court in exercising its discretion to award an injunction or specific performance on the one hand or damages on the other, see the standard texts on equity.

133 (1936) 41 Com. Cas. 90.

to use the soda and suffered further loss. When the damage was finally traced to the soda, the claimants successfully sued for damages in respect of the loss suffered by the firm before the assignment, and later sued again to recover damages in respect of the loss which they had themselves suffered by using the remaining soda after the assignment. The second action failed on the ground of res judicata. In *Furness Withy & Co v Hall*,[134] the claimants, who were under contract with a third party to overhaul a ship, subcontracted the repairing of the ship's refrigerating machinery to the defendants. The defendants failed to complete the work in time, which put the claimants in breach of their contract with the third party, who successfully sued the claimants for damages. The claimants in turn successfully claimed as damages from the defendants the amount that they had had to pay the third party in damages. Subsequently, they brought a further action against the defendants claiming as damages the costs which they had incurred in defending the action brought against them by the third party, costs which were held to have been reasonably incurred and, therefore, prima facie recoverable as damages from the defendants. The second action failed, again on the ground of res judicata. In *Conquer v Boot*,[135] the claimant successfully brought an action for damages for breach of the defendant's contract to build him a bungalow in a good and workmanlike manner, setting forth particulars of the breach. Later he brought another action against the defendant claiming damages for breach of the same contract, setting forth particulars of the breach different from but of the same character as those in the first action. Again the defendant successfully pleaded res judicata.[136] In all these cases the damage had accrued before the trial of the first action, but even if the damage remains prospective at that time it is generally evident that it will accrue in the future, so that there is still no hardship in refusing a second action. This appears to have been the position in *Clarke v Yorke*,[137] where the claimant, who was the defendant's tenant, sued successfully for damages on account of a misrepresentation as to the state of the drainage, and later sued again, and unsuccessfully, in respect of loss sustained from the want of proper drainage since the time of the first action.[138]

**11-032** The second category, which is the important one, best reveals the hardship attached to it in the celebrated old case with a variety of permutations on the parties' names, ranging from *Fitter v Veal*,[139] to *Fetter v Beale*.[140] There a claimant who had recovered in a previous action for assault and battery brought a fresh action upon another piece of his skull coming out; it was held that the former recovery was a bar to the second action. A more modern illustration is afforded by *Derrick v Williams*,[141] where an action was brought by the estate of a deceased person in respect of the death, and no damages were claimed in respect of loss of expectation of life

[134] (1909) 25 T.L.R. 233.

[135] [1928] 2 K.B. 336 CA.

[136] In *Daniels v Carmel Exporters* [1953] 2 Q.B. 242 the defendant failed to deliver goods to the claimant of the quality and description provided for in the contract of sale. The claimant made a successful claim on the ground of defective quality, and later made a second claim on the ground of misdescription. It was held that these facts fell within the rule laid down in *Conquer v Boot* [1928] 2 K.B. 336: the claimant, however, succeeded in respect of the second claim on other grounds connected with arbitration.

[137] (1882) 47 L.T. 381.

[138] It is not completely clear whether the actions were in tort for deceit or in contract for breach of warranty.

[139] (1701) 12 Mod. 542.

[140] (1701) 1 Ld. Raym. 339.

[141] [1939] 2 All E.R. 559 CA.

because in the then state of the law such was not an accepted head of damage in a survival action. It was held to be too late, after the House of Lords had altered the law on the matter,[142] to bring a second action to recover for such loss. This was a mistake of law and not of fact, but the principle is the same.

Certain inroads have indeed been made upon the universality of the requirement that all of a claimant's damages must be awarded at the hearing on damages. Concentration has been on the difficulties encountered by the victims of personal injury. Interim awards were introduced for them in 1970, followed by provisional awards in 1985. Now and most dramatically of all, with the availability of awards of periodical payments from April 2005 the door has been opened to awards stretching into the future which may later be varied should the injured party's condition seriously deteriorate or significantly improve. These forms of awarding damages are considered later in the context of personal injury.[143] And quite apart from the statutory provisions designed for personal injury cases, there is a general greater preparedness today, though it is still exceptional, to postpone the assessment of items of loss which at the time of trial are still in the future and cannot be readily quantified.[144] **11-033**

### (2) Where there is more than one cause of action

Where there is more than one cause of action the corollary of the proposition that recovery for prospective loss can only be given in respect of the particular cause of action that is the subject of the claim is the proposition that a second action can be brought to recover for prospective loss that was not within the ambit of the first cause of action. If, indeed, the claimant could have brought both claims together, the court may exercise its jurisdiction, as it did in *McDougall v Knight*,[145] to stay the second action as an abuse of legal process; alternatively, it may allow the second action to proceed but penalise the claimant in costs for the unnecessary multiplicity of actions.[146] However, it may be that at the time of the first action the claimant was not entitled to sue for prospective loss because the wrong was a continuing one, or because it consisted of a single act not actionable per se causing separate damage on two separate occasions.[147] And where the prospective loss could not have been foreseen or anticipated at the time of the first action, the result is that in both these types of case the difficulties created by the rule in *Fitter v Veal*,[148] are surmounted. **11-034**

Thus, first, in the case of a continuing wrong the corollary of the proposition that damages for prospective loss cannot be awarded is the proposition that a fresh cause **11-035**

---

[142] In *Rose v Ford* [1937] A.C. 826, reversing the Court of Appeal.

[143] See paras 40-004 and following, below.

[144] As in *Deeny v Gooda Walker* [1995] 1 W.L.R. 1206; *A v National Blood Authority* [2002] Lloyd's Rep. Med. 487 and *Cook v Cook* [2011] EWHC 1638 (QB). Not where the loss may not come about at all: *Adan v Securicor Custodial Services Ltd* [2005] P.I.Q.R. P6 at 79. See these cases at para.10-032, above.

[145] (1890) 25 Q.B.D. 1 CA.

[146] This was what the British Columbia Supreme Court did in *Sandberg v Giesbrecht* (1963) 42 D.L.R. (2d) 107 (but see para.11-005, above, indicating that in the particular circumstances there would no longer, in Canada, be two causes of action). Costs are in the discretion of both High Court and county court: see para.12-013, below.

[147] For the circumstances giving rise to more than one cause of action see paras 11-003 to 11-014, above.

[148] (1701) 12 Mod. 542; see para.11-032, above.

of action arises with every minute and that future damage can be sued for as often as it accrues. Indeed practically all the cases dealing with whether there is a continuing wrong or not, cases largely from the 19th century, are concerned with the latter proposition; in other words, the question was not whether or not the claimant could sue now for prospective damage but whether he could bring a second action for loss arising after his first action. Thus in *Holmes v Wilson*,[149] it was held that, after an action had been brought against the defendant in trespass for building buttresses on the claimant's land, it was competent for the claimant to bring a second action in trespass for continuing the erection over the line since it was a continuing wrong.[150] On the other hand, in *Clegg v Dearden*,[151] where the defendant had by an act of trespass made an aperture in the claimant's mine through which water flowed and continued to flow, it was held that, since leaving the aperture open did not amount to a continuing trespass, a recovery in a former action for making the aperture barred all recovery for subsequent damage from its remaining open.[152] And as with trespass, so with nuisance. Thus, in *Shadwell v Hutchinson*,[153] it was held that an action for the continued obstruction of ancient lights lay although an earlier action for damages for their obstruction had already been successfully brought.[154] On the other hand there can be no second action with non-continuing nuisances[155]: there appear to be no illustrations in the cases.[156]

**11-036** Secondly, in the case of a single act not actionable per se causing separate damage on two separate occasions, a situation epitomised by the controversial case of

---

149 (1839) 10 A. & E. 503.

150 It follows further that where the defendant deposits objects on another's land and the claimant gets title to, or an interest in, that land after the making of the deposit, i.e. after the commencement of the tort, he will himself have an action for the fresh tort of continuance: *Hudson v Nicholson* (1839) 5 M. & W. 437, followed in *Konskier v Goodman* [1928] 1 K.B. 421 CA; and also that a defendant getting possession of the offending land after the commencement of the tort will be liable, provided that the object placed on the claimant's land is connected with something on the defendant's, such as shores and timbers which support the defendant's building placed by him over the line.

151 (1848) 12 Q.B. 576.

152 It follows further that a claimant getting title after the act of trespass is complete has no cause of action: *Spoor v Green* (1874) L.R. 9 Ex. 99; and also that a defendant getting title after commission of the act is not liable: see *Greenwell v Low Beechburn Co* [1897] 2 Q.B. 165 and *Hall v Norfolk* [1900] 2 Ch. 493, dealing with nuisance.

153 (1831) 4 C. & P. 333.

154 It follows further that with a continuing nuisance the defendant is liable to a claimant who gets title to the affected land after the commencement of the nuisance: *Thompson v Gibson* (1841) 7 M. & W. 456, applied in *Masters v Brent London Borough Council* [1978] Q.B. 841 (see especially at 848E to H); and also, conversely, a defendant is liable although he does not get title to the offending land until after the commencement of the nuisance. The first of these two rules had not been understood by the trial judge in *Delaware Mansions Ltd v Westminster City Council* [2002] 1 A.C. 321 (facts at para.39-017, below), who dismissed the claimant's action on the ground that the damage had occurred during the previous ownership and the claimant could not show any new damage during its time as owner. He was reversed by Court of Appeal and House of Lords.

155 In *Maberley v Peabody* [1946] 2 All E.R. 192, where the defendant had let debris and earth be piled up against the claimant's adjoining wall, it was held that from the moment the burden was imposed on the wall it sustained damage by being subjected to a strain which must ultimately result in its destruction. An injunction was granted, but Stable J seems to have been of the view that damages for the total injury could have been awarded; yet at the same time he said that there might be a continuing cause of action till the trouble was eradicated, with a fresh cause of action arising as each brick toppled down. It may be that these two propositions are contradictory. The matter cannot be pursued further here.

156 See further at para.11-012, above.

*Darley Main Colliery Co v Mitchell*,[157] it is the act plus damage which constitutes the cause of action, and therefore a new cause of action arises when the second damage occurs. There is thus no difficulty about bringing a second action though the wrong is not a continuing one. This, indeed, was what was successfully accomplished by the claimant in *Darley Main Colliery Co v Mitchell*[158] itself.[159]

---

[157] (1886) 11 App. Cas. 127: facts at para.11-014, above.

[158] (1886) 11 App. Cas. 127.

[159] There is this peculiarity about the type of situation epitomised by *Darley Main Colliery Co v Mitchell* that, while a second action may be brought for the second damage (as in continuing wrongs), no action lies against a defendant getting title after the commission of the act (unlike in continuing wrongs): *Greenwell v Low Beechburn Co* [1897] 2 Q.B. 165; *Hall v Norfolk* [1900] 2 Ch. 493.

# PART 2 NON-COMPENSATORY DAMAGES

Chapter 12

# NOMINAL DAMAGES

Table of Contents



## 1. Circumstances Giving Rise to an Award of Nominal Damages

### (1). Where there is injuria sine damno

**12-001** Technically the law requires not damage (more accurately, a remediable consequence) but an *injuria* or wrong upon which to base a judgment for the claimant. Therefore an actionable *injuria*, although without some consequence, would entitle the claimant to judgment. Since a judgment awarding money was practically the only judgment which the common law could bestow, a judgment for a nominal sum of money or for "nominal damages" was given.

**12-002** The best statement as to the meaning and incidence of nominal damages is given by Lord Halsbury LC in *The Mediana*,[1] where he said:

> "'Nominal damages' is a technical phrase which means that you have negatived anything like real damage, but that you are affirming by your nominal damages that there is an infraction of a legal right which, though it gives you no right to any real damages at all, yet gives you a right to the verdict or judgment because your legal right has been infringed."

Again, the use of "damage" here should today be understood in the sense of a "remediable consequence" because an award will be more than nominal where a claimant is entitled to an award based on a real loss (compensatory damages), a real benefit to the defendant (restitutionary damages), a real profit made by the defendant (disgorgement damages) or a substantial award to deter the claimant and others like him or her (exemplary damages). If none of these circumstances is present, nominal damages may be awarded in all cases of breach of contract[2] and in torts

1 [1900] A.C. 113 at 116.

2 *Marzetti v Williams* (1830) 1 B. & Ad. 415 is a frequently cited illustration. Modern examples are provided by *Surrey County Council v Bredero Homes* [1993] 1 W.L.R. 1361 CA; *Halifax Building Society v Urquart-Dykes and Lord* [1997] R.P.C. 55 (see at 87, line 45) and *North Sea Energy Holdings v Petroleum Authority of Thailand* [1999] 1 Lloyd's Rep. 483 CA.

actionable per se[3]; moreover, at least nominal damages should be awarded in such cases but not all the decisions adhere strictly to this.[4] Sometimes the nominal damages award makes its first appearance on appeal, as in *Brandeis Goldschmidt & Co v Western Transport*,[5] where in a case of detention of goods the Court of Appeal substituted a nominal award for the substantive award made at first instance, in *Grobbelaar v News Group Newspapers Ltd*,[6] where the House of Lords in a libel suit made a nominal award in place of the trial judge's substantive award and the nil award of the Court of Appeal which had reversed on liability, and in *R. (on the application of Lumba (Congo)) v Secretary of State for the Home Department*,[7] where the Supreme Court made a nominal award in a false imprisonment case in which both trial judge and Court of Appeal had held there to be no liability.[8] Sometimes also there may be difficulty in determining whether or not a tort is actionable per se so as to allow a nominal damages award where no remediable consequence is proved—there is no difficulty with contract as all breaches are actionable. In *Watkins v Secretary of State for the Home Department*,[9] which raised the question of whether the tort of misfeasance in public office is a tort actionable per se, there is in the Court of Appeal a wide-ranging learned discussion by Brooke LJ of the authorities, starting with *Ashby v White*,[10] on what constitutes for the purpose of nominal damages torts which are and torts which are not actionable per se. It is a discussion which is unaffected by the Court of Appeal's holding in favour of actionability per se being reversed by the House of Lords.[11]

It is sometimes said that the law presumes or implies "damage" in every breach of contract or in every tortious invasion of a legal right, and that this, therefore, would justify an award of nominal damages in such cases without proof of actual loss. In support of this rationale is often cited Holt CJ's famous dictum in *Ashby v* **12-003**

---

3 *Constantine v Imperial London Hotels* [1944] K.B. 693 is a useful, frequently cited example. A recent example is *Hall v Harris* [2012] EWCA Civ 671 CA where a nominal award for trespass to land was upheld by the Court of Appeal: [2012] EWCA Civ 671 CA at [58].

4 See, e.g. *Gas Light & Coke Co v Towse* (1887) 35 Ch. D. 519; *Pagnan & Fratelli v Corbisa Industrial Agropacuaria* [1970] 1 W.L.R. 1306 CA.

5 [1981] Q.B. 864 CA.

6 [2002] 1 W.L.R. 3024 HL.

7 [2012] 1 A.C. 245. See also *R (O) v Secretary of State for the Home Department (Bail for Immigration Detainees)* [2016] UKSC 19; [2016] 1 WLR 1717.

8 Further awards of nominal damages in false imprisonment cases have followed in *R. (on the application of OM) v Secretary of State for the Home Department* [2011] EWCA Civ 909 CA; *R. (on the application of Abdollahi) v Secretary of State for the Home Department* [2012] EWHC 878 (Admin) (affirmed [2013] EWCA Civ 366 CA); *R. (on the application of Moussaoui) v Secretary of State for the Home Department* [2012] EWHC 126 (Admin) and *R. (on the application of Pratima Das) v Secretary of State for the Home Department* [2013] EWHC 682 (Admin) and *The Queen (on the application of Mohammed) v The Secretary of State for the Home Department* [2014] EWHC 1898 (Admin). All these cases, including *Lumba* in the text, involved claimants, foreign nationals and asylum seekers, who, though unlawfully detained, could and would have been lawfully detained had the correct procedure for their detention been followed. A further case is *Bostridge v Oxleas NHS Foundation Trust* [2015] EWCA Civ 79, where the claimant was a mentally disordered patient and the defendant an NHS trust, which had detained the patient unlawfully, rather than the Secretary of State for the Home Department. In *Bostridge* the Court of Appeal held that for a nominal damages award it mattered not that it was not the NHS trust but a third party that could and would have lawfully detained the claimant.

9 [2005] Q.B. 883 CA.

10 (1703) 2 Ld. Raym. 938; see this leading case in the next paragraph.

11 [2006] 2 A.C. 395.

*White*[12]: "Every injury imports a damage, though it does not cost the party one farthing." This approach is only confusing. In the first place it explains nothing because it is a fiction, as those cases where there is clear evidence of no remediable consequences from the wrong show. In the second place it becomes confused with a very different type of case where the law is said to "presume damage". These are cases where the presumption is based upon the difficulty of assessing the loss, generally a non-pecuniary loss, of which the best example is the injury to the claimant's reputation protected by the tort of libel.[13] In such cases substantial damages may be awarded on the strength of a presumption which is not fictional but is open to rebuttal by the defendant, although indeed rebuttal may be difficult or impossible in the particular circumstances. *Ashby v White*,[14] was itself such a case, substantial damages being awarded. The proper approach is to regard an injuria or wrong as entitling the claimant to a judgment for damages in his favour even without loss or any other remediable consequence, but where there is no loss or consequence such judgment will be for nominal damages only.[15]

### (2). Where loss is shown but its amount is not sufficiently proved

**12-004** Nominal damages may also be awarded where the fact of a loss is shown but the necessary evidence as to its amount is not given.[16] This is only a subsidiary situation, but it is important to distinguish it from the usual case of nominal damages awarded where there is a technical liability but no loss or other remediable consequence. In the present case the problem is simply one of proof, one not of absence of loss but of absence of evidence of the amount of loss.

**12-005** There are a very few scattered illustrations of this type of nominal damages. This paucity of case law warrants the inclusion of *Dixon v Deveridge*,[17] although it was an action for the price of goods sold and delivered and not strictly, therefore, an action for damages. In that case there was evidence which went to show that some amount was due from the defendant, but nominal damages were awarded since the claimant did not give evidence as to what the amount was. And in *Twyman v Knowles*,[18] an action by the claimant lessee against the defendant for trespass to land, it appeared that five days after his trespass the defendant had obtained a lease of the property from the claimant's lessor. In the absence of evidence of the duration of the claimant's lease, it being admitted that the fee was in some third party, the jury concluded that the claimant's lease only lasted till the date of the defendant's lease and awarded nominal damages.

**12-006** In *Greer v Alstons Engineering Sales and Services Ltd (Trinidad and Tobago)*,[19]

---

12 (1703) 2 Ld. Raym. 938 at 955.

13 The discussion in *Watkins v Secretary of State for the Home Department* [2005] Q.B. 883 CA (see previous paragraph *in fin.*) does not really get to grips with the distinction between these two types of case.

14 (1703) 2 Ld. Raym. 938.

15 McCormick, *Damages* (Minnesota, 1935), prefers an even more realistic statement: "The recognition of a right unrelated to detriment sustained is merely a metaphorical prophetical way of stating that in given conditions an adverse judgment will be given without a showing of loss": (p.86).

16 In certain cases where damage is presumed it is not a necessary condition of an award of substantial damages to introduce evidence of the amount of loss. Such cases are not relevant here: they are dealt with at paras 10-008 to 10-010, above.

17 (1825) 2 C. & P. 109.

18 (1853) 13 C.B. 222.

19 [2003] UKPC 46.

the Privy Council held that the appellants were entitled to a substantial award of damages for loss of use of a backhoe despite the failure of the appellants to prove any actual use of the backhoe. The Privy Council said that although

> "loss under this head was unquantified, it is the duty of the court to recognise it by an award that is not out of scale".

However, the award of $5,000 was not disturbed because, although on the low side, it was not contrary to principle.

Another example of the reluctance of courts to award only nominal damages where clear loss had been suffered but where the claimant has not led sufficient evidence of loss is *Karim v Wemyss*.[20] In that case, Mr Wemyss sold a solicitor's practice to Mr Karim. Mr Wemyss misrepresented the turnover and profit of the business. Mr Wemyss represented that the business had a profit earning capacity of £120,000 but, in fact, it had only a profit earning capacity of £92,000. Mr Karim succeeded in a claim for breach of contract and for deceit. In the Court of Appeal, Lewison LJ (with whom Kitchin and Longmore LJJ agreed) explained that the contractual measure of damages was concerned with the difference between the true value of the business and its value if the warranted information had complied with the warranty. The tortious measure was concerned with the difference between the true value and the price paid. But the primary judge had no evidence of either (i) the true value, or (ii) the value of the business if the warranted information had been true. Both of those depended on the value of the goodwill which required a multiplier to be applied to the profit earning capacity to reflect the future years of profitability. The Court of Appeal, without expert evidence, and in a very rough and ready way, examined the breakdown of the sale price and estimated that the goodwill was a fraction of the warranted profit rather than a multiple of it. This might have suggested that there was little reliance on the warranted profit. In any event, the Court of Appeal made an award of damages of only £15,000 for breach of warranty. **12-007**

## 2. Amount Awarded; Nominal and Small Damages Distinguished

"Nominal damages", said Maule J in *Beaumont v Greathead*,[21] "means a sum of money that may be spoken of, but that has no existence in point of quantity". Thus in *Joule v Taylor*,[22] where the claimant sued for a debt of £50 and this amount represented the extent of the court's jurisdiction, it was held that the nominal damages which he claimed for the purpose of obtaining costs did not place the debt beyond the court's jurisdiction. Nevertheless a token sum is awarded, which, after an early period in which the amount could be miniscule,[23] eventually crystallised at the figure of £2, a figure that lasted for a hundred years.[24] For some time at the **12-008**

[20] [2016] EWCA Civ 27 CA.

[21] (1846) 2 C.B. 494 at 499.

[22] (1851) 7 Ex. 58.

[23] *Feize v Thompson* (1808) 1 Taunt. 121 (sixpence, now 2.5p); *Mostyn v Coles* (1862) 7 H. & N. 872 (farthing, now 0.1p); *Sapwell v Bass* [1910] 2 K.B. 486 (shilling, now 5p).

[24] Starting with *Child v Stenning* (1879) 11 Ch. D. 82 CA and running as far as *The Kismet* [1976] 2 Lloyd's Rep. 585; a good number of intermediate cases, all of contract, are listed in earlier editions. Occasionally £1 has been awarded in the latter part of this period, as in *James v Hutton* [1950] 1 K.B. 9 CA; further such cases are listed in earlier editions. In the curious case of *Constantine v Imperial Hotels* [1944] K.B. 693, the award was of 5 guineas (now £5.25): see at 708.

end of the last century £5 had become common if not the norm,[25] but the new century has seen a reversion to £2[26] which amount has even been said to be "the traditional sum",[27] while the House of Lords in *Grobbelaar v News Group Newspapers Ltd*,[28] unaccustomed to having to set a figure for a nominal damages award, reverted to £1, a figure which has since appeared in a number of cases.[29] Yet in the course of the voluminous *Douglas v Hello!* litigation the token sum awarded to each of two claimants for breach of the Data Protection Act 1998 was £50.[30] And in *Checkprice (UK) Ltd v Revenue and Customs Commissioners*,[31] the surprising amount of £500 was awarded.[32] This must be wrong; while £500 may mean little or nothing to the Revenue and Customs Commissioners sued in *Checkprice*, it is for most people even today a considerable amount of money and far from being a nominal sum.

**12-009** This token sum given for nominal damages is to be distinguished from a sum similar in amount which is awarded as compensation calculated for a trifling loss. "Nominal damages", added Lord Halsbury in *The Mediana*,[33] after defining the term, "does not mean small damages". Cases of small damages are not, however, frequent as the law tends not to recognise any distinction between no appreciable damage and no damage at all.[34]

---

25 *Brandeis Goldschmidt & Co v Western Transport* [1981] Q.B. 864 CA (see at 874); *Dean v Ainley* [1987] 1 W.L.R. 1729 (but substantial damages awarded by the Court of Appeal: see at 1729); *Surrey County Council v Bredero Homes* [1993] 1 W.L.R. 1361 CA; *Berkowitz v MW (St John's Wood)* (1993) 48 E.G. 133. £5 as the award reappears in *The Queen on the application of Mohammed) v The Secretary of State for the Home Department* [2014] EWHC 1898 (Admin).

26 See, e.g. *The Football League Ltd v Edge Ellison* [2007] P.N.L.R 2 at 38 (£2 for each of two contract breaches); *Multi Veste 226 BV v NI Summer Row Unitholder BV* [2011] EWHC 2026 Ch.

27 In *Village Investigations Ltd v Gardner* [2005] EWHC 3300 at [77].

28 [2002] 1 W.L.R. 3024 HL.

29 In the two false imprisonment cases of *R. (on the application of OM) v Secretary of State for the Home Department* [2011] EWCA Civ 909 CA at [57] and *R. (on the application of Moussaoui) v Secretary of State for the Home Department* [2012] EWHC 126 (Admin) at [194], and in *Halliday v Creation Consumer Finance Ltd* [2013] EWCA Civ 333 CA, a claim in respect of damage under s.13(1) of the Data Protection Act 1998 (at [6]). In *Hodge Jones & Allen v McLaughlin* [2011] EWHC 2402 (QB) the nominal damages were provisionally assessed at £10 (at [323]).

30 See *Douglas v Hello! Ltd* [2003] 3 All E.R. 996 at [239] and *Douglas v Hello! Ltd* [2004] E.M.L.R. 2 at 13, [12].

31 [2010] EWHC 682 (Admin).

32 [2010] EWHC 682 (Admin) at [63].

33 [1900] A.C. 113 at 116; see also at 118: "not nominal damages ... but a trifling amount".

34 See *St Helens Smelting Co v Tipping* (1865) 11 H.L.C. 642. In actions where the damages tend to be at large because the loss, generally non-pecuniary, is a difficult one to calculate, awards of a token sum are sometimes referred to as "contemptuous damages" or "derisory damages". "Gold-digging" actions of defamation provide the best illustration, e.g. *Newstead v London Express Newspaper* [1940] 1 K.B. 377 CA where one farthing (now 0.1p) was awarded; *Pamplin v Express Newspapers Ltd (No.2)* (1985) 129 S.J. 188 with one halfpenny (now.0.2p) (upheld in the Court of Appeal at [1988] 1 W.L.R. 116 CA) and *Grobbelaar v News Group Newspapers Ltd* [2002] 1 W.L.R. 3024 HL with the substitution of £1, described by Lord Steyn as a "derisory award" (at [36]) and by Lord Millett as "derisory damages" (at [69]). Such damages are in effect nominal damages awarded for the infringement of a right, since the court could presumably have decided for the defendant if damage had been the gist of the action. Such awards differ from other awards of nominal damages of this type only in that the court, having a wide discretion from the damages being at large as to the amount it may award, is not so compelled to give nominal damages as in, say, an action for non-delivery of goods sold where no pecuniary loss is shown, and the "contempt" or "derision" is thus implied in the court's refusal to exercise this discretion in the claimant's favour.

## 3. PRACTICAL FUNCTIONS OF NOMINAL DAMAGES

Apart from the technical truth that an invasion of a right will give the claimant judgment for "a sum of money that has no existence in point of quantity",[35] what are the practical advantages to the claimant of such a barren judgment over an out-and-out judgment for the defendant? There are two. **12-010**

The first is creditable but infrequent today. It is the use of a verdict for nominal damages as a means of establishing, determining or protecting a legal right.[36] Such a right may be of any kind but is generally a property right, whether over land, goods or immaterial things. The very old cases involve rights over land. Thus in *Pindar v Wadsworth*,[37] it was held that the claimant, a commoner, could maintain an action for injury done to the common by taking away manure, although the claimant himself had suffered no damage. The argument which weighed with Grose J was that **12-011**

> "if a commoner could not maintain an action of this sort, a mere wrongdoer might by repeated torts in course of time establish evidence of a right of common".[38]

*Hanfstaengl v W.H. Smith*,[39] was an action for infringement of copyright where the claimant failed to prove that he had suffered any damage. Kekewich J said:

> "I adopt the plaintiff's argument that, if he desires to protect his copyright, he is bound to take action even in a case which is, on the face of it, of a trumpery character, or run the risk of encouraging more serious infringements ... I think the plaintiff is entitled to a verdict for nominal damages."[40]

Today, however, there are generally more direct means available to a claimant for the protection of his property rights than a suit for damages which cannot be more than nominal: in particular, there is the injunction.

The second advantage has been considered the main purpose of an award of nominal damages: nominal damages are, in the picturesque phrase of Maule J in *Beaumont v Greathead*,[41] "a mere peg on which to hang costs". In many cases the **12-012**

---

35 *Beaumont v Greathead* (1846) 2 C.B. 494 at 499.

36 *R. (on the application of Lumba) v Secretary of State for the Home Department* [2012] 1 A.C. 245 is illustrative as is *Bostridge v Oxleas NHS Foundation Trust* [2015] EWCA Civ 79. See *Anglo-Cyprian Agencies v Paphos Industries* [1951] 1 All E.R. 873 at 874, per Devlin J cited at para.12-013 below.

37 (1802) 2 East 154.

38 (1802) 2 East 154 at 162. See too *Patrick v Greenway* (1796) 1 Wms. Saund. 346b (in the notes) and *Bower v Hill* (1835) 1 Bing. N.C. 549. In *Patrick* the claimant brought an action of trespass against the defendant for fishing in the claimant's several fisheries, and obtained a verdict although he neither alleged nor proved that the defendant had taken any fish. A motion to set aside the verdict was refused on the ground that the act of fishing not only was an infringement of the claimant's right but would afterwards be evidence that the defendant had exercised such a right, evidence which would not be available if the act were now overlooked. In *Bower*, where the defendant had erected a permanent obstruction to a drain leading from a river to the claimant's property, the claimant obtained a verdict despite the fact that the part of the drain passing through the claimant's property had for many years been completely choked with mud. Tindal CJ said at 555: "The right of the plaintiff to this way is injured if there is an obstruction in its nature permanent. If acquiesced in for twenty years, it would become evidence of a renunciation and abandonment of the right of way."

39 [1905] 1 Ch. 519.

40 [1905] 1 Ch. 519 at 528.

41 (1846) 2 C.B. 494 at 499.

claimant, unable to show any loss, is spurred on to win solely in order to get his costs paid by the defendant. It is, of course, proper that costs should be awarded against the defendant where the purpose of the action is the creditable one of determining or protecting some right of the claimant, but in all the many other cases a rule that an award of nominal damages carries costs with it serves only to encourage unnecessary litigation.

**12-013** Fortunately this advantage cannot today be reaped by an undeserving claimant, since it is provided by statute and by rules of court that the costs of proceedings both in the High Court and in the county court are in the discretion of the court.[42] It is true that, as Viscount Cave LC said in *Donald Campbell v Pollak*,[43]

> "this discretion, like any other discretion, must of course be exercised judicially, and the judge ought not to exercise it against the successful party except for some reason connected with the case".

However, to deprive a claimant of his costs and to order him to pay those of the defendant in a case where he has been awarded nominal damages but has had no good reason for suing, is surely an exercise of the discretion for a reason connected with the case. Devlin J did just this in *Anglo-Cyprian Agencies v Paphos Industries*,[44] a case of contract,[45] and the words he used there are instructive:

> "No doubt the ordinary rule is that, where a plaintiff has been successful, he ought not to be deprived of his costs, or at any rate, made to pay the costs of the other side, unless he has been guilty of some sort of misconduct. In applying that rule, however, it is necessary to decide whether the plaintiff really has been successful, and I do not think that a plaintiff who recovers nominal damages ought necessarily to be regarded in the ordinary sense of the word as a 'successful' plaintiff. In certain cases he may be, e.g. where part of the object of the action is to establish a legal right, wholly irrespective of whether any substantial remedy is obtained.[46] To that extent a plaintiff who recovers nominal damages may properly be regarded as a successful plaintiff, but it is necessary to examine the facts of each particular case."[47]

Indeed in the usual case in which the claimant has effectively lost, as opposed to the occasional case in which he is seeking to establish a right, the awarding of nominal damages may be seen as a pointless exercise, given the courts' powers and practice on costs. This was certainly the view of Jacob J who, in declining to make an award of nominal damages in a copyright action heard in 1999, *Hyde Park Residence Ltd v Yelland*,[48] said:

---

42 Senior Courts Act 1981 s.51 together with CPR Pt 44 (see especially the now r.44.2(1), which earlier was r.44.3(1)).

43 [1927] A.C. 732 at 811 to 812.

44 [1951] 1 All E.R. 873.

45 For the same result in a case of tort and defamation, see *Pamplin v Express Newspapers Ltd (No.2)* (1985) 129 S.J. 188 (the appeal, at [1988] 1 W.L.R. 116 CA, is not relevant here).

46 This situation is dealt with at para.12-011, above.

47 [1951] 1 All E.R. 873 at 874. Thus in *TCP Europe Ltd v Parry* unreported 23 July 2012 (QB), the claimant, who had been awarded nominal damages on establishing liability, was both deprived of his costs and ordered to pay the defendant his.

48 [1999] R.P.C. 655.

> "It seems to me that the whole question of nominal damages is at the end of this century far too legalistic. A plaintiff who recovers only nominal damages has effectively lost and in reality the defendant has established a complete defence."[49]

With this thought the present chapter may be concluded.

[49] [1999] R.P.C. 655 at 670.

Chapter 13

# EXEMPLARY DAMAGES

Table of Contents



## I. The Exceptional Nature of Exemplary Damages

**13-001** It is often said that exemplary damages are exceptional because the usual object of an award of damages is to compensate the claimant for the harm done to him. However, this statement is a description of the law, not a justification. Moreover, as a description it is not wholly accurate. In separate chapters in this work we see the award of a number of different types of non-compensatory damages: nominal damages, restitutionary damages, and disgorgement damages. The reason for the exceptional nature of exemplary damages is sometimes thought to be that those damages have an object to deter the defendant for his conduct in inflicting that harm and to deter others from similar behaviour. But that object is not unique to exemplary damages. Such an object is achieved by awarding, in addition to the normal compensatory damages, damages which we will see in Ch.15 might be described as disgorgement damages, and which, in equity, were commonly awarded following an account of profits. Further, sometimes damages awards are made to deter but described not as exemplary damages but as punitive damages, vindictive damages or even retributory damages.[1] Some of the circumstances in which it comes into play are whenever the defendant's conduct is sufficiently outrageous to merit punishment, as where it discloses malice, fraud, cruelty, insolence or the like, or as where, should the defendant be a government servant, it is oppressive, arbitrary or unconstitutional.[2] Whether a modern legal system should recognise exemplary damages at all has been much debated, but English law has now settled on the conclusion that, exceptionally, they are justified. The central argument against them is that they are anomalous in the civil sphere, confusing the civil and criminal functions of the law[3]; in particular, it is anomalous that money exacted from a defendant for the object of deterrence should be paid to a claimant rather than to the State. On the other side, a major justification of exemplary damages is that the civil and criminal law have never been entirely distinct; their roots are commingled and the object of deterrence can be seen in numerous areas of the civil law, including both common law and equity (most notably, breach of fiduciary duty). The label "exemplary damages" emphasises the object of deterrence. It is to be preferred to the label "punitive damages" which suggests the legitimacy of objects of punishment in addition to deterrence including retribution, and rehabilitation. The punitive focus of these damages truly conflates crime and civil law and sees justifications for punitive damages on the basis that they are a suitable means for the punishment of minor criminal acts which are in practice ignored by police too caught up in the pursuit of serious crime.[4]

In the 1760s exemplary damages first made their appearance on the English legal scene. The earliest cases arose in the *cause célèbre* of John Wilkes and the *North Briton*. In the Government's effort to stop the *North Briton* from being published, a variety of individuals suffered interference at the hands of public officials, and in two tort actions of 1763 based upon such interference, *Huckle v Money*,[5] a claim for false imprisonment, and *Wilkes v Wood*,[6] a claim for trespass to land, awards of exemplary damages were made. By the end of the decade further awards had appeared in other contexts,[7] and thereafter exemplary damages became a familiar feature of tort—though never contract[8]—law, being awarded not only in cases of **13-002**

---

1 As by Byles J in *Bell v Midland Ry* (1861) 10 C.B. N.S. 287 at 308. In *Broome v Cassell & Co* [1972] A.C. 1027 Lord Hailsham LC thought it desirable to abandon the use of "vindictive" and "retributory" and, as between "exemplary" and "punitive", preferred the former (at 1073C to F); Lord Diplock (at 1124H to 1125A) would have preferred "punitive", but accepted the Lord Chancellor's lead in adhering to Lord Devlin's "exemplary" in *Rookes v Barnard* [1964] A.C. 1129. For these two leading cases, see para.13-003, below.

2 See para.13-017, below.

3 See the remarks of Lord Reid in *Broome v Cassell & Co* [1972] A.C. 1027 at 1087C to F, where he pointed out that "to allow pure punishment in this way contravenes almost every principle which has been evolved for the protection of offenders".

4 The arguments pro and con are fully listed in Street, *Principles of the Law of Damages* (1962), pp.34 to 36.

5 (1763) 2 Wils. K.B. 205.

6 (1763) Lofft 1. The claimant was John Wilkes himself.

7 *Benson v Frederick* (1766) 3 Burr. 1845 (assault); *Tullidge v Wade* (1769) 3 Wils. K.B. 18 (seduction).

8 But things may be changing. See para.13-016, below and the Canadian case of *Royal Bank of Canada v Got*, 178 D.L.R. (4th) 385 (2000) there.

assault, false imprisonment, defamation, seduction and malicious prosecution but also in cases of trespass to land and, eventually, trespass to goods.[9]

**13-003** In the 1960s the situation changed. In *Rookes v Barnard*[10] the House of Lords took the opportunity to review the whole doctrine and held that exemplary damages should be confined to a few categories.[11] However, their Lordships rejected the argument that it was open to them "to remove an anomaly from the law of England".[12] There was an attempt by the Court of Appeal in *Broome v Cassell & Co*,[13] to question the decision, but on the appeal in that case their Lordships put paid to any such questionings.[14] The House was, in the words of the Lord Chancellor,

> "not prepared to follow the Court of Appeal in its criticisms of *Rookes v Barnard*, which ... imposed valuable limits on the doctrine of exemplary damages as they had hitherto been understood in English law and clarified important questions which had previously been undiscussed or left confused."[15]

"We cannot", he added, "depart from *Rookes v Barnard* here. It was decided neither per incuriam nor ultra vires this House."[16]

**13-004** The result is that two centuries of authorities were confined to a limited number of categories. Yet the new thinking does not have such a drastic effect upon the existing case law as would at first sight appear. For as Lord Devlin, who spoke for all their Lordships on the issue of exemplary damages, pointed out in *Rookes v Barnard*,[17] there is a double rationale behind such awards.

> "When one examines the cases in which large damages have been awarded for conduct of this sort",

he said,

> "it is not at all easy to say whether the idea of compensation or the idea of punishment has prevailed".[18]

The House considered that practically all the so-called exemplary damages cases could, and should, be explained as cases of aggravated damage—that is, as cases of extra compensation to the claimant for the injury to his feelings and dignity[19]—and indeed it was the availability of this alternative explanation of the cases which allowed the House to limit exemplary damages to a small number of categories

---

9 The cases are all set out and discussed in the 12th edition (1961) of this work at paras 208 to 211.
10 [1964] A.C. 1129.
11 See paras 13-017 to 13-030, below.
12 [1964] A.C. 1129 at 1221.
13 [1971] 2 Q.B. 354 CA.
14 [1972] A.C. 1027.
15 [1972] A.C. 1027 at 1082E.
16 [1972] A.C. 1027 at 1083D. Out of a full House of seven, only two, Viscount Dilhorne and Lord Wilberforce, favoured the pre-*Rookes* position.
17 [1964] A.C. 1129. Confirming the view advanced in the 12th edition (1961) of this work at paras 212 to 214.
18 [1964] A.C. 1129 at 1221.
19 See in particular Lord Atkin's statement in *Ley v Hamilton* (1935) 153 L.T. 384 HL at 386, that damages for defamation "are not arrived at ... by determining the 'real' damage, and adding to that sum by way of vindictive or punitive damages. It is precisely because the 'real' damage cannot be ascertained that the damages are at large. It is impossible to track the scandal, to know the quarters the poison may reach: it is impossible to weigh at all closely the compensation which will recompense a man or a woman for the insult offered or the pain of a false accusation".

while remaining within the framework of precedent. Lord Devlin hoped that the decision of the House would

> "remove from the law a source of confusion between aggravated and exemplary damages which has troubled the learned commentators on the subject. Otherwise, it will not, I think, make much difference to the substance of the law or rob the law of the strength which it ought to have. Aggravated damages in this type of case can do most, if not all, of the work that could be done by exemplary damages. In so far as they do not, assaults and malicious injuries to property can generally be punished as crimes."[20]

Accordingly, the House did not find it necessary to overrule the earlier authorities en masse. Indeed, only one case, *Loudon v Ryder*,[21] was expressly overruled; the great majority fall now to be explained as awards on account of aggravated damage.[22]

Lord Devlin expressed the view in *Rookes v Barnard*,[23] that exemplary damages were a peculiarity of English law. It is more exact to regard them as a peculiarity of the common law, not accepted by other legal systems. For the English lead of the 1760s was in fact taken up both throughout the Commonwealth and in the United States of America, while the English *volte face* of the 1960s has not been largely followed by other jurisdictions within the common law family.[24] Indeed, in Australia a clear rejection emerged when, in a libel action, the High Court refused to adopt the new English approach.[25] This refusal, moreover, was upheld on appeal by the Judicial Committee of the Privy Council,[26] basing its decision on two factors: that Australia, unlike England before *Rookes*, had already fully accepted the exemplary principle, with all its implications, where damages for libel were concerned; and that it was a matter for Australia, in an area of domestic rather than international significance where the need for uniformity within the Commonwealth is less, to decide whether to change her settled judicial policy on this issue in the law of libel.[27] However, in *Broome v Cassell & Co*,[28] Lord Hailsham LC said that he viewed with dismay the doctrine that the common law should differ in different parts of the Commonwealth, and expressed the hope that, in the light of their Lord- 13-005

---

20 [1964] A.C. 1129 at 1230. As to whether in an insurance context the term "compensatory damages" can cover exemplary damages, see *Charterhouse Development (France) Ltd v Sharp* [1998] Lloyd's Rep. I.R. 266.

21 [1953] 2 Q.B. 202 CA.

22 See, e.g. *Owen and Smith v Reo Motors* (1934) 151 L.T. 274 CA and *Williams v Settle* [1960] 1 W.L.R. 1072 CA, which are so justified at [1964] A.C. 1129 at 1229. But awards in cases falling within the permitted exceptions to the general ban on exemplary damages (paras 13-017 to 13-030, below) may still be upheld on their original basis.

23 [1964] A.C. 1129 at 1221.

24 For case and text references to other jurisdictions, both within and without the common law, see the 13th edition (London: Sweet & Maxwell, 1972) of this work at para.305. Since the new English approach is now settled, it is thought that continued reference to the position elsewhere is no longer needed.

25 *Uren v John Fairfax & Sons Pty* [1967] Argus L.R. 25; (1966) 40 A.L.J.R. 124; *Australian Consolidated Press v Uren* [1967] Argus L.R. 54; (1966) 40 A.L.J.R. 142.

26 *Australian Consolidated Press v Uren* [1969] 1 A.C. 590 PC.

27 [1969] 1 A.C. 590 PC at 637, 641, 642, 644. New Zealand has followed suit, so that the Judicial Committee of the Privy Council continued to be presented with appeals from there which entail decisions on the scope of pre-Rookes exemplary damages; *A v Bottrill* [2003] 1 A.C. 449 PC is an example.

28 [1972] A.C. 1027.

ships' observations on *Rookes*, Commonwealth courts might modify their criticism of it.[29]

**13-006** Although exemplary damages have been limited to various categories now for over half a century in English law—such damages have no place in Scots law—by the efforts of two distinguished courts,[30] there remains a persistent question, consistent with the approach taken elsewhere in the Commonwealth,[31] why the object of deterrence should be confined to three categories. Although these categories might be the dominant and best known examples where deterrence is required, the only limits the depravity requiring deterrence is the boundaries of human ingenuity. In its Report on *Aggravated, Exemplary and Restitutionary Damages*,[32] the Law Commission recommended that exemplary damages be retained and expanded from their current, limited presence in the law, while being put upon a principled basis.[33]

**13-007** The debate continues. In *Kuddus v Chief Constable of Leicestershire*,[34] Lord Nicholls and Lord Hutton favoured the retention of at least the first common law category as they considered that there exemplary damages continued vital and buttressed civil liberties. Lord Slynn and Lord Mackay did not think it appropriate to consider the general question when it was not in issue.[35] But Lord Scott argued that the law did not become fossilised and set in stone when Lord Devlin allowed two common law categories of such damages[36] to survive *Rookes v Barnard*. The common law had not stood still since 1964 and the vast development of judicial review, then in its infancy, could, together with the availability of awards of substantial aggravated damages, take the place of the first category while the latter-day emergence of disgorgement damages (account of profits) as a remedy for wrongdoing provided a substitute for the second.[37] "There is, in my opinion", he concluded, "no longer any need for punitive damages in the civil law".[38]

**13-008** Thus the debate continues and it is not likely to be long before the courts return to this controversial question. Indeed there was a chance that the issue would have been resurrected in *Kuddus* itself. For the House having decided, disagreeing with the courts below, that the claimant's action should not be struck out, the defendants could have gone ahead and responded to the virtual invitation to challenge the existence of exemplary damages in their entirety. But the case settled.

## II. CASES IN WHICH EXEMPLARY DAMAGES MAY BE AWARDED

**13-009** While laying down that, as a general rule, exemplary damages should no longer be awarded, Lord Devlin in *Rookes* considered that their Lordships

---

29 [1972] A.C. 1027 at 1067H and 1083C.

30 The redoubtable Lord Reid was a member of the House of Lords in both *Rookes v Barnard* and *Broome v Cassell & Co*.

31 See *ACB v Thomson Medical Pte Ltd and others* [2017] SGCA 20 at [162]–[175].

32 Law Com. No.247 (1997).

33 Law Com. No.247 (1997), para.5.25.

34 [2002] 2 A.C. 122.

35 In *Gleaner Co Ltd v Abrahams* [2004] 1 A.C. 628 PC the judgment of their Lordships' Board delivered by Lord Hoffmann may be read as being rather sympathetic to exemplary damages although it was with compensatory damages that their Lordships were there concerned.

36 For these see paras 13-017 to 13-027, below.

37 See [2002] 2 A.C. 122 at [107]–[109] (inaccurately described by Lord Scott as "restitutionary damages"). See Ch.15, below.

38 See [2002] 2 A.C. 122 at [110].

> "could not, without a complete disregard of precedent, and indeed of statute, now arrive at a determination that refused altogether to recognise the exemplary principle",[39]

and there remain three categories of cases in which awards of exemplary damages continue to be legitimate, though not mandatory as whether to make an award is in the court's discretion.[40] Lord Devlin in Rookes found two categories of case which he described as categories

> "in which an award of exemplary damages can serve a useful purpose in vindicating the strength of the law and thus affording a practical justification for admitting into the civil law a principle which ought logically to belong to the criminal."[41]

Thus two of the categories are established as part of the common law; to these Lord Devlin had necessarily to add the category of exemplary damages authorised by statute.

However, before turning to the three categories to which exemplary damages have been restricted since 1964, it is important to look at the types of claim in which exemplary damages are available. For the position on this has oscillated between 1964 and today. **13-010**

## 1. Types of Claim in which Exemplary Damages are Possible

As a result of the decision of the House of Lords in *Kuddus v Chief Constable of Leicestershire*,[42] it can confidently be said that today exemplary awards are possible across the whole range of tort. Provided always that there is unacceptable behaviour on the part of the defendant, behaviour that displays features which merit punishment by way of malice, fraud, cruelty, insolence and the like, behaviour referred to, where it is the conduct of government servants that is in issue, as oppressive, arbitrary or unconstitutional,[43] there is no tort where a claim for exemplary damages will not be permitted. Before *Rookes v Barnard*,[44] exemplary damages had become well established in the torts of defamation, false imprisonment and trespass to property. However, it was questioned by some after *Rookes*, with exemplary damages having there been declared anomalous, as to whether the anomaly should be expanded.[45] The Court of Appeal accepted the propriety of these doubts in *A.B. v South West Water Services*,[46] by holding that an award of exemplary damages could only be made where the claimant's cause of action was one in respect of which awards of this kind had already been made before *Rookes* was decided. However, the House of Lords rejected this view in *Kuddus*. It is the features of the defendant's behaviour rather than the cause of action sued upon which determines whether exemplary damages are appropriate. The House did not approve of the need to trawl through the authorities to decipher, in relation to a particular tort, whether pre-*Rookes* damages awards might have included an element of exemplary damages. **13-011**

39 [1964] A.C. 1129 at 1226.
40 See *Holden v Chief Constable of Lancashire* [1987] Q.B. 380 CA at 388D and 389B.
41 [1964] A.C. 1129 at 1226.
42 [2002] 2 A.C. 122.
43 See para.13-017, below.
44 [1964] A.C. 1129.
45 In particular this was the view of Lord Hailsham and Lord Diplock expressed in *Broome v Cassell* [1972] A.C. 1027 at 1076B and 1131A respectively.
46 [1993] Q.B. 507 CA.

It follows that all torts, or more precisely all torts which may contain a wilful element, are now up for consideration in the exemplary stakes.[47]

13-012 Hence it is not necessary in this chapter to examine tort after tort. Mention will be made only of (i) the infrequent torts of intimidation and misfeasance in public office since they featured in the two House of Lords cases which came at the start and towards the end of this whole saga; and (ii) a few others in order to dispel any doubts about their appropriateness for an award of exemplary damages today. As to the former group, it is clear that in *Rookes v Barnard*,[48] where intimidation by trade union members was in issue, Lord Devlin thought that exemplary damages could have been awarded had the facts of the case fallen into one of his announced categories, while in *Kuddus v Chief Constable of Leicestershire*,[49] where a police constable had mishandled in a disgraceful, even fraudulent, manner the investigation of the claimant's complaint about a theft from his flat, it was held that the defendant Chief Constable's acceptance that this amounted to a misfeasance in public office sufficed to allow the case to proceed on the issue of exemplary damages and not be struck out.[50] As to the latter group, the following fall for consideration: deceit, torts arising out of statute and public nuisance.

13-013 Deceit had curiously produced no exemplary awards before *Rookes*. Nor have there been any decisions in either direction since *Rookes* but views have been expressed both in favour and against. On the one hand, Widgery LJ in *Mafo v Adams*,[51] was quite confident that exemplary damages could be awarded and Peter Pain J in *Archer v Brown*[52] thought likewise. On the other hand, Sachs LJ in *Mafo v Adams*,[53] said he still had to be persuaded and *Metallund Rohstoff AG v Acli Metals (London)*,[54] proceeded on the basis that exemplary damages could not,[55] or arguably could not,[56] be awarded. Today the dicta and views in favour must prevail. Indeed Lord Scott in *Kuddus* said specifically that, if exemplary damages were to be retained,[57] deceit should in a suitable case attract them.[58]

---

47 Including torts based upon breach of statutory duty, as in *Design Progression Ltd v Thurloe Properties Ltd* [2005] 1 W.L.R. 1; facts at para.13-025, below. Yet in *Mosley v News Group Newspapers Ltd* [2008] E.M.L.R 20 at 679 Eady J ruled that exemplary damages are not admissible in a claim for invasion of privacy: [2008] E.M.L.R 20 at [197]. However, this was in part due to his doubt as to whether it was proper to classify invasion of privacy as a tort since claims founded on privacy have evolved from claims in equity for breach of confidence: see the discussion in his judgment at [2008] E.M.L.R 20 at [181]–[185]. His further argument that exemplary damages need not be available in all torts (at [187] to [192]) is, after *Kuddus*, not at all convincing. Lindsay J in the earlier *Douglas v Hello! Ltd* [1996] 3 All E.R. 996 had been content to assume, without deciding, that exemplary damages were available in this type of case: [1996] 3 All E.R. 996 at [273]. In any event, both Eady J and Lindsay J considered exemplary damages to be inappropriate on the particular facts.

48 [1964] A.C. 1129.

49 [2002] 2 A.C. 122.

50 However, if the misfeasance in public office claim fails on account of no damage being shown, there is no room for an award of exemplary damages: *Watkins v Secretary of State for the Home Department* [2006] 2 A.C. 395.

51 [1970] 1 Q.B. 548 CA at 558.

52 [1985] Q.B. 401 at 423F.

53 [1970] 1 Q.B. 548 CA at 555.

54 [1984] 1 Lloyd's Rep. 598 CA.

55 [1984] 1 Lloyd's Rep. 598 CA at 612, col.1.

56 [1984] 1 Lloyd's Rep. 598 CA at 603, col.2.

57 Which he regretted: see para.13-007, above.

58 [2002] 2 A.C. 122 at [122].

The statutory torts of sexual and racial discrimination were created after *Rookes*.[59] In *Alexander v Home Office*,[60] the Court of Appeal saw no reason why exemplary damages could not be awarded in a racial discrimination case.[61] In *Wileman v Minilec Engineering*,[62] Popplewell J said the same for sex discrimination,[63] and *Bradford City Metropolitan Council v Arora*,[64] the Court of Appeal restored an award of exemplary damages for discrimination against the claimant on grounds of both sex and race. These views are the state of the law and the dismissal of these cases in *A.B. v South West Water Services*,[65] can be ignored.[66] Outside the discrimination cases, breach of statutory duty under competition law was accepted by Lewison J as an appropriate tort for exemplary damages in *Devenish Nutrition Ltd v Sanofi-Aventis SA*.[67] Two further cases of breach of competition law in which exemplary damages have been claimed, have followed, both being heard by the Competition Appeal Tribunal. These are *2 Travel Group Plc v Cardiff City Transport Services Ltd*,[68] and *Albion Water Ltd v Dwr Cymru Cyfyngedig*.[69] **13-014**

Public nuisance, which also had generated no exemplary awards before *Rookes*, **13-015** was in issue in *A.B. v South West Water Services*,[70] the decision overruled by *Kuddus*. It was an action in negligence and public nuisance and for breach of statutory duty. It would not usually be expected that actions in negligence would lead to exemplary damages, either before or after *Rookes*, since the necessary mental element is not usually present; and this would be true even of gross negligence.[71] But actions in negligence may be combined, as was so in this case, with actions where there may be features of the conduct of the defendant which suffice to allow the use of the exemplary weapon. In *A.B. v South West Water Services*, aluminium sulphate was accidently introduced into the drinking water system at a water treatment works operated by a water authority. A group action was brought by nearly 200 of the authority's customers against the authority's successor claiming damages for injuries suffered as a result of drinking contaminated water. In addition to compensatory damages, exemplary, and also aggravated, damages were sought on the grounds that for some time after the contamination the authority, in its capac-

---

59 By the Sex Discrimination Act 1975 and the Race Relations Act 1976.

60 [1988] 1 W.L.R. 968 CA.

61 [1988] 1 W.L.R. 968 CA at 976.

62 [1988] I.C.R. 318.

63 [1988] I.C.R. 318 at 328.

64 [1991] 2 Q.B. 507 CA.

65 [1993] Q.B. 507 CA.

66 Lord Mackay expressed some reservations in *Kuddus v Chief Constable of Leicestershire* [2002] 2 A.C. 122 at [46] as to whether exemplary damages should now be available in discrimination cases but surely these too can be discounted.

67 [2009] Ch. 390.

68 [2012] C.A.T. 19.

69 [2013] C.A.T. 6.

70 [1993] Q.B. 507 CA.

71 Although there were murmurings in the 19th century that gross negligence might suffice. Indeed the Judicial Committee of the Privy Council has now decided in *A v Bottrill* [2003] 1 A.C. 449 PC that for New Zealand, which retains the pre-*Rookes* law (see para.13-005, above), an exemplary award for outrageous negligence may be appropriate. In *Re Organ Retention Group Litigation* [2005] Q.B. 506, a claim in negligence by parents in respect of the removal and retention of their deceased children's organs by the defendants, no exemplary award was made where the conduct of the defendants did not come anywhere near to being sufficiently outrageous or oppressive; the judge's assumption, without decision, that exemplary damages could be available in negligence claims was hardly necessary: see at [263].

ity as a statutory body and a public servant, had acted in a high-handed and arrogant manner by ignoring customers' complaints, had wilfully and deliberately misrepresented the situation in a circular letter asserting that the water was safe to drink, and had failed to give out proper information or to take precautionary measures so that the contaminated water had been consumed for a longer period and in greater quantities than would otherwise have happened. While the Court of Appeal held that the claim for exemplary damages failed both because on the facts it fell within neither of Lord Devlin's two common law categories[72] and because no awards for exemplary damages had been made before *Rookes* in public nuisance or the other torts concerned, there is nothing to suggest that, in the absence of these factors, the conduct of the water authority would not have sufficed to ground an exemplary award.[73]

**13-016** For contract, on the other hand, the position is less certain. Historically, the law has always set its face against awarding exemplary damages for breach of contract; outrageous conduct is the domain of tort rather than contract. Such a stance was famously taken by the House of Lords in *Addis v Gramophone Co*,[74] in the context of wrongful dismissal of an employee by an employer and continued in the context of wrongful disturbance of a tenant by a landlord right to the verge of the decision in *Rookes*.[75] But may not the new limits on exemplary damages have permitted an enlargement of the situations in which awards may be made? Once the rationale has been changed so as to concentrate upon high-handed public conduct and profit-motivated private conduct, may not such conduct deserve the same sanction whatever the cause of action? Not many years ago exemplary damages were awarded by a Canadian court in *Royal Bank of Canada v Got*.[76] Just as the English courts have now, since *Blake*,[77] countenanced disgorgement damages for breach of contract as well as for tort, so too, it has been rightly said,[78] English courts (probably the Supreme Court) will have to confront the issue of whether exemplary damages are allowable for breach of contract as well as for tort.

## 2. THE THREE CATEGORIES IN WHICH EXEMPLARY AWARDS ARE POSSIBLE

### (1) First common law category: oppressive, arbitrary or unconstitutional conduct by government servants

**13-017** The first of the two common law categories comprises cases in which, in Lord Devlin's words in *Rookes*, there has been "oppressive, arbitrary or unconstitutional action by the servants of the government".[79] This category is based primarily on the 18th century cases which introduced the general doctrine of exemplary damages.[80]

72 See the case further at paras 13-019 and 13-020, below.

73 The holding at first instance in *Catnic Components v Hill & Smith* [1983] F.S.R. 512, that a claim for exemplary damages was not open to the claimant in the absence of any authority that prior to Rookes exemplary damages had been awarded in infringement of patent actions (see at 540 to 541) is no longer acceptable.

74 [1909] A.C. 488.

75 *Perera v Vandiyar* [1953] 1 W.L.R. 672 CA; *Kenny v Preen* [1963] 1 Q.B. 499 CA.

76 178 D.L.R. (4th) 385 (2000).

77 [2001] 1 A.C. 268. For disgorgement damages see Ch.15.

78 In a comment on *Royal Bank of Canada v Got* at 117 L.Q.R. 539 (2001).

79 [1964] A.C. 1129 at 1226.

80 See para.13-002, above.

While the general justification advanced by Lord Devlin in *Rookes* for retaining this, and his other, common law category within the exemplary damages net is that awards under them vindicate the strength of the law,[81] more important, with the first category, is the particular justification which is put by way of a contrast between public servants on the one hand and private corporations and individuals on the other. With the latter:

> "where one man is more powerful than another, it is inevitable that he will try to use his power to gain his ends; and if his power is much greater than the other's, he might, perhaps, be said to be using it oppressively. If he uses his power illegally, he must of course pay for his illegality in the ordinary way; but he is not to be punished simply because he is the more powerful. In the case of the government it is different, for the servants of the government are also the servants of the people and the use of their power must always be subordinate to their duty of service."[82]

Accordingly *Rookes* itself, concerning trade unions and trade disputes, fell outside this category.[83]

Although in *Broome*,[84] Lord Diplock doubted whether today it was necessary to retain this category, it is still with us, and flourishing.

It took some time after *Rookes* for this category to get off the ground. The two editions of this text in the years following *Rookes* despaired of finding any post-*Rookes* decisions in the first category. But then decisions started to appear. Today they are quite numerous. The first was *Attorney General for St Christopher, Nevis and Anguilla v Reynolds*,[85] where unconstitutional action by the Governor of a group of Caribbean Islands causing the wrongful arrest and false imprisonment of the claimant led to an award which included an exemplary element; the Privy Council did not question the propriety of such an award as falling within the first category.[86] Then, on home ground, the Court of Appeal accepted the appropriateness of exemplary damages where there had been a wrongful arrest by a police officer in *Holden v Chief Constable of Lancashire*,[87] and upheld an exemplary award by an industrial tribunal in a case involving discrimination by a local authority in *Bradford City Council v Arora*.[88] It has been police misconduct that has generated most of the awards to date. In addition to *Holden*, important illustrations of exemplary damages for police misconduct are to be found in *Thompson v Commis-* **13-018**

81 See the quotation from his speech at para.13-009, above.

82 [1964] A.C. 1129 at 1226.

83 Lord Hailsham LC in *Broome v Cassell & Co* [1972] A.C. 1027 at 1078B expressed himself as "not prepared to say without further consideration that a private individual misusing legal powers of private prosecution or arrest … might not at some future date be assimilated into the first category"; but, given the motivation of imposing limits on exemplary damages, it is thought that such a development is unlikely.

84 [1972] A.C. 1027 at 1129H to 1130A.

85 [1980] A.C. 637 PC.

86 See [1980] A.C. 637 PC, especially at 662F to G. In *Reynolds* the exemplary award which the Privy Council was upholding was at common law for the false imprisonment and not for the breach of the claimant's constitutional rights. It is the redress sanctioned by the Privy Council in the many similar later Caribbean cases which is in relation to the claimant's constitutional rights, being given by way not of exemplary but of vindicatory damages. The cases are all dealt with in the chapter on vindicatory damages: see para.17-013, below.

87 [1987] Q.B. 380 CA.

88 [1991] 2 Q.B. 507 CA.

*sioner of Police of the Metropolis*,[89] where there had been false imprisonment and malicious prosecution, and in *Hsu v Commissioner of Police of the Metropolis*,[90] where there had been wrongful arrest, false imprisonment and assault. Police misconduct was also in issue in *Kuddus v Chief Constable of Leicestershire*,[91] where in the context of misfeasance in public office the House of Lords accepted that exemplary damages could be awarded.[92] Prison officers and immigration officials featured in *Muuse v Secretary of State for the Home Department*,[93] where substantial exemplary damages for false imprisonment were awarded to a Dutch national born in Somalia who was unlawfully kept in custody for over four months pending deportation to Somalia when it could very easily have been ascertained that there was no right to deport him. The conduct of the prison officers and immigration officials was categorised as an outrageous abuse of executive power. And immigration officers again featured in *Patel v Secretary of State for the Home Department*,[94] where exemplary damages were awarded to a young Indian woman with leave to enter the United Kingdom to visit her family who was treated appallingly by the officers in their attempt to remove her from the country.

**13-019** Two conditions must be satisfied before a first category case can be established. The first concerns the conduct of the defendant. This has to be shown to be, in Lord Devlin's words, oppressive, arbitrary or unconstitutional and, while it was said in *Holden v Chief Constable of Lancashire*,[95] that unconstitutional action would suffice without the need for additional oppressive or arbitrary behaviour, so that in effect the three epithets fall to be read disjunctively, unconstitutional action will not suffice without the presence of aggravating features; the central requirement for exemplary damages has always been, as already said,[96] the presence of outrageous conduct, disclosing malice, fraud, insolence, cruelty and the like.[97] So, the public

---

89 [1998] Q.B. 498 CA.

90 [1998] Q.B. 498 CA; reported together with *Thompson*.

91 [2002] 2 A.C. 122.

92 See para.13-012, above.

93 [2010] EWCA Civ 453 CA.

94 [2014] EWHC 501 (Admin) (see at [343]). See discussion of the case further at paras 42-018 and 40-025, below.

95 [1987] Q.B. 380 CA, at 388C to D.

96 See para.13-001, above.

97 In *Muuse v Secretary of State for the Home Department* [2010] EWCA Civ 453 CA Thomas LJ, in the only reasoned judgment, mistakenly understood the text to be advancing the proposition that the claimant must show not only that the government servant has acted oppressively, arbitrarily or unconstitutionally but also that his action has been motivated by malice, fraud, insolence, cruelty and the like: [2010] EWCA Civ 453 CA at [68]–[71]. This is not at all what is being said in this paragraph. It starts by stating that the first condition that must be satisfied in this category of case concerns the conduct of the defendant which must be shown to be oppressive, arbitrary or unconstitutional and, having so stated, it is concerned to make the point that, the central requirement for the imposition of exemplary damages being, and always having been, the existence of outrageous conduct on the defendant's part, should a claimant be relying on unconstitutional, as distinct from oppressive or arbitrary, action he must show the conduct to be outrageous, for an action which is simply unconstitutional may not constitute a misuse or abuse of constitutional or executive power. The reference to conduct disclosing malice, fraud, insolence, cruelty and the like is made only to emphasise the need for outrageousness in conduct, being the terminology appearing in the heyday of exemplary damages when they were widely available. The oppressive, arbitrary and unconstitutional trilogy simply introduces more suitable terms to indicate outrageousness in the misuse and abuse of power with which actions against government servants are concerned. It is clear that the trilogy takes the place of malice, fraud, insolence, cruelty and the like; it in no way adds to them.

nuisance negligently committed in *A.B. v South West Water Services*,[98] was described by Sir Thomas Bingham MR as being "quite unlike the abuses of power which Lord Devlin had in mind".[99] In *Ministry of Defence v Fletcher*,[100] an award of exemplary damages to a victimised army recruit was set aside by the Employment Appeal Tribunal as the conduct of the army officers, though deplorable, did not cross the high threshold set for a finding of oppressive or arbitrary behaviour. In *R. (on the application of Lumba (Congo)) v Secretary of State for the Home Department*,[101] where the Secretary of State for the Home Department was held liable for the false imprisonment of foreign national prisoners pending their deportation, the Supreme Court was not prepared to award exemplary damages to the claimants since there had not been conduct so outrageous and so unconstitutional, oppressive or arbitrary as to justify such an award. There is a careful analysis of the conduct of the senior Home Office personnel by Lord Dyson[102] with whom, on exemplary damages, the other eight Justices agreed.[103]

The second condition to open the door to a first category award concerns the status of the defendant. Lord Devlin in *Rookes* spoke of servants of the Government[104] but in *Broome* their Lordships were agreed that that term was to be widely interpreted so as to include not only Crown servants but also the police and local and other officials.[105] This wide approach has been suggested to include solicitors, as officers of the court executing an *Anton Piller* order (*Columbia Picture Industries v Robinson*,[106]) and officers of the Agricultural Produce Intervention Board (*R. v Reading J.J. Ex p. South West Meat*).[107] Even where the defendant is clearly within the definition of government servant it must be established that the act complained of has been done in the exercise of a governmental function. In *Bradford City Council v Arora*,[108] the selection of an employee by a local authority, improperly made by reason of sexual and racial discrimination, was held to constitute the exercise of a governmental function and the argument that the authority was acting in a private capacity was rejected. Nevertheless Neill LJ was of the view that there might be cases where the carrying out of a duty by a junior officer of such an authority might not be the exercise of a public function[109] and in *Holden v Chief Constable of Lancashire*,[110] the court was not prepared to accept that every act of a police officer without authority brought the category into play.[111] In *2 Travel Group Plc v Cardiff City Transport Services Ltd*,[112] a bus undertaking owned by, but operated independently of, a local authority was easily held not to fall within the **13-020**

98 [1993] Q.B. 507 CA.
99 [1993] Q.B. 507 CA at 531H.
100 [2010] I.R.L.R. 25.
101 [2012] 1 A.C. 245.
102 [2012] 1 A.C. 245 at [151] to [166].
103 This unanimous view contrasts with the Justices being divided both on the issue of liability and on other aspects of the damages: see paras 17-014 and 42-021, below.
104 See para.13-017, above.
105 See especially [1972] A.C. 1027 at 1077H to 1078B, 1087H to 1088B and 1130B, per Lords Hailsham, Reid and Diplock respectively.
106 [1987] Ch. 38, especially at 87D to F.
107 [1992] Crim. L.R. 672.
108 [1991] 2 Q.B. 507 CA.
109 [1991] 2 Q.B. 507 CA at 518H.
110 [1987] Q.B. 380 CA.
111 [1987] Q.B. 380 CA at 387H to 388B.
112 [2012] C.A.T. 19.

first category as it was not exercising governmental functions of any sort.[113] In *A.B. v South West Water Services*,[114] the defendant, a nationalised body set up under statute for the commercial purpose of supplying water to the public, was held by the Court of Appeal not to be within the first category because in its commercial activities it was not acting as an instrument or agent of government.[115] Moreover, with today's trend towards privatisation such bodies are likely to cease even being government servants; indeed the defendant in A.B., though a public body at the time of the incidents complained of, had since been privatised.

### (2) Second common law category: conduct calculated to result in profit

**13-021** The second of the two common law categories comprises cases in which, again in Lord Devlin's words in *Rookes*,

> "the defendant's conduct has been calculated by him to make a profit for himself which may exceed the compensation payable to the plaintiff."[116]

As with the first common law category, the general justification advanced was that here exemplary damages could serve a useful purpose in vindicating the law's strength,[117] but, as with the first category, it is the particular justification which is the more important. "Where a defendant", said Lord Devlin,

> "with a cynical disregard for a plaintiff's rights has calculated that the money to be made out of his wrongdoing will probably exceed the damages at risk, it is necessary for the law to show that it cannot be broken with impunity".

He added that this category is not confined to money making in the strict sense, extending to

> "cases in which the defendant is seeking to gain at the expense of the plaintiff some object—perhaps some property which he covets—which he either could not obtain at all or not obtain except at a price greater than he wants to put down."[118]

**13-022** This category soon gave rise to case law, the first developments coming in libel. In three cases immediately in the wake of *Rookes* the question was considered whether the publication of defamatory statements by a newspaper in the course of its business for profit could fall within Lord Devlin's second category. In the first, *McCarey v Associated Newspapers*,[119] it was recognised that cases could arise in

---

113 [2012] C.A.T. 19 at [452]–[460]. However, it fell within the second category, thereby allowing exemplary damages to be awarded: see para.13-027, below.

114 [1993] Q.B. 507 CA.

115 [1993] Q.B. 507 CA at 532A, per Sir Thomas Bingham MR; "not an exercise of executive power derived from government": at [525F], per Stuart-Smith LJ In *Re Organ Retention Group Litigation* [2005] Q.B. 506 the judge seems to have taken a National Health Service Trust to be within this first category as he decided that the facts did not bring the claim within the criteria set out in *Rookes v Barnard* [1964] A.C. 1129. But this must be doubtful.

116 [1964] A.C. 1129 at 1226.

117 See para.13-017, above.

118 [1964] A.C. 1129 at 1227. Thus there is no possibility of exemplary damages for the trespass of clamping a car: *Vine v Waltham Forest London Borough Council* [2000] 1 W.L.R. 2383 CA; see at 2390H to 2391D as there is nothing in the headnote.

119 [1965] 2 Q.B. 86 CA.

which this category would be applicable by reason of a newspaper deliberately publishing a defamatory statement in the expectation of increasing its circulation and profit by an amount which would exceed compensatory damages,[120] but it was common ground that no circumstances justifying such exemplary damages had been made out. In *Broadway Approvals v Odhams Press*,[121] it was again held that the second common law category did not apply and that accordingly the judge had misdirected the jury by permitting them to award exemplary damages if they thought fit. On the other hand, in *Manson v Associated Newspapers*[122] Widgery J, while accepting that the two Court of Appeal cases made it

> "perfectly clear that the mere fact that a newspaper is run for profit and that everything published in the newspaper is published, in a sense, with a view to profit, does not automatically bring newspaper defendants into the category of those who may have to pay exemplary damages on the footing that what they have done has been done with a view to profit",[123]

considered that it was equally clear from those authorities that the conditions for the application of Lord Devlin's second common law category were satisfied where it could be inferred that a newspaper had deliberately published a statement

> "conscious of the fact that it had no solid foundation and with the cynical and calculated intention to use it for what it was worth, on the footing that it would produce more profit than any possible penalty in damages was likely to be."[124]

There was evidence in the case from which this inference could be drawn, and the jury were asked to find whether the claimant was entitled to exemplary damages.[125] The jury in fact awarded none.

Libel did not generate an acceptable exemplary award within the second common law category until the important decision in *Broome v Cassell & Co*.[126] A distinguished naval officer sued the publisher and author of a book telling of the wartime destruction of a navy-escorted convoy, and libellous of the claimant in imputing to him responsibility for the disaster. The House of Lords was satisfied that there was a sufficient calculation of profit by both author and publisher to justify an exemplary award. Lord Morris said: **13-023**

> "There may be exemplary damages if a defendant has formed and been guided by the view that, though he may have to pay some damages or compensation because of what he intends to do, yet he will in some way gain (for the category is not confined to money-making in the strict sense) or may make money out of it, to an extent which he hopes and expects will be worth his while. I do not think that the word 'calculated' was used to denote some precise balancing process. The situation contemplated is where someone faces up to the possibility of having to pay damages for doing something which may be held to have been wrong but where nevertheless he deliberately carries out his plan because he thinks that it will work out satisfactorily for him."[127]

---

120 [1965] 2 Q.B. 86 CA at 107, per Diplock LJ giving a film company as another illustration.
121 [1965] 1 W.L.R. 805 CA.
122 [1965] 1 W.L.R. 1038.
123 [1965] 1 W.L.R. 1038 at 1040.
124 [1965] 1 W.L.R. 1038 at 1041.
125 The summing-up on damages is [1965] 1 W.L.R. 1038 at 1042 to 1046.
126 [1972] A.C. 1027.
127 [1972] A.C. 1027 at 1094B to D.

Similar statements to the effect that the term "calculation" is not to be taken as referring to some mathematical process appear in the speeches of Lord Hailsham LC, Viscount Dilhorne and Lord Diplock.[128]

**13-024** Further libel cases where exemplary awards within the second category have been considered appropriate have followed. This was so in *Riches v News Group Newspapers*,[129] where there was held to be a case for the judge to leave to the jury as there was evidence that the defendant newspaper proprietors and publishers had decided that the economic benefits of publishing outweighed the risk of having to pay compensation to the claimants; the jury's award was set aside only on grounds of misdirection and excessiveness.[130] Similarly in *John v MGN*,[131] the evidence of deliberate calculation of profit by the defendant newspaper was very strong and was clearly fit to be left to the jury, going far beyond the bare fact that the newspaper was conducted for profit[132]; in this respect the case, said Sir Thomas Bingham MR delivering the judgment of the court, was "almost a precise counterpart of the *Riches* case".[133] Here the jury's award was set aside only on the ground of excessiveness, the court substituting its own, lower award.[134]

**13-025** Attention has also focused upon cases where the potential profit was made available to a landlord by the departure, tortiously engineered, of a protected tenant, thereby increasing the value to the landlord of the premises formerly occupied by the tenant.[135] In *Mafo v Adams*,[136] the landlord achieved this by trickery, and was held liable in deceit. An award of exemplary damages was made by the county court judge on the basis of the defendant's counsel's admission that such an award was permissible in the circumstances of the case, but the Court of Appeal refused to uphold the award because the judge had found the defendant's motives in tricking the claimant out of possession to be obscure. The claimant was thereby prevented from proving to the satisfaction of the court—and here the Court of Appeal insisted upon the standard of proof in criminal cases[137]—that the defendant's motive was to make a sizeable financial profit by reletting at an unrestricted rent or by selling the premises free of the restriction.[138] On the other hand, in *Drane v Evangelou*,[139] the Court of Appeal upheld the county court's award of exemplary damages. There the landlord engineered the tenant's exclusion from the premises by trespass, forcefully entering them when the tenant was out. On his return the tenant found his furnished maisonette bolted on the inside with several people within and his belongings out in the yard. Eventually, after two applications to the county court and over two months later, he was able to return to the maisonette. Lord Denning MR, with

---

128 [1972] A.C. 1027 at 1078H to 1079D, 1101B to C and 1130E to F respectively. And see Lord Reid, [1972] A.C. 1027 at 1088G to H.

129 [1986] Q.B. 256 CA.

130 See the case further at para.53-009, below.

131 [1997] Q.B. 586 CA.

132 See [1997] Q.B. 586 CA at 623H to 624A.

133 [1997] Q.B. 586 CA at 623G.

134 See the case further at paras 53-010 and 53-022, below.

135 Similar is the potential profit to be made by property owners harassing a neighbouring owner into giving up a right of way over their land, as in *Saxton v Bayliss* unreported 31 January 2014 Central London County Court (facts at para.43-020 fn.82, below).

136 [1970] 1 Q.B. 548 CA.

137 [1970] 1 Q.B. 548 CA at 556, per Sachs LJ expressly, and at 559, per Widgery LJ impliedly.

138 Doubts in *Mafo* whether an exemplary award can be made where the tort is deceit have been dispelled: see para.13-013, above.

139 [1978] 1 W.L.R. 455 CA.

whose judgment the other two members of the court expressed themselves to be in agreement, said that to his mind the second common law category

> "includes cases of unlawful eviction of a tenant. The landlord seeks to gain possession at the expense of the tenant—so as to keep or get a rent higher than that awarded by the rent tribunal—or to get possession from a tenant who is protected by the Rent Acts. So he resorts to harassing tactics. Such conduct can be … punished by the civil law by an award of exemplary damages."[140]

Once again it was stressed, here by Goff LJ, that a "calculation by the defendant of actual money which he hoped to make out of the conduct" was not necessary.[141] And some years after *Drane v Evangelou*,[142] a cache of cases of illegal eviction of tenants by landlords with a view to achieving a higher rent for the premises reached the Court of Appeal. In *Asghar v Ahmed*,[143] and again in *McMillan v Singh*,[144] an exemplary award, in addition to a compensatory award, was upheld where the landlord had resorted to trespass[145] while in *Millington v Duffy*,[146] also a case of trespass, the court indicated that exemplary damages would have been entirely appropriate had they not been expressly disclaimed in the court below. *Guppy (Bridport) v Brookling and James*,[147] differed only in that the tenants' eviction from the premises was effected by nuisance rather than by trespass; an award of exemplary damages was considered appropriate even though it might have been said that the landlord had not wilfully and with calculation set out to commit the tort, the motivation to get rid of the tenants so as to make a profit being sufficient.[148] The appropriateness of mounting the second common law category against evicting landlords having been thus established by the Court of Appeal, cases awarding exemplary damages, cases almost invariably in the county or district court, have continued to appear year in, year out. Their reporting is poor but their existence is clear and, where the profit sought or made merits it, the award can be substantial, as in *Mehta v Royal Bank of Scotland*,[149] and *Daley v Mahmood*.[150] Also, exemplary damages have been awarded where the landlord's moves aimed at achieving a higher rent of the property have been other than by eviction of the tenant. This happened in *Design Progression Ltd v Thurloe Properties Ltd*,[151] where, in breach of its statutory duty to respond in a reasonable time to its tenant's application for a licence to assign, the landlord had pursued a deliberately obstructive policy designed to prevent the assignment so that it could recover the premises with a view to granting a fresh lease at the full market rent.[152]

---

140 [1978] 1 W.L.R. 455 CA at 459F. See *Broome v Cassell & Co* [1972] A.C. 1027 at 1079E to F, per Lord Hailsham LC.

141 [1978] 1 W.L.R. 455 CA at 462B, citing the latter part of the passage from Lord Devlin set out at para.13-021, above.

142 [1987] 1 W.L.R. 455 CA.

143 (1984) 17 H.L.R. 25 CA.

144 (1984) 17 H.L.R. 120 CA.

145 The awards were £1,000 and £250 respectively.

146 (1984) 17 H.L.R. 232 CA.

147 (1983) 14 H.L.R. 1 CA.

148 See especially (1983) 14 H.L.R. 1 CA at 26, 36.

149 [1999] 3 E.G.L.R. 153.

150 [2006] 1 P. & C.R. DG10 at D29. More detail on these two cases at para.39-073, below.

151 [2005] 1 W.L.R. 1.

152 It was suggested by the trial judge in *Al Rawas v Pegasus Energy Ltd (No.2)* [2009] 1 All E.R. 346 that a litigant who misleads the court into granting him search and freezing orders so as to steal a

**13-026** A case outside the normal run is to be found in the Court of Appeal's decision in *Borders (UK) Ltd v Commissioner of Police of the Metropolis*.[153] A street trader had run a racket selling stolen books until apprehended; he was then prosecuted, was given a 30-month prison sentence and was facing a confiscation of proceeds of crime order. A consortium of book retailers had lost some quarter of a million books, some of which had been retrieved. The consortium successfully claimed damages for their losses on the retrieved books, and were awarded £280,000. They also claimed exemplary damages, described as being for part of their losses and the trader's consequent profits, on the unretrieved books. They were awarded £100,000. The trader argued that the £100,000 award lay outside the court's powers. The trader submitted that it was pleaded as an exemplary award (hence it was not compensatory) but it could not be exemplary since it represented actual losses. This submission was not accepted. It was held entirely appropriate to make an exemplary award where the necessary conditions for one were made out, which they clearly were, and the fact that the consortium had sought to justify the exemplary award by reference to facts which could have sustained a further compensatory award did not stand in the way.[154]

**13-027** It will be seen that, as with the first common law category,[155] there could be said, under Lord Devlin's formulation, to be two conditions to be satisfied before a second category case can be established. The wrongdoer must have acted with a cynical disregard for a plaintiff's rights and the wrongdoer must have calculated that the gains from the wrongdoing are likely to exceed the damages at risk. These conditions combine to establish an irrefutable case for deterrence beyond the incidental deterrent effect of a compensatory award. Both conditions are fairly clearly satisfied in the cases of the exemplary awards set out in the previous paragraphs so that no explicit discussion of them appears in the judgments. However, when we come to the three recent cases where breach of statutory duty under competition law is introduced to the exemplary damages scene,[156] there is a difference. Thus in *Albion Water Ltd v Dwr Cymru Cyfyngedig*,[157] which involved the issuing of an anti-competitive, unlawfully high price for water, the two conditions are highlighted and discussed separately in excessive detail—the Competition Appeal Tribunal's judgment on this issue runs to nearly 150 paragraphs[158]—only to arrive at the conclusion that neither condition was satisfied, so that there could be no award of exemplary damages. In *2 Travel Group Plc v Cardiff City Transport Services Ltd*,[159] which concerned anti-competitive behaviour on the part of a city bus undertaking, specific consideration of the two conditions that have to be satisfied is not so marked but, as with Albion Water, nearly 150 paragraphs of the Competition Appeal Tribunal's judgment are devoted to the matter,[160] here coming to the conclusion in favour of awarding exemplary damages. Lewison J in

---

march in litigation could thereby bring himself, in the claim against him for damages under his cross-undertakings, within the second common law category: see at [54]. But this must be doubtful.

153 [2005] EWCA Civ 197 CA.

154 The issue of double jeopardy on account of the impending confiscation of the proceeds is dealt with at para.13-042, below

155 See at para.13-019, above.

156 See the three cases at para.13-014, above.

157 [2013] C.A.T. 6.

158 [2013] C.A.T. 6 at [231]–[355].

159 [2012] C.A.T. 19.

160 [2012] C.A.T. 19 at [461]–[598].

*Devenish Nutrition Ltd v Sanofi-Aventis SA*,[161] which concerned vitamin cartels entered into so as unlawfully to raise prices,[162] was more expeditious. Indeed he could afford to be; he did not have to examine the second category in detail as it was accepted that the case fell within it. A further issue in all three cases was whether, if given a prima facie case for exemplary damages, an award might still be excluded where the defendant was subject to a criminal penalty; this issue is dealt with below.[163]

## (3) Authorisation by statute

In the past, it has been known for statutes expressly to empower the courts to award exemplary damages in respect of particular wrongs where this is justified by the conduct of the defendant. However, the early statutes so providing, which are the Distress for Rent Acts of 1689 and 1737 and the Landlord and Tenant Act of 1730, did not refer to exemplary damages as such but enacted that the claimant should be entitled to double damages[164] or in one case to treble damages.[165] Clearly, the House of Lords in *Rookes* had no option but to accept these dictates of statute, and therefore no question of rationalising the incidence of exemplary damages in this category arose. Nevertheless, statutory provisions of this nature before *Rookes* were extremely few, and beyond these early statutes there existed only two, the Reserve and Auxiliary Forces (Protection of Civil Interests) Act 1951 and the Copyright Act 1956, both of which, as will be seen, were equivocal on the issue. Understandably, now that exemplary damages have been generally confined to limited categories, there have been few subsequent instances of legislative recognition. **13-028**

Lord Devlin's only illustration in *Rookes*,[166] was the Reserve and Auxiliary Forces (Protection of Civil Interests) Act 1951, a statute of a somewhat esoteric nature, which gave by Pt I protection to servicemen against remedies involving interference with goods, such as execution, distress and the like, and provided by s.13(2) that in any action for damages for conversion in respect of such goods the court may take into account the defendant's conduct and award exemplary damages. In *Broome*, Lord Kilbrandon interpreted "exemplary" in s.13(2) as meaning "aggravated", basing this interpretation upon the fact that the subsection applies, by s.13(6), to Scotland where exemplary damages are not recognised.[167] Indeed he expressed himself as "not convinced that any statutory example of the recognition of the doctrine is to be found",[168] and appears to have taken the view that with the confusion of terminology before *Rookes*, all references to exemplary damages in pre-Rookes statutes should be treated as referring to aggravated damages, putting **13-029**

---

161 [2009] Ch. 390.

162 Full facts at para.13-044, below. There was an appeal but none on the issue of exemplary damages: [2009] Ch. 390 CA at 429, [21] and [141].

163 At para.13-042, below. In *Albion Water* it was dealt with in an earlier hearing: [2010] C.A.T. 30.

164 Distress for Rent Act 1689 s.4 (repealed by the Tribunals, Courts and Enforcement Act 2007); Landlord and Tenant Act 1730 s.1 (see the footnote immediately preceding para.28-098, below); Distress for Rent Act 1737 s.3 (repealed by the Tribunals, Courts and Enforcement Act 2007) and s.18 (see the footnote immediately preceding para.28-098, below).

165 Distress for Rent Act 1689 s.3 (repealed by the Tribunals, Courts and Enforcement Act 2007).

166 [1964] A.C. 1129 at 1225.

167 [1972] A.C. 1027 at 1133G.

168 [1972] A.C. 1027 at 1133G at 1133D.

forward the ingenious suggestion that, to make sense of the provision in the survival of actions legislation of 1934[169] prohibiting "exemplary" damages in actions by, but not against, the estate,[170] "exemplary" must be read as "aggravated".[171]

**13-030** Where there is a statute which makes no express reference to exemplary damages but is so phrased as to permit an authorisation to award exemplary damages to be inferred, what is the position? This situation arises with the Copyright, Designs and Patents Act 1988, which by s.97(2) gives the court power, in assessing damages for an infringement of copyright, to award such "additional damages" as the court may consider appropriate in the light of the flagrancy of the infringement.[172] The predecessor of s.97(2), s.17(3) of the Copyright Act 1956 which essentially said the same, had already, before *Rookes* was decided, been held in *Williams v Settle*,[173] to permit an award of exemplary damages. A variety of judicial views has appeared over the years as to whether the Act's reference to flagrancy should be construed as meaning exemplary damages or aggravated damages, many of the views being of their Lordships and most of them supporting the aggravated damages approach. These views are set out when we deal with copyright.[174] Lord Devlin's phrasing this category in terms of exemplary damages which are *expressly* authorised by statute[175] would at first sight appear to put paid to its application to exemplary damages, but at the same time Lord Devlin reserved his opinion as to whether the Act authorised the award of exemplary, as distinct from aggravated, damages.[176] While the argument for aggravated damages appears to be in the ascendant, nevertheless it is thought that today the statutory provision should be interpreted as authorising damages which are exemplary. The reasons for this view are explained when dealing with copyright[177] and need not be repeated here.

## III. Computation of the Exemplary Award[178]

### 1. Various Criteria Applied by the Courts

**13-031** In so far as the object of exemplary damages is to deter, the calculation of the amount to be awarded must clearly be based on criteria different from those employed in the calculation of compensatory damages. Over the years various criteria have been advanced, and some accepted, as relevant to the calculation. In particular, in *Rookes v Barnard*,[179] Lord Devlin, speaking for all their Lordships, stated three considerations[180] which should always be borne in mind when awards

---

169 Law Reform (Miscellaneous Provisions) Act 1934.

170 See paras 23-004 and 23-009, below.

171 [1972] A.C. 1027 at 1133E to F.

172 And also in the light of any benefit accruing to the defendant by reason of the infringement. A provision in similar terms to s.97(2) is introduced for actions for infringement of design right by s.229(3).

173 [1960] 1 W.L.R. 1072 CA.

174 See para.48-064, below.

175 [1964] A.C. 1129 at 1227.

176 [1964] A.C. 1129 at 1225.

177 See para.48-065, below.

178 For the procedural issue of whether separate awards should be made of compensatory damages and exemplary damages, see para.52-047, below.

179 [1964] A.C. 1129 at 1227 to 1228.

180 In *Broome v Cassell & Co* [1972] A.C. 1027, which approved *Rookes*, Lord Hailsham LC said, at 1081E: "It is worth pointing out that neither the Court of Appeal nor any of the counsel who appeared before us attacked these as such. Nor, so far as I am aware, have these been attacked in the

of exemplary damages are in issue; these form the first three of the criteria now to be dealt with.

Before turning to these criteria, of which we identify eight in number, it is valuable to examine one of the decisions of the Court of Appeal on exemplary damages which causes some concern relevant to computation. Other than a faulty reference to the relevance of a compensatory award, none of the following criteria makes an appearance and, more importantly, the criteria relied upon have little or nothing to do with exemplary damages. The case is *Ramzan v Brookwide Ltd.*[181] It involved the deliberate misappropriation of real property, something that happens so rarely that only one other case of it could be found by counsel.[182] Arden LJ alone dealt with exemplary damages, the others simply agreeing with her. She concentrated on the defendant company's conduct in its expropriation of the property having taken place before it had been acquired by the claimant as a gift from his father[183] and on the expropriation having had a deleterious effect on the health both of the claimant of his father.[184] These are matters that go to compensatory damages, even by way of aggravated damages which were here not allowed, and not to deterrence by way of exemplary damages. Nor, with respect, was it correct to say that there is no scope for exemplary damages where an account and disgorgement of profits is claimed,[185] that the fact of making a compensatory award should largely be sufficient in itself[186] and that there is little guidance on the quantification of exemplary damages.[187] On the basis of these various considerations, and primarily on account of the claimant not being the owner of the property at the time of the tort,[188] which can have absolutely nothing to do with deterrence, Arden LJ decided to reduce from £60,000 to £20,000[189] Geraldine Alexander QC's award of exemplary damages in a case which she had described as one of the worst of its kind.[190] 13-032

## (1) The claimant to be the victim of the behaviour requiring deterrence

Lord Devlin's first ruling was that a claimant cannot recover exemplary damages unless he is the victim of the punishable behaviour. It is difficult, however, to see that there is any real scope for the operation of such a rule, which had not previously appeared in the cases. Since causes of action in tort cannot generally be assigned by act of parties, the only important situation in which the victim is not the claimant is where he has died and suit is brought by his estate. But this situation has already been provided for by statute; the Law Reform (Miscellaneous Provisions) Act 1934. That Act, in providing for the survival of tort actions, expressly stated that damages in an action for the benefit of the estate should not include any 13-033

cases in which Commonwealth judges have felt constrained to criticise *Rookes v Barnard*."

181 [2012] 1 All E.R. 903 CA.

182 See para.39-056, below. For the facts of *Ramzan* see para.39-058, below.

183 [2012] 1 All E.R. 903 CA at [78].

184 [2012] 1 All E.R. 903 CA at [78]–[80].

185 [2012] 1 All E.R. 903 CA at [81].

186 [2012] 1 All E.R. 903 CA at [82].

187 [2012] 1 All E.R. 903 CA at [82].

188 [2012] 1 All E.R. 903 CA at [83] *in init.*

189 [2012] 1 All E.R. 903 CA at [83] *in med.*

190 [2011] 2 All E.R. 38 at [69].

exemplary damages.[191] Perhaps Lord Devlin should be taken as intending only to endorse the statutory rule; yet it may be doubted whether the statutory rule is itself a particularly sound one. For why should a defendant whose behaviour merits deterrence escape because his victim has died?

### (2) Moderation in awards

13-034 Next, on a more general note, Lord Devlin considered that awards of exemplary damages should be moderate. Some of the awards that juries have made in the past seemed to him

> "to amount to a greater punishment than would be likely to be incurred if the conduct were criminal; and, moreover, a punishment imposed without the safeguard which the criminal law gives to an offender. I should not allow the respect which is traditionally paid to an assessment of damages by a jury to prevent me from seeing that the weapon is used with restraint. It may even be that the House may find it necessary to follow the precedent it set for itself in *Benham v Gambling*[192] and place some arbitrary limit on awards of damages that are made by way of punishment. Exhortations to be moderate may not be enough."[193]

And in *Broome v Cassell & Co*,[194] Lord Hailsham LC said that, while himself unable to follow Lord Devlin,

> "so far as regards the right of appellate courts to interfere with jury awards on principles different from the traditional nor, I think, with the proposal that *Benham v Gambling* offers a precedent for arbitrary limits imposed by the judiciary in defamation cases,[195] I regard it as extremely important that, for the future, judges should make sure in their direction to juries that the jury is fully aware of the danger of an excessive award."[196]

13-035 In *Broome* itself the House of Lords was upholding a £25,000 exemplary award of February 1970, now worth around £350,000. However, various features of this decision need to be remembered: that the decision was one of a bare majority, three out of a full House of seven being prepared to upset the award as excessive[197]; that the majority was swayed by the great reluctance of the courts to interfere with the damages award of a jury[198] and that Lord Diplock's "doubt if any of your Lordships would have hesitated to interfere with it if it had been awarded by a judge sitting alone"[199] was amply justified from what was said in the speeches; that Lord Morris regarded the "case as exceptional in the sense that the jury must have considered that the conduct of the defendants merited very special condemnation".[200] In *John v MGN*,[201] the Court of Appeal awarded £75,000 by way of exemplary damages in a libel case, a figure which may not appear to be so very

---

191 s.1(2)(a). But see para.13-029, above.
192 [1941] A.C. 157. See para.41-133, below.
193 *Rookes v Barnard* [1964] A.C. 1129 at 1227 to 1228.
194 [1972] A.C. 1027.
195 See his comments on the passage in Lord Devlin's speech, [1972] A.C. 1027 at 1066D to H.
196 [1972] A.C. 1027 at 1081F to G.
197 Lord Wilberforce, Viscount Dilhorne and Lord Diplock.
198 See Ch.53, below.
199 [1972] A.C. 1027 at 1122E.
200 [1972] A.C. 1027 at 1100D. For the facts see para.13-023, above.
201 [1997] Q.B. 586 CA.

moderate, but there were other factors to be taken into consideration such as the wealth of the defendant, a criterion dealt with below[202]; furthermore, the award was in substitution for the far higher one made by the jury of £275,000.

For false imprisonment and malicious prosecution, together with wrongful arrest and assault, the Court of Appeal in two cases heard together, *Thompson v Commissioner of Police of the Metropolis* and *Hsu v Commissioner of Police of the Metropolis*,[203] brought a degree of moderation into assessments which was much greater than had appeared in libel cases. For the jury's award of £200,000 exemplary damages in Hsu £15,000 was substituted; in Thompson £25,000 was preferred to the jury's £50,000, the jury's total award being upheld only because the Court of Appeal increased the compensatory award by nearly £20,000. Lord Woolf, delivering the judgment of the court, said[204]: **13-036**

> "Where exemplary damages are appropriate they are unlikely to be less than £5,000. Otherwise the case is probably not one which justifies an award of exemplary damages at all. In this class of action the conduct must be particularly deserving of punishment for an award of as much as £25,000 to be justified and the figure of £50,000 should be regarded as the absolute maximum, involving directly officers of at least the rank of superintendent."

Thus in *Muuse v Secretary of State for the Home Department*,[205] where there had been outrageous abuse of executive power[206] a false imprisonment award of £27,500 was made and upheld by the Court of Appeal.

For some time moderation was much more in evidence in the cases of trespass and nuisance brought by evicted tenants. *Drane v Evangelou*,[207] and *Guppy (Bridport) v Brookling and James*,[208] produced awards of £1,000 and somewhat later cases ranged from £1,000 to £3,000 with many such awards being of aggravated and exemplary damages combined. Amounts, however, have been going well above this level, starting with an exemplary award of £7,500 in *Mehta v Royal Bank of Scotland*.[209] In *Design Progression Ltd v Thurloe Properties Ltd*,[210] where the claim against the landlord was not by reason of the tenant's eviction but on account of blocking the assignment of the tenant's lease,[211] the award was higher still, at £25,000. Peter Smith J said that the word 'moderate' "is to be assessed in the overall facts of the case and in the light of the conduct and the need to mark disapproval".[212] So too in *Daley v Mahmood*,[213] £30,000 was awarded in exemplary damages for unlawful eviction combined with harassment. It is true, however, that there were four claimants which might increase the level of deterrence required due to the more widespread conduct. As for the trial judge's £60,000 for deliberate **13-037**

---

202 See para.13-038, below.
203 [1998] Q.B. 498 CA.
204 [1998] Q.B. 498 CA at 517C.
205 [2010] EWCA Civ 453 CA.
206 Facts at para.13-018, above.
207 [1978] 1 W.L.R. 455 CA.
208 (1983) 14 H.L.R. 1 CA.
209 [1999] 3 E.G.L.R. 153.
210 [2005] 1 W.L.R. 1.
211 Facts at para.13-025, above.
212 [2005] 1 W.L.R. 1 at [150].
213 [2006] 1 P. & C.R. DG10 at D29.

misappropriation of real property in *Ramzan v Brookwide Ltd*,[214] higher than the general run of exemplary awards and reduced on appeal, this was considered by her to fall within the criterion of moderation in the light of the seriousness of the wrong, the defendant's means and the need to provide a sufficient deterrent.[215]

### (3) The means of the parties

13-038 The third consideration propounded by Lord Devlin was the means of the parties. This is important to deterrence. Clearly, a small exemplary award would go unnoticed by a rich defendant while even a moderate award might cripple a poor defendant, so that for the size of the defendant's bank balance to influence the size of the award is fully appropriate. This has probably always been the implicit practice of the courts; indeed it was explicitly recognised right at the start of exemplary damages in *Benson v Frederick*,[216] and today in *John v MGN*,[217] it was said that it was not there disputed that the defendant's great wealth was a relevant consideration.[218] That the defendant company in *Ramzan v Brookwide Ltd*,[219] together with its associated companies, paid £18 million every year to their parent company was a large factor in the trial judge's decision to award £60,000 in exemplary damages.[220] On the other hand, it is difficult to see how the means of the claimant can have any real relevance to the amount to be awarded on an exemplary basis. Similarly with vicarious liability, it should be the means of the employer rather than of the employee that is relevant. This view was put forward in the 17th edition of this work and, while Lord Mackay indicated in *Kuddus v Chief Constable of Leicestershire*,[221] that he would find this "somewhat difficult to accept", it appears now to be endorsed by the Court of Appeal's decision in *Rowlands v Chief Constable of Merseyside Police*.[222]

### (4) The conduct of the parties

13-039 The parties' conduct has also been taken into account in the past and, though unmentioned by Lord Devlin, would appear to remain today a relevant consideration in assessing exemplary damages. Thus the court may take into account, according to the decision in *Praed v Graham*,[223] the conduct of the defendant right down to the time of judgment, and also, according to the view expressed in *Greenlands v Wilmshurst*,[224] the conduct of the defendant's counsel at the trial. An apology by the defendant in the witness box would make a difference in his favour,

---

214 [2011] 2 All E.R. 38.

215 [2011] 2 All E.R. 38 at [70] to [73]. The reduction of this award to £20,000 by the Court of Appeal, [2012] 1 All E.R. 903 CA, in this curious case, a move unrelated to the specific issue of moderation, is thought somewhat difficult to justify, as is suggested at para.13-032, above.

216 (1766) 3 Burr. 1845.

217 [1997] Q.B. 586 CA.

218 [1997] Q.B. 586 CA at 625E.

219 [2011] 2 All E.R. 38.

220 See [2011] 2 All E.R. 38 at [70]. The reduction of this award to £20,000 by the Court of Appeal, [2012] 1 All E.R. 903 CA, in this curious case, a move unconnected to this question of means, is thought somewhat difficult to justify, as is suggested at para.13-032, above.

221 [2002] 2 A.C. 122 at [47].

222 [2007] 1 W.L.R. 1065 CA; see this case at para.13-046, below.

223 (1890) 24 Q.B.D. 53 CA (libel).

224 [1913] 3 K.B. 507, especially at 532 (libel).

according to Singleton LJ in *Loudon v Ryder*,[225] while persistence in the charge might increase exemplary damages.[226] An important factor in the trial judge's decision to award an exemplary £60,000 in *Ramzan v Brookwide Ltd*,[227] was the defendant's conduct in deliberately expropriating the claimant's property, a most serious type of trespass, followed by no contrition, no apology and attempted cover-up by lying in evidence.[228] Similarly, the conduct of the claimant may be material to the assessment. Thus if the claimant has provoked an assault by the defendant, and assuming circumstances which would today admit of an exemplary award, then, as was said in *Lane v Holloway*,[229] the provocation would be

> "relevant to the question of whether or not exemplary damages should be awarded, and, if so, how much".[230]

And in two cases involving police misconduct heard by juries and then together by the Court of Appeal, *Thompson v Commissioner of Police of the Metropolis* and *Hsu v Commissioner of Police of the Metropolis*,[231] Lord Woolf MR, delivering the judgment of the court, said that in an appropriate case the jury should be told that any improper conduct of the claimant can reduce or even eliminate an exemplary damages award if the jury consider that the claimant's conduct caused or contributed to the behaviour complained of.[232]

### (5) The relevance of the amount awarded as compensation

While the assessment of compensation can never be affected by the amount **13-040**
awarded by way of exemplary damages, the converse is not true. The size of an exemplary award may indeed be influenced by the size of the compensatory one,[233] even to the extent of being eliminated. Lord Devlin in *Rookes v Barnard*,[234] indicated that, in a case where exemplary damages were appropriate,

---

225 [1953] 2 Q.B. 202 CA at 207 (assault).

226 See *Warwick v Foulkes* (1844) 12 M. & W. 507; *Walter v Alltools* (1944) 61 T.L.R. 39 CA (both are false imprisonment; neither is strictly exemplary damages).

227 [2011] 2 All E.R. 38.

228 See [2011] 2 All E.R. 38 at [71] and [74]. The reduction of this award to £20,000 by the Court of Appeal, [2012] 1 All E.R. 903 CA, in this curious case, a move not specifically related to the defendant's conduct, is thought somewhat difficult to justify, as is suggested at para.13-032, above.

229 [1968] 1 Q.B. 379 CA at 391, per Salmon LJ.

230 An exemplary award was eliminated where a detained prisoner provoked a police officer's assault in *O'Connor v Hewitson* [1979] Crim. L.R. 46 CA. But being in arrears of rent did not justify not awarding exemplary damages to an evicted tenant in *McMillan v Singh* (1984) 17 H.L.R. 120 CA.

231 [1998] Q.B. 498 CA.

232 [1998] Q.B. 498 CA at 517D. Perhaps this relevance of the parties' conduct is the best context in which to view Hamilton LJ's statement, made in *Greenlands v Wilmshurst* [1913] 3 K.B. 507 CA at 532 and subsequently cited with approval by Scrutton LJ in *Tolley v Fry* [1930] 1 K.B. 467 CA at 476 and by Goddard LCJ in *Knuppfer v London Express Newspaper* [1943] K.B. 80 CA at 91, that in awarding exemplary damages "there must be some reasonable relation between the wrong done and the *solatium* applied". It is, however, doubtful how important Hamilton LJ's statement is for exemplary damages. Apart from having been treated rather lightly by Lord Atkin in *Ley v Hamilton* (1935) 153 L.T. 384 HL at 386, it was probably directed to aggravated damages rather than exemplary damages proper. This is particularly suggested by the use of the word "*solatium*".

233 As to whether there should be a single award or separate awards see para.52-047, below.

234 [1964] A.C. 1129 at 1228.

"a jury should be directed that if, but only if, the sum which they have in mind to award as compensation (which may, of course, be a sum aggravated by the way in which the defendant has behaved to the plaintiff) is inadequate to punish him for his outrageous conduct, to mark their disapproval of such conduct and to deter him from repeating it, then it can award some larger sum."

There is no reason why the same principle should not apply to awards made by judges sitting alone. Thus the Court of Appeal in *Bradford v Metropolitan City Council*,[235] while emphasising that exemplary damages should be awarded only where compensatory damages would be inadequate to punish the defendant, upheld an exemplary award by an industrial tribunal.[236]

**13-041** The principle was fully endorsed by all seven of their Lordships in *Broome v Cassell & Co*,[237] and its operation is well illustrated by *Drane v Evangelou*,[238] where a landlord resorted to trespass by forcible entry in order to evict his protected tenant and the Court of Appeal upheld the county court judge's decision that such monstrous behaviour called for exemplary damages of £1,000. While Lord Denning MR was content to view the award simply as one of exemplary damages and endorse it as such, Lawton and Goff LJJ thought that it could be justified as an amalgamation of aggravated damages and exemplary damages. Both indeed considered that the award was not excessive as one for aggravated damages only, but said that, even assuming in the landlord's favour that it was excessive as such, they had, in Goff LJ's words,

"not the slightest doubt that the aggregate included an element of punishment which was not in the circumstances excessive".[239]

And in *Guppy (Bridport) v Brookling and James*,[240] where a similar action by tenants against their landlord succeeded in nuisance rather than trespass, an award of £1,000 which combined exemplary and compensatory elements was again upheld by the Court of Appeal.[241] In *John v MGN*,[242] Lord Devlin's "if, but only if" test, as it was there called, was explicitly applied; the result of its application was still to require an exemplary award.[243] But no exemplary damages were awarded in *Sallows v Griffiths*,[244] as it was considered that the compensatory award was adequate for the purpose. Also, that the compensatory damages were sufficiently high to afford adequate punishment, by way of deterrence, of the defendant appears as the justification of no award of exemplary damages by the Jamaican courts in *The Gleaner Co Ltd v Abrahams*.[245] While there was no claimant's appeal on this point to the Privy Council, it is certainly how the position was regarded by Lord

[235] [1991] 2 Q.B. 517 CA.

[236] Thus the Employment Appeal Tribunal's award of £50,000 exemplary damages to a victimised army recruit in order to match its award of £50,000 compensatory damages for aggravated injury to feelings was inappropriate: *Ministry of Defence v Fletcher* [2010] I.R.L.R. 25. In fact the exemplary award was set aside in toto: see para.13-019, above.

[237] [1972] A.C. 1027. It is stated very clearly by Lord Reid: at 1089B to F.

[238] [1978] 1 W.L.R. 455 CA.

[239] [1978] 1 W.L.R. 455 CA at 463D. See similarly Lawton LJ at 461H.

[240] (1983) 14 H.L.R. 1 CA.

[241] See especially (1983) 14 H.L.R. 1 CA at 26.

[242] [1997] Q.B. 586 CA.

[243] See [1997] Q.B. 586 CA at 626A to B.

[244] [2001] F.S.R. 188 CA.

[245] [2004] 1 A.C 628 PC.

Hoffmann, giving the Board's judgment on the defendant's appeal.[246] By contrast, in *Ramzan v Brookwide Ltd*,[247] where the total compensatory damages arrived at were in excess of half a million pounds, the trial judge nevertheless considered it appropriate to make an award of £60,000 in exemplary damages. This she thought was called for because she foresaw the financially powerful defendant company repeating its expropriatory actions elsewhere should it find an opportunity to do so.[248] Since the object of exemplary damages is to deter the defendant and others from wrongful conduct, the realisation of this object will generally require that a potential tortfeasor should know that he may have to pay exemplary damages even if he has not caused any significant loss to the claimant; if, on the other hand, his course of action will clearly cause the claimant substantial damage for which he will be required to pay, that in itself may prove a sufficient deterrent.[249]

### (6) The relevance of any criminal penalty

Somewhat similar to the effect of a substantial compensatory award against the defendant is the effect of a criminal conviction of the defendant. Punishing twice for the same misconduct offends against basic principles of justice and the result here is likely to be not a smaller award but no award at all. The courts have taken this consideration into account. Thus in *Archer v Brown*,[250] the trial judge decided against an award of exemplary damages because the defendant, having been prosecuted, convicted and imprisoned, had already been adequately punished, and in *A.B. v South West Water Services*,[251] while exemplary damages were not awarded for a reason which has since been held to be wrong,[252] Stuart Smith LJ pointed to the defendant's conviction and fine as providing one reason for not making an exemplary award.[253] It is true that in *Asghar v Ahmed*,[254] the fact that the defendant landlord had been prosecuted for evicting his tenant and ordered to pay a fine and costs together amounting to £1,000 was held not to militate against an exemplary award of the same amount, but it seems that the tortious conduct had gone well beyond that on which the conviction was based.[255] On the preliminary issue before the court in *Devenish Nutrition Ltd v Sanofi-Aventis SA*,[256] one of the trial judge's reasons for holding that exemplary damages were not available upon the assumed facts was that the defendants had already been heavily fined for their **13-042**

[246] See [2004] 1 A.C. 628 PC at [40] and [41]. Misfeasance in public office is not to be developed into a tort actionable per se in order to allow exemplary damages on the back of nominal damages: *Watkins v Secretary of State for the Home Department* [2006] 2 A.C. 395.

[247] [2011] 2 All E.R. 38.

[248] See [2011] 2 All E.R. 38 at [73]. The reduction of this award to £20,000 by the Court of Appeal, [2012] 1 All E.R. 903 CA, in this curious case, a move not specifically related to the size of the compensatory award, is thought somewhat difficult to justify, as is suggested at para.13-032, above.

[249] But if the compensatory damages are likely to be paid by the defendant's insurance company, it would seem right to take this into account when fixing the exemplary award. Insurance against exemplary damages may be invalid as contrary to public policy.

[250] [1985] Q.B. 401.

[251] [1993] Q.B. 507 CA.

[252] See para.13-011, above.

[253] [1993] Q.B. 507 CA at 527D to E.

[254] (1984) 17 H.L.R. 25 CA.

[255] (1984) 17 H.L.R. 25 CA at 29.

[256] [2009] Ch. 390.

conduct.[257] By contrast, exemplary damages were awarded in another case of breach of competition law, *2 Travel Group Plc v Cardiff City Transport Services Ltd*,[258] by reason of the defendant company being by statute immune from a fine, and in a third case of breach of competition law, *Albion Water Ltd v Dwr Cymru Cyfyngedig*,[259] the exemplary damages claim was not struck out as no penalty had been exacted.[260] Yet in *Borders (UK) Ltd v Commissioner of Police of the Metropolis*,[261] exemplary damages were awarded although the defendant trader was facing confiscation of the proceeds of his criminal conduct.[262] This was because the court was satisfied that the impending confiscation order would not expose him to double jeopardy as it would take into account the exemplary award in the civil proceedings.[263] Interestingly, the argument that there was double jeopardy on account of the prosecution, conviction and imprisonment of the defendant, the factor which had ousted exemplary damages in *Archer v Brown*,[264] does not appear to have been advanced. This could be attributed to a feeling that with a profit-motivated tort where the profit has been realised, the imposition of imprisonment, as opposed to the ordering of a swingeing fine, should not preclude an exemplary damages award of substantial proportions.[265]

### (7) The position with joint wrongdoers

**13-043** Where joint wrongdoers are sued together, the conduct of one defendant does not allow exemplary damages to be awarded in the single judgment which must be entered against all if the conduct of the other defendant or defendants does not merit punishment. This was the view of Pollock B in *Clark v Newsam*,[266] and is now finally established by the House of Lords in *Broome v Cassell & Co*.[267] However, in so far as an award of aggravated damages is being made, then the aggregate award should take into account both the aggravation engendered by the one defendant and the absence of aggravation on the part of the other or others. This was the view of Alderson B, also in *Clark v Newsam*,[268] and was adopted by Slesser LJ in *Chapman v Ellesmere*.[269] The practical application of these basically complementary rules should be easier now that a clear demarcation between exemplary damages and aggravated damages has been established, but it must be said that in *Broome v*

---

[257] See [2009] Ch. 390 at [64] and [69]; facts at para.13-044, below, dealing with another reason for refusal. On the appeal (at paras 14-028 to 14-029, below) the ruling on exemplary damages was not contested: [2009] Ch. 390 CA at 429, [21] and [141].

[258] [2012] C.A.T. 19.

[259] [2010] C.A.T. 30.

[260] But a later hearing, at [2013] C.A.T. 6, ruled against exemplary damages on the prior ground that the case did not fall within the second common law category: para.13-027, above.

[261] [2005] EWCA Civ 197 CA.

[262] Facts at para.13-026, above. Similarly in *AT, NT, ML, AK v Dulghieru* [2009] EWHC 225 (QB) (facts at para.42-001, below) an award of exemplary damages was held not to be precluded by the making of confiscation orders in criminal proceedings against the defendants: [2009] EWHC 225 (QB) at [71].

[263] [2005] EWCA Civ 197 CA at [60] and [61].

[264] See the case earlier in this paragraph.

[265] But see the discussion at paras 13-048 and following, below.

[266] (1847) 1 Ex. 131 at 141.

[267] [1972] A.C. 1027.

[268] (1847) 1 Ex. 131 at 141.

[269] [1932] 2 K.B. 431 CA; see especially at 471 to 472.

*Cassell & Co*,[270] Lord Wilberforce and Lord Diplock indicated in obiter dicta,[271] apparently not concurred in by Lord Reid,[272] that they would apply the rule that the House was unanimously establishing for exemplary damages to aggravated damages as well.[273]

## (8) The position with multiple claimants

Difficulties have been encountered in awarding exemplary damages where a claim has been brought by a large number of claimants. Thus in *Devenish Nutrition Ltd v Sanofi-Aventis SA*,[274] it was the existence of multiple claimants that provided the trial judge with one of his reasons for holding that exemplary damages were not available.[275] Large vitamin manufacturing companies had entered into worldwide cartels designed to raise prices unlawfully. Many to whom vitamin products had been supplied joined together to seek redress for the illegal overcharges to which they had been subjected, and added to their claim a request for exemplary damages which was not granted, the trial judge noting that the claimants were not the only persons affected by the unlawful conduct and that the remedy would not be available to members of other countries within the European Union.[276] In *A.B. v South West Water Services*,[277] where nearly 200 of the defendant water authority's customers were claiming on account of drinking contaminated water,[278] exemplary damages were not awarded for a reason since held to be wrong.[279] However, Stuart Smith LJ indicated that he regarded the case as peculiarly unsuitable for awarding exemplary damages because of the multiplicity of claimants, asking how one would arrive at the appropriate award and how divide it up.[280] Similarly, in the Supreme Court in *R. (on the application of Lumba (Congo)) v Secretary of State for the Home Department*,[281] where there was false imprisonment of foreign national prisoners pending their deportation, one of the reasons for holding it to be inappropriate to award exemplary damages[282] was the existence of potentially a large number of claimants, and claimants who were not all before the court. Lord Dyson queried how the court was to fix and apportion the punitive element of the damages if all the claims were not quantified by the court at the same time, and how the court was to know that the overall punishment was appropriate if the assessments were made separately at different times for different claimants.[283] **13-044**

---

270 [1972] A.C. 1027.

271 [1972] A.C. 1027 at 1063G and 1131H respectively.

272 [1972] A.C. 1027 at 1090C.

273 For this whole issue see paras 52-062 and following, below.

274 [2009] Ch. 390.

275 For another reason for the refusal see para.13-042, above.

276 See [2009] Ch. 390 at [68] for his various arguments. On the appeal (at paras 14-028 to 14-029, below) the ruling on exemplary damages was not contested: [2009] Ch. 390 CA at 429, [21] and [141].

277 [1993] Q.B. 507 CA.

278 Facts at para.13-015, above.

279 See para.13-011, above.

280 See his arguments at [1993] Q.B. 507 CA at 527A to D.

281 [2012] 1 A.C. 245.

282 The main reason is at para.13-019, above.

283 [2012] 1 A.C. 245 at [167]. In *Borders (UK) Ltd v Commissioner of Police of the Metropolis* [2005] EWCA Civ 197 CA, where exemplary damages were awarded to a consortium of eight book retailer claimants whose books had been stolen by a street racketeer (facts at para.13-026, above), it ap-

This result creates an anomaly if the court determines that a defendant's conduct requires deterrence. For why should defendants be able to escape the need for a deterrent award by the "lucky" chance, for them, that they have injured many rather than one or a few? The best approach would seem to be that deterrence should focus upon the particular conduct of a particular defendant. If there are multiple claimants who have been subjected to the same conduct then the exemplary award should generally be divided amongst them. If the conduct is more serious in relation to some of them, and requires a higher deterrent award, then those claimants should get a greater portion of the award.

## 2. THE QUESTION OF VICARIOUS LIABILITY

**13-045** Claims against the police for exemplary damages under the first common law category appear generally to have been brought, and successfully brought, not against the police officers responsible for the improper conduct but against their superiors, either Chief Constable of a county or Commissioner of Police for the metropolis.[284] Whether it is right thus to award exemplary damages against one who is only vicariously liable and is personally exempt from any improper conduct is a question hardly adverted to before *Kuddus v Chief Constable of Leicestershire*[285] arrived in the House of Lords. While the appropriateness of awarding exemplary damages on a vicarious basis was not even raised by the defendant in *Kuddus*—their Lordships were only concerned with whether an exemplary damages claim for misfeasance in public office should be struck out—Lord Scott came out forcefully against the appropriateness of vicarious liability. The rest of their Lordships preferred to express no view. Lord Scott said that

> "the objection to exemplary damages in vicarious liability cases seems to me to be fundamental"[286]

and later that

> "vicarious punishment via an award of exemplary damages is contrary to principle and should be rejected".[287]

Apart from one comment of Lord Mackay which assumed vicarious liability[288] and Lord Hutton's saying, after citing two Northern Ireland cases favouring vicarious liability, that he reserved his opinion on the matter,[289] their Lordships had nothing to say on the vicarious liability issue as it was not being argued.

**13-046** Following upon *Kuddus* there came two decisions of the Court of Appeal featuring vicarious liability. First in *Manley v Commissioner of Police for the Metropo-*

---

pears that the racketeer had stolen from other booksellers: see [2005] EWCA Civ 197 CA at [10]. No multiple claimant point appears in the case.

[284] The police authority will, however, not be vicariously liable if the conduct leading to the exemplary award is held not to be within the course of the police officer's authority: see *Makanjuola v Metropolitan Police Commissioner*, *The Times*, 8 August 1989.

[285] [2002] 2 A.C. 122.

[286] [2002] 2 A.C. 122 at [131].

[287] [2002] 2 A.C. 122 at [137].

[288] At para.13-038, above.

[289] [2002] 2 A.C. 122 at [93].

*lis*,[290] a claim against the police for assault, false imprisonment and malicious prosecution, no exemplary damages were awarded despite the "high-handed, insulting, malicious and oppressive"[291] conduct of the police officers, and the unpreparedness to make an award appears to have been on the ground that the defendant commissioner of police was not the actual perpetrator whom the court was concerned not to make liable.[292] Then in *Rowlands v Chief Constable of Merseyside Police*,[293] the question was faced four-square by the Court of Appeal. There had again been claims for assault, false imprisonment and malicious prosecution against the police, and exemplary damages of £7,500 for the imprisonment and prosecution were awarded[294] against the defendant chief constable who had in no way participated in the improper conduct.[295] The view was taken that an award of exemplary damages against the head of a particular force was simply a means of expressing strong disapproval of the conduct of the police force as an institution as well as of the individual officers[296] and, since the power to award exemplary damages rested on policy, and exemplary damages are awardable for wrongdoing by government servants of a kind that has a direct effect on civil liberties, it was desirable that awards could be made against those vicariously liable for the conduct of their subordinates as only by this means could awards of an adequate amount be made against those who bear public responsibility for the conduct of the officers concerned.[297] It was also said that this solution removed the constraint imposed by the officers' usually limited means.[298]

This practical and sensible result is to be commended. While at first blush it may appear unfair to impose a deterrent award upon the innocent employer and at the same time allow the guilty employee to escape specific deterrence, there are countervailing considerations as pointed to in *Rowlands*. Apart from the important practical feature that the employee in many, if not most, cases is not going to be worth suing, whether for compensatory or exemplary damages, imposing liability upon employers is likely to provide an incentive for them to control the ways in which their employees operate, thereby producing a certain deterrent purpose.[299] **13-047**

290 [2006] EWCA Civ 879 CA.

291 [2006] EWCA Civ 879 CA at [32].

292 [2006] EWCA Civ 879 CA at [19].

293 [2007] 1 W.L.R. 1065 CA.

294 The damages for the assault had been agreed by the parties.

295 In the light of this decision Eady J in *Mosley v News Group Newspapers Ltd* [2008] E.M.L.R. 20 at 679, while considering exemplary damages inappropriate for other reasons (see the footnote at the end of para.13-011, above), had really no alternative but to conclude that the defendant could be vicariously liable and that any decision to the contrary was now undoubtedly a matter for the House of Lords: see his over-cautious comments at [2008] E.M.L.R. 20 at [203].

296 [2008] E.M.L.R. 20 at [42].

297 [2008] E.M.L.R. 20 at [47].

298 [2008] E.M.L.R. 20 at [47]. It should be noted that the result in *Rowlands* does not impose any burden upon a police force head with greater financial means but no participation in the wrongdoing as the practice in these cases has been to pay the damages out of police funds.

299 However, Lord Scott in *Kuddus* did not accept that the existence of a deterrent purpose provided a sufficient justification for the exemplary element in damages ([2002] 2 A.C. 122 at [129]) and it is true to say that, in the central case of claims against police authorities, the damages will simply end up as a charge on public expenditure. Lord Scott in *Kuddus* also pointed to the rule that against joint wrongdoers sued together there could be no exemplary damages if one of them were innocent of improper conduct (see para.13-043, above) and added that this must be equally true where the innocent wrongdoer is sued alone ([2002] 2 A.C. 122 at [128]). Yet in the unfairness stakes the situation of the normal run of joint and several tortfeasors is materially different from that of employer

Furthermore, the result in *Rowlands* should spill over into other areas of government service. In *Watkins v Secretary of State for the Home Department*,[300] where the claimant did ask for exemplary damages against the individual prison officers—no doubt thinking it politic in the light of Lord Scott's comments in *Kuddus* not to press for an exemplary award against their superior, the Home Office—the issue of who should be sued was not resolved as the House of Lords reversed on liability.[301] Today it is thought that the claimant would succeed against the Home Office rather than have to claim against the individual officers.

### 3. The True Rationale of the Second Common Law Category

**13-048** In earlier editions of this work the idea was put forward that the second common law category was in truth based not upon the punishment or deterrence of defendants but upon the prevention of their unjust enrichment, an idea which found support from Lord Diplock in *Broome v Cassell & Co*,[302] where he recognised the second common law category as being analogous to the civil law concept of *enrichessement indue*,[303] and also from judicial dicta of recent years.[304] The idea had its genesis in the criticism of the limited scope of the second common law category. Thus in *Australian Consolidated Press v Uren*,[305] the unsuccessful appeal from one of the two Australian decisions in which the High Court early refused to follow *Rookes* in libel,[306] counsel for the respondent asked whether Lord Devlin's formulation meant that

> "a defendant who was indifferent to financial results and had had no thought at all of profit but was actuated by venomous malice towards the plaintiff would be absolved from any risk of having to pay exemplary damages?"[307]

This undoubtedly follows from Lord Devlin's formulation, and Taylor J in his judgment in the other of the two Australian libel cases said that he was quite unable to see

> "why the law should look with less favour on wrongs committed with a profit-making motive than upon wrongs committed with the utmost degree of malice or vindictively, arrogantly or high-handedly with a contumelious disregard for the plaintiff's rights."[308]

Lord Reid in *Broome v Cassell & Co*,[309] freely admitted that there was no logical

---

and employee as joint tortfeasors, as the Law Commission has explained in its Report on *Aggravated, Exemplary and Restitutionary Damages*, Law Com. No.247 (1997) at paras 5.222 to 5.224.

300 [2005] Q.B. 883 CA.

301 [2006] 2 A.C. 395.

302 [1972] A.C. 1027.

303 [1972] A.C. 1027 at 1129B.

304 "The rationale of the second category of exemplary damages is, precisely, the confiscation of profits": per Sedley LJ in *Borders (UK) Ltd v Commissioner of Police of the Metropolis* [2005] EWCA Civ 197 CA at [26] (see the case at para.13-026, above). "The rationale behind the second category is not the punishment of the defendant but the prevention of his unjust enrichment": per Treacy J in *AT, NT, ML, AK v Dulghieru* [2009] EWHC 225 (QB) at [68].

305 [1969] A.C. 590 PC.

306 See para.13-005, above.

307 [1969] 1 A.C. 590 PC at 643, per Lord Morris, paraphrasing, without commenting on, counsel's contentions.

308 *Uren v John Fairfax & Sons Pty* [1967] Argus L.R. 25 at 37; (1966) 40 A.L.J.R. 124 at 132.

309 [1972] A.C. 1027.

reason why the malicious tortfeasor should not be punished along with the greedy one,[310] and gave as the reason for excluding the malicious tortfeasor from the second common law category

> "simply that firmly established authority required us to accept this category however little we might like it, but did not require us to go farther".[311]

The difficulties are unanswerable if exemplary damages are recognised, as many cases have done, to be based upon deterrence, both specific and general. However, the narrow formulation by Lord Devlin would now justify a more specific and sharper award of disgorgement damages. However, as a means of deterrence by stripping actual profits, disgorgement damages is a limited method of deterring a tortfeasor from a specific gain, especially as it is dependent on the achievement of profit rather than merely its motivation.[312] **13-049**

While the application of the exemplary damages criteria to the assessment of the award makes sense where the aim of the court is deterrence of the defendant and others, they have little or no relevance where the so-called exemplary damages are designed to operate as an indirect method for extracting profits tortiously obtained by the defendant. This may be tested against any of the eight criteria, but of these it will suffice to take Lord Devlin's three, called by him three considerations.[313] Thus if a defendant's profit is to be disgorged, awards should not be moderate or indeed immoderate, but should be geared to the profit obtained or obtainable by the defendant. Similarly, awards should be influenced not by the overall means of the defendant but by the amount that he stands to gain from his conduct. Moreover, difficult enough as it is to see why a defendant should only be punished where the claimant is the victim of the behaviour, it is even more difficult to be persuaded that he should lose his profit only if he is sued by the person upon whom he has inflicted the wrong. **13-050**

These three considerations were to be borne in mind, said Lord Devlin, "whenever awards of exemplary damages are being considered".[314] It is therefore clear that he intended them to apply to the second common law category as much as to his other two categories. And over the years the courts have consistently follow this advice from on high, as our earlier examination of the criteria has shown. Thus, to take an up-to-date decision, in *Ramzan v Brookwide Ltd*,[315] Geraldine Andrews QC, sitting as a Deputy High Court Judge, took into account, in arriving at her exemplary damages award, the need for moderation in amount[316] and also the means of the defendant.[317] And the same is true of the other criteria that we have set out. Thus, again taking up-to-date decisions, in the three dealing with breach of competition law, *Devenish Nutrition Ltd v Sanofi-Aventis SA*,[318] *2 Travel Group Plc* **13-051**

---

[310] [1972] A.C. 1027 at 1088E.

[311] [1972] A.C. 1027 at 1088E.

[312] Thus exemplary damages were awarded in *Design Progression Ltd v Thurloe Properties Ltd* [2005] 1 W.L.R. 1 where the defendant's design to achieve profits had failed: see especially at [146].

[313] See paras 13-033 to 13-038, above.

[314] [1964] A.C. 1129, 1227.

[315] [2011] 2 All E.R. 38.

[316] See para.13-034, above.

[317] See para.13-038, above. None of this is affected by the reduction of the award by the Court of Appeal, [2012] 1 All E.R. 903 CA, a move, as argued at para.13-032, above, thought difficult to justify.

[318] [2008] 2 W.L.R. 637.

*v Cardiff City Transport Services Ltd*,[319] and *Albion Water Ltd v Dwr Cymru Cyfyngedig*,[320] whether an exemplary damages award could be made turned, among other things, on the presence or absence of a criminal penalty,[321] a consideration irrelevant to the disgorgement of ill-gotten gains. Returning to Geraldine Andrews QC in *Ramzan*, she said that she was unpersuaded in a case such as the one before her by the argument in this text that the award of exemplary damages is simply designed to operate as an indirect method for extracting profits tortiously obtained by the defendant.[322] Now she can be assured that she was right.

319 [2012] C.A.T. 19.
320 [2010] C.A.T. 30.
321 For the details see para.13-042, above.
322 [2011] 2 All E.R. 38 at [69].

CHAPTER 14

# RESTITUTIONARY DAMAGES

TABLE OF CONTENTS



## I. CONCEPT AND MEANING OF RESTITUTIONARY DAMAGES

Another exception to the basic rule that damages are made as compensation for loss has made its appearance in the form of what have been called "restitutionary damages". A conclusive recognition of restitution as a remedy for unjust enrichment took a long time to be recognised by the courts, not being finally accepted until the landmark decision of the House of Lords in *Lipkin Gorman v Karpnale*.[1] The recognition of restitution (or, more accurately, restitutionary damages) for *wrongdoing* rather than for unjust enrichment took even longer. The term restitutionary damages was earlier promoted by respected academic writers, and was adopted by the Law Commission in its Consultation Paper,[2] and later its Report,[3] on *Aggravated, Exemplary and Restitutionary Damages*. **14-001**

What then are restitutionary damages? In a nutshell, restitutionary damages are damages which require a defendant to give back a benefit transferred from the claimant. They focus on the benefit received by the defendant rather than any loss suffered by the claimant. They are the same remedy for a wrong as restitution is for unjust enrichment. In *Sempra Metals Ltd v Inland Revenue Commissioners*,[4] Lord **14-002**

1 [1991] 2 A.C. 548.
2 No.132 (1993).
3 Law Com. No.247 (1997).
4 [2008] 1 A.C. 561 at [116]. See also *Benedetti v Sawiris* [2014] A.C. 938 at [24], per Lord Clarke: "restitution for a wrong".

Nicholls spoke of "restitution for wrongdoing as distinct from restitution for unjust enrichment". In the law of unjust enrichment the rationale for a restitutionary award is

> "to correct normatively defective transfers of value, usually by restoring the parties to their pre-transfer positions".[5]

The same reasoning applies, a fortiori, in the law of wrongs. As Lord Denning put it,

> "the wrongdoer cannot be better off because he did not ask permission. He cannot be better off by doing wrong than he would be by doing right".[6]

**14-003** Only a few decades ago, the suggestion that damages can be restitutionary would have appeared to many as a heresy. But it is now impossible to justify such views. Damages are not tied to loss. They can be exemplary[7]; they can be nominal[8]; and, for a time, it was thought that they could also be vindicatory (although, as we will see,[9] those damages have been mostly eradicated in English law). Further, if we look over from money awards of damages for common law wrongdoing to money awards for wrongdoing in equity we also see a common remedy of disgorgement of profits, discussed in the next chapter as "disgorgement damages". The recognition of restitutionary damages is inevitable once it is acknowledged, as it must be, that damages are not tied to loss and comprise any award in money for a civil wrong.[10]

## II. THE MEASURE OF RESTITUTIONARY DAMAGES

**14-004** The measure of restitutionary damages is very simply stated, although not always so simply applied. It is the benefit wrongfully received by a defendant at the claimant's expense. It is the same measure as is awarded when a defendant is unjustly enriched. In the context of unjust enrichment rather than wrongdoing, Lord Reid has made several important points about the nature of a restitutionary award: (1) it is not compensatory for loss, so the measure is not concerned with any loss suffered by the claimant[11]; (2) it is designed to ensure that a transfer of value is reversed, although the expression "transfer of value" is too general to serve as a legal test[12]; and (3) "a general rule, possibly subject to exceptions, [is] that the claimant must have directly provided a benefit to the defendant".[13]

**14-005** In some cases, the valuation of restitutionary damages will be simple. A defendant who deceives a claimant into paying £100 to the defendant will have obtained

---

5 *Revenue and Customs Commissioners v Investment Trust Companies (In Liquidation)* [2017] UKSC 29 at [42].

6 *Strand Electric and Engineering Co Ltd v Brisford Entertainments Ltd* [1952] 2 Q.B. 246 at 253.

7 Chapter 13, above.

8 Chapter 12, above.

9 Chapter 17, below.

10 See the discussion at paras 1-002 to 1-003, above.

11 *Revenue and Customs Commissioners v Investment Trust Companies (In Liquidation)* [2017] UKSC 29 at [45].

12 *Revenue and Customs Commissioners v Investment Trust Companies (In Liquidation)* [2017] UKSC 29 at [43].

13 *Revenue and Customs Commissioners v Investment Trust Companies (In Liquidation)* [2017] UKSC 29 at [50].

a benefit of £100 at the time of receipt. More difficult are cases where the benefit that the defendant obtained is the opportunity to *use* something of value. The cases in this area have provided numerous examples. One of the most famous was given by Lord Lloyd delivering the advice of the Privy Council in *Inverugie Investments Ltd v Hackett*.[14] He gave the example of a trespasser who takes a concrete mixer without the owner's consent. Just like a man who hires it and must pay the daily hire even if it rains, the trespasser

> "must pay the going rate, even though in the event he has derived no actual benefit from the use of the mixer".

The point is that the benefit which the man obtains is the *opportunity* to use the mixer. That is the benefit for which the market requires others to pay.

Matters become more difficult when determining how one values the benefit to **14-006** the defendant which has been obtained unlawfully from the claimant. In *Seager v Copydex (No 2)*,[15] a case concerning breach of confidence, Lord Denning set out three possible methods of valuation of a benefit received, depending on the type of information involved in the breach of confidence. He said that (1) if there was nothing special about the information then it would be valued by the price that the defendant would reasonably have to pay for a consultant to have obtained that information; (2) if the information was special and could not be obtained from a consultant then the price is the price that a willing buyer would have paid a willing seller for it; and (3) if the information was very special indeed then the price is the capitalisation of a royalty. In cases concerning matters other than breach of confidence, similar valuation questions can arise. Ultimately, the question is the value of the benefit which the defendant has obtained. That value is measured by the price which would be paid by a reasonable person in the defendant's position.

A straightforward case which presents little difficulty is where the defendant **14-007** converts and sells the claimant's property; here the claimant may recover the proceeds of sale even if he himself could only have sold for less. The sale is likely to be the best evidence of the value of the benefit obtained by the defendant. Thus in the very early case of *Lamine v Dorrell*,[16] the sale price of debentures was recovered, then in an action of *indebitatus assumpsit*, without looking to assess any loss to the claimant.

The most common type of claim featuring restitutionary damages is without **14-008** doubt the claim which arises out of the wrongful user of the claimant's property. The cases indicate that here the courts will generally award the market rate of hiring or renting the property in question. Thus in *Strand Electric Co v Brisford Entertainments Ltd*,[17] the claimant was held to be entitled to the full market rate of hire of the detained electrical equipment for the whole of the period of detention.[18] Similarly, the ordinary letting value of the flat was awarded in *Swordheath Properties Ltd v Tabet*,[19] and in *Inverugie Investments Ltd v Hackett*,[20] the market rental of as many as 30 apartments in the hotel for as long a period as 15-and-a-half years.

---

14 [1995] 1 W.L.R. 713 at 718.
15 [1969] 1 W.L.R. 809 at 813.
16 (1705) 2 Ld. Raym. 1216.
17 [1952] 2 Q.B. 246 CA.
18 Facts at para.38-067, below.
19 [1979] 1 W.L.R. 285 CA.
20 [1995] 1 W.L.R. 713 PC.

In *Penarth Dock Engineering Co v Pounds*,[21] the award appears to have been based upon what it would have cost the defendants to have hired a similar dock but, curiously, it was slightly less than the market rent.[22] The market rent may indeed occasionally exceed the benefit to the defendant so that a lower figure falls to be awarded. This was the position in *Ministry of Defence v Ashman*,[23] where the defendant army wife would have moved from the army quarters, which she was wrongfully holding over, into local authority accommodation at a rate below market.[24]

**14-009** Where profits from an interference with the claimant's property rights have been made by the defendant, typically in the cases a land developer, the courts have sometimes awarded a percentage of the defendant's profits. But the percentage has varied from case to case and there have been some wild fluctuations, with the percentage influenced by the size of the profit. Each case has to be taken separately and it appears impossible to lay down any general rules other than to say that the actual profit should really just serve as an illustration of the amount which a reasonable person in the defendant's position would have paid a reasonable claimant. The awards can be illustrated by reference to some of the cases discussed below. Thus in *Wrotham Park Estate Co Ltd v Parkside Homes Ltd*,[25] the award was of only five per cent of the developer's anticipated profit of £50,000 whereas in *Bracewell v Appleby*,[26] as much as 40 per cent was awarded, but since the profit was only £5,000 the total amount was less. These were both cases of the 1970s when the courts may have been feeling their way in this area, but 20 years later in *Jaggard v Sawyer*,[27] the claimant received only £700, although this did represent a potential award of over £6,000 which would have been divisible between the 10 properties in the development other than the defendant's. By contrast, at an even later date in *Amec Developments Ltd v Jury's Hotel Management (UK) Ltd*,[28] where it was a hotel that was being built in breach of a restrictive covenant, the far larger award of £375,000 was reached, being based upon the gain the defendant would make by its breach and the discount which would be applied to that gain in negotiation. Later still in *Tamares (Vincent Square) Ltd v Fairpoint Properties (Vincent Square) Ltd*,[29] where a developer had infringed a right to light, less than one third of the developer's profit, taken at £174,500, was awarded.[30] In *HKRUK II (CHC) Ltd v Heaney*,[31] a further case involving infringement of an easement of light, the trial judge was careful to take a whole batch of factors into account in arriving at the figure of £225,000,[32] which sum he would have awarded had he not been granting an injunction. Certainly factors other than profit and how the parties might have negotiated may influence the court in coming to a view as to the appropriate amount.[33]

---

21 [1963] 1 Lloyd's Rep. 359.
22 These three cases are detailed at paras 37-049 and 39-050, below.
23 (1993) 25 H.L.R. 513 CA.
24 At para.39-051, below.
25 [1974] 1 W.L.R. 798.
26 [1975] Ch. 408.
27 [1995] 1 W.L.R. 269 CA.
28 [2001] 1 E.G.L.R. 81.
29 [2007] 1 W.L.R. 2167.
30 See [2007] 1 W.L.R. 2167 at [37].
31 [2010] EWHC 2245 Ch.
32 [2010] EWHC 2245 Ch at [86] to [94].
33 In the judgment in *Amec Developments Ltd v Jury's Hotel Management (UK) Ltd* [2001] 1 E.G.L.R.

Thus in *Wrotham Park* Brightman J said that he was proceeding with great moderation on account of the fact that the claimants had not warned the developers in advance of their purchase that they, the claimants, would withhold their consent to the proposed development.[34] The Court of Appeal in *Experience Hendrix LLC v PPX Enterprises Inc*,[35] was not required to make an assessment of the appropriate amount of restitutionary damages there, being asked simply to decide whether restitutionary damages, or an account of profits, lay as a matter of principle. Yet it is interesting to see that Mance LJ , without wishing "to fetter any future court in any way", expressed the view that he would be surprised if the appropriate rate of royalty for the restitutionary damages in respect of those of the 63 master recordings which the defendants had licensed in breach of contract were less than twice that agreed in respect of the 33 master recordings which under the settlement contract the defendants were entitled to license.[36] This suggests that Mance LJ considered that the restitutionary damages should not be limited to a reasonable negotiated royalty, no doubt to reflect the fact that the claimants had wished the group of 63 master recordings no longer to see the light of day.

In contrast with these cases, other cases have suggested that a wrongdoer should **14-010**
only have to pay a nominal amount of damages for the value of an opportunity wrongfully obtained. In *Enfield London Borough Council v Outdoor Plus Ltd*,[37] the question concerned whether a trespasser should pay restitutionary damages, measured as a reasonable licence fee as negotiated between a willing buyer and a willing seller. The trespasser had erected advertising hoardings intruding on the claimant's land. The trial judge held that the defendant did not obtain any valuable benefit from the claimant because the defendant could have erected the hoardings lawfully had it known that a trespass had occurred. The Court of Appeal rejected this reasoning and awarded substantial damages. The possibility that the advertising could have been done lawfully is a matter to be taken into account in a hypothetical negotiation to determine the value of the opportunity but it did not mean that the opportunity was worth nothing. However, the opposite result occurred in *Marathon Asset Management LLP v Seddon*.[38] Two employees unlawfully obtained many files containing confidential information from their former employer. The trial judge was critical of the failure by the claimant to bring a case for damages based on the value of the confidential files which were actually used.[39] But, as explained above, that confuses the benefit obtained by the defendant at the claimant's expense (the opportunity to use) with matters from which profit might be determined (actual use). Although the claimant's evidence had valued the price of reasonably obtaining the information at £15 million, the trial judge awarded only nominal damages for the valuable opportunity which the defendants had obtained by taking for free, and unlawfully, confidential information.

---

81 many of the factors to take into account are dealt with at length. So too in *Stadium Capital Holdings (No.2) Ltd v St Marylebone Properties Co Plc* [2011] EWHC 2856(Ch) Vos J, having the task of assessing damages to be based, as the parties were agreed, upon a hypothetical licence fee, conducted a review of the authorities (at [57]–[68]) to ascertain the factors to be taken into account in arriving at the hypothetical licence fee.

[34] [1974] 1 W.L.R. 798 at 815H to 816A.

[35] [2003] 1 All E.R. (Comm) 830 CA.

[36] [2003] 1 All E.R. (Comm) 830 CA at [46]. Facts at para.14-039 and 14-040, below.

[37] [2012] EWCA Civ 608 CA.

[38] [2017] EWHC 300.

[39] [2017] EWHC 300 at [281]–[282].

## III. RESTITUTIONARY DAMAGES DISTINGUISHED FROM COMPENSATORY AND DISGORGEMENT DAMAGES

**14-011** In one of the most commonly cited cases in this field, *Stoke City Council v W&J Wass Ltd*,[40] Nicholls LJ recognised that a person should have a claim against one who has used his property without his consent, a claim to be measured by the amount which could reasonably be required to gain permission for the property's use. Unfortunately, in that case, and a number of cases since, courts have regarded the claimant as suffering loss or damage by virtue of not having received that amount.[41] But it does not matter whether the claimant would have used the property herself or that the claimant is no worse off financially as a result of the use. Restitution of the benefit obtained by the defendant must still be made. In many cases, this award has been described as "compensation".[42] But, as Leggatt J has explained, this is to use "compensation" in the sense only to mean "redress for wrongdoing".[43] The word, "compensation", should not be used in this near-meaningless sense. It can only engender confusion. As Lord Nicholls recognised in *Attorney General v Blake*[44]:

> "These awards cannot be regarded as conforming to the strictly compensatory measure of damage for the injured person's loss unless loss is given a strained and artificial meaning. The reality is that the injured person's rights were invaded but, in financial terms, he suffered no loss."

**14-012** In some cases, an attempt has been made to rationalise restitutionary damages awards as compensation by treating them as cases where the claimant is being compensated for the loss of a bargaining opportunity. This approach is most frequently utilised where the invasion of the proprietary right has been constituted by erecting a building and will continue in the future because injunctive relief to have the building pulled down is unavailable.[45] But it is not convincing. The idea of the bargaining opportunity lost, as Mance LJ pointed out in the contract case of *Experience Hendrix*,[46] involves an element of artificiality if, as is generally the position in this type of case, the opportunity is one that the claimant would in no circumstances have taken. Nothing would have persuaded the claimant to agree to the building that affected the enjoyment of his or her property[47] nor, as in the case before Mance LJ, to agree to the licensing of master recordings which the claimant wished to have removed from the public domain.[48] The best judgments now face up to the fact that these awards are not compensatory for loss at all. They are damages which make restitution of a benefit.

**14-013** It is also necessary to emphasise the distinction between restitutionary damages

---

40 [1988] 1 W.L.R. 1406 CA at 1416D.

41 See [1988] 1 W.L.R. 1406 CA at 1416B, per Nicholls LJ.

42 *WWF World Wide Fund for Nature v World Wrestling Federation Entertainment Inc* [2008] 1 W.L.R. 445 at [58]–[59], per Chadwick LJ.

43 *Marathon Asset Management LLP v Seddon* [2017] EWHC 300 at [202].

44 [2017] EWHC 300 at 279D.

45 See the cases at para.14-022, below.

46 [2003] 1 All E.R. (Comm) 830 CA at [45].

47 As was probably so in *Bracewell v Appleby* [1975] Ch. 408 and *Carr-Saunders v Dick McNeil Associates Ltd* [1986] 1 W.L.R. 922 (both at para.14-022, below) and in the contract case of *Wrotham Park Estate Co Ltd v Parkside Homes Ltd* [1974] 1 W.L.R. 798 (at para.14-036, below).

48 *Experience Hendrix* is at paras 14-039 and 14-040, below.

and disgorgement damages (which are considered in the next chapter). Both are based upon the gain made by a defendant but restitutionary damages focus upon the defendant's gain at the claimant's expense. Disgorgement damages, commonly described as an account of profits, even though the money awarded is not an account, are concerned with the profits made by the defendant, not the benefit received at the claimant's expense. An example can illustrate the point. Suppose a defendant deceives a claimant into paying £1 million to the defendant. The defendant invests the money and makes £2 million net profit in a year. If the defendant repays £1 million at the end of the year, and the claimant cannot show any further consequential loss, is the claimant entitled to any other award? One possible award is an account and then disgorgement of the £2 million profits. Another possible award, irrespective of any profit that the defendant made, is an award of restitution of the time value of the money. The benefit that the defendant received at the claimant's expense is the value of the use of the money. That value is the interest rate that a person in the defendant's position would have been charged for the use of the money. The conclusion that this award of restitution is available for unjust enrichment is now established. In *Sempra Metals Ltd (formerly Metallgesellschaft Ltd) v Inland Revenue Commissioners*,[49] the House of Lords held that the Inland Revenue Commissioners were unjustly enriched by the use that they had of money paid by Sempra earlier than was legally required. Lord Scott, in dissent, said that an award of interest as restitution was a remedy for the recovery of a "wholly conceptual"[50] gain because the Revenue might not have made any actual profits. But the benefit obtained at the claimant's expense was not the actual profit, it was the *opportunity* to use the money. The Revenue in *Sempra* received the opportunity to use the money earlier than it should have done. The opportunity to use millions of pounds without cost is not an illusory benefit, even if it later turns out that no profit was made from the use of the money. The free opportunity to use money is an immediate benefit irrespective of the use to which the money is put.[51] It would be a great surprise to any lender of money that a defendant who obtained the opportunity to use money without paying for it did not immediately obtain any benefit. A bank does not waive interest charges if the borrower squanders the money.

Restitutionary damages must be understood as conceptually separate and distinct **14-014**
from disgorgement of profits following an account of profits. The two awards serve different purposes. The former reverses a benefit obtained wrongfully at the claimant's expense. The latter aims to deter the defendant or others by disgorging profits made wrongfully. Where both awards are available, it should be for the claimant to elect between them, choosing the one which is the most valuable. The award of the higher amount will serve the purposes of the other. Hence, in the example above, if the fraudulent obtaining of the use of the claimant's money gave a defendant a benefit of £100,000 as the price that would have to have been paid for the use of money then disgorgement of the £2 million profits as disgorgement damages would incidentally fulfil the purpose of the restitutionary award. No award of restitutionary damages would be necessary. Alternatively, if only the £5,000 profit were made then a restitutionary award of £100,000 would also incidentally serve

---

49 [2008] 1 A.C. 561.

50 *Sempra Metals Ltd (formerly Metallgesellschaft Ltd) v Inland Revenue Commissioners* [2008] 1 A.C. 561 at [145], per Lord Scott.

51 *Littlewoods Retail Ltd v HM Revenue & Customs* [2014] EWHC 868 (Ch) at [372], per Henderson J. See *Littlewoods Retail Ltd v HM Revenue & Customs* [2015] EWCA Civ 515 at [186] (the Court).

to disgorge all profits made. The better view is that where both awards are available it should be for the claimant to elect between them for the higher award.[52]

14-015 The concern of restitutionary damages is to reverse a benefit wrongfully obtained by the defendant at the claimant's expense. In the law of unjust enrichment, restitution is *always* available, subject to defences, where a defendant is unjustly enriched. The same should be true where a defendant is enriched as a result of a wrong. Hence, just as restitution is prima facie available for unjust enrichment where a defendant receives a benefit at the claimant's expense as a result of a mistake so too should restitution be available where a defendant receives a benefit at the claimant's expense as a result of the defendant's fraud. However, a major part of the difficulty in identifying a rationale for restitutionary damages is that they have been erroneously conflated with disgorgement damages. The circumstances in which disgorgement damages are available are far more limited than restitutionary damages. As explained below, some cases have anomalously restricted restitutionary damages to instances where the wrong is "proprietary". Other cases have repeated common observations that restitutionary damages are only available where compensatory damages are unable to represent "adequate redress for the wrong done to the claimant".[53] It is unclear what is meant by such expressions. The expression is best understood as meaning that if compensatory damages exceed the value of the benefit received by the defendant then there is no need for a restitutionary damages award. Nevertheless, as explained in the paragraph above, the election between the two should be the choice of the claimant.

## IV. Circumstances Giving Rise to Restitutionary Damages

### 1. Liability for Torts and Equitable Wrongs

14-016 Restitutionary damages have long existed in the law of torts, although they have rarely been expressly recognised as such. Sometimes recovery has been regarded as recovery of compensatory damages. Sometimes it has been described with unhelpful labels as money had and received or mesne profits. Sometimes it is described as a "licence fee" or as "licence fee damages". Sometimes it has been described simply as "damages". There have been some advances. One large step forward was taken by Hoffmann LJ in *Ministry of Defence v Ashman*,[54] an action for mesne profits for wrongful occupation of land:

> "It is true that in earlier cases it has not been expressly stated that a claim for trespass can be a claim for restitution. Nowadays I do not see why we should not call a spade a spade."[55]

Hoffmann LJ approached the matter similarly in *Ministry of Defence v Thompson*.[56] This reflects what was said over a half century ago in far sighted remarks by Den-

---

52 *Tang Man Sit v Capacious Investments Ltd* [1996] A.C. 514. See *Vercoe v Rutland Fund Management Ltd* [2010] EWHC 424 (Ch) at [333]–[339]; *Marathon Asset Management LLP v Seddon* [2017] EWHC 300 (Comm) at [223].

53 [2017] EWHC 300 (Comm) at [215].

54 (1993) 25 H.L.R. 513 CA.

55 (1993) 25 H.L.R. 513 CA at 519.

56 (1993) 25 H.L.R. 552 CA.

ning LJ in *Strand Electric Co v Brisford Entertainments*,[57] that the nature of the remedy for detinue in that case was because the defendant "has had the benefit of the goods". But Denning LJ thought that the action resembled one "for restitution rather than an action of tort."[58] We now know that the action is one for restitution (or restitutionary damages) *for* the tort.

Although it is now established that restitutionary damages are available for torts, there is deep confusion about the types of tort for which restitutionary damages can be awarded. One line of cases has suggested that the award should be restricted to "proprietary torts", a label which is problematic in concept as well as in principle. In principle, restitutionary damages should be available for all torts. Like the award of restitution for unjust enrichment, the award of restitutionary damages for a tort aims to reverse a transfer of value. It is very difficult to see why a transfer of value arising from, say, a proprietary tort should be reversed but a transfer of value arising from a tort such as assault should not. **14-017**

## (1) Proprietary torts

In a whole variety of torts directly affecting property, viz., by invasion of what is clearly a proprietary right, there has been recovery of restitutionary damages. **14-018**

### (a) Wrongful interference with land

*(i) Wrongful user and occupation* The greatest number of cases allowing damages which focus on the benefit received by the defendant fall within this category. Starting in the middle of the 19th century with the prolific cases of unauthorised mining of which *Martin v Porter*,[59] was the first and in which a reasonable rent for the use of the passages in the claimant's mine, a so-called wayleave, was awarded as damages, there followed *Whitwham v Westminster Brymbo Coal Co*,[60] where the value of the use of the claimant's land for tipping soil from the defendant's colliery was awarded, *Penarth Dock Engineering Co v Pounds*,[61] where the value of the use of the claimant's dock premises for a pontoon which the defendant failed to remove was given, and *Swordheath Properties v Tabet*,[62] and *Inverugie Investments v Hackett*,[63] where the defendants were liable for the market rental value of, respectively, a flat in which they had held over and a hotel from which they had evicted the claimant, although neither flat nor hotel might have been fully let out during the period of wrongful occupation.[64] In addition, there is the greater complexity of *Ministry of Defence v Ashman*,[65] and *Ministry of Defence v Thompson*,[66] where deserted army wives remained in occupation of married quarters which they had occupied with their husbands at a concessionary rate but which they were now required to vacate for local authority accommodation at a higher rate, **14-019**

---

57 [1952] 2 Q.B. 246 CA.
58 [1952] 2 Q.B. 246 CA at 254 to 255.
59 (1839) 5 M. & W. 351.
60 [1896] 2 Ch. 538 CA.
61 [1963] 1 Lloyd's Rep. 359.
62 [1979] 1 W.L.R. 285 CA.
63 [1995] 1 W.L.R. 713 PC.
64 All these cases are considered in detail at paras 39-048 to 39-050, below.
65 (1993) 25 H.L.R. 513 CA.
66 (1993) 25 H.L.R. 552 CA.

neither rate being as high as the market rate.[67] It has been pointed out above that in these last two cases Hoffmann LJ saw the situation in terms of "restitution",[68] which took him to the local authority accommodation rate, but in the former case Lloyd LJ, in the minority, disagreed with this. For him the claim was simply for compensatory damages, which took him to the concessionary rate. Hoffmann LJ's view, however, won out in *Ashman*, and all these cases should today be seen as being definitely restitutionary in character.[69] The label "restitutionary damages" is, however, better than "restitution" because it directs attention to the fact that these are damages are awarded for a tort rather than as restitution for unjust enrichment.[70] The use of the label "restitution" did not resolve the difficulties in *Ashman* because the award was discounted by Hoffmann LJ to allow for "subjective devaluation", a controversial concept[71] which has been suggested to be available to reduce an award of restitution in unjust enrichment to protect a defendant's freedom of choice. That concept should not available to reduce an award of restitutionary damages for a tort where the award of damages is not concerned with the choice of the defendant, although the benefit to a person in the defendant's position might still have been the local authority rate.

**14-020** An excellent example, albeit very poorly reported, of restitutionary damages for trespass is *Gondal v Dillon Newsagents Ltd*.[72] The Dillons notified the Gondals that they were in breach of a lease but their notice was defective so they committed trespass when they retook possession. In the Court of Appeal, Simon Brown LJ (with whom Pill LJ and Sir John Vinelott agreed) considered a submission that the Gondals were entitled to substantial compensation for a lost opportunity to bargain with the Dillons to allow the Dillons to take possession. Simon Brown LJ explained that the Gondals were not entitled to any compensatory damages because "there is no sensible possibility whatever" that the Gondals would have agreed to any offer that the Dillons might have made.[73] As a result the financial value of that lost possibility was nil. The Gondals also sought restitutionary damages. Historically this award for trespass would have been described as mesne profits. Simon Brown LJ made the award describing it as[74]:

> "a restitutionary award, i.e. damages calculated according to the value of the benefit received by the occupier, is rightly decided not by reference to what subjectively the landlord would have otherwise done with his property, but rather by an objective determination of what the wrongful occupation was worth to the trespasser."

---

67 See the two cases at paras 39-051 to 39-053, below.

68 At para.14-016, above.

69 The tortious remedy in damages available to tenants evicted by landlords under ss.27 and 28 of the Housing Act 1988, being statutory, does not have to be classified as restitutionary damages. Nevertheless the specified measure of recovery is undoubtedly framed in terms of such damages, being based upon the increase in value of the property to the evicting landlord rather than the loss to the evicted tenant. For the statutory action see paras 39-077 and following, below.

70 *Benedetti v Sawiris* [2014] A.C. 938 at [24].

71 [2014] A.C. 938 at [22]–[24].

72 [2001] Restitution Law Review 221 (CA).

73 [2001] Restitution Law Review 221 (CA) at 228.

74 [2001] Restitution Law Review 221 (CA) at 228. See also *Ministry of Defence v Ashman* [1993] 2 E.G.L.R. 102 at 105 (Hoffmann LJ). See also *Ministry of Defence v Thompson* [1993] 2 E.G.L.R. 107.

There has been sporadic recognition in later cases that awards of damages following a trespass can be restitutionary, focusing upon the benefit received by the defendant. For instance, in *Stadium Capital Holdings v St Marylebone Properties Co Plc*,[75] Peter Smith J[76] and Sullivan LJ[77] (Patten LJ agreeing with both) described the award of damages representing the benefit obtained from a trespass as restitutionary. Nevertheless in *Severn Trent Water Ltd v Barnes*,[78] which involved the laying of a water main as a permanent feature by a statutory authority, the Court of Appeal shoehorned the award of the value of the use into compensation for "lost" user or "lost" bargaining opportunity.[79] Recovery was still seen as compensatory rather than restitutionary in the further first instance cases of *Sinclair v Gavaghan*,[80] and *Field Common Ltd v Elmbridge Borough Council*,[81] in both of which the trespass was for a limited period only.[82] **14-021**

*(ii) Wrongful interference involving easements* In *Bracewell v Appleby*,[83] where the defendant had built a house for himself and used the claimants' private road in order to gain access to it, the claimants were awarded damages based upon what would have been payable for the granting of a right of way over the road. In *Carr-Saunders v Dick McNeil Associates*,[84] where the defendants developed their site by building in such a way as to interfere with the claimant's right to light, Millett J considered that he was **14-022**

> "entitled to take account of … the amount of profit which the defendants would look to in the development of their site".[85]

Further infringements of a right to light caused the trial judge in *Deakins v Hookings*,[86] to employ the user principle in assessing the damages, and led to an award based on a substantial proportion of the defendant's profit in *Tamares (Vincent Square) Ltd v Fairpoint Properties (Vincent Square) Ltd*,[87] but without the trial judge expressly taking the restitutionary damages approach. In these cases[88] the defendant is not usually going to be required by mandatory injunction to pull down his building because of economic waste and therefore the damages are based on the assumption that the trespass or nuisance will continue.[89] This differentiates the cases from most of the wrongful user cases dealt with above.

---

75 [2010] EWCA Civ 952 CA.
76 [2010] EWCA Civ 952 CA at [12].
77 [2010] EWCA Civ 952 CA at [17].
78 [2004] 2 E.G.L.R. 95 CA.
79 See the detailed consideration of the case at paras 39-062, below, in a footnote.
80 [2007] EWHC 2256 Ch.
81 [2008] EWHC 2079 Ch.
82 See these two cases at para.39-047, below, in a footnote.
83 [1975] Ch. 408.
84 [1986] 1 W.L.R. 922.
85 [1986] 1 W.L.R. 922 at 931F.
86 [1994] 1 E.G.L.R. 190.
87 [2007] 1 W.L.R. 2167.
88 Detailed at paras 39-061 to 39-063, below.
89 A mandatory injunction was awarded for infringement of an easement of light in *HKRUK II (CHC) Ltd v Heaney* [2010] EWHC 2245 (Ch) but an assessment of damages was also made. This was by the hypothetical licence route with no mention of the restitutionary nature of such awards.

### (b) Wrongful interference with goods

14-023 *(i) Wrongful user* It has long been accepted that if a defendant makes use of the claimant's goods in circumstances where the claimant would not have made use of them himself, the claimant is nevertheless entitled to damages for the tortious use. There are the two familiar classic statements of the Earl of Halsbury and Lord Shaw from the beginning of the last century which speak to this. In *The Mediana*,[90] the Earl of Halsbury envisaged the tortfeasor taking away another's chair for a year and asked rhetorically whether anybody could say that the tortfeasor had a right to diminish the damages by showing that the owner who had plenty of other chairs in the room did not usually sit in the chair taken.[91] Lord Shaw's illustration in *Watson Laidlaw & Co Ltd v Pott, Cassels and Williamson*,[92] moving from chairs to horses, is particularly vivid. He said:

> "If A, being a liveryman, keeps his horse standing idle in the stable, and B, against his wish or without his knowledge, rides or drives it out, it is no answer to A for B to say: 'Against what loss do you want to be restored? I restore the horse. There is no loss. The horse is none the worse; it is the better for the exercise'."[93]

14-024 The award of damages for use often focuses upon the value of the use to the defendant. In those cases the award must be restitutionary. The leading case in this area is *Strand Electric Co v Brisford Entertainments*.[94] There the claimant recovered as damages in detinue the market rate of hire of electrical equipment for the whole period of its tortious detention by the defendant although it was highly unlikely that the claimant, in the absence of its detention, could have hired out all of the equipment for all of the time. Denning LJ said in his forthright and far-sighted way that this was restitution;[95] Somervell and Romer LJJ were content to reserve their opinions as between compensation and restitution.[96] Denning LJ is finally vindicated. Today the award ought now to be regarded as one of restitutionary damages.[97]

14-025 *(ii) Wrongful disposal* Apart from using the claimant's goods, a defendant may dispose of them by sale. It is worth remembering that it has been accepted for over three hundred years, since *Lamine v Dorrell*,[98] that the claimant may claim the price at which the defendant sold. When these cases were decided as part of the form of action for *indebitatus assumpsit* for goods sold it was not necessary to identify the basis upon which the award was made. It was the form which was all important. Today, we can see that the award might be based upon the claimant's loss but it might also be based upon the benefit received by the defendant which is the value of the goods taken. However, if the sale is one that is above the market value of the

---

90 [1900] A.C. 113.

91 [1900] A.C. 113 at 117.

92 (1914) 31 R.P.C. 104 HL.

93 (1914) 31 R.P.C. 104 HL at 119.

94 [1952] 2 Q.B. 246 CA.

95 At para.14-016, above.

96 Details of the case are at para.38-067, below.

97 Loss of so-called user damages were eventually awarded in the long-running *Kuwait Airways Corp v Iraqi Airways Co* [2007] EWHC 1474 (Comm) concerning conversion of aircraft. See the earlier judgments at para.38-071, below.

98 (1705) 2 Ld. Raym. 1216.

goods at the time of conversion, the award of the full value received, including profits, must be explained as either a proprietary award or as disgorgement damages which are considered in the next chapter.

**(c) Wrongful interference with other forms of property** There are also miscellaneous illustrations of wrongful interference involving shares, trademarks, patents and the like. Thus in *Solloway v McLaughlin*,[99] shares of their client, the claimant, were converted by the defendant stockbrokers by selling them but they subsequently bought an equivalent number of shares at a substantially lower price and returned them to the claimant who was still unaware of the conversion. The damages awarded in a later suit could be regarded as restitutionary on the basis that, although the defendant had benefited from the conversion, the claimant had suffered no loss.[100] In *Watson Laidlaw & Co Ltd v Pott, Cassels and Williamson*,[101] Lord Shaw laid down that, to the extent that a claimant whose patent has been infringed has not lost manufacturing profits through the defendant's use of his patent, he should still recover the market value of this use by way of royalty as damages.[102] This again should be seen as a restitutionary recovery. In relation to the analogous infringement of trademarks English authorities were said in earlier editions to be less clear.[103] Today, however, we have the useful decision of Newey J in *32Red Plc v WHG (International) Ltd*[104] awarding damages, although described as the user principle[105] rather than expressly acknowledging the foundation in the benefit gained by the trade mark infringer.[106] The tort of breach of confidence, which may well bring in its train wrongful interference with property rights which results in benefit to the wrongdoer without loss to the victim, has started to make an appearance here, in the Privy Council with *Pell Frischmann Engineering Ltd v Bow Valley Iran Ltd*,[107] and in the Court of Appeal with *Vestergaard Frandsen A/S v Bestnet Europe Ltd*,[108] and *Walsh v Shanahan*.[109] None of the three, however, takes us very far on the damages front as they were concerned with other issues; in *Vestergaared* with a strike out application; in *Walsh* with whether an account of profits should have been allowed; and in *Pell* with whether the Jersey court below had arrived at the correct amount of damages. It is fairly clear that all three courts were thinking of the damages along the lines of the user principle and a hypothetical licence[110] and were not concerned with any restitutionary foundation for these awards. Indeed Lord Walker, giving the speech for the Board in *Pell*, embarked on an extended discussion of how he saw the damages[111] and spoke of damages which exceed the claimant's financial loss as compensatory.[112] 14-026

[99] [1938] A.C. 247 PC.

[100] See the case at para.38-014, below.

[101] (1914) 31 R.P.C. 104 HL.

[102] See the case at para.48-044, below.

[103] Hence an Australian decision, *Colbeam Palmer v Stock Affiliates Pty* (1968) 122 C.L.R. 25, was cited as a good illustration of the recovery of damages in a restitutionary context.

[104] [2013] EWHC 815 Ch.

[105] For which see para.14-008, above.

[106] See the case further at para.48-051, below.

[107] [2011] 1 W.L.R. 2370.

[108] [2013] EWCA Civ 428 CA.

[109] [2013] EWCA Civ 411 CA.

[110] For which see para.14-008, above.

[111] [2011] 1 W.R.R. 2370 at [46]–[54].

[112] [2011] 1 W.R.R. 2370 at [46(1)].

## (2) Other torts

**14-027** The root of the error which sought to confine restitutionary damages to "proprietary torts" comes from *Stoke-on-Trent City Council v W. & J. Wass Ltd.*[113] In that case, the claimant council's right to hold a retail market within the council's area was infringed by the defendant deliberately holding a market within a few miles. An injunction was awarded to prevent further infringement but because the claimant had suffered no loss to its own market the Court of Appeal awarded only nominal damages, reversing Peter Gibson J below who had awarded damages calculated by the licence fee the claimant could have exacted for permission to operate the market. The decision of the Court of Appeal has been universally condemned by commentators. Nourse LJ at the conclusion of his judgment said this:

> "It is possible that the law of tort, more especially of the so-called 'proprietary torts', will in due course make a more deliberate move towards recovery based not on loss suffered by the plaintiff but on the unjust enrichment of the defendant ... But I do not think that that process can begin in this case and I doubt whether it can begin at all at this level of decision."[114]

**14-028** One major development was the decision of the Court of Appeal in *Devenish Nutrition Ltd v Sanofi Aventis SA.*[115] The tort in *Devenish* was breach of statutory duty, the breach being of competition law in which English domestic law and European Community law are interwoven.[116] Large vitamin manufacturing companies had entered into worldwide cartels designed to raise prices unlawfully. Many to whom vitamin products had been supplied joined together in this action claiming repayment of the illegal over-charges to which they had been subjected, over-charges which they had passed on to their own sub-buyers so that loss was going to be difficult or impossible for them to prove. Their claim was rejected by the Court of Appeal, affirming Lewison J below. The central reason for the rejection was this. *Wass* was taken by the majority, Arden and Tuckey LJJ, to have decided that a restitutionary award was not available for a non-proprietary tort and *Wass* had to be followed as the court was of course bound by its own decision.[117] Only the third member of the court, Longmore LJ, took the view that *Wass* was not authority for confining the restitutionary remedy to tortious claims for breach of a proprietary right.[118] Arden LJ does remark in her judgment that the statutory right of the council in *Wass* to license markets in a particular area may well have been a property right by way of incorporeal hereditament.[119] But all three members of the Court of Appeal in *Devenish* undoubtedly regarded *Wass* as dealing with a non-proprietary tort, and then holding by a majority that a restitutionary award for a non-proprietary tort was thereby precluded. This was quite enough to put paid to the claim in *Devenish* for no proprietary tort could possibly be made out.

---

113 [1988] 1 W.L.R. 1406 CA.

114 [1988] 1 W.L.R. 1406 CA at 1415H.

115 [2009] Ch. 390 CA at 429.

116 We need not concern ourselves with the Community law issues.

117 See Arden LJ at [2009] Ch. 390 CA at [70] and [75], Tuckey LJ at [155]. They rightly held that *Wass* could stand with, and was not overruled by, *Attorney General v Blake* [2001] 1 A.C. 268, pointing out that *Wass* had not even been cited in *Blake*. After all it concerned contract and not tort.

118 [2009] Ch.390 CA at 429 at [144].

119 [2009] Ch.390 CA at [70]. It may be that in *Wass* Nourse LJ himself thought that he was dealing with a proprietary tort: see the opening of the citation from his judgment there at para.14-027, above.

Nonetheless the decision in *Devenish* itself is clearly correct, and to be commended, but for somewhat different reasons. In the first place, the claimants were not asking for restitutionary damages from the defendants; they were claiming an account of profits, which as we have seen is a very different thing.[120] Although calling the remedy claimed a restitutionary award, what the claimants sought to recover was the whole of the surplus profit illegitimately made by the defendants. As we will see in the next chapter, an account of profits, or disgorgement damages, should not have been available. Therefore, quite apart from whether *Wass* lay in the way of the Court of Appeal's holding for the claimants, the claimants must still fail. In the second place, and perhaps more controversially, had the claim been limited to one for restitutionary damages, the fact that the claimants had passed down the artificially high prices paid by them to their sub-buyers sufficed to lose them their claim. Longmore LJ put the point tellingly when he said,[121] in words with which Tuckey LJ specifically agreed[122]: **14-029**

> "Neither the law of restitution nor the law of damages is in the business of transferring monetary gains from one undeserving recipient to another undeserving recipient even if the former has acted illegally and the other has not."

While the decision stands in *Wass*[123] that no award of restitutionary damages can be made for the infringement of the right to hold a market, and with it its extension in *Devenish*,[124] banning restitutionary damages for all non-proprietary torts, there is little or no chance that such awards can even be contemplated where it is a non-proprietary right that has been infringed.[125] Yet since a new start has been made in this area of the law,[126] things ought to be different. **14-030**

There continue to be cases where an award which might be explained as restitutionary damages but in which courts nevertheless jump through difficult verbal hoops to give some other explanation for the award. An example which recurs is where there is an infringement of privacy but the claimant suffers no distress or other subjective loss nor any financial loss. In *Representative Claimants (Gulati) v MGN Ltd*,[127] substantial awards of damages were made against MGN Limited, the proprietor of the *Daily Mirror*, *The Sunday People* and *The Sunday Mirror* newspapers for the misuse of private information by "hacking" of telephone messages. The Court of Appeal held that the damages were independent of any distress or financial loss by the claimant and were not made to "vindicate" any right. Instead the award was made **14-031**

> "to compensate for the loss or diminution of a right to control formerly private information and for the distress that the respondents could justifiably have felt because their private information had been exploited".

---

[120] See paras 14-013 to 14-015, above.

[121] [2009] Ch.390 CA at [146].

[122] [2009] Ch.390 CA at [157].

[123] [1988] 1 W.L.R. 1406 CA. See *Wass* at para.14-027, above.

[124] [2009] Ch.390 CA at 429. See *Devenish* at paras 14-028 to 14-029, above.

[125] See also the successful strike out in *Shaw v Medtronic Corevalve LLC* [2017] EWHC 54 (QB) at [31].

[126] Mance LJ's words in *Experience Hendrix v PPX Enterprises Inc* [2003] 1 All E.R. (Comm) 830 CA: see at para.14-045, below.

[127] [2015] EWCA Civ 1291.

The reference to a "lost right of control" was not to a consequence with any assessed effect on the claimant. The justification for an award of damages for the claimant's "lost right to control private information", on a basis independently of any consequence suffered by the claimant, and not as an award of the now-rejected vindicatory damages, is that it is an award of restitutionary damages, representing the benefit that the defendant derived from the wrongdoing. In other words, the defendant wrongfully obtained the opportunity to use information without paying for that opportunity. It is elementary justice that the defendant should have to pay the reasonable price for that opportunity, in addition to an award for the distress to the claimant. Understanding the restitutionary nature of the award will also aid the court in quantifying how the damages can be calculated. For instance, it easily explains why the Court of Appeal rightly accepted that the amount awarded would be affected if the information had become public knowledge anyway.[128] As Mance LJ said in *Experience Hendrix LLC v PPX Enterprises Inc*,[129]

> "the law gives effect to the instinctive reaction that, whether or not the appellant would have been better off if the wrong had not been committed, the wrongdoer ought not to gain an advantage for free, and should make some reasonable recompense."

Similar sentiments were expressed by the primary judge, Mann J, in *Gulati* who said that

> "the defendant will have helped itself, over an extended period of time, to large amounts of personal and private information and treated it as its own to deal with as it thought fit".[130]

This also explains why matters such as (i) the scale of the disclosure and (ii) whether the information would have become public anyway are relevant matters[131] in the assessment of the damages for infringement of the right, irrespective of the consequences suffered. Those matters are concerned with the extent of the advantage obtained by the defendants.

### (3) Equitable wrongs

**14-032** In the preface to this book it was explained that the process of integrating equitable money awards together with common law money awards would take several editions of this book. It is, however, important to mention that restitutionary awards are not confined to common law torts. This provides a further reason why they should not be artificially confined to a category of "proprietary torts".

**14-033** A good example is the equitable wrong of breach of confidence. Most recently, in *Marathon Asset Management LLP v Seddon*,[132] an award of restitutionary damages was considered for a breach of confidence and breach of contract. Two former employees of the claimant (Marathon) had joined a rival firm. Before they departed, they copied many of Marathon's confidential electronic files. One of them, Mr Seddon, helped copy some files which were never subsequently accessed. The other, Mr Bridgeman, unlawfully copied and removed many files and made use of a few

---

[128] [2016] EWHC 294 (Ch) at [45].
[129] [2003] EWCA Civ 323 at [26].
[130] *Gulati v MGN Ltd* [2015] EWHC 1482 (Ch) at [132].
[131] [2003] EWCA Civ 323 at [46].
[132] [2017] EWHC 300 (Comm).

of them. Both acted in breach of confidence and in breach of contract. Marathon suffered no loss. Nevertheless Marathon submitted that it was entitled to £15 million in damages as licence fee damages. In a highly discerning observation, the trial judge, Leggatt J said that the damages could be described as restitutionary

> "if this label is used loosely to refer to an award of money which is assessed by valuing a gain made by the defendant – rather than by valuing a loss suffered by the claimant – from the defendant's wrongful act".[133]

In this case, that gain was made by the employees because they obtained the use of the information without paying a price for it. The trial judge assessed the value of that gain at a nominal amount. That process of assessment in the case was criticised above.[134]

## 2. LIABILITY IN CONTRACT

### (1) Three key authorities

The starting point, and often the end point, in cases of restitutionary damages for breach of contract is the decision in *Wrotham Park Estate Co v Parkside Homes*.[135] In *Attorney General v Blake*,[136] a case considered in the next chapter concerning disgorgement of profits rather than restitutionary damages, Lord Nicholls said that *Wrotham Park*, **14-034**

> "still shines, rather as a solitary beacon, showing that in contract as well as tort damages are not always narrowly confined to recoupment of financial loss".[137]

Later, in his speech in *Sempra Metals Ltd v Inland Revenue Commissioners*,[138] Lord Nicholls (with whom Lord Walker generally agreed) repeated observations he had made earlier in his leading speech in *Kuwait Airways Corp v Iraqi Airways Co (No.6)*[139] that *Wrotham Park* damages are "instances of restitution for wrongdoing as distinct from restitution for unjust enrichment".

The new possibilities opened up by observations in *Blake* in the House of Lords were seized upon and have been developed by the Vice-Chancellor in *Esso Petroleum Co Ltd v Niad Ltd*,[140] and the Court of Appeal in *Experience Hendrix v PPX Enterprises Inc*.[141] Hence we now have three leading cases of awards, in cases factually very different from each other, providing guidance as to the scope and ambit of contractual restitutionary damages. **14-035**

---

133 [2017] EWHC 300 (Comm) at [199].
134 See para.14-010, above.
135 [1974] 1 W.L.R. 798.
136 [2001] 1 A.C. 268.
137 [2001] 1 A.C. 268 at 283H. Lord Walker in *Pell Frischmann Engineering Ltd v Bow Valley Iran Ltd* [2011] 1 W.L.R. 2370 PC failed to understand why Lord Nicholls had referred to *Wrotham Park* as a "solitary beacon", which he said he found "a little surprising": at [48(3)].
138 *Sempra Metals Ltd v Inland Revenue Commissioners* [2008] 1 A.C. 561 at [116].
139 [2002] 2 A.C. 883.
140 [2001] EWHC Ch 458.
141 [2003] 1 All E.R. (Comm) 830 CA.

14-036 **(i) Wrotham Park Estate Co v Parkside Homes**[142] An owner of land sold part of it to a developer. The developer covenanted with the seller and his assignees that he and his successors in title would observe and perform certain covenants restricting the buyer's right to develop the land for building purposes other than in strict accordance with a lay-out plan approved by the seller. The defendants, who were successors in title to the buyer built houses on the purchased land in breach of this restrictive covenant, and the claimants, who had succeeded to a part of the land retained by the seller for the benefit of which the restrictive covenant had been taken, sued for a mandatory injunction seeking demolition of the houses erected and for damages. The injunction was refused because removal of the houses would constitute unpardonable economic waste and the question arose as to whether the award of damages should be nominal, as the defendants contended, because the value of the land, as the claimants accepted, was not reduced in value by the erection of the houses.

14-037 Brightman J regarded this contention as leading to a result of questionable fairness. He asked rhetorically whether

> "it was just that the plaintiffs should receive no compensation and that the defendants should be left in undisturbed possession of the fruits of their wrongdoing"[143]

and proceeded to award as damages in lieu of a mandatory injunction "such a sum of money as might reasonably have been demanded … as a quid pro quo for relaxing the covenant".[144] Although Brightman J described this measure of damages as representing compensation much of his discussion revealed a restitutionary focus. For instance, Brightman J asked whether "the defendants should be left in undisturbed possession of the fruits of their wrongdoing".[145] He compared the recovery with a wayleave award which, as we have seen,[146] is a restitutionary award. And he relied upon the decision of Denning LJ in *Strand Electric Co v Brisford Entertainments*, which imposed reasonable user damages where a wrongdoer had the use of goods for his own purposes. In the light of *Attorney General v Blake*,[147] and *Experience Hendrix v PPX Enterprises Inc*,[148] now to be considered, and of the analysis of *Wrotham Park* in these cases, it should be regarded, together with the tort cases of a similar nature discussed above, as presenting a restitutionary award.

14-038 **(ii) Esso Petroleum Co Ltd v Niad Ltd**[149] In this case, Niad contracted with Esso to sell fuel at daily prices set by Esso in order to match the prices of competitors. In exchange for selling fuel at these low prices, Esso gave Niad financial "price support". Despite claiming the price support under the contract, in breach of contract Niad sold fuel at prices above those set by Esso. However, accepting that proof of lost sales "would not be easy",[150] Esso focussed upon claims for (1) an account of profits as a remedy for the breaches of contract by Niad; and

---

142 [1974] 1 W.L.R. 798.
143 [1974] 1 W.L.R. 79 at 812H.
144 [1974] 1 W.L.R. 79 at 815D.
145 [1974] 1 W.L.R. 79 at 812.
146 Above at para.14-019.
147 [2001] 1 A.C. 268.
148 [2003] 1 All E.R. (Comm) 830 CA.
149 [2001] EWHC Ch 458.
150 [2001] EWHC Ch 458 at [56].

(2) a restitutionary remedy requiring Niad to pay to Esso the amount by which the actual prices charged to customers exceeded the recommended prices.[151] The Vice-Chancellor held that Esso was entitled to both of these remedies and could elect for whichever was the greater. The first remedy, requiring disgorgement of profits, is considered in the next chapter. As for the restitutionary remedy for the breach of contract, although the Vice-Chancellor in *Esso* spoke in terms of unjust enrichment, it is clear that the remedy was imposed for the breach of contract rather than as an action for unjust enrichment based upon, for example, mistake or duress. The Vice-Chancellor said that

> "it appears to me to be the most appropriate remedy in that it matches most closely the reality of the case, namely that Niad took an extra benefit to which it was not entitled."[152]

**(iii) Experience Hendrix v PPX Enterprises Inc**[153] In 1965 the defendants entered into a contract with a rising singer guitarist for him to play and sing exclusively for the defendants. Under the contract the singer guitarist was to receive a very paltry royalty return. He died young a few years later. The defendants sued him, and after his death his estate, for breach of contract. The defendants were met with the formidable defence that the contract was invalid as unconscionable and in restraint of trade. The trial of the action commenced, but after three weeks the defendants, on advice, settled. The settlement agreement dealt with the master titles from which recordings were made. It entitled the defendants to perform existing contractual commitments by way of licence relating to the various masters. For one group of masters, 33 in number, it was provided that existing licences would continue but that in respect of any further licences or extensions of existing licences the estate would be entitled to royalty returns much improved on what had been provided by the original contract. But for a second group of masters, 63 in number, it was provided that no further licences or extensions or renewals of licences were to be granted without consent.[154] The defendants committed deliberate breaches of the settlement agreement in 1995, and again in 1999, by granting licences in respect of 39 master recordings in the second group. From these licences they made substantial profits. In 2001 the claimant, a company effectively owned by the sole beneficiary of the singer guitarist's estate and the assignee of the benefit of the settlement agreement, sued in respect of these breaches for an injunction, damages and an account of profits. 14-039

The trial judge granted an injunction against further licensing of masters of the titles in the second group. But the trial judge dismissed the claimant's claims for damages and for an account of profits, it being conceded that the claimant was unable to show that it had suffered any financial loss as a result of these licensings in breach of contract. On the claimant's appeal against the dismissal of these claims the Court of Appeal decided that the case was not sufficiently exceptional for an account of profits to be appropriate but that the defendant should be required by way of damages to make a reasonable payment for its use of masters in breach of the settlement agreement. The case was, said Peter Gibson LJ, 14-040

151 [2001] EWHC Ch 458 at [58].
152 [2001] EWHC Ch 458 at [64].
153 [2003] 1 All E.R. (Comm) 830 CA.
154 There was a third group of masters, 19 in number, which should have been destroyed by the defendants but nothing turned upon the defendants' failure to destroy them.

"a suitable one ... in which damages for breach of contract may be measured by the benefits gained by the wrongdoer from the breach".[155]

## (2) The later retrograde authority

**14-041** The decision of the Court of Appeal in *WWF World Life Fund for Nature v World Wrestling Federation Entertainment Inc*,[156] was brought about and made complicated largely by the claimant's procedural mismanagement of its claim. The claimant and the defendant had the same initials, WWF. The initials as used by the claimant, the World Wide Fund for Nature, were already extremely well known across the world before the defendant, the World Wrestling Federation, started to use them. This use led to various trade mark proceedings until a settlement agreement was reached containing restrictions on the use of the initials by the defendant. The defendant breached the settlement agreement making profits for itself but without causing any provable loss to the claimant initials holder. The claimant started proceedings for an injunction to enforce the settlement agreement and for damages to be assessed, the basis of its claim for damages not being specified. Application was made for summary judgment and at the hearing of the application the claimant sought to amend by adding a claim for an account and disgorgement of the defendant's profits made by its breach of contract. The application for summary judgment succeeded with an injunction granted and an enquiry as to damages directed, but the application to amend was refused as the case was not of the exceptional nature that *Attorney General v Blake*,[157] had held was required for an account and disgorgement of profits.[158] The claimant in its pleadings, which were not to appear for another three years, claimed damages by way of reasonable licence fee for relaxing its rights under the settlement agreement, damages which throughout the case were referred to as damages on the *Wrotham Park* basis or simply as *Wrotham Park* damages.[159]

**14-042** In the Court of Appeal the defendant's primary contention was that the remedy by way of *Wrotham Park* damages was essentially the same as the remedy by way of an account of profits, both being referred to as gain-based, and that, the claimant's disentitlement to claim such gain-based relief having already been determined with the refusal of the amendment seeking an account, the claimant was not entitled to raise the matter again. This argument required the Court of Appeal to examine the juridical basis of an award of *Wrotham Park* damages and Chadwick LJ, who gave the only reasoned judgment, erroneously concluded after a most extensive review of the authorities[160] that both restitutionary damages and disgorgement damages (an account of profits) were to be regarded as compensatory remedies. The defendant's primary contention was therefore not made out but it had an alternative contention, namely, that for a variety of reasons it would be an abuse of process to allow the claimant to claim *Wrotham Park* damages. The Court of Appeal agreed and struck out the claim.

---

155 [2003] 1 All E.R. (Comm) 830 CA at [58].
156 [2008] 1 W.L.R. 445 CA.
157 [2001] 1 A.C. 268.
158 See para.15-006, below. See further the discussion of *Blake* at para.15-009, below.
159 See *Wrotham Park* at para.14-036, above.
160 Running from [2008] 1 W.L.R. 445 CA at [25]–[56].

A second difficult case is *Garner v One-Step (Support) Ltd*.[161] That case involved deliberate breaches of non-compete and non-solicitation covenants in the sale of a business providing "supported living" services. The primary judge allowed the claimants to elect for *Wrotham Park* damages instead of damages for financial loss. The appellants argued that *Wrotham Park* damages can only be awarded (i) where the injured party is unable to demonstrate identifiable financial loss; and (ii) where to do so is necessary to avoid manifest injustice. The Court of Appeal rejected these submissions. Christopher Clarke LJ (with whom Longmore and King LJJ agreed) held that the absence of financial loss was not a precondition for the award of *Wrotham Park* damages.[162] The ultimate question was said to be whether these damages are a just response and since the just response is, quintessentially, a matter for the judge to decide, in the absence of any error of principle the decision of the primary judge could not be overturned.[163] **14-043**

This approach, while an improvement from *WWF*, still leaves some difficulty. First, it is difficult to see why *Wrotham Park* damages, when based on a defendant's gain, should be any more discretionary than damages based upon a claimant's loss. Secondly, Christopher Clarke and Longmore LJJ saw the remedy as an exceptional form of compensatory award which does not require proof of loss. But it is hard to see why it should be exceptional for a defendant to pay the reasonable value of a benefit that he or she has wrongfully acquired. It should certainly be no more exceptional to require a defendant to pay the reasonable value of a benefit *wrongfully* acquired than it is for a defendant to pay the reasonable value of a benefit acquired without wrongdoing but by unjust enrichment. The reason why the remedy for wrongdoing was thought to be exceptional was because, as Christopher Clarke LJ said,[164] the damages were characterised in *WWF* as *both* "a juridically highly similar remedy to the relief" of an account of profits (where exceptional circumstances are required) and a compensatory remedy. Both of those statements cannot be true. An account of profits requires the calculation and disgorgement of a *defendant's* profits. A compensatory remedy is concerned with a claimant's loss unless compensation is used in a wholly generic sense simply meaning a money award. The reason why *Wrotham Park* damages have some juridical similarity to the account of profits is because they are not compensatory for loss. However, unlike an account and disgorgement of all actual profits made, they focus on the reasonable value of the benefit immediately received by the defendant at the claimant's expense. Disgorgement of profits, as we will see in the next chapter, requires a need for deterrence. Since the rationale and operation of restitutionary damages is quite different from disgorgement of profits there is no reason why the same requirement for exceptional circumstances should exist. **14-044**

Although the decision in *Garner* has attempted to reclaim some territory, the *WWF* decision turned the clock back, attempting to bring the development of restitutionary damages to a complete halt. It contained much dubious reasoning. Doubtless Chadwick LJ had ample support in the cases pre-*Blake* for regarding *Wrotham Park* damages as compensatory, since in the days before restitutionary damages had arrived it was quite natural to seek a compensatory rationale, though not everyone, as we have seen, had done so. But with the clarity that came from **14-045**

[161] [2016] EWCA Civ 180.
[162] [2016] EWCA Civ 180 at [118].
[163] [2016] EWCA Civ 180 at [121].
[164] [2016] EWCA Civ 180 at [106].

*Blake*, followed by *Experience Hendrix v PPX Enterprises Inc*,[165] everything has changed. As Mance LJ said of *Blake* in *Experience Hendrix*, it marked a new start in this area of the law[166] and freed the court from some constraints that prior authority would have imposed. Chadwick LJ's claim that the essentially compensatory nature of *Wrotham Park* damages was endorsed by *Blake* is peculiar in the light of Lord Nicholls, with whom the majority concurred, calling *Wrotham Park* a solitary beacon showing that damages for breach of contract may be measured by the benefit gained by the wrongdoer.[167] Chadwick LJ maintained that this endorsement appears most clearly in a passage from Lord Hobhouse's speech but then Lord Hobhouse was dissenting; he was the sole dissenter. And Chadwick LJ's suggestion that the underlying feature of an account and disgorgement of profits, given in *Blake*, is the need to compensate the claimant is even more peculiar, for it is common knowledge that an account is ordered precisely to strip away profits. He then proposed also to explain *Experience Hendrix* as based on compensation; yet this view hardly accords with the judgments in that case. Not only is Mance LJ, in the leading judgment, concentrating on benefit, but we also find Peter Gibson LJ describing the case as a suitable one for damages for breach of contract to be "measured by the benefits gained by the wrongdoer from the breach".[168] One approach that might be taken, as Leggatt J did in *Marathon Asset Management LLP v Seddon*,[169] is to describe "compensatory" damages as simply meaning "any remedy which is awarded as a response to a wrong done to the claimant". But very great care should be taken with such use of "compensation". Since "damages" are a money award for wrongdoing, the adjective "compensatory" is both redundant and, with its close association with loss, potentially misleading. Another approach is to recognise that *Wrotham Park* damages are not necessarily always restitutionary. The damages might sometimes genuinely compensate for loss. The best approach is that where these damages are awarded for the benefit obtained by the defendant then it should be acknowledged that they are gain-based, and restitutionary.[170]

### (3) Reasonable user fee awards need not always be restitutionary

**14-046** In *Attorney General v Blake*,[171] Lord Nicholls viewed *Wrotham Park Estate Co v Parkside Homes Ltd*,[172] as a solitary beacon lighting the way to an acceptance of damages in contract based upon gain.[173] However, the obvious difficulty with a label such as *Wrotham Park* damages is that it reveals nothing of the nature of the damages. At its narrowest, and ignoring the restitutionary nature of much of Brightman J's reasoning, the award in that case represented a money order for payment of a reasonable sum. In the sense of "reasonable fee damages" then they need not always be restitutionary. Sometimes the same award might be made as a different type of damages. In *Van der Garde v Force India Formula One Team Ltd*,[174] Stadlen

165 [2003] 1 All E.R. (Comm) 830 CA.
166 [2003] 1 All E.R. (Comm) 830 CA at [16].
167 At para.14-034, above.
168 At para.14-040, above.
169 [2017] EWHC 300 (Comm) at [200].
170 See *Vanden Recycling Ltd v Kras Recycling BV* [2017] EWCA Civ 354 at [60].
171 [2001] 1 A.C. 268.
172 [1974] 1 W.L.R. 798.
173 See para.14-034, above.
174 [2010] EWHC 2373 (QB). Facts at para.3-010, above.

J made an award of what he called *Wrotham Park* damages based on the value of the kilometres of driving that the defendant had in breach of contract not allowed to the claimant racing driver, this breach being by way of a short delivery of services and so a form of skimped performance. Stadlen J considered that there was nothing in the authorities to prevent such an award for this breach of contract[175] but the case was one which was inappropriate for his so-called *Wrotham Park* damages, which constituted the claimants' secondary claim for damages, as he had already acceded to their primary claim, awarding them the same amount of $1,865,000 by way of straightforward compensatory damages.[176] Indeed, he upheld this secondary claim just in case he had gone wrong with the primary claim,[177] which it is believed he had not. In the sense in which they were described in *Van der Garde*, the *Wrotham Park* damages were genuinely compensatory for loss in the sense of the normal value of adverse consequences. The breach of contract by the defendant had meant that the claimant had not received the promised services. The compensation represented the money value of the lost performance.

The *Wrotham Park* case has been relied upon in contexts other than *Van der* **14-047**
*Garde* where the award is also one to compensate for loss suffered by adverse consequences to the claimant. In each case it should be necessary to identify the adverse consequence to the claimant and to value it. Most of the cases in this area do little more than assess the amount that a reasonable purchaser would have agreed with a reasonable seller of the relevant right. That simple exercise is usually restitutionary because it measures the benefit received by the defendant by obtaining the relevant use without paying for it. Many of these various cases are fully documented when dealing with sale of land.[178] They can be summarised briefly here. Prior to *Blake*, the Court of Appeal had already on two occasions arrived at this result in the context of restrictive covenants, in *Jaggard v Sawyer*,[179] and again in *Gaffard v Graham*.[180] And in a case subsequent to *Blake*, *Amec Development Ltd v Jury's Hotel Management (UK) Ltd*,[181] the parties agreed in the light of the earlier authorities that damages should be payable where again the breach of a restrictive covenant by building had caused no loss to the claimant. However, the insistence in *Jaggard* that *Wrotham Park* is to be explained on a compensatory basis rather than a restitutionary basis should no longer be acceptable without explanation and valuation of the adverse consequence said to be suffered by the claimant. Yet *Lane v O'Brien Homes*,[182] a further decision after *Blake* following and applying *Wrotham Park*, still tended to look at the damages awarded as compensatory, as being for the loss of a bargaining opportunity although, as the potential of the property was not fully appreciated at the time of contracting, the award is much more simply explained along restitutionary lines.[183] Finally, in *Kettel v Bloomfold Ltd*,[184] a lessor of flats that had granted to its lessees easements of designated car parking spaces

---

175 See the exhaustive, and exhausting, consideration of the authorities from [2010] EWHC 2373 (QB) at [509]–[539].
176 See at para.3-011, above.
177 [2010] EWHC 2373 (QB) at [499].
178 At paras 27-053 to 27-058, below.
179 [1995] 1 W.L.R. 269 CA.
180 (1999) 77 P. & C.R. 73 CA.
181 [2001] 1 E.G.L.R. 81.
182 [2004] EWHC 303 Q.B.
183 See this aspect of *Lane* at para.27-057, below.
184 [2012] EWHC 1422 (Ch).

sought to develop the property by building further flats on the car parking spaces. The lessor made alternative car parking spaces available to the lessees, so that they could be said not to have suffered any loss. The trial judge held the lessees entitled to an injunction preventing the lessor from building but, in case the matter went further and he was held wrong to have granted an injunction, he indicated what damages he would have awarded in lieu. Relying principally on the modern trespass to land cases giving, in effect, restitutionary damages,[185] he would have awarded, in the absence of an injunction, damages on the hypothetical licence fee basis. These he would have assessed at half the value generated by the lessor's development after making an allowance for developer's profit.

**14-048** The controversial decision in *Surrey County Council v Bredero Homes*[186] now stands against this incoming tide of recovery and the decision, poorly received from the start,[187] has effectively been said to be wrong by their Lordships in *Blake*.[188] Mance LJ in *Experience Hendrix v PPX Enterprises Inc*,[189] was rightly of the view that, as he put it in the Court of Appeal,

> "*Blake* ... freed us from some constraints that prior authority in this court (particularly *Surrey County Council v Bredero Homes Ltd* and some of the reasoning in *Jaggard v Sawyer*) would have imposed".[190]

In other words, damages are recoverable in all cases of this type and the damages recoverable can be restitutionary.

## (4) The alternative of injunctive relief

**14-049** In a good number of cases injunctive relief may be available to the claimant and, to the extent that he obtains such relief, the prospective benefit will be removed from the defendant and restitutionary damages, at least for that removed benefit, will not be required. However, the existence of injunctive relief has from time to time been used to argue for greater limitations upon the availability of restitutionary damages than are required. In this connection two particular points should be noted.

**14-050** The granting of a mandatory injunction to remove the benefit from the defendant for the future does not, as was argued in *Experience Hendrix v PPX Enterprises Inc*,[191] preclude an award of restitutionary damages in respect of the past benefit. Thus, to take the illustration given in that case of a restrictive covenant not to use land for a noisy concert breached while the landowner is away, he will be entitled not only to an injunction to prevent repetition but also to restitutionary damages to recover for the financial benefit already obtained by the neighbouring landowner.[192] *Experience Hendrix* was itself a case where an injunction was granted together with restitutionary damages.

**14-051** The fact that injunctive relief has not been claimed when it was available should not preclude a claim for restitutionary damages. Millett LJ's attempt in *Jaggard v*

---

[185] Cases at para.14-019, above.
[186] [1993] 1 W.L.R. 1361 CA.
[187] There is a tide of academic criticism.
[188] For details, see para.27-058, below; facts at para.27-054, below.
[189] [2003] 1 All E.R. (Comm) 830 CA.
[190] [2003] 1 All E.R. (Comm) 830 CA at [16].
[191] [2003] 1 All E.R. (Comm) 830 CA.
[192] [2003] 1 All E.R. (Comm) 830 CA at [35].

*Sawyer*[193] to explain *Surrey County Council v Bredero*[194] on the ground that damages were refused because the claimant had not sought an injunction when it could have had one is misconceived.[195] Not only is there no sign of such reasoning in *Bredero* but the decision itself is now thought to be wrong;[196] Millett LJ was no doubt trying to justify it but for the wrong reason.[197] However, a failure on the part of the claimant to pursue the injunctive route when it was available to him might sometimes be relevant to the amount of damages to be awarded to the claimant since the process of assessment of the price that a reasonable defendant would be required to pay is one which considers all the circumstances. Thus, Brightman J in *Wrotham Park Estate Co v Parkside Homes*[198] said that his award was conservative because of the claimant's failure to warn the developer defendant in advance that no consent to the development would be forthcoming.

[193] [1995] 1 W.L.R. 269 CA.

[194] [1993] 1 W.L.R. 1361 CA.

[195] See the quotation from his judgment at para.27-054, below.

[196] See para.14-048, above.

[197] *Harris v Williams-Wynne* [2006] 2 P. & C.R. 27 CA at 595 is a somewhat confusing decision where damages, which were essentially restitutionary but not so-called, were awarded in equity under Lord Cairns' Act since injunctive relief would have been available. It was stated that resort to equity was necessary as no claim at law was possible in the absence of loss to the claimant (at [27]) but in today's thinking this must surely be wrong. At the same time it was suggested that it may be necessary to consider eliminating differences between claims at law and claims in equity in this area: at [50].

[198] [1974] 1 W.L.R 798 at 815H to 816A.

## CHAPTER 15

# DISGORGEMENT DAMAGES (ACCOUNT OF PROFITS)

TABLE OF CONTENTS



## I. CONCEPT AND MEANING OF DISGORGEMENT DAMAGES

**15-001** The previous chapter was concerned with "restitutionary damages". Those damages are not based upon loss to the claimant. They are based upon a benefit received by the defendant that was obtained at the expense of the claimant. As we saw, restitutionary damages are the same remedy for a wrong as restitution is for unjust enrichment. However, there is another, different, money award based on the gain to the defendant. That award, well-known for centuries in equity as the award following an account of profits, is the disgorgement of all of a defendant's net profits of wrongdoing. Although it is common to refer to an "account of profits" to describe this profit-stripping award for wrongdoing, this is misleading in two senses. The first misleading aspect arises because the account of profits is an equitable remedy. This can suggest that disgorgement of profits is only available in equity. This is incorrect. The second misleading aspect is because the process of accounting is distinct from the disgorgement order stripping the profits. Yet, it is common usage for the term "account of profits" to describe both the process of accounting and the disgorgement of profits found by that account. In this book, the term "disgorgement damages" is preferred for two reasons. First, it emphasises that, like other damages awards, the money award is given for wrongdoing. Secondly, the label is an apt description of the effect of the remedy: it is not a remedy to compensate, nor is it to make restitution, nor is it to punish. Its effect is to disgorge profits.

Disgorgement damages are a different award from restitutionary damages. In *Harris v Digital Pulse Pty Ltd*,[1] the distinguished former Australian judge, Heydon JA (then a judge of the New South Wales Court of Appeal), said that **15-002**

> "the rules relating to an account of profits are not restitutionary in the sense that they do not rest on giving back something which the plaintiff had".

Similarly, Romaine J said in *Maximum Financial Services Inc v 1144517 Alberta Ltd*[2] that disgorgement

> "relief is not available in an action in unjust enrichment, but only if [the defendant] is liable for a civil wrong, and an order requiring it to give up its wrongfully-obtained gains is appropriate".

The epithet "disgorgement"[3] or, to be consistent with any coherent definition of damages, "disgorgement damages",[4] is the appropriate label to describe profit-stripping damages awards for wrongdoing. Indeed, in the leading speech in the House of Lords in the profit-stripping case of *Attorney General v Blake*,[5] Lord Nicholls preferred "to avoid the unhappy expression 'restitutionary damages'"[6] while Lord Steyn spoke of "disgorgement".[7] Lord Millett also emphasised extrajudicially the importance of distinguishing between restitutionary damages and disgorgement damages or, as he described the awards, restitution and disgorgement:

> "[Separating restitution and disgorgement for wrongs] is a valuable insight. Its particular value is that it not only distinguishes between two different categories of gain-based damages, but that it brings out the possibility of concurrent liability [restitution for unjust enrichment and restitution for wrongs] in cases where there has been a transfer of value."[8]

In summary, an award of disgorgement damages (which follows any account that is taken of profits) strips the defendant's profits, irrespective of their source. But a personal award of restitution for unjust enrichment is, in loose terms, "concerned with giving back to someone something that has been taken from them".[9]

---

1 (2003) 56 N.S.W.L.R. 298 at [414].

2 [2015] A.B.Q.B. 646 at [84]. See also *Indutech Canada Ltd v Gibbs Pipe Distributors Ltd* [2011] A.B.Q.B. 38 at [512].

3 *Attorney General v Blake* [2001] 1 A.C. 268 HL at 291–292; *United Pan-Europe Communications NV v Deutsche Bank AG* [2000] 2 B.C.L.C. 461 (CA) at [44]; *Kuwait Airways Corp v Iraqi Airways Co* [2004] EWHC 2603 at [387]; *Westminster City Council v Porter* [2002] EWHC 2179 at [3]; *Mahonia Ltd v JP Morgan Chase Bank (No.2)* [2004] EWHC 1938 at [223]; *Harris v Digital Pulse Pty Ltd* (2003) 56 N.S.W.L.R. 298 at [362], [380], [404], [407]; *Dubai Aluminium Co Ltd v Salaam* [2002] UKHL 48 at [50], [53], [62], per Lord Nicholls, and paras [80], [81], [151]–[167], per Lord Millett.

4 *Hospitality Group Pty Ltd v Australian Rugby Union Ltd* (2001) 110 F.C.R. 157 at [159], per Hill and Finkelstein JJ.

5 [2001] 1 A.C. 268.

6 [2001] 1 A.C. 268 at 284H.

7 [2001] 1 A.C. 268 at 291–292.

8 Millett, [2002] 2 O.U.C.L.J. 291 at 294.

9 *Citadel General Assurance Company v Lloyds Bank Canada* [1997] 3 S.C.R. 805 at [30], per La Forest, Gonthier, Cory, McLachlin, Iacobucci and Major JJ. See also *Sempra Metals Ltd v Inland Revenue Commissioners* [2008] 1 A.C. 561 at [116] to [117], per Lord Nicholls; *Anderson v*

15-003 A simple example can be given to show why the disgorgement of a defendant's profits is a different remedial measure from the restitution of gains received at the claimant's expense. Suppose a defendant deceives a claimant into paying £1,000 to the defendant. The defendant then uses that money to make a profit of £5,000 (including the initial £1,000). The claimant might seek restitution of £1,000 for unjust enrichment (based on the mistake that the claimant made). Or the claimant might seek restitutionary damages for the £1,000 enrichment received by the defendant as a result of the tort of deceit. But the claimant might also seek disgorgement damages of £5,000 based on the profit that the defendant made from the tort of deceit. This chapter is concerned with whether, and when, that award of disgorgement damages is available for wrongdoing. In some instances, including deceit, the common law has not commonly recognised that disgorgement damages are an available remedy. But in *Dubai Aluminium Company Ltd v Salaam*,[10] Lord Millett said that

> "it is increasingly recognised today that the ends of justice sometimes go beyond compensating a plaintiff for his loss and may extend to stripping a defendant of his profits."

15-004 The most well-known instances of disgorgement damages are for equitable wrongdoing. Equity did not use the label "damages" to describe money awards for wrongdoing. The Court of Chancery preferred to make money awards through the language of an account. There was an account of administration in common form. There was an account taken on the basis of wilful default. And there was an account of profits. In each case the taking of the account was a method of assessing the money sum owed by the accounting party. But, as we saw in Ch.1, damages cannot be coherently described other than as a money award for wrongdoing. In relation to wilful default, Brightman LJ said that the payment that the accounting party must make after the account is

> "in reality compensation for loss suffered by the plaintiffs and the settled shares, not readily distinguishable from damages except with the aid of a powerful legal microscope".[11]

As for the *account* of profits, this was no more than the means of obtaining the amount of money owing for wrongdoing, albeit calculated by a defendant's profit rather than a claimant's loss. The label "disgorgement of profits" or "disgorgement damages" is more apt than an account of profits to describe the money award because the account is only the process to ascertain the amount owing. The order for disgorgement of profits or disgorgement damages is the order made following the account.

## II. Rationale of Disgorgement Damages

15-005 The rationale for an award of disgorgement damages can be stated in one word: deterrence. In many of the cases where disgorgement of profits are awarded, this rationale has been emphasised. Lord Herschell said in *Bray v Ford*[12] that "deter-

---

*McPherson (No.2)* [2012] W.A.S.C. 19 at [226], per Edelman J.

10 [2002] UKHL 48 at [164].

11 *Bartlett v Barclays Trust Co. (No.2)* [1980] Ch. 515 at 545.

12 [1896] A.C. 44 at 51. See also *Cadbury Schweppes Inc v FBI Foods Ltd* [1999] S.C.R. 142 at 164

rence is the rationale for stripping a fiduciary of his profit". Lord Keith has also said of disgorgement for a breach of confidence that it serves

> "a useful purpose in lessening the temptation for recipients of confidential information to misuse it for financial gain".[13]

And at common law Lord Hatherley LC, in the context of disgorging profits made as a result of trespass, said that "this Court never allows a man to make a profit by a wrong".[14]

As we saw in the previous chapter, the wrongful receipt of a benefit, at the claimant's expense, presents an immediate justification to make restitution of that benefit to the claimant as restitutionary damages. The same is not true of disgorgement of profits. Other than in instances involving breach of fiduciary duty, where the highest level of deterrence is required, there is no immediate justification for profit-stripping. It is generally unnecessary to deter innocent breaches of duty. Disgorgement damages are therefore a more exceptional measure of damages than restitutionary damages. For instance, in *Experience Hendrix*,[15] where both an account of profits and restitutionary damages were claimed, restitutionary damages were awarded but an account and disgorgement of profits were refused, on the basis that a lesser award by way of restitutionary damages would suffice. Mance LJ was careful to point out that, while Lord Nicholls had emphasised in *Attorney General v Blake*,[16] that an award of an account of profits was only appropriate in exceptional circumstances, "he did not … apply the same epithet or qualification" to an award of restitutionary damages.[17] **15-006**

However, this does not mean that disgorgement damages should be available only for breaches of fiduciary duty or deliberate breaches of other equitable wrongs like breach of confidence. For instance, in the case of the tort of battery the question may be put, where the defendant has been paid handsomely to beat up the claimant, which he does,[18] whether disgorgement damages should be available to the claimant to wrest the assault moneys from the defendant. Why should a deliberate, and profitable, breach of confidence yield a disgorgement award but not a deliberate, and profitable, battery? Or again, the question may be asked, where the defendant has clipped the locks from the head of the claimant, a well-known personality, and sold them for a large sum,[19] whether the claimant should be able to sue for that sum by way of disgorgement damages. Similarly for the tort of defamation, the question may be asked, if the defendant has published a book which libels the claimant and the anticipated sales by reason of the libel are huge and far exceed any dam- **15-007**

---

"the overriding deterrent objective applicable to situations of particular vulnerability"; *Canadian Aero Service v O'Malley* (1973) 40 D.L.R. (3d) 371 (SCC) at 384 "the need to compel obedience … to norms of exemplary behaviour"; *Meinhard v Salmon* (1928) 164 N.E. 545 at 546, per Cardozo CJ. "held to a level higher than that trodden by the crowd".

13 *Attorney General v Guardian Newspapers (No.2)* [1990] 1 A.C. 149 at 262.

14 *Jegon v Vivian* (1871) L.R. 6 Ch. App. 742 at 762. See also *Powell v Aiken* (1858) 4 K. & J. 343 at 351; 70 E.R. 144 at 147.

15 [2003] 1 All E.R. (Comm) 830 CA.

16 [2001] 1 A.C. 268.

17 [2003] 1 All E.R. (Comm) 830 CA at [24].

18 An illustration from Birks, *An Introduction to the Law of Restitution*, edn with revisions (Oxford: OUP, 1989), p.26.

19 An illustration from Street, *Principles of the Law of Damages* (London: Sweet & Maxwell, 1962), p.254.

age done to the claimant's reputation, whether the claimant should be entitled to ignore compensatory damages and sue for disgorgement damages. There is, of course, the means to obtain a measure of recovery obliquely in these cases of battery and defamation by claiming exemplary damages. These are still permitted even after *Rookes v Barnard*,[20] where, in Lord Devlin's words,

> "the defendant's conduct has been calculated to make a profit for himself which may exceed the compensation payable to the plaintiff".[21]

This is, however, a very blunt instrument since recovery is not specifically related to the benefit which has been achieved by the defendant. And there is no reason why disgorgement damages should not be concurrently available for common law wrongs just as they are for wrongs which historically originated in Chancery.

## III. Circumstances Giving Rise to Disgorgement Damages

### 1. Liability for equitable wrongdoing

**15-008** The award of disgorgement damages for equitable wrongdoing, under the label of an account of profits, is extremely common and well-known. The account of profits "is made to provide a remedy for specific equitable wrongdoing".[22] In this edition of this work, the awards of disgorgement damages in equity will not be considered other than for breaches of fiduciary duty that arise in a contractual context. The reader is directed to the standard works on equity and trusts for a consideration of disgorgement in equity generally. It suffices to say that disgorgement of profits is available for conscious breaches of equitable duties such as breach of confidence[23] or dishonest participation in a breach of fiduciary duty.[24] This points up the current gaps in the law. It is impossible to justify the disgorgement of profits made by a dishonest assistant in a breach of fiduciary duty or a person who intentionally breaches a duty of confidence but not from a person who profits from the deceit or wilful assault of another.

### 2. Liability for breach of Contract

#### (1) Attorney General v Blake[25]

**15-009** By far the best known decision concerning disgorgement damages at common law is the decision of the House of Lords in *Attorney General v Blake*.[26] It is commonly thought that this decision is wholly exceptional. It is necessary to consider that decision closely in order to explain why that common perception is false;

20 [1964] A.C. 1129.

21 [1964] A.C. 1129 at 1226. See Ch.13, above, at paras 13-021 and following.

22 *Glazier v Australian Men's Health (No.2)* [2001] N.S.W.S.C. 6 at [36]; *CMS Dolphin Ltd v Simonet* [2001] EWHC Ch 415 at [97].

23 *Attorney General v Guardian Newspapers (No.2) ("Spycatcher")* [1990] 1 A.C. 109 HL.

24 *Novoship (UK) Ltd v Mikhaylyuk* [2015] Q.B. 499 at [71] and *Central Bank of Ecuador v Conticorp SA* [2015] UKPC 11 at [9]. This development was preceded in Canada and Australia by *Cook v Deeks* [1916] 1 A.C. 554 and *Warman International Ltd v Dwyer* (1995) 182 C.L.R. 544. See *Michael Wilson & Partners Ltd v Nicholls* (2011) 244 C.L.R. 427 at [106].

25 [2001] 1 A.C. 268 ("*Blake*").

26 [2001] 1 A.C. 268 ("*Blake*").

although the facts were exceptional, the result was not. It is unexceptional for an order for disgorgement of profits in cases where the claimant owes a contractual duty not to profit from an act, not to be in a position of conflict, or to act in the best interests of the other party. These duties are generally described as fiduciary.

In *Blake*, the House of Lords recognised that an account and disgorgement of profits could be awarded for a breach of contract. An English spy, George Blake, was a Russian double agent. In 1961, he was caught and imprisoned for 42 years, which was then the longest term of imprisonment ever imposed in Britain. Five years later he escaped from his English prison and relocated to Moscow where he has lived ever since in what he has described as "the happiest days of my life". In 1989, Blake wrote his autobiography. The information in his autobiography was no longer confidential. His publishers started paying him royalties. £60,000 had been paid, and £90,000 more was due when the Crown commenced an action to restrain the payments. In the Court of Appeal, an injunction was granted restraining the publisher from sending any royalties to Blake. The difficulty with this order, as the House of Lords later observed, was that in the absence of a private cause of action against Blake there was no right upon which an injunction could be based.[27] So when Blake appealed to the House of Lords, the focus was upon whether any private right existed for disgorgement of Blake's profits. The focus of the submissions of the Attorney General was upon disgorgement of profits for a breach of contract by Blake. Counsel and the court assumed that Blake was an employee.[28] There should have been a simple, and entirely conventional, route to an order for disgorgement of profits. That route was to describe the contractual breach by the label "fiduciary". Indeed, in the leading speech Lord Nicholls explained that the breach of contract, if not a breach of fiduciary obligation, was closely akin to one.[29] But the arguments in the House of Lords were not cast on the basis of fiduciary duties.[30] This was because it was assumed that fiduciary duties could not have survived the termination of Blake's position although the contractual duties did. That assumption is highly questionable. **15-010**

The result of the decision in *Blake* was that the House of Lords held that the profits which Blake made could be disgorged as a remedy for this breach of contract. After a detailed analysis of the authorities, Lord Nicholls, with whose leading speech Lord Goff and Lord Browne-Wilkinson agreed, said, **15-011**

> "[m]y conclusion is that there seems to be no reason, in principle, why the court must in all circumstances rule out an account of profits as a remedy for breach of contract".[31]

An account of profits was awarded. Lord Nicholls refused to lay down rules for the circumstances in which an account and disgorgement of profits would be available for a breach of contract.[32] His Lordship suggested that all the circumstances needed to be considered but that

---

27 As Lord Nicholls and Lord Hobhouse observed, an injunction could not be awarded in support of a power to confiscate proceeds of crime in the absence of a realistic possibility of invoking statutory confiscation powers: [2001] 1 A.C. 268 at 289, per Lord Nicholls and at 298, per Lord Hobhouse.

28 An assumption which was probably incorrect: Simpson, "A Decision Per Incuriam" (2009) 125 L.Q.R. 433.

29 *Attorney General v Blake* [2001] 1 A.C. 268 at 287.

30 [2001] 1 A.C. 268 at 273–275.

31 [2001] 1 A.C. 268 at 284H.

32 [2001] 1 A.C. 268 at 285, per Lord Nicholls and 291, per Lord Steyn, explaining that the principles should be hammered out on the anvil of concrete cases.

"[a] useful general guide, although not exhaustive, is whether the plaintiff had a legitimate interest in preventing the defendant's profit-making activity and, hence, in depriving him of his profit".[33]

The formulation of this principle is important. An express or implied contract term requiring disgorgement of a defendant's profits, irrespective of the claimant's loss, without a legitimate interest in doing so, will be a penalty.[34]

### (2) Where there is a legitimate interest in preventing profit

**15-012** In order to understand when a claimant will have a "legitimate interest" in preventing a defendant's profit making activity by a claim for disgorgement of profits, it is necessary to explain a misconception in much of the subsequent commentary on *Blake*. That misconception is that no claim for breach of fiduciary duty could have succeeded. This view was based upon a belief that contractual duties which are fiduciary will terminate when the contract terminates. It is hard to see why this is the case when other contractual duties can survive termination, such as legitimate restraint of trade clauses, confidentiality clauses, or arbitration clauses. Indeed, by finding that Blake had breached his contract after leaving the security services and publishing his book, the House of Lords implicitly accepted that the contractual duty which was breached had survived termination. It would have been a nonsense to say that the fiduciary duty terminated when the contract terminated, but the contractual duty, with identical content, had not. But this point was not the subject of argument.

**15-013** The most obvious instance where a claimant will have a legitimate interest to prevent a defendant's profit making activity is where the contractual duty can be described as "fiduciary". Usually in these cases the claim for disgorgement of profits is simply expressed as based on breach of fiduciary duty. Unfortunately, the label "fiduciary" is the expression of a conclusion, not a process of reasoning. To describe someone as a fiduciary, without more, is meaningless.[35] So when do fiduciary duties arise?

**15-014** Fiduciary duties are not limited to an incident of a particular status or relationship. Fiduciary duties have been recognised in relationships ad hoc (for the particular relationship in the case). And sometimes even the "archetypal" fiduciary (the trustee)[36] does not owe fiduciary duties.[37] Other trustees, who might usually owe fiduciary duties, will not do so if the express or implied terms of the trust instrument deny those duties.[38] The genesis of a fiduciary duty is an express or implied undertaking made by the fiduciary, usually not to make profit, or not to put himself or herself in a position of conflict, or to act in the best interests of another.[39]

---

33 [2001] 1 A.C. 268 at 285.

34 See Ch.16, below, and *Cavendish Square Holdings v Makdessi* [2016] AC 1172.

35 *Re Goldcorp Exchange Ltd (In Receivership)* [1995] 1 A.C. 74 PC at 98.

36 *Maguire v Makaronis* (1997) 188 C.L.R. 449 at 473, quoting *Hospital Products Ltd v United States Surgical Corporation* (1984) 156 C.L.R. 41 at 68, per Gibbs CJ.

37 *Giumelli v Giumelli* (1999) 196 C.L.R. 101 at [5], per Gleeson CJ, McHugh, Gummow & Callinan JJ.

38 *Sargeant v National Westminster Bank* (1991) 61 P. & C.R. 518; *Hayim v Citibank NA* [1987] A.C. 730; *Citibank NA v QVT Financial LP* [2007] 4 All E.R. 736 CA; *Re Beatty* [1990] 1 W.L.R. 1503 at 1506, per Hoffmann J; *Edge v Pensions Ombudsman* [2000] Ch. 602 at 621, 627–630, per Chadwick LJ for the Court of Appeal.

39 Edelman, "When Do Fiduciary Duties Arise?" (2010) 126 L.Q.R. 302.

In Canada, Cromwell J writing for the unanimous Supreme Court said that

> "the law is, in my view, clear that fiduciary duties will only be imposed on those who have expressly or impliedly undertaken them".[40]

A joint judgment of the High Court of Australia, quoting from McLachlin J, has also emphasised that

> "[t]he essence of a fiduciary relationship… is that one party pledges itself to act in the best interests of the other."[41]

Once a fiduciary duty is seen as a particular express or implied undertaking, it is clear that the genesis of fiduciary duties can be contractual undertakings or non-contractual undertakings. As some English courts have observed, it might therefore be that the rules governing the implication or construction of contractual duties of loyalty are the same as those governing the creation of fiduciary duties[42]; for instance, terms preventing conflicts of interest and duty, or conflicts of duty and duty, or the making of profit from a position.[43] Although dissenting in the result, one of the most widely quoted statements concerning fiduciary duties is that of Mason J in *Hospital Products Ltd v United States Surgical Corporation*[44]: **15-015**

> "…the existence of a basic contractual relationship has in many situations provided a foundation for the erection of a fiduciary relationship. In these situations it is the contractual foundation which is all important because it is the contract that regulates the basic rights and liabilities of the parties."

This passage from Mason J was approved in *Kelly v Cooper*.[45] It was also approved in *Ross River Ltd v Waveley Commercial Ltd*,[46] where Lloyd LJ, with whom the others agreed, added

> "if the relationship is regulated by a contract, then the terms of that contract will be of primary importance, and wider duties will not lightly be implied".

Similarly, in *Henderson v Merrett Syndicates Ltd*,[47] Lord Browne-Wilkinson said that if a contract exists between the parties, the extent and nature of the fiduciary duties are determined by reference to that contract.

This understanding of fiduciary duties makes *Blake* an entirely uncontroversial decision. The claimant Attorney General had a legitimate interest in preventing Blake from profiting from his breach of contract because of an implied undertaking by Blake that he would not use his position as a secret service agent for personal **15-016**

---

[40] *Galambos v Perez* [2009] 3 S.C.R. 247 at [71].

[41] *Youyang Pty Ltd v Minter Ellison Morris Fletcher* (2003) 212 C.L.R. 484 at [40], per Gleeson CJ, McHugh, Gummow, Kirby and Hayne JJ, citing *Canson Enterprises Ltd v Boughton & Co* [1991] 3 S.C.R. 534 at 543, per McLachlin J.

[42] *Ross River Ltd v Waveley Commercial Ltd* [2012] EWHC 81 (Ch) at [241]–[244], per Morgan J; *F&C Alternative Investments (Holdings) Ltd v Barthelemy* [2011] EWHC 1731 (Ch) at [225], per Sales J.

[43] See Edelman, (2010) 126 L.Q.R. 302 at 316, 323–26 (good faith); 316, 318–19 (conflict of interest and duty); 316, 31921 (duties not to make a profit from a position).

[44] (1984) 156 C.L.R. 41 at 97.

[45] [1993] A.C. 205 at 215.

[46] [2013] EWCA Civ 910 at [56], quoting *Ross River Ltd v Cambridge City Football Club Ltd* [2007] EWHC 2115 (Ch) at [197], per Briggs J.

[47] [1995] 2 A.C. 145 at 206.

profit. Indeed, two decades earlier a majority of the United States Supreme Court on similar facts had held that profits should be disgorged by a Central Intelligence Agency operative who had breached a similar duty which was described as fiduciary.[48] In that case, Mr Snepp, a former Central Intelligence Agency operative published a book concerning CIA activities in South Vietnam. The book was published in breach of his contractual obligations to seek pre-publication review from the CIA. The majority of the Supreme Court held that profits could be disgorged because the contract

> "was no ordinary contract; it gave life to a fiduciary relationship and invested in Snepp the trust of the CIA".[49]

The dissentients denied that Snepp should disgorge his profits, but they did so because they considered that the contractual duty could not be described by a label "fiduciary".[50]

**15-017** The most common instances where a claimant will have a legitimate interest in preventing a defendant's profit making activity should therefore be where a claimant has expressly or impliedly undertaken a contractual duty not to profit from an act (in breach of contract) or a contractual duty not to put himself or herself in a position of conflict. The label "fiduciary" is often used to justify the disgorgement of profits. But this need not be necessary to justify disgorgement damages for such breaches of contract. An illustration of this is the decision of the High Court of Australia in *Thornley v Tilley*.[51] In that case, a client instructed the respondent stockbrokers to purchase certain shares for him the price of which would be repaid with interest at 8 per cent until payment. The stockbrokers bought the shares but, in breach of contract with the client, dealt with them on their own behalf. The client sued the stockbrokers, seeking an account and disgorgement of the profits made from the dealings. The High Court held that the client was entitled to account of the profits made from the dealings. Without any consideration of whether the agents were properly to be classified as "fiduciaries", Knox CJ said that the stockbroker had no right to use or deal with the scrip so obtained by them for their own benefit and had to disgorge the profits made.[52]

**15-018** Another example of disgorgement of profits arising from a breach of an implied undertaking not to profit from a position arose in *Reading v Attorney General*.[53] In that case, an army sergeant sat on a truck in uniform to allow alcohol to be smuggled through British checkpoints. The sergeant was paid more than £20,000 in bribes. His profits from these bribes were sought by the Crown. The trial judge, Denning J, focused only on the breach. He said that the profits could be disgorged simply because his acts were

> "in violation of his duty of honesty and good faith, [taking] advantage of his service to make a profit for himself".[54]

The Court of Appeal also held that the profits should be disgorged. In a state-

---

48 *Snepp v United States* 444 U.S. 507 (1980).

49 *Snepp v United States* 444 U.S. 507 (1980) at 510.

50 *Snepp v United States* 444 U.S. 507 (1980) at 519, per Stevens, Brennan and Marshall JJ.

51 (1925) 36 C.L.R. 1.

52 (1925) 36 C.L.R. 1 at 9.

53 [1951] A.C. 507.

54 *Reading v Attorney General* [1948] 2 K.B. 268 at 275.

ment which was endorsed in the House of Lords,[55] Asquith LJ (delivering the judgment of the court) said:

> "[t]here is a well-established class of cases in which [a master or principal] can … recover, whether or not he has suffered any detriment in fact. These are cases in which a servant or agent has realized a secret profit, commission or bribe in the course of his employment; and the amount recoverable is a sum equal to such profit."[56]

The Court of Appeal held that the profits should be disgorged because of an "imputed promise" by Reading that he would pay over any bribes received.[57] The court suggested that Reading was a fiduciary in "a very loose … sense"[58] but said that this fiduciary relationship was not necessary for recovery of the profits.[59] The House of Lords upheld the decision of the Court of Appeal that the profits made by Reading were recoverable by the Crown.[60] In a speech with which Viscount Jowitt LC agreed, Lord Porter said that **15-019**

> "the existence of [a fiduciary relationship] is, in my opinion, not an additional necessity in order to substantiate the claim."[61]

In "complete agreement" with the views of the Court of Appeal, Lord Porter said that the reason was because disgorgement of profits was available to the Crown for Reading's implied contractual promise to repay the bribe money to his employer.[62] The promise might better be characterised as an implied promise by Reading not to profit from his position rather than a fictitious implication that he would repay any bribes received. His duty was not to take bribes; it was not a duty to repay them.

In summary then, the most common instances where a person will have a legitimate interest to prevent a defendant's profit making activity is where there is an express or implied contractual undertaking that (i) the defendant will not profit from the conduct which constitutes the breach; (ii) the defendant will not put himself or herself in a position of conflict by that conduct; and (iii) the defendant will act in the best interests of the claimant. It is unnecessary that the defendant be characterised as a "fiduciary" which is a label that can raise more questions than it answers. But the underlying idea behind the "fiduciary" label points to the effective agreement by a defendant to give up part of his or her ability to act in his or her own self-interest and therefore the legitimacy in depriving the defendant of profits made. Importantly, the existence of a legitimate interest in these circumstances is a reason why an express clause requiring disgorgement of profits would not be a penalty.[63] **15-020**

Outside the common circumstances of an express or implied undertaking not to profit, not to be in a position of conflict, or not to act in the best interests of another, there are very few examples where a legitimate interest in preventing a defendant's profit making activity has been found so as to justify the disgorgement damages **15-021**

---

55 *Reading v Attorney General* [1951] A.C. 507 at 515, per Lord Porter.
56 *Reading v Attorney General* [1949] 2 K.B. 232 at 236.
57 *Reading v Attorney General* at 237.
58 *Reading v Attorney General* at 236.
59 *Reading v Attorney General* at 238.
60 *Reading v Attorney General* [1951] A.C. 507 at 516, per Lord Porter, 517, per Lord Normand.
61 [1951] A.C. 507 at 516, per Lord Porter.
62 [1951] A.C. 507 at 517, per Lord Porter.
63 See generally Ch.16.

which would effectively deprive a defendant of a liberty to act in a self-interested way. A necessary, but not sufficient, condition should be that the breach is of a nature which equity would restrain by injunction. The injunction which could have been granted should relate to a fundamental term of the agreement but the legitimacy of the interest in depriving a defendant of profits should also require that the agreement be one in which the defendant has generally agreed not to act in a self-interested way. One example, is the decision of the Vice-Chancellor in *Esso Petroleum Co Ltd v Niad Ltd*.[64] Under its contract with Esso, Niad was to receive fuel from Esso at a discounted price in return for matching, in its sales, the fuel prices charged by Esso's competitors. Niad repeatedly breached the contract by selling fuel at higher prices. This adversely affected Esso's scheme for controlling their prices so as to steal a march on their competitors, but it was difficult to prove lost sales attributable to Niad's breach. Esso focused instead upon the profits made by Niad. As the Vice-Chancellor put it, the two questions were as follows:

> "(1) Is Esso entitled to an account of profits as a remedy for the breaches of contract by Niad; and (2) Is Esso entitled to a restitutionary remedy requiring Niad to pay to Esso the amount by which the actual prices charged to customers exceeded the recommended prices."[65]

The Vice-Chancellor held that Esso was entitled to both of these remedies and could elect for whichever was the greater. The Vice-Chancellor said that the obligation to implement and maintain the recommended pump prices was fundamental to Esso's scheme and Esso was said to "undoubtedly" have a legitimate interest in preventing Niad from profiting from its breach of contract.[66] The reasons why that legitimate interest existed seemed to be contained in a number of factors to which the Vice-Chancellor made specific mention: (1) the impossibility for Esso to prove loss; (2) the fundamental nature of the obligation to the scheme; and (3) the intentional, and extensive, nature of Niad's breaches indicating a cynical intention to breach the duty and profit from it.[67] The *Niad* decision contrasts with *Morris-Garner v One-Step (Support) Ltd*.[68] In that case, the trial judge refused disgorgement damages, and the Court of Appeal did not doubt that conclusion. The trial judge, Phillips J, held that the circumstances were not sufficiently "exceptional"[69] despite the facts that (1) losses were impossible to quantify; (2) the covenants were a crucial term in the sale of the business; and (3) the profits were made by deliberate breaches of non-compete and non-solicitation covenants in the sale of a business.

**15-022** Another difficult decision is *Stretchline Intellectual Properties Ltd v H&M Hennes & Mauritz (UK) Ltd*,[70] where the court refused disgorgement damages for a breach of an undertaking in a settlement agreement not to infringe a patent. The settlement agreement had substituted contractual remedies for the usual remedies available for a breach of patent. One "normal" order for infringement of patent[71]

64 [2001] EWHC Ch 458.
65 [2001] EWHC Ch 458 at [58].
66 [2001] EWHC Ch 458 at [63].
67 [2001] EWHC Ch 458 at [63].
68 [2016] EWCA Civ 180.
69 [2014] EWHC 2213 (QB) at [103].
70 [2016] EWHC 162 (Pat).
71 [2016] EWHC 162 (Pat) at [34].

is an order for disgorgement of profits. The claimant plainly could have had a legitimate interest in preventing the defendant from profiting from a breach of the settlement agreement by infringing the claimant's patent. However, on its proper construction it seems that the settlement agreement did not manifest an intention to create such an interest. Carr J said that this was not a simple case where there is an undertaking not to infringe a patent because the agreement contained a mutual co-operation and investigation regime if potential infringements were identified.[72]

### (3) Where there is no legitimate interest in preventing profit

The reason why disgorgement damages for a breach of contract are not common is because it is a significant step for the law to take to impose (or recognise, in the case of an express contractual remedy) a remedy which deters a defendant from acting in a way which the law would not otherwise restrain. The cases where this is legitimate have generally involved breaches of express or implied breaches of duties not to profit, or not to be in a position of conflict, or to act in the best interests of another. But there are many contractual duties which will *not* give rise to a legitimate interest in preventing a defendant from profiting from a breach. **15-023**

One example is *Experience Hendrix v PPX Enterprises Inc*.[73] In 1965 the defendants entered into a contract with a rising singer guitarist, Jimi Hendrix, to play and sing exclusively for the defendants. Under the contract Hendrix was to receive a very paltry royalty return. He died a few years later. The defendants who sued him, and after his death his estate, for breach of contract were met with the formidable defence that the contract was in restraint of trade and invalid. The trial of the action commenced, but after three weeks the defendants settled. The settlement agreement dealt with the master titles from which recordings were made. It entitled the defendants to perform existing contractual commitments by way of licence relating to the various masters. For one group of 33 masters existing licences would continue but in respect of any further licences or extensions of existing licences the estate would be entitled to royalty returns much improved on what had been provided by the original contract. For a second group of 63 masters it was provided that no further licences or extensions or renewals of licences were to be granted without consent.[74] The defendants committed deliberate breaches of the settlement agreement in 1995, and again in 1999, by granting licences in respect of 39 master recordings in the second group. From these licences they made substantial profits. In 2001 the claimant company, effectively owned by the sole beneficiary of Hendrix's estate and the assignee of the benefit of the settlement agreement, sued in respect of these breaches for an injunction and damages including disgorgement damages (described in conventional terms as an account of profits). It was conceded that the claimant was unable to show that it had suffered any financial loss as a result of these licenses in breach of contract. The trial judge granted an injunction against further licensing of masters of the titles in the second group but dismissed the claimant's claims for damages and for an account and disgorgement of profits. On the claimant's appeal against the dismissal of these claims, after a very **15-024**

72 [2016] EWHC 162 (Pat) at [25].

73 [2003] 1 All E.R. (Comm) 830 CA.

74 There was a third group of masters, 19 in number, which should have been destroyed by the defendants but nothing turned upon the defendants' failure to destroy them.

full analysis by Mance LJ of *Attorney General v Blake*,[75] the Court of Appeal held that the case was not sufficiently exceptional for an account and disgorgement of profits although the defendant should be required by way of restitutionary damages to make a reasonable payment for its use of masters in breach of the settlement agreement. The case was, said Peter Gibson LJ,

> "a suitable one ... in which damages for breach of contract may be measured by the benefits gained by the wrongdoer from the breach".[76]

But those were the benefits immediately received not all the profits generated. Another way of expressing this conclusion is to say that the claimant did not have a legitimate interest to prevent the defendant's profit making breach.

**15-025** Another circumstance where a defendant does not have a legitimate interest to prevent the claimant's profit making breach arises in cases where the breach consists merely of skimped performance designed to ensure a profit. An example is a case cited by the Court of Appeal in *Blake* which came from Louisiana; this was the old case of *City of New Orleans v Firemen's Charitable Association*.[77] The defendant had provided a firefighting service for the claimant's property with far fewer firemen, horses and hosepipes than had been contractually specified, saving the defendant expense but causing no loss to the claimant because, even with the limited manning, there had been no failure to put out fires. In England, claims based upon skimped performances had not appeared, understandably, before Lord Woolf's pronouncement in *Blake*, although they could have been put forward, but were not, in the well-known *Ruxley Electronics & Construction v Forsyth*,[78] and again in *White Arrow Express Ltd v GUS Catalogue Ltd*.[79] *Ruxley* concerned a swimming pool which was built to a lesser depth than had been contractually specified but which was nevertheless safe and which left the value of the owner's property unaffected. While disallowing the cost of reconstruction the House of Lords did not consider awarding in its place the saving to the builder resulting from having built a shallower pool; the possibility was not even argued.[80] *White Arrow* concerned the delivery and collection of goods by the defendant road transport contractors for the claimants who sold the goods through their mail order business. The defendants had undertaken to provide a de luxe service but had failed to operate the agreed criteria for deliveries and collections, the breach of contract complained of relating to pre-advice of deliveries and timing of collections. In the absence of showing a loss the claimants were held entitled to nominal damages; again, a disgorgement damages claim based upon the defendants' saving by providing an inferior service to that promised was not put forward. Finally, an earlier, controversial, case is the well-known *Tito v Waddell (No.2)*,[81] commonly called the *Ocean Island No.1* case.[82] The defendants failed in their contractual undertaking to replant the claimants' trees on their island. The claimants were unable to recover the cost of replanting themselves

---

75 [2001] 1 A.C. 268.

76 [2001] 1 A.C. 268 at [58].

77 43 La. Ann. 447; 9 So. 486 (1891).

78 [1996] A.C. 344.

79 (1995) 145 N.L.J. 1504; (1996) 15 Tr. L.R. 69.

80 The claimant did receive a comparatively modest award for his disappointment. The case is fully dealt with at paras 31-014 and 31-021, below.

81 [1977] Ch. 106.

82 Facts at para.28-091, below; and see the case also at para.28-084, below.

because of a lack of evidence of an intention to replant and were held to be confined to recovering only the comparatively modest diminution in the value of the land where the trees had initially stood. Megarry VC there stated:

> "[i]t is fundamental to all questions of damages that they are to compensate the plaintiff for his loss or injury … The question is not one of making the defendant disgorge what he has saved by committing the wrong, but one of compensating the plaintiff."[83]

Such a test, which permits only compensatory damages, is no longer correct. But it is unlikely that disgorgement damages would be available in such a case even today. The claimants had a legitimate interest in ensuring compliance with the contract terms but, in light of the findings of fact, it is hard to see how they had a legitimate interest in deterring the defendants from a profit making breach when it was held that objectively there would not have been a basis to infer that they intended to replant.[84]

Another unlikely circumstance for a legitimate interest in preventing a **15-026** defendant's profit making activity is where the defendant profits merely by making a more profitable contract with a third party. This is a situation of a defendant not performing his contract with the claimant because he has entered into, and performed, a similar, more profitable contract with another. This circumstance can arise in the different contexts of money, property and services. First, the defendant contracts to invest money in the claimant's business but uses the money to invest in another business, deriving profits from that investment in excess of the loss to the claimant from the non-investment in his business. This is what happened in the old Scots case of *Teacher v Calder*,[85] where disgorgement damages were refused. Second, the defendant contracts to sell a cargo of oil to the claimant but sells it to a third party for far more when the price of oil increases dramatically; the price of oil then drops equally dramatically, enabling the claimant to buy from another supplier at the original contract price. This is what happened in the Israeli case of *Adras Ltd v Harlow & Jones*.[86] Although disgorgement damages were allowed in that case, it is very doubtful whether an English court would reach the same result. Third, the defendant, in breach of his employment contract, takes a similar job with a rival business at a far higher salary, but the claimant is able to find a substitute at the same salary as he had been paying the defendant.

In *Blake*, the Court of Appeal said that **15-027**

> "the mere fact that the defendant's breach of his contract with the plaintiff has enabled him to enter into a more profitable contract with someone else should … not be sufficient"[87]

to allow a claim for disgorgement damages. The Court of Appeal relied on *Teacher*, although there is no mention of *Adras* which was probably not brought to the court's attention.[88] This stance of the Court of Appeal in *Blake* has since been taken in an

---

83 [1977] Ch. 106 at 332E.

84 [1977] Ch. 106 at 336C–E.

85 (1899) 1 F. (H.L.) 39.

86 (1988) 42(1) P.D., noted in Friedmann, "Restitution of Profits Gained by Party in Breach of Contract" (1988) 104 L.Q.R. 383 and in Finn, *Essays on Restitution* (Sydney: Law Book Company, 1990), pp.8–9.

87 [1998] Ch. 439 CA at 458A.

88 Lord Nicholls in the House of Lords agreed that a claim could not be made against a profiteering

arbitration award, made available by permission of the parties and partly reported as *AB Corporation v CD Co, The Sine Nomine*.[89] In the course of a charterparty the owners withdrew the vessel from the charterers' service and made profits with the vessel elsewhere. The charterers claimed to recover these profits. It is worth setting out what the arbitrators, headed by the former Staughton LJ, had to say in declining to recognise this claim. The award states:

> "It is by no means uncommon for commercial contracts to be broken deliberately because a more profitable opportunity has arisen. Or the contract-breaker takes an over-generous view of his rights, knowing that the law may ultimately be against him. In such a case he may have little or nothing to lose by taking the chance; the downside at worst is that he will have to pay the costs of both sides. International commerce on a large scale is red in tooth and claw. We do not say that the Respondents' action was either deliberate or cynical wrongdoing in this case; they had a respectable argument on liability, although a commercial judge refused their application for leave to appeal."[90]

The award continues:

> "Our solution to the present problem is that there should not be an award of wrongful profits where both parties are dealing with a marketable commodity—the services of a ship in this case—for which a substitute can be found in the market place. In the ordinary way the damages which the claimant suffers by having to buy in at the market price will be equal to the profit which the wrongdoer makes by having his goods or his ships' services to sell at a higher price. It is in the nature of things unlikely that the wrongdoer will make a greater profit than that. And if he does, it is an adventitious benefit which he can keep. The commercial law of this country should not make moral judgments, or seek to punish contract-breakers."[91]

**15-028** The decision in *Niad* can be reconciled with cases like *The Sine Nomine*,[92] on the basis that in *Niad* the parties were not dealing with a marketable commodity for which a substitute could be found in the market and for which a money award would be adequate.

## 3. LIABILITY FOR TORTS

### (1) The principle

**15-029** As a matter of principle, the liability to pay disgorgement damages for a tortious breach should be simple. A tort which is committed intentionally, particularly with a view to profit, should be deterred by disgorgement of the profit made. There is no justification for allowing disgorgement of profits from a conscious wrongdoer who breaches duties which were recognised in the Court of Chancery (including deceit, breach of confidence, and dishonest assistance in a breach of fiduciary duty) but not for a wrongdoer who breaches duties which were, and are, recognised in the common law courts (including similar or identical wrongs of deceit, breach of privacy, and dishonest conspiracy). The proposition was put concisely in 1937, and

defendant (*Attorney General v Blake* [2001] 1 A.C. 268 at 286E) but this was in the context of an account where exceptional circumstances are required.

89 [2002] 1 Lloyd's Rep. 805.

90 [2002] 1 Lloyd's Rep. 805 at [9].

91 [2002] 1 Lloyd's Rep. 805 at [10].

92 [2002] 1 Lloyd's Rep. 805.

reiterated in 2011, in the United States Restatement of Restitution in relation to torts generally:

"[i]f [the defendant] was consciously tortious in acquiring the benefit, he is also deprived of any profit derived from his subsequent dealing with it."[93]

However, as we will see, there are only pockets of the law of torts where this principle has been expressly adopted. Usually, the recognition of profit-stripping damages in the law of torts occurs by the use of antiquated language which obscures the true nature of the award.

Once the different nomenclature used to strip cynical defendant tortfeasors of profits is viewed together it can be seen that disgorgement damages are more widely available than is generally appreciated. The mechanism and language used by courts has been through awards of "money had and received", broad references to "damages", and awards of accounts. In addition, the "blunt instrument" of exemplary damages for cynical breach is sometimes used to effect the same deterrent purposes as disgorgement damages. **15-030**

### (2) Awards using the language of account of profits

In the 19th century, there were a large number of cases concerning the removal, in trespass, of coal under the land of the claimant. The award of disgorgement damages (the value of the coal as a chattel in the defendant's hands) was often made in cases where coal had been removed in a wilful and cynical manner.[94] In *Powell v Aiken*,[95] the Vice Chancellor, Sir William Page Wood stated that the award made effects **15-031**

"an account of profit realised ... by the working of coal to give relief in respect of wrongs attended with profit to the wrongdoer."

Similarly in *Jegon v Vivian*,[96] Lord Hatherley LC (as the Vice-Chancellor had become) explained this award as based upon the fact that "this Court never allows a man to make a profit by a wrong."

The description of profit-stripping as an "account" or "account of profits" was most common in relation to intellectual property wrongs which spanned equity, common law, and statute. An account of profits was commonly awarded for passing off, patent infringement, trade mark infringement and copyright infringement. In *Hogg v Kirby*,[97] Lord Eldon said that the remedy was by an injunction and account because a: **15-032**

"Court of Equity ... is not content with an action for damages; for it is nearly impossible to know the extent of the damage".

---

93 American Law Institute, *Restatement of the Law of Restitution: Quasi Contracts and Constructive Trusts* (St Paul: A.L.I., 1937), Introductory Note to Ch.8 at pp.595–596. See now American Law Institute, *Restatement (Third) of the Law of Restitution and Unjust Enrichment* (St Paul: A.L.I., 2011) at 184.

94 Also *Morgan v Powell* (1842) 3 Q.B. 278; 114 E.R. 513; *Wild v Holt* (1842) 9 M. & W. 672; 152 E.R. 284; *Bulli Coal Mining Co v Osborne* [1899] A.C. 351.

95 *Powell v Aiken* (1858) 4 Kay & J. 343 at 351; 70 E.R. 144 at 147.

96 *Jegon v Vivian* (1871) L.R. 6 Ch. App. 742 at 762.

97 (1803) 8 Ves. Jr. 215, 223; 32 E.R. 336, 339.

It was acknowledged that the account of profits could give the innocent party more than he or she had lost.[98] An example of disgorgement damages for a trade mark infringement is *Colbeam Palmer Ltd v Stock Affiliates Pty Ltd*.[99] The plaintiff produced painting sets under the name "Craft Master" in a number of countries including Australia. The defendant sold painting sets that bore that mark unaware of the plaintiff's existence in Australia. Later, the plaintiff became aware of this and notified the defendant that it was infringing the plaintiff's trade mark. The great Australian judge, Windeyer J reviewed the older authorities on trade mark infringement and explained:

> "The account of profits retains its characteristics of its origin in the Court of Chancery. By it a defendant is made to account for, and is then stripped of, profits which he has made which it would be unconscionable that he retain. These are profits made by him dishonestly, that is by his knowingly infringing the rights of the proprietor of the trade mark ... The account is limited to the profits made by the defendant during the period when he knew of the plaintiff's rights. So it was in respect of common law trade marks. So it still is in respect of registered trademarks: *Edelsten v Edelsten* (1863) 1 De G J & S 185 (46 ER 72); *Slazenger & Sons v Spalding & Bros* (1910) 1 Ch 257; *Moet v Couston* (1964) 33 Beav 578 (55 ER 493). I think that it follows that it lies upon a plaintiff who seeks an account of profits to establish that profits were made by the defendant knowing that he was transgressing the plaintiff's rights."

## (3) Awards using the language of "damages"

15-033 In *Martin v Porter*,[100] the defendant had wilfully removed coal from the claimant's land. The Court *en banc* approved of the order of Baron Parke that the claimant was entitled to both a way leave for the use of the land (restitutionary damages) and to the value of the coal once removed from the land. But the award of the value of the coal when removed from the land was not one of compensatory damages. While the coal was part of the land it had no independent existence. It was just part of the freehold. When taken from the land, it became a chattel. The claim for trespass to land was a claim that the defendant had profited by the trespass and had obtained the valuable coal. As the Lord Chancellor said in *Jegon v Vivian*, when awarding damages for the value of the coal rather than the value of the mere *right* to remove the coal, this Court "never allows a man to make a profit by a wrong".[101] Again, in *Martin v Porter*,[102] Baron Parke said that:

> "I am not sorry that this rule is adopted; as it will tend to prevent trespasses of this kind which are generally wilful".

As Professor Birks[103] and Mr Swadling[104] observed, the same disgorgement award was made in the latter stages of the famous litigation in *Phillips v Homfray*.[105] In that case, Kay LJ described the action for recovery of the value of the coal

---

[98] (1843) 2 Hare 543 at 560; 67 E.R. 224 at 231, per Sir James Wigram VC.

[99] *Colbeam Palmer Ltd v Stock Affiliates Pty Ltd* (1968) 122 C.L.R. 25.

[100] *Martin v Porter* (1839) 5 M. & W. 351; 151 E.R. 149.

[101] *Jegon v Vivian* (1871) L.R. 6 Ch. App. 742 at 761.

[102] *Martin v Porter* (1839) 5 M. & W. 351 at 354; 151 E.R. 149 at 150.

[103] Birks, *Restitution: The Future*, (Sydney: Federation Press, 1992), p.19.

[104] Swadling, "The Myth of Phillips v Homfray" in Swadling and Jones (eds), *The Search for Principle: Essays in Honour of Lord Goff of Chieveley* (Oxford: OUP, 1999), p.277.

[105] [1892] 1 Ch. 465.

obtained by trespass as an action to recover "the benefit they had received from wrongfully taking coal belonging to the plaintiff".[106]

A United States example of a disgorgement damages award for trespass, described only as damages, is the decision of the Kentucky Court of Appeal in *Edwards v Lee's Administrators*.[107] Edwards had built a hotel on his land which attracted numerous tourists who came to visit a cave that lay beneath his land. Edwards was aware that a third of the cave lay beneath Lee's land, but wilfully and cynically trespassed into this part of the cave. In the leading judgment, Stites J did not notice the difference between restitutionary damages (based upon a reasonable rental) and disgorgement damages (stripping the net profit made). Nevertheless, his Honour considered that "profits rather than rent form the basis of recovery" and for the wilful trespasses the recovery was the **15-034**

> "the proportion of profit derived by the trespasser directly from the use of the land itself".[108]

The wilful trespass in *Edwards* contrasts with the innocent trespass considered by the 10th Circuit of the United States Court of Appeals in *Beck and Others v Northern Natural Gas Company*.[109] In that case, "Northern" was a natural gas company which was commissioned by State and Federal Governments to store (by injection) natural gas in a sub-surface area known as the Viola formation. This storage was done by consent of the landowners. However, in trespass, a far greater amount was stored than agreed because of a "migration" of the gas to a lower formation for which permission to store had not been obtained. The Court of Appeals accepted the assessment of the trial judge that the fair market value of the storage was $2.3 million and that the profits generated as a result of the additional storage (through additional sales) was $12 million. However, for the innocent trespass, the court held that the "proper measure of damages was… fair rental value."[110] As we saw in the previous chapter, this is an award of restitutionary damages. An award of disgorgement damages would have required a wilful trespass.

Another example from the United States, this time in the context of the tort of conversion, is the decision in *Olwell v Nye & Nissen Co.*[111] The appellant had purchased the respondents' egg-packing business. The respondents left an egg-washing machine on the premises which had been excluded from the sale of the business. The appellant cynically committed the tort of conversion by using the respondent's egg-washing machine (without the respondent's knowledge) to clean the eggs, a method far more effective than manually washing them. Although using the language of implied contract, the Supreme Court of Washington accepted that the profit must be disgorged. The court referred to arguments of the appellant that an award of disgorgement damages would be excessive as **15-035**

> "any damages awarded to the plaintiff should be based on the use or rental value of the machine and should bear some reasonable relation to market value."[112]

---

106 [1892] 1 Ch. 465 at 473.
107 *Edwards v Lee's Administrators* 96 S.W. 2.d.1028 (1936).
108 *Edwards v Lee's Administrators* 96 S.W. 2.d.1028 (1936).
109 *Beck and Others v Northern Natural Gas Company* 170 F. 3.d.1018 (1999) 10th Cir.
110 *Beck and Others v Northern Natural Gas Company* 170 F. 3.d .1018 (1999) 10th Cir. at 1024.
111 *Olwell v Nye & Nissen Co* 173 P. 2.d. 652 (1946) SCW.
112 *Olwell v Nye & Nissen Co* 173 P. 2.d. 652 (1946) SCW at 653.

Mallery J, with whom the other Justices agreed, rejected these arguments and affirmed a comment from the Restatement of Restitution[113]:

> "the measure of restitution is determined with reference to the tortiousness of the defendant's conduct … If he was consciously tortious in acquiring the benefit, he is also deprived of any profit derived from his subsequent dealing with it."[114]

In the result though it did not matter because the respondent had only sought the restitutionary damages award of the market rate of the use—$25 per month—so the award was limited to that amount.

### (4) Profit-stripping awards described as "money had and received"

15-036 What the United States cases achieved in cases of conversion by reference to "damages", English cases had achieved by the use of the form of *indebitatus assumpsit* known as money had and received. In *Lightly v Clouston*,[115] Mansfield CJ acknowledged that[116]

> "it has now been long settled, that in cases of sale, if the Plaintiff chooses to sue for the produce of that sale, he may do it: and the practice is beneficial to the defendant, because a jury may give in damages for the tort a much greater sum than the value of the goods."

This principle was constantly affirmed and money had and received became the method for disgorging the profits from the sale of converted goods.[117] As we will see below, profits were also disgorged for deceit or fraud under the rubric of "money had and received."[118]

### (5) Awards concealed within exemplary damages

15-037 Disgorgement damages have also been indirectly awarded for a tort in England through a claim for exemplary damages. One category of exemplary damages in *Rookes v Barnard*,[119] is where, in Lord Devlin's words,

> "the defendant's conduct has been calculated to make a profit for himself which may exceed the compensation payable to the plaintiff".[120]

---

[113] American Law Institute, *Restatement of the Law of Restitution: Quasi Contracts and Constructive Trusts* (St Paul: A.L.I., 1937), Introductory Note to Ch.8, at pp.595–596.

[114] *Olwell v Nye & Nissen Co 173 P. 2.d. 652* (1946) SCW at 654. There was a suggestion, however, that the profits in that case might be measured by expenses saved, a concept which English law has not adopted (below, at paras 15-046 and following).

[115] *Lightly v Clouston* (1808) 1 Taunt. 112; 127 E.R. 774; *Lamine v Dorrell* (1705) 2 Ld. Raym. 1216; 92 E.R. 303.

[116] *Lightly v Clouston* 127 E.R. 774 at 775.

[117] *Lightly v Clouston* 127 E.R. 774. See also *Lamine v Dorrell* (1701) 2 Ld. Raym. 1216; 92 E.R. 303; *Oughton v Seppings* (1830) 1 B. and Ad. 241; 109 E.R. 776; *King v Leith* (1787) 2 Term Rep. 141 at 145; 100 E.R. 77 at 78–79; *Parker v Norton* (1796) 6 Term Rep. 695 at 700; 101 E.R. 777 at 779–780; *Feltham Churchwardens v Terry* (1772) Lofft 207 at 208; 98 E.R. 613 at 613.

[118] *Reading v Attorney General* [1951] A.C. 507 HL; *Mahesan S/O Thambiah v Malaysian Government Officers Cooperative Housing Society* [1979] A.C. 374 PC at 376; *Armagas Ltd v Mundogas SA* [1986] A.C. 717 CA at 742–743, per Robert Goff LJ; decision aff'd [1986] A.C. 717 HL; *Petrotrade Inc v Smith* [2000] 1 Lloyds Rep. 486 at 490.

[119] [1964] A.C. 1129.

[120] [1964] A.C. 1129 at 1226. See Ch.13, above, at paras 13-021 and following.

We saw in Ch.13 that exemplary damages in this category have been awarded for torts as varied as libel, trespass, conversion, and breach of statutory duty. However, the award of exemplary damages to deter deliberate, tortious breaches is a blunt instrument since recovery is not specifically related to the benefit which has been achieved by the defendant. Different and wider considerations of deterrence mean that exemplary damages are not tied to the benefit obtained by the defendant. Disgorgement damages might be more limited in achieving a deterrent goal because they are tied to the quantum of profit. But in the measure of the award they are the sharper instrument. In *Borders (UK) Ltd v Commissioner of Police of the Metropolis*,[121] Sedley LJ with whom May LJ agreed, said, referring to an earlier edition of this book, that it may be that the emergence of disgorgement will permit an "attractive synthesis" which

> "allow claimants a more direct recovery without the need to resort to, in this context, the rather clumsy device of exemplary damages."[122]

A classic acknowledgement that the disgorgement award at common law is sometimes described as exemplary damages can be seen in the later treatment of the classic case of *Livingstone v Rawyards Coal Company*.[123] That case is extremely well-known because it also contains the classic statement of how compensatory damages are measured in tort. The defendant had mined for coal under the claimant's land, mistakenly thinking that it had a right to do so. When the claimant realised that the defendant had no such right he sought disgorgement of the value of the coal obtained by the defendant. Although the claim was refused, all the Law Lords in that case said that if the defendant had acted dishonestly (with "bad faith or sinister intention")[124] it would have been required to disgorge the market value of the coal in the defendant's hands, less expenses; in other words, the profit from the tort. In *Broome v Cassell & Co*,[125] Lord Diplock referred to the *Livingstone* case and acknowledged that the goals of this award of disgorgement damages were mirrored in the profit-stripping (second) limb of exemplary damages for cynical breach.[126] However, an award of exemplary damages sometimes goes further than disgorgement damages. Lord Diplock acknowledged in the *Broome* case that the additional refusal often to allow a deduction for the cost of working the coal was a purely punitive element[127] which might be given at common law[128] or in equity.[129] Lord Diplock saw this additional punishment as necessary for additional deterrence: 15-038

> "to restrict the damages recoverable to the actual gain made by the defendant if it exceeded the loss caused to the plaintiff, would leave the defendant contemplating an unlawful act

---

121 [2005] EWCA Civ 197.

122 [2005] EWCA Civ 197 at [25] to [26].

123 (1880) 5 App. Cas. 25 HL at 39. See *British Westinghouse Electric and Manufacturing Co Ltd v Underground Electric Railways Co of London Ltd* [1912] A.C. 673 HL at 689; *Tai Hing Cotton Mill Ltd v Kamsing Knitting Factory* [1979] A.C. 91 PC at 104; *Ruxley Electronics and Construction Ltd v Forsyth* [1996] A.C. 344 HL at 355, 365–366; *Dodd Properties (Kent) Ltd v Canterbury City Council* [1980] 1 W.L.R. 433 CA at 451.

124 *Livingstone v Rawyards Coal Company* (1880) 5 App. Cas. 25 HL at 31, per Earl Cairns LC, at 34 per Lord Hatherley, at 39 per Lord Blackburn.

125 *Broome v Cassell & Co* [1972] A.C. 1027 HL at 1129.

126 *Rookes v Barnard* [1964] A.C. 1129 HL.

127 *Broome & Co* [1972] A.C. 1027 HL at 1129.

128 *Livingstone v Rawyards Coal Company* (1880) 5 App. Cas. 25 HL at 185.

129 *Bulli Coal Mining Co v Osborne* [1899] A.C. 351 HL.

with the certainty that he had nothing to lose to balance against the chance that the plaintiff might never sue him or, if he did, might fail in the hazards of litigation."[130]

## (6) Retrograde authority in relation to deceit

**15-039** In *Halifax Building Society v Thomas*,[131] the appellant building society gave a mortgage to Thomas induced by his fraudulent misrepresentations about his identity and creditworthiness. After Thomas defaulted, the society discovered the fraud, obtained an order for possession of the mortgaged property and sold it. The sale left a surplus of more than £10,000. After the conviction of Thomas the Crown obtained a confiscation order for the value of the surplus.[132] The society argued that the surplus was its property and not the property of Thomas so that the confiscation order could not attach to it.

**15-040** Before the Court of Appeal, the society argued that it owned the surplus in two alternative submissions. The first relied upon a condition of the mortgage which provided that the mortgage was security for "all moneys which may be or become owing." It was argued that because of Thomas' fraud he was liable to account for any profits made and that this liability to account was money "owing" secured by the mortgage. As a result, it was submitted, the surplus from the sale[133] was also secured by the mortgage and belonged to the society. The alternative submission was that the society was entitled to a constructive trust over the profits of fraud in the same manner as such an award is made for a breach of fiduciary duty.[134] This argument was concerned with when a constructive trust will arise and can be put to one side. The Court of Appeal rejected both arguments. The first argument was rejected for two reasons. First, because the provision in the mortgage did not cover liabilities other than debts to the society and so a liability to account for profits did not entitle the society to displace the equity of redemption. Secondly, and much more controversially, because Thomas was not liable to account to the Society for the profits made from his fraud. In the leading judgment, Peter Gibson LJ said that

> "there is an inconsistency between a person being [a contractual] creditor and yet claiming more than that to which he is contractually entitled."[135]

However, there is no inconsistency once it is appreciated that the claim is based upon the tort and not the contract. Further, the House of Lords have allowed disgorgement of profits for breach of fiduciary duty in circumstances in which a contract exists.[136] More fundamentally, Peter Gibson LJ said that there was no decided case that came near the present situation and that

> "the fraud is not in itself a sufficient factor to allow the society to require Mr Thomas to account to it".[137]

On both of these points he was also wrong.

---

130 *Broome & Co* [1972] A.C. 1027 HL at 1130, per Lord Diplock.
131 [1996] Ch. 217 CA.
132 Section 79(3) of the Criminal Justice Act 1988.
133 Pursuant to his equity of reversion under s.105 of the Law of Property Act 1925.
134 *Attorney General of Hong Kong v Reid* [1994] 1 A.C. 324 PC.
135 *Halifax Building Society v Thomas* [1996] Ch. 217 CA at 227.
136 *Gluckstein v Barnes* [1900] A.C. 240 HL.
137 *Halifax Building Society v Thomas* [1996] Ch. 217 CA at 227–228.

The notion that fraud is not sufficient to allow disgorgement of profit is an argument which would not have been entertained for a second in the Court of Chancery. Yet deceit was a wrong which was actionable in either the common law courts as a tort or in equity. In *Peek v Gurney*,[138] Lord Chelmsford said that the loss suffered as a result of fraudulent misrepresentations could be recovered by a suit in Chancery which was "precisely analogous to the common law action for deceit".[139] The same disgorgement existed in the equitable jurisdiction to award "compound interest" including in cases of fraud in order "to disgorge a profit made ... which should not have been made."[140] Indeed, that jurisdiction to strip profits as "compound interest" has recently been described by the Privy Council as subject to the same approach as an account and disgorgement of profits.[141] Moreover, even the common law courts had previously allowed disgorgement of profits made as a result of fraud. **15-041**

In *Mahesan S/O Thambiah v Malaysian Government Officers Co-Operative Housing Society*,[142] an agent took a bribe to purchase land on behalf of his principal at an inflated price. The Privy Council held that the amount of the bribe exceeded the amount by which the price was inflated (the excess which the principal paid). The principal was entitled to elect between recovery of the loss suffered (the excess paid) and recovery of the amount of the bribe as money had and received. Counsel for the principal relied upon the *Reading* case and argued that: **15-042**

> "When an agent has received the bribe his obligation is to hand it to the principal as money had and received and it is recoverable by the principal as such ... By disgorging the bribe the agent loses nothing; the principal receives a windfall but there is nothing in that to preclude him from pursuing his remedy for fraud."[143]

Delivering the advice of the Privy Council, Lord Diplock relied upon the reasoning in the *United Australia* case and accepted that the claimant could elect between compensatory damages for the fraud or disgorgement damages in the form of money had and received.[144] Lord Diplock had difficulty with the notion that no loss might be suffered yet that an award of profits might still be made for the tort of fraud. He considered this "irrebuttable presumption" of loss meant that in cases where disgorgement damages are sought for bribery, loss was not really an element of this common law cause of action.[145] **15-043**

The same should be true of the tort of deceit although there is little authority on **15-044**

---

138 (1873) L.R. 6 H.L. 377.

139 *Peek v Gurney* (1873) L.R. 6 H.L. 377 at 390, 393.

140 *Westdeutsche Landesbank v Islington LBC* [1996] A.C. 669 at 723, per Lord Woolf.

141 *Central Bank of Ecuador v Conticorp SA* [2015] UKPC 11 at [9].

142 *Mahesan S/O Thambiah v Malaysian Government Officers Cooperative Housing Society* [1979] A.C. 374 PC at 376. See also *Armagas Ltd v Mundogas SA* [1986] A.C. 717 CA at 742–743, per Robert Goff LJ; decision aff'd [1986] A.C. 717 HL.

143 *Mahesan* [1979] A.C. 374 at 376.

144 Although at times Lord Diplock seemingly treated money had and received as independent of the law of tort, stating, for example, that "the same facts gave rise in law to two causes of action ... for money had and received and the other for tort": *Mahesan* [1979] A.C. 374 at 382.

145 *Mahesan* [1979] A.C. 374 at 380, 383. See *Fawcett v Whitehouse* (1829) 1 Russ. & M. 132; 39 E.R. 51. Some common law authorities had relied upon the now-rejected concept of implied contract: *Boston Deep Sea Fishing and Ice Co v Ansell* (1888) 39 Ch. D. 339 CA at 367. Others did not: *Salford Corp v Lever* [1891] 1 Q.B. 168 CA; *Armagas Ltd v Mundogas SA* [1986] A.C. 717 CA at 742–743, per Robert Goff LJ; decision aff'd [1986] A.C. 717 HL.

the point. In *Kettlewell v Refuge Assurance Company Ltd*,[146] the claimant sued to recover life insurance premiums paid to a company as a result of fraudulent misrepresentations that if the premiums were paid for four years a policy would be given free thereafter. The claimant clearly obtained a benefit from the payment of the premiums as the insurance company would have been liable to pay out on the contract, despite the fraud if the life assured had died within the insurance period. However, Lord Alverstone CJ and Sir Gorell Barnes thought that all the premiums could be recovered as money had and received as they considered that the benefits conferred upon the claimant could be "ignored". Today, that would probably be rationalised as an award of restitution of the premiums for unjust enrichment based upon a total failure of consideration. But this involved a fiction that the claimant had received no benefit from the insurance company. The approach of Buckley LJ did not take such a fictitious route. Buckley LJ acknowledged that benefits had been received by Mrs Kettlewell. As a result an award to reverse the transaction was not possible. Instead he stated that an award should focus upon the *profit* made by the insurance company. He stated

> "they, having by their agent's fraud got her money into their pocket, cannot be allowed to keep the *profit* as against her".[147]

### (7) Retrograde authority involving breach of statutory duty

**15-045** In the previous chapter we saw that the decision of the Court of Appeal in *Devenish Nutrition Ltd v Sanofi Aventis SA*,[148] misclassified as "restitutionary damages" a claim for disgorgement of profits. The tort in *Devenish* was a breach of statutory duty where vitamin manufacturing companies had entered into worldwide cartels designed to raise prices unlawfully. A claim for disgorgement of the profits was refused because it was erroneously thought that this award was not available for a non-proprietary tort. Nevertheless, the result of the decision must be correct for two reasons. First, because it is elementary economics that an increase in prices does not automatically translate to an increase in profits even in a near-monopoly. Any entitlement to disgorgement of profits would not have entitled the claimants to the whole of the increased prices multiplied by the number of products sold. More fundamentally, the most basic consideration in these cases is deterrence. But, as Arden LJ observed, that goal had already been fulfilled by penalties imposed by the European Commission.[149]

## IV. Measure of Profits, Causation and Remoteness of Profits

### 1. Measure of Profits

**15-046** It is not necessary to descend into the detail of the process of equitable accounting and how profits are determined. Those matters are questions for accounting expertise. However, there is one important matter of principle which must be made. The profit with which disgorgement awards are concerned is the net profit actu-

146 [1908] 1 K.B. 545.
147 [1908] 1 K.B. 545 at 553.
148 [2009] Ch. 390 CA at 429.
149 [2009] Ch. 390 at [102].

ally made and not the expense which is saved by choosing a wrongful, not a proper, action. As a matter of principle it might be thought difficult to separate the two since an expense saved *is* profit made or loss reduced by acting in the wrongful manner rather than acting properly. But courts have refused, on pragmatic grounds, to make an award on the basis of an expense saved.[150] The best attempt to provide a reason for this was given by the Australian judge, McHugh J in *Dart Industries Inc v Decor Corp Pty Ltd*[151]:

> "In a litigious world of unlimited time and resources, the best approach for determining the profit derived from the infringement might be to estimate the profit of the product after allowing a proportion of the overheads and then deduct the opportunity cost of producing the infringing product. This would show the true gain of the infringer from producing or distributing the infringing product instead of the next best alternative. Another but less exact method of determining the profit and preventing the unjust enrichment of the infringer might be to determine what was the best alternative open to the infringer, determine what gross revenue would have been obtained from that alternative, and deduct that sum from the gross revenue obtained from the infringing product. Another suggested method is that there should be a deduction for that part of the overhead which would have been absorbed in producing or selling the alternative to the extent that it was used in producing or selling the infringing product. But to adopt any of these methods would make an often complex subject more complex than it already is. Very likely, it would increase the prospect of contested litigation over the taking of the account and the cost and length of the hearing while the parties and their witnesses investigated and debated the hypothetical ... Lindley LJ, who knew more about accounts of profits than most lawyers, once said ... that he did 'not know any form of account which (was) more difficult to work out, or may be more difficult to work out than an account of profits'. The Court should be slow to adopt a rule which might increase that difficulty."

Unless principle were to prevail over pragmatism, there are numerous cases of expense saved which would not permit disgorgement damages even where those damages were available for that type of breach. One illustration of this type of situation which was cited by the Court of Appeal in *Blake* came from Louisiana; this was the old case of *City of New Orleans v Firemen's Charitable Association*,[152] where the claim was unsuccessful. The defendant had provided a firefighting service for the claimant's property with far fewer firemen, horses and hosepipes than had been contractually specified, saving the defendant expense but causing no loss to the claimant because, even with the limited manning, there had been no failure to put out fires. In England other unsuccessful claims based upon skimped performances include the well-known *Ruxley Electronics and Construction Ltd v Forsyth*,[153] and again in *White Arrow Express Ltd v GUS Catalogue Ltd*.[154] *Ruxley* concerned the swimming pool which was built to a lesser depth than had been contractually specified but which was nevertheless safe and which left the value of the owner's property unaffected. While disallowing the cost of reconstruction the House of Lords did not consider awarding in its place the saving to the builder resulting from having built a shallower pool; the possibility of profits from skimped **15-047**

---

[150] See *Potton Ltd v Yorkclose Ltd* [1990] F.S.R. 11; *Peter Pan Manufacturing Corp v Corsets Silhouette Ltd* [1964] 1 W.L.R. 96; *Siddell v Vickers* (1888) 16 R.P.C. 416; *Celanese International Corp v BP Chemicals Ltd* [1999] R.P.C. 203; *Cala Homes Ltd v Alfred McAlpine Ltd* [1996] F.S.R. 36 at 44.

[151] (1993) 179 C.L.R. 101 at 125.

[152] 43 La. Ann. 447; 9 So. 486 (1891).

[153] [1996] A.C. 344.

[154] (1995) 145 N.L.J. 1504; (1996) 15 Tr. L.R. 69.

performance was not even argued.[155] *White Arrow* concerned the delivery and collection of goods by the defendant road transport contractors for the claimants who sold the goods through their mail order business. The defendants had undertaken to provide a de luxe service but failed to operate the agreed criteria for deliveries and collections, the breach of contract complained of relating to pre-advice of deliveries and timing of collections. In the absence of showing a loss the claimants were held entitled to nominal damages; again, a claim based upon the defendants' saving by providing an inferior service to that promised was not put forward.

**15-048** As noted above,[156] there are obstacles in each of these cases to a conclusion that the claimant had a legitimate interest in preventing the defendant's profit making activity in each of these cases. But, if disgorgement of profits continues, for pragmatic but not principled reasons, to exclude cases of expense saved then these cases would fail *in limine*.

## 2. SCOPE OF DUTY, CAUSATION AND REMOTENESS

**15-049** Like all other awards of damages, questions of scope of duty, causation and remoteness are relevant in cases of disgorgement damages. However, as disgorgement damages have not commonly been recognised by the label of "damages", these considerations have been little explored. However, in principle, there should not be any difference in the tests to be applied for these questions depending upon whether the consequence to which the law responds is the loss of a claimant or the profit of a defendant.

**15-050** As for causation, the starting point is the same as cases of compensatory damages for breach of duty. As we saw in Ch.2,[157] before one can consider the calculation of compensatory damages for loss, it is necessary to determine the kind of loss for which the claimant is entitled to compensation. The same is true for profits. In cases of breach of contract, like those of breach of fiduciary duty, the starting point is what profit the claimant has a legitimate interest in preventing the defendant from making. As the Court of Appeal put the point in a breach of fiduciary duty case,

> "[i]t is sufficient that the profit falls within the scope of his duty of loyalty to the beneficiary."[158]

Once it is determined that the claimant had a legitimate interest in preventing the defendant from profiting in a particular amount then no further question of causation is needed. This point can be illustrated by the decision of the High Court of Australia in *Warman International Ltd v Dwyer*.[159] A manager left his position at Warman and, in breach of fiduciary duty, set up new companies which entered a joint venture agreement with Warman's distributor. Warman claimed an account and disgorgement of all the profits of the new company. In a joint judgment, the High Court of Australia held that Warman was entitled to an account and disgorgement of the net profits before tax of the new companies for the first two years of their operation. The concern of the court was that the "stringent rule requiring a fiduci-

[155] The claimant did receive a comparatively modest award for his disappointment. The case is fully dealt with at paras 31-014 and 31-021, below.

[156] At para.15-025.

[157] At para.2-002.

[158] *Novoship (UK) Ltd v Mikhaylyuk* [2015] Q.B. 499 at [96].

[159] (1995) 182 C.L.R. 544.

ary to account for profits can be carried to extremes".[160] The scope of the new companies' duties determined the extent to which they were liable to disgorge profits.

Even outside cases of breach of contract or breach of fiduciary duty where the wrong consists of the making of the particular profit, questions of the scope of the liability to account remain essential. An English example of this is *Novoship (UK) Ltd v Mikhaylyuk*.[161] A company director and manager took bribes in return for arranging charters of the vessels of his principal. The defendants included dishonest assistants in the breaches of fiduciary duty who also received payments of the bribes. The manager also took bribes for arranging charters to the eighth defendant, which charters proved to be extremely profitable for the sixth and eighth defendants. One issue on the appeal was whether those more remote profits from the charters could be recovered. The Court of Appeal held that they could not. The Court of Appeal accepted that the sixth and eighth defendants' wrong of dishonest assistance in the breach of fiduciary duty caused those profits. In other words, "but for" the dishonest entry into charters, the profits would not have been made. But, using causation in a wider sense which also encompasses remoteness considerations, the Court of Appeal held that the "real or effective cause of the profits" was the unexpected change in the market. For that reason, the Court of Appeal held that there was an "insufficient direct causal connection" between entry into the charters and the profits made and because the account of profits would be "disproportionate".[162] And again in *Gamatronic (UK) Ltd v Hamilton*,[163] the court described disgorgement of profits from a breach of fiduciary duty as irrecoverable because there was "no reasonable relationship" between the breach of duty and the profits. Although the language in each case used was different, the reasoning bears a very strong resemblance to the scope of duty enquiry in relation to compensatory damages in cases where another cause of the loss is the fall in the market.[164] **15-051**

Apart from this preliminary question of the scope of the liability to account for and disgorge profits, questions of remoteness can still arise. The Court of Appeal has said that in those cases **15-052**

> "there is no reason why the common law rules of causation, remoteness and measure of damages should not be applied by analogy".[165]

The use of the remoteness principles can be seen in cases which insist that the profits to be disgorged have "some reasonable connection" with the breach of duty.[166] A good illustration is the United States case of *Frank Music Corp v Metro-Goldwyn Mayer Inc*.[167] The defendant hotel, in breach of copyright, had included a segment from the defendant's musical in its revue. The 9th Circuit Court of Appeals awarded the plaintiff 12 per cent of the profits from the revue (being a total of nine per cent after an allowance to the hotel). The claimants argued that they were also entitled to (i) a share of the profits from the hotel and its gaming operations **15-053**

---

160 (1995) 182 C.L.R. 544 at 561.

161 [2015] Q.B. 499.

162 *Novoship (UK) Ltd v Mikhaylyuk* [2015] Q.B. 499 at [120].

163 [2016] EWHC 2225 (QB) at [192].

164 *Banque Bruxelles Lambert v Eagle Star Insurance Co* [1997] A.C. 191. See Ch.2 at 2-002.

165 *Novoship (UK) Ltd v Mikhaylyuk* [2015] Q.B. 499 at [107].

166 *CMS Dolphin Ltd v Simonet* [2001] EWHC Ch 415 at [97].

167 886 F. 2.d. 1545 (1989) 9th Cir CA.

because the revue enticed people to the hotel and increased those profits; and (ii) a share of additional "downstream corporate benefits" received by the hotel's parent corporation. The 9th Circuit held that the first set of indirect profits could be recovered but that the second were too remote.

CHAPTER 16

# LIQUIDATED DAMAGES

TABLE OF CONTENTS



The parties to a contract may, as part of the agreement between them, fix the amount which is to be paid by way of damages in the event of breach. In some cases this amount will apply to all breaches, in others only to particular breaches. In some cases it will apply to breach by either party, in others only to breach by one particular party. And sometimes different sums may be stipulated for different breaches, whether by one or by both parties. **16-001**

Whether the agreed sum is recoverable from the party in breach depends upon whether it constitutes liquidated damages, when it is recoverable, or a penalty, when it is not. The law as to liquidated damages and penalties has a long involved his- **16-002** tory, and a brief account of the development over the centuries is necessary for a full understanding of the modern law.

### 1. Historical Development of Liquidated Damages and Penalties

## (1) Penal bonds

16-003 The question of penalties originally arose in relation to penal bonds. Such a bond consisted of a promise to pay a stated sum of money if another promise was not fulfilled. The exact form of a penal bond was a promise absolute to pay a stated sum, with a condition inserted to the effect that if the main obligation was performed by a certain day the promise to pay the money would be void. The common law courts originally recognised and enforced these penal bonds, but equity early granted relief by means of restraining any action which was brought for a penalty. This resulted in the common law courts following suit by means of a statute of William III in 1697. This provided[1] that in an action upon a bond the claimant must assign one or more breaches of the obligation upon which the bond was conditioned, and, while he remained entitled on proving a breach to judgment for the full amount of the sum promised in the bond, he could only recover by execution the amount of the damage proved to have been sustained by the breach or breaches assigned, although the judgment would remain as a security for future breaches.[2] Since the judgment was still for the amount promised by the bond, this penal sum was still of some practical importance in that it fixed the maximum amount which could be recovered upon the bond.[3]

16-004 This provision has now disappeared from the statute book[4] and penal bonds have to all intents and purposes disappeared from the present-day scene.[5] The relevance of the historical approach to penal bonds, although influential to the development of the law concerning penalties in Australia,[6] was held to be an historical artefact in the conjoined appeals before the Supreme Court in *Cavendish Square Holdings v Makdessi* and *ParkingEye Ltd v Beavis*.[7]

---

1 8 & 9 Will. 3 c.11 s.8.

2 The particular case of money bonds for the payment of a sum certain at a day certain was specifically dealt with a few years later by a separate statute of 1705, namely, 4 & 5 Anne c.3 ss.12, 13.

3 *White v Sealy* (1778) Doug. 49; *Wilde v Clarkson* (1795) 6 T.R. 303. The best short statements in the cases of the historical development of penal bonds appear in *Beckham v Drake* (1849) 2 H.L.C. 579 at 598, per Williams J; in *Bretts v Burch* (1859) 4 H. & N. 506 at 510, per Bramwell B; and in *Wall v Rederiaktiebolaget Luggude* [1915] 3 K.B. 66 at 72, per Bailhache J.

4 s.8 of 8 & 9 Will. 3 c.11 was repealed by SI 1957/1178 r.7 under the powers conferred by the Supreme Court of Judicature Act 1925 s.99(1)(f), (g) and Sch.1. As for ss.12 and 13 of 4 & 5 Anne c.3 (previous footnote but one), they had already been repealed by the Statute Law Revision Act 1948 s.1 and Sch.1.

5 In repealing the provision of William III, SI 1957/1178 r.7 also introduced into the then *Annual Practice* a new RSC Ord.53G providing that a claimant should claim and recover not the penalty but the amount to which he was entitled under the rules of equity relating to penalties. This provision seems to have disappeared without explanation or trace in the general rearrangement of the Rules of the Supreme Court in 1962: compare *Annual Practice* for 1963 with *Annual Practice* for 1964. Nor does it appear in the new Civil Procedure Rules 1998; one would hardly expect it to.

6 *Andrews v Australia and New Zealand Banking Group Ltd* (2012) 247 C.L.R. 205.

7 [2016] A.C. 1172.

## (2) Sums agreed to be paid as damages for breach of contract

After the penal bond came the sum agreed to be paid for a breach of contract. **16-005** This reversed the position: no longer was the penalty put as the primary obligation in the wording of the agreement. This type of case made its appearance in the course of the 18th century and with Lord Mansfield's judgment in *Lowe v Peers*,[8] in 1768 the law began to take shape. He said there that in the case of

> "covenants secured by a penalty or forfeiture ... the obligee ... may either bring an action of debt for the penalty, and recover the penalty; (after which recovery of the penalty, he cannot resort to the covenant; because the penalty is to be a satisfaction for the whole:) or, if he does not choose to go for the penalty, he may proceed upon the covenant, and recover more or less than the penalty, *toties quoties*."[9]

This laid down, therefore, that the claimant had an election between suing for the penalty or for such damages as he could prove in the ordinary way, but Lord Mansfield did not suggest that the claimant, where he elected to sue for the penalty, would be unable to recover the whole penalty at common law, although he did say that equity would relieve against a penalty as opposed to a covenant "to pay a particular liquidated sum". Not until 1801 in *Astley v Weldon*,[10] a case which may be regarded as establishing the liquidated damages doctrine,[11] was it clearly laid down that if a claimant sued for a penalty he was not entitled even at common law to recover more than the actual damage which he could prove he had incurred.[12] Implied in this decision was the proposition that if the sum were a pre-estimate of loss it would not be regarded as a penalty and could be recovered as liquidated damages. The election given to the claimant in the case of a penalty[13] to sue for the penalty or for breach of contract disregarding the penalty was retained. A different rule from that applying to penal bonds was thus laid down in that the stipulated sum did not fix the maximum amount that the claimant could recover, provided that he ignored the penalty and sued in assumpsit for damages.[14] Only if he sued in debt for the penalty itself would he impose a ceiling on his recovery.[15]

These rules became established without much being said about the statute of William III despite the fact that it applied to such clauses in contracts as much as to penal bonds: thus Lord Mansfield failed to qualify his statements in *Lowe v Peers*,[16] by reference to it. In a number of the cases the court, or one member of the court, **16-006**

---

8 (1768) 4 Burr. 2225.

9 (1768) 4 Burr. 2225 at 2228.

10 (1801) 2 B. & P. 346.

11 In *Wallis v Smith* (1882) 21 Ch. D. 243 CA at 261, Jessel MR called it "the foundation of the subsequent cases on the subject".

12 "It therefore does appear to me that the true effect of this agreement is, to give the plaintiff his option either to proceed upon the covenants toties quoties, or upon the first breach to proceed at once for the £200 out of which he may be satisfied for the damage actually sustained, and which may stand as a security for future breaches": (1801) 2 B. & P. 346 at 353, per Lord Eldon CJ.

13 See Lord Mansfield in *Lowe v Peers* (1768) 4 Burr. 2225, above.

14 *Winter v Trimmer* (1762) 1 Wm. Bl. 395; *Harrison v Wright* (1811) 13 East 343; *Maylam v Norris* (1845) 14 L.J.C.P. 95; *Wall v Rederiaktiebolaget Luggude* [1915] 3 K.B. 66. See paras 16-026 and 16-027, below.

15 *Harrison v Wright* (1811) 13 East 343 at 348, per Lord Ellenborough CJ; *Wall v Rederiaktiebolaget Luggude* [1915] 3 K.B. 66 at 72, per Bailhache J. See paras 16-026 and 16-027, below.

16 (1768) 4 Burr. 2225.

introduced the statute into the decision[17] and sometimes specifically pointed out that the statute applied as much to penalty clauses in a contract as to penal bonds,[18] but generally the statute was ignored. In *Betts v Burch*,[19] Bramwell B commented on this. He said:

> "As to the authorities it is remarkable that from the first to the last the statute is not mentioned. It seems as if, by some singular instinct, the courts have been right, though without referring to the statute by which they ought to have been governed. I believe that the reason is that the judges have considered when equity would have relieved."

This eclipse of the statute had become total in the 20th century even before the repeal in 1957 of the relevant provision in it,[20] so that, although the results reached in the cases were consonant with its requirements, it was in practice a dead letter.[21]

### (3) The criterion of the intention of the parties

**16-007** For a time the courts attempted to justify their interference in these contracts by stating that they were implementing the intention of the parties. Such a claim required them to look to the terminology used in the contract. The contract in *Astley v Weldon*,[22] itself had used neither the term "liquidated damages" nor the term "penalty" but soon after in *Smith v Dickenson*,[23] a clause was held to be a penalty because, it was said, the use of that term clearly prevented the court from holding that the provision was for liquidated damages, while conversely, in *Reilly v Jones*,[24] it was said that no case had been adduced in which a clause had been held to be a penalty where the parties had used the terminology of liquidated damages. However, when in 1829 in *Kemble v Farren*,[25] another milestone case, an amount expressed to be liquidated damages by the parties was held to be a penalty by the court, the bankruptcy of such an interpretation was clear. This, however, was only slowly realised,[26] and, furthermore, there was as yet no clearly developed test to take the place of the test of the parties' intention. As Rigby LJ said at the end of the 19th century in *Willson v Love*[27]:

> "The history of the decisions appears to me to lead to the conclusion that the courts made a mistake when they departed in regard to these cases from the general rule that effect

---

17 It was relied on by Chambre J in *Astley v Weldon* (1801) 2 B. & P. 346 itself at 354; see also *Harrison v Wright* (1811) 13 East 343 at 341, per Lord Ellenborough CJ; *Davies v Penton* (1827) 6 B. & C. 216 at 224, per Holroyd and Littledale JJ. Sometimes it is referred to in order to point out that it did not apply to, and was not required in, Scotland: *Elphinstone v Monkland Iron and Coal Co* (1886) 11 App. Cas. 332 at 346, per Lord Fitzgerald; *Clydebank Engineering and Shipbuilding Co v Don Jose Ramos Yzquierdo y Castaneda* [1905] A.C. 6 at 10, per Lord Halsbury LC.

18 See, e.g. *Betts v Burch* (1859) 4 H. & N. 506 at 510, per Bramwell B; *Wall v Rederiaktiebolaget Luggude* [1915] 3 K.B. 66 at 72, per Bailhache J.

19 (1859) 4 H. & N. 506 at 511.

20 See para.16-004.

21 See *Sparrow v Paris* (1862) 7 H. & N. 594 at 599, per Bramwell B: "We think it is recoverable, and that whether we seek a solution of the question in the statute 8 & 9 Will. 3 c.11, s.8, or elsewhere."

22 (1801) 2 B. & P. 346.

23 (1804) 3 B. & P. 630.

24 (1823) 1 Bing. 302.

25 (1829) 6 Bing. 141.

26 Thus a decade later the court in *Boys v Ancell* (1839) 5 Bing. N.C. 390 was still paying close attention to the terminology.

27 [1896] 1 Q.B. 626 CA at 633.

> ought to be given to the terms of the agreement entered into by the parties, and that, when once the rule was departed from, it became extremely difficult to arrive at any clear rule on the subject."

And, indeed, the numerous 19th century cases show some confusion and not infrequent difficulty in reconciling,[28] a factor which must be recognised when relying on them as precedents. Perhaps today they are of real value only as illustrations of type-situations.[29]

### (4) The modern law

The law was re-stated in a number of authoritative decisions of the House of Lords and Judicial Committee at the beginning of the last century, culminating in 1915 in *Dunlop Pneumatic Tyre Co v New Garage and Motor Co*,[30] where Lord Dunedin reframed in a series of "rules" the principles for ascertaining whether a stipulated sum is liquidated damages or penalty. Upon these cases and upon these rules the modern law rested[31]; at the end of the century the Judicial Committee in *Philips Hong Kong v Attorney General of Hong Kong*,[32] endorsed their approach,[33] while stressing the need for that approach to be realistic.[34] The law concerning penalties was then revisted and rationalised in the important conjoined appeals in *Cavendish Square Holdings v Makdessi* and *ParkingEye Ltd v Beavis*.[35] There, the Supreme Court conducted an extensive review of all of the law and authorities on liquidated damages and penalties. **16-008**

## 2. Nature and Effect of Liquidated Damages and Penalties

### (1) Nature of liquidated damages and penalties

**(a) A summary of the test for a penalty** The most comprehensive review ever undertaken of the law of penalties by an ultimate appellate court was taken in the conjoined appeals in *Cavendish Square Holdings v Makdessi* and *ParkingEye Ltd* **16-009**

---

28 This confusion is epitomised by the different approach taken by the members of the Court of Appeal, particularly James LJ, in *Re Newman* (1876) L.R. 4 Ch. D. 724 CA and, soon after, by the members of the Court of Appeal, particularly Sir George Jessel MR, in *Wallis v Smith* (1882) L.R. 21 Ch. D. 243 CA.

29 See paras 16-061 to 16-098, below.

30 [1915] A.C. 79. The other cases are *Clydebank Engineering Co v Don Jose Ramos Yzquierdo y Castaneda* [1905] A.C. 6; *Public Works Commissioner v Hills* [1906] A.C. 368 PC; *Webster v Bosanquet* [1912] A.C. 394 PC; and, less importantly, *De Soysa v De Pless Pol* [1912] A.C. 194 PC.

31 See *Widnes Foundry v Cellulose Acetate Silk Co* [1931] 2 K.B. 393 CA at 405, per Scrutton LJ: "It is fortunately not necessary to go into all the cases which have discussed particular forms of words and the origin of this penalty jurisprudence … Historically there is a good deal of disagreement as to how it grew up, but personally I consider myself bound by the summary of the cases given by Lord Dunedin in *Dunlop Pneumatic Tyre Co v New Garage & Motor Co*".

32 (1993) 61 B.L.R. 41 PC.

33 "Guidance … is authoritatively set out in the speech of Lord Dunedin in *Dunlop Pneumatic Tyre Co v New Garage and Motor Co.*": (1993) 61 B.L.R. 41 PC at 56. The argument advanced in *Jeancharm Ltd (t/a Beaver International) v Barnet Football Club Ltd* (2004) 92 Con. L.R. 26 CA that Lord Dunedin's approach had been abandoned in *Philips Hong* Kong was roundly dismissed by the Court of Appeal.

34 See *Philips Hong Kong v Attorney General of Hong Kong* (1993) 61 B.L.R. 41 PC at 54, 58–59 and 63.

35 [2016] A.C. 1172.

*v Beavis*.[36] In those cases, the Supreme Court revisited the law of penalties in the context of provisions which (i) disentitled a party from receiving sums of money which without breach he would have received; and (ii) provisions requiring the transfer of property by the party in breach at an undervalue or for no value.

**16-010** In the first appeal before the Supreme Court (*Makdessi*), Mr Makdessi and a colleague held shares in a large advertising and marketing company in the Middle East. Mr Makdessi and his colleague agreed to sell shares to a related company to give it a 60 per cent holding. Cavendish Square Holdings was novated to the related company's rights. The purchase price was to be paid in four instalments. The final two payments could only be calculated in the future, being dependent on the amount of the company's future profits very substantially increased to represent a particularly high figure for goodwill so that the total amount payable could amount to just short of $150 million. Mr Makdessi and his colleague were restricted from trading in the same field in 23 specified countries.

Two crucial provisions of the contract were as follows: if Mr Makdessi breached the restrictive covenants then (i) he would not be entitled to receive the final two instalments of the price paid by Cavendish (cl.5.1); and (ii) Cavendish would have a call option to buy Mr Makdessi's remaining shares, at a price excluding the value of the goodwill of the business (cl.5.6). Mr Makdessi subsequently breached the restrictive covenants. He argued that cll.5.1 and 5.6 were unenforceable penalty clauses. The Supreme Court upheld the validity of the clauses.

**16-011** The second appeal before the Supreme Court (*ParkingEye*) involved parking charges imposed by the claimant company who managed a car park. The car park was intended for motorist customers of a retail store. A parking charge of £85 was imposed on motorists for overstaying the two hour permitted period of free parking. Motorists who entered the car park and parked their cars contracted to adhere to the parking rules. Mr Beavis overstayed the free period by just short of an hour. He refused to pay the £85 charge. One ground was that he alleged that it was a penalty. A majority of the Supreme Court (Lord Toulson dissenting) upheld the validity of the clause.

**16-012** The various judgments in *Makdessi* and *ParkingEye* explained the law of penalties in general terms before applying the reasoning to the two appeals. All of the Supreme Court held that the penalties doctrine was only engaged when there had been a breach of contract. A provision, no matter how extreme, which penalised a party could not be a penalty unless it was consequential upon breach. Lord Neuberger and Lord Sumption (with whom Lord Carnwath agreed) explained that this principle, which had been taken for granted as early as 1939 in *Moss Empires Ltd v Olympia (Liverpool) Ltd*,[37] depended upon a

> "fundamental difference between a jurisdiction to review the fairness of a contractual obligation and a jurisdiction to regulate the remedy for its breach".[38]

Their Lordships rejected the contrary Australian approach[39] as (i) "a radical departure from the previous understanding of the law"; as (ii) an approach which was "entirely historical" but not consistent with history; as (iii) an approach which

---

36 [2016] A.C. 1172.

37 [1939] AC 544. See also *Export Credits Guarantee Department v Universal Oil Products Co* [1983] 1 W.L.R. 399 HL.

38 [2016] A.C. 1172 at [12]–[13].

39 *Andrews v Australia and New Zealand Banking Group Ltd* (2012) 247 C.L.R. 205.

is difficult to apply to the case to which it is supposedly directed; and as (iv) an approach which does not

> "address the major legal and commercial implications of transforming a rule for controlling remedies for breach of contract into a jurisdiction to review the content of the substantive obligations which the parties have agreed".

As to the question of when a clause would be a penalty, the expression of the test was from the judgments of Lord Neuberger and Lord Sumption (with which Lord Carnwath and Lord Clarke agreed, and with the substance of which Lord Mance agreed). The expression by Lords Hodge and Toulson[40] was not substantially different. Lords Neuberger and Sumption recognised that a damages clause may properly be justified by considerations other than the desire to recover compensation for a breach if the innocent party has a legitimate interest in performance extending beyond the prospect of pecuniary compensation flowing directly from the breach. They said: **16-013**

> "The true test is whether the impugned provision is a secondary obligation which imposes a detriment on the contract-breaker out of all proportion to any legitimate interest of the innocent party in the enforcement of the primary obligation."[41]

In summary then, seven points can be made about the likely development of the operation of the law of penalties following the decisions in *Makdessi* and *ParkingEye*: **16-014**

(1) A clause can only be a penalty if it operates conditionally upon breach of contract, in other words if it is a secondary obligation arising upon breach.
(2) Whether a clause operates conditionally upon a breach of contract is a question of substance, not form, and drafting techniques by the parties may not be effective if the true construction of a clause is that it is conditional upon breach.
(3) A penalty is not confined to the payment of money; it can include the transfer of property but it will not include cases where a proprietary or possessory right is transferred but is defeasible upon breach. The only action available in those cases is for relief against forfeiture.
(4) The question whether a clause is a penalty should be asked before asking whether relief against forfeiture should be granted. This is because the penalties doctrine operates at the time the clause comes into operation, not at the time of breach. However, it would be foolish not to plead these doctrines as defences in the alternative to a claim for forfeiture.
(5) The test for whether a clause, conditional on breach, is a penalty is whether it imposes a detriment on the contract-breaker out of all proportion to any legitimate interest of the innocent party in the enforcement of the primary obligation.
(6) In applying this test, courts should consider the circumstances in which the contract was made. A negotiated contract between properly advised parties of comparable bargaining power involves a strong initial presumption that the parties are the best judges of what is legitimate in a provision dealing with the consequences of breach.

---

40 [2016] A.C. 1172 at [255], [294].
41 [2016] A.C. 1172 at [32].

(7) Once a clause is recognised as a penalty then the consequences are that it is void. There is no power for the court partially to enforce the clause to the extent that it might not have been penal, or to enforce it only on terms. To do so would be to rewrite the contract.

**16-015** Applying the law to the facts of *Makdessi*, the Supreme Court unanimously held that neither cl.5.1 nor cl.5.6 was a penalty. As to whether the clause was a secondary obligation which was conditional upon breach, contrary to the press release issued by the Supreme Court, the view on this issue of Lords Neuberger, Sumption and Carnwath was not a majority finding. Their Lordships held that on their proper construction neither clause was a secondary obligation which was conditional upon breach. Both cl.5.1 and cl.5.6 were, in reality, price adjustment clauses which were primary obligations even if the trigger for the price adjustment was a breach. They were not secondary obligations conditional upon breach. None of the other justices reached this conclusion although Lord Hodge and Lord Clarke considered that there was a 'strong argument' that cl.5.1 was a primary obligation. Nevertheless, all of the remaining justices held that these clauses were not penalties because they were not out of proportion to the legitimate interest to be protected.

**16-016** Applying the law to the facts of *Parkingeye*, all of the court held that the parking charge was conditional upon breach. However, eight justices (Lord Toulson dissenting) held that the parking charge was not out of proportion to the legitimate interest to be protected. Lords Neuberger and Sumption (with whom Lords Carnwath and Clarke agreed on this point) said[42] that although *Parkingeye* was not liable to suffer a loss as a result of overstaying motorists, it had a legitimate interest in charging them which extended beyond the recovery of any loss. *Parkingeye* met its costs from the charges for breaches by the motorists. It was also relevant that the landowner had a legitimate interest in the scheme applied by *Parkingeye*, including the receipt of a fee from *Parkingeye* to run the scheme and also to ensure adequate parking for customers of the retailer tenants. The landowner's interest was relevant because the penal character of the scheme could not depend on facts which a motorist might not reasonably know such as whether the landowner operates it himself or employs a contractor like *ParkingEye* to operate it.

**16-017** **(b) The requirement of a breach of contract** A number of cases, prior to *Makdessi* and *ParkingEye*, illustrate the requirement that a clause can only be a penalty if, as a matter of substance, it operates upon a breach of contract. Perhaps the leading example prior to *Makdessi* and *ParkingEye* is *Export Credits Guarantee Department v Universal Oil Products Co.*[43] The defendants there had contracted to construct an oil refinery for a group of Newfoundland companies. Bankers had provided the financing of this project in return for the issue of promissory notes by the companies and for the claimants' guarantee of the promissory notes. By a further contract between the claimants and the defendants the claimants required the defendants, in the event of their default in their performance of the construction contract, to indemnify the claimants against any liability they might incur under the contract of guarantee. Some promissory notes were dishonoured, the claimants duly indemnified the bankers under the contract of guarantee, and then claimed indemnity for themselves from the defendants whom they alleged to be in default under the construction contract. The defendants' argument that the sum claimed

---

42 [2016] A.C. 1172 at [99].

43 *Export Credits Guarantee Department v Universal Oil Products Co* [1983] 1 W.L.R. 399 HL.

constituted a penalty was firmly rejected. Lord Roskill who gave the only reasoned speech said that the clause

> "provided for payment of money on the happening of a specified event other than the breach of a contractual duty owed by the contemplated payer to the contemplated payee."[44]

The breach by the defendants was of their contractual obligations not to the claimants but to third parties.[45]

Another example is *Berg v Blackburn Rovers Football Club & Athletic Plc*,[46] where the manager of a football club was held to be entitled to be paid his remaining salary on termination of his employment by the club prior to the expiry of the contract term. A clause in the manager's service agreement entitled the club to terminate on payment to the manager of the residue of his salary. The termination did not constitute a breach of contract, so no question of penalty arose. A further example is *Cadogan Petroleum Holdings Ltd v Global Process Systems LLC*.[47] That was a complex case concerning the sale and repurchase of two gas plants for very many millions of US dollars. Eder J held that the law as to penalties did not apply to the repurchase price payments, made and to be made, as the obligation to pay was in no way dependent on contractual breach.[48] This decision was referred to, with apparent approval, by Lord Mance in the *Makdessi* and *ParkingEye* appeals.[49]

The situation was different from that in the above cases in *M&J Polymers Ltd v Imerys Minerals Ltd*,[50] where the issue was whether a take or pay clause in a contract could amount to a penalty, such a clause being one which requires buyers of goods to order minimum quantities and to pay for the minimum quantities even if they had not ordered them. It was argued for the suppliers that their claim for the shortfall in goods delivered was simply in debt for the price, being a claim for payment which arose, as it were, on the happening of the specified event of not ordering the goods; therefore no question of penalty arose. Burton J did not agree. He held that the rule as to penalties could apply since the obligation to pay for goods not ordered could only arise where there had been a breach of the obligation to order; the obligation to pay therefore did stem from a breach of contract. Nonetheless the provision was held not to amount to a penalty but to liquidated damages; for one thing, loss to the suppliers to the extent of the value of the shortfall in the goods delivered was on the cards.[51] **16-018**

The situation was again different with the contract in *Euro London Appointments Ltd v Claessens International Ltd*,[52] which was between an employment agency and a client for the agency to introduce, for a fee, personnel for engagement by the client. The contract, which set out a scale of refunds of the introduc- **16-019**

---

44 [1983] 1 W.L.R. 399 HL at 402H. A provision in a sale and leaseback contract that the lessor buyer need not pay the residue of the purchase price, amounting to 30 per cent of it, if it terminated the tenancy pursuant to a contractual right to do so, could not be construed as a penalty: *UK Housing Alliance (North West) Ltd v Francis* [2010] 3 All E.R. 519 CA.

45 It was also pointed out—and this could be of some significance for other cases—that the sum in question represented the actual loss suffered by the claimants: [1983] 1 W.L.R. 399 HL at 403E to G.

46 [2013] EWHC 1070 Ch.

47 [2013] EWHC 214 (Comm).

48 See [2013] EWHC 214 (Comm) at [32] to [35]. There was an additional issue concerning relief from forfeiture; this feature of the case is at para.16-117, below.

49 [2016] A.C. 1172 at [156].

50 [2008] 1 Lloyd's Rep. 541.

51 For Burton J's detailed reasons see [2008] 1 Lloyd's Rep. 541 at [44] and [46].

52 [2006] 2 Lloyd's Rep. 436 CA.

tion fee where personnel who had been engaged left during the first 12 weeks of the engagement, also had a provision that to qualify for any refund the client must pay the agency fee within seven days of being invoiced. This the client failed to do and then maintained that the qualifying provision constituted a penalty. The Court of Appeal, reversing the court below, disagreed; the provision was simply a condition precedent to any right to a refund. Although there was also a provision in the contract making it a contractual obligation to pay the agency within seven days of invoice, the two provisions were held to be completely independent of each other.[53] No question of penalty arose.

16-020 (c) **A penalty can include a required transfer of property on breach** In *Jobson v Johnson*,[54] the defendant had contracted to buy shares in a football club for some £350,000 payable in seven instalments. The agreement contained a clause that, if the defendant defaulted on the payment of the second or any subsequent instalment, he was required to transfer the shares back to the sellers for £40,000, an amount which neither was a genuine pre-estimate of the sellers' loss in the event of the defendant's default nor reflected the true value of the shares. The defendant paid £140,000 towards the purchase price, the shares were transferred to him, and he then defaulted on payment of the instalments. The claimant, the assignee of the sellers of the shares, claimed specific performance of the agreement for the re-transfer of the shares while the defendant claimed that the re-transfer agreement was a penalty and as such unenforceable. The Court of Appeal agreed with the defendant. A majority of the Court of Appeal was, however, prepared to offer the claimant two alternative forms of relief both of which fell short of enforcing the penalty.[55] The decision, as a penalties case, must now be seriously doubted for this reason.[56] However, as to the difference between a money penalty and a penalty comprising other property, Dillon LJ said:

> "There is no distinction in principle between a clause which provides that if a person makes default in paying a sum of £100 on a certain day he shall pay a penalty of £1,000, and a clause which provides that if a person makes default in paying a sum of £100 on a certain day he shall by way of penalty transfer to the obligee 1000 shares in a certain company for no consideration. Again, there should be no distinction in principle between a clause which requires the defaulter, on making default in paying money, to transfer shares for no consideration, and a clause which in like circumstances requires the defaulter to sell shares to the creditor at an undervalue. In each case the clause ought to be unenforceable in equity in so far as it is a penalty clause."[57]

This aspect of the decision in *Jobson v Johnson*, unlike the orders made, was supported in the Supreme Court appeals in *Makdessi* and *ParkingEye*.

## (2) Effect of holding a stipulated sum to be liquidated damages or a penalty

16-021 The same sum cannot, in the same agreement, be treated as a penalty for some purposes and as liquidated damages for others. For if the same sum is extravagant

---

53 Chadwick LJ's leading judgment with its careful analysis deserves perusal.

54 [1989] 1 W.L.R. 1026 CA.

55 As to one of these, see the case further at para.16-026, below.

56 See below at para.16-026.

57 [1989] 1 W.L.R. 1026 CA at 1034H to 1035B.

and unconscionable in relation to one breach to which it applies, and the sum becomes branded as having a penal nature which it cannot lose in relation to other more serious breaches to which it also applies. It adds nothing to say that it would not have been a penalty as to the other breach or breaches, or that it is the other breach or breaches that have in the event occurred.[58] Nor will the court make any severance for the parties, once they have tampered with penal stipulations. The parties should make their own severance at the time of the making of the agreement. They may either stipulate separate sums for the various possible breaches,[59] in which case one sum may be held to be a penalty while another stands as liquidated damages. Alternatively, they may contract that the stipulated sum shall apply to only one or some breaches, and leave the other breaches to be compensated for in the ordinary way by an action for unliquidated damages.[60]

**(a) Sum held to be liquidated damages** The courts implement the intention of the parties in the case of liquidated damages by holding the claimant entitled to recover the stipulated sum[61] on breach, without requiring proof of the actual damage and irrespective of the amount, if provable, of the actual damage. Moreover, it should be appreciated that the concept of a duty to mitigate is entirely foreign to a claim for liquidated damages. Thus in *Abrahams v Performing Right Society*,[62] where an employer summarily dismissed an employee under a contract which provided that the employer could give two years' notice or pay salary in lieu of notice it was held that if the employee's entitlement to claim the payment in lieu of notice was by way of liquidated damages—he was in fact held to be entitled to claim the money as a contractual debt so that no question of damages arose[63]—the full amount would be payable and could not be reduced by any substitute moneys the claimant earned during the two years.[64] **16-022**

In most cases where the claimant has recovered his liquidated damages the stipulated sum has been greater than the actual, or at least the provable, damage. However, just as this cannot diminish his damages, so he cannot increase them by ignoring the liquidated damages clause in the rare case where the actual damage is **16-023**

58 This is best illustrated in those cases where one sum is made to apply to both trifling and serious breaches: see paras 16-062 and following, below. But see the somewhat curious case of *Cato v Cato* (1972) 116 S.J. 138 involving breach of a single obligation—being an obligation to pay money—in which the stipulated sum, though a genuine pre-estimate of damage if the claimant sued for the breach in the USA where he would have to pay his own lawyer even if successful, was held to be a penalty since suit was in fact brought in England.

59 See, e.g. *Imperial Tobacco Co v Parsley* [1936] 2 All E.R. 515 CA.

60 This is well illustrated by many types of contract, e.g. contracts in restraint of trade; the main varieties are set out at paras 16-080 and following, below.

61 The stipulation may, exceptionally, be not for the payment of money but for the transfer of property, whether at no consideration or at an undervalue: see *Jobson v Johnson* [1989] 1 W.L.R. 1026 CA, at para.16-020, above.

62 [1995] I.C.R. 1028 CA.

63 In *Cerberus Software Ltd v Rowley* [2001] I.C.R. 376 CA, on the other hand, where the payment of six months salary in lieu of notice was held to be optional and not to create a contractual debt, dismissal without notice was accordingly a breach giving rise to a requirement to mitigate. There was no suggestion, as there perhaps might have been, that the provision for payment of six months' salary constituted liquidated damages which would have put paid to the defendant's mitigation argument. See *Abrahams* and *Cerberus* further at para.9-023, above.

64 However, as pointed out by Leggatt J in *MSC Mediterranean Shipping Co SA v Cottonex Anstalt* [2015] EWHC 283 (Comm), in assessing whether a stipulated sum is or is not a penalty, the mitigation principle must be taken into account in comparing with the stipulated sum what the claimant would have recovered in the absence of the stipulated sum: see at [113].

demonstrably greater than the stipulated sum,[65] a situation most likely to arise where one sum is stipulated to be paid on a number of varying, yet uncertain, breaches and the most serious breach is the one which occurs. Thus in *Diestal v Stevenson*,[66] where a contract for the sale of coal provided that for every ton not delivered or not accepted the party in default should pay one shilling, the seller, in an action for non-delivery, was held limited to this sum despite his greater loss. And in *Talley v Wolsey-Neech*,[67] where a contract of sale of land provided for liquidated damages on the buyer's failure to complete based on the amount of the loss accruing to the seller on a resale by him, it was held that the seller was confined to this amount[68] and could not claim further damages by way of interest in addition.[69] These cases show that the claimant can neither claim unliquidated damages in addition to the liquidated damages which are designed to deal with the loss that has occurred nor elect to ignore the liquidated damages provision and sue only for unliquidated damages.[70]

**16-024** The claimant will, however, be entitled to sue for unliquidated damages in the ordinary way, in addition to suing for the liquidated damages, if other breaches have occurred outside those which fall within the ambit of the liquidated damages provision or, it seems, if only part of the loss arising from a single breach is regarded as falling within the provision's ambit. The position is illustrated by *Aktieselskabet Reidar v Arcos*.[71] Charterers, in breach of their obligation to load a full and complete cargo by a certain date, took so long to load that the time passed when the ship could carry a summer cargo and she was only able to carry a much smaller winter cargo.

---

[65] It was, however, held in *Bath and North East Somerset DC v Mowlem* (2005) 100 Con. L.R. 1 CA that, where the actual loss is, or is likely to be, greater than the liquidated damages, this may be used as an argument for specific relief—in *Mowlem* by way of an injunction—on the ground that damages would not be an adequate remedy, and further that it is legitimate, in deciding on adequacy of remedy, to consider losses which would be irrecoverable, perhaps because too remote, as well as recoverable losses. Mance LJ said: "The Council accepts—indeed it asserts—that it would be bound in any claim for damages by its contractual agreement regarding liquidated and ascertained damages. The Council is not seeking to avoid that agreement but to rely on it. It is the reason the Council seeks an injunction": at [15]. The Bath case was applied in *AB v CD* [2014] EWCA Civ 229. At [30], Underhill LJ (with whom Ryder and Laws LJJ agreed) said that a claimant will still need to show that if the threatened breach occurs then there is a substantial risk of unrecoverable loss due to the liquidated damages provision. But once this is shown there will be a discretion to award aninjunction. Ryder LJ would have gone further and seen this as one factor in a test for whether it is "just in all the circumstances" to confine a claimant to damages: at [32].

[66] [1906] 2 K.B. 345.

[67] (1978) 38 P. & C.R. 45 CA.

[68] (1978) 38 P. & C.R. 45 CA at 52.

[69] *Cellulose Acetate Silk Co v Widnes Foundry* [1933] A.C. 20 is a clear case in which the stipulated sum was less than the actual damage and the claimant was held entitled to recover only the stipulated sum, but this was interpreted by the House of Lords as a limitation of liability and not as a genuine pre-estimate of probable damage. It is therefore not exactly in point: see para.16-100, below. See too the footnote at the end of para.16-100, below for the curious case of *Temloe v Errill* (1987) 39 B.L.R. 30 CA where the liquidated damages were agreed at nil.

[70] In *Wallace-Turner v Cole* (1983) 46 P. & C.R. 164 the suggestion, at 168, that a claimant may elect between liquidated and unliquidated damages for a single breach of contract, and that this was supported by the similar case of *Talley v Wolsey-Neech* (1978) 38 P. & C.R. 45 CA, seems to be misconceived but is capable of explanation. On breach by the buyer the seller might or might not resell the property and the liquidated damages clause came into operation only if there were a resale; if there were no resale the damages would be unliquidated. The election was therefore not as to the damages but as to the resale. As Stephenson LJ put it in *Talley v Wolsey-Neech*, at 52: "If he decides to sue for damages, he can choose whether to resell or not, and the measure of damages will be different according to his choice."

[71] [1927] 1 K.B. 352 CA.

The charterparty contained the usual provision for demurrage as liquidated damages for the charterers' detention of the ship in loading, but the owners successfully claimed, in addition to the demurrage, unliquidated damages in the ordinary way for loss of freight caused by the charterers' failure to load a full and complete cargo. "The provisions as to demurrage", said Atkin LJ,

> "quantify the damages, not for the complete breach, but only such damages as arise from the detention of the vessel."[72]

And in *Total Transport Corporation v Amoco Trading Co, The Altus*,[73] where the breach of the obligation of charterers to load a full and complete cargo caused the owners to be entitled to demurrage at a lower rate than that to which they would have been entitled had the full and complete cargo been loaded, the owners successfully claimed, in addition to the liquidated damages by way of so-called dead freight representing freight on the amount of cargo which should have been, but was not, loaded,[74] the difference between these two rates. While one may question Webster J's view in *The Altus*,[75] that there had been only a single breach of obligation in both that case and in the earlier *Aktieselskabet Reidar v Arcos*,[76] as there must surely have been a breach not only of the loading obligation but also of the obligation not to delay the ship beyond the lay days,[77] what is important is that, at least in *The Altus*,[78] the loss for which unliquidated damages were being claimed flowed from the same breach as that for which the liquidated damages had been specified. Webster J said that he regarded the ratio decidendi of *Aktieselskabet Reidar v Arcos*,[79] as being that:

> "where a charterer commits any breach, even if it is only one breach, of his obligation either to provide the minimum contractual load or to detain the vessel for no longer than the stipulated period, the owner is entitled not only to the liquidated damages directly recoverable for the breach of the obligation to load (deadfreight) or for the breach of the obligation with regard to detention (demurrage), but also for, in the first case, to [sic] the damages flowing indirectly or consequentially from any detention of the vessel (if it occurs) and, in the second case, to damages flowing indirectly or consequentially from any failure to load a complete cargo if there is such a failure."[80]

Also in some cases an injunction may prove a suitable remedy[81] but, although a claimant may elect[82] whether to ask for an injunction or for his liquidated dam- **16-025**

---

72 [1927] 1 K.B. 352 CA at 363.

73 [1985] 1 Lloyd's Rep. 423.

74 Webster J assumed that a deadfreight clause was properly classified as a liquidated damages clause but was somewhat uncertain whether such a clause should be so treated: see [1985] 1 Lloyd's Rep. 423 at 432, col.2.

75 [1985] 1 Lloyd's Rep. 423.

76 [1927] 1 K.B. 352 CA.

77 Certainly Sargant LJ regarded the charterers in *Aktieselskabet Reidar v Arcos* [1927] 1 K.B. 352 CA as having committed two breaches; see at 366 to 367. And the same was said in *Wallace-Turner v Cole* (1983) 46 P. & C.R. 164 at 168.

78 [1985] 1 Lloyd's Rep. 423.

79 [1927] 1 K.B. 352 CA.

80 [1985] 1 Lloyd's Rep. 423 at 435, col.2.

81 Particularly in the case of covenants in restraint of trade.

82 At first there was a tendency to refuse an injunction because of the very existence of a liquidated damages provision, as in *Young v Chalkley* (1867) 16 L.T. 286. But it soon became established that the claimant might elect for an injunction: this view was taken by the court in *Coles v Sims* (1854)

ages, it is generally held that he cannot have both.[83] Thus in *Sainter v Ferguson*,[84] and again in *Carnes v Nesbitt*,[85] an injunction was refused because liquidated damages had already been awarded, and this view was adopted in *General Accident Assurance Co v Noel*,[86] where the claimant was put to his election. However, it would seem that the claimant should be entitled to have the two remedies where they relate to different breaches. The above three cases, in which an election was insisted upon by the court, concerned covenants in restraint of trade where a single stipulated sum was to become payable if the defendant started business in competition with the claimant, and it was reasonable to regard the two remedies as mutually exclusive. But the situation is different where there is a clause providing a graduated sum to be paid in line with the extent of the breach, as in covenants whereby one party has accepted restrictions on his right to sell his goods and has further agreed to pay the other a specific sum for every item sold in breach of covenant. Here it is reasonable to award liquidated damages for the past, i.e. on the number of items already sold in breach, and an injunction as to the future. This result was reached, without exception being taken,[87] in *Imperial Tobacco Co v Parsley*.[88]

16-026 **(b) Sum held to be a penalty** The courts refuse to implement the intention of the parties in the case of a penalty. The claimant is held entitled to sue and recover for such loss as he can prove in the ordinary way. He cannot even claim to recover the stipulated sum on serious breaches if the clause has been held to be a penalty in respect of some breaches, since, as has been pointed out,[89] the same sum cannot in the same agreement be treated as a penalty for some purposes and as liquidated damages for others. It was said by the Court of Appeal in *Jobson v Johnson*,[90] that strictly the penalty clause remains a term of the contract and is not struck out, but that, if the clause is sued upon, it will not be enforced by the court beyond the amount of the contracting party's loss.[91] This suggested distinction between such a limited suit on the penalty and a claim for unliquidated damages ignoring the penalty, which the contracting party is entitled to pursue, is largely academic, with either approach generally producing the same result. The distinction mattered in *Jobson v Johnson* because the penalty, exceptionally, required not the payment of a stipulated sum but the transfer of a stipulated item of property[92] and the court, by a majority, wished to afford the claimant a decree of specific performance provided

---

5 De G. M. & G. 1 (the view was not, as suggested by Wright J in *General Accident Assurance Co v Noel* [1902] 1 K.B. 377, that both an injunction and liquidated damages could be claimed) and an injunction was awarded in *Howard v Woodward* (1864) 34 L.J. Ch. 47 and *Jones v Heavens* (1877) 4 Ch. D. 636. The claimant can elect for an injunction even if the defendant has offered to pay the stipulated damages: *National Provincial Bank of England v Marshall* (1888) 40 Ch. D. 112 CA.

83 Also he can support his claim for an injunction by reliance on the liquidated damages being lower than his actual loss: *Bath and North East Somerset DC v Mowlem* (2005) 100 Con. L.R. 1 CA, at para.16-023 (first footnote), above.

84 (1849) 7 C.B. 716.

85 (1862) 7 H. & N. 778.

86 [1902] 1 K.B. 377.

87 The only issue before the Court of Appeal was whether the stipulated sum was penalty or liquidated damages.

88 [1936] 2 All E.R. 515 CA.

89 See para.16-021, above.

90 [1989] 1 W.L.R. 1026 CA.

91 Clearly put in this way by Nicholls LJ, [1989] 1 W.L.R. 1026 CA at 1040F to G.

92 See the case at para.16-020, above.

that the value of the stipulated property did not exceed the claimant's loss.[93] The decision in *Jobson v Johnson* on this point must now be in serious doubt. According to Lords Sumption, Neuberger and Carnwath in *Makdessi*, the claim could only have succeeded as a case for relief against forfeiture but a claim for that relief had been struck out in earlier proceedings. Most fundamentally, according to Lords Sumption, Neuberger and Carnwath, the orders made by the Court of Appeal did not merely strike down the clause but had the effect of rewriting the clause. The approach of Lords Mance, Hodge, Clarke and Toulson was not as sceptical about the correctness of *Jobson* as a penalties case although a majority of the Supreme Court all rejected the conclusion in *Jobson* that the court had power to strike down only that part of a penalty clause which was extravagant and unconscionable. Such a partial invalidation of the clause would rewrite the contract.

In most of the cases where the claimant has recovered for actual damage the stipulated penalty sum has been greater in amount. Just as the penalty cannot augment his damages so too the claimant will not be restricted to the penalty in the rare cases where it is less than the actual damage. It might be thought impossible to have what has been categorised as "an extravagant and unconscionable sum" turning out to be less than the actual damage, but such a situation could occur where one sum is stipulated to be paid for a number of breaches of varying importance, as to one of which it is disproportionately large, and a serious breach occurs causing damage greater than the stipulated sum. This has found illustration in charterparties,[94] which early developed a clause stipulating for a single sum to be paid for any non-performance. It was early held in *Winter v Trimmer*,[95] and again in *Harrison v Wright*,[96] that the claimant could ignore this penal stipulation and recover for his greater loss. The same result was reached in the last century in *Wall v Rederiaktiebolaget Luggude*[97] where Bailhache J retraced the law in a very useful judgment which remains the clearest authority for the present rule. However the wording of the clause had become more complex[98] and the earlier cases provide more useful illustrations of circumstances in which a penalty is likely to turn out less than the actual damage. The decision itself was approved soon after as to its interpretation of the particular clause as a penalty by the House of Lords in *Watts v Mitsui*,[99] and, as Scrutton LJ pointed out in *Widnes Foundry v Cellulose Acetate Silk Co*,[100] Lord Sumner clearly took the view that 16-027

> "the clause did not prevent the shipowners or charterers from recovering the actual amount of damage, though it might be more than the estimated amount of freight".[101]

In view of this line of authority, the occasional dicta which state that the penalty

---

[93] See especially Nicholls LJ, [1989] 1 W.L.R. 1026 at 1042D to F and 1045B to F. Other cases where the claim appears to have been on the penalty, *Beckham v Drake* (1849) 2 H.L.C. 579 and *Gerrard v Clowes* [1892] 2 Q.B. 11, are cited by him: [1989] 1 W.L.R. 1026 CA at 1040G to 1041C.

[94] Another illustration is *Maylam v Norris* (1845) 14 L.J.C.P. 95. On a sale of fixtures and fittings for £65, with a stipulation, held penal, that either party should pay £30 on any breach, the seller was held entitled to bring an action in respect of £61 which the buyer had failed to pay him.

[95] (1762) 1 Wm. Bl. 395.

[96] (1811) 13 East 343.

[97] [1915] 3 K.B. 66.

[98] It was held still to constitute a penalty mainly because of its history: see para.16-101, below where the case is considered further.

[99] [1917] A.C. 227.

[100] [1931] 2 K.B. 393 CA.

[101] [1931] 2 K.B. 393 CA at 408.

marks the ceiling of recovery are unacceptable.[102] They are probably based upon the historical fact that the sum in a penal bond fixed the maximum amount recoverable.[103]

## 3. Rules for Distinguishing Liquidated Damages from Penalties

16-028 In *Dunlop Pneumatic Tyre Co v New Garage and Motor Co*,[104] Lord Dunedin formulated four tests for when a clause might be a penalty. Those tests were said to be matters which "may prove helpful". But as Lord Neuberger and Lord Sumption said in *Makdessi*,[105] these were not supposed to be exhaustive considerations although they have proved to be perfectly adequate for dealing with standard damages clauses in consumer contracts.[106] Three useful matters can be highlighted before turning to the verbal formulations which aim to differentiate a penalty from liquidated damages.

### (1) The wording used by the parties is of marginal importance

16-029 Lord Dunedin stated as his first "rule" in *Dunlop Pneumatic Tyre Co v New Garage and Motor Co*,[107] that

> "though the parties to a contract who used the words 'penalty' or 'liquidated damages' may prima facie be supposed to mean what they say, yet the expression used is not conclusive. The court must find out whether the payment stipulated is in truth a penalty or liquidated damages."

It is submitted that today even the term "prima facie" is too strong, for in truth the importance of the wording is but a lingering from the early days before *Kemble v Farren*,[108] when the doctrine that the issue turned on the intention of the parties was still in favour.[109] With that doctrine gone, the wording of the parties cannot provide any answer to the basic test of whether or not the amount is a genuine pre-

---

102 See *Wilbeam v Ashton* (1807) 1 Camp. 78, per Lord Ellenborough: "Beyond the penalty you shall not go; within it, you are to give the party any compensation which he can prove himself entitled to"; *Elphinstone v Monkland Iron & Coal Co* (1886) 11 App. Cas. 332 at 346, per Lord Fitzgerald: "The penalty is to cover all the damages actually sustained but it does not estimate them, and the amount of loss (not, however, exceeding the penalty) is to be ascertained in the ordinary way." In *Cellulose Acetate Silk Co v Widnes Foundry* [1933] A.C. 20 at 26 Lord Atkin wished "to leave open the question whether, where a penalty is plainly less in amount than the prospective damages, there is any legal objection to suing on it, or in a suitable case ignoring it and suing for damages". Diplock LJ in *Robophone Facilities v Blank* [1966] 1 W.L.R. 1428, referring to this express reservation of opinion, said that the matter was "by no means clear": at 1446. Lord Atkin's comments are not, however, quite in point as is shown by his reference to prospective damages; they are more allied to the issue of limitation of liability by way of liquidated damages, which is dealt with elsewhere: see paras 16-099 to 16-103, below.

103 See para.16-003, above. And it did indeed remain true that if the claimant sued in debt for the penalty itself, until this, apparently, ceased to be possible (see para.16-004, above), he would impose a ceiling on his recovery and be entitled to no more than the penal sum. See *Wall v Rederiaktiebolaget Luggude* [1915] 3 K.B. 66 at 72, per Bailhache J: "The result of suing for the penalty is therefore that the claimant recovers proved damages, but never more than the penal sum fixed"; and similarly *Harrison v Wright* (1811) 13 East 343 at 348, per Lord Ellenborough.

104 [1915] A.C. 79 at 86–87.

105 [2016] A.C. 1172 at [21].

106 [2016] A.C. 1172 at [25].

107 [2016] A.C. 1172 at [25].

108 (1829) 6 Bing. 141.

109 See para.16-007, above.

estimate of damage. Ever since the court in *Kemble v Farren*,[110] in 1829 held to be a penalty a sum expressed by the parties to be liquidated damages, there have been numerous cases in which either the like has been held[111] or the converse has been held, i.e. the court has allowed as liquidated damages a provision expressed to be a penalty by the parties,[112] and no cases in which the wording of the parties has turned the scales.[113] It is true that the judges generally go no further in statement than saying that the wording is not "conclusive", a term constantly used by the courts in this connection,[114] but it is submitted that there is more truth in the occasionally found less cautious phrase, such as Bramwell B's "the names ... are immaterial"[115] or Coleridge CJ's "does not depend ... on the words used".[116] However, it remains prudent for parties to use the term "liquidated damages" in framing their contracts, since there is always the slender chance that a court may feel that the other pros and cons so balance out that it is compelled to resort to the wording for its decision.

### (2) The circumstances must be viewed as at the time when the contract was made

Lord Dunedin stated as his third "rule" in *Dunlop Pneumatic Tyre Co v New Garage and Motor Co*,[117] that **16-030**

> "the question whether a sum stipulated is penalty or liquidated damages is a question of construction to be decided upon the terms and the inherent circumstances of each particular contract, judged of as at the time of the making of the contract, not as at the time of the breach."[118]

Similar statements of this principle, which has never been doubted, had already appeared in decisions of the highest authorities,[119] while its practical effect had found illustration in *Clydebank Engineering Co v Don Jose Ramos Yzquierdo y Castaneda*.[120] In that case the defendants had contracted to build for the claimants four torpedo boats to be used in the Spanish-American War of 1898, and the

---

110 (1829) 6 Bing. 141.

111 Early illustrations are *Magee v Lavell* (1874) L.R. 9 C.P. 107; *Re Newman* (1876) 4 Ch. D. 724 CA; *Bradley v Walsh* (1903) 88 L.T. 737; *Public Works Commissioner v Hills* [1906] A.C. 368 PC. See also *Landom v Hurrell* [1955] 1 All E.R. 839 and *Bridge v Campbell Discount Co* [1962] A.C. 600 where sums stated to be "agreed compensation for depreciation" were held penalties.

112 Illustrations are *Crisdee v Bolton* (1827) 3 C. & P. 240; *Sparrow v Paris* (1862) 7 H. & N. 594; *Elphinstone v Monkland Iron Co* (1886) 11 App. Cas. 332; *Clydebank Engineering Co v Don Jose Ramos Yzquierdo y Castaneda* [1905] A.C. 6; *Diestal v Stevenson* [1906] 2 K.B. 345; *Cellulose Acetate Silk Co v Widnes Foundry* [1933] A.C. 20; *Alder v Moore* [1961] 2 Q.B. 57 CA; *Stewart v Carapanayoti* [1962] 1 W.L.R. 34; *Vitol SA v Conoil Plc* [2009] 2 Lloyd's Rep. 466.

113 Of course, before *Kemble v Farren* (1829) 6 Bing. 141 there had been decisions where the terminology had controlled, e.g. *Smith v Dickenson* (1804) 3 B. & P. 630, at para.15-007, above.

114 Lord Atkin in *Cellulose Acetate Silk Co v Widnes Foundry* [1933] A.C. 20 at 25 essayed "far from conclusive".

115 In *Sparrow v Paris* (1862) 7 H. & N. 594 at 599.

116 In *Magee v Lavell* (1874) L.R. 9 C.P. 107 at 114 to 115.

117 [1915] A.C. 79.

118 [1915] A.C. 79 at 86 to 87.

119 *Clydebank Engineering Co v Don Jose Ramos Yzquierdo y Castaneda* [1905] A.C. 6 at 17, per Lord Davey: "You are to consider whether it is extravagant, exorbitant or unconscionable ... at the time when the stipulation is made"; *Public Works Commissioner v Hills* [1906] A.C. 368 PC at 376, per Lord Dunedin: "The circumstances ... must be viewed as at the time the bargain was made."

120 [1905] A.C. 6.

contract stipulated that the defendants should pay the claimants £500 for every week's delay in delivery of each of the four vessels. Delivery was delayed and the claimants successfully claimed the stipulated sums as liquidated damages despite the fact, which was held to be irrelevant, that all four torpedo boats, had they been delivered at the specified time, would have been sunk together with the rest of the Spanish fleet. Similarly, in *Hall v Van Der Heiden*,[121] where in a contract for the refurbishment and remodelling of the claimants' flat the defendant builder was required to pay a specified sum for each day that completion was delayed, the main purpose of this provision was to allow for the cost of alternative accommodation while the work continued, but in the event, tired of their nomadic existence, the claimants had taken re-possession of their flat in advance of the delayed completion. This was not something that would have been anticipated at the time the contract was made and was therefore not capable of turning a perfectly good liquidated damages provision into a penalty.[122]

**16-031** An unusual situation arose in *MSC Mediterranean Shipping Co SA v Cottonex Anstalt*.[123] A contract of carriage by sea provided that for 14 days after the discharge of the cargo in the containers the shipper was entitled to retain the containers without charge, after which time container demurrage was payable indefinitely at a specified daily rate. The Court of Appeal held that the question did not arise because the carrier was not entitled to affirm the contract so that he could obtain demurrage indefinitely. However, as Moore-Bick LJ nevertheless explained,[124] the provision was not penal simply because it fixed no express limit on the period of the charterer's liability. The liability was not unlimited because general principles of law, such as those restraining affirmation, imposed a limit on the scope of the charterer's liability.

## (3) The question of onus

**16-032** Little, if anything, appears to have been said about onus of proof until the 1960s pronouncement of Diplock LJ in the course of his judgment in *Robophone Facilities v Blank*,[125] that the onus of proving that a stipulated sum is a penalty rather than liquidated damages lay upon the party against whom the stipulated sum is claimed.[126] This is now the accepted rule. Thus the judgments in the Court of Appeal decision in *Murray v Leisureplay Plc*,[127] laid emphasis on its being for the party seeking to escape liability to show that the particular provision is a penalty and not for the other party to justify it.[128] Again Blair J in *Azimut-Benetti SpA v Henley*,[129] in arriving at a decision in favour of liquidated damages, referred to the rule as to onus of proof.[130]

---

121 [2010] EWHC 586 (TCC).

122 See [2010] EWHC 586 (TCC) at [70] to [75].

123 [2016] EWCA Civ 789, discussed at paras 9-032 to 9-034.

124 [2016] EWCA Civ 789 at [47].

125 [1966] 1 W.L.R. 1428 CA.

126 [1966] 1 W.L.R. 1428 CA at 1447. He added that the terms under which the sum was to become payable might be sufficient to give rise to an inference of penalty, and that for this purpose Lord Dunedin's "rules" were relevant.

127 [2005] I.R.L.R. 946 CA.

128 Arden LJ at [2005] I.R.L.R. 946 CA at [69] and Clarke LJ at [106(vii]) and [106(xi)].

129 [2011] 1 Lloyd's Rep. 473.

130 [2011] 1 Lloyd's Rep. 473 at [14].

### (4) The test for a penalty

**(a) The old verbal formulations** The early 20th century phrase used to define liquidated damages first appeared in Lord Robertson's speech in *Clydebank Engineering Co v Don Jose Ramos Yzquierdo y Castaneda*.[131] It was later incorporated by Lord Dunedin in his list of "rules" in *Dunlop Pneumatic Tyre Co Ltd v New Garage and Motor Co Ltd*,[132] and since then, as part of these "rules", it was often resorted to.[133] The phrase was that where the parties to a contract, as part of the agreement between them, fix the amount which is to be paid by way of damages in the event of breach, a sum stipulated in this way is liquidated damages where it is in the nature of a genuine pre-estimate of the damage which would probably arise from breach of the contract. The intention behind such a provision is generally to avoid, wherever the amount of the damage which would probably result from breach is likely to be uncertain, the difficulty of proving the extent of the actual damage at the trial of the action for breach.[134] In contrast, it was said that a stipulated sum was a penalty where it was in the nature of a threat fixed *in terrorem* of the other party. This is again found in *Clydebank Engineering Co v Don Jose Ramos Yzquierdo y Castaneda*,[135] this time in Lord Halsbury's speech,[136] and also incorporated by Lord Dunedin in his list of "rules" in *Dunlop Pneumatic Tyre Co*.[137] The intention behind such a penalty provision is generally to prevent a breach of the contract by establishing a greater incentive for its performance. **16-033**

One difficulty with the older verbal formulation is identifying when a clause will be a "genuine pre-estimate of damage" and when it is a threat "in terrorem". In *Dunlop*, Lord Dunedin formulated various indicia.[138] These included the following formulation which became the dominant, almost canonic, statement: **16-034**

> "It will be held to be a penalty if the sum stipulated for is extravagant and unconscionable in amount in comparison with the greatest loss that could conceivably be proved to have followed from the breach."[139]

The application of this test was very different where there was only a single obligation upon the breach of which the sum became payable and where there were several obligations upon the breach of which it became payable. These two situations therefore call for separate consideration.

Perhaps the first call for caution in the application of this verbal formulation was by Lord Woolf, speaking for the court, in *Philips Hong Kong v Attorney General* **16-035**

---

131 [1905] A.C. 6 at 19, taking the phrase from the Lord Ordinary at first instance.

132 [1915] A.C. 79 at 86. He had already made use of the phrase in *Public Works Commissioner v Hills* [1906] A.C. 368 PC at 375 to 376.

133 See, e.g. by Scrutton LJ in *English Hop Growers v Dering* [1928] 2 K.B. 174 CA at 181.

134 Recent authorities, however, indicate that, even if the stipulated sum is not a genuine pre-estimate of loss, it will not be regarded as a penalty if there is a commercial justification for it: see the *Makdessi* and *ParkingEye* cases as referred to at paras 16-009 and following.

135 [1905] A.C. 6.

136 [1905] A.C. 6 at 10. Lord Halsbury had already used it in *Elphinstone v Monkland Iron Co* (1886) 11 App. Cas. 332 at 348.

137 [1915] A.C. 79 at 86.

138 [1915] A.C. 79 at 87.

139 It would seem, however, that the yardstick is the loss that the claimant, rather than the defendant, anticipated: in other words, there is no question of the "second rule" in *Hadley v Baxendale* (1854) 9 Ex. 341 operating against the claimant in this context. See *Robophone Facilities v Blank* [1966] 1 W.L.R. 1428 CA at 1448, per Diplock LJ at para.8-207, above, in a footnote.

*of Hong Kong*,[140] when he said:

> "Except possibly in the case of situations where one of the parties to the contract is able to dominate the other as to the choice of the terms of a contract, it will normally be insufficient to establish that a provision is objectionably penal to identify situations where the application of the provision could result in a larger sum being recovered by the injured party than his actual loss. Even in such situations so long as the sum payable in the event of non-compliance with the contract is not extravagant, having regard to the range of losses that it could reasonably be anticipated it would have to cover at the time the contract was made, it can still be a genuine pre-estimate of the loss that would be suffered and so a perfectly valid liquidated damage provision. The use in argument of unlikely illustrations should therefore not assist a party to defeat a provision as to liquidated damages."[141]

He elaborated on this point later in the judgment in a useful passage, saying:

> "Arguments based on hypothetical situations where it is said that the loss might be less than the sum specified as payable as liquidated damages … should not be allowed to divert attention from the correct test as to what is a penalty provision—namely is it a genuine pre-estimate of what the loss is likely to be?—to the different question, namely are there possible circumstances where a lesser loss would be suffered?"[142]

**16-036** It was contended by the claimant in *Jeancharm Ltd (t/a Beaver International) v Barnet Football Club Ltd*,[143] that *Philips Hong Kong* had departed from *Dunlop* and that it is no longer necessary to find a genuine pre-estimate of loss before holding that a provision constitutes liquidated damages; we had moved on and all that now has to be done is to look at the contract as a whole whenever the parties are of equal bargaining power, as they were in *Jeancharm*. The Court of Appeal disagreed. All that had changed with *Philips Hong Kong* is that, in continuing to apply *Dunlop*, one should be careful in deciding, when parties are of equal bargaining power, whether the clause is a penalty.[144] The rule in *Dunlop* had not been abandoned and, as Keene LJ said,[145] the Privy Council in *Philips Hong Kong* recognised

> "that the situation where one party is dominant is not exhaustive of those contracts where a penalty may be identified".

*Jeancharm* concerned a contract for the supply of football kit to the defendant club in which it was provided that invoices not paid by the club within 45 days of being rendered were to be paid with interest at the rate of five per cent per week, a rate which perhaps at first glance appears innocuous but which, translated to an annual rate, comes out at 260 per cent. There were also some very severe provisions in the contract which applied to the suppliers in the event of breach by them. The Court of Appeal had no difficulty in deciding that the interest provision constituted a penalty as it went far beyond anything that could conceivably be a reasonable pre-estimate of loss.

---

140 (1993) 61 B.L.R. 41 PC.

141 (1993) 61 B.L.R. 41 PC at 58 to 59.

142 (1993) 61 B.L.R. 41 PC at 63. In the light of what Lord Woolf has said, see the various considerations taken into account in *Alfred McAlpine Capital Projects Ltd v Tilebox Ltd* (2006) 104 Con. L.R. 39 at [94] in holding the specified sum there to be liquidated damages and not a penalty, and see too *CFW Architects v Cowlin Construction Ltd* (2006) 105 Con. L.R. 116, at [177]–[191]. Facts of both cases at para.16-089, below.

143 (2004) 92 Con. L.R. 26 CA.

144 See (2004) 92 Con. L.R. 26 CA at [15].

145 (2004) 92 Con. L.R. 26 CA at [21].

**(b) Revised test: a legitimate interest in enforcement** The observations of Mance LJ in *Cine Bes Filmcilik Ve Yapimcilik v United International Pictures*,[146] that the language of stipulations *in terrorem* sounds unusual to modern ears, indicated that the time had come to recast the test in terms more suitable for today. This recasting was to be found in the judgment of Colman J in *Lordsvale Finance Plc v Bank of Zambia*,[147] in a passage[148] cited with approval both by Mance LJ in *Cine* and by all three members of the court in *Murray v Leisureplay Plc*,[149] to the effect that **16-037**

> "whether a provision is to be treated as a penalty is a matter of construction to be resolved by asking whether at the time the contract was entered into the predominant contractual function of the provision was to deter a party from breaking the contract or to compensate the innocent party for breach".

In *Lordsvale*, the clause in question was a provision which required the payment of a greater rate of interest when a borrower was in default. Colman J held that the clause was valid because its predominant contractual function was to reflect in interest the greater credit risk of the borrower. In *Murray* the claimant chief executive director had a service agreement under which he was entitled to a year's notice but which provided that should the employer wrongfully terminate the contract with insufficient notice, the employee became entitled to a year's gross salary, pension and other benefits in kind. Stanley Burnton J held that this provision constituted a penalty, but the Court of Appeal unanimously upheld it. Different approaches were taken by Arden LJ on the one hand and by Buxton LJ on the other, with Clarke LJ expressing a preference for the broader approach of Buxton LJ. Although Arden LJ came to the conclusion that the contractual provision was not a penalty, she adopted the conventional approach which requires a comparison between the amount put forward as liquidated damages and common law damages and, if there was a discrepancy, requires a justification of it. Buxton LJ however considered that this introduced "a rigid and inflexible element into what should be a broad and general question".[150] Citing Lord Dunedin's test of extravagance and unconscionability for ascertaining a penal sum,[151] he said that it was clear that neither the literal wording nor the spirit of the test applied to the case before the court; indeed for him the general impression created by it was that **16-038**

> "the traditional learning as to penalty clauses is very unlikely to fit into the dynamics of an employment contract, at least when the penalty is said to be imposed on the employer".[152]

The new broad approach proposed by Buxton LJ was followed in *Azimut-* **16-039**

---

146 [2003] EWCA Civ 1669 CA. This was not a decision between liquidated damages and penalty but a summary judgment case involving no more than the identification of a triable issue. The same is true of *Cantor Fitzgerald LP v Drummond* unreported 4 August 2009.

147 [1996] Q.B. 752.

148 [1996] Q.B. 752 at 762G.

149 [2005] I.R.L.R. 946 CA.

150 [2005] I.R.L.R. 946 at [114].

151 See para.16-034, below.

152 [2005] I.R.L.R. 946 CA at [115]. Chadwick LJ delivering the principal judgment in *Euro London Appointments Ltd v Claessens International Ltd* [2006] 2 Lloyd's Rep. 436 CA, took up the new learning. While prepared there to decide against penalty on the basis of condition precedent (see the case at para.16-019, above), he went on to hold that, even if it were necessary to investigate whether the condition precedent was a disguised penalty, it could not be so treated because its dominant contractual purpose was compensatory rather than deterrent: see generally at [24]–[40].

*Benetti SpA v Healey*.[153] The claimant yacht builder contracted to construct and sell to a company wholly owned by the defendant a luxury yacht for £38 million, the defendant giving his personal guarantee for payment of the purchase price, which was payable in instalments. The contract provided that the claimant could terminate the contract upon a failure to pay the instalments whereupon 20 per cent of the purchase price was to be due by way of liquidated damages and also provided, importantly, that instalments paid before the termination were to be returned to the extent that they exceeded the 20 per cent. The defendant, when sued on the guarantee, argued that this was a penalty. Blair J was satisfied that the predominant function of this contractual provision was not to deter from breach but to compensate for breach. He did not agree with the defendant that he had to form a view as to the maximum possible loss that the parties would have expected to flow from any determination of the contract and the extent to which the stipulated sum exceeded that maximum possible loss, and stated that in his view the provision was not even arguably a penalty.[154]

**16-040** The reformulation of the test for a penalty was completed in the decision of the Supreme Court in the conjoined appeals in *Makdessi* and *ParkingEye*. Lord Neuberger and Sumption rationalised the test as asking whether, if the clause goes beyond compensation for breach, the innocent party

> "has a legitimate interest in performance extending beyond the prospect of pecuniary compensation following directly from the breach in question".[155]

Notions of whether the clause is "in terrorem", or whether it has a deterrent purpose, or whether it is a "genuine pre-estimate of loss" should be ultimately subsumed by the overarching enquiry into legitimacy of the interest that supports the provision. As Lords Neuberger and Sumption explained[156]:

> "The true test is whether the impugned provision is a secondary obligation which imposes a detriment on the contract-breaker out of all proportion to any legitimate interest of the innocent party in the enforcement of the primary obligation. The innocent party can have no proper interest in simply punishing the defaulter. His interest is in performance or in some appropriate alternative to performance. In the case of a straightforward damages clause, that interest will rarely extend beyond compensation for the breach, and we therefore expect that Lord Dunedin's four tests would usually be perfectly adequate to determine its validity. But compensation is not necessarily the only legitimate interest that the innocent party may have in the performance of the defaulter's primary obligations."

This test was expressly supported by a majority of their Lordships. Lord Carnwath agreed with the whole of the judgment of Lords Neuberger and Sumption and Lord Clarke agreed with their Lordships on this point.

### 4. Application of the "legitimate interest" test

**16-041** One reason why the decisions in the conjoined appeals in *Makdessi* and *ParkingEye* have not wholly displaced every earlier decision is because an innocent party will always have a legitimate interest in a clause which provides for compensation for breach. Hence, it will often remain useful to ask whether the

153 [2011] 1 Lloyd's Rep. 473.
154 [2011] 1 Lloyd's Rep. 473 at [29].
155 [2016] A.C. 1172 at [28].
156 [2016] A.C. 1172 at [32].

clause, at the time of contracting, did no more than estimate for compensation for breach. These cases can usefully be divided into (i) those where there is only a single obligation upon the breach of which a sum is payable or property must be transferred; and (ii) those where there are several obligations upon the breach of which the sum is payable or property transferrable.

**(a) Where there is only a single obligation upon the breach of which the sum becomes payable or the property transferrable**

*(i) Where the loss is reasonably calculable at the time of contracting* If the loss accruing to the claimant from the breach in question can, at the time when the contract was made, be accurately or reasonably calculated in money, the fixing of a larger sum will prima facie be treated as a penalty. **16-042**

The loss which can be most accurately calculated is that arising from a breach which itself consists of a failure to pay money, and therefore the clearest, and the classic, example of a penalty is a provision that, upon failure to pay a sum of money in breach of contract, a larger sum shall become payable. Although there are no clear examples of this principle in cases where the only event upon which the larger sum becomes payable is the non-payment of the smaller sum,[157] there are plenty of statements of it in the authorities. In Lord Dunedin's speech in *Dunlop Pneumatic Tyre Co v New Garage and Motor Co*,[158] he called it "one of the most ancient instances".[159] However, it is important to emphasise that the basis of this rule depended in turn upon another principle, namely that non-payment of money attracted only nominal damages or at least none beyond simple interest[160] and that, starting with *Muhammad v Ali*,[161] through *Trans Trust SPRL v Danubian Trading Co*,[162] to *Wadsworth v Lydell*,[163] this principle has been emasculated and now in *Sempra Metals v Inland Revenue Commissioners*,[164] abandoned; this ought in turn to have a corresponding effect on the principle at present under discussion.[165] The breach consisted of a failure to pay the purchase price in *Muhammad* of land and in *Trans Trust* of goods and, if there had been a provision that upon failure to pay **16-043**

---

[157] All the illustrations are to be found, not unexpectedly, in the cases where there are several other breaches to which the penalty applies: see para.16-053, below. But See *Cato v Cato* (1972) 116 S.J. 138 at para.16-021, above.

[158] [1915] A.C. 79 at 87. It appears as rule 4(b), and he called it a corollary to the principal test of extravagant and unconscionable sum in comparison with the greatest possible loss.

[159] [1915] A.C. 79 at 87. Earlier statements of this rule are really only of historical interest now; it is to be found as early as *Astley v Weldon* (1801) 2 Bos. & P. 346 at 354, per Chambre J, the decision which initiated the modern law on the subject. In *Galsworthy v Strutt* (1848) 1 Ex. 659 at 665 Parke B had said: "It would be competent for the parties to make a stipulation to pay a certain sum on the non-performance of a covenant to pay a smaller sum; but they must do so in express terms; and if that be done I do not see how the courts can avoid giving effect to such a contract"; while Alderson B said (at 667) that he was "not prepared to say" that this was not the law. Such statements are entirely against the current of authority.

[160] See paras 30-002 and 30-005, below.

[161] [1947] A.C. 414 PC.

[162] [1952] 2 Q.B. 297 CA.

[163] [1981] 1 W.L.R. 598 CA.

[164] [2008] 1 A.C. 561; at para.19-061, below.

[165] The relationship between the two principles is brought out by the fact that it was in a case where the issue was whether a provision constituted liquidated damages or a penalty, *Wallis v Smith* (1882) 21 Ch. D. 243 CA, that Jessel MR delivered a strong attack upon the then rule that only nominal damages are recoverable for non-payment of money: (1882) 21 Ch. D. 243 CA at 257. His remarks are quoted at para.30-005, below.

the price a larger sum should become payable, it is submitted that the larger sum could properly have been considered as liquidated damages.[166]

**16-044** As to a breach other than a failure to pay money, cases had not formerly appeared in which a sum payable only on a single breach has been held to be a penalty on the ground that the loss was reasonably calculable in money at the time of the making of the contract, until an illustration of this was provided by *Lansat Shipping Co Ltd v Glencore Grain BV, The Paragon*.[167] Breach of a time charter by the late redelivery of the ship would in the normal course allow damages to the shipowner at the difference between market and contract rates of hire for the overdue period. The time charterer in *The Paragon* was late in redelivery of the ship by six days and a clause in the time charter provided, where there was breach by late redelivery at a time when the market rate of hire exceeded the contractual rate of hire, which was the position in *The Paragon*, that the rate was to be adjusted to that market rate for the 30 days preceding the contractual redelivery date. This was held to be a penalty.

**16-045** *(ii) Where the loss is not reasonably calculable at the time of contracting* If on the other hand the loss accruing to the claimant from the breach in question cannot, at the time when the contract was made, be accurately or even reasonably calculated in money, it becomes far less easy to class the sum to be paid on breach as extravagant and unconscionable, and here it is likely that the stipulated sum will be held to be liquidated damages.[168] Indeed the difficulty of precise estimation is positively in favour of a holding of liquidated damages, for, as Lord Dunedin pointed out in *Dunlop Pneumatic Tyre Co v New Garage and Motor Co*[169]:

> "It is no obstacle to the sum stipulated being a genuine pre-estimate of damage, that the consequences of the breach are such as to make precise estimation almost an impossibility. On the contrary that is just the situation when it is probable that pre-estimated damage was the true bargain between the parties."

A complementary, but slightly different, approach is also frequently found in the cases; this takes the point that the parties are entitled to make provision to bypass the problems set by the difficulty and the expense of proving certain types of damage. Thus Lord Halsbury LC said in *Clydebank Engineering Co v Don Jose Ramos Yzquierdo y Castaneda*[170]:

> "The very reason why the parties do in fact agree to such a stipulation is that sometimes ... the nature of the damage is such that proof of it is extremely complex, difficult and expensive".[171]

**16-046** It was found difficult, in earlier editions of this work, to put one's finger on a clear-cut case where only a single possible breach leading to a finding of no penalty

---

166 The full facts of *Muhammad* and *Trans Trust* are at para.24-015, below.

167 [2009] 2 Lloyd's Rep. 688 CA.

168 [2009] 2 Lloyd's Rep. 688 CA at [50].

169 [1915] A.C. 79 at 87 to 88. This statement appears as r.4(d).

170 [1905] A.C. 6 at 11.

171 Statements stressing the difficulty or expense of proof or both have appeared from early days, as in *Crisdee v Bolton* (1827) 3 Car. & P. 240 at 243, per Best CJ; *Kemble v Farren* (1829) 6 Bing. 141 at 148, per Tindal CJ; *Green v Price* (1845) 13 M. & W. 695 at 701, per Parke B; *Webster v Bosanquet* [1912] A.C. 394 PC at 398, per Lord Mersey; *Robophone Facilities v Blank* [1966] 1 W.L.R. 1428 CA at 1447, per Diplock LJ.

was involved. But one example is *Keegan v Newcastle United Football Co Ltd*.[172] The £2 million to which the manager of a football club became entitled on his constructive dismissal was held not to be a penalty, the court saying that, in view of the near impossibility of estimating precisely what the manager's loss would be, it considered the amount agreed upon to represent a reasonable pre-estimate to the extent that it was possible to carry out such an exercise at all.

**(b) Where there are several obligations upon the breach of which the sum becomes payable or property transferrable** If there are several breaches upon the occurrence of which the stipulated sum is to become payable, the test for assessing the nature of the sum is still whether it is extravagant and unconscionable in comparison with the greatest possible loss, but there is a much larger chance of its being held a penalty since, as Lord Dunedin pointed out in *Dunlop Pneumatic Tyre Co v New Garage and Motor Co*,[173] 16-047

> "if there are various breaches to which one indiscriminate sum to be paid in breach is applied, then the strength of the chain must be taken at its weakest link".

This rigorous rule is capable of casting many a stipulated sum into the category of a penalty since practically every contract may be broken more than once, in more ways than one, and by more than one party. Its rigour has been tempered, however, in various ways, all of which have in common that they tend to make the stipulated sum payable only on breach of a single obligation, thus removing it from the ambit of the present category and moving it back into the last. A preliminary step, therefore, is to deal with these various methods before proceeding to deal with the cases which fall four-square within the present category.

In the first place, the parties may be careful to delimit the field in which the sum becomes payable. Thus they may specify that the sum is intended to cover only certain breaches or even only certain aspects of a single breach. There are many common cases: thus where a seller of a business enters into a covenant not to engage in a similar business within a specified radius, there are many other breaches that he may commit in connection with the sale of the business, e.g. a failure to complete or a breach of warranty of quiet enjoyment, and there are all the possible breaches which the buyer may commit: clearly the stipulated sum is not intended to have reference to any of these breaches, and for these, if they occur, an ordinary action for damages will lie.[174] One of the main distinctions between *Dunlop Pneumatic Tyre Co v New Garage and Motor Co*,[175] and *Ford Motor Co v Armstrong*,[176] two cases concerning resale price maintenance agreements where the courts came to different conclusions on very similar facts, is to be found here. In both cases the defendant dealer had contracted not to resell the goods below certain prices, not to sell them to certain prohibited persons, and not to exhibit them without the claimant's permission; in both, his breach consisted of a breach of the first obligation. But whereas in *Dunlop Pneumatic Tyre Co v New Garage and Motor* 16-048

[172] [2010] I.R.L.R. 94.

[173] [1915] A.C. 79 at 89.

[174] For good illustrations because the issue was controverted see *Aktieselskabet Reidar v Arcos* [1927] 1 K.B. 352 CA and *Total Transport Corp v Amoco Trading Co (The Altus)* [1985] 1 Lloyd's Rep. 423 at para.16-024, above.

[175] [1915] A.C. 79; facts at para.16-092, below.

[176] (1915) 31 T.L.R. 267 CA: facts at para.16-092, below.

*Co*,[177] the sum stipulated to be paid on breach, which was held to be liquidated damages, did not apply to the third and minor obligation not to exhibit without permission,[178] the stipulated sum in *Ford Motor Co v Armstrong*,[179] which was held to be a penalty, applied equally to all three obligations.

**16-049** Alternatively, the parties may stipulate that different sums shall be paid for different breaches. This was done for breaches of different stipulations in *Imperial Tobacco Co v Parsley*,[180] and the court was, therefore, able to concentrate upon the particular breach which occurred and the particular sum stipulated in relation to it. This sum was in the circumstances held to constitute liquidated damages. And in the case of a different magnitude of breach of the same stipulation, parties commonly introduce graduated sums increasing in proportion to the size of the breach. This method has proved particularly useful where the breach has consisted of delay in performance. Thus in a number of cases of building contracts, of which *Clydebank Engineering Co v Don Jose Ramos Yzquierdo y Castaneda*,[181] is the chief,[182] the courts have upheld as liquidated damages a provision that the amount to be paid by the builder in the event of his breach by delay shall be so much for each day, week or other specified short period beyond the time fixed for completion of the construction.[183] Others have successfully adopted the graduated sum where the breach enlarges itself in space rather than in time. Thus the following two provisions were held to constitute liquidated damages. In *Elphinstone v Monkland Iron and Coal Co*,[184] lessees, granted the privilege of placing slag from blast-furnaces on land let to them, covenanted to pay £100 for every acre of the land that was not restored at a particular date; in *Diestal v Stevenson*,[185] a contract for the sale of coal provided that one shilling for every ton should be paid for that part of the contract which was not executed, whether by failure to deliver by the seller or failure to accept by the buyer. A number of cases have dealt with covenants whereby one party has accepted restrictions on his right to sell his goods and has further agreed to pay the other a specific sum for every item sold in breach of covenant. Generally the court has allowed recovery of such sums as liquidated damages, as in *Dunlop Pneumatic Tyre Co v New Garage and Motor Co*[186]; the cases reaching a contrary result have turned on further factors: in *Ford Motor Co v Armstrong*,[187] the stipulated sum became payable also upon a minor breach other than sale, and

---

177 [1915] A.C. 79.

178 And indeed the House of Lords was of the view that it did not apply to the second obligation either.

179 (1915) 31 T.L.R. 267 CA.

180 [1936] 2 All E.R. 515 CA: facts at para.16-092, below.

181 [1905] A.C. 6.

182 The other cases are *Law v Redditch Local Board* [1892] 1 Q.B. 127 CA; *Cellulose Acetate Silk Co v Widnes Foundry* [1933] A.C. 20; and *Philips Hong Kong v Attorney General of Hong Kong* (1993) 61 B.L.R. 41 PC.

183 But a provision for graduated sums will be a penalty if it operates in such a way that the sums decrease in proportion to the size of the breach, as has been a feature of many hire-purchase contracts: see especially *Bridge v Campbell Discount Co* [1962] A.C. 600 at para.16-076, below, and Lord Radcliffe's remark there that "it is a sliding scale of compensation, but a scale that slides in the wrong direction": at 623.

184 (1886) 11 App. Cas. 332.

185 [1906] 2 K.B. 345.

186 [1915] A.C. 79. Other cases are *English Hop Growers v Dering* [1928] 2 K.B. 174 CA; *Imperial Tobacco Co v Parsley* [1936] 2 All E.R. 515 CA.

187 (1915) 31 T.L.R. 267 CA.

in *Willson v Love*,[188] it became payable upon the sale of either of two commodities of substantially different value.

In the second place, the courts do not favour the attempts of defendants to give a narrow meaning to what constitutes a single obligation. Most stipulations can be broken in a number of ways: a former employee who has covenanted not to trade within a certain radius can set up in business five miles away or 10. To use Lord Parker of Waddington's analysis in *Dunlop Pneumatic Tyre Co v New Garage and Motor Co*,[189] there is at one end of the scale the case of **16-050**

> "a single stipulation, which if broken at all, can be broken once only, and in one way only, such as a covenant not to reveal a trade secret to a rival trader".[190]

At the other end of the scale there is the case of a number of different stipulations, whether or not of varying importance. Between lies the case of the stipulation which,

> "though still a single stipulation, is capable of being broken more than once, or in more ways than one, such as a stipulation not to solicit the customers of a firm".[191]

The courts tend to regard any and all breaches of such stipulations as a breach of a single obligation. Thus in *Law v Redditch Local Board*,[192] a sum payable on the non-completion of a building contract was held to be liquidated damages as it was payable upon breach of a single obligation or, as it is often put, upon a single event. Kay LJ said:

> "I cannot agree with the ingenious argument that because there may be many matters, some very small, which would constitute non-completion, these sums may be regarded as payable on several events. According to that argument, there must be considered to be several different non-completions of the works. There may be different causes of non-completion; but non-completion is only one single event."[193]

There are many illustrations of this principle in relation to covenants in restraint of trade. The point was made in the first case establishing that a sum stipulated for breach of such covenants is generally one for liquidated damages, *Crisdee v Bolton*,[194] where Best CJ said:

> "The sum of £500 is to be paid for the doing of one thing only, viz., setting up a victualling house within one mile."

Similar statements are to be found in the later cases on restraint of trade

---

[188] [1896] 1 Q.B. 626 CA.
[189] [1915] A.C. 79.
[190] [1915] A.C. 79 at 97.
[191] [1915] A.C. 79 at 98.
[192] [1892] 1 Q.B. 127 CA.
[193] [1892] 1 Q.B. 127 at 136. See, too, *Sparrow v Paris* (1862) 7 Hurl. & N. 594, where the defendant had agreed to pay a sum equal to a half of the freight should the ship upon which the claimant had shipped goods not sail before any other vessel then in berth. This sum was held to be liquidated damages and the ingenious argument rejected that the covenant was that the ship should not be the second, or the third, or the fourth to sail. "It is a sum payable on one event", said Bramwell B: at 599.
[194] (1827) 3 Car. & P. 240.

covenants.[195] And a very valuable and authoritative statement of the principle is provided in Lord Atkinson's speech in *Dunlop Pneumatic Tyre Co v New Garage and Motor Co*,[196] a case of sale of goods in which the buyer had agreed not to resell below certain listed prices. He said:

> "The object of the appellants in making this agreement, if the substance and reality of the thing and the real nature of the transaction be looked at, would appear to be a single one, namely, to prevent the disorganisation of their trading system and the consequent injury to their trade in many directions."[197]

He then pointed out that the parties' object was akin in some respects to that of an employer taking from an employee a covenant in restraint of trade, and continued:

> "It is, I think, quite misleading to concentrate one's attention upon the particular act or acts by which, in such cases as this, the rivalry in trade is set up, and the repute acquired by the former employee that he works cheaper and charges less than his old master, and to lose sight of the risk to the latter that old customers, once tempted to leave him, may never return to deal with him, or that business that might otherwise have come to him may be captured by his rival … In many cases a person may contract to do or abstain from doing an act which is a composite act, the product or result of almost numberless other acts … It would be quite illegitimate to … disintegrate the obligations to do what the parties regarded as a single whole into a number of obligations to do a number of things of varying importance, and treat the [stipulated sum] as prima facie a penalty, because these individual breaches of the agreement did not cause, in many instances, any injury commensurate with that sum."[198]

**16-051** If, however, none of the above methods applies so as to make the stipulated sum payable only on breach of a single obligation, then the case will remain one of a sum payable on breach of several obligations; such cases must now be considered.

**16-052** *(i) Where the loss is reasonably calculable at the time of contracting* If the loss accruing to the claimant from any one of the several possible breaches can, at the time when the contract was made, be accurately or reasonably calculated in money, the fixing of a larger sum will prima facie be treated as a penalty as to all the possible breaches and it is equally immaterial that some or all the other breaches were not so calculable or would involve a greater loss and that it was one of these other breaches that in the event occurred.

**16-053** This re-introduces the most accurately calculable loss of all, the loss arising from breach of a promise to pay money. If one of the several possible breaches is of this type and the stipulated sum, payable on any breach, is greater than the sum due in performance of the contract, the case is one of penalty. This is well illustrated by the facts of the two cases which established the whole doctrine, *Astley v Weldon*,[199]

---

195 See, e.g. *Price v Green* (1847) 16 M. & W. 346 at 354, per Patteson J: "It is the sum named in respect of the breach of this one covenant only, and the intention of the parties is clear and unequivocal. There is but one thing to which the £5,000 relates, viz. the restriction of trade though extended to two different districts"; and *Reynolds v Bridge* (1856) 6 El. & Bl. 528 at 545, per Crompton J: "Clearly this is all one covenant. If the covenant is once broken as to any provision which it contains, the whole is at an end, the liquidated sum is to be recovered."

196 [1915] A.C. 79; full facts at para.16-092, below.

197 [1915] A.C. 79 at 92.

198 [1915] A.C. 79 at 92–93.

199 (1801) 2 Bos. & P. 346.

and *Kemble v Farren*.[200] In the first an actress was engaged by a theatre manager, who agreed to pay her a weekly salary with travelling expenses if she should perform at his theatre, complying with all its rules and subject to all its fines, and it was further provided that if either should fail to perform the agreement he or she should pay the other £200. In the second an actor was similarly engaged under a contract which provided, inter alia, that he should be paid about £3 every night that the theatre was open, and that £1,000 should become payable by either if he failed to perform the agreement, or any part of it, or any stipulation contained in it. In both cases, in a suit brought by the manager for a refusal to appear on the stage, the stipulated sum was held to be a penalty; in the first since an act by the actress in contravention of the theatre rules rendered her liable to a fine, and in the second since the manager's neglect to pay the actor for one night's performance would have entailed the entire liability.

As to a breach other than a failure to pay money, there appear to be no cases in which a sum, payable upon breach of several different obligations, has been held to be a penalty on the ground that the loss for one of the possible breaches was reasonably calculable at the time of the making of the contract. This is probably because in most of the cases of this type one of the obligations has been to pay money.[201] **16-054**

*(ii) Where the loss is not reasonably calculable at the time of contracting* If on the other hand the loss accruing to the claimant from all the several breaches cannot, at the time when the contract was made, be accurately or even reasonably calculated in money, it becomes less easy to class the sum to be paid on breach as extravagant and unconscionable. The principle that where there is difficulty of precise estimation and of proof of the damage the stipulated sum is likely to be liquidated damages operates here as well as with cases where there is only a single breach upon which the sum becomes payable. However, one final rule comes in, in the case of a stipulated sum covering several breaches, which may swing the pendulum away from liquidated damages back to penalty even though there may be difficulty of estimation and proof on all breaches. This rule was definitively stated by Lord Dunedin, once again in *Dunlop Pneumatic Tyre Co v New Garage and Motor Co*.[202] He said: **16-055**

> "There is a presumption (but no more) that it is penalty when a single lump sum is made payable by way of compensation, on the occurrence of one or more or all of several events, some of which may occasion serious and others but trifling damage."

Numerous statements to this effect have appeared in the early reports,[203] and the principle is well illustrated in the decisions. In *Ford Motor Co v Armstrong*,[204] car manufacturers had sold cars to a dealer under an agreement whereby the dealer agreed, first, not to sell the cars under a listed price, secondly, not to sell them to

---

200 (1829) 6 Bing. 141.

201 See para.16-055, below, and the cases cited in the footnote at the end of it which, in relation to the seller's or lessor's obligations, come the nearest to falling within this category.

202 [1915] A.C. 79 at 87. It appears as r.4(c).

203 e.g. *Boys v Ancell* (1839) 5 Bing. N.C. 390 at 396, per Coltman J; *Elphinstone v Monkland Iron and Coal Co* (1886) 11 App. Cas. 332 at 343, per Lord Watson (as explained in *Dunlop Pneumatic Tyre Co v New Garage and Motor Co* [1915] A.C. 79); *Betts v Burch* (1859) 4 Hurl. & N. 506 at 511, per Bramwell B; *Magee v Lavell* (1873–74) L.R. 9 C.P. 107 at 115, per Coleridge J.

204 (1915) 31 T.L.R. 267 CA.

other car dealers, and thirdly, not to exhibit them without the manufacturers' permission, and had further agreed that for every breach he would pay £250. The Court of Appeal held this to be a penalty on the ground that the damage which would arise under the third clause was different in kind from that which would arise under the first two. It is submitted that difference in kind between two breaches is not enough to make the stipulated sum a penalty unless there is also a substantial difference in the amount of the probable loss arising from each breach, a requirement which would seem to have been satisfied on the facts of *Ford Motor Co v Armstrong*.[205] In *Willson v Love*,[206] the lessees of a farm had covenanted not to sell hay or straw off the premises during the last year of the term but to consume it on the premises and to pay, as additional rent, £3 for every ton of hay or straw so sold. This was held to be a penalty because payable upon two different events, the sale of hay and the sale of straw, there being a substantial difference between the manurial value of the two commodities.[207] In *CMC Group Plc v Zhang*,[208] by a settlement agreement the defendant undertook not to make derogatory or unfavourable communications about the claimant company and, if he committed any breach of his undertaking, to repay the sum of US $40,000 paid to him under the settlement and be liable in addition for damages. The Court of Appeal held this sum to constitute a penalty, relying on Lord Dunedin's presumption of penalty where a single sum is payable whatever the breach.[209] In *Boys v Ancell*,[210] the defendant had agreed to grant a lease to the claimant in consideration of the claimant's promise to execute the counterpart and to pay the expenses, and each party had bound himself to pay £500 should he be in breach. In holding this a penalty Coltman J pointed out that

> "the sum specified here is applicable equally to the refusal to grant a lease, and the omission to pay the expenses of it".[211]

In *Magee v Lavell*,[212] the claimant sold his tenancy in a public house to the defendant together with the goodwill, with the provision for the payment of £100

> "if either party shall refuse or neglect to perform all or every part of this agreement".

This was held to be a penalty,[213] Coleridge J saying that it involved "several events of various degrees of importance".[214] Indeed the most frequent illustration of this category is to be found in cases concerning the sale or lease of land and businesses where the stipulated sum, which has been held to be a penalty, was to become payable if either party did not comply with each and every part of the

---

205 (1915) 31 T.L.R. 267 CA. The case should be contrasted with the very similar *Dunlop Pneumatic Tyre Co v New Garage and Motor Co* [1915] A.C. 79, where a different result was reached: see para.16-048, above.

206 [1896] 1 Q.B. 626 CA.

207 However, in *Dunlop Pneumatic Tyre Co v New Garage and Motor Co* [1915] A.C. 79 Lord Dunedin was a little dubious about this result: at 89.

208 [2006] EWCA Civ 408 CA.

209 See [2006] EWCA Civ 408 at [14] and [22]. Nor could the provision be rescued by construing the settlement agreement as being for a payment conditional upon certain events not occurring: see [2006] EWCA Civ 408 at [19]–[21], per Dyson LJ.

210 (1839) 5 Bing. N.C. 390.

211 (1839) 5 Bing. N.C. 390 at 396.

212 (1873–74) L.R. 9 C.P. 107.

213 Following the similar much earlier case of *Davies v Penton* (1827) 6 B. & C. 216.

214 (1873–74) L.R. 9 C.P. 107 at 115.

contract.[215]

However, the tendency of the courts in the most modern cases has been to enclose this final rule within reasonable bounds and to assert that variety in the possible losses does not necessarily preclude a proper provision for liquidated damages. This has been done in two related ways: either by holding that the probable loss following on all the breaches is so uncertain that it is equally uncertain that the loss from one breach would be greater or less than that from the next, or by holding that the provision is a sort of averaging out of the probable loss to be sustained from all the breaches, provided always there is not too great a disparity between the greatest possible loss and the smallest possible loss. **16-056**

The first method is to be found in *Dunlop Pneumatic Tyre Co v New Garage and Motor Co*.[216] Lord Atkinson there said that: **16-057**

> "although it may be true … that a presumption is raised in favour of a penalty where a single lump sum is to be paid by way of compensation in respect of many different events, some occasioning serious, some trifling damage, it seems to be that the presumption is rebutted by the very fact that the damage caused by each and every one of those events, however varying in importance, may be of such an uncertain nature that it cannot be accurately ascertained."[217]

The same idea had been put in more concrete form much earlier by Alderson B in *Galsworthy v Strutt*,[218] where he said in relation to a covenant in restraint of trade on the sale of a solicitor's practice:

> "The act of damage … by another's practising within 50 miles for the period of seven years, would not be the same in amount as if he were to practise within 40 miles, or next door, nor the same if he had set up in business in the first, second, or sixth year, … but the parties have agreed to a certain fixed sum, in order to prevent the necessity of being at the expense of procuring the attendance of witnesses for the purpose of giving evidence upon those matters."[219]

This method is more likely to prove efficacious if the probable damage varies in degree, and not also in kind, with each breach, a point put forward by Lord Parker of Waddington in *Dunlop Pneumatic Tyre Co v New Garage and Motor Co*,[220] and acted upon by the Court of Appeal in *Ford Motor Co v Armstrong*.[221]

The second method, which is more radical perhaps, is also to be found in *Dunlop Pneumatic Tyre Co v New Garage and Motor Co*.[222] Lord Parker of Waddington there took the view that the presumption of penalty would be displaced by an express statement in the contract that, since the breach of one stipulation would result in loss between £5 and £15 and the breach of another in loss between £2 and £12, the parties have, therefore, settled on £8 as liquidated damages. Here the **16-058**

---

215 Such cases are *Betts v Burch* (1859) 4 Hurl. & N. 506; *Bradley v Walsh* (1903) 88 L.T. 737; *Lock v Bell* [1931] 1 Ch. 35; *Michel Habib v Sheikh Suleiman* [1941] 1 All E.R. 507 PC. Some of these may fall, like *Astley v Weldon* (1801) 2 Bos. & P. 346 and *Kemble v Farren* (1829) 6 Bing. 141, into the category where one at least of the possible breaches was accurately calculable: see paras 16-042 to 16-044, above. Either way the result here is the same.

216 [1915] A.C. 79.

217 [1915] A.C. 79 at 95 to 96.

218 (1848) 1 Ex. 659.

219 (1848) 1 Ex. 659 at 666 to 667.

220 [1915] A.C. 79 at 98.

221 (1915) 31 T.L.R. 267 CA.

222 [1915] A.C. 79 at 99.

stipulated sum is explicitly calculated as a mean figure. Similarly, Scrutton LJ in *English Hop Growers v Dering*,[223] considered it to be reasonable that "damages of the same kind, but difficult to value exactly, may be averaged".[224]

**16-059** The application of these two methods has assisted in the upholding of sums as liquidated damages in several modern decisions, although the situation has generally been a hybrid one in which the same result has been reached also on the alternative, but related, ground that the stipulated sum was payable only on breach of a single stipulation. *Dunlop Pneumatic Tyre Co v New Garages and Motor Co*,[225] provides, once again, the most useful illustration.[226]

**16-060** In connection with these two routes for the upholding of stipulated sums as liquidated damages the authoritative, and contemporary, remarks of Lord Woolf in *Philips Hong Kong v Attorney General of Hong Kong*,[227] are particularly valuable. He there said:

> "There is always going to be a variety of different situations in which damage can occur and even though long and detailed provisions are contained in a contract it will often be virtually impossible to anticipate accurately and provide for all the possible scenarios. Whatever the degree of care exercised by the draftsman it will still be almost inevitable that an ingenious argument can be developed for saying that in a particular hypothetical situation a substantially higher sum will be recovered than would be recoverable if the plaintiff was required to prove his actual loss in that situation. Such a result would undermine the whole purpose of parties to a contract being able to agree beforehand what damages are to be recoverable in the event of a breach of contract. This would not be in the interest of either of the parties to the contract."[228]

## 5. MAIN TYPES OF CONTRACT IN WHICH THE OLDER RULES WERE APPLIED

**16-061** To reiterate, although the older cases have now been subsumed into a broader enquiry which asks whether the innocent party has a legitimate interest in performance, there remains considerable utility in considering these cases and the older rules upon which they relied. One reason is the insistence by Lord Neuberger and Sumption in *Makdessi* and *ParkingEye* that the older approaches, applying Lord Dunedin's four tests in *Dunlop*, would usually be "perfectly adequate".[229] Another is that the focus in the older cases upon tests for whether the provisions involved a "genuine pre-estimate of loss" is of assistance in determining whether the innocent party has a legitimate interest since a clause which has only the purpose of providing compensation for loss will always reflect a legitimate interest. In the decided cases there appear again and again certain types of contract in which are contained provisions for the payment of a stipulated sum upon breach: this is

---

223 [1928] 2 K.B. 174 CA at 182.

224 And see *Robophone Facilities v Blank* [1966] 1 W.L.R. 1428 CA at 1449, per Diplock LJ, quoted at para.16-096, below.

225 [1915] A.C. 79.

226 See, too, the other cases dealt with at para.16-050, above, where the factor of the sum being held payable only on breach of a single obligation was involved. One case where that factor was not present is *Wallis v Smith* (1882) 21 Ch. D. 243 CA, which must stand on the present ground alone. See para.16-088, below, for the facts.

227 (1993) 61 B.L.R. 41 PC.

228 (1993) 61 B.L.R. 41 PC at 54. But nothing in what Lord Woolf said is to be construed as affecting the time-honoured rule that to avoid being held to be a penalty the agreed sum or sums must be a genuine pre-estimate of loss, as *Jeancharm Ltd (t/a Beaver International) v Barnet Football Club Ltd* (2004) 92 Con. L.R. 26 CA has confirmed: see the case at para.16-036, above.

229 [2016] A.C. 1172 at [32].

because liquidated damages are more suited to some types of contract than to others. Some contracts were tested out in this regard over 100 years ago,[230] and whether the clauses were rejected as penalties, as in the cases concerning leases of public houses,[231] or accepted as liquidated damages, as in the cases concerning restraint of trade,[232] such contracts appear little in litigation today as the law is taken to be settled. Other contracts have made their appearance for consideration only in the 20th century; the prime illustrations concern covenants restricting the terms on which goods may be sold or resold[233] and contracts of hire-purchase.[234]

## (1) Types of contract where the stipulated sum or property to be transferred is generally a penalty

**(a) Charterparties: failure to carry out general provisions on either side** In charterparties these appeared early, and soon became common form, a clause which ran: "Penalty for non-performance of this agreement estimated amount of freight." Even before the general doctrine of liquidated damages and penalties had become established, this clause was treated as a penalty since it covered all breaches, whether serious or trifling, and by either party: an early illustration is *Winter v Trimmer*.[235] Eventually the clause developed into an extended form which ran: 16-062

> "Penalty for non-performance of this agreement proved damages, not exceeding estimated amount of freight";

but it had become so established as a penalty clause that in *Wall v Rederiaktiebolaget Luggude*,[236] it was held that it retained this nature despite the milder form of wording.[237] There is little sign in any of these authorities of a legitimate interest which might support such a clause.

**(b) Employment contracts: failure to carry out general provisions on either side** The two early 19th century cases which laid the foundation for the modern law, *Astley v Weldon*,[238] and *Kemble v Farren*,[239] concerned the engagement by a theatre management of an actress and an actor respectively who in breach of contract refused to appear. Both cases contained a clause that, if either party to the contract should fail to perform in any way, a stipulated sum should be paid to the other party.[240] In both cases the stipulated sum was held to be a penalty and irrecoverable, for the sum might become due on a large number of breaches of substantially differing degrees of importance, such as complete non-performance 16-063

---

[230] The contract between charterer and shipowner in which the charterer promises to pay at a certain rate during the period in which he improperly detains the ship, commonly called demurrage, has always been accepted without any testing in the courts: see para.16-081, below.

[231] See para.16-064, below.

[232] See para.16-083, below.

[233] See paras 16-090 to 16-092, below.

[234] See paras 16-066 to 16-079, below.

[235] (1762) 1 Wm. Bl. 395. Followed in *Harrison v Wright* (1811) 13 East 343.

[236] [1915] 3 K.B. 66. This case is fully considered at para.16-101, below.

[237] For a holding of penalty other than in relation to general provisions on either side of a charterparty, see *Lansat Shipping Co Ltd v Glencore Grain BV, The Paragon* [2009] 2 Lloyd's Rep. 688 CA at para.16-044, above.

[238] (1801) 2 B. & P. 346.

[239] (1829) 6 Bing. 141.

[240] £200 in *Astley v Weldon* (1801) 2 B. & P. 346; £1,000 in *Kemble v Farren* (1829) 6 Bing. 141.

by either party as against the actress's failure to pay a trifling fine or the management's failure to pay the actor one night's salary.[241] Further, these cases illustrate that type of contractual provision which stipulates one identical sum for breach by either party: such a stipulation can hardly ever constitute liquidated damages. These two decisions became an object lesson, and this type of case does not reappear in the reports.

16-064 **(c) Sale and lease of land and buildings: failure to carry out general provisions on either side** A similar type of provision to the above, in that the same sum is stipulated to be paid both on all the possible breaches of contract and on breaches by either party, does persist through the 19th century before being eventually put to rest. That is the case of the sale, or more generally the lease, of land and buildings[242] with a provision that, upon failure by either party to carry out any part of the agreement, the one in breach should pay the other a single stipulated sum. It may be said today that, after a little fluctuation, such is universally held to be a penalty. Most of the cases have concerned leases, public houses, liability of either party to pay the same stipulated sum on his breach, and breach by the buyer.[243] The only case in which the sum was held to be liquidated damages was the early *Reilly v Jones*,[244] but this was based on the words used, a doctrine soon afterwards overruled by *Kemble v Farren*.[245] It is difficult to state the most important as they are much on a par. One might perhaps take *Magee v Lavell*,[246] since it explained a possible inconsistency[247] and has Denman J's point that but for authority he might have construed the clauses as making the sum payable only upon a total refusal to perform. Such a construction has never been adopted: most of the cases talk about every and any part of the agreement, and in a number of them it was pointed out that the same sum could apply to varying breaches.[248]

16-065 The cases trail in a desultory way into the 20th century[249]: the result was always penalty.

**(d) Hire-purchase contracts: breach by failure by hirer to pay instalments**

16-066 *(i) The developing law* The position with the application of the law on liquidated damages and penalties to failures to pay instalments by hirers under hire-purchase contracts is extremely complex and calls for a preliminary analysis before turning to the detail of the cases. We may start by drawing attention to the peculiarity that

---

241 For more details on these cases, see para.16-053, above.

242 And fixtures, stock in trade, goodwill, etc.

243 Such are *Reilly v Jones* (1823) 1 Bing. 302; *Betts v Burch* (1859) 4 H. & N. 506; *Magee v Lavell* (1874) L.R. 9 C.P. 107; *Bradley v Walsh* (1903) 88 L.T. 737; *Lock v Bell* [1931] 1 Ch. 35. Other cases are *Davies v Penton* (1827) 6 B. & C. 216; *Boys v Ancell* (1839) 5 Bing. N.C. 390.

244 (1823) 1 Bing. 302.

245 (1829) 6 Bing. 141. It is true that in *Lea v Whittaker* (1872) L.R. 8 C.P. 70 it seems as if the court was approving and following *Reilly v Jones* (1823) 1 Bing. 302, but the case was explained in *Magee v Lavell* (1874) L.R. 9 C.P. 107 upon the ground that there was a deposit there. *Hinton v Sparkes* (1868) L.R. 3 C.P. 161 was also based on deposit.

246 (1874) L.R. 9 C.P. 107.

247 See preceding footnote but one.

248 See, e.g. *Boys v Ancell* (1839) 5 Bing. N.C. 390 at 396, per Coltman J; *Betts v Burch* (1859) 4 H. & N. 506 at 511, per Bramwell B; *Magee v Lavell* (1874) L.R. 9 C.P. 107 at 115, per Coleridge J.

249 There are three cases, all in the first half of the last century: *Bradley v Walsh* (1903) 88 L.T. 737; *Lock v Bell* [1931] 1 Ch. 35; and *Michel Habib v Sheikh Suleiman* [1941] 1 All E.R. 507 PC.

there is a whole series of important cases over a five-year period in the early 1960s but hardly anything either before or after, indeed apparently nothing at all for more than the last 25 years.[250] During those five years the case law saw very substantial development, going even to House of Lords level, on the applicability of the law as to penalties in this situation. Indeed the barrage on the Court of Appeal was so intensive as to elicit the comment from Lord Denning MR in 1966 in opening his judgment in *Robophone Facilities v Blank*,[251] itself a case, and the only case, of penalties in a contract of hire[252]: "We have become used to hire-purchase agreements in these courts". What then were the reasons for this concentration of the cases within a five year period so long ago? They appear to be two-fold, the first explaining the absence of earlier decisions, the second explaining their absence later.

The first reason stems from the typical hire-purchase agreement providing that it was the termination, or determination, of the agreement that gave rise to the stipulated sum become payable. It had become common practice to provide that on the hirer's default in paying instalments the owner, generally a finance company, might determine the contract, retake the goods, and claim from the hirer a stipulated sum, often expressed to be by way of agreed compensation for depreciation in the value of the goods, the clause in the contract providing for payment of this sum coming to be known as the "minimum payment" clause. Here there was breach of the hire-purchase contract by the hirer but despite this it was at first thought that the law as to liquidated damages and penalties could have no application to such clauses in these contracts because the event upon which the sum became payable was the determination, and not the breach, of the contract. Thus it was early held in *Elsey v Hyde*,[253] that a stipulated sum, although unconscionable and extravagant, was still recoverable by the owner and could not be classed as a penalty even if it was the hirer's breach that gave the owner his option to determine, since the sum became due as a result of the election to determine and not because of the breach. This view was accepted in *Re Apex Supply Co*.[254] Then in 1953 the Court of Appeal held the view to be misconceived, and the conclusion on the inapplicability of the law as to penalties to be wrong, in *Cooden Engineering Co v Stanford*,[255] a decision followed in *Landom Trust v Hurrell*,[256] and later approved by the House of Lords in *Bridge v Campbell Discount Co*.[257] Hodson LJ expressed his difficulty in seeing **16-067**

> "the validity of the distinction between a claim to receive payment of a sum of money because of a right to determine arising from breach of contract and a claim to receive payment of the same sum by reason of breach of contract giving a right to determine."[258]

Serious consideration of the question of the amount payable on a termination on account of breach did not therefore start till, with *Cooden Engineering*, it became one

[250] For the details of what has appeared after the five year period see para.16-069, below.
[251] [1966] 1 W.L.R. 1428 CA.
[252] See the important *Robophone* at para.16-096, below.
[253] 1926 unreported, but referred to in *Re Apex Supply Co* [1942] 1 Ch. 108 and in *Cooden Engineering Co v Stanford* [1953] 1 Q.B. 86 CA both of which are dealt with below.
[254] [1942] 1 Ch. 108, but only by way of dictum since in that case the owner had determined the contract upon the hiring company going into liquidation, which was not considered to amount to a breach.
[255] [1953] 1 Q.B. 86 CA, Jenkins LJ dissenting.
[256] [1955] 1 All E.R. 839.
[257] [1962] A.C. 600, where, however, the argument proceeded on a somewhat more advanced point.
[258] [1953] 1 Q.B. 86 CA at 116.

of practical importance. After *Cooden Engineering* had shown the way, the cases soon took off.

**16-068** The second reason relates to the presence of legislative control of hire-purchase agreements as it existed after 1964. Again, the position is complex and needs to be traced historically. Legislative control started well before 1964 with the Hire-Purchase Act 1938. This initial statute in the field gave the hirer a right to terminate at any time before the final payment fell due and, if he did so, he could not be required to pay more than the amount by which one-half of the hire-purchase price exceeded the total of the sums paid and due before the termination,[259] and the statute further provided that the hirer could not be subjected to a liability to pay an amount greater than this after the termination in any manner whatsoever of the agreement, which clearly included termination on account of breach.[260] This degree of protection given to the hirer was then massively enlarged by the Hire-Purchase Act 1964 which, in provisions repeated in the consolidating Hire-Purchase Act 1965, while otherwise following the 1938 Act, reduced the entitlement of the owner from recovery of one-half of the hire-purchase price to recovery of its actual loss where the court was satisfied that this was less.[261] Thus from 1964 every stipulated sum, or at least every stipulated sum greater than actual loss, was effectively turned into an irrecoverable penalty. The Consumer Credit Act 1974, which of course is the statute that now matters, continued these provisions, but in a curiously different fashion. The restriction of the owner's recovery to actual loss was itself restricted to cases where the termination had been by the exercise by the hirer of his statutory right to terminate[262]; the great significance of this different approach will be addressed later.[263] And it should be noted here that the Consumer Credit Act 1974 also introduced provisions as to extortionate credit bargains where the court could afford relief to the hirer from payment in excess of what was fairly due and reasonable,[264] provisions which the Consumer Credit Act 2006 has now replaced with somewhat similar provisions on so-called unfair relationships.[265]

**16-069** Not only did the Hire-Purchase Act 1964 introduce this power of the court to restrict the owner to its actual loss but it also extended the catchment of the legislation by substantially increasing the amount that the hire-purchase price must not exceed in order to constitute a regulated agreement, as a hire-purchase agreement under the legislative control is termed. This amount went to £2,000 from £300[266] and this was carried over into the Hire-Purchase Act 1965 until it was increased to £5,000 in 1978 at a time when that statute was still the controlling statute in these matters, the equivalent provisions of the Consumer Credit Act 1974 for the protection of the hirer not coming into force until May 1985.[267] Thus while the cases of the five-year period of the early 1960s could easily fall outside the statutory control, this now became far less likely and helps explain why there are only two reported

---

[259] By s.4(1) of the 1938 Act.

[260] By s.5(c), read with s.4(1) of the 1938 Act.

[261] See ss.27 to 29 at s.28(1)(a) and (2), and especially s.29(2)(c) of the Hire-Purchase Act 1965.

[262] s.99 together with s.100(1) and (3) of the Consumer Credit Act correspond to s.27(1) together with s.28(1)(c) and (2) of the earlier Hire-Purchase Act, but there is no section corresponding to s.29 with its vital subs.(2)(c).

[263] See para.16-072, below.

[264] In ss.137 to 140.

[265] In ss.140A to 140D.

[266] £300 had been introduced by the Hire-Purchase Act 1954. The initial statutory limit in the Hire-Purchase Act 1938 was £100, with only £50 for cars.

[267] By SI 1983/1551 arts 2 and 6.

cases involving agreements concluded during the 20-year reign in this area of the Hire-Purchase Act 1965. *Capital Finance Co v Donati*,[268] saw the hire-purchase of a car for £2,310 under an agreement concluded in 1973 when the limit still stood at £2,000; *Lombard North Central v Butterworth*,[269] concerned a computer for which over £10,000 was to be paid under an agreement made, it would seem, in 1982 or even before[270] when the statutory limit had moved to £5,000. Section 8 of the Consumer Credit Act 1974, in defining agreements that were to be covered, started life also with a £5,000 limit but when its provisions for the protection of hirers came into force in 1985 the limit was pitched higher at £15,000[271] and higher still at £25,000 in 1998,[272] which suffices to explain why there have been no cases, or certainly no reported cases, since *Lombard v Butterworth* of agreements falling outside the relevant statutory control. Now the Consumer Credit Act 2006 by s.2(1) has removed the financial limit completely from s.8 of the 1974 Act[273] so that for the future no agreement whatsoever can escape the legislative control on account of the level of the hire-purchase price specified in it.

In these circumstances, with the disappearance of the financial limit and the limitation to recovery of actual loss, it might seem that there is no longer any need to set out the details of the earlier authorities. But there are two essential reasons, and a tangential one, for still dealing with them. **16-070**

The first reason is straightforward. While the initial Hire-Purchase Act of 1938 covered agreements made by every type of hire-purchaser, the Hire-Purchase Act 1964 introduced an exclusion for agreements made by a body corporate as the hirer,[274] an exclusion continued in the Hire-Purchase Act 1965.[275] This was taken up, and indeed widened, by the Consumer Credit Act 1974, which is the statute that now matters. Section 8, in defining agreements to be covered, specifies agreements with the hire-purchaser as an individual, and the sections of the Consumer Credit Act 1974 on extortionate credit bargains, now on unfair relationships, are also couched in terms of individuals.[276] No doubt it was thought that it was only individuals that needed protection. Yet there could be hire-purchasers other than individuals, such as trusts as well as companies, to whom, unprotected by statute, it might be important to know their position as between liquidated damages and penalty. **16-071**

The second reason is more subtle. As we have seen,[277] the Consumer Credit Act 1974, like the Hire-Purchase Acts 1964 and 1965 before it, has provision whereby recovery against the hirer can be restricted to the owner's actual loss but that such provision is, oddly, of a much more restricted nature than formerly in that it applies only where there is a determination by the hirer under his statutory right. Therefore a termination for breach by the owner is no longer covered by the **16-072**

---

268 (1977) 121 S.J. 270 CA. See the case at para.16-079, below.

269 [1987] Q.B. 527 CA. See the case at paras 16-079 and 26-017, below.

270 The report does not reveal the date of the agreement but states that the finance company commenced its action in May 1984 which was well after the agreement, as by that date the deposit and two three-monthly instalments had been paid, there had been a failure to pay the third on a number of occasions, and the computer had been repossessed and sold.

271 SI 1983/1878.

272 SI 1998/996.

273 Brought into effect by SI 2008/831.

274 By s.2 of the 1964 Act.

275 By s.4 of the 1965 Act.

276 See formerly s.137(2) and now s.140C(1).

277 At para.16-068, above.

legislation. This point never seems to have been taken but it is undoubtedly there for the taking. It is true that a hirer faced with a termination on account of breach might still seek relief under the provisions on unfair relationships, but these provisions and the similar ones on extortionate credit bargains which they have replaced appear to be untested, and in any event the case would have to be an extreme one before a court would be prepared to interfere.

**16-073** The tangential reason can be briefly stated. It is that what has been held to be the legal position unencumbered by statute may be applicable by analogy to other types of contract. It is therefore interesting to see that in *Dalkia Utilities Services Plc v Celtech International Ltd*,[278] a decision of 2008 concerning termination after breach of a contract other than of hire-purchase, many of the Court of Appeal cases of the five-year period of the early 1960s were cited by Christopher Clarke J.[279]

**16-074** We therefore turn finally to these authorities. They require an analysis of some detail.

**16-075** *(ii) The case law* The stipulated sum which the owners claimed under the provisions of the contract for the hire-purchase of a car in *Cooden Engineering Co v Stanford*,[280] was the full balance of instalments remaining unpaid, together with all costs, charges and expenses incurred by the owners in the exercise of their powers under the agreement and in the retaking of possession of the car upon determination. The Court of Appeal, in holding this a penalty, pointed to various factors: (1) only 40 per cent of unpaid instalments was to become payable where it was the hirer who determined; (2) the sum could become due upon a trivial and very early breach; (3) the owner would get the full price and the car as well, so that unless the car was valueless, an exceptional contingency which could be ignored, the sum "must always exceed any damage to the owners".[281] Indeed it was not difficult to hold that a "minimum payment" clause which, in addition to out-of-pocket expenses, exacted the maximum payment under the contract constituted a penalty, but in the next case, *Landom v Hurrell*,[282] the "minimum payment" was down to three-quarters of the full price for the car. Nevertheless Denning LJ still held this to be a penalty, listing the following pointers: (1) the three-quarters of the price was a sum inserted by rule of thumb, for it was the same whatever the breach; (2) the sum was payable on the assumption of good repair since the owner was entitled to further damages for bad condition of the car under another clause; (3) the value of the car could not have dropped to the extent of three-quarters of the price in one month, when the first payment fell due and breach by non-payment was a possibility, or even in six months, when such breach had become a fact; (4) for a simple hire of a car, whether for one month or even six, the hiring charge would have been nowhere near the figure represented by three-quarters of the purchase price, and yet the hiring charge would in such a case have to cover depreciation. This last argument was introduced probably because the stipulated sum was stated to be agreed compensation for depreciation.

---

[278] [2006] 1 Lloyd's Rep. 599.

[279] In date order *Yeoman Credit Co v Waragowski* [1961] 1 W.L.R. 1124 CA; *Overstone v Shipway* [1962] 1 W.L.R. 117 CA; *Financings v Baldock* [1963] 2 Q.B. 104 CA; *Lombard North Central v Butterworth* [1987] Q.B. 527 CA.

[280] [1953] 1 Q.B. 86 CA.

[281] [1953] 1 Q.B. 86 CA at 109.

[282] [1955] 1 All E.R. 839.

In *Bridge v Campbell Discount Co*,[283] the question of the validity of a "minimum payment" clause reached the House of Lords, their Lordships holding that the owner had terminated upon the hirer's breach. The "minimum payment" in the particular contract had now fallen to two-thirds of the full price; this too was held to be a penalty. Once again the stipulated sum was stated to be agreed compensation for depreciation and their Lordships considered it specifically in this light. They pointed out that the stipulated sum could clearly not be treated as a genuine pre-estimate of the damage suffered by depreciation since the amount payable on breach was in inverse proportion to the depreciation.[284] Their Lordships then went on to hold that the sum, looked at other than as agreed compensation for depreciation, was still a penalty. Lord Radcliffe, after pointing to the now familiar argument that the car came back into the owner's hands with a realisable value that might well exceed the balance of the purchase price which the owner had not yet got in, introduced the hitherto dormant argument that the full hire-purchase price contained a considerable interest element which the owner did not forego, and expressed the general doubt as to whether an owner **16-076**

> "could ever validly protect himself on the scale of up to two-thirds that is envisaged here, without much more elaborate provisions for adjustment according to the circumstances in which the claim falls due."[285]

This group of cases culminating in *Bridge v Campbell Discount Co*,[286] established that a "minimum payment" clause where the minimum payment is two-thirds or higher of the full price has slender, if any, chance of being classified other than as a penalty.[287] However, total acceptance of this proposition is barred by the decision of the Court of Appeal in *Phonographic Equipment (1958) Ltd v Muslu*.[288] The claim there was under a clause, in a hire-purchase contract for a juke box, providing for the payment by the hirer on breach **16-077**

> "by way of agreed depreciation of the goods a sum equal to … 50 per cent of the total hire-purchase price payable … plus … a further 5 per cent of such total hire-purchase price for each month which has elapsed between the date of the agreement and the receipt of the goods by the owners up to 75 per cent of the said total price",

less the sums already paid and the sums already fallen due. The Court of Appeal held that this was not a penalty. This decision, although only cited in argument in *Bridge v Campbell Discount Co*,[289] and not touched upon in their Lordships' speeches, appears to be wholly contradictory to the ratio decidendi of that case. And indeed Veale J in *E.P. Finance Co v Dooley*[290] considered *Muslu* no longer binding for this reason,[291] and held a clause in the same form as that in *Muslu* a penalty.

---

283 [1962] A.C. 600.

284 [1962] A.C. 600 at 621, 623 ("it is a sliding scale of compensation, but a scale that slides in the wrong direction") and 626.

285 [1962] A.C. 600 at 625.

286 [1962] A.C. 600.

287 In *United Dominions Trust (Commercials) Ltd v Ennis* [1968] 1 Q.B. 54 CA, it was accepted without argument that, following Bridge, a "minimum payment" clause for two-thirds of the purchase price constituted a penalty.

288 [1961] 1 W.L.R. 1379 CA.

289 [1962] A.C. 600.

290 [1963] 1 W.L.R. 1313.

291 [1963] 1 W.L.R. 1313 at 1321.

However, in *Lombank Ltd v Excell*,[292] the Court of Appeal, surely with over-abundant caution, only partially accepted this view. The court there ruled, per curiam, that it was impossible to say that the *Muslu* decision had as a matter of law precluded the court from holding that a clause in such a form in a hire-purchase agreement was a penalty[293]: the resolution of the question depended not solely upon the construction of the clause but also on the subject-matter of the contract and all relevant surrounding circumstances, and the matter was remitted to the judge below for the appropriate evidence to be called.[294] At the same time the court, while admitting that if the *Muslu* case had not been decided they might have held this type of clause to be always invalid as a penalty, did not think that it was open to them to say that *Bridge v Campbell Discount Co*,[295] had shown the *Muslu* case to be wrong in law in every case and had in effect overruled it.[296] They pointed to the fact that the form of the clause in the two cases differed and that the sliding scale of depreciation in *Muslu* did not slide in the wrong direction as in *Bridge*.[297] Nevertheless, this is true only for the early months of the hiring, namely until the monthly increments of five per cent have reached 75 per cent of the total price; after that point has been reached the situation is similar to that in *Bridge* and in the earlier cases of *Cooden Engineering Co v Stanford*,[298] and *Landom Trust v Hurrell*.[299] Thus assuming that the contract was determined and the goods repossessed in the sixth month of the hiring, the position would be precisely the same as that in *Landom Trust v Hurrell*,[300] where the determination came after six months and 75 per cent of the full price was payable upon determination.

**16-078** It might be thought that these "minimum payment" clauses would cease to be interpreted as penalties once the various arguments of the courts for holding them to be such are met by appropriate modifications of the hire-purchase agreement, but this is not borne out by *Anglo-Auto Finance Co v James*.[301] In that case a clause which provided that on default the owner should be entitled to the balance of the hire-purchase price less the net amount realised by the owner's sale of the vehicle was held by the Court of Appeal to be a penalty in the light of the decision in *Bridge v Campbell Discount Co*.[302] It seemed, however, to pass unnoticed that, though the particular clause might be framed in terms of the full hire-purchase price, the provisions for the deduction of the amount realised on sale changed its whole tenor and went most of the way to removing the force of the earlier arguments in favour of penalty. Moreover, two years earlier in *Yeoman Credit Co v Waragowski*,[303] the Court of Appeal had calculated the claimant owner's unliquidated damages in respect of the defendant hirer's breach at precisely the amount which, without reference to the earlier case, it now declared to be a penalty. It is true that the calcula-

---

292 [1964] 1 Q.B. 415 CA.

293 [1964] 1 Q.B. 415 CA at 424 to 426.

294 As to some of the factors which may be considered relevant, see [1964] 1 Q.B. 415 CA at 427 to 428. *Lombank v Cook* [1962] 1 W.L.R. 1133 and *Lombank v Archbold* [1962] C.L.Y 1409, in both of which the judge held himself bound by the *Muslu* case to hold a clause in this form not a penalty, were overruled.

295 [1962] A.C. 600.

296 [1964] 1 Q.B. 415 CA at 424, 426.

297 [1964] 1 Q.B. 415 CA at 425 to 426.

298 [1953] 1 Q.B. 86 CA; see para.16-075, above.

299 [1955] 1 All E.R. 839; see para.16-075, above.

300 [1955] 1 All E.R. 839.

301 [1963] 1 W.L.R. 1042 CA.

302 [1962] A.C. 600.

303 [1961] 1 W.L.R. 1124 CA.

tion of unliquidated damages in *Yeoman Credit Co v Waragowski* had already, in two cases immediately following it, *Overstone v Shipway*,[304] and *Yeoman Credit Co v McLean*,[305] been shown to be faulty in so far as it failed to make a deduction in respect of the earlier return to the owner of his capital outlay,[306] but there is nothing in *Anglo-Auto Finance Co v James* to suggest that the court there, in holding the "minimum payment" clause to be a penalty, was relying exclusively on the point of interest not foregone.

It is considered that the resolution of this apparent inconsistency between *Anglo-Auto Finance Co v James*,[307] on the one hand and *Yeoman Credit Co v Waragowski*,[308] on the other is to be found in the later cases on unliquidated damages which have made much smaller awards to claimants. Starting with *Financings v Baldock*,[309] the courts began to limit the owner's damages to recovery of the instalments which were in arrear when the contract was terminated[310]; the termination, it was said, arose by virtue of the exercise by the owner of the option which the contract expressly gave him to terminate on non-payment of instalments and not, as in the earlier cases, by virtue of his acceptance of a repudiation of the contract by the hirer. Thus only where the hirer's breach is insufficiently serious to entitle the owner to terminate the contract otherwise than by virtue of its contractual option, so that the *Financings v Baldock* measure of damages controls, will a "minimum payment" clause of the *Anglo-Auto Finance Co v James*,[311] variety undoubtedly be regarded as a penalty. Certainly, the Court of Appeal have continued to hold such clauses in such circumstances to be penalties, both in *Capital Finance Co v Donati*,[312] and in *Lombard North Central v Butterworth*,[313] the sole cases which appear to have come up for decision since.[314] Only where the contract excludes termination under an owner's option exercisable without repudiation by the hirer will such a clause have any chance of being accepted as providing for liquidated damages rather than as constituting a penalty when there is a repudiatory breach.[315] **16-079**

### (2) Types of contract where the stipulated sum is generally liquidated damages

There are two large categories into which most of the provisions which have been successfully upheld as liquidated damages can be placed. The first is defined by the form of breach upon which the provision operates; this is breach by delay, generally[316] by improper detention of a ship by a charterer[317] or by the failure of a builder **16-080**

304 [1962] 1 W.L.R. 117 CA.
305 [1962] 1 W.L.R. 131.
306 See para.26-013, below.
307 [1963] 1 W.L.R. 1042 CA.
308 [1961] 1 W.L.R. 1124 CA.
309 [1963] 2 Q.B. 104 CA.
310 See paras 26-014 and following, below.
311 [1963] 1 W.L.R. 1042 CA.
312 (1977) 121 S.J. 270 CA.
313 [1987] Q.B. 527 CA; a case of hire but akin, in the particular circumstances, to hire-purchase.
314 For the reason that these are the only two decisions see para.16-068, above.
315 For further discussion of these issues see the consideration of unliquidated damages in hire-purchase contracts at paras 26-012 to 26-017, below.
316 There are a few other isolated instances, such as *Elphinstone v Monkland Iron Co* (1886) 11 App. Cas. 332 and *Diestal v Stevenson* [1906] 2 K.B. 345.
317 See para.16-081, below.

to complete a construction on the due date,[318] and generally involving[319] a stipulated sum graduated in relation to the length of the delay. The second is defined by the form of protection that the contractual promise is designed to afford; this is protection from competition to one party's business[320] by securing a covenant whereby the other party restricts his own business activities whether by promising not to compete with his employer on leaving his employment or with the buyer of his business after the sale,[321] by accepting restrictions on the terms upon which he may resell goods bought from the promisee,[322] or by agreeing that all his goods shall be sold to the promisee.[323]

16-081 **(a) Charterparties: improper detention of ship by charterer** It has long been an everyday provision in a charterparty that if the charterer improperly detains the ship, whether at the port of loading or the port of discharge, he shall pay the shipowner at a certain rate for every day of improper detention. Such a stipulated sum, graduated to the size of the breach, is always referred to as demurrage. Stipulated sums payable to carriers of goods in their shipping containers, graduated to the length of time after they should have been returned to the carrier, have today come to be classified as demurrage, specifically as container demurrage. *MSC Mediterranean Shipping Co SA v Cottonex Anstalt*,[324] is such a case, and probably the first such case. This familiar term has tended to obscure that this is a straightforward case of liquidated damages, but that it is so is clearly recognised by the Court of Appeal in *Aktieselskabet Reidar v Arcos*,[325] Atkin LJ referring to the demurrage provisions there as quantifying the damages,[326] and by the House of Lords in *President of India v Lips Maritime Corporation*,[327] Lord Brandon saying simply that the effect of a demurrage clause "is to liquidate the damages payable."[328] The true analysis has also been obscured by the long acceptance of demurrage

318 See para.16-085, below.

319 Except in *Wallis v Smith* (1882) 21 Ch. D. 243 CA: see para.16-088, below.

320 Business is here used to include professions.

321 See para.16-083, below.

322 See para.16-092, below. In *Dunlop Pneumatic Tyre Co v New Garage and Motor Co* [1915] A.C. 79 Lord Atkinson compared this type of case with the last one: at 92.

323 See para.16-091, below. Sale of goods cases, though falling outside these two categories, also provide illustrations of stipulated sums which have been held to be liquidated damages. In *Smith Bros v Gosta Jacobsson* [1961] 2 Lloyd's Rep. 522 the contract provided that, in respect of claims against the sellers for non-delivery, the buyers should be paid as liquidated damages a sum equal to 10 per cent of the c.i.f. value of the goods, and this sum was held recoverable as liquidated damages as at the time of the contract the sellers knew that the buyers required the goods for general trading: at 525. In *Stewart v Carapanyoti* [1962] 1 W.L.R. 34 the contract provided that in calculating the damages a penalty of not less than 2 per cent or more than 10 per cent should on a seller's default be added to, and on a buyer's default be deducted from, the estimated market value of the goods, and on the seller's default this was held to be liquidated damages since it was "a perfectly reasonable, business like way of providing machinery for dealing with a practical, concrete problem, namely, how is the innocent party to be compensated for certain items of loss which are not covered by an award based merely on the difference between contract price and market price": at 39. In *M&J Polymers Ltd v Imerys Minerals Ltd* [2008] 1 Lloyd's Rep. 541 a take or pay clause in a sale of goods contract was held to amount to a provision for liquidated damages; see the case at para.16-018, above. And see, too, contracts of hire of goods at paras 16-093 to 16-098, below.

324 [2015] EWHC 283 (Comm), see [2016] EWCA Civ 789 on appeal, discussed at paras 9-032 to 9-033 and para.16-031, above.

325 [1927] 1 K.B. 352 CA.

326 [1927] 1 K.B. 352 CA at 363. The case is considered at para.16-024, above.

327 [1988] A.C. 395.

328 [1988] A.C. 395 at 422F.

clauses even before liquidated damages clauses in general were accepted and understood. The result has been that this type of clause has never gone through a thorough testing in the courts,[329] but there can be no doubt that it is properly held to constitute liquidated damages since the sum is payable only on one form of breach and is graduated in line with the size of that breach.[330]

**(b) Employment contracts: failure to carry out a particular provision by one of the parties** We have seen that the early 19th century had already put paid to holding a stipulated sum to be liquidated damages where it was payable by either of the parties and on breach of any of the contractual provisions.[331] The situation, however, is very different, as has been recognised in modern times, where the stipulated sum is to be paid by one party and in respect of one category of breach. Thus in *Neil v Strathclyde Regional Council*,[332] the stipulation was of this nature and was also for a graduated sum—an employee had undertaken to remain in the service of her employers for a minimum of two years after completion of a training course and, if she failed to do so, to pay them a proportion of the amount they had expended in putting her through the course, such proportion being governed by how much of the minimum period she failed to fulfil—and this was held to be a provision for liquidated damages rather than a penalty. And in two later cases, which both had an unusual feature, the stipulated sum, which again was to be paid by one party only and was in respect of one category of breach, was held to be liquidated damages. The unusual feature in *Murray v Leisureplay Plc*,[333] was that the stipulated sum was to be paid not by the employee but by the employer,[334] while the unusual feature in *Tullett v Prebon Group Ltd v Ghaleb-el-Hajjali*,[335] was that the breach of contract was by the prospective employee failing to work at all for the employer.[336] Yet from time to time in this context penalty will be decreed. So in *Giraud UK Ltd v Smith*,[337] a provision that an employee leaving without giving notice must pay his employers the equivalent of his pay for the period of notice was held to be a penalty. 16-082

**(c) Covenants in restraint of trade between buyer and seller of a business or between employer and employee** The earliest type of case to become established in the courts as one which lent itself to a provision for liquidated damages concerned the sale of a business or professional practice in which the seller had entered into a covenant in restraint of trade in favour of the buyer; and the same principles were applied to the similar covenants entered into in employment contracts by a servant in favour of his master. The first case, *Crisdee v Bolton*,[338] concerned the sale of a public house but the stipulated sum was payable not on any breach by either party but only by the seller for breach of a covenant not to carry on the same trade within a mile of the public house. Best CJ pointed out that 16-083

[329] But see *MSC Mediterranean Shipping Co SA* [2016] EWCA Civ 789 at [46].

[330] In the absence of graduation a sum payable on detention beyond the due time for redelivery could well be a penalty, as in *Lansat Shipping Co Ltd v Glencore Grain BV, The Paragon* [2009] 2 Lloyd's Rep. 688 CA; see the case at para.16-044, above. More is said in relation to building contracts on graduated sums at para.16-085, below; see too para.16-049, above.

[331] See para.16-063, above.

[332] [1984] I.R.L.R. 14 (a Scottish case). See the case further at para.33-038, below, in a footnote.

[333] [2005] I.R.L.R. 946 CA.

[334] Facts at para.16-038, above.

[335] [2008] I.R.L.R. 760.

[336] Facts at para.16-102, below.

[337] [2000] I.R.L.R. 763.

[338] (1827) 3 C. & P. 240.

"the sum of £500 is to be paid for the doing of one thing only, viz. setting up a victualling house within one mile".[339]

This doctrine became established in a number of mid-19th century decisions. These concerned primarily sales of surgeons' practices or of moieties of such partnerships,[340] but they also included cases dealing with sales of a coach service business,[341] of a perfumier's shop,[342] and of a solicitor's practice.[343] *Reynolds v Bridge*,[344] which, decided in 1856, formed the last of this group, is the most important. The courts have construed such covenants as a single whole entailing a single obligation,[345] and have accorded no brief to the argument that because there are varying ways of committing the breach the stipulated sum must be a penalty.[346]

**16-084** The law was thus clearly established by 1856; after this date cases fall away.

**16-085** **(d) Building contracts: failure to complete construction on time** From 1876 on, there have been decisions on building contracts in which there have been clauses stipulating the amount to be paid by the builder should he fail to complete construction upon the due date. The contracts have variously been for the erection of buildings,[347] ships,[348] railways,[349] sewerage works[350] and industrial plant[351]; a contemporary contract in the line was for a computerised supervisory system for the approaches to a highway under construction.[352] In most of the cases the stipulated amount has been held to be liquidated damages.[353]

**16-086** Such clauses have been readily interpreted as providing for liquidated damages because the amount of loss arising from a delay in completion of a building project is generally difficult to estimate and because the agreement has generally provided that the amount to be paid shall be so much for each week, or other period of time, beyond the time fixed for completion of the construction, thus graduating the stipulated sum in line with the seriousness of the breach. Thus in *Clydebank Engineering Co v Don Jose Ramos Yzquierdo y Castaneda*,[354] the leading case in this connection, the Spanish Government, in expectation of war, contracted for the construction and delivery of four torpedo-boats by the defendants within a certain time, £500 to be paid for each vessel for every week of delay. This was held to constitute liquidated damages. A similar result was reached in two cases a century

---

339 (1827) 3 C. & P. 240 at 243.

340 *Rawlinson v Clarke* (1845) 14 M. & W. 187; *Sainter v Ferguson* (1849) 7 C.B. 716; *Atkyns v Kinnier* (1850) 4 Ex. 776; *Reynolds v Bridge* (1856) 6 E. & B. 528. See *Mercer v Irving* (1858) E.B. & E. 563, decided on a question of form and therefore not a direct authority.

341 *Leighton v Wales* (1838) 3 M. & W. 545.

342 *Price v Green* (1847) 16 M. & W. 346.

343 *Galsworth v Strutt* (1848) 1 Ex. 659.

344 (1856) 6 E. & B. 528.

345 See *Price v Green* (1847) 16 M. & W. 346 at 354, per Patteson J, and *Reynolds v Bridge* (1856) 6 E. & B. 528 at 545, per Crompton J, both quoted in a footnote to para.16-050, above.

346 See *Galsworthy v Strutt* (1848) 1 Ex. 659 at 666 to 667, per Alderson B, quoted at para.16-057, above.

347 *Wallis v Smith* (1882) 21 Ch. D. 243 CA; *Re Newman* (1876) 4 Ch. D. 724 CA.

348 *Clydebank Engineering Co v Don Jose Ramos Yzquierdo y Castaneda* [1905] A.C. 6.

349 *Public Works Commissioner v Hills* [1906] A.C. 368 PC.

350 *Law v Redditch Local Board* [1892] 1 Q.B. 127 CA.

351 *Cellulose Acetate Silk Co v Widnes Foundry* [1933] A.C. 20.

352 *Philips Hong Kong v Att Gen of Hong Kong* (1993) 61 B.L.R. 41 PC.

353 The exceptions are *Public Works Commissioner v Hills* [1906] A.C. 368, PC and *Re Newman* (1876) 4 Ch. D. 724 CA. The reasons are indicated at para.16-087, below.

354 [1905] A.C. 6.

apart. In *Law v Redditch Local Board*,[355] the provision was that, if the construction of sewerage works was not completed within the contractual time, the contractor should pay £100 and then £5 for every week during which the works should remain incomplete; in *Philips Hong Kong v Attorney General of Hong Kong*,[356] the provision was that, if certain key dates were not met in the installation of a computerised supervisory system for a highway project, and if the whole project were not completed within the specified time, agreed sums would become payable at a daily rate.[357]

On the other hand where there is no provision for graduation of the sum, the clause is in danger of being held a penalty. The principal illustration of this is *Public Works Commissioner v Hills*,[358] where in a contract for the construction of a railway for a colonial government it was provided not only that the contractors were to deposit £50,000 as security but that the government was to retain 10 per cent of the payments which it was required to pay from time to time as the construction work progressed, and that all these amounts would be forfeited[359] should the contractors fail to complete the railway line. This was held to be a penalty; not only was there no sum graduated in proportion to the seriousness of the breach but a diametrically opposite result would have been achieved since the amount of money retained by the government depended on what it was due to pay, which in turn depended on the amount of construction work done, so that as the seriousness of the breach decreased the amount that the contractors stood to lose on breach grew higher. However, it was only the failure to work out a suitable provision which resulted in the clause being labelled a penalty, and Lord Dunedin specifically said that their Lordships had 16-087

> "no doubt that the case of the non-completion of a railway would be a natural and proper case in which to make such a stipulation".[360]

And again in *Re Newman*,[361] although in a contract to erect buildings it was agreed that the contractors should pay £10 for each week's delay after the due completion date, the effect of this graduated sum was cancelled out by a final stipulation that the contractors should pay £1,000 if they should fail to perform the contract in all respects; the whole was held to constitute a penalty.

In one case, *Wallis v Smith*,[362] a sum has been held to be liquidated damages despite the fact that no provisions for graduation were included in the contract. The case is, therefore, a difficult one, and indeed was decided at a controversial time when the doctrine was still not fully free from the shackles of its history.[363] The relevant facts were these. The claimant contracted to sell an estate to the defend- 16-088

---

355 [1892] 1 Q.B. 127 CA.

356 (1993) 61 B.L.R. 41 PC.

357 Also in *Cellulose Acetate Silk Co v Widnes Foundry* [1933] A.C. 20 a provision for the payment of £20 for each week's delay in the delivery and erection of industrial plant was held to constitute liquidated damages. This, however, is not so cogent an authority in this connection as the amount was well below the estimated loss, and the clause was interpreted as involving a limitation of liability: see para.16-100, below.

358 [1906] A.C. 368 PC.

359 Strictly the case is one of money paid in advance and as such is considered at para.16-109, below.

360 *Public Works Commissioner v Hills* [1906] A.C. 368 PC at 375.

361 (1876) 4 Ch. D. 724 CA.

362 (1882) 21 Ch. D. 243 CA.

363 The Court of Appeal indeed launched into an exhaustive consideration of the whole subject but most of their deliberations are, for practical purposes today, superseded by the speeches in the House of

ant for £70,000 which was to be expended by the defendant in building thereon. A deposit of £5,000 was to be paid by the defendant over a period of seven months. If the claimant could not make a good title he would pay £5,000 as liquidated damages; if the defendant should commit a substantial breach of the contract, either in not proceeding with the building or in failing to perform any of the contract's provisions, the £5,000 deposit should, if paid, be forfeited and, if not paid, become payable as liquidated damages. The defendant altogether failed in carrying out his side of the contract and the claimant successfully sued for the £5,000 as liquidated damages.[364]

**16-089** The new century has produced further decisions on delay in building contracts. In *Alfred McAlpine Capital Projects Ltd v Tilebox Ltd*,[365] a provision for payment at the rate of £45,000 for every week of delay in completion of building works was held to constitute liquidated damages. Apart from an extended review of all the leading authorities on the subject,[366] the lengthy judgment is taken up with attempting to assess what losses were likely to have been foreseeable at the time of contracting in order to come to a view on whether the weekly £45,000 constituted a genuine pre-estimate of loss. In *CFW Architects v Cowlin Construction Ltd*,[367] the provision for payments on delay in the construction of houses under a design and build contract was upheld as liquidated damages despite being potentially harsh on the builder.[368] In *Hall v Van Der Heiden*,[369] a sum to be paid for each day's delay by the builder in his work on the claimant's flat was without difficulty held to be liquidated damages.

**16-090** **(e) Covenants restricting the terms upon which goods may be sold or resold**[370] The most modern type of contract clearly attracting the doctrine of liquidated damages concerns the imposition by contractual agreement of restrictions on one party upon his right to sell and market his goods and produce.

**16-091** *Webster v Bosanquet*,[371] opened the field of liquidated damages to contracts in which one party has agreed to sell to the other all of his goods of a particular type and description. In that case the claimant and defendant had been partners in selling tea, and on the dissolution of the partnership the claimant took over the assets at a sum. It was provided in the contract that the defendant should for 10 years sell to the claimant the whole of his crop on the two estates where as partners they had grown their tea, if the claimant should pay the defendant £75 a year for the use of the names of the two estates. The defendant sold elsewhere, and the claimant successfully sued him for the sum which the parties had stipulated would become pay-

---

Lords and the Judicial Committee decisions at the beginning of the last century: see para.16-008, above.

364 Although the contract provided that the defendant should deposit the £5,000 over the period of seven months and although Jessel, MR said emphatically that any agreement that a deposit should be forfeited would be implemented even if the sum were penal ((1882) 21 Ch. D. 243 CA at 258), the court did not treat the case as one concerning a deposit. This aspect of the case should be reconsidered in the light of the modern developments in deposit cases: see paras 16-104 and following, below.

365 (2006) 104 Con. L.R. 39.

366 (2006) 104 Con. L.R. 39 at [35]–[49].

367 (2006) 105 Con. L.R. 116.

368 (2006) 105 Con. L.R. 116 at [177] to [191].

369 [2010] EWHC 586 (TCC). Facts at para.16-030, above.

370 Or bought; but there are no cases. This type of covenant is now subject to the legislation dealing with restrictive trade practices.

371 [1912] A.C. 394 PC.

able upon breach by selling other than to the claimant. Lord Mersey said:

> "That such a sale might seriously affect his [i.e. the claimant's] business was obvious, and the very uncertainty of the loss likely to arise made it most reasonable for the parties to agree beforehand as to what the damages should be."[372]

Similarly, in *English Hop Growers v Dering*,[373] the defendant was a member of the claimant society which had been formed to organise the marketing of home-grown hops by their sale through the society, and the defendant had agreed to deliver to the society all the hops grown or produced by him in 1926 on a certain 63-acre piece of land and, if he failed to sell them to the claimant or disposed of them elsewhere, to pay to the claimant £100 for each of the 63 acres, or, if his default were partial, proportionately on a smaller acreage. Upon the defendant's total failure to perform, the claimant society successfully claimed the full stipulated sum of £6,300. Sankey LJ said:

> "The damage is really the undermining of the market and the undermining of the existence of the plaintiff company.... The maintenance of an artificial price is a difficult and delicate operation. It may be upset by a trivial or unexpected occurrence, for example, by one important member deserting the combine or a small untied amount being placed on the market."[374]

*Dunlop Pneumatic Tyre Co v New Garage and Motor Co*,[375] provided the finishing touches, by adding one further type of case to those which lend themselves to the proper inclusion of a provision for liquidated damages, the case of a sale of goods in which the buyer has agreed to restrictions on his rights of resale. The claimants sold tyres to the defendant car dealer who agreed not to tamper with the marks on the tyres, not to sell them below certain listed prices, not to sell them to persons on a certain suspended list, and not to exhibit or export them without the claimant's consent; in addition the defendant agreed to pay £5 for every tyre, tube or cover which he sold or offered in breach of the contract. The defendant sold below the listed price and the claimants recovered the stipulated sum as liquidated damages. And in *Imperial Tobacco Co v Parsley*,[376] the same result was reached in similar circumstances, but the covenant upon which the sum operated was directed solely to resale price maintenance. In that case Lord Wright said: **16-092**

> "Where you have a price-maintaining system, which is an ordinary incident of this modern life in this type of business, any departure by a retailer from the terms which he has undertaken as to maintaining the schedule prices may have the most serious and widespread effect."[377]

But on the facts of *Ford Motor Co v Armstrong*,[378] which concerned the sale of cars by a manufacturer to a car dealer, the Court of Appeal reached a different result. This, however, was not because this type of contract was not considered suitable for a liquidated damages clause, but because the manufacturer had drawn the net too wide: the stipulated sum was to become payable by the dealer not only for a

---

372 [1912] A.C. 394 PC at 398.
373 [1928] 2 K.B. 174 CA.
374 [1928] 2 K.B. 174 CA at 188 to 189.
375 [1915] A.C. 79.
376 [1936] 2 All E.R. 515.
377 [1936] 2 All E.R. 515 at 519.
378 (1915) 31 T.L.R. 267 CA.

breach by reselling a car below the listed price or to a prohibited person but also for a breach by exhibiting the car without the manufacturer's permission, which was a stipulation different in kind as well as in importance. The amount payable for any one breach was also substantially higher than in *Dunlop Pneumatic Tyre Co v New Garage and Motor Co*,[379] £250 per item as opposed to £5 per item, but the court laid less stress on this: it was only important in that it highlighted the penal nature of the sum in relation to the trivial breach of exhibiting without permission.

16-093 **(f) Contracts of hire: failure by hirer to pay instalments** It was said in the 13th edition of this work in 1972 that it was really somewhat premature to say of contracts of hire that they are of a type where the stipulated sum is generally liquidated damages, since there was only one case dealing directly with the issue and favouring the liquidated damages solution, having been decided between that edition and the previous one. It remains premature today for, although we have arrived at the 20th edition, there is still only this one decision. It is *Robophone Facilities v Blank*.[380]

16-094 The reason for this singularity of decision is the same as that to be attributed to the drying up of the hire-purchase cases resulting from the impact of legislative control of agreements.[381] Whereas with hire-purchase this control started with the Hire-Purchase Act 1938, followed by various later Hire-Purchase Acts and leading to the Consumer Credit Act 1974 now in force in place of the earlier statutes, contracts of hire had to await till the Consumer Credit Act before finding themselves also controlled. Section 15(1) of that Act defined as a regulated consumer hire agreement any agreement for the hire of goods made by an individual as hirer, capable of subsisting for more than three months, and not requiring the hirer to make payments in excess of a statutory limit.[382] Section 132 then provided that where the owner under such an agreement recovered possession of the goods hired, then if their recovery was otherwise than by action and the hirer applied to the court for an order, or if their recovery was sought by action and the court made an order for their delivery to the owner, the court might order that the obligation to pay the whole or part of any sum owed by the hirer to the owner in respect of the goods should cease if it appeared just to the court so to order in the light of the extent to which the goods had been enjoyed by the hirer. There remained scope for the law outside the statute to apply where the amount payable under an agreement exceeded the statutory limit, fixed initially at £5,000 and rising over the years to £15,000 and then to £25,000.[383] But no cases appeared. And the Consumer Credit Act 2006 by s.2(2) has removed the financial limit completely from s.15(1) of the 1974 Act[384] so that today every single hire agreement with an individual debtor is caught by the legislation.

16-095 With the financial limit removed, it might seem that there is no longer any need

[379] [1915] A.C. 79.

[380] [1966] 1 W.L.R. 1428 CA.

[381] For the position with hire purchase see paras 16-066 and following above.

[382] *Lombard North Central v Butterworth* [1987] Q.B. 527 CA fell outside the ambit of the Consumer Credit Act 1974 as the payments to be made under the contract were well above the prescribed limit at the time; the clause in question was held to be a penalty. However, it is not considered to be in point here as the contract was analogous to one of hire-purchase rather than to one of hire: see the case at para.26-017, below.

[383] This mirrors the increases made to the statutory limit in the hire-purchase cases: see para.16-069, above.

[384] Brought into effect by SI 2008/831.

to look at any law that preceded the legislative intervention. But one of the reasons for doing so with hire-purchase contracts[385] applies here too, that is, that the restrictions imposed by the Consumer Credit Act 1974 on the damages recoverable by lenders are only in favour of individual hirers[386] and there could be hirers other than individuals, such as companies or trusts, to whom it may be important to know their position as between liquidated damages and penalty.[387] It therefore falls for us still to consider the solitary decision in *Robophone Facilities v Blank*.[388]

The stipulated sum in *Robophone* was held by the Court of Appeal to be liquidated damages, although only by a majority. The contract, which was for a seven-year hiring of a telephone-recording machine, provided that if the agreement was terminated for any reason (other than one not in the event relevant) the hirer should pay to the owner company all rentals accrued due and also by way of liquidated damages a sum equal to 50 per cent of all rentals which would subsequently have become payable. The defendant hirer failed to take delivery of the machine and the claimant owners, having terminated the contract on account of the defendant's breach, successfully claimed damages calculated at half of the total rentals payable over the seven year period of the hire. In a detailed and careful analysis Diplock LJ worked out a formula for ascertaining an approximation of the claimants' actual loss, a formula which sought to express the loss as a percentage of the rent for the unexpired period of the contract. He first calculated the profit element in each instalment of rent as the gross amount of the instalment less a deduction for the cost of maintaining the goods and a deduction for their depreciation in value calculated on a straight-line basis over the period of hire. This gave a profit rental of some 59 per cent of the gross rent, but this percentage fell to be further reduced by the fact that the damages would be received in a lump sum payable at once and not over the seven year period of hire. The discount to be made for this accelerated receipt would, however, fall progressively as the unexpired period of the contract decreased, and the calculation ended with a figure for the amount of the actual loss, which loss was within the range of 47 per cent to 58 per cent of the gross rents for the unexpired period of the contract.[389] Accordingly the figure of 50 per cent chosen by the contracting parties was **16-096**

> "reasonably close to the actual loss likely to be occasioned to the plaintiffs so far as it is capable of prediction, and if this figure will tend to operate slightly to the advantage of the plaintiffs if the contract is terminated early in its life, it will tend to operate rather more heavily to the advantage of the defendant if it is terminated late in its life."[390]

This decision, in holding to be liquidated damages a provision in a contract of hire for the payment, in addition to the hire rentals accrued due before breach, of 50 per cent of the total hire rentals falling due in the future, is in interesting contrast to the position with hire-purchase contracts where at the time a "minimum payment" clause had been condemned as a penalty by the courts if requiring two- **16-097**

---

[385] For the position with hire-purchase contracts see para.16-071, above.

[386] See at para.16-094, above.

[387] Contracts where the hiring is only up to three months, and which are still outside the legislation, are hardly likely to cause a problem and can be ignored.

[388] [1966] 1 W.L.R. 1428 CA; see the reference to the case at para.16-093, above.

[389] [1966] 1 W.L.R. 1428 CA at 1444 to 1445.

[390] [1966] 1 W.L.R. 1428 CA at 1449.

thirds, and by statute if requiring 50 per cent, of the full hire-purchase price to be paid.[391]

16-098 The crucial difference between the two types of contract is that, while upon the breach of either contract the goods in fact come back into the possession of the owner, it is only in the case of the contract of hire that it is envisaged that this would have happened in any event upon the natural termination of the agreement by full performance; accordingly, the full hire rentals in the one contract are substantially lower than the full hire-purchase price in the other since they alone are calculated on the assumption of the eventual return of the goods. Beyond this, the owner's actual loss can be estimated at around the 50 per cent mark only on the basis that the loss could not have been mitigated by his re-hiring the goods because, his supply exceeding the demand, he has lost the profit on the transaction. Indeed Lord Denning MR dissented largely because he considered that, in assessing the recoverable actual loss, the principles of remoteness of damage required the fact that the claimants' supply might exceed demand to be ignored.[392] However, while this proposition, itself in conflict with earlier authority,[393] was in no way agreed to by the other two members of the court, Diplock LJ considered that it was not in any event in point since he was of the view that a stipulated sum which is a genuine pre-estimate of a contracting party's actual loss cannot be a penalty merely because that actual loss may flow, in part or in whole, from special circumstances of which the other contracting party may not be aware.[394]

## 6. RELATED SITUATIONS

### (1) Limitations of liability by way of liquidated damages

16-099 In the normal case, an assessment of whether a clause is supported by a legitimate interest will involve an assessment of whether it provides only for compensation for loss. In turn this will invite consideration of whether the sum stipulated in the contract to be paid in the event of breach is unreasonably large in proportion to the probable loss. Occasionally, however, the situation may arise where the stipulated sum is disproportionately small in relation to the probable loss. Here it is still true that the stipulated sum is disproportionate to, and cannot be said to be a genuine pre-estimate of, the probable loss; but it cannot realistically be called a penalty in the traditional sense of an extravagant and unconscionable sum which is not supported by a legitimate interest. The only manner in which it might be said that a sum substantially smaller than the probable loss could be a penalty is in relation not to the party paying but to the party to be paid the sum: he has agreed to accept as compensation for breach a completely inadequate amount. Yet it is hard to see why he does not have a legitimate interest in accepting a smaller sum, and the courts have not been astute to see oppression where a party has agreed to cut down on his prima facie rights, as is clear from the many limitation of liability clauses which have been upheld in the courts. A small agreed sum of this type is indeed akin to a clause limiting the extent in damages of a party's liability; it differs from such a clause only in that it does not represent a ceiling beyond which the recoverable dam-

391 See, respectively, *Bridge v Campbell Discount Co* [1962] A.C. 600 at para.16-076, above, and the Hire-Purchase Act 1965 at para.16-068, above.

392 [1966] 1 W.L.R. 1428 CA at 1437; see further at para.26-011, below.

393 See paras 25-130 and 26-010, below.

394 [1966] 1 W.L.R. 1428 CA at 1448.

ages cannot rise but forms the exact amount that may be recovered even if in the result the actual damage is less than the stipulated figure.

*Cellulose Acetate Silk Co v Widnes Foundry*,[395] a decision of the House of Lords, deals with this very situation. The parties there agreed, after protracted negotiations, that the defendants should deliver and erect an acetone recovery plant for the claimants in 18 weeks and should pay £20 for each week's delay. Far greater damage than could be fully compensated for by this amount was likely to and did result from the defendants' delay, and the claimants claimed that they were entitled to disregard the agreed sum as being a penalty and to sue for the actual damage that they had suffered. This contention was not accepted by the House of Lords. Lord Atkin in his speech said that the defendants had agreed to supply an accessory to a business over which they had no responsibility or control and the extent of which might be enormous. He said: **16-100**

> "I agree that this is not a pre-estimate of actual damage; I think it must have been obvious to both the parties that the actual damage would be much more than £20 a week, but it was intended to go towards the damage, and it was all that the sellers were prepared to pay."[396]

In the Court of Appeal Slesser LJ had said:

> "One cannot perhaps take the view that it is a pre-estimate of the damage, because being a limitation it is possible that it might be said to be a limitation of the pre-estimate; that is to say, the parties may, and it is perfectly open to them to do so if they please, agree that the party who is to suffer from the breach will accept as damages a sum less than that which would have been payable on a pre-estimate. The question of the amount being unconscionable, exorbitant or extravagant does not arise."[397]

Against the view that a limitation of liability rather than a penalty is constituted by a stipulated amount which is too small to be a genuine pre-estimate of the probable loss is, at first sight, *Wall v Rederiaktiebolaget Luggude*,[398] a decision made more authoritative by its approval by the House of Lords in *Watts v Mitsui*.[399] This case, and the later one in the House of Lords also, concerned a charterparty which the owners of the ship had failed to perform and which contained a clause that ran: **16-101**

> "Penalty for non-performance of this agreement proved damages, not exceeding estimated amount of freight".

The owners unsuccessfully contended that this clause was not a penalty but was effective to limit their liability to the charterers to the estimated amount of freight which would become payable to them had they performed the charterparty. However, in holding the clause to be a penalty and awarding the charterers damages for their actual greater loss, Bailhache J relied to a large extent on the long history of this clause in charterparties. Originally the clause had read: "Penalty for non-performance of this agreement estimated amount of freight", while alongside it

---

395 [1933] A.C. 20.

396 [1953] 1 Q.B. 86 CA.

397 *Widnes Foundry v Cellulose Acetate Silk Co* [1931] 2 K.B. 393 CA at 414 to 415. In *Temloe v Errill* (1987) 39 B.L.R. 30 CA it was held that the parties to a building contract had agreed that liquidated damages for delay by the builder should be not even a small sum but nil.

398 [1915] 3 K.B. 66.

399 [1917] A.C. 227. The approval was obiter because, although the facts were similar, the damages were in the event proved to be less than the stipulated sum.

there had grown up a commonly inserted limitation of liability clause which was very different in phraseology. In these circumstances Bailhache J took the view that the nature of the clause, which in its original form was clearly a penalty, had not been changed by the addition of four words. The expanded form merely spelled out the effect of a penalty clause, i.e. that a claimant suing on a penalty clause could sue for his actual damage up to the limit of the penal sum. The new clause, concluded Bailhache J, "is nothing more than the common form writ large".[400] Furthermore,

> "it would never strike [businessmen] that a clause beginning in that way was a limitation of liability clause, the very appearance of which is usually totally different, and is one to which they must pay attention or put up with the consequences."[401]

Thus it may fairly be said that this clause in a charterparty is exceptional, a view adopted both by Lord Finlay LC in *Watts v Mitsui*,[402] and by Scrutton LJ.in the Court of Appeal in *Widnes Foundry v Cellulose Acetate Silk Co*,[403] the former going so far as to say that

> "if this clause had appeared for the first time I think it might have been construed as imposing a limitation on the damages to be recovered".

**16-102** What is said in the above paragraphs did not suffice to convince Nelson J in *Tullett v Prebon Group Ltd v Ghaleb-el-Hajjali*[404] of the merits of the limitation argument. He considered that the cases cited above show that the determination of whether a clause is a penalty clause is fact specific

> "and do not perhaps permit one to conclude that a small stipulated sum could never be a penalty clause".[405]

*Tullett* concerned an employment contract into which the claimant employer had entered with the defendant specialist broker, the contract providing that if the broker failed to take up the employment, which in fact happened, he would have to pay a sum equal to half his net basic salary and half the signing on payment the employer had contracted to pay him. There were many good reasons to hold that this provision constituted liquidated damages rather than a penalty. The employer and employee had equal bargaining power, both were legally represented, they had concluded the contract after tough negotiation, and the potential loss from the employee's breach was uncertain and could be very substantial if the employer were unable to find—as indeed turned out to be the case—a suitable replacement employee to generate the profits that it was anticipated the defendant's brokerage would have brought in. The stipulated sum having accordingly been held to amount to liquidated damages, the argument that a small sum could still constitute a penalty fell away. Yet it is important to note that the argument had been that the stipulated sum was not prevented from being a penalty by reason of its being "on one scenario

---

400 [1915] 3 K.B. 66 at 74. The penalty used to be an upper limit only if the claimant sued on the penalty. This is considered at para.16-027, above.
401 [1915] 3 K.B. 66 at 74 to 75.
402 [1917] A.C. 227 at 235.
403 [1931] 2 K.B. 393 CA at 407.
404 [2008] I.R.L.R. 760.
405 [2008] I.R.L.R. 760 at [39].

of damages"[406] considerably smaller than the damages that the claimant might recover; this scenario might be a showing that the experienced broker defendant would have generated profits for the employer far in excess of 50 per cent of his salary and signing on fee. Now the limitation argument has no application and is not intended to apply in such a situation; it applies only where in *all* circumstances, rather than on one scenario, the loss is bound to be greater than the stipulated sum, as with the £20 for each day of delay in *Cellulose*.[407]

If the sum stipulated in the contract turns out to be less than the actual damage in fact although disproportionately large for the probable damage, this is likely to be a penalty in the ordinary way. The situation where the probable loss is less than the stipulated sum but the actual loss is more may sound a somewhat academic one; but it can arise where one sum is stipulated to be paid for a number of breaches of varying importance. It is likely to be a penalty if as to one breach it is disproportionately large, and it is immaterial that, in the events that happen, another breach occurs which involves greater damage than the stipulated sum: the sum remains a penalty, and no questions of limitation of liability can arise.[408] This, indeed, provides another interpretation for *Wall v Rederiaktibolaget Luggude*,[409] one which was indicated by Scrutton LJ in *Widnes Foundry v Cellulose Acetate Silk Co*,[410] where he said that in his view Lord Sumner's support of the case in *Watts v Mitsui*,[411] **16-103**

> "turned largely upon the fact that there was one clause purporting to fix one damage for every sort of breach".[412]

## (2) Money paid or payable before breach: deposits and forfeiture clauses

A contract may call for the immediate deposit of a sum of money rather than requiring payment of that sum upon breach.[413] The contract might then provide that upon the depositor's breach of contract the deposited sum shall be forfeited to the other. In effect, this can give the same result as a penalty in the conventional sense, and therefore it should follow that the same treatment be given by the courts to such clauses. The courts have, until comparatively recently, been slow to afford any relief in such a situation. One obvious explanation is that the innocent party has a legitimate interest in the provision of a clause which requires forfeiture of a genuine deposit which is an earnest for performance. The recipient has become entitled to **16-104**

---

406 See [2008] I.R.L.R. 760 at [39].

407 See *Cellulose* at para.16-100, above.

408 Whether the claimant is restricted to suing for the penalty has already been considered: see para.16-027, above.

409 [1915] 3 K.B. 66; facts at para.16-101, above.

410 [1931] 2 K.B. 393 CA at 408.

411 [1917] A.C. 227.

412 Aside from limiting liability by way of liquidated damages, contracting parties may agree that the liability of one or other of them shall be limited to particular heads of loss. Any such agreement requires very clear language. Thus in *Bem Dis A Turk Ticaret v International Agri Trade Co, The Selda* [1998] 1 Lloyd's Rep. 416, affirmed [1999] 1 Lloyd's Rep. 729 CA (facts at para.25-129, below), it was held that a provision in a contract for the sale of tapioca that the damages "shall be based on" the normal measure of the difference between contract price and market price, together with a further provision that no damages for loss of profit were to be recoverable, was insufficient to exclude a claim for wasted expenditure.

413 It is assumed throughout the text that the money is deposited with the other party, but it is possible that it might be deposited with a third party.

retain those amounts. If they are later to be forfeit then provided that they were genuinely a deposit at the time of contracting, their recovery should be governed by the rules concerning relief against forfeiture. This was the approach of Hoffmann LJ in *Else (1982) Ltd v Parkland Holdings*,[414] which attracted some support of Lords Neuberger and Sumption (with whom Lords Carnwath and Clarke agreed on this point) in *Makdessi* and *ParkingEye*.[415] The cases discussed below might now best be reinterpreted as concerned with the equitable doctrine of relief against forfeiture rather than the doctrine concerning penalties, although some of the cases prior to *Makdessi* had analysed the claims for recovery in terms of whether the clause was a penalty at common law.

**16-105** The first issue which falls to be decided where a party to a contract has paid over money to the other party in pursuance of the contract and has then defaulted is whether the parties had or had not provided that such money should not be recoverable upon the payer's default: for at this stage may be solved the question of whether the payer can recover the money he has transferred. A provision that money paid shall not be recoverable on the payer's default may be either express or implied. An express provision of this type generally takes the form of a forfeiture clause, a clause stating that the money shall be forfeited on default; on the other hand a provision of this type is generally implied from the fact that the money is stated to be paid as a deposit. Although there have been separate lines of cases dealing with forfeiture clauses and with deposits, Denning LJ properly equated these two modes in *Stockloser v Johnson*.[416] The use of the term "deposit" is not conclusive to support an implication of an agreement that money shall be forfeited on default, but in the particular case of sale of land it is now so commonly understood that by a deposit *eo nomine* the parties intend to indicate forfeiture on default as to be always acted upon. This has been so ever since the crucial case of *Howe v Smith*,[417] where the Court of Appeal exhaustively considered the earlier, and rather uncertain, authorities and held that the deposit was paid as earnest and as a guarantee of the performance of the contract, the parties intending that the claimant on default should have no right to its return.

**16-106** If there is no agreement, whether express or implied, that money paid shall not be returnable on default, then nothing in the nature of agreed liquidated damages exists in the contract and the defaulter is entitled, if the other party terminates on the basis of the default and does not keep the contract open and available for performance, to recover the money he has paid over in part performance in an action for restitution of unjust enrichment on the basis of a failure of consideration. Clear decisions to this effect, decided in the older language of money had and received, are *Mayson v Clouet*,[418] and *Dies v British and International Mining Corporation*,[419] where a buyer of land and a buyer of goods respectively defaulted

---

414 [1994] 1 B.C.L.C. 130.
415 [2016] A.C. 1172 at [16]–[17].
416 [1954] 1 Q.B. 476 CA at 490: "But when there is a forfeiture clause or the money is expressly paid as a deposit (which is equivalent to a forfeiture clause)".
417 (1884) 27 Ch. D. 89 CA.
418 [1924] A.C. 980 PC.
419 [1939] 1 K.B. 724.

in their instalments of the purchase price,[420] and the law is so stated by Somervell and Denning LJJ in the Court of Appeal in *Stockloser v Johnson*.[421]

If, on the other hand, there is such an agreement that money paid shall not be returnable upon default, then it was thought that the common law adhered to this expressed intention and in all circumstances refused any redress to the claimant payer,[422] and that this was so whether the payments to be forfeited or the moneys deposited were or were not out of all proportion to the actual or probable loss accruing to the payee; in other words, whether they were in the nature of a penalty or of liquidated damages paid before the event.[423] The law appeared to have been settled in this way by the Court of Appeal in *Stockloser v Johnson*,[424] but everything has been put into a state of some uncertainty by the decision, welcome though it is, of the Judicial Committee of the Privy Council in *Workers Trust and Merchant Bank v Dojap Investments*.[425] Before dealing with this case it is necessary to explore and understand how far *Stockloser v Johnson*[426] had taken the common law. **16-107**

In *Stockloser*, in two contracts for the sale of plant and machinery between the same parties it was agreed by them that, if the buyer defaulted for a period of 28 days in the payment of any instalment of the purchase price, the seller would be entitled to rescind the contract, forfeit the already paid instalments, and retake possession of the plant and machinery. The purchase price was in each contract £11,000 and the claimant defaulted in his instalments after he had paid £4,750 on one contract and £3,500 on the other and after he had received royalties which the Court of Appeal held that he was not due to pay back under the agreement properly construed. The claimant was unable and unwilling to complete the performance of the contract and he sued to recover the amount of the instalments he had paid. The court held that, even if the claimant could show that the forfeiture clause had a penal character, he could not argue that it should be ignored so as to enable him to recover the money at common law by an action for money had and received. If this applies where the parties' intention to allow forfeiture is express, it will apply a fortiori where such an intention is to be implied from the language of deposit, and indeed Denning LJ included both in his unequivocal statement of the rule. He said: **16-108**

> "Where there is a forfeiture clause or the money is expressly paid as a deposit (which is equivalent to a forfeiture clause), then the buyer who is in default cannot recover the money at law at all."[427]

Before this decision the law had not been stated clearly and there were strands of authority moving in either direction; in the cases using the language of deposit rather than of forfeiture the courts tended to concentrate upon the prior question of whether or not the parties intended that the money should not be recoverable on **16-109**

[420] Other cases involving sale of land support the proposition but as decisions are somewhat equivocal: see especially *Palmer v Temple* (1839) A. & E. 508 and *Harrison v Holland* [1922] 1 K.B. 211 CA.

[421] [1954] 1 Q.B. 476 CA at 483, 489 to 490 respectively.

[422] Equity is dealt with later: see paras 16-112 and following, below.

[423] Money deposited by one contracting party in a joint account, to be released on that party's breach to the other contracting party, was treated without argument in *Forrest v Davies* (1971) 220 E.G. 345 CA as money payable, to which the normal rules as to liquidated damages and penalties applied, and not as money paid, to which the rules now under consideration would apply.

[424] [1954] 1 Q.B. 476 CA.

[425] [1993] A.C. 573 PC.

[426] [1954] 1 Q.B. 476 CA.

[427] [1954] 1 Q.B. 476 CA at 490.

default. On the one side was a strong dictum of Jessel MR in *Wallis v Smith*,[428] that

> "where a deposit is to be forfeited for the breach of a number of stipulations, some of which may be trifling, some of which may be for the payment of money on a given day, in all those cases … the bargain of the parties is to be carried out."[429]

Combined with this were two cases, *Hinton v Sparkes*,[430] and *Lock v Bell*,[431] in which recovery of a deposit, which the contract stated should be forfeited on default, was refused. These decisions, both of which concerned a sale of a public house and a deposit by the buyer, were particularly strong because they also contained a provision that a further sum should be paid upon default by the buyer, and the court in both, while allowing the seller to forfeit the deposit, refused to allow him to recover the further sum on the ground that it was a clear penalty. *Stockloser v Johnson*,[432] thus supported and confirmed these authorities.[433] On the other side were the cases of *Public Works Commissioner v Hills*[434] in the Privy Council and *Barton v Capewell Continental Patents Co*.[435] In the former the claimant, who had contracted to carry out construction work for the defendants, deposited £50,000 as security and also allowed the defendants to retain, as agreed, 10 per cent from the payments which they made under the contract to the claimant as the construction work progressed. Upon the claimant's default he successfully sued to recover both amounts from the defendants, the court holding that each constituted a penalty. In the latter a contract for the sale of patent rights, in which the purchase price was to be paid in instalments, provided that if the claimant buyer should default either in paying the instalments or in certain other ways all payments already made to the seller should be forfeited. Again the sums paid before default were treated as a penalty and the buyer recovered them. These two cases were summarily dealt with in *Stockloser v Johnson*,[436] Denning LJ saying briefly that the point was not argued in either,[437] and have since been disregarded until *Workers Trust and Merchant Bank v Dojap Investments*,[438] to which we can now turn.

**16-110** In that case, an appeal from Jamaica, the Judicial Committee of the Privy Council

---

[428] (1882) 21 Ch. D. 243 CA at 258. Indeed the case might have been decided on this ground: see para.16-088 above.

[429] Rigby LJ in *Willson v Love* [1896] 1 Q.B. 626 CA at 633 indicated that he was of the same view. Bigham J in *Pye v British Automobile Commercial Syndicate* [1906] 1 K.B. 425 was more cautious, giving only qualified support to Jessel MR's statement of the law, but nevertheless holding in the circumstances before him that the claimant was not entitled to recover the money he had deposited with the defendant.

[430] (1868) L.R. 3 C.P. 161.

[431] [1931] 1 Ch. 35.

[432] [1954] 1 Q.B. 476 CA.

[433] *Hinton v Sparkes* (1868) L.R. 3 C.P. 161 is also authority for another point of importance. Instead of paying the deposit as agreed the buyer had given an IOU. It was held that the fact that this forced the seller into the position of claimant made no difference to his rights and that he could recover the money promised by the IOU, Willes J took the view that the seller could have claimed the money which the buyer had failed to deposit even in the absence of an IOU: at 166. This is clearly right; as Willes J said, it would be wrong if the seller's position could be prejudiced and the buyer's position ameliorated by reason of the buyer committing two breaches of contract instead of only one: see para.16-104, above.

[434] [1906] A.C. 368 PC.

[435] (1893) 68 L.T. 857.

[436] [1954] 1 Q.B. 476 CA.

[437] [1954] 1 Q.B. 476 CA at 488. Counsel for the defendant put the case for not regarding these two decisions as compelling authorities in more detail: at 482.

[438] [1993] A.C. 573 PC.

held that a deposit is subject to forfeiture only if it is of a reasonable amount. The claimants had bought premises at auction from the defendant bank. The contract required the payment of a 25 per cent deposit and of the balance of the purchase price within 14 days, and provided for forfeiture of the deposit upon a failure by the claimants to comply with their contractual obligations. The claimants having failed to complete on time, the bank rescinded the contract and forfeited the deposit. The Judicial Committee, while accepting that the law allowed forfeiture of the conventional deposit, generally of 10 per cent, even if it bore no relation to the contemplated loss to the seller, held that the 25 per cent deposit was unreasonable and could therefore be recovered by the claimants after deducting the sum, if any, at which, on an inquiry, the damage suffered by the defendant bank was put.

There is no suggestion that the relief thus afforded was other than at common law. **16-111**
Indeed Lord Browne-Wilkinson who delivered the Judicial Committee's judgment cited *Public Works Commissioner v Hills*,[439] in support of the decision, saying it was clear authority that payment given for security is not forfeitable.[440] He further relied upon Denning LJ's suggestion in *Stockloser v Johnson*[441] that a substantial payment on account of the purchase price of land ought to be recoverable by the buyer; yet there is no indication that he appreciated that Denning LJ was indisputably speaking only of the position in equity.[442] If then *Workers Trust Bank v Dojap*,[443] is intended to state the common law position *Stockloser v Johnson*[444] is departed from, although the departure is confined to the matter of deposits; Lord Browne-Wilkinson specifically said that the court did not wish to decide anything beyond the case of the deposit.[445]

The approach of equity now falls to be examined; this requires a return to the **16-112**
examination of the key decision in *Stockloser*,[446] which here too reconsidered and restated the position and which made at this point its most positive contribution to the law. The Court of Appeal started off by recognising that equity has a general right to relieve against penalties, not only by refusing to enforce them but also by giving affirmative relief to the victim by decreeing recovery of money already paid by him. Denning LJ said:

> "He may … have a remedy in equity, for, despite the express stipulation in the contract, equity can relieve the buyer from forfeiture of the money and order the seller to repay it on such terms as the court thinks fit."[447]

This jurisdiction, although generally considered in relation to express forfeiture clauses, should now apply equally where the intention of forfeiture is implied generally by the language of deposit. Indeed Denning LJ clearly equated the two modes

439 [1906] A.C. 368 PC. See the case at para.16-109, above.
440 [1993] A.C. 573 PC at 582D.
441 [1954] 1 Q.B. 476 CA.
442 He had after all said that with deposits the buyer "cannot recover the money at law at all": [1954] 1 Q.B. 476 CA at 490; the full sentence is at para.16-108, above. And the reference to reasonable deposits by Lord Hailsham in *Linggi Plantations v Jagatheesan* [1972] 1 Malayan L.J. 89 PC, at 94E to G, on which Lord Browne-Wilkinson also relied, may too have been in the context of equitable relief, there being a mention by Lord Hailsham both of equity and of *Stockloser v Johnson* there; it is not clear.
443 [1993] A.C. 573 PC.
444 [1954] 1 Q.B. 476 CA.
445 See the passage from the judgment at para.16-117, below.
446 [1954] 1 Q.B. 476 CA.
447 [1954] 1 Q.B. 476 CA at 490.

in *Stockloser v Johnson*.[448] However, it is clear that equity is more guarded in giving affirmative relief by decreeing recovery of money than in refusing to enforce penalties,[449] and, as Denning LJ pointed out in *Stockloser v Johnson*,[450] there is only one case in which the equitable jurisdiction has been exercised in the affirmative manner. This was *Steedman v Drinkle*,[451] a decision of the Judicial Committee of the Privy Council, in which the court allowed a defaulting buyer of land to recover, before the seller had accepted the repudiation implicit in the default, instalment payments which he had already made. Being the only decision it loomed large in *Stockloser v Johnson*,[452] and the members of the Court of Appeal, in finally establishing the existence and extent of the equitable jurisdiction, devoted a large part of their judgments to its interpretation.

**16-113** The first question which arose upon the earlier decision was whether or not it permitted the exercise of the equitable doctrine to allow recovery after, as well as before, rescission by the other party on the basis of the default. On this the members of the Court of Appeal disagreed. However, the majority, constituted by Somervell and Denning LJJ, adopted the more liberal view that *Steedman v Drinkle*,[453] had established a general doctrine of relief from forfeiture by allowing recovery of money and that it was not limited to the case where the other party had not yet rescinded. The narrower view taken by Romer LJ, that it was so limited, was based upon the rule that before rescission by a seller of land on the buyer's default the buyer if now ready and willing to perform can claim specific performance,[454] but that no such claim can be made by him after the seller's rescission. Romer LJ took the view that whether this rule applied to an action to recover money already paid had never been argued in *Steedman v Drinkle*,[455] itself concerning a sale of land, and he held that the rule should apply. The majority, in coming to the opposite conclusion, pointed out that the requirement that there should have been no rescission was relevant only to a case where specific performance was being asked for by the claimant, and the fact that in *Steedman v Drinkle*[456] the seller had not rescinded and the buyer had been at the time ready and willing to complete was immaterial to let in the equitable doctrine in the first place. The doctrine itself therefore applies even after rescission and even though the claimant is at the time of suit for the recovery of the money not ready and willing to perform.[457]

**16-114** Although this limitation upon the equitable doctrine was successfully scotched, the majority of the Court of Appeal required the presence of two conditions for the doctrine's applicability. Denning LJ said:

"Two things are necessary, first, the forfeiture clause must be of a penal nature, in this

---

448 [1954] 1 Q.B. 476 CA at 490. See para.16-105, above.

449 Probably for the reasons already considered generally: see para.16-104, above.

450 [1954] 1 Q.B. 476 CA at 490.

451 [1916] 1 A.C. 275 PC.

452 [1954] 1 Q.B. 476 CA.

453 [1916] 1 A.C. 275 PC.

454 *Re Dagenham (Thames) Dock Co* (1873) L.R. 8 Ch. 1022; *Kilmer v British Columbia Orchard Lands* [1913] A.C. 319 PC.

455 [1916] 1 A.C. 275 PC.

456 [1916] 1 A.C. 275 PC.

457 The majority interpreted the decision in *Mussen v Van Diemen's Land Co* [1938] Ch. 253, where a claimant who was not ready and willing to complete at the time of suit had been refused recovery of money already paid, as being based upon another proper prerequisite of the applicability of the equitable doctrine, i.e. the claimant must show that it would be unconscionable to refuse recovery and this he had failed to do. For this prerequisite, see para.16-114, below.

> sense, that the sum forfeited must be out of all proportion to the damage, and, secondly, it must be unconscionable for the seller[458] to retain the money."[459]

It is plain that the first is a condition in conformity with the ordinary case where only negative relief is being claimed, i.e. suit is brought for the payment and not for the repayment of money. In *Stockloser v Johnson*[460] itself the majority of the Court of Appeal seemed to assume the amount to be a penalty without discussion[461]; presumably they were viewing the circumstances as at the time when the contract was made, since this is the established rule in the ordinary case where negative relief is claimed.[462] But whereas the first condition is all that both law and equity require when asked to give negative relief, this second condition of unconscionability comes in when affirmative relief, by way of the recovery of money already paid, is claimed, and it was on this condition that the claimant's action foundered both in *Stockloser v Johnson*,[463] and in the similar[464] earlier case of *Mussen v Van Diemen's Land Co*.[465] At first sight it would seem that, since unconscionability is also the basis of the test of what is a penalty, the court was merely applying the same criterion twice over: yet the conclusion reached on the first condition was in the claimant's favour but that on the second was against him. The explanation of this lies in the time factor. Whether a penalty is involved is to be tested by the circumstances existing at the time of the formation of the contract; whether unconscionability is involved is to be tested by the conditions existing when the equitable doctrine is invoked, i.e. at the time of suit.[466] In *Stockloser v Johnson*,[467] the claimant was held to have failed to satisfy the second condition because he had himself received substantial benefits by way of royalties[468]; in *Mussen v Van Diemen's Land Co*,[469] he failed partly through his own delay in bringing suit.[470] A great deal will therefore turn, in cases in which a buyer is paying the purchase price by instalments, upon how many instalments have already been paid at the time of the buyer's default: as Denning LJ suggested in *Stockloser v Johnson*,[471] there would be no equity to reclaim a five per cent payment of the purchase price, but it would be very different if 90 per cent had been paid.

---

458 These principles are of course not limited to contracts of sale.
459 [1954] 1 Q.B. 476 at 490; similarly at 484, per Somervell LJ.
460 [1954] 1 Q.B. 476 CA.
461 Denning LJ expressly said he was prepared to regard the forfeiture clause as penal: [1954] 1 Q.B. 476 CA at 492. Romer LJ in his dissent, however, said that it was not really so, as the claimant had had the advantages and fruits of the income-producing property: [1954] 1 Q.B. 476 CA at 494; on the other hand Somervell LJ, more properly, made this factor go to unconscionability: [1954] 1 Q.B. 476 CA at 484.
462 See para.16-030, above.
463 [1954] 1 Q.B. 476 CA.
464 Except that the sale was of land and not plant and machinery.
465 [1938] Ch. 253, as interpreted by the Court of Appeal majority in *Stockloser v Johnson* [1954] 1 Q.B. 476 CA.
466 *Stockloser v Johnson* [1954] 1 Q.B. 476 CA at 492, per Denning LJ; similarly at 488, per Somervell LJ The action, which is in restitution, is really based upon the doctrine of unjust enrichment; see [1954] 1 Q.B. 476 CA at 492, Denning LJ: "The equity operates, not because of the plaintiff's default, but because it is in the particular case unconscionable for the seller to retain the money. In short, he ought not unjustly to enrich himself at the plaintiff's expense."
467 [1954] 1 Q.B. 476 CA.
468 [1954] 1 Q.B. 476 CA at 484, 492, per Somervell and Denning LJ respectively.
469 [1938] Ch. 253.
470 Denning LJ made this point in *Stockloser v Johnson* [1954] 1 Q.B. 476 CA at 492.
471 [1954] 1 Q.B. 476 CA at 492.

**16-115** Unfortunately, this holding by the majority in *Stockloser v Johnson*,[472] that on the facts of the case the claimant was not entitled to relief led Sachs J in *Galbraith v Mitchenall Estates*,[473] to regard as obiter the views expressed that a claimant could be entitled to recover payments already made by him, and, accordingly, to consider himself free to adopt the dissenting view of Romer LJ. Indeed he felt that a court of first instance had to come to its own conclusion on the matter because he regarded Romer LJ's view as being supported by all the members of the Court of Appeal in *Campbell Discount Co v Bridge*.[474] In the case before him the claimant, after making an initial payment of £550 under a contract of hire of a caravan with a retail price of £1,050, had failed to pay the monthly rentals, and the defendant finance company had repossessed the caravan after a few months, at which date it was worth £800, and sold it for £775; the contractual terms enabled the defendants both to retain the initial payment and have repossession of the caravan.[475] In the claimant's action for recovery of the initial payment on the ground that its retention constituted a penalty, Sachs J held that, although the contractual position enabling the defendants to have both the initial payment and the repossessed caravan was one of undue harshness so as to be of a penal nature, there was no equity of restitution where the contract had been freely entered into without fraudulent or unconscionable conduct,[476] and accordingly the claim must fail.[477]

**16-116** Sachs J's approach is open to criticism. In the first place, it is strongly arguable that the views which he held obiter constituted part of the ratio decidendi of *Stockloser v Johnson*.[478] By deciding that equity had the power to afford affirmative relief to a contracting party, after the other party's rescission, by way of restitution of moneys paid, the majority was breaking new ground, and it therefore is difficult to regard the endorsement of such a power as mere dictum merely because it was held further that the facts of the particular case did not admit of its exercise. *Campbell Discount Co v Bridge*,[479] did not deal with the same issue, so that the judgments of the Court of Appeal there lend only indirect support to Romer LJ's view; they do so only in so far as the court did not favour affording equitable relief against the exaction of a penalty from a hirer defendant, and their decision on this was reversed in the House of Lords.[480] Moreover, even taking the matter as *res integra*, it is submitted that Sachs J should have decided for the claimant. A penalty should be a penalty still whether it be a sum payable or a sum retainable, and the courts should afford relief from both. Unsatisfactory distinctions would thereby be avoided, and the result would be in line with the historical roots of the doctrine

---

472 [1954] 1 Q.B. 476 CA.

473 [1965] 2 Q.B. 473.

474 [1961] 1 Q.B. 445 CA.

475 The contract also entitled the defendants to enforce payment of a proportion of the outstanding rentals, but they made no claim under these provisions as they would have been met with the defence, after *Bridge v Campbell Discount Co* [1962] A.C. 600, that these provisions constituted a penalty.

476 The contract of hire was a long document in small print which the claimant had signed without reading and had assumed to be a contract of hire-purchase, but there was no sharp practice or unconscionable conduct on the part of the defendant finance company.

477 Some 10 years after Sachs J's decision contracts of hire became legislatively controlled, thereby ameliorating the position of most hirers. For details see para.16-094, above.

478 [1954] 1 Q.B. 476 CA.

479 [1961] 1 Q.B. 445 CA.

480 *Bridge v Campbell Discount Co* [1962] A.C. 600.

protecting against penalties, for these display no technical limitations on the availability of relief.[481]

To have reached such a progressive conclusion would have been possible for the Judicial Committee of the Privy Council in *Workers Trust and Merchant Bank v Dojap Investments*,[482] but the opportunity was not taken. While it is not clear whether the court there was intending, in relation to deposits, to change the common law position as laid down in *Stockloser v Johnson*,[483] or, again in relation to deposits, to adopt the equity position as propounded by the majority there,[484] it is clear that the court did not wish to commit itself beyond the case of the deposit. Referring to the differing stances taken in the earlier case by Somervell and Denning LJJ on the one hand and Romer LJ on the other, Lord Browne-Wilkinson said: **16-117**

> "Their Lordships do not find it necessary to decide which of these two views is correct in a case where a party is seeking relief from forfeiture for breach of contract to pay a price by instalments, the party in default having been let into possession in the meantime. This is not such a case."[485]

Yet it is a little difficult to see, once it is accepted that deposits may be recovered wherever they smack of penalty, how the courts can stop short of accepting a general principle that moneys paid before breach may not be forfeited if their retention by the payee would have penal consequences. *Workers Trust Bank v Dojap* should be interpreted as marking the beginning of the demise of any rule that moneys paid before breach, as opposed to moneys payable upon breach, fall outside the protection from penalties of contracting parties.[486]

---

481 See paras 16-003 and following, above.

482 [1993] A.C. 573 PC.

483 [1954] 1 Q.B. 476 CA. See para.16-108, above.

484 See paras 16-112 and following, above.

485 [1993] A.C. 573 at 582C.

486 No question of forfeiture arose in *Euro London Appointments Ltd v Claessens International Ltd* [2006] 2 Lloyd's Rep. 436 CA (facts at para.16-019, above): see [2006] 2 Lloyd's Rep. 436 at [44], per Lawrence Collins J. Whether in *Cadogan Petroleum Holdings Ltd v Global Process Systems LLC* [2013] EWHC 214 (Comm) (see the case at para.16-017, above) the court had jurisdiction to grant relief against forfeiture, which was said to depend in part on how *Stockloser v Johnson* was interpreted, did not have to be decided by Eder J as counsel had accepted that there was jurisdiction; in the event Eder J, held that on the facts there was no call to relieve from forfeiture: see [2013] EWHC 214 (Comm) at [37] and following.

Chapter 17

# VINDICATORY DAMAGES

Table of Contents



**17-001** Vindicatory damages are a feature of the modern era, unheard of in the past. Indeed their first appearance was not even under that name; we had to wait many years before vindicatory damages began to be talked of as such. Vindicatory damages emerged in various pockets of the law, particularly in defamation to protect a person's reputation, by showing publically through a substantial award of damages that his or her reputation is secure. These damages go beyond compensation for loss. Indeed they go beyond responding to any consequence at all. They respond to the infringement of a right. In 2016, vindicatory damages were rejected by the Supreme Court. But the pockets of law where they had been specifically recognised, particularly defamation and privacy, have yet to be fully rationalised.

## 1. Early Pockets of Vindicatory Damages

**17-002** For this principal purpose of vindicatory damages the story starts, effectively, with the decision during the Second World War of *Rook v Fairrie*,[1] where the wartime practice for libel cases to be heard by a judge sitting alone was followed. Sir Wilfred Greene MR who gave the only reasoned judgment in the Court of Appeal agreed with the holding of Atkinson J below that, whereas a jury cannot mark their sense of the grossness of a libel in any other way than by awarding heavy damages, a judge may take into account, as a ground for awarding less than a jury would probably allow, that he has been able to express his views in his judgment.[2] Thus both the comments made by the judge and the further damages given by the jury are to be seen as providing vindication for the claimant, although the term vindication is to be found neither in the judgment of Sir Wilfred Greene MR nor in that of Atkinson J and the term vindicatory damages was hardly to be expected in these early days.

**17-003** While tortious injury to a person's reputation comes about primarily through defamation, sometimes it makes its appearance where the action brought is for false imprisonment, another of the few torts still susceptible to jury trial. Thus injury to the reputation was in issue in *Hook v Cunard S.S. Co*,[3] where again, as in the earlier defamation case of *Rook v Fairrie*, the action was tried by a judge without a jury. Here too it was held that a smaller amount of damages may be awarded where the

1 [1941] 1 K.B. 507 CA.
2 [1941] 1 K.B. 507 CA 514–515.
3 [1953] 1 W.L.R. 682.

action is tried not by a jury but by a judge sitting alone. The claimant, a lounge steward on a liner, was falsely accused by a passenger of assaulting his daughter, and the defendants, who ran the liner, imprisoned the claimant to placate the passenger and to avoid publicity. On the issue of damages, Slade J said:

> "It is fortunate for the defendants that I, not sitting with a jury, am able to make it clear that there is no vestige of ground, nor has any vestige of ground been suggested by the defendants, for casting the slightest aspersion on the plaintiff's character. I am, therefore, able to vindicate him in this court, and it is not necessary for me to vindicate him by visiting a heavy sum of damages on the defendants for their conduct in this matter as a jury might well have done, that being the only way in which they could have made it clear that there is no stain of any kind on his character."[4]

This does for false imprisonment what *Rook v Fairrie*,[5] had already done for defamation, except that here there was a specific reference to vindication by Slade J. The vindication is effected by what the judge says in his judgment and, by implication, by what damages the jury awards beyond pure compensation for loss.

The approach taken in respect of libel in *Rook v Fairrie*, after a cold reception **17-004** by the Court of Appeal soon after in the further wartime defamation cases, heard by judges alone, of *Knuppfer v London Express Newspaper*,[6] and *Bull v Vazquez*,[7] was eventually disapproved by the House of Lords in *Dingle v Associated Newspapers*,[8] where we are merely told that the claimant chose not to have his case tried before a jury.[9] This disapproval, however, was obiter dicta as it did not appear that the judge at first instance had awarded smaller damages because he had expressed his views in his judgment. Lord Morton, with whose remarks the rest of their Lordships agreed, and also Lord Denning, pointed out that the judge could not know what effect his vindication would have, as he could neither ensure that the newspapers would give it adequate publicity nor know how far the claimant's general reputation would be improved by his complimentary remarks.[10] Their Lordships were also concerned over the introduction of two tiers of libel damages.

One further, much later case also gave rise to a consideration of the question of **17-005** whether what a judge said in his judgment could take the place of vindicatory damages. *Purnell v Business F1 Magazine Ltd*,[11] was a curious case in that there was a judgment by a judge on liability followed by a jury deciding on quantum only, and this brought up the unusual question of how far the judge's judgment should be taken into account by the jury in its award. Eady J had struck out a defence of justification and entered judgment for the claimant for damages to be assessed, after which the case proceeded to trial on damages before Gray J and a jury. The defendant's appeal on quantum concerned only vindicatory damages, the conten-

---

4 [1953] 1 W.L.R. 682 at 686.

5 [1941] 1 K.B. 507 CA.

6 [1943] K.B. 80 CA; see at 91, per Goddard LCJ.

7 [1947] 1 All E.R. 334 CA; see at 336 to 337, per Lord Greene MR.

8 [1964] A.C. 371.

9 [1964] A.C. 371 at 376.

10 [1964] A.C. 371 at 404 and 408 respectively. Lord Denning also sketched various administrative inconveniences that would follow upon the acceptance of *Rook v Fairrie*: defendants would find it impossible to assess what sums they should pay into court since they could not know in advance whether the judge would castigate the defendant in his judgment, while claimants would be discouraged from bringing before a judge alone actions which were more suitable for trial by him than by a jury: [1964] A.C. 371 at 408 to 409.

11 [2008] 1 W.L.R. 1 CA.

tion being that Gray J had been wrong to allow the jury to include any element of vindication in its award as the judgment of Eady J fully vindicated the claimant. Against this the claimant argued that Eady J's judgment should not be taken into account at all.[12] After a detailed analysis of all the authorities including those cited above, Laws LJ, giving the principal judgment with which the other two members of the court expressed agreement, took an intermediate position; the judgment could be taken into account but not to the extent of eliminating a vindicatory award. Thus Laws LJ thought it

> "inescapable that the existence of a prior reasoned judgment rejecting a justification defence and so holding that the claimant has indeed been libelled is at least capable of providing some vindication of a claimant's reputation."[13]

Nonetheless Laws LJ expressed the view that the effect in relation to vindication of a judgment in the claimant's favour was, generally speaking, most likely to be marginal and that there will be cases where the judgment will provide no, or no significant or reckonable, vindication.[14] This means that *Purnell* brings us far nearer to the *Dingle* position than to that championed in *Rook*,[15] and that the concern of their Lordships in *Dingle* over the introduction of two tiers of libel damages is largely removed.[16]

**17-006** After *Dingle*, despite the obiter nature of their Lordships' views, the way appeared to be open for the awarding by judges of defamation damages to vindicate a claimant, and this might even have been thought to apply to damages given in vindication of a person wrongfully imprisoned, thereby departing from *Hook v Cunard S.S. Co*.[17] Indeed if vindicatory damages had survived they might have been extended to a person maliciously prosecuted or a person the subject of certain other maliciously instituted proceedings, as here too the principal head of damage tends to be the injury to reputation.[18]

**17-007** Yet in many years after *Dingle* awards by way of vindication by judges sitting alone have not appeared in the cases, or at least not in the reported cases. This is because jury trials have for long been the prevailing rule in this field. It is likely that juries have increased their awards to show that the claimant's reputation is secure but one has no proof of this since juries do not give judgments. Even where the judge in his summing up directs the jury to their entitlement to vindicate the claimant, as Gray J did in *Purnell v Business F1 Magazine Ltd*,[19] one cannot know for certain if the jury has obliged. All one can point to are the statements at the highest level in cases which were with a jury at first instance, considered in dealing with defamation,[20] in particular Lord Hailsham's in *Broome v Cassell & Co*,[21] where he said, though without any specific reference to vindication, that the sum awarded by the jury must be sufficient to convince bystanders that the charge was baseless,[22]

---

12 [2008] 1 W.L.R. 1 CA at [24].
13 [2008] 1 W.L.R. 1 CA at [27].
14 [2008] 1 W.L.R. 1 CA at [29]–[30].
15 See at paras 17-002 and 17-004, above.
16 See *Purnell* further at para.53-034, below.
17 [1953] 1 W.L.R. 682.
18 See paras 44-002, 44-004 and 44-009, below.
19 [2008] 1 W.L.R. 1 CA.
20 At para.46-034, below.
21 [1972] A.C. 1027.
22 [1972] A.C. 1027 at 1071C. This statement was alluded to in *Rantzen v Mirror Group Newspapers*

and Lord Hoffmann's in *The Gleaner Co Ltd v Abrahams*,[23] where the claim had been heard by a Jamaican jury, that

> "the damages must be sufficient to demonstrate to the public that the plaintiff's reputation has been vindicated."

By the end of the last century, however, trials of defamation actions by judge and jury were becoming uncommon, and have become increasingly so in the new century.[24] Thus we find Eady J saying in *Culla Park Ltd v Richards*,[25] that as a matter of public policy the emphasis is now against trial by jury,[26] and statements to the same effect have appeared generally. The award of damages as vindication by a judge as distinct from a verdict of a jury is now directly in the spotlight since s.11 of the Defamation Act 2013 has amended s.69(1) of the Senior Courts Act 1981[27] so as to take away completely the right to jury trial for claimants bringing actions for libel or slander. **17-008**

The result is that vindicatory damages—though still referred to in this context as damages by way of vindication[28]—came into the open. In case after case the vindication issue was raised, and generally concentrated on, by judges in their judgments. Key cases on this are collected when dealing with defamation damages,[29] and it is interesting to find that none of the judges appear to have awarded smaller damages on account of what they have said in their judgments. This is significant evidence that in this area the award of damages to "vindicate" is really concerned with compensating for adverse consequences which have been, or are likely to be experienced, by the claimant. **17-009**

Indeed from what has now been said by the Court of Appeal in *Cairns v Modi*,[30] where a world-famous professional cricketer had been falsely accused of match fixing, it may be that the days of damages reduction always for judicial comments are all but numbered. Lord Judge CJ, giving the judgment of the court, said that the court was disinclined to accept any such general principle that damages should always be less where there is vindication through the judge's reasoned judgment.[31] He added that he thought it unlikely that cricket fans will have downloaded the judgment of the trial judge and read it with close attention. Their interest was rather to find out just how much the trial judge had awarded the cricketer.[32] **17-010**

In all these cases with a vindicatory element in the damages awarded, there is rarely a clear breakdown between (i) the damages for injury to feelings or pecuniary loss; (ii) exemplary damages to deter such breaches; and (iii) the damages by **17-011**

---

[1994] Q.B. 670 CA, 695G by Neill LJ, who did include a reference to vindication.

23 [2004] 1 A.C. 628 PC at [55].

24 Enquiry of Andrew Caldecott QC, a distinguished practitioner in this field, has told me that there have been no jury trials yet in 2013, two in 2012 (*Luke Cooper v ANL* and *Boyle v MGN*), with the last before these in 2009 (*Bower v Desmond*).

25 [2007] EWHC 1687 (QB).

26 [2007] EWHC 1687 (QB) at [38].

27 And s.66(3) of the County Courts Act 1984.

28 Vindicatory damages as a term has arrived where damages for infringement of a right are concerned: see para.17-015, below.

29 Which see, at para.46-036, below.

30 [2013] 1 W.L.R. 1015 CA.

31 [2013] 1 W.L.R. 1015 CA at [30].

32 [2013] 1 W.L.R. 1015 CA at [32].

way of "vindication", these three being the regular heads of damages in libel cases.[33] This combination of the vindicatory element with other heads of damages appears to suggest that the vindicatory element represents a type of substantial damages which go beyond the circumstances in the other heads. However, we will see in the defamation chapter that "vindication" here really repeats other heads of damages including compensation for future adverse consequences and potentially exemplary damages.

**17-012** The rejection of vindicatory damages as a general concept, explained below, has left this small part of the law in an unsatisfactory state. The reference to vindication awards in these defamation cases might best be re-rationalised as cases where compensation is awarded for likely future consequences if the libel "emerges from its lurking place at some future date".[34] In extreme cases the award should be rationalised as one of exemplary damages.

## 2. VINDICATORY DAMAGES FOR INFRINGEMENT OF A RIGHT GENERALLY

**17-013** The express, and general, recognition of a category of vindicatory damages in vindication of a right first made itself felt in a series of cases from the Caribbean coming, over the last decade, before the Judicial Committee of the Privy Council and concerning the infringement of constitutional rights. Many of these cases concern gross misconduct by the police forces of one Caribbean island or another, with arrests, assaults, imprisonments and degrading treatment, and the main constitutional rights infringed are the right of liberty and freedom and the right to security of the person. The first and principal case, involving appalling behaviour on the part of a police officer, is *Attorney General of Trinidad and Tobago v Ramanoop*.[35] Lord Nicholls in a passage of the judgment of the Judicial Committee which he delivered, a passage invariably quoted and relied upon in subsequent judgments, said that in these cases a compensatory award might not suffice to vindicate the infringed constitutional right, and added:

> "The fact that the right violated was a constitutional right adds an extra dimension to the wrong. An additional award, not necessarily of substantial size, may be needed to reflect the sense of public outrage, emphasise the importance of the constitutional right and the gravity of the breach, and deter further breaches."[36]

Vindicatory damages were awarded, although the references to deterrence looked a lot like the award was one of exemplary damages. Soon after, they were also awarded, again on account of police misconduct, in *Merson v Cartwright and the Attorney General of the Bahamas*,[37] and in *Subiah v Attorney General of Trinidad and Tobago*.[38] Next came *Takitota v Attorney General of The Bahamas*,[39] where the claimant after arrest by the police was detained in custody in inhumane conditions for eight years. The Privy Council upheld the Court of Appeal's exemplary award

---

33 See para.46-030, below.

34 *Broome v Cassell & Co Ltd* [1972] A.C. 1027 HL at 1071, per Lord Hailsham, cited with approval in *R. (on the application of Lumba) v Secretary of State for the Home Department* [2012] 1 A.C. 245 at [223], per Lord Collins.

35 [2006] 1 A.C. 328 PC.

36 [2006] 1 A.C. 328 PC at [19].

37 [2005] UKPC 38.

38 [2008] UKPC 47. Here the vindicatory element was contained in a global award.

39 [2009] UKPC 11.

as a vindicatory award, regarding the vindicatory damages, which had also been awarded, as having much the same effect in financial terms as exemplary damages, so that both should not be awarded.[40] Interestingly, in these cases the term vindicatory damages at last emerges[41] and continues to be used in further Privy Council decisions on Caribbean appeals.[42] Their nature as disguised exemplary damages, reflected in the emphasis on the gravity of the breach and the need for deterrence, is vividly illustrated in *B v Attorney General of St Helena*.[43] In that case, vindicatory damages were refused for the most extraordinary breach involving non-consensual sterilisation. These damages were refused because the damages for financial loss as well as damages for pain and suffering were sufficient and there was no further need to make an award of vindicatory damages where the St Helena government was not shown to be complicit in what had occurred.[44]

The apparent sanctioning by the Privy Council of awards of vindicatory dam- **17-014**
ages for infringement of a constitutional right in the Caribbean cases stands in stark contrast with the decision of the Supreme Court in *R. (on the application of Lumba) v Secretary of State for the Home Department*,[45] a case of false imprisonment, that the infringement of a right does not lead in our law to an entitlement to vindicatory damages, though the decision on this was not unanimous but by a majority of six to three.[46] In *Lumba* the defendant Secretary of State was held liable for the false imprisonment of foreign national prisoners pending their deportation as she had applied an unpublished policy which was unlawful when exercising her power to detain them but, since they would have been detained in any event if she had applied the lawful published policy, they had suffered no loss so that compensatory damages were out of the question, it being accepted that they were entitled to nominal damages as false imprisonment is a tort actionable per se.[47] Now we have seen that vindicatory damages of the sort designed to make manifest that a reputa-

---

40 [2009] UKPC 11 at [13] and [15]. *Inniss v Attorney General of St Christopher and Nevis* [2008] UKPC 42 is a further case of an award of vindicatory damages, one which did not involve police misconduct.

41 *Ramanoop* at [9]; *Merson* at [20] and [21]; *Subiah* at [10] and [14]; *Takitota* at [15].

42 The Privy Council may decline to make an award of vindicatory damages when not thought to be necessary, as in *James v Attorney General of Trinidad and Tobago* [2010] UKPC 23 and in *Graham v Police Service Commission and Attorney General of Trinidad and Tobago* [2011] UKPC 46. Neither involved police misconduct and in both the infringement of constitutional right was of a more minor nature. Alternatively, there may be no claim for vindicatory damages, even in police misconduct cases, but only for declarations that there has been infringement, as in *Webster v Attorney General of Trinidad and Tobago* [2011] UKPC 22. And see the most recent appeal to the Privy Council from the Caribbean, *EW v Attorney General of Antigua and Barbuda* [2013] UKPC 21, which is touched upon in the last footnote but one to para.17-015, below.

43 [2017] see 2015 WL 12660052.

44 [2017] see 2015 WL 12660052 at [7].

45 [2012] 1 A.C. 245.

46 The majority was made up of Lords Phillips, Kerr, Collins, Brown, Rodger and Dyson, the minority of Lord Hope, Lord Walker and Lady Hale.

47 The Court of Appeal in *Bostridge v Oxleas NHS Foundation Trust* [2015] EWCA Civ 79 CA held that where, unlike the defendant Secretary of State for the Home Department in *Lumba*, the defendant NHS trust had no power lawfully to detain the claimant, a mentally disordered patient, but he could and would have been lawfully detained anyway by a third party, there was still an entitlement only to nominal damages as there was no loss. Delivering the only reasoned judgment in the Court of Appeal, Vos LJ recorded that the appellant's counsel had disavowed any argument based upon the Earl of Halsbury's famous dictum in *The Mediana* [1900] A.C. 113 at 117, discussed at para.37-047, below.

tion is unsullied can be available to a claimant suing for false imprisonment,[48] but this did not avail the claimants in *Lumba* as they were without reputation and were thus left with claiming vindicatory damages on account of infringement of a right, that is, the right to liberty.

**17-015** The leading speech on the damages issues in *Lumba* was that of Lord Dyson, with whom on the issues of damages all of the other Justices in the majority basically agreed. He dealt with the matter in some detail,[49] citing, and stating his agreement with, what was said in the 18th edition of this work and rightly regarding the Caribbean cases in the Privy Council as special since they were limited to claims involving the infringement of constitutional rights. He pointed out that the implications of allowing vindicatory damages in the case before the court would be far reaching and lead to undesirable uncertainty, he asked rhetorically where it would all end if the court granted the claimed vindicatory damages against the state for false imprisonment, and he boldly concluded that he saw "no justification for letting such an unruly horse loose on our law".[50] And somewhat less stylistically, Lord Collins made the bare statement that he did not

> "consider that the concept of vindicatory damages should be introduced into the law of tort".[51]

This should put an end to the idea of awarding, in the common law, vindicatory damages for infringement of a right.[52] Thus, ironically, just as the term vindicatory damages at last comes into use in English case law—use of it is made in six of the lengthy nine speeches in *Lumba*—the term is, in this context, left with nothing upon which to operate.

**17-016** Any doubt that remained has now been removed by the unanimous application of the decision in *Lumba* in *R. (on the application of O) v Secretary of State for the Home Department (Bail for Immigration Detainees)*.[53] The Supreme Court held that although the Home Secretary had unlawfully failed to apply her policy to the

---

48 See in particular *Hook v Cunard Steamship Co* [1953] 1 W.L.R. 682 at para.17-003, above.

49 [2012] 1 A.C. 245 at [97]–[101].

50 All this at [2012] 1 A.C. 245 at [101].

51 [2012] 1 A.C. 245at [232]. Lord Collins's conclusions on vindicatory damages are specifically endorsed by Lord Phillips: [2012] 1 A.C. 245 at [335]) while Lord Brown, in a speech with which Lord Rodger associated himself, said (at [362]) that he was in respectful agreement with Lord Dyson outside his stated disagreement with it, this being as to the scope of the tort of false imprisonment and unrelated to the question of vindicatory damages. Only Lord Kerr of the majority on this issue had a qualified approach, saying that if there were any scope for vindicatory damages it must be very limited indeed and could only be justified if a declaration that there has been infringement provided insufficiently emphatic recognition of the seriousness of the default: at [256]. (He repeated this in giving the judgment of the Privy Council in *W v Attorney General of Antigua and Barbuda* [2013] UKPC 21, a decision following on from *Lumba* and also concerning detention under an improper procedure, without in any way indicating that he was talking, as in the light of *Lumba* he surely must have been, only of infringements of Caribbean constitutional rights.) However, even without Lord Kerr we still have a majority deciding firmly that vindicatory damages are not going to be introduced into the common law.

52 Thus Davies J, in arriving at £15,000 for her award of damages in *AAA v Associated Newspapers Ltd* [2012] EWHC 2103 (QB), a case involving the Human Rights Act, was wrong to take into account (at [126] and [127]) Eady J's support in Mosley of vindicatory damages in privacy cases. What Eady J said there on vindicatory damages and privacy has surely been overtaken by the Supreme Court's decision in *Lumba*. Nothing on damages is said, as not in issue, in the appeal in *AAA*: [2013] EWCA Civ 554 CA.

53 [2016] 1 W.L.R. 1717.

claimant's detention, if the claim for judicial review were permitted to proceed the result would be a declaration that detention was unlawful and an award of only nominal damages. Since the decision of the Supreme Court provided sufficient vindication, the Court of Appeal had been correct to refuse permission for the claim to proceed.

### 3. VINDICATORY DAMAGES FOR INFRINGEMENT OF A RIGHT TO PRIVACY

At about the same time as vindicatory damages for infringement of constitutional rights were being introduced, back in England Eady J introduced vindicatory damages in a very different type of case, one involving invasion of privacy. *Mosley v News Group Newspapers Ltd*,[54] concerned the publication of articles containing details of a gathering featuring a well-known person indulging in sado-masochistic practices[55] and Eady J made an award in damages of £60,000, in which was included an amount, possibly large, on account of vindicatory damages. He considered that recent jurisprudence showed that a legitimate consideration in awarding damages is that of vindication,[56] not in the familiar sense used in defamation of vindication of reputation, which as we have seen might be understood as compensating for future loss, but in the sense of vindication to mark the infringement of a right.[57] As we have seen,[58] the possible purpose of vindicatory damages in defamation as compensating for future loss is impossible with invasions of privacy, for once the information is out things cannot be put right. The award of damages cannot easily be seen as a payment for future distress because the award in this case of infringement of privacy marked only the act of obtaining the information. Therefore, it was said, vindicatory damages were called for, and that Eady J's award contained an unknown quantity of vindicatory damages is made clear from his conclusion. He said: **17-017**

> "It seems to me that the only realistic course is to select a figure which marks the fact that an unlawful intrusion has taken place while affording some degree of *solatium* to the injured party. That is all that can be done in circumstances where the traditional object of restitutio is not available."[59]

It is the case, however, that neither can there be precise restitution to the everyday victim of a traffic accident as far as his non-pecuniary loss is concerned; yet he will not be given vindicatory damages.

The Court of Appeal has now recognised that these damages for misuse of private **17-018**

---

54 [2008] E.M.L.R. 20 at 679.

55 For the full facts of the case see para.47-006, below.

56 In support of bringing vindication into the damages frame Eady J cited passages from two House of Lords cases, from Lord Scott's speech in *Ashley v Chief Constable of Sussex* [2008] A.C. 962 at [21] and [22] and Lord Hope's in *Chester v Afshar* [2005] 1 A.C. 134 at [87]. But neither of these cases ran to the awarding of damages by way of vindication. Ashley was concerned with whether a claimant should be allowed to continue with an action in order to establish whether an assault had been committed, an action which could not result in the award of further compensatory damages because these had already been fully paid. As for Lord Hope's espousal in *Chester* of the vindicatory principle, this was simply for the purpose of justifying the imposition of liability despite a very tenuous causal connection between act and damage (see the case at para.8-028, above).

57 [2008] E.M.L.R. 20 at [216].

58 See paras 17-002 and following, above.

59 [2008] E.M.L.R. 20 at [231].

information cannot be vindicatory damages after *Lumba*. In *Gulati v MGN Ltd*,[60] appeals were brought by MGN Limited, the proprietor of the *Daily Mirror*, *The Sunday People* and *The Sunday Mirror* newspapers, against awards of damages to eight claimants for misuse of private information by "hacking" of their telephone messages. The damages included (i) separate awards for hacking which did not lead to publication; (ii) hacking which led to publishing of articles; (iii) general distress; and (iv) aggravated damages. The awards ranged in total from £72,500 to £260,250. The highest single award for hacking (although combined in this instance with distress) was £85,000 for Mr Yentob, a BBC executive who made extensive use of his voicemail. His voicemail contained an enormous amount of entertainment-related material of interest to journalists. His phone was hacked at least twice a day for a period of about seven years.

**17-019** One ground of appeal was that the awards should have been limited to damages for distress. *MGN* submitted that by making an award of both damages for distress and damages for misuse of private information the primary judge's approach was contrary to the rejection of vindicatory damages by a majority of the Supreme Court in *Lumba*. The primary judge had held that an award for the mere infringement of the claimants' rights should be made because if damages were limited to an award for distress, a person who suffered no distress or died before the discovery of the wrong would receive no compensation. Delivering the judgment with which the other members of the Court of Appeal agreed, Arden LJ said that the damages were not to "vindicate" a right but were

> "to compensate for the loss or diminution of a right to control formerly private information and for the distress that the respondents could justifiably have felt because their private information had been exploited".[61]

**17-020** The award of damages for the loss of a right to control information in cases like *Gulati* looks a lot like an award of vindicatory damages.[62] A loss of control, or loss of autonomy, occurs in almost every tortious or contractual wrong. By itself, "loss of autonomy" is not necessarily a loss in the sense of an adverse consequence. If I am about to step off the curb into the path of an oncoming car and you push me backwards then I will have lost autonomy as a result of your actions. But my loss of the autonomy to walk where I pleased with the consequence that I would be run over by a car is not a loss in the sense of being factually worse off. Your actions subtracted from my autonomy but made me better off by saving my life. It is therefore necessary to identify the sense in which the loss of control that a person encounters over his or her life has adverse consequences as an undesired intrusion into the person's life. In other words, the concept of damages simply for the loss of a "right to control formerly private information" should not be understood as suggesting, literally, that the compensation is for the loss or impairment of a right. A right is a normative concept. A loss or impairment of a right could only be a normative loss. It is not a loss experienced in the real world. The position of the representative claimants is not affected in any way merely as a result of loss of any normative right. The real loss is a consequential loss such as distress suffered, or any other consequences experienced by the claimant as a result of the infringement.

---

60 [2017] Q.B. 149 CA.

61 [2017] Q.B. 149 CA at [46] and [48].

62 *AAA v Associated Newspapers Ltd* [2012] EWHC 2103 (QB), *Weller v Associated Newspapers Ltd* [2014] E.M.L.R. 24 (appeal dismissed on other grounds: [2015] EWCA Civ 1176 CA.

If there are no real consequences then there should be no damages for loss. Hence, in *Murray v Ministry of Defence*,[63] Lord Griffiths, with whom the remainder of the House of Lords agreed, said that only nominal damages would be awarded where a person is falsely imprisoned but suffered no loss and no distress because he was released before he found out that he had been falsely imprisoned. The discussion above is not to express any doubt about the result in *Gulati*. The award of damages in *Gulati* for the claimant's "lost right to control private information" can comfortably be justified as restitutionary, representing the benefit that the defendant derived from the wrongdoing. The defendant acted wrongfully, obtaining the benefit of the opportunity to use the information without paying for it. This is why the Court of Appeal accepted that the amount awarded would be affected if the information had become public knowledge anyway.[64] This point is explained in Ch.14.

---

63 [1988] 1 W.L.R. 692.

64 [2016] EWHC 294 (Ch) at [45].

# PART 3 VARIOUS GENERAL FACTORS IN THE ASSESSMENT OF DAMAGES

Chapter 18

# THE INCIDENCE OF TAXATION

Table of Contents



**18-001** For a little over 50 years the tax element has been a factor of major significance in damages awards. While nearly all the problems have been concerned with the incidence of income tax, the introduction of a capital gains tax, now more than 40 years ago, added a further dimension to the difficulties in this area, and separate consideration must be given to both taxes.[1]

## I. INCOME TAX

### (A) THE RULE IN GOURLEY'S CASE

Until the decision in *British Transport Commission v Gourley*,[2] the English courts had not reduced awards of damages on the ground that the amount, for the loss of which the damages represented compensation, would have been diminished in the claimant's hands by the incidence of taxation.[3] But in this case the House of Lords held that, in an action for damages for personal injuries tortiously inflicted, the calculation of the claimant's damages in respect of his loss of earnings, both past and prospective at the time of trial, must take into account the tax which would have been payable upon them. The early cases to the contrary were overruled. **18-002**

The presence of two factors was necessary to set the stage for the problem which was posed for their Lordships' decision in *Gourley*'s case[4]: (1) the sums for the loss of which the damages awarded constitute compensation would have been subject to tax; and (2) the damages awarded to the claimant would not themselves be subject to tax. For there cannot be any reason for taking tax into account in calculating damages given in compensation for a loss which would never itself have been taxed: this would let in a taxation where no taxation would have been, which would be unfair to the claimant. Equally there cannot be any reason for taking tax into account in calculating the damages if the damages themselves will then be taxed in the same manner as the loss compensated would have been taxed: this would result in a double taxation, equally unfair to the claimant. In *Gourley*'s case,[5] the first factor was indisputably present; and the second factor was admitted by both sides to be present.[6] Accepting the correctness of this admission,[7] the question which thus unfolded itself was whether the amount of taxation which the claimant would have had to pay upon earnings was or was not too remote to be considered in the assessment of the damages. A full House of seven held, with one dissent,[8] that it was not too remote. Their Lordships thought that to consider whether the matter of taxation was or was not *res inter alios acta* was of no assistance,[9] misleading,[10] and the **18-003**

---

1 For an unusual and complex case concerning tax, involving the ascertainment of the measure of damages in a claim against the Revenue which had been held by the Court of Justice of the European Communities to have exacted tax in a manner contrary to Community law, and therefore a claim unrelated to any of the claims, issues and authorities dealt with in this chapter, see *Pirelli Cable Holding NV v Inland Revenue Commissioners* [2006] 1 W.L.R. 400 HL.

2 [1956] A.C. 185.

3 *Fairholme v Firth & Brown* (1933) 149 L.T. 332; 49 T.L.R. 470 (wrongful dismissal); *Jordan v Limmer & Trinidad Lake Asphalt Co* [1946] K.B. 356 (personal injury); *Billingham v Hughes* [1949] 1 K.B. 643 CA (personal injury). But the Scottish cases were divided: *Blackwood v Andre*, 1947 S.C. 333 was in line with the English cases, *McDaid v Clyde Navigation Trustees*, 1946 S.C. 462 stood out alone as *contra*; both were cases of personal injury.

4 [1956] A.C. 185.

5 [1956] A.C. 185.

6 [1956] A.C. 185 at 197, 205, 211.

7 Its correctness is considered at para.18-026, below.

8 The dissent was by Lord Keith.

9 [1956] A.C. 185 at 215, per Lord Tucker.

10 [1956] A.C. 185 at 206–207, per Lord Goddard, with whose speech Lords Somervell and Radcliffe agreed.

wrong approach.[11]

> "The mere fact that the item arises as between the claimant and a third party would not seem to be the test",[12]

said Lord Goddard. The decision was come to squarely upon the question of remoteness.[13] It is, of course, very often a difficult question to determine what is and what is not too remote, but the factor uppermost in their Lordships' minds in holding that the incidence of taxation was not too remote appears to have been that tax is imposed by law upon all and is not peculiar or personal to the claimant. Thus Earl Jowitt quoted Lord Sorn in *McDaid v Clyde Navigation Trustees*,[14] the one Scottish case which had foreshadowed *Gourley*'s case:

> "When you get a liability to which all earnings are subject and which depends not upon any circumstances peculiar to the individual but upon a general law of the land universal in its application, it would be wrong to ignore the existence of the liability."[15]

Similarly, Lord Reid said that "taxation is not something purely personal to the plaintiff",[16] while Lord Tucker spoke of an

> "expenditure which—although not actually a charge on earnings—is imposed by law as a necessary consequence of their receipt".[17]

Finally, on a less analytical note, Earl Jowitt and Lord Goddard stated that it would be "out of touch with reality"[18] to ignore the tax element.[19]

**18-004** One question falls for detailed discussion: in what types of case will the rule in *Gourley*'s case,[20] apply. Subsidiary questions concern the practical application of the rule: on whom lies the burden of proof and how is the quantum of damages to be assessed in regard to tax.[21]

---

11 [1956] A.C. 185 at 212, per Lord Reid.

12 [1956] A.C. 185 at 207. Lord Goddard gave as an illustration of a transaction between the claimant and a third party which is held not to be *res inter alios acta* the substitute contract which the claimant has entered into after a wrongful dismissal in respect of which he is suing for damages. And Earl Jowitt gave as an illustration the contract of a claimant, suing for personal injuries, with his employer which forms the basis of the damages for loss of earnings: [1956] A.C. 185 at 199. Neither illustration is, however, analogous to the case of taxation.

13 [1956] A.C. 185 at 203, 207, 212, per Earl Jowitt, Lord Goddard and Lord Reid respectively. But remoteness of a rather different kind to that dealt with in Ch.8, above: see *Parry v Cleaver* [1970] A.C. 1 at 15, per Lord Reid.

14 1946 S.C. 462.

15 [1956] A.C. 185 at 200.

16 [1956] A.C. 185 at 214.

17 [1956] A.C. 185 at 215.

18 [1956] A.C. 185 at 203 and 207 respectively. They took the phrase from Lord Sorn's judgment in *McDaid v Clyde Navigation Trustees*, 1946 S.C. 462.

19 The *Gourley* principle that the incidence of taxation is relevant in the calculation of a claimant's damages may apply in situations outside that with which we are concerned here. This was so in *Capita Alternative Fund Services (Guernsey) Ltd v Drivers Jonas* [2012] EWCA Civ 1417 CA where, in awarding in a professional negligence case the difference between the price paid and the price that would have been paid on proper advice, these prices fell to be calculated after deduction of the tax credits to which they would give rise: see [2012] EWCA Civ 1417 CA at [49] and following.

20 [1956] A.C. 185.

21 Interest on damages may also fall to be awarded, quite apart from the *Gourley* rule, not on their gross amount but their net amount after tax. The propriety of this important result was first revealed by *Tate & Lyle Food and Distribution v Greater London Council* [1982] 1 W.L.R. 149 and later

### (B) Type-Situations in Which the Rule in Gourley's Case May Apply

### 1. General Considerations

The presence of the two factors present in *Gourley*'s case[22] itself is enough to bring the rule into operation; in other words, they are sufficient conditions for it to apply. And for some time after *Gourley* came on the scene, and still in general today, it can be said that the two factors in *Gourley*'s case must be present before the rule will be applicable to any situation; in other words, they are not only sufficient but also necessary conditions.[23] This is what may be called pure or mainstream *Gourley* with which practically all the cases are concerned and with which therefore this chapter is largely concerned. At their simplest the two factors can be stated as: 18-005

(1) the amount of the loss compensated would have been subject to tax
(2) the damages would not be subject to tax

and will be referred to as factor (1) and factor (2). However, over the years and particularly within the last 20 years, a modified form of *Gourley* has made its appearance; it will be referred to as modified *Gourley*. This is where factor (2), as stated, is inapplicable because the damages will indeed be taxed but the tax will differ from the tax that the amount of the loss compensated would have suffered. Should *Gourley* still apply, albeit in modified form? To deal with this question it was initially intended simply to expand factor (2) so as to refer, in the alternative, to damages not subject to tax and to damages not subject to the same tax, and then deal with the two situations separately. The difficulty with this approach is that, since we shall have to speak frequently of factor (2) when dealing with mainstream *Gourley*, it would become confusing to have to use a term that covered the two formulations which are alternative and in effect inconsistent with each other as the damages cannot at the same time be subject to no tax and subject to some tax. It is therefore best if we give another name to the other formulation of the second requirement and, since it represents a modified factor (2), it may be referred to as factor (2M). There will be little need to have resort to the term in its operation as an alternative to the true factor (2).

## (1) Mainstream Gourley

The great majority of the cases in which the rule has been held to be applicable have involved situations where the damages were subject to no tax whatsoever. The home ground of the rule lies here; it is pure *Gourley*. Both factors (1) and (2) are applicable; these two factors require some closer attention. 18-006

**(a) Factor (1): the amount in respect of the loss of which the damages awarded constitute compensation would have been subject to tax** At one end of the scale, no award in respect of a non-pecuniary loss can be regarded as 18-007

developed in *O'Sullivan v Management Agency and Music* [1985] Q.B. 428 CA, a case which also brought to light even further tax implications in the exceptional context of an award, in equity, of compound interest. *Tate & Lyle* has been followed and applied in *Deeny v Gooda Walker* [1996] L.R.L.R. 168 and again in *Amstrad Plc v Seagate Technology Inc* (1998) 86 B.L.R. 34 and *BSkyB Ltd v HP Enterprise Services UK Ltd* [2010] EWHC 86 (TCC). The matter of interest and tax is fully dealt with at paras 19-135 to 19-140, below.

22 [1956] A.C. 185.

23 See, e.g. *Hall v Pearlberg* [1956] 1 W.L.R. 244 at 247.

compensation for a sum which would have been subject to tax. Such a loss is in no way concerned with earnings, income, or indeed a money loss at all. Thus claims in respect of pain and suffering, injury to feelings and to reputation, and all other non-pecuniary losses will not satisfy the first requirement; and in *Gourley*'s case[24] the separate substantial assessment[25] for the claimant's pain and suffering and loss of amenities of life was in no way brought into issue.

**18-008** At the other end of the scale, awards in respect of loss of personal earnings will constitute compensation for sums which would have been subject to tax. This was *Gourley*'s case[26] itself, where tort had incapacitated the claimant; equally, compensation for breach of contract by wrongful dismissal of the claimant from service will satisfy this factor. Where, however, there are other failures to pay money in breach of contract, it will be necessary to ascertain whether the payment, if made properly under the contract, would or would not have constituted taxable income in the claimant's hands.

**18-009** In between falls the difficult case where the loss to the claimant is in relation to a loss of property, whether land or goods or shares. Here the claimant is deprived of what will generally be a capital asset, in the case of tort by misappropriation, by destruction, or sometimes by damage, in the case of contract by failure to deliver or transfer at the agreed time or at all. In so far as the claimant recovers damages in respect of the capital value of such an asset no question of income tax will generally arise, but if he also claims damages for loss of profits or loss of use there would then appear to be a situation where compensation is recovered in respect of something which, had there been no tort or breach of contract, could have been subject to income tax in his hands. This will be given further consideration when dealing with particular cases.

**18-010** **(b) Factor (2): the damages awarded to the claimant would not themselves be subject to tax** The bare proposition, sometimes stated, that damages are not subject to tax on income is entirely false. The leading case which demonstrates this is *Riches v Westminster Bank*,[27] where the House of Lords held that interest, although awarded by way of damages, was nevertheless taxable.[28] Whether damages are taxable turns upon the nature of the loss for which they are awarded and upon the complexities of the Income Tax Acts, the annual Finance Acts, and any other relevant taxing legislation.

**18-011** Once again it is clear that damages awarded in respect of non-pecuniary losses can never be taxable since the loss for which they are awarded could never have been taxed; such awards satisfy equally the second factor and are therefore right outside the rule in *Gourley*'s case.[29] However, when it comes to pecuniary losses, all will generally turn upon the complexities of tax law as to whether a sum awarded in damages as compensation for a particular pecuniary loss is or is not liable to tax on income. In many cases the answer is reasonably straightforward but by no means

---

24 [1956] A.C. 185.

25 The figure was £9,000 which was high, and not generally separated, at that date.

26 [1956] A.C. 185.

27 [1947] A.C. 390.

28 Interest on damages for personal injury and wrongful death is however exempted by statute: see paras 18-026 and 18-029, below together with para.19-087, below.

29 [1956] A.C. 185. The suggestion, made and rejected, in *Orthet Ltd v Vince-Cain* [2005] I.C.R. 374 EAT, that damages for injured feelings awarded in a claim under s.65 of the Sex Discrimination Act 1975 could be subject to tax seems very odd.

always. Thus the question of whether the damages constituted a taxable income receipt of a trade was taken all the way to the Lords in *Deeny v Gooda Walker*,[30] and the court got the answer wrong so that the matter had to be revisited in *Pennine Raceway v Kirklees Metropolitan Council (No.2)*.[31] One reason for the uncertainties lies in the fact that from the start our taxing of income has not been done globally but source by source. Types of income have been classified by reference to the source from which they come and to constitute taxable income or profit the sum in question must be traceable to one of these sources. This may be referred to as the source doctrine. Thus it has been held, in a variety of cases, that if the taxpayer has ceased to possess a source of income he could not be taxed upon delayed receipts from that source. This is why damages paid to a wrongfully dismissed employee were held not taxable—before statute intervened—because the source, which was the employment, had *ex hypothesi* gone before the damages were awarded. It also helps to explain why in *Gourley*'s case[32] itself, where the loss was of personal earning capacity of a claimant no longer able to earn, it was conceded that the damages would not be taxable: it has never been argued. Further consideration of when damages are taxable and when not must await the treatment of particular type-situations.

Exceptionally, the damages will escape taxation not because of the provisions of tax law but because of the practicalities of the situation. This was the position in *Finley v Connell Associates*,[33] where no tax would be raised on the award because the company entitled to the damages was in insolvent liquidation. The case also had another unusual feature in relation to the taxability of the damages. The claimant was not the company but an individual director who had taken an assignment of the company's right of action, and it was held that the fact that she might have to pay tax on the damages was neither here nor there. The claim was essentially the company's and only its tax position fell to be taken into account.[34] **18-012**

**(c) The relation between the two factors** From the above considerations of the two factors, this important conclusion may be reached. Basically the two factors cover the same ground, and the courts are considering much the same question twice over. If both questions are answered the same way, whether the answer be that under neither factor would the sum be taxable or that it would be taxable under both,[35] then the problem in *Gourley*'s case would vanish because it could never arise.[36] What, of course, prevents the same answers being given to the two questions are the intricacies and limits of the taxing provisions of the relevant legisla- **18-013**

---

30 [1995] S.T.C. 439; [1996] L.R.L.R. 109 CA; [1996] 1 W.L.R. 426 HL. See the case at para.18-048, below.

31 [1989] S.T.C. 122 CA. See the case four footnotes below.

32 [1956] A.C. 185.

33 [2002] Lloyd's Rep. P.N. 62.

34 The tax and damages issues are dealt with at [2002] Lloyd's Rep. P.N. 62 at [217] and following.

35 It is of concern that the courts do not always get this answer right. Thus in *Pennine Raceway v Kirklees Metropolitan Council (No.2)* [1989] S.T.C. 122 CA, compensation under the Town and Country Planning Act 1971 was held to be payable net of tax on the basis that the compensation would not be taxable in the claimant's hands but, when the Revenue then proceeded to demand tax, the decision had to be altered so that the compensation became payable gross.

36 A mistaken application of the rule in *Gourley*'s case was made in *The Telemachus* [1957] P. 47, which concerned an award for salvage services, where it was held that because the amount awarded would be taxable (i.e. factor (2) did not apply) it should therefore be increased accordingly. This case was rightly not followed in *Island Tug & Barge Co Ltd v S.S. Makedonia* [1958] 1 Q.B. 365. See *Parsons v B.N.M. Laboratories* [1964] 1 Q.B. 95 CA at 138, per Pearson LJ.

tion, in particular the rule that to constitute taxable income or profit the sum in question must be traceable to a source[37]; what the court can regard as taxable under factor (1) the Inland Revenue cannot always hold taxable under factor (2). It may, however, be questioned whether, as a matter of policy, it is wise for the courts to take upon themselves the task of taxing where the Inland Revenue authorities have feared to tread, and, it should be noted, thereby reaching a result which benefits not the Inland Revenue but the wrongdoer or his insurance company. The State's preparedness not to tax the damages for loss of earning capacity in personal injury claims must surely be intended to assist the victims of the injuries rather than their perpetrators. Indeed the defendant may find it more profitable to commit the wrong, intentionally and with the tax position in mind, as by wrongfully dismissing his employee and paying damages with the resultant saving of the amount of the tax upon the employee's salary.[38] It may be that the solution should be found in a legislative addition to the statutory tax law, whereby power is given to tax the type of damages to which, without such a provision, the rule in *Gourley*'s case would apply.[39] This has indeed been done, soon after *Gourley*'s case, for wrongful dismissal[40]; there is no likelihood, after all these years, of doing it for personal injury.

## (2) Modified Gourley

18-014 When we turn to modified *Gourley* it is factor (1) and factor (2M) that must be applicable before *Gourley* can apply. Whatever the permutation should be, factor (1) has always to be present. Factor (2M), however, has to be substituted for the far commoner factor (2).

18-015 **(a) Factor (1): the amount in respect of the loss of which the damages awarded constitute compensation would have been subject to tax** Nothing further need be said about factor (1). It has already been examined[41] and it presents no differences as between mainstream *Gourley* and modified *Gourley*.

### (b) Factor (2M): the damages would be subject to a different level of tax

18-016 *(i) The damages are subject to less tax* What if there will be tax charged on the damages but in a lesser amount than the tax which the moneys lost to the claimant would have borne? Is *Gourley* in a modified form to be applied? This question initially arose in *Julien Praet et Cie v H.G. Poland*,[42] and was there answered in the negative. Damages had to be assessed for the wrongful termination of an agency relating to Belgian motor insurance. The case was unusual in two respects which in combination may have influenced the decision: the tax in question was foreign and the tax rates involved were very small. The loss for which damages were being awarded was of insurance premiums to be collected in Belgium which, if

---

37 On the source doctrine see para.18-011, above.

38 This illustration does not lose its practical force by reason of the statutory provisions for taxing "golden handshakes" (see para.18-043, below) since the first £30,000 is exempt.

39 Lord Keith in *Gourley*'s case said in his dissent that if the claimant must have his damages reduced by taxation it should be effected by legislation which would put the money into the Revenue's hands: [1956] A.C. 185 at 218.

40 See para.18-043, below.

41 See paras 18-007 to 18-009, above.

42 [1962] 1 Lloyd's Rep. 566.

received, would have been subject to tax at a two per cent rate in Belgium. When, however, it appeared in evidence that the damages themselves would be subject to tax in Belgium, albeit at an amount well below the two per cent figure, that was held to be an end of the matter. The rule in *Gourley*'s case did not apply because factor (2) was not present, namely the damages awarded would be subject to tax, and it was immaterial that it was likely that the tax which would be levied on the damages would be less than that which would have been levied on the income in respect of the loss of which the damages constituted compensation. Mocatta J said:

> "Once it is agreed or provided that the damages awarded will be subject to tax, the court inquires no further and does not consider whether the tax liability on the damages would be heavier or lighter than the tax liability on the lost income."[43]

*Gourley* did not apply. This decision was approved by the Court of Appeal in *Parsons v B.N.M. Laboratories*.[44] The argument had been put forward there, as it had in *Julien Praet et Cie v H.G. Poland*, that taxation should be taken into account on both sides, by first calculating the damages on the net income or profits after tax and then adding to this figure a sum equal to the expected taxation of the damages. Sellers LJ rejected this outright, finding it a wholly unacceptable argument.[45] Harman LJ, while conceding that the argument was a logical conclusion from the *Gourley* principle, considered it an impracticable conclusion. "It is better," he said,

> "where the Crown has taken a hand and actually taxed the damages in the recipient's hands, to leave the two taxes to set themselves off one against the other. There may be some roughness in this justice but it does at least make an end of the matter … No account should be taken of tax at either end. This may be a matter largely dictated by expediency but it strikes me as preferable in an imperfect world to an over-assiduous search after perfection."[46]

Pearson LJ agreed that the practice of ignoring taxation in cases where both the lost earnings or profits and the damages are taxable was sound and should not be disturbed.[47]

It is somewhat ironic that *Parsons v B.N.M. Laboratories*,[48] was the decision to cement the rule of no *Gourley* where there was to be some degree of tax on the damages since *Gourley* was in fact applied in that case. The issue before the court was whether the rule applied in an action for wrongful dismissal where the first £5,000 of a damages award for wrongful dismissal was exempt from tax[49] and the claimant's loss of salary before tax for which damages were to be awarded was well below this amount. The court held that, since factor (2) therefore applied as much as factor (1), the *Gourley* rule did apply and the damages must be appropriately reduced. What caused the court to discuss the question of the applicability or inapplicability of the *Gourley* rule if the tax on the damages awarded should be at a lower rate than the tax which would have been payable on the moneys lost through the breach of contract was the argument raised by the claimant that all awards for **18-017**

43 [1962] 1 Lloyd's Rep. 566 at 595.
44 [1964] 1 Q.B. 95 CA.
45 [1964] 1 Q.B. 95 CA at 114.
46 [1964] 1 Q.B. 95 CA at 130.
47 [1964] 1 Q.B. 95 CA at 137–139.
48 [1964] 1 Q.B. 95 CA.
49 See para.18-043, below.

wrongful dismissal were in fact within the charge to tax and that the legislation merely provided a relief from that tax, rather than an exemption from tax, for amounts not exceeding £5,000. Had this argument been accepted, then the question of whether the *Gourley* rule could apply where factor (2) was not present would have had to be decided—even though in reality no tax would have fallen to be paid on the damages—and it is clear that the court would have decided the question in the claimant's favour and have held the *Gourley* rule inapplicable to the case in the absence of factor (2).[50] However, everything that was said on this question became obiter by reason of the majority's rejection of the argument that the statutory provisions provided only a relief and not an exemption from tax.[51]

**18-018** Nevertheless the courts soon moved away, in wrongful dismissal cases, from the *Parsons* view that *Gourley* could not apply where the damages were partly taxable. They did so the moment that cases appeared where the damages awarded exceeded the then £5,000 threshold. Otherwise a marked disparity and unfairness would result between claimants whose loss of salary before tax fell just on either side of the £5,000 mark.[52] Thus the *Parsons* view was abandoned in England in *Bold v Brough, Nicholson & Hall Ltd*,[53] and in Scotland in *Stewart v Glentaggart Ltd*,[54] and again not followed later in *Shove v Downs Surgical Plc*,[55] where Sheen J stressed the disparity, saying that an approach which applied the *Gourley* rule to an award which was a few pounds under £25,000, the then exemption limit, but some other principle to an award a few pounds over this limit "must lead to problems bordering on the absurd".[56] These three cases all applied the *Gourley* rule without difficulty to the exempted amount but not to the excess[57]; their principal concern was with the method of working out the statutory tax on the damages, a task made difficult and controversial by the infinitely complex legislative formula which controlled the computation until 1988.[58] But this development was not thought necessarily to place in doubt the validity of the general rule applied in *Praet* and approved in

---

50 See the references to the judgments at para.18-016, above. The further solution suggested by counsel for the defendant, namely that taxation should be taken into account on one side only, by calculating the damages on the net income or profits after tax and then making no addition in respect of the expected taxation of the damages, received short shrift at the hands of the court. This is clearly unfair to the claimant, resulting in a double taxation and at variance with the cardinal principle that damages are to put the claimant in the position he would have been in had the wrong never been committed: see [1964] 1 Q.B. 95 CA at 130 and 137, per Harman and Pearson LJJ respectively. So too the same argument by the defendant's counsel was summarily dismissed by the Court of Appeal in *Capita Alternative Fund Services (Guernsey) Ltd v Drivers Jonas* [2012] EWCA Civ 1417 CA (see at [60] per Gross LJ) in a different context, for which see para.18-003, above.

51 [1964] 1 Q.B. 95 CA at 128 and 140, per Harman and Pearson LJJ respectively; on this Sellers LJ dissented: [1964] 1 Q.B. 95 CA at 119.

52 Explained in more detail at para.18-045, below.

53 [1964] 1 W.L.R. 201.

54 1963 S.C. 300.

55 [1984] 1 All E.R. 7.

56 [1984] 1 All E.R. 7 at 10a–b.

57 The majority in *Parsons v B.N.M. Laboratories Ltd* [1964] 1 Q.B. 95 CA, would not necessarily have disagreed with this result, for Pearson LJ not only qualified his conclusion that it was sound practice to ignore tax where both the lost profits and the damages were taxable with the proviso that "there may be exceptional cases in which a departure from the practice may be required for the doing of justice in special circumstances" ( see at 139) but also gave an award for wrongful dismissal in excess of £5,000 as a possible illustration of the type of case where, even though factor (2) was not present, "there might be special hardship or other exceptional features to be taken into account … for the purpose of doing justice" (at 137).

58 See para.18-045, below.

*Parsons*[59]—the wrongful dismissal cases could be explained either by regarding the damages award as divisible, with factor (2) applying to the first tranche of the award but to the first tranche only, or, if this is considered too esoteric an approach, by regarding the situation presented by these cases as exceptional—and what was said in both cases, especially *Parsons*, and in the following wrongful dismissal cases continued to be extensively cited in the later cases outside the wrongful dismissal field.

While it would of course simplify the position if the courts could adopt the rough and ready assumption that the effects of taxation cancel out, the facts of a particular case may make such an assumption entirely unjustified. The most obvious cause of tax on damages being lower than tax on loss is falling tax rates between the time of the loss and the time of the award. This was the position in the forward-looking and important, but ill-reported, decision in *Amstrad Plc v Seagate Technology Inc.*[60] Damages had been awarded for the loss of profits which would have been made from the sale in 1989 and 1990 of some 50,000 computers. The tax on the damages when received would be at a rate of 33 per cent but the tax on the profits had they been received at the proper times would have been at rates of 34 and 35 per cent. His Honour Judge Humphrey Lloyd held that the damages, as he put it, "should be adjusted to take into account the incidence of taxation".[61] In other words, *Gourley* was applied to the difference between the tax rates which, although small as a matter of rates, was large as a matter of amount, making a difference of about £1 million to the claimants. Here was a sensible shift away from the *Praet* and *Parsons* approach; indeed the five reasons which Pearson LJ had propounded in *Parsons* for the rule which was there approved are all neatly and fully answered in Judge Humphrey Lloyd's extensive and excellent judgment.[62] In the end he found no reason, as he put it, "why expediency and pragmatism should override logic and justice".[63] **18-019**

But things went differently in *Deeny v Gooda Walker*,[64] an episode in the extensive litigation initiated by Lloyd's names against their managing and underwriting agents for subjecting their syndicates to excessive exposure to risk by failure to arrange reinsurance cover to protect them against losses. While the principal question there, which was taken to the Lords, was whether the damages were taxable,[65] there was a second question, but at first instance only,[66] which was whether, if it were decided that the damages were taxable, there should still be taken into account the fact that the damages would be taxed at a lower rate than would have been the losses for which compensation was given. The reason for this was that many of the Names would have been able to set-off losses on other income against tax at a higher rate than the rate applicable to the award at the date of recovery. Potter J was not prepared to depart from what he called the traditional approach of simply regarding the effects of taxation as cancelling out; he was not so prepared because of the complexity of examining the different tax positions of over **18-020**

59 See para.18-016, above.

60 (1998) 86 B.L.R. 34. The report at (1998) Mason's C.L.R. Rep. 1 is of HH Judge Humphrey Lloyd's earlier decision on the issues of liability and damages.

61 (1998) 86 B.L.R. 34 at 57I.

62 (1998) 86 B.L.R. 34 at 54H to 57H.

63 (1998) 86 B.L.R. 34 at 54G.

64 [1995] S.T.C. 439.

65 [1996] 1 W.L.R. 426 HL; affirming [1996] L.R.L.R. 109 CA; affirming [1995] S.T.C. 439; see the decision at para.18-048, below.

66 [1995] S.T.C. 439.

3,000 individuals, particularly when the whole approach to the case had been on a group syndicate basis.[67] The case may therefore be considered somewhat special but there is no doubt that here logic and justice took second place to expediency and pragmatism.

**18-021** In *BSkyB Ltd v HP Enterprise Services UK Ltd*,[68] the claimant satellite broadcaster, claiming for breach of contract and misrepresentation in relation to the provision of a new customer relationship management system, was awarded damages for benefits lost. These benefits, had they been achieved rather than lost, would have been taxable at 30 and 29.5 per cent over the years, whereas because of a reduction in the rate of corporation tax the damages representing them would be taxed at a rate of 28 per cent and, while the reduction in the corporation tax rate was fairly small, given the overall sums in issue the potential sum resulting from the change in corporation was, as in *Amstrad*,[69] substantial. After a full review of the authorities,[70] with a concentration on what was said in the Court of Appeal in *Parsons*, Ramsey J elected to follow *Amstrad* rather than *Deeny* and the obiter views expressed in *Parsons*, adopting Judge Humphrey Lloyd's rejection of Pearson LJ's reasons in *Parsons* for not applying *Gourley* where some tax fell on the damages,[71] and concluding that in the damages assessment

> "an allowance should be made for the difference between the corporation tax treatment which the lost benefit would have received and the corporation tax treatment which the sums awarded as damages are likely to receive".[72]

**18-022** *Amstrad*,[73] *Deeny*,[74] and *BSkyB*,[75] are all first instance decisions. So are the various wrongful dismissal cases other than *Parsons*,[76] and in *Parsons*, with the award being below the then exempt threshold of £5,000, it had been possible to apply *Gourley* in its full rigour. What then is likely to be the approach of the Court of Appeal, and indeed of the Supreme Court, to these developments? That the wrongful dismissal cases are not exceptional but mark a shift away, supported by *Amstrad* and now *BSkyB*, from the rule first enunciated in *Praet* is indicated by the Court of Appeal in *O'Sullivan v Management Agency and Music*.[77] Though primarily concerned with an accounting for profits rather than damages, the Court of Appeal was there prepared to apply the *Gourley* rule to amounts awarded to a composer of songs in respect of royalties which would not be subject to United Kingdom tax in his hands, because they were attributable to years outside the six-year period in respect of which the Inland Revenue could still claim tax, while not applying the rule to amounts representing royalties which would have accrued to the claimant

---

67 See [1995] S.T.C. 439 at 456g–457d.

68 [2010] EWHC 862 (TCC).

69 See para.18-019, above.

70 [2010] EWHC 862 (TCC) at [53]–[67].

71 [2010] EWHC 862 (TCC) at [75]; and referring to what he called our critical acclaim of the *Amstrad* decision appearing in the 18th edition of this work: at [67].

72 [2010] EWHC 862 (TCC) at [77]. For his full discussion of the issue see at [68] to [77] together with [46].

73 (1998) 86 B.L.R. 34.

74 [1996] 1 W.L.R. 426.

75 [2010] EWHC 862 (TCC).

76 [1964] 1 Q.B. 95 CA.

77 [1985] Q.B. 428 CA.

within the immediately preceding six-year period.[78] A contrary result was subsequently reached at first instance by Nicholls LJ in *John v James*,[79] but his reasons for not adhering to the *O'Sullivan* approach are not impressive. *O'Sullivan* and not *John v James* was followed by Laddie J in *Celanese International Corporation v BP Chemicals Ltd*.[80]

*(ii) The damages are subject to more tax* If then, as considered above, the courts are prepared to reduce the damages when they are subject to less tax, it should follow that, if the damages will bear more, rather than less, tax than the amount lost, for which damages are being given, would have borne, the amount awarded should be appropriately increased. This should happen in a case such as *Amstrad Plc v Seagate Technology Inc*,[81] if the rates of tax had been increasing rather than reducing over the relevant years so that the tax on the damages would be greater than that on the lost profits. It is true that in *Tate & Lyle Food and Distribution v Greater London Council*,[82] Forbes J refused to adjust the damages upwards on account of the rate of corporation tax having risen between cause of action and judgment, but it was early days when *Tate & Lyle* was decided, very little was said or argued on the point,[83] and, in any event, Forbes J was, as we shall see, being innovative enough in relation to tax.[84] In the early wrongful dismissal cases after the introduction by statute of tax on the damages,[85] the possibility of the damages being adjusted upwards, because one of the methods used by the courts to compute the statutory tax under the complex formula provided[86] could lead to that tax being higher than would otherwise have been payable, had already been contemplated, though occasion does not seem to have arisen to call for implementation. And this could still happen today in wrongful dismissal cases because, with the statutory formula gone, it is provided, for the purposes of the statutory tax, that the damages are to be chargeable to statutory tax as income of the year of assessment in which they are paid but with the first £30,000 exempt.[87] But if the damages represent lost salary over a number of years and not a single year, the statutory tax combined with the *Gourley* tax paid on the exempt £30,000[88] could well exceed the total amount that would have been payable in tax in the absence of a wrongful dismissal, and if rates of tax are falling from the time of dismissal to judgment in the action, this would be inevitable. **18-023**

If the courts are prepared, as they should be, to increase damages in such cases, they become illustrations of *Gourley* in reverse. This apt term was originally coined **18-024**

[78] The position taken by the Court of Appeal is of course clearer in relation to the accounting with which it was primarily concerned.

[79] [1986] S.T.C. 352; both in relation to damages and accounting.

[80] [1999] R.P.C. 203 at [128]–[137].

[81] (1998) 86 B.L.R. 34, at para.18-019, above.

[82] [1982] 1 W.L.R. 149.

[83] Forbes J's conclusion on the point is contained in part of a single sentence in his judgment: [1982] 1 W.L.R. 149 at 156H to 157A.

[84] See at paras 19-135 and following, below.

[85] See para.18-043, below.

[86] Used in *Stewart v Glentaggart Ltd*, 1963 S.C. 300 and in *Shove v Downs Surgical Plc* [1984] 1 All E.R. 7, cases referred to in para.18-018, above.

[87] Now by Income Tax (Earnings and Pensions) Act 2003 s.403(1) and (2). For further detail on all this see para.18-046, below.

[88] See further para.18-046, below.

by Lord Reid in *Taylor v O'Connor*[89] where, in the context of an award for loss of dependency in a fatal accident claim, the increase in the damages was brought about by the need to counteract the shortfall created by the high tax borne by the annual income which the award would generate. "This case", said Lord Reid, "is in a sense *British Transport Commission v Gourley* in reverse".[90] Quite apart from the fact that the damages were getting an increase, rather than suffering the far commoner diminution, on account of tax, this type of case, which concerns personal injury equally with fatal accidents, differs from the normal run of *Gourley* cases in that the adjustment for tax is not made by adding an appropriate sum to, or deducting it from, what would otherwise be the figure of damages, but by increasing what would otherwise be the multiplier.[91] But whatever the method by which *Gourley* in reverse operates, it can only apply in the context of modified *Gourley*. *Gourley* in reverse can never apply where the damages are subject to no tax whatsoever, in other words to mainstream *Gourley*.[92]

## 2. TORT

### (1) Personal injury

**18-025** Personal injury is covered by the decision in *Gourley*'s case.[93] The heads of damage which were held to be calculable with tax taken into account were the loss of earning capacity in the future, awarded as general damages, and the loss of earnings from the time of injury to the time of judgment, awarded as special damages. No deduction was to be made on account of tax in the calculation of the other heads of damage, i.e. pain and suffering and loss of amenities, and out-of-pocket expenses. It was also held to be immaterial whether the tax would have been deducted from the claimant's earnings at source or whether he would receive his gross earnings and then be required to pay the tax himself to the Inland Revenue.[94] *Gourley*'s case[95] was of the latter type.

**18-026** The only feature which is not actually decided by *Gourley*'s case,[96] is whether these particular damages would themselves be liable to tax, for it was agreed that they would not be.[97] Earl Jowitt alone gave his opinion on the correctness of this,

---

89 [1971] A.C. 115.

90 [1971] A.C. 115 at 129F.

91 Dealt with on the tax issue at paras 18-027 and 18-029, below, respectively.

92 *Gourley* in reverse can, however, apply, in either its mainstream or its modified form, if the damages are subject to tax but the loss compensated would not have been, i.e. where neither Factor 1 nor Factor 2 is present. Such a possibility may be thought to be an impossibility in practice, but it did arise in *4 Eng Ltd v Harper* [2009] Ch. 915, a case of deceit: facts at para.49-025, below. The loss was of tax-free dividends, free of tax because paid out of company profits already taxed, and David Richards J ordered the damages attributable to the loss of dividends to be grossed up to take account of the tax to which they might be subject. It was not, however, established that the damages would be taxable, or if taxable to what extent. In these circumstances the order was made on the basis of the claimant company's undertaking to seek a ruling from the Revenue as to its tax liability and, if no tax or tax less than the grossed-up element were payable, to return the damages paid to the extent that the grossed-up amount was in excess of the tax payable, if any. See [2009] Ch. 915 at [104] and [105].

93 [1956] A.C. 185.

94 [1956] A.C. 185 at 198, 207, per Earl Jowitt and Lord Goddard respectively.

95 [1956] A.C. 185.

96 [1956] A.C. 185.

97 [1956] A.C. 185 at 197, 205, 211.

saying that he thought that it was rightly agreed.[98] And indeed it would seem that there is no "source" from which the amount given as damages can be said to come as income,[99] for it represents not so much loss of earnings as the loss of future earning capacity, which is a capital value.[100] Further, no distinction was taken in *Gourley*'s case,[101] between the special damages for loss of earnings up to the time of judgment and the general damages for loss of future earning capacity. This is correct, and it would be fallacious to regard the special damages as taxable on the ground that they are loss of income and the general damages as not taxable on the ground that they are loss of a capital asset. For both are of the same nature, and it is only the accident of the time when the action is heard that will put a particular sum into the one category or the other. If the general damages for loss of future earning capacity are to be regarded as not taxable, then the same should be said in respect of the special damages, which in this case only represent a portion of the general damages for loss of earning capacity in a crystallised form. And indeed the claimant has not specifically earned, by working for them, the sums of damages awarded as special.

In the context of fatal accidents the House of Lords in *Taylor v O'Connor*,[102] promoted the idea of *Gourley* in reverse; an increase in the damages was required to counteract the shortfall created by the high tax borne by the annual income which the award would generate.[103] Subsequently, in the personal injury context, the House of Lords in *Hodgson v Trapp*,[104] has poured cold water upon this idea and no personal injury case of *Gourley* in reverse has so far survived to Court of Appeal level. The matter is considered in more detail when dealing with personal injury and fatal accidents.[105] **18-027**

## (2) Injuries resulting in death

Even before *Gourley*'s case it had been accepted in actions by or on behalf of a deceased's dependants under the Fatal Accidents Act that what the deceased would have had to pay in tax must be taken into account in assessing the damages. While in a physically injured claimant's claim for his loss of earnings it was possible to regard any tax which would be levied on them as representing a collateral liability which should be ignored—which was indeed the approach of the English courts before *Gourley*[106]—as the claim of a deceased's dependants is for their loss of that portion of the deceased's earnings which would have been used for their support, and therefore for an amount which would already have suffered tax in the deceased's hands before it came to be applied for their benefit, no question of the **18-028**

---

98 [1956] A.C. 185 at 197.

99 See paras 18-011 and 18-013, above.

100 Mirroring the earlier legislation from 1960 onwards, s.406(b) of the Income Tax (Earnings and Pensions) Act 2003 exempts from the charge to tax on termination of employment a payment provided "on account of injury to, or disability of, an employee". And following upon legislation from 1971, s.751 of the Income Tax (Trading and Other Income) Act 2005 exempts from tax the interest given on personal injury damages, whether by court order or by settlement (see para.19-087, below). This latter exemption does not justify awarding a lower rate of interest: *Mason v Harman* [1972] R.T.R. 1.

101 [1956] A.C. 185.

102 [1971] A.C. 115.

103 See in this connection para.18-029, below.

104 [1989] A.C. 807.

105 See paras 40-146 and following, and para.41-077, below.

106 See para.18-002, above.

liability to tax being merely collateral could ever arise. Authority for this solution is provided by Lord Goddard CJ in *Zinovieff v British Transport Commission*,[107] a decision before *Gourley*, where he said that counsel had agreed that he was

> "bound to take into account the taxation which the intestate would have had to pay, because one has to find the net value which the intestate was to the dependants whom he has left behind."

A fortiori tax is taken into account after *Gourley*.[108]

18-029 While it is clear that the dependants' damages are not taxable as such,[109] the House of Lords indicated in *Taylor v O'Connor*,[110] that, where the size of the figures involved warranted it, account should be taken, in deciding upon the amount of the annual dependency and the multiplier to apply to it,[111] not only of the fact that the lump sum in damages, in so far as it is still unspent, will earn interest over the years but also of the fact that that interest will be subject to income tax. "The damages", said Lord Reid, "will therefore have to be increased by an amount necessary to counteract this short-fall",[112] namely the shortfall created by the tax borne by the annual income; this was, as he put it, "in a sense *British Transport Commission v Gourley* in reverse".[113] However, a later House of Lords, in *Hodgson v Trapp*,[114] has seriously qualified, indeed all but departed, from this view. Pointing out that everything said on this issue in *Taylor v O'Connor*[115] was obiter,[116] their Lordships held, in the analogous personal injury context, that except in exceptional cases the future incidence of taxation is satisfactorily taken care of by the conventional assumption of an interest rate applicable to a stable currency and the selection of a multiplier appropriate to that rate. No such exceptional fatal accident case has yet appeared and it seems that *British Transport Commission v Gourley* in reverse in this context has little chance of making an appearance.

### (3) Defamation

18-030 The position for defamation was early considered by the House of Lords in *Lewis v Daily Telegraph Ltd*.[117] It was there held that the *Gourley* rule applied to an action of defamation so as to require a direction to the jury to make an allowance, in

---

107 *The Times*, 1 April 1954; also reported in Kemp and Kemp, *The Quantum of Damages*, 2nd edn (London: Sweet & Maxwell, 1962), at p.132 (not in later editions).

108 This appears by implication in all the cases; see, e.g. *Taylor v O'Connor* [1971] A.C. 115.

109 Mirroring earlier legislation from 1960 onwards, s.406(a) of the Income Tax (Earnings and Pensions) Act 2003 exempts from the charge to tax a payment provided "in connection with the termination of employment by the death of an employee". And following upon legislation from 1971, s.751 of the Income Tax (Trading and Other Income) Act 2005 exempts from tax the interest given on damages for wrongful death, whether by court order or by settlement. This latter exemption does not justify awarding a lower rate of interest: *Mason v Harman* [1972] R.T.R. 1.

110 [1971] A.C. 115.

111 For the general method of calculating wrongful death damages see paras 41-038 and following, below.

112 [1971] A.C. 115 at 129B. Lords Guest and Pearson considered it appropriate to increase the multiplier (at 136 and 143 respectively) while Lords Reid and Morris together with Viscount Dilhorne made the increase in the figure of annual dependency (at 130, 134 and 139 respectively).

113 [1971] A.C. 115 at 129F.

114 [1989] A.C. 807.

115 [1971] A.C. 115.

116 [1989] A.C. 807 at 830G, per Lord Oliver who gave the speech, with which his brethren agreed, on this issue.

117 [1964] A.C. 234; facts at para.46-077, below.

assessing the damages for loss of profit arising from the defamation, for the obligation to pay tax on it had it been earned. The jury would not be expected to make mathematical calculations but to deal with the matter on broad lines.[118]

There may not be all that much scope for the operation of *Gourley* in defamation because most claims are by individuals rather than companies and the huge awards that have appeared over the years, now somewhat curbed by the rulings of the Court of Appeal,[119] have been for loss of a good reputation without being in any way related to money matters. Claims by corporations, on the other hand, are geared to financial loss. As it happened, in the particular case of *Lewis* one of the claimants was a company and the other an individual, and the difference between the two is well brought out by Lord Reid who distinguished between the two thus. He said: **18-031**

> "A company cannot be injured in its feelings, it can only be injured in its pocket. Its reputation can be injured by a libel but that injury must sound in money. The injury need not necessarily be confined to loss of income. Its goodwill may be injured. But in so far as the company establishes that the libel has, or has probably, diminished its profits, I think that *Gourley*'s case applies ... The position with regard to an individual plaintiff is rather different. He may be entitled to very substantial damages although his income has not been affected by the libel. But if he does attempt to prove loss of income as a result of the libel, then I think that a similar direction must be given to the jury, and it may be necessary to mention surtax[120] as well as income tax."[121]

There may be even less scope for *Gourley* here than Lord Reid in *Lewis v Daily Telegraph Ltd*[122] thought. It will be seen that their Lordships assumed that, should any of the libel damages be awarded for loss of profit, admittedly not common, those damages would not be taxable in the hands of the claimant. "There can be no difference in principle", said Lord Reid, **18-032**

> "between loss of income caused by negligence and loss of income caused by a libel",[123]

and it may be assumed that, in saying this, the negligence he had in mind was negligence resulting in personal injury. Yet it is not at all clear that damages specifically awarded for loss of business profits, particularly to a company, would not be taxable in the defamed claimant's hands, unless, which is unlikely, the business has been brought down by the defamation.[124] Defamation does not appear to have produced any cases since *Lewis*,[125] in which *Gourley* has been applied. The law has moved on since *Gourley*'s day and it is not difficult to find cases in which damages have been held subject to tax where they represent business profits lost through negligence, whether involving property[126] or of a professional nature.[127]

### (4) Goods: misappropriation, destruction, and damage

In relation to tortious conduct affecting goods the question of the incidence of tax on damages has arisen in two different contexts, both where a claimant has been **18-033**

---

118 [1964] A.C. 234 at 262.
119 See paras 46-023 to 46-028, below.
120 Now higher rate tax.
121 [1964] A.C. 234 at 262.
122 [1964] A.C. 234.
123 [1964] A.C. 234 at 262.
124 So that the taxable source disappears: see para.18-011, above.
125 [1964] A.C. 234.
126 See the authorities at paras 18-033 to 18-041, below.
127 In particular *Deeny v Gooda Walker* [1996] 1 W.L.R. 426 HL, at para.18-048, below.

claiming damages for the tort and where the Inland Revenue has been claiming tax from the claimant on the damages recovered by him in his action. Clearly, it is only in the first context that the application of the *Gourley* rule is directly in issue, but this does not mean that the decisions of the courts falling within the second are irrelevant to the question of the scope of the *Gourley* rule in torts affecting goods. For, in the first place, if the Inland Revenue has succeeded in its claim for tax, this proves that factor (2) is absent and that it would therefore be inappropriate to apply the *Gourley* rule in any comparable claim for damages. And, in the second place, if the Inland Revenue has failed to exact the tax claimed, this result may have been arrived at by the court by first deciding that that which the claimant has lost through the tort, and for which the damages awarded constituted compensation, would not have been subject to tax; in other words, the court's decision may have been based upon the absence of factor (1), so that once again it would be inappropriate to apply the *Gourley* rule in any comparable claim for damages. Moreover, since the Inland Revenue was vigilant in the pursuit of the exaction of tax from damages awards long before the *Gourley* rule had made its debut in 1955[128] there is in the sphere of claims for tax a much longer line of authority available to assist in marking out the proper application of the *Gourley* rule in claims for damages.

**18-034** Where a chattel is tortiously misappropriated, destroyed or damaged, the claimant's primary claim is for the value or the diminished value, as the case may be, of the chattel. If the chattel is a capital asset in the hands of the claimant, then factor (1) will be inapplicable. This is brought out clearly in certain dicta of Lord President Clyde in *Burmah S.S. Co v IRC*,[129] a case in the Scottish Court of Session which involved not tort but contract, the Inland Revenue there claiming that the appellant shipowner was liable to tax on the damages awarded him for breach of contract.[130] Lord Clyde said:

> "Suppose ... that one of the appellant's vessels was negligently run down and sunk by a vessel belonging to some other ship-owner, and the appellant recovered as damages the value of the sunken vessel, I imagine that there could be no doubt that the damages so recovered could not enter the appellant's profit and loss account because the destruction of the vessel would be an injury inflicted, not on the appellant's trading, but on the capital assets of the appellant's trade, making (so to speak) a hole in *them*, and the damages could therefore ... only be used to fill *that* hole."[131]

Thus it was accepted without dispute in *London & Thames Haven Oil Wharves v Attwooll*,[132] that the damages awarded to the taxpayer company for the diminution in value of its tortiously damaged deep-water jetty, measured by the cost of repair, were not taxable. However, if the chattel is not a capital asset of the claimant's business but is part of his stock in trade, e.g. furniture in the hands of a furniture dealer, this reasoning would not apply. Factor (1) would therefore be introduced into the situation but by the same stroke factor (2) would be excluded, so that the *Gourley* rule is still ousted.[133] Accordingly, in relation to the primary claim for the value or diminished value of the chattel, the practical importance of deciding whether the

---

[128] Thus the leading case was decided over 90 years ago: *Glenboig Union Fireclay Co v IRC* (1922) 12 T.C. 427 HL (Sc.), at para.18-036, below.

[129] (1931) 16 T.C. 67, Court of Session.

[130] See this case at para.18-053, below.

[131] (1931) 16 T.C. 67 at 71 to 72.

[132] [1967] Ch. 772 CA; see this case at para.18-036, below.

[133] See *Diamond v Campbell-Jones* [1961] Ch. 22 at para.18-055, below.

inapplicability of the rule stems from the absence of factor (1) or factor (2) tends to disappear. Thus in *Hall v Pearlberg*,[134] where hay had been converted by the defendant, it was held that no tax element fell to be taken into account in assessing the damages for conversion, principally because it was thought that factor (1) was absent but alternatively because the presence of factor (1) would mean the absence of factor (2).

The claimant may, however, also claim damages for the loss of use of the chattel, or for the loss of profits by its use, or for interest upon its capital value; and this head of damage, in whichever of the three ways stated, produces more problems as to the application of the *Gourley* rule. The easiest case is where the damages are awarded specifically and separately as interest, for it is now fairly clear that such damages themselves can be taxable. The authority for this proposition is the instructive decision in Admiralty of *The Norseman*.[135] The claimant's ship was damaged in the defendant's harbour and on the damages interest was awarded, which was the already common practice in Admiralty. It was held that this interest was taxable, applying *Riches v Westminster Bank*,[136] and indeed the same result should be reached where interest is awarded as damages other than in Admiralty, whether at common law or by statute.[137] Since, therefore, in such cases factor (2) is not satisfied, the *Gourley* rule will not be applicable. **18-035**

On the other hand, if the damages are given under the head of loss of use value or of loss of profits, the matter is more complicated. If the loss for which the damages are awarded is of trading profits which would have been made through the use of the chattel, then factor (2) would appear to be inapplicable because the damages would have to be entered into the claimant's revenue or profit and loss account. The claimant's business continues after the tort, and forms the "source"[138] from which the amount given as damages can be said to come as income. Thus both in *Pryce v Elwood*,[139] where the claimant claimed for damage to a car which he used in his car-hire business, and in *Morahan v Archer and Belfast Corporation*,[140] where the claimant claimed for damage to his taxi-cab, it was held that tax should not be deducted in assessing damages for loss of profits which the claimants would have made during the period while the vehicles were being repaired, since these damages would be received as revenue and hence be taxable in the claimants' hands.[141] Both these decisions were cited and approved by Willmer LJ in *London and Thames Haven Oil Wharves v Attwooll*.[142] In that case the taxpayer company, as a result of tortious damage to its deep-water jetty, suffered loss by reason of having to incur the costs of repairing the jetty, and also loss due to the jetty being out of use for 380 **18-036**

---

[134] [1956] 1 W.L.R. 244.

[135] [1957] P. 224.

[136] [1947] A.C. 390; see para.18-010, above.

[137] See Ch.19, below.

[138] See paras 18-011 and 18-013, above.

[139] (1964) 108 S.J. 583.

[140] [1957] N.I. 61.

[141] While in *Herring v British Transport Commission* (1958) 37 A.T.C. 382, where the claimant haulier claimed for earnings lost through the withdrawal of a motor lorry from his fleet as a result of tortious damage to it, the gross loss of earnings was again awarded as damages, this was because Donovan J considered factor (1) absent where the profits for which compensation was being awarded derived from only part of a business, and in *McGhie & Sons v British Transport Commission* [1963] 1 Q.B. 125 at 150, Phillimore J rightly expressed doubts as to the correctness of this conclusion. It would seem, however, that the decision itself was correct because the damages would have been taxable, i.e. because of the absence of factor (2) rather than of factor (1).

[142] [1967] Ch. 772 CA.

days, which loss was computed as a percentage of the original cost of the jetty over the 380 days. The Court of Appeal, reversing Buckley J, held that such part of the total amount received by the taxpayer company as represented the excess over the amount of the physical damage to the jetty was a taxable revenue receipt because it was in effect a payment for loss of trading profits. However it does not necessarily follow, as the court agreed, that damages will constitute a trading receipt wherever their calculation is based upon profits lost to the trader. This was made clear in the leading case of *Glenboig Union Fireclay Co v IRC*.[143] There the taxpayer company, which was a lessee of certain fireclay fields utilised by it in its business of manufacturing fireclay goods and merchanting raw fireclay, received compensation upon the exercise by a railway company of its statutory powers to require part of the fireclay to be left unworked, and the House of Lords held that the amount received in compensation, although calculated by the profits lost, constituted a capital receipt, being a payment made for the sterilisation of a capital asset. "There is no relation", said Lord Buckmaster,

> "between the measure that is used for the purpose of calculating a particular result and the quality of the figure that is arrived at by means of the application of that test".[144]

The Court of Appeal in *London and Thames Haven Oil Wharves v Attwooll*[145] distinguished this decision as turning on the fact that the taxpayer company had been permanently deprived of its capital asset, which had ceased to be one which could be used or exploited in the company's trade.[146] However, the *Gourley* rule is probably also inapplicable in the context of *Glenboig Union Fireclay Co v IRC*,[147] since the presence of factor (2) would seem to bring in its train the exclusion of factor (1); this is supported by the reasoning of the decisions dealing with statutory compensation for the compulsory acquisition of land.[148]

**18-037** Distinctions along these lines may not, however, be called for where the chattel is not utilised by its owner with a view to profit, generally in a trade or business carried on by him, for it may be that even damages which are clearly awarded for loss of use value or loss of profits will in such circumstances not be taxable because of the absence of a "source".[149] Thus in *Simpson v Executors of Bonner Maurice*,[150] a case arising out of the First World War and involving compensation awarded under the Peace Treaty in respect of German stocks and shares owned by a British national, Rowlatt J at first instance appeared to be of the view that damages for the detention of a chattel could not be called rent or hire for it during the period of detention so as to be taxable,[151] a proposition which the Privy Council in *Raja's Commercial College v Gian Singh & Co*,[152] has stated to be

143 (1922) 12 T.C. 427 HL.
144 (1922) 12 T.C. 427 HL at 464.
145 [1967] Ch. 772 CA.
146 [1967] Ch. 772 CA at 807 to 808, 813 and 817.
147 (1922) 12 T.C. 427 HL.
148 See para.18-041, below.
149 See paras 18-011 and 18-013, above.
150 (1929) 14 T.C. 580 CA.
151 (1929) 14 T.C. 580 CA at 593.
152 [1977] A.C. 312 PC.

"no doubt quite accurate in relation to chattels which, if not detained, would have been used by the owner for his own purposes but … not applicable to chattels which the owner would have let out on hire".[153]

However, it may be that the lack of a source, which introduces factor (2), also eliminates factor (1), so that the *Gourley* rule would remain excluded.

### (5) Land: wrongful occupation, wrongful use and damage

With torts affecting land, as with torts affecting goods, the question of the incidence of tax can arise both in claims for damages and in claims for tax on damages; while cases of the latter as well as the former type are of relevance in dealing with the *Gourley* rule,[154] the post-*Gourley* period has produced more of the former type for land than for goods. **18-038**

In relation to the primary claim for the diminished value of the land, factor (1) will be inapplicable where the land is a capital asset in the claimant's hands. Thus in *Hall v Pearlberg*,[155] where the defendant had entered into unlawful possession of the claimant's farm, and the land, buildings and equipment were depreciated by the defendant's bad husbandry, the damages representing diminished value were awarded in full.[156] On the other hand, if the claimant should be dealing in the buying and selling of land, so that the land is trading stock in his hands, then the *Gourley* rule would not apply because of the absence not of factor (1) but of factor (2).[157] **18-039**

Where the claim is specifically for interest upon the capital value of the land, then, as with goods,[158] the *Gourley* rule is ousted because the damages are taxable. Where the claim was for loss of user value, it was held in *Hall v Pearlberg*,[159] that the damages awarded in lieu of rent for the period of the defendant's wrongful occupation of the claimant's farms must be reduced by the amount of tax to which the rent would have been liable. This case, however, is rendered doubtful in the light of the Privy Council's decision in *Raja's Commercial College v Gian Singh & Co*,[160] again a claim for loss of rent. Landlords successfully brought an action for possession and for damages against tenants who had not complied with a valid notice to quit and had hence become trespassers, the damages being calculated at the difference between the amount of rent paid by the tenants and the rent the landlords could have obtained had the tenants left on time. The tenants argued that the damages were not subject to income tax and should therefore be reduced by the amount of income tax which the landlords would have had to pay on the rent, but the Privy Council dismissed their appeal from the Court of Appeal in Singapore, holding that the damages were indeed taxable. The tenants had sought to distinguish the trading taxpayer, who would be taxable on damages received as compensation for loss **18-040**

---

153 [1977] A.C. 312 PC at 322B. That case concerned land and not chattels, an investor and not a trader: see para.18-040, below.

154 For the reasons for this, see para.18-033, above.

155 [1956] 1 W.L.R. 244.

156 See the case at para.18-034, above. See too the comment of Earl Jowitt in *British Transport Commission v Gourley* [1956] A.C. 185 at 202, concurred in by Lord Morton in *West Suffolk CC v Rought* [1957] A.C. 403 at 414, on *Comyn v Att Gen* [1950] Ir. R. 142, a case of compensation for compulsory acquisition of land.

157 See para.18-034, above, and *Diamond v Campbell-Jones* [1961] Ch. 22 at para.18-055, below.

158 See *The Norseman* [1957] P. 224, at para.18-035, above.

159 [1956] 1 W.L.R. 244.

160 [1977] A.C. 312 PC. *Hall v Pearlberg* was not cited, but see four footnotes below.

of trading profits, from the investing taxpayer, but the Privy Council could see no logical reason why the treatment of damages for income tax purposes should depend on whether the recipient was a trader or was, as here, an investor, and therefore the damages which were awarded in place of lost income fell to be treated as income which was taxable.[161] In *Hall v Pearlberg*,[162] it would appear that the claimants, who had just purchased the farms in question, had not in fact let them out before the defendant's trespass but they undoubtedly had the intention of doing so,[163] and it is difficult to see how the holding in that case can survive *Raja's Commercial College v Gian Singh & Co*.[164] The situation could be different with a claimant owner who is awarded the market rental value of his land although he would not himself have let it out during the period of the trespasser's occupation; indeed this seems to be accepted by Lord Fraser, delivering the judgment of their Lordships, in *Raja's Commercial College v Gian Singh & Co*.[165] But again[166] the introduction of factor (2) may eliminate factor (1) and keep the *Gourley* rule still out of the picture.

**18-041** Where the claim is for loss of profits, the first cases indicated that, even where the recipient of the damages is utilising the land in a trade or business, there is room for the application of the *Gourley* rule despite the fact that, with goods, this does not appear to be so. In *West Suffolk County Council v Rought*,[167] and again in *McGhie v British Transport Commission*,[168] two cases of claims for statutory compensation for the compulsory acquisition of land rather than for damages, but to which the same principles must apply, the opportunity to apply the *Gourley* rule arose from the fact that in both it was accepted that the statutory compensation would not be taxable in the hands of the recipient.[169] In the first case a manufacturing company claimed compensation for loss of profits in the period before it was able to recommence operations in alternative accommodation, and in the second case a mineowner, who was required to abstain from working minerals because they were within the area necessary for the protection of a railway, claimed compensation for what was held to be not the loss of the capital value of the minerals or the sterilisation of a capital asset but the loss of the profits to be made out of working the minerals. Accordingly, in each case both factor (1) and factor (2) were present, and the awards of statutory compensation made to the claimants fell to be reduced by the amount of tax they would have paid on the profits. On the other hand, in *Re*

---

[161] *Simpson v Executors of Bonner Maurice* (1929) 14 T.C. 580 CA (see para.18-037, above), which was the decision upon which the tenants founded their argument ([1977] A.C. 312 PC at 321B), was distinguished as involving facts of a "very special and unusual nature" (at 322F).

[162] [1956] 1 W.L.R. 244.

[163] See the statement of facts at [1956] 1 W.L.R. 244 at 245. The claimants were in fact a trading company but they were not dealing in land but in the sand and gravel to be extracted from it.

[164] [1977] A.C. 312 PC. It may be that *Hall v Pearlberg* can be justified on the basis that it was just not possible to bring the damages within the complex mechanism for taxing rents and other receipts from land then in force, consisting of assessments on the annual value of land together with so-called "excess rent" assessments. But that would not justify it today as these complexities were abandoned in later charging provisions which, from 1970, have moved much nearer to the provision of the Singapore Income Tax Act in issue in the *Raja's Commercial College* case. Income from property is now charged under Pt 3 of the Income Tax (Trading and Other Income) Act 2005.

[165] [1977] A.C. 312 PC at 322B; see his comment cited at para.18-037, above.

[166] See para.18-037, above.

[167] [1957] A.C. 403.

[168] [1963] 1 Q.B. 125.

[169] See [1957] A.C. 403 at 407, 412 and [1963] 1 Q.B. 125 at 137.

*Associated Portland Cement Manufacturers Ltd's Application*,[170] Buckley J declined to apply the *Gourley* rule and distinguished *McGhie v British Transport Commission*,[171] because the statutory compensation claimed was not for the loss caused by minerals remaining unworked but for the loss of the minerals themselves and therefore of a capital asset. And in *Stoke-on-Trent City Council v Wood Mitchell & Co*,[172] the Court of Appeal indicated that the principle in *Rought*,[173] is no longer applicable to statutory compensation for compulsory acquisition, and held that the *Gourley* rule cannot apply to that part of the compensation received for loss of profits because this falls to be treated as a trading receipt and may accordingly be taxable income. In arriving at this conclusion the court was assisted by the refusal of the Inland Revenue, in contrast to their preparedness in *Rought*,[174] to commit themselves to the non-liability to tax of the income element of the compensation.[175]

## 3. CONTRACT

### (1) Contracts of employment: wrongful dismissal

In *Gourley*'s case Lord Goddard, with whose speech Lord Somervell and Lord Radcliffe agreed, stated that he was dealing, as to the principles involved, with the cases both of personal injury and of wrongful dismissal.[176] Following this, the rule was soon applied, without further argument, in a series of cases involving wrongful dismissal,[177] and its applicability in this context was finally endorsed, after argument, by the majority of the Court of Appeal in *Parsons v B.N.M. Laboratories*.[178] **18-042**

The correctness of this result of course depends upon the presence, in the context of wrongful dismissal, of both factor (1) and factor (2). There was never any doubt over factor (1): clearly the salary for the loss of which the damages are given would have been subject to tax. And at the time *Gourley*'s case was decided, and for a few years after, the presence of factor (2) was also assured: there could not be said to be a source from which the amount given as damages arose as income,[179] for by the **18-043**

170 [1966] Ch. 308.

171 [1963] 1 Q.B. 125.

172 [1980] 1 W.L.R. 254 CA.

173 [1957] A.C. 403.

174 [1957] A.C. 403

175 The court was also assisted by a statutory provision in relation to capital gains tax, with the construction of which it was indeed primarily concerned. See, too, *Pennine Raceway v Kirklees Metropolitan Council (No.2)* [1989] S.T.C. 122 CA, dealt with, under onus of proof, at para.18-057, below.

176 [1956] A.C. 185 at 210.

177 *Beach v Reed Corrugated Cases* [1956] 1 W.L.R. 807 (where issue was calculation of quantum after taking tax into account); *Phipps v Orthodox Unit Trusts* [1958] 1 Q.B. 314 CA (where question was of defendant's entitlement to particulars of claimant's tax position); *Shindler v Northern Raincoat Co* [1960] 1 W.L.R. 1038, especially at 1050 (where the tax issue was not main one). See also *Re Houghton Main Colliery Co* [1956] 1 W.L.R. 1219, where a company under contractual obligation to pay pensions to the claimants, two of its employees, went into liquidation, and it was held that tax must be deducted from the lump sums at which the pensions had been valued for the purpose of proving in the liquidation.

178 [1964] 1 Q.B. 95 CA, Sellers LJ dissenting. While Harman LJ doubted whether it was open to the court not to apply the rule in wrongful dismissal cases (at 123), Sellers LJ thought the issue was still in the realm of obiter dicta and that precedent did not require the court to apply the *Gourley* rule (at 110).

179 On the source doctrine see paras 18-011 and 18-013, above.

very dismissal the existing source disappeared.[180] But the non-taxability, that resulted from this analysis of payments of compensation, which had become a familiar pattern wherever a person retired, or otherwise amicably departed, from an employment, led in 1960 to legislative intervention, and while the provisions of ss.37 and 38 of the Finance Act of that year,[181] provisions now in somewhat different form in ss.401 to 404A of the Income Tax (Earnings and Pensions) Act 2003,[182] were directed primarily to catch these so-called "golden handshakes", they were phrased in terms sufficiently wide to apply to damages awarded for loss of earnings for wrongful dismissal.[183] At first sight this would appear undeniably to remove the rule in *Gourley*'s case from the scene: the damages being now taxable, factor (2) is no longer present.[184] However, an unqualified statement that the damages are now taxable is precluded by the fact that the first tranche of any award was exempted, initially the first £5,000 and today the first £30,000, from the taxation imposed by the statutory provisions,[185] and it is this exemption which in this context has at once allowed the *Gourley* rule to continue to flourish and given rise for many years to difficulties in its application.

**18-044** Initially it was open to the courts to decide that the rule in *Gourley*'s case was ousted even in relation to the then first £5,000 which escaped tax: it could have been held that factor (2) was absent because the whole award was indeed within the scope of the statutory tax although relieved in part from bearing any actual tax. This simple and straightforward solution was, however, rejected by the majority of the Court of Appeal in *Parsons v B.N.M. Laboratories*[186] itself, where the claimant's loss of earnings was well below the £5,000 threshold. Pearson LJ there said:

> "When Parliament has expressly provided that tax shall not be charged in respect of a payment such as this it is in my view impossible to contend successfully that a payment such as this is chargeable to tax. Section 38(3) [of the Finance Act 1960] does not create a relief from tax in the ordinary sense. It leaves a small or medium-sized payment of the relevant character outside the scope of the taxation imposed by the Act: such a payment is not brought into charge, and does not become taxable subject-matter."[187]

Accordingly factor (2) was present and *Gourley* was applied.

---

180 This, however, may not be so where the claimant is a person exercising a profession. His dismissal will not terminate his profession, the existing "source" will not disappear, and accordingly factor (2) and the Gourley rule should be inapplicable. But it is exceptional that a person exercising a profession can be wrongfully dismissed; it could, however, happen, for instance, in the case of an actor. And see para.18-047, below.

181 Together with Sch.4 to the Act.

182 Previously, Income and Corporation Taxes Act 1988 s.148, as substituted in 1998.

183 Today the legislation of 2003 simply provides, in s.401(1), that it applies to payments "received at the termination of an employment". The earlier legislation, from the Finance Act 1960 onwards, also made specific reference to payments made "in pursuance of an order of a court in proceedings for wrongful dismissal or otherwise for breach of a contract of employment".

184 Since s.401(1) is in terms of employments (see previous note), it has no application to professions. However, a person following a profession cannot generally be wrongfully dismissed; and in the exceptional case where this is possible, as with an actor, the dismissal will not terminate the profession, so that it seems that the *Gourley* rule would be inapplicable quite apart from s.401(1).

185 The progression, today only of historical interest, was as follows: £5,000: Finance Act 1960 s.38(3); £10,000: Finance Act 1978 s.24(1); £25,000: Finance Act 1981 s.31(1); £30,000: Finance Act 1988 s.74(1), now in Income Tax (Earnings and Pensions) Act 2003 s.403(1). No increase has been made since 1988.

186 [1964] 1 Q.B. 95 CA. It appealed, however, to Sellers LJ who dissented on this point too (for the anterior point, see the footnote at the end of para.18-042, above).

187 [1964] 1 Q.B. 95 CA at 140; see too at 128, per Harman LJ.

It would still have been possible to hold the *Gourley* rule inapplicable to a case in which the loss of earnings before tax was over £5,000, distinguishing *Parsons v B.N.M. Laboratories*,[188] on the ground that the *Gourley* rule was relevant only to the situation where the total award escaped tax under the statutory provisions. But while this would once again have the merit of simplicity, and indeed appealed to Harman LJ in *Parsons v B.N.M. Laboratories*,[189] it would now lead to unjust results as between claimants, in particular as between the claimant whose loss of earnings before tax fell just below £5,000 and the claimant whose loss of earnings before tax was slightly in excess of £5,000. For while the full rigour of the *Gourley* rule would apply to the former, the latter would escape it entirely, at the cost only of paying tax under the statutory provisions upon the slight excess over £5,000. In the result the courts have applied *Gourley* to the exempted amount but not to the excess and for many years had to battle, in a series of cases, with the more complex solutions which were available, solutions made complex by the introduction in the legislation of an elaborate formula for calculating the statutory tax. **18-045**

Fortunately these cases, and these solutions, are now history with the abandonment of the statutory formula in 1988[190] and need no longer be rehearsed here.[191] Since that date a much more straightforward solution has prevailed and today s.403 of the Income Tax (Earnings and Pensions) Act 2003 provides, by subs.(1) combined with subs.(2), that the first £30,000 does not suffer tax and the balance is subject to income tax in the ordinary way as employment income of the assessment year in which the payment is received.[192] With the statutory formula gone, there is no longer any difficulty in calculating the appropriate amount to be deducted on account of the tax element. It is the amount of tax which the individual would have paid on £30,000 regarded as the highest part of his total income which for this purpose must be taken to include the damages awarded in excess of £30,000 upon which he will be taxed.[193] **18-046**

## (2) Contracts for professional and other services, including agency

In *Lyndale Fashion Manufacturers v Rich*,[194] the defendant's business was that of a travelling salesman for the claimants, he being remunerated by commission and taxed on his profits of that business. In an action against him by the claimants, who had wrongly dispensed with his services, the defendant claimed damages in respect of commission he would otherwise have earned. In issue was the calculation of the deduction on account of tax,[195] it being common ground that the *Gourley* rule required such a deduction,[196] and the Court of Appeal stating that "the principle laid **18-047**

188 [1964] 1 Q.B. 95 CA.

189 [1964] 1 Q.B. 95 CA at 130; but not so much to Pearson LJ: see at 137. See the case further at paras 18-016 to 18-018, above.

190 The statutory formula was repealed by Finance Act 1988 s.74(2).

191 For those interested the cases and their solutions are fully documented in earlier editions, most recently in the 16th edition at [603] to [605]. The cases applying the statutory formula are referred to at para.18-018, above.

192 The provision was formerly in Income and Corporation Taxes Act 1988 s.148, as substituted in 1998.

193 For details see Income Tax (Earnings and Pensions) Act 2003 s.403(1) and (4) combined with s.404. See para.18-062, below, on the propriety of considering the amount subject to *Gourley* as the top slice of the claimant's income.

194 [1973] 1 W.L.R. 73 CA.

195 See para.18-062, below.

196 [1973] 1 W.L.R. 73 at 76A.

down in *Gourley*'s case plainly applies".[197] Yet it may be questioned whether it is incontrovertible that the damages would not be subject to tax since it is accepted in general that damages received by traders as compensation for loss of trading receipts are taxable as income,[198] and it is difficult to see why an agent working on a commission basis should be treated any differently. Only if it could be said that the claimant's business itself was brought to an end by the breach of contract and did not continue in any way whatsoever might it be argued that the "source" had gone and that accordingly the damages could not be taxable.[199]

**18-048** The converse case of the provider of the services being in breach and not the victim of the breach appeared in *Deeny v Gooda Walker*,[200] and tends to support, at House of Lords level, the view that the uncritical acceptance of the application of the *Gourley* rule in *Lyndale Fashion Manufacturers v Rich*,[201] was misconceived.[202] The claimants, underwriting members of Lloyd's, were awarded damages against the defendants, their so-called members' agents and managing agents, for conducting the claimants' underwriting business negligently by their failure to arrange adequate reinsurance cover against losses. The damages were assessed at the amount that the claimants would have received had the appropriate reinsurance cover been in place, which would have either increased the claimants' profits or reduced their losses. The House of Lords, affirming the courts below, held that the damages did not fall to be reduced on account of tax because the damages would themselves be taxable. Factor (2) was absent and *Gourley* did not apply. Entering into agency agreements with their members' agents and managing agents was in the course of the claimants' underwriting business so that, where the agents performed their duties negligently resulting in the claimants realising less money, the damages payable by the agents were a receipt of the claimants' business. Lord Hoffmann, who gave the leading speech, gave a second ground for his decision; he was prepared to take a wider view of when a receipt arose out of a trade, considering that it need not become payable by virtue of a pre-existing trade relationship, thereby applying the rule to that effect as formulated by Diplock LJ in *London and Thames Haven Oil Wharves v Attwooll*.[203] Though none of Lord Hoffmann's brethren was prepared to endorse this approach, deciding the case solely on the first ground as stated above, their views were strictly obiter and those of Lord Hoffmann, together with Diplock LJ, are to be preferred.[204]

**18-049** On the basis of this decision, at three levels, that the damages were fully taxable so that mainstream *Gourley* did not apply because factor (2) was not present,

---

197 [1973] 1 W.L.R. 73 at 76F.

198 See paras 18-036 and 18-041, above and paras 18-051 and following, and para.18-055, below.

199 For the source doctrine see para.18-011, above.

200 [1996] 1 W.L.R. 426 HL.

201 [1973] 1 W.L.R. 73 CA.

202 Curiously the *Lyndale* decision does not feature in any of their Lordships' speeches.

203 [1967] Ch. 772 CA at 815. His formulation went thus: "Where, pursuant to a legal right, a trader receives from another person compensation for the trader's failure to receive a sum of money which, if it had been received, would have been credited to the amount of profits (if any) arising in any year from the trade carried on by him at the time when the compensation is so received, the compensation is to be treated for income tax purposes in the same way as that sum of money would have been treated if it had been received instead of the compensation." For the *Attwooll* case see paras 18-034 and 17-036, above.

204 See, too, *Dickinson v Jones Alexander & Co* [1993] 2 F.L.R. 321 where, in a claim against solicitors for the mishandling of a wife's divorce proceedings, it was assumed that the damages awarded, which represented the wife's lost income, would be taxable in her hands and therefore no deduction for tax was made from them.

it was then further contended, but not beyond first instance, in *Deeny v Gooda Walker*,[205] that modified *Gourley* was still applicable in the presence of factor (2M)[206] so that the rule should apply to the difference in tax that would have been paid in normal circumstances and the lower tax that would be paid on the damages.[207] This contention also failed; the reasons for this decision, and its correctness, have already been considered.[208]

*Finley v Connell Associates*[209] is a further case of an award of damages for a loss of trading profits, here of a company, stemming from the negligence of a professional adviser, here a solicitor. In the normal way such damages would have been taxable as representing trading receipts, again ousting *Gourley*, but because the company was in insolvent liquidation and had therefore ceased to trade, no tax would fall to be paid on the award. Accordingly *Gourley* applied and a deduction of 25 per cent was made from the damages. This decision also has already been considered, together with the implications for the *Gourley* rule of the further peculiar feature of the case that the claimant was the assignee of the company's right of action.[210] **18-050**

## (3) Contracts affecting goods

With one important exception,[211] none of the authorities dealing with the tax element in relation to contracts affecting goods appears to be a claim to obtain damages. The law has therefore to be gleaned from cases of claims by the Inland Revenue for tax upon damages already received.[212] **18-051**

While the primary claim may occasionally be in respect of the market value of the chattel, generally at the time and place of due delivery, as in the case of breach by non-delivery of goods contracted to be carried, it is commoner to find that the primary claim is in respect of the difference either between the market value of the goods and the contract price, as in the case of breach by non-delivery or non-acceptance of goods contracted to be sold, or between the market value at the time of due delivery and the market value at the time of actual delivery, as in the case of breach by delayed delivery of goods contracted to be sold or carried, or between the market value of goods as warranted and their market value as is, as in the case of breach of warranty in a contract for sale of goods. In any of these cases, if the chattel represents or would represent trading stock in the hands of the recipient of the damages, then those damages will constitute a taxable revenue receipt, factor (2) will accordingly be absent, and there will be no room for the application of the *Gourley* rule. Thus in *Sommerfelds v Freeman*,[213] where the Ministry of Supply paid £50,000 for failure to deliver to a purchaser certain surplus war material which would have been trading stock in the purchaser's hands, this amount, which was taken to have been calculated by the parties on the basis of the profit the purchaser would have made on reselling the material, was held to be a taxable revenue receipt **18-052**

---

205 [1995] S.T.C. 439.
206 For the meaning of modified *Gourley* and factor (2M), see para.18-005, above.
207 See para.18-020, above.
208 See paras 18-020 to 18-022, above.
209 [2002] Lloyd's Rep. P.N. 62.
210 See para.18-012, above.
211 See para.18-054, below.
212 For the reasons why such cases are relevant see para.18-033, above.
213 (1966) 44 T.C. 43.

in his hands.[214] On the other hand, if the chattel is a capital asset in the hands of the recipient of the damages, the damages will not be a taxable receipt so that factor (2) will be present; however, factor (1) will now be absent, and there will again be no call to apply the *Gourley* rule in a claim for damages.

**18-053** As to a claim beyond the normal measure of damages for consequential loss by way of loss of use or of profits, or for interest, it would seem that the *Gourley* rule is again totally eliminated because of the absence either of factor (1) or of factor (2). Even where the chattel is a capital asset in the hands of the recipient of the damages, it will be the absence of factor (2) which ousts the rule if the profits which would have been made but for the deprivation of the chattel, and which are the subject of the claim, would have been trading profits. This is well illustrated by *Burmah S.S. Co v IRC*,[215] in the Court of Session in Scotland. In that case a shipping company had placed a ship in the hands of repairers for overhaul, the repairers delayed her redelivery and the company claimed damages from them based upon the estimated loss of trading profit. The claim was compromised, and it was held in the present action that the settlement figure could be included as a trading receipt in the computation of the company's profits for tax purposes. So too damages received by a shipowner for breach of a charterparty are as likely to be a taxable receipt in his hands as are damages for breach of a repair contract. This was the familiar illustration given by Lord President Clyde in his judgment. He said:

> "Suppose someone who chartered one of the appellant's vessels breached the charter and exposed himself to a claim of damages at the appellant's instance, there could, I imagine, be no doubt that the damages recovered would properly enter the appellant's profit and loss account for the year. The reason would be that the breach of the charter was an injury inflicted in the appellant's trading, making (so to speak) a hole in the appellant's profits, and the damages recovered could not therefore be reasonably or appropriately put by the appellant—in accordance with the principles of sound commercial accounting—to any other purpose than to fill that hole."[216]

**18-054** The one important case of a contract affecting goods which is a claim for damages rather than a tax appeal about damages is *Amstrad Plc v Seagate Technology Inc*,[217] and its importance lies in its being not a case of mainstream *Gourley* involving factors (1) and (2) but a case of modified *Gourley* involving factors (1) and (2M).[218] The award of damages was in respect of loss of profits from the sale of a large number of computers and it was undoubted both that the damages would be taxable and that the lost profits would have been taxable. The *Gourley* issue arose because, on account of timing, the damages were to suffer some £1 million less tax than the lost profits. Accordingly, factors (1) and (2M) were applicable and *Gourley* in its modified form was applied.[219]

---

214 Following *Bush, Beach and Gent v Road* (1939) 22 T.C. 519. There are many cases on the general point of when compensation for the loss of a beneficial contract is a trading receipt as opposed to a capital receipt: see the standard texts on income tax.

215 (1931) 16 T.C. 67, Court of Session.

216 (1931) 16 T.C. 67 at 71.

217 (1998) 86 B.L.R. 34.

218 For the meaning of modified *Gourley* and factor (2M), see para.18-005, above.

219 See the case further at para.18-019, above.

### (4) Contracts affecting land

Much the same principles apply to contracts affecting land as to contracts affecting goods.[220] Once again, the primary claim where there has been non-performance is for the difference between the market value of the land and the contract price. Again, the *Gourley* rule will be excluded because of the absence of factor (1) where the recipient of the damages is not dealing in the buying and selling of land, and because of the absence of factor (2) where he is. Thus in *Diamond v Campbell Jones*,[221] where the claimant, a dealer in real estate, bought a London town house from the defendant, who then repudiated, Buckley J, in awarding the normal measure of damages for non-acceptance, namely market price less contract price, said: **18-055**

> "Such a profit in the hands of the plaintiff would undoubtedly have attracted income tax ... On the other hand, it appears to me that any damages recovered by the plaintiff are liable to attract tax as part of the profits or gains of his business ... I must, I think, award him a gross sum in damages equal to the gross amount of the profit which he would be likely to have made had there been no breach of contract."[222]

As to an additional claim for loss of user value or of profits, or for interest in lieu, it would seem that again the *Gourley* rule is totally eliminated; this is indicated by the analogous cases dealing with goods.[223] Only if the tax on the amount of the damages differs from the tax on the amount of the loss compensated could *Gourley* make a limited appearance; again there is the analogy in the context of goods.[224]

## (C) *THE PRACTICAL APPLICATION OF THE RULE IN GOURLEY'S CASE*

## 1. BURDEN OF PROOF

### (1) Application of the Gourley rule

There was for long little clarity on where the onus of proof lay in relation to the application of the rule in *Gourley*'s case. Does the claimant have to prove that factor (1) is not present or the defendant prove that it is? Similarly, does the claimant have to prove that factor (2) is not present or the defendant prove that it is? It is true that, in the wake of *Gourley*, the Official Referee adopted the view in *Hall v Pearlberg*,[225] that the onus remained upon the claimant to prove his damage, and therefore required him to show that either factor (1) or factor (2) was inapplicable to his claim.[226] But the law has moved on since then. **18-056**

After a period of uncertainty the Court of Appeal eventually in *Stoke-on-Trent City Council v Wood Mitchell*,[227] held that it was the defendant's onus to show that factor (2) is satisfied, so that his failure to do so ousts the *Gourley* rule. The court **18-057**

---

220 See paras 18-051 and following, above.

221 [1961] Ch. 22.

222 [1961] Ch. 22 at 37.

223 See para.18-053, above.

224 See *Amstrad Plc v Seagate Technology Inc* (1998) 86 B.L.R. 34 at para.18-054, above.

225 [1956] 1 W.L.R. 244.

226 [1956] 1 W.L.R. 244 at 247; see similarly Lord Morton, soon after, in *West Suffolk CC v Rought* [1957] A.C. 403 at 413: "It is ... incumbent on them [the plaintiffs] to prove their loss after taking into account the incidence of taxation."

227 [1980] 1 W.L.R. 254 CA; see the case at para.18-041, above.

took the view that the rule could only be applied if "it is clear beyond peradventure"[228] that the sum received by the claimant—in the particular case statutory compensation rather than damages but to which the same principles apply—would not be taxable in the claimant's hands[229]; otherwise the dangers of double taxation are too great. Indeed it is of some concern that the courts do not always get the tax position right. Thus in *Pennine Raceway v Kirklees Metropolitan Council (No.2)*,[230] the compensation—again the case was one of statutory compensation rather than damages—was held to be payable net of tax on the basis that it would not be taxable in the claimant company's hands and, after the time of appealing this decision had run out, the Revenue turned round and demanded tax. Fortunately, faced with this double taxation the claimant company was able to obtain an extension of time for requiring a case to be stated and the decision was changed, the Court of Appeal by then adopting the same approach to factor (2) onus as it had done in *Stoke-on-Trent City Council v Wood Mitchell*.[231] But none of this would have happened in *Pennine Raceway v Kirklees Metropolitan Council*,[232] if the onus had firmly been on the defendant to show that factor (2) applied. These considerations suggest that it may be wise in some cases to try to join the Revenue but it may prove difficult to obtain the Revenue's consent.[233] Indeed it was said by the Court of Appeal in *Deeny v Gooda Walker*,[234] that the court had been told that it was the first time that the Revenue had been joined by consent to argue the tax issue before the trial judge in relation to a dispute over damages, not being a tax appeal.[235]

**18-058** There is likely to be far less difficulty with proof that factor (1) does or does not apply but it is nonetheless thought that the onus should be also on the defendant here. There seems little point in splitting the onus between the two factors and in any event it may be said that there should be no issue of taxation until a defendant raises it. This certainly was the view taken by Ouseley J in *Finley v Connell Associates*.[236] "It is for the defendants", he said,

> "to show that both factors are satisfied so as to bring the rule in *Gourley* into play because it is the Defendants that seek an exception to the normal rule in relation to the incidence of taxation on damages".[237]

---

228 [1980] 1 W.L.R. 254 CA at 259G.

229 See especially [1980] 1 W.L.R. 254 at 258H to 259H.

230 [1989] S.T.C. 122 CA.

231 [1980] 1 W.L.R. 254 CA.

232 [1989] S.T.C. 122 CA. As the court pointed out, the problem may be solved by the Revenue's acceptance that the compensation would not be taxable, as happened in two further cases of statutory compensation, *West Suffolk County Council v Rought* [1957] A.C. 403 and *McGhie v British Transport Commission* [1963] 1 Q.B. 125 (both at para.18-041, above).

233 The CPR confirms that the Revenue is not to be added as a party to any proceedings except with their consent. They may, however, themselves apply to be joined as a party.

234 [1996] L.R.L.R. 109 CA.

235 [1996] L.R.L.R. 109 CA at 111, col.1. The burden of proof apart, where there is uncertainty whether the damages are to be taxable, it might be possible to award damages without any deduction of tax on the claimant's undertaking to return the amount of damages attributable to the tax element should the damages turn out not to be taxable This was done in the somewhat exceptional case of *4 Eng Ltd v Harper* [2009] Ch. 91, considered at para.18-024, above.

236 [2002] Lloyd's Rep. P.N. 62.

237 [2002] Lloyd's Rep. P.N. 62 at [218].

### (2) Computation for the Gourley rule

18-059 Onus for the computation of the tax to be deducted where *Gourley* applies would seem to present less difficulty. It could well be said that here the onus should be on the claimant on the basis that it is he rather than the defendant who has the knowledge and information necessary for the assessment of the amount to be deducted in respect of tax and that the court, with no material for assessing the proper amount of the deduction, would be in difficulty in arriving at an appropriate amount. While the edge is taken off this argument since the Court of Appeal decided in *Phipps v Orthodox Unit Trusts*[238] that the defendant is entitled to details of the claimant's tax position in a case where the *Gourley* rule applies, it still seems sensible that it should be for the claimant to produce the necessary material for the court; material concerning his other income, his tax allowances, his financial plans for the future.[239]

## 2. CALCULATION OF THE TAX

18-060 In *Gourley*'s case, the House of Lords made it plain that mathematical exactness and accuracy were not required in assessing the deduction to be made on account of tax. Earl Jowitt said it would be unfortunate if their Lordships' decision

> "were to involve an elaborate assessment of tax liability.[240] ... An estimate will be none the worse if it is formed on broad lines, even though it may be described as rough and ready. It is impossible to assess with mathematical accuracy what reduction should be made by reason of the tax position."[241]

Lord Goddard further said[242] that

> "in complicated cases it is to be hoped that the parties, with the help of accountants, will be able to agree figures".

In its Report which followed hard on the heels of the *Gourley* decision[243] the Law Reform Committee pointed out that the figure for tax liability can normally be calculated before trial and is rarely the subject of argument in court.[244] But there are exceptional cases, and the Law Reform Committee did not approve of a proposal that the question should be settled in chambers by an assessor before trial, since in the exceptional case where figures cannot be agreed by the parties it will not be so much a questions of figures

---

238 [1958] 1 Q.B. 314 CA.

239 For the relevance of these see paras 18-061 and 18-062, below.

240 His observations were confined to damages for personal injury, but they are of general application. Wynn-Parry J in *Re Houghton Main Colliery Co* [1956] 1 W.L.R. 1219 at 1224 considered them applicable to damages for wrongful dismissal. And see Lord Reid in *Lewis v Daily Telegraph* [1964] A.C. 234 at 262: "damages for libel have to be assessed by a jury, and juries are not expected to make mathematical calculations, so they can only deal with this matter on broad lines."

241 [1956] A.C. 185 at 203–204. See, too, at 208, 215, per Lord Goddard and Lord Reid respectively.

242 [1956] A.C. 185 at 208.

243 (1958) Cmnd. 501.

244 (1958) Cmnd. 501 at [13].

> "as of an imponderable arising from the plaintiff's future pattern of life, and a matter no less suitable for decision by a judge than by an assessor".[245]

In any event nothing has come of any such proposal.

**18-061** There seems little doubt that the assessment of tax liability will be based upon present rates of tax, and also on present rates of reliefs and allowances.[246] Lord Goddard in *Gourley*'s case said that, in so far as no one can foresee whether rates of tax will go up or down, he would, in directing a jury, advise them "not to speculate on the subject but to deal with it as matters are at present".[247] The court should of course take into account any changes which have already occurred between the date the cause of action arose and the date of judgment to the extent that they are relevant to assessing the claimant's loss.[248] In *Daniels v Jones*,[249] the court properly took note of the fact that the introduction of substantial surtax reliefs on earned income had been proposed in the current Budget, although there was no certainty at the time of the court's judgment that these proposals would become law.[250] In *Amstrad Plc v Seagate Technology Inc*,[251] Judge Humphrey Lloyd went further and, in the context of ascertaining the tax not on the lost profits or earnings but on the damages, ordered that no judgment should be entered until after it was known whether the imminent Budget statement brought in a change in the rate of corporation tax.[252] Difficulties, however, arise when the question of the future pattern of the claimant's life falls to be considered. Thus, if a bachelor is likely to marry and have a family, his allowances would in future increase. Whether any investment income of the claimant is likely to continue, or whether he is likely to become entitled to investment income in the future, would be relevant. Particularly important is the question whether the claimant would probably have taken steps to reduce his future tax liability by taking tax avoidance measures within the law. A dictum in Lord Goddard's speech in *Gourley*'s case gives some assistance here. He said:

> "In cases where surtax[253] is payable and the rate has been affected by private income, the nature of that private income will be relevant. If it is a life annuity under a will or settlement it may well be expected to continue. If it is disposable investments which might be sold at any time or transferred to a child less, perhaps little, regard should be had to it."[254]

This dictum was applied in *Beach v Reed Corrugated Cases*,[255] a case of wrongful dismissal. The claimant had a large private income consisting of disposable investments. Out of his total income, earned and unearned, he paid away substantial

---

245 (1958) Cmnd. 501 at [13].

246 Occasionally, however, it is an assessment of foreign tax liability that will have to be made: see, e.g. *Winkworth v Hubbard* [1960] 1 Lloyd's Rep. 150 where the figures appear to have been agreed between the parties.

247 [1956] A.C. 185 at 209. Citing in *Johnson v Fourie* [2011] EWHC 1062 (QB) this ruling of Lord Goddard, Owen J declined to take into account statements of the Chancellor of the Exchequer of his intent to reduce rates of income tax and of corporation tax in the future: at [140]–[145].

248 In *Hall v Pearlberg* [1956] 1 W.L.R. 244 the court was in error in deducting at the tax rate prevailing at judgment as opposed to the rate at the earlier date when the loss in respect of which damages were being given was incurred.

249 [1961] 1 W.L.R. 1103 CA.

250 [1961] 1 W.L.R. 1103 CA at 1116, per Pearson LJ.

251 (1998) 86 B.L.R. 34.

252 For the relevance of this, see para.18-019, above.

253 Now higher rate tax.

254 [1956] A.C. 185 at 209.

255 [1956] 1 W.L.R. 807.

amounts under covenant to his ex-wife and to friends and relatives, and Pilcher J accepted his evidence that he intended in the immediate future both substantially to increase these amounts and to hand over substantial sums of capital to his wife and children. In these circumstances it was held that comparatively little regard should be had to the claimant's private income when arriving at the amount by which the damages should be reduced on account of tax. Pilcher J said that there was nothing to prevent the claimant, after making his proposed capital gifts, from setting aside sufficient income-producing investments to pay the covenanted sums, and investing the rest of his capital in non-income-bearing investments with prospects of capital appreciation, provided he kept enough ready money in the bank for immediate requirements.[256] Today the likelihood of substantial Gift Aid payments by the claimant could be relevant.

In calculating the amount to be deducted on account of income tax, it is clear that the gross sum to which the *Gourley* rule is to be applied is to be treated as spread over the years in which the moneys would have accrued to the claimant but for the tort or breach of contract.[257] To the amount so deducted it may, however, be occasionally necessary to calculate, and add in, a further amount where the damages are themselves taxable and modified *Gourley* in reverse ought to apply.[258] What the cases have not made so clear is how far the calculation is affected by other income which the claimant may possess. In *Re Houghton Main Colliery Co*,[259] Wynn-Parry J was not prepared to accept that the amount in respect of which damages were being awarded should be regarded as the top slice of the claimant's income, preferring to regard it as neither the top nor the bottom slice.[260] Logically, however, as was first pointed out in the 13th edition of this work in 1972, the contention that it should be regarded as the top slice is correct, and this was accepted by the Court of Appeal in *Lyndale Fashion Manufacturers v Rich*.[261] Orr LJ, with whom the other members of the court agreed, said that the relevant question, namely how much larger would the claimant's tax have been had he received the commission for the loss of which he was suing, **18-062**

> "admits of only one answer, for if a comparison is to be made between a given income and that income with something added, the addition must be treated as the top part of the income"[262];

and to the extent that Wynn-Parry J's view in *Re Houghton Main Colliery Co* was to the contrary, he, Orr LJ, rightly would not accept it.[263] Now rather late in the day, in the context of damages claims by employees for wrongful dismissal, the income

---

256 [1956] 1 W.L.R. 807 at 815.

257 See *Re Houghton Main Colliery Co* [1956] 1 W.L.R. 1219 where the spreading technique was used in relation to the calculation of damages for loss of pension rights.

258 For explanation of modified *Gourley* and *Gourley* in reverse, see paras 18-005 and 18-023 to 18-024, above, respectively.

259 [1956] 1 W.L.R. 1219.

260 [1956] 1 W.L.R. 1219 at 1224 to 1225.

261 [1973] 1 W.L.R. 73 CA; facts at para.18-047, above.

262 [1973] 1 W.L.R. 73 CA at 79E.

263 [1973] 1 W.L.R. 73 CA at 79F. In *Bold v Brough, Nicholson & Hall Ltd* [1964] 1 W.L.R. 201, Phillimore J misguidedly went even further and, in a claim for wrongful dismissal, made the calculation in respect of the £5,000 which was not subject to tax on the footing that it was the bottom slice of the claimant's income. See *Hartley v Sandholme Iron Co* [1975] Q.B. 600 where the need to deduct from the damages for loss of earnings a rebate of tax made because too much tax had now been deducted at source for the part of the tax year preceding the claimant's injury can only have arisen because the damages otherwise being awarded had not been regarded as the top slice of the

tax legislation imposing tax on such damages has provided indirect support for this clearly correct position. In 2007 there has been inserted in the Income Tax (Earnings and Pensions) Act 2003 a new s.404A[264] which provides, in subs.(1), that a payment to a person which is subject to the statutory tax is treated as the highest part of his total income. If then the amount awarded as damages for wrongful dismissal is to be regarded as the highest part of the employee's income for the purposes of the statutory tax, it must be equally so regarded for the purposes of the £30,000 which escapes the statutory tax and is subject to the *Gourley* rule.[265]

## II Capital Gains Tax

### 1. General Considerations

**18-063** Capital gains tax was introduced by the Finance Act 1965 and is now the subject-matter of a legislative consolidation in the Taxation of Chargeable Gains Act 1992. Charged upon gains accruing on the disposal of assets, capital gains tax does not cause damages awards to be reduced in the way that income tax does: there is no equivalent for capital gains tax to *Gourley*'s case[266] for income tax. The reason for this is that there would seem to be no circumstances in which the amount in respect of the loss of which the damages awarded constitute compensation would have been subject to capital gains tax but the damages themselves will not be—no circumstances, in other words, in which both factor (1) and factor (2)[267] are present. Generally speaking, where property is not involved and frequently even where it is, the damages will represent compensation for an income loss or for a non-pecuniary loss, and accordingly factor (1) is absent. Where, on the other hand, the loss is in respect of property, that property may have been a capital asset which was available for disposal, thus making the presence of factor (1) a possibility; but it is reasonably clear that if on any occasion factor (1) should be present, by the same token factor (2) will be absent and the award will be subject to capital gains tax. For, although the general charging section of the Taxation of Chargeable Gains Act 1992, which is s.1, makes it clear that there can be no liability to capital gains tax in the absence of a disposal of assets and it might be thought that the mere receipt of a damages award in respect of a property loss could not constitute such a disposal, the meaning given to disposal of assets by s.22(1) of the Act is sufficiently wide to catch such an award. That subsection provides that for the purposes of capital gains tax there is a disposal of assets

> "where any capital sum is derived from assets notwithstanding that no asset is acquired by the person paying the capital sum",

and specifies in sub-paragraph (a) the case of:

> "capital sums received by way of compensation for any kind of damage or injury to assets or for the loss, destruction or dissipation of assets or for any depreciation or risk of depreciation of an asset."

---

claimant's income.

264 By Sch.1 Pt 2 para.437 to the Income Tax Act 2007.

265 For the details of the statutory tax and its impingement on damages awards see paras 18-042 to 18-046, above.

266 [1956] A.C. 185.

267 See paras 18-005 to 18-024, above.

Indeed the problem which is posed by the introduction of capital gains tax is not whether damages awards need be reduced in order to ensure that claimants are not over-compensated but whether, in the light of the wide meaning given to disposal of assets by s.22(1), the damages awards themselves may be taxable. For if s.22(1) treats the deriving of capital sums from assets as disposals[268] and if, as is clear from the provision of s.21(1)[269] that all forms of property shall be assets for capital gains tax purposes, rights of action are assets, it would seem that every damages award constitutes a disposal of an asset.[270] And this proposition finds dramatic support from the important decision in *Zim Properties v Procter*.[271] Solicitors had settled a claim against them for negligence which had lost the taxpayer company an advantageous sale of certain properties which it owned and Warner J, following the lead of the House of Lords in *O'Brien v Benson's Hosiery (Holdings)*,[272] held that, where there was a right to bring an action to seek to enforce a claim which might not succeed but which was neither frivolous nor vexatious and that right could be turned to account by negotiating a compromise yielding a capital sum, the right constituted an asset for capital gains tax purposes and the settlement figure was a capital sum subject to capital gains tax.[273] This gives rise to the further question whether, if the occasion should arise where a claimant can show that damages awarded will be subject to capital gains tax but that there would have been no charge to capital gains tax in respect of the loss for which those damages represented compensation, such claimant may then claim an appropriate increase in the award, praying in aid, in a somewhat unusual context, the principle that a wrongdoer must take his victim as he finds him.[274] Such a situation could have arisen in *Zim Properties v Procter*,[275] where the capital gains tax fell on the amount by which the properties had declined in value between the date of the contract and the date set for the completion which never took place,[276] an amount which in no way represented a potential chargeable gain available to the company. The case indicates, however, that if the ultimate value of the claim is precisely the value it has at the moment that the right to claim is deemed to have been acquired, the charge to tax is reduced to nil, and it may be that this feature would eliminate any charge to capital gains tax in the vast majority of cases. Yet no such elimination may now be possible since changes in the capital gains tax legislation would seem to entail that, in the tax computation, the value of the claim is no longer to be deductible. **18-064**

Fortunately the danger of damages falling into these deep and murky tax waters has been largely avoided since the publication by the Revenue some four years after **18-065**

---

268 The particular capital sums specified in the four sub-paragraphs of s.22(1) are only to be regarded as illustrations of the general provision of the subsection; sub-para.(c) does, however, specify capital sums received in return for the surrender of rights.

269 Enacting that "all forms of property shall be assets … including (a) … incorporeal property generally, and … (c) any form of property … coming to be owned without being acquired".

270 This would explain why it was thought necessary to enact in s.51(2) of the Taxation of Chargeable Gains Act 1992 that "it is hereby declared" that certain damages awards are not chargeable gains: see para.18-067, below.

271 (1985) 58 T.C. 371.

272 [1980] A.C. 562.

273 See, too, *Pennine Raceway v Kirklees Metropolitan Council (No.2)* [1989] S.T.C. 122 CA where compensation awarded under the Town and Country Planning Act 1971 was held to be a capital sum derived from assets within the subsection, then s.20(1) of the Capital Gains Tax Act 1979.

274 A principle which, though normally associated with tort, has application also to contract: see paras 8-092 and following and paras 8-187 and following, above.

275 (1985) 58 T.C. 371.

276 The facts are set out at para.18-076, below.

the decision in *Zim Properties v Procter*,[277] of an Extra-Statutory Concession, now D33,[278] which almost entirely nullifies the effect of the decision. The concessionary treatment differs depending upon whether the cause of action giving rise to the damages does or does not relate to an underlying asset. If an underlying asset is involved, as where there is tortious damage to or misappropriation of property, failure to deliver or accept property sold or negligent professional advice in relation to a sale of property, any gain accruing on the disposal of the right of action giving rise to the damages is to be computed as if the damages derived from the asset itself[279] and not from the right of action.[280] Where there is no underlying asset involved, any gain accruing on the disposal of the right of action giving rise to the damages is exempted from capital gains tax.[281] Not surprisingly the result of this huge concession is that *Zim* has had no progeny and does not appear to have been heard of in the 25 years since the promulgation of the Extra-Statutory Concession.[282]

**18-066** Nonetheless a text on damages needs to be sure that no damages problems still lurk darkly in the interstices of taxation. Accordingly, we must examine particular type-situations in which the problem of the taxability of damages awards may arise. The concessionary treatment is of course what now matters but for clarity, and concessions being concessions, it is sensible, in dealing with the various type-situations, first to set out the strict position and then to turn to the impact, if any, of the concession upon that position.[283]

## 2. TORT

### (1) Torts affecting the person

**18-067** Any possible argument that damages for personal injury, wrongful death, defamation and the like are subject to capital gains tax is avoided by the express declaration, in s.51(2) of the Taxation of Chargeable Gains Act 1992, that

> "sums obtained by way of compensation or damages for any wrong or injury suffered by an individual in his person or in his profession or vocation are not chargeable gains."

**18-068** The concession therefore has no application. Indeed the Revenue recognises this in the concession itself, referring to s.51(2) and specifically stating that it covers, in relation to individuals, physical injury, unfair or unlawful discrimination, libel and slander and, in relation to relatives and personal representatives, fatal accidents.[284] With or without the concession no damages problem can arise.

---

277 (1985) 58 T.C. 371.

278 Entitled *Capital gains tax on compensation and damages*, issued in, and effective from, December 1988, and still appearing under the same title in HMRC's list of Extra-Statutory Concessions as at 6 April 2013.

279 The taxpayer had unsuccessfully argued that this was the true position in *Zim*.

280 Extra-Statutory Concession D33, para.9.

281 Extra-Statutory Concession D33, para.11.

282 Apart from *Zim*'s being applied in *Pennine Raceway v Kirklees Metropolitan Council (No.2)* [1989] S.T.C. 122 CA, a case decided at the very beginning of the month in which concession D33 was issued and became effective, cases in which *Zim* has even been cited have not been found.

283 D. Wilde, "Damages and Capital Gains Tax" (1991) *British Tax Review* 5, suggests that even with the concession difficulties remain and argues that it would be best if *Zim* were declared by the courts to be wrongly decided.

284 Extra-Statutory Concession D33, para.12.

## (2) Torts affecting property

If damages received in relation to a property loss tortiously inflicted constitute a trading receipt,[285] no question of capital gains tax can arise,[286] and even if the receipt is a capital receipt the exemptions from capital gains tax for private residences, for chattels disposed of for £6,000 or less, or for chattels which are wasting assets[287] will apply in appropriate cases. However, aside from this, by virtue of the provision of s.22(1)(a) of the Taxation of Chargeable Gains Act 1992 that there is a disposal of assets where a capital sum is received by way of compensation for any kind of damage or injury to assets or for the loss, destruction or dissipation of assets or for any depreciation or risk of depreciation of an asset,[288] it follows that if the claimant is holding property of a market value higher than at the date he acquired it so that he has a potential capital gain in his hands, then if he recovers damages for the tortious misappropriation, destruction or damage of the property which reflect the increased market value, he will be required to pay capital gains tax on the increase in value of the whole, if destroyed or misappropriated, or of part, if damaged. He has in effect been forced by the tort to realise his potential capital gain. **18-069**

There are, however, certain ways of postponing, though not of escaping, the capital gains tax. By s.23 of the Act provision is made for the recipient of the damages, where he uses the whole sum to replace or repair the property, to claim in effect to postpone the capital gains tax charge until a subsequent disposal by him of the replacement or of the repaired property.[289] If he only uses part of the damages towards replacement or repair, then the intention is that he pay capital gains tax on the part not so used.[290] If in the case of repair the part not used is not reasonably required and is small compared with the whole damages, postponement until subsequent disposal is again allowed,[291] and even if none of the damages is used in repair, the capital gains tax charge can be postponed in this way should the amount of the damages be small compared with the value of the property.[292] These provisions as to repair do not, however, apply to wasting assets.[293] **18-070**

What then is the tax position in respect of any gain that has not been postponed in one of the above ways? The concession does not appear to give any benefit here. The right of action will have arisen at the time of misappropriation, destruction or damage and its value is likely to be represented by the value of the property misappropriated or destroyed, or the diminution in the value of the property damaged. The tax computation will therefore be the same whether the damages are regarded as derived from the asset itself or as derived from the right of action The question that **18-071**

---

285 See paras 18-033 to 18-041, above.

286 See s.37 of the Taxation of Chargeable Gains Act 1992 expressly provides that sums chargeable to income tax are outside the charge to capital gains tax.

287 See Taxation of Chargeable Gains Act 1992 ss.222 to 226B, 262 and 45 respectively.

288 See para.18-063, above.

289 See s.23(4) as to replacement and s.23(1)(a) as to repair.

290 See s.23(5) as to replacement and s.23(3) as to repair. There are similar provisions in ss.152 to 159 in relation to the replacement, as opposed to the repair, of a limited class of business assets, but it does not appear to be necessary to resort to the relief afforded by these in view of the wider provisions of s.23.

291 Section 23(1)(b).

292 Section 23(1)(c).

293 Section 23(8). This subsection has been substituted for the original s.23(6) which had excluded wasting assets entirely from the section. Wasting assets are broadly defined as assets with a predictable life not exceeding 50 years: see s.44.

then arises is whether the claimant can successfully argue for an increase in the damages to cover the payment of this tax. It would not appear to be appropriate simply to add the tax to the damages since this would eliminate the taxpayer's eventual liability to tax on an actual disposal of the property. The most that could be awarded would be some form of interest to mark the disadvantage of paying the tax now rather than at a later date. But at what later date would there have been disposal, if at all? It is thought to be improbable that courts would wish to become entangled in such difficulties of computation and that no addition to the damages would be made on account of tax.

## 3. CONTRACT

### (1) Contracts of employment: wrongful dismissal

**18-072** No charge to capital gains tax falls upon damages awarded for wrongful dismissal. This must clearly be so in respect of any award in excess of £30,000 since this excess is subject to income tax under the provisions now in ss.401 to 404A of the Income Tax (Earnings and Pensions) Act 2003.[294] It is also, but less clearly, so in respect of the initial £30,000 which is exempted from income tax.[295] The reason why this disposal, within the meaning of that term in s.22(1) of the Taxation of Chargeable Gains Act 1992,[296] does not attract capital gains tax is to be found in s.52 which, read together with s.37, extends the exemption from capital gains tax of amounts taken into account in computing the profits or gains of an employment for the purposes of income tax to amounts which would be so taken into account but for the fact that the profits or gains are not chargeable to income tax.

**18-073** The concession therefore is not required to ensure that the damages will not be subject to capital gains tax. Since also the amount in respect of the loss of which the damages constitute compensation would clearly not have suffered capital gains tax, no damages issue presents itself.

### (2) Contracts for the sale of property: failure to perform

**18-074** Damages for breach of contract awarded to the seller or buyer of property may be outside the charge to capital gains tax, in the first place, because they constitute a trading receipt subject to income tax[297] or, in the second place, because the property is of a type which falls within one of the general exemptions from capital gains tax.[298] However, in so far as the deriving of capital sums from assets is treated as a disposal of assets,[299] it would seem that, where there is a sale of property and a failure to accept by the buyer at a time when the market price has dropped below the contract price, the normal measure of damages for non-acceptance could, under the strict position, be subject to a charge to capital gains tax. And in the converse case of a failure to deliver by the seller at a time when the market price has risen above the contract price, the normal measure of damages for non-delivery could similarly, again under the strict position, be subject to a charge.

---

[294] See para.18-043 above; and therefore outside the charge to capital gains tax: see para.18-069, above.
[295] See para.18-043, above.
[296] See paras 18-063 and 18-064, above.
[297] See paras 18-051 to 18-055, above.
[298] See para.18-069, above.
[299] See para.18-063, above.

Under the concession the seller here should be liable to tax as upon a part disposal of the asset; it may be that under the strict position he would be liable for less, but consideration of this need not delay us. The important point, for damages, is that no argument is available for an increase in the damages to cover the payment of the tax because, had the buyer not been in breach, the sale would have gone through and the seller would have been liable to the tax upon the full purchase price. On the other hand, in the converse case there would have been no tax for the buyer to pay had the sale gone through without breach by the seller since he was only acquiring and not disposing of the asset, but now with the damages it would seem that he will be liable as on a part disposal of it. The question that then again arises is whether the buyer can successfully argue for an increase in the damages to cover the payment of this tax. It is thought that he cannot, because the charge to tax will only be anticipating the potential gain that he would have had on his hands had the purchase gone through, and it is virtually impossible for the court to afford compensation for the early charge to tax which has been forced upon him since it cannot be known or judged when in the normal course the gain might have been realised.[300] **18-075**

### (3) Contracts for professional services: negligent advice

In *Zim Properties v Procter*,[301] the taxpayer company had contracted in July 1973 to sell certain properties for £175,000 but the negligence of the company's solicitors gave the purchasers the opportunity properly to refuse to complete in July 1974, by which time the property market had collapsed. The company's claim against the solicitors for some £100,000, almost all of which represented the difference between the purchase price and the market value at July 1974, was eventually settled at a figure of £60,000. This amount in settlement was held to be a capital sum derived from the company's right to sue the solicitors and was therefore subject to capital gains tax but after deducting—by virtue of the provision of the then s.22(4) of the Finance Act 1965, now varied by s.17 of the Taxation of Chargeable Gains Act 1992, that an asset not acquired by arm's length bargain is deemed to be acquired at its market value—the value of the right to sue at the time of its acquisition by the company, which was held to be in July 1973. On the assumption that the contract price of £175,000 represented the market value of the properties at the time of contracting, then that acquisition value would be virtually nil making the whole £60,000 chargeable to tax. Yet it is difficult to see this as a potential chargeable gain that the taxpayer company would have made. A later disposal of the properties could, if the market were not to recover, give the company an allowable loss but that might be something that the company could not utilise. Moreover, there is the curiosity that, had the acquisition been held to be at July 1974, as was unsuccessfully argued, rather than at July 1973, the charge to capital gains tax would have been eliminated.[302] And there is the further concern that the substitution of what is **18-076**

---

300 The position is analogous to that with torts affecting property where it is analysed in somewhat more detail: see para.18-071, above.

301 (1985) 58 T.C. 371.

302 The July 1973 acquisition date was arrived at in reliance on *Forster v Outred & Co* [1982] 1 W.L.R. 86 CA, a decision which has since been heavily distinguished and which has been said to be difficult to reconcile with the later House of Lords decision in *Pirelli General Cable Works v Oscar Faber & Partners* [1983] 2 A.C. 1. See paras 11-019 and 11-020, above.

now s.17 of the Taxation of Chargeable Gains Act 1992[303] for the former s.19(3) of the Capital Gains Tax Act 1979,[304] made with certain tax avoidance schemes in mind, whereby the rule of acquisition at market value where acquisition is by non-arm's length bargain no longer applies to an acquisition unaccompanied by a corresponding disposal,[305] suggests that there will necessarily always be a nil acquisition cost whatever is held to be the time of acquisition of the right to claim damages.

**18-077** Here the concession does ameliorate the taxpayer's position. Under it the taxpayer company in *Zim*,[306] would not be liable to tax on a capital gain of the whole £60,000 of the settlement figure but would be entitled to deduct, as on a part disposal, a proportion of the price at which it had acquired the property. The Revenue gives just this type of case as an example of how the concession would work and talks of an entitlement to deduct "an appropriate part of the cost of the building".[307] It is thought that this should be that part of the acquisition cost as bears to the total acquisition cost as the £60,000 received bears to the £175,000 at which the taxpayer company had sold. While this indicates the amount of tax to which a damages award would have been subject, the question remains as to whether the claimant can successfully argue for an increase in the damages to cover the payment of this tax. It is thought that this is unlikely since, had the solicitor not been negligent, the sale would have gone through and the taxpayer company would have been paying tax upon its capital gain by reference to the full contract price. The effect of the negligence is simply to give rise to a charge to tax on a lower figure, upon £60,000 rather than £175,000. On the other hand, had the solicitor's negligence caused a purchase rather than a sale by the claimant to go off at a time when prices had soared, the position should be the same as with the buyer who has lost his profitable bargain not by reason of his solicitor's negligence but because of his seller's non-delivery.[308]

---

303 Which had started life as s.29A of the Capital Gains Tax Act 1979.

304 Which had started life as s.22(4) of the Finance Act 1965.

305 See s.17(2)(a).

306 (1985) 58 T.C. 371.

307 Extra-Statutory Concession D33, para.9.

308 For this, see para.18-075, above. What is said on the topic of tax on damages in *Youlton v Charles Russell* [2010] EWHC 1918 Ch at [2]–[9], where the assignment to the claimant of a cause of action featured, is probably of little or no general value. The reference to *Zim* (at [6]) suggests that the court was concerned with capital gains tax rather than income tax.

CHAPTER 19

# THE AWARDING OF INTEREST

TABLE OF CONTENTS

## I. Introductory

**19-001** In editions of this book before 2008 the chapter on interest, in opening, declared that the early case law upon the recovery of interest is riddled with inconsistency, that this stemmed from the gradual weaning away of the law from the stigma attached by the religion and thought of an earlier day to the taking of usury, that Calvinism by tracing out the narrow distinction between interest and usury had provided the first effective means for the removal of this stigma, but that the law had been slow to follow and had moved haltingly between allowance and disallowance of interest. The chapter proceeded to set out, as best it could, the way this halting process continued over the years up to the present, thereby lending detailed support to Lord Goff's comment in *Westdeutsche Landesbank Girozentrale v Islington Borough Council*,[1] that "our law of interest has developed in a fragmentary and unsatisfactory manner".

**19-002** Then upon an unsuspecting and unexpecting legal world there burst the decision of the House of Lords in *Sempra Metals Ltd v Inland Revenue Commissioners*,[2] a decision which could claim to be about the most important in the law of damages in quite some time. Their Lordships were, in the words of Lord Mance,[3] invited radically to reshape the law and radically reshape it they have. This called for a substantial rewriting of this chapter; indeed it was entirely recast.

**19-003** It was a complicated task. This may be said to be because their Lordships' decision knocked the existing law sideways. Whereas before *Sempra Metals* statutory interest awards tended to hold the day with what may be called common law interest awards staying on the sidelines, their Lordships brought the latter into clear prominence. Not only was this so but the relationship between the two was much clarified. Beforehand, in many minds the two were not clearly distinguished and were seen as running into one another. While it may be that the real and proper terminological distinction remained, that between statutory interest and common law interest, we now had a neat, sensible and easy distinction, one which was already becoming known and which had previously featured somewhat in this text. This is the distinction between interest *on* damages, for statutory interest, and interest *as* damages, for common law interest. We built on this distinction.

**19-004** In these circumstances it was thought best to examine the law as it stood at the time of *Sempra Metals*, looking separately at interest at common law in a range of particular cases and particular type situations, and then at interest under the statute, generally less generous, in a greater number of cases and in the same type situations. This was, and is, followed by an examination of *Sempra Metals* itself and of its impact on all that has gone before. That done, we turn to the rules concerning the calculation of the interest to be awarded. These required far less emendation so that the structure of the second half of the chapter remains as before.

1 [1996] A.C. 669 at 682F.
2 [2008] A.C. 561.
3 [2008] A.C. 561 at [205].

## II. THE POSITION BEFORE SEMPRA METALS[4]

### (A) INTEREST OUTSIDE STATUTE: INTEREST AS DAMAGES

### (1) CONTRACT: OBLIGATIONS TO PAY MONEY

**(i) Common law** The first cases on interest and damages practically all concern failures to pay moneys due under a contract and so could be said to be more concerned with debt than with damages. They start by allowing interest to be recovered. Thus in the very early *Blaney v Hendrick*,[5] it was held that "when money lent becomes due, it carries interest from the day it becomes payable"[6] and in *Mountford v Willes*,[7] interest was similarly awarded on the unpaid price of goods sold. Yet even at that time it was by no means all one way and we find in 1807 in the reporter's notes to *De Havilland v Bowerbank*,[8] in the English Reports the comment that **19-005**

> "it would unfortunately be a very difficult matter to fix upon another point of English law on which the authorities are so little in harmony with each other".[9]

Indeed in that case Lord Ellenborough showed himself to be generally against interest, giving a very limited list of cases, all in contract, in which interest might be recovered,[10] and thereby ushered in the trend towards the refusal of interest as damages for the failure to pay money, a trend which became established in the next quarter of a century. In contradistinction to the earlier cases, interest was thus refused in *Gordon v Swan*,[11] upon a failure to pay the price of goods sold on the due date and in *Page v Newman*,[12] upon a failure to repay a loan.[13] *Page* was the real turning point.[14] It was a decision that was particularly relied upon by the House of

4 For the effect on a claimant's entitlement to interest of his being indemnified against his loss by his insurers, see the varying results in *Harbutt's "Plasticine" v Wayne Tank and Pump Co* [1970] 1 Q.B. 447 CA and *Cousins & Co v D. and C. Carriers* [1971] 2 Q.B. 230 CA (at para.19-044, below) and *Metal Box v Currys* [1988] 1 W.L.R. 175 (at para.19-046, below).

5 (1771) 3 Wils. 205.

6 (1771) 3 Wils. 205 at 206.

7 (1800) 2 B. & P. 337.

8 (1807) 1 Camp. 50.

9 170 E.R. 872 at 873.

10 "Interest ought to be allowed by law," he said, "only in cases where there is a contract for the payment of money on a certain day, as on bills of exchange, promissory notes, etc.; where there has been an express promise to pay interest; or where, from the course of dealing between the parties, it may be inferred that this was their intention; or where it can be proved that the money has been used, and interest has actually been made": (1807) 1 Camp. 50, 51. The legislature added somewhat to Lord Ellenborough's contractual list in s.28 of the Civil Procedure Act 1833 (see at para.19-030, below) but many cases slipped through that narrowly drawn provision, including the important *London, Chatham & Dover Ry v S.E. Ry* [1893] A.C. 429 itself.

11 (1810) 12 East 419.

12 (1829) 9 B. & C. 378.

13 Interest was also refused in *Higgins v Sargent* (1823) 2 B. & C. 348 upon a failure to pay money due under an insurance policy and in *Foster v Weston* (1830) 6 Bing. 709 upon a failure to pay money due under a deed.

14 In this development the influence of the old usury stigma (see para.19-001, above) is here subtly present. The ground for the refusal of interest given by *Bullen & Leake* 3rd edn (1868), p.51 was that it was "generally presumed not to be within the contemplation of the parties", so that if interest were not expressly or impliedly contracted for when this course was open to the parties, as here, the law was not to give interest by way of damages. It is this rationale of the rule that lends cohe-

Lords in holding at the end of the 19th century in *London, Chatham & Dover Ry v S.E. Ry*[15] that, although this common law rule was to be regretted, it was now ingrained and only legislation could effect a change.[16]

**19-006** In 1934 the legislature did effect a change and it might be thought that, once a general entitlement to be awarded interest on damages had been introduced, the inability to award interest as damages on the payment of money would cease to matter. This however is not so. Apart from the new entitlement lying in the court's discretion, statutory interest suffered, as we shall see,[17] from two limitations: it was restricted to interest that was simple and it was restricted to interest on the amount of damages awarded. So there was still scope for cases challenging the decision in *London, Chatham & Dover Ry v S.E. Ry*,[18] which lay across the path of progress in the law of damages.[19]

**19-007** Such a case made its appearance in the House of Lords in *The President of India*

---

sion to the exceptions to it which developed in the 19th century. Thus in *Petre v Duncombe* an annuity was not paid by the grantor, so that his surety had to pay it. Not only did the surety recover from the grantor the amount he had paid the third party but he was awarded interest as damages, Erle J saying that "the cases upon direct contracts for the payment of money which omit mention of interest are well distinguished on the ground that the intention of the parties is presumed to be expressed in the terms of their contract". Another more general exception appears where the defendant has promised to pay a certain sum on a certain day with interest at a fixed rate till then; in a number of cases, mainly concerning mortgage deeds and of which *Cook v Fowler* is the chief, interest has been allowed as damages upon failure to pay the principal on the due date. That such an award was in the nature of damages has been highlighted by the fact that the fixed contractual rate has been too high to be adopted as the rate for failure to pay upon time: *Cook v Fowler* (1874) L.R. 7 H.L. 27 (contractual rate 60 per cent, damages rate 5 per cent); *Re Roberts* (1880) 14 Ch. D. 49 CA (contractual rate 10 per cent, damages rate 5 per cent).

15 [1893] A.C. 429.

16 It is interesting to find that there are scattered dicta in several 19th century cases which state generally that interest is recoverable as damages for non-payment of money. These cases are of two types. First, there are those where the defendant's default was a failure to deliver goods, and the court referred to the analogous case of a defendant's failure to pay money where, it was said, interest is included in the damages: *Fletcher v Tayleur* (1855) 17 C.B. 21 at 29, per Willes J, and *British Columbia Saw Mill Co v Nettleship* (1868) L.R. 3 C.P. 499 at 507, per Bovill CJ: see para.30-002, below. Secondly, there are cases of non-payment of money where the claimant has successfully recovered damages going well beyond mere interest by showing that the contract was a special one and that the special loss claimed was within the parties' contemplation, in all of which the court assumed that in the normal case of non-payment of money interest is recoverable: *Prehn v Royal Bank of Liverpool* (1870) L.R. 5 Ex. 92 at 100, per Pigott B, and *Larios v Bonany y Gurety* (1873) L.R. 5 P.C. 346 at 357: see paras 30-007 and 30-008, below. Any suggestion built upon such dicta that interest was generally awardable at common law could not stand against the cases in the text culminating in the authoritative *London, Chatham & Dover Ry v S.E. Ry* [1893] A.C. 429. See *Trans Trust S.P.R.L. v Danubian Trading Co* [1952] 2 Q.B. 297 CA at 306, where Denning LJ said that the law "did undoubtedly refuse to award interest until the recent statute". There was however one never doubted exception to the general rule. Damages for failure to pay a bill of exchange or promissory note have always included interest, and s.57 of the Bills of Exchange Act 1882 gave legislative sanction to this particular rule: see paras 30-012 and following, below where the measure of damages for the dishonour of bills and notes is fully dealt with.

17 At paras 19-036 to 19-042, below.

18 [1893] A.C. 429.

19 Where the failure to pay money is not by the defendant but by a third party, the *London, Chatham & Dover Ry* rule does not stand in the way of the recovery of interest as damages. This was the position in *WM Nelson Cladding Ltd v Murray Williamson Builders Ltd* (2000) 16 Const. L.J. 75 where a main contractor claimed damages from a sub-contractor on account of the sub-contractor's failure to carry out work properly. This failure had caused the employer's architect to decline to issue a certificate certifying payment to the main contractor who as a result suffered financing charges by way of overdraft interest which he was able to recover as damages.

*v La Pintada Compania Navigacion*,[20] sometimes referred to simply as the *La Pintada* case,[21] where the claimants sought to recover interest on moneys paid to them after commencement of proceedings. Because of the then restriction of the 1934 Act to awarding interest on the amount of judgment,[22] recovery of interest was only possible at common law. However, the insidious influence of *London, Chatham & Dover Ry v S.E. Ry*,[23] continued to prevail and the House of Lords was unprepared, though reluctantly, to depart from it. Lord Brandon in the leading speech gave three reasons for this, all of which are connected to the legislative intervention and none of which, as we shall later see, is at all convincing. His first and main reason was that the injustice of the decision had been largely removed by the legislative introduction of statutory interest.[24] His second was, in effect, that one could not go outside the statute within which the particular case technically could not fall.[25] His third was that it would not be right to admit two rival systems for the recovery of interest, statutory and non-statutory.[26]

Yet a few years before *La Pintada* was decided, the Court of Appeal had been **19-008** more bold and, presented in *Wadsworth v Lydall*[27] with another situation where statutory interest was restricted, here on account of the limitation to simple interest, had made an award at common law of interest as damages, an award which was not restricted to simple interest. Relying on earlier observations made by Denning LJ in *Trans Trust S.P.R.L. v Danubian Trading Co*,[28] that the only real ground for not awarding interest on the non-payment of money was that it was not in the contemplation of the parties and therefore too remote,[29] the Court of Appeal held that the *London, Chatham & Dover Ry* decision did not preclude an award of interest as damages for breach of an obligation to pay money where the defaulting payer had been well aware that not having the money would put the payee into difficulties with a purchase he had made on the strength of its expected receipt, requiring him to pay interest charges to his purchaser.[30] The interest awarded was effectively compound interest, unavailable under the statutory regime. Nothing indeed is specifically said by the Court of Appeal of compound interest in *Wadsworth v Lydall* but the whole object of the claim must have been to obtain interest that was compounded, as there is no reason to think that the claimant would not have been entitled to claim statutory simple interest.

*Wadsworth v Lyall* came before *La Pintada* and Lord Brandon clearly had to deal **19-009** with it in his speech. While approving it, he interpreted Brightman LJ's reasoning there, it has always been thought without any justification, as referring only to special damages within the second rule in *Hadley v Baxendale* and excluding general damages under the first rule. It may be that this interpretation was forced

---

20 [1985] A.C. 104.

21 As in the speeches in *Sempra Metals Ltd v IRC* [2008] A.C. 561.

22 It had been amended by the time their Lordships had reached their decision: see para.19-040, below.

23 [1893] A.C. 429.

24 [1985] A.C. 104 at 129H.

25 See [1985] A.C. 104, 130A to 131A. For the reason that the statute was inapplicable see para.19-040, below.

26 [1985] A.C. 104, 131A to D.

27 [1981] 1 W.L.R. 598 CA.

28 [1952] 2 Q.B. 297 CA.

29 The passage is cited at para.38-003, below.

30 For the full facts see para.25-133, below.

upon Lord Brandon to conform with his reasons[31] for not departing from the *London, Chatham & Dover Ry* rule, but, as has been said in earlier editions, it is an odd conclusion that interest should be irrecoverable although obviously foreseeable and yet recoverable where foreseeable only because of special circumstances brought to the knowledge of the defendant. Lord Brandon's approach came to be much criticised.[32] But for the moment the law rested there.

**19-010** **(ii) Equity** The common law's inhibitions over interest never affected equity. Equity's preparedness to award interest where the obligation is to pay money, in particular where there has been an unpaid purchase price, can be seen in a number of early cases. In *Re Pigott and the Great Western Rly Co*,[33] which concerned a rather special type of contract, it is said in the headnote that the ordinary rules as between vendor and purchaser applied,

> "including the liability for the purchasing company, in a proper case, to pay interest on their unpaid purchase price".

In *Re Shaw and the Corporation of Birmingham*,[34] interest fell to be paid on what was there regarded as purchase money. In *Marsh v Jones*,[35] where a lessor had agreed to buy machinery from his outgoing tenant, the latter recovered interest as damages for delay in paying for the machinery. Cotton LJ said[36] that the case was not one of interest as incidental to specific performance[37] but of damages and in his opinion the plaintiff was "entitled by way of damages to interest" from the time the defendant took possession.[38] These are all very early cases; nothing later in the same vein seems to have appeared. Interest of course will have remained available in precisely the same way after the 1934 introduction of statutory interest as before.

**19-011** **(iii) Admiralty** We shall see that there has been a long tradition of awarding interest in ship collision cases in the Admiralty courts[39] so that it would not be surprising to find these courts awarding interest where there has been a contractual failure to pay money. That this was so may be suggested by a ruling of the House of Lords in *The President of India v La Pintada Compania Navigacion*,[40] appearing in the speech of Lord Brandon on whom the other Lords largely relied, to the effect that the Admiralty Court had never had power to award interest on debts already paid before judgment,[41] which at that time could not be done by way of statutory interest.[42] This may imply that there were other circumstances in which

---

31 At para.19-007, above.

32 Notably by Staughton J in *President of India v Lips Maritime Corp* [1985] 2 Lloyd's Rep. 180 at 185.

33 (1881) 18 Ch. D. 146.

34 (1884) 27 Ch. D. 614.

35 (1889) 40 Ch. D. 563 CA.

36 (1889) 40 Ch. D. 563 CA at 566.

37 It appears to have been accepted that in a claim for specific performance there would be interest for the period from breach to performance.

38 For recovery of interest in equity rather than at common law, but in the context of tort, see also *Phillips v Homfray* [1892] 1 Ch. 465 CA.

39 See paras 19-020 and 19-023, below.

40 [1985] A.C. 104.

41 Thereby overruling *Tehno-Impex v Geb Van Weelde Scheepvaartkantoor* [1981] Q.B. 648 CA and reinstating *The Medina Princess* [1962] 2 Lloyd's Rep. 17.

42 See para.19-040, below.

the Admiralty Court was properly awarding interest as damages under its own jurisdiction; an alternative interpretation, however, is that awards in other circumstances would have had to be under the statutory power.[43]

### (2) CONTRACT: OBLIGATIONS RELATING TO PROPERTY

**(a) Goods** In obligations relating to goods interest did feature in the early cases in a limited way thus. Where the defendant has failed to deliver goods, as under a contract of sale, manufacture or carriage, or has failed to deliver them upon time, the claimant is entitled to claim the loss of the value of the use of the goods up till the time when he could reasonably have obtained substitute goods or during the period of delay, as the case may be. This award of the value of the use of the goods takes the place of interest, namely the value of the use of money, and accordingly it is not required, and would be improper, to award interest as well. The analogy between loss of use value and interest appears very clearly in two cases. In *Fletcher v Tayleur*,[44] the defendant was in breach of a contract to construct a ship for the claimant and in awarding loss of profit Willes J took the analogy of interest, saying that in non-payment of money the measure of damages was the interest of the money,[45] and **19-012**

> "it might be a convenient rule if the measure of damages in such a case as this was held by analogy to be the average profit made by the use of such a chattel".[46]

In *British Columbia Saw Mill Co v Nettleship*,[47] a case of goods lost by the defendant carrier, Bovill CJ regarded the value of the use of the goods specifically as interest. He said:

> "It is difficult to see any proper way of compensating the plaintiffs for the delay they have suffered, except by applying the rule which obtains in the case of non-payment of money, namely by allowing interest on the value of the goods which had been replaced."[48]

Where the defendant has failed to deliver goods and the contract is one of sale or manufacture, there may be, apart from the loss of use while substitute goods are acquired, a further loss which should attract interest. On the assumption that there is an available market for the goods, the claimant will claim the normal measure of market price less contract price on the basis that he can immediately buy substitute goods in the market.[49] To the extent that the market price is higher than the contract price, the claimant will have had to expend more money than he anticipated, and should therefore be entitled to interest on the damages awarded. Such a recovery appears in *Panchaud Frères v Pagnan and Fratelli*,[50] and in *Zijden* **19-013**

---

43 Thus the suggestion in *Tehno-Impex* that the Admiralty Court might award compound interest was firmly scotched by Lord Brandon in *La Pintada*.

44 (1855) 17 C.B. 21.

45 But see footnote at the end of para.19-005, above.

46 (1855) 17 C.B. 21 at 29.

47 (1868) L.R. 3 C.P. 499.

48 (1868) L.R. 3 C.P. 499 at 507. But see footnote at the end of para.19-005, above.

49 See paras 25-004 and following, below. Generally, where there is failure to deliver under a contract of carriage of goods, there will be no need to buy substitute goods but only to arrange alternative carriage; aliter, however, if the carrier loses the goods.

50 [1974] 1 Lloyd's Rep. 394 CA.

*Wildhandel v Tucker and Cross*,[51] both claims in the commercial court for non-delivery of goods resulting in damages based on the difference between market price and contract price. In the former, Lord Denning MR said

> "In a commercial transaction, if the plaintiff has been out of his money for a period, the usual order is that the defendant should pay interest for the time for which the sum has been outstanding. No exception should be made except for good reason."[52]

These cases concerned commercial arbitrations. In both of them the court held the arbitrators to have been wrong to have awarded no interest and there is no indication in either that the interest that the arbitrators should have awarded was dependent on statutory authority.

19-014 **(b) Land** In many contracts for the sale or lease of land the operation of the restrictive rule in *Bain v Fothergill*[53] formerly prevented the purchaser or lessee on a failure of title from claiming damages for the loss of his bargain, limiting him to a restoration of the *status quo ante*. He thus had to sue to recover money which he had deposited in part payment of the price, and as early as 1776, in *Flureau v Thornhill*,[54] which established the restrictive rule, Blackstone J laid down that interest on the deposit was recoverable as damages. When at the beginning of the 19th century the courts began to refuse interest as damages for failure to pay money, the allowance of interest in the present situation became questioned, but its recovery was vindicated in *De Bernales v Wood*,[55] and *Farquhar v Farley*,[56] since when it was never doubted.[57]

19-015 However, such awards of interest are now a matter of history as the rule in *Bain v Fothergill*,[58] was removed by statute in 1989.[59] Interest is therefore no longer required to be awarded to purchasers and lessees now able to sue, whatever the breach of contract of sale or lease, for loss of their bargain. The situation with obligations relating to land is in some ways similar to that with obligations relating to goods. Thus where there has been no, or delayed, conveyance of land under a contract of sale or lease, the value of the loss of use or loss of profits has been awarded as damages in some early cases which were outside the restrictive rule in *Bain v Fothergill*.[60] It would give a double recovery to award interest as well.

19-016 Yet *Bushwall Properties v Vortex Properties*,[61] a case which has not received the attention it deserves, provides an important illustration of a recovery of interest by a buyer where there has been a failure to convey. The defendants sold land to the

---

51 [1976] 1 Lloyd's Rep. 341.

52 [1974] 1 Lloyd's Rep. 394 CA at 411. See, too, *Myron (Owners) v Tradax Export* [1970] 1 Q.B. 527 at 536F, per Donaldson J.

53 (1874) L.R. 7 H.L. 158.

54 (1776) 2 Wm. Bl. 1078.

55 (1812) 3 Camp. 258.

56 (1817) 7 Taunt. 592.

57 Other cases in which it was accepted that deposit plus interest thereon was recoverable are *Hodges v Litchfield (Earl)* (1835) 1 Bing. N.C. 492 and *Keen v Mear* [1920] 2 Ch. 574. In the later case, however, interest on that part of the purchase money which the claimant purchaser had placed on deposit at his bank was not allowed.

58 (1874) L.R. 7 H.L. 158.

59 See para.27-005, below.

60 See *Ward v Smith* (1822) 11 Price 19 (lease); *Jaques v Millar* (1877) 6 Ch. D. 153 (lease); *Royal Bristol Permanent Building Society v Bomash* (1877) 35 Ch. D. 390 (sale).

61 [1975] 1 W.L.R. 1649; reversed on another ground: [1976] 1 W.L.R. 591 CA.

claimants with the purchase price payable in stages but then refused to proceed with the contract unless the claimants paid the full purchase price immediately. The claimants, instead of attempting to buy elsewhere, accepted this offer in mitigation of their loss,[62] borrowing money in order to find the full purchase price, and claimed damages representing the interest which they had incurred on the moneys borrowed. It was held that to award, in addition, interest on these damages would not offend against the statutory prohibition of compound interest, at the time referred to in the statute as interest upon interest.[63] Oliver J argued that

> "although what is claimed here is simply a replacement of a sum of money, the quantum of which is calculated by reference to interest which the plaintiffs have had to pay, the sum so claimed is not in any relevant sense interest itself; it is the sum payable by way of damages for breach of contract."[64]

Nevertheless despite Oliver J's wording, in effect the totality of his award was an award of interest, and compound interest, as damages. The reality is that the statute with its permission of simple interest was being by-passed and the award of the claimed interest together with the interest on that interest represented an award of interest as damages at common law.

### (3) CONTRACT: OBLIGATIONS RELATING TO SERVICES

In the case of the defendant's breach of contract to render services there was for long no authority for awarding interest as damages at common law. It may be that there simply was not seen to be any need for interest to be awarded. In latter days, however, the gauntlet thrown down by *Wadswoth v Lydall*,[65] seen as interpreted in *La Pintada*,[66] has been picked up in cases of professional services negligently performed. Thus by formulating the claim within the second rule in *Hadley v Baxendale* and pleading the claim for interest as special damage, compound interest was recovered in *Hartle v Laceys*.[67] A solicitor's negligence had caused his client to lose the opportunity of a profitable resale of property in the purchase and the sale of which the client had instructed the solicitor. The solicitor well knew that his client had borrowed heavily from his bank and that the anticipated resale proceeds were to be used to bring down his borrowing. In these circumstances, and with the appropriate pleading, the Court of Appeal held that the client was entitled to recover in respect of his loan the interest compounded monthly and the bank charges for servicing the loan which continued in the absence of any resale proceeds payment. The defendant solicitor had unsuccessfully contended that, since most com- **19-017**

---

62 The defendants had, in fact, transferred the land to an associated company, which company it was that made the offer.

63 "Nothing in this section—(a) shall authorise the giving of interest upon interest ...": Law Reform (Miscellaneous Provisions) Act 1934 s.3 proviso.

64 [1975] 1 W.L.R. 1649 at 1660B–C. In *Crewe Services & Investment Corp v Silk* [1998] 2 E.G.L.R. 1 CA where the damages for a tenant's breach of his covenant to repair were assessed in the usual way at the diminution in the value of the landlord's reversion, there being no expectation that the landlord would enter and carry out the repairs as he was entitled under the lease, the Court of Appeal, without giving reasons, disallowed the trial judge's award of interest. It may be assumed that the reason was that the claimant landlord had not been kept out of any money during the litigation.

65 [1981] 1 W.L.R. 598 CA.

66 For this see paras 19-008 and 19-009, above.

67 [1999] Lloyd's Rep. P.N. 315 CA.

mercial activity involved the regular use of borrowing, the claimant client's loss was foreseeable without the communication of any special circumstances. By contrast, in *Birmingham Midshires Mortgage Services v Phillips*,[68] a claim by mortgage lenders against solicitors, the claimants were denied compound interest on the moneys they had borrowed to fund the loan in the absence of evidence of the extent of the defendants' knowledge of how the claimants as centralised lenders financed their business.

**19-018** Two House of Lords cases in which lenders have recovered from negligent valuers interest which goes beyond the level of statutory interest, *Swingcastle v Gibson*,[69] and *Nykredit Mortgage Bank Plc v Edward Erdman Group Ltd (No.2)*,[70] are here of some concern in the then state of the authorities. In the absence of any evidence as to how the lenders financed the loss or evidence showing how the money could have been properly employed by them if not lent to the borrowers, the House of Lords took a not ungenerous rate of 12 per cent as the proper rate to apply. The Court of Appeal in *IM Properties v Cape & Dalgleish*,[71] accepted that this was to be regarded as an award of special damages[72] but it was undoubtedly not pleaded and the rate awarded was one plucked from the air without any particular proof by the lenders as to how they had financed the loss or, alternatively, as to how the money, if not lent to the borrowers, would have been profitably employed by them. In *Nykredit* the House of Lords effectively allowed interest at the rate at which the lenders had borrowed to fund the loan up until such time as the lenders' total loss by way of money lent plus such interest reached the limit of the valuers' liability. Could it be said that in either case that this was interest awarded as damages under the second rule in *Hadley v Baxendale*? It certainly seems doubtful.[73]

### (4) TORTS AFFECTING PROPERTY OTHER THAN LAND

#### (a) Destruction

**19-019** *(i) Common law* The position is simple. No cases appear at common law which specifically award interest where the claimant's goods have been destroyed. However, another course is open. The value of the loss of use may be awarded as damages on general principles and this would be equivalent to interest.

**19-020** *(ii) Admiralty* By contrast, it can be said, as by Sir Charles Butt P in *The Kong Magnus*,[74] that "a clear and uniform rule has long existed"[75] that interest is awarded in the case of the total destruction of a ship, in a collision or otherwise.[76] Sir Robert Phillimore put it thus in *The Northumbria*.[77] He said:

---

68 [1998] P.N.L.R. 468.

69 [1991] 2 A.C. 223.

70 [1997] 1 W.L.R. 1627 HL.

71 [1999] Q.B. 297 CA.

72 [1999] Q.B. 297 CA at 452 and 465, per Waller and Hobhouse LJJ respectively.

73 The claimant's recovery in *Saigol v Cranley Mansion* (2001) 72 Con. L.R. 54 CA in respect of her liability to interest on her borrowing to fund a contract for the reconstruction of her premises may also be questionable on the then state of the authorities as there does not appear to have been reliance upon the second rule in *Hadley v Baxendale*. No argument on the issue appears in the report.

74 [1891] P. 223 at 235.

75 Also in *The Joannis Vatis (No.2)* [1922] P. 213 at 223, Sir Henry Duke P talked of the rule as "well established and proper to be taken into account".

76 Different views, however, were expressed as to the merits of the Admiralty practice. Sir Charles Butt

> "The Admiralty, in the exercise of an equitable jurisdiction, has proceeded upon another and a different principle from that on which the common law authorities appear to be founded. This principle adopted by the Admiralty Court has been that of the civil law, that interest was always due to the obligee when payment was not made, *ex mora* of the obligor; and that, whether the obligation arose *ex contractu* or *ex delicto*."[78]

*The Dundee*,[79] in 1827 is often cited as one of the first cases accepting this doctrine while its rationale is best set out in *The Amalia*,[80] where Dr Lushington considered whether the practice of awarding interest was a good one and held that it was. He said:

> "Interest was not given by reason of indemnification for the loss, for the loss was the damage which had accrued, but interest was given for this reason, namely that the loss was not paid at the proper time. If a man is kept out of his money, it is a loss in the common sense of the word, but a loss of a totally different description and clearly to be distinguished from a loss which has occurred by damage done at the moment of a collision."[81]

The amount of interest was affected by whether the ship had or had not a cargo on board at the time of the collision. In the latter case the interest was awarded upon the value of the ship from the date of the collision, as in *Straker v Hartland*.[82] In the former case the interest was awarded upon the value of the ship plus the value of the freight from the conclusion of the voyage, which was taken as being the date when the freight would have been paid, as in *The Amalia*,[83] and in *The Northumbria*.[84] The reason behind these two measures was well explained in the latter case by Sir Robert Phillimore. Interest was given from the conclusion of the voyage where the ship was with cargo because

> "by giving freight you had already given the interest on the use of the vessel during the interval between the collision and her arrival in port; whereas in the case of there being no cargo, there was no freight to represent the interest, and it was therefore expressly given",[85]

---

in *The Kong Magnus* [1891] P. 223 at 235, was not very sure that it was a good one; Sir J Hannen in *The Gertrude* (1887) 12 P.D. 204 at 206, could only regret that the Admiralty rule was not the common law rule.

77 (1869) L.R. 3 A. & E. 6.

78 (1869) L.R. 3 A. & E. 6 at 10. Cited with approval in *The Berwickshire* [1950] P. 204 at 209, and in *The Norseman* [1957] P. 224 at 231.

79 (1827) 2 Hagg. Adm. 137.

80 (1864) 5 New Rep. 164n.

81 (1864) 5 New Rep. at 164n. He added that he agreed with what Lord Stowell had expressly said in *The Dundee* (1827) 2 Hagg. Adm. 137 that he gave interest "by reason of detention of payment and not by way of damages", and he entirely agreed with this principle. But it is difficult to see the difference; the reason of the statement was the statutory limitation on the amount of damages recoverable: see the next footnote but two. In effect "such interest represents in theory the value of the capital to the owner": Roscoe, *Measure of Damages in Maritime Collisions*, 3rd edn (Stevens, 1929), p.37.

82 (1864) 2 Mar. L.C. 159. Also, but less well, reported in *5 New Rep. 163; 34 L.J. Ch. 122*.

83 (1864) 5 New Rep. 164n.

84 (1869) L.R. 3 A. & E. 6. The last three cases all concerned the question of the effect on the measure of damages of the limitation of liability introduced by a statute of 1813 and replaced by the Merchant Shipping Act 1854; see now the Merchant Shipping Act 1995 s.185 as amended. This, however, does not basically affect the question of interest.

85 (1869) L.R. 3 A. & E. 6 at 12.

that is from the date of the collision. To have given interest from the time of collision in the first case would, with the addition of the award for loss of freight, have been to put the claimant in a better position than if the tort had not been committed; not to have given interest from the time of collision in the second case would have been to put him in a worse position.[86] In *Liesbosch Dredger v S.S. Edison*,[87] the practice was applied by the House of Lords in a case celebrated for other reasons.[88] The claimants, having had their dredger sunk by the defendants, recovered its value to them as a profit-earning chattel, capitalised as at the date of loss; this value was assessed by taking into account the market price of a substitute, costs of adapting and transporting it to the place of sinking, and the loss in carrying out a contract with a third party. "It is on the true value so ascertained", said Lord Wright,

> "that the interest ... from the date of the collision will run, as further damages, ... that is, damages for the loss of the money representing the lost vessel as from the date of the loss until payment."[89]

**19-021** The same principles were applied where the loss has been of the ship's cargo rather than loss of the ship itself. Interest was awarded for loss of cargo in *The Gertrude*.[90]

### (b) Damage

**19-022** *(i) Common law* As with destruction the position is again simple. No cases appear at common law that specifically award interest where the claimant's goods have been damaged. Again too, damages may, as an alternative, be claimed for loss of use of the goods.

**19-023** *(ii) Admiralty* The cases in Admiralty allowed interest from an early date also in the case of damage to ships. Thus in *The Hebe*,[91] Dr Lushington held that, in order to carry out restitutio in integrum, interest must be awarded upon the costs of repairs from the date at which the bill for repairs had been paid by the claimant. From that date the claimant will have lost the use of the money paid for the repairs. Also, upon damages for loss of profits or upon demurrage[92] there would seem to be good reason to award interest from the date, before trial, at which the moneys would or should have been paid to the claimant.

**19-024** In the rather special case of damage to non-profit-earning ships, it has become established that damages for loss of use are generally to be calculated on the basis of interest on the capital value of the damaged ship.[93] This was worked out in cases in the House of Lords, particularly *Admiralty Commissioners v S.S. Chekiang*,[94] and

---

86 (1869) L.R. 3 A. & E. 6 at 12.

87 [1933] A.C. 449.

88 See para.8-111, above for the full facts.

89 [1933] A.C. 449 at 468. See, too, *The Berwickshire* [1950] P. 204, where, however, the argument was on a different point: see para.19-082, below.

90 (1887) 12 P.D. 204; affirmed (1888) 13 P.D. 105 CA.

91 (1847) 2 W. Rob. 530.

92 Which is in effect liquidated damages: see para.16-081, above.

93 For the details see paras 37-056 to 37-061, below.

94 [1926] A.C. 637.

*Admiralty Commissioners v S.S. Susquehanna*,[95] and this would appear to be done in exercise of the Admiralty jurisdiction of the court though this is not specifically said.

**(c) Misappropriation** Since the Admiralty jurisdiction was unlikely to be invoked for misappropriation of ships, neither common law nor Admiralty provides us with any cases where interest is awarded.[96] As far as the common law is concerned the very early dictat of the legislative provision giving power to the jury to award interest in cases of trover and of trespass *de bonis asportatis*[97] implies that interest could not be awarded at common law for the misappropriation of chattels. **19-025**

## (5) TORTS AFFECTING LAND

**(a) Wrongful occupation or user** In so far as the normal measure of damages in cases of wrongful occupation or wrongful use of land is the reasonable rental value of the occupation or user,[98] there is no call to award interest; if given, it would spell a double recovery. So in *Whitwham v Westminster Brymbo Co*,[99] Chitty J refused to award interest upon the damages given for wrongful user of land; this, he said, **19-026**

> "would be to treat the plaintiffs as having invested their damages at interest in the hands of the defendants".[100]

**(b) Damage** The same principles were applied as with tortious damage to goods. In *Whitwham v Westminster Brymbo Co*,[101] interest was also refused upon the damages for injury to the land, the same reason being given.[102] **19-027**

## (6) TORTS AFFECTING THE PERSON

At common law no question of interest as damages arose whatever the tort. Only claims for personal injury or loss of life in a ship collision or ship sinking could give rise to an award of interest and this was by reliance on the Admiralty jurisdiction. **19-028**

Yet even in Admiralty interest was ordinarily awarded to run only from the date of the report of the registrar adjudicating on the claim, which of course represented **19-029**

---

95 [1926] A.C. 655.

96 The nearest case is *Phillips v Homfray* [1892] 1 Ch. 465 CA but analysis shows it to run along equitable rather than common law lines. Minerals had been tortiously removed from under the claimant's farm by the deceased and the claimant, having successfully claimed to recover their value from the deceased's estate, now claimed interest in addition. In the then state of the law actions in tort did not survive against the estate of the tortfeasor, and therefore the action had to be treated as an equitable action on the basis of unjust benefit (see the similar litigation on the same facts: *Phillips v Homfray* (1883) 24 Ch. D. 439 CA). Even so, interest was refused because of the claimant's delay in claiming it: only Kay LJ expressed the view that the claimant, but for the delay, could have claimed interest in the equitable action (at 475), the other two members of the court reserving their opinions.

97 Civil Procedure Act 1833 s.29: see para.19-030, below.

98 See paras 39-046 and following, below.

99 [1896] 1 Ch. 894; affirmed without reference to the present point at [1896] 2 Ch. 538 CA.

100 [1896] 1 Ch. 894 at 899.

101 [1896] 1 Ch. 894.

102 No statutory interest was awarded in *British Coal Corp v Gwent County Council* [1995] N.P.C. 103 CA.

interest not upon the damages but upon the judgment debt and was perfectly permissible apart from present considerations. That this was clear, normal Admiralty practice was accepted in two cases of 1938 involving fatal injuries in collisions at sea, *The Theems*,[103] and *The Aizkarai Mendi*[104]; in the latter the claimant had contended that the interest should run from the date of the collision, namely when the cause of action accrued, and cited *The Northumbria*[105] in support, but this contention was rejected by Langton J, though without reasons.[106] The defendant had argued that claims for loss of life differed from claims for loss of property—where, as we have seen, interest from the date of loss has for long been awarded—in that

> "the dependants are maintained by a lump sum which is taken to represent what the deceased would have earned during his life, and not a sum, therefore, which would earn interest".[107]

### (B) *INTEREST CONFERRED BY STATUTE: INTEREST ON DAMAGES*

**19-030** For long statute did very little to ameliorate the position on interest. All that was enacted by the legislature[108] were two sections in the Civil Procedure Act 1833, commonly called Lord Tenterden's Act, giving a power, which was discretionary, to award interest in actions of debt, where certain special circumstances existed, by s.28[109] and in actions of trover and trespass *de bonis asportatis* and in actions on policies of insurance by s.29. When declining to expand common law recovery of interest in *London, Chatham & Dover Ry v S.E. Ry*,[110] the narrowness of these provisions was criticised by the House of Lords.

**19-031** One hundred years later a general power to award interest on damages in all cases was finally conferred on the courts by s.3(1) of the Law Reform (Miscellaneous Provisions) Act 1934.[111] Today the power is contained in the much expanded s.35A of the Senior Courts Act 1981,[112] subs.(1) of which runs thus:

> Subject to rules of court, in proceedings (whenever instituted) before[113] the High Court[114] for the recovery of a debt or damages there may be included in any sum for which judg-

---

103 [1938] P. 197; see especially at 200.

104 [1938] P. 263; see especially at 269.

105 (1869) L.R. 3 A. & E. 6.

106 [1938] P. 263 at 279 to 280.

107 [1938] P. 263 at 269.

108 Spurred into activity by Bentham's writings on utilitarianism, according to Lindley LJ in *London, Chatham & Dover Ry v S.E. Ry* [1892] 1 Ch. 120 CA at 140.

109 Interest might be awarded as damages where money was due under a written instrument at a certain time, or where payment of money due was demanded, together with interest, in writing.

110 [1893] A.C. 429; see at para.19-005, above.

111 The two sections in Lord Tenterden's Act were repealed by s.3(2).

112 Inserted into the Senior Courts Act 1981 by the Administration of Justice Act 1982 s.15(1) and Sch.1, Pt I.

113 Section 35A goes beyond s.3 in specifying "proceedings before", rather than "proceedings tried in", a court, thereby removing the contortions which had been necessary to hold that judgments in default and the like fell within the statutory provision.

114 For the county courts there is a section equivalent to s.35A, currently County Courts Act 1984 s.69, its predecessor, County Courts Act 1959 s.97A having been inserted in that statute by the Administration of Justice Act 1982 s.15(1) and Sch.1, Pt II. There is no difference between s.35A and s.69 other than procedural, s.35A having a subsection on rules of court (subs.(5)) and s.69 a subsection on level of jurisdiction (subs.(8)). The original s.3 applied to proceedings in any court of record and, rather

ment is given simple interest, at such rate as the court thinks fit or as rules of court may provide, on all or any part of the debt or damages in respect of which judgment is given, or payment is made before judgment,[115] for all or any part of the period between the date when the cause of action arose and (a) in the case of any sum paid before judgment, the date of the payment and (b) in the case of the sum for which judgment is given, the date of the judgment.

To this, subs.(6) adds that interest under the section may be calculated at different rates in respect of different periods. The court is thus given by these two subsections a fivefold discretion: apart from the main discretion whether to award interest at all, the court has a discretion as to at what rate, on what part of the damages, and for what period between accrual of action and judgment or payment, to award interest and whether, in doing so, to take different rates for different periods.

Where personal injury or wrongful death is concerned this fivefold discretion is **19-032** reduced to a fourfold one, and it is the main discretion, namely whether to award interest at all, that is taken away. Subsection (2) of s.35A provides that in such cases the award of interest is today mandatory unless the court considers that there are special reasons for declining interest.[116]

It will be necessary to examine how the statutory interest provision has come to **19-033** be applied in practice, and to do so by taking separately the various types of contractual and tortuous obligation, as has already been done above with interest outside statute. Before this, certain limits of the statutory provision need to be looked at, limits which do not necessarily apply to where interest outside statute is in issue.

In what follows in this chapter reference will be made only to the statutory provi- **19-034** sion applicable to proceedings in the High Court, viz., s.35A of the Senior Courts Act 1981. However there can simply be substituted, where necessary, a reference to the equivalent statutory provision applicable to proceedings in the county court, viz., s.69 of the County Courts Act 1984.[117]

Also apart from the general provision for the awarding of statutory interest with **19-035** its total coverage, there is a separate corner of legislation, supported by regulations, permitting the awarding of interest in the statutory torts of discrimination. This is dealt with at appropriate places in what follows.

## 1. LIMITS OF THE STATUTORY PROVISION

### (1) Limited to simple interest only

The interest to be awarded under s.35A of the Senior Courts Act 1981 is simple **19-036** interest; subs.(1) specifically refers to interest being simple. This is the same as under the earlier s.3 of the 1934 Act.[118] To date no legislative thought has been given

curiously, it remains in force for courts of record other than the High Court and county courts; its retention to this extent is by virtue of the Administration of Justice Act 1982 s.15(4) and (5).

115 For the significance of the references to payments made before judgment, which did not appear in the original s.3, see para.19-040, below.

116 This provision did not appear in the original s.3, being later inserted in the section as s.3(1A) by the Administration of Justice Act 1969 s.22. See further para.19-050, below.

117 For which see the preceding footnote but two.

118 The superseded s.3 of the 1934 Act had achieved the same result by means of a proviso that "nothing in this section shall authorise the giving of interest upon interest". The precise scope of this proviso in relation to damages was considered in *Bushwall Properties v Vortex Properties* [1975] 1

to allowing compound interest, necessary though that may be in order to achieve full compensation for claimants. But things are changing in the common law[119] and legislation should no longer be required to achieve this end.

### (2) Limited to interest on amount of judgment[120]

19-037 Section 3(1) of the 1934 Act permitted interest to be awarded only on the amount for which judgment was given. This gave rise to difficulties in three situations.

19-038 **(a) Payments before judgment and before commencement of proceedings** Payments made before proceedings commenced would not feature in the judgment eventually given so that interest could not be awarded on such payments either under s.3(1) or under its successor, s.35A of the 1981 Act. Accordingly, Hobhouse J was, not surprisingly, unprepared to allow statutory recovery in *Chiswell Shipping v National Iranian Tanker Co, The World Symphony*.[121] However, that case dealt with debt—a failure to pay moneys under a contract when due—rather than with damages and an attempt was made in *IM Properties v Cape & Dalgleish*[122] to persuade the Court of Appeal that s.35A could be construed so as to allow statutory interest on payments made before commencement of proceedings where the claim was for damages. The attempt failed. Accountants were sued for negligence by their clients whose initial loss was cut down by their acceptance of shares before the commencement of proceedings. The Court of Appeal, reversing the court below, held them entitled to statutory interest not on the initial loss up until acceptance of the shares and thereafter upon the initial loss as reduced by the value of the shares accepted but only upon the initial loss as so reduced from initial loss to judgment, which represented the amount of the damages awarded.

19-039 The Law Commission had recommended that this lacuna in the now s.35A should be filled by a change in the law[123]; both Lord Scarman and Lord Roskill agreed with this in *The President of India v La Pintada Compania Navigacion*.[124] However, Parliament has made no move in this direction. But change should no longer be required, as we shall see.[125]

19-040 **(b) Sums paid after commencement of proceedings and before judgment** Payments made before judgment but after proceedings commenced would also not feature in the judgment eventually given and interest could not be awarded on such payments under s.3(1) of the 1934 Act. Accordingly, the House of Lords

---

W.L.R. 1649 and what was there said is equally applicable to the new formulation. See, for this case and for its potential scope, para.19-016, above.

[119] See paras 19-058 and following, below.

[120] There is one situation—proceedings for the recovery of a debt and the defendant pays the whole debt to the claimant otherwise than in pursuance of a judgment in the proceedings—where this limitation does not apply: see s.35A(3). Also, interest can be claimed on debts under the Late Payment of Commercial Debts (Interest) Act 1998 but not under s.35A where the debt is not included in a judgment. This is neatly illustrated by *Fitzroy Robinson Ltd v Mentmore Towers Ltd* [2009] B.L.R. 165: see [55] and following. But it is not damages.

[121] [1991] 2 Lloyd's Rep. 251.

[122] [1999] Q.B. 297 CA.

[123] Law Commission, *Law of Contract. Report on Interest* (HMSO, 1978), Law Com. No.88, Cmnd.7229.

[124] [1985] A.C. 104.

[125] See para.19-069, below.

was unable in *The President of India v La Pintada Compania Navigacion*,[126] to allow recovery of statutory interest on a payment made in the course of the litigation.[127] But by the time of their Lordships' decision the successor section, s.35A, which came into effect after the arbitrators' award with which the *La Pintada* case was concerned, had permitted such recovery.[128] To this extent s.35A(1) is wider than the earlier s.3(1).

Whether s.35A covers a payment not by the defendant but by a third party has **19-041**
been called in question. It was indeed held in *Seaconsor Far East v Bank Markazi*[129] that s.35A allowed interest upon payment after commencement of proceedings but before judgment even if the payment was made by a third party but doubt was cast on this conclusion in *IM Properties v Cape & Dalgleish*,[130] where Waller LJ said obiter[131] that in his view s.35A contemplated a payment by the defendant and that the court would have no power to award statutory interest on any amounts provided by a third party.[132] Hobhouse LJ, however, preferred to leave the point open.[133]

**(c) Other amounts which go to reduce the damages award** A further limita- **19-042**
tion on the awarding of statutory interest also stemming from the fact that it may only be recovered on the damages awarded and not on any higher amount[134] has come to the fore. Where the defendant's negligence causes the claimant to lose a particularly profitable sale of a property which he is only able to sell later but before judgment at a reduced price or which he is still retaining at judgment at a reduced value, and his damages are calculated at the profitable resale price less the reduced price or value, statutory interest falls to be given on this net figure and is not available on the profitable resale price lost despite the fact that this loss has continued for some considerable time after its accrual. This result the claimants had eventually to concede in *Blue Circle Industries v Ministry of Defence*,[135] where their property, damaged by the defendants' breach of statutory duty, had not, as anticipated, been profitably sold and was still retained at judgment.[136]

---

126 [1985] A.C. 104.

127 The House also confirmed that the Admiralty Court had never had power to award interest on debts already paid before judgment, thereby overruling *Tehno-Impex v Gebr. Van Weelde Scheepvaartkantoor* [1981] Q.B. 648 CA, and reinstating *The Medina Princess* [1962] 2 Lloyd's Rep. 17.

128 See the wording of s.35A(1)(a) at para.19-031, above. The wording of the subsection is such that the awarding of interest is not precluded by payment of the whole of the damages: *Edmunds v Lloyd Italico & L'Ancora Compagnia di Assicurazione e Riassicurazione* [1986] 1 W.L.R. 492 CA.

129 [1997] 2 Lloyd's Rep. 89.

130 [1999] Q.B. 297 CA.

131 Obiter because *IM Properties* (at para.19-038, above) concerned a payment before commencement of proceedings.

132 [1999] Q.B. 297 CA at 306E to F.

133 [1999] Q.B. 297 CA at 308B. Whichever interpretation prevails may not now matter: see para.19-069, below.

134 Except (see para.19-040, above) where s.35A applies to allow interest on payments after commencement of proceedings.

135 [1999] Ch. 289 CA.

136 See [1999] Ch. 289 CA. at 324F and following. But today the claimant would be in a better position: see para.19-069, below.

## 2. Categories to which Statutory Interest Applies

### (1) Contract: obligations to pay money

**19-043** Statutory interest has been awarded in a number of cases where an obligation to pay money has not been met. *Miliangos v George Frank (Textiles)*,[137] and subsequently *Miliangos v George Frank (Textiles) (No.2)*,[138] cases familiar in another connection,[139] are illustrations of interest being awarded on an unpaid purchase price.[140] To decide whether interest ought to be awarded in these cases, one first looks to see whether the claimant would have money available to him which he now, by the breach of contract, has not, and this is clearly the case where the defendant's breach has consisted in a failure to pay the price of goods sold and delivered to him by the claimant. In awarding interest in such a case in *Kemp v Tolland*,[141] Devlin J said that he did so

> "on the simple commercial basis that if the money had been paid at the appropriate commercial time, the other side would have had the use of it".[142]

So too where in a contract for the sale of land the purchaser fails to pay the deposit, which is a regular feature of such contracts, it was held in *Ng v Ashley King (Developments) Ltd*[143] that the seller, though not entitled to contractual interest, was entitled to statutory interest from the time that the deposit should have been paid.[144] The situation would be similar where the defendant had failed to repay a loan to the claimant, but if his breach was in failing to make a loan to the claimant it might be different, as the claimant should take steps to procure another loan in the market. The situation might also be different where the defendant's breach was in failing to pay a third party, as where a banker fails to honour the claimant's drafts. Secondly, one looks to see whether the claimant nevertheless retains property which, had the defendant paid over the money, would have been transferred by the claimant to the defendant or some third party. Thus in the case of a sale of land by the claimant to the defendant, the rents from the land which the claimant will reap by continuing possession of the land will offset the amount of interest that could have accrued to him on the purchase money. Where, on the other hand, the property has already been handed over by the claimant before the price was paid him, as will often be the case in a sale of goods, interest should be recoverable on the price.

### (2) Contract: obligations relating to property

**19-044** Where the defendant has failed to deliver goods, as under a contract of sale or manufacture, and there is an available market for the goods, the claimant can claim the normal measure of market price less contract price[145] on the basis that he can

---

137 [1975] Q.B. 487.
138 [1977] Q.B. 489.
139 See para.20-024, below.
140 See the two cases at para.19-121, below.
141 [1956] 2 Lloyd's Rep. 681.
142 [1956] 2 Lloyd's Rep. 681 at 691.
143 [2011] Ch. 115.
144 See [2011] Ch. 115 at [53] to [60].
145 See paras 25-004 and following, below.

immediately buy substitute goods in the market.[146] To the extent that the market price is higher than the contract price, the claimant will have had to expend more money than he anticipated, and should therefore be entitled to interest on the damages awarded.[147] Similarly, interest may be called for where there is not a failure to deliver goods but a breach of warranty in respect of delivered goods leading to expenditure by the claimant for which he claims damages. This is illustrated by *Harbutt's "Plasticine" v Wayne Tank and Pump Co*,[148] where, because of defects in a heating system for the claimants' factory which the defendants had contracted to supply and install, the installation went up in flames destroying the factory, which had to be rebuilt. The claimants were awarded not only damages for the cost of replacement of the factory but also, under the then s.3 of the 1934 Act, the interest thereon. However, since the claimants had at an early date been indemnified by their insurers as to part of their loss, the Court of Appeal, stressing the discretionary nature of an award of interest on damages, allowed the interest only on the balance not covered by the insurance moneys. On the other hand, in *Cousins & Co v D. and C. Carriers*,[149] where the defendant carriers lost in transit certain goods belonging to the claimants, statutory interest was awarded them although they were indemnified by their insurers, being held entitled to claim interest to the extent that they had to account for any interest recovered to the insurers. On the insurance aspect *Harbutt's "Plasticine"* was distinguished.[150]

### (3) Contracts: obligations relating to services

In looking at common law interest as damages in obligations relating to services we have seen that authorities allowing interest have not appeared until latterly when there has been a sprinkling of cases seeking compound interest.[151] Authority is also lacking, and to this day, where statutory interest on damages is concerned. However, the cases allowing interest as damages may assist in showing what circumstances may give rise to an interest claim, although with statutory interest there can be no question of compounding the interest. **19-045**

### (4) Torts affecting property other than land

**(a) Destruction** Statutory interest was awarded in *Metal Box v Currys*,[152] where goods stored by the claimants with the defendants were negligently destroyed in a fire for which the defendants were responsible. The claimants would not have made profitable use of the goods over the period for which interest was awarded but this was held in no way to debar them from claiming interest. Counsel for the claimants put the case of a work of art or Ming vase which was destroyed and submit- **19-046**

---

146 Generally, where there is failure to deliver under a contract of carriage of goods, there will be no need to buy substitute goods but only to arrange alternative carriage; aliter, however, if the carrier loses the goods.

147 See the cases at para.19-013, above where the interest awarded in this type of situation appears not to have been statutory, the cases being commercial arbitrations not under the then s.3 of the 1934 Act.

148 [1970] 1 Q.B. 447 CA.

149 [1971] 2 Q.B. 230 CA.

150 See on the insurance aspect *Metal Box v Currys* [1988] 1 W.L.R. 175, at para.19-046, below.

151 See paras 19-017 and 19-018, above.

152 [1988] 1 W.L.R. 175.

ted that the fact that it had no profit-earning capacity was irrelevant to the question of the awarding of interest, which should not depend on the use to which the chattel was put.[153] McNeill J agreed. He said that he was aware of

> "no authority for the proposition that the plaintiff who has been deprived of his chattel by the defendant's tort and who is kept out of the value of the chattel ... should not be awarded interest on the judgment sum. To my mind to hold otherwise would be to confuse damages for consequential loss with interest. Indeed it may well be that in some circumstances there can be interest on damages for consequential loss."[154]

It was further held that, the claimants being insured, the interest would not be restricted to the period after the insurer had settled the claimants' claim on the basis that it was the insurer, by subrogation, who was seeking to recover the loss against the defendant.[155]

19-047 **(b) Damage** Statutory interest was held to be justified in *Metal Box v Currys*,[156] also in respect of those of the claimants' goods which had been damaged, rather than destroyed, in the fire; the case has already been considered when dealing with destruction of goods.[157] The claimants there had been kept out of the value of the goods damaged as well as of those destroyed. By contrast, it was held by the House of Lords, reversing the courts below, that no interest should be awarded on the facts of *Giles v Thompson*.[158] While their cars, which had been damaged by the negligence of the defendants, were being repaired, replacement cars were made available to the several claimants by car hire companies on the understanding that the hire charges would be paid once they had judgment in their claims against the defendants. The decision not to allow interest on the awards of damages for car hire is clearly correct as the claimants had not been kept out of their money during the time that their claims were being litigated; there was no provision, as Lord Mustill pointed out,[159] requiring the claimants to pay interest on the hire charges to the car hire companies.[160] Similarly, no interest was awarded, either under contract, as damages or by virtue of the statute, in *Pattni v First Leicester Buses Ltd*,[161] where interest on the credit car hire charges had not been paid by the claimant.[162]

19-048 **(c) Misappropriation** Where the misappropriation consisted of the infringement by the defendants of the claimants' patent and damages were awarded based on the royalties which the defendants would have had to pay had they taken a licence, interest was given under the then 1934 Act on these damages in *General*

---

153 [1988] 1 W.L.R. 175 at 180A to B.

154 [1988] 1 W.L.R. 175 at 180B to C.

155 Compare on this insurance aspect *Cousins & Co v D. and C. Carriers* [1971] 2 Q.B. 230 CA where *Harbutt's "Plasticine" v Wayne Tank and Pump Co* [1970] 1 Q.B. 447 CA was distinguished: see at para.19-044, above.

156 [1988] 1 W.L.R. 175.

157 See para.19-046, above.

158 [1994] 1 A.C. 142.

159 [1994] 1 A.C. 142 at 168D.

160 And it has now been held that even the full hire charges are not recoverable (*Dimond v Lovell* [2002] 1 A.C. 384, at para.37-020, below) unless the claimant is impecunious (*Lagden v O'Connor* [2004] 1 A.C. 1067 at para.37-021, below).

161 [2011] EWCA Civ 1384 CA.

162 For the case see para.37-024, below.

*Tire & Rubber Co v Firestone Tyre & Rubber Co*,[163] since the claimants were receiving the royalties later than they would have done had the defendants acted properly.[164] However, if the claimant is claiming as special damage the value of the use of the goods from the time of their conversion, he ought not to be given interest as well. Where the claim was formerly in detinue *Strand Electric Co v Brisford Entertainments*[165] made it clear that the value of the use of the goods is recoverable and the same result was later reached in *Hillesden Securities v Ryjack*,[166] an action, necessarily in conversion since the abolition of detinue,[167] where the market rate of hire of the goods between conversion and judgment was awarded.[168] To such a head of recovery interest must surely be only alternative.[169] So too, in refusing interest on the value of goods converted in *Trafigura Beheer BV v Mediterranean Shipping Co SA*,[170] where for the purpose of the damages the value at judgment higher than the value at conversion had been taken, the Court of Appeal, reversing the court below on this, pointed out that to give the increase in value of the goods and interest in addition would confer a double benefit on the claimants.[171] Longmore LJ likened damages based on increased value of the goods to damages for loss of their use, seeing a compelling analogy between them, and then in relation to loss of use adopted the argument put forward here in the then current edition of this text that loss of use and interest must be alternative.[172] However, where as in *Checkprice (UK) Ltd v Revenue and Customs Commissioners*,[173] the award was of market value at the time of conversion with no special damage or consequential loss, it was appropriate to allow interest on the market value.[174]

## (5) Torts affecting land

In looking at interest as damages in relation to wrongful occupation of land, we have seen that, the rental value of the land being generally awarded, there is then no call to award interest as well,[175] and the same will apply here. However, an award of statutory interest may occasionally be needed. Thus in *Carr v Boxall*,[176] where the claimant had been denied occupation of a kiosk of which he was proved to be the tenant and the action was decided in his favour in mid-1958 whereupon he reoccupied the premises, but the assessment of damages was delayed till the end of 1959, interest was awarded on the damages to run from the time of his reoccupation.[177] Most recently, in *Dobson v Thames Water Utilities Ltd*,[178] interest **19-049**

[163] [1975] 1 W.L.R. 819 HL: see the case at paras 48-042 and 48-045, below.
[164] For the period for which interest was awarded, see para.19-080, below.
[165] [1952] 2 Q.B. 246 CA: facts at para.38-067, below.
[166] [1983] 1 W.L.R. 959.
[167] See para.38-002, below.
[168] Facts at para.38-067, below.
[169] See *Whitwham v Westminster Brymbo Co* [1896] 1 Ch. 894, the analogous land case decided before the arrival of statutory interest, at para.19-026, above.
[170] [2007] 2 Lloyd's Rep. 622 CA.
[171] See [2007] 2 Lloyd's Rep. 622 CA at [43].
[172] See [2007] 2 Lloyd's Rep. 622 CA at [41]–[44] and the details of the case at para.38-020, below.
[173] [2010] EWHC 682 (Admin). Facts at para.38-009, below.
[174] [2010] EWHC 682 (Admin) at [55].
[175] See para.19-026, above.
[176] [1960] 1 W.L.R. 314.
[177] See especially at 318.
[178] [2012] EWHC 986 (TCC).

was awarded by Ramsey J on the damages for loss of amenity where the claimants' land was adversely affected by a serious nuisance, such damages being calculated by taking an annual percentage of the rental value of the land as representing the loss of its amenity value.[179] This is correct if the courts are prepared to award interest on the non-pecuniary loss element in torts generally, but this has not yet been done in torts at common law outside the field of personal injury and wrongful death.[180] Indeed the Court of Appeal has declined in a deceit action to award interest on non-pecuniary loss in *Saunders v Edwards*,[181] and also in a claim for wrongful arrest and false imprisonment, *Holtham v Commissioner of Police for the Metropolis*.[182] The fact that the calculation was by way of the land's rental value makes no difference as this does not turn the loss into a pecuniary one. Ramsey J said[183] that he considered the governing principle to be that set out by Lord Herschell LC in *London, Chatham & Dover Ry v S.E. Ry*,[184] to the effect that an interest award to a claimant is to be regarded as compensation for being kept out of the money which should have been paid him. This, however, refers to a monetary loss, to a pecuniary benefit of which the claimant has been deprived by the defendant—indeed London, Chatham & Dover was a case of debt—and not to a non-monetary loss which is not truly calculable in money but where a monetary award is the best that the law can do by way of compensation. Neither *Saunders* nor *Holtham* appears to have been cited to Ramsey J.

## (6) Torts affecting the person

19-050 **(i) Personal injury and wrongful death** Despite the discretionary power to make awards of interest on damages conferred by the 1934 Act, it was not the practice of the courts before 1970 to do so in claims arising out of personal injury and wrongful death. The situation was then radically changed by the legislative intervention of 1969 making the award of interest mandatory, in the absence of special reasons, in all personal injury and wrongful death claims.[185] It then became a matter of urgency for the courts to consider upon what principles they were to act in carrying out this mandate of Parliament, and guidelines were laid down at an early date by Lord Denning MR delivering the judgment of the Court of Appeal in *Jefford v Gee*,[186] itself a personal injury action. Detailed provision was made by him for how interest was to be calculated on both the pecuniary loss and the non-pecuniary loss in personal injury cases and on the pecuniary loss in cases of fatal injury where at that date no award for non-pecuniary loss was allowed. The details are best left until we reach the whole issue of how the interest awarded falls to be calculated.[187]

---

179 See this aspect of the matter at para.39-021, below.

180 Which Ramsey J rightly considered not to be a useful analogy: [2012] EWHC 986 (TCC) at [10].

181 [1987] 1 W.L.R. 1116 CA.

182 [1987] C.L.Y. 1154 CA: These two cases are at para.19-056, below.

183 [1987] C.L.Y. 1154 CA at [17].

184 [1893] A.C. 429.

185 Achieved today by subs.(2) of s.35A of the Senior Courts Act 1981 providing for the substitution of "shall be included" for "may be included" and the addition of "unless the court is satisfied that there are special reasons to the contrary" in subs.(1) in its application to judgments given for personal injury and death. See the current legislative provisions at paras 19-031 and 19-032, above.

186 [1970] 2 Q.B. 130 CA.

187 See paras 19-087 and following, below.

One matter which does not go to the calculation or computation of the damages should be looked at here and that is the question of whether there should be any interest at all awarded on non-pecuniary loss of a person physically injured. One of Lord Denning MR's guidelines in *Jefford v Gee*, as we shall see when we come to consider the calculation of interest, was related to the awarding of interest on the non-pecuniary loss, but when in *Cookson v Knowles*[188] he came once again to deliver the judgment of the Court of Appeal he said, though obiter, that his guideline should be changed so that in future no interest be given on the damages awarded for non-pecuniary loss. He pointed out that, in awarding damages for non-pecuniary loss, **19-051**

> "the courts invariably assess the lump sum on the 'scale' for figures current at the date of the trial—which is much higher than the figure current at the date of the injury or at the date of the writ",[189]

and that, since the claimant thus stands to gain by the delay in bringing the case to trial, he ought not to gain still more by having interest from the date of service of the writ.[190]

However, the House of Lords, while declining in that case[191] to adjudicate on this issue,[192] later refused in *Pickett v British Rail Engineering*[193] to agree with the Court of Appeal when it proceeded there to apply its new guideline. Lord Wilberforce pointed to what he regarded as the fallacy in the Court of Appeal's argument. "Increase for inflation", he said, **19-052**

> "is designed to preserve the 'real' value of money: interest to compensate for being kept out of that 'real' value. The one has no relation to the other. If the damages claimed remained, nominally, the same, because there was no inflation, interest would normally be given. The same should follow if the damages remain in real terms the same."[194]

This refusal to adopt the no interest solution was endorsed by their Lordships in *Wright v British Railways Board*,[195] and the guideline for non-pecuniary loss initially laid down in *Jefford v Gee*[196] has remained unchanged to this day.

Yet it appears that the only reason advanced before their Lordships for not awarding interest was the inflation argument and it is thought that there are other, and cogent, reasons for proscribing any interest on the damages for non-pecuniary loss. There is much to be said for regarding the purpose behind the awarding of interest as damages as being to compensate a claimant for the delay, which the process of litigation makes inevitable, in reimbursing a money loss which he has suffered as a result of the tort or breach of contract. Accordingly, interest can have no relevance where monetary damages are being awarded not as replacement for other money but as representing the best that the law can do in the face of incommensurable loss which is not truly calculable in money. It is accepted that any award for pain and **19-053**

---

188 [1977] Q.B. 913 CA.
189 [1977] Q.B. 913 CA at 921C.
190 [1977] Q.B. 913 CA at 921D.
191 [1979] A.C. 556.
192 [1979] A.C. 556 at 573G, per Lord Diplock.
193 [1980] A.C. 136.
194 [1980] A.C. 136 at 151D.
195 [1983] 2 A.C. 773.
196 [1970] 2 Q.B. 130 CA.

suffering and loss of amenities must be in the nature of a conventional sum,[197] and to award interest upon such a conventional sum surely becomes supererogatory. Indeed it is suspected that their Lordships' further endorsement of the reduction in the rate of interest for non-pecuniary loss to, as we shall see, two per cent in *Wright v British Railways Board*,[198] reflects an uneasiness at making any award at all. Fortunately, the Court of Appeal has now had the good sense to refuse to award any interest on the damages for non-pecuniary loss in an action of deceit[199]; it would be wise, but is probably too late, to do the same with personal injury and also wrongful death.[200]

**19-054** **(ii) Other torts affecting the person** Claims by claimants for interest on damages in actions of defamation, false imprisonment, malicious prosecution and the like have been somewhat slow to surface. Courts have therefore had little opportunity to consider the appropriateness of such claims. The principal case in this context in fact concerns an action of deceit, for while deceit may be regarded as a proprietary tort in its primary protection of a claimant's pecuniary interests it can be seen as a tort affecting the person in so far as it allows damages for non-pecuniary loss. This case is *Saunders v Edwards*,[201] where the seller of a flat had fraudulently misrepresented that it included a roof terrace and the damages awarded the buyer included a sum for the disappointment and inconvenience suffered throughout their occupation of it.

**19-055** Indeed the reason why there has been a paucity of cases is that actions of defamation, false imprisonment and malicious prosecution are frequently not brought to recover for pecuniary as opposed to non-pecuniary loss,[202] and it is pecuniary loss with which interest is primarily concerned. There can be no doubt, if a past pecuniary loss is proved in any such case, that interest should be awarded, and interest at the commercial rate. Indeed in *Saunders v Edwards* it was not disputed that interest should run on the pecuniary loss measured by the difference between the price of the flat and its actual value.

**19-056** The difficulty comes with non-pecuniary loss. In various earlier editions the hope was expressed that interest on non-pecuniary loss might be avoided,[203] and this indeed happened in the context of deceit in *Saunders v Edwards*.[204] The Court of Appeal there wisely declined to follow the personal injury analogy in refusing to award any interest on damages for such loss, whether past or future, and indeed about the same time the Court of Appeal refused interest on damages for non-pecuniary loss in a claim for wrongful arrest and false imprisonment, *Holtham v*

---

197 See para.40-253, below.

198 [1983] 2 A.C. 773; see para.19-127, below.

199 *Saunders v Edwards* [1987] 1 W.L.R. 1116 CA. See the case at paras 19-054 to 19-056, below.

200 At least, however far compound interest may advance after the decision in *Sempra Metals* (which see at paras 18-058 and following), the reasoning of their Lordships in that case makes it clear that compound interest could never be awarded on the damages for non-pecuniary loss. See too the recommendation of the Law Commission in its Report on *Pre-Judgment Interest on Debt and Damages* that, should a power to award compound interest be introduced, interest on damages for non-pecuniary loss in personal injury cases should continue to be single: (2004), Law Com. No.287, paras 7.8 to 7.12.

201 [1987] 1 W.L.R. 1116 CA.

202 See, generally, Chs 42 to 46, below.

203 And see para.19-053, above.

204 [1987] 1 W.L.R. 1116 CA.

*Commissioner of Police for the Metropolis*.[205] Bingham LJ's comments in *Saunders* on this issue are valuable. He said of the award to compensate for the claimant's inconvenience and disappointment:

> "It was a single global award, modest in amount but intended to cover the past and the future. It is somewhat analogous to an award of general damages to a defamation plaintiff for mental distress and suffering, which has never, as I think, been augmented by interest up to the date of trial. I consider this approach to be correct in principle, because in neither case can the damages be realistically seen as having accrued due to the plaintiff at a certain time in the past and as having thereafter been wrongly withheld from him."[206]

Kerr LJ also said that, as it seemed to him, it was

> "generally better to award a global sum under this head of damages, without the addition of interest."[207]

One distinction with interest on personal injury and wrongful death damages that was pointed to is that s.35A of the Senior Courts Act 1981 made the awarding of interest mandatory in such cases but discretionary in others.

**(iii) Statutory torts of discrimination** The damages in the statutory torts involving discrimination, which are generally only for the non-pecuniary loss by way of injury to feelings, are awarded by virtue of statute, with the legislation expressly permitting awards of interest on compensation for injured feelings in discrimination cases in the employment field but saying nothing on interest in other cases of discrimination. This legislation, which merits criticism, is best dealt with when we turn to consider discrimination cases generally.[208] **19-057**

## III. The Position After Sempra Metals

We come at last to *Sempra Metals v Inland Revenue Commissioners*.[209] We must now examine this landmark decision, the analysis which brought their Lordships to it, and how it affects, and impacts upon, all that has gone before. **19-058**

### 1. The Decision

Domestic legislation provides that a United Kingdom resident company is required to pay advance corporation tax on distributions by way of dividend and is then entitled to have tax so paid later set off against the company's mainstream corporation tax. The legislation further provides that a subsidiary company resident in the United Kingdom is not obliged to account in this way on dividends paid to its parent company if a group income election is made and, more importantly for our purposes, if the parent company is also United Kingdom resident. The European Court of Justice however held in *Metallgesellschaft Ltd v Inland Revenue Commissioners*,[210] that a tax regime which allowed resident parent companies but not non- **19-059**

205 [1987] C.L.Y. 1154 CA.
206 [1987] 1 W.L.R. 1116 CA at 1135E to F.
207 [1987] 1 W.L.R. 1116 CA at 1129G.
208 In Ch.43, below
209 [2008] A.C. 561.
210 Reported at [2001] Ch. 620.

resident ones to receive dividends from their resident subsidiaries without payment of advance corporation tax was contrary to the article of the EC Treaty which guarantees freedom of establishment. This breach of Community law would entitle a resident subsidiary adversely affected to bring a claim under domestic law for redress, the Court of Justice identifying in the most general terms that there could be a restitutionary right or, in the alternative, a right by way of damages to claim interest on moneys prematurely paid.[211]

**19-060** *Sempra Metals Ltd v Inland Revenue Commissioners*,[212] was such a claim by the United Kingdom resident subsidiary of a German parent, being for interest accruing on amounts of tax paid during the period between making the payments and the date on which mainstream corporation tax became payable. The Revenue did not dispute the liability to pay simple interest on these amounts and the sole issue of substance was whether the award should be calculated on the basis of compound interest; as far as damages were concerned this could only be by an award of interest at common law, statutory interest being restricted to simple interest. The House of Lords, affirming the courts below, decided in the claimant's favour.

**19-061** Before their Lordships there was not only a claim to recover the interest as damages but also as restitution for unjust enrichment. Moreover, the restitutionary cause of action was in the vanguard since the claimant Sempra was said to prefer it[213] because it presented fewer limitation problems.[214] We are not of course concerned with this principal restitution claim where there was disagreement among their Lordships ending up with, in the claimant's favour, a majority of three and a minority of two. We are concerned only with the damages claim and fortunately not only was the House prepared to come to a decision on it but also there was here unanimity. Thus Lord Nicholls of the restitution majority concluded his detailed examination of the law on the damages aspect of the case with

> "I consider the court has a common law jurisdiction to award interest, simple and compound, as damages on claims for non-payment of debts as well as on other claims for breach of contract and in tort"[215]

while Lord Scott of the restitution minority expressed his concurrence with the conclusion, which appeared to him to have been unanimously accepted, that

> "interest losses caused by a breach of contract or by a tortious wrong should be held to be in principle recoverable, but subject to proof of loss, remoteness of damage rules, obligations to mitigate damage and any other relevant rules relating to the recovery of alleged losses."[216]

**19-062** It will be seen that Lord Scott mentions that proof of loss is required. On this Lord Nicholls is more detailed. He said that

> "the House should hold that, in principle, it is always open to a claimant to plead and prove his actual interest losses caused by late payment of a debt".[217]

---

211 See the discussion in Lord Hope's speech in *Sempra Metals* at [2008] A.C. 561 at [10]–[15].
212 [2008] A.C. 561.
213 [2008] A.C. 561 at [18], per Lord Hope.
214 See [2008] A.C. 561 at [16] and [21], per Lord Hope and at [192] and [229], per Lord Mance.
215 [2008] A.C. 561 at [100].
216 [2008] A.C. 561 at [132].
217 [2008] A.C. 561 at [94].

He then went on to say:

> "But an unparticularised and unproved claim simply for 'damages' will not suffice. General damages are not recoverable. The common law does not *assume* that delay in payment of a debt will of itself cause damage. Loss must be proved."[218]

As for the proof required, Lord Nicholls said that this would depend on the nature of the loss and the circumstances of the case. He explained:

> "The loss may be the cost of borrowing money. That cost may include an element of compound interest. Or the loss may be loss of an opportunity to invest the promised money. Here again, where the circumstances require the investment loss may need to include a compound element if it is to be a fair measure of what the plaintiff lost by the late payment. Or the loss flowing from the late payment may take some other form."[219]

## 2. THE ANALYSIS

The starting point in the analysis reshaping the law for the 21st century is their Lordships' desire to be rid of the rule laid down by them in *London Chatham & Dover Ry*[220] at the end of the 19th century and adhered to by them in *La Pintada*[221] towards the end of the 20th. This rule was, in the words of Lord Nicholls, an anomalous, unprincipled exception to the broad common law principle that a claimant can recover damages for losses caused by a breach of contract or a tort which satisfy the usual remoteness tests.[222] Recognising that an action in debt for a failure to pay money amounts to the same thing as an action for damages for breach of a contract to pay a debt,[223] the removal of the exception would necessarily carry over to all other breaches of contract, and to tort as well. There was indeed no stopping place before the whole of the law of contract and tort was brought into the net, as the above citations from the speeches of Lord Nicholls and Lord Scott show.[224] **19-063**

An essential feature of the analysis was that, by opening the whole of the law of contract and tort to awards of interest, it went counter to the unpreparedness of Lord Brandon in *La Pintada* to allow interest under the first rule in *Hadley v Baxendale* while accepting awards of interest awarded under the second. Their Lordships were rightly very critical of this distinction of Lord Brandon. Lord Nicholls explained very clearly why it was misconceived.[225] Lord Mance agreed with him that it was difficult to follow or accept,[226] and Lord Walker agreed with him that the distinc- **19-064**

---

218 [2008] A.C. 561 at [96]; his italics.

219 [2008] A.C. 561 at [95].

220 [1893] A.C. 429.

221 [1985] A.C. 104.

222 [1985] A.C. 104 at [74].

223 [1985] A.C. 104 at [96].

224 While not dealing specifically with interest, *Parabola Investments Ltd v Browallia Cal Ltd* [2011] Q.B. 477 CA shows that recovery of damages for the loss of the use of money, in that case resulting from deceit, is now fully accepted: see this aspect of *Parabola* at para.49-038, below. As Toulson LJ put it there (at [50] and [51]), the hostile view of such claims has gone with *Sempra Metals* and the ghost of Lord Tenderden who, as we have seen, in 1829 launched this view upon the law in *Page v Newman* (see para.19-005, above) has been laid to rest.

225 [1985] A.C. 104 at [85]–[89].

226 [1985] A.C. 104 at [215].

tion was unsound and should no longer be used.[227] It can now be forgotten and interest can be awarded across the board.

**19-065** Lord Brandon had given as one reason for holding against the claimants in *La Pintada* that it would be wrong to have two competing systems for the recovery of interest, one under statute and one at common law.[228] But as Lord Nicholls pointed out in *Sempra Metals*, their Lordships' decision did not lead to a result which conflicts with the legislation because the legislative provision, s.35A, is not an exhaustive code,[229] being concerned with interest on debts and damages and saying nothing about the principles to be applied when assessing damages.[230] Here he is in effect making the distinction between interest as damages and interest on damages, and this is taken up by Lord Walker who refers to the distinction in these very terms.[231] The recovery of interest at common law, now established, is entirely different, and separate, from the recovery of interest under statute.[232]

**19-066** In a nutshell, all of Lord Brandon's reasoning in *La Pintada*[233] has been shown to be unpersuasive and has been abandoned.

## 3. THE RESULTS

**19-067** **(a) Cases where compound interest is sought** Compound interest is now to be available across the board wherever the claimant can prove a loss of compound interest. No longer is compound interest to be confined to equity, prepared to award it where there is a fiduciary relationship or money obtained by fraud,[234] to arbitrators, given a power to award compound interest by an imaginative statutory innovation,[235] and to the very occasional case at common law. There is no need now to implement the Law Commission's recommendation in its recent Report on interest[236] to introduce compound interest by legislation, a recommendation which ran thus:

> "The courts should be given power to award compound (rather than simple) interest in appropriate circumstances. In broad terms, we think that compound interest is usually appropriate in large cases, and recommend that in payments of £15,000 or more there should be a rebuttable presumption in favour of compound interest. For payments of less than £15,000 the rebuttable presumption would be that interest is simple."[237]

This could be said to fit, very roughly, with the cases where claimants are likely to

---

227 [1985] A.C. 104 at [165].

228 His other reasons are at para.19-007, above.

229 [1985] A.C. 104 at [98]. He drew attention to s.35A(4) which provides that "interest in respect of a debt shall not be awarded under this section for a period during which, for whatever reason, interest on the debt already runs".

230 [1985] A.C. 104 at [99].

231 [1985] A.C. 104 at [164], adopting what he called Ward LJ's apt expression of the point in *Hartle v Laceys* [1999] Lloyd's Rep. P.N. 315 CA at 327, col.2.

232 See too Moore-Bick LJ in a conflict of laws case, *Maher v Groupama Grand Est* [2010] 1 W.L.R. 1564 CA, at [36]: "There is no necessary inconsistency between the existence of a substantive right to interest and the existence of a statutory discretion. Substantive rights to recover interest were already well known to the law when the 1934 Act was passed."

233 For which reasoning see para.19-007, above.

234 For compound interest in equity see the next paragraph.

235 Arbitration Act 1996 s.49(1).

236 Law Commission, *Pre-Judgment Interest on Debt and Damages*, (2004), Law Com. No.287.

237 (2004), Law Com. No.287, para.1.18.

be able, or to wish, to make a claim for compound interest, but it is far better to take the *Sempra Metals* route than to have such legislative amounts and presumptions imposed.

A further word should be said here about compound interest in equity today. Equity has shown itself prepared to award compound interest in order to ensure that a person does not make a profit from his own wrongdoing if that person is in a fiduciary position.[238] Such a recovery of interest constitutes an accounting or is by way of disgorgement and is considered in Chapter 15. More uncertain is whether there is jurisdiction in equity to award compound interest against those obtaining money or other benefit through fraud. The question was raised but left undecided by the Court of Appeal in *Clef Aquitaine SARL v Laporte Materials (Barrow) Ltd*,[239] though it was accepted that the matter will need decision one day.[240] A decision in favour would in effect be allowing compound interest upon compensation rather than as disgorgement, being similar to compensation for fraudulent misrepresentation, but historically speaking the award would need to be classified as one not for damages but for equitable compensation so as to attract the equitable jurisdiction. Since *Clef Aquitaine* the question has reappeared more than once but with no very clear answer. In *Black v Davies*,[241] which was an action in deceit, McCombe J would have been prepared to award compound interest but for his belief that the equitable remedy of compound interest should be ancillary to an equitable cause of action. Instead, the Court of Appeal, while not sharing this belief, refused compound interest because the defendant's fraudulent representation had not caused him to obtain and retain money belonging to the claimants but had simply caused them to lose money.[242] Subsequently, an award of compound interest was made in the complicated fraud case of *Man Nutzfahrzeuge AG v Freightliner Ltd*,[243] but it is not entirely clear whether this was based on the benefit obtained by the fraudulent defendant or on the loss to the claimant.[244] These difficulties of where exactly equity lies in this area of damages can now be by-passed, it is suggested, by applying *Sempra Metals* so as to allow, where appropriate, compound interest at common law in deceit actions. 19-068

**(b) Cases where statutory interest is limited to the amount for which judgment is given** We have seen that statutory interest is not available in respect of amounts paid before commencement of proceedings which therefore do not feature in the judgment.[245] In one such case, *IM Properties v Cape & Dalgleish*,[246] Hobhouse LJ recognised that the claimants might have included a claim for com- 19-069

---

[238] See especially the treatment of the interest issue by Buckley LJ in *Wallersteiner v Moir (No.2)* [1975] Q.B. 373 CA at 397 to 399, and by Hobhouse J and Lord Browne-Wilkinson in *Westdeutschebank Landesbank Girozentrale v Islington Borough Council* at, respectively, [1994] 4 All E.R. 972, 990 to 995 and [1996] A.C. 669, 701D. See too *O'Sullivan v Management Agency and Music* [1985] Q.B. 428 CA and see *Miliangos v George Frank (Textiles) (No.2)* [1977] Q.B. 489 at 495A to D, per Bristow J.

[239] [2001] Q.B. 488 CA.

[240] [2001] Q.B. 448 CA at 503H to 506B.

[241] [2004] EWHC 1464 (QB).

[242] See [2005] EWCA Civ 531 CA, especially at [87]–[89].

[243] [2006] EWHC 2347 (Comm).

[244] See [2006] EWHC 2347 (Comm) at [318]–[321]. The claim in deceit, and therefore the issue of interest, does not appear in the appeal at [2008] P.N.L.R. 6 at 117.

[245] See para.19-038, above.

[246] [1999] Q.B. 297 CA.

mon law interest with reliance, then in vogue, on the second rule in *Hadley v Baxendale*, but since they had not done so he did not commit himself as to whether such a claim would have succeeded.[247] We have also seen that there can be other amounts which go to reduce the award and on which statutory interest therefore cannot be claimed.[248] In one such case, *Blue Circle Industries v Ministry of Defence*,[249] Simon Brown LJ regarded a similar claim for common law interest as a possibility but a remote one.[250] After *Sempra Metals* both of these claims should succeed provided that the claimant were able to show that it was in the contemplation of the parties that the defendant's breach of contract would cause him to borrow onerously or to lose out on lending attractively. Moreover, if successful in his proof of loss, the claimant should be entitled to the great advantage of compound interest.

**19-070** **(c) Cases generally** It is of course the truth that the great majority of cases will be unaffected by the *Sempra Metals* breakthrough. This is particularly true of personal injury and fatal accident cases, which probably account for most of the awards of interest on damages today. These will remain under the statutory umbrella. Yet should a claimant in a particular case be able to bring proof that he has borrowed extensively to cover his medical expenses, or has been unable to invest earnings which he has lost, compound interest ought to be available to him. Recovery would of course be subject, as was made clear in *Sempra Metals*, to remoteness, mitigation, and all the other general rules of damages, but remoteness and mitigation would not be likely to stand in the claimant's way. For mitigation to apply, the defendant would have to show that the claimant had acted unreasonably in borrowing as he had done, or that the way in which he claimed he would have invested was unreasonable. As for remoteness, the claimant is protected by the familiar maxim that you take your victim as you find him. New territory has been mapped out for the shabby millionaire.[251]

## IV. CALCULATION OF THE AMOUNT OF INTEREST

### 1. PERIOD OF TIME FOR WHICH INTEREST IS AWARDED

**19-071** Section 35A of the Senior Courts Act 1981 allows the court to award interest on damages for any part of the period between the date when the cause of action arose and the date of judgment.[252] That this is the maximum period for which interest may be awarded is consonant with general principle, and this period should also govern in any case in which interest is to be awarded apart from statute. Put shortly, the same period governs both for interest awarded on damages under statute and interest awarded as damages at common law.[253]

---

[247] [1999] Q.B. 297 CA at 307G.

[248] See para.19-042, above.

[249] [1999] Ch. 289 CA.

[250] [1999] Ch. 289 CA at 324E to 325A.

[251] For the shabby millionaire see para.8-104, above.

[252] Or, now, to the date of payment if before judgment: see para.19-040, above.

[253] Where in *Youlton v Charles Russell* [2010] EWHC 1032 Ch damages had been awarded by Warren J for loss of a chance (dealt with at para.34-044 below), he had then to consider the periods to which and from which interest should be awarded on the lost chance claim: see his later judgment on consequential matters at [2010] EWHC 1918 Ch at [32] and following.

### (1) Time to which interest runs

Cases of unwarrantable delay by the claimant apart,[254] there can be no objection to awarding interest down to the date of judgment[255] since damages for loss arising from a single cause of action cover all past loss and even in the exceptional case of a continuing cause of action damages are assessable as far as the date of judgment.[256] By contrast, in so far as interest awarded as damages represents compensation for being out of pocket in relation to losses already accrued there is no reason for it to continue after judgment, for the damages will have given the claimant the money value of those losses. **19-072**

This, of course, is on the assumption that the defendant paid the judgment debt forthwith, an assumption which the court must make when awarding damages. If he does not, the claimant's recovery cannot be by way of damages. Instead he must rely on the provision of s.17 of the Judgments Act 1838[257] that every judgment debt shall carry interest from the time of entering the judgment.[258] This suffices to make the award of interest to a claimant continuous till the moment he is paid the compensation. But it is not necessarily a continuous award at the same rate. Until 1971 the interest rate on judgments had throughout remained pegged at four per cent[259] so that by that date it was well below the various rates that damages were attracting.[260] Then the other extreme was reached in 1985 when the judgment rate leapt to 15 per cent,[261] placing it, as time went on, so far above the various damages rates that it led to attempts by claimants, in the common case of split trials in personal injury actions, to obtain the judgment rate from the date of the judgment on liability rather than from the later date of judgment on damages. Such attempts were finally scotched by the House of Lords in *Thomas v Bunn*,[262] holding that the judgment referred to in s.17 of the 1838 Act was the final judgment which quantified the amount the defendant was required to pay as a result of his liability.[263] Of course the post-judgment part of the award of interest not being damages, it falls outside the scope of this text. It is included here simply to complete the picture.[264] **19-073**

---

254 Delay by the claimant and its effect are dealt with at paras 19-096 to 19-102, below.

255 Or to the date of payment before judgment; on this, as far as statutory interest is concerned, see para.19-040, above.

256 It is thought that this is still possible even without a specific provision, as there was formerly: see para.11-027, above. The fact that the claimant has requested an adjournment is no reason for not awarding interest down to the date of judgment: *May v A.G. Basset & Son* (1970) 114 S.J. 269.

257 The Judicial Committee of the Privy Council has a common law jurisdiction to award interest on judgments when dealing with cases from Commonwealth countries which do not have statutory provisions comparable to s.17: *Central Electricity Board of Mauritius v Bata Shoe Co (Mauritius)* [1983] 1 A.C. 105 PC.

258 For "the time of entering up the judgment" in s.17 there was substituted in 1998 "such time as shall be prescribed by rules of court": Civil Procedure (Modification of Enactments) Order 1998 (SI 1998/2940). This alteration has not affected the discussion in the text.

259 See para.19-105, below.

260 See paras 19-104 and following, below. See *Cook v J. L. Kier & Co* [1970] 1 W.L.R. 774 CA, where the Court of Appeal found a way, ingenious but perhaps difficult to justify, of avoiding this disparity in relation to the amount by which it increased the trial judge's award.

261 See para.19-106, below.

262 [1991] 1 A.C. 362.

263 In contrast to costs, upon which interest runs not from the date of assessment quantifying the amount payable but from the earlier date of judgment: *Hunt v Douglas (Roofing)* [1990] 1 A.C. 398.

264 Under Pt 36 of the CPR which provides for offers to settle by claimants, the court is given power, where judgment against the defendant is at least as advantageous to the claimant as the claimant's

**19-074** Where it will not be appropriate for interest to run as far as judgment is where interim payments are made before judgment,[265] and today interim payments are becoming much more common than in former days. The position should then be that the claimant is entitled to interest on the total of the award up until the time of any interim payment, thereafter to interest on the remaining balance, and so on after each further interim payment. The Court of Appeal, dealing with the issue in *Bristow v Judd*,[266] a personal injury action, was faced with the added complication that in such actions the time from which interest runs and the rate of interest differ as between the special damages for pre-trial pecuniary losses and the general damages for non-pecuniary loss.[267] It was held there that an interim payment should be attributed first of all to the special damage which has been incurred up to the date of the interim payment and only when an interim payment exceeded the amount of the special damage incurred at the date of such payment would the balance be taken in diminution of the general damages. While the court did not respond to the request to give general guidance on the calculation of interest where interim payments have been made, on the ground that the award of interest is discretionary and the facts of each case are likely to differ widely,[268] nevertheless the method adopted seems sensible and should be followed.

**19-075** It was held in *Mamidoil-Jetoil Greek Petroleum Co SA v Okta Crude Oil Refinery AD*,[269] a successful claim for breaches of contract for the supply by the claimants to the defendant of crude oil and for the handling of crude oil at the defendant's terminal by one of the claimants,[270] that the usual award of interest from the date of accrual of cause of action to the date of judgment was not to be cut down because the decree of a foreign court had made it illegal for the defendant to pay any damages awarded against it.[271] This issue appearing in *Mamadoil-Jetoil* has received more consideration in the context of the time from which interest runs rather than the time to which interest runs.[272] The result here follows the result in *The Berwickshire*,[273] there, although that case was not cited, and is clearly correct.

## (2) Time from which interest runs

**19-076** It is incontrovertible, in the first place, that interest cannot run for any period of time which is anterior to the accrual of the claimant's cause of action.[274] In the

---

offer, to award the claimant interest up to 10 per cent above base rate under r.36.14(3)(a). *The Vergina (No.3)* [2002] 1 Lloyd's Rep. 238 is such a case, where interest was awarded under the somewhat differently worded former r.36.21(2) which applied up until April 2007. This again is not damages and falls outside the scope of this text.

265 Indeed where any payment is made before judgment.

266 [1993] P.I.Q.R. Q117 CA.

267 See paras 19-129 and 19-131, below.

268 [1993] P.I.Q.R. Q117 CA at 128.

269 [2003] 1 Lloyd's Rep. 42.

270 The judgment on liability is at [2003] 1 Lloyd's Rep. 1.

271 [2003] 1 Lloyd's Rep. 42 at [10]–[12].

272 See para.19-082, below.

273 [1950] P. 204.

274 For the purposes of awarding interest the cause of action may, exceptionally, arise at a time before the claimant is entitled to bring proceedings in respect of it. This was the position in *General Tire and Rubber Co v Firestone Tyre and Rubber Co* [1975] 1 W.L.R. 819 HL (facts at para.19-084, below), where, although the claimants could not, until their patent was sealed, sue for its infringement, their cause of action arose some years earlier on the occasion of the first infringement after

second place, it would seem that, cases of unwarrantable delay by the claimant apart,[275] in principle interest should commence to run from the moment the cause of action does accrue in respect of loss which also then accrues,[276] and, in respect of loss which accrues at a later date falling before the date of judgment, then from such later date.[277] In very many cases loss and cause of action will accrue simultaneously.

**(a) Ascertaining the time of accrual of the cause of action** Very occasionally there may be difficulty in ascertaining the moment at which the cause of action accrues. This problem came to the fore in relation to interest in the well-known *SAAMCO* litigation,[278] the question being when does interest start to run in favour of a mortgage lender with an inadequate security because of a combination of a negligent overvaluation and a collapse in the property market. The question of interest was not raised in the original *SAAMCO* decision itself, *Banque Bruxelles Lambert v Eagle Star Insurance Co*,[279] and the matter awaited a later adjudication of the House of Lords in *Nykredit Mortgage Bank v Edward Erdman Group (No.2)*.[280] It was there held that the cause of action arose and the loss accrued not when the claimants realised their security and the loss crystallised, as the defendants contended, but at the much earlier time when it was clear that there was going to be a loss, in the particular case immediately as the borrower had instantly defaulted and the security was already worth less than the amount borrowed. The situation is more difficult where there is no immediate default by the borrower. One then has to estimate the strength of his covenant, and the cause of action does not arise, and the loss accrue, until one can say that he is clearly going to default—a far from easy question to resolve—or has defaulted. 19-077

**(b) Interest from a time after accrual of the cause of action** Cases are today becoming much commoner in which interest is held not to run from the time of the accrual of the cause of action but from a later time because the loss does not immediately arise. These cases cover a whole variety of circumstances and merit examination. 19-078

One case, early in this context, is *Kaines v Österreichische Warrenhandelsgesellschaft*[281] where sellers of goods were in anticipatory breach, accepted by the buyers, and the buyers then bought in substitute goods at a price higher than the contract price. The Court of Appeal held that interest ran not from the time when the breach occurred and the cause of action accrued but from the later time, which was even after the issue of the writ, when the buyers were required to make payment for the substitute goods. Not until then were they out of pocket, to the extent that they then paid out more than they would have done had the sellers performed the contract. 19-079

---

publication of the complete specification: see at 836B to G and 841A to C.

[275] Delay by the claimant and its effect are dealt with at paras 19-096 to 19-102, below.

[276] That interest on demurrage—and demurrage is in effect liquidated damages—should run from the time that demurrage is incurred was taken for granted in *Galaxy Energy International Ltd v Bayoil SA, The Ama Ulgen* [2001] 1 Lloyd's Rep. 512.

[277] No interest was awarded where the damages for breach of contract related to remedial works not yet carried out: *Hunt v Optima (Cambridge) Ltd* [2013] EWHC 1121 (TCC); see at [3].

[278] For which, see para.34-073, below.

[279] [1997] A.C. 191.

[280] [1997] 1 W.L.R. 1627 HL.

[281] [1993] 1 Lloyd's Rep. 1.

The Court of Appeal in *Kuwait Airways Corp v Iraqi Airways Co*,[282] considered that the claimant's submission that interest should be awarded, upon the price of the substitutes for aircraft converted, not from the date of conversion but from the date of replacement was "intuitively correct".[283] In *Martini Investments v McGinn*,[284] a claim on an insurance policy, interest was awarded from the date that repairs on a holiday home damaged in a volcano became feasible, having for a time been prohibited. In *The Vergina (No.3)*,[285] another claim on an insurance policy, it was held that the starting date for interest was the date when the insurer was in breach of his obligation to hold the insured harmless, a date which might well be moved forward to give the insurers a reasonably short time to consider whether there was a valid claim under the policy.[286] Indeed it was said in *Quorum A/S v Schramm (No.2)*,[287] that in claims under insurance policies the court would not necessarily follow the basic principle that interest is awarded from the date of loss but, on unusual and complex insurance claims, would exercise its discretion on the basis that it was proper to allow insurers some time to consider the claim, the time given varying according to the nature of the loss, the manner of presentation of the claim and the circumstances requiring investigation by the insurer. On the other hand, in *Kinetics Technology International v Cross Seas Shipping Corp, The Mosconici*,[288] where cargo of parts of a furnace carried on the defendant's vessel was lost overboard, interest was awarded from the date of the loss and not from the later time that the parts were replaced. Similarly, in *Aerospace Publishing Ltd v Thames Water Utilities Ltd*,[289] where damaged and destroyed archives were reinstated, interest was held by the Court of Appeal, reversing the trial judge, to run from the time of damage or destruction and not from the later time of reinstatement.[290]

19-080 (c) **Interest from a time after the loss is felt** The period between cause of action and judgment for which interest under statute is awarded is specifically stated to lie in the discretion of the court so that the court may choose to award interest from a date later than that at which the claimant's loss accrued. However, it is thought that a court awarding interest as damages at common law may, where it finds good reason, do likewise. The obvious case for such treatment is where there has been an unjustifiable delay on the part of the claimant in bringing his action to trial but this is dealt with separately for reasons which will appear.[291] An illustration in the commercial field of an award of interest for less than the usual period is afforded by *General Tire and Rubber Co v Firestone Tyre & Rubber Co*.[292] The complete specification for a patent was published in 1951 but the patent was not finally granted until 1963. Upon grant the claimant patentees became entitled to

282 [2002] 2 A.C. 883 CA at 896. Facts at para.38-071, below.

283 [2002] 2 A.C. 883 CA at [630]; this matter was not passed upon by the House of Lords [2002] 2 A.C. 883 HL at 1075.

284 [2001] Lloyd's Rep. I.R. 374.

285 [2002] 1 Lloyd's Rep. 238.

286 [2002] 1 Lloyd's Rep. 238 at [29].

287 [2002] 2 Lloyd's Rep. 72.

288 [2001] 2 Lloyd's Rep. 313.

289 (2007) 110 Con. L.R. 1.

290 (2007) 110 Con. L.R. 1 at [92]–[95]. Similar is *Woodlands Oak Ltd v Conwell* [2011] EWCA Civ 254 CA where interest was awarded on damages for defects in building works which had not been remedied by the time of judgment: see at [35] to [37].

291 See paras 19-096 to 19-102, below.

292 [1975] 1 W.L.R. 819 HL.

claim in respect of infringing use at any time after the publication of the specification and brought an action for damages against the defendants for infringing use over the period from 1958 onwards. The trial judge awarded interest on the damages from the commencement of infringing use in 1958, was upheld by the Court of Appeal, but the House of Lords only allowed interest to run from the grant in 1963. Lord Wilberforce, in the leading speech, started by recognising that justice, in principle, required that a wrongdoer who has failed to pay money he ought to have paid should pay interest over the period for which he has withheld the money, and continued:

> "But other considerations may enter into it. In a commercial setting, it would be proper to take account of the manner in which and the time at which persons acting honestly and reasonably would pay. Correspondingly, account ought to be taken of any unreasonable or delaying or obstructive conduct of the debtor, for example, in a patent context, any delaying or facetious opposition to a patent grant."[293]

In the instant case he found no such conduct imputable to the defendants, while, on the other hand, he was satisfied that there was independent evidence that in normal commercial practice royalties in respect of use before grant were not expected to be paid until grant and that there was no evidence of interest being expected or paid for the period until grant.[294]

**19-081** In *B.P. Exploration Co (Libya) v Hunt (No.2)*,[295] Robert Goff J exercised his discretion as to the period for which interest should run by awarding it only from the time, some two years after the claimants' cause of action had accrued, that the defendants knew that a claim was to be made against them; this exercise of judicial discretion was upheld both by the Court of Appeal[296] and by the House of Lords.[297] Similarly, in both *Kleinwort Benson v South Tyneside Borough Council*,[298] and *Westdeutsche Landesbank Girozentrale v Islington Borough Council*[299] Hobhouse J held, where causes of action accrued to the claimants at the time payments had been made by them to the defendants, that the starting date for the award of interest should not be before the time that the defendants realised that the payments which they had received from the claimants had been improperly received. It was thought that these three cases might be distinguished on the basis that they were not claims for damages but claims in unjust enrichment—the first one for benefits conferred under a contract subsequently frustrated, the later two for moneys paid under contracts subsequently held void—and, further, that these claims were novel ones—the earliest one was the first after very many years to be brought before the courts under the Law Reform (Frustrated Contracts) Act 1943 while the later ones were based on contracts which both parties had taken to be completely valid—so that the court in each case considered that the defendant initially could not have reasonably expected any claim to be made. Fortunately the need to find a distinc-

293 [1975] 1 W.L.R. 819 HL at 836H to 837A.

294 Lord Salmon dissented on the interest point because he considered there was no evidence that interest was not expected to be paid for the period until grant: [1975] 1 W.L.R. 819 HL at 841G.

295 [1979] 1 W.L.R. 783.

296 [1981] 1 W.L.R. 232 CA; see at 245C to F.

297 [1983] 2 A.C. 353. However, at this stage the appeal was only by the defendant who argued, unsuccessfully, that the interest should have run from an even later date because he could not know before judgment the extent of his liability: see at 373C to 374D.

298 [1994] 4 All E.R. 972.

299 [1994] 1 W.L.R. 938.

tion has evaporated since Hobhouse J's decision in the *Westdeutsche Landesbank* case has been reversed, the House of Lords holding, as did the Court of Appeal, that interest should run from the date of the receipt of the moneys by the defendant, in other words from the date when the cause of action arose,[300] and it may fairly be said that the reversal in this case must put the other two in doubt.[301]

**19-082** There remains the question of the date from which interest will be awarded where, at the date when the cause of action arose and continuing until a later date falling between accrual of the cause of action and judgment in the action, the defendant could not lawfully have paid money to the claimant because, for instance, the claimant was an alien enemy. In *The Berwickshire*,[302] a case of tort which involved the sinking of a ship owned and manned by then alien enemies, it was held that the usual award of interest as damages from date of accrual of cause of action to date of judgment was not to be cut down because payment could not have been lawfully made until the claimants ceased, almost four years after the commission of the tort, to be alien enemies. Lord Merriman P said:

> "The true principle underlying the award of interest in Admiralty is that in every £'s worth of damage in respect of which interest is ultimately awarded, the interest has accrued potentially from the moment when the damage was suffered until the liability has been adjudged and the amount finally ascertained."[303]

It was submitted in earlier editions that this is not restricted to cases in Admiralty and also applies to breach of contract as much as to tort, a submission which now derives support from *Mamidoil-Jetoil Greek Petroleum Company SA v Okta Crude Oil Refinery AD*,[304] a decision considered in the context of the time to which interest runs rather than the time from which interest runs.[305] A doubt was introduced in the case of contract because interest as damages for failure to pay a bill of exchange has been refused in two cases, *Biedermann v Allhausen*,[306] and *Ledeboter v Hibbert*,[307] where at the time payment of the bill fell due it could not have been made because the rightful payee was then an alien enemy. These cases are fully considered later in connection with bills and notes,[308] where it is submitted that, although correct, they are exceptional in that the act which would have constituted the breach of duty was the very thing which the defendant could not lawfully do, and that therefore no question of default or of damages could arise at all until payment once again became lawful.

**19-083** This then leaves, apart from the peculiar case of non-pecuniary loss in personal injury considered below,[309] *General Tire and Rubber Co v Firestone Tyre and Rubber Co*[310] as the only clear illustration—outside delay yet to be dealt with[311]—of an

---

300 [1996] A.C. 669, affirming [1994] 1 W.L.R. 938 CA.
301 The awarding of interest in *McGlinn v Waltham Contractors Ltd* (2007) 112 Con. L.R. 148 on the cost of repairs which had not been carried out (see at [5]–[8]) appears wrong.
302 [1950] P. 204.
303 [1950] P. 204 at 217.
304 [2003] 1 Lloyd's Rep. 42.
305 See para.19-075, above.
306 (1921) 37 T.L.R. 662.
307 [1947] K.B. 964.
308 See para.30-022, below.
309 See paras 19-094 and 19-095, below.
310 [1975] 1 W.L.R. 819 HL.
311 See paras19-096 to 19-102, below.

award of interest from a time after the accrual of the cause of action or, if later, after the time when the loss is felt. What permitted this result in that case was a rather special commercial practice in the field of patent royalties.[312]

**(d) Interest where the loss is a continuing one** Where there has been a continuing loss to a claimant which has accrued, at regular or irregular intervals, over the years, then, strictly speaking, for each separate slice of loss the time from which the interest should run will differ, being from when that slice accrues. However, a particular short-hand method has been developed for the computation where the claim is for personal injury and fatal injury; this is considered below.[313] **19-084**

It would not seem that this short-hand method has much relevance for commercial cases or in other fields. With much larger figures of past loss likely to be involved, it makes it important to take the slices of loss separately.[314] A typical case is *Tate & Lyle Food and Distribution v Greater London Council*,[315] where Forbes J accepted the basis for the computation of interest put forward by the claimants in an action, heard in 1981, where they were claiming dredging costs incurred by them between 1967 and 1974. This computation first assumed that all the dredging invoices paid during any one calendar year had been paid halfway through that year, then aggregated these costs year by year, and finally took interest year by year on the accumulating total.[316] The resulting figure was two thirds of a million pounds.[317] Also instructive is *Deeny v Gooda Walker (No.3)*,[318] one of the many aspects of the claims by Lloyd's Names against their managing and underwriting agents for exposing them to excessive risks of liability to third party insurers. While it was held that the claimants sustained losses as and when the funds of their syndicates were used by the agents to discharge the claimants' liabilities, as there would have been an interval between payment of each claim and a recovery of an indemnity in respect of it from the reinsurers, taken as being 105 days, interest should start to run only from the end of that interval; the loss was not felt until then. **19-085**

Nevertheless in *Ramzan v Brookwide Ltd*,[319] the Court of Appeal, on being offered by counsel, for the remedying of the trial judge's incorrect award of a constant rate of interest, the alternatives of calculating the interest on each element of the loss from the time at which it arose and of using the short-hand personal injury method of halving the interest,[320] chose the latter alternative. Arden LJ in the leading judgment said without more: **19-086**

> "There is no reason not to apply the practice in *Dexter v Courtaulds Ltd* to cases other than personal injury."[321]

---

312 See the case at para.19-080, above.

313 See paras 19-091 to 19-093, below.

314 Occasionally, where there is a loss of profits or an incurring of expenditure over a period of time it may be appropriate to take interest on half the amount for the whole of the period, following the accepted pattern in personal injury cases. This was done in relation to loss of profits in *Blayney v Clogau St Davids Gold Mines Ltd* [2002] F.S.R. 233: case at para.48-055, below.

315 [1982] 1 W.L.R. 149; decision later reversed but on liability only: see [1983] 2 A.C. 509.

316 [1982] 1 W.L.R. 149 at 155H.

317 See [1982] 1 W.L.R. 149 at 157E, and on the case see further paras 19-112 and 19-135, below.

318 [1996] L.R.L.R. 168.

319 [2012] 1 All E.R. 903 CA.

320 [2012] 1 All E.R. 903 CA at [87].

321 [2012] 1 All E.R. 903 CA at [88].

It would seem that the commercial cases favouring, and using, the former alternative[322] cannot have been brought to the court's attention.[323] A rough and ready method was used by the Court of Appeal in *Driver v Air India Ltd*,[324] to deal with interest in an employee's claim for unpaid overtime over a number of years.[325]

### (3) Application of the above principles to personal injury and wrongful death cases

19-087 **(a) The general rules** The starting point is with the guidelines of Lord Denning MR in *Jefford v Gee*.[326] He there laid down that, in relation to the claimant's pecuniary losses, interest should be awarded on the special damages, namely the claimant's loss of wages and medical expenses down to trial,[327] from the date of the injury to the date of judgment in the action, but that no interest at all should be awarded on the general damages for future pecuniary loss, whether in respect of future loss of earnings or future medical expenses.[328] A distinction along similar lines cannot, however, be made in respect of the claimant's non-pecuniary loss since this loss, being by its nature indivisible, does not admit of a neat division between pre-trial deprivation and post-trial deprivation; accordingly compensation in respect of it falls to be awarded, as general damages, in one lump sum. So, too, in every Fatal Accidents Act claim, although here by practice rather than by necessity, the court at that time awarded one lump sum for the pecuniary loss of dependency and made no breakdown between special damage to the date of trial and future loss after the date of trial. In these circumstances the Court of Appeal's solution was that, in relation both to awards for non-pecuniary loss in personal injury claims and to awards for loss of dependency in Fatal Accidents Act claims, interest should be awarded as from the date of service of the writ until the date of judgment.[329] Such should be the general rules, with rules also prescribed for payment into court[330] and deduction of tax[331]; in exceptional cases however—"as when", said Lord Denning

---

[322] At para.19-086, above.

[323] Nor does this personal injury practice stem from the *Dexter* case, which presented a rather special situation and is not now generally followed (see paras 19-092 and 19-093, below), but from the earlier, more important *Jefford v Gee* [1970] 2 Q.B. 130 CA (see paras 19-091 to 19-093, below). The facts of this curious case of *Ramzan* are at para.39-058, below.

[324] [2011] EWCA Civ 986 CA.

[325] [2011] EWCA Civ 986 CA at [7], [12] and [13].

[326] [1970] 2 Q.B. 130 CA.

[327] This includes damages in respect of the gratuitous care and attendance of the claimant, generally by his or her relatives, rightly held by the Court of Appeal in *Roberts v Johnstone* [1989] Q.B. 878, reversing the court below, to be special rather than general damages for the purpose of awarding interest.

[328] [1970] 2 Q.B. 130 CA at 147A to C.

[329] [1970] 2 Q.B. 130 CA at 147E to 148C. The Admiralty practice of awarding interest from the date of the registrar's report (see para.19-029, above) should be changed so as to award interest from the date of service of the writ: at 148D.

[330] The rule laid down that a payment into court should not take interest into account ([1970] 2 Q.B. 130 CA at 149 to 150) has been changed. The current position provides for offers to settle to be treated as inclusive of interest.

[331] The legislature has since intervened (initially in 1971) to provide that interest awarded by courts in the United Kingdom in personal injury and wrongful death claims is not to be taxable (now Income Tax (Trading and Other Income) Act 2005 s.751(1)(a)), an exemption extended to such claims which have been settled (s.751(2)) and to equivalent foreign court awards where the interest is tax exempt in the foreign country (s.751(1)(c) replacing an earlier Extra Statutory Concession).

MR, "one party or the other has been guilty of gross delay"[332]—the court may diminish or increase the rate at which interest is awarded[333] or the period for which it is allowed.[334]

Less than a decade later, the Court of Appeal in *Cookson v Knowles*,[335] changed, for Fatal Accidents Act claims, the guidelines laid down by it in *Jefford v Gee*,[336] and in this was upheld, on appeal, by the House of Lords.[337] What led to the change was the effect on damages awards of the relentless and continuing inflation of the 1970s. The first issue before both the Court of Appeal and the House of Lords was whether the damages by way of loss of dependency should be based on what the deceased was earning at his death or what he would have been earning had he still been alive at the time of the trial; the decision was in favour of the latter because of its practical reliability, though it was accepted that the former would in strict juristic theory have been the correct choice, and this issue is dealt with elsewhere.[338] **19-088**

Such a conclusion, however, necessitated that the court should make separate assessments for the past loss of dependency to trial and the future loss of dependency after trial in precisely the same way as has been the established practice for a claimant's pecuniary losses in personal injury claims.[339] This then gave the opportunity to follow the *Jefford v Gee*[340] guidelines as to the pecuniary losses in personal injury claims[341] and to hold, as was indeed done, that interest should be awarded on the past loss but none on the future loss. This new refusal to allow interest on the future loss was indeed integrated with the decision to base the computation of that loss on the anticipated earnings at trial rather than on the actual earnings at death. Lord Diplock dealt with the matter in some detail thus: **19-089**

> "Once it has been decided to split the damages into two components which are calculated separately, the starting point for the second component, the future loss … is the present value not as at the date of death but *at the date of the trial* of an annuity equal to the dependency starting then and continuing for the remainder of the period for which it is assumed the dependency would have enured to the benefit of the widow if the deceased had not been killed. To calculate what would have been the present value of that annuity at the date of death, its value at the date of trial would have to be discounted at current interest rates for the 2½ years which had elapsed between the death and trial. From the juristic standpoint it is that discounted amount and no more to which the widow became entitled at the date of her husband's death. Interest on that discounted figure to the date of trial would bring it back up to the higher figure actually awarded. To give in addition interest on that higher figure would be not only to give interest twice but to give interest on interest."[342]

This general solution for awarding interest on damages for pecuniary loss is **19-090**

---

332 [1970] 2 Q.B. 130 CA at 151E.
333 See paras 19-103 and following, below as to rate generally.
334 See paras 19-071 and following, above as to period generally.
335 [1977] Q.B. 913 CA.
336 [1970] 2 Q.B. 130 CA.
337 [1979] A.C. 556.
338 See para.41-042, below.
339 See [1979] A.C. 556 at 575D, per Lord Fraser.
340 [1970] 2 Q.B. 130 CA.
341 See para.19-087, above.
342 [1979] A.C. 556 at 572B to D; italics his. See Lord Denning MR in the Court of Appeal at [1977] Q.B. 913 at 921F.

unimpeachable,[343] for personal injury claims and since *Cookson v Knowles*, as varied by the decision of the Supreme Court in *Knauer (Widower and Administrator of the Estate of Sally Ann Knauer) (Appellant) v Ministry of Justice (Respondent)*,[344] in relation to calculation of the multiplier at the date of trial for fatal accident claims. With personal injury the special damages represent the past loss to the date of trial and must therefore attract interest. The general damages represent the future loss, both in relation to earnings and medical expenses, so there can be no entitlement to interest on what in effect is compensation received in advance; indeed the courts in assessing the general damages, far from giving interest, invariably discount the future loss to its present value at the time of judgment.[345] These principles apply mutatis mutandis to fatal accident claims. All that remains for consideration is the particular method used for calculating the interest on the past loss together with the peculiar manner in which the non-pecuniary loss is calculated.

**19-091** **(b) The particular method of calculation for past loss** As Lord Denning MR pointed out in laying down guidelines in *Jefford v Gee*,[346] a personal injury claimant should be entitled to interest on any past loss as from the date when it occurred[347] but it was there decided that with these special damages awarded for loss to trial the court should avoid having to go into the tedious detail of calculating interest on salary from accrual and on medical expenses from date of payment and should deal with the matter broadly, taking interest on the whole of the special damages at the normal rate from the period from the date of injury to the date of judgment and awarding half of this amount. This could be described, with the same result, as awarding interest on half of the special damages, or at half the normal rate—Lord Denning MR's preferred formulation[348]—or for half of the period from injury to judgment. This method of computation was extended to Fatal Accidents Act claims after it was decided that a separate assessment for the pre-trial pecuniary loss should be made in such claims also.[349]

**19-092** In *Ichard v Frangoulis*,[350] this halving procedure was not followed because, since all, or virtually all, of the medical expenses claimed had been incurred at the date of the accident, it was only fair to the claimant to take, at the full rate, the whole period from the time he might be assumed to have paid his medical bills down to trial.[351] However, the Court of Appeal in *Dexter v Courtaulds*,[352] was critical of this decision. Declining also to endorse the similar approach in similar circumstances of Forbes J in a number of unreported personal injury cases to which the court had

---

343 However the decision in *Wadey v Surrey County Council and Wisely v John Fulton (Plumbers) Ltd* [2000] 1 W.L.R. 820 HL, two conjoined appeals, that interest is to be awarded on the damages for the past pecuniary loss before deducting social security benefits received by the claimant derogates from the statement in the text that the solution for awarding interest on the past pecuniary loss is unimpeachable. For details, see para.40-173, below.

344 [2016] A.C. 908.

345 See paras 40-066 and 40-209, below.

346 [1970] 2 Q.B. 130 CA; see para.19-087, above.

347 [1970] 2 Q.B. 130 CA at 146B. For the position on interest where no loss in earnings has been incurred because they have been made up to the claimant voluntarily by his employer, see *Davies v Inman* [1999] P.I.Q.R. Q26 CA, at para.40-160, below.

348 [1970] 2 Q.B. 130 CA at 146F to 147A.

349 See *Cookson v Knowles* [1979] A.C. 556 at para.19-089, above.

350 [1977] 1 W.L.R. 556.

351 Again the judge talked of departing from half rate rather than half period; see previous paragraph.

352 [1984] 1 W.L.R. 372 CA.

been referred and failing to note the earlier, unreported Court of Appeal decision in *Prokop v Department of Health and Social Security*,[353] which took the same line as these cases but which was not brought to the court's attention, the Court of Appeal held that in the typical personal injury case the principles laid down in *Jefford v Gee*,[354] should be adhered to. It was recognised that Forbes J's

> "way of thinking has its attractions and it may well be that in some cases it is the appropriate way of dealing with special damage",[355]

and there was instanced the high earner off work for only a few months but with a very substantial loss of income or the seriously injured victim paying for an expensive, successful operation which allowed him back to work very soon and, in both cases, the trial not coming on for four or five years. Fortunately, the court in *Dexter v Courtaulds*,[356] indicated that there was a way around its decision, saying that if there were special circumstances which would make it unfair for the claimant to apply the *Jefford v Gee*[357] rule, circumstances which would be known to the claimant but not necessarily to the defendant, the claimant should by his pleadings so state when claiming interest and set out the facts on which he relied.[358] This seemed a sensible result since it dealt with the difficulty, also adverted to by the court,[359] that it allowed defendants properly to gauge any offer to settle, which must today include interest though not separately itemised.

As time goes on, the courts are becoming more prepared to abandon the halving procedure and follow *Prokop* where there has been a decidedly irregular loss of special damages over the years between cause of action and trial. In *Hobin v Douglas (No.1)*,[360] where with over eight years between accident and trial the claimant's loss of earnings was attributable largely to the years immediately prior to the trial rather than the years immediately following the accident, the trial judge was prepared to calculate the interest for each year separately. Roch LJ, giving the judgment of the court upholding the award, said: **19-093**

> "The judge commented in the course of discussion with counsel: 'That [namely, his making a calculation by separate years] seems to me a very fair way of doing it. I would be surprised if the Court of Appeal took the view that there was a fairer way of doing it.' We agree."

In *Johnson v Fourie*,[361] the claimant's earnings loss fell to be calculated from the turnover of a company and the turnover had massively increased from some £3 million at the time of her injury to £20 million at the time of trial. Since applying the *Jefford v Gee* method would substantially over-compensate the claimant, Owen J had no difficulty in holding that the defendant's approach, which was to calculate the interest on an annual basis, was correct.[362] *Dexter* was not mentioned in the

---

353 *Prokop v Department of Health and Social Security* unreported 5 July 1983.
354 [1970] 2 Q.B. 130 CA.
355 [1984] 1 W.L.R. 372 CA at 375C.
356 [1984] 1 W.L.R. 372 CA.
357 [1970] 2 Q.B. 130 CA.
358 [1984] 1 W.L.R. 372 CA at 377C.
359 [1984] 1 W.L.R. 372 CA at 376H.
360 *The Independent*, 26 October 1998 CA.
361 [2011] EWHC 1062 (QB).
362 [2011] EWHC 1062 (QB) at [138] and [139].

judgment.[363] Not applying *Dexter* in these cases avoided not under-compensation but substantial over-compensation, the greater loss coming late rather than early in the period between cause of action and trial. Whether in these cases the special circumstances were pleaded or required to be pleaded, here by the defendant rather than the claimant, is not known; indeed this could be rather difficult for a defendant who was not apprised of the claimant's special circumstances. In any event it is thought that the days of the *Dexter* decision are numbered.

19-094 **(c) The peculiar method applied to non-pecuniary loss** Giving the judgment of the court in *Jefford v Gee*,[364] Lord Denning MR laid down[365] in respect of the non-pecuniary loss of a claimant in a personal injury claim that, as a general rule, interest should be given on the award not from when the cause of action accrued, or if later from when the loss was felt, but only from the date of service of the writ, continuing until the date of judgment.[366] This solution of the court stemmed from the principle, culled by Lord Denning MR from his survey of the various strands of authority, that interest

> "should only be awarded to a plaintiff *for being kept out of money* which ought to have been paid to him"[367]

and that the defendant ought to have paid once the writ had been served.[368] This, however, seems a very dubious principle since, if the defendant, as will frequently happen, considers that the claim against him should be contested, he cannot be blamed for not paying before the time that judgment is eventually entered against him. It is true that his obligation to pay then relates back, not however to the time that the writ was issued but to the time that the cause of action accrued. Lord Denning MR pointed to Sir Robert Phillimore's statement in *The Northumbria*[369]—that the Admiralty courts held that interest was due when payment was not made *ex mora*—as showing that there must have been a wrongful withholding by the defendant,[370] but the fact remains that the Admiralty courts, in awarding interest when a ship was lost as in *The Northumbria*, allowed interest to run not from the date of the writ but from the date of the loss.[371] Nor is Lord Diplock's restatement

---

363 See too *Horton v Evans* [2007] EWHC 315 (QB) where the claimant claimed interest on lost earnings at half rate from the time of her injury, saying that this was in accordance with *Dexter*, but Keith J had no doubt that interest was to be awarded at the half rate only from the later time when the loss of earnings commenced: at [8].

364 [1970] 2 Q.B. 130 CA.

365 [1970] 2 Q.B. 130 CA at 147F to H.

366 And, in relation to an additional party, only from the time of the service of the third party notice which apprises him of the proceedings: *Slater v Hughes* [1971] 1 W.L.R. 1438 CA. This solution was also applied by Lord Denning MR to the pecuniary loss in Fatal Accidents Act claims until, as we have seen (at para.19-089, above), the decision in *Cookson v Knowles* [1979] A.C. 556 made it possible to follow the pattern adopted for pecuniary loss in personal injury claims by giving interest from the death on the pre-trial loss and no interest at all on the post-trial loss.

367 [1970] 2 Q.B. 130 CA at 146A. The italics are his.

368 [1970] 2 Q.B. 130 CA at 147G. He applied the same principle in the context of a contractual claim in *Harbutt's "Plasticine" v Wayne Tank & Pump Co* [1970] 1 Q.B. 447 CA; facts at para.19-044, above.

369 (1869) L.R. 3 A. & E. 6; see para.19-020, above.

370 [1970] P. 130 CA at 144F.

371 See the cases at para.19-020, above.

in *Wright v British Railways Board*[372] of the considerations which have led to the awarding of interest only from the date of issue of the writ any more convincing; as for the important practical consideration that the current rule encourages claimants not to delay in bringing claims, the encouragement is already present by virtue of the discretion as to how far interest may be given or may be withheld.[373] And it may be noted that Lord Denning MR's principle has been departed from at first instance for the limited non-pecuniary loss which has since become available in Fatal Accidents Act claims.[374]

The courts' solution would appear to be an uneasy and unsatisfactory compromise between awarding no interest and awarding too much interest, a compromise dictated by the fact that awards for non-pecuniary loss in personal injury claims do not, and probably cannot, provide a breakdown between the past loss to judgment and the prospective loss thereafter.[375] Interest is therefore effectively being given in respect of future loss, which in itself is an argument for affording no interest at all, as has already been suggested should be the case,[376] to the victim of personal injury.[377] **19-095**

### (4) Effect of delay on time to and from which interest runs

For very many years after interest became statutorily available, while the very occasional statement could be found that a claimant might be deprived of interest if he dragged his heels in pursuing his action—in particular the comment of Watkins J in *Birkett v Hayes*[378]—there appear to have been no decisions, or at least no reported decisions, giving effect to such exhortations. Not until the late 1980s did decisions begin to appear, after which time they have made rapid progress. **19-096**

**(a) Types of claim in which reduction of interest for delay has been considered** There is of course no limit to the types of claim which can give rise to the issue of whether there should be a reduction in the interest which would normally **19-097**

372 [1983] 2 A.C. 773 at 779A to G.

373 See the cases on delay at paras 19-096 to 19-102, below.

374 See at para.19-133, below the unreported *Khan v Duncan* and *Prior v Hastie*. Along the same lines is *Derby Specialist Fabrication Ltd v Burton* [2001] 2 All E.R. 840 EAT, a case of the statutory tort of racial discrimination. This was the result of the regulations governing such claims, the Employment Tribunals (Interest on Awards in Discrimination Cases) Regulations (SI 1996/2803) providing in reg.6(1)(a) that interest on damages for injury to feelings is to run from the date of the act of discrimination to the day of calculation. See *Derby*, at [36] and following.

375 See para.19-087, above. In *Slater v Hughes* [1971] 1 W.L.R. 1438 CA Davies LJ conceded that there was a certain illogicality in allowing interest on the general damages to run only from the date of service of writ while allowing interest on the special damages from the date of injury: at 1444.

376 See para.19-053, above.

377 Some curious arguments for the defendant appeared in respect of damages for personal injury non-pecuniary loss in *Manning v King's College Hospital NHS Trust* [2008] EWHC 3008 (QB). It was argued that interest should run not from service of the writ but from the later service of the particulars of claim, argued that interest should run not to the date judgment was given but to the earlier date the trial commenced, and argued at one point, but later dropped, that interest should run not to the judgment on damages but to the much earlier judgment on liability. Naturally none of the arguments succeeded; they should have been given short shrift by the trial judge, yet were addressed by him at length: see at [71]–[81].

378 [1982] 1 W.L.R. 816 CA at 825E to F, with whom Lord Denning MR and Eveleigh LJ agreed. Lord Denning MR in the seminal *Jefford v Gee* [1970] 2 Q.B. 130 at 151E had said that gross delay could affect interest, but in either direction: see at para.19-087, above.

be awarded, but those which have to date arisen in the decided cases may be worth noting. Thus interest has been cut down for delay in claims for breach of contract,[379] claims in tort for interference with property,[380] claims for professional negligence[381] and claims on insurance policies.[382] But what has produced the commonest type of claim where interest has been reduced is not any of these types of business claim but claims for personal injury, starting with *Pritchard v Cobden*,[383] and under the Fatal Accidents Act, starting with *Corbett v Barking Health Authority*.[384] Many of these cases have involved either injured young children or dependent young children so that there has been entitlement to bring an action at any time before three years from the attainment of the child's majority, but it has been invariably held that this did not protect the child from being penalised in interest,[385] even where the court has assured the claimant that the delay was no cause for criticism.

**19-098** There is, however, the occasional case in which delay, though pleaded, is not held to cut down the interest award. Thus delay was held not relevant so as to defer the running of interest on demurrage due under a charterparty in *Galaxy Energy International Ltd v Bayoil SA, The Ama Ulgen*.[386] In *Seashore Marine SA v Phoenix Assurance Plc*,[387] there was held to have been no significant delay so as to justify interrupting the period of interest.[388] In *Headford v Bristol and District Health Authority*,[389] with as much as 30 years between personal injury and trial, the Court of Appeal refused to strike out or limit the claimant's pleaded claim for interest, which the trial judge must have been prepared to allow, but it is fair to say that it is unclear how many years of interest were being claimed. Again, delay did not feature sufficiently to limit the claim for interest in *Hunt v Optima (Cambridge) Ltd*.[390]

---

379 *Fast Ferries One SA v Ferries Australia Pty Ltd* [2000] 1 Lloyd's Rep. 534 (breach of shipbuilding contract). *Costain Ltd v Charles Haswell & Partners Ltd* [2010] 128 Con. L.R. 154 (breach of building contract by defective design for foundation works); *Cooper v National Westminster Bank Plc* [2010] 1 Lloyd's Rep. 490 (breach of banking contract, where the reduction in interest for delay was tempered by the defendant bank's high-handed conduct towards the claimant customer: see at [91]–[95]).

380 *Metal Box v Currys* [1988] 1 W.L.R. 175 (negligent damage in fire of goods stored by three claimants); *Blayney v Clogau St Davids Gold Mines Ltd* [2002] F.S.R. 233 (infringement of copyright).

381 *Hamilton-Jones v David & Snape* [2004] 1 W.L.R. 924; solicitor's negligence.

382 *Adcock v Co-operative Insurance Society* [2001] Lloyd's Rep. I.R. 657 CA; *Kuwait Airways v Kuwait Insurance* [2001] Lloyd's Rep. I.R. 678; *Hellenic Industrial Development Bank SA v Atkin, The Julia* [2003] Lloyd's Rep. I.R. 365.

383 [1988] Fam. 22 CA; see at 44D to F, the headnote having nothing on interest. Also *Spittle v Bunney* [1988] 1 W.L.R. 847 CA; *Nash v Southmead Health Authority* [1993] P.I.Q.R Q156; *Fairhurst v St Helen's and Knowsley Health Authority* [1995] P.I.Q.R. Q1; *Read v Harris* [1995] P.I.Q.R. Q34; *Eagle v Chambers (No.2)* [2004] 1 W.L.R. 3081 CA.

384 [1991] 2 Q.B. 448 CA. Also *Cresswell v Eaton* [1991] 1 W.L.R. 1113.

385 First stated at first instance in *Corbett v Barking Health Authority* [1991] 2 Q.B. 408 CA, that from "the fact that the child is protected by limitation, it does not follow he is therefore protected as regards to interest": see at 431H to 432A. But the child may become protected in another way: see the footnote at the end of para.19-102, below.

386 [2001] 1 Lloyd's Rep. 512.

387 [2002] 1 Lloyd's Rep. 238.

388 [2002] 1 Lloyd's Rep. 238 at 244 at [31]–[35].

389 [1995] P.I.Q.R. P180 CA.

390 [2013] EWHC 1121 (TCC); see at [8]–[12]. *Network Rail Infrastructure Ltd v Hardy* [2015] EWHC1460 TTC is a case other than of personal injury where delay, which was pleaded, was held not to cut down the interest award. The earlier judgment on the damages to be awarded is at para.39-029, below.

**(b) Manner in which delay affects the calculation of the interest award** Delay by a claimant may affect the time from, or the time to, which interest runs; interest may be cut down either at the beginning or at the end of the period of accrual of cause of action to judgment. One might think that delay should operate upon the time to which, rather than from which, interest is to run, on the basis that the claimant is awarded interest up until the time when he would have obtained judgment had he pursued his claim with all due diligence; this was how the matter was resolved in *Read v Harris*,[391] and *Blayney v Clogau St Davids Gold Mines Ltd*.[392] Other cases have lopped off the period at the beginning. Thus the starting point for interest was taken at a date well after cause of action but continuing to judgment in *Adcock v Co-operative Insurance Society*,[393] and in *Hamilton-Jones v David & Snape*,[394] while in the third of the three claims which were before the court in *Metal Box v Currys*,[395] interest was awarded from the time of issue of writ to judgment. This approach probably stems from the fact that the largest element in delay is often tardiness on the part of the claimant in instituting proceedings. **19-099**

The commonest approach is not to have any specified period from one point in time to another but simply to take the interest for the years from accrual of cause of action to judgment and then to disallow the interest for a number of these years. Either the trial judge will state that he is deducting a specified number of years of interest, as in *Corbett v Barking Health Authority*,[396] and in *Eagle v Chambers (No.2)*,[397] or will specify the number of years, fewer than the years from accrual of cause of action to judgment, for which he will award interest, as in the first two of the three claims in *Metal Box v Currys*,[398] and in *Hellenic Industrial Development Bank SA v Atkin, The Julia*.[399] **19-100**

With interest rates naturally varying over time, these different methods of going about the reduction on account of delay have repercussions on the calculation of the interest. Where the court is prepared to award, say, seven years of interest in a case with a nine-year period between accrual of cause of action and judgment, there will be a difference in amount between interest for the seven years from accrual of cause of action, for the seven years preceding judgment and for seven-ninths of the interest from accrual of cause of action to judgment.[400] **19-101**

**(c) Periods by which interest is reduced** By reason of the discretionary nature of the trial court's decision to reduce interest, it is impossible to lay down any general rules as to the degree of reduction in particular cases. This is well emphasised by the fact that, whenever the matter has gone higher, the trial judge's **19-102**

---

391 [1995] P.I.Q.R. Q34.

392 [2002] F.S.R. 233 at [128]–[130].

393 [2001] Lloyd's Rep. I.R. 657 CA.

394 [2004] 1 W.L.R. 924.

395 [1988] 1 W.L.R. 175.

396 [1991] 2 Q.B. 408 CA.

397 [2004] 1 W.L.R. 3081 CA. Also in *Pritchard v Cobden* [1988] Fam. 22 CA, *Spittle v Bunney* [1988] 1 W.L.R. 847 CA and *Cresswell v Eaton* [1991] 1 W.L.R. 1113.

398 [1988] 1 W.L.R. 175.

399 [2003] Lloyd's Rep. I.R. 365.

400 See *Spittle v Bunney* [1988] 1 W.L.R. 847 CA at 860F ("the judge … was unable to adjudicate on which the … years were") and 860I ("the difficulty of identifying which were the two years which had to be deducted"). One of counsel's arguments for an increase in the interest awarded by the trial judge in *Adcock v Co-operative Insurance Society* [2001] Lloyd's Rep. I.R. 657 CA was that the claimant was prejudiced by the disallowance of interest for the early years of the claim.

reduction of the period of interest awarded by him has invariably been left untouched by the Court of Appeal.[401] The range of periods involved is all that can be documented. Thus the cases reveal that to date the minimum number of years between cause of action and judgment that has brought intervention has been seven,[402] around nine years quite commonly leads to reduction,[403] with the high point coming at 24 years where the claimant was a child injured at birth.[404] As for the period for which interest is not awarded, nine months appears to be easily the shortest,[405] two to four years is common,[406] seven years has appeared,[407] and in the cases involving children 10 or 11 years of reduction have been known in the context of exceedingly long intervals between cause of action and judgment.[408]

## 2. Rate of Interest Awarded

**19-103** As already indicated,[409] the rules governing the period of time for which interest may be awarded do not vary as between interest under statute and interest at common law. However, when it comes to the question of the rate of interest the difference between the two forms of interest is stark. This is because, while, as we shall see, various rates have competed with one another in the calculation of the simple interest allowed by statute, with a case deserving interest as damages at common law the interest to be awarded is most likely to be compound where not only are commercially based rates invariably used but also, and certainly in the new world of *Sempra Metals*, the courts will concern themselves with the actual rate at which the claimant has had to borrow or at which he has been unable to invest.[410] Thus

---

401 *Pritchard v Cobden* [1988] Fam. 22 CA; *Spittle v Bunney* [1988] 1 W.L.R. 847 CA; *Corbett v Barking Health Authority* [1991] 2 Q.B. 408 CA; *Adcock v Co-operative Insurance Society* [2001] Lloyd's Rep. I.R. 657 CA; *Eagle v Chambers (No.2)* [2004] 1 W.L.R. 3081 CA.

402 *Read v Harris* [1995] P.I.Q.R. Q34; and see the 7½ years in *Spittle v Bunney* [1988] 1 W.L.R. 847 CA and *Hamilton-Jones v David & Snape* [2004] 1 W.L.R. 924.

403 *Cresswell v Eaton* [1991] 1 W.L.R. 1113 (nine years); *Adcock v Co-operative Insurance Society* [2001] Lloyd's Rep. I.R. 657 CA (nine years); *Metal Box v Currys* [1988] 1 W.L.R. 175 (two claims nine years, one claim 914); *Pritchard v Cobden* [1988] Fam. 22 CA (9½ years); *Hellenic Industrial Development Bank SA v Atkin, The Julia* [2003] Lloyd's Rep. I.R. 365 (eight years); *Corbett v Barking Health Authority* [1991] 2 Q.B. 408 CA, went up to 11½ years.

404 In *Fairhurst v St Helen's and Knowsley Health Authority* [1995] P.I.Q.R. Q1. Not far behind was *Nash v Southmead Health Authority* [1993] P.I.Q.R Q156 with 17 years.

405 In *Blayney v Clogau St Davids Gold Mines Ltd* [2002] F.S.R. 233.

406 *Pritchard v Cobden* [1988] Fam. 22 CA (two years); *Spittle v Bunney* [1988] 1 W.L.R. 847 CA (two years); *Metal Box v Currys* [1988] 1 W.L.R. 175 (two claims two years but a third claim seven); *Cresswell v Eaton* [1991] 1 W.L.R. 1113 (2½years); *Read v Harris* [1995] P.I.Q.R. Q34 (three years); *Hamilton-Jones v David & Snape* [2004] 1 W.L.R. 924 (3½years); *Corbett v Barking Health Authority* [1991] 2 Q.B. 408 CA (four years); *Hellenic Industrial Development Bank SA v Atkin (The Julia)* [2003] Lloyd's Rep. I.R. 365 (four years).

407 *Eagle v Chambers (No.2)* [2004] 1 W.L.R. 3081 CA. Being out of a total of 14½ years from injury to judgment, the Court of Appeal accepted that the judge had taken "a tough view" but did not interfere. See at [99]–[101] (no reference to interest in report's catchwords or headnote).

408 *Nash v Southmead Health Authority* [1993] P.I.Q.R. Q156 (10 years); *Fairhurst v St Helen's and Knowsley Health Authority* [1995] P.I.Q.R. Q1 (11 years). Buxton LJ in *Eagle v Chambers (No.2)* [2004] 1 W.L.R. 3081 CA said that in cases where the inordinate delay was due not to the claimant—particularly where a child or a patient—but to the claimant's solicitors, the need to deprive the claimant of his full compensation might some day be reconsidered but for the present the claimant's only remedy would be an action based on negligence against his solicitors: see at [110]–[112].

409 See para.19-071, above.

410 See especially at para.19-062, above.

we find in *West v Ian Finlay and Associates*,[411] where the claimants had to borrow to meet the cost of remedying the defects occurring in the renovation of their house undertaken by the defendant, that Edward-Stuart J awarded them, though with no mention of *Sempra Metals*, interest at 7 per cent over base rate as this was needed to cover their borrowing.[412]

### (1) General overview: the various rates of interest

No firm rate of interest on damages can of course be laid down for all cases since interest rates constantly change and the award of interest under statute is discretionary. But beyond this there fall to be considered two matters which introduce complications. First, it is necessary to look separately at the development in commercial and analogous cases, commercial matters being dealt with largely by the Commercial Court, in ship collision cases, which have been dealt with in Admiralty, and in cases of personal injury and wrongful death. Secondly, it is necessary to look at three different types of rate, which are the commercial rate, used in the Commercial Court, in Admiralty and elsewhere; the special investment account rate on money paid into court, which is used in cases of personal injury and wrongful death; and the rate on judgment debts, or the Judgments Act rate, which has been used in a variety of damages cases. Only with compound interest are these complications not encountered for the reasons indicated in the previous paragraph. **19-104**

The Law Commission in its Consultation Paper on *Compound Interest*,[413] in proposing for compound interest that a standard rate, applicable in all cases, should be prescribed, proposed also that this rate apply to simple interest[414] and that the prescribed rate should be the commercial rate, a rate set by reference to bank base rate.[415] These recommendations have followed through to the Law Commission Report entitled *Pre-Judgment Interest on Debt and Damages*.[416] This proposal to have a single rate is a very sensible one. The reasons for the use of one of the various rates today in play as against another are largely historical. The judgment debts rate goes back to s.17 of the Judgments Act 1838 when interest on judgment debts was introduced, with a rate fixed at 4 per cent. It stood unchanged for well over a hundred years until power was conferred by s.44(1) of the Administration of Justice Act 1970 to substitute rates other than 4 per cent in the section. By then 4 per cent could no longer be regarded as a realistic rate, and the courts very rightly rejected any argument that it should be taken as an appropriate yardstick for determining the rate of interest to be awarded on damages themselves. When after 1969 it became mandatory to award interest in personal injury claims, Lord Denning MR chose to take the special, then called short-term, investment account as his model on account of the judgment debt rate being by then unrealistically low.[417] At the same time the courts in commercial and all other cases began to reject judgment debt **19-105**

---

411 [2013] EWHC 868 (TCC).

412 [2013] EWHC 868 (TCC) at [388] and [389].

413 Law Commission, *Compound Interest* (2002), Law Com. No.167.

414 *Compound Interest* (2002), Law Com. No.167 at Pt V, para.5.4.

415 *Compound Interest* (2002), Law Com. No.167 at Pt V, para.5.5.

416 *Pre-Judgment Interest on Debt and Damages* (2004), Law Com. No.287at para.1.18 and paras 10.1 and 10.2.

417 *Jefford v Gee* [1970] 2 Q.B. 130 CA at 148.

interest for the same reason[418] and to fashion their own rate based upon what happened in commerce.[419] However for some little time now, as will be seen, a practice has crept into some courts to award judgment rate interest in commercial and analogous cases[420] and also in personal injury cases.[421] Yet there is no rational distinction to be found between the various rates. They are all intended to achieve the same purpose which is to compensate the claimant who has been kept out of his money. Moreover, the uncertainty about which rate will be chosen in a particular case is unhealthy. Thus personal injury cases today have been encountered in which the defendant has argued for the special investment account rate when standing at 6 per cent,[422] the claimant for the higher judgment debt rate when standing at 8 per cent,[423] and the trial judge, unsure of the true position, has simply split the difference. Such a result is most unsatisfactory; one simply does not know where one is.[424]

**19-106** The proposal that the single rate should be the commercial rate rather than one of the other two rates in the field is also very sensible. The judgment rate in particular should be avoided by reason of its entire failure to keep up with market rates over the years. As we have already seen in dealing with the question of to what time interest on damages should run,[425] not only did the judgment rate remain at 4 per cent from its 19th century inception until 1971,[426] by which time it was well below the market rate—only in 1970 had statute given the power to raise the rate—but it went to a high of 15 per cent in 1985 when market rates were already somewhat lower and remained there while market rates began to tumble. Righting the position in 1993 by a reduction to 8 per cent,[427] the figure at which the special investment account rate then stood, the judgment rate is still at that figure today although market rates are lower. Indeed, that the rate has not moved again is curious in the light of the special investment account rate having been reduced on three occasions[428] in response to further falls in interest rates. One would have thought that, once parity between the two rates had been achieved in 1993, they would have been kept the same. Yet today the disparity is far greater with, as we shall see, the special investment account rate recognising today's dramatic economic downturn by announcing reduction after reduction and the judgment rate so far ignoring it by making no change.

**19-107** The rate on the short-term, now special, investment account used for interest on damages in cases of personal injury and wrongful death[429] has also moved in fits and starts, but the fits used to be less severe and the starts have been more frequent. It was already down to 8 per cent when judgment debt rate caught up with it in 1993

---

418 See, e.g. *The Mecca* [1968] 665 at 674, per Brandon J.

419 See paras 19-109 and following, below.

420 At para.19-118, below.

421 At para.19-130, below.

422 Which it no longer does. See para.19-129, below.

423 Which it still does. See para.19-130, below.

424 Interest awarded may be at an enhanced rate—thus in *The Vergina (No.3)* [2002] 1 Lloyd's Rep. 238 it was LIBOR plus 3 per cent and in *Kinch v Rosling* [2009] EWHC 286 (QB) it was 10 per cent—but consideration of such cases falls outside the scope of this text as the interest given is not interest on damages.

425 See para.19-073, above.

426 When 7.5 per cent was substituted.

427 SI 1993/564.

428 See next paragraph.

429 See para.19-126, below.

and since then it has responded to falls in market rates by a reduction to 7 per cent in 1999, to 6 per cent in 2002, and in 2009 first to 3 per cent, then to 1 per cent and finally to the all time low of 0.5 per cent where it still stands. It has thus been more realistic than judgment debt rate but it has tended to follow the market rather than to keep up with it although, as can be seen, it has moved fairly speedily in today's recession.[430]

The case, in moving to a uniform rate, for using the commercial rate is therefore a strong one. Staughton LJ was absolutely right when some time ago he summed up the position, at once pointedly and concisely, in *United Bank of Kuwait v Hammond*,[431] with the comment that the commercial rate is **19-108**

> "more sophisticated and accurate than the slow moving special account rate, or the even slower moving Judgment [sic] Act rate".

Precisely what is meant by the commercial rate is considered below.[432] In its Report, *Pre-Judgment Interest on Debt and Damages*, in 2004 the Law Commission proposed a rate of 1 per cent over bank rate but with a discretion in the court to award a higher or a lower rate.[433]

## (2) Cases in the Commercial Court and analogous cases

**(a) Development over the years** While it has always been recognised that in commercial transactions the award of interest should reflect the current commercial value of money,[434] there was for long a prevalent practice of awarding 5 per cent, which stretched back well into the 19th century[435] and continued into the second half of the 20th. It is true that occasionally, when there had been a tendency in the market towards lower interest rates, interest at 4 per cent[436] and even 3.5 per cent[437] had been awarded, but before the 1960s there appear to be no cases in which interest on damages was awarded at a rate exceeding 5 per cent. Change came about the middle of the decade[438] and by 1973 in *Cremer v General Carriers*,[439] Kerr J was awarding interest at 7.5 per cent, saying that this was the rate which he had been awarding generally in other cases.[440] **19-109**

But even before this a more flexible approach was emerging, perhaps first evidenced by Donaldson J's award in *F.M.C. Meat v Fairfield Cold Stores*[441] of interest at 1 per cent over bank rate, an award of which, he said, was his "usual course".[442] In *Miliangos v George Frank (Textiles)*,[443] the parties agreed that, if the **19-110**

---

430 For the various rates over the years see the 2013/2014 edition of *Facts and Figures, Tables for the Calculation of Damages*.

431 [1988] 1 W.L.R. 1051 CA at 1064.

432 See paras 19-109 and following, below.

433 (2004), Law Com. No.287, Pt III para.343 and para.333 respectively. The prescribed rate is intended for simple and compound interest alike.

434 See *Re Roberts* (1880) 14 Ch. D. 49 CA at 52, per Jessel MR.

435 Illustrations are *Petre v Duncombe* (1851) 20 L.J.Q.B. 242; *Re Roberts* (1880) 14 Ch. D. 49 CA; *Mellersh v Brown* (1890) 45 Ch. D. 225.

436 *Kemp v Tolland* [1956] 2 Lloyd's Rep. 681; see especially at 691.

437 *Neumann v I.R.C.* (1933) 148 L.T. 457; see especially at 461.

438 For the detail in figures see the 14th edition of this work (1980) at para.477.

439 [1974] 1 W.L.R. 341.

440 [1974] 1 W.L.R. 341 at 358A.

441 [1971] 2 Lloyd's Rep. 221.

442 [1971] 2 Lloyd's Rep. 221 at 227.

interest was to be awarded in accordance with appropriate sterling rates,[444] then 7.5 per cent should be awarded for a particular period and 1 per cent over minimum lending rate—as bank rate had then become—thereafter.[445] And by the time of *Miliangos v George Frank (Textiles) (No.2)*,[446] Bristow J is found to be assuming that this more flexible approach has become the norm, as he there said:

> "The court fixes a rate applicable for plaintiffs in general and has done so in the sterling context[447] by applying its judicial knowledge of what is from time to time the bank rate or minimum lending rate, and its judicial knowledge of the fact that in practice, by and large, it costs about one per cent more than that to borrow the money."[448]

Donaldson J in *F.M.C. Meat v Fairfield Cold Stores*,[449] had been prepared to use the bank rate as the basis for awarding interest although appreciating that it presented complications whenever the computation stretched over a long period[450]; and the courts should not be deflected from use of the minimum lending rate on account of the fears expressed by Kerr J in *Cremer v General Carriers*,[451] that the complications could increase with its use, since the object of the move from the one rate to the other was apparently to enable changes in rate to be made more flexibly and frequently than formerly.[452] In fact the 7.5 per cent rate which Kerr J awarded in that case was very near to the 7.9 per cent rate at which the claimants had arrived using bank rate and minimum lending rate, the period covered being from late 1968 to mid-1973.[453] However, much higher rates were in store after the oil crisis of late 1973; indeed by 1980 the minimum lending rate had risen above 16 per cent. In 1979 in *B.P. Exploration Co (Libya) v Hunt (No.2)*,[454] Robert Goff J, in awarding interest "on the basis of bank rate or minimum lending rate plus one per cent", did so "in accordance with the usual practice" in the Commercial Court,[455] and in 1984 Kerr LJ said in *Polish S.S. Co v Atlantic Maritime Co, The Garden City*,[456] that base rate—by then the equivalent of the former minimum lending rate—plus 1 per cent remained the practice in the Commercial Court.

**19-111** Cases other than those heard in the Commercial Court also began to attract interest at base rate plus one per cent. Thus in *Tate & Lyle Food and Distribution v Greater London Council*,[457] where dredging costs were incurred by the claimants to deal with a nuisance perpetrated by the defendants,[458] Forbes J preferred the commercial rate to the personal injury rate, saying that it seemed to him that the rate at which a commercial borrower could borrow money was the safest guide.[459]

443 [1975] Q.B. 487.
444 It was subsequently decided that Swiss rates were the appropriate ones: see para.19-121, below.
445 [1975] Q.B. 487 at 492H.
446 [1977] Q.B. 489.
447 He refers to the sterling context because the case itself had foreign overtones: see para.19-121, below.
448 [1977] Q.B. 489 at 496A.
449 [1971] 2 Lloyd's Rep. 221.
450 [1971] 2 Lloyd's Rep. 221 at 227.
451 [1974] 1 W.L.R. 341.
452 [1974] 1 W.L.R. 341 at 357E.
453 [1974] 1 W.L.R. 341 at 357H to 358A.
454 [1979] 1 W.L.R. 783.
455 [1979] 1 W.L.R. 783.
456 [1985] Q.B. 41 CA at 67B.
457 [1982] 1 W.L.R. 149.
458 See the case further at paras 19-112 and 19-135, below.
459 See [1982] 1 W.L.R. 149 at 154F to 155D. Followed by Slade J in *International Military Services*

Similarly in *Metal Box v Currys*,[460] where goods were tortiously destroyed in a fire and the owners' insurers were entitled to claim by subrogation, McNeill J, while noting counsel's submission that the case did not involve "a commercial dispute in the strict sense", took the view that

> "if insurers have to borrow at a commercial rate or apply their own funds and so lose their investment value to meet a claim by their insured, then recovery of that amount against a wrongdoer in an action by subrogation would carry interest at the commercial rate."[461]

Once the courts had accepted this approach of gearing the award of interest to commercial borrowing, the point was made in *Miliangos (No.2)*,[462] that the court is not concerned with the rate of interest at which the particular claimant may in fact have borrowed.[463] Bristow J there said: **19-112**

> "The court is not concerned with the actual cost of borrowing to the individual concerned in the individual case. Depending on many variables, some people can borrow cheaper than others. The court fixes a rate applicable for plaintiffs in general."[464]

Forbes J's approach in *Tate & Lyle Food and Distribution v Greater London Council*,[465] was, however, more flexible. While also saying that the appropriate rate was that at which claimants in general could borrow, he added that this did not

> "mean that you exclude entirely all attributes of the plaintiff other than that he is plaintiff. There is evidence here that large public companies of the size and prestige of these plaintiffs could expect to borrow at one per cent. over the minimum lending rate, while for smaller and less prestigious concerns the rate might be as high as three per cent. over the minimum lending rate. I think it would always be right to look at the rate at which plaintiffs with the general attributes of the actual plaintiff in the case (though not, of course, with any special or peculiar attribute) could borrow money as a guide to the appropriate interest rate."[466]

In *Shearson Lehman Hutton v Maclaine Watson & Co (No.2)*,[467] Webster J took the view that the cases talking of the Commercial Court's practice—cases already cited[468]—did not

> "have the effect of precluding evidence as to the rate at which persons with the general attributes of the plaintiff could have borrowed money",[469]

---

*Ltd v Capital & Counties Plc* [1982] 1 W.L.R. 575; see at 587 to 588.

460 [1988] 1 W.L.R. 175.

461 [1988] 1 W.L.R. 175 at 183A.

462 [1977] Q.B. 489.

463 Nor with the rate of profit that the claimant would have achieved with the money: *Tate and Lyle Food and Distribution v Greater London Council* [1982] 1 W.L.R. 149 at 155D, per Forbes J.

464 [1977] Q.B. 489 at 495H to 496A.

465 [1982] 1 W.L.R. 149.

466 [1982] 1 W.L.R. 149 at 154E to F. Citing this passage Ramsey J awarded interest at 3 per cent over base rate in *Bridge UK.Com Ltd v Abbey PynfordPlc* [2007] EWHC 728 TCC, being satisfied that the claimant was a company within the category of smaller businesses which had to borrow at higher rates: see at [145] and [146]. Also, Forbes J's comments about small concerns having to borrow at 3 per cent over base rate fits with the holding, 20 years later, in *Jaura v Ahmed* [2002] EWCA Civ 210 CA: see the case at para.19-114, below.

467 [1990] 3 All E.R. 723.

468 See para.19-110, above.

469 [1990] 3 All E.R. 723 at 733f.

and he went on:

> "I conclude, therefore, that the practice of the Commercial Court amounts to no more than a presumption which can be displaced if its application would be substantially unfair to either party".[470]

There was, however, no evidence in the case before him to displace the presumption.[471] In *Fiona Trust & Holding Corp v Privalov*,[472] where very substantial sums of interest were in issue, Andrew Smith J was prepared to consider the personal circumstances of the claimants and examined at some length[473] the defendants' contention that the LIBOR plus 2.5 per cent rate that he had taken as a starting point[474] was higher than the rate of interest that the claimants had in fact paid on their borrowings. Even so, he concluded that the defendants' contention was not made out.[475]

**19-113** For quite some years interest at base rate plus 1 per cent continued to be the norm.[476] Thus Webster J in *Shearson Lehman v Maclaine Watson (No.2)*,[477] applied what he regarded as the general rule and awarded 1 per cent over base rate. In the familiar negligence claims by mortgage lenders against valuers and solicitors, base rate plus 1 per cent has from time to time been awarded, as in *Banque Bruxelles Lambert v Eagle Star Insurance Co*,[478] and on the consequential loss in *Hartle v Laceys*.[479] Base rate plus 1 per cent was also awarded in *Martini Investments v McGinn*,[480] and in *Adcock v Co-operative Insurance Society*,[481] while, with foreign interest rates involved, in *Kuwait Airways v Kuwait Insurance*,[482] and in *Hellenic Industrial Development Bank SA v Atkin, The Julia*,[483] United States prime rate was awarded because it was the nearest equivalent to base rate plus 1 per cent.[484] Interest was awarded at 2 per cent over base rate in *Brown v K.M.R. Services*,[485] and *Deeny v Gooda Walker (No.3)*,[486] claims in the Commercial Court

---

470 [1990] 3 All E.R. 723 at 733g. Occasionally application of the usual rule would be unfair to the defendant as in *UCB Bank v Edwin Watson & Sons* unreported 9 March 1999, where the rate at which the claimants had to borrow was rightly awarded even though, in that case, it fell below rather than rose above the general rate.

471 [1990] 3 All E.R. 723 at 733h. The Commercial Court in *Kinetics Technology International v Cross Seas Shipping Corp, The Mosconici* [2001] 2 Lloyd's Rep. 313 rapidly scotched what was called the novel proposition that a discount be made to the commercial rate of interest to bring it in line with the 2 per cent utilised for non-pecuniary loss in personal injury claims: see at 316, col.2–317, col.1.

472 [2011] EWHC 664 (Comm).

473 [2011] EWHC 664 (Comm) at [23]–[31].

474 Foreign rates of interest were involved. See the case at para.19-120, below,

475 [2011] EWHC 664 (Comm) at [32].

476 Interest at base rate less 1 per cent was all that was awarded in *University of Keele v Price Waterhouse* [2004] P.N.L.R. 8 at 112 but that was because the claimant had conceded that this was the rate it would have earned on the moneys; see at [70] and [71]. No issue on interest appears in the appeal: [2004] P.N.L.R. 43 CA at 888.

477 [1990] 3 All E.R. 723.

478 [1995] 2 All E.R. 769 at first instance; not in issue on appeal.

479 [1999] Lloyd's Rep. P.N. 315 CA; for interest on the main award, see para.19-017, above.

480 [2001] Lloyd's Rep. I.R. 374.

481 [2001] Lloyd's Rep. I.R. 657.

482 [2001] Lloyd's Rep. I.R. 678; see the case at para.19-120, below.

483 [2003] Lloyd's Rep. I.R. 365.

484 These last cases were claims on an insurance policy, not claims for damages.

485 [1995] 2 Lloyd's Rep. 513. This does not appear from this report but from the report of the second case; see at the next footnote but one.

in the litigation by Lloyd's Names against their agents. The reason given was that this "represented what individual Names were likely to have to pay when borrowing money".[487]

**(b) The position today on rate level** With the turn of the century higher rates, still measured from base rates, slowly started to appear, the movement to higher rates receiving an initial boost from the decision of the Court of Appeal in *Jaura v Ahmed*.[488] The claimant suffered a wrongful forfeiture of the lease that he had taken of business premises. Because of reduced profits in the business he had entered into sub-leases of substantial parts of the premises in order to help service the bank overdraft which to the knowledge of his lessor, the defendant, he had incurred in order to finance the purchase. The wrongful termination deprived the claimant of the rents from the sub-leases so that he incurred a liability for accumulating interest on the overdraft. The Court of Appeal held him entitled to interest at 3 per cent over base rate to reflect the interest incurred on the overdraft. Rix LJ, who gave the only judgment on interest, with which the other two members of the court agreed, said: **19-114**

> "It is right that defendants who have kept small businessmen out of money to which a court ultimately judges them to be entitled should pay a rate which properly reflects the real cost of borrowing incurred by such a class of businessmen. The law should be prepared to recognise, as I suspect evidence might well reveal, that the borrowing costs generally incurred by them are well removed from the conventional rate of 1% above base (and sometimes even less) available to first class borrowers."

This sensible decision was then prayed in aid by claimants but not always successfully. This was so with the third claimant, a magazine publisher, in *Douglas v Hello! Ltd*,[489] because the trial judge was not satisfied that it had borrowed money at all, in which case the rate at which it could have invested, on which there was no evidence, would have been appropriate; in the result the judge awarded the amount claimed discounted by 20 per cent. *Jaura v Ahmed* was also unsuccessfully prayed in aid by the claimants in *Aerospace Publishing Ltd v Thames Water Utilities Ltd*,[490] the trial judge's award of 1 per cent over base despite the claimants having had to borrow at 2.5 per cent over base being held by the Court of the Appeal to be within his discretion.[491] By contrast, though without any reference to *Jaura v Ahmed*, 3 per cent over base rate was awarded in *Bridge UK.Com Ltd v Abbey Pynford Plc*,[492] the claimant having an overdraft facility with interest payable at that rate.[493] The trial judge in *Ramzan v Brookwide Ltd*,[494] regarded as typical a rate of 2 per cent over base rate, which she would have been prepared to award had not the defendant been prepared to accept an average rate of 6 per cent per annum over a nine-year period, a period which started with base rate, it was said, at 7.25

486 [1996] L.R.L.R. 168.
487 [1996] L.R.L.R. 168 at 175, col.1.
488 [2002] EWCA Civ 210 CA.
489 [2004] E.M.L.R. 14 at 230; see at [22].
490 (2007) 110 Con. L.R. 1.
491 (2007) 110 Con. L.R. 1 at [98].
492 [2007] EWHC 728 TCC.
493 [2007] EWHC 728 TCC at [146].
494 [2011] 2 All E.R. 38.

per cent and ended with it at 0.5 per cent.[495] The use of the rate of 6 per cent was not challenged in the Court of Appeal,[496] though the trial judge's use of a constant rate of interest was.[497] In *Driver v Air India Ltd*,[498] the Court of Appeal awarded to an employee interest at 8 per cent for one period and at 5 per cent for another when overtime had not been paid him[499]: this was at somewhat more than 3 per cent higher than base rate had been during the two periods. In *Attrill v Dresdner Kleinwort Ltd*,[500] a claim for breach of employment contracts by two individual employees of an employer bank, Owen J not only took borrowing rate but recognised that the awards of 5 per cent over the bank's base rate.[501] In *West v Ian Finlay and Associates*[502] Edwards-Stuart J went as far as 7 per cent over base rate.[503] From these cases it will be seen that courts are becoming prepared to endorse higher percentages over base rate now that, with the economic recession, base rate has fallen to an all-time low, standing since the middle of 2009 at a mere 0.5 per cent. Yet despite this, courts can still be found not going beyond 2 per cent over base rate, as in *Hunt v Optima (Cambridge) Ltd*.[504]

**19-115** The London Inter-Bank Offered Rate, generally referred to as LIBOR, has very much come to the fore as an appropriate interest rate to award. However, it has tended to have been utilised by agreement of the parties rather than by adjudication of the court, as in *Nykredit Mortgage Bank v Edward Erdman Group (No.2)*,[505] and *Birmingham Midshires Mortgage Services v Phillips*.[506] LIBOR was also accepted as appropriate in *Portman Building Society v Bevan Ashford*.[507] In *Eronpark Ltd v Secretary of State for the Environment*,[508] interest on compensation for acquisition of land awarded by the Lands Tribunal was based on the cost of borrowing money at LIBOR plus 2 per cent. These may have represented the rates at which the claimants had borrowed in the particular cases. Certainly the award of LIBOR plus 3 per cent in *Pgf II SA v Royal & Sun Alliance Insurance Plc*[509] was on the assumption that this was the rate at which the claimant would have borrowed.[510]

**19-116** It has been seen that the commercial rate to which courts tend to look in fashioning their awards is the rate at which money would have been borrowed. But the wrong done to a claimant may cause him to miss out on investments rather than cause him to borrow and the return on investments could well fall short of the cost of taking up a borrowing facility. In dealing with how the prescribed rate of interest that is proposed should be set, the Law Commission stated in its *Consultation*

---

495 [2011] 2 All E.R. 38 at [79].
496 [2012] 1 All E.R. 903 CA at [85].
497 See para.19-086, above. The facts of this curious case are at para.39-058, below.
498 [2011] EWCA Civ 986 CA.
499 See [2011] EWCA Civ 986 CA at [7], [12] and [13].
500 [2012] EWHC 1468 (QB).
501 [2012] EWHC 1468 (QB) at [2]–[5].
502 [2013] EWHC 868 (TCC).
503 See the case at para.19-103, above.
504 [2013] EWHC 1121 (TCC); see at [5] and [14]. Also *2 Travel Group Plc v Cardiff City Transport Services Ltd* [2012] C.A.T. 19 at [415] and *Albion Water Ltd v Dwr Cymru Cyfyngedig* [2013] C.A.T. 6 at [226].
505 [1997] 1 W.L.R. 1627 HL: 0.4 per cent above LIBOR.
506 [1998] P.N.L.R. 468: three month LIBOR.
507 [2000] Lloyd's Rep. P.N. 354 CA. The contest was between simple and compound interest.
508 [2001] 3 E.G.L.R. 133.
509 [2010] EWHC 1459 (TCC). Facts at para.28-072, below.
510 See [2010] EWHC 1459 (TCC) at [343] to [348].

*Paper*[511] that the rate should

> "reflect the market investment rates available to, or the mortgage rates payable by, private individuals"[512]

and, more concisely in its following Report,[513] that "the rate should reflect the commercial reality of borrowing and investing".[514] But investment rates and borrowing rates are not going to be the same and if they are intended to be alternatives no choice is made by the Law Commission between them. In *Fiona Trust & Holding Corp v Privalov*,[515] Andrew Smith J recognised that the rate of interest achievable on investment was likely to fall below the rate exacted on borrowing but, citing cases, regarded the court's consistent practice to be to use the borrowing rate whatever the particular claimant's position, whether as a result of the wrong he had to borrow or had less to invest.[516] This approach is unfortunate, not being realistic. And there is also the question of what rate of interest should be utilised where no borrowing or loss of investment is involved. This would have been the position in *Metal Box v Currys*,[517] had the claimants not carried insurance and McNeill J's judgment there suggests that this factor should not make a difference, not disentitling the claimant to an award of interest.[518]

**(c) The commercial rate and compound interest** It is important to appreciate that while it is said, as by Rix LJ, importantly, in the Court of Appeal in *Jaura v Ahmed*,[519] that rates higher than 1 per cent over bank rate are generally required in order to reflect the real cost of a claimant's borrowing, higher rates are not likely in themselves to suffice to make the claimant whole as there is not taken into account that it is generally the case that interest on a bank or other borrowing is compounded. Indeed *Jaura v Ahmed* itself makes this entirely clear. The appellant started by claiming in the alternative interest at common law as of right and interest under statute in the court's discretion, both at an enhanced rate to cover borrowing costs, but ended up claiming only the latter. The claim for statutory interest was necessarily for simple interest but the abandoned claim must also have been for simple interest since the trial judge's holding that compound interest was not available was accepted by the appellant's counsel and endorsed by Rix LJ.[520] Thus rates may be enhanced without being compounded.[521] The same may have been the position in *Xena Systems Ltd v Cantideck*,[522] where on account of patent infringement the holder of a patent had had to borrow at 8 per cent. His claim, citing *Sempra Metals*, for interest at this rate as a head of damage was preferred to the defendant's argument for 1 per cent over bank base rate, a rate commonly used for statutory 19-117

511 (2002), Law Com. No.167. For this see para.19-105, above.
512 (2002), Law Com. No.167, Pt.V, para.5.5.
513 (2004), Law Com. No.287.
514 (2004), Law Com. No.287, Pt III para.3.25.
515 [2011] EWHC 664 (Comm).
516 [2011] EWHC 664 (Comm) at [14].
517 [1988] 1 W.L.R. 175.
518 See the case at para.19-046, above.
519 [2002] EWCA Civ 210 CA. See the case at para.19-114, above.
520 For all this see his judgment at [2002] EWCA Civ 210 CA at [14] to [16].
521 So too the enhanced rate of 3 per cent over LIBOR in *Pgf II SA v Royal & Sun Alliance Insurance Plc* [2010] EWHC 1459 (TCC) (see para.19-115, above) was not compounded.
522 [2013] EWPCC 1.

interest. His Honour Judge Birss specifically referred to the distinction between interest as damages, the claimant's contention, and interest on damages, the defendant's, but whether the award was of compound interest is not made clear.[523] Also in *West v Ian Finlay & Associates*, where the claimants on account of the defective renovation of their house borrowed to fund remedial work at 8 per cent, Edwards-Stuart J awarded them interest at this rate. Again it is unclear whether this was compounded, although it is fair to say that lenders generally compound the interest that they charge.[524]

### (d) Deviations from the commercial rate

**19-118** *(i) Judgment rate* The commercial rate has from time to time been departed from, in cases not in the Commercial Court itself, in favour of the rate awarded on judgment debts and for the Court of Appeal to have declined to interfere with the trial judge's discretion so to award. This happened in *Watts v Morrow*,[525] following in this respect a case not in the law reports, *Pinnock v Wilkins & Son*.[526] This departure from the norm is not to be encouraged. Bingham LJ in *Watts*[527] admitted that:

> "there is much to be said for applying a rate of interest which reflects the cost or value of money over the relevant period rather than a flat rate under the Judgments Act 1838 which has remained fixed over a number of years despite fluctuations in interest rates during that time."[528]

Nonetheless awards at the judgment rate continue to appear. This happened again, with no reasons given, in *Crédit Lyonnais SA v Russell Jones & Walker*,[529] in *Hamilton-Jones v David & Snape*,[530] and in *Kinch v Rosling*.[531] By contrast, the trial judge in *Ramzan v Brookwide Ltd*,[532] said rightly that judgment rate was inappropriate for pre-judgment interest.[533] In *Perry v Raleys Solicitors*,[534] the Court of Appeal awarded interest at the judgment rate for a lengthy period of more than a decade pre-judgment. However, in that case, the only other alternative which had been proposed was the special investment account rate which Gloster LJ, with whom the other judges agreed, considered would be insufficient to compensate the

---

523 [2013] EWPCC 1 at [34], [35] and [47].

524 With awards of compound interest there is no settled rule as to how frequently the compounding is to be done, whether monthly, annually or for any other period of time. For example, in *Fiona Trust & Holding Corp v Privalov* [2011] EWHC 664 (Comm) Andrew Smith J adopted three-monthly rests: at [19].

525 [1991] 1 W.L.R. 1421 CA; see at 1443H to 1444B and 1446A to B.

526 *The Times*, 29 January 1990.

527 [1991] 1 W.L.R. 1421 CA.

528 [1991] 1 W.L.R. 1421 CA at 1446A. See the discussion at para.19-106, above.

529 [2003] Lloyd's Rep. P.N. 7.

530 [2004] 1 WL.R. 924.

531 [2009] EWHC 286 (QB). But in *Nicholson v Knox Ukiwa & Co* [2008] P.N.L.R. 33 at 782 Saunders J did give a reason for preferring judgment rate for interest over an extremely long period of 15 years; the reason was that the high rate offset the lack of compounding: see at [106]–[109]. Facts at para.34-086, below.

532 [2011] 2 All E.R. 38.

533 [2011] 2 All E.R. 38 at [78]. For her award as to rate of interest, accepted by the Court of Appeal ([2012] 1 All E.R. 903 CA), see para.19-114, above

534 [2017] EWCA Civ 314 CA.

appellant for the loss suffered by being out of his money.[535] Another reason given, however, was that the higher judgment rate should be preferred as a sanction for the conduct of the respondent in how the litigation was conducted.[536] This effectively adds a punitive element to the assessment of the monetary interest award. If it were the only justification for the higher award then it would amount to a sanction for post-breach conduct. This approach is consistent with the practice that is permitted following an offer of settlement that is more favourable than the judgment.[537]

*(ii) Special investment account rate* With the comments of Bingham LJ in mind in *Watts v Morrow*,[538] encouraging the award of the commercial rate over the judgment rate,[539] Neuberger J in *Harrison v Bloom Camillin (No.2)*,[540] declined to award interest at the judgment debt rate. Instead he made his award at the special investment account rate, used in personal injury cases, on the basis that this rate better reflected changes in the value of money and interest rates.[541] While this is of course true, it is even more true of the commercial rate.[542] Yet Neuberger J's use of the special investment account rate was adopted in *Griffiths v Last Cawthra Feather*.[543] **19-119**

**(e) Applicability of foreign rates** Commercial cases have appeared in which the interest rate has had to be arrived at with reference not to sterling but to foreign rates; the courts have been prepared to be guided by the rate at which a person could "reasonably have borrowed"[544] the foreign currency in the foreign country. Thus United States prime rate was awarded in *Kuwait Airways v Kuwait Insurance*,[545] and the same rate was given, following the *Kuwait* case, in *Kinetics Technology International v Cross Seas Shipping Corp, The Mosconici*,[546] the rate there being referred to as the Federal rate plus basis points. A like result was arrived at in *Mamidoil-Jetoil Greek Petroleum Company SA v Okta Crude Oil Refinery AD*.[547] Aikens J there said: **19-120**

> "When the currency of the loss and the currency of damages is US dollars, then the Commercial Court will consider the cost of borrowing US dollars. That is the position in this case. The cost of borrowing US dollars is usually expressed by reference to the US Prime Rate. That is the rate that commercial banks charge their most creditworthy customers if they are borrowing US dollars."[548]

---

535 [2017] EWCA Civ 314 at [68].

536 [2017] EWCA Civ 314 at [68].

537 *OMV Petrom SA v Glencore International AG* [2017] EWCA Civ 195 at [32]–[35].

538 [1991] 1 W.L.R. 1421 CA.

539 See previous paragraph.

540 [2000] Lloyd's Rep. P.N. 404.

541 Interest is dealt with at [2000] Lloyd's Rep. P.N. 404 at 408 to 410. But without reasons he reverted to judgment debt rate in *Hamilton-Jones v David & Snape* [2004] I WL.R. 924.

542 See the discussion at para.19-106, above.

543 [2002] P.N.L.R. 27 at 612; see at [46]–[47].

544 Bristow J's words in *Miliangos (No.2)* [1977] Q.B. 489 at 497E. And Kerr J spoke of "the commercial borrowing rate which prevailed" in the foreign country in *Helmsing Schiffahrts v Malta Drydocks Corp* [1977] 2 Lloyd's Rep. 444 at 449.

545 [2001] Lloyd's Rep. I.R. 678.

546 [2001] 2 Lloyd's Rep. 313.

547 [2003] 1 Lloyd's Rep. 42.

548 [2003] 1 Lloyd's Rep. 42 at [16]. In the absence of evidence to the contrary Aikens J assumed the claimants would be regarded by a lending bank as most creditworthy: at [17].

By contrast, in *Fiona Trust & Holding Corp v Privalov*,[549] where the award to the claimants, who were very many Russian ship-owning groups, was to be in US dollars, Andrew Smith J, while stating that it had become conventional in commercial cases to award US Prime Rate,[550] considered it more appropriate in the case before him to award US LIBOR plus 2.5 per cent rather than US Prime Rate. This was because those operating outside the United States were unaccustomed to Prime Rate and, more importantly, because borrowings by shipping companies were generally effected using LIBOR.[551] Citing *Fiona Trust*, Leggatt J regarded the same approach as being appropriate in *VIS Trading Co Ltd v Nazarov*,[552] where he was awarding interest on damages given in US dollars for breach of contract against one defendant and for tort against another. He pointed to the fact that for borrowings in US dollars LIBOR has become the most widely used benchmark in international commerce generally as well as in shipping[553] and awarded US LIBOR plus the slightly lower 2.25 per cent.[554]

**19-121** Two earlier decisions which followed immediately upon the House of Lords holding in *Miliangos v George Frank (Textiles)*,[555] that an English court may make its award of damages in a foreign currency are also illustrative. In *Miliangos v George Frank (Textiles) (No.2)*,[556] the claimant, a Swiss carrying on business in Switzerland, who had sold goods to the defendants at a price payable in Swiss francs and had successfully claimed for that purchase price in Swiss francs, was held entitled to interest in Swiss francs at the rate Swiss francs could have been borrowed in Switzerland during the relevant period. In *Helmsing Schiffahrts v Malta Drydocks Corp*,[557] the claimant shipowners, who carried on business in Germany and had had ships built for them in Malta by the defendants for a price payable in Maltese pounds, became entitled, in the events which had happened, to the return of part of the moneys they had paid to the defendants and successfully claimed the amount due in Maltese pounds. Interest was awarded which was also to be payable in Maltese pounds but was to be based on the prevailing commercial borrowing rates in Germany. Maltese pounds were indeed the currency of account under the contract but German marks were the currency of the claimants since the defendants' failure to repay the moneys due had caused, and foreseeably caused, the claimants to find an equivalent sum from other sources in Germany.[558]

---

549 [2011] EWHC 664 (Comm).

550 [2011] EWHC 664 (Comm) at [15].

551 The claim was for equitable compensation, there being breaches of fiduciary duty, but the same reasoning must be applicable to claims for common law damages.

552 [2013] EWHC 491 (QB).

553 [2013] EWHC 491 (QB) at [14].

554 Lower for reasons given at [2013] EWHC 491 (QB) at [17]. In *Slocom Trading Ltd v Tatik Inc* [2013] EWHC 1201 Ch. interest on the damages was awarded in euros.

555 [1976] A.C. 443; see paras 20-024 and following, below.

556 [1977] Q.B. 489.

557 [1977] 2 Lloyd's Rep. 444.

558 Contrast *Les Laboratoires v Apotex Inc* [2008] EWHC 3289 (Pat) where interest was awarded in sterling as it was unclear that the loss would have emerged in Canadian dollars. See, too, from the 1970s *B.P. Exploration Co (Libya) v Hunt (No.2)* [1979] 1 W.L.R. 783 where there was a dollar as well as a sterling element in the award and Robert Goff J made his interest computation on the basis that the claimants would have borrowed on the London Eurodollar market: see at 849E to 850B. The claim for interest was in US dollars in *Somasteel SARL v Coresteel DMCC* unreported 20 April 2015, an action for non-delivery of goods sold, but, since the buyer's interests were in Morocco and its financial interests arose in Morocco, interest was awarded at the historical Moroccan rate.

**(f) Effect of delay on rate of interest** In *La Pintada Compania Navigacion v President of India*,[559] Staughton J put forward the suggestion that unjustifiable delay on the part of the claimant could be dealt with by reducing the rate of interest to which he would otherwise be entitled[560] but the suggestion has not received general acceptance. In *Metal Box v Currys*,[561] McNeill J said that he did not consider it suitable for application to the case before him.[562] Delay has been dealt with, as it was in *Metal Box v Currys* itself, by reducing the period of interest and not the rate. There is occasionally to be found a case, generally in the commercial court as was *La Pintada*, where interest is awarded at a lower rate on account of delay.[563] 19-122

## (3) Cases in Admiralty

**(a) The developing position** Litigation over ship collisions in the past provided the greatest number of cases in which interest had been awarded as damages since in Admiralty awards of interest dated back to the first half of the 19th century.[564] The Admiralty courts started by awarding at 4 per cent[565] and not establishing a normal rate of 5 per cent until the 1920s or 1930s.[566] Nor was this 5 per cent rate overtaken by a higher rate as early as it was in the Commercial Court[567]—in 1968 in *The Mecca*[568] which was a limitation action, namely an action brought to establish the amount of damages liability by a person entitled to the benefit of the provisions for limitation of liability under the Merchant Shipping Acts, Brandon J spoke of the Admiralty rate of 5 per cent as against a commercial court rate ranging from 5 to 7 per cent.[569] A few years later in *The Funabashi*,[570] another limitation action, Dunn J awarded 6.5 per cent. He did so by praying in aid the analogy of personal injury claims where, two years earlier, awards of interest on damages had become mandatory and where the Court of Appeal had chosen for the appropriate rate that obtained on short-term, in 1987 renamed special, investment account.[571] "There is no difference in principle", said Dunn J, "between interest on a limitation fund and 19-123

559 [1983] 1 Lloyd's Rep. 37.

560 [1983] 1 Lloyd's Rep. 37 at 44, col.2.

561 [1988] 1 W.L.R. 175.

562 [1988] 1 W.L.R. 175 at 181H.

563 *Derby Resources AG v Blue Corinth Marine Co, The Athenian Harmony* [1998] 2 Lloyd's Rep. 410 (award at half rate); *Quorum A/S v Schramm (No.2)* [2002] 2 Lloyd's Rep. 72 (agreed rate 9.37 per cent rate awarded 6.5 per cent).

564 See paras 19-020 and 19-023, above. Cases concerning bills of exchange may also be numerous, but these are somewhat of a law unto themselves and are treated separately: see paras 30-012 and following, below.

565 See, e.g. *The Kong Magnus* [1891] P. 223.

566 It was said in *The Joannis Vatis (No.2)* [1922] P. 213 at 223, that "during recent years" interest has been awarded at 5 per cent; this rate was awarded in *Liesbosch Dredger v S.S. Edison* [1933] A.C. 449, and Bucknill J in *The Theems* [1938] P. 197 at 200 said that 5 per cent was "now the usual Admiralty rate".

567 See para.19-109, above.

568 [1968] P. 665.

569 [1968] P. 665 at 673. Bucknill J in *The Theems* [1938] P. 197 at 200 had distinguished between interest in ordinary actions and interest in limitation actions on the ground that in the latter an award of interest as part of the damages would contravene the statutory limit placed on the damages, but Brandon J in *The Mecca* [1968] P. 665 at 674 was unimpressed by this and said that in his view "the supposed distinction between interest on damages and interest as part of damages is unreal", a view which he reiterated in *The Aldora* [1975] Q.B. 748 at 752G.

570 [1972] 1 W.L.R. 666.

571 See para.19-126, below.

interest on damages for personal injury",[572] and his 6.5 per cent rate marked the average rate on short-term investment account over the relevant period. Again in *The Aldora*,[573] a case in Admiralty but concerning a salvage award rather than an award of damages, the court utilised the prevailing short-term investment account rates.

**19-124** However, Kerr J in *Cremer v General Carriers*,[574] in declining to embrace for commercial transactions the analogy of interest awards in personal injury cases, said that he thought that the object of Dunn J in *The Funabashi*[575] was to bring the Admiralty Court more closely into line with the practice of other courts and that he relied upon the developments in personal injury claims as a means of achieving this,[576] without in any way seeking to say that these developments laid down any practice which was to be generally binding as a matter of authority.[577] Indeed Dunn J had recognised that

> "a rate of interest which is broadly based on the bank rate during the period in question, but adding something towards the actual cost of borrowing over that period, represents a rational approach to the award of interest in commercial cases"[578]

and that the Admiralty cases were to follow and adopt the pattern of commercial cases[579] rather than that of personal injury ones soon began to appear. This began with two cases of salvage awards[580] of the late 1970s, *The Rilland*,[581] and *The Ben Gairn*,[582] and by 1984 the analogy of the personal injury cases appearing in *The Funabashi*,[583] had been decisively rejected in favour of the commercial ones by the Court of Appeal in *Polish S.S. Co v Atlantic Maritime Co, The Garden City*.[584]

**19-125** **(b) The position today** In *The Garden* City Kerr LJ pointed to the fact that the Commercial Court had adopted base rate plus 1 per cent and added:

> "The practice in that court and the practice of the Admiralty Court is now the same. In my view there is good reason for equating the rates of interest awarded in both of these courts, since both deal with commercial disputes, and much of the litigation in the Commercial Court is also concerned with shipping."[585]

This has remained the position ever since. Any variation from, or qualification of, the general rule in Commercial Court cases[586] will apply equally here.[587]

---

572 [1972] 1 W.L.R. 666 at 671C.
573 [1975] Q.B. 748.
574 [1974] 1 W.L.R. 341.
575 [1972] 1 W.L.R. 666.
576 [1974] 1 W.L.R. 341 at 356D to E.
577 [1974] 1 W.L.R. 341 at 356D to E.
578 [1974] 1 W.L.R. 341 at 355H.
579 See paras 19-109 and following, above.
580 Which followed the Admiralty rules in ship collision cases: see para.19-020, above.
581 [1979] 1 Lloyd's Rep. 455.
582 [1979] 1 Lloyd's Rep. 410.
583 [1972] 1 W.L.R. 666.
584 [1985] Q.B. 41 CA, especially at 66 to 67.
585 [1985] Q.B. 41 CA at 67C.
586 See paras 19-109 and following, above.
587 The interest will generally be payable gross but is then likely to be taxable in the claimant's hands: see para.18-010, above. For an unusual case where the Crown as defendant in a ship collision case unsuccessfully argued that it should pay the claimant the interest net of tax, see *Esso Petroleum Co*

## (4) Cases of personal injury and wrongful death

**(a) The developing position** Where damages were claimed in respect of a person's physical injury or death, awards of interest, as we have seen, had neither been made at common law nor initially in practice under the 1934 Act but took on a new importance by becoming mandatory in 1969.[588] In the first case to reach the Court of Appeal, *Jefford v Gee*,[589] where, as we have also seen, Lord Denning MR laid down his guidelines, the claimant suing for personal injury was awarded interest at 6 per cent. The approach of the court was somewhat different from that of the Commercial Court in the matter of interest,[590] arriving at the 6 per cent figure by reference to the rate of interest prescribed under the Supreme Court Fund Rules as accruing on money paid into court and placed on short-term investment account, renamed special investment account in 1987, and laying down that this should be the rate to be used in future cases of this type.[591] When this form of investment for money paid into court was introduced in 1965 under the provisions of the Administration of Justice Act of that year, the rate of interest was fixed at 5 per cent, but this was gradually increased by rules made by the Lord Chancellor to reach a height of 15 per cent in 1980; while remaining very high through the 1980s, it then began in the 1990s to fall substantially back. The court had arrived at 6 per cent in *Jefford v Gee*[592] by taking an average of the rates prevalent during the period from late 1966 to mid-1969 in respect of which interest was being awarded.[593] This approach was not questioned in *Cookson v Knowles*,[594] a decision involving a Fatal Accidents Act claim and important because it changed the *Jefford v Gee*,[595] guidelines for awarding interest in such claims,[596] the rate of interest there taken being 9 per cent as this was the prevailing rate for practically the whole of the period from the end of 1973 to mid-1976 in respect of which interest was being awarded.[597] 19-126

Initially, interest was awarded at the same rate upon the damages for pecuniary loss and non-pecuniary loss alike. However, in 1982 the Court of Appeal decided in *Birkett v Hayes*,[598] that the rate of interest on that part of the personal injury award which represented non-pecuniary loss should be reduced from the then over 10 per cent figure to a mere 2 per cent[599]; both this result and the reasoning on which it was based were endorsed in the following year by the House of Lords in *Wright v Brit-* 19-127

---

*v Ministry of Defence* [1990] Ch. 163.

588 See paras 19-032 and 19-050, above.

589 [1970] 2 Q.B. 130 CA.

590 See paras 19-109 and following, above.

591 [1970] 2 Q.B. 130 CA at 151A and D. Nor was the rate to be reduced because the interest became exempted from tax by statute (see para.19-087, above): *Mason v Harman* [1972] R.T.R. 1.

592 [1970] 2 Q.B. 130 CA.

593 [1970] 2 Q.B. 130 CA at 149B.

594 [1979] A.C. 556.

595 [1970] 2 Q.B. 130 CA.

596 See paras 19-088 and following, above.

597 Since it was also decided that in future a separate assessment for the past pecuniary loss should be made in Fatal Accidents Act claims as much as in personal injury claims (see para.19-089, above), the rule that interest for such loss should run at half-rate (see para.19-091, above) now applies to both types of claim: see the detailed treatment of Lord Diplock, [1979] A.C. 556 at 572D to 573A.

598 [1982] 1 W.L.R. 816 CA.

599 This reduction does not affect damages for a relative's gratuitous care, rightly held in this connection to be special damage: *Roberts v Johnstone* [1989] Q.B. 878 CA.

*ish Railways Board*.[600] In *Wright*, Lord Diplock, with whose speech the other Law Lords agreed, traced out the distinction, recognised since medieval times, between two elements in the object to be achieved by the giving of interest:

> "one, a reward for taking a risk of loss or reduction of capital; the other, a reward for foregoing the use of the capital sum for the time being."[601]

Only the latter element fell to be regarded in arriving at the proper rate of interest for non-pecuniary loss and, since the former element loomed large in times of steep inflation, the rate to award should be less than 4 per cent and, once the fact that the award would be exempt from income tax was also taken into account, 2 per cent was held to be the appropriate rate. Lord Diplock accepted that, were inflation to tumble, the Court of Appeal's 2 per cent guideline in *Birkett* might have to be changed upwards but, since guidelines of this sort were designed to promote predictability and so facilitate settlements, they should not be lightly changed and it was therefore unrealistic to suppose that this particular guideline would be changed in the immediate future while the long-term future of inflation was unknown.[602]

**19-128** One was thus left after *Wright* with a somewhat curious difference between the rate for pecuniary loss in these cases, then standing at 12.5 per cent,[603] and the 2 per cent rate for non-pecuniary loss. One can see that taking the level of non-pecuniary awards at the time of trial can provide a justification for eliminating the risk factor, although it should be noted that the level of the pecuniary awards by way of special damages takes into account such increases as occur in lost earnings and medical expenses from injury to trial. Nor is there any very good reason—other than a desire indirectly to emasculate the non-pecuniary award—why the tax exemption afforded by s.751 of the Income Tax (Trading and Other Income) Act 2005 to interest given by way of damages to the victims of personal injury should not lead to a lower rate of interest with pecuniary loss,[604] so that the advantage of the exemption goes to those for whom it was intended, and yet should do so with non-pecuniary loss.

### (b) The position today

**19-129** *(i) Pecuniary loss: personal injury and wrongful death* The position today has not changed since the use of the now special investment account rate was established at the start in *Jefford v Gee*,[605] for personal injury and somewhat later in *Cookson v Knowles*,[606] for wrongful death.[607] Interest is to be awarded at this rate which, with falling rates, was back by February 2002 at the 6 per cent where it started, and with the current economic downturn fell dramatically in the first half of 2009 from 3 per cent through 1.5 per cent to 0.5 per cent, where it still stands.

**19-130** What needs to be avoided is resort to the Judgments Act rate. The former

---

600 [1983] 2 A.C. 773.

601 [1983] 2 A.C. 773 at 781F.

602 [1983] 2 A.C. 773 at 785G to 786A.

603 The rate from April 1983 to 1984, Wright having been decided by the Lords in June 1983. When the Court of Appeal decided the earlier Birkett, the rate was even higher at 14 per cent.

604 So decided in *Mason v Harman* [1972] R.T.R. 1.

605 [1970] 2 Q.B. 130 CA.

606 [1979] A.C. 556.

607 See para.19-126, above.

*Supreme Court Practice* used to state that it was becoming common to award this rate instead of the special investment account rate in personal injury and wrongful death cases, but there is no justification for such a practice[608] although, as we have seen, it has been creeping in.[609] To resist any such trend is all the more important while the judgment rate ignores the market place and remains stolidly at 8 per cent despite massive reductions elsewhere.

*(ii) Non-pecuniary loss: personal injury* The position today is no different from what it has been since 1982.[610] Interest is awarded to claimants at a rate of 2 per cent. **19-131**

Whether, in the wake of *Wells v Wells*,[611] establishing a discount rate of 3 per cent for the calculation of future financial loss,[612] 3 per cent should here replace 2 per cent is a matter upon which there was disagreement at first instance, some favouring a move to 3 per cent[613] and others thinking it inappropriate for a judge at first instance to depart from the 2 per cent rate.[614] The Court of Appeal has now hopefully closed the discussion by endorsing, in *L v Chief Constable of Staffordshire*,[615] the view that 2 per cent should be retained, saying rightly that there is no intrinsic reason why the rate of return to be used for future pecuniary loss should be the same as the rate on general damages for non-pecuniary loss. And whether there will now be calls, in the wake of the reduction in the rate for pecuniary loss from 6 per cent to 3 per cent[616] for an equivalent reduction to 1 per cent for non-pecuniary loss is not known. If such calls appear, they should be resisted. There is much to be said for leaving the rate for general damages at the 2 per cent at which it has stood for nearly two decades, neither raising it nor lowering it, in light of the fact that the assessment of interest is on a conventional sum unrelated to financial loss—so that there is a cogent argument, as put elsewhere, for awarding no interest at all—and indeed on a conventional sum which combines compensation for past loss, which can properly attract interest, and future loss, which should not. **19-132**

*(iii) Non-pecuniary loss: wrongful death* By contrast with personal injury, the 2 per cent rate does not appear to have been carried through to the awards for bereavement, which were statutorily introduced from 1983, into claims under the Fatal Accidents Act.[617] Two cases, unfortunately unreported, speak to this. In *Khan v Duncan*[618]—the other case is *Prior v Hastie*[619]—Popplewell J, awarding 11.5 per cent, said that it seemed to him that this non-pecuniary loss was one **19-133**

---

608 Certainly no order has been made under the Senior Courts Act 1981 s.35A(5) giving power to apply the Judgments Act rate.

609 The reasons for avoiding the rate on judgment debts have already been set out at paras 19-105 and 19-106, above.

610 See para.19-127, above.

611 [1999] 1 A.C. 345.

612 See paras 40-122 and following, below.

613 As in *Burns v Davies* [1999] Lloyd's Rep. Med. 215 and *Taylor v Shropshire Health Authority* [2000] Lloyd's Rep. Med. 96.

614 As in *Cox v Allison Engineering Ltd*, 29 June 1999, N.L.J.C.C. 107 and *Barry v Ablerex Construction (Midlands) Ltd* [2000] P.I.Q.R. Q263.

615 [2000] P.I.Q.R. Q349 CA.

616 See para.19-107, above.

617 See para.41-019, below.

618 *Khan v Duncan* unreported 9 March1989.

619 [1987] C.L.Y. 1219.

"which is incurred as at the moment of death, that unlike general damages upon which two per cent is paid, the figure does not increase as the years go by so that interest is to be reduced for that reason",

and was "more akin to special damage". Apart from this reasoning, just as one may suspect that the reduction to 2 per cent in personal injury cases reflects an uneasiness at awarding any interest for non-pecuniary loss,[620] so the preparedness to allow a full commercial rate in wrongful death cases may reflect a converse uneasiness that the statutory entitlement to bereavement damages is set at such a low, some feel derisory, level.[621]

### (5) Cases of nuisance

19-134 Deciding on the rate of interest to take for pecuniary losses arising from nuisance, a tort affecting land, presents no particular problem but, interest having been awarded by Ramsey J in *Dobson v Thames Water Utilities Ltd*,[622] on the damages for non-pecuniary loss by way of loss of amenity in the enjoyment of land caused by a nuisance,[623] the difficult question arose as to the appropriate rate of interest to apply. Ramsey J awarded the special account rate sought by the claimants, which rate, though not generally used outside personal injury claims, he regarded as representing a suitable commercial rate.[624] At the same time he rejected the 2 per cent rate used for non-pecuniary loss in personal injury claims advocated by the defendant as he rightly regarded the analogy with general damages for personal injury an irrelevance. For one thing the claims for loss of amenity on account of the nuisance were only for the past years up to the trial and not, as with personal injury, also for future years, which may be very many. It is thought, however, that the better solution is to award no interest at all for the reasons already set out[625] so that no question of rate arises.

## 3. AMOUNT ON WHICH INTEREST IS AWARDED: INTEREST AND TAXATION

19-135 To counteract the effects of a nuisance committed by the defendants, costs of dredging a riverbed were incurred by the claimants in *Tate & Lyle Food and Distribution v Greater London Council*,[626] over a seven and a half year period from 1967 to 1974; judgment for damages in respect of these costs was given in 1981. The claimants had properly treated these costs as trading expenses and had deducted them in arriving at their trading profits for corporation tax purposes. In these circumstances it was held that the claimants must bring into the interest computation the amount of corporation tax that they had saved; as they had ceased to be kept out of their money, represented by their expenditure on dredging over a seven and a half year period, to the extent of the amounts saved annually in tax, those amounts would no longer carry interest from the time that the tax became payable. In effecting the necessary calculation Forbes J considered that he was entitled to adopt a

620 See para.19-053, above.
621 See para.41-019, below.
622 [2012] EWHC 986 (TCC).
623 See para.19-049, above.
624 [2012] EWHC 986 (TCC) at [19].
625 At para.19-049, above.
626 [1982] 1 W.L.R. 149.

very broad approach.[627] He took the mid-point of the seven and a half year period from 1967 to 1974, advanced this by the 21 months which, because tax was not immediately payable, it took the tax benefit to materialise in each year, and calculated interest from that date to the date of judgment at the full rate.[628] The resulting figure was then deducted from the figure of interest already arrived at before bringing the tax benefit into consideration and the net amount awarded. It may be, however, that in fairness to the claimants some credit, again broadly assessed, should have been given to reflect the fact that, because the rate of corporation tax had risen, the claimants would be likely to pay more tax on their damages in respect of their dredging costs than they had saved by charging those costs as an expense. Forbes J declined to make any such adjustment.[629]

This decision has far-reaching consequences.[630] It was so stated in earlier editions of this work and the proposition is adhered to in this. In *Deeny v Gooda Walker (No.3)*,[631] it was said that the *Tate & Lyle*[632] case stands alone with no progeny, thereby suggesting a more muted significance to it. There are of course two aspects to the significance of a decision on damages: the size of its impact on the figures awarded in subsequent cases, and the size of its impact on the number of cases following and applying it. As to the former there is no doubt that it is significant. The combination of substantial interest rates, substantial tax rates, and the passing of many years between the accrual of causes of action and the hearing of the resultant claims means that very large reductions in damages on account of interest can be envisaged: thus in the *Tate & Lyle* case itself the reduction was by over a third, bringing the interest award down by nearly a quarter of a million pounds.[633] As to the latter the fault would seem to be that, perhaps through unfamiliarity with Forbes J's innovative decision, defendants have not hurried to take advantage of it. **19-136**

Moreover, the *Tate & Lyle*[634] case does have a following and one in the Court of Appeal; this is to be found in the important decision of *O'Sullivan v Management Agency and Music*.[635] Before turning to that case, three ways in which Forbes J's decision may be applied, beyond that in which it was applied in the *Tate & Lyle*[636] case, may be set out. First, the principle applies not only where expenditure claimed by the claimant has been set by him against his tax but also where he is awarded loss of trading or other profits which, had they been achieved, would have been taxable in his hands, provided always in this case that the award is of the profits before tax because the damages representing the lost profits will also be taxable in the claimant's hands.[637] Secondly, where damages, as they occasionally do, take into account the profits made by the defendant out of his wrongdoing should these be **19-137**

---

[627] [1982] 1 W.L.R. 149 at 156F.

[628] This was not quite the same method as he had used to calculate the interest before bringing in the tax factor (see para.19-085, above) and which would have been more precise.

[629] [1982] 1 W.L.R. 149 at 156H to 157A.

[630] Unaffected by its reversal on liability only: see [1983] 2 A.C. 509.

[631] [1996] L.R.L.R. 168.

[632] [1982] 1 W.L.R. 149.

[633] [1982] 1 W.L.R. 149 at 157E.

[634] [1982] 1 W.L.R. 149.

[635] [1985] Q.B. 428 CA.

[636] [1982] 1 W.L.R. 149.

[637] There is thus no call to make a deduction on account of tax in the interest awarded on the pre-trial loss of earnings in personal injury actions or in respect of any other claim to which the rule in *British Transport Commission v Gourley* [1956] A.C. 195 (see paras 18-002 and following, above) applies.

greater than those lost to the claimant,[638] it is again the loss of profits after the tax paid on them, here by the defendant, upon which the interest calculation falls to be made. Thirdly, although compound interest has not in the past been generally awarded by way of damages but mainly in equity on an accounting,[639] the compounding should be done on the interest generated after that interest has borne tax, with an upward adjustment to cater for the tax payable on the interest award itself, a method of computation which, because the compounding of interest brings such spectacular increases in the figures, is likely to make even greater inroads on the interest to be awarded. These matters all make their appearance in *O'Sullivan v Management Agency and Music*,[640] and the view expressed by Phillips J in *Deeny v Gooda Walker (No.3)*,[641] that, contrary to what was said in this book, the report of the case did not indicate that the principle of *Tate & Lyle*[642] was being applied[643] is clearly incorrect. That tax was taken into account in the interest computation is specifically stated by both Dunn and Waller LJJ.[644]

**19-138** Notwithstanding all this, Phillips J in a finely reasoned judgment decided to follow Forbes J in the *Tate & Lyle* case.[645] *Deeny v Gooda Walker (No.3)*,[646] was another of the many aspects of the claims brought by Lloyd's Names against their managing and underwriting agents for failure to arrange adequate insurance cover for them against losses. The damages were based upon what the claimants would have received with appropriate insurance cover, receipts which would have increased the claimants' profits or reduced their losses. Two principal arguments for ignoring tax in the computation of the interest on these damages had been put forward by the defendants there. First, there was the argument from logic that, since tax was ignored in the computation of the damages, themselves taxable,[647] tax should equally be ignored in the computation of the interest awarded, which would also be taxable when received. In correctly countering this argument Phillips J said:

> "Damages are awarded to compensate for the loss of money or its equivalent. Interest is awarded to compensate for the loss of use of money. In accounting terms damages compensate for the effect of wrongdoing on profit and loss, interest compensates for the effect of wrongdoing on cashflow. If in year one loss is caused which is shared between the plaintiff and Inland Revenue and in year five damages fall to be awarded which will be shared between the plaintiff and the Inland Revenue, it can be logical to disregard the effect of taxation when assessing the damages. But it does not follow that the plaintiff should receive an award of interest which compensates not only for his loss of use of

---

638 See Ch.14 above.

639 See para.19-068, above.

640 [1985] Q.B. 428 CA.

641 [1996] L.R.L.R. 168.

642 [1982] 1 W.L.R. 149.

643 [1996] L.R.L.R. 168 at 172, col. 2.

644 [1985] Q.B. 428 CA at 462C and 473F to G respectively. Dr McGregor was counsel for the defendants who argued the interest point in the case. He confirmed, in earlier editions of this work, that the report is correct.

645 *John v James* [1986] S.T.C. 352, where Nicholls J declined to adopt the *O'Sullivan* approach, does not seem to have been brought to the attention of Phillips J, but the Court of Appeal is more compelling both in its authority and in its reasoning.

646 [1996] L.R.L.R. 168.

647 This being decided at House of Lords level in yet another aspect of the Lloyd's Names' litigation: see *Deeny v Gooda Walker (No.2)* [1996] 1 W.L.R. 426 HL, at para.18-048, above.

money but in addition for the loss of use of the share which should have been received by the Inland Revenue."[648]

Secondly, there was the pragmatic argument that exceedingly complex calculations would often be required to ascertain the effect that taxation would have had on the claimant's cashflow,[649] thereby making it difficult to assess the net figure upon which interest should be awarded. Phillips J was not, however, prevailed upon to accept this argument. He said:

> "If the Court proceeds on the artificial premise that the plaintiff has been deprived of the use of the whole of the damages notwithstanding the effect of taxation the interest awarded will provide the plaintiff with a substantial unjustified windfall at the expense of the defendant. In my judgment the Court should approach each claim to interest on its own merits, placing a sensible pragmatic restraint on attempts to conduct a detailed investigation of a plaintiff's tax position but, at the same time, refraining from awarding interest for loss of use of money if it appears that the plaintiff is unlikely to have suffered the loss of use in question."[650]

In the event Phillips J awarded interest on only 75 per cent of the damages to which all of the group claimants had been held entitled.

The defendant in *Mamidoil-Jetoil Greek Petroleum Co SA v Okta Crude Oil Refinery AD*[651] attempted to make use of this valuable path to a reduced liability in damages but without success. Aikens J there declined to apply *Deeny*,[652] which he distinguished. He was entitled to do so on the basis that he had been afforded no evidence as to the claimant's tax position, but to have been entitled to do so also on the basis of requiring the claimant to have followed the position in *Deeny* and have set up special losses to reduce or nullify its tax liabilities on other income,[653] which it had not done, is unconvincing. All that should have been required was to show that the tax liabilities which would have arisen on the profits had they been received between accrual of cause of action and judgment had been deferred until such time as the damages were received. Aikens J purported to apply what he said was known as "the rule in *Parson's case*"[654] but the result in *Parsons*[655] has been substantially modified over the years.[656] **19-139**

By fortunate contrast, in *BSkyB Ltd v HP Enterprise Services UK Ltd*,[657] Ramsey J adopted and applied the reasoning of Phillips J in *Deeny v Gooda Walker (No.3)*,[658] so as to base the award of interest on the net amount of damages after the deduction of tax. Ramsey J, unlike Phillips J, did not regard the *Tate & Lyle*[659] case as standing alone with no progeny but took into account, with the assistance of this work, the Court of Appeal's decision in *O'Sullivan v Management Agency and* **19-140**

---

648 [1996] L.R.L.R. 168 at 173.

649 Although, as the learned judge noted, [1996] L.R.L.R. 168 at 173, col.2, the calculations were "relatively simple" in the *Tate & Lyle* case.

650 [1996] L.R.L.R. 168 at 173–174.

651 [2003] 1 Lloyd's Rep. 42; facts at para.19-075, above.

652 [1996] L.R.L.R. 168.

653 [2003] 1 Lloyd's Rep. 42 at [13] and [14].

654 [2003] 1 Lloyd's Rep. 42 at [14], note 6.

655 [1964] 1 Q.B. 95 CA.

656 See Ch.18, above at paras 18-018 to 18-022.

657 [2010] EWHC 862 (TCC).

658 [1996] L.R.L.R. 168.

659 [1982] 1 W.L.R. 149.

*Music*,[660] together with *Amstrad Plc v Seagate Technology Inc*.[661] As in *Deeny* the damages were awarded for lost profits, referred to in *BSkyB* as lost benefits.[662]

660 [1985] Q.B. 428 CA. On all this see paras 19-135 to 19-137, above.
661 (1998) 86 B.L.R. 34, which dealt with a related tax issue: see para.18-019, above.
662 See *BSkyB* on the related tax issue at para.18-021, above.

CHAPTER 20

# THE EFFECT OF CHANGES IN VALUE

TABLE OF CONTENTS



All pecuniary losses stem from loss in relation to property, to services, or to money. It is therefore necessary, in order to assess damages, to set a value upon the property, services or money involved, a task which gives rise to problems where the value of the property, services or money has been subject to change, whether gradual or sudden. This forms an area of the law of damages which has been little explored. **20-001**

## 1. CHANGES IN THE VALUE OF PROPERTY

Where damages are awarded for a loss in relation to property, the normal measure is based upon the market value of the property at the time of the wrong, whether tort or breach of contract. Thus in the case of the tort of conversion of goods the appropriate time is the time of conversion, while in the case of breach of a contract to sell goods the appropriate time is the time of due delivery, whether the breach be by seller or buyer. Difficulties may arise, however, where, by reason of a fluctuation in the supply and demand position of the property, its market value changes between the time of the wrong and the time that judgment is entered in the claimant's action for damages.[1] **20-002**

This problem, which has already been considered in greater detail in relation to mitigation,[2] appears more in tort than in contract because a person whose goods have been converted is not required to go into the market and seek a replacement. While, on the one hand, the measure of damages will not be less than the normal measure where the market value has decreased between the time of conversion and the time of judgment if the claimant can show that he would have sold the goods **20-003**

---

[1] The market value may also change because of a fluctuation in money values; this is dealt with at para.20-014, below.

[2] See paras 9-042 to 9-044, above.

before the market fell,[3] on the other hand, where the market value has increased, it has been held in *Sachs v Miklos*,[4] that to the normal measure of the market value at the time of conversion may be added as consequential loss any market increase in value between then and the earliest time that the action should reasonably have been brought to judgment.[5] And if the market value should fluctuate both up and down during this period, the claimant may be entitled to the highest intermediate value but only if he can show that he would have sold, or has in fact repurchased, at the time when such value was reached.[6] Similar principles should apply to misappropriation of land and to destruction of goods.

**20-004** In contract, however, the normal measure is generally not affected because a party to a contract of sale is on the other's breach required to go forthwith into the market and find another buyer or another seller, as the case may be. But if a buyer of goods should pay the price in advance, there is some authority for the proposition that he is not required to seek a replacement in the market, as the seller now has possession of the money which the buyer should otherwise have used for a replacement, and that therefore he is entitled to claim damages in respect of any increase in the market value between the time of the breach of contract and the earliest time that the action should reasonably have been brought to judgment.[7] And with a buyer of land it is now becoming recognised that he is not required, on the seller's default by failure to complete, to buy other land in replacement until such time as he has taken steps to obtain specific performance if such steps, though eventually unsuccessful, have been reasonably taken[8]; or indeed until such time as he has received his damages if inflationary trends have made it too difficult for him to finance a repurchase.[9] Here again there is justification for awarding damages based upon market value at a point in time after the date of breach and even up to the date of judgment.

**20-005** Changes in the value of property in relation to place as opposed to time also give rise to occasional difficulty. This is so where the claimant's goods are being carried under contract and are converted or destroyed while in transit, either by the carrier or by a third party. The little authority that exists suggests that the damages would be assessed with reference to the market value at the place of due delivery rather than at the place of conversion, at least where the former was the higher. Thus in *Ewbank v Nutting*,[10] goods had been converted by an improper sale during transit, the sale fetching a very low price. The court was clear that what the goods had sold at was no fair test of what the claimant should recover. Wilde CJ said that the measure was "the amount of damage the plaintiff had sustained by the unauthorised sale".[11] This was taken as the cost price of the goods plus the freight, because the

---

3 See paras 38-014 to 38-017, below.

4 [1948] 2 K.B. 23 CA: facts at para.38-018, below.

5 A similar result was reached in the former detinue by another route in *Rosenthal v Alderton* [1946] K.B. 374 CA. The court gave the higher market value at the time of judgment subject to the claimant being required to mitigate by bringing an action within a reasonable time after he knew or ought to have known of the defendant's wrong.

6 See para.38-022, below.

7 The authorities from which this proposition is derived are all dealt with at para.9-044, above.

8 See *Malhotra v Choudhury* [1980] Ch. 52 CA at para.27-008, below; approved in *Johnson v Agnew* [1980] A.C. 367 dealing with the converse case of a claim by a seller of land: see para.27-040, below.

9 See *Wroth v Tyler* [1974] Ch. 30 at para.27-009, below.

10 (1849) 7 C.B. 797.

11 (1849) 7 C.B. 797 at 809.

jury had been so directed and the court's primary concern was to decide whether this could be wrong. Nevertheless the trend of the judgments suggests that the market value at the place of due delivery would have been acceptable as a measure.[12] And in the similar case of *Acatos v Burns*,[13] though it was admitted that the price at which the goods sold at the place of conversion was not controlling and a higher figure was agreed by the parties, Brett LJ said in his judgment that the true measure was "the value of the goods to the owner",[14] while Bramwell LJ said it was "what it would be worth to the owner if it had not been sold".[15] It is true that in both of these cases it was the carrier who was the converter so that a flavour of contract is introduced, but there is no reference to this factor in either. It is submitted that the proper analysis of these cases is that the market value at the place of the conversion is taken as the normal measure and to this is added as consequential loss the amount by which the market is higher at the place of due delivery.

## 2. Changes in the Value of Services

Where damages are awarded in relation to a loss of services, the same difficulties may arise where there is a change in the value of services between the time of the wrong and the time of judgment.[16] **20-006**

In contract, once again, the normal measure is generally not affected because a party to a contract of service or for services is on the other's breach required to go forthwith into the market and find another employer or another employee or independent contractor, as the case may be. In tort on the other hand, in the common case of physical injury to the claimant depriving him of his earning capacity, it is clear that changes in the value of services are reflected in the awards of damages without any conscious analysis of the problem here considered. Thus if by the time of trial and judgment the value of the claimant's services has risen on the market, the court, in assessing the damages, will go upon the basis that, had the injury not prevented his continuing in his work, his wages or salary would have risen correspondingly. Occasionally, indeed, where there is an unusually long gap in time between the cause of action accruing and the action being heard, express mention may be made of the fact that the court will take into account any change in the value of services, as in *The Swynfleet*,[17] where, in a claim in respect of the death of two English seamen in 1939, damages were assessed on the basis of the far higher seamen's wages of 1947 when the claim was heard. **20-007**

---

12 This appears most clearly from a passage in the argument: "[Cresswell J. Suppose the conversion had been by throwing the cargo overboard what would have been the measure of damage in that case? What would the cargo have been worth to the owner?] What it would have sold for at the port of destination, minus the freight. [Cresswell J. May we not reasonably conclude that the goods would be worth the invoice price and the cost of carriage?] That might or might not be. [Wilde CJ. It would not be more than actual indemnity]": (1849) 7 C.B. 797 at 805.

13 (1878) 3 Ex. D. 282.

14 (1878) 3 Ex. D. 282 at 291–292.

15 (1878) 3 Ex. D. 282 at 288.

16 The market value may also change because of a fluctuation in money values; this is dealt with at para.20-015, below.

17 (1947) 81 Ll. L. Rep. 116.

## 3. Changes in the Value of Money

**20-008** Fluctuations, often dramatic, in the real value of money, i.e. its purchasing power, became prevalent in the 20th century, and it is therefore particularly important today to have clear rules as to the time at which the claimant's loss is to be assessed or measured. This problem resolves itself into a number of situations. First, there is the general problem of change in the value of sterling over the years; secondly, there are particular changes in the internal value of sterling between the time of accrual of the cause of action and the time of judgment in the action; thirdly, there are particular fluctuations of foreign currencies in relation to sterling between the time of accrual of the cause of action and the time of judgment.[18]

### (1) General change in the internal value of sterling over the years

**20-009** The spectacular decline in the purchasing power of sterling has normally been reflected in awards of damages without any special consideration of this factor, because the cost of property and of services rises correspondingly and any award of damages in respect of property or services is based upon their present-day market value. Similarly, where the damages are awarded for a failure to pay money, the amount of the money which will be awarded against the defendant will be the same nominal sum as he has promised and failed to pay.

**20-010** If, however, the damages are given as compensation for a non-pecuniary loss the decline in the purchasing power of sterling cannot in the same way be automatically reflected in the award. In such cases the courts have expressly said that permanent changes in the value of sterling must be taken into account. Very frequently, it is true, damages for non-pecuniary loss are at large or at least give, in the nature of things, scope for ample variations in the assessment as between one case and another, so that any direct consideration of change in the value of sterling tends to be avoided and its effect to be masked. However, the updating of awards for non-pecuniary loss on this account does undoubtedly occur, especially in personal injury cases.

**20-011** With personal injury in the past the impact of change in the value of sterling was made particularly clear when it came to awards for loss of expectation of life because the scope for variation between assessments had been strictly curtailed ever since the House of Lords in *Benham v Gambling*[19] laid down that only very moderate sums should be awarded for this head of damage, there reducing to £200 the Court of Appeal's award of £1,000 in respect of a child whose circumstances were very favourable. Though no longer of practical significance the development here is still worth recording because it is instructive on the manner in which courts operate in this field. In *Hart v Griffiths-Jones*[20] Streatfeild J, in awarding damages for loss of expectation of life in the case of a child whose circumstances were less fortunate, expressly took the decline in money values into account and held that,

---

[18] The succeeding discussion is concerned only with inflation occurring before judgment. Questions of the relevance of the prospect of future inflation after judgment have arisen in personal injury and wrongful death claims, and are considered in those contexts: see paras 40-144 and 41-076, below.

[19] [1941] A.C. 157; see para.40-262, below.

[20] [1948] 2 All E.R. 729.

"although I should have awarded less than £200 had I been considering like values, the depreciation of the pound justifies me making an award under this head of £200".[21]

In *Naylor v Yorkshire Electricity Board*,[22] the House of Lords accepted unanimously that a quarter of a century's inflation since *Benham v Gambling*,[23] justified an increase in the conventional award, which the trial judge had made, from £200 to £500.[24] Lord Upjohn did indeed question the relevance of expert evidence which had been introduced to show that the value of the pound in real terms had fallen by about two-and-a-half times in the interim; he did however accept that

"over the years the conventional sum to be awarded for such head of damages rises no doubt but by fits and starts rather than by estimation of the purchasing power of the pound".[25]

Accordingly, by 1973 in *McCann v Sheppard*,[26] the Court of Appeal was advocating an increase to £750, in *Gammell v Wilson*,[27] that court held the conventional sum to be £1,250 in 1979,[28] and in *Kralj v McGrath*,[29] it was agreed that in 1985 the conventional figure was £1,750.[30] Any further rise cannot be documented as loss of expectation of life as a separate head of damage has been removed by statute.[31]

As for the elements of non-pecuniary loss that remain with us in personal injury **20-012**
cases—pain and suffering and, now the principal head, loss of amenities—we find an updating in 1978 in *Walker v John McLean & Sons*,[32] and again in 1985 in *Housecroft v Burnett*,[33] on account of awards falling behind the value of money.[34] These stepped increases were followed in 1992 by the arrival of the Judicial Studies Board's *Guidelines for the Assessment of General Damages in Personal Injury Cases* which has continued, at two-yearly intervals since, to provide for particular injuries bands of figures which reflect the changes in the value of sterling.[35] A further leap forward in awards came in 2000 with *Heil v Rankin*,[36] but the increases there set out were not designed to reflect declines in the value of sterling but rather resulted from a reappraisal of the general level at which non-pecuniary awards for personal injury should be set.[37] And now, moving on well beyond personal injury,

---

21 [1948] 2 All E.R. 729 at 730.
22 [1968] A.C. 529.
23 [1941] A.C. 157.
24 The House's rejection of the Court of Appeal's increase of Ashworth J's award to £1,000 was on another ground.
25 [1968] A.C. 529 at 552. Similarly in *Glasgow Corp v Kelly* [1951] 1 T.L.R. 345 HL, an appeal to the House of Lords from Scotland in connection with the peculiarly Scottish head of damage of *solatium* for wounded feelings caused by the death in respect of which action is brought, Lord Normand re-affirmed his view that "permanent changes in the value of money must be considered in making awards for *solatium*": at 347.
26 [1973] 1 W.L.R. 540 CA.
27 [1982] A.C. 27 CA.
28 [1982] A.C. 27 CA at 42G.
29 [1986] 1 All E.R. 54.
30 [1986] 1 All E.R. 54 at 59f.
31 See para.40-263, below.
32 [1979] 1 W.L.R. 760 CA.
33 [1986] 1 All E.R. 332 CA.
34 See para.40-279, below (in a footnote).
35 See para.40-275, below.
36 [2001] Q.B. 272 CA.
37 See paras 40-278 and following.

the Court of Appeal in its final decision in *Simmons v Castle*,[38] authorised a 10 per cent increase in damages for non-pecuniary loss across the board, in contract as well as in tort, effective from 1 April 2013.[39] This 10 per cent uplift is not discretionary. Claimants are entitled to it, unless they entered into a conditional fee arrangement.[40]

### (2) Particular changes in the internal value of sterling between the time of accrual of the cause of action and the time of judgment

**20-013** The period between the time a cause of action accrued and the time judgment in the action was given used generally not to be long enough for the decline in the purchasing power of sterling to assume sufficient proportions to have any practical effect on the damages; latter-day experiences with inflation, however, have made this far less true today. And even in monetarily more stable times, the length of time allowed by the Statute of Limitations before action need be brought, together with the possible existence of factors such as mistake and fraud which may hold up its running against the claimant, combined with the further possible delay between issue of the writ and trial of the action to present cases where many years separated accrual and judgment. Thus the decline in the real value of sterling can become important. Different considerations may apply depending upon whether the damages are being awarded in respect of a pecuniary or a non-pecuniary loss, and whether, in the case of a pecuniary loss, in relation to property, services or money.

**20-014** Where the damages are awarded for a property loss, the nominal cost of the property in sterling will have risen in inverse proportion to the fall in the real value of sterling. The market value of the property can therefore be regarded as having increased, and although this has happened because of a change in money values and not a change in the supply and demand position of the property, the courts treat the problem as involving a change in the value of property and not in the value of money. This seems to follow from *Rosenthal v Alderton*,[41] and *Sachs v Miklos*,[42] actions in the former detinue and in conversion respectively, where the goods were misappropriated during the Second World War. The rise in the market value of the goods at the time of judgment was probably attributable, in part at least, to the decline in the purchasing power of sterling during the war. In both cases the Court of Appeal was prepared to assess the damages at the market value of the goods at the time of judgment provided the claimant had not delayed unreasonably in bringing his action; in the case of detinue the damages were held specifically to be the market value at judgment, while in the case of conversion they were taken as the market value at the time of accrual of action with the increase in market value to judgment added as consequential loss.[43] On the other hand, in the case of a failure to deliver goods in breach of a contract of sale, the market value is generally taken at the time of breach, and this would not be affected by any subsequent increase in market value even if it were the result solely of a decrease in the value of sterling. The reason is that in these circumstances the claimant is required to seek upon

---

38 [2013] 1 W.L.R. 1239 CA; final decision from 1243.

39 For the procedural history and reasons for this development, stemming from the package of reforms appearing in the Jackson Report on Civil Litigation Costs, see para.51-044, below.

40 *Summers v Bundy* [2016] EWCA Civ 126 CA.

41 [1946] K.B. 374 CA.

42 [1948] 2 K.B. 23 CA.

43 Both cases are dealt with more fully at paras 38-018 and 38-021, below.

breach an immediate replacement in the market. These situations have already been fully dealt with.[44]

Where the damages relate to a loss of services the claimant is similarly required, if the failure to render the services is in breach of contract, to seek a replacement of these services in the market, so that he cannot claim in respect of any subsequent increase in market value of such services even if it were the result solely of a decrease in the value of sterling. Whether the same would apply in tort turns on whether the claimant is required to replace. But where there can be no question of replacement, as where the claimant is claiming in respect of services which he himself would have rendered, as in the common case of physical injury where damages are sought for loss of earnings and earning capacity, there seems no reason why the market value of the claimant's earning capacity at the time of judgment should not be taken where this has increased nominally in sterling in correspondence with a fall in sterling's real value. The courts have shown themselves prepared to accept this position.[45] **20-015**

Where the claimant's claim is in respect of a failure to pay money,[46] or is for loss of money paid out by himself, such as money paid for repairs upon a chattel wrongfully damaged by the defendant, the position is different. Where the loss is a money loss, the fact that a change in the value of money is involved is unmasked: it is no longer latent as in the cases of loss of property and of services. It is submitted that there is a good argument for basing the award to the claimant on the value of the money at the time of breach in the case of contract and at the time that the loss was determined in the case of tort. This fits the general rule of damages that they are to be assessed as at the date of the wrong rather than the date of trial and judgment, is consistent with the established rule where foreign currency is involved,[47] and provides for the claimant a hedge against the inflationary dangers of the law's delays to which he ought to be entitled, always provided that he is not responsible himself for culpable delay in suing.[48] However, the trend of authority is the other way. In *The Baarn*,[49] Scrutton LJ said: **20-016**

> "I take it that if a tort had been committed in England before England went off the gold standard, the plaintiffs could not say: 'We insist, after England has gone off the gold standard and the pound has depreciated in international purchasing power, on being paid the value of the gold standard pound at the time of the commission of the tort.' A pound in England is a pound whatever its international value."[50]

Denning LJ in *Treseder-Griffin v Co-operative Insurance Society*,[51] put forward

---

44 See paras 20-002 to 20-004, above, indicating that the position may be different with a pre-paid price or a sale of land.

45 See especially *Cookson v Knowles* [1979] A.C. 556, at para.41-042, below. See *The Swynfleet* (1947) 81 Ll. L.R. 116 at para.20-007, above.

46 Such an action may be for debt as opposed to damages; this however seems to be immaterial for the present argument. See the equivalent foreign currency cases at para.20-022, below.

47 See paras 20-019 and following, below.

48 See the effect of culpable delay in suing in relation to goods at para.20-014, above.

49 [1933] P. 251 CA.

50 [1933] P. 251 CA at 265. It is because this view does not clearly fit with the parallel rule where foreign currency is involved that he added: "I do not think the results of the decision in *The Volturno* [1921] 2 A.C. 544 have yet been thoroughly elucidated": at 266. See paras 20-019 and following, below.

51 [1956] 2 Q.B. 127 CA at 144: "In England we have always looked upon a pound as a pound, whatever its international value. Sterling is the constant unit of value by which in the eye of the law

similar views; the case itself concerned the effect of a "gold clause" in a domestic contract and therefore dealt in questions of construction rather than of the amount to be awarded in an action for damages or for debt. It is true that these statements take into account the international value of sterling, but that Scrutton LJ's view was similar in relation to the internal value of a currency appears from his further illustration that

> "the difficulty may be tested by considering an action in Germany for a foreign tort brought to judgment during the period when the German mark had become practically worthless though it was of value when the tort was committed."[52]

**20-017** Finally, there is the case of the non-pecuniary loss. In *Bishop v Cunard White Star*,[53] in a claim for damages in 1950 for loss of expectation of life resulting from a tort committed in 1942, it was held that these damages had crystallised in 1942, the general fall in the value of sterling between 1942 and 1950 was therefore not relevant and the damages must be assessed on the basis of sterling in 1942. This conclusion has for long not been supportable. Widgery LJ indicated that he was of the contrary view when he said in *Mitchell v Mulholland (No.2)*[54]:

> "No one doubts that an award of damages must reflect the value of the pound sterling at the date of the award and conventional sums attributed to, say, the loss of an eye, have been adjusted upwards in recent years on that account. Inflation which has reduced the value of money at the date of the award must, thus, be taken into account."

And Lord Denning MR said categorically in *Cookson v Knowles*,[55] that

> "the courts invariably assess the lump sum [namely for the non-pecuniary loss to an injured plaintiff] on the 'scale' for figures current at the date of the trial",

and the propriety of this was in no way challenged by the House of Lords in that case.[56] This position is maintained today.

### (3) Particular changes in the external value of sterling between the time of accrual of the cause of action and the time of judgment[57]

**20-018** Where a foreign element appears in a case, bringing with it questions involving payments in foreign currency, the problems to which changes in the value of money give rise become both more acute and more common because of the frequent large fluctuations in the rates of exchange, together with wholesale devaluations of one currency in relation to another. Moreover, the law in this area has undergone a sea change with the House of Lords decision in *Miliangos v George Frank (Textiles)*.[58]

---

everything is measured. Prices of commodities may go up or down, other currencies may go up and down, but sterling remains the same." He further developed these views in *Re United Railways of Havana and Regla Warehouses* [1961] A.C. 1007 at 1069 to 1070.

52 [1933] P. 251 CA at 266 to 267.

53 [1950] P. 240; see especially at 256.

54 [1972] 1 Q.B. 65 CA at 83.

55 [1977] Q.B. 913 CA at 921C.

56 [1979] A.C. 556.

57 How the general problems of private international law are solved in relation to damages cannot be dealt with in this book: see the standard texts on the subject.

58 [1976] A.C. 443.

**(a) The general rule before the Miliangos decision** The general rule, which for long prevailed and which was said to be settled[59] and beyond doubt,[60] was that the damages fell to be assessed in sterling according to the rate of exchange at the date of breach in the case of contract, and in the case of tort at the date that the loss was determined. This was established first as to breaches of contract other than by failure to pay a foreign debt in *Di Ferdinando v Simon, Smits & Co*,[61] then as to tort in *S.S. Celia v S.S. Volturno*,[62] approving the earlier case, and finally as to breaches of contract by failure to pay a foreign debt in *Re United Railways of Havana and Regla Warehouses*.[63] **20-019**

The decisions in these three cases, and indeed in the cases which they approved or which followed them, still merit attention as they have not completely lost their relevance under the new regime which the *Miliangos* decision[64] has ushered in. They are therefore dealt with first. **20-020**

*(i) Contract* The problem initially came to the fore at Court of Appeal level in *Di Ferdinando v Simon, Smits & Co.*[65] The defendant had agreed to carry the claimant's goods to Italy and to deliver them there. He failed to deliver them at all and the claimant claimed as damages for breach of contract the value of the goods at the time and place of due delivery.[66] The Court of Appeal, in assessing this value, based its calculation upon the market value of the goods both at the time and place of due delivery, i.e. the value in Italy at the time of breach, this value being converted into sterling as at that time and ignoring subsequent changes in the exchange rate between sterling and Italian currency. Further decisions involving breaches of contract where the claim was not based solely on a failure to pay money due under the contract arrived at a similar result.[67] **20-021**

If the action was based solely upon the failure to pay money, so that, had the defendant contracted to pay the money in sterling, the action would be in debt and no longer for damages, the general rule again applied, but this was not finally settled until the House of Lords decision in *Re United Railways of Havana and Regla Warehouses*.[68] The facts of that case were very complicated and it will suffice to set out only those of direct relevance here. A railway company in 1921, in raising **20-022**

59 *Vionnet v Wills* [1940] 1 K.B. 72 CA at 78; See *Re United Railways of Havana & Regla Warehouses* [1961] A.C. 1007 at 1048 to 1049, 1060.

60 *Salim Nasrallah Khoury v Khayat* [1943] A.C. 507 PC at 513.

61 [1920] 3 K.B. 409 CA.

62 [1921] 2 A.C. 544.

63 [1961] A.C. 1007. The general rule was extended to salvage awards in *The Teh Hu* [1970] P. 106 CA.

64 [1976] A.C. 443.

65 [1920] 3 K.B. 409 CA.

66 The defendant had also converted the goods but the available action in tort does not appear to have been pursued.

67 They dealt with claims for non-delivery of goods sold (*Lebeaupin v Crispin* [1920] 2 K.B. 714); claims for non-acceptance of goods sold (*Barry v Van der Hurk* [1920] 2 K.B. 709); claims for wrongful dismissal (*Ottoman Bank v Chakarian* [1930] A.C. 277 PC); claims proved in company's compulsory winding up in respect of non-payment of money by banks (*Re British American Continental Bank, Goldzieher's Claim* [1922] 2 Ch. 575; *Re British American Continental Bank, Lisser's Claim* [1923] 1 Ch. 276). For further details, see the 13th edition (1972) of this work at paras 473 to 474.

68 [1961] A.C. 1007. Their Lordships rejected the technical argument that the claim was for debt and not for damages (at 1046, 1059, 1069): the court in converting the debt into sterling is in effect assessing the damages and not awarding the debt.

money in the United States of America to finance the acquisition of rolling stock for its railway in Cuba, entered into an elaborate scheme whereby it assigned the rolling stock to trustees for the lenders who leased it back to the company, the rentals being payable in dollars and being fixed so as to cover repayment of the loan with interest over the 15 years of the lease, after which time the company would become owner of the rolling stock. From 1931 the company ceased to pay the dollar rentals to the trustees, but it was not until 1954 that the matter came before the English courts when the trustees sought to prove in the company's voluntary liquidation following upon the acquisition of the railway by the Cuban Government. The House of Lords held that the provable sum in dollar rentals[69] was to be converted into sterling at the rates of exchange prevailing at the dates when the several sums fell due and were not paid. This decision thus confirmed the earlier authorities which had reached a similar result.[70]

**20-023** *(ii) Tort* With tort, on the other hand, the time when the wrong occurred was not necessarily the time when the conversion into sterling was made because this is not always the time when the particular loss, which is being translated, accrues. It is true that, if a chattel is destroyed or damaged beyond repair, then the market value or the diminution in the market value respectively would be taken for conversion into sterling at the moment of the tort. As Lord Sumner said in *S.S. Celia v S.S. Volturno*,[71] where a ship had been damaged by collision in foreign waters:

> "If the damages were such as need not be repaired at all, the whole loss might have been measured by the immediate depreciation of the ship … if there was any conversion into sterling, it would have been calculated at the rate current at the time of the collision."[72]

But the case itself concerned losses arising after the commission of the tort, the disputed claim being for the loss of payments in foreign currency for hire of the ship while the ship was being repaired. The date at which it was held that the conversion into sterling must be made was referred to variously as "the date when the loss was incurred"[73] and "the date at which the loss is suffered".[74]

---

[69] A possible alternative action for conversion proved of little value to the claimants: see [1961] A.C. 1007 at 1042, 1056, 1061–1062, 1065 to 1066.

[70] They dealt with claims for the price of goods sold (*Uliendahl v Pankhurst Wright* (1923) 39 T.L.R. 629; *Peyrae v Wilkinson* [1924] 2 K.B. 166; *Vionnet v Wills* [1940] 1 K.B. 72 CA); claims for the price of goods resold to seller (*Cummings v London Bullion Co* [1952] 1 K.B. 327 CA); claims for freight for the charter of a ship (*Mehmet Dogan Bey v Abdeni* [1951] 2 K.B. 405); claims for failure to pay bills of exchange on maturity (*Salim Nasrallah Khoury v Khayat* [1943] A.C. 507 PC); claims for debts proved in company's compulsory winding up (*Re British American Continental Bank, Credit General Liegeois' Claim* [1922] 2 Ch. 589); claims on a foreign judgment (*East India Trading Co v Carmel Exporters & Importers* [1952] 2 Q.B. 439 CA). For further details see the 13th edition (1972) of this work at para.476.

[71] [1921] 2 A.C. 544 at 554 to 555.

[72] See too *The Canadian Transport* (1932) 43 Ll. L. Rep. 409 CA (at para.20-049, below) where the claim was in respect not of a ship in collision but of a cargo of logs aboard a ship in collision.

[73] [1921] 2 A.C. 544 at 548, per Lord Buckmaster.

[74] [1921] 2 A.C. 544 at 559, per Lord Parmoor. See too *The Baarn* [1933] P. 251 CA, where the loss was by way of expenditure incurred in repairing the damaged ship, and the time for conversion into sterling was held to be the time when the expenditure was effected.

**(b) The Miliangos decision** This general rule[75] was rooted in the basic assumption that all claims and all judgments had to be in sterling, and that the amount awarded as damages in an English court must be expressed in English currency.[76] It is in complete accord with principle that damages should be calculated in contract at the date of breach and in tort at the date of determination of loss even if the loss, contractual or tortious, is a loss incurred in a foreign currency. The important feature is the conversion of the damages to sterling at the same date as that at which the damages were calculated, and this stemmed from the necessity to arrive at a figure in sterling for the loss proved in terms of a foreign currency. It was the need for the conversion following on the normal calculation that produced the rule. **20-024**

In *Miliangos v George Frank (Textiles)*[77] the House of Lords "revolutionised the position"[78] and "transformed"[79] the law in this field by disposing once and for all of the assumption, which had been universally held for so long, that an English court had always to confine itself in its judgments to sterling and could never give judgment in a foreign currency. The possibility of change had been heralded in the two years preceding this decision of late 1975. The Court of Appeal in *Jugoslavenska Oceanska Plovidba v Castle Investment Co Inc*,[80] had held valid an award of experienced commercial arbitrators in London expressed in a foreign currency, it having become the practice of such arbitrators for some time past to express their awards in the appropriate foreign currency, and then, in blatant disregard of the precedent of *Re United Railways of Havana and Regla Warehouses*,[81] had held, first in *Schorsch Meier v Hennin*,[82] and later in the *Miliangos* case itself,[83] that an English court could also give a judgment in a foreign currency.[84] **20-025**

The facts of *Miliangos*,[85] were, as Lord Wilberforce said in the leading majority speech in the House of Lords, **20-026**

> "as simple as in *Re United Railways of Havana and Regla Warehouses*[86] they were complex".[87]

The claimant, a Swiss national, sold goods to the defendants, an English company, at a price expressed to be payable in Swiss francs to a Swiss bank within 30 days of the date of invoice, the proper law of the contract being Swiss. The goods

---

75 See para.20-019, above.

76 *S.S. Celia v S.S. Volturno* [1921] 2 A.C. 544 at 549, 555, 560, 566; *Re United Railways of Havana & Regla Warehouses* [1961] A.C. 1007 at 1043, 1052, 1059, 1068–1069. In *Miliangos v George Frank (Textiles)* [1976] A.C. 443 at 466H, Lord Wilberforce, with whom Lord Cross agreed (at 491H), referred to this assumption as a "modern self-imposed limitation" of which the *fons et origo* was clearly Lindley MR's judgment in *Manners v Pearson* [1898] 1 Ch. 581 CA at 586 to 587.

77 [1976] A.C. 443.

78 *Barclays Bank International v Levin Bros (Bradford)* [1977] Q.B. 270 at 282D, per Mocatta J.

79 *Services Europe Atlantique Sud (SEAS) v Stockholms Rederiaktiebolag, The Folias* [1979] Q.B. 491 at 498D, per Robert Goff J.

80 [1974] Q.B. 292 CA.

81 [1961] A.C. 1007.

82 [1975] Q.B. 416 CA.

83 [1975] Q.B. 487 CA.

84 Also, the Admiralty court in *The Halcyon the Great* [1975] 1 W.L.R. 515, departing from former Admiralty practice, ordered the sale of a ship for a sum in a foreign currency and for the price obtained to be lodged in a separate foreign currency account.

85 [1976] A.C. 443.

86 [1961] A.C. 1007.

87 [1976] A.C. 443 at 457F.

and invoices were delivered, but no part of the price was paid and two bills of exchange drawn in Switzerland and accepted by the defendants were dishonoured on presentation. The claimant brought a claim for the price or, alternatively, for the amount due on the bills of exchange expressed, in each case, in the sterling equivalent of the sum due in Swiss francs as at the dates when payment should have been made, but later applied to amend his statement of claim so as to claim the sums due to him in Swiss francs. This amendment, duly allowed, put in issue for the House of Lords the continuing correctness of their earlier, but not much earlier, decision in the *Havana Railways*[88] case.

**20-027** Lord Wilberforce quoted extensively from the speeches in the *Havana Railways*[89] case[90]

> "in order to make clear what … appears from all of them to be the basic presupposition … [namely] that procedurally an action cannot be brought here for recovery or payment of a sum expressed in foreign currency, and that, in effect, it can only be brought for a sum expressed in sterling, recoverable by way of damages."[91]

The question which then arose was whether "any fresh considerations of any substance" had emerged to induce the House to depart from this presupposition and adopt a different rule.[92] Lord Wilberforce found that there had, and the key to such consideration was undoubtedly the monetary uncertainties which had afflicted the world in the 1970s. He said:

> "The situation as regards currency stability has substantially changed even since 1961. Instead of the main world currencies being fixed and fairly stable in value, subject to the risk of periodic re- or de-valuations, many of them are now 'floating', i.e. they have no fixed exchange value even from day to day. This is true of sterling. This means that, instead of a situation in which changes of relative value occurred between the 'breach date' and the date of judgment or payment being the exception, so that a rule which did not provide for this case could be generally fair, this situation is now the rule. So the search for a formula to deal with it becomes urgent in the interest of justice."[93]

**20-028** The new formula which was adopted was, again in Lord Wilberforce's words, to depart from the former "adherence to the 'breach date' " by "awarding delivery *in specie* rather than by giving damages".[94] The result was that, while the breach date was still used for the calculation, in foreign currency, of the claimant's loss, the need to convert into sterling the amount so calculated for the purposes of the judgment theoretically disappeared if the claim was for the foreign currency.[95] However, a conversion date is still required to be inserted in the judgment of the

---

88 [1961] A.C. 1007.

89 [1961] A.C. 1007.

90 [1976] A.C. 443 at 460D to 462F.

91 [1976] A.C. 443 at 462G.

92 [1976] A.C. 443 at 462H.

93 [1976] A.C. 443 at 463E to G. See too at 497F and 510D, per Lord Cross and Lord Edmund-Davies respectively. Both Lord Wilberforce and Lord Cross expressed themselves as strongly influenced by the introduction of foreign currency awards in commercial arbitrations—awards which the Court of Appeal had held to be enforceable as judgments (see para.20-025, above)—regarding it as unacceptable that different rules should apply as between arbitrations and actions: 464C to D and 497F to G respectively.

94 [1976] A.C. 443 at 466D.

95 Lord Wilberforce insisted that the claim "must be specifically for the foreign currency": [1976] A.C. 443 at 468G.

court, or could even be inserted in the claim itself,[96] for, as Lord Fraser put it, "there must be some provision for converting the foreign currency into sterling so that it can be enforced in this country".[97] This practical necessity caused Lord Edmund-Davies to take the view that

> "the core of this litigation is not in reality whether judgments given by the courts of this country must always be expressed in sterling, though that point was expansively canvassed",[98]

but that "the real question" was

> "what is the proper date to take for the purpose of converting into sterling the amount of foreign currency found due from the defendant?"[99]

While this may be said to be true if one looks only at the end result, it ignores the fact that it is the acceptance of the ability to give judgment in a foreign currency that makes the date of judgment, rather than the date of breach, appear as the appropriate date for effecting the conversion just as, formerly, it was the acceptance of the necessity to give judgment in sterling which caused the courts to look to the date of breach when making the conversion.[100]

In fact, it was not the date of judgment that was chosen by their Lordships but the date of payment in the sense of the date when the court authorises the claimant to enforce the judgment by levying execution for a sum expressed in sterling.[101] The choice, said Lord Wilberforce, "is between (i) the date of action brought, (ii) the date of judgment, (iii) the date of payment" in the sense indicated.[102] Of these the date of payment undoubtedly "gets nearest to securing to the creditor exactly what he bargained for".[103] Lord Fraser put the matter thus: **20-029**

> "Any conversion date earlier than the date of payment would, in my opinion, be open to the same objection as the breach date, namely that it would necessarily leave a considerable interval of time between the conversion date and the date of payment. During that interval currency fluctuations might cause the sterling award to vary appreciably from the sum in foreign currency to which the creditor was entitled. In my opinion, it would not be justifiable to disturb the existing rule of taking the breach date, merely to substitute for it some other date rather nearer to the date of payment but still more or less distant from it. If the date of raising an action in this country were taken for conversion, a period of a year or more might easily elapse, allowing for appeals, before payment was made. The date of judgment would be better[104] but there seems no reason why one should stop short

---

96 By claiming in the alternative the sterling equivalent at a specified date: see [1976] A.C. 443 at 468G, per Lord Wilberforce.

97 [1976] A.C. 443 at 501F.

98 [1976] A.C. 443 at 498C.

99 [1976] A.C. 443 at 498F to G.

100 See para.20-024, above.

101 [1976] A.C. 443 at 469C (together with 468H), 497H to 498A and 501H, per Lords Wilberforce, Cross and Fraser respectively. See Lord Edmund-Davies, at 501C. In the arbitration case of *Jugoslavenska* (see para.20-025, above) the date of the arbitration award had been taken for conversion, but Lord Wilberforce could see no reason why this minor discrepancy between arbitrations and actions could not be removed by adjusting the practice so as to have conversion at the date of leave to enforce in sterling: at 469D.

102 [1976] A.C. 443 at 468G to H.

103 [1976] A.C. 443 at 469A.

104 But here too, as Lord Wilberforce pointed out, [1976] A.C. 443 at 469C, an appeal could again

of the latest practicable date, which seems to be the date when the court authorises enforcement of the judgment."[105]

Lord Fraser indeed rightly pointed out that the conversion date should theoretically be at the still later point in time of the date of actual payment of the debt by the defendant as this would give to the claimant exactly the cost in sterling of buying the foreign currency,

> "but theory must yield to practical necessity to this extent that, if the judgment has to be enforced in this country, it must be converted before enforcement".[106]

20-030 In coming to this decision their Lordships did not think that they were, in Lord Wilberforce's words,

> "called upon, or would be entitled in this case, to review the whole field of the law regarding foreign currency obligations".[107]

Lord Wilberforce therefore saw

> "no need to overrule or criticise or endorse such cases as *The Volturno* or *Di Ferdinando v Simon, Smits & Co*"[108]

and wished to make it clear that

> "for myself, I would confine my approval at the present time of a change in the breach-date rule to claims such as those with which we are here concerned, i.e. to foreign money obligations, sc. obligations of a money character to pay foreign currency arising under a contract whose proper law is that of a foreign country and where the money of account and payment is that of that country, or possibly of some other country but not that of the United Kingdom."[109]

Lord Cross and Lord Fraser also expressed themselves as desirous of not exploring the ground beyond foreign debts and foreign money obligations,[110] but did not make any reference to the requirements, which were satisfied on the *Miliangos* facts themselves, as to proper law, money of account and money of payment.[111] However, it was clear that it would not be long before some at least of the issues which were left unresolved by their Lordships would come before the courts, and indeed in the

impose on a creditor a considerable currency risk.

105 [1976] A.C. 443 at 502B to D.

106 [1976] A.C. 443 at 501G; but see para.20-053, below. It was said that, where the foreign money obligation was the subject of a liquidation or a proof in bankruptcy the date for conversion should be the date when the creditor's claim in terms of sterling is admitted to proof (see at 469C and 498B, per Lord Wilberforce and Lord Cross respectively), but in a subsequent company liquidation case, *Re Dynamics Corp of America* [1976] 1 W.L.R. 757, Oliver J declined to adopt such a date and took instead, basing himself on other earlier authority, the date of the winding-up order.

107 [1976] A.C. 443 at 467H to 468A.

108 [1976] A.C. 443 at 486D. For these two cases see paras 20-021 and 20-023, above.

109 [1976] A.C. 443 at 467G to H.

110 [1976] A.C. 443 at 497H to 498A and 503C respectively.

111 All three were Swiss in *Miliangos*. Money of account differs from money of payment in that the former represents the subject-matter of the obligation while the latter indicates the mode of discharging the obligation: it is the difference between in *obligatione* and *in solutione*. Thus if the purchase price of goods sold is expressed to be "1,000 US dollars payable in Swiss francs", the money of account is dollars, the money of payment francs. See Mann, *The Legal Aspect of Money*, 7th edn (2012), paras 7-65 to 7-67.

time that has passed since the *Miliangos*[112] decision substantial developments have taken place. These developments must now be examined.

**(c) The working out of the Miliangos decision** It is useful, in examining these developments, to start with claims for moneys due in the performance of a contract or due as contractual damages liquidated by the parties' prior stipulation, because with such claims the three factors of proper law of contract, money of account and money of payment are all prominent. With claims for unliquidated damages for breach of contract, only the factor of proper law of contract can be of significance, while with claims arising out of tort not even this factor remains. **20-031**

*(i) Contract debt and liquidated damages* The *Miliangos*[113] case concerned a claim for the price of goods sold and delivered[114] and will clearly apply to all payments made by a defendant in performance of his side of the contract. What is not so clear is whether their Lordships intended their ruling to cover the case of a claim for liquidated damages. While they wished it, in Lord Wilberforce's words, to **20-032**

> "be open for future discussion whether the rule applying to money obligations, which can be a simple rule, should apply as regards claims for damages for breach of contract",[115]

it would seem that a claim for liquidated damages could be regarded as a claim in respect of a money obligation as well as a claim for damages for breach of contract.[116] However, the "future discussion" which Lord Wilberforce envisaged led to an early application of the new rule to liquidated damages at Court of Appeal level. In *Federal Commerce and Navigation Co v Tradax Export*,[117] where there was a claim for demurrage under a charterparty for the carriage of grain from North America to Europe, with the demurrage expressed to be payable in US dollars at the rate of US$3,000 a day, the Court of Appeal held that the claimant shipowners were entitled to judgment in US dollars for the demurrage claimed.[118] It is true that

---

[112] [1976] A.C. 443.

[113] [1976] A.C. 443.

[114] Facts at para.20-026, above.

[115] [1976] A.C. 443 at 468A.

[116] Strictly, probably not a money obligation in the sense, to which Lord Wilberforce was confining himself (para.20-030, above), of an obligation of a money character "arising under a contract".

[117] [1977] Q.B. 324 CA.

[118] The House of Lords allowed the charterer's appeal on the issue of liability, nothing being said on damages: *Federal Commerce and Navigation Co v Tradax Export* [1978] A.C. 1. See too *Veflings Rederi A/S v President of India, The Bellami* [1978] 1 W.L.R. 982 and *Monrovia Tramp Shipping Co v President of India, The Pearl Merchant* [1978] 2 Lloyd's Rep. 193 in both of which Donaldson J rightly applied the reasoning of *Miliangos* so as to hold, where a payment in sterling had been made by charterers on account of demurrage which had fallen due and which was expressed at a rate to be calculated in US dollars, that the charterers were only entitled to credit for such amount in US dollars as the sterling payment represented if converted at the rate of exchange prevailing at the date of such payment. The rate of exchange at the earlier date of default, namely when the demurrage fell due, for which the charterers contended, and which produced a larger credit because sterling was falling as against the US dollar, was rejected. As Donaldson J pointed out in the first of these two cases, it would be improper to permit the debtor to improve his position by making payment well after default but just before judgment: [1978] 1 W.L.R. 982 at 985D to F. Both decisions, together with a similar third entitled *Marperfecta Compania Naviera v President of India, The Doric Chariot*, were affirmed by the Court of Appeal at [1979] 1 W.L.R. 59 CA, but with only two or three sentences (at 62F) devoted to this point. The new rule was again held applicable to demurrage in *President of India v Taygetos Shipping, The Agenor* [1985] 1 Lloyd's Rep. 155. See the cases further at para.20-

Lord Denning MR treated demurrage as "a debt due under the contract",[119] but there is no doubt that Brandon J was right in questioning this in *The Despina R*,[120] when he said that liability for demurrage is to be classified as a liability for liquidated damages rather than for debt.[121]

**20-033** Accepting therefore that the *Miliangos*[122] decision applies equally to claims for debt and claims for liquidated damages, the question then arises how far the courts have travelled, if at all, beyond Lord Wilberforce's limits of requiring a foreign proper law, a foreign money of account and a foreign money of payment.[123] It soon became clear that the fact that the proper law of the contract was English was not to deter the courts from giving judgment in the stipulated foreign currency which was the money of account and of payment. *Barclays Bank International v Levin Brothers (Bradford)*[124] involved, as had *Miliangos*[125] itself, English buyers dishonouring bills of exchange expressed in a foreign currency, here US dollars, and drawn in respect of goods sold to them by foreign sellers, here a New York corporation. While the claimants were not the foreign sellers themselves but their indorsees of the bills of exchange, the important difference from *Miliangos*[126] was that, though the currency of account and the currency of payment were both the same foreign currency, the proper law of the contract was English. Mocatta J nevertheless held that the case was a proper one for judgment to be given in the currency of the bills of exchange.[127] He said that he did not

> "read the opinions of the other members of the House of Lords as approving the limitations of the new rule by such restrictions as are mentioned by Lord Wilberforce.... The very great weight attached in the majority opinions of the House of Lords to the decision in *Jugoslavenska Oceanska Plovidba v Castle Investment Co Inc*[128] indicates clearly in my opinion that it cannot be a sine qua non to a judgment being entered in a foreign currency that the proper law of the contract giving rise to the obligation must be other than the law of England. My reason for saying this is that, ... in the cases where commercial

034, below.

119 [1977] Q.B. 324 CA at 342E.

120 [1978] Q.B. 396 at 407F.

121 See para.16-081, above. The repeal of s.2(3) of the Foreign Judgments (Reciprocal Enforcement) Act 1933 by s.4 of the Administration of Justice Act 1977 allowed judgments given in a foreign currency and registrable for enforcement by the English courts to be registered in the foreign currency, whereas formerly they had to be registered in sterling on the basis of the rate of exchange prevailing at the date of the original judgment.

122 [1976] A.C. 443.

123 [1976] A.C. 443 at 467G to H, at para.20-030, above.

124 [1977] Q.B. 270.

125 [1976] A.C. 443.

126 [1976] A.C. 443.

127 A further difficulty in the way of the claimants was the provision of the Bills of Exchange Act 1882 s.72(4), that, where the sum payable under a bill, drawn out of but payable in the UK, is expressed in a foreign currency, the amount is to be calculated according to the rate of exchange on the day the bill is payable. It was held, however, that the subsection merely provided a formula to ascertain the amount of sterling an acceptor should pay at maturity if he chose to pay in sterling, and had no statutory effect on the sum recoverable where the acceptor failed to pay at maturity and had to be sued. Mocatta J accepted ([1977] Q.B. 270 at 282F) that *Salim Nasrallah Khoury v Khayat* [1943] A.C. 507 PC, where the Privy Council had placed reliance on the Palestinian equivalent of s.72(4), is, since *Miliangos* [1976] A.C. 443, of no continuing authority upon the issue of enforcement of action of bills of exchange expressed in a foreign currency. However, the problem presented to Mocatta J was resolved at source by the repeal of s.72(4) itself by s.4 of the Administration of Justice Act 1977.

128 [1974] Q.B. 292. See para.20-027, above.

arbitrators in the City of London and elsewhere in the country give awards in foreign currencies, the proper law of the contracts under which such awards are made is almost invariably English."[129]

Similarly, where in *Federal Commerce and Navigation Co v Tradax Export*,[130] the demurrage was awarded in the US dollars which the contract stipulated,[131] this was done despite the fact that the proper law of that contract was English. When presented with the proposition that judgment in a foreign currency required that the proper law of the contract be that of a foreign country, Lord Denning MR, with whose reasons the other members of the court agreed,[132] said:

> "I think that the power should not be so confined. Once it is recognised that judgment can be given in a foreign currency, justice requires that it should be given in every case where the currency of the contract is a foreign currency: otherwise one side or the other will suffer unfairly by the fluctuations of the exchange."[133]

He too said he relied greatly on the practice of commercial arbitrators in London.[134]

The need for a foreign proper law having thus been disposed of, there remain the two questions of whether both money of account and money of payment need be foreign and, if so, whether they need be of the same foreign country.[135] There seems to be no good reason why Lord Wilberforce's restrictions[136] should apply here any more than on the issue of proper law. In three cases—*Veflings Rederi A/S v President of India, The Bellami*,[137] *Monrovia Tramp Shipping Co v President of India, The Pearl Merchant*[138] and *Marperfecta Compania Naviera v President of India, The Doric Chariot*[139]—each of which concerned a charterparty under which any demurrage which became due was to be calculated at a rate expressed in US dollars, the Court of Appeal, hearing appeals in all three together, took the view that the currency in which the demurrage fell to be paid under the agreements was also US dollars[140]: accordingly, neither of these two remaining questions arose. However, Donaldson J, who had heard the first two of the cases below,[141] and whose decisions in both were affirmed by the Court of Appeal, appears to have regarded the **20-034**

---

129 [1977] Q.B. 270 at 279B to D.

130 [1977] Q.B. 324 CA.

131 See para.20-032, above.

132 [1977] Q.B. 324 CA at 349A and 354A.

133 [1977] Q.B. 324 CA at 342A.

134 [1977] Q.B. 324 CA at 342B. Accordingly both Mocatta J and the Court of Appeal departed from the first limb of the restriction in para.3 of the then Practice Note, *Practice Direction (Judgment: Foreign Currency)* [1976] 1 W.L.R. 83, requiring writ or statement of claim to specify "(i) that the contract under which the debt is claimed in the foreign currency is governed by the law of some country outside the United Kingdom; and (ii) that under that contract the money of account in which the debt was payable was the currency of that country or of some other foreign country." This paragraph, which was clearly based on Lord Wilberforce in *Miliangos* (para.20-030, above), was later amended so as to eliminate any reference not only to proper law but also to moneys of account and payment: [1977] 1 W.L.R. 197.

135 For the distinction between money of account and money of payment, see para.20-030, above.

136 See para.20-030, above.

137 [1979] 1 W.L.R. 59 CA.

138 [1979] 1 W.L.R. 59 CA.

139 [1979] 1 W.L.R. 59 CA.

140 [1979] 1 W.L.R. 59 CA at 63A.

141 [1978] 1 W.L.R. 982 and [1978] 2 Lloyd's Rep. 193 respectively.

money of payment, as opposed to the money of account, as sterling[142]: the demurrage, like the freight for which express provision had been made, fell to be paid in British external accounts sterling in London. This would mean that, in effect, Donaldson J was answering the first of the two questions in the negative, with the result that the second of the questions can no longer be in issue. While the issue actually before the court in these cases was as to the relevant date to take the exchange rate in order to ascertain the extent to which a payment by the defendants made between default and judgment discharged their liability,[143] an important feature of Donaldson J's approach, though perhaps not of the Court of Appeal's, is that it implicitly accepts that, even where sterling is the money of payment, the claimant is entitled to judgment in the foreign money of account. This indicates that, as between currency of account and currency of payment, it is the former which controls, so that in the converse situation, where it is the currency of account which is sterling, it would seem that judgment would simply be given in sterling and no attention would fall to be paid to the exchange rate as between sterling and the US dollar—or indeed any other foreign currency—at any point in time. And adopting a similar process where the moneys of account and of payment are different but are both foreign, it would seem that judgment would be given in the foreign currency of account for the sum specified in that currency of account, and the currency of payment, here itself also foreign, would again have no contribution to make in the calculation. Should however the parties to a charterparty stipulate that demurrage is to be paid in sterling at the exchange rate ruling at the date of the bills of lading, as was the case in *President of India v Taygetos Shipping, The Agenor*,[144] the position is different. Staughton J there said that in his judgment

> "a different solution is appropriate where the contract provides, as it does here, an agreed exchange rate between the money of account and the money of payment. In such a case I consider that the judgment or award should prima facie be in the money of payment."[145]

This, he added, was what the creditor has lost if payment is not made, is what the debtor might have tendered and is what the creditor would have been bound to accept.[146]

**20-035** *(ii) Contract: unliquidated damages* The first case to come up in the courts after the House of Lords had given their judgment in *Miliangos*,[147] involved a claim for damages for breach of contract as well as one for debt. In *Kraut v Albany Fabrics*,[148] there was, once again, a sale of goods by Swiss sellers to English buyers payable

[142] See especially [1978] 1 W.L.R. 982 at 984E and 985A.

[143] See para.20-032, above.

[144] [1985] 1 Lloyd's Rep. 155.

[145] [1985] 1 Lloyd's Rep. 155 at 158, col.2.

[146] Nor can the parties, as the House of Lords rightly decided in *President of India v Lips Maritime Corp* [1988] A.C. 395 reversing the Court of Appeal, claim the exchange loss as special damages. On the unavailability to the claimant, in these circumstances, of the benefit of *Miliangos* see at 426B to D, per Lord Brandon. Where in *Fearns v Anglo-Dutch Paint & Chemical Co Ltd* [2011] 1 W.L.R. 366 in the context of the operation of set-off the issue arose as to the proper date for conversion of a debt in euros and damages in pounds into a common currency, the judge's view that damages can be recovered for a currency exchange loss caused by the late payment of a debt appears inconsistent with the Lips decision despite the judge's citing it as illustrating his view (see at [52]–[57]).

[147] [1976] A.C. 443.

[148] [1977] Q.B. 182.

in Swiss francs. Not only did the buyers refuse to pay for such of the goods as had been delivered but they also refused to accept any further consignments. The sellers, having sued for moneys owing for the goods delivered and for damages for breach of contract for the goods rejected, wished to amend their claim to ask for judgment in Swiss francs. The defendants raised no objection in relation to the moneys owing, conceding that this part of the claim was covered by the *Miliangos*[149] decision, but opposed the amendment in relation to the damages for breach of contract.[150] Eveleigh J nevertheless granted the claimants leave to amend in order to make the claim for damages in Swiss currency. While accepting that *Di Ferdinando v Simon, Smits & Co*[151] was[152] binding upon him[153] he rightly regarded that case as not in any way being concerned with deciding whether or not damages could be awarded in a foreign currency—it being assumed without argument that judgment must be in sterling—but simply with arriving at a figure in sterling for a loss proved in terms of foreign currency.[154] In *Federal Commerce and Navigation Co v Tradax Export*,[155] Lord Denning MR assumed that the court could give judgment in the appropriate foreign currency

> "both when [the claim] is for a debt due under the contract (as demurrage) or damages for breach of contract (as of the implied term)".[156]

And in *Services Europe Atlantique Sud (SEAS) v Stockholms Rederiaktiebolag*,[157] generally referred to as *The Folias*,[158] where charterers sued shipowners on account of damaged cargo, it was not even contended, in the words of Robert Goff J at first instance, that the arbitrators were not

> "free to make an award in a foreign currency simply because the claim is one for damages".[159]

In commenting on this he pointed out that:

> "any other conclusion would lead to absurd results. It is not only possible, but common, that in one commercial arbitration claims for both debt and damages may arise out of closely related facts; for example, to take a case close to the present, in a time charter dispute there are often claims both for balance of hire, which is a contract debt, and for damages relating to the condition of the ship on redelivery. It would be most undesirable if the award in respect of the claim in debt could be made in a foreign currency, whereas in respect of the claim in damages the award could only be made in sterling."[160]

---

149 [1976] A.C. 443.
150 [1977] Q.B. 182 at 186C to D.
151 [1920] 3 K.B. 409 CA: see para.20-021, above.
152 Together with *S.S. Celia v S.S. Volturno* [1921] 2 A.C. 544, the corresponding tort decision: see para.20-023, above.
153 [1977] Q.B. 182 at 187D.
154 [1977] Q.B. 182 at 188C to F.
155 [1977] Q.B. 324 CA: facts at para.20-032, above.
156 [1977] Q.B. 324 CA at 342E. Demurrage is strictly liquidated damages and not debt: see para.20-032 *in fin*, above.
157 [1979] A.C. 685: full facts at para.20-037, below.
158 As in the report at [1979] 1 Lloyd's Rep. 1 HL.
159 [1979] Q.B. 491 at 498H.
160 [1979] Q.B. 491 at 498H to 499B.

The reversal of Robert Goff J's decision by the Court of Appeal[161] and the House of Lords[162] in no way affected this point, Lord Wilberforce, who delivered the leading speech in the House, saying

> simply that "the effect of … *Miliangos v George Frank (Textiles)* is that in contractual as in other cases a judgment (in which for convenience I include an award) can be given in a currency other than sterling".[163]

**20-036** Once the hurdle of whether judgment for unliquidated damages for breach of contract can be awarded in a foreign currency has been successfully cleared, there comes the more difficult problem of what is the appropriate foreign currency to use. While the proper law of the contract cannot be controlling here any more than it is with debt and liquidated damages[164]—and indeed the proper law of the charterparty in *The Folias*[165] was English law—there is no longer the same assistance to be derived from the money of account and the money of payment. For there will be no specified money of payment in relation to unliquidated damages as there is where debt or liquidated damages is in issue, and the money of account which is applicable to the discharge of contractual obligations, such as the payment of the price of goods that are purchased or the hire of a ship that is chartered, may have little or no relevance to the damage or loss which in fact occurs and for which damages are being sought.

**20-037** It was this issue of the appropriate foreign currency for the award that formed the real point of dispute in *The Folias*.[166] The claimants, a French corporation having their place of business in Paris, chartered a ship from Swedish owners, the defendants, under a charterparty which provided for the hire and other payments to be made in US dollars but, in any general average adjustment, for disbursements in a foreign currency to be exchanged in a European convertible currency, in pounds sterling or in US dollars. During a voyage from Spain to Brazil the refrigeration machinery failed and some of the cargo arrived in Brazil in a damaged condition. Claims were made by the cargo receivers and the claimants used French francs in order to acquire the Brazilian cruzeiros needed to settle these claims for which they were liable. The claimants then claimed in turn from the defendants in respect of this expenditure, the action being for breach of the warranty of seaworthiness in the charterparty. The issue was whether the award should be in Brazilian cruzeiros as the defendants contended, in French francs as the claimants primarily contended and as the arbitrators had awarded, or in US dollars as the claimants secondarily contended, the contentions of the parties reflecting, predictably, the result or results that favoured them in the light of the currency fluctuations which had come about.

**20-038** The argument for US dollars was based on the proposition that US dollars was the currency of the parties' implied choice. By making US dollars money of account and money of payment in respect of the obligations arising under the contract, the parties, it was said, had evinced an intention that, except for the purposes of general average, all payments, whether by way of debt or by way of damages,

---

161 [1979] Q.B. 491 CA.
162 [1979] A.C. 685.
163 [1979] A.C. 685 at 700D. See, too, at 702C.
164 See para.20-033, above.
165 [1979] A.C. 685.
166 [1979] A.C. 685.

should be made in US dollars as the currency of the contract. Robert Goff J at first instance rejected this submission of the claimants. He said:

> "I do not consider that, simply because the parties have agreed upon the U.S. dollar as the currency of account and currency of payment of the hire and other monetary obligations arising under the contract, they have therefore agreed that damages for breach of any obligation under the contract should be calculated and paid in dollars, regardless of the currency in which the loss was incurred. There is no express agreement to this effect; and no such agreement can, in my judgment, be implied. That being so, the suggestion becomes completely artificial. Where, as here, a French charterer incurs a loss in cruzeiros, it cannot be assumed that he will either expend US dollars to purchase the necessary cruzeiros, or buy in an equivalent amount of dollars to hedge against his contingent liability, and there is thus no connection between the loss and the US dollar at all."[167]

Robert Goff J's reasoning here, though not passed upon by the Court of Appeal, was accepted by the House of Lords where Lord Wilberforce said:

> "The first step must be to see whether, expressly or by implication, the contract provides an answer to the currency question. This may lead to selection of the 'currency of the contract'. If from the terms of the contract it appears that the parties have accepted a currency as the currency of account and payment in respect of all transactions arising under the contract, then it would be proper to give a judgment for damages in that currency. But there may be cases in which, although obligations under the contract are to be met in a specified currency, or currencies, the right conclusion may be that there is no intention shown that damages for breach of the contract should be given in that currency or currencies. In the present case the fact that US dollars have been named as the currency in which payments in respect of hire and other contractual payments are to be made, provides no necessary or indeed plausible reason why damages for breach of the contract should be paid in that currency. The terms of other contracts may lead to a similar conclusion."[168]

But the major question remained: should the award be in the currency of direct **20-039**
loss, namely the Brazilian cruzeiros which were used by the claimants to discharge their liability to the cargo receivers, or in the currency of indirect loss, namely the French francs which were used to acquire the cruzeiros with which to discharge this liability? Robert Goff J decided in favour of the former, largely guided to this conclusion by *The Canadian Transport*,[169] a decision of the Court of Appeal which was soon to be unsuccessfully put forward, in the context of tort,[170] as a binding authority in favour of the currency of direct loss solution. The Court of Appeal however took a more robust view and reversed Robert Goff J,[171] a reversal endorsed by the House of Lords.[172] Damages for breach of contract in respect of sums expended in a foreign currency should be calculated, in the words of Lord Wilberforce,

> "in the currency in which the loss was felt by the plaintiff or 'which most truly expresses his loss.' This is not limited to that in which it first and immediately arose. In ascertaining which this currency is, the court must ask what is the currency, payment in which will

---

167 [1979] Q.B. 491 at 506C to E.
168 [1979] A.C. 685 at 700E to 701B.
169 (1932) 43 Ll. L. Rep. 409 CA.
170 See para.20-049, below.
171 [1979] Q.B. 491 CA.
172 [1979] A.C. 685.

as nearly as possible compensate the plaintiff in accordance with the principle of restitution, and whether the parties must be taken reasonably to have had this in contemplation."[173]

Not only the no longer authoritative *Di Ferdinando v Simon, Smits & Co*,[174] but also *The Canadian Transport*,[175] depended

"on the sterling-breach-date rule which was thought to prevent a choice between the currency of expenditure and the currency of the plaintiff".[176]

The true principles were those applied in *Kraut v Albany Fabrics*[177] by Eveleigh J.

**20-040** Applying then the true principles to the instant case, the appropriate currency for the damages award was held to be French francs. "The essential question", said Lord Wilberforce,

"is what was the loss suffered by the respondents. I do not find this to be identical with that suffered by the cargo receivers: the charterers' claim against the owners is not one for indemnity in respect of expenditure sustained but is one for damages for breach of contract. ... I think it must follow from this that their loss, which they claim as damages, was the discharge of the receivers' claim, together with the legal and other expenses they incurred. They discharged all these by providing francs—until they provided the francs to meet the receivers' claim they suffered no loss. Then secondly was this loss the kind of loss which, under the contract, they were entitled to recover against the owners? The answer to this is provided by the arbitrators' finding that it was reasonable to contemplate that the charterers, being a French corporation and having their place of business in Paris, would have to use French francs to purchase other currencies to settle cargo claims arising under the bills of lading."[178]

**20-041** *Société Française Bunge SA v Belcan NV, The Federal Huron*,[179] is a further contract case involving damage to a ship's cargo; here the shipowners were sued by the cargo receivers. It was the practice of the claimants, a French corporation which traded in and processed soya beans, to purchase and send cargoes of beans to a plant in France for processing. They purchased mainly in the United States of America and Brazil, and in small quantities in France. Purchase prices were always fixed in US dollars but sale prices were made in dollars, in French francs if the sale was in France, or in the national currency of the buyer. Where the currency of a sale was not in US dollars the claimants would, on spot sales, convert the sale proceeds immediately into dollars and, on forward sales, sell the currency forward and buy dollars at the same value on that date. Indeed because the dominant currency of the soya trade was US dollars, the corporation's financial affairs were arranged so that all expenses and receipts were quantified in that currency. The claimants shipped a cargo of soya beans from the United States of America to Bordeaux; on arrival it was found to be damaged, and was sold for a price expressed in French francs by the claimants who incurred additional local expenditure, which they paid in francs. The contract of carriage giving rise to the claimants' claim for this damage

[173] [1979] A.C. 685 at 701B to C.
[174] [1920] 3 K.B. 409 CA.
[175] (1932) 43 Ll. L. Rep. 409 CA.
[176] [1979] A.C. 685 at 701G.
[177] [1977] Q.B. 182: see para.20-035, above.
[178] [1979] A.C. 685 at 702D to G.
[179] [1985] 3 All E.R. 378.

expressed the freight in US dollars payable in dollars and the demurrage as a daily dollar rate, and had English as its proper law. The claimants asked that judgment should be in dollars but the defendants contended for francs on the ground that, since damages are calculated at the diminution in the value of the damaged cargo at the port of destination and discharge,[180] these damages should prima facie be measured in the currency used there and the claimants had failed to show that their special circumstances sufficed to displace this rule. Bingham J decided in the claimants' favour. He first rightly held[181] that the contract of carriage, even though the only currency mentioned therein was dollars, could not be said either expressly or by implication to specify dollars as the currency which the parties had agreed upon as the currency in which damages should be paid—Lord Wilberforce's "currency of the contract"[182]—and he went on to consider, as between dollars and francs, in which currency the claimants' loss was felt and which currency most truly expressed their loss, again using the terminology of Lord Wilberforce in *The Folias*.[183] On this he concluded that the claimants' main claim for damage to the cargo could only be fairly expressed in dollars. He referred to the fact that they had paid for the cargo in dollars and to their practice in relation to both spot and forward sales, and added:

> "It is plain that the cargo receivers were prepared to take the risk that the dollar would depreciate against other currencies but were not prepared to take the risk that any other currency, including the franc, would depreciate against the dollar. To give judgment in francs in these circumstances ... would mean that the shipowners' breach and the intervention of the court had imposed on the cargo receivers an exchange loss which they would not otherwise have suffered and against which, as a matter of routine commercial practice, they took careful measures to protect themselves. A dollar loss is what the cargo receivers would have foreseen as a result of cargo damage. I have no direct evidence of what the shipowners contemplated but have no reason to doubt that they also would have foreseen a loss in dollars if a commodity bought in and shipped from the United States were damaged."[184]

He then held similarly, although he considered the solution to be less plain, that the dollar was the appropriate currency for the award for the incidental expenses which had been discharged in francs, persuaded by the claimants' practice of quantifying all costs and expenses in dollars.[185] And similarly in *The Food Corp of India v Carras (Hellas), The Dione*,[186] where shipowners and charterers had, on entering into a charterparty, agreed to share equally any overtime incurred during loading at Buenos Aires and the owners had paid the stevedores in pesos, having remitted dollar funds to their agents in Buenos Aires to make the payment, it was held in the owners' damages claim for reimbursement of half the payment from the charterers, that the award should be in their own currency, the dollar, rather than in the currency, the peso, in which the repairs had been incurred.

There may however be a question beyond that of what currency most truly expresses the claimant's loss, and that is the question whether such other currency **20-042**

---

[180] See paras 32-002 to 32-004, below.
[181] [1985] 3 All E.R. 378 at 383b.
[182] See para.20-038, above.
[183] [1979] A.C. 685.
[184] [1985] 3 All E.R. 378 at 383e–g.
[185] [1985] 3 All E.R. 378 at 383h.
[186] [1980] 2 Lloyd's Rep. 577.

was within the contemplation of the contracting parties. This appears from *Metaalhandel Magnus v Ardfields Transport*.[187] Metal dealers in Holland bought a large quantity of tungsten rods packed in sealed drums from sellers in England. The sellers, who had undertaken to store the goods in the warehouse of a third party,[188] were in breach of contract in failing to use reasonable care in the storage of the goods which were removed by an unauthorised person and never traced. Gatehouse J posed for himself the two questions, of currency and of contemplation, and concluded:

> "The fact that a foreign plaintiff will necessarily have his bank accounts in, keep his financial books in, and funds his purchases of other currencies from the currency of his own currency cannot automatically result in an award in our Courts in that currency. It must depend on the particular circumstances of the case. … The parties to this contract cannot be said to have had in contemplation that damages payable … if damage or loss of the goods should occur … should be measured in guilders."[189]

On the other hand, in *Virani Ltd v Manuel Revert y Cia SA*,[190] the currency of loss and the contemplation of the parties coincided. The claimant, an English company which had sold a quantity of cloth it had imported from Pakistan to the defendant, a Spanish company, at a price expressed in pesetas contended that the damages in its action for breach of contract on the defendant's refusing to take delivery should be expressed in US dollars; the defendant contended for euros (pesetas no longer being a currency in use), which conversion was much more favourable to it. Since the contract was of no assistance in arriving at the correct solution—that the price was expressed in pesetas was in no way controlling—the proper approach was to inquire which currency most truly expressed the claimant's loss. This was held to be US dollars, for which currency the evidence was said to be all one way. The price of the claimant's purchase from Pakistan had to be paid in dollars. Its contract price to Spain was based on its internal costings calculated in dollars. Dealing in the international market it was anxious to protect itself against fluctuations in exchange rates and it had provided itself with cover by selling forward the expected amount of pesetas in exchange for dollars. Next, it had to be established that the parties must be taken reasonably to have had a dollar currency in their contemplation, and this too was answered in the claimant's favour since the defendant, being a large dealer in cloth as familiar as was the claimant with the vagaries of rising and falling exchange rates, must have expected of anyone engaged in foreign transactions that steps would be taken to protect the value of a transaction by covering it in the way the claimant had done.

**20-043** Once the currency in which the claimant's loss is effectively felt has been identified, it only remains for the court to calculate that loss in that currency, generally using the breach date for the calculation, and following this by the necessary conversion into sterling as at the date of judgment[191]; to this process therefore fluctuations in the currency of loss between breach and judgment can have no relevance. That this is so was dramatically highlighted in the further decision of the House of Lords in *Attorney General of the Republic of Ghana v Texaco Overseas*

---

[187] [1988] 1 Lloyd's Rep. 197.

[188] The third party was the second defendant but took no part in the proceedings.

[189] [1988] 1 Lloyd's Rep. 197 at 205, col.1.

[190] [2004] 2 Lloyd's Rep. 14 CA.

[191] See para.20-028, above.

*Tankships, The Texaco Melbourne*.[192] The claimants shipped fuel oil on the defendants' vessel for transport along the Ghanaian coast for some 150 miles. The cargo never arrived at its destination where the claimants had intended to sell it. There was therefore no fuel oil to sell and the claimants did not replace the fuel oil by a further purchase. In the claimants' claim for damages for non-delivery the crucial question was the identification of the appropriate currency for the award in view of the catastrophic decline of the Ghanaian cedi against the US dollar between the time of breach of contract in 1982 when the rate of exchange was 2.75 cedis to the dollar and the time of judgment in the trial before Webster J in 1991 when the rate was 375 cedis to the dollar.[193] The claimants naturally wished that the currency of the award should be dollars; one argument for saying that their loss had been felt in dollars was that the cost of obtaining a replacement cargo in Italy, the nearest available market,[194] for shipment to Ghana would have had to be incurred in dollars.

Nevertheless it was held by the House of Lords, affirming a majority of the Court of Appeal which had reversed Webster J, that the Ghanaian cedi was the currency in which the claimants had felt their loss, a conclusion to which a number of factors led their lordships. The claimants' business was conducted in Ghana in Ghanaian currency and, consistently with this, their bank accounts and their business accounts were maintained in Ghanaian currency, and, perhaps most importantly, the cargo of fuel oil, had it arrived, would have been sold in Ghana to Ghanaian companies for Ghanaian currency.[195] Nor was the claimants' argument for a loss felt in US dollars supported by the fact that, without a cargo of fuel oil to sell, they might have obtained a replacement cargo in Italy with US dollars because, by virtue of Ghana's stringent exchange control legislation, the claimants, in order to obtain the necessary dollars, would have had to expend cedis to acquire them from the Bank of Ghana; and indeed no replacement cargo had been sought. It having been decided that the loss was felt in cedis, that was an end of the matter, Lord Goff stating categorically early in his leading speech that subsequent depreciation, or indeed appreciation, of the relevant currency was to no avail.[196] **20-044**

It was little consolation to the claimants that they were entitled to interest upon the amount awarded from breach date to judgment date but, as Lord Goff rightly said, it was important not to be mesmerised by the striking difference in the figures, by the fact that an award in US dollars would have amounted for the claimants to nearly $3 million whereas one in cedis amounted, when translated into dollar terms, to some $20,000. Webster J had been wrong to have been influenced by this immense disparity so as to consider himself entitled to take into account subsequent **20-045**

---

[192] [1994] 1 Lloyd's Rep. 473 HL.

[193] Not 3.75 cedis as is said both in the headnote and in the speeches in the Lloyd's report.

[194] For the available market aspect of *The Texaco Melbourne* see the discussion at para.32-005, below.

[195] See Lord Goff at [1994] 1 Lloyd's Rep. 473 HL at 478, col.2. Nonetheless *The Texaco Melbourne* was distinguished by Gloster J in *Milan Nigeria Ltd v Angeliki B Maritime Co* [2011] EWHC 892 (Comm), where the defendant shipowners were liable for damage to, rather than for the loss of, the claimants' cargo, arbitrators having found no difficulty in holding that the loss was felt in US dollars and not in Nigerian naira, the currency where the cargo would, if not lost, have been discharged and sold, and where replacement goods might have been acquired. The arbitrators had so decided because they saw the cargo owners' claim as being related to international trade where the primary currency was US dollars, with the cost of the goods and the ocean freight being in that currency, and this conclusion was reached regardless of the fact that cargo, once discharged, would invariably be sold in the local currency. Gloster J held that the arbitrators' decision must stand and that there could be no appeal against it: see generally at [46] to [68].

[196] [1994] 1 Lloyd's Rep. 473 HL at 476, col.2.

events in the shape of the collapse of the cedi. Had the claim been pursued with more vigour and not taken nine years to come on, the claimants would have fared much better; thus three years after the breach the decline in the cedi had advanced only to an exchange rate of 60 to the US dollar, nowhere near to the 375 at the time of Webster J's judgment. Better still would it have been for the claimants if they had had a clause in the contract specifying that damages be awarded in, or with reference to, US dollars or other hard currency, but that is perhaps asking for too much foresight and indeed a preparedness on the part of the defendants to agree to such a clause. There was no reason for making the calculation at a date later than the breach, when the cedi would have further declined to the claimants' advantage, as might have been the case had the claimants in fact acquired a replacement cargo but had been unable, acting reasonably, to do so for some time.[197] Had the claimants been able to show that they would have used the proceeds from their sale of the fuel oil in further projects which would have cushioned them against a catastrophic decline in the cedi and that such action was within the contemplation of the parties, this might have been a ground for a more favourable award,[198] but no such evidence was led or such possibility suggested.

**20-046** *(iii) Tort* Once it became accepted that unliquidated damages for breach of a contract, and whether a contract with a foreign proper law or not, could be awarded in a foreign currency, a parallel extension of the *Miliangos* development[199] in relation to damages for tort was inevitable. This extension came with *The Despina R*,[200] the decision in which at first instance[201] came close upon that in *The Folias*[202]; the final appeals in both were heard together.

**20-047** Two Greek ships were damaged in a collision off Shanghai. Ensuing litigation between the owners of the two ships was settled on the basis that the defendant owners were liable to the claimant owners to the extent of 85 per cent of the damage suffered by the claimants. The claimants had incurred expenses, mainly in respect of temporary and then permanent repairs, in Chinese, Japanese and US currencies,[203] their ship having moved from Shanghai to Yokohama to Los Angeles, and had also lost, through detention of the ship, freight on charterparties in performance or already contracted for, such freight being payable in US dollars in New York. The claimants' ship was managed by agents in New York, where there was a US dollar bank account which was used for all payments in and out in respect of the ship, and the moneys expended in currencies other than US currency were acquired for the purpose with sums in US dollars transferred from New York.

**20-048** The first question that arose for decision was whether judgment could be given for the claimants in a currency other than sterling where the claim was for damages in tort. Just as in *Kraut v Albany Fabrics*,[204] Eveleigh J had to consider whether *Di Ferdinando v Simon, Smits & Co*,[205] required him to embrace the sterling solu-

---

197 There is now substantial authority for looking to times subsequent to the wrong for the purposes of the damages assessment: for instances see paras 27-009, 27-049 and 39-017 to 39-018, below.
198 See para.20-053, below.
199 [1976] A.C. 443.
200 [1979] A.C. 685.
201 [1978] Q.B. 396; see above for CA.
202 [1979] Q.B. 491.
203 There was also £6 worth of expenditure in sterling.
204 [1977] Q.B. 182; see para.20-035, above.
205 [1920] 3 K.B. 409 CA.

tion for unliquidated damages for breach of contract, so their Lordships in *The Despina R*,[206] had to consider whether *The Volturno*,[207] required them to do likewise in relation to tort damages. Once again it was held that the earlier decision did not prevent adoption of the foreign currency solution. The question, said Lord Russell, was whether, after *Miliangos*,[208] "the approach in *The Volturno* should still be adhered to"[209] in claims for tort damages, a salient feature of that decision being the theory that a claim could only be made in sterling.[210] "The *Miliangos* case", he continued,

> "was one for debt in a foreign currency, and it may rightly be said that the parties were in agreement that the payment should be made in that currency, whereas in the case of damages for tort it is at least highly unlikely that there should be such agreement, and it was not so here. But the rule that a claim here must be made only in sterling and judgment given only in sterling is basically a rule of procedure, and in my opinion it is undesirable that the rule of procedure should be retained for a claim for damages (whether in tort or for breach of contract) while departed from in a case of debt."[211]

Then came the more difficult question: what was the appropriate foreign currency or currencies in which to give judgment? It was the same question as had arisen in *The Folias*,[212] except that, there being no contract between the claimants and defendants, the choice of the currency of the contract was at least eliminated. The claimants argued for US dollars as the currency to which was attributable not only direct expenditure and loss but also indirect expenditure in so far as US dollars had been used to obtain the other currencies in which the direct payments had been made. The defendants, on the other hand, argued for the various currencies, Chinese, Japanese and US, in which the expenditure or loss had been directly and immediately incurred. In deciding in favour of the argument of the claimants neither the House of Lords[213] nor the Court of Appeal, differing from Brandon J below,[214] viewed *The Canadian Transport*,[215] an earlier tort decision by which the Court of Appeal[216] was bound, as having considered and rejected the contention that the initial valuation of the damage to the claimant should be made in the currency in which the claimant had effectively felt the loss rather than the currency in which the expenditure or loss had been directly incurred. *The Canadian Transport*,[217] again involved a claim in tort arising out of a ship collision, but it was a claim by the owners of cargo being carried on one of the ships against the owners of the other ship. The cargo, which was lost, was of logs purchased in the Argentine before shipment from there and paid for with the Argentine pesos which the claimants, being French, had acquired with French francs. The claimant cargo owners had put forward their claim in a somewhat curious way, first valuing their loss in Argentine **20-049**

[206] [1979] A.C. 685.
[207] [1921] 2 A.C. 544.
[208] [1976] A.C. 443.
[209] [1979] A.C. 685 at 703G.
[210] [1979] A.C. 685 at 703H. See, too, at 696D to H.
[211] [1979] A.C. 685 at 704A to B.
[212] [1979] A.C. 685; see para.20-039, above.
[213] [1979] A.C. 685.
[214] [1978] Q.B. 396; see above for CA.
[215] (1932) 43 Ll. L. Rep. 409 CA.
[216] [1978] Q.B. 396; see above for CA.
[217] (1932) 43 Ll. L. Rep. 409 CA.

pesos, then converting to pounds sterling, then converting the pounds sterling into French francs, and finally re-converting the francs to sterling at a different date and at a considerable profit to themselves.[218] In the view of Lord Wilberforce in the House of Lords in *The Despina R*,[219]

> "the decision of the Court of Appeal, against the cargo owners, was based in part on their rejection of the treble exchange manoeuvre and in part on their acceptance of the necessity of giving judgment in sterling".[220]

In his opinion the question was to be solved by applying the normal principles, of restitutio in integrum and of reasonable foreseeability of loss,[221] governing the assessment of damages in tort cases.[222] "It appears to me", he added,

> "that a plaintiff who normally conducts his business through a particular currency, and who, when other currencies are immediately involved, uses his own currency to obtain those currencies, can reasonably say that the loss he sustains is to be measured not by the immediate currencies in which the loss first emerges but by the amount of his own currency, which in the normal course of operation, he uses to obtain those currencies. This is the currency in which his loss is felt, and is the currency which it is reasonably foreseeable he will have to spend."[223]

Accordingly, US dollars was the appropriate currency for the damages award in *The Despina R*.[224] At the same time Lord Wilberforce said that he wished to make it clear that he

> "would not approve of a hard and fast rule that in all cases where a plaintiff suffers a loss or damage in a foreign currency the right currency to take for the purpose of his claim is 'the plaintiff's currency.' I should refer to the definition I have used of this expression and emphasise that it does not suggest the use of a personal currency attached, like nationality, to a plaintiff, but a currency which he is able to show is that in which he normally conducts trading operations. Use of this currency for assessment of damage may and probably will be appropriate in cases of international commerce. But even in that field, and still more outside it, cases may arise in which a plaintiff will not be able to show that in the normal course of events he would use, and be expected to use, the currency, or one of several currencies, in which he normally conducts his operations (the burden being on him to show this) and consequently the conclusion will be that the loss is felt in the currency in which it immediately arose."[225]

**20-050** After *The Despina R*[226] had thus laid down the ground rules in the context of tortious damage to property, tortious injury to the person arose for consideration in *Hoffman v Sofaer*.[227] A national of the United States of America claimed damages for negligent medical treatment, seriously affecting his right arm, received while holidaying in England. In deciding on the appropriate currency of the award the

---

218 See *The Despina R* [1978] Q.B. 396 at 412D, per Brandon J at first instance.
219 [1979] A.C. 685.
220 [1979] A.C. 685 at 697D.
221 See para.2-002 and Ch.8, above, respectively.
222 [1979] A.C. 685 at 697F.
223 [1979] A.C. 685 at 697G to H.
224 [1979] A.C. 685.
225 [1979] A.C. 685 at 698F to H.
226 [1979] A.C. 685.
227 [1982] 1 W.L.R. 1350.

judge, after citing extensively from their Lordships' speeches in *The Despina R*,[228] asked himself the question "with what currency is the plaintiff's loss closely linked?" and answered it by saying that in his judgment

> "undoubtedly all the losses in effect for which I have awarded damages other than that for pain and suffering are closely linked with the currency of his country, namely, dollars";[229]

judgment for all the pecuniary losses was accordingly given in US dollars. The claimant was back in his home in Wisconsin and it was clear that his medical expenses had been incurred there, the necessary modifications to his car had been carried out there, the loss of his ability to carry out work in the home would require the employment of others there, and the degree of salary which he was no longer capable of earning would have to be replaced there. Similar is *Bordin v St Mary's NHS Trust*,[230] a Fatal Accidents Act claim on behalf of a child for the death of its mother in childbirth. Most of the award was made in Italian lire since the child was to be cared for by his father and grandparents who all lived in Italy.

In *Hoffman v Sofaer*,[231] it could be said that the non-pecuniary element in the **20-051** judgment, awarded as a solace to the claimant for his injuries, would also be spent in Wisconsin and in connection with pain and suffering which would continue to be incurred there. Since the parties had agreed that this part of the award should be in sterling[232] the matter of the appropriateness of sterling was not argued, but the result is correct. The award for non-pecuniary loss in a personal injury claim is a conventional figure[233] and one to be ascertained by the principles and practices of English law,[234] so that it would be entirely improper to attempt to award the equivalent American conventional figure,[235] which would in all probability be a very great deal higher. Once this is accepted, then the court having arrived at the appropriate English conventional figure for the case, which would be one based upon the level of conventional figures prevailing at the time of the judgment,[236] there is no point in the court converting this into dollars since any conversion to dollars will require to be immediately reconverted to sterling for the enforcement of the judgment.

After *Hoffman v Sofaer*,[237] there was a return to the home ground of *The Despina* **20-052** *R*,[238] in *The Lash Atlantico*.[239] Repairs of damage inflicted, in a collision, upon the claimant's ship were paid for by the managers of the ship in several currencies but these payments were converted into Greek drachmas in order to render an account to the claimants. Accordingly, it was held that, since the claimants operated in Greek currency, this was the currency in which they felt their loss, and the award should

---

228 [1979] A.C. 685.
229 [1982] 1 W.L.R. 1350 at 1358D.
230 [2000] Lloyd's Rep. Med. 287.
231 [1982] 1 W.L.R. 1350.
232 [1982] 1 W.L.R. 1350 at 1357A.
233 See para.40-253.
234 In conflict of law terms the proper law of the tort would, for reasons unnecessary to explore here, be English.
235 Or, more precisely, the conventional figure in the state of Wisconsin.
236 See para.20-017, above.
237 [1982] 1 W.L.R. 1350.
238 [1979] A.C. 685.
239 [1985] 2 Lloyd's Rep. 464.

be in Greek drachmas rather than in US dollars as the Registrar below had held because dollars had been the currency used by the managers in the management of the ship.[240] And still in the context of shipping is *Kinetics Technology International v Cross Seas Shipping Corp, The Mosconici*,[241] but it concerned not the ship herself but her cargo. There was lost overboard the defendant's vessel cargo of the Italian corporate claimant. The replacements in respect of which the claim was brought were manufactured in Italy and paid for in Italian currency. Nevertheless these features were wholly overwhelmed by a series of countervailing features: in particular, the Italian claimant was part of a substantial United States group of companies, the Italian contract to which the claimant was party was a US dollar transaction, the claimant was paid in US dollars and there was provision in the contract for damages for non-delivery in US dollars. Accordingly, the currency which most justly expressed the loss was US dollars.

20-053 **(d) The effect of the Miliangos[242] decision** The effect of the *Miliangos*[243] decision and of its early imaginative development by the courts is most salutary. Claimants are now protected against falls in the external value of sterling in relation to their own currency. In the days when the former rule was established, the cases almost invariably involved a rise in the value of sterling in relation to the foreign currency—this was true in particular of *Di Ferdinando v Simon, Smits & Co*,[244] and *The Volturno*[245]—and it was not until the position was reversed, as in *Re United Railways of Havana and Regla Warehouses*[246]—that the inequity of the rule for claimants became apparent, and then, with the continuing erosion of the pound sterling in world markets, became a matter which called for radical re-appraisal of the law.[247] The new rule will therefore not assist claimants if sterling is rising. But this is as it should be; indeed the former rule may sometimes have unfairly advantaged claimants suing in a climate of appreciating sterling. As Mocatta J succinctly put the position in *Barclays Bank International v Levin Bros (Bradford)*,[248] in relation to a contracting party suing on dishonoured bills of exchange given for the price due in dollars for goods sold:

> "The old rule … lead[s], when sterling falls, to the creditor receiving most unfairly a sum in sterling when he comes to enforce his judgment far less in value than the dollars due

---

[240] In both to blame ship collision cases the Admiralty rule is that the two claims are set off against each other, leaving a single claim for the balance with only one judgment of the court. If one liability is in one currency and one in another, the currency of the lesser liability is converted into the currency of the greater and the set-off then effected at the date on which the amounts of the two liabilities are established by agreement or decision: *The Transoceanica Francesca* [1987] 2 Lloyd's Rep. 155. In *The Botany Triad and Lu Shan* [1993] 2 Lloyd's Rep. 259, applying the same rule, it was decided that interest was to be added to each claim before, rather than after, the balance was struck.

[241] [2001] 2 Lloyd's Rep. 313.

[242] [1976] A.C. 443.

[243] [1976] A.C. 443.

[244] [1920] 3 K.B. 409 CA.

[245] [1921] 2 A.C. 544.

[246] [1961] A.C. 1007.

[247] The unfairness is particularly well illustrated in *The Teh Hu* [1970] P. 106 CA, which concerned a salvage award rather than damages.

[248] [1977] Q.B. 270: facts at para.20-033, above.

at the date of maturity, whereas if sterling should have appreciated after the date of maturity, the creditor would under the old rule … receive an uncovenanted bonus."[249]

Now, under the *Miliangos*[250] solution, the claimant will only suffer, as Lord Wilberforce pointed out in *The Despina R*,[251] the effect of depreciation in the internal value of his own currency.[252] If this should bring an advantage to the defendant, this is merely incidental and fortuitous; what matters is that the claimant should be fully compensated. Thus, as Ormrod LJ said in the Court of Appeal in *The Folias*,[253] if the Brazilian cruzeiro had appreciated in relation to the French franc, the defendants "might have insisted on an award expressed in francs rather than cruzeiros".[254] Only if the claimant might have hedged himself against the fall in his own currency and if this was within reasonable foresight or reasonable contemplation, to use the remoteness terminology of tort and contract respectively,[255] might it be necessary to afford him further redress in damages. So, too, it might be necessary to ensure that delaying tactics in relation to the hearing of the action would bring no financial advantage.[256] And ideally there should also be provision to cater for delay by the defendant in the payment of the judgment until there had been a change in the rate of exchange in his favour.[257] In such circumstances the claimant could be given an entitlement to claim by a further action for any loss which he thereby incurred; this appears to be possible in, for instance, Germany.[258]

There remain some live areas of controversy in the working out of the boundaries of the *Miliangos* decision. One of those concerns whether a court has the power, in making a costs award, to compensate for any exchange rate losses incurred in paying costs. The issue arose in *Elkamet Kunststofftechnik GmbH v Saint-Gobain Glass France SA*,[259] where Arnold J considered, in a summary assessment of costs, that a German company could be compensated for losses incurred when exchanging euros to pounds in order to pay its solicitors' bills. This was said to follow because an order for costs is designed to compensate the successful party for its expenditure so that exchange rate losses can be compensated in the same way as it is entitled to be compensated by way of interest for being kept out of the money.[260] But in *MacInnes v Gross*,[261] Coulson J declined to make an order in similar terms. One reason was that he was **20-054**

[249] [1977] Q.B. 270 at 278F.

[250] [1976] A.C. 443.

[251] [1979] A.C. 685 at 697B.

[252] The point is also made in the Court of Appeal at [1978] Q.B. 396 CA at 436, per Stephenson LJ; at first instance [1978] Q.B. 396 CA at 410G, per Brandon J; and in *The Folias* [1979] Q.B. 491 CA at 524E, per Geoffrey Lane LJ.

[253] [1979] Q.B. 491 CA: facts at para.20-037, above.

[254] [1979] Q.B. 491 CA at 520F.

[255] See Ch.8, above.

[256] See again the related decisions in *Rosenthal v Alderton* [1946] K.B. 374 CA, and *Sachs v Miklos* [1948] 2 K.B. 23 CA, at para.20-003, above.

[257] See para.20-029, above.

[258] So indicated in Mann, *The Legal Aspect of Money* 5th edn (1992) (the last of the editions produced by Dr Mann himself), p.345, fn.23. This excellent book is now in its 7th edition (2012): see a reference to its content at para.20-030, above.

[259] [2016] EWHC 3421 (Pat).

[260] [2016] EWHC 3421 (Pat) at [11] to [13].

[261] [2017] EWHC 127 (QB).

> "uncomfortable with the idea that an award of costs should be treated as an order for compensation, as if it were a claim for damages".[262]

262 [2017] EWHC 127 (QB) at [20].

CHAPTER 21

# COSTS, DAMAGES AND FINES IN PREVIOUS PROCEEDINGS

TABLE OF CONTENTS



One item of loss for which damages are claimed in a heterogeneous group of cases concerns expenditure incurred in previous legal proceedings. Here it is important to analyse the general principles which lie behind the many and diverse decisions. The expenditure in question is of three varieties. It can consist of whatever damages have been awarded against the now claimant in the earlier proceedings together with the other party's costs which he is required to pay and the costs he himself has incurred. It can consist, though but rarely, of fines imposed upon the now claimant in the earlier proceedings, together once again with any costs he has been required to pay and any costs he has himself incurred. Or it can consist of costs only, being the costs that the now claimant has incurred which he is unable to recover from the other party to the earlier proceedings.[1] **21-001**

[1] There are also two types of case in which costs, damages and fines are awarded otherwise than as damages, and it is important to isolate these since they do not fall within the ambit of this book and are governed by different principles. (1) The important case is that of contracts of indemnity whereby one party agrees to indemnify the other against all damages, costs and expenses arising out of

**21-002** There is not much difficulty about the recovery by the now claimant of damages and costs awarded against him in the earlier proceedings. Recovery is subject only to remoteness in the largest sense of that term; the various aspects of remoteness are dealt with *in extenso* below.[2] Much the same goes for the occasional now claimant fined in the previous proceedings; once again he may recover both fine and costs imposed on him subject to the rules of remoteness, the policy aspect of which predominates here.[3] It was also for long accepted that the now claimant could recover as damages all of his own costs, where reasonable, to the extent that they were not recovered from the other party to the previous proceedings. However, copious doubt has now been cast upon the propriety of such a recovery of the totality of the now claimant's earlier costs. A serious difficulty has thus arisen in the law and it is important to address it in some detail in advance of covering the rest of the ground. This is fully justifiable for two related reasons: the new approach is believed to be flawed and the courts are not yet committed to it.

## I. THE PRELIMINARY QUESTION AS TO THE AMOUNT OF THE NOW CLAIMANT'S OWN COSTS RECOVERABLE AS DAMAGES

**21-003** In a civil action the successful party will generally recover costs against the other party. In earlier days these were called party and party costs, or taxed costs, to be distinguished from solicitor and client costs, which was the term formerly used for the greater amount of costs, however reasonable, payable by the client to his solicitor. It would make nonsense of the rules about costs if the successful party in an action who has been awarded costs could claim in a further action by way of damages the amount by which the costs awarded him fell short of the costs actually incurred by him. This has naturally never been allowed, and it is hardly surprising that there is a dearth of authority on the point. *Cockburn v Edwards*,[4] is probably the only case in which such a claim was attempted but without success, the refusal being at Court of Appeal level[5] as, curiously, the extra costs had been allowed as damages below.[6] Since in those days only costs necessarily incurred were

---

transactions with a third party, such contractual indemnity being express or implied and not always referring to costs and damages by name. The action is not one for damages but one to recover money payable under the terms of a contract, the main example being the action by a surety against the principal debtor after the surety has been sued for the debt by the creditor (see the standard texts on suretyship) with another frequent example being an action by an agent against a principal in respect of costs, and possibly damages, incurred in a prior action by or against the agent in a matter concerning the agency (see the standard texts on agency). (2) A further case, not involving contract, is where the now claimant is sued by a third party for debt or damages for which the now defendant is primarily liable. The action is not one for damages but one in restitution, historically by way of the common count for money paid, to recover the debt or damages paid and, if the principles of restitution and unjust enrichment allow, the costs incurred, the main example being of a quasi-suretyship on a bill of exchange (see the standard texts on suretyship and negotiable instruments).

2 See paras 21-048 to 21-076, below.

3 See paras 21-067 to 21-072, below.

4 (1881) 18 Ch. D. 449 CA.

5 See (1881) 18 Ch. D. 449 CA at 463, per Cotton LJ: "The difference between solicitor and client costs and party and party costs in an action cannot be given by way of damages in the same action, the latter costs being all that the claimant is entitled to"; also at 462, per Brett LJ. Similar, but not quite damages, is *Barnett v Eccles Corp* [1900] 2 Q.B. 423 CA.

6 On this Fry J was reversed; see the headnote at 450. The case was prayed in aid in the complicated and confusing *Corbett v Bond Pearce* [2006] EWHC 909 to deny recovery by the claimant from the defendant of costs that the claimant had been ordered to pay to the defendant at an earlier stage in

allowed as taxed costs, this left a wide margin between such costs and costs reasonably incurred by the client to his solicitor. It is therefore not surprising that the law developed so as to allow this substantial shortfall in a litigant's costs in litigation with one party to be claimable as damages in an action against another party whose wrong has been the cause of the earlier action. This has been so for over a century and a half and, as we shall see, there is a wealth of supporting authority.[7]

In 1986 there was a sea change; the move was made from necessary costs to reasonable costs. The then RSC Ord.62 on costs was entirely recast to enable the successful party in litigation to recover costs either on what was termed the standard basis, which allows costs reasonably incurred and reasonable in amount, or on what was termed the indemnity basis, which allows costs except where unreasonable in amount or unreasonably incurred, standard basis costs being the norm in civil litigation. When the Civil Procedure Rules 1998 took over from the RSC the provision reappeared in equivalent form as CPR r.44.4,[8] retaining the position that the burden of proof of reasonableness is on the claimant for standard basis costs and on the defendant for indemnity basis costs, but introducing the further important requirement for standard basis costs that they be not only reasonable but also proportionate to the matters in issue. The terminology also changes; while the RSC had specifically referred to "taxed costs", the CPR simply speaks of the court making an assessment of costs. Taxed costs now become known as assessed costs,[9] and the terminology of party and party costs and solicitor and client costs of former times effectively disappears.[10] Party and party costs, which represented taxed costs, are now the assessed costs, and for solicitor and client costs which are in excess of the assessed costs the term extra costs will be used, mirroring the usage of courts from a very early date right up to modern times where in case after case they have spoken of the excess of the solicitor and client costs over the party and party costs, whether they were allowing recovery of such excess or refusing it, as the extra costs.[11] **21-004**

In 1996 in the key decision of *British Racing Drivers' Club v Hextall Erskine & Co*,[12] Carnwarth J decided that this sea change in the rules for the recovery of costs justified the abandonment of the old learning on the recovery of the costs of an earlier action as damages. Claimants, claiming against their solicitors all of the costs that they had incurred in a previous action against different defendants which had been settled with the claimants and the principal two defendants paying their own **21-005**

the proceedings: see at [78].

7 For the many cases see paras 21-037 to 21-047, below. There is also some, but more uncertain, authority for the shortfall to be claimable against the same party to the earlier litigation provided that it has been caused by that party's wrong: see paras 21-015 to 21-030, below.

8 Replaced by CPR r.44.3 from 1April 2013.

9 In modernising fashion the terms assessed costs and assessment of costs will be used in references to the myriad of cases in which costs will have appeared, in the terminology of the day, as taxed costs, except of course that in quotations from judgments the terms taxed costs and taxation of costs will be retained.

10 The solicitor and client basis does still feature, now in CPR r.46.9 (earlier in CPR r.48.8), but this is for working out costs payable as between solicitor and client and has nothing to do with the solicitor's costs of a party which the other party may be required to pay.

11 As in *Hathaway v Barrow* (1807) 1 Camp. 151; *Sandback v Thomas* (1816) 1 Stark. 306; *Grace v Morgan* (1836) 2 Bing. N.C. 534; *Quartz Hill Gold Mining Co v Eyre* (1883) 11 Q.B.D. 674 CA (Brett LJ has "the theory of extra costs": at 682); *Berry v British Transport Commission* [1962] 1 Q.B. 306 CA (Devlin LJ uses "extra costs" throughout his judgment).

12 [1996] 3 All E.R. 667.

costs, were held by Carnwath J limited to such costs as they would have received in the previous action on an assessment of costs on the standard basis. Several first instance judges since have followed Carnworth J[13] but simply on the grounds of judicial comity.[14]

**21-006** A few years earlier the Court of Appeal had on two occasions, in *The Tiburon*,[15] and in *Lonrho Plc v Fayed (No.5)*,[16] expressed the same view, thereby helping Carnwarth J to champion the standard basis, but in neither case did this view form the basis of the decision. Since *The Tiburon* was not a case of two separate actions and since there was no power to review the decision below on costs, it has been pointed out that the Court of Appeal's view was doubly obiter.[17] In *Lonrho*, since the third party was being maintained by the defendants in his future action against the claimants, both actions were regarded as being between the same parties to which the normal costs rules would apply, again making the Court of Appeal's view, here advanced only by a majority,[18] obiter. So the position is open, with no Court of Appeal decision in the way, as was appreciated by the first instance judges following Carnwarth J.[19] In one of the first instance decisions, that of Warren J in *Dadourian Group International Inc v Simms*,[20] there was an appeal[21] but unfortunately the appeal did not run to this issue.[22]

**21-007** It is believed that the abandonment of the old learning, which has prevailed for so many years, is mistaken. Of course if costs assessed on the standard basis are the same thing as costs on the equivalent of the former solicitor and client basis, the issue disappears, and at a cursory glance it might be thought that this is so since reasonableness is brought in as a criterion for both standard and indemnity bases and since it has always been the case that a litigant's extra costs to be recoverable must be reasonable as the authorities dealt with below[23] clearly demonstrate. It is not to the point to say, as do some of the judges in the cases,[24] that there could be recovery of costs which are by any standards unreasonable, as by hiring the most

---

[13] In chronological order, they are Ferris J in *Yudt v Leonard Ross & Craig* unreported 24 July 1998, Evans-Lombe J in *Mahme Trust Reg v Lloyds TSB Bank Plc* [2006] EWHC 1321 Ch, HHJ Behrens in *Redbus LMDS Ltd v Jeffrey Green & Russell* [2007] P.N.L.R. 12 at 287, Warren J in *Dadourian Group International Inc v Simms* [2007] EWHC 454 Ch and Foskett J in *Swain v Geoffrey Osborne Ltd* [2010] EWHC 3118 (QB).

[14] In *Sifti v Clough & Willis* [2007] EWHC 985 Ch, where costs of a probate action were being claimed against negligent solicitors, none of these cases was cited to the trial judge; it appears that the claimant may have been content with costs of the probate action on the standard basis: compare [21] with [22]. Warren J also in *Youlton v Charles Russell* [2010] EWHC 1032 Ch regarded Carnwarth J's decision as changing the law (at [529] and [539]), but it is not at all clear where this gets him in his consideration of costs as damages, either in his judgment here (at [528] and following) or in his later judgment on consequential matters ([2010] EWHC 1918 Ch at [44] and following).

[15] [1992] 2 Lloyd's Rep. 26 CA.

[16] [1993] 1 W.L.R. 1489 CA.

[17] By Sir Anthony Colman in *National Westminster Bank Plc v Rabobank Nederland* [2008] 1 Lloyd's Rep.16 at [16]. See this case at para.21-027, below.

[18] Not including Dillon LJ.

[19] For these judges and the case references see the previous paragraph. Thus the judge said in *Yudt* (unreported) that further consideration must "be done by the Court of Appeal", in *Redbus* (at [83]) that we have an "area ripe for consideration by the Court of Appeal" and in *Dadourian* (at [38]) that the issue "would benefit from consideration by a higher court".

[20] [2007] EWHC 454 Ch.

[21] [2009] EWCA Civ 169 CA; [2009] 1 Lloyd's Rep. 601 CA.

[22] This comes out at [2009] EWCA Civ 169 CA at [128] and [129].

[23] At paras 21-055 and following, below.

[24] As by Evan-Lombe J in *Mahme* [2006] EWHC 1321at [686].

expensive solicitors in a run of the mill case. For these would not have been recoverable under the prior law. It was well established that, if it were shown to have been unreasonable for the now claimant to have brought or defended the earlier proceedings because, say, there was no arguable defence or valid claim, no recovery whatsoever of costs of the proceedings would have been allowed,[25] and the same must surely go for the incurring of unreasonable costs in the earlier action as for bringing or defending the earlier action in the first place. So if there were substantial equivalence between costs incurred and costs recoverable one could be prepared to live with the new learning but three factors, which are cumulative, go to show that there is not a substantial equivalence.

In the first place, standard basis costs have to be not only reasonable but proportionate to the matters in issue. This was not a requirement at the time of Carnwarth J's decision and the earlier Court of Appeal dicta but, with the introduction of the proportionality principle into the standard basis by the CPR, it is a requirement today. Thus costs, though reasonable, will be disallowed if not proportionate, a limitation which has no application to the indemnity basis, or to the former solicitor and client basis. As Sir Anthony Colman put it in *National Westminster Bank Plc v Rabobank Nederland*,[26] "the introduction of the component of proportionality ... displaces the basis of the argument" of substantial equivalence.[27] Secondly, the indemnity basis of assessment can offer a significantly higher measure of costs recovery than does the standard basis by virtue of the incidence of proof of reasonableness. Although, as Parker LJ commented in *The Tiburon*,[28] the only difference between the standard and indemnity bases lies in the burden of proof, it is a vital difference. Thirdly, there is the difference in the meaning of reasonableness between the former solicitor and client costs and indemnity costs. Warren J considered in *Dadourian*,[29] that it was **21-008**

> "arguably not the case that the test of reasonableness under CPR 44.4[30]—at least as applied by Costs Judges—is the same as the test of reasonableness which applies when assessing damages at common law",

an argument that is particularly convincing when participation in the earlier proceedings is seen, as it has been in quite a few of the cases, as a step in mitigation.[31] For not only, as with the indemnity basis, is the burden of proof on the issue of reasonableness reversed but in addition the standard of reasonableness is an unexacting one.[32] Moreover, experience in practice lends support to these

---

25 See paras 21-055 and following, below.

26 [2008] 1 Lloyd's Rep. 16.

27 [2008] 1 Lloyd's Rep. 16 at [26].

28 [1992] 2 Lloyd's Rep. 26 at 34, col.1.

29 [2007] EWHC 454 Ch at [34].

30 Now, since 1April 2013, CPR r.44.3.

31 By Carnwarth J in *British Racing Drivers' Club* [1996] 3 All E.R. 667 at 691f (passage cited in the next footnote); Evans-Lombe J in *Mahme* [2006] EWHC 1321 Ch at [65]; Colman J in *National Westminster Bank Plc v Rabobank Nederland* [2008] 1 Lloyd's Rep. 16 at [16].

32 See Lord Macmillan's well-known statement in *Banco de Portugal v Waterlow* [1932] A.C. 452 at 506 that measures taken in extrication from a difficult situation "ought not to be weighed in nice scales" at the instance of the party occasioning the difficulty. Even Carnwarth J himself said in *British Racing Drivers' Club* ([1996] 3 All E.R. 667 at 691f): "The expenditure on the professional fees of solicitors and accountants was, as I have held, expenditure incurred by the plaintiffs in reasonably mitigating their loss. Prima facie therefore it is claimable under the ordinary rules relating to mitigation."

differences. Thus it is unusual for more than 80 per cent of the costs actually incurred by the claimant to be allowed him on a standard basis assessment and for more than 90 per cent on an indemnity basis, and all this within the bounds of reasonableness as variously interpreted.

**21-009** Given that there is far from being a substantial equivalence between what would have been awarded in the past and what is to be awarded under the changed approach, any further argument for abandoning the established law in favour of what Carnwarth J has brought in would have to be based on public policy. Thus we find Hart J saying in *Pearce v European Reinsurance Consultants and Run-Off Ltd*,[33] that there are "plainly strong arguments of legal policy in favour" of going for the standard basis[34] but, as so often happens when public policy is invoked in an attempt to justify a position, one is not told what the particular policy in mind is. One suggested policy reason that has emerged, adverted to by His Honour Judge Behrens in *Redbus*,[35] is based upon the steadily increasing amount of legal costs being a matter of great public concern, but this cannot be a good reason for depriving a claimant of proper compensation. Sir Anthony Colman, giving judgment in *National Westminster Bank Plc v Rabobank Nederland*,[36] said that he seriously doubted whether the reasoning in the decisions using the standard basis could be supported on public policy grounds.[37]

**21-010** At least Carnwarth J in *British Racing Drivers' Club*,[38] was clear as to how he saw the public policy. To him the distinction between costs in proceedings between the same parties and costs in proceedings with third parties should never have been made, not even in the days of great disparity between party and party costs and solicitor and client costs; the distinction "was anomalous, given that similar policy considerations applied in each case".[39] The former great costs disparity had persuaded the courts to introduce an anomaly and the change in the costs rules simply "enables the anomaly to be resolved".[40] Yet it is surely curious that the courts should have been prepared to perpetrate an anomaly and live with it happily for a century and a half. One need only look at the two 19th century cases which firmly established the law on costs as damages, *Collen v Wright*,[41] and *Hammond v Bussey*,[42] to see how sensible the courts have been. In the first case the now claimant was one to whom an apparent agent had warranted his authority to enter into a contract on behalf of a principal and who in reliance on this warranty of authority had sued the alleged principal but failed. He was held entitled to recover as damages all his expenses of his suit against the alleged principal since they had been occasioned by the assertion of authority having been persisted in, never withdrawn

33 [2006] P.N.L.R. 8 at 142, [30]. In Pearce Hart J was influenced by the new learning but was unprepared to come to a decision summarily on the issue: see at [22]–[30].

34 Also *Dadourin* [2007] EWHC 454 Ch at [38], per Warren J ("there are serious policy issues here").

35 [2007] P.N.L.R. 12 at 287, [87(2)] when referring to Hart J's invocation of policy reasons for the new approach.

36 [2008] 1 Lloyd's Rep. 16.

37 [2008] 1 Lloyd's Rep. 16 at [25].

38 [1996] 3 All E.R. 667.

39 [1996] 3 All E.R. 667 at 691g.

40 [1996] 3 All E.R. 667 at 691h.

41 (1858) 8 E. & B. 647.

42 (1888) 20 Q.B.D. 79 CA. As to how the law was established by these two cases, see para.21-032, below.

and therefore reasonably acted upon by him.[43] In the second case the now claimant was a buyer of goods to whom their quality had been warranted by his seller and who, having sold on with the same warranty, was sued by his sub-buyer but lost. Having reasonably defended since his seller had denied all liability and had insisted that the goods were according to contract,[44] he was held entitled to recover as damages his full costs of the sub-buyer's claim against him. Why should the now claimant in these cases be under-compensated in respect of two sets of costs when it is the now defendant's wrong which has involved him in two actions rather than one? There is nothing anomalous in allowing the now claimant, provided he has acted reasonably, to be made whole in relation to the action into which he has been forced by the now defendant's breach of contract or tort. In the one action his loss in costs has to be looked at through the glass of costs but in the other it can be, and should be, looked at through the glass of damages. In the one action the Civil Procedure Rules on costs must prevail; in the other Lord Blackburn's age-old principle—one might here say his overriding principle—in *Livingstone v Rawyards Coal Co*,[45] that the party suffering the wrong is to be put into the position he would have been in had he not suffered the wrong.

There are now signs that the decision of Carnworth J may soon be a thing of the past, that its days are numbered. Various factors deserve mention. First, it is notable that the judges following Carnwarth J on account of judicial comity[46] did not do so with great eagerness. Thus Ferris J in *Yudt*, while feeling compelled to follow Carnwarth J, confessed to being impressed by the criticism of the new approach in the then current edition of this work.[47] Judge Behrens in *Redbus* considered that he was required to follow the Carnworth J lead.[48] Warren J in *Dadourian*, while feeling constrained to do the same, did so without a great deal of enthusiasm.[49] Foskett J in *Swain* felt obliged, though again somewhat unenthusiastically, to follow Carnworth J.[50] Secondly, there is the appearance after the turn of the century of three contract cases, yet to be considered,[51] where the two sets of proceedings were between the same parties and costs of the first were fully allowed as damages in the second, the prior costs being incurred in a foreign court or in a domestic arbitration. Indeed in relation to one of these cases, *National Westminster Bank Plc v Rabobank Nederland*,[52] a decision of Sir Anthony Colman, Foskett J in *Swain v Geoffrey Osborne Ltd*,[53] went so far as to express sympathy with the claimant's contention in *Swain* that Carnworth J's decision was inconsistent with Sir Anthony Colman's and that the law had moved on.[54] Thirdly, in *Occidental Chartering Inc v Progress Bulk Carriers Ltd*,[55] we find a reference, by Cooke J, to costs being claimed as dam- **21-011**

43 See Willes J, delivering the judgment of the full Court of Exchequer, (1857) 8 E. & B. 647 at 658.
44 This appears less from the judgments than from the headnote and the facts as stated at (1888) 20 Q.B.D. 79 at 81.
45 (1880) 5 App. Cas. 25.
46 For these judges and cases see para.21-005, above.
47 The passage from *Yudt* unreported 24 July 1998, is set out in *Mahme* [2006] EWHC 1321 Ch at [66].
48 [2007] P.N.L.R. 12 at [87].
49 [2007] EWHC 454 Ch at [38].
50 [2010] EWHC 3118 (QB) at [44]. Only Evans-Lombe J in *Mahme* followed Carnworth J willingly: [2006] EWHC 1321 Ch at [68].
51 At paras 21-024 to 21-030, below.
52 [2008] 1 Lloyd's Rep. 16.
53 [2010] EWHC 3118 (QB).
54 [2010] EWHC 3118 (QB) at [43].
55 [2012] EWHC 3515 (Comm).

ages in arbitrations "on the basis of the line of authorities from *Hammond v Bussey* onwards" without any suggestion that these authorities were adversely affected by Carnwarth J's decision.[56] Finally, and most importantly, in *Herrmann v Withers LLP*,[57] Newey J, citing approvingly from the previous paragraph as it appeared similarly in an earlier edition of this work, has boldly decided in favour of awarding indemnity basis costs, rather than costs on the standard basis argued for by the defendants, as damages to claimants who had reasonably instructed solicitors to advise on a problem arising out of the negligence of the defendant solicitors.[58] The *British Racing Drivers' Club* decision of Carnwarth J was doubted and not followed.[59] It is true that Newey J did not go as far as awarding a full indemnity equivalent to the costs that would have been awarded under the former solicitor and client basis, but it appears that indemnity basis costs were all that the claimants had asked him for. Perhaps the neatest solution would be for the courts to ensure, whenever in these types of case costs reasonably incurred earlier are claimed as damages, that a full indemnity is awarded with no percentage shortfall, however small. We await the Court of Appeal's solution.

## II. Costs in Previous Proceedings between the Same Parties

21-012 We have already adverted to the obvious rule that a claimant's extra costs in excess of the costs awarded him by the court cannot be claimed in a further action brought by him with the object of recovering these extra costs as damages.[60] What, however, if he should be bringing a second action, arising out of the same cause of action as the first, for purposes other than simply to recover the extra costs incurred in the first action? Or if he should be bringing a second action which is based upon a separate cause of action independent of the first? These two possibilities need separate consideration.

### 1. Further Proceedings where No Separate Independent Cause of Action is Available

21-013 If, as could in the past happen, a claimant was involved necessarily in two separate actions with the defendant, this made no difference; he could not claim as damages in the second action the costs incurred by him in the first action, which went beyond those awarded by the court therein. This was true with an action of ejectment followed by one for mesne profits, or with a claim for specific performance followed by one for damages. However, for long it has been possible to claim all relief in one action, a position encapsulated for today in the wide words of r.7.3 of the Civil Procedure Rules.[61] This makes the early cases involving two separate actions between claimant and defendant, all from the earlier part of the 19th century, largely of historical interest for us.[62]

---

56 [2012] EWHC 3515 (Comm) at [22].

57 [2012] EWHC 1492 Ch.

58 Facts at para.9-107, above.

59 See Newey J's extended discussion at [2012] EWHC 1492 Ch at [105]–[116].

60 See para.21-003, above.

61 "A claimant may use a single claim form to start all claims which can be conveniently disposed of in the same proceedings."

62 Since, however, they might prove of some assistance in analogy they are appended here. (1) The now claimant may have brought two successful actions against the now defendant. This was so in an ac-

The issue has, however, reappeared in the context of an unsuccessful attempt to recover costs incurred in proceedings brought in another jurisdiction as damages in an action in England between the same parties in respect of the same claim. This occurred in *The Ocean Dynamic*,[63] where the claimant had brought an action in England for breach of a carriage contract against the defendant, a United States company carrying on business in Wisconsin. The defendant having disputed the jurisdiction of the English court, the claimant issued a protective writ in Wisconsin. The defendant's challenge to the English court was dismissed and the claimant's proceedings in Wisconsin were discontinued. The claimant then attempted unsuccessfully to recover in the English proceedings, as damages for breach of the carriage contract, its costs of the abortive proceedings in Wisconsin. This case is to be distinguished from the various breach of contract cases which have now started to appear where a different result has been reached on account of the claimant having a separate and independent cause of action.[64] In *The Ocean Dynamic* the only cause of action available to the claimant was for breach of the contract of carriage and the costs sought to be recovered by the claimant were in no sense caused by any breach of that contract. Rather they arose out of the claimant's own decision to issue the protective writ in Wisconsin. **21-014**

## 2. Further Proceedings where a Separate Independent Cause of Action is Available

It may be that the claimant has a free-standing cause of action which exists independently of the proceedings in which the costs sought to be recovered as damages have been incurred. If the claimant is thus capable of establishing a separate cause of action, it may be said that he has found a sufficient peg upon which to claim as damages costs incurred by him in the earlier proceedings. Devlin LJ in *Berry v British Transport Commission*,[65] the leading case in this area, certainly **21-015**

---

tion of ejectment followed by an action for mesne profits or in an action of replevin followed by an action for a wrongful distress. It was held that none of the extra costs incurred in the first action was recoverable in the second: *Grace v Morgan* (1836) 2 Bing. N.C. 534 (replevin/distress); *Doe v Hare* (1833) 2 Dowl. 245 and *Doe v Filliter* (1844) 13 M. & W. 47 (both ejectment/mesne profits). Exceptionally, where the courts did not in practice award costs in certain ejectment actions such costs were allowed in the subsequent mesne profits action: *Symonds v Page* (1830) 1 Cr. & J. 29; *Doe v Huddart* (1835) 2 C.M. & R. 316; and also where the ejectment action, decided first against the claimant, was reversed in error and costs could not be awarded by the Court of Error, then they were permitted to be recovered in the mesne profits action: *Nowell v Roake* (1827) 7 B. & C. 404. (2) The now claimant may have brought and lost the first action, then brought and succeeded in the second. This could happen formerly where a buyer of land brought first an action for specific performance which, because the seller had no title, was dismissed without costs according to the practice in Chancery; then in the second action for damages for breach of contract the buyer could not recover the costs of the former Chancery proceedings: *Malden v Fyson* (1847) 11 Q.B. 292. (3) The now claimant may have won the first action in the role of defendant and then succeeded in the second as claimant. Thus in *Hodges v Litchfield* (1835) 1 Bing. N.C. 492 the seller of land had brought a suit for specific performance against the purchaser which had failed owing to his lack of title, the purchaser being awarded the usual costs. The purchaser then sued for damages for breach of contract based on the defect in title and claimed as one item of his damages the extra costs as between solicitor and client which he had incurred in successfully defending the suit for specific performance. This was refused.

63 [1982] 2 Lloyd's Rep. 88.

64 These cases are at paras 21-024 to 21-030, below.

65 [1962] 1 Q.B. 306 CA at 322.

thought this should be so. He said:

> "I find it difficult to see why the law should not now recognise one standard of costs as between litigants and another when those costs form a legitimate item of damage in a separate cause of action flowing from an additional wrong."

The separate cause of action may arise from a tort or from a breach of contract.

## (1) Tort

**21-016** A separate tort may be involved in instigating, assisting or causing the previous proceedings. Such torts could be malicious prosecution, false imprisonment or conspiracy. The question in issue has received the most consideration in the case of malicious prosecution.

**21-017** **(a) Malicious prosecution** There are two cases of importance. The much earlier one is *Quartz Hill Gold Mining Co v Eyre*,[66] where a petition had been maliciously brought against the now claimant company and dismissed without costs. It was held in the Court of Appeal that the costs incurred by the company in defending itself in the prior proceedings did not constitute legal damage to ground an action for malicious prosecution. As to the costs which the court in the prior action was entitled to have awarded the now claimant, Bowen LJ said, correctly, that the now claimant will get these costs in the prior action unless he does not deserve them, in which case he ought not to get them in the subsequent action.[67] As to the extra costs which the now claimant has incurred over and above those the court might have awarded, Brett MR said, unconvincingly, that the extra costs, not being considered necessary, cannot have been caused by the malicious litigation.[68]

**21-018** The later case is *Berry v British Transport Commission*.[69] Here the Court of Appeal refused to extend the decision in *Quartz Hill Gold Mining Co v Eyre*[70] to costs in criminal proceedings, and held, where the claimant brought an action for malicious prosecution against the British Transport Commission which had prosecuted her for pulling a train communication cord, that the expenses which the claimant had incurred, in the course of her defence and of her successful appeal, in excess of the sum awarded her by the recorder, were sufficient to support her action. The court, which by its decision reversed what had formerly been understood to be the law,[71] distinguished criminal cases from civil on the ground that the provisions, and more particularly the practice, relating to costs differ between the two types of case. In the words of Danckwerts LJ:

> "In a civil action, the successful party is almost always awarded costs. A successful party can only be deprived of his costs by the exercise of a judicial discretion and for good

---

66 (1883) 11 Q.B.D. 674 CA.

67 (1883) 11 Q.B.D. 674 CA at 690.

68 (1883) 11 Q.B.D. 674 CA at 682–683, where it is put more elaborately than this.

69 [1962] 1 Q.B. 306 CA.

70 (1883) 11 Q.B.D. 674 CA.

71 That such additional costs would not ground an action for malicious prosecution was considered as both well established and binding on it by the Court of Appeal in *Wiffen v Bailey and Romford U.D.C.* [1915] 1 K.B. 600 CA (see at 607 and 610), though counsel had conceded the point. This had been followed by Diplock J at first instance in *Berry v British Transport Commission* [1961] 1 Q.B. 149.

> reason. In criminal cases, in practice a person who is acquitted is not necessarily, or indeed it would appear usually, awarded any costs. And even if a sum is awarded for costs, it appears to be no real compensation for the expenses to which the party has been put, and even sometimes to be a mere nominal amount."[72]

Similar statements were made by Ormerod and Devlin LJJ.[73]

The most important feature of *Berry* for the law of damages is to be found in the rightly critical approach of Devlin and Danckwerts LJJ of the law as laid down for civil cases in the *Quartz Hill* case. Devlin LJ, after attempting to rationalise the general rule of no recovery for the extra costs on the ground that such a rule helps keep down extravagance in litigation and is therefore of benefit to all who have to resort to the law, added: **21-019**

> "But the last person who ought to be able to share in that benefit is the man who *ex hypothesi* is abusing the legal process for his own malicious ends."[74]

Danckwerts LJ said similarly:

> "The theory that taxed costs are a sufficient compensation for a successful defendant, at any rate in a civil action, seems to me an unreal or perhaps even a cynical view, which ought not to have any place in the conditions of an action for malicious prosecution."[75]

Moreover, the rule of no recovery of the extra costs may not be established beyond recall, as is rather suggested by Danckwerts LJ in *Berry*.[76] For he had discovered, through his diligence in looking at the report of *Quartz Hill* in the Weekly Notes, that the reason for the claimant company being awarded no costs in that case was that its appearance in the prior proceedings was considered to have been unnecessary.[77] This was more than sufficient ground for disallowing the extra costs; if the costs which the court could have awarded as costs had been incurred unreasonably, the same must go for the extra costs. And the court in *Quartz* may well not have been apprised of the very early but somewhat similar cases of *Sandback v Thomas*,[78] and *Gould v Barratt*,[79] where the extra costs beyond court costs were easily awarded, by Lord Ellenborough and Lord Abinger respectively in judgments each, refreshingly, of a single sentence.[80] **21-020**

---

72 [1962] 1 Q.B. 306 CA at 338.

73 [1962] 1 Q.B. 306 CA at 317 and 325–326, respectively. Devlin LJ indeed held for the claimant on the narrower ground that the particular costs awarded the claimant in the criminal prosecution did not represent an order for costs even according to the conventional measure in civil cases: at 332. This was because he thought that the court might be prevented by *Barnett v Eccles Corp* [1900] 2 Q.B. 423 CA from holding that the rule as to costs in civil cases should not be extended to costs in criminal cases: [1962] 1 Q.B. 306 CA at 329. However, he expressed no opinion on the case which involved neither an action for malicious prosecution nor an action for damages proper.

74 [1962] 1 Q.B. 306 CA at 323.

75 [1962] 1 Q.B. 306 CA at 336.

76 [1962] 1 Q.B. 306 CA at 338.

77 Referred to by Devlin LJ at [1962] 1 Q.B. 306 CA at 319.

78 (1816) 1 Stark. 306; malicious holding to bail.

79 (1838) 2 Mood. & Rob. 171; malicious arrest.

80 Even if the decision in *Quartz* is adhered to, what may just be possible is that, where there is other damage sufficient to ground the action, such extra costs can be added thereto. This is a question of policy and a question of the scope of the protection of the tort; it is dealt with generally elsewhere. See para.8-125, above

21-021 Of course with today's much more generous costs regime[81] a claimant's position on costs is much ameliorated since the days when Devlin and Danckwerts LJJ were speaking. This amelioration has caused first instance courts, as we have seen,[82] to deny recovery of the extra costs in the very many cases, yet to be considered in detail,[83] where the previous proceedings have been between the now claimant and a third party. This denial of recovery must apply a fortiori to cases where both sets of proceedings are between the same parties but if, as has been argued, this denial of recovery is misplaced, it is surely equally misplaced where, as with malicious prosecution, the two sets of proceedings are between the same parties.

21-022 **(b) False imprisonment** In false imprisonment the prior proceedings in which the now claimant incurs costs are those whereby he procures his discharge. What law there is upon the recovery of such costs is very old, being contained in a few mid-19th century cases. These together sketch out the rule that recovery is allowed subject to three provisos: that the action brought to gain release was necessary, that the costs had not been refused by the court in that action, and that the costs incurred were reasonable ones. *Pritchet v Boevey*,[84] is the case which established that costs incurred in procuring discharge from a false imprisonment are recoverable; it would seem that all three provisos were satisfied. As to the second proviso, there had been no adjudication as to these costs by the judge who ordered the claimant's release; he would have given the claimant his costs if he had undertaken not to bring an action, and on the claimant's refusal no order had been made as to costs. Similarly, in *Foxall v Barnett*,[85] where the claimant, committed to prison for manslaughter by a coroner's warrant, had been admitted to bail and had subsequently got the inquisition under which he had been committed quashed, it was held that in an action against the coroner for false imprisonment he might recover the cost of quashing the inquisition, Lord Campbell insisting that the first proviso had to be shown to be satisfied.[86] By contrast, with the second proviso not satisfied in *Loton v Devereux*,[87] where the claimant had been refused costs in the prior action as opposed to there being no order as to costs, the claimant failed to recover them as damages. And it is submitted that a failure to satisfy the third proviso gives the proper explanation of *Bradlaugh v Edwards*.[88] The jury not having awarded the claimant damages in respect of his expenses in procuring bail before the magistrates and in getting together evidence for the defence of the charge, Erle CJ indicated that these costs may have been unreasonably incurred.[89]

---

81 See para.21-004, above.
82 See para.21-005, above.
83 See paras 21-031 and following, below.
84 (1833) 1 Cr. & M. 775.
85 (1853) 23 L.J.Q.B. 7.
86 See (1853) 23 L.J.Q.B. 7 at 8: "If the claimant had been discharged on habeas corpus, instead of being admitted to bail, and had afterwards got the inquisition quashed, I should have thought that he could not have included the cost of quashing in his damages. But here he was only released from prison upon his giving bail to appear and take his trial. He was still liable to surrender on his recognisances, and was not a perfectly free man till he had got rid of the inquisition. By doing that he was restored to his original state, but until then the effects of the wrongful imprisonment were not done away with. Therefore this is damage which flows from the wrongful act of the defendant."
87 (1832) 3 B. & Ad. 343; distinguished in *Pritchet v Boevey* on this ground
88 (1861) 11 C.B. N.S. 377.
89 (1861) 11 C.B. N.S. 377 at 384: "Where a party has been illegally imprisoned, and has been put to expense in procuring his discharge, he may very well urge that fact before the jury as an aggravation:

**(c) Conspiracy** In *Hathaway v Barrow*[90] conspiracy made a solitary appearance as a tort which was the cause of the previous proceedings. The conspiracy was to prevent the claimant from obtaining his certificate under what was called a commission of bankrupt and for these purposes the conspirators had unsuccessfully petitioned the Lord Chancellor, who had ordered them to pay the claimant's costs; these had been taxed but not discharged. Sir James Mansfield ruled that no part of the claimant's costs could be recovered in his action. This makes sense as far as the party and party costs are concerned as they might at any time be paid by the conspirators and "must, therefore, be considered as satisfaction". But the judgment continues: 21-023

> "Nor could he admit proof of the extra costs; as it would be incongruous to allow a person one sum as costs in one Court, and a different sum for the same costs in another Court."[91]

This shows that the judge thought it a plain case of simply attempting in a second action to obtain as damages the costs not awarded in the first, without appreciating that the presence of an independent tort could make all the difference. Moreover, this decision of 1807 was long before the general principles had been worked out by the courts[92] and is at odds with the important views expressed by Devlin and Danckwerts LJJ in the leading case in this area of *Berry v British Transport Commission*.[93]

## (2) Contract

Whereas the authorities in the field of tort, with the exception of *Berry v British Transport Commission*,[94] are old, those in contract are very much up to the moment. They concern breaches of exclusive jurisdiction clauses, of anti-suit clauses and of agreements to arbitrate. Importantly, they are to be distinguished from *The Ocean Dynamic*,[95] where both actions were in respect of the same claim.[96] 21-024

**(a) Breach of exclusive jurisdiction clause** In *Union Discount Co Ltd v Zoller*,[97] where contracting parties had agreed that the English courts should have exclusive jurisdiction over their contractual disputes but the defendants brought proceedings in New York in breach of the exclusive jurisdiction clause, the now claimant was held entitled to recover as damages the costs incurred in securing the striking out of the New York proceedings, the practice in New York being not to award costs to a party successfully applying for a strike-out. Schiemann LJ, giving the only judgment, said that the situation was akin to malicious prosecution and 21-025

but he has not right to demand to be reimbursed ex debito justitiae. It is in the discretion of the jury to give him such damages as they may consider a sufficient compensation for the wrong the party has sustained, irrespective of any expense he may, perhaps needlessly, have incurred in his defence."

90 (1807) 1 Camp. 151.

91 (1807) 1 Camp. 151 at 152.

92 Interestingly, the decision came at a time when the courts on occasion were prepared, as in *Sandback v Thomas* (1816) 1 Stark. 306, to award the extra costs where a separate tort could be spelt out, especially if a tort involving malice: see at para.21-020, above.

93 [1962] 1 Q.B. 306 CA. See at para.21-019, above.

94 [1962] 1 Q.B. 306 CA. See at para.21-018, above.

95 [1982] 2 Lloyd's Rep. 88.

96 Considered at para.21-014, above.

97 [2002] 1 W.L.R. 1517 CA.

that the same rule as in *Berry v British Transport Commission*,[98] should prevail. The *Ocean Dynamic*[99] was specifically distinguished.

21-026 The Court of Appeal was eager, as Schiemann LJ put it, to tread cautiously in a field little explored in the litigation of today. He offered two illustrations of what he called more doubtful cases, which, he said, should be left for the future. The future has already made one of these illustrations a reality—a court action brought in breach of an arbitration agreement—and this is dealt with in due course.[100] The other illustration is of breach of an exclusive jurisdiction clause where the costs rules of the foreign jurisdiction are similar to the English costs rules. This illustration may be thought to reflect the development in the purely English cases spearheaded by the decision of Carnwarth J in *British Racing Drivers' Club*,[101] which has been extensively criticised at the beginning of this chapter and to which, curiously, no reference is made in *Zoller*. Since it is believed that the Carnwarth J approach is flawed,[102] the same result here as that reached in *Zoller* is favoured here.

21-027 **(b) Breach of anti-suit clause** In *National Westminster Bank Plc v Rabobank Nederland*,[103] a complex novation agreement had been entered into by two banks in connection with their very substantial loans to a now failing company. The novation agreement contained a clause by which the defendant bank agreed not to bring any claims against the claimant bank in relation to various matters. In breach of this anti-suit clause the defendant bank brought proceedings in California which the claimant bank successfully defended but without being awarded as costs more than the very limited items of expenditure allowable in California. It was held that the very substantial shortfall in costs was recoverable as damages by the claimant bank, there being no good reason why English courts should impose upon California their own CPR costs rules and extend CPR principles to the conduct of litigation in a jurisdiction to which the CPR was wholly inapplicable, as distinct from simply applying the test of whether the costs had been reasonably incurred.[104]

21-028 Sir Anthony Colman had no doubt that the series of first instance decisions awarding standard basis costs as damages[105]

> "should have no application to a case such as this where the former proceedings were in a foreign jurisdiction with a costs regime under which the winning party was unable to recover all such costs on a basis equivalent to that which would have been applied to a damages claim: that is to say on the basis that the winning party would be entitled to recover all costs reasonably incurred and in a reasonable amount."

He added:

> "If the winning party can formulate a claim for the whole or part of such costs in the English courts as a claim for damages for breach of a separate cause of action … there is, in my judgment, no reason as a matter of public policy or otherwise, why he may not

---

98 [1962] 1 Q.B. 306 CA; at para.21-018, above.
99 [1982] 2 Lloyd's Rep. 88; at para.21-014, above.
100 At para.21-029, below.
101 [1996] 3 All E.R. 667. For these cases, all at first instance, see para.21-005, above.
102 See paras 21-007 to 21-011, above.
103 [2008] 1 Lloyd's Rep. 16.
104 [2008] 1 Lloyd's Rep. 16 at [24].
105 At para.21-005, above.

recover them subject to ordinary damages rules. Under those rules the burden of proof of failure to mitigate rests on the party in breach."[106]

**(c) Breach of agreement to arbitrate** Improper resort to the courts in breach of contract has also made an appearance where, as is common, a contract has provided for disputes to be submitted to arbitration and one of the contracting parties has impleaded the other party in the courts. This situation arose in *A v B (No.2)*[107] and brings to life one of the Schiemann LJ's two case situations in *Union Discount Co Ltd v Zoller*,[108] in which he was uncertain as to what should be the result. A party to an arbitration agreement which provided for a Swiss arbitration attempted without success to invoke the supervisory jurisdiction of the English courts and the other, successful party was held by Colman J entitled to recover its costs of the proceedings in the English courts on an indemnity basis. It would appear that he was awarding these costs as costs but, as he said in his later decision of *Rabobank* just considered, his award reflected the measure of damages which that party could recover in proceedings for breach of the arbitration agreement.[109] The case differs from, and goes beyond, *Zoller*,[110] and *Rabobank*,[111] in two important respects, but nevertheless it leads to a result which is to be commended. **21-029**

The first difference is that the claim in breach of contract was brought in England rather than in a foreign jurisdiction so that it was English rather than foreign court costs that were in issue. The doubt as to the proper result in this situation felt by Schiemann LJ in *Zoller*,[112] is thus resolved in the claimant's favour and, it is thought, rightly so. The second difference is that there was only one claim and not two. The result in the two-party situation of this case therefore mirrors what was formerly the clear result in three-party situations, yet to be dealt with, where the now claimant brings in the now defendant by third party procedure rather than by bringing a separate action against him.[113] Colman J saw no good reason, of policy or otherwise, why the claimant should be required to bring a separate action for the extra costs rather than have them awarded to him in the existing action. To require a separate action, he said, **21-030**

> "would involve delay in obtaining compensation properly due and a formalistic and cumbersome procedure which would in itself involve more costs and judicial time."[114]

---

106 [2008] 1 Lloyd's Rep. 16 at [25].

107 [2007] 1 Lloyd's Rep. 358.

108 [2002] 1 W.L.R. 1517 CA. See at para.21-026, above.

109 [2008] 1 Lloyd's Rep. 16 at [8]. But it is thought that the measure of damages should go beyond the indemnity basis for the reasons set out at para.21-008, above.

110 At para.21-025, above.

111 At para.21-027, above.

112 [2002] 1 W.L.R. 1517 CA. See at para.21-026, above.

113 See paras 21-034 to 21-036, below.

114 [2007] 1 Lloyd's Rep. 358 at [10]. There was no hope of costs being allowed as damages in *Carroll v Kynaston* [2011] Q.B. 959 CA., a case of persistent litigants which Ward LJ described as the worst and most dreadful kind of litigation. One of the litigants first unsuccessfully sued to have a settlement declared not contractually binding and then, undaunted, sued for breach of the settlement contract, claiming as damages the costs incurred in his first action. In this he clearly failed. He was not claiming for costs which he had been unable to recover in the first action, having not asked for them in that action as he should have done and, if unsuccessful, have appealed: see at [20]–[22]. Yet to reach this result Ward LJ, felt obliged to go through, in careful detail, most of the cases appearing in this section, from para.21-015 to para.21-030, of this chapter: at [23]–[31].

## III. Costs, Damages and Fines in Previous Proceedings between the Now Claimant and Third Parties

### 1. The Rule as it has Developed

21-031 **(a) In general** Where the costs that are now being claimed as damages have been incurred in previous proceedings between the now claimant and some third party, it was for long the rule that all costs incurred in such actions by the now claimant were recoverable subject only to the costs having been reasonably incurred and to all other aspects of remoteness of damage.[115] Where the now claimant has been the successful party in the previous proceedings, he would generally be claiming only the extra costs above the assessed costs that the unsuccessful party must pay him. Where, however, he has been the unsuccessful party in the previous proceedings—and this is the commoner case since it is exceptional, if the now claimant has been successful in the previous proceedings, that he should have an action at all against the now defendant—then there was much more to be claimed by him as damages in respect of costs. For it is not only a question of the extra costs above the assessed costs that are to be claimed but the whole of the now claimant's own costs in the prior proceedings and also the assessed costs that he will have had to pay to the third party.[116]

21-032 *Hammond v Bussey*,[117] decided in 1888, is generally regarded as the authority from which the recovery of costs as damages in third party cases stems. Yet there are cases well before that decision in which it can be seen that the full costs incurred by the now claimant have been held recoverable as damages; such very early cases are *Smith v Compton*,[118] *Bramley v Chesterton*,[119] and, most importantly, *Collen v Wright*.[120] These cases, in which the issue was not fully spelt out, seem to have been ignored in preference to *Hammond v Bussey* because the issue of recovery as damages of any costs at all was highlighted in *Hammond* on account of a series of cases in the 1870s in which the matter had become controversial.[121] Now however, as we have seen, the rule in *Hammond v Bussey*, though long established, is in peril,[122] and the recovery of costs beyond standard basis costs is in the balance.[123]

21-033 Furthermore, if the now claimant has been unsuccessful as defendant in the previous proceedings with the third party, which is the commonest case of all, he will

---

115 Remoteness in its various aspects relevant here is considered in detail at paras 21-048 to 21-076, below. Costs incurred by an accused in criminal prosecutions have also been claimed, both where the accused has been acquitted and, more commonly, where convicted and fined; for details see paras 21-067 and following.

116 The amount of costs recoverable in these various situations is given detailed consideration at paras 21-077 to 21-089, below.

117 (1888) 20 Q.B.D. 79 CA.

118 (1832) 3 B. & Ad. 407.

119 (1857) 2 C.B. N.S. 592.

120 (1857) 8 E. & B. 647. On this aspect of the decision, which of course is known for being the first to recognise the liability of an agent for breach of warranty of authority, see para.21-010, above.

121 *Mors-le-Blanch v Wilson* (1873) L.R. 8 C.P. 227; *Baxendale v London, Chatham & Dover Ry* (1874) L.R. 10 Ex. 35 and *Fisher v Val de Travers Asphalte Co* (1876) 1 C.P.D. 511. For the details see the 17th edition (2003) at para.18-013.

122 Although *Hammond* is still cited in *Occidental Chartering Inc v Progress Bulk Carriers* [2012] EWHC 3515 (Comm) as the basis for the entitlement to claim costs paid in one arbitration as damages in another; at [22].

123 See the discussion at paras 21-005 and following, above.

be claiming not only costs but also the damages he has been required to pay to the third party. That, subject to the rules of remoteness, these are recoverable has never been doubted; even the cases before *Hammond v Bussey*,[124] which engendered uncertainty as to the recovery of costs as damages,[125] allowed the recovery of the damages themselves which had been awarded in the previous proceedings.[126]

**(b) Where there have been no strictly previous proceedings** In a number of first instance cases it has been held that the rule still applies where there have not been two separate actions between different parties but a single action comprising claims between different parties. This is particularly important, in effect only important, for the recovery of the extra costs as damages. The cases have all concerned a chain of sales of goods where liability for breach of warranty was passed down the chain not by separate actions but by use of third party procedure. In the earliest case, *Kasler & Cohen v Slavouski*,[127] breach of warranty of quality of dyed rabbit skins featured, in *Butterworth v Kingsway Motors*[128] and in *Bowmaker (Commercial) v Day*,[129] breach of warranty of title to a car. That solicitor and client costs were awarded down the chain is clearly shown in *Butterworth* in Pearson J's detailed explanation of his award.[130] This seemed a sensible result as it involved only third party procedure and non-action costs; it could probably be held unreasonable, Branson J suggested in *Kasler*, for each claim along the line to be separately defended in a separate court action.[131] 21-034

In *Penn v Bristol and West Building Society*[132] a solicitor had warranted to a building society that he had the authority of a wife to negotiate the sale of a house held jointly by herself and her husband, the purported sale of which was designed, by way of a mortgage fraud of which the wife knew nothing, to obtain a loan from the building society. When the wife successfully sued the building society to establish that the charge over the house in its favour was void, the building society brought in the solicitor, claiming successfully against him for breach of warranty of authority, by way of third party procedure and counterclaim rather than by suing him in a separate action.[133] It was held by the Court of Appeal that, because there was only one set of proceedings though including more than one claim, this did not suffice to allow, in respect of one of the claims, more than standard basis costs, although it accepted that greater costs would have been recoverable as damages had a separate action been brought, thus being uninfluenced by, perhaps because unaware of, what earlier, in *The Tiburon*,[134] and *Lonrho Plc v Fayed (No.5)*,[135] the 21-035

---

124 (1888) 20 Q.B.D. 79 CA.

125 See these in the previous paragraph.

126 Also with criminal prosecutions where the now claimant has been the unsuccessful accused, he may recover, again subject to the rules of remoteness, the fine that has been the measure of his conviction. For details see paras 21-067 and following.

127 [1928] 1 K.B. 78.

128 [1954] 1 W.L.R. 1286.

129 [1965] 1 W.L.R. 1396.

130 [1954] 1 W.L.R. 1286 at 1297–1300.

131 [1928] 1 K.B. 78 at 88–89.

132 [1997] 1 W.L.R. 1356 CA.

133 Actions for breach of warranty of authority have constituted the commonest case of a separate action where the now claimant has been claimant also in the earlier action: for details see para.21-044, below.

134 [1992] 2 Lloyd's Rep. 26 CA.

135 [1993] 1 W.L.R. 1489 CA.

Court of Appeal had said.[136] Waller LJ, who gave the only reasoned judgment in *Penn*, accepted that it could be said that this result would discourage the bringing of third party and other claims in the one action but did not think this a serious risk having regard to the many other benefits of proceeding in one action and having all issues tried at the same time.[137] But surely claimants would be more persuaded to proceed in one action if they knew that their position on costs as damages was as good as it would be in a separate action and could even be held to be unreasonable if they failed to take the more cost-effective route.[138]

**21-036** To reach the result in *Penn* Waller LJ was required to give a dubious interpretation to the costs rule in RSC Ord.62 r.3(2), which then provided that:

> "No party to any proceedings shall be entitled to recover any of the costs of those proceedings from any other party to those proceedings except under an order of the court."

The interpretation is dubious because there is nothing in the provision to suggest that it requires the court to order that the costs need be on the standard basis only and that the costs cannot be awarded as damages.[139] Indeed not only is this decision, somewhat ironically, contrary to the whole focus of the Court of Appeal judgments in *The Tiburon*, a claim against two defendants in the alternative[140] where the same costs rule was before the court but which, while only five years earlier, was not even referred to by Waller LJ.[141] It may just be possible to regard the two Court of Appeal decisions as inconsistent with one another, allowing a later court to choose between them, even to consider the later case to have been decided per incuriam as made in apparent ignorance not only of *The Tiburon* but of the earlier first instances cases of *Kasler*, *Butterworth* and *Bowmaker* cited above.[142] Alternatively, the *Penn* case can be regarded as no longer controlling on the ground that it was based on an interpretation of RSC Ord.62 r.3(2) and this rule has now entirely disappeared in today's CPR without an equivalent provision replacing it.

## 2. Main Type-situations in which Costs, Damages and Fines have been Claimed as Damages

**21-037** In analysing the main type-situations in which costs, damages and fines have been claimed as damages, the division is made according to the legal relationship, whether by way of contract or tort, between the now claimant and the now defendant: that between the now claimant and the third party is here of minor importance. And a further division can be usefully made according to the now claimant's role in the previous proceedings, whether as defendant, claimant or accused.

---

136 For which see para.21-006, above.

137 [1997] 1 W.L.R. 1356 CA at 1366A.

138 See Branson J's comment on unreasonableness in *Kasler & Cohen v Slavouski* [1928] 1 K.B. 78 at 88–89 referred to at para.21-034, above.

139 See Waller LJ's reasoning at [1997] 1 W.L.R. 1356 CA at 1365F–H.

140 For *The Tiburon* see para.21-006, above.

141 Indeed Waller LJ, in saying that he had not found it easy to establish the correct approach to the problem, added that he was "surprised to find that there is apparently no authority to guide in what must be a not unfamiliar situation": [1997] 1 W.L.R. 1356 at 1365C.

142 At para.21-034, above. And see also, in this connection, the interesting *A v. B (No.2)* [2007] 1 Lloyd's Rep. 358 at para.21-029 above.

### (a) Costs and damages where the now claimant has been sued

*(i) Sale of goods* The commonest type of case giving rise to the issues dealt with in this chapter is that in which the now claimant has bought goods from the defendant, has resold them, and has then been sued by his sub-buyer because the defendant's breach of contract has involved him in a similar breach of his sub-contract. Generally the breach has been a breach of warranty of quality, as in the leading case of *Hammond v Bussey*,[143] but there are also cases of breach by delayed delivery,[144] of breach of warranty of title,[145] and of fundamental breach by reason of the article delivered not representing the contract article at all.[146] A second type of case is that in which the now claimant has bought goods from the defendant and, while using them, has caused physical damage to a third party who has then sued him; this has arisen both where the damage has been to the third party's person[147] and where it has been to his property.[148] A further type of case is that in which the now claimant, having bought from the defendant goods which were not the defendant's to sell, has then been faced with claims against him by third parties in respect of the goods.[149] **21-038**

*(ii) Sale of land* The only type of case appearing in the reports is that in which the claimant has bought land from the defendant and then has been sued, usually for possession, by a third party with a superior title.[150] **21-039**

*(iii) Lease of land* Similarly, there are cases where the claimant has taken a lease of land from the defendant and has then been sued, usually for possession, by a third party with a superior title.[151] There are also cases in which the claimant has taken **21-040**

---

143 (1888) 20 Q.B.D. 79 CA (costs). Other cases are *Randall v Raper* (1858) E.B. & E. 84 (damages); *Bostock v Nicholson* [1904] 1 K.B. 725 (damages; resale not of the goods but of their product); *Pinnock v Lewis & Peat* [1923] 1 K.B. 690 (damages and costs); *Bennett v Kreeger* (1925) 41 T.L.R. 609 (costs); *Kasler & Cohen v Slavouski* [1928] 1 K.B. 78 (costs; a chain of actions involving third-party procedure); *Dobell v Barber* [1931] 1 K.B. 219 CA (damages); *Parker v Oloxo* [1937] 3 All E.R. 524 (damages and costs); *Biggin v Permanite* [1951] 2 K.B. 314 CA (damages and settlement); *Marles v Philip Trant* [1954] 1 Q.B. 29 CA (damages and costs). Cases decided before *Hadley v Baxendale* (1854) 9 Ex. 341 (*Lewis v Peake* (1816) 7 Taunt. 153 (damages and costs); *Pennell v Woodburn* (1835) 7 C. & P. 117 (damages and costs) and *Wrightup v Chamberlain* (1839) 7 Scott 598 (costs)) were said by Lord Esher MR in *Hammond v Bussey* (1888) 20 Q.B.D. 79 CA at 91 to be now of no value whichever way decided.

144 *Agius v Great Western Colliery Co* [1899] 1 Q.B. 413 CA (costs); *Contigroup Companies Inc v Glencore AG* [2005] 1 Lloyd's Rep. 241 (damages and settlement). See *Alison v Wallsend Slipway & Engineering Co* (1927) 43 T.L.R. 323 CA, where the seller's delay in delivery caused the buyer to be in breach of his contract to repair a third party's ship.

145 *Butterworth v Kingsway Motors* [1954] 1 W.L.R. 1286; *Bowmaker (Commercial) v Day* [1965] 1 W.L.R. 1396 (damages and costs, with a chain of actions involving third-party procedure, in both cases).

146 *British Oil & Cake Co v Burstall* (1923) 39 T.L.R. 406 (damages).

147 *Kiddle v Lovett* (1885) 16 Q.B.D. 605 (settlement); *Mowbray v Merryweather* [1895] 2 Q.B. 640 CA (damages); *Vogan v Oulton* (1899) 81 L.T. 435 CA (costs); *Scott v Foley* (1899) 15 T.L.R. 55 (costs).

148 *Britannia Hygienic Laundry Co v Thornycroft* (1925) 41 T.L.R. 667 (costs).

149 See *Lloyds and Scottish Finance v Modern Cars and Caravans (Kingston)* [1966] 1 Q.B. 764 (costs of interpleader proceedings).

150 *Smith v Compton* (1832) 3 B. & Ad. 407 (costs); *Sutton v Baillie* (1891) 65 L.T. 528 (costs); *G.W. Ry v Fisher* [1905] 1 Ch. 316 (costs).

151 *Rolph v Crouch* (1867) L.R. 3 Ex. 44 (damages and costs).

a lease and, by reason of the lessor's failure to repair, has been sued by a third party to whom he has sub-let or assigned,[152] or by a third party to whom physical damage has been caused by the non-repair.[153]

21-041 Conversely, there are cases where the lessor is the now claimant. The most frequent type of case is that in which, the lessee having failed to repair, the lessor is sued for non-repair by his superior landlord.[154] There is also the situation where, the lessee having failed to relinquish possession at the end of his lease, the lessor is sued by the person to whom he has relet for not giving him possession of the premises.[155]

21-042 *(iv) Miscellaneous* Other situations involve contracts of carriage of goods, whether the action by the third party be against the consignee[156] or against the carrier[157]; contracts of building or manufacture, whether the action by the third party be against the one doing the work[158] or the one commissioning the work[159]; contracts between solicitor and client for lending advice where the action is by the third party lender against the client[160]; collateral contracts of warranty made between the person hire-purchasing and the person supplying goods, where the action is by the third party finance company against the hire-purchaser[161]; contracts of agency[162]; contracts of warranty of authority[163]; the tort of deceit[164]; torts resulting in damage to or destruction of goods[165]; and bankruptcy proceedings.[166]

21-043 **(b) Costs where the now claimant has himself sued** Where the now claimant was also claimant in the previous proceedings, his present claim can only be in respect of costs: *ex hypothesi* damages and fines cannot be involved.

21-044 *(i) Contract of warranty of authority* Easily the most frequently occurring type of case where the now claimant has been claimant in the previous action is that in which the now defendant has warranted his authority to contract as agent on behalf of a professed principal and has so induced the claimant, first, to enter into an apparent contract, and then unsuccessfully to sue the apparent principal, both in reliance on this assertion of authority. A series of important cases between 1856 and

---

152 *Short v Kalloway* (1839) 11 A. & E. 29 (damages and costs).

153 *The Kate* [1935] P. 100 (damages and costs).

154 *Walker v Hatton* (1842) 10 M. & W. 249; *Clare v Dobson* [1911] 1 K.B. 35 (both costs).

155 *Bramley v Chesterton* (1857) 2 C.B. N.S. 592 (damages and costs).

156 *Baxendale v London, Chatham & Dover Ry* (1874) L.R. 10 Ex. 35 (costs); *The Ocean Dynamic* [1982] 2 Lloyd's Rep. 88 (settlement and costs).

157 *Mors-le-Blanch v Wilson* (1873) L.R. 8 C.P. 227 (damages and costs).

158 *Dixon v Fawcus* (1861) 3 E. & E. 537 (damages and costs).

159 *Fisher v Val de Travers Asphalte Co* (1876) 1 C.P.D. 511 (settlement and costs).

160 *Gold v Mincoff Science & Gold* [2001] Lloyd's Rep. P.N. 423 (costs).

161 *Smith v Spurling Motor Bodies* (1961) 105 S.J. 967 CA (damages and costs); *Yeoman Credit v Odgers* [1962] 1 W.L.R. 215 CA (damages and costs).

162 *Mainwaring v Brandon* (1818) 8 Taunt. 202 (damages and costs); *Osman v J. Ralph Moss* [1970] 1 Lloyd's Rep. 313 CA (damages and costs).

163 *Pow v Davis* (1861) 1 B. & S. 220 (costs); *Oliver v Bank of England* [1901] 1 Ch. 652 (damages and costs).

164 *Dadourian Group International Inc v Simms* [2009] 1 Lloyd's Rep. 601 CA (costs, in an arbitration).

165 *Tindall v Bell* (1843) 11 M. & W. 228; *Ronneberg v Falkland Islands Co* (1864) 17 C.B. N.S. 1; *The Wallsend* [1907] P. 302 (all costs).

166 *Pearce v European Reinsurance Consultants and Run-Off Ltd* [2006] P.N.L.R. 8 at 142 (costs).

1870 illustrates this type-situation[167]; examples of it continue to appear.[168] And the same situation may arise where the agent has induced the now claimant to act on the faith of the warranty in a matter of business other than that of entering into a contract with the professed principal.[169]

*(ii) Miscellaneous* The cases remaining after those on warranty of authority form only a miscellany. They involve leases, whether the action against the third party be by the lessee[170] or the lessor[171]; contracts of agency, whether the agent is employed to enter into contracts on behalf of the principal[172] or to deal with the principal's property[173]; contracts of insurance[174]; sales of goods where the buyer has sued the true owner or the seller[175]; torts resulting in damage to or destruction of goods[176] infringement of patent rights[177] deceit[178] and a variety of heterogeneous claims.[179] **21-045**

### (c) Costs and fines where the now claimant has been prosecuted

*(i) Sale of goods* The most frequently occurring type of case where the now claimant has been prosecuted is that in which a tradesman has bought from the defendant food or drink which has failed to satisfy a warranty of quality and has then been prosecuted for having food or drink unfit for human consumption on his premises,[180] or for reselling it under a false description[181] or above the permitted price.[182] **21-046**

*(ii) Miscellaneous* Other situations involve contracts of agency where the agent has in breach of contract acted so as to lead to his principal's prosecution,[183] and also the torts of fraud, conspiracy and negligence where the victim has been induced to act in such a way that he has been prosecuted.[184] **21-047**

---

167 *Randell v Trimen* (1856) 18 C.B. 786; *Collen v Wright* (1857) 8 E. & B. 647; *Hughes v Graeme* (1864) 33 L.J.Q.B. 335; *Spedding v Nevell* (1869) L.R. 4 C.P. 212; *Godwin v Francis* (1870) L.R. 5 C.P. 295.

168 *Rasnoimport V/O v Guthrie* [1966] 1 Lloyd's Rep. 1; *Chitholie v Nash & Co* (1974) 229 E.G. 786.

169 *Yonge v Toynbee* [1910] 1 K.B. 215 CA.

170 *Child v Stenning* (1879) 11 Ch. D. 82 CA.

171 *Henderson v Squire* (1869) L.R. 4 Q.B. 170; followed in *Henderson v Van Cooten* (1923) 67 S.J. 228.

172 *Salvesen v Rederi Aktiebolaget Nordstjernan* [1905] A.C. 302.

173 *Re United Service Co* (1870) L.R. 6 Ch. 212.

174 *Seavision Investment SA v Evennett, The Tiburon* [1992] 2 Lloyd's Rep. 26 CA (costs).

175 *Bowmaker (Commercial) v Day* [1965] 1 W.L.R. 1396 and *Browning v Brachers* [2005] EWCA Civ 753 CA respectively.

176 *The Solway Prince* (1914) 31 T.L.R. 56.

177 *Morton-Norwich Products v Intercen (No.2)* [1981] F.S.R. 337.

178 *KBC Bank v Industrial Steels (UK) Ltd* [2001] 1 Lloyd's Rep. 370; see at 376–377.

179 *British Racing Drivers' Club v Hexall Erskine & Co* [1996] 3 All E.R. 667 (settlement and costs); *Mahme Trust Reg v Lloyds TSB Bank Plc* [2006] EWHC 1321 Ch (costs); *Redbus LMDS Ltd v Jeffrey Green & Russell* [2007] P.N.L.R.12 at 287 (costs); *Swain v Geoffrey Osborne Ltd* [2010] EWHC 3118 (QB) (costs).

180 *Crage v Fry* (1903) 67 J.P. 240; *Cointat v Myham* [1913] 2 K.B. 220.

181 *Payne v Ministry of Food* (1953) 103 L.J. 141.

182 *Proops v Chaplin* (1920) 37 T.L.R. 112 (costs only, as there was an acquittal).

183 *Leslie v Reliable Advertising Agency* [1915] 1 K.B. 652; *Osman v J. Ralph Moss* [1970] 1 Lloyd's Rep. 313 CA.

184 *Askey v Golden Wine Co* [1948] 2 All E.R. 35 (fraud and conspiracy); *Osman v J. Ralph Moss* [1970]

## 3. The Various Aspects of Remoteness of Damage Involved

**21-048** Whether or not a person who in previous proceedings with a third party has incurred costs, has had costs or had damages awarded against him, or has had a fine imposed on him, can recover for these expenditures in an action for damages against the defendant turns upon principles of remoteness of damage. Four separate aspects of the remoteness issue are found; in particular cases they appear sometimes alone and sometimes in various combinations. These four aspects straddle the causal and the policy sides of remoteness.[185]

### (1) Contemplation of the parties in contract; foreseeability in tort

**21-049** **(a) Contract** The first remoteness question is whether, in the case of breach of contract, it was in the contemplation of the parties that the now claimant would become involved in a legal action with a third party. This is but a particular application of the rule in *Hadley v Baxendale*.[186] This issue has made a pronounced appearance only in cases of sale of goods where the buyer has sued to recover in respect of damages and costs he has had to pay when himself sued by his sub-buyer. At the one end of the scale is *Bostock v Nicholson*,[187] where the defendant sold to the claimant sulphuric acid warranted commercially free from arsenic. The claimant used the acid in the manufacture of brewing sugar, which was one well-recognised and ordinary use for it but an intended use not expressly made known by him to the defendant, and then sold this sugar to brewers who used it in brewing beer. Because the sulphuric acid had not been commercially free from arsenic the beer was rendered poisonous and the brewers successfully claimed damages from the claimant. The claimant then sued the defendant to recover, inter alia, in respect of the damages he had been compelled to pay the brewers: this part of his claim failed on the ground that

> "no liability is incurred in the ordinary case of a separate and distinct collateral contract with a third person uncommunicated to the original contractor or wrongdoer".[188]

At the other end of the scale is the leading case, *Hammond v Bussey*,[189] where the defendant sold coal to the claimant knowing that the claimant intended to resell it for use in steamers. The claimant did resell it, was successfully sued by his sub-buyer on account of its bad quality, and then himself brought an action against the defendant to recover the damages he had paid to the third party and the costs of defending the action. The Court of Appeal held that the parties must have contemplated that a sub-sale would be made, since the rule in *Hadley v Baxendale*[190] would apply to the case of a sub-contract which within the knowledge of the defendant was in the ordinary course of business sure to be made,[191] and that

---

1 Lloyd's Rep. 313 CA (negligence).

185 For the distinction between causation and policy in remoteness, see Ch.8, above.

186 (1854) 9 Ex. 341.

187 [1904] 1 K.B. 725.

188 [1904] 1 K.B. 725 at 742, per Bruce J. The rule as thus stated by him was taken from Smith's notes to *Vicars v Wilcocks* (1806) 8 East 1.

189 (1888) 20 Q.B.D. 79 CA.

190 (1854) 9 Ex. 341.

191 (1888) 20 Q.B.D. 79 CA at 89, per Lord Esher MR.

therefore a breach by the seller would mean a claim against the buyer by his sub-buyer.[192] The defendant indeed admitted that he was liable for the damages that the claimant had had to pay the third party and contested only his liability for the costs incurred by the claimant in the prior action. Nevertheless there could properly be a recovery for neither such damages nor such costs unless the sub-sale was in the contemplation of the parties.

Each case must be taken on its own facts in deciding whether it falls within *Bostock v Nicholson*,[193] or within *Hammond v Bussey*.[194] It is, however, significant that there is a large number of sale of goods cases which follow the latter authority in allowing recovery of damages and costs that the buyer has had to pay to his sub-buyer when sued by him, while *Bostock v Nicholson*[195] stands alone, without progeny.[196] This suggests that the courts tend to hold that the parties to a sale of goods will generally contemplate that resale may be effected. On the other hand, a different conclusion might be reached in the case of a contract of carriage of goods since, as Lord Upjohn pointed out in *The Heron II*,[197] in relation to the somewhat similar claim for loss of profits by reason of the non-delivery, late delivery or defective delivery of goods, **21-050**

> "it must be remembered when dealing with the case of a carrier of goods by land, sea or air, he is not carrying on the same trade as the consignor of the goods and his knowledge of the practices and exigencies of the other's trade may be limited and less than between buyer and seller of goods who probably know far more about one another's business."

However, *The Pegase*[198] has since established that no rule of policy prevents the recovery of damages from a carrier assessed with reference to a sale by the consignee,[199] and in *The Ocean Dynamic*,[200] where the claimants, importers of block frozen cherries, had sold them on to a manufacturer of filling for cherry pies and had then been sued by the manufacturer for the defective condition of the cherries which had come about during their carriage, it was held that they could claim against the carrier for the amount paid to the manufacturer in settlement together with their costs of defending this claim since, in the words of Robert Goff J,

> "it must have been within the general knowledge of any reasonable person involved in the business of carriage of goods by sea that cartons of block frozen cherries were not unlikely to be the subject of processing after arrival at their destination, and that the importer was not unlikely to sell them on to a manufacturer for that purpose."[201]

There are also a few sale of goods cases in which the buyer has been prosecuted for deficiencies in the quality of the goods, the offence sometimes consisting in his **21-051**

---

192 (1888) 20 Q.B.D. 79 CA at 90, per Lord Esher MR.

193 [1904] 1 K.B. 725.

194 (1888) 20 Q.B.D. 79 CA.

195 [1904] 1 K.B. 725.

196 The case, however, has ancestors in *Portman v Middleton* (1858) 4 C.B. N.S. 322 and *Williams v Reynolds* (1865) 6 B. & S. 495.

197 [1969] 1 A.C. 350 at 424, echoing a very similar comment of Asquith LJ in *Victoria Laundry v Newman* [1949] 2 K.B. 528 CA at 537.

198 [1981] 1 Lloyd's Rep. 175.

199 See paras 32-019 and 32-039, below.

200 [1982] 2 Lloyd's Rep. 88.

201 [1982] 2 Lloyd's Rep. 88 at 93 to 94.

reselling them, as in *Proops v Chaplin*,[202] and sometimes in exhibiting them for sale, as in *Cointat v Myham*.[203] In both these cases, the fact that the buyer might be prosecuted if the goods proved defective was held to be within the contemplation of the parties, so that loss consisting in costs incurred or fines imposed was held not too remote. In the former Rowlatt J said that the claimant and the defendant

> "both knew if the whisky was described as 30 per cent under proof when it was not, the result would be a prosecution"[204];

in the latter Lord Coleridge J similarly said that

> "the defendants must have known that the claimant relying on the implied warranty would naturally expose the meat for sale and that a conviction for so doing might reasonably follow without any negligence on his part."[205]

Similarly, where in *Leslie v Reliable Advertising & Addressing Agency*,[206] a moneylender was prosecuted because his agent had sent circulars to a minor, the judge thought the damage in costs and fine resulting from the prosecution was not too remote to be recoverable in an action by the moneylender against the agent in so far as[207]

> "a possible breach of the law, if a mistake was made in the list, must have been within the contemplation of the parties".[208]

21-052 **(b) Tort** In tort the extent of liability is generally confined by doctrines of foreseeability[209] and where this is so, as in the all-pervasive tort of negligence, it is necessary for the claimant to show that the defendant could reasonably have foreseen that the claimant might become involved in legal proceedings with a third party. Thus in *Morton-Norwich Products v Intercen (No.2)*,[210] an action for infringement of a patent, the claimants successfully recovered as damages the costs incurred in bringing a discovery action against HM Customs since it was held to be reasonably foreseeable to the defendant infringers that the claimant would take all necessary steps to find out the extent of the defendants' activities and thereby incur expense in investigation and discovery of the full facts. On the other hand, in *Dormeuil Frères v Feraglow*,[211] an action for both passing off and infringement of trade mark in which the claimant claimed reimbursement of unrecovered legal costs expended in pursuing manufacturers of infringing cloth, recovery was allowed, as being foreseeable, for legal costs of putting unsuspecting manufacturers on notice but not, as being too remote, for costs of preventing further infringements by them

---

202 (1920) 37 T.L.R. 112.

203 [1913] 2 K.B. 220. Also *Crage v Fry* (1903) 67 J.P. 240.

204 (1920) 37 T.L.R. 112 at 114.

205 [1913] 2 K.B. 220 at 222.

206 [1915] 1 K.B. 652.

207 Recovery was, however, refused on other remoteness grounds: see para.21-069, below.

208 [1915] 1 K.B. 652 at 661. The matter of contemplation of the parties is considered generally in Ch.8, above, and in particular relation to the sale of goods in Ch.25, below.

209 But with the tort of deceit no foreseeability is required for the recovery of costs: *KBC Bank v Industrial Steels (UK) Ltd* [2001] 1 Lloyd's Rep. 370; see at 376 to 377.

210 [1981] F.S.R. 337.

211 [1990] R.P.C. 449.

after notice, or of pursuing manufacturers aware of the true position from the start, as the defendants could not be held responsible for such wrongful acts.

### (2) Reasonableness in the conduct of the previous proceedings

The aspect of remoteness upon which the arguments in the majority of the cases turn concerns the reasonableness of the now claimant in having defended the action brought against him or in having brought the previous action himself. This issue of reasonableness does not affect his recovery from the defendant of damages awarded against him in the previous proceedings, since his liability in respect of damages does not depend upon his having contested the action. The same is true of fines imposed upon the now claimant after being prosecuted; the fine would be there whether or not he sought to defend himself in the prosecution. Settlements and costs, however, are a different matter and need to be looked at. **21-053**

**(a) Settlements** Where the now claimant has made a payment by way of settlement of a claim brought against him, he can recover this amount as damages from the now defendant provided that the settlement represented a reasonable figure. *Biggin v Permanite*,[212] which established this and that a settlement was a relevant consideration,[213] is the leading case. At the time when Biggin was decided, over 60 years ago, settlements of damages claims were not so common but, now that they are practically the order of the day, there has been a number of first instance decisions on the matter around the turn of the century, some of which have relied heavily on *Biggin*.[214] Recovery of the amount paid out in settlement was allowed in *General Feeds Inc Panama v Slobodna Plovidba Yugoslavia*,[215] the court holding that it was for the claimant to prove that the fact and the amount of settlement were reasonable in all the circumstances. Similarly, in *Ascon Contracting Ltd v Alfred McAlpine Construction Isle of Man Ltd*,[216] main contractors claiming from their subcontractors the amount in liquidated damages they had paid their employer were required to show that such payment had been made in reasonable settlement of the employer's claim. In *Contigroup Companies Inc v Glencore AG*,[217] where there was delay in delivery of goods sold, the amount paid in settlement was held to be reasonable and therefore recoverable. *Siemens Building Technologies FE Ltd v Supershield Ltd*[218] takes us to the Court of Appeal where Biggin again made its inevitable appearance and again the amount paid in settlement was held to be recoverable as reasonable.[219] **21-054**

**(b) Costs** The issue of reasonableness assumes a much greater importance when it arises in connection with the now claimant's claim to recover as damages costs which he has paid in the previous proceedings. Reasonableness in bringing claims, **21-055**

---

212 [1951] 2 K.B. 314 CA.

213 Thereby reversing Devlin J's decision, [1951] 1 K.B. 422, that the claimant's settlement with the third party was irrelevant to the determination of the defendant's liability.

214 True in *P. & O. Developments v The Guy's and St Thomas' National Health Service Trust* [1999] B.L.R. 3 and in *The Royal Brompton Hospital v Hammond & Lerche* [1999] B.L.R. 162.

215 [1999] 1 Lloyd's Rep. 688.

216 (2001) 16 Con. L.J. 316.

217 [2005] 1 Lloyd's Rep. 241.

218 [2010] 1 Lloyd's Rep. 349 CA.

219 Full facts at para.8-181, above.

successfully and unsuccessfully, and in defending claims, successfully and unsuccessfully, falls to be considered, and also reasonableness in the costs incurred themselves.

**21-056** *(i) Successful claim or defence* Where the now claimant has been the successful party in the previous proceedings, it can hardly be said that costs were incurred by him unreasonably, and he will therefore recover in respect of them.[220] He will be held to have acted reasonably even although he does not succeed in all the courts through which the proceedings are taken, provided that he succeeds in the final court to which the original claim is taken; this was the position in *Britannia Hygienic Laundry Co v Thornycroft*.[221] He will also be held to have acted reasonably where, although liable to the third party for a certain amount in damages, he has defended a claim made against him by the third party which he has then succeeded in showing at the trial to be exorbitant, whether he has paid into court a sum which in the event is sufficient, as in *Agius v Great Western Colliery*,[222] or has paid nothing into court, as in *Great Western Ry v Fisher*.[223]

**21-057** *(ii) Unsuccessful defence* Where the now claimant has unsuccessfully defended a civil action, his claim for costs will fail if the defence is held unreasonable. As was said in *Short v Kalloway*,[224]

> "no person has a right to inflame his own account against another by incurring additional expense in the unrighteous resistance to an action which he cannot defend."

**21-058** Illustrations of reasonableness are nevertheless more common in the cases than of unreasonableness. This is so particularly where the action in which the costs are claimed is brought against a seller of goods or a seller or lessor of land for breach of contract. In such cases the seller or lessor is generally in a better position to know about the condition, quality and title of the goods or the land than the buyer or lessee, who may therefore be considered to be entitled to rely, when sued by a third party in relation to the goods or land, upon his seller or lessor not being in breach of contract. As Lord Esher MR put it in *Hammond v Bussey*,[225] a case of breach of warranty in a sale of coal in which the unsuccessful defence was held reasonable,

> "the reasonable course to be pursued by the vendees might be that they should not at once submit to the claim but that, unless they could get information from the vendor that there was really no defence, they should defend the action."

And in *Rolph v Crouch*,[226] it was held that a lessee's unsuccessful defence of an action for possession brought against him by a third party was reasonable, he having notified his lessor who paid no attention to the notice. Kelly CB said:

---

220 In *Morton-Norwich Products v Intercen (No.2)* [1981] F.S.R. 337 (see para.21-052, above) where the previous action was of the somewhat unusual nature of a discovery action successfully taken against HM Customs, it might possibly have been held that to have brought such an action was not reasonably justified; certainly this was the contention of the defendants. The contention, however, failed.

221 (1925) 41 T.L.R. 667; reversed on the facts: (1925) 95 L.J.K.B. 237 CA.

222 [1899] 1 Q.B. 413 CA.

223 [1905] 1 Ch. 316.

224 (1839) 11 A. & E. 29 at 31.

225 (1888) 20 Q.B.D. 79 CA at 90.

226 (1867) L.R. 3 Ex. 44.

"The claimant, being left to himself, acted for the best, upon his own judgment. He acted bona fide, giving credence to the defendant's warranty"

of quiet enjoyment. He was thus "justified in the course which he took".[227] Furthermore, the now claimant's contention that his defence was reasonable is frequently reinforced by the now defendant's vigorous denial that he has committed a breach of contract. This was the position in *Hammond v Bussey*,[228] and in *Bennett v Kreeger*,[229] where the defendant had insisted that the goods sold were in accordance with the warranty given, and in *Sutton v Baillie*,[230] where the defendant had insisted that no right of way in a third party's favour existed over the land sold.

**21-059** Indeed the very fact that the now defendant may be able to contest his liability for the damages paid to the third party if the now claimant fails to defend the third party's claim is in itself a factor to be taken into account in determining reasonableness. Thus in *Kasler & Cohen v Slavouski*,[231] where there was a chain of buyers of certain skins to be made into fur collars, it was held that, an analyst's report having exonerated the particular fur collar from an allegation that it contained deleterious matter, the penultimate buyer had reasonably defended an action for damages brought by the ultimate buyer and user, for if he had paid the amount claimed after the analyst's report "one can well imagine what the parties higher up the line would have said".[232] Similarly, in *Oliver v Bank of England*,[233] a case not of sale or lease but of breach of warranty of authority, where the Bank of England had transferred certain securities upon the presentation by the defendant stockbroker of a power of attorney on which the name of the owner of the securities was forged, it was held by Kekewich J that the bank had been well advised to defend the action brought against them by the owner, since, if they had taken judgment by consent or allowed judgment to go by default, they would have been liable to have been called upon by the now defendant to justify their conduct.[234] Moreover, even where the defence undertaken by the now claimant was not a well advised one, he may still be entitled to claim that it was reasonable if it was undertaken at the instigation of the now defendant himself. Thus in *Yeoman Credit v Odgers*,[235] the Court of Appeal refused to upset the county court's award of an indemnity against the costs of defence incurred by a hire-purchaser of a car in relation to a claim brought against him by the finance company because, although inept in the extreme, it was fostered and encouraged by the car dealer who had been joined as a third party in the finance company's action against him.[236]

---

227 (1867) L.R. 3 Ex. 44 at 49.

228 (1888) 20 Q.B.D. 79 CA.

229 (1925) 41 T.L.R. 609.

230 (1892) 65 L.T. 528.

231 [1928] 1 K.B. 78.

232 [1928] 1 K.B. 78 at 88. See, too, *Bowmaker (Commercial) v Day* [1965] 1 W.L.R. 1396 where the breach of warranty in question was of title to a car.

233 [1901] 1 Ch. 652. The case went to the House of Lords on the main issue of liability where it was affirmed sub nom. *Starkey v Bank of England* [1903] A.C. 114.

234 [1901] 1 Ch. 652 at 664 to 665.

235 [1962] 1 W.L.R. 215 CA.

236 See [1962] 1 W.L.R. 215 CA at 222–223 and 225, per Holroyd Pearce and Harman LJJ respectively. See similarly *Lloyds and Scottish Finance v Modern Cars and Caravans (Kingston)* [1966] 1 Q.B. 764: facts at para.9-104, above. The unsuccessful defence of a claim may form a reasonable course of action in part or up to a certain point in time; see such a holding in respect of an unsuccessful claim in *Godwin v Francis* (1870) L.R. 5 C.P. 295 at para.21-062, below.

**21-060** A few cases do appear in the books of defences which have been held unreasonable. Thus in *Smith v Spurling Motor Bodies*,[237] where a finance company sued the now claimant under an agreement for the hire-purchase of a car, and the now claimant in turn sued the car dealer for breach of warranty, it was held that the now claimant could not claim an indemnity for the costs of his defence as no defence could have been a reasonable one. However, most of the cases of unreasonable defences have concerned damage to or destruction of goods, with the now defendant liable in tort or in contract. Tort is illustrated by *The Wallsend*.[238] The claimant's ship, sunk by the defendant's fault, was raised by the river conservancy, which claimed from the claimant the expenses of raising the ship, a claim which the now claimant unsuccessfully contested. It was held that, although the claimant could recover from the defendant the expenses of raising, he could not recover the costs incurred by him in the action brought by the conservancy against him, since it was not reasonable to have defended this clear-cut claim.[239] Similarly, in *Tindall v Bell*,[240] the claimant, whose ship had been damaged by the defendant's negligence, had had to employ a tug to rescue her and he unsuccessfully defended a claim brought by the tug-owners for salvage. Here too it was held that he could not recover the costs incurred by him in an unreasonable defence. The case, however, differs from *The Wallsend*,[241] in that the third party had claimed substantially more than the court had awarded him, although the award was greater than the amount which the now claimant had paid into court. In such circumstances the amount claimed is cut down by the claimant, so that he is to a limited extent successful, and it is submitted that today, after cases like *G.W. Ry v Fisher*,[242] such a defence could be held reasonable so as to allow recovery of these costs as damages in the succeeding action, although the smallness of the payment into court would not justify their recovery as costs in the first action itself.[243]

**21-061** A somewhat different tort case is *Ronneberg v Falkland Islands Co*,[244] where the defendant caused the loss of a third party's goods, which the claimant was carrying by sea under a contract with the third party. It was held that the claimant could not recover from the defendant the costs incurred by him in defending the third party's action because the defence was an untenable one. Breach of contract is illustrated by *Baxendale v London, Chatham & Dover Ry*.[245] The claimant had again contracted to carry goods for the third party, had then sub-contracted the carriage to the defendant who damaged the goods, and the claimant was held to have acted unreasonably in defending the action brought against him by the third party, since he had been repeatedly advised that the only available line of defence was unsound. He therefore could not recover these costs as damages from the now defendant. And

---

237 (1961) 105 S.J. 967 CA.

238 [1907] P. 302.

239 Bargrave Deane J stressed the fact that the claimant did not inform the defendant, but this can only be one factor in determining reasonableness.

240 (1843) 11 M. & W. 228.

241 [1907] P. 302.

242 [1905] 1 Ch. 316; see para.21-056, above.

243 Since *Tindall v Bell* (1843) 11 M. & W. 228 was decided before the general principles of damages were laid down in *Hadley v Baxendale* (1854) 9 Ex. 341, its authority is weakened: see *Hammond v Bussey* (1888) 20 Q.B.D. 79 CA at 91, per Lord Esher MR.

244 (1864) 17 C.B. N.S. 1.

245 (1874) L.R. 10 Ex. 35. Although dicta in this case were overruled in *Hammond v Bussey* (1888) 20 Q.B.D. 79 CA (see para.21-032, above), the decision is not affected.

*Osman v J. Ralph Moss*[246] provides an illustration of an unreasonable defence to a third party's claim where the now defendant's liability to the now claimant was both in tort and in contract. The liability arose out of the failure of the defendants, who were motor insurance brokers, to obtain third party insurance cover for the claimant; the costs which were not allowed as damages were those which would have been saved had the now claimant submitted to judgment in the third party's claim.

*(iii) Unsuccessful claim* Similar principles apply where the now claimant has unsuccessfully brought a civil action. Once again, the main illustrations, if not all of them, are of circumstances in which the now claimant was held to have acted reasonably. Easily the most prevalent type of case is that in which an agent has warranted his authority to enter into a contract on behalf of a principal, and, in reliance on this warranty, the claimant has sued unsuccessfully the purported principal on the contract or for breach of the contract.[247] Costs thus incurred have been recovered from the agent where he has persisted throughout in the assertion of authority, as in *Randell v Trimen*,[248] *Collen v Wright*,[249] and *Hughes v Graeme*.[250] But circumstances other than persistence of this nature on the part of the now defendant may render the claimant's suit reasonable; such circumstances were held to exist in *Spedding v Nevell*,[251] where the agent, who purported on behalf of the lessor to renew the claimant's lease, was the lessor's brother and had for some time past received the rents on behalf of his brother. The warranty of authority cases also show that the unsuccessful bringing of a claim may form a reasonable course of action in part or up to a certain point in time. Thus in *Godwin v Francis*,[252] it was held that it was reasonable for the now claimant to have acted on the warranty of authority and commenced proceedings against the purported principal, but that he should have discontinued after receipt of answers to interrogatories in which answers not only the principal but the agent swore on oath that the latter lacked authority. **21-062**

*(iv) The level of the costs incurred* Apart from the question of the reasonableness of incurring the costs claimed as damages, the amount of incurred costs, as formerly assessed as between solicitor and client, themselves attract a test of reasonableness but one which is more expansive than that applying to the now standard based and indemnity based costs. There are no specific cases on this, but it has been pointed out earlier that this represented the law.[253] **21-063**

## (3) Causation

A minor aspect of remoteness on which there is a little authority is that if the costs **21-064**

246 [1970] 1 Lloyd's Rep. 313 CA.

247 There is also in the sale of goods field *Bowmaker (Commercial) v Day* [1965] 1 W.L.R. 1396, where the unsuccessful claim in conversion by the buyer of a car against its true owner was held to have been reasonably bought.

248 (1856) 18 C.B. 786.

249 (1857) 8 E. & B. 647.

250 (1864) 33 L.J.Q.B. 335.

251 (1869) L.R. 4 C.P. 212. In *Rasnoimport V/O v Guthrie* [1966] 1 Lloyd's Rep. 1 it is not made clear for what reasons the now claimant had been persuaded to claim against the principal; in any event the recovery of costs as damages is barely touched upon in the judgment, other issues preponderating in the case.

252 (1870) L.R. 5 C.P. 295.

253 See para.21-007, above.

would have been incurred by the now claimant even if the defendant had not committed the tort or breach of contract against him, he cannot claim damages in respect of them from the defendant[254]; the same must go for damages and fines although cases of these involving causation may be hard to envisage. This is a straight question of causation, and appeared in *Pow v Davis*,[255] a case involving a breach of warranty of authority. The claimant, having been let into possession of a third party's property under a purported lease which the defendant agent had warranted he had authority from the third party to conclude, unsuccessfully defended an action of ejectment brought against him by the third party. He then claimed the costs of this unsuccessful defence from the defendant in an action for breach of warranty of authority. Recovery was denied because, even had the defendant had the purported authority, the now claimant's defence in the ejectment action must still have failed as the agreement for the lease was oral only, the now claimant, in defending, having acted on an erroneous view of the law.

**21-065** Lack of causation reappeared in the complexities of *Vrinera Marine Co Ltd v Eastern Rich Operations Inc, The Vakis T*[256] as a ground for refusing recovery. The now defendant had time-chartered a vessel to the now claimant who sub-chartered her to a third party on a voyage charter. The now defendant claimed against the now claimant for breach of the obligation to provide a safe port and berth leading to bottom damage to the vessel and in turn the now claimant claimed similarly against the third party. The now claimant counterclaimed against the now defendant for breach of the obligation of seaworthiness and the third party did likewise against the now claimant. It turned out that all the damage had resulted from the unseaworthiness of the vessel with no question of its being due to an unsafe port and berth, so that the now defendant's claim against the now claimant was discontinued and this resulted in discontinuance of the now claimant's claim against the third party. The now claimant then attempted to recover from the now defendant the costs incurred in its claim against the third party and failed because no causal link could be found between the breach by the now defendant of the obligation of seaworthiness and the now claimant's failed claim against the third party for breach of a different obligation, viz. the obligation to provide a safe port and berth.[257]

## (4) Policy

**21-066** Where the now claimant has himself committed a wrong, which he will have done *ex hypothesi* wherever his role in the previous proceedings has been that of unsuccessful defendant in a civil action or unsuccessful accused in a criminal prosecution, the question arises whether he is thereby debarred by the courts by reasons of policy from recovering the costs, damages or fines incurred.

**21-067** **(a) Now claimant prosecuted** Where the wrong is a crime for which the now claimant has been successfully prosecuted, the law on whether he is entitled to recover from the now defendant the costs and fines which have been extracted from

[254] But as *KBC Bank v Industrial Steels (UK) Ltd* [2001] 1 Lloyd's Rep. 370 shows, if the defendant's breach is the direct, though not the only, cause of the incurring of the costs, recovery is allowed; see at 376 to 377.

[255] (1861) 1 B. & S. 220.

[256] [2004] 2 Lloyd's Rep. 465.

[257] See [2004] 2 Lloyd's Rep. 465 at [17] and [19].

him was for long in a state of flux. The authorities do not start until the opening of the 20th century and end in 1970 with a decision which may be said finally to settle what the law is. Since then nothing has appeared; the cases have dried up. It remains therefore simply to trace the development of the law over this period and show the current position.

The authorities start with two cases, *Crage v Fry*,[258] and *Cointat v Myham*,[259] in which the now claimant was successfully prosecuted for having on his business premises food, sold to him by the defendant, which was unfit for human consumption. The offence was one which did not require proof of mens rea, in the sense that the accused knew or ought to have known of the unfit nature of the food. In both he recovered his costs of defence and the costs of the prosecution which he had been ordered to pay. However the two courts reached different results on the recovery of the fine which the now claimant had been ordered to pay. In the former, recovery was refused in the absence of evidence as to what influenced the magistrate in imposing it, although the now claimant had neither known nor had any means of discovering that the food was unfit. In the latter, recovery was allowed since the jury had found that the imposition of the fine was "not brought about wholly or in part by the claimant's own negligence".[260] **21-068**

The allowance or refusal of recovery of the fine in these two decisions turned in effect on the presence or absence of fault in the now claimant; in neither was there raised the broader point of public policy that a law which imposed a punishment, as opposed to compensation, would be defeated by the punishment being passed on to another. This point was, however, raised in *Leslie v Reliable Advertising Agency*.[261] The now claimant, a moneylender, engaged the defendants to issue circulars to the public, requiring them to take care not to send any to minors. The defendants addressed one to a minor and the claimant was convicted and fined for knowingly causing it to be sent to a person he knew to be a minor, it being provided by statute that if in such proceedings it was proved that the person to whom it was sent was a minor the person charged should be deemed to have known that fact unless he proved he had reasonable grounds for believing that the minor was of full age. The now claimant's belief was based on his instructions to the defendants to strike out all minors from the list, but the magistrate held that this was not sufficient ground for the belief. Rowlatt J held that the now claimant could not recover as damages the fines and the costs he had incurred. He based his decision on the narrower ground of the claimant's fault, but his own view was that **21-069**

> "a law which imposes a punishment as distinguished from a payment of compensation is defeated by the punishment being passed on to another. The object sought to be secured by such a statute in the public interest is not that so much money shall be collected by way of fine but that a person who puts himself in such and such a position shall be punished by way of fine in order to make such persons prevent such things happening again, and I should have thought that the statute could not have its effect if the convicted person could obtain compensation in a civil court for the punishment inflicted upon him in the criminal court."[262]

---

258 (1903) 67 J.P. 240.

259 [1913] 2 K.B. 220.

260 [1913] 2 K.B. 220 at 222. The decision was reversed on other grounds: (1914) 84 L.J.K.B 2253 CA.

261 [1915] 1 K.B. 652.

262 [1915] 1 K.B. 652 at 658 to 659. Later, at 661, he stated the principle aphoristically: "The question is not whether the conviction involves guilty knowledge but whether the fine is punitive."

In support of his view Rowlatt J was able to point to the similar opinion stated by the judges in the much earlier *Colbourn v Patmore*.[263] This was an action by a newspaper proprietor against his editor to recover damages in respect of a fine imposed on him when convicted for a libel which the editor had inserted in the paper: the action failed on a point of pleading, thus making the judges' remarks dicta. Against his view Rowlatt J had that of Kennedy J in *Burrows v Rhodes*,[264] a decision which did not involve either a claim in respect of costs, damages or fines or a conviction of the claimant, although he had committed an offence. Despite the fact that Rowlatt J thought that Kennedy J did not

> "consider the question whether criminal punishments are not by their nature incapable of being the subject of indemnity",

he was sufficiently swayed by Kennedy J's view to decide the case before him without resort to the broad ground of policy.

21-070 Later, in *Askey v Golden Wine Co*,[265] where the now claimant had been prosecuted for selling cocktails unfit for human consumption, the ingredients for them having been supplied to him by a seller whose agents had induced him to buy by fraud and conspiracy, it was held that he could not recover the fine and the costs he had had to pay. Denning J said:

> "It is, I think, a principle of our law that the punishment inflicted by a criminal court is personal to the offender, and that the civil courts will not entertain an action by the offender to recover an indemnity against the consequences of that punishment."[266]

Yet, once again, it was a case of mens rea, since Denning J found that the now claimant had been guilty of gross negligence, and indeed he diluted his general statement as to non-recovery by introducing the concept of mens rea in such terms as personal responsibility, deterrence, reformation.[267] On the other hand, in *Payne v Ministry of Food*,[268] in which the now claimant had been convicted of selling milk under a false description, the description being that under which it was sold to him by the now defendant, the recovery of both fines and costs was refused without mention of the issue of mens rea.

21-071 This was the somewhat open state of the various first instance authorities when *Osman v J. Ralph Moss*,[269] came to be decided in the Court of Appeal. There, the defendant insurance brokers having led the claimant motorist to believe he was properly insured, the claimant was prosecuted for the absolute offence of driving without an insurance policy, and both the fine imposed and the costs of entering a plea in mitigation were held recoverable because no fault could be attributed to the claimant. Sachs LJ said:

> "Having examined the authorities as to cases where the person fined was under an absolute liability, it appears that such fine can be recovered in circumstances such as the present as damages unless it is shown that there was on the part of the person fined a degree of

---

263 (1834) 1 C.M. & R. 73.

264 [1899] 1 Q.B. 816 at 831 to 832. Rowlatt J discounted *Crage v Fry* (1903) 67 J.P. 240 and *Cointat v Myham* [1913] 2 K.B. 220 because in neither was the point of policy raised.

265 [1948] 2 All E.R. 35.

266 [1948] 2 All E.R. 35 at 38.

267 [1948] 2 All E.R. 35 at 38.

268 (1953) 103 L.J. 141.

269 [1970] 1 Lloyd's Rep. 313 CA.

mens rea or of culpable negligence in the matter which resulted in the fine. The onus in cases such as the present is on the defendants, who were the true cause of the sequence of events leading to the fine, to show that there are circumstances which make that fine irrecoverable as damages by the claimant."[270]

Edmund Davies LJ accepted that "as to the recoverability of a fine in civil proceedings there are conflicting decisions",[271] but as between *Cointat v Myham*,[272] and *Leslie v Reliable Advertising Agency*,[273] he expressed a preference for the former.[274]

Thus the cases all agree that where the now claimant's conviction has involved mens rea he cannot recover as damages the fine which he has been ordered to pay. The later cases also support the view that there can be no recovery of the costs incurred where there is mens rea, neither the costs which the now claimant has been ordered to pay to the prosecution nor the costs of his own defence. Where, however, there has been no showing of mens rea in the now claimant the law was for long uncertain, but now, since *Osman*,[275] appears to be settled, at Court of Appeal level, in favour of recovery both of fines and of costs.[276] **21-072**

**(b) Now claimant sued** Where the wrong is a tort or breach of contract for which the now claimant has been successfully sued, the position is different. Here the general rule is that public policy does not stand in the way of recovery of the damages and costs incurred; indeed, as the substance of this chapter has shown, most of the cases involve unsuccessful defences of civil actions.[277] In two, possibly three, exceptional cases, however, the issue of policy makes an appearance as a potential bar to recovery. Again, these cases are of an early vintage, with some from the 19th century, and again they have dried up, with nothing in the reports for over 50 years. **21-073**

The first exception is this. Where the now claimant's tort or breach of contract for which he has been successfully sued has entailed the commission of a criminal offence for which he is not however prosecuted, his claim against the now defendant may be objected to on the ground that the damage is the consequence of his own illegal act.[278] Here the question of whether the now claimant was at fault or not may be even more relevant. Thus in *Askey v Golden Wine Co*,[279] which has already been considered in relation to the now claimant's conviction and his claim to recover the fine and costs, there was a further claim in respect of the amount that he had had **21-074**

---

270 [1970] 1 Lloyd's Rep. 313 CA at 316. See, too, Phillimore LJ who thought, since the claimant had incurred the liability through no fault, negligence or dishonesty on his part but because he was grossly misled by the defendants, that "it would … be quite wrong in such circumstances if he was not able to recover the amount of this fine as a just debt": at 320.

271 [1970] 1 Lloyd's Rep. 313 CA at 318.

272 [1913] 2 K.B. 220.

273 [1915] 1 K.B. 652.

274 [1970] 1 Lloyd's Rep. 313 CA at 318.

275 [1970] 1 Lloyd's Rep. 313 CA.

276 *Safeway Stores Ltd v Twigger* [2011] 2 All E.R. 841 CA is a rather special case considering whether a company could recover from its directors and employees a penalty, or fine, exacted from it by the Office of Fair Trading for anti-competition activities.

277 See the cases at paras 21-038 to 21-042, above. The leading authority of *Hammond v Bussey* (1888) 20 Q.B.D. 79 CA was itself such a case.

278 That this defence to a claim is different from that where the now claimant has been prosecuted and is claiming the fine and costs is made clear from Rowlatt J's judgment in *Leslie v Reliable Advertising Agency* [1915] 1 K.B. 652.

279 [1948] 2 All E.R. 35: facts at para.21-070, above.

to refund to his sub-buyers. This claim also failed, Denning J saying that

> "speaking generally, public policy requires that no right of indemnity or contribution or damages should be enforced in respect of expenses which the claimant has incurred by reason of being compelled to make reparation for his own crime."[280]

However, he clearly considered the claimant's negligence a vital factor and distinguished *Crage v Fry*,[281] on the ground that in that case there was no negligence.[282] Somewhat similar is *Marles v Philip Trant*,[283] where a buyer of wheat resold it under a contract which, though not illegal, was performed illegally by his failure to deliver to his sub-buyer certain particulars as required by statute. The sub-buyer successfully claimed damages for breach of warranty from the buyer, who in turn claimed from his own seller both the damages and costs that he had had to pay in the action against himself. The Court of Appeal allowed this latter claim despite the buyer's having committed a statutory offence, since the offence was one of mere inadvertence and also the damage did not result from the omission which constituted the offence. The accent was indeed on the latter of these two grounds.

**21-075** The second exception arises where the now claimant's wrong was not one which followed but one already in existence at the time of the now defendant's tort or breach of contract. This situation is illustrated by cases of a now defendant's breach of a contractual obligation not to disclose information which revealed that the now claimant had committed a wrong against a third party who, by the now defendant's breach, gained the information which allowed him successfully to sue the now claimant. Such cases, of which the most important is that of *Weld-Blundell v Stephens*,[284] have already been fully considered in dealing with the requirements of policy in remoteness of damage generally.[285] It is pointed out there that grounds of causation and of policy vied with each other in forming the true ratio decidendi of *Weld-Blundell v Stephens* and the reasons are given for preferring the ground of policy, which is epitomised in Lord Dunedin's words that

> "a man cannot recover damages because he has had to make reparation for a wrongful act committed by himself".[286]

**21-076** There is also a third type of case where the refusal of recovery would seem to have to be based on policy grounds but where it is difficult to see what policy grounds might be legitimately invoked. In *Walker v Hatton*,[287] it was held, settling a conflict of authority,[288] that where an underlessor was successfully sued by the

---

280 [1948] 2 All E.R. 35 at 38.

281 (1903) 67 J.P. 240.

282 [1948] 2 All E.R. 35 at 39; See *Burrows v Rhodes* [1899] 1 Q.B. 816, a case not involving costs, damages and fines, which Rowlatt J distinguished in *Leslie v Reliable Advertising Agency* [1915] 1 K.B. 652.

283 [1954] 1 Q.B. 29 CA.

284 [1920] A.C. 956. The others are *Bradstreets v Mitchell* [1933] Ch. 190 and *Howard v Odhams Press* [1938] 1 K.B. 1 CA.

285 See para.8-007, above.

286 [1920] A.C. 956 at 976. Analogous to this present exception is the formerly important *Neville v London Express Newspaper* [1919] A.C. 368, where the result was properly framed in terms of policy: see the footnote at the end of para.8-131, above.

287 (1842) 10 M. & W. 249.

288 See, e.g. *Neale v Wyllie* (1824) 3 B. & C. 533, which was overruled, the court having there allowed costs as damages, and *Penley v Watts* (1841) 7 M. & W. 601, which was followed, the court having

head lessor for damages for breach of his covenant to repair, he was not entitled to recover the costs incurred by him in defence of this action in a claim against his underlessee for a similar breach of his covenant to repair. The rationale, which was put forward by Parke B for this result,[289] is thought to lose its force with the developments on the recovery of costs as damages considered above and, although the decision was followed after these developments in *Clare v Dobson*,[290] it is submitted that these authorities should not be followed on Parke B's ground today. The matter is explained in detail later when dealing with the contract of lease of land.[291]

## 4. Amount Recoverable

Once all the hurdles presented by the issues of remoteness have been crossed so that the claimant has established his claim to recover the costs, damages and/or fines incurred in the previous proceedings, the question arises of the measure of his recovery, of how much he is entitled to as damages. This question has already been addressed in relation to the recovery of costs.[292] **21-077**

**(a) Damages and fines** Generally, with damages and fines the claimant will recover the amount thereof that he has had to pay. The same will usually apply to settlements made with third parties, subject to reasonableness.[293] The only point to be made in relation to damages is that occasionally the damages paid to the third party may not represent the amount that the now claimant is entitled to claim from the defendant. This was the position in *Dexters v Hill Crest Oil Co*,[294] where a commodity sold by the defendant to the claimant was resold by him under a more valuable description and therefore at a substantially higher price. The Court of Appeal, although deciding against the claimant on other grounds, took the view that he could not recover from his seller the damages he had had to pay his sub-buyer. This is a question of causation or contemplation of the parties. **21-078**

**(b) Costs** A much more elaborate analysis is needed where the claim is for costs as damages. Here it is again useful to treat separately cases where the now claimant has been successful and cases where he has been unsuccessful in the previous proceedings, and also, to a degree, whether he has been claimant or defendant, or accused, in the previous proceedings. **21-079**

*(i) Failure as claimant or defendant in the previous proceedings* Where the now claimant has unsuccessfully but reasonably defended an action against him, he will generally recover, as well as the damages he has been adjudged to pay the third party suing him, the assessed costs he has had to pay him and, under the old approach,[295] his own costs of defending the action formerly assessed as between solicitor and client. The costs recovered as damages are not always detailed in the cases **21-080**

---

there refused costs as damages.

289 (1842) 10 M. & W. 249 at 258; set out at para.28-083, below.

290 [1911] 1 K.B. 35.

291 At para.28-083, below.

292 See paras 21-003 and following, above.

293 Reasonableness, and its relevance, have been dealt with at para.21-054, above.

294 [1926] 1 K.B. 348 CA.

295 For which see paras 21-003 and following, above.

decided under the old regime, but this amount was clearly awarded in *Scott v Foley*,[296] in *Bennett v Kreeger*,[297] and in *The Kate*.[298] Under the new approach,[299] which is not yet set in stone and may well not survive,[300] his own costs of defending the action are to be assessed on the standard basis.[301]

**21-081** The same result is to be found, endlessly magnified, in a chain of sales where the liability is passed along the chain, generally not by separate actions but by the use of third party procedure. This appears in *Kasler & Cohen v Slavouski*,[302] in *Butterworth v Kingsway Motors*,[303] and in *Bowmaker (Commercial) v Day*.[304] In the latter two cases, third party procedure was in operation and each party received as damages the damages and assessed costs he had to pay the party next along the line, plus his costs assessed between solicitor and client of that claim.[305] In the first case, only the claim at the end of the line reached the courts, the other parties incurring small non-action costs. All these were taken into account in the final assessment. Yet these cases are in danger today, subject to attack from two different directions. They were all decided under the old approach to costs as damages and, were the new approach to prevail[306] or, alternatively, should the dubious decision in *Penn v Bristol and West Building Society*,[307] be adopted, only standard basis costs will be allowed right down the line. As argued earlier, on neither ground should this happen.[308]

**21-082** Where, conversely, the now claimant has unsuccessfully but reasonably brought a claim, he has again been held entitled to the assessed costs paid by him to the other party and, under the old approach to costs as damages, to his own costs assessed as between solicitor and client. Again this is not spelt out in all the cases; on this, *Hughes v Graeme*[309] and *Chitholie v Nash and Co*[310] are clear however. Under the new approach,[311] his own costs of bringing the action are to be assessed on the standard basis.[312]

---

296 (1899) 15 T.L.R. 55.

297 (1925) 41 T.L.R. 609.

298 [1935] P. 100; and where the claimant compromised the suit, he recovered this amount and his own costs as between solicitor and client: *Smith v Compton* (1832) 3 B. & Ad. 407.

299 For which see paras 21-003 and following, above.

300 See para.21-011, above.

301 To achieve this the court will itself have to make an assessment—or order an assessment, which means further proceedings—of the costs of the prior action so as to arrive at a figure for standard basis costs that the claimant may claim as damages from the defendant. The wisdom of such complications may be doubted. It is not known if any court has yet dealt with such a case; the nearest the courts have come to it appears to have been in cases which have settled or been compromised with the parties paying their own costs: see Carnwarth J, the author of the new approach, in *British Racing Drivers' Club* and Ferris J, following Carnwarth J, in *Yudt* (these cases are at para.21-005, above) who both directed an enquiry to determine what the costs would have been on the standard basis in the earlier proceedings.

302 [1928] 1 K.B. 78.

303 [1954] 1 W.L.R. 1286.

304 [1965] 1 W.L.R. 1396.

305 Worked out in detail by Pearson J in *Butterworth v Kingsway Motors* [1954] 1 W.L.R. 1286 at 1297–1300.

306 For the two different approaches see paras 21-003 and following, above

307 [1997] 1 W.L.R. 1356 CA.

308 See paras 21-008 and following, and para.21-036, respectively, above.

309 (1864) 33 L.J.Q.B. 335.

310 (1974) 229 E.G. 786.

311 For the old and the new approaches see paras 21-003 and following, above.

312 To achieve this the court will itself have to make an assessment—or order an assessment, which

The position is, however, more complex where the unsuccessful claimant or defendant has been legally aided in the previous proceedings—today an ever diminishing possibility—so that it is unlikely that the costs awarded against him will be paid over either by him or by the Legal Aid Agency[313] on his behalf. This is because the costs order is not to be enforced without an order of the court and a court will not make an order in the absence of a significant change in the legally aided person's circumstances, which in effect requires that he has come into money. There would therefore seem to be little point in requiring the now defendant to pay over these costs as damages. This situation arose in *Browning v Brachers*.[314] A legally aided action by buyers against their seller for breach of warranty was dismissed, with costs ordered against them, on account of the negligent handling of the litigation by their solicitor. In their subsequent claim against the solicitor it was argued for the solicitor that, four years having passed since the costs order had been made with presumably no major change in the buyers' financial circumstances, there was little chance that the costs would be pursued. Rather than making an award which reflected this chance, Jack J rightly preferred the course of ordering the solicitor to indemnify the buyers should they be required to pay their seller the costs.[315] What however may not have been appreciated by the court is that, in the wake of the buyers' recovery of substantial damages from the solicitor, the costs order could certainly be enforced. This follows from the decision of the Court of Appeal in the context of a solicitor's negligence claim in *Wraith v Wraith*,[316] where the Court of Appeal held that the improvement in the legally aided person's financial circumstances, which would allow for enforcement of the order, could be as a result not of winning the football pools—the standard illustration of financial amelioration justifying enforcement—but of winning damages in litigation, even if it were in litigation connected with—indeed here arising out of—the litigation in which the order for costs had been made.[317] **21-083**

*(ii) Failure as accused in the previous proceedings* Where the now claimant has unsuccessfully defended a prosecution, he has been held entitled to his costs of defence, as in *Crage v Fry*,[318] and *Cointat v Myham*[319]: this probably included the costs ordered to be paid to the prosecution, but it is not clear from any of the reports. In *Osman v J. Ralph Moss*,[320] where the now claimant had been prosecuted both for careless driving and for driving without insurance, only the costs of that part of the **21-084**

---

means further proceedings—of the costs of the prior action so as to arrive at a figure for standard basis costs that the claimant may claim as damages from the defendant. The wisdom of such complications may be doubted. It is not known if any court has yet dealt with such a case; the nearest the courts have come to it appears to have been in cases which have settled or been compromised with the parties paying their own costs: see Carnwarth J, the author of the new approach, in *British Racing Drivers' Club* and Ferris J, following Carnwarth J, in *Yudt* (these cases are at para.21-005, above) who both directed an enquiry to determine what the costs would have been on the standard basis in the earlier proceedings.

313 Replacing the Legal Services Commission, which ceased to exist on 4 March 2013.

314 [2004] P.N.L.R. 28 at 517. Full facts at para.10-096, above.

315 See [2004] P.N.L.R. 28 at [94], [95] and [98]. On the appeal, [2005] EWCA Civ 753 CA, this part of the award was not challenged: see at [149].

316 [1997] 1 W.L.R. 1540 CA.

317 [1997] 1 W.L.R. 1540 CA at 1545H to 1546D.

318 (1903) 67 J.P. 240.

319 [1913] 2 K.B. 220.

320 [1970] 1 Lloyd's Rep. 313 CA.

defence attributable to the now defendant's wrong, namely causing the claimant to drive without insurance, were held recoverable. The new thinking, if adopted, that only standard basis costs are to be allowed[321] should have no application to a criminal prosecution in the light of the decision, in a slightly different context, of *Berry v British Transport Commission*.[322]

21-085 *(iii) Failure cases: costs where there is an appeal in the previous proceedings* In the above types of case, any of the costs involved in an unsuccessful appeal in the prior proceedings by the now claimant after his failure at first instance will generally not be recoverable because they will not be held to have been reasonably incurred, and thus the now defendant should not be liable for them. Thus costs of the first hearing only and no appeal costs were allowed in *Vogan v Oulton*,[323] and also in *G.W. Ry v Fisher*.[324] In *Vogan v Oulton*,[325] Wright J said he knew of no such case allowing appeal costs, and

> "it would be going a long way when a man has had a decision against him on a matter which is largely a question of fact, if not altogether a question of fact, to allow those to be recovered".[326]

However, in one exceptional case, *Sutton v Baillie*,[327] it was held reasonable to appeal, since there had been a difference of opinion among the judges below,[328] and the costs of the unsuccessful appeal against the third party were allowed as damages against the now defendant. A further possibility, on which there is no authority, is that the now claimant may have succeeded at first instance in the prior proceedings and then lost on an appeal brought against him. Such appeal costs ought prima facie to be recoverable, since the appeal was not at the instigation of the now claimant and in view of his success below it could hardly but be reasonable for him to contest the appeal.

21-086 *(iv) Success as claimant or defendant in the previous proceedings* In the sparser cases of a now claimant who was successful in the prior proceedings, the amount of costs recoverable as damages will naturally be different. Where the now claimant has successfully brought or successfully defended an action, the amount recoverable under the old approach to costs as damages[329] consisted of his costs assessed as between solicitor and client less the assessed costs which will generally be recovered by him from the other party to the prior litigation. This amount was given in *The Solway Prince*,[330] where the claimant had successfully sued and in *Agius v Great Western Colliery*,[331] where the claimant had successfully defended.

---

321 See paras 21-005 and following, above.
322 [1962] 1 Q.B. 306 CA. at para.21-018, above.
323 (1898) 79 L.T. 384; affirmed (1899) 81 L.T. 435 CA, but only on the question of whether the costs of the action at first instance were recoverable.
324 [1905] 1 Ch. 316.
325 (1898) 79 L.T. 384.
326 (1898) 79 L.T. 384 at 385.
327 (1892) 65 L.T. 528.
328 The matter had been adjudicated upon by two judges of first instance in two separate actions.
329 See paras 21-003 and following, above.
330 (1914) 31 T.L.R. 56.
331 [1899] 1 Q.B. 413 CA.

Under the new approach[332] he will have no claim since all he is entitled to by way of damages are standard basis costs and these will have been paid to him by the other party to the previous proceedings.

Where, however, payment by the other party or on his behalf of the costs ordered against him is not forthcoming, they are recoverable from the now defendant. This was decided some time ago in *Britannia Hygienic Laundry Co v Thornycroft*[333] at first instance.[334] Three sets of costs had been awarded to the now claimant by the Court of Appeal in the prior action[335] but they had not been paid by the other party[336] because he was a man of straw. It was held that the claimant could recover his full costs as between solicitor and client without any deduction in respect of the costs awarded but practicably irrecoverable. The same situation can arise if the other party in the previous proceedings is legally aided—today an ever diminishing possibility—where the general position is that the legally aided person cannot, and the now Legal Services Commission will not, pay the costs awarded against him. In these circumstances the Court of Appeal awarded the unrecovered costs as damages in *Grocutt v Khan*,[337] a somewhat unusual and complex case. The claimant and the defendant doctors, when hiring a car together for an outing for themselves and their companions in the course of a medical conference abroad, agreed that the defendant would take out a comprehensive insurance policy for them against accident. An accident occurred when the claimant was driving and the defendant's mother, who was injured, brought a legally aided action for damages against the claimant which was dismissed with costs awarded to him. Unable to recover these costs from the mother or the Legal Services Commission[338] or from the insurance company because the defendant had lost the policy, he claimed them from the defendant as damages for breach of contract and succeeded. Lord Phillips MR said that all that was at stake was the claimant's unrecovered costs in the earlier action and, while he found the facts unusual raising interesting questions of legal analysis, he was in no doubt as to the result though he thought the precise route to it somewhat uncertain.[339] There was no suggestion that the new approach to costs as damages,[340] which was unmentioned, should apply so as to limit the doctor's recovery to the costs ordered, which would have been standard basis costs, but then this was a special case in that the insurance company, absent the loss of the policy, would have underwritten the doctor's full costs. **21-087**

*(v) Success as accused in the previous proceedings* Where the now claimant has successfully defended a prosecution he will generally recover as damages the full costs of the defence, as in *Proops v Chaplin*[341]: the question of deducting costs which will have been paid by the other side will arise only where the court can, and does, order the prosecutor to contribute towards the defence costs. Moreover, no further deduction from the full costs of the defence is appropriate since the new **21-088**

---

332 See paras 21-005 and following, above.
333 (1925) 41 T.L.R. 667.
334 The decision was reversed on the facts: (1925) 95 L.J.K.B. 237 CA.
335 For the details of this see the case at para.21-089, below.
336 Except as to £30 security.
337 [2003] Lloyd's Rep. I.R. 464 CA.
338 Which ceased to exist on 4 March 2013, being replaced by the Legal Aid Agency.
339 [2003] Lloyd's Rep. I.R. 464 CA at [1].
340 See paras 21-005 and following, above.
341 (1920) 37 T.L.R. 112.

thinking, if adopted, that only standard basis costs are to be allowed in civil suits[342] should have no application to criminal prosecutions in the light of the analogous decision of *Berry v British Transport Commission*.[343]

21-089 *(vi) Success cases: costs where there is an appeal in the previous proceedings* In *Britannia Hygienic Laundry Co v Thornycroft*,[344] the claimant had incurred three sets of costs as there had been a double appeal and it was held that all were recoverable as "the probable and even direct consequence"[345] of the now defendant's breach of contract. On the particular facts the now claimant had failed at first instance but had been upheld both in the Divisional Court and in the Court of Appeal. It would not seem to matter, however, which party won in any of the lower courts; the only important question is that the now claimant should have won in the final court to which the original action was taken.

342 See paras 21-005 and following, above.

343 [1962] 1 Q.B. 306 CA at para.21-018, above.

344 (1925) 41 T.L.R. 667.

345 (1925) 41 T.L.R. 667 at 668; see the case further at para.21-087, above.

CHAPTER 22

# BREACH OF UNDERTAKINGS AS TO DAMAGES

TABLE OF CONTENTS



## 1. THE ISSUE

Suppose that in pre-trial, interlocutory proceedings a claimant or a defendant is restrained from acting in a particular way or compelled to act in a particular way. The price which the restraining party usually has to pay for the restraint is to give an undertaking as to damages. The common form of such an undertaking is as follows: **22-001**

"If the court later finds that this order has caused loss to the respondent, and decides that the respondent should be compensated for that loss, the applicants will comply with any order the court may make".

The undertaking as to damages can be extremely significant. In some instances, such as freezing orders, a restraint upon a party using his or her funds can lead to losses which vastly exceed the amount involved in the restraint. As we will see, those amounts are recoverable in a similar way as they would be if the losses from the restraint flowed from a breach of contract. In one respect this analogy is apt. The undertaking is a promise, given to the court but for the benefit of the restrained party. The promise is one, however, which amounts to a contempt of court if not honoured.

## 2. THE GIVING OF AN UNDERTAKING AND WHETHER IT WILL BE ENFORCED

An undertaking cannot be compelled by the Court. It is voluntarily offered by a party seeking a restraint. In *Hoffmann-La Roche & Co AG v Secretary of State for Trade and Industry*,[1] Lord Diplock explained that all the court has a power to do is to refuse an application for an injunction or freezing order if a party declines to give an undertaking. Lord Diplock continued: **22-002**

"Non-performance of it is contempt of court, not breach of contract, and attracts the remedies available for contempts, but the court exacts the undertaking for the defendant's benefit. It retains a discretion not to enforce the undertaking if it considers that the conduct

[1] [1975] A.C. 295, 361.

of the defendant in relation to the obtaining or continuing of the injunction or the enforcement of the undertaking makes it inequitable to do so, but if the undertaking is enforced the measure of the damages payable under it is not discretionary. It is assessed on an inquiry into damages at which principles to be applied are fixed and clear. The assessment is made upon the same basis as that upon which damages for breach of contract would be assessed if the undertaking had been a contract between the plaintiff and the defendant that the plaintiff would *not* prevent the defendant from doing that which he was restrained from doing by the terms of the injunction."

**22-003** The question whether a court will exercise its discretion to enforce an undertaking as to damages is not the central concern of a work such as this, which focuses upon the rules concerning damages rather than the liability to pay them. The general rule is that prima facie a person who has suffered loss as a result of an interim order being wrongly made against him is entitled to be compensated for his loss. It has even been said that this is "virtually as of right".[2] However, there are circumstances in which discretion will not be exercised to order an inquiry as to damages. The most common include delay in seeking the inquiry or a trifling amount of damage.[3] Others, which we have seen in the quotation from Lord Diplock above, include the conduct of the defendant in relation to the obtaining or continuing of the injunction or the enforcement of the undertaking.

## 3. THE ASSESSMENT OF DAMAGES UPON AN ENFORCED UNDERTAKING

**22-004** The most comprehensive consideration of this issue came in *Fiona Trust and Holding Corporation v Privalov*.[4] The claimants brought claims against Mr Nikitin and his companies for in excess of US $577 million. At the outset of the litigation, the claimants obtained a freezing order in respect of assets up to the value of $225 million. The freezing order was discharged shortly afterwards but two years later, the claimants obtained a further freezing order for assets worth US $377 million, with the claimants giving the usual undertakings as to damages. Mr Nikitin and his companies were ultimately held liable for only US $16 million plus interest. The primary judge ordered an inquiry as to the damages suffered by the defendants as a result of the freezing orders. The ultimate result of the inquiry was an award of damages based on the undertaking of $59.8 million.[5] The inquiry was made by Males J who started from the proposition that if the discretion to enforce the undertaking was to be exercised then the defendants are entitled to recover damages for the losses suffered by them as a result of the freezing orders assessed by reference to ordinary contractual principles, including principles of causation, mitigation and remoteness.[6] However, Males J recognised that the analogy with breach of contract was not exact. The undertaking is given to the Court although it remains a promise for the benefit of the other party. Further, since the assessment of damages suffered as a result of a freezing order is often "inherently imprecise"[7] a "liberal assessment" of the defendants' damages should be adopted. The expres-

2 *Lunn Poly Ltd v Liverpool & Lancashire Properties Ltd* [2006] EWCA Civ 430 at [42], per Neuberger LJ; *Fiona Trust and Holding Corporation v Privalov* [2014] EWHC 3102 (Comm) at [12], per Andrew Smith J.

3 *Smith v Day* (1882) 21 Ch. D. 421 CA.

4 [2016] EWHC 2163 (Comm).

5 *Fiona Trust & Holding Corporation v Privalov* [2016] EWHC 2451 (Comm).

6 [2016] EWHC 2163 (Comm) at [47].

7 [2016] EWHC 2163 (Comm) at [51].

sion "liberal assessment" is probably best avoided because it carries the false implication that the imprecision of facts permits the application of principles which are more generous than they would be in relation to any other enforced promise. The expression derives from Lord Wilberforce in a patent infringement case where he spoke of a liberal assessment of damages against defendants to an infringement of patent suit because they were wrongdoers.[8] Several points should be made about the calculation principles in *Fiona Trust*.

**Loss of a chance** The difficulty in calculation in *Fiona Trust* was that it was not obviously clear whether the defendants would have realised a profit by investing the assets that were the subject of the freezing order: there was a boom in the shipping market from 2005 to mid-2008, followed by a crash of unprecedented severity. This is not a difficulty unique to cases involving calculation of damages which flow from an undertaking. The same issue often arises in loss of chance cases. As Males J recognised, referring to the recovery in some cases of profits quantified on the basis of a lost chance: **22-005**

> "The true position is that in principle damages can be awarded for loss of profits even if a claimant might have made a loss. The approach which the court will adopt is to ask whether the claimant has proved to a sufficient standard (which may be the balance of probabilities, or sometimes merely that there was a real and substantial chance as in loss of a chance cases) that its trading would have been profitable. If so, the court will make the best assessment of the damages that it can, applying if necessary a discount to reflect whatever uncertainty exists, while recognising that a party seeking to show what might have happened is not required to perform an impossible task with unrealistic precision."[9]

The only matter in this paragraph of Males J's decision which one might doubt is the suggestion that there are competing standards of balance of probabilities and real and substantial chance. More accurately, there is a single standard of balance of probabilities but a claimant is entitled to a quantified loss of chance by proving, to that standard, that there was a real and substantial chance which was lost.

**Causation and remoteness** As to these issues, the same principles apply as for a breach of contract. Those principles were summarised by Males J thus: the freezing order need not be the sole or exclusive cause of the loss in question, but must be an effective cause; the burden is on the party who obtained the freezing order to demonstrate a failure to mitigate; and the type of loss (but not the particular loss within that type) must be within the reasonable contemplation of the parties.[10] All of these propositions have been considered in detail in other chapters in this book. However, it is necessary to reiterate the unfortunate suggestion, not confined to this case, that a cause need not be the "sole or exclusive cause of the loss in question". In a but-for sense, there is almost no cause in life, perhaps save for God for those who believe, which is the sole or exclusive cause of anything else. In relation to mitigation, the context of the undertaking is important. As Males J explained,[11] the potentially catastrophic effect of the "nuclear weapon" of a freezing order is such that courts will take a realistic approach to a submission that a defendant should **22-006**

8 *General Tire & Rubber Co Ltd v Firestone Tyre & Rubber Co Ltd* [1975] 1 W.L.R. 819 at 824.
9 *Parabola Investments Ltd v Browallia Cal Ltd* [2011] Q.B. 477. See paras 10-037 and 10-047, above.
10 [2016] EWHC 2163 (Comm) at [48].
11 [2016] EWHC 2163 (Comm) at [48].

have approached the claimant or made an application to the court for a variation of the freezing order. This nuclear weapon having been deployed, it may suggest that the claimant might not have a reasonable response, and in any event an application for a variation is often "far from straightforward".[12]

## 4. EXEMPLARY DAMAGES

**22-007** One difference between the assessment of damages upon the undertaking and assessment of damages for breach of contract is that there is authority which suggests that if the Court concludes that the injunction had been obtained fraudulently or maliciously, the Court might award exemplary damages. This observation was made obiter dicta by Brett LJ who drew an analogy with the case of fraudulent or malicious breach of contract for which he considered that exemplary damages were available.[13] The authority is weakened by the current state of authority that exemplary damages are not available for such a breach of contract. Nevertheless, the breach of an undertaking given for an interlocutory injunction which is obtained fraudulently or maliciously is quite different from a breach of a contractual obligation. The breach of the undertaking is a breach of a duty to the Court, punishable by contempt. Where the undertaking was given in circumstances of fraud or malice, it is suggested that this is entirely a suitable vehicle for the deterrent order of exemplary damages subject to existing constraints on exemplary damages considered in Chapter 13.

12 [2016] EWHC 2163 (Comm) at [48], quoting *Hone v Abbey Forwarding Ltd* [2014] EWCA Civ 711 at [65].

13 *Smith v Day* (1882) 21 Ch. D. 421 at 427.

CHAPTER 23

# DAMAGES IN ACTIONS SURVIVING DEATH

TABLE OF CONTENTS



## 1. DAMAGES IN ACTIONS SURVIVING DEATH

At common law the basic maxim was *actio personalis moritur cum persona*, which operated to bar the survival of actions either against the deceased's estate or for the benefit of the deceased's estate. Actions founded upon contract formed a general exception to the rule, actions based upon torts by which the deceased had enriched his estate at another's expense could be pursued against the deceased's estate, and the operation of the maxim was further limited by various statutes.[1] The operation of the rule or maxim left much to be desired: it was unduly constricting, particularly in preventing a living claimant from obtaining compensation merely because a defendant had died, however large his estate, and in preventing the estate of a deceased potential claimant from recovering compensation from a defendant for what represented a pecuniary loss to that deceased and therefore a loss to his estate. **23-001**

The maxim has, however, all but totally ceased to have effect since 1934, and the modern law is contained in s.1 of the Law Reform (Miscellaneous Provisions) Act of that year, somewhat amended since, as we shall see. It is enacted by s.1(1), which subsection apart from its proviso remains unchanged to the present day, that **23-002**

> "on the death of any person after the commencement of this Act all causes of action subsisting against or vested in him shall survive against, or, as the case may be, for the benefit of, his estate."

Then one cause of action is excluded from the operation of the subsection, namely defamation; this is by virtue of the proviso to s.1(1), or, more precisely, by virtue of that part of the proviso as has not since been repealed.[2] The rationale of the exclu-

---

[1] The details are all now past history.

[2] The proviso to the original s.1(1) also excluded three further causes of action, namely seduction, inducement of one spouse to leave or remain apart from the other and claims for damages on the ground of adultery. Since these causes of action have all been abolished (Law Reform (Miscellaneous Provisions) Act 1970 ss.4 and 5; Administration of Justice Act 1982 s.2), the references to them in the proviso have become otiose and have accordingly been removed (Law Reform (Miscellaneous Provisions) Act 1970 s.7(2) and Sch. thereto; Administration of Justice Act 1982 s.75(1) and Sch.9). The statutory claim for damages for bereavement, introduced in 1982, does not survive for the benefit of the estate: see para.23-011, below.

sion of defamation appears to be that this tort primarily involves non-pecuniary loss to the person wronged and there is no good reason why the deceased's estate should recover for non-pecuniary loss to the deceased.[3] But, conversely, there is no good reason why the living victim of the tort should not be able to claim against the tortfeasor's estate in this action, and the legislature, it is submitted, has drawn its exception too wide. The law, however, is clear.[4]

## 2. Measure of Damages in Such Actions

23-003 Generally speaking, the measure of damages will be the same as where the action has been pursued between the two parties when alive. All that calls for discussion are the few differences arising from the fact that the action is now being brought by the estate or against the estate of a deceased party.

### (1) Actions against the estate: death of the wrongdoer

23-004 Since the aim of an award of damages is to compensate the person wronged there is no reason why the measure of damages should be in any way affected or limited by the death of the wrongdoer, and s.1 of the 1934 Act introduces no limitations on the measure to be awarded in actions against the estate. The only type of damages which might have been reasonably excluded is exemplary damages, in so far as these represent an anomalous form of punishment of a wilful wrongdoer; it might have been thought unnecessary and improper to visit the sins of such a person upon his estate. But that the legislature did not intend to exclude such damages appears impliedly from the express exclusion of exemplary damages only in actions brought for the benefit of the estate.[5] Moreover, while the incidence of exemplary damages has become much restricted as a result of the decision in *Rookes v Barnard*,[6] to the extent that exemplary damages are now used as an indirect means of disgorging the profits from a wrongdoer[7] it is certainly appropriate that they should not be excluded by reason of the wrongdoer's death.

23-005 One limitation there is of course: the estate is only liable to the extent of the assets. But then this practical limitation exists equally in an action against a wrongdoer who is still alive.[8]

### (2) Actions for the benefit of the estate: death of the person wronged

23-006 Compensation and not penalty being the gist of compensatory damages, it is not so compelling that an action for the benefit of the estate should lie for all damage suffered by the deceased personally. If the estate has suffered loss by reason of the

---

3 But it can involve pecuniary loss: see paras 46-005 and 46-038, below.

4 In 1991 after consultation (*Defamation: Death of a Party to Defamation Proceedings* (1990)) no change in the law was recommended by the Lord Chancellor's Department.

5 See s.1(2)(a); since 1982, s.1(2)(a)(i). See para.23-009, below. But see para.13-029, above.

6 [1964] A.C. 1129. See Ch.13, above.

7 See para 13-048 and 13-050, above.

8 In certain cases the executor is not only liable in his representative capacity, a liability to the extent of the assets, but is liable personally. In such a case he is in the position of an ordinary defendant and is fully liable to the extent of his own personal assets. The circumstances in which an executor can be sued personally, and not merely qua executor, do not properly fall for discussion here.

loss to the deceased being pecuniary, an action to recover such loss is proper,[9] but if the loss is non-pecuniary, as it may be, for instance, in torts involving injury to reputation or to the person, the recovery of such a loss by the estate is more dubious. It is not surprising, therefore, that s.1 of the 1934 Act imposes certain limitations on recovery by the estate. These limitations have, as will be seen, a somewhat erratic impact, and it is thought that the law would be both simplified and improved if the Act of 1934 were amended so as to allow all actions to survive for the benefit of the deceased's estate but at the same time to limit the estate's recovery in all cases to accrued items of a pecuniary nature, non-pecuniary losses of the deceased being personal to him and having no proper entitlement to a place in the assessment of damages which come to his estate. The reference to accrued items keeps out prospective earnings of the victim of a fatal accident,[10] and the reference to items of a pecuniary nature, rather than to pecuniary losses, is designed to allow the estate to claim, under the guise of an award of exemplary damages, in respect of profits made by the defendant through intentionally wrongful conduct which was calculated by him to make such profits.[11]

**(a) Contract** Contract has not presented much of a problem since recovery for breach of contract has been almost invariably for pecuniary loss only. A long-standing exception appears where the breach of contract results in physical injury or death to the contracting party.[12] The heads of damage are the same as where physical injury or death is caused by a tort, and indeed there will practically always be a concurrence of contract and tort actions in such circumstances: the matter is therefore better considered under tort. However, a pattern of limited recovery in contract for mental distress has developed, a development rooted in the early 1970s, and, though the matter has not so far been in issue, it is difficult to see how a court could resist a claim by the estate for such damages where they might properly have been awarded to the deceased himself had he lived.[13] **23-007**

**(b) Tort** Tort frequently involves a non-pecuniary loss, and even damages beyond any loss, pecuniary or non-pecuniary, suffered by the victim of the tort are recoverable in certain limited circumstances as exemplary damages.[14] **23-008**

*(i) Exemplary damages* The 1934 Act provides that the damages in an action for the benefit of the estate "shall not include any exemplary damages".[15] Yet in one **23-009**

---

9 Where in *Fox v British Airways Plc* [2013] EWCA Civ 972 CA an employee claiming for discrimination and unfair dismissal died before suit, his estate was held entitled to claim for his loss of death-in-service benefit. This was a loss that he had suffered personally and therefore was a loss that had accrued to him before he died.

10 See para.23-011, below.

11 See para.23-009, below.

12 Another long-standing exception to the basic pecuniary flavour of contract damages appeared in the anomalous breach of promise of marriage where damages for non-pecuniary loss and even exemplary damages were recoverable (see Ch.30 of the 12th edition (1961) of this work), and the 1934 Act, by s.1(2)(b), expressly excluded such damages in actions by the estate. However, no action now lies for breach of promise of marriage and s.1(2)(b) has accordingly been repealed: Law Reform (Miscellaneous Provisions) Act 1970 ss.1, 7(2) and Sch.

13 See paras 5-023 and following, above. And the same would be true of the occasional recovery in contract for physical inconvenience and discomfort: see paras 5-017 to 5-019, above.

14 See Ch.13, above.

15 See s.1(2)(a); since 1982, s.1(2)(a)(i).

sense these are the only damages beyond pecuniary loss that could properly be allowed, as being for punishment and not for compensation; at least it would be more appropriate to exclude damages intended for punishment from actions against the estate, which the Act does not do.[16] However, since the strength of the exemplary principle has been largely sapped after the decision in *Rookes v Barnard*,[17] the statutory exclusion is in line with the new thinking; indeed Lord Devlin in that case, in stating various considerations to be borne in mind wherever exemplary damages are in issue, gave as one of them that exemplary damages cannot be recovered by a claimant unless he is the victim of the punishable behaviour.[18] At the same time, to the extent that exemplary damages are now used as an indirect means of preventing the unjust enrichment of a wrongdoer,[19] the statutory exclusion of exemplary damages in actions by the estate ought to be reconsidered.

**23-010** *(ii) Torts affecting dignitary interests* The Act takes a bold approach towards a particular tort which generally involves substantial recoveries for non-pecuniary loss: defamation is eliminated completely from its operation. As has been indicated,[20] this would seem to go too far in throwing out the baby of pecuniary loss with the bathwater of non-pecuniary loss. The Act, on the other hand, is silent in relation to all other torts which are primarily for the protection of dignitary rather than proprietary or economic interests, such as false imprisonment, malicious prosecution and the like, and presumably damages for non-pecuniary as well as pecuniary loss may be recovered by the estate in any of these torts. This would therefore seem not to go far enough. Put shortly, the Act makes the mistake of concentrating on the types of tort rather than on the heads of damage.[21]

**23-011** *(iii) Torts causing death* The Act then provides, in relation to the specific and all-important case of torts causing personal injury which has proved fatal, that the damages

> "shall be calculated without reference to any loss or gain to his estate consequent on his death".[22]

This oddly phrased provision appears to have been intended only to exclude the kind of damages which the deceased could not himself have recovered had he not died. Lord Wright so explained the statutory provision in *Rose v Ford*,[23] giving the accrual of insurance moneys on the death as an obvious example of such a gain and the cessation of an annuity on the death as an obvious example of such a loss,[24] but his latter instance was not approved of in *Gammell v Wilson*,[25] where the alternatives of the cost of obtaining a grant of probate or administration and a liability to

---

16 See para.21-004, above. But see para.13-029, above.
17 [1964] A.C. 1129; see Ch.13, above.
18 [1964] A.C. 1129 at 1227.
19 See para.13-048, above.
20 See para.23-002, above.
21 See Street, *Principles of the Law of Damages* (1962), p.143: "the fundamental error is in basing distinction on causes of action rather than on heads of damages".
22 See s.1(2)(c); "except that a sum in respect of funeral expenses may be included".
23 [1937] A.C. 826.
24 [1937] A.C. 826 at 842.
25 [1982] A.C. 27.

capital transfer tax were preferred.[26] The view, originally propounded in 1936 by MacKinnon J in *Slater v Spreag*,[27] that the provision of s.1(2)(c) has the effect of excluding the recovery of the prospective earnings that the deceased could have recovered had he lived, was eventually shown to be wrong in 1981 in *Gammell v Wilson*.[28] This revelation was so long delayed because the issue had been dormant while it was thought, until the 1961 decision in *Oliver v Ashman*,[29] was overruled in *Pickett v British Rail Engineering*,[30] in 1978, that the deceased, had he lived, could not have claimed prospective earnings[31]; clearly if he could not do so, his estate could not either. However, the very large awards to the estate to which the unfortunate, but after *Pickett* inevitable, decision in *Gammell* inexorably led, brought about a further legislative intervention, and s.4 of the Administration of Justice Act 1982 amended s.1(2) of the 1934 Act so that it now provides, by a new sub-subsection (a)(ii) that damages in an action for the benefit of the estate

> "shall not include any damages for loss of income in respect of any period after that person's death".[32]

In addition s.1 of the Administration of Justice Act 1982 eliminates any right of the estate to claim damages for the non-pecuniary loss of expectation of life,[33] so that the estate may now claim, apart from the entirely proper accrued losses of the deceased by way of lost earnings and medical expenses before death, only for his pain and suffering, generally minimal or even non-existent in a fatal injury, and for his loss of amenities of life which may loom quite large as the courts have given an objective quality to this head of damage.[34] As for the new limited right to claim non-pecuniary loss by way of bereavement in the dependants', as opposed to the survival, claim arising out of a tortiously inflicted death,[35] the legislature has sensibly seen to it that this right is not to survive for the benefit of the claimant's estate upon his or her death.[36]

---

26 [1982] A.C. 27 (CA and HL).
27 [1936] 1 K.B. 83 at 87–88.
28 [1982] A.C. 27.
29 [1962] 2 Q.B. 210 CA.
30 [1980] A.C. 136.
31 See para.40-109, below.
32 See para.41-126 below.
33 See paras 40-263 and 41-133, below.
34 See especially *Andrews v Freeborough* [1967] 1 Q.B. 1 and *Murray v Shuter* [1976] Q.B. 972 CA, at para.41-134, below.
35 See para.41-019, below.
36 Law Reform (Miscellaneous Provisions) Act 1934 s.1(1A), inserted by the Administration of Justice Act 1982 s.4(1).

# PART 4 PARTICULAR CONTRACTS AND TORTS

Chapter 24

## THE MEASURE OF DAMAGES IN CONTRACT AND TORT COMPARED

**24-001** Is the measure of damages in contract and tort the same? This is a question frequently posed. Sometimes it is said that it is, sometimes that it is not. Before any clear answer can be found it is necessary to break down this omnibus question, for the term "measure of damages" may refer to a number of things.

**24-002** The clearest and undoubted distinctions between contract and tort lie in the exceptional cases where damages are not given strictly on the principle of awarding compensation.[1] On the one hand, since liquidated damages can only result from agreement,[2] they apply to contract and cannot in the nature of things refer to tort. On the other hand, exemplary damages, though now explicitly confined to three categories of case, continue to be awarded only in tort and have not yet spread to contract,[3] although they may well do so.[4] Similarly, restitutionary and disgorgement damages have long existed in tort though their presence has been heavily disguised, and are now being specifically heralded as available in contract[5] but to a more limited degree.[6] To the extent that vindicatory damages have not yet been abolished, for protection of reputation or interference with privacy their availability is confined to tort.[7] Nominal damages have application to all contracts but only to some torts.[8]

**24-003** Turning to the case of compensatory damages, which is much more important because it represents the norm, there is at the very start a basic, though somewhat latent, distinction between contract and tort. This distinction is in the general rule which is the starting point for resolving all problems as to measure of damages. The distinction is latent because the leading formulation of the general rule is sufficiently wide to cover contract and tort equally: this formulation is that the claimant is entitled to be put into the same position, as far as money can do it, as he would have been in had the wrong not been committed.[9] In contract, however, the wrong

---

1 See Chs 12 to 17, above.

2 See Ch.16, above. Liquidated damages apart, a contracting party may attempt to limit his liability to particular heads of loss, as in *Bem Dis A Turk Ticaret v International Agri Trade Co, The Selda* [1999] 1 Lloyd's Rep. 729 CA (see footnote at the end para.16-103, above). This too can happen only in contract and not in tort.

3 See Ch.13, above.

4 Having already appeared in Canada: *Royal Bank of Canada v Got* 178 D.L.R. (4th) 385 (2000). See para.13-016, above.

5 See Chs 14 and 15, above.

6 See paras 14-034 and 15-023, above.

7 See Ch.17, above.

8 See Ch.12, above.

9 The most widely accepted statement is that of Lord Blackburn in *Livingstone v Rawyards Coal Co*

consists not in the making but in the breaking of the contract and therefore the claimant is entitled to be put into the position he would have been in if the contract had never been broken or, in other words, if the contract had been performed.[10] The claimant is entitled to recover damages for the loss of his bargain. In tort, on the other hand, no question of loss of bargain can arise: the claimant is not complaining of failure to implement a promise but of failure to leave him alone. The measure of damages in tort is therefore to be assessed on the basis of restoring as far as possible the status quo ante. This distinction does not stand out in the great majority of cases since contract and tort have such widely different areas of application, but in cases involving misrepresentations there is an overlap of contract and tort which is instructive in this connection. Where the claimant has been induced to enter into a contract by a misrepresentation of fact on the defendant's part, then if the representation constitutes a term of the contract, whether condition or warranty, he can sue for breach of contract and, in claiming for loss of his bargain, is entitled to such damages as will put him into the position he would have been in had the misrepresentation been true. If, however, the representation does not constitute a term of the contract, then, although the claimant may be entitled to rescind on the ground of misrepresentation, there is no breach of contract for which he can get damages, and his only common law action for damages can be in tort, in deceit if the misrepresentation has been fraudulently made, in negligence where it has been carelessly made.[11] It is sometimes assumed that if the claimant can show fraud he is in as good a position as far as damages are concerned as if he had been able to sue for breach of contract on the ground that the representation was a term of the contract.[12] This is fallacious, for the proper measure of damages in deceit—a measure adopted in the late 19th century and now firmly established by the Court of Appeal in *Doyle v Olby (Ironmongers)*[13]—is to put the claimant in the position he would have been in, not if the representation had been true, but if the representation had never been made. This is a more restrictive rule: the action in tort does not take into account the loss of a bargain. Conversely, cases of breach of warranty of authority are sometimes regarded as, in effect, giving damages for innocent misrepresentation. That this is not the proper view is shown by the fact that it has been consistently decided in the cases, of which *Re National Coffee Palace Co Ex p. Panmure*,[14] is perhaps the most important, that the measure of damages is based upon putting the claimant in the position he would have been in, not if the representation had never been made, but if the representation had been true.

Further general distinctions between contract and tort damages, if any, must lie in the limits which are placed upon the general rule which is the starting point in assessing compensatory damages.[15] No distinctions appear to exist in the rules as **24-004**

(1880) 5 App. Cas. 25, 39: for details see para.2-002, above.

10 The best-known statement of this formulation as to contract damages on their own is that of Parke B in *Robinson v Harman* (1848) 1 Ex. 850 at 855; for details see para.2-003, above.

11 Negligent misrepresentation also gives damages under the Misrepresentation Act 1967 s.2(1) where it is now established that the tortious measure of damages applies but, unfortunately, the measure for deceit rather than for negligence, as was held in the much criticised decision in *Royston Trust v Rogerson* [1991] 2 Q.B. 297 CA: see paras 49-052 to 49-056, below.

12 See *Bain v Fothergill* (1874) L.R. 7 H.L. 158 at 207, per Lord Chelmsford.

13 [1969] 2 Q.B. 158 CA, and confirmed by the House of Lords in *Smith New Court Securities v Scrimgeour Vickers* [1997] A.C. 254. See Ch.47, below.

14 (1883) 24 Ch. D. 367 CA; see especially at 374 to 375, per Bowen LJ See para.36-002, below.

15 These limits are dealt with in Chs 6 to 11, above.

to mitigation of damage, or as to certainty of proof, or as to the extent to which recovery for past and prospective loss is allowed.[16] Nor does any distinction make itself felt in the further limitation to recovery for losses within the scope of the defendant's duty, a limitation which has today been much canvassed[17]; indeed many of the cases where this limitation has been in issue have been cases of professional negligence where the liability lies both in contract and in tort.[18] But with contributory negligence the position is different. While damages can be reduced by apportionment in the case of the claimant's contributory negligence when he is suing in tort, this is not possible in contract except where there is concurrent liability in contract and tort.[19] This would appear to be settled law but its wisdom has been questioned.[20]

**24-005** There remains to consider the limits imposed by the all-important rules of remoteness of damage.[21] And indeed it is this issue which has given rise to all the discussions and all the real difficulties: is the law as to remoteness of damage the same in tort and in contract? There are dicta to the effect that they are precisely the same,[22] and that this is settled law,[23] dicta that the liability in tort is the wider[24] and dicta that the liability in contract is the wider.[25] This last type of dictum has over the years been the most frequent,[26] but nevertheless a measure of the confusion is pointed to when Scrutton LJ is seen to say that the contract liability is wider in *The Edison*,[27] and soon after in *The Arpad*,[28] to say the opposite. How do these basically divergent views arise?

**24-006** Damage may be too remote in one of two ways: either because it is not caused by the defendant's act, or because, even if so caused, it is not within the scope of the protection afforded to the claimant.[29] The principles of causation, however, cannot alter with the boundaries of contract and tort: in particular, what is a direct consequence for tort is a direct consequence for contract and causation remains

---

16 These matters are dealt with in Chs 9, 10 and 11 respectively.

17 Since the decision of the House of Lords in *Banque Bruxelles Lambert v Eagle Star Insurances Co Ltd* [1997] A.C. 191, commonly called *SAAMCO*.

18 As was the decision in *SAAMCO* itself. For the canvassing of the idea specifically in contract see *The Achilleas* [2009] 1 A.C. 61 at paras 8-168 and following, above, especially at para.8-172.

19 See Ch.7, above.

20 See paras 7-014 and 7-015, above, and the Law Commission's Report on *Contributory Negligence as a Defence in Contract*, (1993) Law Com. No. 219.

21 See Ch.8, above.

22 *The Notting Hill* (1884) 9 P.D. 105 at 113, per Brett MR. See *Addis v Gramophone Co* [1909] A.C. 488 at 497, per Lord Collins, dissenting; *The Susquehanna* [1926] A.C. 655 at 661, per Lord Dunedin.

23 *H.M.S. London* [1914] P. 72 at 77, per Evans J.

24 *The Arpad* [1934] P. 189 CA at 205, per Scrutton LJ, dissenting; *The Heron II* [1969] 1 A.C. 350 at 385, per Lord Reid.

25 *The Argentino* (1888) 13 P.D. 191 CA at 200 to 201, per Bowen LJ, and again in *Cobb v G.W. Ry* [1893] 1 Q.B. 459 CA at 464; the dictum in *Cobb* was cited with approval by Lord Sumner in *Weld-Blundell v Stephens* [1920] A.C. 956 at 979, by Lord Atkin in *East Suffolk Catchment Board v Kent* [1941] A.C. 74 at 92 to 93, and by Greer LJ in *The Edison* [1932] P. 52 CA at 68 and again referred to by him in *The Arpad* [1934] P. 189 CA at 216.

26 See previous note.

27 [1932] P. 52 CA at 61.

28 [1934] P. 189 CA at 205.

29 See Ch.8, above.

immutable.[30] Hence, if the law as to remoteness of damage is not the same in contract and tort, the differences must arise in relation to scope of protection.

24-007 The view that the liability in tort is wider than in contract used to rely primarily upon the proposition that the decision in *Re Polemis*,[31] by extending liability in negligence beyond foreseeable damage so as to encompass unforeseeable damage directly caused, imposed in tort a wider liability than had been imposed in contract by the general rule in *Hadley v Baxendale*.[32] But the disapproval of *Re Polemis*,[33] by the Privy Council in *The Wagon Mound*,[34] a disapproval soon afterwards endorsed by the House of Lords,[35] eliminated this divergence between remoteness in contract and remoteness in tort at what was generally regarded as the critical point. It is true that the so-called "egg-shell skull" rule, long established in tort, has survived *The Wagon Mound* decision[36] but this rule should apply equally in contract on the comparatively rare occasions when it can be relevant. Indeed that this is so was well demonstrated by *Parsons (Livestock) v Uttley Ingham & Co*,[37] where the claimants were allowed recovery for the death of a valuable pig herd smitten, through the defendants' contractual negligence, with an intestinal infection which could not have been anticipated.[38] However, the demise of *Re Polemis*,[39] has not removed the only support for the proposition that circumstances may dictate a wider liability in tort than in contract. For since in contract the scope of protection is bounded by the all-important doctrine of the contemplation of the parties established by *Hadley v Baxendale*,[40] liability for unforeseeable damage is virtually eliminated; yet, the special case of negligence apart, in a tort action most damage is actionable once the causation hurdle is over, and indeed in torts of strict liability the defendant is ex hypothesi liable for unforeseeable damage.[41] But quite apart from the fact that liability in tort may well extend beyond foreseeable damage, the House of Lords in *The Heron II*[42] has declared that liability in contract does not extend even to all foreseeable damage. The court in *Hadley v Baxendale*, said Lord Reid,

> "did not intend that every type of damage which was reasonably foreseeable by the parties when the contract was made should either be considered as arising naturally, i.e. in

---

30 For the treatment of direct consequences in relation to causation, see paras 8-031 to 8-034 and 8-142, above. It was accepted in the contract case of *Galoo v Bright Grahame Murray* [1994] 1 W.L.R. 1360 CA at 1369H that the principles relating to causation were the same in contract and tort. Thus *Galoo* was applied in a tort context in *Saddington v Colleys Professional Services* [1999] 1 Lloyd's Rep. P.N. 140 CA and *Moore v Zerfah* [1999] 1 Lloyd's Rep. P.N. 144 CA (see these two cases at para.8-051, above) while Staughton LJ in *Total Transport Corp v Arcadia Petroleum, The Eurus* [1998] 1 Lloyd's Rep. 351 CA, dealing with cause in a contractual context, cited from this book the general rule on causation primarily in its tortious aspect: see para.8-034, above. To be contrasted with *Galoo* are and, from Northern Ireland, *MacMahon v Hamilton* [2002] Lloyd's Rep. P.N. 93 (see these two cases at para.8-154, above).

31 [1921] 3 K.B. 560 CA.

32 (1854) 9 Ex. 341. See *Sunley v Cunard White Star* [1939] 2 K.B. 791 at 800, per Hallett J.

33 [1921] 3 K.B. 560 CA.

34 [1961] A.C. 388 PC; except in so far as it deals with causation.

35 In *Hughes v Lord Advocate* [1963] A.C. 837, an appeal from Scotland: see para.8-090, above.

36 See paras 8-092 to 8-096, above.

37 [1978] Q.B. 791 CA: facts at para.8-189, above.

38 For more details, see paras 8-187 to 8-189, above.

39 [1921] 3 K.B. 560 CA.

40 (1854) 9 Ex. 341; see paras 8-158 and following, above.

41 Although, as *Cambridgeshire Water Co v Eastern Counties Leather* [1994] 2 A.C. 264 shows, the rule in *Rylands v Fletcher* (1868) L.R. 3 H.L. 330 is not entirely devoid of issues of foreseeability.

42 [1969] 1 A.C. 350.

> the usual course of things, or be supposed to have been in the contemplation of the parties. Indeed the decision makes it clear that a type of damage which was plainly foreseeable as a real possibility but which would only occur in a small minority of cases cannot be regarded as arising in the usual course of things or be supposed to have been in the contemplation of the parties … The modern rule of tort is quite different and it imposes a much wider liability."[43]

This has now been taken further in the direction of limiting the liability in contract by the introduction, by Lords Hoffmann and Hope in the controversial House of Lords decision in *The Achilleas*,[44] of the further requirement in relation to contract damages that the party in breach must have assumed responsibility for losses even if they are losses not unlikely to result. As indicated elsewhere, it is thought that there will be few cases—there have been none so far—where this further test will lead to a reduction in the damages.[45]

**24-008** Their Lordships' adoption in *The Heron II* of a test of remoteness framed in terms of what the defendant should have realised was not unlikely to result may indeed produce no different result in the great majority of cases than would an application of the reasonable foreseeability test, but there is bound to be at least a residual area of difference.[46] Would not, for instance, the subsequent charter fixture in *The Achilleas*,[47] which was held to be not likely to result for the purposes of contractual liability, have been held to have been reasonably foreseeable had there been a liability in tort?[48] And it is the consideration that contracting parties may contemplate liability on a narrower range than what is reasonably foreseeable that largely explains the general disallowance of recovery for non-pecuniary loss in contract, contract being concerned primarily with commercial matters. Recovery for non-pecuniary loss has indeed been long available in the shape of damages for physical inconvenience and discomfort,[49] and for pain and suffering and loss of amenities,[50] and has at a later date appeared in the field of mental distress,[51] but damages for mental distress remain unavailable in commercial contracts[52] as opposed to

---

43 [1969] 1 A.C. 350 at 385. See at 423, per Lord Upjohn: "it is better to use contemplate or contemplation in the case of contract, leaving foresee or foreseeability to the realm of tort". See too [1969] 1 A.C. 350 at 411, 413, 422, 425.

44 [2009] 1 A.C. 61.

45 The whole matter is considered in detail at paras 8-168 and following.

46 Scarman LJ's view that the difference between the "reasonably foreseeable" tort test and the "reasonably contemplated" contract test is semantic, a view expressed in *Parsons (Livestock) v Uttley Ingham & Co* [1978] Q.B. 791 CA at 807B, is unacceptable.

47 [2009] 1 A.C. 61.

48 For more detail on all this see paras 8-164 and following, above.

49 *Hobbs v L.S.W. Ry* (1875) L.R. 10 Q.B. 111; *Bailey v Bullock* [1950] 2 All E.R. 1167; *Stedman v Swan's Tours* (1951) 95 S.J. 727 CA; *Calabar Properties v Stitcher* [1984] 1 W.L.R. 287 CA; *Elmcroft Developments v Tankersley-Sawyer* (1984) 15 H.L.R. 61 CA. The matter is considered fully at paras 5-017 to 5-019, above.

50 *Summers v Salford Corp* [1943] A.C. 282; *Griffin v Pillett* [1926] 1 K.B. 17; *Porter v Jones* (1943) 112 L.J.K.B. 173 CA; even where the deterioration in health stems from compensation neurosis: *Wales v Wales* (1967) 111 S.J. 946; *Malyon v Lawrence Messer & Co* (1968) 112 S.J. 623. The matter is considered fully at paras 5-020 and 5-022, above.

51 Initially for the disappointment resulting from a ruined holiday in *Jarvis v Swan's Tours* [1973] Q.B. 233 CA and *Jackson v Horizon Holidays* [1975] 1 W.L.R. 1468 CA, with holiday cases continuing to this day, culminating in *Milner v Carnival Plc* [2010] 3 All E.R. 701, CA. A different type of case of importance is *Heywood v Wellers* [1976] Q.B. 446 CA. The matter is considered fully at paras 5-023 and following, above.

52 *Hayes v Dodd* [1990] 2 All E.R. 815 CA; *Watts v Morrow* [1991] 1 W.L.R. 1421 CA; *Branchett v*

consumer and personal contracts,[53] and there are still denied to a claimant complaining of breach of contract damages for non-pecuniary injury to reputation.[54] The most satisfactory rationale of the exclusion of these heads of damage, which are frequent in tort, is that they are not within the contemplation of the parties to a contract, and this rationale is now supported by the fact that the breakthrough in allowing damages for mental distress occurred in contracts where the parties may be taken to have contemplated such damage, as the contracts have not primarily been commercial ones but ones affecting also the claimant's personal and social interests.[55] Also, damages are seldom given in contract for injury to reputation even where the loss is pecuniary, and in the few types of case where they have been allowed, as wrongful dismissal of an actor,[56] failure to advertise properly for the claimant's business,[57] and failure to honour the claimant's drafts[58] or otherwise sustain his financial credit,[59] the loss has been one that was particularly contemplated by the contract. All these cases illustrate where the liability in tort is wider because of the limiting doctrine in contract of the contemplation of the parties.

Difficulties can arise where actions in contract and tort lie concurrently and, on the particular facts, the damages are wider in tort than in contract. Since the tort of negligence has been expanded to allow recovery for pure economic loss so that in cases of professional negligence there is concurrent liability in contract and in tort, the question arises whether, where it would make a difference, the victim of the negligence may rely on the wider tortious test of reasonable foreseeability and ignore the stricter and more limiting contractual test of contemplation of the parties. It is thought that there is much to be said for not allowing this to be done. Where the claim in tort is in the context of a contractual relationship, the parties are not strangers, as most tortfeasors and tort victims are, and they should be bound by what they have brought to their contractual relationship in terms of what risks have been communicated by the one and undertaken by the other. **24-009**

The approach suggested in the previous paragraph would not entail depriving the victim of contractual and tortious negligence of the entitlement to take advantage of the longer limitation period available in the tort. The exclusion of the tort remedy on remoteness grounds is geared to what risks the contracting parties have **24-010**

*Beaney* [1992] 3 All E.R. 910 CA; *Channon v Lindley Johnstone* [2002] P.N.L.R. 41 CA, p.884; *Howell-Smith v Official Solicitor* [2006] P.N.L.R. 21 CA, p.394; *Wiseman v Virgin Atlantic Airways Plc* [2006] EWHC 1566 (QB): all at paras 5-027 and 5-028, above.

53 *Farley v Skinner* [2002] 2 A.C. 732; *Ruxley Electronics v Forsyth* [1996] A.C. 344; *Herrmann v Withers LLP* [2012] EWHC 1492, Ch; see too *Haysman v MRS Films Ltd* [2008] EWHC 2494 (QB) and *Demarco v Perkins* [2006] P.N.L.R. 27 CA at 512: all at paras 5-029 and 5-030, above. The position with employment contracts is uncertain after *Johnson v Gore Wood & Co* [2002] 2 A.C.1 and *Johnson v Uniysis Ltd* [2003] 1 A.C. 518: see at paras 5-031•to 5-034, above.

54 *Groom v Crocker* [1939] 1 K.B. 194 CA; *Bailey v Bullock* [1950] 2 All E.R. 1167; See *Addis v Gramophone Co* [1909] A.C. 488. But the law may change for employment contracts in the light of *Johnson v Gore Wood & Co* [2002] 2 A.C.1 and *Johnson v Unisys Ltd* [2003] 1 A.C. 518. The matter is considered fully at para.5-035, above.

55 See paras 5-025 to 5-030, above.

56 *Marbé v George Edwardes* [1928] 1 K.B. 269 CA; *Clayton v Oliver* [1930] A.C. 209.

57 *Marcus v Myers* (1895) 11 T.L.R. 327; *Aerial Advertising Co v Batchelors Peas* [1938] 2 All E.R. 788.

58 *Rolin v Steward* (1854) 14 C.B. 595; *Kpohraror v Woolwich Building Society* [1996] 4 All E.R. 119 CA; *Nicholson v Knox Ukiwa & Co* [2008] P.N.L.R. 33 at 782.

59 *Wilson v United Counties Bank* [1920] A.C. 102.

undertaken, a consideration that has no application to the availability of limitation periods.

**24-011** The approach suggested in the previous paragraph was approved in *Wellesley Partners LLP v Withers LLP*,[60] and applied with the effect that the test for recoverability of damage for economic loss was held to be the same whether the action was brought for a tort or for breach of contract. The test to be applied in cases of concurrent liability was the contractual one because the existence of concurrent liability should not upset the agreed consensus particularly given that the tortious duty arose out of the same assumption of responsibility as exists under the contract.[61]

**24-012** Two of the judges in *Wellesley Partners* suggested that the principle might even go further. Roth J and Longmore LJ said that the contractual test might apply even if there were no concurrent liability but if the tortious liability were based on the *Hedley Byrne* principle of liability based on an assumption of responsibility in a "relationship equivalent to contract".[62] There is great merit in this suggestion. As Murphy JA and I explained in *Swick Nominees Pty Ltd v Leroi International Inc (No.2)*,[63] the *Hedley Byrne* doctrine reaffirmed a very old principle that would today be seen as contractual, not tortious.

**24-013** Broadly, *Wellesley Partners* involved negligence by a firm of solicitors in drafting the changes to a partnership agreement for a headhunting firm to provide for a partnership share for an investment bank. The solicitors had been told by Mr Channing, a star operator for the headhunting firm, to include an option permitting the bank to reduce its share *after* 42 months. Instead, the solicitors included a clause permitting the reduction *within* 41 months. The investment bank reduced its share, and withdrew capital, within 12 months. The headhunters said that they lost profits including a loss because Mr Channing's time had been occupied with the dispute with the investment bank which caused them to lose a chance of obtaining lucrative business with an investment bank called Nomura. The trial judge awarded around £1 million for that head of damages for the lost chance of obtaining Nomura's business.

One ground of appeal was whether that loss was too remote. The Court of Appeal considered that there were differences between the remoteness test for breach of contract and the test for a tort. Floyd LJ explained that there were parallels between the test in cases of breach of contract and in cases of torts.[64] In both there were two limbs. The first limb in contract ("reasonable contemplation") is comparable, although more restrictive, than it is for torts ("reasonable foreseeability" which could include highly unusual or unlikely damage). The second limb involving "assumption of responsibility" in contract and "scope of duty" for a tort, also involves similar, but not identical, enquiries. But where the liability was concurrent, and possibly also where the liability was *Hedley Byrne* liability based on an assumption of responsibility in a relationship akin to contract, the contractual approach should prevail.

**24-014** There are, however, authorities, and over a very long period, where the concur-

---

60 [2016] Ch. 529 CA at [74], per Floyd LJ, at [145]–[163], per Roth J, and at [183]–[187] per Longmore LJ.

61 [2016] Ch. 529 CA at [76] and [80], per Floyd LJ; [186], per Longmore LJ. (Floyd LJ); [186] (Longmore LJ).

62 At [163] and [187].

63 [2015] WASCA 35 at [369]–[372].

64 [2015] EWCA Civ 1146 at [74].

rent liability is for breach of contract and in the tort of conversion. Here it is thought that a claimant should be entitled to tortious damages where these are higher than the contractual. This is because the two claims are not for the same type of default, as with negligence, but with different types of default, the one being the breaking of a contract concerning goods, the other being the conversion of those goods The cases have concerned, as defendant, a seller or a carrier of goods who has so dealt with them as to be liable in conversion to the other contracting party. Actions of conversion have been brought where a seller of goods has, after the property has passed to the buyer, refused to deliver them[65] or has resold them to a third party,[66] and where a carrier of goods has delivered them on their arrival to the wrong person,[67] has improperly sold them in transit[68] or has made a short delivery to the claimant.[69] In such cases the market value of the goods at the time and place of due delivery, which is the normal contractual measure, will generally be the measure for conversion, since the latter measure also looks to market value and since the time and place of conversion is generally the time and place at which the goods should have been delivered. There are, however, two possible variants that could arise. (1) In the first place the goods may have been sold by the claimant to a third party at a price higher than the market value at due delivery and the claimant, without a market available to him in which he could buy equivalent goods, has been unable to carry out this contract. In the absence of knowledge of this contract, the defendant seller or carrier would not generally be liable to the claimant for his loss of profit in an action for breach of contract. Until the Court of Appeal decision in *The Arpad*,[70] however, there was authority for saying that such consequential loss was recoverable in conversion. That authority lay primarily in *France v Gaudet*,[71] where a buyer recovered from his seller, as damages for conversion, his resale price which was well in excess of the market price at due delivery. Mellor J, in delivering the court's judgment, said that in conversion, irrespective of the market value, the resale price was recoverable since it represented the special value that the goods had for the claimant.[72] But in *The Arpad*,[73] the Court of Appeal, by a majority, interpreted *France v Gaudet*[74] restrictively, taking the view that the resale price was adopted there because it formed evidence of the market value of the goods, and Greer LJ specifically said that "the reasons stated for the decision by Mellor J can-

65 *France v Gaudet* (1871) L.R. 6 Q.B. 199.

66 *Aronson v Mologa Holzindustrie* (1927) 32 Com. Cas. 276 CA.

67 *Brandt v Bowlby* (1831) 2 B. & Ad. 932; *Braun v Bergenske S.S. Co* (1921) 8 Ll. L. Rep. 51.

68 *Ewbank v Nutting* (1849) 7 C.B. 797; *Acatos v Burns* (1878) 3 Ex. D. 282.

69 *The Arpad* [1934] P. 189 CA. Maugham LJ was not satisfied that a short delivery constituted a conversion since mere omission or negligence was not then conversion (see now Torts (Interference with Goods) Act 1977 at paras 38-002 to 38-004, below, especially s.2(2)), but he was not prepared to decide the case on this technical ground: at 231 to 232. There was a good deal to be said for his doubts, but the point becomes academic in view of the decision itself that the measure of damages is not greater in conversion than for breach of contract.

70 [1934] P. 189 CA.

71 (1871) L.R. 6 Q.B. 199.

72 (1871) L.R. 6 Q.B. 199 at 204 to 205. Also in *Braun v Bergenske S.S. Co* (1921) 8 Ll. L. Rep. 51, where the defendant carrier had converted the goods by delivering them to the wrong person, Bailhache J, although awarding damages on the basis of the claimant's sale price to a third party as there was no evidence of market value, said that in any event he would have given the sale price.

73 [1934] P. 189 CA.

74 (1871) L.R. 6 Q.B. 199.

not be supported".[75] Scrutton LJ dissented on this issue, saying that *France v Gaudet*[76] had stood unchallenged for 60 years.[77] It has already been submitted[78] that there is much to be said for this view and that there is hope now that it will prevail, not, it is true, for all conversions but at least for those which are deliberately motivated. For while the Court of Appeal in *Saleslease Ltd v Davis*,[79] followed *The Arpad*,[80] and did so again in *Kuwait Airways Corp v Iraq Airways Co*,[81] considering itself bound by it, Lord Nicholls in the leading speech in the House of Lords in *Kuwait Airways*[82] drew a distinction between the converter who is knowing and dishonest and the converter who is not and said that, while the remoteness test for the latter should be foreseeability, the test for the former should be whether the loss arose directly and naturally. This view, though obiter, had the agreement of both Lord Hope and Lord Hoffmann.[83] (2) In the second place the goods may have been sold by the defendant at a time prior to that of due delivery and probably also at a place different from that of due delivery. The market value of the goods at the time and place of due delivery will form the measure of damages where it is higher than that at the time and place of conversion; in contract because this is the normal measure, and in tort by taking the market value at conversion as the normal measure and adding the rise as consequential loss. This view, in relation to tort, is supported by the two carriage cases of *Ewbank v Nutting*,[84] and *Acatos v Burns*.[85] On the other hand, where the market value of the goods at the time and place of due delivery is lower than the market value at the time and place of conversion, it is arguable that while the former gives the contractual measure, the latter forms the measure in tort. Thus in *Aronson v Mologa Holzindustrie*,[86] where a seller of goods converted them by a resale before the time of due delivery and the market value fell between conversion and the time of due delivery, the buyer recovered damages based upon the higher price at conversion. Scrutton LJ said that "the measure of damages is the price of the goods at the time when the conversion took place".[87] The question whether this could also have formed the contractual measure was not tackled because it was held that the amount awarded was also recoverable on a restitutionary basis, and indeed this result can generally be achieved in such cases. Thus, although the contractual measure is in strict theory less, the question of whether it is becomes academic.

**24-015** The contemplation of the parties may on occasion work the other way and lead to the opposite and frequently expressed view that the liability in contract is the wider. This stems from the second rule in *Hadley v Baxendale*,[88] that, where special

---

75 [1934] P. 189 CA at 219.
76 (1871) L.R. 6 Q.B. 199.
77 [1934] P. 189 CA at 204.
78 See para.8-108, above.
79 [1999] 1 W.L.R. 1664 CA.
80 [1934] P. 189 CA.
81 [2002] 2 A.C. 883 CA at 896.
82 [2002] 2 A.C. 883 HL at 1075.
83 For the details see para.38-070, below. In *Sandeman Coprimar SA v Transitos y Transportes Integrales SL* [2003] Q.B. 1270 CA the Court of Appeal simply accepted that in a negligent conversion the test was reasonable foreseeability: see at [25] to [31].
84 (1849) 7 C.B. 797.
85 (1878) 3 Ex. D. 282; see these two cases at paras 32-010 and 38-042, below.
86 (1927) 32 Com. Cas. 276 CA.
87 ((1927) 32 Com. Cas. 276 CA at 285.
88 (1854) 9 Ex. 341.

circumstances are at the making of the contract communicated to the party subsequently in breach, damages may be given in respect of these special circumstances since they were within the parties' contemplation. There can be no such communication beforehand to a tortfeasor, and therefore it is said that the liability in contract can be greater in this connection. It should, however, be remembered, as Devlin J carefully pointed out in *Biggin v Permanite*,[89] that, although the rule as to special circumstances tends to be referred to as giving the claimant an increased amount or as embodying a specially beneficial measure for him, it is capable of working to his detriment. Yet it generally works in his favour, and this may enlarge the contemplation of the parties beyond the scope of the protection that would be afforded to the victim of a tort. Such a situation could arise where, as in *The Arpad*,[90] there is a loss of goods which constitutes both a breach of contract and a conversion. The Arpad has held that the claimant cannot recover in conversion for the loss of the exceptionally high profit at which he has sold the goods to a third party; in that case he also failed to recover in contract for the loss of this profit, but the conclusion could have been different, yet different in contract alone, if the defendant had been informed by the claimant of his sale to a third party and so brought it within the contemplation of the parties. An even more illuminating illustration used to be afforded by the cases where the claimant is beset and harassed by impecuniosity. This stemmed from the famous decision in *Liesbosch Dredger v S.S. Edison*,[91] where claimants, with insufficient money to buy a new dredger to replace the one which the defendants had negligently sunk, were denied recovery in tort for the loss arising out of their financial inability. In later cases, by contrast, damages have been awarded in contract in respect of loss arising from the claimant's impecuniosity because his impecuniosity was within the contemplation of the parties. In *Muhammad v Ali*,[92] the claimants agreed to sell land to the defendant which they had already contracted to sell to a third party, the defendant agreeing to indemnify the claimants against claims made by the third party. Upon the claimants transferring the land to the defendant they were sued by the third party and damages were awarded against them. The third party, to enforce this judgment, had other land of the claimants sold in execution proceedings at a price substantially below its value, and out of the proceeds satisfied his judgment debt. In the claimants' subsequent action for damages against the defendant it was held that, in the circumstances, the damage to the claimants resulting from the execution sale, amounting to the market value of the land less the price at which it was sold, was not too remote, for, in the words of Lord Uthwatt,

> "the vendors' impecuniosity was not a separate and concurrent cause of the land being sold in execution".[93]

---

[89] [1951] 1 K.B. 422 at 435 to 436; see too *Trans Trust S.P.R.L. v Danubian Trading Co* [1952] 2 K.B. 297 CA at 301, per Somervell LJ.

[90] [1934] P. 189 CA.

[91] [1933] A.C. 449.

[92] [1947] A.C. 414 PC.

[93] [1947] A.C. 414 PC at 417. Lord Wright, in contrasting this case with *The Liesbosch* [1933] A.C. 449 in *Monarch S.S. Co v Karlshamns Oljefabriker* [1949] A.C. 196 at 224, said that "the difference in the result did not depend on the differences (if any) between contract and tort in this connection".

In *Trans Trust S.P.R.L. v Danubian Trading Co*,[94] the defendants bought steel from the claimants who were to buy it from a third party. Neither claimants nor defendants were in a position to provide the money necessary to obtain its delivery. It was a term of the contract that payment by the defendants should be by cash against shipping documents from a confirmed credit to be opened in favour of the third party by a fourth party to whom the defendants had in turn contracted to sell the steel. The defendants failed to procure the opening of the credit, and the claimants lost the profit they would have made on the transaction although if they had had sufficient money and already bought the steel at the time of breach they would have suffered no loss as the market price at breach was higher than the contract price. Nevertheless they recovered the profit they had failed to make. Somervell LJ said:

> "The real question is what was the loss contemplated by the parties rather than the reason for it. Even if the plaintiffs had been very rich it might still have been 'contemplated' that if the defendants did not procure the obtaining of the credit the plaintiffs could not and would not themselves have used their resources for the opening of a credit for this steel."[95]

However, after a growing preparedness to allow recovery within the framework of the foreseeability of tort despite financial difficulties besetting the claimant, the impecuniosity principle of *The Liesbosch*[96] has been declared false by the House of Lords in *Lagden v O'Connor*,[97] and abandoned.[98] This illustration of a greater damages liability in contract than in tort therefore now loses much of its force. However, the introduction in *The Achilleas*[99] of the new test of assumption of responsibility[100] has produced, somewhat unexpectedly, a further illustration of contractual liability which would not have founded recovery had the liability been in tort. This new test which was initially seen as exclusionary of liability was held by the Court of Appeal in *Siemens Building Technologies FE Ltd v Supershield Ltd*,[101] also to be inclusionary, thereby imposing liability in contractual negligence for a flood which would not have led to tortious liability as not reasonably foreseeable.[102]

**24-016** In summary, the law as to remoteness of damage would appear to be the same in contract and in tort as far as the causation limiting aspect of remoteness is concerned, but the scope of the protection afforded to the claimant is sometimes wider in tort and sometimes wider in contract, depending upon the voluntary factor in contract, varying from agreement to agreement, of the contemplation of the parties.

---

94 [1952] 2 Q.B. 297 CA.

95 [1952] 2 Q.B. 297 CA at 302. See *Aruna Mills v Dhanrajmal Gobindram* [1968] 1 Q.B. 655 (facts at para.25-056, below) where the claimant recovered for loss arising from devaluation of the Indian rupee because, although at that time damage from fluctuations in currency values was ordinarily too remote, this devaluation was in the circumstances in the contemplation of the parties.

96 [1933] A.C. 449.

97 [2004] 1 A.C. 1067.

98 See paras 8-110 to 8-113, above.

99 [2009] 1 A.C. 61.

100 See at para.22-007, above.

101 [2010] 1 Lloyd's Rep. 349, CA.

102 The case is fully considered at para.8-181, above.

# PART 4A CONTRACT

CHAPTER 25

# SALE OF GOODS

TABLE OF CONTENTS



**25-001** Together with the general law on the sale of goods, and with one significant exception, the law relating to damages in such contracts has been codified in what is now the Sale of Goods Act 1979.[1] Sections 50, 51, 53 and 54 which contain the relevant law form the starting point in considering damages for various types of breach, but since the statute consists of a codification of the common law, the bulk of the material remains case law.[2] The exception to the codification of sale of goods law by the Sale of Goods Act is the Consumer Rights Act 2015. That legislation provides for numerous additional remedies for contraventions involved in a sale of goods by a trader to a consumer including a right to reject (s.20), and a right to repair and replacement (s.23). In addition, by s.19(11)(a), the Consumer Rights Act permits a consumer to claim at common law for damages which are preserved for breach of contract (s.19(9)(c)) as well as damages for breach of the terms required

1 Replacing its classic forbear, the Sale of Goods Act 1893.

2 These damages provisions of the Sale of Goods Act can be applied to the sale of what are not, strictly speaking, goods, as in *Deutsche Bank AG v Total Global Steel Ltd* [2012] EWHC 1201 (Comm) where the sale was of carbon emission units: see the case at para.25-062, below.

by the Act to be treated as part of the contract (s.19(9)(a)) or if the goods do not conform to the contract (s.19(9)(b)). The Consumer Rights Act does not provide the rules which govern the award of damages. Those rules must be intended to be those which have developed carefully in the context of the Sale of Goods Act, discussed below.

## I. BREACH BY SELLER

### 1. NON-DELIVERY

The measure of damages for non-delivery of goods sold is prescribed by s.51 of the Sale of Goods Act 1979 thus: **25-002**

(1) Where the seller wrongfully neglects or refuses to deliver the goods to the buyer, the buyer may maintain an action against the seller for damages for non-delivery.

(2) The measure of damages is the estimated loss directly and naturally resulting, in the ordinary course of events, from the seller's breach of contract.

(3) Where there is an available market for the goods in question the measure of damages is prima facie to be ascertained by the difference between the contract price and the market or current price of the goods at the time or times when they ought to have been delivered, or, if no time was fixed, then at the time of the refusal to deliver.

(4) This section does not apply to a contract to which Ch.2 of Pt 1 of the Consumer Rights Act 2015 applies (but see the provision made about such contracts in s.19 of that Act).

To this, s.54 adds that nothing in the Act shall affect the buyer's right to recover interest or special damages where by law it is recoverable. However, excluded from s.51, by s.51(4), are contracts including those by a trader to supply goods to a consumer (broadly a person acting outside that person's business).

Section 51(2) is framed in terms of the first rule in *Hadley v Baxendale*,[3] excluding the element of the defendant's knowledge of special circumstances; s.51(3) states the normal measure of damages under the first rule; s.54 brings in the second rule in *Hadley v Baxendale*,[4] and will in appropriate cases displace s.51(2) and (3) and allow increased damages. **25-003**

#### (1) Normal measure

The normal measure of damages, as stated in s.51(3) thereby incorporating the common law as stated in *Barrow v Arnaud*,[5] is the market price of the goods at the contractual time for delivery[6] less the contract price,[7] since this represents the amount that the buyer must obtain to put himself in the position he would have been **25-004**

---

3 (1854) 9 Ex. 341. See paras 8-158 and following, above.

4 (1854) 9 Ex. 341.

5 (1846) 8 Q.B. 595 at 609 to 610.

6 And also at the contractual place for delivery: *Aryeh v Kostoris & Son* [1967] 1 Lloyd's Rep. 63 CA at 73, col.1, per Diplock LJ. This, however, seldom leads to problems, but it may be in issue where the goods are to be transported between the parties: see para.25-015, below. See also *Aronson v Mologa Holzindustrie* (1927) 32 Com. Cas. 276 CA, where the action was conversion.

7 This is on the normal assumption that the contract price has not been paid over. *Bunge S.A. v Nidera B.V.* [2013] EWCA Civ 1628 CA, a claim for the difference between market price and contract price

in had the contract been carried out.[8] For, to put himself in such a position, he must go into the market and buy equivalent goods[9]; and even if he does not choose to rebuy in the market his loss will remain the same.[10] If, therefore, there is no difference between the contract and the market prices the buyer will have lost nothing and the damages will be nominal.[11]

25-005 The ascertainment of the contract price will not present great difficulty,[12] but in ascertaining the market price questions arise as to what it is, how it is evidenced, and at what time it is taken.

25-006 **(a) The need for an available market** Market price less contract price is laid down as the prima facie measure in s.51(3)[13] only where there is an "available market". The essential requirement is that the buyer should be able to go out and buy equivalent goods in the market. If he can do this, then the court awards damages by way of "available market" and an application of s.51(3) on the basis of the price at which he can buy. If, on the other hand, there is a holding of no "available

---

on account of the non-delivery of a cargo of a large amount of milling wheat, may perhaps be mentioned at this early stage of the non-delivery section of the text. While in the absence of argument the Court of Appeal did not commit itself, those below expressed the view that they doubted if the decision in *The Golden Victory* (for which see paras 10-117 and following, above) applied to the sale of a single parcel of goods of the kind with which the case was concerned: see at [8], [9] and [26]. See too, in contrast, *Novasen SA v Alimenta SA* [2013] EWHC 345 (Comm) in the footnote at the end of para.10-121, above.

8 This remains the measure even if the buyer is a non-profit-making organisation: *Diamond Cutting Works Federation v Triefus* [1956] 1 Lloyd's Rep. 216. A somewhat curious illustration of the application of the measure is provided by *Barry v Davies* [2000] 1 W.L.R. 1962 CA, where an auctioneer refused to sell two machines to the highest bidder who was awarded, applying s.51(3), the amount required to purchase similar machines elsewhere, and not just the amount that the machines had fetched at a later auction sale, less the amount of his bid.

9 The normal measure may, exceptionally, become unavailable to the buyer should he have failed to mitigate, as was held in *The Solholt* [1983] 1 Lloyd's Rep. 605 CA: facts at para.9-053, above.

10 Exceptionally it may be unreasonable for the buyer to seek equivalent goods, as was held in the curious case of *Sealace Shipping Co v Oceanvoice (The Alecos M)* [1991] 1 Lloyd's Rep. 120 CA. A ship was sold together with a spare propeller but the propeller was not delivered. The buyer claimed for the cost of having a special one manufactured, in the absence of an available market, together with the cost of its transportation and installation but it was considered that the buyer was unlikely, and did not need, to obtain a replacement propeller, presumably because the ship could function without a spare, and his damages were accordingly held to be limited to the propeller's scrap value. By contrast, in *Times Newspapers Ltd v George Weidenfeld & Nicolson Ltd* [2002] F.S.R. 463 where the claimant had bought serialisation rights in a Prime Minister's memoirs for £100,000 from the defendant who failed to deliver, and the claimant eventually bought for £220,000 directly from the copyright owner who should have sold the publication rights to the defendant, the difference between these two sums was awarded as damages.

11 *Valpy v Oakeley* (1851) 16 Q.B. 941; *Griffiths v Perry* (1859) 1 E. & E. 680. Both these cases were complicated by the buyer's bankruptcy and the fact that he had prepaid by bill subsequently dishonoured, but both were cited with approval in *Erie County Natural Gas Co v Carroll* [1911] A.C. 105 PC at 118 as authority for the proposition in the text. Nominal damages were awarded for breach by non-delivery under the second of two contracts for the sale of steel billets in *Somasteel SARL v Coresteel DMCC* unreported 29 April 2015, as the market price had fallen well below the contract price.

12 Where the contract provided that any new or additional export duties were to be for the account of the buyer and an export duty was imposed after the making of the contract of sale, the contract price was held to include this subsequent duty for the purpose of measuring the damages: *Produce Brokers New Co (1934) v British Italian Trading Co* [1952] 1 Lloyd's Rep. 379.

13 See para.25-002, above.

market" within the meaning of the subsection, leading to an application of s.51(2), the price at which the buyer can buy can still be regarded[14] as the market price.

Over the years varying views have been put forward by the courts as to the meaning to be attached to the term available market, but the general run of these cases have concerned the converse situation of non-acceptance where the same term is used in the equivalent s.50(3).[15] Since in this connection the principles are the same for non-delivery and non-acceptance, there is no need here to discuss the reasons not to accept these varying views, beyond stating that the outcome of a case never appears to have been affected by whether a narrow or a wide interpretation of the statutory term "available market" has been adopted. Now, two decisions where breach is by non-delivery have appeared, *M&J Marine Engineering Services Co Ltd v Shipshore Ltd*,[16] and *Air Studios (Lyndhurst) Ltd v Lombard North Central Plc*.[17] None of the problems in relation to non-acceptance are referred to in either judgment, other than in *Air Studios* to Webster J's approach in the *Shearman* case,[18] and these views should still be kept in mind. In both cases there was held to be no available market. In *M&J Marine* Field J was of the opinion that an available market involves a reasonably available supply of the contract goods and a reasonably available source of demand for such goods and held that there was no such market in the case before him for machined wheel rollers.[19] In *Air Studios*, where there had been a failure to deliver second-hand electrical equipment, Males J, while satisfied that the relevant available market was comprised of equivalent, and not restricted to identical, such equipment, decided that there was not a market of this nature existing at or within a reasonable time of the seller's breach.[20] 25-007

Apart from the general problem, there is one particular point which has come up for decision in the non-delivery cases. It arose in *British Motor Trade Association v Gilbert*,[21] and again, on similar facts, in *Mouat v Betts Motors*.[22] At a time when cars were in short supply and the price at which they could be sold was controlled, the defendant gave the claimant an option to buy a car at the controlled price.[23] On the defendant's breach of this covenant by selling the car to a third party, the much higher open market price was taken in calculating the normal measure of damages, for, as Lord Denning said in the latter case, the rule that the buyer is entitled to go into the market and buy equivalent goods at the market price 25-008

> "applies even though the only available market is a surreptitious market which is fed by persons who have broken their covenants".[24]

The question remains as to when the court will hold that the buyer is able to go out and buy equivalent goods. Generally this admits of an easy answer, but oc- 25-009

---

14 See para.25-002, above.

15 See paras 25-118 to 25-120, below. The cases are *Dunkirk Colliery Co v Lever* (1878) 9 Ch. D. 20 CA; *Thompson v Robinson* [1955] Ch. 177; *Charter v Sullivan* [1957] 2 Q.B. 117 CA; *Lazenby Garages v Wright* [1976] 1 W.L.R. 459 CA; *Shearson Lehman Hutton v Maclaine Watson & Co* [1990] 3 All E.R. 723.

16 [2009] EWHC 2031 (Comm).

17 [2012] EWHC 3162 (QB).

18 At para.25-120, below.

19 [2009] EWHC 2031 (Comm) at [30]. Facts of the case are at para.25-031, below.

20 See his useful discussion from para 25-095 to 25-100.

21 [1951] 2 All E.R. 641.

22 [1959] A.C. 71 PC.

23 Less depreciation. The full facts of these two cases are at para.25-012, below.

24 [1959] A.C. 71 PC at 82.

casionally equivalent goods are not immediately available or are not available near at hand. In such circumstances whether the buyer should wait or should buy from afar is to be tested by what is reasonable. In *Lesters Leather and Skin Co v Home and Overseas Brokers*,[25] snakeskins had been bought for delivery at a United Kingdom port but on arrival they were rejected by the buyer as not merchantable, thus making in effect a failure to deliver. The seller contended that the buyer should have bought other skins which were available in India, and that therefore the normal measure of damages applied and the buyer's claim for consequential loss of profit must fail. This contention was rejected on the ground that it was not reasonable to expect such a repurchase, Lord Goddard CJ saying that

> "the buyers were not bound to go hunting the globe to find out where they can get skins".[26]

25-010 **(b) Relevant and irrelevant prices in ascertaining the market price** The price at which a third party has agreed to buy the goods from the buyer may be treated as evidence of the market price where it is difficult to assess,[27] but generally it is irrelevant and should not be taken in lieu of the market price: this is so whether such a price is higher or lower than the market price. If this price is higher it may possibly be taken to inflate the normal measure by way of consequential losses[28] but will not by that fact represent the normal measure. If it is lower it cannot be taken so as to decrease the damages. This latter proposition was established by the important case of *Williams v Agius*[29] in the House of Lords. The claimant, having bought from the defendant a cargo of coal to be shipped to Genoa, resold before the time fixed for delivery a cargo of similar amount and description to a third party at a price higher than the contract price but lower than what turned out to be the market price at the time when the defendant failed in breach of contract to deliver. It was held that the normal measure of damages applied and that the price at which the claimant had contracted to resell was irrelevant.[30] The short answer to the contention that the lower resale price is relevant is that the only way in which

---

25 (1948) 64 T.L.R. 569 CA.

26 (1948) 64 T.L.R. 569 CA. See, too, at 570, per Singleton LJ quoting Sellers J below: "It is one thing to enter into a contract. It would be another thing to have got the goods actually here." *Contrast Att-Gen of the Republic of Ghana v Texaco Overseas Tankships (The Texaco Melbourne)* [1994] 1 Lloyd's Rep. 473 HL, at para.32-005, below, where the non-delivery was of goods carried rather than sold.

27 See the equivalent cases in non-acceptance where the seller has resold at para.25-121, below; see *France v Gaudet* (1871) L.R. 6 Q.B. 199, where the action was conversion, as interpreted in *The Arpad* [1934] P. 189 CA, at para.38-069, below; and at para.29-006, below *Luxe Holding Ltd v Midland Resources Holding Ltd* [2010] EWHC 1908 Ch, a sale of shares rather than of goods and an application for a freezing order rather than an action for damages, where the seller's resale price was taken as evidence of market value. The price of an offer by a third party not yet crystallised into a contract may also be evidence of the market price. And in *Hong Guan & Co v R. Jumabhoy & Sons* [1960] A.C. 684 PC, where nine years had elapsed between the sale and the hearing of the action, the Judicial Committee took, as evidence of the market price, the amount paid by the claimants in settlement with their sub-buyers, Lord Morris saying that as a matter of business common sense it was a reasonable inference that the sum paid in settlement would certainly not be more, and would probably be less, than the market price less the sub-sale contract price: at 703. When the place of delivery is not the same under the sub-contract as under the contract, the sub-sale price may afford no evidence of relevant market price: *Aryeh v Kostoris & Son* [1967] 1 Lloyd's Rep. 63 CA at 72 to 73, per Diplock LJ.

28 See paras 25-028 to 25-030, below.

29 [1914] A.C 510; approving and following *Rodocanachi v Milburn* (1886) 18 Q.B.D. 67 CA, the equivalent case in a contract of carriage: see para.32-007, below.

30 The case was complicated by a purported assignment of the sub-contract by the sub-buyer to the

a buyer can carry out his sub-contract is by buying similar goods in the market at the higher price. If indeed his sub-sale was of the identical goods then he cannot satisfy his sub-contract by re-buying in the market, but in such a case he is necessarily put in breach of his sub-contract and, as Lord Dunedin pointed out,[31] might be liable in damages to his sub-buyer to an extent far beyond the sub-sale price.[32]

Yet, as has been pointed out earlier, on the somewhat unusual facts of *Williams v Agius*,[33] there was no possibility either of the buyer being sued by the sub-buyer or of the buyer rebuying in the market. There have indeed been signs of discontent, particularly in *Oxus Gold Plc v Templeton Insurance Ltd*,[34] with the absolute nature of the rule propounded by the House of Lords, so that it is considered that the time may have come for its reconsideration, possibly along the lines proposed elsewhere.[35] **25-011**

*Williams v Agius*[36] has been applied so as to hold irrelevant the price, lower than the market price at due delivery, at which the buyer could lawfully resell the goods. This unusual situation arose in *Mouat v Betts Motors*.[37] The defendant, in buying a new car from the claimant dealers at the controlled price, covenanted not to resell the car within two years unless he first offered it back to the claimants at the original controlled price less depreciation. In breach of this covenant the defendant resold the car within two years at the much higher, because inflated, price prevailing on the open market. The claimant dealers successfully claimed the normal measure of damages represented by the open market price less the repurchase price of the option. The defendant argued that the only damage suffered by the claimants was that represented by the controlled price less the repurchase price, because, if the defendant had performed his covenant and offered to resell the car to the claimants, they could only have resold it, under Board of Trade regulations, at the controlled price. This contention was rejected by the Judicial Committee of the Privy Council. Lord Denning said: **25-012**

> "It does not lie in Mouat's mouth to say that, if he had fulfilled his covenant, the dealers could only resell the car [at the controlled price]. That was a matter peculiar to the dealers which was no concern of his. The dealers were entitled in law to be put into as good a position as if he had fulfilled his covenant: and to do this they were entitled to go into the market and buy a similar car at the market price."[38]

And where the buyer would probably have resold the car at the controlled price

defendant, the original seller.

31 [1914] A.C. 510 at 523.

32 In *Finlay v Kwik Hoo Tong* [1929] 1 K.B. 400 CA, all three members of the Court of Appeal spoke of the difficulties of reconciling *Williams v Agius* [1914] A.C. 510 with *Hall v Pim* (1928) 33 Com. Cas. 324 HL. However, even if there may be difficulties in accepting *Hall v Pim* in so far as it allowed a buyer to recover a greater sum than the normal measure by reason of his having lost a resale contract at a price higher than the market price, the decision stands or falls on the question of what the parties must be taken to have contemplated in the way of resale. Whether accepted or not, it does not affect *Williams v Agius*, where the seller was attempting to hold the buyer to a smaller sum than the normal measure by reason of the buyer's sub-sale at a price lower than the market price, an issue on which the seller's contention was clearly wrong and for which the contemplation of the parties as to sub-sales is an immaterial consideration.

33 [1914] A.C. 510. Their unusual nature is brought out in para.9-174 combined with para.9-181, above.

34 [2007] EWHC 770 (Comm).

35 For this proposal see para.9-183, above. The whole problem is given extended consideration in the context of mitigation and avoided loss at paras 9-171 to 9-183, above.

36 [1914] A.C. 510.

37 [1959] A.C. 71 PC.

38 [1959] A.C. 71 PC at 82.

although not bound by law to do so, this is, a fortiori, an irrelevant factor. This appears to have been the position in the earlier case of *British Motor Trade Association v Gilbert*,[39] which was similar[40] to *Mouat v Betts Motors*[41] in other respects.[42]

25-013 Similarly, the price at which the buyer has bought equivalent goods may be evidence of the market price but again it is generally irrelevant and is not to be taken in preference to the market price. Some difficulty may be experienced in this connection on account of *Erie County Natural Gas Co v Carroll*,[43] a case which is generally cited for the proposition that if the buyer succeeds in getting substitute goods without cost to himself the damages will be nominal. This case, however, properly understood, dealt not with a claim for the normal measure of damages based on market price but with a claim for consequential loss represented by the expense of procuring a substitute for the gas which the defendant had failed to supply; it is therefore dealt with later.[44] What is important here is that it does not follow from this decision that, where the buyer makes a straightforward claim for market price less contract price, the seller could maintain that the damages were nominal because by some good fortune the buyer had acquired equivalent goods, as by gift from a third party. This would be *res inter alios acta*.[45]

25-014 On the other hand, if the buyer should later buy the self-same goods from the self-same seller at a price lower than the market price at the time of breach, the market price does become displaced by the price payable under the renegotiated contract. It was so held in *Pagnan & Fratelli v Corbisa Industrial Agropacuaria*,[46] where this somewhat unusual situation arose. The claimant buyers, having properly rejected because of partial damage the cargo of maize which was the subject-matter of the sale from the defendants, brought an action for damages for non-delivery although

---

39 [1951] 2 All E.R. 641.

40 A difference not affecting the issue of damages was that the defendant in *British Motor Trade Association v Gilbert* [1951] 2 All E.R. 641 covenanted not only with the dealer from whom he bought the car but also under seal with the trade association, and it was the trade association which sued.

41 [1959] A.C. 71 PC.

42 Danckwerts J, in the earlier case, was not completely satisfied with the appropriateness of the normal measure of damages. He said that it was a little strange that "the plaintiffs should be entitled to demand payment of a sum of money which can only be considered at the present time, so far as dealings at the present time are concerned, on the footing that the scheme of the plaintiffs is not being carried out, but is being, surreptitiously or otherwise, evaded": [1951] 2 All E.R. 641 at 644. It is this that suggests that the court was assuming that the claimants, had they been given the opportunity to exercise the option, would have resold the car at the list price at which they had sold originally to the defendant. This would have been in line with their general policy, of which the covenant was a manifestation, to check the inflation of the price of cars which were at the time in limited supply. In these cases there is indeed this further consideration that the claimants may have suffered damage, not so much in their role as buyers deprived of an option to purchase, but because the sale in breach of covenant was liable to have an inflationary effect on the price of cars. It would, therefore, be not unreasonable to use the normal measure as a suitable amount to award for a loss which would have been very difficult to assess. There may, too, be restitutionary possibilities in such a situation.

43 [1911] A.C. 105 PC.

44 See para.25-026, below. That the claim was regarded by the court as one for consequential loss is made particularly clear by the passage in Lord Atkinson's speech beginning: "It would have been competent for the plaintiffs to have abstained from procuring gas in substitution for that which the defendants should have supplied to them, and have sued the defendants for damages for breach of their contract": at 116 to 117.

45 The general principles involved are those of mitigation and avoided loss. These, together with *Erie County Natural Gas Co v Carroll* [1911] A.C. 105 PC, are considered in Ch.9 at paras 9-108 and following, above; for what follows see in particular paras 9-121 to 9-123 and 9-133 to 9-138.

46 [1970] 1 W.L.R. 1306 CA.

they had in fact subsequently bought the whole cargo from the defendants at a reduced price, which had the result of turning their loss into a handsome profit in excess of the difference between the price under the original contract and the prevailing market price at all relevant times. In these circumstances the Court of Appeal refused to award any damages, rejecting the claimants' argument that they were entitled to the normal measure by way of market price at breach less original contract price. Salmon LJ pointed out that the later purchase at the reduced price was certainly not *res inter alios acta* and that the arbitration tribunal had found as a fact that it was not an independent or disconnected transaction but formed part of a continuous dealing between the parties.[47] Accordingly, the initial failure to deliver a sound cargo could not properly be looked at in isolation but must be linked with the later purchase, thereby showing that the claimants had suffered no loss and displacing the measure of damages of s.51(3) which, as Megaw LJ was careful to point out, is only stated to be a prima facie measure.[48]

**(c) Time at which the market price is to be taken** The time at which the market price is to be taken is, as stated in the first limb and the second limb respectively of s.51(3),[49] the time fixed for delivery or, if no time is fixed, the time of refusal to deliver. In two somewhat special sets of circumstances, however, the question has arisen as to whether this time is an appropriate time to adopt. (1) Where the market price has risen between the time of breach and the time of judgment in the action and the purchase price has been prepaid by the buyer, it is arguable that the buyer should be entitled to the higher value at the time of judgment in order to put him into the position he would have been in had the contract been performed. This argument gained acceptance mainly in actions for not replacing stock[50] and was impliedly recognised for sale of goods in *Gainsford v Carroll*.[51] In that case the court refused to allow the buyer damages based upon the higher market price at the time of judgment on the ground that, having still the money with which he had intended to pay the purchase price, he should have gone into the market and rebought at the time of the failure to deliver. Clearly on this rationale the result would be different where the buyer had already paid over the purchase price. Yet when this situation arose in *Startup v Cortazzi*,[52] the court rejected the claimant's argument that he was entitled to the higher market price at the date of judgment. The members of the court, however, dealt with the issue rather woollily,[53] and it is significant that Atkin LJ in *Aronson v Mologa Holzindustrie*,[54] treated the question as an open one. Moreover, case law in the analogous field of sale of land has 25-015

47 [1970] 1 W.L.R. 1306 CA at 1315.

48 [1970] 1 W.L.R. 1306 CA at 1318. On the case considered from the aspect of mitigation and avoided loss, see para.9-137, above. Interestingly, in *Somasteel SARL v Coresteel DMCC* unreported 29 April 2015, an action for non-delivery of goods sold where there was held to be an available market, the trial judge arrived at a market price not by concentrating on the buyer's actions, as the cases preceding above do, but by taking the average price based on similar contracts that the seller had made around the time of the contract.

49 See para.25-002, above.

50 See paras 29-013 to 29-015, below. The general issue is basically one of mitigation and is treated in Ch.9, above.

51 (1824) 2 B. & C. 624.

52 (1835) 2 C.M. & R. 165.

53 This was not from want of its being put clearly by counsel.

54 (1927) 32 Com. Cas. 276 CA at 289–291.

provided accumulating support for the argument which in *Startup v Cortazzi*,[55] did not succeed.[56] (2) Where the seller sends the goods some distance to the buyer, especially if by a long sea voyage, it seems to be generally assumed, as in *Melachrino v Nickoll*,[57] and in *A.B.D. (Metals and Waste) v Anglo Chemical and Ore Co*,[58] that the time[59] of final arrival rather than that of shipment constitutes the time of delivery.[60] On the other hand it was held in *Sharpe v Nosawa*,[61] that where the goods were to be shipped under a c.i.f. contract the time of due delivery was not when the goods would finally have arrived but the earlier time at which the shipping documents ought to have been delivered, since their delivery was a constructive delivery of the goods giving the claimant the power to deal with them.

**25-016** There remains the question of what is the appropriate time to adopt outside these special cases. One exact time fixed for delivery generally poses no difficulties: the calculation is made as of that time. However, more difficult situations have arisen.

**25-017** *(i) Where a specific period or a succession of times is fixed for delivery* The last possible moment within a specific period fixed for delivery is the time to be taken, since the seller is entitled to tender delivery up until that moment.[62] Where delivery is to be by instalments so that there is a number of successive times fixed for delivery, each fixed time is taken as to each instalment.[63]

**25-018** *(ii) Where the seller repudiates before the time fixed for delivery* The fact that the seller has repudiated the contract before the time fixed for delivery does not affect the prima facie rule that the market price at the time so fixed is the relevant one. In the first place, if the seller's repudiation is not accepted by the buyer it is a nullity and there is no breach till there is non-performance, i.e. at the time fixed for delivery,[64] and the buyer, with no duty to mitigate,[65] is entitled to sit back on a rising market, and then claim the normal measure based on the market price at the time fixed for delivery: the authorities for this proposition are *Leigh v Paterson*,[66] and

---

55 (1835) 2 C.M. & R. 165.

56 See the cases at para.27-009, below.

57 [1920] 1 K.B. 693.

58 [1955] 2 Lloyd's Rep. 456.

59 These cases are also authority for taking the place of final arrival as the place at which the market price is to be taken.

60 *Van den Hurk v Martens* [1920] 1 K.B. 850 shows that this may indeed not even be the time of final arrival in the buyer's hands but the time of final arrival in the buyer's sub-buyer's hands where the seller was aware that the buyer was buying for resale elsewhere. This, however, would seem to be a case of consequential loss.

61 [1917] 2 K.B. 814.

62 See *Leigh v Paterson* (1818) 8 Taunt. 540. This case involved problems of anticipatory breach and mitigation which are dealt with at para.25-018, below.

63 See *Brown v Muller* (1872) L.R. 7 Ex. 319; *Roper v Johnson* (1873) L.R. 8 C.P. 167. Both these cases also involved problems of anticipatory breach and mitigation which are dealt with at para.25-018, below.

64 See *Stocznia Gdanska v Latvian Shipping Co* [1997] 2 Lloyd's Rep. 228 in the first footnote to para.25-124, below for the equivalent position when it is the buyer who repudiates.

65 The dicta suggesting the contrary, of Mathew J in *Nickoll v Ashton* [1900] 2 Q.B. 298 at 305 and, on appeal, of Vaughan Williams LJ dissenting, [1901] 2 K.B. 126 CA at 138 cannot be accepted, unless one takes Lord Collins MR's view in *Tredegar Iron Co v Hawthorn* (1902) 18 T.L.R. 716 CA that Mathew J's dictum was based on an *accepted* repudiation.

66 (1818) 8 Taunt. 540.

*Brown v Muller*.[67] The buyer is not holding the seller to ransom here: the sanction is that the contract is still open and not only may the seller still perform but subsequent events may even, unexpectedly, relieve him of the necessity to perform.[68] In the second place, if the seller's repudiation is accepted[69] by the buyer so that there is then and there a breach, the damages are still prima facie calculated at the time fixed for delivery, a point settled by *Roper v Johnson*,[70] and confirmed by the House of Lords in *Garnac Grain Co v Faure & Fairclough*,[71] but the buyer is now under a duty to mitigate and cannot therefore sit back with impunity on a rising market. It is indeed the seller's onus to prove that the buyer has failed to mitigate by not going into the rising market and repurchasing, so that in the absence of any such evidence from the seller the prima facie rule will still be applied in the buyer's favour, as in *Roper v Johnson*,[72] and again in *Garnac Grain Co v Faure & Fairclough*.[73] If the seller discharges this onus and shows that the buyer could in the interim between the acceptance of the repudiation and the time fixed for delivery have repurchased in the market at a price lower than that prevailing at the time fixed for delivery, he is entitled to have the damages assessed by reference to this lower price.[74] Where the buyer fails to repurchase when he ought to have done, the market price at the date fixed for delivery will be taken against him where it proves to be lower than the market price at the date when he could and should have repurchased. This was the position in *Melachrino v Nickoll*,[75] where the market price was above the contract price at the time of the acceptance of the repudiation but below the contract price at the time fixed for delivery: only nominal damages were awarded. Where the buyer fails to repurchase when he ought to have done and no evidence is tendered as to the price prevailing at the time fixed for delivery, the price at which he should have repurchased is to be taken, as opposed to either any lower price to which the goods later, but before the time fixed for delivery, fell or the higher price at which the buyer subsequently, but again before the delivery time, did repurchase. All of this is illustrated by *Kaines v Osterreichische Warrenhandelsgesellschaft*.[76] Finally, if the buyer repurchases, in a reasonable attempt to mitigate, at a market

---

67 (1872) L.R. 7 Ex. 319.

68 *Avery v Bowden* (1855) 5 E. & B. 714 (affirmed (1856) 6 E. & B. 953) is a classic example of this situation: see the standard texts on contract.

69 For what constitutes an acceptance of a repudiation, see the standard texts on contract. Suing the seller is a clear example.

70 (1873) L.R. 8 C.P. 167. Brett J in a very clear judgment put the matter thus: "The election to take advantage of the repudiation of the contract goes only to the question of breach, and not to the question of damages; and.... when you come to estimate the damages, it must be by the difference between the contract price and the market price at the day or days appointed for performance, and not at the time of breach": at 180. See, too, *Melachrino v Nickoll* [1920] 1 K.B. 693 at 699, per Bailhache J.

71 [1968] A.C. 1130; see especially at 1140.

72 (1873) L.R. 8 C.P. 167. The prima facie measure was taken even although the trial took place before the time fixed for delivery had arrived. In such circumstances the court must arrive at the market price on that future date "as best it can": *Melachrino v Nickoll* [1920] 1 K.B. 693 at 699, per Bailhache J. It presumably must be estimated on the basis of the market price at and before the trial and the trend of the market. The situation is seldom likely to arise: if there is a market and the due date is well ahead the seller will probably be able to show that the buyer should have repurchased.

73 [1968] A.C. 1130; see at 1140.

74 *Melachrino v Nickoll* [1920] 1 K.B. 693 at 697. Bailhache J's judgment in this case contains a very clear exposition of the various situations involved. See the equivalent non-acceptance case of *Roth v Taysen* (1896) 12 T.L.R. 211 CA, at para.25-124, below.

75 [1920] 1 K.B. 693.

76 [1993] 1 Lloyd's Rep. 1 CA. See the non-acceptance case of *Metelmann & Co v N.B.R. (London)*

price which in the event turns out to be higher than that at the time fixed for delivery, he is entitled, on general principles of mitigation, to have the damages assessed with reference to his repurchase price.[77]

25-019 *(iii) Where the time fixed for delivery is postponed at the request of one of the parties* Where the time fixed for delivery has been postponed at the request of the seller, but nevertheless he ultimately fails to deliver in the extended period, this has the effect of deferring the point in time at which the breach takes place and therefore alters the date with reference to which the damages are to be calculated. The old contract continues but the date of breach is shifted, and the damages will be calculated at the market price on the last day to which the contract was extended if a date was fixed, or at the date when the buyer refused to grant further indulgence, or at a reasonable period after his last grant of indulgence. This was established in *Ogle v Vane*.[78] A contract for the sale of iron had a delivery date in July and the buyer waited for delivery at the seller's request until February, when, refusing to wait any longer, he rebought in the market which since July had risen. The buyer's claim to have the damages measured according to the higher market price when he rebought in February succeeded. Kelly CB said:

> "It would be contrary to common sense and justice, when there has been a series of proposals by the defendant involving delay for his own benefit, and acquiescence on the part of the plaintiff, that because there may be no binding contract, varying the terms of the former contract, the plaintiff is to be tied down to the strict letter of the rule as to the measure of damages for the non-delivery of goods, and not to be entitled to the damages consequent upon the delay."[79]

However, it was held in *Ex p. Llansamlet Tin Plate Co*,[80] that there must be a clear request to wait by the seller and a holding out of a promise that delivery in the future will be achieved; the buyer cannot just "forbear" on his own on a rising market and then claim on the basis of the risen market price. More recently, in *Johnson Matthey Bankers v The State Trading Corp of India*,[81] it was held that the sellers' request for an extension of the delivery dates under 34 contracts for the sale of silver was, though clearly not express,[82] nevertheless a proper business conclusion to draw from the facts and documents[83] and that this sufficed, being acquiesced in or assented to by the buyers,[84] to defer for over a year the time at which the market price of the silver fell to be taken. Indeed Staughton J went further and adopted Lord Wilberforce's formulation, in a somewhat different context, in *Johnson v Agnew*,[85] that

> "in cases where a breach of a contract for sale has occurred, and the innocent party reasonably continues to try to have the contract completed, it would to me appear more logical

[1984] 1 Lloyd's Rep. 614 CA, at para.25-124, below.

77 *Melachrino v Nickoll* [1920] 1 K.B. 693 at 697.

78 (1868) L.R. 3 Q.B. 272.

79 (1868) L.R. 3 Q.B. 272 at 279. Applied to similar facts in *Blackburn Bobbin Co v Allen* [1918] 1 K.B. 540; see especially at 553 to 554 (affirmed [1918] 2 K.B. 467 CA, but this point was not appealed).

80 (1873) L.R. 16 Eq. 155, distinguishing *Ogle v Vane* (1868) L.R. 3 Q.B. 272.

81 [1984] 1 Lloyd's Rep. 427.

82 See (1873) L.R. 16 Eq. 155 at 437, col.2.

83 (1873) L.R. 16 Eq. 155 at 438, col.1.

84 See (1873) L.R. 16 Eq. 155 at 438, col.1.

85 [1980] A.C. 367 at 401A to B.

and just rather than tie him to the date of the original breach, to assess damages as at the date when (otherwise than by his default) the contract is lost."[86]

This represents an application to this particular situation of the growing tendency to allow damages to be assessed at a date later than breach if in all the circumstances this appears to be reasonable.[87]

Where the request to postpone delivery comes from the buyer and the seller at first concurs, but subsequently refuses to deliver on the basis of the buyer's unpreparedness to accept at the date originally fixed by the contract, the matter is more complex. The general rule as to liability evolved by the courts is that the seller cannot suddenly retract his forbearance but must give reasonable notice to the buyer, thereby placing the buyer under an obligation to accept the goods within a reasonable time of the retraction.[88] On the seller's peremptory refusal to deliver, it would seem that this will constitute the breach and the damages will be assessed with reference to the market price at that date. This appears from *Tyers v Rosedale & Ferryhill Co*,[89] which was, however, complicated by the fact that the delivery under the contract was to be by instalments. Iron sold by the defendant to the claimant was to be delivered in monthly instalments over the year 1871. The claimant at various periods in 1871 requested the defendant to forbear from delivering the entire quantity contracted for and then in December required delivery of the whole balance, upon which demand the defendant repudiated the contract and refused to deliver any further iron. The claimant's claim for damages, assessed with reference to the market price in December, succeeded. The question whether the defendant was bound to deliver the whole balance in December, or was entitled to deliver by monthly instalments or to demand a reasonable time for delivery, and the question whether therefore the damages should be assessed with reference to the market price in December or at subsequent monthly periods, did not fall for decision since the December price was claimed by the claimant and happened to be advantageous to the defendant, presumably because the market had risen thereafter. On principle the court would have to decide at what time the seller would be bound to deliver and the market price would be taken at that time, subject to the buyer's duty to mitigate where the seller had repudiated and he had accepted the repudiation.[90] **25-020**

*(iv) Where no time is fixed for delivery* The situations dealt with so far have all involved the first limb of s.51(3) as there has been a fixed time or times for delivery. Where no time is fixed for delivery, the second limb of s.51(3) specifically provides that the time to be taken is that of the refusal to deliver.[91] This would clearly apply to a contract to deliver goods on demand or as required by the buyer: an illustra- **25-021**

[86] See [1984] 1 Lloyd's Rep. 427 at 437, col.1 to 438, col.1.

[87] See, e.g. the cases at paras 27-009 and 25-049, below.

[88] Technical difficulties arise here as to the validity of the seller's forbearance on both the question of consideration and the necessity in certain cases that the alteration be in writing. To overcome these difficulties the courts have constructed a rather unsatisfactory distinction between variation and waiver, for details of which see the standard texts on contract. All that is of concern here is the measure of damages if the seller is successfully sued for breach (waiver); if the buyer's action fails (variation), no question of damages will arise.

[89] (1875) L.R. 10 Ex. 195.

[90] Compare the comments on the case in *Tai Hing Cotton Mill v Kamsing Knitting Factory* [1979] A.C. 91 PC at 103G to H together with the decision there.

[91] See para.25-002, above.

tion is provided by *Tai Hing Cotton Mill v Kamsing Knitting Factory*.[92] It is not, however, settled whether the case is one in which no time is fixed within s.51(3) should the contract provide expressly or by implication for delivery at a time fixed by the happening of a certain event, such as the arrival of a ship as in *Melachrino v Nickoll*,[93] or within a reasonable time of the making of the contract, or, combining the two, within a reasonable time of the happening of an event, as in *Millett v Van Heek*,[94] which provided for delivery within a reasonable time of the removal of a Government embargo. Differing views have been expressed in the courts on this question[95] but it seems largely an academic one since, apart from anticipatory breach, any refusal by the seller to perform must necessarily fall at approximately the same time as what on one view is the time fixed,[96] while it was rightly held in *Millett v Van Heek*,[97] that the refusal to deliver which brings the measure prescribed by the second limb of s.51(3) into operation cannot be by an anticipatory breach, i.e. by a repudiation before the arrival of the time for performance as opposed to a non-performance itself.

**25-022** The correctness of *Millett v Van Heek*[98] was unsuccessfully challenged in *Tai Hing Cotton Mill v Kamsing Knitting Factory*,[99] where the Judicial Committee of the Privy Council

> "affirm[ed] the principle that the second limb of s.51(3) does not apply in any case of anticipatory breach of contract".[100]

While recognising that

> "there may be great difficulty in determining when the contract ought to have been performed, and [that] there could be much convenience in assessing damages as at the date of repudiation by the seller, assuming the buyer accepts it",[101]

their Lordships were nevertheless persuaded that *Millett v Van Heek*,[102] should be upheld as

---

92 [1979] A.C. 91 PC.

93 [1920] 1 K.B. 693.

94 [1921] 2 K.B. 369 CA.

95 Bray and Sankey JJ in the Divisional Court in *Millett v Van Heek* [1920] 3 K.B. 535 took the view that a contract for delivery within a reasonable time of a specified event was one in which no time was fixed for delivery. Bailhache J in *Melachrino v Nickoll* [1920] 1 K.B. 693 had taken the contrary view in a case where the goods sold were to be shipped and the ship's arrival date could only be estimated within the period of a month. The Court of Appeal, in affirming *Millett v Van Heek* [1921] 2 K.B. 369 CA, on another ground, reserved their opinion on this question, although Atkin LJ rather tended to Bailhache J's view: at 378.

96 See *Tai Hing Cotton Mill v Kamsing Knitting Factory* [1979] A.C. 91 PC at 104C where their Lordships accepted that "it may well be … that the enactment [namely, the second limb] was introduced into the subsection without consideration in depth of the juristic position, and that on analysis it proved, exceptionally, to have no content whatever".

97 [1921] 2 K.B. 369 CA.

98 [1921] 2 K.B. 369 CA.

99 [1979] A.C. 91 PC.

100 [1979] A.C. 91 PC at 105A.

101 [1979] A.C. 91 PC at 104B.

102 [1921] 2 K.B. 369 CA.

"it would be surprising if the first limb of one and the same subsection were intended to be a specific application of the general principle in the preceding subsection, and the second limb to be a radical departure from it".[103]

## (2) Consequential losses

In cases of non-delivery consequential losses are not likely to arise where there is a market available in which the buyer can buy equivalent goods against his use or resale.[104] But in the absence of an available market[105] consequential losses are frequent.[106] **25-023**

### (a) Loss through loss of use

*(i) Loss of user profits* The cases dealing with the recovery of user profits concern, fortuitously, actions for delayed delivery and not for non-delivery. Their proper place therefore comes later.[107] However, as they involve the same principles they remain the relevant authorities for non-delivery also and apply here mutatis mutandis. That a claim for loss of user profits can be in addition to the normal measure of damages[108] is illustrated by *Vanda Compania of Costa Rica v Société Maritime Nationale of Paris, The Ile aux Moines*,[109] a case involving the non-delivery of a ship where it was accepted that the buyers could have claimed not only the difference between the market price and the contract price but also loss of user profits until such time as a substitute ship could be found by them, there being no available market. **25-024**

*(ii) Expenses made necessary* Recovery for expenses made necessary by the breach is illustrated for non-delivery by cases in which the buyer has successfully claimed as damages the cost of acquiring the nearest substitute at a higher price where there has been no market in which he could buy exactly equivalent goods. Thus in *Hinde v Liddell*,[110] the seller failed to deliver a large purchase of grey shirting. The buyer, in order to fulfil a sub-contract, bought other shirting of a somewhat superior quality and at an increased price, since it was impossible to get exactly equivalent shirting on the market and this was the nearest obtainable in quality and price. The buyer recovered as damages the price he paid for the substitute **25-025**

---

[103] [1979] A.C. 91 PC at 104D. This point had already been fully and forcefully made in a passage, which their Lordships cited (at 101D to 102B), from Atkin LJ's judgment in *Millett v Van Heek* [1921] 2 K.B. 369 CA at 376 to 377.

[104] Thus in *Peterson v Ayre* (1853) 13 C.B. 353, where the buyer claimed loss of profits on a resale and also damages paid by him to his sub-buyer, the claim for such an amount was peremptorily dismissed by Maule J who said that he should have gone into the market and repurchased (at 365, *arguendo*). In *Coastal International Trading v Maroil* [1988] 1 Lloyd's Rep. 92 there was held to be no available market, thereby permitting recovery to the claimants of their contemplated loss of profit on a resale.

[105] See paras 25-006 to 25-008, above, for discussion of the meaning of available market.

[106] One item of recovery in the complex damages case of *Thai Airways International Public Co Ltd v KI Holdings Co Ltd* [2015] EWHC 1250 (Comm), where there was non-delivery of a number of economy class seats sold for installation in aircraft, was the additional cost of purchasing of replacement seats, subject to certain credits. See at [2015] EWHC 1250 (Comm) at [20] and [141] and following, and the case in detail at para.9-007, above.

[107] See paras 25-045 to 25-047, below.

[108] See para.25-004, above.

[109] [1974] 2 Lloyd's Rep. 502.

[110] (1875) L.R. 10 Q.B. 265.

shirting less the contract price. This decision was accepted in *Blackburn Bobbin Co v Allen*,[111] where on non-delivery of timber from Finland the buyer bought English timber which was the best available substitute but which entailed more expense and waste in cutting. McCardie J was prepared to award damages on the basis of the extra expense.[112]

**25-026** If the buyer, faced with non-delivery and a consequent inability to carry on his business, buys substitute goods which, after use in the business, are sold at a profit, this profit is to be taken into account in any claim by the buyer for the cost of obtaining the substitute. This was established in *Erie County Natural Gas Co v Carroll*.[113] The claimant sold gas leases to the defendant reserving to himself the right to the supply of sufficient gas for the operation of his business. The defendant in breach of contract cut off the gas and the claimant thereupon procured gas to run his business by the acquisition of other gas leases from third parties and by the construction of works to produce gas. Subsequently when he sold his business the claimant sold the gas leases and works for more than they had cost him. In these circumstances the Judicial Committee of the Privy Council held that the claimant was entitled only to nominal damages, in an action against the defendant for failure to supply the reserved gas, on the ground that the substitute gas had been procured, as events turned out, at no cost to himself. In such a claim for expenses the defendant is entitled to require that any equivalent gains to the claimant be deducted.[114]

**25-027** **(b) Loss on a resale** Loss on a resale, like damage through loss of use, is most likely to arise where there is no market in which similar goods can be bought. But, in addition, loss can arise here despite the existence of a market generally, because this market is not available to the buyer himself. As Salter J pointed out in *Patrick v Russo-British Grain Export Co*,[115] there are two such cases.

> "One is when the sale is of specific goods, and the buyer has resold the same goods. The other is where the contract of resale has the same delivery date as the contract of sale."[116]

Yet although in these two cases the buyer will not fail to mitigate his loss by not buying in the market, he will not necessarily recover in respect of his loss. For, as was made clear by Devlin J in *Kwei Tek Chao v British Traders*,[117] damages for loss on a resale are not recoverable merely because the seller knows that the buyer is a merchant buying generally for resale, as what is contemplated on non-delivery where there is a market is that the buyer will go out into the market and buy.[118] Only if the seller contemplated that the buyer could only carry out his sub-sale by deliver-

---

111 [1918] 1 K.B. 540.

112 [1918] 1 K.B. 540 at 554. The same sum of damages was arrived at and awarded on a different ground, while on appeal the damages question was not considered.

113 [1911] A.C. 105 PC. The case is considered further in the context of mitigation and avoided loss at para.9-123, above. Compare the breach of warranty case of *British Westinghouse Co v Underground Ry* [1912] A.C. 673 at para.25-080, below.

114 See, too, *Hinde v Liddell* (1875) L.R. 10 Q.B. 265 at 270, where Field J suggested that, if the buyer, having bought more expensive goods in substitution in order to fulfil a sub-contract, had been given a higher price by his sub-buyer, this factor should have been taken into account.

115 [1927] 2 K.B. 535.

116 [1927] 2 K.B. 535 at 541.

117 [1954] 2 Q.B. 459 at 489–490.

118 See *Aryeh v Kostoris & Son* [1967] 1 Lloyd's Rep. 63 CA, where the Official Referee was held to have erred in awarding to the claimant, where there was an available market, the loss of his sub-sale profit and the compensation paid to his sub-buyer.

ing the very same goods will he be liable for loss on a resale where there is a market.[119]

*(i) Loss of profit on a resale* The earlier cases did not allow the buyer to recover the loss of profit on a resale, whether made before or after the purchase, where all the seller knew was that the buyer had bought with a general intention to resell, as in *Thol v Henderson*,[120] or even where it was the practice, known to the seller, for buyers to resell before delivery, as in *Williams v Reynolds*.[121] Later cases, however, have shown a more liberal tendency and allowed loss of such profit where the defendant knew the buyer would resell,[122] or even where it was probable that the buyer would resell.[123] The cases where the resale was only a probability need closer consideration. In *Patrick v Russo-British Grain Export Co*,[124] wheat was bought and resold at a higher price. The seller failed to deliver, and there was no market available to the buyer at the time of breach or subsequently. The parties contemplated that the wheat would probably be resold. In awarding as damages the resale price less the contract price, Salter J held that in order for the buyer to get his loss of profit on a resale it was not necessary **25-028**

> "that the seller should have known, when he sold, that the buyer was buying to implement a contract already made or that the buyer would certainly resell; it is enough if both parties contemplate that the buyer will probably resell and the seller is content to take the risk. I think, therefore, that the arbitrators' finding [that the probability of resale was contemplated] is sufficient to support a claim for loss of profit on a resale."[125]

In *Hall v Pim*,[126] the claimant bought from the defendant an unascertained cargo of wheat which he resold without awaiting delivery, and further resales of the cargo took place by a series of string contracts. The defendant failed to deliver and the

---

119 See *Hall v Pim* (1928) 33 Com. Cas. 324 HL, at para.25-028, below, and *Aryeh v Kostoris & Son* [1967] 1 Lloyd's Rep. 63 CA at 68, 72, per Wilmer and Diplock LJJ respectively.

120 (1882) 8 Q.B.D. 457.

121 (1865) 6 B. & S. 495. 19th century cases allowing the recovery of loss of profit on a resale are not strong authorities because the seller, having known of the sub-contracts, admitted his liability for the loss of profit and the argument was on other matters: *Borries v Hutchinson* (1865) 18 C.B. N.S. 445; *Grebert-Borgnis v Nugent* (1885) 15 Q.B.D. 85 CA. Yet Asquith LJ in *Victoria Laundry v Newman* [1949] 2 K.B. 528 CA at 536 gave *Borries v Hutchinson* as his sole illustration of recoverable loss of profit on a resale: this itself suggests a lack of authority in favour of the buyer.

122 *Lyon v Fuchs* (1920) 2 Ll. L.R. 333; *Frank Mott v Muller* (1922) 13 Ll. L. Rep. 492; *Household Machines v Cosmos Exporters* [1947] 1 K.B. 217; *Coastal International Trading v Maroil* [1988] 1 Lloyd's Rep. 92.

123 *Patrick v Russo-British Grain Export Co* [1927] 2 K.B. 535; *Hall v Pim* (1928) 33 Com. Cas. 324 HL.

124 [1927] 2 K.B. 535.

125 [1927] 2 K.B. 535 at 540. He distinguished *Williams v Reynolds* (1865) 6 B. & S. 495 on the ground that "the court, though satisfied that the parties contemplated resale by the buyer, were not satisfied that they contemplated a resale on such terms that, if the seller made default, the buyer must be unable to satisfy his sub-buyer. It was a case in which the parties contemplated that, in the event of non-delivery, the buyer would buy against the seller, and only nominal damages were recoverable": .at 542 to 543. If, indeed, the buyer could have gone into the market and rebought in *Williams v Reynolds* after the seller's breach and still been in time to carry out the sub-sale which he had made before the failure to deliver, then the decision would be the same today (see *Kwei Tek Chao v British Traders* [1954] 2 K.B. 459 at 489 to 490, per Devlin J, at para.25-027, above). But whether the buyer was in a position to rebuy in time is not clear from the report; if he were not, then the real explanation is that times had changed between the decision in *William v Reynolds* and that in *Patrick v Russo-British Grain Export Co*.

126 (1928) 33 Com. Cas. 324 HL.

House of Lords allowed the claimant the loss of profit on his resale, even though the arbitrators had found that the chance of the buyer keeping the goods for himself and the chance of his reselling them were approximately equal. Viscount Dunedin, alluding to the need to show that the resale was probable, said that

> "to make a thing probable, it is enough, in my view, that there is an even chance of its happening".[127]

However, there was this special factor in the case: the contract contained clauses providing for a series of sub-sales. This appears to have made the question of the probability of resale much less important. Thus Lord Shaw of Dunfermline said that it appeared to him that

> "the chance of a not unlikely thing [i.e. a resale] happening … [was] one of those chances which must be reckoned to have been within the contemplation of the parties when sub-contracts or transfers were the matter of express agreement between them."[128]

Viscount Haldane went even further. He said:

> "Whether the latter [i.e. the plaintiff] was likely to enter into such sub-contracts and pass the cargo down a chain of resales is not material. It is enough that the contract contemplated by its terms that he should have the right to do so if he chose."[129]

**25-029** Scrutton and Sankey LJJ criticised this decision in *Finlay v Kwik Hoo Tong*,[130] and explained it on its special facts. Nevertheless, although *Hall v Pim*[131] is rather a special case by reason of the provision for sub-sales, this factor is only sufficient to oust the rule, subsequently stated in *Kwei Tek Chao v British Traders*,[132] that resale profits are not recoverable where there is a market, since what is contemplated on non-delivery is that the claimant will go into the market and buy. Beyond this the remarks in the case are still generally relevant on the issue of how probable a resale must be before it may be said to be within the contemplation of the parties and so let in a claim for loss of profit. Greer LJ indeed said in *Finlay v Kwik Hoo Tong*,[133] that the decision in *Hall v Pim*,[134]

> "commends itself to my mind as a reasonable and sound view of what ought to be the law on the subject of taking into account sub-contracts in estimating damages arising out of the principal contract",

and, more importantly, much of what was said in the decision has now received general endorsement by the House of Lords in *The Heron II*.[135] It is submitted further that the difficulty of reconciling *Hall v Pim*,[136] with *Williams v Agius*,[137] a difficulty of which all the members of the Court of Appeal in *Finlay v Kwik Hoo*

---

127 (1928) 33 Com. Cas. 324 HL at 330.
128 (1928) 33 Com. Cas. 324 HL at 335.
129 (1928) 33 Com. Cas. 324 HL at 326.
130 [1929] 1 K.B. 400 CA at 411 to 412, 417 to 418, respectively. Sankey LJ quoted counsel's remark that *Hall v Pim* was a decision which had "astonished the Temple and surprised St Mary Axe".
131 (1928) 33 Com. Cas. 324 HL.
132 [1954] 2 Q.B. 459 at 489–490; see para.25-027, above.
133 [1929] 1 K.B. 400 CA at 415.
134 (1928) 33 Com. Cas. 324 HL.
135 [1969] 1 A.C. 350; see at 387–388, 405–406, 410, 414, 424.
136 (1928) 33 Com. Cas. 324 HL.
137 [1914] A.C. 510.

*Tong*[138] spoke, fails to take account of the fact that in *Williams v Agius*[139] the sub-contract was being introduced by the defendant to cut down the normal measure of damages that the claimant was claiming, while in *Hall v Pim*[140] it was introduced by the claimant to show consequential loss beyond the normal measure. Different considerations may well apply in these very different situations.[141]

Where damages are allowed for loss of profit on a resale of which the seller knew the actuality or the probability, he will not be liable for an exceptional loss of profits unless he has been informed of the details of the sub-contracts and only then if he can be said to have taken the risk of such loss on his shoulders. This appears from the speeches in *Hall v Pim*.[142] Lord Dunedin said: **25-030**

> "The contracts … must be contracts in accordance with the market, not extravagant and unusual bargains."[143]

And Lord Shaw said:

> "It is not suggested that these prices were out of the ordinary course of business. Had this been so, different considerations might quite well have arisen."[144]

Thus in *Household Machines v Cosmos Exporters*,[145] where the seller knew of the claimant's intention to resell but did not know the details of the sub-contract, Lewis J did not award the claimant the 12 per cent by which the sub-contract price was higher than the contract price, but gave only 10 per cent. Similarly, in *Coastal International Trading v Maroil*,[146] where the sub-contract, of which the defendants were fully aware, contained unusual terms rendering the claimants' profit under it unreasonable and such as would not have been within the contemplation of the parties, the profit awarded to the claimants was arrived at after eliminating the extravagant effect of the unusual terms.

*(ii) Cost of acquiring substitute goods* The loss on a resale may not be caused by the resale itself being lost but be represented by the cost of acquiring at a price higher than the initial purchase price the nearest substitute goods should there be no market in which exactly equivalent goods can be bought, with which substitute goods the resale is then carried through. Here the buyer should recover as damages the price paid for the substitute goods less the contract price, in the same manner as has been held where the substitute goods are required not for resale but for use.[147] *M&J Marine Engineering Services Co Ltd v Shipshore Ltd*,[148] was a case of this nature. Machined wheel rollers, for which there was held to be no available market,[149] had been sold at a profit to a third party by the buyer who on the seller's non-delivery had acquired substitute goods for its resale at a much higher price than **25-031**

138 [1929] 1 K.B. 400 CA at 410, 415, 417.
139 [1914] A.C. 510.
140 (1928) 33 Com. Cas. 324 HL.
141 See the footnote at the end of para.9-174, above.
142 (1928) 33 Com. Cas. 324 HL.
143 (1928) 33 Com. Cas. 324 HL at 330.
144 (1928) 33 Com. Cas. 324 HL at 331. See *Victoria Laundry v Newman* [1949] 2 K.B. 528 CA in relation to loss of user profits at para.25-046, below.
145 [1947] 1 K.B. 217.
146 [1988] 1 Lloyd's Rep. 92.
147 See the cases at para.25-025, above.
148 [2009] EWHC 2031 (Comm).
149 See the case at para.25-007, above.

that at which it had bought. It is a curious case because the buyer renegotiated with the third party an amount for it to pay which was even slightly above the price the buyer had paid for the substitute goods. In these circumstances the buyer was awarded as damages, apart from its costs in renegotiating the resale, the initial loss of profit on its resale—viz., the difference between the price the third party had initially agreed to pay and the contract price—less the small profit eventually made on the resale—viz., the difference between the price the third party had finally paid and the cost of the substitute goods.[150] Yet it is thought that a better method of assessment would have been not to award the initial profit less the final profit but to award the cost of the substitute goods less the initial contract price and then to deduct from this, as a form of mitigation,[151] the difference between what the third party finally paid and what it had initially contracted to pay. The result mathematically is the same.

**25-032** *(iii) Compensation paid to a sub-buyer* The buyer may also recover damages in respect of compensation which he has had to pay to his sub-buyer for his breach of the sub-contract. The authorities, however, are conflicting. In *Borries v Hutchinson*,[152] the seller sold caustic soda knowing that the buyer was buying for resale on the Continent. In an action for damages for non-delivery the seller admitted liability for the loss of profit on the resale, but successfully contested the buyer's claim for the amount he had paid his sub-buyer by reason of his breach of the sub-contract occasioned by the defendant's non-delivery. On the other hand, in *Grébert-Borgnis v Nugent*,[153] the seller sold sheepskins to the claimant, knowing that, except as to price, the contract was substantially the same as the claimant's sub-contract with a French customer. In an action for damages for non-delivery the seller again did not dispute liability for the loss of profit on the resale, but here the buyer successfully recovered the damages he had paid his sub-buyer in a suit in a French court. The Court of Appeal said that the damages given by the French court were not as a matter of law the exact amount the claimant was entitled to, but that this amount might be treated as a not unreasonable one at which the damages might be assessed. It is difficult to see how these two cases can be satisfactorily reconciled,[154] and it is submitted that *Grebert-Borgnis v Nugent*[155] is to be preferred as a decision of the Court of Appeal and a decision showing the later more liberal tendency to allow recovery for loss on a resale. If the sub-sale is sufficiently within the parties' contemplation to allow loss of profits, it must surely also let in recovery in respect of compensation paid to the sub-buyer.[156]

**25-033** Where no claim has yet been made by the sub-buyer it was held in *Household*

---

150 See the discussion at [2009] EWHC 2031 (Comm) at [25]–[31] where the figures are a little difficult to work out.

151 See the mitigation principles set out at paras 9-117 and following, above.

152 (1865) 18 C.B. N.S. 445.

153 (1885) 15 Q.B.D. 85 CA.

154 Unless it be upon the ground suggested by Brett LJ in *Grebert-Borgnis v Nugent* (1885) 15 Q.B.D. 85 CA at 90 that the buyer in *Borries v Hutchinson* had been liable under his sub-contract for some extraordinary penalties of which his seller did not know. But there is no evidence of any such penalties. Bowen LJ thought that Borries v Hutchinson was wrong and irreconcilable with *Elbinger Aktiengesellschaft v Armstrong* (1874) L.R. 9 Q.B. 473, a case of delayed delivery: see para.25-052, below.

155 (1885) 15 Q.B.D. 85 CA.

156 This view is lent support by Lord Dunedin's remarks in *Hall v Pim* (1928) 33 Com. Cas. 324 HL at 330. On the other hand Salter J in *Patrick v Russo-British Grain Export Co* [1927] 2 K.B. 535 at 540 thought that the probability of a resale "might well have been insufficient to support a claim for

*Machines v Cosmos Exporters*,[157] that the buyer was entitled to a declaration of indemnity, limited to such damages as in law were due to him from the seller, in respect of damages which he might in the future be held liable to pay or might reasonably pay in respect of the discharge of his legal liability to the sub-buyer. But in *Trans Trust S.P.R.L. v Danubian Trading Co*,[158] the Court of Appeal expressed the view obiter, in the converse situation where the seller was claiming from the buyer the amount by which he might be liable over to his own seller, that the proper course was not to award a declaration of indemnity but to reserve this head of damages for calculation if and when it arose.[159]

*(iv) Costs incurred in defending a sub-buyer's action* If there is non-delivery to the buyer so that he cannot deliver to his sub-buyer he is so clearly in breach that he will seldom have any ground for defending an action brought against him by his sub-buyer. The costs of such a defence will therefore generally be on his own head since he cannot claim that they were incurred as the probable result of his seller's breach. The costs of a defence which succeeds in cutting down an exorbitant claim by the sub-buyer should, however, be recoverable.[160] **25-034**

*(v) Other expenses made necessary* There may be other miscellaneous expenses in connection with a resale which the buyer incurs as a result of the breach. There are no illustrations in non-delivery.[161] **25-035**

*(vi) Loss of profit on further sales* There are so far, in the context of non-delivery, no clear successful claims for loss of custom generally, stemming from the loss of particular sub-sales of the goods sold by the defendant. Thus in *Doe v Bowater*,[162] the defendant sold coal to the claimant, knowing that the claimant had a coal retail business. The defendant made a short delivery and the claimant, unable to fulfil his contracts with his customers, lost the customers but this loss was held irrecoverable. However, the Court of Appeal has since in *G.K.N. Centrax Gears v Matbro*,[163] in the context of a sale of defective goods, opened up the way to recovery for loss of goodwill and of repeat orders; all that is required is that, applying *Hadley v Baxendale*,[164] such loss be shown to be in the particular circumstances in the contemplation of the contracting parties. **25-036**

**(c) Expenses rendered futile by the breach** As an alternative to claiming for loss of profits a buyer may sometimes claim, as consequential loss, for expenses **25-037**

---

costs incurred in litigation with a sub-buyer or for penalties or damages paid to him": this was cited with apparent approval by Devlin J in *Heskell v Continental Express* [1950] 1 All E.R. 1033 at 1049.

157 [1947] 1 K.B. 217.

158 [1952] 2 Q.B. 297 CA; see especially at 303, 307, per Somervell and Denning LJJ respectively. See para.10-032, above.

159 See *Deeny v Gooda Walker* [1995] 1 W.L.R. 1206 at para.40-280, below, endorsing, in a different context, the jurisdiction to order postponement of the adjudication of part of the damages.

160 See the equivalent case in delayed delivery of *Agius v Great Western Colliery Co* [1899] 1 Q.B. 413 CA, at para.25-053, below. But today the buyer successful against his sub-buyer may find himself entitled to no costs recovery from the seller for the reasons explained when breach of warranty of quality and fitness by the seller is reached: see paras 25-086 and 25-087, below.

161 See delayed delivery at para.25-054, below, and breach of warranty at para.25-106 below.

162 [1916] W.N. 185.

163 [1976] 2 Lloyd's Rep. 555 CA.

164 (1854) 9 Ex. 341.

rendered futile by the breach. Illustrations however must be sought in cases of delayed delivery and breach of warranty.[165]

## 2. DELAYED DELIVERY

**25-038** No rule is prescribed by the Sale of Goods Act 1979 for the measure of damages where the goods sold are delayed and ultimately accepted by the buyer after the delay. The consequential losses are much the same as in non-delivery, but the normal measure of damages is necessarily quite different and is indeed more in line with the normal measure for breach of warranty.[166]

### (1) Normal measure

**25-039** The normal measure of damages, subject to the qualification made below,[167] is the market value at the contractual time[168] for delivery less the market value at the time[169] of actual delivery,[170] since this represents the amount that will put the buyer into the position he would have been in had the contract been carried out.[171] Authoritative statements of this measure seem to be non-existent: the most commonly referred to, that appearing in Blackburn J's judgment in *Elbinger Aktiengesellschaft v Armstrong*,[172] deals in value and not in market value, since the situation under discussion was that in which there was no market.[173]

**25-040** Where delay in delivery has caused the buyer either reasonably to go into the market and acquire equivalent goods so that, when the contractual goods eventually arrive, he has no need for them and disposes of them or, alternatively, to await the goods and then dispose of them as he may originally have intended, then the normal loss as stated makes sense. But as Parker J rightly pointed out in *Croudace Construction v Cawoods Concrete Products*,[174] where the delay in delivery was of masonry blocks to a builder, it may have no relevance to the case in which the buyer waits for the delivery and then proceeds to use the goods in the way he intended. For as he said:

> "When selling building materials to a contractor for delivery on a building site, the difference in the value of the materials is, as a matter of common sense, wholly irrelevant. If between the date when the goods should have been delivered and the date when they were in fact delivered, there is a fall in the value, that is, as a matter of commercial real-

---

165 See paras 25-057 and 25-109, below, respectively.

166 See paras 25-061 and following, below.

167 See para.25-040, below.

168 And also at the contractual place for delivery: see *Aryeh v Kostoris & Son* [1967] 1 Lloyd's Rep. 63 CA at 73, col.1, per Diplock LJ.

169 And place; see previous note.

170 This is on the normal assumption that the contract price will have been paid over.

171 The suggestion in *Smeed v Foord* (1859) 1 E. & E. 602, similar to that formerly appearing in the corresponding contracts of carriage by sea (see paras 32-029 to 32-031, below), that the defendant is not liable for a fall in the market value, cannot be accepted.

172 (1874) L.R. 9 Q.B. 473 at 477, citing Willes J in *Borries v Hutchinson* (1865) 18 C.B. N.S. 455 at 465.

173 In *Galaxy Energy International Ltd v Murco Petroleum Ltd* [2013] EWHC 3720 (Comm) this measure was put forward by the claimant in quantification of its loss and was not disputed by the defendant: at [26]. The dispute turned on how market value of the cargo of fuel oil sold was to be determined: see at [29] and following.

174 [1978] 2 Lloyd's Rep. 55.

ity, of supreme indifference to the contractor and in no real sense does he suffer any loss or damage as a result of the fall."[175]

Inevitable increased expenses inflicted upon the buyer by reason of the lateness of the delivery, as were there claimed, would then appear to constitute the normal measure; unless they do, as Parker J said, there would in such a case be no normal loss at all. Even where the buyer awaits the delivery and uses the goods, however, the normal measure of market value at due delivery and market value at actual delivery may be applied, as in *Fletcher v Tayleur*,[176] where the difference between these two values was a seasonal one. The defendant, building for the claimant a passenger ship for the Australian trade, failed to deliver it at the contractual date in August when freights to Australia were at their seasonal peak and delivered it the following March when freights had fallen low. The claimant successfully claimed the diminution in value by the fall in freights for passenger-carrying ships, and this was measured by the profits the ship would have made less the profits she did make on her first voyage.[177]

**(a) Relevant and irrelevant prices in ascertaining the market value at the contractual time for delivery** The contract price may be taken as evidence for the market value of the goods at the contractual time for delivery where this is difficult to assess, but it is generally irrelevant and is not to be taken in lieu of the market value where this is clearly different. Similarly the price at which a third party has agreed to buy the goods from the buyer may be taken as evidence of such market value, but again is generally irrelevant and is no proper substitute where the market value is clearly different. These principles do not find illustration in the cases of delayed delivery, and authority must be sought in the equivalent breach of warranty cases.[178] 25-041

**(b) Relevant and irrelevant prices in ascertaining the market value at the time of actual delivery** The price at which the buyer has resold the goods to a third party may be taken as evidence of their value at the time of actual delivery where this is difficult to assess: once again authority must be sought in the equivalent breach of warranty cases.[179] Yet with a resale after the delayed goods have reached the buyer, the resale price should be held to be irrelevant where clearly different from the market value at actual delivery. If the resale price is lower than the market value at delivery it cannot be relied on by the buyer to augment his damages nor should his damages be decreased if he is able to sell at a price higher than the market value at actual delivery.[180] The position may be different, however, where the resale has been made in advance of the seller's breach. Thus the resale price higher than the market value at delivery was held to control in *Wertheim v* 25-042

175 [1978] 2 Lloyd's Rep. 55 at 58, col.2. The decision, which was primarily concerned with the ambit of a clause excluding liability for consequential loss (see para.3-013, above, in a footnote), was affirmed by the Court of Appeal: above.

176 (1855) 17 C.B. 21.

177 This has overtones of consequential loss but, strictly, it is loss of market.

178 See paras 25-063 and 25-064, below.

179 See paras 25-065 and 25-066, below.

180 For the reasons for this result see the cases on mitigation and avoided loss at paras 9-135 and 9-136, above.

*Chicoutimi Pulp Co.*[181] The seller delivered late the contractual load of wood pulp, the market price at the port of delivery having dropped considerably between the time fixed for delivery and the time of actual delivery. The buyer had resold the goods, some under contracts anterior to the contract sued upon and some under contracts anterior to the time of actual delivery but all at a price substantially higher than the market price at the port of delivery on the date of actual delivery. All these sub-contracts appear to have been successfully performed, possibly because the delivery date under them was later than the date of actual delivery to the buyer. The measure of damages was held to be limited to the market price at the port of delivery at the time specified for delivery less the resale price.[182] Lord Atkinson stated that

> "the market value [i.e. at the time of actual delivery] is taken because it is presumed to be the true value of the goods to the purchaser … but if in fact the purchaser, when he obtains possession of the goods, sells them at a price greatly in advance of the then market value, that presumption is rebutted and the real value of the goods to him is proved by the very fact of this sale to be more than market value, and the loss he sustains must be measured by that price, unless he is, against all justice, to be permitted to make a profit by the breach of contract, be compensated for a loss he never suffered, and be put, as far as money can do it, not in the same position in which he would have been if the contract had been performed, but in a much better position."[183]

This argument was criticised by Scrutton LJ in *Slater v Hoyle & Smith*,[184] pointing out, inter alia, that the buyer was under no obligation to deliver the contract goods on the sub-contract and that, if he had bought other goods and used them for the sub-contract, he would have been left with the original goods on his hands so that their market price at actual delivery would have been the relevant figure in measuring the damages. The answer to this would seem to be simply that in *Wertheim*,[185] the buyer had in fact not bought other goods for his sub-contract.[186]

**25-043** The issue is one of mitigation and avoided loss[187] and the sale of goods cases, dealing variously with non-delivery and breach of warranty of quality as well as delayed delivery, move in different directions. They are given an extended analysis elsewhere[188] and a solution to the difficulties they present is there proposed.[189]

## (2) Consequential losses

**25-044** As with non-delivery, consequential losses in delayed delivery are not likely to arise where there is a market available in which the buyer can buy similar goods

---

181 [1911] A.C. 301 PC.

182 The seller had also contended that the normal measure was inapplicable because there was no market at Chicoutimi, the contractual port of delivery; however the court was prepared, in the circumstances of the case and for the purpose of the measure of damages, to take the market price at Manchester, to which the buyer intended to send the goods, as fairly representing the market value at the contractual port of delivery: [1911] A.C. 301 PC at 315–316.

183 [1911] A.C. 301 PC at 307–308.

184 [1920] 2 K.B. 11 CA at 23–24.

185 [1911] A.C. 301 PC.

186 See similarly for breach of warranty paras 25-068 and 25-069, below. The matter is further considered on a more general basis in Ch.9, above, at paras 9-171 and following.

187 Dealt with at paras 9-108 and following.

188 At paras 9-171 to 9-183, above.

189 For this see para.9-183, above.

against his use or resale.[190] If no such market exists, consequential losses are frequent.[191]

### (a) Loss through loss of use

*(i) Loss of user profits* Cases awarding damages for loss of user profits by reason of delayed delivery start with two decisions of 1868.[192] The first of these, the important *Cory v Thames Ironworks Co*,[193] was complicated by the fact that the parties had not in contemplation the same use for the article to be supplied. The claimants, who were coal merchants, bought the hull of a large floating boom derrick from the defendants, intending to place in the hull hydraulic cranes for the purpose of transhipping their coals direct from the colliers into barges, a purpose which was entirely novel and unknown to the defendants, who assumed the claimants intended to use the hull for a coal store, its most obvious use for coal merchants. The delivery of the hull was delayed, and this resulted in a large loss of profits to the claimants by reason of their being unable to put the derrick to their intended use. In so far as this use was exceptional, they did not attempt to claim for the large loss they incurred, but claimed instead the smaller loss of profits that would follow from the inability to put the hull to its obvious use for storing coal. The defendants argued that if the claimants succeeded they would be recovering damages for what they had neither suffered nor contemplated suffering. The court, in rejecting this argument, pointed out that the result of this reasoning would have been that, when a buyer intended to apply a thing to a purpose which would make the damage greater than that which would have resulted from its application to the purpose which the seller supposed that the buyer intended, the seller would not be liable in damages at all. The court held that, since the sellers had contemplated that the derrick was to be employed in its most obvious profit-earning manner and the buyers had lost more than they would if they had so employed it, the latter were entitled to be compensated to the extent of the loss from the obvious use. This case was followed in the same year in *Re Trent and Humber Co Ex p. Cambrian Steam Packet Co*,[194] where the claimant's vessel, which the defendant had contracted to repair, was redelivered to the claimant late, and the court awarded as damages the net profit which the claimant would have obtained by chartering the vessel had she been delivered at the proper time. Lord Cairns said: 25-045

> "If a profit would arise from a chattel, and it is left with a tradesman for repair, and

---

[190] They are not necessarily so limited, however. Thus in *Smeed v Foord* (1859) 1 E. & E. 602, although there was evidence that the buyer could have hired another threshing-machine when the seller delayed in delivery, the main evidence was that he was prevented from doing so by the seller's continued assurances that the machine would shortly be coming. The buyer was held entitled to recover for consequential loss: see para.25-048, below.

[191] One item of recovery in the complex damages case of *Thai Airways International Public Co Ltd v KI Holdings Co Ltd* [2015] EWHC 1250 (Comm), where there was delayed delivery of a number of economy class seats sold for installation in aircraft, was the additional cost of purchasing, before delivery had taken place, of replacement seats, subject to certain credits. See at [18], [19] and [141] and following, and the case in detail at para.9-007, above.

[192] The earlier case of *Fletcher v Tayleur* (1855) 17 C.B. 21 is essentially a case of loss of market (see para.25-040, above), while *Waters v Towers* (1853) 8 Ex. 401, allowing the buyer's loss of profit through inability to perform a contract for the supply of bobbins by reason of the seller's late delivery of machinery at his mill, is hardly a reliable authority as decided before *Hadley v Baxendale* (1854) 9 Ex. 341 (see para.8-158, above).

[193] (1868) L.R. 3 Q.B. 181.

[194] (1868) L.R. 3 Ch. App. 112.

detained by him beyond the stipulated time, the measure of damages is prima facie the sum which would have been earned in the ordinary course of employment of the chattel in the time."[195]

Similar is the decision in *Steam Herring Fleet v Richards*,[196] in which Kennedy J allowed loss of fishing profits where the defendant delayed delivery of a steam drifter built for the claimant company's fishing fleet, although the year before in *Watson v Gray*,[197] he had refused loss of profits by the use of the claimant's barges where the defendant had delayed delivery of steel plates sold by him to the claimant, the plates being required for the building of the barges.[198]

**25-046** No other straight decision appears on this issue until the landmark case of *Victoria Laundry v Newman*,[199] where Asquith LJ, delivering the judgment of the Court of Appeal, reconsidered the whole question of damages for breach of contract.[200] The claimants, launderers and dyers, wishing to extend their business and having in view, inter alia, the prospect of certain highly profitable dyeing contracts, purchased a boiler from the defendants, an engineering company, who were aware of the claimants' business and that they required the boiler for the business, and who had been informed during the negotiations that the claimants intended to put the boiler into use in the shortest possible space of time. The defendants did not know at the material time the precise role for which the boiler was cast in the claimants' economy, e.g. whether, as the fact was, it was to function in substitution for an existing boiler of inferior capacity, or in replacement of an existing boiler of equal capacity, or as an extra unit to be operated side by side with and in addition to any existing boiler.[201] In an action arising out of a five-month delay in delivery the claimants claimed to include in their damages their loss of business profits, no similar goods having been available on the market. The Court of Appeal held that the defendants could have foreseen that loss of business profits would be liable to result to the claimants from a long delay in delivery, and that, although the defendants did not know of the highly lucrative dyeing contracts so that in the absence of such knowledge the claimants could not "recover specifically and as such the profits expected on these contracts", the claimants were not thereby

"precluded from recovering some general (and perhaps conjectural) sum for loss of business in respect of dyeing contracts to be reasonably expected, any more than in respect of laundering contracts to be reasonably expected".[202]

---

[195] (1868) L.R. 3 Ch. App. 112 at 117.

[196] (1901) 17 T.L.R. 731.

[197] (1900) 16 T.L.R. 308.

[198] See, too, *Saint Line v Richardsons* [1940] 2 K.B. 99 where the defendant had installed engines in the claimant's ship and on delivery the claimant properly rejected them as unfit and had others installed. Atkinson J took the view, although the point was not for his decision, that loss of profit due to delay (not actually here in delivery) would be recoverable. "If one takes loss of profit", he said, "it is quite clear that such a claim may very well arise directly and naturally from the breach based on delay. The vessel was a trading vessel and the owners were deprived of the possession and use of the vessel for many months, and thereby of the obvious opportunity of making profit": at 104.

[199] [1949] 2 K.B. 528 CA.

[200] See paras 8-162 and following, above.

[201] [1949] 2 K.B. 528 CA at 534.

[202] [1949] 2 K.B. 528 CA at 543. In these circumstances the court may insist on having evidence of what would constitute a reasonable and normal profit: see *North Sea Energy Holdings v Petroleum Authority of Thailand* [1997] 2 Lloyd's Rep. 418, a case of non-acceptance by a buyer, at para.25-129, below. The Court of Appeal, in affirming ([1999] 1 Lloyd's Rep. 483 CA), did not have to address

This decision has broadened and clarified[203] the law as to loss of business profits in contracts for the sale of goods. In the first place, the earlier cases allowing recovery had all concerned delayed delivery of obviously profit-earning ships[204]; any possible limitation of recovery to such cases is now past. In the second place, the Court of Appeal rejected the argument, relied on by the judge below, that there is a critical difference, as far as damages for default in delivery are concerned, between a self-contained profit-earning whole and a part of that whole. "In our view," said Asquith LJ, **25-047**

> "there is no intrinsic magic, in this connection, in the whole as against a part. The fact that a part only is involved is only significant in so far as it bears on the capacity of the supplier to foresee the consequences of non-delivery."[205]

None of the important cases in which recovery for consequential loss has been refused where there has been default in delivery of a part of a profit-making whole has concerned loss of user profits by a buyer.[206] They have concerned loss of user profits by the owner of the part through breach of a contract for its carriage,[207] or loss incurred by the buyer of the part on the resale of the whole into which the part was incorporated.[208] In other words, there has been either a different type of contract or a different type of loss.

*(ii) Expenses made necessary* Apart from loss of user profits, expenses may be incurred as a result of the loss of use. Thus in *Smeed v Foord*,[209] where a threshing-machine was sold and delivered late, the buyer recovered the resultant expense in stacking his crops and also, the stacked crops having been damaged by rain, the expense of drying them. In *Watson v Gray*,[210] where steel plates were sold and their delivery delayed, the buyer recovered for the increased cost of building barges for which the plates had been intended. And in *Henderson v Meyer*,[211] a crane manufacturer sold cranes to a timber importer for use in his timber yard and delivered them late so that the buyer suffered loss in loading by hand. The buyer recovered as damages the extra labour costs of handling his timber by hand instead **25-048**

this point.

203 In the light of the House of Lords criticism of the terminology of foreseeability in *The Heron II* [1969] 1 A.C. 350 (see paras 8-164 to 8-167, above) a certain amount of rephrasing of the reason for the result reached is perhaps required (see para.8-183, above), but not even Lord Reid, who was the most critical of the Court of Appeal's terminology, cast any doubt on the correctness of the decision: see especially at 389.

204 See, e.g. *Cory v Thames Ironworks Co* (1868) L.R. 3 Q.B. 181; *Re Trent and Humber Co Ex p. Cambrian Steam Packet Co* (1868) L.R. 4 Ch. App. 112; *Steam Herring Fleet v Richards* (1901) 17 T.L.R. 731; see, too, *Fletcher v Tayleur* (1855) 17 C.B. 21 and *Saint Line v Richardsons* [1940] 2 K.B. 99. All these have been referred to above and they were cited by Asquith LJ in delivering the Court of Appeal's judgment in *Victoria Laundry v Newman* [1949] 2 K.B. 528 CA at 536. He also cited *Wilson v General Ironscrew Colliery Co* (1878) 47 L.J.Q.B. 239 which was, however, a case of breach of warranty.

205 [1949] 2 K.B. 528 CA at 543–544.

206 *Watson v Gray* (1900) 16 T.L.R. 308 provides an illustration but it is rather an unimportant case.

207 *Hadley v Baxendale* (1854) 9 Ex. 341; *British Columbia Saw Mill Co v Nettleship* (1868) L.R. 3 C.P. 499.

208 *Portman v Middleton* (1858) 4 C.B. N.S. 322. Resale losses were however allowed in *Elbinger Aktiengesellschaft v Armstrong* (1874) L.R. 9 Q.B. 473 and in *Hydraulic Engineering Co v McHaffie* (1878) 4 Q.B.D. 670 CA; see paras 25-051 and 25-052, below.

209 (1859) 1 E. & E. 602.

210 (1900) 16 T.L.R. 308.

211 (1941) 46 Com. Cas. 209.

of by cranes and also the extra cost of loading his lorries by hand. He failed, however, to recover damages in respect of additional demurrage on barges kept waiting to be unloaded and rent for storage of some timber awaiting unloading. Such items were held too remote: the seller as a crane manufacturer could not be expected to have contemplated such expenses as they depended on the length of the timber-importing season.

**25-049** **(b) Loss on a resale** What has already been said in relation to loss on a resale occasioned by non-delivery[212] applies also to delayed delivery. There are, however, several cases involving delayed delivery which serve to fill in details and further illustrate the relevant principles.

**25-050** One useful and interesting point that the delayed delivery cases add is by way of dictum in *Elbinger Aktiengesellschaft v Armstrong*,[213] where wheels and axles were delivered late so as to put the buyer in breach of his contract to make wagons for a railway company. It was pointed out that even if the seller could not be taken to have contemplated loss through a sale by the buyer he could have contemplated loss of user profits, and therefore the buyer was entitled to recover for his actual loss to the extent of the loss that would have been incurred had he intended to use the goods himself. Blackburn J said:

> "It is obvious that both parties contemplated that the wheels and axles were to be put into immediate use. Under such circumstances, the natural and almost inevitable consequence of a delay in delivering a set of wheels would be that the plaintiffs, if they meant the waggon for their own use, or their customers, if the waggon was bespoke, would be deprived of the use of a waggon for a period equal to that for which the set of wheels was delayed. At all events the plaintiffs were entitled to recover at a rate per day equal to whatever the jury should find to be reasonable compensation for the loss of the use of the waggons."[214]

The situation is similar to that illustrated by *Cory v Thames Ironworks Co*,[215] except that here the actual loss is not due to an uncontemplated use but to an uncontemplated sale.[216]

**25-051** *(i) Loss of profit on a resale* *Hydraulic Engineering Co v McHaffie*,[217] illustrates, for delayed delivery, the recovery of loss of profit on a sub-sale because the sub-sale was one contemplated by the seller. It was indeed the sub-buyer himself who introduced the buyer to the seller as a person capable of manufacturing and selling a special part for a machine which the buyer was in turn manufacturing for and selling to the sub-buyer. Thus the seller knew at the time of contracting that the contract was the basis for the buyer's sub-sale[218]; furthermore, he was informed by the buyer of the date when the latter was due to deliver the entire machine to the sub-buyer. In the buyer's action for damages for delayed delivery of the special part he recovered, inter alia, his loss of profit on the sub-sale, the sub-buyer having refused to take the machine which was now useless.

---

212 See paras 25-027 and following, above.

213 (1874) L.R. 9 Q.B. 473.

214 (1874) L.R. 9 Q.B. 473 at 477.

215 (1868) L.R. 3 Q.B. 181; see para.25-045, above.

216 The court may sometimes insist on having adequate evidence of the actual loss before making an award: see *North Sea Energy Holdings v Petroleum Authority of Thailand* [1997] 2 Lloyd's Rep. 418, a case of non-acceptance by a buyer, at para.25-129, below. The Court of Appeal, in affirming ([1999] 1 Lloyd's Rep. 483 CA), did not have to address this point.

217 (1878) 4 Q.B.D. 670 CA.

218 (1878) 4 Q.B.D. 670 CA at 675, per Brett LJ.

*(ii) Compensation paid to a sub-buyer* Two further early cases deal with sales in which the goods were not to be resold in the same form by the buyer but were first to be incorporated by him into some other article which was then to be sold.[219] In these two, however, the claim went beyond one for loss of profit to one for recovery in respect of damages paid to the sub-buyer: yet the test is still whether or not the seller contemplated the resale. In the first case, *Portman v Middleton*,[220] the claimant, having contracted to repair a threshing-machine for a third party by harvest time, needed a new fuse box. The defendant undertook to make him one in a fortnight but he delivered it late. The claimant was thus put in breach of his contract to repair, but he failed to recover the damages which he had had to pay the third party, since he had not told the defendant of his contract to repair the machine and the loss he claimed was not an ordinary consequence of the defendant's breach. The second case, the important *Elbinger Aktiengesellschaft v Armstrong*,[221] provides an intermediate situation between that in *Portman v Middleton*,[222] and that in *Hydraulic Engineering Co v McHaffie*.[223] The defendant agreed to supply the claimants with a large number of wheels and axles which the claimants were to use in making wagons for a railway company. The defendant delivered late and the claimants, unable to complete their sub-contract as there was no market in which to buy other wheels and axles, became liable to pay to the railway company liquidated damages. The railway company exacted only part, amounting to £100. At the time of contracting the defendant had been informed of the sub-contract but not of the delivery dates nor of the amount of liquidated damages payable on breach. In these circumstances the defendant contended that his liability was only for nominal damages; the claimants contended that, as a matter of law, the defendant was liable for the exact amount which the claimants had been compelled to pay for breach of their sub-contract. The court accepted neither of these contentions but held that the jury might properly have given general damages to the amount of £100 without reference to the liquidated damages actually incurred, and therefore the claimants' verdict for £100 might stand. Blackburn J said that if the jury had been told that 25-052

> "the plaintiffs were entitled to such damage as in their opinion would be fair compensation for the loss which would naturally arise from the delay, including therein the probable liability of the plaintiffs to damages by reason of the breach through the defendant's default of that contract to which, as both parties knew, the defendant's contract with the plaintiffs was subsidiary, the direction would not, at all events, have been too unfavourable to the defendant."[224]

This has remained the position up to the present day. Thus compensation paid to a sub-buyer was allowed as damages in *Contigroup Companies Inc v Glenmore AG*,[225] where there was no available market for the buyer to acquire equivalent goods, a sub-sale was within the contemplation of the parties, and the compensation to the sub-buyer was by way of settlement.

---

[219] See *Victoria Laundry v Newman* [1949] 2 K.B. 528 CA, where the Court of Appeal, after considering the authorities, rejected the argument relied upon by the judge below that there is a critical difference, as far as default in delivery is concerned, between a self-contained profit-earning whole and a part of that whole; see para.25-047, above.

[220] (1858) 4 C.B. N.S. 322.

[221] (1874) L.R. 9 Q.B. 473.

[222] (1858) 4 C.B. N.S. 322.

[223] (1878) 4 Q.B.D. 670 CA.

[224] (1874) L.R. 9 Q.B. 473 at 479.

[225] [2005] 1 Lloyd's Rep. 241.

**25-053** *(iii) Costs incurred in defending a sub-buyer's action* With delayed delivery which puts the buyer in breach of his sub-contract he will be so clearly in breach that he will seldom have any ground for defending an action brought against him by his sub-buyer, and the costs of such a defence will therefore be his own responsibility and irrecoverable as damages from his seller. *Agius v Great Western Colliery Co*,[226] does, however, illustrate one type of case in which costs of defence can be regarded as reasonably incurred. In this case the buyer admitted that he was liable to the sub-buyer for a certain amount of damages which he paid into court, and then defended the sub-buyer's claim for a greater amount which he successfully showed at the trial to be exorbitant. Not only was it obvious, said Lord Halsbury LC, that a claim by the sub-buyer against the buyer would follow a breach by the sellers[227] but

> "it would be reasonable for the plaintiff, if, as was the case, he could not show that he was not liable, to take such steps as might be necessary to ensure that, at all events, the damages recovered should not be extravagant."[228]

Chitty LJ further pointed out that

> "the defence was one which in the result was for the benefit of the defendants".[229]

Yet today the buyer who is successful against his sub-buyer may, where standard basis costs have been awarded him against, and paid him by, the sub-buyer, find himself entitled to none of his extra costs for the reasons which will be explained when breach of warranty of quality by the seller is dealt with.[230]

**25-054** *(iv) Other expenses made necessary* Other miscellaneous expenses in connection with a resale may be recoverable. Thus in *Borries v Hutchinson*,[231] the buyer recovered for the extra freight and insurance in sending the delayed goods to Russia to his sub-buyer at a season of the year when such costs were higher.

**25-055** *(v) Loss of profit on further sales* The position with claims for loss of custom generally, which has stemmed from the loss of particular sub-sales of the goods sold by the defendant, has been subject to development. In *Simon v Pawsons & Leafs*,[232] the defendant delivered late certain material to the claimant which she required to make up certain clothes for a school, with the result that she was put in breach of this sub-contract and consequently lost her position as dressmaker for the school. She failed, however, to recover damages for loss of this post. Scrutton LJ, expressing disagreement with the first instance decision in *Cointat v Myham*,[233] which was an equivalent case of breach of warranty, said that in all his considerable experience of contracts for the sale of goods he did not remember any cases of claims "for loss of repeat orders from the customer".[234] However, Scrutton LJ's view received

---

226 [1899] 1 Q.B. 413 CA.
227 The buyer had expressly stated to the sellers that he would resell.
228 [1899] 1 Q.B. 413 CA at 420.
229 [1899] 1 Q.B. 413 CA at 424.
230 See paras 25-086 and 25-087, below.
231 (1865) 18 C.B. N.S. 445.
232 (1933) 38 Com. Cas. 151 CA.
233 [1913] 2 K.B. 220.
234 (1933) 38 Com. Cas. 151 CA at 158.

a somewhat cool reception in *G.K.N. Centrax Gears v Matbro*[235]—Lord Denning MR ventured to differ from it[236] while Stephenson LJ thought it not in accord with the general principles of contract damages[237]—and recovery for the loss of repeat orders was there allowed but in the context of a sale of defective goods and breach of warranty.[238] The approach taken in *Cointat v Myham*,[239] is thus re-instated.

**(c) Other losses** Consequential losses not related to either use or resale of the goods sold are difficult to find, but one appeared in *Aruna Mills v Dhanrajmal Gobindram*.[240] A contract for the sale of cotton at a price in Indian rupees contained a provision for a variation in the purchase price should the prevailing rate of exchange vary between the date of the contract and the date of payment. The sellers were in breach by late shipment of the cotton, but the buyers nevertheless accepted the goods and thereby became liable to pay an enhanced price because between contract and payment the Indian rupee had been devalued. They, however, successfully claimed to be entitled to damages equal to the difference between the original and the enhanced price if they could show that, but for the sellers' delay, they would have been able to have paid for the cotton before the devaluation and hence at the lower original price.[241] 25-056

**(d) Expenses rendered futile by the breach** The buyer's expenses of hiring staff whose services were rendered useless by the delayed delivery of the goods were allowed without question in *Waters v Towers*,[242] were also recovered in *Steam Herring Fleet v Richards*,[243] and were stated to be recoverable in *Saint Line v Richardsons*.[244] "Expenses thrown away", said Atkinson J in this last case, "may well be recoverable under the general law".[245] Care, however, must be taken in allowing recovery of expenses rendered futile by the breach, for such recovery is alternative, and not additional, to a claim for loss of profits. Thus in *Hydraulic Engineering Co v McHaffie*,[246] where the seller failed to deliver on time a part for a machine which the buyer was making for a third party, the court fell into error by allowing the buyer to recover both the expense incurred in making the machine and the profit which he lost when the third party refused to take the machine because it was not ready on time.[247] 25-057

## 3. Breach of Condition: Goods Properly Rejected

If the buyer has lawfully rejected the goods the case becomes in effect one of 25-058

---

235 [1976] 2 Lloyd's Rep. 555 CA.
236 [1976] 2 Lloyd's Rep. 555 CA at 573, col.2.
237 [1976] 2 Lloyd's Rep. 555 CA at 577, col.2.
238 See para.25-107, below.
239 [1913] 2 K.B. 220.
240 [1968] 1 Q.B. 655.
241 Recovery was under the second rule in *Hadley v Baxendale* (1854) 9 Ex. 341 because of the special circumstances contemplated by the parties; see the case further in a footnote to para.8-207, above.
242 (1853) 8 Ex. 401.
243 (1901) 17 T.L.R. 731.
244 [1940] 2 K.B. 99.
245 [1940] 2 K.B. 99 at 105.
246 (1878) 4 Q.B.D. 670 CA.
247 Unless it was the case—which does not appear from the report—that the award was of net rather than gross profit: see paras 4-024 to 4-049, above, where the basis for the recovery of expenses rendered futile by the breach of contract is discussed. See the breach of warranty case at para.25-109, below.

non-delivery and the measure of damages is therefore the same as that applicable to non-delivery,[248] with the one addition of recovery for expenses which stem from the receipt of the defective goods. Thus where the seller wrongfully refuses to take back the goods the buyer may recover expenses incurred in keeping them either until the seller does receive them or until they can be resold on the market by the buyer. Available authority in illustration of this is old, ever concerning the sale of horses, but remains sound today. In *Chesterman v Lamb*,[249] and again in *Ellis v Chinnock*,[250] the seller of a horse wrongfully refused to take it back and the buyer recovered for the expenses of its keep for the period which elapsed before he could reasonably resell it; on the other hand in *Caswell v Coare*,[251] the expenses of a horse's keep were disallowed as the buyer had failed to tender the horse back to the seller. In today's more complex age a more complex recovery of such expenses appears in *Truk (UK) Ltd v Tokmakidis GmbH*.[252] The buyers, who were in the business of buying and selling vehicles used for the recovery of vehicles in distress, bought from their sellers the underlift for such a recovery vehicle, which underlift was then fitted to the chassis of the recovery vehicle. In properly rejecting the underlift as not having been correctly installed and returning it to the sellers, costs were incurred in removing the underlift from the chassis and in repairing the chassis after the underlift had been removed; in addition there had been the cost of commissioning an engineer to report on the condition of the recovery vehicle. All these expenses were allowed as damages, and in addition to the loss of resale profit which could here have been recovered in a straightforward non-delivery claim. And in *Clegg v Andersson t/a Nordic Marine*,[253] where a yacht sold was rejected by the buyer as not of satisfactory quality because of an overweight keel, the buyer was awarded as damages the price, other acquisition costs and consequential losses.[254]

### 4. BREACH OF CONDITION OR WARRANTY AS TO QUALITY, FITNESS OR DESCRIPTION: GOODS ACCEPTED

**25-059** The measure of damages for breach of warranty generally, and for breach of condition treated as warranty, is prescribed by s.53 of the Sale of Goods Act 1979 thus:

(1) Where there is a breach of warranty by the seller, or where the buyer elects, or is compelled, to treat any breach of a condition on the part of the seller as a breach of warranty, the buyer is not by reason only of such breach of warranty entitled to reject the goods; but he may
  - (a) set up against the seller the breach of warranty in diminution or extinction of the price; or
  - (b) maintain an action against the seller for damages for the breach of warranty.

(2) The measure of damages for breach of warranty is the estimated loss directly and naturally resulting, in the ordinary course of events, from the breach of warranty.

---

248 See paras 25-002 and following, above.
249 (1834) 2 A. & E. 129.
250 (1835) 7 C. & P. 169.
251 (1809) 1 Taunt. 566.
252 [2000] 1 Lloyd's Rep. 543.
253 [2003] 2 Lloyd's Rep. 32 CA.
254 No useful detail is available on the assessment of the damages as this was referred to a Master: see at [2003] 2 Lloyd's Rep. 32 CA at [67] to [69].

(3) In the case of breach of warranty of quality such loss is prima facie the difference between the value of the goods at the time of delivery to the buyer and the value they would have had if they had answered to the warranty.
(4) The fact that the buyer has set up the breach of warranty in diminution or extinction of the price does not prevent him from maintaining an action for the same breach of warranty if he has suffered further damage.

To this s.54 adds that nothing in the Act shall affect the buyer's right to recover interest or special damages where by law recoverable. However, again, this time by s.53(4A), contracts for sale of goods between a trader and a consumer are excluded. Those contracts are dealt with by the Consumer Rights Act 2015 which, as explained at the start of this chapter, preserves the same common law rules as to damages but also supplements them with additional remedies.

Section 53(2) is framed in terms of the first rule in *Hadley v Baxendale*,[255] excluding the element of the defendant's knowledge of special circumstances; s.53(3) states the normal measure of damages under the first rule in the case of breach of warranty of quality, but it would appear to be equally the normal measure for other breaches of warranty, such as those in relation to description and fitness; s.54 brings in the second rule in *Hadley v Baxendale*, and in appropriate cases will displace s.53(2) and (3) and allow increased damages.[256] **25-060**

## (1) Normal measure

The normal measure of damages, as stated in s.53(3), is the value of the goods as warranted less their value as they are, both values being generally taken at the contractual time for delivery,[257] since this represents the amount that will put the buyer into the position he would have been in had the warranty been satisfied.[258] Many everyday cases illustrate this rule; probably the clearest illustration in the reports is the early case of *Dingle v Hare*.[259] A modern application of this measure to the sale of a business rather than to a sale of goods, is found in *Senate Electrical Wholesalers Ltd v Alcatel Submarine Networks Ltd*,[260] where, by overstating the profits of the business sold, the seller was in breach of warranty and it was common ground that **25-061**

"if [the claimants] established a loss, the measure of damages was the difference between the price actually paid ... and the true value of the business at the time of the agreement".[261]

If the value at actual delivery is nil, then the market value of the goods as war-

255 (1854) 9 Ex. 341. See paras 8-158 and following, above.

256 A buyer is entitled to recover for consequential losses arising from the breach of warranty on top of recovery for the normal measure. The arbitration award was therefore held to be wrong in *Saipol SA v Inerco Trade SA* [2014] EWHC 2211 (Comm) as it had limited the buyer of sunflower seed oil, contaminated in the shipping of it, to the normal measure by applying s.53(3 instead of s.53(2)).

257 And the contractual place for delivery. This is the case with breach by non-delivery (see second footnote to para.25-004, above) and Diplock LJ's suggestion in *Aryeh v Kostoris & Son* [1967] 1 Lloyd's Rep. 63 CA at 73, col.1 that it is different for breach of warranty is surely misconceived.

258 This is on the normal assumption that the contract price will have been paid over.

259 (1859) 29 L.J.C.P. 143; 7 C.B. N.S. 145. See too *Curtis v Hannay* (1800) 3 Esp. 82 at 84, per Lord Eldon CJ.

260 [1999] 2 Lloyd's Rep. 423.

261 [1999] 2 Lloyd's Rep. 423 at 429, col.1. The difficulty lay in ascertaining what was the business's true value; the various contentions on value are elaborately examined in the judgment of the court.

ranted forms the measure of damages[262]; conversely, the damages are nil if the breach of warranty does not affect the value of the goods.[263]

25-062 That the time, and place, taken for assessing the value of the goods is the time, and place, of delivery is, however, only a prima facie rule and in *Choil Trading SA v Sahara Energy Resources Ltd*,[264] the rule was held displaced. Delivery to the buyer of a cargo of contaminated naphtha took place at the time of its shipment, but it was not until tests carried out on board the ship had revealed the contamination some two weeks later that there was rejection of the cargo by the buyer's sub-buyer. It was held that the difference between the values of sound and contaminated naphtha fell to be assessed as at the later date.[265] Similar is *Bominflot Bunkergesellschaft für Mineralole mbH Co v Petroplus Marketing AG*.[266] The defect in gasoil sold to the claimant buyer did not become patent until some time after it had been delivered from the ship transporting it, whereupon the buyer promptly proceeded to find for the unsound gasoil a sub-buyer who as part of the arrangement sold to the buyer a cargo of replacement, sound gasoil. It was held that the time to ascertain the value of both sound and unsound gasoil was the time of the later sale and repurchase.[267] So too in *Deutsche Bank AG v Total Global Steel Ltd*,[268] a time later than that of delivery was taken as the buyer of the carbon emission units had delayed in order to give the seller a chance to put things right.[269]

25-063 (a) **Relevant and irrelevant prices in ascertaining the value of the goods as warranted** The contract price may be taken as evidence of the value of the goods as warranted where it is difficult to assess, but it is generally irrelevant and is not to be taken in lieu of the value as warranted. Where the contract price has been taken without argument, this has probably been because it represented the market value. Thus the headnote and all the judgments in one report of *Dingle v Hare*,[270] speak of the contract price while the headnote and all the judgments in another report of the same case[271] speak of the market value: clearly they must have been the same. That the contract price, however, cannot control where clearly different from the value as warranted is established by *Loder v Kekule*.[272] Between the making of a contract for the sale of tallow and the contractual date for its delivery the market fell. In an action for breach of warranty the buyer unsuccessfully contended that the contract price was the relevant sum to be subtracted from; the court held that the market value at the date of due delivery was the relevant sum and, further, that the fact that the purchase price had been paid made no difference.

25-064 Similarly, the price at which a third party has agreed to buy the goods from the buyer may be evidence of their value as warranted,[273] but again it is generally ir-

262 See, e.g. *Bridge v Wain* (1816) 1 Stark. 504.

263 See, e.g. *Bramhill v Edwards* [2004] 2 Lloyd's Rep. 653 CA where buyers of a motor home failed to prove that its width marginally in excess of the permitted width had any effect on its value.

264 [2010] EWHC 374 (Comm).

265 See [2010] EWHC 374 (Comm) at [115] and following, together with [131].

266 [2012] EWHC 3009 (Comm).

267 See the discussion at [2012] EWHC 3009 (Comm) at [60] to [66].

268 [2012] EWHC 1201 (Comm).

269 See [2012] EWHC 1201 (Comm) at [166].

270 (1859) 29 L.J.C.P. 143.

271 (1859) 7 C.B. N.S. 145.

272 (1857) 3 C.B. N.S. 128.

273 So, too, is the price of an offer not yet crystallised into a contract. But, as was pointed out in *Aryeh v Kostoris & Son* [1967] 1 Lloyd's Rep. 63 CA, the damages paid by the claimant to a sub-buyer

relevant and should not be taken in preference to the value as warranted. Thus in *Cox v Walker*,[274] the jury were directed that the price of an offer made by a third party to the buyer of a horse was some evidence of its value[275]; but the resale price cannot be utilised to assess the normal measure of damages where clearly different from the value as warranted. Thus in *Clare v Maynard*,[276] which again concerned the sale of a horse, the court refused to take the price at which the buyer had contracted to resell where this price was higher than the value at delivery of a horse answering the warranty. This price may be relevant to increase the damages by way of consequential loss[277] but cannot represent the normal measure of damages. Conversely, where the resale price is lower than the value of the goods as warranted, this will not diminish the damages. Cases of recent years go both ways, being fact dependent. In *Choil Trading SA v Sahara Energy Resources Ltd*,[278] the price at which the buyer had sold the cargo of naphtha as sound to a third party could not be taken as its sound value at the time six weeks later at which warranted value had to be assessed.[279] On the other hand, in *Bominflot Bunkergesellschaft für Mineralole mbH Co v Petroplus Marketing AG*,[280] the best evidence of value as warranted was held to be the price paid by the buyer for replacement sound gasoil under the contract made at the very time value was to be assessed.[281]

**(b) Relevant and irrelevant prices in ascertaining the value of the goods as they are** The price at which the buyer has resold the defective goods may be taken as evidence of their value where this is difficult to assess.[282] Such evidence can play a more important part here than in other situations since, where goods are defective, it is likely that there will be no market for them.[283] Devlin J, dealing with a case of such goods in *Biggin v Permanite*,[284] there said: **25-065**

> "It seems to me that one can rarely arrive at an accurate figure of unsound value. Where the breach is non-delivery, there is often a market price which can be quoted, or evidence can be given of the price at which at the relevant date similar goods were changing hands, but there is rarely any market price for damaged goods, since their value depends on the extent of the damage. If the actual damaged goods are sold with all faults, good evidence

who has properly rejected the goods and sued for non-delivery cannot be evidence of the value as warranted less the value as is. For the damages of a sub-buyer who has properly rejected the goods would be based on the value of the goods as warranted less the sub-contract price (see paras 25-004 and 25-058, above) and, as Diplock LJ said, this amount "would be the same whether the diminution in value of the goods due to the breach of warranty of quality was 1 per cent or 99 per cent of the value which they would have had if they had answered to the warranty": at 71 to 72; and see at 70, per Willmer LJ.

274 (1835) 6 A. & E. 523n.

275 The case was finally compromised.

276 (1837) 6 A. & E. 519.

277 See para.25-096, below.

278 [2010] EWHC 374 (Comm).

279 See the lengthy discussion by Christopher Clarke J at [2010] EWHC 374 (Comm) at [132]–[150]. Facts at para.25-062, above.

280 [2012] EWHC 3009 (Comm).

281 See [2012] EWHC 3009 (Comm) at [64]. Facts at para.25-062, above.

282 See *Slater v Hoyle & Smith* [1920] 2 K.B. 11 CA at 17 per Warrington LJ.

283 In the absence of an available market it was difficult to assess the value of the carbon emission units sold in *Deutsche Bank AG v Total Global Steel Ltd* [2012] EWHC 1201 (Comm): see at [167] and following.

284 [1951] 1 K.B. 422, reversed on a ground not affecting the present issue: [1951] 2 K.B. 314 CA.

can be obtained of the difference in value, but such a sale is not always possible, and a claim for substantial damages cannot be limited to goods which have been sold."[285]

In *Choil Trading SA v Sahara Energy Resources Ltd*,[286] where the buyer had sold the cargo of naphtha in its contaminated condition to a third party Christopher Clarke J held that the price at which this sale was made could be taken as the value of the naphtha in its contaminated condition at the date, two weeks earlier, on which contaminated value had to be assessed.[287] Similarly, in *Bominflot Bunkergesellschaft für Mineralole mbH Co v Petroplus Marketing AG*,[288] the best evidence of value of the unsound gasoil was held to be the price paid for it to the buyer under the contract made at the very time value was to be assessed.[289]

**25-066** Nevertheless the price at which the buyer has sold defective goods is generally not to be taken in lieu of their market value at delivery where clearly different. If, therefore, such resale price is lower than the market value of the goods at delivery it cannot be relied on by the buyer to augment his damages. To this there is to be added one slight qualification: where the market has fallen between breach and the time when the buyer sells the defective goods at the then market price, the court will take his selling price, as in *Powell v Horton*,[290] and in *Loder v Kekule*,[291] if the sale is held to have been within a reasonable time in the circumstances. Conversely, if the buyer's resale price is higher than the value of the defective goods at delivery, it cannot be relied on by the seller to reduce the normal measure of damages.[292] Thus in *Jones v Just*,[293] first quality hemp was bought but second quality was delivered. The market price of hemp rose, enabling the buyer to resell the hemp delivered at substantially the same price as first quality hemp had stood in the market at the time of delivery. It was held nevertheless that the normal measure applied: although this gave the buyer the benefit of the rise in the market he would have had this benefit in any event. Indeed he would probably have resold the hemp at an even greater price had it been of first quality.[294]

**25-067** In *Slater v Hoyle & Smith*,[295] the matter was taken a step further and perhaps a step too far in relation to higher resale prices but, importantly, in respect of a resale which had been made before, rather than after, the seller was in breach. The case concerned a sale of cotton cloth where the buyer was buying in order to fulfil a

---

[285] [1951] 1 K.B. 422 at 438. In the case itself there was no resale to assist Devlin J in assessing the depreciated value of the goods. Evidence of hypothetical sub-buyers as to what they would have been prepared to pay for the goods at the date of breach, goods "which they never saw and of whose defects they have learnt only at second-hand" (at 439), would, he said, have been of no use to him. He thought that in these circumstances a method of calculation which could be legitimately followed by the court was by way of a price allowance. This was "a common practice of the commercial world to deal with this type of case…. and claims for damaged goods are constantly met to the satisfaction of both parties by the fixing of an allowance by an adjuster or some person skilled in the trade": at 439.

[286] [2010] EWHC 374 (Comm).

[287] See [2010] EWHC 374 (Comm) at [151]–[155]. Contrast Christopher Clarke's holding on value as warranted at para.25-064, above. Facts of the case at para.25-062, above.

[288] [2012] EWHC 3009 (Comm).

[289] See [2012] EWHC 3009 (Comm) at [61]. Facts at para.25-062, above.

[290] (1836) 3 Scott 110.

[291] (1857) 3 C.B. N.S. 128.

[292] For the reasons for this result see the cases on mitigation and avoided loss at paras 9-135 and 9-136, above.

[293] (1868) L.R. 3 Q.B. 197.

[294] See the decision in the context of mitigation and avoided loss at para.9-133, above.

[295] [1920] 2 K.B. 11 CA.

contract of sale already made by him to a third party. The cloth delivered by the seller was of inferior quality but the buyer had used it to fulfil his sub-contract and had received the full contract price from his sub-buyers without their having taken legal proceedings against him.[296] This sub-contract price was higher than the market value at delivery of the inferior cloth although lower than the market value at delivery of cloth of the warranted quality. In these circumstances the buyer claimed the normal measure of damages. Against this the seller contended not merely that the resale price should be taken instead of the market price at delivery but that the buyer had suffered no damage whatsoever, since had the cloth been as warranted he would still have got the same price for it in fulfilment of his sub-contract. The Court of Appeal rejected this contention. Scrutton LJ said that sub-contracts were *res inter alios acta*; they were

> "'circumstances peculiar to the plaintiff', which cannot affect his claim one way or the other. If the buyer is lucky enough, for reasons with which the seller has nothing to do, to get his goods through on the sub-contract without a claim against him, this on principle cannot affect his claim against the seller any more than the fact that he had to pay very large damages on his sub-contract would affect his original seller."[297]

He said further that the buyer might have bought other and merchantable goods to use for the sub-contract and would then have had the original goods on his hands, so that their market price at delivery would have been the relevant figure for the damages assessment.[298]

Doubt has now been cast upon the correctness of this approach in *Bence Graphics International v Fasson UK*.[299] Vinyl film used to make identification decals for bulk containers was supplied by the defendants to the claimants who printed words or numbers on the film and cut it to size so that it could be applied to the containers. By reason of defects in its manufacture the film supplied tended to degrade so that the decals became illegible and the buyers to whom the claimants had sold the decals made by them with the vinyl film registered complaints about the poor labelling. A claim by one buyer was settled; the claimants' major buyer gave intimation of a claim but this so far had not been pursued. At first instance the claimants were held entitled to the difference between the value of the goods at the time of delivery and the value they would have had if they had fulfilled the warranty. The issue before the Court of Appeal was whether the correct measure of damages was this prima facie measure or was the actual loss suffered by the claimants which appeared in the circumstances to be less. The majority favoured the actual loss. Auld **25-068**

---

296 It appears from Scrutton LJ's judgment that "the sub-buyer made oral complaints but did not reject the goods, and though at the time of the trial he was claiming on the buyers, he had not taken any actual proceedings": at 19. Nevertheless the Court of Appeal judgments proceeded on the assumption that the buyer had been fortunate enough to evade compensating his sub-buyer.

297 [1920] 2 K.B. 11 CA at 23.

298 [1920] 2 K.B. 11 CA at 23–24, CA. There was the further point that the original sale was of unbleached cloth and the sub-sale of bleached: Bankes LJ decided the case on this ground. Also the seller did not know of the sub-sale. While both these factors would have provided hurdles to a buyer claiming more than the normal measure (see paras 25-092 and following, below), and are in similar fashion hurdles to a seller claiming to hold the damages at an amount below the normal measure, the removal of these hurdles in the case of the seller would still not suffice in the view of Scrutton LJ (but see now para.25-068, below) to support the contention that the resale price was relevant, unless the seller could bring his case within the limited field suggested by Devlin J in *Biggin v Permanite* [1951] 1 K.B. 422 at 436; see para.8-195, above.

299 [1998] Q.B. 87 CA.

LJ considered that the time had come for *Slater v Hoyle & Smith*,[300] to be reconsidered, at least in the context of claims by a buyer for damages for breach of warranty where he had successfully sold on the subject-matter of the contract in its original or modified form.[301] Otton LJ, agreeing in the result, did so by distinguishing *Slater*,[302] narrowly on its facts; there the sub-sale was of the identical goods, here the goods had been substantially processed or converted by the buyer and the seller knew of the precise use to which the goods were to be put.[303] Thorpe LJ dissented, because of a particular finding of fact by the trial judge and there is no mention of *Slater* in his judgment.[304]

**25-069** How then should the position be resolved? It is submitted that Auld LJ's approach is to be preferred, according as it does with the reality of the situation. It is difficult to see how Otton LJ can justify a different result depending upon whether the goods are sold on in the same condition or after an anticipated modification, and one suspects that were he presented with a situation similar to that in *Slater*,[305] he would wish to decide the case as he decided *Bence Graphics*.[306] And surely the answer to Scrutton LJ's attempted justification of the result in *Slater*,[307] on the ground that the buyer might have bought substitute goods for the sub-contract is that, if the buyer, acting reasonably, had preferred not to foist the defective goods upon his sub-buyer but had supplied him with substitute goods and retained the defective ones, then the difference in value of the goods as they are and as they ought to have been does mark his real loss and, accordingly, the measure of his damages.[308] However, in *OMV Petrom SA v Glencore International AG*,[309] the Court of Appeal, without deciding, seemed to indicate a preference for the view of the Court of Appeal in *Slater v Hoyle & Smith*,[310] over that of the later Court of Appeal in *Bence Graphics v Fasson*.[311] The Court of Appeal in *OMV Petrom* observed that the reliance by Auld LJ in *Bence* on the Privy Council decision in *Wertheim v Chicoutimi Pulp Co*,[312] was upon a decision which Scrutton LJ thought was erroneous.[313] But, as we have seen above there is a simple explanation which answers the concerns that Scrutton LJ had about the decision in *Wertheim*.[314]

**25-070** The issue is one of mitigation and avoided loss[315] and the sale of goods cases, dealing variously with non-delivery and delayed delivery as well as breach of war-

---

300 [1920] 2 K.B. 11 CA.
301 [1998] Q.B. 87 CA at 102G.
302 [1920] 2 K.B. 11 CA.
303 [1998] Q.B. 87 CA at 99B. He regarded the sale in *Slater* to be of the same goods although the cloth, unbleached in the original sale, had been bleached before being sold on; contra Auld LJ, at 103C. Indeed, in *Slater* it was precisely because Bankes LJ considered the sale and sub-sale to be of different goods that he decided that the sub-sale fell to be ignored.
304 [1998] Q.B. 87 CA at 99B at 109C and following.
305 [1920] 2 K.B. 11 CA.
306 [1998] Q.B. 87 CA.
307 [1920] 2 K.B. 11 CA.
308 See similarly for delayed delivery para.25-042, above. The matter is further considered on a more general basis in Ch.9, above, at paras 9-171 and following.
309 [2016] EWCA Civ 778 CA.
310 [1920] 2 K.B. 11 CA.
311 [1998] Q.B. 87 CA.
312 [1911] A.C. 301.
313 [2016] EWCA Civ 778 CA at [45].
314 See para.25-042, above.
315 Dealt with at paras 9-108 and following.

ranty of quality, move in different directions. They are given an extended analysis elsewhere[316] and a solution to the difficulties they present is there proposed.[317]

### (2) Consequential losses

The consequential losses over and above the normal measure of damages are likely to be more numerous in cases of breach of warranty than in cases of non-delivery and delayed delivery. The reason is this. Where there is non-delivery or delayed delivery the breach is in the nature of things immediately obvious to the buyer, and consequential losses only arise where there is no market available to him in which he can buy other goods against his use or resale. Where there is breach of warranty the breach frequently neither is nor ought to have been obvious to the buyer on delivery of the goods, and consequential losses may arise not only because of the absence of an available market but because, before the breach is discovered, some further damage occurs through use of the goods either by the buyer or by other parties, including the buyer's sub-buyers. 25-071

**(a) The preliminary question whether the buyer should have known of the breach** These considerations raise the issue of whether the buyer knew or ought to have known that the goods were defective[318] and that therefore the seller was in breach of warranty. 25-072

Some defects are patent, and for damage resulting from such defects there can be no recovery. As Rowlatt J said in *British Oil and Cake Co v Burstall*[319]: 25-073

> "If a buyer received from his seller an article which was 'patently' not the article contracted for, he could not use it at the risk of the seller."

Some defects the astute buyer will see immediately, and some he will discover after a time. Here it is futile for the buyer to plead his ignorance of the defect, for the seller is not liable for any damage which the buyer could have avoided by appropriate steps taken after the time he should have known of the defect. Thus in *Biggin v Permanite*,[320] Devlin J found that the buyer ought to have known of the defect by a certain date, after which he should have notified his sub-buyer. Any damage caused to the sub-buyer, for which the buyer was liable, by use of the goods after he should have been informed of the defect was therefore attributable to the buyer's failure to give the necessary notification. Devlin J said:

> "A claimant cannot pass on his liability to an outside party for bad quality if, before the sale to the outside party, he had notice of the defect in quality… . Similarly, if the knowledge of the defects comes to the claimant after the sale to the outside party, and if, by passing on that knowledge to the outside party, he can diminish his liability to that party, he is bound to do so."[321]

Many defects, however, are not patent or easily discoverable without examina- 25-074

---

316 At paras 9-171 to 9-183, above.

317 For this see para.9-183, above.

318 The terms "defect" and "defective" are used throughout for ease of reference, although strictly the goods are not always physically defective but defective only in the sense that they do not come up to the warranty.

319 (1923) 39 T.L.R. 406 at 407.

320 [1951] 1 K.B. 422; reversed on another ground: [1951] 2 K.B. 314 CA.

321 [1951] 1 K.B. 422 at 435, citing Rowlatt J in *British Oil and Cake Co v Burstall* (1923) 39 T.L.R. 406 at 407, and Lawrence LJ in *Dobell v Barber* [1931] 1 K.B. 219 CA at 238.

tion of the goods. Here the buyer is entitled to rely on the warranty and is not to be expected to make a thorough examination of the goods for latent defects in order to ascertain whether the warranty has been complied with. There appear to be no cases in which the buyer's action has failed on the ground that he ought to have examined the goods before using them or reselling them.[322] On the contrary, in two types of case it has been held no defence for the seller to say that the buyer should have examined the goods.

**25-075** The first type of case finds illustration in three cases of sales of cake to be used ultimately for feeding cattle, *Pinnock v Lewis*,[323] *British Oil and Cake Co v Burstall*,[324] and *Dobell v Barber*.[325] In all of these the buyer successfully claimed that he was entitled to rely on the warranty without examination and therefore could recover for the damages and costs which he had had to pay his sub-buyer.[326] Roche J said in *Pinnock v Lewis*[327]:

> "The buyers were entitled, if they chose, without being guilty of negligence or unreasonable conduct, to rely on their contract with the sellers rather than to rely on any precautions of their own."

*Dobell v Barber*,[328] differed from the other two cases in that the warranty was a statutory one from which the seller had made a futile attempt to escape by stating to the buyer that he disclaimed the responsibility the statute cast on him. The buyer was still held entitled to rely on the warranty without examination, since otherwise, as Lawrence LJ pointed out, the

> "seller could always protect himself against the full consequences naturally flowing from the warranty by stating that he did not accept the responsibility which the Act casts upon him".[329]

**25-076** The second type of case is that in which the buyer has claimed to recover for the damages which he has had to pay a third party who has been physically injured by the defective condition of the goods. Both the illustrations of this situation, *Mowbray v Merryweather*,[330] and *Scott v Foley*,[331] are very strong cases because the buyer's liability to the third party had been based on his negligence, vis-à-vis him, in failing to inspect the goods.

---

322 The cases in which the buyer has been refused damages to compensate him for fines and costs incurred in a criminal prosecution (paras 25-088 and 25-104, below) get near to this, but the issue has been the broader one of policy.

323 [1923] 1 K.B. 690.

324 (1923) 39 T.L.R. 406.

325 [1931] 1 K.B. 219 CA.

326 And see *Hardwick Game Farm v Suffolk Agricultural Poultry Producers Association* [1969] 2 A.C. 31 at para.25-097, below.

327 [1923] 1 K.B. 690 at 698.

328 [1931] 1 K.B. 219 CA.

329 [1931] 1 K.B. 219 CA at 237. In *Wrightup v Chamberlain* (1839) 7 Scott 598 the claimant, who had bought a horse warranted sound and resold it with a similar warranty to a sub-buyer who brought an action against him for breach of warranty which he unsuccessfully defended, failed in his subsequent suit against his own seller for the costs incurred by him in this unsuccessful defence only because he could by reasonable examination have discovered the defect, not before he resold, but before he defended the action brought by the sub-buyer.

330 [1895] 2 Q.B. 640 CA.

331 (1899) 15 T.L.R. 55.

### (b) Loss through use and through loss of use

*(i) Loss of user profits* The simplest case of loss of profits which would have been made through use of the goods is represented by the situation where the buyer proposes to make some product out of them. Here the value of the goods is not to be taken. Thus in *Wagstaff v Shorthorn Dairy Co*,[332] where inferior seeds were sold and planted so that an inferior crop resulted, the damages were assessed at the value of the crop which would have come up had the seed answered to the warranty less the value of the inferior crop.[333] Similarly, in *Ashworth v Wells*,[334] where an orchid was sold warranted white and flowered purple two years later, purple orchids being practically valueless, the value of a white orchid already in flower was taken in assessing the damages as against the much lower selling value of a white orchid which would flower only in two years' time. In *Holden v Bostock*,[335] where sugar was sold to brewers to be used for brewing beer and because of arsenic in the sugar the beer was rendered poisonous and was destroyed by the brewers, the value of the beer at its market price in their cellars was allowed, inter alia, in damages.[336] And precisely 100 years after this decision it has been replicated in two related cases. In *Britvic Soft Drinks Ltd v Messer UK Ltd*,[337] the two claimants, Britvic and Bass, had purchased from the defendant suppliers bulk carbon dioxide, otherwise CO2, for the carbonisation of the, respectively, soft and alcoholic carbonated drinks that they manufactured and sold, which CO2 had become contaminated with benzene. In *Bacardi-Martini Beverages Ltd v Thomas Hardy Packaging Ltd*,[338] the claimant had purchased from the defendant manufacturers the alcoholic carbonated drinks which it sold, such drinks similarly containing CO2 that had been contaminated with benzene. Successful claims were made, inter alia,[339] for the value of the stock of drinks that the claimants had to destroy.[340] **25-077**

In these cases it is vital that the use to which the goods have been put in order to derive the product was a use which the seller either knew or must be taken to have contemplated: otherwise the damage will be too remote. Thus in *Bunting v Tory*,[341] where a bull was sold at an auction and the buyer used him for breeding, he failed to recover the value of the bull's progeny as it would have been had the bull satisfied the warranty less the value of the bull's progeny as it was, since the seller had **25-078**

[332] (1884) Cab. & Ell. 324.

[333] See the analogous result in *Randall v Raper* (1858) E.B. & E. 84 and *Wallis v Pratt* [1911] A.C. 394 at para.25-097, in a footnote, below, where the buyer recovered this amount of damages from the seller where he himself had had to pay this amount by way of damages to his sub-buyer, who was the one who had done the sowing of the seeds. In the latter case the facts relevant here appear better in the lower court: [1910] 2 K.B. 1003 CA; the argument was on another point.

[334] (1898) 14 T.L.R. 227 CA.

[335] (1902) 18 T.L.R. 317 CA.

[336] The seller had contended for a measure of damages calculated not by the value of the sugar at delivery but by the cost to the buyer of making the equivalent amount of fresh beer. This case differs from those of the seeds and the plants in that the goods were mixed with other materials to make the product.

[337] [2002] 1 Lloyd's Rep. 20.

[338] [2002] 1 Lloyd's Rep. 62.

[339] Other claims are at paras 25-085, 25-090, 25-098 and, but unsuccessful, para.25-107, below.

[340] *Britvic* [2002] 1 Lloyd's Rep. 20 at 47 to 49 at [115]–[121]; *Bacardi-Martini* [2002] 1 Lloyd's Rep. 62 at 64, [2], [66] and [13]. Both decisions were affirmed by the Court of Appeal, at [2002] 2 Lloyd's Rep. 368 and 379 respectively, without anything being said about damages.

[341] (1948) 64 T.L.R. 353.

not been informed that the buyer purposed using the bull for breeding and since breeding was not the only purpose for which the bull might have been required.[342]

**25-079** A more sophisticated case is loss of general business profits. This has its most interesting illustration in *Cullinane v British "Rema" Manufacturing Co*.[343] The seller of a clay pulverising plant warranted that it would pulverise the buyer's clay at a specified rate. On its failure to pulverise at the warranted rate the buyer claimed damages in respect of the capital expended and also for loss of business profits for a period of three years, the estimated useful life of the plant being 10 years. The primary importance of this case is that the Court of Appeal held that the buyer could not recover for both of these items even though the loss of profits claimed was for three years and not for the full 10-year life of the plant.[344] However, throughout the judgments[345] it was taken for granted that the buyer was entitled to claim for his loss of business profits.[346] "The plant", said Jenkins LJ,

> "having been supplied in contemplation by both parties that it should be used by the claimant in the commercial production of pulverised clay, the case is one in which the claimant can claim as damages for the breach of warranty the loss of the profit he can show that he would have made if the plant had been as warranted."[347]

**25-080** If the buyer, finding the goods deficient in use and therefore unable to yield the intended business profits, should replace them with others which because of their superiority result in greater profits, these profits must be taken into account in any claim by the buyer for loss of profits incurred before the goods had been replaced. This was established, in relation to a sale of turbines, in *British Westinghouse Co v Underground Ry*,[348] a case of great importance in the general field of mitigation and avoided loss.[349]

**25-081** *(ii) Physical damage to the buyer's interests* The seller is frequently held liable for physical damage to the goods themselves, or to the buyer, or to persons or property in which the buyer has an interest.

**25-082** Inherent vice in the goods causing their physical decay or destruction can generally be calculated within their market value at the time of delivery. This, however, is not always the case, as for example where a horse, warranted sound, runs amok by reason of its vicious nature and kills itself. Presumably the value of a sound horse would be recoverable without deducting the value that the vicious horse had at the time of delivery.

---

342 But see *Bostock v Nicholson* [1904] 1 K.B. 725 and *Hardwick Game Farm v Suffolk Agricultural Poultry Producers Association* [1969] 2 A.C. 31 at paras 25-083 and 25-084, below, where it was held that damage consequent upon use, which in the first case was not the only ordinary use and in the second case was not even the predominant use, was not too remote.

343 [1954] 1 Q.B. 292 CA.

344 This aspect of the case, which has its difficulties, is dealt with at paras 4-044 to 4-049, above.

345 Including that of the dissenting Morris LJ.

346 [1954] 1 Q.B. 292 CA at 303, 308, 316.

347 [1954] 1 Q.B. 292 CA at 308. In *Borealis AB v Geogas Trading SA* [2011] 1 Lloyd's Rep. 482 the claimant recovered for profits lost during repairs necessitated by the damage caused to its plant and equipment by the contaminated goods sold to it (facts of the case at para.8-150, above). Moreover, this was without reduction, or even elimination, of the award on account of the claimant's having taken the opportunity to effect repairs to other equipment at the plant, the analogy of the shipping cases as dealt with at para.37-044, above being referred to: see at [156] to [160].

348 [1912] A.C. 673.

349 The case is considered further in that context at para.9-121, above. Compare *Erie County Natural Gas Co v Carroll* [1911] A.C. 105 PC at para.25-026, above.

Beyond the case of physical damage to the goods sold themselves, the goods may cause physical damage to persons or property other than themselves. Thus where food is sold for consumption the buyer can recover damages for any illness caused to himself by its consumption,[350] and also for the illness or death of his wife, as in *Jackson v Watson*,[351] his children,[352] his birds, as in *Hardwick Game Farm v Suffolk Agricultural Poultry Producers Association*,[353] and his animals.[354] The same principle applies where coal is sold which causes injury when burned, as in *Wilson v Rickett Cockerill*,[355] and where clothes are sold which cause injury when worn.[356] Again, where the goods sold are defective so that, when put to the contemplated use, accident results and the buyer is injured or his property is damaged or lost, he can recover for such injury, damage or loss. Illustrations are *Randall v Newson*,[357] where a pole sold by a coach-builder for the buyer's carriage broke in use, thus frightening and injuring the horses, and *Borrodaile v Brunton*,[358] where an anchor cable sold to a shipowner broke, thereby causing the loss of his anchor. Another type of case is that in which the goods sold are in their contemplated use placed with others, or used in combination with others to give a new product, so as to damage or destroy those others. Thus in *Smith v Green*,[359] where a diseased cow was sold to a farmer which he placed together with other cows and a number of them, including the cow sold, died from the disease, the seller was held liable for the entire loss. And in *Bostock v Nicholson*,[360] where commercial sulphuric acid warranted free from arsenic was used by the buyer for making brewers' sugar, one of its ordinary uses, he recovered not only the price paid for the acid rendered worthless to him by the breach of warranty but the value of the other ingredients spoilt by being mixed with the acid. Somewhat similarly, in *Harbutt's "Plasticine" v Wayne Tank & Pump Co*,[361] where the defendants contracted to supply and install a heating system for the claimants' factory and, because of defects, the installation went up in flames destroying the factory, the claimants were held entitled to recover for this loss. Moreover, the damages were measured not by the value of the destroyed factory but by the higher cost of replacing it, no allowance being made to the defendants for any benefit to the claimants for having a new factory in place of the old one.[362] The same result appears in *Bacon v Cooper (Metals)*,[363] where the defendants sold the claimant a quantity of steel which broke up his fragmentiser, thereby bringing his main business of producing and selling fragmentised scrap steel to a halt, and **25-083**

[350] See *Square v Model Farm Dairies* [1939] 2 K.B. 365 CA; the point was so clearly accepted it was hardly argued. The damages will be calculated as in any other personal injury case (see Ch.40, below); indeed under the rule in *Donoghue v Stevenson* [1932] A.C. 562 the consumer may sue in tort parties other than his own seller.

[351] [1909] 2 K.B. 193 CA.

[352] There are no cases but there would seem to be little doubt.

[353] [1969] 2 A.C. 31.

[354] See at paras 25-093 and 25-097, below, the cases involving sales of cattle food where it was the ultimate buyer's animals which were injured: *Pinnock v Lewis* [1923] 1 K.B. 690; *British Oil and Cake Co v Burstall* (1923) 39 T.L.R. 406; *Dobell v Barber* [1931] 1 K.B. 219 CA.

[355] [1954] 1 Q.B. 598 CA.

[356] See *Grant v Australian Knitting Mills* [1936] A.C. 85 PC (tort case).

[357] (1877) 2 Q.B.D. 102 CA.

[358] (1818) 8 Taunt. 535. This case was regarded as of doubtful authority in *Hadley v Baxendale* (1854) 9 Ex. 341, but it is difficult to see why.

[359] (1876) 1 C.P.D. 92.

[360] [1904] 1 K.B. 725.

[361] [1970] 1 Q.B. 447 CA.

[362] On the "new for old" damages issue, see para.2-007, above.

[363] [1982] 1 All E.R. 397.

in his successful claim for, inter alia, the cost of repairing the fragmentiser there was included the whole cost of a replacement rotor, which made up most of the total repair cost, despite the fact that the claimant was obtaining a new rotor in place of one which had seen nearly half of its useful life.[364] In addition, because the claimant had obtained the new rotor on hire purchase as his resources could in no way stretch to an outright purchase at some £40,000, he was allowed the high finance charges of the hire purchase as part of his damages; the profits lost while the fragmentiser went unrepaired were also awarded.

**25-084** In all these cases, it is once again vital that the use to which the goods have been put by the buyer is one that the seller either contemplated or must be taken to have contemplated: otherwise the damage will be too remote. If the buyer adopts the ordinary use of the goods, as where food sold for human consumption is eaten by him, or adopts one of the ordinary and well-recognised uses although not the only one, as in *Bostock v Nicholson*,[365] or adopts even a use which is not the predominant one provided it is a use which is sufficiently common, as in *Hardwick Game Farm v Suffolk Agricultural Poultry Producers Association*,[366] where contaminated ground-nut extractions were supplied for compounding into a poultry food and the compound was fed to pheasants and partridges,[367] he will recover under the first rule in *Hadley v Baxendale*.[368] If, however, he puts them to some special use, he will recover only if this intention is communicated to the seller,[369] i.e. under the second rule in *Hadley v Baxendale*.[370] Here, as elsewhere, the dividing line between the first and second rules is not always clear in the cases.[371]

**25-085** *(iii) Compensation paid to a third party for physical or other damage to his interests; costs incurred in defending the third party's action.*[372] Where goods sold to the buyer have proved defective and have resulted in an accident causing physical damage to the person or property of a third party to whom the buyer has been held liable,[373] the buyer may recover, as damages from his seller, the damages paid to the third party. This result was reached in *Mowbray v Merryweather*,[374] where a defective chain broke and injured a stevedore, the buyer's servant. Nor is recovery for compensation paid to third parties limited to compensation in respect of physical damage to them. Thus in *Bacardi-Martini Beverages Ltd v Thomas Hardy Packaging Ltd*,[375] one of the cases arising out of the so-called benzene incident,[376] damages were allowed in respect of the compensation paid by the claimants to their retailers who had been left with defective goods on their hands. The damages were

---

[364] See the preceding note but one.
[365] [1904] 1 K.B. 725.
[366] [1969] 2 A.C. 31.
[367] See especially [1969] 2 A.C. 31 at 86, per Lord Reid, and 91, per Lord Morris. The main question before the court, as these passages show, was not whether the ultimate buyer could recover for physical damage to his interests but whether intermediate buyers could recover for damages they had to pay in respect of such physical damage: see the case further at para.25-097, below.
[368] (1854) 9 Ex. 341.
[369] As, semble, in *Randall v Newson* (1877) 2 Q.B.D. 102 CA.
[370] (1854) 1 Ex. 341.
[371] Thus it is not clear within which category *Smith v Green* (1876) 1 C.P.D. 92 falls.
[372] See further on the general principles, Ch.20, above, passim.
[373] Whether in tort or contract is immaterial.
[374] [1895] 2 Q.B. 640 CA.
[375] [2002] 1 Lloyd's Rep. 62.
[376] Facts at para.25-077, above.

in fact agreed in *Bacardi-Martini* and so are set out by Tomlinson J[377] without discussion.

In addition to such damages the buyer may recover the costs paid to the third party as assessed by the court and his own costs if he has reasonably but unsuccessfully defended the action brought against him by the third party, as in *Scott v Foley*,[378] but not generally the costs of an unsuccessful appeal brought by him.[379] Formerly, recovery of the buyer's own costs incurred in such a defence was of these costs assessed as between solicitor and client; now, solicitor and client costs no longer exist in this context and the buyer should instead simply be entitled to all his costs if reasonably incurred. There is, however, a growing move at first instance, one not to be encouraged, which would restrict the buyer to what, if assessed, would have been his standard basis costs; this unfortunate development has already been fully examined in an earlier chapter to which reference should be made.[380] If the buyer has settled with the third party out of court and there is no evidence of negligence on his part so as to make him liable to the third party for the latter's injury, then only nominal damages can be recovered by the buyer from his seller.[381] Should the buyer's liability to the third party be a strict one independent of his negligence, then a fortiori he should be able to recover damages paid to the third party and costs reasonably incurred.[382] **25-086**

In addition, where the third party's action has failed because he has not succeeded in proving that the buyer was negligent or in proving that the buyer's liability was a strict one, costs incurred by the buyer have been held recoverable; *Britannia Hygienic Laundry Co v Thornycroft*,[383] was such a case. However, whether today the buyer can recover any costs where standard basis costs have been awarded to him, and paid to him by the seller, depends upon whether or not the new regime referred to in the preceding paragraph takes hold.[384] **25-087**

*(iv) Fines paid; costs incurred in defending a prosecution*[385] In *Crage v Fry*,[386] and again in *Cointat v Myham*,[387] the buyer of food was convicted of having in his shop food unfit for human consumption. In both it was recognised to be within the contemplation of the parties that the buyer might be prosecuted if the goods should **25-088**

---

377 [2002] 1 Lloyd's Rep. 62 at 66, [13]. No damages issues arose in the Court of Appeal which affirmed: [2002] 2 Lloyd's Rep. 379 CA.

378 (1899) 15 T.L.R. 55 (defective ladder injured stevedore); see, too, *Vogan v Oulton* (1899) 81 L.T. 435 CA (sack gave way and fell on workman) which was hire not sale, but the principle is the same.

379 *Vogan v Oulton* (1899) 81 L.T. 435 CA; hire not sale, but the principle is the same.

380 See the discussion at paras 21-003 and following, above. For the amount of costs recoverable in these circumstances under the old regime and under the new see para.21-009 together with para.21-081, above.

381 *Kiddle v Lovett* (1885) 16 Q.B.D. 605 (platform fell on and injured the claimant's workman); again not strictly sale.

382 The Court of Appeal in *Stacey v Autosleeper Group Ltd* [2014] EWCA Civ 1551 (facts in note to para.8-150, above) endorsed the trial judge's allowing recovery of costs paid to the third party, but not in full as they had been increased by the buyer's unreasonable conduct: at [24]–[25].

383 (1925) 41 T.L.R. 667; reversed on the facts: 42 T.L.R. 198 CA.

384 See again the discussion at paras 21-003 and following, above. For the amount of costs recoverable in these circumstances under the old regime and under the new see para.21-008 together with para.21-086, above. The *Britannia Hygienic* case was unusual in that the seller was unable to pay the costs awarded against him and the buyer had to sue the third party also for these; see this aspect of the case at para.21-087, above.

385 See further on the general principles, Ch.21, above, passim.

386 (1903) 67 J.P. 240.

387 [1913] 2 K.B. 220; new trial ordered on another ground: (1914) 110 L.T. 749 CA.

prove defective. But in the former case the buyer failed, in the absence of evidence as to what influenced the magistrate in imposing the fine, to recover it as damages from the seller, while in the latter he did recover it, Lord Coleridge J pointing out that the jury had been entitled to find that the fine was neither wholly nor in part brought about by the buyer's own negligence.[388] Thus whether the fine was recoverable turned, in the cases, on the presence or absence of fault in the buyer. Although later decisions, in actions other than for breach of contract of sale of goods, raised the broader point of public policy that a law which imposed a punishment, as opposed to awarding compensation, would be defeated by the punishment being passed on to another,[389] the current position appears to be that the key to a denial of recovery does indeed lie in a showing of mens rea on the part of the now claimant.[390]

**25-089** Beyond the fine are the costs which the buyer has incurred in the prosecution. *Crage v Fry*,[391] and *Cointat v Myham*,[392] agreed at this point, and both allowed recovery of the buyer's costs of defence and the costs of the prosecution he had been ordered to pay. However, the criteria which apply to the recovery of fines ought surely to govern also in relation to the recovery of costs, and these cases must be viewed in the light of the decisions on this issue generally.[393] If, of course, the prosecution fails and the buyer is acquitted, then nothing intervenes to prevent his properly recovering his costs as damages.[394]

**25-090** *(v) Other expenses made necessary* There may be other, miscellaneous, expenses made necessary by the breach of warranty which will also be recoverable. In *Smith v Johnson*,[395] inferior lime had been sold to a builder so that the mortar for which it was used did not come up to statutory requirements and the wall in the construction of which the mortar was used was condemned. The builder recovered as damages from the seller the cost of pulling down and rebuilding the wall. Similarly in *Britvic Soft Drinks Ltd v Messer UK Ltd*,[396] and *Bacardi-Martini Beverages Ltd v Thomas Hardy Packaging Ltd*,[397] the cases arising out of the so-called benzene incident,[398] the costs incurred in destroying the defective goods were awarded. And a good number of other expenses featured in the damages.[399]

---

388 [1913] 2 K.B. 220 at 222.

389 See paras 21-069 and 21-070, above.

390 See paras 21-071 and 21-072, above.

391 (1903) 67 J.P. 240.

392 [1913] 2 K.B. 220.

393 See paras 21-066 and following, above.

394 See *Proops v Chaplin* (1920) 37 T.L.R. 112 at para.25-105, below. Whether the prosecution succeeds or fails the buyer should be entitled to recover all of his costs reasonably incurred and the limits that are now coming in for parties in a civil suit (see paras 21-003 and following, above) should have no application to criminal prosecutions in the light of the Court of Appeal's decision in *Berry v British Transport Commission* [1962] 1 Q.B. 306 CA, which see at para.21-018, above.

395 (1899) 15 T.L.R. 179.

396 [2002] 1 Lloyd's Rep. 20.

397 [2002] 1 Lloyd's Rep. 62.

398 Facts at para.25-077, above.

399 See the broad heads of claim set out in *Britvic* [2002] 1 Lloyd's Rep. 20 at 46, [112] and the agreed damages listed in *Bacardi-Martini* [2002] 1 Lloyd's Rep. 62 at 66, [13]. Both decisions were affirmed by the Court of Appeal, at [2002] 2 Lloyd's Rep. 368 and 379 respectively, but no issue of damages arose in either.

**(c) Loss on a resale**[400] We have seen[401] that Devlin J in *Kwei Tek Chao v British Traders*,[402] in relation to breach by non-delivery made clear that damages for loss on a resale are not recoverable merely because the seller knows that the buyer is a merchant buying generally for resale since what is contemplated is that the buyer on breach will go out into the market and buy substitute goods. Only where substitute goods cannot be bought on the market does loss of profit become the appropriate measure of damages. In *Choil Trading SA v Sahara Energy Resources Ltd*,[403] this rule of Devlin J was applied by Christopher Clarke J to breach of warranty of quality.[404] 25-091

Where there is breach of warranty there is more likely to be a series of subsales than with non-delivery or delayed delivery since the defect may not be discovered for some time. The terms "chain of buyers" and "string contracts" are frequently found in this connection. An important issue which arises here that does not apply to the non-delivery and delayed delivery situations is whether the warranties in the sub-sales must be the same as that in the principal sale between the claimant and defendant before loss to the claimant arising out of such sub-sales is recoverable. This matter was first given detailed consideration by the Court of Appeal in *Dexters v Hill Crest Oil Co.*[405] Scrutton LJ there said: 25-092

> "Those cases where there has been a chain of sales and sub-sales often present complications and difficulties; but one point I have always understood as clear, namely that in order to make a sum recovered for breach of the last contract in the chain the measure of damages for a similar breach of a contract higher up in the chain, it is essential that the contracts along the chain connecting them should be the same."[406]

In the case itself the defendants had sold dark cotton seed grease to the claimant; this was followed by a number of sub-sales. The claimant claimed for a sum equal to the amount recovered by the ultimate buyer from his seller by whom it had been sold as black cotton seed grease, which was apparently more valuable and was thus sold at a substantially higher price. The Court of Appeal decided against the claimant on grounds not relevant here, but all thought that the claimant could not have recovered the damages claimed as in the circumstances it was impossible to apply the amount recovered by a sub-buyer as the measure of damages recoverable against the original seller.

Scrutton LJ's dictum would however seem to be a little too strict. *British Oil & Cake Co v Burstall*[407] had already suggested that recovery was possible where the difference between the warranties was immaterial. There the defendant had sold copra cake to the claimant who had resold it as free from castor. Since copra cake 25-093

---

400 In *Marles v Philip Trant* [1954] 1 Q.B. 29 CA, it was decided that a buyer was not precluded from recovering his loss on a resale that he had performed illegally (by failing to deliver to his sub-buyer a statement concerning certain particulars of the goods required by statute) "unless either (1) the contract was an illegal contract, or (2) the damage resulted from the omission": at 35, per Singleton LJ.

401 At para.25-027, above.

402 [1954] 2 Q.B. 459.

403 [2010] EWHC 374 (Comm).

404 See [2010] EWHC 374 (Comm) at [128]–[130]. Facts of *Choil* are at para.25-062, above.

405 [1926] 1 K.B. 348 CA.

406 [1926] 1 K.B. 348 CA at 359.

407 (1923) 39 T.L.R. 406.

not free from castor cannot be described as copra cake at all,[408] the claimant had added nothing in his sub-sale by warranting it free from castor, and it was said, though the point was not up for decision, that this would not preclude the claimant recovering from the defendant the amount he had to pay in compensation to his sub-buyer. The true principle, it is submitted, is stated by Devlin J in *Biggin v Permanite*.[409] He adopted the principle as expounded by Scrutton LJ but went on to consider what degree of variation in description would prevent recovery. Starting from the broad general rule of contract damages he arrived at the conclusion that

> "if the variation to a description is such that it is impossible to say whether the injury that ultimately results would have flowed from the breach of the original warranty, the parties must as reasonable men be presumed to have put the liability for the injury outside their contemplation as a measure of compensation."[410]

He drew a distinction, in the application of this principle, between market loss and physical damage. In the former

> "any variation that is more than a matter of words is likely to be fatal, because there is no way of telling its effect on the market value. In the latter case the nature of the physical damage will show whether the variation was material or not".[411]

He suggested, by way of illustration, the situation where a buyer in his sub-sale had added to the original warranties given him by his seller that the article

> "could be used at any time within two years, whereas in fact it was usable only for one year after manufacture. Looked at generally, that is a material addition, but if, in fact, it had been used within one year with injurious results, the additional warranty ought not, I apprehend, to bar the claim. If, however, it were sold with all faults, it would generally be impossible to prove what part of the market loss was due to … breaches of the original warranties, and what part to its shorter life in breach of the hypothetical warranty."[412]

**25-094** The facts of the case to which Devlin J had to apply the principles he outlined were these. Manufacturers of an adhesive for use in the laying of felt roofs sold a large quantity to the defendant roofing contractors. The defendants sold it to the claimants, who were specialists in roofing materials, for sale to the Dutch Government, who in turn sold to numerous Dutch roofing contractors. The adhesive proved defective, the Dutch contractors claimed damages against the Dutch Government, who in turn claimed against the claimants both in respect of their liability to the Dutch contractors and for loss in the disposal of adhesive still unused in their hands. The claimants settled the claim against them and then sued the defendants for the amount they had paid the Dutch Government, the defendants claiming over against the manufacturers whom they brought in as third parties. It was not disputed that the necessary similarity existed in the contracts between the defendants and the claimants, and the claimants and the Dutch Government respectively.[413] What was in issue was whether there was the necessary similarity (1) in these two contracts and the contracts between the Dutch Government and the Dutch contractors in rela-

---

408 So held in *Pinnock v Lewis* [1923] 1 K.B. 690.
409 [1951] 1 K.B. 422; reversed on another ground: [1951] 2 K.B. 314 CA.
410 [1951] 1 K.B. 422 at 433.
411 [1951] 1 K.B. 422 at 434.
412 [1951] 1 K.B. 422 at 434.
413 [1951] 1 K.B. 422 at 432.

tion to the claimants' claim against the defendants, and (2) in the contracts between the third party manufacturers and the defendants, and the defendants and the claimants respectively, in relation to the defendants' claim against the third parties. The first issue could not be determined until the contracts between the Dutch Government and the Dutch contractors were produced and the relevant principles of Dutch law ascertained,[414] but Devlin J expressed his view that it would not be "necessarily fatal"[415] if, as was likely, the specifications in all the Dutch Government's subsales were not in exactly the same form as in the contract of sale to the Dutch Government, and if, as was equally likely, the Dutch law as to implied conditions of quality was not exactly the same as the English.

> "The test will be whether the Dutch Government could show that the whole of its liabilities to the contractor arose from the failure of the compound to behave as warranted by the claimants."[416]

The second issue, however, allowed of immediate determination. The third party manufacturers had warranted the adhesive to be good, except for slight creepage; the defendants had passed on the warranty without the exception and added to it that the adhesive could be used with bitumen felt and needed little drying time. In these circumstances Devlin J held that the liability of the third party manufacturers to the defendants could not be measured by the defendants' liability to the claimants, for

> "no one can say how far the deficiency … is due to the original defect or to the curtailment of the drying time, or, perhaps, to its incompatibility with bitumen felt".[417]

The same principles will apply when the chain of contracts involves not differences in the warranties but differences in the goods themselves. Thus the goods may have been processed by the buyer, as with the bleaching of the unbleached cloth sold in *Slater v Hoyle & Smith*,[418] or they may have been incorporated into another product, as with the use of the vinyl film sold in the identification decals in *Bence Graphics International v Fasson UK*.[419] Taking the sale of the identification decals into account in the later case had the effect of reducing rather than increasing the damages,[420] but the principles laid down in *Biggin v Permanite*,[421] by Devlin J[422] were cited, approved and followed by Auld LJ.[423] **25-095**

*(i) Loss of profit on a resale* None of the cases appears to involve a disputed claim for loss of profit on a resale: they are all on the further advanced points of whether damages, fines or costs in litigation arising out of the breach are **25-096**

---

414 [1951] 1 K.B. 422 at 432.
415 [1951] 1 K.B. 422 at 434.
416 [1951] 1 K.B. 422 at 434.
417 [1951] 1 K.B. 422 at 434–435.
418 [1920] 2 K.B. 11 CA. Facts at para.25-067, above.
419 [1998] Q.B. 87 CA. Facts at para.25-068, above.
420 For this, see para.8-195, above.
421 [1951] 1 K.B. 422.
422 At para.25-093, above.
423 See [1998] Q.B. 87 CA at 106C–107D. The buyer's sub-sale was not taken into account in *Slater* but that was on the ground that it had already been entered into before the sale itself, and in any event the decision is now being doubted: see para.25-068, above.

recoverable. If, however, such items are recoverable, loss of profit should be allowed in damages a fortiori.[424]

25-097 *(ii) Compensation paid to a sub-buyer* Frequently damages or other compensation paid to a sub-buyer have been recovered. Some of these cases are of no great assistance because decided before *Hadley v Baxendale*,[425] established the general principles of contract damages,[426] because liability for such was admitted,[427] because there was little or no argument on the point,[428] or, finally, because the damages payable to the sub-buyer were the same amount as the normal measure of damages[429] or as the measure which the buyer could have recovered apart from a resale.[430] It is indeed true that the cases where there is admission, or little or no argument, as to these damages imply that they may well be recoverable. However, several cases deal with the matter directly, and together illustrate the general principle that recovery is allowed where the sub-contract was within the contemplation of the parties. The first case was *Bostock v Nicholson*.[431] The defendants sold commercial sulphuric acid warranted free from arsenic to the claimant, who used it for making brewers' sugar which he then sold to brewers. This was one of such acid's ordinary uses. It was held that the claimant could not recover the damages he was liable to pay to the brewers. Bruce J gave as his reasons that

> "no special circumstances were communicated to the defendants as to make them responsible for damages which would not ordinarily flow from their breach of contract,[432] … [and that] no liability is incurred in the ordinary case of a separate and distinct collateral contract with a third party uncommunicated to the original contractor or wrongdoer."[433]

On the other side of the line lies *Pinnock v Lewis*.[434] The defendant sold copra cake to the claimant who resold it to another, who manufactured part into cakettes and dairy meal and sold the manufactured and the unmanufactured parts to dealers, who sold it to farmers whose cattle fell ill. There were claims along the line, and the

---

424 See the non-delivery and delayed delivery cases at paras 25-028 to 25-030 and 25-051, above, respectively.

425 (1854) 9 Ex. 341.

426 As in *Lewis v Peake* (1816) 7 Taunt. 153 (sale and resale of horse with warranty); *Pennell v Woodburn* (1835) 7 C. & P. 117 (sale and resale of picture; claimant failed on other grounds). When stating in *Hammond v Bussey* (1888) 20 Q.B.D. 79 CA, that the pre-*Hadley v Baxendale* cases are now not reliable, Lord Esher MR cited *Lewis v Peake* as an example: at 91.

427 As in *Hammond v Bussey* (1888) 20 Q.B.D. 79 CA; *Kasler v Slavouski* [1928] 1 K.B. 78. In *Biggin v Permanite* [1951] 2 K.B. 314 CA, where the seller contemplated a resale by the buyer, it was admitted that the damages were to be assessed on the basis of the buyer's liability to his sub-buyer.

428 As in *Bennett v Kreeger* (1925) 41 T.L.R. 609; *Alison v Wallsend Slipway Co* (1927) 43 T.L.R. 323 CA; *Parker v Oloxo* [1937] 3 All E.R. 524.

429 This can be so where the sub-buyer also has sued for breach of warranty but not, as in *Aryeh v Kostoris & Son* [1967] 1 Lloyd's Rep. 63 CA, where the sub-buyer has properly rejected the goods and sued for non-delivery: see first footnote in para.25-064, above.

430 As in *Randall v Raper* (1858) E.B. & E.84 and *Wallis v Pratt* [1911] A.C. 394, where, in a sale and resale of seeds, the amount of damages paid to the sub-buyer was the value of the crop that would have resulted had the warranty been adhered to, less the value of the resulting inferior crop. This amount the buyer would have been able to recover even had he not resold but had used the seeds himself: see para.25-078, above.

431 [1904] 1 K.B. 725.

432 [1904] 1 K.B. 725 at 736.

433 [1904] 1 K.B. 725 at 742.

434 [1923] 1 K.B. 690.

claimant sued and recovered from the defendant damages[435] he had had to pay to his own sub-buyer. *Bostock v Nicholson*,[436] was distinguished on the ground that it was in the parties' contemplation that the copra cake would be used for cattle food and for nothing else. The same result was reached on similar facts in *Dobell v Barber*.[437] Linseed cake was sold and the buyer resold it to his customers for their cattle. The cattle fell ill on eating it, and the buyer recovered from his seller the damages he had paid his customers. Scrutton LJ put the case squarely on the second rule in *Hadley v Baxendale*,[438] saying that Lord Esher's words in *Hammond v Bussey*,[439] that the second rule applied to a sub-contract which in the defendant's knowledge was in the ordinary course of business sure to be made, exactly covered the case. On the other hand, in *Hardwick Game Farm v Suffolk Agricultural Poultry Producers Association*,[440] recovery appears to have been under the first rule. There ground-nut extractions were sold for compounding into a poultry food and the buyer sold the compound to a game farm for feeding to pheasants and partridges. The ground-nut extractions were contaminated and the pheasants and partridges either died or grew up stunted. The buyer successfully claimed to recover in respect of the damages he had to pay to the game farm, while the seller in turn recovered similarly against his own seller.[441]

*Biggin v Permanite*,[442] deals with a further point, a settlement made by the buyer with his sub-buyer. The claimant bought from the defendant an adhesive for use with roofing felt which, as the defendant knew, he intended to resell. The goods proving unsatisfactory, the claimant's sub-buyer claimed damages from him. Acting on legal advice, the claimant settled the case for £43,000 and the costs of the proceedings; this amount the Court of Appeal[443] awarded as damages against the defendant. Here it was necessary for the claimant to show not only that the possibility of a settlement was within the contemplation of the parties but that it was a reasonable settlement. As to the first, Somervell LJ cited Bowen LJ's remark in *Hammond v Bussey*,[444] that parties have been held to contemplate litigation in the sort of circumstances before the court, and took the view that it would "be unfortunate if they were not also held to contemplate reasonable settlements".[445] As to the second, he said that, although he did not regard the settlement as conclusive, **25-098**

> "the fact that it is admittedly an upper limit would lead to the conclusion that, if reasonable, it should be taken as the measure … The law, in my opinion, encourages reasonable settlements, particularly where, as here, strict proof would be a very expensive matter. The question, in my opinion, is: what evidence is necessary to establish reasonableness? I think it relevant that the settlement was made under advice legally taken."[446]

In the circumstances the evidence established reasonableness. And in *Britvic Soft*

---

435 And costs; for their recovery see para.25-099, below.
436 [1904] 1 K.B. 725.
437 [1931] 1 K.B. 219 CA.
438 (1854) 9 Ex. 341.
439 (1888) 20 Q.B.D. 79 CA.
440 [1969] 2 A.C. 31.
441 See [1969] 2 A.C. 31 at 91 and 103, per Lord Morris.
442 [1951] 2 K.B. 314 CA.
443 Reversing Devlin J at [1951] 1 K.B. 422.
444 (1888) 20 Q.B.D. 79 CA.
445 [1951] 2 K.B. 314 CA at 321–322.
446 [1951] 2 K.B. 314 CA at 322.

*Drinks Ltd v Messer UK Ltd*,[447] one of the cases arising out of the so-called benzene incident,[448] damages were awarded in respect of the compensation paid by the claimants to their retailers to whom they had sold the defective goods and who had been left with them on their hands. In assessing this head of damages Tomlinson J had to be satisfied, along the lines of *Biggin v Permanite*,[449] that the amounts paid out to retailers by the claimants were reasonable.[450]

**25-099** *(iii) Costs incurred in defending a sub-buyer's action*[451] A number of cases in the last section dealt not only with damages paid to the sub-buyer but with costs incurred in defending the sub-buyer's action. Sometimes liability for both damages and costs has been contested[452]; sometimes liability for the damages has been admitted and only liability for costs contested.[453] Whereas damages paid to the sub-buyer are recoverable if the sub-sale was in the contemplation of the parties, costs paid in defending an action brought by the sub-buyer are recoverable only if two hurdles are cleared. The claimant must show both that the sub-sale was in the parties' contemplation and that the costs of defending were reasonably incurred.[454]

**25-100** The leading case in relation to such costs is *Hammond v Bussey*.[455] Coal of a particular description sold by the defendant to the claimant was resold by the claimant with the same warranty, the defendant knowing that it was the claimant's business to supply coal to steamships. The coal did not answer the description, but this was discovered only on use and not on inspection. When the claimant was sued by his sub-buyer, he notified the defendant who insisted that the coal was in accordance with the contract. The claimant defended unsuccessfully, and claimed as damages from the defendant the damages and costs he had had to pay his sub-buyer. The defendant admitted the damages but contested unsuccessfully the costs. The Court of Appeal held first that the sub-sale was in contemplation of the parties within the second rule in *Hadley v Baxendale*.[456] Lord Esher did not think that

> "the second branch of the rule must be confined to the case of a sub-contract already actually made at the time of the making of the contract, and would not apply to the case of a sub-contract not yet actually made, but which will probably be made."[457]

He was, however, clear that it applied to

---

447 [2002] 1 Lloyd's Rep. 20.

448 Facts at para.25-077, above.

449 [1951] 2 K.B. 314 CA.

450 See the discussion at [2002] 1 Lloyd's Rep. 20 at 50–51at [125] to [126]. No damages issues arose in the Court of Appeal which affirmed: [2002] 2 Lloyd's Rep. 368 CA. There is a useful passage by Toulson LJ in the building contracts case of *Siemens Building Technologies FE Ltd v Supershield Ltd* [2010] 1 Lloyd's Rep. 349 CA at [28] on how the reasonableness of a settlement is to be assessed.

451 See further on the general principles, Ch.21, above.

452 As in *Pinnock v Lewis* [1923] 1 K.B. 690 and *Bennett v Kreeger* (1925) 41 T.L.R. 609, although in the latter the main argument was as to costs. Sometimes both have been but faintly contested, as in *Parker v Oloxo* [1937] 3 All E.R. 524. The pre-*Hadley v Baxendale* decisions of *Lewis v Peake* (1816) 7 Taunt. 153 and *Pennell v Woodburn* (1835) 7 C. & P. 117 also deal with damages and costs, but as said at para.25-097, above, they can no longer be relied upon.

453 As in *Hammond v Bussey* (1888) 20 Q.B.D. 79 CA, and *Kasler v Slavouski* [1928] 1 K.B. 78.

454 Although this second factor does appear in the case of compensation paid to the sub-buyer where the compensation is not by way of damages but by way of settlement; see para.25-098, above.

455 (1888) 20 Q.B.D. 79 CA.

456 (1854) 9 Ex. 341.

457 (1888) 20 Q.B.D. 79 CA at 89.

> "a sub-contract which within the knowledge of the defendant was in the ordinary course of business sure to be made."[458]

The court then held that the parties must have further contemplated as being the inevitable result of a breach by the defendant that

> "there would be a lawsuit by the sub-vendees, and that the reasonable course to be pursued by the vendees might be that they should not at once submit to the claim but that, unless they could get information from the vendor that there was really no defence, they should defend the action."[459]

Similar is *Bennett v Kreeger*,[460] where a coat was sold by the defendant manufacturer to the claimant, a ladies' tailor, for resale. The customer to whom the claimant resold the coat contracted skin disease from it and sued the claimant for damages. The claimant requested his seller to undertake the defence but the latter denied liability, although without ever suggesting that the claimant would have no answer to his customer's action. Thereupon the claimant defended the action unsuccessfully. His claim to recover as damages from the defendant the costs thereby incurred was allowed. Not only was the sub-sale within the parties' contemplation but the claimant's defence was in the circumstances reasonable. On the other hand, in the much earlier case of *Wrightup v Chamberlain*,[461] it was held that the claimant's defence of his sub-buyer's action was unreasonable. The claimant bought a horse from the defendant with a warranty of soundness and resold it with the same warranty. The sub-buyer returned it as unsound and sued the claimant for damages. The claimant notified the defendant of this, the defendant disregarded the notice, and the claimant unsuccessfully defended the action of the sub-buyer. It was held that the claimant could not recover from the defendant his costs incurred in defence since he could, before embarking on the defence, have discovered that the horse was unsound by reasonable examination after its return to him.

*Kasler & Cohen v Slavouski*,[462] introduces the complex situation presented by a "chain of buyers" or a series of "string contracts",[463] and in relation thereto deals with both the issue of the contemplation of the parties as to the various sub-sales and the issue of the reasonableness of the various defences. The defendant sold dyed rabbit skins to the claimant, a wholesale furrier, knowing that the claimant intended to make them into fur collars. The claimant made them into collars which he sold to a third party, who sold them to a fourth party, who sold them to a draper. The draper sold a coat, to which he had attached one of the fur collars, to a customer, who contracted dermatitis from the collar. The customer sued the draper for breach of warranty and, one by one, each earlier seller was brought in. The draper defended his customer's action and lost, but none of the other claims down the line was defended. At the end of the line the claimant sued the defendant for the cumulative costs that he had paid as damages to his own sub-buyer.[464] On the issue of whether the sub-sales were within the contemplation of the parties it was contended 25-101

---

458 (1888) 20 Q.B.D. 79 CA.

459 (1888) 20 Q.B.D. 79 CA at 90.

460 (1925) 41 T.L.R. 609.

461 (1839) 7 Scott 598.

462 [1928] 1 K.B. 78.

463 See para.25-092, above.

464 The extent to which the cumulative costs can mount up in these circumstances is well illustrated. The claimant claimed £699 and was awarded over £650; yet the damages awarded to the customer

by the defendant that the rule allowing recovery of costs as damages extended to enable the first buyer to recover from the original seller what he might have had to pay his sub-buyer, and that it might entitle the sub-buyer, if he had sold on, to recover from the first buyer, but that it was never permissible to go back more than two steps.[465] This contention was rejected by Branson J on the ground that the defendant could foresee that the claimant as buyer of the rabbit skins would not "wear them round his own neck"[466] but would make them up into collars which he would sell, and that there would necessarily be a line of wholesalers and retailers through whose hands the collars would pass before reaching the ultimate wearer.[467] On the issue of the reasonableness of the defence, the interesting feature is that the defence in question was not that of the claimant when sued by his own sub-buyer but that of the first person sued at the end of the line, here the draper sued by his customer. His defence was held to be reasonable because an analyst's report had exonerated the particular fur collar from the allegation that it contained deleterious matter: as the court pointed out, if the draper had paid the amount claimed by his customer after this analyst's report "one can well imagine what the parties higher up the line would have said".[468] Branson J further said, however:

> "There may well be a difference on the question of adding costs to damages, or treating costs incurred as part of the damages between those costs which were incurred originally in the course of contesting the validity of the claim made for damages by reason of the breach, and the intermediate costs incurred by one party or another resisting an attempt to pass the claim back. Whether a particular amount of resistance is or is not reasonable is, I think, a question of fact, and it seems to me that in so far as resistance is reasonable in the circumstances, then each person who so resists has suffered extra damage measured by the amount of resistance … I think it must be reasonable for anybody before submitting to a liability of this kind to see a solicitor and have advice."[469]

This problem, however, did not arise in the particular case as the parties other than the draper did not contest the claims against them.[470]

**25-102** The amount which the buyer may recover under this head in the simple case of a single claim by his sub-buyer, reasonably but unsuccessfully defended, consists of the costs paid to the sub-buyer assessed by the court and his own costs then assessed as between solicitor and client. This amount was clearly held recoverable in *Bennett v Kreeger*.[471] Where there is the complication of a chain of sub-sales with claims along the line, the same result is reached, with costs snowballing as li-

at the end of the line amounted only to £67.

465 [1928] 1 K.B. 78 at 85.

466 [1928] 1 K.B. 78 at 87.

467 *Borries v Hutchinson* (1865) 18 C.B. N.S. 445, a non-delivery case, and dealing with compensation paid to a third party and not with costs incurred, was distinguished on the ground that loss of profit twice over was not in the parties' contemplation there. Branson J's view was adopted by Devlin J in *Biggin v Permanite* [1951] 1 K.B. 422 (reversed on grounds not affecting the present considerations: [1951] 2 K.B. 314 CA), again a case dealing with compensation and not costs. He there said: "I do not think that the application of the principle is to be determined by the number of links in the chain. If what happened at the end was within the contemplation of the parties, I do not think it matters how long the chain is": at 432.

468 [1928] 1 K.B. 78 at 88.

469 [1928] 1 K.B. 78 at 88–89.

470 Other cases where the costs in claims along the line were recovered are *Pinnock v Lewis* [1923] 1 K.B. 690 (sale of cattle food) and *Butterworth v Kingsway Motors* [1954] 1 W.L.R. 1286 (sale of a car).

471 (1925) 41 T.L.R. 609. The cases do not always detail what costs are being given as damages.

ability follows liability. Thus in *Butterworth v Kingsway Motors*,[472] third-party procedure was in operation and each party received as damages the damages and assessed costs he had to pay the party next along the line, plus his own costs in the claim against him[473] then assessed as between solicitor and client. In *Kasler & Cohen v Slavouski*,[474] only the claim at the end of the line was defended in court, but the other parties incurred small non-action costs which were all taken into account in the final assessment.

In all the above cases the buyer's own costs which he was held entitled to recover were his costs assessed as between solicitor and client. Today solicitor and client costs no longer exist in this context and it might be thought that the buyer should simply be entitled to all his costs if reasonably incurred. There is, however, a growing move at first instance, one not to be encouraged, which would restrict the buyer to what, if assessed, would have been his standard basis costs; this unfortunate development has already been fully examined in an earlier chapter to which reference should be made.[475] **25-103**

*(iv) Fines paid; costs incurred in defending a prosecution*[476] In *Payne v Ministry of Food*,[477] a buyer of milk, having resold it under the same description as it was sold to him, was prosecuted for selling milk under a false description and convicted. He failed to recover as damages from his seller either the fine imposed on him or the costs incurred by him. The court did not consider whether mens rea had been present or not, and the ground of the decision would appear to be that it is against public policy to allow the monetary loss involved in a criminal conviction to be passed on to another party. The case, however, must be viewed in the light of the decisions on this issue generally, and these indicate that the current key to the denial of recovery is not policy but the presence of mens rea.[478] **25-104**

In *Proops v Chaplin*,[479] on the other hand, a buyer of whisky, having resold it in reliance on a warranty that it was 30 per cent under proof, was prosecuted for selling it above the permitted price and acquitted. Here neither mens rea nor any ground of public policy could bar his claim and he recovered as damages from his seller the costs of his successful defence.[480] **25-105**

*(v) Other expenses made necessary* Other miscellaneous expenses in connec- **25-106**

---

472 [1954] 1 W.L.R. 1286.

473 The various awards of damages along the line are set out in impressive detail, [1954] 1 W.L.R. 1286 at 1297–1300 by Pearson J. Further illustrations of such a succession of awards are provided by *Godley v Perry* [1960] 1 W.L.R. 9 (see especially at 16 to 17) and *Bowmaker (Commercial) v Day* [1965] 1 W.L.R. 1396.

474 [1928] 1 K.B. 78.

475 See the discussion at paras 21-003 and following, above. For the amount of costs recoverable in these circumstances under the old regime and under the new see para.20-009 together with para.21-080, above.

476 See further on the general principles, Ch.21, above, passim.

477 (1953) 103 L.J. 141.

478 See paras 21-066 and following, above, and the sale of goods cases where the prosecution stemmed from use and not from resale at paras 25-088 and 25-089, above.

479 (1920) 37 T.L.R. 112.

480 Whether the prosecution succeeds or fails the buyer should be entitled to recover all of his costs reasonably incurred and the limits that are now coming in for parties in a civil suit (see para.21-003 and following, above) should have no application to criminal prosecutions in the light of the Court of Appeal's decision in *Berry v British Transport Commission* [1962] 1 Q.B. 306 CA, which see at para.21-018, above.

tion with a resale may be recoverable. Thus, in *Molling v Dean*,[481] where the seller knew that the buyer intended to send the goods to a sub-buyer in America and the goods were properly rejected there by the sub-buyer, the buyer recovered, inter alia,[482] the cost of bringing the goods back from America.

**25-107** *(vi) Loss of profit on further sales* Initially, successful claims were not to be found in respect of loss of custom generally, which has stemmed from the loss of particular sub-sales of the goods sold by the defendant. In *Bostock v Nicholson*,[483] poisonous sulphuric acid was sold which the buyer used in the manufacture of brewers' sugar which he then sold to brewers for the brewing of beer. The beer brewed was thus rendered poisonous causing illness, and sometimes death, to the drinkers of it. One of the buyer's unsuccessful heads of claim was for loss of his business goodwill and credit. In refusing damages on this head Bruce J relied upon the fact that the poisonous acid had not been sold as such by the buyer to the brewers but had been manufactured by him into another substance.[484] Had he, however, taken a wider view of the contemplation of the parties in relation to the particular sub-sales,[485] the general trend of decisions at that time would still have been against awarding damages for loss of profit on potential further sales.[486] However, the Court of Appeal in *G.K.N. Centrax Gears v Matbro*[487] took the view that loss of repeat orders was as much a matter for claim as any other loss if shown to be within the contemplation of the contracting parties, and there allowed recovery in respect of such a loss since it must have been seen not only as probable but as almost inevitable that the supply of defective axles by manufacturers to specialist makers of forklift trucks for incorporation by them into the trucks would cause much damage to their goodwill, with their customers becoming dissatisfied and refraining from placing further orders.[488] And in *Britvic Soft Drinks Ltd v Messer UK Ltd*,[489] there was a claim for the loss of future business profits on the basis that the publicity engendered by what was referred to as the benzene incident[490] had caused its sales of carbonated soft drinks in later trading periods to be substantially less than they would otherwise have been. This claim failed but only on the matter of proof, the claimant in the judgment of the court having not come close to demonstrating that the publicity had had any measurable impact upon the demand for its products.[491] It is quite clear, however, that a downturn in demand caused by the delivery of a defective product would, if shown, have brought an entitlement to damages.[492]

---

481 (1902) 18 T.L.R. 216.

482 The cost of sending the goods to America was also recovered; this is dealt with at para.25-109, below.

483 [1904] 1 K.B. 725.

484 [1904] 1 K.B. 725 at 741–742.

485 The decision came at a time when the more liberal trend in relation to loss on a resale had not been established: see para.25-028, above.

486 See *Doe v Bowater* [1916] W.N. 185 and *Simon v Pawsons & Leafs* (1933) 38 Com. Cas. 151 CA, at paras 25-036 and 25-055, respectively, above.

487 [1976] 2 Lloyd's Rep. 555 CA.

488 The contrary view expressed by Scrutton LJ in *Simon v Pawsons & Leafs* (1933) 38 Com. Cas. 151 CA was disapproved.

489 [2002] 1 Lloyd's Rep. 20.

490 Facts at para.25-077, above. There were two claimants, Britvic and Bass, but only Britvic included a claim for loss of future business profits.

491 [2002] 1 Lloyd's Rep. 20 at 57 at [147].

492 See the analysis at [2002] 1 Lloyd's Rep. 20 at 51 to 57 at [129]–[147]. No damages issues arose in

**(d) Other losses** In *Borealis AB v Geogas Trading SA*,[493] the buyer was held entitled to recover for expenditure on managerial and staff time taken up in dealing with remedial work to plant and equipment damaged by the goods sold being contaminated.[494] Similarly, in *Azzurri Communications Ltd v International Telecommunications Equipment Ltd*,[495] where telephone handsets purchased in bulk by the claimant turned out to be faulty in operation, recovery was allowed in respect of management and staff time taken up in investigating the problem.[496] **25-108**

**(e) Expenses rendered futile by the breach** In *Molling v Dean*,[497] the buyer recovered not only the cost of bringing back the goods from America where his sub-buyer had rejected them,[498] but also the cost of sending them to America to the sub-buyer. These two costs did not call for separate treatment in the particular decision but the principle behind the one is not the same as that behind the other. Whereas the cost of bringing the goods back was an expense incurred as a result of the breach, the cost of sending them was an expense which would have been incurred even if there had been no breach, the breach merely serving to render it futile. Thus while the cost of bringing the goods back was an out-of-pocket loss which the buyer could properly claim, along with other out-of-pocket losses like damages or fines or costs incurred in other actions or prosecutions, in addition to his loss of profit so as to put him into the position he would have been in had the contract been performed, the cost of sending the goods was an out-of-pocket loss which could only properly be claimed in lieu of the loss of profit. Care is required here to avoid giving a double and sometimes inconsistent recovery.[499] **25-109**

## 5. BREACH OF CONDITION AS TO TITLE OR OF WARRANTY OF QUIET POSSESSION

Where the buyer is evicted from possession of the goods by a person with a superior title the normal measure of damages is the market value of the goods, and this value should be taken at the time of eviction thereby incorporating any increase in the value of the goods, whether due to ordinary market changes or to reasonable improvements made by the buyer. This measure was adopted in *Mason v Burningham*,[500] where the buyer of a typewriter for £20 had spent £11 on overhauling it. Later the typewriter was discovered to have been stolen and had to be returned to the owner, and the buyer successfully claimed to recover as damages not only the £20 but the £11,[501] the judge holding that in making this improvement to the typewriter he had behaved in a common sense way and done the ordinary and natural thing.[502] In *Louis Dreyfus Trading Ltd v Reliance Trading Ltd*,[503] the damages were necessarily different from those in *Mason v Burningham* since the buyer **25-110**

---

the Court of Appeal which affirmed: [2002] 2 Lloyd's Rep. 368 CA.

493 [2011] 1 Lloyd's Rep. 482; facts at para.8-150, above.

494 See [2011] 1 Lloyd's Rep. 482 at [144] to [149].

495 [2013] EWPCC 17.

496 [2013] EWPCC 17 at [85] to [88]. This head of damages is already well established in the field of tort; see the cases at the end of para.4-059, above.

497 (1902) 18 T.L.R. 216.

498 See para.25-106, above.

499 This whole question is considered from general principles at paras 4-024 to 4-049, above.

500 [1949] 2 K.B. 545 CA.

501 Applying s.53(2) of the then Sale of Goods Act 1893; see para.25-059, above.

502 The analogous land cases, *Bunny v Hopkinson* (1859) 27 Beav. 565 and *Rolph v Crouch* (1867) L.R. 3 Ex. 44 (at paras 27-020 and 28-018, below, respectively) were relied upon, Singleton LJ saying that he thought they were "in point".

had eventually obtained possession of the goods sold. Discharge of a cargo of sugar from the vessel upon which it was being shipped was delayed by reason of an injunction restraining discharge obtained by a third party—it was this that gave rise to the breach of the warranty of quiet possession—and when the injunction was finally lifted and the claimant received the sugar, its price in the market had fallen. The prima facie measure of damages, which arbitrators awarded, was held to be, using the analogy of damages for breach of warranty of quality, the difference between the contract price and the value of the sugar when it was eventually received. On the appeal this as the correct prima facie measure was not challenged.[504]

**25-111** Recovery for consequential losses is illustrated by *Bowmaker (Commercial) v Day*,[505] where the buyer on eviction reasonably but unsuccessfully sued the person evicting him in conversion. His costs in this suit then assessed as between solicitor and client were held recoverable as damages in his action against his seller.[506]

## 6. Breach of Condition: Loss of the Right to Reject the Goods

**25-112** A breach of condition by the seller entitles the buyer to reject the goods but unless a decision to reject is taken and is implemented speedily the right of rejection is lost. Sometimes the right is lost because the buyer, through no fault of his own, learns too late of the seller's breach. In three cases damages have been claimed by buyers arising out of the loss of the right to reject where the contract has been one in which the seller has undertaken to ship the goods to the buyer on a certain date and has shipped them late. In such cases no damage would have resulted from the loss of the right to reject had not the market price fallen after the date of the seller's breach; the buyer's action for damages is therefore unusual in that he is claiming to be put into the position he would have been in not if the contract had been performed but if it had never been made. It may be that a claimant is not entitled to elect between these two bases for damages as this would give him the right to claim damages for entering into a bad bargain.[507] If, however, he repudiates for breach of condition he does get the opportunity to resile from a bad bargain,[508] and the issue that is posed by the buyer's loss, through no fault of his own, of the right to repudiate the contract and reject the goods, is whether he may claim by way of damages to be put into the position he would have been in had he been able to repudiate. In theory, the issue is arguable either way: in practice, the courts appear to have reached a middle solution which is based on compromise rather than on logic.

---

503 [2004] 2 Lloyd's Rep. 243.

504 Strictly, it should have been phrased as the difference between the value as warranted and the value received, which may well have given the same result. The issue in the Court of Appeal was as to whether the prima facie measure was appropriate in the light of a pre-contract sub-sale: see the case at para.8-196, above.

505 [1965] 1 W.L.R. 1396.

506 But today the buyer may find himself confined to recovery of only his standard basis costs: see the discussion at paras 18-003 and following, above and the *Bowmaker v Day* case at para.21-081, above.

507 He may claim on this alternative restitutionary basis when he is not attempting to escape from a bad bargain but is compelled by law or by circumstances to do so: this is not election but Hobson's choice. See paras 4-024 to 4-049, above, where the scope of this alternative measure is considered.

508 He may, indeed, claim damages in addition to repudiating but these are assessed upon the normal basis of giving him the benefit of his bargain.

In the first case, *Taylor v Bank of Athens*,[509] beans were to be shipped by the seller under a c.i.f. contract in July or August. On their arrival in late September the buyer resold them, and only later discovered that they had been shipped in early September and that the bills of lading had been misdated. There was no difference in value between an August and a September shipment but the market had been falling heavily from July onwards. In these circumstances the buyer claimed damages for the seller's breach in not shipping within the contract period; this was a breach of condition giving the right to reject the goods but their resale had removed the possibility of rejection. Nominal damages only were awarded. McCardie J said: **25-113**

> "It is vital to observe that the loss must result from the breach of warranty, as distinguished from a loss through having entered into the contract. It does not extend, I think, to a case where the loss results not from the breach of warranty but from an unfortunate or improvident bargain which the buyer may have made. Market falls are not generally due to the vendor's fault. A buyer cannot, I think, save in very exceptional circumstances, attribute to his seller a loss which, in substance and in fact, arises not from the seller's breach, but from a fall in market values."[510]

However in the second case, *Finlay v Kwik Hoo Tong*,[511] the Court of Appeal on similar facts[512] reached a different conclusion, and awarded the buyer as damages the contract price less the fallen market price because the action was not for breach in not shipping within the contract period but for breach in failing to deliver a genuine bill of lading. Greer LJ, distinguishing *Taylor v Bank of Athens*,[513] on this ground of reliance upon a different breach, specifically said that he would have agreed to nominal damages if there had been no "distinct breach of contract by tendering a wrongly dated bill of lading".[514] The principle of this decision was carried a step further in *Kwei Tek Chao v British Traders*,[515] where again the facts were similar, except that the buyer knew of the breach as to the bill of lading by the time of delivery so that he could have rejected the goods as distinct from the documents.[516] He chose, however, not to reject the goods and was still successful in his claim to recover as damages the contract price less the fallen market price. The seller's contention was rejected that not he but the buyer himself was responsible for the loss of the latter's right to reject. Devlin J held that there were two rights to reject, first the documents and then the goods, and that very different considerations would govern the buyer's mind when considering rejection of the goods as distinct from rejection of the documents. For if he rejects the goods and goes into the market again, he is left only with an unsecured claim against the seller since by now he has paid the price. He was therefore entitled to claim for the loss of his right to reject the documents, and Devlin J pointed out that the damages which the seller was liable to pay on this basis were exactly the same as if the buyer had rejected, the only difference being that the seller and not the buyer would have

509 (1922) 27 Com. Cas. 142.

510 (1922) 27 Com. Cas. 142 at 147.

511 [1929] 1 K.B. 400 CA.

512 There was a difference in connection with the sub-contract but it is not relevant here: see the case at para.9-096, above.

513 (1922) 27 Com. Cas. 142.

514 [1929] 1 K.B. 400 CA at 414.

515 [1954] 2 Q.B. 459.

516 There was another difference from the two earlier cases in that the buyer lost a profitable resale because of the late shipment. For this loss he did not recover for reasons that are considered elsewhere: see para.25-027, above.

been handling the goods.[517] Beyond this the case decided two minor points in relation to the damages. First, it was held that the market price was to be taken not at the time of breach by tender of the false documents but at the time of the buyer's discovery of the breach, since

> "if the market has fallen, a buyer will, if he is considering only economic conditions, exercise his right to reject, because he can then go out into the market and buy the same goods at the market price ... and he can put the difference in his pocket".[518]

Secondly, it was held that the market price to be taken was the selling and not the buying price, between which in the particular case there was a considerable margin, since

> "the buyer has received the goods, and a calculation which supposes, incorrectly and notionally, that he should go out and buy another quantity of the same goods, has nothing to do with the reality of the matter".[519]

## II. BREACH BY BUYER

**25-114** One of the most frequently brought actions against the buyer of goods is an action for the price.[520] This, however, is not an action for damages and is therefore not dealt with.

### 1. NON-ACCEPTANCE

**25-115** The measure of damages for non-acceptance of goods is prescribed by s.50 of the Sale of Goods Act 1979 thus:

(1) Where the buyer wrongfully neglects or refuses to accept and pay for the goods, the seller may maintain an action against him for damages for non-acceptance.
(2) The measure of damages is the estimated loss directly and naturally resulting, in the ordinary course of events, from the buyer's breach of contract.
(3) Where there is an available market for the goods in question the measure of damages is prima facie to be ascertained by the difference between the contract price and the market or current price at the time or times when the goods ought to have been accepted, or, if no time was fixed for acceptance, then at the time of the refusal to accept.

To this s.54 adds that nothing in the Act shall affect the seller's right to recover interest or special damages where by law recoverable.

**25-116** Section 50(2) is framed in terms of the first rule in *Hadley v Baxendale*,[521] excluding the element of the defendant's knowledge of special circumstances; s.50(3) states the normal measure of damages under the first rule; s.54 brings in the second

---

517 [1954] 2 Q.B. 459 at 483. But it is thought that the extension of the availability of this measure of damages in *Kleinjan and Holst v Bremer Handelsgesellschaft* [1972] 2 Lloyd's Rep. 11 to a buyer who, had he wished, could have rejected both documents and goods is misconceived.

518 [1954] 2 Q.B. 459 at 479.

519 [1954] 2 Q.B. 459 at 497–498.

520 This action is dealt with by s.49 of the Sale of Goods Act 1979.

521 (1854) 9 Ex. 341. See paras 8-158 and following, above.

rule in *Hadley v Baxendale*,[522] and will in appropriate cases displace s.50(2) and (3) and allow increased damages.

## (1) Normal measure

The normal measure of damages, as stated in s.50(3) thereby incorporating the common law as stated in *Barrow v Arnaud*,[523] is the contract price less the market price at the contractual time[524] for acceptance.[525] This represents the amount the seller must obtain to put himself in the position he would have been in had the contract been carried out, since he can sell the goods in the market.[526] If, however, there is clearly no available market, then, consequential losses apart, the damages will be assessed at the contract price less the value of the goods to the claimant at the time of breach, which value is likely to be based, as in *Harlow and Jones v* **25-117**

522 (1854) 9 Ex. 341.

523 (1846) 8 Q.B. 595 at 610.

524 And at the contractual place for acceptance. See Diplock LJ, but dealing with the converse case of delivery by the seller, in *Aryeh v Kostoris & Son* [1967] 1 Lloyd's Rep. 63 CA at 73, col.1.

525 This is on the normal assumption that the contract price has not been paid over.

526 The criticised decision in *Braithwaite v Foreign Hardwood Co* [1905] 2 K.B. 543 CA, causes some difficulty, as the amount of damages awarded was smaller than the contract price less the market price by reason of a deduction being made for the inferiority of the goods tendered by way of first instalment. Properly understood the case was this. The contract was one to sell rosewood by instalments and while the first consignment was on the sea the buyer refused to accept; this refusal the court subsequently held to be wrongful. The seller did not there and then accept the repudiation but offered to tender the first instalment which was, in fact, of inferior quality. This the buyer refused on the basis of his earlier repudiation; there was never an actual tendered delivery. The facts of the case were explained in this way by Greer J in *Taylor v Oakes* (1922) 38 T.L.R. 349 at 351, basing himself on the leading judgment in the case of Lord Collins MR Bankes LJ in the Court of Appeal ((1922) 38 T.L.R. 517 at 518) expressed agreement with Greer J's interpretation. There was thus, as Greer J said, no actual breach by the seller since by refusing delivery the buyer had waived all further acts of performance by the seller. The seller could, therefore, sue for damages, and these should be the normal measure, i.e. contract price less market price of rosewood of the contract standard. This was Lord Collins MR's view in the case itself ([1905] 2 K.B. 543 CA at 552), but he went on to say that "the learned judge has assessed the damages from the point of view of common sense rather than of strict law, and has made an allowance, of which the defendants cannot complain" (at 552). It thus appears that the deduction was not made as of right, and the decision becomes one on its special facts. On this explanation of the case, even Lord Sumner, who criticised it in *British and Beningtons v North-Western Cachar Co* [1923] A.C. 48 at 70–71, would probably accept it: his point did not really go to the question of the measure of damages. But while a contracting party, after acceptance of an anticipatory breach, is relieved of his obligation to perform his side of the bargain, that his ability or inability to perform is relevant to the damages recoverable is usefully illustrated by *North Sea Energy Holdings v Petroleum Authority of Thailand* [1997] 2 Lloyd's Rep. 418 (a point which did not arise on the appeal: [1999] 1 Lloyd's Rep. 483 CA); see the case at para.25-129, below. How far after a repudiation by a buyer of goods the seller's ability, or willingness, still to perform can affect the damages was much in issue in the complicated case of *Acre 1127 Ltd v De Montfort Fine Art* [2011] EWCA Civ 87 CA where the contract was for the supply of valuable items of contemporary art and in which the *Braithwaite* case (above in this note) was extensively referred to.

*Panex (International)*,[527] and *AerCap Partners Ltd v Avia Asset Management AB*,[528] upon the price at which they are eventually sold by the claimant.[529]

25-118 **(a) The need for an available market** Contract price less market price is laid down as the prima facie measure in s.50(3)[530] only where there is an "available market". Various definitions of what constitutes an available market have been given in the authorities. The earliest is that of James LJ in *Dunkirk Colliery Co v Lever*.[531] He said that what he understood by an available market was that, upon the buyer's refusal to accept the coal he had bought, the sellers

> "might have sent it in wagons somewhere else, where they could sell it, just as they sell corn on the Exchange, or cotton at Liverpool: that is to say, that there was a fair market where they could have found a purchaser either by themselves or through some agent at some particular place."[532]

Later, however, wider views have been expressed in two cases which involved the sale of cars by dealers where the manufacturers had laid down a fixed retail selling price.[533] In the first, *Thompson v Robinson*,[534] Upjohn J, while holding himself bound by the earlier definition, gave his own view that

> "an available market merely means that the situation in the particular trade in the particular area was such that the particular goods could freely be sold, and that there was a demand sufficient to absorb readily all the goods that were thrust on it, so that if a purchaser defaulted, the goods in question could readily be disposed of."[535]

In the second, *Charter v Sullivan*,[536] Jenkins LJ thought James LJ's definition too narrow, but he also found Upjohn J's too wide[537] since he doubted if there could be an available market for goods within the subsection

> "unless those goods are available for sale in the market at the market or current price, in the sense of the price, whatever it may be, fixed by reference to supply and demand as the price at which a purchaser for the goods in question can be found, be it greater or less than or equal to the contract price. The language of s.50(3) seems to me to postulate that in the cases to which it applies there will, or may, be a difference between the contract

527 [1967] 2 Lloyd's Rep. 509. Some of the goods were in fact taken back by the claimants' own sellers. In relation to these the damages were based upon the contract price as between claimants and defendants less the contract price as between claimants and their own sellers: see [1967] 2 Lloyd's Rep. 509 at 531. A seller cannot obtain more than the contract price less his resale price by transferring to his buyer a liability for demurrage and reducing the resale price pro tanto: *Cerealmangini SpA v Toepfer* [1981] 3 All E.R. 533.

528 [2010] EWHC 2431 (Comm).

529 Provided always that there is not a failure to mitigate which, as was held in *Robbins of Putney v Meek* [1971] R.T.R. 345, is not constituted by a sale which, though in normal circumstances premature, is dictated by the claimant's impecuniosity (see para.9-097, above).

530 See para.25-115, above.

531 (1878) 9 Ch. D. 20 CA.

532 (1878) 9 Ch. D. 20 CA at 25.

533 These two cases involved new cars. For second-hand cars there can be no available market as each such car is unique and is different from the next one: *Lazenby Garages v Wright* [1976] 1 W.L.R. 459 CA.

534 [1955] Ch. 177.

535 [1955] Ch. 177 at 187.

536 [1957] 2 Q.B. 117 CA.

537 He spoke of the former as not exhaustive and of the latter as not entirely satisfactory: [1957] 2 Q.B. 117 CA at 128.

price and the market or current price, which cannot be so where the goods can only be sold at a fixed retail price."[538]

It is submitted that this trend to a definition wider than that of James LJ is sound, since it is not realistic to limit the term "available market" to the few basic commodities, such as grains and metals, which are quoted and sold on an official exchange. As for the wider definitions themselves, it is submitted that Jenkins LJ's limitation upon Upjohn J's suggestion is a sound one but the difference is little more than academic. For if, where there is a fixed retail price for goods such as cars, the seller is still in a position to sell all the cars he can obtain and stock, then while Upjohn J would regard this as an available market and apply s.50(3)[539] to give nominal damages, Jenkins LJ, while rejecting the possibility of an available market, would reach the same result of nominal damages by the application of s.50(2).[540] **25-119**

To give a wide meaning to the term "available market" derives new support from the decision in *Shearson Lehman Hutton v Maclaine Watson & Co.*[541] In determining whether in the circumstances of the case before him there was an available market Webster J, after referring to, and citing from, all three of the earlier cases above, namely *Dunkirk Colliery*,[542] *Thompson*,[543] and *Charter*,[544] among others,[545] said: **25-120**

> "The answer seems to me to be: that if the seller actually offers the goods for sale there is no available market unless there is one actual buyer on that day at a fair price; that if there is no actual offer for sale, but only a notional or hypothetical sale for the purposes of s.50(3), there is no available market unless on that day there are in the market sufficient traders potentially in touch with each other to evidence a market in which the actual or notional seller could if he wished sell the goods."[546]

Webster J went on to hold that, since it could be reasonable or sensible for the seller to have waited before going into the market and selling the goods, in this case some seven-and-a-half tonnes of standard grade tin, the market price could take into account the price which might have been negotiated within a few days of the breach with other potential buyers who earlier were not part of the market because of difficulties of communication.[547] There is thus a temporal aspect to "available market"; the market does not necessarily have to be available on the date of breach itself.[548]

**(b) Relevant and irrelevant prices in ascertaining the market price** The **25-121**

---

538 [1957] 2 Q.B. 117 CA at 128.

539 See para.25-115, above.

540 See para.25-115, above.

541 [1990] 3 All E.R. 723. There are also, at last, two cases discussing available market where the breach has been by non-delivery rather than by non-acceptance. See them at para.25-007, above.

542 (1878) 9 Ch. D. 20 CA.

543 [1955] Ch. 177.

544 [1957] 2 Q.B. 117 CA.

545 The other three cases referred to, and cited from, concerned breach by sellers rather than buyers or sale of shares rather than goods.

546 [1990] 3 All E.R. 723 at 730j. Passage cited and adopted by David Steel J in the charterparty case, at para.25-068, below, of *Zodiac Maritime Agencies Ltd v Fortescue Metals Group Ltd* [2011] 2 Lloyd's Rep. 360 at [56].

547 [1990] 3 All E.R. 723 at 731a to b.

548 See *Garnac Grain Co v Faure & Fairclough* [1968] A.C. 1130 at 1138. Where there was a so-called forward freight swap agreement, rather than a conventional sale, in *Dampskibsselskabet Norden A/S v Andre & Cie SA* [2003] 1 Lloyd's Rep. 287, there was held to be an available market in which the claimant could have found a buyer and replaced its contract; see at 290 to 292.

price at which the seller has resold the goods to a third party, clearly after the buyer's non-acceptance,[549] may be treated as evidence of the market value where it is difficult to assess,[550] but generally it is irrelevant and should not be taken in preference to the market price. The occasional case in which the resale price has been taken, such as *Maclean v Dunn*,[551] and *Re Nathan, Ex parte Stapleton*,[552] can only be supported on the ground that it afforded evidence of the market price, and indeed there is no suggestion in these cases that the market and resale prices differed at all.[553] So too the seller of two Boeing aircraft was held entitled in *AerCap Partners Ltd v Avia Asset Management AB*[554] to the difference between the contract price and the substantially lower price at which it resold the aircraft a good many months after the buyer's repudiation of the contract, this apparently on the basis that the resale price was good evidence of the market value, though possibly on the basis that no available market had appeared until the time of the resale.[555] But apart from being evidence of market price the resale price, where clearly different, cannot control. Thus in *Campbell Mostyn v Barnett*,[556] it was held that the damages could not be reduced because the market had risen after the breach and the seller had resold at the market price higher than at the time of the buyer's breach.[557] Conversely, the damages will not be increased because the market falls after breach and the seller waits before reselling, at least if he waits more than a reasonable time.[558]

25-122 **(c) Time at which the market price to be taken** The time at which the market price is to be taken is, as stated in the first limb and the second limb respectively of s.50(3),[559] the time fixed for acceptance or, if no time is fixed, the time of refusal to accept. It is however generally accepted today that the law gives the seller a reasonable period of time after breach in which to make the substitute sale, as was the case in *AerCap Partners Ltd v Avia Asset Management AB*.[560] One exact time fixed for acceptance poses no difficulties: the calculation is made as of that time. As for the more difficult situations, they have been before the courts mostly in con-

---

549 When dealing above with the various cases of seller's as opposed to buyer's breach, it had been necessary to deal with resales by the buyer both before and after breach.

550 So too may the price of an offer not yet crystallised into a contract.

551 (1828) 4 Bing. 722. Best CJ said that "it is most important that when a party refuses to take goods he has purchased, they should be resold, and that he should be liable to the loss, if any, upon the resale": at 729.

552 (1879) 10 Ch. D. 586 CA, Jessel MR said that "the damages for the breach are plainly, if the market is falling, the difference between the contract price and the price obtained on the resale": at 590.

553 The resale price will not afford evidence of the market price where the terms of the resale differ substantially from the terms of the original sale, as in *Macklin v Newbury Sanitary Laundry* (1919) 63 S.J. 337, where a horse sold with a warranty was resold without the warranty at a much smaller price.

554 [2010] EWHC 2431 (Comm).

555 See the lengthy analysis of Gross LJ at [2010] EWHC 2431 (Comm) at [90] and following.

556 [1954] 1 Lloyd's Rep. 65 CA; following *Jamal v Moolla Dawood* [1916] 1 A.C. 175 PC, the equivalent case in sale of shares: see para.29-010, below. It is not thought that these decisions are affected by *Bence Graphics v Fasson UK* [1998] Q.B. 87 CA: see para.25-068, above.

557 See the decision in the context of mitigation and avoided loss at para.9-134, above.

558 See at para.25-066, above, the breach of warranty cases where the buyer was held to have resold the defective goods within a reasonable time.

559 See para.25-115, above.

560 [2010] EWHC 2431 (Comm); facts in the preceding paragraph.

nection with the equivalent non-delivery cases,[561] but the principles established in those cases should apply mutatis mutandis here.

*(i) Where a specific period or a succession of times is fixed for acceptance* Unlike the case of non-delivery the last possible moment within a specified period fixed for acceptance would not be the time to be taken[562]; rather would it be the time within that period at which the goods are tendered by the seller. Where delivery is by instalments so that a number of successive times is fixed for acceptance, each fixed time is taken as to each instalment.[563] **25-123**

*(ii) Where the buyer repudiates before the time fixed for acceptance* The fact that the buyer has repudiated the contract before the time fixed for acceptance does not affect the prima facie rule that the market price at the time so fixed is the relevant one. In the first place, if the buyer's repudiation is not accepted by the seller it is a nullity and there is no breach till there is non-performance, i.e. at the time fixed for acceptance,[564] and the seller, with no duty to mitigate, is entitled to sit back on a falling market and then claim the normal measure based on the market price at the time fixed for acceptance: this result was reached in *Philpotts v Evans*,[565] and *Tredegar Iron & Coal Co v Hawthorn*.[566] This latter case did not involve a repudiation not accepted at all but a repudiation accepted only after some time during which the market was falling, and it was held that there was no duty to mitigate during the period which elapsed between repudiation and its acceptance. In the second place, if the buyer's repudiation is accepted by the seller so that there is then and there a breach, the damages are still prima facie calculated at the time fixed for acceptance,[567] but subject to a duty to mitigate on the seller's part with the onus on the buyer to prove that the seller has failed in this duty.[568] Thus it was held in *Roth v Taysen*[569] that, where the buyer showed that the seller could in the interim between the acceptance of the repudiation and the time fixed for acceptance have resold in the market at a price higher than that at the time fixed for acceptance, he was **25-124**

---

[561] See paras 25-015 to 25-022, above.

[562] See for non-delivery *Leigh v Paterson* (1818) 8 Taunt. 540 at para.25-017, above.

[563] See the equivalent non-delivery cases of *Brown v Muller* (1872) L.R. 7 Ex. 319 and *Roper v Johnson* (1873) L.R. 8 C.P. 167 at para.25-017, above.

[564] In *Stocznia Gdanska v Latvian Shipping Co* [1997] 2 Lloyd's Rep. 228 it was held at first instance that the repudiatory anticipatory breach by the buyers had not been accepted so that there was no entitlement to sue for damages. While this decision on acceptance of breach was set aside by the House of Lords ([1998] 1 Lloyd's Rep. 609; see at 623) it remains illustrative of the position.

[565] (1839) 5 M. & W. 476.

[566] (1902) 18 T.L.R. 716 CA. See too *Kyprianou v Pim & Co* [1977] 2 Lloyd's Rep. 570.

[567] See the equivalent non-delivery cases of *Roper v Johnson* (1873) L.R. 8 C.P. 167 and *Garnac Grain Co v Faure & Fairclough* [1968] A.C. 1130, at para.25-018, above. It was said, however, in *Tredegar Iron and Coal Co v Hawthorn* (1902) 18 T.L.R. 716 CA at 717 that "the damages were to be calculated as on the date of the acceptance of the repudiation"; and similarly in *Sudan Import Co v Société Générale de Compensation* [1957] 2 Lloyd's Rep. 528. Strictly, in view of *Roper v Johnson* (1873) L.R. 8 C.P. 167 this is not correct: the calculation is at the date fixed for acceptance, subject to a duty to mitigate from the date of the acceptance of the repudiation. In the particular two cases no argument was addressed on any difference in the market price between these two dates; the sole argument was between the seller's successful contention for the market price at the date of the acceptance of the repudiation and the buyer's unsuccessful contention for the market price at the date of the unaccepted repudiation.

[568] See *Roper v Johnson* (1873) L.R. 8 C.P. 167 and *Garnac Grain Co v Faure & Fairclough* [1968] A.C. 1130 at para.25-018, above, in relation to non-delivery.

[569] (1896) 12 T.L.R. 211 CA.

entitled to have the damages assessed by reference to this higher market price. Where in *Metelmann & Co v N.B.R. (London)*,[570] sellers of 2,000 tonnes of sugar which had not been specifically appropriated to the contract, after acceptance of their buyers' repudiation on a then rapidly falling market, had immediately sold 2,000 tonnes on the terminal market, the deduction to be made from the contract price in assessing their damages was held to be the price at which they had so sold rather than the somewhat higher price at which the market later stood on the date of due delivery under the contract[571] or the substantially higher price at which the buyers had contended the sellers should have sold on the physical market at a date between repudiation and due delivery when the volatile sugar market had temporarily and unexpectedly rallied. The sellers were found to have acted as any reasonable trader would have done in effecting an immediate sale on the terminal market, which could be achieved more speedily than a sale on the physical market, so as to stem the losses which would increase as the market continued, as was then anticipated, to fall.[572]

25-125 *(iii) Where the time fixed for acceptance is postponed at the request of one of the parties*[573] Where the time fixed for acceptance has been postponed at the buyer's request and he ultimately fails to accept in the extended period, the point in time at which breach takes place is deferred and the damages will be calculated at the market price on the last day to which the contract was extended if a date was fixed, or at the date when the claimant refused to grant further indulgence, or at a reasonable period after his last grant of indulgence. This appears from *Hickman v Haynes*.[574]

25-126 In the legally more complex situation[575] where the request to postpone acceptance comes from the seller, and the buyer at first concurs but subsequently refuses to accept on the basis of the seller's unpreparedness to deliver at the date originally fixed by the contract, the measure of damages[576] will presumably be calculated with reference to the market price at the time of the buyer's peremptory refusal to accept which will constitute the breach.[577] In *Hartley v Hymans*,[578] the measure was so calculated, the market having fallen.[579]

25-127 *(iv) Where no time is fixed for acceptance* So far only the first limb of s.50(3) has been involved as there has been a fixed time or times for acceptance. Where no time is fixed for acceptance, the second limb of s.50(3) specifically provides that

570 [1984] 1 Lloyd's Rep. 614 CA.

571 This was the market price which had been taken by the judge at first instance.

572 See Sir John Donaldson MR [1984] 1 Lloyd's Rep. 614 at 632, col.1, Browne-Wilkinson LJ, at 633, col.2–634, col.1. Matters of mitigation have been worked out by the courts in greater detail in the non-delivery cases which will apply mutatis mutandis here: see para.25-018, above.

573 This again has been worked out in more detail in the non-delivery cases: see paras 25-019 and 25-020, above.

574 (1875) L.R. 10 C.P. 598; applying the equivalent non-delivery case of *Ogle v Vane* (1868) L.R. 3 Q.B. 272.

575 See non-delivery at para.25-020, above.

576 Assuming the buyer can be said to be in default: see non-delivery at para.25-020, above.

577 Unless the breach is still anticipatory, in which case the principles discussed in para.25-124, above, will apply. See the comments on *Hartley v Hymans* (see next note) in *Tai Hing Cotton Mill v Kamsing Knitting Factory* [1979] A.C. 91 PC at 103F to G together with the decision there.

578 [1920] 3 K.B. 475.

579 McCardie J relied (at 496) on the equivalent non-delivery case of *Tyers v Rosedale and Ferryhill Co* (1875) L.R. 10 Ex. 195.

the time to be taken is that of the refusal to accept.[580] The question of exactly what contracts can be described as having no time fixed for acceptance within the meaning of the subsection has already been considered in the equivalent non-delivery cases,[581] and the reasons for regarding the question as largely academic apply equally here, especially since here too the measure prescribed by the end of s.50(3) cannot be brought into operation by an anticipatory breach, i.e. a repudiation before the arrival of the time for acceptance as opposed to a non-acceptance of a tendered delivery itself.[582]

## (2) Consequential losses

**(a) In general** Consequential losses are as infrequent in actions by the seller for non-acceptance as they are common in actions by the buyer for non-delivery, delayed delivery or breach of warranty. This is because a person is less likely to incur consequential loss where goods are not taken off his hands under a contract than where he does not receive goods as contracted. Illustrations are however to be found. **25-128**

Thus where the claimant incurred storage charges during the period before he succeeded in selling the goods to a third party, such charges were held recoverable in *Harlow and Jones v Panex (International)*.[583] So too sellers of tapioca, who had in *Bem Dis A Turk Ticaret v International Agri Trade Co, The Selda*,[584] chartered a vessel in which to ship the tapioca to the buyer, upon the buyer's non-acceptance recovered as damages the sums which they had to pay to the owners of the vessel for the cancellation of the charter, the arbitrators having found this to be a loss arising naturally from the buyer's breach. In *Vitol SA v Conoil Plc*,[585] where the seller sold large cargoes of gasoil under a number of contracts with delivery ex-ship and the buyer first delayed in taking them up and eventually did not take them up at all, a whole series of consequential losses was awarded. In addition to the normal measure of contract price less market price, the seller was awarded damages for losses caused by the delay, which were covered by a liquidated damages provision,[586] damages in respect of various demurrage payments, and damages for storage charges incurred for the gasoil until it could be resold. And an interesting, and uncommon, consequential loss appeared in *North Sea Energy Holdings v Petroleum Authority of Thailand*,[587] where the claim by the seller was the converse of the claim frequently met with, that of a buyer for loss of profit on a resale of goods not delivered.[588] A contract to supply 70 million barrels of Arabian crude oil to be delivered over a five-year period was wrongfully repudiated by the defendant buyers. The claimant sellers accepted the repudiation and claimed their anticipated profit which was huge, being the difference between the price at which they were **25-129**

---

[580] See para.25-115, above.

[581] See para.25-021, above.

[582] See the equivalent non-delivery cases of *Millett v Van Heek* [1921] 2 K.B. 369 CA and *Tai Hing Cotton Mill v Kamsing Knitting Factory* [1979] A.C. 91 PC.

[583] [1967] 2 Lloyd's Rep. 509; even though the claimant's own sellers had agreed with the claimants not to charge them for storage if they failed to recover in respect of storage charges from the defendants: see at 531.

[584] [1999] 1 Lloyd's Rep. 729 CA.

[585] [2009] 2 Lloyd's Rep. 466.

[586] Although called a penalty, it was construed as providing for liquidated damages.

[587] [1997] 2 Lloyd's Rep. 418.

[588] See paras 25-028 to 25-030, above.

selling to the defendants and the very much lower price at which they were to acquire the oil under their contractual arrangements with their own suppliers, from whom they had not yet acquired the oil. Apart from holding that in fact the claimants would have been unable to get the oil from their suppliers, in which case there would be no loss to them, Thomas J held, after citing *Victoria Laundry v Newman*,[589] and Lord Dunedin in *Hall v Pim*,[590] that, even if they could have got the oil, their damages could not be calculated by reference to the apparent contract with their suppliers because it was an extravagant and unusual bargain, one of which the defendants had no cognisance.[591] Nor was the learned judge prepared to apply the rule first appearing in *Cory v Thames Ironwork Co*,[592] and award the normal profit on such a contract. There were so many price possibilities in the world of oil sales that evidence of what that normal profit would be was required, and there was none; accordingly, it was concluded, the claimants were not entitled to substantial damages.[593] This the Court of Appeal interpreted as meaning nominal damages which, in affirming, it said the trial judge was right to award.[594] This endorsement of the trial judge's nominal award was arrived at on the basis of his first holding, namely that the claimants would have been unable to get the oil from their suppliers,[595] and all the other points dealt with by the trial judge stand, being set out without adverse comment and without being passed upon by the Court of Appeal.[596]

25-130 **(b) The impact of supply and demand** One important situation giving rise to a consequential loss is illustrated by the case of *Thompson v Robinson*.[597] The defendant refused to accept a Vanguard car which he had bought from the claimant car dealers at the retail selling price fixed by the manufacturers. The claimants returned the car to their suppliers, but nevertheless successfully claimed from the defendant their loss of profit on the repudiated sale since, as Vanguards were readily available for sale, they had sold one less Vanguard than they otherwise would have done. In awarding this loss of profit to the claimants, Upjohn J applied *Re Vic Mill*.[598] In that case the claimants had contracted to manufacture for and sell to the defendant certain machines, and the defendant became unable to accept the machines, in circumstances discharging the contract by breach, at a time when the claimants had manufactured some of the machines but not others. The claimants sold the machines already manufactured, after making small alterations to them, to a third party at a price similar to the contract price. Nevertheless they were held entitled to the profit they would have made on their sale to the defendant and were not confined to recovering the trivial cost of alteration, since it was fallacious to suppose that, in the words of Hamilton LJ,

---

589 [1949] 2 K.B. 528 CA; at para.25-046, above.

590 (1928) 33 Com. Cas. 324 HL at 330; at para.25-028, above.

591 [1997] 2 Lloyd's Rep. 418 at 437–438.

592 (1868) L.R. 3 Q.B. 181; at para.25-045, above.

593 [1997] 2 Lloyd's Rep. 418 at 439, col.2.

594 [1999] 1 Lloyd's Rep. 483 CA.

595 A conclusion reached by the Court of Appeal in a much more elaborate way; for this aspect of the case see para.10-093, above.

596 There were claims by the sellers in both *Toprak Mahsulleri Ofisi v Finagrain Compagnie Commerciale Agricole et Financière* [1979] 2 Lloyd's Rep. 98 CA and *Cerealmangimi SpA v Toepfer* [1981] 3 All E.R. 533 for losses in excess of the normal measure but these were held to be precluded because a clause, identical in both contracts, limited the sellers' claim to the normal measure, namely, contract price less market price.

597 [1955] Ch. 177.

598 [1913] 1 Ch. 465 CA.

"the second customer was a substituted customer, [and] that, had all gone well, the makers would not have had both customers, both orders, and both profits".[599]

Similarly, the profit that the claimants would have made on the sale to the defendant of the machines that had not been manufactured at the time of the breach was also held recoverable, because, as Buckley LJ said, the defendant

"failed to produce any evidence to show that if the works had been employed to execute the orders under the contract they (i.e. the plaintiffs) would have been unable to execute other orders which they had received".[600]

However, in contrast to *Thompson v Robinson*,[601] it was held in *Lazenby Garage v Wright*,[602] where the defendant refused to accept a second-hand car which he had bought from the claimant second-hand car dealers, that the dealers, having resold the car at a price higher than the contract price, were entitled to no damages as the defendant could not have contemplated that they would have sold one car less. Second-hand cars are unique, with each one different from the next, and

"there was no basis for any proper inference as to what effect on the plaintiffs' trade would have been felt if the car in question had been sold and delivered to the defendant, instead of to the buyer who in fact eventually bought it."[603]

On the other hand, if the state of the market or the state of the defendant's manufacturing facilities was such that demand exceeded supply, the position is different, any further contract is truly a substituted contract, and the claimant cannot recover his profit on the sale to the defendant. The converse of *Thompson v Robinson*[604] is provided by *Charter v Sullivan*,[605] in which only nominal damages were awarded for a defendant buyer's non-acceptance of a Hillman Minx, sold to him at a fixed retail price, where the claimant dealer could sell all the Hillman Minxes he could get: the converse of *Re Vic Mill*[606] is provided by *Hill v Showell*,[607] in which, the defendant having failed to accept steel cartridge clips which the claimant had contracted to manufacture and sell, evidence was held admissible to show that the claimant was thereby enabled to execute other profitable orders.[608] **25-131**

## 2. FAILURE TO PROCURE THE OPENING OF A LETTER OF CREDIT

Breach by non-acceptance is by far the most common ground of an action for damages against the buyer of goods. Of other possible breaches which could give **25-132**

---

599 [1913] 1 Ch. 465 CA at 473; similarly at 474, per Buckley LJ.

600 [1913] 1 Ch. 465 CA at 474; see, too, at 472, per Hamilton LJ, where the onus of proof is clearly placed on the defendant. *Re Vic Mill* was applied in *Sony Computer Entertainment Ltd v Cinram Logistics UK Ltd* [2008] EWCA Civ 955 CA to allow, similarly, recovery of the profit lost on a sale by a seller not of unaccepted goods but of stolen goods, stolen when in the charge of the defendant distributor and carrier: see the case at para.32-020, below. Here too the onus of proof was held to be on the defendant, the analysis being that the case was one of mitigation; see at para.9-045, above.

601 [1955] Ch. 177.

602 [1976] 1 W.L.R. 459 CA.

603 [1976] 1 W.L.R. 459 CA at 463, per Bridge LJ.

604 [1955] Ch. 177.

605 [1957] 2 Q.B. 117 CA.

606 [1913] 1 Ch. 465 CA.

607 (1918) 87 L.J.K.B. 1106 HL.

608 The trial judge had ruled such evidence inadmissible and the House of Lords upheld the Court of Appeal's consequent grant of a new trial on the issue of damages.

rise to problems of damages that of failure to procure the opening of a letter of credit is singled out for treatment[609] because it has practical commercial importance and because it has produced a decision, *Trans Trust S.P.R.L. v Danubian Trading Co*,[610] which deserves study both inside and outside the framework of the sale of goods.[611]

**25-133** In this case the defendants contracted to buy steel from the claimants who were to buy it from a third party who had an option to buy from the manufacturers. Neither the claimants, the defendants nor the third party were in a position to provide the money necessary to obtain delivery of the steel. It was a term of the contract between the claimants and the defendants that payment by the defendants should be by cash against shipping documents from a confirmed credit to be opened in favour of the third party by a fourth party to whom the defendants had in turn contracted to sell the steel. The defendants failed to procure the opening of the credit and then repudiated the contract at a time when the market price was higher than the contract price. In these circumstances the normal measure of damages for non-acceptance would have been nominal, and therefore the claimants sued instead for breach of the defendant's covenant to procure the opening of the letter of credit, claiming (1) the profit they would have made had the transaction been carried through; and (2) an indemnity against damages which they might subsequently have to pay the third party, their seller. The first claim succeeded on the ground that the parties must have contemplated that the loss upon breach would be the claimants' profit because both knew that the claimants had not the necessary money with which to buy the steel.[612] Thus, as Denning LJ said,

> "even if the market price … has risen, he will not be able to take advantage of the rise because he will not have any goods to resell."[613]

Nor was the claimants' impecuniosity a vital factor, for, in the words of Somervell LJ,

> "even if the plaintiffs had been very rich it might still have been contemplated that if the defendants did not procure the opening of the credit the plaintiffs could not and would not themselves have used their resources for the opening of a credit for this steel".[614]

The second claim, however, failed on the ground of remoteness, because the defendants did not know that the third party depended on the credit in order to get the goods and it therefore could not have been in the parties' contemplation that the third party might have a claim against the claimants similar to the claimants' successful first claim against the defendants.[615]

---

609 See, also, *British Motor Trade Association v Gilbert* [1951] 2 All E.R. 641 and *Mouat v Betts Motors* [1959] A.C. 71 PC, which were an amalgamation of a breach of covenant not to resell the goods and a breach of an option given to the seller to repurchase. Regarded from the latter angle, they become cases of breach by a seller and are treated accordingly: see para.25-012, above.

610 [1952] 2 Q.B. 297 CA.

611 For the importance of this decision outside sale of goods itself, see paras 8-207 and 24-015, above and paras 30-003 and 30-006, below.

612 Followed on this point in *Ian Stach v Baker Bosley* [1958] 2 Q.B. 130; see especially at 145.

613 [1952] 2 Q.B. 297 CA at 305.

614 [1952] 2 Q.B. 297 CA at 302. The Court of Appeal regarded the failure to procure a letter of credit as something more than a mere failure to pay money, so that it was not necessary for them to come to any conclusion on the validity of the old rule, which has since been departed from, that damages for non-payment of money are only nominal: see paras 30-002 and following.

615 Apart from the question of remoteness, the Court of Appeal was not prepared to give a declaration

## 3. OTHER BREACHES

Other types of breach may occasionally occur: *Addax Ltd v Arcadia Petroleum Ltd*,[616] provides an illustration. While there was delayed delivery of the barrels of crude oil which were the subject of the sale, this was exceptionally the fault not of the seller but of the buyer who had been late in providing the vessel upon which the oil was to be loaded. The seller had attempted to cover its position by buying in from its own suppliers, and the issue of damages, which was somewhat complicated, concerned losses of the seller in respect of the hedging contracts caused by the delay. It was held that these losses were recoverable. **25-134**

of indemnity in respect of a then unassessed liability. This is dealt with at para.10-032, above.

616 [2000] 1 Lloyd's Rep. 493.

CHAPTER 26

# HIRE AND HIRE-PURCHASE OF GOODS

TABLE OF CONTENTS



## I. BREACH BY LENDER

### 1. NON-DELIVERY

**26-001** There appear to be no cases which concern themselves with the measure of damages where there is non-delivery of goods to the hirer under a hiring or a hire-purchase agreement, and it is necessary, therefore, to look to lease of land cases as presenting the nearest analogy to hire of goods[1] and to sale of goods cases as presenting the nearest analogy to hire-purchase of goods.[2] It is submitted that the normal measure of damages for non-delivery of hired goods is the price at which equivalent goods can be hired in the market for the contractual period of hire less the contract rate of hire; and for non-delivery of hire-purchased goods the price at which equivalent goods can be bought in the market less the total amount that must be paid by the hire-purchaser under the contract before he can become the purchaser. In both cases the appropriate market price should be taken at the time of breach by non-delivery.

**26-002** Any consequential losses beyond this should also follow the pattern of lease of land and sale of goods.

### 2. BREACH OF WARRANTY

#### (1) Hire

**26-003** There is also an absence of authority on the measure of damages for breach of

---

1 See paras 28-004 to 28-006, below.

2 See paras 25-002 and following, above.

warranty where goods have been hired. In principle, the normal measure should be the amount of hire the goods as warranted could command in the market less the amount of hire they can command as they are. In practice, this is likely to work out at the rentals which the claimant has paid under the contract less the value of such use as he has had of the goods; this would probably be so where, for instance, he has hired an unroadworthy car. The cost of repairing the goods will not be an appropriate measure. As Donovan LJ said in *Charterhouse Credit Co v Tolly*,[3] itself a case of hire-purchase:

> "If I hire a car which turns out to be useless for the purpose by reason of defects, it is not for me to repair the car; and to treat the estimated cost of repairs as the measure of my damage does not really meet the requirements of the case."[4]

With consequential losses, as indeed with the normal measure, the analogy of the hire-purchase cases can be of some value.[5] Thus the hirer of a defective car should be able, in appropriate circumstances, to claim for physical injury incurred as a result of the defects.[6] The hirer was held entitled in *U.C.B. Leasing v Holtom, Bell and Colvill*,[7] to the cost, over different periods, of public transport and of a substitute car and also to a small amount for inconvenience and distress, but the latter award would not stand today in the light of the later restrictions on damages for non-pecuniary loss in contract.[8] Where in *Lobster Group Ltd v Heidelberg Graphic Equipment Ltd*,[9] a printing press which proved defective was hired, a claim for loss of profits was held to be available to the hirer.[10] **26-004**

## (2) Hire-purchase

The normal measure of damages for breach of warranty in the case of hire-purchased goods cannot be simply stated because it varies according to whether, upon discovery of the breach, the hirer continues with the contract so that he still contemplates the eventual purchase of the goods or whether the contract is terminated so that the goods are returned to the owner. Moreover, there is the additional complication to be contended with that the hirer's action will frequently not be for breach of the hire-purchase contract, into which he will have entered with a finance company, but for breach of the collateral warranty made between him and the dealer who has supplied the goods. The measure of damages will, however, follow the same lines, whether the claim be against the finance company or dealer. **26-005**

The simplest situation is where the hiring has run its course and the hirer has exercised his option to purchase before the breach of warranty is revealed and action is brought. In such circumstances the normal measure of damages, as was held in *Brown v Sheen and Richmond Car Sales*,[11] is the market value of the goods as **26-006**

---

3 [1963] 2 Q.B. 683 CA.
4 [1963] 2 Q.B. 683 CA at 705.
5 See para.26-013, below.
6 See *Andrews v Hopkinson* [1957] 1 Q.B. 229.
7 [1987] R.T.R. 362 CA.
8 See paras 5-027 and following, above.
9 [2009] EWHC 1919 (TCC).
10 It, however, failed both on causation and on proof (at [2009] EWHC 1919 (TCC) at [199] and following) and the hirer had to be content with the recovery of certain rectification costs (at [2009] EWHC 1919 (TCC) at [234] and following).
11 [1950] 1 All E.R. 1102 (claim against dealer). See *Andrews v Hopkinson* [1957] 1 Q.B. 229 at 235

warranted less their market value as they are; since the claimant has by now purchased the goods, it becomes appropriate to award the same normal measure as is attracted by a breach of warranty in a sale of goods.[12] And even where the breach of warranty is revealed and action is brought before the hiring has run its course, this same measure can be appropriate where it is anticipated that the hirer will still purchase the goods or where, as in *Jackson v Chrysler Acceptances*,[13] he is required to purchase them by virtue of his being held to have affirmed the contract. Alternatively, in such circumstances, the cost of repairs may be awarded. This was done in relation to a car in *Yeoman Credit Co v Apps*,[14] and although in *Charterhouse Credit Co v Tolly*,[15] doubts were thrown upon the correctness of this decision, the doubts were based solely upon the fact that the hirer had not gone on to purchase the car but had returned it to the owners.[16] Upjohn LJ pointed out that in *Yeoman Credit Co v Apps*,[17] the Court of Appeal had not really considered the impact of the hirer's subsequent, and proper, rejection of the car upon the assessment of damages, but had merely upheld the assessment below which had been

> "on the hypothetical basis that the agreement would continue in force and the hirer would complete the purchase".[18] With the mode of assessment on that footing he respectfully agreed.[19]

**26-007** The difference between the market value of the goods as warranted and as they are, or the cost of repairing the goods, becomes an inappropriate measure where in the course of the hiring the hirer becomes entitled, by virtue of the seriousness of the owner's breach, to return the goods and in fact does so. In such circumstances, as is made clear by Donovan LJ in *Charterhouse Credit Co v Tolly*,[20] which concerned the acquisition of an unroadworthy second-hand car at a hire-purchase price of somewhat below £500, the normal measure becomes the amount of the moneys paid by the hire-purchaser to the finance company under the agreement as this will put him into the position he would have been in had the contract been performed by giving him the cost of hiring similar goods on similar terms as to the eventual option to purchase for the usual nominal sum. This measure follows the accepted contractual approach by giving the hire-purchaser the benefit of his bargain and is not to be regarded as aiming to put him into his pre-contract position by returning to him his abortive payments.[21] The position in *Charterhouse*, however, was complicated by the fact that, while the car provided under the hire-purchase agreement had such serious defects as to put the owner finance company in fundamental breach of contract, the hire-purchaser treated the contract as still subsisting, effected some minor repairs, and then himself fell into breach by fail-

---

to 236.

12 See paras 25-061 and following, above.

13 [1978] R.T.R. 474 CA.

14 [1962] 2 Q.B. 508 CA.

15 [1963] 2 Q.B. 683 CA.

16 Lord Wilberforce's guarded reference to the case in *Doobay v Mohabeer* [1967] 2 A.C. 278 PC at 288 should probably be taken to be attributable to the same doubts.

17 [1962] 2 Q.B. 508 CA.

18 [1963] 2 Q.B. 683 CA at 712.

19 [1963] 2 Q.B. 683 CA at 712; adding only that damages from loss of use during repair, a consequential loss, could also be recovered.

20 [1963] 2 Q.B. 683 CA.

21 See on all this Donovan LJ [1963] 2 Q.B. 683 CA at 705 to 706.

ing to pay instalments, so that in the event it was the finance company which terminated the contract and repossessed the car. In these circumstances Upjohn LJ put forward the view that the hire-purchaser could not complain about the loss of his option to purchase for a nominal sum as this resulted from his own breach,[22] by which he presumably meant that he was no longer entitled to claim to be put into a position to be able to make a similar hire-purchase contract by being awarded the instalments paid which of course well exceed a normal hiring charge by having built into their amount the element of the effectively free option to purchase at the end of the contractual term. Yet Upjohn LJ agreed with Donovan LJ that the hire-purchaser could recover by way of damages the moneys he had paid under the contract, making the rather odd comment that the finance company could not complain if the court took a somewhat severe view of its failure to implement its promise and made the punishment fit the crime.[23] The hire-purchaser recovered as damages not only the deposit he had paid but also the damages payable to the finance company on its counterclaim, consisting of the instalments in arrears at the time of termination, together with the cost of the minor repairs, all subject to a small deduction for the use that the hire-purchaser had had of the goods, being of £5.[24] The *Charterhouse* decision was applied by the Judicial Committee of the Privy Council in *Doobay v Mohabeer*,[25] which concerned an unusual hire-purchase agreement of a rice mill in disrepair that the owner undertook, and failed, to repair. Again the cost of repair was rejected as being an incorrect measure of damages and again the damages awarded to the hire-purchaser were based on the moneys paid by him and included such damages as he was liable to pay to the owner for his own failure to pay the hire-purchase instalments. The scenario alternative to that in *Charterhouse* and *Doobay* is of the hire-purchaser's claim being not against the finance company for breach of the hire-purchase contract but against the dealer for breach of the collateral warranty; here it is likely that the damages recoverable by the hire-purchaser will take into account damages for which he himself will have been liable to the finance company. This is illustrated by *Yeoman Credit Co v Odgers*,[26] where the defendant had entered into an agreement with the claimant finance company for the hire-purchase of a car in reliance on the warranty of the car dealers, who were brought into the suit as third parties. The car was unroadworthy from the start and, after payment of four monthly instalments of the hire-purchase price, the claimant finance company at the defendant hire-purchaser's request terminated the agreement, retook and sold the car and sued under the agreement for arrears of instalments and for damages for various losses to be calculated at the amount necessary to make the aggregate of the defendant's payments equal to half of the hire-purchase price. The claimant finance company having got judgment against the defendant hire-purchaser for its whole claim, the court allowed recovery as between the defendant hire-purchaser and the third party dealers of the whole loss suffered by the defendant, including his liability under the hire-purchase contract.[27]

After very many years devoid of cases of hire-purchasers claiming damages for **26-008**

---

22 [1963] 2 Q.B. 683 CA at 710.
23 [1963] 2 Q.B. 683 CA at 711.
24 Even considered on the high side by Upjohn LJ: [1963] 2 Q.B. 683 CA at 710.
25 [1967] 2 A.C. 278 PC.
26 [1962] 1 W.L.R. 215 CA.
27 Whether in view of the decisions considered at paras 16-075 to 16-079, above, the court below had been right in awarding the finance company all the damages claimed by it was not in issue.

breach of warranty arising out of the faulty condition of the item the subject-matter of the hire-purchase agreement, one such case has appeared on the scene, bringing many complications in its train as it moved from first instance to Court of Appeal. *Brewer v Mann*,[28] had as the claimant a lady who bought on hire-purchase at a price of £425,000 a vintage Bentley motor car dating from 1930 for the use of her husband and herself. After the two of them had made use of the car for some 14 months she became aware that the car might not be as vintage as she had been led to believe and brought actions for damages against both the finance company and the dealer, having ceased to pay further due instalments which had resulted in the finance company terminating the contract, repossessing the car and counter-claiming for moneys due to it under the contract provisions. His Honour Judge Thornton decided completely in the claimant's favour and awarded her damages which, while being worked out in a somewhat complicated and unclear fashion,[29] were based on recovery of the initial deposit and the instalments already paid, together amounting to £94,555, which the judge said were being claimed by the claimant as reliance damages.[30] No deduction was to be made for the benefit to the claimant for her use of the car and the finance company's counterclaim was dismissed in fairly summary fashion.

**26-009** The Court of Appeal would have none of this. On the defendants' appeal the errors were carefully brought to light in the necessarily long judgment of the court delivered by Rix LJ. The finance company not being in breach of contract, the court said that there was no answer to its counterclaim, which was allowed. This left the claim for damages against the dealer. The court did not adjudicate on the proper measure against the dealer because, finding the judge to have shown bias against the defendants and favour for the claimant, leading to unfairness and revealing a total lack of objectivity, a retrial was ordered in which the damages would have to be re-assessed. What the Court of Appeal did was to give detailed indications of how the damages were likely to go, following on from its analysis of the relevant cases of the 1960s, the heyday of damages claims arising out of hire-purchase contracts, in particular *Charterhouse Credit Co v Tolly*,[31] but also *Yeoman Credit Co v Odgers*,[32] and *Yeoman Credit Co v Apps*,[33] all of which cases are dealt with in the preceding paragraphs and all of which cases also concerned cars though far less prestigious ones.[34] The court first pointed out that the tortious measure of damages, which the reliance damages that the judge had purported to give effectively are, were inappropriate in this contractual setting.[35] The court then went so far as to suggest that the claimant might have suffered no loss at all. This was on the basis that, whereas in the three 1960s cases considered by the court the car had been unroadworthy and a nuisance from the start, here the Bentley was in good condition and the claimant and her husband had had long enjoyable motoring with it, and on the further basis that the court considered correct Upjohn LJ's suggestion in

---

28 [2012] EWCA Civ 246 CA, on appeal from [2010] EWHC 2444 (QB).

29 [2010] EWHC 2444 at [217] and following.

30 [2010] EWHC 2444 at [218].

31 [1963] 2 Q.B. 683 CA.

32 [1962] 1 W.L.R. 215 CA.

33 [1962] 2 Q.B. 508 CA.

34 Damages are considered by the court at [309] to [328].

35 For the concept and the proper use of reliance damages, which are in effect constituted by a claimant's wasted expenditure, see the full discussion at paras 4-025 above.

*Charterhouse*, the consequence of which has been explained,[36] that the hire-purchaser could not rely for his damages on having the option to purchase at a nominal sum when it had been lost to him by virtue of his own breach.[37] On one matter the Court of Appeal was adamant. From whatever sum the claimant might be awarded on the retrial there must be deducted, again disagreeing with the judge below, an amount for the benefit to the claimant of her use of the car, calculated by the court at £45,000.[38]

There is one aspect of the Court of Appeal's judgment with which one might cavil. This is its endorsement of Upjohn LJ's suggestion that in effect a hire-purchaser should be denied the normal measure of damages where by himself being in breach he has lost the option to purchase for a nominal sum. In these hire-purchases of cars the breaches by the finance company and dealer as to the condition of the car have inevitably preceded any breach by the hire-purchaser in discontinuing instalment payments and the breaches by finance company and dealer remain present for him to sue upon. Indeed when held liable under the contract provisions to the finance company it has been held that he may recover for this liability from the dealer under the collateral warranty, as we have seen happened in *Yeoman Credit Co v Odgers*.[39] Also in these cases it is likely to be the breach by the faulty condition of the car which has led to the hire-purchaser's decision to pay no more. In this connection it is worth noting what the Court of Appeal in *Brewer v Mann* said about *Odgers*. According to the court the finance company in *Odgers* bamboozled—the Court of Appeal's own word—the hire-purchaser into following the suggestion of the finance company that it should terminate the contract, thereby giving it rights to damages as on a hire-purchaser's repudiation, rather than terminating it himself on the finance company's repudiation.[40] Although this would seem to be a misinterpretation of what had happened in *Odgers* as it is clear from the case report that it was the hire-purchaser's suggestion that the finance company should terminate the agreement.[41] There is therefore no indication of bamboozling. Nonetheless it would seem odd if the hire-purchaser in this way should lose his claim for the normal measure of damages. **26-010**

In any event where there is no question of breach by the hire-purchaser himself his damages will fall to be measured by the amount of the instalments he has already paid under the hire-purchase agreement, as was allowed at first instance and not challenged in the Court of Appeal in *Farnworth Finance Facilities v Attryde*,[42] where the court was not directly concerned with the damages awarded except to the extent that the dealer in *Farnworth* argued that credit ought to be given for the use of the motor cycle hire-purchased. Here the court declined to make a deduction for use on the ground that the value of such use of the motor cycle which the hire-purchaser had had was offset by the great amount of trouble which the motor cycle had given him.[43] Indeed it is for consideration whether it is necessarily and in all cases appropriate to make a deduction for use, particularly when it would be in a **26-011**

---

36 See at para.26-007, above.
37 See [2012] EWCA Civ 246 CA at [323].
38 [2012] EWCA Civ 246 CA at [325] and [326].
39 [1962] 1 W.L.R. 215 CA.
40 [2012] EWCA Civ 246 CA at [313] and [314].
41 See Odgers at para.26-007, above.
42 [1970] 1 W.L.R. 1053 CA.
43 [1970] 1 W.L.R. 1053 CA at 1059 to 1060, per Lord Denning MR.

substantial amount, as this fails to give to the hire-purchaser the wherewithal to enter into an equivalent hire-purchase contract.

**26-012** Thus on any retrial of the *Brewer v Mann* case there was bound to be great difficulty in finding the correct damages solution. In a hearing[44] listed before Master Fontaine to give directions for the retrial, she was able to deal only with the question of how far the claimant was to be permitted to rely on her amended particulars of claim for the retrial and, applying the test of reasonable prospect of success used on applications for amendment of a pleaded case, Master Fontaine concluded on the question of damages that the draft amended claim had no prospect of success on a retrial and ordered that the claim be struck out. So there will now be no retrial. We therefore must await a further case of this nature. On past experience this could take up to 50 years.

**26-013** In addition to the normal measure of damages, various items of consequential loss have been held recoverable in the cases. It is clear that, where the damages are based on the cost of repair, because the hire-purchaser continues with the contract despite the owner's breach and retains the goods, he is further entitled to claim damages for loss of the use of the goods during repair.[45] And, indeed, even where the normal measure is arrived at on the basis of the goods being returned to the owner, there may still be recovery for the cost of repairs incurred by the hire-purchaser which have now been rendered futile for him,[46] or indeed for any other abortive expenses, such as the cost of installation of the goods on the hire-purchaser's premises.[47] Consequential losses of a different order appeared in *Andrews v Hopkinson*,[48] and in *Jackson v Chrysler Acceptances*,[49] where, respectively, the hire-purchaser recovered, beyond the normal measure, for injuries incurred by him in an accident caused because the car he was driving, which was the subject of the hire-purchase contract, was defective, and in respect of a spoilt holiday caused by the breakdown of the car hire-purchased from the defendants. And in *Yeoman Credit Co v Odgers*,[50] where the finance company sued the hire-purchaser who in turn brought in the dealer as third party, the damages awarded to the hire-purchaser against the dealer included the cost of all the proceedings. The contention that

> "the judgment should not have ordered the third party to pay the defendant's costs of defending, since … the defence was hopeless and unnecessary"[51]

failed because,

> "although his defence was inept in the extreme, it was fostered and encouraged by the third party, who was there".[52]

---

44 *Brewer v Mann* unreported 11 April 2013.

45 *Charterhouse Credit Co v Tolly* [1963] 2 Q.B. 683 CA at 712, per Upjohn LJ; *Smith v Spurling Motor Bodies* (1961) 105 S.J. 967 CA.

46 As in *Charterhouse Credit Co v Tolly* [1963] 2 Q.B. 683 CA.

47 As in *Doobay v Mohabeer* [1967] 2 A.C. 278 PC.

48 [1957] 1 Q.B. 229 (claim against dealer); see at 235 and 236.

49 [1978] R.T.R. 474 CA.

50 [1962] 1 W.L.R. 215 CA.

51 [1962] 1 W.L.R. 215 CA at 222.

52 [1962] 1 W.L.R. 215 CA at 255. On the other hand, in *Smith v Spurling Motor Bodies* (1961) 105 S.J. 967 CA it was held that the hire-purchaser could not claim an indemnity for the costs of his defence as no defence could have been a reasonable one.

## II. Breach by Hirer

### 1. Non-acceptance and Related Breaches

#### (1) Hire

The normal measure of damages for non-acceptance in the case of hired goods is, it is submitted, the contract rate of hire less the market rate at which the lender can make a substitute contract for the contractual period of hire. And where the goods are in fact delivered but are subsequently repossessed by the owner on the hirer's default, the normal measure is again the contract rate of hire less the market rate at which a substitute contract can be made, but limited to the unexpired part of the contractual period of hire. If the market rate is no lower than the contract rate, then the normal measure will produce an award of nominal damages only.[53] Where the lender elected to terminate the agreement by reason of the hirer's failure to pay the hire instalments, the lender was held in *U.C.B. Leasing v Holtrom, Bell and Colvill*,[54] entitled to the instalments due only up to the time of termination as damages, thereby following the cases in the equivalent situation in hire-purchase.[55] Where in *Bulkhaul Ltd v Rhodia Organique Fine Ltd*,[56] in a contract of lease and hire for the 10-year working life of bespoke tanks for carrying chemicals the lessee-hirer returned the tanks about halfway through the contract as not requiring them any longer, the measure of damages was accepted as being not the contract rate less the market rate of hire but rather the contract rate of hire over the contract period less the price at which the tanks could be sold. The issue before the Court of Appeal was whether the lessor-lender had failed to mitigate in not selling and whether the price at which a third party had offered to purchase the tanks, an offer made before the breach of contract, could be taken as evidence of selling value. As in the case of breach by non-delivery of hired goods, the analogy of lease of land can prove useful[57]; so too can the analogy of sale of goods.[58] **26-014**

The lender will also be entitled, by way of damages for consequential loss, to the contractual rate of hire during the period, if any, which elapses between the breach and the time he succeeds, or ought to have succeeded by virtue of reasonable mitigating steps, in hiring out the goods to a new hirer; this is so whether the hirer's breach has been by an initial failure to accept the goods or by a later default leading to their repossession by the lender.[59] The requirement of mitigation will generally stand in the way of any claim by the lender based upon the total hire charges or the total outstanding hire charges, as the case may be,[60] but this need not be so **26-015**

---

53 In *National Cash Register v Stanley* [1921] 3 K.B. 292 it was held that only an action for damages lay for non-acceptance and the claimant could not elect to sue in debt for the whole hire. *Wright v Melville* (1828) 3 C. & P. 542, which had held that, once the goods were accepted, the hirer was liable for the whole hire, was distinguished, but it would seem that this decision must now be read in the light of more modern decisions such as *Bentworth Finance v Jennings* (1961) 111 L.J. 488; see this case at para.26-015 (first two footnotes), below.

54 [1987] R.T.R. 362 CA.

55 See para.26-019, below.

56 [2008] EWCA Civ 1452 CA.

57 See para.28-039, below.

58 See paras 25-115 and following, above.

59 See, e.g. *Bentworth Finance v Jennings* (1961) 111 L.J. 488 (three months' rental on hired car).

60 In refusing the claimants' claim for the total outstanding hire less the price at which they had sold the car upon repossessing it, the court in *Bentworth Finance v Jennings* (1961) 111 L.J. 488 pointed

where the claimant's supply of goods of the type hired out exceeds the demand for them. That there may be a consequential loss in these circumstances was first revealed by *Interoffice Telephones v Freeman*.[61] In 1950 the claimants agreed to install, let and maintain, and the defendants agreed to hire, an office telephone installation for 12 years. In 1956 the defendants repudiated the contract and the claimant sued for damages. On the authority of *British Automatic Stamp Machine Co v Haynes*,[62] it was contended that, even though the claimants' supply exceeded demand, their damages should be limited to the hire from breach until such time as they could reasonably have relet the goods. The contention was rejected and the earlier case disapproved, on the ground that the claimants, having installations readily available for hire, had by the breach let one installation less than they would otherwise have done. Therefore they were entitled to their loss of profit on the transaction.[63] This was calculated on the following lines. The basis was the amount of future rentals which the defendants were due to pay under the terms of the contract, and from this was deducted (1) the amount which the claimants would have incurred in performance of the contract, here represented by future maintenance charges, (2) an amount representing the benefit to the claimants in receiving now the rentals due only in the future, and (3) an amount representing the benefit to the claimants in receiving back their property now instead of in 1962, which amount was measured by the depreciated value of the goods minus the costs of the reconditioning.[64]

**26-016** *Interoffice Telephones v Freeman*[65] was further considered by the Court of Appeal in *Robophone Facilities v Blank*,[66] where the claimants had hired out for a period of seven years a telephone-recording system machine to the defendant who had failed to take delivery of it. Harman and Diplock LJJ were on the whole content to accept the correctness of the assessment of damages adopted in the earlier case,[67] but were not required to decide the point as they considered that the contracting parties had stipulated for the payment of a sum which could properly be regarded as liquidated damages.[68] Lord Denning MR, on the other hand, dissenting because he held the stipulated sum to be a penalty, had to come to a view on the measure of damages and would have limited recovery to the loss incurred in the few weeks which it would have taken the claimants to relet the machine, not only because he regarded as lacking any evidence that the claimants' supply exceeded the demand but also because he thought that, applying the rule in *Hadley v Baxendale*,[69] the defendant need only contemplate that his suppliers' stock would be such as to meet

---

out that "if they had taken the steps to mitigate their damages which they should have taken they would have hired out the car to a new hirer": at 488.

61 [1958] 1 Q.B. 190 CA.

62 [1921] 1 K.B. 377.

63 Thus applying the sale of goods cases of *Re Vic Mill* [1913] 1 Ch. 465 CA and *Thompson v Robinson* [1955] Ch. 177; see para.25-130, above. *Re Vic Mill* had already, in the previous year, been followed in preference to *British Automatic Stamp Machine Co v Haynes* [1921] 1 K.B. 377 by Barry J in *Telephone Rentals v R.C.A. Photophone* unreported 1957.

64 See [1958] 1 Q.B. 190 CA at 195 to 196, per Jenkins LJ.

65 [1958] 1 Q.B. 190 CA.

66 [1966] 1 W.L.R. 1428 CA.

67 Harman LJ more than Diplock LJ who in the end reserved his opinion: [1966] 1 W.L.R. 1428 CA at 1439 to 1440 and 1449.

68 For this aspect of the decision see para.16-096, above.

69 (1854) 9 Ex. 341.

current demand.[70] He accordingly doubted Parker LJ's statement in *Interoffice Telephones v Freeman*,[71] that

> "the defaulting party must contemplate that damages will vary according to the state of the market, including questions of supply and demand".[72]

It should, however, be remembered that any questioning of this proposition must contend not only with the decision in *Interoffice Telephones v Freeman*,[73] but also with the corresponding authorities on sale of goods[74]; and certainly, in so far as Lord Denning MR may have been influenced by his concern, evinced throughout the cases, for the protection of hirers and hire-purchasers, the proposition he has espoused should not be accepted as a general principle.

### (2) Hire-purchase

Considering the proper measure of damages for breaches by the hire-purchaser is complicated by the presence in what has been the typical hire-purchase agreement of a provision requiring the hire-purchaser to make what is referred to as a "minimum payment" in the event of, among other things, breach, thereby bringing into play the law as to penalties and liquidated damages together with, in practically all the cases, the restrictions imposed by the Consumer Credit Act 1974. This aspect of the law has already been fully dealt with[75] and the inter-connection between it and our present concern is emphasised, indeed explained, by the fact that the question of the proper measure of unliquidated damages comes up not because there is no "minimum payment" clause in the particular agreement but because the "minimum payment" clause which the agreement contains is held to be a penalty, or to fall foul of the dictates of the Consumer Credit Act 1974, so that the court must then have regard to what unliquidated damages to award. Hence the cases earlier considered which, as we have seen, all but entirely fall within the narrow compass of a five-year period in the early 1960s,[76] are the cases which reappear here. There are no others. 26-017

The cases do not indeed deal with breach by initial non-acceptance of the goods by the hire-purchaser but with the analogous situation where subsequently he is in breach by defaulting upon his instalment payments. It might be thought that the normal measure of damages would be the full hire-purchase price, namely the total of the amounts payable by the hire-purchaser under the agreement, less the price at which the owner can make a similar hire-purchase contract upon similar terms, always of course giving credit for the instalments already paid. The courts, however, started off by being more generous in their assessments, deducting from the full hire-purchase price only the amount at which the goods had sold in the market, a measure which suggests that what is being given is the loss of the profit on the transaction.[77] The first case was *Yeoman Credit Co v Waragowski*,[78] where the 26-018

70 [1966] 1 W.L.R. 1428 CA at 1437.
71 [1958] 1 Q.B. 190 CA.
72 [1958] 1 Q.B. 190 CA at 202.
73 [1958] 1 Q.B. 190 CA.
74 See para.25-130, above; See also para.8-203, above.
75 See paras 16-066 and following, above.
76 See paras 16-075 to 16-079, above.
77 See the hire cases dealt with at paras 26-014 to 26-016, above.

claimant, having retaken and sold the van hire-purchased because of non-payment of rentals, sued for rentals due and damages; the Court of Appeal assessed the damages at the unpaid balance of the hire-purchase price less the amount realised by the van's sale. This was taken a stage further in *Yeoman Credit Co v McLean*,[79] where it was held that a discount must be allowed in respect of the earlier return to the claimants of their capital outlay, a point not argued in the earlier case. Master Jacob said:

> "The accelerated receipt of the proceeds of sale represents moneys in the hands of the plaintiffs which they would, in the ordinary course of their business as a finance company, put to use again to earn a further profit or interest ... If, therefore, in assessing the damages suffered by the plaintiffs, no reduction is to be made in the amount of their hire charges, the plaintiffs would, in effect, be receiving two amounts of profit or interest at the same time on the same sum of money."[80]

Soon afterwards *Yeoman Credit Co v Waragowski*,[81] was followed in *Overstone v Shipway*,[82] adopting the qualification introduced in *Yeoman Credit Co v McLean*.[83]

**26-019** Then in the following year the damages assessments suddenly became more restrictive, and the earlier cases were interpreted as dealing only with the situation where the hirer's failure to pay instalments has amounted to a repudiation of the contract by him. In *Financings v Baldock*,[84] the Court of Appeal held that there was no repudiation by the hirer since, although in default in the payment of two instalments of hire, he had not indicated any unwillingness or inability to pay either these or any future instalments when the claimants retook the vehicle. Accordingly, the retaking by the claimants was not by virtue of their acceptance of a repudiation of the contract but merely by virtue of the express stipulation in the contract giving them a right to terminate on non-payment of instalments. The claimants could therefore recover damages only for breaches up to the date of the termination and not thereafter, and their damages were held to be limited to the two instalments in arrears with interest. This decision was followed twice within a few months, first in *Brady v St Margaret's Trust*,[85] and then in *Charterhouse Credit Co v Tolly*[86]; subsequently, the decision was applied in *United Dominions Trust (Commercial)*

---

78 [1961] 1 W.L.R. 1124 CA.

79 [1962] 1 W.L.R. 131.

80 [1962] 1 W.L.R. 131 at 135. He went on to consider how the calculation of the discount should be achieved, and said "One approach, and it is by no means the only one, is to calculate the hire-charges on the amount received from the proceeds of sale from the date of its receipt until the expiry of the agreement at the percentage charged in the agreement ... But ... the function of the court is not to act as a mathematician": at 135.

81 [1961] 1 W.L.R. 1124 CA.

82 [1962] 1 W.L.R. 117 CA.

83 [1962] 1 W.L.R. 131. In *Lombank v Beal* [1962] C.L.Y. 1395 no discount was made because any advantage to the claimants from accelerated receipt was more than offset by the extent to which the defendant was in arrears in paying instalments.

84 [1963] 2 Q.B. 104 CA.

85 [1963] 2 Q.B. 494 CA. The award included, in addition to the arrears of the instalments, damages for breach of the contract to keep the vehicle in good repair, the court being careful to point out that in assessing such damages neither the initial price of the vehicle in a hire-purchase transaction nor the price obtained for it after it has been retaken by the owners was a guide.

86 [1963] 2 Q.B. 683 CA. See para.26-007, above where this case is dealt with because the owner was also in breach, indeed in fundamental breach, by having provided a defective car; the hirer had treated the contract as subsisting and had then himself fallen into breach by failure to pay instalments.

*Ltd v Ennis*,[87] so as to hold for the defendant hire-purchaser where the claimant finance company had failed to sue for the non-payment of one instalment which marked their sole right to damages.

In the earlier cases of *Yeoman Credit Co v Waragowski*,[88] and *Overstone v Shipway*,[89] the Court of Appeal had indicated that the measure of damages might be different from the one they were applying where it would be unreasonable for the claimant to exercise his right to terminate the agreement; however, in the later cases of *Financings v Baldock*,[90] and *Brady v St Margaret's Trust*,[91] the Court of Appeal held that the observations to this effect should not be taken too literally and that the question was not whether the right to terminate the contract had been exercised reasonably or unreasonably, an issue which could not affect the measure of damages, but whether the right to terminate had been exercised by virtue of a repudiation or by virtue of an express stipulation in the contract. At the same time, Lord Denning MR in *Financings v Baldock*,[92] voiced concern that there should be a difference in the assessment of damages between cases where there is a repudiation by the hirer and cases where there is not, and expressed himself as disturbed about the assessment of damages in the two earlier cases. He said: 26-020

> "Take the present case. A hirer does not pay two instalments, whereupon the owners retake the vehicle. There is no repudiation. The damages are limited to the unpaid instalments with interest. But take another case. If he had been more courteous and had written: 'I cannot pay any more instalments', that would have been a repudiation and the damages would be multiplied tenfold."[93]

Pointing out that in what he called "repudiation" cases no regard seemed

> "to have been paid to the fact that the hirer had the right to terminate the hiring at any time and thus bring to an end his obligation to pay any more instalments",[94]

he stated that the hirer should not, in his view, be liable for any more damages than if he had himself given notice to terminate,[95] and that if he had given notice himself the damages would have been limited to the breaches up to the date of termination unless the owners could rely on the "minimum payment" clause.[96]

While at first sight this argument looks compelling, it in fact contains a serious flaw, for Lord Denning MR fails to take into account the full impact of the "minimum payment" clause. The hirer is given an entitlement to terminate at any time only in conjunction with the owner's entitlement in that event to payment under the "minimum payment" clause. In practice no hire-purchase agreement without a "minimum payment" clause gives the hirer an option to terminate at will, and it is only to a contract of this academic nature that Lord Denning's reasoning can properly apply. The difficulty arises, of course, where the amount payable under the "minimum payment" clause is found, upon an application of the relevant criteria 26-021

87 [1968] 1 Q.B. 54 CA.
88 [1961] 1 W.L.R. 1124 CA.
89 [1962] 1 W.L.R. 117 CA.
90 [1963] 2 Q.B. 104 CA.
91 [1963] 2 Q.B. 494 CA.
92 [1963] 2 Q.B. 104 CA.
93 [1963] 2 Q.B. 104 CA at 113.
94 [1963] 2 Q.B. 104 CA at 113.
95 Citing *Withers v General Theatre Corp* [1933] 2 K.B. 536 CA; see para.10-106, above.
96 [1963] 2 Q.B. 104 at 113.

laid down in the case law, to be of penal proportions. In such circumstances the courts have so far hesitated to hold that the law as to penalties applies where it is the hirer who exercises his option to terminate; if this hesitation should ripen into a refusal to apply the law as to penalties, then the owner will be entitled to claim the stipulated sum, however penal. However, the law as to penalties should apply provided that the substance of the event upon which the stipulated sum may become payable is a breach, but then only if the owner is entitled to compensation for his actual loss; otherwise the law would be penalising the owner for having inserted a penalty clause, a step which has so far never been taken and which ought not to be taken. Since it would seem that the owner's actual loss should be calculated on the principles first laid down in *Yeoman Credit Co v Waragowski*,[97] the anomalies which Lord Denning MR envisaged disappear, however by applying throughout not the lower measure of damages of *Financings v Baldock*,[98] which he favours but the higher measure of damages of *Yeoman Credit Co v Waragowski*.[99] In one set of circumstances only may the lower measure of damages remain appropriate, namely where the owner terminates the agreement under a contractual option and the hirer's breach is insufficiently serious to have entitled the owner to terminate the agreement otherwise than by virtue of the contractual option.

**26-022** After a very considerable lull in the case law following upon the intense activity of the early 1960s the Court of Appeal returned to the damages issue in *Lombard North Central v Butterworth*.[100] The agreement for the hire of a computer by the defendant provided that his failure to make punctual payment of instalments should entitle the claimant finance company to terminate the agreement and also provided, independently of this, that the punctual payment of instalments was to be of the essence of the agreement. The case was thus one of hire rather than hire-purchase, but it had more affinities with the latter in so far as it was anticipated that at the end of the period of hire the computer would be sold to the hirer and the selling price would go to reduce the rentals paid[101]; moreover, it was the hire-purchase rather than the hire cases on damages which were relied upon by the court. It was first held that the claimants' termination of the contract and repossession of the computer on the defendant's repeated failure to pay the instalments not amounting to a repudiation entitled them to damages only for breaches up to the time of termination—in effect to damages along the lines of *Financings v Baldock*[102]—so that a stipulation in the contract that in these circumstances a "minimum payment" clause obliging the defendant to pay the remaining instalments was unenforceable as a penalty[103]; it was then further held that, punctual payment being of the essence of the contract, the claimants were entitled to treat default in one payment as a repudiation by the defendant of the agreement, thereby enabling them nevertheless to recover their loss in respect of the whole transaction—in effect to recover damages along the lines of *Yeoman Credit Co v Waragowski*.[104] The court viewed this result with some distaste. Nicholls LJ, after referring to the damages available under *Financings v*

---

97 [1961] 1 W.L.R. 1124 CA. Subject only to the qualification raised at para.26-018, above.

98 [1962] 2 Q.B. 104 CA.

99 [1961] 1 W.L.R. 1124 CA.

100 [1987] Q.B. 527 CA.

101 See [1987] Q.B. 527 CA at 543G–H.

102 [1963] 2 Q.B. 104 CA; see para.26-019, above.

103 See para.16-079, above.

104 [1961] 1 W.L.R. 1124 CA; see para.26-018, above.

*Baldock*,[105] to an owner determining a hire-purchase agreement in exercise of a power so to do given to him by the agreement on non-payment of instalments, said:

> "There is no practical difference between (1) an agreement containing such a power and (2) an agreement containing a provision to the effect that time for payment of each instalment is of the essence, so that any breach will go to the root of the contract. The difference between these two agreements is one of drafting form, and wholly without substance. Yet under an agreement drafted in the first form, the owner's damages claim arising upon his exercise of the power of termination is confined to damages for breaches up to the date of termination, whereas under an agreement drafted in the second form the owner's damages claim, arising upon his acceptance of an identical breach as a repudiation of the agreement, will extend to damages for loss of the whole transaction."[106]

This conclusion, as he pointed out,

> "emasculates the decision in *Financing v Baldock*, for it means that a skilled draftsman can easily sidestep the effect of that decision."[107]

Indeed it was precisely what had happened in *Lombard North Central v Butterworth*.[108]

## 2. Damage to the Goods or their Destruction

Where the hirer causes physical destruction of the goods by unauthorised user constituting a breach of contract, the lender's measure of damages will be the value of the goods. There is hardly any authority, merely a few minor and very old cases, such as *Roberts v McDougall*,[109] where a hired cart was destroyed and *Stead v Bligh*,[110] where a hired horse was injured so that he had to be killed. These cases turned only on liability, presumably because the issue of the measure of damages hardly seemed arguable. **26-023**

Where the hire has caused physical damage to the goods, whether by unauthorised user or by failure to keep them in good condition so that they are returned in disrepair, the lender's measure of damages will be either the amount by which the value of the goods has diminished or the cost of their repair. Here an authority, *Sunrock Aircraft Corporation Ltd v Scandinavian Airlines System*,[111] has at last appeared. Two leased aircraft were redelivered at the end of the lease in an unrepaired condition. In the Court of Appeal it was said to be **26-024**

> "common ground that the measure of damages for redelivering a hired chattel in a damaged condition was the cost of repairs, unless it was unreasonable to effect repairs; if it was unreasonable to effect repairs, then the measure was the diminution of value."[112]

Since in *Sunrock* it would have been unreasonable to repair—no repairs had in fact been effected—and since there was no diminution in value—the lessor had sold on

105 [1963] 2 Q.B. 104 CA.
106 [1987] Q.B. 527 CA at 546E–F.
107 [1987] Q.B. 527 CA at 546G.
108 [1987] Q.B. 527 CA.
109 (1887) 3 T.L.R. 666.
110 (1898) 62 J.P. 458.
111 [2007] 2 Lloyd's Rep. 612 CA.
112 [2007] 2 Lloyd's Rep. 612 CA at [32].

the aircraft at a price which did not reflect any disrepair—nominal damages were awarded.[113]

26-025 Where it is the hire-purchaser who causes physical destruction of, or damage to, the goods by unauthorised user, different considerations apply. The damages should be the same as with hire if the hire-purchaser does not exercise his option to buy; if he does, there will, of course, be no action for damages at all.

## 3. FAILURE TO SURRENDER THE GOODS

26-026 Where the hirer fails to surrender the goods at the end of the contractual period of hire he is liable for the market value of the goods at the time of breach by failure to surrender. On the other hand where the hire-purchaser fails to surrender the goods, not wishing, or being in a position, to exercise his option to buy, the measure of damages is the total amount payable under the hire-purchase agreement less the amount of hire instalments already paid. This follows from *Wickham Holdings v Brooke House Motors*,[114] in which this amount was recovered in conversion from a third party to whom the hire-purchaser had wrongfully transferred the goods for value[115]: the hire-purchaser's liability in contract can hardly be greater.[116]

---

113 The case was complicated by matters of construction of the contract and by a failure of the lessee to participate in an agreed mediation process, which had persuaded the trial judge to make a cost of repairs award ([2006] EWHC 2834 (Comm)); on this he was reversed.

114 [1967] 1 W.L.R. 295 CA.

115 Resolving a conflict of authority; for details see para.38-063, below.

116 For the measure of damages in a related situation, namely where a fraudulent hirer absconds with the vehicle on hire-purchase and the finance company sues the dealer on the dealer's warranty that the particulars given by the hirer were true, see *Liverpool and County Discount Co v A.B. Motor Co (Kilburn)* [1963] 1 W.L.R. 611 CA.

Chapter 27

# SALE OF LAND

Table of Contents



## I. Breach by Seller

Breaches of contract by a seller of land fall into two categories corresponding to the division of the transaction into contract and conveyance. Thus breach by failure to convey and breach by delay in conveying fall within the first category, while into the second fall breaches of the covenants in the conveyance.[1] The distinction **27-001**

[1] Occasionally there may be covenants in the contract itself, as with the undertakings to carry out work in *Dean v Ainley* [1987] 1 W.L.R. 1729 CA, *Strange v Westbury Homes (Holdings) Ltd* [2009] 128 Con. L.R. 26 CA and *Howard-Jones v Tate* [2012] 2 All E.R. 369 CA at paras 27-031 and 27-032,

continues to have analytical importance; its former great practical importance is no more after the demise of the rule in *Bain v Fothergill*,[2] a rule which had applied solely to the first category.[3]

27-002 The first category is subdivisible into cases where the seller fails completely to convey so that the buyer never gets the property, and cases where he merely delays conveyance.[4] The measure of damages will clearly be different in these two cases and they are therefore dealt with separately.

### (A) *FAILURE TO COMPLETE*

27-003 Where the seller refuses to proceed with the contract in such circumstances as amount to a repudiation or discharging breach, several remedies are available to the buyer. In the first place he may resort to the equitable remedy of specific performance. Or, secondly, he may treat the breach as discharging the contract, restore benefits received, if any, and recover back in an action of restitution his deposit, any further part of the price he has paid, and the expenses properly incurred in the investigation of title.[5] The recovery of this amount by the buyer is sometimes erroneously called damages.[6] This is perhaps to be explained by the fact that, in the days when the rule in *Bain v Fothergill*,[7] flourished, the buyer would often recover the same amount in an action for damages as he would in the restitution action.

27-004 Thirdly, the buyer may sue for damages, a course of action most commonly pursued where the seller has no title to convey.[8] While the remedy in damages, which is alone the preserve of this book, should in no way be prejudiced by the existence or the pursuit, other than to finality, of the other remedies,[9] case law had introduced here a degree of confusion. In *Horsler v Zorro*,[10] Megarry J held that, where a buyer had abandoned his claim for specific performance before judgment, he could not substitute a claim for damages for his loss of bargain because he was to be regarded as now having rescinded the contract ab initio and so precluded himself from pursuing his damages remedy. This erroneous holding gained a certain credence from the later decision of the Court of Appeal in *Capital and Suburban Properties v Swycher*,[11] that the damages remedy was precluded where an order for

---

below.

2 (1874) L.R. 7 H.L. 158; for details of the rule and its demise see the footnotes to para.27-005, below.

3 See para.27-014, below.

4 For another form of breach there is a seller's derogation from grant. In *Carter v Cole* [2009] EWCA Civ 410 CA sellers of land had stipulated for a right of way over the land sold to allow vehicular access to land retained and let out by them. Interference with this access by the buyers, who were in effect sellers of the right of way, put paid for a time—there was a mandatory injunction to restore the position—to the intended commercial use of the land. The damages were based on the value of that use: at paras [19] and following.

5 See, e.g. *Re Hare and O'More's Contract* [1901] 1 Ch. 93.

6 See, e.g. in *Compton v Bagley* [1892] 1 Ch. 313.

7 (1874) L.R. 7 H.L. 158.

8 In *Tye v House and Jennings* (1998) 76 P. & C.R. 188 there was not a sale but only an exclusivity agreement, viz. no commitment to sell but only an agreement not to deal with others during a specified period; the purchaser's costs thrown away were awarded.

9 Even if an order of specific performance is obtained and enforced, the buyer may yet be able to claim damages in addition. As to the measure of damages in such circumstances, this is in effect that for delay in completion, dealt with at paras 27-010 and following, below.

10 [1975] Ch. 302.

11 [1976] Ch. 319 CA, involving the converse case of a buyer of land in breach. See further at para.27-035, below.

specific performance had been obtained but not complied with. Fortunately, following upon the Court of Appeal's assertion in *Buckland v Farmar & Moody*,[12] that the holding in *Horsler v Zorro*,[13] was wrong, the House of Lords in *Johnson v Agnew*,[14] in this connection overruled both *Horsler v Zorro*,[15] and *Capital and Suburban Properties v Swycher*.[16]

## (1) Normal measure

The normal measure of damages is the market value of the property at the contractual time for completion less the contract price. In cases where the failure to complete has been other than through a defect in title, this measure has been awarded from *Engell v Fitch*,[17] in the 1860s down to *Diamond v Campbell-Jones*,[18] in the 1960s[19] and will continue to be awarded.[20] The same is now true for all cases, including those where it is a defect in title which has caused the failure to complete, the restrictive rule in *Bain v Fothergill*,[21] having been abolished in 1989.[22] **27-005**

---

12 [1979] 1 W.L.R. 221 CA.

13 [1975] Ch. 302.

14 [1980] A.C. 367.

15 [1975] Ch. 302.

16 [1978] Ch. 176 CA.

17 (1869) L.R. 4 Q.B. 659. Kelly C.B., delivering the judgment of the court, said at 665: "What we then have to consider is, when a vendor, not by reason of any want of title, but by reason of not choosing to oust the mortgagor, refuses to complete, and the action is really for a breach of contract to deliver possession, whether under such circumstances the vendee is entitled to recover the difference between the contract price and the market value at the time of breach. We think the vendee is entitled to this difference." And later he said: "If an increase in value has taken place between the contract and the breach, such an increase may be taken to have been in the contemplation of the parties within the meaning of *Hadley v Baxendale*": at 668.

18 [1961] Ch. 22.

19 But the runaway inflation of the 1970s began to erode the ubiquity of this basic measure: see para.27-009, below.

20 There do not appear to be any further cases deciding on this measure after *Diamond v Campbell-Jones*, probably because the position is now entirely clear. Other earlier cases are *Godwin v Francis* (1870) L.R. 5 C.P. 295 and *Re Daniel* [1917] 2 Ch. 405. The former was not against a seller but against the alleged agent of a seller for breach of warranty of authority, but the damages on this head were calculated on the basis of the damages the claimant could have recovered from the seller had he refused to convey under a binding contract. The measure stated in the text was also implicitly accepted in *Goffin v Houlder* (1921) 90 L.J. Ch. 488 and in *Ridley v De Geerts* [1945] 2 All E.R. 654 CA. See too *Strutt v Farlar* (1847) 16 M. & W. 249, where the claimant contracted to withhold execution of a judgment debt owed him by a third party in consideration of the defendant leasing him a house and, the consideration being executed, the claimant recovered the value of the lease.

21 This is the rule, which prevailed for over two centuries from 1776 to 1989 and formed a celebrated exception to the principle of contract damages that the claimant is entitled to be put in the same position as if the contract had been performed, that damages in respect of loss of bargain were not recoverable, in the absence of fraud or bad faith, by the buyer against the seller who failed to complete through a defect in title. The damages were held to recovery of the buyer's deposit and his expenses of investigating title. The rationale of the rule was the difficulty of showing a good title to land in England, with defects in title lying concealed in title deeds which were, in the amusing phrase attributed to Lord Westbury, "difficult to read, disgusting to touch, and impossible to understand", but this rationale could no longer stand up to examination as registered conveyancing, following upon the great property legislation of 1925, gradually became the order of the day. After many calls for reform (including in this work) the legislature finally obliged: see next note.

22 Law of Property (Miscellaneous Provisions) Act 1989 s.3 provided for the rule to be "abolished in relation to contracts made after this section comes into force".

**27-006** Ascertaining the contract price will not present difficulty but arriving at the market value may. No similar body of case law has grown up here as in the analogous case of sale of goods around the question of the market price; only on a few points are there direct decisions.[23] (1) Because of the difficulties in forming an exact estimate of the market value of a piece of land, on which opinions may well differ, the price at which the claimant had contracted to resell the property, though strictly irrelevant per se, has been taken as prima facie evidence of the market value. This was done in *Engell v Fitch*,[24] where the claimant had given evidence of the resale and the defendant had not countered with any evidence that the resale price did not represent the market price.[25] (2) Because of the same difficulties the resale price obtained by the defendant, who has backed out of his contract with the claimant on making a better bargain with another party, has been taken as evidence of the market price at the time due for completion. This was so in *Godwin v Francis*,[26] in *Goffin v Houlder*,[27] and in *Ridley v De Geerts*.[28] (3) On the other hand, apart from being evidence of the market price, the price at which the claimant has contracted to sell the land to a third party is irrelevant; accordingly it was held in *Brading v McNeill*,[29] that such a resale price, lower than the market price, could not decrease the damages below the normal measure.[30]

### (2) CONSEQUENTIAL LOSSES

**27-007** For long there were no decided cases in which clear items of consequential loss had been allowed.[31] *Godwin v Francis*,[32] provides an illustration of a loss held too remote, namely the loss on the resale by the claimant of animals bought by him for the purpose of stocking the land in question. Such damage, it was held, did not flow naturally from the breach and was not shown as being distinctly contemplated by the parties. As to loss of profit on a resale of the land itself, the trend of authority is against allowing recovery. Cockburn CJ in *Engell v Fitch*,[33] did indeed give an

---

23 Where required, the details worked out in the sale of goods cases should be referred to: see Ch.25, above.

24 (1869) L.R. 4 Q.B. 659.

25 (1869) L.R. 4 Q.B. 659 at 665, 667. Lord Chelmsford's criticism of this case in *Bain v Fothergill* (1874) L.R. 7 H.L. 158 at 203 is misdirected, as he assumed that the court was awarding damages for loss of profit on a resale rather than taking the resale price as the best evidence in the circumstances of the market value.

26 (1870) L.R. 5 C.P. 295. "The price at which it was resold is prima facie evidence of its market value": at 307, per Bovill CJ.

27 (1921) 90 L.J. Ch. 488 (case of an option to purchase).

28 [1945] 2 All E.R. 654 CA. And in *Day v Singleton* [1899] 2 Ch. 320 CA at 335. Sir F. H. Jeune said the fact that the defendant had resold the property at a higher price "will be material in estimating the amount of the damages".

29 [1946] Ch. 145. The contract was for the sale of a lease together with a business, but the court regarded the case as one concerning real property: see at 150, per Evershed J.

30 The fact that the subsale had been made before the main contract was held immaterial, as was the fact that with contracts concerning land the claimant has a remedy by way of specific performance. Beyond this, however, Evershed J did express the view that it might not be "just or logical strictly to apply the principle of *Rodocanachi v Milburn* in all cases" ([1946] Ch. 145 at 152), this being the equivalent case in contracts of carriage: see para.32-007, below.

31 The loss in *Day v Singleton* [1899] 2 Ch. 320 CA, may be a loss of user of the hotel contracted to be sold.

32 (1870) L.R. 5 C.P. 295.

33 (1868) L.R. 3 Q.B. 314 at 334.

emphatic view that

> "the purchase of real property sold by auction for the purpose of resale is a matter of everyday occurrence; and the possibility of a resale cannot be taken to be beyond the contemplation of the parties to such a contract",

but the Court of Exchequer Chamber, in affirming,[34] was not prepared to adopt his view, although not expressly dissenting from it, and considered that there was no general rule of law that a buyer of land could recover the loss of profit on a resale[35]; or that it could be said that the parties must be taken to have contemplated a resale.[36] In *Bain v Fothergill*,[37] Lord Chelmsford and Lord Hatherley contrasted sales of goods with sales of land and suggested that loss on a resale of land will be too remote as land is not generally bought with a view to resale.[38] And in *Diamond v Campbell-Jones*,[39] the buyer of the leasehold of a London town house, who was a dealer in real estate and had already bought and converted several such houses, failed to recover as damages, in an action against the repudiating seller, the profit that he would have made upon the conversion of the house into flats and offices. Not only was it found that the defendant seller had no actual knowledge at the time of the making of the contract as to how the claimant proposed to deal with the house, but the court was unprepared to impute any such knowledge to him. "Special circumstances", said Buckley J,

> "are necessary to justify imputing to a vendor of land a knowledge that the purchaser intends to use it in any particular manner".[40]

The possibility of recovering for loss of profit eventually became an actuality in *Cottrill v Steyning & Littlehampton Building Society*.[41] The defendants granted the claimant an option to purchase certain land, the option to be exercised as soon as reasonably possible after the claimant, with a view to permitting his intended development of the land, had obtained planning permission for houses and flats together with the rescission of a tree preservation order. After the claimant had satisfied these requirements, the defendants in breach of contract sold the land to a third party, and the court held that, since there could be no doubt that the defendants knew that the claimant intended to develop the land, special circumstances were established which entitled the claimant to have the damages assessed by reference to the profits which both parties contemplated he would make.[42] Accordingly the damages were assessed at the market value of the land at the date of completion of the development less the expenses attributable to the carrying out of the development.[43] Subsequently, in *Malhotra v Choudhury*,[44] where the defendant had **27-008**

---

34 (1868–69) L.R. 4 Q.B. 659.

35 (1868–69) L.R. 4 Q.B. 659 at 665.

36 (1868–69) L.R. 4 Q.B. 659 at 668.

37 (1874) L.R. 7 H.L. 158.

38 (1874) L.R. 7 H.L. 158 at 202 and 211, respectively.

39 [1961] Ch. 22.

40 [1961] Ch. 22 at 36; see the full quotation at para.8-198, above, where the difference in this connection between sale of land and sale of goods is enlarged upon.

41 [1966] 1 W.L.R. 753.

42 [1966] 1 W.L.R. 753 at 756.

43 [1966] 1 W.L.R. 753 at 757. The fact that the claimant might have resold the land to a company which he controlled without taking, for tax reasons, a profit on the resale was held not to affect the measure of damages: at 757.

granted an option to the claimant to purchase a house and surgery should the defendant cease to be a partner in the medical partnership upon which the two were then embarking, the Court of Appeal held, upon the defendant's failure to comply with the option when exercised by the claimant upon the dissolution of the partnership, that the claimant was entitled to damages for loss in his medical practice arising from his inability to practise from the surgery, as distinct from loss arising as a consequence of competition from the defendant. "The parties must have contemplated", said Cumming-Bruce LJ,

> "that if the plaintiff decided to exercise his option, he would exercise the option with the intent to use the surgery for the purpose for which it had been built and for which it had been used from the date of the partnership deed."[45]

**27-009** The galloping inflation of the 1970s brought into sharp focus a new form of what is essentially consequential loss. As has been seen, for the normal measure the value of the land is taken, following general principle, at the time contractually fixed for completion,[46] but such a measure could be grossly unfair to a buyer if prices had escalated between the contractual date for completion and the date of judgment in his action for damages, as the award he obtains will fall far short of giving him the means of acquiring an equivalent property. Of course he cannot complain of this if he ought to have acquired an equivalent property before the escalation of prices, but he may be able to show good reason why he did not do so. Thus if he brought a claim for specific performance in circumstances where he had a reasonable chance of obtaining such a decree but in the event was refused one and awarded damages instead, it would clearly be pointless for him to have acquired an equivalent property while he was awaiting the outcome of his specific performance suit. Again, prices might already have substantially increased between the making of the contract and the date fixed for its completion, and the buyer might not be in a position to raise the funds which even at that date he would require, in addition to those he had earmarked for the transaction, to acquire an equivalent property. Both these points were available to the buyers in *Wroth v Tyler*[47]—the claim for specific performance might well have succeeded, as there were possible ways of dealing with the seller's wife's rights under the Matrimonial Homes Act 1967 which constituted the stumbling block in the case,[48] and the value of the property at the date fixed for completion was already 25 per cent up on the contract price of £6,000, with the buyers, a young couple about to be married and buying their first house, having, to the seller's knowledge, no further financial resources—but it was the second point that was emphasised by Megarry J in coming to the conclusion that a proper application of the general principle of compensation required that the normal measure be departed from and the value of £11,500, which the property had at the time of judgment, be taken rather than its £7,500 value at the time of breach.[49] He then proceeded to award damages on such a basis not by a direct departure from the normal measure at common law but by invoking the equitable jurisdiction established by Lord Cairns' Act to grant damages in substitution for specific

44 [1980] Ch. 52 CA.

45 [1980] Ch. 52 CA at 80D.

46 See para.27-006, above.

47 [1974] Ch. 30.

48 See Megarry J's judgment, [1974] Ch. 30 at 47G to 53B.

49 See [1974] Ch. 30 at 57A to B.

performance,[50] being further of the view that a valuation as at the time of judgment was not precluded, as being outside the contemplation of the parties, because, though a rise in house prices was contemplated, a rise of such dramatic proportions as in fact took place was not.[51] Nonetheless there seems no good reason why similar damages should not be available at law in appropriate circumstances, and this has been accepted by higher authority in two cases where once again, before having had to turn to the damages remedy, a reasonable and proper attempt to compel the defendant specifically to perform had been made, namely in *Malhotra v Choudhury*,[52] by the Court of Appeal, where however the valuation was moved back from the date of judgment by one year because of the buyer's delay in pursuing his claim, and in *Johnson v Agnew*,[53] by the House of Lords, where the converse case of a buyer's failure to complete was involved.[54]

Starting from 1980 cases have dried up both on whether a loss of profits can be claimed[55] and on whether a date later than the date of breach can be taken in the determination of market value.[56] This may simply be because the existing authorities are generally regarded as having sufficiently settled the law to discourage further litigation. **27-010**

### (B) *DELAY IN COMPLETION*

If the seller delays in effecting a conveyance of the property in circumstances which allow the buyer to regard the breach as discharging the contract and justifying him in refusing the property, then, since he will not have the property transferred to him, the situation is the same as with a failure to complete as far as the measure of damages is concerned. More often he will have the property transferred to him late, either because the delay does not discharge the contract or he elects not to treat the delay as a discharge, or because he forces the seller's hand by successfully suing for a decree of specific performance. In such a situation the measure of damages is properly regarded as damages for delay.[57] **27-011**

#### (1) NORMAL MEASURE

The normal measure of damages is the value of the user of the land, which will generally be taken as its rental value, for the period from the contractual time for completion to the date of actual completion. This is so whether the delay is brought **27-012**

[50] See para.1-014, above. The decision was followed and applied in *Grant v Dawkins* [1973] 1 W.L.R. 1406 (facts at para.27-013, below) where the damages were awarded in addition to specific performance.

[51] On this remoteness issue, see further para.8-191, above.

[52] [1980] Ch. 52 CA: facts at para.27-008, above.

[53] [1980] A.C. 367.

[54] See the case at para.27-040, below and also *Radford v De Froberville* [1977] 1 W.L.R. 1262 at para.27-049, below.

[55] See para.27-008, above.

[56] See para.27-009, above. One case on the second issue has recently appeared where it is the buyer who is in breach; see *Hooper v Oates* [2013] EWCA Civ 91 CA at para.27-040, below.

[57] The restrictive rule in *Bain v Fothergill* (1874) L.R. 7 H.L. 158 applied to delay in completion as well as to failure to complete (*Rowe v School Board for London* (1887) 36 Ch. D. 619 at 623) but with delay there was little scope for its operation, probably not beyond the case where a defect in title was removed after the contractual date of completion had passed. In any event the rule may now be ignored here, having been abolished: see para.27-005, above.

to an end by the voluntary action of an indolent seller or by a decree of specific performance against a recalcitrant seller. This measure was applied in *Royal Bristol Permanent Building Society v Bomash*,[58] where the claimant purchaser had agreed to let the property within five days of due completion and the delay resulted in this sub-contracting falling through: the damages were assessed at the rent that the claimant would have received from his tenant on the basis that this represented the value of the user of the property.[59]

### (2) CONSEQUENTIAL LOSSES

**27-013** *Jones v Gardiner*,[60] illustrates recovery for consequential damage. The claimant there successfully claimed damages for loss of rent on the buildings which he would have erected or converted on the premises, Byrne J saying:

> "I bear in mind that one of the lots was sold as for a building site, that both were sold as with possession, and that the purchasers intended to build and have been delayed in their work by the defendant's default."[61]

And in *Grant v Dawkins*,[62] the buyer, who had obtained specific performance but had had to pay off certain mortgages on the land, was held entitled to damages in respect of his payments up to the amount by which the value of the land exceeded the purchase price.[63]

### *(C) BREACH OF COVENANTS*

**27-014** After the property has been conveyed to the purchaser there can be no question of specific performance, and it will generally be too late for rescission. The purchaser is thus confined to an action for damages should a failure of title or some other flaw appear after conveyance. The restrictive rule in *Bain v Fothergill*[64] had never applied once the contract had been completed by conveyance,[65] so its abolition[66] is of no concern in the context of breach of covenants in the conveyance.

#### 1. THE FOUR USUAL COVENANTS OF TITLE

58 (1887) 35 Ch. D. 390.

59 If the claimant fails to ask for damages when he obtains his decree for specific performance, he may ask later for damages in respect, but in respect only, of further delay: *Ford-Hunt v Singh (Raghbir)* [1973] 1 W.L.R. 738.

60 [1902] 1 Ch. 191.

61 [1902] 1 Ch. 191 at 196. This case was followed in *Phillips v Lamdin* [1949] 1 All E.R. 770, although the report does not indicate how the damages for the delay there were assessed. See the analogous lease case of *Jacques v Millar* (1877) 6 Ch. D. 153, at para.28-009, below.

62 [1973] 1 W.L.R. 1406.

63 The value was taken not at the date of breach but at the date the damages fell to be assessed: see para.27-009, above. A further liability that should be mentioned shortly is that a seller in occupation may be liable for damage occurring to the premises, as in *Royal Bristol Permanent Building Society v Bomash* (1887) 35 Ch. D. 390, *Phillips v Silvester* (1872) L.R. 8 Ch. App. 173 and *Clarke v Ramuz* [1891] 2 Q.B. 456 CA.

64 (1874) L.R. 7 H.L. 158.

65 See per Lord Blackburn in *Locke v Furze* (1866) L.R. 1 C.P. 441 at 454: "This ... is not the case of a contract for the sale of land but the case of a conveyance ... [*Bain v Fothergill*] does not apply to the case of an executed contract."

66 See para.27-005, above.

Analogous to the warranties in the sale of goods are the various convenants for title which are commonly found in sales of land. The four usual covenants for title are (1) for good right to convey, (2) for quiet enjoyment, (3) for freedom from incumbrances, and (4) for further assurance. 27-015

The first two are those to which most consideration need be given here. The main difference between the two is this. The first covenant operates *in praesenti* and therefore, if there is a defect in title,[67] the covenant is broken immediately on conveyance and an action lies there and then without any interference with the buyer's possession; furthermore, it has been held that the breach is single, entire and complete upon the execution of the conveyance.[68] The second covenant operates prospectively and there is no breach until some disturbance of the buyer's enjoyment of the land takes place; and it is a continuing covenant upon which damages may be recovered from time to time as they accrue. Where there has been disturbance of possession, by eviction and the like, there will generally be a breach of both covenants and therefore it is best to deal with the covenant for quiet enjoyment first, as it will bring in many cases where the action was also on the covenant for a good right to convey. 27-016

The third covenant, like the first, operates *in praesenti* and in many respects may be considered as part of, or a continuation of, the first.[69] But, also like the first, it will often be joined with an action under the second covenant, namely for quiet enjoyment, where the buyer's enjoyment has been disturbed by an incumbrancer. It will therefore be best to consider the third covenant partly in conjunction with the second and partly in conjunction with the first.[70] 27-017

The fourth covenant does not need consideration on the question of damages.[71] 27-018

## 2. COVENANT FOR QUIET ENJOYMENT[72]

### (1) Total eviction

Where the buyer is evicted[73] from the whole property the normal measure of 27-019

[67] As to the extent of the obligation incurred by the seller under these covenants, see the standard texts.

[68] *Turner v Moon* [1901] 2 Ch. 825, following the view of Bramwell B in *Spoor v Green* (1874) L.R. 9 Ex. 99 at 110 in preference to the view taken by Kelly CB in the same case at 117, and by the court in *Kingdom v Nottle* (1815) 4 M. & S. 53, that the breach is a continuing breach.

[69] See e.g. *Turner v Moon* [1901] 2 Ch. 825 where the action for breach of the implied covenant of title was based upon the existence of a right of way to which a third party was entitled; followed in *Great Western Ry v Fisher* [1905] 1 Ch. 316.

[70] One point, however, that should be separately dealt with in respect of incumbrances is that there is sometimes found, instead of the general covenant against incumbrances, a special covenant to pay off or remove incumbrances. In *Lethbridge v Mytton* (1831) 2 B. & Ad. 772 it was held that the measure of damages for breach of such a covenant was the full amount of the incumbrances even though the claimants had paid nothing themselves. This has been best explained on the ground that "the covenant is assumed to be covered by the consideration paid for the land, or in other words, the value of the land in the plaintiff's hands is diminished by the amount of the incumbrance": Sedgwick, *Damages*, 9th edn (New York, 1913), Vol.3, para.972, at p.2009.

[71] A failure to execute assurance is in itself unlikely to give rise to further loss or damage.

[72] As indicated in paras 27-016 and 27-017, above, this is taken to include such breaches of the covenant for quiet enjoyment as involve breaches of the covenant for good right to convey or of the covenant against incumbrances.

[73] It is generally accepted that if a third party is in possession at the time of conveyance the purchaser can be said to have been "evicted" although never in possession.

damages is the market value of the land.[74] This has been held in two cases, *Jenkins v Jones*,[75] and *Bunny v Hopkinson*,[76] although in neither was the matter given much consideration, perhaps because everyone concerned was certain that this was undoubtedly the proper measure. In the former the main question was on another matter; but the result in damages is quite striking since, although the land, worth £500, had been sold to the claimant for £10, nevertheless he was held entitled on eviction to recover £500, as this was what he had "lost by the breach". In the latter, the main question was whether the claimant could in addition recover the expenses he had incurred in making improvements on the land; it was undisputed that he could recover the value of the land.

**27-020** *Bunny v Hopkinson*[77] is indeed the main authority for the further important point on the measure of damages, that the market value of the land is to be taken at the time neither of contract nor of conveyance but of eviction, and that therefore any increase in its value, whether due to ordinary market changes or to improvements made on the land by the purchaser, will fall within the assessment figure. In that case the land had been sold for building purposes and after some houses had been built by the purchaser he was evicted; he recovered as damages not only the value of the land but

> "the amount expended in converting the land into the purpose for which it was sold".[78]

No distinction is taken between the expenses of improving and the value of the improvements; probably they were considered to be the same, but the latter would be more strictly correct. There is also a suggestion that the improvements made must be such as were within the contemplation of the parties at the time of contracting if their value is to be recovered: this seems right, as otherwise the damages would not be such as the seller could have foreseen as flowing from a breach of his covenant. Yet in the brave new world of restitutionary and disgorgement damages for breach of contract heralded by the Court of Appeal in *Attorney General v Blake*,[79] the buyer could attempt to side-step any remoteness limitation by claiming to recover for the value of improvements as constituting gain to the seller.[80]

---

[74] The purchase price will generally have been paid. If not, then of course it falls to be deducted from the value of the land in assessing the damages.

[75] (1882) 9 Q.B.D. 128 CA.

[76] (1859) 27 Beav. 565.

[77] (1859) 27 Beav. 565.

[78] (1859) 27 Beav. 565 at 568.

[79] [1998] Ch. 439 CA; the approach of the House of Lords, [2001] 1 A.C. 268 was somewhat different. On restitutionary and disgorgement damages generally, see Chs 14 and 15, above.

[80] The cases on leases also provide authority for taking the value of the land at the time of eviction, with improvements if any, as they are based on the same principle. Thus see *Rolph v Crouch* (1867) L.R. 3 Ex. 44 where the expense of erecting a building for the claimant's trade was recovered; and *Lock v Furze* (1866) L.R. 1 C.P. 441 where there appears to have been a rise in the market value of the land which was allowed for in the damages: see paras 28-018 and 28-021, below, respectively. Against this, in *Lewis v Campbell* (1819) 8 Taunt. 715 (sale or assignment of a leasehold interest), Dallas CJ said: "I very much doubt whether in any case a plaintiff can recover for the improvements and buildings he may choose to make and erect upon the lands": at 727. And Richardson J (at 729) thought that there should be no recovery in respect of additions to the property, while reserving his opinion as to improvements to the land itself. Perhaps what these judges had in mind was the question whether the particular improvements had been in the parties' contemplation. Not only however is this all dicta but comes from a decision long before *Hadley v Baxendale* (1854) 9 Ex. 341 established an authoritative measure of damages for breach of contract.

## (2) Partial eviction

If eviction[81] is from part only of the land, because title has failed only as to part of the land, the same measure applies mutatis mutandis. Thus in *Eastwood v Ashton*,[82] it was held, in a case where the claimant buyer never obtained possession of a strip of the land sold, that the true measure of damages was well settled as **27-021**

> "the difference in value between the land as purporting to be conveyed and the land as it actually passes to the purchaser".[83]

The contention that the measure was restricted to the difference in price which would have been obtained at the sale had the disputed strip been omitted was rejected. Similarly, where the title has failed to part of the land in time as opposed to in space, as where there is an unexpired lease to run, the measure should be the value of the use of the land for the period during which the buyer is deprived of its use.

In an analogous case where the defendant had agreed to sell a house to the claimant with vacant possession, and after conveyance failed to give possession because a tenant protected by the Rent Acts refused to quit the premises, the claimant recovered, inter alia, the purchase price less the value of the house subject to the tenancy in *Beard v Porter*.[84] A strictly correct measure would have taken not the purchase price but the value of the house freed from the tenancy, but perhaps in the circumstances these were the same. Damages based upon the difference in value of the house bought with and without vacant possession were indeed awarded in *Strutt v Whitnell*,[85] though the issue before the court was a difficult one of mitigation.[86] In *Beard v Porter*,[87] the main argument had been on other items, namely whether the claimant could recover the expenses incurred in buying a second house and in taking lodgings in the interim. It was held that he could.[88] **27-022**

## (3) Disturbance by the exercise of incumbrances

Next come incumbrances which disturb the buyer's enjoyment without resulting in his loss of any part of the possession, as where a right of way is exercised rightfully by a third party. In such circumstances it was held in *Sutton v Baillie*[89] that the damages should be measured by the value of the land free from the right of way less its value fettered.[90] **27-023**

---

81 See first footnote to para.27-019, above.

82 [1913] 2 Ch. 39. On the issue of liability it was first reversed ([1914] 1 Ch. 68 CA) and then restored ([1915] A.C. 900).

83 [1913] 2 Ch. 39 at 55, per Sargant J.

84 [1948] 1 K.B. 321 CA.

85 [1975] 1 W.L.R. 870 CA.

86 As to whether the buyer's entitlement to such damages had been lost by a failure to resell: see paras 9-053 and 9-054, above.

87 [1948] 1 K.B. 321 CA.

88 Evershed MR dissenting.

89 (1892) 65 L.T. 528.

90 Contrast the lease case of *Child v Stenning* (1879) 11 Ch. D. 82 CA, where only nominal damages were allowed in similar circumstances: the measure was not the permanent injury to the land but only the damage sustained up to the commencement of the action, since the covenant for quiet enjoy-

### (4) Payments, compromises, damages and costs

27-024 Where the buyer is threatened with eviction or disturbance by the third party, he may get rid of the outstanding interest by paying for it, whether by buying in a superior title, securing the release of a servitude, or paying off an incumbrance which is not a servitude but only a money charge, and whether by voluntary compromise or under a court judgment against him. The sum so paid he can then recover as damages from his seller, as in *Smith v Compton*,[91] a case of buying in a superior title under a voluntary compromise, and in *Great Western Ry v Fisher*,[92] a case of securing the release of a right of way by payment under a court judgment. The amount recoverable could not on principle exceed the value of the interest bought in; conversely, the claimant can only recover the amount paid by him to the third party even though it is less than the value of such interest.

27-025 Further, if the buyer has to pay damages to the person with the superior title and is nonetheless evicted by him, he will be able to recover the amount paid as damages from his seller in addition to the value of the land lost.[93]

27-026 Lastly, the buyer may recover court costs reasonably incurred by him in unsuccessfully defending an action brought against him by the person with the superior title, as in *Smith v Compton*,[94] and *Sutton v Baillie*,[95] or an arbitration on the same issue, as in *Great Western Ry v Fisher*.[96] Whether such a defence is reasonable will depend on all the facts; it is likely to be so where it succeeds in bringing down the figure paid to the third party from the figure claimed by him,[97] where the seller insists that the buyer is in the right,[98] and even, if otherwise reasonable, where the buyer fails to inform the seller of the action and defends entirely on his own initiative.[99] In the past the costs recoverable included the costs paid to the other party and the now claimant's costs assessed as between solicitor and client,[100] but solicitor and client costs, at least in this context, have now gone, and a series of first instance cases in other areas have held, it is thought wrongly, that the now claimant may recover his own costs only on the new standard basis.[101] The costs of an appeal are generally not allowed,[102] exceptionally they may be, as in *Sutton v Bail-*

ment was a continuing one and there might be no interference in the future. The distinction between the cases is considered at para.28-019, below. See the analogous case of failure to give vacant possession by the seller's leaving heaps of rubbish on the premises in *Cumberland Consolidated Holdings v Ireland* [1946] 1 K.B. 264. The measure of damages was held to be the cost of removal of the rubbish.

91 (1832) 3 B. & Ad. 407.

92 [1905] 1 Ch. 316.

93 The only illustrations are provided by the lease cases of *Williams v Burrell* (1845) 1 C.B. 402 and *Rolph v Crouch* (1867) L.R. 3 Ex. 44: see para.28-022, below.

94 (1832) 3 B. & Ad. 407.

95 (1892) 65 L.T. 528.

96 [1905] 1 Ch. 316.

97 *Great Western Ry v Fisher* [1905] 1 Ch. 316.

98 *Sutton v Baillie* (1892) 65 L.T. 528.

99 *Smith v Compton* (1832) 3 B. & Ad. 407; although in this case there may have been a covenant to indemnify against actions brought.

100 As in *Great Western Ry v Fisher* [1905] 1 Ch. 316.

101 For a full discussion see paras 21-003 to 21-011, above.

102 As in *Great Western Ry v Fisher* [1905] 1 Ch. 316.

*lie*,[103] where there had been disagreement in the lower court and the seller had insisted there was no incumbrance.[104]

## 3. COVENANT FOR GOOD RIGHT TO CONVEY[105]

Cases of this sort present more difficulty than the preceding in one respect, namely that the nature of the damage is in general still hypothetical, and not finally crystallised and ascertained. Where the claimant has entered into possession and then a defect is discovered, it may be that there is little or no chance that he will be evicted in the case of a superior title or that his enjoyment of the premises will be interfered with in the case of an incumbrance. In such circumstances it is arguable that the damages should be nominal, on the ground that until eviction or other interference the injury is merely hypothetical. Against this it may be said with force that the covenant for good right to convey would thus be watered down to one for quiet enjoyment and that, to avoid this, the claimant should get full damages here and now. It is suggested that a middle course is the correct one. The claimant should be able to recover damages representing the diminution in the value of the property as a saleable asset by reason of the possibility of interference, and the more remote the possibility the less will the selling value be diminished. But further, if subsequently an unexpected turn of events brings eviction or other interference, the claimant has a residual action under the covenant for quiet enjoyment, in assessing the damages under which the court would take into account the amount recovered earlier under the other covenant.[106] **27-027**

Authority is almost non-existent. The only case that deals with the problem is *Turner v Moon*,[107] and is therefore of some importance although only a first instance decision. Land was sold for building and conveyed. After a house had been built by the buyer claimant a right of way over the property was discovered, but there was no evidence that its grantee had ever sought to exercise it. In the claimant's action for breach of an implied covenant of title it was held by Joyce J that the proper measure of damages was **27-028**

> "the difference between the value of the property as purported to be conveyed, and that which the vendor had power to convey".[108]

---

103 (1892) 65 L.T. 528.

104 The whole question of the recovery of damages and costs paid in previous proceedings is considered generally in Ch.21, above.

105 As indicated in para.27-017, above, this is taken to include such breaches of the covenant for good right to convey as involve a breach of the covenant against incumbrances, but exclude such breaches thereof as involve a breach of the covenant for quiet enjoyment as they have already been covered in paras 27-019 to 27-026, above.

106 See the somewhat analogous cases of cumulative actions by a lessor for breach of covenant to repair during the term and then at its end: *Henderson v Thorn* [1893] 2 Q.B. 164; *Ebbetts v Conquest* (1900) 82 L.T. 560; see para.28-074, below.

107 [1901] 2 Ch. 825.

108 [1901] 2 Ch. 825 at 829 to 830, citing the old case of *Gray v Briscoe* (1607) Noy. 142. It is true that Joyce J's full statement as to the measure of damages runs thus: "The proper measure of damages … is the difference between the purchase money … and the value of the premises as conveyed … that is to say, the difference between the value of the property as purported to be conveyed, and that which the vendor had power to convey": [1901] 2 Ch. 825 at 829 to 830. This suggests that he regarded the purchase price and the value the property would have had if unfettered as the same in the case before him: price can, of course, be evidence of value.

This supports the view suggested that the present diminution in saleable value is the proper measure, although the judgment does not indicate what amount was given.[109] The fact too that, in rejecting the claimant's claim in respect of the loss of the improvements he had made on the land by building the house, Joyce J distinguished *Bunny v Hopkinson*,[110] where a similar loss was recovered, on the ground that there had been eviction and the claim had been made on the covenants of title generally, including the covenant for quiet enjoyment, may rather suggest that he would have allowed a further action in respect of subsequent damage beyond the amount for which recovery was given in the present one. Nothing appears as to what point in time the value should be taken but, since the covenant operates *in praesenti* and is broken at the moment of conveyance, the value at that time should be taken and not that at the time of action.

**27-029** In certain cases, however, it will be possible to calculate the damages once and for all with reasonable accuracy although there has been no present disturbance of the buyer. This would be so if what has been conveyed is an estate less than freehold, as, for instance, a leasehold property or a life estate: in such a case the difference in value between the two estates would be given. Thus, in an old case, *Gray v Briscoe*,[111] where the defendant had covenanted that the land was freehold but it was copyhold, the court's judgment runs briefly:

> "The jury shall give damages, in their consciences, according to that rate, that the country values fee-simple land more than copy-hold land."[112]

**27-030** Finally, where the buyer's title has been perfected after conveyance without any expense on his part, as where the grantor, having conveyed without title, subsequently acquired a title which enures to the grantee by the process known as "feeding the estoppel", only nominal damages can be recovered in the absence of special loss. So also if part of the title is thus acquired after conveyance, the recoverable damages will be reduced to the extent of the title acquired.

### 4. COVENANTS OTHER THAN OF TITLE

**27-031** A seller may covenant in the contract to carry out work on the premises after conveyance to the buyer. In *Howard-Jones v Tate*,[113] the work that the seller contracted to carry out on the premises within six months of completion of the sale, and failed to do in that time, was the provision of electricity and mains water supplies. Directing that damages against the seller be re-assessed on account of the trial judge's assessment on the wrong basis of restoring the pre-contractual position, Kitchin LJ in the leading Court of Appeal judgment indicated that the recoverable losses would comprise the cost of having the services installed and any other losses suffered as a result of their not being installed in due time.[114] In the earlier

[109] In *Kingdon v Nottle* (1815) 4 M. & S. 53, where the question at issue was not the measure of damages, the special damage laid, and which was considered adequate to support the action, was that the land was thereby of less value to the claimant and that he was prevented from selling it so advantageously.
[110] (1859) 27 Beav. 565.
[111] (1607) Noy. 142.
[112] (1607) Noy. 142.
[113] [2012] 2 All E.R. 369 CA.
[114] [2012] 2 All E.R. 369 CA at [31] to [36].

*Dean v Ainley*,[115] the defendant, in selling a house to the claimant, had undertaken to carry out work to prevent the leaking of water from a terrace, referred to as a patio, into a cellar beneath. Subsequently it was found that insufficient work had been carried out to prevent water leaking into the cellar from the patio and, specific performance of the covenant no longer being available, an action for damages was brought in which the Court of Appeal held that the proper measure of damages was the cost of waterproofing the patio, the alternative measure, though not expressly adverted to, being the diminution in value of the house. Glidewell LJ so held because he was satisfied that the claimant fully intended to waterproof the cellar itself and to use the damages awarded for the waterproofing of the patio[116] to contribute to the cost of this work; by contrast Kerr LJ thought the claimant's intentions in this regard immaterial.[117] Glidewell LJ's approach is to be preferred. Diminution in value rather than the generally higher cost of putting matters right should surely be the appropriate measure where there is no intention to incur that cost. Such a solution is indeed supported by the decisions in *Radford v De Froberville*,[118] which was applied, and in the contrasting *Wigsell v School for Indigent Blind*,[119] which was distinguished, these being the two analogous cases, dealt with later,[120] which concern covenants by the buyer rather than by the seller of land.

The seller may also undertake to carry out, or to have carried out, work on the premises before conveyance and it then turns out, after conveyance, that the work is inadequate, indeed defective. In *Strange v Westbury Homes (Holdings) Ltd*,[121] a developer sold a number of plots to a number of buyers and it was a term of each contract that the developer had completed, or soon would complete, the erection of the plots in a thorough and workmanlike manner. This the developer failed to do. The Court of Appeal upheld the trial judge's award of damages for the cost of remedial work and in addition for the diminution in value of the properties following the remedial work's completion.[122] **27-032**

[115] [1987] 1 W.L.R. 1729 CA.

[116] The greater cost of waterproofing the cellar, which would have solved the problem entirely, was not awarded since on general principle the claimant was only entitled to damages equal to the cost of the less expensive solution, though Kerr LJ decided on the ground that the defendant had undertaken to waterproof not the cellar but only the patio: see at 1737A to B.

[117] The third member of the court, Sir George Waller, is silent on this point.

[118] [1977] 1 W.L.R. 1262.

[119] (1882) 8 Q.B.D. 357.

[120] See paras 27-044 to 27-048, below.

[121] [2009] 128 Con. L.R. 26 CA.

[122] The trial judge had also made an award for distress and inconvenience but there was no appeal against this. And see here, in connection with work to be done before conveyance, *Rushton v Worcester County Council* [2002] H.L.R. 188 CA, which concerned not a seller's breach of contract but a breach, in the course of a sale of land, of the seller's statutory duty. A tenant had acquired her house under a right to buy where the landlord council in breach of statutory duty had failed to disclose a defect in the house which rendered it valueless. Had there been no such breach the tenant would have required the council to repair the house before her buying it at the discounted price to which she was entitled. The tenant's damages were held to consist not only of the expenditure wasted upon the actual purchase of the house but also of the discount which she would have received on the purchase of the house once repaired. The trial judge was, however, held to have been wrong to award the tenant damages for the alternative accommodation and removal costs required, and the inconvenience and disruption suffered, in the course of the repairs to the house that the tenant would have had done by the council as these were never now to happen.

## II. Breach by Buyer

**27-033** Breaches of contract by a buyer fall into the same two categories as those by a seller, breach by failure to accept a conveyance or by delay in doing so,[123] and breach of the covenants in the conveyance once accepted.

### (A) *Failure to Accept*

**27-034** Where the buyer refuses to proceed with the contract in such circumstances as amount to a repudiation or discharging breach, a number of remedies are available to the seller. In the first place, he may resort to the equitable remedy of specific performance; or, secondly, he may treat the breach as discharging the contract, forfeit any deposit but restore any payments made on account of the purchase price, and proceed to deal with the property as he desires. Each particular contract must be construed to ascertain whether money already paid by the buyer is a deposit in earnest or guarantee of performance and therefore to be forfeited, or a part payment of the price and therefore to be restored.[124] The deposit is rather analogous to liquidated damages; how far it affects the measure of damages in the seller's action is considered later.

**27-035** The seller's third course is to sue for damages. This remedy should in no way be prejudiced by the existence or the pursuit, other than to finality, of the other remedies. However, the case law of the 1970s had introduced here a degree of confusion. Thus in *Capital and Suburban Properties v Swycher*,[125] where the seller had obtained a decree of specific performance with which the buyer failed to comply, the Court of Appeal held that, although the seller was not prevented from electing to be released from his obligations under the contract with consequent retention of the land and forfeiture of the buyer's deposit, it was too late for him to treat the contract as discharged so as to sue at law for damages for the loss of his bargain. This seemed an odd halfway house position, allowing in effect to the buyer the second of his three remedies but not the third. However, Foster J was able in *Biggin v Minton*,[126] neatly to get round this refusal of damages by invoking Lord Cairns' Act and awarding the damages in equity in lieu of specific performance[127]; subsequently the Court of Appeal in *Johnson v Agnew*,[128] though endorsing the common law position as laid down by them in *Capital and Suburban Properties v Swycher*,[129] nevertheless also applied *Biggin v Minton*,[130] and awarded damages under Lord Cairns' Act to a seller no longer able to carry through the decree of specific performance, that inability being in the circumstances the primary responsibility of the buyer. Fortunately, the House of Lords has finally brought clar-

123 Delay is of little importance here and is not given separate treatment. It did however feature in *Anglo Continental Educational Group (GB) Ltd v ASN Capital Investments Ltd* [2010] EWHC 2649 Ch where in issue was, inter alia, the compensation payable by the buyer for late completion which was governed by the provisions of the Law Society's *General Conditions of Sale*: see at [53] and following.

124 *Howe v Smith* (1884) 27 Ch. D. 89 CA, is the leading case on this question.

125 [1976] Ch. 319 CA.

126 [1977] 1 W.L.R. 701.

127 For damages in equity see para.1-014, above.

128 [1978] Ch. 176 CA.

129 [1976] Ch. 319 CA.

130 [1977] 1 W.L.R. 701.

ity to the subject. In the appeal in *Johnson v Agnew*,[131] their Lordships held that, where an order for specific performance obtained by the buyer has not been complied with, the buyer is entitled to apply to the court to put an end to the contract and then to pursue, at common law, his damages remedy.[132] Resort to Lord Cairns' Act was unnecessary; *Capital and Suburban Properties v Swycher*,[133] was overruled.[134]

## (1) NORMAL MEASURE

The normal measure of damages is the contract price less the market price at the contractual time fixed for completion.[135] This measure is first clearly stated in *Laird v Pim*,[136] by Parke B: **27-036**

> "The measure of damages ... is the injury sustained by the claimant by reason of the defendants not having performed their contract. The question is, how much worse is the plaintiff by the diminution in the value of the land, or the loss of the purchase-money, in consequence of the non-performance of the contract?"[137]

The first relevant price, therefore, is the contract price; the market value at the moment of contracting is not relevant, however much lower than the contract price.[138] The second relevant price is the market price at the contractual time fixed for conveyance; if no time is fixed it will presumably be at the time of refusal to accept a conveyance,[139] and if there is an anticipatory repudiation by the buyer accepted by the seller this event can provide a proper time to take the market value, but a time before such repudiation cannot be taken.[140] The price at which the seller has resold is strictly not to be taken in preference to the market price, but it has been taken in most cases, of which *Noble v Edwards*,[141] is the prime illustration and *Keck v Faber*,[142] and *York Glass v Jubb*,[143] are others.[144] This would seem to be on the ground that the resale price affords good evidence of the market price, and there is no suggestion in these cases awarding the difference between the contract price and the resale price that the latter differed at all from the market price. In the second of these cases the principal point decided was that the price to be taken was the selling price realised within a reasonable time of the breach and not the higher selling **27-037**

131 [1980] A.C. 367.

132 See further at para.27-004, above.

133 [1976] Ch. 319 CA.

134 The difficulties have arisen largely because the term "rescission" has been used in two entirely different senses. See the valuable articles by Albery (1975) 91 L.Q.R. 337 and Dawson (1977) 93 L.Q.R. 232, since in effect endorsed by the speech of Lord Wilberforce in *Johnson v Agnew* [1980] A.C. 367.

135 See the similar measure in the analogous sale of goods: paras 25-117 and following, above.

136 (1841) 7 M. & W. 474.

137 (1841) 7 M. & W. 474 at 478. The claimant unsuccessfully claimed the whole purchase price while retaining the land.

138 *York Glass Co v Jubb* (1926) 134 L.T. 36 CA; see especially at 42, per Warrington LJ.

139 Compare to the analogous sale of goods in Ch.25 where these points have been worked out in more detail: see paras 25-122 and following, above.

140 *York Glass Co v Jubb* (1926) 134 L.T. 36 CA. See for the analogous sale of goods para.25-124, above.

141 (1877) 5 Ch. D. 379; reversed on another point, at 392 CA.

142 (1915) 60 S.J. 253.

143 (1926) 134 L.T. 36 CA.

144 In all these cases the resale price was lower than the contract price.

price which could have been realised later by slowly nursing the property for speculative building. And in the third of the cases it was held that it was proper to take the break-up price at which the property and the business thereon were sold since it had become no longer possible to sell the property and business at a higher price as a going concern. The Court of Appeal has now considered these three cases, citing them from this work, in *Hooper v Oates*.[145] Lloyd LJ, who gave the leading judgment, rightly said that, while the resale price taken in these cases was on the basis that it reflected the market price, the question of the correct date for assessment of the market price was not addressed, the choice being between the date of breach and the date of resale when the value was less. How this choice should be made is considered later when dealing with consequential losses.[146]

### (2) Consequential losses

**27-038** Beyond this normal measure there may be consequential losses. "These damages", said Pollock MR in *York Glass Co v Jubb*,[147]

> "are not confined to the actual margin between the sum realised and the contract price; there may be incidental expenses which have necessarily flowed from the breach of contract".

One expense commonly encountered is the expense of the abortive sale to the defendant; in *Essex v Daniell*,[148] the seller recovered damages representing the auctioneer's charges for the abortive sale and the costs incurred by him in preparing to complete the sale. It is true that this case concerned special conditions of sale, but Brett J said that "under ordinary circumstances"[149] the seller's expenses in preparing for the sale are recoverable. This head of damage requires to be analysed rather carefully, since the expenses of the abortive sale would have been incurred even had the buyer not defaulted; putting the seller into the position he would have been in had the contract been performed still entails his having incurred these expenses. The true analysis is this. The seller recovers the full contract price less the net market value of the property left on his hands, i.e. the amount at which a resale has been or could be made deducting therefrom the costs of resale. Thus the expenses to be looked at are not those of the abortive sale but those of the resale, or, where there has been no resale, the estimated costs of a resale. Since the costs will tend to vary proportionately with the selling price, and the claimant is presumably claiming damages in respect of a fall in the market value, the costs, actual or estimated, of a resale will be less than those of the original sale to the defendant.[150]

**27-039** Profits lost, as distinct from expenditures incurred, do not make an appearance as they do when it is the seller that is in breach, since here the claimant, the seller, is parting with the land rather than acquiring it. Loss of profits was indeed claimed

---

145 [2013] EWCA Civ 91 CA.

146 See para.27-040, below.

147 (1926) 134 L.T. 36 CA at 40, citing Parke B's general rule in *Robinson v Harman* (1848) 1 Ex. 850 at 855.

148 (1875) L.R. 10 C.P. 538.

149 (1875) L.R. 10 C.P. 538 at 553.

150 Thus it is submitted that *Essex v Daniell* (1875) L.R. 10 C.P. 538 should be taken to turn on its particular conditions of sale. The case was not followed in *Ng v Ashley King (Developments) Ltd* [2011] Ch. 115 but this was on a different point: see para.27-042, below.

in *Strategic Property Ltd v O'Se*,[151] but the claim, which was unsuccessful, was for loss of profits not on a later sale but on the sale in question itself. In back-to-back sales of a flat the intermediate seller claimed for the loss of profit on its sub-sale, having sold at a higher amount than that at which it had bought in the head sale. This profit was lost because when the defendant sub-buyers failed to complete, the claimant intermediary seller did not complete the head sale, thereby losing its profit on the sub-sale. The trial judge held that the claim for loss of the sub-sale profit failed because the claimant should have completed the head sale and claimed the normal measure of damages from the sub-buyers. Yet it is fair to say that, the completion date being the same for the head sale and the sub-sale, a claim by the intermediary seller on completion of the sub-sale for the normal measure of damages was very likely to have given it the sub-sale profit.

Just as with a seller's breach recovery may be allowed to the buyer for the es- **27-040**
sentially consequential loss emanating from a market rise at a time after that contractually fixed for completion,[152] so too there can be recovery for the equivalent consequential loss which may result to the seller from a market fall after the completion date, which is the breach date. Such a recovery is well illustrated by the important House of Lords decision in *Johnson v Agnew*.[153] In that case their Lordships decided that, where the seller has reasonably and properly pursued his remedy by way of specific performance but has had subsequently to abandon the attempt to have the contract performed, he was entitled to claim[154] damages in respect of the fall in the market value of the land between the contractual time for completion and the abandonment of specific performance.[155] The possibility of going beyond the normal measure of contract price less market price at the completion date has very recently been further considered by the Court of Appeal in *Hooper v Oates*.[156] Lloyd LJ, giving the leading judgment, pointed out that, under our procedures and legislation, the sale of land invariably requires time. and that, whatever the position may be with items of personal property, such as commodities and listed shares, it is hardly ever the case that there is an immediate available market for the sale, or purchase, of land in the sense that the seller can go out into the market at the date of breach and find a purchaser who is prepared to enter into contract there and then. It therefore must be appropriate to take the market value at the time a resale is entered into, always provided that the seller has not taken unreasonably long in finding an alternative purchaser, and if the market has fallen in the interim between completion date and resale date there is a loss to the seller beyond the normal measure. Indeed the decision in *Hooper v Oates* goes further than this as the court was dealing with a situation where there had been no resale. The claimants, a husband and wife, contracted in 2008 to sell their freehold property to the defendant and moved to another property which they had acquired elsewhere. When the defendant did not complete, the claimants accepted his repudiation and proceeded to market the property extensively through estate agents but were unable to find a buyer. After three years, by which time the value of the property had substantially declined, they gave up and moved back into the property themselves.

---

151 [2009] EWHC 3512 Ch.
152 On this see para.27-009, above.
153 [1980] A.C. 367.
154 At common law as much as in equity, on which see para.1-014, above.
155 [1980] A.C. 367 at 400H to 401E.
156 [2013] EWCA Civ 91 CA.

In the damages claim the defendant argued for taking the value of the property at the date of breach in which case the claimants had suffered no loss that was not covered by the forfeited deposit. This argument was firmly rejected. Even though there had been no resale the appropriate date at which to take the market valuation was the date when the claimants brought to an end their reasonable attempts to resell and took the property back for their own use.[157]

**27-041** Any other consequential losses will be recoverable if they fall within general principles. Thus where the buyer had been put into possession of the land and had taken from it a quantity of brick clay, the value of the clay was included in the damages in *Laird v Pim*.[158]

### (3) EFFECT OF A DEPOSIT ON THE DAMAGES

**27-042** How far the existence of a deposit, given as earnest and therefore forfeited on breach, will affect the damages is an important question. In the first place, it was held in *Icely v Grew*,[159] where the deposit was to be forfeited on failure to comply with the conditions of sale, that this applied only to a breach of the conditions of sale and not to a breach of the entire contract to buy, so that on a wrongful abandonment of the purchase the seller was not restricted to forfeiting the deposit but could sue in addition for damages. One of course could draw up contracts where the forfeiture of the deposit was to be the sole remedy but they do not appear in the reports or in practice and it might be suggested that any such provision constituted a penalty.[160] In the second place, it was held in *Ockenden v Henly*,[161] that, where the conditions of sale provided for the forfeiture of the deposit and for the recovery of the deficiency in price on a resale together with the expenses of resale, the deposit must be brought into account in assessing the damages for a failure to accept conveyance[162] and it is thought that the same would apply to a buyer's suit for breach of contract in the absence of special conditions. Next came *Essex v Daniell*,[163] where there had been no resale and the expenses of the abortive sale were held recoverable in addition to the forfeiture of the deposit, the court distinguishing *Ockenden v Henly*,[164] on the ground that it applied only where the power of resale given by the conditions had been exercised. It has been said in earlier editions of this work that it is difficult to see why this should make any difference[165] and now in *Ng v Ashley King (Developments) Ltd*,[166] Lewison J has agreed with this,[167] declining to follow *Essex v Daniell* and applying *Ockenden v Henly*. Pointing out that since its Victorian genesis *Essex v Daniell* has not been referred to in

---

157 See Lloyd LJ at [2013] EWCA Civ 91 CA at [37]–[40].

158 (1841) 7 M. & W. 474.

159 (1836) 6 Nev. & M. 467.

160 On the penalty possibility see paras 16-104 and following, above.

161 (1858) E.B. & E. 485.

162 Approved by Fry LJ in *Howe v Smith* (1884) 27 Ch. D. 104 to 105 CA. Whether the deposit was taken into account in *Icely v Grew* (1836) 6 Nev. & M. 467(above) is not clear.

163 (1875) L.R. 10 C.P. 538.

164 (1858) E.B. & E. 485.

165 Inasmuch as the deposit is a type of liquidated damages, it is difficult to reconcile with the principles developed as to liquidated damages any suggestion that the deposit can be retained and damages claimed in addition. See paras 16-104 and following, above.

166 [2011] Ch. 115.

167 [2011] Ch. 115 at [35].

a single English judgment,[168] Lewison J held that, where the buyer is in repudiatory breach of a contract for the sale of land and the seller forfeits the deposit, the buyer must give credit for the deposit in his claim for damages even where no resale of the land has been made by him.[169]

### (B) BREACH OF COVENANTS

The covenants made in the conveyance by the buyer are not nearly so numerous or important as those made by the seller. Such covenants are normally positive or restrictive covenants as to the user of the premises taken by the seller for the protection of adjoining property retained by him, and the seller is generally more interested in their enforcement by means of an action for specific performance or for an injunction. An action for damages is, however, also available, and will become important whenever, for one reason or another, neither specific performance nor an injunction is available[170] or is granted.[171] The measure of damages will generally be the diminution in the value of the adjoining land caused by the breach, but there may be alternative measures which will give to the claimant a greater recovery. With breaches of covenants in leases the ubiquitous alternative to the diminution in value of the reversion was the cost to the lessor of performing the covenant of which the lessee is in breach,[172] but such an alternative is much less appropriate in the present context. Indeed it can never arise where the covenant is a restrictive one as no outlay of expenditure is called for, but even with a positive covenant the fact that the land upon which it is intended that the covenant be performed is forever out of the hands of the seller—which is not the case with the lease where of course the land eventually reverts to the lessor—generally makes it impossible for the seller to carry out the covenant either in substance or at all, except occasionally where he can effectively carry it out on the land which he has himself retained. In the great majority of cases, therefore, it may be necessary to seek in some other direction for a measure which is alternative to the diminution in value of the adjoining land. Moreover, the fact that relief by way of specific performance or injunction is available to the victim of the breach but is not sought by him is of importance in deciding whether any damages beyond the diminution in value of this adjoining land should properly be awarded, since the failure to claim the specific relief may show disinterest in whether the covenant, positive or restrictive, is conformed with. **27-043**

## 1. POSITIVE COVENANTS

### (1) Where the seller is himself able in substance to perform the covenant

There appear to be only two cases in which the measure of damages appropriate for the breach of a positive covenant has been investigated. Both cases, moreover, have concerned the same type of covenant, namely a covenant by the **27-044**

[168] [2011] Ch. 115 at [31].

[169] See his very full and helpful discussion from [16] to [52].

[170] As in *Radford v De Froberville* [1977] 1 W.L.R. 1262: see para.27-046, below.

[171] As in *Wrotham Park Estate Co v Parkside Homes* [1974] 1 W.L.R. 798: see para.27-053, below.

[172] See paras 28-045 and following, and 28-084 and following, below.

buyer to build a separating wall between the land bought by him and the land retained by the seller. This produces the special situation where it is possible for the seller, in the presence of the buyer's refusal or failure to build, effectively to carry out the covenant himself by constructing a wall of the type specified in the contract on his own side of the boundary between the two closes.

**27-045** The earlier case is *Wigsell v School for Indigent Blind*,[173] a late Victorian case which, although relied on fairly extensively in earlier editions of this text in relation to both sales and leases of land, received virtually no attention from the courts[174] until it came very much to the fore in two cases decided in 1977.[175] It concerned a purchase by the defendants of a plot of some 12 acres of land for the erection of a school or asylum for the blind, and a covenant by them to keep the plot, which the seller's remaining estate wholly surrounded, enclosed by a brick wall or an iron railing seven feet high. Neither asylum nor wall was built and, the project having been abandoned, the defendants offered the land back to the claimants, the seller's executors, in accordance with a provision in the conveyance, which offer was refused. The claimants then gave notice to the defendant to build, but the notice was not complied with and an action for damages was brought. The failure to build resulted in some 20 acres of the claimants' retained land becoming less valuable; the defendants admitted liability in damages for that diminished value, but successfully argued that they were not liable for the cost of erecting the wall or railing. Field J, delivering the judgment of the Divisional Court, said:

> "It must be remembered that remedies for a breach of contract such as this are of two kinds. First, the plaintiffs, if they really wished to have the wall built in accordance with the contract, so that they might have the very thing contracted for, and nothing else, might have claimed in the Chancery Division specific performance of the covenant, and in that event, if the Court had come to the conclusion that the damages to be recovered in an action for damages, upon the principles applicable to such actions, would not adequately protect the plaintiffs' rights and interest, it might have ordered the defendants to build the wall, and so no question could have arisen as to the extent or otherwise of any injury sustained by the plaintiffs from the absence of it. But it was also open to the plaintiffs to do what they have done, viz. bring this action for damages, in which event they will be under no obligation whatever to expend the amount recovered in erecting the wall, and most probably would never think for a moment of any such expenditure, which to us, at least, would seem a simple waste of the money. The effect, however, of electing to bring the action for damages, is to convert the right to the performance of the contract into a right to have compensation in money, and the rule in such a case, stated in its most general terms, is that the plaintiff is entitled to have his damages assessed at the pecuniary amount of the difference between the state of the plaintiff upon the breach of the contract and what it would have been if the contract had been performed."[176]

**27-046** A different result, however, was much later arrived at in *Radford v De Froberville*.[177] The claimant, who lived in Dorset, owned a house in London which was subdivided into flats and let by him to tenants. The house had, for London, a

[173] (1882) 8 Q.B.D. 357.

[174] "Suprisingly modest in its judicial progeny": per Megarry VC in *Tito v Wadell (No.2)* [1977] Ch. 106 at 331F; "has enjoyed modest obscurity": per Oliver J in *Radford v De Froberville* [1977] 1 W.L.R. 1262 at 1273H to 1274A.

[175] *Tito v Waddell (No.2)* [1977] Ch. 106 and *Radford v De Froberville* [1977] 1 W.L.R. 1262.

[176] (1882) 8 Q.B.D. 357 at 363 to 364.

[177] [1977] 1 W.L.R. 1262.

very large garden, and a plot forming part of the garden and fronting on to the highway was sold by the claimant to the defendant on terms that she, the defendant, would build a house on the plot and erect a wall to specification, so as to divide the plot sold from the land retained by the claimant, and to maintain such wall in repair. The defendant built neither house nor wall, and sold the plot to a third party from whom she took, by way of indemnity, a covenant to observe and perform the covenants into which she herself had entered. The third party also built neither house nor wall. The claimant having obtained a judgment for damages, the issue of the correct measure came before Oliver J, the effective choice lying between the cost to the claimant of erecting a wall to the contract specifications on his own land and the much lesser amount by which the value of the claimant's retained land was diminished, as an investment property, by the absence of the wall. Counsel for the defendant argued that the cases allowing the cost of doing the stipulated work had all concerned leases, in all of which

> "the plaintiff is concerned with a covenant to do something on the plaintiff's land and something which, at least in cases where the lease had expired, is solely for the *plaintiff's* benefit",[178]

and, basing himself on the decision in *Wigsell*,[179] submitted that there was

> "a fundamental distinction between such a case and a case where that which is contracted to be done is the erection of something wholly on the *covenantor's* land, therefore, wholly or mainly for the *covenantor's* benefit albeit there may be some concomitant advantage, aesthetic, protective or functional to the plaintiff [and that in the latter type of case] … there can, as a matter of principle, be no other approach than that of seeking to assess in monetary terms the value which the provision of the advantage would have had to the plaintiff and, where that advantage is one which he enjoys as a landowner, the only yardstick of assessment is the amount by which the enjoyment of the advantage would increase the value of the land."[180]

Oliver J rejected this submission, considering that there was no such general principle and that, if there were, it would run contrary to contract damages' underlying aim of putting the victim of the breach in the same situation, as far as money could do it, as if the contract had been performed.[181] The purpose of the wall, said the learned judge, **27-047**

> "was to provide for the plaintiff in a form acceptable to him, but at the defendant's expense, that which otherwise the plaintiff would have been bound to provide for himself on his own land. He could, of course, when he parted with his adjoining land, have reserved a right of entry and liberty to construct a wall himself and extracted a covenant from the defendant to reimburse him the cost or charged it on the land. If that had been done and the defendant had failed to pay there could, I think, be no doubt that the plaintiff would have recovered the cost from him. In the event, he trusted the defendant to do the work herself and extracted a covenant from her to do it. But, in either case, viewed realistically, the answer to the question 'What has the plaintiff actually lost by the breach?' seems to me to be, as a practical matter, the same. The plaintiff contracted for the supply of a

[178] [1977] 1 W.L.R. 1262 at 1271E; counsel's emphasis.

[179] [1977] 1 W.L.R. 1262 at 1273H.

[180] [1977] 1 W.L.R. 1262 at 1271E to G; counsel's emphasis.

[181] The principle as it appears in the early, much cited statement of Parke B in *Robinson v Harman* (1848) 1 Ex. 850 at 855: see para.2-003, above.

wall bounding his property as part of the consideration for the transfer and the effect of the transaction was that he paid for it in advance, because he transferred his land before the work was done. That price cannot of course be restored to him nor can the defendant's part of the bargain be specifically performed, because she has sold the land to a stranger to the contract. Why should he not now be compensated by awarding him the sum which is required to enable him to carry out, as nearly as possible, for himself what the defendant has failed to do for him?"[182]

Accordingly, Oliver J held that the claimant was entitled to the cost of erecting the wall provided that he intended to erect it and that he was acting reasonably in doing so. As to the first of these conditions the judge declared himself

"entirely satisfied that the plaintiff genuinely wants this work done and that he intends to expend any damages awarded on carrying it out"[183];

as to the second condition he said that he knew

"of no principle of damages which would dictate that a plaintiff who has stipulated for an article of a certain quality should be fobbed off with an inferior substitute merely because it is cheaper for a defendant who has broken his contract to supply it."[184]

Furthermore, it was no reason to award less by way of damages that the claimant was not in personal occupation of the retained land but was motivated by a desire to confer a benefit on his tenants.[185]

**27-048** That contrary results were reached in these two cases is not to be attributed in any way to the separation of a century but stems from two points of difference between them which are themselves related. In the earlier case, the claimants could have claimed, but chose not to claim, specific performance, and it seems to have been accepted on all sides that they had no intention themselves of building the wall, it being no longer really required as the asylum project had been abandoned. In the later case, a claim for specific performance would have been futile as the property sold had been resold to a third party against whom the covenant, being of a positive nature, was unenforceable, and the court was convinced that the claimant had every intention of building the wall, and expending any damages awarded in doing so. Of these two differences it is clearly the second which is the key one—there can be no justification in awarding damages to do something which is not going to be done—but the existence of the first difference, which is capable of objective proof, gives some assistance in establishing whether the second difference, of a more subjective nature, is also present. For the failure to claim specific performance where it is not likely to be barred, whether by the intervention of a third party or for some other reason, may indicate a certain disinterest in the performance of the covenant.[186]

---

182 [1977] 1 W.L.R. 1262 at 1269D to G.

183 [1977] 1 W.L.R. 1262 at 1284E.

184 [1977] 1 W.L.R. 1262 at 1284H.

185 [1977] 1 W.L.R. 1262 at 1285B to E.

186 Compare *Dean v Ainley* [1987] 1 W.L.R. 1729 CA, at para.27-031, above, concerning a seller's rather than a buyer's covenant, where there was disagreement as to the need to show that the claimant intended to do the relevant work. Glidewell LJ considered, it is submitted rightly, that such an intention had to be there in order to permit recovery of the cost of effecting the work, but Kerr LJ thought otherwise.

A further important point arose for decision in *Radford v De Froberville*,[187] namely whether the damages were to be based upon the cost of building the wall at the date of the breach of contract or at the date of judgment, inflation having pushed the later cost far higher than the earlier. Faced with the general rule at common law that damages are to be assessed at the date of breach of contract, but at the same time with the assessment at the date of judgment in *Wroth v Tyler*,[188] where damages had been awarded for a seller of land's breach of contract under the equitable jurisdiction, heralded by Lord Cairns' Act, to give damages in lieu of specific performance,[189] Oliver J rightly held that damages at common law could be similarly based, saying that **27-049**

> "if the function of an award is to put the plaintiff in as good a position as if the contract had been performed, I do not see why, in principle, the same should not equally apply in an appropriate case of the breach of a contract which cannot be specifically performed."[190]

He pointed out that the earlier cases had been decided in times of relative financial stability in which the date of assessment made little or no difference and, to the extent that it did, adequate compensation was afforded by awarding interest. Now it was necessary to think again if one was to keep the law abreast of the times. When it is reasonable for a claimant to seek specific performance, he can hardly be under a duty to act in mitigation until he knows whether the court is going to grant him the decree sought, but when specific performance is out of the question, as in the instant case because of the sale to a third party,

> "the proper approach is to assess the damages at the date of the hearing unless it can be said that the plaintiff ought reasonably to have mitigated by seeking an alternative performance at an earlier date, in which event the appropriate measure would … be the cost of the alternative performance at that date."[191]

Oliver J did not have sufficient material before him to resolve the question of date, but he did express some general views on how the matter should be approached. First, he did not think that it could be the claimant's duty to expend money in building on his own land while there remained a reasonable probability that the work would be carried out by the owner of the plot; and secondly, once proceedings were commenced because this reasonable probability had come to nothing, he thought that the defendant could not complain that it was unreasonable for the claimant to delay carrying out the work for himself before the damages had been assessed, more particularly where his right to any damages at all was being contested so that he might never recoup the cost, provided always that the claimant conducts the proceedings with due expedition.[192]

---

187 [1977] 1 W.L.R. 1262.

188 [1974] Ch. 30; see para.27-009, above.

189 See para.1-014, above.

190 [1977] 1 W.L.R. 1262 at 1286F.

191 [1977] 1 W.L.R. 1262 at 1286H.

192 [1977] 1 W.L.R. 1262 at 1287A to B, E to F. See further at paras 27-009 and 27-040, above, for the confirmation of this approach in *Johnson v Agnew* [1980] A.C. 367.

### (2) Where the seller is debarred from himself performing the covenant

27-050 In many, if not most, cases, however, the seller will not be able to take over the performance of the covenant by effecting a substitute performance through the execution of comparable work on his own land. Here the possibility of a claim for specific performance becomes particularly important, as only by bringing such a claim will the seller be able to ensure that the covenant is carried out. If he fails to invoke such relief when it is available and to ask the court to direct the work to be carried out by the buyer or by others at his expense, then it is difficult to see how the damages can properly be assessed other than by the diminution in value in the retained land by the non-performance of the covenant, although this may be substantially less than the cost of performance or even lead to a nominal award.

27-051 There remains, however, the situation where the court is not prepared to award the claimant seller a decree of specific performance. There may be just no point in the claimant's attempting to pursue this remedy, as where it is clearly unavailable because the burdened land has been resold to a third party, or, while it may not be unreasonable for the claimant to initiate such a claim, yet the court in the event declines to grant specific performance because, say, of the difficulties of supervision of performance, or of great hardship to the defendant, or because the claimant has shown a lack of speed in pursuing his rights.[193] In *Radford v De Froberville*,[194] Oliver J said that, even if the court were satisfied that a claimant wanted the work done, he could

> "readily see that there may be cases in which, … because the plaintiff cannot mitigate by carrying out comparable work on his own land …, diminution in value is the only appropriate measure".[195]

And the same thought may have partly lain behind his apparent acceptance of the submission of counsel that,

> "if I sell a plot of land adjoining my house and stipulate for the erection on it of some ornamental feature (for instance a pool and a fountain), all that I lose by the breach of that stipulation is the view of the pool and fountain, the economic measure of which is the amount by which its presence next-door would enhance the value of my premises."[196]

It is submitted, however, that there is no reason why the claimant should not argue, where the diminution in value of his retained land caused by the breach of the covenant is insignificant or even non-existent, that he is entitled to the type of measure which has emerged in analogous fields[197] and which here would be based upon the amount which the defendant would have been prepared to pay to gain release from the obligation of performing the covenant. If such a measure is available to the beneficiary of a restrictive covenant to whom an injunction has not been granted,[198] it should surely also be available to the beneficiary of a positive covenant

---

193 For the general grounds for refusing a decree of specific performance, see the standard texts on contract and equity.

194 [1977] 1 W.L.R. 1262.

195 [1977] 1 W.L.R. 1262 at 1273G.

196 [1977] 1 W.L.R. 1262 at 1269A.

197 See paras 27-053 to 27-055 and 39-060 and following, below.

198 As in *Wrotham Park Estate Co v Parkside Homes* [1974] 1 W.L.R. 798; *Jaggard v Sawyer* [1995]

who cannot obtain specific performance and who is in no position to effect a substitute performance himself.[199]

## 2. Restrictive Covenants

Where the covenant is restrictive in nature the diminution in the value of the adjoining or retained land will still form the starting point in the assessment of damages, but the search for alternative measures will not take one down the same road as with positive covenants. For there is no longer any overt action to be taken in pursuance of the covenant whether by the buyer under his contractual obligations or by the seller in lieu, so that any measure based on the cost of doing the work contracted for can have no relevance. The covenantor's breach is no longer in failing to do what he has contracted to do, but in doing what he has contracted not to do. Here it might seem at first sight that the measure by way of diminution of value of the land retained must now hold the field, as there can never be any question of the seller, as covenantee, taking steps to remedy the situation by incurring the cost of carrying out the covenant himself. A measure of damages which is alternative to diminution in value has, however, emerged for restrictive covenants, although it is radically different from the alternative measure which has been applied where a positive covenant was in issue.[200] This measure is based upon the sum of money which the seller might reasonably have demanded of the buyer for releasing him from his covenant. **27-052**

Such a measure made its appearance in *Wrotham Park Estate Co v Parkside Homes*.[201] An owner of land sold part of it to a developer who covenanted with the seller and his assigns that he and his successors in title would observe and perform certain covenants restricting the buyer's right to develop the land for building purposes other than in strict accordance with a layout plan approved by the seller. Successors in title to the buyer built houses on the purchased land in breach of this restrictive covenant, and the claimants, who had succeeded to a part of the land retained by the seller for the benefit of which the restrictive covenant had been taken, sued for a mandatory injunction seeking demolition of the houses erected and for damages. The injunction having been refused because removal of the houses would constitute unpardonable economic waste, it fell to Brightman J to deal with the defendant's contention that the award of damages should be nominal because the value of the claimants' land, as they conceded, was not one whit diminished by the erection of the houses. The judge, regarding this contention as leading to a result of questionable fairness, said: **27-053**

> "If, for social and economic reasons, the court does not see fit in the exercise of its discretion, to order demolition of the 14 houses, is it just that the plaintiffs should receive no compensation and that the defendants should be left in undisturbed possession of the fruits of their wrongdoing? Common sense would seem to demand a negative answer to this question."[202]

---

1 W.L.R. 269 CA and *Gafford v Graham* (1999) 77 P. & C.R. 73 CA at paras 27-053 to 27-058, below.

[199] With the advent of restitutionary damages in contract, stemming from *Attorney General v Blake* [1998] Ch. 439 CA, this is even more likely to be the case. See Ch.14 generally.

[200] See paras 27-046 and 27-047, above.

[201] [1974] 1 W.L.R. 798.

[202] [1974] 1 W.L.R. 798 at 812H.

In the event Brightman J, accepting that damages are usually measured by reference to the amount that would place the claimants in the same position as if the covenant had not been broken but focusing on the benefit to the defendants who could have avoided a breach by seeking a relaxation of the covenant, decided that

> "a just substitute for a mandatory injunction would be such a sum of money as might reasonably have been demanded by the plaintiffs from [the defendants] as a quid pro quo for relaxing the covenant".[203]

He rejected the claimants' submission that the sum should be a substantial proportion of the development value of the land, and awarded instead five per cent of the developers' anticipated profit of £50,000. A proportion of the development value was rejected because the layout covenant was not an asset which the owner of the seller's estate had ever contemplated having the opportunity or desire to turn to account and, in addition, the breach of covenant in question had taken place over a very small area of the land originally sold.[204] As to the appropriate percentage of developers' profit to be awarded, Brightman J considered that he should, on the particular facts of the case, act with great moderation because the claimants could have made it clear to the developers, before the developers had committed themselves to the purchase of the land, that they, the claimants, were not going to consent to the development in question.[205]

**27-054** A different result was reached in *Surrey County Council v Bredero Homes*,[206] where the Court of Appeal confined their award to nominal damages, the claimant council having complained that the defendant developers, to whom they had sold land for a housing estate, had built 77 houses on the site whereas the covenant in the contract allowed them only to build 72. To a large extent the Court of Appeal here was looking at the situation from the point of view of restitution—which in the circumstances it was not prepared to allow—rather than damages. Thus Dillon LJ said that the remedy at common law for breach of contract is damages which are to compensate the claimant for his loss and

> "not to transfer to the victim, if he has suffered no loss, the benefit which the wrongdoer has gained by his breach of contract",[207]

and Steyn LJ said[208] that the award in *Wrotham Park*,[209] was "only defensible on the basis of the ... restitutionary principle". However, in the later *Jaggard v Sawyer*,[210] the Court of Appeal was of the erroneous view that the award in *Wrotham Park*,[211] was justified on compensatory and not restitutionary principles. The award of no more than nominal damages in *Bredero Homes*,[212] was to be explained on the ground that no injunction had been sought against the defendants in that case by

203 [1974] 1 W.L.R. 798 at 815D.
204 [1974] 1 W.L.R. 798 at 815E to G.
205 [1974] 1 W.L.R. 798 at 815H to 816A. Compare the 40 per cent of profit awarded in *Bracewell v Appleby* [1975] Ch. 408, which involved trespass to land (see para.39-061, below), but there the total profit was only £5,000.
206 [1993] 1 W.L.R. 1361 CA.
207 [1993] 1 W.L.R. 1361 CA at 1364G.
208 [1993] 1 W.L.R. 1361 CA at 1369F.
209 [1974] 1 W.L.R. 798.
210 [1995] 1 W.L.R. 269 CA.
211 [1974] 1 W.L.R. 798.
212 [1993] 1 W.L.R. 1361 CA.

the claimants, it being too late for them to do so because the defendants had already disposed of all the houses to buyers. Millett LJ pointed out that:

> "It is the ability to claim an injunction which gives the covenant much of its value. If the plaintiff delays proceedings until it is no longer possible for him to obtain an injunction, he destroys his own bargaining power and devalues his right. The unavailability of the remedy of injunction at one and the same time deprives the court of jurisdiction to award damages under the Act [i.e. Lord Cairns' Act] and removes the basis for awarding substantial damages at common law."[213]

The situation in *Jaggard v Sawyer*,[214] was such that it was once again, as in *Wrotham Park*,[215] appropriate to award more than nominal damages to the claimant. In a residential development of 10 properties in plots lining a private cul-de-sac, each property including an area of roadway immediately in front of it, the defendant owners of one of the properties had commenced to build a further house at the back of the one they already owned with access over the common roadway, and the claimant, the owner of another of the properties in the cul-de-sac, brought an action for an injunction to restrain the proposed user over her section of the roadway on the ground that it involved breach of the covenants[216] subject to which each property had been conveyed. The court declined to grant an injunction but awarded damages in lieu. The amount awarded, which was of damages regarded as compensation and not restitution, was some £700, being on the basis that the defendants should have been prepared to pay £6,250 for a right of way and the release of their covenant; this £6,250 would have been divisible between all the owners other than the defendants, thereby entitling the claimant to one ninth of that amount. Moreover, it was held to be proper for the court to award damages once and for all in respect of future wrongs, because it awarded them in substitution for the grant of an injunction and to compensate for those future wrongs which an injunction would have prevented. This possibility had not been in issue in either *Wrotham Park*,[217] or *Bredero Homes*,[218] because, as Millett LJ pointed out in *Jaggard v Sawyer*,[219] both cases were concerned with a single past breach of covenant.[220] **27-055**

*Wrotham Park*,[221] as interpreted in *Jaggard*,[222] as being explainable on compensatory rather than restitutionary principles,[223] was applied in *Gafford v Graham*,[224] so as to assess the damages for breach of a restrictive covenant by reference to the sum that the claimant might reasonably have demanded as a quid pro quo for relaxing the restrictions in perpetuity. The court arrived at a figure of £25,000 which is far greater than was awarded in either *Wrotham Park* or *Jaggard*. In *Amec Develop-* **27-056**

---

213 [1995] 1 W.L.R. 269 at 291G. But see para.14-051, above.
214 [1995] 1 W.L.R. 269 CA.
215 [1974] 1 W.L.R. 798.
216 And also trespass.
217 [1974] 1 W.L.R. 798.
218 [1993] 1 W.L.R. 1361 CA.
219 [1995] 1 W.L.R. 269 CA.
220 [1995] 1 W.L.R. 269 CA at 291E.
221 [1974] 1 W.L.R. 798.
222 [1995] 1 W.L.R. 269 CA.
223 See para.27-054, above.
224 (1999) 77 P. & C.R. 73 CA.

*ments Ltd v Jury's Hotel Management (UK) Ltd*,[225] where a hotel was built in breach of a restrictive covenant, the parties had agreed, in the light of *Wrotham Park* and *Jaggard*, that the damages should be such sum as might reasonably have been demanded for permitting the encroachment. This produced the even larger, indeed much larger, award of £375,000. The principal issue had been to arrive at the gain the defendant would have made in being allowed to breach the covenant, and then at the discount from that sum which would have been applied in negotiation, many relevant factors to take into account in arriving at a final figure being dealt with at length in the judgment.[226]

**27-057** *Lane v O'Brien Homes*,[227] is a further illustration of a claim by a seller of land against his buyer concerned with overbuilding, in this case building a fourth house on the land when the buyer had agreed to build only three. The case differs from the general run in two respects. First, the building had not been built by the time of the litigation; only planning permission for it had been applied for and had been granted. Secondly, the breach was of a collateral contract and not of a covenant in the sale contract itself. The defendant buyer argued, on the strength of the recovery allowed in *Wrotham Park*, that he should be liable for only five per cent of the profit to be made on the fourth house, while the claimant argued that he was entitled to the whole of the profit on the fourth house. The trial judge awarded in the region of half of this profit[228] and was upheld on appeal.[229] The appeal dealt also with the time at which the percentage of the profit to be paid over in damages fell to be assessed. When the contract of sale was entered into, the prospect of obtaining planning permission for a fourth house was not thought promising by either contracting party so that at that time the defendant would have had to pay a good deal less than half of his notional profit to the claimant for his permission. However the appeal judge, in upholding the trial judge's award, said that he was

> "satisfied that the *Wrotham Park* principle requires the court to consider the course of hypothetical negotiations for the release from the prohibition not at the time of the sale, but later."[230]

The later time chosen as the relevant time was the time the defendant would have sought release from his contractual commitment, namely, when planning permission had been granted, and with planning permission a certainty "the stakes had become very much higher".[231] It could of course be said that, if the damages are still to be regarded as compensation for loss of a bargaining opportunity, then for the purposes of an assessment of the damages one should look to the time of contract-

---

225 [2001] 1 E.G.L.R. 81.

226 An award of damages for a buyer's breach of a covenant not to build based on what the parties were likely to have agreed to for the release of the covenant was upheld by the Court of Appeal in *Harris v Williams Wynne* [2006] 2 P. & C.R. 27 CA at 595. But some dubious reasoning was involved: see *Harris* at para.14-051, in a footnote, above.

227 [2004] EWHC 303 (QB).

228 In arriving at this result the trial judge entered, unnecessarily, the lists of loss of a chance doctrine, saying that the court must assess the degree of probability that the benefit lost as a result of the breach of contract would accrue to the claimant. But all that was needed was to assess the percentage of the profit which should in fairness accrue to the claimant, and this was indeed accepted on the appeal in *Lane*: see at [22].

229 The appeal was to the High Court from the county court.

230 [2004] EWHC 303 (QB) at [25].

231 [2004] EWHC 303 (QB).

ing, which is when the bargaining would have taken place. If, however, one regards the damages award, as one today should, as one of restitutionary damages, there is no difficulty in basing the damages on the profit that the defendant is expected to make.[232]

Indeed all the above successful claims by covenantees arising out of breaches of restrictive covenants which have redounded to the advantage and benefit of defaulting covenantors have to be looked at again from a restitutionary rather than a compensatory angle in the light of the arrival on the legal scene and the better explanation of these cases based on the concept of restitutionary damages for breach of contract. In particular *Bredero Homes*,[233] the one case in which the claimant failed is at risk from this angle. It has been much criticised not only in the legal literature but by the House of Lords in *Attorney General v Blake*,[234] itself. Lord Nicholls, with whose speech Lord Goff and Lord Browne-Wilkinson agreed, as much as said that he thought the decision wrong,[235] and Lord Hobhouse agreed with him that *Wrotham Park*,[236] was to be preferred to it.[237] A separate chapter is devoted to the whole issue of restitutionary damages.[238] **27-058**

Finally, there is the situation where there is no diminution in the value of the claimant's land attributable to the defendant's breach of covenant not because the breach may even have enhanced its value but because the character of the neighbourhood has deteriorated due to a general disregard and failure to comply with restrictive covenants in which the claimant himself has acquiesced. Here there seems no good reason to award him the measure of damages thus fashioned in *Wrotham Park*,[239] and followed in the later cases. No damages were awarded in such a situation in *Sayers v Collyer*,[240] and this should remain true today. And although it was there said in the Court of Appeal, differing from the court below,[241] that the change in the character of the neighbourhood was no ground for refusing relief, whether by way of injunction or damages, because it was not caused by the claimant's conduct, this factor would still be bound to negate recoverable damage as the diminution in value of the claimant's land would remain unattributable to the defendant's breach of covenant. **27-059**

---

232 See paras 14-036 to 14-037, above and Ch.14 generally.
233 [1993] 1 W.L.R. 1361 CA; at para.27-054, above.
234 [2001] 1 A.C. 268.
235 [2001] 1 A.C. 268 at 283G to H.
236 [1974] 1 W.L.R. 798.
237 [2001] 1 A.C. 268 at 298G to H. Lord Steyn, who had been a member of the Court of Appeal in *Bredero Homes*, not surprisingly attempted a justification: at 291B to F.
238 See Ch.14. See in particular para.14-047, above.
239 [1974] 1 W.L.R. 798.
240 (1884) 28 Ch. D. 103 CA.
241 (1883) 24 Ch. D. 180.

CHAPTER 28

# LEASE OF LAND

TABLE OF CONTENTS

## I. BREACH BY LESSOR

Breaches of contract by a lessor fall into two categories corresponding to the division of the transaction into the agreement to lease and the execution of the lease.[1] Thus breach by failure to execute the lease and breach by delay in doing so fall within the first category, while into the second fall breaches of the covenants in the lease as executed. The distinction continues to have analytical importance; its former great practical importance is no more after the demise of the rule in *Bain v Fothergill*,[2] a rule which, while applying to leases as well as to sales of land,[3] applied solely to the first category.[4] **28-001**

The first category is subdivisible into cases where the lessor fails completely to execute the lease so that the lessee never gets the property and those where he merely delays execution. The measure of damages will clearly be different in these two cases and, therefore, they are dealt with separately. **28-002**

### (A) FAILURE TO COMPLETE

Where the lessor refuses to proceed with the contract in such circumstances as amount to a repudiation or discharging breach, a number of remedies are available to the lessee. In the first place he may resort to the equitable remedy of specific performance. Or, secondly, he may treat the breach as discharging the contract and recover back in an action of restitution any moneys paid by him, at the same time restoring any benefits received. His third alternative is an action for damages.[5] This remedy is most commonly invoked where the lessor has no longer title to convey: otherwise specific performance would be sought.[6] **28-003**

#### (1) NORMAL MEASURE

The normal measure of damages is the value of the term, which will be calculated as the rental value of the premises less the contractual rent reserved by the lease. This is now true for all cases, including those where it is a defect in title which has caused the failure to complete, the restrictive rule in *Bain v Fothergill*,[7] which applied to leases as much as sales, having been abolished in 1989.[8] **28-004**

There are no direct authorities.[9] Where the claimant succeeded in obtaining a new **28-005**

---

1 This is exactly analogous to breaches by a seller of land: see para.27-001, above.

2 (1874) L.R. 7 H.L. 158.

3 For the rule and its demise see the footnotes to para.27-005, above.

4 See para.27-014, above.

5 See the fuller treatment in the parallel case of sale of land at paras 27-003 and 27-004, above.

6 He may be able to claim damages in addition to specific performance. As to the measure of damages in such circumstances this is in effect that for delay in completion, dealt with at paras 28-007 and following, below.

7 (1874) L.R. 7 H.L. 158.

8 For the rule and its demise see the footnotes to para.27-005, above.

9 See *Williams v Burrell* (1845) 1 C.B. 402 and *Jaura v Ahmed* [2002] EWCA Civ 210 CA at para.28-015, below, providing the nearest analogy. In *Paris Oldham & Gijlstra v Staffordshire Building Society* [1988] 27 E.G. 71 CA, where headlessees failed to assign their headlease to their sub-lessees but, in breach of contract, surrendered it to the freeholder thereby making the sub-lessees the direct tenants of the freeholder, their loss was the value of the headlease over the value of their sub-lease which had more frequent rent review clauses, more restrictive user provisions and no option to renew. It is not clear precisely how this was to be worked out, the Court of Appeal simply saying that the trial judge had got it wrong and ordering a retrial.

lease of the same premises from a third party at a higher rent in *Hollington Bros v Rhodes*,[10] it was said obiter that the claimant would be entitled to the difference between the contractual rent and the amount he was paying the third party.

### (2) CONSEQUENTIAL LOSSES

**28-006** As to consequential losses, loss of trade profits to be derived from the use of the premises and like losses ought to be recoverable on general principles provided they are within the ordinary rules of remoteness as to the contemplation of the parties. This derives support from the decision in *Wall v City of London Real Property Co.*[11] By reason of the lessor's inability to give title to the premises which were intended to constitute an entrance to a hotel run by the claimant lessee, the claimant was unable to obtain entrance to a luncheon bar which he had erected so that he lost money expended on it and profits to be made from it. Damages were awarded to cover the net loss, the lessee being held entitled to the amount which represented the difference between the state of things as they were and as they would have been had the contract been carried out.[12]

## *(B) DELAY IN COMPLETION*

**28-007** If the lessor delays in executing the lease, in circumstances which allow the lessee to regard the breach as discharging the contract and justifying him in refusing the property, then, since he will not have the property transferred to him, the situation is the same as with a failure to complete as far as the measure of damages is concerned. More often he will have the property transferred to him late, either because the delay does not discharge the contract or he elects not to treat it as a discharge or because he forces the lessor's hand by successfully suing for a decree of specific performance. In such a situation the damages are properly regarded as damages for delay.[13]

### (1) NORMAL MEASURE

**28-008** The normal measure of damages is the value of the user of the land, which will generally be taken as its rental value, for the period between the contractual date set for execution of the lease and the date of actual execution. There are no direct authorities.[14]

### (2) CONSEQUENTIAL LOSSES

---

10 [1951] 2 All E.R. 578n.

11 (1874) L.R. 9 Q.B. 249. See, too, *Ward v Smith* (1822) 11 Price 19, but the case is of little value as the argument was practically all on other points and it was decided before *Hadley v Baxendale* had settled the rules as to remoteness of damage in contract. Compare to *Jaques v Millar* (1877) 6 Ch. D. 153 at para.28-009, below.

12 The claimant could not recover both the expenses rendered futile and the loss of anticipated profits: see para.4-024, above.

13 The restrictive rule in *Bain v Fothergill* (1874) L.R. 7 H.L. 158 applied to delay in completion as well as to failure to complete. While delay gave little scope for its operation, the rule may now be ignored here, as it has been abolished by statute: see para.27-005, above.

14 See *Royal Bristol Permanent Building Society v Bomash* (1887) 35 Ch. D. 390 at para.27-012, above, which provides the nearest analogy.

As to consequential losses, loss of trade profits by use of the property and the like are recoverable if they were contemplated by the defendant within the ordinary rules of remoteness. In *Jaques v Millar*,[15] the lessor, who knew that the lessee was taking the premises to carry on a trade on them, wilfully refused to perform the contract and the lessee successfully sued for a decree of specific performance. He also claimed damages and Fry J considered that he was entitled to recover **28-009**

> "the value of the possession of the premises to the plaintiff for the period between [the date of the contract] and the time which he actually obtained possession of other premises".[16]

Although he would not explain in detail the motives operating on his mind,[17] this value would appear to have been based upon the loss of profits to the claimant in his trade.[18] Loss of trade profits, however, will not be recoverable where such loss was at the time of the contract being made not within the contemplation of the parties.

### (C) BREACH OF COVENANTS

Once the lease has been executed there can be no suit for the contract's specific performance and it will generally be too late for rescission. The lessee is thus confined to an action for damages should his possession be interfered with in some way. He will also be entitled to damages should the lessor break any other covenant into which he has entered, particularly those connected with the future condition of the premises,[19] and, with the important covenant to repair, may even be able to obtain specific performance.[20] The restrictive rule in *Bain v Fothergill*,[21] which applied to leases as much as to sales, had never applied once the lease was executed,[22] so that its abolition[23] is of no concern in the context of breach of covenants in the lease. **28-010**

Apart from specific covenants, breach of the overarching obligation of the lessor not to derogate from his grant may give rise to the issue of damages. In *Platt v London Underground*,[24] loss of profits resulting from the derogation from grant were awarded; the issue in the case was whether there had been mitigation of the loss of profits.[25] The loss of a right to park on land retained by the lessor was **28-011**

---

15 (1877) 6 Ch. D. 153 (overruled on another point in *Marshall v Berridge* (1881) 19 Ch. D. 233 CA).

16 *Jaques v Millar* (1877) 6 Ch. D. 153 at 159–160.

17 (1877) 6 Ch. D. 153 at 160.

18 See *Wall v City of London Real Property Co* (1874) L.R. 9 Q.B. 249 at para.28-006, above.

19 Which may allow damages for non-pecuniary loss by way of loss of amenity, as in *Newman v Framewood Manor Management Co Ltd* [2012] EWCA Civ 159 CA where the Court of Appeal made a modest award against the lessor of a flat in breach of covenant in the provision of the leisure facilities of swimming pool, jacuzzi and gym: at [42] and following. Covenants in respect of the future condition of the premises do not tend to appear in the case of a breach by a seller of land since sale is an out and out transfer.

20 *Jeune v Queens Cross Properties* [1974] Ch. 97. Contrast the position of the lessor at para.28-041, below.

21 (1874) L.R. 7 H.L. 158.

22 See para.27-014, above.

23 For the rule and its abolition see the footnotes to para.27-005, above.

24 [2001] 2 E.G.L.R. 121.

25 See the case at para.9-153, above.

regarded as a derogation from grant in *Saeed v Plustrade Ltd*,[26] and led to an award based upon rental value of the parking lot but discounted by 10 per cent in recognition of the possibility that the lessee, in competition with other tenants, might not always find the parking lot available. And there may be other varieties of breach. Thus in *U.Y.B. Ltd v British Railways Board*,[27] water had penetrated from the lessor's contiguous property making it impossible for the lessees to use the premises for their projected business. The Court of Appeal endorsed the trial judge's award of lost profits, though only for a limited period as the claimants did not seek alternative accommodation to carry on their business,[28] together with his award of the value of the business as at the time that the carrying on of the business became impossible.[29]

### 1. Covenant for Quiet Enjoyment and Covenant Against Incumbrances

**28-012** The covenant for quiet enjoyment, and the covenant against incumbrances which may be regarded as part of it or a continuation of it, operate equally in leases as in sales of land, again operating prospectively. But a covenant for good title does not generally make its appearance and therefore breaches of the other two covenants, which occur only where there has been some interference with the lessee's enjoyment of the premises, are all that require consideration.

**28-013** If, after execution of the lease, the lessee is compelled to give up possession to the real owner, or never enters into possession by reason of a third party being the real owner, the measure of damages follows general principles and allows, and has always allowed, the lessee compensation for the loss of his bargain. The now abolished rule in *Bain v Fothergill*[30] had never applied after completion.

**28-014** Where the disturbance is by the landlord himself, there was a time when damages for mental distress might be allowed to a harassed and evicted tenant. The suggestion that such damages could be awarded came first from Lord Denning MR in *McCall v Abelesz*[31]; an application of it is found in *Sampson v Floyd*.[32] With the retreat from a wide-ranging recovery for mental distress in contract,[33] however, the Court of Appeal held in *Branchett v Beaney*,[34] which was a case of disturbance without loss of possession,[35] that breach of the covenant of quiet enjoyment did not

---

26 [2002] 2 E.G.L.R. 19 CA.

27 (2001) 81 P. & C.R. DG19 CA.

28 Which was regarded as a failure to mitigate. The claim was also brought in tort, probably nuisance. It would seem that the Court of Appeal also endorsed the trial judge's award of the value of the business as at the time the carrying on of the business became impossible. Decided in a different field, *MMP GmbH v Antal International Network Ltd* [2011] EWHC 1120 (Comm), relying on the trial judge's award in *U.Y.B. v British Railways Board*, indicates that a claim for the value of a business runs only where the business has ceased or been abandoned. If it is continuing, the claim must be for lost future business profits.

29 Compare to *MMP GmbH v Antal International Network Ltd* [2011] EWHC 1120 (Comm), at para.4-018, above, which indicates that where a business continues after the breach of contract, the claim must be for loss of profits and not for the value of the business as diminished by the breach.

30 (1874) L.R. 7 H.L. 158; for which see para.27-005, above.

31 [1976] Q.B. 585 CA.

32 [1989] 2 E.G.L.R. 49 CA.

33 See paras 5-026 and 5-027, above.

34 [1992] 3 All E.R. 910 CA.

35 Facts at para.5-027, above.

permit the award of damages for mental distress; *Sampson v Floyd*,[36] was departed from. "Enjoyment" referred to the exercise, use and benefit of the right and not to the derivation of pleasure.[37] Of course in cases of eviction the tenant may be able to have recourse to an action in tort, where he can recover without difficulty for non-pecuniary loss, and there is also a statutory action which is very generous in its awards; these are dealt with in due course.[38]

### (1) Total eviction

28-015 The normal measure of damages where the lessee is evicted from the whole property, or fails ever to get possession of it at all,[39] is the value of the unexpired term, which will be calculated as the rental value of the premises less the contractual rent which would have fallen to be paid in the future. The early direct authority for this proposition is the decision in *Williams v Burrell*,[40] where the claimant was ejected by the rightful owner and recovered, inter alia, the value of the term lost; Lord Tindal CJ, who delivered the court's judgment, said that it was too clear to require discussion.[41] This decision was approved in *Lock v Furze*,[42] and continues to find application today. Thus where the lessor had entered in *J.S. Bloor (Measham) Ltd v Calcott*,[43] the lessee was held entitled to the rental value of the land leased up to the expiry of the lease.[44] And the Court of Appeal in *Jaura v Ahmed*,[45] recognising that the normal measure of damages for wrongful eviction is the value of the unexpired term calculated by rental value less contractual rent,[46] allowed recovery for the loss of anticipated profit rental from sub-lettings but not, as duplication, for the capital value of the lease. Furthermore, principle dictates that the value of the unexpired term should be taken at the time of eviction, which is the moment of breach, and not at the time of contract, so that any increase in the value of the land due to ordinary market changes or to improvements made thereon by the lessee will fall within the assessment figure. There are no cases on total eviction of a lessee dealing with this, but the authorities on the analogous situations of partial eviction of a lessee,[47] of buying in the superior title by the lessee,[48] and of total eviction of a purchaser of land,[49] all point to this result.[50]

---

36 [1989] 2 E.G.L.R. 49 CA.

37 In *Grange v Quinn* [2013] EWCA Civ 24 CA (at para.28-017, below) the recorder's award based on mental distress was annulled by the Court of Appeal: see Gloster J at [123] and [129].

38 See paras 39-044 and following, below; the statutory remedy has generated awards in excess of pecuniary loss rather than provided for non-pecuniary loss. Nor have damages for non-pecuniary loss by way of physical discomfort and inconvenience appeared in claims for breach of the covenant for quiet enjoyment in the way that they have in claims for breach of the covenant to repair: see the latter at para.28-031, below.

39 It is generally accepted that if a third party is in possession at the time of execution of the lease, the lessee can be said to have been "evicted" although never in possession.

40 (1845) 1 C.B. 402.

41 (1845) 1 C.B. 402 at 433.

42 (1866) L.R. 1 C.P. 441. Early sale of land cases provide analogous authority: see *Jenkins v Jones* (1882) 9 Q.B.D. 128 CA and *Bunny v Hopkinson* (1859) 27 Beav. 565 at para.27-019, above.

43 [2002] 1 E.G.L.R. 1.

44 There was also a claim in trespass: see para.39-049, below (in a footnote).

45 [2002] EWCA Civ 210 CA; facts at para.19-114, above.

46 [2002] EWCA Civ 210 CA at [9].

47 *Rolph v Crouch* (1867) L.R. 3 Ex. 44; see para.28-018, below.

48 *Lock v Furze* (1866) L.R. 1 C.P. 441; see para.28-021, below.

49 *Bunny v Hopkinson* (1859) 27 Beav. 565; see para.27-020, above.

28-016 Consequential losses, if not too remote, are also recoverable. Thus in *Grosvenor Hotel Co v Hamilton*,[51] where the lessee was obliged to leave the premises and remove his business elsewhere, not by reason of eviction but because of the vibration of the lessor's machines on the adjoining property,[52] the expenses of setting up in other premises were included in the damages awarded. Lindley LJ said:

> "If the term were of value the defendant could recover its value by way of damages; but to say that the damages are confined to the value of the term is erroneous in point of law. The damages are whatever loss results to the injured party as a natural consequence of the wrongful act of the defendant. The expense of setting up in a new place is such a natural consequence."[53]

In *Jaura v Ahmed*,[54] it was the expenditure on fixtures and fittings, which remained on the premises and were thus lost to the lessee on account of the eviction, for which recovery was allowed. Also, in appropriate circumstances a lessee might recover loss of profits in a business which the lessor knew he was to carry on upon the premises.[55]

28-017 In lieu of claiming damages which put him into the position as if the lease had run its course without his being evicted, that is for his expectation interest, a lessee who is wrongly evicted can claim the alternative measure based on expenditure rendered futile by the breach, generally referred to as wasted expenditure, though not if it is shown that he has made a bad bargain. In modern times this measure has made an appearance twice in the Court of Appeal, in *Grange v Quinn*,[56] expressly and in *Sampson v Floyd*,[57] on a proper analysis of the case,[58] allowing recovery to the lessee of the purchase price for the lease together with any incidental expenses less, unless de minimis, the benefit received from the lease before the wrongful eviction. These two cases have already been analysed when considering generally this alternative way of going about claiming damages for breach of contract.[59]

## (2) Partial eviction

28-018 If eviction[60] is from part only of the land, whether in space or in time, the same measure applies mutatis mutandis. In *Rolph v Crouch*,[61] the eviction was from a strip of the total land, on which strip the lessee had built a conservatory for use in

---

50 With the exception of dicta in the very old *Lewis v Campbell* (1819) 8 Taunt. 715 as to improvements: see footnote at the end of para.27-020, above.

51 [1894] 2 Q.B. 836 CA.

52 This amounts to the same thing for the purpose of the measure of damages. Nor was the covenant broken the covenant for quiet enjoyment but the covenant that the lessor should not derogate from his grant; again the measure of damages is not affected in this regard.

53 [1894] 2 Q.B. 836 CA at 840.

54 [2002] EWCA Civ 210 CA; facts at para.19-114, above.

55 See the close analogy of *Rolph v Crouch* (1867) L.R. 3 Ex. 44 at para.28-018, below and also *Jaques v Millar* (1877) 6 Ch. D. 153 at para.28-009, above. See, too, the much more modern loss of profit cases where there is disturbance without eviction, at para.28-020, below.

56 [2013] EWCA Civ 24 CA.

57 [1989] 2 E.G.L.R. 49, CA.

58 This is well explained by Gloster LJ in *Grange v Quinn* at [95]–[97].

59 See paras 4-037 to 4-038, above.

60 See the first footnote in para.28-015, above.

61 (1867) L.R. 3 Ex. 44.

his trade of florist. Damages were held recoverable in respect of[62] the loss of the value of the strip of land, the expense of building the conservatory—which may alternatively be regarded as representing the improvement in the value of the premises—and also loss of profit or, as it was put,[63] what the strip of land might reasonably have been expected to be worth to the claimant.

### (3) Disturbance by the exercise of incumbrances

Where there is no eviction, total or partial, but the lessee's enjoyment of the premises is disturbed without loss of possession to him, as where a right of way or other incumbrance is exercised rightfully by a third party, the measure of damages is more difficult to assess. A covenant for quiet enjoyment is a continuing covenant upon which damages may be recovered from time to time as they accrue, so that a claimant cannot sue for future unascertained damage. In *Child v Stenning*,[64] where the breach of covenant consisted in the fact that other persons had established a right of way over the demised premises, it was held that the measure of damages was not the permanent injury to the land but only the damage sustained up to the commencement of the action,[65] and, since no such damage had been proved nominal damages were awarded. Jessel MR said: **28-019**

> "It has been held that where there has been eviction, so that you can never have another action under the covenant for quiet enjoyment, but are evicted for ever, there, of course, the damages must be assessed once for all. But where there has been no eviction the damages are only the damages actually sustained; because you cannot tell what may happen in the future, or how far persons who have a right to interfere and disturb the quiet enjoyment may choose to avail themselves of that right or whether they will interfere at all."[66]

In an equivalent case of sale of land, *Sutton v Baillie*,[67] it has been held on the other hand that the damages are the difference between the value of the land free and its value fettered. The difference here would seem to lie in the fact that on sale there is in addition to the covenant for quiet enjoyment the covenant for good right to convey. This view is supported by further remarks of Jessel MR in *Child v Stenning*,[68] when he said:

> "The evidence ... as to the diminished value of the land as building land ... would be available, no doubt, if the action had been on a covenant for title, that is, a covenant that the vendor was seised, or that the lessor had a good right to convey, but which is not admissible in an action merely for breach of the covenant for quiet enjoyment."[69]

Claims for loss of profits on account of interference with the lessee's quiet enjoyment made an appearance in the 1990s. In *Mira v Aylmer Square Investments*,[70] tenants holding long leases in blocks of flats were subjected to serious interference by **28-020**

62 Inter alia: the other items are dealt with at paras 28-022 and 28-023, below.
63 (1867) L.R. 3 Ex. 44 at 49.
64 (1879) 11 Ch. D. 82 CA.
65 Later, by what became RSC Ord.37 r.6, down to the assessment of damages. But there is no equivalent provision in the CPR; for the effect of this see para.11-027, above.
66 (1879) 11 Ch. D. 82 CA at 85.
67 (1892) 65 L.T. 528; see para.27-023, above.
68 (1879) 11 Ch. D. 82 CA.
69 (1879) 11 Ch. D. 82 CA at 86.
70 [1990] 1 E.G.L.R. 45 CA.

the landlord's construction of penthouses on the roofs of the flats and in their action for breach of the covenant of quiet enjoyment they successfully claimed for the loss of profits that they would have made on sub-lettings; although the landlords had no knowledge of sub-lettings, recovery was held to fall within the first rule in *Hadley v Baxendale*.[71] In *Lawson v Hartley-Brown*,[72] where retail premises were leased to the claimants, it was accepted that a claim for their loss of profits lay; it failed only on account of not being properly pleaded and proved. In *Connaught Restaurants v Indoor Leisure*,[73] on the other hand, where the lessees had taken the premises to run the business of a private snooker club, a claim for loss of profits succeeded.[74]

## (4) Payments, compromises, damages and costs

28-021 Where the lessee is threatened with eviction or disturbance by the third party, he may get rid of the outstanding interest by paying for it, whether by buying in a superior title, by securing the release of a servitude, or by paying off an incumbrance which is not a servitude but only a money charge, and whether by voluntary compromise or by a court judgment against him. The sum so paid he can then recover as damages from his lessor less any amount he will be saved from paying him under the lease.[75] *Lock v Furze*,[76] illustrates this proposition. The claimant was in possession under a lease expiring in 1864. In 1860, in consideration of a £400 premium, the claimant obtained a further lease of 21 years from his lessor commencing from the end of the former term. In 1863 on the lessor's death it was discovered that as life tenant he had only had the power to grant leases in possession, so that the new lease was void. The claimant therefore obtained from the reversioners a fresh lease for seven years at a considerable increase of rent, presumably because the market value had risen in the interim, and sued his lessor's executors for damages on the covenant for quiet enjoyment in the void lease. It was held that the measure of damages included the value of what the claimant had lost by the breach, i.e. the difference between the value of the void lease and the value of the lease from the reversioners.[77] On the other hand, where in the basically similar circumstances of *Jones v Hawkins*,[78] the lessee negotiated a new lease from the reversioners at a lower rent than that of the lease of which the defendant lessor was in breach, only nominal damages were recovered as the lessee had suffered no loss.

28-022 Further, if the lessee has to pay damages to the person with the superior title and is nonetheless evicted by him, he may recover the amount paid as damages from his lessor in addition to the value of the unexpired term lost, as in *Williams v Burrell*,[79] and in *Rolph v Crouch*.[80]

---

71 (1854) 9 Ex. 341.

72 (1995) 71 P. & C.R. 242 CA.

73 [1992] 2 E.G.L.R. 252.

74 The interference with an easement granted to lessees by their lessor took the trial judge to restitutionary damages in *Kettel v Bloomfold Ltd* [2012] EWHC 1422 Ch. See the case at para.14-047, above.

75 See the sale of land cases at para.27-024, above.

76 (1866) L.R. 1 C.P. 441.

77 Also included in the damages were the £400 premium and the costs of the void lease, but to award the loss of the bargain and at the same time the expenses that the claimant would have had to incur in order to get it, is wrong. See para.4-024, above.

78 (1886) 3 T.L.R. 59.

79 (1845) 1 C.B. 402.

Lastly, the lessee may recover court costs incurred in defending, unsuccessfully but reasonably, an action brought against him by the party with the superior title. This is again supported by *Williams v Burrell*,[81] and *Rolph v Crouch*.[82] Whether a defence is reasonable will depend on the facts of each particular case.[83] It was held to be so in the former case where the lessor had, "by directing a defence, admitted that there was reasonable ground for defending"[84]; and also in the latter case where the lessee gave notice of the action to the lessor who failed to make any communication with the lessee, so that he, being left to himself, acted for the best upon his own judgment, giving credence to the lessor's warranty of quiet enjoyment.[85] Even the costs incurred by the lessee in an action unsuccessfully brought by him against the third party may be recoverable as in *Child v Stenning*.[86] The action was in order to establish whether the third party had a right of way as he claimed, and the Court of Appeal said that the lessor, in insisting that no right of way existed, incited, almost requested, the lessee to sue. The costs recoverable formerly included the costs paid by the now claimant to the other party and his own costs assessed on the old solicitor and client basis[87] but a movement, thought to be misguided, is on foot to limit claimants to the new standard basis in their recovery of costs as damages.[88] Exceptionally the costs of an appeal may be allowed.[89] 28-023

## 2. COVENANT TO REPAIR

### (1) Normal measure

The extent of any repairing obligation clearly affects the estimation of the amount of damages but what is comprised in the term repair goes to liability rather than damages[90]: the distinction between repair and improvement is in each case a question of degree.[91] In *Hewitt v Rowlands*,[92] the Court of Appeal held that, in the words of Bankes LJ, with which Atkin and Scrutton LJJ agreed, the normal measure of damages is 28-024

> "the difference in value to the tenant of the premises, from the date of the notice to repair down to the date of the assessment of damages, between the premises in their present

---

80 (1867) L.R. 3 Ex. 44.

81 (1845) 1 C.B. 402.

82 (1867) L.R. 3 Ex. 44.

83 "The question in these cases is whether or not the defence is such as a prudent man might be expected to set up": per Erle J, arguendo, in *Williams v Burrell* (1845) 1 C.B. 402 at 427.

84 (1845) 1 C.B. 402 at 433–434.

85 Kelly CB was firm in his view but Channell and Pigott BB were a little dubious.

86 (1879) 11 Ch. D. 82 CA.

87 Authority on this is to be found in the sale of land cases: see para.27-026, above.

88 For a full discussion see paras 21-003 to 21-011, above.

89 Authority on this is to be found in the sale of land cases: see para.27-026, above.

90 The curious case of *Bluestorm Ltd v Portvale Holdings Ltd* [2004] H.L.R. 49 CA at 939 shows not only that the lessor will not be liable on its repairing covenant where the lessee's breach causes the lessor to be unable to effect the repairs but also that any loss thereby caused to the lessor is recoverable from the lessee.

91 *Elmcroft Developments v Tankersley-Sawyer* (1984) 15 H.L.R. 63 CA. Compare *Ravenseft Properties v Davstone Holdings* [1980] Q.B. 12 at para.28-044, below, on the equivalent covenant by a lessee where there is far more case law on the issue of damages.

92 (1924) 93 L.J.K.B. 1080 CA.

condition and their value, if the landlord on receipt of the tenant's notice had fulfilled the obligations of the covenant."[93]

This suggests that what the court had in mind was the diminution in market value engendered by the lack of repair—no specific assessment was required to be made or upheld by the court which simply sent the case back to the registrar for damages to be assessed in accordance with the court's directions—but a subsequent Court of Appeal in *Calabar Properties v Stitcher*,[94] doubted whether this could have been what the earlier court had in mind in the case before it in view of the fact that the claimant there had a tenancy which was statutory and, therefore, not marketable.[95] Stephenson LJ thought that the registrar would not have gone far wrong in *Hewitt v Rowlands*,[96] in assessing the difference in value between repaired and unrepaired premises

> "if he had equated it with what the plaintiff might have to spend on performing the landlord's covenant (assuming the landlord would not perform it himself)".[97]

In *Calabar Properties v Stitcher*,[98] where the lessee held the residue, of over 80 years, of a long lease of a high class flat and, due to the lessor's breach of repairing covenant, had had to endure dampness and damage to the flat from the penetration of water, the judge below had awarded her the cost of decorating and making good the interior of the flat,[99] coupled with an order that the lessor should carry out the necessary external work to prevent a recurrence of the damage; the Court of Appeal endorsed this award.[100]

**28-025** At the same time the court in *Calabar*,[101] held that the judge was right to refuse to award, additionally, to the lessee the amount of the diminution in value of the flat as a marketable asset, a claim that was said to have the support of *Hewitt v Rowlands*.[102] To submit that this represented part of the lessee's loss was, in Stephenson LJ's view, "to ask the court to take a wholly unreal view of the facts".[103] If, said Griffiths LJ, she

> "did not wish to sell the flat but to continue to live in it after the [lessor] had carried out the necessary structural repairs it was wholly artificial to award her damages on the basis of loss in market value, because once the [lessor] had carried out the repairs and any consequential redecoration of the interior was completed there would be no loss in market value."[104]

---

93 (1924) 93 L.J.K.B. 1080 CA at 1082. That Bankes LJ prefaced a similar formulation somewhat earlier in his judgment (at 1082) with the words "prima facie" underlines that it was the normal measure of damages that he had in mind.

94 [1984] 1 W.L.R. 287 CA.

95 [1984] 1 W.L.R. 287 CA at 295C to D and 299C.

96 (1924) 93 L.J.K.B. 1080 CA.

97 He added to this "substantial general damages for inconvenience and discomfort" but it is doubtful whether a court in 1924 would have thought of this.

98 [1984] 1 W.L.R. 287 CA.

99 See, similarly, *Bradley v Chorley Borough Council* (1985) 17 H.L.R. 305 CA.

100 But indicated, rightly, that the one-third reduction made for betterment need not, on the authorities, have been made: see [1984] 1 W.L.R. 287 CA at 291D, per Stephenson LJ and 298H, per Griffiths LJ No such reduction was made in *Bradley v Chorley Borough Council* (1985) 17 H.L.R. 305 CA.

101 [1984] 1 W.L.R. 287 CA.

102 (1924) 93 L.J.K.B. 1080 CA.

103 [1984] 1 W.L.R. 287 at 293D.

104 [1984] 1 W.L.R. 287 at 298A.

It would have been different if the failure to repair had caused the lessee to choose to sell the flat and move elsewhere; then, Griffiths LJ said, the measure of damages would indeed have been the difference in the price she received for the flat in the damaged condition and that which it would have fetched if the lessor had observed the repairing covenant.[105] This view was endorsed in *Wallace v Manchester City Council*,[106] where the Court of Appeal laid down, in the form of propositions of which there were four, certain principles and guidelines for the assessment of damages for breach of landlords' repairing covenants.[107] The fourth proposition[108] was that, if the tenant is forced by the failure to repair to sell or sublet, he may recover for the diminution of the price or of the recoverable rent occasioned by the landlord's breach of covenant.

From all this it would seem that the normal measure can be cost of repairs or diminution in value, sometimes the one and sometimes the other being the appropriate measure for the particular circumstances of the particular claimant.[109] However, *Wallace v Manchester City Council*,[110] has further shown[111] that any award of diminution in value, where the tenant remains in occupation, may simply reflect the lessee's non-pecuniary loss by way of discomfort and inconvenience. This manner of going about the damages will be examined in dealing with non-pecuniary loss.[112] **28-026**

It appears that, when diminution in value is considered the appropriate award, it is often calculated in practice by reference to the rent paid during the relevant period; thus it was taken as a percentage of the total rent in *Sturolson & Co v Mauroux*.[113] Where in *Electricity Supply Nominees v National Magazine Co*,[114] no non-pecuniary award was possible for a corporate tenant,[115] so that the damages fell to be assessed at the diminution in value to the tenant of its occupation of the premises, it was held that the rent payable was admissible evidence of such value. Alternatively, where in *City and Metropolitan Properties v Greycroft*,[116] it was envisaged that a company taking the lease of a flat might be able to claim the profit realisable upon a sale of the lease, it was held that this could be regarded as a measure of diminution in value.[117] **28-027**

---

105 See [1984] 1 W.L.R. 287 at 297H to 298A.

106 (1998) 30 H.L.R. 1111 CA.

107 (1998) 30 H.L.R. 1111 CA at 1120–1121.

108 For the third see para.28-032, below.

109 *Calabar Properties v Stitcher* [1984] 1 W.L.R. 287 CA at 296B and 297F to G. In *Hawkins v Woodhall* [2008] EWCA Civ 932 CA the cost of repairs appears to have simply been taken as marking the diminution in value: see at [48] and [49].

110 (1998) 30 H.L.R. 1111 CA.

111 As have the cases following it, viz., *Shine v English Churches Housing Group* [2004] H.L.R. 42 CA at 727 and *Niazi Services Ltd v Van der Loo* [2004] H.L.R. 34 CA at 562.

112 See para.28-032, below.

113 (1988) 20 H.L.R. 332 CA. In *Lubren v London Borough of Lambeth* (1988) 20 H.L.R. 165 CA, the award for living with ever-escalating defects over a five-year period seems to have been about half of the rent.

114 [1999] 1 E.G.L.R. 130. The breach was not of a covenant to repair but of a covenant to provide certain services, including the installation of lifts and air-conditioning; but the principles are the same.

115 As a company can only suffer financial loss: see para.5-014, above and Lord Reid at para.18-031, above.

116 [1987] 1 W.L.R. 1085.

117 Compare the normal measure in the far commoner cases of breach of a lessee's repairing covenant at paras 28-045 and following, below. Where diminution in value is awarded it is not right to make

**28-028** The period taken into account is only that up to the assessment of damages because the covenant to repair is a continuing covenant upon which damages may be recovered from time to time as they accrue and a claimant cannot sue for future unascertained damage.[118] Subsequent actions for breach of the same covenant will not be barred, but the damages recovered in the first action will be relevant in assessing those in the later action. So in *Coward v Gregory*,[119] the defendant pleaded that the lessee had in an earlier action on the covenant recovered a sum which, if he had expended it in putting the premises into repair, would have prevented the want of repair now complained of. It was held that this did not bar the second action but went in mitigation of damage.[120]

## (2) Consequential losses

**28-029** Consequential losses, not too remote, are also recoverable. Items for which recovery has been allowed are physical injury to the claimant,[121] and physical damage both to the claimant's chattels on the premises[122] and to other parts of the premises not covered by the covenant to repair.[123] In *Marshall v Rubypoint*,[124] the tenant, having suffered three burglaries made possible by the state of disrepair of the front door to the building which amounted to a breach of the landlord's repairing covenant, recovered for items stolen and consequential expenses as well as for personal injury. Another possible consequential loss is loss of profits. In *Savva and Savva v Hussein*,[125] the tenant claimed for profits of the business which he conducted on the premises. This the trial judge would have been prepared to award but for the fact that he seems not to have been satisfied by the tenant's figures for business losses and instead he awarded two months' rent by way of damages. This award was upheld in the Court of Appeal, Staughton LJ rationalising it as having been made on the basis that the tenant was carrying on sufficient business to make at least enough profit to pay his rent; there was therefore a reasonable inference that he had suffered loss to this extent.[126] In *Hawkins v Woodhall*,[127] while the Court of Appeal accepted that as a matter of law a claim lay for lost profits and for diminu-

---

a reduction in the damages on account of the fact that the property was not important to the lessee: *McCoy & Co v Clark* (1982) 13 H.L.R. 87 CA.

[118] Damage accruing between the commencement of the action and the assessment of the damages at its hearing used to be taken into account under RSC Ord.37 r.6, but it is unclear whether this is still possible in the absence of an equivalent provision in the CPR: see para.11-027, above. And contrast to the old case of *Shortridge v Lamplugh* (1702) 2 Ld. Raym. 798, especially at 802–803, where, in the converse situation of breach of the lessee's covenant to repair, the jury were permitted to consider in assessing damages the fact that the premises had become more out of repair since the commencement of the action.

[119] (1866) L.R. 2 C.P. 153.

[120] Compare to the equivalent cases on breach of the lessee's covenant to repair at para.28-074, below.

[121] *Griffin v Pillett* [1926] 1 K.B. 17; *Porter v Jones* (1943) 112 L.J.K.B. 173 CA; and see *Berryman v Hounslow London Borough Council* (1998) 30 H.L.R. 567 CA (no recovery for physical injury only because held not foreseeable). Physical injury to the claimant's family, in so far as it represents a damage to the claimant on the lines of *Jackson v Watson* [1909] 2 K.B. 193 CA (see para.4-021, above), should also be recoverable.

[122] *Hewitt v Rowlands* (1924) 93 L.J.K.B. 1080 CA (furniture).

[123] *Green v Eales* (1841) 2 Q.B. 225, especially at 238.

[124] [1997] 1 E.G.L.R. 69 CA.

[125] (1997) 73 P. & C.R. 150 CA.

[126] (1997) 73 P. & C.R. 150 CA at 155 to 156.

[127] [2008] EWCA Civ 932 CA.

tion in the value of the tenancy,[128] there was held to be no proper basis on the evidence for the trial judge to have made an award of lost profits[129] so that only an award for diminution in the value of the tenancy was appropriate.[130]

Some difficulty has been experienced with expenses incurred in taking another house while the leased premises were uninhabitable pending completion of the repairs. These were held in principle not to be recoverable in the early case of *Green v Eales*.[131] The court pointed out[132] that, although the defendant covenanted to repair, he did not covenant to find the lessee another house while repairs were going on, but went on to suggest that damages might be recovered in respect of the additional time that the lessee was obliged to be in another house on account of the defendant's delay in commencing repairs. This was interpreted by Griffiths LJ in *Calabar Properties v Stitcher*,[133] as simply pointing to the fact that the lessor would not be in breach if he set about effecting the repairs promptly but that delay could put him in breach,[134] and the Court of Appeal therefore there held that the cost of alternative accommodation constituted an appropriate head of damage where the lessee had been forced to leave her flat because the lessor's failure to repair had rendered it uninhabitable.[135] What in fact had been claimed there were the outgoings of the unrepaired flat during the period that it was vacated and the Court of Appeal upheld the judge's refusal to make an award in respect of these, pointing out that it was the cost of the alternative accommodation that was the relevant expense—the judge below had regarded the one set of expenses as comparable to the other[136]—and declining to award the lessee her expenditure on alternative accommodation only because no claim for such had been pleaded.[137] 28-030

### (3) Non-pecuniary loss

Where physical injury lets in an award by way of consequential loss,[138] such an award will cover the non-pecuniary as well as the pecuniary side of the injury. More importantly, as damages for non-pecuniary loss in contract expanded to include damages for mental distress,[139] awards came to be made for any disappointment, discomfort, loss of enjoyment and ill health which living with the lack of repair might have produced. In the 1980s such awards became quite common and were generally endorsed by the Court of Appeal. Thus the £3,000 awarded on this ground was upheld in *Calabar Properties v Stitcher*,[140] an award for inconvenience, 28-031

---

128 [2008] EWCA Civ 932 CA at [44].
129 [2008] EWCA Civ 932 CA at [53].
130 There was also held to have been a failure to mitigate. The basis of the assessment in *Earle v Sotos Charalambous* [2007] H.L.R. 8 CA at 93 is not clear. The damages are said to have taken account of rental value and it may be that the lessee was claiming for his inability to sublet by reason of the disrepair from the time he had been apprised of it by the lessor.
131 (1842) 2 Q.B. 225.
132 (1842) 2 Q.B. 225 at 238.
133 [1984] 1 W.L.R. 287 CA.
134 [1984] 1 W.L.R. 287 CA at 298C–F.
135 [1984] 1 W.L.R. 287 CA at 291H and 298B.
136 [1984] 1 W.L.R. 287 CA at 291G–H, per Stephenson LJ.
137 See para.51-022, below, on the pleading point. Compare and contrast with *Calabar* the complex case of *Bella Casa Ltd v Vinestone Ltd* [2006] B.L.R. 72 at para.31-019, below.
138 See para.28-029, above.
139 See para.5-026, above.
140 [1984] 1 W.L.R. 287 CA. Also the £2,000 in *Elmcroft Developments v Tankersley-Sawyer* (1984)

discomfort and injury to health was endorsed on appeal in *Sturolson & Co v Mauroux*,[141] and, though regarding an award of £5,460 for three-and-a-half years of inconvenience and distress as on the high side, the Court of Appeal nevertheless upheld it in *Chiodi v de Marney*.[142] Nor has the subsequent confinement of mental distress damages[143] affected this category of case seriously or at all because everything can be put down to discomfort and inconvenience. Indeed in *Watts v Morrow*,[144] the leading Court of Appeal authority on the restrictions placed on mental distress damages,[145] Bingham LJ expressed the view that someone having to put up with repairs all around him was entitled to damages

> "for physical inconvenience and discomfort caused by the breach and mental suffering directly related to that inconvenience and discomfort".[146]

Thus in *Wallace v Manchester City Council*,[147] the trial judge awarded £3,500 which worked out at approximately £1,000 for each year of the non-pecuniary loss there. Such an annual figure was said by the claimant's counsel, without being specifically accepted by the Court of Appeal, to be at the bottom of the then unofficial tariff for discomfort and inconvenience which, after allowing for revaluation of the amounts awarded so as to arrive at current values, an extensive review of the cited cases—being those appearing in the text above—indicated. The £2,750 figure which was there said to be at the top of the tariff would appear to be derived from *Brent London Borough Council v Carmel*,[148] where the Court of Appeal refused to interfere with an award of over £50,000 which was said, rather vaguely and unhelpfully, to include general damages, special damages and interest.

**28-032** In *Wallace v Manchester City Council*,[149] the proper application of the third of the Court of Appeal's guiding propositions on damages[150] was in issue, that proposition being that for periods when the tenant remained in occupation despite the breach of the repairing obligation the loss requiring compensation was the loss of comfort and convenience resulting from living with the lack of repair. Three methods of assessment of the sum required to compensate the tenant for this loss were set out by Morritt LJ[151] in the only reasoned judgment. It could be arrived at not only by making what was called a global award for discomfort and inconvenience—and in *Wallace* itself the trial judge had sensibly taken this approach[152]—but also by making a notional reduction of the rent, or indeed by a mixture of these two methods. There was no need to assess the damages separately under the heads

15 H.L.R. 63 CA; see at 77 and following. That the lessee had a comfortable time in hospital is no ground for awarding less for illness: *McCoy & Co v Clark* (1982) 13 H.L.R. 87 CA.

141 (1988) 20 H.L.R. 332 CA. Other illustrations are *Minchburn v Peck* (1988) 20 H.L.R. 392 CA and *Shine v English Churches Housing Group* [2004] H.L.R. 42 CA at 727 in which also failure to mitigate reduced the non-pecuniary award: see the two cases on this at para.9-050, above.

142 (1989) 21 H.L.R. 6 CA; see at 10. This amount was based on £30 a week; yet the rent was only £8 a week. There was also a further award of £1,500 for injury to health which was not appealed.

143 See para.5-027, above.

144 [1991] 1 W.L.R. 1421 CA.

145 See para.5-028, above.

146 [1991] 1 W.L.R. 1421 CA at 1445H.

147 (1998) 30 H.L.R. 1111 CA.

148 (1996) 28 H.L.R. 203 CA.

149 (1998) 30 H.L.R. 1111 CA.

150 These propositions are referred to at para.28-025, above.

151 (1998) 30 H.L.R. 1111 CA at 1121.

152 See para.28-031, above.

both of discomfort and of diminution in value since it was said that in this type of case these were alternative ways of expressing the same loss.[153] This approach is thought to be rather odd, but the Court of Appeal in *Shine v English Churches Housing Group*,[154] nevertheless purported to follow Morritt LJ[155] and there adopted his method of assessment based upon a notional reduction of the rent. While the court accepted that

> "there will be cases in which the level of distress or inconvenience experienced by a tenant may require an award in excess of the level of rental payable"[156]

*Shine* was not such a case and, since the trial judge had awarded an amount well beyond the rental figure, his award for discomfort and inconvenience was very substantially reduced, from £19,000 to £8,000. The court put forward an explanation of why it considered it proper to have regard to financial considerations in arriving at damages for non-financial loss by saying that it was

> "in our judgment logical that the calculation of the award of damages for stress and inconvenience should be related to the fact that the tenant is not getting proper value for the rent, which is being paid for defective premises".[157]

This approach is borne out by the further Court of Appeal decision in *Niazi Services Ltd v Van der Loo*,[158] where the method of assessment by a notional reduction of the rent payable was again used in the assessment of the damages for the non-pecuniary loss.[159] Since the breaches of covenant to repair were on a comparatively small scale, of a much less serious nature than in *Shine*, the defendants argued for a smallish sum, but because the property was a high-class flat in a very high-class neighbourhood with a high rent—£34,800 per annum as compared with the £2,600 per annum in *Shine*—the tenant was paying for and entitled to expect high-class standards, and this argument was rejected.[160]

Where the claimant is a company rather than an individual there is no requirement to award damages in the form of a sum for distress, inconvenience and disruption; a company can only suffer financial loss.[161] Thus in *Electricity Supply Nominees v National Magazine Co*,[162] no non-pecuniary award was made to the trading company tenant. The court was thus forced back upon an assessment of diminution in value.[163] **28-033**

---

[153] It had already been repeated in *Larksworth Investments v Temple House and Beach* [1999] B.L.R. 297 CA that diminution in value and general inconvenience can be regarded as in the alternative and it was also said that a mathematical approach was needed in that case even if only as a check.

[154] [2004] H.L.R. 42 CA at 727.

[155] *Wallace* was stated to be "plainly the leading case" on awards for discomfort and inconvenience in this context: see [2004] H.L.R. 42 CA at 727 at [94].

[156] [2004] H.L.R. 42 CA at 727 at [104].

[157] [2004] H.L.R. 42 CA at [105]. There was also held to have been a failure to mitigate: see the case on this at para.9-050, above.

[158] [2004] H.L.R. 34 CA at 562.

[159] [2004] H.L.R. 34 Cab at [27]–[30].

[160] [2004] H.L.R. 34 CA at [31].

[161] See para.18-031, per Lord Reid; also para.5-014, above.

[162] [1999] 1 E.G.L.R. 130. The breach was not of a covenant to repair but of a covenant to provide certain services, including the installation of lifts and air-conditioning; but the principles are the same.

[163] See the case at para.28-027, above.

## 3. COVENANT OF FITNESS FOR HABITATION

**28-034** There is at common law an implied covenant of fitness for habitation at the commencement of the tenancy in leases of furnished premises, and statute has imposed a similar covenant, but applying not only to the commencement but throughout the tenancy, in leases of dwelling-houses under a certain rent.[164] Nothing appears as to the measure of damages in such cases. All that can be said is that it is clear that damages are recoverable in respect of physical illness and injury caused by breach of the covenant,[165] and also, it seems, in respect of removing to other premises.[166]

## 4. COVENANT TO RENEW AND OPTION TO PURCHASE

**28-035** Covenants to renew leases and options to purchase in leases are but agreements to lease and agreements to sell respectively superimposed upon an existing lease between the same parties. A breach of such covenant or option is thus in effect a failure to complete a contract to lease or to sell, and therefore the damages will follow the pattern appearing in claims for such contractual breaches.[167] This is reflected in such authorities as there are.

**28-036** As to renewal, the principal case, in the absence of better, is *Gas Light and Coke Co v Towse*.[168] The covenant to renew at a specified rent was granted by a lessor who was only empowered to lease at the best rent obtainable. When the time for renewal arrived the rent specified in the covenant was far below the best rent. It was held that the covenant was good when it was made but that it could not be carried out for want of title when the time arrived. Because the restrictive rule in *Bain v Fothergill*[169] was applicable, the claimant was not entitled to claim the normal contract measure[170] but, with the rule in *Bain v Fothergill* gone,[171] the measure of damages would have been represented by the loss of the claimant's bargain, to be measured by the rental value that the premises could command at the date of breach less the contractual rent which had been specified for the renewed lease.[172] Thus in *Spedding v Nevell*,[173] not only was recovery had for the value of the term but, the lessee having made improvements contemplated by the agreement, that value was taken as enhanced thereby for the purpose of assessing the damages; there was, however, no recovery in respect of the lessee's liability arising from his sale of the lease as this was not within the contemplation of the parties.[174] In *Plummer v Tibsco*

164 Now Landlord and Tenant Act 1985 s.8.

165 See, e.g. *Summers v Salford Corp* [1943] A.C. 283.

166 See *Charsley v Jones* (1889) 53 J.P. 280, where the claimant who had moved with his family to other premises recovered damages, but the report is not clear as to what items formed the damages.

167 Failure to complete in lease of land is at paras 28-003 and following, and in sale of land at paras 27-003 and following.

168 (1887) 35 Ch. D. 519.

169 (1874) L.R. 7 H.L. 158.

170 In the particular circumstances no damages could be recovered by him.

171 See para.27-005 and para.28-001, above.

172 Contrast to *Wright v Dean* [1948] Ch. 686 on options to purchase at para.28-037, below.

173 (1869) L.R. 4 C.P. 212.

174 *Spedding* was not a claim by a lessee against his lessor for breach of a covenant to renew but a claim against the lessor's agent for breach of warranty of authority; but the principles involved are the same. For more on this case see under breach of warranty of authority at paras 36-007, 36-013 and 36-014, below.

*Ltd*,[175] the lessee had an option to renew a five-year lease which option he exercised but was left, upon the lessor's refusal to grant the lease, with a lease in equity which he then surrendered in return for a 20-year lease on different terms. Only nominal damages were awarded on the basis that the only breach of contract was the failure to provide the legal title.

As to options to purchase, the law is contained in *Wright v Dean*.[176] In that case the claimant in 1937 had taken a 21-year lease from the defendant with an option to purchase. In 1944 the defendant sold the reversion to a third party in circumstances which made the option unenforceable against the third party, and in 1947 the claimant purported to exercise the option. The restrictive rule in *Bain v Fothergill*,[177] being inapplicable in the circumstances, the claimant was entitled—and would be today with the rule in *Bain v Fothergill* gone[178]—to damages for the loss of his bargain, the normal measure for breach of contract. There being no consequential losses in the case, the normal measure represented the full recoverable sum. It was calculated at the value of the property in the market if offered for sale at the date of the purported exercise of the option, deducting the amount payable under the option, and, since the claimant would still have the 11-year residue of the lease which he would not have had as such had the option contract been performed, deducting also a sum representing the value of the remainder of the lease, namely the rent that could be obtained for the lease in the market less the contractual rent reserved by the lease. **28-037**

## II. BREACH BY LESSEE

Breaches of contract by a lessee fall into the same two categories as those by a lessor, breach by failure to accept a lease or by delay in doing so[179] and breach of the covenants in the lease once accepted. **28-038**

### (A) FAILURE TO ACCEPT

Where the lessee refuses to proceed with the contract the lessor may claim specific performance, or treat the contract as discharged, or sue for damages.[180] If he pursues his remedy in damages the normal measure is represented by the contractual rent reserved by the lease less the rental value of the premises at the time of breach. This was applied in *Marshall v Mackintosh*,[181] where the claimant had relet the premises at a lower rent, which was all they would now command, and damages were assessed on the basis of the difference between the contractual rent under the broken agreement and the new rent. Where, however, the claimant had succeeded in reletting at a higher rent than the contractual rent because of market **28-039**

---

175 [2002] 1 E.G.L.R. 29 CA.

176 [1948] Ch. 686.

177 (1874) L.R. 7 H.L. 158.

178 See para.27-005 and para.28-001, above.

179 Delay is of little importance here since delay in the acceptance of property is not likely to cause damage: it does not require separate treatment.

180 See the fuller treatment in the parallel case of sale of land at paras 27-034 and 27-035, above.

181 (1898) 78 L.T. 750. This and the following case concerned building leases; see further as to them paras 28-084 and following, below.

improvements, he was held only entitled to nominal damages in *Oldershaw v Holt*.[182]

**28-040** Beyond this there are no authorities.[183] Consequential losses will be recoverable under ordinary principles but are not very likely to arise.

### (B) BREACH OF COVENANTS

**28-041** A lessee generally enters into a large number of covenants principally in respect of the user and of the possession of the property, and it is therefore not surprising that it is here that questions relating to damages in leases have been most litigated. The principal covenant is the covenant to repair, and here damages are made the more important since an order for specific performance of a repair covenant has long been held to be unavailable to a lessor against his lessee.[184]

**28-042** A preliminary matter to deal with is the lessor's action for the rent that the lessee has contracted to pay. This is an action upon the contract itself. If the rent is, as generally, for a fixed sum, difficulty as to its calculation will hardly arise: difficulties as to the amount to be received by the lessor are prone to appear, first where the rent is claimed in an action for use and occupation because no fixed rent has been agreed, secondly, where the lessee sets up a right to an apportionment of the rent, and, thirdly, where certain deductions in respect of outgoings paid by the lessee are permitted to be made from the rent due.[185] The question of damages is in no case involved.

#### 1. COVENANT TO REPAIR

**28-043** A lessee's covenant to repair[186] may take various forms but the two main types are (1) a covenant to keep the premises in repair during the tenancy and so deliver up and (2) a covenant only to leave or put in repair at the expiration or sooner determination of the term. With regard to (1), a breach of covenant by failure to repair is a continuing breach and an action may be brought for breach of covenant at any time during the continuance of the term as well as an action at its expiration or sooner determination[187]; but with regard to (2), only an action at the expiration or sooner determination of the term will lie as there is no breach of covenant till that time.

**28-044** The extent of repair that the lessee is obliged to perform is clearly important in estimating the amount of the damages. Essentially, however, the question as to what is meant by the term repair goes to liability and obligation and only a few basic

---

182 (1840) 12 A. & E. 590. As to the correctness of this see the case dealt with in connection with mitigation and avoided loss in the footnote at the end of para.9-134, together with para.9-135, above.

183 In *Foster v Wheeler* (1888) 38 Ch. D. 130 CA at 134 Bowen LJ said that if there was a wanton refusal to accept the lease the damages might be substantial. But the wantonness cannot affect the measure in contract where exemplary damages are not yet allowed: see Ch.13, above, especially at para.13-016.

184 *Hill v Barclay* (1810) 16 Ves. Jun. 402, approved in *Jeune v Queens Cross Properties* [1974] Ch. 97. Contrast the position of the lessee at para.28-010, above.

185 For details see the standard texts on landlord and tenant.

186 Repair may include decorate: *Latimer v Carney* [2007] 1 P. & C.R.13 at 213.

187 An action brought in the term does not prevent a further action on its termination: *Henderson v Thorn* [1893] 2 Q.B. 164 and *Ebbetts v Conquest* (1900) 82 L.T. 560 are illustrations of such a second action being brought. Of course the measure of damages is affected: see para.28-074, below.

points need be made here.[188] (1) The covenant to repair embraces the renewal of a subordinate part of the whole building, such as a roof, a floor or a wall.[189] But a renewal involving the reconstruction of the entirety of the fabric is outside the covenant to repair, the antithesis being apparently between the renewal and replacement of a defective part and the renewal and replacement of substantially the whole building.[190] In *Ravenseft Properties v Davstone Holdings*,[191] it was confirmed, on a review of the earlier authorities, that the question of into which category a case fell was one of degree. (2) The expression "keep in repair" embraces to put in repair[192]; this was decided in *Payne v Haine*,[193] and, therefore, since this case a tenant cannot justify keeping premises in bad repair because they happened to be in that state when he took them. (3) Evidence of disrepair would seem to be admissible to show how far the premises were capable of being repaired at all and what amount of repair could have been contemplated by the covenant. The class of a house will vary according to its original construction and to its age. (4) It was held in *Proudfoot v Hart*,[194] that the expression "tenantable repair", which is frequently used, was properly defined as meaning

> "such repair as, having regard to the age, character and locality of the house, would make it reasonably fit for the occupation of a reasonably-minded tenant of the class who would be likely to take it".[195]

A qualification upon this definition was stated in *Anstruther-Gough-Calthorpe v McOscar*,[196] to the effect that the fact that the neighbourhood had deteriorated during a long term,[197] so that the class of persons who would take a lease of the property at the end of the term had deteriorated and their requirements by way of repairs were less, could not alter the character of the covenant or the standard of repair which it envisaged when made.[198]

### (1) General rules as to measure of damages

The measure of damages at common law for breach of the lessee's covenant to repair differed according to whether the action was brought during the term or at 28-045

[188] For details see the standard texts on landlord and tenant. *Ultraworth Ltd v General Accident Fire & Life Assurance Corp Plc* [2000] L. & T.R. 495 illustrates also the detail a court may go into in assessing disrepair.

[189] As in *Ultraworth Ltd v General Accident Fire & Life Assurance Corp Plc* [2000] L. & T.R. 495. Since renewal there might have been achieved in more than one manner, it was for the tenant to choose the method to be adopted. And the lessee's repair of the roof was held to be adequate without requiring its complete replacement, which had been effected by the lessor on the lease's termination, in *Riverside Property Investments Ltd v Blackhawk Automotive* [2005] 1 E.G.L.R. 114.

[190] *Lurcott v Wakeley* [1911] 1 K.B. 905.

[191] [1980] Q.B. 12.

[192] As presumably does the expression "leave in repair" in the second type of covenant above.

[193] (1847) 16 M. & W. 541.

[194] (1890) 25 Q.B.D. 42 CA.

[195] (1890) 25 Q.B.D. 42 CA at 55, per Lopes LJ.

[196] [1924] 1 K.B. 716 CA, following *Morgan v Hardy* (1886) 17 Q.B.D. 770, affirmed on this point at (1886) 35 W.R. 588 CA.

[197] The lease was 95 years; in *Proudfoot v Hart* it had only been three years.

[198] It would seem, however, that since the passing of s.18(1) of the Landlord and Tenant Act 1927 the damages may be affected since they are no longer necessarily the cost of the repairs but are limited to the diminution in the value of the reversion. Plainly the deterioration of the neighbourhood will affect the value of the reversion: the matter is considered at para.28-066, below.

its determination. The normal measure in the former case was the diminution in the value of the reversion; in the latter the cost of repairs[199] was the measure.[200] Both rules were worked out in the course of the 19th century and were regarded as established by the Court of Appeal in 1895 in *Ebbetts v Conquest*.[201] Rigby LJ gave a clear statement of the position thus:

> "The authorities ... clearly show that as a general rule there is a difference in the assessment of damages in an action for breach of a covenant to yield up in repair brought after the determination of the term, and in an action for breach of a covenant to keep in repair brought during the continuance of the term. In the first case, an arbitrary rule is laid down upon grounds of convenience, that whether or not the lessor in fact loses by the want of repair, he shall be paid the amount which would be necessary to place the premises in good repair. It may happen that a payment of that amount would not induce him to repair—it may be far more to his interest to let the building be pulled down; but these considerations are not taken into account, principally because they depend upon the arrangements which the lessor has made with other persons, with which the lessee has nothing at all to do, as to which in general he will have no information, and as to which at the time he enters into the bargain he can have none.[202] In the second case the rule is that on a covenant to keep in repair you are to take the effect upon the value of the reversion, treating it as though it were carried into the market for sale under such circumstances that the purchaser might do whatever he liked with the property and turn it to the best advantage."[203]

**28-046** Superimposed upon the common law position is s.18(1) of the Landlord and Tenant Act 1927. This was enacted with the intention of limiting the damages to the diminution in the value of the reversion, particularly in cases where the cost of repairs in an action at the end of the term was recoverable at common law although it was quite clear that the money would not be expended on repairs by the lessor. The full subsection runs thus:

> "Damages for a breach of a covenant or agreement to keep or put premises in repair[204] during the currency of a lease, or to leave or put premises in repair at the termination of a lease, whether such covenant or agreement is express or implied, and whether general or specific, shall in no case exceed the amount (if any) by which the value of the reversion (whether immediate or not) in the premises is diminished owing to the breach of such covenant or agreement as aforesaid; and in particular no damage shall be recovered for a breach of any such covenant or agreement to leave or put premises in repair at the termination of a lease, if it is shown that the premises, in whatever state of repair they might be, would at or shortly after the termination of the tenancy have been or be pulled down, or such structural alterations made therein as would render valueless the repairs covered by the covenant or agreement."

**28-047** The first half of s.18(1) in its terms applies equally to actions brought during the

---

199 Plus occasionally damages for loss of use during repairs.

200 This measure was unaffected by a further covenant to insure against fire for a specific sum; the defendant's liability is not limited to that sum since the covenant to insure is only intended as an additional security to the lessor: *Digby v Atkinson* (1815) 4 Camp. 276.

201 [1895] 2 Ch. 377 CA; affirmed sub nom. *Conquest v Ebbetts* [1896] A.C. 490.

202 But compare the remarks of Megarry VC in *Tito v Waddell (No.2)* [1977] Ch. 106 at 329F to–G, dealt with at para.28-055, below.

203 *Ebbetts v Conquest* [1895] 2 Ch. 377 CA at 385–386. Similarly, though more shortly, per Lopes LJ at 384.

204 Where it is a covenant to decorate which is breached, the poor decorative state of the premises may constitute a breach of the repairing covenant so that s.18(1) will apply: *Latimer v Carney* [2007] 1 P. & C.R.13 at 213; see at [58] to [61].

currency of the lease and to actions brought at its determination. Since, however, in actions brought during the currency of the lease the normal measure of damages at common law is the diminution in the value of the reversion, this is the same as the amount allowed to be recovered by the first half of s.18(1). On the other hand, it has been held in *Re King*,[205] that the second half of s.18(1) does not even in its terms apply to actions brought during the currency of the lease. "It seems to me", said Buckley J there,

> "that the distinction between the language of the first half of the subsection and the language of the second half of the subsection is so clear that it is impossible to extend the second half of the subsection by inference to make it apply to a covenant to keep or put premises in repair during the currency of the lease."[206]

However, the measure of damages in actions brought at the determination of the lease is undoubtedly affected by s.18(1), both first half and second. It might therefore be thought that, as far as such actions were concerned, the pre-1927 law should now be regarded purely as past history and omitted from a statement of the modern law. Two factors, however, require a brief treatment of the pre-1927 measure of damages. First, the modern law is only made completely clear in the light of it, and, secondly, it has been said that the Act did not change the law permitting recovery of the cost of repairs: "all that it has done is to impose a limit on the amount of those damages".[207] It is true that it has also been said that the real question is what is the injury to the reversion,[208] but this is, as will be seen, in order to circumvent the necessity of assessing two separate figures in every case, i.e. cost of repairs and injury to reversion; if a case could arise in which the cost of repairs was less than the damage to the reversion then only the cost of repairs is recoverable. Such a case may be unlikely to arise but it is important to have a strictly correct understanding of the combination of common law and statute for such an eventuality. Indeed the eventuality did arise in *Culworth Estates v Society of Licensed Victuallers*,[209] where the claimants contended that the damage to their reversion was greater than the costs of repair combined with professional fees and loss of rent during the repair period. However, since they limited their claim to these costs, in which claim they were successful, the issue of awarding the greater diminution in value of the reversion did not arise, but the Court of Appeal appeared to accept, rightly, that the claimants had the entitlement to claim this higher amount.[210] 28-048

## (2) Measure of damages in action during tenancy[211]

The normal measure of damages is the amount by which the marketable value of the reversion has been diminished. This measure, originally laid down in 1841 28-049

205 [1962] 1 W.L.R. 632; facts at para.28-054, below.

206 [1962] 1 W.L.R. 632 at 648; reversed on grounds not touching damages.

207 See Luxmoore J in *Hanson v Newman* [1934] Ch. 298 at 300–301; and see per Jenkins LJ in *Jones v Herxeimer* [1950] 2 K.B. 106 CA at 119.

208 See Denning LJ in *Smiley v Townshend* [1950] 2 K.B. 311 CA at 323.

209 (1991) 62 P. & C.R. 211 CA.

210 *Elite Investments v Bainbridge Silencers* [1986] 2 E.G.L.R. 43 is a further illustration of repair cost less than diminution in value establishing claim for cost of repair as damages.

211 See, e.g. where the tenant covenants to keep in repair or put in repair during the term.

by Coleridge J in *Doe d. Worcester School Trustees v Rowlands*,[212] was gradually accepted in the latter half of the century in preference to the measure of damages calculated by the cost of the required repairs,[213] and, since *Ebbetts v Conquest*,[214] in 1895, has been regarded[215] as established. *Crewe Services & Investment Corp v Silk*,[216] provides a contemporary decision confirming that the test at common law is the diminution in value of the reversion. The claim was by the landlord against the tenant of a protected agricultural holding who had allowed the farm premises to fall into substantial disrepair. The tenancy being protected, it was uncertain when the reversion would fall in and the court assessed the damages by taking the cost of the repairs and discounting by three-quarters.[217] The value of the reversion should be taken as at the date of assessment of damages rather than at any earlier date.[218]

**28-050** Two alternative measures which had been put forward are no longer law, at least so far as they attempt a general rule. (1) On the one hand there is the measure of nominal damages laid down by Rolfe B in *Marriott v Cotton*,[219] on the ground that if substantial damages were awarded in an action during the term the claimant might put the money in his pocket and then bring a subsequent action for non-repair in which he would again be entitled to recover substantial damages. The fallacy of this argument is that it assumes that the court in the later action cannot take into account the damages awarded in the first action: that this is a wrong assumption is

---

212 (1841) 9 C. & P. 734, 739: "The true question therefore is—to what extent is the reversion injured by the non-repair of the premises?"

213 See per Martin B in *Smith v Peat* (1853) 9 Ex. 161 at 166: "It seems to me that the criterion of damage is the loss which the landlord would sustain by the non-repair if he went into the market to sell the reversion"; per Lord Coleridge CJ in *Williams v Williams* (1874) L.R. 9 C.P. 659 at 666: "No substantial damages can be recovered under the general covenant where no damage has been done to the reversion" (applying the rule, but with perhaps a wrong result, to an action by underlessor against underlessee: see para.28-079, below); per Keating J in *Mills v East London Union* (1872) L.R. 8 C.P. 79 at 85: "I think the rule laid down in the more recent cases, viz. that the true measure of damages is the extent to which the lessor's reversion is damnified by the want of repair, is the sounder rule"; per Denman J similarly at 87; and finally per Lopes and Rigby LJJ in *Ebbetts v Conquest* [1895] 2 Ch. 377 at 384, 386 respectively, regarding the matter as settled. All these were actions during the term but none represents a clear application of the normal measure: the nearest of them is *Mills v East London Union* (1872) L.R. 8 C.P. 79.

214 [1895] 2 Ch. 377 CA; affirmed sub nom. *Conquest v Ebbetts* [1896] A.C. 490.

215 An authoritative statement of the rule is to be found in *Gooderham and Worts v Canadian Broadcasting Corp* [1947] A.C. 66 PC at 83, per Lord Macmillan: "The measure of damages is the diminution in the value of the reversion resulting from the breach, without prejudice to any further claim which the landlord may have at the termination of the tenancy."

216 [1998] 2 E.G.L.R. 1 CA.

217 For the effect of a landlord's entitlement by the lease to enter and repair see para.28-052, below. In the *Crewe Services* case where the landlord was so entitled but did not propose to exercise his right, the court said that it was unnecessary to come to a concluded view as to the possible significance of an actual intention of the landlord to enter and repair. In so saying the Court of Appeal would seem not to have been apprised of *Jervis v Harris* [1996] Ch. 195 CA (at para.28-052) where it had decided the point a year earlier.

218 Indeed this was long ago done in the old case of *Shortridge v Lamplugh* (1702) 2 Ld. Raym. 798; see especially at 802–803. The question was also raised without decision in *Gooderham and Worts v Canadian Broadcasting Corp* [1947] A.C. 66 PC; see especially at 84. Also it would seem that the value of the reversion should be taken at assessment on account of the action during the term being a continuing cause of action. Damages could therefore formerly be calculated to the date of assessment under RSC, Ord.37 r.6, and hopefully can still be despite the absence of an equivalent provision in the CPR (on this see para.11-027, above).

219 (1848) 2 C. & K. 553.

seen from the decisions in *Henderson v Thorn*,[220] and *Ebbetts v Conquest*.[221] The court is therefore not limited to nominal damages.[222] (2) At the other end of the scale there is the measure of damages based on the cost of the required repairs put forward by Lord Holt in *Vivian v Champion*.[223] The impropriety of this measure is pointed out by Coleridge J in *Doe d. Worcester School Trustees v Rowlands*,[224] where he said:

> "In estimating the damages in cases where the lease has a long time to run, it is not fair to take the amount that would be necessary to put the premises into repair as the measure of damages; for in such cases, when the damages are awarded to the landlord he is not bound to expend them on repairs, neither can he do so without the tenant's permission to enter on the premises."

So too Alderson B said in *Turner v Lamb*[225]:

> "The damage by non-repair may surely be very different if the reversion comes to the landlord in six months, or in 900 years. Lord Holt's doctrine would startle any man to whom the proposition was stated."

Subsequent dicta affirm that the court is not bound to give as damages the cost of repairs,[226] and that there is no general rule that the damages must always be the cost of repairs.[227]

It does not follow, however, because neither nominal damages nor the cost of repairs is the criterion to apply, that very small damages on the one hand or the cost of repairs on the other may not be awarded in particular cases where such represent the diminution in the value of the reversion. (1) Thus, since **28-051**

> "the loss which is occasioned to the lessor's reversion [is] a loss which will be greater or less according as the term of the tenant at the time of the breach has a less or greater time to run",[228]

the damages may be very small where the expiration of the term is very far in the future. In *Doe d. Worcester School Trustees v Rowlands*,[229] Coleridge J said that

> "if the lease had ninety-nine years to run, it could not make much difference in the value of the reversion whether the premises were now in repair or not".

However, as pointed out by Lord Herschell in *Conquest v Ebbetts*,[230] this is not necessarily true of all 99-year leases since

---

220 [1893] 2 Q.B. 164; see para.28-074, below.

221 (1900) 82 L.T. 560; see para.28-074, below.

222 See per Wright J in *Joyner v Weeks* [1891] 2 Q.B. 31 at 36. Indeed it appears that in a subsequent unreported stage of *Marriott v Cotton* itself, the ruling of nominal damages was reversed and substantial damages entered up. This is according to O'Brien J in the Irish case of *Bell v Hayden* (1859) 9 Ir. C.L.R. 301 who said he had discovered this from copies of the orders made in the case procured by him from the offices of the Queen's Bench in England.

223 (1705) 2 Ld. Raym. 1125.

224 (1841) 9 C. & P. 734 at 739.

225 (1845) 14 M. & W. 412 at 414, arguendo. So, too, Parke B at 414, also arguendo.

226 See Wright J in *Joyner v Weeks* [1891] 2 Q.B. 31 at 36.

227 See Lord Herschell in *Conquest v Ebbetts* [1896] A.C. 490 at 494.

228 See Lopes LJ in *Ebbetts v Conquest* [1895] 2 Ch. 377 at 384.

229 (1841) 9 C. & P. 734 at 739.

230 [1896] A.C. 490 at 493.

"there are circumstances in which it might be of the utmost importance to the reversioners that the buildings should be in a proper state of repair".

And in *Joyner v Weeks*[231] Wright J was of the view that it was settled that the court was not limited to nominal damages

"even where the length of the term unexpired is so great that no real damage can be proved or the accumulated proceeds of investment of a nominal sum[232] would at the end of the term provide more than a sufficient fund."

(2) Conversely, where the end of the term is very near, the diminution in the value of the reversion may well be calculated by the cost of the repairs. More particularly the cost of repairs, with a discount for immediate payment, has been allowed where the defendant was an underlessee and the claimant an underlessor liable over for repairing to the head lessor. This amount was awarded in the important case of *Conquest v Ebbetts*.[233] Lord Herschell there said:

"If the premises were now in good repair, the reversion of the respondents [i.e. the underlessors] would secure them the improved rent of £100 a year, to the end of the term, without any liability on their part, unless it were to the extent to which repairs subsequently became necessary. As matters stand they can only receive this rent subject to the liability of restoring the premises to good repair, so that they may in that condition redeliver them to their lessor. The difference between these two positions represents the diminution in the value of their reversion owing to the breach of covenant, and on this basis the damages seem to me to have been properly assessed."[234]

**28-052** A question which has long lain open is whether a lessor can recover the cost of repairs where he has himself entered the premises and executed them during the term under a right reserved by him in the lease. Wright J in *Joyner v Weeks*,[235] was of the view that he could and, a century later, his view appears to be confirmed by the Court of Appeal in *Jervis v Harris*,[236] though there the recovery was held to be by way of debt rather than damages. In a term of 999 years it was provided that, in default of the tenant remedying the situation within three months of being given notice of want of repair, the landlord could do the repairs himself and recover the cost from the tenant. The landlord was held entitled to claim the amount he had expended as a debt. The court further said that this was not a case of a penalty because the contract provided for the payment of a sum of money on the happening of a specified event, namely, repair by the landlord, other than a breach of a contractual duty owed by the party liable, namely, failure to repair by the tenant. This was hardly consistent with much earlier but now obsolete developments in the

231 [1891] 2 Q.B. 31 at 36.

232 He probably meant £2 or the like.

233 [1896] A.C. 490.

234 [1896] A.C. 490 at 494. Earlier, in another case of underlessor versus underlessee, *Davies v Underwood* (1857) 2 H. & N. 570, Bramwell B had said that the damage to the reversion, though one very good test, was not an exclusive test, and Watson B had taken a similar view: at 574. But this must be read now in the light of *Conquest v Ebbetts* [1896] A.C. 490; also, since the head landlord had ejected both his lessee and the underlessee, the action was rather one brought at the expiration of the term than during it. The whole question of underleases is dealt with at paras 28-076 to 28-083, below.

235 [1891] 2 Q.B. 31 at 35.

236 [1996] Ch. 195 CA.

hire-purchase field.[237] What goes for hire-purchase contracts should go for leases and it is thought that there are better reasons for not regarding the cost of repair as a penalty. While the cost of repair clearly cannot be said to represent the diminution in the value of the reversion on a 999-year lease, repairing is what the tenant has agreed to do so that the cost of the repairs could be regarded as the equivalent in money of a decree of specific performance. That the court was clearly eager to decide the way it did is seen from the comment that the court was being asked for the first time to strike down a standard clause familiar to property lawyers for generations which had been enforced on countless occasions.[238] Of course if it is known that the landlord, entitled under the terms of the lease to enter and carry out repairs, does not propose to exercise this right, the normal measure of diminution in value will be applied, as in *Crewe Services & Investment Corp v Silk*.[239]

Little has been decided on how the diminution in the value of the reversion should be worked out in figures.[240] All that can be said is that in the ordinary case of the freeholder claimant who will be in a position to deal with the reversion as he likes and give similar rights to a purchaser, the measure of damages will be the value of the reversion repaired less its value unrepaired.[241] The fact therefore that the best or most likely use for the property will involve pulling down the buildings or altering their structure so that the repairs would not be executed even at the end of the term will be a matter which will enter into the calculation of the diminution in the reversion's value. And when the claimant is himself a lessee, i.e. under a superior lease, the application of the general rule requires the special circumstances to be kept in mind, circumstances that give to the claimant's reversion a special value to him.[242] **28-053**

The general statutory limitation on the measure of damages introduced by the first half of s.18(1) of the Landlord and Tenant Act 1927[243] should not have any practical effect upon the damages here since the measure of the limitation and the common law measure are one and the same, namely the diminution in the reversion's value. Even where the cost of repairs has been allowed in these cases, as in *Conquest v Ebbetts*,[244] this will still be so, since the cost of repairs has only been taken in the particular circumstances as marking the amount by which the reversion's value has been diminished for the claimant. As for the particular limitation introduced by the second half of s.18(1)[245]—which enumerates specific instances in which no damages should be recovered—this has been held to have no application to actions brought during the currency of the lease in *Re King*.[246] In that case the lessee of a long lease covenanted to keep in repair a factory built on the **28-054**

---

237 For these see paras 16-066 and following, but see now para.16-014.

238 [1996] 1 E.G.L.R. 78 CA at 81 col.2.

239 [1998] 2 E.G.L.R. 1 CA. See the case at para.28-049, above.

240 See, at para.28-049, above, *Crewe Services & Investment Corp v Silk* [1998] 2 E.G.L.R. 1 CA where, the time when the reversion would fall in being uncertain, cost of repairs discounted by three-quarters was taken for the diminution in value.

241 "Treating it as though it were carried into the market for sale under such circumstances that the purchaser might do whatever he liked with the property and turn it to the best advantage": *Ebbetts v Conquest* [1895] 2 Ch. 377 CA at 386, per Rigby LJ.

242 See *Conquest v Ebbetts* [1896] A.C. 490 at para.28-051, above. Underleases are dealt with at paras 28-076 to 28-083, below.

243 Quoted at para.26-046, above.

244 [1896] A.C. 490: see para.28-051, above.

245 Quoted at para.28-046, above.

246 See para.28-047, above.

demised property. In 1944 the factory was burnt down and was not reinstated by the lessee. In 1953 the lessor started an action for damages for breach of the covenant to keep the factory in repair during the currency of the lease. Later that year the property was acquired under a compulsory purchase order by the London County Council who entered into possession in 1957, pulled down the ruin of the factory, and redeveloped the property. Subsequently, in 1960, the Lands Tribunal fixed the price to be paid by the London County Council to the lessee for his leasehold interest and to the lessor for his freehold reversion. In the lessor's action for damages, Buckley J awarded the diminution in the value of the reversion by reason of the non-repair, this being represented by the difference, if any, between the price

> "a willing purchaser might have been expected to have given for his interest in this property in the open market, with all the rights incident to it, including any right of action against the tenant for failure to keep the property in repair"

and the price

> "a willing purchaser might have been expected to have given for the same interest if the covenant to repair had been fully performed by the tenant".[247]

The date for assessment was to be the last day on which the reversion belonged to the claimant, namely the day before that on which he agreed with the London County Council the price they should pay him for his interest in the property. The second half of s.18(1) did not apply, so there was no question of no damages being recovered on the ground that the factory had been pulled down.

### (3) Measure of damages in action at determination of tenancy[248]

28-055 **(a) At common law: pre-1927** Where the action is commenced after the expiration or earlier determination of the term the damages at common law are such a sum as will put the premises into the state of repair in which the tenant was bound to leave them. The first clear judicial holding that this was the proper measure is that of Denman J in *Morgan v Hardy*,[249] followed by the Court of Appeal in the leading case of *Joyner v Weeks*.[250] In this latter case the choice between the two measures of cost of repairs and diminution in the reversion's value was directly before the court, and it was decided that the former represented the true measure: whether or not it exceeded the latter was a question that need not be explored.[251] Lord Esher MR said that to award the cost of repairs was such an inveterate practice as to amount to a rule of law,[252] while Fry LJ regarded such a rule as one of great practical convenience since it was far simpler than the alternative one and he had

---

247 [1962] 1 W.L.R. 632 at 649. The decision was reversed on grounds not touching the issue of damages: [1963] Ch. 459 CA.

248 See, e.g. whether under a covenant to keep or put in repair during the term and so deliver up, or under a covenant only to leave or put in repair at the term's determination.

249 (1886) 17 Q.B.D. 770; reversed on another point: see (1886) 18 Q.B.D. 646 CA, and sub nom. *Hardy v Fothergill* (1888) 13 App. Cas. 351.

250 [1891] 2 Q.B. 31 CA. Earlier dicta to the same effect appear in *Woodhouse v Walker* (1880) 5 Q.B.D. 404 at 408 and in *Whitham v Kershaw* (1885) 16 Q.B.D. 613 CA at 616–617, but both concerned the analogous action of waste, and indeed the former was not a contract case but tort.

251 Thereby reversing the Divisional Court.

252 *Joyner v Weeks* [1891] 2 Q.B. 31 CA at 43.

no hesitation in endorsing it.[253] Megarry VC in *Tito v Waddell (No.2)*[254] questioned whether this case did indeed lay down that cost of repairs was the invariable rule of damages,[255] but that this was the universal interpretation is clear from the decisions dealt with below[256] and from the intervention of statute, otherwise uncalled for, in the form of s.18(1) of the Landlord and Tenant Act 1927.[257]

The cost of repairs is the short way of expressing the normal measure; more precisely it should be expressed, as by Wright J in *Joyner v Weeks*,[258] as the cost of repairs with some allowance for loss of rent or occupation during repair and with some deduction, where proper, by reason of substitution of new for old. There is some authority for both limbs of this proposition. Thus in *Woods v Pope*,[259] and again in *Birch v Clifford*[260] damages were allowed for the loss of the use of the premises during repair[261]; and in *Yates v Dunster*,[262] a deduction was made from the cost of repairs of the amount by which the premises would, after repair, be more valuable than they had been before they fell into disrepair.[263] **28-056**

The cost of repairs would in the normal case properly represent the extent to which the lessor has been injured by the breach. But where the circumstances were such that the loss to the lessor was less by reason of the fact that the repairs were not to be done at all or did not require to be done completely or so thoroughly or were to be done by a third party at no expense to the lessor, the normal measure still applied: all these factors were in effect held to be collateral and did not go in mitigation. Thus no reduction of the damages was made in all the following circumstances: (1) where the landlord had decided before the end of the lease to pull down the buildings and had done so before action: *Inderwick v Leech*[264]; (2) where the lessor had made an agreement with a third party to grant him at the end of the defendant's term a new lease under which the buildings were to be pulled down and new ones erected, and they had been pulled down by the third party, the condition of the premises having formed, it was said, no ingredient in the price: *Rawlings v Morgan*[265]; (3) where, owing to a deterioration in the neighbourhood, the premises **28-057**

253 [1891] Q.B. 31 CA at 46. The Court of Appeal thus held that the cost of repairs is the ordinary and general rule: whether this rule is affected by rules of mitigation where the lessor has already relet to a third party who has covenanted to repair was a further and separate question decided in the case: see para.28-057, below.

254 [1977] Ch. 106.

255 [1977] Ch. 106 at 329F–G.

256 See para.28-057, below.

257 See para.28-046, above and paras 28-058 and following, below. Indeed in the context of the repair covenant this statutory provision has made otiose Megarry VC's general analysis (see paras 28-084 and following, below) as to when a lessor may recover for the cost of work which the lessee in breach of covenant has failed to do.

258 [1891] 2 Q.B. 31 at 37.

259 (1835) 6 C. & P. 782.

260 (1891) 8 T.L.R. 103.

261 And was also admitted to be correct in *Proudfoot v Hart* (1890) 25 Q.B.D. 42 at first instance; see especially at 47.

262 (1855) 11 Ex. 15.

263 The action was during the term, but the same result would have been achieved had it been at the end of the term. A similar result was achieved in *Soward v Leggatt* (1836) 7 C. & P. 613; see especially 617. Compare to para.2-007, above.

264 (1885) 1 T.L.R. 484.

265 (1865) 18 C.B. N.S. 776. The court laid stress on the fact that the agreement with the proposed new lessee was oral only and therefore not binding on the other party, but *Joyner v Weeks* [1891] 2 Q.B. 31 CA, shows this to be unimportant: see later in this paragraph.

would command as high a rent even though the covenant to repair was not strictly complied with: *Morgan v Hardy*,[266] followed in *Anstruther-Gough-Calthorpe v McOscar*[267]; (4) where the claimant had granted a new lease to a third party to run from the expiration of the defendant's lease under which the third party covenanted to repair, so that the performance of the defendant's covenant to repair was a matter of pecuniary indifference to the claimant: *Joyner v Weeks*.[268]

28-058 **(b) As limited by statute: post-1927** The terms of s.18(1) of the Landlord and Tenant Act 1927[269] do not enact a new measure of damages in substitution for the old one of cost of repairs but set a ceiling upon the old measure. That ceiling is the diminution in the value of the reversion. It has therefore been said that the old measure applies subject to a limit,[270] but since this would involve the ascertainment of two figures, a practice which would be unnecessarily cumbersome,[271] and since it is highly unusual for the cost of repairs to be less than the diminution in the value of the reversion, common sense and practicality suggest that the court ought generally to go straight to the basic test of what is the diminution in the reversion's value.[272] This approach was laid down as correct by the Court of Appeal in *Smiley v Townshend*[273]—where Denning LJ said that in calculating the damages one must do so "remembering that the real question is: what is the injury to the reversion?"[274]—and confirmed by the Court of Appeal in *Culworth Estates v Society of Licensed Victuallers*.[275] Occasionally, the repair costs will fall below the diminution in the value of the reversion. This happened in *Sunlife Europe Properties Ltd v TigerAspect Holdings Ltd*,[276] where it became necessary to calculate both figures.[277]

28-059 The reversion that falls to be valued is the estate, freehold or leasehold, of the

266 (1886) 17 Q.B.D. 770; affirmed on this point at (1886) 35 W.R. 588 CA.

267 [1924] 1 K.B. 716 CA. The question of liability and the question of measure of damages come very close here. The first question is: does the deterioration in the neighbourhood lower the standard of repair for which the defendant is liable under his covenant? The answer to this being no, the second question is: does the said deterioration diminish the measure of damages? The Court of Appeal in this case was concentrating on the first question and it is with regard to it that the court distinguished the earlier *Proudfoot v Hart* (1890) 25 Q.B.D. 42 CA. See para.28-044, above.

268 [1891] 2 Q.B. 31 CA. This case is also dealt with on the general question of mitigation and avoidance of loss at para.9-185, above where it is suggested that it might not be followed today, a view adopted in *Pgf II SA v Royal & Sun Alliance Insurance Plc* [2010] EWHC 1459 (TCC) (facts at para.28-056, above) in the light of *Ruxley Electronics & Construction Ltd v Forsyth* [1996] A.C. 344: see para.9-186, above.

269 Quoted at para.28-046, above.

270 *Hanson v Newman* [1934] Ch. 298 at 300–301, per Luxmoore J; see *Jones v Herxeimer* [1950] 2 K.B. 106 CA at 119, per Jenkins LJ.

271 As pointed out by Fry LJ in *Joyner v Weeks* [1891] 2 Q.B. 31 CA at 46.

272 This does not always happen. Thus in *Ultraworth Ltd v General Accident Fire & Life Assurance Corp Plc* [2000] 2 L. & T.R. 495 the court went into great detail as to the cost of repair, coming to a figure of £150,000, and then proceeded to award no damages as there was held to be no diminution in the value of the reversion. Again in *Mason v Totalfinaelf UK Ltd* [2003] 3 E.G.L.R. 91 there was a finding of cost of repair as well as of diminution in value, and with a substantial difference between the two; the repair cost for a petrol filling station of £134,738 was nearly double the diminution in value of £73,500.

273 [1950] 2 K.B. 311 CA.

274 [1950] 2 K.B. 311 CA at 323.

275 (1991) 62 P. & C.R. 211 CA.

276 [2013] EWHC 463 (TCC).

277 [2013] EWHC 463 (TCC) at [204]–[205] and [213].

lessor subject to the lease.[278] Since the action is being brought at the determination of the lease the reversion will generally be in possession, namely in the claimant's possession. But it has been held that the reversion is still to be valued as at the determination of the defendant's lease even though it does not then fall into the claimant's possession by reason of his having granted a reversionary lease to a third party[279] or his having agreed to a surrender of the tenancy only upon finding a new lessee,[280] or by reason of the property having been requisitioned by a public authority[281]; this follows from the reference in s.18(1) to "the value of the reversion (whether immediate or not)".[282] Furthermore, the fact that the term has ended not by effluxion of time but by the claimant's forfeiture for the defendant's breach of covenant, repairing or otherwise, does not prevent the reversion from being valued at the date of forfeiture, and the lessee cannot claim a set-off by reason of the acceleration of the reversion. As Lawrence LJ said in *Hanson v Newman*,[283] which decided this point:

> "One of the provisions of the lease is that the landlords may determine the term on a breach of covenant by the tenant. The term granted by the lease is therefore subject to determination in that event under the express provisions of the lease. In these circumstances it cannot properly be said that the reversion has been accelerated when the landlords re-enter for breach of covenant."

It may therefore be in the interests of the lessor to enforce a forfeiture where possible so as to enable him to bring his action as on the term's determination and not during its currency, thereby gaining higher damages.

The most obvious mode of valuing the reversion, or rather the diminution in its value, is by finding the marketable value of the property had the repairs been executed and by deducting from this its marketable value in its unrepaired state. This test was approved and applied in *Hanson v Newman*,[284] and in *Jones v Herxeimer*,[285] the court said that this calculation was "no doubt the right criterion to apply in many if not most cases".[286] Illustrative for today of this way of going about ascertaining the diminution in value is *Hammersmith Properties (Welwyn) Ltd v Saint-Gobain Ceramics & Plastics Ltd*,[287] where there was much argument on the assessment both of value in repair and value unrepaired.[288] In assessing the market value of the property in its unrepaired state it is the property as it reverts to the lessor that is to be taken, so that the Court of Appeal in *Van Dal Footwear Ltd v Ryman Ltd*,[289] held the trial judge to be wrong to have increased that value because **28-060**

---

278 *Hanson v Newman* [1934] Ch. 298 CA; see at 306, per Lawrence and Romer LJJ.

279 *Terroni v Corsini* [1931] 1 Ch. 515.

280 *Jaquin v Holland* [1960] 1 W.L.R. 258 CA; see especially at 266–267, per Devlin LJ.

281 *Smiley v Townshend* [1950] 2 K.B. 311 CA.

282 Whether these factors affect the measure of damages in assessing this value is considered at paras 26-067 to 26-069, below.

283 [1934] Ch. 298 CA at 304.

284 [1934] Ch. 298 CA; see especially at 305, per Lawrence LJ, citing Luxmoore J below at 302.

285 [1950] 2 K.B. 106 CA.

286 [1950] 2 K.B. 106 CA at 118. It was followed and applied in *Smiley v Townshend* [1950] 2 K.B. 311 CA. The calculation of diminution in value, being less than the cost of repair so that s.18(1) applied, was also in issue in *Craven (Builders) Ltd v Secretary of State for Health* [2000] 1 E.G.L.R. 128 and *Sun Life Assurance Plc v Racal Tracs Ltd* [2000] 1 E.G.L.R. 138.

287 [2013] EWHC 1161 (TCC).

288 Taking up a very large part of Ramsey J's judgment: [2013] EWHC 1161 (TCC) at [85]–[146].

289 [2010] 1 W.L.R. 2015 CA.

the former tenant might have taken a further lease of the property in its unrepaired condition.

**28-061** The cost of repairs, however, though not providing the ultimate test any longer, will nevertheless frequently be a strong guide to, if not represent, the diminution in the market value of the reversion. This is most likely to be so where the lessor is in possession at the determination of the defendant's lease and will forthwith carry out himself the repairs required by the covenant. In this connection *Jones v Herxeimer*[290] is an important decision. There the lease in question was of some five rooms in a house; the lessee had left them in disrepair, the lessor had repaired them and the Court of Appeal gave him as damages the cost of these repairs. Jenkins LJ, delivering the court's judgment, said:

> "There must be many cases in which it is in fact quite obvious that the value of the reversion has, by reason of a tenant's failure to do some necessary repair, been damaged precisely to the extent of the proper cost of effecting the repair in question."[291]

*Hanson v Newman*,[292] had not laid down

> "an invariable rule of law to the effect that in all circumstances the procedure of placing values on the reversion repaired and the reversion unrepaired, and ascertaining the difference, must necessarily be gone through in order to ascertain the diminution in the value of the reversion attributable to the want of repair."[293]

Although, he added, this calculation is valid in many if not most cases,

> "we certainly deprecate its introduction as a sine qua non into all cases, including a small and simple case like the present concerned with the letting of some of the rooms in a house, where it becomes a purely hypothetical calculation wholly removed from the practical realities of the matter."[294]

It is true that in this case the lease in question was only of part of a house so that, as the court said, the evidence of the capital value of that part was beside the point since

> "there could be no question as a practical matter of a sale of the five rooms let to the tenant ... separately from the rest of the house".[295]

Nonetheless it would seem that on similar facts, with the exception that the lease was of a whole house, the cost of the repairs would come near to representing the damage. The Court of Appeal expressly disapproved[296] Lynskey J's dictum in *Landeau v Marchbank*,[297] that

> "the fact that repairs are necessary is not in itself even prima facie evidence of damage to the value of the reversion"[298];

---

290 [1950] 2 K.B. 106 CA.
291 [1950] 2 K.B. 106 CA at 117.
292 [1934] Ch. 298 CA.
293 *Jones v Herxeimer* [1950] 2 K.B. 106 CA at 117.
294 [1950] 2 K.B. 106 CA at 118.
295 [1950] 2 K.B. 106 CA at 118.
296 [1950] 2 K.B. 106 CA at 116.
297 [1949] 2 All E.R. 172 at 175.
298 And see Devlin LJ's remarks in *Jaquin v Holland* [1960] 1 W.L.R. 258 CA at 266 that although a

and Denning LJ has said that where the repairs have been or are going to be done the cost may be a very real guide[299] and indeed is usually the measure of damages.[300] In *Smiley v Townshend*,[301] the premises had been requisitioned during the term, were still so at its end when the action was brought, and it was not known when the requisition would end, before which time the requisitioning authority might have done some of the repairs. Denning LJ said that in cases like this, where it was uncertain whether or not the lessor would effect the repairs, their cost still might afford a starting figure which would, however, have to be scaled down according to the circumstances.[302] Conversely, in *Culworth Estates v Society of Licensed Victuallers*,[303] s.18(1) was held to be no impediment to the lessor's claim based on the cost of repairs as it was likely that the damage to the reversion was at least as great as, if not greater than, that cost.[304]

On the other hand, where it is clear that the repairs are not going to be done by the lessor, their cost forms little or no guide in assessing the injury to the reversion.[305] It was this type of case that the legislature had in mind when s.18(1) of the Landlord and Tenant Act 1927 was passed,[306] since it was thought unfair that the cost of repairs should be recovered by the lessor and put into his pocket. It is therefore important to deal carefully with the effect of s.18(1) here, since it is here, and practically only here, that it has resulted in changing the amount recoverable. **28-062**

---

buyer of the reversion might disregard the disrepair, because what might be an appreciable sum for repairs if looked at from the viewpoint of the rent the landlord was getting might not matter very much from the viewpoint of capital value, it did not necessarily follow that such disrepair "should be disregarded altogether, or that a landlord will just have to put up with what is in effect a real loss".

299 In *Smiley v Townshend* [1950] 2 K.B. 311 CA at 322.

300 In *Haviland v Long* [1952] 2 Q.B. 80 CA at 84.

301 [1950] 2 K.B. 311 CA.

302 [1950] 2 K.B. 311 CA at 322 to 323. But the fact that the lessees had repaired did not entitle them to the cost of repairs in *Crown Estate Commissioners v Town Investments* [1992] 1 E.G.L.R. 61; in principle they were entitled only to nominal damages. There was no diminution in the value of the reversion because of the existence of statutory sub-tenants who would pay a rent based upon premises in repair.

303 (1991) 62 P. & C.R. 211 CA. Also in *Elite Investments v Bainbridge Silencers* [1986] 2 E.G.L.R. 43.

304 In *Latimer v Carney* [2007] 1 P.& C.R. 13 at 213, a case with a very full and careful judgment by Arden LJ, the claimant landlords had effected repairs but were said by the Court of Appeal to have failed to present their case properly by not producing expert valuation evidence or clear evidence of repair costs: at [26]. Nevertheless the trial judge was held to have been wrong to have awarded no damages on account of insufficient evidence. The damage to the reversion should have been inferred from the estimated cost of repairing the roof necessary before the premises could be relet and from the estimated cost of doing the other repairs necessary before the new tenant would take his lease. There had however to be a 60 per cent discount in respect of the other repairs to take account of the fact that the landlords had carried out more extensive work than was necessary, having effected improvements and modernisation at the same time as doing the repairs.

305 See per Denning LJ in *Smiley v Townshend* [1950] 2 K.B. 311 CA at 322. Thus an extremely advantageous sale by the lessor of the premises in their unrepaired state resulted in *Simmons v Dresden* (2005) 97 Con. L.R. 81, after a protracted consideration of values for the premises if repaired (at [93]–[102]), in a holding of no diminution in the value of the reversion despite very substantial breaches by the lessee of the repairing covenant.

306 See per Somervell LJ in *Haviland v Long* [1952] 2 Q.B. 80 CA at 82 as to pulling down and as to structural alteration, and per Denning J in *Westminster v Swinton* [1948] K.B. 524 at 534 as to repairs done by third parties. Somervell LJ thought that the legislature did not have the latter in mind. Clearly they did not in s.18(1) in fin., but it could be argued that they did in the subsection's general statement. Yet the decision in *Haviland v Long* itself rather suggests that Somervell LJ is right.

28-063 (1) Where the premises at or shortly after the termination of the tenancy have been or will be pulled down whatever their state of repair, the lessor can recover no damages and the verdict will be for the defendant: this is expressly provided by s.18(1). Whether they are to be pulled down by the claimant or by some third party would seem to be immaterial. Therefore *Inderwick v Leech*,[307] and *Rawlings v Morgan*,[308] are no longer law. It is sufficient that a firm intention existed at the determination of the term on the part of the lessor to pull down the premises, and a subsequent revocation of this intention does not remove the case from the operation of the section[309]; on the other hand a merely provisional intention of the lessor at the end of the term will not suffice to bring the case within the statutory provision.[310] The onus of proving that the facts are within the subsection is on the lessee.[311] And where in *Hibernian Property Co v Liverpool Corp*,[312] the lessee of a house was a local authority which so failed to repair that it was able to declare the house unfit for human habitation and to include it in a slum clearance area order, it was held that s.18(1) had no application. Caulfield J said:

> "The last part of s.18 certainly, I think, contemplates the lessor making a decision to pull down or so structurally alter the premises that any repairs that would be shown to be necessary to achieve compliance with the covenants in the lease would be rendered nugatory. I do not, however, think that the section is even capable of being construed as enabling a municipal corporation, by its own failure to comply with covenants to repair so that the house has to be demolished, to contend that the second part gives it relief in a claim for damages for breach of covenant."[313]

The damages were assessed as the value of the reversion if the repairing covenant had been complied with.

28-064 (2) Where the premises at or shortly after the termination of the tenancy, whatever their state of repair, would have structural alterations made therein as would render valueless the repairs covered by the covenant, the lessor can recover no damages and the verdict will be for the defendant: this also is expressly provided for by s.18(1). The defendant established that it was the position in *Mather v Barclays Bank*,[314] but failed to do so in *Culworth Estates v Society of Licensed Victuallers*.[315] What is said under (1) above will apply here mutatis mutandis.

28-065 (3) Where structural alterations were to be made in a house by its conversion into flats and maisonettes so that only some, but not all, of the repairs were rendered valueless, it was held in *Landeau v Marchbank*,[316] that only nominal damages were recoverable as there was no evidence of diminution in the value of the reversion.[317]

---

307 (1885) 1 T.L.R. 484: see para.28-057, above.

308 (1865) 18 C.B. N.S. 776: see para.28-057, above.

309 *Salisbury v Gilmore* [1942] 2 K.B. 38 CA.

310 *Cunliffe v Goodman* [1950] 2 K.B. 237 CA. The trial judge in *Pgf II SA v Royal & Sun Alliance Insurance Plc* [2010] EWHC 1459 (TCC) concerned himself very much with the question of the date at which a lessor's intention about what to do with the property is to be considered, concluding rightly that it had to be taken as the date of the termination of the lease and no later: see at [41] and following.

311 *Cunliffe v Goodman* [1950] 2 K.B. 237 CA.

312 [1973] 1 W.L.R. 751.

313 [1973] 1 W.L.R. 751 at 755H.

314 [1987] 2 E.G.L.R. 254.

315 (1991) 62 P. & C.R. 211 CA.

316 [1949] 2 All E.R. 172.

317 Lynskey J, however, assumed that the fact that repairs were necessary was not even prima facie

(4) Where, owing to a deterioration in the neighbourhood, the premises would let at as high a rent even though the covenanted repairs were not carried out in all strictness, then, although the lessee remains under an obligation to carry out the repairs at the covenanted standard,[318] it would seem that the measure of damages will be affected to the extent that the deterioration must have diminished the value of the reversion. *Portman v Latta*,[319] points to this conclusion. In that case the premises at the end of the lease in 1940 could not be let as a dwelling-house and would have to be put to some other use, such as use by housing institutions. The value repaired less the value unrepaired was given as damages and not the cost of repair. **28-066**

(5) Where, on the other hand, owing to the high demand for property in the particular area, the premises were relet to a third party at the same rent although only part of the repairs had been carried out by the claimant lessor, it was held in *Jaquin v Holland*,[320] that the damages were not limited to the cost of the partial repairs. The high demand for property in the area was a consideration that, said Devlin LJ, "must be extraneous to the true principle on which the value should be arrived at".[321] **28-067**

(6) Where the covenanted repairs were to be carried out in full although not by the lessor himself, the cost of repairs was held to be recoverable in *Haviland v Long*.[322] The defendant being in breach of his repairing covenants, the claimant lessor shortly before the end of the lease entered into a fresh lease with a third party who, while paying a full economic rent, agreed to carry out the repairs, the claimant undertaking to reimburse him out of any sum recovered from the defendant by way of dilapidations. It was contended for the defendant that having regard to the terms of the new lease the value of the reversion had not been diminished and that the lessor had therefore suffered no loss. The court, however, held that at the time of the new lease the claimant had a contingent right to recover damages should the defendant eventually be in breach, that he did not lose that right by reason of the new bargain with the third party, and allowed the cost of repairs as the measure of damages. Somervell LJ said: **28-068**

> "The damage to the reversion would be measured by the cost of the repairs, because it was everybody's intention to go on using the building as it was before, and it was economic to do so. I cannot see why that right should be lost because it is made a term in a bargain."[323]

In this case the claimant had arranged to pay over to the third party any sum that he obtained on this account from the defendant, and if there had been no such arrangement it is unlikely that the third party would have been prepared to pay the full economic rent for the property. Nevertheless, even if the lessor stood to benefit

---

evidence of diminution in the value of the reversion ([1949] 2 All E.R. 172 at 175); this view was soon after disapproved by the Court of Appeal in *Jones v Herxeimer* [1950] 2 K.B. 106 CA.

318 As laid down in *Morgan v Hardy* (1886) 17 Q.B.D. 770 and *Anstruther-Gough-Calthorpe v McOscar* [1924] 1 K.B. 716 CA: see para.28-044, above.

319 [1942] W.N. 97.

320 [1960] 1 W.L.R. 258 CA.

321 [1960] 1 W.L.R. 258 CA at 268. He also expressed the view that "in general the rent which could have been obtained for the house is not any very valuable guide to the value of the reversion": at 267.

322 [1952] 2 Q.B. 80 CA.

323 [1952] 2 Q.B. 80 CA at 83.

by dint of an advantageous bargain with the third party, it would seem from the reasoning of all three members of the Court of Appeal in *Haviland v Long*,[324] that the cost of repairs would still be recoverable. Thus Somervell LJ, quoting the judge below, said:

> "It is the fact that … the repairs require to be done and not the circumstances in which the landlord and his new tenant agree upon the manner of meeting the charge, which is the governing consideration."[325]

Denning LJ said quite categorically:

> "The fact that the landlord has an undertaking from a new tenant to do the repairs does not go in diminution of damages. It is res inter alios acta."[326]

And Roxburgh J said[327] that to decide otherwise would be contrary to the principle which Lawrence LJ had enunciated in *Hanson v Newman*,[328] that reversionary leases must be disregarded.[329] In the light of this, ironically enough, *Joyner v Weeks*,[330] could be decided the same way today.[331] Yet in view of the decision in *Ruxley Electronics Construction Ltd v Forsyth*,[332] it has been suggested by His Honour Judge Toulmin in *Pgf II SA v Royal & Sun Alliance Insurance Plc*,[333] that it would now not be followed.[334]

**28-069** (7) Where it is not clear whether the repairs will be effected by the lessor by reason of the fact that at the end of the tenancy in question the property is requisitioned and it is possible that the requisitioning authority may themselves do some of the repairs before derequisitioning, it was held in *Smiley v Townshend*,[335] that such possible future events might be relevant in the assessment of damages. The future events could not in themselves reduce the damages since what repairs the authority might do was entirely a matter of speculation, nor could repairs done by the authority before action brought effect a reduction since this was the lessor's lucky chance and res inter alios acta. But the possibility of future repairs might be taken into account in so far as it threw light on the value of the reversion at the end of the lease.[336] The cost of repairs might be taken as a starting figure but would require to be scaled down in the light of the circumstances.[337] The relevant circumstances in such a case would be the possibility of repairs by the requisition-

---

324 [1952] 2 Q.B. 80 CA.

325 [1952] 2 Q.B. 80 CA at 83.

326 [1952] 2 Q.B. 80 CA at 84.

327 [1952] 2 Q.B. 80 CA at 84

328 [1934] Ch. 298 CA; see para.28-059, above.

329 It had already been held in *Terroni v Corsini* [1931] 1 Ch. 515 that reversionary leases must be disregarded, but that case was more concerned with the moment in time at which the value of the reversion had to be taken in assessing damages: see the footnote reference to the case at para.28-059, above.

330 [1891] 2 Q.B. 31 CA; see para.28-057, above.

331 Despite Denning J's dictum in *Westminster v Swinton* [1948] K.B. 524 at 534 that s.18 was enacted "in order to remedy *Joyner v Weeks*".

332 [1996] A.C. 344, at para.31-014, below

333 [2010] EWHC 1459 (TCC).

334 See his discussion at [2010] EWHC 1459 (TCC) at [23] and following, and see too para.9-186, above.

335 [1950] 2 K.B. 311 CA.

336 See especially at 320–321, per Denning LJ.

337 [1950] 2 K.B. 311 CA at 322–323, per Denning LJ.

ing authority and also the inability of the lessor to give possession to a new lessee or purchaser while the requisition remained: both these factors would minimise the extent to which the lack of repair affected the value of the reversion.

(8) Where a public authority before the end of the lease had resolved to make a compulsory purchase order but the order itself was not made until after the lease had ended, no damages were awarded in *London County Properties v Wallis-Whiddett*,[338] since there was no diminution in the reversion's value. The key factor was not the making of the order but the decision to make it, for from that time, which was before the end of the lease, the property became virtually unsaleable in the market. Nor was there any evidence that the price paid under the compulsory purchase was in any way affected by the lack of repairs. **28-070**

(9) No account is to be taken of latent development value of the property so as to increase its market value in its unrepaired state since the repairs would become unnecessary if the development were proceeded with. A lessor's damages are not to be reduced, or eliminated, because of a development value which at the date of the termination of the lease the lessor had no intention of realising. As was pointed out by His Honour Judge Toulmin in *Pgf II SA v Royal & Sun Alliance Insurance Plc*,[339] this had not been argued successfully since s.18(1) of the Landlord and Tenant Act 1927 had been passed, and it was not successfully argued before him.[340] **28-071**

At common law the exact measure of damages was not the cost of repairs but their cost plus, where relevant, a sum for loss of use during repair, and less, where relevant, a sum in respect of the extent that the new was more valuable than the old.[341] Although the cost of repairs is no longer the test, it would seem that these two factors in appropriate cases will be relevant in assessing the amount by which the value of the reversion has been diminished. Indeed both factors made an appearance in *Pgf II SA v Royal & Sun Alliance Insurance Plc*,[342] where the lessee and the sub-lessee of a prestigious six-storey office block in London's financial centre built in the early 1970s were in breach of their repairing covenants. It was undisputed that the lessor had carried out a scheme of refurbishment which went well beyond that for which the lessees could have been expected to pay to put the premises into repair,[343] which meant that from the cost of the scheme as carried out fell to be deducted the cost of the element of improvement. For the loss of the use of the premises during repair, loss of rent was in principle recoverable but the lessor's inability to prove that the carrying out of the repairs had prevented the letting of the premises for the whole of the claimable period of repair led to a limited recovery for lost rent.[344] **28-072**

One final possible head of damages is the surveyor's expenses incurred by the lessor in preparing a schedule of dilapidations and thereby ascertaining the extent of the injury, but recovery of such expenses was not allowed by way of damage to the reversion in *Maud v Sandars*.[345] Although the injury to the reversion marks only **28-073**

---

338 [1950] W.N. 180. Perhaps nominal damages should in strictness have been awarded as the case did not fall within those specific instances in s.18(1) of "no damage [sic] recoverable".

339 [2010] EWHC 1459 (TCC).

340 See [2010] EWHC 1459 (TCC) at [55] to [68].

341 See para.28-056, above.

342 [2010] EWHC 1459 (TCC).

343 [2010] EWHC 1459 (TCC) at [54].

344 See [2010] EWHC 1459 (TCC) at [256] to [269].

345 [1943] 2 All E.R. 783, but there was little or no argument on the issue. *Skinner v Knight* [1891] 2 Q.B. 542 CA, gives support to the same conclusion.

the upper limit of the damages, this limit will have been reached without the inclusion of surveyor's expenses, and they would seem therefore to fall outside the scope of the damages, at least since the statutory change of 1927. Nevertheless such damages were allowed in *Pgf II SA v Royal & Sun Alliance Insurance Plc*,[346] where it may be that they did not extend the award beyond the diminution in value ceiling.[347] While one is sympathetic to allowing such damages even should they exceed the diminution in value, it is thought that *Maud v Sandars* is right in disallowing the cost of the schedule of dilapidations. It may be that here s.18(1) has gone too far in its limiting of the damages recoverable.

### (4) Measure of damages in action at determination of tenancy when there has been a prior action during tenancy

**28-074** Two cases give guidance on the measure of damages where an action at the end of the term follows upon one during it. In *Henderson v Thorn*,[348] the lessor had recovered damages in an action during the term but had not expended the amount awarded on repairs. In this subsequent action at the end of the term he was awarded the cost of repairs less the amount recovered in the prior action.[349] In *Ebbetts v Conquest*,[350] the facts and result were similar except that the actions were between an underlessor and an underlessee. Because the lease in question was an underlease, the assessment of damages in the action during the term had taken into account the cost of the repairs as the diminution in the value of the claimant's reversion,[351] but Bigham J held that the fact that the liability to repair had been taken into account in the prior action did not prevent recovery in the later action since the questions in issue in the two actions were different: then it was a question of damage to the reversion, now it was a question of the state of disrepair. Nevertheless it is difficult to see how substantial damages could be awarded in the second action, since in the first the damages had been measured by the cost of repairs subject to a deduction for immediate payment.[352]

### (5) Measure of damages where there is an assignment or underlease

**28-075** **(a) Assignment** Where the lessee assigns his term the position at common law is that the assignee may be sued by the lessor[353] for breaches of the repairing covenant which are committed during his holding[354]; the measure of damages will be the same as in the ordinary case of lessor suing lessee. The lessee remains liable throughout the term despite any assignment and may therefore be sued by the lessor[355] in respect of breaches committed by the assignee, being in effect liable in

346 [2010] EWHC 1459 (TCC); facts in the previous paragraph.
347 See [2010] EWHC 1459 (TCC) at [328]–[342].
348 [1893] 2 Q.B. 164.
349 Also deducted was an amount representing depreciation.
350 (1900) 82 L.T. 560.
351 *Conquest v Ebbetts* [1896] A.C. 490.
352 See the prior action at para.28-051, above.
353 Or the assignee of the reversion, if any.
354 In default of evidence it may be assumed that the disrepair happened during the defendant assignee's holding: *Smith v Peat* (1853) 9 Ex. 161; it is no defence to an assignee that the premises were in disrepair when he took them: *Plummer v Johnson* (1902) 18 T.L.R. 316.
355 Or the assignee of the reversion, if any.

the nature of a surety. If the lessor recovers from the lessee, the lessee may then sue his assignee for an indemnity, which may be express or implied, and being an indemnity will include any costs properly incurred by him in the defence of the action brought against him by the lessor.[356] This is not a question of damages: it is a suit upon an express or implied contract of indemnity. However, because of the perceived unfairness of the lessee remaining liable, frequently for many years, for breaches of covenant by his assignee, or indeed his assignee's assignee, statute has now removed the right of the lessor to proceed against his lessee after an assignment. This result is achieved by the Landlord and Tenant (Covenants) Act 1995 which provides by s.5(2) that a tenant who assigns the whole of the premises demised to him is released from the tenant covenants of the tenancy. However, the section operates only in relation to leases granted on or after the date of the Act's coming into force, so that the common law rule will still have relevance for some time to come. Of course, in any claim for breach of the repairing covenant by the lessor against the assignee, whether by choice under the old law or by necessity under the new, the damages will simply follow the lines already considered.

**(b) Underlease** Where the lessee underlets the underlessee cannot be sued by the lessor:[357] there is no privity of estate between them. The underlessor is the only person who can sue him[358] and the measure of damages here gives rise to some problems.[359] **28-076**

*(i) Cost of repairs* The leading case in regard to underleases is *Conquest v Ebbetts*.[360] The claimant, the lessee of a 61-year term, sub-let to the defendant for a period extending up to 10 days before the expiration of his own lease, at an improved rent and with identical repairing covenants, the sub-lease giving full notice of the existence and terms of the head lease. The damages for breach of the repairing covenants fell to be assessed in an action brought during the term, three-and-a-half years before the termination of the lease. Evidence was given that, when the lease fell in, the only profitable way of dealing with the ground would be to pull down the house and treat the land as building ground. The house, if repaired, would be worth £200 more to pull down than if left unrepaired, and it was contended that this was all that the original lessor could recover against the original lessee and therefore all that the latter could recover against his sub-lessee. The damages awarded, however, amounted to the full cost of the repairs less a discount by reason of the fact that the claimant was getting an immediate payment and not one at the end of the sub-lease. A number of points appear from this decision. **28-077**

(1) The damages are not nominal merely because the sub-lessor has only a nominal reversion, in this case one of 10 days. Indeed it had already been held in **28-078**

---

356 If he has no defence the proper course will be for him to let judgment go by default.

357 Or the assignee of the reversion, if any.

358 The original lessor may also be able to sue the underlessor but in *Crown Estate Commissioners v Town Investments* [1992] 1 E.G.L.R. 61 the existence of the underlease caused there to be no diminution in value of the lessor's reversion: see the case also in the last footnote but two at para.28-061, above.

359 Where the underlessor's reversionary interest had a negative value, diminution in value was held in *Shortlands Investments v Cargill* [1995] 1 E.G.L.R. 51 to be the difference between the amount which the underlessor would pay to a transferee of his interest and the greater amount he would pay because the repairing covenant had been broken.

360 [1896] A.C. 490; affirming *Ebbetts v Conquest* [1895] 2 Ch. 377 CA.

*Clow v Brogden*,[361] and in *Davies v Underwood*,[362] that it was no answer to a sub-lessor's claim that his interest in the premises had ceased by reason of his eviction by the head lessor.

**28-079** (2) The diminution in the value of the reversion in such a case is best measured by the cost of repairs, less the discount for immediate payment, since the claimant is liable over for repairing to the head lessor. A similar measure had been awarded earlier in *Davies v Underwood*.[363] Bramwell and Watson BB had regarded this as not based upon the test of damage to the reversion's value but the present decision of the House of Lords clearly regards it as answering to this test.[364] The cost of repairs is thus recoverable whether the action is during the term[365] or at its determination,[366] and even since the enactment of s.18(1) of the Landlord and Tenant Act 1927. One decision, however, is difficult to reconcile with the principle that the sub-lessor's liability over to the head lessor is a relevant consideration: that is *Williams v Williams*.[367] In that case the head lease contained a general covenant to repair followed by a special covenant to repair within three months after notice; the sub-lease was in similar terms except that the special covenant was limited to two months' notice. The head lessor served a notice to repair in three months and, the defendant sub-lessee not having complied with it, the claimant the following year served a notice on him to repair within two months. The head lessor threatened forfeiture proceedings after three months had elapsed from his notice but before two months had elapsed from the claimant sub-lessor's. To avoid forfeiture the claimant entered, did the repairs, and sued the defendant for damages, all before the two months were up. It was therefore properly held that the claimant's action on the special covenant failed,[368] but it was also held that his action on the general covenant failed as the premises were not out of repair when suit was commenced, even though it was the claimant who had executed the repairs. It is submitted that this is inconsistent with *Conquest v Ebbetts*, unless the decision is explainable on the ground that it was thought that the notice calling on the defendant to repair within two months under the special covenant operated as an election under that covenant.[369]

**28-080** (3) Whether the defendant's knowledge of the existence and terms of the head lease was a necessary factor in the claimant's recovery of damages based on the cost of repairs is a matter upon which the House of Lords is silent. All three members of the Court of Appeal, however, laid great stress upon this knowledge. Lindley LJ said:

> "It is important to notice that the underlessee knew the position of his immediate lessor, for the underlessee disclosed the fact that it was an underlease. ... The plaintiffs' li-

---

361 (1840) 2 M. & G. 39.

362 (1857) 2 H. & N. 570.

363 (1857) 2 H. & N. 570.

364 See para.28-051, above.

365 As in *Conquest v Ebbetts* [1896] A.C. 490.

366 As in *Davies v Underwood* (1857) 2 H. & N. 570 (determination by forfeiture).

367 (1874) L.R. 9 C.P. 659.

368 In *Colley v Streeton* (1823) 2 B. & C. 273, where the action on the special covenant succeeded because the sub-lessee had proper notice to repair before the commencement of the action, the cost of repairs necessary to avoid a forfeiture was awarded as damages: see especially per Bayley J at 280.

369 Foa, *Landlord and Tenant*, 8th edn (1957), p.223, agrees with this criticism of *Williams v Williams*. The 8th is the last edition of Foa to appear.

ability over to their lessor must be taken into account, for it was one of the circumstances, special if you like, but known to and reasonably within the contemplation of the underlessee."[370]

This and similar statements by the rest of the court[371] show that the case was regarded as falling under the so-called second rule in *Hadley v Baxendale*.[372] The necessity of knowledge, however, may be largely academic since an underlessee is surely to know that he is taking an underlease and know also, or at least reasonably assume, what were the covenants in the head lease.

(4) Since the claimant might have to pay the full cost of repairs under his covenant with the head lessor, the evidence that the only profitable way of dealing with the property at the end of the lease was to pull down the premises was irrelevant. Lord Herschell said: **28-081**

"The duty of the appellants as between themselves and the respondents was to fulfil the obligation of the covenant into which they had entered, and to keep the premises in repair. If they had done so the present question would not have arisen. They have broken their covenant, and when sued for the breach they have, in my opinion, no right to demand that a speculative inquiry shall be entered upon as to what may possibly happen, and what arrangements may possibly be come to, under the special circumstances of the case, when the superior lease expires by effluxion of time."[373]

However, since the enactment of s.18(1) of the Landlord and Tenant Act 1927 the claimant would not have to pay any damages to his head lessor if at the end of the lease the latter intended to pull down the premises,[374] and if this were so in the circumstances of the particular case it would seem that it could substantially reduce, if not reduce to nominal, the damages recoverable by the sub-lessor against the sub-lessee.

*(ii) Value of the term lost* Another head of damage, beyond the cost of repairs, is the value of the term lost to the underlessor where, by reason of the underlessee's failure to repair, the head lessor enforces forfeiture and both underlessee and underlessor are evicted. The question would be largely academic if the claimant sub-lessor was only claiming the value of a nominal reversion of, say, 10 days as is the position so often with underleases; the substantial claim will however be for the loss to the underlessor of the difference between the rent that the underlessee was paying him and the rent he was paying the head lessor. In *Clow v Brogden*,[375] Maule and Bosanquet JJ expressed doubt[376] whether the value of the term forfeited could be recovered and whether the sub-lessee could be liable in such an action for all the consequences to his own lessor of a breach of covenant contained in a lease to which he was not himself a party. And in *Logan v Hall*,[377] it was held that, although the defendant had had knowledge of the existence and terms of the head lease, the **28-082**

370 [1895] 2 Ch. 377 CA at 383.
371 [1895] 2 Ch. 377 CA at 384, 387.
372 (1854) 9 Ex. 341.
373 [1896] A.C. 490 at 495.
374 See para.28-063, above.
375 (1840) 2 Scott N.R. 303.
376 See arguendo (1840) 2 Scott N.R. 303 at 314. The report of *Clow v Brogden* at (1840) 2 M. & G. 39 does not contain their statements.
377 (1847) 4 C.B. 598.

claimant could not recover the value of his reversionary interest[378] since this loss was not the natural consequence of the defendant's breach of his covenants but resulted rather from the claimant's breach of his own covenants with the head lessor. But, on the assumption that the sub-lessee was aware of the existence and terms of the head lease, such a consequential loss would seem to be as much within the rule in *Hadley v Baxendale*,[379] as were the cost of repairs in the view of the Court of Appeal in *Ebbetts v Conquest*.[380] In *Logan v Hall*,[381] Coltman J had relied[382] on the cases refusing the recovery of costs as damages[383] and therefore the reasoning applied there may apply here, namely that the covenants in the two leases are necessarily different, even if in the same words, because made at different times, by reason of the fact that a covenant to repair must in each case be construed with reference to the age and character of the premises at the time of the demise. Coltman J was also influenced by the fact that to hold for the claimant would give the same result as a contract of indemnity.[384] In this uncertain state of the authorities the wise course for the claimant to take is to exact a covenant of indemnity in the lease itself.

**28-083** *(iii) Costs incurred in defending action by head lessor* Where the underlessor has already been successfully sued by the head lessor for damages for breach of his own covenant to repair, another possible head of damage makes its appearance, namely the costs which the underlessor has incurred in the defence of that action. It was held, however, in *Walker v Hatton*,[385] that the claimant was not entitled to recover these costs from the defendant even though the covenants in the sub-lease were, with one small exception, the same as those in the head lease, and even though the claimant had defended the action brought against him by the head lessor only after the defendant had denied that any notice of repair had been given, had insisted that the premises were not in disrepair, had refused to assent to the claimant's offer to suffer judgment by default, and had then been notified by the claimant that in these circumstances he would defend the action by the head lessor and would hold the defendant responsible for the costs: nor did it affect the claimant's position that he had put it out of his power to enter during the term for the purpose of repairing.[386] The rationale put forward by Parke B[387] was that, since a covenant to repair has reference to the condition of the premises when the covenant begins to operate, the covenants in the head and sub-leases, even if identical in words, must necessarily be different in substance and would vary substantially in their operation. This argument, however, is perhaps only conclusively directed to the question of whether there could be said to be an implied contract of indemnity on the part of the sub-lessee,[388] and there was a certain tendency in the mid-19th

378 Indeed it was only one day.
379 (1854) 9 Ex. 341.
380 [1895] 2 Ch. 377 CA.
381 (1849) 4 C.B. 598.
382 (1849) 4 C.B. 598 at 624.
383 See para.28-083, below.
384 (1849) 4 C.B. 598 at 624.
385 (1842) 10 M. & W. 249.
386 This case followed and approved the similar case of *Penley v Watts* (1841) 7 M. & W. 601 (where the claimant had let judgment go by default in the action against him and was only claiming as damages against the defendant the costs incurred in the assessment of the damages in the prior action); and overruled *Neale v Wyllie* (1824) 3 B. & C. 533 which had allowed recovery of costs as damages.
387 (1842) 10 M. & W. 249 at 258.
388 Thus in *Pontifex v Foord* (1884) 12 Q.B. D. 152 this argument is used to show that there is no

century not to allow the recovery of costs as damages for breach of contract but only under an express or implied contract of indemnity. This trend was discontinued in sale of goods cases with the important decision in *Hammond v Bussey*,[389] but it was held in *Clare v Dobson*,[390] by Lord Coleridge J that this development had not shaken the authority of the earlier sub-lease cases, and, accordingly, he considered himself bound to hold in the case before him that the claimant sub-lessor could not recover as damages the costs incurred by him in proceedings brought by him for relief against forfeiture threatened by the head lessor, such proceedings being successful by reason of the repairs having been executed in the interim.[391] It is suggested that the question should be reconsidered by higher authority, for *Clare v Dobson*,[392] seems to be out of line with the modern trend allowing recovery of costs as damages.[393] Yet it must be stated in conclusion that an objection of a totally different nature can be put forward to the recovery today of such a head of damages, namely the limiting of the recoverable damages to the diminution in the reversion's value by s.18(1) of the Landlord and Tenant Act 1927. It is difficult to press these damages within the statutory limitation.

## 2. OTHER COVENANTS ON THE CONDITION AND USE[394] OF THE PREMISES

In a valuable part of a judgment of unusual length delivered by Megarry VC in *Tito v Waddell (No.2)*,[395] otherwise known as the *Ocean Island No.1* case,[396] the learned judge, in the absence of clear authority, considered "as a matter of principle" the measure of damages **28-084**

> "in relation to the breach of a contract to do work on the land of another, whether to build, repair,[397] replant or anything else."[398]

He expounded the position in a series of five points, of which the essential one for the purposes of the particular problem is the third. After stating the fundamental tenet of damages that they are to compensate the claimant for loss by putting him in the position he would have been had he not suffered the wrong, and emphasising that any gain or saving to the defendant by not doing what he has contracted to do is as such irrelevant,[399] he said:

---

contract of contribution or indemnity so as to allow the operation of third-party procedure to bring in the sub-lessee in the action by the head lessor against his lessee under the then Rules of Court.

389 (1888) 20 Q.B. D. 79 CA. See at para.21-032, above.

390 [1911] 1 K.B. 35.

391 He relied on a dictum of Lindley L J in *Ebbetts v Conquest* [1895] 2 Ch. 377 CA at 382.

392 [1911] 1 K.B. 35.

393 See Ch.21, above, passim.

394 For how damages fall to be assessed for breach of a covenant to keep a retail shop open on the demised premises, the closure of which resulted in a diminution in the value of the reversion, see, and contrast, *Costain Property Developments v Finlay* (1989) 57 P. & C.R. 345 and *Transworld Land Co v J Sainsbury* [1990] 2 E.G.L.R. 255.

395 [1977] Ch. 106.

396 There were two cases, *Ocean Island No.1* and *Ocean Island No.2*, heard and dealt with in the judgment in reverse order. Only *No.1* involved issues of damages.

397 While covenants to repair are dealt with separately elsewhere in this chapter (at paras 28-043 and following, above), Megarry VC's more general analysis is there taken into account so far as it is relevant to the repair obligation: see para.28-055, above.

398 [1977] Ch. 106 at 332D.

399 [1977] Ch. 106 at 332E–G. But things have started to change. With the advent of a possibly wide

> "Third, if the plaintiff can establish that his loss consists of or includes the cost of doing work which in breach of contract the defendant has failed to do, then he can recover as damages a sum equivalent to that cost. It is for the plaintiff to establish this: the essential question is what his loss is."[400]

There were various ways, he continued, in which a claimant might establish that the cost of doing the work constituted his loss, whether in whole or in part. The work may have already been done by him or he may be able to satisfy the court that the work will be done by him. He may do the latter by showing that he is under some contractual or statutory obligation to carry out the work, or, being under no coercion, he may merely state that he intends to do the work which, after all, he had contracted for consideration to have done. In the latter case everything will turn on whether the court believes that this is his intention, and here he may be aided by the circumstances, which may

> "demonstrate a sufficient fixity of intention in the plaintiff's resolve, as where the property is his home and will be highly inconvenient or nearly uninhabitable until the work is done".[401]

If the intention is satisfactorily shown, then it should not matter that

> "the house could be made convenient or inhabitable by doing cheaper or less idiosyncratic work: what matters is the work to which the plaintiff is entitled under the contract".[402]

The fact that there can be no certainty about the doing of work which has not yet been done cannot affect the position;

> "the court ought to be ready to act on evidence which, without assuming certainty, nevertheless carries conviction".[403]

Again, Megarry VC said in relation to the covenant to repair that

> "if the circumstances fail to indicate sufficiently that the work will be done, the court might accept an undertaking by the plaintiff to do the work; and this ... would surely compel fixity of intention".[404]

**28-085** It will be seen that Megarry VC's analysis is based upon the assumption that the claimant is going to do the work himself, so that it must follow that, as lessor, he has got the property back in his own hands. Accordingly, the analysis has no proper relevance where the action for damages is during the term of the lease[405] and only comes into its own where the tenancy has determined before action is brought. The two situations must therefore be examined separately.

---

swathe of gain-based damages for breach of contract, in the light of the Court of Appeal's approach in *Attorney General v Blake* [1998] Ch. 439 CA, the result in *Tito v Waddell (No.2)* (facts at para.28-091, below) could well be different. On this see generally Chs 14 and 15.

[400] [1977] Ch. 106 at 332H.

[401] [1977] Ch. 106 at 333D.

[402] [1977] Ch. 106 at 333E.

[403] [1977] Ch. 106 at 334D.

[404] [1977] Ch. 106 at 333F–G.

[405] This assumes that there is no question of the lessor being entitled to re-enter, and in fact re-entering, to do the work himself while at the same time allowing the lease to continue.

## (1) Measure of damages in action during tenancy

If the action is brought while the term is continuing, the damages will be measured by the amount of the diminution in the value of the lessor's reversionary interest. The damages cannot consist of the cost to the lessor of carrying out the covenant himself as he is not, if out of possession, in a position to do so.[406] A decree of specific performance would be the only method of having the covenant carried out, but, if specific performance is regarded as not generally being available for breach of a lessee's covenant to repair,[407] it would seem that it can hardly be sought in respect of other covenants requiring the lessee to carry out work on, or to maintain the condition of, the premises.[408] **28-086**

The position is illustrated by the covenant against waste, a covenant much akin to the covenant to repair, where the only case on damages appears to be *Whitham v Kershaw*.[409] The defendant lessee had committed an act of waste in removing soil, and the claimant lessor brought an action for damages during the currency of the term. It was held that "the true measure of damages is the injury done to the reversion",[410] and that **28-087**

> "it would be wrong to say that the reversionary value had necessarily been diminished by the cost of restoring the property to its original condition".[411]

This is exactly as with actions during the term on covenants to repair. Similarly, in *Stephens v Junior Army and Navy Stores*,[412] where there was an action during the term for breach of a covenant to build, it was held that the measure of damages was the loss occasioned to the lessor's reversion,[413] applying *Ebbetts v Conquest*,[414] which contains the basic rules as to damages for the covenant to repair.[415]

Neither of these cases gives any specific guidance as to how the precise calculation is to be made. Sometimes, however, as in *Watson v Charlesworth*,[416] which involved an action during the term for breach of a mining covenant, the contracting parties will have effectively provided the answer in the agreement itself. There the rent to be paid by the lessees was nominal until they started mining and from then on at a substantial figure. On the lessees ceasing to work, it was held that the lessors were entitled to such rent as they would probably have received if the lessees had continued working.[417] *Pell v Shearman*,[418] is a somewhat similar case of a mining covenant, but it requires careful reading. There the covenant was to sink a shaft in search of coal, which would have cost £2,600, and, if the defendants found **28-088**

---

406 See preceding footnote.

407 See *Hill v Barclay* (1810) 16 Ves. Jun. 402, a principle accepted in *Jeune v Queens Cross Properties* [1974] Ch. 97. Compare paras 28-010 and 28-041, above.

408 Contrast to *Tito v Waddell (No.2)* [1977] Ch. 106 at 331D, per Megarry VC.

409 (1885) 16 Q.B.D. 613 CA.

410 (1885) 16 Q.B.D. 613 CA at 618, per Bowen LJ; similarly at 616, per Lord Esher MR.

411 (1885) 16 Q.B.D. 613 CA at 616, per Lord Esher MR; similarly at 617, per Cotton LJ.

412 [1914] 2 Ch. 516 CA.

413 See especially [1914] 2 Ch. 516 CA at 529, per Swinfen Eady LJ.

414 [1895] 2 Ch. 377 CA.

415 See para.28-045, above.

416 [1905] 1 K.B. 74 CA; affirmed sub nom. *Charlesworth v Watson* [1906] A.C. 14, but nothing is said on damages.

417 Stirling LJ ([1905] 1 K.B. 74 CA at 88) stated the general rule about putting the covenantee into as good a pecuniary position as if the contract had been performed.

418 (1855) 10 Ex. 766.

a vein of marketable coal, they would pay the claimant £2,500.[419] On the defendants' failure to sink a shaft the claimant sued for damages and was awarded £2,500, the judge telling the jury that the claimant had a right to have a pit sunk to the depth agreed on at the defendants' cost and that they either ought to estimate the damages with reference to the expense of so doing or might give the amount which would have become payable on the contingency. A rule to enter nominal damages was refused and the court did not indicate which of the judge's alternatives was correct. But Field J in *Wigsell v School for Indigent Blind*,[420] took the view that the court thought that the correct alternative was the loss of the chance of finding marketable coal. This, it is submitted, is the proper explanation of *Pell v Shearman*.[421] If all possibility of a mine being found could have been negatived the damages must have been nominal, since no damage could accrue from breach of the covenant as no benefit would flow from its performance.[422]

### (2) Measure of damages in action at determination of tenancy

28-089 Where the premises are back in the hands of the lessor because the term has come to an end, either by effluxion of time or because the lessor has validly exercised a right of re-entry on breach, the lessor is now in a position to do the work which the lessee had contracted, and failed, to do on the premises—e.g. to build or to mine—or to undo the work which the lessee has done on, or the harm he has done to, the premises—e.g. by converting from residential to industrial use or by incompetent farming. It, therefore, becomes a practical proposition for the lessor to incur the cost of doing or undoing, as the case may be, the lessee's work and to claim his expenditure as damages; for ease of reference such cost will here be referred to as the cost of reinstatement, although the term reinstatement does not strictly cover alterations to the condition of the premises at the commencement of the lease which the lessee had contracted to bring about, as by building or mining.

28-090 Nevertheless, even though the cost of reinstatement may be an available measure of damages, the normal measure remains the diminution in the value of the reversion which, it is true, will in many cases be properly assessed by taking the cost of reinstatement. As Denning J rightly said in *Westminster v Swinton*[423]:

> "In cases in which there are not breaches of covenant to deliver up in repair, the law has always been and still is that there is no rigid rule that damages are the cost of reinstating the premises. It depends on the particular case."[424]

---

419 The covenant was not strictly between lessor and lessee. The defendants had agreed that, if the claimant would surrender to his lessor the land then in his possession, they would, on obtaining a lease of it themselves, sink a shaft and pay £2,500 to the claimant if they found coal.

420 (1882) 8 Q.B.D. 357 at 365–366.

421 (1855) 10 Ex. 766.

422 In *Radford v De Froberville* [1977] 1 W.L.R. 1262 at 1278H, Oliver J said that *Pell v Shearman* "certainly supported the cost of the work as a possible measure of damages". This is no doubt true, but it can hardly form the proper measure where the award clearly cannot be expended in carrying out the work.

423 [1948] 1 K.B. 524 at 534.

424 In saying, in *Tito v Waddell (No.2)* [1977] Ch. 106 at 331E, that he regarded as unsound the footnote comment in the 13th edition of this work that the analogy of covenants to repair cannot be used in respect of other covenants as the rule allowing cost of repairs was a special rule not applied elsewhere, and that he further regarded the comment as not being supported by the authority cited, namely Denning J's statement quoted in the text, Megarry VC failed to appreciate that both com-

Certainly there are cases in which there has been no claim for the cost of reinstatement. Thus in *Marshall v Mackintosh*,[425] where the claimant lessor had re-entered the premises on the defendant lessee's failure to build and relet, it was held that he might recover the difference between the contractual rent, which was the equivalent of the market rent with the buildings that the defendant had covenanted to erect, and the rent at which he relet, lower by reason of the failure to build, taking 25 years' purchase. Conversely, in *Oldershaw v Holt*,[426] where the claimant had been able to relet at an increased rent as the market had improved, this was taken into account in assessing the damages with the result that the damages were nominal.[427] And moving from building to farming covenants, in *Williams v Lewis*,[428] the measure of damages awarded was the injury to the reversion which, it was there said, will in practice amount to the diminution in rent that the claimant will obtain in reletting.[429]

Where the lessor does make a claim for the cost of reinstatement, then the principles set out by Megarry VC in *Tito v Waddell (No.2)*,[430] will fall to be applied. The possibility that such a claim could properly be made had been appreciated long before, but not necessarily in the context of a sharp difference in figures as between diminution in value and cost of reinstatement. Thus as early as *Whitham v Kershaw*,[431] where the action for breach of the covenant against waste by removing soil was during the term,[432] Lord Esher MR recognised that **28-091**

> "if there were a covenant to leave the premises in the same condition as when taken, the damages in an action which could only be brought after the termination of the lease would obviously be the cost of replacing the house by a house of equal value",[433]

but it is doubtful if the cost of reinstatement would there have been allowed had an action been brought at the end of the term since, as Cotton LJ pointed out, there was no evidence that anyone would have thought it worthwhile to bring back the soil at the cost required.[434] And precisely the same conclusion was reached in *Tito v Waddell (No.2)*[435] itself. In that case, by virtue of an agreement of 1913 between the native landowners of Ocean Island and a British company interested in mining phosphate on the island, together with deeds executed between individual landown-

---

ment and authority were directed to pointing out simply that the cost of reinstatement was not necessarily and always the appropriate measure of damages. What led him to this misunderstanding may have been his belief that cost of reinstatement was not the invariable common law rule for damages for breach of the repair covenant (see at 329F–G), but, if that had been so, there would have been no point in the legislation which appeared as s.18(1) of the Landlord and Tenant Act 1927: see paras 28-046 and 28-055 to 28-057, above.

425 (1898) 78 L.T. 750.

426 (1840) 12 A. & E. 590.

427 As to the correctness of this see the case dealt with in connection with mitigation and avoided loss in the footnote at the end of para.9-134, together with para.9-135, above.

428 [1915] 3 K.B. 493.

429 [1915] 3 K.B. 493 at 497.

430 [1977] Ch. 106; see para.28-084, above.

431 (1885) 16 Q.B.D. 613 CA.

432 See para.28-087, above.

433 (1885) 16 Q.B.D. 613 CA at 616–617. Contrast to *Woodhouse v Walker* (1880) 5 Q.B.D. 404 at 408; but the case is tort rather than contract.

434 (1885) 16 Q.B.D. 613 CA at 617.

435 [1977] Ch. 106.

ers and the company consequent on such agreement,[436] the landowners agreed to grant to the company the right to remove phosphate together with trees and other plants from their land for an extensive term of years. It was provided that, when the land ceased to be used by the company for the exercise of the rights granted, it should revert to the particular landowners freed from all rights of the company, and the company undertook to replant the land as nearly as possible to the extent to which it had been planted in the first place. In claims by a number of the landowners for specific performance of the covenant to replant or, in the alternative, for damages for its breach, claims brought against the British Phosphate Commissioners who in 1920 had taken over from the company, Megarry VC, having held that the case was not one for specific performance,[437] further refused to give damages based on the cost of replanting because he could find no satisfactory evidence of any intention on the part of the claimants, who owned scattered plots of land on the island, to replant those plots.[438] Accordingly, the damages fell to be assessed on the basis of the diminution in value of the various plots.[439]

**28-092** So far no case has appeared where cost of reinstatement well in excess of diminution in value has been awarded. For this it is necessary to turn to another type of situation where at the end of the term the premises are in a different structural condition from that in which they should have been, either because the lessee has altered their condition in breach of contract or because, though alteration was permissible, he has failed to restore them to their original condition. Here one leaves the replanting of the vegetation of Ocean Island and comes nearer home to the less exotic changing the use of urban premises from residential to commercial or from a single dwelling-house to a number of flats. In this type of situation the difference between diminution in the value of the reversion and the cost of reinstatement can be far more marked than in the case of a repair covenant broken, because the lessee may have increased rather than diminished the market value of the reversion by his breach. Yet the lessor has expressly stipulated that the premises should revert to him in a particular condition and questions of market value may not count with him: for instance, he may wish to occupy the premises himself as a private dwelling-house and not be interested in the increased value that would be given to the property by conversion to commercial use or conversion into flats. Here therefore it would seem that, while the prima facie measure of damages remains the diminution in the value of the reversion, the claimant ought to be awarded as damages the cost of reinstatement if he intends to alter the condition of the premises to comply with the contract and if this can be regarded as a reasonable course for him to take in the circumstances.

**28-093** Such a measure was awarded to the claimant lessor in *Eyre v Rea*.[440] The assignee of a lease had converted the premises into five flats in breach of covenant

---

[436] The text of the deeds used is set out [1977] Ch. 106 at 146G–149C.

[437] [1977] Ch. 106 at 321E–328F.

[438] [1977] Ch. 106 at 336D–G. Nor was cost of reinstatement available by awarding the damages, as was here possible, under the equitable jurisdiction established by Lord Cairns' Act: see at 334H to 335B.

[439] The figure was not an easy one to arrive at (see [1977] Ch. 106 at 336H to 337F), and eventually Megarry VC quantified the damages by the exercise of a rusticum judicium: see *Tito v Waddell (No.2)* [1977] Ch. 106 at 340, where the difficulties arising from co-ownership of plots by some of the claimants were also dealt with.

[440] [1947] 1 K.B. 567. Curiously this important case appears not to have been referred to in *Tito v Waddell (No.2)* [1977] Ch. 106.

to use as a private dwelling-house. The lessor successfully claimed forfeiture and damages. The argument of the lessee that the lessor had now got something more valuable financially than a house for single occupation since he could let it at a higher rent and had therefore suffered no damage, was rejected. The claimant was held entitled to the cost of restoring the house to an unconverted one and in addition to the rent lost for the period it would take for the work to be done. Cost of reinstatement was also allowed in *Westminster v Swinton*,[441] but, because of the different fact situation, in a somewhat modified form. The claimant had let to the defendant, who had underlet to a third party, who in turn had underlet to a fourth party, who had converted the premises into flats in breach of covenant to use and keep as a private dwelling-house. Denning J declared forfeiture as to the fourth party and held that the third party should recover as damages from the fourth party the cost of reinstatement less the financial benefit to him of the property being flats for the period up to the time when he must reinstate. Denning J said that *Eyre v Rea*,[442] must not be taken as deciding that in every breach of this kind the full cost of reinstatement was the measure of damages; in that case it had represented the measure because the right course was to reinstate at once and that was what the lessor intended to do. On the other hand *James v Hutton*,[443] illustrates well the situation where the normal measure of diminution in the reversion's value continues to apply. The defendant lessee of a shop made certain alterations to the shop front under licence and covenanted to restore the premises to their original condition at the end of the term. He failed so to restore them. No evidence appeared that the restoration of the old shop front would make the premises suitable for any particular purpose or business, or that the premises were made less valuable by the substitution of the new and modern front; nor was there any evidence that the claimant had any reason for desiring that the new front be altered. In these circumstances nominal damages were awarded, the court pointing out that there was no true analogy with the case of a breach of a covenant to repair and the common law measure of damages there, i.e. the cost of repair, because a dilapidated building must necessarily be worth less than a house in a proper state of repair.[444] But the court expressly disclaimed that they were suggesting that the claimant could not give evidence that he desired to use the premises for a purpose for which the new front was unsuitable. Similarly in *Espir v Basil Street Hotel*,[445] nominal damages were awarded. The claimant was himself a lessee of part of certain premises and he sub-let this part to the defendant, retaining to himself a reversion of only 15 days. The defendant then acquired from the head lessor a 999-year lease of the whole premises subject to the claimant's interest in part. In breach of his covenant in the sub-lease he made structural alterations, having acquired the total property with the unitary purpose of running an hotel. The true measure, said Scott LJ, is

> "the injury to the reversion in the sense of the present depreciation in the present value of the ultimate reversion"[446];

and this was nil.

---

441 [1948] 1 K.B. 524.
442 [1947] 1 K.B. 567.
443 [1950] 1 K.B. 9 CA.
444 [1950] 1 K.B. 9 CA at 16.
445 [1936] 3 All E.R. 91 CA.
446 [1936] 3 All E.R. 91 CA at 96.

## 3. COVENANT AGAINST ASSIGNMENT OR UNDERLETTING

28-094 The measure of damages for breach of a covenant not to assign or underlet, or not to assign or underlet without consent, follows general principles and aims to

> "put the plaintiff, as far as possible, in the same position so far as money will do it, as if the covenant had not been broken".[447]

Since, however, the lessor's complaint will generally be in respect of an act which would form a breach of one of the other covenants in the lease, and since the lessee's own liability for breach of these covenants does not generally cease on assignment or underletting, the lessor will generally be able to sue him for breach of the particular covenant. Thus frequently there is no need for the lessor to resort to suing on the present covenant; only in certain special circumstances does it come into play.

28-095 The commonest case of resort to this covenant has been where the defendant is himself an assignee of the lease and therefore has ceased to be generally liable for the future on the covenants in the lease where he himself has made a further assignment, such assignment being in breach of the present covenant. A further practical ingredient of the situation is that the defendant's own assignee, himself liable on the general covenants of one or more of which he is in breach, is not worth suing because insolvent. These circumstances arose in *Williams v Earle*,[448] the leading case, and also in *Langton v Henson*,[449] and *Cohen v Popular Restaurants*,[450] and in all three it was held that the lessor was entitled to recover such amount as would put the claimant in the position he would have been in had he retained the liability of the defendant instead of an inferior liability. In making this assessment it was held in the first case that account must be taken both of past breaches of covenant by the insolvent and possible future ones. Blackburn J agreed with the defendant's counsel that the assessment would be a matter of some difficulty and suggested that the parties would do well to agree that the lease be surrendered to the claimant so that the damages would then become crystallised. In the third case the lessor had elected to avoid the lease, and it was held therefore that the action was for damages for breach of covenant in a lease that had come to an end so that the damages must be assessed once and for all.[451] In the second case the claimant appears to have recovered in respect of past breaches by the insolvent; the question of future liability was not considered. Thus there is no clear authority about how damages in relation to the future are to be assessed: whether they are or are not recoverable should depend upon whether the breach of the covenant not to assign or underlet is or is not a continuing breach.

28-096 Another special situation is that where the lessee remains liable on all the other covenants but is not in breach of any of them. The lessor has been then able to make use of the present covenant to protect himself not from an insolvent assignee or underlessee but from one who is objectionable by reason of the use to which he has put the premises. The position here was fully considered in *Lepla v Rogers*.[452] The

---

447 *Williams v Earle* (1868) L.R. 3 Q.B. 739 at 751, per Blackburn J.
448 (1868) L.R. 3 Q.B. 739.
449 (1905) 92 L.T. 805.
450 [1917] 1 K.B. 480.
451 [1917] 1 K.B. 480 at 484.
452 [1893] 1 Q.B. 31.

defendant lessee sub-let without permission, and so in breach of covenant, to a person for the known purpose of carrying on the highly dangerous business of a turpentine distillery. The premises were burnt down by a fire arising from such use and the defendant was held liable, in breach of his covenant not to sub-let, for the full loss caused by the fire since it was "the natural result of the letting for the hazardous purpose".[453] Hawkins J expressed the view, however, that if the premises had been sub-let for the ordinary purpose of occupation to a tenant who was not known by previous experience to be reckless or dangerous in his habits, the defendant would not have been liable had the premises been burnt down by the sub-lessee acting recklessly or using the property for a dangerous purpose; for in such a case, in as much as a refusal of the lessor to consent to the sub-letting would at the time have been unreasonable and capricious, the defendant would have been entitled to sub-let as if no such covenant existed.[454] On the other hand, where the sub-lessee was in fact an unsuitable tenant at the time of the sub-letting but unknown to the defendant lessee, it was said in *Mackusick v Carmichael*,[455] that the costs incurred by the claimant in getting rid of the nuisance created by the sub-lessee's use of the premises for immoral purposes would be recoverable as being the natural consequence of the breach.[456]

A further special situation is where the lessee both remains liable on the other covenants and is in breach of one or more of them, but the lessor would have had a better remedy against him had he remained in possession, as by way of distress. Such a loss should be recoverable as damage flowing from breach of the present covenant. And an entirely different type of claim by a lessor for breach of the covenant not to underlet appeared in *Crestfort Ltd v Tesco Stores Ltd*,[457] being a claim for compensatory damages in the amount that the lessor would have demanded for relaxing the covenant against underletting.[458] This is analogous to the many more authorities dealing with claims by a seller of land where covenants against building have been breached by the buyer.[459] **28-097**

## 4. Covenant to Deliver up Possession[460]

The normal measure of damages is the value of the use of the property until such **28-098**

---

453 [1893] 1 Q.B. 31 at 38; applying the general rule in *Hadley v Baxendale* (1854) 9 Ex. 341.

454 *Lepla v Rogers* [1893] 1 Q.B. 31 at 37–38.

455 [1917] 2 K.B. 581.

456 [1917] 2 K.B. 581 at 586 to 587. This was only dicta as it was held that there was no breach of covenant by the defendant.

457 [2005] L. & T.R. 20 at 413.

458 See the case at [2005] L. & T.R. 20 at [72] and following.

459 Considered at paras 27-052 to 27-057, above.

460 Where the lessee fails to give vacant possession of the premises to the lessor at the determination of the term the legislature has provided for the recovery by the lessor of double rent in a holding over after notice given by the tenant (s.18 of the Distress for Rent Act 1737) and of double the yearly value in a holding over after notice given by the landlord (s.1 of the Landlord and Tenant Act 1730). These two provisions, which are still resorted to occasionally today as, unsuccessfully, in *Ballard (Kent) Ltd v Oliver Ashworth (Holdings) Ltd* [1999] 2 E.G.L.R. 23 CA, are with a view to securing recovery of premises; but an action for damages is also available. These two provisions, connected as they are with leases, have survived the legislative abolition of distress for rent in its tortious role, where goods are taken and where again double, or even treble, damages have been statutorily allowed, the repeals in question being by the Tribunals, Courts and Enforcement Act 2007: see para.38-089, below, and the first footnote to para.13-028, above.

time as the lessor regains possession, in effect the rent lost[461]: this was awarded in *Henderson v Squire*.[462] Of consequential losses, two have been adjudicated upon and allowed. First, the costs incurred by the lessor in an action brought to eject the lessee's sub-tenant who refused to vacate the premises were also allowed in *Henderson v Squire*[463];

> "for we must take it that was the best mode of recovering possession: and these costs follow as a necessary consequence of letting to an under-tenant if he refuses to go out of possession".[464]

Secondly, the lessor in *Bramley v Chesterton*,[465] recovered the reasonable damages and costs which he had had to pay in an action brought against him by a new tenant to whom he had relet the premises at the end of the defendant's term and to whom he had been unable, in breach of contract, to deliver possession. Such a successful claim later became familiar in sale of goods cases,[466] but this appears to be the only one, and an early one at that, resulting from failure to give up possession after a lease. Nevertheless there is no reason why the modern general rule allowing recovery of damages and costs[467] should not apply in appropriate circumstances. Thus recovery of the damages and costs paid by the lessor in the action against him will depend upon whether the parties contemplated a reletting by him upon such terms as he did relet, while recovery of the costs will further depend upon whether it was reasonable for the lessor to defend the action. In *Bramley v Chesterton*,[468] the defendant knew that the claimant had relet; this, said Cockburn CJ, was a "not unimportant fact",[469] but at the same time he indicated that the knowledge would be imputed in any event, since he referred to the reletting as "the common and ordinary course of dealing on the part of an owner of land".[470] As to the terms of the reletting, both Lord Cockburn CJ and Cresswell J refused to say that there would be any liability where the new contract was in some way special, extraordinary or peculiar,[471] while Willes J specifically said that it was not suggested that the damages paid by the claimant to the new tenant were compensation for the loss of a good bargain.[472]

**28-099** If the lessor is not full beneficial owner he can only recover to the extent of his

---

461 With no deduction of tax from the damages as they will be taxable: *Raja's Commercial College v Gian Singh & Co* [1977] A.C. 312 PC.

462 (1869) L.R. 4 Q.B. 170; and also in *Ibbs v Richardson* (1839) 9 A. & E. 849. The action is as much tort (namely the action for mesne profits) as contract: indeed in *Bramley v Chesterton* (1857) 2 C.B. N.S. 592 some of the judges were rather dubious about the action in contract. As far as the rent lost is concerned, it would seem that the action can also be framed in quasi-contract, now unjust enrichment, upon waiver of the tort: see *Ibbs v Richardson* (1839) 9 A. & E. 849.

463 (1869) L.R. 4 Q.B. 170.

464 Per Blackburn J, (1869) L.R. 4 Q.B. 170 at 174. Followed and applied in *Henderson v Van Cooten* (1923) 67 S.J. 228, where the person retaining possession was not even a sub-tenant but only a caretaker.

465 (1857) 2 C.B. N.S. 592.

466 See para.21-038, above.

467 See paras 21-031 and following, above.

468 (1857) 2 C.B. N.S. 592.

469 (1857) 2 C.B. N.S. 592 at 605.

470 (1857) 2 C.B. N.S. 592 at 605.

471 (1857) 2 C.B. N.S. 592 at 604 and 605, respectively.

472 (1857) 2 C.B. N.S. 592 at 606. Further, three of the judges regarded the action as based on tort rather than contract, but the measure of damages should be the same on this issue.

interest. Thus it was held in *Watson v Lane*[473] that, where the lessor was a mortgagor and three days after the lessee's breach the mortgagee demanded possession of the premises from the lessor, only the damage sustained by the claimant by being deprived for these three days was recoverable.

473 (1856) 11 Ex. 769.

CHAPTER 29

# SALE OF SHARES AND LOAN OF STOCK

TABLE OF CONTENTS



**29-001** Although the Sale of Goods Act 1979 does not apply to contracts for the sale of shares,[1] the principles relating to damages in sale of goods have been applied, as far as the subject-matter permits, to such contracts.[2] Therefore all that need be done is to set out the relevant cases on sale of shares, leaving any gaps to be filled in by reference to the corresponding parts in the chapter on sale of goods.

**29-002** The lending of shares is not a common transaction. There are however a number of old cases dealing with damages in actions for not replacing stock lent.

## I. BREACH BY SELLER

### 1. NON-DELIVERY

**29-003** The normal measure of damages is the market price of the shares at the contractual time for delivery less the contract price.[3] This represents the amount that the buyer must obtain to put himself in the position he would have been in had the contract been carried out, since to do so he must buy equivalent shares in the market. This measure was established as far back as *Shaw v Holland*,[4] Parke B taking the analogy of sale of goods.[5]

---

1 By s.61 "“goods” includes all personal chattels other than things in action and money"; shares are things in action.

2 The similarity to sale of land, stemming from the fact that by the contract of sale the seller of the shares becomes a trustee for the buyer and the buyer becomes the owner in equity, thus entitling him to a decree of specific performance, does not go to the issue of damages. Except occasionally: see para.29-005, below.

3 This assumes that the contract price has been paid.

4 (1846) 15 M. & W. 136; similarly *Powell v Jessop* (1856) 18 C.B. 336. Contrast *Manchester and Oldham Bank v Cook* (1883) 49 L.T. 674.

5 (1846) 15 M. & W. 136 at 145. The Privy Council accepted in *Sentinel International Ltd v Cortes* [2008] UKPC 60 that the appropriate measure of damages was the difference between the contract price and the value of the shares sold, and not the measures of nominal damages and loss of income proposed in the Bahamian Court of Appeal (at [45]), but there being no market price for the shares the question discussed (at [46]–[52]) was their proper valuation.

Thus while the price at which a third party has agreed to buy the shares from the buyer, and the price at which the buyer has bought equivalent shares, may be evidence of the market value where it is difficult to assess, these prices are generally irrelevant and should not be taken in preference to the market price. This is in line with the law relating to sale of goods.[6] So in the somewhat complex *Bear Stearns Bank Plc v Forum Equity Ltd*,[7] the analogy of sale of goods was taken[8] and the price at which the buyers had sold to a third party below the market price was held to be irrelevant and not to be preferred to the market price. The claimant buyers had contracted with the defendant sellers to acquire from them certain notes, initially representing corporate debt and coming to be represented by shares, and then, before the seller was in breach by failing to deliver, had sold on half of their interest in the notes, later to be shares, at a price which was substantially lower than the market price of the shares. In ignoring the resale price Andrew Smith J took his cue from the important House of Lords decision in *Williams v Agius*,[9] establishing this rule for goods sold and not delivered.[10] Somewhat similar is *Oxus Gold Plc v Templeton Insurance Ltd*,[11] where the same measure was applied; the fact that, had the shares there been delivered, the buyer would have immediately sold them at a price substantially below the price at which they had been bought was again held irrelevant. However, while Langley J came to this result because he said the law was "clear and settled at the highest level",[12] which was a reference to *Williams v Agius* and to the corresponding case in carriage of goods of *Rodocanachi v Milburn*,[13] he was clearly unhappy with the result. It is suggested elsewhere that the absolute rule in *Agius* and *Rodocanaci*, whether in the context of sale of goods or sale of shares, may be due for re-examination.[14] 29-004

The time at which the market price is to be taken is the contractual time for delivery. In general the principles worked out in the sale of goods cases apply here: of the several possible situations[15] few have been adjudicated upon in relation to the sale of shares, but the cases that there are indicate an application of common principles while at the same time bringing out small differences. (1) Where the market price has risen between the date of breach and the date of judgment in the action, it was held in *Shaw v Holland*,[16] that the time of judgment was not to be taken in preference to the time of breach by not delivering. Parke B said that the action was more akin to one for non-delivery of goods than to one for not replacing stock,[17] since 29-005

---

6 See paras 25-010 to 25-014, above.
7 [2007] EWHC 1576 (Comm).
8 [2007] EWHC 1576 (Comm) at [197].
9 [1914] A.C. 510.
10 See [2007] EWHC 1576 (Comm) at [200]–[ 209]. He was right to see the *Agius* case as relevant rather than *Bence Graphics International v Fasson UK* [1998] Q.B. 87 CA which dealt with defective delivery rather than non-delivery. See the full discussion at paras 9-171 to 9-183, above.
11 [2007] EWHC 770 (Comm).
12 [2007] EWHC 770 (Comm) at [83].
13 (1886) 18 Q.B.D. 67 CA.
14 See the full consideration of the problem in the context of mitigation and avoided loss at paras 9-171 to 9-183, above.
15 See paras 25-015 to 25-022, above.
16 (1846) 15 M. &. W. 136.
17 See paras 29-013 to 29-015, below.

"the plaintiff had his money in his own possession, and might have gone into the market and bought other shares as soon as the contract was broken".[18]

This rationale disappears where the purchase price has been paid in advance; and it has been submitted that in the case of goods the buyer should then be entitled to recover for any increase in the market price between breach and judgment.[19] Here, however, it is submitted that there is no call for such a rule, as the buyer of shares has in his own hands the power to right his position by suing for specific performance which will give him the shares themselves.[20] (2) Where the buyers in *Bear Stearns Bank Plc v Forum Equity Ltd*[21] had acted reasonably in initially pursuing a claim for specific performance, abandoned for a damages claim upon knowledge that the sellers had disposed of the shares elsewhere, they were held entitled to have the market price taken at a date many months later than the contractual time of delivery, by which date the market price had risen.[22] (3) Where the time fixed for delivery is postponed at the request of the seller, it has been held in *Wilson v London and Globe Finance Corp*,[23] that the date of the breach is postponed until the buyer no longer will grant indulgence and the market price on that date will therefore be the relevant one.[24] This is the same as with sale of goods.[25] (4) Where the contract is for the sale of shares not yet in existence at the time of the contract, the delivery required by the contract may be not the shares when issued but the earlier letter of allotment. In such a case it was held in *Tempest v Kilner*[26] that, failure to deliver the letter of allotment constituting the breach, the damages were to be calculated at the market price on that date and the buyer could not claim on the basis of the rise in price at the time of the later issue of the shares themselves.

**29-006** With the sale of a shareholding in a company, whether of a tranche of the shares or of them all, there may be no open market for the shareholding and therefore no market value upon which to rely. In these circumstances in *Plumbly v BeatthatQuote.com Ltd*,[27] where there was a refusal to allot the 10 per cent holding in a company to which there was an entitlement under a share option agreement, for the damages for non-delivery the value of the shares was arrived at by applying first a multiplier of 1.2 to the company's annual revenue and then a 65 per cent discount as the holding sold was a minority one.[28] Alternatively, the court may be prepared to take the resale price by the seller in breach as providing good evidence of market value, as in *Luxe Holding Ltd v Midland Resources Holding*

[18] (1846) 15 M. & W. 136 at 146. He relied on *Gainsford v Carroll* (1824) 2 B. & C. 624, which gave the same reason for goods: see para.25-015, above.

[19] See para.25-015, above.

[20] And, in damages, the dividends paid between breach and judgment: *Sri Lanka Omnibus Co v Perera* [1952] A.C. 76 PC, at para.29-007, below.

[21] [2007] EWHC 1576 (Comm); facts in the preceding paragraph.

[22] See [2007] EWHC 1576 (Comm) at [210]–[ 216]. In the different context of sale of land the important *Johmson v Agnew* [1980] A.C. 367 (at para.27-040, above) is along the same lines.

[23] (1897) 14 T.L.R. 15 CA. This ratio decidendi was on the facts adopted by only a majority of the Court of Appeal; there was a second ratio in which all concurred.

[24] It had previously been recognised in *Shaw v Holland* (1846) 15 M. & W. 136 at 146 that the buyer's indulgence at the seller's request postpones the breach, but the point had not been argued.

[25] The equivalent sale of goods case, *Ogle v Vane* (1867) L.R. 2 Q.B. 275, was indeed applied in *Wilson v London and Globe Finance Corp* (1897) 14 T.L.R. 15 CA.

[26] (1845) 3 C.B. 249.

[27] [2009] EWHC 321 (QB).

[28] See [2009] EWHC 321 (QB) at [131] and following.

*Ltd*,[29] which was an action not for damages but for a freezing order, a company having contracted to sell to a company its shareholdings in 20 foreign companies and then selling them to another company at a higher price.[30]

## 2. OTHER BREACHES

The nearest approach to delayed delivery comes in the cases where the buyer forces delivery on an unwilling seller by successfully suing for specific performance. If the market value has fallen he would be wise not to pursue this remedy, and if the market value has risen or remained unaltered the normal measure of market price at due delivery less market price at actual delivery will yield only nominal damages. However the buyer who has been awarded a decree of specific performance can recover as damages the equivalent of the dividends at the rates declared by the company between the date when the shares should have been delivered or allotted and the date of actual delivery or allotment together with interest on the dividends during non-payment. This result was reached in *Sri Lanka Omnibus Co v Perera*.[31] **29-007**

Where the shares are in some way not up to the promised standard this is in the nature of a breach of warranty of quality and the normal measure is of value as warranted less value in fact. This is confirmed and applied in all of three cases in the circumstances of which it was held that events subsequent to the breach were not to be taken into account. These are *Ageas (UK) Ltd v Kwik-Fit (GB) Ltd*,[32] *Hut Group Ltd v Nobahar-Cookson*,[33] and *Bir Holdings Ltd v Mehta*,[34] considered in detail at para.10-121, above. **29-008**

In *Lion Nathan v CC Bottlers*,[35] the whole of the share capital in a soft drinks company was sold with a warranty not that the profits for a number of months would be a specified figure but that the forecast of profits for those months had been calculated with all due care. It was said by Lord Hoffmann that, had there been a warranty as to the level of profits, which he referred to as a warranty of quality, then

> "the damages would prima facie have been the difference between what the shares would have been worth if the earnings had been in accordance with the warranty and what they were actually worth".[36]

Since, however, the breach of warranty was only in relation to the forecast, the damages were held to be the difference between the price agreed on the basis of the forecast as made and the price it would have been had the forecast been properly made.[37] Where the seller delivered partly paid instead of fully paid shares in *Re*

29 [2010] EWHC 1908 Ch.

30 See [2010] EWHC 1908 Ch at [57] and following, especially at [59].

31 [1952] A.C. 76 PC.

32 [2014] EWHC 2178 (QB).

33 [2014] EWHC 3842 (QB).

34 [2014] EWHC 3903 (Ch).

35 [1996] 1 W.L.R. 1438 HL.

36 [1996] 1 W.L.R. 1438 HL at 1441G.

37 See the case also at para.10-113, above. Limited warranties in respect of the shares were also in issue in *Bottin International Investments Ltd v Venson Group Plc* [2006] EWHC 3112 Ch. Great difficulty was experienced in valuation of the shares on the basis that the warranties were true and accurate, which was needed in order to arrive at the normal contract measure of value as represented less value as is. It was not however necessary for Blackburne J to come to a view on this since it

*Government Security Fire Insurance, Mudford's Claim*,[38] the buyer successfully claimed the amount unpaid.

## II. BREACH BY BUYER

### 1. NON-ACCEPTANCE

29-009 The normal measure of damages is the contract price less the market price at the contractual time for acceptance. This represents what the seller must obtain to put himself in the position he would have been in had the contract been carried out, since he can sell the shares in the market. The authority for this measure is *Jamal v Moolla Dawood*[39] in the Privy Council.[40]

29-010 The price at which the seller has resold the shares to a third party may be evidence of the market value where it is difficult to assess, but it is generally irrelevant and should not be taken in preference to the market price. It was thus held in *Pott v Flather*,[41] that the damages could not be increased because the market had fallen after breach and the seller had waited before reselling. One slight qualification is to be engrafted upon this rule in the case where the seller does not resell at the very moment of breach in the hope that the buyer will still complete or because he cannot be expected to move instantly, and the market has fallen by the time he does resell. In these circumstances it was held by Alderson B in *Stewart v Cauty*,[42] where eight days had elapsed between the buyer's refusal to accept and the seller's resale, that the damages were to be calculated

> "at the difference between the contract price and the price to be obtained within a reasonable time after the breach of the contract".[43]

Where, on the other hand, the market has risen after breach and the seller has resold at a price higher than that at the time of breach, it was held in *Jamal v Moolla Dawood*,[44] that the damages could not be decreased for this reason. "If the seller", said Lord Wrenbury,

> "retains the shares after the breach, the speculation as to the way the market will subsequently go is the speculation of the seller, not of the buyer; the seller cannot recover

was clear that the value as represented by the warranties was going to be no greater, and in all probability a good deal less, than the purchase price of the shares, and the normal tort measure, of price paid less value as is, had already been awarded in a deceit claim brought concurrently. See at [418]–[424].

38 (1880) 14 Ch. D. 634. Followed in *Ex p. Appleyard* (1881) 18 Ch. D. 587. In both these cases the claimant was proving in the liquidation of the company.

39 [1916] 1 A.C. 175 PC.

40 The fact that the broker who was the buyer's agent to buy the shares has become a defaulter before the final settlement and his personal liability has been ascertained under the Stock Exchange rules as between himself and the jobber who sold, does not affect the measure of damages as between the buyer and seller: *Anderson v Beard* [1900] 2 Q.B. 260; *Levitt v Hamblet* [1901] 2 K.B. 53; *Beckhuson v Hamblet* [1901] 2 K.B. 73.

41 (1847) 16 L.J.Q.B. 366.

42 (1841) 8 M. & W. 160.

43 (1841) 8 M. & W. 160 at 162–163. In *Pott v Flather* (1847) 16 L.J.Q.B. 366 the market price was taken on the day following the breach as the breach had occurred so late in business hours as not reasonably to allow a sale to be made that day.

44 [1916] 1 A.C. 175 PC.

from the buyer the loss below the market price at the date of the breach if the market falls, nor is he liable to the purchaser for the profit if the market rises."[45]

The time at which the market price is to be taken is the contractual time for acceptance. In the absence of direct authorities assistance must be sought in the equivalent cases in the sale of goods.[46] 29-011

### 2. Other Breaches

The case law does not include any other types of breach by the buyer. *Platt v Platt*[47] approaches being an illustration of a type of breach other than non-acceptance but the case in contract failed. Instead the claim succeeded in tort, the purchase of the shares having been induced by misrepresentation.[48] 29-012

## III. Breach by Lender

Actions for not replacing at the due date stock which has been loaned by the claimant to the defendant are not a prominent feature of modern litigation, but some early cases of this type are important since they provide the fullest treatment of an issue that appears in a number of other places in the law of damages.[49] This is the issue of whether a claimant who has been deprived of goods or shares by the defendant's tort or breach of contract is entitled to recover as damages their value at the time of judgment in the action where this is higher than at the time of breach. The argument for giving the higher market value at the time of judgment is that the claimant has until this time been deprived of the goods or shares or of the money, given as damages, with which he can replace them.[50] This argument has been fully accepted in actions for not replacing stock. In *Shepherd v Johnson*,[51] the court gave as damages the risen value of the stock as it stood at the time of the trial and the same result has since been reached in a number of cases, with little argument.[52] As Grose J said in *Shepherd v Johnson*[53]: 29-013

> "The true measure of damages in all these cases is that which will completely indemnify the plaintiff for the breach of the engagement. If the defendant neglect to replace the stock at the day appointed, and the stock afterwards rise in value, the plaintiff can only be indemnified by giving him the price of it at the time of the trial."[54]

It is submitted that the proper analysis of this measure of damages is that the 29-014

---

45 [1916] 1 A.C. 175 PC at 179. See the decision in the context of mitigation and avoided loss at paras 9-134 to 9-136, above.

46 See paras 25-122 to 25-127, above.

47 [1999] 2 B.C.L.C. 745.

48 See the case at para.49-026, below.

49 See. e.g. in the sale of goods (see para.25-015, above), in the sale of shares (see para.29-005, above), in contracts for professional services involving stockbrokers (see paras 34-089 to 34-091, below) and in the tort of conversion (see paras 38-011 and following, below). See, too, paras 9-042 to 9-044, above, for a discussion of the general principles involved.

50 In the case of sale of goods or of shares the buyer will generally not have prepaid the purchase price. He is, therefore, in a position to replace and the present issue does not arise.

51 (1802) 2 East 211.

52 *Downes v Back* (1816) 1 Stark. 318; *Harrison v Harrison* (1824) 1 C. & P. 412; and admitted in *Owen v Routh* (1854) 14 C.B. 327.

53 (1802) 2 East 211.

54 (1802) 2 East 211 at 212.

normal measure is the market value at the time of breach, i.e. the time of failure to replace the stock, and that the subsequent rise in value is given by way of consequential loss. This way of stating the measure of damages is important as it makes clear that the measure where the market value has fallen between breach and trial remains the higher value at the time of breach, a measure awarded apparently without argument in *Sanders v Kentish*.[55] This is clearly correct because the claimant might have sold the stock before the market fall,[56] but that this is the measure in such a situation is not always clear from the above cases where the market has risen: they tend to state simply that the market value at the time of trial is the proper measure without any reference to whether the market has risen or fallen. It is put more clearly in the headnote to *McArthur v Seaforth*,[57] which states that the measure of damages is the market price at the time of breach or at the time of trial at the option of the claimant.

**29-015** A claimant's simple election between market price at breach and at trial, however, fails to take into account two further possible factors. (1) In the first place the claimant may, with a rising market, be dilatory in bringing an action. On general principles the damages should be limited to the price to which the market had climbed at the time when the trial would have taken place had the claimant acted with reasonable speed. Yet in *Shepherd v Johnson*,[58] Grose J said that it was

> "no answer to say that the defendant may be prejudiced by the plaintiff's delaying to bring his action; for it is his own fault that he does not perform his engagement at the time; or he may replace it at any time afterwards so as to avail himself of a rising market".

It is submitted that this view, which has never been tested, is inconsistent with general principles of mitigation.[59] (2) In the second place the market price of the stock may at some time between breach and trial have reached a height above both the price at breach and the price at trial. In such circumstances the court in *McArthur v Seaforth*[60] was of the view that the claimant was not entitled to the highest intermediate value; such a measure involves the purely speculative assumption that the claimant would have sold out on that day. On the other hand it might be said that since the defendant is in breach the claimant is entitled to have this assumption made on his behalf.[61]

---

55 (1799) 8 T.R. 162. Compare to *Forrest v Elwes* (1799) 4 Ves. 492.
56 See *Forrest v Elwes* (1799) 4 Ves. 492 at 497.
57 (1810) 2 Taunt. 257.
58 (1802) 2 East 211 at 212.
59 See Ch.9, above, especially paras 9-043 and 9-044.
60 (1810) 2 Taunt. 257.
61 In the case itself, however, the higher value of the stock between breach and trial was given to it not by a rise in the market but because the holders were given the option to be paid off at par or to commute their 5 per cent stock for 3 per cent stock. Furthermore the court was influenced by the fact that the claimant had asked the defendant to replace the stock so that he might be paid at par, giving no indication that he wished to take the new stock.

CHAPTER 30

# CONTRACTS TO PAY OR TO LEND MONEY

TABLE OF CONTENTS



## I. BREACH BY PARTY PROMISING TO PAY

**30-001** Practically all modern contracts contain a promise by one party to pay a sum of money.[1] Where the contract involves the transfer of property, whether permanently or temporarily, as in the preceding chapters on contract,[2] the money payment represents the price of the property; where the contract involves the rendering of services, as in succeeding chapters on contract,[3] the money payment represents the price of the services. Such contracts take their names from the property transfer or the service rendering and not from the money payment: they are sales of goods or contracts of carriage and are not referred to as contracts for the payment of money. Nevertheless the promise to pay money in all these contracts sometimes becomes an important one where damages are concerned. It is true that generally, upon a failure to pay, the other party has an action for damages arising out of non-acceptance of the property or services[4] in which he may recover either the normal measure of damages or[5] consequential losses; and occasionally the other party may have some further action for damages, such as for failure to open a letter of credit.[6] But where the other party brings an action in debt for the price, either so electing or because in the circumstances it is the only action available to him, this action is

[1] This does not include money lent, as opposed to money paid outright. For the reasons see the last footnote in this paragraph.

[2] Chs. 23 to 27.

[3] Chapters 29 to 33. The contract dealt with in Ch.34 is a rather special one.

[4] See, e.g. non-acceptance by buyer or hirer in the case of goods, failure to complete by buyer or lessee in the case of land, failure to supply cargo in carriage contracts, wrongful dismissal in employment contracts.

[5] As in *Thompson v Robinson* [1955] Ch. 177.

[6] As in *Trans Trust S.P.R.L. v Danubian Trading Co* [1952] 2 Q.B. 297 CA.

based solely upon the failure to pay, and although itself an action in debt and not for damages it may involve a claim for damages for the wrongful detention of the debt. Indeed in *Sempra Metals v Inland Revenue Commissioners*,[7] Lord Nicholls has equated the two forms of action, in the non-technical sense of that term, with his reference to

> "claims at common law for … interest losses as damages for breach of a contract to pay a debt and, which today comes to the same, claims for payment of a debt with interest."[8]

Furthermore, there are the few contracts not involving the transfer of property or the rendering of services which do bring into prominence the promise to pay, and which are more likely to be properly called contracts to pay money: these are mainly transactions involving bills of exchange and promissory notes.[9] Whatever the consideration for the promise to pay money, all actions for failure to pay fall for consideration here.[10] Such actions in general are dealt with first, and then actions for the dishonour of bills and notes: these are taken separately only because they form a special category and are also affected by statutory provisions.

## 1. FAILURE TO PAY MONEY IN GENERAL

### (1) Recovery of interest as damages

**30-002** The normal measure of damages for failure to pay money has been stated in the cases sometimes to be nominal damages and sometimes to be interest for the detention of the debt. This curious inconsistency arises from the law's vacillation between the allowance and the disallowance of interest. This general problem of interest is fully treated in an earlier chapter[11] where it is pointed out that, starting from the early 19th century, courts began to refuse to allow interest as damages at common law for the non-payment of money, a rule that was reluctantly confirmed by the House of Lords at the end of that century in *London, Chatham & Dover Ry v S.E. Ry*,[12] and reconfirmed by the House of Lords in *The President of India v La Pintada Compania Navigacion*,[13] towards the end of the following century. It was thus said until the 17th edition of this book that all statements in the cases that interest is awardable for the non-payment of money had to be regarded either as misconceived, as made in reference to one of the possible common law exceptions, in particular the undoubted case of the dishonour of bills and notes,[14] or as made in reference to the statutory provisions for the award of interest on debts. Now all that

---

7 [2008] A.C. 561.

8 [2008] A.C. 561 at [96].

9 Some, however, fall easily within the description of contracts for professional services: para.34-084, below.

10 Actions for failure to lend money under a contract of loan are alone excluded and are dealt with later. This is partly because a loan is not a permanent but a temporary payment and the money must be repaid although not, of course, *in specie*; and partly because the action has affinities to an action for non-delivery of property. On the other hand, actions for failure to repay money lent are included here.

11 See Ch.19, above.

12 [1893] A.C. 429.

13 [1985] A.C. 104.

14 See paras 30-012 and 30-018, below.

has gone with the further decision of the House of Lords in *Sempra Metals Ltd v Inland Revenue Commissioners*,[15] effectively overruling its two earlier decisions.

30-003 As a result of *Sempra Metals*, interest, including compound interest, is today recoverable as damages at common law in appropriate circumstances. The impact of that decision has been fully considered in the chapter on interest, to which reference should accordingly be made,[16] and little more need be added here. As was held in *Sempra Metals*, proven interest losses from a failure to pay money should now be recoverable subject to the general rules of damages, in particular those on remoteness of damage. It was Denning LJ in *Trans Trust S.P.R.L. v Danubian Trading Co*[17] who, as Lord Nicholls said in *Sempra Metals*,[18] not for the first time showed the way forward. In the *Trans Trust* case Denning LJ said of the belief that interest was not allowable:

> "I do not think that the law has ever taken up such a rigid standpoint. It did undoubtedly refuse to award interest till the recent statute ... but the ground was that interest was 'generally presumed not to be within the contemplation of the parties'.[19] That is, I think, the only real ground on which damages can be refused for non-payment of money. It is because the consequences are as a rule too remote."[20]

30-004 *Trans Trust*, as we shall see, did not itself concern the awarding of interest, simple or compound; also, it was only somewhat indirectly concerned with a failure to pay money. The breakthrough decision for the recovery of compound interest, which therefore deserves pride of place, is the decision of the Court of Appeal in *Wadsworth v Lydall*.[21] Upon the dissolution of a partnership under which the claimant had run a farm owned by the defendant it was agreed that the claimant should vacate the farm in consideration of the defendant paying him £10,000. The claimant, with nowhere else to live, contracted to purchase another property on terms that £10,000 of the purchase price was to be paid on completion. He vacated the farm but the defendant failed to pay, thereby putting him in difficulties with his contract of purchase. Five months later he succeeded in extracting £7,200 from the defendant and this enabled completion to take place, the balance still due remaining outstanding on mortgage. Apart from claiming the £2,800 still unpaid by the defendant the claimant successfully sought to recover the interest charges he had had to pay to his purchaser as a result of the delayed completion. The defendant prayed in aid *London, Chatham & Dover Ry v S.E. Ry*,[22] but the Court of Appeal preferred to rely upon the obiter dicta in *Trans Trust*. Brightman LJ said that:

> "if a plaintiff pleads and can prove that he has suffered special damage as a result of the defendant's failure to perform his obligation under a contract, and such damage is not too remote on the principle of *Hadley v Baxendale*,[23] I can see no logical reason why such special damage should be irrecoverable merely because the obligation on which the

15 [2008] A.C. 561.
16 See in particular paras 19-058 and following, above.
17 [1952] 2 Q.B. 297 CA.
18 [2008] A.C. 561 at [81].
19 Citing Bullen & Leake, 3rd edn (1868), p.51.
20 [1952] 2 Q.B. 297 CA at 306.
21 [1981] 1 W.L.R. 598 CA.
22 [1893] A.C. 429.
23 (1854) 9 Ex. 341.

defendant defaulted was an obligation to pay money and not some other type of obligation."[24]

Here the damage was not too remote. "I find it inconceivable", said Ormrod LJ,

> "that this particular defendant did not contemplate and fully understand the plaintiff's position. He must have known as a fact that the plaintiff was dependent upon this £10,000 to make arrangements for alternative accommodation for himself and his family. Moreover, if he did not know, no reasonable person in 1976 looking at the facts could come to any other conclusion but that £10,000 was vital to the plaintiff and that, if he could not get the £10,000 immediately, he was bound to be put to expense in arranging alternative sources of finance—assuming that he could do so."[25]

The correctness of this approach is now amply confirmed for today by *Sempra Metals*.[26]

## (2) Recovery of damages other than interest

**30-005** A claimant may wish to claim more than interest. Here he has been faced in the past with an even more rigorous attitude of the common law towards damages for non-payment of money. "No matter what the amount of inconvenience sustained by the plaintiff", said Willes J in *Fletcher v Tayleur*,[27]

> "in case of non-payment of money, the measure of damages is the interest of the money only".

This refusal to go beyond interest has not always received approval, and the rule was soundly criticised by Jessel MR in *Wallis v Smith*,[28] where he said:

> "It has always appeared to me that the doctrine of the English law as to non-payment of money—the general rule being that you cannot recover damages because it is not paid by a certain day, is not quite consistent with reason. A man may be utterly ruined by the non-payment of the sum of money on a given day, the damages may be enormous, and the other party may be wealthy."[29]

---

24 [1981] 1 W.L.R. 598 CA at 603F–G.

25 [1981] 1 W.L.R. 598 CA at 605D–E.

26 In earlier editions *Alsabah Maritime Services Co v Philippine International Shipping Corp* [1984] 1 Lloyd's Rep. 291, another, but unsuccessful, claim for interest on account of a failure to pay money, was unfavourably contrasted with *Wadswoth v Lydall*. Today it is thought that *Alsabah* would be decided differently, but it is useful to keep it in mind. Neill J there refused, though with some reluctance, to award interest to the claimants, shipping agents operating in Saudi Arabia who were suing for moneys owing them under an agency contract, the defendant shipowners, their principals, having fallen very much behind with the payments due in respect of the claimant's disbursements to port authorities and others for which they had had to borrow at high rates of interest. In so refusing the judge took various matters into account: the specific provision in the agency contract that no other charges would be made except as specifically agreed by the defendants, the vigorous protests of the defendants as soon as the question of charging interest was raised, the prohibition on awarding interest under Saudi Arabian law. Yet the contractual provision against any further charges can be amply explained as referring to payments which could be held to be due under the contract as opposed to damages for its breach, protests when asked to pay out money are surely equivocal, while the Saudi Arabian prohibition should only be relevant if, as is nowhere suggested, Saudi Arabian law were the proper law of the contract.

27 (1855) 17 C.B. 21 at 29.

28 (1882) 21 Ch. D. 243 CA.

29 (1882) 21 Ch. D. 243 CA at 257. The wealth of the defendant is hardly relevant. He added, rather

This rule that no damages beyond interest can be recovered, though at one time frequently stated, effectively met its quietus with the Court of Appeal's decision in *Trans Trust S.P.R.L. v Danubian Trading Co.*[30] Put briefly—the full facts of the case are set out when dealing with sale of goods[31]—a buyer's failure to open a letter of credit, by which payment was to be made for the goods sold, resulted in a foreseeable loss of profit to the seller, and for this loss of profit damages were awarded. **30-006**

Indeed, the important *Trans Trust* case apart, there is a series of cases in which the defendant has contracted to sustain the claimant's financial credit and has been held liable, upon his failure to pay the claimant's creditors, well beyond interest. Thus in *Rolin v Steward*,[32] a trader recovered substantial damages for injury to his credit from his banker who had failed to meet his cheques and drafts although he had money of the trader with which to meet them; and this has been widened with the removal of the limitation to traders in *Kpohraror v Woolwich Building Society*.[33] Damages for loss of credit were also recovered in *Wilson v United Counties Bank*,[34] where a banker had expressly contracted to sustain the claimant's credit, and in *Larios v Bonany y Gurety*,[35] where a defendant was in breach of an agreement to open a credit in the claimant's favour and to honour his drafts to the amount of the credit. In the latter the defendant argued unsuccessfully that **30-007**

> "being merely the breach of an agreement to pay a sum of money, nothing could be recovered by way of damage, except the principal money contracted to be paid, and interest".[36]

In *Prehn v Royal Bank of Liverpool*,[37] a similar breach of a similar contract led to recovery for a different type of loss. The defendant bankers in Liverpool undertook by their letter of credit to the claimant to accept drafts of the claimant in Alexandria, the claimant promising to put the defendants in funds for their payment. Bills were duly accepted by the defendants, the claimant provided the necessary funds, but before the bills became due the defendants notified the claimant that they would be unable to meet them. The claimant thereupon arranged that the bills should be taken up by other bankers to whom he had to pay 2.5 per cent commission, was also obliged to pay the holders the expenses of protesting the bills, and incurred expenses in telegraphic communication between Liverpool and Alexandria. It was held that the claimant could recover for all three items of expenses. **30-008**

These results were reached because the damage which occurred was in the particular circumstances within the contemplation of the parties at the time the contract was made. It is for this reason that the contracts in these cases have often **30-009**

---

quaintly: "However that is our law. If, however, it were not our law the absurdity would be apparent."

30 [1952] 2 Q.B. 297 CA.

31 At para.25-133, above.

32 (1854) 14 C.B. 595.

33 [1996] 4 All E.R. 119 CA. And see the curious case of *Nicholson v Knox Ukiwa & Co* [2008] P.N.L.R. 33 at 782 where substantial damages were awarded for injury to credit together with even more substantial interest on them. The cases of dishonour of clients' cheques by bankers are fully considered at paras 34-085 to 34-087, below.

34 [1920] A.C. 102.

35 (1873) L.R. 5 P.C. 346.

36 (1873) L.R. 5 P.C. at 357.

37 (1870) L.R. 5 Ex. 92.

been referred to as special ones.[38] This factor is brought out well by a comparison of these cases with actions on bills and notes in respect of their dishonour, in which actions certain strict limits are imposed upon the measure of damages by s.57 of the Bills of Exchange Act 1882.[39] Thus in *Re English Bank of River Plate*,[40] which was such an action and in which the expenses incurred by the claimant were practically the same as those incurred by the claimant in *Prehn v Royal Bank of Liverpool*,[41] damages in respect of the expenses were refused and the earlier case distinguished on the ground that it was not an action on a bill but on a special contract.[42]

**30-010** All these decisions now gather strength from the ruling of the House of Lords in *Sempra Metals*. They are in effect illustrations of what is now the general rule, and there should be no need any more to speak of special contracts.

**30-011** A somewhat different case of the recovery of damages unaffected by *Sempra Metals* is *Cooper v National Westminster Bank Plc*,[43] where there was failure to pay over money in the form of a bank draft. The defendant bank did not deliver, but cancelled, a bank draft in euros issued by it in the claimant's favour at his request. Damages were assessed by taking the value at the time of failure to deliver less the value at the time of issue, thereby taking the foreign exchange profit away from the bank and giving it to the claimant. The analogy of damages for non-delivery in a sale of goods contract was employed.[44]

## 2. DISHONOUR OF BILLS OF EXCHANGE AND PROMISSORY NOTES

**30-012** In the particular case of failure to pay money due on a bill of exchange or promissory note, the law has been put into statutory form by the Bills of Exchange Act 1882. The measure of damages is stated in s.57 as to bills of exchange, and its provisions are applied mutatis mutandis to promissory notes by s.89(1).[45] The former section originally ran in full thus:

> "Where a bill is dishonoured, the measure of damages, which shall be deemed to be liquidated damages,[46] shall be as follows:

---

38 See, e.g. *Prehn v Royal Bank of Liverpool* (1870) L.R. 5 Ex. 92 at 100, per Pigott B ("an action on a special contract"). Contrast *Larios v Bonany y Gurety* (1873) L.R. 5 P.C. 346 at 357; *Re English Bank of River Plate* [1893] 2 Ch. 438 at 446.

39 See paras 30-012 and following, below.

40 [1893] 2 Ch. 438.

41 (1870) L.R. 5 Ex. 92.

42 [1893] 2 Ch. 438 at 446. Banker's commission was again refused in *Banque Populaire de Bienne v Cave* (1895) 1 Com. Cas. 67 because there was "no special contract" (at 69) as in *Prehn v Royal Bank of Liverpool* (1870) L.R. 5 Ex. 92.

43 [2010] 1 Lloyd's Rep. 490.

44 See [2010] 1 Lloyd's Rep. 490 at [82] to [89].

45 Section 89(2) provides that, in applying to notes the provisions of the Act as to bills, the maker of a note is deemed to correspond with the acceptor of a bill (these being the persons primarily liable), and the first indorser of a note with the drawer of an accepted bill payable to drawer's order. The only particular difference in relation to damages between bills and notes is that protest is not necessary for a foreign note but is required for a foreign bill appearing on the face of it to be such: see s.89(4) and para.30-025, below.

46 Deeming the damages liquidated allowed the claim to be specially indorsed on the writ under the then RSC Ord.3 r.6, enabling use of the summary procedure under the then RSC Ord.14 (even if a claim was included for interest "until payment": *Lawrence v Willcocks* [1892] 1 Q.B. 696 CA; or "until payment or judgment": *London & Universal Bank v Clancarty* [1892] 1 Q.B. 689). This,

(1) The holder may recover from any party liable on the bill, and the drawer who has been compelled to pay the bill may recover from the acceptor, and an indorser who has been compelled to pay the bill may recover from the acceptor or from the drawer, or from a prior indorser—
   (a) The amount of the bill;
   (b) Interest thereon from the time of presentment for payment if the bill is payable on demand, and from the maturity of the bill in any other case;
   (c) The expenses of noting, or, when protest is necessary, and the protest has been extended, the expenses of protest.

(2) In the case of a bill which has been dishonoured abroad, in lieu of the above damages, the holder may recover from the drawer or an indorser, and the drawer or an indorser who has been compelled to pay the bill may recover from any party liable to him, the amount of the re-exchange with interest thereon until the time of payment.

(3) Where by this Act interest may be recovered as damages, such interest may, if justice require it, be withheld wholly or in part, and where a bill is expressed to be payable with interest at a given rate, interest as damages may or may not be given at the same rate as interest proper."

Section 57(2) was repealed by s.4 of the Administration of Justice Act 1977, a repeal which followed the decision in *Miliangos v George Frank (Textiles)*,[47] that English courts are not debarred, as had been formerly assumed, from making their awards of damages in foreign currencies[48]; accordingly, the amount of re-exchange has disappeared as a statutorily prescribed measure of damages[49] and s.57(1) is therefore left commanding the field.[50] However, should there arise any situation which is not covered by subs.(1), or which was not formerly covered by subss.(1) and (2), it is provided by s.97(2) that the rules of common law, including the law merchant, shall continue to apply to bills and notes where not inconsistent with the express provisions of the Act. **30-013**

From the cases that follow it will be seen that reported litigation on the domestic front is confined entirely to the 19th century. The rather few authorities of the 20th century have all contained a foreign element. This has been because either foreign currencies or alien enemies in wartime have been involved. As for the 21st century it has produced one case containing, like all the 20th century cases, a foreign element, but since the proper law was also foreign it does not concern us, the damages having to be assessed according to the provisions of the proper law.[51] **30-014**

---

however, has long ceased to be of importance by reason of RSC changes. Today under the CPR particulars of claim may be placed within the claim form (CPR r.7.4(1)(a)) and summary judgment is available for all damages claims (CPR r.24.3). In *Re Gillespie Ex p. Robarts* (1886) 16 Q.B.D. 702, Cave J at first instance held that the purpose of inserting the provision as to liquidated damages was to fix the amount which could properly be claimed on a specially indorsed writ, thus allowing the claimant to sue for unliquidated damages beyond the measure specified in s.57: at 706. The Court of Appeal affirmed this decision on other grounds ((1886) 18 Q.B.D. 286 CA: see para.30-027, below) without commenting on this interpretation, but it cannot stand against subsequent cases refusing damages beyond the measure laid down by s.57 when s.57 applied: see para.30-026, below.

47 [1976] A.C. 443.

48 See paras20-018 and following, above. The reason for the repeal is indicated at para.30-015.

49 For what precisely was meant by the amount of re-exchange, see Byles J's clear exposition in *Suse v Pompe* (1860) 8 C.B. N.S. 538 at 564–565. See, too, counsel *arguendo* in *De Tastet v Baring* (1809) 11 East. 265 at 269–270 and North J in *Re Commercial Bank of South Australia* (1887) 36 Ch. D. 522 at 528.

50 The former law will be found in the 13th edition (1972) of this work at paras 795 and following.

51 The case is *Karafarin Bank v Mansoury-Dara* [2010] 1 Lloyd's Rep. 236. Iranian law had to be ap-

## (1) The preliminary problem of the proper law of the contract

30-015 Bills and notes generally give rise to a number of separate and different contracts between the various parties to the instrument,[52] and frequently one or more of these several contracts will involve problems of a conflict of laws. The solution of such problems is strictly outside the scope of this book, but since they are intertwined in some of the cases with problems of the domestic law of damages, it is important to set them apart at the outset. Generally speaking,[53] the proper law of the contract, both as to formal validity and as to interpretation, is the *lex loci contractus* which, since the contract is generally incomplete without delivery of the instrument,[54] will generally be the place of delivery. Hence if all the contracts, namely the drawing, the making, the acceptance, the indorsements, are made in this country,[55] s.57 of the Act will apply; if they are all made abroad, s.57 can have no application since the proper law will be a foreign one.[56] When some of the contracts are made in this country[57] and some abroad, s.57 will apply only to the former, but nevertheless the fact that the latter are made abroad may have an effect upon the damages recoverable in relation to the former. It was with this situation in mind that s.57(2) was enacted, giving a separate measure of damages for bills and notes dishonoured abroad, although this provision has now been repealed. Where dishonour occurs abroad the proper law of the contract of the acceptor of a bill or of the maker of a note is presumably that of the foreign country, and therefore no mention was made of the acceptor in s.57(2) or, by implication, of the maker. The proper law of the drawer's or indorsers' contracts may however be that of this country, and the measure of damages was to be calculated by the amount of re-exchange which was needed to compensate the holder in a claim against drawer or indorsers if it was assumed, as would frequently be the case, that the bill or note fell to be discharged in the currency of the country of dishonour where payment was primarily due.[58]

---

plied, under which interest is prohibited but an amount was awarded by reference to an inflation index.

52 "A congeries of contracts dependent on one original contract, which always has a certain effect on the others": Dicey and Morris, *The Conflict of Laws*, 15th edn (London: Sweet & Maxwell, 2012), para.33-328.

53 The following generalisations, looked at from the point of view of conflict of laws and not of domestic damages, necessarily suffer from over-simplification. For a full treatment, see the standard works on conflict of laws.

54 Section 21(1); but see the proviso.

55 To avoid further complication, it is assumed that "this country" for the purposes of the conflict of laws in relation to bills and notes has the same meaning as "this country" has for the purpose of the domestic law of damages in relation to bills and notes. While it is true that there was no definition of "abroad" for the purpose of s.57(2), and accordingly of "this country" for the purpose of s.57(1), the distinction was probably the same as that made in s.4(1), in a somewhat different connection, between "British Islands" and "foreign", "British Islands" being there defined for the purposes of the Act as "any part of the United Kingdom of Great Britain and [Northern] Ireland, the islands of Man, Guernsey, Jersey, Alderney, and Sark, and the islands adjacent to any of them being part of the dominions of Her Majesty".

56 As was the case in *Karafarin Bank v Mansoury-Dara* [2010] 1 Lloyd's Rep. 236: see the preceding paragraph.

57 See the last footnote but one, above.

58 Of course, the currency in which dishonour occurs and the country in the currency of which payment is expressed need not necessarily be the same. See, for example, the three cases dealt with in para.30-017, below.

However, now that, since *Miliangos*,[59] the holder can claim the amount of such a bill or note in the foreign currency itself, it was presumably considered that the purpose of s.57(2), with its provision of a special measure of damages for this situation, was spent. Conversely, where the proper law of the contract of the acceptor or maker is that of this country and dishonour consequently occurs here, but the proper law of the drawer's or indorsers' contracts is that of a foreign country, the amount that the drawer or indorsers need to recover from the acceptor or maker to compensate them after being sued according to the foreign law by the holder will be the amount of the re-exchange. This situation is not catered for by s.57, since s.57(1) does not give the amount of re-exchange, and s.57(2) never applied to bills and notes dishonoured in this country. The Court of Appeal in *Re Gillespie Ex p. Robarts*[60] held it to be a *casus omissus*, and allowed recovery under the rules of common law, which by s.97(2) continue to apply to bills where not inconsistent with the express provisions of the Act. This is a measure of the complexities involved.

### (2) Bills and notes[61] to which s.57 applies

Today the only measure of damages prescribed by s.57, now that its second subsection has gone,[62] is the measure appearing in subs.(1), namely the amount of the bill or note together with interest and the expenses of noting and protest.[63] **30-016**

**(a) The amount of the bill or note** The amount of the bill or note is of the order of debt rather than damages. Its calculation hardly needs explanation. If expressed in a foreign currency the rate of exchange, where translation into sterling for the award was formerly necessary, was taken at the time of the breach by failure to pay on maturity or on demand; this was held in *Salim Nasrallah Khoury v Khayat*.[64] **30-017**

---

59 [1976] A.C. 443; see paras 20-018 and following, above.

60 (1886) 18 Q.B.D. 286 CA.

61 The provisions of s.57(1) apply to notes by virtue of s.89(1).

62 See paras 30-012 to 30-013 and, above.

63 Provided always that the section can be regarded as capable of applying (see the *casus omissus* dealt with at para.30-027, below), no question has ever arisen as to whether a claimant may, in appropriate circumstances, be entitled to claim a different measure of damages to that prescribed by s.57(1). See, however, the conflicting authorities on the former s.57(2), the court in *Suse v Pompe* (1860) 8 C.B. N.S. 538 holding inadmissible evidence of a custom which would allow the holder suing the indorser to elect for the amount he had paid him for the bill rather than the amount of re-exchange prescribed by s.57(2) because the custom contradicted the instrument (at 567), but the court in *Willans v Ayers* (1877) 3 App. Cas. 133 PC, pointing out (at 144 to 145) that the custom there in issue, which allowed the holder to claim a fixed percentage of the amount of the bill in substitution for the amount of re-exchange based upon a fluctuating exchange rate, had been recognised by the courts in other countries even when it depended solely on usage and also by the early case of *Auriol v Thomas* (1787) 2 T.R. 52. It was suggested in the 13th edition of this work, at para.810, that, provided that s.57(2) did not prevent any custom from varying the statutory measure of damages, the solution lay in deciding whether the custom fell to be regarded as liquidated damages or a penalty: the custom in *Willans v Ayers* would come within the accepted principles of liquidated damages because it could work both for and against the claimant since it substituted the customary for the general measure, but the custom in *Suse v Pompe* would be a penalty as it could only operate in the claimant's favour since it entitled him to elect between the customary and general measures. And contrast *Re Commercial Bank of South Australia* (1887) 36 Ch. D. 522 where it was held that a claimant could not avoid claiming the measure prescribed by s.57(2), which applied to his case, by claiming under s.57(1).

64 [1943] A.C. 507 PC.

Now, since *Miliangos*,[65] the award may be of the amount of the bill or note in the foreign currency, and this indeed was the situation in *Miliangos*[66] itself,[67] and in *Barclays Bank International v Levin Brothers (Bradford)*.[68] In the latter case *Salim Nasrallah Khoury v Khayat*[69] was regarded as being of no continuing authority upon the issue of the enforcement by action of bills and notes expressed in a foreign currency.[70]

**30-018** **(b) Interest** It has for very long been accepted that interest, where not expressly made payable by the terms of the bill or note, could be awarded by way of damages for detention of the debt. Such a rule was laid down as early as 1746 by Lord Hardwicke in *Ex p. Marlar*,[71] and was practically the sole survivor of the attack made upon the propriety of awards of interest as damages for failure to pay money.[72] Its survival is witnessed by a series of cases around 1820, *Re Burgess*,[73] *Cameron v Smith*,[74] and *DuBelloix v Waterpark*,[75] in all of which the rule was taken as settled. Now it is incorporated in section 57(1).

**30-019** *(i) A discretionary award* The award of interest as damages was stated to be a matter for the jury's discretion in *DuBelloix v Waterpark*[76] and, although soon after it was said in *Laing v Stone*[77] that

> "it would be inconvenient if it were left to the discretion or rather the caprice of the jury to say whether interest should be paid or not",

the discretionary nature of the award has been retained by s.57(3), which allows the withholding of interest in whole or in part if justice requires it. As pointed out by Lord Esher MR in *Ex p. Charman*,[78] the discretion is no longer that of the jury, but of the judge.

**30-020** *(ii) Period of time for which interest is given* Following general principles, interest is calculated from the date when the cause of action arose. Thus, in the first place, where the bill or note has a fixed time[79] for payment, interest runs from that time. This common law rule is now incorporated in s.57(1)(b). If the maturity date

---

65 [1976] A.C. 443; see paras 20-018 and following, above.
66 [1976] A.C. 443.
67 Facts at para.20-026, above.
68 [1977] Q.B. 270; facts at para.20-033, above. A conversion into sterling is still required, however, in the court's judgment in order that it may be enforced here; for details of this see paras 19-028 and 19-029, above.
69 [1943] A.C. 507 PC.
70 And s.72(4) of the Bills of Exchange Act 1882, now repealed, was held not to prevent the court from awarding the amount of the bill in the foreign currency: see first long footnote at para.20-033, above.
71 (1746) 1 Atk. 150.
72 See the cases at paras 19-005 and following, above.
73 (1818) 2 Moore 745.
74 (1819) 2 B. & Ald. 305.
75 (1822) 1 Dow. & Ry. 16.
76 (1822) 1 Dow. & Ry. 16 at 19, per Abbott CJ and Bayley J.
77 (1828) 2 Mann. & Ryl. 561 at 562–563.
78 [1887] W.N. 184 CA.
79 In *Blake v Lawrence* (1802) 4 Esp. 147 a note was payable by instalments, with a provision that on failure to pay any instalment the whole amount was to become due. It was held that interest was to be calculated upon the whole amount remaining due after default, and not upon the respective instalments at the time when they would otherwise have become payable.

of the bill or note has arrived it will thus be immaterial, for the award of interest, that payment is not demanded till some time later, as happened in *Bank Polski v Mulder*,[80] or that the defendant, if drawer or indorser, has not received notice of dishonour.[81] On the other hand, where money was due to an estate before the appointment of an administrator, so that there existed no one to whom the interest could properly be paid, it was held in *Murray v East India Co*,[82] that interest did not run till demand by the administrator. The ground of this decision was that no cause of action arose until there was a party capable of suing; the same result should be reached under the Act today.[83] In the second place, where the bill or note is payable on demand, the cause of action arises on demand by presentment for payment, and interest therefore runs from this time. This is also incorporated in s.57(1)(b), but earlier cases remain useful on some points. Thus in *Pierce v Fothergill*,[84] the issue of the writ was considered a sufficient demand to allow the award of interest from that time, while a demand was dispensed with as a useless formality in *Re East of England Banking Co*,[85] where a bank had closed its door and thereby intimated to all the world its refusal to pay bills.

Again following general principles, interest is calculated down to the date of **30-021** judgment. As early as 1760 Lord Mansfield in *Robinson v Bland*,[86] pointed out the justice of carrying down the interest beyond the commencement of the action to judgment. "It takes from defendants", he said,

> "the temptations to make use of all the unjust dilatories of chicane. For, if interest is to stop at the commencement of the suit, where the sum is large, the defendant may gain by protracting the cause in the most expensive and vexatious manner, and the more the plaintiff is injured the less he will be relieved."

This common law rule is not expressly covered by s.57; it clearly still stands. If, however, there has been a valid tender by the defendant it has been held in *Dent v Dunn*,[87] that interest does not run after this; since interest represents compensation for being deprived of money it should not be awarded where payment of that money has been tendered. As to interest after judgment, this is not within the realm of damages, and, once again following general principles, is awarded under the separate provisions of the Judgments Act 1838.[88]

Where, at the time the bill or note would in the ordinary course have become pay- **30-022** able, whether on maturity or on demand, it has been illegal to pay money to the person entitled because he was an alien enemy, interest has been held to run only

---

80 [1942] 1 K.B. 497 CA; see especially at 500.

81 The decision in *Walker v Barnes* (1813) 5 Taunt. 240, that a drawer was liable for interest only after notice of dishonour, cannot stand now against s.57(1).

82 (1821) 5 B. & Ald. 204.

83 See the cases on alien enemies at para.30-022, below. Alternatively the same result might be reached today by invoking the court's discretionary powers under s.57(3).

84 (1835) 2 Bing. N.C. 167.

85 (1868) L.R. 6 Eq. 368; see especially at 375–376. Although strictly not within the wording of s.57(1) this would probably still be considered good law today.

86 (1760) 2 Burr. 1077 at 1087. The claimant sued both for dishonour of a bill and for failure to repay a loan in respect of which the bill had been given. He succeeded only on the second limb of his action because the bill was held to be void. The court's award of interest was, therefore, for the failure to repay the loan, but it is clear that the court would have held similarly as to interest awarded for dishonour of the bill.

87 (1813) 3 Camp. 296.

88 As now amended: see paras 19-105 and 19-106, above.

from the time payment again became legal. This result was suggested in *DuBelloix v Waterpark*,[89] in relation to the French Revolutionary and Napoleonic Wars, and was reached in *Biedermann v Allhausen*,[90] and *Ledeboter v Hibbert*,[91] cases following upon the First and Second World Wars respectively. Some difficulty, however, has arisen because of the treatment of these decisions in *The Berwickshire*.[92] In that case, which involved the tortious sinking of a ship owned and manned by then alien enemies, interest was awarded as damages on the value of the ship and of the seamen's effects from the date of the tort in 1940 and not from the date in 1944 when the claimants ceased to be alien enemies. Lord Merriman P, although declaring himself not to be concerned to express any opinion whether the bills and notes cases were rightly decided,[93] treated them unenthusiastically and in particular pointed out that the dicta in their Lordships' speeches in *Stevenson v Aktiengesellschaft für Cartonnagen Industrie*[94] were hardly in their favour.[95] It is submitted, however, that the bills and notes cases present an exceptional situation, and are properly decided for the reason that the act which would have constituted the breach of duty was the very thing which the defendant could not lawfully do. The defendant was therefore not in default[96] and consequently did not become liable to pay damages at all until the claimant ceased from being an alien enemy. This rationale appears from Morris J's judgment in *Ledeboter v Hibbert*,[97] where he said that there seemed to him

> "to be something incongruous in asking the court to award damages against a man for failing to do what the law forbade him to do",

and also in Lord Atkinson's speech in *Stevenson v Aktiengesellschaft für Cartonnagen Industrie*,[98] where he said that the principle upon which the bills and notes cases[99] appeared to him to be based was

> "that interest is in the nature of damages payable by the debtor by reason of his withholding his debt, his default in not paying his debt, and since during war he cannot lawfully pay his debt to an alien enemy without committing a crime, he is not in any default in omitting to pay it, and should not therefore be mulcted in damages for not doing what he cannot do lawfully."[100]

This reasoning can only apply where the defendant's primary obligation is itself to

89 (1822) 1 Dow. & Ry. 16. The case was decided in the defendant's favour on the ground that the award of interest had properly been left to the jury's discretion. Abbott CJ, however, added as a second ground the fact that the claimant had been an alien enemy for most of the relevant period.

90 (1921) 37 T.L.R. 662.

91 [1947] K.B. 964.

92 [1950] P. 204.

93 [1950] P. 204 at 217.

94 [1918] A.C. 239.

95 [1950] P. 204 at 216–217.

96 The fact that the defendant could and should have paid the money to the Custodian of Enemy Property was not considered to be a default vis-à-vis the claimant in *Ledeboter v Hibbert* [1947] K.B. 964.

97 [1947] K.B. 964 at 967.

98 [1918] A.C. 239 at 256.

99 At that time *DuBelloix v Waterpark* (1822) 1 Dow. & Ry. 16 was the only English case but two American cases had also been relied upon by the defendant there.

100 See, too, *Biedermann v Allhausen* (1921) 37 T.L.R. 662 at 663, per Darling J.

pay money and reaches neither cases of tort, such as *The Berwickshire*,[101] where the duty imposed by the general law is invariably something other than the payment of money, nor all other cases of breaches of contract where the duty arising from the promise is not to pay money but, for instance, to deliver or accept goods under a contract of sale. And, even where the primary obligation is to pay money, this reasoning should not apply where the defendant is in breach in not paying before payment became illegal; it is therefore submitted that a different conclusion might be reached where the claimant became an alien enemy after his cause of action had arisen by reason of a failure to pay the bill or note on maturity or on demand.[102] Nor, finally, does this reasoning apply where, although the primary obligation is to pay money, the claim is not one for damages so that no default need be shown.[103] Indeed in cases such as *Biedermann v Allhausen*,[104] and *Ledeboter v Hibbert*,[105] themselves, the principles of restitution and unjust enrichment might profitably be explored by claimants for a possible ground of recovery.

*(iii) Rate of interest* In the 19th century, within which all of the authorities not involving a foreign element lie,[106] interest was usually awarded at five per cent because this was taken to represent the commercial value of money at the time.[107] However, even then it was accepted that this rate should vary with the general rate of interest which reflects the current value of money.[108] Of course in the latter part of the 20th century a steep rise took interest rates for a time into double figures, since when rates have fallen further and further back, and these fluctuations will be reflected in awards of interest where bills or notes are dishonoured. Where a bill or a note is expressed to be payable with interest at a given rate up to the date of maturity, interest awarded as damages after this date is presumably calculated upon the initial amount of the bill or note plus the interest expressly payable at maturity,[109] and by s.57(3) may or may not in the discretion of the court be given at the same rate as the contractual rate of interest. There are early cases in which interest has **30-023**

---

[101] [1950] P. 204.

[102] This is one ground (there are others: see, for one other, the next note) upon which *Wolff v Oxholm* (1817) 6 M. & S. 92 may be distinguished, although it was not a distinction which appealed to Lord Merriman P in *The Berwickshire* [1950] P. 204 at 213. It also represents the position in *DuBelloix v Waterpark* (1822) 1 Dow. & Ry. 16.

[103] Thus interest was awarded in *Wolff v Oxholm* (1817) 6 M. & S. 92 where interest was payable by the express terms of the bill; and in *Stevenson v Aktiengesellschaft für Cartonnagen Industrie* [1918] A.C. 239 (which was a claim not on a bill but for a share of the profits of a partnership) where there was a fiduciary relationship between the parties. Contrast Lord Parmoor in the latter case, where he said that in his opinion the view expressed in *DuBelloix v Waterpark* (1822) 1 Dow. & Ry. 16 against the award of interest during the period in which it could not lawfully be paid "would not apply either to a case in which there is a stipulation for interest, or where there is a fiduciary relationship between the parties on the dissolution of a partnership": [1918] A.C. 239 at 259–260.

[104] (1921) 37 T.L.R. 662.

[105] [1947] K.B. 964.

[106] See para.30-014, above.

[107] In *Re Commercial Bank of South Australia* (1887) 36 Ch. D. 552 at 529, North J spoke of five per cent as "being the rate of interest payable in this country when the rate is not specially agreed upon".

[108] See *Cameron v Smith* (1819) 2 B. & Ald. 305 at 308–309, per Bayley J: "It is competent for them [i.e. the jury] either to allow 5 per cent or 4 per cent according to their judgment of the value of money."

[109] This would seem to be so despite the fact that statutory interest under the Senior Courts Act 1981 s.35A(1) is confined to simple interest.

been awarded as damages at a contractual rate higher than the commercial rate,[110] and cases where this has been refused.[111] In strictness, it would seem that the courts should lean in favour of whatever is currently the commercial rate and not the contractual rate, since the parties have failed to make express provision and the commercial rate gives the court's view of the value of money.

30-024 **(c) Expenses of noting and protest** Section 57(1)(c) includes in the damages the expenses of noting. This is a charge made by a notary public, to whom the holder has handed the bill or note on its dishonour, for re-presenting it and on its redishonour noting this fact on the bill or note itself.[112] Whether noting is necessary or not in the circumstances, the expenses of it are recoverable.

30-025 Section 57(1)(c) also includes in the damages the expenses of protest, but only where protest is necessary. This is a charge made by a notary public for issuing a certificate setting out the facts of presentation and dishonour and protesting against all parties liable on account of the dishonour.[113] By the provisions of the Act there is no necessity to protest an inland bill or note,[114] a foreign bill not appearing on the face of it to be such,[115] or a foreign note.[116] Only in the case of a foreign bill appearing on the face of it to be such is protest necessary,[117] and therefore only in such a case are the expenses of protest recoverable as damages. Thus in *Re English Bank of River Plate*,[118] the expenses of protest for better security were held to be irrecoverable.

30-026 **(d) Other losses** Section 57(1) appears to mark the limits to the recoverable damages in the cases to which it applies. Thus not only does it prevent, by direct implication, recovery of the expenses of a protest declared by the Act to be an unnecessary one, as was held in *Re English Bank of River Plate*,[119] but it stands in the way of recovery for losses of which it makes no mention. This is also illustrated by *Re English Bank of River Plate*,[120] where recovery in respect of the commission paid by the claimant drawers to their bankers for accepting the bill for honour and for providing money to meet it, was also refused.[121] Similarly, in *Banque Populaire de Bienne v Cave*,[122] the holder failed to recover from the acceptor for expenses incurred by way of banker's commission, brokerage and stamps for postage.[123] The trend of these decisions suggests that, even if further loss can be said

110 See, e.g. *Keene v Keene* (1857) 3 C.B. N.S. 144.
111 See, e.g. *Ward v Morrison* (1842) Car. & M. 368.
112 For further details, see the standard texts on bills and notes. In *Dando v Boden* [1893] 1 Q.B. 318 the words "bank charges" were held a sufficient description of expenses of noting in a specially indorsed writ.
113 Protest is a continuation of the noting; this continuation of the process is what is meant in s.57(1)(c) by the term "the protest has been extended".
114 See ss.51(1) and 89(1) respectively.
115 See s.51(2) *in fin*.
116 See s.89(4).
117 See s.51(2).
118 [1893] 2 Ch. 438.
119 [1893] 2 Ch. 438.
120 [1893] 2 Ch. 438.
121 See, especially, [1893] 2 Ch. 438 at 445.
122 (1895) 1 Com. Cas. 67.
123 Both cases distinguished *Prehn v Royal Bank of Liverpool* (1870) L.R. 5 Ex. 92: see para.30-008, above. Such expenses may be recoverable where the defendant is liable for re-exchange, by virtue

to have been in the contemplation of the parties in the particular circumstances, recovery will not be allowed.[124] Although the general common law rule which refused damages for non-payment of money might be displaced where the parties contemplate further loss, it is submitted that the measure for bills and notes, which is indeed more generous, could not, being statutory, be similarly displaced. In practice, however, where further loss is contemplated it would have been possible to regard the agreement as a special one so that the claimant could found his action upon this special contract as distinct from suing on the bill or note itself. This must be all the truer after the decision in *Sempra Metals Ltd v Inland Revenue Commissioners*.[125]

### (3) Bills and notes to which s.57 does not apply

If s.57 should not make provision for a particular situation, then, by virtue of s.97(2), the common law[126] applies. Such a situation arose in *Re Gillespie Ex p. Robarts*.[127] A bill was drawn abroad payable in this country. On the acceptor's dishonour of the bill in this country the drawer became liable by the law of the foreign country to pay the amount of re-exchange to the holder as damages, and it was held that he was entitled to recover the amount of re-exchange to which he became liable from the acceptor, for, as Lindley LJ said, **30-027**

> "the acceptor of a bill drawn abroad knows that, in the event of dishonour, there is a liability for re-exchange".[128]

This recovery was neither under s.57(1), which does not include the amount of re-exchange in the damages, nor under s.57(2), which applied only to bills dishonoured abroad, but was by virtue of s.97(2) which saves the rules of common law in so far as they are not inconsistent with the express terms of the Act.[129] As far as the Act was concerned, the situation raised by the facts of *Re Gillespie Ex p. Robarts*,[130] was treated as a *casus omissus*. "Section 57(1)", said Lindley LJ,

> "does not appear to be addressed to the case of a bill the drawer of which is liable in damages for re-exchange".[131]

Therefore, since before the Act it had been held a number of times that the

---

of s.97(2), at common law: see paras.30-015, above, and 30-027, below.

124 Cave J's holding in *Re Gillespie Ex p. Robarts* (1886) 16 Q.B.D. 702 (affirmed on other grounds: (1886) 18 Q.B.D. 286 CA), that the provision as to liquidated damages in s.57 was intended to allow the claimant to sue for unliquidated damages beyond the measure specified by the section, cannot stand against the decisions in the text. It would also seem that s.57(1), as interpreted in these decisions, would require a different result today on the facts of *Dickinson v Hatfield* (1831) 1 Moo. & Rob. 141, in which costs of postage were allowed where the defendant had by letter directed the claimant to charge the postage to his account. It might, however, be possible to regard such a direction as giving rise to a separate contractual obligation.

125 [2008] A.C. 561. See at paras 30-002 and following, above.

126 Including the law merchant.

127 (1886) 18 Q.B.D. 286 CA.

128 (1886) 18 Q.B.D. 286 CA at 292 to 293.

129 See para.30-015, above, where the complexities discussed indicate the reason why this situation was not brought within the ambit of s.57 by the framers of the Act.

130 (1886) 18 Q.B.D. 286 CA.

131 (1886) 18 Q.B.D. 286 CA at 292.

amount of re-exchange was recoverable as damages in such circumstances,[132] these decisions were applied by virtue of s.97(2). Nor is the position affected by the repeal of s.57(2) with its prescription of the amount of re-exchange as the measure of damages for bills dishonoured abroad.[133] That prescription is no longer needed because English law can now award the amount of the bill or note in the foreign currency itself, but in *Re Gillespie Ex p. Robarts*[134] the need to award the amount of re-exchange arose because of the foreign law—the drawer was required to pay the amount of the re-exchange when sued by the holder under the foreign law and accordingly required a similar measure to recoup himself in his action against the acceptor here. That this was how the amount of re-exchange came to be relevant is clearly enunciated by Lindley LJ. "The liability", he said,

> "of the drawer in the present case to pay damages to the holder for re-exchange depends on the law of Tobago, and not on s.57 of the Bills of Exchange Act."[135]

**30-028** This is the only situation in which s.57 has been held to be inapplicable and the pre-existing common law has been resorted to. If other situations should arise in which the measure of damages laid down by s.57(1) seems inappropriate, the common law is always there to fill the gap.

## II. BREACH BY LENDER

**30-029** In contracts for the loan of money the normal measure of damages for the lender's failure to provide the money is the amount required by the borrower to go into the market and effect a substitute loan for himself less the amount that the contractual loan had required. It has been said by Day J in *Manchester & Oldham Bank v Cook*,[136] that

> "nominal damages … are usually given in the case of breach of contract to lend money, for the reason that usually if a man cannot get money in one quarter he can in another".

Thus in *South African Territories v Wallington*,[137] since the claimant gave no evidence showing a loss beyond this, nominal damages were awarded. But the Court of Appeal recognised that the damages could be substantial for failure to provide the loan. Chitty LJ said that

> "the damages in such a case may be large or small, or merely nominal, according to the circumstances".[138]

They will be nominal if the claimant, as a man of good credit, can readily obtain a loan elsewhere, but

---

132 *Francis v Rucker* (1768) Amb. 672; *Walker v Hamilton* (1860) 1 De G.F. & J. 602; *Re General South American Co* (1877) 7 Ch. D. 637. Whether the earlier cases of *Woolsey v Crawford* (1810) 2 Camp. 445 and *Napier v Schneider* (1810) 12 East 420 were overruled is not clear.

133 See paras 30-012 and 30-013, above.

134 (1886) 18 Q.B.D. 286 CA.

135 (1886) 18 Q.B.D. 286 CA at 292.

136 (1883) 49 L.T. 674 at 678. See, too, Chitty J in *Western Wagon Co v West* [1892] 1 Ch. 271 at 277, giving as illustration the claimant who goes straight into the market and obtains another loan. This was cited with approval by Lopes LJ in *South African Territories v Wallington* [1897] 1 Q.B. 692 CA at 695.

137 [1897] 1 Q.B. 692 CA; affirmed [1898] A.C. 309.

138 [1897] 1 Q.B. 692 CA at 696.

> "if he cannot obtain the money except at a higher rate of interest, or for a shorter term of years, or upon other more onerous terms, the damages would be greater and might be very substantial. The burden of proving the amount of the loss sustained rests on the plaintiff".[139]

A qualification of this appears in *Bahamas Sisal Plantation v Griffin*,[140] which like the previous case concerned a failure by the defendant to fulfil his contract to take debentures from the claimant company. It was pointed out there that

> "in measuring the damages it must be assumed that when the company applied elsewhere for an advance it still remained a company with ordinary credit. If by reason of circumstances, the company had fallen into disrepute and bad financial odour, the defendant was not responsible for that."[141]

Since this was the cause of the company's failure to find another person to take the debentures, the claim for damages failed. So too in *Blue Sky One Ltd v Mahan Air*,[142] the trial judge, after citing all the above cases of early date and also referring to this work, held that in the case before him there was no reason to depart from the rule denying damages where the inability of the borrower to secure alternative funding was not made out.[143]

There may also be consequential losses. Thus the damages may include the cost of raising the money elsewhere. However, where two sets of such costs were claimed in *Astor Properties v Tunbridge Wells Equitable Friendly Society*,[144] one for a temporary and the other for a permanent loan, two sets were held not to be in the reasonable contemplation of the parties and only one was allowed in damages.[145] Further, the claimant may recover for the loss of any contract which hinged upon the loan if the defendant was aware of the purpose for which the claimant was entering into the loan. The authority for this is the decision in *Manchester & Oldham Bank v Cook*.[146] The claimant asked the defendant bank for a loan to enable him to purchase an interest in a colliery. The defendant agreed but failed to find the money, and the claimant was unable, apparently, to obtain the money elsewhere and so unable to complete the purchase. It was held that he could recover damages in respect of the loss of the colliery purchase, the court stressing that "the bank had express notice of the purpose for which the money was required".[147] And in *Astor Properties v Tunbridge Wells Equitable Friendly Society*,[148] where the money to be lent was to be used by the claimant for a purchase-money mortgage, damages were allowed for the estimated loss of the rents that the claimant would have obtained from the property for the period of delay before the claimant obtained the property by means of a substitute loan. **30-030**

---

139 [1897] 1 Q.B. 692 CA at 696 and 697.
140 (1897) 14 T.L.R. 139.
141 (1897) 14 T.L.R. 139 at 140.
142 [2010] EWHC 631 (Comm).
143 See [2010] EWHC 631 (Comm) at [144]–[148].
144 [1936] 1 All E.R. 531.
145 Contrast *Duckworth v Ewart* (1864) 2 H. & C. 129, with a complex set of facts and not precisely a contract of loan, where the cost of an abortive mortgage was allowed as damages but, by a majority, nothing further.
146 (1883) 49 L.T. 674.
147 (1883) 49 L.T. 674 at 678, per Day J; similarly, at 679, per Smith J.
148 [1936] 1 All E.R. 531.

## III. BREACH BY BORROWER

**30-031** Conversely, the normal measure of damages for the borrower's failure to accept the money contracted to be lent is the profit the lender would have made on the loan less the profit he can make on a substitute loan made by him in the market. There appear to be no cases dealing with the question.

CHAPTER 31

# CONSTRUCTION CONTRACTS

TABLE OF CONTENTS



Construction or building contracts form a halfway house between contracts for the transfer of property[1] and contracts for the rendering of services.[2] Classified with exactness they are contracts for work and materials, contracts involving the application of labour to an end-product. It is not necessary to deal exhaustively with all such contracts, for if the accent is on the end-product rather than on the work the contract tends to fall within contracts for the sale of goods in relation to damages,[3] while if the accent is on the work rather than on the end-product the contract tends to fall within contracts of agency[4] in relation to damages, using agent in this connection to cover the independent contractor[5] and the professional adviser. Contracts of construction, however, are given special consideration since they occur frequently and since they have certain special features in relation to damages. **31-001**

Apart from cases on defective construction, the authorities on the measure of damages in construction contracts are not numerous, which in view of the importance of such contracts and the existence of so many is surprising. It is, **31-002**

---

1 See Chs.25 to 29.

2 See Ch.Chs.32 and 35.

3 See, e.g. *Re Vic Mill* [1913] 1 Ch. 465 CA and *Hill v Showell* (1918) 87 L.J.K.B. 1106 HL: see paras25-130 and 25-131, above.

4 Contrast *Robinson v Graves* [1935] 1 K.B. 579 CA at 9 (contract to paint a lady's portrait) laying down the modern test that if the accent was on the work or skill the contract was not for sale of goods, and therefore did not fall within the now repealed s.4 of the Sale of Goods Act 1893.

5 Whether in relation to sale of goods or to contracts of agency, all contracts for work and materials are contracts entered into with an independent contractor.

therefore, sometimes necessary to have recourse, in the absence of direct guidance, to general principles and to the cases on the sale of goods,[6] the contract which is probably the most analogous.

31-003 In the normal run actions for breaches of construction contracts are between builder and owner, but there may also be actions which bring in those in the building team. Thus there are cases in which the building owner is claiming against the architect[7] or against the construction manager.[8] There are also cases between members of the building team not involving the building owner, as between main contractor and sub-contractor[9] or as between sub-contractor and sub-sub-contractor.[10]

## I. BREACH BY BUILDER

### 1. FAILURE TO BUILD AT ALL OR IN PART

#### (1) Normal measure

31-004 The normal measure of damages is the cost to the owner of completing the building in a reasonable manner less the contract price,[11] and possibly, in addition, the value of the use of the premises lost by reason of the delay. This measure of cost of completion less contract price is laid down by the Court of Appeal in *Mertens v Home Freeholds Co*,[12] which is to be regarded as the leading case since it still proves to be the only one dealing with this issue of the normal measure of damages where a building is not built or not completely built.[13] The defendant contracted to build a house for the claimant and was to begin work immediately after possession of the site was given to him. The defendant worked well for a month, but then deliberately failed to proceed with due dispatch in the knowledge that a government embargo on building without licence was to be imposed. Had he worked according to contract, the roof could have been on the house before the embargo descended. Two or three years later the claimant completed the work himself, when building was again permitted but when costs had risen. It was held that the proper measure of damages was the cost to the claimant of completion in a reasonable

6 The analogy of sale of goods has, however, its dangers: See *Mertens v Home Freeholds Co* [1921] 2 K.B. 526 CA, at para 31-004, below.

7 As in *Earl's Terrace Properties Ltd v Nilsson Design Ltd* [2004] B.L.R. 273 (at para.31-011, below), *Imperial College of Science and Technology v Norman & Dawbarn* (1986) 2 Constr. L.J. 280 (at para. 31-012, below) and *John Harris Partnership v Groveworld Ltd* [1999] P.N.L.R. 697 (in footnote at the end of para.31-019, below).

8 As in *Great Eastern Hotel v John Laing Construction* (2005) 99 Con. L.R. 45 (at para.31-011, below).

9 As in *Floods of Queensferry Ltd v Shand Construction Ltd* [1999] B.L.R. 319 (at para.31-008, below) and *Aldgate Construction Co Ltd v Unibar Plumbing & Heating Ltd* (2010) 130 Con. L.R. 190 (in footnote preceding para.31-012, below).

10 As in *Johnson Control Systems Ltd v Techni-Track Europa Ltd* (2004) 91 Con. L.R. 88 CA. The details on the damages are very confusing.

11 Or that part of the contract price, if any, remaining unpaid.

12 [1921] 2 K.B. 526 CA.

13 It was accepted in *Ferguson v Sohl* (1992) 62 B.L.R. 95 CA, where the claimant was able to have the works completed for a total expenditure of less than the contract price, that the damages were nominal. This, however, it was held, did not preclude an action of restitution for the amount the claimant was held to have overpaid the defendant; the difficulties of this result cannot be explored here.

manner at the earliest moment that he was allowed to proceed with building, less the amount he would have had to pay the defendant had the defendant completed the house as far as the roofing-in at the time agreed by the terms of the contract. The Court of Appeal reversed the Divisional Court, which had taken for its basic figure not the cost of completion but the market value that the completed building would have had at the contractual time due for completion. Of this Lord Sterndale MR said:

> "They [the Divisional Court] have treated the contract as if it were one for the sale of goods and have held that the measure of damages is the difference between the market price of the day of what the plaintiff ought to have had and what he got. In my humble opinion that is an entirely wrong way of looking at the contract. There is no contract to deliver goods, and there is no market price for a roofed house."[14]

*Mertens v Home Freeholds Co*,[15] is also authority for taking the cost of completion as at the time when it became once again legal to build, although between breach and the removal of the government embargo on building two or three years afterwards costs had risen substantially. And conversely, as Younger LJ pointed out, **31-005**

> "if the cost of building had decreased in that time the damages would have been correspondingly diminished".[16]

This rule is, however, subject to the general principles of mitigation so that, in the words of Lord Sterndale,

> "the building owner must set to work to build his house at a reasonable time and in a reasonable manner, and is not entitled to delay for several years and then, if prices have gone up, charge the defaulting builder with the increased price."[17]

No authority exists for the proposition that the claimant should also recover for the value of the loss of the use of the building and property by reason of the delay involved before he could complete the building himself. No such claim was made in *Mertens v Home Freeholds Co*,[18] but Younger LJ clearly considered it an open question whether the claimant could have recovered for the loss and inconvenience in being kept out of the house for two or three years.[19] **31-006**

Other than a contract to build a building there is the contract in *De Beers UK Ltd v Atos Origin IT Services UK Ltd*,[20] which was for information technology suppliers to build and deliver a software system to a diamond trader. The suppliers were in repudiatory breach of their contract with the result that no system was provided **31-007**

---

14 [1921] 2 K.B. 526 CA at 534; see, too, at 539, per Warrington LJ. Lord Sterndale said that the Divisional Court took the market price of what the claimant should have got less the market price of what he did get. This is, of course, breach of warranty damages and assumes that the price is paid. The Court of Appeal, in reversing the Divisional Court, restored the Official Referee's order, but the restored measure does not appear quite correct because from the cost of completion the Official Referee had deducted not only the contract price but also the market value of the work already done. This last deduction, although right when starting with a basic figure of market value of what the claimant should have got, is wrong when starting from cost of completion as the base.

15 [1921] 2 K.B. 526 CA.

16 [1921] 2 K.B. 526 CA at 543.

17 [1921] 2 K.B. 526 CA at 535 to 536.

18 [1921] 2 K.B. 526 CA.

19 [1921] 2 K.B. 526 CA at 543.

20 [2010] EWHC 3276 (TCC); [2011] B.L.R. 274.

by them to the trader. It was held that the trader was entitled in damages to the cost of upgrading its existing software system and the cost of purchasing a new system elsewhere.[21] These software system costs were allowed as it was accepted that the claimant had need for a new system although there was no certainty that the claimant would acquire one.[22] There is a hint here of the interesting argument that, in a different context, had succeeded in *Van der Garde v Force India Formula One Team Ltd*.[23]

### (2) Consequential losses

**31-008** Decisions on consequential losses are also lacking, so that, in order to gauge whether such items as loss of business profits or loss of sale profits would be recoverable in a particular case, reliance must be placed upon analogies from other contracts and upon the general principles of contract damages. *Floods of Queensferry Ltd v Shand Construction Ltd*,[24] may be seen as a case involving consequential loss, being a claim for additional plant and management costs brought by a sub-contractor for earthworks against the main contractor in a building contract relating to a highway. It would seem that these losses were considered to be recoverable, the main issue being whether mitigation principles required that credit notes of third parties be taken into account.[25]

## 2. DELAY IN COMPLETING BUILDING

### (1) Normal measure

**31-009** If the builder fails to complete the building by the time required by the contract the normal measure of damages should be the value of the use of the building during the period of delay, the value generally being taken as the rental value. Unfortunately, there appear to be no cases on this.

### (2) Consequential losses

**31-010** By contrast, cases of recovery for consequential losses resulting from delay have appeared though only in this century. There are three such.

**31-011** In *Earl's Terrace Properties Ltd v Nilsson Design Ltd*,[26] the claim made was against the architect rather than the builder. The claimants were developers who were refurbishing on a grand scale a row of London terrace houses. Their architect's inadequate design resulted in faulty installations which required remedial work delaying the completion of the houses and their handover to the claimants for sale by 15 months. This caused delay in the return to the claimants of their capital locked into the project[27] and they successfully claimed for their loss on account of their

---

[21] At the same time the trial judge was unprepared to allow employee costs to the claimant trader; these would have constituted a consequential loss.

[22] See [2010] EWHC 3276 (TCC) at [342] and following.

[23] [2010] EWHC 2373 (QB): see the case at para.3-010, above.

[24] [1999] B.L.R. 319. This was the first claim under this name; the second is in the footnotes at paras 49-079 and 49-080, below.

[25] On this issue see the case at para.9-131, above.

[26] [2004] B.L.R. 273.

[27] [2004] B.L.R. 273 at 72.

funds being held within the development project and not released by the selling of the houses. In *Great Eastern Hotel v John Laing Construction*,[28] the claim based on delay was against the construction manager[29] rather than the building contractor. The claimant was one of the major railway hotels in London and succeeded in recovering in respect of loss of profits, professional fees and miscellaneous costs.[30] The defendant company also invoked unsuccessfully causation principles, arguing that it should not be liable for delay for which it might not be responsible, but material contribution was held to be the acid test.[31] In *Bridge UK.Com Ltd v Abbey Pynford Plc*,[32] in the performance of the contract for the construction and installation of a foundation for the claimant's printing press, the defendant builder ran into difficulties leading to the need for remedial measures and a consequent failure to complete the work on time. For this delay the claimant recovered for its loss of profit on printing work which it had to send out to other companies and on printing work it was unable to carry out, for various expenditures[33] and for management time taken away from other activities, a head of damage which has already appeared in various tortious contexts.[34]

## 3. DEFECTIVE BUILDING[35]

### (1) Normal measure

The authorities effectively start with *East Ham Corp v Bernard Sunley*,[36] in the House of Lords, a case of defective building where the claimants had acted reasonably in effecting the necessary repairs, and the House of Lords accepted and applied as the normal measure of damages the cost of reinstatement,[37] this cost being **31-012**

[28] (2005) 99 Con. L.R. 45.

[29] For the role of the construction manager see (2005) 99 Con. L.R. 45 at [20].

[30] Dealt with at great length in a judgment running to 400 paragraphs.

[31] See (2005) 99 Con. L.R. 45 at [297] and following.

[32] [2007] EWHC 728 TCC.

[33] As to the proprietary of awarding some of these see para.4-024, above.

[34] See paras. 37-014, 37-027, and para.48-022, below.

[35] Though not exactly a case of defective performance *Aldgate Construction Co Ltd v Unibar Plumbing & Heating Ltd* (2010) 130 Con. L.R. 190 can be seen to fit in here. The sub-contractor sued by the developer owner had not done poor work on the property but had negligently caused a fire there so that further work needed to be done on the property. Yet the question on damages was not the usual one concerning repair and reinstatement (for which see the text below) but was as to how far damages were available to the developer owner if prevented by the fire from developing other properties. This was elaborately considered by the trial judge in the light of the facts and the very many legal authorities which were not the ones generally found in defective performance cases but those dealing in causation, scope of duty, remoteness and the like.

[36] [1966] A.C. 406.

[37] See, especially, [1966] A.C. 406 at 434 and 444–445. In the then absence of authority, it was submitted in the 12th edition of this work in 1961 that the cost of reinstatement should form the normal measure of damages, and support for this was found in two cases, which may still be worth keeping in mind, where the builder had brought an action under the terms of the contract for the price, and the owner had been allowed to set up in reduction of the price the amount of damage he had sustained through the builder's breach by defects or deviations in construction, the amount of damage being taken as the cost of remedying the defect or deviation. This appeared first from *Thornton v Place* (1832) 1 Moo. & Rob. 218, a case of a contract to slate a house, where Parke J laid down that the builder was entitled to recover the price "subject to a deduction; and the measure of that deduction is the sum which it would take to alter the work, so as to make it correspond with the specification" (at 219). It appeared again in *Dakin v Lee* [1916] 1 K.B. 566 CA, where Sankey J in

taken as at the time the defects were discovered.[38] There followed *Imperial College of Science and Technology v Norman & Dawbarn*,[39] a claim against the designer of a building, where many years later tiles began to fall from the building and the claimants were held entitled to the cost of remedial work in recladding the building although by then the useful life of the tiles was nearly over.[40] In *Minscombe Properties v McAlpine*,[41] the court, although not exactly concerned with construction of a building under contract, allowed the cost of removing soil which had been dumped on the claimant's land in breach of an agreement, giving the defendants the right to dump in connection with the construction of a new road, because the claimants intended to develop the land and would have to remove the soil to do so, no discount being made for the possibility that planning permission would not be allowed.[42] More decisions have appeared in recent years. In *Linklaters Business Services v Sir Robert McAlpine Ltd*,[43] solicitors claimed for the faulty installation by contractors of insulated air conditioning pipework in the solicitors' office premises, of which they were lessees, pipework which had become extensively corroded on failure of the insulation. The solicitors had, on proper expert advice, replaced the corroded pipework throughout the building, rather than attempting a less costly remedial scheme for which the contractors contended, and were held to have acted wholly reasonably in so doing,[44] thereby entitling them to damages measured by the cost of replacement.[45] What was termed the usual rule was applied in *Hall v Van Der Heiden*,[46] so as to allow as damages the costs, which were not shown to be in any way unreasonable, of putting right defective and incomplete performance by the builder.[47] In *Brit Inns Ltd v BDW Trading Ltd*,[48] the trial judge set out, with authorities, the proper approach to a claim for reinstatement costs,[49] stating that, where the work was already done by trial, the actual costs were almost always the starting point in assessing what was reasonable and were particularly significant where carried out on professional advice, but holding that the claim before him had been grossly exaggerated. In *Hunt v Optima (Cambridge) Ltd*,[50] where over the years defects had appeared in a block of flats poorly constructed by

---

the Divisional Court (at 576) quoted Parke J's statement with approval, and Pickford LJ in the Court of Appeal said that the owner, sued for the price, was entitled "to deduct such an amount as is sufficient to put that insufficiently done work into the condition in which it ought to have been according to the contract" (at 582).

38 The question which arose of whether it was the cost of reinstatement at that time or at an earlier time that must be within the contemplation of the parties is dealt with at para.8-184, above.

39 (1986) 2 Constr. L.J. 280.

40 (1986) 2 Constr. L.J. 280 at 286. The case illustrates the entitlement to replace new for old: see para.2-007, above. But entitlement to a so-called betterment is not available where the claimant has gone further than necessary: *Scott Wilson Kirkpatrick & Partners v Ministry of Defence* [2001] 73 Con. L.R. 52 CA.

41 (1986) 2 Constr. L.J. 303 CA.

42 Compare the authorities on loss of a chance at paras 10-040 and following, above, which were held to have nothing to do with this case: see (1986) 2 Constr. L.J. 303 CA at 311, per O'Connor LJ.

43 [2010] EWHC 2931 (TCC).

44 Akenhead J's extended reasons are set out by him at [2010] EWHC 2931 (TCC) at [145].

45 *Skandia Property v Thames Water* [1999] B.L.R. 338 CA, a tort case at para.39-007, below, was distinguished.

46 [2010] EWHC 586 (TCC).

47 See [2010] EWHC 586 (TCC) at [62]–[67].

48 [2012] EWHC 2143 (TCC).

49 [2012] EWHC 2143 (TCC) at [54]–[58].

50 [2013] EWHC 681 (TCC).

the defendant developer, it was accepted that reinstatement should form the basis of the award of damages to the various claimants who had acquired flats, with the claimants being required to show that the remedial solutions proposed by them were reasonable.[51]

31-013 *Cory & Son v Wingate Investments*,[52] went beyond all these decisions by allowing as damages the cost of reinstatement at the time when the claimants' claim was heard and when prices had risen steeply. The reinstatement had still not been effected at the date of trial since the claimants had felt unable to incur the considerable expenditure needed before they were assured of recovering this amount from the defendants, who had vigorously disclaimed liability right to the door of the court. This decision is in line with others appearing when inflation was severe, though not in the context of building contracts, where claimants have been held justified in deferring reinstatement up to the time of trial without being branded with a failure to mitigate.[53]

31-014 If, however, the cost of remedying the defect is disproportionate to the end to be attained, the damages fall to be measured by the value of the building had it been built as required by the contract[54] less its value as it stands.[55] This measure was in effect first awarded in *Applegate v Moss*,[56] being the full value of the building, properly built, as it was valueless and would have to be pulled down[57]; was adopted in *Atkins v Scott*,[58] where the expense of completely stripping defective tiling was not allowed; and has now received the imprimatur of the House of Lords in *Ruxley Electronics v Forsyth*,[59] reversing the majority decision of the Court of Appeal.[60]

---

51 See [2013] EWHC 681 (TCC) at [139]–[141] of a long judgment.

52 (1980) 17 B.L.R. 104 CA.

53 See especially *Dodd Properties (Kent) v Canterbury City Council* [1980] 1 W.L.R. 433 CA, at paras 39-018 and 39-026, below. A New Zealand case appearing in the English reports, *Bevan Investments v Blackhall & Struthers* (1978) 11 B.L.R. 78 CA, is a further illustration of an award in respect of defective performance in a building contract of the cost of reinstatement at trial.

54 As *Deosaran v Barrow* [2006] UKPC 33 shows, a value that needs to be satisfactorily proved to permit recovery of this measure.

55 In the then absence of authority, it was submitted in the 12th edition of this work in 1961 that where the cost of reinstatement was uneconomic the measure as stated in the text should apply, and it was pointed out that one possible reason for the lack of English cases is that, where the defect is of such a type, there will probably not be a sufficiently substantial performance by the builder to allow him to sue for the price (under the rule established in *Dakin v Lee* [1916] 1 K.B. 566 CA), and, being himself in substantial breach, he will be unable to sue even for the value of the work already done by him (under the rule in *Sumpter v Hedges* [1898] 1 Q.B. 673 CA). The owner will thus have the part performance for nothing and will hardly care to trouble to sue for damages when in all probability he will have gained and not lost. It is true that the rule in *Sumpter v Hedges*, which effectively bars a restitutionary rather than a damages remedy, has been widely criticised but the Court of Appeal in *Cleveland Bridge UK Ltd v Multiplex Constructions (UK) Ltd* [2010] EWCA Civ 139 CA considered that the case "remains intact and binding, at least for the moment": at [138], and see the extended discussion around the case from [82]–[140].

56 [1971] 1 Q.B. 406 CA.

57 Again (see para.31-012, above), the time at which the defects were discovered was taken as the relevant time for valuation.

58 (1990) 7 Constr. L.J. 215 CA.

59 [1996] A.C. 344.

60 [1994] 1 W.L.R. 650 CA. If in *Tomlinson v Wilson*, Q.B. TCC unreported 11 May 2007, where there was defective building of a house extension, the trial judge had held the builder to be in breach rather than the owner (for the owner's damages liability see para. 31-023 below), he would not have awarded the cost incurred by the owner in the demolition and rebuilding of the extension since he held this to be unreasonable as the building done was susceptible of repair at a much lower figure: see at [68] and [69]. The repair cost would, however, have been awardable: see at [75] to [78].

In *Ruxley* the claimant companies contracted to build a swimming pool for the defendant in his garden. While the pool contractually should have had a maximum depth of seven-and-a-half feet, its maximum depth as built was six-and-three-quarter feet and its depth where most would dive was only six feet. The defendant, sued for the contract price, counterclaimed for damages for breach of contract based on the cost, which was over £20,000, of reconstructing the pool to the contractual specification. The trial judge found that the shortfall in depth neither was unsafe nor decreased the value of the pool. The House of Lords held that, since it was unreasonable for the defendant to insist on reinstatement because the expense of the work involved would be out of all proportion to the benefit to be obtained, he was confined to the difference in value, which here was nil, and that this was so whether or not he had an intention, given available damages, to reinstate. This is an eminently sensible decision, providing the result which had already been reached by the Court of Appeal in *Atkins v Scott*,[61] and which had been put forward in previous editions of this work.[62] The limitations of the principle that the decision contains should however be recognised and indeed were recognised by Lord Jauncey in his speech. He said[63]:

> "Where the contract breaker has entirely failed to achieve the contractual objective it may not be difficult to conclude that the loss is the necessary cost of achieving that objective. Thus if a building is constructed so defectively that it is of no use for its designed purpose the owner may have little difficulty in establishing that his loss is the necessary cost of reconstructing. Furthermore, in taking reasonableness into account in determining the extent of loss it is reasonableness in relation to the particular contract and not at large. Accordingly, if I contracted for the erection of a folly in my garden which shortly thereafter suffered a total collapse it would be irrelevant to the determination of my loss to argue that the erection of such a folly which contributed nothing to the value of my house was a crazy thing to do."[64]

**31-015** *Freeman v Niroomand*,[65] is a case somewhat similar to *Ruxley*.[66] The defendant had built not according to specifications a porch at the front of the claimant's house. No diminution in the value of the house arose from this breach of contract and to alter the porch to conform to the specifications was unreasonably costly and was not something that the claimant intended to do. In these circumstances the trial judge awarded not nominal damages but of £130, which represented the amount saved by the builder; this award was upheld by the Court of Appeal. He had, said Millett LJ, been

61 (1990) 7 Constr. L.J. 215 CA. In *Ruxley* Lord Jauncey and Lord Lloyd also relied in support of their conclusion on the valuable *Jacob & Youngs Inc v Kent*, 230 N.Y. 239 (1921) in the Court of Appeals of New York and *Bellgrove v Eldridge* (1954) 90 C.L.R. 613 in the High Court of Australia.

62 As in 15th edition (1988) at para.1092, cited by Lord Jauncey in *Ruxley*.

63 [1996] A.C. 344 at 358.

64 The possibility of a claim by the pool owner in restitution based on the saving to the builder resulting from having built a pool shallower than specified was not explored. This might now be available: see Ch.14, especially at para.14-033, above. And compare the next paragraph in fin.

65 (1996) 52 Con. L.R. 116 CA.

66 See also *Fulham Leisure Holdings Ltd v Nicholson Graham & Jones* [2007] P.N.L.R.5 at 83, at para.34-045, below, where *Ruxley* was applied in a very different type of case. Damages were not considered by the Court of Appeal which reversed on liability: [2008] EWCA Civ 84 CA.

"attempting, in a difficult situation, to quantify the loss which the householder had suffered, and he chose to equate that loss with the amount which the builder had saved by not providing a porch in accordance with the contractual specifications".[67]

This can be interpreted as allowing damages for non-pecuniary loss along the "consumer surplus" lines that Lord Mustill outlined in *Ruxley*.[68] It does not appear to have been intended as an early manifestation of disgorgement damages, with the award being aimed at removing from the defendant profit made from his breach of contract.[69]

The value of the building as it should have been less its value as it is becomes the appropriate measure also where the claimant sells it without remedying the defects.[70] In *Rawlings v Rentokil Laboratories*,[71] where the contract was to install a damp-proof system in a house, this amount was in effect awarded—more precisely, it was the value the house would have had but for the breach less the reduced price the claimant was able to obtain for it—and he was held entitled to this measure of damages even though by the time of the sale the defects had been put right, the history of the defects having spoiled the market for the disposal of the house. In *Birse Construction Ltd v Eastern Telegraph Company Ltd*,[72] where a residential training college was built with defects by the defendant construction company for the claimants who intended to sell the college, it was held that there could be no recovery of the cost of remedying defects which the claimants were not proposing to remedy before they sold.[73] **31-016**

## (2) Consequential losses

Recoverable consequential losses should include such items as loss of use of the building during the repairs[74] and also loss of profits in appropriate circumstances.[75] Physical damage caused by the defective nature of the building should be recoverable, such as damage to the contents of the building by the weather or losses caused through fire or flood. Thus in *Sainsbury Plc v Broadway Malayan*,[76] the claimants recovered for damage caused by a fire on their premises, a fire which they maintained would have been contained had the defendants constructed a fire wall properly, though their damages were subject to reduction on account of contributory negligence and because there was only a chance that the wall properly constructed would have contained the fire.[77] In *Raflatac v Eade*,[78] the claimant's **31-017**

[67] (1996) 52 Con. L.R. 116 at 121.

[68] See para.31-021, below.

[69] See Ch.15 especially at para.14-033, above. The whole subject of restitutionary and disgorgement damages needs to be considered in the present context.

[70] It may be that there was no intention in *Saigol v Cranley Mansion* (2001) 72 Con. L.R. 54 CA, to remedy the defects but it is not clear from the Delphic statement that the measure of damages awarded was the diminution in the claimant's interest. As to the claimant's additional recovery in respect of her liability to interest, see footnote at the end of para.19-018, above.

[71] [1972] E.G.D. 744.

[72] [2004] EWHC 2512 TCC.

[73] See [2004] EWHC 2512 TCC at [51]–[54].

[74] In *Applegate v Moss* [1971] 1 Q.B. 406 CA (see the case at para.31-014, above) interest was awarded from the date the claimants went out of occupation to the date of judgment.

[75] As in the New Zealand case, available in our reports, of *Bevan Investments v Blackhall & Struthers* (1978) 11 B.L.R. 78 CA.

[76] (1998) 61 Con. L.R. 31.

[77] On the correctness of this latter point see the cases on loss of a chance at para.10-040 and follow-

employees were used to clean up the flood that was caused by effectively defective building and the claimant recovered for the wages thus thrown away.

31-018 Fees of various kinds have also been claimed, not invariably successfully, as items of consequential loss. In *Rawlings v Rentokil Laboratories*,[79] recovery was allowed for legal fees incurred in abortive attempts to sell the defective house. In *George Fischer Holding v Multi-Design Consultants*,[80] the claimants, suing the defendants for the faulty design and construction of a building, recovered as part of their damages professional fees incurred in preparing a remedial scheme which it was proposed not to adopt and implement before the action had been heard. In *Gemma Ltd v Gimson*,[81] recovery was allowed for fees of quantity surveyors supervising the remedial work[82] and of security guards protecting the empty building.[83] But in *Johnston v W. H. Brown Construction (Dundee) Ltd*,[84] a case from Scotland, the pursuer unsuccessfully claimed for the cost of an architect's report investigating the defects, for the cost of a solicitor's advice on the contractual aspects of the defects and also for management costs. None of these items was held to constitute consequential losses for which there could be recovery. In principle, it was said, the cost of taking technical and legal advice in the preparation of a claim is not recoverable as damages. As for the claim for management costs, there was no clear proof of any such costs related to the disruption of the pursuer's business by the defective work itself or by the process of remedying the defects.

31-019 An unusual claim made its appearance in *Bella Casa Ltd v Vinestone Ltd*.[85] The claimant company had acquired, for a capital sum, a long lease of a London flat. Of the three defendants the first was the company which had granted the claimant the lease, a company which had agreed with the claimant to procure the carrying out of refurbishment works on the flat, the second defendant was the architect and the third the contractor. Claims were made on account of defects in the construction work. While these claims were for breach of contract against the first defendant and for breach of common law and statutory duty against the second and third, and were in different amounts, all three had an important element in common which was that they sought recovery for a loss of use of the flat amounting to some £350,000, this amount being based upon interest on the claimant's purchase price of the lease for the period that the flat was not fit for occupation. After a magisterial review of the authorities in all the fields of relevance, the trial judge sensibly decided against this claim for loss of use. While he accepted that the authorities supported loss of use claims, generally in modest amounts, and also claims for loss of enjoyment through inability to use,[86] he considered the claim as here presented as

---

ing, above.

78 [1999] 1 Lloyd's Rep. 506; [1999] B.L.R. 261. In the Lloyd's report this issue does not appear in the headnote, only in the report (511, col.2), the case principally concerning contributory negligence.

79 [1972] E.G.D. 744; facts at para.31-016, above.

80 (1998) 61 Con. L.R. 85.

81 (2005) 97 Con. L.R. 165.

82 (2005) 97 Con. L.R. 165 at [214].

83 (2005) 97 Con. L.R. 165 at [213].

84 [2000] B.L.R. 243.

85 [2006] B.L.R. 72.

86 Recovery for loss of enjoyment may be questionable: see para.31-020, below. *Bayoumi v Protim Services Ltd* (1998) 30 H.L.R. 785 CA was cited as illustrative ([2006] B.L.R. 72 at [29] and [30]), but that was a case of breach of statutory duty rather than of contract.

taking a step too far. There were no building contract cases allowing such a claim,[87] cases involving non-repair of premises by lessors were, if anything, against recovery[88] and the extensive shipping cases, generally allowing interest on capital value, have to do with non-profit-making use of depreciating assets in the public domain[89] as has the single case concerning not a ship but a municipal corporation bus.[90] At the same time the learned judge was prepared to hold in favour of the claimant's far smaller claims for the service charges and for the costs of utilities paid during the period of non-occupation, these being effectively wasted.[91] There is however merit in the defendant's argument that these expenses would have been incurred in any event so that the wrong could not be said to be causative of these losses, but it may be possible to regard such costs as representing the loss of use for which the authorities do allow recovery although, the flat having been taken only for the very occasional use, which had not materialised, of a director of the claimant company, there was no direct claim along such lines.[92]

## (3) Non-pecuniary losses

*Rawlings v Rentokil Laboratories*,[93] allowed damages for the discomfort and inconvenience caused to the claimant in living in the house in its defective state but, by contrast, it was held in *Hutchinson v Harris*,[94] where the work was to the claimant client's[95] house which she was acquiring not to live in as her home but to resell at a profit, that there was no reasonable contemplation that distress or vexation would be caused so that an award for such should not be made. The occasional case which has allowed damages for the distress and disappointment caused by not having the building contracted for properly built[96] did appear for a time to have been overtaken by the now current thinking on non-pecuniary loss for breach of contract that damages for distress, vexation and disappointment arising out of a breach are **31-020**

87 See [2006] B.L.R. 72 at [38]–[42].

88 See [2006] B.L.R. 72 at [31] together with [35] and [36].

89 [2006] B.L.R. 72 at [50]–[63].

90 [2006] B.L.R. 72 at [64]–[65]. Indeed there was cited one Court of Appeal case, *Alexander v Rolls Royce Motors* [1996] R.T.R. 95 CA (at para.37-054, below), holding that these cases involving assets in the public domain have no application to a private hired car: [2006] B.L.R. 72 at [66] to[68]. The cases on loss of use of non-profit-earning goods are considered at paras 37-045 and following, below.

91 See [2006] B.L.R. 72 at [32]–[34]. In his extensive consideration of the authorities the learned judge fell into only one error. He was not right to say (at [39]–[42]) that *Applegate v Moss* [1971] 1 Q.B. 406 CA is not an authority for the proposition for which it is cited as he failed to note that it is there stated that interest was awarded not for the period of the claimants' occupation but from the date when they went out of occupation, which is exactly what the Court of Appeal in *Applegate*, disagreeing with the court below, decided.

92 On the question of mitigation and avoided loss (see paras 9-108 and following, above). In *Design 5 v Kensington Housing Association* (1986) 34 B.L.R. 92 the judge held that he was not required to take into account in computing the damages the collateral benefit of a government grant received by the claimant housing association which might eliminate its loss. This decision was applied in *John Harris Partnership v Groveworld Ltd* [1999] P.N.L.R. 697, where the claim was against the architect rather than the builder and it was the partial funding by a third party of the claimant's development that was not required to be taken into account.

93 [1972] E.G.D. 744; see the case at para.31-016, above.

94 (1978) 10 B.L.R. 19 CA.

95 The defendant was not the builder but the architect.

96 *Inglis v Cant* [1987] C.L.Y. 1132; *Wilkin v Bower* [1987] C.L.Y. 1133; *Jones v Derval* [1988] C.L.Y. 1048; *Appleton v Murten* [1993] C.L.Y. 1386.

not recoverable unless the object of the contract was to provide peace of mind or freedom from distress[97] and accordingly are not recoverable for distress, vexation and disappointment arising out of the breach of a purely commercial contract.

31-021 However the House of Lords in *Ruxley Electronics v Forsyth*,[98] somewhat unexpectedly, endorsed the awarding of damages for non-pecuniary loss in a building contract, stating that, where there has been a breach of performance resulting in loss of expectation of performance, loss of satisfaction of a personal preference or loss of a pleasurable amenity, the court may award damages at a modest level for non-pecuniary loss. Lord Mustill said[99]:

> "The law must cater for those occasions where the value of the promise to the promisee exceeds the financial enhancement of his position which full performance will secure. This excess, often referred to in the literature as the 'consumer surplus' ...[100] is usually incapable of precise valuation in terms of money, exactly because it represents a personal, subjective and non-monetary gain. Nevertheless, where it exists the law should recognise it and compensate the promisee if the misperformance takes it away."

It is clear that their Lordships were eager to see the victim of the breach of contract with some degree of recovery once they had decided, rightly, that for pecuniary loss he was entitled, with reinstatement unreasonable and value undiminished, to only nominal damages.[101] How far their Lordships' views will allow damages for non-pecuniary loss, and in what amount,[102] to be awarded in contracts to build, which are essentially commercial contracts, is still not known. It may be considered that the only need for such awards, outside those for discomfort and inconvenience, will be in cases where there is a combination of undiminished value and unreasonable, or uneffected, reinstatement,[103] and the award in *Freeman v Niroomand*,[104] can be seen as being for non-pecuniary loss along *Ruxley* lines.[105] Guidance from the higher courts is indeed needed as inconsistent first instance decisions are now appearing. Thus no damages were awarded in *Eribo v Odinaiya*,[106] for "the stress, inconvenience and overall unpleasantness" during the course of design and refurbishment works at the claimant's home which went badly wrong.[107] By contrast, recovery was allowed for distress as well as inconvenience in *Hall v Van Der Heiden*.[108]

---

97 See paras 5-023 and following, above.
98 [1996] A.C. 344.
99 [1996] A.C. 344 at 360–361.
100 Citing the valuable discussion at (1979) 95 L.Q.R. 581 (Harris, Ogus and Phillips).
101 See the case at para.31-014, above.
102 The House of Lords did not have to decide whether the trial judge's award for non-pecuniary loss of £2,500, thought to be generous, was appropriate as it was unchallenged by the building companies and there was no appeal against it.
103 See further at para.5-030, above on the effect of *Ruxley*.
104 (1996) 52 Con. L.R. 116 CA.
105 Facts at para.31-015, above.
106 [2010] EWHC 301 (TCC).
107 See [2010] EWHC 301 (TCC) at [141] and [142].
108 [2010] EWHC 586 (TCC): see at [90]–[92]. The first instance award for distress and anxiety in *Gemma Ltd v Gimson* (2005) 97 Con. L.R. 165 not only for the claimants themselves but in respect of their children (at [218]) surely goes too far.

## II. BREACH BY OWNER

### 1. PREVENTION RESULTING IN NON-COMPLETION

On the measure of damages where the owner acts so as to bar completion there is, surprisingly, a dearth of authority.[109] General principles would put the normal measure at the contract price less the cost to the builder of executing or completing the work.[110] In calculating the builder's costs the indirect as well as the direct costs must be included, especially overheads. This measure, however, should be subject to reduction if the defendant can show that the time made available to the claimant by the breach has been, or could have been, used by him in executing other profitable contracts with which he would not otherwise have been able to contend. This is analogous to the cases of manufacturing and erecting machinery dealt with under sale of goods.[111] **31-022**

Two other measures, alternative to this basic measure, may be suggested. They are (1) the net profit which the builder could have made on the whole contract plus his expenditure in part performance; and (2) for the work done, such proportion of the contract price as the cost of the work done bears to the total cost of the whole contract, plus, for the work remaining, the profit that would have been made upon it.[112] If there is adequate proof of the cost to the builder of completing the unfinished part of the work and also if the entire contract can be done at a profit to the builder, all three formulae, i.e. the basic measure and the two alternatives, yield the same result. It is when one or other of these two factors is lacking that the alternatives assume importance. Thus if the first factor is lacking and the claimant cannot prove the cost of completion, often a difficult matter for proof, it may not be unreasonable to allow him to recover at least the cost of the work done. If, however, it is the second factor that is lacking and the contract could only have been completed by the builder at a loss to himself, then while the basic measure favours the defendant entirely the first alternative favours the claimant entirely, and perhaps therefore the second alternative measure with its intermediate result is the most fair in such circumstances. Another, perhaps simpler, approach open to a claimant who is unable to complete except at a loss is to treat the contract as discharged by the breach and sue in restitution on a quantum meruit for the cost of the work done, an action which does not depend upon the contract and therefore will not be trammelled or limited by the contract rate. This will give the claimant more than the second alternative measure and as much as the first alternative measure, calculated however not as contractual damages but as restitution.[113] This conclusion has the support of the decision in *Lodder v Slowey*.[114] The contract in that case was to construct a tun- **31-023**

---

[109] *Stocznia Gdanska SA v Latvian Shipping Co* [2002] 2 Lloyd's Rep. 436 CA, which concerned a shipbuilding contract, is a case of this nature but there is no clarity on the measure of damages in the report of the case before the Court of Appeal. The matter below, at [2001] 1 Lloyd's Rep. 537, did not deal with damages.

[110] If, of course, the builder has completed the building he can sue under the terms of the contract for the price.

[111] See paras 25-130 and 25-131, above, especially *Re Vic Mill* [1913] 1 Ch. 465 CA, and *Hill v Showell* (1918) 87 L.J.K.B. 1106 HL.

[112] This second alternative measure was adopted by the trial judge, after resolution of his doubts, in *Tomlinson v Wilson*, Q.B. TCC unreported 11 May 2007: see at [44] to [46].

[113] From this point of view the matter is, therefore, strictly not dealing with damages at all.

[114] [1904] A.C. 442 PC.

nel and other works on certain land, and the builder was prevented from completing. The judge at first instance had held[115] that the measure of damages was the amount which the claimant builder had lost by exclusion from the works before their completion,[116] and not the value of the work done by the claimant whether at the market price[117] or at the contract price.[118] This had been reversed on appeal and the proper measure held to be the actual value of the work and materials, the court considering it immaterial whether the claimant, had he been allowed to complete, would have made a profit or a loss.[119] This was affirmed by the Judicial Committee of the Privy Council and at the same time put on the correct analytical basis. "Their Lordships also agree", said Lord Davey,

> "as to the proper measure of damages, or (more accurately) as to the right of the respondent [builder] to treat the contract as at an end and sue for work and labour done instead of suing for damages for breach of the contract."[120]

**31-024** There being no cases on the normal measure of damages, a fortiori there are none on consequential losses. One such loss would be the damages that the building contractor is compelled by the owner's breach to pay to his sub-contractors; this, however, might well be held to be too remote.

## 2. PREVENTION RESULTING IN DELAY

**31-025** There appear to be no English authorities on the measure of damages where the owner acts so as to delay completion, but on general principles the builder should be allowed to recover for such losses as the necessary payment of wages during the delay, the increased cost of labour or materials when work is resumed, and deterioration of the building materials during the delay. In a Canadian case appearing in the English reports, *Ellis-Don v The Parking Authority of Toronto*,[121] where the contractors had been delayed in building by the owner's failure to procure a permit, they were held entitled to recover as damages their extra costs[122] including overhead costs, the calculation being by way of a weekly sum in respect of overheads and loss of profit.[123]

---

115 [1904] A.C. 442 PC at 443.

116 Meaning the basic measure.

117 Similar to the first alternative measure.

118 Similar to the second alternative measure.

119 [1904] A.C. 442 PC at 444.

120 [1904] A.C. 442 PC at 453.

121 (1978) 28 B.L.R. 98.

122 See too *Penvidic Contracting Co v International Nickel Co of Canada* (1975) 53 D.L.R. (3d) 748, Supreme Ct. of Canada, where, though there was no specific reference to delay as such, the builder recovered for additional expenses incurred by reason of the owner's breach of his obligation to facilitate the work.

123 The elaborate calculation and complex formula in relation to overhead costs advanced in Hudson, *Building and Engineering Contracts*, 10th edn (1970), pp.596 and following, was there cited: (1978) 28 B.L.R. 98 at 124 to 127. See now 12th edn (2012), paras 6-072 to 6-074, discussing the usage of the even more complex Hudson and Eichleay formula in relation to overhead costs.

## 3. Other Breaches

A further type of breach appears in *Rees & Kirby v Swansea City Council*,[124] where there was a failure by the owners to make valuations and to certify amounts due to the builders so that there was a consequent failure to provide the sums properly due to them. Nevertheless the court refused to award the builders interest on these sums as damages, considering that here it was not possible "properly to find a way round"[125] the decision in *London, Chatham & Dover Ry v S.E. Ry*,[126] prohibiting interest damages for a failure to pay money.[127] In *Department of Environment for Northern Ireland v Farrans (Construction)*,[128] on the other hand, interest was included in the damages awarded to the building contractor upon the owner's failure to pay on the due date, applying *Wadsworth v Lydall*,[129] which had refused, where the claim for interest was by way of special damage within the second rule in *Hadley v Baxendale*,[130] to have regard to the *LLondon, Chatham & Dover Ry* prohibition. Now with the final overruling by the House of Lords in *Sempra Metals Ltd v Inland Revenue Commissioners*,[131] of *London, Chatham & Dover Ry*, all is changed. Interest would today be awardable in *Rees & Kirby*, and awarding interest in *Farrans (Construction)* would no longer require a dubious and unnecessary reliance on the second rule in *Hadley v Baxendale*.[132] **31-026**

---

[124] (1983) 25 B.L.R. 129.

[125] (1983) 25 B.L.R. 129 at 147.

[126] [1893] A.C. 429.

[127] In the appeal the interest issue was not addressed as there was held to be no breach of contract: see (1985) 30 B.L.R. 1 CA at 24–25.

[128] (1981) 19 B.L.R. 1.

[129] [1981] 1 W.L.R. 598 CA.

[130] (1854) 9 Ex. 341.

[131] [2008] A.C. 561.

[132] See the revolution in the awarding of interest damages fully examined at paras 19-058 and following, above.

Chapter 32

# CONTRACTS OF CARRIAGE

Table of Contents



**32-001** Contracts for the carriage of goods give rise to more problems in damages than do contracts for the carriage of persons, and the bulk of the case law deals in contracts to carry goods by sea. Such contracts are generally by way of charterparty, of which there are three different varieties: charterparties by demise, time charterparties, and voyage charterparties. Charterparties by demise differ from the other two in that the shipowner parts with the possession of the ship to the charterer; thus they are not properly contracts for the rendering of services but for the hire of goods. No reference has been made to them when dealing with hire of goods[1] only because such charterparties have today fallen into disuse. Time and voyage charterparties, on the other hand, are properly considered as contracts for the rendering of services since the shipowner remains in possession of the ship and as employer of the master and crew: the shipowner contracts to render services by his master and crew to carry the goods provided, during a specified period in a time charterparty and for a specified voyage or voyages in a voyage charterparty. It is true that the contract price in a time charterparty is frequently referred to as "hire",

[1] See Ch.26, above.

but it is universally accepted that such a term is inappropriate.[2] And whether the time or voyage charterer intends to supply cargo himself, or to enter into sub-contracts with other shippers who provide the cargo, does not affect the nature of such charterparties as contracts for the rendering of services. What it is important to appreciate with charterparties is that it is the shipowner who is in effect the carrier and the charterer who is in effect the cargo owner.[3]

## I. BREACH BY CARRIER

### (A) CARRIAGE OF GOODS

#### 1. NON-DELIVERY INCLUDING DELIVERY IN A DAMAGED CONDITION

In contracts for the carriage of goods[4] breach by non-delivery may refer to a number of situations. Principally the cases are concerned with the situation where the goods are lost or destroyed in transit,[5] but there are also cases of misdelivery either in the sense of delivery to someone other than the proper consignee[6] or in the sense of delivery of the wrong goods to the consignee.[7] The same measure of damages applies because in each case there is a non-delivery to the claimant of the goods contracted to be carried, although in the unusual last type of case there is a delivery of a substitute which will have to be returned or its value deducted from the damages. Damage, as opposed to loss or destruction, in transit does not of course amount to non-delivery; it is not, however, given separate treatment because it has given rise to virtually no authorities on damages—a clutch of cases in the 1980s, *The Ocean Dynamic*,[8] *The Good Friend*,[9] and *The Sanix Ace*,[10] provide three excep- **32-002**

---

[2] As are the terms "hiring", "letting", "delivery" and "redelivery" which are also used. Contrast *Tankexpress A/S v Compagnie Financiere Belge des Petroles* [1949] A.C. 76 at 90, per Lord Porter: "It is a commonplace that the phraseology still adopted in the case of the charter of a ship where her services are put at the disposal of a charterer but she is not demised, is deceptive."

[3] For further details on the general law as to the types of charterparty, see *Scrutton on Charterparties*, 23rd edn (London: Sweet & Maxwell, 2015).

[4] The claim may not always fall within the main categories of claim dealt with below. Thus in *The Timawra* [1996] 2 Lloyd's Rep. 166, which concerned a time charterparty, the claim was for a failure by the owners to provide the charterers with dry docking. In the charterers' action for damages arising out of the failure to dry dock the chartered vessel in January, it was held that credit for the later dry docking in July did not have to be given; also at para.9-132, above.

[5] The loss or destruction must, of course, be one for which the carrier is liable; this includes one type of case which lies on the tenuous borderline between liability and remoteness of damage. Thus, a carrier will be liable for loss or destruction after he has improperly dealt with the goods (as by deviation or improper stowage) where but for the improper dealing the immediate cause of the loss or destruction would have been one for which he would not have been liable (as jettison, act of God and the like), unless he can positively show that the loss from this cause would have occurred even in the absence of improper dealing by him. This point was originally decided in *Davis v Garrett* (1830) 6 Bing. 716 (deviation) and later applied in *Scaramanga v Stamp* (1880) 5 C.P.D. 295 (deviation; see especially at 299), *Royal Exchange Shipping Co v Dixon* (1886) 12 App. Cas. 11 (improper stowage) and *Morrison v Shaw Savill* [1916] 2 K.B. 783 CA (deviation). Compare the same result in contracts concerning principal and agent at para.35-010, below.

[6] As in *Brandt v Bowlby* (1831) 2 B. & Ad. 932 and *Braun v Bergenske S.S. Co* (1921) 8 Ll. L. Rep. 51.

[7] As in *Montevideo Gas Co v Clan Line* (1921) 37 T.L.R. 866 CA.

[8] *Jack L. Israel v Ocean Dynamic Lines SA, The Ocean Dynamic* [1982] 2 Lloyd's Rep. 88.

[9] *Empresa Cubana Importadora de Alimentos Alimport v Iasmos Shipping Co SA, The Good Friend* [1984] 2 Lloyd's Rep. 586.

tions—and the principles to be applied are much the same as with the far more important non-delivery, except that the normal measure of damages takes not the market value of the goods but the diminution in that value. In awarding in *The Good Friend* the market value of a substitute cargo less the price at which the claimants had sold the damaged cargo, Staughton J was not prepared to take the higher price at which the claimants had repurchased on a rising market although their delay in repurchasing was reasonably explainable.[11]

## (1) Normal measure

**32-003** The normal measure of damages for non-delivery is the market value of the goods at the time and place at which they should have been delivered less the amount it would have cost to get them to the place of delivery. The clearest statements of this measure are to be found in the leading case of *Rodocanachi v Milburn*,[12] where Lindley LJ spoke of it as a well-settled rule.[13] The rule is fully endorsed by the House of Lords in *Attorney General of the Republic of Ghana v Texaco Overseas Tankships, The Texaco Melbourne*,[14] where the essential dispute was as to the currency in which the market value of the goods should be assessed.[15] That the market value is to be taken at the contractual place of delivery by the carrier and not at the place where the goods were delivered to the carrier was first clearly laid down and applied in *Rice v Baxendale*.[16] That the cost of carriage must be deducted was established by *Rodocanachi v Milburn*[17]: this is, however, on the assumption that the carriage freight has not been paid. If the freight has already been paid then nothing falls to be deducted from the market value of the goods,[18] and, if the advance freight has been paid, then only the accruing freight is to be deducted.[19]

---

10 *Obestain Inc v National Mineral Development Corp Ltd, The Sanix Ace* [1987] 1 Lloyd's Rep. 465.

11 He was not persuaded that the principle of *Dodd Properties (Kent) v Canterbury City Council* [1980] 1 W.L.R. 433 CA, allowing deferment of reinstatement of a loss on a rising market (see para.39-018, below), applied: see [1984] 2 Lloyd's Rep. 586 at 596, col.2, 597, col.1.

12 (1886) 18 Q.B.D. 67 CA: "the value of the goods upon their arrival at the port of discharge less what he [i.e. the claimant] would have to pay in order to get them": at 76, per Lord Esher MR; "the value of the goods at the port of discharge, minus the accruing freight": at 78, per Lindley LJ.

13 (1886) 18 Q.B.D. 67 CA at 78.

14 [1994] 1 Lloyd's Rep. 473 HL.

15 This controversial issue is considered in detail elsewhere: see paras 20-043 to 20-045, above.

16 (1861) 7 H. & N. 96. This was adopted earlier in *Brandt v Bowlby* (1831) 2 B. & Ad. 932 (see especially at 939, per Parke J) but the action was in tort for conversion, and it was not till *The Arpad* [1934] P. 189 CA, that the relationship of the contractual and tortious measures of damages was considered in this connection: see para.24-009, above.

17 (1887) 18 Q.B.D. 67 CA.

18 In *Taylor & Son v Bowden Transport* [1966] 1 Lloyd's Rep. 207 and *Pye v B.G. Transport Service* [1966] 2 Lloyd's Rep. 300 (both carriage by land) the court simply awarded the value of the goods lost; this may have been because the carriage charges had been paid.

19 *Rodocanachi v Milburn* (1887) 18 Q.B.D. 67 CA. The fact that the goods were insured and the loss was caused by the defendant in such a way as to prevent the insurance moneys from being payable does not allow the claimant to claim as part of his damages the insurance premium he has paid: *Parker v James* (1814) 4 Camp. 112. As Lord Ellenborough said in that case, no new value was given to the goods by insuring them (at 114); looked at another way, one may say that, in order to put the claimant into the position he would have been in had the goods arrived and been properly delivered, it is not necessary to reimburse him his insurance premium since he would have had to pay this even had there been no breach of contract. On the other hand, the fact that the freight has been paid by the claimant and has been insured by him does not entitle the defendant to deduct the paid freight from the damages on the ground that the claimant has been or will be reimbursed for that amount

Where part only of the goods is not delivered the same measure applies mutatis mutandis.[20]

Where goods are delivered in a damaged condition the normal measure looks to the amount by which the market value of the goods has been diminished by the damage; whether or not there need be a deduction for the freight depends upon whether or not it has been paid over. This measure was awarded in *Vinmar International Ltd v Theresa Navigation SA*,[21] and in *Exportadora Valle de Collina SA v AP Moller-Maersk A/S*.[22] In awarding the sound arrived value of the goods less the amounts for which the goods had been resold or could be salvaged, that value was assessed in *The Ocean Dynamic*,[23] on the basis that a higher rate of customs duty would be payable upon them than the claimants had paid on the goods actually imported.[24] 32-004

**(a) Market value ascertained through the existence of an available market; meaning thereof** 32-005 In *Attorney General of the Republic of Ghana v Texaco Overseas Tankships, The Texaco Melbourne*,[25] where a cargo of fuel oil was never delivered by the carriers, Lord Goff indicated that there was

> "in the cases some divergence of opinion on the question whether, in cases where there is an available market for the goods, it is the buying price or the selling price which is the relevant price".[26]

As he pointed out, since a market presupposes a place where goods can either be bought or be sold,[27] the difference, if any, between the two prices on that market is likely to be only marginal, so that generally it will not matter whether one takes a selling price or a buying price.[28] While in *The Texaco Melbourne* there was a substantial divergence between the two prices, the difficulty there arose from the fact that fuel oil could not be freely bought and sold in Ghana, where the fuel oil was to be delivered and where the claimants would have sold it, so that there was no available market in Ghana, but it was accepted that the Italian market was an available market for the purchase of replacement fuel oil. It therefore became crucial to know which was the relevant price to take to ascertain whether there indeed was an available market. The difficulty did not have to be resolved by their

---

by his insurers: *Dufourcet v Bishop* (1886) 18 Q.B.D. 373; he may claim it on behalf of his insurers who are subrogated to his rights on paying him. The same will apply where it is the goods themselves that the claimant has insured.

[20] *British Columbia Saw Mill Co v Nettleship* (1868) L.R. 3 C.P. 499 and *The Arpad* [1934] P. 189 CA are illustrations of partial non-delivery; these cases primarily concern consequential losses: see paras 32-013 and 32-018, below, respectively. In cases of short delivery of a cargo carried by sea, on the question of how the extent of short delivery is worked out, see *Spaight v Farnsworth* (1880) 5 Q.B.D. 115 and *Mediterranean and New York S.S. Co v Mackay* [1903] 1 K.B. 297 CA; and on the question of whether the carrier is estopped by the bill of lading from denying that the whole cargo was shipped, see *Lishman v Christie* (1887) 19 Q.B.D. 333 and *Crossfield v Kyle Shipping Co* [1916] 2 K.B. 885. Neither of these questions is strictly one of damages.

[21] [2001] 2 Lloyd's Rep. 1; see at 15–16.

[22] [2010] EWHC 3224 (Comm); see at [188].

[23] [1982] 2 Lloyd's Rep. 88; facts at para.21-014, above.

[24] See [1982] 2 Lloyd's Rep. 88 at 93.

[25] [1994] 1 Lloyd's Rep. 473 HL.

[26] [1994] 1 Lloyd's Rep. 473 HL at 480, col.1.

[27] Citing Scrutton LJ in *The Arpad* [1934] P. 189 CA at 202.

[28] For the decision in its primary context of the proper currency of an award, see paras 20-043 to 20-045, above.

Lordships since their decision was unaffected by whether or not there was an available market,[29] but surely it must be correct to take the buying price rather than the selling price. For this is what the claimant must expend if he wishes to provide himself with substitute goods which he may then sell; he cannot claim a higher selling price as he could have achieved a sale by buying in at the lower price.[30]

32-006 **(b) Relevant and irrelevant prices in ascertaining the market value** The price at which a third party has agreed to buy the goods from the claimant[31] may be treated as evidence of the market value at due delivery where it is difficult to assess.[32] However, this sale price will not afford evidence of the market value where it is clearly different, as in *The Arpad*.[33] The defendant shipowners contracted to carry a cargo of wheat for the claimant. This wheat the claimant had bought in August and resold immediately at about the same price under advance contracts, but the defendants had no knowledge of this sale. On the cargo's arrival the following January a short delivery was discovered. There was no market at the port of delivery in which the claimant could buy against the short delivery,[34] and he therefore claimed damages on the basis of the price at which he had sold the cargo under the advance contracts. His first contention[35] was that this price was evidence of the market value. The Court of Appeal recognised the rule that in a proper case sub-contracts may, where there is no market, be put in evidence to show the value of the goods at non-delivery. Nevertheless the court refused to accept the price at which the claimant had sold in August as evidence of the market value the following January, i.e. the time of due delivery, when it was well known that the price of all wheat had fallen during that period.[36]

32-007 However, apart from being evidence of the market value of the goods, the price at which a third party has agreed to buy the goods from the claimant is irrelevant and should not be taken in lieu of the market value: this is so whether such a price is higher or lower than the market value. If this price is higher it may possibly be taken to inflate the normal measure by way of consequential losses, as was also argued by the claimant in *The Arpad*,[37] but will not by that fact represent the normal measure. If it is lower it has been held that it cannot be taken so as to decrease the damages, a point established in the leading case of *Rodocanachi v Milburn*,[38] a deci-

---

29 See preceding note.

30 See further on available market *Derby Resources AG v Blue Corinth Marine Co, The Athenian Harmony* [1998] 2 Lloyd's Rep. 410 at para.32-011, below.

31 In *Pye v B.G. Transport Service* [1966] 2 Lloyd's Rep. 30, where there was a loss of radio sets in transit to the London docks for onward transmission to the claimants' Persian buyers, the claimants were held not to be restricted, in their claim based on the value of the radio sets, to recovery of the fake price, substantially lower than the market value, at which they had been invoiced to the buyers with a view to defrauding the Persian customs. The sale contract was illegal, but the claimants did not have to rely on it in suing for breach of the carriage contract.

32 In *Braun v Bergenske S.S. Co* (1921) 8 Ll. L.R. 51, where the goods were delivered to the wrong person, damages were awarded on the basis of the claimant's sale price to a third party as there was no evidence of market value. The action however was in tort for conversion, but it has been held that the same measure applies in tort and in contract in this connection: see para.24-009, above.

33 [1934] P. 189 CA.

34 Although there was one in which he could sell.

35 He also claimed to recover the sale price as consequential loss: see para.32-018, below.

36 [1934] P. 189 CA at 210, 230, per Greer and Maugham LJJ respectively. Scrutton LJ delivered a dissenting judgment but it is not clear if he dissented on this exact point.

37 [1934] P. 189 CA: see at para.32-018, below.

38 (1886) 18 Q.B.D. 67 CA.

sion which, as Maugham LJ said in *The Arpad*,[39] "has constantly been cited and always approved"; in particular it was approved and followed by the House of Lords in *Williams v Agius*,[40] which presented the corresponding situation in sale of goods.[41] In *Rodocanachi v Milburn*, charterers had consigned a cargo for carriage by the defendant's ship and it was lost by the master's negligence. The charterers had sold the cargo at a price which turned out to be less than the market price prevailing at the port of delivery at the time when the cargo should have arrived, and it was held by the Court of Appeal that the relevant price was the market price and not the charterers' sale price, for the value must be taken "independently of any circumstances peculiar to the plaintiff".[42] Generally speaking, to fulfil their contract the charterers would have had to purchase similar goods in the market at the market price, and if their sale were of the identical goods, so that they could not satisfy the contract by buying in the market, they would necessarily be put in breach of their contract and might be liable in damages to their buyer to an extent far beyond the sale price.[43] Yet on the facts of *Rodocanachi v Milburn*, there was no possibility either of the charterers being sued by their buyer or of the charterers repurchasing in the market. This was because the cargo consigned for carriage by the defendant's ship had been sold by the charterers at the lower price on a "to arrive" basis so that non-delivery by the defendant shipper relieved them of all liability to their buyer without any need to go into the market to repurchase. There have indeed been signs of discontent, particularly in *Oxus Gold Plc v Templeton Insurance Ltd*,[44] with the absolute nature of the rule propounded by the Court of Appeal in *Rodocanachi v Milburn*, so that it is considered that the time may have come for its reconsideration, possibly along the lines proposed elsewhere.[45]

Another method of assessing the value of the goods where there is no market at the time and place of due delivery is to take the claimant's cost price, i.e. the market price at the place where the goods were delivered to the carrier, and add to this the cost of carriage[46] and an amount to cover the reasonable profit in the ordinary course of business of a person transporting goods to the particular place of due delivery. This calculation was adopted in *O'Hanlan v G.W. Ry*.[47] **32-008**

Delivery of the goods in a damaged condition, as opposed to a failure to deliver, will require the market value of the damaged goods to be ascertained.[48] There is less likely to be an available market for damaged goods than for sound goods. Thus, as Colman J rightly said in *Derby Resources AG v Blue Corinth Marine Co, The* **32-009**

---

39 [1934] P. 189 CA at 227.

40 [1914] A.C. 510.

41 See para.25-010, above.

42 (1886) 18 Q.B.D. 67 CA at 77, 80, per Lord Esher MR and Lopes LJ respectively.

43 See in relation to the corresponding situation in other types of contract Lord Dunedin in *Williams v Agius* [1914] A.C. 510 at 523 (sale of goods) and Evershed J in *Brading v McNeill* [1946] Ch. 145 at 151–152 (sale of business with lease).

44 [2007] EWHC 770 (Comm).

45 For this proposal see para.9-183, above. The whole problem is given extended consideration in the context of mitigation and avoided loss at paras 9-171 to 9-183, above.

46 Although this cost would be included to give the market value, it would generally fall to be deducted again to give the normal measure of market value of goods less market rate of freight.

47 (1865) 6 B. & S. 484. See *Parker v James* (1814) 4 Camp. 112 where the defendant had paid the cost price and shipping charges into court, and the court said that there was no evidence that the goods were worth more.

48 See para.32-004, above.

*Athenian Harmony*,[49]

"where the damaged goods are actually resold, the resale price will often be strong evidence of the market price of those goods in their damaged condition".

32-010 **(c) Time and place at which the market value is to be taken** The market value is to be taken at the time and place of due delivery. The fact that the goods are lost, destroyed or converted during transit does not make the time and place of such loss, destruction or conversion the relevant time and place to assess the market value of the goods. Thus in *Ewbank v Nutting*,[50] the goods, converted during transit, had sold at very low prices and the jury were directed to give as damages not the sale price but the cost price together with the expenses of shipping the goods. The court was quite clear that what the goods had sold at was no fair test and that, as Wilde CJ put it, the measure was "the amount of damage the plaintiff had sustained by the unauthorised sale".[51] The court did not specifically look to the market value at the time and place of due delivery, being primarily concerned with whether a measure based upon cost price plus freight could be wrong. But the trend of the judgments suggests that the market value at due delivery would have been acceptable as a measure.[52] Similarly in *Acatos v Burns*,[53] where again there was conversion by sale during transit, Brett LJ said that the true measure was "the value of the goods to the owner"[54] and Bramwell LJ agreed.[55] In both these cases the price at which the goods were sold was lower than the market value at the time and place of due delivery. There is, however, no reason why the normal measure of damages should not equally apply where the selling price was higher.[56]

32-011 Evidence of the market price of the goods at a different place and a different time may be the only means of quantification where there is no available market for the goods shipped at the time and place of due delivery. It is only if the evidence is of prices at places and times so remote that it is of no probative value in arriving at the sound value of the goods—and also, in the case of delivery in a damaged condition, in arriving at the damaged value of the goods—that it can be said that market prices do not help and that there is thus no available market. This was the approach taken by Colman J in *Derby Resources AG v Blue Corinth Marine Co, The Athenian Harmony*,[57] where the cargo was delivered in a damaged condition and at the place of delivery there was in operation a command economy where goods could not be freely bought and sold.

---

49 [1998] 2 Lloyd's Rep. 410 at 416, col.2.

50 (1849) 7 C.B. 797. The action was in tort for conversion, but in this connection the measure of damages in tort and contract would seem to be the same in taking the higher value at due delivery: see para.24-014, above.

51 (1849) 7 C.B. 797 at 809.

52 This appears most clearly from a passage in the argument: "[Cresswell J. Suppose the conversion had been by throwing the cargo overboard, what would have been the measure of damage in that case? What would the cargo have been worth to the owner?] What it would have sold for at the port of destination, minus the freight. [Cresswell J. May we not reasonably conclude that the goods would be worth the invoice price and the cost of carriage?] That might or might not be. [Wilde CJ. It would not be more than an actual indemnity.]": (1849) 7 C.B. 797 at 805.

53 (1878) 3 Ex. D. 282. Again the action was conversion: see the preceding footnote but two.

54 (1878) 3 Ex. D. 282 at 291, 292.

55 (1878) 3 Ex. D. 282 at 288.

56 These cases are further considered at para.24-014, above and para.38-042, below.

57 [1998] 2 Lloyd's Rep. 410.

## (2) Consequential losses

In cases of non-delivery consequential losses are not likely to arise where there is a market available in which the buyer can buy equivalent goods against his use or sale. One type of loss where there is a market available to a buyer consists in expenses incurred in inquiry and search for the goods. Consequential losses, however, frequently appear in the absence of an available market.[58] 32-012

### (a) Loss through loss of use

*(i) Loss of user profits* The leading case concerning the loss of user profits by reason of non-delivery is *British Columbia Saw Mill Co v Nettleship*.[59] The defendant contracted with the claimant to carry by sea from England to Canada several cases of machinery, the claimant intending the machinery for the erection of a sawmill in Canada. On the arrival of the defendant's ship in Canada one of the cases, which contained parts of the machinery without which the mill could not be erected, was found to be missing, and the claimant was obliged to replace the missing parts from England with a consequent year's delay. The claimant claimed to recover a year's loss of profit. This claim was disallowed since, although the defendant carrier knew generally that the cases contained machinery, he neither knew that the mill could not be erected at all without the missing parts nor that the missing parts could only be replaced by sending to England. The only damages for loss of user that the court was prepared to give was the user value of the goods as represented by interest on their value for the time that it would take the claimant to obtain replacements.[60] 32-013

The judgments of both Bovill CJ and Willes J in this case indicate a stricter approach in awarding loss of user profits, and business profits generally, against a carrier of goods than is to be found in cases where the defendant was a seller of goods. For they suggest that the defendant would still not have been liable even had he known that the missing parts were essential for the mill's erection and were replaceable only from England. In support of this view are strong dicta from two of a trilogy of important modern cases on the question of remoteness of damage in contract cases, *Victoria Laundry v Newman*,[61] and *Monarch S.S. Co v Karlshamns Oljefabriker*.[62] Thus in the former Asquith LJ, delivering the judgment of the court, said that in the case of a carrier, as opposed to a seller, the courts are less ready to imply liability for loss arising from the claimant's inability to use the goods in order to earn profits.[63] And in the latter, Lord Porter said that if the claim had been for loss of profits in the claimant's business he would have thought the defendant's contention that the damage was a result of circumstances peculiar to the claimant was a sound one.[64] In *The Heron II*,[65] the third case in the trilogy, Lord Upjohn, 32-014

---

58 For an unusual consequential loss see *Sandeman Coprimar SA v Transitos y Transportes Integrales SL* [2003] Q.B. 1270 CA at para.8-215, above.

59 (1868) L.R. 3 C.P. 499.

60 See, especially, (1868) L.R. 3 C.P. 499 at 507. See the defendant's contention in *Montevideo Gas Co v Clan Line* (1921) 37 T.L.R. 544 at 545 (affirmed at 866 CA) that the claimant's damages were limited to the cost price plus interest. See para.19-012, above.

61 [1949] 2 K.B. 528 CA.

62 [1949] A.C. 196.

63 [1949] 2 K.B. 528 CA at 536–537.

64 [1949] A.C. 196 at 216; similarly at 222, per Lord Wright.

echoing a very similar comment of Asquith LJ in *Victoria Laundry v Newman*,[66] gave the reason for this. "It must be remembered", he said,

> "when dealing with the case of a carrier of goods by land, sea or air, he is not carrying on the same trade as the consignor of the goods and his knowledge of the practices and exigencies of the other's trade may be limited and less than between buyer and seller of goods who probably know far more about one another's business."[67]

**32-015** This does not, however, mean that in no circumstances can damages for loss of business profits through use be recovered, and indeed Robert Goff J in *The Pegase*,[68] has said, although in the context of delayed delivery, that

> "there appears to be no rule of policy excluding, or restricting, the recovery of such damages; everything depends on the circumstances of the particular case".[69]

*Montevideo Gas Co v Clan Line*,[70] being the one case where the claimant has successfully claimed something akin to profits of this nature, is accordingly one of substantial interest. The defendants contracted with the claimants to carry and deliver at Montevideo a quantity of gas coal which they knew the claimants urgently required for the manufacture of gas. They mistakenly delivered a smaller quantity of steam coal which the claimants reasonably used to keep their plant running. In the absence of a market at Montevideo in which they could buy gas coal, the claimants successfully claimed what they had lost in the manufacture of gas by the use of the inferior steam coal and also by the short delivery. The Court of Appeal pointed out that the value had to be arrived at by some other method when there was no market and was content to take the value to the claimants. Roche J's judgment below,[71] which the Court of Appeal affirmed, is however more illuminating. After agreeing with the claimants' contention that the contemplation of the parties is more rigidly applied to carriers than to sellers as

> "a natural result of the fact that a carrier is supposed to know less about the commodity he carries and to undertake less responsibility in connection with it",[72]

he proceeded to point out that the defendants knew the gas coal was urgently required to make gas, that gas coal was probably not quickly obtainable, and that steam coal would not be an adequate substitute, a matter which should be generally known. On the basis of these facts the defendants were therefore liable for the claimants' loss; for

> "in truth distinctions between the liability of a carrier and a seller depend on matters of fact and not of law".[73]

---

65 [1969] 1 A.C. 350.
66 [1949] 2 K.B. 528 CA at 537.
67 [1969] 1 A.C. 350 at 424. See, too, *Montevideo Gas Co v Clan Line* (1921) 37 T.L.R. 544 at 545, per Roche J, quoted in para.32-015, below.
68 [1981] 1 Lloyd's Rep. 175.
69 [1981] 1 Lloyd's Rep. 175at 184, col.1. See the case at para.32-033, below.
70 (1921) 37 T.L.R. 866 CA.
71 (1921) 37 T.L.R. 544.
72 (1921) 37 T.L.R. 544 at 545.
73 (1921) 37 T.L.R. 544 at 545.

*(ii) Expenses made necessary* An illustration of an expense that could be made necessary by the breach is that of acquiring goods which in the absence of a market are the nearest substitute though exacting a higher price. The authorities are all cases of delayed delivery and therefore are considered later[74]; however, they apply mutatis mutandis here. **32-016**

**(b) Loss on a sale** Loss on a sale of the goods to a third party, like damage through loss of use, is most likely to arise where there is no market in which similar goods can be bought.[75] But in addition loss can arise here despite the existence of a market generally, because this market is not available to the claimant himself, either because he has sold the specific goods or because the contract of sale has the same delivery date as the contract of carriage.[76] **32-017**

*(i) Loss of profit on a sale* Loss of sale profits are, like loss of user profits and for the same reason,[77] less likely to be recoverable in contracts of carriage of goods than in contracts of sale of goods. The authority for non-delivery in carriage contracts is the important decision in *The Arpad*.[78] In an action for non-delivery of part of a cargo of wheat, the Court of Appeal held by a majority that the law did not take account of sub-contracts even where there was no market in which the claimant could buy against his sale to a third party. Maugham LJ went through a lot of familiar authorities[79] to support his conclusion that **32-018**

> "the exclusion from consideration of sub-contracts does not depend on the existence of a market".[80]

And quite apart from the authorities he took the view that:

> "it would be very unfortunate if shippers and purchasers of goods carried by sea were in a position, during a perhaps prolonged period, to enter into contracts of sub-sale, and to please themselves as to whether these were disclosed in the event of a dispute arising such as one based on short delivery."[81]

Later, however, Robert Goff J said in *The Pegase*,[82] that he knew **32-019**

> "of no rule of policy excluding or restricting recovery of damages from a carrier assessed with reference to a loss of resale profits, if on the ordinary principles of law such damages should be awarded".[83]

How far the defendant's actual or implied knowledge of an actual, probable or pos-

[74] See para.32-035, below.
[75] The cargo owners' loss on their resale contract was not awarded in *Vinmar International Ltd v Theresa Navigation SA* [2001] 2 Lloyd's L.R. 1 as they could have gone into the market to buy a substitute cargo; see at 15 to 16.
[76] Contrast the corresponding situation in sale of goods at paras 25-027 and following, above.
[77] See para.32-014, above.
[78] [1934] P. 189 CA.
[79] [1934] P. 189 CA at 223–230.
[80] [1934] P. 189 CA at 227.
[81] [1934] P. 189 CA at 222; similarly at 209 to 210. See, too, *The Saint Cloud* (1863) Br. & Lush. 4 where loss on a sale was not allowed: the goods had not been lost but only damaged.
[82] [1981] 1 Lloyd's Rep. 175; facts at para.32-039, below.
[83] [1981] 1 Lloyd's Rep. 175 at 185, col.2.

sible sale by the claimant will alter the position as stated in *The Arpad*,[84] is considered later under delayed delivery where there are cases on the point.[85]

32-020 An interesting question in the context of a claim for profit on a sale of goods lost before they could be delivered arose in *Sony Computer Entertainment UK Ltd v Cinram Logistics UK Ltd*.[86] The claimants were the manufacturers of memory cards which they sold on a continuing basis to one of their most important customers. The defendants were responsible for the warehousing, carriage and distribution of the memory cards. A consignment of them from the claimants to their customer was stolen when in the defendants' charge. Because of the close trading relationship between claimants and customer, the sale thereby lost had been at a discounted price, and therefore below the market price, so that at first glance there would appear to be no difficulty in claiming for this particular loss of profit.[87] The defendants however argued that no sale had been lost on the basis that the customer had replaced its order, thereby entitling the claimants only to the cost price to them of acquiring replacement memory cards. The Court of Appeal held against the defendants, deciding that any further orders by the customer had not been replacement orders but extra ones. In achieving this result the analogous cases of claims against a buyer rather than a carrier of goods were strongly relied upon.[88]

32-021 *(ii) Compensation paid to a buyer; costs incurred in defending the buyer's action*[89] If the claimant is unable to recover his loss of profit on a sale of the goods, a fortiori he will be unable to recover any compensation he has paid to his buyer or any costs incurred in defending an action brought against him by his buyer. On the other hand, if the court should hold that the claimant may recover for his loss of profit on his sale, he ought also to be able to recover as damages both compensation paid to his buyer and costs incurred in defending the buyer's action, provided always these outlays were reasonably incurred. Thus in *The Ocean Dynamic*,[90] where the cargo had been delivered but in a damaged condition,[91] while no loss of profit on the sale of the cargo by the consignees was claimed, such a sale was held to have been within the contemplation of the parties, and recovery for compensation paid and costs incurred was allowed. Yet the position on the recovery of costs may be changing. Where the claimant has reasonably but unsuccessfully defended a claim brought by his buyer, formerly recovery of his own costs incurred in a reasonable defence was of these costs assessed as between solicitor and client; now, solicitor and client costs no longer exist in this context and the claimant should instead simply be entitled to all his costs reasonably incurred. There is, however, a

---

84 [1934] P. 189 CA.

85 See paras 32-037 to 32-042, below.

86 [2008] EWCA Civ 955 CA.

87 Whether the market value of the memory cards could have been claimed was not in issue as the claimants contented themselves with the discounted price. The issue is adverted to by Rix LJ at [50] and its resolution in the claimant's favour would be dependent on the continued adherence to the leading case of *Rodocanachi v Milburn* (1886) 18 Q.B.D. 67 CA. See the discussion at para.32-007, above.

88 In particular *Re Vic Mill* [1913] 1 Ch. 465 CA and *Hill v Showell* (1918) 87 L.J.K.B. 1106 HL See the various cases at paras 25-130 and 25-131, above.

89 See the delayed delivery case of *Heskell v Continental Express* [1950] 1 All E.R. 1033 (para.32-043, below) and also the sale of goods cases in Ch.25 where the issues involved here have been considered more thoroughly.

90 [1982] 2 Lloyd's Rep. 88; facts at para.21-014, above.

91 See para.32-002, above.

growing move at first instance, one not to be encouraged, which would restrict the claimant to what, if assessed, would have been his standard basis costs in the action with the buyer; this unfortunate development has already been fully examined in an earlier chapter to which reference should be made.[92]

*(iii) Loss of profit on further sales* No successful claims for loss of general custom due to loss of goodwill appear in the cases. The possibility of such a claim has been considered, in the context of delayed delivery, in *The Pegase*.[93] **32-022**

**(c) Other expenses made necessary by the breach** In actions for breach of contract by a carrier one common illustration of the recovery of expenses made necessary by the breach is of reasonable expenditure in inquiring and searching for the goods when they have failed to arrive at the due date. The authorities on this are of cases of delayed delivery and are therefore considered later[94] but they apply mutatis mutandis here.[95] **32-023**

**(d) Expenses rendered futile by the breach** As an alternative to claiming for loss of profits a claimant may sometimes claim, as consequential loss, for expenses rendered futile by the breach. These are generally not allowed in carriage contracts,[96] but illustrations of non-recovery must be sought in cases of delayed delivery.[97] **32-024**

## (3) Claimant with a limited interest in the goods

The person who contracts for the carriage of goods which are not his own property is nevertheless entitled to their full value in an action for breach of contract arising out of their loss or destruction.[98] This is borne out by *Crouch v L.N.W. Ry*,[99] where the claimant was himself a carrier of parcels and had sub-contracted certain carriage to the defendant. He was held entitled to the full value of the goods upon their loss. The court pointed out that he would himself be liable to the owner, and that it was not necessary that he should have paid the owner since he "will be liable to account for whatever may be received by him".[100] Even if he were not contractually liable to the owner by reason of, say, some exemption clause in the contract, it is submitted that he would still be under an obligation to account to the **32-025**

92 See the discussion at paras 21-003 and following, above.

93 [1981] 1 Lloyd's Rep. 175. See the case at para.32-039, below.

94 See para.32-046, below.

95 In *Papera Traders Co Ltd v Hyundai Merchant Marine Co Ltd, The Eurasian Dream (No.2)* [2002] 2 Lloyd's Rep. 692, where goods carried by sea had been damaged, the expense of a contingency fee paid to a claims handler was held not recoverable as too remote: see the case at para.8-215, above.

96 But see *Club Coffee Co v Moore-McCormack Lines*, a case in the Canadian Exchequer Court reported at [1968] 2 Lloyd's Rep. 103, where the damages awarded included customs duty that the claimant had paid on bags of coffee not delivered, being liable for duty on bags imported into Canada whether ultimately received by him or not. Compare *S.S. Ardennes (Cargo Owners) v S.S. Ardennes (Owners)* [1951] 1 K.B. 55, at para.32-046, below, which was cited by the court; there the extra duty was an expense made necessary, rather than one rendered futile, by the breach.

97 See para.32-047, below. For the general principles involved see paras 4-024 and following, above.

98 There is more authority for this principle in actions of tort for conversion than in actions for breach of a contract of carriage: see paras 38-050 and following, below.

99 (1849) 2 C. & K. 789.

100 (1849) 2 C. & K. 789 at 801–802.

owner for moneys received by him as damages over and above his own qualified interest in the goods. Similarly, where the property in the goods is still in the person contracting for their carriage but the risk has passed to others, that contracting party remains entitled to the full value of the goods if lost or destroyed or to the diminution in their value if damaged. This is borne out by *Obestain v National Mineral Development Corp, The Sanix Ace*,[101] where the charterers, while they still had the property in the goods which had been delivered in a damaged condition, had passed the risk to 11 end users who had each paid them their purchase price. The court held that the owners' contention that the charterers were entitled only to nominal damages, on the basis that they had suffered no loss because they had been able to collect the price, was unsustainable. The claimants' property in the goods gave them the right to recover substantial damages. Again, it is thought that there would be an obligation to account to the 11 end users for any damages received.

## 2. Delayed Delivery

### (1) Normal measure

**32-026** The normal measure of damages is the market value of the goods at the place of delivery at the time they should have been delivered less their market value there at the time they were in fact delivered.[102] Where the delay has caused physical damage to the goods by reason of their being perishable, the loss in market value is clearly recoverable, a result so solidly established that the cases do not trouble to argue the point.[103] Where, however, the loss is due to a general fall in the market, difficulties have arisen where the carriage is by sea.

**32-027** **(a) Carriage by land** Where the carriage of the goods is by land and the market price has fallen during the period of delay, the normal measure of damages applies and damages are given for the fall in the market price. This was held in *Collard v S.E. Ry*,[104] which concerned the carriage of hops by rail. The delay in that case was partly because the hops were delivered late and partly because, being also damaged by exposure by the defendant carrier, they had to be dried before they could be put into a saleable condition.[105] The claimant successfully claimed the amount by which the market had depreciated between the time the hops should have been delivered and the time he was in a position to put them on the market. Martin B said:

---

[101] [1987] 1 Lloyd's Rep. 465.

[102] The best illustrations, for carriage by land, are *Collard v S.E. Ry* (1861) 7 H. & N. 79 and *Heskell v Continental Express* [1950] 1 All E.R. 1033 (see especially at 1046) and, for carriage by sea, *The Heron II* [1969] 1 A.C. 350. See paras 32-027 and 32-030, below, respectively.

[103] Illustrations where such loss has been given as damages are *Hawes v S.E. Ry* (1884) 54 L.J.Q.B. 174 (fish) and *Glynn v Margetson* [1893] A.C. 351 (oranges). *Collard v S.E. Ry* (1861) 7 H. & N. 79 provided a slight refinement; the depreciation in quality had affected only the price at which the goods (hops) could be sold while they were still as good for use. "Not a legal distinction", said Pollock CB (at 82), although he added that the jury could consider it on the actual facts of the case.

[104] (1861) 7 H. & N. 79.

[105] Only a part of the hops in each parcel had been damaged so as to need drying, and that part might have been replaced by good hops or the uninjured part might have been sold separately. But it was the custom to sell hops in their original bags marked by the excise, and any transfer or filling up would have been looked on with suspicion. In these circumstances the defendant was held liable for the delay to the whole bulk.

"We are to assume that the hops ought to have been delivered on a certain day, and that by reason of the defendants' breach of duty they could not be delivered until another day. It was proved that if they had been brought to market they would have fetched a certain price, but, not being brought until a later day, the market price in the meantime fell, and the value of the hops was diminished by the amount of £65. If that be not a direct, immediate and necessary consequence of the defendant's breach of duty, it is difficult to understand what would be."[106]

A more modern illustration is *Heskell v Continental Express*.[107] There Devlin J awarded

"the ordinary measure of damages for delay in delivery, namely the fall in market value of the goods".[108]

The matter is taken a step further by *Wilson v Lancashire & Yorkshire Ry*,[109] in which the decrease in market value was allowed where it was due to the season for the goods being over before they were delivered. The defendant so delayed the claimant's cloth, which the claimant had bought to make into caps, that the season had passed before he could execute the orders his travellers had obtained. In allowing his claim for damages for loss of this season, the court was careful to point out that the damages awarded did not represent the "loss of profits of the season" but the "loss by depreciation in market value".[110] This was followed in *Schulze v G.E. Ry*,[111] where the claimant again recovered his loss of season through the delayed carriage of his samples.[112] There was no suggestion that the defendant in either case was aware that the market was seasonal. **32-028**

**(b) Carriage by sea** Where in a contract of carriage by sea, on the other hand, the market has fallen between due delivery and actual delivery, it was held in the 19th century in *The Parana*,[113] that this fall could not be recovered as damages within the normal measure. Mellish LJ distinguished the case of carriage by land on the ground that the court there considered the goods to be consigned for immediate sale on delivery, and said that to give damages for a market fall the court must be able to come to two conclusions, **32-029**

"first, that it was reasonably certain that the goods would not be sold until they did arrive; and, secondly, that it was reasonably certain that they would be sold immediately after they arrived, and that that was known to the carrier at the time when the bills of lading were signed."[114]

These two assumptions he thought most uncertain in the case before him.[115]

---

106 (1861) 7 H. & N. 79 at 86. There was also a successful claim for a depreciation in quality which remained even after the hops had been dried.

107 [1950] 1 All E.R. 1033.

108 [1950] 1 All E.R. 1033 at 1046.

109 (1861) 9 C.B. N.S. 632.

110 (1861) 9 C.B. N.S. 632 at 644. See too at 646, per Byles J: "Profits include the increased value arising from the purpose to which the plaintiff intended to apply the goods: whereas diminution in exchangeable value is only something subtracted from the inherent value of the articles themselves."

111 (1887) 19 Q.B.D. 30.

112 Both cases were approved in *Wertheim v Chicoutimi Pulp Co* [1911] A.C. 301 PC at 308.

113 (1877) 2 P.D. 118 CA.

114 (1877) 2 P.D. 118 CA at 123.

115 (1877) 2 P.D. 118 CA at 123.

**32-030** The implications of this decision were far reaching. Since, outside consequential losses, the loss suffered by the claimant is contained in the extent of the fall in the market price,[116] the normal measure of damages becomes nil,[117] and it is a short step from this to the proposition that there is no action for damages for delay in delivery in carriage by sea at all.[118] The decision however gained no real acceptance in the courts, was never applied in the course of almost a century in favour of a defendant sued for breach of contract[119] by late delivery of goods carried by sea,[120] and was finally rejected by the House of Lords in *The Heron II*.[121] In that case their Lordships held that there was no good reason to exempt contracts of carriage by sea where the breach was by delay from the general operation of the remoteness rule laid down in *Hadley v Baxendale*,[122] and that, under the so-called "first rule", the defendant carriers were liable in damages to the extent that the market value of the goods when they should have been delivered exceeded their market value when they were in fact delivered. Lord Reid pointed out that Mellish LJ's test of reasonable certainty that such a loss would occur was far too strict; although such a test might have been right at the time, since for a considerable period after *Hadley v Baxendale*,[123] there had been a tendency to set narrow limits to damages awards,[124] it had long been obsolete.[125] It was also pointed out by Lord Upjohn that Mellish LJ may well have been influenced by the great uncertainties in the timings of sea transport in a day when the sailing ship was still predominant, a situation that was soon to be altered as the age of sail gave way to the age of the steam engine.[126]

---

[116] Apart always from cases where there is physical damage to the goods.

[117] Or, at most, interest on the value of the goods during the period of delay, which was the measure contended for by the unsuccessful carrier in *The Heron II* [1969] 1 A.C. 350.

[118] This argument is indeed found, in the House of Lords and as late as 1949, in *Monarch S.S. Co v Karlshamns Oljefabriker* [1949] A.C. 196; see Lord Porter's speech at 219.

[119] It was followed and applied within a few years where the action was in tort in *The Notting Hill* (1884) 9 P.D. 105 CA.

[120] Various ways were found for distinguishing *The Parana* and awarding damages for loss caused by a market fall during the period of delay. In *Smith v Tregarthan* (1887) 56 L.J.Q.B. 437 where the goods had been shipped on the wrong vessel which arrived three days later, the court said that the case was one not of delayed delivery but of non-delivery, with the later acceptance of the goods going in reduction of the damages. In *Sargant v E. Asiatic Co* (1915) 32 T.L.R. 119 where, on the arrival of the goods at London, the carrier wrongly refused their delivery to the claimant and carried them on to Copenhagen and back again to London, it was held that *The Parana* did not apply to delay which occurred not in the course of the contractual transit but after the goods had arrived at their proper contractual destination. Most importantly, in *Dunn v Bucknall* [1902] 2 K.B. 614 CA, where the goods were for the supply of British troops in South Africa in the Boer War, and in *S.S. Ardennes (Cargo Owners) v S.S. Ardennes (Owners)* [1951] 1 K.B. 55 where mandarin oranges were delayed in transit from Spain to London, the court held that the goods were to the actual or imputed knowledge of the defendant carrier intended for a particular market or season which would be missed if the goods were delayed. Moreover, the courts had no difficulty in awarding damages for delay in delivery of goods carried by sea where there has been consequential loss not resulting from a fall in the market: see, e.g. *Monarch S.S. Co v Karlshamns Oljefabriker* [1949] A.C. 196, at para.32-050, below.

[121] [1969] 1 A.C. 350. In the 12th edition (1961) of this work it was submitted that the rule in *The Parana* was due for reconsideration.

[122] (1854) 9 Ex. 341: for the rule see paras 8-160 and following, above.

[123] (1854) 9 Ex. 341.

[124] [1969] 1 A.C. 350 at 387.

[125] [1969] 1 A.C. 350 at 392. See similarly at 411 to 412, per Lord Hodson and 418 and 420, per Lord Pearce.

[126] [1969] 1 A.C. 350 at 428.

Indeed by the turn of the century Lord Collins MR in *Dunn v Bucknall*,[127] a decision referred to by all of their Lordships, was pointing out that

> "as the means of sea transport improve, voyages of three and four weeks' duration may be, and are now accomplished with almost absolute certainty, and the state of the market at the reasonably calculated date of arrival may well be a vital factor present to the minds of both parties at the time of making the contract."[128]

In *Dunn v Bucknall*,[129] however, the Court of Appeal was able to base its decision for the claimant on the "second rule" in *Hadley v Baxendale*[130]; now in *The Heron II*,[131] the House of Lords has rendered unnecessary a finding of special circumstances known to the defendant and established the fall in market value as the normal measure of damages.[132]

Their Lordships were content to hold that *The Parana*,[133] in so far as it sought to lay down a general proposition or rule of law, must in the words of Lord Upjohn "be regarded as either obsolete, being overtaken by events or as overruled"[134]; with whether or not the decision was wrong on its particular facts they stated they were not really concerned.[135] Indeed, even today, "it may be", in the words of Lord Pearce, **32-031**

> "that in some unusual cases it will be found that the situation between the parties showed that the shipper was indifferent to the time of arrival and that the parties did *not* contract on the basis that in case of deviation or delay the shipowner should be liable for loss of market."[136]

But this, of course, would go to liability rather than to damages for, as Lord Morris pointed out,

> "if the parties for some particular reason have contracted on the basis that there is no obligation to proceed normally to a destination, then delay would not constitute a breach".[137]

At the same time, Lord Upjohn was careful to stress that the normal measure is not ousted merely because the time of a ship's arrival at her destination is not precisely predictable. "Even today", he said,

> "when very long journeys half-way round the world are undertaken, the estimate of the time which a ship ought to take may vary within wide limits",

---

127 [1902] 2 K.B. 614 CA.

128 [1902] 2 K.B. 614 CA at 623. See similarly *Monarch S.S. Co v Karlshamns Oljefabriker* [1949] A.C. 196 at 219, per Lord Porter.

129 [1902] 2 K.B. 614 CA.

130 (1854) 9 Ex. 341.

131 [1969] 1 A.C. 350.

132 Thereby bringing English law into line with that of the USA where the courts have declined, as Lords Hodson and Pearce pointed out (at 412 and 418–419), to follow *The Parana* since *US v Middleton*, 3 F. (2d) 384 (1924).

133 (1877) 2 P.D. 118 CA.

134 [1969] 1 A.C. 350 at 428.

135 [1969] 1 A.C. 350 at 392, 413, 420, 428. Lord Pearce however stated (at 420) that he considered *The Notting Hill* (1884) 9 P.D. 105 CA, to be wrongly decided; this was the one case, and a case in tort, in which *The Parana* had been followed.

136 [1969] 1 A.C. 350 at 419. His emphasis.

137 [1969] 1 A.C. 350 at 403.

and

> "if the ship greatly exceeds the larger estimate through breach of contract and the cargo owner thereby misses his market he is entitled to damages for loss of market".[138]

## (2) Consequential losses

32-032 As with non-delivery, consequential losses in delayed delivery are not likely to arise where there is a market available in which the claimant can buy equivalent goods against his use or sale. The most commonly illustrated type of loss where there is a market available to the claimant consists in expenses incurred in inquiry and search for the goods. The most frequent consequential losses, however, remain those which result from the absence of an available market to the claimant.

### (a) Loss through loss of use

32-033 *(i) Loss of user profits* The leading case concerning the loss of user profits by reason of delayed delivery is the *fons et origo* of the modern case law on contract damages, *Hadley v Baxendale*,[139] itself. The claimant's millshaft was broken and he gave it to the defendant carrier to take to the makers as a model for a new one. On making the contract, the defendant's clerk was informed that the article to be carried was the broken shaft of a mill and that the claimant was the owner of the mill.[140] The defendant delayed the millshaft's delivery, and the claimant claimed to recover for the loss of profits while the mill, as a result of the delay, remained idle. The court rejected the claim on the ground that the facts which the defendant was held to know were, in the words of Alderson B, not sufficient to

> "show reasonably that the profits of the mill must be stopped by an unreasonable delay in the delivery of the broken shaft by the carrier to the third person".[141]

Again, in *Gee v Lancashire & Yorkshire Ry*,[142] the claimant's mill was stopped by a carrier's delay in delivery, this time in the carriage of cotton. The loss of profits from the mill standing idle was once again held irrecoverable, since the defendant had not been informed that any particular inconvenience would be likely to result from the delay and since, further, the loss was sustained, not in consequence of the non-arrival of the cotton alone, but in consequence of the claimant's having no other cotton in stock, the latter being a fact which the defendant was not bound to expect. Wilde B said that the decision might have been different

---

138 [1969] 1 A.C. 350 at 429. He referred to two cases in the USA (which does not follow *The Parana*: see footnote at the end of para.8-032, above) where damages for loss of market were awarded where the limits within which the time of the voyage could be estimated were very broad: *US v Middleton*, 3 F. (2d) 384 (1924) (60 to 90 days) and *The Iossifoglu*, 32 F. (2d) 928 (1929) (46 to 66 days).

139 (1854) 9 Ex. 341.

140 As was pointed out by Asquith LJ in *Victoria Laundry v Newman* [1949] 2 K.B. 528 CA at 537–538, the headnote in *Hadley v Baxendale* is misleading in so far as it says that the defendant's clerk was informed that the mill was stopped and the shaft must be sent immediately. This again appears in the statement of the facts ((1854) 9 Ex. 341 at 344). One can only assume that the claimant gave evidence to this effect which was not accepted by the court. For if it had been accepted the court must surely, said Asquith LJ, have decided for the claimant under the second rule as propounded there: [1949] 2 K.B. 528 CA at 537.

141 (1854) 9 Ex. 341 at 355.

142 (1860) 6 H. & N. 211.

"if it were the practice to work all the cotton mills in the neighbourhood from hand to mouth".[143]

But there are no cases where loss of business profits has been granted in this type of case and Asquith LJ in *Victoria Laundry v Newman*,[144] after giving cases where loss of profits has been allowed, put this type "at the other end of the scale",[145] saying that "in such cases the courts have been slow to allow loss of profit as an item of damage".[146] Yet, more recently, Robert Goff J in *The Pegase*,[147] in relation to damages for the loss of user profits, has said that

"there appears to be no rule of policy excluding, or restricting, the recovery of such damages".[148]

While accepting that sellers were likely to have more knowledge than carriers so as to appreciate the effect of late delivery, he added:

"It is not difficult to envisage a carrier being held responsible for damages for loss of user profits in a case where, for example, a railway locomotive consigned by sea to a railway company was delivered late, even though nothing specific was communicated at or before the time of making the contract concerning the use to which the goods were to be put."[149]

Although the courts have generally shown themselves unprepared to allow the claimant his loss of user profits, damages for loss of use can be given on a much smaller scale by an award calculated by interest on the value of the goods for the period of delay. This has been done in non-delivery,[150] and also in delayed delivery where the loss has arisen from a sale.[151] This amount is permitted even if during the period of delay it is proved or admitted that the claimant would not have put the goods to profit-making use. This position arose in *Sunley v Cunard White Star*.[152] There the defendants agreed to collect by road, and transport by sea by one of their ships sailing on a specified date, a tractor belonging to the claimants, which was to be used in work which the claimants had undertaken to perform in Guernsey. The defendants' sub-contractors delayed the collection by road, and the tractor had to be sent by a later ship, thus causing loss of use for a week in Guernsey. There was no evidence that the claimants suffered any loss of profit on their work in Guernsey, or that the tractor's special work would have been finished earlier had it not been delivered a week late. The claimants, said the court, having **32-034**

"failed to prove any facts on which their damages could be estimated … relied on the law",[153]

143 (1860) 6 H. & N. 211 at 220; and Pollock CB talked of "actual notice … or notice from the well understood course of business": at 216.

144 [1949] 2 K.B. 528 CA.

145 [1949] 2 K.B. 528 CA at 536, citing *Hadley v Baxendale* (1854) 9 Ex. 341 and *Gee v Lancashire and Yorkshire Ry* (1860) 6 H. & N. 211.

146 [1949] 2 K.B. 528 CA at 536–537. For his explanation of this slowness, see para.8-214, above; and contrast para.32-014, above.

147 [1981] 1 Lloyd's Rep. 175; facts at para.32-039, below.

148 [1981] 1 Lloyd's Rep. 175 at 184, col.1.

149 [1981] 1 Lloyd's Rep. 175 at 184, col.2.

150 See para.32-013, above.

151 See para.32-042, below.

152 [1940] 1 K.B. 740 CA.

153 [1940] 1 K.B. 740 at 747.

but in such circumstances

> "their only possible claim must rest on the fact that by the machine being thrown suddenly on their hands for a week[154] they were prevented from earning its keep, and had to put up with current outgoings uncompensated by earnings".[155]

The Court of Appeal considered that four legitimate heads of damage could be claimed:

> "(1) depreciation which was running on, (2) interest on the money invested which was being wasted, (3) some trivial amount of maintenance which was no doubt involved, (4) some expenditure of wages which were thrown away."[156]

It may be questioned whether the third and fourth items were properly allowed in addition to the first two, since wages and maintenance would have been incurred even had the contract been properly performed[157]; the total amount awarded was very small, however, in all £14.[158]

32-035 *(ii) Expenses made necessary* Claims for expenses made necessary by the breach are illustrated for delayed delivery by cases in which the claimant has sued for the cost of acquiring the nearest substitute at a higher price where there has been no market in which he could buy exactly equivalent goods. In *Millen v Brasch*,[159] the claimant's trunk was sent by the defendant carrier to New York instead of to Rome, thus causing delay in its delivery. The trunk, as the defendant could have surmised, contained clothes, and the claimant bought other clothes in Rome at an enhanced price and recovered for his expenditure, the judge applying the test[160] of whether this was the reasonable thing to do. On the other hand, in *Romulus Films v William Dempster*,[161] where the claimant film company chartered the defendant's aircraft to carry film equipment from Africa to London and delivery in London was delayed, McNair J refused damages to cover the expenditure in having the properties and wardrobes duplicated in London to enable the shooting of the film, which had been arranged on a tight schedule, to continue. "I am unable to find", he said,

> "that these circumstances—the necessity for immediate shooting in England following upon the completion of shooting in the field—formed any part of the ordinary practices and exigencies of a film company's trade or business."[162]

However, he allowed for the extended hire of cameras, which might mean cameras duplicated in London but more probably referred to the fact that cameras hired to take to Africa could not be returned in time to the London suppliers from whom they had been hired. A further illustration of recovery other than for the expense of

---

154 Meaning before its collection by the defendants' sub-contractors.
155 [1940] 1 K.B. 740 CA at 748.
156 [1940] 1 K.B. 740 CA.
157 See para.4-024, above.
158 Depreciation on a pure sinking fund basis would have been £29, but, since it would be less when the tractor was idle than when working, £20 was held sufficient. Under the other three heads, £10 was allowed. From this total of £30 there was deducted £16 which represented the receipts during the week while awaiting collection, thus making a final sum of £14.
159 (1882) 10 Q.B.D. 142.
160 Put forward in *Le Blanche v L.N.W. Ry* (1876) 1 C.P.D. 286 CA: see para.32-057, below.
161 [1952] 2 Lloyd's Rep. 535.
162 [1952] 2 Lloyd's Rep. 535 at 540.

acquiring a substitute is provided by *The Subro Valour*,[163] where a fire on the chartered vessel had required the cargo to be rescued and transhipped. The charterers successfully claimed for, inter alia,[164] the salvage expenses and transhipment costs incurred by them.

**(b) Loss on a sale** Loss on a sale of goods to a third party, like damage through loss of use, is most likely to arise where there is no market in which similar goods can be bought. But, in addition, loss can arise here despite the existence of a market generally, because this market is not available to the buyer himself, either because he has sold the specific goods or because the contract of sale has the same delivery date as the contract of carriage.[165] **32-036**

*(i) Loss of profit on a sale* Loss of sale profits are, like loss of user profits and for the same reason,[166] less likely to be recoverable in contracts of carriage of goods than in contracts of sale of goods. The general rule was established soon after *Hadley v Baxendale*,[167] in a number of cases which, without much discussion, refused the claimant loss of profit he would have made on a sale which was lost to him by reason of the delay.[168] Then in *Horne v Midland Ry*,[169] the whole question was discussed at length before seven judges in the Exchequer Chamber, and this case remains the leading one on loss of sales by reason of delayed carriage. The claimants were under a contract to supply to a firm in London shoes for the use of the French Army, the price being an unusually high one. They contracted with the defendants for their carriage to London stating that they were under a contract to deliver by 3 February, and that unless the shoes were so delivered they would be thrown on their hands, but not stating the special nature of the contract. The shoes were delayed, in consequence of which the buyers refused to take delivery, and the sub-contract was lost. The claimants had to sell them at the ordinary market price, which was well below the special contract price. The court[170] refused to hold the defendants liable for the difference between the ordinary market value of the shoes and the special contract price, on the ground that, since they did not know of the exceptional nature of the claimants' sale contract, damages of such an exceptional nature could not have been in the contemplation of the parties at the time the contract was made, and the mere notice that there was a contract did not put the defendants upon inquiry as to its nature. **32-037**

There can be no doubt about this decision, for the sub-contract was exceptionally lucrative and this factor was uncommunicated to the defendants. Some uncertainty has, however, centred on what the position is (1) where the sub-contract is in no way exceptional and its existence, although not expressly communicated to the defendant by the claimant, is not unlikely[171]; (2) where the claim- **32-038**

---

163 [1995] 1 Lloyd's Rep. 509.

164 See the case in the fn. at the end of para.32-042, below.

165 See the corresponding situation in sale of goods at paras 25-049 and following, above.

166 See para.32-014, above.

167 (1854) 9 Ex. 341.

168 *Le Peintur v S.E. Ry* (1860) 2 L.T. 170; *Simmons v S.E. Ry* (1861) 7 Jur. 849; *Hales v L.N.W. Ry* (1863) 4 B. & S. 66; *G.W. Ry v Redmayne* (1866) L.R. 1 C.P. 329.

169 (1873) L.R. 8 C.P. 131.

170 By a majority of five to two.

171 "Not unlikely" adopts the new vogue in terminology ushered in by *The Heron II* [1969] 1 A.C. 350: see para.8-164, above.

ant informs the defendant of a contract which is in no way exceptionally lucrative; and (3) where the claimant informs the defendant that he has an exceptionally lucrative contract the performance of which hinges on prompt delivery by the defendant.

**32-039** The first situation was considered in *Heskell v Continental Express*.[172] Here it was held that the claimant could not recover his loss on his sale,[173] not the whole loss because it was an exceptionally lucrative sale,[174] and not any part of it as the defendant had, it seems, neither actual nor imputed knowledge of the sale. Counsel for the claimant had, however, argued that the defendant should have known in the ordinary course of business that a contract of the type in question would be involved. As to this Devlin J said:

> "Lord Macnaghten in *Stroms v Hutchison*[175] seems to think that this degree of knowledge should be imputed to the carrier as an ordinary business man. I think that the decision in *The Arpad*[176] and the earlier authorities referred to in it, preclude me from taking this view of a carrier's liability. I am, for my part, willing to hold that a carrier should recognise sub-sale by a consignor or consignee as a serious possibility, but that is not enough, as the leading case of *Horne v Midland Ry*[177] shows. In *The Arpad*,[178] Maugham LJ said: 'I suppose most vendors of goods and most carriers might be taken to know that if the purchaser or consignee is a trader the goods will probably be sold or are bought for sub-sale, but the authorities seem to show conclusively that something more than that is necessary to enable the damages to be assessed by reference to a contract of sub-sale entered into before the date of delivery.' … To make the carrier liable for any higher measure of damages it seems to me to be necessary that he should have knowledge, actual or imputed, of something that makes the ordinary measure inadequate. Such knowledge may be derivable from the terms of the sub-contract, or, possibly, from the market conditions at the place of delivery."[179]

Support for the recovery of loss of resale profits later appeared in *The Pegase*,[180] where the claimant receivers of a cargo of chromite sand purchased for processing and resale lost substantial profits because the arrival of the shipment was delayed for 65 days. The position there was that, although the defendant carriers had no detailed knowledge of the receivers' business, they were aware of the possibility of resale and the possibility that there would be no available market for buying in substitute goods. Accordingly, a conclusion that the carriers should be liable for some resale profits was unobjectionable in principle.[181] However, the whole loss of profit did not necessarily fall to be awarded for there should be taken into account two matters: first, since the actual resale contracts were not known to the carriers, whether the profits lost to the receivers were in any way out of the ordinary, and second, since the carriers knew nothing of the receivers' storage facilities or stocks,

---

172 [1950] 1 All E.R. 1033.

173 The loss claimed was not a loss of profit but the damages that the claimant had had to pay for breach of his sub-contract. This aspect of the decision is considered later: see para.32-043, below; however, the court considered the more general issue of loss on a sale, whatever exact form it might take in a particular case.

174 Following *Horne v Midland Ry* (1873) L.R. 8 C.P. 131.

175 [1905] A.C. 515: facts at para.32-051, below.

176 [1934] P. 189 CA.

177 (1873) L.R. 8 C.P. 131.

178 [1934] P. 189 CA.

179 [1950] 1 All E.R. 1033 at 1048–1049.

180 [1981] 1 Lloyd's Rep. 175.

181 [1981] 1 Lloyd's Rep. 175 at 186, col.1.

that the carriers could not be taken to have contemplated that the receivers would have an immediate need for the sand because they had run down their stocks to provide storage space for the expected shipment.[182] As for breach by shipowners resulting in delay in making the ship available to charterers for the loading of cargo, loss to the charterers from loss of a fixture, and the consequent loss of the profit from that fixture, have been held recoverable as loss which is not unlikely to result from the breach of contract. Latter-day illustrations are *The Amer Energy*,[183] and *Sylvia Shipping Co Ltd v Progress Bulk Carriers Ltd*.[184] These two decisions are not adversely affected by the controversial House of Lords decision in *The Achilleas*,[185] which they followed in time, as has been shown in the earlier discussion on remoteness of damage.[186]

The second situation arose in *Simpson v L.N.W. Ry*.[187] The claimant, who was in the habit of exhibiting samples of his goods at cattle shows, delivered certain parcels of goods to the defendant at the Bedford showground to be carried to the Newcastle showground, having written on the consignment note that the goods must be at Newcastle "on Monday certain". Delivery was delayed till the Newcastle show was over, and the claimant successfully claimed profits that he lost as a result. This authority stands, it is submitted, on the ground that the sub-contract was an ordinary one and that the defendant necessarily knew that delay by him would result in its breach. An essentially similar case, and of the same period, is *Jameson v Midland Ry Co*,[188] where the defendant carriers were held liable for loss of profits where they had delayed delivery of a parcel of cutlery which they knew, or ought to have known, was being sent to a show for sale; a modern illustration is *Panalpina International Transport v Densil Underwear*,[189] where a consignment of shirts sent by air to Nigeria was delayed and recovery for loss of the Christmas market was allowed, the carrier having been told that the shirts were destined for a purchaser who wanted the goods before Christmas for this market. **32-040**

The third situation was discussed in the judgments in *Horne v Midland Ry*,[190] and the view was expressed, particularly by Martin B, that a notice that exceptional damage will result from delay will only render the defendant liable for the exceptional damage if given under such circumstances as to make it a term of the contract that the defendant will be so liable in the event of breach.[191] Kelly CB thought such a term was well nigh impossible since in his view the defendants, being common carriers, had no option but to carry the goods.[192] On the other hand Lush J, dissenting, thought that the defendants were entitled to demand extraordi- **32-041**

182 See [1981] 1 Lloyd's Rep. 175 at 185, col.2–186, col.2.
183 [2009] 1 Lloyd's Rep. 293.
184 [2010] 2 Lloyd's Rep. 81.
185 [2009] 1 A.C. 61. See the decision at paras 8-168 and following, above.
186 See paras 8-176 and following, above, especially at para.8-178. Contrast the situation where it is the charterer that loses a fixture: para.32-078, below.
187 (1876) 1 Q.B.D. 274.
188 (1884) 50 L.T. 426.
189 [1981] 1 Lloyd's Rep. 187.
190 (1873) L.R. 8 C.P. 131.
191 (1873) L.R. 8 C.P. 131 at 139–140.
192 (1873) L.R. 8 C.P. 131 at 136–137.

nary remuneration for extraordinary risk.[193] This aspect of the second rule in *Hadley v Baxendale*,[194] is still in general a somewhat unsettled one.[195]

**32-042** In any case where the court refuses loss of profit to the claimant on his sale, damages may still properly be given for loss of use calculated by interest on the value of the goods for the period of delay. Thus in *Heskell v Continental Express*,[196] Devlin J gave a sum as

> "compensation in respect of the period for which the plaintiff was out of his money or lost the commercial use of the goods, whichever way one likes to put it".[197]

**32-043** *(ii) Compensation paid to a buyer; costs incurred in defending the buyer's action* *Heskell v Continental Express*[198] decided that, in the circumstances of that case, the claimant could not recover from the defendant carrier the damages he had paid to the party to whom he had sold the goods carried, having been put in breach of his contract by reason of the defendant's delay in delivery. Devlin J considered the issue on the basis of the principles involved in allowing any recovery arising from loss on a sale in a carriage contract: hence the case has already been given consideration.[199] Had the circumstances been such that the claimant might properly have recovered his loss of profit on a sale of the goods, it is submitted that he ought also to be able to recover as damages any compensation paid to his buyer. Devlin J indeed took the view that it did not necessarily follow that if loss of profit was awarded compensation paid to the buyer would also be allowable[200]; for this he cited Salter J in *Patrick v Russo-British Grain Export Co*.[201] It is submitted, however, that the contrary view expressed by Lord Dunedin in *Hall v Pim*,[202] is the true one.[203]

**32-044** Similarly, it would seem that any costs incurred by the claimant in defending an action brought by his buyer should, if reasonably incurred, be recoverable in circumstances where other losses arising from a sale would be recoverable.[204] Yet the position on the recovery of costs may be changing. Where the claimant has reasonably but unsuccessfully defended a claim brought by his buyer, formerly recovery of his own costs incurred in a reasonable defence was of these costs assessed as between solicitor and client; now, solicitor and client costs no longer exist in this context and the claimant should instead simply be entitled to all his costs

---

193 (1873) L.R. 8 C.P. 131 at 145.

194 (1854) 9 Ex. 341.

195 The general issue is considered at paras 8-205 to 8-207, above.

196 [1950] 1 All E.R. 1033.

197 [1950] 1 All E.R. 1033 at 1046. Somewhat similar to the loss of a resale profit is the loss for which a successful claim was made in *The Subro Valour* [1995] 1 Lloyd's Rep. 509. The value to the claimant charterers of the cargo, which they had purchased, upon the delayed delivery was less than it would have been upon the contractual delivery because an EC subsidy was no longer available to them. Although the defendants would not have had any special knowledge of what was referred to as an EC relief levy, it was held that they must be taken to have known that the value of goods might be affected by variations in EC subsidies, so that it was reasonably foreseeable that the net amount payable by buyers for goods might for that reason be affected by delay: at 520, col.1.

198 [1950] 1 All E.R. 1033.

199 See para.32-039, above.

200 [1950] 1 All E.R. 1033 at 1049.

201 [1927] 2 K.B. 535 at 540 (sale of goods).

202 (1928) 33 Com. Cas. 324 HL at 330 (sale of goods).

203 See the sale of goods cases in Ch.25 where the issues involved have been considered more thoroughly.

204 See preceding paragraph.

reasonably incurred. There is, however, a growing move at first instance, one not to be encouraged, which would restrict the claimant to what, if assessed, would have been his standard basis costs in the action with the buyer; this unfortunate development has already been fully examined in an earlier chapter to which reference should be made.[205]

*(iii) Loss of profit on further sales* There appear to be no illustrations of successful claims for loss of general custom due to loss of goodwill. In *The Pegase*,[206] the receivers of the shipped goods failed to recover for such a head of damage. Robert Goff J said that there were no facts found which would support a conclusion that the carrier defendants ought reasonably to have contemplated any loss of goodwill as likely to result from their breach and that, without any knowledge on their part of the claimant receivers' business or of the circumstances in which the claimants traded, any loss of goodwill must have been so speculative as to be too remote.[207] **32-045**

**(c) Other expenses made necessary by the breach** Recovery of expenses other than those arising through loss of use or out of a sale has sometimes been allowed in the cases. Thus in *S.S. Ardennes (Cargo Owners) v S.S. Ardennes (Owners)*,[208] the increase in import duty which had been imposed during the period of delay was allowed as damages. However, the principal illustration of this type of recoverable expenditure is that of expenses reasonably incurred in inquiring and searching for the missing goods. These have been allowed without much argument in a number of cases, starting with *Hales v L.N.W. Ry*,[209] and ending with *Heskell v Continental Express*,[210] the amount generally being small and being concerned with such items as telegrams and hire of transport.[211] **32-046**

**(d) Expenses rendered futile by the breach** As an alternative to claiming loss of profit a claimant may sometimes claim, as consequential loss, for expenses rendered futile by the breach. Not only, however, is this alternative to a recovery for loss of profit[212] but will not be available at all where a claim for loss of profit itself would have been too remote, a situation which, as has been seen, is common in carriage contracts. This, it is submitted, is the explanation of the unpreparedness of the courts to allow as damages wages and expenses of the claimant's employees rendered fruitless by reason of the late delivery of the goods. Thus wages of the claimant's workmen were not allowed in *Gee v Lancashire & Yorkshire Ry*,[213] or in *Le Peintur v S.E. Ry*,[214] nor were the expenses of travellers employed by the **32-047**

---

205 See the discussion at paras 21-003 and following, above.
206 [1981] 1 Lloyd's Rep. 175; facts at para.32-039, above.
207 [1981] 1 Lloyd's Rep. 175 at 186, col.2.
208 [1951] 1 K.B. 55.
209 (1863) 4 B. & S. 66 (£5 in inquiry and search).
210 [1950] 1 All E.R. 1033 (£10 in endeavour to trace goods; see at 1046).
211 *Giachetti v Speeding* (1899) 15 T.L.R. 401 (expenditure on telegrams) is another case. See, too, *Woodger v G.W. Ry* (1867) L.R. 2 C.P. 318 which has a dictum that recovery was allowable for "cab-hire or other reasonable expenses if the plaintiff had to call several times at the company's office in endeavouring to recover the goods": at 321.
212 See paras 4-024 and following, above, where the basis for the recovery of expenses rendered futile by the breach of contract is discussed.
213 (1860) 6 H. & N. 211.
214 (1860) 2 L.T. 170.

claimant, such as their hotel expenses while waiting for the goods, in *Wilson v Lancashire & Yorkshire Ry*,[215] or in *Candy v Midland Ry*.[216] Similarly the claimant's own hotel expenses, when he was himself a commercial traveller, were not allowed in *Woodger v G.W. Ry*.[217]

### 3. FAILURE TO CARRY OR TO CARRY TO THE RIGHT PLACE

**32-048** Where the defendant has failed to carry the goods at all[218] or has carried them to the wrong place, two alternative measures appear to be open to the claimant to put him in the position he would have been in had the carriage contract been performed. First, he may engage substitute transport to get the goods to the contractual place for delivery and claim as damages the cost of so doing less the price he would have paid under the contract with the defendant, i.e. market rate of freight less contract rate of freight, and in addition the amount by which the price at the place of delivery has fallen between the contractual time for delivery and the arrival of the goods by the substitute transport when this is necessarily later.[219] Or, secondly, he may buy similar goods at the contractual place for delivery and claim the cost of so replacing less the sum of the value of the goods at the place of loading, the amount of freight and the amount of insurance.[220]

**32-049** If the circumstances allow of either course of action on the claimant's part, i.e. engaging other transport or replacing with other goods, it would seem that on general principles of mitigation he will be bound to adopt that which is less costly, subject always to the consideration that all that is required of him is to act

---

215 (1861) 9 C.B. N.S. 632.

216 (1878) 38 L.T. 226. *Contra Black v Baxendale* (1847) 1 Ex. 410, but Bovill CJ expressed doubts about this decision in *Woodger v G.W. Ry* (1867) L.R. 2 C.P. 318, pointing out that it had been decided before *Hadley v Baxendale* (1854) 9 Ex. 341.

217 (1867) L.R. 2 C.P. 318.

218 A failure to carry may be constituted in a time charterparty by a delay in providing the ship. This is not a case of delayed delivery of the goods, because the charterer's complaint is not that the goods were delivered late but that there was not time to carry as many goods. This situation is illustrated by *Adamastos Shipping Co v Anglo-Saxon Petroleum Co* [1959] A.C. 133, although the issue before the court was limitation of liability. Viscount Simonds described the charterers' claim thus: "Owing to the delay … [the ship] was able to complete fewer voyages than she otherwise would have done within the period of charter. The charterers, therefore, claimed damages in a very large sum, the claim being for the difference between the charter and market rates of freight on cargo-carrying voyages which might have been performed within the eighteen months if she had been continuously fit for service": at 157. And where in a time charter the owners wrongfully repudiated so that they failed to provide the ship for the charter for the entire period, it was held in *Koch Marine v D'Amica Societa di Navigazione, The Elena d'Amico* [1980] 1 Lloyd's Rep. 75 that the difference between the contract rate for the balance of the charter period and the market rate of a substitute ship for that period constituted the normal recovery. In *The Wave* [1981] 1 Lloyd's Rep. 521, where the owners' wrongful repudiation amounted to a failure to provide the ship for the time charter from the start, a gloss was put on this normal recovery so as to award as damages the difference between the contract rate of hire and the market rate not at but shortly after the repudiation, this being on the basis that it would take the charterers a little time to obtain a replacement fixture: at 532, col.1.

219 *Monarch S.S. Co v Karlshamns Oljefabriker* [1949] A.C. 196. And see *The Kaliningrad* [1997] 2 Lloyd's Rep. 35, at paras 48-006 and 48-007, below, where the damages were for loss of business and profits in addition to the cost of a substitute vessel in a claim in tort for procuring the breach of the claimant's sub-charter with the charterer.

220 *Stroms Bruks Aktie Bolag v Hutchison* [1905] A.C. 515; see especially at 529, per Lord Davey.

reasonably. Thus if neither course is clearly the more favourable one he will not at his peril adopt the course which in the result may turn out to be the more costly.[221]

The first measure is the relevant one where the second course of action is not open to the claimant because no market exists at the place of delivery in which he can buy replacements. The fact that there is a market at the place of delivery where the goods could be sold will not prevent this measure from being correct, for the claimant is not bound to accept as damages the difference between the market selling price at the place of delivery and the place of loading. This was established by *Monarch S.S. Co v Karlshamns Oljefabriker*,[222] where there was not a total but a partial failure to carry the goods in the sense that they were carried to a destination other than the contractual destination: the same principles, however, apply to both types of case. A British ship, in which the defendant was carrying a cargo of beans to Sweden, was forced by Admiralty orders to go to Glasgow,[223] and the claimants, a Swedish company who were consignees of the cargo, transhipped it to neutral vessels and claimed as damages from the defendant carrier the cost of transhipment. The defendant's contention that the claimants could only claim the selling price in Sweden less the selling price in Glasgow was rejected by the House of Lords. Lord Wright said: **32-050**

> "What the respondents wanted was the consignment of beans; their value either at Glasgow or Sweden where no beans were on the market, would have been a poor consolation. But as transhipment could be effected, the extra cost incurred for transhipment was the proper subject of monetary compensation."[224]

And Lord Porter said:

> "I cannot think that they were obliged to accept any such substituted performance. They appear to me to have had the right to require the goods to be delivered at the place stipulated, and if the shipowner failed to carry out his bargain to deliver there, the direct and natural consequence is that the merchant should arrange for the carriage forward and charge the shipowner with the reasonable cost of doing so. Nor do I think it improves the appellants' position to say that it is the respondent's duty to minimise or nullify his damages by selling elsewhere. He is entitled to have his contract fulfilled in the manner stipulated and is under no obligation to accept some undesired method of performance."[225]

This may be subject, it is submitted, to its having been impossible to replace the goods in Sweden; Lord Wright, in his statement of the proper measure just quoted, specifically referred to the fact that there was no market in Sweden in which beans could be bought. Somewhat similarly, in *Blackgold Trading of Monrovia v Almare SpA di Navagazione of Genoa, The Almare Seconda and Almare Quinta*,[226] where the owners failed to make the ship available, the charterers successfully claimed the

221 Contrast Lord Davey in *Stroms Bruks Aktie Bolag v Hutchison* [1905] A.C. 515 at 529, where the claimant successfully claimed the cost of replacement and not the cost of reshipment: "There was evidence that it would have been a speculative and very risky thing to send that quantity to Cardiff [i.e. the contractual destination] or elsewhere for sale without having secured a purchaser, and that prices subsequently fell."

222 [1949] A.C. 196.

223 The breach in this case was based on delay, and there is a separate and important point as to remoteness in its causation aspect: see para.8-156, above.

224 [1949] A.C. 196 at 220.

225 [1949] A.C. 196 at 217–218.

226 [1981] 2 Lloyd's Rep. 433.

extra cost of shipping the cargo in question by making alternative arrangements; they kept the charter on foot for a while but eventually cancelled, and this was held not to constitute a failure to mitigate.

**32-051** The second measure is the relevant one where the first course of action is not open to the claimant because no suitable substitute transport is available. This was the position in *Stroms Bruks Aktie Bolag v Hutchison*,[227] the leading case on failure to carry. The defendant contracted to carry for the claimant woodpulp from Sweden to Cardiff but failed to do so. The claimant had sold the woodpulp to a third party, who bought in against the claimant who reimbursed him for this outlay. The claimant's allowing his buyer to buy in this way was treated by the court as equivalent to the claimant's buying himself; further, the purchase price was taken as evidence of the cost of replacing the goods in Cardiff.[228] It was not possible to procure a substitute vessel in time to deliver the goods to Cardiff, and in these circumstances it was held that the measure of damages was, in the words of Lord Davey, the

> "cost of replacing the goods at their place of destination at the time when they ought to have arrived, less the value of the goods in Sweden and the amount of the freight and insurance".[229]

This measure was applied in *Nissho Co v Livanos*,[230] where the claimant chartered the defendant's ship to carry a cargo of salt from the Red Sea to Japan, having obtained a permit from the Japanese Government which only covered a cargo on the defendant's ship. Upon the defendant's failure to carry, the claimant was unable to employ a substitute vessel because the Japanese Government refused to change the name of the ship in the permit. Thus the circumstances which made no other vessel available to the claimant were peculiar to the claimant and were neither known to nor could reasonably have been anticipated by the defendant. Nonetheless Lord Caldecote CJ held this immaterial.[231]

**32-052** A similar result was correctly reached in *Fyffes Group v Reefer Express Lines Pty, The Kriti Rex*.[232] It was there held, where the defendants failed to tender the chartered vessel, on account of unseaworthiness, for the loading of the claimants' cargo of bananas, that the claimants were

> "entitled to recover damages assessed by reference to the replacement value of the goods at the time when they would otherwise have arrived at their destination, less any residual value of the goods at the port of loading and savings on freight, insurance and other voyage expenses."[233]

---

[227] [1905] A.C. 515.

[228] See [1905] A.C. 515 at 529, per Lord Davey. Thus there was no question of the claimant trying to claim his profits on the sale: the purchase price was merely taken as evidence of market value. A connected point decided by their Lordships was that the measure was not affected if the date of due delivery under the sale was such that it could not have been carried out even if the defendant had delivered in the proper contractual way.

[229] [1905] A.C. 515 at 529.

[230] (1941) 57 T.L.R. 400. And also in *Heimdal A/S v Questier* (1949) 82 Ll. L. Rep. 452, in which case the price at which the claimant had sold the goods was taken as evidence of the cost of replacement at the contractual place of delivery: see at 473. This case is further dealt with at para.32-053, below.

[231] (1941) 57 T.L.R. 400 at 401.

[232] [1996] 2 Lloyd's Rep. 171.

[233] [1996] 2 Lloyd's Rep. 171 at 194, col.2. There was also a claim over by the defendants, who had sub-chartered to the claimants, against the owners who had initially time-chartered the vessel to the

The court would have none of the argument that the claimants should be confined to the additional cost of obtaining alternative transport because substitute transportation was available and the defendants could not have envisaged at the time of contracting that the claimants, for their own particular reasons, would not have been in a position to engage it.[234]

To both measures consequential losses may be added. Thus in *Featherston v Wilkinson*,[235] where the defendant failed to carry a cargo of coal, the claimant recovered, under the first measure, the amount by which the price of coal at the port of loading had risen before he was able to charter another ship, since by the custom of the colliery trade there he was not allowed to secure a cargo until he had a ship ready for its carriage. And in *Heimdal A/S v Questier*,[236] where the cargo which the defendant failed to carry perished in the prevailing conditions at the port of loading, the claimant recovered, under the second measure, the value of this cargo, or, put more precisely,[237] the cargo possessed no value which fell to be deducted from the cost of replacement at the port of destination.[238] **32-053**

A third measure may make an appearance where neither reshipment nor replacement is possible. In such circumstances it would seem that the market selling price at the place of delivery less the market selling price at the place of loading would, after deducting freight and insurance, measure the damages. This will be very similar in most cases to the second measure. A variation on this appeared in the interesting decision of *Watts v Mitsui*,[239] where, even if the defendant had not failed to provide a ship to carry the claimant's goods from the Black Sea to Japan, the contract would never have been performed as war would have prevented the vessel getting out of the Dardanelles. The House of Lords held that the claimant was entitled to claim the loss incurred by being deprived by the defendant's default of the opportunity of insuring the goods, it being established that the claimant could, and would as a reasonable man, have effected insurance against sea and war risks on the value of the cargo at the port of destination. The measure of damages awarded was the market price in Japan at the expected date of arrival after deduction of the insurance premium and expenses, less the price to be paid by the claimant to his seller for the goods. This latter price was adopted in preference to the market price at the port of loading at the time of breach for two reasons: (1) because this gave the claimant's loss and (2) because there was no evidence of the market price at breach and the claimant's buying price could therefore be taken as evidence thereof. The second reason is completely acceptable, but the first may be questioned.[240] **32-054**

---

defendants. In this claim credit had to be given for losses avoided by the defendants in not completing the voyage under the sub-charter to the claimants but not for losses saved thereafter: see at 204.

234 Perhaps this decision and the earlier *Nissho Co v Livanos* (at para.32-051, above) indicate that principles of remoteness cannot cut down a normal measure of damages as opposed to recovery for consequential losses.

235 (1873) L.R. 8 Ex. 122.

236 (1949) 82 Ll. L.R. 452.

237 The court did not use this precision, awarding the market price at destination less cost, freight, insurance and the like, and then adding the cost of the perished cargo. The claimant also recovered the freight in respect of the uncarried cargo: such a recovery depends upon whether freight has been prepaid or not.

238 Consequential losses may sometimes be too remote, as in the strange case of *Walton v Fothergill* (1835) 7 C. & P. 392.

239 [1917] A.C. 227.

240 Contrast the more considered law in sale of goods cases as to the relevance of the price at which

### (B) CARRIAGE OF PERSONS

#### 1. INJURY AND DEATH IN CARRIAGE

**32-055** Far and away the most actions brought in respect of the carriage of persons are for injury or death in transit. Such actions sound as much in tort as in contract; either way the measure of damages will follow the lines of all cases of personal injury and death however caused, a matter fully dealt with in other chapters.[241]

#### 2. DELAY IN CARRIAGE

**32-056** Where delay is not such as to lead the claimant reasonably to engage other transport to get him to his destination, there will probably be no damage other than consequential losses. There is no real authority on these, but much the same principles will apply as with failure to carry.[242]

**32-057** Where delay is such as to lead the claimant reasonably to engage other transport to get him to his destination, the normal measure of damages is the cost of obtaining substitute transport less the contract price. Thus in the case of *Romulus Films v Dempster*,[243] where the carriage was by air, the cost of a substitute flight was allowed in the damages. The cost of other transport will however be disallowed where the delay is not such as to make its engagement reasonable. This is well illustrated by *Le Blanche v L.N.W. Ry*.[244] The claimant contracted with the defendant for his carriage by rail from Liverpool to Scarborough. The train arrived too late to catch the proper connection at York, and instead of waiting for the next train he hired a special train which got him to Scarborough an hour and a half earlier in the evening. He claimed to recover the cost of hiring the special train. The Court of Appeal considered that the test to be applied was whether the claimant had acted reasonably and took the view that he had not done so, particularly in view of the fact that he had no engagement at Scarborough necessitating his arrival at any particular time. Mellish LJ laid down a useful test, concurred in by the other members of the court, for ascertaining what was reasonable in this regard: whether, according to the ordinary habits of society, a person in the claimant's position would have incurred the expenditure on his own account and at his own cost had the circumstances been such that the defendant was not responsible.[245] This test was applied in the similar case of *Bright v P. & O. Navigation Co*,[246] where the expense of a special train from Dover to London was not allowed as damages, although the circumstances were slightly more in the claimant's favour than in *Le Blanche v L.N.W. Ry*.[247]

---

the goods have been sold to, or equivalent goods bought from, a third party by the claimant: see Ch.25, passim.

241 See Chs 40 and 41, below.

242 See para.32-059, below. The most that can be pointed to is a rhetorical dictum of Willes J in *British Columbia Saw Mill Co v Nettleship* (1868) L.R. 3 C.P. 499 at 510, as to whether a barrister en route for the Calcutta bar, to the knowledge of the shipping company taking him there, could possibly recover in respect of lucrative briefs lost through delay in arrival.

243 [1952] 2 Lloyd's Rep. 535.

244 (1876) 1 C.P.D. 286 CA.

245 (1876) 1 C.P.D. 286 CA at 313.

246 (1897) 2 Com. Cas. 106.

247 (1876) 1 C.P.D. 286 CA. But in *Buckmaster v G.E. Ry* (1870) 23 L.T. 471 the cost of hiring a special train for a morning journey from Suffolk to London was allowed. The point, however, was not argued and the decision came before *Le Blanche v L.N.W. Ry* (1876) 1 C.P.D. 286 CA.

**3. Failure to Carry or to Carry to the Right Place** Where the defendant has failed to carry at all or has carried to the wrong place, the normal measure of damages is the cost of obtaining substitute transport less the contract price. Thus Blackburn J in *Hinde v Liddell*,[248] spoke of: **32-058**

> "the case of a carrier who fails to carry a passenger to a given place, in which case the passenger has been held over and over again to be entitled to take the best substitute in the shape of a conveyance he can get, no matter that it costs much more than the fare."

Such a multitude of decisions appears to be a mirage, but the principle is clear and there are frequent similar dicta to be found.[249] Furthermore, the cases of delay in which substitute transport is engaged deal with a very similar situation.[250]

As to consequential losses, expenses of hotels and the like while waiting for the substitute transport have been allowed, as in *Cranston v Marshall*,[251] and *Hamlin v G.N. Ry*[252]; but loss of appointments with customers was held not recoverable in the latter case.[253] In *Anglo-Continental Holidays v Tybaldos*,[254] where the claimants were not the persons to be carried but the travel agents who had arranged a cruise, and where the breach in question was a failure to carry in the agreed transport, a smaller and less attractive ship having been substituted by the defendant shipowners with a less attractive timetable of stopovers at ports in the course of the cruise, damages were awarded for the claimant's loss of goodwill.[255] The most considered case of consequential losses is *Hobbs v L.S.W. Ry*.[256] The claimant and his wife and children were set down by the defendants at the wrong station so late on a wet night that they could find neither conveyance nor hotel and had therefore to walk several miles home in the rain. The claimant's claim for damages for physical inconvenience was granted, but not his claim in respect of a cold caught by his wife, whereby he incurred loss by way of medical expenses and temporary deprivation of her assistance in business. Catching cold was regarded as too remote, but this conclusion was soon doubted by the Court of Appeal in *McMahon v Field*.[257] **32-059**

## II. Breach by Cargo Owner

Practically all the cases of breach by the party contracting to have goods carried concern carriage by sea, but the principles apply mutatis mutandis to carriage by land and by air. **32-060**

Various actions may be available to the carrier, some of which do not involve damages. The principal action not involving damages is the action for freight, an **32-061**

---

[248] (1875) L.R. 10 Q.B. 265 at 268.

[249] See, e.g. *Hamlin v G.N. Ry* (1856) 26 L.J. Ex. 20 at 23, per Alderson B (not in the report at 1 H. & N. 408); *Le Blanche v L.N.W. Ry* (1876) 1 C.P.D. 286 CA at 302–303, per Brett J; both approved in *Erie County Natural Gas Co v Carroll* [1911] A.C. 105 PC at 117.

[250] See para.32-057, above, especially *Le Blanche v L.N.W. Ry* (1876) 1 C.P.D. 286 CA.

[251] (1850) 5 Ex. 395.

[252] (1856) 26 L.J. Ex. 20 at 184, col.1.

[253] In *Buckmaster v G.E. Ry* (1870) 23 L.T. 471 loss of custom was held recoverable but, in the absence of argument, this is doubtful.

[254] [1967] 2 Lloyd's Rep. 61 CA.

[255] Lord Denning MR saying that such awards were exceptional in such cases: [1967] 2 Lloyd's Rep. 61 CA at 66. See para.4-020, above.

[256] (1875) L.R. 10 Q.B. 111.

[257] (1881) 7 Q.B.D. 591 CA. Damages were given here where horses had caught cold; the case, however, did not concern a contract of carriage.

action under the terms of the contract equivalent to the action for the price in sale of goods.[258] The only difference is that, whereas in sale of goods it is generally simple to ascertain the price, in contracts of carriage by sea the question of how the freight is calculated can be very complicated, being essentially a matter of construction of the contract. But it is not damages.[259] Also there may be circumstances in which the carrier may claim freight in part, *pro rata itineris*, either under the terms of the contract if divisible or in restitution in the case of discharging breach. Again this is not damages.[260]

## 1. FAILURE TO SUPPLY CARGO

**32-062** Within breach by failure to supply cargo is included both a failure to supply any cargo and a failure to supply the full amount which the contract obliges the defendant to supply. It also includes failure to load when the ship is supplied by the claimant.

### (1) Normal measure

**32-063** **(a) Growth of the modern measure** The normal measure of damages may be stated today as the contract rate of freight[261] less the market rate of freight.[262] This is calculated by taking not the gross amounts of the contract and the market freights but the net amounts after the cost of earning the freights.[263] The market freight is deducted on the ground that this sum either was or could have been earned by the defendant on the claimant's refusal to supply cargo.[264] This is in accordance with general principles and in particular with the measure of damages in an action for non-acceptance of goods sold.[265] However, this measure allowing for the deduction of market freight developed slowly in carriage contracts.

---

258 See para.25-114, above.

259 For details of how the amount of freight due is ascertained, see the standard texts on carriage of goods by sea.

260 Late payment does not lead to a claim for damages for an exchange loss: *President of India v Lips Maritime Corp* [1988] A.C. 395.

261 The principles which the courts apply for calculating the freight in an action under the terms of the contract for the freight are equally relevant for calculating the contract freight in an action for damages. For details see the standard textbooks on carriage of goods by sea. *Thomas v Clarke* (1818) 2 Stark. 450 is important in this connection as deciding that, in an action for not supplying the cargo, an average value is taken in order to arrive at the proper measure of damages.

262 It may of course not be the market rate of freight for the whole length of the charter: see, e.g. *Petroleum Shipping v Vatis, The Riza and Sun* [1997] 2 Lloyd's Rep. 314 at para.32-071, below. Demurrage payments may sometimes be included within the claim for the lost profit: *Odfjell Seachem A/S v Continentale des Petroles et d'Investissements* [2005] 1 Lloyd's Rep. 275, distinguishing *SIB International v Metallgesellschaft Corp, The Noel Bay* [1989] 1 Lloyd's Rep. 361 CA.

263 The defendant, where he has the right to elect between a number of ports for the discharge of the cargo, is entitled to have the damages assessed on the assumption that he would have opted for discharge at the port where discharge would have cost the claimant carrier the most; this was decided in relation to the deduction of wharfage dues in *Kaye Steam Navigation Co v Barnett* (1932) 48 T.L.R. 440. For the general principles involved here see paras 10-106 to 10-113, above.

264 For the exceptional position where the market rate is higher than the contract rate, see the interesting *Omak Maritime Ltd v Mamola Challenger Shipping Co* [2011] 1 Lloyd's Rep. 47 at para.4-032, above.

265 See paras 25-115 to 25-117, above.

Early, in *Hunter v Fry*,[266] where the breach was only a failure to supply the full quantity of cargo, it was laid down that the measure of damages was the sum the ship would have earned had the full and complete cargo been loaded deducting the freight earned on the goods actually shipped by the defendant. This will not be the gross amount of freight on the deficiency since the cost of earning the freight falls to be deducted, a point taken in *Morrison v Levison*,[267] another case of failure to supply the full cargo.[268] As a measure of damages this did not take into account, however, any substitute amount which the claimant has earned or ought to have earned by reason of his ship becoming free or partly free for the contract period through the defendant's default. It is true that where the defendant has supplied a good part of the cargo it is less likely that the claimant did or could have taken a substitute amount of goods than where the defendant has failed to supply any cargo at all: nevertheless the measure as stated in *Hunter v Fry*,[269] would apply as much to total failure as to partial failure to supply. **32-064**

The next step was to remedy this deficiency in part, and the measure was held to be the amount that the claimant would have earned under the contract less the amount he has in fact earned elsewhere. This general rule was stated and applied in *Smith v McGuire*[270]; in Martin B's words the measure of damages was **32-065**

> "the freight to be earned, and deduction of the expenses which the shipowner would be put to in earning it; and what the ship earned (if anything) during the period which would have been occupied in performing the voyage, ought also to be deducted".[271]

Before this in *Staniforth v Lyall*,[272] where the claimant had earned more on the substitute voyage than he would have earned under the contract, he was awarded only nominal damages. By the time of *Aitken Lilburn v Ernsthausen*,[273] the claimant was prepared to admit that his substitute earnings must be deducted; but it is significant that A.L. Smith LJ[274] and Kay LJ, while both referring to the general rule laid down in *Smith v McGuire*,[275] stated it differently. For A.L. Smith LJ the ordinary measure was

> "the difference between the charterparty freight and the net freight actually earned, after deducting expenses".[276]

Kay LJ on the other hand put it thus:

> "The general rule is, that when such a breach by non-delivery of [i.e. failure to supply] cargo occurs the owners are entitled to damages to the amount of the freight thereby lost,

---

[266] (1819) 2 B. & Ald. 421.

[267] (1876) 1 C.P.D. 155.

[268] The expression "dead freight" is used to define the damages claimed for breach of contract to furnish a full cargo in accordance with charter: Compare *McLean v Fleming* (1871) L.R. 2 Sc. & D. 128 HL.

[269] (1819) 2 B. & Ald. 421.

[270] (1858) 3 H. & N. 554.

[271] (1858) 3 H. & N. 554 at 567; similarly at 565, per Watson B.

[272] (1830) 7 Bing. 169.

[273] [1894] 1 Q.B. 773 CA.

[274] A joint judgment with Lindley LJ.

[275] (1858) 3 H. & N. 554.

[276] [1894] 1 Q.B. 773 CA at 781.

> but if they fill up the ship on their own account, the amount of freight so earned goes in reduction of such damages."[277]

In the former the mitigating result of other earnings is incorporated within the normal measure; in the latter it is pure mitigation, imposed *ab extra* on the normal measure.

**32-066** Apart from actual substituted earnings nothing had yet been heard of the effect, on normal measure or on mitigation, of substitute earnings which the claimant has not, but should have, made. There is a hint of this *en passant* in Parke B's statement in *Harries v Edmonds*,[278] that

> "the plaintiff is entitled to recover what the defendant ought to have paid minus what he might have got";

but in *Smith v McGuire*,[279] Martin B stated the view that the claimant will not suffer for his failure to take mitigating steps. "It may be doubtful", he said,

> "whether a party who breaks a contract has a right to say 'I will not pay you the damage arising from my breach of contract, because you ought to have done something for the purpose of relieving me.' I am not prepared to say that a shipowner, who has lost his freight by reason of a breach of contract by the charterer, is bound to go and look for employment for his ship so as to relieve the charterer from the consequences."[280]

This must today be wrong now that the rules as to mitigation have been worked out, and the contrary view is stated in later cases.[281] Thus in *Aitken Lilburn v Ernsthausen*,[282] A.L. Smith LJ is found to say:

> "It is not disputed that, when the defendants refused to perform this obligation, it was incumbent upon the plaintiffs to do what was reasonable to mitigate the damages which the defendants would have to pay by reason of their breach of contract, and that, if the plaintiffs could reasonably obtain other cargo to fill up the space which the defendants had wrongfully refused to fill up, they were bound to do so."[283]

And in *Wallems Rederij A/S v Muller*,[284] Mackinnon J went so far as to hold that the master's delay on the voyage to take other cargo in order to mitigate the damage was impliedly authorised by the charterparty and therefore constituted no deviation. He said:

> "It is clear that he [i.e. the shipowner] is, in his own interest, bound to do it [i.e. search out other cargo], because otherwise he will not be able to recover his full damages."[285]

**32-067** It may be thought that there is no basic difference between the measure of damages as contract rate of freight subject to mitigation and as contract rate less market rate of freight. The difference lies in the very practical matter of onus of proof. If

---

277 [1894] 1 Q.B. 773 CA at 777.
278 (1845) 1 C. & K. 686 at 688.
279 (1858) 3 H. & N. 554.
280 (1858) 3 H. & N. 554 at 567.
281 Some of the earlier texts were uncommitted on this issue, such as Maclachlan, *Merchant Shipping*, 4th edn (1892), p.615.
282 [1894] 1 Q.B. 773 CA.
283 [1894] 1 Q.B. 773 CA at 781.
284 [1927] 2 K.B. 99.
285 [1927] 2 K.B. 99 at 105.

the measure is the first stated, all the claimant need prove is the contract price and the defendant is then required to prove, if he wishes to reduce the damages, that the claimant has, or should have, earned substitute freight. But if the measure is the second stated, the claimant will recover only contract rate less market rate unless he can prove that in the particular circumstances he neither has, nor could reasonably have, earned substitute freight. This, which has been submitted here to be the modern rule, gives the defendant the better position and appears to be supported by *Rheinoel v Huron Liberian Co, The Concordia C*[286]: on a failure by charterers to supply cargo there was awarded the net revenue which the owners would have earned under the charterparty less the net revenue in fact earned during its currency, plus the deviation expenses incurred to earn the alternative charter rate. So too in *SIB International v Metallgesellschaft Corp, The Noel Bay*,[287] Staughton LJ spoke of the now well-settled rule of earnings lost less substitute earnings achieved, pointing out in this connection that

> "one problem that almost invariably arises, and does in this case, is that the substitute voyage lasts for longer than the voyage under the original charterparty. The solution commonly adopted is to take a proportion of the profits on the substitute voyage to set off against the profits lost on the original voyage."[288]

In that case there had been a wrongful repudiation by the charterers, accepted by the owners, of a voyage charterparty and the owners recovered for the profit which they would have made on the voyage but giving the necessary credit for any profit they made on the substitute charter which they were able to conclude.

In a number of cases over the last few years where the charterparty has been repudiated by the charterer, issues have arisen in connection with the availability or non-availability to the shipowner of a market in charterparties. The first issue on this in *Zodiac Maritime Agencies Ltd v Fortescue Metals Group Ltd*,[289] where the charterer had repudiated a five-year voyage charter about a year after its commencement, was whether there was an available market so that, in the shipowner's claim for damages, the normal measure of contract rate less market rate, these rates here being expressed in terms of so many US dollars per day, could be applied. It was held on the facts that there was no available market.[290] In *Dalwood Marine Co v Nordana Line SA*,[291] there was again a premature wrongful termination of a charterparty by the charterers with no available market in the relevant area. The shipowner sailed the ship to another location and delivered her pursuant to another charterparty which had a hire rate significantly higher than that under the breached charterparty. The earnings of the ship after the date on which she would have been notionally redelivered under the breach charterparty were taken into account, entitling the shipowner to no damages as a gain rather than a loss had been made.[292] In *Glory Wealth Shipping PTE Ltd v Korea Line Corp*,[293] where a charterer's 32-068

[286] [1985] 2 Lloyd's Rep. 55.
[287] [1989] 1 Lloyd's Rep. 361 CA.
[288] [1989] 1 Lloyd's Rep. 361 CA at 363, col.1.
[289] [2011] 2 Lloyd's Rep. 360.
[290] See [2011] 2 Lloyd's Rep. 360 at [56] to [61]. For more on available market in the context of contracts of carriage see para.32-005, above, and for issues concerning mitigation arising in consequence of this holding of no available market see para.9-132, above.
[291] [2010] 2 Lloyd's Rep. 315.
[292] The case is seen from a mitigation angle at para 9-131, above.
[293] [2011] 2 Lloyd's Rep. 370.

repudiation of a time charter took place when there was no market for the unexpired period of the charter but the market revived at a much later date, it was held that, mitigation apart,[294] the revived market rate was not to be taken in assessing the owners' damages, their actual loss forming the correct measure.[295]

32-069 **(b) Circumstances in which substitute freight which has or could have been earned is not deducted** The authorities illustrate how in certain circumstances no deduction falls to be made of other freight which was earned or could have been earned. These circumstances arise out of familiar general principles in relation to liquidated damages, mitigation of damage and the effect of anticipatory breach on damages.

32-070 No deduction is made of substitute freight earned where the damages are liquidated. This statement of clear principle[296] is made only because of some difficulty which has been experienced in reconciling the decisions in *Bell v Puller*,[297] and *Puller v Staniforth*.[298] In *Bell v Puller*,[299] the claimant contracted to carry a cargo of lead to St Petersburg and to bring back to England other cargo. The contract provided that if from political circumstances the ship should remain 40 days at St Petersburg without unloading the lead, and consequently without loading the return cargo, she was to return to England and the claimant was to be paid a stipulated sum which was less than the freight payable for performance of the contract. The cargo of lead could not be unloaded before the 40 days had passed and the ship returned to England bringing back the lead but earning further freight on the return voyage. It was held that the claimant was entitled to the stipulated sum without deducting the money earned on the return voyage, Mansfield CJ pointing out that the claimant, when making the contract,

> "would doubtless insist on more or less liquidated damages, according to the chance he foresaw of getting freight home from the place where he was going".[300]

On the other hand, in *Puller v Staniforth*,[301] which was similar except that the original cargo was sold at the foreign port and not brought back to England, it was held that the freight earned on the return voyage must be deducted from the damages. This case may have been decided on its special facts, since the right to the liquidated sum may not have vested absolutely[302]; otherwise it should be regarded as doubtful.

32-071 No deduction is made of substitute freight which could have been earned where the failure to earn has not constituted a failure to mitigate. Thus in *UBC Chartering Ltd v Liepaya Shipping Co, The Liepaya*,[303] where there was a redelivery of the vessel by the charterers which was premature by 14 days, the owners were held not to have failed to mitigate by not finding substitute employment for the vessel over

294 Mitigation was not an issue in the case: [2011] 2 Lloyd's Rep. 370 at [28].
295 [2011] 2 Lloyd's Rep. 370 at [31].
296 See Ch.16, above, passim.
297 (1810) 2 Taunt. 285.
298 (1809) 11 East 232.
299 (1810) 2 Taunt. 285.
300 (1810) 2 Taunt. 285 at 299.
301 (1809) 11 East 232.
302 *Staniforth v Lyall* (1830) 7 Bing. 169 shows that the claimant must have carried out the contract in the manner required in order to make him absolutely entitled to the liquidated sum.
303 [1999] 1 Lloyd's Rep. 649.

this very short period, either from third parties or from the charterers themselves,[304] and were awarded damages representing their loss of net hire for the whole of the 14 days. Again, it may be that the owner has negotiated substitute charters but, as will often be the case, not covering the whole period of the original, breached charterparty. In these circumstances if the court holds the shortfall in substitute charters not to be attributable to a failure to mitigate, the only substitute freight to deduct will be that actually earned. Thus in *Petroleum Shipping v Vatis, The Riza and Sun*,[305] where there was an immediate wrongful repudiation of two four-and-a-half month time charterparties by the charterers accepted by the owners, the trial judge held that there was no failure to mitigate by the owners in taking only four fixtures for one of the vessels and two for the other, which fixtures clearly covered only a portion, possibly small, of the four-and-a-half months, and accordingly awarded the freight due on the charterparties less the earnings in fact made, and not the earnings that might have been made, on substitute fixtures.

No deduction is made of substitute freight earned where the steps taken by the claimant have not cut down the loss for which the defendant was liable, where the apparently substitute earnings are not truly a substitute since they could still have been realised even had there been no breach. This situation arose in *Aitken Lilburn v Ernsthausen*.[306] By a charterparty containing the usual exception as to fire, the defendant charterers contracted to load the claimants' ship with a full cargo of bales of jute. The defendants loaded a portion of the bales but most of these were burnt immediately after loading. This caused considerable delay, and the defendants in breach of contract refused to supply any further cargo. The claimants, with the defendants' unburnt bales still on board, filled up the rest of the ship with other cargo on their own account. The claimants admitted that the defendants were not liable to pay freight for the bales which had been burnt, and the defendants admitted that they were liable for freight on the bales which they had never shipped. They contended, however, that in estimating the damages they were entitled to deduct the entire sum earned by the claimants on their own account. The claimants accepted this contention in relation to the space which the defendants had never attempted to fill but successfully disputed it in relation to the space occupied by the bales which had been burnt. The fire had taken the latter space out of the contract; it had become a space which the defendants were not bound to fill up again and out of which the claimants could derive no benefit under the charterparty. Any freight earned by filling up that space, therefore, was the claimants' own. As A.L. Smith LJ said: 32-072

> "For that jute [i.e. the bales that were burned] the shipowners were under no obligation to try and find other cargo, for, as regards this, there were no damages to be mitigated."[307]

No deduction is made of substitute freight which could have been earned before breach although after an anticipatory repudiation by the defendant which, being 32-073

[304] On the mitigation aspect of substitute employment offered by the charterers see para.9-058, above.

[305] [1997] 2 Lloyd's Rep. 314.

[306] [1894] 1 Q.B. 773 CA.

[307] [1894] 1 Q.B. 773 CA at 782. Compare *Stewart v Rogerson* (1871) L.R. 6 C.P. 424 where, after a breach by failure to accept the cargo after its carriage had been completed, both ship and cargo were arrested with the result that the freight became due under the contract and the claimant had perforce to sue for damages. The measure awarded was the contract freight; the carriage being over, there was no contract time available to the claimant in which he could earn other freight.

unaccepted by the claimant, has not ripened into a breach. *Hudson v Hill*,[308] is the principal case on this issue. The defendants declined to provide a cargo at the port stipulated in the charterparty and offered to provide a cargo at another port 90 miles off. The claimant's captain refused this offer, insisting upon performance of the charterparty, and it was held that he was not bound to accept as he might reasonably think that acceptance would put an end to the original charterparty. It is true that "the defendants' agents were insisting that there was no breach by them of the charterparty",[309] and that the court stressed the reasonableness of the captain's conduct, Brett J saying that he was

> "not prepared to say that in every case of this kind a captain can wait until the lay-days are over; circumstances may render it unreasonable in him to stay until they have expired".[310]

Yet Lord Coleridge CJ said that he had summed up at the trial on the basis of the anticipatory breach cases[311] and that the result of these was that

> "a declaration of an intention not to perform a contract need not be accepted, and the contract will remain in force at the option of the party against whom the breach is intended to be committed".[312]

This case concerned an alternative offer by the defendant himself: in two other cases, *Harries v Edmonds*,[313] and *Dimech v Corlett*,[314] the offer was from a third party, and in both it was held that it was not obligatory on the claimant's captain to accept this offer and that its refusal did not therefore cut down the claimant's damages. The offer, said the court in the latter case, being before the expiration of the lay-days, was made

> "during the time, therefore, for which the captain of the vessel, who insisted on the liability of the respondent to perform the charterparty, was bound to keep the vessel ready to receive cargo offered by him."[315]

As against these cases there is the decision in *Wilson v Hicks*,[316] where the facts were similar to those in *Hudson v Hill*,[317] and where it was held to be a proper direction to the jury that the damages could be less than the full freight if the jury thought that the master's conduct in refusing the defendant's alternative offer was unreasonable. In so far as this suggests that an anticipatory repudiation by the defendant must be accepted by the claimant, it must be wrong.

32-074 **(c) Normal measure not always recoverable to end of contractual period** Where there is breach of a charterparty by its wrongful cancellation by the charterers, the normal damages measure of charter rate of freight less market rate

---

308 (1874) 43 L.J.C.P. 273.
309 (1874) 43 L.J.C.P. 273 at 279.
310 (1874) 43 L.J.C.P. 273 at 279.
311 He referred, inter alia, to the leading case of *Avery v Bowden* (1855) 5 E. & B. 714 (affirmed (1856) 6 E. & B. 953).
312 (1874) 43 L.J.C.P. 273 at 281.
313 (1845) 1 C. & K. 686.
314 (1858) 12 Moo. P.C. 199; see especially at 230 to 231.
315 (1858) 12 Moo. P.C. 199 at 231.
316 (1857) 26 L.J. Ex. 242.
317 (1874) 43 L.J.C.P. 273.

may not be available for the full remaining contractual period. This can be so if the charterers would have become entitled rightfully to cancel the charterparty, and would have done so, at a point in time later than the wrongful cancellation. In *Maredelanto Compania Naviera SA v Bergbau-Handel GmbH, The Mihalis Angelos*,[318] breach came even before performance by the charterers was due to commence, the wrongful cancellation having been an anticipatory breach accepted by the shipowners, and only nominal damages were awarded since rightful cancellation would have immediately and inevitably followed. So too where the charterers' right to cancel was anticipated as a near certainty in *B.S.& N. Ltd v Mikado Shipping Ltd, The Seaflower*,[319] the damages only extended to the time that rightful cancellation would have happened. More difficulty was encountered in *Golden Strait Corporation v Nippon Yusen Kubishika Kaisha, The Golden Victory*,[320] where it was not known at the time of wrongful cancellation that the possibility of rightful cancellation would arise in the future. The great question therefore was whether or not, in assessing the shipowners' damages, the court could regard and take into account events after the wrongful cancellation, being events which gave the charterers a right to cancel. On this there was a sharp division of view, three of their Lordships deciding in the charterers' favour, two in the shipowners'. These three cases are considered in more detail in the chapter on certainty of damage.[321]

## (2) Consequential losses

Authority is lacking on consequential losses. They will arise infrequently, as a person is less likely to incur such losses where his services are not accepted than where services are not rendered to him.[322] An illustration is however provided by *Total Transport Corp v Amoco Trading Co, The Altus*,[323] where there was awarded the difference between the demurrage rate which would have been payable had the minimum required cargo been supplied and the lower demurrage rate payable on the short cargo.[324] **32-075**

In *Louis Dreyfus Commodities Suisse SA v MT Maritime Management BV, "MTM Hong Kong"*[325] Males J considered whether damages should be restricted to the losses suffered up until the point when the contract voyage would have come to an end. The charterers submitted that *Smith v McGuire*[326] permitted only the recovery of losses until the point that the contract voyage had ended, although there was no claim in that case for losses beyond the point when the contract voyage had ended. The difference was substantial. The *Smith v McGuire* measure would have led to an award in favour of the shipowner of US$478,386. The amount which was awarded by the arbitral tribunal resulted in an award of almost three times this amount. **32-076**

The reason for the difference was that additional consequential loss was suf-

---

318 [1971] 1 Q.B. 164 CA.

319 [2000] 2 Lloyd's Rep. 37.

320 [2008] A.C. 353.

321 See at paras 10-115 and following, above.

322 See sale of goods at paras 25-128 to 25-131, above.

323 [1985] 1 Lloyd's Rep. 423.

324 The main issue was as to whether such damages were recoverable in addition to liquidated damages: see para.16-024, above.

325 [2015] EWHC 2505 (Comm).

326 (1858) 3 H & N 554.

fered by the owners because performance of the contract voyage would not only have enabled the owners to earn the freight payable under the voyage charter but it would also have ensured that the vessel was situated in Europe without delay at the conclusion of the voyage, ready to take advantage of the higher freights available in the North Atlantic market. The charterers' repudiation meant that the owners had to mitigate by taking a different charter, which delayed the repositioning of the vessel causing the loss of two lucrative transatlantic charters that could have been performed in the same time as the mitigation charter. The primary judge upheld the arbitral tribunal's award of these consequential losses.

## 2. DETENTION OF THE TRANSPORT

### (1) Normal measure

**32-077** Where in a charterparty the charterer detains the ship either at the port of loading or the port of discharge beyond the allowed contractual period of the lay-days, it has long been provided that he will pay demurrage at a certain rate for every day of improper detention. This provision for demurrage is a form of liquidated damages.[327] The result of this well-established practice of pre-estimating the damages for detention in this way has prevented the growth of case law on the measure of unliquidated damages for the detention by the cargo owner of the transport.[328] The normal measure of such damages will be constituted by the amount lost through loss of use of the ship. For this, one illustration—they are quite numerous—is provided by *Gatoil Anstalt v Omenial, The Balder London (No.2)*,[329] where the owners of a ship, wrongfully prevented by the charterers from withdrawing her from a charter, were awarded as damages the difference between the charter rate and the market rate of hire for the period in question.[330]

### (2) Consequential losses

**32-078** Before *The Achilleas*[331] appeared claims for the late redelivery of a ship under a charterparty had been concerned for the purpose of damages, where more than demurrage was in issue, only with the appropriate rate of hire for the overrun period. *The Achilleas* at last raised the question of the damages to be awarded where late redelivery has meant that a subsequent charter fixture could not be fulfilled on time. Because the shipowners were unable to deliver at the contractual date, the new charterers were in a position to renegotiate downwards the daily rate and the shipowners' claim was for the difference between the original daily rate and the revised daily rate over the period of the new charter. None of the many authorities on late delivery threw any light on an issue which in this context was novel. It was

---

327 The proposition that demurrage is liquidated damages is considered at para.16-081, above.

328 There may indeed be unliquidated damages in addition to demurrage in certain circumstances. This is well illustrated by *Aktieselskabet Reidar v Arcos* [1927] 1 K.B. 352 CA, and *The Altus* [1985] 1 Lloyd's Rep. 423: see para.16-024, above.

329 [1983] 1 Lloyd's Rep. 492.

330 There are analogies in cases dealing with other contracts, such as *Re Trent and Humber Co Ex p. Cambrian Steam Packet Co* (1868) L.R. 4 Ch. App. 112 (delay in repairing a ship) at para.25-045, above and *Jebsen v East and West India Dock Co* (1875) L.R. 10 C.P. 300 (delay in discharging a ship) at para.9-153, above.

331 [2009] 1 A.C. 61.

essentially a question of remoteness and of whether the loss satisfied the rule in *Hadley v Baxendale*. A majority of experienced arbitrators and judges of great commercial experience at first instance and in the Court of Appeal[332] held for the shipowners. Somewhat surprisingly, the House of Lords unanimously reversed. The decision has been fully analysed when dealing with remoteness of damage,[333] to which analysis reference should be made.

## 3. Damage to the Transport

Occasionally the cargo owner is liable to the shipowner for damage to the ship. **32-079** Here the diminution in the value of the ship is normally measured by the cost of repair and this approach was adopted at first instance in *Meredith Jones v Vangemar Shipping Co, The Apostolis No.2*,[334] thereby applying the rule established for tortious damage to ships.[335] However, the Court of Appeal, reversing on liability[336] but nevertheless expressing its view on damages,[337] considered that in reality the diminution in value was far below the cost of repair. In these circumstances the shipowners would be entitled to claim the cost of repair only if it was reasonable to repair the vessel[338] and all the evidence, in the court's view, was against this. It is true that the repairs had not been carried out by the shipowners—and that this on its own would not prevent recovery was a proposition that was not challenged[339]—but if the new owners' allegation that the price they paid on purchasing the vessel was reduced by a very substantial amount to reflect the need for repair had any truth, surely the diminution in value would indeed be similar to the repair cost.

---

332 The arbitrators and the judges were so described in the House of Lords by Lord Walker: [2009] 1 A.C. 61 at [65].

333 See paras 8-168 and following, above.

334 [1999] 2 Lloyd's Rep. 292.

335 At para.37-003, below.

336 [2000] 2 Lloyd's Rep. 337 CA.

337 See at [2000] 2 Lloyd's Rep. 337 CA at 48, col.2.

338 See para.37-004, below in relation to tort.

339 See para.37-007, below in relation to tort.

CHAPTER 33

# CONTRACTS OF EMPLOYMENT

TABLE OF CONTENTS



## I. BREACH BY EMPLOYER

### 1. INTRODUCTORY: WRONGFUL DISMISSAL AND UNFAIR DISMISSAL

**33-001** For an employee to have a claim for damages on dismissal by his or her employer, it is necessary to show that the dismissal was wrongful, that is, in breach of contract. If there is no contractual bar to the employee's dismissal, the employer is entitled to dismiss without having any good reason for doing so. Since very many employees, particularly workers, do not have contracts with their employers which are for a term of years or other period, or which require the employer to give more than a very short period of notice, they are effectively at the mercy of their employers. To counter this disparity between employer and employee, a right to compensation for a dismissal that was unfair but did not constitute a breach of contract, and therefore was not a wrongful dismissal, was introduced some time ago by the Industrial Relations Act 1971 and continues to be available today.[1]

**33-002** The question arises as to whether the now substantial law on compensation for unfair dismissal should be included in this book. In the introductory chapter, with its definition of damages as an award in money for a civil wrong,[2] it is pointed out that actions claiming money under statutes where the claim is made independently of a wrong are not actions for damages,[3] and therefore fall outside this book, whereas actions claiming money which are based upon statutes which have cre-

1 The present law is contained in the Employment Rights Act 1996 Pt. X.
2 At para.1-001, above.
3 Such as actions in respect of benefits under the Social Security Acts.

ated a tort, and are therefore dependent on a wrong, are actions for damages,[4] and are therefore well within this book. It is thought difficult to classify the action made available for unfair dismissal as a statutory tort. We are not in the realm of wrongs but only of unfairness in industrial practices, an unfairness which it was thought right to address.[5]

Aside from this, and more importantly, the calculation of compensation is on a somewhat different basis to that of common law damages. This was made clear from the very start by Sir John Donaldson as President of the National Industrial Relations Court. He said in *Norton Tool Co v Tewson*,[6] the first decision of that court in relation to unfair dismissal: **33-003**

> "In our judgment the common law rules and authorities on wrongful dismissal are irrelevant. That cause of action is quite unaffected by the Industrial Relations Act 1971 which has created an entirely new cause of action, namely the 'unfair industrial practice' of unfair dismissal. The measure of compensation for that statutory wrong is itself the creature of statute and is to be found in the Act of 1971 and nowhere else."

Two issues in *Norton Tool* concerning damages saw a radical departure from the common law approach, the one taking the damages to a higher level, beyond compensation for loss, and the other to a lower level, under-compensating loss. Thus it was held in *Norton Tool* that there should be no deduction, from the compensation for loss of wages for the whole of the six-week notice period to a claimant who had been summarily dismissed, of the wages earned in another job which he had found four weeks after dismissal. After many decisions following this rule, it was finally confirmed by the Court of Appeal in *Burlo v Langley*.[7] *Norton Tool* also held that the term loss in the statute did not include injury to feelings for which there could be no compensation under the statute. This was later confirmed by the House of Lords in *Dunnachie v Kingston upon Hull City Council*.[8] Accordingly, it seems inappropriate that the case law which has built up over the period from 1971 is dealt with in this book[9]; the standard texts and monographs on employment law should be consulted. At the same time cases of unfair dismissal are occasionally dealt with in the text should they evidence a principle which applies equally to wrongful dismissal.[10]

## 2. WRONGFUL DISMISSAL

Where an employer by wrongfully dismissing his employee discharges the contract by his breach, a number of alternatives lie open to the employee. If he has **33-004**

4 Such as actions by a deceased's dependants under the Fatal Accidents Act 1976.

5 It is fair to say that Sir John Donaldson, who was much involved at the time the scheme was launched, thought that there was a statutory wrong: see the next paragraph.

6 [1973] 1 W.L.R. 45 at 48F.

7 [2007] 2 All E.R. 462, CA; see at [66].

8 [2005] 1 A.C. 226.

9 Note from the careful judgment of Lady Justice Smith in *Burlo v Langley* [2007] 2 All E.R. 462 CA the complexities involved in arriving at the correct unfair dismissal compensation under the statute.

10 See, e.g. *Wilding v British Telecommunications Plc* [2002] I.C.R. 1079 CA, at para.33-020, below. It is the case that separate claims for unfair dismissal and for wrongful dismissal may be made, as in *O'Laoire v Jackel International (No.2)* [1991] I.C.R. 718 CA (in the footnote at the end of para.33-015, below) and in the first instance *Burlo v Langley* [2006] 2 All E.R. 1104 EAT (at para.33-006, below). Also claims for wrongful dismissal can be combined with claims for discrimination in employment, for which see Ch.44, below.

completed his part of the contract he can sue for his wages under the terms of the contract. If he is dismissed during the period covered by the contract of service he cannot sue for wages under its terms unless the contract is divisible,[11] but he may either sue in restitution on a quantum meruit for the services already rendered, or he may bring an action for damages for breach of contract.

### (1) Normal measure

**33-005** The measure of damages for wrongful dismissal is prima facie the amount that the claimant would have earned had the employment continued according to contract subject to a deduction in respect of any amount accruing from any other employment which the claimant, in minimising damages, either had obtained or should reasonably have obtained.[12] The rule has crystallised anomalously in this form. It is not the general rule of the contract price less the market value of the claimant's services that applies; instead the prima facie measure of damages is the contract price, which is all the claimant need show. This is then subject to mitigation by the claimant who is obliged to place his services on the market, but the onus here is on the defendant to show that the claimant has or should have obtained an alternative employment.

**33-006** **(a) The amount the employee would have earned under the contract** Basically, the amount that the claimant would have earned under the contract is the salary or the wages which the defendant had agreed to pay.[13] Thus where in *Burlo v Langley*,[14] the employer had agreed to pay only statutory sick pay to the employee when absent ill and the employee would have been unable to work during the notice period on account of sickness, the damages entitlement in her wrongful dismissal claim was to sick pay and not to full pay.[15] In addition there may be benefits in kind, the value of which must also be taken into account, such as a rent-free residence,[16]

---

11 Or the Apportionment Act 1870 applies. *Re BCCI* [1994] I.R.L.R. 282 provides an illustration of how the Act operates; see at 290 to 291. It was held at one early time that an employee improperly dismissed during the contractual period might wait till its expiry and then sue in indebitatus assumpsit for the whole period under the doctrine of constructive service. That doctrine was, however, tacitly overruled in *Elderton v Emmens* (1853) 4 H.L.C. 625.

12 *Beckham v Drake* (1849) 2 H.L.C. 579 at 607–608, per Erle J advising their Lordships. His still remains the best and fullest statement of the measure to be found in the reports, and runs thus: "The measure of damages … is obtained by considering what is the usual rate of wages for the employment here contracted for, and what time would be lost before a similar employment could be obtained. The law considers that employment in any ordinary branch of industry can be obtained by a person competent for the place, and that the usual rate of wages for such employment can be proved, and that … it is the duty of the servant to use diligence to find another employment." As to its pleading as special damage, see *Monk v Redwing Aircraft Co* [1942] 1 K.B. 182 CA and *Hayward v Pullinger* [1950] 1 All E.R. 581, at para.51-021, below.

13 Including any bonus: *Lake v Campbell* (1862) 5 L.T. 582. But as to bonuses which the employer is not under a contractual obligation to pay, see *Lavarack v Woods of Colchester* [1967] 1 Q.B. 278 CA and *Horkulak v Cantor Fitzgerald International* [2005] I.C.R. 402 CA at, respectively, paras 33-010 and 33-011, below.

14 [2006] 2 All E.R. 1104 EAT.

15 The employee's appeal to the Court of Appeal, at [2007] 2 All E.R. 462 CA, was only in respect of the damages entitlement in her unfair dismissal claim.

16 *Re English Joint Stock Bank, Yelland's Case* (1867) L.R. 4 Eq. 350.

board and lodging,[17] luncheon vouchers[18] and the like,[19] and also benefits under pension schemes[20] and by way of stock options.[21]

Where the claimant has been entitled to be paid commission on work done or sales effected by him, or in relation to the profits made by the defendant in his business, or on orders received from customers introduced by him, this must also be taken into account, provided always that the defendant's failure to provide the claimant with an opportunity to earn the commission constitutes a breach of contract. This proviso is important, and on the facts of a particular case it is often difficult to ascertain whether there has been such a breach, especially where the wrongful dismissal is occasioned by the defendant closing down his business.[22] The failure to pay the wages or salary constitutes a breach, but the failure to give an opportunity to earn the commission may not.[23] If, however, there is a breach as to commission, and this is more likely to be so where the commission depends on the claimant's own work and efforts than on the defendant's profits,[24] the claimant will be entitled to recover damages in respect thereof, and not only commission proper[25] but also money paid on piecework,[26] and tips.[27] The average amount the claimant has previously earned by way of commission may be taken as evidence of what he **33-007**

---

17 *Lindsay v Queen's Hotel Co* [1919] 1 K.B. 212. Usage, however, established a special rule in the case of domestic servants, as they were then called, which allowed them to recover a month's wages without board. In *Lindsay* it was held that this rule did not apply in the case of a wrongful dismissal during the currency of a month's notice already given by the domestic servant. In such a case the damages are the actual loss sustained and will include loss of board and lodging from the date of wrongful dismissal to the date of termination under the notice.

18 Recognised in *McGrath v De Soissons* (1962) 112 L.J. 60, although in the particular circumstances of that case the loss of luncheon vouchers did not feature in the damages because the claimant was not entitled to them during the period the defendants could pay him a salary in lieu of notice; he was entitled to them only for the days he was actually working for the defendants and the defendants were not obliged to find him work during the period he was entitled to notice.

19 On the other hand, expenses connected with the service that the claimant would have had to pay himself, and of which he is, therefore, relieved by the dismissal, must be deducted.

20 *Bold v Brough, Nicholson & Hall* [1964] 1 W.L.R. 201. In *Silvey v Pendragon* [2001] I.R.L.R. 685 CA, recovery was allowed by the Court of Appeal, reversing the court below, for loss of enhanced pension rights which the claimant had lost when his employment was terminated without due notice a few days before the birthday upon which such pension rights would have accrued. The Court of Appeal easily found, agreeing with the court below, that the damage was not too remote, applying the usual authorities on remoteness in contract. However, the employer's right to discontinue the pension scheme may defeat the employee's claim in this respect, as in *Beach v Reed Corrugated Cases* [1956] 1 W.L.R. 807. See further para.33-009, below.

21 Recognised in *O'Laoire v Jackel International (No.2)* [1991] I.C.R. 718 CA, but in the particular circumstances no damages were awarded in respect of the stock options as the claimant was held to have no contractual right to them. See further para.33-009, below.

22 The question is often put in the form of whether the case falls within *Turner v Goldsmith* [1891] 1 Q.B. 544 CA, on the one hand or within *Rhodes v Forwood* (1876) 1 App. Cas. 256 on the other.

23 It did not, e.g. in *Re Newman, Raphael's Claim* [1916] 2 Ch. 309 CA, so that the claimant had no claim in respect of the commission. Many of these cases concern agents rather than employees: see para.35-003, below.

24 Compare *Reigate v Union Manufacturing Co* [1918] 1 K.B. 592 CA at 603, per Bankes LJ.

25 As in *Addis v Gramophone Co* [1909] A.C. 488; *Re Rubel Bronze Co and Vos* [1918] 1 K.B. 315; *Reigate v Union Manufacturing Co* [1918] 1 K.B. 592 CA; and *Roberts v Elwells Engineers* [1972] 2 Q.B. 586 CA. In the last case, because the commission was due on all orders received from customers introduced by the claimant, commission had to be taken into account beyond the date at which the contract could have been lawfully determined by the defendant.

26 *Devonald v Rosser* [1906] 2 K.B. 728; *Bauman v Hulton Press* [1952] 2 All E.R. 1121.

27 *Manubens v Leon* [1919] 1 K.B. 208.

would have earned subsequently but for the dismissal.[28] So, too, what the claimant's substitute has earned on commission since the dismissal would constitute evidence of the claimant's loss.[29] The state of the defendant's business and general business conditions also may go to show how much or little the claimant has lost, whether the commission turns on the profits of the business or on the sales that the claimant effects or on other work he does for the business. Thus in *Reigate v Union Manufacturing Co*,[30] it was held that the defendant might show that, as matters and prices stood and might be anticipated, there was very little prospect of any large quantity of business being done and that damages were not necessarily to be assessed on the assumption of a flourishing business. And, somewhat similarly, where the amount the claimant would have earned under the contract turns on a contingency depending on the will of a third person, the contingency must be evaluated. This was the position in the early case of *Richardson v Mellish*.[31]

**33-008** That the amount which the employee would have earned under the contract may be subject to the loss of a chance doctrine is shown, as is the computation of the damages when this is so, by *Ministry of Defence v Wheeler*.[32] The loss of a chance doctrine, however, must not be carried too far in wrongful dismissal, as indeed in other, cases.[33] Thus the court in *Janciuk v Winerite*[34] held that a claimant has no entitlement in an action for wrongful dismissal to be compensated for the loss of the chance that, had a contractual disciplinary procedure been operated, he might not have been dismissed and, in so holding, said emphatically and rightly:

> "We regard the [claimant's] attempt to introduce the loss of a chance into the calculation of the damages as a heresy".[35]

The statement by the trial judge in *Bank of Credit and Commerce International v Ali*,[36] that *Allied Maples*,[37]

> "clearly lays down that, in the case of applications for jobs to be made in the future after the date of the trial, the court must adopt the 'loss of the chance' approach"[38]

is misconceived.

**33-009** Where the amount the employee would have earned under the contract turns on a contingency depending on the will of the employer himself, the situation is more complicated by reason of the operation of the rule that damages against a contract breaker must be assessed on the basis that he will perform the contract in the man-

---

[28] As in *Devonald v Rosser* [1906] 2 K.B. 728 (piecework).

[29] Though he may be able to show that he would have earned more than his successor, as in *Addis v Gramophone Co* [1909] A.C. 488.

[30] [1918] 1 K.B. 592 CA (a case of agency).

[31] (1824) 2 Bing. 229; facts at para.10-050, above.

[32] [1998] 1 W.L.R. 637 CA, at para.10-105, above and at para.33-021, below.

[33] There was an unsuccessful attempt to carry it too far in *Harper v Virgin Net Ltd* [2004] I.R.L.R. 390 CA by claiming, in the employee's action for damages for wrongful dismissal, for the loss of a chance of recovering compensation for unfair dismissal: see the case in the footnote at the end of para.10-092, above.

[34] [1998] I.R.L.R. 63.

[35] [1998] I.R.L.R. 63 at 64.

[36] [1999] 4 All E.R. 83; see the case at para.33-031 (in a footnote), below.

[37] [1995] 1 W.L.R. 1602 CA; see at paras 10-058 and following, above.

[38] [1999] 4 All E.R. 83 at 110d.

ner most beneficial to himself.[39] Accordingly in *Beach v Reed Corrugated Cases*,[40] where a company director claimed damages for wrongful dismissal, no damages were awarded for loss under the company's retirement benefit scheme for directors, as the defendant company had the right to discontinue either the whole scheme or any participant's assurance under it at any time. So, too, in *O'Laoire v Jackel International (No.2)*,[41] there was no recovery in respect of the hope of taking up stock options exercisable by the employee only with the consent of the board of the employer company; "given the attitude of the defendants towards the plaintiff", said Sir Nicolas Browne-Wilkinson VC,

> "in my judgment there is no value of such hope and accordingly no damages are recoverable".[42]

On the other hand, in *Bold v Brough, Nicholson & Hall*,[43] the employee was held entitled to claim for loss of the chance of obtaining benefits under his employers' pension scheme because, although the employers had a right to discontinue the scheme as a whole, they had no discretion to withhold contributions in respect of the claimant employee so long as the scheme continued. Here

> "the employers' discretion to continue or discontinue the pensions scheme was not a discretion as to the manner of performing their contract of service with the plaintiff but a discretion as to the way in which they would conduct their business as a whole. Upon this the amount which they would be under a legal liability to pay to the plaintiff under his contract of service depended—in the same way as the amount which they would be under a legal liability to pay to employees remunerated in whole or in part by commission would depend upon the exercise of their discretion as to expansion or contraction of their trade in a particular article or as to its price. The plaintiff was accordingly entitled to be recompensed for the likelihood that his employers would have continued to conduct their business as a whole in such a way as to produce the event which would have entitled him to claim pension contributions under his service agreement if it had been performed."[44]

In *Lavarack v Woods of Colchester*,[45] the Court of Appeal was faced with a **33-010** similar problem in relation to an employers' bonus scheme rather than an employers' pension scheme and with the further difference that, before the employee's action came to trial, the scheme had in fact been legitimately discontinued by the defendant employers and replaced, in the case of most employees, by increased salaries. In these circumstances the majority of the court held that the claimant employee was not entitled to damages representing the probable increase in salary which would have come to him had he continued to be employed by the defendants. A claimant suing for wrong dismissal, said Russell LJ,

---

39 See paras 10-106 to 10-108, above.

40 [1956] 1 W.L.R. 807.

41 [1991] I.C.R. 718 CA.

42 [1991] I.C.R. 718 CA at 730E. Contrast *Withers v General Theatre Corp* [1933] 2 K.B. 536 CA, where a second reason for refusing damages to a wrongfully dismissed actor complaining of loss of opportunity to appear at a famous theatre (the first, dealt with at para.33-028, below, is no longer law) was that the defendant had an option as to the theatres at which the claimant should appear.

43 [1964] 1 W.L.R. 201.

44 *Lavarack v Woods of Colchester* [1967] 1 Q.B. 278 CA at 296–297, per Diplock LJ. This explanation of the distinction between the *Beach* and the *Bold* cases merely elaborates that put forward by Phillimore J in *Bold* itself: see [1964] 1 W.L.R. 201 at 211–212.

45 [1967] 1 Q.B. 278 CA.

> "can rely only on the fact that the defendant was obliged to carry out the contract sued upon. His prospects in terms of money or money's worth resulting from the carrying out of the contract may be conditioned by the estimated impact of external events on the results of the carrying out. But it has never been held that the plaintiff can claim any sum on the ground that the defendant might after the repudiation date have voluntarily subjected himself to an additional contractual obligation in favour of the plaintiff."[46]

Diplock LJ admitted that, if the defendants had continued their bonus scheme, the claimant might well have been entitled to be recompensed for the loss of bonus, but it was unnecessary to decide this.[47] However, Lord Denning MR, in a cogent dissent, considered that the claimant should be entitled in respect of the loss of future bonuses whether the bonus scheme had been discontinued or not, pointing to the clear finding of the master that, had the employment continued, the claimant would have received an increase of salary in lieu of bonus on the discontinuance of the scheme.[48]

**33-011** In *Horkulak v Cantor Fitzgerald International*,[49] at first instance *Lavarack* was distinguished since in *Horkulak* the claimant employee had the benefit of a term in his contract which entitled him to receive a discretionary bonus.[50] On the appeal,[51] the Court of Appeal agreed that the ratio of *Lavarack* was not decisive of the case, *Lavarack* not being concerned with the true construction of a discretionary bonus clause.[52] The issue for the trial judge was therefore whether, in line with the employer defendant's obligation to exercise its discretion reasonably and in good faith, the discretionary bonus would have been paid, and he held that it would have been.[53] The Court of Appeal was of the view that the judge was correct to hold that the claimant would have been entitled, had he remained in the employment, to a bona fide and rational exercise by his employers of their discretion and further that the judge's holding that the discretion would have been exercised in his favour had not been shown to be wrong.[54]

**33-012** There remained the question of the level of bonus that would have been paid. The Court of Appeal examined the judge's approach to this vital question in the utmost detail[55] and, while not upholding any of the criticisms of it put forward by the employer, took the view that the judge had not explained his reasons adequately for arriving at his bonus figures and sent the matter back to him for further consideration and elucidation.[56] Of particular importance in this connection is the Court of Appeal's dealing with the relationship between the rule that a defendant is entitled to perform the contract in the least onerous manner and the rule that the freedom of choice of method of performance is limited by reasonableness.[57]

---

46 [1967] 1 Q.B. 278 CA at 298.

47 [1967] 1 Q.B. 278 CA at 297.

48 [1967] 1 Q.B. 278 CA at 288–289.

49 [2003] I.C.R. 697.

50 [2003] I.C.R. 697 at [85] and [86].

51 [2005] I.C.R. 402 CA.

52 [2005] I.C.R. 402 CA at [31]–[36].

53 See [2003] I.C.R. 697 at [86] and [89] and following.

54 See [2005] I.C.R. 402 CA at [46] and [50]. *Lavarack* and *Horkulak* come under discussion in *IBM United Kingdom Holdings Ltd v Dalgleish* [2015] EWHC 389 Ch where there was not wrongful dismissal but breach of the duty of trust and confidence. See the case at para.33-031, below.

55 [2005] I.C.R. 402 CA at [60]–[92].

56 [2005] I.C.R. 402 CA at [93] and [105].

57 Issues fully considered at paras 10-106 and following, above. For a further aspect of the damages

The employee is entitled to recover for prospective loss and there is no need to wait until the end of the term before suing. There is no more uncertainty in the assessment than in personal injury cases. Strictly there should be a deduction in respect of immediate payment and, though much less importantly, in respect of the contingencies of life: this was made in *Re English Joint Stock Bank, Yelland's Case*,[58] where Sir W. Page-Wood VC directed that the proper course was to ascertain the present value of an annuity of £500 (the annual salary under the contract) terminating at the date the contract would have ended, regard also being had to the risk to life and health.[59] Such elaborations are not found to the same extent as in the far commoner cases of personal injury, but doubtless these considerations weigh with the judges when arriving at their awards. Yet in *Edwards v Society of Graphical & Allied Trades*,[60] which concerned dismissal on account of the claimant's wrongful expulsion from his trade union, while the trial judge accepted the invitation to adopt the practice in personal injury cases and calculate the damages by applying a multiplier to the claimant's annual loss of earning capacity,[61] the Court of Appeal held this to be misguided as there was a great difference between permanent incapacity from personal injury and loss of trade union membership where there could be reinstatement.[62] The date to be taken as the termination of the contract generally presents no difficulty. When the defendant has a right to terminate the contract before the end of the term, damages should only be awarded to the end of the earliest period at which the defendant could have so terminated the contract, a conclusion accepted in *Marsh v National Autistic Society*[63]; conversely, where the claimant has an option to extend the contract, the probability of his exercising this option, and the value thereof, may be taken into account. **33-013**

In the short period between the decision in *British Transport Commission v Gourley*[64] in 1955, establishing that awards for loss of earning capacity in personal injury cases are to be based upon the claimant's salary after tax, and the Finance Act 1960, introducing for the first time taxability of awards of damages for wrongful dismissal, it was accepted in a number of cases that the calculation of the damages for the claimant's loss of earnings, both past and prospective, must take into account the tax which would have been payable upon them.[65] The situation was, however, complicated by the provision in ss.37 and 38 of the Finance Act 1960 for the taxation under the then Sch.E, in terms sufficiently wide to apply to damages awarded for loss of earnings for wrongful dismissal, of payments in excess of £5,000 on a person's retirement or removal from any office or employment; the **33-014**

---

in *Horkulak*, one that was only before the trial judge, see para.10-106, above.

58 (1867) L.R. 4 Eq. 350.

59 (1867) L.R. 4 Eq. 350 at 351–352.

60 [1971] Ch. 354, High Court and CA.

61 See, for personal injury, paras 40-066 and following, below.

62 [1971] Ch. 354 CA at 378A, per Lord Denning MR; see also 379C, per Sachs LJ. While the Ogden Tables have been prepared for use in personal injury and fatal accident cases, there is no good reason why they should not be used in appropriate wrongful dismissal cases. It has been held in *Kingston upon Hull City Council v Dunnachie (No.3)* [2004] I.C.R. 227 that they may be used in employment tribunal cases but that their use should be rare and confined to calculations of career-long losses.

63 [1994] I.C.R. 453; see, too, *O'Laoire v Jackel International (No.2)* [1991] I.C.R. 718 CA at 730F. This, however, should be read in the light of the cases discussed at paras 33-009 and 33-010, above. And see, too, *Rigby v Ferodo* [1987] I.R.L.R. 61 CA, at para.33-034, below.

64 [1956] A.C. 185.

65 *Beach v Reed Corrugated Cases* [1956] 1 W.L.R. 807; *Phipps v Orthodox Unit Trusts* [1958] 1 Q.B. 314 CA; *Shindler v Northern Raincoat Co* [1960] 1 W.L.R. 1038.

£5,000 exemption has stood at £30,000 since 1988[66] and now is to be found in s.403(1) of the Income Tax (Earnings and Pensions) Act 2003.[67] In the first case to come before the English courts, *Parsons v B.N.M. Laboratories*,[68] the loss of earnings before tax was well below £5,000, thus bringing the statutory relief in respect of the first £5,000 into play, and the Court of Appeal, after confirming that the *Gourley* rule applied to cases of wrongful dismissal as well as personal injury,[69] held that, since the award fell completely outside the taxation provisions of the statute, the court must continue to calculate the damages upon the claimant's earnings after taking into account the tax he would have paid upon them. For a time the application of the *Gourley* rule became exceptionally complicated when the claimant's loss of earnings was above the exempt limit, so that the amount awarded would be taxed, though only in part, under the statutory provisions. However, these complications have disappeared since 1988 when s.74 of the Finance Act of that year provided that the excess over the exempt amount would simply be taxed in the ordinary course rather than under the statutory formula which had prevailed in varying guises of elaboration over some 30 years. This simplification is today set out in s.403(1) of the Income Tax (Earnings and Pensions) Act 2003. The mode of calculation, and the effect of taxation on damages for wrongful dismissal generally, are fully considered elsewhere.[70]

**33-015** There remains the question of how far deductions should be made in respect of any collateral benefits which the claimant has obtained as a result of his wrongful dismissal. This difficult area has been far more fully explored in the analogous context of personal injury.[71] It would seem that, as with personal injury and for the same reasons, there would be no deduction in respect of insurance moneys to which the employee is entitled or of monetary contributions made gratuitously to him by charities and others. The same should generally be true of pensions and indeed the Court of Appeal so held in *Hopkins v Norcross*,[72] relying upon the House of Lords cases in the personal injury field[73]; the employee's pension, it was said, flowed from work which the employee had done and belonged to a category of collateral benefit which was exempt from the general principle that credit should be given for benefits received by the claimant as a consequence of the defendant's breach of contract. There remain social security benefits, many of which in the personal injury field have since 1989 been dealt with by statute[74] so that they can no longer provide an analogy for wrongful dismissal. One such benefit which has been fully adjudicated upon in the area of wrongful dismissal is unemployment benefit. In *Parsons v B.N.M. Laboratories*,[75] the Court of Appeal held that the sum of unemployment benefit paid to the claimant under the then National Insurance Act 1946 fell to be

---

66 Introduced by s.74 of the Finance Act 1988. There had been intermediate rises to £10,000 by the Finance Act 1978 s.24(1) and to £25,000 by the Finance Act 1981 s.31(1).

67 Previously in Income and Corporation Taxes Act 1988 s.148, as substituted in 1998.

68 [1964] 1 Q.B. 95 CA. The impact of the statutory provisions on damages for wrongful dismissal had already been considered in Scotland in *Stewart v Glentaggart*, 1963 S.C. 300.

69 Although this had already been stated in *Gourley* itself by Lord Goddard, with whose speech Lords Somervell and Radcliffe agreed. Sellers LJ dissented on this issue.

70 See Ch.18, above, especially paras 18-042 to 18-046.

71 See paras 40-149 and following, below.

72 [1994] I.C.R. 11 CA.

73 *Parry v Cleaver* [1970] A.C. 1 and *Smoker v London Fire Authority* [1991] 2 A.C. 502; see paras 40-154 and following, below.

74 See paras 40-162 and following, below.

75 [1964] 1 Q.B. 95 CA.

deducted from the damages for loss of earnings for wrongful dismissal. The court distinguished the private insurance policy, moneys from which are not deducted from damages, on various related grounds: that receipt of unemployment benefit was "as a matter of general right under the system of State insurance", that the contribution towards unemployment insurance is one that the claimant was

> "bound to make with the very object of mitigating the damage which inability to work will do him",

that the employer was a contributing party to the unemployment insurance.[76] Doubts about whether this decision would survive were generated in *Parry v Cleaver*,[77] where the majority of the House of Lords, while not calling *Parsons* in question, nevertheless indicated that the matter would require reconsideration when it again arose,[78] but these doubts were dispelled by *Westwood v Secretary of State for Employment*,[79] where the House endorsed the taking into account of unemployment benefit in mitigation of damages. Lord Bridge, speaking for all their Lordships, said that he could see no

> "analogy at all between the generosity of private subscribers to a fund for the victims of some disaster, who also have claims for damages against a tortfeasor, and the State providing subventions for the needy out of funds which, in one way or another, have been subscribed compulsorily by various classes of citizen."[80]

Nor did he consider the "argument for the view that unemployment benefit is the fruit of insurance" as more than "superficially plausible",[81] and reached "the conclusion that *Parsons* was rightly decided".[82] Indeed the trend to general deductibility in personal injury cases initiated in *Hodgson v Trapp*,[83] primarily also by Lord Bridge,[84] should spill over into the field of wrongful dismissal. Thus it would seem that the non-deduction of supplementary benefit, now income support, in *Basnett v J. & A. Jackson*,[85] is no longer acceptable. It is only with redundancy payments that the position may continue to be somewhat uncertain. The earlier authorities are conflicting; no deduction was made in *Basnett v J. & A. Jackson*,[86] in this not following the earlier *Stocks v Magna Merchants*.[87] Moreover, in this field of benefit

---

76 These three grounds are to be found, respectively, [1964] 1 Q.B. 95 CA at 144, per Pearson LJ, at 121, per Harman LJ and at 131, per Sellers LJ.

77 [1970] A.C. 1.

78 [1970] A.C. 1 at 19 and 39, per Lords Reid and Wilberforce respectively.

79 [1985] A.C. 20.

80 [1985] A.C. 20 at 43F.

81 [1985] A.C. 20 at 43G.

82 [1985] A.C. 20 at 44A. However, the claimant was required to account only for the net gain accruing to him which, in the particular case where the wrongful dismissal was in respect of a 12-week period after which the claimant continued unemployed, was constituted not by the unemployment benefit, together with earnings-related supplement, received during those 12 weeks but by the lesser sum received in supplementary benefit for the first 12 weeks after the period of entitlement to unemployment benefit expired. See [1985] A.C. 20 at 39G–40A and 44G–H for how this was worked out.

83 [1989] A.C. 807.

84 See paras 40-163 and 40-238, below.

85 [1976] I.C.R. 63.

86 [1976] I.C.R. 63.

87 [1973] 1 W.L.R. 1505; preferring to follow two first instance unfair dismissal cases holding for no deduction. The arguments put forward on both sides are set out at length in the judgment at [1976]

the analogy of the personal injury cases does not point the way to a clear solution, *Mills v Hassell*[88] having refused the deduction and *Wilson v National Coal Board*,[89] an appeal to the House of Lords from Scotland, having allowed it. Not that these form two inconsistent decisions: the contrasting results stemmed from the fact that in *Wilson*, which their Lordships regarded as presenting somewhat exceptional facts, the employee would not have been dismissed at all, and made redundant, but for the incapacity caused by the injury, since he would have been offered, and would have accepted, another job from his employers, whereas there was no evidence for a similar conclusion in *Mills*.[90] Yet on this footing can it not be said, wherever there is wrongful dismissal coupled with redundancy, that the employee would not have been made redundant had he not been wrongfully dismissed and that therefore redundancy payments made to him should always be deducted from his damages? Alternatively, it may be argued that wrongful dismissal cannot here be equated with personal injury, for the redundancy does not *result* from the wrongful dismissal as it may do from the personal injury: in a sense the wrongful dismissal and the redundancy are one and the same thing. Wrongful dismissal gives rise to a right to claim for loss of earnings over a necessarily limited period and the employee would still have received his redundancy payment if, without being wrongfully dismissed, his services had been dispensed with at the end of his contractual term.[91] This points to making no deduction on account of redundancy payments and is thought to be the better approach.[92]

33-016 **(b) The amount the employee has or should have earned in alternative employment** Any amount that the claimant has earned in substituted[93] employment since the breach will be deducted[94] and the loss incurred will vanish where the claimant has immediately passed into other employment on equally good terms. This is well illustrated by *Reid v Explosives Co*.[95] In that case the claimant was entitled to six months' notice by his employers, the defendant company. The appointment of a manager by order of the Chancery Court at the instance of the

I.C.R. 63 at 67D–73H.

88 [1983] I.C.R. 330.

89 1981 S.L.T. 67 HL (Sc).

90 See further at para.40-177, below.

91 If however, as in *Baldwin v British Coal Corp* [1994] I.R.L.R. 139, the employee would never have become entitled to a redundancy payment but for the dismissal, deduction is appropriate. It was accepted in *Baldwin* that redundancy payments are normally not to be deducted.

92 *O'Laoire v Jackel International (No.2)* [1991] I.C.R. 718 CA shows that a compensatory award for unfair dismissal does not fall to be deducted from damages awarded for wrongful dismissal unless a double recovery for the same loss can be proved. In *Aspden v Webbs Poultry & Meat Group (Holdings)* [1996] I.R.L.R. 521 it was held proved and the full amount of the sum paid by the defendants to the claimant by way of settlement of his unfair dismissal claim was brought into account against the damages for wrongful dismissal since the court was satisfied that there would otherwise be a double recovery.

93 It must be truly a substitute. If the claimant could have taken the new employment in addition to the old, as where the claimant was not required to give his time exclusively to the defendant, the damages will not be affected by the amount earned in the new employment.

94 See, e.g. *Collier v Sunday Referee Publishing Co* [1940] 2 K.B. 647, where the claimant was held entitled to damages amounting to sums payable under the contract less any remuneration earned in other employment after breach, and *Cerberus Software Ltd v Rowley* [2001] I.R.L.R. 160 CA, a somewhat controversial decision on whether the employee was required to take the substituted employment: see first footnote in para.33-018, below.

95 (1887) 19 Q.B.D. 264 CA.

debenture holders was held to be a wrongful dismissal of the claimant; but by the instructions of the manager he continued his duties at the same salary for over six months. In these circumstances it was held that he was entitled to no damages. The court will look at the facts that have occurred up till the date of trial and gauge the probabilities of the future. So in *Re Newman, Raphael's Claim*,[96] where the claimant, dismissed during a one-year contractual term, had obtained other employment at the same salary but subject to a week's notice, it was held that the claimant had suffered no damage after he had entered upon this new employment, for there was no substantial doubt that the claimant would keep his new job till the end of the one-year contractual term, the trial being only a few weeks before this date.

The amount which the employee earns in the substituted employment encompasses commissions, benefits in kind, benefits from pension schemes and the like in the same way as does the amount which he would have earned under the contract that has been broken.[97] A somewhat unusual illustration of this appears in *Lavarack v Woods of Colchester*,[98] where the claimant, after his wrongful dismissal by the defendant company, had taken employment with another company as manager at a comparatively small salary and purchased half of the company's share capital. It was held that, since the claimant's release from his duties under his contract with the defendant company gave him the time to work for and manage the other company and by that work and management to enhance the value of his shareholding in the other company, the amount by which his equity in it had increased up to the time when his contract with the defendants would, but for the breach, have come to an end fell to be taken into account in assessing the damages. "His salary of £1,500", said Lord Denning MR, **33-017**

> "was very low for a man of his ability: and it looks as if he was getting, in addition, a concealed remuneration by a profit on his shares in the company".[99]

At the same time, the requirement that benefits conferred by reason of the substituted employment are to be taken into account must not be pressed too far. This is again illustrated by the *Lavarack* case, for the claimant there had purchased shares also in a third company, one which was in serious competition with the defendants, and in which he would therefore, under the terms of his contract with the defendants, have been unable to take a financial interest. It was held, however, that the value to the claimant of this investment did not fall to be taken into account in assessing the damages as it could not be attributed to his release from his employment with the defendants. Lord Denning MR said:

> "He might have invested his money in any other company and made similar profits. It is sheer speculation whether he would do better in [this company] than in others. I realise that the plaintiff was only at liberty to invest in [this company] because his employment

---

96 [1916] 2 Ch. 309 CA.

97 See paras 33-006 and 33-007, above. And if the claimant has been entitled to commission from the defendant on all orders received from customers introduced by him, which would give an entitlement to commission even after his contract of employment has been determined, the assessment of damages has to take account of the likelihood of the defendant's finding that his customers cease to deal with him as they are now open to being canvassed by the claimant on behalf of a new employer: see *Roberts v Elwells Engineers* [1972] 2 Q.B. 586 CA, especially per Lord Denning MR (with whom the other members of the court expressed agreement) at 596D.

98 [1967] 1 Q.B. 278 CA.

99 [1967] 1 Q.B. 278 CA at 291.

was terminated. But nevertheless the benefit from that investment was not a direct result of his dismissal. It was an entirely collateral benefit, for which he need not account to his employers."[100]

**33-018** Any amount that the claimant ought to have earned where he could reasonably have obtained alternative suitable employment also falls to be deducted,[101] and again may cause the loss incurred to vanish. This is well illustrated by *Brace v Calder*.[102] Two persons out of a partnership of four employing the claimant resigned from the partnership, which operated as a technical dismissal of the claimant. The remaining two, however, offered to keep the claimant on in his employment but the claimant refused this offer. It was held that he should have accepted it in mitigation and he was awarded only nominal damages. Alternatively, the employee does take up other employment but for reasons unconnected with his wrongful dismissal is dilatory in doing so. This was the position in *Horkulak v Cantor Fitzgerald International*,[103] with the result that two months of the basic salary claimed was deducted by the Court of Appeal.[104]

**33-019** The general principles of how far a claimant is required to act in mitigation[105] apply. In particular, an employee is not expected to accept employment in a lower status. Thus in *Yetton v Eastwoods Froy*,[106] the claimant, dismissed as managing director of the defendant company, was held to have acted reasonably in refusing the defendants' offer of employment as assistant managing director, a position which was a significant step down[107]; in *Edwards v Society of Graphical & Allied Trades*,[108] it was held that the claimant, dismissed from his employment as a skilled worker in a printing business,[109] could not reasonably have been expected to accept offers of work as a general labourer having regard to his standing, experience and personal history[110]; and in *Basnett v J. & A. Jackson*,[111] it was held not to be

---

100 [1967] 1 Q.B. 278 CA at 290.

101 See, e.g. *Re Gramophone Records Ltd* [1930] W.N. 42. But the claimant is not required to mitigate in this way where he has not accepted a repudiation, so that there is still no breach of contract; this is illustrated by *Shindler v Northern Raincoat Co* [1960] 1 W.L.R. 1038. So, too, where the contract provides for notice or payment in lieu, the summary dismissal of the claimant may not constitute a breach of contract but an election by the defendant between two modes of performance so as, again, to impose on the claimant no requirement of mitigation by seeking substitute employment. This is illustrated by *Abrahams v Performing Rights Society* [1995] I.C.R. 1028 CA, but a different, and unfortunate, result was reached in *Cerberus Software Ltd v Rowley* [2001] I.C.R. 376 CA, because the court found that the summary dismissal constituted a breach of contract giving rise to a requirement to mitigate. The issue being one of mitigation, these two cases are considered in that context at para.9-023, above.

102 [1895] 2 Q.B. 253 CA.

103 [2005] I.C.R. 402 CA.

104 See [2005] I.C.R. 402 CA at [93]–[99].

105 See Ch.9, above; especially the question of whether an offer by the defendant to take the claimant back need be accepted: see paras 9-060 to 9-062.

106 [1967] 1 W.L.R. 104.

107 This, although perhaps the most important, was only one of the factors taken into account: see [1967] 1 W.L.R. 104 at 118 to 119, and the further reference to the case at para.33-020, below.

108 [1971] Ch. 354 CA.

109 The claimant's action was not against his employer for wrongful dismissal but against his trade union for wrongful expulsion resulting in legitimate dismissal by his employer. But the principle is the same.

110 See, similarly, *Clayton-Greene v de Courville* (1920) 36 T.L.R. 790 where an actor, having been refused an important part which he had been engaged to play, reasonably refused to accept a minor part although at the same salary.

111 [1976] I.C.R. 63; see, especially, at 66C–67C.

unreasonable for the claimant, dismissed as works manager, to refuse the defendants' offer of a position as works clerk, which was a lower-paid as well as a lower-grade job. Nor will an employee necessarily be expected to accept employment in a different part of the country, or in a different type of work even if of an equal status with that from which he has been dismissed.

It may, however, be reasonable for the employee in the state of the labour market to accept a lower salary, although he may be regarded as continuing to act reasonably, as in *Yetton v Eastwoods Froy*,[112] if he continues for some time to seek employment in the same class of post as that from which he has been dismissed before turning to apply for less well-paid posts. It may be unreasonable to refuse an offer by the defendant himself as was held to be so in *Brace v Calder*.[113] The refusal of an offer of re-employment was also held to be a failure to mitigate in *Wilding v British Telecommunications Plc*,[114] and by all three courts hearing the case.[115] At the same time it was said there by the Court of Appeal that it was not enough for the employer to show that it would have been reasonable to take the mitigating step; the employer must show that it would have been unreasonable for the employee not to take it.[116] The refusal of an offer by the defendant at a lower salary is very likely to be permitted, as in *Jackson v Hayes*,[117] and also of offers made on the terms that the claimant should not act on his legal rights against the defendant or on terms requiring the claimant to work under the direction of persons with whom he has quarrelled in the course of his dismissal, as in *Shindler v Northern Raincoat Co*.[118] So, too, one of the factors which led the court in *Yetton v Eastwoods Froy*[119] to hold that the defendant's offer to the claimant of alternative employment was reasonably refused was that the dismissal had taken place in an arbitrary and high-handed fashion.[120] **33-020**

An important point is decided by *Ministry of Defence v Wheeler*.[121] It is that, where the amount that the employee would have earned in the employment from which he has been dismissed is subject to the loss of a chance doctrine, fairness requires that for the purposes of the damages computation the amount that he has or ought to have earned in alternative employment should, effectively, also be so subject.[122] **33-021**

## (2) Consequential losses

**(a) In general** Cases in the reports as to general consequential losses are negligible but various items can be imagined. Thus expenses incurred in finding a **33-022**

112 [1967] 1 W.L.R. 104.

113 [1895] 2 Q.B. 253 CA.

114 [2002] I.C.R. 1079 CA.

115 It was a claim for unfair rather than wrongful dismissal but the same principles apply.

116 See especially Sedley LJ at [2002] I.C.R. 1079 CA at [53]–[55].

117 [1938] 4 All E.R. 587.

118 [1960] 1 W.L.R. 1038.

119 [1967] 1 W.L.R. 104.

120 See the various factors taken into account, [1967] 1 W.L.R. 104 at 118–119. If, of course, a claimant does accept an engagement, the non-acceptance of which would not have constituted a failure to mitigate, the amount earned will be deducted: see paras 9-108 and 9-117 and following, above.

121 [1998] 1 W.L.R. 637 CA.

122 See the case at para.10-105, above.

new post ought to be recoverable,[123] or expenses of coming to the job and then going home on dismissal.[124]

33-023 **(b) The particular case of injured feelings or reputation** One head of damage has, however, received a great deal of consideration, that of injury to the claimant's feelings or reputation stemming from the dismissal. In the leading case of *Addis v Gramophone Co*,[125] the House of Lords decisively rejected such a claim and the influence of this holding has persisted up until the present day. Nevertheless it is now, and at the highest level, showing signs of weakening.[126]

33-024 *(i) Injury to feelings* In *Addis* the claimant had been dismissed in a harsh and humiliating manner, and it was held that the manner of the dismissal could in no way affect the damages. While two of their Lordships talked in terms of exemplary damages,[127] which have never yet been awarded for breach of any contract,[128] it was the injury to the feelings that lay at the heart of the other speeches.[129] The decision indeed mirrors, and confirms, what Erle J, advising their Lordships, said in *Beckham v Drake*[130]:

> "No allowance would be made in the nature of *pretium affectionis*, nor any reference to any pain that might be felt by the [employee] on the ground that he was attached to the place."

*Addis v Gramophone Co*[131] was applied at first instance in *Shore v Downs Surgical*,[132] to refuse damages for distress caused by a brusque and uncivilised dismissal, and again, similarly, by the Court of Appeal in *O'Laoire v Jackel International (No.2)*.[133] This remains the position today for wrongful dismissal despite obiter indications of their Lordships in *Mahmud v Bank of Credit and Commerce International SA*,[134] that damages for mental distress might one day be available for breach of an employment other than by wrongful dismissal.[135]

33-025 *(ii) Injury to reputation* This stands on a slightly different footing from injury to feelings. In so far as the injury to reputation results in a non-pecuniary loss it is irrecoverable in the same way as non-pecuniary loss from the injury to feelings. However, it is possible that the injury to reputation may cause a pecuniary loss if

123 But not, it seems, if due to loss of reputation, at least as the law now stands: see para.33-025, below.

124 Some cases deal with this but they concern provisions in the contract itself and are therefore not relevant to damages. This amount would be alternative to the normal measure: See paras 4-024 and following, above.

125 [1909] A.C. 488.

126 After having "cast a long shadow over the common law", as Lord Nicholls put it in *Eastwood v Magnox Electric Plc* [2005] 1 A.C. 503 at [1].

127 Lord James of Hereford, [1909] A.C. 488 at 492 and Lord Collins, dissenting at 497 and 500 to 501.

128 Neither before *Rookes v Barnard* [1964] A.C. 1129 nor, for the time being, after *Rookes*: see Ch.13, above, passim. Yet, curiously, Lord Collins's dissent in *Addis* was on the basis that it had been competent for the jury to award exemplary damages.

129 Lord Atkinson [1909] A.C. 488 at 493, Lord Gorell, at 501, 502, Lord Shaw, at 504.

130 (1849) 2 H.L.C. 579 at 608.

131 [1909] A.C. 488.

132 [1984] 1 All E.R. 7.

133 [1991] I.C.R. 718 CA.

134 [1998] A.C. 20.

135 On this see paras 33-026 and 33-032, below and for the whole issue of non-pecuniary loss see Ch.5, above.

it means that the claimant has more difficulty in obtaining new employment. In *Addis v Gramophone Co*,[136] the House of Lords had to deal with the prior case of *Maw v Jones*,[137] where it was held that

> "the plaintiff was entitled to recover for all the damage flowing naturally from the breach, and in considering what that would include the jury might take into account the difficulty that the plaintiff as discharged apprentice would have in obtaining employment elsewhere."[138]

Although on its facts *Maw v Jones*[139] can survive as falling within the special category of contracts of apprenticeship,[140] it is generally thought that the decision, so far as it depends on the generality of the principle stated, is to be regarded as no longer supportable since *Addis v Gramophone Co*.[141] For this view reliance is placed upon the emphatic words of Lord Loreburn that the damages

> "cannot include compensation either for the injured feelings of the servant, or for the loss he may sustain from the fact that his having been dismissed of itself makes it more difficult for him to obtain fresh employment"[142];

the cases where a banker is sued by a customer for dishonouring his cheques, which must be regarded as a pecuniary loss caused through injury to credit and reputation, were exceptional.[143] In *O'Laoire v Jackel International (No.2)*,[144] the Court of Appeal held that *Addis v Gramophone Co*[145] precluded damages for the diminution in the claimant's employment prospects; "the headnote in that case", said Sir Nicolas Browne-Wilkinson VC, "accurately reflects the decision".[146] This is, however, not strictly true for Lord Loreburn was the only one of their Lordships specifically to refer to employment prospects. The rest confined themselves to the non-pecuniary aspects of the case; indeed Lord Atkinson said expressly that whether there was an entitlement to damages for the harsh and humiliating way in which the claimant had been dismissed, including the pain experienced by reason of the imputation conveyed by the manner of his dismissal, was the only point necessary to deal with and the only circumstance which made the case of general importance.[147] It could be argued therefore that the decision in *O'Laoire*,[148] was ar-

---

136 [1909] A.C. 488.

137 (1890) 25 Q.B.D. 107.

138 (1890) 25 Q.B.D. 107 at 109 per Lord Coleridge J.

139 (1890) 25 Q.B.D. 107.

140 The rescue operation has been effected by the Court of Appeal in *Dunk v George Waller & Son* [1970] 2 Q.B. 163 CA (see para.33-030, below) although, oddly, none of the judgments refers to the case despite its citation by counsel.

141 [1909] A.C. 488.

142 [1909] A.C. 488 at 491.

143 There is also implied support in *Dunk v George Waller & Son* [1970] 2 Q.B. 163 CA (see para.33-030, below) for the view that *Addis v Gramophone Co* stands for the principle that even pecuniary injury to reputation is not generally recoverable in an action for wrongful dismissal since it was felt necessary in that case to distinguish *Addis v Gramophone Co*; see especially at 168, per Lord Denning MR See, too, *Withers v General Theatre Corp* [1933] 2 K.B. 536 CA (at para.33-028, below) where, however, the accent was on the failure to afford future publicity rather than on the manner of the breach as causing the inability to get fresh work.

144 [1991] I.C.R. 718 CA.

145 [1909] A.C. 488.

146 [1991] I.C.R. 718 CA at 731B.

147 [1909] A.C. 488 at 493.

rived at per incuriam and that the court there would have been pleased to have felt able to decide differently; Sir Nicolas Browne-Wilkinson VC said that he felt

> "considerable sympathy for [the] argument ... in relation to the adverse impact of the dismissal on the plaintiff's chances of re-employment".[149]

**33-026** All this comes before the decision in *Mahmud v Bank of Credit and Commerce International SA*,[150] yet to be dealt with under breach of the trust and confidence obligation.[151] The House of Lords there held that *Addis v Gramophone Co*,[152] did not preclude recovery for financial loss given a relevant breach of an employment contract, and it might be thought that this inroad upon the common understanding of *Addis* overtakes everything that has been said above. The decision has not, however, been interpreted as overruling, in the context of financial loss, *Addis* or as endorsing recovery for financial loss where the breach in question is simply wrongful dismissal.[153] This is clear from their Lordships' further decision in *Johnson v Unisys Ltd*.[154] There the employee, suing for wrongful dismissal, claimed that because of the manner in which he had been dismissed he had since been unable to work, with the result that he had suffered, and would continue to suffer, a very substantial loss of earnings. His claim failed. In the absence of breach of the trust and confidence term or any other term, their Lordships were unprepared to extend any such recovery to cases simply of wrongful dismissal, because they regarded any extension of the law of wrongful dismissal as being precluded by the legislation giving employees a remedy for unfair dismissal, a remedy which the claimant in *Unisys* had already successfully pursued. And it follows that if damages for reputation loss arising from wrongful dismissal are not available with a financial loss, the same must be true, and a fortiori, of damages for non-financial loss.[155]

**33-027** *Johnson v Unisys Ltd* was held to govern in *Edwards v Chesterfield Royal Hospital NHS Foundation Trust*.[156] The claimant was appointed as consultant surgeon at a National Health Service hospital under a contract providing that either party could terminate it on three months' notice to the other, and providing expressly that the consultant was entitled to a formal disciplinary hearing where allegations of misconduct were made against him. He was wrongfully dismissed on the grounds of personal and professional misconduct and was on this account unable to obtain similar employment elsewhere. His claim was for damages for the defendant's failure to implement the contractual disciplinary procedure properly, arguing that but for this failure there would have been no finding of misconduct and therefore no dismissal. It was held by the Supreme Court that *Johnson* prevented the recovery of damages not only for loss arising from dismissal but also for loss arising from failures in the steps leading to dismissal even if these failures amounted to a breach of contract, unless the loss claimed could be regarded as occurring quite independently of the dismissal. This result was however a close thing, being ar-

---

148 [1991] I.C.R. 718 CA.

149 [1991] I.C.R. 718 CA at 731A.

150 [1998] A.C. 20.

151 See para.33-031, below.

152 [1909] A.C. 488.

153 Thus *Addis* was again considered to stand in the way of recovery in *Disney v France Luxury Group SA* [2004] EWHC 2303 (QB).

154 [2003] 1 A.C. 518.

155 The whole issue in respect of non-pecuniary loss is further considered in Ch.5, above.

156 [2012] 2 A.C. 22.

rived at by a bare majority of four Justices to three and by their reversing the Court of Appeal. *Botham v Ministry of Defence*, which was heard by the Supreme Court together with *Edwards*, was factually more in the employer's favour and the appeal in *Botham* was allowed by the court with only a single dissent.

*(iii) Loss of publicity* There is one clear exceptional case in which, in the context of wrongful dismissal, damages for loss of reputation, or, as it is more often put, loss of publicity, is recoverable by the claimant. This is where the enhancement of the claimant's reputation by publicity was particularly contemplated by the contract, so that it might be regarded here as a head of damage contemplated by the parties themselves when entering into the contract. This was first established with regard to actors in *Marbé v George Edwardes*,[157] which case was tested and confirmed by the House of Lords in *Clayton v Oliver*.[158] The main point decided in these two cases was that such a contract imposed on the defendant an obligation to allow the claimant to appear before the public as an actor, and not a great deal was said about damages, except that Lord Buckmaster in *Clayton v Oliver*[159] said that he thought that "loss of reputation" was not the exact expression but "loss of publicity" should be used. More assistance is given by the later case of *Withers v General Theatre Corp*,[160] where, the anterior point of liability being by then settled, concentration fell on the question of the basis of the assessment of the damages. The position is put most clearly by Greer LJ: **33-028**

> "When a proprietor of a music-hall or theatre engages an artiste to perform, he is promising two things: he is giving a consideration which consists of two different elements; first, a salary which he promises the artiste for his services, and secondly, the opportunity to play in public some part which will attract attention.... For the loss of the opportunity ... and so enhancing or maintaining his reputation, he is also entitled to recover damages."[161]

Nevertheless it was held by the Court of Appeal that no damages were recoverable where the claimant's only loss was injury to his already existing reputation as an actor. In an edition of this work in 1997 it was submitted that this limitation could be discarded and this has now happened. On this point *Withers* was overruled in *Mahmud v Bank of Credit and Commerce International SA*.[162]

This head of damage for loss of publicity was extended from actors to authors, or at least to an author of a screenplay entitled to a screen credit, in *Tolnay v Criterion Films*.[163] Goddard J pointed out that **33-029**

[157] [1928] 1 K.B. 269 CA.

[158] [1930] A.C. 209; followed in *McLaren v Chalet Club* (1951) 1 C.L.C. 2508. *Turpin v Victoria Palace* [1918] 2 K.B. 539 was overruled, but only on the anterior issue of whether such a contract imposed an obligation on the defendant to provide the claimant actor with the opportunity to appear. Had he come to a positive conclusion on this issue, McCardie J would in that case have been perfectly prepared to give damages for loss of publicity. Earlier in *Bunning v Lyric Theatre* (1894) 71 L.T. 396 it had been held that such damages were recoverable where the actor's contract had express provisions for his securing publicity.

[159] [1930] A.C. 209 at 220.

[160] [1933] 2 K.B. 536 CA.

[161] [1933] 2 K.B. 536 CA at 554.

[162] [1998] A.C. 20. See this case at para.33-031, below.

[163] [1936] 2 All E.R. 1625. Similarly *Ackland v World Screenplays*, *The Times*, 23 February 1950.

> "all persons who have to make a living by attracting the public to their works, be they … painters or … literary men … or … pianists and musicians, must live by getting known to the public".[164]

He thought that the loss of publicity to an actor, whose worth the public can only estimate by seeing him perform, is more serious than in the case of the author.[165] On the other hand, in *Collier v Sunday Referee Publishing Co*,[166] it was held that a chief sub-editor of a newspaper could not recover damages for loss of publicity, there being no implied stipulation in the contract for publicity; in *Moss v Chesham UDC*,[167] such a claim by a surveyor to a local authority failed; in *Disney v France Luxury Group SA*,[168] it was considered that loss of publicity damages were not recoverable by a fashion designer; and in *Re Gollomb*,[169] the Court of Appeal refused to give damages to a company director for the loss of the publicity or prestige he would have got by being in the defendant's service, where the contract had been wrongfully determined before his service had commenced.[170] The approach of the Court of Appeal suggests that damages for loss of publicity are germane only to theatrical or closely analogous contracts; Greer LJ thought that very special considerations apply to theatrical contracts since the consideration to the artist, certainly to the artist in the early stages of his career, is as much, if not more, the opportunity to appear as it is the mere wages.[171]

**33-030** Somewhat similar to a dismissed actor's loss of publicity is a dismissed apprentice's loss of training. In *Dunk v George Waller & Son*,[172] the claimant, whose contract of apprenticeship had been wrongfully terminated during its course, was held entitled, apart from loss of earnings, to damages for his loss of training and also for the diminution of his future prospects by reason of his loss of

> "status of a man who has completed an apprenticeship, which might be important in acquiring a new job".[173]

The Court of Appeal regarded an apprenticeship agreement as being of a special character, significantly different from an ordinary contract of service,[174] and, accordingly, there was no room for the application of the rule in *Addis v Gramophone Co*,[175] as currently understood,[176] that the prejudice to the prospects of future

---

164 [1936] 2 All E.R. 1625 at 1626 to 1627.

165 [1936] 2 All E.R. 1625 at 1626.

166 [1940] 2 K.B. 647.

167 (1945) 172 L.T. 301.

168 [2004] EWHC 2303 (QB).

169 (1931) 144 L.T. 583 CA.

170 Wrongful determination before entering performance was held to be on a footing with wrongful dismissal during performance.

171 (1931) 144 L.T. 583 CA at 590. In *Fielding v Moiseiwitsch* (1946) 175 L.T. 265 an impresario was held not entitled to damages for loss of publicity caused by the contractual failure of the defendant, a famous pianist, to appear at a concert. This was of course not wrongful dismissal—the employer was claimant and not defendant—but the decision is interesting in that the court, in refusing damages under this head, stressed the fact that an impresario promoting concerts is a businessman rather than a creative artist: see at 270.

172 [1970] 2 Q.B. 163 CA.

173 [1970] 2 Q.B. 163 CA at 169, per Karminski LJ.

174 [1970] 2 Q.B. 163 CA at 167 and 169, per Lord Denning MR and Widgery LJ, respectively. And for the purpose of these damages contract of apprenticeship is not to be narrowly construed: *Flett v Matheson* [2006] I.C.R. 673 CA.

175 [1909] A.C. 488.

employment engendered by the dismissal is to be ignored. As Lord Denning MR said:

> "The very object of an apprenticeship agreement is to enable the apprentice to fit himself to get better employment."[177]

## 3. Breach of Obligation of Trust and Confidence

Today there have come into prominence claims by employees for breach of an implied term in the contract of employment of trust and confidence and these have important repercussions upon the issue of damages. The leading case is *Mahmud v Bank of Credit and Commerce International SA*[178] in the House of Lords. The claimants, who were two long-serving employees of the defendant bank which collapsed as a result of a massive and notorious fraud perpetrated by those controlling the bank and who, having been made redundant by the bank's liquidators, thereafter found difficulty in obtaining employment because of their association with the bank, made a claim for what was referred to as "stigma compensation" arising from their having been put at a disadvantage in the labour market. The House of Lords allowed their claim. It was held that, provided a relevant breach of contract was established, financial loss in respect of damage to reputation could be recovered for breach of a contract of employment. Here the employer was in breach of its obligation to its employees not to conduct a dishonest or corrupt business, this obligation being one particular aspect of the general obligation not to engage in conduct likely to undermine the trust and confidence required in the employment relationship. Thus if it was reasonably foreseeable that conduct in breach of the trust and confidence term would prejudicially affect employees' future employment prospects and loss of that type was sustained in consequence of such a breach, damages for such loss would be recoverable.[179] In so holding the House reversed the courts below, both the Court of Appeal[180] and Evans-Lombe J at first instance[181] who had confessed to "considerable sympathy" with the argument for damages for loss of employment prospects but had felt himself precluded by Addis from accepting it. Breach of the implied term of trust and confidence was again found at first instance in *Horkulak v Cantor Fitzgerald International*,[182] but the Court of Appeal treated the case simply as one of wrongful dismissal[183] and the damages in both **33-031**

---

[176] See para.33-025, above.

[177] [1970] 2 Q.B. 163 CA at 168. Two old cases which indicated that a dismissed apprentice could sue only for his loss up to the bringing of the action, *Addams v Carter* (1862) 6 L.T. 130 and *Parker v Cathcart* (1886) 17 Ir. C.L.R. 778, were held overruled.

[178] [1998] A.C. 20.

[179] But in further actions brought against BCCI by its employees—there was a total of 369 claims of which five were selected as being representative—all five claimants failed because they were unable to cross what were called the evidential hurdles lying in the way of success in "stigma compensation" claims, it being said that the reliable and tested evidence of a prospective employer was necessary and that vague allegations of being hampered in the employment market were not enough: *Bank of Credit and Commerce International SA v Ali* [1999] 4 All E.R. 83; affirmed [2002] 3 All E.R. 750 CA. This is the only one of a whole batch of cases, seven in all, with this title which is relevant to damages.

[180] Where it appeared as *Malik v BCCI* [1995] 3 All E.R. 545 CA.

[181] Where it appeared as *Re BCCI* [1994] I.R.L.R. 282.

[182] [2003] I.C.R. 697; see at [27] and [79].

[183] [2005] I.C.R. 402 CA; see at [2].

courts followed conventional wrongful dismissal lines.[184] Also the House of Lords in *Eastwood v Magnox Electric Plc*[185] was concerned with breach of trust and confidence but it was its relationship with the legislative remedy for unfair dismissal that was in issue and nothing was said, or required to be said, on matters of damages.[186]

33-032 The decision in *Mahmud*[187] is of great importance as it recognises for the first time that damages may be recoverable for financial loss arising from damage to an employee's reputation resulting from breach of the employment contract, thereby making an inroad upon the common understanding of *Addis v Gramophone Co.*[188] And although their Lordships' decision was concerned with pecuniary loss, much was said about the general applicability today of *Addis* also to non-pecuniary loss. As the law stands, there can be no recovery for mental distress whether regarded as arising from injury to feelings or injury to reputation, even where there is breach of the implied term of trust and confidence. This was initially held in *Bliss v South East Thames Regional Health Authority*,[189] then in *French v Barclays Bank*,[190] and accepted as the law in *Gogay v Hertfordshire County Council*.[191] But this could now change.[192]

## 4. INJURY AND DEATH

33-033 A large body of case law exists upon the duty owed by the employer to the employee in respect of the latter's physical safety and the duty encompasses the psychiatric.[193] The actions sound as much in tort as in contract[194]; either way the measure of damages will follow the lines of all cases of personal injury and death however caused, a matter fully dealt with elsewhere.

---

184 For the damages awarded see paras 10-106 and 33-011 to 33-012, above.

185 [2005] 1 A.C. 503.

186 Breach of the obligation of trust and confidence again features in *IBM United Kingdom Holdings Ltd v Dalgleish* [2015] EWHC 389 Ch, which involved an employer's scheme to vary the contractual rights of employees by making their salaries non-pensionable in return for salary increases. Warren J's judgment is concerned with the entitlement to damages rather than with their assessment but there is much discussion on damages (at [139]–[178]). See the references to the case at paras.10-113 and 33-011, above.

187 [1998] A.C. 20.

188 [1909] A.C. 488.

189 [1987] I.C.R. 700 CA.

190 [1998] I.R.L.R. 646 CA.

191 [2000] I.R.L.R. 703 CA; there was psychiatric injury and recovery for mental distress was allowed.

192 For further consideration of the problems of non-pecuniary loss in this field see paras 5-031 to 5-035, above.

193 The damages awarded for psychiatric injury in *Gogay v Hertfordshire County Council* [2000] I.R.L.R. 703 CA, were in the context of a breach of the term of trust and confidence: see this at paras 33-031 and 33-032, above.

194 The Court of Appeal confirmed in *Matthews v Kuwait Bechtel Corp* [1959] 2 Q.B. 57 CA, that the employee may sue in contract for physical injury.

### 5. Miscellaneous Breaches

**33-034** Breaches other than by wrongful dismissal are few and far between.[195] In *Rigby v Ferodo*,[196] there was no dismissal, the employee continuing to work at the lower figure to which his employers had wrongfully reduced his wages. The claimant's entitlement to damages was held by the Court of Appeal not to be limited to the 12-week period of notice by which the contract could have, but had not, been lawfully determined by the employers. In *Cox v Philips Industries*,[197] the breach consisted in the employers' relegating the employee to a position of less responsibility with very vague duties in breach of their express contractual obligation to afford him a better position with greater responsibility and an increased salary, this obligation having been undertaken in order not to lose him to a rival company. However, as the claimant had been fully paid, his only claim was for the non-pecuniary loss arising from the depression, anxiety, frustration and illness suffered by him. To the extent that recovery for this mental distress was allowed in *Cox* the decision is no longer law.[198] In *Clark v Nomura International Plc*,[199] the breach consisted of not awarding the employee a discretionary bonus for the nine-month period before his dismissal, during which time he had earned profits for his employer of over £6 million and had set up a further transaction likely to bring in £16 million. The discretion, though on the face of the contract unfettered, could not be exercised in a perverse or irrational fashion, so the court considered what would have been the bonus that the employee should have got and awarded that sum, amounting to £1.35 million, as damages.[200]

## II. Breach by Employee

**33-035** Little authority exists on the measure of damages where the employee is in breach. There would seem to be a number of reasons for this. First, one is more likely to find that, if anyone is suing, it is the employee claiming his wages since it is he who stands to lose by his own breach, and the employer can often benefit by the employee forfeiting his right to his wages.[201] Secondly, the employer, rather than suing for damages, is more likely to dismiss the employee summarily with or without forfeiture of wages. Thirdly, in the case of an employee's breach of contract in restraint of trade, the employer is more likely to claim an injunction or to be able to sue for liquidated damages.[202]

---

195 Even breach of the trust and confidence term, dealt with separately at para.33-031, above, has so far not made much of an appearance.

196 [1987] I.R.L.R. 61 CA.

197 [1976] 1 W.L.R. 638.

198 In line with the restrictions which have developed on damages for mental distress in contract: see paras 5-026 and 5-027, above. Cox was specifically overruled in *Bliss v South East Thames Regional Health Authority* [1987] I.C.R. 700 CA.

199 [2000] I.R.L.R. 766.

200 A discretionary bonus was also in issue in the wrongful dismissal case of *Horkulak v Cantor Fitzgerald International* [2005] I.C.R. 402 CA: see the case at paras 33-011 and 33-012, above.

201 Only if the contract is divisible or the Apportionment Act 1870 applies can an employee in default sue for his wages.

202 See para.16-083, above.

## 1. Failure or Refusal to Work

**33-036** The prima facie measure of damages will be the cost of procuring another person to do the work, less the amount that would have been paid under the contract to the defendant.[203] This is usefully illustrated by *Richards v Hayward*,[204] although there was no argument on the question of damages. The claimant employed the defendant as a ship's surgeon on a voyage for which, as payment, the defendant was to be carried at half fare. On the defendant's failure to appear, the claimant hired a substitute whom in payment he had to carry at no fare at all. The damages were measured by the half fare.[205]

**33-037** Beyond this the employer may claim, as consequential loss, the value of the work lost by reason of the employee's defection less, once again, the amount that would have been paid to him under the contract. This situation will arise when a substitute is not immediately available; *Ebbw Vale Steel Co v Tew*,[206] an action against a face-worker in a coal mine, provides an illustration, the damages being assessed at the value of the output lost less the expenses which would have been incurred in obtaining it. But where in *National Coal Board v Galley*,[207] the defendant was a supervisor who did not work at the coal-face, it was held that his defection had not contributed to loss of output and no damages in respect of such loss could be recovered against him. The loss of output had been caused by reason of the refusal of others to work the particular shift, and the defendant, though acting in concert with them, was not liable for damages caused by their breaches of contract in the absence of any claim in tort for conspiracy or inducement of breach of contract.[208]

**33-038** Moreover, the claimant may sometimes wish to claim for expenditure rendered futile by the defendant's breach of contract, and his right to elect for this alternative measure was endorsed by the Court of Appeal, in the context of employment contracts broken by the employee, in *Anglia Television v Reed*.[209] The claimant television company employed the defendant actor to play the leading role in a film which the claimants had decided to make for television. When later the defendant repudiated the contract and refused to perform, the claimants were unable to find a suitable substitute for the defendant, and the film was abandoned. Being unable to prove what profit they would have obtained had the film been made with the defendant in it, the claimants claimed to recover their expenditure which had been wasted by the defendant's breach. The issue in the case was whether the claimants could recover the expenditure which they had already incurred in employing other personnel for the projected film before entering into the contract with the defendant,[210] and it was held that they could recover for such pre-contractual expenditure as well as

---

203 Where in *Giraud UK Ltd v Smith* [2000] I.R.L.R. 763 the employee was in breach by leaving without giving notice, a clause in the contract that he should pay his employers an amount equivalent to his pay for the period of notice was held to be not a liquidated damages clause but a penalty and accordingly unenforceable: see the case at para.16-082, above.

204 (1841) 2 M. & G. 574.

205 See, too, *National Coal Board v Galley* [1958] 1 W.L.R. 16 CA, where the cost of obtaining a substitute worker was awarded as damages.

206 (1935) 79 S.J. 593 CA.

207 [1958] 1 W.L.R. 16 CA.

208 Another instance of coalminers refusing to work is *Bowes v Press* [1894] 1 Q.B. 202, but it is not of much assistance on the question of damages.

209 [1972] 1 Q.B. 60 CA.

210 The propriety of allowing the pre-contractual expenditure is considered in a general context at para.4-027, above.

for their post-contractual expenditure since it was reasonably within the contemplation of the parties that all the expenditure would be wasted if the contract was broken by the defendant.[211]

## 2. CARELESS OR DEFECTIVE WORK

Where the employee does careless or defective work he will be liable for loss resulting to the employer's person or property, as by physical injury and damage, or loss to the employer by reason of his liability in damages to a third party. The latter type of damage is dramatically illustrated by the decision of the House of Lords in *Lister v Romford Ice Co*,[212] where a third party recovered damages from the employer for negligent injury inflicted by the employee in the course of his employment and the employer in turn recovered this amount from the employee as damages for breach of contract. The measure of damages in the case of physical injury or damage will follow the lines of other cases on physical injury or damage[213] and, in the case of liability in damages to a third party, it will be the amount of such damages.[214] **33-039**

## 3. MISCELLANEOUS BREACHES

A variety of other breaches by the employee has appeared. Such as there are tend to revolve around actions which seek to deprive the employer of profit by competition or otherwise. Thus in *Sanders v Parry*,[215] the defendant, who had been engaged as an assistant solicitor by the claimant, made a secret agreement with one of the claimant's clients that he would leave the claimant's employ and set up in practice on his own account, whereupon the client would transfer to him from the claimant all the client's legal work. This agreement having been duly carried through, the claimant successfully claimed for breach of the implied term of the employment contract that the defendant would serve him with good faith and fidelity, and was awarded damages for the loss of the chance of retaining the legal work of the departed client.[216] In *S.B.J. Stephenson Ltd v Mandy*,[217] the solicitation of the employer's clients by the employee's possession of confidential information led to damages for the loss of the chance of retaining those clients, but no loss was held to have been shown of lost management fees, loss of goodwill or loss of reputation. **33-040**

---

211 In the *Scottish Neil v Strathclyde Regional Council* [1984] I.R.L.R. 14 recovery was also by way of wasted expenditure except that this measure had been enshrined in what was held to be a liquidated damages clause: see the case at para.16-082, above; the court pointed out (at 16) that "*National Coal Board v Galley* is not an authority for holding in all cases the only measure of damages for the withdrawal of labour by an employee is the cost of hiring a substitute." Further, the employers' entitlement to such damages was unaffected by the fact that, as a local authority, they could also be entitled to reimbursement of the cost of their expenditure on the employee through the medium of a credit in their rate support grant; this was a collateral arrangement which did not permit the employee to escape paying damages for her breach of contract.

212 [1957] A.C. 555.

213 See Chs 37, 39 and 40, below.

214 But, where the employer has been prosecuted for a fine, whether he can recover this amount from his employee turns upon considerations which are examined at paras 21-068 to 21-072, above.

215 [1967] 1 W.L.R. 753.

216 The calculation of this loss appears at [1967] 1 W.L.R. 753 at 767. See further on damages for loss of a chance paras 10-048 and following, above.

217 [2000] F.S.R. 286.

In *CMS Dolphin Ltd v Simonet*,[218] the defendant had resigned both as employee and director of the claimant company without giving proper notice and set up business in competition. While it was accounting for profits and equitable compensation that dominated the action, the claimant company as employer was nonetheless held entitled to damages for the lost chance of a lucrative contract which might have been obtained had the defendant not improperly resigned.[219] In *Merlin Financial Consultants v Cooper*,[220] where the employee was in breach of a restrictive covenant by setting up a competing business on the termination of his employment, the employer was awarded damages based on the profits that it would have made from the clients who had left, subject to a deduction, as an expense, of the amount payable to a replacement employee, and subject in addition to a percentage deduction from these profits as the trial judge was of the view that some of the clients would have left anyway, even if the employee had not been in breach of his contractual obligations.[221]

**33-041** A somewhat different situation arose in *Nottingham University v Fishel*,[222] in that the employee was not seeking to take profit from his employer.[223] The defendant, who was scientific director and senior lecturer at the claimant university, was held to be in breach of his employment contract by doing outside work without obtaining the university's consent. However, no damages were awarded as the university was unable to prove any loss. The court was unprepared to award restitutionary or disgorgement damages[224] in respect of the gain made by the defendant from his outside work, although the court did consider[225] the decision of the Court of Appeal in *Attorney General v Blake*,[226] which had just about then introduced the idea of gain-based damages into the law of contract.[227] In *Blake* the House of Lords affirmed[228] on somewhat different grounds[229] and it may be that *Fishel* is overtaken by that affirmation.[230]

---

218 [2001] 2 B.C.L.C. 704.

219 See [2001] 2 B.C.L.C. 704 at [141].

220 [2014] EWHC 1196 (QB).

221 [2014] EWHC 1196 (QB) at [74]–[83].

222 [2001] R.P.C. 367.

223 This was also the position in *Noble Resources SA v Gross* [2009] EWHC 1435 (Comm) where there was recovery by an employer of huge losses on unauthorised speculative trading in aluminium futures concealed by an employee in breach of his employment contract. However, claims for conspiracy (see at para.48-020, below) and in deceit (see at para.49-006, below, in a footnote) against the employee and others took more prominence over the breach of contract claim.

224 On these, see Ch.15, above.

225 At [2001] R.P.C. 367 at 392–394.

226 [1998] Ch. 439 CA.

227 See Ch.15, above.

228 [2001] 1 A.C. 268.

229 See para.14-025, above.

230 And by the further developments in this expanding area of contract damages: see Ch.15, above. An unusual, and unsuccessful, claim for an employee's breach is *Dennis & Co v Campbell* [1978] Q.B. 365 CA. The manager of a betting shop contravened his employer's instructions not to accept bets on credit and was sued for money lost on a bet and not received by the shop. The action failed because, the bet being void, the employer could not recover against the employee what he could not recover against the person placing the bet.

# CHAPTER 34

# CONTRACTS FOR PROFESSIONAL AND OTHER SERVICES

TABLE OF CONTENTS



A basic distinction is made by the common law between, in its traditional nomenclature, the contract of service and the contract for services. The former is the contract made with an employee, in earlier days referred to as a servant; contracts of employment are dealt with in the previous chapter.[1] The latter is the contract made with an agent, sometimes referred to as an independent contractor; contracts of agency, in editions before 2000, were compendiously dealt with in a single chapter. However, with the tremendous growth of claims for professional negligence, the time had more than come to erect the contract for professional and indeed other services into a chapter of its own. In earlier days it was possible to contain the then very limited case law on professional negligence in a corner of a general chapter on agency contracts, but the explosion of such claims has put them into a position of dominance. And since it is true that professional and other advisers are not necessarily thought of as agents, it was thought better and clearer to deal with them outside contracts of agency as such. Rather is the agent thought of as one who is required to enter into a contract for a principal, and to a lesser extent as one who is entrusted with his principal's property. The agent proper, as such an agent may perhaps be called, is now the subject of a separate, later chapter.[2] 34-001

[1] See Ch.33, above.

[2] See Ch.35, below.

## I. Breach by the Party Engaging the Services

34-002 Whereas with contracts of employment the accent is on damages claims by employees rather than by employers, with contracts for services it is the other way round. A cornucopia of claims by those who have engaged the services of others is met by virtual silence on the part of those others who have provided them. He whose services have been improperly dispensed with has a number of alternative remedies open to him, similar to those available to the employee[3] and also to the agent acting on behalf of a principal.[4] He may sue on the contract for such remuneration or fees as have been agreed and, if suit on the contract is not available, he may sue on a quantum meruit for the value of the services already rendered.[5] With these actions at his command, an action for damages may not prove necessary. When it is brought into play the measure of damages is likely to be the amount that he would have earned from the services had he not been prevented from continuing to act; consequential losses are somewhat difficult to envisage.[6] As with the employee, he will be required to mitigate his damage by seeking alternative remunerative occupation. However, since he has a freer hand in performing the services and may not have to devote his time exclusively to the contract, other services upon which he embarks will not be truly alternative if he could have performed both concurrently, and will therefore not go in mitigation of damage.[7]

## II Breach by the Party Rendering the Services

### (A) In General

34-003 Where the performance of services, whether or not of a professional nature, is such that there is breach of contract and also physical injury or death to the person engaging the services, the damages will be assessed as with other cases of physical injury or death, whether breach of contract or tort, and the chapters on personal injury and fatal injuries are to be referred to.[8] Indeed since practically all of these cases are grounded in negligence, there will generally be concurrent liability in tort and contract. The predominant field is of course that of medical negligence, or clinical negligence as it tends to be called today; it is the physical nature of the damage

---

3 See para.33-004, above.

4 See para.35-002, below.

5 The early, well-known case of *Planché v Colburn* (1831) 8 Bing. 14 which paved the way for quasi-contractual, now unjust enrichment claims in this field is of the nature of a contract for services: the defendant had commissioned articles from the claimant and had then refused to publish them. Factually similar is *Sadler v Reynolds* [2005] EWHC 309 (QB) where the claimant had contracted with the defendant to write the defendant's autobiography but was unable to do so as the defendant in breach of contract had agreed with another to write it; he received a modest amount in damages for the loss of the opportunity to enhance his reputation. Compare the position where the contract is one of employment, at para.33-029, above.

6 The loss in *Sadler v Reynolds* [2005] EWHC 309 (QB) (in preceding note) can be seen as a consequential loss.

7 Whether tax should be deducted from any award of damages is a matter which hovers between the decision in *Lyndale Fashion Manufacturers v Rich* [1973] 1 W.L.R. 73 CA, the equivalent case of an agent suing his principal, and the decision in *Deeny v Gooda Walker (No.2)* [1996] 1 W.L.R. 426 HL, the converse case of breach by the provider of the services. See the general discussion at paras 18-047 to 18-050, above.

8 See Chs 40 and 41, below.

which sets apart such negligence from the main run of professional negligence liability.

The basic principles concerning breach by a party rendering services ought to be the same as the principles concerning breach by a party providing goods. The similarity is most apparent where the services involve the provision of work which needs to be obtained elsewhere due to non-performance. **34-004**

In *Gartell & Son (a firm) v Yeovil Town Football & Athletic Club Ltd*,[9] Gartell & Son carried out work for Yeovil Football and Athletic Club Limited on their athletic pitches. Yeovil refused to pay saying that the work was defective and counterclaimed for the cost of works rendered necessary by the breach of contract. The Court of Appeal upheld the conclusion of the primary judge that the work performed had been so defective that there had been no improvement to the pitch. This meant that Yeovil was discharged from its obligation to pay the contract price. However, the primary judge had awarded Yeovil the entire costs of the performance of the work by another party. The Court of Appeal held that this was an error. The damages are to be assessed by reference to

> "the additional cost to Yeovil of arranging for the work contracted for to be done by someone else, but Gartell cannot be denied payment and then rendered liable for the entire cost of obtaining a substitute performance".

The Court of Appeal explained that the situation is analogous to the case of non-delivery of goods. There, the purchaser's damages are

> "the additional amount he reasonably has to pay for the goods from another supplier. The purchaser does not get the substitute goods for nothing."[10]

Where the injury to the person engaging the services is a pecuniary one resulting from negligent performance of the services by way of wrong advice or wrong information, the heart of the matter is reached.[11] Before turning to particular categories of defendant well documented in the authorities, it may be useful to catalogue a miscellany of other defendants, partly to indicate who has made an occasional appearance in the case law and partly to show that resort has frequently been had to general principles in working out the damages in these cases. And the results in the more familiar areas of professional negligence, which are afforded extended treatment below, can also assist in solving damages issues posed by negligent advice and information given in these other fields of expertise. There is of course the professionally negligent defendant, such as the barrister, who is not in contractual relations with the claimant and who therefore falls outside this chapter.[12] Conversely, the breach of contract for services is not always based on negligence, professional or other.[13] **34-005**

---

[9] [2016] EWCA Civ 62 CA.

[10] [2016] EWCA Civ 62 at [33].

[11] There is in addition, as will be seen, a limited scope for recovery for non-pecuniary loss by way of distress, disappointment and the like.

[12] Claims against barristers with damages issues make an appearance in the chapters dealing with general principles: see *Green v Alexander Johnson* [2005] EWCA Civ 775 CA, in footnote at the end of para.8-138, above (cause and scope of duty), *Luke v Wansbroughs* [2005] P.N.L.R. 2 at 15 at para.10-081, above (loss of earning capacity and loss of a chance) and *Gascoine v Ian Sheridan & Co and Latham* (1994) 5 Med. L.R. 437 at para.10-081, above (loss of a chance).

[13] This was the position in *Transafrik International Ltd v Venus Corp Ltd* (2008) 121 Con L.R. 78

**34-006** Claims by members of Lloyd's against their agents feature prominently. In *Bates v Barrow*,[14] and *Brown v K.M.R. Services*,[15] the issue was remoteness of damage while a whole series of *Deeny v Gooda Walker* claims dealt with matters ranging from certainty of damage to tax and interest on damages.[16] Insurance brokers feature in *Osman v J. Ralph Moss*,[17] where the claimant, prosecuted for uninsured driving, recovered as damages the fine imposed and his costs incurred,[18] in *Arbory Group Ltd v West Craven Insurance Services*,[19] where there was recovery of loss of profits resulting from the broker's failure to provide adequate business interruption insurance, and in the important case of *Aneco Reinsurance Underwriting v Johnson & Higgins*,[20] where there was negligence as to £11 million and liability for £35 million.[21] Against architects there has been recovery for the loss of marketing opportunity because of culpable delay in obtaining planning consent in *Hancock v Tucker*,[22] for expenditure on planning permission, planning consultants and other architects in *John Harris Partnership v Groveworld Ltd* and for losses resulting from the inadequate design of terrace houses in *Earl's Terrace Properties Ltd v Nilsson Design Ltd.*[23] The claim was against financial advisers in *Hale v Guildarch*,[24] trade mark agents in *Halifax Building Society v Urquart-Dykes and* Lord,[25] auctioneers in *Thomson v Christie Manson & Woods Ltd*,[26] computer consultants in *Stephenson Blake (Holdings) Ltd v Streets Heaver Ltd*,[27] and computer system designers in *De Beers UK Ltd v Atos Origin IT Services UK Ltd.*[28] The claim in *Van der Garde v Force India Formula One Team Ltd*,[29] was for failure to provide services to a motor racing driver.

---

where the defendant was an aviation technical consultant holding itself out as a specialist in the repair of damaged aircraft. The damages for the failure adequately to effect the repairs and on time, based on loss of use of the aircraft and the diminution of their value, were calculated simply by resort to general principles.

14 [1995] 1 Lloyd's Rep. 680; at para.8-186, above.

15 [1995] 2 Lloyd's Rep. 513 CA; at para.8-191, above.

16 *Deeny v Gooda Walker* [1995] 1 W.L.R. 1206: certainty, at para.10-039, above; *Deeny v Gooda Walker (No.2)* [1996] 1 W.L.R. 426 HL: tax, at para.18-048, above; *Deeny v Gooda Walker (No.3)* [1996] L.R.L.R. 168: interest, at para.19-138, above.

17 [1970] 1 Lloyd's Rep. 313 CA.

18 See the case at para.21-071, above.

19 [2007] 2 Lloyd's Rep. I.R. 491.

20 [2002] 1 Lloyd's Rep. 157 HL.

21 See too *George Barkes (London) Ltd v LFC (1988) Ltd* [2000] P.N.L.R. 21 (inadequate cover arranged; nominal damages as not causative but, if causative, saving in premium deductible) and *Bollom & Co Ltd v Byas Mosley & Co* [2000] Lloyd's Rep. I.R. 136 (inadequate cover advised, leading to limited recovery from insurers).

22 [1999] Lloyd's Rep. P.N. 814.

23 [2004] B.L.R. 273, at para.31-011, above. See, too, *P. & O. Developments v The Guy's and St Thomas' National Health Service Trust* [1999] B.L.R. 3, and *The Royal Brompton Hospital v Hammond & Lerche* [1999] B.L.R. 162 where the claims were against not only the architect but also the project manager, quantity surveyor and engineers of the professional team acting for a hospital in a building contract.

24 [1999] P.N.L.R. 44: advice on home income plan; no liability.

25 [1997] R.P.C. 55: nominal damages.

26 [2005] P.N.L.R. 38 CA at 713: alleged misdescription of auction lot.

27 [2001] Lloyd's Rep. P.N. 44: purchase of alternative system to that negligently advised.

28 [2010] EWHC 3276 TCC.

29 [2010] EWHC 2373 (QB).

### (B) PARTICULAR CATEGORIES

Apart from the miscellany of persons providing professional and other services catalogued in the previous paragraph, there are particular categories that have given rise to a wealth of litigation on damages. Easily in front is the solicitor; the damages case law there is now huge. Close behind come the surveyor and the valuer. Others fall to be dealt with more briefly.[30] **34-007**

## 1. SOLICITORS

Solicitors can be negligent in a variety of ways as the cases on damages show; indeed cases against solicitors are becoming legion, thereby making it difficult to deal with them in an organised fashion and to categorise them satisfactorily. An attempt is here made to place the decisions into various categories but this is intended purely for the purposes of exposition, and decisions appearing in one category may well prove useful in relation to another category.[31] Moreover, many of the decisions are dealt with again in other parts of this book, as they tend to give rise to general problems on damages, particularly on questions of certainty[32] and of recovery for non-pecuniary loss in contract.[33] **34-008**

### (1) Pecuniary loss

**(a) Negligent advice on points of law** In a number of cases the solicitor has given wrong advice or failed to give correct advice to his client upon a point of law.[34] In *Otter v Church, Adams, Tatham & Co*,[35] a solicitor misinformed his client as to the latter's interest in certain property, thus depriving him of the opportunity of increasing his estate by making the property, which was settled property, his own absolutely. The error was discovered only after his death when it was too late to effect a remedy, and in his personal representatives' successful claim for damages the measure was calculated as the loss to the estate occasioned by the passing of the settled property to the next tenant in tail. Due allowance was made for the possibility that the deceased on being properly advised might not have disentailed but it is thought that no discount was required; the reasons are explained elsewhere.[36] In *Hall v Meyrick*,[37] a solicitor failed to advise or warn his client that her marriage would revoke a will made in her favour by her intended husband. The marriage took place, and two years later the husband died intestate. At first instance **34-009**

---

30 While the great bulk of the case law concerns professional negligence in advising, informing and the like, the separate treatment of bankers and stockbrokers (at paras 34-088 to 34-089 and 34-084 to 34-091, below, respectively) is each in relation not to negligent advice or information but to a somewhat special type of contract and contract breach and the separate treatment of travel agents (at para.34-093, below) is in relation to mismanagement rather than to advice.

31 There may also be claims in tort where there is no contractual relationship between the claimant and the solicitor, as in *Al-Kandari v Brown & Co* [1988] Q.B. 665 CA and *White v Jones* [1995] 2 A.C. 207 CA.

32 See Ch.10, above.

33 See Ch.5, above.

34 Or mixed law and fact.

35 [1953] Ch. 280.

36 See para.10-072, above.

37 [1957] 2 Q.B. 455.

the claimant successfully claimed damages[38] for the loss of the opportunity of taking steps to obtain a new will from her husband after their marriage; but on account of the various contingencies, particularly the contingency of whether her husband would have been willing to execute a new will, she was not awarded the full difference between the value of her interest under a will leaving her everything and the value of her interest on intestacy. In *Griffiths v Evans*,[39] a solicitor failed to advise an injured workman of his right to sue at common law in contradistinction to his right under the Workmen's Compensation Acts, with the result that the claimant workman was now left with a claim against his employers which they disputed on the ground that by inaction the claimant had lost his common law rights, whereas formerly his claim had been undisputed by them. The majority of the Court of Appeal held that the solicitor had not been negligent, since the decisions upon whether the common law right was lost by inaction were conflicting. Denning LJ however dissented on the issue of liability, and there is therefore an assessment of damages from him. In his opinion the claimant could not recover the full amount that he could have claimed against his employers, since allowance must be made for the chance that he might still recover from them. The damages should be assessed

> "by taking into account the inconvenience and expense to which the plaintiff will be put in suing the employers and the risk of failure."[40]

In *Berry v Laytons*,[41] a solicitor failed to advise his client that his rights under EU legislation were far better than his rights under his employment contract. In the absence of this advice the employee came to an agreement with his employer, and in his ensuing claim for damages the solicitor was held liable for the employee's loss of the opportunity of doing a better deal than he had done.

**34-010** Negligent advice on a point of law led to no liability on the part of solicitors in *Haugesund Kommune v Depfa ACS Bank*,[42] because the loss that occurred was held not to fall within the scope of their duty as solicitors. The decision was approved by the Supreme Court in *BPE Solicitors v Hughes-Holland*.[43] In the former, the claimant, an Irish bank, instructed the defendant solicitors to advise on whether two Norwegian municipalities with which it wished to enter into swap contracts had the capacity to do so, the practical effect of such contracts being to achieve a form of borrowing by the municipalities and of lending by the bank. The solicitors advised, wrongly and negligently, that there was capacity, but also advised, correctly, that it was not possible for the bank to obtain execution in any form against the municipalities. The result of the contracts being ultra vires and void was that the apparent contractual obligation to repay the moneys advanced at various times in the future became a genuine restitutionary obligation to repay at once. Over the next years both of the municipalities made disastrous investments with the moneys borrowed so that, having become very short of funds, they declined to make any further payments under the contracts, and the bank claimed against its solicitors damages based on the moneys which it might no longer receive. The Court of Appeal, depart-

38 The Court of Appeal, [1957] 2 Q.B. 455 reversed the decision on other grounds.
39 [1953] 1 W.L.R. 1424 CA.
40 [1953] 1 W.L.R. 1424 CA at 1432.
41 [2009] EWHC 1591 (QB).
42 [2011] 3 All E.R. 655 CA.
43 [2017] UKSC 21 at [42].

ing from the court below, held the solicitors not liable for the bank's loss as it fell outside the scope of their duty. The bank's claim against the municipalities would founder either on the municipalities' impecuniosity or on the municipalities' reliance on their immunity from execution, both of which risks—the credit risk and the no execution risk—lay squarely on the bank and not on the solicitors. As Rix LJ put it, liability of the solicitors for the bank's loss could arise only if the municipalities were prevented from repaying the bank by something that arose from their legal incapacity and from the invalidity of the transactions, and there was nothing to indicate that this was so.[44] Indeed the reality was that an equal, or even more than equal, claim in restitution had risen up in place of the claim in contract.

Finally, as with all loss, negligent advice by solicitors can lead to a reduction in liability if the client fails to mitigate the loss. This occurred in *LSREF III Wight Ltd v Gateley LLP*,[45] where a firm of solicitors negligently omitted from their advice to a lender any reference to the effect of an insolvency forfeiture clause in a lease over a property provided as security. The loss of value was £240,000. But the lessor offered to remove the clause for £150,000. The lender unreasonably refused and therefore failed to mitigate its loss. 34-011

**(b) Negligence in the acquisition of property by purchase** This category of case has produced a vast amount of authority. The question of the proper assessment of damages where the solicitor has been acting for his client in the purchase of property,[46] whether freehold or leasehold, has arisen again and again, making very difficult an orderly presentation of the material; there is no clear way through the wood.[47] The plan is to look first at what is the normal measure, next to consider the principal consequential losses, and then to throw general analysis aside with a listing in some detail of the decisions which remain. 34-012

*(i) Normal measure* In *Lake v Bushby*,[48] the claimant was buying property with a bungalow which he planned to convert into a dwelling-house, and the defendant solicitor failed to pass on to him information that no plans had been approved for the original bungalow so that the local council might require that it should be pulled down. The damages awarded were assessed at the purchase price less the value of the property diminished by the possibility that the local council might require the building to be pulled down. This correct measure is suggested in the judgment, 34-013

---

44 See his whole discussion at [2017] UKSC 21 at [73]–[87].

45 [2016] EWCA Civ 359 CA.

46 *Swindle v Harrison* [1997] 4 All E.R. 705 CA, is an important case of a solicitor handling a purchase for a client, here of a hotel, together with lending her money on the security of her home to complete the purchase, but the claim, which was unsuccessful, was not one for damages but for equitable compensation for breach of fiduciary duty, which is not covered by this text (as to which coverage see para.1-017, above). The somewhat similar case of *Collins v Brebner* [2000] Lloyd's Rep. P.N. 587 CA, also involved equitable compensation.

47 It can at least be said that no damages would fall to be awarded if, the negligence apart, the claimant would still have proceeded with the acquisition and suffered the same loss; the action would fail on account of the negligence not being causative. This is conveniently illustrated by *BDG Roof-Bond Ltd v Douglas* [2000] 1 B.C.L.C. 401; see at 424–426. Solicitors' negligent advice was held by the Court of Appeal, reversing the judge below, to be causative of their client's pursuing of a claim against a third party in *Levicom International Holdings BV v Linklaters* [2010] P.N.L.R. 29 CA at 566, but the question of loss was not addressed and the assessment of damages was remitted. The case therefore need not detain us.

48 [1949] 2 All E.R. 964.

which refers to the contract price; the headnote, however, states the measure to be the value of the property with a "secure" building, less its value as diminished by the possibility of the building being pulled down. This latter measure, though on the particular facts probably giving the same result, is strictly incorrect, for it confuses giving the claimant the benefit of his bargain with the solicitor with giving him the benefit of his bargain with the third person from whom he has bought the property. Since, if he had not been misinformed by the solicitor, he would presumably not have bought the property at all, he cannot claim that the solicitor's breach has caused him to lose the benefit of the property bargain.[49] This error reappears in the similar case of *Pilkington v Wood*,[50] and this time in the ratio decidendi and not merely in a faulty headnote, though again on the particular facts it made no practical difference. The defendant solicitor had acted for the claimant in the purchase of certain property and had negligently failed to discover that the seller's title was defective. The claimant recovered as damages the market value of the property at the time of purchase with a good title less its market value at the same time with a defective title. It was further held that the claimant was under no duty to mitigate this damage by embarking on a complicated and difficult piece of litigation against his seller.[51] On the other hand his claim for consequential losses arising from his inability to resell the property except at a loss, in particular hotel and travelling expenses in connection with his new employment in a different part of the country incurred by reason of his not having the financial resources to buy other accommodation, was held too remote.[52]

**34-014** The error appearing in *Lake v Bushby*,[53] and *Pilkington v Wood*,[54] was exposed, and the correct normal measure of damages clearly established, by *Ford v White & Co*.[55] There the claimants negotiated to purchase a dwelling-house together with an adjoining vacant plot of land which were offered at a price which reflected the existence of a restriction against building on the land. The defendants, their solicitors, negligently stated that the land was not so restricted, and acting on this advice the claimants bought at the offered price. The claimants claimed damages against the defendants measured by the difference between the market value of the land subject to the restriction and the market value of the land free from the restriction, but were held limited to the difference between the market value subject to the restriction and the purchase price paid, which was nil. The court applied the principles laid down in the closely analogous situation arising in the important cases of *Cassa-boglou v Gibb*,[56] and *Salvesen v Rederi Aktiebolaget Nordstjernan*,[57] and explained *Lake v Bushby*,[58] and *Pilkington v Wood*[59] on the lines suggested above

---

[49] The position is, of course, different where the solicitor, instructed to acquire a house for his client, negligently fails to do so. Here the normal measure of damages encompasses the market value less the purchase price of the lost house, the case falling within the principles dealt with at para.35-006, below. *Nash v Phillips* [1974] E.G.D. 57 provides an illustration of such a recovery.

[50] [1953] Ch. 770.

[51] For more detail on the mitigation aspect of the case, see para.9-090, above. On this, see too *Gregory v Shepherds* [2000] P.N.L.R. 44 where, had the claim been successful, issues of failure to mitigate would have arisen; see at 63D–64E.

[52] The remoteness issue is the anterior one: see paras 6-011 and following, above.

[53] [1949] 2 All E.R. 964.

[54] [1953] Ch. 770.

[55] [1964] 1 W.L.R. 885.

[56] (1883) 11 Q.B.D. 797 CA; facts at para.35-008, below.

[57] [1905] A.C. 302; facts at para.35-009, below.

[58] [1949] 2 All E.R. 964.

as being cases where the price paid was taken to be synonymous with the value as represented, whereas in the present case the two substantially diverged.[60]

These principles concerning recovery of the normal loss are, of course, subject to the usual rules including mitigation and remoteness. Hence, in *Bacciottini v Gotelee and Goldsmith (A Firm)*,[61] the normal measure of loss suffered was not recovered when solicitors failed to advise the appellant purchasers of a planning restriction on property they purchased for development. The reason that the normal recovery was denied was because the purchasers mitigated their loss by successfully removing the planning restriction. **34-015**

*(ii) Consequential losses* While the price paid for the purchase of the property less its market value represents the normal measure of damages, the particular circumstances of the case may require that the claimant be awarded damages beyond this by way of recovery for consequential loss.[62] A whole variety of such possible or actual recoveries appears in the authorities. In *Allied Maples v Simmons & Simmons*[63] the claimants purchased the shares in a company which owned business and shop properties which the claimants were eager to acquire. The defendant solicitors acting for the claimants allowed the purchase to proceed without advising the claimants of the dangers of the lack of a warranty from their vendors that no contingent liabilities existed, such a warranty having been removed from the draft contract by the other side's solicitors. It turned out that some of the properties which had been previously owned by the company had potential liabilities on leases which the company had assigned and, subsequent to the acquisition by the claimants, these liabilities materialised and resulted in claims against the company, and hence the claimants, as a consequence of defaults by the assignees of the leases. The case had not proceeded to an assessment of damages because the Court of Appeal was concerned with the anterior issues of causation and loss of a chance[64] but, to the extent that the claimants could overcome these hurdles, it seems clear that they would be entitled to damages in respect of the liabilities which they **34-016**

---

59 [1953] Ch. 770.

60 [1964] 1 W.L.R. 885 at 890–891 (but the correct measure may not have been applied in *Collard v Saunders* [1971] C.L.Y. 11161). On the other hand, where the solicitor's negligence led to the claimant's failure to acquire land, the sellers having cancelled the contract, the claimant was held entitled in *Stinchcombe v Addison* (1971) 115 S.J. 368 to the price at which the land was now available to him less the price he would have had to pay under the cancelled contract. The position in this case approached that referred to at para.34-013, second footnote, above; see, too, *Wapshott v Davis Donovan & Co* [1996] P.N.L.R. 361 CA, at para.34-029, last footnote but one, below. While it was agreed in *Cottingham v Attey Bower & Jones* [2000] Lloyd's Rep. P.N. 591 that the damages were to be measured by the costs of remedying the defects in the property acquired (limited, however, to defects additional to ones of which the purchasers had already been apprised by their surveyor), it seems that these costs were taken to represent the difference between the price paid for the property and the value of the property in its actual condition: see at 602, col.1.

61 [2016] EWCA Civ 170 CA.

62 This was not the case in *Jenmain Builders Ltd v Steed & Steed* [2000] Lloyd's Rep. P.N. 549 CA, where the solicitor's negligence had lost the claimant property developers the opportunity to purchase a property. Their damages were held to be limited to the difference between the market value of the property and the price at which they could have bought, which on the evidence available was nil, and did not include the development profit that they would have made. As Chadwick LJ pointed out (at 555, col.1), the profit potential of the property is an element that a properly informed market will take into account in fixing the market value and, accordingly, the purchase price on offer.

63 [1995] 1 W.L.R. 1602 CA.

64 See the case at paras 10-057 and following, above.

had been compelled to satisfy upon the assigned leases. In *Hayes v James and Charles Dodd*,[65] the claimant husband and wife bought, with the assistance of a bank loan, a leasehold workshop and yard for their motor repair business, together with a freehold maisonette which was part of the property, having been told, wrongly, by their solicitor that there was a right of access over land at the rear of the property. Such access was vital to the success of the claimants' business, there being very restricted access at the front, and without it the business eventually failed and was closed down. The claimants, having attempted unsuccessfully to sell the property as a single unit, eventually sold the maisonette and a year later the workshop and plant. They were held entitled to recover damages on the basis of the capital expenditure thrown away on the purchase of the business together with the expenses incurred, of which the rent and the bank loan interest loomed largest, credit being given for the increase in value of the maisonette before it was sold; no failure to mitigate because of the time taken by the claimants to sell was found. Factually similar is *Scott v Kennedys and Vertex Law*.[66] A husband and wife bought a guest house and its associated business which they would not have bought but for their solicitor's negligent failure to inform them that the planning permission which had been given required the guest house and its adjoining, attached property to be in the same occupation. Vos J in a full judgment considered many items of the claimed damages, this taking him to general principles involving remoteness, foreseeability and contemplation of the parties, and ended up awarding the claimants, who had eventually sold the property, their capital loss, thereby following and applying the earlier decision in *Hayes v Dodd*.

34-017 In *Buckley v Lane Herdman & Co*,[67] where the claimants, husband and wife, were buying a new home and their solicitors negligently exchanged contracts for the sale of the old home before they had exchanged contracts for the new in breach of an express term that the two transactions must be simultaneous in order to protect the claimants, with the result that, after proceedings for specific performance had been brought against them in respect of the old home, they were forced to buy the only other house available, damages were awarded for expenses in finding the alternative house and making it habitable, for loss of earnings and for costs incurred in the specific performance proceedings.[68] In *Gregory v Shepherds*,[69] and again in *Patel v Daybells*,[70] the measure of damages was in issue where a property, respectively an apartment abroad and a sports club, was purchased subject to a charge which was unknown because the defendant solicitors had failed to discover it. In neither case would damages assessed at the diminution in value of the property have availed the claimants because, in each case, the price at which the property was eventually sold after the charge had been removed appears to have been no less than the amount at which the claimants could have sold earlier had the property been unencumbered from the start. Nevertheless the claimants in *Gregory* were held entitled to recovery of the costs incurred in attempting to procure the removal of the charge and interest upon the sale price of the apartment from the time they could have sold in the

65 [1990] 2 All E.R. 815 CA.

66 [2011] EWHC 3808 Ch.

67 [1977] C.L.Y. 3143.

68 The inclusion of the expense of a removal van is, however, dubious, as this expense would have been incurred in any event.

69 [2000] Lloyd's Rep. P.N. 724 CA.

70 [2000] Lloyd's Rep. P.N. 844.

absence of the charge until the time of actual sale, and the claimants in *Patel* would have been entitled, had they succeeded on liability, to damages compensating them for the losses occasioned by the delay in selling the sports club, principally in respect of a liability on a loan taken out to fund the purchase. In *Joyce v Bowman Law Ltd*,[71] the claimant who was not a developer, through the negligence of a licensed conveyancer advising him on the purchase of a dilapidated cottage, failed to secure a buyer's option over adjacent land. The profit he would have made had he been able to develop the whole property to its fullest was allowed.[72]

*Ladenbau (UK) v Crawley & de Reya*[73] is a complex case which further supports recovery for consequential loss. There the defendants' failure to discover an incumbrance over land the claimants were buying caused them not a loss of profit on a resale but a delay in the receipt of that profit while the incumbrance on the title was being removed, for which delay damages were awarded. The reasoning which would entitle the court to reach this result is not however immediately clear—while *Ford v White*[74] appears to have been cited in argument[75] no authorities were referred to in the short part of Mocatta J's judgment which dealt with the issue of damages,[76] save the classic ones on remoteness directed to the question of whether or not the defendants were to be taken to have had a resale in contemplation—and the facts, and in particular the timescale of events, need to be examined with some care. In August 1972 the claimants retained the defendants, a firm of solicitors, to act for them in the purchase of a site of several acres, intending, as they informed the defendants, to build a factory for their own use and to develop and dispose of the rest. In October the defendants made the usual inquiries before contract and a local land charges register search, but they failed to requisition an official search of the register of common land, an omission which was held to be negligent. The contract of sale between the claimants and their sellers was signed in November; completion took place in May 1973. Shortly before completion, and also in May 1973, the claimants had negotiated a resale at a very handsome profit; completion of this sale to the sub-purchasers was due to take place in September 1973. However, a search of the register of common land requisitioned by the sub-purchasers' solicitors elicited, in August 1973, a response from the local authority that part of the site had been registered on the application of a company which had included it in its application in error. This put paid to the completion intended for September. Fortunately, the registering company, recognising that the registration of the site had taken place by mistake, was prepared to assist in securing the necessary amendment to the register but the local authority took time to effect it so that not until April 1974 were the sub-purchasers' solicitors able to verify that the register had been cleared of the offending entry, after which in May 1974 completion of the sub-sale took place. Thus had the defendants not been negligent they would have discovered the entry in the register at much the same time as they made their other inquiries, namely in October 1972, but this would not have deflected the claimants from seeking to purchase the site as they would have been negotiating for an amendment of the register. Moreover, since in the event only eight months **34-018**

---

71 [2010] EWHC 251 Ch.

72 Although heavily discounted on loss of a chance principles: see the case at para.10-104, above.

73 [1978] 1 W.L.R. 266.

74 [1964] 1 W.L.R. 885.

75 This appears from the report at [1978] 1 All E.R. 682; see at 684j.

76 [1978] 1 W.L.R. 266 at 289B–H.

elapsed between the discovery of the entry on the register in August 1973 and the register's amendment and its verification in April 1974, there would have been ample time for the defendants, with the aid of the registering company, to have secured the necessary amendment so as not to put in jeopardy the completion of the sub-sale 11 months later in September 1973. It is therefore correct to say that the loss to the claimants caused by the delayed receipt of their profits was directly attributable to the defendants' negligence.[77]

**34-019** *(iii) Further illustrative decisions* Many decisions remain after these above which have been analysed into cases showing the normal measure of damages and those showing consequential losses. With these the best that can be done is to set them out, and in some detail, as they may prove helpful in the consideration of other fact situations that may arise.

**34-020** *Stanley K. Oates v Anthony Pitman & Co*[78] is a valuable case dealing with the various approaches to damages in this type of case. The solicitor defendant, acting for the claimants in the purchase of a property which they were to use both as a home and as a business of holiday lettings, failed to discover that the planning permission attaching to the property did not entitle it to be used for holiday lettings. The claimants embarked on a costly programme of refurbishment and used the property for holiday lettings for a time before the lack of planning permission was discovered. They then applied for planning permission retrospectively but because the permission granted was of a limited nature and required the expenditure of substantial sums, which they could not afford, to comply with fire and building regulations they sold the property. They were successful in recovering for the diminution in the value of the property and the cost of applying for planning permission but unsuccessful in their claim for loss of profits. As to the profits, these could not have been earned had the transaction not been entered into, and it would not have been entered into had the solicitor not been negligent. As to the diminution in value, it was agreed that this represented the correct measure, but the court pointed out that the diminution in value rule could not be applied indiscriminately. In a claim against a solicitor for negligence, it was said, the damages could be approached in at least three possible ways: first, the simple one where there was evidence as to the market value of comparable properties; secondly, the more difficult one where the property was unusual or to be used for a particular purpose or where time had elapsed before the discovery of the defects, which was the right approach for the present case; and thirdly, the cost of extrication from the transaction, a method inappropriate for the present case.

**34-021** Again various approaches to damages were in play in *Dent v Davis Blank Furniss*,[79] where it turned out that the property purchased by the claimants at auction was registered as common land, the defendant solicitor having failed to carry out a search of the commons register, and where the claimants had expended a great deal in improving the property, an expenditure which was quite unmatched by any commensurate increase in the property's value. The claimants' contention that they were entitled to this expenditure less the value of the land as improved, on the basis

[77] Compare the discussion of *Perry v Sidney Phillips & Son* [1982] 1 W.L.R. 1297 CA (surveyors' negligence), at para.34-059, below. And see *County Personnel (Employment Agency) v Alan R. Pulver & Co* [1987] 1 W.L.R. 916 CA, at para.34-029, below.

[78] [1998] P.N.L.R. 683 CA.

[79] [2001] Lloyd's Rep. P.N. 534.

that otherwise they would not have entered into the transaction and should be entitled to the cost of extricating themselves from it, was rejected. There was no suggestion that the claimants wished to extricate themselves from the transaction for they remained living at the property, and in any event to compensate them for this element of improvement of the property was not within the scope of the defendants' duty of care. The defendants' contention that the damages should be assessed by reference to the diminution in the value of the property assessed at the date of the claimants' purchase—the price paid by the claimants at the auction was held to have been greater than the property's value—was also rejected. Diminution in value was indeed awarded but, since to have taken it at the date of breach would have under-compensated the claimants because in ignorance of the common land registration they had expended money on the property that they would not otherwise have done, the appropriate date to take for the application of the diminution in value rule was the date, some five years later, when the claimants had achieved deregistration of sufficient of the property for their purposes.

In *Havenledge Ltd v Graeme John & Partners*,[80] the defendant solicitor, engaged by the claimants when purchasing a derelict property for renovation and then operation as a nursing home, failed to discover that mining took place underneath the property. Not until after it had been renovated and the nursing home opened was the mining discovered after the appearance of cracks in the property. Continuing repair works followed which adversely affected the business and it had eventually to be closed down. Damages would have been nominal if diminution in value was taken as the measure since the price paid was no greater than the value of the property at the time of purchase. However, it was held that the claimants should be entitled to claim both their wasted expenditure in renovation and their lost profits. This was not an inconsistent recovery because the lost profits for which the damages were obtained were not those of the nursing home that eventually failed but of the notional nursing home that the claimants would have started elsewhere had they been properly advised by the defendant.[81] Had there been no negligence there would have been no wasted outlays and also profits on another site. **34-022**

In *Griffiths v Last Cawthra Feather*,[82] the defendant firm of solicitors had acted for the claimants in the purchase of a house and had failed to advise them that there was a water culvert under the garden which the owner was under a statutory liability to maintain and repair. The judge found that, had the purchasers been told of the culvert, they would not have proceeded with the purchase. Over the 13 years which had elapsed to trial there had been no need to do any work on the culvert, but it was held that the existence of the obligation had resulted in a substantial diminution in the value of the property. The amount of that diminution, calculated as at the date of the breach of contract rather than at the date of trial, was awarded as damages. **34-023**

A similar result to that in *Havenledge*[83] was reached in *Keydon Estate Ltd v Eversheds LLP*.[84] The claimant, a small commercial investment company, was minded to acquire the freehold reversion of an office building with the object, **34-024**

---

80 [2000] P.N.L.R. 804.

81 See [2000] P.N.L.R. 804 at 817C–D. Contrast *East v Maurer* [1991] 1 W.L.R. 461 CA, at para.49-031, below.

82 [2002] P.N.L.R. 27 at 612.

83 See para.34-022, above.

84 [2005] P.N.L.R. 40 at 817.

known to its solicitors who were the defendants, of obtaining a source of income by way of rents from the lessee of the property, a substantial tenant. However, the lessee had created a sub-lease and the claimant wished to be assured that the lessee would nonetheless remain liable on the covenants in the lease. The defendants' assurance that this would be so was negligent since the sub-lease had operated as an assignment releasing the lessee as assignee from liability on the covenants. The sub-lessee soon after went into administration, the lessee refused to pay the rents, and the claimant's income stream dried up. The trial judge concluded that, had the claimant been correctly advised, it would not have proceeded with the purchase but would have spent the money thereby released in acquiring an equivalent property generating a similar rental income stream, there being held to be other such properties available on the market. It was emphasised that the loss for which the damages were to be awarded was not the anticipated loss of the income stream from the freehold reversion bought, but the loss of a similar stream from the alternative property that would have been bought in the absence of the defendants' negligent advice.[85] Accordingly, the claimant's damages amounted to the difference between the position it would have been in had it bought an alternative property and its current position, between the likely result of such a purchase and what in fact had transpired.[86]

**34-025** In *Powell v Whitman Breed Abbot & Morgan*[87] the defendant solicitors, acting for the claimant in the purchase of the leasehold of a town house which the claimant planned to renovate and resell profitably, were asked to advise her whether it would impede the resale of the house if she took the leasehold interest not in her own name but in that of a company. Their advice was held to be wrong in that it would take considerably longer to sell a company lease than an individual lease. After considering at length a myriad of figures and calculations submitted by the parties directed at ascertaining the proper measure of damages,[88] the trial judge eventually held that the award should amount to six per cent of the value at the time of the claimant's purchase as a rough estimate of the loss by having the resale delayed.[89] It is however for consideration whether, for this calculation, the value should be rather at the date when the resale would have taken place had the lease been in the claimant's own name.

**34-026** *Greymalkin Ltd v Copleys*[90] involved the purchase of a property where the solicitor had been negligent in failing to discover that the property was encumbered but the judgment in the case is found to be somewhat convoluted and not particularly helpful on the damages issues. The purchase was by a property development company of a decrepit hotel with the intention of converting it into flats but, because the property was subject to charges not overreached by the sale and thus creating a cloud on the title, charges which the defendant solicitor had negligently failed to uncover, the planned conversion could not come to fruition. The claimant, after spending substantial sums in preserving and repairing the property, eventually sold it at a substantial loss and claimed, under a whole series of heads, an amount in excess of half a million pounds. In this milieu the trial judge set out the principles

85 [2005] P.N.L.R. 40 at [31].
86 [2005] P.N.L.R. 40 at [30].
87 [2005] P.N.L.R. 1 at 1.
88 [2005] P.N.L.R. 1 at [36]–[58].
89 [2005] P.N.L.R. 1 at [59]–[60].
90 [2004] P.N.L.R. 44 at 901.

of damages which he purported to apply in somewhat confusing detail, after having set out, also in detail, the complex rival contentions of claimant and defendant on damages, and then sought to apply these principles so as to end up with awarding what he called the prima facie measure of damages, which he stated as the difference at the time of purchase between the property's value without, and its value with, the cloud on title, and which amounted to under £50,000, on the basis that "there is no alternative basis of assessment that can do justice in this case".[91] He was undoubtedly right to reject most of the myriad and dubious heads of loss put forward by the claimant[92]; and in particular to hold that the case was not a suitable one for awarding either the costs of remedying the defects as the charges clouding the title had been met, by the insurers of another solicitor, without any cost to the claimant, or the costs of extrication as the ultimate sale of the property was not effected by way of extrication from the situation in which the claimant found itself.[93] But it is difficult to see why a claim for the claimant's wasted expenditure, subject here to the problems of proof, up until the time of knowledge of the cloud on title should not have been allowed. Moreover, what does not appear to have been noticed is that, as the claimant had bought at a price which was nearly twice the market value of the property with an unencumbered title and as the judge held that the claimant would not have bought at all had the cloud on title been revealed by the defendant,[94] the true measure of damages that could be claimed was this purchase price less the value with the cloud on title,[95] a much higher sum, at over £150,000, than was awarded to the claimant.[96]

**(c) Negligence in the acquisition of property by lease** Clients suing solicitors for negligence in relation to the leasing of property to them have produced far fewer cases on damages than have solicitor clients suing over the sale of property to them. In *Sykes v Midland Bank Executor and Trustee Co*,[97] the defendant solicitors, in advising the claimant firm of architects and surveyors in relation to an underlease of part of a building in central London which the claimants were proposing to take for the expansion of their business from Hull, negligently failed to explain to the claimants that, while under the provisions of the underlease their lessor could not arbitrarily withhold consent to their assigning or subletting, the superior lessors could. The defendant solicitors were also aware that the claimants might wish to assign or sublet in the future. In the event, the superior lessors did refuse consent to a later proposed subletting, but the claimants were awarded only nominal damages in their action against the solicitors, not indeed because the Court of Appeal was unprepared to award damages for loss of the opportunity to sublet but because the claimants had failed to establish that, had they been properly advised, they would probably not have entered into the underlease or at least not on the terms on which they did.[98] **34-027**

---

91 [2004] P.N.L.R. 44 at [86].
92 [2004] P.N.L.R. 44 at [98].
93 [2004] P.N.L.R. 44 at [86].
94 [2004] P.N.L.R. 44 at [85].
95 For this see paras 34-013 and 34-014, above.
96 No such point appears to have been taken on the appeal, which was dismissed: [2005] P.N.L.R. 20 CA at 334.
97 [1971] 1 Q.B. 113 CA.
98 That it was not a loss of chance case but one requiring proof on the balance of probabilities is explained at para.10-059, above.

**34-028** Failure of a solicitor to apply for a renewed tenancy for his client has given rise to claims. Again in *Clark v Kirby-Smith*,[99] only nominal damages were awarded. There the claimant tenants had instructed the defendant, their solicitor, to apply for a new tenancy, their lessor having served a notice upon them under the Landlord and Tenant Act 1954 that he would not oppose an application by them for the grant of a new tenancy. The defendant failed to take the necessary steps and the claimants claimed damages (1) for the loss of the asset represented by a new lease granted under the Landlord and Tenant Act 1954 and (2) for the settlement, and the costs of settlement, of a claim for dilapidations which the claimants had to meet in consequence of their failure to apply for a new lease. The court held as to (1) that only nominal damages could be awarded as it was impossible to say what value, if any, the new lease which might be granted would have had, and as to (2) that the sums claimed for dilapidations and costs resulted from the claimants' own breach of covenant and not from the defendant's negligence. On the other hand, the claimant in *Aran Caterers Ltd v Stepien Lake Gilbert & Paling*[100] succeeded in obtaining damages. As a result of the solicitor's failure to apply for the grant of a new tenancy of business premises, the lessee had to negotiate a less favourable and less secure lease of the premises and later, because of the insecurity, acquired a leasehold in another property in a much less favourable position for business. He was awarded compensation for disturbance and for lost profits of his business.

**34-029** Another useful decision is *County Personnel (Employment Agency) v Alan R. Pulver & Co*.[101] The defendant solicitors, in negotiating for the claimants a sub-lease of two ground floor rooms for their business use, negligently failed to advise the claimants of a particularly onerous rent review clause in the sub-lease. When the claimants later attempted to sell the underlease and business the sale fell through partly because of the rent review clause, and the claimants then surrendered the underlease on the payment by them of a substantial sum. While the case was remitted to the judge below for the assessment of damages, the Court of Appeal indicated the principles to be applied, holding that the sum paid by the claimants to extricate themselves from the unfavourable sub-lease would represent a fair assessment of their recoverable loss unless the payment was shown to be unreasonable,[102] but that there would be no entitlement to claim for the loss on the abortive sale because on the judge's findings the claimants would not have entered into the sub-lease at all if they had been properly advised.[103] The court was particularly concerned to point out that the measure of damages proposed by the defendants of price paid less actual value, which is now recognised as the normal measure where the acquisition of the freehold is concerned,[104] should not be mechanistically applied.[105] It was not always

---

[99] [1964] Ch. 506.

[100] [2002] 1 E.G.L.R. 69.

[101] [1987] 1 W.L.R. 916 CA.

[102] See [1987] 1 W.L.R. 916 CA at 926C, and generally Bingham LJ's lengthy formulation of the principles to be applied at 925C–927A.

[103] It would have been different if the claimants could have negotiated the sublease without the onerous clause: see [1987] 1 W.L.R. 916 CA at 926E.

[104] See paras 34-013 and 34-014, above.

[105] [1987] 1 W.L.R. 916 CA at 926A, per Bingham LJ. It was argued unsuccessfully in *Wapshott v Davis Donovan* [1996] P.N.L.R. 361 CA, a case of purchase rather than lease by the claimant, that what was said in the *County Personnel* case justified a departure in *Wapshott* from the normal measure. The case is complex and confusing; it is submitted that the rejection of the contention that values at a date later than the breach should there have been taken is unconvincing.

appropriate and was certainly inappropriate, indeed artificial, here where the claimants were acquiring an asset, an underlease at a market rent, which would have no capital value for them.[106]

There was much the same result as in the *County Personnel* case in *Funnell v Adams & Remer*,[107] which again had an onerous rent review clause at its centre, but the parties were there in agreement that the appropriate measure of damages was not the normal measure but the costs of extrication[108]; the argument turned on issues of valuation and causation. The negligence of the defendant solicitors, instructed by the claimant tree surgeons and landscape gardeners to negotiate a 25-year lease of premises to which they wished to move their expanding business, consisted of a failure to advise the claimants on the effect that a change made to the lease would have on the rent review clause. Under a clause in the lease as initially drafted, the claimants were obliged to carry out certain works of improvement to the premises. During the negotiations the claimants indicated that they wished to have permission from the lessor to carry out substantial further works for their own benefit and to enhance their business. Unfortunately the lease was changed to provide for this by adding the further works to the clause dealing with the works required by the lessor, with the result that not only were the claimants now obliged to carry out the further works but, by their being so obliged, the lessor became entitled to take the further works into account when it came to rent review. This meant that the claimants would be both paying for the further works and paying rent for them. When, shortly before the first of the five-year rent reviews was due, this position was revealed to the claimants, they realised that they could not afford to continue in the premises at what would be the higher rent, and therefore assigned the lease and moved out. In these circumstances the appropriate measure of damages was 34-030

> "the cost of extrication from the predicament and coupled with costs wasted by embarking on a venture which had to be aborted at an early stage."[109]

**(d) Negligence in the disposition of property by sale** The case of the negligent solicitor concerned in selling property owned by his client presents a paucity of authority on damages in contrast to the weight of authority which has overwhelmed the converse case of the negligent solicitor purchasing property for his client.[110] There is *Ramsey v Owen White & Catlin*,[111] where little of value can be culled from either counsel's argument or court's judgment as reported. There is *Stovold v Barlows*,[112] where the vendor claimed that he lost a sale through his solicitor's delay in sending the intending purchaser the deeds, and damages were awarded for the loss of this chance.[113] There is *Johnson v Bingley Dyson & Finney*,[114] where the solicitor had failed to advise the obtaining of a proper valuation of the property before selling, and the true value of the property at the date of sale less the sum in 34-031

106 [1987] 1 W.L.R. 916 CA at 926B, 927H–928A.
107 [2008] B.L.R. 206.
108 See [2008] B.L.R. 206 at [16] and [17].
109 [2008] B.L.R. 206 at [16].
110 See paras 34-012 to 34-026, above.
111 (1976) 241 E.G. 611.
112 [1996] P.N.L.R. 91 CA.
113 See the case at para.10-070, last footnote, above.
114 [1997] P.N.L.R. 392.

fact realised by the sale was taken as the appropriate measure of damages. There is *Matlaszek v Bloom Camillin*,[115] where the solicitor negligently failed to advise of the risks to the sellers of a company business of relying on the credit of the purchaser and of the guarantor. The damages were assessed as the value of the company with which the sellers would not have parted had they been properly advised, and in coming to a value the net asset basis was rejected in favour of average annual earnings multiplied by an appropriate price earnings ratio. And there is *Tom Hoskins Plc v EMW Law*,[116] where damages were allowed for a company's trading losses which had not been avoided by reason of the negligent handling by its solicitor of the sale of its businesses.

34-032 (e) **Rights to property lost by negligence** In quite a number of cases the negligence of the solicitor has consisted in a failure to take steps, timeously or otherwise, to protect the property rights of his client and has led to some substantial awards.[117] In *Hodge v Clifford Cowling & Co*,[118] and again in *Ricci v Masons*,[119] in *Matlock Green Garage Ltd v Potter Brooke-Taylor & Wildgoose*[120] and in *Nahome v Last Cawthra Feather Solicitors*,[121] it was the claimant lessee's right to apply for a new tenancy that was lost. This was because the application was not made within the statutory time limit or, in the *Nahome* case, was not made in proper form. In *Ricci* the claimant, who ran the business of a restaurant on the premises, had succeeded in agreeing a new but, of course, less satisfactory tenancy with the landlord. Nevertheless he had lost the opportunity, which he had been minded to take, of selling the restaurant together with the lease. It was held that to take a date later than the date of breach for the assessment would be an injustice to the claimant; he recovered in damages, inter alia, the difference between the value of the lease he would and should have acquired and the value of the one that he was able to negotiate with loss of statutory protection. In *Nahome* the claimants maintained that their jewellery business which they ran from the leasehold premises would have developed into a highly successful, largely internet-based, business, and claimed the very large profits they allegedly would have made had the business not had to close down. The trial judge came to the somewhat uncertain conclusion that the appropriate way to compensate the claimants was by reference to the value of the business of which they had been deprived[122] and held profits from the internet business to be too remote as the defendants had not been made aware either of its existence or of its dependence on the leasehold premises.[123] In *Murray v Lloyd*,[124] the claimant's right to apply for a statutory tenancy was again lost but for a rather different reason. The loss of the opportunity for the claimant, who had purchased a leasehold property, to acquire a statutory tenancy was as a result of her solicitor's negligence

---

115 [2004] P.N.L.R. 17 at 309.

116 [2010] EWHC 479 Ch.

117 *Clark v Kirby-Smith* [1964] Ch. 506, at para.34-028, above can also be put into this category but the award there was of nominal damages only.

118 [1990] 2 E.G.L.R. 89 CA.

119 [1993] 2 E.G.L.R. 159.

120 [2000] Lloyds's Rep. P.N. 925.

121 [2010] EWHC 76 Ch.

122 [2010] EWHC 76 Ch at [71]; after a lengthy analysis in which many of the cases in the text of this work were cited.

123 See [2010] EWHC 76 Ch at [91] and following.

124 [1989] 1 W.L.R. 1060.

in allowing her to take the lease in the name of an offshore company for tax purposes, so that an assignment of the leasehold interest to her required the landlord's consent which was refused. In these circumstances she was held entitled to damages assessed by reference to what it would cost her to acquire what she had lost, that is to the cost of acquiring similar rights of occupation on similar terms in similar alternative accommodation. This was assessed at the amount by which the effect of a lease on terms similar to those which the claimant would have enjoyed as a statutory tenant would depreciate the value of a similar freehold property.[125] In *Snipper v Enever Freeman & Co*,[126] the claimant lessee lost her enfranchisement rights to purchase the freehold. She nevertheless achieved an extension to her lease four years later and it was held that, while this was a benefit to be taken into account, it was only fair that the values of the enfranchisement right lost and of the extended lease gained should be taken as at the same date and that the date should be that of the lease extension. In *Layzell v Smith Morton & Long*,[127] the claimant lost his succession rights on the death of his father to the farm on which they had worked. The assessment of the damages was based upon the cost of his acquiring the freehold of a similar farm and then selling that freehold and entering into a tenancy agreement similar to the one he had lost. There was held to be no significant chance that the claimant would have been held ineligible or unsuitable to succeed his father to the farm and therefore no discount fell to be made from these damages. These are multifarious cases. Not only do they need to be scrutinised for the detail and the reason of the recovery allowed in each but also it is difficult to say that they present any clear common principle other than the grand overriding one of the claimant being put in the position he would have been in had no breach of contract occurred. Moreover, factual changes can easily change the damages to be awarded; in particular, there may be relevance in identifying the time when the claimant became aware of his loss of rights.[128]

**(f) Negligent conduct of litigation** Where the solicitor fails to defend, or to defend properly, an action brought against his client so that a verdict goes against his client, the damages will be the whole amount for which the client is made liable in the lost suit where he had a clear defence to it: this is illustrated by the old case of *Hoby v Built*.[129] Even if the defence succeeds but the solicitor has failed to obtain adequate security for his client's costs, he can be liable, as in *Martin Boston & Co v Roberts*,[130] for the irrecoverable costs. If the defence is not so certain, the court must estimate the chance of its succeeding and assess damages on this basis.[131] *Cook v Swinfen*,[132] perhaps comes nearest to illustrating this position. There the defendant solicitor's negligent defence of the divorce proceedings in which the now claimant was respondent resulted in her being adjudicated the guilty party and **34-033**

---

125 This came to £115,000; the lease had been purchased, some eight years earlier, for £50,000. It may be that a discount should have been made to take into account the seven years of the lease which remained to run at the time of judgment.

126 [1991] 2 E.G.L.R. 270.

127 [1992] 1 E.G.L.R. 169.

128 See the discussion in the analogous context of surveyors and valuers at para.34-059, below.

129 (1832) 3 B. & Ad. 350.

130 [1996] P.N.L.R. 45 CA; see the case at para.10-075, above.

131 Compare at para.34-034, below, the cases where it is the chance of a claimant's succeeding that must be assessed.

132 [1967] 1 W.L.R. 457 CA.

obtaining maintenance neither for herself nor for her son, and damages were awarded for loss of the chance of obtaining not only such maintenance but also a more favourable outcome of the divorce suit. *Channon v Lindley Johnstone*,[133] was another claim, here by the husband, for the solicitor's negligent defence of divorce proceedings. Again, a better outcome of the proceedings for the claimant would have resulted had the defence been competently handled, the deficiencies in the material put before the judge hearing the divorce proceedings having led him wrongly to assume a large disparity of income between the parties. The award for the loss of a chance of achieving the better outcome was increased by the Court of Appeal.[134] Where, of course, no diligence could have been effectual, as where the client had no ground of defence, then the client will have lost nothing but will still be entitled to nominal damages for the breach of contract.[135] So, too, only nominal damages were awarded to the claimant in *Groom v Crocker*,[136] where he had lost nothing because the damages awarded against him in the earlier action had been paid by his insurance company.

**34-034** Where, conversely, the solicitor is employed to bring an action which is lost by his negligence, he may on similar principles be liable in damages to the full amount that his client would have recovered from the person sued. Again, at the other end of the scale, if the client had no ground of action, he will have lost nothing and be entitled only to nominal damages.[137] The most common situation, however, is where it is uncertain whether the client's action, if properly pursued, would or would not have succeeded, a situation which, starting with *Kitchen v Royal Air Force Association*,[138] has come to be illustrated by suits against solicitors for negligently allowing potential actions in respect of personal injury or wrongful death to become statute-barred. Here the damages are to be based upon the value of the loss of the chance of success in the personal injury or wrongful death claim; the cases are dealt with in the discussion of the problem of certainty of damage and need not be repeated here.[139]

**34-035** Solicitors employed to bring an action may also be liable for damage to their client which falls short of the loss of the action itself. If the amount recovered is less than it would have been had the claim been properly handled, the solicitor will be liable for the shortfall. Thus in *Dickinson v Jones Alexander & Co*,[140] where a solicitor, conducting proceedings for divorce for a wife, settled her claim for a grossly inadequate amount, the damages were held to be the difference between the financial provision the claimant would have obtained from a proper award and what she did obtain, the risk being negligible that she would have obtained less than the proper award had her claim proceeded without settlement. In *Pearson v Sanders*

133 [2002] P.N.L.R. 41 CA at 884.

134 From £25,000 to £35,000.

135 Recognised in *Godefroy v Jay* (1831) 7 Bing. 413.

136 [1939] 1 K.B. 194 CA. At one time the court tended to grant a new trial when a defendant lost an action through his solicitor's negligence but this has not been the practice for very many years.

137 In *Aitcheson v Madock* (1793) 1 Peake 218 he was non-suited in such circumstances. More up-to-date illustrations are *Hatswell v Goldbergs* [2002] Lloyd's Rep. P.N. 359 CA, where the claimant's action for medical negligence, which the defendant solicitor allowed to become statute-barred, would have had no real chance of success, and *Mount v Barker Austin* [1998] P.N.L.R. 493 CA, where the claimant, being bound to fail in his original action, was held entitled to no recovery from the solicitor in respect of it.

138 [1958] 1 W.L.R. 563 CA.

139 See para.10-076, above.

140 [1993] 2 F.L.R. 321.

*Witherspoon*,[141] the action was not lost but the solicitor pursued the claim with such little vigour that the judgment eventually obtained was valueless by reason of supervening insolvency; the Court of Appeal engaged in a detailed assessment of what the claimant would have gained from a timeous judgment.[142] In *McGrath v Kiely and Powell*,[143] the claimant was awarded against her solicitor[144] the whole of the extra damages she would have obtained in her successful personal injury claim had the full extent of her injuries been revealed to the court. Where the solicitor compromises a suit against his client's instructions, he will be liable in respect of the amount by which the compromise was too low, but if the compromise was in the client's favour he will get only nominal damages; these were the holdings, respectively, in the two old cases of *Butler v Knight*,[145] and *Fray v Voules*.[146] So too the solicitor will be liable where he settles his client's claim at an undervalue; this was the position, as alleged, in *Luke v Wansbroughs*,[147] and the position, as clearly established, in *Hickman v Blake Lapthorn*.[148] The damages will run to the extent of the undervalue, but subject to a discount where, as in *Hickman*, there is uncertainty as to whether the claimant would have succeeded at trial. A somewhat different type of solicitor's negligence appeared in another old case, *Hawkins v Harwood*.[149] This consisted in not properly instructing counsel for the claimant and not attending court, so that the claimant's counsel was obliged to withdraw the record. The solicitor was liable for the claimant's expenses needlessly thrown away; this included the expense of conveying the witnesses to the trial. Moving closer to the present day, there is *Maden v Clifford Coppock & Carter*[150] where the solicitor's negligence consisted in giving the wrong advice to his client on the costs consequences of a claim being brought against the client with the result that the client fought the case unsuccessfully whereas, with the right costs advice, he would have settled on favourable terms. The damages were based on the difference between the client's position after the unsuccessful outcome of the litigation and his position as it would have been had he settled, although subject to discounting the award for the possibility that the settlement might not have come about.[151]

Differences have arisen over the question whether it is proper for the court to take into account events that have occurred between the time the claim negligently conducted by the solicitor would have been heard and the often much later time that the claim against the solicitor is heard so as to permit either an increase or a decrease on the damages to be awarded. The difficulties have been thrice considered **34-036**

---

141 [2000] P.N.L.R. 110 CA.

142 The court's valuation of the lost chance is at para.10-097, above.

143 [1965] I.R. 497.

144 And her doctor.

145 (1867) L.R. 2 Ex. 109.

146 (1859) 1 E. & E. 839.

147 [2005] P.N.L.R. 2 at 15.

148 [2006] P.N.L.R. 20 at 371.

149 (1849) 4 Ex. 503.

150 [2005] P.N.L.R. 7 CA at 112.

151 See para.10-073, above for the discount aspect of the case. And see, at para.10-074, *Feakins v Burstow* [2006] P.N.L.R. 6 at 94 where the solicitor's negligent conduct of proceedings, particularly in the assembling of evidence, meant that the client could not prove that he was not liable to certain payments to the authorities over his export of sheep; he was entitled in damages to the amount of these payments but subject to a substantial discount.

by the Court of Appeal[152] and the matter is fully examined earlier when dealing with loss of a chance.[153]

34-037 **(g) Negligence in connection with the acquisition of property by mortgage** While the landmark decision in *Banque Bruxelles Lambert v Eagle Star Insurance Co*[154]—commonly called *SAAMCO*—was itself directed towards valuers and surveyors being sued by mortgage lenders seeking to recover often catastrophic losses emanating from the collapse of the property market at the end of the 1980s, the progeny has consisted mainly of mortgage lender claims for such losses, claims in huge numbers, against solicitors. Thus 13 claims against solicitors or solicitors' firms were heard in *Bristol and West Building Society v May, May & Merrimans*,[155] eight out of 87 in *Bristol and West Building Society v Fancy & Jackson*,[156] and 12 out of a far larger number in *Nationwide Building Society v Balmer Radmore*.[157] However, they are not all devoted to issues of negligence, even in part. The claims against *May, May & Merrimans* to recover the shortfall in proceeds of sale were all for breach of trust and breach of fiduciary duty, and the importance for damages lies in the sequel, *Bristol and West Building Society v May, May & Merrimans (No.2)*,[158] where it was held that no credit had to be given by the claimant lenders for moneys received by them under a mortgage indemnity guarantee policy since no question of double recovery arose.[159] The claims against *Balmer Radmore*, were mainly concerned with breach of fiduciary duty and, while *Bristol and West Building Society v Mothew*,[160] concerned breach of contract as well as breach of trust, the contractual decision was devoted to whether a causal link had been shown and damages were left to the future. *Target Holdings v Redferns*[161] is a key case of a solicitor handling a mortgage loan for a client, but the claim, which only had a limited success, was not one for negligence but for breach of trust, and therefore currently outside the remit of this text.[162] Cases also sometimes deal not only with the general measure of damages but also with individual aspects of it, in particular contributory negligence and mitigation,[163] or with individual aspects only, as in *Birmingham Midshire Mortgage Services v Phillips*,[164] where the primary issue was interest.[165]

34-038 An initially important decision, following upon *SAAMCO*, on the general

---

152 *Charles v Hugh James Jones & Jenkins* [2000] 1 W.L.R. 1278 CA; *Dudarec v Andrews* [2006] 1 W.L.R. 3002 CA; *Whitehead v Hibbert Pownall & Newton* [2008] P.N.L.R. 25 at 625.

153 At paras 10-098 to 10-102.

154 [1997] A.C. 191. See para.34-073, below.

155 [1996] 2 All E.R. 801.

156 [1997] 4 All E.R. 583.

157 [1999] Lloyd's Rep. P.N. 241.

158 [1998] 1 W.L.R. 336.

159 The decision was applied in *Portman Building Society v Bevan Ashford* [2000] Lloyd's Rep. P.N. 354 CA; see the cases on this issue at para.9-168, above.

160 [1998] Ch. 1 CA.

161 [1996] A.C. 421.

162 As is the somewhat similar case of *Collins v Brebner* [2000] Lloyd's Rep. P.N. 587 CA.

163 Aspects which are dealt with elsewhere: see paras 7-017 to 7-018 and para.9-051 respectively. Indeed the importance today of contributory negligence and mitigation in reducing damages awards to mortgage lenders is such that the issue deserves some detail. This is given at paras 34-077 to 34-080, below, when dealing with claims against surveyors and valuers, to which reference may be made as the same principles apply.

164 [1998] P.N.L.R. 468.

165 At para.19-017, above; contributory negligence and mitigation also featured.

measure of damages where the suit is by mortgage lender against solicitor was the eight cases dealt with by Chadwick J and reported as *Bristol and West Building Society v Fancy & Jackson and others*.[166] However, the reasoning of Chadwick J in that case was disapproved in *BPE Solicitors and another v Hughes-Holland*.[167] It should be put to one side.

The most important post-*SAAMCO* case involving negligence in connection with acquisition of a property by mortgage is *BPE Solicitors and another v Hughes-Holland*.[168] That case involved a businessman who lent £200,000 to a developer labouring under the misapprehension that the developer owned the property, Building 428, which was to be developed. In fact, the loan was used for a shell company owned by the developer to buy Building 428 and to pay VAT. Solicitors were instructed to act for the businessman in drawing up a facility agreement and a charge. However, they drew up the facility agreement negligently, and in a way which confirmed the businessman's incorrect assumptions. The project was a failure and all money was lost. The businessman would not have entered the agreement but for his misapprehension that the finance he was providing was to be used for development of Building 428. Nevertheless, even if the finance had been used as the businessman intended, the project would still have been a complete failure. **34-039**

The Supreme Court held that the businessman could not recover any damages from the solicitors. The solicitors did not assume responsibility for the businessman's decision to lend. Lord Sumption, with whom the others agreed, explained the "fundamental features" of the decision in SAAMCO. A defendant who provides advice which will be used in making a decision does not assume legal responsibility for the decision. The decision maker must show that he is worse off than he would have been if the advice were correct.[169] One does not start with the proposition that the adviser is responsible for the decision and then determine whether there is a basis in the rules of causation to limit recovery of the foreseeable loss.[170] The question is whether the loss flowed from the feature which made the conduct wrongful.[171] **34-040**

In addition to the plethora of cases involving a fall in the market, there are others where the feature causing loss is something other than a market fall. As the Supreme Court explained in *BPE Solicitors and another v Hughes-Holland*,[172] there can be other extraneous sources of loss outside the scope of a defendant's duty other than a market fall. *Omega Trust Co v Wright Son & Pepper*[173] was one such case. *SAAMCO* was indeed raised by counsel and discussed in the judgment,[174] and the claimants were held entitled to recover, though subject to a swingeing discount for their contributory negligence, the whole of the money they had lent. *Portman Building Society v Bevan Ashford*,[175] is another such case, and one dealing with a variety of damages issues. It was there held that, where the solicitor had negligently failed to provide information which showed that the transaction was not viable and indeed **34-041**

---

166 [1997] 4 All E.R. 583.
167 [2017] UKSC 21 at [49]–[50].
168 [2017] UKSC 21 at [49]–[50].
169 [2017] UKSC 21 at [35].
170 [2017] UKSC 21 at [36] and [38].
171 [2017] UKSC 21 at [38].
172 [2017] UKSC 21 at [46].
173 [1998] P.N.L.R. 337.
174 [1998] P.N.L.R. 337 at 358 to 359.
175 [2000] Lloyd's Rep. P.N. 354 CA.

that the borrowers might be fraudulent, the lender was entitled to recover the whole of its loss as falling within the scope of the solicitor's duty. This decision was disapproved by the Supreme Court in *BPE Solicitors and another v Hughes-Holland*,[176] where the court explained that the failure of a solicitor to report on some fact was not a breach of duty which scope extended to liability for losses arising from fraud by the counterparty.

**34-042** A new slant can be seen in *Lloyds Bank Plc v Burd Pearse*,[177] in that, had the defendant solicitor advised of the existence of two restrictive covenants affecting the property in question, the potential borrower would not have bought rather than that the lender claimant would not have been prepared to lend. The evidence was that the claimant, knowing of the restrictive covenants, would have invited the borrower to try to negotiate a reduced price and that, depending on the outcome, might have lent a lesser sum; the borrower was not one to whom the claimant was unwilling to lend. In these circumstances the claimant was not entitled to recover for its whole loss but only to the extent that the value of the property with the restrictive covenants fell below the value it would have had if unencumbered. The case thus differed from that against *Steggles Palmer*,[178] in the conjoined decision in *Bristol and West Building Society v Fancy & Jackson and others*.[179] The better view of this decision after *BPE Solicitors v Hughes-Holland* should not be that the facts are distinguishable from *Steggles Palmer* (which should be regarded as wrongly decided) but that the defendant's duty did not extend to liability for these losses. The defendant did not assume responsibility for the extent of the losses.

**34-043** **(h) Miscellaneous** There is to be noted a miscellany of cases not falling within any of the categories dealt with above; they may prove of some assistance when dealing with other instances of solicitor's negligence. *Day v Cook*[180] provides an elaborate assessment of damages,[181] for negligent failure to advise the claimant to obtain independent advice in respect of disadvantageous transactions. In *Gold v Mincoff Science & Gold*,[182] where the defendant solicitor failed to advise the claimant, a partner in a property-dealing partnership, that he had committed himself to the partnership's bankers for the liabilities not only of the partnership but also for the indebtedness outside the partnership of his partner, Neuberger J considered a whole series of heads of damage as being recoverable in principle,[183] from the loss of the claimant's interest in the partnership, the loss of a property of his mortgaged to the bank, the costs of defending a claim brought by the bank, the loss of earnings suffered as a result of his investigative work into the bank's claim against him, to the loss of the chance of his extricating himself from the unnecessary commitment to the bank. Both *Worby v Rosser*,[184] and *Corbett v Bond Pearce*,[185] accept that, where a solicitor's negligence in the preparation and execution of a will leads to expensive probate proceedings after the testator's death, there may be a claim for

[176] [2017] UKSC 21 at [52].
[177] [2001] Lloyd's Rep. P.N. 452 CA.
[178] At para.34-038, above.
[179] [1997] 4 All E.R. 582.
[180] [2000] P.N.L.R. 178.
[181] But substantially varied in the Court of Appeal: [2002] 1 B.C.L.C. 1 CA.
[182] [2001] Lloyd's Rep. P.N. 423.
[183] He was not being asked to assess damages.
[184] [1999] Lloyd's Rep. P.N. 972 CA.
[185] [2001] 3 All E.R. 769 CA.

damages at the suit of the testator's personal representatives for these litigation costs, although in neither of these cases was the claim successful. In *MacMahon v Hamilton*,[186] the solicitor, who had been instructed to issue proceedings against a third party, assured his client not only that this had been done but also that judgment had been entered for £20,000 with enforcement proceedings commenced, and on the strength of this entirely false information the client went into substantial overdraft which required him to remortgage the family home; the claim against the third party eventually becoming statute-barred, the client recovered from the solicitor his losses connected with the overdraft and remortgage.[187]

Loss of a chance is the principal feature in the damages in a number of these cases. In the difficult and complex *Ball v Druces & Attlee (No.2)*[188] the claimant had retained the defendants to safeguard his interests in a project of which he was an originator and which became enormously successful. He successfully sued the defendants for negligence in allowing the project to be set up as a charitable trust, thereby preventing him from claiming any right to share in the profits generated by the project. Here there were very many acts of third parties that had to be performed before those profits would have come the claimant's way.[189] Nelson J held that, in assessing the damages where there are various outcomes, **34-044**

> "the right approach is to evaluate the chance of success of each of the possible outcomes, giving a percentage assessment for each category of lost chance".[190]

While it is no doubt true that the different chances lost have then to be amalgamated, Nelson J appears to have allowed recovery in respect of outcomes which should have been regarded as alternative rather than cumulative.[191] Even more complex is *Farrukh v Irwin Mitchell*,[192] where the loss of a chance was in relation to the acquisition of shares and where both the ascertainment and the relevance of their market price was very much to the fore. In the end the trial judge held on a whole series of elaborate grounds that, while a loss of £9 million was claimed, there would be no recovery. In *Susan Finley v Connell Associates*,[193] the solicitor, acting for the client in relation to a property development, failed to advise her that the terms of the building licence granted by the City Council permitted the nature of the development to be changed without the payment of a premium to the Council, and, had she been properly advised, the property development would have proceeded more swiftly and in a more favourable market so that a greater profit would have been made. Ouseley J, in a lengthy judgment and in a manner somewhat difficult to follow, applied the principles enunciated on loss of a chance in *Allied Maples*,[194] so as to arrive at a recoverable loss of profit which was substantially discounted. Where in *Youlton v Charles Russell*,[195] solicitors were negligent in failing to ensure that agreements between a company and the trustees of its pension scheme were not open to challenge on grounds of want of authority and conflict of

---

186 [2002] Lloyd's Rep. P.N. 93.
187 See the case also at para.8-154, above.
188 [2004] P.N.L.R. 39 at 745.
189 See them set out in the judgment: [2004] P.N.L.R. 39 at [201] and [202].
190 [2004] P.N.L.R. 39 at [275].
191 See his conclusions on quantum at [2004] P.N.L.R. 39 at [309]–[311] and [313].
192 [2006] EWHC 1541.
193 [2002] Lloyd's Rep. P.N. 62.
194 See paras 10-057 and following, above.
195 [2010] EWHC 1032 Ch.

interest, damages were to be assessed on the basis of the lost chance of the trustees enforcing their claims had the agreements been beyond challenge. However, no question of loss of a chance arose in *Martin v Triggs Turner Bartons*,[196] where a power of advancement to a deceased's widow granted a life interest in residue was negligently drafted by the deceased's solicitors so as to apply only to £100,000 from the estate rather than to the whole of the estate except for £100,000. There was no loss of a chance because the widow suffered an immediate loss in that the value of the benefit she received was reduced.[197] The court's task was therefore the difficult one of valuing the widow's loss, a matter of quantification.[198]

**34-045** A final addition to this miscellany of forms of solicitor's negligence[199] is *Fulham Leisure Holdings Ltd v Nicholson Graham & Jones*.[200] The claimant company, which was a vehicle of Mohammed Al Fayed and which had a 75 per cent shareholding in another company through which the then insolvent Fulham football club had been acquired, sued the defendant, its firm of solicitors, for negligence in removing, from the shareholder agreement with the two individuals holding the remaining 25 per cent in that other company, the claimant's right, in certain circumstances which came about, to dilute the shares held by the two individuals. When some years after the club's acquisition this was discovered, in order to give Mr Al Fayed, through the claimant company, the control that he no longer could obtain by dilution of the individuals' shareholding, he decided to buy out the two individuals and claimed as damages the £7.75 million that he had paid them to achieve this, a payment referred to in the case as the cost of cure. Nothing was said of the familiar diminution in value test, no doubt because it would have been difficult or impossible to put any value on the bundle of rights the claimant company acquired under the shareholder agreement and the rights it should have had. In a careful judgment Mann J, while decreeing that it was legitimate to use cost of cure as the measure of damages in solicitors' negligence cases, held against the claimant on two grounds. First, and principally, he held that buying out the two individuals went well beyond the cost of cure, cure requiring only the reinstatement of the right to dilute.[201] Secondly, and alternatively, he held, applying *Ruxley*,[202] that a payment of £7.75 million was not reasonable and went far beyond, and was entirely disproportionate to, the rights the company acquired and the benefits it achieved.[203]

## (2) Non-pecuniary loss

**34-046** At one time mental distress did not ground recovery in contract but, when change came in the early 1970s,[204] one of the early cases to allow such damages involved

196 [2009] EWHC 1920 Ch.
197 See [2009] EWHC 1920 Ch at [73] and [74].
198 See [2009] EWHC 1920 Ch at [75]–[92].
199 See, too, *The Guild (Claims) Ltd v Eversheds* [2000] Lloyd's Rep. P.N. 910 where the defendants were retained by the claimants in their purchase of a company which resulted in a loss on the acquisition; no loss was suffered by the company.
200 [2007] P.N.L.R 5 at 83.
201 See [2007] P.N.L.R 5 at [279]–[287].
202 At para.31-014, above.
203 See [2007] P.N.L.R 5 at [288]–[302]. The Court of Appeal, reversing on liability ([2008] EWCA Civ 84 CA), found no need to address issues of quantum, "interesting as those issues are": at [120].
204 See para.5-025, above.

solicitor defendants. This was *Heywood v Wellers*,[205] decided in 1975. Solicitors, instructed by the claimant to bring proceedings to restrain a man from molesting her, so bungled the proceedings that the molestation continued causing the claimant mental distress and upset for which the Court of Appeal allowed her damages. There then came in the late 1980s a more restricted approach to the allowing of damages for mental distress in contract,[206] and solicitor defendants were once more in the vanguard of this further development, again featuring in one of the early cases thereof. This was *Hayes v James and Charles Dodd*,[207] decided in 1988. The sale to a husband and wife of business premises went disastrously wrong, with their business failing, because the access to the premises of which they had been assured by their solicitor was lacking.[208] Since this was essentially a commercial contract the Court of Appeal decided that it was inappropriate to award damages for mental distress. Such damages were to be confined to cases where the purpose of the contract was to give enjoyment or peace of mind on the one hand or to remove stress and worry on the other. *Heywood v Wellers*[209] was not affected as the mental distress in that case was, in the words of Bridge LJ, the result of the failure to obtain the very relief to secure which had been the sole purpose of engaging the solicitor.[210] Thus the Court of Appeal in *Channon v Lindley Johnstone*,[211] has refused to uphold the trial judge's award of damages for distress and disappointment to a claimant who would have had a better outcome to the divorce proceedings initiated by his wife had his case been better handled by the solicitor defendant. Such a situation, said the court, did not provide an exception to the general rule that such damages were not recoverable for breach of a solicitor's retainer.[212] Similarly, in *Howell-Smith v Official Solicitor*,[213] no damages for disappointment or frustration from the Official Solicitor's bad handling of litigation were awarded.[214]

Nevertheless there still remains a fair scope for obtaining against solicitors damages for non-pecuniary loss. In the first place, there has always been a preparedness to award such damages where physical illness has resulted. Thus in both *Wales v Wales*,[215] and *Malyon v Lawrence Messer & Co*,[216] the court allowed damages for the deterioration of the claimant's physical and nervous condition during the period of delay, due to the solicitor's incompetence, in hearing the claimant's personal injury action.[217] In the second place, damages for physical inconvenience and **34-047**

205 [1976] Q.B. 446 CA.
206 See para.5-027, above.
207 [1990] 2 All E.R. 815 CA.
208 See the case at para.34-016, above.
209 [1976] Q.B. 446 CA.
210 [1976] Q.B. 446 CA at 463H–464A.
211 [2002] P.N.L.R. 41 CA at 884.
212 Applying Bingham LJ's well-known principle formulated, in the context of claims against surveyors, in *Watts v Morrow* [1991] 1 W.L.R. 1421 CA, and set out at para 5-028, above.
213 [2006] P.N.L.R. 21 CA at 394.
214 What were called general damages awarded in *Fraser v Gaskell* [2004] P.N.L.R. 32 at 613, which concerned solicitors being negligent in relation to a bankruptcy, appear to be for non-pecuniary loss: see at [121]. Whether, in the light of the way the law has developed, such damages were correctly awarded may be questioned.
215 (1967) 111 S.J. 946.
216 (1968) 112 S.J. 623.
217 Contrast *Cook v Swinfen* [1967] 1 W.L.R. 457 CA, at para.34-033, above (breakdown in health held too remote). Contrast *Al-Kandari v Brown & Co* [1988] Q.B. 665 CA, at para.8-058, above, where solicitors not in contractual relationship with the claimant were held liable, in the amount of £20,000, for severe physical and mental injury to her from a kidnapping sparked off by their negligence.

discomfort have always been allowed.[218] In *Bailey v Bullock*,[219] the claimant had instructed the defendant solicitor's managing clerk to take immediate steps to regain possession of his house for his own occupation from the tenant to whom he had let it, but the managing clerk deliberately took no such steps while deceiving the claimant into thinking that a summons had been issued and that there were genuine reasons for the failure of the matter to come before the court. The claimant having been forced meanwhile to live in discomfort with his wife and child in the small house of his wife's parents, damages for the inconvenience and discomfort were awarded. Somewhat similar is *Buckley v Lane Herdman & Co*,[220] in that the claimant husband and wife, through their solicitor's negligence, found themselves with their old home sold and no new home into which to move. As there was another available house which the claimants bought, it may be that no real inconvenience and discomfort is revealed, in which case the decision to award damages for non-pecuniary loss would not be followed today. Provided that there is indeed physical inconvenience and discomfort arising out of living in an unsuitable house, the award may stretch to giving compensation for the accompanying distress and mental suffering which is directly related to that inconvenience and discomfort. This was accepted in *Watts v Morrow*,[221] an equivalent case concerning surveyors,[222] and would appear to explain the Court of Appeal's decision in *Wapshott v Davis Donovan & Co*.[223] The leasehold flat which a young married couple had acquired became too small for them when they started a family and they needed to move to larger accommodation. However, when they put the flat on the market it turned out to be unsaleable, a defect in title not having been appreciated by their solicitors, so that they were forced to continue living in now cramped conditions. Damages were awarded for the inconvenience and the distress in having to remain in confined accommodation when they started having children.[224]

**34-048** *Hamilton-Jones v David & Snape*[225] takes us back to the situation, which has survived the ups and downs of recovery for non-pecuniary loss, that is, to the situation, initially found in *Heywood v Wellers*,[226] where the provision of peace of mind and the avoidance of mental distress form an important object of the contract. The claimant, suing her solicitor for negligence in allowing her children to be removed to Tunisia by their Tunisian father, was held entitled to damages for the distress from being deprived of the company of, and the ability to bring up, her children and from knowing that they would be brought up in a culturally and linguistically different foreign country. The claimant feared that the children's father would attempt to spirit them out of the country and had instructed the defendant to take the necessary steps, which he failed to do, specifically to ensure that the father would be un-

---

218 Even inconvenience which is not of a strictly physical nature may ground recovery, as in *Piper v Daybell, Court-Cooper & Co* [1969] E.G.D. 535 where the defendant solicitor failed to reveal to the claimant a right of way existing over the premises which he was contemplating buying as a home and damages were awarded to him for the inconvenience of having his neighbour crossing and recrossing in front of his windows.

219 [1950] 2 All E.R. 1167.

220 [1977] C.L.Y. 3143; see the case further at para.34-017, above.

221 [1991] 1 W.L.R. 1421 CA.

222 See para.34-061, below.

223 [1996] P.N.L.R. 361 CA.

224 See, especially, Beldam LJ at [1996] P.N.L.R. 361 CA at 378H–379A.

225 [2004] 1 W.L.R. 924.

226 [1976] Q.B. 446 CA; see the case at para.34-046, above.

able to do so; thus part of the reason for the contract was to protect the claimant's peace of mind. Neuberger J conducted a careful review of the relevant authorities[227] and considered a whole variety of factors in arriving at the figure of £20,000 for the non-pecuniary loss.[228] Since then we have the decision of Newey J in the solicitor's negligence case of *Herrmann v Withers LLP*,[229] in which he held the claimant purchasers of a residential property entitled to damages from their solicitors for the disappointment and the loss of amenity in being unable to use a communal garden, this being in addition to the damages awarded representing the diminution in value of the property from the lack of garden use.[230]

## 2. SURVEYORS AND VALUERS

Claims against surveyors and valuers by clients may be by those who have bought property on the strength of a negligent survey or valuation or by those who have lent money on mortgage in reliance on a negligent survey or valuation of the property mortgaged. The measure of damages is substantially different in the two cases so that they call for separate treatment. And also to be dealt with are the occasional illustrations of a surveyor's or valuer's negligence in relation to the disposal rather than the acquisition of property.[231] **34-049**

### (1) Purchasers of property negligently surveyed or valued[232]

**(a) Pecuniary loss: normal measure** The first important case is *Philips v Ward*,[233] where the claimant's purchase of a house had been made in reliance upon the report submitted to him by the defendant surveyor, and the Court of Appeal held that the normal measure of damages in such cases is the difference between the value of the property in the condition described in the surveyor's report and its value as it should have been described. Subsequent cases continued to apply this measure,[234] but, as was rightly pointed out in *Ford v White & Co*,[235] which concerned in relation to the purchase of property professional negligence by a solicitor rather than a surveyor,[236] the normal measure is more accurately expressed as the difference between the purchase price paid and the value as properly described. For while the application of the normal measure as stated in *Philips v Ward*[237] and in the decisions following it may never have led to an incorrect result, as in none **34-050**

---

227 See [2004] 1 W.L.R. 924 at [43]–[64].

228 See [2004] 1 W.L.R. 924 at [66] to [69]. And see, in the context of awards for non-pecuniary loss against professionals, the important *Farley v Skinner* [2002] 2 A.C. 732 at para.34-062, below.

229 [2012] EWHC 1492 Ch.

230 See the case further on this at para.5-030, above.

231 For a case where the negligence consisted of an undervaluation of the claimant's land for the purposes of compensation for compulsory acquisition, see *Weedon v Hindwood, Clarke & Esplin* (1974) 234 E.G. 121.

232 Occasionally there will be no contract between the purchaser and the valuer when the claim can only be in tort. *Scullion v Bank of Scotland Plc* [2011] 1 W.L.R. 3212 CA was such a case, considered at para.49-067, below.

233 [1956] 1 W.L.R. 471 CA.

234 *Hood v Shaw* (1960) 176 E.G. 1291; *Hardy v Walmsley-Lewis* (1967) 203 E.G. 1039; *Daisley v Hall* (1972) 225 E.G. 1553; *Morgan v Perry* (1974) 229 E.G. 1737.

235 [1964] 1 W.L.R. 885.

236 See para.34-014, above.

237 [1956] 1 W.L.R. 471 CA.

of the cases had there been any suggestion that the value of the property as it had in fact been described differed from the purchase price paid, it was nevertheless incorrectly stated as it confuses giving the claimant the benefit of his bargain with his surveyor and giving him the benefit of his bargain with his seller. For had the surveyor not presented an inaccurate report the claimant would presumably have declined to buy the property, and he therefore cannot claim that the breach of the surveying contract has caused him to lose the benefit of the sale contract.[238]

**34-051** Fortunately the Court of Appeal returned to the problem in *Perry v Sidney Phillips & Son*,[239] and made the normal measure of damages crystal clear in this context. In that case the claimant bought a house in reliance on the defendant surveyors' report. Serious defects soon made their appearance but only minor repairs were effected by the claimant as he could not afford major ones. On the claimant's claim for damages the judge awarded, improperly,[240] the cost of repair; however, by the time the matter reached the Court of Appeal, the claimant had sold the house at a price well in excess of what he had paid for it, and therefore the question of assessing damages by the cost of repair fell away. The Court of Appeal had no doubt but that the measure of damages which represented the claimant's financial loss was constituted by the price he had paid for the house less its market value in its actual condition at the time of purchase; on this amount interest was awarded. To Kerr LJ's mind this result was "entirely concluded" by the trilogy of similar cases where property had been bought in reliance on negligent professional advice,[241] namely *Philips v Ward*,[242] *Ford v White & Co*,[243] and the further case of *Simple Simon Catering v Binstock Miller & Co*.[244] The Court of Appeal confirmed, and awarded, in *Watts v Morrow*,[245] the normal measure, there described as the diminution in value rule though, as Staughton LJ recognised,

> "more accurately to be expressed as the difference between the price paid and the value in [the property's] true description".[246]

Diminution in value was again the description of the award in *Patel v Hooper & Jackson*.[247] And in *Oswald v Countrywide Surveyors*,[248] the normal measure of damages was again wrongly taken as the difference between the value of the property in the condition described in the surveyor's report and the property's actual value, relying on *Philips v Ward* and *Watts v Morrow* for this proposition. In fact the price of £225,000 that the claimants paid was marginally above the surveyor's negligent valuation of £215,000 and, since the court took the former figure for the

238 Compare the earlier appearance of this fallacy in the arguments in the very analogous cases of *Cassaboglou v Gibb* (1883) 11 Q.B.D. 797 CA, and *Salvesen v Rederi Aktiebolaget Nordstjernan* [1905] A.C. 302, dealt with at paras 35-005 and 35-009, below. And see also paras 34-013 and 34-014, above, for the cases dealing with solicitors where the fallacy has also been exposed.

239 [1982] 1 W.L.R. 1297 CA.

240 See para.34-052, below.

241 [1982] 1 W.L.R. 1297 CA at 1306D. But see para.34-059, below.

242 [1956] 1 W.L.R. 471 CA.

243 [1964] 1 W.L.R. 885.

244 (1973) 117 S.J. 529.

245 [1991] 1 W.L.R. 1421 CA.

246 [1991] 1 W.L.R. 1421 CA at 1430A. He added: "at least where no point is taken, as in this case, that the plaintiff chose to pay above market value". But it is thought that the fact that the claimant may have bought above market is irrelevant; it can hardly be put down to contributory negligence.

247 [1999] 1 W.L.R. 1792 CA; together with certain other losses: see paras 34-058 and 34-060, below.

248 [1996] 50 Con. L.R. 1 CA.

value in the condition described, and did not bring in the higher value of the property once repairs had been effected, the correct result seems eventually to have been reached.[249]

The cost of putting the property into the condition as described in the surveyor's report was sometimes accepted as representing the normal measure of damages, both before the decision in *Perry*,[250] as in *Freeman v Marshall*,[251] and after *Perry*,[252] in *Hipkins v Jack Cotton Partnership*,[253] and *Syrett v Carr & Neave*.[254] However, as was stated in earlier editions, such cost should not be allowed if it is clear that it would exceed the amount by which the value as is falls short of the value as described or, more accurately, of the price paid. Accordingly, in *Philips v Ward*,[255] the claimant's claim for the cost of putting the property into the condition described in the defendant's report was disallowed; this amount was not required to put the claimant in the position he would have been in had the surveying contract been properly fulfilled. **34-052**

The choice between so-called diminution in value and cost of repairs came up again for specific adjudication in *Watts v Morrow*.[256] The claimants, who were husband and wife, purchased a country house for £177,500 in reliance on the defendant's survey which failed to reveal substantial defects in the property. The claimants carried out repairs to remedy the defects at a cost of some £34,000 and brought an action against the defendant claiming the cost of the repairs. It was common ground that at the date of the purchase the value of the house in its true condition was £162,500 and therefore £15,000 below the price which the claimants had paid for it. The trial judge found that the claimants acted entirely reasonably in retaining and repairing, rather than reselling, the house and awarded them the cost of repairs as claimed. The Court of Appeal reversed. Ralph Gibson LJ said: **34-053**

> "The fact that it is reasonable for the plaintiff to retain the property and to do the repairs seems to me to be irrelevant to determination of the question whether recovery of the cost of repairs is justified in order to put the plaintiff in the position in which he would have been if the contract, i.e. the promise to make a careful report, had been performed. The position is no different from that in *Philips v Ward*[257]: either the plaintiff would have refused to buy or he would have negotiated a reduced price. Recovery of the cost of repairs after having gone into possession … is not a position into which the plaintiff could have been put as a result of proper performance of the contract."[258]

Bingham LJ put the position succinctly thus:

---

[249] It was common ground in *McKinnon v e.surv Ltd* [2003] 2 E.G.L.R. 57 that the purchaser was entitled to the difference between the purchase price and the value of the property at the date of the purchasing valuation and the oddity of the case lay in the fact that the suspected defect did not exist although this could not have been known at the time of valuation. For how this affected the damages see the case at para.9-116, above.

[250] [1982] 1 W.L.R. 1297 CA.

[251] (1966) 200 E.G. 777.

[252] [1982] 1 W.L.R. 1297 CA.

[253] [1989] 2 E.G.L.R. 157.

[254] [1990] 2 E.G.L.R. 161.

[255] [1956] 1 W.L.R. 471 CA.

[256] [1991] 1 W.L.R. 1421 CA.

[257] [1956] 1 W.L.R. 471 CA.

[258] [1991] 1 W.L.R. 1421 CA at 1435H–1436B.

"If Mr and Mrs Watts were to end up with the house and an award of £34,000 damages they would have obtained the house for £143,500. But even if the defendant had properly performed his contract this bargain was never on offer. The effect of the judge's award is not to put Mr and Mrs Watts in the same position as if the defendant had properly performed but in a much better one."[259]

**34-054** Much the same was said, and in a more striking context, in *Smith and Smith v Peter North*,[260] where once again the Court of Appeal, agreeing with the trial judge, held that the appropriate measure of damages was diminution in value and not cost of repair. The context was more striking for two reasons. The one was that the single joint expert's report valued the property, which the claimants had bought as a residence, at precisely the same amount with and without the defect of which complaint was made; the other was that the actual and the proper valuations came out at £10,000 more than the claimants had paid for the property. To obtain recovery of the cost of repair was therefore essential for them[261]; but it was not to be. Jonathan Parker LJ, who gave the leading judgment, said:

"To apply the cost of repairs measure ... would be to place the Appellants in a substantially better position than they would have been in had [the respondent surveyor] given a proper report ... An award of damages which enabled the Appellants in effect to carry out repairs to the property to a minimum pleaded cost of £130,000 entirely at the Respondent's expense would mean that the Appellants had acquired the property, with the benefit of the repairs, for a net outlay of (at most) some £200,000—that is to say, some £130,000 less than the market value of the property at the date of purchase."[262]

**34-055** *Hipkins v Jack Cotton Partnership*,[263] and *Syrett v Carr & Neave*,[264] both awarding the cost of repairs,[265] were held in *Watts v Morrow*,[266] to have been wrongly decided. The most that the cost of repairs can provide, as *Steward v Rapley*[267] indicates, is material evidence as to what would be a proper price for the property. Thus in that case the Court of Appeal considered the cost of repairs as the most reliable method of market valuation and reversed the judge below who had awarded a lower amount because, it was said, he had failed to distinguish between recovering cost of repairs as a head of damage and as a method of arriving at market value.[268]

**34-056** Although these cases concern the normal measure of damages, that normal measure is not immutable. In *Bacciottini v Gotelee and Goldsmith (A Firm)*,[269] Davis LJ (Lloyd Jones and Underhill LJJ agreeing) explained that the normal loss at the date of breach suffered by the appellants might have been the difference

---

259 [1991] 1 W.L.R. 1421 CA at 1445A–B.

260 [2002] Lloyd's Rep. P.N. 111 CA.

261 There was only a small claim for accommodation costs in addition: see at para.34-057, below.

262 [2002] Lloyd's Rep. P.N. 111 CA at [50].

263 [1989] 2 E.G.L.R. 157.

264 [1990] 2 E.G.L.R. 161.

265 See para.34-052, above.

266 [1991] 1 W.L.R. 1421 CA.

267 [1989] 1 E.G.L.R. 159 CA.

268 Compare *Bigg v Howard Son & Gooch* [1990] 1 E.G.L.R. 173 at para.34-057, below. Again in *Rushmer v Countrywide Surveyors* (1994) Ltd [2000] P.N.L.R. 529 the court was assiduous in applying the Court of Appeal authorities so as to base the award on diminution in value, while being prepared to look at the cost of rectification as an assistance in arriving at the diminution in value.

269 [2016] EWCA Civ 170.

between the price they paid and the value of the property without the planning restriction but the appellants had successfully had the planning restriction removed. Therefore the normal loss could not be recovered. The Court of Appeal observed that the question really is whether, in all the circumstances of the case, the normal measure properly reflects the overriding compensatory rule.[270]

**(b) Pecuniary loss: consequential losses** Claimants deciding to put right rather than to dispose of the property negligently surveyed have been held entitled to recover for consequential losses during the time when the necessary repairs were being done. In *Hood v Shaw*,[271] the claimant recovered his costs of moving out of the house for this period, in *Freeman v Marshall*,[272] his loss of rent from the letting of flats in the house during this period.[273] It is however thought that, just as repair costs in excess of the normal measure of damages are not recoverable, such costs or losses should not be recoverable in addition to the normal measure; otherwise the claimant is again put into a better position than if the defendant had properly performed. Indeed the trial judge concluded in *Bigg v Howard Son & Gooch*[274] that "no separate award for cost of accommodation during repair is appropriate"[275] at the same time he considered that **34-057**

> "the likely need for and cost of vacating the premises during repair can readily be taken into account, with the repair costs themselves, in arriving at the price which a properly advised purchaser would have paid".[276]

Yet as early as *Cross v David Martin & Mortimer*[277] it was being said that, although it might be illogical to give the cost of alternative accommodation during repair if the cost of repair itself was being turned down, it had become a well-established practice.[278] And while continuing to recognise the illogicality, such awards are still being made today, as in *Holder v Countrywide Surveyors*.[279] There was a claim for accommodation costs during repair in *Smith and Smith v Peter North*,[280] which appears to have been successful at first instance but, since there was no appeal against it, the matter has not yet reached the Court of Appeal.

If, however, the claimant adopts the course which is alternative to repairing and disposes of his house, the situation will be different. In the first place, he should be entitled in these circumstances, as was contemplated by Romer LJ in *Philips v Ward*,[281] to "his costs and expenses of moving in and moving out and of the resale"[282] in addition to the normal measure of damages; these are costs of extricating himself from the transaction. Romer LJ's view that such costs thrown away **34-058**

---

270 [2016] EWCA Civ 170 at [48], referring to *Pankhania v London Borough of Hackney* [2004] EWHC 323 Ch at [21].

271 (1960) 176 E.G. 1291.

272 (1966) 200 E.G. 777.

273 And in *Morgan v Perry* (1974) 229 E.G. 1737 the costs of finding out what precisely was wrong with the property were allowed as a consequential loss.

274 [1990] 1 E.G.L.R. 173.

275 [1990] 1 E.G.L.R. 173 at 175E.

276 [1990] 1 E.G.L.R. 173 at 175B.

277 [1989] 1 E.G.L.R. 154.

278 [1989] 1 E.G.L.R. 154 at 159D.

279 [2003] P.N.L.R. 3 at 29.

280 [2002] Lloyd's Rep. P.N. 111 CA; see the case at para.34-054, above.

281 [1956] 1 W.L.R. 471 CA.

282 [1956] 1 W.L.R. 471 CA at 478.

were recoverable in addition to the normal measure was expressly accepted by Bingham LJ in *Watts v Morrow*.[283] Indeed the costs of resale were allowed to the claimant in *Hardy v Walmsley-Lewis*,[284] although not the costs of purchase. It is, however, difficult to see the basis for this latter denial of recovery. For on the assumption that the claimant would not have bought the property had the defendant submitted a true report, the cost of neither purchase nor resale would have been incurred by him. True, he had contemplated incurring costs in purchasing a house, but such costs will still have to be incurred by him in acquiring a substitute for the defective house now disposed of. And in the second place, he should be entitled, where he sells rather than repairs, to the cost of temporary accommodation in the course of acquiring an alternative house. This result was reached in *Patel v Hooper & Jackson*.[285] The claimants, who decided to dispose of the uninhabitable house bought as they could not afford to put it into proper condition, recovered from the negligent surveyor the cost of accommodation until such time as the house should have been sold. However, since it was found that, if properly advised, they would have bought another, and habitable, house the Court of Appeal held[286] that the recorder's award of damages equivalent to an indemnity for past and future mortgage interest payments, endowment policy premiums and household insurance premiums was misconceived as these would all have been incurred in respect of the alternative house which the claimants would have bought.

**34-059** The claimant had contended in the appeal in *Perry v Sidney Phillips & Son*[287] for, as the appropriate measure of damages, the value that the house would have had at the date of the trial had it been in the condition in which, on the basis of the defendant surveyors' report, it should have been less its value in its defective condition. Oliver LJ rightly said that there was nothing to justify this contention because the claimant had there "chosen … to retain the property and not to cut his loss by reselling it".[288] This, however, depends upon the claimant being aware of his loss soon after the time of purchase, and such a contention as was put forward in *Perry* could take on weight if the defects, and the defendant's negligence, should not come to light for some long time during which property prices had been climbing. If a claimant can in these circumstances show that, had he been properly advised, he would have bought not the property negligently valued but an equivalent property in good condition at the then market price, it would be necessary, in order to satisfy the fundamental principle of putting a claimant in the position he would have been in had he not sustained the wrong, to award as damages the value that such equivalent property in good condition would have had, not necessarily at the time of trial but rather at the time when the defects ought reasonably to have been discovered, less the value at that same time of the property in fact acquired and less also the difference, if indeed there was any, between what the claimant would have needed to pay for an equivalent property in good condition at the time he bought the defective property and the purchase price that he did pay for the defective property.[289] Ralph

---

283 [1991] 1 W.L.R. 1421 CA at 1445B. And probably implicitly by Ralph Gibson LJ: see at 1435D.

284 (1967) 203 E.G. 1039.

285 [1999] 1 W.L.R. 1792 CA.

286 Distinguishing *Hayes v Dodd* [1990] 2 All E.R. 815 CA, where no other property would have been bought in the place of that acquired through the solicitor's negligent advice: see para.34-016, above.

287 [1982] 1 W.L.R. 1297 CA; see para.34-051, above.

288 [1982] 1 W.L.R. 1297 CA at 1304G.

289 Compare the discussion of *Ladenbau (UK) v Crawley & de Reya* [1978] 1 W.L.R. 266 (solicitors'

Gibson LJ in *Watts v Morrow*,[290] said that he considered it to be arguable that, if the defects had been discovered only some years after the purchase and if the value of the property, both in its described state and in its defective state, had increased by 25 per cent as a result of inflation of house prices, the measure of damages should be taken as the difference between the values so increased.[291] If, however, the market has collapsed in the years following upon the purchase, it would seem, in the light of the House of Lords decision in *Banque Bruxelles Lambert v Eagle Star Insurance Co*, otherwise known as *SAAMCO*,[292] that the normal measure of damages should apply so that the amount to be deducted from the claimant's purchase price is the value of the property in its defective state at the time of the purchase rather than its value at the later time of discovery of the defects after the collapse in the market. The valuer can surely be no more liable to a purchaser than to a mortgagee for loss caused by a collapse in the market.[293]

Further cases have appeared where, at first instance, *SAAMCO* has been invoked successfully by surveyor and valuer defendants with purchaser claimants. In *Capita Alternative Fund Services (Guernsey) Ltd v Drivers Jonas*,[294] where surveyors had negligently advised the purchasers of a shopping centre development as to its value and commercial prospects, the trial judge applied *SAAMCO*, limiting the damages to the difference between what the purchasers had paid and what they should have paid on the basis of correct advice and not extending the damages to all the business losses that followed purchase.[295] In the affirming Court of Appeal[296] the *SAAMCO* issue was not appealed.[297] The trial judge also in *Scullion v Bank of Scotland Plc*,[298] applied *SAAMCO*, where there was an overstatement by the defendant valuer of the capital value of, and the potential income from, the flat that the claimant was buying,[299] so as not to allow recovery for loss caused by a collapse in the market. In the Court of Appeal, reversing on liability,[300] this point was not touched on. **34-060**

**(c) Non-pecuniary loss** Successful claims for non-pecuniary loss also made their appearance with *Perry v Sidney Phillips & Son*,[301] where the claimant was in addition awarded damages for the distress, vexation, anxiety and inconvenience suffered as a result of having to live for a lengthy period in a defective house without **34-061**

negligence) at para.34-018, above.

290 [1991] 1 W.L.R. 1421 CA.

291 [1991] 1 W.L.R. 1421 CA at 1438A.

292 [1997] A.C. 191.

293 See the case at para.34-073, below. Conversely, the normal measure based upon the value of the property in its defective state at acquisition may still be awarded although the defects have later been cured by the action of a third party. This happened in *Gardner v Marsh and Parsons* [1997] 1 W.L.R. 489 CA, but the result is thought to be questionable: see the case, in the context of mitigation, at para.9-162, above.

294 [2011] EWHC 2336 (Comm).

295 See [2011] EWHC 2336 (Comm) at [298]–[309].

296 [2012] EWCA Civ 1417 CA.

297 [2012] EWCA Civ 1417 CA at [20]. The Court of Appeal reversed only on a question of tax deduction which, as pointed out in the footnote at the end of para.18-003, above, is not of relevance to the damages issues involving tax dealt with in Ch.18, above.

298 [2010] EWHC 2253 Ch.

299 Full facts at para.49-067, below. With no contract between valuer and buyer the claim lay only in tort, but this does not affect the result.

300 [2011] 1 W.L.R. 3212 CA.

301 [1982] 1 W.L.R. 1297 CA.

being sure when repairs would be executed. This decision led to similar recoveries[302] until the onset of a more restricted approach, with the decision in *Watts v Morrow*,[303] to the allowing of damages for mental distress in what are essentially commercial contracts,[304] *Perry* was interpreted in *Watts* as giving damages only for the physical inconvenience and discomfort together with any mental suffering directly related thereto; mental distress beyond this, it was held by the Court of Appeal in *Watts*, was not recoverable in a claim under a contract with a negligent surveyor.[305] Further recoveries since *Watts* for non-pecuniary loss in actions against surveyors and valuers[306] are generally to be interpreted as being similarly restricted. Decisions, however, are still to be found allowing damages for inconvenience and the distress associated with it, as with the claimants in *Holder v Countrywide Surveyors*,[307] who had bought a house in which because of defects they could not live. And in *Patel v Hooper v Jackson*,[308] where the claimants had for long had to live in much less desirable accommodation than the property bought would have afforded had it been as described by the surveyor defendant, a modest award of £2,000 for the years of living in relative discomfort was made.

**34-062** In *Farley v Skinner*,[309] where the defendant surveyor negligently failed to discover that a house was subject to much aircraft movement, a matter upon which he had been specifically asked to advise, the surveying contract was eventually held by the House of Lords, after disagreement below, not to be regarded as a commercial contract precluding recovery for the distress caused to the claimant purchaser by the excessive aircraft noise over the house. Nor was the claimant precluded, as a Court of Appeal majority had held, from recovering for the annoyance caused by the aircraft noise as amounting to physical inconvenience and discomfort. At the same time their Lordships endorsed the view expressed by Bingham LJ in *Watts v Morrow*,[310] that awards in this area should be restrained and modest. The trial judge's figure of £10,000 in *Farley* was considered to be high and at the very top end of the scale but, because the case was regarded as special and exceptional, their Lordships declined to interfere with the award.[311]

**34-063** In *Perry v Sidney Phillips & Son*,[312] the argument was rejected that the damage emanating from the distress and discomfort was too remote because it was only the claimant's lack of means which prevented him from repairing the house and thereby bringing the distress and discomfort to an end; this argument stemmed from the familiar contention based upon impecuniosity and the ruling in *Liesbosch Dredger v S.S. Edison*.[313] Lord Denning MR viewed *The Liesbosch* impecuniosity rule as not

---

302 See, e.g. *Westlake v Bracknell District Council* (1987) 19 H.L.R. 375; *Hipkins v Jack Cotton Partnership* [1989] 2 E.G.L.R. 157; *Bigg v Howard Son & Gooch* [1990] 1 E.G.L.R. 173; *Syrett v Carr & Neave* [1990] 2 E.G.L.R. 161.

303 [1991] 1 W.L.R. 1421 CA.

304 See paras 5-026 and following, above.

305 Compare Bingham LJ's remarks in the case at para.5-018 and at para.5-028, above.

306 See, e.g. *Ezekiel v McDade* (1994) 37 Con. L.R. 140.

307 [2003] P.N.L.R. 3 at 29.

308 [1999] 1 W.L.R. 1792 CA.

309 [2002] 2 A.C. 732.

310 [1991] 1 W.L.R. 1421 CA at 1445H.

311 See [2002] 2 A.C. 732 at [28], [61] and [110], and the further discussion of *Farley* at paras 5-018, 5-029 and 5-030, above. For amount awarded, contrast the nuisance case of *Dennis v Ministry of Defence* [2003] 2 E.G.L.R. 121 at para.39-020 in a footnote, below.

312 [1982] 1 W.L.R. 1297 CA.

313 [1933] A.C. 449.

of general application[314] and Kerr LJ remarked that its authority was being consistently attenuated by the judiciary.[315] Now it has gone, finally overturned by the House of Lords in *Lagden v O'Connor*,[316] and the decision in *Perry* can rest in peace.

## (2) Mortgagees of property negligently surveyed or valued

Claims by lenders to intending purchasers or to owners on the strength of a negligent survey or valuation of the property to be purchased or already owned have produced a different pattern of damages. For one thing, the emphasis shifts from the purchase price of the property to the amount loaned on the security of the property. For another thing, claims for non-pecuniary loss in the shape of distress and discomfort have naturally not arisen. 34-064

**(a) Normal measure** Little has been said about what is the normal measure of damages where the claimant is mortgagee rather than purchaser.[317] An attempt needs to be made, however, as with other breaches of contract,[318] to identify the normal measure, even if only to set the scene for the consideration of consequential losses with which the major cases, as we shall see, have been concerned. 34-065

A distinction is sometimes drawn between the case of the lender who with knowledge of the true position would not have lent at all to the borrower and the lender who with such knowledge would have lent the borrower less. It is the distinction between so-called "no transaction" cases and so-called "successful transaction" cases, terminology introduced, in a different type of case, by Staughton LJ in *Hayes v James and Charles Dodd*,[319] and resorted to in a number of decisions thereafter. The distinction was rejected by Lord Hoffmann in the leading case in the field of *Banque Bruxelles Lambert v Eagle Star Insurance Co Ltd*,[320] otherwise known as *South Australia Asset Management Corp v York Montague* or simply *SAAMCO*.[321] That rejection, in the context of the scope of the duty that is owed by a claimant, has been reiterated by the Supreme Court in *BPE Solicitors and another v Hughes-Holland*.[322] The reason why the "no transaction" or "successful transaction" distinction cannot be a governing principle is because it does not answer the question of whether the defendant assumed responsibility for all the losses suffered. Instead, it is directed to a different question which is the extent of the losses which were caused. 34-066

Quite apart from the limitation imposed upon damages arising from the need to confine them to the scope of the defendant's duty, the role that the "no transaction" or "successful transaction" distinction can still play in the law of damages is as a way of determining whether the normal measure of loss is the appropriate 34-067

---

314 [1982] 1 W.L.R. 1297 CA at 1302H.

315 [1982] 1 W.L.R. 1297 CA at 1307C. Oliver LJ merely pointed out that there were other reasons for the claimant's failure to repair, in particular that the defendants were strenuously resisting any suggestion that they were liable for the repairs: at 1305E.

316 [2004] 1 A.C. 1067: see paras 8-110 to 8-113, above.

317 See for purchaser claimants paras 34-050 and following, above.

318 There is, of course, here generally a concurrent liability in tort.

319 [1990] 2 All E.R. 815 CA at 818j–819a.

320 [1997] A.C. 191.

321 [1997] A.C. 191 at 218G.

322 [2017] UKSC 21 at [51]–[52].

measure based on rules of causation. Where, had a correct valuation been given, the claimant would not have lent at all, the normal measure will be contained within the difference between the defendant's negligent valuation and what would have been the correct valuation, otherwise described as the shortfall in the claimant's security. The normal measure is said to be contained within this difference, which forms its ceiling, rather than being the difference itself, since the claimant's actual loss is prima facie[323] the difference between the amount which has in fact been lent and the realised proceeds of the mortgaged property. Thus with a negligent valuation of £150,000 and a true valuation of £100,000 together with a loan on the strength of the negligent valuation of £130,000 and an ultimate sale of the mortgaged property for £70,000, the actual loss is £60,000 but what we have called the normal measure is limited to £50,000. But if the market has not fallen and the proceeds of the ultimate sale are £100,000, then actual loss and normal measure will be the same at £30,000. Thus cases can be cited, in the wake of *SAAMCO*,[324] in which the damages have been based upon the difference between the defendant's valuation and the correct valuation; this was so in *Coventry Building Society v William Martin & Partners*,[325] and again in *UCB Bank v David J. Pinder*.[326] To the normal measure interest at a reasonable commercial rate falls to be added.

**34-068** Where, had a correct valuation been given by the surveyor or valuer, the claimant would still have lent to the borrower but would have lent less, the normal measure will be contained within a different difference, here the difference between the amount in fact lent and the amount that would have been lent on a correct valuation. Here the normal measure is said to be contained within this difference rather than being this difference itself since, once again, the claimant's actual loss is prima facie[327] the difference between the amount which has in fact been lent and the realised proceeds of the mortgaged property. Thus if, on the figures in the previous paragraph's illustration, the claimant would have lent £85,000 on being given a true valuation of £100,000, then where, as in the earlier illustration, he sells the property for £70,000 suffering a loss of £60,000, his damages will be limited to £45,000, being the difference between the £130,000 that he did lend and the £85,000 that he would have lent. But where, again as in the earlier illustration, the market has not fallen and the sale proceeds are £100,000, he would have suffered no loss on an initial loan of £85,000 and, accordingly, actual loss and normal measure will be the same at £30,000. This type of situation is illustrated in the cases by *Singer & Friedlander v John D. Wood & Co*,[328] and *Corisand Investments v Druce & Co*,[329] where damages were assessed by reference to the difference between the amount of the loan in fact made and the amount that would have been lent on a proper valuation, together with interest at a reasonable commercial rate[330] which, once again, falls to be added to the normal measure.

---

323 Prima facie because there may be consequential losses, dealt with below, in addition.

324 [1997] A.C. 191.

325 [1997] 2 E.G.L.R. 146; contributory negligence and time from which interest ran were in issue.

326 [1998] 2 E.G.L.R. 203; establishing the actual value of the property at the time of the faulty valuation was the main concern.

327 Prima facie because there may be consequential losses, dealt with below, in addition.

328 [1977] 2 E.G.L.R. 84; see at 93M.

329 [1978] 2 E.G.L.R. 86; see at 98B and 101B.

330 But from the said difference there was deducted the contractual interest which had in fact been received by the claimants, and the interest at a reasonable commercial rate was computed on the amount remaining after that deduction. The deduction of the whole of the contractual interest

The normal measure may well lead to a smaller award where an alternative loan by the claimant to the mortgagor borrower, rather than no loan at all, is in issue.[331] An important aspect of this is that it is for the defendant to prove on the balance of probabilities that an alternative loan would have taken place and, if so, of what amount and upon what terms; today's much utilised loss of a chance has no place here. Thus where the defendant had satisfied this burden of proof in *The Mortgage Corp v Halifax (SW)*,[332] the claimant was not entitled to argue, in an attempt to augment the damages, that the court should simply evaluate, necessarily at over 50 per cent, the chance of an alternative loan.[333] Conversely, a defendant unable to adduce proof on the balance of probabilities cannot seek to reduce the damages by seeking an evaluation, at 50 per cent or under, of the chance of an alternative loan. **34-069**

**(b) Consequential losses: what is generally recoverable** There are no really clear illustrations of recovery for consequential losses. The best that can be done is to refer to *Baxter v Gapp & Co*,[334] which was the only case of any importance in this field until the last quarter of the last century. The decision there appears to be based upon the assumption that the claimant, had he not been misled into lending by the defendants' negligent valuation, would not have lent at all,[335] and the lender was held entitled to recover for the whole loss sustained by him which included various consequential losses by way of the cost of insuring the property and of maintaining it in repair while in the claimant's possession, legal charges during that period, expenses of the abortive attempts to sell, estate agents' commission on the eventual sale price and legal charges in connection with the sale. It is true that there was little or no discussion of these particular items of damage either at first instance[336] or in the Court of Appeal,[337] Goddard LJ below merely listing the items as being included in the claimant's whole loss for which he held that there should be recovery[338] and the Court of Appeal, in affirming, making no mention of the various items at all. But such recovery accords with principle. Moreover, it is important not to be diverted by the fact that *Baxter* is said to have been disapproved by the House of Lords in *Swingcastle Ltd v Gibson*.[339] This disapproval was only on a point relating to interest and may not even have been a point that was concerning the court in *Baxter*.[340] In any event, Lord Lowry, who gave the only reasoned speech in *Swingcastle*, was clear. In *Baxter*, he said, **34-070**

> "the real issue … was whether, in addition to the difference between the capital amounts, the plaintiff could recover as damages his consequential loss".[341]

received was, however, surely too great.

331 As in the illustrations in paras 34-067 and 34-068, above.

332 [1999] Lloyd's Rep. P.N. 159.

333 [1999] Lloyd's Rep. P.N. 159 at 174, col.1.

334 [1939] 2 K.B. 271 CA.

335 See Mackinnon LJ at [1939] 2 K.B. 271 CA at 273 referring to the assessment of damages on the basis that the claimant made the loan "which he would not have done but for the valuation".

336 [1938] 4 All E.R. 457.

337 [1939] 2 K.B. 271 CA.

338 [1938] 4 All E.R. 457 at 466G.

339 [1991] 2 A.C. 223; in the headnote.

340 See the footnote at the end of para.34-075, below.

341 [1991] 2 A.C. 223 at 235B. Indeed damages were awarded for the cost of estate agents and solicitors relating to repossession and sale in *Swingcastle* itself but such damages were not in issue: see the case at para.34-075, below.

**34-071** Consequential losses of the nature appearing in *Baxter v Gapp*,[342] may, however, not all be appropriate as items for recovery in cases where the lender, had he been given a proper valuation, would have lent the borrower less rather than not at all. This is because there now would be a loan in any event, leading to the need to take steps to enforce the security when things go wrong with the loan and the borrower. It is particularly true where the lender would still have lost out on the transaction because the amount that would have been lent moved above the market value of the mortgaged property. Thus, for instance, costs of repossession proceedings and of the sale of the property should not feature in the award where these expenses would have been incurred in any event with a smaller loan.[343]

**34-072** (c) **Consequential losses: what is generally irrecoverable** The principal cases in the field are concerned with losses for which recovery is not available. In particular, there is loss arising out of a property market collapse, a true consequential loss, and there is loss of interest at a high rate which may be, but is generally not, a true consequential loss. The key case dealing with the former is *Banque Bruxelles Lambert v Eagle Star Insurance Co Ltd*,[344] commonly known as *SAAMCO*, the name we shall now use for it. The key case dealing with the latter is *Swingcastle v Gibson*.[345]

**34-073** *(i) Losses from fall in market* The effect on damages of the collapse of the property market was addressed by the House of Lords in *SAAMCO*.[346] Claimants in three separate actions required the defendants to value properties on the security of which the claimants were minded to advance money on mortgage. In each case the defendants considerably overvalued the properties and the amounts lent by the claimants were influenced by the overvaluations. The property market then collapsed, greatly increasing the losses eventually suffered by the claimants. The trial judge and the Court of Appeal held that the claimants were entitled by way of damages to their entire loss represented by the amount lent, together with contractual interest, less the amount for which the properties sold. This, therefore, included the loss attributable to the market fall. The House of Lords did not agree with this result and gave a more limited recovery to the claimants. Lord Hoffmann, who gave the only reasoned speech with which his brethren expressed agreement, said that the real question was for what kind of loss were the claimants entitled to compensation, and concluded that the damages should be limited to the consequences of the valuation being wrong. In each case the damages should be limited to the amount by which the faulty valuation of the defendants exceeded the figure which a reasonable valuer would have arrived at as the amount the property would be most likely

---

342 [1939] 2 K.B. 271 CA.

343 Little assistance on damages is derived from the early decisions of *Crabbe v Brinsley* (1888) 5 T.L.R. 14 (where the full amount of the advance was recovered) and *Scholes v Brook* (1891) 64 L.T. 674 CA (where the basis of the damages assessment is unclear: see the discussion of the case by MacKinnon LJ in *Baxter v Gapp & Co* [1939] 2 K.B. 271 CA at 273). On the entitlement of a mortgage lender to recover hedging costs from a negligent valuer see the leading judgment of Longmore LJ in *Mortgage Agency Services Number One Ltd v Edward Symmons LLP* [2013] EWCA Civ 1590 CA.

344 [1997] A.C. 191.

345 [1991] 2 A.C. 223.

346 [1997] A.C. 191.

to have fetched if sold on the open market.[347] This was limited in effect to the shortfall in the claimants' security. Thus in the first of the three cases, where the difference between the defendants' valuation and the true value at the time of breach was £10 million and the difference between the amount lent, with interest, and the realised proceeds of the property was £9.75 million, the claimants were entitled to their whole loss[348]; the judgment below was affirmed. By contrast, in the second and third cases the shortfall in the security between what, at breach, the claimants thought they had and what they in fact had was not so great as the claimants' whole loss and their damages fell to be limited to the extent of that shortfall; the appeals were allowed.

The importance of this decision is well known and the limits that it imposes upon damages have been well rehearsed. The decision was effectively endorsed by the Supreme Court in *BPE Solicitors and another v Hughes-Holland*.[349] It is, however, equally important to notice that there are two situations when recovery will not be denied a lender claimant for the consequential loss arising from the collapse in the property market. Both situations are adverted to by Lord Hoffmann in *SAAMCO*.[350] The first is easy, being where the information is provided fraudulently.[351] The imposition of liability here is no more than a reflection of what Lord Lindley said long ago in *Quinn v Leathem*,[352] that "the intention to injure the plaintiff … disposes of any question of remoteness of damage".[353] The second is more difficult, being where the duty is not just to provide information to enable someone to decide on a course of action but to advise someone as to what course of action to take.[354] The difficulty is not in stating the distinction, which is simply that between giving information and giving advice, but in deciding within which category a particular case falls. Cases, after *SAAMCO*, have sometimes had to grapple with this problem. The difficulty has now been removed by the decision of the Supreme Court in *BPE Solicitors v Hughes-Holland*,[355] in which Lord Sumption, giving the opinion of the court, explained that the crucial distinction is not between whether what is given is "information" or "advice" but, rather, whether the person providing the service has assumed responsibility for the risk of the whole transaction (as is usually the case where advice is sought generally) or just for part of it (as is usually the case where only information is sought).[356] **34-074**

*(ii) Losses from non-payment of interest* The question of the measure of damages where there has been default in payment of interest claimed the attention of the House of Lords in *Swingcastle v Gibson*.[357] The claimants, a finance company, lent £10,000 on mortgage to the owners of a dwelling-house in reliance upon a valu- **34-075**

---

[347] The court rightly did not accept the argument advanced by the defendants that the limit should be to the excess over the highest valuation which would not have been negligent: see [1997] A.C. 191 at 221E to 222A.

[348] Subject to a deduction made by the trial judge on account of contributory negligence.

[349] [2017] UKSC 21.

[350] [1997] A.C. 191.

[351] [1997] A.C. 191 at 215E–F.

[352] [1901] A.C. 495.

[353] [1901] A.C. 495 at 537.

[354] [1997] A.C. 191 at 214E–F.

[355] [2017] UKSC 21.

[356] [2017] UKSC 21 at [40]–[41].

[357] [1991] 2 A.C. 223.

ation commissioned by them from the defendant surveyor. The survey was conducted negligently and the valuation given, of £18,000, was much too high. It was accepted that, had a proper valuation been made, the claimants would not have lent any money to the house owners. The owners quickly fell into arrears and the claimants repossessed and sold the house just over two years later for £12,000. This, of course, was appreciably above the amount that the claimants had lent but interest under the terms of the loan was payable at an annual rate initially of over 36 per cent and on default of over 45 per cent so that the amount owing, adding loan to contractual interest alleged due, was not far short of twice what had been lent. The House of Lords, reversing the Court of Appeal, held that the claimants were not entitled to claim, after giving credit for the price realised on the sale of the house, this amount. For the claimants so to claim constituted a failure, once again,[358] to distinguish between obtaining the benefit of their bargain with the borrowers and obtaining the benefit of their bargain with the defendant surveyor. Where the lenders went wrong, said Lord Lowry, delivering the only reasoned speech with which the other members of the court agreed, was to claim

> "incorrectly that the valuer by his negligence deprived them of the interest which they would have received from the borrowers if the borrowers had paid up. The security for the loan was the property but the lenders did not have a further security consisting of a guarantee by the valuer that the borrowers would pay everything, or indeed anything, that was due from them to the lenders at the date, whenever it occurred, on which the loan transaction terminated. The fallacy of the lenders' case is that they are trying to obtain from the valuer compensation for the borrowers' failure and not the proper damages for the valuer's negligence."[359]

Instead, the claimants were entitled to be compensated at a proper rate of interest, held to be a not ungenerous 12 per cent,[360] for being deprived of £10,000 for an appropriate period,[361] possibly two years but perhaps somewhat less as they could have realised their security more quickly,[362] together with their estate agents' and solicitors' costs in connection with the repossession and sale of the property. Since the total was likely not to exceed, or to exceed only marginally, the sale price of £12,000 for which credit had to be given, judgment was entered for the defendant.[363]

---

358 As in the first cases involving claims against surveyors or valuers by purchaser claimants (see para.34-050, above) or against solicitors by the same (see para.34-013, above).

359 [1991] 2 A.C. 223 at 238G–H.

360 [1991] 2 A.C. 223 at 239B.

361 The sometimes difficult question of the time from which interest, properly due, runs was tackled by the House of Lords in *Nykredit Mortgage Bank v Edward Erdman Group (No.2)* [1997] 1 W.L.R. 1627 HL and is addressed here when dealing with interest generally: see para.19-079, above. It should also be noted, in relation to interest, that the results in both *Swingcastle* and *Nykredi* may not be entirely consistent with the thinking at the time about how far interest might be recovered as damages: see in particular para.19-018, above.

362 [1991] A.C. 197 at 239C.

363 In so holding, their Lordships departed from *Baxter v Gapp & Co* [1939] 2 K.B. 271 CA, to the extent that that decision supported the lenders' claim for their contractual interest. The Court of Appeal in *Swingcastle v Gibson* [1990] 1 W.L.R. 1223 CA, had been not unsympathetic to the result at which their Lordships arrived but had considered themselves bound by the earlier decision, also of the Court of Appeal, to hold that the lenders were entitled to claim the lost interest at the rate at which the borrowers had contracted to pay. Yet it is fair to say that this was not a proposition for which *Baxter v Gapp* was formerly renowned; indeed Lord Lowry was not sure if "that proposition can be teased out of it": [1991] 2 A.C. 223 at 236G. The dispute was on other matters considered at para.34-070, above.

The one situation where a lender might properly claim interest at the rate at which he had contracted with his borrower is where he can show that, had he been properly advised by the surveyor or valuer, he would indeed not have lent to that particular borrower but would have been able to find a substitute borrower to whom he could have lent on the same terms. Lord Lowry in effect recognised some such possibility when he awarded his 12 per cent interest **34-076**

> "in the absence of any evidence as to how the lenders financed the loan or evidence showing how the money, if not lent to the borrowers, could have been profitably employed".[364]

However, the lender would need to be able to show that he had limited funds available for lending and that the new borrower was one not only who would have agreed to the same terms but to whom he would not otherwise have been able to lend. Such a case is likely to be rare.

**(d) Effect on damages of contributory negligence and failure to mitigate** Issues of mitigation of damage and of how far contributory negligence affects damages do not generally appear in this book when dealing with particular contracts and particular breaches, being comprehensively dealt with in chapters on these specific topics.[365] What has given rise to an exception here is simply the weight of cases in which contributory negligence and mitigation have featured ever since mortgage lenders began their assault on negligent surveyors and valuers to retrieve their vast losses consequent upon the catastrophic collapse in the property market.[366] **34-077**

Thus those claimant lenders in *SAAMCO*,[367] who were unaffected by the ruling in that case limiting recovery to the shortfall in the security taken because the shortfall was greater than their actual loss and they therefore were prima facie entitled to recover for their whole loss represented by the amount they had lent less the proceeds the mortgaged property had realised,[368] nevertheless did not achieve as great an award because that amount was made subject to a deduction by the trial judge for contributory negligence. In deciding in the claim against the negligent valuers in *Platform Homes Loans Ltd v Oyston Shipways Ltd*,[369] upon a particular method of effecting an apportionment on account of contributory negligence,[370] the House of Lords was resolving a point upon which there had been a wide difference of judicial opinion, and the large number of cases evidencing this difference which are cited by Morritt LJ in the Court of Appeal[371] goes to show just how often contributory negligence had been causing an award, in one way or another, to be reduced. Contributory negligence can in this context take a variety of forms; frequently met is where the level of lending has been much too high even on the basis of the negligent valuation being correct or has been unwise in the light of the **34-078**

---

364 [1991] 2 A.C. 223 at 239B.

365 See Chs 7 and 9.

366 Although the brunt of the attacks on professional advisers has been taken by solicitors rather than valuers: see para.34-037, above. Interest is also dealt with separately, in Ch.19, and the difficult interest question arising in *Nykredit Mortgage Bank v Edward Erdman Group (No.2)* [1997] 1 W.L.R. 1627 HL, in the context of mortgage lenders' losses is considered there: see para.19-077, above.

367 [1997] A.C. 191.

368 See para.34-073, above.

369 [2000] 2 A.C. 190.

370 For which, see para.7-010, above.

371 [1998] Ch. 466 CA at 474.

poor creditworthiness of the borrower. Contributory negligence can lead to a whole range of percentage reductions.[372]

**34-079** The requirement of mitigation operates in a similar way to cut down awards; indeed in some cases both doctrines are brought to bear, so that the claimant's transfer of the mortgage debt at a distinct undervalue in *Skipton Building Society v Lea Hough & Co*,[373] caused the action to fail upon grounds both of contributory negligence and failure to mitigate. Similar is *Europe Mortgage Co Ltd v GA Property Services Ltd*,[374] which can also be seen as involving an absence of mitigation though the court did not speak of mitigation in holding for the defendant. It was there decided that there could be no recovery where the loss arose from the lender's selling of the loan to a third party at an erroneously low price rather than resorting to the security which was at the time more than adequate. The use of the mitigation doctrine in this way is becoming much commoner. In particular, the failure to effect an earlier sale of the security when market prices were more favourable and the failure first to take action on the security before claiming against the surveyor or valuer have been seen as failures to mitigate. While such holdings have appeared more where the negligent defendant has been a solicitor,[375] actions, or inactions, of this nature by a mortgagee lender will be considered equally unreasonable, for the purposes of mitigation, in claims against surveyors and valuers.

**34-080** An earlier case of importance in which mitigation featured strongly, in the form of a failure to pursue borrowers on their personal covenants, is *London Building Society v Stone*.[376] It was agreed that the starting point there in arriving at the damages was the full amount of money lent since none would have been lent on a proper valuation[377] but the question was whether there was a need to make a deduction from this amount on account of the lenders' rights over against the borrowers. A couple about to get married and wishing to buy a particular house approached the claimant building society for a mortgage. The defendant valuer reported the property to be worth the amount for which the couple wished to buy it whereas because of the property's physical condition it was commercially worthless. When soon after it was discovered that the property was subject to subsidence and that, if nothing were done, part of the house would collapse, the buyers turned for help to the claimants who put the necessary remedial work in hand. The cost of this escalated to a figure far greater than the initial purchase price of the house, but the borrowers were thereby enabled to sell the house at a price sufficient for them to repay their loan. Should then the claimants have mitigated their loss by claiming against the borrowers upon their covenants and undertakings appearing in the mortgage? The majority of the Court of Appeal thought not.[378] Stephenson LJ was of the view that it was for the defendant to show that it would have been unreasonable for the claimants not to have enforced the borrowers' covenants and that he could not be said to have so shown where, as here, the borrowers were unable to provide additional payments and the claimants felt that they were morally

---

372 For apportionment patterns, see para.7-018, above.

373 [2000] P.N.L.R. 545.

374 [1999] Lloyd's Rep. P.N. 709.

375 See *Bristol and West Building Society v Fancy & Jackson* [1997] 4 All E.R. 582 (failure to sell earlier) and *Western Trust & Savings Ltd v Travers & Co* [1997] P.N.L.R. 295 (failure to enforce security) at para.9-084, above.

376 [1983] 1 W.L.R. 1242 CA.

377 [1983] 1 W.L.R. 1242 CA at 1249E.

378 Sir Denys Buckley dissented.

responsible for the loss of the borrowers' home and that enforcement of the covenants would have injured their public relations.[379] Indeed O'Connor LJ adopted a more extreme view and said that there was no need for the claimants to attempt to mitigate their loss by extracting money from the borrowers and that any contribution by them to the cost of repairs would have fallen to be ignored[380]; but it is thought that this goes too far, particularly in the light of today's preparedness to find that a failure to pursue the security constitutes a failure to mitigate.[381] *Eagle Star Insurance Co v Gale & Power*,[382] where the borrower's covenants had been taken into account, was a still earlier decision which O'Connor LJ wished to overrule but it may now be seen as reinstated.[383]

## (3) Vendors of property negligently advised as to value or otherwise

The principles which we have seen applied in the many cases where too high a valuation has been advised by the surveyor or valuer to one about to buy[384] apply equally where too low a valuation is provided to an intending seller. This was the position in *Montlake v Lambert Smith Hampton Group*,[385] which concerned the disposal by a well-known football club, Wasps, of its ground, together with its team and its goodwill, in an arrangement whereby it acquired shares. For the purposes of this disposal the ground was valued by the defendants at under £1 million. This was a negligent valuation because the defendants had failed to make proper enquiries as to the prospects of obtaining residential planning permission. The ground was eventually sold for £11.9 million once planning permission for residential development had been obtained. A proper valuation by the defendants at the time of the disposal by Wasps would have produced a valuation of £3.25 million, and the damages were based on the difference between this figure and the actual disposal figure of under £1 million. It was held not to be appropriate to base the damages on the much higher figure at which the ground had ultimately sold as the trial judge considered it to be improbable that Wasps, if properly advised, would have decided to go it alone by keeping the ground out of its disposal and taking the chance of itself obtaining the planning permission.[386] **34-081**

The negligence may however be in matters other than advice on the value of the property concerned. Thus in *Francis v Barclays Bank Plc*,[387] the surveyor's negligence lay in failure to make enquiries as to the likelihood of residential development on land which the bank he was advising was considering selling. Loss of a chance featured in the bank's damages and these are dealt with elsewhere.[388] In *Malmesbury v Strutt & Parker*,[389] chartered surveyors were engaged by owners of land adjoining an airport to negotiate a lease with the airport of part of their land **34-082**

---

379 [1983] 1 W.L.R. 1242 CA at 1263D–E.
380 [1983] 1 W.L.R. 1242 CA at 1257A–B.
381 See para.34-079, above.
382 (1955) 166 E.G. 37.
383 Indeed O'Connor LJ was alone in his wish to overrule *Eagle Star*, Stephenson LJ not passing on it and the dissenting Sir Denys Buckley adopting it.
384 See paras 34-050 and following, above.
385 [2004] 3 E.G.L.R. 149.
386 [2004] 3 E.G.L.R. 149 at [205]–[211].
387 [2005] P.N.L.R. 18 at 297.
388 See para.10-080, above.
389 [2007] P.N.L.R.29 at 571.

for airport car parking. The surveyors were negligent in not seeking to negotiate a rent that reflected the earnings of the car parks, referred to as a turnover rent. The evaluation of the chance of the airport's agreeing to a turnover rent had first to be decided[390]; afterwards came the question of the measure of the loss. The landowners contended for the difference between the rents that they would have obtained under a lease with a turnover rent and the rents that they would obtain under the lease as negotiated. The surveyors contended for the difference in the value of the reversions—the reversion that they should have had and the reversion that they did have—the reversions to be valued as at the time of the transaction as there was nothing in subsequent events to justify taking a later date. Jack J, after a full examination of a wide sweep of authorities, in a careful judgment sensibly upheld the surveyors' contentions.

## 3. ACCOUNTANTS

**34-083** Claims against accountants are today not uncommon, and claims against actuaries and auditors have also appeared. They are dealt with very briefly here only because practically all the cases have already appeared at other parts of the text, to which reference may be made. In *First Interstate Bank of California v Cohen Arnold*,[391] recovery against the defendant accountants turned on issues of certainty of damage and loss of chances.[392] In *Downs v Chappell*,[393] the defendant accountants' liability was based upon negligent misrepresentation over a business's profitability.[394] In *Cossey v Lonnkvist*,[395] the issue was whether the accountants' misinformation about a business's turnover had caused the damage.[396] In *Andrews v Barnett Waddingham*,[397] there was failure of the defendant actuary to advise on one aspect of an annuity, but there was here no recovery as the loss arose otherwise.[398] In *University of Keele v Price Waterhouse*,[399] the accountants' negligence lost the claimant university the chance of implementing a tax-saving scheme.[400] Claims have also been made against accountants for their failure to advise their clients on the availability of tax reliefs. In *Slattery v Moore Stephens*,[401] there was failure to advise the claimant, entitled to be taxed on the remittance basis, that he should have his salary paid offshore; this led to recovery of the amount of tax that would have been saved had he done so.[402] In *BE Studios Ltd v Smith & Williamson Ltd*,[403] there was failure to advise the client company of new statutory provisions for claiming relief for expenditure on research and development, but here no tax loss was proved.

---

390 See this at para.10-080, above.
391 [1996] P.N.L.R. 17 CA.
392 See the case at para.10-079, above.
393 [1997] 1 W.L.R. 426 CA.
394 See the case at para.49-030 and especially at para.49-051, below.
395 [2000] Lloyd's Rep. P.N. 885 CA.
396 See the case at para.8-153, above
397 [2006] P.N.L.R. 24 CA at 432.
398 See the case at para.8-157, above.
399 [2004] P.N.L.R. 8 at 112.
400 See the case at para.10-078, above. Damages were not appealed: [2004] P.N.L.R. 43 CA at 888.
401 [2004] P.N.L.R. 14 at 241.
402 Subject, in one tax year, to a reduction for contributory negligence.
403 [2006] S.T.C. 358.

## 4. Bankers

Bankers, like other professionals, may be liable for giving negligent advice. In *Woods v Martins Bank*,[404] the claimant recovered as damages capital lost in investments made upon the bank's advice and money paid under a guarantee of a small private company's overdraft, the bank also having advised that the claimant enter into the guarantee.[405] Poor financial advice from an investment bank engaged to manage the profits of a family shipping business led to the claim in *JP Morgan Chase Bank v Springwell Navigation Corporation*,[406] where the false argument that recovery for two losses—for the resulting decline in value of the claimant's portfolio and for lost shipping profits as fewer vessels than planned were acquired with the reduced portfolio—would amount to double recovery was rejected by the Court of Appeal.[407] In *Rubenstein v HSBC Bank Plc*,[408] the claimant had told the defendant that he wished to invest without risk and have easy access to his money, but the bank advised him to invest in a form of bond which was subject to market losses while telling the claimant that the investment was the same as a cash deposit. When the risk materialised on the collapse of the market, the Court of Appeal held the bank liable for the claimant's losses.[409] There are, however, types of breach of contract other than by the giving of negligent advice. **34-084**

**(a) Failure to honour cheques** What calls for separate and particular consideration is breach of contract by a banker's failure to honour his customer's cheques and drafts when he has moneys of the customer to meet them. The important characteristic of such cases is that the claimant can recover substantial damages for injury to his credit without proof of actual damage. This was established, where the claimant was a trader, by *Rolin v Steward*,[410] still the leading case on damages though decided over a century and a half ago.[411] The clearest explanation appears in Lord Birkenhead's speech in *Wilson v United Counties Bank*,[412] which itself concerned a banker's failure to sustain credit, where he said that **34-085**

> "the ratio decidendi in such cases is that the refusal to meet the cheque, under such circumstances, is so obviously injurious to the credit of a trader that the latter can recover, without allegation of special damage, reasonable compensation for the injury done to his credit."[413]

---

404 [1958] 1 W.L.R. 1018.

405 There was no argument on damages.

406 [2006] P.N.L.R. 28 at 528.

407 On a strike out application.

408 [2012] EWCA Civ 1184 CA.

409 The main issue in *Rubenstein* turned on causation and remoteness and on this is considered at para.8-157, above.

410 (1854) 14 C.B. 595.

411 *Marzetti v Williams* (1830) 1 B. & Ad. 415 had already established that damages for injury to credit could be awarded in such a case, but gave nominal damages as only the question of liability was in issue.

412 [1920] A.C. 102 at 112.

413 See, too, Cresswell J in *Rolin v Steward* (1854) 14 C.B. 595 at 606, citing Lord Tenterden in *Marzetti v Williams* (1830) 1 B. & Ad. 415: "'I cannot forbear to observe that it is a discredit to a person, and therefore injurious in fact, to have a draft refused payment for so small a sum; for, it shows that the banker had very little confidence in the customer. It is an act particularly calculated to be injurious to a person in trade.' His Lordship, therefore, assumes as a thing not to be disputed, that a breach of contract of this sort must of necessity be injurious to a person in trade."

Subsequently in *Gibbons v Westminster Bank*,[414] it was held that the rule did not apply where the customer was not a trader, so that actual injury to credit would have to be proved to give an entitlement to more than nominal damages, but that limitation has been departed from by the Court of Appeal in *Kpohraror v Woolwich Building Society*.[415] Evans LJ, in a judgment with which his brethren agreed, there said:

> "History has changed the social factors which moulded the rule in the nineteenth century. It is not only a tradesman of whom it can be said that the refusal to meet his cheque is 'so obviously injurious to [his] credit' that he should recover, 'without allegation of special damage, reasonable compensation for the injury done to his credit'[416] … The credit rating of individuals is as important for their personal transactions, including mortgages and hire-purchase as well as banking facilities, as it is for those engaged in trade, and it is notorious that central registers are now kept. I would have no hesitation in holding that what in effect is a presumption of some damage arises in every case, in so far as this is a presumption of fact."[417]

**34-086** The question of what was the appropriate level for an award where no special loss by way of loss of credit could be shown arose in *Nicholson v Knox Ukiwa & Co*.[418] It was an unusual case in many ways. It was unusual in the very high number of cheque dishonours; while the number alleged by the claimant, in the 200s, was probably an over-estimate, more than 40 dishonours were admitted. It was unusual in that, while the dishonours had taken place as far back as 1973 and 1974, the case in which they were in issue was not heard until 2008, with the result that the question of interest dominated the issue of damages. It was unusual in that the claim was not against the bank itself but against solicitors for having at a mediation agreed a settlement figure inclusive of interest which the claimant understood to be exclusive of interest and which, being inclusive of interest, was alleged to be at an undervalue. And it was unusual in that the claimant's claim against the bank had over the years been mishandled by solicitor after solicitor, with the claimant suing each in turn on a loss of a chance basis and finally suing the ultimate solicitor for mishandling the mediation.

**34-087** In the event Saunders J decided against the claimant on the basis that he well knew that the settlement figure was inclusive of interest so that the question of whether the settlement was at an undervalue fell away. Since however that question had been at the forefront of much of the argument, Saunders J thought that he ought to give his view on what would have been the appropriate measure of damages against the bank to which interest, in an amount many times the damages, would have had to be added. Since it was agreed that the likely trial date for the action against the bank would have been January 1984, it was the level of damages that would have been awarded at that date which was in issue. Saunders J rightly

414 [1939] 2 K.B. 882.

415 [1996] 4 All E.R. 119 CA. *Gibbons* was effectively overruled; *Rae v Yorkshire Bank* [1988] B.T.L.C. 35 CA, where only nominal damages were allowed, was explained on the basis that the claim there was only for non-pecuniary loss, for "inconvenience and humiliation", which is seldom awarded in contract.

416 From Lord Birkenhead's speech in the text above.

417 [1996] 4 All E.R. 119 CA at 124a–c. Although damages for injury to credit were awarded, the claimant's further, and much larger, claim for specific trading losses was disallowed as there was nothing to indicate to the defendant that the one-day delay in payment of the claimant's cheque would result in trading losses to him.

418 [2008] P.N.L.R. 33 at 782.

said that he found little assistance from the very few and scattered authorities which showed awards, when adjusted to 1984 figures, in the mid-thousands.[419] He concluded that the appropriate bracket was wide and, in his judgment, between £10,000 and £20,000, but his view was that the award here would have been much more likely to have been closer to £10,000 than to £20,000.[420] Since today this bracket would be between £25,000 and £50,000, as Saunders J recognised,[421] it is thought that the bracket may have been pitched rather too high. It was however, as we have pointed out, a highly unusual case and there is little doubt that Saunders J was influenced by the fact that cheques had been dishonoured in droves and by the effect that this was bound to have on the claimant's business.

**(b) Failure to sustain credit** Where a banker had expressly contracted to sustain a trader's financial credit, substantial damages were held recoverable without proof of actual damage in *Wilson v United Counties Bank*.[422] Their Lordships regarded the situation as analogous to the cases of dishonour of cheques, and indeed a fortiori since there was express agreement to protect the claimant's credit.[423] The position will now be the same for non-traders.[424] **34-088**

## 5. Stockbrokers

A stockbroker's failure to enter into a contract for the purchase or sale of shares on behalf of his principal simply forms a particular example of an agent's failure to enter into a contract as instructed, dealt with in the next chapter.[425] The present concern, in this chapter devoted to professional service contracts, is with a rather special and difficult type of case where the stockbroker, having in his hands shares which he has bought for his principal or which the principal has deposited with him as margin, proceeds to sell them without instructions. There will frequently be conversion as well as breach of contract in such cases, but the measure of damages may well be the same in both.[426] The difficulties arise where the market value of the shares fluctuates between the time of the broker's wrongful sale, the time the news of it comes to the principal's ears, and the time that action is brought by the principal and judgment entered for damages. **34-089**

Where the broker sells shares which have been deposited with him as margin by the principal, this will constitute at the moment of such sale both a breach of contract and a conversion. Commonly a fair interval of time will elapse before the principal comes to hear of the broker's default and therefore before he can bring **34-090**

---

419 *Rolin v Steward* (1854) 14 C.B. 595: £6,900; *Davidson v Barclays Bank* [1940] 1 All E.R. 316 (where the bank was sued in libel): £4,350; *Kpohraror v Woolwich Building Society* [1996] 4 All E.R. 119 CA: £3,200.

420 [2008] P.N.L.R. 33 at 782, [92]. Nevertheless he opted for £15,000 because he was required to be generous to a claimant suing his solicitor for losing him his case. This approach is misconceived because the requirement to be generous to such a claimant is in relation to the evaluation of his chances of success in his claim (see on this para.10-095, above) and not in the evaluation of the damages recoverable therein.

421 [2008] P.N.L.R. 33 at [84].

422 [1920] A.C. 102.

423 The general problems to which all these cases give rise are dealt with at paras 30-007 and 30-009, above.

424 See para.34-085, above.

425 On the coverage of this and the next chapter, see para.34-001, above.

426 Contrast para.24-009, above.

an action. In such circumstances, where the market had fallen in the interval, it was held in *Solloway v McLaughlin*,[427] that the principal was still entitled in conversion to the market value at the time of conversion, and there is no reason why in an action for breach of contract he should not equally be entitled to the market value at the time of breach. This award may represent more than the claimant has lost as he had clearly not intended to sell the shares during the interval; but any other rule would allow the broker to profit from his default.[428] Where on the other hand the market has risen during the interval between default and knowledge, the claimant's loss would be less than satisfied by an award of the market value at the time of default. It is submitted that the claimant should be entitled to claim the market value to which the shares have risen at the time of judgment, provided he brings an action with all reasonable speed upon learning of the sale. This proposition derives support from the cases on conversion of goods,[429] and also from *Ellis and Co's Trustee v Dixon-Johnson*,[430] which concerned such a situation, but was highly complicated by questions of bankruptcy. Where, further, the market value has fluctuated both up and down between breach, knowledge and judgment, there is little clear authority. It is submitted that, as elsewhere,[431] whether to give the highest intermediate value between knowledge and judgment should be dependent upon whether the claimant can show that he himself would have sold at the height of the market.[432] It was said in editions of this work to the 16th in 1997 that some support for such an award was to be found in Wills J's decision in *Michael v Hart*,[433] but that against allowing any intermediate value were *Simmons v London Joint Stock Bank*,[434] and *Mansell v British Linen Co*.[435] Since then the Court of Appeal in *Ata v American Express Bank Ltd*,[436] has declared Wills J's decision overruled, stating it to be inconsistent with *Simmons* and *Mansell*.[437] Yet this overruling supports rather than contradicts the submission in the above text because it was on the basis that there would have been no sale at the market height. Hirst LJ, who gave the only reasoned judgment, specifically stated:

> "If, of course, a claimant in the position of the plaintiff in *Michael v Hart* could prove on the balance of probabilities that he would have sold at the height of the market if his shares had not been sold earlier, then he would indeed be able to recover damages calculated on that hypothesis."

**34-091** Where the broker sells shares that he has purchased for the principal and agreed to carry over till a certain settlement day, this is probably breach of contract without

---

427 [1938] A.C. 247 PC: facts at para.38-014, below.

428 See [1938] A.C. 247 PC at 259, per Lord Atkin: quoted at para.38-014, below.

429 See *Sachs v Miklos* [1948] 2 K.B. 23 CA at para.38-018, below.

430 [1925] A.C. 489.

431 See para.38-022, below.

432 To give the value at breach if this is higher than the value between knowledge and judgment would be in effect the same as the situation where a steady fall occurs.

433 [1901] 2 K.B. 867; affirmed on another ground [1902] 1 K.B. 482 CA.

434 [1891] 1 Ch. 270; see especially at 284, per Kekewich J.

435 [1892] 3 Ch. 159, a somewhat analogous decision.

436 *The Times*, 26 June 1998.

437 And also with *The Playa Larga*, for which case see para.38-022, below, sub nom. *Industria Azucarera Nacional SA v Empresa Exportada de Azucar* [1982] Com. L.R. 171. In *Ata the Court Appeal reference of* [1983] 2 Lloyd's Rep. 171 is given but the Court of Appeal did not pass on this damages issue.

conversion. In *Michael v Hart*,[438] the defendant broker improperly sold such shares at a time when prices were falling and informed the principal that he had closed his account. The principal, instead of buying on the falling market or bringing an action, informed the broker that he would insist on performance of the defendant's contract when the settlement date arrived. By this date the prices had recovered and gone even higher, and it was held that the claimant's contention that the damages were to be measured with reference to the higher market value at the settlement date was correct.[439] Here the breach by the broker was an anticipatory breach which the principal was entitled not to accept,[440] and it was this factor which made it proper to award the claimant the higher value, although he had taken no steps to buy or to sue upon knowledge, and which posed a different situation from that dealt with in the last paragraph.[441]

## 6. Estate Agents

Claims against their estate agents by clients who have acquired property, by purchase or lease, on the strength of misinformation negligently given to them by the estate agent should follow the same lines as similar claims against solicitors[442] and against surveyors and valuers.[443] *Carreras v Levy*[444] is a case in point. In finding office accommodation for the claimants, the defendant estate agents misrepresented the area of the premises which in the event the claimants took on lease. The claimants succeeded in proving that, but for the misrepresentation, they would have rejected the lease, and thereby avoided the finding which led to a nominal damages award in *Sykes v Midland Bank Executor and Trustee Co.*[445] Nevertheless nominal damages were still given as the landlords might have obtained for the space on offer any amount within a very wide price range, and the claimants had therefore failed to show that they had been induced to pay more than the market value of the premises. "Prima facie", said John Stephenson J, **34-092**

> "the measure of damages is the difference between the rent actually agreed and paid for the lease and the market value of that leasehold interest expressed in rent".[446]

This precisely states the measure as laid down in the critical case, cited by the judge,[447] of *Ford v White & Co.*[448] In *Duncan Investments Ltd v Underwood*,[449] the claimant was more successful where a portfolio of properties was bought in reliance upon the defendant estate agents' negligent advice as to the prices which the

---

438 [1902] 1 K.B. 482 CA.

439 It is important to appreciate that the Court of Appeal's overruling in *Ata v American Express Bank Ltd of Michael v Hart* (see para.34-090, above) is only of that decision at first instance. The other ground dealt with here upon which the Court of Appeal affirmed is unaffected by *Ata*.

440 The familiar cases on anticipatory breach are dealt with in Lord Collins MR's judgment.

441 See, similarly, *Murray v Hewitt* (1886) 2 T.L.R. 872 where damages were assessed by reference to the market value at the time of action brought. Contrast paras 9-021 to 9-023, above.

442 See paras 34-012 to 34-026, above.

443 See paras 34-050 to 34-063, above.

444 [1970] E.G.D. 618.

445 [1971] 1 Q.B. 113 CA, which was expressly distinguished ([1970] E.G.D. 618 at 626). See the case at para.34-027, above.

446 [1970] E.G.D. 618 at 623.

447 [1970] E.G.D. 618 at 632.

448 [1964] 1 W.L.R. 885. See para.34-014, above.

449 [1998] P.N.L.R. 754 CA.

individual properties would realise. The value of the properties if sold individually was substantially greater than if sold *en bloc* and the Court of Appeal, reversing the court below, took the former value since the parties had only had that value in mind. The defendants had advised on individual prices and knew that the claimant proposed to sell the properties individually. In *John D Wood & Co (Residential and Agricultural) v Knatchbull*,[450] the negligence was of a rather different nature. The defendant estate agent, who had been instructed by the claimant to find a buyer for his property with the asking price set at £1.5 million, failed to inform the claimant that the asking price for a similar neighbouring property was £1.95 million. Damages were awarded the claimant for loss of the chance of selling at a figure higher than his asking price.

## 7. TRAVEL AGENTS

**34-093** A contract with a travel agent to provide a holiday differs from most of the contracts so far considered in that it has much less of a commercial flavour. Pecuniary loss may not therefore be uppermost in the mind of the customer whose complaint against the travel agent is for mismanagement of the holiday arrangements. It is true that the travel agent may be liable for any increased cost incurred by the customer in making alternative holiday arrangements, or for the amount by which the holiday arranged turns out to be worth less in money terms than the customer has paid for it. But the real loss in many cases will simply be marked by the fact that the whole holiday has been ruined. In *Jarvis v Swan's Tours*,[451] in a decision which has brought into prominence the whole question of how far recovery for non-pecuniary loss is allowable in contract,[452] the Court of Appeal held that the claimant was entitled to damages for the disappointment of a spoiled holiday. Already some 20 years earlier that court had, in *Stedman v Swan's Tours*,[453] given damages for the inconvenience and discomfort caused to the claimants by their travel agent's reservation of very inferior hotel rooms at their holiday destination,[454] but it was not until *Jarvis*,[455] that damages were openly and explicitly given for disappointment. The claimant there had booked a winter sports holiday in Switzerland in reliance on what Edmund Davies LJ called the defendant travel agents' "lavishly illustrated brochure with its ecstatic text",[456] only to discover that the "great time"[457] which had been promised did not materialise and the many facilities which he had been led to expect were simply not there. There was no clear physical inconvenience or discomfort because, as Lord Denning MR pointed out, the claimant had been conveyed to Switzerland and back and had been provided with meals and bed in the hotel. But the holiday had been a grave disappointment, and the Court of Appeal gave the claimant damages for the disappointment, distress, annoyance and frustration caused by the breach of contract, regarding as espousing limitations which were no longer acceptable the 19th century statements[458] that

---

450 [2003] 1 E.G.L.R. 33.
451 [1973] Q.B. 233 CA.
452 See para.5-025, above.
453 (1951) 95 S.J. 727 CA.
454 See para.5-018, above.
455 [1973] Q.B. 233 CA.
456 [1973] Q.B. 233 CA at 239B.
457 [1973] Q.B. 233 CA at 239B.
458 In *Hamlin v Great Northern Ry* (1856) 1 H. and N. 408 at 411 and *Hobbs v L.S.W. Ry* (1875) L.R.

damages are not available to a claimant for inconvenience stopping short of physical inconvenience, such as annoyance, vexation and disappointment of mind occasioned by a breach of contract. In a proper case damages for mental distress can be recovered in contract, and a contract for a holiday was a proper case.

Soon after *Jarvis* came *Jackson v Horizon Holidays*,[459] where a holiday had been spoiled for a whole family. The Court of Appeal, in upholding the judge's award,[460] specifically analysed it as being, in part, of damages for the diminution in value of the holiday and, in part, of damages for mental distress. Lord Denning MR said that in *Jarvis* it had been **34-094**

> "held by this court that damages for the loss of a holiday may include not only the difference in value between what was promised and what was obtained, but also damages for mental distress, inconvenience, upset, disappointment and frustration caused by the loss of the holiday."[461]

In addition, there may be a claim for further expenses incurred by the claimant; indeed one interesting feature of the decision in *Jarvis* is that the amount awarded was twice the cost of the holiday.

Cases now can be found every year in which damages along these lines are awarded for spoilt or ruined holidays. In the 18th edition of this work it was pointed out that, while these were generally county court decisions and ill-reported, *Current Law Yearbooks* had been providing examples from 1980 onwards, in earlier years in profusion, of otherwise unreported cases on loss of holidays; they have gradually decreased in number and have now virtually disappeared.[462] It was said that these awards for the non-pecuniary loss, which were generally in hundreds of pounds with the occasional leap into the thousands, appeared unnecessarily modest, especially as they tended to be made for division between all the members of the family or, very occasionally, other holiday group. The Court of Appeal in *Milner v Carnival Plc*,[463] subsequently addressed the question of what is the correct measure of damages for a ruined holiday, the ruined holiday in *Milner* being that of a husband and wife who had embarked on a cruise on a Cunard luxury liner. The many county court decisions in the *Current Law Yearbooks* were before the court, having been marshalled by counsel, and Ward LJ in a valuable judgment, the only reasoned one given, commented that they tended on the whole to show rather low awards.[464] In the result the Court of Appeal arrived at the much higher award of £12,000,[465] being £3,500 for the diminution in the value of the cruise by about a **34-095**

---

10 Q.B. 111 at 122; for these, see para.5-023, above.

459 [1975] 1 W.L.R. 1468 CA.

460 The extension of the decision in *Jarvis* to allow, on similar facts, to the claimant in Jackson recovery not only for his own disappointment but also for that of his wife and children raises the further question as to how far a party making a contract which is, at least in part, for the benefit of third parties can recover damages in respect of the loss to them.

461 [1975] 1 Ll. L. R. 1468 CA at 1472B–C. On the whole development of recovery in contract for mental distress see paras 5-023 and following, above.

462 The awards used to be found in the lengthy section entitled "Damages" but since about the turn of the century have been in the small section entitled "Hospitality and Leisure". But in the seven years from 2007 no cases of this nature have appeared in the "Hospitality and Leisure" section.

463 [2010] 3 All E.R. 701 CA.

464 [2010] 3 All E.R. 701 CA at [37], where the various amounts of damages in the cases are usefully set out by him. He also praised counsel for their industry in producing up to 56 cases of this nature (at [35]) and for their diligent analyses (at [37]).

465 Although a reduction of the trial judge's even higher £22,000.

third,[466] together with £4,000 to the husband and £4,500 to the wife for their inconvenience and distress.[467] Yet this must not be taken as a representative award for today. For Ward LJ not only was careful to point out that each case presented different facts and different holiday features which would affect the damages awarded[468] but also regarded *Milner* as an exceptional case[469]—the cruise was billed in ecstatic terms as a legendary experience while for the claimants it was the unrepeatable holiday of a lifetime—calling for an exceptional award.[470] Nonetheless the impression gained from his judgment is that in the future awards are likely to be somewhat higher than in the few cases in the law reports and the many in the earlier *Current Law Yearbooks*.[471]

466 [2010] 3 All E.R. 701 CA at [46].

467 [2010] 3 All E.R. 701 CA at [60].

468 See his useful analysis of types of holiday at [2010] 3 All E.R. 701 CA [37].

469 [2010] 3 All E.R. 701 CA at [52].

470 [2010] 3 All E.R. 701 CA at [55].

471 Since *Milner* was decided, there is *Antcliffe v Thomas Cook Tour Operations Ltd* unreported 4 July 2012 Birmingham County Court. Only £3,000 to be divided between five claimants, being a mother and her children, was awarded for diminution in the value of the holiday and loss of enjoyment, but counsel do not seem to have been arguing for higher sums: at [123]–[126]. *Milner* was cited tangentially.

## Chapter 35

# CONTRACTS CONCERNING PRINCIPAL AND AGENT

Table of Contents



Contracts of agency were, in editions before 2000, compendiously dealt with in a single chapter. However, as explained at the beginning of the previous chapter and for reasons there set out,[1] contracts for professional and other services have now been taken out of this omnibus category and dealt with separately in that chapter. This has left what we have called the agent proper for this chapter which, as in the editions since 2000, is confined to the agent, together with the corresponding principal, engaged to contract for his principal or entrusted with his principal's property. **35-001**

## I. Breach by Principal

Like the employee, the agent whose services have been improperly dispensed with has a number of similar alternative remedies open to him. He may sue on the contract for his commission or salary, either if his work is completed or if the agreement was to pay him in any event. If a suit on the contract is not available, he may sue on a quantum meruit for the value of the services already rendered[2] or he may bring an action for damages. Whether an agent is entitled to his commission or salary if he does not achieve the required result, e.g. finding a purchaser for the principal's house, or if he is prevented by the principal from continuing his efforts to achieve that result, e.g. by the principal taking the house out of the market, and whether such prevention constitutes a breach of contract letting in a claim for damages, is all a question of the construction of the particular agreement and is not germane to a work on damages.[3] **35-002**

---

1 See para.34-001, above.

2 As in *Prickett v Badger* (1856) 1 C.B. N.S. 296. The headnote states that Willes J refers to the measure of damages but neither he nor his brethren have a word about damages; they are concerned only with the common counts. It was, of course, early days for damages; the decision in *Prickett* came in the year in which *Mayne on Damages* was first published.

3 See the standard texts. Further, and additionally, the agent can claim to be indemnified and reimbursed for outlays, expenses and losses incurred in the performance of his agency. Although the

35-003 With these various alternatives available to a dismissed agent, the action for damages makes infrequent appearances. The measure of damages will be the amount that the agent might reasonably have earned under the contract had he not been prevented from continuing to act.[4] Thus in *Inchbald v Western Neilgherry Coffee Co*,[5] the claimant was a stockbroker employed by the defendant company to allot the shares of the company, and the claimant, after an initial payment of £100, was to be paid £400 upon the allotment of the whole of the shares. After a good number had been allotted, the company, in breach of the contract with the claimant, was wound up. In the claimant's action for damages he was awarded £250. Willes J said that he was "entitled to receive the £400, less an allowance for the risk".[6] In *Trollope v Martyn*,[7] the defendant instructed the claimant, a house agent, to find a purchaser for certain property. The claimant found a would-be purchaser, who signed an agreement to buy subject to contract and subsequently approved and signed the draft formal contract proposed by the defendant. The defendant then withdrew and refused to proceed with the matter. The Court of Appeal awarded as damages the amount of commission the claimant would have earned had the transaction been completed.[8] On the other hand, in *Trollope v Caplan*,[9] the Court of Appeal held that before an estate agent can get damages equal to the commission he would have earned had the transaction gone through, it must be found as a fact that but for the defendant's breach a binding contract with the purchaser would have been entered into. This, as Greene LJ said, had been established to the court's satisfaction in *Trollope v Martyn*,[10] but in the case before the court there was no such proof, since, except as to price, none of the terms of the contract of sale had been agreed by the parties. Yet Greene LJ also pointed out that it did not follow that, because the agent cannot get damages equal to his commission, he can only get nominal damages, saying that

> "the measure of damages ... must depend on the value of the chance of earning the commission, and that value may be great or small or nominal according to the circumstances."[11]

---

amount and the extent of this indemnity may be difficult to calculate, it is not to be classified as damages; it is implied contractual indemnity, an implied liability on the contract.

4 In *Lyndale Fashion Manufacturers v Rich* [1973] 1 W.L.R. 73 CA, it was common ground that, under the *Gourley* rule (see paras 18-002 and following, above), the incidence of tax fell to be taken into account in assessing the claimant's damages, the issue being as to the proper amount of tax to be deducted: see para.18-062, above). It is, however, thought not necessarily to be correct to deduct tax in agency cases, a view supported by *Deeny v Gooda Walker (No.2)* [1996] 1 W.L.R. 426 HL, where the contract was for professional services with the converse case of breach by the provider of the services. See the general discussion at paras 18-047 to 18-050, above.

5 (1864) 17 C.B. N.S. 733.

6 (1864) 17 C.B. N.S. 733 at 742. The action was for damages; yet the quantum meruit cases of *Planché v Colburn* (1831) 8 Bing. 14 and *Prickett v Badger* (1856) 1 C.B. N.S. 296 were cited.

7 [1934] 2 K.B. 436 CA. On the issue of liability both this and the following decision of *Trollope v Caplan* [1936] 2 K.B. 382 CA, are generally discredited since their treatment by the House of Lords in *Luxor v Cooper* [1941] A.C. 108; but they remain illustrative on the issue of damages.

8 Scrutton LJ dissented, but only on the issue of liability.

9 [1936] 2 K.B. 382 CA.

10 [1934] 2 K.B. 436 CA.

11 [1936] 2 K.B. 382 CA at 401, per Greene LJ. If this chance is slender, the claimant might be well advised to take the quasi-contractual, or today restitutionary, approach and sue on a quantum meruit for the value of services rendered, as in *Prickett v Badger* (1856) 1 C.B. N.S. 296.

In contrast to *Trollope v Martyn*,[12] is the much later *Nicholas Prestige Homes v Neal*,[13] where the estate agent claimants had a sole agency agreement with the defendant house owner who was in breach of the agreement by selling the house through another estate agent, and the Court of Appeal held the claimants entitled to their full commission as damages since the chance they had lost of selling the house was considered to be a certain one.[14] Nor need the damages be limited to commission on a single lost deal. Thus in *IRT Oil and Gas Ltd v Fiber Optic Systems Technology (Canada) Inc*,[15] the claimant company, the exclusive sales agent for the defendant company under a five year contract, recovered for its loss of profit following upon the defendant principal's repudiation of the contract in the course of the five years, although that loss of profit was difficult to calculate.[16]

Like the employee, the agent will be required to mitigate his damage by seeking alternative work and, to the extent that he achieves this, any amount earned will fall to be deducted from his lost commission. Thus in *Duffen v Frabo SpA*,[17] moneys earned as a consultant were taken into account as reducing the agent's potential loss[18]; in *Lyndale Fashion Manufacturers v Rich*,[19] the agent without argument brought into the computation of his damages claim moneys earned in mitigation from a new principal. However, since an agent has a freer hand in carrying out the contract and may not have to devote his working time exclusively to his principal, other work which he takes on will not be truly alternative if he could have done both concurrently, and will therefore not go in mitigation of damage. **35-004**

## II. BREACH BY AGENT[20]

### (A) AGENTS EMPLOYED TO ENTER INTO CONTRACTS ON BEHALF OF THE PRINCIPAL

The damages, which here aim to put the principal in the position he would have been in had the agent carried out his agency properly, will differ depending upon whether the agent could have concluded the contract that he was engaged to conclude, and it is important to keep this distinction well in mind. (1) If the breach consists in a failure to enter into the required contract properly or at all, the principal must be put in the position he would have been in if that contract had been **35-005**

12 [1934] 2 K.B. 436 CA.

13 [2010] EWCA Civ 1552 CA.

14 [2010] EWCA Civ 1552 CA at 32.

15 [2009] EWHC 3041 (QB).

16 See the case further at para.10-005, above. Where a contract, upon which the principal has defaulted, has been concluded between the principal and the buyers to whom the agent has introduced the principal, and a term is implied into the contract of agency to the effect that the principal will not fail to perform the contract with the buyers so as to deprive the agent of his remuneration under the agency contract, then, as in *Alpha Trading v Dunnshaw-Patten* [1981] Q.B. 290 CA, damages of an equivalent amount to the commission he would have earned will be available to the agent: at 296C–D. Only liability, and not damages, was in issue before the Court of Appeal in *Alpha Trading*; for the case below see [1980] 2 Lloyd's Rep. 284.

17 [2000] 1 Lloyd's Rep. 180.

18 [2000] 1 Lloyd's Rep. 180 at 196, col.2 ("would probably have been in no position to take on the extra work of the consultancy"). It was conceded that earnings from employment as managing director of a company had to be taken into account: at 195, col.2.

19 [1973] 1 W.L.R. 73 CA.

20 In certain cases the agent may be liable to account for profits to the principal. Such actions, which result from the agent's fiduciary relationship to the principal, have a flavour of equity about them, and to include them here would only confuse the common law principles as to measure of damages.

concluded; in many cases this will give the principal the benefit of the bargain that would have been made with the third party.[21] (2) If on the other hand the breach does not consist in such a failure because such a contract was not available to the agent, but consists in entering into the wrong type of contract or in informing the principal that he has entered into the right type of contract, the principal must be put in the position he would have been in if the wrong contract had not been concluded[22] or if he had not been misinformed that the right contract was made.[23]

## 1. Breach by Failure to Conclude the Contract as Instructed

**35-006** Where the breach consists in a failure to conclude the required contract, the rather few authorities, many of which are also old, all support the proposition that the principal is generally entitled to recover for the loss of the bargain that he would have gained. Thus where the agent has been employed to sell property and fails to do so or to do so properly, the principal would be entitled to recover as damages the amount the property had depreciated before he could make a sale himself, or, if the contract should have been concluded by the agent at a particular price, that contract price less the market value This proposition is illustrated by two cases, one concerning a sale of shares and the other a sale of a house. In *Neilson v James*,[24] a stockbroker, commissioned to sell shares, worded the contract in such a manner that it was void by statute and he was held responsible to his client for the full contractual price of the shares, where the buyer repudiated the contract, the shares being now valueless since the bank in which they were held had stopped payment and been ordered to be wound up.[25] In *Keppel v Wheeler*,[26] the principal employed the agent to sell a house. After the principal had accepted an offer made through the agent subject to contract but before the exchange of formal contracts, the agent received a higher offer which he did not communicate to his principal. The measure of damages was held to be the higher offer less the original contract price.[27] Conversely, where the defendant has been employed to buy property and fails to do so properly or at all, the claimant would recover the amount by which the property had appreciated. Thus, where an agent, directed to invest the funds of his principal in a particular stock, neglects to do so, and the stock thereupon rises, the principal is entitled to recover the enhanced value as if the stock had been purchased.[28] Lastly, where the defendant has been employed to effect an insurance

---

21 *Neilson v James* (1882) 9 Q.B.D. 546 CA; *Keppel v Wheeler* [1927] 1 K.B. 577 CA; and the cases concerning agents employed to effect insurances. All these are dealt with at paras 35-006 and 35-007, below.

22 *Cassaboglou v Gibb* (1883) 11 Q.B.D. 797 CA.

23 *Salvesen v Rederi Aktiebolaget Nordstjernan* [1905] A.C. 302.

24 (1882) 9 Q.B.D. 546 CA.

25 It made no difference that the broker had adopted the form of contract which was customary at the Stock Exchange.

26 [1927] 1 K.B. 577 CA.

27 The agent was allowed to set off his commission as he acted in complete good faith.

28 In *Battern v Wedgwood Coal and Iron Co* (1886) 31 Ch. D. 346, where the defendant had failed to invest the principal's funds, it was held that he was bound to make good the loss of interest, but that he was entitled to a set-off in respect of a gain that had resulted from a fall in the price of Consols between the time when the investment should have been made and the date of the order dealing with the matter. For a case of a solicitor failing to buy a house, see *Nash v Phillips* [1974] E.G.D. 57 at para.34-013 (in a footnote), above.

for the claimant and has failed to insure at all, or has insured so carelessly that the claimant cannot recover against the underwriters under the policy, the claimant in the event of a loss will recover as damages the amount that he could have successfully claimed from the underwriters on a valid policy, deducting the necessary premiums he would have to have paid.[29] Where an underwriter has paid the claimant despite the policy's invalidity the claimant cannot recover this again as damages from the agent,[30] though it has been held that, where the principal returned policy moneys so paid by an underwriter without suit, he might recover from the agent in respect of these amounts.[31] If, however, no loss that was intended to be insured against has occurred, the measure of damages, of course, would not be the amount of the insurance moneys; and in *Charles v Altin*,[32] the court held that in any event it was not a positive rule of law that the claimant must recover from the agent the amount of the insurance moneys.[33] So too, where the insurance had been validly entered into by a sub-agent who, upon the loss, collected the insurance moneys and wrongfully refused to hand them over to the head agent it was said that this unlawful detention could not give the principal a right of action against the head agent for the whole amount received by the sub-agent: this was in *Cahill v Dawson*.[34]

But if the principal could have derived no benefit in law from the required contract even had the agent carried out his instructions, as where the contract would not have been enforceable against the third party because in some way vitiated, or, though enforceable, would not have given the claimant any pecuniary benefit by reason of the third party's insolvency, no damages will be recoverable from the agent. The first branch of this proposition is supported by three decisions, the very old case of *Webster v De Tastet*,[35] followed and applied in *Cohen v Kittell*,[36] and *Cheshire v Vaughan*.[37] In the first and the last case the claimant had employed the defendant to effect an insurance, which in the first was illegal because the objects of the insurance were slaves, in the last was void because the policy was a p.p.i. one.[38] In the middle case the claimant had employed the defendant to make void bets.[39] It was said to make no difference that in practice such losses were always paid by underwriters or bookmakers as debts of honour: the claimant could not recover against the agent more than he could have recovered in an action against **35-007**

---

29 *Mallough v Barber* (1815) 4 Camp. 150 ("the sum directed to be insured, deducting the premiums"); *Park v Hammond* (1815) 4 Camp. 344; *Smith v Price* (1862) 2 F. & F. 748.

30 *Park v Hammond* (1815) 4 Camp. 344.

31 *Maydew v Forrester* (1814) 5 Taunt. 615.

32 (1854) 15 C.B. 46.

33 The issue in the case was one of set-off; all that was decided on the measure of damages was that it was not necessarily the full amount of the policy.

34 (1857) 3 C.B. N.S. 106.

35 (1797) 7 T.R. 157.

36 (1889) 22 Q.B.D. 680.

37 [1920] 3 K.B. 240 CA.

38 The Court of Appeal did not stop in *Cheshire v Vaughan* [1920] 3 K.B. 240 CA, to decide whether such a policy might not be void but illegal. If the policy were illegal there would have been the additional ground that the contract of agency would itself become illegal: see at 250, 258. Although spelt out nowhere in the report of the case, it would appear that p.p.i. stands for policy proof of interest and that it is the fact that an insurable interest is thereby taken for granted which causes the policy to be void or even illegal.

39 Void bets also featured in *Dennis & Co v Campbell* [1978] Q.B. 365 CA, where they were taken by an employee in a manner contrary to his instructions: see the footnote at the end of para.33-041, above.

the third party.[40] It was submitted as far back as the 1961 edition of this work that, at least absent illegality, this last point was questionable though the onus would be on the claimant to show that he would have been paid by the third party, and this submission has since gained some support from the success of claims against insurance brokers in the somewhat different context of a contract which could be repudiated by the underwriter.[41] These cases suggest that the denial of any recovery in *Cheshire v Vaughan* could be wrong and that there should have been a partial, or even full, recovery depending upon the degree of likelihood that the claimant would in practice have been paid on the policy even though the policy was void.[42] The second branch of the above proposition is illustrated by *Park v Hammond*,[43] where it was held that since the claimant could not have recovered against the underwriter, even had the agent properly concluded the insurance contract, by reason of the underwriter's bankruptcy, he could not recover the policy moneys as damages from the agent.[44]

## 2. Breach Other than by Failure to Conclude the Contract as Instructed

**35-008** *Cassaboglou v Gibb*,[45] the leading case, introduces the more complex situation where the required contract was not available to the agent. The claimant instructed the defendant to buy on his account, and ship to him from Hong Kong, a particular sort of opium. No such opium was procurable. The defendant shipped an inferior opium as being that which he had been commissioned to buy, and advised the claimant to that effect, who resold the opium to a third party. On arrival the inferiority was discovered and the third party buyer made a successful claim for damages upon the claimant, who then sold the opium for whatever it would fetch. The claimant argued that he was entitled to be put in the same position as he would have been in if the opium he ordered had been supplied, and claimed as damages the market value of the superior opium less the market value of the inferior. But the court held that he was only entitled to be repaid the money he had expended in purchasing an article which he had never ordered, the damages which he had to pay to his buyer, and all incidental expenses to which he had been put in the transaction.[46] Here the damages are cut down in two stages. The claimant's claim for the market value of the superior opium less the market value of the inferior would have put him in a better position than he would have been in if his instructions had been carried out, assuming for the moment that the superior opium had been available; for he would

---

40 *Webster v De Tastet* (1797) 7 T.R. 157; *Cohen v Kittell* (1889) 22 Q.B.D. 680 at 683, per Huddleston B.

41 These cases are at para.10-077, above.

42 It is true that Diplock LJ in the first of these insurance broker cases, *Fraser v B.N.Forman (Productions)* [1967] 1 W.L.R. 898 CA, distinguished the three cases in the text, which were naturally cited to the court, on the ground that they concerned void contracts and not valid contracts which might be repudiated, but one suspects that he may have simply been looking for a distinction as he considered the Court of Appeal bound by them.

43 (1815) 4 Camp. 344.

44 Compare the similar results arrived at in the case of breach of warranty of authority: see para.36-004, below.

45 (1883) 11 Q.B.D. 797 CA.

46 In *Mainwaring v Brandon* (1818) 8 Taunt. 202 also, a sub-agent bought inferior goods and in an action against him by the original agent the latter recovered the damages and costs he had had to pay his own principal for breach of the head contract of agency.

then have paid a purchase price in relation to superior opium instead of the lower purchase price that he had paid for the inferior.[47] But further than this, the fact that no opium of the proper description was available reduced the damages even more, to the amount which the claimant was out of pocket by reason of the erroneous purchase, namely the amount awarded by the court.[48]

The irrecoverability of loss of profits where the required contract could not have been concluded by the principal is brought out in clearer focus by the decision in *Salvesen v Rederi Aktiebolaget Nordstjernan*,[49] where the House of Lords followed and applied *Cassaboglou v Gibb*.[50] The claimant had employed the defendant to find freight at a certain rate per ton for one of his ships. The defendant informed the claimant that he had got a charter, but three days later the claimant learned that the proposed charterers refused to proceed with the contract. The claimant made no effort to look elsewhere for equally advantageous freight, but used the ship under a current contract at a much lower rate, and brought an action against the alleged charterers which he lost. It was held that when an agent, employed to conduct negotiations for a principal, makes an incorrect statement to him that he has concluded a contract on his behalf, the measure of damages for the breach of contractual duty is the loss actually sustained in consequence of the misrepresentation, and does not include profits which the principal would have made if the representation had been true.[51] The claimant was therefore not entitled to recover the rate of freight at which the defendant had been instructed to contract less the rate actually earned by the claimant, but was awarded only damages for trouble incurred, outlay on telegrams and the like, and also the costs of the action against the alleged charterers down to the closing of the record, since these costs were held to have been reasonably incurred. There had been no evidence that the claimant had lost any opportunity of profitably employing the ship owing to his belief that a charter had been arranged,[52] but Lord Robertson stated that if, misled into inaction, the claimant had missed other chances for the ship, this would be a head of damage. This is illustrated by *Johnston v Braham and Campbell*,[53] where the claimant, an actress, was induced to enter into a certain theatrical engagement at Northampton by the misrepresentation of the defendant, her theatrical agent, as to the takings of the theatre, she being entitled under the contract to receive 60 per cent of the takings. That she could recover her out-of-pocket expenses was admitted, but 35-009

---

[47] Watkin Williams J in the Divisional Court makes this point by illustration: (1882) 9 Q.B.D. 220 at 224. The claimant has instructed the defendant to bid at a sale for a valuable picture, and in breach of his instructions he buys a poor one for £100. The claimant resells it for £90; the original would have been worth £1,000. Are then the damages to be £910?

[48] Had the defendant been in a position to buy superior opium, it follows from the cases in para.35-006, above, that the claimant would have been entitled to recover the loss of profit on a purchase by him of the superior opium, namely the difference between the two prices of such opium at Hong Kong and London minus all costs and charges. Brett MR refused to commit himself on the measure of damages if the opium of the proper description could have been bought (1883) 11 Q.B.D. 797 CA at 804, but the cases at para.35-006, above, are conclusive.

[49] [1905] A.C. 302.

[50] (1883) 11 Q.B.D. 797 CA.

[51] Note the interesting difference between this measure, where the action is against the agent by his own principal, i.e. breach of contract of agency, and that where the action is against the agent by the other party to the proposed contract, i.e. breach of contract of warranty of authority: see Ch.36, below. *Collen v Wright* (1857) 8 E. & B. 647 is indeed expressly distinguished in *Salvesen v Rederi Aktiebolaget Nordstjernan* [1905] A.C. 302.

[52] [1905] A.C. 302 at 311, per Lord Davey.

[53] [1917] 1 K.B. 586 CA.

she also recovered for her loss of time in going to Northampton, the evidence of her other engagements being taken as evidence of the value of her time. Such damages are indeed on the basis of putting the claimant into the position he would have been in had the misrepresentation not been made, the status quo ante position. Only if the defendant could and should have concluded the contract that the claimant thought he had, would the claimant be entitled to be put into the position he would have been in had the representation been true. And in such a case the breach would be more than the misrepresentation: it would be the failure to conclude the required contract.

### (B) AGENTS DEALING WITH THE PRINCIPAL'S PROPERTY

**35-010** Where the principal's property entrusted to the agent is physically destroyed by reason of the agent's default, the measure of damages is prima facie the market value of the goods. In the absence of cases on this matter, reference should be made to the general principles in relation to damages for the destruction of goods, which will apply.[54] An agent will be liable for loss or destruction after he has improperly dealt with the goods where, but for the improper dealing, the immediate cause of the loss would have been one for which he would not have been liable, unless he can positively show that the loss from this cause would have occurred even in the absence of improper dealing by him. Thus if an agent should deposit goods in an improper place, and fire accidentally destroy them there, he will be liable for the loss. This was the position in the important case of *Lilley v Doubleday*,[55] where the defendant was a bailee of the claimant's goods.[56]

**35-011** Where the principal's property entrusted to the agent is improperly parted with by the agent so that, though not physically destroyed, it is lost to the principal, the principal may recover the value of the property,[57] or the value of that which should have been obtained in exchange.[58] This is especially so where the property acts as security to the principal for some other item owing to him. The simplest case of this type is *Stearine Co v Heintzmann*,[59] where the agent parted with the possession of the principal's goods in breach of his instructions not to do so before receiving the price; the principal recovered the value of the goods from him. In *Pape v Westacott*,[60] the principal was a lessor, who had put into his agent's hands a licence to the lessee to assign the term, with instructions to the agent not to hand it over to the lessee till the latter had paid the last quarter's rent, then in arrears. The agent accepted a cheque instead of cash from the lessee and handed over the licence; the cheque was subsequently dishonoured. In an action against his agent the lessor recovered as damages the amount of the unpaid quarter's rent. In *Matthews v Discount Corp*,[61] weight notes were deposited with the agent, which notes were security for an advance made by the principal to a third party. The agent wrong-

---

54 See Ch.37, below.

55 (1881) 7 Q.B.D. 510.

56 Compare the same result in contracts of carriage at para.32-002 (in a footnote), above.

57 In many cases the principal will be able to sue alternatively in conversion; the measure of damages in such a case is dealt with in Ch.38, below. The most interesting cases are those dealing with brokers carrying stock on margin. These are more conveniently dealt with at paras 34-089 to 34-091, above.

58 See preceding note.

59 (1864) 17 C.B. N.S.

60 [1894] 1 Q.B. 272 CA.

61 (1869) L.R. 4 C.P. 228.

fully gave them up to the third party, thereby depriving the principal of the security. It was held, without working out details of the damages, that the principal was entitled to substantial damages. A somewhat different situation is presented by *Compania Financiera "Soleada" v Hamoor Tanker Corp, The Borag*,[62] and one in which recovery for the particular loss was denied. Here the agents caused to be wrongfully arrested the ship which they were managing for the owners who, to obtain her release, had to provide a bank guarantee and who submitted to heavy bank interest charges in order to obtain it. It was held that these charges were too remote to be recoverable; they were wholly unreasonable and should never have been incurred.

62 [1981] 1 W.L.R. 274 CA.

## Chapter 36

# CONTRACTS OF WARRANTY OF AUTHORITY BY AGENT

Table of Contents



### 1. The Contractual Measure of Damages

36-001 One who professes to act as agent for a principal is taken to warrant the existence of his authority in consideration of the representee acting in a matter of business on the faith of it, and will be liable for breach of contract if that authority does not exist. This was originally recognised, and has its most frequent illustration, where the agent warrants his authority to contract on behalf of his professed principal and thereby induces the other party to enter into an apparent contract on the faith of this assertion of authority,[1] but it has been held to apply to all cases where the agent induces the other to act in a matter of business on the warranty.[2]

36-002 It has often been thought difficult to press the relationship between the agent and the other party into the framework of contract, the consideration for the warranty of authority being somewhat tenuous. As a result, the situation has sometimes been rationalised, at a time when neither the law of tort nor statute imposed any liability in damages for non-fraudulent misrepresentation,[3] as a legal means of providing a remedy for an innocent misrepresentation in a particular set of circumstances; on the other hand in *Dickson v Reuter's Telegraph Co*,[4] Bramwell B said that, properly understood, the present action did not constitute an exception to the rule that an action of deceit lay only for fraudulent misrepresentation, but formed a separate and independent rule. This latter view, and the formal analysis of contract, become important in formulating the proper measure of damages. This measure is now established as not that for the tort of deceit, i.e. restoring the status quo ante,[5] but the general contract measure. Lord Esher MR put the measure for breach of warranty of authority concisely in *Firbank's Executors v Humphreys*. He said[6]:

---

1 So laid down in the well-known case of *Collen v Wright* (1857) 8 E. & B. 647.

2 Established by *Starkey v Bank of England* [1903] A.C. 114, approving *Firbank's Executors v Humphreys* (1886) 18 Q.B.D. 54 CA.

3 Compare para.49-001, below.

4 (1877) 3 C.P.D. 1 CA at 5.

5 See paras 49-002 to 49-006, below.

6 (1886) 18 Q.B.D. 54 CA at 60.

"The damages under the general rule are arrived at by considering the difference in the position he [the person acting in reliance on the warranty] would have been in had the representation been true and the position he is actually in in consequence of its being untrue."[7]

## 2. WARRANTY OF AUTHORITY TO CONTRACT ON THE PRINCIPAL'S BEHALF

### (1) The amount that would have been recoverable from the alleged principal

In this, the commonest case of warranty of authority, the basis of the damages is the amount that the claimant has lost by being unable, by reason of falsity of the warranty, to sue the alleged principal.[8] For what the agent has promised is not that the principal will perform the contract but that he will be bound by it. **36-003**

If therefore the claimant would have been unable to sue the principal even if the agent had had the warranted authority, he has been deprived of no gain by the agent's breach and can recover no damages for the loss of his bargain.[9] Further, even if the claimant would have had a cause of action against the alleged principal had the agent's authority existed but this would have given him no pecuniary benefit by reason of the principal's insolvency, he has again been deprived of no gain by the agent's breach and can recover no damages for loss of his bargain. This point of insolvency is stressed in a number of cases, though proved in none.[10] Whether, however, the claimant in such circumstances of legal or financial unenforceability can abandon the normal contractual measure of recovery for loss of bargain and claim upon the basis of his out-of-pocket expenses is uncertain. In *Pow v Davis*,[11] part of the claim was to recover as damages the amount which the claimant had expended in effecting repairs to premises which the defendant had purported to have authority to let to him; on this particular issue the claimant succeeded, but the matter was hardly considered by the court. *Heskell v Continental Express*,[12] points the other way. In that case the agent had falsely warranted that he had authority to sign a bill of lading, and the claimant on the strength of this had assumed that goods had been forwarded to his buyer, to whom he had to pay damages when the goods did not duly arrive. His claim for damages against the agent failed because even if the agent had signed the bill of lading with authority there would still have been no contract of carriage with the shipowner in the circumstances. These two cases **36-004**

7 A fuller analysis, in so far as it considers the alternative measure and rejects it as not law, appears in Bowen LJ's judgment in *Re National Coffee Palace Co Ex p. Panmure* (1883) 24 Ch. D. 367 CA at 374–375.

8 *Richardson v Williamson* (1871) L.R. 6 Q.B. 276 at 279, per Blackburn J; *Heskell v Continental Express* [1950] 1 All E.R. 1033 at 1043, per Devlin J.

9 No such damages were, therefore, awarded in *Pow v Davis* (1861) 1 B. & S. 220 or *Heskell v Continental Express* [1950] 1 All E.R. 1033, and it was for this reason that whether the claimant would have been able to sue the principal became the main issue in *Rasnoimport V/O v Guthrie* [1966] 1 Lloyd's Rep. 1.

10 *Simons v Patchett* (1857) 7 E. & B. 568 at 574, per Crompton J; *Spedding v Nevell* (1869) L.R. 4 C.P. 212 at 226, per Montague Smith J; *Godwin v Francis* (1870) L.R. 5 C.P. 295 at 308, per Montague Smith J; *Richardson v Williamson* (1871) L.R. 6 Q.B. 276 at 279 to 280, per Blackburn J; *Re National Coffee Palace Co Ex p. Panmure* (1883) 24 Ch. D. 367 CA at 372, per Brett MR.

11 (1861) 1 B. & S. 220.

12 [1950] 1 All E.R. 1033.

however differ in that while the claim in *Pow v Davis*[13] was for expenditure rendered futile by the breach,[14] that in *Heskell v Continental Express*[15] was for expenditure caused by the breach, and it may be that the latter might have been regarded as too remote to be recoverable even in an action based on the normal contractual measure.[16]

**36-005** Given an enforceable contract had the agent had authority and given a solvent principal, the damages will be based on the measure of damages that the claimant could have recovered in an action for breach of contract against the principal had the principal been bound, and this will generally give him damages for the loss of his bargain. The particular measure falls to be judged in accordance with the particular type of contract that the defendant had warranted his authority to negotiate, and illustrations in the cases range over a variety of contract types.

**36-006** (1) Where the contract was one of purchase of goods by the claimant it was held in *Hughes v Graeme*[17] that he could recover[18] the value of the goods less the contract price. The property in question was wool imported from California which gave it a special value as it could be exported to America duty-free, and the claimant had intended to avail himself for his profit of this special character by so exporting the wool: in assessing the damages this factor was taken into account.

**36-007** (2) Where the contract was one of purchase of land by the claimant it was held in *Godwin v Francis*[19] that he could recover[20] the market value of the land less the contract price, the price at which the alleged principal had resold the land being taken as prima facie evidence of its market value. Similarly, where the contract was an agreement to renew a lease by the claimant lessee it was held in *Spedding v Nevell*[21] that he could recover[22] the value of the term, a value taken as enhanced by improvements made by the claimant, such expenditure being contemplated by the agreement itself.[23] In *Chitholie v Nash & Co*,[24] market value less contract price was again awarded to the claimant buyer, but Talbot J refused to take for the assessment of damages the market value of the land purchased at the time of judgment, which value, because of inflation, was much higher than the market value at breach. This would appear to be wrong as the higher damages could, as *Wroth v Tyler*[25] had already shown, have been awarded against the principal where specific performance

---

13 (1861) 1 B. & S. 220.

14 There is authority for allowing recovery of such expenditure rendered futile by the breach where there are no circumstances of legal or financial unenforceability: this authority is the root case of *Collen v Wright* (1857) 8 E. & B. 647, where again the claimant had gone into possession under a purported lease and effected repairs. The claimant's difficulty there was one of proof; he had abandoned his claim for loss of bargain at the suggestion of the court, Crompton J saying that it was "too vague": at 314. See, too, *Spedding v Nevell* (1869) L.R. 4 C.P. 212, where on similar facts the outlay in effecting repairs was incorporated in the damages for loss of bargain by taking the value of the term at the time of eviction.

15 [1950] 1 All E.R. 1033.

16 For the relationship between expenses rendered futile and expenses caused by the breach see Ch.4, above.

17 (1864) 33 L.J.Q.B. 335.

18 Inter alia: see para.36-014, below.

19 (1870) L.R. 5 C.P. 295.

20 Inter alia: see para.36-014, below.

21 (1869) L.R. 4 C.P. 212.

22 Inter alia: see para.36-014, below.

23 (1869) L.R. 4 C.P. 212 at 227.

24 (1974) 229 E.G. 786.

25 [1974] Ch. 30.

was refused.[26] Talbot J regarded himself as bound by the normal measure based on market value at breach since market value at judgment had been taken in a buyer of land's action against his seller only where the equitable jurisdiction under Lord Cairns' Act to award damages in substitution for specific performance was being invoked[27]—and clearly damages against the seller's agent are not being so awarded—but this limitation has since been departed from in the converse case of a seller of land's action against his buyer where damages at common law have been awarded based on market value at judgment,[28] and the propriety of this departure has indeed been endorsed at appellate level.[29] Accordingly, market value at judgment less contract price was awarded in *Suleman v Shahsavari*,[30] there being no delay in the claimant buyer of a house pursuing his claim against the solicitor agent of the sellers, the claimant knowing that the contract was lost to him only after the court had decided that the solicitor lacked authority.[31] The same result was arrived at in *Greenglade Estates Ltd v Chana*,[32] where the defendant auctioneer sold long leasehold properties to the claimant consortium without, as it turned out, authority. The formula in *Suleman* was followed and applied by postponing the date of valuation of the properties for as long as the claimant was acting reasonably in trying to have the contract enforced.[33]

In all these cases concerning land the principal had had a good title, so that in an action against him the ordinary contract measure of damages would have applied and not the restrictive rule in *Bain v Fothergill*,[34] then in operation. Had this rule applied by reason of the seller or lessor having a defective title, this would consequently affect the measure of damages in the claimant's action against the agent. However, this possibility is now a thing of the past with the statutory abolition of the rule in *Bain v Fothergill* in 1989.[35] **36-008**

(3) All the prior cases involved a claimant at the purchasing end of the transaction: it is similar with a sale by the claimant. Two cases with a seller claimant from the 19th century are complemented by a third case of the 21st. In *Simons v Patchett*,[36] the sale was of a ship, and the claimant was held entitled to recover from the defendant, when it appeared that he had no authority to buy for his principal, the contract price less the lower price at which the claimant had resold, this being taken as the best price attainable. "If direct evidence had been given", said Lord Campbell CJ, **36-009**

> "of the fall in the market price of ships between the time of making of the supposed bargain and the time at which the plaintiff might reasonably resell the ship that fall in price

[26] See para.27-009, above.
[27] Namely the position in *Wroth v Tyler* [1974] Ch. 30.
[28] *Radford v De Froberville* [1977] 1 W.L.R. 1262: see para.27-049, above.
[29] *Malhotra v Choudhury* [1980] Ch. 52 CA (buyer of land as claimant) and *Johnson v Agnew* [1980] A.C. 367 (seller of land as claimant); see paras 27-009 and 27-041, above.
[30] [1988] 1 W.L.R. 1181.
[31] [1988] 1 W.L.R. 1181 at 1184A and para.27-009, above.
[32] [2012] EWHC 1913 Ch.
[33] However, this was done only at the instance of counsel for both parties ([2012] EWHC 1913 Ch at [14]), the trial judge expressing himself as finding serious difficulty in subscribing to the approach of the judge in *Suleman*, giving reasons for this which are not convincing and somewhat unclear (at [12]).
[34] (1874) L.R. 7 H.L. 158.
[35] See the footnotes at the end of para.27-005, above.
[36] (1857) 7 E. & B. 568.

would be recoverable. Might not the jury reasonably infer such a fall in price from the difference in price obtained in this case?"[37]

In *Re National Coffee Palace Co Ex p. Panmure*,[38] where the Court of Appeal approved and acted upon all the prior cases, the sale was of shares. A company sold and allotted shares to the alleged principal of a broker. On the company's liquidation, the liquidator sued the broker for breach of his warranty of authority to buy the shares for the principal and recovered the full nominal value, the court having found that the shares were totally unsaleable in the market at the time the allotment to the principal had been made. This was the normal measure for non-acceptance, namely the contract price less the market price, the market price here being nil. In *Habton Farms v Nimmo*,[39] the sale was of a horse. Purportedly acting on behalf of a wealthy racehorse owner as principal, the defendant agent concluded a contract for the purchase from the claimant sellers of a racehorse for £70,000. The racehorse owner declined to accept delivery on the basis that he had not authorised the transaction but the sellers nevertheless sought to enforce the contract, suing both principal and agent, and did not therefore attempt to sell the horse elsewhere, the horse remaining in their ownership. Four weeks after the date upon which delivery and payment under the contract had been due, the horse unexpectedly contracted a disease and had to be put down. In the proceedings brought by the sellers against principal and agent, the trial judge held for the racehorse owner on the ground of no authority but awarded damages against the agent for breach of warranty of authority, the seller being held entitled to recover the full market value of the horse which from the time of the alleged contract until its death had not varied from £70,000. The defendant's argument for a nil award in accordance with the normal measure of damages where an agent warranted the authority of a solvent principal to buy a chattel, namely the difference between the contract price and the market price at the time of due completion, was rejected. The Court of Appeal affirmed. Had the contract proceeded, the sellers would have divested themselves of the ownership, possession and risk of harm to the horse in return for the price well before the horse's death; they should not be in a worse position than they would have been, had there been a contract, simply because they were entitled to damages from the agent for breach of warranty of authority rather than to the sale price from the principal. The sellers had lost a valuable contract and their loss from the death of the horse was no different than a loss from a general fall or collapse in the market price for horses of a similar calibre or, as was suggested by Lord Campbell CJ in *Simon v Patchett*,[40] from a fall in the market price of ships.[41] Although the normal measure of damages in this type of claim is the difference between the contract price and the market value at the time of due completion, this is not an absolute rule so that damages can be assessed at some other date if it be more just to do so.[42]

**36-010** (4) Where the contract was one of loan of money to a company where the direc-

---

[37] (1857) 7 E. & B. 568 at 572.

[38] (1883) 24 Ch. D. 367 CA.

[39] [2004] Q.B. 1 CA.

[40] (1857) 7 E. & B. 568 at 572.

[41] See earlier in this paragraph.

[42] Jonathan Parker LJ dissented, largely because he took a different view as to the claimant's intention to resell. Clarke LJ cited at length from this chapter in the 16th edition, bringing in the two 19th century cases, appearing in the text above, of *Simon v Patchett* and *Re National Coffee Palace Co*.

tors had no power to bind the company, the claimant in *Richardson v Williamson*,[43] recovered the amount of money lent from the directors.[44]

36-011 (5) Where in *Rasnoimport V/O v Guthrie & Co*,[45] the contract was one of carriage of goods under a bill of lading, and the defendant, the shipowner's agent, had signed a bill of lading which greatly overstated the amount of goods in fact shipped, the claimant, as indorsee of the bill of lading, was held entitled to recover the value of the goods undelivered together with interest.

36-012 (6) A final case is provided by *Meek v Wendt*.[46] The claimant brought an action against an insurance company which carried on business in America and obtained judgment for £1,000 in default of appearance. The claimant negotiated a settlement with the defendants who were the company's English agents, and agreed to accept £300 in settlement, which amount was to be paid by a bank in London. In an action for the defendants' breach of warranty of authority to conclude a settlement it was held that the claimant was entitled to £300.[47] The court judgment was of no value as the insurance company had no assets in England and it could not be enforced in the circumstances in America; further, the value of the claimant's remedy on the insurance policy could not be estimated. Thus the claimant had sold something which was worth nothing for a price of £300, and therefore the measure of damages was the contract price of £300 less the market price which was nil.

36-013 These cases all illustrate the recovery from the purported agent of what would have represented only the normal measure of damages in an action against the principal,[48] but such consequential losses as would not, on general principles, have been too remote to be recoverable in an action against the principal may also be properly included in the damages. On the other hand, there can be no recovery for losses which would have been held too remote to be claimed in such an action, since they do not constitute something that the claimant has lost by being unable to sue the alleged principal. Thus in *Godwin v Francis*,[49] the claimant could not recover the loss on the resale of horses and cattle he had bought to stock the land, which was the subject of the main contract, since this was not contemplated by the parties. And in *Spedding v Nevell*,[50] the claimant could not recover in respect of the damages and costs that he had had to pay to his sub-buyer of the leasehold interest he had contracted to buy, since a resale had not been contemplated by the parties[51] at the time the contract was entered into.

---

43 (1871) L.R. 6 Q.B. 276.

44 Contrast *McCollin v Gilpin* (1880) 5 Q.B.D. 390 where the claimant should have known from the articles of association that the defendant directors had no authority.

45 [1966] 1 Lloyd's Rep. 1.

46 (1888) 21 Q.B.D. 126.

47 He also recovered his expenses of negotiating the settlement, but to award this item in addition is wrong since the claimant would have had to incur this expense in order to obtain the settlement. See paras 4-024 and following, above.

48 Thus the damages by way of interest which the claimant would have claimed against the principal were held recoverable in the action against the agent in *Rasnoimport V/O v Guthrie* [1966] 1 Lloyd's Rep. 1 (facts at para.36-011, above); the arguments in the case, however, appear all to have been on issues of liability.

49 (1870) L.R. 5 C.P. 295.

50 (1869) L.R. 4 C.P. 212.

51 For this purpose the agent and alleged principal will be taken to be one and the same.

### (2) Costs of unsuccessful action with the alleged principal

**36-014** Beyond this, the claimant may be entitled to recover, in addition, damages that he could not have recovered from the principal in the event of a binding contract between them. This is so with regard to the costs of an unsuccessful action brought by him against the principal, in reliance on the warranty of authority, whether an action for the price,[52] for specific performance,[53] or for damages.[54] Whether such costs are recoverable turns on whether it was reasonable for the claimant to embark on the litigation with the alleged principal. In the first three cases where such costs were awarded in the damages, *Randell v Trimen*,[55] *Collen v Wright*[56] and *Hughes v Graeme*,[57] the agent had persisted throughout in the assertion of authority. In the later case of *Spedding v Nevell*,[58] however, this was extended to a situation where the defendant had in no way persisted in his assertion—it would seem that the claimant had not consulted him—and it only came out at the trial of the action against the principal that the agent had had no authority, the agent admitting this when examined on behalf of the principal. He was in fact the principal's brother, who owned the land the lease of which he purported to renew to the claimant lessee, and he had for some time past received the rents on behalf of his brother. In these circumstances Montague Smith J said that, considering the relations of the parties and the prior acting of the defendant on his brother's behalf, the claimant might still have been justified in going on with the action even if the defendant had stated before suit to the claimant that he had had no authority.[59] *Godwin v Francis*,[60] took the law a little further by allowing the costs in part, namely down to the receipt by the claimant of answers to interrogatories, in which answers not only the principal but the agent swore on oath that the latter lacked authority. Bovill CJ said:

> "The plaintiff was fully justified in acting on this implied representation, and commencing proceedings against the vendors. The plaintiff was entitled, at least, to the distinct denial of the defendant himself of his authority before he gave up his claim to the estate."[61]

But after such denial on oath by the agent, the claimant should have discontinued his action against the principal; he had in fact continued the action relying upon another ground, namely the apparent authority of the agent, so that he failed

> "because he acted on a wrong view of the law, and not because he was mistaken in respect of the authority in fact given by the vendors to the defendant".[62]

Another connection in which reasonableness must appear is that the claimant must have brought the right type of action against the principal. Thus in *Hughes v*

52 As in *Randall v Trimen* (1856) 18 C.B. 786.
53 As in *Collen v Wright* (1857) 8 E. & B. 647; *Hughes v Graeme* (1864) 33 L.J.Q.B. 335; *Spedding v Nevell* (1869) L.R. 4 C.P. 212 and *Chitholie v Nash & Co* (1974) 229 E.G. 786.
54 As in *Rasnoimport V/O v Guthrie* [1966] 1 Lloyd's Rep. 1.
55 (1856) 18 C.B. 786.
56 (1857) 8 E. & B. 647.
57 (1864) 33 L.J.Q.B. 335.
58 (1869) L.R. 4 C.P. 212.
59 (1869) L.R. 4 C.P. 212 at 226. And see, too, *Chitholie v Nash & Co* (1974) 229 E.G. 786.
60 (1870) L.R. 5 C.P. 295.
61 (1870) L.R. 5 C.P. 295 at 305–306.
62 (1870) L.R. 5 C.P. 295 at 306.

*Graeme*,[63] a suit for specific performance of a contract for the sale of goods of a special character, the court said that the costs would not have been recoverable if it could have been shown that the Chancery Court had no jurisdiction in respect of goods, especially if the suit had been dismissed on that ground, which was not in fact the case.

Similarly, the costs of unsuccessfully defending an action brought by the alleged principal against the claimant may be recoverable. Such a situation, which is likely to be less frequent, arose in *Pow v Davis*,[64] where the claimant had been let into possession of the principal's property by the agent, and the principal brought an action of ejectment. In this case, however, the claimant failed on this head of damage because on the facts, even if the agent had had authority, the claimant would have had no defence to the principal's ejectment action; he had continued to defend on a wrong view of the law put to him by his attorney. **36-015**

As to what costs are recoverable where the whole action against the principal down to its conclusion is held to be reasonable, was dealt with in *Hughes v Graeme*,[65] and, a century later, in *Chitholie v Nash & Co.*[66] The costs which were allowed as damages in these two cases were, in the terminology of the day, the taxed costs paid by the claimant to the principal and the claimant's own costs taxed as between solicitor and client. Today, however, not only has the terminology changed but the law may be changing. On the one side, the taxed costs of the principal have become assessed costs; this is purely a change in terminology with no substantive implications. On the other side, solicitor and client costs as between parties to an action have disappeared and the new thinking, which is considered to be flawed, is that, in cases like *Hughes* and *Chitholie*, the claimant should recover his own costs assessed on the standard basis with no entitlement to the extra costs which would bring him up to the former level of costs taxed as between solicitor and client. This whole matter has been extensively considered at an earlier point in the text, where it is suggested that the new thinking may be overtaken by good sense.[67] **36-016**

## 3. Other Warranties of Authority by an Agent

Occasionally claims are made against agents who have warranted authority other than to contract on a principal's behalf. The few cases here are divisible into three groups, dependent upon whether the claim involves damages only, damages and costs, or only costs. These are given separate consideration. **36-017**

First, damages only. *Firbank's Executors v Humphreys*[68] shows that recovery by the claimant may depend as much upon the alleged principal's insolvency as upon his solvency. The defendants, the directors of a company, issued company debenture stock without authority to the claimant, who was constructing a railway for the company, in order to save him pressing for cash and to induce him to carry on with the railway. When the lack of authority was later discovered the company was insolvent and in the claimant's action against the directors he recovered as dam- **36-018**

63 (1864) 33 L.J.Q.B. 335.
64 (1861) 1 B. & S. 220.
65 (1864) 33 L.J.Q.B. 335.
66 (1974) 229 E.G. 786.
67 In Ch.20, above; see especially paras 21-003 to 21-011.
68 (1886) 18 Q.B.D. 54 CA.

ages the full amount of the debenture stock. *Weeks v Propert*,[69] is similar, except that, instead of the company being insolvent, the debenture issued by the directors was void as against the company. The recovery of costs in previous proceedings did not feature in either of these cases as in neither were there any previous proceedings.

**36-019** Next, damages and costs. *Oliver v Bank of England*,[70] shows that the claim for breach of warranty of authority may arise out of the claimant's unsuccessful defence of a suit brought by an alleged principal rather than an unsuccessful action brought by the claimant against the principal. The Bank of England had transferred certain securities upon the presentation by the defendant stockbroker of a power of attorney on which the name of the owner of the securities was forged. The Bank, in a suit by the owner, was ordered to replace the transferred securities with the back dividends on them and also to pay to the owner his costs of the action. The Bank then sought indemnity from the stockbroker on the ground of breach of warranty of authority and Kekewich J, deciding for the Bank on liability,[71] held that the defendant should

> "pay to the bank all that the bank are bound to pay the plaintiff in the original action, including of course the costs which they have been ordered to pay".[72]

In *British-Russian Gazette v Associated Newspapers*,[73] the now defendant and another party had sued the now claimant for libel. Without authority from the other party the defendant purported on behalf of both of them to make a settlement with the claimant of both actions for 1,000 guineas. Because of the lack of authority the purported settlement was of no effect, and the defendant and the other party both continued suit successfully at first instance; the claimant then appealed and his appeal was allowed as to the other party. Since the award of damages to the now defendant in the libel action, namely £1,000, was slightly below the amount of the purported settlement, the loss which the now claimant had suffered by the breach of warranty of authority did not in the event include the libel action damages, otherwise recoverable from the now defendant, and was marked out by the costs incurred by the now claimant in the litigation which the settlement was designed to avoid. The details of how these damages were worked out are complex,[74] but those costs which the claimant was considered to have reasonably incurred were held recoverable.

**36-020** Finally, and most interestingly, costs only. The recovery as damages of only the costs of litigation is in issue where it is the litigation itself that the defendant, who will be a solicitor, has warranted that he has authority to conduct on behalf of his alleged principal. The main case here is *Yonge v Toynbee*.[75] The principal, against whom the claimant was bringing a libel action, had gone insane, a fact which was initially unknown to the claimant or to the solicitor who had warranted his authority to act for the principal in the action. There was no discussion of what costs were

---

69 (1873) L.R. 8 C.P. 427.

70 [1901] 1 Ch. 652.

71 The case went to the House of Lords on the issue of liability only, and was affirmed sub nom. *Starkey v Bank of England* [1903] A.C. 114.

72 [1901] 1 Ch. 652 at 664. Kekewich J had held that it had been reasonable for the Bank to have defended the action brought against it by the owner; on this aspect of the case see para.21-059, above.

73 [1933] 2 K.B. 616 CA.

74 See, for the details of working out, Scrutton LJ at [1933] 2 K.B. 616 CA at 646–647 and Greer LJ at 655–656. They were not quite in agreement and Slesser LJ, at 657, supported Scrutton LJ.

75 [1910] 1 K.B. 215 CA.

recoverable from the solicitor by the Court of Appeal; Buckley LJ was simply confident that

> "the measure of damages is, no doubt, the amount of the plaintiff's costs thrown away in the action".[76]

This must mean costs on the then solicitor and client basis. A few years later in *Fernée v Gorlitz*,[77] the measure was spelt out. Solicitors had brought an action on behalf of an infant acting, as was legally necessary, by her next friend, the action being to set aside a contract on the ground that it was not for her benefit. When it later turned out that the infant's next friend was also an infant, and therefore incompetent to have authorised the solicitors to commence the proceedings, the parties sued by the infant succeeded in having the action dismissed and in recovering from the solicitors their costs incurred in defending the action. As to which costs, effectively claimed as damages, were recoverable by them, Eve J asked:

> "Is it the costs which they might have recovered from a competent and solvent next friend if they had succeeded in the action, or is it the expense to which they have been put in consequence of this futile proceeding?"[78]

and decided that it should be the latter, which would be, as in, and therefore following, the preceding *Yonge v Toynbee*,[79] costs on the then solicitor and client basis. Had Eve J chosen the former measure, he would have been awarding costs on the then party and party basis since this is what would have been recovered from the infant's next friend had there been no breach of warranty of authority and had the action proceeded to an unsuccessful conclusion for the infant. Put in today's terms, a party suing for breach of warranty of authority—the promisee of the warranty—is here held entitled to recover all of the costs reasonably incurred by him and not merely standard basis costs.[80]

It will be seen that this result assumes that the promisee of the warranty is not here claiming the normal measure of contract damages to put him in the position he would have been in if the contract had been performed, in other words, if the warranty had been true. While this may not seem strange in this context as the contract of warranty of authority is a very peculiar sort of contract, one with overtones of tort, it is in any event as it should be since, whatever the contract, a contracting party, faced with a breach by the other contracting party, is entitled to elect to claim for wasted expenditure, otherwise called expenditure rendered futile by the breach, and ignore claiming for the benefit of his bargain. This was called by Hutchinson J in *C.C.C.Films (London) Impact Quadrant Films*,[81] an unfettered **36-021**

---

76 [1910] 1 K.B. 215 CA 229; Swinfen Eady J simply said that the defendant was "liable to pay the costs of the party misled": at 231. Actions for breach of warranty of authority apart, the court has an inherent jurisdiction to order solicitors commencing proceedings without the authority of their apparent client to pay the costs incurred by the opposing party in consequence of the solicitors' unauthorised conduct. *Yonge v Toynbee* appears to have been such a case. See too, coming to the same result, *Simmons v Liberal Opinion Ltd* [1911] 1 K.B. 966 CA and *Babury Ltd v London Industrial Plc* (1989) 189 N.L.J. 1596.

77 [1915] 1 Ch. 177.

78 [1915] 1 Ch. 177 at 181.

79 [1910] 1 K.B. 215 CA.

80 This should still be so today even if the new regime with its allowance of standard basis costs only—the regime explained and criticised at paras 21-003 to 21-011, above—is finally accepted.

81 [1985] Q.B. 16 at 32A–D.

choice.[82] Thus Colman J, in stating in *Skylight Maritime SA v Ascot Underwriting Ltd*[83] that it is important not to lose sight of the fact that the court is concerned to quantify what benefit has been lost by reason of the fact that the alleged principal is not after all a party to the proceedings,[84] himself loses sight of the entitlement of the promisee of the warranty to elect for the alternative measure of wasted expenditure.

**36-022** It should be noted, however, that Eve J in *Fernée v Gorlitz*,[85] referred to the promisee succeeding in the action with the alleged principal and to the alleged principal being solvent.[86] Thus it is thought that the promisee of the warranty of authority may not be entitled to claim his costs thrown away if in the action against the alleged principal he would have been the loser. For here it may be said that by the premature ending of the claim he will have been spared having to pay costs, or even damages and costs, to the other party. Of course it would be for the party warranting authority to show that the promisee would have lost and this may be difficult, or impossible, for him to do. Nor may the promisee be entitled to the costs thrown away if, though he would have won the action, he would have won it against an alleged principal who was insolvent. Here it may be said that he would have been faced with the inability to obtain any costs from the alleged principal. Both situations have affinities with the important qualification on the entitlement of a contracting party to claim reliance expenditure, which is that he cannot do so in order to escape from a bad bargain; he cannot put himself in a better position than if the contract had been properly performed.[87] These situations have not yet appeared in the case law.

82 See generally paras 4-024 and following and especially *Anglia Television v Reed* [1972] 1 Q.B. 60 CA.
83 [2005] P.N.L.R. 25.
84 At [2005] P.N.L.R. 25 at [16].
85 [1915] 1 Ch. 177.
86 See para.36-021, above.
87 Established for English law in *C. & P. Haulage v Middleton* [1983] 1 W.L.R. 1461 CA. See para.4-029, above.

# PART 4B TORT

CHAPTER 37

# TORTS AFFECTING GOODS: DAMAGE AND DESTRUCTION

TABLE OF CONTENTS



**37-001** Physical damage to or destruction of goods may result from a large variety of very different torts of which trespass is the oldest and negligence the most prolific, and which includes torts involving, or bordering upon, strict liability, as where the damage or destruction results from nuisance, by reason of dangerous premises, goods or animals in the defendant's control, from his non-natural user of land under the rule in *Rylands v Fletcher*,[1] or from breach of statutory obligation giving rise to an action in tort. Although most of the decisions are drawn from the tort of negligence, they will equally cover the whole gamut of the relevant torts and the measure of damages will be calculated in the same manner throughout.[2] Indeed the Torts (Interference with Goods) Act 1977 uses the term "wrongful interference" or

[1] (1868) L.R. 3 H.L. 330.

[2] Exemplary damages may, however, be given to augment the award but now only in the limited circumstances fully dealt with in Ch.13, above. Two other general qualifications to the statement that the damages are calculated in the same manner throughout are: (1) they may be reduced by the claimant's contributory negligence; (2) they may have a ceiling placed on them by statute, e.g. under the Merchant Shipping Act 1995 ss.185 (as amended) and 186, or by contract between the parties. Although of general application, these two qualifications are in practice particularly important in torts causing physical damage.

"wrongful interference with goods" to refer to torts affecting goods generally, and includes in that term negligence and any other tort so far as that tort "results in damage to goods or to an interest in goods".[3] However the Act's provisions affecting damages cannot have any practical application to damage or destruction,[4] as opposed to misappropriation,[5] except in relation to claims by claimants with limited interests in the goods affected.[6]

Not only are most of the cases actions of negligence but most of those in which questions of the measure of damages have been worked out have over the years involved damage to or destruction of ships, generally by collision. The principles expounded in these cases are, however, of universal application. "There is no special measure of damages applicable to a ship", said Pickford LJ in *The Kingsway*,[7] **37-002**

> "different from the measure of damages applicable to any other chattel. The nature of the thing damaged may give rise to more difficult questions in the assessment of damages but it does not change the assessment in any way."[8]

The decisions involving ships are, therefore, relevant ones where it is something other than a ship which has been damaged or destroyed. However, as time has gone on, damages cases have appeared arising from road traffic accidents where cars are damaged, or occasionally destroyed and written off, and the 21st century has provided us also with an ever-expanding series of cases involving damage to cars where the owner, while the car is being repaired, has hired a replacement from a credit car hire company. These latter cases have special features in relation to damages and call for separate consideration.[9]

## I. DAMAGE

### (A) NORMAL MEASURE

The normal measure of damages is the amount by which the value of the goods damaged has been diminished. This, in the ship collision cases, has invariably been taken as the reasonable cost of repair. As Greer LJ said in *The London* **37-003**

---

3 Section 1(c) and (d).

4 It is assumed that the statutory reference to "damage to goods" will include their destruction.

5 For the provisions in relation to misappropriation see Ch.38, passim.

6 See paras 37-012 and 37-068, below. The other provisions affecting damages deal principally with claims for goods detained and claims for goods improved.

7 [1918] P. 344 CA at 356.

8 See, somewhat similarly, Bowen LJ in *The Argentino* (1888) 13 P.D. 191 CA at 201: "There is no difference in principle between such a loss [i.e. by disablement of a ship through collision] and the loss which the owner of a serviceable threshing machine suffers from an injury which incapacitates the machine." See too Devlin LJ in the Court of Appeal in *The Hebridean Coast* [1961] A.C. 545 at 562, and Harman LJ in *Darbishire v Warran* [1963] 1 W.L.R. 1067 CA at 1071.

9 See paras 37-018 to 37-024, below. There also used to be a mountain of small cases involving damaged, sometimes destroyed, cars reported briefly in the *Current Law Yearbooks*, which acquire these reports, ex relatione, from the barristers or solicitors handling the cases. Thus the 1994 and 1995 *Yearbooks* between them had over 40 reported under the sub-heading to Damages entitled "Loss of Use of Car". These reports have since much diminished in number and the sub-heading "Loss of Use of Car" has been abandoned. Indeed small cases of this nature have all but disappeared from the *Yearbooks*, none making an appearance in them from 2008 to 2013. In any event, while these reports may prove useful to those seeking assistance with a case, they are not of sufficient significance, or indeed undoubted reliability, for incorporation here.

*Corporation*[10]:

> "Prima facie, the damage occasioned to a vessel is the cost of repairs—the cost of putting the vessel in the same condition as she was in before the collision, and to restore her in the hands of the owners to the same value as she would have had if the damage had never been done; and prima facie, the value of a damaged vessel is less by the cost of repairs than the value it would have if undamaged."

In the case of goods other than ships the cost of repair has now become established as, prima facie, the correct measure of the claimant's loss. Accepted some time ago in a number of first instance cases,[11] this was confirmed by the Court of Appeal in *Darbishire v Warran*,[12] where it was said by Harman LJ that

> "it has come to be settled that in general the measure of damage is the cost of repairing the damaged article."[13]

Moreover if, despite the repairs, the market value of the goods is less than before, the claimant should be entitled to such diminution in value in addition to the cost of repair. Thus in *Payton v Brooks*,[14] Roskill LJ said:

> "There are many cases … where the cost of repairs is a prima facie method of ascertaining the diminution in value. It is not, however, the only method of ascertaining the loss. In a case where the evidence justifies[15] a finding that there has been, on top of the cost of repairs, some diminution in market value … I can see no reason why the plaintiff should be deprived of recovery under that head of damages also."[16]

Thus in *The Georgiana v The Anglican*,[17] the claimant was held entitled to recover, in addition to the cost of partial repairs to a yacht which did not make her as strong and seaworthy as formerly, the amount by which the value of the partially repaired yacht was less than before the damage occurred.[18]

**37-004** The cost of repair is, however, appropriate only if in the circumstances it is reasonable for the claimant to effect the repair; it might be cheaper to buy a replacement on the market and sell the damaged item for what it will fetch.[19] The cost of repair is expected to reflect the diminution in the value of the ship, or other chattel, so that, if it can be shown that the diminution in value is below, possibly well below, the cost of repair, then it may be inappropriate to award the cost of repair. This appears to have been the view which the Court of Appeal took of the damaged ship in *Meredith Jones v Vangemar Shipping Co, The Apostolis, No.2*,[20] a decision based in contract but equally relevant here.[21] On the other hand, in *Aerospace*

---

10 [1935] P. 70 CA at 77.

11 See, e.g. *London Transport Executive v Court* [1954] C.L.Y. 888 and *London Transport Executive v Foy Morgan* [1955] C.L.Y. 743.

12 [1963] 1 W.L.R. 1067 CA.

13 [1963] 1 W.L.R. 1067 CA at 1071.

14 [1974] R.T.R. 169 CA.

15 Which it did not in the instant case.

16 [1974] R.T.R. 169 CA at 176.

17 (1873) 21 W.R. 280.

18 See too *Cooper v Kirby (Harboro)* [1972] C.L.Y. 810.

19 When this is so, the replacement value is to be based on the figures before the court: *Thatcher v Littlejohn* [1978] R.T.R. 369 CA.

20 [2000] 2 Lloyd's Rep. 337 CA.

21 See the case at para.32-079, above.

*Publishing Ltd v Thames Water Utilities Ltd*,[22] where archives utilised in a business had been damaged by flooding, the cost of restoration rather than the lesser diminution in value was to be awarded since the claimant had a genuine, and reasonable, intention of reinstating the damaged collection. The test is whether it is reasonable or not for the person whose item of personal property has been damaged to decide to repair it. If so, the cost of repair is recoverable. If not, only the diminution in value is to be awarded.

The question of the reasonableness of repairing has arisen in the common case of the damaged motor car. Thus in *Darbishire v Warran*,[23] Harman LJ pointed to the exception to the prima facie rule of cost of repair where **37-005**

> "it can be proved that the cost of repair greatly exceeds the value in the market of the damaged article"[24]

and applied the exception in the particular case before the court. The claimant's second-hand shooting brake, which was reliable, suited his needs, and had been kept in good repair by him, was damaged by the defendant, and the claimant repaired it at a cost of £192 despite advice from the repair garage and his insurers that repairs would be "uneconomic". There was evidence that it would have been difficult to get a replacement of the particular model in the second-hand market, but that similar shooting brakes could be had for £80 to £100. The Court of Appeal held that in the circumstances the claimant, in having the car repaired at a cost exceeding its market value instead of trying to replace it with a comparable car at the market price, had failed to mitigate his loss and was entitled to recover, not the cost of repair, but only the lower market value.[25] The court pointed out that the claimant may have acted reasonably as far as he was concerned in having the car repaired, but that the relevant question was whether he had acted reasonably as between himself and the defendant in view of his duty of mitigation, a question which had to be considered from the point of view of a businessman.[26] Two members of the court also thought that *O'Grady v Westminster Scaffolding*,[27] where repair costs had been allowed although well in excess of the car's market value, could, if necessary, be distinguished on the ground that the car there, which was the apple of its owner's eye, had, through special work done on it, become a unique article thus making the standard market value irrelevant.[28] The third however preferred not to commit himself to

> "any view of the measure of damage which falls upon a party unfortunate enough to injure a freak article".[29]

The method of assessing the cost of repair has been elaborated in a number of cases. (1) The cost of repair must be reasonable, both in that the work must be **37-006**

---

22 (2007) 110 Con. L.R. 1 CA.

23 [1963] 1 W.L.R. 1067 CA.

24 [1963] 1 W.L.R. 1067 CA at 1071.

25 Hiring charges during the repair period were also allowed, but the appropriateness of this recovery was not argued.

26 See [1963] 1 W.L.R. 1067 CA at 1072 and 1076, per Harman and Pearson LJJ respectively.

27 [1962] 2 Lloyd's Rep. 238.

28 [1963] 1 W.L.R. 1067 CA at 1072 and 1077, per Harman and Pearson LJJ.

29 [1963] 1 W.L.R. 1067 CA at 1079, per Pennycuick J.

necessary and the charges must not be extravagant.[30] Both tests were applied in *The Pactolus*,[31] the first being decided in the circumstances in the claimant's favour, and the second in the defendant's. (2) The cost of a complete repair of all the damage is recoverable by the claimant notwithstanding that the result of a complete repair may be to render the ship more valuable than she was before the collision. This was laid down in *The Gazelle*,[32] where Dr Lushington held, apparently in opposition to prior practice, that the deduction in insurance cases of one third of the value of the material, since the new material is more valuable than the old, had no proper application to a case of tort, and no such deduction could be permitted to the defendant.

> "The measure of the indemnification is not limited by the terms of any contract but is coextensive with the amount of the damage. The right against the wrongdoer is restitutio in integrum, and the restitution he is bound to make without calling upon the party injured to assist him in any way whatsoever … If [the injured] party derives incidentally a greater benefit than mere indemnification, it arises only from the impossibility of otherwise effecting such indemnification without exposing him to some loss or burden, which the law will not place on him."[33]

(3) In addition to the cost of labour and materials in effecting the repairs, the claimants in *London Transport Executive v Foy Morgan*,[34] were held entitled to claim a sum for overhead charges where they had repaired a damaged motor vehicle themselves by reason of their maintaining a repair and maintenance depot. However, in *London Transport Executive v Court*,[35] it was held that such a sum must be a reasonable and proper one and that there cannot be recovery for overhead expenses that would have existed in any event.

**37-007** The fact that the repairs have not yet been executed before the hearing of the action, or will never be executed at all, does not prevent the normal recovery. Since damages may on general principles be given for prospective loss, it is immaterial that the repairs are not yet executed. Thus in *The Kingsway*,[36] where only temporary repairs had been effected before the trial, and the permanent repairs had been postponed owing to the exigencies of wartime, the claimants recovered, inter alia, a sum in respect of such permanent repairs on proving with reasonable certainty that they would have to be done. And, more importantly, since the cost of repair is adopted as being equivalent to the diminution in the ship's value, it is immaterial

---

[30] Even where notional because repairs had not been effected: see *Meredith Jones v Vangemar Shipping Co Ltd (The Apostolis) (No.2)* [1999] 2 Lloyd's Rep. 292 at para.37-007, below, a matter unchallenged on appeal: [2000] 2 Lloyd's Rep. 337 CA.

[31] (1856) Swab. 173.

[32] (1844) 2 W. Rob. (Adm.) 279. Applied in *The Munster* (1896) 12 T.L.R. 264.

[33] (1844) 2 W. Rob. (Adm.) 279 at 281. He cited *Hare v Beckington* (unreported) at 282 as a case at common law which supported him in his decision and awarded the same measure in *The Pactolus* (1856) Swab. 173 where he repeated the rule: at 174. Dr Lushington had to reject the analogy of the marine insurance rule of deducting one third new for old, but would no longer be required to do so since modern policies either exclude the rule or subject it to important exceptions, as is said in *British Shipping Laws*, Vol.4, 11th edn (1961), para.529. This is not included in the latest edition of the equivalent volume of *British Shipping Laws, Marsden on Collisions*, 13th edn (2003) which simply states, at para.15-41, that "no deduction is made from the damages in respect of unavoidable betterment".

[34] [1955] C.L.Y. 743.

[35] [1954] C.L.Y. 888.

[36] [1918] P. 344 CA.

that, as circumstances turn out, the repairs will never be executed. Thus in *The Glenfinlas*,[37] where the ship was lost from other causes before the claim for damages was heard, liability for the estimated cost of repairs was admitted. This was approved by Scrutton LJ in *The York*,[38] where he said that the owners had properly claimed the cost of permanent repairs

> "because the ship when sunk was of less value to them, for she was in such a condition that required permanent repairs".

In *The London Corporation*,[39] where after the collision the claimant's ship was not repaired but was sold to be broken up, it was held that this factor did not discharge the onus on the defendant to prove that the claimant had suffered no damage, for the vessel might not have been sold to ship-breakers had she not been damaged; and further it was held that

> "the prima facie damage is the cost of repair, and circumstances which are peculiar to the plaintiffs—namely, that they have, before the damage has been determined, sold the vessel to be broken up, is an accidental circumstance which ought not to be taken into account in the way of diminution of damages."[40]

Somewhat similarly, in *The Endeavour*,[41] the repairs had been executed but before paying them the claimant had gone bankrupt; the defendant's contention that the claimant could not claim the cost of repair from him because it would only go to swell the creditors' fund, was rejected. The court pointed out that

> "if somebody out of kindness were to repair the injury and make no charge for it, the wrongdoer would not be entitled to refuse to pay as part of the damages the cost of the repairs to the owner".[42]

And these two decisions have found later applications. *The Endeavour* was applied, but in the context of damage to land, in *Jones v Stroud District Council*,[43] where the cost of the repairs had been met by a third party.[44] *The London Corporation* was applied, but in a contractual context, in *Meredith Jones v Vangemar Shipping Co Ltd, The Apostolis No.2*,[45] at first instance to allow the cost of repairs not executed; in the Court of Appeal,[46] which reversed on liability, there was no challenge to the proposition that recovery of the cost of repair was not prevented by the fact that the repairs had not been carried out.[47] In *Coles v Hetherton*,[48] 13 test cases arising out of minor road traffic accidents were brought before the Court of Appeal, being the latest of the now many cases in the great battle between large mo-

---

37 [1918] P. 363n.
38 [1929] P. 178 CA at 184–185.
39 [1935] P. 70 CA.
40 [1935] P. 70 CA at 78, per Greer LJ. He took the analogy of the normal measure of damages in sale of goods which disregards circumstances peculiar to the claimant.
41 (1890) 6 Asp. M.C. 511.
42 (1890) 6 Asp. M.C. 511 at 512.
43 (1986) 34 B.L.R. 27 CA.
44 See the case at para.39-011, below.
45 [1999] 2 Lloyd's Rep. 292.
46 [2000] 2 Lloyd's Rep. 337 CA.
47 [2000] 2 Lloyd's Rep. 337 CA at 348, col.2. Had it not reversed on liability, the Court of Appeal would not have awarded the cost of repair but for other reasons. See the case at para.32-079, above.
48 [2013] EWCA Civ 1704 CA.

tor insurers.[49] Insurers for the various owners of negligently damaged vehicles indemnified them by having the vehicles repaired for them and then brought subrogated claims in the names of the owners as the policyholders. The insurers were able to have the repairs done at a lower cost than the policyholders would have had to pay on the open market and the defendants, insurers for the tortfeasors, maintained that the lower cost to the claiming insurers should form the measure of damages. The Court of Appeal disagreed, as had Cooke J below. It was the policyholders who had suffered the loss, it was their asset that was diminished in value, and the loss was suffered at the outset when the accident occurred and before any decision had been made about repair. A claimant's loss is assessed by the reasonable cost of repair in the open market, this measure being only a means of ascertaining the diminution in the value of the vehicle.[50]

**37-008** These various cases have fortunately remained unaffected by the decision of the House of Lords in *Dimond v Lovell*,[51] yet to be considered.[52] It having been in that case decided that, where, while her tortiously damaged car was being repaired, the claimant hired a replacement car from a credit car hire company, now more commonly called a credit hire company,[53] under a credit agreement which was unenforceable, she was not entitled to recover damages for the notional hire of the replacement car, the question arose whether the same result should follow where the unenforceable contract is not for the hire of another car but for the repair of the damaged car. The argument that it should was accepted by Gray J in *Burdis v Livsey*,[54] since he was persuaded that *Jones v Stroud*,[55] was no longer good law, being overruled by implication by *Hunt v Severs*,[56] and, more particularly, *Dimond v Lovell*.[57] However, a different view was taken by the Court of Appeal.[58] The court saw that there was a fundamental distinction to be drawn between repair costs and hire charges. When the vehicle is damaged the owner suffers an immediate loss representing the diminution in its value and the cost of carrying out the repair simply represents the prima facie, but not the essential, measure of this loss. By contrast, the hire charges represent a potential loss which, when the charges are not incurred by the claimant, never materialises. The distinction to be drawn is between a loss that has never been suffered and a loss that has been suffered but is subsequently reduced or eliminated. Put another, and simpler, way it is the distinction between a direct loss and a consequential loss.

**37-009** The decision of the Court of Appeal in *Burdis* is to be applauded. The court was not deflected by the consideration that the claimant was better off than before the accident, as she had her car in as good a condition as before together with the money representing the cost of the repairs to it. This may seem like over-compensation but it is not. The reason that the claimant is better off is not because she has been given

---

49 More on this battle when dealing with the credit car hire company cases at para.37-018 and following, below.

50 The detailed judgment of the court, delivered by Aikens LJ, in which most of the cases in the text above are cited, repays study.

51 [2002] 1 A.C. 384.

52 Considered at para.37-019, below.

53 The rationale for such companies is explained at para.37-018, below.

54 [2001] 1 W.L.R. 1751.

55 The principal case of those considered in para.37-007, above.

56 [1994] 2 A.C. 350.

57 [2002] 1 A.C. 384.

58 *Burdis v Livsey* [2003] Q.B. 36 CA.

too much in damages but because she has benefited from a contract which cannot be enforced against her. There is no reason why her protection as a consumer should be diverted to the tortfeasor.[59]

*Performance Cars v Abraham*,[60] shows that the cost of repair is not, however, recoverable if the work which will repair the defendant's damage is required to repair other damage to the chattel already existing before the defendant's tort. In that case the defendant damaged the front wing of the claimant's Rolls Royce motorcar, and to make good the damage it was necessary to respray the whole lower part of the car. At the time the damage was inflicted the rear wing had already been damaged by a third party, and this required a similar re-spray of the whole lower part of the car. The claimant had sued the third party and recovered judgment for the cost of the re-spray but this judgment was unsatisfied, and the claimant now claimed to recover similarly from the defendant. The Court of Appeal however, reversing the judge below, held that the defendant was not liable to the claimant for the cost of re-spraying because he had damaged a car which already required to be re-sprayed in any event, so that the need for re-spraying was not the result of the defendant's act and imposed no extra burden on the claimant.[61] The same principle finds a slightly different application in *Organic Research Chemicals v Ricketts*.[62] A car broke down and was towed to a garage for repair. The garage negligently caused further damage to the engine. The Court of Appeal, reversing the judge below who had given as damages against the garage the cost of a reconditioned engine, held that, since the installation of a new engine remedied the existing defect as well, the proper measure of damages was the difference between the cost of a new engine and the cost of repairing the defect which caused the first breakdown. **37-010**

In addition to the cost of repairing the ship, interest upon this amount is awarded in Admiralty practice. This practice was established primarily in cases dealing with destruction of ships but applies equally to damage. Thus as early as *The Hebe*,[63] Dr Lushington, to effect restitutio in integrum, awarded interest on the cost of repair from the time the claimant had paid the repair bill, while in *The Norseman*,[64] the appropriateness of such an award of interest was accepted without question. Where cars rather than ships are concerned, so that Admiralty practice is irrelevant, inter- **37-011**

---

59 Lord Hope's stating at the start of his speech in *Lagden v O'Connor* [2004] 1 A.C. 1067 at [14], that Lagden was an appeal against the Court of Appeal's decision in *Burdis v Livsey* [2003] Q.B. 36 CA may confuse. The two cases were part of a number of test cases which had been heard together at Court of Appeal level and the issue in the *Lagden* appeal to the House of Lords was entirely different from what had been the issue in the *Burdis* appeal to the Court of Appeal. Indeed leave to appeal to the House of Lords was granted in *Lagden* and refused in *Burdis*: see [2003] 1 W.L.R. 394.

60 [1962] 1 Q.B. 33 CA.

61 Lord Evershed MR said ([1962] 1 Q.B. 33 CA at 39) that he thought the defendant derived assistance from *The Haversham Grange* [1905] P. 307 CA and *Carslogie S.S. Co v Royal Norwegian Government* [1952] A.C. 292, but it is submitted that the principles applied in these cases, dealing with claims for expenses of docking and loss of user profits where other repairs had been effected concurrently, have no direct application where, as in *Performance Cars v Abraham*, it is the liability for the cost of repair itself, forming the basic measure of damages, which may be attributable to another tortfeasor. *Performance Cars* was however held to be directly in point in *Steel v Joy* [2004] 1 W.L.R. 3002 CA, which concerned two consecutive physical injuries (see para.8-026, above), and was there approved and followed.

62 *The Times*, 16 November 1961, CA.

63 (1847) 2 W. Rob. (Adm.) 530.

64 [1957] P. 224.

est may be awarded in appropriate circumstances under statute; indeed this must be true for all other chattels damaged.[65]

37-012 That the claimant had only a limited interest in the goods damaged did not prevent him, if in possession of them, from recovering at common law the normal measure of damages. This was established for destruction of goods in *The Winkfield*[66]: the same principles must apply in the case of damage. However, this position has been undermined by the Torts (Interference with Goods) Act 1977 which effectively permits the defendant to ensure that the claimant does not recover beyond the extent of his limited interest. Where the limited interest in the goods is a reversionary interest, the damages are confined to damage to the reversion; this requires permanent damage. Thus in *HSBC Rail (UK) Ltd v Network Rail Infrastructure Ltd*,[67] the claimant lessor of several railway carriages which had been severely damaged in the Hatfield rail crash of October 2000 failed in its action to recover damages because, the carriages having been repaired at no cost to the claimant, permanent damage to the reversion could not be shown.[68] The law has been far more fully worked out in relation to misappropriation of goods, and the details are collected there.[69]

## (B) CONSEQUENTIAL LOSSES

### 1. EXPENSES OTHER THAN THE COST OF REPAIR

#### (1) Expenses made necessary

37-013 **(a) In general** The cost of repair will include a variety of expenses beyond the contractual price paid to the repairer and in particular, with ships, docking expenses. Many such expenses will be considered as part of the cost of repair.[70] Expenses marginal to the repair itself, however, will generally be given separate treatment. Thus the expense of hiring a tug to take the ship into port after the collision, even although the tug might have been employed in any event for this purpose, was held recoverable in *The Inflexible*.[71] Dr Lushington said:

> "The incurring of such expense in ordinary cases is purely optional, and most clearly is not a measure of necessity but one of expediency, which may or may not be adopted according to the judgment of the master, and according to the state of the wind and weather, and indeed other circumstances. I am of the opinion that a merely probable, but discretionary, outlay cannot be deducted from a charge made indispensable by the collision."[72]

---

65 The awarding of interest is fully considered in Ch.19, above; see in relation to damage to goods paras 19-022 to 19-024 and para.19-047.

66 [1902] P. 42 CA: see para.37-068, below, where it is also pointed out that a claimant who is part owner may have been in a different position.

67 [2006] 1 W.L.R. 643 CA.

68 See on the damages as between bailor and bailee, in relation to chattels destroyed, *O'Sullivan v Williams* [1992] 3 All E.R. 385 CA and *Re-Source America International Ltd v Platt Site Services Ltd* [2005] 2 Lloyd's Rep. 50 CA in a footnote to para.37-068, below.

69 See paras 38-050 and following, below.

70 See, e.g. *The Black Prince* (1862) Lush. Adm. 568, where graving dock dues were allowed, without argument, as part of the repair costs. When assessing damages there may be dangers in including docking expenses within the cost of repair; see the last footnote but one in para.37-040, below.

71 (1857) Swab. 200.

72 (1857) Swab. 200 at 201.

Recovery for expenses which clearly cannot be subsumed within the term repair costs is variously illustrated, both where ships are concerned and where they are not. Thus in *Carisbrooke Shipping CV5 v Bird Port Ltd*,[73] where a ship suffered substantial damage in port, damages were awarded for both employee costs and management costs, the long-standing practice in ship collision cases of allowing 1 per cent of the value of the claim for disruption of business and expenditure of management time being followed.[74] In *Aerospace Publishing Ltd v Thames Water Utilities Ltd*,[75] recovery was allowed for the staff costs occasioned by diversion of the claimant's employees from their normal profit-earning duties to counter flooding causing damage to archives,[76] thereby disrupting the claimant's business in which the archives were used.[77] And a rather different form of recovery appeared in *Ironfield v Eastern Gas Board*,[78] where the claimant's car had been insured against damage so that the cost of repair fell on his insurance company. Here the claimant was still held entitled to recover from the defendant as special damage the first £10 of the loss which he had to pay under the terms of his insurance policy and £15 for loss of his "no claims" bonus. **37-014**

**(b) Hire of substitute vehicles** As far back as 1826 the cost of the hire of a substitute ship during the period of repair was held recoverable in *The Yorkshireman*.[79] In modern times, however, it is the hire of substitute cars that commands the damages field. For many years the cases were concerned with perfectly ordinary hirings from conventional car hire companies; latterly, hirings from credit car hire companies, with their special features, have been mounting and have nearly overtaken conventional hirings. While some of the issues are the same for both—such as the issue of whether there is any need to hire at all or of whether the period of hire is too long—it is nevertheless convenient, and also makes for clarity, to consider separately the ordinary, straightforward hiring cases and the credit car hiring cases. **37-015**

*(i) Conventional car hiring* The earliest issue that arose in this field was as to whether the claimant is entitled to hire a car of equally high quality to the one damaged and being repaired. In *Watson Norie v Shaw*,[80] where the Jensen car with which the claimant company, with an eye to prestige, had supplied its managing director had been damaged, and the company hired first a Rover and then a Jaguar during the period when the Jensen was being repaired, it was held that the full cost of hire should not be allowed but only the amount that it would have cost to hire a Ford Zephyr, the court being of the opinion that a Ford Zephyr was quite adequate for the company's needs while its prestige car was being repaired. By contrast, in *H.L. Motorworks v Alwahbi*,[81] where the claimant company was repairing a Rolls Royce for its owner and became involved in a collision when taking the car out for a trial run, damages were awarded in respect of the claimants' reimbursement of the **37-016**

73 [2005] 2 Lloyd's Rep. 626.
74 See [2005] 2 Lloyd's Rep. 626 at [153]–[171].
75 (2007) 110 Con. L.R. 1 CA.
76 And also destruction of archives: see para.37-069, below.
77 See (2007) 110 Con. L.R. 1 CA at [73] and following.
78 [1964] 1 W.L.R. 1125n.
79 (1826) 2 Hagg. Adm. 30n.
80 [1967] 1 Lloyd's Rep. 515 CA.
81 [1977] R.T.R. 276 CA.

owner's cost in hiring a substitute Rolls Royce until his own could be made available to him. Cairns LJ said:

> "It is essential to bear in mind that this was not the plaintiff company's own car … It does not seem to me that there was imposed on them a duty of querying the amount of [the owner's] claim unless it was plainly an excessive one. … On the face of it, the customer was entitled to have … another Rolls Royce. It might have been very damaging to the relationship of the plaintiff company as car repairers and the owner as their customer if they had endeavoured to cut down the amount of his claim … *Watson Norie v Shaw* was quite a different case, among other things, because there the car in question was the plaintiff company's own car."[82]

Where, as is usual, the damaged car is owned by the claimant, it has been held, as in *Daily Office Cleaning Contractors v Sheffard*,[83] to be reasonable to hire another prestige car, and indeed it has now been said in *Brain v Yorkshire Rider Ltd*,[84] where the cost of the car hired by the claimant was eventually held recoverable on an appeal because he had acted reasonably in hiring the particular car, that what was called the ill-reported *Watson Norie v Shaw*,[85] was not authority for the proposition that the cost of a prestige car is not to be allowed where a more modest vehicle is adequate for the claimant's needs. Once need is established, the starting point is an equivalent car.[86] While this must be generally true it is salutary to remember the words of Russell LJ in *Watson Norie* where he said:

> "In a case like this, where hire is necessary for a short period, I do not think it is correct to say that the plaintiff is entitled, as an axiom, to put upon the defendants the burden of the cost of hiring a car equal or substantially equal in quality, value and prestige to the damaged car. The test is whether the hiring cost is no more than reasonably necessary to fill the time gap, having regard to the purposes for which the plaintiff company needed to hire a car."[87]

Thus in *Singh v Yakubi*,[88] where, the claimant's Rolls Royce having been damaged, he hired first a Bentley and then another Rolls Royce for use in a business partnership and claimed as much as £99,000 by way of hire charges, the trial judge refused the claim as need for the business partnership, which had a fleet of other cars, had not been shown. He was upheld by the Court of Appeal, which decreed that such high claims should be scrutinised carefully by the court to see whether need existed.[89]

---

82 [1977] R.T.R. 276 CA at 280G–281D; and see similarly at 282F–J, per Roskill LJ.

83 [1977] R.T.R. 361.

84 [2007] Lloyd's Rep. I.R. 564.

85 [1967] 1 Lloyd's Rep. 515 CA.

86 That the claimant was entitled to have hired a comparable replacement for his luxury car was not challenged in *Heap-Hammond v TNT UK* unreported 15 June 2007 CC District Judge.

87 [1967] 1 Lloyd's Rep. 515 CA, 518. See too *Mattocks v Mann* [1993] R.T.R. 13 CA where the claimant had first hired a four door saloon at 130 a week and then changed this for a smaller two-door car at a lower rate of hire, the defendant's argument that she could have done with the smaller car throughout was rejected, particularly in the light of the fact that to have hired a car equivalent to the one damaged would have cost £354 a week. For hiring when the car is a write-off, see *Moore v D.E.R. Ltd* [1971] 1 W.L.R. 1476 CA, at para.37-069, below.

88 [2013] EWCA Civ 23 CA.

89 [2013] EWCA Civ 23 CA at [39].

Next come cases dealing with the period of hire for which the claimant is entitled to claim. It was held in *Martindale v Duncan*,[90] by the Court of Appeal that the claimant was not debarred by mitigation principles from claiming for the full 22 weeks that he had hired a substitute car although, being impecunious, he had delayed having repairs done pending approval of them by the defendant's and his own insurers. Similarly in *Mattocks v Mann*,[91] the Court of Appeal allowed the claimant hire charges not only during the period of repair, which itself took little short of a year from the damage,[92] but for some months thereafter until her repossession of the car; the delay in repossession was due to the claimant's inability to pay from her own resources and consequent need to await payment by the insurers.[93] **37-017**

*(ii) Car hiring on credit: the credit car hire imbroglio* The arrival on the market of credit car hire companies, which are sometimes called accident car hire companies, has led to litigation making for a veritable confusion of cases and case law. These companies work in this way. Because motor insurance policies generally do not cover the cost of hiring a substitute car during the repair of the car tortiously damaged, such companies have stepped in and come to the aid of the car owner. They allow the hirer credit on their charges until the conclusion of the hirer's claim for damages and also take on the burden of conducting that claim. The companies then collect from the damages. In these circumstances as would be expected, these companies have substantially higher hire charges than ordinary car hire companies. Also because credit given to a consumer is involved, there is a chance that under legislation designed to protect the consumer the contract of hire is unenforceable by the credit hire company. Both of these features appeared in the leading case in this field, a case which went to the House of Lords. **37-018**

*Dimond v Lovell*,[94] concerned a claimant who had hired a substitute car from a credit car hire company while her negligently damaged car was being repaired. The hiring agreement was held to be a credit agreement within the Consumer Credit Act 1974 and to be unenforceable against the claimant because it was not properly executed. The question was whether the claimant was entitled to recover damages for the notional cost of hire and the answer, undoubtedly correct, was that she could not. She had, somewhat fortuitously, suffered no loss, having received a collateral benefit which it was appropriate to take into account in assessing her damages and it would be contrary to the intention of the 1974 Act to allow her to recover the hire **37-019**

---

90 [1973] 1 W.L.R. 574 CA.

91 [1993] R.T.R. 13 CA.

92 Contrast [1993] R.T.R. 13 CA at 18L: "The plaintiff had put the car with reputable and well known repairers. She was not … to be criticised because they were overworked or had taken on too much work."

93 Contrast *Ramwade v W.J. Emson & Co* [1987] R.T.R. 72 CA, where the basic reason for the vehicle hire charges there being held not recoverable was remoteness; it was unnecessary for Parker LJ to have invoked, at 75L to 76A, impecuniosity and *The Liesbosch* (now departed from) to support the court's conclusion. Also there was no recovery of hire charges in *Agheampong v Allied Manufacturing (London) Ltd* unreported 30 June 2008 CC Circuit Judge, where the claimant had been driving his car illegally because uninsured and, but for the damage to it, would have continued to do so throughout the period of hire for which he was claiming; it was held that the case fell squarely within the ambit of the ex turpi causa principle as applied, in a different context, in *Hewison v Meridian Shipping Services PTE Ltd* [2003] I.C.R. 766 CA (at para.40-078, below).

94 [2002] 1 A.C. 384.

charges as trustee for the credit car hire company.[95] A different result, in different circumstances, was later reached by His Honour Judge Mackie in *W v Veolia Environmental Services (UK) Plc*,[96]where the hiring agreement was again held to be unenforceable against the hirer claimant.[97] Here the credit hire charges had actually been paid to the credit hire company, not by the claimant himself but, as is usual in these cases, by his insurers,[98] and damages were allowed, there being no possibility of double recovery by the claimant as he would have to account for the damages to the insurers.[99]

**37-020** The further question in *Dimond* was whether the claimant would be entitled to recover the higher charges of the credit car hire company or be confined to the charge that an ordinary car hire company would have made. Of course, this further question had become academic because of their Lordships' unanimous decision to reject the claim entirely. Nevertheless, because of its practical importance for hirings from credit car hire companies, *Dimond* gave consideration to the question. The view adopted, but only by a majority of their Lordships and in disagreement with the Court of Appeal, was that the claimant would, if the agreement with the car hire company had been enforceable, have been limited to the rate for the hire of a car from an ordinary car hire company.[100] The refusal to allow the full hire charges of the credit car hire company was on the basis that it was providing additional services and, as Lord Hoffmann who gave the leading speech put it, in reliance upon the principle enunciated in *British Westinghouse Co v Underground Ry*,[101] additional benefits obtained as a result of taking reasonable steps to mitigate loss are to be brought into account in the assessment of the damages.[102]

**37-021** Later, in *Lagden v O'Connor*,[103] the House of Lords, again by a majority, held that, because he could not afford to hire a car at all, the claimant was entitled to recover the higher charges of the credit car hire company. "Common fairness", said Lord Nicholls,

> "requires that if an innocent plaintiff cannot afford to pay car hire charges, so that left to himself he would be unable to obtain a replacement car to meet the need created by the negligent driver, then the damages payable under this head of loss should include the reasonable costs of a credit hire company."[104]

Nor was the claimant required to account for the additional benefits that hiring from

---

95 The situation is to be distinguished from a claim for the cost of repair itself for which cost, even if notional, there can be recovery: see para.37-008, above.

96 [2011] EWHC 2020 (QB).

97 This was by reason of regulations directed against agreements concluded at the hirer's home or place of work.

98 As to whether making the payment could be regarded as a failure to mitigate see para.9-100, above.

99 Because the insurers had, curiously, paid over the full hire charges despite their being a good deal higher than the insurance cover, the judge limited the recovery to the amount of that cover: see at [40].

100 Lord Nicholls thought there should be no such limit and Lord Saville preferred to express no view.

101 See para.9-108, above.

102 Only the basic hire rate and not the credit hire rate was allowed in *Heap-Hammond v TNT UK* unreported 15 June 2007 CC District Judge, on the basis of a failure to mitigate. In *McLaren v Hastings Direct* unreported 1 July 2009 CC District Judge, the issue of no recovery for additional benefits and the issue of mitigation were sensibly kept separate so that, the credit hire company hiring apart, the claimant was held to have hired at an unreasonably expensive rate.

103 [2004] 1 A.C. 1067.

104 [2004] 1 A.C. 1067 at [6].

a credit car hire company brought. The evidence showed, said Lord Hope, that he

> "had no choice but to use the services of the credit hire company and that, if he was to make use of these services, he had no way of avoiding the additional benefits that were provided to him."[105]

The impecuniosity of the claimant made the case different from *Dimond* which the House of Lords distinguished.[106]

This sensible decision raises the question of what constitutes impecuniosity for these purposes. While it can be said that there is now a brisk business in the many cases heard at county court level of claimants who have hired cars from credit hire companies alleging impecuniosity, there is little reported authority to date on the issue. There is *W v Veolia Environmental Services (UK) Plc*,[107] where His Honour Judge Mackie was prepared to hold impecunious, so as to allow entitlement to recover the credit car hire charges incurred in their entirety, an actuary living in a good part of London whose damaged car was an old Bentley but whose finances were in a very poor state.[108] And the trial judge in *Opoku v Tintas*,[109] was satisfied that the claimant, who had occasionally driven his damaged car as a minicab, had a tiny bank balance and had quite large debts, was impecunious for these purposes, and this holding was not challenged by the Court of Appeal.[110] **37-022**

There is a great deal of litigation stemming from these developments, litigation fuelled by the long and continuing war, or "long running battle"[111] between credit car hire companies and motor insurance companies where many attempts have been made to by-pass the difficulties presented by the part of the decision in *Dimond v Lovell*,[112] disallowing recovery of reasonably incurred credit car hire charges by a claimant who is pecuious. Dealing with all this litigation in an orderly fashion is not easy. We may first note the various hire rates that are being claimed, both by the impecunious and by those who are now being called the pecunious. The impecunious are entitled to the credit hire rate but the pecunious are only entitled to what for long was called the spot rate, but is now called the basic hire rate. This follows on from the Court of Appeal's expressing a preference, in both of the two appeals brought together of *Pattini v First Leicester Buses Ltd* and *Bent v Highways and Utilities Construction*,[113] for the terminology of basic hire rate to that of spot rate as being more accurate. The court explained that spot rate is a misnomer, being more appropriately applied to rates of freight or charter hire or to the open market price of a commodity where the service or commodity is for immediate rather than future delivery.[114] With both basic hire rates and credit hire rate there is a bracket of rates from which claimants may choose.[115] **37-023**

---

105 [2004] 1 A.C. 1067 at [35].

106 For the abandonment by *Lagden* of the celebrated impecuniosity rule of *The Liesbosch* [1933] A.C. 449 see paras 8-110 to 8-113, above.

107 [2011] EWHC 2020.

108 See the judge's analysis of the claimant's position at [2011] EWHC 2020 at [60] and [61].

109 [2013] EWCA Civ 1299.

110 The appeal was concerned with the funding of repair costs: see at para.37-028, below.

111 *McBride v UK Insurance Ltd* [2017] EWCA Civ 144 at [1].

112 [2002] 1 A.C. 384.

113 [2011] EWCA Civ 1384 CA.

114 Pattini at [2011] EWCA Civ 1384 CA at [30(4)].

115 There is such a large and profitable market in this area that it has led to fraud and dishonesty in providing evidence of rates to courts, as happened in *Dickinson v Tesco Plc* [2013] EWCA Civ 36

**37-024** A miscellany of cases, reaching Court of Appeal, have sought to resolve further difficulties arising from this basic principle. First in time was *Bee v Jenson (No.2)*.[116] A method had been devised to avoid the problems presented by the Consumer Credit Act 1974 which had surfaced in *Dimond v Lovell*,[117] whereby the claimant, whose car had been damaged, entered into a hiring agreement for a replacement car with the hiring company at what was held to be a suitable basic hire rate[118] but it was arranged that an insurance company was liable to pay, and did pay, the hire charges to the hire company which had offered a financial inducement to the insurance company to commit itself in this way.[119] It was decided that the claimant was entitled to recover the cost of hire in the hire contract[120] which, once indemnified, would be held by him for the insurer's benefit; the defendant was liable not merely for the true cost of the hire to the insurers, viz., the hire cost less the financial inducement received. As Longmore LJ who gave the only reasoned judgment said, this was the logical result of *Bradburn v G.W. Ry*,[121] the classic case establishing early that a claimant's insurance cover is to be ignored when assessing the damages to which he is entitled.[122] In *Bent v Highways and Utilities Construction*,[123] the pecunious claimant, a well-known footballer, had hired a car on credit hire terms. It was accepted that it was reasonable for him to have hired the particular make and model of car but, because he was not entitled to recover as damages the credit hire rate, it fell to the court to consider the method to use to find, on the evidence available, the basic hire rate for the car to which he was entitled.[124] As the trial judge was considered not to have carried out this task properly,[125] the Court of Appeal decided for itself, coming up with a different figure.[126] *Pattni v First Leicester Buses Ltd*,[127] concerned interest which claimant had contracted to pay on the credit hire charges for the period between the end of the hire of the replacement car and the date when the claim against the defendant driver was finalised. The Court of Appeal held him not entitled to recover this contractual interest charge as it constituted the cost of an additional benefit within the reasoning of the House of Lords in *Dimond v Lovell*.[128]

**37-025** There being a whole range of basic hire rates offered on the market for vehicles generally and therefore for vehicles of the type that it was reasonable for the

---

CA.

116 [2007] 4 All E.R. 791 CA.

117 [2002] 1 A.C. 384; see at para.37-020, above.

118 The judge had decided the rate was reasonable and good value for money compared with other basic hire rates and there was no appeal against this finding: see [2007] 4 All E.R. 791 CA at [4].

119 Whether the claimant was also personally liable for the hire charges did not have to be decided as it would have made no difference to the result: see at [14]–[17].

120 By way of general damages rather than special damages. For this aspect of the *Bee* case, see footnote at end of para.37-054, below.

121 (1874) L.R. 10 Ex. 1.

122 Dealt with at para.9-166, above. That *Bee* does not affect the House of Lords' holding in *Dimond* is illustrated by *Wei v Cambridge Power and Light Ltd* unreported 9 September 2010 County Court, (see at [21] and [26]).

123 The second of the two appeals heard together at [2011] EWCA Civ 1384 CA.

124 See [2011] EWCA Civ 1384 CA at [73]–[80].

125 See [2011] EWCA Civ 1384 CA at [80]–[85].

126 [2011] EWCA Civ 1384 CA at [86] and following.

127 The first of the two appeals heard together at [2011] EWCA Civ 1384 CA.

128 [2011] EWCA Civ 1384 CA at [50] to [63]. For that reasoning see para.37-020, above. Nor was interest recoverable as damages or under the statute, it having been a finding of fact that no interest had been paid: at [64]–[70].

particular claimant to hire, judges at the lower level have had much difficulty in deciding on the basic hire rate appropriate in the case before them. The Court of Appeal in *Stevens v Equity Syndicate Management Ltd*,[129] has now given guidance. The claimant there had entered into a credit hire agreement but, being held not to be impecunious, was entitled to claim only the basic hire rate. Accordingly, the Court of Appeal started by considering how the basic hire element in the total charged under the credit hire agreement was to be ascertained. But it was impractical to find this out because it would require disclosure and analysis at a cost in excess of the value of the claim. So the court resorted to looking at basic hire rates available in the claimant's locality, which is what the lower courts in the case had attempted to do.[130] If, as is likely, there is a range of rates, the court must seek out the lowest reasonable rate quoted by a mainstream supplier, or in the absence of a mainstream supplier by a local reputable supplier, for a vehicle of the kind in issue to a reasonable person in the position of the claimant.[131]

A claim that *Stevens v Equity Syndicate Management Ltd* was inconsistent with earlier decisions of the Court of Appeal,[132] and wrongly decided, was rejected in *McBride v UK Insurance Ltd*.[133] Counsel for one of the appellants in *McBride*,[134] argued that the requirement to obtain the lowest reasonable rate, was inconsistent with a passage from *Pattni v First Leicester Buses Ltd*,[135] in which Aikens LJ said that **37-026**

> "even if the credit hire rate for the car hired is *at the top of the range of credit hire rates*, so long as it is reasonable to hire that car and the credit hire rate is reasonable, then the court has to calculate the BHR on the basis that the claimant notionally went round to an equivalent non-credit hire company".

In *McBride* Flaux LJ explained, however, that what Aikens LJ said was subject to the requirement that the claimant had acted reasonably. In other words,

> "if the defendant can show that a basic hire rate at the top end of the range exceeds the lowest reasonable rate within the range charged by a mainstream supplier or reputable local supplier, then the claimant will not recover more than that lowest reasonable rate, unless he or she can demonstrate that it was appropriate on the facts of the particular case to take some higher rate, which is extremely unlikely ever to be the case."[136]

The assumption here is that the reasonable person in the position of the claimant would normally be willing to pay no more than the lowest reasonable rate available locally from a reputable car hire company.[137]

A further issue, also considered in *McBride v UK Insurance Ltd*, concerned the effect of excesses on identifying the basic hire rate. If a claimant, like the claimant in the *McBride* appeal, would always pay to reduce an insurance excess to nil then how should that additional cost be provided for? Flaux LJ held that the correct ap- **37-027**

---

129 [2015] EWCA Civ 93 CA.

130 [2015] EWCA Civ 93 CA at [30]–[32].

131 [2015] EWCA Civ 93 CA at [32]–[40].

132 In particular, *Pattni v First Leicester Buses Ltd* [2011] EWCA Civ 1384 CA and *Burdis v Livsey* [2003] Q.B. 36 CA.

133 [2017] EWCA Civ 144 CA.

134 The case concerning two appeals from the county courts.

135 [2011] EWCA Civ 1384 CA at [76] (emphasis added).

136 [2017] EWCA Civ 144 CA at [53].

137 [2017] EWCA Civ 144 CA at [40].

proach where there was no reasonably available product with no excess was to make an adjustment to the damages recoverable to reflect the cost of the nil excess provided that, having regard to stand-alone products which offer an elimination of the insurance excess on a hired car, it was reasonable to purchase the nil excess.[138] Where mainstream or reputable local car hire companies do offer a product with a nil excess, this separate assessment exercise is unnecessary.[139]

**37-028** As already said,[140] there are indeed issues, such as the need to hire and the length of hiring, which are the same whether the hiring be from a conventional car hiring company or from a credit car hire company. Illustrative of this is *Opoku v Tintas*.[141] Because of impecuniosity the claimant was entitled to, and did, hire from a credit car hire company but the hiring period was lengthy because he did not have his car repaired until his insurer had paid him the repair costs on a without prejudice basis. It was held that he should have had the car repaired once it had been inspected by his insurer's engineer, thereby bringing the need for the hired car to an end. It was said by the Court of Appeal that the courts had to exercise particular control where damages claims involved credit hire because of the very high rates charged—in *Opoku* the total cost of car hire from accident to repair claimed had been some £130,000. Also in *Opoku* there was held to be nothing inconsistent, as had been argued, between allowing the claimant credit hire charges on account of impecuniosity and requiring him to repair well before he had been paid by his insurer.[142] The Court of Appeal has now made it crystal clear in *Zurich Insurance Plc v Sameer*,[143] that a claimant's entitlement to rely on impecuniosity goes to the duration of hire as much as to the rate of hire. Impecuniosity could justify a higher level of award where the claimant continued to hire due to inability to pay for repairs or to buy a replacement car.[144] The case itself was concerned only with the interpretation of an order debarring the claimant, whose car was a write-off, from relying on his impecuniosity and with whether the order covered the duration of hiring as well as the rate of hire. A further issue mentioned but not argued was whether the rules of mitigation required the claimant to claim on his insurance policy and with the proceeds buy a replacement car. The court said that, while this was an interesting question of some importance, it was for another day.[145]

### (2) Expenses rendered futile

**37-029** Apart from the hiring of substitute goods there are the expenses rendered futile by the loss which may sometimes be included in the damages: thus it was held in *The Inflexible*,[146] that the wages of the ship's officers and crew were recoverable if it were customary to retain them during the standstill period. In *Edmund Handcock v "Ernesto" (Owners)*,[147] the crew's wages were paid and boiler furnaces were kept

---

138 [2017] EWCA Civ 144 CA at [76]–[77] and [81].
139 [2017] EWCA Civ 144 CA at [79].
140 At para.37-015, above.
141 [2013] EWCA Civ 1299.
142 Compare the cases on period of hire where the hiring is from a conventional car hiring company at para.37-017, above.
143 [2014] EWCA Civ. 357 CA.
144 [2014] EWCA Civ. 357 at [9(4)].
145 [2014] EWCA Civ. 357 at [41]–[43].
146 (1857) Swab. 200; see especially at 204.
147 [1952] 1 Lloyd's Rep. 467 CA. The case was contract, but the same principles would apply to tort.

burning while repairs lasting three days were effected upon the claimant's damaged tug, and it was held that these expenses were recoverable although they would have been incurred whether the tug had been detained in dock or not and although there would have been no work for the tug during the three days even if she had been available. Somervell LJ, delivering the Court of Appeal judgment, said:

> "They were moneys normally expended in order that there might be an available tug. Owing to the collision they were expended, but the tug was not available, and the plaintiffs were deprived of her use."[148]

If indeed there is a successful claim for loss of profits, this head of expenses rendered futile would disappear: otherwise damages would be given twice over. Thus it is sometimes found, as in *The City of Peking*,[149] that such expenses as the crew's wages and maintenance are held to be properly recoverable where the claim for loss of profits is disallowed.[150]

## 2. Loss of Profits of Profit-Earning Chattels

### (1) Ships

The case law has developed entirely around ships and damage to ships. This development has been elaborate and is to be traced from the middle of the 19th century. 37-030

It was recognised in *The Clarence*,[151] by Dr Lushington that a sum for loss of profits is a proper item in damages where a ship is detained for repair if such loss is proved by the claimant, an onus which was held not to have been discharged in that case.[152] The early cases usually allowed damages for loss of freight under the term "demurrage"; this term was used, and is occasionally still used, in this connection as indicating the sum which would represent the generalised loss through deprivation of use of the ship during a period of detention for repairs.[153] Thus freight not earned was allowed in *The Betsy Caines*[154] and "demurrage" was awarded in *The Gazelle*,[155] with the proper qualification that it must be calculated by 37-031

> "deducting … from the gross freight so much as would in ordinary cases be disbursed on account of expenses in earning of the freight".[156]

---

Indeed many tort cases were referred to.

148 [1952] 1 Lloyd's Rep. 467 CA at 469.

149 (1890) 15 App. Cas. 438 PC.

150 See, especially, (1890) 15 App. Cas. 438 PC at 449. The disallowance of the loss of profits claim is dealt with at para.37-037, below.

151 (1850) 3 W. Rob. (Adm.) 283. This case is taken as a starting point because it contrasts with the contemporaneous decision in *The Columbus* (1849) 3 W. Rob. (Adm.) 158 in relation to destruction: see para.37-071, below.

152 (1850) 3 W. Rob. (Adm.) 283 at 286–287.

153 See Lord Herschell in *The Argentino* (1889) 14 App. Cas. 519 at 523–524, where he talked of the damages "under the name of demurrage in respect of the loss of earnings which it must reasonably have been anticipated would ensue during the time of detention". The commonest use of the term "demurrage" is in contract, being a provision in charterparties for payment by the charterer to the shipowner at a certain rate for every day of improper detention of the ship: see para.32-077, above.

154 (1826) 2 Hagg. Adm. 28.

155 (1844) 2 W. Rob. (Adm.) 279.

156 (1844) 2 W. Rob. (Adm.) 279 at 284.

"As to the time for which such compensation must be made", said Dr Lushington in *The Inflexible*,[157]

> "it ought to be reckoned from the period when the vessel, in the ordinary course, would have been ready for sea if there had been no collision, up to the period when with due diligence the repairs ought to have been completed."

Subsequently in *The Black Prince*,[158] it was further held that the measure was to be calculated with reference to the length of time the ship had by the collision been thrown out of her usual employment: not to the longer time of repairs, nor to the shorter difference between the usual and the actual time in port.[159] And where only temporary repairs have been carried out by the time of the action and permanent repairs remain to be carried out in the future, it was held in *The Kingsway*,[160] that the claimant was entitled not only to demurrage damages in respect of the temporary repairs but also to recover for the prospective loss of time during the execution of the permanent repairs.

**37-032** Damages under the name of demurrage, however, merely represent the amount of earnings that a ship would generally lose through being detained. Frequently the damages under this head may rise or fall below this figure: either it is shown that the ship would, but for the damage, have earned more than the demurrage rate, or it cannot be shown that the damage has caused any loss of profit at all.[161] At this point the authorities enter the difficult field of remoteness of damage, and some of the cases are not too easy to reconcile.[162]

**37-033** Thus, on the one hand, the principle of demurrage damages was extended to give damages for more specific losses of earnings, such as the loss of part of a fishing season, as in *The Risoluto*,[163] or for the loss of a charterparty. The latter was first allowed in *The Star of India*,[164] and firmly established by the House of Lords in *The Argentino*.[165] In *The Star of India*,[166] the collision occurred as the claimant's ship was about to go to the loading port to load under the charterparty, and as a result of the collision the charterers acquired, and exercised, the right to cancel the charterparty. It was held that the claimant could recover damages for the loss of the charterparty, the granting of the option to cancel by the claimant to the charterers not being the proximate cause of the loss. In estimating the loss, various deductions were made from the amount that would have been earned under the charterparty, namely the wear and tear saved, a figure in respect of the uncertainties and perils of the voyage, and the like. *The Argentino*,[167] extended the recovery of damages to include the loss of a future charterparty for a voyage which, although

---

157 (1857) Swab. 200 at 205.
158 (1862) Lush. Adm. 568.
159 See, especially, (1862) Lush. Adm. 568 at 574–575.
160 [1918] P. 344 CA.
161 Compare *The Argentino* (1888) 13 P.D. 191 CA at 201–202, per Bowen LJ.
162 Most of them are also considered in connection with the general problem of remoteness at paras 8-105 to 8-108, above.
163 (1883) 8 P.D. 109.
164 (1876) 1 P.D. 466. Followed in *The Consett* (1880) 5 P.D. 229, although the main question in that case was whether the charterparty had really been lost or whether the claimant could still reasonably have fulfilled it.
165 (1889) 14 App. Cas. 519.
166 (1876) 1 P.D. 466.
167 (1889) 14 App. Cas. 519.

contracted for, would not be embarked upon until the completion of the voyage in the course of which the collision occurred. Lord Herschell said in delivering the leading speech:

> "The loss of the use of a vessel and of the earnings which would ordinarily be derived from its use during the time it is under repair, and therefore not available for trading purposes, is certainly damage which directly and naturally flows from a collision. But, further than this, … the damage is not necessarily limited to the money which could have been earned during the time the vessel was actually under repair. It does not appear to me to be out of the ordinary course of things that a steamship, whilst prosecuting her voyage, should have secured employment for another adventure. And if at the time of a collision the damaged vessel had obtained such an engagement for an ordinary maritime adventure, the loss of the fair and ordinary earnings of such a vessel on such an adventure appear to me to be the direct and natural consequence of the collision."[168]

He further pointed out that there could be no general demurrage claim in addition to the special loss of the charterparty since otherwise damages would be given twice over, and that against the sum allowed for the lost charterparty must be set the sum the claimant earned, or could have earned, between the completion of the repairs and the end of the period during which he would have been engaged on the lost charterparty.[169]

That a more restricted recovery in respect of profitable charterparties may, **37-034** however, be appropriate, particularly where the fact situation is of greater complexity, appears from a trilogy of more modern cases, *The Soya*,[170] *The World Beauty*[171] and *The Naxos*.[172] In *The Soya*,[173] a collision, requiring the claimants' ship to be laid up for repairs for 20 days, took place at the very end of 1950 as she was proceeding to a port of loading under a charterparty from London to the Far East. The net profit to be made on this charterparty was at a daily rate of £150. The first half of 1951 saw an extraordinary rise in rates for Far Eastern voyages which reached its peak in May of that year. Thus when the ship had duly completed, after repair and 20 days later than otherwise, the charterparty earning her £150 daily, she completed further charterparties in the Far East, entered into after the collision, earning net profits at daily rates exceeding £800. The claimants claimed loss of profit for the 20 days' detention based on approximately the £800 figure; the defendants contended that the loss of profit should be calculated at the average daily rate under the charterparty from London to the Far East. The Court of Appeal accepted the defendants' contention. The first unusual feature of the case was that the charterparty to which the ship was proceeding at the time of collision was eventually performed despite the collision, the ship reaching the loading point just in time to prevent its cancellation. In these circumstances the profit on that charterparty was

---

168 (1889) 14 App. Cas. 519 at 523.

169 (1889) 14 App. Cas. 519 at 524. Contrast *The Daressa* [1971] 1 Lloyd's Rep. 60 where the claimants successfully claimed for the loss of an operating subsidy payable by the US Federal Maritime Board and withheld on the ground that the claimants could recover it from the defendants; also *Owners of the Ship "Front Ace" v Owners of "Vicky 1"* [2008] 2 All E.R. (Comm) 42 CA which considered what was the appropriate method for arriving at the lost profit, that used in *The Argentino* not being controlling: see at [58] and following.

170 [1956] 1 W.L.R. 714 CA.

171 [1970] P. 144 CA.

172 [1972] 1 Lloyd's Rep. 149.

173 [1956] 1 W.L.R. 714 CA.

not lost, and the daily rate was not relevant qua specific lost profit. The second new feature then came into play, i.e. the extraordinary rise in freight rates over the following six months, and the claimants argued that the loss of 20 days should therefore be calculated in relation to what the ship would have been earning had it not been put 20 days behind schedule by the collision. The court said of this argument that it

> "must result in the postponement for an indefinite period, perhaps to the end of the ship's career, of the point of time at which the loss, if any, due to the 20 days' detention, could be ascertained, and the ultimate result in terms of profit or loss would necessarily be influenced or indeed determined by causes and factors wholly independent of the collision."[174]

This, however, would seem unnecessarily to magnify the difficulties of assessment, and it is submitted that the proper period to be taken in these circumstances for ascertaining the claimant's loss by the 20 days' detention is the 20 days following the end of the ship's commitments already in existence at the time of the collision: it was for these 20 days that the claimants had been deprived by the tort of the profitable use of their ship.

**37-035** However, in *The Naxos*,[175] Brandon J was not prepared to accept that *The Soya*,[176] had laid down an inflexible rule that the damages must always be calculated on the basis of the rate of freight earned on the charterparty the commencement of which was delayed, but which was not lost, by the detention of the vessel for repair, such charterparty being there designated the "instant charterparty".[177] The particular instant charterparty was at an exceptionally high rate and Brandon J thought it would not be fair to the defendants to base the calculations of loss on that rate, preferring to take an average of the voyages before and after so as

> "to arrive at a representative figure for the earning capacity of the vessel at that period".[178]

While, looked at in conjunction with *The Soya*,[179] this appears rather to be unfair to the claimants who were given the low rate of the instant charterparty in the earlier case and refused the high rate of the instant charterparty in the later one, it is thought that Brandon J was right not to base his award on the high rate, in effect detecting the flaw in *The Soya*,[180] with its acceptance of the rate earned on a charterparty which was never lost. However, but for a further special feature existing in *The Naxos*,[181] this should have led him not to average but, as has already been submitted, to look forward to the period after the completion of the instant charterparty and of any other charterparties already contracted at the time of the collision. The further special feature of the case was that the claimants had been advised by surveyors that they could safely defer permanent repairs to suit their convenience, and indeed they were not effected until some nine months after the collision, during which period the vessel had completed five charterparties. If then the claim-

---

174 [1956] 1 W.L.R. 714 CA at 726, per Jenkins LJ.
175 [1972] 1 Lloyd's Rep. 149.
176 [1956] 1 W.L.R. 714 CA.
177 [1972] 1 Lloyd's Rep. 149 at 155–156.
178 [1972] 1 Lloyd's Rep. 149 at 156.
179 [1956] 1 W.L.R. 714 CA.
180 [1956] 1 W.L.R. 714 CA.
181 [1972] 1 Lloyd's Rep. 149.

ants had chosen to do the permanent repairs at a time of particularly high freight rates, they might properly be regarded as having failed to mitigate their loss.

In the third case, *The World Beauty*,[182] the more restricted recovery was attributable to mitigating steps which the claimants had successfully taken in reduction of their losses. The collision damage inflicted on the claimants' ship occurred in the course of the performance of a charterparty which had been negotiated nine months earlier when freight rates had been very much higher. The claimants chartered another ship at the low rates then prevailing, employing her as a substitute ship to perform the charter, and on completion of the necessary repairs to the damaged ship advanced by some 100 days her employment under a seven-year time charter, which had been arranged to follow upon the earlier charter and which had also been negotiated when rates had been very high. The Court of Appeal held that the claimants could not simply claim their loss of profit on the earlier charter for the period during which the damaged ship was out of use but must give credit, first, for the profit made by the substitute ship under the remainder of the earlier charter and, second, not indeed for the 100-day profit made on the follow-up charter but for the benefit of achieving this profit seven years earlier than they otherwise would have done. The court was, however, divided as to the proper method of calculating this benefit. The majority considered that the calculation should be based on the profit the ship would have earned if she had been available on the market from the completion of repairs to the date of due delivery under the follow-up charter. Winn LJ, dissenting on this, preferred to take the figure which represented the present value of an amount equal to the 100-day profit payable seven years in the future.[183] **37-036**

At the other end of the scale are the cases in which the circumstances have led to an award less than the demurrage rate. Many and varied cases fall within this category and present difficulties of analysis.[184] **37-037**

(1) Just as the claimant's position at the time of the tort may have been that he had concluded a profitable charterparty for the ship, so too it may be that he had been operating the ship unprofitably. This was the position in *The Bodlewell*,[185] where the ship was at the time running at a loss in order to establish a new trade. It was held that nothing could be allowed for the loss of the use of the ship during the repair period, the contingent profit which might later have been earned when the trade was established being held too remote. Somewhat similarly in *Admiralty Commissioners v S.S. Valeria*,[186] where the claimant had hired the ship from the Dutch Government at a larger rate of hire than the profit he was making by the use of the vessel, it was held that the latter and not the former sum was the relevant one in assessing the damages.[187]

---

182 [1970] P. 144 CA.

183 Willmer LJ at first instance had put forward yet a third method which was akin to that of Winn LJ: at [1970] P. 144 CA at 154. For the mitigation aspects of the case, see paras 9-115 and 9-125, above.

184 The analysis in the text follows the lines adopted in dealing with remoteness generally: see Ch.8, above, especially paras 8-009 and 8-010.

185 [1907] P. 286.

186 [1922] 2 A.C. 242.

187 These two cases were decided after the House of Lords had decided, in *The Greta Holme* [1897] A.C. 596 and *The Mediana* [1900] A.C. 113, that damages for loss of use were recoverable even where the ship was not profit-earning: see paras 37-045 to 37-049, below. The claimant argued for their application both in *The Bodlewell* [1907] P. 286 and in *Admiralty Commissioners v S.S. Valeria* [1922] 2 A.C. 242 to profit-earning vessels which were not making so much profit as the demur-

(2) A state of affairs other than the unprofitable operation of the ship may exist at the time of the tort so as to make the demurrage rate too high a measure, as in *S.S. Strathfillan v S.S. Ikala*.[188] In that case the claimants used the damaged vessel to import oil, but owing to the war the Government had fixed an annual quota as to the amount importable. The claimant owned one other ship for the purpose of this trade, and hired outside tonnage to carry the bulk of the quota. After the completion of the collision repairs the ship made one further voyage which enabled the claimants to complete the quota and, apart from the collision, she could not have made a second voyage to bring in part of the quota during the year. In these circumstances a majority of the House of Lords held that the assessment was wrong as the registrar had wrongly inferred that the extra tonnage was hired as a result of the collision. A rather different situation arose in *The City of Peking*,[189] where it was held, on somewhat complicated facts, that a claim for demurrage failed because a substituted vessel, belonging also to the claimant company, took the place of the damaged ship on her homeward route. "The profits of her homeward voyage," said Sir Barnes Peacock, "though earned by other steamers, were earned by other steamers of the company and for the company".[190]

(3) So, too, matters subsequent to the tort may prevent the claimant from showing that the damage by the defendant has been the cause of any such loss. The simplest situation is where the ship has been lost from other causes between the date of collision and the date the claim for damages is heard. In these circumstances it was held in *The Glenfinlas*,[191] that no damages could be recovered for loss of use by reason of detention during the prospective permanent repairs, since the repairs never could be done and the loss of time could not occur.[192] In *The York*,[193] the damage did not render the claimants' ship unseaworthy and she continued trading without effecting repairs; while so trading the claimants contracted to sell her, and during the period required for inspection by the buyer the collision repairs were executed. It was held that, since the claimants' contract prevented them from using the ship as a profit-earning vessel during the time the repairs were executed, they had suffered no loss under this head.[194] On the other hand,

---

rage rate: this attempt was unsuccessful. *The Greta Holme* [1897] A.C. 596. *The Mediana* [1900] A.C. 113 and *The Marpessa* [1907] A.C. 241 were expressly distinguished in *Admiralty Commissioners v S.S. Valeria* [1922] 2 A.C. 242 on the ground that the ships in question were not profit-earning.

188 [1929] A.C. 196.

189 (1890) 15 App. Cas. 438 PC.

190 (1890) 15 App. Cas. 438 PC at 446. Just as *The Mediana* [1900] A.C. 113, where damages for the loss of use of a non-profit-earning ship were awarded, was distinguished in *The Bodlewell* [1907] P. 286 and *Admiralty Commissioners v S.S. Valeria* [1922] 2 A.C. 242 (see preceding footnote but two), similarly *The City of Peking* (1890) 15 App. Cas. 438 PC, was distinguished in *The Mediana* [1900] A.C. 113 itself. The difference would seem to lie in the substitute ship being an idle ship in the former case and a stand-by ship in the latter. See further on non-profit-earning ships paras 37-045 and following, below.

191 [1918] P. 363n.

192 Approved by Pickford LJ in *The Kingsway* [1918] P. 344 CA at 358–359, and by Scrutton LJ in *The York* [1929] P. 178 CA at 184–185.

193 [1929] P. 178 CA.

194 Other illustrations put by Scrutton LJ may concern either preceding or subsequent events. "Sup-

in *H.M.S. London*,[195] where the repairs were delayed by a dockworkers' strike,[196] the claimant recovered damages for the loss of use of the ship during the whole period she was laid up for repair.

The situation where the claimant effects the collision repairs to his ship at the same time as other repairs to her, and in such a manner as not to increase the repair period, may be fitted into the preceding analysis of the cases. It seems better, however, to give this situation separate treatment for two reasons: because the cases form a homogeneous group, and because the recovery of expenses incurred as well as profits lost is involved. **37-038**

## (2) Chattels other than ships

Where other than ships are concerned authority is sparse, virtually non-existent, but the shipping world cannot have a monopoly on the recovery for lost profits which must be available for other chattels Thus at first instance in *Aerospace Publishing Ltd v Thames Water Utilities Ltd*,[197] loss of income from damaged archives used in a business until such time as they were restored was awarded as consequential loss and this does not appear to have been in issue, or challenged, in the Court of Appeal.[198] **37-039**

## 3. Expenses and Loss of Profits where other Repairs have been Effected Concurrently

On this issue we are concerned only with ships.[199] The question which has arisen is as to the defendant's liability for the expenses of docking during repair and for the loss of use and profits during repair when other repairs have been effected concurrently with the collision repairs caused by the defendant's tort in such a manner as not to increase the repair period or to increase the dock expenses. As a result of the decision in *The Haversham Grange*,[200] it was for a long time the law that there was a distinction in this regard between a defendant's liability for dock expenses, where apportionment might be allowed, and a defendant's liability for loss of use and profits, where no apportionment was permitted. This illogical and unsatisfactory distinction was removed by the House of Lords in *Carslogie S.S. Co v Royal* **37-040**

pose", he said, "that a vessel caught in the Baltic, and detained by ice so that she could not trade at all, takes the opportunity of doing repairs. She may recover the cost of repairs, but in my view she is not entitled to say: 'I have lost so many days' trading profit,' because the pre-existing condition, which has nothing whatever to do with the collision, is that however much she wanted to trade, she could not, because she was held up by ice. Another case which occurred to me was the case of an embargo preventing any ship from moving or trading, and the shipowner, taking advantage of his ship being held up by the embargo, deciding to do repairs due to a previous collision … Again I do not think it would be possible for him to say: 'I claim from you the loss of profit on trading,' because it was quite impossible, owing to circumstances not connected with the collision at all—namely, the embargo—that he should trade, and consequently he never lost any profits of trading because of the collision": [1929] P. 178 CA at 185–186.

[195] [1914] P. 72.

[196] The strike was presumed legal in the absence of evidence to the contrary: for the general relevance of this see paras 8-045 and following, above.

[197] [2005] EWHC 2987 (QB).

[198] (2007) 110 Con. L.R. 1 CA; see its decision at para.37-004, above.

[199] For a solitary illustration involving a chattel other than a ship see the footnote at the end of para.37-042, below.

[200] [1905] P. 307 CA: facts at para.37-043, below.

*Norwegian Government*,[201] where their Lordships were unanimous in condemning the distinction,[202] accepting the earlier decision in so far as it related to liability for loss of use and profits and rejecting it in so far as it related to liability for dock expenses.[203] It would seem, therefore, that now no question of apportionment will arise; the defendant either will be liable in full or will not be liable at all for whichever head of damage is claimed.[204] In any event, both heads of damage may now be considered together on this issue.

**37-041** The first situation is where the damage caused by the defendant has, by making the ship unseaworthy, necessitated the docking of the ship for repairs and the claimant has seized the opportunity to effect concurrently other repairs, which were not caused by the collision and which there was no necessity for him to carry out at that particular time. In these circumstances in *The Acanthus*,[205] where the claimant had taken the advantage of the opportunity to fit the ship with bilge keels without causing delay or increase of dock expenses, it was held that the defendant remained liable for the whole of the dock expenses. It was immaterial that the claimant had already had it in mind to effect this addition, since he had been under no obligation or necessity to do so. Similarly, in *Admiralty Commissioners v S.S. Chekiang*,[206] where advantage had been taken of the docking to give the ship her annual overhaul without adding to the repair period, it was held by the House of Lords that the defendant was nevertheless liable for damages for loss of use during the whole period of docking. And in *The Ferdinand Retzlaff*,[207] where the claimants had already arranged at the time of the collision for their ship to go for her first four-yearly survey and owners' repairs in some three weeks' time, it was held that the defendants were not entitled to credit for the saving of cost and of time in bringing these forward and doing them together with the collision repairs, as this had increased neither the cost, as by way of dock dues, of the collision repairs nor the time occupied in effecting them.[208]

**37-042** The converse situation, i.e. where repairs are necessitated by the ship being rendered unseaworthy by factors other than the damage caused by the collision for which the defendant is responsible, arose in *Carslogie S.S. Co v Royal Norwegian Government*.[209] The claimant's ship, after being damaged by the defendant, had temporary repairs effected which rendered her seaworthy, and subsequently proceeded to New York in order to carry out permanent repairs. En route she was rendered unseaworthy by heavy weather, thus requiring immediate repair. At New York both sets of repairs were effected concurrently, and the period taken would

---

201 [1952] A.C. 292. It had already come in for criticism by Lord Phillimore in *Admiralty Commissioners v S.S. Chekiang* [1926] A.C. 637 at 643.

202 [1952] A.C. 292 at 303, 312, 315, 317.

203 The fallacy with regard to dock expenses appears to have arisen because they tended to be considered as part of the cost of repair: see *The Chekiang* [1925] P. 80 CA at 95, per Atkin LJ.

204 Whether the decision in *Marine Insurance Co v China Transpacific S.S. Co* (1886) 11 App. Cas. 573 (sometimes called *The Vancouver*), properly interpreted, may today justify an apportionment in an insurance claim may perhaps be doubted. In any event, it does not affect claims for damages where the rules have now been worked out more fully.

205 [1902] P. 17.

206 [1926] A.C. 637.

207 [1972] 2 Lloyd's Rep. 120.

208 The starting point of these cases had been *Ruabon S.S. Co v London Transport Insurance Co* [1900] A.C. 6, which also concerned dock dues, in relation, however, not to a claim for damages in respect of a tortious collision but to an insurance claim. The principle of this decision was thus applied in the three cases in the text.

209 [1952] A.C. 292.

have been no less had only the heavy weather repairs been carried out. It was held by the House of Lords, reversing the Court of Appeal, that the claimant was not entitled to any damages for loss of profit in respect of the 10 days which would have been required to repair the collision damage separately. Even if the collision was a cause of the detention, which their Lordships were prepared to assume,[210] the detention for collision repair did not result in any loss of profit; where the Court of Appeal erred, said Lord Normand, was

> "in thinking that the issue could be settled by determining whether there was a causal connection between the collision damage and the detention … for 10 days".[211]

"The real issue", he continued,

> "is whether in these ten days the vessel was a potential profit-earning vessel or not",[212]

and the answer to this was in the negative because the ship,

> "though not disabled from trading by the collision damage, was necessarily disabled from trading by the weather damage".[213]

It did not matter at all that the weather damage occurred after the collision damage. "If the fact is", said Lord Normand,

> "that one of two casualties made the vessel unseaworthy and the other did not, the problem of liability is solved and the time sequence is irrelevant."[214]

And since the House of Lords put claims for loss of profits and for dock expenses on the same footing,[215] it is clear that the same result would follow where the claimant's claim was for the expenses of docking. In such a case the payment of dock dues would not be a loss by reason of the collision damage, because such payment would be "in order to carry out the immediately necessary weather damage repairs".[216]

Where, however, each set of repairs, taken separately, would have been immediately necessary because each casualty by itself would have rendered the ship unseaworthy, then the sequence of casualties becomes important and the loss of profits and the dock expenses will be properly attributed to the first in time. This was the situation in *The Haversham Grange*,[217] where the claimant's ship was damaged in two independent collisions by two independent tortfeasors, and each collision would by itself have rendered the ship unseaworthy. At first instance, Gorell Barnes P held that the claimant had no claim against the tortfeasor second in time in respect either of loss of profits or of dock expenses.[218] In so far as the Court of Appeal reversed this decision as to the dock expenses, holding the defendants li- **37-043**

---

[210] [1952] A.C. 292 at 301, 311, 317.

[211] [1952] A.C. 292 at 310 to 311; similarly at 317, per Lord Tucker.

[212] [1952] A.C. 292 at 311.

[213] [1952] A.C. 292 at 311 at 313.

[214] [1952] A.C. 292 at 311 at 311.

[215] See para.37-040, above.

[216] [1952] A.C. 292 at 313. The decision of the House of Lords was applied, in the context of the repair of an item of equipment in a factory, in *Beoco v Alfa Laval Co* [1995] Q.B. 137 CA.

[217] [1905] P. 307 CA.

[218] The claimant had previously sued the tortfeasor first in time, but since as to that collision the claimant had been contributorily negligent he had only recovered 50 per cent of the damages. He now tried, unsuccessfully, to recover the remaining 50 per cent from the second tortfeasor, having not been

able for an apportioned part of the loss, it can no longer be accepted after the strictures of the House of Lords in *Carslogie S.S. Co v Royal Norwegian Government*,[219] and Gorell Barnes P's decision stands in full as correct. The basis of the decision is made clear by their Lordships in *Carslogie S.S. Co v Royal Norwegian Government*.[220] Viscount Jowitt said:

> "That rule [i.e. in *The Haversham Grange*[221]] … rightly treats the first wrongdoer who renders the vessel unseaworthy as responsible for the consequent delay, notwithstanding the act of a second wrongdoer who also rendered the ship unseaworthy."[222]

And Lord Normand said:

> "In *The Haversham Grange*[223] the time sequence was important because the damage suffered … in each of the two collisions was enough to make her unseaworthy."[224]

It would therefore seem clear that even where only one casualty is caused tortiously and the other without liability upon anyone, as by heavy weather, the dock expenses and loss of profits will be attributable solely to the casualty first in time. If that is the casualty caused by the tortfeasor he will be wholly liable, but if it is the casualty caused by the heavy weather the claimant will have no redress.

**37-044** Finally, the ship may have remained seaworthy throughout, neither injury having necessitated immediate repair. As far as the tortfeasor sued is concerned, such circumstances would seem to be similar to the first situation. Where he is the sole tortfeasor, the other damage not having been caused tortiously, he is liable to pay for the repairs of the damage inflicted by him, which must be carried out at some time, and will be wholly liable for dock expenses and loss of profits. The other repairs done by the claimant concurrently will just be an opportunity seized by him: in this respect the situation is similar to that in *The Acanthus*,[225] *Admiralty Commissioners v S.S. Chekiang*,[226] and *The Ferdinand Retzlaff*.[227] It is true that in *The Royal Fusilier*,[228] an apportionment was decreed in such circumstances so that the defendant was made liable only in part for dock expenses, but the decision was based upon the Court of Appeal's holding in *The Haversham Grange*,[229] and must therefore be taken, after *Carslogie S.S. Co v The Royal Norwegian Govern-*

contributorily negligent in the second collision.

219 [1952] A.C. 292.

220 [1952] A.C. 292.

221 [1905] P. 307 CA.

222 [1952] A.C. 292 at 306. Compare Lord Phillimore in *Admiralty Commissioners v S.S. Chekiang* [1926] A.C. 638 at 652 to 653, speaking of *The Haversham Grange* [1905] P. 307 CA: "The claim against the second ship was disallowed, because the first ship had got to pay it."

223 [1905] P. 307 CA.

224 [1952] A.C. 292 at 311.

225 [1902] P. 17.

226 [1926] A.C. 637.

227 [1972] 2 Lloyd's Rep. 120. But contrast this case (at para.37-041, above) with *The Hassel* [1962] 2 Lloyd's Rep. 139, where there was no second infliction of damage in addition to the damage caused by the tort but before the collision the shipowner had intended to lay off the ship for inspection and repairs at or about the time she was laid off for the repairs from the collision damage, and it was held, upon the collision and owner's repairs being effected simultaneously, that the shipowner could recover loss of profits only for the total period of detention less the amount of time required to effect the owner's inspection and repairs. The court said that the claimant must satisfy it that "but for the collision the vessel would have continued trading": at 144.

228 (1926) 25 Ll. L. Rep. 566.

229 [1905] P. 307 CA.

*ment*,[230] to fall with it. And where there are two tortfeasors in these circumstances, each causing one set of damage, it would seem that the claimant may take his choice between them and recover the whole of these two heads of damage from either; he cannot, of course, recover twice.

## 4. Loss of Use of Chattels which are Not Profit-Earning

### (1) General damages for loss of use

Where the chattel damaged is not profit-earning, there may be a claim for loss of use rather than for loss of profits. Again, ships dominate the authorities. **37-045**

**(a) Ships** Where the ship which has been damaged is not profit-earning either because she is used for utility by public bodies or because she is used for pleasure, and the claimant does not hire a substitute during the period of repair, difficulties arise with regard to the head of damage representing loss of use.[231] The argument put forward by defendants in such cases is that the claimants, since they were not using their ship for the acquisition of profits, have not suffered any pecuniary loss, beyond out-of-pocket expenses, by being deprived of the use of the ship during the time required for repair. They ought therefore to be limited to damages representing out-of-pocket expenses, such as costs of repair and wages still paid to the crew. **37-046**

This view prevailed until 1897. In that year the decision of the House of Lords in *The Greta Holme*,[232] **37-047**

> "corrected the error, and decided that in such a case general damages might be recovered"[233];

and it was soon followed and clarified by two further decisions of the House of Lords in *The Mediana*,[234] and *The Marpessa*.[235] In all three cases the claimant was the Mersey Docks and Harbour Board, a public authority deriving its funds from the rates and not entitled to make or distribute profits. In *The Greta Holme*,[236] and *The Marpessa*,[237] the damaged ship was a dredger, in *The Mediana*,[238] it was a lightship.

In the first case, *The Greta Holme*,[239] the damage to the dredger resulted in a delay in the dredging, the claimants not having gone to the cost of substituting a new dredger while the damaged one was repaired. The House of Lords, reversing the Court of Appeal, allowed general damages for the loss of use while the dredger was undergoing repairs. Lord Watson said that the principles applied by the Court of Ap- **37-048**

---

230 [1952] A.C. 292.

231 No difficulties arise with the other heads. Thus the propriety of recovery for expenses incurred was not doubted or disputed in any of the cases now to be dealt with. See, e.g. *The Mediana* [1900] A.C. 113 at 121; *The Astrakhan* [1910] P. 172 at 181; *Admiralty Commissioners v S.S. Chekiang* [1926] A.C. 637 at 640; *Admiralty Commissioners v S.S. Susquehanna* [1926] A.C. 655 at 658. see *Edmund Handcock v "Ernesto" (Owners)* [1952] 1 Lloyd's Rep. 467 CA at 469.

232 [1897] A.C. 596.

233 *The Marpessa* [1907] A.C. 241 at 244, per Lord Loreburn.

234 [1900] A.C. 113.

235 [1907] A.C. 241.

236 [1897] A.C. 596.

237 [1907] A.C. 241.

238 [1900] A.C. 113.

239 [1897] A.C. 596.

peal would entail the result

> "that a corporation who invest large sums of money in a dredger, or in any other article which they intend to use, and do use continuously, for purposes which are of interest to them, and protect the pocket of the ratepayers, although they are not productive of private gain, can recover from a wrongdoer the cost of repairing injury done to these articles, but are not entitled to recover damages from the person who deprives them of the use of such articles without lawful cause."[240]

Lord Herschell pointed out that had the damaged dredger not been one bought but hired by the claimants, and they had been bound to pay for its hire during the time they were deprived of its use, they could have recovered the sums so paid as damages from the defendant.

> "How can they the less be entitled to damages because, instead of hiring a dredger, they invested their money in its purchase? The money so invested was out of their pockets, and they were deprived of the use of the dredger, to obtain which they had sacrificed the interest on the money spent on its purchase. A sum equivalent to this, at least, they must surely be entitled to. But I think they are also entitled to general damages in respect of the delay and prejudice caused to them in carrying out the works entrusted to them."[241]

*The Marpessa*,[242] was a similar decision on similar facts.[243]

**37-049** *The Mediana*,[244] introduced a different situation. In that case the place of the damaged lightship was taken during her repair by another lightship belonging to the claimant harbour board, the substituted ship being kept expressly for the purpose of such an emergency. The House of Lords, applying the principle in *The Greta Holme*,[245] held that the claimants were entitled to substantial damages for the loss of the use of the damaged lightship. Lord Halsbury LC regarded *The Greta Holme*,[246] as based upon a broad principle which he stated thus:

> "Where by the wrongful act of one man something belonging to another is either itself so injured as not to be capable of being used or is taken away so that it cannot be used at all, that of itself is a ground for damages."[247]

And later he said:

> "The broad principle seems to me to be quite independent of the particular use the plaintiffs were going to make of the thing that was taken, except—and this I think has been the fallacy running through the arguments at the Bar—when you are endeavouring to establish the specific loss of profit, or of something that you otherwise would have got which the law recognises as special damage. In that case you must show it, and by precise evidence … But when we are speaking of general damages no such principle applies at all, and the jury might give whatever they thought would be the proper equivalent for the unlawful withdrawal of the subject-matter then in question."[248]

Lord Shand and Lord Brampton further pointed out that if the claimants had hired

---

240 [1897] A.C. 596 at 604.
241 [1897] A.C. 596 at 605.
242 [1907] A.C. 241.
243 The main question there was quantum, and is therefore treated at para.37-057, below.
244 [1900] A.C. 113.
245 [1897] A.C. 596.
246 [1897] A.C. 596.
247 [1900] A.C. 113 at 116.
248 [1900] A.C. 113 at 117–118.

another lightship to replace the damaged one, the defendants must have been liable for the cost of the hire.[249]

These three decisions in respect of ships owned by local public bodies employed in local public services were later applied to ships owned by the State and employed in national public services. The first reported case is *The Astrakhan*,[250] where damages were given for loss of use of a warship belonging to the Danish State, although the ship would not have been used during the period taken up by the repairs. And in 1926 the House of Lords set the seal of its approval to such an extension in two decisions. In the first, *Admiralty Commissioners v S.S. Chekiang*,[251] general damages were allowed for the loss of use of a damaged cruiser belonging to the Admiralty[252]; in the second, *Admiralty Commissioners v S.S. Susquehanna*,[253] similar damages were given in respect of damage to an oil tanker belonging to the Admiralty and engaged in supplying oil fuel to the Fleet.[254] **37-050**

A good many years later, in 1960, we have a further House of Lords decision in *The Hebridean Coast*,[255] with a public electricity authority as claimant. Here their Lordships simply applied the principles worked out in the earlier cases without seeking to elaborate upon them.[256] After this decision the cases just fall away. No case of this nature involving ships has troubled the courts in over 50 years.[257] **37-051**

**(b) Public service buses, company cars and private cars** In place of cases of collisions at sea have come cases of collisions on land, with the principles developed in the former being applied to the latter. The cases deal first with vehicles which, like the ships above, are in the public domain. There follow, somewhat later, cases from the private sector, involving cars in a company business or in private use. **37-052**

The authorities start with *Birmingham Corporation v Sowsbery*.[258] A bus belonging to that city's corporation, a non-profit-making organisation, was in collision with the defendant's car and, while the bus was being repaired, the corporation replaced it with another bus from the spare fleet which it maintained for emergencies. The corporation was held entitled to general damages for loss of use of the damaged vehicle. Much more recently, the same situation appeared in *West Midlands Travel Ltd v Aviva Insurance UK Ltd*,[259]with the same result.[260] A bus of the claimant company, which provided public transport services, was damaged in a road traffic accident but the company was able to cover the loss of the bus from the spare capac- **37-053**

[249] [1900] A.C. 113 at 122 and 123, respectively.

[250] [1910] P. 172.

[251] [1926] A.C. 637.

[252] See, especially, [1926] A.C. 637 at 650, per Lord Phillimore.

[253] [1926] A.C. 655.

[254] A later illustration is *The West Wales* [1932] P. 165 (British battleship); the main question was on quantum and is, therefore, treated at para.37-060, below.

[255] [1961] A.C. 545.

[256] The main issue was whether the loss of the claimants' ship had necessitated their chartering other ships, and this they failed to prove.

[257] Similar situations in respect of ships used by their owners for pleasure, such as yachts, have not claimed the attention of the courts. However, general damages were apparently allowed in *The Zoroaster* (1903), unreported but cited in Roscoe, *Measure of Damages in Maritime Collisions*, 3rd edn (1929), p.107; in *The Broderick Castle* (1906), also cited (Roscoe. at p.108), there was a special loss as the claimant lived on the yacht.

[258] [1970] R.T.R. 84.

[259] [2013]EWCA Civ 887 CA.

[260] A third case, also with the same situation and the same result, is the unreported *West Midlands Passenger Transport Executive v AJS Pressings*, 11 November 1988.

ity which, as is common, it maintained. There could therefore be no claim for special damages but general damages for loss of use were recovered.[261]

**37-054** *Beechwood Birmingham Ltd v Hoyer Group UK Ltd*,[262] then moves us into the private sector. The claimant was a motor dealing company with an available pool of cars. On one of its cars being damaged in an accident, a replacement car was taken on credit hire. It was held that there could be no recovery of the hire charges as special damages since a car from the available pool should have been used[263] but that general damages for loss of use could be awarded.[264] So here we have general damages awarded for loss of use not of a non-profit earning chattel, as in the shipping and corporation bus cases, but of a chattel which was profit-earning but which would not have been used for earning profits during the period of repair.[265] This is an important development. The distinction is drawn in *Beechwood Birmingham* between claims by a company for loss of use of a car employed in the course of the company's business and claims by an individual owner of a car used solely for convenience and not for profit. It had already been said in *Alexander v Rolls Royce Motors*,[266] that private cars were different from items of transport in the public service in that, where no substitute car is hired, there can be no recovery of general damages of a financial nature. This was on the basis that with the individual car owner there is no business loss that calls for compensation.[267] The distinction is not between the corporate claimant and the individual claimant but between the claimant with a business and the claimant without, so that the individual running a business using cars, either alone or in partnership, is in the same position as to general damages of a financial nature as is the equivalent company.[268]

**37-055** At the same time *Beechwood Birmingham* confirms that the private car owner should be entitled to general damages for non-pecuniary loss. For, as it was put by the Court of Appeal, he should be entitled to compensation for

> "the lack of advantage and inconvenience caused by not having the use of a car ready at hand and at all hours for personal and/or family use".[269]

This is of course a far cry from all the cases dealt with above in this section, but the point should be noted.[270]

---

261 The main question was quantum, and is treated at para.37-062, below.

262 [2011] Q.B. 357 CA.

263 For the full facts see under mitigation at para.9-067, above.

264 This follows on from Lord Reid's saying in *The Hebridean Coast* [1961] A.C. 545, which again involved a non-profit earning claimant, an electricity authority, that he did "not proceed on any supposed distinction in principle between a profit-earning ship and a non-profit-earning ship": at 577.

265 For the computation of the damages which were allowed see para.37-062, below.

266 [1996] R.T.R. 95 CA.

267 See *Beechwood Birmingham* at [2011] Q.B. 357 CA at [48].

268 In *Bee v Jenson (No.2)* [2007] 4 All E.R. 791 CA general damages were awarded to the claimant for loss of use of his tortiously damaged private car where he had hired a replacement car with the hire charges paid by his insurer (full facts at para.37-024, above); this meant that he could not claim the hire charges by way of special damages. The general damages for the loss of use which Court of Appeal therefore awarded him in lieu were not of the same nature as those being considered here.

269 [2011] Q.B. 357 CA at [48].

270 This is probably the best place also to note that perusal of the *Current Law Yearbooks* had revealed in *Beechwood Birmingham* that county courts up and down the land have for quite a number of years been awarding modest sums for non-pecuniary loss along these lines, said to be £40 to £50 a week in 1995 rising to £100 per week in 2005 (at [49]) and no doubt higher now. It may be taken that the Court of Appeal was confirming this approach of the county courts.

## (2) Amount of such damages

**(a) Ships** *The Greta Holme*,[271] and *The Mediana*,[272] established the rule that the claimant was entitled to general damages for the loss of the use of the ship but, concerned as their Lordships were with the issue of whether such damages were allowable at all, they give no real assistance as to how the measure of such damages is to be calculated, no argument being directed to this point. This was left to be worked out by the later cases in the House of Lords, first *The Marpessa*,[273] and, more particularly, the two cases of 1926, *Admiralty Commissioners v S.S. Chekiang*,[274] and *Admiralty Commissioners v S.S. Susquehanna*.[275] **37-056**

From these decisions it is now established that the amount of damages awarded under this head, where there is no substitute ship hired and no stand-by ship kept available, is generally to be calculated on the basis of interest upon the capital value of the damaged ship at the time of the collision, this value being ascertained by taking the original cost and deducting depreciation. This measure was first sketched out by Lord Loreburn delivering the leading speech in *The Marpessa*,[276] where the facts were like those in *The Greta Holme*.[277] He said that, failing evidence that a substitute for the damaged ship had been hired, **37-057**

> "the plaintiffs were entitled to put their case in another way. They might say: The cost to us of maintaining and working this dredger, while it is working, amounts to so much per day, and its depreciation daily amounts to so much more. We take the total daily sum which it costs us as a fair measure of the value of its daily service to us. Those services are at least worth what we are habitually paying for them year after year, including what we sacrifice in depreciation."[278]

Similarly, in *Admiralty Commissioners v S.S. Chekiang*,[279] the House of Lords refused to disturb the registrar's award in which damages for loss of use of an Admiralty light cruiser had been calculated on the basis of five per cent interest upon the capital value of the ship at the time of the collision, this value being ascertained by taking the original cost and deducting depreciation.[280] This, as Lord Sumner pointed out,[281] was in effect the measure applied in *The Marpessa*.[282]

Where, on the other hand, a stand-by ship has been kept available by the claimant, the calculation is made upon the value of the stand-by itself. Thus in *Admiralty Commissioners v S.S. Susquehanna*,[283] where the House of Lords held wrong the registrar's award for the loss of use of an Admiralty oil tanker, which he had based upon the tanker's commercial value if profitably chartered, because the tanker would not have been hired out during the period of repair, Viscount Dunedin **37-058**

[271] [1897] A.C. 596.
[272] [1900] A.C. 113.
[273] [1907] A.C. 241.
[274] [1926] A.C. 637.
[275] [1926] A.C. 655.
[276] [1907] A.C. 241.
[277] [1897] A.C. 596.
[278] [1907] A.C. 241 at 244–245.
[279] [1926] A.C. 637.
[280] A similar calculation is to be found in the case of a ship used by the claimant for his pleasure in the unreported case of *The Zoroaster* (1903), referred to in Roscoe, *Measure of Damages in Maritime Collisions*, 3rd edn (1929), p.107.
[281] [1926] A.C. 637 at 646.
[282] [1907] A.C. 241.
[283] [1926] A.C. 655.

outlined the considerations which the registrar, on the case being remitted to him, should have in mind. He said:

> "If their fleet were sufficient to provide a stand-by, then the expenses of keeping that stand-by may fairly be taken into consideration. Such expenses mean not only the daily upkeep but something representing the amount of capital which had been parted with in order to have another ship, but the initial figure of cost does not necessarily represent that capital. Not only has there been necessary deterioration by lapse of time, but a vessel's condition may not be worth what was originally paid for it, quite apart from the deterioration."[284]

Interest on the value of the stand-by ship forms the correct calculation, however, only if the stand-by ship is in fact substituted for the damaged ship. Lord Sumner pointed out that there is no presumption of a stand-by,[285] and on the particular facts of the case he took the view that no stand-by had been used and that therefore the claimants could

> "not get damages based on the use of a stand-by when in fact they did very well without one".[286]

**37-059** In any event it cannot be said that the damages will always be calculated on the basis of interest on the value of the damaged or stand-by vessel. In *Admiralty Commissioners v S.S. Chekiang*,[287] Lords Dunedin and Sumner held there was no absolute rule that the damages in such cases must be calculated on a percentage of the ship's capital value at the time of collision,[288] while later in *The Hebridean Coast*,[289] where damages were again awarded on the basis of interest, it was said in the Court of Appeal that

> "there is no special sanctity about any particular method of arriving at the appropriate sum",[290]

and that

> "if the damages had been sought in some ampler form they might have been obtained".[291]

Lord Sumner in the earlier case went into great detail as to why an award based on interest might not always be appropriate with ships in public service, saying that interest has little to do with non-commercial transactions and, outside contract cases is a highly fictitious factor in calculations. It is a very long passage, cited in earlier editions of this work, but it now seems better simply to refer readers to it[292] for

---

284 [1926] A.C. 655 at 662.
285 See [1926] A.C. 655 at 663.
286 [1926] A.C. 655 at 663.
287 [1926] A.C. 637.
288 [1926] A.C. 637 at 642 and 649, respectively.
289 [1961] A.C. 545.
290 [1961] A.C. 545 at 559, per Willmer LJ.
291 [1961] A.C. 545 at 565, per Devlin LJ. The award based on interest on capital value was accepted by the House of Lords without any real discussion, the propriety of this as the general mode of calculating the damages for loss of use not being the main issue, for which see the footnote at the end of para.37-056, above.
292 It is to be found at [1926] A.C. 637 at 647–648.

consultation should a case involving a damaged ship in public service come their way, of which there has been none since 1960.[293]

Where interest is properly awarded, deviations from the method of calculation laid down in the cases in the House of Lords have not been accepted by the courts. In *The West Wales*,[294] it was held that the registrar was wrong to calculate interest on half the capital value because the ship, with a 20-year effective life, was four years old at the time of the collision. "What the several Lords [in *Admiralty Commissioners v S.S. Chekiang*[295]] insist upon", said Bateson J, **37-060**

"is that the deprivation to the complainant is a deprivation of interest on money spent on the thing purchased."[296]

And in *The Hebridean Coast*[297] it was held that, where the registrar had rightly rejected the claimant's claim for damages based upon the cost of chartering a substitute ship to take the place of the damaged ship during repair, it was improper to allow as damages the identical amount by way of interest on the capital value of the ship, which amount worked out at interest at 30 per cent. "The two measures of damage … are quite distinct", said Hodson LJ in the Court of Appeal, "and should not be confused".[298]

Interest in the past was generally awarded at five per cent[299] as in *Admiralty Commissioners v S.S. Chekiang*.[300] Occasionally the more generous award of seven per cent was allowed, as in *The Marpessa*,[301] in 1907 and *The Hebridean Coast*,[302] in 1960.[303] These were higher rates than the Admiralty Court was in those days awarding on damages generally.[304] While it is known that starting in the 1970s substantially higher interest rates began to be reflected in damages awards generally[305] and from the 1990s the Admiralty rate has fallen back in line with interest rates generally,[306] we have no knowledge of the impact on shipping cases of this nature since, as has been pointed out,[307] litigation on this front has entirely dried up after the decision in *The Hebridean Coast*. **37-061**

**(b) Public service buses, company cars and private cars** In applying these rules evolved in the cases concerning ships to the assessment of the proper award in respect of damage to a city corporation's bus, Geoffrey Lane J in *Birmingham Corporation v Sowsbery*,[308] assumed that the earlier authorities had established two possible methods of calculation of the damages, which he stated as "the interest on **37-062**

---

293 See para.37-051, above.
294 [1932] P. 165.
295 [1926] A.C. 637.
296 [1932] P. 165 at 171.
297 [1961] A.C. 545.
298 [1961] A.C. 545 at 554, adopting Lord Merriman P at first instance. See, too, Devlin LJ at 565–566.
299 See *The Hebridean Coast* [1961] A.C. 545 at 551, per Lord Merriman P at first instance.
300 [1926] A.C. 637.
301 [1907] A.C. 241. This appears from the formulation of the registrar's award, which was upheld, [1906] P. 14 at 18.
302 [1961] A.C. 545.
303 The award of only 2.5 per cent in *The West Wales* [1932] P. 165 was there held to be misconceived.
304 Up to about 1920 four per cent, up to about 1970 five per cent.
305 See paras 19-104 and following, above.
306 For interest rates in Admiralty awards see paras 19-123 to 19-125, above.
307 See para. 37-051, above.
308 [1970] R.T.R. 84; see para.37-053, above.

capital and depreciation method exemplified by *The Chekiang*"[309] and "*The Marpessa* method of cost of maintenance and operation"[310] which he called the "standing charge" cost basis. He then proceeded to apply the latter since he said

> "the standing cost basis of calculation did not suffer from possible fluctuations in capital value and interest rates, and provided a reasonably stable basis for calculation as fair to both sides as could be devised".[311]

Accordingly, he held the claimants entitled to the aggregate daily standing cost charge for the days when the use of the vehicle was lost, there being no suggestion that the daily rate was other than an accurate estimate of the cost of running an omnibus by a reasonably efficient organisation.[312] Yet, however sensible a calculation based upon cost of maintenance and operation may be, it is doubtful whether this method was in fact applied in *The Marpessa*.[313] Certainly, as already indicated, Lord Sumner did not think so,[314] and Moore-Bick LJ has now said the same in his judgment in *West Midlands Travel Ltd v Aviva Insurance UK Ltd*.[315] Accordingly in that case, after reviewing at length, in the only reasoned judgment, all of the many Admiralty authorities mainly in the House of Lords dealt with above,[316] came to the conclusion that the method to be used should be based on the capital tied up, wasted expenditure and depreciation.[317] Also in *Beechwood Birmingham Ltd v Hoyer Group UK Ltd*,[318] which has extended the rule as to non-profit-earning ships and buses to cars which, though held for the generation of profit, are not being used for profit at the time of the tortious damage[319] the Court of Appeal preferred the method of taking interest on capital and depreciation over that of taking the cost of maintenance and operation.[320] So Geoffrey Lane J's choice of the latter method in *Birmingham Corporation v Sowsbery*,[321] can now be consigned to history.

## II. Destruction

### 1. Normal Measure

**37-063** The normal measure of damages is the market value of the goods destroyed at the time and place of destruction. In the ship collision cases, it has always been said that the owners of the lost ship are entitled to restitutio in integrum: this was said to be "the leading maxim" by Dr Lushington in *The Clyde*,[322] and its applicability was not questioned by the defendant in *Liesbosch Dredger v S.S. Edison*.[323] The basis of putting the claimant into the position he would have been in had the collision not occurred, which is what is required to effect restitutio in integrum, is the

---

309 [1970] R.T.R. 84 at 86I.
310 [1970] R.T.R. 84 at 86K.
311 [1970] R.T.R. 84 at 86G.
312 (1969) 113 S.J. 877.
313 [1907] A.C. 241.
314 At para.37-057, above.
315 [2013] EWCA Civ 887 CA at [27].
316 [2013] EWCA Civ 887 CA at [5]–[22].
317 [2013] EWCA Civ 887 CA at [28] and following. See also *Bee v Jenson* [2007] EWCA Civ 923.
318 [2011] Q.B. 357 CA.
319 See para.37-054, above.
320 See [2011] Q.B. 357 CA at [52].
321 [1970] R.T.R. 84.
322 (1856) Swab. 23 at 24; and similarly in *The Columbus* (1849) 3 W. Rob. (Adm.) 158 at 162.
323 [1933] A.C. 449; see, especially, at 459.

award of the market value of the lost ship[324]: this was accepted in *Liesbosch Dredger v S.S. Edison*,[325] where Lord Wright stated the rule to be that the measure of damages was

> "the value of the ship to her owner as a going concern at the time and place of the loss".[326]

With this sum the claimant can generally obtain a replacement. Arriving at the value of the destroyed ship can, however, be a difficult task, frequently because of the dramatically different valuations of the experts in the litigation. This was the case in *Voaden v Chapman, The Baltic Surveyor*,[327] where the claimant's ship and pontoon at which she was moored both sank together with the defendant's negligently moored yacht. On valuation the judgment of Colman J is thorough and painstaking.

Should the replacement cost be more than the market value, that cost is still recoverable if it is reasonable to replace. Thus in *Aerospace Publishing Ltd v Thames Water Utilities Ltd*,[328] where archives utilised in a business had been damaged by flooding, the cost of restoration rather than the lesser diminution in value was to be awarded since the claimant had a genuine, and reasonable, intention of reinstating the damaged collection. However Colman J in *Voaden v Champion, The Baltic Surveyor*,[329] was not prepared to award the cost of a replacement ship which would necessarily have a substantially longer life than the destroyed ship on the ground that the principle that new for old requires no deduction applies only to damaged property repaired and not to destroyed property replaced. But it is doubtful whether such a rigid distinction between these two categories is justified—certainly the distinction does not exist where real property is concerned.[330] **37-064**

Nor is it relevant that the replacement cost should exceed the amount at which the claimant had acquired the goods. Thus in *Dominion Mosaics and Tile Co v Trafalgar Trucking*,[331] where a fire caused by the defendants' negligence destroyed a quantity of machines used by the claimants for carpet display in their business selling floor coverings and acquired by them only a few months earlier at a special price, the cost of replacement was recovered. Both the earlier acquisition at the special price and the fact that the claimants had not yet replaced the machines were held irrelevant. Of the earlier acquisition, Taylor LJ said: **37-065**

> "Had the machines been an outright gift instead of a mere bargain, logic could not have denied them any damages at all on the footing that, as they had paid nothing, they had lost nothing."[332]

The principle of restitutio in integrum did not mean restoring to the claimants the

---

[324] In *The Ironmaster* (1859) Swab. 441 it was held that, in the absence of a clear market value, the best evidence of value is the opinion of those who knew the vessel shortly before, the next best evidence is the opinion of those who are well conversant with shipping generally, while the original cost, the cost of repairs due and the sum at which insurance had been taken out, though evidence of value, were of inferior weight. This was approved in *The Harmonides* [1903] P. 1 at 5–6. The question of the best evidence of value is also dealt with in *The Clyde* (1856) Swab. 23.

[325] [1933] A.C. 449.

[326] [1933] A.C. 449 at 464. The relevance of the phrase "to her owner as a going concern" will appear later: see paras 37-073 and 37-074, below.

[327] [2001] 1 Lloyd's Rep. 739.

[328] (2007) 110 Con. L.R.1 CA.

[329] [2001] 1 Lloyd's Rep. 739.

[330] See the cases at para.2-007, above.

[331] [1990] 2 All E.R. 246 CA.

[332] [1990] 2 All E.R. 246 CA at 254h.

amount they had paid for the machines but putting them in the position that they had been before the fire as owners of machines which it would take a particular amount to buy.

**37-066** However, the claimant will not be entitled to the cost of a replacement where it is unreasonable to demand an exact replacement. Thus in *Uctkos v Mazzetta*,[333] the owner of a totally destroyed motorboat was held not entitled to its replacement, since the motor-boat was of an unusual type requiring a very large expenditure to construct a similar one and since there were boats of comparatively similar design, construction and performance available. The damages awarded the claimant were therefore assessed at

> "the reasonable cost of another craft which reasonably meets his needs and which is reasonably in the same condition".[334]

So too with the replacement of the machines in *Dominion Mosaics and Tile Co v Trafalgar Trucking*,[335] where the Court of Appeal agreed with the trial judge that, had the machines been virtually worn out with a month's life left in them, it would have been inappropriate to award the full replacement value.[336] Similarly, where in *Southampton Container Terminals Ltd v Schiffahrtgesellschaft Hansa Australia & Co mbH, The Maersk Colombo*,[337] a crane had been demolished in a ship collision, the damages were held limited to the crane's market or resale value and did not extend to the very much higher replacement cost. Not only was it unreasonable to replace as the expense would be out of all proportion to the benefit obtained but also replacement cost was never going to be incurred, the claimant having ordered larger cranes for installation before the collision. Clarke LJ's detailed examination of many authorities[338] is valuable.

**37-067** In addition to the market value of the ship, interest on that value is awarded in Admiralty practice. It was said in *The Kong Magnus*,[339] that a clear and uniform rule had long existed that interest is awarded in the case of total destruction of a ship whether by collision or otherwise, and this practice was applied by the House of Lords in *Liesbosch Dredger v S.S. Edison*.[340] If the ship has no cargo at the time of destruction, the interest is awarded on the value of the ship from that time, as in *Straker v Harland*.[341] If the ship has a cargo at the time of destruction, the interest is awarded on the value of the ship plus the value of the freight from the conclusion of the voyage, which is taken as being the date when the freight would have been paid, as in *The Amalia*,[342] and *The Northumbria*.[343] Ships and Admiralty practice apart, awards may also be made in respect of other chattels under the statutory provisions for the giving of interest. This was done, where the goods of three

---

333 [1956] 1 Lloyd's Rep. 209.

334 [1956] 1 Lloyd's Rep. 209 at 216.

335 [1990] 2 All E.R. 246 CA; see para.37-065, above.

336 [1990] 2 All E.R. 246 CA at 255b.

337 [2001] 2 Lloyd's Rep. 275 CA.

338 [2001] 2 Lloyd's Rep. 275 CA at [28]–[79]. At [43] he stated that the principle of *Ruxley* (for which see para.31-014, above) applies equally to tortious destruction as to breach of contract.

339 [1891] P. 223 at 235, per Sir Charles Butt P.

340 [1933] A.C. 449.

341 (1864) 2 Mar. L.C. 159.

342 (1864) 5 New Rep. 164n.

343 (1869) L.R. 3 A. & E. 6. Interest is awarded similarly in claims for loss not of the ship but of the cargo, as in *The Gertrude* (1887) 12 P.D. 204 (affirmed (1888) 13 P.D. 105 CA) and *The Berwickshire* [1950] P. 204.

claimants had been destroyed by fire in a warehouse through the defendants' negligence, in *Metal Box v Currys*.[344]

A claimant with only a limited interest in the goods was still entitled at common law, where in possession of the goods, to recover the normal measure of damages. This was decided in the leading case of *The Winkfield*,[345] where mails in charge of the Postmaster General were sunk when the ship carrying them came into collision with another ship. The Postmaster General was held entitled to recover the full value of the mails in an action against the owners of the latter ship, and this even though he was under no liability for the loss of the mails to the persons interested in them.[346] This common law position, however, has now been statutorily departed from in the Torts (Interference with Goods) Act 1977, s.8 together with s.7 of which effectively permit the defendant to ensure that the claimant cannot recover beyond the extent of his limited interest. Where the limited interest in the goods is a reversionary interest, the damages are confined to damage to the reversion and this requires permanent damage. Thus in *HSBC Rail (UK) Ltd v Network Rail Infrastructure Ltd*,[347] the claimant who was the lessor of railway carriages, two of which had been damaged beyond economic repair—so effectively destroyed—in the Hatfield rail crash of October 2000, failed in its action to recover damages because, the claimant having been paid the value of the two carriages by the lessee under its contractual obligation, permanent damage to the reversion could not be shown.[348] The whole question of claimants with a limited interest is fully dealt with, and both *The Winkfield*,[349] and the Torts (Interference with Goods) Act 1977 further considered, in relation to misappropriation of goods, where the matter has been principally before the courts.[350] The complications which bedevil the case law where claimants with a limited interest in goods have sued for their misappropriation[351] have not appeared in relation to damage and destruction. This is because where both the claimant and the defendant have an interest in the goods, litigation is more likely to arise between them over the misappropriation of the goods than over their damage or destruction. **37-068**

344 [1988] 1 W.L.R. 175; see the case at para.19-046, above. The awarding of interest is fully considered in Ch.19, above; see in relation to destruction of goods paras 19-019 to 19-021 and para.19-046.

345 [1902] P. 42 CA.

346 *Overruling Claridge v South Staffordshire Tramway Co* [1892] 1 Q.B. 422. It seems, however, that where the claimant's limited interest consisted of a part ownership in the goods destroyed, he could only recover to the extent of his interest: *Addison v Overend* (1796) 6 T.R. 766; *Sedgworth v Overend* (1797) 7 T.R. 279. But this situation has been of minor importance in the development of the law.

347 [2006] 1 WL.R. 643 CA.

348 *O'Sullivan v Williams* [1992] 3 All E.R. 385 CA, shows that, where the bailor of a destroyed chattel, able to show permanent damage to himself, has recovered full damages against the tortfeasor, in *O'Sullivan* by way of settlement, the bailee has no cause of action; the bailor would then be accountable to the bailee for any interest, lacking in *O'Sullivan*, that the bailee had. Conversely, if the bailee recovers full damages he must account for these to the bailor to the extent that the damage is to the bailor while retaining any amount which he can show represents damage to himself: this is illustrated by *Re-Source America International Ltd v Platt Site Services Ltd* [2005] 2 Lloyd's Rep. 50 CA.

349 [1902] P. 42 CA.

350 See paras 38-050 and following, below.

351 See paras 38-050 and following, below.

## 2. CONSEQUENTIAL LOSSES

### (1) Expenses

**37-069** There is a scarcity of illustrations of the recovery of expenses made necessary or rendered futile by the tort. The most useful case here, as elsewhere, is *Liesbosch Dredger v S.S. Edison*,[352] where the damages awarded included not only the market value of a dredger comparable to that sunk but also the costs of adapting it to the claimant's needs, of transporting it to the place where the original dredger had been sunk, and of insuring it for this journey. In addition, in assessing loss of profits, the court included

> "such items as overhead charges, expenses of staff and equipment and so forth thrown away".[353]

It is true that the House of Lords attempted to include all such loss within the normal measure of market value of the ship,[354] but it makes for a clearer analysis to spell out the various items in the total figure of damages awarded.[355] In *Aerospace Publishing Ltd v Thames Water Utilities Ltd*,[356] recovery was allowed for the staff costs occasioned by diversion of the claimant's employees from their normal profit-earning duties to counter flooding causing the destruction of archives,[357] thereby disrupting the claimant's business in which the archives were used.[358] In *Moore v D.E.R. Ltd*,[359] where the claimant's Rover car, which was used by him in his practice as a dentist, was rendered a total loss in an accident caused by the defendant's negligence, the Court of Appeal held that the claimant was entitled to recover for the cost of hiring another Rover car for the 18 weeks which it took to obtain a new Rover, the long wait being in part due to a strike at the factory.[360] The argument that the claimant should have hired a less expensive car was rejected on the ground that he was entitled to a comparable car[361]; also rejected was the argument that the claim for the cost of a substitute car should be substantially cut down because the claimant could have bought a secondhand Rover within two weeks of the accident. In buying a new Rover, the court held, the claimant had acted in a sensible and businesslike way; he had a busy practice and needed to be certain his car was reliable, he did not trust secondhand cars, and moreover his practice was to change his car every two years so that he would in any event have expected to purchase a new Rover within six months of the accident.

### (2) Loss of profits of profit-earning chattels

**37-070** **(a) Ships** The case law has developed entirely around ships and the destruc-

352 [1933] A.C. 449.
353 [1933] A.C. 449 at 468.
354 Compare para.37-074, below, in relation to loss of profits.
355 Contrast too the corresponding cases in relation to damage at paras 37-013 to 37-029, above.
356 (2007) 110 Con. L.R. 1 CA.
357 And also damage to archives: see para.37-014, above.
358 See (2007) 110 Con. L.R. 1 CA at [73] and following.
359 [1971] 1 W.L.R. 1476 CA.
360 The constructive total loss of the car in *Agheampong v Allied Manufacturing (London) Ltd* unreported 30 June 2008 CC Circuit Judge, led to no recovery of hire charges because of illegality: see the case in the footnote at the end of para.37-017, above.
361 Compare and contrast the cases on hiring where the car is damaged at para.37-016, above.

tion of ships. This development has been elaborate and is to be traced from the middle of the 19th century.

Recovery for loss of profits should follow the same pattern with destruction as with damage; yet Dr Lushington laid down in *The Columbus*,[362] that such a recovery could not be permitted where a ship was totally lost, although at the same time ruling in *The Clarence*,[363] that loss of profits was a permitted head of damage where a ship was only damaged. He put forward a somewhat tenuous distinction: in cases of damage, he said, such loss was capable of being accurately calculated depending upon no contingency,[364] while in cases of destruction it would involve too many contingencies and extend to endless ramifications.[365] Today loss of profits is no longer excluded from the damages in cases of the destruction of ships but it took some time to eradicate what Lord Wright in *Liesbosch Dredger v S.S. Edison*,[366] called "an arbitrary rule", and the rule has influenced the way in which the succeeding case law developed and in which the modern rule is framed. **37-071**

Recovery for loss of profits was first allowed in cases in which at the time of the collision the claimant's ship was operating under a profitable charterparty. First in *The Kate*,[367] and then in *The Racine*,[368] it was held that the measure of damages included not only the market value of the ship but also the profits lost under the charterparty. In the former, Jeune P referred to the measure of damages as stated by Sir Robert Phillimore in *The Northumbria*,[369] where he said that the practice was to effect restitutio in integrum, in the case of total loss of a ship with a cargo, by calculating the value of the ship at the end of the voyage and the value of freight that would have been earned less expenses which would have had to be incurred to complete the voyage, whereas, if no cargo was on board, then interest on the value of the ship from the day of collision was given.[370] Jeune P pointed out that the difference between Dr Lushington and Sir Robert Phillimore was more apparent than real. **37-072**

> "Dr Lushington indicates that the value of the vessel is to be taken at the time of the collision, which does not ... exclude a fact such as the existence of a profitable charter from being allowed to enhance the value of the vessel as at that time. Sir Robert Phillimore states that the value should be taken as at the end of the voyage, and therefore lets in freight or interest as an additional compensation."[371]

He then extended these principles from a ship with cargo to a ship without cargo but under charter, and awarded the profits lost under the charterparty.[372] This was

---

362 (1849) 3 W. Rob. (Adm.) 158.

363 (1850) 3 W. Rob. (Adm.) 283; see para.37-031, above.

364 (1849) 3 W. Rob. (Adm.) 158 at 165.

365 (1849) 3 W. Rob. (Adm.) 158 at 164. He repeated this view in *The Clyde* (1856) Swab. 23 at 24.

366 [1933] A.C. 449 at 462, 463.

367 [1899] P. 165.

368 [1906] P. 273 CA.

369 (1869) L.R. 3 A. & E. 6 at 12.

370 *The Northumbria* (1869) L.R. 3 A. & E. 6 concerned the question of awarding interest: see para.37-067, above.

371 [1899] P. 165 at 174. Indeed, as Stirling LJ pointed out in *The Racine* [1906] P. 273 CA, Dr Lushington in *The Amalia* (1864) 34 L.J. Adm. 21 at 22, another interest case, had expressly stated that in the case of total loss the practice was to give the value of the ship and freight with interest.

372 He cited from Pritchard's *Admiralty Digest* various claims similarly dealt with by registrars: [1899] P. 165 at 175–176.

followed by the Court of Appeal in *The Racine*,[373] where the loss of profits on three successive charters was allowed as damages less a reasonable percentage for contingencies. Fletcher Moulton LJ said he saw no difference in principle between one voyage and a chain of voyages under the same charterparty, or, as there, a chain of voyages under separate charterparties.[374] Future profits were however discounted, said Vaughan Williams LJ,

> "by taking the possibility of accidents into consideration; and if you have a chain of charterparties, of course the possibility of earning the profits not being defeated increases with the lapse of time".[375]

These two cases were further applied in *The Empress of Britain*,[376] to a ship sunk in the second year of a charterparty in force for seven years on seven different voyages, the charterparty being cancellable at the charterers' annual option: it was held that the whole charterparty was to be taken into account in assessing the damages, and also the contingencies and the charterparty's special terms, i.e. presumably the annual option to cancel. This goes a long way: one may suspect that there is this limitation, namely that the period over which loss of profit is allowed does not extend beyond the time when the claimant could reasonably have procured a substitute vessel.

**37-073** The cases culminate in the famous *Liesbosch Dredger v S.S. Edison*.[377] The former importance of this case on the issue of remoteness of damage[378] has overshadowed its importance as the leading case on the measure of damages for the tortious destruction of a profit-earning chattel. The claimant's dredger, sunk by the defendant, was required by them for the performance of a contract, the case differing from earlier cases in that the dredger was not under charter but was "employed by the owners in the normal course of their business as civil engineers".[379] The House of Lords recognised that, if immediate replacement had been possible, the measure of damages would be calculated by taking the market price of a replacement, but held that, since immediate replacement was a merely fanciful idea in the circumstances,[380] the claimants were entitled to damages for the delay and prejudice to their contract[381] and it was immaterial that the particular dredger was neither named in the contract nor appropriated to it: it was sufficient that it was actually being used and intended to be used for the contract work.[382] Lord Wright, delivering the leading speech, cited the earlier cases on charterparty losses, concluding that it was now clear "that the arbitrary rule suggested by Dr Lushington[383] is not law".[384] He said:

> "The true rule seems to be that the measure of damages in such cases is the value of the

---

373 [1906] P. 273 CA.

374 [1906] P. 273 CA at 281.

375 [1906] P. 273 CA at 278; similarly at 281, per Fletcher Moulton LJ.

376 (1913) 29 T.L.R. 423.

377 [1933] A.C. 449.

378 This aspect is dealt with at paras 8-110 to 8-113, above.

379 [1933] A.C. 449 at 465, per Lord Wright.

380 Not because of the claimant's impecuniosity, which led them to the expensive hire of another dredger—this was what was held too remote—but because to purchase one would take time.

381 [1933] A.C. 449 at 465.

382 [1933] A.C. 449 at 466.

383 See *The Columbus* (1849) 3 W. Rob. (Adm.) 158; see para.37-071, above.

384 [1933] A.C. 449 at 463.

ship to her owner as a going concern at the time and place of the loss. In assessing that value regard must naturally be had to her pending engagements, either profitable or the reverse."[385]

The measure awarded was stated by him thus:

"1. The value of the *Liesbosch* to the appellants, capitalised as at the date of the loss, must be assessed by taking into account: (1) the market price of a comparable dredger in substitution; (2) costs of adaptation, transport, insurance, etc., to Patras [the place of the collision]; (3) compensation for disturbance and loss in carrying out their contract over the period of delay between the loss of the *Liesbosch* and the time at which the substituted dredger could reasonably have been available for use in Patras, including in that loss such items as overhead charges, expenses of staff and equipment, and so forth thrown away, but neglecting any special loss due to the appellants' financial position. On the capitalised sum so assessed, interest will run from the date of the loss.[386]"

*Liesbosch Dredger v S.S. Edison*,[387] thus establishes the modern law. The rule in *The Columbus*,[388] is discredited, and with it falls, it is submitted, the decision itself and those following it, like *The City of Rome*,[389] and *The Anselma de Larrinaga*,[390] in all of which recovery was refused for the loss of fishing till a replacement ship could be obtained. It is true that such profits are stated in the decisions to be more speculative than specific contracts lost,[391] but it is never an answer that, because it is difficult to assess the damages precisely, none should be given.[392] At the same time, the influence of the rejected rule in *The Columbus*,[393] is subtly present in the formulation of the modern rule in *Liesbosch Dredger v S.S. Edison*.[394] Instead of adopting the conventional separation between market value of the property as representing normal measure and loss of profits as representing consequential loss, the rule fuses the two heads: this leads to a danger of a duplication of damages if the two heads are not viewed in relation to each other, a danger recognised by Lord Wright. He said: **37-074**

"The rule ... requires some care in its application; the figure of damage is to represent the capitalised value of the vessel as a profit-earning machine, not in the abstract but in view

385 [1933] A.C. 449 at 463–464.

386 [1933] A.C. 449 at 468–469.

387 [1933] A.C. 449.

388 (1849) 3 W. Rob. (Adm.) 158.

389 (1887) 8 Asp. M.L.C. 542n.

390 (1913) 29 T.L.R. 587.

391 *The Anselma de Larrinaga* (1913) 29 T.L.R. 587 distinguished the authorities allowing loss of profits from charterparties on the ground of "there being a contract for an ascertainable amount—a very different thing from the speculative question of the possibility of catching fish": at 587. See, too, *The Fortunity* [1961] 1 W.L.R. 351 where Hewson J, while accepting that, for ocean shipping, engagements not already contracted for and fixed were too uncertain for consideration, awarded the loss of profits that a motorcruiser, hired out on the Broads, would have made throughout the 1959 season had she not been sunk, although only 16 out of the 25 weeks of this season had been booked at the time of the sinking. This result was based on the finding that "vessels on the Broads ... are employed in one small defined area, whose seasonal employment at scheduled rates, not subject to fluctuation, can be fairly accurately determined by comparison with what actually occurred in the hiring of other craft similarly employed by the same owners": at 354.

392 See para.10-002, above. Compare *The Risoluto* (1883) 8 P.D. 109, where in the case of a damaged ship damages for the loss of a fishing season were awarded.

393 (1849) 3 W. Rob. (Adm.) 158.

394 [1933] A.C. 449.

of the actual circumstances. The value of prospective freights cannot simply be added to the market value but ought to be taken into account in order to ascertain the total value for purposes of assessing the damage, since if it is merely added to the market value of a free ship, the owner will be getting pro tanto his damages twice over. The vessel cannot be earning in the open market, while fulfilling the pending charter or charters."[395]

**37-075** The cutting out of the loss of profits figure for this reason is well illustrated by *The Llanover*.[396] In that case the collision occurred during the Second World War when a free ship, as the claimant's was, had a virtual certainty of profitable employment due to the acute shipping shortage, and it was held that damages for loss of trading profits did not form a head of damage as these were already reflected in the enhanced market value of the ship. By contrast in *The Fortunity*,[397] where one of the claimants' fleet of motorcruisers, which they hired out on the Broads, was sunk in 1958 and could not be replaced till 1960 so that the profits of the whole of the 1959 season were lost, these profits together with the market value of the vessel to the trade were awarded as damages. This did not amount in the circumstances to a duplication of damages because, although

> "someone in the trade would pay a price which would be governed by what the trade purchaser estimated [the vessel] would earn",

it would be a price based upon

> "the expectation of a reasonable return on his capital, and not taking into account the fact that she was already fixed with considerable bookings for the next season, with a virtual certainty of full employment throughout the season."[398]

*Voaden v Champion, The Baltic Surveyor*,[399] however, returned to the result in *The Llanover* by refusing the claim for loss of chartering income and loss of use of the claimant's ship sunk through the defendant's negligence.[400] Having analysed *The Liesbosch* in some detail, Colman J said that

> "the claim for loss of chartering profits … is, in my judgment, wrong in principle. [The ship] had no pending charter commitments at the date of the loss, which was at the end of the chartering season … Her potential as a profit-earning engine in future chartering seasons would be reflected in her replacement value. If interest were to run on that sum from the date of the loss, the owner would be sufficiently compensated".[401]

**37-076** Conversely, it may be necessary, when applying Lord Wright's rule, to avoid placing too high a figure on the ship's market value. This point is brought out in

395 [1933] A.C. 449 at 464.
396 [1947] P. 80.
397 [1961] 1 W.L.R. 351.
398 [1961] 1 W.L.R. 351 at 356.
399 [2001] 1 Lloyd's Rep. 739.
400 Facts at para.37-063, above.
401 [2001] 1 Lloyd's Rep. 739 at 749, col.1. For a further decision on loss of profits where aircraft had been converted rather than destroyed by the defendant, see *Kuwait Airways Corp v Iraq Airways Co* [2002] 2 A.C. 883 CA. All the above authorities concerning ships destroyed were relied upon (see at CA [621] to [626]) but the Court of Appeal was more prepared to award loss of profits: see the case at para.38-071, below. The House of Lords at [2002] 2 A.C. 883 affirmed the award for loss of profits (see Lord Nicholls at HL [95], Lord Hoffmann at HL [130]) without, however, any reference to these shipping authorities.

*The Philadelphia*,[402] where the value of the ship on the market had risen between the time of the collision and the time at which the voyage would have ended. It was contended on the authority of *The Kate*,[403] and *The Racine*,[404] that the higher market value at the end of the voyage was the appropriate figure, both those cases having said that that was the relevant time at which to take the market value. An augmented market value at the end of the voyage, however, has been taken only in the sense of including the loss of profit as represented by the freight lost on the cargoes carried,[405] and the Court of Appeal pointed out that in *The Kate*,[406] and *The Racine*,[407] where the loss of charterparty profits was awarded separately, the market value which was taken at the end of the voyage was not an augmented value at all but the value as diminished by wear and tear and the like, a diminution in value which the ship must necessarily have undergone in order to complete the charterparties.[408] Thus any increase after the tort in the market value of ships of the type destroyed is generally irrelevant to the normal measure of damages.[409]

**(b) Chattels other than ships** Where other than ships are concerned authority is sparse, virtually non-existent, but the shipping world cannot have a monopoly on the recovery for lost profits which must be available for other chattels Thus at first instance in *Aerospace Publishing Ltd v Thames Water Utilities Ltd*,[410] loss of income from destroyed archives used in a business until such time as they were restored was awarded as consequential loss and this does not appear to have been in issue, or challenged, in the Court of Appeal.[411] **37-077**

## (3) Loss of use of non-profit-earning chattels

All the cases dealing with recovery for the loss of use of non-profit-earning ships concern ships that were damaged and not ships that were destroyed. The principles developed in relation to damage are nevertheless the same principles as must apply to destruction. This was in effect recognised by Scrutton LJ in *The Edison*,[412] where he said: **37-078**

> "The claims for damage to a ship by collision fall into two classes: (1) where the ship is not lost but damaged so that for a time she cannot be used; (2) where the ship is totally lost. In each of these cases there may be a subdivision, according as the injured ship is one commercially used for profit, or is a ship used by bodies which do not carry on business to earn commercial profits."

---

402 [1917] P. 101 CA.
403 [1899] P. 165.
404 [1906] P. 273 CA.
405 See para.37-072, above.
406 [1899] P. 165.
407 [1906] P. 273 CA.
408 Lawrence J said that more properly the allowance for wear and tear and the like should not have been deducted from the market value of the ship at the time of collision but from the profits lost on the charterparty, which by such deduction would be calculated net: [1917] P. 101 CA at 113.
409 Rise in market value after the tort might, however, be relevant in another connection, i.e. the inability of the claimant to replace immediately may allow him the market price at the time of proper replacement.
410 [2005] EWHC 2987 (QB).
411 (2007) 110 Con. L.R. 1 CA; see its decision at para.37-064, above.
412 [1932] P. 52 CA at 61.

Also, on appeal, in *Liesbosch Dredger v S.S. Edison*,[413] there is a hint in Lord Wright's speech that non-profit-earning ships require separate treatment from profit-earning ships. Having laid down a measure based on the value of a ship to the owner as a going concern, he warned against a rule that will cover all cases and listed a number of instances of ships which "may all raise different questions before the true value can be ascertained".[414] In this list he included ships of war, lightships, and dredgers employed by public authorities.[415]

---

413 [1933] A.C. 449.
414 [1933] A.C. 449 at 465.
415 [1933] A.C. 449 at 465.

CHAPTER 38

# TORTS AFFECTING GOODS: MISAPPROPRIATION

TABLE OF CONTENTS



## I. INTRODUCTORY: AND IN PARTICULAR OF THE DEMISE OF DETINUE

Misappropriation of goods may, like damage or destruction, result from a number of torts, but whereas with damage or destruction the measure of damages is calculated in the same manner whatever the tort, with misappropriation certain differences in relation to damages have appeared as between the various possible torts **38-001** in the field. The three common law torts have been conversion, detinue and trespass. Actions for wrongful distress and actions of replevin are largely based on trespass, or on conversion in the alternative, but in some cases of wrongful distress the liability has for centuries been purely statutory.[1]

**38-002** The law on damages for misappropriation of goods was substantially amended by the Torts (Interference with Goods) Act 1977. The Act sought to implement the recommendations made by the Law Reform Committee in its 18th Report.[2] However, while the Committee proposed that

> "the three remedies of detinue, conversion and trespass to chattels will be superseded by a single tort of wrongful interference with chattels",[3]

the 1977 Act retained conversion and trespass as separate torts although using the term "wrongful interference" or "wrongful interference with goods" to refer to, inter alia,[4] both of them,[5] and has simply abolished detinue.[6] One minor comment on this approach is that, while the Act's provisions affecting damages must apply to conversion and trespass, they will not in strictness apply to cases of wrongful distress in which the liability was already purely statutory.[7] Fuller comment is, however, called for on how the disappearance of detinue impinges on issues of damages.

**38-003** Detinue took a claimant beyond the confines of conversion in two respects: it gave him a marginally larger right, and a substantially larger remedy. The right made its appearance wherever goods bailed were lost or destroyed through the negligence of the bailee: this was detinue but not conversion. The remedial difference, on the other hand, applied across the whole gamut of the overlap between conversion and detinue: conversion was no more than an action for damages; detinue was primarily an action for the return of the goods. In *General & Finance Facilities v Cooks Cars (Romford)*,[8] Diplock LJ pointed out that

> "an action in detinue today may result in a judgment in one of three different forms: (1) for the value of the chattel as assessed and damages for its detention; or (2) for return of the chattel or recovery of its value as assessed and damages for its detention; or (3) for return of the chattel and damages for its detention."[9]

The judgment was generally in the second form which gave the claimant the opportunity of deciding between enforcing specific restitution of the goods and claiming their value,[10] and the third form of judgment was in fact unusual, depending

---

1 Distress is about to be superseded by a novel statutory remedy, as is replevin. For distress see para.38-089, below and for replevin para.38-090, below.

2 (1971) Cmnd. 4774.

3 (1971) Cmnd. 4774 at para.27.

4 An owner of goods who had neither possession nor an immediate right to possession could not sue in conversion, trespass or detinue, but had to resort to a special action on the case for injury done to his reversionary interest. This situation seems now to be within the ambit of wrongful interference as that term is to include "any other tort so far as it results in damage to goods or to an interest in goods": Torts (Interference with Goods) Act 1977 s.1(d). However, claims in respect of reversionary interests have so far hardly surfaced.

5 Torts (Interference with Goods) Act 1977 s.1(a) and (b).

6 Torts (Interference with Goods) Act 1977 at s.2(1).

7 See para.38-001, above.

8 [1963] 1 W.L.R. 644 CA.

9 [1963] 1 W.L.R. 644 CA at 650.

10 In the case cited the claimants in their action of detinue had obtained leave to sign summary judgment for the return of a crane or its value, with damages for its detention to be assessed, but the

upon the claimant's showing the importance to him of restoration *in specie*; the first form gave the same result as did conversion, and was appropriate where the chattel was an ordinary article of commerce. Where a defendant was required to redeliver the goods, the court had a discretionary power to compel him to do so, a power which did not exist at common law despite the fact that detinue was brought primarily for the return of the goods, but was originally given by s.78 of the Common Law Procedure Act of 1854, was continued in Ord.45 r.4 of the Rules of the Supreme Court[11] and appears today re-enacted by Pt 50 of the Civil Procedure Rules. The fact that the action was primarily for the return of goods made for basic differences from the measure of damages in conversion even where the goods were not ordered to be returned. Thus normal measure and consequential losses were different because damages for the detention of the goods were included within the former and not the latter,[12] the time of assessing the value of the goods was different,[13] and the effect of redelivery or proffered redelivery was different.[14]

The Torts (Interference with Goods) Act 1977, in abolishing detinue,[15] is careful to ensure that what was formerly available to a claimant only in detinue shall now be available to him in conversion itself. In the first place, an action in conversion is to lie for loss or destruction of goods which a bailee has allowed to happen in breach of his duty to his bailor.[16] In the second place, in proceedings for wrongful interference—which includes both conversion of goods and trespass to goods[17]—against a person in possession or control of goods, relief, so far as appropriate, may be given in accordance with s.3 of the Act.[18] That section, by subs.(2), provides that: **38-004**

"The relief is—

(a) an order for delivery of the goods, and for payment of any consequential damages, or
(b) an order for delivery of the goods, but giving the defendant the alternative of paying damages by reference to the value of the goods, together in either alternative with payment of any consequential damages, or
(c) damages"

and further, by subs.(3), that:

"Subject to rules of court—

master had failed to assess separately the value of the crane and the damages. The Court of Appeal held, on the claimants' appeal, that they were entitled to separate assessments because the judgment in detinue did not divest the claimants of their ownership of the crane but gave them a right to decide, after the assessment of the crane's value, whether they would apply for leave to enforce specific restitution of the crane itself rather than claim recovery of its value.

11 Section 78, together with most of the Common Law Procedure Act 1854, was repealed when the Rules of the Supreme Court came into force in 1883.

12 See para.38-006, below.

13 See paras 38-011 and following, below.

14 See para.38-075 and para.38-081, below.

15 Torts (Interference with Goods) Act 1977 s.2(1).

16 Torts (Interference with Goods) Act 1977 s.2(2).

17 Torts (Interference with Goods) Act 1977 s.1.

18 Torts (Interference with Goods) Act 1977 s.3(1). It is sufficient for s.3 to apply that the defendant has been in possession and control of the goods at the time the proceedings began even if the goods were subsequently returned to the claimant or disposed of: *Hillesden Securities v Ryjack* [1983] 1 W.L.R. 959.

(a) relief shall be given under only one of the paras (a), (b) and (c) of subs.(2),
(b) relief under para.(a) of subs.(2) is at the discretion of the court, and the claimant may choose between the others."[19]

The same range of possible judgments, which had applied formerly only to detinue,[20] is thus opened up for conversion, and the power to order redelivery will come to be invoked in conversion rather than in detinue. The damages, however, will now always fall to be assessed according to the methods appropriate to conversion and not, where different,[21] to those appropriate to detinue.

**38-005** In the light of these developments, the scheme of this chapter is to deal first with conversion, earlier called trover, which has for long been the principal action, and to include, where the principles applied are the same, cases based upon trespass and indeed, wherever relevant, upon wrongful distress and replevin; this allows a consolidation of the pertinent case law and saves unnecessary repetition. Former detinue cases are considered, in so far as they may still be of assistance.[22] Trespass is then dealt with in so far as there are differences, established or possible, between it and conversion. The chapter is then rounded off with a note on wrongful distress and replevin, now being replaced by statutory alternatives.

## II. Conversion

### 1. Normal Measure

#### (1) In general

**38-006** The normal measure of damages for conversion is the market value of the goods converted.[23] This is well settled[24] and is based upon the ground that, as Greer LJ put it in *Hall v Barclay*,[25]

---

[19] CPR r.40.14, re-enacting but in different wording. RSC Ord.42 r.1A, provides that, notwithstanding anything in s.3(3), a claim relating to the detention of goods by a partial owner whose right is not founded on a possessory title can result in a judgment or order for payment of damages only, partial owner being defined as one of two or more persons with interests in the goods who does not have written authority of all the others to sue on their behalf. This rule has been said to be aimed at claims in respect of reversionary interests in goods; presumably, however, an order for delivery of the goods will generally be inappropriate in respect of all other part owners: See paras 38-050 and following, below.

[20] See para.38-003, above.

[21] See para.38-003, above.

[22] For details of the previous law, if required, see the 13th edition (1972) of this work.

[23] In the former (see paras 38-002 to 38-004, above) action of detinue, which was primarily for the return of the goods, the normal measure consisted, in addition to the value of the goods where they were not ordered to be returned, of the loss arising through the detention of the goods and whether they were ordered to be returned or not. In conversion, this is only recoverable by way of consequential loss: see paras 38-066 and following, below.

[24] "The principle on which damages for conversion should be awarded ... is well settled": *Caxton Publishing Co v Sutherland Publishing Co* [1939] A.C. 178 at 190, per Lord Macmillan; the parties had agreed that the proper measure was the value at conversion. In *Checkprice (UK) Ltd v Revenue and Customs Commissioners* [2010] EWHC 682 (Admin) the trial judge held the market value of the cider there converted (facts at paras 38-009 and following, below) formed the proper measure of damages, and left the parties to try to agree it: at [51]–[53].

[25] [1937] 3 All E.R. 620 CA at 623.

> "where you are dealing with goods which can be readily bought in the market, a man whose rights have been interfered with is never entitled to more than what he would have to pay to buy a similar article in the market".[26]

The rule is strikingly illustrated by *Chubb Cash v John Crilley & Son*,[27] a case which is dealt with elsewhere.[28]

The value of the goods is, however, the basic criterion,[29] this being most commonly and most simply calculated by taking the market value.[30] Calculation becomes more difficult where there is no market value.[31] It is sometimes said that the value to the owner must then be looked to, but this term, though in one sense correct,[32] is not in itself clear and is, therefore, likely to lead to inaccuracy.[33] Situations that may here arise have now been before the courts in a variety of cases, the decisions in which go to clarify the law. **38-007**

In *Hall v Barclay*,[34] certain davits and testing apparatus had been converted by the defendant and sold as scrap. There was no current market price at which the goods could have been bought or sold, and the Court of Appeal held that the claimant was not limited to the selling value the goods possessed, i.e. the scrap value, but could recover the cost of obtaining replacements in the absence of a market in which such goods could be bought ready made. There was evidence that the claimant would want to use such replacements[35] so that he could not be said to be claiming on the basis of replacement value just in order that the defendant should pay him damages. *Hall v Barclay* was applied in *Wilson v Robertsons (London) Ltd*,[36] awarding the cost of replacement of a ring with a special engraving wrongfully sold by the defendant pawnbroker.[37] On the other hand, where in *Fairfax Gerrard Hold-* **38-008**

---

26 "Never" is too strong a word; there may be consequential losses: see paras 38-066 and following, below. Sometimes, however, and depending on the circumstances, it may be more appropriate to award the selling price than the buying price, the wholesale price than the retail price. The fact that the parties in *Zabihi v Janzemini* [2009] EWCA Civ 851 CA (facts at para.38-049, below) may have envisaged a private sale of converted jewellery at a substantially higher price than the market value was neither here nor there: see at [42]–[44] and [60].

27 [1983] 1 W.L.R. 599 CA; see at 604B where the passage in the then text is referred to.

28 See para.38-050, below.

29 See *Hall v Barclay* [1937] 3 All E.R. 620 CA at 623, per Greer LJ; and see *Caxton Publishing Co v Sutherland Publishing Co* [1939] A.C. 178 at 192 and 203.

30 Calculating the market value is not always simple, as in the endlessly complex case of *Kuwait Airways Corp v Iraq Airways Co* [2002] 2 A.C. 883 CA (facts at para.38-071, below) where the Court of Appeal held that the appropriate value to take of aircraft which had been converted and destroyed was not what was called the fair market value, which the trial judge had adopted, but the current market price which reflected the cost that would need to be incurred to replace converted aircraft with like aircraft: see CA at [599]–[ 604]. Moreover, no discount fell to be made from that value on account of the fact that the aircraft were, already at the time of the conversion, in grave danger of destruction: see CA at [606] to [619]. The House of Lords at [2002] 2 A.C. 883 HL, affirmed the Court of Appeal without going into questions of how the aircraft should be valued.

31 The question in *Cumberbatch v Lambeth LEC* [2006] R.T.R. 2 CA at 21 was how to arrive at a valuation of converted unroadworthy vehicles due to be made roadworthy by the claimant vehicle repairer.

32 See *Caxton Publishing Co v Sutherland Publishing Co* [1939] A.C. 178 at 192.

33 [1939] A.C. 178 at 203.

34 [1937] 3 All E.R. 620 CA.

35 [1937] 3 All E.R. 620 CA at 626.

36 [2006] EWCA Civ 1088 CA.

37 [2006] EWCA Civ 1088 CA at [43]–[45]. Conversion by seizure of two luxury cars led to an award of replacement cost in *Lightning Bolt Ltd v Elite Performance Cars Ltd* unreported 2 November 2011. This measure was described as the replacement cost of the value without warranty with a 12

*ings Ltd v Capital Bank Plc*,[38] the converted property, a very particular machine not boasting a market value, had been purchased under a finance agreement not for the claimant finance company's own use but for its customer's, the award was not of the cost of buying a replacement but of the amount that a sale of the machine would have yielded; the last thing the finance company would have wanted was an additional machine to sell in the market.[39] In the absence of any other evidence of the market value of the two items of industrial plant and equipment converted in *Tanks and Vessels Industries Ltd v Devon Cider Co Ltd*,[40] it was ruled that the market value for which the company owning them could claim was to be taken as the value for which it could have disposed of them at the time of their conversion[41]; the problem before the court lay in discovering what that value was.[42] In *Caxton Publishing Co v Sutherland Publishing Co*,[43] value had to be calculated in a "highly artificial situation".[44] The defendants published a book which contained extracts from material in which the claimants had a copyright. The conversion was constituted by the act of binding together the infringing sheets so as to form the book produced by the defendants. It was held that it would ignore the realities of the case to measure the value of the sheets by the cost of printing them; the fact that they were to be inserted in a book must be taken into account, and the value should then be calculated by taking a proportion of the book's value.[45] In *Jabir v HA Jordan & Co Ltd*,[46] the value required to be ascertained was of a remarkable pearl which the claimant dealer in pearls had bought from another dealer and sold on at a higher price to a third dealer to be mounted in a ring. The defendants whom the claimant entrusted to do the mounting lost the pearl. The Court of Appeal upheld the trial's judge's award of damages at the price that the claimant had sold on, preferring the practical views on market value of the three experienced dealers who had all seen the very unusual pearl, and were informed buyers and sellers, over the substantially lower valuation views of the defendant's experts who had not seen the pearl.

**38-009** Exceptionally, a claimant may find that the normal entitlement to damages based on market value falls away. This was so in *Checkprice (UK) Ltd v Revenue and Customs Commissioners*,[47] where quantities of alcoholic beverages held for sale by the claimant company were taken by Revenue and Customs under its power to

---

per cent mark-up to reflect retail value.

38 [2007] 1 Lloyd's Rep. 171.

39 See [2007] 1 Lloyd's Rep. 171 at [34]–[42]. In *Kuwait Airways Corp v Iraq Airways Co* [2002] 2 A.C. 883 CA (facts at para.38-071, below) the decision to buy new, as opposed to used secondhand, aircraft as replacements for the planes converted was held not to be caused by the conversion. Indeed the cost of the new aircraft was not claimed, thereby preventing recovery for the financing of their purchase: see at CA at [644]–[650]. The House of Lords [2002] 2 A.C. 883 HL, agreed that replacement with new aircraft was not caused by the conversion and that the financing charges were not recoverable: see Lord Nicholls at HL at [96]–[98] and Lord Hoffmann at HL at [130]. Compare the further aspects of the case at paras 38-067 and 38-071, below.

40 [2009] EWHC 1360 Ch.

41 [2009] EWHC 1360 Ch at [58].

42 [2009] EWHC 1360 Ch at [59]–[61].

43 [1939] A.C. 178.

44 [1939] A.C. 178 at 190, per Lord Macmillan.

45 And see *Building and Civil Engineering Holidays Scheme Management v Post Office* [1966] 1 Q.B. 247 CA, at para.38-046, below, dealing with the question of whether the market value of holiday stamps should be taken as their face value or their value as pieces of paper; the action, however, was not in conversion but was a statutory one.

46 [2011] EWCA Civ 816 CA.

47 [2010] EWHC 682 (Admin).

detain goods to investigate whether they are liable to forfeiture because customs duty has not been paid on them. If this is not established by the end of a reasonable period, the goods must be returned or proceedings for forfeiture commenced in the magistrates' court. As Revenue and Customs after a reasonable period did neither, there was a conversion of the beverages which then either passed their sell-by date or became infected and had to be destroyed. While on a quantity of cider among the detained beverages the claimant was held entitled to damages based on market value since it was established that duty had been paid, and paid at a time when the cider was still saleable, so that the powers both of detention and of seizure had come to an end, it was also held that there was no entitlement to damages based on the market value of all the other detained beverages. This was because it had not been established that customs duty had been paid on them, so that the loss suffered by the claimant was the loss of the opportunity to prove such payment to the magistrates' court. Since it was held that the chance of doing so was speculative, there was no loss for which compensatory damages could be awarded.[48] The appropriate award was of nominal damages.[49]

### (2) The particular case of conversion by infringement of copyright

From early till late in the 20th century infringement of copyright provided a special case in which the general rule that the measure of damages is the value of the goods converted was applied in circumstances where there was a strong chance that the claimant was thereby overcompensated. What gave rise to this curiosity was the statutory provision appearing as s.18(1) of the Copyright Act 1956, which replaced s.7 of the Copyright Act 1911, that subject to the provisions of the Act **38-010**

> "the owner of any copyright shall be entitled to all such rights and remedies, in respect of the conversion or detention by any person of any infringing copy, or of any plate used or intended to be used for making infringing copies, as he would be entitled to if he were the owner of every such copy or plate and had been the owner thereof since the time when it was made".

In *Caxton Publishing Co v Sutherland Publishing Co*,[50] the House of Lords accepted, and later endorsed in *Infabrics v Jaytex*,[51] that the notional ownership thus conferred on the copyright owner led to a measure of damages represented by the value of the goods which constituted infringing copies. What caused this to reflect overcompensation is that it in no way follows, from the fact that the defendant has produced and marketed goods in breach of the claimant's copyright, that the claimant has suffered loss to the extent of the value of the goods. Following the recommendations of the *Whitford Committee Report* in 1977[52] and subsequent judicial criticism[53] of the law as it stood, the entitlement to claim in conversion was abandoned. No equivalent provision appears in the Copyright, Designs and Patents Act 1988 which replaces the Copyright Act 1956, and since s.18(1) of the 1956 Act

[48] [2010] EWHC 682 (Admin) at [56]–[62].

[49] Conversion, though an action on the case, is nevertheless a tort actionable per se.

[50] [1939] A.C. 178; see para.38-008, above.

[51] [1982] A.C. 1.

[52] Cmnd. 6732; see, especially, para.943.

[53] Particularly in *Infabrics v Jaytex* [1982] A.C. 1 and *Lewis Trusts v Bamber Stores* [1983] F.S.R. 453 CA.

does not apply after the 1988 Act came into force except for the purpose of proceedings commenced before then,[54] it has lost its practical importance. If by some highly improbable chance a claim might still be meandering its way down the legal process, reference can be made to the 15th edition of this work for the former law with all its complexities.[55]

## 2. TIME AT WHICH VALUE IS TO BE TAKEN: CHANGES IN THE VALUE OF THE GOODS

**38-011** There is a good deal of authority for taking the time of the conversion as the time at which the market value is to be assessed. This was originally laid down in *Mercer v Jones*,[56] an action for conversion of a bill of exchange, where Lord Ellenborough directed that interest on the bill should only be allowed up to the time of conversion. He said:

> "In trover the rule is, that the plaintiff is entitled to damages equal to the value of the article converted at the time of the conversion."[57]

The same rule has been restated both in the Court of Appeal in *Henderson v Williams*,[58] and by the Judicial Committee of the Privy Council in *Solloway v McLaughlin*,[59] and again in *BBMM Finance (Hong Kong) v Eda Holdings*.[60]

**38-012** On the other hand, Abbott CJ in *Greening v Wilkinson*,[61] an action for conversion of cotton warrants, denied that the rule laid down in *Mercer v Jones*,[62] was good law, and on a rising market he ruled that the jury

> "may give the value at the time of the conversion, or at any subsequent time, in their discretion, because the plaintiff might have had a good opportunity of selling the goods if they had not been detained."[63]

Lord Porter in *Caxton Publishing Co v Sutherland Publishing Co*,[64] reserved his opinion on whether Abbott CJ's view could be supported. Subsequently, in the decisions in *Sachs v Miklos*,[65] and in *Munro v Willmott*,[66] there has been a tendency to

---

54 Copyright, Designs and Patents Act 1988 s.170 and Sch.1 para.31(2).

55 15th edn, 1988, paras 1302 to 1305.

56 (1813) 3 Camp. 477.

57 (1813) 3 Camp. 477 at 477.

58 [1895] 1 Q.B. 521 CA at 530 and 532, per Lord Halsbury and Lindley LJ respectively.

59 [1938] A.C. 247 PC at 257, per Lord Atkin, in relation to shares; and undisputed by the parties in *Caxton Publishing Co v Sutherland Publishing Co* [1939] A.C. 178: see at 192 and 203, per Lord Roche and Lord Porter respectively.

60 [1990] 1 W.L.R. 409 PC at 413D–E, per Lord Templeman, again in relation to shares. This measure also derives support from the wording of s.29 of the Civil Procedure Act 1833 which, in allowing the court a discretion to award interest in actions of trover and trespass, stated that it should be given "over and above the value of the goods at the time of the conversion or seizure". This clearly assumed that the time of conversion was the time at which the goods were to be valued. The modern provisions as to interest, contained in s.35A of the Senior Courts Act 1981, throw no light on this issue.

61 (1825) 1 C. & P. 625.

62 (1813) 3 Camp. 477.

63 (1825) 1 C. & P. 625 at 626.

64 [1939] A.C. 178 at 203.

65 [1948] 2 K.B. 23 CA.

66 [1949] 1 K.B. 295.

state that the value at the date of judgment is the relevant figure, but, as will be seen, this is given serious qualification by the results of both cases.[67]

It is submitted that the soundest approach is to start off with the value at the time of conversion as the prima facie measure; this is in accord with the general principle that damages are to be assessed as at the date of the wrong. The effect upon this measure of damages of increases or decreases in the value between wrong and judgment must then be considered. Increases must be divided into those that would have happened without intervention by the defendant, i.e. rises in the market value, and those that are due to acts done or expenses incurred by the defendant in relation to the goods.[68] **38-013**

## (1) Market fluctuations

**(a) Fall** Where the goods fall in value after the time of conversion, the defendant was held in *Solloway v McLaughlin*,[69] still to be liable for the market value at the time of conversion. The defendant stockbrokers converted shares of their claimant client by selling them. Subsequently, when the claimant closed his account with them, they bought the same number of shares in the same company at the substantially lower price to which the market had fallen since the sale and conversion, and handed these over to the claimant, who took them without knowledge of the conversion. Later he discovered about the conversion, sued for damages, and was awarded the value of the shares at the date of conversion, less the value of the shares bought in replacement as at the time when he accepted them. The defendants argued for nominal damages on the ground that the claimant had suffered no loss as he had intended to retain his original shares and these would have fallen to the price of the repurchase. This contention was rejected by the House of Lords. Lord Atkin said: **38-014**

> "It is objected that this will be to put him in a better position than if he had not been defrauded at all .... All this amounts to is to recognise that fraudulent brokers have often sounder judgment than their clients as to the future course of markets. If the shares had been converted and not returned, there can be no question that the client would have been entitled to receive the proceeds of the conversion, though he himself had planned to hold and thought he had succeeded in holding the shares until a time when the value was nothing. Fortunately for the commercial community the law has many effective forms of relief against dishonest agents, and no injustice is done if the principal benefits, as he occasionally may, by the superior astuteness of an unjust steward in carrying out a fraud."[70]

Any other rule would allow the converter to profit, certainly in the case of a stockbroker, and as against a wrongdoer who would make a profit if the market

---

67 See the similar statement in *Beaman v A.R.T.S.* [1948] 2 All E.R. 89 at 93, per Denning J. In the former (see paras 38-002 to 38-004, above) action of detinue where damages were given in lieu of the return of the goods, it was logical that the market value should be taken at the time when they would have been ordered to be returned, namely at the time of judgment, and that this represented the law was finally established by *Rosenthal v Alderton* [1946] K.B. 374 CA: facts at para.38-021, below.

68 In relation to increases and decreases in value, and indeed elsewhere, it is important to note that mitigation principles apply as much to conversion as to any other tort, this having been unsuccessfully challenged in *Uzinterimpex J.S.C. v Standard Bank Plc* [2008] EWCA Civ 819 CA. See the case at paras 9-072 and 9-078, above.

69 [1938] A.C. 247 PC.

70 [1938] A.C. 247 PC at 259.

value at the time of the wrong were not awarded the law is prepared to award such market value.

**38-015** That the defendant has made a profit is not essential, however, to an award of market value at conversion of goods of which the value on the market has subsequently fallen. The Judicial Committee of the Privy Council in *BBMM Finance (Hong Kong) v Eda Holdings*,[71] applied its earlier decision in *Solloway v McLaughlin*,[72] so to hold. There the defendants converted over 10 million shares of the claimants by disposing of them to a third party when they stood in the market at Hong Kong $5.75 per share, and later purchased shares to replace the shares so sold when their price in the market had more than halved, standing at only Hong Kong $2.40 per share. No profit had in fact been made by the defendants on account of their not having presented the cheque which they had received from the third party on the sale but, Lord Templeman said,

> "the inexplicable failure ... to collect the sale price cannot mitigate or reduce the damages recoverable".[73]

> "The general rule ... that a plaintiff whose property is irretrievably converted has vested in him a right to damages for conversion measured by the value of the property at the date of conversion"[74]

applied.

**38-016** Detinue cases of the 19th century reached the same result as *Solloway v McLaughlin*,[75] by ordering the return of the goods where these had not already been delivered up and by then awarding as damages for detention the difference between the market value at default and the market value at judgment. These detinue cases were *Williams v Archer*,[76] and *Williams v Peel River Co*[77]; damages based on the market fall were also awarded in *Barrow v Arnaud*,[78] an action on the case similar to detinue.[79] However, in *Brandeis Goldschmidt & Co v Western Transport*,[80] decided after the Torts (Interference with Goods) Act 1977 with its abolition of detinue had come into force,[81] the Court of Appeal, in assessing damages after a Master's order for the delivery up of a consignment of copper had been complied with, awarded a nominal amount only and rejected the claimants' contention that they were entitled to recover as of right under a general rule of law the amount of the fall in the market value of the copper during the period of the defendants' detention. The claimants had imported the copper to refine and sell as cathodes and it had been detained by the defendant transporters en route for the refining process. Since it was thus clear that, as Brandon LJ put it,[82] the claimants had not acquired the copper with the intention of selling it on the market and would not in any event

71 [1990] 1 W.L.R. 409 PC.
72 [1938] A.C. 247 PC.
73 [1990] 1 W.L.R. 409 PC at 413G.
74 [1990] 1 W.L.R. 409 PC at 412B.
75 [1938] A.C. 247 PC.
76 (1847) 5 C.B. 318; approved in *Rosenthal v Alderton* [1946] K.B. 374 CA at 378.
77 (1887) 55 L.T. 689 CA.
78 (1846) 8 Q.B. 595.
79 Facts at para.9-044, above.
80 [1981] Q.B. 864 CA.
81 See para.38-002, above.
82 [1981] Q.B. 864 CA at 869B.

or at any time have used it for that purpose but, on the contrary, would have used it as a raw material for their business with the purpose of making profits from the sale of the finished product, an award based on the fall in the market value was inappropriate; the claimants had not been deprived of the opportunity of selling the copper on the market on the date when the detention began or been compelled to sell the copper on the date when it was delivered up. It is true that the claimants might have suffered a loss of profit on the sale of their finished products but they had expressly abjured this alternative way of putting their case.[83] They did indeed claim bank interest paid during the period of detention on the basis of their practice of reducing the bank borrowings which financed the purchases of the copper by the proceeds of the cathode sales; but this claim also failed because they adduced no evidence that the receipt of sale proceeds would have been advanced had there been no detention of the copper.[84] Brandon LJ examined the three earlier cases in which the fall in market value had been awarded and concluded that it had been a reasonable inference that the claimants in each of these had acquired the goods in question with the intention of selling them at a profit on the market.[85] Damages based on the fall in market value therefore on the facts represented the loss suffered. Brandon LJ, delivering the leading judgment, said that he could not

> "see why there should be any universally applicable rule for assessing damages for wrongful detention of goods, whether it be the rule contended for by the plaintiffs or any other rule. Damages in tort are awarded by way of monetary compensation for a loss or losses which a plaintiff has actually sustained, and the measure of damages awarded on this basis may vary infinitely according to the individual circumstances of any particular case. It is for plaintiffs to prove what loss, if any, they have suffered by reason of a tort, and when, as here, the effect of the tort is potentially adverse interference with the course of their business operations, it is for them to establish by evidence that there was in fact such adverse interference, and that they suffered a properly quantifiable loss by reason of it."[86]

This sensible decision in *Brandeis Goldschmidt & Co v Western Transport*,[87] may appear to sit oddly with the Judicial Committee's awards in *Solloway v McLaughlin*,[88] and in *BBMM Finance (Hong Kong) v Eda Holdings*,[89] of the amounts by which the market value of the shares had fallen after the date of the conversion although the claimant had in the first case missed, and in the second had apparently missed, no chance of selling them before their fall.[90] The distinction, it was suggested in an earlier edition of this work, between the *Solloway* and *Brandeis* decisions, is that in the one, but not in the other, the defendants made a profit by themselves selling the goods; and it may be said that one could distinguish the *BBMM Finance* and *Brandeis* decisions along similar lines in that the defendants in *BBMM Finance*,[91] had had a profit on their hands but one which they had inexplicably failed to realise.[92] However, the decision in *BBMM Finance* reveals **38-017**

83 [1981] Q.B. 864 CA at 873B.
84 [1981] Q.B. 864 CA at 873C–G.
85 [1981] Q.B. 864 CA at 870G–872G.
86 [1981] Q.B. 864 CA at 870D–E.
87 [1981] Q.B. 864 CA.
88 [1938] A.C. 247 PC.
89 [1990] 1 W.L.R. 409 PC.
90 See paras 38-014 and 38-015, above.
91 [1990] 1 W.L.R. 409 PC.
92 See para.38-015, above.

that the true distinction is somewhat different. As Lord Templeman explained:

> "The *Brandeis Goldschmidt* case[93] … [was] concerned with damages caused by temporary deprivation of possession and use of property. A different consideration will apply when the property is irreversibly converted and the plaintiff loses that property."[94]

Here then is the distinction between conversion where the claimant sues for the value of the goods and detinue where he claims and obtains their return, a claim which he is now entitled to make in conversion as it has taken over from detinue.[95] In the first claim he will obtain the value at conversion, in the second he may obtain less. Yet the issue of defendant's profit is still not far away. For wherever the goods have been delivered up, whether voluntarily or under a court order, by the defendant to the claimant, as was the position not only in *Brandeis* but also in the three 19th century cases which the Court of Appeal there distinguished,[96] no question of the defendant's making a profit can arise; and even where the order for delivery up gives the defendant the alternative of paying damages, which alternative he adopts, he will not have made a profit by a disposal of the goods as such an order must assume him still to be in possession. Where, by contrast, the claim is necessarily not for the goods themselves but for their value because the defendant's conversion has arisen from a disposal of them, he may have made a profit on that disposal but whether he has done so or not is immaterial for the measure of damages to which the claimant is entitled.

**38-018** **(b) Rise** *Greening v Wilkinson*,[97] where Abbott CJ laid down that the jury had a discretion to award the value at any time subsequent to the conversion, was a case where the market rose between conversion and trial, but it is not clear from the report what time the jury chose. Similarly in *Johnson v Hook*,[98] the market was rising, but, although the time at which Stephen J assessed the market value is clear, it is not clear at what time he regarded the conversion as taking place.[99] The matter was, however, fully considered by the Court of Appeal in the important case of *Sachs v Miklos*.[100] The defendants had in 1940 allowed the claimant to store his furniture in their house free of charge, and subsequently lost touch with him, owing to his failure to keep them informed of his whereabouts. In 1943 the defendants, requiring the space taken up by the furniture, wrote two letters to the claimant at an address supplied by his bank. Receiving no reply to these letters, which were not returned, the defendants sold the furniture. In 1946 the claimant demanded the furniture from the defendants who tendered the £15 for which it had been sold. The market value having risen greatly since the sale, the claimant brought an action in conversion, and also in detinue, claiming as damages the increased value. The Court of Appeal stated first that

93 And also, added Lord Templeman, *Williams v Peel River Co* (1887) 55 L.T. 689 CA, one of the Victorian detinue cases: see para.38-016, above. Counsel for the defendants had relied on a passage from Bowen LJ's judgment in this case.

94 [1990] 1 W.L.R. 409 PC at 413D.

95 See paras 38-002 to 38-004, above.

96 See para.38-016, above.

97 (1825) 1 C & P. 625.

98 (1883) Cab. & Ell. 89.

99 To this extent the headnote, which states that a time after the conversion could be taken at which to assess the value, is misleading.

100 [1948] 2 K.B. 23 CA.

"the measure of damages is the same in conversion as it is in detinue where the facts are only that the defendant has the goods in his possession and could hand them over but would not".[101]

This, however, does not necessarily mean that the value is prima facie taken as at the time of judgment, as it was in detinue[102] before that form of action was abolished,[103] although the result may be the same. For the court said later:

"The value of the goods converted, at the time of their conversion, is one thing ... but it does not follow that that sum is the measure of the plaintiff's loss. The question is what is the plaintiff's loss, what damage he has suffered, by the wrongful act of the defendants."[104]

If the claimant received the letters and, therefore, knew or ought to have known that the goods would be sold, then

"this great rise in value which has taken place since is not damage which he can recover as flowing from the wrongful act"[105];

but if he did not know of the sale until 1946

"it is impossible to say that he is not entitled to recover the value of the goods at that time".[106]

This suggests that the increase till knowledge is to be treated as consequential damage. The fact that the claimant cannot claim the value after knowledge removes the criticism that a shrewd and unscrupulous claimant might delay bringing his action upon a rising market. For in *Sachs v Miklos*,[107] the Court of Appeal remitted the case to the county court judge to find, not only whether the claimant knew or ought to have known of the conversion before 1946, but whether there was undue delay on his part in bringing an action between 1946 and 1947.[108]

Similarly, in *Industria Azucarera Nacional SA v Empresa Exportado de Azucar*,[109] where at a time of political upheaval the Cuban sellers of a cargo of sugar paid for by the Chilean buyers converted it by wrongfully retaking possession from the carrier, the buyers were held entitled to the value at conversion of the sugar together with essentially consequential damage measured by the increase in market price in the succeeding month by the end of which **38-019**

"it would have been practical for [the buyers] to cover themselves by making purchases in the market".[110]

The possibility of awarding the greater value at the time of the arbitrators' award—on the basis that a claimant is not required to replace until he has obtained

---

101 [1948] 2 K.B. 23 CA at 38 to 39.
102 See footnote at the end of para.38-012, above.
103 See paras 36-002 to 36-004, above.
104 [1948] 2 K.B. 23 CA at 39.
105 [1948] 2 K.B. 23 CA at 40.
106 [1948] 2 K.B. 23 CA at 40.
107 [1948] 2 K.B. 23 CA.
108 [1948] 2 K.B. 23 CA at 41.
109 [1982] Com. L.R. 171.
110 [1982] Com. L.R. 171 at 176, col.2. The Court of Appeal, at [1983] 2 Lloyd's Rep. 171, did not pass upon the damages issue.

his damages[111]—was not fully explored as the buyers had unsuccessfully claimed not this but the highest value to which the sugar market had climbed between conversion and judgment.[112]

**38-020** In *Trafigura Beheer BV v Mediterranean Shipping Co SA*,[113]cargo owners sued shipowners for the conversion of a cargo of copper in containers on the cargo's arrival at its Shanghai destination. The conversion came about by the issuing of a delivery order to fraudsters on their presentation of a false bill of lading or, on the following day, by the failure to deliver the cargo to the cargo owners on their presentation of the true bill of lading. The shipowners were able to ensure that the fraudsters did not get delivery but were refused delivery themselves. So the cargo remained in the container terminal with the volatile price of copper rising, and would remain there until the outcome of litigation in the Maritime Court of Shanghai over the cargo's ownership was known. In the cargo owners' damages claim the trial judge held the proper measure of damages to be the value of the cargo at the date of judgment rather than at the date of conversion because it was reasonable for the cargo owners not to get in a replacement cargo while the fate of the cargo was in the balance as they could be left with two parcels of copper with no certain buyers and continuing uncertainty as to the movement of copper prices, and also because if the shipowners only had to pay damages equal to the value of the cargo at conversion they would gain the benefit of the increase in value as title to the cargo would pass to them on payment of the damages.[114] The Court of Appeal upheld this award and stated agreement with the reasons given.[115] However, Longmore LJ said correctly[116] that, had the judge taken the value at conversion for his damages, he could have awarded the increase in value between conversion and judgment as consequential loss along *Sachs v Miklos* lines,[117] and also that this consequential loss could equally be described as damages for loss of use of the copper between conversion and judgment and therefore recoverable as such.

**38-021** The equivalent case to *Sachs v Miklos*,[118] under the former[119] detinue was *Rosenthal v Alderton*,[120] where the facts were similar, there having been a conversion by sale of the goods left for wartime care with the defendant. The court assessed the value of the goods at the time of judgment[121] but made the reservation that the election to sue in detinue despite a conversion was available to a claimant "at any rate where he was not aware of the conversion at the time".[122] Probably the claim in detinue continued to lie but the calculation of the value recoverable by the claimant would be subject to his duty to mitigate from the moment he was aware that the defendant was in breach of duty. This analysis is indeed supported by *Sachs*

---

111 The argument had ranged over what was called the *Startup v Cortazzi* (1835) 2 C.M. & R. 165 line of cases (for which see para.9-044, above) as well as the *Sachs v Miklos* [1948] 2 K.B. 23 CA line.
112 See para.38-022, below for this aspect of the case.
113 [2007] 2 All E.R. 149 (Comm).
114 [2007] 2 All E.R. 149 (Comm) at [136]–[138].
115 [2008] 1 All E.R (Comm) 385 CA at [38] together with [40].
116 At [2008] 1 All E.R (Comm) 385 CA at [41].
117 See para.38-018, above.
118 [1948] 2 K.B. 23 CA; at para.36-018, above.
119 See paras 38-002 to 38-004, above.
120 [1946] K.B. 374 CA.
121 See footnote at the end of para.38-012, above.
122 [1946] K.B. 374 CA at 379.

*v Miklos*,[123] where the suit was brought, and the same result in effect reached in detinue as well as conversion. Today with the abolition of detinue[124] the value will undoubtedly be taken at the date of detention and conversion, with the recoverable loss arising out of any subsequent rise in value being treated as consequential.[125]

**(c) Rise and fall** *Industria Azucarera Nacional SA v Empresa Exportado de Azucar*,[126] also dealt with the possibility of a market rise followed by a market fall between wrong and judgment. After the conversion the price of sugar had risen first slowly, later astronomically, and had then fallen away before the arbitrators made their award. The court rejected the buyers' claim to be awarded the highest intermediate value and their contention that **38-022**

> "the damages should reflect [their] loss of opportunity to sell the goods at the top of the market"[127]

in the absence of evidence that they would have so sold.[128] Had there been such evidence the position might have been different.[129]

## (2) Value increased

Formerly, if a person whose goods had been misappropriated wanted damages he sued in conversion but if he wanted the goods returned he sued in detinue. Now that conversion has supplanted detinue,[130] his claim must be in conversion whichever remedy he wishes to pursue. Where increased value has been given to the goods through the acts of the defendant or of third parties, it is now necessary, in dealing with conversion, to examine separately the situation where the claimant receives damages only and the situation where he has the goods returned to him with consequential damages, if any. **38-023**

**(a) Where the claimant's claim is for damages only[131] and physical additions are made to the goods** If the damages are calculated by the value at the time of the conversion, then any increased value given to the goods through **38-024**

---

123 [1948] 2 K.B. 23 CA.

124 See paras 38-002 to 38-004, above.

125 See paras 38-066 and following, below.

126 [1982] Com. L.R. 171; facts at para.38-019, above.

127 [1982] Com. L.R. 171 at 177, col.1. *McArthur v Seaforth* (1810) 2 Taunt. 457 (see para.29-015, above) was said to be to the "contrary effect".

128 In the former (see paras 38-002 to 38-004, above) detinue cases, *Williams v Peel River Co* (1887) 55 L.T. 689 CA and *Archer v Williams* (1846) 2 C. & K. 26, the claims for damages for detention appear to have been limited to the overall fall in value and ignored the intermediate rise, though Cresswell J in the latter at first instance directed the jury (at 27 to 28) that the highest intermediate value constituted the measure of damages.

129 See further on this award para.38-019, above. The general principles involved are considered at paras 9-042 to 9-044, above.

130 See paras 38-002 to 38-004, above.

131 This is to be taken as covering the situation where the claimant claims the return of the goods but the court either (1) declines to order the defendant to return them and awards damages only or (2) gives the defendant the option of returning the goods and paying consequential damages or of paying damages only, and the defendant elects the second alternative. For the various possibilities that are open to the court and the claimant, see Torts (Interference with Goods) Act 1977 s.3(2) and (3) at para.38-004, above.

improvements made to them by the defendant or third parties will not be included in the measure of damages. To include such an increase in value would give the claimant more than compensation, for his loss was of the goods as unimproved. The claimant is not forced to pay for improvements he does not want, since he is suing not for specific restitution but for damages only. The cases support this result, at least where the increased value has been the work of the defendant[132]; statute has now in part adopted and in part qualified it, making no distinction as between value increased by the defendant and value increased by third parties.

**38-025** The two cases of *Reid v Fairbanks*,[133] and *Munro v Willmott*,[134] exclude the value of the defendant's physical additions to the goods from the calculation of damages.[135] In *Reid v Fairbanks*,[136] the claimant brought an action for the conversion of a ship which had been in an unfinished state at the time of the conversion, but was afterwards completed and sent to sea by the defendant. The claimant claimed her full value when finished, but the Court of Common Pleas ruled that the damages were her value at the time of conversion. This value might be ascertained by taking the value the ship would have had when completed according to contract less the cost of completion after the conversion. In argument Maule J said:

> "Although it be true that in trover the owner may recover for the conversion of the improved chattel, it does not follow that he is entitled to recover the improved value as damages. The proper amount of damages is the amount of pecuniary loss which the plaintiffs have been put to by the defendant's conduct."[137]

In *Munro v Willmott*,[138] the defendant permitted the claimant to leave her car for a short time without charge in his hotel yard, but the car remained there for several years. On its becoming an obstacle owing to the conversion of the yard into a garage, the defendant, after unsuccessful efforts to communicate with the claimant, spent £85 in renovating the car to make it saleable, and sold it at £100. Subsequently the claimant sued the defendant in conversion. Lynskey J found that at the date of judgment the car was worth £120, whereas, but for the defendant's work on it, it would have been worth only some £20 as scrap. He awarded £35, saying that he must "assess the plaintiff's property in the car as it is", but

> "in assessing that value, I must have regard to what the defendant has spent in making the vehicle saleable".[139]

---

132 There being a dearth of authority where the work has been that of a third party.

133 (1853) 13 C.B. 692.

134 [1949] 1 K.B. 295.

135 There is also a third case, the very early one of *Green v Farmer* (1768) 4 Burr. 2214, an action of trover against a dyer for cloths given to him to be dyed, which he contended he was entitled to retain till the price of dyeing other goods was paid. This contention was rejected and the claimant had a verdict, but only for the value of the cloths when they were sent to the defendant in their white state. This, however, is not conclusive, as the work was done by the claimant's orders and the defendant had a lien to that extent.

136 (1853) 13 C.B. 692.

137 (1853) 22 L.J.C.P. 206 at 209–210. This is a clearer statement than that appearing in the report at (1853) 13 C.B. 692 at 729.

138 [1949] 1 K.B. 295.

139 [1949] 1 K.B. 295 at 298. The claimant sued also in detinue (now abolished: see paras 38-002 to 38-004, above) but fared no better there despite the fact that, since the damages were calculated at the time of the judgment, it was not so easy to exclude the value as increased by the defendant's labour as it was in conversion. Lynskey J said, at 299: "The measure of damages in detinue, it seems

Statute has since introduced specific provisions to deal with improvements made to the goods. Subsection (1) of s.6 of the Torts (Interference with Goods) Act 1977 states: **38-026**

> "If in proceedings for wrongful interference[140] against a person ('the improver') who has improved the goods, it is shown that the improver acted in the mistaken but honest belief that he had a good title to them, an allowance shall be made for the extent to which, at the time as at which the goods fall to be valued in assessing damages,[141] the value of the goods is attributable to the improvement."[142]

Subsections (2) and (4) then go on to make provision for an equivalent allowance where the claim for wrongful interference is made against the transferee from the improver or from an intermediate transferee, provided again that it is shown that the transferee who is sued acted in good faith.[143]

This statutory provision clearly covers the case of the defendant who knows nothing of the claimant's existence or of the claimant's title, such as the defendant who has bought goods from one who has stolen them from the claimant. However the introduction of a test of bona fides—honest belief in title in the case of the improver, acting in good faith in the case of the transferee from the improver—is a little disturbing; certainly it had made no appearance in the cases and seems to be a backward step. Thus in *Reid v Fairbanks*,[144] the defendant, who had purchased the ship from a third party, had been aware, before he completed her, that the claimant was disputing his title to her,[145] and in the ensuing litigation the claimant's title was vindicated. Could it necessarily be said here that the defendant had an honest but mistaken belief in his title when the position as to title was complicated and he knew that the matter remained to be resolved by proceedings in court? And in *Munro v Wilmott*,[146] the defendant clearly had no honest but mistaken belief that he had good title; on the contrary, he was well aware of the claimant's title but wished to rid himself of the goods which were becoming an embarrassment to him. It is true that, for the type of circumstances that arose in *Munro v Wilmott*,[147] s.12 of the Torts (Interference with Goods) Act 1977 would now give to the defendant bailee the right to sell goods of his bailor without being liable in conversion if he has taken reasonable, though unsuccessful, steps to trace or communicate with him, but the **38-027**

---

to me, must be similar if not the same. At any rate, when I am asked to give damages in detinue for the value of a motor car as at today and when I find that a large sum of money has been spent on it for the purpose of making it even saleable, I must take that into account in assessing what is the value of the property which the plaintiff has lost." See, too, *Greenwood v Bennett* [1973] Q.B. 195 CA where, in interpleader proceedings, the principle of *Munro v Willmott* [1949] 1 K.B. 295 was accepted by the Court of Appeal in relation to both conversion and detinue.

140 Which includes conversion: see para.38-002, above.

141 This implication that the goods may be required to be valued at a time later than the date of conversion may not, however, be justified: see paras 38-011 to 38-013, above.

142 It also may be questioned whether it is right that the allowance should be to the extent of the increase in value where this is greater than the expense incurred by the improver.

143 And subs.(3) completes the picture by providing that a transferee who has bought the goods and who, on being sued, has received an allowance in respect of the improvement must submit to a similar allowance being made in any claim brought by him against his own bona fide seller in respect of the failure of consideration.

144 (1853) 13 C.B. 692; facts at para.38-025, above.

145 This appears from the statement of facts, (1853) 13 C.B. 692 at 715 and also from the argument, at 728.

146 [1949] 1 K.B. 295; facts at para.38-025, above.

147 [1949] 1 K.B. 295.

bailee remains liable to account to the bailor for the proceeds of sale less any costs of sale[148] and no mention is made of any further permitted deduction on account of improvements effected. It would seem therefore that the bailee must now improve the goods at his peril, even if the goods as improved can command a far better price in the market.

38-028 **(b) Where the claimant's claim is for damages only[149] and expenses are incurred in making the goods saleable: cases of unauthorised mining** If the damages are calculated by the value at the time of conversion, then any increased value given to the goods through the incurring of expenses which are necessary to make them saleable will again[150] not be included in the measure of damages. Inclusion of such an increase in value over compensates the claimant and, where he is suing for damages and not claiming specific restitution, such necessary expenses should be deducted in order to arrive at the value of the goods which forms the normal measure. This is well illustrated by *Clark v Nicholson*,[151] where goods of a bankrupt had been seized by the sheriff after the bankruptcy and sold by him bona fide but wrongfully, and it was held that in an action of trover against the sheriff by the trustees in bankruptcy the jury might deduct the expenses incurred by the sheriff in selling, since these were expenses that the trustee, under a duty to sell, would in any event have had to incur himself.[152] The provisions of s.6 of the Torts (Interference with Goods) Act 1977, which now regulate the position on deductions for improvements—and which in effect allow a deduction for improvements only where the defendant can show bona fides[153]—would not seem to apply to expenses in making the goods saleable: such expenses can hardly be properly categorised as improvements. Accordingly, the authority of the prolific 19th century cases of unauthorised mining, where the rule that expenses are deducted finds its fullest application, would appear to remain unimpaired.

38-029 Where mineral in the earth is wrongfully severed and raised by the defendant, its value at the pit's mouth is greater by virtue of the severance and raising than its value in the earth, since it is of no use to anyone until severed and raised. Therefore the exact loss to the claimant, whether in an action of trover for wrongfully converting his minerals or in an action of trespass to goods for wrongfully taking them away, is measured by the price at the pit's mouth less both the cost of severing and

---

148 At s.12(5).

149 This is to be taken as covering the situation where the claimant claims the return of the goods but the court either (1) declines to order the defendant to return them and awards damages only or (2) gives the defendant the option of returning the goods and paying consequential damages or of paying damages only, and the defendant elects the second alternative. For the various possibilities that are open to the court and the claimant, see Torts (Interference with Goods) Act 1977 s.3(2) and (3) at para.38-004, above.

150 See para.38-024, above.

151 (1835) 6 C. & P. 712.

152 Dicta in former (see paras 38-002 to 38-004, above) detinue cases support this result: see *Peruvian Guano Co v Dreyfus* [1892] A.C. 166 where the defendant had paid for the transport of certain cargoes of guano to the required market and Lord Macnaghten stated obiter in a vigorous speech (at 174 to 177, reviewing all the analogous conversion and trespass to land cases), with which Lord Watson concurred (at 186), that the freight charges paid by the defendant should be deducted from the market value of the goods in fixing the measure of damages, and *Glenwood Lumber Co v Phillips* [1904] A.C. 405 PC where it was said that expenses in cutting down timber, sawing it into logs and floating it downstream to the market "might properly, but would not necessarily, be taken into account" (at 412) if damages were being assessed in detinue for the logs.

153 See paras 38-026 and 38-027, above.

the cost of raising.[154] If the defendant is not allowed to deduct these costs, the claimant is paid for expenditure which he has never incurred. On the other hand, if the defendant is allowed to deduct this outlay, it may be said that he is being paid for his own unlawful act.

A technical rule,[155] however, comes in to mark a distinction between the cost of severance and the cost of raising. The former is incurred before the mineral, originally part of the realty, has become a chattel; the latter is incurred after this. The action of trover or of trespass to goods can only apply to chattels and does not crystallise until the moment of severance, and the value of the mineral at that moment will, therefore, be the first possible value that it has qua chattel. There is thus this second objection to allowing the defendant the cost of severance, an objection which has no application to the cost of raising. And indeed it is with the problems arising from this second, and technical, difficulty that the courts are concerned in the numerous cases. **38-030**

*(i) Deduction of the cost of severing the mineral* The rule was originally laid down in *Martin v Porter*,[156] in 1839 that the value of the mineral as soon as it existed as a chattel formed the measure of damages and that no deduction could be made for the cost of severance. Within three years this had been twice followed and applied.[157] **38-031**

But already a qualification on this general rule had been introduced in *Wood v Morewood*.[158] In that case Parke B directed the jury that **38-032**

> "if there was fraud or negligence on the part of the defendant, they might give, as damages under the count in trover, the value of the coals at the time they first became chattels, on the principle laid down in *Martin v Porter*; but that if they thought the defendant was not guilty of fraud or negligence, but acted fairly and honestly in the full belief that he had a right to do what he did, they might give the fair value of the coals as if the coalfield had been purchased by the plaintiff."[159]

The jury found for the latter sum.[160] This milder rule, which thus allows deduction of the cost of severance, was accepted and applied in the equity courts a quarter of

---

154 Damage to the claimant's land, as by letting down the surface, and wayleave rent are recoverable also, but this is the trespass to land count: see paras 39-015 and 39-048, below, respectively.

155 Lord Blackburn called it "a technical rule" in *Livingstone v Rawyards Coal Co* (1880) 5 App. Cas. 25 at 39.

156 (1839) 5 M. & W. 351.

157 In *Wild v Holt* (1842) 9 M. & W. 672 and *Morgan v Powell* (1842) 3 Q.B. 278.

158 (1841) 3 Q.B. 440n.

159 (1841) 3 Q.B. 440n at 441. The measure as so stated may, however, go to the other extreme and be too small: see para.38-038, below.

160 The action in *Wood v Morewood* (1841) 3 Q.B. 440n was trover whereas in the other three early cases it had been trespass, but this can make no difference.

a century later, the principal case being *Jegon v Vivian*,[161] which was itself approved by the House of Lords in *Livingstone v Rawyards Coal Co.*[162]

38-033 It is important to ascertain the extent to which the rule in *Wood v Morewood*,[163] qualified the rule in *Martin v Porter*.[164] The decided cases have established the application of the milder rule, allowing deduction of the cost of severance, in the following circumstances: (1) where the defendant had a bona fide belief in his title to the land in which the minerals lay: as in *Wood v Morewood*,[165] itself and in three later cases[166]; (2) where the defendant had inadvertently worked into the mine of the claimant, his adjoining owner: as in *Re United Merthyr Collieries*[167]; (3) where there was a bona fide dispute as to title between the claimant and the defendant, which dispute was in course of a long litigation that was finally decided against the defendant so as to make him ab initio a wrongdoer: as in *Jegon v Vivian*[168]; (4) where the defendant had begun work in a mine vested in trustees in the bona fide expectation that a contract would be concluded between them giving him a licence to work the mine and having given one of the trustees notice that that expectation would be immediately acted upon by an entry on the property, but no contract was afterwards entered into and the trustees had no power to make one: as in *Trotter v Maclean*[169]; (5) where the defendants had begun to work the claimant's mine in the bona fide expectation that an order granting permission to work it would be made in their favour by the Railway and Canal Commission, the application for the order having been filed before their trespass and the expected order being subsequently made, but the defendants had given no notice to the claimant that they were to commence working the mine as they did not know who was the owner: as in *Townend v Askern Coal Co.*[170]

38-034 The trend of these decisions and of the dicta in them indeed suggests that the strict rule in *Martin v Porter*,[171] will now apply only where the trespass is wilful or fraudulent, and that the qualification as stated by Parke B in *Wood v Morewood*,[172] is now to be enlarged so as to include cases of negligence. This trend stems from the approach laid down by Lord Halsbury LC in *Jegon v Vivian*.[173] He said:

> "Now it strikes me as a strong measure to give a man, instead of the value of his coal, the great advantage of having it worked without any expense for getting and hewing … It

---

161 (1871) L.R. 6 Ch. App. 742. The milder rule made a first appearance in equity in *Powell v Aiken* (1858) 4 K. & J. 343 and was applied in *Hilton v Woods* (1867) L.R. 4 Eq. 432. Cases applying the milder rule subsequent to *Jegon v Vivian* are *Re United Merthyr Collieries* (1872) L.R. 15 Eq. 46; *Ashton v Stock* (1877) 6 Ch. D. 719; *Trotter v Maclean* (1879) 13 Ch. D. 574; *Townend v Askern Coal Co* [1934] 1 Ch. 463; also *Job v Potton* (1875) L.R. 20 Eq. 84 (not tort but an accounting between co-tenants) and *Brown v Dibbs* (1877) 37 L.T. 171 PC (again not tort but breach of contract for sale of working mine).

162 (1880) 5 App. Cas. 25.

163 (1841) 3 Q.B. 440n.

164 (1839) 5 M. & W. 351.

165 (1841) 3 Q.B. 440n.

166 *Hilton v Woods* (1867) L.R. 4 Eq. 432; *Ashton v Stock* (1877) 6 Ch. D. 719; and *Livingstone v Rawyards Coal Co* (1880) 5 App. Cas. 25.

167 (1872) L.R. 15 Eq. 46.

168 (1871) L.R. 6 Ch. App. 742.

169 (1879) 13 Ch. D. 574.

170 [1934] 1 Ch. 463.

171 (1839) 5 M. & W. 351.

172 (1841) 3 Q.B. 440n.

173 (1871) L.R. 6 Ch. App. 742.

seems a rough and ready mode of doing justice, though the remark that a wilful trespasser ought to be punished is worthy of observation and it seems to me that the judges have founded their decisions upon the ground of wilful trespass."[174]

And later he said:

"I think that the milder rule of law is certainly that which ought to guide this court, subject to any case made of a special character which would induce the court to swerve from it. Otherwise, on the one hand, a trespass might be committed with impunity if the rule *in poenam* were not insisted upon; so, on the other hand, persons might stand by and see their coal worked, being spared the expense of winning and getting it."[175]

This has been interpreted by the courts as putting the burden on the claimant of showing that the stricter rule applies. *Re United Merthyr Collieries*,[176] is a strong case, for it was one not of bona fide belief in title or expected title but of inadvertently crossing the boundary of the claimant's adjoining mine: yet the milder rule was applied in the absence of any evidence of fraud. So, too, in *Livingstone v Rawyards Coal Co*,[177] all their Lordships spoke of the stricter rule as applying in cases of trespass which was wilful or fraudulent.[178]

Perhaps it may be put this way. The rationale of the decisions is that the technical rule has been maintained in cases where the conduct of the defendant has been wilful and therefore such as formerly to have permitted exemplary damages to be visited upon him, and the costs of severance that he has incurred thus came to represent a kind of crystallised measure of exemplary damages; on the other hand, where exemplary damages have not been appropriate, the technical rule has been abandoned and the defendant has been allowed to deduct the costs of severance. The difficulty with this rationale today is that, valid though it may be as an explanation of the cases at the time they were decided, it would now need to be made consistent with the restrictions that the decision in *Rookes v Barnard*,[179] has imposed a general ban on the awarding of exemplary damages.[180] However, one of the three exceptional categories of case in which exemplary damages are still permitted is where the defendant has calculated that he would profit from his tortious conduct,[181] and it would seem that cases of unauthorised mining wilfully committed can with ease be brought within this category. It is true that the application of the technical rule will not serve to wrest an actual profit from the defendant since the costs of severance constitute only an expense incurred by him, but it will presumably be clear that he will have calculated upon achieving a profit out of his tortious mining.[182] **38-035**

In the light of this analysis, the earlier decisions applying the stricter measure should now be read as dealing with defendants who were wilful trespassers. Most **38-036**

174 (1871) L.R. 6 Ch. App. 742 at 760 to 761.

175 (1871) L.R. 6 Ch. App. 742 at 762.

176 (1872) L.R. 15 Eq. 46.

177 (1880) 5 App. Cas. 25.

178 (1880) 5 App. Cas. 25 at 31, 34, 39, per Earl Cairns LC, Lord Hatherley and Lord Blackburn respectively. Only these three appear to have been present.

179 [1964] A.C. 1129.

180 See Ch.13, above.

181 See paras 13-021 and following, above.

182 The unauthorised mining cases were explained along similar lines by Lord Diplock in *Broome v Cassell & Co* [1972] A.C. 1027 at 1129B. Today they may come to be re-categorised as cases of disgorgement damages: on these see, generally, Ch.15.

of them are indeed equivocal upon this point in so far as they were decided at a time when the question of the defendant's state of mind was not considered a vital matter. Of the cases in which the stricter measure was awarded to the claimant, it is not clear that the defendant knew that he was trespassing either in the first common law cases, establishing the rule of no deduction,[183] or in some of the later cases in equity.[184] Indeed, the only cases adopting the stricter measure where there was no uncertainty as to the defendant's state of mind are cases in which his conduct was clearly fraudulent: these are *Phillips v Homfray*,[185] and also *Trotter v Maclean*,[186] in respect of the time after the defendant knew that no contract would be concluded giving him a licence to work the mine.[187]

**38-037** *(ii) Deduction of the cost of raising the mineral* No technical objection intervenes to prevent the deduction of the cost of raising the mineral. The only argument against it is that the defendant should not be allowed to deduct value added to the goods by his expenditure when this arose out of his own wrongful act. Such a contention has, however, never found favour, and the cost of raising has invariably been deducted in all those cases in which argument has raged around the question of the cost of severance. In *Morgan v Powell*,[188] the court specifically allowed the cost of raising to be deducted where the judge below had refused the deduction, for, said the court, although the defendant cannot, properly speaking, charge the claimant for his labour,[189] the coal could have no saleable value without being taken from the pit. And even when the distinction between wilful and innocent conduct on the defendant's part was developed in relation to the cost of severance, it had no operation upon the cost of raising which even a fraudulent defendant could claim to deduct: this is clearly stated in *Joicey v Dickinson*.[190] Thus all the cases dealt with in connection with the cost of severance strongly support the rule that any increase in the value due to the cost incurred in raising the mineral may be deducted: or, stated more properly, that any subsequent increase in value by reason of the defendant's expenditure in transporting the goods to a place where they can be sold does not form part of the value that the claimant has lost or is entitled to claim.

---

183 *Martin v Porter* (1839) 5 M. & W. 351; *Wild v Holt* (1842) 9 M. & W. 672; *Morgan v Powell* (1842) 3 Q.B. 278.

184 *Llynvi Coal Co v Brogden* (1870) L.R. 11 Eq. 188; *Ecclesiastical Commissioners for England v N.E. Ry* (1877) 4 Ch. D. 845 (disapproved on this ground in *Bulli Coal Mining Co v Osborne* [1899] A.C. 350 at 364). In *Joicey v Dickinson* (1881) 45 L.T. 643 CA, it appears that the defendant's servants had committed the trespass without the defendant being aware of it: but the defendant was only arguing that the cost of raising be deducted, and was not claiming that the cost of severance should be also. It, therefore, does not form a decision on the point.

185 (1871) L.R. 6 Ch. App. 770.

186 (1879) 13 Ch. D. 574.

187 *Taylor v Mostyn* (1886) 33 Ch. D. 226 CA may be considered another such case, but there are overtones of contract by reason of the fact that accounts were being taken as against a mortgagee in possession who was claimant not defendant.

188 (1842) 3 Q.B. 278.

189 The cost of raising refers only to the defendant's out-of-pocket expenses and not also to the value of his services: see para.38-038, below.

190 (1881) 45 L.T. 643 CA.

*(iii) Further possible deductions* The non-penal measure as laid down originally in *Wood v Morewood*,[191] was **38-038**

> "the fair value of the coals as if the coalfield had been purchased from the claimant",[192]

and in the first two equity cases accepting and applying the non-penal measure, *Hilton v Woods*,[193] and *Jegon v Vivian*,[194] it was stated as

> "the fair value of such coal and other minerals, at the same rate as if the mines had been purchased by the defendants at the fair market value of the district".[195]

Such a measure would not be as great as the value at the pit's mouth less the costs of severance and raising. For no buyer would give a price for undug minerals as, with the addition of costs of severance and raising, would be exactly the value of the coal when brought to the surface: such a price would leave him without any profit on the transaction. However in the next case, *Re United Merthyr Collieries*,[196] the court awarded the value at the pit's mouth less the costs of severance and raising without apparently realising that they were awarding a higher rate of damages than had been laid down in the earlier three cases. This transition, thus peaceably made, has been consistently maintained, and all subsequent cases giving the non-penal measure[197] have gone on the lines of *Re United Merthyr Collieries*,[198] and not of the prior cases. The difference between these two measures is that, while the later one deducts from the value at pit's mouth only the expenditure incurred by the defendant in severing and raising, the earlier one in effect deducts, in addition to the out-of-pocket expenses, the market value of the defendant's services in carrying out the severance and raising of the minerals. The later rule would appear correctly to measure the claimant's loss, since it is he and not the defendant who is entitled to make any profit through the severance, raising and sale of his mineral. As Bacon VC said in *Re United Merthyr Collieries*[199]:

> "The plaintiff is to be put in the same situation as he would have been in, neither better nor worse, if he himself had severed the coal and brought it to the pit's mouth."

In some circumstances, however, it would be unrealistic to award as much as the value at the pit's mouth less the costs of severing and raising. This was so in *Livingstone v Rawyards Coal Co*,[200] where the claimant, under whose land the minerals lay, owned such a small area of land that he could neither have profitably **38-039**

---

191 (1841) 3 Q.B. 440n.
192 (1841) 3 Q.B. 440n at 441, per Parke B.
193 (1867) L.R. 4 Eq. 432.
194 (1871) L.R. 6 Ch. App. 742.
195 *Hilton v Woods* (1867) L.R. 4 Eq. 432 at 441; *Jegon v Vivian* (1871) L.R. 6 Ch. App. 742 at 762. The latter was quoted with approval by Lord Blackburn in *Livingstone v Rawyards Coal Co* (1880) 5 App. Cas. 25 at 40, but not applied due to the special circumstances of the case.
196 (1872) L.R. 15 Eq. 46.
197 See the post-1872 cases cited in the last footnote but one to para.38-032, above. In *Attorney General v Tomline* (1877) 5 Ch. D. 750 Fry J adopted a measure which is like that awarded in the early cases, i.e. "the net returns from the saleless such a sum of money by way of profit as would induce a third party to undertake the enterprise": at 768. But the case was a very peculiar one in that the copyholder claimant had no right to the minerals other than that of forbidding their being taken.
198 (1872) L.R. 15 Eq. 46.
199 (1872) L.R. 15 Eq. 46 at 49.
200 (1880) 5 App. Cas. 25.

worked the mine himself nor disposed of the right to work it to any except the adjacent owners, the defendants, who had carried away his coal under the bona fide belief that it was included in their lease. The House of Lords held in these circumstances that the measure of damages was the value the claimant could have obtained from the persons who were able to work the mine, and that this was to be ascertained by taking the royalty the adjacent owners would reasonably pay for the privilege of mining.[201] And in *Townend v Askern Coal Co*,[202] Farwell J held that, having regard to *Livingstone v Rawyards Coal Co*,[203] the proper method of arriving at the measure of damages in the case before him was to take the royalties which would have been payable.

38-040 **(c) Where the claimant's claim is for the return of the goods**[204] Rather more difficult was the situation in former[205] detinue cases where the court was prepared to accede to the claimant's demand for the return of the goods. Here it was not just a question of giving damages on the basis of unimproved value, but of compelling the claimant to pay to the defendant the amount by which he had increased the value. The clue would seem to lie in the fact that the remedy of specific restitution is an equitable and discretionary one, the court since 1854 having the discretion, and not the defendant.[206] It was, therefore, probable that the claimant, assuming that he was not refused outright an order for redelivery,[207] would be put on such terms as seemed necessary to the court to do complete justice between the parties; such terms would presumably be that the claimant should make a reasonable payment to the defendant in respect of the increase in value. This was vigorously suggested obiter by Lord Macnaghten in *Peruvian Guano Co v Dreyfus*.[208] He took the view that equity, with its power to order restitution of the goods, would not "assist the claimant if he refused to do equity by making just allowances"[209]; and as to the similar power given, since 1854, to the common law courts,[210] he said:

> "I should doubt whether it was incumbent upon the court to order the defendant to return the goods *in specie* where the plaintiff refused to make a fair and just allowance and so claimed the interposition of the court, under the Common Law Procedure Act, for the purpose of obtaining an advantage not consistent with the justice of the case."[211]

Yet the contrary view was put forward and acted upon by the Judicial Committee

[201] Lord Blackburn pointed out that the royalty was not itself the measure but evidence of the value which constituted the measure: (1880) 5 App. Cas. 25 at 43.

[202] [1934] 1 Ch. 463.

[203] (1880) 5 App. Cas. 25.

[204] This is to be taken as applying to the situation where the claimant claims the return of the goods and the court either (1) orders the defendant to return the goods, or (2) gives the defendant the option of returning the goods and paying consequential damages or of paying damages only, and the defendant elects the first alternative. For the various possibilities that are open to the court and the claimant, see Torts (Interference with Goods) Act 1977 s.3(2) and (3) at para.38-004, above.

[205] See paras 38-002 to 38-004, above.

[206] See para.38-003, above.

[207] As in *Whiteley v Hilt* [1918] 2 K.B. 808 CA, which not only involved an ordinary article of commerce, a piano, but also the claimant had a limited interest so that his measure of damages would not in the circumstances have been the full value. See para.38-063, below.

[208] [1892] A.C. 166.

[209] [1892] A.C. 166 at 176.

[210] See para.38-003, above.

[211] [1892] A.C. 166 at 176.

of the Privy Council in *Glenwood Lumber Co v Phillips*.[212] "Their Lordships", said Lord Davey,

> "think that the judgment is in the form usual in actions for detinue, and it would not be right to impose on the respondent the obligation of paying the appellants the expenses of their wrongful acts as a condition of recovering what must be considered in this action as his property."[213]

The working out of these difficulties has now shifted to conversion with the statutory abolition of detinue.[214] However, in the wake of abolishing detinue, the same statute has specifically provided that the court may now in conversion require the claimant to pay for any improvements made to the goods if he is to obtain their return to him. Section 3(7) of the Torts (Interference with Goods) Act 1977 enacts that where under s.6 an allowance falls to be made in assessing damages in proceedings for wrongful interference[215] for the extent to which the value of the goods is attributable to any improvement made to them,[216] and the goods are ordered to be returned to the claimant,[217] **38-041**

> "the court may assess the allowance to be made in respect of the improvement, and by the order require, as a condition for the delivery of the goods, that allowance to be made by the claimant".

This then confirms, for improvements made to the goods, the position taken by Lord Macnaghten in *Peruvian Guano Co v Dreyfus*,[218] but again[219] leaves open the position where expenses have been incurred in making the goods saleable.[220] In fact the conflicting dicta in the detinue cases as to whether the claimant should be required to make an appropriate allowance to the defendant appeared in cases where the defendant had incurred expenses in making the goods saleable.[221] Unauthorised mining is not heard of today, but should a latter-day case appear it is to be hoped that, especially in the light of the new statutory provision permitting an allowance for improvements, the same solution will be reached, without statutory aid, where expenses rather than improvements are in issue.

## 3. Place at Which Value is to be Taken

The place at which the value of the goods is to be assessed is generally the place at which the conversion occurs. In the cases two types of circumstances indicate variants to this rule; but they are apparent rather than real variants. (1) In *Burmah* **38-042**

---

212 [1904] A.C. 405 PC.

213 [1904] A.C. 405 PC at 412. However, it was Lord Macnaghten's approach in *Peruvian Guano Co v Dreyfus* [1892] A.C. 166 which appealed, in the context of interpleader proceedings, to the Court of Appeal in *Greenwood v Bennett* [1973] Q.B. 195 CA.

214 See paras 38-002 to 38-004, above.

215 Which includes conversion: see para.38-002, above.

216 See para.38-026, above.

217 With or without giving the alternative of paying damages in lieu.

218 [1892] A.C. 166; see para.38-040, above.

219 See para.38-028, above.

220 As for improvements which may not be covered by s.6 (see para.38-027, above), the court would now seem to be prohibited from making an allowance to the defendant.

221 See para.38-040, above.

*Trading Corp v Mirza Mahomed*,[222] where logs were converted when lying felled in a forest, it was held that the damages might properly be assessed at the market value at the nearest available market less the cost of transporting the goods there. This measure, however, is still the value at the place of conversion: the logs could not be sold in the forest and therefore an assessment of their value in situ requires a deduction of transport costs to a place where they could be sold.[223] (2) Both in *Ewbank v Nutting*,[224] and in *Acatos v Burns*,[225] where goods were converted in the course of their sea transit and sold at prices lower than their market value at the place to which they were being carried, the court refused to accept the defendant's contention that the damages were to be measured by the sale price and looked rather to the value that the goods had to the claimant. In neither case did the court specifically look to the market value at the place of due delivery but both lend support to the correctness of such a measure.[226] It is true that both cases have a flavour of contract, the goods having been converted by their carrier, but it is submitted that the same result should be reached where the conversion is by a stranger. The strict analysis, however, of the tort damages is that they are still based upon the market value at the place of conversion as the normal measure, with the amount by which the market value is greater at the place of due delivery being added as consequential loss. This approach leaves open the way to awarding the market value at the place of conversion where this is higher than the market value at the place of due delivery, a measure to which, it is submitted, the claimant is fully entitled: otherwise the defendant benefits from the tort.

## 4. SOME SPECIAL CASES OF VALUE[227]

### (1) Value of bills of exchange, promissory notes and similar instruments

**38-043** In actions for the conversion of negotiable instruments, such as bills and notes, the amount of the instrument is prima facie the measure of damages. This was well established by a series of cases culminating in *Morison v London County & Westminster Bank*,[228] which concerned the conversion by a bank of a customer's cheque. It is true that there are no specific coins in the converting bank belonging to the claimant customer and, as Lord Reading said,

> "it may be that the claim in trover of the cheque is a somewhat artificial and cumbrous way of arriving at the remedy".[229]

---

222 (1878) L.R. 5 Ind. App. 130.

223 This principle is also illustrated by the unauthorised mining cases: they are special only in that the goods were transported by the defendant himself. See paras 38-028 to 38-039, above.

224 (1849) 7 C.B. 797.

225 (1878) 3 Ex. D. 282.

226 More details of the judgments are given in the discussion of these cases at para.32-010, above.

227 Law Reform Committee, proposal in its 18th Report (1971) Cmnd.4774 that a claimant's loss should not necessarily be measured by the value of the chattel, particularly where it is a document or token of small inherent value but constituting or evidencing a right to property or other benefits (see, especially, paras 90 to 91), finds no implementation in the provisions of the Tort (Interference with Goods) Act 1977.

228 [1914] 3 K.B. 356 CA. The prior cases are referred to at 365 and 379 by Lord Reading CJ and Phillimore LJ respectively; they do not all touch directly on the question of measure of damages.

229 [1914] 3 K.B. 356 CA at 365.

Phillimore LJ, while saying that the rule was so well established as to make it unnecessary to inquire into the principles underlying it, nevertheless offered an explanation. He said:

> "The principal problem is that, though the plaintiff might at any moment destroy the cheques, while they remained in his possession they are potential instruments whereby the sums they represent may be drawn from his bankers, and if they get into any other hands than his, he will be the loser to the extent of the sums they represent. It may be also that anyone who has obtained its value by presenting a cheque is estopped from asserting that it has only a nominal value."[230]

Generally the face value of the negotiable instrument indicates its real value. Even where this is not so, the measure will still be the face value of the instrument if it is the defendant who has diminished its value by procuring its payment in part to himself, as in *Alsager v Close*,[231] or by erasing a signature on it, as in *McLeod v McGhie*,[232] or if the claimant can show, as in *Delegal v Naylor*,[233] that the instrument, although at a discount at the place where payable and of no value at the place where sued upon, was worth its full amount in his hands since backed by the British Government. Where, however, the instrument was void, although not without value, it was held in *Matthew v Sherwell*,[234] that, in trover for a cheque by assignees in bankruptcy against the bankrupt's bank, the assignees were not entitled to the face value since they were proceeding on the ground that the cheque was worthless because drawn without their authority.[235] *Smith v Lloyds TSB Group Plc*,[236] confirms that damages for the conversion of a cheque are represented by its face value but in the particular case there was no entitlement to the face value because material alteration had caused the cheque to become void. **38-044**

It has not been decided whether the face value controls when the instrument is not negotiable. The Court of Appeal took the view that it did in *Bavins v London & South Western Bank*,[237] where the document converted was an order for payment of money conditional on the signature of an appended receipt. The point was not decided, as the Court of Appeal held that the defendant bank, to whom the document had been paid with a forged indorsement and receipt and the money received by them for their customer, were liable to the claimant in the alternative count of money had and received. The Court of Appeal's view as to the conversion damages seems right, falling within the reason of the rule as given by Phillimore LJ in *Morison v London County & Westminster Bank*.[238] **38-045**

Whether face value could be regarded as market value was considered in relation to privately issued holiday credit stamps in *Building and Civil Engineering* **38-046**

---

[230] [1914] 3 K.B. 356 CA at 379.

[231] (1842) 10 M. & W. 576.

[232] (1841) 2 Scott N.R. 605. If the instrument is returned with a diminished value this on general principles will go in mitigation of damages: see *Alsager v Close* (1842) 10 M. & W. 576 at 584.

[233] (1831) 7 Bing. 460.

[234] (1810) 2 Taunt. 439.

[235] Compare *Wills v Wells* (1818) 8 Taunt. 264, which concerned a void insurance policy. The claimant recovered only nominal damages, although the defendant had been paid a gratuity on the policy by the insurance company.

[236] [2000] 1 W.L.R. 1225.

[237] [1900] 1 Q.B. 270 CA.

[238] [1914] 3 K.B. 356 CA.

*Holidays Scheme Management v Post Office*,[239] where postal packets containing such stamps were lost by the defendant's negligence. The stamps entitled employees holding them to holiday pay and the claimant company which managed the scheme, selling stamps at their face value to employers and reimbursing them at face value when stamped cards were received back from them, was under obligation to, and did, replace the lost stamps. Under the scheme the stamps were not to be bought and sold and were not negotiable in any way, but there was fraudulent trafficking in unused stamps stolen or otherwise improperly acquired. In an action under s.9(2) of the Crown Proceedings Act 1947 allowing recovery for negligent loss of postal packets provided, inter alia, that the amount should not exceed their "market value", both sides argued that there was no market value, the defendant contending that therefore the amount recoverable was nil and the claimants contending that therefore there was no limit on the recoverable amount. Alternatively, the defendant contended that the market value was the value as pieces of paper, which was negligible, and the claimants that the market value was the face value. The Court of Appeal held that the stamps did have a market value and that that value was their face value. "I do not think", said Lord Denning MR,

> "that the word 'market' here is used in the sense of the Sale of Goods Act 1893. It does not connote a market where buyers and sellers congregate. The 'market value' here means the price at which the goods could be expected to be bought and sold as between willing seller and willing buyer, even though there may be only one seller or one buyer, and even though one or both may be hypothetical rather than real."[240]

For the purposes of the case Pearson LJ thought that market value

> "could be sufficiently defined as the uniform or average price or consideration for which the article in question is ordinarily bought and sold or acquired and disposed of in legitimate transactions."[241]

Market value, however, represented not the measure of damages but a statutory ceiling on them, and accordingly in the circumstances the claimant's loss was to be assessed by making appropriate discounts from the market value on account of the possibility of the non-presentation to the claimants for payment of all or some of the stamps, and of the fact that the claimants were being paid now in respect of liabilities of theirs which would only arise in the future.[242]

## (2) Value of title deeds

**38-047** In actions for the conversion of title deeds, the court may give as the measure of damages the full value of the estate, but to be reduced to a nominal sum on the redelivery of the deeds. If subsequently the claimant should refuse to accept the deeds and insist on the full damages awarded, the court will presumably exercise its discretion to make him accept, as in *Coombe v Sansom*.[243]

---

239 [1966] 1 Q.B. 247 CA.
240 [1966] 1 Q.B. 247 CA at 264.
241 [1966] 1 Q.B. 247 CA at 269.
242 [1966] 1 Q.B. 247 CA at 267, per Pearson LJ. There was a further statutory limit upon the claimant's recovery which in fact reduced the damages even more.
243 (1822) 1 Dow. & Ry. 201; see *Loosemore v Radford* (1842) 9 M. & W. 657 at 659, per Alderson B.

### (3) Value of goods which the claimant must sell in any event

Where goods have been converted by seizure and sale after a bankruptcy, it has been held, in *Whitmore v Black*,[244] and in *Whitehouse v Atkinson*,[245] that where the sale was bona fide the trustee in bankruptcy was entitled only to the amount produced by the sale since he himself was bound to sell.[246] It is otherwise if the claimant was under no necessity to sell: then, as was held in *Glasspoole v Young*,[247] the full value is recoverable although the sale price was less. **38-048**

### (4) Value of goods where the defendant fails to produce them

Although generally the claimant must strictly prove the amount of the goods taken and their value, even though conversion is admitted by the pleadings,[248] it was held in the very old case of *Armory v Delamirie*,[249] where a boy chimney-sweep sued a jeweller for the conversion of a jewel he had found in a chimney, that, since the defendant had the jewel in his possession and would not produce it, it was to be presumed against him to be of the greatest value that a jewel of that type could be.[250] Nearly three hundred years after this decision the need to ascertain the value of missing converted jewellery about which little was known[251] reappeared in *Zabihi v Janzemini*,[252] and, while the principle in *Armory v Delamirie* has today gained a new lease of life in contexts other than the valuation of jewellery,[253] the Court of Appeal considered that some limitation must be placed upon the principle and that it could not apply to the case before the court. In *Zabihi* the claimant had handed over to the defendant for the purposes of sale four sets of gold and diamond jewellery which the defendant converted by his failure to produce and account for them. The Chancellor relied on factual differences, pointing out that in *Armory v Delamirie* the size of the jewel to be replaced was known, the jewel having been in a socket returned to the boy chimney-sweep, whereas in *Zahibi* all that was known was that the jewellery comprised diamonds mounted in gold so that an application of the principle would lead to little more than guesswork.[254] Moore-Bick LJ went further. He thought the assuming of the existence of facts most favourable to the claimant difficult to reconcile with the indemnity principle and with the **38-049**

---

244 (1844) 13 M. & W. 507 (execution creditor defendant).

245 (1828) 3 C. & P. 344 (sheriff defendant).

246 There is, of course, no logic in this, and indeed the contrary appears to be assumed in *Smith v Baker* (1873) L.R. 8 C.P. 330.

247 (1829) 9 B. & C. 696.

248 See, e.g. *Cook v Hartle* (1838) 8 C. & P. 568.

249 (1722) 1 Strange 505.

250 The further old, though not quite so old, case of *Mortimer v Cradock* (1843) 12 L.J.C.P. 166 takes much the same line. Part of a diamond necklace, which had been lost by the claimant, was traced into the possession of the defendant who could not account satisfactorily for having it and did not show positively that the whole set had not come into his hands. The jury was directed to presume that the whole necklace had been in his custody and to give damages accordingly.

251 Contrast *Jabir v HA Jordan & Co Ltd* [2011] EWCA Civ 816 CA (at para.38-008, above) where the missing pearl had been seen by three experienced dealers in pearls.

252 [2009] EWCA Civ 851 CA.

253 See para.10-095, above.

254 See his remarks at [2009] EWCA Civ 851 CA at [32]. He also pointed out that the claimant was hardly in the same position as the boy chimney-sweep since he, as well as the defendant, had given dishonest evidence as to the jewellery's value. Thus any presumption against the defendant was matched by an equal and opposite presumption against the claimant: at [32].

requirement that a claimant must prove his loss.[255] While he accepted that the principle might be justified where the defendant has wilfully suppressed evidence that would otherwise have been available to the claimant to enable him to prove his case—which was of course the position in *Armory v Delamirie* itself—he found it difficult to accept that the inability to make the goods available for inspection is of itself sufficient to invoke the principle, and that to assume the goods to be of fair average quality was more logical.[256]

## 5. Claimant with a Limited Interest in the Goods[257]

**38-050** The issue of damages where the claimant has a limited interest in the goods is whether he is thereby restricted to claiming less than the normal measure of the market value of the goods. Such decisions as do allow recovery only to the extent of the claimant's limited interest—buyer of goods may sue converting seller for market value less contract price, finance company may sue converting hire-purchaser for outstanding balance of contract instalments[258]—are no authority for increasing the damages beyond market value should, exceptionally, the claimant's limited interest appear to be greater than the market value. This is well illustrated by *Chubb Cash v John Crilley & Son*.[259] The defendants, whose debtor was in possession of a cash register under a hire-purchase agreement with the claimants, in execution of a distress warrant seized the cash register and realised £178 for it at a public auction in rooms where cash registers were regularly sold. The claimants had assigned the benefit of the instalments payable under the hire-purchase agreement and, when the debtor defaulted in the payment of instalments, were obliged to pay £951 to their assignee under the terms of the assignment. The claimants claimed damages for conversion against the defendants in the amount of £1,232 which was the balance outstanding under the hire-purchase agreement; the judge awarded them the £951 they had had to pay their assignee. The Court of Appeal would have nothing of either of these amounts and awarded only £178 as representing the market value of the cash register, the amount realised at the auction being in the circumstances the best evidence of market value and there being no evidence of any change in the market value or the condition of the cash register between the date of conversion and the date of sale. Bush J pointed out that the loss claimed

---

[255] [2009] EWCA Civ 851 CA at [50] and [51].

[256] [2009] EWCA Civ 851 CA at [51].

[257] The text deals only with situations in which the division between the interest of the claimant and the interest of the other person, whether defendant or third party, in the goods is between ownership and a right less than ownership. The situation in which the claimant is part owner of goods with another is excluded. To include it in the text would overburden an already complex analysis and, since it has not given rise to many problems in the cases, it can be dealt with briefly in a footnote. Thus it would seem, principally from *Bloxham v Hubbard* (1804) 5 East 407, that a part owner, whether relying on possession or a right to possession and whether suing a stranger or his co-owner, is only entitled to recover to the extent of his interest, and not even this if the defendant takes proper steps to require him, in an action against a stranger, to join his co-owner as claimant: see para.38-057, below. There is therefore no need for a defendant to pray in aid the provisions of the Torts (Interference with Goods) Act 1977 dealt with at para.38-052, below.

[258] See paras 38-058 and following, below.

[259] [1983] 1 W.L.R. 599 CA.

"does not in this case flow from the conversion but flows from the failure of the debtor to perform his obligations under the agreement".[260]

## (1) Defendant a stranger with no interest in the goods, but a jus tertii

At common law a defendant sued in conversion was not permitted to set up as a defence a *jus tertii* against a claimant who was in actual possession of the goods, although such a defence was available to him against a claimant who relied only on an immediate right to possession.[261] This inability to plead the *jus tertii* necessarily had repercussions on the damages which a claimant might claim: if the defendant could not set up the *jus tertii* as a defence to the claim, he could not set up in diminution of damages the fact of the third party's interest in the goods, and therefore could not defeat a claim for their full value. Indeed, even where the defendant was permitted to set up by way of defence the *jus tertii* because the claimant was relying only upon an immediate right to possession but this turned out not to be a complete defence as the claimant did himself have a degree of interest in the goods, the better view was thought to be that such a claimant was still entitled to claim the full value of the goods.[262] And a further consequence of these rules was that a defendant could find himself subjected to a double liability by having to pay the full value of the goods to more than one claimant.[263] **38-051**

The Torts (Interference with Goods) Act 1977 introduced, by s.7, provisions for avoiding any such double liability[264] of a person liable for conversion. This is achieved by apportioning the damages, in proceedings where there is more than one claimant, according to the interests of the claimants,[265] by requiring a separate claimant, who has recovered more than what would on an apportionment have been his proper share of the value of the goods, to account for the excess to any other person having a right to claim,[266] and further by requiring the person to whom such account has been made, and who has himself made a successful claim for damages against the converter, to reimburse the converter to the extent that he has in **38-052**

---

260 [1983] 1 W.L.R. 599 CA at 604D. The cases on which the claimant relied, namely, *Wickham Holdings v Brooke House Motors* [1967] 1 W.L.R. 295 CA and *Belvoir Finance Co v Stapleton* [1971] 1 Q.B. 210 CA (see para.38-063, below), were doubly irrelevant in that they concerned the situation where the defendant held the remaining interest in the goods; where the defendant is a stranger with no interest in the goods—as was the position here—the limited interest of the claimant does not affect his damages at common law: see paras 38-051 and following, below.

261 See the standard books on tort. The same was true for trespass and probably also for the former (see paras 38-002 to 38-004, above) detinue.

262 See para.38-057, below.

263 While it seemed that full recovery by bailor or bailee would bar subsequent action by the other (a view accepted in *The Winkfield* [1902] P. 42 CA at 61), it was not clear that the same was true where the limited interest arose other than by bailment.

264 A term which is stated in s.7(1) to mean "the double liability of the wrongdoer which can arise— (a) where one of two or more rights of action for wrongful interference is founded on a possessory title, or (b) where the measure of damages in an action for wrongful interference founded on a proprietary title is or includes the entire value of the goods, although the interest is one of two or more interests in the goods". The introduction of paragraph (b) supports the view expressed in the text (para.38-051, above)—or at least shows an unwillingness to reject it as an unacceptable view— that even a claimant relying only upon an immediate right to possession may be able to claim the full value of the goods.

265 See s.7(2).

266 See s.7(3).

total been overpaid.[267] While these rules ensure that persons liable for conversion will in the end escape an imposition of double liability, they do not, except in the case of proceedings brought by all the persons interested in the goods, make any inroad upon the common law position that a claimant in conversion is entitled to the full value against a defendant who is a stranger to the goods with himself no interest in them. This is left for the more direct measures of s.8, the first subsection of which enacts thus:

> "The defendant in an action for wrongful interference[268] shall be entitled to show, in accordance with rules of court, that a third party has a better right than the plaintiff as respects all or any part of the interest claimed by the plaintiff, or in right of which he sues, and any rule of law (sometimes called *jus tertii*) to the contrary is abolished."

It is then provided that rules of court relating to proceedings for wrongful interference may, inter alia,

> "authorise the defendant to apply for directions as to whether any person should be joined with a view to establishing whether he has a better right than the plaintiff, or has a claim as a result of which the defendant might be doubly liable".[269]

Appropriate provision was made by RSC Ord.15 r.10A, thereby enabling a defendant, by raising the issue of *jus tertii*, to bring the third party into the proceedings which, in turn, enabled the court to divide the damages as between the various contenders under the provisions of s.7. RSC Ord.15 r.10A was one of the rules that the Civil Procedure Rules 1998 failed to include in their initial partial re-enactment of Ord.15; the position was eventually rectified by the introduction in 2001 of a new CPR r.19.5A in terms similar to those of RSC Ord.15 r.10A.[270]

**38-053** One may now turn to an examination of the authorities read in the light of these statutory changes.

**38-054** (a) **Where the claimant relies on possession** That the claimant in conversion was entitled at common law, where he relied on possession, to recover the full value of the goods against a stranger with no proprietary interest in them, even though he had only a limited interest in them, was the case whether he was the bailee of the goods or the owner in possession. The common case was where he was a bailee. This is illustrated, for misappropriation of goods, by *Swire v Leach*,[271] an action of trespass for an illegal distress. The defendant, the landlord of the claimant pawnbroker, had wrongfully taken in distress pledges in the claimant's possession, and it was held that the claimant could recover from the defendant the full value of the pledges.[272] However the leading case on normal measure of damages at common law where the claimant is a bailee is *The Winkfield*,[273] which concerned not conversion of goods by misappropriation but physical destruction of goods by negligence: but the case, in which all the authorities on both types of loss were considered, applies in principle to conversion as well. It goes beyond *Swire v*

---

267 See s.7(4), together with the illustration there given.

268 Which includes conversion: see para.38-002, above.

269 See s.8(2)(c).

270 Introduced by Civil Procedure (Amendment) Rules 2001 (SI 2001/256).

271 (1865) 18 C.B. N.S. 479.

272 It was a strong court, as Collins MR pointed out in *The Winkfield* [1902] P. 42 CA at 57.

273 [1902] P. 42 CA.

*Leach*,[274] in that it established that the bailee is entitled to the full value even though he would have had a good answer to an action by the bailor for damages for loss of the thing bailed.[275] The facts of the case were these. Mails in charge of the Postmaster-General were sunk when the ship carrying them was in collision with another ship, the owners of which admitted liability for negligence but contested the Postmaster-General's claim to recover for the loss of the mails on the ground that he was under no liability for their loss to the persons interested in them. The Court of Appeal held that this was no defence, for "as against a wrongdoer, possession is title".[276] The situation is not so much that a bailee is liable over to the bailor and therefore entitled to the full value, as that the bailee is entitled to the full value and, in consequence, has to account over. Thus where the bailee recovers, he will hold the proceeds of his action, beyond his own interest therein, on behalf of the bailor.

Conversely in the case of the owner of goods in possession, some interest in the goods may be carved out in favour of another. Nevertheless, such owner can at common law recover the full value of the goods from a stranger who has converted them. Thus in *Turner v Hardcastle*,[277] the claimant had bought plant and stock and had defaulted in paying the seller the instalments of purchase money, but the seller had not taken any steps consequent upon this default. The defendant converted the goods, and as against this wrongdoer not claiming under the seller the claimant recovered the full value, being on receipt thereof accountable to his seller in respect of the amount of unpaid purchase money. **38-055**

The position is unaltered by the Torts (Interference with Goods) Act 1977 if the defendant does not, when sued, seek to show that the claimant has only a limited interest in the goods, but he is unlikely not to take advantage of the provisions of the Act permitting him to do so. Rules of court now enable him to ensure that the third party with an interest in the goods is brought into the action, and the court can then, in awarding damages, make an appropriate division of the value of the goods between claimant and third party.[278] **38-056**

**(b) Where the claimant relies on an immediate right to possession** It is sometimes said that where the claimant relies on a right to possession he can recover only to the extent of his limited interest. *Bloxham v Hubbard*,[279] is then cited as authority for this, but all that that case established was that a claimant with only a part share in a chattel, although he would be defeated completely in an action for conversion if the defendant took the point by plea in abatement that he was only part owner, will succeed to the extent of his interest if there is no such plea.[280] No suggestion is made that the fact that the claimant is relying on an immediate right to possession is material in such a case, and it seems that a claimant who is only a **38-057**

[274] (1865) 18 C.B. N.S. 479.

[275] The contrary decision in *Claridge v South Staffordshire Tramway Co* [1892] 1 Q.B. 422 was overruled.

[276] [1902] P. 42 CA at 60.

[277] (1862) 11 C.B. N.S. 683.

[278] For details of the relevant provisions see para.38-052, above.

[279] (1804) 5 East. 407.

[280] This was already laid down in the 17th century in *Nelthorpe v Dorrington* (1674) 2 Lev. 113 and *Dockway v Dickenson* (1696) Skinn. 640, and established for torts causing destruction of goods just before *Bloxham v Hubbard* in *Addison v Overend* (1796) 6 T.R. 766 and *Sedgworth v Overend* (1797) 7 T.R. 279.

part owner of the goods converted would be in the same position even if he relied on actual possession. *Bloxham v Hubbard*,[281] is no authority for limiting the recovery of a claimant who relies on an immediate right to possession of the whole of a chattel, and it is submitted that *The Winkfield*,[282] which is stated in terms wide enough to cover such a claimant, would apply so as to allow recovery at common law of the full value of the converted goods. And in *Chabbra Corp Pte v Jag Shakti (Owners)*,[283] the Judicial Committee of the Privy Council, on appeal from Singapore, has held claimants, who were pledgees of a cargo of salt on account of having indorsed to them bills of lading by the persons financing the purchase of the salt, entitled to claim by way of damages from the defendant shipowner, who had converted the salt by delivering it to the purchasers without the production of bills of lading, the full market value of the salt at the time and place of conversion; it was irrelevant that the claimants might be under a liability to account to the buyers for part of the amount recovered. The court founded itself upon *Swire v Leach*,[284] and *The Winkfield*[285]; no reference appears to the fact that the claimants were relying not on possession, as in those cases, but on an immediate right to possession.[286] However, the decision does not assist the English claimant since the Torts (Interference with Goods) Act 1977, which of course has no application in Singapore, now permits the defendant to ensure that the claimant cannot recover beyond the value of the limited interest.[287]

### (2) Defendant the person holding the remaining interest in the goods, and no jus tertii[288]

38-058 If the defendant is himself the other person holding an interest in the property, no third party interest is involved and accordingly the provisions of the Torts (Interference with Goods) Act 1977 have no application.[289] It is sometimes assumed that in these circumstances the claimant will not be entitled to claim the full value, but must allow a reduction by the amount of the defendant's interest. The rationale of this is that the claimant, if he recovered the full value from the defendant, would be holding the amount of the defendant's interest on the defendant's account: this on the face of it seems an absurd result. The matter, when examined,

---

281 (1804) 5 East. 407.

282 [1902] P. 42 CA: see para.38-054, above.

283 [1986] A.C. 337 PC.

284 (1865) 18 C.B. N.S. 479: see para.38-054, above.

285 [1902] P. 42 CA: see para.38-054, above. And held *London Joint Stock Bank v British Amsterdam Maritime Agency* (1910) 16 Com. Cas. 102, to the extent that it was to the contrary, to be wrongly decided.

286 And compare the first footnote in para.38-052, above. While the Singapore Court of Appeal's award, limited to the amount of the financing contributed to the purchase, was thus held to be on an incorrect legal basis, it was nevertheless upheld, and the appeal dismissed, because the Judicial Committee regarded this as the only amount it could justifiably arrive at on the different legal basis on account of the claimants' failure to adduce reliable evidence of market value.

287 See para.38-052, above; and contrast para.38-056, above.

288 The defendant must have acquired his interest before the conversion to qualify for inclusion at this point. If he acquires his interest after the conversion, *Edmondson v Nuttall* (1864) 17 C.B. N.S. 280 shows that he cannot claim a reduction in damages. This position and this case are dealt with at para.38-079, below.

289 Section 7 deals with double liability of a defendant to two or more claimants, s.8 entitles the defendant to show that a third party has a better right than the claimant: see para.38-052, above.

is however not as simple as this, and some rather careful distinctions have to be drawn.

**(a) Where the claimant relies on possession** Where a bailor retakes goods from his bailee, the bailee can recover only to the extent of his limited interest. Generally the bailee's limited interest will arise from his holding the goods as security for a debt owed to him by the owner-bailor; this is the position in the case of pledge. The matter has, however, been considered in the cases in a somewhat more complex situation where it is the creditor who is made owner of the goods under a mortgage bill of sale to give him security and it is the debtor who remains in possession, and, subsequently, the creditor wrongfully takes the goods from the debtor before default in payment. In such a case it was held in *Brierly v Kendall*,[290] that, although trespass lay,[291] the full value of the goods was not the measure of damages. The claimant could only recover an amount proportioned to his interest in them at the time of taking. This has been followed in a number of cases[292]: but in two of these, *Massey v Sladen*,[293] and *Moore v Shelley*,[294] substantial damages were nevertheless awarded. This is properly explained, it is submitted, on the ground that the mode of seizure aggravated the damages or, formerly, even justified an exemplary award.[295] In such circumstances the practical effect of deducting the amount of the defendant's interest is cancelled out. **38-059**

In the security cases it may not be the owner who has wrongfully taken, whether as the debtor giving the security or as the creditor taking it, but the non-owner out of possession. Presumably if a mortgagor takes from a mortgagee in possession the same result will be reached, limiting the mortgagee's damages to the extent of his interest, subject to increase for aggravation or possibly by an exemplary award.[296] If, however, the non-owner out of possession no longer has any proprietary interest in the goods, it would seem that, the whole proprietary interest being in the owner in possession, he can recover the full value of the goods. It was so held in *Gillard v Brittan*,[297] where an unpaid seller retook the goods from the buyer, who sued him successfully for the full value without any deduction for the unpaid purchase price. The court pointed out that the seller's action for the price was still available to him and not affected by his wrongful act.[298] This seems correct as it discourages people from taking the law into their own hands without resort to the further sanction of aggravated or, if appropriate, exemplary damages.[299] **38-060**

**(b) Where the claimant relies on an immediate right to possession** Greater difficulties arise where the claimant relies on an immediate right to possession. In **38-061**

---

290 (1852) 17 Q.B. 937.

291 The court said that trover would equally have lain.

292 *Toms v Wilson* (1863) 4 B. & S. 455; *Massey v Sladen* (1868) L.R. 4 Ex. 13; *Moore v Shelley* (1883) 8 App. Cas. 285.

293 (1868) L.R. 4 Ex. 13.

294 (1883) 8 App. Cas. 285.

295 For the modern approach to exemplary damages see Ch.13, above.

296 See the preceding paragraph.

297 (1841) 8 M. & W. 575.

298 In *Johnson v Lancashire and Yorkshire Ry* (1878) 3 C.P.D. 499 at 507, Denham J doubted whether *Gillard v Brittan* (1841) 8 M. & W. 575 could stand after *Chinery v Viall* (1860) 5 H. & N. 288, but this latter type of case (facts at para.38-063, below) differs in that the seller is no longer in a position to sue for the price.

299 See the preceding paragraph.

these cases it will always be the owner who is suing by reason of something the person in possession has done.

**38-062** In the cases concerning goods held by a bailee as security, it has been held in the case of pledge that the pledge is not determined by an improper sub-pledge or premature sale, so that the pledgor is not thereby entitled to immediate possession and cannot, therefore, bring conversion[300] at all until he has paid or tendered the debt due so as to entitle him to that immediate possession: this result was reached in *Donald v Suckling*,[301] and in *Halliday v Holgate*.[302] On the other hand, it has been held in the case of lien that the lien is determined by an improper sale,[303] thereby entitling the owner to immediate possession and to an action of conversion in which he can recover the full value of the goods without any deduction in respect of the debt due to the defendant: this result was reached in *Mulliner v Florence*.[304] There would, therefore, seem to be no room for an intermediate position in which the claimant has a right of action but will not recover the full value, and in so far as this was held to be so in an earlier case of pledge, *Johnson v Stear*,[305] it is questionable whether this decision can now stand. It is true that only nominal damages were awarded because the value of the goods pledged did not exceed the amount of the debt, but in view of *Donald v Suckling*,[306] and *Halliday v Holgate*,[307] it would seem that the claimant should have had no right of action at all till payment or tender.[308]

**38-063** There are, however, cases outside the security cases, where it has been held that an owner with a limited interest can bring conversion but subject to a deduction in respect of the other party's interest. This has arisen in contracts of sale and of hire-purchase. In the case of sale, it was held in *Chinery v Viall*,[309] that, where a buyer who had not paid the purchase money sued his seller in conversion for reselling the goods to another, the full value of the goods less the agreed price[310] was the measure of damages.[311] This rule should apply equally to carriage contracts, so that the carrier converting the goods would be liable for the full value at the time and place of

300 Nor could he bring the former (see paras 38-002 to 38-004, above) detinue.

301 (1866) L.R. 1 Q.B. 585.

302 (1868) L.R. 3 Ex. 299.

303 There is now a statutory power of sale.

304 (1878) 3 Q.B.D. 484 CA. It is true that in this case the defendant's lien was in respect of a debt due to him not from the claimant but from a third party, but it does not seem that this point affected the decision.

305 (1863) 15 C.B. N.S. 330.

306 (1866) L.R. 1 Q.B. 585.

307 (1868) L.R. 3 Ex. 299.

308 In *Donald v Suckling* (1866) L.R. 1 Q.B. 585 the conclusion in *Johnson v Stear* (1863) 15 C.B. N.S. 330 that the sale did not determine the pledge was accepted and applied: the further conclusion in *Johnson v Stear* that the wrongful conversion immediately entitled the pledgor to an action was glossed over. Bramwell LJ in *Mulliner v Florence* (1878) 3 Q.B.D. 484 CA at 490 interpreted Blackburn J in *Donald v Suckling* (1866) L.R. 1 Q.B. 585 as doubting whether *Johnson v Stear* (1863) 15 C.B. N.S. 330 was right, and Brett LJ said (*Mulliner v Florence* at 493) that *Johnson v Stear* would require "a very great consideration" before it was acted upon.

309 (1860) 5 H. & N. 288.

310 This is also the contractual measure of damages for non-delivery by a seller: there was also indeed a count in contract.

311 If on the other hand there is no privity between the parties, as where the defendant sells to another who sells to the claimant, then the claimant can sue the defendant in conversion for the full value although he has not paid the price to his own seller: *Johnson v Lancashire & Yorkshire Ry* (1878) 3 C.P.D. 499.

due delivery less the freight.[312] In the case of hire-purchase, it was held in *Belsize v Cox*,[313] that, where the hirer wrongfully sold or pledged the goods to a third party, the owner might bring conversion[314] against either hirer or third party, but could only recover the full value less the amount of hire instalments already paid him, both hirer and third party having the option, even after the conversion which it was held did not determine the proprietary part of the agreement merely because the bailment was determined, to purchase the goods by tendering the remaining unpaid instalments. In *United Dominions Trust v Parkway Motors*,[315] McNair J distinguished these two cases by reason of the fact that, in the contract before him, the hirer was prohibited from assigning either the goods or the benefit of the agreement, and therefore the owner could recover the full value from the third party assignee; but this decision has now fortunately been overruled by the Court of Appeal in *Wickham Holdings v Brooke House Motors*,[316] where the claimant finance company, claiming the full value of the car which the hirer under the hire-purchase agreement with it had wrongfully sold to the defendant dealer, was awarded only the balance outstanding under the hire-purchase agreement at the date of conversion. Lord Denning MR, after noting that in the 12th edition of this work it had been suggested that McNair J's decision "seemed inconsistent with the principles of the earlier cases",[317] said:

> "I base my decision on this: In a hire-purchase transaction there are two proprietary interests: the finance company's interest and the hirer's interest. If the hirer wrongfully sells the goods or the benefit of the agreement, in breach of the agreement, then the finance company are entitled to recover what they have lost by reason of his wrongful act. That is normally the balance outstanding on the hire-purchase price. But they are not entitled to more than they have lost."[318]

*Wickham Holdings* was followed and applied in this century in *VFS Financial Services (UK) Ltd v Euro Auctions*.[319]

In *Belvoir Finance Co v Stapleton*,[320] the Court of Appeal once again had to deal with the conversion of cars under hire-purchase agreements between hirer and finance company but with this variation, that the hire-purchase agreements entered into by the finance company and also the prior sale contracts under which the finance company had acquired the cars were illegal. In these circumstances the court again awarded as damages the balances outstanding under the hire-purchase agreements at the date of conversion, overruling the defendant's contention that the claimant finance company was entitled to no damages at all because it could not prove what these balances were without reference to the illegal hire-purchase **38-064**

312 Compare *Rew v Payne, Douthwaite* (1885) 53 L.T. 932.
313 [1914] 1 K.B. 244. Also in *Whiteley v Hilt* [1918] 2 K.B. 808 CA.
314 Or, formerly (see paras 38-002 to 38-004, above), detinue.
315 [1955] 1 W.L.R. 719.
316 [1967] 1 W.L.R. 295 CA. Winn LJ, however, preferred to reserve his opinion upon the correctness of the earlier decision rather than to join with his brethren in overruling it: at 302.
317 [1967] 1 W.L.R. 295 CA at 300. See 12th edition (1961), para.706, fn.46.
318 [1967] 1 W.L.R. 295 CA at 300–301.
319 [2007] EWHC 1492 (QB). This result could have been easily reached without, at [93]–[110], the lengthy consideration of, and lengthy citations from, Lord Nicholls's speech in *Kuwait Airways Corp v Iraqi Airways Co* [2002] 2 A.C. 883.
320 [1971] 1 Q.B. 210 CA.

agreements.[321] Sachs LJ, however, indicated that the finance company's profit under the illegal hire-purchase agreements should be eliminated in the assessment of the damages wherever there was evidence to establish it.[322]

**38-065** The distinction between the sale and hire-purchase cases on the one hand and the security cases proper on the other is, it is suggested, this: that in the former, if the owner was allowed to recover the full value as damages neither would the seller in sale be able to sue for the price[323] nor would the hirer, or third party, in hire-purchase be able to sue for the recovery of paid instalments; in the cases of security specifically taken for a debt, it is only the security that is lost to the defendant, who is still entitled to sue in personam for the debt. This distinction derives support from *Blue Sky One Ltd v Mahan Air*,[324] a case so complex that Beatson J's elaborate judgment needs to be read rather than being vainly summarised here. In essence several highly valuable aircraft connected with Iran had been converted and one of the claimants who had mortgaged one of the aircraft was held entitled to recover its full value. A whole raft of cases on recovery of limited damages by claimants with a limited interest was introduced by the defendants' counsel but after full consideration of them Beatson J dismissed them as not in point, differentiating between cases of defendants precluded and defendants not precluded, after the conversion suit, from claiming payment of the moneys owing to them.[325]

## 6 Consequential Losses

**38-066** Loss beyond that represented by the market value of the goods may be incurred by the claimant through being deprived of their use.[326] Whether he can recover for such consequential loss turns on the principles of remoteness of damage.[327]

**38-067** Thus it has been held in *Davis v Oswell*,[328] that expenditure in hiring a substitute is recoverable. In that case, the claimant, suing for the conversion of his pony, successfully claimed as consequential loss the cost of hiring other horses less the expense saved in not having to keep and feed his own pony.[329] In *Kuwait Airways*

---

321 [1971] 1 Q.B. 210 CA at 218 and 221, per Lord Denning MR and Megaw LJ respectively.

322 [1971] 1 Q.B. 210 CA at 221; there was no such evidence in the case before the court. This and the preceding case were distinguished in the very different circumstances of *Chubb Cash v Crilley & Son* [1983] 1 W.L.R. 599: see para.38-050, above.

323 This point was made in *Chinery v Viall* (1860) 5 H. & N. 288.

324 [2010] EWHC 631 (Comm).

325 See the discussion at [2010] EWHC 631 (Comm) [97] and following, with Beatson J's conclusion at [115].

326 Where the trial judge in *Trafigura Beheer BV v Mediterranean Shipping Co SA* [2007] 2 All E.R. 149 (Comm) had awarded the value of the goods at the time of judgment which was higher than the value at conversion, Longmore LJ pointed out in the Court of Appeal, [2008] 1 All E.R. (Comm) 385 at [41], that alternatively the judge could have awarded the increase in value between conversion and judgment as damages for loss of use. The case is at para.38-020, above.

327 Compare *Re Simms* [1934] Ch. 1 CA at 17, per Lord Hanworth: "Special damage may in certain cases be allowed, but it must be, as in all other cases of damages, the direct result of the tort." Remoteness apart, the claimant has the burden of proving that consequential loss has been suffered. This the claimant failed to do in *Checkprice (UK) Ltd v Revenue and Customs Commissioners* [2010] EWHC 682 (Admin) in respect of the conversion of cider for which there was an entitlement to compensatory damages: see at [54] to [55] and the facts at para.38-009, above.

328 (1837) 7 C. & P. 804.

329 Contrast *Strand Electric Co v Brisford Entertainments* [1952] 2 Q.B. 246 CA at 254 (a former detinue case dealt with later in this paragraph), per Denning LJ: "Suppose a man used a car in his business, and owing to its detention he had to hire a substitute at an increased cost, he would clearly

*Corp v Iraq Airways Co*,[330] an airline's aircraft had been converted, with four planes destroyed and six detained, and the claim for the acquisition of substitute capacity until replacement or return was held by the Court of Appeal allowable in principle.[331] The House of Lords[332] affirmed the award for cost of substitution for the detained aircraft.[333] And it has already been submitted[334] that the claimant should be allowed to recover as consequential loss the amount by which the market value of the goods has risen between conversion and judgment.[335] Moreover, and particularly now that detinue has been absorbed by conversion,[336] it would seem that the claimant should be able to recover the market rate of hire for the goods between conversion and judgment, certainly where he was in the habit of hiring out the goods and possibly even where he was not. In *Hillesden Securities v Ryjack*,[337] recovery was allowed in conversion, in an action brought after the abolition of detinue, of the full market hire of a Rolls Royce motorcar, which the hirer from the claimant had wrongfully sold to the defendants, from the date of its conversion by the defendants until the date of its return, before judgment, to the claimant; the case concerned a profit-earning chattel and one which the claimant would have hired out, and the defendants did hire out, at a profit.[338] And in the important detinue case of *Strand Electric Co v Brisford Entertainments*,[339] where the defendants had refused to return to the claimants certain profit-earning electrical equipment which the claimants hired out in the course of their business, and which the defendants had made use of during the detention for their own ends, the Court of Appeal held that the claimants were entitled in the circumstances to recover as damages[340] the full market rate of hire of such equipment for the whole of the period of detention.[341] It was held immaterial that the claimants might not have realised the full hire during the detention period by reason of the fact that only 75 per cent of their stock of equipment was generally out on hire, that not infrequently some of it was loaned gratis and that some of it might have been accidentally damaged or destroyed. As for the refusal of the trial judge in *Tanks and Vessels Industries Ltd v Devon Cider Co Ltd*,[342] after a detailed consideration of the *Kuwait Airways* and *Strand Electric* cases, to award to the claimant company damages for loss of use of its industrial plant and equipment converted, this was surely wrong. The trial judge was so persuaded by her drawing some, in this context irrelevant, distinctions between

---

be able to recover the cost of the substitute."

330 [2002] 2 A.C. 883 CA; facts at para.38-071, below.

331 See at [2002] 2 A.C. 883 CA at [628] and following, for the aircraft destroyed and at [634] and following, for the aircraft detained. The claim in respect of the destroyed aircraft failed for other reasons.

332 [2002] 2 A.C. 883 HL.

333 See Lord Nicholls at [95], Lord Hoffmann at [130].

334 See para.38-018, above.

335 Provided he brings an action within a reasonable time after he knew or ought to have known of the conversion: see para.38-018, above.

336 See paras 38-002 to 38-004, above.

337 [1983] 1 W.L.R. 959.

338 [1983] 1 W.L.R. 959 at 962A.

339 [1952] 2 Q.B. 246 CA.

340 A recovery which, however, would not be by way of consequential loss but would represent the normal measure of damages in detinue.

341 Somervell and Denning LJJ adopted the analogy of recovery of mesne profits in the case of detention of land: [1952] 2 Q.B. 246 CA at 252, 253–254, respectively.

342 [2009] EWHC 1360 Ch.

conversion and the former detinue and between the claimant electing for redelivery and electing for damages.[343]

**38-068** Of the argument that the claimants might not have found hirers, Romer LJ in *Strand Electric* said, in a passage the reasoning of which must apply equally to conversion as to detinue:

> "A defendant who has wrongfully detained and profited from the property of someone else cannot avail himself of such a hypothesis as this. It does not lie in the mouth of such a defendant to suggest that the owner might not have found a hirer."[344]

This was an attempt, concurred in by Somervell LJ, to press the result into the strait-jacket of loss to the claimant. For this reason both Lords Justices reserved their opinions, "in this comparatively virgin field",[345] as to whether the claimant would be entitled to a similar measure of damages if the property had not been profit-earning, or if the claimant had never applied it for the earning of profit.[346] Denning LJ on the other hand, recognising that even the measure the Court of Appeal was giving went far beyond the claimants' loss, did not limit his view of the defendant's liability in this way. "It is an action against him", he said,

> "because he has had the benefit of the goods. It resembles, therefore, an action for restitution rather than an action of tort. But it is unnecessary to place it in any formal category."[347]

Looked at from this angle, the claimant could always recover, beyond his proved loss, to the extent of the benefit conferred on the defendant by his use of the goods, and it would seem that for Denning LJ this same result could have been arrived at in an action of conversion as much as in one of detinue.[348] And with the arrival of restitutionary damages on the scene[349] it may be that such claims are destined to move into their orbit and become one of the major illustrations of this new-found category of damages.

**38-069** By contrast, the claimant's loss of profits on contracts made with third parties has tended to form too remote an item of damage. That such a loss may be recoverable is undoubtedly recognised,[350] but it has been allowed only where it could have been anticipated by the defendant. Thus in *Cash and Brown v Chief Constable of*

---

[343] See the judgment at [2009] EWHC 1360 Ch at [62] to [67].

[344] [1952] 2 Q.B. 246 CA at 257. The *Mediana* [1900] A.C. 113 and similar cases (see paras 38-034 and following, above) were distinguished on the ground that where the tort involved damage and not misappropriation the defendant did not have the use of the goods although the claimant was deprived of them for a time. Lord Halsbury's dictum there (at 118), that damages are to be assessed on the same principle whatever the cause of action, trover, detinue or negligence, was not approved by Somervell LJ ([1952] 2 Q.B. 246 CA at 251). This way of distinguishing *The Mediana* by Somervell and Denning LJJ shows that the Court of Appeal must have been thinking not only of loss to the claimant but of benefit to the defendant.

[345] [1952] 2 Q.B. 246 CA at 257, per Romer LJ.

[346] [1952] 2 Q.B. 246 CA at 252, per Somervell LJ, and at 257, per Romer LJ.

[347] [1952] 2 Q.B. 246 CA at 255.

[348] See, too, his statement that "if the goods are retained by the wrongdoer up till judgment the hiring charge runs up to that time … but if the goods have been disposed of by the wrongdoer the hiring charge will cease at the time of such disposal": at 255.

[349] See Ch.14, above.

[350] Contrast *Re Simms* [1934] Ch. 1 CA at 29, per Romer LJ: "It may be conceded that in an action for the conversion of chattels a plaintiff may in certain cases recover by way of special damage any loss of profit from the use of the chattels that he may have suffered by the conversion."

*Lancashire*,[351] where the first claimant's horse had been improperly detained by the police for some three months, he was held entitled to damages for the lost sales of foals which would have been sired by the horse during this period of detention.[352] Here the profits would have been made by a sale not of the item converted itself but of its product. In *Bodley v Reynolds*,[353] the claimant recovered for his loss of custom by reason of the defendant's conversion of the tools of his trade, but of this decision it was said in *France v Gaudet*,[354] that the defendant must be shown to have known that in the nature of things inconvenience beyond the loss of the tools would be caused to the claimant.[355] The leading case in this connection is *The Arpad*,[356] where the Court of Appeal[357] held that the claimant could not recover as damages for conversion of part of a cargo of wheat his loss of profit on a sale of the wheat before the conversion. The Court of Appeal explained *France v Gaudet*,[358] where a buyer had successfully claimed in conversion against his seller, who refused to deliver, the price at which he had resold the goods to a third party, as turning on the fact that the resale price had been taken merely because it was evidence of the market price in the particular circumstances of the case.[359] It may be, however, that *The Arpad*,[360] does not accord entirely with the general rules of remoteness in tort damages and it has been suggested elsewhere[361] that, if the matter should come up before the House of Lords, their Lordships may well prefer the strong dissent of Scrutton LJ.[362]

*The Arpad* was nevertheless followed by the Court of Appeal in *Saleslease Ltd* **38-070**

---

351 [2008] EWHC 396 Ch.

352 Various other items claimed were disallowed, such as the cost of acquiring another horse as the detained horse was still owned by the first claimant and its value had not been shown to be diminished.

353 (1846) 8 Q.B. 779.

354 (1871) L.R. 6 Q.B. 199 at 205.

355 It was also held in *Wood v Bell* (1856) 5 E. & B. 772, where *Bodley v Reynolds* (1846) 8 Q.B. 779 was cited and approved, that special damage was recoverable but it is not clear in what the special damage consisted.

356 [1934] P. 189 CA.

357 Scrutton LJ dissenting.

358 (1871) L.R. 6 Q.B. 199.

359 In *France v Gaudet* (1871) L.R. 6 Q.B. 199 the court had given these damages not exactly as consequential loss but because the sale price represented "a special value, attached by special circumstances to the article converted": at 205, per Mellor J. Greer LJ in *The Arpad* [1934] P. 189 CA at 219 said that Mellor J's reasons could not be supported.

360 [1934] P. 189 CA.

361 See paras 8-106 to 8-108, above.

362 *Moon v Raphael* (1835) 2 Bing. N.C. 310 and *Re Simms* [1934] Ch. 1 CA, are two further cases where somewhat similar consequential losses were refused, but on grounds of pleading and causation respectively. They are, therefore, only of indirect assistance. In the former recovery was refused as the damage was not specially pleaded, but Tindal CJ expressed the view that the special damage, which consisted of rent paid for the premises in which the goods converted were lying in charge of the defendant sheriff, was irrecoverable, "not being a damage necessarily consequent" upon the conversion. In the latter the defendant, a receiver, converted plant and machinery of a bankrupt, a builder, and used them to complete a number of the bankrupt's building contracts. The trustee in bankruptcy failed to recover the profits on these contracts from the defendant, but there was no evidence to show to what extent the plant and machinery were essential to carrying out the contracts: see, especially, at 22. Compare also *Archer v Williams* (1846) 2 C. & K. 26, where in detinue (now abolished: see paras 38-002 to 38-004, above) for scrip certificates, it was held that the loss caused by the claimant's being deprived of a further allotment of shares by reason of the detention of the scrip certificates was too remote.

*v Davis*[363]; again, however, there was a dissent though on the basis of the foreseeability of the damage. The court held that, in assessing damages for the tort of conversion, a consequential loss above the market value which was special to the circumstances of the particular claimant but not made known to the tortfeasor was too remote and therefore irrecoverable. It followed that the claimant could not recover damages for the loss of a lucrative leasing contract fortuitously available with only one particular customer since the defendant could not have foreseen that by his retaining the goods the only possibility of entering into a leasing contract would be lost. The issue of remoteness and foreseeability was again considered by the Court of Appeal in *Kuwait Airways Corp v Iraq Airways Co*,[364] where it was accepted that the court was bound by *The Arpad* and *Saleslease* to require foreseeability for recovery. However, in the House of Lords[365] Lord Nicholls, in the leading speech, drew a distinction between the converter who is knowing and dishonest and the converter who is not, and expressed the opinion—though, as he said, this was not strictly necessary for his decision in the case—that, while the remoteness test for the latter should be that of foreseeability, the test for the former should be the wider one of whether the loss arose directly and naturally.[366] Lord Hope said specifically that he wished to associate himself with Lord Nicholls's approach on this[367] while Lord Hoffmann expressed agreement with Lord Nicholls's speech in general.[368] In *Nigerian National Shipping Lines v Mutual Ltd, The Windfall*,[369] on the other hand, it appears to have been accepted that the loss of profit on the sale of a vessel was recoverable once it was shown that that loss resulted from the wrongful detention. It may be that the sale price reflected the market price at the time of the sale, so that only the normal measure was being awarded, but there is no indication that this was the case or was considered to be relevant.[370] Where cargo owners claimed to recover from converting shipowners costs and other losses arising from hedging which the owners had arranged for the cargo in order to safeguard against fluctuations in the volatile copper prices, their claim failed at first instance in *Trafigura Beheer BV v Mediterranean Shipping Co SA*,[371] these losses being held to be too remote. That cargo owners would enter into hedging arrangements was not reasonably foreseeable by shipowners.[372]

**38-071** *Kuwait Airways Corp v Iraq Airways Co*,[373] affirmed by the House of Lords,[374] is a decision of enormous complexity—the judgment of the Court of Appeal runs to over 100 pages and to just short of 700 paragraphs—raising many issues of damages among which is that of recovery for lost profits. After the invasion and occupation of Kuwait by Iraq in 1990, 10 aircraft of the Kuwait airline were converted by the Iraqi airline. Four of the planes were subsequently destroyed in a bombing

---

363 [1999] 1 W.L.R. 1664.
364 [2002] 2 A.C. 883 CA; facts at para.38-071, below.
365 [2002] 2 A.C. 883 HL.
366 [2002] 2 A.C. 883 HL at [99]–[104].
367 [2002] 2 A.C. 883 HL at [169].
368 [2002] 2 A.C. 883 HL at [125].
369 [1998] 2 Lloyd's Rep. 664.
370 See [1998] 2 Lloyd's Rep. 664 at 672, col.2 to 673, col.1.
371 [2007] 2 All E.R. 149 (Comm).
372 [2007] 2 All E.R. 149 (Comm) at [127]–[131]. This issue was not pursued in the appeal, [2008] 1 All E.R. (Comm) 385 CA, which was by the shipowners. The case is at para.38-020, above.
373 [2002] 2 A.C. 883 CA.
374 [2002] 2 A.C. 883 HL.

attack by international forces; the other six were taken out of Kuwait and detained until their eventual return to the Kuwait airline in 1992. The Court of Appeal rightly considered that a claim for loss of profits was appropriate for the destroyed aircraft, and could have succeeded[375] but for the fact that the claim failed for other reasons,[376] and that a claim in respect of the detained aircraft was also appropriate in principle but remained subject to proof.[377] While reliance was placed upon the many cases concerning destruction of ships,[378] including in particular *The Liesbosch*,[379]the *Kuwait* case properly seems to go beyond them in its preparedness to allow loss of profits.[380] However, the period for which the loss of profit would be allowable did not extend beyond the time when the destroyed four aircraft could have been replaced and when the detained six were returned. The House of Lords affirmed[381] this award for loss of profits in respect of the detained aircraft[382] without, however, any reference to the authorities on the destruction of ships.[383]

Outside loss of profits *Sandeman Coprimar SA v Transitos y Transportes Integrales SL*,[384] produced a consequential loss for which there was no recovery because it was of a type that was not reasonably foreseeable. The claimants, exporters of whisky to Spain, acquired from the Spanish tax authorities tax seals of nominal value for use in sealing their whisky bottles to indicate that Spanish excise duty had been duly paid by them. They contracted with a carrier for the carriage by road from Spain to Scotland of cartons containing these tax seals. This carrier sub-contracted the carriage to a second carrier who in turn subcontracted it to a third carrier. The cargo was lost in the course of carriage and the claimants were required to pay to the Spanish tax authorities under a guarantee an amount equivalent to the excise duty which would have been recovered on the bottles to which the seals should have been attached. The claimants failed to recover this amount from the second and third carriers, who were liable as sub-bailees in conversion, as neither could reasonably have appreciated the nature of the goods in the cartons or the consequences of their loss. While recognising that **38-072**

> "there can be problems in applying a test of foreseeability to carriers who handle consolidated containers of many different varieties of goods",

Lord Phillips delivering the judgment of the court concluded that

> "no carrier without specific knowledge of the nature of [tax seals] and of the guarantee that has to be given to the Spanish authorities for their release, could envisage that the loss of a number of cartons could give rise to the type of liability experienced by [the claimants] in this case".[385]

---

375 See [2002] 2 A.C. 883 at CA at [627].

376 See [2002] 2 A.C. 883 at CA at [404].

377 See [2002] 2 A.C. 883 at CA at [652].

378 [2002] 2 A.C. 883 at CA at [587]–[598] and [621]–[626]. These cases are at paras 37-065 to 37-070, above.

379 [1933] A.C. 449.

380 See, especially, [2002] 2 A.C. 883 CA at [623].

381 [2002] 2 A.C. 883 HL.

382 See Lord Nicholls at [2002] 2 A.C. 883 HL at [95], Lord Hoffmann at [130].

383 Damages for lost profits, user damages and damages to cover the cost of replacement aircraft were eventually assessed and awarded in this very long-running case: *Kuwait Airways Corp v Iraqi Airways Co* [2007] EWHC 1474 (Comm).

384 [2003] Q.B. 1270 CA.

385 [2003] Q.B. 1270 CA at [28]; see also at [25]–[31]. The claim against the second and third carriers,

**38-073** The problem of the limits within which policy will allow recovery arose in conversion in another, less usual, form in *Thurston v Charles*.[386] The defendant, a member of a town corporation, wrongfully communicated to the other members a letter written to the claimant by a third party which contained statements defamatory of the claimant. A claim in defamation failed because the communication was held privileged, but the claimant succeeded in his claim for trespass and conversion, and compensation for the injury to his reputation was, in effect, given in the damages. On the other hand Lord Esher MR stated categorically in *Dixon v Calcraft*,[387] that such damages in an action for seizing a chattel were unknown to English law. Somewhat similarly in *Brewer v Dew*,[388] an action of trespass for seizing goods under an unfounded claim for debt, damages were given for the annoyance and disturbance to the claimant in his business, and although this was applied to give such compensatory damages in *Smith v Enright*,[389] it appeared to have been interpreted as a case of exemplary damages in *Owen & Smith v Reo Motors*,[390] and so applied; however, Lord Devlin in *Rookes v Barnard*,[391] interpreted the award in *Owen & Smith v Reo Motors*[392] itself, as being one of compensatory damages.

**38-074** In *Lonrho v Fayed (No.5)*,[393] a case of conspiracy, the Court of Appeal has now preferred the view expressed in *Dixon v Calcraft*,[394] to the decision arrived at in *Thurston v Charles*.[395] However, it may be that the other cases involving actions for misappropriating goods are not affected by the overturning of *Thurston* for either of two reasons, namely that they are not cases where protection from claims other than in defamation was needed or that they are not cases where the damages were given for non-pecuniary loss of reputation but only for the pecuniary loss and for injured feelings. The arguments are set out fully when dealing with remoteness of damage.[396] It cannot be said that the law has yet clearly committed itself to deciding whether no such damages should be allowed in actions for misappropriation of goods.[397]

---

which was in negligence as well as conversion, could not have been in contract because of the absence of privity. For the successful claim in contract against the contracting carrier see para.8-215, above. There were also complex claims under the Convention scheduled to the Carriage of Goods by Road Act 1965 not relevant here.

386 (1905) 21 T.L.R. 659.

387 [1892] 1 Q.B. 458 CA. The action was not in tort but upon a statute.

388 (1843) 11 M. & W. 625.

389 (1893) 63 L.J.Q.B. 220.

390 (1934) 151 L.T. 274 CA.

391 [1964] A.C. 1129 at 1229.

392 (1934) 151 L.T. 274 CA.

393 [1993] 1 W.L.R. 1489 CA.

394 [1892] 1 Q.B. 458 CA.

395 (1905) 21 T.L.R. 659.

396 See paras 8-128 to 8-130, above.

397 Damages for injury to feelings were held to be unavailable in *Cash and Brown v Chief Constable of Lancashire* [2008] EWHC 396 Ch where the first claimant's horse had been wrongfully detained for three months: see at [57].

## 7. Effect on Damages of Redelivery of the Goods or Their Equivalent

### (1) Where the claimant accepts redelivery

Where the defendant offers and the claimant accepts redelivery of the goods at any time before the action has proceeded to judgment,[398] this does not go to bar the action but goes only in reduction or mitigation of the damages.[399] Thus the claimant may proceed for damages resulting from his being out of possession of the goods, and although he may succeed in recovering only nominal damages he is entitled at least to this.[400] Thus nominal damages were awarded in *Moon v Raphael*,[401] and *Hiort v L.N.W. Ry*,[402] Bramwell LJ saying in the latter that the claimant was so entitled **38-075**

> "because a conversion cannot be purged, and if a defendant is guilty of conversion he must pay some damages".[403]

The position is the same where there has been redelivery to the claimant before any action by him has been brought,[404] as in *Kani v Barnet LBC*,[405] where the claimant's cars were seized by the defendant borough council but eventually returned to him before any claim for damages had been made by him.[406]

With a straightforward redelivery of the goods no difficulties arise.[407] However, more subtle situations have come before the courts. **38-076**

(1) A notional redelivery can go in reduction of the damages. The authority for this is *Hiort v L.N.W. Ry*.[408] The defendant warehousemen converted corn which **38-077**

[398] The text is concerned with redelivery before judgment. Where the claimant accepts an offer by the defendant at the trial for redelivery after judgment, judgment may then be entered by consent and will be for the value of the goods, to be reduced to a nominal sum upon their being given up: *Wintle v Rudge* (1841) 5 Jur. 274. In such circumstances it would seem that the claimant cannot refuse to take the goods when tendered after judgment.

[399] See *Edmondson v Nuttall* (1864) 17 C.B. N.S. 280 at 294, per Willes J, cited with approval by the Judicial Committee in *Solloway v McLaughlin* [1938] A.C. 247 PC at 258. This principle has been long recognised.

[400] On the other hand, in the former (see paras 38-002 to 38-004, above) detinue acceptance of the goods before judgment went to bar further maintenance of the action for the goods or their value, since the action of detinue was primarily for the return of the goods: *Crossfield v Such* (1852) 8 Ex. 159. An action for damages for detention then lay only if the claimant could prove he had suffered loss.

[401] (1835) 2 Bing. N.C. 310. There was a claim for special damage at the trial, but the court refused to allow it as it had not been pleaded.

[402] (1879) 4 Ex. D. 188 CA.

[403] (1879) 4 Ex. D. 188 CA at 195. *Evans v Lewis* (1838) 3 Dowl. 819 is not inconsistent with the rule that an action lies for nominal damages, for in that case there had not been redelivery but payment into court and, as Lord Abinger said, the jury may have found for the defendant because they thought the amount paid in covered any damages beyond the value of the goods themselves.

[404] This principle also has been long recognised; see, e.g., Bull. N.P. 46: "If a man take my horse and ride him, and after deliver him to me, yet I may have trover against him, for the riding was a conversion, and the redelivery will only go in mitigation of damages."

[405] [2010] EWCA Civ 818 CA.

[406] Damages awarded were in respect of damage to the cars during their detention but not in respect of the claim that the cars, if not detained, could have been sold before the market fell as the claimant was unable to prove this: see at [2010] EWCA Civ 818 CA at [31] and following.

[407] It is immaterial that the redelivery is not made by the defendant; in the case of a series of conversions the return of the goods by one of the converters will go in reduction of damages in an action against another of the converters.

[408] (1879) 4 Ex. D. 188 CA.

they held for the claimant by delivering it to the claimant's agent in anticipation of, but without, a delivery order. Later, a third party who had bought the corn from the claimant obtained from the claimant a delivery order to himself, and this he indorsed to the claimant's agent who forwarded it to the defendants as the delivery order he had promised to send them. This was held to be, in the words of Bramwell LJ,

> "equivalent to a return of the goods. I do not mean to say that it is a return, but it is in the nature of a return of the goods, and the same reason for reducing the damages to a nominal amount applies."[409]

**38-078** (2) A delivery to the claimant of an equivalent article will go in reduction of damages. This appears from *Solloway v McLaughlin*.[410] The defendant stockbrokers converted shares of the claimant, their client, by selling them. Later, when the claimant closed his account with them, they bought the same number of shares in the same company at the lower price to which the market had fallen, and handed them over to the claimant who took them without knowledge of the conversion. The damages awarded in the claimant's subsequent action were the value of the shares at the date of the conversion less the value of the shares bought in replacement at the time when the claimant accepted them.[411]

**38-079** (3) Where the claimant's debts to the defendant have been paid by the goods or the proceeds of the goods converted, the situation is generally that in which the defendant at the time of the conversion has an interest in the goods: whether he is entitled to a reduction in the damages awarded against him has already been considered in connection with claims by claimants with a limited interest in the goods.[412] Where, however, the defendant has no interest in the goods at the time of the conversion, it is clear that the acquisition of such an interest subsequently, and the consequent use of the goods in satisfaction of the claimant's debt to him, will not limit the claimant's damages: he will be entitled to the full value of the goods. This point was decided in *Edmondson v Nuttall*.[413] The defendant, having converted goods by refusing to give them up in anticipation of levying execution on them in respect of a judgment obtained by him against the claimant, issued execution the following day, caused the goods to be seized and sold, and applied the proceeds in satisfaction of the debt. It was held that the claimant was entitled in trover to recover the full value of the goods without taking into account, in reduction of the damages, the fact that the goods had been subsequently applied in satisfaction of the claimant's debt to the defendant.

**38-080** (4) Where the claimant's debts to a third party have been paid by the goods or the proceeds of the goods converted, there is authority that this may sometimes go in reduction of the damages. This is clear where the defendant is compelled to pay the claimant's debt, a situation which may arise where the goods converted are properly taken by a third party, as by distress or in execution, in satisfaction of a debt owed to him. In *Plevin v Henshall*,[414] such a reduction was allowed even where the distress, by which the claimant's landlord took the goods converted by the

409 (1879) 4 Ex. D. 188 CA at 196.

410 [1938] A.C. 247 PC.

411 The claimant indeed did not dispute this deduction, the argument being on another point: see para.38-014, above.

412 See paras 38-058 to 38-065, above.

413 (1864) 17 C.B. N.S. 280.

414 (1833) 10 Bing. 24.

defendant in satisfaction of the claimant's rent, occurred after judgment in the claimant's conversion action. A more elaborate situation has arisen where the defendant has converted the claimant's cheques by transferring them to a third party who has then used them in discharge of the claimant's debts. In *Underwood v Bank of Liverpool*,[415] the defendant bank had converted cheques of the claimant company by crediting them to the company's sole director. Though the question of damages was not directly up for decision, Scrutton LJ took the view, with which Atkin LJ agreed, that the fact that the sole director had used some of the proceeds of the cheques to discharge the claimant company's liabilities might go in reduction of damages, and an inquiry as to the exact facts in this regard was directed. He referred to Byles J's view in *Edmondson v Nuttall*,[416] that

> "you could not mitigate damages for conversion of a bag of money by showing that the defendant had out of the bag of money converted paid the debt of the plaintiff",

but added that he was

> "not sure that the learned judge had in his mind the Equity doctrines under which a person who had in fact paid the debts of another without authority was allowed the advantage of his payments".[417]

On the other hand, in *Lloyds Bank v Chartered Bank*,[418] where again a claimant was suing for conversion of cheques by a defendant bank, in this case by paying them to the claimant's accountant, the fact that the accountant had used some of the cheques to pay his debts to the claimant was held not to go in reduction of the damages. Scrutton LJ said that

> "whether any particular payment to the plaintiff by one of the wrongdoers reduces the damages for conversion must depend on the facts of each case, and cannot be settled by mere proof of receipt without more".[419]

It would seem that the vital difference between these two cases is that in *Underwood v Bank of Liverpool*,[420] the party to whom the defendant bank paid the cheque, himself also a converter, paid debts of the claimant owing to others, whereas in

---

415 [1924] 1 K.B. 775 CA.

416 (1864) 17 C.B. N.S. 280 at 297.

417 *Underwood v Bank of Liverpool* [1924] 1 K.B. 775 CA at 794, referring to *Bannatyne v MacIver* [1906] 1 K.B. 103 CA and *Reid v Rigby* [1894] 2 Q.B. 40 (Atkin LJ agreed at 799). The equity doctrine to which Scrutton LJ was referring deals with the situation where an agent has borrowed money on his principal's behalf but without his authority and used it to pay off liabilities of the principal. In these circumstances the lender, who cannot sue the principal on the contract of loan, is subrogated to the rights of the principal's creditors who have been paid with the money lent, and to this extent the lender can recover: see, in particular, *Brooks & Co v Blackburn Benefit Society* (1882) 22 Ch. D. 61 CA (affirmed (1884) 9 App. Cas. 857); *Reid v Rigby* [1894] 2 Q.B. 40; *Bannatyne v MacIver* [1906] 1 K.B. 103 CA; *Reversion Fund and Insurance Co v Maison Cosway* [1913] 1 K.B. 364 CA. Wright J, in an analogous claim for money had and received by the claimant company against the defendant bank who had paid the company's cheques signed by only one director, approved of the Court of Appeal's judgments in *Underwood v Bank of Liverpool* [1924] 1 K.B. 775 CA, on this point, and applied them to the analogous situation: *Liggett (Liverpool) v Barclays Bank* [1928] 1 K.B. 48.

418 [1929] 1 K.B. 40 CA.

419 [1929] 1 K.B. 40 CA at 61.

420 [1924] 1 K.B. 775 CA.

*Lloyds Bank v Chartered Bank*,[421] he appropriated the money in payment of debts he himself owed to the claimant. However, the details have in no way been worked out by the courts: a clear rule awaits further decisions.

## (2) Where the claimant refuses to accept redelivery

**38-081** Since the claimant in conversion is suing not for the goods but for their value, it is logical that he should be entitled to demand their value as damages and to reject any offer, made by the defendant before the action has proceeded to judgment,[422] to return them, even though the goods have in no way deteriorated since the time of conversion.[423] The courts however soon tempered logic with practicality, and as early as 1762 in *Fisher v Prince*,[424] it was laid down that, if the goods were brought into court by the defendant in the same condition as before the tort, and the claimant was claiming no consequential loss above the value of the goods, the court would stay proceedings upon the goods being handed over and costs paid. Lord Mansfield and Wilmot J concurred in the distinction

> "that where trover is brought for a specific chattel, of an ascertained quantity and quality, and unattended with any circumstances that can enhance the damages above the real value, but that its real and ascertained value must be the sole measure of the damages, there the specific thing demanded may be brought into Court ... [But] where there is an uncertainty either as to the quantity or quality of the thing demanded, or that there is any tort accompanying it that may enhance the damages above the real value of the thing, and there is no rule whereby to estimate the additional value, there it shall not be brought in."[425]

And where, in conversion for several chattels, the defendant offered to redeliver one of them in *Earle v Holderness*,[426] the court stayed the proceedings in respect of the one chattel and allowed the action to continue as to the rest. But in *Tucker v Wright*,[427] it was firmly laid down that proceedings would not be stayed where there was uncertainty as to the value of the goods which might have been materially injured, thus justifying a claim for more than nominal damages even if the goods were returned.[428] Yet in such circumstances the court may, as in *Earle v Holder-*

---

421 [1929] 1 K.B. 40 CA.

422 The text is concerned with refusal of an offer made before judgment. If the claimant refuses an offer of redelivery after judgment and insists on levying execution on the judgment for damages, it would seem to be too late for the defendant to compel the claimant to take the goods. One exception to this is where the judgment of the court is specifically aimed at compelling the defendant to make redelivery. This is the case with actions for the conversion of title deeds where the court may award as damages the full value of the estate, but to be reduced to a nominal sum on redelivery of the deeds. Where, in *Coombe v Sansom* (1822) 1 Dow & Ry. 201, the claimant then refused to accept the deeds and insisted on the full damages awarded, the court made him accept.

423 On the other hand, in the former (see paras 38-002 to 38-004, above) detinue it was completely logical for the court to stay proceedings since the action of detinue was primarily for the return of the goods. Alternatively, as in *Phillips v Hayward* (1835) 3 Dowl. 362, the court would put the claimant on terms that he pay the costs in the action for damages for detention should he fail to prove that he had suffered loss.

424 (1762) 3 Burr. 1363.

425 (1762) 3 Burr. 1363 at 1364. That the rule applies equally to trespass is shown by *Pickering v Truste* (1796) 7 T.R. 53.

426 (1828) 4 Bing. 462.

427 (1826) 3 Bing. 601.

428 In *Whitten v Fuller* (1773) 2 Wm. Bl. 902 the court refused a stay for the same reason, but it is not clear upon what the court based its refusal in *Makinson v Rawlinson* (1822) 9 Price 460, the applica-

*ness*,[429] put the claimant on terms that he pay the costs in the action for damages if he should fail to prove that he has suffered loss.

## 8. Exemplary Damages

The whole approach to exemplary damages was changed by the decision in *Rookes v Barnard*,[430] since approved in *Broome v Cassell & Co*,[431] and is treated in detail elsewhere.[432] Yet for conversion, it was said in the 13th edition of this work in 1972, the result may be to enlarge rather than to limit the scope for exemplary damages, and this has now proved to be the case. For formerly, it used generally to be said, though for no very good reason, that at common law exemplary damages could not be recovered in conversion as opposed to trespass[433] and no cases of exemplary awards had appeared before *Rookes v Barnard*.[434] Since *Rookes* however, although exemplary damages are recoverable only if the circumstances of the case bring it within one of the three categories set out by Lord Devlin,[435] and although it is only the second common law category directed to profit-motivated torts which is likely to prove relevant for conversion,[436] exemplary damages should now be awardable in torts where formerly they had not run. And this argument has been accepted by the House of Lords in *Kuddus v Chief Constable of Leicestershire*,[437] overruling the Court of Appeal's adoption of the contrary view in *A.B. v South West Water Services*,[438] and holding that it is the features of the defendant's behaviour rather than the cause of action sued upon which have to be looked at in order to decide upon the appropriateness of an exemplary award.[439] **38-082**

The tort of conversion also provides the only clear example of the category of exemplary damages authorised by statute: the Reserve and Auxiliary Forces (Protection of Civil Interests) Act 1951, which by Pt I gives protection to servicemen against remedies involving interference with goods, such as execution, distress and the like, provides by s.13(2) that in any action for damages for conversion in respect of such goods the court may take into account the defendant's conduct and award exemplary damages. But Lord Kilbrandon in *Broome v Cassell & Co*,[440] sought to interpret the "exemplary" in the subsection as referring to aggravated damages. **38-083**

---

tion by the defendant being on an affidavit that the condition of the animal converted had improved since the tort.

429 (1828) 4 Bing. 462.

430 [1964] A.C. 1129.

431 [1972] A.C. 1027.

432 Ch.13, above.

433 The argument for treating conversion and trespass alike in relation to exemplary damages under the former law is set out in the 12th edition of this work (1961) at para.713.

434 [1964] A.C. 1129.

435 See paras 13-017 to 13-030, above.

436 See the comments in connection with the unauthorised mining cases at para.38-035, above.

437 [2002] 2 A.C. 122.

438 [1993] Q.B. 507 CA.

439 See paras 13-011 and following, above.

440 [1972] A.C. 1027 at 1133G.

## III. Trespass

38-084 Trespass to goods straddles the boundaries of loss by misappropriation and of loss by damage or destruction. Hence it bears affinities on the one hand to conversion and on the other hand to the tort of negligence. The damages are, of course, to be worked out on different principles in the case of loss by misappropriation and in the case of loss by damage or destruction. Only the former falls for consideration here.[441]

38-085 In the case of loss by misappropriation the measure of damages in trespass is in general the same as in conversion. The two torts are, indeed, frequently coincident, with either action available to the claimant. The same rules will apply as to the time and place at which the value of the goods is to be assessed, as to the measure of damages where the claimant has a limited interest in the goods, and as to recovery for consequential losses.[442] The cases, however, do point to some possible differences, but none of these either is convincing in principle or, now that the forms of action have gone, should be important in practice.

38-086 One possible difference arises where the item in question has been severed from land and has thus become a chattel. If its value is greater as a chattel than as part of the land, there is no difference in respect of damages between trespass to goods and conversion: this is amply illustrated by the cases of unauthorised mining.[443] But if its value is greater as part of the land than as a chattel, the greater value has been disallowed in conversion but allowed in trespass. Thus, in relation to the seizing of fixtures under an illegal distress, it was held in *Clarke v Holford*,[444] that the claimant can only recover their value as chattels in conversion, while in *Moore v Drinkwater*,[445] he was allowed their greater value as fixtures in trespass. "Fixtures *in situ*," said Erle CJ,

> "are worth far more than they are when severed, and the very wrong complained of was for the severance."[446]

Outside distress cases it was held in *Thompson v Pettit*,[447] that where trustees in bankruptcy seized and sold fixtures which the bankrupt had assigned to the claimant as security for a loan, the fixtures being in a house of which the bankrupt was lessee, the claimant could recover in trespass the greater value the fixtures had if valued between incoming and outgoing tenant, since he would have been entitled, on non-payment of the loan, to sell them to the eventual purchaser of the term and might well have done so. However, a strict analysis shows that these cases allowing the value as fixtures were actions of trespass to land, where the measure is properly the fall in the value of the land. If the claim was for trespass to goods, the

---

441 The latter is considered in Ch.37, above. There will, occasionally, be trespass to goods without either physical damage to the goods or a sufficient appropriation to ground conversion which requires a wrongful interference with title. Moving goods from one place to another without in any way seeking to deny the claimant's title, as in *Fouldes v Willoughby* (1841) 8 M. & W. 540, is trespass without conversion. Apart from any aggravated damages, the damages in such cases are likely to be nominal.

442 See, respectively, paras 38-011 and following, 38-042, 38-050 and following, and 38-066 and following, above.

443 See paras 38-028 and following, above.

444 (1848) 2 C. & K. 540.

445 (1858) 1 F. & F. 134.

446 (1858) 1 F. & F. 134 at 135.

447 (1847) 10 Q.B. 103.

measure should be the smaller one in conversion, as there is no trespass to goods till the fixtures have been severed and hence already have the smaller value. However, the compendious word trespass has been used in the cases, and no close analysis has been made. Where the action was trover the different word brought in the different measure, and, with the forms of action strict, all Rolfe B could say in *Clarke v Holford*,[448] where trover for the goods was brought, was that

> "probably the defendant may be liable to another action for having brought them into that state".[449]

Today, the claimant could recover the larger amount without having to resort to a new action.

38-087 Another possible difference is that redelivery of the goods or of their equivalent or proceeds does not go in reduction of damages in trespass as in conversion. This appears to be the result of the decision in *Rundle v Little*,[450] where in an action for trespass to goods it was held that the defendant could not claim to reduce the damages by giving in evidence a repayment by him to the claimant, after action brought, of money produced by the sale of the goods. This was on the technical ground that, in the words of Lord Denman CJ,

> "a plaintiff is entitled to recover by way of damages all that at the commencement of the suit he has lost through the wrongful act for which the defendant is sued".[451]

It is submitted that this decision must either be taken as going on a matter of pleading or be regarded as wrong and unacceptable.

38-088 A further difference related to exemplary damages but this difference has now evaporated. Prior to the new approach to exemplary damages initiated by *Rookes v Barnard*,[452] it was generally accepted that, while the propriety of an award of exemplary damages in conversion remained a matter of argument untranslated into actuality, exemplary damages were certainly recoverable in trespass to goods, a conclusion which in effect rested upon the decision in *Owen & Smith v Reo Motors*.[453] And it is further accepted, since *Kuddus v Chief Constable of Leicestershire*,[454] overruling *A.B. v South West Water Services*,[455] that provided the circumstances of the case bring it within one of the three categories set out by Lord

---

448 (1848) 2 C. & K. 540.
449 (1848) 2 C. & K. 540 at 544.
450 (1844) 6 Q.B. 174.
451 (1844) 6 Q.B. 174 at 178.
452 [1964] A.C. 1129. See Ch.13, above.
453 (1934) 151 L.T. 274 CA. In that case the defendants supplied to the claimant a motor chassis for display purposes, with an option to purchase it on stated terms and with liberty to attach to it a body belonging to the claimant. The defendants were to be entitled to remove the chassis at any time, but if it had been attached to the body the claimant was to be entitled to dismantle it before such removal. The defendants, without notice, entered the claimant's garage and seized the chassis and body, which they took into the street where they dismantled the body in the view of a number of dealers and one of the claimant's creditors. The Court of Appeal, Greer LJ dubitante, held the claimant entitled to damages which appear to have been assessed on an exemplary basis.
454 [2002] 2 A.C. 122.
455 [1993] Q.B. 507 CA.

Devlin in *Rookes v Barnard*,[456] exemplary damages may be awarded whatever the cause of action.[457] Trespass and conversion therefore stand on the same footing.[458]

## IV. WRONGFUL DISTRESS

**38-089** Distress, through statutory intervention no longer to be so called,[459] is a process of self-help by which a person takes possession of another's goods and retains them as a security for the payment of a debt or of damages by the latter. If goods are distrained in circumstances which make the distress in some manner wrongful, an action for damages will lie against the distrainor in respect of this wrongful distress, with double and triple damages being brought in by some very old statutes.[460] There are various forms of distress, both at common law and statutory, but easily the most important from the point of view of damages is wrongful distress for rent; other forms of distress have received no attention in the authorities in relation to damages. Former editions of this work dealt in detail with the cases on the assessment of damages where the wrongful distress was for rent, the damages being very different as between illegal, irregular and excessive distress, though it is rather doubted that much, if any, attention has been paid to what this substantial section of this chapter contained since damages for wrongful distress for rent have not been a feature of the modern world, as is shown by the bulk of the cases dating from the 19th century and before, with only a small handful in the 20th and none in the 21st. Now s.71 of the lengthy and complex Tribunals, Courts and Enforcement Act 2007 states shortly that "the common law right to distress for arrears of rent is abolished", the Government's Explanatory Note to the section tells us that the repeals dealt with in Schs 14 and 23 to the Act "will sweep away the existing law on distress for rent", and these provisions have been brought into force on 6 April 2014. Accordingly, no more on damages for distress for rent need be said. It is very unclear as to what the position will be for the future, the 2007 statute providing in its elaborate Pt 3, entitled "Enforcement by Taking Control of Goods",[461]that the former common law distraint for rent is now, with many other actions involving the taking of goods, in the hands of so-called enforcement agents[462] who may be required to pay damages for loss to him whose goods are wrongly taken,[463] but how this loss is to be assessed it is impossible to say, particularly as the rules distinguishing illegal, irregular and excessive distress appear to have been removed by the statute.[464] In the highly unlikely event that a case involving damages for wrongful distress for rent has surfaced before 6 April 2014, reference can be made to the full treatment of damages in the previous edition to this one, it being specifically provided in the statute that pre-commencement distraints are not affected.[465]

---

456 [1964] A.C. 1129. For the categories see 13-017 to 13-030, above.

457 See paras 13-011 and following, above.

458 See the discussion on conversion at para.38-082, above.

459 See later in this paragraph.

460 Details at para.13-028, above.

461 Which runs from s.62 to s.90.

462 The new regime for taking control of goods is set out in great detail in Sch.12, most of the provisions of which are implemented by the Taking Control of Goods Regulations 2013 (SI 2013/1894) in force from 6 April 2014.

463 Schedule 12 para.66(5)(b).

464 See s.65(2)(a).

465 See s.66, in particular s.66(b).

## V. Replevin

When goods are taken out of a person's possession he may by way of proceedings in replevin obtain their immediate return until the right to their possession has been decided by action. In this action of replevin he claims to retain the goods and to recover damages.[466] Just as the common law rules on distress are replaced by a new procedure under the Tribunals, Courts and Enforcement Act 2007,[467] so are the rules of replevin,[468] with the result that the cases, such as they are, disappear in the same way as those covering distress for rent. **38-090**

[466] The other party is also a claimant, generally claiming satisfaction for some demand out of which the seizure arose, but he is not claiming damages.

[467] See para.38-089, above.

[468] Tribunals, Courts and Enforcement Act 2007 s.65(1) and (2)(c).

Chapter 39

# TORTS AFFECTING LAND

Table of Contents



**39-001** The two central torts affecting land are trespass and nuisance; beyond these there are, more peripherally, trespass by livestock[1] and torts injuring reversionary interests in land. Generally, the measure of damages is calculated in the same way whatever the tort, but separate treatment is occasionally necessary for particular torts on particular points. It is the form of the injury and not the form of the tort which gives the important division in relation to damages: wrongful damage to the land on the one hand and wrongful occupation and user of the land on the other.[2]

**39-002** Occasionally a case will arise which fits into neither category, involving neither

[1] Which has replaced cattle trespass: Animals Act 1971 ss.1(1)(c) and 4.

[2] These correspond to the torts relating to goods in Ch.37 and Ch.38 respectively.

wrongful damage nor wrongful occupation and user. Such was *Berry v Newport Borough Council*,[3] where the claim was for breach of statutory duty by a local housing authority in failing to inform the purchaser of a council house from the authority that the house had been designated as a defective dwelling. The measure of damages was correctly held to be the purchase price less the price the claimant would have paid had she been informed that the dwelling was in the defective category, and not the very much higher cost of repair and reinstatement. In coming to this result the Court of Appeal applied the reasoning in the similar contract claims of purchasers of property negligently valued by surveyors.[4]

## I. Damage

### 1. Normal Measure

#### (1) In general

The principal issue is whether damages should be measured by diminution of the value of land or by the cost of reinstatement. The discussion which follows illustrates that this question is "highly fact sensitive".[5] However, the historical treatment by the courts of the distinction between the two measures, reveals the relevant factors and guidelines which inform the appropriate measure. The overarching principle is one of reasonableness. **39-003**

It was for long said that the normal measure of damages was the amount of the diminution of the value of the land, a proposition based on what was generally considered to be the leading, but somewhat ancient, case of *Jones v Gooday*,[6] where the alternative measure of cost of replacement or repair, i.e. the sum which it would take to restore the land to its original state, was rejected. The facts of the case were that the defendant had cut a ditch in the claimant's field and carried away the soil. Lord Abinger CB said he could not assent to the proposition that the claimant whose soil had been taken away was entitled to the **39-004**

> "amount which would be required to restore the land to its original condition. All that he is entitled to is to be compensated for the damage he has actually sustained".[7]

And Alderson B said that, if the claimant was right, one who let sea in on land worth £20 would have to pay for excluding it by expensive engineering operations.[8]

However, as was pointed out as far back as the 1961 edition of this work, the first written by Dr McGregor, *Jones v Gooday*,[9] was the sole case where a claimant in possession and with full ownership[10] had been refused the cost to him of replace- **39-005**

---

3 (2001) 33 H.L.R. 197 CA. See too *Adamson v Halifax Plc* [2003] 1 W.L.R. 60 CA, where a mortgagee in breach of its statutory duty sold the mortgaged property at an undervalue. The measure of damages was the reduction in value of the equity of redemption. The case is also illustrative of the clear general rule that the court, in making its assessment, takes into account and does not ignore whatever has happened up until the time of the trial.

4 See these at paras 34-050 and following, above.

5 See *Lea Valley Developments Ltd v Derbyshire* [2017] EWHC 1353 (TCC) at [37].

6 (1841) 8 M. & W. 146.

7 (1841) 8 M. & W. 146 at 146.

8 (1841) 8 M. & W. 146 at 147.

9 (1841) 8 M. & W. 146.

10 Claimants with limited interests are dealt with at paras 39-036 to 39-041, below.

ment or repair of the damage done. Further, Alderson B's remark there suggested that the cost of replacement or repair may be an inappropriate measure only because it is out of all proportion to the injury to the claimant. That this is the true reason of the result in *Jones v Gooday*,[11] was, very soon after the 1961 edition, supported by *Hollebone v Midhurst and Fernhurst Builders*,[12] a decision which was almost immediately adopted by the Court of Appeal, in the context of a claim for breach of contract, in *Harbutt's Plasticine v Wayne Tank and Pump Co*.[13] In *Hollebone* the claimant's house had been damaged by fire, and the judge allowed the cost of reinstating the damage because

> "by reason of its size, its position, its features, its seclusion and the area in which it is located the property is properly termed unique or of a nature that comparable properties are few and far between".[14]

*Jones v Gooday* was distinguished on the ground that there the damage was minimal,[15] while other cases where the cost of repair had not been allowed were explained[16] as turning upon the fact that the claimant was the reversioner[17] or upon the fact that rebuilding was not possible[18]; indeed, in addition, the judge was able to point to various cases where the cost of repair had been allowed, although generally without argument.[19]

**39-006** Since the contract case of *Harbutt's Plasticine*, cases allowing reinstatement, or even replacement, have in the present context become quite common. In *British Coal Corp v Gwent County Council*,[20] a claim for statutory compensation to which damages principles were applied, the owners of a seriously damaged building were held entitled to recover the cost of a replacement building, the cost of replacement being less than the cost of repair and reinstatement of the damaged building. In *Bryant v Macklin*,[21] the Court of Appeal, setting aside the trial judge's award of diminution in value, substituted a substantially higher figure based on partial reinstatement.

---

11 (1841) 8 M. & W. 146.

12 [1968] 1 Lloyd's Rep. 38.

13 [1970] 1 Q.B. 447 CA.

14 [1968] 1 Lloyd's Rep. 38 at 39.

15 [1968] 1 Lloyd's Rep. 38 at 40.

16 [1968] 1 Lloyd's Rep. 38 at 40.

17 *Hosking v Phillips* (1848) 3 Ex. 168 and *Moss v Christchurch R.D.C.* [1925] 2 K.B. 750, dealt with at para.39-038, below.

18 *Spicer v Smee* (1946) 175 L.T. 163; see especially at 170.

19 As in *Duke of Newcastle v Broxhowe* (1832) 4 B. & Ad. 273, a claim in respect of the felonious destruction of Nottingham Castle, and *Nitrophosphate and Odam's Chemical Manure Co v London and St Katharine Docks Co* (1878) 9 Ch. D. 503 CA, where it was not disputed that the cost of repair was the proper measure (at 520). The most interesting case cited by the judge in *Hollebone* is the Scottish *Hutchison v Davidson*, 1945 S.C. 395, where the whole issue was aired and the conclusion reached that sometimes diminution in value is appropriate and sometimes cost of repair: see, especially, at 408, per Lord Russell; in fact, in the particular circumstances it was considered that the proper measure was the amount of diminution in value, but the point became academic on the court's view that both measures led to much the same result. And indeed there are other cases of earlier days in which it seems that the cost of repair, which was allowed, represented the measure of the diminution in the property's value, thus leaving no scope for disagreement: see *Rust v Victoria Graving Dock Co* (1887) 36 Ch. D. 113 CA, and *Marsden v Colnbrook Trading Co* [1954] C.L.Y. 890 CA; and compare *Mayfair Property Co v Johnston* [1894] 1 Ch. 508 at para.39-038, below.

20 (1995) 71 P. & C.R. 482 CA.

21 [2005] EWCA Civ 762 CA; facts at para.39-013, below.

In the claim in *Bole v Huntsbuild Ltd*,[22] for the defendant's breach of statutory duty under the Defective Premises Act 1972 by the construction of badly designed foundations for the claimant's house which rendered it uninhabitable, the Court of Appeal upheld the trial judge's award covering the cost of remedying all of the defects and damage to the house attributable to the badly designed foundations; this amounted to foreseeable loss well within the damage contemplated by the statute. The Court of Appeal would have nothing of the defendant's argument that the award should have been limited to covering only that which was necessary to render the house fit for habitation.[23] Further decisions allowing reinstatement are dealt with in later paragraphs.

Also in the years since *Harbutt's Plasticine*, there have been cases in the present context where the cost of reinstatement was not allowed because it was clear that reinstatement was not contemplated. In *Hole & Son (Sayers Common) v Harrisons of Thurnscoe*,[24] the defendant's lorry demolished a terrace of three cottages belonging to the claimants, causing the statutory tenant inhabiting one of the cottages to move out. The claimants had intended to demolish the cottages when the opportunity presented itself, and the accident damage together with the departure of the statutory tenant provided the opportunity, so that they had no intention of repairing the cottages. The cost of reinstatement was therefore rightly refused, and the claimants' recovery was held restricted to a small sum for repairs to an internal wall and some loss of rent. In *Taylor (Wholesale) v Hepworths*,[25] where fire gutted the claimants' billiard hall on a site which they held for its potential redevelopment value and which they had no intention of using as a billiard hall, diminution in value was again rightly held to win out over cost of reinstatement as the appropriate measure of damages.[26] Moreover, even this degree of recovery was eliminated because it was less than the costs of clearing the site for redevelopment, which costs the claimants had been saved. The claimants' entitlement to damages thus comprised only the cost of removal of the debris, of immediately necessary remedial works and of securing the premises against trespassers, together with a sum for damage to trade fixtures and fittings.[27] Furthermore, recovery is unlikely to be allowed for reinstatement to the extent that it goes beyond what is required. Thus in *Skandia Property (UK) Ltd v Thames Water Utilities Ltd*,[28] the cost of installing a new waterproof system, after a flood, was not allowed because this went beyond repairing the damage caused. It was said that, for a claimant to recover damages beyond the cost of repair and reinstatement, he must show that it was reasonable to incur expenditure beyond this cost and that it would be a rare case in which this burden could be discharged; mere reliance by the claimant upon his expert was not enough.[29] *Harrison v Shepherd Homes Ltd*,[30] was a claim under the Defective **39-007**

---

22 (2009) 127 Con. L.R. 154 CA.

23 (2009) 127 Con. L.R. 154 CA at [36] and following.

24 [1973] 1 Lloyd's Rep. 345.

25 [1977] 1 W.L.R. 659.

26 Certain passages taken from this section of the 13th edition (1972) of this work were cited and, it was said, "correctly reflect the state of the law": [1977] 1 W.L.R. 659 at 667D.

27 See [1977] 1 W.L.R. 659 at 669E to 670E. It was held to be irrelevant that the claimant's insurers, who were the effective claimants by the normal process of subrogation, had paid the claimants the cost of reinstatement under the terms of the insurance contract.

28 [1999] B.L.R. 338 CA.

29 *Skandia* was distinguished in *Linklaters Business Services v Sir Robert McAlpine Ltd* [2010] EWHC 2931 (TCC), a contract case at para.31-012, above.

Premises Act 1972 by owners of houses on an estate built by the defendant which suffered significant cracking as a result of defective piling. At first instance the judge concluded that it was not reasonable to award the cost of reinstatement by the repiling of the houses as this cost would exceed the value of the houses in their undamaged state. Instead, he awarded diminution in value together with the cost, appropriately discounted, of two sets of remedial works over the next 20 years. The defendant's appeal on the judge's calculation of the diminution in value and on whether there was double counting in awarding diminution in value and remedial costs as well was unsuccessful.[31]

**39-008** Where the claimant's claim cannot be for reinstatement, whether because it is not practical or not sensible, it will be important to be sure that the right figure for diminution in value is arrived at. Indeed in *Farmer Giles v Wessex Water Authority*,[32] where the wall of the claimant's building collapsed into a river and the diminution in the value of the site was £10,000 with the cost of reinstatement coming out, on one calculation, at the impossible figure of £155,000, the Court of Appeal said that it was not restricted to a choice between the two figures and upheld the trial judge's award of £34,000. This figure of £34,000 reflected the fact that the building had been about to be redeveloped and refurbished for commercial purposes and it was held to be correct to take the value with regard to this potential development in the future. In reality, therefore, the court was not discovering a third measure but was making an assessment of diminution in value. Russell LJ said:

> "The real difference between the parties here is as to how one goes about measuring that diminution in value. Does one have regard to the potential of the building? Or is one disqualified from so doing?"[33]

The court decided that it was not so disqualified, there being a specific finding of the claimant's intention to develop the property which formed part of a larger plot where precisely the form of development which the claimant planned was occurring.[34]

**39-009** Reinstatement was again allowed but with a variation in *Ward v Cannock Chase District Council*.[35] The claimant owned two cottages, where he lived with his wife and nine children, at the end of a terrace of cottages belonging to the defendant council. The area was zoned for industrial development and the policy of the council was to board up the cottages that it owned as they became vacant so that they fell into disrepair and were being damaged by vandals. The claimant continued to live at the premises but, as conditions became impossible, was eventually forced to

---

30 [2012] EWCA Civ 904 CA.

31 In the context of a claim for an interim payment it was held in *Trebor Bassett Holdings Ltd v ADT Fire and Security Plc* [2012] EWHC 3365 (TTC) that in arriving at an appropriate amount it was necessary to take what was called the irreducible minimum as between diminution in value and cost of reinstatement, an oddity of the case being that the defendant was arguing for diminution in value based not on the value of the land but on the value of the business carried on there: see at [39]–[51].

32 [1990] 1 E.G.L.R. 177 CA.

33 [1990] 1 E.G.L.R. 177 CA at 179E.

34 In the rather peculiar circumstances of *McAreavey v Coal Authority* (2000) 80 P. & C.R. 41 CA, the claimants were awarded statutory damages represented by diminution in value through mining subsidence and were held not limited to loss caused by delay in reinstatement by the defendant, a reinstatement indeed which never took place.

35 [1986] Ch. 546.

move out of them, after which they deteriorated rapidly and soon became beyond repair so that demolition was ordered by the court. In his negligence action against the council, which had consistently failed to effect repairs, he claimed, inter alia, the cost of rebuilding and Scott J held that a claimant should be so entitled where, as here, he could establish that he reasonably intended to rebuild and that his was an exceptional case.[36] The premises constituted a land holding of special and particular value to the claimant with his large family,[37] and an award of the diminution in value would never enable the claimant to rebuild and, when combined with the proceeds of sale of his two cottages, would also be hopelessly inadequate for the purchase elsewhere of anything remotely similar.[38] Moreover, *Ward*,[39] introduced a new dimension to the choice, in making the damages assessment, between diminution in value and cost of reinstatement. Scott J's preparedness there to award the reinstatement cost, as he considered the claimant's desire to reinstate to be reasonable, ran into the difficulty that planning permission might be required and, if so, might not be forthcoming. In these circumstances it might be thought that the claimant would have to be content with damages based on the diminution in value, but the claimant nevertheless contended that, if planning permission were needed and unavailable, damages should be assessed at a sum equal to the reasonable cost of purchasing reasonably equivalent accommodation. Scott J rejected this as an impossible contention: where would the substitute property be and how would its equivalence be measured?[40] A contrary conclusion was, however, rightly reached in the subsequent case of *Dominion Mosaics and Tile Co v Trafalgar Trucking Co*,[41] where the buildings in which the claimants conducted their business were severely damaged in a fire caused by the defendants' negligence and had to be demolished. The diminution in value amounted to £60,000 while the cost of rebuilding was £570,000. The claimants considered rebuilding but decided that it was impractical and instead acquired other premises for £390,000. Accordingly, their claim was not for the cost of reinstatement but for the cost of acquiring the alternative property; they were held entitled so to claim. They required premises to carry on their business and it was a reasonable course to purchase the new premises. Not only was the price of the new building well below that of the cost of rebuilding but its early acquisition mitigated the damage which would have been caused them by loss of annual profits of £30,000 during the rebuilding. Returning to *Ward*,[42] and Scott J's unpreparedness to allow the cost of an equivalent property, this left the claimant there undeterred and he proceeded to claim instead for the cost of adapting, as suitable accommodation for himself and family, a third, adjacent cottage which he also owned; in this he was successful. This alternative award was made subject to any necessary planning permission being obtained and to the imposition of a ceiling

---

36 [1986] Ch. 546 at 576G to 577B.

37 [1986] Ch. 546 at 574F to G.

38 [1986] Ch. 546 at 573G. In contrast is the Irish case, there referred to, of *Munnelly v Calcon* [1978] I.R. 387 where only diminution in value was awarded, the position being that the claimant's house in Dublin, from which he carried on business, was irreparably damaged by the defendant's negligence but it was established that for the market value of the house he could purchase elsewhere in Dublin a comparable house and that the move would not materially affect his business.

39 [1986] Ch. 546.

40 [1986] Ch. 546 at 578A.

41 [1990] 2 All E.R. 246 CA.

42 [1986] Ch. 546.

represented by the cost of reinstating the two cottages damaged by the defendant council's negligence.[43]

**39-010** The claimant who is allowed the cost of reinstatement is not required to submit to the deduction of the amount by which the property as renewed or repaired is more valuable than it was in its condition before the tort. While there was early authority in favour of making such a deduction,[44] this restriction was overthrown by *Hollebone v Midhurst and Fernhurst Builders*,[45] where the judge preferred to follow decisions to the contrary in the context of damage to ships,[46] and in this the decision was followed by the Court of Appeal in *Harbutt's Plasticine v Wayne Tank and Pump Co*.[47] To require such a deduction, said Widgery LJ there, would effectively force the claimants to invest money in modernising their property which might be highly inconvenient for them.[48] And where in *Dominion Mosaics and Tile Co v Trafalgar Trucking Co*,[49] the claimants were held entitled to acquire new premises rather than rebuild the damaged premises, no discount was required for the fact that the new premises had 20 per cent more floor space; "this", said Taylor LJ, "falls within the sort of betterment for which no reduction should be made".[50]

**39-011** Nor is the claimant to be denied recovery of the cost of reinstatement because payment for the reinstatement has come from elsewhere. This appears from *Jones v Stroud District Council*,[51] where the Court of Appeal held that it could award the owner of a house tortiously damaged the cost of repair where it was satisfied that the house had been repaired, and was not further concerned with the fact that the owner had not had to pay for the repair because the funds had come from a company which had executed the repairs without invoicing him for them. In *Burdis v Livsey*,[52] Gray J had been persuaded that *Jones v Stroud* was no longer good law after the House of Lords decisions in *Hunt v Severs*,[53] and, more particularly, *Dimond v Lovell*,[54] but on the appeal[55] *Jones v Stroud* was properly reinstated. Neill LJ had said in *Jones* that

> "if property belonging to [a claimant] has been damaged to an extent which is proved and the court is satisfied that the property has been or will be repaired I do not consider that

---

43 [1986] Ch. 546 at 583C–G.

44 *Lukin v Godsall* (1795) Peake Add. Cas. 15; *Hide v Thornborough* (1846) 2 C. & K. 250. Lord Kenyon's analogy, in the former case, of the marine insurance rule of deducting one-third new for old has no longer any force if, as is said in *British Shipping Laws*, Vol.4, 11th edn (1961), para.529, modern policies either exclude the rule or subject it to important exceptions. This does not appear in the latest edition of the equivalent volume of *British Shipping Laws, Marsden on Collisions*, 13th edn (2003) which simply states, at para.15-41, that "no deduction is made from the damages in respect of unavoidable betterment".

45 [1968] 1 Lloyd's Rep. 38.

46 *The Pactolus* (1856) Swab. 173; *The Munster* (1896) 12 T.L.R. 264. See para.37-006, above.

47 [1970] 1 Q.B. 447 CA; a contract case which, as we have seen (para.39-005, above), is important in the present context.

48 [1970] 1 Q.B. 447 CA at 473. See para.2-007, above.

49 [1990] 2 All E.R. 246 CA.

50 [1990] 2 All E.R. 246 CA at 252d. Nor were the claimants required to account for the profit that they had made on the resale of the new premises after they had taken a lease of still further premises for their business: see para.9-144, above.

51 [1986] 1 W.L.R. 1141 CA, applying *The Endeavour* (1890) 6 Asp. M.C. 511 which dealt with damage to goods: see para.37-007, above.

52 [2001] 1 W.L.R. 1751.

53 [1994] 2 A.C. 350.

54 [2002] 1 A.C. 384.

55 [2003] Q.B. 36 CA.

> the court is further concerned with the question whether the owner has had to pay for the repairs out of his own pocket or whether the funds have come from some other source",[56]

and the Court of Appeal in *Burdis*, after examining the cases, concluded[57] that

> "Neill LJ's judgment in *Jones v Stroud* represents a modern restatement of a principle established by the earlier authorities",

these earlier authorities being largely of cases of damage to goods.[58]

The difficulty in deciding between diminution in value and cost of reinstatement arises from the fact that the claimant may want his property in the same state as before the commission of the tort but the amount required to effect this may be substantially greater than the amount by which the value of the property has been diminished. The test which appears to be the appropriate one is the reasonableness of the claimant's desire to reinstate the property; this will be judged in part by the advantages to him of reinstatement in relation to the extra cost to the defendant in having to pay damages for reinstatement rather than damages calculated by the diminution in value of the land.[59] That reasonableness is the criterion is well brought out by *Lodge Holes Colliery Co v Wednesbury Corp*,[60] where the court gave neither the amount of the diminution in value nor the expense incurred in reinstatement but awarded the cost of a partial and limited replacement. In that case the defendant, while working a mine under the highway, let down its surface, which the claimant local authority, bona fide and on the opinion of skilled advisers, restored to its former level at great cost, although an equally commodious road might have been made more cheaply. It was held that the claimants were only entitled to recover the lesser cost. Lord Loreburn LC, delivering the leading speech, pointed out that a court should be 39-012

> "very slow in countenancing any attempt by a wrongdoer to make captious objections to the methods by which those whom he has injured have sought to repair the injury",

and that

> "in judging whether they [i.e. the claimants] have acted reasonably, I think a court should be very indulgent and always bear in mind who was to blame".[61]

Nevertheless

> "the point of law which was advanced by the claimants, namely that they were entitled to raise the road to the old level, cost what it might and whether it was more commodious to the public or not, will not, in my opinion, bear investigation. Such a rule might lead to a ruinous and wholly unnecessary outlay."[62]

Lord Loreburn's further comment that 39-013

---

56 [1986] 1 W.L.R. 1141 CA at 1150H–1151A.

57 [2003] Q.B. 36 CA at [97].

58 Cases dealt with at para.37-007, above. See *Burdis* further at paras 37-008 and 37-009, above.

59 Compare *Hutchison v Davidson*, 1945 S.C. 395 at para.39-005, above (in a footnote).

60 [1908] A.C. 323, reversing the Court of Appeal [1907] 1 K.B. 78 CA.

61 [1908] A.C. 323 at 325. Anticipating by quite a number of years Lord Macmillan's more famous remarks in *Banco de Portugal v Waterlow* [1932] A.C. 452 quoted at para.9-079, above.

62 [1908] A.C. 323 at 326.

> "even those who have been wronged must act reasonably, however wide the latitude of discretion that is allowed to them within the bounds of reason"[63]

was cited and applied at first instance in *Dodd Properties (Kent) v Canterbury City Council*,[64] to deny damages to the claimants based upon their proposals for the repair of their building damaged by the defendants' pile-driving operations, the court preferring the defendants' more modest proposals as the basis for a proper assessment of the claimants' damages. Cantley J said:

> "The claimants are … not bound to accept a shoddy job or put up with an inferior building for the sake of saving expense to the defendants. But I do not consider that they are entitled to insist on complete and meticulous restoration when a reasonable building owner would be content with less extensive work which produces a result which does not diminish to any, or any significant, extent the appearance, life or utility of the building, and when there is also a vast difference in the cost of such work and the cost of meticulous restoration."[65]

In *Scutt v Lomax*,[66] and *Bryant v Macklin*,[67] it was the reinstatement of trees that was in issue, and in both the court allowed the cost of only a partial reinstatement. In *Scutt* land of the claimant in front of his home had been laid bare by the defendant, a devastation which included the uprooting of several mature trees. The diminution in the value of the land was minimal. In *Bryant* the claimants' trees had been damaged by the defendants' animals breaking through the boundary between their two properties. The trial judge based damages on diminution of value which was less than any of the replacement costs being contended for. In both cases the Court of Appeal considered that it was reasonable only to incur the cost of planting smaller trees which would mature over the years, and allowed damages accordingly.[68]

39-014 The further issue which has become prominent is one of timing: at what point in time should the cost of reinstatement, or even the diminution in value, be taken? Since the cases have been largely in the area of nuisance the relevant law is collected below when dealing with this particular tort.[69] Also cases may arise in which there is a degree of additional recovery for non-pecuniary loss, loss which tends to be classified in this context of damage to land as a loss of amenity, constituted by annoyance, inconvenience, discomfort and the like. Again, the principal examples come from the law of nuisance, and again they are separately dealt with under nuisance together with the few illustrations produced by the analogous tort of trespass to land.[70]

### (2) The particular case of trespass by unauthorised mining

39-015 The old cases of unauthorised mining which occupy a large place in conver-

---

63 [1908] A.C. 323 at 326.

64 [1980] 1 W.L.R. 433.

65 [1980] 1 W.L.R. 433 at 441F–G. In the claimants' appeal to the Court of Appeal (at para.39-018, below) this issue was not raised by them: see at 448B–C, per Megaw LJ.

66 (2000) 79 P. & C.R. D31 CA.

67 [2005] EWCA Civ 762 CA.

68 At the same time both Courts of Appeal boosted the claimants' recovery by awarding further sums for loss of amenity, through having for a time no trees and then smaller trees, and by awarding aggravated damages: see at paras 39-020 and 39-042, below.

69 See paras 39-017 to 39-019, below.

70 See paras 39-020 and 39-021, below.

sion[71] reappear at this point. Although the main head of loss is the value of the severed minerals removed, there may also be recovery for damage to the land. Thus in *Morgan v Powell*,[72] compensation was given "for all injury done to soil by digging"[73]; in *Jegon v Vivian*,[74] and *Phillips v Homfray*,[75] damage in working the mine was also made part of the inquiry; in *Ecclesiastical Commissioners v N.E. Ry*,[76] and *Llynvi Coal Co v Brogden*,[77] an inquiry was directed as to whether any damage had been caused by the defendant's breaking through the boundary; in *Taylor v Mostyn*,[78] damage by flooding of the mine was taken into account; in *Livingstone v Rawyards Coal Co*,[79] recovery for damage done to houses on the surface was allowed. None of the cases deals in details of how the damages are assessed, but presumably the general principle of diminution in value of the land applies unless it should be appropriate to award the cost of reinstatement.

Damages awarded in such cases under the count for conversion may eliminate the loss suffered by way of the damage to the land,[80] as was pointed out by Lord Blackburn in *Livingstone v Rawyards Coal Co.*[81] He said: **39-016**

> "As it would necessarily follow, when you took away the coals that were below the land, that the surface of the land would come down, you must not take the sum which would be given as compensation for the injury to the surface twice over. You must not take that sum as being a matter which you are to be paid for, and also take the coals as if they had been got out without damage."[82]

## (3) The particular case of nuisance[83]

A nuisance may only cause physical damage to the land, as to which the normal measure of damages will be, as in other cases, the diminution in the value of the land.[84] If in the case of physical damage the damages are measured by the cost of replacement this will generally be termed, in relation to nuisance, the cost of abating it.[85] Indeed *Bunclark v Hertfordshire C.C.*,[86] where extensive and continuing **39-017**

---

71 See paras 38-029 to 38-039, above. The unauthorised mining cases are also relevant to wrongful occupation and user of land: see para.39-048, below.

72 (1842) 3 Q.B. 278.

73 (1842) 3 Q.B. 278 at 284, per Denman CJ.

74 (1871) L.R. 6 Ch. App. 742.

75 (1871) L.R. 6 Ch. App. 770.

76 (1877) 4 Ch. D. 845.

77 (1870) L.R. 11 Eq. 188.

78 (1886) 33 Ch. D. 226 CA. It was an action by mortgagee against mortgagor and not straight tort.

79 (1880) 5 App. Cas. 25.

80 They may also eliminate the loss suffered by way of occupation and user of the land: see paras 39-048 and 39-049, below.

81 (1880) 5 App. Cas. 25.

82 (1880) 5 App. Cas. 25 at 41.

83 That the damages are generally the same in nuisance and in negligence is illustrated by *Network Rail Infrastructure Ltd v Conarken Group Ltd* [2010] EWHC 1852 (TCC) at first instance, the Court of Appeal ([2011] EWCA Civ 644 CA) dealing only with negligence: facts at para.39-029, below.

84 Compensation under statute where the claimant's land has been injuriously affected by works which, but for being carried out under statutory authority, would have constituted a nuisance may be calculated somewhat differently: *Wildtree Hotels Ltd v Harrow LBC* (2001) 81 P. and C.R. 97 HL.

85 Where in *Abbahall Ltd v Smee* [2003] 1 W.L.R. 1472 CA the damages consisted of expenditure in abating a nuisance by repairing the roof of a building of which the claimant owned the ground floor and the defendant the upper floors, the main issue for the court was to decide upon the proper division of the expenditure between the parties.

damage was caused to a block of flats by neighbouring tree roots, illustrates a recovery both in respect of diminution in value, because the bad reputation given to the block by the nuisance had reduced the amount the flats would fetch on the market, and in respect of the cost of repair and reinstatement. Also, other remedial expenditure in respect of physical damage may be comprised in the cost of abatement or elimination, as in *Delaware Mansions Ltd v City of Westminster*,[87] where the House of Lords held that the failure of the defendant council to remove a tree the roots of which, to the defendant's knowledge, were causing damage to three blocks of flats of the claimant, entitled him to recover the costs of the expensive but necessary work of underpinning the foundations of the blocks which had been undertaken in order to eliminate the nuisance.[88] Where the nuisance does not entail physical damage to the land, diminution in value and cost of abatement again appear as acceptable measures of damages. Thus in *Snell & Prideau v Dutton Mirrors*,[89] where the claimants' right of way was obstructed and narrowed by building by the defendants, the claimants' entitlement to damages was said to amount to the difference between the value of their property with the full right of way, including the right of passageway for vehicles, and its value with the more limited right now existing.[90] Alternatively, in *Wandsworth London Borough Council v Railtrack Plc*,[91] where a public nuisance was caused by pigeon droppings from the defendants' railway bridge bringing considerable inconvenience to pedestrians passing below, the claimants were held entitled to the reasonable cost of abatement.[92] It was there specifically said that no distinction was to be drawn between nuisance causing physical damage to property and nuisance causing inconvenience and interfering with comfort.[93] And when it came to the damages assessment in *Dobson v Thames Water Utilities Ltd*,[94] claimants with a proprietary interest in the land affected by smells from the defendant's works[95] were held entitled to recover the cost of de-odourisers and fans purchased to overcome the nuisance.[96]

**39-018** Not only was the cost of repair and reinstatement awarded in *Bunclark v Hertfordshire C.C.*,[97] but it was awarded on the basis of building costs in 1976 and 1977 when the work was done rather than the much lower costs of 1969 when the nuisance commenced. This was for two reasons, first, because reinstatement had not been worth carrying out while the defendants' trees still stood, and, secondly,

---

86 (1977) 243 E.G. 381 and 455.

87 [2002] 1 A.C. 321

88 Again in *L.E. Jones Ltd v Portsmouth City Council* [2003] 1 W.L.R. 427 CA, underpinning foundations to counteract nuisance by tree roots was held recoverable; there was no failure to mitigate by adoption of less expensive measures. *Loftus-Brigham v London Borough of Ealing* (2006) 103 Con. L.R. 102 CA also involved nuisance by tree roots but the issue was causation not measure: for the case see the footnote at the end of para.8-018, above.

89 [1995] 1 E.G.L.R. 259 CA.

90 The defendants were not to be ordered, by mandatory injunction, to pull their building down. Cases such as this may be looked at as wrongful user rather than as wrongful damage, thereby pointing to a rather different measure of damages: see the authorities at paras 39-048 and following, below.

91 [2001] 1 W.L.R. 368.

92 However, mitigation principles prevented the full costs incurred being recoverable: see at para.9-073, above. The damages were basically affirmed on appeal: [2002] Q.B. 756 CA at [27].

93 [2001] 1 W.L.R. 368 at 384D.

94 [2001] 1 W.L.R. 368 at 384D.

95 Facts at para.39-021, below.

96 See the details at [2001] 1 W.L.R. 368 at [1018].

97 (1977) 243 E.G. 381 and 455.

because the claimants did not have the financial resources to effect an earlier reinstatement. So, too, in *Dodd Properties (Kent) v Canterbury City Council*,[98] the Court of Appeal, reversing Cantley J, accepted the claimants' contention that, because they had not been financially able to effect repairs at the time the defendants' pile-driving operations damaged their building and because it would not have made commercial sense for them to spend the money needed for repair on a property which would not produce corresponding additional income before being sure of recovering the cost from the defendants, they should be entitled to damages based upon the much higher cost of repairs at the time, some 10 years later, when the claim was heard. Megaw LJ said that

> "the true rule is that, where there is a material difference between the cost of repair at the date of the wrongful act and the cost of repair when the repairs can, having regard to all relevant circumstances, first reasonably be undertaken, it is the latter time by reference to which the cost of repair is to be taken in assessing damages."[99]

It was held, differing from Cantley J, that *The Liesbosch*,[100] with its talk of impecuniosity had no application in this situation[101]; today of course there would be no need for the court to have troubled itself with this aspect of that case as it has gone.[102]

39-019 This issue of the propriety of adopting a higher cost eventually reached the Judicial Committee of the Privy Council in *Alcoa Minerals of Jamaica Plc v Broderick*,[103] where their Lordships, in the circumstances of the case before them, agreed that the damages should be based upon the cost of repair or reinstatement at the time that this was effected rather than upon the much lower cost prevailing at the time that the nuisance was committed. The case concerned a nuisance caused by the dispersal of pollutants, gases and dust from the defendant's smelting plant which damaged the roof of the claimant's nearby house; injury to other property of the claimant and to his health also ensued.[104] Unable to pay for the repairs to the roof at the time that the damage occurred, the claimant waited until the successful outcome of the litigation to do so, by which time the cost of repairing the roof had increased some fourfold because of rapid inflation in Jamaica and, in consequence, a Jamaican dollar greatly fallen in value. Once again the decision in *The Liesbosch*,[105] which has haunted this type of case and made its sensible solution difficult to reach, was side-stepped. But no longer is there a need to side-step[106] as the impecuniosity rule of *The Liesbosch* is dead and buried.[107]

---

98 [1980] 1 W.L.R. 433 CA; see the case further at para.39-013, above.

99 [1980] 1 W.L.R. 433 CA at 451C–D.

100 [1933] A.C. 449.

101 See [1980] 1 W.L.R. 433 at 452G–453E.

102 See paras 8-110 to 8-113, above.

103 [2002] 1 A.C. 371 PC.

104 As to the latter see para.39-020, below.

105 [1933] A.C. 449.

106 Nor to attempt, as did Lord Slynn, to formulate a not convincing distinction: see [2002] 1 A.C. 371 PC at 382G.

107 See paras 8-110 to 8-113, above. In *Ward v Cannock Chase District Council* [1986] Ch. 546, a case of negligence rather than of nuisance, where, the cost of reinstatement being held in the particular circumstances the appropriate award (see para.39-009, above), it was accepted with little or no argument that that cost fell to be measured as at the date of the inquiry into damages: at 577E–G. And the court also held that if the damages had to be assessed on the basis of diminution in value, because reinstatement was prevented by planning permission being needed and not obtainable, the date at

39-020 Beyond physical and other damage to the land leading to pecuniary loss,[108] a nuisance may cause annoyance, inconvenience, discomfort, or even illness to the claimant occupier. Recovery in respect of these principally non-pecuniary losses is allowable[109] and may be regarded as part of the normal measure of damages.[110] In the cases the claimant has been disturbed in the occupation of his home. Early illustrations are afforded by *Halsey v Esso Petroleum Co*,[111] where the claimant suffered noise and smell from an oil-distributing depot, *Bone v Seale*,[112] where the claimant had to endure persistent smells emanating from a pig farm, and *Bunclark v Hertfordshire C.C.*,[113] where the spreading of tree roots inflicted upon the claimant cracked walls, dust and general anxiety.[114] *Bone v Seale*,[115] was taken to appeal, and the Court of Appeal reduced the award for 12 years of discomfort from £6,000 to £1,000, Stephenson and Scarman LJJ considering that the award below must be too high in the light of awards for loss of the sense of smell in personal injury cases.[116] In *Ward v Cannock Chase District Council*,[117] a case of negligence rather than nuisance,[118] the court held the claimant entitled to damages for the discomfort, and any attendant anxiety and distress, experienced by himself and his large family, first in living in a house which the defendant council had failed to repair and later in living in temporary, and unsatisfactory, accommodation while the house was being rebuilt.[119] In *Scutt v Lomax*,[120] and *Bryant v Macklin*,[121] cases of

---

which the diminution in value should be measured was not the normal time of commission of the tort but the later time of demolition of the property to which the tortious conduct had eventually led: see at 578D.

108 At para.39-017, above.

109 Recovery for the non-pecuniary loss should be in addition to any damages awarded for any pecuniary loss should, for instance, reinstatement of the premises to its former condition be required. To the extent that Stuart-Smith J in *Arroyo v Equion Energia Ltd* [2013] EWHC 3150 TCC may say to the contrary at [67] of a judgment dealing wholly with procedure and amendment of pleadings, it should not be accepted. *Arroyo* was a claim in England by farmers in Colombia for damage to their farmlands against an offshoot of a company involved in the construction of a pipeline which passed over their lands. Colombian law applied to the heads of damage, though English to their quantification, and the damages claimed in the pleadings included "moral damages" and for "loss of amenity/quality of life": see at [4]. As for moral damages, these have already come into English law, through the European Union, in the field of intellectual property, there called moral prejudice: see para.48-070 and, for an explanation of the term, para.48-074, below.

110 See *Bone v Seale* [1975] 1 W.L.R. 797 CA at 804F, where Scarman LJ adopted this statement from the 13th edition (1972) of this work. Damage by way of profits lost or expenses incurred falls within consequential losses: see para.39-026, below.

111 [1961] 1 W.L.R. 683; see especially at 702–703.

112 [1975] 1 W.L.R. 797 CA.

113 (1977) 243 E.G. 381 and 455.

114 *Bunclark* has, a good deal later in time, found itself a progeny. In *Berent v Family Mosaic Housing* [2012] EWCA Civ 961 CA the Court of Appeal considered the level of awards for distress and inconvenience caused by tree root damage, regarding *Eiles v London Borough of Southwark* [2006] All E.R. (D) 237 as establishing the benchmark for such damages and confirming that, as was said in *Eiles*, the general damages for having to live in a house structurally damaged by tree roots should provide modest, not generous, compensation: at [39] and [40]. Following these decisions a modest amount was awarded in the further tree roots case of *Khan v Harrow Council* [2013] EWHC 2687 (TCC): see at [100].

115 [1975] 1 W.L.R. 797 CA.

116 [1975] 1 W.L.R. 797 CA at 803G–804A and 805A–C respectively. But Ormerod LJ was not impressed by the analogy: at 806A.

117 [1986] Ch. 546.

118 Facts at para.39-009, above.

119 [1986] Ch. 546 at 579B–H. A degree of the anxiety and distress suffered was held too remote.

trespass rather than nuisance, awards were made to the claimants to compensate them for their unhappiness at the loss, for a time, of the amenity of trees to look out upon.[122] The Court of Appeal's award in *Scutt* was of £3,000 but in *Bryant* the trial judge's award was increased by the Court of Appeal to £12,000 as the loss of the amenity of the trees affected the enjoyment of the claimants' home very directly and more severely than in the earlier case.[123] In *Alcoa Minerals of Jamaica Plc v Broderick*,[124] where the defendant's smelting plant affected the claimant's nearby house, the general damages of Jamaican $30,000 awarded below went unchallenged in the appeal to the Privy Council,[125] but this amount related mainly to the injury to health and, although looking very large, was the equivalent at the time of the award of under £600.[126] In *Barr v Biffa Waste Services Ltd*,[127] damages were claimed in nuisance by over 150 households on account of the smell from pre-treated waste coming from the defendant's landfill site. While the claims all failed as the defendant's user was held to be reasonable and therefore not a nuisance[128] and, this apart, while practically all of the household claims would have failed as the smell was not shown to have exceeded a permissible threshold,[129] any household which could prove that for it the threshold had been exceeded would have been held entitled to £1,000 per annum for loss of enjoyment of the property,[130] there being no diminution in value of any of the properties. Similarly, in *Anslow v Norton Aliminium Ltd*,[131] 132 households largely succeeded in claiming nuisance damages on account of odours emanating from an aluminium foundry operated by the defendant but did not succeed on account of dust, smoke and noise as there had been an insufficiency of interference. Awards were to be of modest amounts ranging from £750 to £2,000 per annum.[132] All these amounts of course need to be updated to cur-

---

120 (2000) 79 P. & C.R. D31 CA.

121 [2005] EWCA Civ 762 CA.

122 In a further case of trespass, *Cash and Brown v Chief Constable of Lancashire* [2008] EWHC 396 Ch, only a modest award of £150 was made to the second claimant as the temporary trespass by the police had caused minimal injury to his feelings.

123 See [2008] EWHC 396 Ch at [27]; facts of both cases at para.39-013, above. Tree roots damage on its own commands far smaller awards: see the cases earlier in this paragraph.

124 [2002] 1 A.C. 371 PC.

125 See [2002] 1 A.C. 371 PC at 376H; facts at para.39-019, above.

126 See, too, *Jan de Nul (UK) v NV Royale Belge* [2000] 2 Lloyd's Rep. 700 where the court recognised that in both public nuisance and private nuisance—silt had been deposited in an estuary through dredging operations—damages might be awarded for infringement of a claimant's rights even where the effects of the infringement could not be assessed with any precision in monetary terms: at 716.

127 [2011] 4 All E.R. 1065.

128 [2011] 4 All E.R. 1065 at [582].

129 [2011] 4 All E.R. 1065 at [583].

130 [2011] 4 All E.R. 1065 at [584] as explained at [542]–[559].

131 [2012] EWHC 2610 (QB).

132 [2012] EWHC 2610 (QB) at [476]. The damages in *Dennis v Ministry of Defence* [2003] 2 E.G.L.R. 121, where the level of aircraft noise created by the airfield operated by the defendant constituted a very serious interference with the claimant's enjoyment of his property, were dealt with curiously and it is thought improperly by the trial judge who awarded an "overview" figure of £950,000 for loss of use, loss of capital value and loss of amenity, saying enigmatically that his total was not just simply an addition of the three elements (see at [88]) and adding that for the noise there would have been needed to be "not less than £50,000 to do justice to this loss of amenity if this aspect stood alone" (see at [89]). The cases in the text show that no other nuisance case has come anywhere near so high a non-pecuniary award, and the £50,000 is in stark contrast to the £10,000 for aircraft noise in the important *Farley v Skinner* [2002] 2 A.C. 732 (*Farley* is at para.34-062, above) which their Lordships there considered to be at the very top end of the scale. The judge did not consider *Farley*

rent prices in order to appreciate the level of the awards; in particular, the ruling in the ultimate Court of Appeal hearing of *Simmons v Castle*,[133] that damages for all types of non-pecuniary loss in all civil claims should be increased by 10 per cent needs to be kept in mind.[134]

**39-021** Particularly in relation to the recovery of damages for non-pecuniary loss in nuisance, *Dobson v Thames Water Utilities Ltd* is an important case, both in the hearing in the Court of Appeal[135] and in the following assessment of damages before Ramsay J.[136] Occupiers of properties in the vicinity of the defendant's sewage treatment works were adversely affected by odours and mosquitoes from the defendant public authority's negligent operation of those works. A class action was brought by the occupiers claiming common law damages for nuisance and damages for breach of the Human Rights Act, only the occupiers with a proprietary interest being entitled to claim in nuisance. At Court of Appeal level, while assessing the nuisance damages was not in issue,[137] the court nevertheless emphasised that it was damage to the land and not damage to the person that was the essence of recovery in nuisance. Interference with the claimant's enjoyment of his property is the gist of the claim here; it is the proprietary loss of amenity not the personal loss of amenity, as in personal injury claims, for which the damages are awarded.[138] This then led Ramsey J when the assessment of damages came to him not, as before, to assess the non-pecuniary loss by reference to precedent and to the amounts awarded in preceding cases[139] but to use an alternative method and, in the many claims before him, to go on the basis of the loss of the amenity value of the land. He assessed percentage reductions in rental value year by year to take account of the loss of amenity caused by the nuisance, the percentages used by him running from 5 per cent down to 1.25 per cent.[140]

**39-022** There remains the question of whether there can be recovery in nuisance for personal injury. This issue appeared, somewhat tangentially, in *Jones v Ruth*,[141] another case of a dispute between neighbours in adjoining properties. The claimants were two women living together in a house adjacent to that of the defendant. The development of his property on which the defendant embarked caused exces-

---

an apt comparison, the noise nuisance in *Dennis* "testing the limits of tolerance" ([85]), but this can hardly justify the level of his damages increase.

133 [2013] 1W.L.R. 1239 CA; this hearing is from p.1243.

134 For the procedural history and reasons for this development, stemming from the package of reforms appearing in the *Jackson Report on Civil Litigation Costs*, see para.40-280, below. In the first Court of Appeal hearing of *Simmons v Castle* [2013] 1 W.L.R. 1239 CA at 1240, where the ruling was confined to torts causing suffering, inconvenience or distress, two torts were specifically mentioned of which nuisance was one: see at [20].

135 [2009] 3 All E.R. 319 CA.

136 [2011] EWHC 3253 TCC.

137 See the progression of the case explained at para.39-023, below.

138 From this it would seem to follow that, when land is owned in joint names by two or more, the nuisance award should be only for the total loss of the amenity of enjoyment of the land rather than for the personal loss of amenity of each joint owner.

139 As in the cases in the preceding paragraph.

140 [2011] EWHC 3253 (TCC) at [1019] and following, especially at [1020] and [1032]. The same approach had been taken in *Lawrence v Fen Tigers Ltd* [2011] EWHC 360 (QB) so as to award as damages the notional diminution in the amenity value of residential property resulting from a nuisance by the noise of racing cars from a nearby stadium and track: see at [310]–[323]. HH Judge Richard Seymour QC specifically relied for this approach on what had been said in the Court of Appeal hearing in *Dobson*.

141 [2012] 1 W.L.R. 1495 CA.

sive and persistent noise and vibration, took four years rather than one to complete, involved an invasion of the adjoining property to achieve a further storey for the defendant's own building, and all this with no consideration given to the two neighbouring women to whom the defendant acted throughout in a bullying and unpleasant manner.[142] One of the women claimants had suffered psychiatric injury causing her a loss of earnings for a number of years. The trial judge had refused recovery for this loss of earnings apparently on the basis that the law is that recovery for personal injury cannot arise out of nuisance. This was not considered by the Court of Appeal, nuisance being hardly touched upon as the appeal turned on the question of harassment, and the Court of Appeal held, departing from the trial judge, that the claimant could recover for her lost earnings in her harassment claim. It is considered that on nuisance the trial judge goes too wide and that, if the personal injury and its financial and other consequences are attributable to the enjoyment, or lack of enjoyment, of property, damages should be recoverable.[143]

## (4) The particular case of infringement of human rights

Damage by repeated flooding of the claimant's house and garden by the failure of the defendant public authority and statutory sewerage undertaker to carry out works to prevent the flooding led in *Marcic v Thames Water Utilities Ltd*, as the case went up the courts ladder, to a variety of holdings between liability in nuisance and liability under the Human Rights Act 1998. At first instance His Honour Judge Richard Havery decided for liability under the Human Rights Act and rejected liability in nuisance,[144] the Court of Appeal held for nuisance and not for the Human Rights Act liability[145] while the House of Lords held that the claimant could sustain neither a claim in nuisance nor one under the Human Rights Act.[146] Although alone in deciding in favour of the nuisance claim, the Court of Appeal was not asked to address the computation of the damages in nuisance.[147] The interaction of damages for infringement of human rights and damages for nuisance was considered again in *Dobson v Thames Water Utilities Ltd*,[148] where it was of unpleasantness from a public authority's negligently operated sewage treatment works that occupiers of nearby properties were complaining. The Court of Appeal was there concerned not with nuisance damages as such but with how far any common law award of damages in nuisance impinged upon the entitlement to have damages under the Human Rights Act.[149] The nuisance damages, decided by Ramsay J in two later hearings, are dealt with elsewhere.[150] **39-023**

---

142 The details of the appalling behaviour are graphically listed by the trial judge in his findings on nuisance set out by the Court of Appeal at [9].

143 The Privy Council seems to have endorsed recovery for injury to health in the *Alcoa Minerals* case set out at para.39-020, above.

144 [2002] Q.B. 929; HH Judge Havery at 935. *Marcic v Thames Water Utilities Ltd (No.2)* [2002] Q.B. 1003 has his assessment of Human Rights Act damages.

145 [2002] Q.B. 929; Court of Appeal at 973.

146 [2004] 2 A.C. 42.

147 *Marcic* in its human rights aspect is considered in the chapter on that topic, at para.50-147, below.

148 [2009] 3 All E.R. 319 CA.

149 *Dobson* in its human rights aspect is considered in the chapter on that topic, at para.50-069, below.

150 See para.39-017 (pecuniary loss), para.39-021 (loss of amenity) together with paras 19-049 and 19-134 (interest).

## 2. Prospective Loss

39-024 Damages for prospective loss are, in general, recoverable, but an exception arises in the case of continuing wrongs where damages cannot be given at common law for loss beyond the time of commencement of the action or, formerly expressly by rule of court[151] and now hopefully impliedly under the new rules of civil procedure,[152] for loss beyond the time of assessment.[153] Damage to land is an area where continuing torts flourish, and it becomes important to ascertain when the tort is continuing and when not. Only a summary statement is necessary here, as the matter has already been fully considered in dealing with prospective loss generally.[154]

39-025 Nuisances are generally continuing torts so that prospective damages for prospective loss cannot be claimed at law[155]; such losses will therefore be the subject of fresh actions whenever they occur.[156] Nuisances which fall within the principle of *Darley Main Colliery Co v Mitchell*,[157] are indeed not continuing, but prospective losses will not be claimed because they are unexpected, and if they do later occur a further action can be brought. Trespasses constituted by placing and leaving some object on the claimant's land are continuing; prospective losses therefore cannot be claimed at law,[158] but will ground fresh actions when they occur.[159] On the other hand trespasses constituted by making a hole in the claimant's land are over and done the moment the hole is made; prospective losses therefore can be claimed, and indeed must be, as a second action will necessarily fail.[160]

## 3. Consequential Losses

### (1) Loss of profits and expenses incurred

39-026 Loss of user profits have over the years been allowed as damages by way of consequential loss in several cases. In the early case of *Rust v Victoria Graving Dock Co*,[161] the claimant, suing the defendant in respect of the flooding of his building estate, recovered for the loss of rental on the houses in his possession for the period that they were being repaired and also for the delay in letting that part of the land in his possession which was vacant. In *Dodd Properties (Kent) v Canterbury*

---

151 RSC Ord.37 r.6.

152 There appears to be no equivalent RSC provision in the CPR: see para.11-027, above.

153 Equity, however, has more power to assist a claimant complaining of a continuing wrong: see para.11-029, above.

154 See Ch.11, above.

155 As in *Battishill v Reed* (1856) 18 C.B. 696.

156 As in *Shadwell v Hutchinson* (1831) 4 C. & P. 333.

157 (1886) 11 App. Cas. 127: see para.11-014, above.

158 Compare *Battishill v Reed* (1856) 18 C.B. 696.

159 As in *Holmes v Wilson* (1839) 10 A. & E. 503.

160 As in *Clegg v Dearden* (1848) 12 Q.B. 576. It was held at first instance in *Marcic v Thames Water Utilities Ltd (No.2)* [2002] Q.B. 1003 that an award of damages in respect of future wrongs was consistent with the principles applied by the European Court of Human Rights and was necessary to afford the claimant just satisfaction even though damages at common law would not be available: see at [13]–[17]. The appropriateness of such damages was not addressed by either the Court of Appeal or the House of Lords as they held against Human Rights Act liability. See *Marcic* further at para.37-022, above and in the Human Rights Act context at para.50-147, below.

161 (1887) 36 Ch. D. 113 CA.

*City Council*,[162] recovery was allowed in respect of the dislocation of the business of the second claimants, who were the tenants of the land, during the execution by the first claimants, who were the owners, of the repairs necessitated by the nuisance committed by the defendants, the computation being based upon the assumption that the repairs were carried out not at or soon after the accrual of the cause of action, which they had not been, but at the very much later date to which the court considered that it had been reasonable for the first claimants to defer carrying out the repairs and at which the figure of the second claimants' loss of profits through the dislocation of their business was nearly three times as great.[163]

Beyond this, loss of profits has been allowed in some cases of public nuisance to a highway causing special damage to the claimant sufficient to ground recovery in tort.[164] Thus in *Rose v Groves*,[165] and in *Campbell v Paddington Corp*,[166] where, respectively, the access to and the view from the claimant's house were obstructed, he recovered the loss of profit he would have made by using the house as, again respectively, a place for refreshments and a place from which a royal funeral procession could be watched.[167] **39-027**

Recovery in respect of a claimant's expenditure, beyond the expenditure in repair or reinstatement subsumed under the normal measure of damages,[168] has also been accepted by the courts in public nuisance cases. In *Rose v Miles*,[169] where the defendant obstructed a canal, the claimant was held entitled to recover for costs incurred in unloading his goods from barges and having them carried by land. In *Tate & Lyle Food and Distribution v Greater London Council*,[170] where construction work by the defendants had caused deposits of silt to form in a river thereby preventing access to the barge moorings for the claimants' riverside trading premises, it was held that, in addition to claiming for the cost of the remedial work of dredging undertaken by the claimants, they could in principle recover for expenditure on managerial time in initiating and supervising the remedial work[171] and were only prevented from doing so by reason of a lack of proof of such loss on their part. In *Ward v Cannock Chase District Council*,[172] a case in negligence **39-028**

---

162 [1980] 1 W.L.R. 433 CA.

163 For this timing aspect of the case see paras 9-097 and 39-018, above. Loss of profits was also awarded, but only for a limited period, for inability to use the claimant's premises for a projected business in *U.Y.B. Ltd v British Railways Board* (2001) 81 P. & C.R. DG19 CA. This appears to be a case brought in nuisance although, there being the relation of lessor and lessee between the parties, the claim was also founded in contract: see the facts at para.28-011, above.

164 Many such cases do not of course involve torts affecting land, e.g. those of physical injury to the claimant on the highway.

165 (1843) 5 M. & G. 613.

166 [1911] 1 K.B. 869.

167 Contrast *Moore v Buchanan* (1966) 197 E.G. 565 where, in a claim for nuisance caused by unlawful obstruction of a right of way, no damages were awarded for the claimant's reduced prospects of finding a purchaser for his house. Damages may also be claimed for loss of use and enjoyment of, as distinct from loss of profit from, the premises, as in *Bayoumi v Protim Services Ltd* (1998) 30 H.L.R. 785 CA.

168 See paras 39-003 and following, above.

169 (1815) 5 M. & S. 101.

170 [1982] 1 W.L.R. 149.

171 That the House of Lords eventually held that this public nuisance did not constitute a private nuisance to the claimants as riparian owners ([1983] 2 A.C. 509) in no way affects the points decided at first instance on damages.

172 [1986] Ch. 546.

rather than nuisance,[173] the claimant was held entitled to recover for the extra cost incurred by him by reason of living with his family in other accommodation and also, on the assumption that his demolished house was to be rebuilt, for the cost of removal back there on completion,[174] but not, as too remote, for the loss of use of his adjoining land for various money-making activities carried on by him there.[175] In *Bayoumi v Protim Services Ltd*,[176] a case of breach of statutory duty under the Defective Premises Act 1972 where work carried out by the defendant on a house rendered it uninhabitable, the claimant, a later purchaser, recovered, inter alia, for the expenses of travel to and from the premises to oversee repairs.[177]

**39-029** In *Network Rail Infrastructure Ltd v Conarken Group Ltd*,[178] the expenditure held recoverable by the Court of Appeal was expenditure which led to a loss of profits for Network Rail, the claimant. Road drivers employed by the defendants had inflicted damage to the railway tracks of Network Rail causing severe disruption of rail services, thereby disabling Network Rail from making the affected sections of track available to the companies operating the trains. Network Rail generates its revenue by making the rail network available to these companies for a fee and is at the same time liable to make compensation payments to these companies, under contracts made with them, in respect of periods when the rail network is unavailable to them. The defendants argued that, on grounds of remoteness and scope of duty, there should be no liability in respect of the compensation payments, payments which were calculated by reference to an agreed formula that took into account the effect of the disruptions on the public's confidence in the service and its preparedness to travel by rail, and which represented very substantial loss to the train operating companies going well into the future. This argument did not prevail. The defendants could undoubtedly foresee that financial damage would result from the loss of the use of the tracks and it did not matter that they did not know how the loss would be made up, the extent of the loss or the precise manner in which the loss would come about.[179]

In *Network Rail Infrastructure Ltd v Handy*,[180] Akenhead J described the proceedings as involving a sense of "*déjà vu*". Again, when the defendants damaged the railway track in this case several different points were raised that had not been previously raised, or had been conceded. Again, the defendants were found to be liable to pay damages for the losses suffered by Network Rail under the agreed formula.

---

173 Facts at para.39-009, above.

174 [1986] Ch. 546 at 579H–580D.

175 [1986] Ch. 546 at 578G–579B.

176 (1998) 30 H.L.R. 785 CA.

177 The claimant also recovered for loss of use and enjoyment of the premises for four years and for damage to goods, in this case furniture. But in an action again for, inter alia, breach of statutory duty the claim for so-called loss of use in the form of interest on the capital value of the premises failed in *Bella Casa Ltd v Vinestone Ltd* [2006] B.L.R. 72: see the case at para.31-019, above.

178 [2011] EWCA Civ 644 CA.

179 It was also unsuccessfully argued by the defendants that the contracts between Network Rail and the train operating companies, to which they were not parties, could not bind them to pay the compensation amounts specified therein. Yet here was a genuine, reasonable pre-estimate of the financial loss that the train operating companies would suffer from disruption of the rail services and that the compensation payments represented the best assessment that could be made of the commercial damage done to them, it was appropriate to utilise these payments for the assessment of the damages payable

180 [2015] EWHC 1175 (TCC).

One argument made by the defendants was that the imposition of damages based on a formula that was agreed between the claimant and third parties could be unreasonable. Akenhead J, following comments in the Court of Appeal in the *Conarken Group* case, explained that there is no overarching or separate principle that requires damages to be reasonable as between claimant and defendant. However, if the amount of agreed damages were extremely large, then even if those damages had been suffered they might be reduced based on principles of causation, remoteness, mitigation, or a focus on the scope of the tortious duty.

Another issue was whether economic loss was recoverable in a trespass action when there was no physical damage to land. It was held that neither in negligence nor in trespass was physical damage necessary. In negligence cases it is sufficient if the breach of duty results in substances or physical things being deposited on the property in question in more than a de minimis manner such that the property cannot be used or enjoyed as it otherwise would or could be if the substances or physical things had not been so deposited. In trespass cases, economic losses can be recovered even if there is no damage to, or fouling of, the land. An example given was a defendant who trespasses by parking a fleet of lorries on the claimant's land. Even if there is no physical damage to the land a reasonable charge could be recovered based on the income the claimant land-owner might reasonably have charged for lorries to park there. This would be equivalent to a loss of income.

### (2) Losses grounding a separate cause of action

Apart from the above cases and heads of loss, the authorities on consequential losses are mainly very old, decided in a day when the principles upon how damages are worked out hardly existed. They all concern losses which might have been made a distinct ground of action. On the one hand, it has been held that in the action for trespass to land the claimant could recover as a separate head of consequential loss for damage, caused in the course of the trespass, by reason of the defendant seducing the claimant's daughter as in *Bennett v Allcott*,[181] the claimant's cattle being infected as in *Anderson v Buckton*,[182] or the claimant's goods being taken as is clear from *Pritchard v Long*.[183] On the other hand, in *Bracegirdle v Orford*,[184] where the defendant had broken into the claimant's house under a false and unfounded charge that the claimant was keeping stolen property there, it was considered that the claimant could not recover for slander as a separate head of consequential loss in the trespass action. It is not clear why there should be a difference. It is true that the objection was taken in *Bracegirdle v Orford*,[185] that trespass and slander had different periods of limitation, and indeed, if the only reason for allowing such consequential losses in trespass is to obviate the necessity of a further action for the separate tort,[186] their disallowance would but be **39-030**

[181] (1781) 2 T.R. 166.

[182] (1719) 1 Strange 192; this involved cattle trespass which has its special problems: see paras 39-034 and 39-035, below.

[183] (1842) 9 M. & W. 666, where it was assumed that the claimant could have recovered in respect of the goods if he had only alleged and shown that they were his property.

[184] (1813) 2 M. & S. 77.

[185] (1813) 2 M. & S. 77.

[186] If indeed this is the only reason it has little practical importance now that the forms of action are gone and amendment is allowed so freely.

proper if otherwise a limitation period would be circumvented. This, however, is not how the court arrived at its decision in *Bracegirdle v Orford*.[187]

39-031 It might be thought that the distinction between *Bracegirdle v Orford*,[188] and the cases on the other side of the line reflects the type of interests that the tort of trespass to land is designed to protect.[189] In this connection another very old case can be added to the *Bracegirdle v Orford* side: it was stated by the court in *Huxley v Berg*,[190] that the loss to the claimant by the ill health and death of his wife resulting from her terror when the defendant broke into the house could not constitute a separate head of damage. But there seems no valid reason why trespass to land should be regarded as protecting incidentally the claimant's interest in his cattle and his daughter, and not that in his wife and his reputation. The cases are virtually irreconcilable.

39-032 Yet from a practical viewpoint it does not really matter which group is preferred, since in those cases where the additional damages have been refused by way of specific consequential loss, they have been allowed by a different route as representing an aggravation of the damage. This was what was decided both in *Bracegirdle v Orford*,[191] and in *Huxley v Berg*.[192] And in *Davis v Bromley U.D.C.*,[193] where the defendants had entered upon the claimant's land and demolished a wall in an arbitrary and high-handed manner, a new trial was granted because the damages had been awarded upon the basis of the claimant's pecuniary loss. As Mathew LJ put it, "a material part of the claimant's case was the insult which he had suffered".[194]

39-033 Taking all the cases together, therefore, it would appear that consequential losses will be recoverable either specifically or by way of aggravation, subject as always to their not being too remote in the causal sense.

## (3) The special case of trespass by livestock

39-034 Cattle trespass, since 1971 replaced[195] by a statutory liability for trespassing livestock,[196] presented problems of its own.[197] Where it was the defendant's cattle which went upon the claimant's land and not the defendant himself, it was still the damage to the land, and in particular to crops in the case of cattle trespass, that formed the basic measure of damages; indeed "there seems no doubt", said Lord Goddard CJ in *Wormald v Cole*,[198]

---

187 (1813) 2 M. & S. 77.

188 (1813) 2 M. & S. 77.

189 It could be said that the decision in *Bracegirdle*, involving reputation, now derives support from the Court of Appeal's departure in *Lonrho v Fayed (No.5)* [1993] 1 W.L.R. 1489 CA, from *Thurston v Charles* (1905) 21 T.L.R. 659. But it is thought not; the reasons for this view appear at para.8-129, above.

190 (1815) 1 Stark. 98.

191 (1813) 2 M. & S. 77.

192 (1815) 1 Stark. 98. The terror and consequent death of the wife were received in evidence as showing the violence of the defendant's conduct.

193 (1903) 67 J.P. 275 CA.

194 (1903) 67 J.P. 275 CA at 276. The headnote misleadingly talks of punitive damages.

195 Animals Act 1971 s.13(3).

196 Animals Act 1971 ss.1(1)(c) and 4.

197 For the statutory definition of "livestock", superseding the common law meaning of "cattle", see Animals Act 1971 s.11.

198 [1954] 1 Q.B. 614 CA at 621.

> "that originally the damage in an action of cattle trespass was confined to damage to the surface trespassed upon and to the depasturing of the crop".

It became established, however, that liability in cattle trespass could include damages in respect of injury to other animals, whether by impact, as in *Lee v Riley*,[199] and *Ellis v Loftus Iron Co*,[200] or by infection, as in *Theyer v Purnell*,[201] and also in respect of injury to the person, as in *Wormald v Cole*,[202] while as to damage to goods it was conceded, and Devlin J clearly considered it to be rightly conceded, in *Cooper v Railway Executive*,[203] where trespassing cattle damaged a train by derailment and also the railway track, that such damage was recoverable in cattle trespass. These cases made it quite clear therefore that the interests protected by cattle trespass were in no way limited to those in the land and crops alone, so that any failure to recover for loss beyond injury to land and crops could only be because the damage was too remote in the causal sense. However, the statutory liability for trespassing livestock is restricted to damage "to the land or to any property on it",[204] so that the interest of the owner or occupier of land in his physical safety is no longer protected by this tort.[205]

It would seem that, whenever the trespassing cattle infect the claimant's animals **39-035**
with disease, this damage will not causally be too remote as there is nothing intervening between the act and the damage: the defendant's cattle were already diseased before the trespass.[206] In *Theyer v Purnell*,[207] where the claimant recovered for loss resulting from the infection of his sheep with scab by the defendant's trespassing sheep, the court appeared to regard this as a reasonably foreseeable consequence, A.T. Lawrence J saying that

> "every owner of sheep must be aware that his sheep are liable to develop scab"[208]

but it would seem that the same result should be reached whether the infection is regarded as reasonably foreseeable or not.[209] More difficult are the cases where the trespassing animal causes injury by impact. There are dicta both in cattle trespass cases[210] and in negligence cases[211] that the defendant's liability does not extend beyond damage resulting from acts of the animal in accordance with its ordinary

---

199 (1865) 18 C.B. N.S. 722: mare kicked horse.

200 (1874) L.R. 10 C.P. 10: stallion kicked mare.

201 [1918] 2 K.B. 333. The early case of *Anderson v Buckton* (1719) 1 Strange 192 is similar but the court held that a separate action would have lain for the infecting of the claimant's cattle without any allegation of trespass.

202 [1954] 1 Q.B. 614 CA.

203 [1953] 1 W.L.R. 223.

204 Animals Act 1971 s.4(1)(a).

205 This adopts a recommendation of the Law Commission, *Civil liability for animals* (HMSO, 1967), Law Com. No.13,para.65.

206 See on this aspect of causation para.8-009, above.

207 [1918] 2 K.B. 333.

208 [1918] 2 K.B. 333 at 336.

209 The disapproval of *Re Polemis* [1921] 3 K.B. 560 CA, in *The Wagon Mound* [1961] A.C. 388 PC, does not affect the causation aspect of that decision: see paras 8-012 and 8-014, above.

210 *Manton v Brocklebank* [1923] 2 K.B. 212 CA at 227, per Warrington LJ; *Buckle v Holmes* [1926] 2 K.B. 125 CA at 130, per Atkin LJ.

211 *Cox v Burbidge* (1863) 13 C.B. N.S. 430 at 436 to 437, per Erle CJ; *Aldham v United Dairies* [1940] 1 K.B. 507 CA at 514, per du Parcq LJ (a view repeated by him in *Searle v Wallbank* [1947] A.C. 341 at 360); see too at 511, per Lord Greene MR, according to whom the defendant may not be liable in negligence for an animal's "spontaneous act".

nature. Thus there is no case in which recovery has been given where an animal has injured another animal of the same sex; and in *Wormald v Cole*,[212] where the claimant recovered for physical injuries inflicted by a trespassing heifer, the point was left open whether the claimant could have recovered had she been attacked. Lord Goddard CJ, however, inclined to the view that in such circumstances the claimant would still have succeeded,[213] and the 1971 legislation, while putting an end to all claims for personal injury in this context,[214] appears to confirm that the damage need not result from acts in accordance with the animal's ordinary nature.[215]

### 4. CLAIMANT WITH A LIMITED INTEREST

**39-036** Where the claimant has only a limited interest in the land his damages are confined to the extent of his interest.[216] Such claimants may be divided into two groups, those in present occupation of the land such as lessees and life tenants, and those with a reversionary or security interest in the land.

#### (1) Persons in occupation

**39-037** Of present occupiers, a lessee should recover the amount by which the value of the lease has been diminished and, beyond this, any particular loss in his enjoyment of the land. Where the defendant dug and removed brick earth from the land the lessee was held entitled in *Attersoll v Stevens*,[217] to recover the full value of the brick earth removed because he was entitled by the terms of the lease to the whole brick earth. On the complicated facts there was a disagreement among the judges as to the lessee's interest in the brick earth, but all accepted the principle that he could not recover more than the amount of his interest. Similarly, a life tenant should be awarded the diminished value of the net rents and profits to the extent of his life expectation, except that he could recover for the full damage if liable to the reversioner in respect of it. A mere occupant, however, will recover only nominal damages if he fails to give evidence of the time for which he was entitled to occupy: this result was reached in *Twyman v Knowles*.[218]

#### (2) Persons not in occupation

**39-038** **(a) Persons with a reversionary interest** Reversioners, on the other hand, may only recover damages to the extent of the injury to the reversion. Most of the cases are indeed concerned only with the prior question of whether the reversion had been injured, for without an injury to the reversion no action lies, and establish that permanent physical damage to the land, as by the destruction of houses or the cutting down of trees, is generally[219] necessary to create such an injury.[220] There are,

---

212 [1954] 1 Q.B. 614 CA.

213 [1954] 1 Q.B. 614 CA at 625. The causal and policy limits on recovery generally are discussed in Ch.6, above; in the present connection see, especially, paras 8-040 and 8-127.

214 See the wording of the Animals Act 1971 s.4(1)(a) at para.39-034, above.

215 Implied in the Animals Act 1971 s.4(1)(a).

216 Compare torts affecting goods: see paras 37-012, 37-068 and 38-050 and following, above.

217 (1808) 1 Taunt. 183.

218 (1853) 13 C.B. 222.

219 Exceptionally the reversion may be injured without permanent physical damage to the land as in *Bell v Midland Ry* (1861) 10 C.B. N.S. 287.

however, some few cases which bear directly on the assessment of damages. In the old case of *Bedingfield v Onslow*,[221] where trees were cut down, it was held the reversioner could recover the value of the timber, the tenant being entitled only to damages in respect of the shade, shelter and fruit. In *Mayfair Property Co v Johnston*,[222] where the defendant had encroached upon the claimant's land in setting the foundations of a new wall, the damages awarded to the claimant, a reversioner, were based on the cost of removing the encroachment.[223] The other cases concern the destruction of houses. In *Hosking v Phillips*,[224] where the claimant's house, which stood on land he had leased to a third party, had been destroyed by the defendant, the proper measure of damages was held to be the amount by which the selling price of the claimant's reversion had been reduced. "The reversion", said Parke B,

> "is rendered less valuable, because, instead of the house and land, the claimant had the land alone without the house", and the question was "how much less the land was worth".[225]

In *Moss v Christchurch R.D.C.*,[226] where the claimant's cottage, which he had let, was almost completely destroyed by fire caused by the defendant, the measure of damages awarded was the diminution in the value of the claimant's reversion.

The fullest consideration of the damages recoverable by a reversioner, however, appears in the complex situation presented in *Rust v Victoria Graving Dock Co*.[227] The claimant, the owner of a building estate, sued the defendant in respect of damage caused by a flood to, inter alia,[228] houses erected by builders under building leases. Although admitting that none of the flood damage would last to the end of the leases, the claimant put forward a contention which is best stated in the words of Cotton LJ who said: **39-039**

> "When a man buys land for the purpose of letting it out on building leases the usual course is, that when some of the houses are built and the ground rent is secured, he sells the reversion, or, according to a common expression, sells the ground rent, in order to raise money to go on with the speculation. It is said that, this being so, any depreciation in the selling value of the ground rents is a ground for giving damages to the reversioner."[229]

This contention of the claimant was rejected, because, as Cotton LJ said:

> "On the general rule he cannot get any damages for any wrongful act of the defendants unless the damage is one which will endure and be continuing when the reversion becomes an estate in possession. Now sale is not the natural way of dealing with a reversion, and if it were admitted that every wrongful act which lessens its selling value gives the

[220] There are cases, mostly very early, in which the reversioner failed to establish a cause of action, succeeded on liability but with nothing said on measure of damages, or claimed an injunction rather than damages. It seems unnecessary to continue to cite these numerous cases; they can be found in earlier editions at this juncture of the book.

[221] (1685) 3 Lev. 209.

[222] [1894] 1 Ch. 508.

[223] See, especially, [1984] 1 Ch. 508 at 516.

[224] (1848) 3 Ex. 168.

[225] (1848) 3 Ex. 168 at 182.

[226] [1925] 2 K.B. 750.

[227] (1887) 36 Ch. D. 113 CA.

[228] The other items of damage are considered at paras 39-026, above and 39-041, below.

[229] (1887) 36 Ch. D. 113 CA at 131 and 132.

> reversioner a right to damages, the general rule I have mentioned that a reversioner can only recover damages for permanent injury, would entirely be done away with. The argument for the claimant would be forcible if it could be established that this was a regular understood business, and that ground rents and reversions only existed in a case like this for the purpose of bringing them into the market as recognised saleable articles, to be dealt with as any other saleable article would be."[230]

But no such recognised trade or business had been made out.

**39-040** A few further cases have appeared in modern times. That the claimant was a reversioner in *Abbahall Ltd v Smee*,[231] did not stand in his way in his claim for expenditure in abating the nuisance.[232] In *Irontrain Investments Ltd v Ansari*,[233] where damage had been caused to property held under lease, the lessor reversioner was entitled to recover damages from the tortfeasor for rent lost through its lessee's ceasing to pay rent in consequence of the damage. In so deciding, the court stated that it was following its earlier decision in *Ehlmer v Hall*.[234]

**39-041** **(b) Persons with a security interest** A suit by a claimant with only a security interest in the land is also illustrated by *Rust v Victoria Graving Dock Co*.[235] Part of the land flooded was the subject of building agreements under which houses were in course of erection, and the claimant was bound to make, and had made, advances to the builders on the security of them. Since the claimant was only interested in them as security for his advances, the proper course, said Cotton LJ, was

> "to ascertain what sum would have been required to repair the injury to the structure of the houses caused directly by the flood, and then to ascertain how far the houses before they were repaired would have been a sufficient security for the claimant's advances, and if there was a deficiency then to give to the claimant so much of the sum required to repair the damage to the houses, as in addition to the value of the houses in their damaged state would have been sufficient to make good the advances."[236]

## 5. Aggravation and Mitigation; Exemplary Damages

**39-042** The issue of aggravation and mitigation of damage does not assume the same proportions in damage to land as it does in defamation and in other torts affecting dignitary interests.[237] It was formerly specifically mentioned because some of the old cases dealt with under consequential losses, which losses might have been made a distinct ground of action,[238] may find their true niche as cases of aggravation of damage. Now *Scutt v Lomax*,[239] and *Bryant v Macklin*,[240] provide two factually similar modern illustrations of awards of aggravated damages where land around the claimants' homes had been laid bare of trees by the defendant. The Court of Appeal's award in *Scutt* was £1,000 but in *Bryant* the trial judge's award was increased

---

230 (1887) 36 Ch. D. 113 CA at 132.
231 [2003] 1 W.L.R. 1472 CA; facts at para.39-017, above.
232 See [2003] 1 W.L.R. 1472 CA at [6] and [7].
233 [2005] EWCA Civ 1681 CA.
234 [1993] 1 E.G.L.R. 137 CA.
235 (1887) 36 Ch. D. 113 CA.
236 (1887) 36 Ch. D. 113 CA at 133.
237 See Chs 42 to 47, below.
238 The cases are all dealt with at paras 39-030 to 39-032, above.
239 (2000) 79 P. & C.R. D31 CA.
240 [2005] EWCA Civ 762 CA.

by the Court of Appeal to £4,000 since the aggravation by the defendants' deliberate and high-handed conduct was far greater than in the earlier case.[241] In *Owers v Bailey*,[242] aggravated damages were awarded for interference with a neighbour's right of way involving conduct which was intimidatory, unpleasant and malicious.[243]

39-043 The whole approach to exemplary damages was changed by the decision in *Rookes v Barnard*,[244] since approved in *Broome v Cassell & Co*,[245] and is treated in detail elsewhere.[246] Exemplary damages are now recoverable only where the circumstances of the case bring it within one of the three categories set out by Lord Devlin.[247] Thus decisions spanning well over a century from *Merest v Harvey*,[248] to *Lavender v Betts*,[249] in which exemplary damages have been awarded for wilful damage inflicted upon land fall now to be interpreted as decisions involving awards on account of aggravated damage or, in the single case of *Loudon v Ryder*,[250] as overruled.[251] It is not thought that any of these earlier decisions would have fallen within any of Lord Devlin's categories and it may be doubtful if any will today.[252] Thus no exemplary damages could be awarded in *Scutt v Lomax*,[253] or in *Lawrence v Fen Tigers Ltd*,[254] as the defendant's trespass in the one case and the defendant's nuisance in the other had not been shown to be profit motivated.[255]

## II. OCCUPATION AND USER

39-044 Where the defendant wrongfully deprives the claimant of his land, the claimant will generally wish to recover not the value of the land but the land itself. The principal action is therefore an action for the recovery of the land, historically better known as the action of ejectment. Damages will thus generally be limited to loss arising from the period of wrongful occupation by the defendant. Such damages are recoverable in the action for mesne profits, in origin an action of trespass. This action was formerly brought after judgment in ejectment but it may now be joined

---

241 Facts of both cases at para.39-013, above.

242 [2007] 1 P. & C.R. DG17.

243 No aggravated damages were awarded in the nuisance case of *Lawrence v Fen Tigers Ltd* [2011] EWHC 360 (QB) (facts at para.39-021, above (in a footnote)) as the defendants' conduct was eventually considered not to have justified them: see the very lengthy examination of the evidence at [247]–[299].

244 [1964] A.C. 1129.

245 [1972] A.C. 1027.

246 See Ch.13, above.

247 See paras 13-017 and following, above.

248 (1814) 5 Taunt. 442.

249 [1942] 2 All E.R. 72.

250 [1953] 2 Q.B. 202 CA.

251 See para.13-004, above. However, it is likely that the exemplary damages in *Loudon v Ryder*, which involved a combined trespass to the person and trespass to land, were awarded only for the trespass to the person—the jury's award was "for trespass, £1,500, and the combined assault and exemplary damages, £4,000, in the proportion of assault, £1,000, and exemplary damages, £3,000". If so, there is no overruling applicable to the present context.

252 *Aliter* with trespass by occupation and user, as distinct from trespass causing damage, where cases within Lord Devlin's second category, involving profit-making activity, are easily found: see at para.39-075, below.

253 (2000) 79 P. & C.R. D31 CA. Despite the trial judge's attempt to give exemplary damages; facts at para.39-013, above.

254 [2011] EWHC 360 (QB); facts at para.39-021, above (in a footnote).

255 See *Lawrence* at [300]–[309].

with the action for the recovery of the land itself.[256] If, however, the court declines to order recovery of the land, the claimant will be entitled to its value as well as to mesne profits.[257]

**39-045** Where the defendant merely uses the claimant's land or part of it without depriving him of its possession, no question of recovering the land or its value arises. Damages are necessarily limited to loss arising from the period of wrongful user.[258]

## 1. NORMAL MEASURE

### (1) Where the occupation or user has come to an end

**39-046** The normal measure of damages is the market rental value of the property occupied or used for the period of wrongful occupation or user.[259] Authority is somewhat sparse but this measure is consonant with general principles and with the name of the action for wrongful occupation as one for mesne profits,[260] and as a measure has been confirmed by the Judicial Committee of the Privy Council in the unusual case of *Inverugie Investments v Hackett*,[261] where the claim was not of the normal modest proportions but ran into millions of dollars.[262] An award of mesne profits for trespass by occupiers holding over for a limited period after notice to vacate in *London Development Agency v Nidai*,[263] is illustrative.[264] If the rental value varies due to market fluctuations during the period of wrongful occupation, these fluctuations should be taken into account. If the defendant makes improvements on the land, the rental value should be assessed upon the unimproved value.[265] In the claim for mesne profits in *Earlrose Golf & Leisure Ltd v Fair Acre Investments*

---

256 See the wide provision of CPR r.7.3: "A claimant may use a single claim form to start all claims which can be conveniently disposed of in the same proceedings".

257 This was the final position in *Horsford v Bird* [2006] 1 E.G.L.R. 75 PC: see the case at para.39-057, below. See also the complicated case of *Ramzan v Brookwide Ltd* [2012] 1 All E.R. 903 CA at para 39-058, below.

258 This loss was held to be trivial by the Judicial Committee of the Privy Council in *Stanford International Bank Ltd v Lapps* [2006] UKPC 50, making a dramatic reduction from $270,000 to $500 of the damages for trespass, the matter having been much mishandled by the courts of Antigua and Barbados; see at [39].

259 This assumes no damage or injury to the land, actions for wrongful damage to land usually arising independently of wrongful occupation. But if there should be wrongful damage during wrongful occupation it should be recoverable in the action for mesne profits, and the damages for such will be assessed as in actions for wrongful damage simpliciter.

260 Contrast *Clifton v Huntley* [1948] 2 All E.R. 283 at 284, per Denning J.

261 [1995] 1 W.L.R. 713 PC.

262 See the case at para.39-050, below.

263 [2009] EWHC 1730 Ch.

264 See too *Marsden v Colnbrook Trading Co* [1954] C.L.Y. 890 CA where the Court of Appeal, reversing the court below, awarded the claimant damages for loss due to deprivation of the use of his land by reason of the defendant having vehicles on it, and *The Mayor and Burgesses of the London Borough of Lewisham v Masterson* (2000) 80 P. & C.R. 117 CA where the value of the use of the property was awarded, the relevant value being held to be not the commercial value to the defendant of the use to which he put the property but the value of the occupation he had chosen to enjoy, and the rent at which the defendant might have leased the premises being considered germane to establishing that value.

265 The land itself will of course be recovered in its improved state, and there is no clear machinery whereby the claimant may be made to pay for these improvements even if there are sufficient damages for wrongful occupation from which the value of the improvements could be deducted. Contrast the analogous position with goods at paras 38-040 and 38-041, above.

*Ltd*,[266] where the defendants had by trespass stored plant, equipment and waste material on the claimant's land for a limited period, the Court of Appeal emphasised that the correct approach to determining rental value is by reference to comparables, and the master's award was substantially reduced by the court on account of his reliance on inappropriate and unsuitable rentals.[267]

In *Eaton Mansions (Westminster) Ltd v Stinger Compania de Inversion SA*[268] the lessee of two flats in a mansion block had by trespass installed on its roof air-conditioning apparatus but had before the time of trial removed the apparatus, thereby bringing the wrongful occupation and user to an end. In the suit for damages the trial judge, instead of awarding mesne profits in the usual way, awarded damages by way of a hypothetical licence fee which, as we shall see, is how so-called negotiating damages have come to be awarded where the occupation and user continues into the future without its being brought to an end voluntarily or by mandatory injunction.[269] It is thought that this is not the right approach to the damages for an occupation and user which has already ceased. The trial judge pointed out that a normal feature of negotiating damages is that they look forward in so far as they reflect the compulsory acquisition of the land for the future, and he indeed admitted that what he had done could be said **39-047**

> "simply to quantify what is traditionally known as mesne profits through use of the negotiating damages model".[270]

But this way of going about the damages award is confusing. It can also lead to the wrong result as the computation of mesne profits may well differ from computation of a hypothetical licence fee. Other first instance cases where only user for a temporary period, preceding judgment in the litigation, has been in issue have also taken the hypothetical licence route when the mesne profits route would have been the proper one.[271] As for the appeal to the Court of Appeal in *Eaton Mansions*,[272] there was no argument on whether the hypothetical licence approach was the right one, it being assumed that it was. The issue before the court was as to whether one looked to a hypothetical licence that would have been negotiated at the time of the trespass, when it was expected to be a trespass continuing into the future, or at the time of trial, when it was known that the trespass had come to an end. This the court found somewhat difficult to resolve,[273] eventually opting for time of trial and thereby dismissing the appeal. Had the correct approach by way of mesne profits been taken, there would have been no difficulty in deciding that the mesne profits claimable were limited to the period of actual trespass.

One issue which has received much attention by the courts, and upon which there **39-048**

266 [2009] EWCA Civ 1295 CA.

267 See [2009] EWCA Civ 1295 CA at [37] and following.

268 [2012] EWHC 3354 Ch.

269 See paras 39-060 and following, below.

270 [2012] EWHC 3354 Ch at [48].

271 Such are *Sinclair v Gavaghan* [2007] EWHC 2256 Ch where the defendants, in order to gain access to a property they were developing, trespassed on the apex of a triangle of land which was not used by, and had minimal value for, the claimant owner, and *Field Common Ltd v Elmbridge Borough Council* [2008] EWHC 2079 Ch where a local authority, in constructing a private road with a tarmac surface, encroached on a strip of the claimant's land. For the temporary nature of the trespass in these cases see *Sinclair* at [16] and *Elmbridge* at [18].

272 [2013] EWCA Civ 1308 CA.

273 See Patten LJ's extended discussion at [2013] EWCA Civ 1308 CA at [12] to [24].

is a great deal of authority, is whether the claimant is entitled to the market rental value where he cannot be said to have lost this amount because he would not have let out the land during the period of occupation or, more particularly, would not have let out its use during the period of user.[274] This issue has arisen principally in the prolific cases of trespass by unauthorised mining which occupy a large place in conversion; the authorities all come from the 19th century.[275] In the first of these cases, *Martin v Porter*,[276] and in several subsequent ones[277] a reasonable rent for the use of the passages in the mine, generally called wayleave, has been granted as damages, even though no injury has been done to the land. These damages have been allowed whether the defendant was acting wilfully or innocently,[278] and apparently whether the passages were used to transport the defendant's own minerals from his adjoining mine[279] or the converted minerals of the claimant.[280] For two reasons, however, these cases do not give such firm authority as their number would suggest. First, in all of them the primary issue was whether the costs of severance might be deducted in assessing the damages in respect of the minerals taken and therefore little was said on this point; secondly, the propriety of this award, since no damage had been done to the claimant, was doubted by the court in two of the cases,[281] and even by the House of Lords in *Livingstone v Rawyards Coal Co*.[282] Nevertheless, on the strength of these decisions as establishing the principle, it was held in *Whitwham v Westminster Brymbo Coal Co*,[283] where the defendant had trespassed on the claimant's land by tipping soil from his colliery upon it, that the principle of the wayleave cases applied so that the damages were not to be assessed merely by taking the diminution of the value of the land but by the higher value of the user to which the defendant had put it. Lindley LJ said[284] the law was settled by *Jegon v Vivian*.[285] He put the matter thus:

> "The claimants have been injured in two respects. First, they have had the value of their land diminished; secondly, they have lost the use of their land, and the defendants have had it for their own benefit. It is unjust to leave out of sight the use which the defendants

---

274 That the property was of little or no commercial value to the defendant occupier cannot take the damages below market value: *The Mayor and Burgesses of Lewisham v Masterson* (2000) 80 P. & C.R. 117 CA.

275 See paras 36-028 to 36-039, above. The unauthorised mining cases are also relevant to damage to land: see paras 39-015 and 39-016, above.

276 (1839) 5 M. & W. 351.

277 See *Morgan v Powell* (1842) 3 Q.B. 278; *Hilton v Woods* (1867) L.R. 4 Eq. 432; *Jegon v Vivian* (1871) L.R. 6 Ch. App. 742; *Phillips v Homfray* (1871) L.R. 6 Ch. App. 770.

278 *Hilton v Woods* (1867) L.R. 4 Eq. 432 and *Jegon v Vivian* (1871) L.R. 6 Ch. App. 742 are cases of trespasses which were not wilful. The distinction is important on the connected question of the measure of damages for the minerals taken and converted: see paras 38-031 to 38-036, above.

279 As in *Martin v Porter* (1839) 5 M. & W. 351; *Morgan v Powell* (1842) 3 Q.B. 278 and *Hilton v Woods* (1867) L.R. 4 Eq. 432.

280 As in *Jegon v Vivian* (1871) L.R. 6 Ch. App. 742. Yet this ought surely to be wrong as the defendant is already paying the value of these minerals to the claimant in the same action.

281 See *Hilton v Woods* (1867) L.R. 4 Eq. 432 at 441 and *Phillips v Homfray* (1871) L.R. 6 Ch. App. 770 at 780.

282 (1880) 5 App. Cas. 25 at 38, per Lord Hatherley; concurred in by Lord Blackburn: at 43. The claim was precluded because not pursued in the court below.

283 [1896] 2 Ch. 538 CA.

284 [1896] 2 Ch. 538 CA at 542.

285 (1871) L.R. 6 Ch. App. 742. The other wayleave cases referred to were *Martin v Porter* (1839) 5 M. & W. 351 and *Phillips v Homfray* (1871) L.R. 6 Ch. App. 770.

> have made of this land for their own purposes, and that lies at the bottom of what are called the wayleave cases."[286]

In the result, it was held that as to so much of the claimant's land as was covered by the soil tipped thereon by the defendant, the value of the land by using it for tipping purposes was the correct measure, this value being much greater than the diminution in the land's value since it was the only land procurable for tipping purposes.

In more modern times the courts have applied *Whitwham v Westminster Brymbo Coal Co*,[287] to reach a similar result. In *Penarth Dock Engineering Co v Pounds*,[288] the defendant, having bought a pontoon or floating dock from the claimants, failed to have it removed within a reasonable time from the dock premises of which the claimants were lessees and which were in the course of being closed down by their lessors. In the claimants' action, which was framed as trespass or breach of contract, Lord Denning MR assessed the damages at the benefit obtained by the defendant by having the use of the dock premises after he should have removed the pontoon, although the claimants had lost nothing since the dock premises were of no use to them and their lessors had not required them to pay extra rent.[289] In *Swordheath Properties v Tabet*,[290] the claimants, having let a flat to the first defendant for a three-month term, found at the end of the term that the first defendant had departed and that the remaining defendants, whom he had left in occupation, refused to go. He brought an action, therefore, against all the defendants claiming possession and against the defendants other than the first for damages for trespass, but at first instance the judge refused damages on the ground that it had not been shown that the claimant would have been able to relet during the period of wrongful occupation. The Court of Appeal reversed the decision. Megaw LJ, with whom the other members of the court agreed, said: **39-049**

> "It appears to me to be clear, both as a matter of principle and of authority, that in a case of this sort the claimant, when he has established that the defendant has remained on as a trespasser in residential property, is entitled, without bringing evidence that he could or would have let the property to someone else in the absence of the trespassing defendant, to have as damages for the trespass the value of the property as it would fairly be calculated; and, in the absence of anything special in the particular case it would be the ordinary letting value of the property that would determine the amount of the damages."[291]

These cases were applied by the Judicial Committee of the Privy Council in the very exceptional circumstances of *Inverugie Investments v Hackett*.[292] The claimant, the lessee of a hotel containing 30 apartments situated on Grand Bahama, was evicted from the hotel by the defendants. Lengthy court proceedings followed, with **39-050**

---

[286] [1896] 2 Ch. 538 CA at 541.

[287] [1896] 2 Ch. 538 CA.

[288] [1963] 1 Lloyd's Rep. 359.

[289] It was unsuccessfully argued in *J.S. Bloor (Measham) Ltd v Calcott* [2002] 1 E.G.L.R. 1 that, because Lord Nicholls in *Attorney General v Blake* [2001] 1 A.C. 268 in the context of gain-based damages (for which see Ch.12, above) had referred to *Whitwham* and *Penarth* as "no loss" cases (see 278F–G), the principle behind them did not run to situations where the trespass caused not no loss but a lesser loss than the benefit. The claim was also brought in contract for breach of quiet enjoyment: see para.28-015, above.

[290] [1979] 1 W.L.R. 285 CA.

[291] [1979] 1 W.L.R. 285 CA at 288D–E.

[292] [1995] 1 W.L.R. 713 PC.

the result that the defendant did not give up possession to the claimant until 15-and-a-half years had elapsed. A very substantial claim for damages was made and their Lordships held, disagreeing with the majority of the Bahamian Court of Appeal, that the claimant was entitled to recover the market rent of all 30 apartments over the full 15-and-a-half years. That not all of the apartments could have been let out for all of the time and, indeed, that the hotel might have been run unprofitably could not operate to reduce this entitlement. Lord Lloyd, giving the judgment of the Board, said that the cases

> "establish, beyond any doubt, that a person who lets out goods on hire, or the landlord of residential property, can recover damages from a trespasser who has wrongfully used his property whether or not he can show that he would have let the property to somebody else, and whether or not he would have used the property himself."[293]

**39-051** In so far as these decisions may look beyond even market rental value of the land to the benefit which the defendant had extracted from its user, they are moving away from compensatory to restitutionary damages.[294] Lord Lloyd's view was that the so-called "user principle", as the underlying principle of these cases had been called by Nicholls LJ in *Stoke-on-Trent City Council v W. & J. Wass Ltd*,[295]

> "need not be characterised as exclusively compensatory, or exclusively restitutionary; it combines elements of both".[296]

Yet the choice between compensation and restitution had already been directly faced by the Court of Appeal in *Ministry of Defence v Ashman*.[297] The defendant was an army wife deserted by her husband. She remained in occupation of their married quarters, which were owned by the claimant Ministry, after her husband's licence to occupy them had been terminated until such time as she could be, and was, rehoused in local authority accommodation. The licence fee, or rent, for the married quarters was at the concessionary rate of £95 a month; the local authority accommodation suitable for the defendant's needs stood at £145 a month; and the market rent was approaching £500 a month. The Ministry claimed the market rent. Hoffmann LJ said, with a degree of boldness but also of good sense, that the landowner's claim could be on two alternative bases. He agreed that it was true that

> "it has not been expressly stated that a claim for mesne profits for trespass can be a claim for restitution. Nowadays I do not see why we should not call a spade a spade. In this case the Ministry of Defence elected for the restitutionary remedy."[298]

Lloyd LJ was opposed to this outcome. For him the claim was simply for compensation; the restitutionary route was not open to the court. However, since Kennedy LJ took, though less forcefully, the same stance as Hoffmann LJ—he spoke of the approach being "somewhat analogous to quasi-contractual restitution"[299]—the award made was based upon the benefit to the defendant. Since the

---

293 [1995] 1 W.L.R. 713 PC at 717F.

294 Compare in relation to goods, *Strand Electric Co v Brisford Entertainments* [1952] 2 Q.B. 246 CA, at para.38-067, above.

295 [1991] 1 W.L.R. 1406 CA at 1416D.

296 [1995] 1 W.L.R. 713 PC at 718C.

297 (1993) 25 H.L.R. 513 CA.

298 (1993) 25 H.L.R. 513 CA at 519.

299 (1993) 25 H.L.R. 513 CA at 518.

defendant would never have considered paying a market rent but at the same time was no longer entitled to the married quarters at the Ministry's concessionary rate, the benefit at which the majority arrived was the middle figure of the cost of appropriate local authority accommodation. Then in no time a differently constituted Court of Appeal, but still one containing Hoffmann LJ, followed *Ashman*[300]; the fact pattern in *Ministry of Defence v Thompson*,[301] was identical and the conclusion reached the same. Hoffmann LJ said that the law now was that an owner might today choose to found his mesne profits claim in restitution; this was no doubt a correct statement in view of the majority ruling in *Ashman*.[302]

Where do these two decisions leave the damages claim for mesne profits? That it still exists is undoubted. Hoffmann LJ clearly stated that a claimant was entitled to elect between the compensation claim and the restitution claim[303] and said further that the owner was not in any way prejudiced by being afforded a restitutionary claim since, if his loss were greater than the benefit to the defendant, he could claim that loss by way of compensation.[304] However, this concentration on loss seems to suggest that a claimant could be held strictly to what he can show that he has lost, now that through restitution he can reap the benefit gained by the defendant without resort to a compensation claim. This, however, might be thought to be inconsistent with the result in *Inverugie Investments v Hackett*,[305] which is a result to be commended. It may be that the simple answer is that restitutionary damages focus on the benefit received by the defendant, not the use or profit made from it. He will be able to claim full market value by way of mesne profits damages. **39-052**

*Ministry of Defence v Ashman*,[306] and *Ministry of Defence v Thompson*,[307] themselves are also useful illustrations of a special, possibly unusual, situation where the market rental value not only does not provide the measure of the defendant's benefit but also is an inappropriate measure for the claimant's damages. As was said in *Ashman*[308] by Lloyd LJ, the champion of the right to damages only approach, the market rent will prevail in the vast majority of cases but not where there are abnormal features, which he considered the case before the court had. He was therefore of the view that the claimants should be entitled only to the concessionary rate of £95 a month, the lowest of the three proposed figures, the rate at which they had allowed occupation by the defendant and her husband and at which they would presumably continue to allow other married army personnel to occupy.[309] This of course was not as generous as the award by way of restitution espoused by Lloyd LJ's brethren. **39-053**

In *Shi v Jiangsu Native Produce Import & Export Corp*,[310] the interrelation of compensatory damages and restitutionary damages in the context of mesne profits was in issue. A company, sued by its employee for arrears of salary, counterclaimed for mesne profits in respect of the employee's occupation of a house for over five **39-054**

[300] (1993) 25 H.L.R. 513 CA.
[301] (1993) 25 H.L.R. 552 CA.
[302] (1993) 25 H.L.R. 513 CA.
[303] (1993) 25 H.L.R. 513 CA at 519.
[304] (1993) 25 H.L.R. 513 CA at 520.
[305] [1995] 1 W.L.R. 713 PC; see para.39-050, above.
[306] (1993) 25 H.L.R. 513 CA.
[307] (1993) 25 H.L.R. 522 CA.
[308] (1993) 25 H.L.R. 513 CA.
[309] (1993) 25 H.L.R. 513 CA at 522.
[310] [2010] EWCA Civ 1582 CA.

years after the termination by notice of his licence to occupy it rent-free, after which he had been a trespasser. On his treatment of the counterclaim, which was by way of a cross-appeal, the trial judge was roundly reversed by the Court of Appeal. He had made no award by way of damages because he had assumed, wrongly, that the company's counterclaim was on a restitutionary basis. He then had made a nil award by way of restitution because of exceptional circumstances which he held, again wrongly, subjectively devalued the benefit to the employee of occupying the premises to the extent of eliminating it. These exceptional circumstances were that the employee was an employee of the company, had lived in the house rent-free, believed that he had a right to occupy it and may have had nowhere else to move to, and that the company had long delayed claiming possession and was a foreign company that had wound up its domestic operations. Dyson LJ, whose judgment was the only one to deal with the counterclaim and cross-appeal, pointed out that the counterclaim was clearly pleaded as a claim for compensation and held the company was entitled to damages by way of mesne profits based on the rental market value of the house as that amount represented the company's loss.[311] While this disposed of the company's cross-appeal, and in its favour, Dyson LJ sought to indicate what should have been the decision of the trial judge had the counterclaim indeed been advanced on a restitutionary basis. Dyson LJ rightly saw none of the factors listed by the trial judge as being exceptional circumstances, so that there was no basis for treating the value to the employee of the benefit of occupation as being less than the rental market value.[312] The decisions in *Ministry of Defence v Ashman* and the similar *Ministry of Defence v Thompson*,[313] were very much to the fore, both at first instance and in the Court of Appeal, and Dyson LJ specifically referred to Hoffmann LJ's saying in the former case that the value of the right of occupation to a former licensee who has occupied at a concessionary rent is not in itself a special, or exceptional, circumstance though it may become one when taken in conjunction with the fact that the occupant has no choice but to stay in the premises until he or she is rehoused in cheaper accommodation.[314] That was not however the employee's position here; he could have moved to alternative accommodation had he been so minded. This valuable decision of the Court of Appeal thus accepts that it is now recognised that recovery for mesne profits may be on a damages basis or on a restitution basis and that whether the one route or the other is pursued lies in the election of the party claiming. In addition, it affords an illustration of the situation where recovery will be the same on either basis, and also an illustration of the situation where either recovery will be of rental market value because that constitutes both the loss to the landowner and the benefit to the trespasser. The decision further indicates that there is only limited scope for reduction of the value of the benefit to the trespasser by way of subjective devaluation.

### (2) Where the occupation or user is continuing

39-055 **(a) Occupation or user without expropriation** Should, without expropriation of the land, the wrongful occupation or user continue into the future and beyond the time of action brought because a mandatory injunction has been refused or,

---

311 [2010] EWCA Civ 1582 CA at [23].
312 [2010] EWCA Civ 1582 CA at [25] and [26].
313 At para.39-051, above.
314 [2010] EWCA Civ 1582 CA at [25].

alternatively, has not been claimed, it is thought that, strictly speaking, the normal measure of damages should still be regarded as mesne profits up to the time of action and thereafter damages for the prospective future loss which the courts now calculate by way of a hypothetical licence fee. This is today a developing area of law and the ever-growing weight of authority is collected below under the rubric of prospective loss.[315]

**(b) Expropriation** Should the wrongful occupation and user go as far as expropriation of the land and again a mandatory injunction restoring it to the claimant is refused or not claimed, awarding a hypothetical licence fee becomes inappropriate so that the normal measure of damages becomes the value of the expropriated land together with mesne profits up until the time that judgment in the case gives the claimant that value in lieu of an injunction. This was the result in both *Horsford v Bird*,[316] and *Ramzan v Brookwide Ltd*,[317] it being said at first instance in *Ramzan*,[318] that deliberate misappropriation of property was so rare that counsel had found no case of it other than *Horsford*. **39-056**

In *Horsford v Bird*,[319] where a mandatory injunction to remove a boundary wall and fence encroaching upon the claimant's land had been refused, the Judicial Committee of the Privy Council held that the claimant had a claim for damages representing the value of the expropriated land and **39-057**

> "a clear claim to damages in the form of mesne profits for the use of his land by"

the defendant, the mesne profits being up until the time that judgment in the case gave the claimant the value of the land in lieu of an injunction.[320] The trial judge and the Court of Appeal awarded the claimant the market value of the expropriated land as an undeveloped plot but the Judicial Committee doubled this figure to reflect the value of the land to the defendant as part of his garden.[321]

*Ramzan v Brookwide Ltd*,[322] is a complicated case, both factually and legally. Two adjoining buildings belonged, the one to an individual who ran a restaurant in his building, and the other to a financially powerful company which was in the process of converting its building into several flats. By way of a so-called flying freehold the restaurateur owned a store room on the first floor of the company's building. Access to this store room was from, and only from, the first floor part of the restaurant, the store room also providing access to a fire escape which ended up at the back of the restaurateur's building. By trespass the company, acting in a high-handed and highly unpleasant manner, incorporated the store room into its building in order to provide extra space for the flats it was constructing, at the same time knocking down the fire escape. By these actions of the company the use of the first floor part of the restaurant was barred since there was no longer available to it a fire escape as was required by regulations. **39-058**

---

315 At paras 39-060 and following.
316 [2006] UKPC 3.
317 [2012] 1 All E.R. 903 CA.
318 [2011] 2 All E.R. 38.
319 [2006] UKPC 3.
320 See [2006] UKPC 3 at [15].
321 There is no explicit discussion in the judgment, delivered by Lord Scott, as to whether this award is to be regarded as compensatory or restitutionary. See at [2006] UKPC 3 at [13] and [14].
322 [2012] 1 All E.R. 903 CA.

**39-059** Among the various items of damages claimed were, as in *Horsford*, the capital value of, and the mesne profits from, the expropriated property, being in this case the store room with the appendage of the fire escape. The trial judge had awarded £55,000 for the capital value of the store room and £23,000 for mesne profits. The £55,000 was a figure agreed by the experts and was not appealed, but the figure for mesne profits was first drastically reduced by agreement of the parties and then total eliminated by the Court of Appeal.[323] This refusal to allow any amount for mesne profits could be misconceived. Arden LJ and also Lloyd LJ said that since the claimant needed the store room for access to the fire escape he could not let it out.[324] This fails to take account of the host of authorities, dealt with above, that it is irrelevant that the claimant would not, or could not, have let out or otherwise used the property.[325]

## 2. PROSPECTIVE LOSS

**39-060** The problems which arise in cases of damage to land in relation to continuing wrongs[326] are not repeated in cases of occupation and user. This is because in the cases of claims for mesne profits by owners of land already considered,[327] and indeed in nearly every such case, the wrongful user will either have ceased by the time of action or, if it is still persisted in by the defendant, will be put a stop to for the future by the court granting to the claimant an injunction requiring the defendant to desist from any continuance of his trespasses. Neither a question of whether the wrong is or is not a continuing one nor a question of damages for loss in future periods of wrongful user will arise. But what measure of damages will the court award in the case where, for one reason or another, an injunction to prevent a continuance of the trespass is refused?[328]

**39-061** This issue first arose in the 1970s in *Bracewell v Appleby*.[329] Six houses built on an estate formed a cul-de-sac around a private road, each of the six properties comprising part of the road with appropriate grants and reservations of rights of way over the road for the purpose of access to the houses. The defendant, who owned

---

323 [2012] 1 All E.R. 903 CA at [89] and [95]. The trial judge's award for the rebuilding of the fire escape was rightly eliminated, Lloyd LJ pointing out, at [97] that claiming the cost of rebuilding within the expropriated property was inconsistent with recovery of its capital value.

324 [2012] 1 All E.R. 903 CA at [67] and [95].

325 There was a further complication. The expropriated store room had for a good many years before the trial formed part of one of the flats constructed and let out by the defendant company in its building The trial judge had made an award of £20,000 as the rent from that flat and, recognising that this effectively doubled up with her award of mesne profits, deducted the £20,000 from her mesne profits award. The reason for this seemingly odd approach was that in her earlier judgment on liability she had found the defendant to be a trustee of the expropriated property so that there was not only a claim in tort but also one for breach of trust, and it was for this breach of trust that the £20,000 was being awarded, The Court of Appeal, by giving no amount for mesne profits (see text of this paragraph), had therefore to turn to the much larger award for lost restaurant profits (see para.39-067, below) to make an appropriate adjustment, and it took Arden LJ a lengthy analysis (at [49]–[64]) to reach the clearly correct conclusion that the claim for breach of trust and the claim for loss of profit were not cumulative but alternative remedies, thereby eliminating the award for breach of trust. It is to be hoped that this trust complication can now be put to rest and not appear again.

326 See paras 39-024 and 39-025, above.

327 See paras 39-044 and following, above.

328 These will tend to be damages given under the jurisdiction originally conferred on the equity courts by Lord Cairns' Act in 1858: see para.1-015, above.

329 [1975] Ch. 408.

one of the houses and who had acquired a plot of land adjoining its grounds, proceeded to build on the plot a new house, access to which could only be over the private road and the grounds of the defendant's existing house. The claimants, who each owned another of the six houses on the cul-de-sac, brought an action claiming a declaration that there was no right of way over the private road for the purpose of gaining access to the new house and seeking an injunction restraining the defendant from using the road to reach the house. The declaration was granted, but the injunction was nevertheless refused because the claimants had delayed proceedings until the building of the new house was at an advanced stage. Graham J accordingly proceeded to award damages in lieu, and took the view that

> "the defendant must be liable to pay an amount of damages which in so far as it can be estimated is equivalent to a proper and fair price which would be payable for the acquisition of the right of way in question."[330]

While he accepted that the claimants were reluctant to accommodate the defendant as they did not want an extra house on the cul-de-sac, he thought that, for the purpose of assessing damages, the claimants

> "must not be treated as if they were in the extremely powerful bargaining position which an interlocutory injunction would have given them if it had been obtained before the defendant started operations."[331]

The figure to aim at was that which, in negotiation, the claimants would have accepted as adequate to compensate them for the loss of amenity and the increased user of the road, but which at the same time would not be so high as to deter the defendant from building at all. Graham J considered that the defendant would have been prepared to pay a relatively high proportion of his profit for the right of way needed to achieve the building of the new house in which he wanted to, and now did, live, and he awarded damages based on 40 per cent of that profit.[332] In this decision Graham J adopted the approach taken only a year earlier by Brightman J in *Wrotham Park Estate Co v Parkside Homes*,[333] a case which involved not trespass to land but sale of land,[334] and by being a year late lost his place in legal history as damages of this nature are now, 40 years on, universally referred to as "*Wrotham Park* damages" whatever the tort or contract concerned.

Before turning to the many cases which have appeared since *Bracewell v Appleby*,[335] it is worth indicating briefly how in this context the courts have rationalised the recovery of damages. Two attempts have surfaced. The one relies on the so-called user principle whereby a person whose property has been used by another without consent should be entitled to claim the amount that giving permission for use of the property would have cost. The other is that the property owner has been deprived of a bargaining opportunity. The two rationalisations attempt to justify what has now become the accepted way of calculating the damages by way of a hypothetical licence fee. The difficulty is that neither approach is easy to square with 39-062

330 [1975] Ch. 408 at 419D–E above.
331 [1975] Ch. 408 at 419H–420A.
332 [1975] Ch. 408 at 420B–C.
333 [1974] 1 W.L.R. 798, where only 5 per cent of profit was awarded. But then the profit was £50,000 as compared with the £5,000 in *Bracewell*.
334 See details of the case at para.27-053, above.
335 [1975] Ch. 408.

the compensatory role of damages; as to the first there is no loss to the claimant where he would not have used the property himself and as to the second the bargaining opportunity is in most cases one that the claimant property owner would have refused.[336] However, the turn of the century has seen the arrival of restitutionary damages which permits a new rationalisation for future cases, a rationalisation which can lead to different levels of recovery.

**39-063** In a number of the cases adopting the same approach in awarding damages in lieu of a mandatory injunction as appeared in the opening case of *Bracewell* it was a right to light that had been infringed.[337] This was so in *Carr-Saunders v Dick McNeil Associates*,[338] where, evidence of the amount of profit the defendants would have made from development of their site being lacking, £8,000 was awarded by way of general damages.[339] In *Deakins v Hookings*,[340] where the infringement had reduced the value of the property by an estimated £1,500, damages were assessed at £4,500 on what was referred to by the trial judge as the user principle.[341] A mandatory injunction was indeed granted here, the assessment of damages being a precaution should there be a successful appeal against the injunction. So too in *HKRUK II (CHC) Ltd v Heaney*,[342] a mandatory injunction was awarded but a computation of damages for the infringement was also made, the trial judge taking into account a number of factors to reach £225,000 as the amount that he considered right for the hypothetical licence between the dominant and servient owners. In *Tamares (Vincent Square) Ltd v Fairpoint Properties (Vincent Square) Ltd*,[343] infringement of a right to light led to an award based on a substantial proportion of the defendant's profit, but the trial judge simply followed the earlier

---

[336] For all this in more detail see paras 14-011 and 14-012, above. *Severn Trent Water Ltd v Barnes* [2004] 2 E.G.L.R. 95 CA is an interesting case among the cases about to be considered because, unusually, it is a case where the rationale of loss of business opportunity makes some sense. In laying a water main in the exercise of its statutory functions the defendant water undertaker committed a trivial, accidental and unintentional trespass by placing part of the main under the extreme corner of an over two acre parcel of the claimant's grazing land. As a statutory undertaker the defendant had been entitled to enter on land and do the mains work subject only to service of notice on the landowner affected and, later, to payment to him of compensation which, in the absence of agreement, would be assessed by the Lands Tribunal. The defendant had not served notice on the claimant because unaware of his land ownership and, when the true position was discovered after the main had been constructed, it was too late for an injunction and damages were claimed. Here the water undertaker under its statutory powers could require a landowner to give up to it the use of his land, in which circumstances it is right to say that the landowner has lost the opportunity to negotiate compensation before the trespass, and, with no choice but to let the defendant proceed, would have bargained for as much compensation as he could muster. At the same time the fact that the defendant could require the claimant to give up the use of his land serves to explain why the amount finally awarded was small compared with awards in other cases. This was, as the Court of Appeal pointed out (at [39]), not only because loss and benefit were insignificant but also because in all the authorities cited the defendant would have been unable to proceed without the claimant owner's permission thereby placing him in a much stronger position to negotiate a price or licence fee prior to trespass, being constrained only by market forces.

[337] In *Snell & Prideau v Dutton Mirrors* [1995] 1 E.G.L.R. 259 CA, the infringement of the easement, there a right of way rather than a right to light, was dealt with as wrongful damage rather than wrongful user: see the case at para.39-017, above.

[338] [1986] 1 W.L.R. 922.

[339] [1986] 1 W.L.R. 922 at 931C–932A.

[340] [1994] 1 E.G.L.R. 190.

[341] Contrast for this principle para.39-051, above.

[342] [2010] EWHC 2245 Ch.

[343] [2007] 1 W.L.R. 2167.

*Bracewell* and *Carr-Saunders*; the possibility of a restitutionary approach does not appear to have been even raised with him.

Most of the cases have involved a defendant who has built, or otherwise interfered, over the line. In *Stadium Capital Holdings v St Marylebone Properties Co Plc*,[344] the trespass arose from the defendant's advertising hoarding intruding into the airspace of the claimant's land. Here the Court of Appeal accepted that the damages should be awarded on a restitutionary basis but regarded this as generally meaning a hypothetical licence fee for the trespasser's occupation of the land. The judge was considered wrong, in the circumstances of the case, to have thought in terms of awarding all of the defendant's gains; this amounted to an account of profits. The case was sent back for a reassessment which it fell to Vos J to make in *Stadium Capital Holdings (No.2) Ltd v St Marylebone Properties Co Plc*.[345] On damages Vos J started from the position that the parties were in agreement that a hypothetical licence fee was the appropriate way of going about the assessment[346] and that what was in dispute concerned the factors to be taken into account in arriving at the hypothetical licence fee. Vos J proceeded to conduct a useful review of the relevant authorities[347] and concluded that, in the light of the claimant's holding the trump card of being able to stop the defendant's retention of the hoarding in its place, the hypothetical licence fee should be half of the expected net revenue that the defendant would receive from a particular advertiser. A further case of an advertising hoarding encroaching on to the claimant's land went to the Court of Appeal, His Honour Judge Seymour below having awarded only nominal damages. The defendants in *Enfield London Borough Council v Outdoor Plus Ltd*,[348] did not own the land upon which the advertising hoarding was erected but had entered into a licence agreement with a Mr Shah entitling them to erect it on his land. The hoarding was duly erected on that land but inadvertently it was built with its steel supports extending over the boundary of Mr Shah's land on to waste land belonging to the claimant. This marginal invasion of the claimant's land did not come to light for several years. Judge Seymour had awarded nominal damages on the ground that, had the parties appreciated the position before erection, no trespass would have occurred as the hoarding would have been built wholly within Mr Shah's land. The Court of Appeal rightly saw this as the wrong approach to the damages question. What mattered was that the trespass had occurred and it was necessary to ascertain the value of the benefit to the defendant of that trespass, which was the function of the hypothetical negotiation,[349] the court being in no doubt that the hypothetical negotiation approach was the right one to adopt.[350] The court then turned to what, in place of nominal damages, should be awarded. Split ownership of the site used for an erection being unprecedented in the authorities, the Court of Appeal accepted the evidence of the joint expert in the case that it was likely that the licence fee would be split evenly between the parties, here the claimant and Mr Shah. **39-064**

Cases of building over the line continue but without anything new in legal **39-065**

---

344 [2010] EWCA Civ 952 CA.
345 [2011] EWHC 2856 Ch.
346 [2011] EWHC 2856 Ch at [56].
347 [2011] EWHC 2856 Ch at [57]–[68].
348 [2012] EWCA Civ 608 CA.
349 [2012] EWCA Civ 608 CA at [47].
350 [2012] EWCA Civ 608 CA at [53].

analysis. *Seeff v Ho*,[351] was a dispute between neighbouring householders where the defendants built an extension slightly encroaching over the claimants' property without decreasing its value and possibly–it is nowhere stated–without increasing the value of the defendants' property. The Court of Appeal moved up the trial judge's award of damages from £200 to £500 but the basis of this award is not made at all clear in the only reasoned judgment of Thomas LJ.[352] Hypothetical licence fees were not mentioned. In *Jones v Ruth*,[353] where by trespass and nuisance the defendant had added an extra storey to his building, Patten LJ in the Court of Appeal's one reasoned judgment went along the now familiar route of the hypothetical negotiated licence and came up with one third of the increased value of the defendant's property,[354] thereby correcting the trial judge's award of the amount by which the value of the defendant's property had been increased

**39-066** A very different form of intrusion upon a claimant's property made its appearance before the Supreme Court in *Bocardo SA v Star Energy UK Onshore Ltd*,[355] where modern technology had produced a dramatic variant on the cases of unauthorised mining which dominated in the 19th century, already considered,[356] with the important difference that here the intrusion was set to continue into the future after judgment. The defendant company in the construction of oil wells entered the substrata beneath the surface of the claimant company's land at 800 to 2,900 feet below ground level and, despite the fact that the entry was at such a very great depth, it was held to constitute a trespass. Yet the case does not take the law further on the damages front as the parties were agreed that damages assessed on user are based on the negotiated price for the grant of a licence, and because the main argument on quantum revolved around the assessment of compensation under statute. Lord Clarke set out at some length how he saw the law as having developed in this area[357]; but there is nothing new in what he said. In particular, no mention is made of whether the damages at common law are to be regarded as compensatory or as restitutionary.

## 3. Consequential Losses

**39-067** The pattern of recovery for consequential losses will be similar to that in cases of misappropriation of goods.[358] Again there is not a great deal of authority but the position is clear. In *Barclays Bank v Jones*,[359] the defendant refused to vacate a single room in the claimant's flat and, since this prevented the claimant from letting the whole flat, damages were assessed on the rent thus lost by the claimant. In *Whitwham v Westminster Brymbo Coal Co*,[360] just considered, as to that part of the claimant's land which was uncovered by soil tipped by the defendant from his colliery, the claimant recovered the diminution in its value, since by covering one part of the land with soil the defendant had made the rest useless for any other purpose

[351] [2011] EWCA Civ 186 CA.

[352] See [2011] EWCA Civ 186 CA at [44] to [46].

[353] [2012] 1 W.L.R. 1495 CA. Facts at para.39-022, above.

[354] See his reasoning at [39] to [41].

[355] [2011] 1 A.C. 380.

[356] At para.39-048, above.

[357] [2011] 1 A.C. 380 at [118]–[124].

[358] See Ch.38, above.

[359] [1955] J.P.L. 822.

[360] [1896] 2 Ch. 538 CA.

than that of tipping soil. Where in the curious and difficult case of *Ramzan v Brookwide Ltd*,[361] the claimant, barred by the defendant's expropriation of his flying freehold from using the first floor of his restaurant had lost profits, recovery was allowed him for many years of restaurant profits amounting to over £200,000.[362] In all these cases the loss of profits relates to property other than the property directly affected by the tort, whether trespass, nuisance or other wrong.

In addition, claims for non-pecuniary loss would seem to be in order; to be dispossessed of one's property, or to have its use interfered with, may well cause inconvenience, discomfort and distress. However, such claims will generally give rise to an entitlement to aggravated damages since they will stem from culpable and unattractive conduct of the defendant; such damages are dealt with later.[363] **39-068**

## 4. CLAIMANT WITH A LIMITED INTEREST

Where the claimant's limited interest consists in rights over the defendant's land, the damages will be limited to the period of wrongful interference. This was the position in *Moore v Buchanan*,[364] where there was a wrongful obstruction of a right of way. Cases of this nature, but where the wrongful interference has not come to an end, also dominate where recovery for prospective expense is in issue; such cases have already been considered.[365] **39-069**

Where the claimant's limited interest is by virtue of being occupier but not owner of the land, the claim could no doubt be for mesne profits where the defendant is someone other than the owner; but there are no cases. There is, however, an abundance of authority where the owner is the defendant, generally being a landlord who has evicted his tenant. Here damages are given for the loss of use and for inconvenience, the award thus comprising elements of pecuniary and of non-pecuniary loss. It is indeed the aggravation of the damages for non-pecuniary loss, frequently combined with an exemplary award, that is the controlling feature of these cases; they accordingly fall for consideration below.[366] **39-070**

What is important, however, for the evicted tenant today is not so much his entitlement at common law but rather the additional statutory remedy which has been available to him since the Housing Act 1988 introduced a tortious liability in damages against a landlord evicting his tenant. The damages recoverable in the statutory action, which have proved substantial, are considered later so that their interplay with the damages at common law may be examined at the same time.[367] **39-071**

---

361 [2012] 1 All E.R. 903 CA.

362 Full facts and the other, more difficult but lesser, items of damages are at paras 39-058 and 39-059, above.

363 See para.39-072, below.

364 (1966) 197 E.G. 565.

365 At paras 39-060 and following, above.

366 See paras 39-072 and following, below. For a case setting out various elements of the damages see *Sampson v Wilson* (1997) 29 H.L.R. 18 CA, at para.39-085, below.

367 See paras 39-077 and following, below.

## 5. AGGRAVATION AND MITIGATION; EXEMPLARY DAMAGES

**39-072** In *Drane v Evangelou*,[368] where a landlord resorted to trespass in order to evict his protected tenant[369] and the Court of Appeal upheld the county court judge's decision that such monstrous behaviour called for exemplary damages of £1,000, two members of the court saw the award as much as one of aggravated damages. Lawton LJ said:

> "It seems to me that my task here is to look at the facts and to start by asking the question what sort of sum would it have been proper to award for aggravated damages in this case, which undoubtedly was one for aggravated damages. To deprive a man of a roof over his head in my judgment is one of the worst torts which can be committed. It causes stress, worry and anxiety."[370]

He concluded that he would not have thought the sum awarded as excessive for aggravated damages,[371] and Goff LJ agreed.[372]

**39-073** Further claims by harassed tenants evicted in a highly unpleasant manner by unscrupulous landlords[373] have followed and again reached Court of Appeal level. Another award of £1,000 with combined compensatory and exemplary elements was upheld by that court against a landlord sued by two tenants in nuisance in *Guppy (Bridport) v Brookling and James*.[374] In *Asghar v Ahmed*,[375] separate awards for aggravated damages and exemplary damages were upheld, the one to compensate the claimant for what was described as enormous suffering, distress and intolerable anxiety and the other to punish the defendant, and in the respective amounts of £500 and £1,000. In *McMillan v Singh*,[376] the Court of Appeal stepped in where the judge below had declined to make an award, being deflected, wrongly,[377] by the fact that the tenant had been in arrears of rent, and gave £250 each for aggravated and exemplary damages, while in *Millington v Duffy*,[378] the distress and inconvenience suffered by the claimant was considered to be inadequately compensated at £150 and an award of £500 was substituted, exemplary damages having been expressly disclaimed by the claimant in the court below though they were in the Court of Appeal's view available. Cases of tenants suing for illegal eviction, often with a change of locks, have continued to appear but, being generally county court decisions for still comparatively small sums, they are ill reported; their existence however is undoubted. Amounts have increased, which is in part due to

---

[368] [1978] 1 W.L.R. 455 CA.

[369] Facts at para.13-025, above.

[370] [1978] 1 W.L.R. 455 CA at 461E–F.

[371] [1978] 1 W.L.R. 455 CA at 461G.

[372] [1978] 1 W.L.R. 455 CA at 463C. He said, with more precision, that "the award could be justified as compensation with the addition of aggravated damages". Contrast *Thompson v Commissioner of Police of the Metropolis* and *Hsu v Commissioner of Police of the Metropolis* [1998] Q.B. 498 CA, cases of wrongful arrest, false imprisonment, assault and malicious prosecution, where the Court of Appeal said that, contrary to the practice current at the time, separate awards should be made for the basic damages and the aggravated damages: at 516E.

[373] The eviction was not by the landlord in *Islam v Yap* [2009] EWHC 3603 (QB); aggravated and exemplary damages were awarded as well as damages based on the claimant's rental rate.

[374] (1983) 14 H.L.R. 1 CA.

[375] (1984) 17 H.L.R. 25 CA.

[376] (1984) 17 H.L.R. 120 CA.

[377] See (1984) 17 H.L.R. 120 CA at 124.

[378] (1984) 17 H.L.R. 232 CA.

inflation, but, since the exemplary award has been frequently combined with the aggravated damages and even the general damages in one global figure, it is then impossible to allocate as between the various elements in the award.[379] Quite substantial awards are not unknown. Thus the tenant suing his landlord and two others for unlawful eviction in *Mehta v Royal Bank of Scotland*,[380] achieved separate awards of £7,500 in exemplary damages together with £10,000 general damages and £10,000 aggravated damages. The comparatively high exemplary award and aggravated damages are to be explained, respectively, by the tortfeasors' having made "much larger profits" than usual and by "the element of distress" continuing well after the eviction.[381] *Daley v Mahmood*,[382] said in the judgment to be "one of the most serious cases of harassment followed by unlawful eviction", appears at first sight to go further than *Mehta* as a total of £16,000 aggravated damages for the harassment and eviction together with a total of £30,000 exemplary damages were awarded, but these amounts were to be divided between four tenants, being allocated equally between them.

Claims between adjoining occupiers as well as between tenants and landlords can give rise to aggravated and exemplary damages but so far have not been particularly successful. In *Ketley v Gooden*,[383] an occupier trespassed upon his neighbour's land in order to assist in the construction of a development from which he expected to make a profit. The trial judge awarded, in addition to general damages and £1,000 aggravated damages, £1,500 exemplary damages, but the Court of Appeal refused to uphold the exemplary element in the damages though it is difficult to see why.[384] In *Horsford v Bird*,[385] the Judicial Committee of the Privy Council endorsed the Court of Appeal of Antigua and Barbuda's reversal of the trial judge in so far as it was held that the defendant's conduct in building a boundary wall over the line was not such as to justify an award of aggravated damages against him.[386] **39-074**

The exemplary element in the awards in all of these cases is attributable to their falling within the second of the three categories where exemplary damages are still permissible, as set out by Lord Devlin in *Rookes v Barnard*,[387] namely the category comprising cases in which the defendant has acted tortiously with a view to profit.[388] If therefore, exceptionally, profit motivation cannot be shown in a wrongful eviction case, exemplary damages cannot be given. With the landlord himself the profit **39-075**

379 See the list referred to in the footnote at the end of para.39-082, below as to the aggravated and exemplary part of the awards, then being made, which combined common law and statutory awards; this list also shows that much more is available to the tenant under the statutory action (dealt with at paras 39-077 and following, below).

380 [1999] 3 E.G.L.R. 153.

381 [1999] 3 E.G.L.R. 153 at 162, col.2.

382 [2006] 1 P. & C.R. DG 10 at D29.

383 (1997) 73 P. & C.R. 305 CA.

384 Pill LJ simply said, without giving reasons, that the case was not a suitable one for exemplary damages: at 313.

385 [2006] 1 E.G.L.R. 75 PC.

386 [2006] 1 E.G.L.R. 75 PC at [14]. Facts at para.39-057, above.

387 [1964] A.C. 1129. The whole approach to exemplary damages has been changed by this decision, confirmed in *Broome v Cassell & Co* [1972] A.C. 1027. For the details of the changed approach see Ch.13, above.

388 This category is prominent with occupation and user of land though not with damage to land as a defendant who occupies and uses land is more likely to be profit-motivated than one who does damage to it.

motivation should be obvious but in *Ramdath v Oswald Daley*,[389] where the eviction was engineered not only by the landlord but also by his managing agent and both were sued, the Court of Appeal set aside the additional exemplary award against the agent since any profit from the eviction was not to enure to him and, accordingly, he did not fall within Lord Devlin's second category.[390]

**39-076** Lord Devlin's other two categories[391] do not appear so far to have produced any exemplary damages awards in this area of tort. Nor is it anticipated that the third category, where there has to be express authorisation by statute, will do so. As for the first category, encompassing government servants acting oppressively, arbitrarily or unconstitutionally, it may be that the appearance of questionable raids on private premises by the police and other organs of government could give scope for exemplary damages. Indeed there is a precedent for this in one of the two earliest cases of an exemplary award, *Wilkes v Wood*.[392]

## 6. THE STATUTORY ACTION

### (1) The statutory measure of damages

**39-077** **(i) In general** Statute introduced, by ss.27 and 28 of the Housing Act 1988, a tortious liability in damages against a landlord who unlawfully deprives a residential occupier of his occupation, either by evicting him or by acting in such an unreasonable way that the tenant gives up his occupation. Just as the common law action to redress wrongful occupation and user of land, namely the action for mesne profits, can be seen as an action in restitution as well as an action for damages,[393] so also the recovery which is available in the statutory tort has distinct overtones of restitution. For the damages are measured not by the deprivation of the evicted tenant but by the increase in the value of the property to the evicting landlord.[394] The amounts awarded by the courts can, for the particular context, be substantial.[395] Thus in one of the earliest decisions on the Act, *Tagro v Cafane*,[396] the Court of Appeal refused to interfere with an award of £31,000 though regarding the amount as high; "the appeal", said Lord Denning MR, "is a cautionary tale for landlords who are minded unlawfully to evict their tenants".[397] In *Murray v Aslam*,[398] the award was just short of £35,000. While set aside by the Court of Appeal this was because, the tenant having been reinstated, the case was held not to be properly within s.27; the propriety of the award, provided the valuations were right, was not in question. In

389 (1993) 25 H.L.R. 273 CA; [1993] 1 E.G.L.R. 82 CA.

390 Whether the award against the landlord as joint tortfeasor can then be supported may be questioned: see further on this aspect paras 52-062 and following, below. Nor can the agent be sued for profit under the statutory action (dealt with at paras 39-077 and following, below): *Sampson v Wilson* (1997) 29 H.L.R. 18 CA.

391 For treatment of the categories and exemplary damages generally, see Ch.13, above.

392 (1763) Lofft. 1.

393 See para.39-051, above.

394 Section 28 sets out the measure of damages; it is so titled.

395 Interest, however, is not added. See Dillon LJ in *Jones and Lee v Miah and Miah* (1992) 24 H.L.R. 578 CA at 591: "justice did not require the award according to the special formula to be topped up by an award of interest."

396 [1991] 1 W.L.R. 378 CA.

397 [1991] 1 W.L.R. 378 CA at 380B.

398 (1995) 27 H.L.R. 384 CA.

*Mehta v Royal Bank of Scotland*,[399] the statutory damages amounted to £45,000. The award was said to be higher than the general run of statutory damages because

> "much larger profits were made by the tortfeasors and the element of distress … continued for some months after [the eviction]".[400]

But only the profit, and not the distress, is relevant for the statutory, as distinct from any compensatory, award.[401]

39-078 On all of the issues that are about to be considered there was much uncertainty over the appropriate damages for quite some time after the legislation made its debut in 1988. As will be seen, it took a series of Court of Appeal cases appearing right through the 1990s to answer all the questions and so establish the law firmly. The result has been that since the end of 2001 the case law, unreported as well as reported, is devoid of decisions on damages.[402]

39-079 **(ii) The importance of correct valuations** That the valuations, which are effectively of the premises not subject to the tenancy and the premises subject to the tenancy, should be right is of great importance for the proper assessment of the damages. The Court of Appeal has made it clear that the exercise is not to be performed in the abstract but by reference to the rights of the landlord and the tenant. In a number of cases valuations have been made by the parties on the wrong basis, and these errors have produced at first instance statutory damages assessments in five figures when they should have been far less or even nil. The result has been to impose a fine whereas the statute is directed only at depriving landlords of their profit.

39-080 In *Melville v Bruton*,[403] it was the calculation of the value of the premises as not subject to the tenancy that was wrong. For this valuation the valuers had assumed vacant possession whereas the eviction of the tenant made no difference to the value as two others were still left in occupation. The Court of Appeal therefore reduced the statutory award from £15,000 to nil. However, it is commoner for it to be the valuation of the premises as subject to the tenancy that is wrong, because it is made on the assumption of a secure tenancy when in fact the tenancy is highly precarious. Thus in *King v Jackson*,[404] where the tenant at the time of eviction had been entitled to remain on the premises for only a further six days, the award of £11,000 was reduced to £1,500. In *Osei-Bonsu v Wandsworth London Borough Council*,[405] valuations of a precarious tenancy had again been made upon the wrong basis of a secure tenancy which entitled the claimant to a statutory award of £30,000, but here the Court of Appeal refused, because the values had been agreed below between the parties, to rectify the error and reduce the damages to the £2,000 that it would

---

399 [1999] 3 E.G.L.R. 153.

400 [1999] 3 E.G.L.R. 153 at 162, col.2. The £49,500 awarded in *Kalas v Farmer* [2010] EWCA Civ 108 CA was an agreed sum.

401 See the useful list of high awards at p.62, n.222 of the Law Commission's Consultation Paper, *Aggravated, Exemplary and Restitutionary Damages* (HMSO, 1993), Law Com No.132; not reproduced in the resulting Law Commission Report, (1997), *Law Com. No.247*. Of course, lower awards also appear where the valuations dictate: see, e.g. £1,500 in *King v Jackson* (1998) 30 H.L.R. 541 CA (at para.39-080, below), £2,500 in *Nijar v Mann* (2000) 32 H.L.R. 223.

402 A solitary case is *Kalas v Farmer* [2010] EWCA Civ 108 CA, at para.39-081, below.

403 (1997) 29 H.L.R. 319 CA.

404 (1998) 30 H.L.R. 541 CA.

405 [1999] 1 W.L.R. 1011 CA.

otherwise have awarded.[406] This is then a further cautionary tale for landlords, revealing the dangers of not getting the valuations right in the first place.

39-081 **(iii) The claimant's conduct: mitigation** It is provided by s.27(7) of the Act that, if it appears to the court that it is reasonable to mitigate the damages on account of the conduct of the tenant or of any one living with him, the court may reduce the award by whatever amount it considers appropriate. Little or nothing was heard of this provision in the early years of the statutory action but eventually it began to take effect. In *Regalgrand Ltd v Dickerson and Wade*,[407] the trial judge's reduction of the prima facie award of £12,000 based on valuations[408] right down to £1,500 was upheld by the Court of Appeal who said that the decision on the appropriate reduction was in the discretion of the trial judge. It was held that all aspects of the tenant's conduct could be taken into account, including non-payment of rent and the evincing of an intention to vacate the premises. In *Osei-Bonsu v Wandsworth London Borough Council*,[409] the damages were reduced on account of the tenant's conduct from £30,000 to £10,000, but the size of the reduction may have been influenced by the fact that the Court of Appeal took the view that the proper statutory award, without mitigation, should have been £2,000 rather than £30,000.[410] In *Kalas v Farmer*,[411] the Court of Appeal held the trial judge to be entirely right to refuse mitigation of the damages where the point was not taken in the defence, in correspondence, at the trial, or indeed anywhere at any time before the appeal.

## (2) The interrelation of common law and statutory damages

39-082 Section 27(5) of the Housing Act 1988 makes clear that the statutory action is additional to the entitlement at common law but at the same time provides that there shall not be double recovery for the same loss. The question therefore arises as to how far an award under the statute prevents an award of common law damages, the statutory award in practice being almost invariably the higher of the two. Common law damages, as we have seen, will be for loss of use of the premises and for inconvenience, supplemented by both aggravated and exemplary damages.[412] And for a time it was common practice to make awards of aggravated damages, of exemplary damages or of both in addition to awards under ss.27 and 28.[413]

39-083 Then came the decision of the Court of Appeal in *Nwokorie v Mason*.[414] In that case the claimant was awarded £500 of general damages, £1,000 of aggravated damages[415] and statutory damages of £4,500. At first instance the general damages

406 Although able to make a reduction for another reason: see para.39-081, below.

407 (1997) 74 P. & C.R. 312 CA.

408 See para.39-079, above.

409 [1999] 1 W.L.R. 1011 CA.

410 See para.39-080, above.

411 [2010] EWCA Civ 108 CA.

412 See para.39-070 together with para.39-072, above.

413 See the useful list of combined awards of aggravated and/or exemplary damages and of damages under ss.27 and 28 of the Housing Act 1988 at p.62, n.223 of the Law Commission's Consultation Paper, (HMSO, 1993) Law Com No.132 (not reproduced in the resulting Law Commission Report, (1997), *Law Com. No.247*) by which time the aggravated and exemplary awards were beginning to be set off against the statutory award: see paras 39-083 and 39-084, below.

414 (1994) 26 H.L.R. 60 CA; [1994] 1 E.G.L.R. 59 CA.

415 Interpreted as such by the Court of Appeal although in the court below the £1,000 had been described

were, by agreement of the parties, set off against the statutory award but the aggravated damages were not; the Court of Appeal held that these must be set off too as representing compensation for the same loss. Of the £1,000 thus awarded to the claimant Dillon LJ said:

> "It is still … damages in respect of his loss of the right to occupy the premises as his residence, damages aggravated by the manner in which he lost that right, the loss of the right to occupy the premises as his residence."[416]

It was said in the 16th edition (1997) of this work that what applies to aggravated damages should apply also to exemplary damages; both should be set off against the statutory award. In *Nwokorie v Mason*,[417] the court distinguished *Jones and Lee v Miah and Miah*,[418] where no set off of an exemplary award had been made against the statutory damages, on the ground that it had simply been accepted by the parties that a set off was not called for so that the case was not authoritative on the point; this suggests that the Court of Appeal in *Nwokorie*,[419] would have approached exemplary damages in the same way as it approached aggravated damages. If Lord Devlin's second category of exemplary damages is regarded as a form of disgorgement[420] and the remedy of ss.27 and 28 of the Housing Act 1988 is grounded in disgorgement, then the exemplary award on top of the statutory award does constitute a double recovery. It could be argued *per contra*—but it is not thought to be the better argument—that the issue to which the statute addresses itself is only that of "the same loss" and neither of these two awards is strictly concerned with loss at all. Subsequently, the desired result was achieved in the more complex case of *Francis v Brown*.[421] There the tenant sued not only the landlord mother but also her daughter who had assisted in the eviction and had later had the property transferred to her. The Court of Appeal, on the appeal only of the daughter against the trial judge's very muddled award against the two of them as joint tortfeasors of statutory damages, exemplary damages, aggravated damages and special damages, confirmed that the statutory award of £40,000 against the mother necessarily eliminated the award of £40,000 exemplary damages against her; the result of this was that no exemplary damages could be awarded against the appealing daughter.[422] As for the aggravated damages of £1,000 for which the daughter remained liable, the mother's liability was not in issue but it is thought that, had it been, the court would have had these also set off against the statutory award, leaving only the daughter's liability for them.[423] Since then there has been a correct adjudication at first instance on the whole range of the common law damages. In *Mehta v Royal Bank of Scotland*,[424] the separate awards for compensatory, aggravated and exemplary damages were all three set off against the greater statu- **39-084**

---

as exemplary.

416 (1994) 26 H.L.R. 60 CA at 68; [1994] 1 E.G.L.R. 59 CA at 62G.

417 (1994) 26 H.L.R. 60 CA; [1994] 1 E.G.L.R. 59 CA.

418 (1992) 24 H.L.R. 578 CA; [1992] 2 E.G.L.R. 50 CA.

419 (1994) 26 H.L.R. 60 CA; [1994] 1 E.G.L.R. 59 CA.

420 As to which see Ch.15, above.

421 (1998) 30 H.L.R. 143 CA.

422 See para.52-065, below.

423 See, again, para.52-065, below. Except that in the particular case, because the amount of the exemplary damages was as great as the amount of the statutory award, there would have been none of it left for set-off.

424 [1999] 3 E.G.L.R. 153.

tory award, following *Nwokorie v Mason*,[425] for the set-off of the aggravated damages and citing this paragraph in the 16th edition for the set-off of the exemplary damages.[426]

39-085 It seems however that the common law damages may not be entirely submerged in a statutory award. Thus *Nwokorie*,[427] was distinguished by the Court of Appeal in *Kaur v Gill*,[428] on the basis, according to the very short report, that the £500 general damages there awarded

> "related to the tenant's complaints of harassment against the landlord and not to her claim for statutory damages for unlawful eviction".

Yet it might be thought that the harassment was all part and parcel of the eviction process, so that the common law damages were attributable to, in Dillon LJ's phrase in *Nwokorie*,[429] the manner of her eviction. It may be, however, that the interesting *Sampson v Wilson*,[430] helps to give the explanation. While the Court of Appeal's single concern in that case was with deciding that only the landlord can be liable under the statute, Sir Thomas Bingham MR recited the elements in the trial judge's award without criticism. Apart from damages for loss of amenity over three years from breach of the landlord's repairing covenant, there were damages for loss suffered by harassment and exemplary damages; but these were only for the time before the tenants had been evicted. Undoubtedly conscious of the need to avoid a double recovery, the trial judge said:

> "However I can give [the claimants] damages for what they had to put up with before they left. There was … substantial deprivation of beneficial enjoyment. In principle, if all else fails, they arise in trespass—entering premises without permission and doing detrimental works, exceeding any permission."[431]

Accordingly, he held that each tenant had

> "suffered damage equivalent to the whole of his rent; that is, having an uninhabitable home and losing the whole value of it".[432]

As for the exemplary award—it was "a proper case for exemplary damages"—the trial judge said:

> "I am of course limiting myself to the period before the tenants go and not, because of the overlap provisions, to the effect of their leaving."[433]

---

425 (1994) 26 H.L.R. 60 CA; [1994] 1 E.G.L.R. 59 CA.

426 But it is important to remain vigilant in the light of decisions like *Fairweather v Ghafoor* [2001] C.L.Y. 4164. While purporting to follow *Francis v Brown* (in text of this paragraph) it is stated that there was an award under the Act and that aggravated damages were also awarded.

427 (1994) 26 H.L.R. 60 CA; [1994] 1 E.G.L.R. 59 CA.

428 *The Times*, 15 June 1995, CA.

429 (1994) 26 H.L.R. 60 CA at 68; [1994] 1 E.G.L.R. 59 CA at 62G.

430 (1997) 29 H.L.R. 18 CA.

431 (1994) 26 H.L.R. 486 at 505.

432 (1994) 26 H.L.R. 486 at 506.

433 (1994) 26 H.L.R. 486. The suggestion is also made in the report of *Kaur v Gill* that the damages there, in addition to the statutory award, could be upheld as being for breach of the covenant for quiet enjoyment. If the loss is regarded as non-pecuniary only, this suggestion faces the difficulty that damages for non-pecuniary loss have not run for this breach of contract: see para.28-014, above.

### (3) The lack of a need for exemplary damages

The result of the high level of recovery where the statutory remedy is invoked is that increasing use has come to be made of these actions. Moreover, it may be questioned whether, with statutory damages assessed at the difference between the values of the landlord's interest with and without the tenant's occupation,[434] there is any longer even a need for exemplary damages to discourage profit motivated evictions. Certainly, current exemplary damages awards are falling far short of fulfilling their function in this context when they can be as low as £1,000 to £3,000 and the statutory awards can exceed, and well exceed, £30,000.[435] And if any exemplary damages are, in any event, to be set off against the statutory award,[436] they have no practical function at all. **39-086**

434 See para.39-077, above.

435 Compare para.39-073, above with para.39-077, above.

436 See para.39-084, above.

Chapter 40

# TORTS CAUSING PERSONAL INJURY

Table of Contents

**40-001** Personal injuries[1] may be inflicted by means of a large number of very different torts. Although the tort of negligence qualifies to take easily the largest share, personal injuries may result from trespass to the person or from nuisance, by reason of dangerous premises, chattels or animals in the defendant's control, from his non-natural user of land, from breach of statutory obligation giving rise to a claim in tort. Personal injury may indeed also occasionally arise from breach of contract, as a contract of carriage or sale of goods, but there will generally be a concurrent tort in such cases.[2] Whatever the ground of the defendant's liability however, the measure of damages will be calculated in the same manner throughout.[3]

---

1 Which can include pre-natal injuries, under statute if occurring after the passing of the Congenital Disabilities (Civil Liability) Act 1976 (see especially s.4(3)) and at common law if occurring before: see *Burton v Islington Health Authority* and *De Martell v Merton and Sutton Health Authority* [1993] Q.B. 204 CA. How far, for the purposes of art.17 of the Warsaw Convention 1929 scheduled to the Carriage by Air Act 1961, the term "bodily injury" or "*lésion corporelle*" covers psychiatric illness was considered in *Morris v KLM Royal Dutch Airlines* and *King v Bristow Helicopters Ltd* [2002] 2 A.C. 628.

2 Where the liability is in tort, only the person physically injured now has a claim. The *actio per quod consortium et servitium amisit* was abolished by the Administration of Justice Act 1982 s.2, for injuries falling after the end of that year; *Hodgson v Trapp* (1988) 18 Fam. L.R. 60 winds up the cases. The damages formerly recovered in the action *per quod* will now be recovered, at least in their *servitium* aspect, by the physically injured person himself: see paras 40-225 and following, below.

3 Two general qualifications to the statement that the damages are calculated in the same manner throughout are: (1) they may be reduced by the claimant's contributory negligence; (2) they may have a ceiling placed on them by statute, e.g. under the Merchant Shipping Act of the day, or by contract between the parties. Although of general application, these two qualifications are in practice particularly important in torts causing physical damage. A third qualification is that in certain limited circumstances exemplary damages may be awarded for injury intentionally inflicted; but this is assault and is dealt with in Ch.42, below. Aggravated damages for injury by negligence, however outrageous, are not available: *Kralj v McGrath* [1986] 1 All E.R. 54.

For long the common law relating to damages for personal injury was untroubled by legislation. Then in the 1990s statutory change came[4] with s.10 of the Civil Evidence Act 1995,[5] dealing with actuarial evidence in personal injury cases,[6] and with a statute which for the first time takes this important subject for its title. This is the Damages Act 1996. For the purposes of this text it deals with aspects of multipliers,[7] periodical payments[8] and, to an extent, with provisional damages[9] and structured settlements.[10] Finally we have two sections of the lengthy Courts Act 2003 which return to the question of periodical payments but in more dramatic fashion.[11] **40-002**

A preliminary question of fact in every personal injury case is whether actionable damage has been suffered. In instances such as pleural plaques, no actionable damage was found to have occurred.[12] In *Rothwell v Chemical and Insulating Company Ltd*,[13] Lord Hoffmann explained that actionable damage is "an abstract concept of being worse off, physically or economically". This could not be proved by sensitisation from exposure at work to platinum salts in *Greenway v Johnson Matthey Plc*,[14] any more than with the pleural plaques in *Rothwell v Chemical and Insulating Co*.[15] However, the decision in *Carder v The University of Exeter*,[16] emphasises that the conclusion reached will be highly dependent upon particular facts. In that case, the Court of Appeal considered whether the negligent exposure of Mr Carder by the appellant to 2.3 per cent of the total lifetime dose of asbestos was "actionable damage". The appellant submitted that the exposure had made and would make no difference to his symptoms, disability or prognosis. The Master of the Rolls (with whom Gross and Christopher Clarke LJJ agreed) held that on the facts there had been actionable damage because the severity of the disease had been increased to a small, albeit not measurable, extent. **40-003**

## I. Forms of Award and of Compensation

While the final lump sum award has dominated in personal injury cases as elsewhere, inroads upon it have been made as time has gone by and as more concern has been felt about its twin weaknesses in this vital and dominant area of damages awards, namely, first, that the amount awarded will be too great or too little because of the uncertainty of how the claimant's life will in fact develop in the future and, **40-004**

---

4 The only earlier statutory change was the abolition by the Administration of Justice Act 1982 of the right to damages for loss of expectation of life (see para.40-263, below) and of the *actio per quod consortium et servitium amisit* (see last footnote but one, above).

5 But still not in force.

6 See para.40-072, below.

7 See s.1; see para.40-121, below.

8 See s.2; see para.40-010, below.

9 Section deals with provisional damages only in relation to fatal accident claims; see para.40-010, below.

10 Section dealt only with protection for structured settlement annuitants. Its replacement now provides, similarly, for periodical payments.

11 Replacing s.2 of the Damages Act; see para.40-011, below.

12 *Rothwell v Chemical and Insulating Company Ltd* [2008] 1 A.C. 281.

13 [2008] 1 A.C. 281 at [7].

14 [2014] EWHC 3957 (QB). See at [13] and following, and the facts at para.8-137, above.

15 See para.5-012, above. See also the decision of the same judge (Jay J) in *Saunderson v Sonae Industria (UK) Ltd* [2015] EWHC 2264 (QB) at [178].

16 [2016] EWCA Civ 790.

secondly, that the amount awarded may be exhausted and not run the course of the injury by reason of overspending or under-investing. As a preliminary to dealing generally with the measure of damages here, these developing inroads will be considered, and considered in the order in which they have arrived on the scene.

## 1. Interim Awards

**40-005** This first inroad was not designed to cater for the uncertainty of the lump sum but nevertheless it assists to a degree. Awards of interim payments are intended to tide over claimants who have lost earnings and incurred medical and other expenses, or need to incur further expenses,[17] while the slow process of litigation unwinds.[18] Interim payments were introduced for personal injury as far back as 1970. They are available today in any action for damages[19] under CPR rr.25.6 to 25.9, but it is in the field of personal injury that their greatest importance lies.

**40-006** The availability of interim payments can help with the problem of the uncertainty of the future because the need to proceed with great speed to the end of the litigation is reduced. This is particularly true where advantage is taken, where appropriate, of splitting the claim into two parts, so that the issue of liability is decided first and the assessment of damages is arrived at later, with provision for the awarding at the hearing on liability of interim payments on account of the final award; this helps to deal with perhaps the most frequent cause of a damages award turning out to be wrongly based, namely a substantial change in the claimant's condition, which in the nature of things is most likely to occur within the first years after the injury. Interim payments may also be awarded where liability is admitted[20] and where the court is satisfied that at trial the claimant would obtain judgment for substantial damages.[21] No more than a reasonable proportion of the likely amount of the final judgment should be ordered.[22]

## 2. Provisional Awards

**40-007** The next inroad on the final lump sum award was specifically designed to deal with the uncertainties of a claimant's future in his injured condition. A claimant is now entitled, where it is anticipated that his condition may in the future change

---

17 As by acquiring special accommodation in which a catastrophically injured claimant can live and be cared for: *Osunde v St Guy's and St Thomas' Hospital* [2007] EWHC 2275 Fam; *Brewis v Heatherwood & Wrexham Park Hospital NHS Trust* [2008] EWHC 2526 (QB). It may not always be possible to have an interim payment sufficient to acquire alternative accommodation, whether special or not, as in *Mabirizi v HSBC Insurance (UK) Ltd* [2011] EWCA Civ 1280 (QB).

18 Need is not, however, a prerequisite for an interim award: *Stringman v McCardle* [1994] 1 W.L.R. 1653 CA.

19 And have been since 1980.

20 CPR r.25.7(1)(a).

21 CPR r.25.7(1)(c). Where with liability admitted the court is satisfied that substantial damages will be awarded but it is currently difficult to conclude accurately what sum will be recovered, the assessment must be carried out on a conservative basis and the risk of overpayment avoided: *AS v West Suffolk Hospital Trust* unreported 1 May 2015.

22 CPR r.25.7(4); as to the interpretation of this see *Spillman v Bradfield Riding Centre* [2007] EWHC 89 (QB). Pt IV of the Law Commission's Report on *Structured Settlements and Interim and Provisional Damages* (Law Com. No.224 (1994)) has a valuable discussion of the various issues concerning interim payments. The practice which developed has had to be modified to accommodate the periodical payments regime along the lines set out by the Court of Appeal in *Eeles v Cobham Hire Services Ltd* [2010] 1 W.L.R. 409 CA.

substantially for the worse, to claim damages on the provisional basis that his condition will remain stable but with the right to return to the court for further damages should this prove not to be the case.[23] More precisely, it is enacted by s.32A of the Senior Courts Act 1981[24] that, where there is a chance that at some time in the future a person will, as a result of his injury, develop a serious disease or suffer a serious deterioration physically or mentally,[25] the court may award him damages assessed on the assumption that he will not develop the disease or suffer the deterioration in his condition, and award further damages at a future date if he develops the disease or suffers the deterioration.[26]

One limitation on provisional damages which has met with criticism is that a claimant may only make one application for further damages in respect of each disease or type of deterioration specified in the order for the award of provisional damages.[27] It is also unfortunate that the court is not given the power, as it now is with periodical payments,[28] to award provisional damages in an appropriate case rather than to make a final award. A claimant is not required to claim provisional damages rather than a final lump sum award and the trial judge in *Cowan v Kitson Insulations Ltd*,[29] was very clear that the choice should be the claimant's. "It is his [decision] and his alone", he said, **40-008**

> "and he wants to put this matter entirely behind him, and in my view he is entitled to adopt that attitude".[30]

The claimant in *Cowan* was a workman who had developed pleural plaques which could lead to one of the serious asbestos-related diseases and, at the time the decision was arrived at, the prevailing view was that pleural plaques on their own sufficed to give a cause of action.[31] The decision in the case may, however, have

---

23 In *Kotula v EDF Energy Networks (EDN) Plc* [2011] EWHC 1546 (QB) the claimant was awarded provisional damages allowing him to return for a further lump sum should his condition substantially worsen while retaining the right to seek, in the same eventuality, to have his periodical payments varied upwards. In *Woodward v Leeds Teaching Hospitals Trust* [2012] EWHC 2167 (QB) there was held to be a real risk of the claimant's condition deteriorating disastrously so as to allow an award of provisional damages in respect of part of her personal injury claim. In *Loughlin v Singh* [2013] EWHC 1641 (QB) an order for provisional damages was made where there was a significant risk of post-traumatic epilepsy developing: see at 98].

24 Introduced by s.6 of the Administration of Justice Act 1982. The equivalent provision for the county court is s.51 of the County Courts Act 1984.

25 On the interpretation of chance and serious deterioration see *Willson v Ministry of Defence* [1991] 1 All E.R. 638. What was said in *Willson* was approved by the Court of Appeal in *Curi v Colina* unreported 29 July 1998, and was applied so as to make no provisional award in *Davies v Bradshaw* [2008] EWHC 740 (QB). By contrast, *Willson* was applied so as to allow a provisional award to be made in *Kotula v EDF Energy Networks (EDN) Plc* [2011] EWHC 1586 (QB). Provisional damages are not available where the chance is not deterioration in condition but the need for care and accommodation that will no longer be free: *Adan v Securicor Custodial Services Ltd* [2005] P.I.Q.R. P6 at 79.

26 It is enacted by s.32A(2) that provision was to be made by rules of court for enabling the court to award provisional damages. While the introduction of detailed procedural rules took some time, s.32A applies to actions whenever commenced: Administration of Justice Act 1982 s.73(2). The procedural rules are now contained in CPR Pt 41.

27 CPR r.41.4(2).

28 See para.40-011, below.

29 [1992] P.I.Q.R. Q19.

30 [1992] P.I.Q.R. Q19 at 21.

31 It is quite clear from the headnote and the judgment that calcified pleural plaques were all that had developed with no sign in the workman, who remained healthy, of asbestosis or mesothelioma.

proved to have been a very short-sighted one for the claimant who would find himself massively under-compensated if he later contracted the asbestos-related disease, because it would be too late for him to claim the very large compensation to which he would then be entitled had he not already sued to final judgment. And the making of a final rather than a provisional award may have turned out also to be have been unfair to the defendant, for the serious disease may in the event never have been contracted by the claimant so that the damages which the defendant will have paid will represent pure over-compensation. However, these difficulties would now seem to have disappeared in respect of asbestos-related disease with the decision of the House of Lords in *Rothwell v Chemical & Insulating Co Ltd*.[32] In a series of appeals in respect of claims for personal injury where the claimants had developed pleural plaques from exposure to asbestos, a condition which while not constituting physical injury gives rise to the chance or risk of future asbestos-related disease together with concomitant mental anxiety, it was rightly held, departing from two decades of first instance decisions, that three heads of claim which individually would not found a cause of action—viz., physiological change short of injury, risk or chance, and anxiety—could not be aggregated so as to constitute sufficient damage to give rise to a legal claim. Accordingly, there could be no possibility of provisional damages. Therefore no claim at all for damages could be brought until the time that the dreaded disease materialised, if it did, when the award then made would be a final award.[33]

## 3. PERIODICAL PAYMENTS AWARDS

### (1) Introductory

**40-009** The disadvantages of the lump sum award in personal injury cases are well known and have been much discussed; the twin weaknesses which it exhibits—that it cannot be accurately calculated and that it may not be properly used—have already been referred to.[34] With no assistance from the legislature, the structured settlement was invented by those caught up in the problems and difficulties of personal injury litigation in order to meet the difficulties of spending or investing awards inappropriately and of dying at a time earlier or later than anticipated. Periodical payments can provide the same benefits and can be made to do even better.

**40-010** The first step towards the use of periodical payments was taken by s.2(1) of the Damages Act 1996 empowering the court awarding damages in a personal injuries action to order that the damages wholly or partly take this form. However, the subsection did not go very far since it provided that the power to award periodical payments was to be exercised only with the consent of the parties. So little use was made of this facility by litigants that Lord Steyn in *Wells v Wells*,[35] described the power to order periodical payments as a dead letter. But he added:

> "The solution is relatively straightforward. The court ought to be given the power of its own motion to make an award for periodic payments rather than a lump sum in appropri-

---

32 [2008] A.C. 281.

33 Part V of the Law Commission's Report on *Structured Settlements and Interim and Provisional Damages* (HMSO, 1994), Law Com. No.224 has a valuable discussion of the various issues concerning provisional damages.

34 See para.40-004, above.

35 [1999] 1 A.C. 345 at 384C.

ate cases. Such a power is perfectly consistent with the principle of full compensation for such pecuniary loss."

And the time for this has finally arrived.

By s.100 of the Courts Act 2003 there is substituted for s.2 of the Damages Act 1996 three new sections which commence, by s.2(1), with the conferring on the court of the power, without the need for any consent from the parties, to award periodical payments for future pecuniary loss rather than the traditional lump sum. There follows a host of other provisions, of immense detail and complexity, appearing not only in new sections of the Damages Act 1996 but also in a statutory instrument, Civil Procedure Rules and Practice Directions. This legislation was finally brought into force on 1 April 2005.[36] **40-011**

Thus the structured settlement, which has had a good innings since its initial implementation received judicial approval back in 1989 in the unreported case of *Kelly v Dawes*, is no longer needed. It has been overtaken and is ignored by the new regime; the original ss.4 and 5 of the Damages Act 1996 dealing with various aspects of structured settlements and the Practice Direction on structured settlements have gone. Structured settlements, arrived at consensually, do remain available but they do not now merit consideration here. Indeed it was only their former immense importance that brought them in for treatment since a structured settlement is not an award of damages. If required, what was said in the last edition but one may be referred to.[37] **40-012**

The new rules on periodical payments intertwine substance and procedure. Much is procedural in nature. Since in this book procedural aspects of damages are now being addressed by another mind, in the book's final chapters, there have been dangers for us of unnecessary repetition and of overlap. We have arranged therefore for the key parts of the legislation, both primary and secondary, to be set out in full in the procedural chapters while only being referred to here, but with cross-references to where they will be found there set out. Matters purely procedural are left for later. Where, however, substance and procedure cannot be neatly separated, there will be cross-references to any later commentary[38] in dealing with the substantive matters. These will now be addressed. **40-013**

## (2) Matters in issue

Two short but important matters of substance may be covered before the detail is attacked. Periodical payments arising out of personal injury are not subject to income tax[39] and assignment or charge of the right to receive periodical payments is forbidden unless the court approves.[40] **40-014**

**(a) Losses to which awards apply** The central feature of the power given to the courts to award periodical payments is that it is limited to "awarding damages **40-015**

---

36 SI 2005/910 para.3(w); with the power to award periodical payments exercisable in proceedings whenever begun: SI 2005/911 para.11. For the inglorious procedural details see para.52-025, below (in a footnote).

37 17th edition (2003) paras 38–008 to 38–010.

38 The procedural part will be found at paras 51-033 to 51-034 and paras 52-025 and following, below.

39 Income Tax (Trading and Other Income) Act 2005 s.731.

40 Damages Act 1996 s.2(6).

for future pecuniary loss".[41] The power is not intended to deal with either past pecuniary loss or with non-pecuniary loss.[42] Thus damages for the loss of congenial employment—essentially non-pecuniary loss—cannot be awarded by the court, of its own motion,[43] in the form of periodical payments. On the other hand, it would seem that *Smith v Manchester* awards for handicap in the labour market—essentially a future pecuniary loss though only a potential one—could technically be made by way of periodical payments,[44] though the generally small size of such awards makes this highly unlikely in practice.

40-016 **(b) Matters considered in making awards** In deciding whether or not to make a periodical payments award the court must look at all the circumstances, in particular at what best suits the needs of the claimant, and also have regard to specified factors, listed as the size of the payments, the incidence of contributory negligence, and the wishes of both claimant, suitably advised, and defendant, together with their reasons for their preference.[45]

40-017 In earlier years some concern has been expressed in this work about these factors to be taken into account. While the size, legislatively termed the scale, of the payments is to be considered by the court, it was thought to be unfortunate that there was not introduced, as had been proposed by some, a presumption in favour of periodical payments for large cases, cases in excess of a specified sum, with a countervailing presumption against them where the award for future pecuniary loss falls below the specified figure. Then it is not made clear how the existence of contributory negligence is to affect decisions as between lump sum and periodical payments. Contributory negligence is particularly important where the damages are being awarded to cover the cost of long-term care. Does the fact that periodical payments significantly reduced for contributory negligence will not cover the ongoing cost mean that the court should be moved towards awarding a traditional lump sum? Or can the court raid, as it were, the lump sum award for non-pecuniary loss, or possibly the lump sum for past gratuitous care which will not have been spent, in order to increase the level of periodical payments given for the future long-term care? And what of the award, where there is one, for loss of earnings, whether by lump sum or periodical payments? Can it too be raided? Also, it is not clear how much attention the court must pay to the wishes of the parties. Remembering that claimants may be eager to have their damages under their immediate control and defendants may be eager to have the litigation put immediately and finally to rest, allowing the parties' wishes to carry the day could prove the death knell to the whole new system. Fortunately, with the new system now in place for nearly 10

---

41 Damages Act 1996 s.2(1) (as substituted for the original).

42 It is nevertheless provided, in Damages Act 1996 s.2(2) (as substituted for the original), that "other damages in respect of personal injury", which presumably means damages other than damages for future pecuniary loss, may be awarded by way of periodical payments if the parties consent. Our stated view in the last edition that very little use was likely to be made of this entitlement is being borne out in practice.

43 See previous note.

44 Despite the contrary being stated in the then Judicial Studies Board's guidance document prepared by Judge Oliver-Jones QC and Master Ungley (at para.13).

45 Damages Act 1996 s.2A(1)(a) combined with CPR r.41.7 and PD41B, para.1. These provisions are set out at paras 52-025 to 52-027, below. In *Morton v Portal Ltd* [2010] EWHC 1804 (QB) (at paras 40-019 and 40-020, below) there is a valuable consideration of the operation of the various matters and factors that a court is required to take into account in deciding whether or not to make a periodical payments order: see at [10]–[ 22].

years, decisions have arrived showing how the courts are interpreting the various requirements.

Practically all of the decisions concern awarding of periodical payments to cover future care costs rather than future earnings loss. In *Godbold v Mahmood*,[46] where periodical payments were awarded for recurring care and related costs, Mitting J indicated that there were two reasons which justified his doing so. These were the uncertainty as to the claimant's life expectation, over which there was disagreement, and the security of the income stream which would not be dependent on investment returns.[47] In *Walton v Calderdale Healthcare NHS Trust*,[48] where care costs were awarded by way of periodical payments, this being in accordance with the wishes of both parties, it would seem that again there must have been disagreement about life expectation since Silber J indicated concern that a lump sum might not provide sufficient compensation.[49] **40-018**

Contributory negligence was in issue in *Rowe v Dolman*.[50] The claimant, aged 55 at the time of trial, was seriously injured in a road accident for which he was held 20 per cent to blame. He was eager to be awarded a lump sum for his care and related living costs as, with an entitlement to only 80 per cent of his damages, these costs could not be met by an award of periodical payments. In a short judgment Simon J agreed. With periodical payments the claimant would not be able to live his life as he wished, still in his own home, whereas with a lump sum he would be able to do so for a substantial part of his remaining life.[51] This was said by May LJ, in dismissing the appeal to the Court of Appeal,[52] to be a solid reason for the judge's decision.[53] By contrast, an award of periodical payments was made in *Sarwar v Ali and Motor Insurers' Bureau*,[54] for the cost of future care to a claimant, injured in a car crash at the age of 17, who had been 25 per cent contributorily negligent for not wearing a seat belt and who had himself expressed a wish for a lump sum, Very little indeed is said on the issue by Lloyd Jones J in his lengthy judgment, which is taken up with the question of indexation, *Sarwar* being one of the string of cases departing from the retail prices index, or RPI, and the only one of these which was not appealed.[55] It is however clear from the judgment that there was going to be an award of periodical payments, contributory negligence or no. It may be significant that the claimant had changed his mind at the last minute on whether he wanted periodical payments or a lump sum for the future cost of his care. The case had been conducted right up to the conclusion of the evidence on a periodical payments preference and it was only at the adjourned hearing for final submissions that a lump sum was put forward as the claimant's preference.[56] It may also be significant that periodical payments were also awarded for loss of earnings, a further feature of **40-019**

---

46 [2005] Lloyd's Rep. Med. 379.

47 [2005] Lloyd's Rep. Med. 379 at [34].

48 [2005] Lloyd's Rep. Med. 398.

49 His reasons for making the award are at [2005] Lloyd's Rep. Med. 398 at [11].

50 [2007] EWHC 2799 (QB).

51 [2007] EWHC 2799 (QB) at [9].

52 [2008] EWCA Civ 1040 CA.

53 [2008] EWCA Civ 1040 CA at [22]. See the useful discussion at [19]–[26] where the figures are carefully analysed. An equity release scheme, the availability of which was said by the defendant to justify a periodical payments award, was held to be in the circumstances inappropriate. The other members of the court concurred with May LJ's judgment.

54 [2007] LS Law Med. 375.

55 The indexation cases are dealt with at paras 40-023 to 40-026, below.

56 This appears at [2007] LS Law Med. 375 at [100]–[105].

*Sarwar* distinguishing it from the other cases, and this again against the final wishes of the claimant. In the penultimate paragraph of his judgment[57] Lloyd Jones J said that he had in mind the evidence of one of the claimant's indexation experts that the periodical payments for cost of care and loss of earnings, discounted for contributory negligence, would come close to covering the actual costs of care until the claimant reached the age of 65.[58] So this shows that the damages for loss of earnings were indeed going to be raided to pay for the costs of care. The earnings periodical payments would of course cease at the claimant's projected retirement date and would not be available to carry him through to 72, which was the age to which the judge had found[59] that he would live.[60] Since *Rowe* and *Sarwar* we have *Morton v Portal Ltd*,[61] where, in making a periodical payments order to cover future care, Walker J expressed himself as satisfied that the 25 per cent deduction for contributory negligence would not present too great a difficulty for the claimant who at 55 had suffered serious injuries in a work accident.[62]

**40-020** As for the preferences of claimant and defendant as between lump sum and periodical payments, the courts have been clear that these preferences must always take second place to what is in the best interests of the claimant. This was well put by Waller LJ giving the judgment of the Court of Appeal in *Tameside and Glossop Acute Services NHS Trust v Thompstone*,[63] the indexation appeal about to be considered. He said:

> "In the end, it is for the judge to decide what order best meets the claimant's needs. The judge's mind should be focused not on what the claimant prefers but on what best meets the claimant's needs; the two are not necessarily the same."[64]

In *Morton v Portal Ltd*,[65] where a claimant of full age and capacity wished to have periodical payments for his future care to which the defendant had no objection, Walker J rightly regarded this as not conclusive in its favour as the court must be satisfied that a periodical payments order was in the claimant's best interests, and in addition there was the requirement that the court had to be satisfied that continuity of payment was secure. Nonetheless, independently of these considerations, he was satisfied that a periodical payments order was appropriate.[66]

---

57 [2007] LS Law Med. 375 at [218].

58 See the figures in the Summary of Judgment at [2007] LS Law Med. 375 at [219].

59 Lloyd Jones J in an earlier judgment had adjudicated on the claimant's life expectancy: [2007] EWHC 274 (QB).

60 Curiously, according to the figures in the Summary of Judgment, at [2007] LS Law Med. 375 at [219], the loss of earnings payments were to cease at age 67, not 65.

61 [2010] EWHC 1804 (QB).

62 [2010] EWHC 1804 (QB) at [12].

63 [2008] 1 W.L.R. 2207 CA.

64 [2008] 1 W.L.R. 2207 CA at [108]. Further consideration of some of the above cases will be found in the procedural section at the end of this work: see para.52-029, below. Two further cases, though not specifically concerned with matters required to be taken into account, may best be dealt with here. Both concern uncertainty of the required level of future care costs. In *Taylor v Chesworth and The Motor Insurers' Bureau* [2007] EWHC 1001 (QB) where care costs were going to fluctuate over the years, periodical payments were awarded to cover the cost of the underlying level of support which the claimant would always need, with a lump sum added for the periods when he would need more support: see at [160(3)] and [161].

65 [2010] EWHC 1804 (QB).

66 See [2010] EWHC 1804 (QB) at [22].

**(c) Indexation of awards** It is clear that orders for periodical payments will commonly extend for many years—it was 49 years in *Sarwar v Ali and Motor Insurers' Bureau*,[67] where the claimant was injured at 17 and in cases of children injured at birth it is likely to be longer still—and the amounts specified in an order will soon become outdated by reason of inflation. The legislation therefore provides for indexation of awards. Subsection (8) of the new s.2 of the Damages Act 1996 enacts that orders for periodical payments are to be treated as providing for the amount of the payment ordered to vary with the retail prices index, the RPI. **40-021**

There is however a very serious problem with retail price indexation. It was well recognised that the provision of long-term medical care and treatment for the very seriously injured is the principal use for which periodical payments are intended by the legislation, and it is also recognised that health care inflation, reflecting the earnings of carers, is greater than retail price inflation. It would, therefore, be appropriate for a court to order, for a claimant requiring long-term medical care and treatment, periodical payments which will increase in line with health care inflation. The same should be true for the other head of future loss for which periodical payments are designed, namely, loss of earnings. Earnings inflation too is greater than retail price inflation but to a lesser extent than is health care inflation. Thus we find in *A v B Hospitals NHS Trust*,[68] Lloyd Jones J concluding that the form of award that best met the claimant's needs was the lump sum award for which the claimant was contending on the basis that periodical payments linked to the retail prices index would be most unlikely to meet his future care costs.[69] Later in *A v Powys Local Health Board*,[70] Lloyd-Jones J did precisely the same thing and for the same reason for a claimant again arguing for a lump sum; here he felt committed to the retail prices index—by this time, as we shall see, other indices were beginning to be used by the courts—because the claimant would be living in Ireland and the evidence was that there was no earnings series appropriate to use for indexing carers' earnings in Ireland.[71] **40-022**

Subsection (8) specifying retail prices indexation is however immediately followed by subs.(9) stipulating that an order for periodical payments may include provision disapplying subs.(8) or modifying its effect. The question of the proper interpretation of subs.(9) came before the Court of Appeal on a strike out application in *Flora v Wakom (Heathrow) Ltd*.[72] The claimant filed a statement of case, with expert financial evidence, contending that an average earnings index and not the retail prices index should be applied to the periodical payments in respect of future loss of earnings and care, and the defendant applied for a strike out on the basis that the claimant had no realistic prospect of arguing for any index other than the one specified in s.2(8). Sir Michael Turner dismissed the defendant's application as procedurally misconceived[73] and the Court of Appeal upheld this refusal of a strike out, rejecting the defendant's contention that s.2(8) established the normal court order and that s.2(9) could be triggered only in exceptional circumstances, it being common ground that there was nothing particularly exceptional about a case **40-023**

67 [2007] LS Law Med. 375.
68 [2007] LS Law Med. 303.
69 See [2007] LS Law Med. 303 at [12] and [33].
70 [2007] EWHC 2996 (QB).
71 [2007] EWHC 2996 (QB) at [21]–[23].
72 [2007] 1 W.L.R. 482 CA.
73 [2006] LS Law Med. 80.

of severe physical injury. However, the Court of Appeal did not discuss the minutiae of the various indices and contented itself with saying that it was up to the trial judge to make such order for index linking as he considered appropriate and fair.[74]

**40-024** *Flora* resulted in a series of first instance decisions tackling the question of indexation, being in date order *Thompstone v Tameside & Glossop Acute Services NHS Trust*,[75] *Corbett v South Yorkshire Strategic Health Authority*,[76] *Sarwar v Ali and Motor Insurers' Bureau*,[77] and *RH v United Bristol Healthcare NHS Trust*.[78] All four have much in common, in the arguments put forward by either side, in the indices put forward to be substituted for the retail prices index, in the experts on indexation appearing, in the detailed and careful consideration of the issues and in the conclusions reached, all in judgments of great length. Three measures other than the retail prices index were put forward. There was the Annual Earnings Index, AEI, and the Annual Survey of Hours and Earnings, ASHE; both of these were aggregate measures which included data from all occupations. Disaggregated earnings data from broad occupational groups were also available under both AEI and ASHE, and the third measure offered to the court was taken from a disaggregated sub-set of the ASHE data, the Annual Survey of Hours and Earnings: Occupational Earnings for Care Assistants and Home Carers, ASHE 6115. Perhaps not unsurprisingly, in each of the four cases ASHE 6115 was chosen by the trial judge as coming the nearest to measuring the claimant's loss with accuracy.

**40-025** In three of the four cases an appeal was taken to the Court of Appeal, reported under the name of the lead case *Thompstone*.[79] After a decidedly thorough and painstaking consideration of the appellants' many contentions against the use of indices other than the retail prices index and against the trial judges' use of ASHE 6115 in particular, none of which contentions was found to be impressive, the Court of Appeal entirely endorsed the judgments below, all of which were commended. It is hardly necessary here to consider the detail of the various contentions and of their rebuttal in view of the final outcome. For not only did Waller LJ, delivering the judgment of the court, conclude by saying that the appellants' contentions on all issues were rejected[80] but earlier in relation to indexation he specifically said this:

> "We hope that as a result of these proceedings the National Health Service, and other defendants in proceedings that involve catastrophic injury, will now accept that the appropriateness of indexation on the basis of ASHE 6115 has been established after an exhaustive review of all the possible objections to its use, both in itself and as applied to the recovery of costs of care and case management. It will not be appropriate to reopen that issue in any future proceedings unless the defendant can produce evidence and argument significantly different from, and more persuasive than, that which has been deployed in the present cases. Judges should not hesitate to strike out any defences that do not meet that requirement."[81]

This then can be said to be the end of the line for defendants, as the NHS appeal to the House of Lords was abandoned.

---

74 [2007] 1 W.L.R. 482 CA at [37].
75 [2007] LS Law Med. 71.
76 [2007] LS Law Med. 430.
77 [2007] LS Law Med. 375.
78 [2007] LS Law Med. 535.
79 [2008] 1 W.L.R. 2207 CA.
80 [2008] 1 W.L.R. 2207 CA at [145].
81 [2008] 1 W.L.R. 2207 CA at [100].

Of the four cases above, *Sarwar v Ali and Motor Insurers' Bureau*,[82] differed from the other three in four respects. It was the only one which was not appealed,[83] it involved injury to a teenager[84] and not brain damage at birth, the order for periodical payments was against the wishes of the claimant, and periodical payments were ordered not only for the cost of care but also for the loss of earnings. It is this last difference with which we are concerned here. It was clear that for the loss of the claimant's future earnings the disaggregated earnings data for care workers would not be appropriate and the measure chosen by Lloyd Jones J was the ASHE aggregated earnings data for male full-time employees. Had it been possible to determine the occupation of the claimant, an appropriate disaggregated sub-set of the ASHE data could have been used to provide a more accurate assessment, but this was not feasible as the claimant had at the time of his injury not entered the labour market. While this decision on earnings lacks the support of the Court of Appeal, there is no reason to think that it would not have endorsed the decision on earnings as well as on cost of care. 40-026

**(d) Security of continuity of awards** Subsection (3) of the amended s.2 of the Damages Act 1996 provides that the court may not make an order for periodical payments unless it is satisfied that continuity of payment is reasonably secure. Subsection (4) then gives three cases where continuity of payment is to be regarded as reasonably secure.[85] These are: where payment is protected by a guarantee given for a public sector settlement,[86] where payment is protected by a guarantee given under the financial services compensation scheme,[87] as extended to periodical payment orders,[88] and where the source of the payment is a government or health service body designated by order made by the Lord Chancellor.[89] 40-027

In most of the cases which have awarded periodical payments, cases considered above, the court has been satisfied on the issue of security of continuity. No difficulty can arise where the defendant is the NHS Litigation Authority itself since it has been designated as a health service body by the Lord Chancellor, but in none of the above cases does it appear as defendant. With other health service defendants one needs to look elsewhere since the NHS Litigation Authority is the only health service body designated by the Lord Chancellor,[90] other than certain health trusts and boards in Wales and Northern Ireland.[91] In *Walton v Calderdale Healthcare NHS Trust*,[92] Silber J said that he was satisfied on the security of payments continuing because a health service body would be making the payments,[93] but this would seem to be misguided in view of the fact that the defendant was a NHS Trust located in England. With such a trust the route to satisfaction as to 40-028

---

82 [2007] LS Law Med. 375.

83 This appears at *Thompstone v Tameside & Glossop Acute Services NHS Trust* [2008] 1 W.L.R. 2207 CA at [8].

84 Facts at para.40-019, above.

85 The two subsections are set out at para.52-040, below.

86 Such guarantees are given under the now s.6 of the Damages Act 1996.

87 Under s.213 of the Financial Services and Markets Act 2000.

88 By the new s.4 of the Damages Act 1996.

89 Designated in the Schedule to the Damages (Government and Health Service Bodies) Order 2005 (SI 2005/474).

90 SI 2005/474 Pt 1.

91 SI 2005/474 Pt 2.

92 [2005] Lloyd's Rep. Med. 398.

93 [2005] Lloyd's Rep. Med. 398 at [9].

continuity of payment being secure seems rather to be found in Forbes J's judgment in *YM v Gloucestershire Hospitals NHS Foundation Trust*.[94] Had the defendant there been an NHS Trust rather than an NHS Foundation Trust, with which Forbes J had to deal, it seems that he would have been satisfied on security of payment as the Secretary of State was obliged to take over an NHS Trust's liabilities should it cease to exist. Not so with an NHS Foundation Trust, so that Forbes J was able to satisfy himself on the security front only by a feat of *legerdemain* whereby he contrived to bring the NHS Litigation Authority itself into the proceedings.

**40-029** Where other than health service defendants have been concerned, there has been a variety of ways of looking at the question of security of continuity of payment. In *Godbold v Mahmood*,[95] which involved a road accident, Mitting J said he was satisfied that continuity of payment would be reasonably secure because he considered the matter to fall within the second of the three cases in s.2(4) where continuity of payment is to be regarded as reasonably secure, viz., under the financial services compensation scheme as extended.[96] In *Taylor v Chesworth and The Motor Insurers' Bureau*,[97] which can be seen from the named defendants also to have involved a road accident, Ramsey J recognised that the Motor Insurers' Bureau did not fall within the designated government and health service bodies under s.2(4) but was satisfied that it had

> "the necessary financial, statutory and organisational status to provide assurance that continuity of periodical payments is reasonably secure both in terms of duration and level of payment."[98]

The same must go for *Sarwar v Ali and Motor Insurers' Bureau*,[99] where the security issue was not specifically raised,[100] and all other cases with the Motor Insurers Bureau as a defendant.[101]

**40-030** The moment it is decided, as it now has been,[102] that the courts may utilise indices which take into account higher inflationary trends than appear in the retail prices index, difficulties can arise where the paying defendant is an insurance company. This is because defendants' insurers are required, by so-called close matching regulations under the Financial Services and Markets Act 2000, to hold assets to match their liabilities, and there are no assets which are linked to health care inflation, or to earnings inflation, for the insurers to acquire. The best they can do is to acquire index-linked government stocks, ILGS, which protect against inflation but only against inflation as measured by the retail prices index.[103] Therefore a defendant's liability insurer would not be in a position to acquire an annuity product

---

94 [2006] LS Law Med. 309.

95 [2005] Lloyd's Rep. Med. 379.

96 [2005] Lloyd's Rep. Med. 379 at [32]. For the three cases see para.40-027, above.

97 [2007] EWHC 1001 (QB).

98 [2007] EWHC 1001 (QB) at [162] and [163].

99 [2007] LS Law Med. 375.

100 There is just what was said at [2007] LS Law Med. 375 at [214].

101 In *Taylor* [2007] EWHC 1001 (QB) at [163] Ramsey J mentions the earlier case of *Daniel Thacker* where the status of the MIB was considered.

102 See para.40-025, above.

103 At one time the money could have run out well before many periodical payments awards will have come to an end as the Government had not issued any such stocks maturing beyond 2035. However, there were issued in 2005 index-linked stocks maturing in 2055, in 2011 index-linked stocks maturing in 2062 and in 2013 index-linked stocks maturing in 2068. This takes us a bit further.

which would allow it to make payments linked to health care or earnings inflation, and following from this, since the court is required by s.2(3) to be satisfied that the continuity of payments is secure, it can be forcefully argued that the court would not be able to make an order for payments linked to health care or earnings inflation but be restricted to ordering payments linked only to the lower retail price inflation. This is a very unfortunate situation which needs to be remedied. Short of the Government issuing stocks linked to health care and earnings inflation, which is probably an impracticality, the solution to this problem can only be for the Government not indeed to guarantee the payments themselves but, in the case of insured defendants, to take on a limited liability for periodical payments for the costs of medical care and treatment and for the loss of earnings to the extent that they outstrip the retail prices index. When the difficulty that the retail prices index would be forced on the courts by the close matching regulations was raised with the Court of Appeal in the strike out case of *Flora v Wakom (Heathrow) Ltd*,[104] Brooke LJ, apart from declaring that this matter was best left to the trial, simply posited that the regulations might change as new average earnings index related instruments are devised.[105] But this is no more than wishful thinking. Brooke LJ also noted that the difficulty was overcome in *Flora* itself because the defendant's insurance company had a self-funding policy in relation to periodical payments orders.[106] That is true, the insurance company in *Flora* being the well-established Norwich Union, but the day may well come when the defendant insurance company is a small, financially vulnerable one which may go to the wall.

**(e) Variation of awards** It is a feature of most legal systems which provide for **40-031** the award of periodical payments that they allow for their variation in the future should circumstances radically change, and s.2B of the Damages Act 1996, as inserted by the Courts Act 2003, does indeed provide that the court may in the future vary its order in specified circumstances.[107] The section however leaves it to statutory instrument to specify the circumstances, and we have the provision by statutory instrument two years later[108] that variation may be applied for if there is a chance that at some future time the injured claimant's condition will seriously deteriorate or significantly improve.[109] Four criticisms of this provision, and those which follow it in the statutory instrument, may be advanced.

The first and major criticism is that the scope for variation is restricted to changes **40-032** in the claimant's condition. Why should this be the only change of circumstances envisaged by the legislation? Indeed it may be said that changes in the medical condition of the victims of a seriously disabling injury are rare. What is far more important is change in the care needs of the injured person. There may, for instance, be change of needs for equipment for the disabled, but perhaps the most important potential change is that caused by the unexpected death or departure of a spouse who has shouldered the caring and whose departure makes necessary for the injured

104 [2007] 1 W.L.R. 482 CA; see the case at para.40-023, above.

105 [2007] 1 W.L.R. 482 CA at [30].

106 [2007] 1 W.L.R. 482 CA at [30].

107 The principal part of the section is set out at para.52-032, below.

108 Damages (Variation of Periodical Payments) Order 2005 (SI 2005/841).

109 SI 2005/841 para.2; set out at para.52-033, below. In *Kotula v EDF Energy Networks (EDN) Plc* [2011] EWHC 1546 (QB), the claimant, in addition to having the right, should his condition substantially worsen, to seek to have the periodical payments awarded him varied upwards, was awarded provisional damages allowing him, in the same eventuality, to return for a further lump sum.

person hospital or other institutional care which could be either very costly or, alternatively, free. Secondly, the requirement that the change in the claimant's condition be envisaged[110] seems too limited. Surely these provisions should deal with the unexpected as well as the anticipated and variation should be intended to provide for what cannot be predicted. Thirdly, while it is provided that the court's order must specify the disease or type of deterioration or improvement envisaged,[111] it may not be possible to be sure of the disease or deterioration which may come about. Fourthly, the provision that only one application to vary may be made in respect of the specified deterioration or improvement[112] is also unnecessarily restrictive. Indeed it may be said generally that there is too much of an attempt simply to mirror the earlier provisions on entitlement to provisional damages[113] which are in the nature of things bound to have a smaller compass and, moreover, have found little use in the near 30 years that they have been in force.[114]

40-033 **(f) Dependants' rights in awards** No provision was made in the original legislation to protect the dependants on the death of the claimant whose expectation of life has been cut down by the injury received. The courts having taken the view—it has been suggested unnecessarily—that a successful claim by an injured person precluded a further dependants' suit after his death, they took the precaution of making lump sum awards to cover the lost years for the dependants' protection.[115] Since periodical payments will cease on death, some replacement of the former award for the lost years was needed. It was suggested in the last edition but one, which was at a time when the legislation was in the course of reaching the statute book, that what was required was a provision, similar to that already enacted for provisional damages awarded for an injury which proves fatal,[116] that, where a person dies from his injuries after having obtained an award of periodical payments, the award is not to operate as a bar to a dependants' action under the Fatal Accidents Act. No doubt as a result of representations made, the lacuna has been filled, but it has been filled in a curious way. Instead of the dependants being afforded an action after the death has come about, the court is to make provision for the dependants, should death eventually result from the injury, at the time of the claim by the injured party. This is achieved by a combination of civil procedure rule and practice direction[117] which, read together, stipulate that the periodical payments order is to provide that a part of the award is to continue after the claimant's death for the benefit of his or her dependants specifying the amount to be paid and the duration of payments. But it surely would have been better, and wiser, to wait until after the death before coming to a view as to what will be needed by the dependants and indeed as to who the dependants will then be.

---

110 SI 2005/841 para.2 requires proof or admission of a chance of deterioration or improvement.
111 SI 2005/841 para.5(b); the complete para.5 is set out at para.52-034, below.
112 SI 2005/841 para.7.
113 See paras 40-007 and 40-008, above.
114 See further on variation paras 52-032 to 52-037, below.
115 See para.40-109, below.
116 See para.41-009, below.
117 CPR r.41.8(2) and 41B PD 2.1.

## II. CERTAINTY OF LOSS

As a further preliminary to dealing with the general measure of damages here, the issue of certainty of damage and loss in the early stages falls to be examined. By early stages is meant the period from the injury itself to the adjudication by the final court. **40-034**

In an action for personal injury the damages are in the first place limited by the general doctrines of remoteness and mitigation of damage which play a large part in this type of action. These have already been fully considered in this general context and do not need further treatment[118]; this chapter deals only with such damage as has got through the net of both doctrines. However, something further must be said in the context of personal injury about the third limiting doctrine, that of certainty of damage. For while damages awarded for loss resulting from personal injury may well fall to be reduced because of the rules relating to remoteness and mitigation of damage, there is in general no similar attempt at reduction on the ground that the requirement of certainty of damage is not satisfied. **40-035**

This refusal of the courts to sacrifice physically injured claimants on the altar of the certainty principle does, however, lead them into difficulties. For with damage caused by a physical injury the prediction of the exact course which it will take is generally of far greater difficulty than is the case with most other types of damage and loss emanating from tortious conduct or breach of contract. Nevertheless, courts may be helped to a limited extent by the fact that the events which throw new light on the extent of the claimant's loss have occurred before their adjudication. Accordingly, it becomes necessary to look separately at changes of circumstances taking place before the judgment of the court of first instance, changes during the period where appeals are in process or still available to the parties, and changes after the litigation is at an end and damages have been awarded. **40-036**

### 1. CHANGES BEFORE THE DECISION OF THE COURT OF FIRST INSTANCE

There is today universal acceptance of the sensible and realistic rule that trial courts must look at the position at the time of their judgments and take account of any changes of circumstances which may have taken place since the injury was inflicted. This applies both to change which increases the claimant's loss and to change which diminishes it. There are, however, certain differences in effect between aggravation and amelioration of loss, so that it is best to deal with these two facets separately. **40-037**

**(a) Loss increased** It may be that the claimant's loss can be shown to be greater than had been initially anticipated because of increases in the salary he is now prevented from earning through incapacity resulting from the injury. Such increases are relevant to the assessment of the damages for loss of earning capacity, and whether they are due to general inflation, to factors special to the field of employment in which the claimant had been working, or indeed to any other cause.[119] Or again, the claimant's own physical condition may have worsened unexpectedly, so as to produce an increased incapacity before his case is heard; if so, the court would **40-038**

[118] See Chs 8 and 9, above.

[119] Well illustrated in the field of fatal accidents by *The Swynfleet* (1947) 81 Ll. L. Rep. 116; facts at para.41-032, below.

certainly take this into account and award damages on the basis of the degree of incapacity as it is now known to be,[120] the passage of time having provided better evidence of the seriousness of his injury and the extent of his loss.[121]

**40-039** The fact that courts are prepared to look at the facts as they stand at the date of judgment does not mean that responsibility for all developments between injury and trial are to be laid at the tortfeasor's door, and an aggravation of the claimant's physical condition from causes in no way connected with the defendant's tortious act must not be taken into account. If, for example, the defendant blinds the claimant in one eye and the claimant, before trial, loses his other eye in some later accident, his incapacity is not measured as at the date of judgment and the defendant is responsible only for turning him into a one-eyed man, not for completely blinding him; should the second eye be lost tortiously, the claimant will have a further action against that tortfeasor based on blinding a one-eyed man. However, should the nature of the second injury suffered by the claimant before the trial in respect of the first be such that on its own it would have inflicted the total injury, it may seem that this should be taken into account so as to make inappropriate any damages at all against the defendant for his infliction of the first injury for the period subsequent to the infliction of the second, since from that time he cannot properly be regarded as having caused an injury which would not have occurred without his participation. On two occasions this very difficult question has come before the House of Lords only to receive very different solutions.

**40-040** In *Baker v Willoughby*,[122] the claimant's leg had been severely injured in a car accident but, before his claim in respect of this injury had been heard, he was involved in an armed robbery in which his injured leg was shot and as a result had to be amputated. The House of Lords upheld the claimant's contention that his damages should in no way be decreased by the fact of the second injury, and rejected the defendant's argument that by reason of the shooting and resulting amputation the damages should be limited to those relevant to the period between the injuries. Their Lordships advanced, and relied upon, the proposition that the tortfeasor does not have his liability reduced if, as Lord Reid put it,

> "the later injuries merely become a concurrent cause of the disabilities caused by the injury inflicted by the defendant"[123];

in other words, the defendant will be held to have caused the damage if his participation would have been necessary to bring it about in the absence of other factors sufficient to do so. The House was thereby able to avoid placing the victim of injuries sustained by two successive and independent torts in a worse position than the victim of the self-same injuries sustained at the hands of a single

[120] Implicitly supported by *Jenkins v Richard Thomas & Baldwins* [1966] 1 W.L.R. 476 CA and *Murphy v Stone-Wallwork (Charlton)* [1969] 1 W.L.R. 1023 HL, dealt with at paras 40-047 and 40-048, below.

[121] See, somewhat similarly, the South African case of *Wigham v British Traders Insurance Co*, 1963 (3) S.A. 151 where the court based the damages upon the claimant's expectancy of life at the time of judgment, when she was 84, although the actuarial figure at the time of the injury, when she was 81, would have provided a prediction of a substantially shorter life span. Contrast *Wormald v Cole* [1954] 1 Q.B. 614 CA.

[122] [1970] A.C. 467.

[123] [1970] A.C. 467 at 494. Lord Reid's speech was concurred in by Viscount Dilhorne, Lord Donovan and Lord Guest; only Lord Pearson delivered a separate speech.

tortfeasor.[124] It was, however, suggested in some earlier editions of this work that it did not necessarily follow from the decision in *Baker v Willoughby*,[125] that damages should equally be awarded against the tortfeasor inflicting the original injury where the further injury is non-tortious and that it was questionable whether the victim of a tort whose injury is swallowed up in a supervening heart disease or other non-tortious illness or injury should be entitled to claim damages for the loss arising subsequently to the time that he is overcome by the later affliction. There is a world of difference between protecting the victims of multiple torts from falling between two stools and affording protection from non-tortious loss by requiring the defendant to pay even where the claimant would in any event have fallen ill or been incapacitated. The difficulty in the acceptance of this approach lay in *Baker v Willoughby*[126] itself: reliance there upon *Harwood v Wyken Colliery Co*[127]—where an employee successfully claimed workmen's compensation in respect of an accident which had made him fit only for light work although a heart disease had supervened which also caused him to be fit only for light work—suggested that the House of Lords was accepting that the result should be the same, and in favour of the claimant, with a non-tortious as with a tortious supervening event.

The House of Lords returned to the problem in *Jobling v Associated Dairies*,[128] **40-041**
and there endorsed the view that a non-tortious supervening event must be brought into account to reduce the damages to which there would otherwise, and in the absence of such event, have been an entitlement to claim against the tortfeasor. The claimant suffered an accident at work which left him with a back injury and a consequent reduction in earning capacity. A few years later, but before the trial of his action against his employers took place, he was found to be suffering from myelopathy, a condition with which the accident had no connection but which rendered him very soon after its discovery totally unfit for work. The House of Lords, upholding the Court of Appeal which had reversed the trial judge, held that there could be no recovery for loss of earnings from the time of total incapacity; the myelopathy was not to be disregarded since the court must recognise that the supervening illness would have overtaken the claimant in any event. In so deciding, their Lordships considered it to be immaterial whether the inception of the myelopathy had preceded the accident, being then dormant, or had followed upon it. *Baker v Willoughby*,[129] was questioned. The reliance there on causation principles alone was disapproved,[130] and the particular reliance on *Harwood v Wyken Colliery Co*,[131] was considered to be misconceived since workmen's compensation had been based on different principles from those prevailing in tort; instead, there were prayed in aid two tenets of accepted doctrine, first, what was called the vicissitudes principle which requires that allowance, generally by way of a discount, be made in assessing future earnings loss for the normal contingencies of life, of which

---

[124] This does not apply when the second tort is hypothetical rather than real: see *Heil v Rankin* [2001] P.I.Q.R. Q3 CA at 16, at para.8-027, above. And the *Baker v Willoughby* principle has no application where a first accident has left the injured party with a residual earning capacity obliterated by a second accident: *Brazier v Wolverhampton City Council* [2007] EWCA Civ 1479 CA.

[125] [1970] A.C. 467.

[126] [1970] A.C. 467.

[127] [1913] 2 K.B. 158 CA.

[128] [1982] A.C. 794.

[129] [1970] A.C. 467.

[130] [1982] A.C. 794 at 802E–F, 806D, 811A, 815B and 820G.

[131] [1913] 2 K.B. 158 CA.

illness is generally regarded as one,[132] and, second, the rule that the court does not speculate where it knows,[133] so that, if one of the contingencies becomes actual before the date of the trial, this actuality must be taken into account.[134]

**40-042** Despite the strictures cast upon *Baker v Willoughby*,[135] none of their Lordships was prepared positively to disagree with the decision.[136] All that was decided was that, in the words of Lord Edmund-Davies,

> "where, as in the present appeal, the question in issue relates to the assessment of damages when, a tort having been committed, the victim is overtaken before trial by a wholly unconnected and disabling illness, the decision in *Baker v Willoughby* has no application."[137]

Others in the House had pointed to the difficulties inherent in drawing a distinction between tortious and non-tortious supervening events; how could one be sure of whether there was or was not a second tort, particularly in the absence of the alleged second tortfeasor? Only Lord Keith was prepared to accept that to the extent that *Baker v Willoughby* had decided that

> "in proceedings against the first tortfeasor alone, the occurrence of the second tort cannot be successfully relied on by the defendant as reducing the damages which he must pay … the decision … was correct."[138]

His reasons for taking this stance where there are successive and independent tortious acts are cogent. He said:

> "In that situation it is necessary to secure that the claimant is fully compensated for the aggregate effect of all his injuries. As Lord Pearson noted in *Baker v Willoughby* it would clearly be unjust to reduce the damages awarded for the first tort because of the occurrence of the second tort, damages for which are to be assessed on the basis that the claimant is already partially incapacitated."[139]

Lord Keith recognised that the difficulties of ascertaining whether or not the subsequent event was of a tortious character were real, but rightly concluded that they were not sufficient to preclude the acceptance of the distinction between tortious and non-tortious supervening events.[140] Nor does the suggestion of Lord Edmund-Davies that compensation in respect of the second tort would have been available to the claimant under the Criminal Injuries Compensation Scheme on the facts of *Baker v Willoughby*,[141] or that of Lord Wilberforce that social security benefits should be looked at to see what compensation they would have provided for the second tort, take one further because, apart from the fact that neither of these forms of financial assistance would have been likely to have matched the damages available in tort, both forms of compensation would have started from the premise

---

132 See para.40-131, below.

133 See, inter alia, paras 40-053 and 41-033, below.

134 For a different approach to consecutive injuries, see *Reaney v University Hospital of North Staffordshire NHS Trust* [2014] EWHC 3016 (QB) at para.8-092 fn.448, above.

135 [1970] A.C. 467.

136 [1982] A.C. 794 at 804C, 809D, 810H, 821G.

137 [1982] A.C. 794 at 809E.

138 [1982] A.C. 794 at 815G–H.

139 [1982] A.C. 794 at 815D.

140 [1982] A.C. 794 at 816B.

141 [1970] A.C. 467.

of a claimant already partially incapacitated by the earlier tort. Lord Keith's point is therefore not met. It is true that the Court of Appeal in *Baker v Willoughby* had, through the adoption of the alternative solution of placing the total liability on the second tortfeasor, seen to it that the claimant there was not prejudiced; this had been achieved by a somewhat unusual application of the principle that the tortfeasor must take his victim as he finds him, it being said that the damages recoverable by the claimant from the second tortfeasor included as a head of damage the diminution of the damages recoverable by him from the first tortfeasor.[142] While the solution of the House of Lords is to be preferred over that of the Court of Appeal in that not only is it fairer as between the two tortfeasors but also it provides a greater measure of protection for the victim since, should the whole burden be placed upon the second tortfeasor and he is a man of straw—as would appear to have been the position in *Baker v Willoughby*[143]—or cannot be traced, then the victim is left without tortious redress, Lord Pearson in that case in any event thought that the head of damage suggested by the Court of Appeal was not an admissible one because too remote[144]; moreover, Lord Keith in *Jobling v Associated Dairies*,[145] implicitly indicated the same as he went on the assumption that damages against the second tortfeasor fell to be assessed to a claimant already incapacitated by the first tort.[146]

Furthermore, the result reached by the House of Lords in *Baker v Willoughby*,[147] does not require the retention of liability upon the first tortfeasor where the initial injury gives rise to the need for an operation at such time in the future as the victim may choose and the later tortious injury forces him immediately into hospital for the identical operation. In these circumstances the first tortfeasor should escape liability for both the loss of earning capacity and the medical expenses attributable to the operation because the victim at the time of the second tort was neither incapable of continuing to earn nor obliged to incur medical expenses. A series of decisions involving damage to ships, which are dealt with elsewhere,[148] can be applied by analogy to endorse this reasoning and this result.[149] However, this category of case is clearly a very limited one, and Lord Reid rightly did not find the shipping cases of real value in solving the problem posed in *Baker v Willoughby*.[150] **40-043**

**(b) Loss reduced** As with subsequent aggravations of the claimant's loss, so with subsequent ameliorations: these too must be taken into account. Thus in *Rouse v Port of London Authority*,[151] where the claimant was a docker and between his injury and the trial there was a decline in employment in the docks, the court took into consideration the probability that the claimant would not have earned his pre- **40-044**

142 [1970] A.C. 467 at 480–481, 482 and 483, per Widgery, Fenton Atkinson and Harman LJJ respectively.

143 [1970] A.C. 467.

144 [1970] A.C. 467 at 496A.

145 [1982] A.C. 794.

146 [1982] A.C. 794 at 815D.

147 [1970] A.C. 467.

148 See paras 37-040 to 37-044, above.

149 The process of application in this way is undertaken in Street, *Principles of the Law of Damages* (1962), at pp.175 to 177.

150 [1970] A.C. 467 at 493. For further consideration of *Baker v Willoughby* and *Jobling v Associated Dairies* in a somewhat different context see *Rahman v Arearose Ltd* [2001] Q.B. 351 CA, at para.8-026, above, and see the two consecutive injuries in *Steel v Joy* [2004] 1 W.L.R. 3002 CA, also at para.8-026, above, where *Baker v Willoughby* was rightly considered not to be in point.

151 [1953] 2 Lloyd's Rep. 179.

accident wages during this period.[152] So, too, in *Carter v British India Steam Navigation Co*,[153] the claimant was held not entitled, after he had voluntarily taken a severance payment and left work under a voluntary severance scheme, to claim for loss of future earnings.

**40-045** There is, however, this difference between aggravations and ameliorations of loss, that, while it is necessary to distinguish between those increases in the damage which are and those which are not to be taken into account, all ameliorations in the damage are relevant to the assessment of the damages, whatever form the amelioration may take. In particular—since in contrast to the position in respect of aggravation of damage—where subsequent events unconnected with the tortious act so affect the victim's condition that the loss to him is diminished, the defendant is entitled to have these events taken into account since the actual damage is less.[154] This is neatly illustrated by a decision from Australia where between the injury and the trial the claimant had been convicted of a crime and sentenced to 10 years' imprisonment, and the court rightly took into account, in assessing his damages, his diminished earning capacity both in prison itself and on the labour market after his release.[155] But the most dramatic illustration in practice of this type of event is, ironically, the death of the potential claimant. This makes for an amelioration of the loss suffered in the sense that the death acts as a deliverance for the victim, wiping out all future damage by way of pain, loss of earning capacity and medical expenses, and it is accepted that death from causes other than the tortious act limits the damages claimable by the estate to the period that the claimant has lived since the wrong done to him.[156]

## 2. Changes Before the Decision of the Appeal Court

**40-046** Difficulties, however, appear where the changes in the claimant's loss manifest themselves after the decision of the court of first instance but before the process of litigation has come to an end in one or other of the appellate courts available to the parties. Thus the Court of Appeal may be faced with knowledge of a change of circumstances which was still in the future when the High Court came to the decision which is now under appeal; the House of Lords may know something to be a certainty which was to the Court of Appeal only a possibility or did not even constitute a factor in that court's decision. Although logically a change of circumstances coming before an appellate court's decision is as relevant as one coming before the decision of the court at first instance or of a lower appellate court, the judges are not eager to allow the introduction of new evidence at the appeal stage, generally basing themselves upon the principle *interest reipublicae ut sit finis litium*.

**40-047** In *Jenkins v Richard Thomas & Baldwins*,[157] the change occurred between the

152 And see *Ashcroft v Curtin* [1971] 1 W.L.R. 1731 CA, especially at 1738, where the chance of the claimant being thrown on the labour market had not materialised in the five-and-a-half years between injury and trial.

153 [1974] 1 Lloyd's Rep. 419.

154 Subject always to the qualification that some collateral benefits may have to be ignored: see paras 40-149 and following, and 40-221 and following, below.

155 *Leschke v Jeffs and Faulkner* [1955] Queensland Weekly Notes 67.

156 Well illustrated in the field of fatal accidents by *Williamson v Thornycroft* [1940] 2 K.B. 658 CA; facts at para.41-033, below.

157 [1966] 1 W.L.R. 476 CA.

decision of the High Court and that of the Court of Appeal. The claimant, employed by the defendants as a pitman, had sued his employers for an eye injury which prevented his continuing his former work. After the accident the defendants had continued to employ the claimant but only as a labourer, and at the trial the judge asked the defendants if they were in a position to give the claimant a better job than this. This overture led the defendants to suggest and agree to employ the claimant as a grinder, and the trial judge accordingly based his assessment of damages for loss of earning capacity on the difference between the claimant's former wage as a pitman and the wage which he would now earn as a grinder. However, after the trial, the claimant turned out to show no aptitude for the work as a grinder and, since he never became proficient, continued to receive only a labourer's wage. He therefore sought, by notice of appeal dated more than a year after the trial, to have the damages increased on the ground that his loss of earnings was greater than had been assessed, and at the hearing of the appeal sought leave to introduce the new evidence which supported his contention. The Court of Appeal agreed to hear the new evidence and as a result increased the claimant's damages.[158] The court was, however, careful to point out that evidence of new facts on appeal would only be allowed in exceptional circumstances, and that it was prepared to look at the facts emerging since the trial only because the claimant could show that immediately after the trial the damages assessment had been proved wrong. Salmon LJ was also influenced by the fact that the false assumption upon which the trial judge relied was largely based upon the defendants' representations, honest but mistaken, at the trial that the claimant would be employable as a grinder.[159]

In *Murphy v Stone-Wallwork (Charlton)*,[160] the change occurred between the decision of the Court of Appeal and that of the House of Lords. Again, the claim was by a claimant workman against his employer arising out of a work injury which resulted in the claimant's becoming incapable of as remunerative work as before. In this case the claimant, disabled from heavy work, had been re-employed by the defendants after a short absence on lighter work at a lower wage, and the damages were assessed by the trial judge, and later re-assessed at a higher figure by the Court of Appeal, on the assumption throughout that the claimant would continue to be employed by the defendants on the lighter work despite his disability. No account was therefore taken of the possibility that the claimant, in his partially disabled condition, might be thrown upon the open labour market, with consequent loss to him. Some two weeks after the hearing before the Court of Appeal the defendants, although in no way acting mala fide, dismissed the claimant because his continued employment in his weakened condition might be a source of danger to his fellow **40-048**

[158] By the then Rules of the Supreme Court an appeal was by way of rehearing with the Court of Appeal specifically empowered to receive evidence as to matters occurring after the date of the trial. These rules however were not relied upon in the judgments; *aliter* in *McCann v Sheppard* [1973] 1 W.L.R. 540 CA (at para.40-050, below) and in the analogous Fatal Accidents Act case of *Curwen v James* [1963] 1 W.L.R. 748 CA (at para.41-035, below). Today the Civil Procedure Rules require appeals to be by way of review rather than re-hearing (see para.53-024, below) and say nothing as to the admission of evidence of post trial matters. Yet the position appears to be unaltered, CPR r.52.10(1) giving the appeal court all the powers of the lower court and CPR r.52.11(2), through its stipulation that the appeal court will not, unless it orders otherwise, receive evidence which was not before the lower court, implying that these powers of the appeal court must include the power to admit such evidence.

[159] 1966] 1 W.L.R. 476 CA at 479–480.

[160] [1969] 1 W.L.R. 1023 HL.

employees. The claimant thereupon appealed to the House of Lords within the time limited for appeal, asking for a further increase in his damages and for leave to introduce the new evidence before the House. Once again, the new evidence was admitted[161] on the basis that the case was an exceptional one. Here the exceptional feature lay in the course taken by the defendants which had engendered the belief, upon which the conduct of the trial on both sides had been based, that the defendants would not dismiss the claimant, coupled with the decision to dismiss him within weeks of the Court of Appeal's judgment, although such a decision, if it was going to be taken at all, could and should have been taken at a much earlier point in time.

**40-049** Although arriving at the same result as the Court of Appeal in *Jenkins v Richard Thomas & Baldwins*,[162] their Lordships expressed varying degrees of concern over that decision. Lord Pearson, it is true, only went so far as to say that he thought the question was more difficult on the facts of that case,[163] but Lord Pearce regarded it as very near the borderline,[164] and Lord Upjohn said that he was "not happy about the case … which may require consideration in the future".[165] Lord Upjohn sought to distinguish the case before the House and also *Curwen v James*[166]—where the Court of Appeal, in a Fatal Accidents Act claim, had allowed evidence of the claimant widow's remarriage between trial and appeal[167] and which the Court of Appeal had itself relied upon in *Jenkins v Richard Thomas & Baldwins*[168]—on the ground that in both the basis for the damages assessment was falsified, however innocently, by the act of the party who would benefit from a refusal to allow the introduction of the new evidence,[169] or, in the more telling phrase of the appellant's counsel, "by a deliberate act of the respondents within their sphere of action".[170] On the other hand, this element was entirely lacking in *Jenkins v Richard Thomas & Baldwins*,[171] where, as Lord Pearce pointed out, "it was only the appellant's condition which had caused the alteration of circumstances".[172]

**40-050** However, *Mulholland v Mitchell*,[173] which also reached the House of Lords, showed that a distinction along these lines cannot be controlling. There the change of circumstances affected not the earning capacity of the claimant, whom a car accident had permanently incapacitated both mentally and physically, but the medical expenses which would be incurred on his behalf for the rest of his life. The judge had awarded damages under this head on the basis that the claimant would be nursed by his wife at home at a cost of £1,312 a year, but took into account that the

---

[161] There were no rules of procedure as to admission of evidence governing the House of Lords similar to those governing the Court of Appeal (see footnote to para.40-047, above), but the House was satisfied that it had ample power to admit whatever evidence it thought proper: see at 1027 and 1031, per Lord Upjohn and Lord Pearce respectively.

[162] [1966] 1 W.L.R. 476 CA.

[163] [1969] 1 W.L.R. 1023 HL at 1036.

[164] [1969] 1 W.L.R. 1023 HL at 1028.

[165] [1969] 1 W.L.R. 1023 HL at 1031.

[166] [1963] 1 W.L.R. 748 CA.

[167] See para.41-035, below. Although a widow's remarriage is, since 1971, to be disregarded (see para.41-069, below), the authority of this decision in the present context is unimpaired.

[168] [1966] 1 W.L.R. 476 CA.

[169] [1969] 1 W.L.R. 1023 HL at 1031. See, too at 1027, per Lord Pearce.

[170] [1969] 1 W.L.R. 1023 HL at 1026.

[171] [1966] 1 W.L.R. 476 CA.

[172] [1969] 1 W.L.R. 1023 HL at 1028.

[173] [1971] A.C. 666.

strain might be too much for her and that the claimant might therefore have to go into a nursing home where the cost was £903 a year. Notice of appeal was duly given by the claimant against the assessment of damages but, before the time for a hearing of the appeal had come and indeed within a few weeks of his returning home after the trial, it had become clear that it was impossible for him to continue there due to the deleterious effect on his own health, and he was moved to the only suitable nursing home the cost of which was £1,827 a year, the nursing home contemplated at the trial being no longer in existence. The Court of Appeal granted application for leave to introduce evidence of these new matters at the hearing of the appeal, and the House of Lords upheld the Court of Appeal's exercise of its discretion to give such leave, once again stressing that the circumstances of the case were exceptional. While Lord Wilberforce, in drawing a distinction between evidence which

> "ought not to be admitted when it bears upon matters falling within the field or area of uncertainty, in which the trial judge's estimate had previously been made"

and evidence which

> "may be admitted if some basic assumptions, common to both sides, have clearly been falsified by subsequent events","

added "particularly if this has happened by the act of the defendant",[174] it will be seen that there was no such act of the defendant in the case before the House. Subsequently, in *McCann v Sheppard*,[175] where the claimant, aged only 26 at the time of his injury, had been awarded damages on the basis of an expectation of long years of suffering and loss of earnings but died of an overdose of painkilling drugs four-and-a-half months after the trial and three months after the giving of notice of appeal but before the hearing of the appeal, the Court of Appeal admitted evidence of the death so as to reduce the damages. Here it is true that the claimant's deliberate conduct had brought about his death but the death was not deliberately engineered, and in any event there is nothing in the Court of Appeal judgments to suggest that the situation would have been any different had the claimant died from a cause totally unconnected with the injury and unassisted by conduct on his own part. To Lord Denning MR the case seemed to come within Lord Wilberforce's words in *Mulholland v Mitchell*,[176] that "it would affront common sense" if the court were to shut its eyes to the fact of death,[177] and James LJ put the position very broadly, saying that

> "where notice of appeal has been served within the time prescribed by the rules and an event has taken place at a time reasonably proximate to the date of the trial, which event falsifies the facts upon which judgment proceeded, the court should not rehear the matter upon the basis of the fiction that the event has not taken place."[178]

In *Lim Poh Choo v Camden and Islington Area Health Authority*,[179] it was again, **40-051**

---

174 [1971] A.C. 666 at 679 to 680.
175 [1973] 1 W.L.R. 540 CA.
176 [1971] A.C. 666 at 680.
177 [1973] 1 W.L.R. 540 CA at 546B.
178 [1973] 1 W.L.R. 540 CA at 549H.
179 [1980] A.C. 174 at 183D–G.

as in *Mulholland v Mitchell*,[180] the course of the claimant's medical care which changed. At first instance it was anticipated that the claimant, rendered by negligent hospital treatment into a persistent vegetative state, would be cared for by her mother in Malaysia for a good many years. But by the time the case had reached the Court of Appeal the mother's health had deteriorated so that it was becoming likely that the claimant would have to be transferred to an English nursing home; by the time of the hearing before the House of Lords this transfer had taken place. Each appellate court in turn allowed fresh evidence to be called so that the cost of future care could be assessed upon the changed factual basis, and no difficulty seems to have been felt by either court in allowing the introduction of this fresh evidence.[181]

**40-052** If the decision in *Jenkins v Richard Thomas & Baldwins*,[182] is to be regarded as suspect,[183] it must therefore be for a reason other than that propounded in *Murphy v Stone-Wallwork (Charlton)*.[184] And such a reason is to hand in *Murphy* itself, where their Lordships indicated that the position of the claimant in the case before them would not have been so persuasive had his dismissal occurred at some stage later than the time within which notice of appeal could be served. Lord Upjohn said that, where the time allowed for appeal has run out, whether it be to the Court of Appeal or to the House of Lords, he would apply "a very strict rule indeed", and would allow the matter to be reopened only "in very special and exceptional cases indeed"[185]; Lord Pearce also contrasted the position before with the position after the expiry of the period for appealing, saying that the burden on the appellant who has launched his appeal in time was "less severe than it would have been had he come later".[186] Now *Jenkins v Richard Thomas & Baldwins*,[187] was indeed a case in which the claimant appears to have launched his appeal outside the prescribed time-limit, the notice of appeal being dated more than a year after the trial, and would therefore seem to be distinguishable on this ground not only from *Murphy v Stone-Wallwork (Charlton)*,[188] but also from *Mulholland v Mitchell*,[189] *Lim Poh Choo v Camden and Islington Area Health Authority*,[190] and *McCann v Sheppard*.[191] These last three cases, however, go further than the earlier House of Lords decision since in each the appeal had been launched in time for reasons unconnected with the change of circumstances, which—certainly in *Mulholland* and in *McCann*—did not come about until some while after notice of appeal had been given.

---

180 [1971] A.C. 666.

181 See [1980] A.C. 174 at 183D–G, per Lord Scarman. The decision below is reported at [1979] Q.B. 196 CA. *Vernon v Bosley (No.2)* [1999] Q.B. 18 CA, is a somewhat unusual case where further medical evidence was admitted, applying *Mulholland v Mitchell* [1971] A.C. 666.

182 [1966] 1 W.L.R. 476 CA.

183 It was accepted *en passant* by Lord Wilberforce and Lord Pearson in *Mulholland v Mitchell* [1971] A.C. 666 at 679, 681 that there were doubts about the correctness of this earlier case.

184 [1969] 1 W.L.R. 1023 HL; see para.40-049, above.

185 [1969] 1 W.L.R. 1023 HL at 1031.

186 [1969] 1 W.L.R. 1023 HL at 1028. In *Curwen v James* [1963] 1 W.L.R. 748 CA, the court also reserved its opinion on the admissibility of evidence of a remarriage occurring after the time for appealing had run out: see para.41-036, below.

187 [1966] 1 W.L.R. 476 CA.

188 [1969] 1 W.L.R. 1023 HL.

189 [1971] A.C. 666; especially at 681–682, per Lord Pearson: "This is not a case of application being made after the time for appealing has expired. In such a case a very strict rule should be applied."

190 [1980] A.C. 174.

191 [1973] 1 W.L.R. 540 CA.

The "very strict rule" of Lord Upjohn therefore appears only to apply where there has been failure to appeal within the prescribed time-limit, and even where an appeal is late their Lordships in *Murphy v Stone-Wallwork (Charlton)*,[192] were unanimous that the assessment of damages could and should be reopened if there has been bad faith or underhand dealing by the party who would benefit from a refusal to upset the decision of the lower court—if, for instance, the defendants in that case had already had the intention to dismiss the claimant in their mind during the course of the trial.[193]

With lump sum awards not subject to revision it would clearly be inappropriate, at least in the absence of fraud or bad faith, to allow cases to be reopened after the period for appealing has expired; otherwise there could indeed never be an end to the litigation. This apart, however, there is much to be said for applying the broad general principle, enunciated by Harman LJ in *Curwen v James*,[194] that "the court should never speculate where it knows",[195] so as to allow, in appeals brought within the prescribed time, the introduction in evidence of all new facts which materially affect the size of the damages awarded, and that this should be so whether the appeal has or has not been launched by reason of the new facts and whether the new facts are or are not attributable to deliberate conduct on the part of either appellant or respondent. **40-053**

Of course, however powerful in this connection may be this principle that the court should never speculate where it knows, there remains ever present the countervailing principle with which this discussion started, namely *interest reipublicae ut sit finis litium*.[196] This comes out in the context of a claimant's medical state. While in all the cases dealt with so far, including the three in the House of Lords, the new evidence has been admitted, there is a number of cases in the Court of Appeal, all involving medical evidence indicating that the claimant's condition is worse than had been anticipated, where the new evidence has been disallowed. These stretch from *Pursell v Railway Executive*,[197] before the other authorities, to *Hunt v Severs*,[198] the last of the cases.[199] They are in effect illustrations of what Lord Wilberforce in *Mulholland v Mitchell*,[200] called evidence bearing on matters within the area of uncertainty taken into account by the judge in his assessment.[201] Medical condition will undoubtedly vary over the years and in these cases such changes have been considered to be within the risks taken into account in the trial court's adjudication so that the new evidence has been refused. **40-054**

---

[192] [1969] 1 W.L.R. 1023 HL.

[193] [1969] 1 W.L.R. 1023 HL at 1026, 1030 and 1034, per Lords Pearce, Upjohn and Pearson respectively.

[194] [1963] 1 W.L.R. 748 CA.

[195] [1963] 1 W.L.R. 748 CA at 753. Compare with this Lord Wilberforce and James LJ at para.40-050, above.

[196] See para.40-046, above. And see *Hunt v Severs* [1993] Q.B. 815 CA at 832A–C, per Sir Thomas Bingham MR.

[197] [1951] 1 All E.R. 536 CA.

[198] [1993] Q.B. 815 CA. While the decision was reversed by the House of Lords, the present issue did not feature in the appeal.

[199] The other cases, unreported, are *Bull v Richard Thomas & Baldwins* [1960] CA. Transcript 202 and *Gordon v Windle* [1978] CA. Transcript 21.

[200] [1971] A.C. 666.

[201] See the passage at para.40-050, above.

### 3. Changes After the Litigation has Ended

**40-055** Once the damages have been fully assessed, and no further appeal against the assessment is possible, there is today no method available—unless the circumstances have permitted resort to a claim for provisional damages[202]—for altering the award. An award to a disabled man of 30, based upon normal life expectancy, cannot be reduced even if another accident kills him within a very short time; nor can he have his damages increased upon proof that his disablement has now turned out to be much greater than had been anticipated.[203] It was said in earlier editions of this work that this result of the system of lump sum awards not subject to revision might one day lead to the adoption of the proposal, advocated in 1978 by the Pearson Commission, by a majority, in respect of the future pecuniary loss caused by serious and lasting injury[204] that the courts should in general make their awards in the form of periodical payments[205] and that the periodical payments should be subject to later revision when there is a material change in circumstances.[206] While little or nothing was done about the Pearson Commission's recommendations for many years, they have, from 2005, come to fruition.[207]

## III. Heads of Damage: Function and Interrelation

**40-056** The person physically injured may recover both for his pecuniary losses and his non-pecuniary losses. Of these the pecuniary losses themselves comprise two separate items, namely the loss of earnings and other gains which the claimant would have made had he not been injured and the medical and other expenses to which he is put as a result of the injury, and the courts have sub-divided the non-pecuniary losses into two heads or categories, namely pain and suffering, and loss of amenities of life.[208] While all these heads of damage are given separate consideration in this chapter, it is useful to start by examining their function and how they interrelate.[209]

### 1. Function

**40-057** The function of the pecuniary heads of damage is to ensure that the claimant recovers, subject to the rules of remoteness and mitigation, full compensation for the loss that he has suffered. This is today a clear principle of law. Unfortunately there appears to be at variance with this view an obiter dictum of Brett J in *Rowley*

[202] See paras 40-007 and 40-008, above.

[203] *Fitter v Veal* (1701) 12 Mod. 543, alias *Fetter v Beale* (1701) 1 Ld. Raym. 339 (facts at para.11-032, above) is a classic illustration.

[204] See *Royal Commission on Civil Liability and Compensation for Personal Injury* (the Pearson Commission) (HMSO, 1978), Cmnd.7054 to 1, paras 555 to 576; contrast non-pecuniary loss: at paras 612 to 614.

[205] See the Pearson Commission at para.580 giving a discretion to the court where the injuries are not serious and lasting.

[206] See the Pearson Commission at paras 586 to 589.

[207] See paras 40-011 and following, above on the introduction of periodical payments.

[208] There was formerly a third, loss of expectation of life: see paras 40-262 and 40-263, below.

[209] The Judicial Committee of the Privy Council, allowing the appeal in *Patel v Beenessreesingh* [2012] UKPC 18, saw the Court of Appeal of Mauritius as having got it wrong with every single head of damage.

*v L. & N.W. Ry*,[210] reflecting an earlier obiter dictum of Parke B in *Armsworth v S.E. Ry*,[211] to the effect that a jury

> "must not attempt to give damages to the full amount of a perfect compensation for the pecuniary injury, but must take a reasonable view of the case, and give what they consider, under all the circumstances, a fair compensation."

While both these cases not only are old but also concerned claims under the Fatal Accidents Act, the dictum of Brett J for long continued to be cited in personal injury actions by high authority.[212] Much less has been heard of it, however, since Edmund Davies LJ said in *Fowler v Grace*,[213] in 1970:

> "I confess to having been troubled for years by the oft-quoted direction of Brett J to the jury in *Rowley v L. & N.W. Ry*."

It was submitted in earlier editions of this work that these dicta are misleading and cannot be accepted at face value; at most, the approval of them should be interpreted only as endorsing that contingencies and the like must be taken into account[214] or, alternatively, should be seen in the context of non-pecuniary loss where indeed perfect compensation is impossible.[215] Indeed this approach finds support in a judgment of Brett LJ himself, when sitting, not long after *Rowley*, in the Court of Appeal in the then leading personal injuries case of *Phillips v L. & S.W. Ry*.[216] He there made it clear that it is simply the need to take contingencies and the like into account which makes arithmetical perfection in assessment impossible.[217] And the matter was eventually put on an unambiguous basis by Lord Scarman in *Pickett v British Rail Engineering*,[218] where, after commenting that all a court can give for non-pecuniary loss is fair compensation, he said:

> "But, when a judge is assessing damages for pecuniary loss, the principle of full compensation can properly be applied. Indeed anything else would be inconsistent with the general rule.[219] … Though arithmetical precision is not always possible, though in estimating future pecuniary loss a judge must make certain assumptions (based upon the evidence) and certain adjustments, he is seeking to estimate a financial compensation for a financial loss. It makes sense in this context to speak of full compensation as the object of the law."[220]

There has been no regress from this position since.

The function of the non-pecuniary heads of damage is very different. The concept **40-058**

---

[210] (1873) L.R. 8 Ex. 221 at 231.

[211] (1847) 11 Jur. 758 at 760; cited in the long footnote to para.41-027, below.

[212] *Rose v Ford* [1936] 1 K.B. 90 CA at 102 and *Owen v Sykes* [1936] 1 K.B. 192 CA at 198, both per Greer LJ; *British Transport Commission v Gourley* [1956] A.C. 185 at 209, per Lord Goddard; *West v Shephard* [1964] A.C. 326 at 356, per Lord Devlin; *Watson v Powles* [1968] 1 Q.B. 596 CA at 603 and *Fletcher v Autocar and Transporters* [1968] 2 Q.B. 322 CA at 335 per Lord Denning MR.

[213] (1970) 114 S.J. 193 CA at 193.

[214] See paras 40-128 to 40-141, below.

[215] See para.40-253, below.

[216] (1879) 4 Q.B.D. 406; (1879) 5 Q.B.D. 78 CA; (1879) 5 C.P.D. 280 CA.

[217] See (1879) 5 C.P.D. 280 CA at 290–292.

[218] [1980] A.C. 136.

[219] As formulated by Lord Blackburn in *Livingstone v Rawyards Coal Co* (1880) 5 App. Cas. 25 at 39; set out at para.2-002, above.

[220] [1980] A.C. 136 at 168B–D.

of full compensation, central to pecuniary loss, cannot operate here. It is not possible to give full compensation as no amount in money can fully compensate for a serious physical injury; indeed with all physical injuries one is not, when arriving at a compensatory figure, comparing like with like. The best that the law can do is put a monetary value upon the deprivation which the injured person has suffered; the values which English law has adopted here are given consideration later.[221] Another function of the non-pecuniary award is sometimes said to be as a solace to the injured person, the money enabling him to obtain a degree of satisfaction from the acquisition of goods and services which he enjoys. This latter function—which indeed has been called "the functional approach"[222]—is only relevant where the injured person is aware of his plight; the approach by way of monetary value of the deprivation applies objectively as well as subjectively, to the unconscious claimant who knows not of his condition as well as to the conscious one, and therefore fits more with how English law has developed.[223]

## 2. INTERRELATION

**40-059** It was for long difficult to assess any interrelationship between the various heads of damage because of the erstwhile practice, strongly advocated and endorsed by the Court of Appeal as late as *Watson v Powles*,[224] in 1968, of making global awards. All this was soon to change, under the influence of the new need to award interest and a new preparedness to facilitate appeals; these developments are set out in dealing with interest[225] and with appeals.[226] Indeed today the breakdown of awards in personal injury cases is detailed and meticulous.[227]

**40-060** As one justification for the former practice of making global awards, there was the alleged danger of overlap between the various heads of damage where computed separately. Lord Denning MR touched on this aspect in *Watson v Powles*[228] itself,[229] but the high point of the overlap concept is *Fletcher v Autocar and Transporters*.[230] There the majority of the Court of Appeal held that the trial judge, who had itemised his award, had erred in considering the loss of earnings, the expenses and the non-pecuniary loss as separate heads of damage which could simply be added together, for, especially in a case—as was the one before the court—in which a claimant's life had been transformed by his injuries, there is a danger of overlapping between the various heads. In particular, if, having awarded the claimant damages for the additional expenses incurred by the accident and for his loss of amenities of life, the court then went on to award his future loss of earnings in total, this would mean that he was being compensated on the basis that his earnings, after deduction of board and lodging, would have been saved and that he would not have spent his future earnings on any pleasures which made life enjoyable. The claimant, in Lord Denning MR's words,

[221] See paras 40-253 and following, below.
[222] By Ogus in a valuable article: (1972) 35 M.L.R. 1.
[223] See, especially, *West v Shephard* [1964] A.C. 326, at para.40-260, below.
[224] [1968] 1 Q.B. 596 CA.
[225] See para.19-050, above.
[226] See paras 53-036 and following, below.
[227] See para.53-038, below.
[228] [1968] 1 Q.B. 596 CA.
[229] [1968] 1 Q.B. 596 CA at 603.
[230] [1968] 2 Q.B. 322 CA, Salmon LJ dissenting.

"should not be given compensation for being deprived of those pleasures and recreations unless account is taken of the fact that he would have had to pay for them".[231]

Moreover, after *Jefford v Gee*,[232] made itemisation of damages necessary, Lord Denning MR indicated in *Smith v Central Asbestos Co*,[233] that it was still necessary to bear in mind the danger of overlapping, and there held the judge below to be justified in giving a smaller amount for non-pecuniary loss in the light of the high figure awarded by him for loss of earnings.[234] Subsequently, however, in *Lim Poh Choo v Camden and Islington Area Health Authority*,[235] in a speech with which the other members of the House of Lords expressed agreement, Lord Scarman, while giving no final opinion on the point of principle of whether overlap could exist as between the damages for pecuniary loss and the damages for non-pecuniary loss,[236] confessed that he doubted the possibility.[237] Moreover, this case, by confirming that a claimant who had been reduced to a persistent vegetative state is still entitled to a full recovery for loss of earning capacity,[238] shows that there is no real overlap issue as between the two heads of pecuniary damage, namely loss of earning capacity and medical expenses. All that is necessary, where an award for a lifetime's cost of care is made, is to ensure that the saving in the claimant's living expenses is taken into account in the computation of that award; where no such award is made because the cost of care is to be borne by the National Health Service or by local authorities, the saving attributable to maintenance at the public expense is set off against the recovery for loss of earnings. Lim[239] itself, is authority for the first of these propositions[240]; s.5 of the Administration of Justice Act 1982[241] is authority for the second.[242]

The hope was expressed in earlier editions of this work that this dubious concept of overlap would simply fade discreetly away. With little or nothing heard of it in the cases for very many years, it would seem that the hope has been realised. **40-061**

## IV. Loss of Earning Capacity and Related Benefits

The claimant is entitled to damages for the loss of his earning capacity resulting from the injury; catastrophic injuries, where cost of care predominates, apart, this generally forms the principal head of damage in a personal injury action. Both earnings already lost by the time of trial and prospective loss of earnings are included. While the rules of procedure require that the past loss be pleaded as special dam- **40-062**

---

231 [1968] 2 Q.B. 322 CA at 337.
232 [1970] 2 Q.B. 130 CA.
233 [1972] 1 Q.B. 244 CA.
234 [1972] 1 Q.B. 244 CA at 261H–262A.
235 [1980] A.C. 174.
236 It did not arise for decision on the facts: [1980] A.C. 174 at 192C.
237 [1980] A.C. 174 at 192D. The Pearson Commission, agreeing with the Law Commission, regards the overlap argument as misconceived, considering assessment of pecuniary and non-pecuniary loss to be totally independent of each other: the Pearson Commission (HMSO, 1978), Cmnd.7054, para.759.
238 See [1980] A.C. 174 at 190D–192A, per Lord Scarman.
239 [1980] A.C. 174.
240 See para.40-200, below.
241 *Reversing Daish v Wauton* [1972] 2 Q.B. 262 CA.
242 See para.40-182, below.

age and the prospective loss as general damage,[243] there would appear to be no substantive difference between the two, the dividing line depending purely on the accident of the time that the case comes on for hearing. Thus it has been accepted that the rule in *British Transport Commission v Gourley*,[244] in relation to the incidence of taxation applies equally to the loss of income till judgment and the loss of earning capacity in the future.[245] Similarly, the courts must take account of relevant changes of circumstances occurring before and after judgment, the only difference being that the former are a reality and the latter a matter of estimate.[246] However, interest is to be awarded on the past loss[247] but not on the prospective loss of earnings.[248]

**40-063** The claimant is also entitled to any other loss by way of gains prevented which he can show resulted from the injury. Thus an employee can recover for the loss of benefits connected with employment, such as free accommodation, free produce, free use of a car, the right to a share of profits, or an entitlement to an option on shares, in the employing company. Claims are also commonly made for the loss of value of work that the claimant was accustomed to do around the house, generally styled DIY,[249] or in the garden. While a claimant commonly claims for the loss of value of work that he was accustomed to carry out domestically, it was held in *Swain v London Ambulance Service NHS Trust*,[250] that he cannot claim if the work has been done solely for a member of the family. In that case the claimant recovered for the cleaning only of his own car and not also of his wife's, although it was said that the position could have been different with a two-car family in which the use of both vehicles benefited the household. That there is no legislative provision in England allowing damages to an injured person for the loss of his capacity gratuitously to render services to his relatives was commented upon critically by the Court of Appeal in the light of such recovery having been not only recommended by the Pearson Commission and the Law Commission but also enacted for Scotland in s.9 of the Administration of Justice Act 1982. However, the Court of Appeal has since succeeded in allowing an action to lie at common law by an imaginative application of *Daly v General Steam Navigation Co*.[251] In *Lowe v Guise*,[252] the claimant, who lived with his mother and disabled brother, had provided gratuitous carer services for his brother for many hours a week, which he was no longer capable of giving in full so that the mother had taken over. It was held that

---

243 *British Transport Commission v Gourley* [1956] A.C. 185 at 206, per Lord Goddard. For the difference between general and special damage in pleading, see paras 51-016 and following, below.

244 [1956] A.C. 185.

245 See [1956] A.C. 185 at 197, 205, 211.

246 Compare paras 40-037 to 40-045 with para.40-055, above.

247 Interest on past earnings lost is not on the gross earnings but on the net amount after the tax and national insurance contributions which the employer would have been obliged to deduct: *Bentwood Bros (Manchester) Ltd v Shepherd* [2003] I.C.R. 1000 CA.

248 *Jefford v Gee* [1970] 2 Q.B. 130 CA. Nor is interest to be awarded on damages for handicap in the labour market (see para.40-096, below): *Clarke v Rotax Aircraft* [1975] 1 W.L.R. 1570 CA. For the reason for the difference between past loss and prospective loss, see para.19-090, above. For the recovery of interest on loss of earnings where the employer has voluntarily made up the earnings to the employee claimant, see *Davies v Inman* [1999] P.I.Q.R. Q26 CA, at para.40-160, below.

249 But care must be taken that the multiplier used for the DIY assessment is not too high: see *Chase International Express Ltd v McCrae* [2004] P.I.Q.R. P21 CA at 314.

250 [1999] All E.R. (D) 260 CA.

251 [1981] 1 W.L.R. 120 CA; for which see paras 40-086 and 40-087, below.

252 [2002] Q.B. 1369 CA.

the claimant was entitled to claim damages for the loss of his ability to look after his brother as he had lost something of real value to himself. *Swain* can now hopefully be dismissed as an aberration.[253]

Other losses arising in rather special cases have appeared or could appear.[254] One loss may be taken from the analogous case of wrongful dismissal: there seems no reason why a physically injured actor should not be entitled to recover damages for loss of publicity in the same way as a wrongfully dismissed one.[255] This, however, is very akin to loss of earnings, and a more instructive illustration is provided by the loss of opportunity of marriage, and the consequent deprivation of the support of a husband, that may be suffered by a girl or young woman seriously injured. Recovery for such a loss was allowed by O'Connor J in *Moriarty v McCarthy*,[256] but it has become the practice in later cases to allow for this loss simply by the court's declining to use a lower multiplier for loss of earning capacity than would be appropriate for a man.[257] A somewhat analogous illustration appears in *Lampert v Eastern Omnibus Co*.[258] A wife claimed damages on the ground that her husband had left her as a result of her disfigurement caused by the injury inflicted by the defendant. Hilbery J took the view that this loss formed an acceptable head of damage,[259] and refused recovery only on the ground that the wife had failed to establish that she had lost anything of value by the desertion of her husband with whom she had already been on bad terms, or indeed that his reason for deserting her had been the disfigurement. On the other hand, in *Oakley v Walker*,[260] the costs of providing home help and care for the children of a marriage were awarded to a husband as a recoverable head of damage where his wife had left not only him but also the children after he had suffered disfigurement and change of personality in an accident. In *Kralj v McGrath*,[261] where the claimant sued for personal injury caused through medical negligence and occurring at the delivery of her twin sons, one of whom died as a result soon after birth, there was no loss of earning capacity as such but the claimant nevertheless was held entitled to recover in respect of earnings which she anticipated losing over a five-year period when she had a further child to replace the twin who had died.[262] **40-064**

A somewhat unusual, but now fortunately historical, situation in which it was stated obiter by the Court of Appeal that a claimant could recover for a particular pecuniary loss other than loss of earnings arose in *Hassall v Secretary of State for Social Security*.[263] Two claimants, in receipt of unemployment benefit at the time **40-065**

---

253 For more detail on this whole matter, see paras 40-090 to 40-094, below.

254 In *Horton v Evans* [2007] EWHC 315 (QB) the loss was represented by the fall in the value of shares in a business due to the claimant's injury precluding her essential participation in the business, the valuation of the shares being taken at the time when the claimant would have realised them.

255 See para.33-028, above.

256 [1978] 1 W.L.R. 155.

257 See para.40-104, below.

258 [1954] 1 W.L.R. 1047.

259 Following Lord Campbell's view in *Lynch v Knight* (1861) 9 H.L.C. 577, as interpreted by the High Court of Australia in *Wright v Cedzich* (1930) 43 C.L.R. 493, which interpretation was approved by Lord Goddard in *Best v Fox* [1952] A.C. 716 at 732.

260 (1977) 121 S.J. 619.

261 [1986] 1 All E.R. 54.

262 The cases dealing with failed sterilisations and the like, which are somewhat similar and may even be regarded as involving personal injury, are dealt with separately at paras 40-282 and following, below.

263 [1995] 1 W.L.R. 812 CA.

of injury, continued to collect much the same amount in benefit after injury but now because of incapacity to work. In the Secretary of State's successful claim to recoup this benefit from the claimants' general damages, which was held possible because of the then unfortunate wording of the recoupment legislation,[264] the Court of Appeal indicated that the claimants could and should have claimed in their action against the tortfeasor special damages for their loss of entitlement to benefit, which would not have been recoupable because it would have been paid by virtue of their unemployment rather than by virtue of their injury. The Court of Appeal in *Neal v Bingle*,[265] reversing the judge below, applied the obiter suggestion in *Hassall* so as to allow the claimant, who also had no claim for loss of earnings being unemployable, to recover by way of special damages a sum equivalent to the benefits he would have received but for the accident. However, the need for such decisions has gone for the future. Now that the Secretary of State can recoup benefits relating to earning capacity only from damages awarded for loss of earning capacity, and not from either general damages or damages for care,[266] the *Hassall* and *Neal* situation cannot arise, but these cases remain illustrative of how far losses under the head of loss of earning capacity and related benefits can be taken.

### *(A) General Method of Assessment*

**40-066** The courts have evolved a particular method for assessing loss of earning capacity, for arriving at the amount which the claimant has been prevented by the injury from earning in the future. This amount is calculated by taking the figure of the claimant's present annual earnings less the amount, if any, which he can now earn annually, and multiplying this by a figure which, while based upon the number of years during which the loss of earning power will last, is discounted so as to allow for the fact that a lump sum is being given now instead of periodical payments over the years.[267] This latter figure has long been called the multiplier; the former figure has come to be referred to as the multiplicand.[268] Further adjustments, however, may or may not have to be made to multiplicand or multiplier on account of a variety of factors, namely the probability of future increase or decrease in the annual earnings, the so-called contingencies of life, and the incidence of inflation and taxation.[269]

**40-067** There are, exceptionally, situations in which the court is entitled, because there are too many imponderables in the case, to regard this conventional method of computation as inappropriate and to arrive simply at an overall figure after consideration of all the circumstances. In *Blamire v South Cumbria Health Author-*

---

264 See para.40-273, below.

265 [1998] Q.B. 466 CA.

266 For the statutory provision achieving this, see paras 40-168 and 40-241, below.

267 But for the Employment Tribunal to take account of accelerated receipt merely by making a 5 per cent deduction from the total figure for two and a half years' earnings and 10 years' pension is unacceptable: *Bentwood Bros (Manchester) Ltd v Shepherd* [2003] I.C.R. 1000 CA.

268 In many cases it will be necessary to have separate multiplicands and multipliers for the earnings which the claimant would have made but for the injury and the earnings which he can make after the injury. A good illustration is afforded by *XYZ v Portsmouth Hospitals NHS Trust* [2011] EWHC 243 (QB) (facts at para.10-089, above) where there is dealt with separately the claimant's loss of future earnings (at [42] and following) and his residual earning capacity (at [221] and following).

269 These various factors are discussed in detail below. Compare the similar method used in Fatal Accidents Act claims at paras 41-038 and following, below.

*ity*,[270] the trial judge was held justified in rejecting the conventional approach employing multiplicand and multiplier because the uncertainties of what the claimant would have earned had she not been injured and what over time she would now earn in her injured state were so great that, as Steyn LJ said, "inevitably one is driven to the broad brush approach".[271] This case is now regarded as having brought this type of award to the fore so that it has become common for courts to speak of *Blamire* awards or the *Blamire* type of award. Such awards have been made, or considered, in a variety of circumstances.

Claims brought on behalf of children on account of their education being alleged to be inadequate present very difficult problems for damages assessment as was said in *Liennard v Slough BC*,[272] and again in *Keating v London Borough of Bromley*,[273] and in such cases the *Blamire* approach may be particularly appropriate. Indeed it was said in *Liennard* that, had the case not failed, *Blamire* would have applied. In *Chase International Express Ltd v McRae*,[274] the Court of Appeal overturned the assessment of the trial judge, who had used the conventional multiplicand/multiplier method, in favour of, as it was put, a round sum as was done in *Blamire*, there being little or no reliable evidence before the judge of the claimant's pre-accident employment history or his post-accident earning capacity.[275] The *Blamire* approach was also taken, though "in a more calculated way", in *Van Wees v Karkour and Walsh*[276] where the future career path was very uncertain,[277] ending up with an award for lost earnings and pension of a million pounds.[278] In *Ward v Allies and Morrison Architects*,[279]where the likely career pattern and earning capacity of the claimant, just out of university, could not be ascertained and proved, neither but for the accident nor as a result of the accident, the Court of Appeal, affirming the trial judge, considered that he was "driven" to adopt the *Blamire* approach.[280] **40-068**

Also, where a claimant's handicap in the labour market requires a separate award, which, as we shall see, courts have been making since *Smith v Manchester Corporation* was decided,[281] this is generally achieved without resort to multiplicand and multiplier.[282] The Court of Appeal expressly endorsed the trial judge's **40-069**

270 [1993] P.I.Q.R. Q1 CA.
271 [1993] P.I.Q.R. Q1 CA at Q6.
272 [2002] E.L.R. 527; see at [167]–[172].
273 [2003] E.L.R. 590; see at [199]–[204].
274 [2004] P.I.Q.R. P21 CA at 314.
275 [2004] P.I.Q.R. P21 CA at [14]–[16].
276 [2007] EWHC 165 (QB).
277 [2007] EWHC 165 (QB) at [133] and [134].
278 See [2007] EWHC 165 (QB) at [155].
279 [2012] EWCA Civ 1287 CA.
280 See [2012] EWCA Civ 1287 CA at [20]–[26]. In making an assessment of loss of earnings over a lifetime by the employment of a global lump sum, it may nevertheless be prudent to check the proposed sum against the method of multiplicand and multiplier. By so doing in *Sharpe v Addison* [2004] P.N.L.R. 23 CA at 426, what would have been an annual figure of £4,000 for the multiplicand was seen to be much too small: see at [37]–[39], per Rix LJ.
281 See paras 40-096 and following, below.
282 A statement of the difference between a *Blamire* award and a *Smith v Manchester* award is at *Ronan v Sainsbury's Supermarkets Ltd* [2006] EWCA Civ 1074 CA at [22], per Hughes LJ. But *Smith v Manchester* awards may be becoming less common: see para.40-100, below.

rejection of this method in favour of a lump sum approach in both *Dhaliwal v Hunt*,[283] and *Goldborough v Thompson and Crowther*.[284]

**40-070** In the past the courts were for long been pressed to pay more attention to actuarial evidence in coming to their assessments. This proposal was, also for long, received unenthusiastically and a line of cases, from *Watson v Powles*,[285] decided in 1967 to *Auty v National Coal Board*,[286] decided in 1984, rejected the use of actuarial tables as the primary method of assessment though admitting, generally rather grudgingly, their value as a cross-check of the calculations carried out without them.[287] However, the situation gradually changed for the better and, as will be seen, has now been transformed. It is therefore no longer necessary, happily, to burden the text with the to-ings and fro-ings of decades of outmoded authority.[288]

**40-071** The first step was the appointment of a working party chaired by Sir Michael Ogden QC to produce suitable actuarial tables, and in 1984 there was published by the Government Actuary's Department the Ogden Tables as they are generally called, the full title being

> "Actuarial Tables with explanatory notes for use in Personal Injury and Fatal Accident cases".

A second and much expanded edition appeared in 1994, a fourth in 2000 was further expanded,[289] and the Tables reached their seventh edition in 2011. This is the edition to which references here are made. As the years went by, Ogden became more and more cited in personal injury litigation so that by the time of *Hunt v Severs*,[290] Lord Bridge, who gave the only speech in the House of Lords, had to accept that practice had changed and that actuarial tables—and he had the Ogden Tables in mind—were featuring more prominently in the evidence on which courts relied.[291]

**40-072** Technically, the introduction of the Ogden Tables before a court needed an actuary to be called to prove them and, although objection was seldom taken by courts or counsel to their introduction without such strict proof, it seemed sensible to make provision by legislation for their direct admissibility. Hence s.10(1) of the Civil Evidence Act 1995 was enacted providing for the Ogden Tables to be admissible in evidence.[292] This subsection is still not in force, and it seems now that it will be left to wither, having been overtaken by events.

---

283 [1995] P.I.Q.R. Q56 CA.

284 [1996] P.I.Q.R. Q86 CA.

285 [1968] 1 Q.B. 596 CA.

286 [1985] 1 W.L.R. 784 CA.

287 The use of combined annuity and life expectation tables to assist in the damages calculation was approved as long ago as *Phillips v L. & S.W. Ry* (1879) 5 Q.B.D. 78 CA, the leading case of the 19th century on personal injury damages; see, too, Slesser LJ's summary in *Roach v Yates* [1938] 1 K.B. 256 CA at 268–269.

288 For these, see the 15th edition (1988) of this work at paras 1454 to 1456.

289 Expanded to deal with an issue relating to fatal accidents: see para.41-054, below.

290 [1994] 2 A.C. 350.

291 [1994] 2 A.C. 350 at 366. Indeed the Court of Appeal in *Hunt v Severs* [1993] Q.B. 815 CA called upon counsel to produce a further actuarial table to assist in making a calculation for a fixed number of years: [1993] Q.B. 815 CA at 841G–H. Such a table was later provided by Ogden; today it appears as Table 28.

292 This was as a result of a recommendation of the Law Commission in its Report on *Structured Settlements and Interim and Provisional Damages* (HMSO, 1994), Law Com. No.224, paras 2.9–2.15.

For the House of Lords in *Wells v Wells*,[293] apart from its famous prescription of a new discount rate,[294] laid down, equally famously, that the rate was to be derived from, and by use of, the Ogden Tables. Lord Lloyd put it beyond further argument. "The tables", he said, "should now be regarded as the starting point, rather than a check".[295] And he added by way of warning: **40-073**

> "A judge should be slow to depart from the relevant actuarial multiplier on impressionistic grounds."[296]

Moreover, it is implicit in the speeches of Lord Steyn and Lord Hope that they agreed.[297] Thus the Ogden Tables have triumphed. They are now established in the damages lexicon, the order of the damages day and a prerequisite for the damages calculation.[298]

Moreover, this triumph of the Ogden Tables has resulted in the multipliers in use becoming far more precise and exact. From the somewhat arbitrary round numbers of earlier days courts now adopt the Ogden detailed figures for specific ages, even interpolating between them, so as to end up with multipliers which run to two decimal points. Not only can there be this degree of precision and exactness but also the competing multipliers advanced by claimant and defendant turn out on some issues to be very close. Thus in *Tinsley v Sarkar*,[299] where there was a dispute over whether to use Ogden Table 1 or Ogden Table 28 to assess the cost of lifetime care for a claimant whose life expectation had been cut down, the competing multipliers argued for were 23.76 by the claimant and 22.92 by the defendant.[300] **40-074**

### (B) CALCULATION OF THE MULTIPLICAND AND OF THE MULTIPLIER

#### 1. DIMINUTION IN EARNINGS: THE BASIC FACTOR FOR THE MULTIPLICAND

The starting point in the calculation of the multiplicand[301] has long been the **40-075**

---

293 [1999] 1 A.C. 345.

294 See paras 40-122 and 40-123, below.

295 [1999] 1 A.C. 345 at 379F.

296 [1999] 1 A.C. 345 at 379F.

297 See [1999] 1 A.C. 345 at 388E and 393C respectively.

298 There seems to be little point in considering here the alternative Duxbury Tables because it looks as if the courts dealing with personal injuries are choosing generally to ignore them. Styled the Duxbury Tables after the name of the decision which adopted them in matters of divorce in the Family Division where they have made their mark, they appear more sophisticated because of their reliance on the computer and computer software, and were indeed proposed for use in personal injury claims by the Court of Appeal in *Wells v Wells* [1997] 1 W.L.R. 652 CA, Thorpe LJ dealing with them at length in an appendix to the court's judgment in which he compared the Ogden approach unfavourably with Duxbury. In view of this, what was crucial was the attitude of the House of Lords on the appeal in *Wells*. But Duxbury made little impact and all but passed their Lordships by. Only Lord Lloyd and Lord Steyn referred to the Duxbury Tables in their speeches and then not with any intention of utilising them in arriving at their decision on discount rate: [1999] 1 A.C. 345 at 375A and 387C respectively. Little further has been heard of Duxbury in the personal injury context, appearing only in relation to a tax issue: see footnote at the end of para.40-148, below; it is clear that Ogden has prevailed.

299 [2006] P.I.Q.R. Q1 at 1.

300 See [2006] P.I.Q.R. Q1 at [29]. The case is at para.40-220, below.

301 Lord Lloyd commented in *Wells v Wells* [1999] 1 A.C. 345 at 377F that, since the effect of reducing the rate of discount (see paras 40-119 and following, below) will be to increase the multiplier in every case, it is all the more important to keep firm control of the multiplicand.

amount earned by the claimant before the injury. However, since the decision in *Cookson v Knowles*,[302] in the related field of fatal accidents,[303] the starting point, through the stimulus of inflationary conditions, became the amount that the claimant would have been earning at the date of trial had he not been injured; as Waller LJ put it in *Auty v National Coal Board*,[304]

> "the limit to which inflation should influence the assessment of future loss is to take the loss at date of trial and not at date of accident, and no more".[305]

From this is deducted the amount that the claimant is capable of earning in the future; if the injury has brought total incapacity, then nothing falls to be deducted.[306] A loss of pension rights falls to be included in the same way as an earnings loss, taking the annual pension which the claimant would have received less the annual pension he will now receive after the injury; *Auty v National Coal Board*,[307] also deals with the computation of such a loss.[308]

**40-076** In *Parry v Cleaver*,[309] Lord Reid drew attention to the two questions which arise when the financial loss suffered as a result of an inability to work by reason of injuries has to be assessed. He said:

> "First, what did the claimant lose as a result of the accident? What are the sums which he would have received but which by reason of the accident he can no longer get?"[310]

This first question—the second dealt with the deductibility of collateral benefits and is considered in due course[311]—was the one in issue in the landmark decision in *British Transport Commission v Gourley*,[312] in which it was established by the House of Lords that the computation is to be made on the earnings after deduction of the income tax which would have been payable on them.[313] Similarly, contributions under the Social Security Acts and formerly under the National Insurance Acts which they replaced—generally referred to as national insurance contributions—were also deducted in arriving at earnings; *Cooper v Firth Brown*,[314] which so held, while open to review by the higher courts, has not been challenged and is clearly right. In *Dews v National Coal Board*,[315] the House of Lords expanded these deduc-

---

302 [1979] A.C. 556.
303 See para.41-042, below.
304 [1985] 1 W.L.R. 784 CA.
305 [1985] 1 W.L.R. 784 CA at 796F.
306 This is, however, subject to the deduction of collateral benefits (see paras 40-149 and following, below) which now include the saving attributable to free maintenance in a National Health Service institution (see para.40-182, below).
307 [1985] 1 W.L.R. 784 CA.
308 But the discount of 27 per cent made for contingencies in *Auty* is not for approval: see this issue at para.40-135, below.
309 [1970] A.C. 1.
310 [1970] A.C. 1 at 13.
311 See paras 40-149 and following, below.
312 [1956] A.C. 185; fully considered in relation to personal injury claims at paras 18-025 to 18-027, above.
313 Which may entail that there must also be deducted from the damages any payment by way of rebate of tax arising from the fact that too much tax has now been collected in respect of the period preceding the injury: *Hartley v Sandholme Iron Co* [1975] Q.B. 600; Contrast also *Brayson v Wilmot-Breedon* [1976] C.L.Y. 682. But see the reference to *Hartley* in a footnote to para.18-062, above.
314 [1963] 1 W.L.R. 418.
315 [1988] A.C. 1.

tions to include employees' contributions to a compulsory pension scheme. Following an injury at work the claimant, a miner employed by the defendant board and required by his contract of employment to make to a pension scheme a weekly contribution of a percentage of his earnings which the board was entitled to deduct from his pay, was off work and for several weeks received no pay. Accordingly, no deductions could be made in respect of contributions but their non-payment entailed no loss to the claimant of his pension rights. Damages were awarded based on the claimant's take home pay net of the compulsory pension contribution. The House rejected the contention of the claimant's counsel that the true view of *British Transport Commission v Gourley*,[316] was that tax was held to be deductible only on the ground that the liability to pay tax was part of the general law of the land[317] and that a mandatory contractual liability to pay was quite different.[318] Indeed Lord Griffiths, in a speech with which his brethren expressed agreement, said that he did not regard it as a critical feature that the pension scheme was a compulsory one[319] so that contributions under a voluntary scheme would also fall to be deducted.[320] Although the general principle was recognised that it is no concern of the tortfeasor how the physically injured claimant chooses to dispose of his earnings, nevertheless in the words of Lord Mackay with whose speech also there was general agreement

> "the tortfeasor is concerned with the disposal of any part of the claimant's remuneration which is applied to obtain benefits which may be affected by the claimant's injury and, if affected, would be a proper subject of claim against the tortfeasor. If a claimant is entitled to a benefit such as, for example, pension rights which is damaged as a result of his inability to work consequent upon an accident and the tortfeasor is bound to compensate him for the reduction in the value of that benefit[321] the tortfeasor must be concerned with the extent to which the injured claimant's remuneration required to be devoted to obtaining that benefit. Otherwise, where a claim for such a loss is made, there would be a double recovery."[322]

Thus accident insurance premiums paid by an employee stand on a different footing because, as Woolf LJ in the Court of Appeal[323]—which the House of Lords was affirming—pointed out in discussing them,[324] neither are the benefits from such a policy taken into account in the damages[325] nor is there recoverable in the damages the loss of any such benefits by inability to continue paying premiums.[326] In

---

316 [1956] A.C. 185.

317 There was direct support for such a limitation only in the speech of Lord Tucker: see [1956] A.C. 185 at 215.

318 See [1988] A.C. 1 at 13H–14D, per Lord Griffiths.

319 [1988] A.C. 1 at 16G.

320 This is subject only to the point that an employee under a voluntary pension scheme might be able to show that he has suffered loss in the amount of the contributions because he would have chosen to cease participation therein: see [1988] A.C. 1 at 16H.

321 For recovery of loss of pension rights, see *Auty v National Coal Board* [1985] 1 W.L.R. 784 CA at para.40-075, above.

322 [1988] A.C. 1 at 18A–C.

323 [1987] Q.B. 81 CA.

324 [1987] Q.B. 81 CA at 102E–F.

325 See para.40-150, below.

326 In the Court of Appeal (affirmed by the House of Lords) union dues were also discussed; it was conceded that no deduction should be made as they were not compulsory ([1987] Q.B. 81 CA at 102B) and Sir John Donaldson MR agreed (at 90G); but Woolf LJ would say, rightly, that whether the dues were voluntary or compulsory was immaterial (at 102C), thinking on the whole that they

any event, in all these cases it is immaterial whether the income tax or the contribution towards State or private pension has been deducted at source and so never received by the claimant or has been made directly by the claimant out of the earnings once received.[327] Moreover, it must be right that, if the employee's contributions do not come into the computation, neither, and a fortiori, do the contributions, matching or otherwise, of the employer.[328]

**40-077** It very occasionally may happen that the earnings utilised for the multiplicand have some impropriety or illegality attached to them. In *Newman v Folkes and Dunlop Tyres Ltd*,[329] the claimant had never paid tax or national insurance upon his substantial earnings and it was argued that this disentitled him from any recovery for loss of earnings. Garland J however correctly held that since the claimant's earnings were derived from a lawful source he was entitled, despite the collateral illegality, to rely on the loss of that source to found a claim, but it might be necessary to make an adjustment for unpaid tax and national insurance. The multiplicand should thus be based upon the earnings so adjusted rather than upon the gross earnings that the claimant had been accustomed to retaining. The position would have been different had the earnings come from an illegal source; there could then have been no recovery. This follows a fortiori from the decisions disallowing claims for loss of dependency based upon illegal earnings of the deceased.[330]

**40-078** *Hewison v Meridian Shipping Services PTE Ltd*,[331] raised the issue of the effect of illegality upon a lost earnings claim, and hence upon the appropriate multiplicand, in a more difficult context. The claimant was injured at work in an accident for which the defendants, his employers, admitted liability. He had been employed for many years as a merchant seaman but he had indicated, falsely, to his employers that he did not suffer from epilepsy, a condition which prohibited his working as a seafarer. Some time after the accident he was dismissed after suffering an epileptic seizure at work. By a majority the Court of Appeal held that he was not entitled to claim for loss of earnings on the basis of his continuing to work until retirement age as a seaman. Although he would not be disentitled to damages for loss of the earnings that he would otherwise have received by reason only of a collateral or insignificant illegality or unlawful act, here his deception of his employers was neither collateral, being central to his obtaining the earnings in question, nor insignificant, because of the potential risks involved.[332]

---

were not to be deducted (at 102C).

327 See *British Transport Commission v Gourley* [1956] A.C. 185 at 198, 207, 213; *Dews v National Coal Board* [1988] A.C. 1 at 17E.

328 Contrast *Dews v National Coal Board* [1988] A.C. 1 at 12A–B, per Lord Griffiths. While it was also recognised that a deduction has to be made of the expenses of earning the lost income, it was suggested that this should not generally be taken so far as to require a deduction of the expense of travelling to and from work: see at 12H–13E.

329 [2002] P.I.Q.R. Q2 at 13.

330 See *Burns v Edman* [1970] 2 Q.B. 541 and *Hunter v Butler* [1996] R.T.R. 396 at para.41-013, below.

331 [2003] I.C.R. 766 CA.

332 *Gray v Thames Trains Ltd* [2009] A.C. 1339 is another personal injury claim for loss of earnings which was held by the House of Lords, reversing the Court of Appeal (also at [2009] A.C. 1339 CA), to be prevented by the ex turpi causa maxim. See the case at para.8-065, above.

## 2. Earnings of Different Categories of Person

### (1) Employees

What the claimant is earning per annum at the time of injury will generally be easy to calculate where he is employed at a wage or salary; similarly, the amount which he is capable of earning in the future is often made clear by the terms of such post-injury employment as he has entered into before his claim is brought to trial. Only a few points need be noted. In *Behrens v Bertram Mills Circus*,[333] it was held, where the claimant was earning jointly with another in a circus act, that the calculation could be properly based on half this amount as the claimant had been receiving half the benefit of the earnings although, commercially speaking, the claimant's contribution to the act was worth less than half.[334] In *Donovan v Cammell Laird*,[335] where a widower had been prevented by the injury from earning for 12 months during which time he did domestic work in his house and thus saved paying for the domestic assistance which, had he been earning at work, he would have required, a deduction was made in respect of this sum. In *Ronan v Sainsbury's Supermarkets Ltd*,[336] where the injury caused the young claimant to give up his job in banking and take a university course, he was held entitled to his three years' loss of earnings during the degree course. An issue of some difficulty, that of how far loss of a chance comes into the assessment of an employee's lost earnings,[337] is considered elsewhere in relation to certainty of damage.[338] **40-079**

### (2) Self-employed persons

Where the claimant is self-employed the calculation, though rather more complex, follows similar lines. If he is in professional practice, either alone or in partnership, then it will be necessary to assess his earnings from that practice together with any earnings of which he is still capable, whether in the practice or elsewhere.[339] A difficulty, however, arose in assessing the true loss of earning capacity in *Ward v Newalls Insulation Co*.[340] The claimant was a partner in what was initially a two-man partnership which owned and controlled a number of companies. The partners drew their income from the partnership, which received the company profits, on an equal basis. The two partners then introduced their wives as further partners and, by agreement with the Inland Revenue, paid tax on the basis of four separate and equal incomes from the partnership profits, although the wives contributed no capital and did no work for the partnership. In assessing the **40-080**

---

[333] [1957] 2 Q.B. 1.

[334] See [1957] 2 Q.B. 1 at 27.

[335] (1949) 82 Ll. L. R. 642.

[336] [2006] EWCA Civ 1074 CA.

[337] See *Doyle v Wallace* [1998] P.I.Q.R. Q146 CA; *Langford v Hebran* [2001] P.I.Q.R. Q160 CA; *Heil v Rankin* [2001] P.I.Q.R. Q3 CA at 16; *Herring v Ministry of Defence* [2004] 1 All E.R. 44 CA; *Brown v Ministry of Defence* [2006] P.I.Q.R. Q9 at 109; *Appleton v El Safti* [2007] EWHC 631 (QB); *Collett v Smith* [2009] EWCA Civ 583 CA; *Clark v Maltby* [2010] EWHC 1201 (QB) and *XYZ v Portsmouth Hospitals NHS Trust* [2011] EWHC 243 (QB).

[338] See paras 10-082 to 10-090, above where all the cases in the preceding note are considered.

[339] See e.g. *Phillips v L. & S.W. Ry* (1879) 5 Q.B.D. 78 CA; *Fletcher v Autocar and Transporters* [1968] 2 Q.B. 322 CA. Paucity of evidence of earnings loss did not prevent an award to a self-employed joiner in *Eden v West & Company* [2003] P.I.Q.R. Q2 CA at 16.

[340] [1998] 1 W.L.R. 1722 CA.

claimant's damages in his personal injury claim the Court of Appeal reached the conclusion that his real loss of earning capacity was 50 per cent of the partnership profits and that it did not, as the trial judge had held, have to be reduced to 25 per cent.

**40-081** A self-employed businessman is not entitled to recover in respect of gratuitous services performed by his wife for his business as a result of his injury; it was so held in *Hardwick v Hudson*.[341] Such services fell into a different category from caring services provided voluntarily by a relative or friend where recovery is allowed.[342] With a business the circumstances were different in that the services would normally be provided under a contract of employment even if performed by a relative or friend. If then such services were provided gratuitously without a contract, the loss saved by the business would not ground any recovery since it was to be attributed to the voluntary intervention of the relative or friend in circumstances where a contractual arrangement was to be expected.

**40-082** More difficult is the case of the claimant who is self-employed in the sense that he controls and manages, to one degree or another, a family company.[343] In *Lee v Sheard*,[344] where the claimant's absence from the business of a private company, of which he was a director holding nearly half the share capital, caused a substantial reduction in the company's turnover and profits, it was held that the claimant under this head of damage was entitled to recover in respect of the diminution of the profits distributed to him. Similarly in *Jason v Batten (1930)*,[345] the court considered that it was entitled to take into account the undoubted effect of the claimant's absence on the profits of his corporate business, holding that the true loss fell to be measured by the reduction in the net profit of the company, the turnover, gross profit and overheads of which were all down in the year in which the claimant was injured.[346] Such a straight calculation, however, may not always be correct, as the deterioration in company or business profits may not be completely due to the claimant's absence: general business and trade conditions may have been an operative factor. On the other hand, the fact that company or business profits are produced not only as a result of the claimant's services but also from other labour and from capital should not affect any diminution in the damages.[347]

---

341 [1999] 1 W.L.R. 1770 CA.

342 See paras 40-225 and following, below.

343 That the courts regard as unattractive any technical argument that a loss may have been suffered not by the claimant but by the claimant's one-man company is shown, in another context, by *Esso Petroleum Co v Mardon* [1976] Q.B. 801 CA: see para.49-062, below.

344 [1956] 1 Q.B. 192 CA. *Lee v Sheard* was expressly adopted and approved in a somewhat different context in *Gerber Garment Technology Inc v Lectra Systems* [1997] R.P.C. 443 CA (see the case at para.48-047, below) and impliedly in the personal injury context in *Ward v Newalls Insulation Co* (see the case in the last paragraph but one, above).

345 [1969] 1 Lloyd's Rep. 281.

346 But a claimant claiming for diminution in the profits of his one-man business cannot succeed in this claim if, though the evidence points to a decrease in the company's profitability which is due to the injury, the records kept are too rudimentary and the accounts too unreliable to quantify the loss: *Ashcroft v Curtin* [1971] 1 W.L.R. 1731 CA.

347 In *Bellingham v Dhillon* [1973] Q.B. 304, where the claimant owned 500 out of the 501 shares in the company carrying on his driving school business, both sides agreed that for the purpose of the action the company's loss was his loss: at 305E. For the facts, see para.9-126, above.

## (3) Non-employed persons

Where the claimant is not employed, it is necessary to look first at the reason for the lack of employment. The claimant may not need to work because he is of independent means or he may not be able to find work. Again, the claimant may not be working because supported by a relative, as in the case of an injured wife or child. **40-083**

**(a) Persons of independent means** If the claimant is not earning any income because he is a gentleman of leisure, living wholly on a private unearned income,[348] the position is somewhat unclear. If the true basis of recovery is for loss of earning capacity rather than loss of earnings, then it could be argued that he is entitled to the market value of his lost time; there is, however, no authority on the point.[349] **40-084**

**(b) Persons who cannot find employment** If the claimant was out of work at the time of the injury and was therefore not earning because he could not find work rather than because he did not care to work, the court has to estimate his prospects of gaining employment in the future, and at what level, and assess the damages accordingly. In *Meah v McCreamer*,[350] it was held to be necessary, in assessing damages, to take into account the claimant's previous criminal tendencies, which would probably have resulted in his spending periods in prison, and his previous poor employment record, which could indeed eliminate any continuing loss of earnings when combined with the fact that he would receive free board in prison. In *Hassall v Secretary of State for Social Security*,[351] no claim was even made for loss of earning capacity because the two injured claimants accepted that for the period of their incapacity they would not have been able to find work even if fit. Similarly, no award for loss of earning capacity featured in *Neal v Bingle*,[352] where the facts were like those in *Hassall*. **40-085**

**(c) Wives** In *Daly v General Steam Navigation Co*,[353] the claimant housewife became, as a result of her injuries, partially incapable of undertaking housekeeping duties and ran her home with the assistance of her husband but without employing a home help as the family did not, before the award of damages, have the resources to have one. The claimant was held to be entitled to recover the value of her domestic services and the argument that, before doing so, she must show a firm intention of employing an assistant in the house was firmly rejected by the Court of Appeal. Bridge LJ said: **40-086**

> "Once the judge had concluded, as this judge did, that, to put the claimant, so far as money could do so, in the position in which she would have been if she had never been injured, she was going to need, in the future, domestic assistance for eight hours a week, it seems to me that it was entirely reasonable and entirely in accordance with principle in assess-

[348] Which in itself is irrelevant to reduce the damages for loss of earning capacity: see para.40-142, below.

[349] Should a claimant's pattern of life have been to live on social security benefits rather than to seek gainful employment, it must be doubtful if he could then appropriately claim for loss of earning capacity. Contrast *Lowe v Guise* [2002] Q.B. 1369 CA, at para.40-094, below.

[350] [1985] 1 All E.R. 367.

[351] [1995] 1 W.L.R. 812 CA; facts at para.40-065, above.

[352] [1998] Q.B. 466 CA.

[353] [1981] 1 W.L.R. 120 CA.

> ing damages, to say that the estimated cost of employing labour for that time … was the proper measure of her damages under this head. It is really quite immaterial, in my judgment, whether having received those damages, the claimant chooses to alleviate her own housekeeping burden … by employing the labour which has been taken as the basis of the estimate on which damages have been awarded, or whether she chooses to continue to struggle with the housekeeping on her own and to spend the damages which have been awarded to her on other luxuries which she would otherwise be unable to afford."[354]

At the same time it was held that the wife was not entitled to claim the cost of employing the labour which was no doubt needed, but not engaged, between the time of accident and the time of trial; this was an expense which was known not to have been incurred. Instead an addition was made to the non-pecuniary award.[355]

**40-087** This inconsistency of approach in *Daly*,[356] as between the past and the future loss, whereby the Court of Appeal, while objecting to the artificiality of regarding as a pecuniary loss past housekeeping incapacity where no help is taken on, applied that artificiality to the future, is to be deprecated. Surely it would be better to allow no damages for pecuniary loss for either the past or the future, unless the claimant satisfies the court that she will take on help, but to make an addition to the non-pecuniary award, as the Court of Appeal indeed did for the past,[357] for both the past and the future.[358] In any event the impact of *Daly* is somewhat limited as it posits a claimant who is not going to accept assistance from others; certainly after the damages have been awarded, most wives would be likely to utilise part of their damages to pay for domestic assistance. If the claimant does hire paid domestic help the defendant will clearly be liable for this cost and, if relatives give gratuitous assistance, a claim for this assistance may also be lodged. Indeed in *Daly* itself, where the claimant's husband had given up his part-time employment to help carry out the housework, an amount representing his lost earnings was awarded to the claimant.[359]

**40-088** **(d) Children** In the case of a child[360] wholly or partially incapacitated for life, the court must make an estimate of how well the child, if uninjured, would have fared as an earner on attaining adulthood. The court is here faced with the difficulty that it has little or no material upon which to assess future earning potential where the injury is incurred, and especially where the trial comes on, at a time when the child is still too young for its ability to be measured with any degree of objectivity and certainty.[361] In many of the earlier cases, even into the 1980s, the problem was not specifically addressed. Sometimes it was not at all clear how the court had

---

354 [1981] 1 W.L.R. 120 CA at 127C–E.

355 See para.40-258, below.

356 [1981] 1 W.L.R. 120 CA.

357 Indeed all that the Court of Appeal did in relation to the past loss was to add to the non-pecuniary award the amount which had been awarded by the trial judge, in the Court of Appeal's view wrongly, as a pecuniary loss for past incapacity: see [1981] 1 W.L.R. 120 CA at 128.

358 This was the criticism and proposed solution of the Law Commission, first in its consultation paper requesting views, *Damages for Personal Injury: Medical, Nursing and Other Expenses*, Consultation Paper (1996) No.144, and then in its following report, ibid. (1999), *Law Com. No.262*, criticism and solution having the support of almost all of the consultees who responded to the consultation paper on this issue: see No.144 at paras 3.73 to 3.78 and *Law Com. No.262* at paras 3.87 to 3.91.

359 Today, however, after *Hunt v Severs* [1994] 2 A.C. 350, the claimant would be required to hold these damages on trust for her husband: see para.40-228, below.

360 The damages recovered by a child are under the control of the court: see CPR r.21.11.

361 In the case of an irreversibly brain-damaged child, the time at which the trial comes on is not likely to be of significance in this connection.

arrived at the multiplicand, as in *S v Distillers Co (Biochemicals)*,[362] and *Connolly v Camden and Islington Area Health Authority*.[363] Sometimes the multiplicand/multiplier method made no appearance, as in *Jones v Lawrence*,[364] or was indeed expressly abandoned, as in *Joyce v Yeomans*,[365] where the Court of Appeal stated that the court was not bound to calculate the loss of earning capacity on a mathematical basis by applying a multiplier to a multiplicand, and indeed the majority even went as far as to say that it was inappropriate where the circumstances produced so many imponderables.[366] This, however, is too extreme; more sensible counsels have since prevailed.

The start was to look to the national average wage: this was adopted for the multiplicand by the trial judge, and approved by the Court of Appeal, in *Croke v Wiseman*,[367] with Lord Denning MR's contention that there should be no award at all for loss of future earnings for so young a claimant being roundly, and rightly, rejected by the majority of the court. In *Almond v Leeds Western Health Authority*,[368] one-and-a-half times the national average wage was adopted where the child came from an excellent home with parents who would have seen to it that he was properly educated and trained.[369] Then in *Cassel v Riverside Health Authority*,[370] where the child claimant was born suffering from cerebral palsy, a much higher multiplicand appeared, based upon the propitious omens to be derived from the evidence of the child's heredity and environment, the family pattern on both sides being one of effort and success. The contention of the defendant that it was not open to the judge to make the assumptions, for a child damaged at birth, that he would have pursued the career of an able and ambitious earner in continuous and demanding work was rejected. The Court of Appeal upheld Rose J's chosen multiplicand of £35,000, which represented two-and-a-half times the national average wage for non-manual workers. While Ralph Gibson LJ considered this to be "at the upper reaches",[371] Farquharson LJ thought it "not particularly high"[372] and Purchas LJ said it was **40-089**

> "a reasonable middle of the range figure in the very special circumstances which prevailed in this case."[373]

And it is now becoming common to take into account parental backgrounds and achievements, as in *M (A Child) v Leeds Health Authority*,[374] where a multiplicand

---

362 [1970] 1 W.L.R. 114 CA; see at 126C and 128A.

363 [1981] 3 All E.R. 250; see at 255d–f.

364 [1969] 3 All E.R. 276; see at 271C–272A.

365 [1981] 1 W.L.R. 549 CA.

366 Brandon LJ, however, expressed the correct view that the court would not be erring in law by adopting the multiplicand/multiplier method: [1981] 1 W.L.R. 549 CA at 557B.

367 [1982] 1 W.L.R. 71 CA. In *Daish v Wauton* [1972] 2 Q.B. 262 CA, the multiplicand was based on a labourer's wage; at 272G.

368 [1990] 1 Med. L.R. 370.

369 Following the unreported *Taylor v Glass*, 1979. In *Taylor v British Omnibus Co* [1975] 1 W.L.R. 1054 CA, the child's father's favourable employment position was taken as a yardstick.

370 [1992] P.I.Q.R. Q168 CA.

371 [1992] P.I.Q.R. Q168 CA at 179.

372 [1992] P.I.Q.R. Q168 CA at 183.

373 [1992] P.I.Q.R. Q168 CA at 189.

374 [2002] P.I.Q.R. Q4 at 46.

of £16,000, which represented a modest uplift on the then average female earnings, was taken.[375]

40-090 **(e) Other family members rendering gratuitous services** *Lowe v Guise*,[376] expanded the law of damages by deciding that, where a family member had looked after another family member and could no longer do so, or do so to the same extent, because of his injury, he could recover damages. The claimant, who lived with his mother and disabled brother, had provided gratuitous carer services for his brother for many hours a week, most of which hours he was no longer capable of giving. For these hours the mother was now providing the gratuitous care. In these circumstances it was held that the claimant was entitled to claim damages for the loss of his ability to look after his brother as he had lost something of real value to himself.

40-091 Two difficulties had lain in the path of the Court of Appeal's coming to this sensible result. The first was that Parliament had, in s.9 of the Administration of Justice Act 1982, enacted for Scotland, but excluding England, a provision allowing a reasonable sum by way of damages to an injured person for the loss of his or her capacity gratuitously to render services to his or her relatives; this suggested that no similar claim would lie in England. The second was the decision in *Swain v London Ambulance Service NHS Trust*,[377] where an injured husband's claim for the loss of value of the work of cleaning his wife's car was denied.

40-092 The court dealt with the first difficulty by taking the view that Parliament's failure to extend s.9 to England was on the basis that England could reach the same result through the common law, and indeed had already done so in *Daly v General Steam Navigation Co*,[378] in relation to wives' services.[379] It is, however, doubtful whether the court in *Daly* had this general situation of relatives' services in mind and, despite what is said in *Lowe v Guise*,[380] the Law Commission in its Report on *Damages for Personal Injury: Medical, Nursing and Other Expenses*[381] did not so regard *Daly*. The court dealt with the second difficulty by regarding *Swain* as a special case on its own facts. It is indeed doubtful if *Swain* would now be followed.[382]

40-093 The question of the level of recovery was not fully explored by the Court of Appeal in *Lowe v Guise*.[383] Rix LJ simply said that, even though the claimant was providing his care gratuitously, his loss "can and ought as a matter of policy to be measured in money's worth".[384] Potter LJ went further. He said that,

> "where the services have been supplied gratuitously and are therefore performed by another, also gratuitously, a subsidiary problem arises as to the basis upon which the loss or value of the services is to be assessed","[385]

---

375 See [2002] P.I.Q.R. Q4 at [50]–[58].
376 [2002] Q.B. 1369 CA.
377 [1999] All E.R. (D) 260 CA.
378 [1981] 1 W.L.R. 120 CA.
379 See paras 40-086 and 40-087, above.
380 [2002] Q.B. 1369 CA.
381 (1999), *Law Com. No.262*.
382 See the whole question further at para.40-063, above.
383 [2002] Q.B. 1369 CA.
384 [2002] Q.B. 1369 CA at [38].
385 [2002] Q.B. 1369 CA at [53].

and considered[386] that the judge who would eventually have to assess the damages would be bound to follow the differentiation made by the Court of Appeal in *Daly* between financial loss in respect of general damages for the future and none in respect of special damages for the past.[387] This would be unfortunate as that distinction has been rightly criticised, as by the Law Commission.[388] As to the amount to be awarded, the choice seems to be between the commercial rate for the services and a discounted rate along the lines of the recovery for gratuitous services rendered not by, but to, a family member.[389] Scottish courts, in assessing "the reasonable sum" required by statute,[390] generally base their awards upon the commercial rate; it should, however, be remembered that the payment to the claimant is by way of damages which are not subject to tax, as a payment to a professional carer would be. The matter still awaits resolution.

It was also argued by the claimant in *Lowe v Guise*,[391] that, since his injuries had **40-094** taken away not only his ability to look after his brother but his capacity to earn a living, he should be compensated for the latter. That he had chosen for good reason not to exploit his earning capacity did not mean that he had not had the capacity to earn, which was an asset of value. Unlike the man who has chosen not to work because rich or idle and who will remain rich or idle after being injured, the claimant's injuries were now the sole cause of his unemployment. This argument had no success.[392]

## 3. ADJUSTMENTS FOR VARIATION IN ANNUAL EARNINGS LOSS

### (1) In general

The amount which the claimant was presently earning may not be the amount **40-095** which he would have continued to earn in the future. It will often be the case that the claimant's earnings would have increased over the years as he progressed in his career, and this factor has always been taken into account[393]; conversely, the court in other cases will have to take note of the fact that the claimant's earnings are liable to diminish in the future, as where he was in an occupation with a high rate of unemployment[394] or where he had reached an age when he was due to continue working only on a part-time basis. Again, there is the possibility that the earnings which the claimant is now making may be cut down because the injury has depreciated his value as an employee, for a partial disability frequently does not affect a man's wages or salary immediately but nevertheless puts him at a disadvantage in the labour market should he have to look for fresh employment[395]; the courts have

[386] [2002] Q.B. 1369 CA at [57].
[387] For this, see para.40-087, above.
[388] See again para.40-087, above.
[389] See paras 40-233 and 40-234, below.
[390] See para.40-091, above.
[391] [2002] Q.B. 1369 CA.
[392] [2002] Q.B. 1369 CA at [43]–[47].
[393] *Roach v Yates* [1938] 1 K.B. 256 CA at 269, per Slesser LJ for an early statement to this effect.
[394] Compare *Rouse v Port of London Authority* [1953] 2 Lloyd's Rep. 179, at para.40-044, above.
[395] Contrast *Lau Ho Wah v Yau Chi Biu* [1985] 1 W.L.R. 1203 PC, a case involving not damages but a form of employees' compensation in Hong Kong, where the Judicial Committee, in holding the claimant entitled to compensation for his loss of earning capacity despite the fact that he had obtained employment in which he earned more than at the time of the accident, noted that such a recovery would protect him from the risk of subsequently finding himself thrown on the labour market with

accepted that this factor too must be taken into account and, as will be seen, deal with it in a special way.[396] Conversely, there may in a particular case be a significant chance that the earnings which the claimant is now making will increase.[397] In all these cases if adjustment is to be made by changing, up or down, the multiplicand or the multiplier, it has been said that the adjustment should be to the multiplicand[398]; yet not infrequently today the adjustment is made to the multiplier.[399] Of course it will be the multiplicand which is adjusted where there is no immediate loss in earnings but only a potential loss in the future, as with a child or with a person suffering a handicap in the labour market, since nothing is achieved by adjusting the multiplier. If, indeed, it should be possible to identify with some degree of precision the times in the future at which the multiplicand will change, then different multiplicands may be taken for different periods with the multiplier then split between however many periods there should happen to be. Such an identification of changes is more likely to be possible with medical expenses than with earnings; the manner in which the exercise requires to be carried out is therefore set out later when dealing with medical expenses.[400]

### (2) Handicap in the labour market: then and now

40-096 **(a) The introduction of Smith v Manchester awards** With the claimant disadvantaged in the labour market, an alternative course is to make a separate award for this head of damage, distinguishing between the loss of actual earnings—of which indeed there will be none if the claimant has continued in employment at the same salary as formerly—and the loss of earning capacity represented by the physical handicap produced by the injury. This is the course which the courts have been taking in this area. The development along these lines is said to have started in the mid-1970s with the decision of the Court of Appeal in *Smith v Manchester Corporation*,[401] but there are cases of the same nature which came before it.[402] Although, ironically, not achieving the status bestowed by appearance in the official or any other of the well-known law reports, the case gave its name to this head of damages, an award for handicap in the labour market being known as a *Smith v Manchester* award and such damages as *Smith v Manchester* damages.

---

a then genuine earnings loss: see 1207GH.

396 See para.40-096, below.

397 See, e.g. *Hoffman v Sofaer* [1982] 1 W.L.R. 1350, especially at 1352G–1353B and 1354B–E; *Long v Mercury Communications* [2002] P.I.Q.R. Q1 at 1, especially at [47].

398 *Mallett v McMonagle* [1970] A.C. 166 at 175, per Lord Diplock, but with reference to the analogous calculation of loss of dependency in Fatal Accidents Act claims. The multiplicand cannot be increased to take into account wage inflation in excess of retail price inflation: see *Cooke v United Bristol Healthcare NHS Trust* [2004] 1 W.L.R. 251 CA at para.40-125, below.

399 See, e.g. *Long v Mercury Communications* [2002] P.I.Q.R. Q1 at 1, [47] (multiplier reduced as earnings claimant will now make likely to increase); *Newman v Folkes and Dunlop Tyres Ltd* [2002] P.I.Q.R. Q2 at 13, [51] (multiplier reduced as earnings claimant would have made likely to decrease).

400 See para.40-218, below. With Duxbury calculations (for these see footnote at the end of para.40-073, above) the anticipated changes in earnings would be incorporated by the computer software, thereby bypassing today's less accurate methods of calculation. But Duxbury is not being used in personal injury claims (see above).

401 (1974) 17 K.I.R. 1 CA.

402 *Gardner v Dyson* [1967] 1 W.L.R. 1497 CA; *Cheesman v Furness Withy & Co* [1969] 1 Lloyd's Rep. 315; *Patel v Edwards* [1970] R.T.R. 425 CA; *Ashcroft v Curtin* [1971] 1 W.L.R. 1731 CA. Contrast Browne LJ in *Moeliker v Reyrolle & Co* [1977] 1 W.L.R. 132 CA at 139H: "a head ... long recognised".

A cluster of four further Court of Appeal decisions appeared very soon after[403] and showed that *Smith v Manchester* had put the head of damage on the map.[404] Handicap in the labour market assessed as a separate item of damages took off after these cases of the mid-1970s. Further unreported Court of Appeal decisions of the 1980s are witness to this and cases, reported and unreported, have continued[405] in fair number until recently.[406]

The most typical situation is that of the employee continuing to work after the injury for the same employer at the same rate of pay. This was *Smith v Manchester*,[407] itself. The claimant was a domestic worker in one of Manchester Corporation's old people's homes and the Corporation had undertaken to continue with her services at the same wage as long as they could properly do so, but there was "a real risk" that she would lose her job.[408] There are, however, well recognised permutations. Thus the claimant at the date of trial may be working for the same employer at a lower wage, which was the position in *Nicholls v National Coal Board*,[409] where the pitman coal cutter had been kept on in a lighter job with his wages cut. In these circumstances there will be a claim in respect of the reduced earnings as well as for the handicap in the labour market, and in *Clarke v Rotax Aircraft*,[410] the need to avoid any overlap between the awards for loss of earnings and for loss of earning capacity was stressed. Or the claimant may be working for a different employer or working for himself; in either case his earnings are likely to be at a different level. Thus in *Tait v Pearson*,[411] the claimant, who was working at a new job on an oil rig, was even making more than before the injury,[412] but the work was intermittent and was not work that the claimant would be able to continue doing indefinitely. And, early on, *Cook v Consolidated Fisheries*,[413] made it clear that the claimant's being in employment at trial is not a prerequisite of an award. In *Cook* a deckhand on a trawler decided that in future he would drive lorries but was not driving at the time of the trial as he had not yet gained the necessary qualifications. Indeed in *Dhaliwal v Hunt*,[414] where the court purported to use a *Smith v Manchester* calculation, the claimant was too young to have been in employment, being still a child. **40-097**

Many times the court has spoken of the problem of arriving at an appropriate **40-098**

---

403 Namely *Clarke v Rotax Aircraft* [1975] 1 W.L.R. 1570 CA; *Nicholls v National Coal Board* [1976] I.C.R. 266 CA; *Moeliker v Reyrolle & Co* [1977] 1 W.L.R. 132 CA; *Cook v Consolidated Fisheries* [1977] I.C.R. 635 CA.

404 "Although [the case] laid down no new principle of law ... it seems to have made claims under this head more fashionable": Browne LJ in *Moeliker v Reyrolle & Co* [1977] 1 W.L.R. 132 CA at 140E.

405 But a claimant should not be confined to a *Smith v Manchester* award where there is adequate evidence of future lost earnings to justify the use of the usual multiplicand/multiplier method: *Stefanovic v Carter* [2001] P.I.Q.R. Q6 CA at 55.

406 For the reason for the decline see para.40-100, below.

407 (1974) 17 K.I.R. 1 CA.

408 *Moeliker v Reyrolle & Co* [1977] 1 W.L.R. 132 CA; *Foster v Tyne and Wear County Council* [1986] 1 All E.R. 567 CA and *Gunter v John Nicholas & Sons* [1993] P.I.Q.R. P67 CA, are further cases where the employee was in the same job and had sustained no loss of wages.

409 [1976] I.C.R. 266 CA.

410 [1975] 1 W.L.R. 1570 CA.

411 [1996] P.I.Q.R. Q92 CA.

412 As in *Lau Ho Wah v Yau Chi Biu* [1985] 1 W.L.R. 1203 PC: see the case at the third footnote in para.40-095, above.

413 [1977] I.C.R. 635 CA.

414 [1995] P.I.Q.R. Q56 CA.

figure. Thus Auld LJ referred in *Dhaliwal v Hunt*,[415] to a remark of Megaw LJ in an unreported case that the assessment of damages under this head usually involves "nothing but a guess"[416] while in the early *Moeliker v Reyrolle & Co*,[417] Browne LJ said:

> "It is impossible to suggest any formula for solving the extremely difficult problems involved in … the assessment. A judge must look at all the factors which are relevant in a particular case and do the best he can."[418]

In that case Stephenson LJ said that if the risk were substantial the award should generally be in hundreds of pounds and if serious then in thousands,[419] figures which today would require to be increased by a factor of five for inflation. In quite a number of cases the court has taken a number of years of the claimant's pre-injury earnings as the basis for the calculation. Thus in *Foster v Tyne and Wear County Council*,[420] the trial judge awarded five times the claimant's annual salary, an award which was upheld by the Court of Appeal though said to be on the high side; generally when this method has been used the number of years taken has been lower, even as low as half a year in *Moeliker v Reyrolle & Co*.[421] Quite high amounts in the context of the level of the claimant's pre-injury earnings do appear. In *Goldborough v Thompson and Crowther*,[422] the Court of Appeal upheld an award of £30,000; in *Herbert v Ward*,[423] £50,000 was awarded where the same employer had fitted in the employee despite his grave disabilities, but his tenure was "very much in the balance" and if his employment ceased he had a "very poor prospect of competing in the labour market". Awards can also be very much lower and have come to be cut down by the Court of Appeal. Thus an award of two or three years' earnings was held too much in the circumstances of *Ronan v Sainsbury's Supermarkets Ltd*,[424] and awards were reduced to one of four months' earnings in the circumstances of *Brown v Ministry of Defence*,[425] and to one which amounted to about seven months' earnings in the circumstances of *Evans v Tarmac Central Ltd*.[426] The evidence may not justify any award; it did not, for example, in *Hoffman v Sofaer*,[427] or in *Johnson v Warren*.[428]

**40-099** In *Moeliker v Reyrolle & Co*,[429] the Court of Appeal emphasised the need to show a substantial, rather than a negligible, risk of the claimant's being thrown on the

---

415 [1995] P.I.Q.R. Q56 CA.
416 [1995] P.I.Q.R. Q56 CA at Q60.
417 [1977] 1 W.L.R. 132 CA.
418 [1977] 1 W.L.R. 132 CA at 142C. Occasionally the court still arrives at its award by use of multiplicand and multiplier, as in *Gunter v John Nicholas & Sons* [1993] P.I.Q.R. P67 CA.
419 [1977] 1 Ll.L.R. 132 CA at 144D–E.
420 [1986] 1 All E.R. 567 CA.
421 [1977] 1 W.L.R. 132 CA.
422 [1996] P.I.Q.R. Q86 CA.
423 *Herbert v Ward* unreported 25 July1982.
424 [2006] EWCA Civ 1074 CA.
425 [2006] P.I.Q.R. Q9 CA at 109.
426 [2005] EWCA Civ 1820 CA. The one year taken in *Green v DB Group Services (UK) Ltd* [2006] I.R.L.R. 764 was on earnings in a future career: see at [182] and [183].
427 [1982] 1 W.L.R. 1350; see at 1354F1355E.
428 [2007] EWCA Civ 595 CA: claimant, though unable to do physical work, could do clerical work which was freely available to her and was work she had previously done.
429 [1977] 1 W.L.R. 132 CA.

labour market. This need has since been stressed again in *Frost v Palmer*,[430] and *Robson v Liverpool City Council*,[431] but that the requirement that there be a real risk of future unemployment is not to be interpreted too strictly is also evidenced by both of these cases. Nonetheless some concern has been expressed that the tendency is for courts to underestimate the likely loss and to err on the ungenerous side in their awards.[432] *Morgan v UPS Ltd*,[433] highlights the uncertainty in arriving at an appropriate figure for these damages. The trial judge, having awarded £12,500 "for impairment of … future earning capacity", gave a further £10,000 "as *Smith v Manchester* damages". It was not at all clear how the figure of £10,000 had been arrived at and the Court of Appeal, while upholding the judge's total award, was concerned that there might have been an element of double counting.[434]

**(b) The impact of the new Ogden method of contingencies assessment** All the above may now be history. A fairer method of dealing with handicap in the labour market may now have been provided through the radically new methodology for assessing discounts for the contingencies of life which has been introduced in the Ogden Tables 6th edition of 2007 and repeated in the current 7th edition of 2011. This new methodology, explained at a later point,[435] introduces three entirely different factors from formerly in the assessment of contingency discounts, and it is the factor of disability status that matters here. Thus the earnings loss of a claimant suffering a degree of disability from the injury suffered will fall to be assessed at salary discounted for contingencies in his pre-accident non-disabled condition less salary discounted at a much higher percentage for contingencies in his post-accident disabled condition, thereby taking any handicap into account.[436] No reported cases of *Smith v Manchester* awards later than the arrival of the new Ogden discount factors have appeared[437] and the cases of this nature since that time, none of which has reached the Court of Appeal, have attempted to apply the new Ogden guidelines.[438] Certainly, it is clear from the commentary in the Ogden Tables that the Working Party envisages that the new methodology should be used in place of the *Smith v Manchester* approach.[439] So it might be said that the *Smith v Manchester* award is now dead.[440] Yet against a verdict of death it is thought that two rather dif- **40-100**

---

430 [1993] P.I.Q.R. Q14 CA.

431 [1993] P.I.Q.R. Q78 CA.

432 See the interesting study, going beyond simply the issue of *Smith v Manchester* awards, of Lewis, McNabb and Wass, Methods of Calculating Damages for Loss of Future Earnings [2002] J.P.I.L. 151.

433 [2008] EWCA Civ 375 CA.

434 See generally the three judgments, and particularly at [2008] EWCA Civ 375 CA at [29]–[34] and [37].

435 See at para.40-134, below.

436 Compare the discounted figures set out in Table A with those in Table B for males and the discounted figures set out in Table C with those in Table D for females at para.42 of the Explanatory Notes to the 7th edition (2011) of the Ogden Tables.

437 In the last of the above cases in which a *Smith v Manchester* award was made, *Morgan v UPS* (see preceding paragraph), the Court of Appeal in its hearing (17 April 2008) made no mention of the new approach, but then the hearing below (11 May 2007) came before Ogden 6th edition was out.

438 See them at para.40-137 to 40-139, below. Thus in one of these cases, *Conner v Bradman & Co* [2007] EWHC 2789 (QB), Judge Peter Coulson QC considered a *Smith v Manchester* award inappropriate. Instead, he took into account the new Ogden discounts based on disability so as to end up with a substantial discount in assessing the claimant's post-accident earnings: at [63]–[74]. See *Conner* further at para.40-139, below.

439 See in particular the Ogden Tables Explanatory Notes, para.31.

440 Although it seems that trial judges may still be thinking along these lines, as was HH Judge Red-

ferent considerations can be put forward. First, a court might exceptionally decide that, despite Ogden's very wide definition of disability the particular claimant did not fall within it and yet was considered by the court of be handicapped in the labour market. Secondly, although it seems unlikely, the courts might take against the new Ogden approach—which has been said judicially to be controversial[441]—and return to *Smith v Manchester*.

**40-101** The discussion in the immediately preceding paragraph supporting the survival of *Smith v Manchester* is also supported by the Explanatory Notes made by the Ogden Working Party that there will be circumstances in which the *Smith v Manchester* approach would still be appropriate. One of those circumstances arose in *Billett v Ministry of Defence*.[442] There, the claimant had suffered an injury to his feet whilst serving in the army. The trial judge had made an award of £99,062.04 based upon the Ogden Tables for loss of earning capacity. The Court of Appeal held that the Ogden Tables should not have been applied because there was no evidence of how the claimant would be classified within a scale of degree of impairment and if the Ogden Tables were applied without adjustment the award for future loss of earning capacity would be hopelessly unrealistic for the claimant who was pursuing his chosen career as a lorry driver without hindrance. The exercise of making an adjustment to the reduction factors in the Ogden Tables would be no more scientific than the broad brush judgment that the court makes when taking the *Smith v Manchester* approach. It was preferable to apply *Smith v Manchester* because: (i) the claimant was at the very margins of the definition of disability; (ii) his disability affected his activities outside work much more than it affected his work; and (iii) there was no rational basis for determining how the reduction factor should be adjusted. Applying *Smith v Manchester*, the Court of Appeal awarded an amount of £45,000 for the future earning capacity in place of the trial judge's award of £99,062.04.

### 4. Period of Years of Claimant's Disability: the Basic Factor for the Multiplier

**40-102** The starting point in the calculation of the multiplier is the number of years that it is anticipated the claimant's disability will last[443]; the calculation falls to be made as from the date of trial, a practice which was unsuccessfully challenged in *Pritchard v J. H. Cobden*.[444] In that case the Court of Appeal rightly held that damages for loss of earnings of a living claimant should continue to be assessed as special damages for the earnings lost between injury and trial, with a calculation of the future loss of earnings from trial by selecting a multiplier for the multiplicand from the date of trial to compensate the claimant for the likely loss of earnings for his future working life, and that the delay between injury and trial, however great, was not a sufficient reason for ceasing the practice, even if it did tend to result in

dihough in *Ecclestone v Medway NHS Foundation Trust* [2013] EWHC 790 (QB) who would have made a *Smith v Manchester* award had he not found for the defendant: see at [76].

441 As in *XYZ v Portsmouth Hospitals NHS Trust* [2011] EWHC 243 (QB) at [229], by Spencer J.

442 [2015] EWCA Civ 773 CA.

443 Where the court was unable to form a reasonable view as to the claimant's chances of obtaining employment in the future, the chances of his doing so were taken into account in *O'Keefe v John Stewart & Co Shipping* [1979] 1 Lloyd's Rep. 182 by reducing the multiplier: see at 189–190.

444 [1988] Fam. 22 CA.

higher awards in personal injury cases, in favour of that adopted in cases of fatal injuries of selecting, on dubious reasoning, a multiplier from the date of death.[445]

The calculation of how long the claimant's disability is likely to last may require medical testimony, the latest data at the time of trial being taken, frequently an agreed medical report based on an examination of the claimant as near as practicable to the time of the trial, though disagreement between the medical experts is not uncommon.[446] If the medical testimony establishes that the injury is permanent but without a shortening of the claimant's expectation of life, it becomes necessary to assess the expectation of the claimant's working life. In earlier days the parties not uncommonly introduced in evidence tables of average life expectancies, accepted by the courts as of some assistance, but now we have the Ogden Tables[447] thereby rendering unnecessary the tables formerly put in. These have life expectancies and working life expectancies built into them and today are invariably relied upon.[448] Initially the Ogden Tables contained only tables based upon historic mortality rates, and later there were added tables with the higher projected mortality rates which were recommended for use as being more realistic. Later still, it having become common practice for the courts to use the projected mortality tables,[449] Ogden boldly discarded the historic mortality tables, so that today the current, 7th edition of 2011 carries, for the use of the courts, only the tables, somewhat expanded, based on the projected mortality rates.[450] **40-103**

Where the claimant is a young unmarried female, account was taken by the Court of Appeal in *Harris v Harris*,[451] and again by O'Connor J in *Moriarty v McCarthy*,[452] so as to give a multiplier lower than would be appropriate for a male of the same age, of the likelihood that she would have married and, at least for a period while bringing up children, would have ceased to work. At the same time a separate sum was awarded in both these cases for the claimant's loss of her prospects of marriage; indeed in *Moriarty*,[453] the precise sum by which the damages for loss of earning capacity were less by the reduction of the multiplier was added to the general damages to take account of the loss of marriage prospects. By contrast, in *Hughes v McKeown*,[454] the trial judge preferred to make no reduction in the multiplier from that which would have been appropriate if the claimant had been a man, but on the basis that no account be taken of the economic loss of marriage prospects in the general damages for loss of amenity.[455] This approach in *Hughes* was approved by **40-104**

---

445 See paras 41-052 and following, below.

446 The court has power to stay a claim until the claimant has submitted to a medical examination: *Edmeades v Thames Board Mills* [1969] 2 Q.B. 67 CA; *Lane v Willis* [1972] 1 W.L.R. 326 CA; *Starr v National Coal Board* [1977] 1 W.L.R. 63 CA (reviewing all the authorities).

447 See para.40-071, above.

448 For the acceptance of the Ogden Tables fully and finally by the courts, see para.40-073, above.

449 They were used first in *Worrall v Powergen Plc* [1999] Lloyd's Rep. Med. 177.

450 If of interest, details of how these moves were made in the various editions of the Tables, together with some of the early cases adopting the projected mortality rates, can be found at para.35-102 of the previous, 18th edition.

451 [1973] 1 Lloyd's Rep. 445 CA.

452 [1978] 1 W.L.R. 155.

453 [1978] 1 W.L.R. 155.

454 [1985] 1 W.L.R. 963.

455 The reference to general damages for loss of amenity may suggest that it is the non-pecuniary aspect of loss of marriage prospects that is in contemplation (compare para.40-258, below) but it is clear from the cases that it is the pecuniary loss that, one way or the other, is being compensated here. If a separate sum should be awarded (now, it is true, no longer required under the new approach) it

the Court of Appeal in *Housecroft v Burnett*,[456] where O'Connor LJ said that he did not consider it to be in conflict with *Harris v Harris*,[457] and was indeed

> "a convenient way of assessing the claimant's economic loss in this very limited class of case".[458]

However, where the general damages for loss of amenity are an agreed figure, as in *Thomas v Wignall*,[459] it may be that there is a danger of double counting, but the Court of Appeal there nevertheless felt able to uphold the trial judge's award because the multiplicand adopted by him had been on the low side, so that the end result did not appear to be unfair.[460] There have been no further significant developments in this class of case since.[461]

## 5. Adjustments Where Life Expectancy is Cut Down by the Injury

### (1) In general

**40-105** Determining the extent to which a claimant's life has been cut down by his injury is an important feature in the assessment of personal injury damages. In case after case its determination is crucial to the determination of the multiplier and can have a sometimes dramatic effect where the multiplier has to be applied to a very high multiplicand. This issue was for long dormant but has over the past half century been pushed into prominence by advancing medical skills which have allowed greater certainty in prediction of diminution of life expectancy sufficient to satisfy the courts' requirements of proof. Nor will the arrival of periodical payments necessarily help as, so far, most cases awarding periodical payments have concentrated on medical expenses by way of cost of care[462] other than on the basis of earning capacity; the issue is still with us.

**40-106** Greater certainty there has been over life expectancy, it is true, but nevertheless the issue of how far the claimant's expectation of life has been cut down is very often the subject of a significant conflict of medical testimony, a conflict which needs to be resolved by the trial judge and is not always easy for him. Thus we find, for instance, Flaux J in *Burton v Kingsbury*,[463] devoting over 20 paragraphs[464] of his careful judgment to examining the rival contentions of the medical experts before forming his concluded view on the number of years of life expectation to take. It is of course clinical evidence that counts, it having been held in *Ruff v The Royal*

would be better to give it as a separate item of pecuniary loss rather than add it to the general damages. For financial overtones of the essentially non-pecuniary award for loss of amenities, see footnote at the end of para.40-258, below.

[456] [1986] 1 All E.R. 332 CA.

[457] [1973] 1 Lloyd's Rep. 445 CA.

[458] [1986] 1 All E.R. 332 CA at 345d.

[459] [1987] Q.B. 1098 CA; see especially at 1110, per Nicholls LJ.

[460] In this case the claimant was in fact already a wife; she had married at the early age of 17 and the accident had happened very soon after the wedding. It would seem that the same principles can apply here; certainly all the previous cases in the text were cited and relied upon.

[461] All that can be said is that sometimes judges will refer to loss of marriage prospects as something they take into account in awarding general damages (see para.40-258, below) but this does not touch on pecuniary loss which is what we are dealing with here.

[462] See paras 40-018 and following, above.

[463] [2007] EWHC 2091 (QB).

[464] [2007] EWHC 2091 (QB) at [19]–[42].

*Victoria Infirmary*,[465] that, for resolving a conflict, clinical evidence is to be preferred to statistical evidence.

An issue which has in recent years come to the fore in the context of assessing cost of a lifetime's care, an issue on which there has been some dispute, is whether, once the judge has come to a decision on the number of years of the claimant's life expectation, he should for his assessment utilise Tables 1 and 2 of the Ogden tables, which give multipliers for pecuniary loss for life for males and females respectively, or turn to what is now Table 28, which provides what Ogden calls multipliers for pecuniary loss for term certain. The current thinking with lifetime care costs is, as we shall see, that Table 28 should be used on the basis that the medical experts in the case will in their predictions of life expectation already have taken mortality into account.[466] This issue does not as yet seem to have appeared in the calculations of loss of earnings of a claimant with a reduced life expectation, and here we come up against a difficulty in applying Table 28. The difficulty arises from the fact that earnings do not last till death but take a claimant only up to retirement, and, even if a pension, which will be for life, follows, the amount of the pension will not match the amount of the pre-retirement earnings, thereby requiring separate calculations for earnings and for pension to be made. Here as with costs of lifetime care it will be appropriate to use Table 28, and assess the loss by way of a term certain, wherever the claimant's reduced life expectation does not extend beyond the time when he or she would have retired in the normal course. On the other hand, where the claimant's reduced life expectation moves past his or her normal retirement age, the calculation is necessarily somewhat more complex. The loss of earnings up to retirement age falls to be calculated in the usual way, that is, by using the appropriate table, from Tables 3 to 14, for multipliers for the loss of earnings to a variety of pension ages. The pension after retirement can then be calculated by using Table 28, ignoring Tables 15 to 26 which give multipliers for loss of pension commencing at a variety of retirement ages, the term certain for these purposes being the number of years the claimant is now expected to live less the number of years appearing in the calculation, under Tables 3 to 14, of the pre-retirement earnings loss. **40-107**

## (2) The question of the lost years

The question which falls for consideration here is whether the court should award the prospective loss of earnings for the period that the claimant's working life would have lasted but for the injury or only for the period to which his life has been shortened by the injury. Ascertaining the claimant's reduced expectation of life is of course important whichever of these two routes is taken because the multiplier is in both cases based upon the claimant's post-injury expectation. The knotty problem is whether there has to be the addition of a separate amount in respect of earnings in the so-called lost years. **40-108**

In 1962 in *Oliver v Ashman*,[467] the Court of Appeal came down in favour of making the assessment on the post-injury life expectancy, thereby resolving for a period the uncertainty which had by then been generated by conflicting decisions of courts of first instance.[468] In so deciding, the Court of Appeal regarded the matter as **40-109**

---

465 [2001] Lloyd's Rep. Med. 530.

466 See para.40-220, below generally.

467 [1962] 2 Q.B. 210 CA.

468 In *Harris v Brights Asphalt Contractors* [1953] 1 Q.B. 617 damages had been awarded on the post-

concluded for itself by the decision in *Benham v Gambling*,[469] and by the remarks of Viscount Simon who delivered a speech with which all the other Law Lords concurred.[470] That case, however, was concerned with the awarding of damages for loss of expectation of life to the estate of a person fatally injured[471] and the House of Lords in *Pickett v British Rail Engineering*,[472] concluded that *Benham* "was no authority compelling the decision in *Oliver v Ashman*"[473] because Viscount Simon

> "did not have in mind a claim by a living person for earnings during the lost years".[474]

Authority therefore not standing in its way, the House proceeded to overrule[475] *Oliver v Ashman*.[476] While, in choosing to base the damages upon the post-injury life expectancy, *Oliver v Ashman* may have avoided an award to the claimant of "wages in heaven" and may appear consequently to have faithfully followed the compensatory principle which underlies the whole law of damages, the decision was now seen as a short-sighted one because it ignored the fact that it left no moneys available to the claimant out of which to make provision after his death for his dependants, who are generally assumed to be precluded by the claimant's successful action from themselves making any claim under the Fatal Accidents Act. It had indeed been urged upon their Lordships that, the real loss being to the victim's dependants, the right way to compensate them was to change the law by statute to enable the dependants to recover their loss independently of any action by the victim. This approach was also urged in all earlier editions of this work, although it was felt that it could be achieved within the existing framework and therefore without the need for legislation.[477] However their Lordships would have none of this. Since there was no Fatal Accidents Act claim in *Pickett v British Rail Engineering*,[478] Lord Wilberforce said that they must proceed upon the basis that the assumption that no dependants' claim could follow upon the injured party's claim was correct, while pointing out that it was unsupported by any decision of the House[479]; the assumption accepted, it then

> "provides a basis, in logic and justice, for allowing the victim to recover for earnings lost during his lost years".[480]

Yet 25 years later we find, again in the House of Lords, Lord Phillips had this to say in *Gregg v Scott*[481]:

> "It would be much better if the claimant had no right to recover for such loss of earnings and the dependants' right to claim under s.1(1) of the Fatal Accidents Act 1976 subsisted

injury life expectancy, but in *Pope v Murphy* [1961] 1 Q.B. 222 and at first instance in *Oliver v Ashman* [1961] 1 Q.B. 337 itself, the awards were based on the pre-injury life expectancy.

469 [1941] A.C. 157.

470 See [1962] 2 Q.B. 210 CA at 229, 238, 244.

471 See para.41-133, below.

472 [1980] A.C. 136.

473 [1980] A.C. 136 at 148E, per Lord Wilberforce.

474 [1980] A.C. 136 at 148E.

475 Lord Russell dissenting.

476 [1962] 2 Q.B. 210 CA.

477 As explained at para.41-008, below.

478 [1980] A.C. 136.

479 [1980] A.C. 136 at 146H.

480 [1980] A.C. 136 at 146G.

481 [2005] 2 A.C. 176 at [182].

despite the claimant's recovery of damages for his injury. I am not persuaded that this result could not be achieved by a purposive construction of that section."

This comment of Lord Phillips thus takes up what has been proposed here in the earlier editions.

*Pickett v British Rail Engineering*,[482] rather than *Oliver v Ashman*,[483] is the decision that has not been far-sighted and it has created serious difficulties in the assessment of damages here. While it was no doubt come to with the interests of the claimant's dependants in mind, it was inevitable that it would have similar application where the claimant had none. Worse still, its equally inevitable application to fatal accidents where it was not needed, as the dependants of deceased victims have since the mid-19th century been provided for, created a chaotic situation to which legislation mercifully put an eventual end.[484] This legislation, however, did not touch claims by living claimants and it was of concern that the attempts to contain awards to the estate suing after a fatal accident, so as to limit the receipt of undeserved windfalls—and of the then reported cases, apart from one or two dealing with young children, all had concerned victims who had been killed with consequent claims by their estates[485]—would adversely affect those deserving claims by living claimants which have the dual purpose of providing support for claimant and dependants alike. **40-110**

In *Pickett v British Rail Engineering*,[486] Lord Wilberforce accepted that the amount to be recovered in respect of earnings in the "lost years" should require a deduction of an estimated sum to represent the victim's probable living expenses during these years. That, in Lord Wilberforce's opinion, was right **40-111**

"because the basis, in principle, for recovery lies in the interest which [the claimant] has in making provision for dependants and others, and this he would do out of his surplus."[487]

To take account of the change in the law introduced by *Pickett*,[488] therefore, it is not simply a question of increasing the multiplier from one formerly based upon the post-injury life expectancy to one appropriate for the pre-injury life expectancy. The change necessitates reducing the multiplicand to take into account the deduction for living expenses and then applying separate multipliers, one for the period that the claimant is still expected to live applied to the initial multiplicand, one for the lost years applied to the multiplicand as reduced by the living expenses; alternatively the court may prefer the simpler, but less exact, method of leaving the multiplicand untouched and adjusting downwards the initial multiplier.[489] Neither *Pickett*,[490] nor

---

482 [1980] A.C. 136.

483 [1962] 2 Q.B. 210 CA.

484 See para.41-126, below.

485 *Chambers v Karia* unreported 2 February 1979, is one case with a living and adult claimant; considered at para.40-115, below.

486 [1980] A.C. 136.

487 [1980] A.C. 136 at 151A. Even before *Oliver v Ashman* [1962] 2 Q.B. 210 CA, but after the same result as that in *Oliver* had appeared at first instance in *Harris v Brights Asphalt Contractors* [1953] 1 Q.B. 617, a claim by a claimant based, because of the reduced life expectation, upon the deprivation of the ability to provide for his dependants had been advanced in *Richards v Highways Ironfounders* [1955] 1 W.L.R. 1049 CA, but, after acceptance by Devlin J, had been rejected on appeal.

488 [1980] A.C. 136.

489 Contrast *Housecroft v Burnett* [1986] 1 All E.R. 332 at 345e–f, per O'Connor LJ.

490 [1980] A.C. 136.

*Gammell v Wilson*,[491] which decided that the *Pickett* principle applied to claims by the estate of a deceased victim,[492] gave any guidance as to the proper method of computing the deduction for living expenses and therefore did not assist in the task of determining the adjusted multiplicand for the lost years or the adjusted multiplier for the totality of the loss of earnings claim. First instance courts adopted different approaches to the question and three solutions emerged. Some judges deducted only that which the victim expended upon himself personally and ignored all joint expenditure on himself and his family, thus arriving at the same deduction as would be made in the assessment of a Fatal Accidents Act dependency[493]; other judges took as the criterion the cost of maintaining the deceased in his station in life, thereby deducting what he had expended upon himself together with a proportion of the general family expenditure as might properly be attributed to him[494]; still other judges took as the criterion what the deceased would have saved, thereby deducting as living expenses all that he spent, whether on himself, on his family or elsewhere.[495] It will be seen that this is in ascending order of deduction, with awards becoming smaller as one proceeds from one solution to the next.[496] Eventually the disparity came before the Court of Appeal for resolution in *Harris v Empress Motors*.[497] O'Connor LJ considered that three principles emerged which he stated thus:

> "1. The ingredients that go to make up 'living expenses' are the same whether the victim be young or old, single or married, with or without dependants. 2. The sum to be deducted as living expenses is the proportion of the victim's net earnings that he spends to maintain himself at the standard of life appropriate to his case. 3. Any sums expended to maintain or benefit others do not form part of the victim's expenses and are not to be deducted from the net earnings."[498]

The middle solution was thus favoured and there the matter has rested.

**40-112** This development of the law, culminating in *Harris* and reached in cases involving essentially unmeritorious claims by the estates of deceased victims, leads in the context of the living claimant to either under-compensation or over-compensation, depending upon the family circumstances of the particular case. If, on the one hand, the person suffering the injuries is a married man without children, or without dependent children, his widow, were he killed, would generally be entitled in a claim for loss of dependency under the Fatal Accidents Act to 66.6 per cent of his earnings, this being on the broad basis that one third was personal expenditure of the husband—which forms the sole amount to be deducted—one-third personal

---

[491] [1982] A.C. 27.

[492] See para.41-126, below.

[493] See paras 41-041 and 41-080, below. Illustrations are *Benson v Biggs Wall & Co* [1983] 1 W.L.R. 72; *Harris v Empress Motors* [1983] 1 W.L.R. 65 (at first instance); *Clay v Pooler* [1982] 3 All E.R. 570.

[494] See, especially, *White v London Transport Executive* [1982] Q.B. 489.

[495] See, especially, *Sullivan v West Yorkshire Passenger Transport Executive* unreported 17 December 1980, but judgment cited in *Harris v Empress Motors* [1983] 1 W.L.R. 65 at 68 (first instance).

[496] Contrast the 25 per cent deduction in *Harris v Empress Motors* [1983] 1 W.L.R. 65 (at first instance), applying the first solution to a deceased who had been a husband and father of two children, with the 85 per cent deduction in *Sullivan v West Yorkshire Passenger Transport Executive* (see previous note) applying the third solution to a deceased who had been a young bachelor.

[497] [1984] 1 W.L.R. 212 CA.

[498] [1984] 1 W.L.R. 212 CA at 228G–H.

expenditure of the wife and one-third expenditure on the two jointly[499] but, where suit is brought by the still living husband, half of this joint expenditure requires, under Harris, also to be deducted, thereby reducing what is intended to be available to the wife, after the anticipated premature death of her husband, to 50 per cent of his earnings. Where there are, or are likely to be, young children of the marriage, the disparity will not be so great because, the joint expenditure being attributable to a larger number, a smaller slice of it falls to be deducted from the 75 per cent of earnings which is generally taken as the family dependency for Fatal Accidents Act purposes while the children are at home.[500] And as the number of children increases so does the disparity lessen, but there must always remain a degree of under-compensation, as is reflected in the practice which has developed where there are children of the marriage or union of deducting 33.3 per cent so as to give a dependency based on 66.6 per cent of earnings as opposed to the 75 percent in Fatal Accidents Act cases. Moreover, this computation assumes that the claimant's life expectation after the injury is shorter than the minorities of any children there may be; after the children have left home the wife's Fatal Accidents Act dependency will generally revert to 66.6 per cent[501] and the lost years claim, after deducting the husband's living expenses, to 50 per cent of earnings, so that this amount of disparity will return. If, on the other hand, the claimant is a confirmed young single person, or one who because of catastrophic injuries will clearly never now marry, an award in respect of the lost years will necessarily over-compensate, however high the deduction for his or her living expenses may be pitched, as there is no one for whose support the money awarded is needed.

Yet even before the Court of Appeal had arrived at the decision in *Harris v Empress Motors*,[502] in mid-1983 the law had been changed: statute had prohibited claims by the estate for the income of the lost years of persons dying after the end of 1982.[503] The decisions which involve claims by the estate of a deceased victim need no longer be examined further. Apart from there appearing to be no reported cases after *Harris*, and the cases before *Harris*, though substantial in number, being no longer authoritative, because of *Harris*, on the major issue of the computation of living expenses, in truth these many estate actions, where because of the anomalous nature of the claim the courts have been eager to contain the awards, are essentially inappropriate as precedents for the generally meritorious claims made by the still living accident victim. Indeed in these changed circumstances, with estate claims prohibited, it was suggested, in the editions of this work since 1982, that the courts should depart from the ruling in *Harris* and restore the first, and most generous, of the three solutions at which some first instance courts arrived before Harris, namely that which calls only for the same deduction as would be made in the assessment of a Fatal Accidents Act dependency.[504] This would be fairer for the dependants but of course could also have the effect of exacerbating the problem of over-compensation of those claimants without dependants. **40-113**

In those few cases where living claimants without dependants had sued, the courts had already begun successfully to contain awards or even to eliminate them **40-114**

499 See para.41-043, below.
500 See again para.41-043, below.
501 See again para.41-043, below.
502 [1984] 1 W.L.R. 212 CA.
503 See para.41-126, below.
504 See para.40-111, above.

entirely. With children it was elimination. In *Connolly v Camden Area Health Authority*,[505] the trial judge, and in *Croke v Wiseman*,[506] the Court of Appeal, made a nil award in respect of the lost years of a child claimant; the two children were, respectively, five and seven-and-a-half years old at the time of trial. Where the victim is a young child the court can justify giving nothing, or at least a very small amount, on the basis that the future for a child is speculative and that, if the expectation of life is cut down substantially, the lost years would not have been years of earning while, if the expectation of life is not cut down substantially, the lost years are themselves so very far in the future. Griffiths LJ in *Croke v Wiseman*,[507] took a principled line, saying:

> "In the case of a child, however, there are no dependants, and … if the injuries are catastrophic … there will never be any dependants … In such circumstances, it seems to me entirely right that the court should refuse to speculate as to whether in the future there might have been dependants for the purpose of providing a fund of money for persons who will in fact never exist."[508]

Since then, however, the Court of Appeal in *Iqbal v Whipps Cross University Hospital NHS Trust*,[509] has claimed that what had been said in the House of Lords in *Pickett v British Rail Engineering*,[510] and in *Gammell v Wilson*,[511] had been misunderstood in *Croke* and that an award for the lost years should have been made there. However, the Court of Appeal considered itself bound to follow *Croke* and reversed the judge below who had made an award for the lost years.[512] Gage LJ, who gave the leading judgment, said in concluding that "the error, if error it be, must be corrected by the House of Lords."[513] The suggestions that *Croke* is an error and involves a misunderstanding of *Pickett* is an unfortunate approach to the issue. It having been again emphasised, in *Gregg v Scott*,[514] by Lord Phillips, that the decision in *Pickett* to allow damages for earnings in the lost years was justified because

> "only in this way could provision be made for the loss to be suffered by the dependants",[515]

the refusal to award such damages in the case of a child where there are clearly to be no dependants should continue and, hopefully, will continue. Wages in heaven should not be awarded when they are not needed on earth. Nevertheless, the clamour to overrule *Croke* continues apace, despite the recognition that a case will need to be taken to the Supreme Court for this to occur.[516] The decision in *Croke*

---

505 [1981] 3 All E.R. 250.
506 [1982] 1 W.L.R. 71 CA.
507 [1982] 1 W.L.R. 71 CA.
508 [1982] 1 W.L.R. 71 CA at 82G.
509 [2008] P.I.Q.R. P9 CA at 161.
510 [1980] A.C. 136.
511 [1982] A.C. 27.
512 The making of an award by the trial judge ([2006] EWHC 3111 (QB)) is to be contrasted with the making of no award by another trial judge in *Massey v Tameside Glossop Acute Services NHS Trust* [2007] EWHC 317 (QB) (Admin).
513 [2008] P.I.Q.R. P9 CA at 161 at [64].
514 [2005] 2 A.C. 176.
515 [2005] 2 A.C. 176 at 180.
516 *Totham v King's College Hospital NHS Foundation Trust* [2015] EWHC 97 (QB); *JR v Sheffield*

was also distinguished in *JR v Sheffield Teaching Hospitals NHS Foundation Trust* where a claim could have been made when the claimant was seven (the same age as James Croke) but the claimant delayed bringing action until he was 24, albeit for reasons which had nothing to do with creating a lost years claim.[517] One ground upon which *Croke* was distinguished was said to be the time when the claimant had brought his claim, namely 20 years after the accident. That distinction is unprincipled. The point of principle is that the lost years award does not apply where there is no real prospect of dependancy, including the need to make provision for others. That applies as much to adults as it does to children. This ground of distinction was, in any event, unnecessary because the claimant had real prospects of a dependancy.[518]

Containment of awards with adult living claimants began with *Chambers v Karia*,[519] a case from the early days when the action was still available to the estate. The claimant was a man without dependants who was approaching 34 years of age at the time of trial. O'Connor J needed to calculate the claimant's earnings less living expenses only for the years which lay at the end of the period covered by the multiplier, so that under 9 per cent was added to the award that he would have made for lost earning capacity in the absence of the lost years portion thereof. Later in *Housecroft v Burnett*,[520] where the claimant had attained nearly 20 years of age by the date her action was heard, the selfsame judge, now O'Connor LJ, decided upon a different approach to working out the earnings less living expenses for the lost years. These, he said, **40-115**

> "because of their remoteness in time, are highly speculative and I think are better dealt with by some small adjustment in the multiplier, such as a factor of one, or even a half, as applied to the full multiplicand, rather than trying to speculate what proportion of notional earnings 30 years hence would not form part of the claimant's then living expenses."[521]

Indeed, since he regarded the multiplier adopted by the judge below as appropriate had there been no shortening of life, O'Connor LJ considered that there was no need to make any provision for the lost years.[522] Then in *Hunt v Severs*,[523] where the claimant was nearly 29 years of age at trial and did have a dependant—she had married the defendant himself—the trial judge increased the multiplier of 12 for loss of earnings by only one-half and in this was upheld by the Court of Appeal.[524] The containment of awards that these three cases evidence is of course due to the fact that in each of them the post-accident expectation of life was of a significant length—20, 27 and 25 years respectively. To move to a substantial award one would need an expectation of life that has been cut down to a short remaining span. It would then be necessary to make a calculation of earnings less expenses, probably

---

*Teaching Hospitals NHS Foundation Trust* [2017] EWHC 1245 (QB).

517 *JR v Sheffield Teaching Hospitals NHS Foundation Trust* [2017] EWHC 1245 (QB).

518 [2017] EWHC 1245 (QB) at [36].

519 *Chambers v Karia* unreported 2 February 1979.

520 [1986] 1 All E.R. 332 CA.

521 [1986] 1 All E.R. 332 CA at 345f.

522 See [1986] 1 All E.R. 332 CA at 345e.

523 [1993] Q.B. 815 CA.

524 This issue was not taken to the House of Lords.

along *Harris v Empress Motors*,[525] lines, and not simply to make a reduction in the multiplier.

**40-116** Not until *Phipps v Brooks Dry Cleaning Services*,[526] did such a case, in which the issue arose,[527] make an appearance. A married man of 51 at trial with only a few months to live made a claim in respect of both his lost earnings and his lost pension. It was accepted that a calculation of the claimant's living expenses was required in what was essentially a lost years claim and the Court of Appeal held that even with a living claimant whose expectation of life does not extend much beyond the trial date the *Harris v Empress Motors*,[528] approach was to be followed for the calculation. This gave a discount in the lost years claim for what the claimant would have spent on himself which is substantially greater than the discount in a Fatal Accidents Act claim for what the deceased would have similarly spent. The appropriate discount was accordingly 50 per cent in respect of both earnings and pension, resulting in an award of £45,000 for the earnings and a little over £20,000 for the pension. At the same time the court held that the claimant could not claim for his inability to carry out gardening and DIY activities over the lost years.[529] While damages in respect of the lost years are not confined to recovery for lost earnings and extend to all pecuniary loss,[530] the claimant here had not lost any value by being deprived of the opportunity of saving himself expense in doing work which he would now never do.

**40-117** A further case of a claimant with a very short life expectancy appeared with *Shanks v Swan Hunter Group Plc*.[531] As is well known, mesothelioma from exposure to asbestos takes very many years after contraction to become evident and, once it does, is likely very soon to prove fatal. In *Shanks* the sufferer from mesothelioma was a married man supporting grandchildren, his earnings at the time coming from employment in Australia. He had reached the age of 59 at trial, by which time his life expectation was a mere 1.67 years. It was held, by His Honour Judge Hickinbottom J, that he would have worked till 70, thereby giving a near decade of working life's earnings for the lost years. Once again, as in *Phipps*, the calculation for loss of earnings followed the *Harris v Empress Motors* model but at least the judge recognised the anomaly of this approach, showing himself to be fully cognisant of the arguments against *Harris* expressed above.[532] He said:

> "The difference between the conventions as to deductions for living expenses in a claim under the Fatal Accidents Act on the one hand and a claim by a living claimant on the other has no obvious rational basis, given the principle behind allowing lost years claims by a living claimant expressed by Lord Wilberforce and the merit (as he saw it) of bringing lost

---

525 [1984] 1 W.L.R. 212 CA; see para.40-111, above.

526 [1996] P.I.Q.R. Q100 CA.

527 In the marginally earlier *Gabriel v Nuclear Electric* [1996] P.I.Q.R. Q1 with a claimant expected to die within nine months of trial, the parties had agreed that the loss of earnings claim was subject to a 50 per cent reduction.

528 [1984] 1 W.L.R. 212 CA; see para.40-111, above.

529 Overruling on this *Bateman v Hydro Agri (UK)* unreported 15 September 1995, and *Gabriel v Nuclear Electric* [1996] P.I.Q.R. Q1.

530 Thus it should be noted that a claimant might have a claim for an inheritance, or some other financial advantage other than earnings, which he will now no longer obtain. Contrast *Adsett v West* [1983] Q.B. 826, a claim of earlier days brought by the estate of a deceased dealing with recovery for the prospect of inheritance during the lost years.

531 [2007] EWHC 1807 (QB).

532 See paras 40-112 and 40-113, above.

years claims into line with amounts recoverable under the Fatal Accidents Act (see *Pickett* at page 151A).[533] Why should a married man without children recover only 50 per cent of his earnings if he sues for lost years himself, when his estate would recover 66 per cent if he dies and his estate sues in respect of the same loss? Of course, the former is not a dependency claim in form or substance .... but the disparity in these potential results is curious and difficult to justify rationally."[534]

Nonetheless His Honour Judge Hickinbottom accepted that the starting point for the deduction for living expenses was 50 per cent for a married man without children and 33.3 per cent for a married man with children, stating that this was supported by both parties,[535] but since the claimant was financially supporting grandchildren who were not living with him, the cost to him of which was less great than if he had had children living with him, the judge considered that the claimant fell between these two figures and opted for a deduction of 40 per cent,[536] thus reducing the award for earnings in the lost years from 1,638,000 Australian dollars to 982,800 Australian dollars. Had the claim been a Fatal Accidents Act claim, where the conventional discounts are 33.3 per cent for dependent wife without children and 25 per cent for dependent wife with children, the discount would presumably have worked out at around 28 per cent, with a consequent increased lost years award, coming out at somewhat short of 1,200,000 Australian dollars.

It would seem therefore that escape from the rigours of the *Harris v Empress Motors*,[537] computation of deductions for living expenses will require a decision of the Supreme Court. Of course were the Supreme Court to go further by eliminating the claim for the lost years and allowing a claim by dependants under the Fatal Accidents Act, as already proposed,[538] such a solution would also have brought a fairer result for the dependent wife in *Phipps v Brooks Dry Cleaning Services*,[539] and the dependent wife and grandchildren in *Shanks v Swan Hunter Group Plc*.[540] And this solution would have the added advantage of avoiding unmeritorious claims by injured persons without dependants. An equivalent solution has already been statutorily found for provisional damages and fatal accidents.[541] **40-118**

## 6. THE APPROPRIATE DISCOUNT RATE FOR THE MULTIPLIER

The claimant's annual loss—the multiplicand—is not multiplied by the number of years during which his incapacity is expected to last; this would clearly overcompensate him as it would put the future lost earnings into his hands long before he would otherwise have received them, and would enable him to enjoy the interest accruing in the intervening period. It is the present value of the future lost earnings that is to be awarded. The multiplicand is therefore to be multiplied by the appropriate figure—the multiplier—to arrive at that present value. A question of immense importance then arises: what is the appropriate discount rate for the court to adopt? This is crucial for the multiplier. For the greater the assumed return on the **40-119**

533 See Lord Wilberforce and Pickett at para.40-111, above.
534 [2007] EWHC 1807 (QB) at [35].
535 [2007] EWHC 1807 (QB) at [39(iii)].
536 [2007] EWHC 1807 (QB) at [39(iii)] and [40].
537 [1984] 1 W.L.R. 212 CA.
538 See para.40-109, above.
539 [1996] P.I.Q.R. Q100 CA.
540 [2007] EWHC 1807 (QB).
541 Damages Act 1996 s.3; on this see para.41-009, below.

damages awarded, the smaller the multiplier, and vice versa. Claimants therefore argue for low discount rates, defendants for high ones.

## (1) The historical background

**40-120** The issue of the appropriate discount rate for the multiplier in personal injury cases has had an interesting and chequered history. This history has been spelt out at some length in earlier editions of this work but it is thought that, in view of the knowledge that readers are primarily interested in how the law stands today, the time has come to give here the history in summary form. Full detail can be found in the previous edition.[542]

**40-121** For very many years it had been common practice to take a discount rate of 4.5 per cent, a net return which in the inflationary days of 1978 the Lords in *Cookson v Knowles*,[543] stated that claimants could achieve by investment in gilts for interest at fixed rates and in equities for income and capital return. Change, though it was to take many years, was on its way, heralded by the 1981 arrival on the market of index-linked government stock, acronymically ILGS. The 1984 edition of the Ogden Tables[544] and a 1994 Law Commission Report[545] recommended that claimants should have the complete protection from inflation that ILGS would give them, the Law Commission Report further recommending legislation providing that courts be required, when choosing a discount rate in a personal injury case, to take account of the net return on ILGS. Then came the Damages Act 1996 which did not so provide but only went as far as to provide that the rate to be taken for the discount was

> "such rate of return (if any) as may from time to time be prescribed by an order made by the Lord Chancellor".[546]

**40-122** Before the Lord Chancellor acted, the House of Lords did. In three combined appeals heard in 1998, *Wells v Wells, Thomas v Brighton Health Authority* and *Page v Sheerness Steel Co*,[547] it adopted investment in ILGS as the most accurate method of calculating the present value of the financial loss which claimants would suffer. An injured person, it was said, was not in the same position as the ordinary prudent investor, who could afford to take risks in his investment strategy. An injured person could not so afford and therefore should be entitled to the greater security and certainty achievable by investment in ILGS. This was seen as the ideal solution as it gives claimants the possibility of ensuring that, if they invest in ILGS, the moneys awarded will last throughout the estimated period of loss and not run out beforehand. The House decided upon 3 per cent as the appropriate net after tax return; this represented the then return on ILGS.

**40-123** Three years later, in 2001, the Lord Chancellor set a rate of 2.5 per cent. The rate then set was unequivocally based upon ILGS, being based upon the three year average gross redemption yield on ILGS, an approach which followed that of the House

---

542 18th edn (2009), paras 35-119 to 35-132.

543 [1979] A.C. 556.

544 For these, of which this was the first edition, see para.40-071, above.

545 Law Commission, *Structured Settlements and Interim and Provisional Damages* (HMSO, 1994), Law Com. No.224.

546 By s.1(1).

547 [1999] 1 A.C. 345.

of Lords in *Wells v Wells*. While the Damages Act 1996 entitled him to prescribe different rates of return for different classes of case,[548] he set a single rate. He stated further that he intended that the rate set should obtain for the foreseeable future, rightly pointing out that it would be detrimental to the certainty necessary to promote the proper resolution of disputes to make frequent changes to the discount rate. So in 2014 we are still living with the 2.5 discount rate.

## (2) The present position

Much has happened since the Lord Chancellor set the discount rate in 2001 and of prime importance is the collapse of the rate of return on ILGS. His discount rate of 2.5 per cent no longer reflects reality and has not done so for years. This is dramatically shown by a case from Guernsey which went to the Privy Council, the Lord Chancellor's discount rate not applying in Guernsey as the Damages Act 1996 does not extend to the Channel Islands. Accordingly, the common law stemming from *Wells v Wells*,[549] fell to be applied. In *Simon v Helmot*,[550] the Privy Council upheld the award of the Guernsey Court of Appeal to a young man with very grave injuries, using a rate of minus 1.5 per cent for his earnings-related losses, being his own earnings and his carers' earnings, and a rate of 0.5 per cent for costs that were not earnings-related, presumably being such items as transport costs and accommodation costs. This 0.5 per cent was arrived at by first taking the 1.25 per cent rate of return then current in Guernsey on index-linked securities, reducing this to 1 per cent for the incidence of tax, and reducing further to 0.5 per cent on account of the extent that inflation was higher in Guernsey than in the United Kingdom. The minus 1.5 per cent was then achieved by taking the 0.5 per cent and reducing it by 2 per cent to mark the extent that earnings inflation was higher than price inflation. The court was aware that today the position is reversed, certainly in the United Kingdom, with price inflation greater than earnings inflation, but relied on the strong unchallenged evidence that over the long term the annual average works out at 2 per cent, though with considerable fluctuations from year to year.[551] **40-124**

There was one way open to the English courts to depart in a particular case from the 2.5 per cent discount rate laid down. This stemmed from the provision of s.1(2) of the Damages Act 1996 that the court may take a different rate of return than that prescribed by the Lord Chancellor if any party "shows that it is more appropriate in the case in question", with the Lord Chancellor stating, when announcing his decision on rate, that he had borne in mind this provision allowing resort to a rate other than that prescribed by him "if there are exceptional circumstances which justify it". However, the attempts that have been made over the years by claimants invoking s.1(2) and arguing, on a variety of grounds, for a lower rate than 2.5 per cent to be applied have all failed.[552] In *Warriner v Warriner*,[553]an unsuccessful at- **40-125**

---

548 By s.1(3).

549 [1999] 1 A.C. 345.

550 [2012] UKPC 5.

551 [2012] UKPC 5 at [64] (Lady Hale), [84] (Lord Clarke) and [108] (Lord Dyson). Once one is into minus figures, it is inapt to speak of the rate as a discount rate and, while Lord Dyson was content with "negative discount" though accepting that the term was somewhat odd (at [118]), Lord Hope, who gave the leading judgment with which the others agreed, preferred to describe the exercise simply as a process of adjustment (at [14]).

552 There was an earlier case, before the Lord Chancellor's pronouncement, of such a failure. The claimant in *Warren v Northern General Hospital NHS Trust (No.2)* [2000] 1 W.L.R. 1404 CA wished to

tempt was made to persuade the court to apply lower discount rates because the rate of return on ILGS had been continuing to fall. The Court of Appeal saw nothing unusual about the case which it regarded as typical of many others in which large sums and long life expectancies are involved. The report of the claimant's expert forensic accountant, said Dyson LJ, had not identified any special features of the case taking it outside the classes of case that the Lord Chancellor took into account when fixing the rate. In truth, he added, it was on analysis more a criticism of the Lord Chancellor's rate itself.[554] In a trilogy of appeals heard and reported together, *Cooke v United Bristol Healthcare NHS Trust* together with *Sheppard v Stibbe and Page v Lee*,[555] the argument for a lower rate to be used was on the basis that, earnings inflation and health care inflation being greater than retail price inflation, use of a discount rate geared to ILGS and therefore to inflation measured by the retail price index did not reflect the true loss, and an attempt to bypass the proscription of adjustment of the multiplier for higher earnings inflation and the even higher health care inflation was made by proposing adjustment of the multiplicand. The Court of Appeal would have none of this. The discount rate was intended to be the only factor in the computation yielding the claimant's lump sum to allow for future inflation and the multiplicand could not be taken as allowing for the same thing without usurping the basis on which the multiplier had been fixed. To Laws LJ what was being argued constituted an assault on the Lord Chancellor's discount rate and on the efficacy of the Damages Act.[556] In *Harries v Stevenson*,[557] the argument for a lower discount rate was that, since periodical payments orders, unaffected by the discount rate, gave full compensation, the same should be made true of lump sum payments by an appropriate adjustment of the discount rate. It was pointed out by the claimant's counsel that the legislation empowering the courts to order periodical payments had come after the decisions in *Warriner* and *Cooke*, and the result in the Privy Council's *Helmot v Simon*,[558] was also prayed in aid. Once again the argument failed. Morgan J, after a very full discussion of the authorities, was satisfied that the approach in *Warriner* and *Cooke* still controlled and that the *Helmot* case had no application to a decision, as he had to make, under the Damages Act 1996.

**40-126** From these cases it has become clear that the courts are not prepared to depart from the Lord Chancellor's discount rate by resort to their power to do so where use of a different rate of return is considered appropriate. So there is nothing for it but to have the discount rate changed if it is still intended that it should reflect returns on ILGS. It is good to know that already the Lord Chancellor of the day has set up consultations on changing the rate, perhaps propelled into it by the Privy Council's decision in *Helmot v Simon*, but this move is taking a long time, not unexpectedly, to produce a result. The Government Consultation Paper which was issued called for responses by late October 2012 but nothing has appeared since then and we are well into 2017. What will eventually come out of it all cannot yet

have the discount rate of 3 per cent as set in *Wells v Wells* [1999] 1 A.C. 345 (see para.40-122, above) lowered on account of the very heavy incidence of taxation on the damages, but the Court of Appeal did not consider this justified.

553 [2002] 1 W.L.R. 1703 CA.

554 [2002] 1 W.L.R. 1703 CA at 1712B.

555 [2004] 1 W.L.R. 251 CA.

556 [2004] 1 W.L.R. 251 CA at 30.

557 [2012] EWHC 3447 (QB).

558 See this at para.40-124, above.

be known and speculation is dangerous. One thing is thought to be certain and that is that the Lord Chancellor will not be prepared to sanction discount rates as low as those endorsed in *Helmot v Simon* which went even beyond 0.5 per cent into the negative, down to minus 1.5 per cent.[559] Such rates would lead to higher and higher multipliers, giving, in the most serious of cases, awards in many more millions of pounds than they already are today. Ogden in its Tables in the current, 7th edition has for the first time taken its multipliers into the negative, down as far as minus 2 per cent, and, as illustrative, multipliers for pecuniary loss for life for males has for a 25-year-old a multiplier of 30.92 at 2.5 per cent and a multiplier of 106.33 at minus 1.5 per cent. It is thought that the time has come to return to a sense of normality and this can only be done through an abandonment of gearing awards to the returns on ILGS.

If, instead, awards are geared, as before the decision in *Wells v Wells*,[560] to investment in other than ILGS, the way to finding a reasonable discount rate is made out, and it is significant that the Government Consultation Paper indicates that consultees should be considering this as a possibility. The justification for going in this direction is that application of a discount rate based on ILGS leads to over-compensation of the injured victim, certainly the very severely injured one. For the thinking based on ILGS returns ignores the hard fact that claimants, like the Court of Protection for their patient claimants, are not in reality going to invest their awards in ILGS and do better with their money elsewhere. Lord Lloyd in *Wells*, cited this view as put forward in the then current edition of this text[561] and said that he did not agree with it, adding that the House had not been referred to any commentary or book, other than this text, which disagreed with the use of ILGS as recommended by both Ogden and the Law Commission.[562] Now it looks as if this text may have been right after all. 40-127

## 7. Adjustments to the Multiplier for Contingencies

In addition to the discount because the award is by way of lump sum, it is common practice for the courts to make a further discount on account of the general contingencies of life or, as they may be called, the vicissitudes of life. It is said that the multiplier must suffer some reduction to cater for the possibility that the claimant will die earlier than expected, the possibility that he will meet with some accident that will keep him out of work for a lengthy period or even result in his premature retirement, the possibility that he may lose his job and become temporarily or even permanently unemployed, and the like.[563] 40-128

### (1) Mortality

It has been argued in earlier editions of this work that the court's insistence upon the need to make a discount for the possibility of earlier death is misconceived. For 40-129

[559] See this at para.40-124, above.
[560] [1999] 1 A.C. 345.
[561] That edition fell between the Court of Appeal and House of Lords hearings of the case.
[562] [1999] 1 A.C. 345 at 371. For Ogden and the Law Commission see para.40-121, above.
[563] Discounting for contingencies appears as early as *Phillips v L. & S.W. Ry*; see Field J's direction to the jury, (1879) 5 Q.B.D. 78 at 81–82 and the statements on appeal, (1879) 5 C.P.D. 280 CA at 290–291, 293.

there is no more reason to assume that the claimant will die earlier than expected than to assume that he will outlive his life expectancy, and the eventuality of earlier decease is already taken into account in the actuarial tables themselves. The Court of Appeal's attempt in *Mitchell v Mulholland (No.2)*,[564] to answer this,

> "the chances are equal either way, but as a matter of calculation it can be shown that the impact of the chance of shorter life is of greater significance than that of longer life"[565]

is equally misconceived. For this consideration is also effectively taken into account in the formulation of the actuarial tables which allow earnings to be cut off at an age, as of retirement, which is in advance of the statistically expected death; this is true of the Ogden Tables in providing, as they do, tables of multipliers for loss of earnings to a variety of ages for both men and women[566] and also for loss of pension commencing thereafter.[567]

**40-130** These difficulties have all disappeared. The Ogden Tables, blessed by the House of Lords, are today in full use[568] and they have long been clear on the matter. The explanatory notes state that the tables

> "make reasonable provision for the levels of mortality which members of the population of the United Kingdom alive today may expect to experience in future."[569]

In addition, the view that the need to make a discount for the possibility of earlier death is a misconception has been robustly championed by the House of Lords in *Thomas v Brighton Health Authority*,[570] one of the cases in the *Wells v Wells* trilogy.[571] While this holding of their Lordships was in the context of the cost of care,[572] it must apply equally where loss of earnings is concerned.[573]

## (2) Contingencies other than mortality

**40-131** (a) **In general** Some degree of discount is appropriate for factors other than mortality, for such possibilities as unemployment or failure in business, illness or accident of a non-fatal kind. As Diplock LJ pointed out some time ago in *Whit-*

---

564 [1972] 1 Q.B. 65 CA.

565 [1972] 1 Q.B. 65 CA at 86B, per Sir Gordon Willmer; see similarly at 76, per Edmund Davies LJ.

566 *Ogden Tables*, 7th edn (2011), Tables 3 to 14.

567 *Ogden Tables*, 7th edn (2011), Tables 15 to 26. Yet in the days before the appearance of these Tables the Court of Appeal continued to adhere to its reasoning in *Mitchell*. In *Auty v National Coal Board* [1985] 1 W.L.R. 784 CA. Waller LJ stated that he agreed with what had been said there, adding that "when making the calculation which the judge had to make, those who die early are the only ones which matter because the fact of living longer than the expectation is immaterial" [1985] 1 W.L.R. 784 CA at 798F; and Waller LJ's brethren in turn agreed with him. [1985] 1 W.L.R. 784 CA at 803F and 811H, per Oliver and Purchas LJJ respectively. Yet living longer than the life expectation would result in the claimant's pension being payable for longer, and *Auty* itself indeed concerned a loss of pension entitlement.

568 See para.40-073, above.

569 7th edn (2011) Explanatory Notes, para.19.

570 [1999] 1 A.C. 345.

571 See para.40-122, above.

572 See para.40-219, below.

573 And indeed it was an earnings award that the Privy Council had to increase in *Eaton v Johnston* [2008] UKPC 1 on account of the Court of Appeal of the Cayman Islands having, in using Ogden, made a further discount for the possibility of earlier death: see at [35]–[40].

*tome v Coates*,[574] even the second pair of these factors—sickness and accidental injury—are

> "not reflected in the Registrar-General's tables, because he is concerned with life and death, not with healthy life and unhealthy life so long as life continues".[575]

The same is true of the Ogden Tables which, mortality apart,

> "do not take account of the other risks and vicissitudes of life, such as the possibility that the claimant would for periods have ceased to earn due to ill-health or loss of employment."[576]

That a discount is required on such grounds is fully recognised by the courts. Thus at the highest level this was accepted by their Lordships in the *Wells v Wells* trilogy[577]; in *Thomas v Brighton Health Authority*,[578] the concession by counsel for the claimant that there is room for a judicial discount when calculating loss of earnings was taken to be correct[579] and in *Page v Sheerness Steel Co*,[580] discounts in respect of the claims for loss of earnings and for loss of pension, of a level yet to be considered,[581] were made.

Before turning to the question of the appropriate level of discount, a word should be said about the manner in which the courts effect the discount. The method is of course well known; the multiplier is simply reduced by a specified number. In earlier days courts used to produce a number on impressionistic lines without any real explanation of how it has been arrived at. The alternative method, which has come to be used, has been for the court to relate the number by which it is reducing the multiplier to a percentage by which the multiplier is discounted.[582] This is by far the better method as it alone makes clear the precise amount of discount that is being applied. Also, it may not have been appreciated that what appears as a small impressionistic decrease in the multiplier will constitute a large percentage decrease in the multiplier. Thus it only needs a reduction of one in the multiplier to produce a 4 per cent discount on a multiplier of 25 moving up to a 10 per cent discount on a multiplier of 10, while a reduction of two in the multiplier gives an 8 per cent discount on a multiplier of 25 moving up to a 20 per cent discount on a multiplier of 10. In any event, the days of impressionistic reductions of the multiplier have fortunately gone and are a thing of the past. **40-132**

The Ogden Tables, since the second edition in 1994, have given guidance on how **40-133**

---

574 [1965] 1 W.L.R. 1285 CA; a wrongful death case.

575 [1965] 1 W.L.R. 1285 CA at 1292; cited by Edmund Davies LJ in *Mitchell v Mulholland (No.2)* [1972] 1 Q.B. 65 CA at 76–77. As Lord Diplock he made the same point in *Mallett v McMonagle* [1970] A.C. 166 at 176.

576 7th edn (2011) *Explanatory Notes*, para.19.

577 See para.40-122, above.

578 [1999] 1 A.C. 345.

579 [1999] 1 A.C. 345 at 378D. Lord Lloyd, only in whose speech the issue of contingencies was fully considered (at 377H to 379G), accepted the concession on the basis that in the case of loss of earnings, as opposed to costs of care, "the contingencies can work in only one direction—in favour of the defendant" (at 378D); yet it is not thought that this is entirely correct in the light of the quotation at para.40-141, below, from *Bresatz v Przibilla* (1962) 108 C.L.R. 541 (High Ct. of Australia).

580 [1999] 1 A.C. 345.

581 See paras 40-135 and following, below.

582 Though it has sometimes been a little difficult to marry the reduction in the multiplier with the percentage discounted.

to adjust for contingencies other than mortality, use this better method and arrive at the discount by specified percentages set out in Tables appearing in Section B of the *Explanatory Notes*. However, Ogden goes about the exercise in a different way, though one ending up with the same results. Instead of applying a percentage discount, say 10 per cent, to the multiplier, the method used is to multiply the multiplier by a figure which represents the percentage remaining after the discount. Thus to achieve a discount of, say, 8 per cent, Ogden will multiply the multiplier by 0.92. It is done this way to make for ease in calculation; only one operation has to be carried out, viz., multiply by the figure given, rather than two operations, viz., multiply by the discount and subtract the resulting figure from the multiplier. Nevertheless we shall continue here to speak generally in terms of percentage discounts as this makes clearer what is the precise effect of the contingencies adjustment to the multiplier.

**40-134** A methodology for assessing contingencies other than mortality is set out in the Ogden Tables. Initially, from 1994, the factors of occupational types and geographic location were thought to be the ones important for the making of the assessment. Later, a new methodology, which has very important consequences, was introduced in the 6th edition of 2007 and repeated in the current 7th edition, replacing the methodology set out in earlier editions with Section B of the explanatory notes entirely recast. The new approach was based upon recent research, the findings of which have shown that educational attainment is a key factor which, when allowed for, makes relatively small the effect of the earlier factors of occupational types and geographic location, which were discarded. In addition to educational attainment, employment status and disability status, both at the time of injury and at the time of trial, are of central importance. Gender is the one previous factor that is retained. The research has also demonstrated that after injury more time is spent out of employment than earlier research had suggested. The overall result is that the new methodology produces significantly higher percentage discounts.[583] The discounts are higher than before for the fit, well-educated male in employment, are higher still for the female, the less well-educated and the unemployed, and for the disabled mount very high.[584]

**40-135** **(b) Level of discount** What amounts to an appropriate percentage discount to take is a controversial question to which widely different answers have been given over the years. In *Mitchell v Mulholland (No.2)*,[585] decided at a time when courts were still looking askance at all actuarial evidence, the 2 per cent discount which the claimant's expert witnesses there proposed as appropriate was regarded not only suspiciously but as much too small.[586] At the other end of the scale there is the also comparatively early *Auty v National Coal Board*,[587] which has been much criticised for the Court of Appeal's endorsement of the trial judge's huge discount for contingencies of 27 per cent. However in *Auty* since it was death that was regarded

---

583 Compare the detailed tables at para.42 of Section B of the explanatory notes in the 7th edition (2011) with the tables at paras 32 to 34 of the equivalent Section B of the *Explanatory Notes* in the 5th edition (2004), the last edition before the change.

584 See Tables A to D at para.42 of the 7th edition (2011).

585 [1972] 1 Q.B. 65 CA.

586 See [1972] 1 Q.B. 65 CA at 76F, per Edmund Davies LJ.

587 [1985] 1 W.L.R 784 CA.

as the major factor in arriving at this discount[588] and as the impropriety of a discount for the possibility of earlier death became later established by the House of Lords in *Thomas v Brighton Health Authority*,[589] it would seem that a discount of 27 per cent in the circumstances of *Auty* is consigned to oblivion. Nevertheless in *Page v Sheerness Steel Co*,[590] one of the *Wells v Wells* trilogy,[591] Dyson J, presented by the defendant with the Auty discount of 27 per cent and by the claimant with the suggestion of a 2 per cent discount proposed by the Ogden Tables for the contingency discount for the loss of earnings, made the 2 per cent discount and then, saying that he was bound by Auty, reluctantly discounted by 10 per cent.[592] The Court of Appeal without reasons substituted 15 per cent[593] but the House of Lords said there was no sound reason for this increase and restored the 10 per cent.[594]

In the days of these decisions the guidance given by the Ogden Tables was not much in evidence, guidance which put forward much lower rates of discount. Thus Ogden produced a discount of no more than 2 per cent for a male in his 20s retiring at 65 or for a male in his 30s retiring at 60. Once the House of Lords in *Wells v Wells*,[595] had endorsed the use of Ogden, with Lord Lloyd saying that Ogden should be the starting point for arriving at the appropriate multiplier,[596] it might be expected that things would be different. However, over-high discount rates continued, particularly where very young claimants were concerned. Thus in *M (A Child) v Leeds Health Authority*,[597] the defendant contended for a discount of 30 per cent and the court adopted 22.5 per cent[598]; no mention of the Ogden tables is made in Sullivan J's judgment. Appreciably lower discounts can indeed be found though not as low as the Ogden ones would indicate. Thus in *Parkhouse v Northern Devon Healthcare NHS Trust* and also in *Massey v Tameside Glossop Acute Services NHS Trust*,[599] 5 per cent was taken[600]; again, no mention of the Ogden tables appears in either Gage J's or Teare J's judgment. So it looks as if it was only the tables of multipliers that came into prominence with *Wells v Wells* and not the tables which give appropriate discounts for contingencies other than mortality. **40-136**

Interestingly, with the sea change in the Ogden approach through the move to entirely new criteria bringing significantly higher contingency discounts,[601] things have changed. The courts are now showing themselves fully prepared to utilise the new material. A number of cases can be found illustrative of this in relation to the claimant's pre-injury earnings and there may indeed, as in *Connery v PHS Group Ltd*,[602] be no dispute between the parties over the discount figure to be taken from **40-137**

588 See [1985] 1 W.L.R. 784 CA at 798E.
589 [1999] 1 A.C. 345. See paras 40-129 and 40-130, above.
590 [1996] P.I.Q.R. Q26.
591 See para.40-122, above.
592 [1996] P.I.Q.R. Q26 at 38.
593 [1997] P.I.Q.R. Q1 at 54.
594 [1999] 1 A.C. 345 at 381G.
595 [1999] 1 A.C. 345.
596 See para.40-073, above.
597 [2002] P.I.Q.R. Q4 at 46.
598 Stating that this was the percentage used by the Court of Appeal in *Thomas v Brighton Health Authority*: see paras [59]–[62]. The discount for the earnings multiplier was not in issue in the Lords in *Thomas*.
599 [2007] EWHC 317 (QB) (Admin).
600 See [2007] EWHC 317 (QB) (Admin) at [107] and [108].
601 See para.40-134, above.
602 [2011] EWHC 1685 (QB).

the new Ogden.[603] It may be, however, that a claimant argues that his or her circumstances gives an entitlement to a lower contingency discount, thereby increasing the damages for loss of earnings. This was so in *Crofts v Murton*.[604] It was argued that the Ogden discount of 19 per cent that would apply to the figure of the claimant's pre-injury earnings was too high as he was not typical of the broad population upon which the Ogden figure was based, and contended for a 5 per cent discount.[605] The judge agreed, citing the commentary in Ogden[606] that the figures suggested under the new methodology are intended as a "ready reckoner" which provides an initial adjustment to the multiplier but which cannot take into account all circumstances so that it may be appropriate to argue for higher or lower adjustments in particular cases.[607]

**40-138** The bulk of the cases, however, are concerned with disputes over the contingencies discount on the claimant's post-injury earnings, generally referred to as the residual earnings. This concentration on the position with residual earnings results from the introduction of disability status as one of the factors to be taken into account in the assessment of the impact on the damages of contingencies other than mortality. When formerly under Ogden the factors with which one was concerned were occupation and geographical location, the claimant's position was likely to be the same, for the reduction of the multiplier for contingencies, both pre-injury and post-injury. But once disability is in as a relevant factor, a multiplier much reduced for contingencies may well be needed for the post-injury earnings. Moreover, there is not only a need for a post-injury multiplier but also a distinct probability that the use of it to heighten claimants' damages will be disputed by defendants. This probability arises from the low threshold for disability as defined by Ogden. Persons are to be regarded as disabled if the condition of disability or illness lasts over a year or is progressive, substantially limits their ability to carry out normal day-to-day activities, and affects the kind or amount of paid work they can do.[608] This low threshold for disability means that cases will arise where significant adjustments to, and modifications of, the post-injury contingencies multiplier will be required.

**40-139** The issue first came before the courts in *Conner v Bradman & Co Ltd*.[609] Having found that the 51-year-old male claimant had, under the Ogden criteria, been rendered disabled by the injury, the trial judge applied for his calculation of the claimant's pre-accident earning capacity the contingency discount for an employed non-disabled man, which was not disputed, but for his calculation of the claimant's residual earning capacity he took for the contingency discount a figure which fell halfway between the discount for the disabled person and that for the non-disabled person.[610] So too in *XYZ v Portsmouth Hospitals NHS Trust*,[611] for the 40-year-old male claimant's residual earnings the difference between the non-disabled and disabled discounts was again taken at the halfway mark in circumstances where the trial judge thought it was a borderline decision as to

603 See at [2011] EWHC 1685 (QB) at [61].
604 *Crofts v Murton* unreported 8 September 2008.
605 In Ogden terms, the multiplier fell to be multiplied by 0.95 rather than 0.81.
606 *Explanatory Notes*, Section B, para.32 of the 7th edition (2011).
607 *Crofts*, paras [140]–[142].
608 For the full definition, with explanation in detail, see explanatory notes, Section B, para.35.
609 [2007] EWHC 2789 (QB).
610 See HH Judge Peter Coulson QC at [2007] EWHC 2789 (QB) at [63]–[74].
611 [2011] EWHC 243 (QB).

whether the claimant met in full the criteria for disability set out in Ogden.[612] By contrast, in *Leesmith v Evans*,[613] where the defendant argued similarly for taking the mid-point between the non-disabled and disabled discounts in calculating residual disability, the trial judge settled for a discount some five-sixths of the way from the non-disabled to the higher disabled discount, thus favouring the 28-year-old male claimant.[614] In the other direction goes *Connery v PHS Group Ltd*.[615] The trial judge said that he was adopting the approach taken in *Conner v Bradman* by the judge there,[616] but the contingency discount for the 47-year-old female claimant's residual earnings of one-third at which he arrived was only one-seventh of the way from Ogden non-disabled to Ogden disabled, being therefore much in favour of the defendant.[617] And in *Clarke v Maltby*,[618] the trial judge found that the 45-year-old female claimant's residual disabilities did not justify any higher contingencies discount on her residual earnings multiplier. In some cases the Ogden criteria might not be applied at all. These cases will be where the degree of disability is very small, the effect upon a claimant's work is not significant, and there is no rational basis for determining how the reduction factor should be adjusted.[619]

So far there have not been found cases in which the contingencies discount laid down by Ogden for post-injury earnings has been applied precisely; the court has preferred to modify it to suit the circumstances of the case. Moreover, no case has yet reached the Court of Appeal and it would be useful to have that court's views on the correct application of the new Ogden contingency discounts based on disability when it comes to assessing the degree of discount appropriate in these cases. **40-140**

As a last word, this may be said. In *Herring v Ministry of Defence*,[620] a decision which came before the new Ogden criteria had been introduced and in which the trial judge's discount of 25 per cent on pre-injury earnings had been reduced to 10 per cent,[621] the figure of 25 per cent being said to be "a gross departure from that appropriate simply in respect of future illness and unemployment",[622] Potter LJ. commented[623] that **40-141**

> "the observations of Windeyer J in *Bresatz v Przibilla*[624] have for long been quoted but perhaps insufficiently recognised so far as deductions for contingencies are concerned".

This text has directed attention to these observations in every edition since they appeared in 1962, and in conclusion on the general issue of contingencies we would

612 See Spencer J at [2011] EWHC 243 (QB) at [229]–[233], especially at [232].
613 [2008] EWHC 134 (QB).
614 See Cooke J. at [2008] EWHC 134 (QB) at [106].
615 [2011] EWHC 1685 (QB).
616 Although he gets his name wrong: [2011] EWHC 1685 (QB) at [65].
617 See HH Judge Platts at [2011] EWHC 1685 (QB) at [62]–[68]. The figures are not entirely clear. The judge stated that he had been urged to use a more conventional method of assessment and to ignore the Ogden tables (at [64]) and that he did not wish to tinker with them (at [65]). Yet at the end he comes up with a contingency discount requiring a multiplication by 0.66 (at [68]), although this is not specifically related to his having earlier (at [63]) given the pre-injury discount as requiring a multiplication by 0.72 and the post-injury discount as requiring a multiplication by 0.28.
618 [2010] EWHC 1201 (QB).
619 *Billett v Ministry of Defence* [2015] EWCA Civ 773 CA, discussed above at para.40-101.
620 [2004] 1 All E.R. 44 CA.
621 [2004] 1 All E.R. 44 CA at [38].
622 [2004] 1 All E.R. 44 CA at [31].
623 [2004] 1 All E.R. 44 CA at [29].
624 (1962) 108 C.L.R. 541.

do so again. Windeyer J said:

> "The generalisation that there must be a 'scaling down' for contingencies seems mistaken. All 'contingencies' are not adverse: all 'vicissitudes' are not harmful. A particular claimant might have had prospects or chances of advancement and increasingly remunerative employment. Why count the possible buffets and ignore the rewards of fortune? Each case depends upon its own facts. In some it may seem that the chance of good fortune might have balanced or even outweighed the risk of bad."[625]

This strongly underlines the need for a cautious approach to the adjustment of the multiplier for the contingencies of life.

## 8. No Specific Adjustments for Unearned Income

**40-142** The fact that the claimant has a substantial and secured private income is irrelevant to the assessment of damages under this head.[626] This was decided in the various stages of the early leading case of *Phillips v L. & S.W. Ry*,[627] and has not been doubted since. In the appeal in the Court of Appeal[628] from the second trial Cotton LJ said:

> "It has been urged that independent income ought to be taken into account in estimating the pecuniary loss. I cannot agree to that. The fact that he has an independent income does not make the claimant's pecuniary loss less. … In estimating the pecuniary loss the independent income of the claimant is not to be taken as a kind of set-off, so as to reduce the amount which the jury would otherwise award."[629]

The same type of statement can be found in the judgment of Field J at the first trial,[630] and in the judgment of James LJ, with which his brethren concurred, in the appeal in the Court of Appeal from the first trial.[631] The point has never been disputed since.

**40-143** There is one respect in which a rule of no adjustments for unearned income could be unfavourable to a claimant. This is in relation to tax. For even Lord Reid, with his preparedness to put Gourley into reverse[632] and increase an award to counteract the incidence of higher tax upon it because of its size, would not allow into the calculation any private income of the claimant.[633] Of course a claimant is only disadvantaged where he is attempting to increase his damages on the basis that the income generated by the award will attract very high rates of tax—the *Gourley* in reverse situation—and it seems that the courts are unlikely to be prepared to increase the multiplier on this account, outside income or no outside income.[634]

## 9. No Specific Adjustments for Inflation

625 (1962) 108 C.L.R. 541 at 544.
626 Although it may be relevant in assessing damages for non-pecuniary loss: see para.40-270, below.
627 (1879) 4 Q.B.D. 406; 5 Q.B.D. 78 CA; 5 C.P.D. 280 CA.
628 At this date a motion for a new trial went first to the Queen's Bench Division.
629 (1879) 5 C.P.D. 280 CA at 294.
630 (1879) 5 Q.B.D. 78 at 82.
631 (1879) 5 Q.B.D. 78 at 87.
632 See paras 18-029, above and 38-144, below.
633 *Taylor v O'Connor* [1971] A.C. 115 at 129D; similarly Viscount Dilhorne: [1971] A.C. 115 at 139E.
634 See para.40-148, below.

The courts were beginning in the 1960s to be urged to take the prospect of future inflation into account in making their damages assessments. After the Court of Appeal in *Mitchell v Mulholland (No.2)*,[635] attempted, but failed, in a personal injury claim "to give for the first time a definitive ruling on the point",[636] House of Lords and Court of Appeal in three cases of the 1970s dealing with fatal accidents got to grips with the problem, *Taylor v O'Connor*,[637] *Young v Percival*,[638] and *Cookson v Knowles*[639]; the solution reached was that, provided that the discounting to give the present value of the future lost earnings was done at the 4 to 5 per cent rate considered appropriate in times of stable currency, no specific adjustment on account of inflation was required, to either multiplicand or multiplier. This solution was then further endorsed in the 1980s, once more in the personal injury context, by the House of Lords in *Lim Poh Choo v Camden and Islington Area Health Authority*,[640] and later by the Court of Appeal in *Auty v National Coal Board*,[641] a claim for a loss of pension rights maturing well into the future. **40-144**

These details are set out so that the development of the law on this point is understood, but there is today no need further to consider either the details or the views expressed by so many eminent judges—they are all set out in some earlier editions[642]—for by the decision of the House of Lords in *Wells v Wells*,[643] that in future the discount rate should reflect the net return on index-linked government stock, the problem of inflation is *ex hypothesi* largely solved. And the Lord Chancellor's adoption of their Lordships' ruling in his specification of a discount rate[644] cements the solution. At least for the time being this is true but, should change in the discount rate which is in the air today abandon reliance on ILGS,[645] the inflation issue may return. **40-145**

## 10. ADJUSTMENTS FOR TAXATION

It was the decisions which in the past got to grips with the inflation issue[646] that brought forward the related issue of the need to take account of the possibility of the incidence of high taxation on the income generated by the lump sum awarded in damages. In *Taylor v O'Connor*,[647] the earliest of the House of Lords cases, Lord Reid aptly described the situation as "Gourley in reverse", requiring an increase rather than a reduction in the damages awarded.[648] Eventually the suggestion was put into practice in *Thomas v Wignall*,[649] in relation not to an award for lost earnings but to an, in this respect analogous, award for the expenses of medical care; the Court of Appeal increased the multiplier by one from 14 to 15. **40-146**

---

635 [1972] 1 Q.B. 65 CA.
636 [1972] 1 Q.B. 65 CA at 86F, per Sir Gordon Willmer.
637 [1971] A.C. 115.
638 [1975] 1 W.L.R. 17 CA.
639 [1979] A.C. 556.
640 [1980] A.C. 174.
641 [1985] 1 W.L.R. 784 CA.
642 The latest of which is the 15th edition (1988), at para.1478 and paras 1573 to 1575.
643 [1999] 1 A.C. 345; see para.40-122, above.
644 See para.40-123, above.
645 See para.40-127, above.
646 Compare para.40-144, above.
647 [1971] A.C. 115.
648 [1971] A.C. 115 at 129F. It was a case of a fatal accident but the same principles apply.
649 [1987] Q.B. 1098 CA.

**40-147** A year later in *Hodgson v Trapp*,[650] the House of Lords, departing from its earlier expressed views, overruled *Thomas v Wignall*.[651] Lord Oliver, who gave the leading speech on the taxation issue, said:

> "In my opinion, the incidence of taxation in the future should ordinarily be assumed to be satisfactorily taken care of in the conventional assumption of an interest rate applicable to a stable currency and the selection of a multiplier appropriate to that rate. Both in *Cookson v Knowles* and in *Lim*'s case this House was prepared to envisage that there might be very exceptional cases, where it could be positively shown by evidence that justice required it, in which special allowance might have to be made ... for tax. ... Tax is merely one of the imponderables that are taken care of in the conventional method of assessing damages. There may, I suppose, be cases—although, again, I cannot for my part readily imagine one arising in an exercise in its nature imprecise—where the considerations pointing to the selection of one of two possible multipliers are so finely balanced that the future incidence of taxation may be taken into account as one, but only one, of the factors which might properly tip the balance in favour of selecting the higher rate rather than the lower, but the course sanctioned in *Thomas v Wignall* of making a specific addition on account of this factor alone is, in my judgment, as incorrect as would be a specific addition to cover the risk of future inflation."[652]

**40-148** The door has therefore not been entirely closed upon the prospect of an addition to the multiplier on account of taxation[653] but, although illustrations can be constructed to show that, where high levels of income are generated by a damages award, a claimant may be disadvantaged in comparison with a claimant receiving a lower income, it was said in earlier editions of this work that, in the light of *Hodgson v Trapp*,[654] it was not going to be easy in practice to persuade a court that there should therefore be an increase in the multiplier. And this prediction has so far been justified. In *Warren v Northern General Hospital NHS Trust (No.2)*,[655] despite the evidence that compensation of between £1.25 million and £3.5 million would be reduced by taxation to within 0.5 per cent of 3 per cent which was the discount rate set by *Wells v Wells*[656]—the award for financial loss in *Warren* was in the region of £3 million—such a reduction did not, in the view of the Court of Appeal, make the case very exceptional so as to justify increasing the multiplier.[657] And in *Van Oudenhoven v Griffin Inns Ltd*,[658] where it was the incidence of Dutch tax which was relied upon as making the case exceptional, the Court of Appeal held that it was bound to look at whether there were corresponding advantages in Holland, including the availability of a higher return from the foreign equivalent of index-linked government securities, the level of indirect taxation and the cost of living, and that the fact that Dutch tax was higher than United Kingdom tax, which was the only information before the court, did not alone render the case suf-

---

650 [1989] A.C. 807.

651 [1987] Q.B. 1098 CA.

652 [1989] A.C. 807 at 835.

653 The alternative route of increasing the multiplicand, much earlier put forward by three of their Lordships in *Taylor v O'Connor* [1971] A.C. 115—Lord Reid, Lord Morris and Viscount Dilhorne at 129E, 134D and 139D, respectively—would appear to have been abandoned. It was Lord Guest and Lord Pearson who would have increased the multiplier: at 136A and 143A respectively.

654 [1989] A.C. 807.

655 [2000] 1 W.L.R. 1404 CA.

656 [1999] 1 A.C. 345.

657 Or lowering the discount rate. For this aspect of the case see the first footnote in para.40-125, above.

658 [2000] 1 W.L.R 1413 CA.

ficiently exceptional. What the Court of Appeal would have made of *Biesheuvel v Birrell*,[659] with Dutch tax again involved, a much higher award in the region of £7 to £8 million, and a multiplier increased as the judge put the case in the very exceptional category, is not known.[660] The appeal in the case was settled.[661]

### *(C)* THE DEDUCTIBILITY OF COLLATERAL BENEFITS

Before the House of Lords decision in *British Transport Commission v Gourley*,[662] in 1955 that an award for loss of earning capacity must take into account the income tax which the claimant would have had to pay on the earnings because the award itself would not be taxable,[663] no deductions were made at common law by the courts from the damages to be awarded to a physically injured claimant for the loss of his earning capacity because part of his loss had been or would be recouped by reason of benefits conferred upon him by third parties with whom the defendant had nothing to do.[664] Such benefits were described as completely collateral matters, as *res inter alios acta* or as too remote to be brought into consideration. However, *British Transport Commission v Gourley*,[665] initiated a trend which favoured deductions. *Gourley* itself was not directly concerned with collateral benefits: the question there in issue was the first of the two questions which, as Lord Reid later pointed out in *Parry v Cleaver*,[666] arise when assessing the financial loss of a physically injured claimant, namely, **40-149**

> "what are the sums which he would have received but for the accident but which by reason of the accident he can no longer get?",[667]

rather than the second question, namely,

> "what are the sums which he did in fact receive as a result of the accident but which he would not have received if there had been no accident?",[668]

---

659 [1999] P.I.Q.R. Q40.

660 *Biesheuvel* was cited in *Warren* in argument, and in *Van Oudenhoven* in the judgments but without being commented upon except to say that it involved much higher figures.

661 It was pointed out in earlier editions that the need to adjust the multiplier on account of increased tax could well be eliminated if in place of the Ogden Tables the Duxbury Tables (for these, see footnote at the end of para.40-073, above) were used, since they have a more sophisticated, computer-based method for dealing with the tax element. But since Duxbury appears to be largely a dead letter as far as personal injury damages are concerned, with Ogden prevailing (see above), it is thought unnecessary to consider Duxbury further here. It is true that in *Van Oudenhoven v Griffin Inns Ltd* [2000] 1 W.L.R. 1413 CA, counsel appears to have introduced a Duxbury calculation in support of his argument for a lower discount rate in the particular case, but the reaction was rather negative, the Court of Appeal simply saying that on the basis of the Duxbury calculation it reached the conclusion that a lower discount rate was not justified: see para.22. We are not told what the Duxbury calculation was. The examination, backed by illustrations in figures, of how Duxbury would operate to improve the damages computation in this regard can be found, if required, in the 16th edition (1997) at paras 1613 to 1615.

662 [1956] A.C. 185.

663 See paras 18-002 and 40-076, above.

664 A degree of deduction of social security benefits was however required by statute from 1948: see para.40-162, below.

665 [1956] A.C. 185.

666 [1970] A.C. 1.

667 [1970] A.C. 1 at 13B.

668 [1970] A.C. 1 at 13C.

which second question gives rise to the further question "whether the latter sums must be deducted from the former in assessing the damages".[669] The belief in such deductibility has increased as the years have gone by, but only in respect of certain categories of benefit; moreover, with social security benefits a whole new regime has legislatively appeared introducing the new concept of deductibility with accountability to the State of the deductions made.[670] Each particular type of benefit requires to be examined separately.

### 1. Insurance Moneys

**40-150** As early as 1874 it was decided in *Bradburn v G.W. Ry*,[671] that, where the claimant had taken out accident insurance, the moneys received by him under the insurance policy were not to be taken into account in assessing the damages for the injury in respect of which he had been paid the insurance moneys. This decision has withstood time and is solidly endorsed at House of Lords level by *Parry v Cleaver*,[672] not only by the majority who relied upon it by analogy[673] but also by the minority who sought to distinguish it,[674] and more recently by Lord Bridge speaking for the whole House in *Hussain v New Taplow Paper Mills*,[675] and in *Hodgson v Trapp*,[676] and by Lord Templeman similarly in *Smoker v London Fire Authority*.[677] The matter is clearly now incontrovertible. The argument in favour of non-deduction is that, even if in the result the claimant may be compensated beyond his loss, he has paid for the accident insurance with his own moneys, and the fruits of this thrift and foresight should in fairness enure to his and not to the defendant's advantage.[678]

**40-151** This rationale is not available to the claimant who has not taken out, and paid the premiums under, the insurance policy which generates the payments to him. Accordingly, where in *Hussain v New Taplow Paper Mills*,[679] the employer defendants had covered by insurance their liability to their employees for wages during illness so that the source of the payment of wages made to the claimant employee was the insurance policy towards which he had made no contribution by way of premiums, it was held that he could not invoke the established rule that insurance moneys paid are not to be deducted from damages for loss of earnings; the sums received by him were not to be regarded in his hands as insurance moneys but simply as wages which, as will be seen,[680] do fall to be deducted. "The fact", said Lord Bridge,

---

[669] [1970] A.C. 1 at 13C.

[670] See paras 40-164 and following, below.

[671] (1874) L.R. 10 Ex. 1.

[672] [1970] A.C. 1.

[673] [1970] A.C. 1 at 38.

[674] [1970] A.C. 1 at 31 and 49.

[675] [1988] A.C. 514 at 527G.

[676] [1989] A.C. 807 at 819H.

[677] [1991] 2 A.C. 502 at 539B–F.

[678] See *Parry v Cleaver* [1970] A.C. 1 at 14 and 31, per Lords Reid and Morris respectively; *Smoker v London Fire Authority* [1991] 2 A.C. 502 at 539F, per Lord Templeman, citing Asquith LJ in *Shearman v Folland* [1950] 2 K.B. 43 CA at 46.

[679] [1988] A.C. 514.

[680] See para.40-152, below.

> "that the defendants happen to have insured their liability to meet these contractual commitments as they arise cannot affect the issue in any way".[681]

This decision was applied in *Page v Sheerness Steel Co*,[682] by Dyson J who held that moneys payable to an employee under his employer's insurance policy fell to be deducted as they represented sick pay, which was always deductible,[683] and not insurance; his decision was affirmed, and his reasoning supported, by the Court of Appeal[684] and by the House of Lords,[685] both concerned in the case with weightier issues.[686] There has then followed *Gaca v Pirelli General Plc*,[687]where, now in the Court of Appeal, Dyson LJ, in a fully reasoned judgment concurred in by the other members of the court, ruled that payments made to the employee claimant under a group personal accident insurance policy held by the employer defendant must be deducted unless it was shown, as it was not in *Gaca* any more than in the earlier cases, that the employee had paid or contributed to the insurance premiums directly or indirectly. Neither the employer's arranging the insurance for the benefit of the employee nor the fruits of the employee's work enabling the employer to pay for the insurance could be regarded as constituting an indirect contribution.[688]

## 2. Wages, Salary, Sick Pay

It is fully accepted today that, where an injured claimant continues to be paid his wages by his employer as of right, or part of his wages, and whether under the name of sick pay or otherwise, these sums fall to be deducted from the damages for loss of earnings. In *Hussain v New Taplow Paper Mills*,[689] Lord Bridge said: **40-152**

> "It has always been assumed as axiomatic that an employee who receives under the terms of his contract of employment either the whole or part of his salary or wages during a period when he is incapacitated for work cannot claim damages for a loss which he has not sustained",[690]

citing *Metropolitan Police District Receiver v Croydon Corp*,[691] as an example of this. Certainly, the matter was treated as obvious both in that case[692] and in the companion case heard together with it on appeal, *Monmouthshire County Council*

---

681 [1988] A.C. 514 at 530C.

682 [1996] P.I.Q.R. Q26.

683 See para.40-152, below.

684 [1997] P.I.Q.R. Q1 CA at 56 to 58. This part of the Court of Appeal's judgment is not included in the report at [1997] 1 W.L.R. 652.

685 [1999] 1 A.C. 345 at 381H–382A.

686 Page was the third of the three cases together generally known as *Wells v Wells*.

687 [2004] 1 W.L.R. 2683 CA.

688 See the useful discussion on indirect contributions at [2004] 1 W.L.R. 2683 CA at [56] to [59]. In *McCamley v Cammell Laird Shipbuilders* [1990] 1 W.L.R. 963 CA, where no deduction was allowed of moneys which had come to the claimant through the medium of a personal accident insurance policy taken out by the holding company of the company employing him, the Court of Appeal was applying the benevolence exception to the rule of deduction rather than the insurance exemption. In any event McCamley has been held in *Gaca v Pirelli* (see text) to have been wrongly decided: see para.40-161, below.

689 [1988] A.C. 514.

690 [1988] A.C. 514 at 530D.

691 [1957] 2 Q.B. 154 CA.

692 See per Lord Goddard CJ at [1957] 2 Q.B. 154 CA at 163.

*v Smith*[693]; was taken to be established by Lord Denning MR in *Browning v War Office*,[694] dealing with, and since overruled on, pensions; and was implicitly accepted by all their Lordships in *Parry v Cleaver*,[695] despite their sharp disagreement on the deductibility of pensions with which the case also dealt.

**40-153** *Turner v Ministry of Defence*,[696] eventually provided the first clear decision on the point, Lord Denning MR there saying that it was plain to him that

> "the loss was not the full wages but the wages less sick pay and on that account credit must be given for it".[697]

Since then the House of Lords in *Hussain v New Taplow Paper Mills*[698] has held, confirming the Court of Appeal, that, even where employers had set up an insurance scheme whereby sick pay paid by them to their employees was reimbursed to them under the scheme, the sick pay received by one of their employees must still be taken into account in arriving at the assessment of loss of earning capacity in the employee's personal injury claim. The employers, who were the defendants, had offered the claimant another job at a lower wage so that amounts representing half-pay would continue to be made to him under the scheme though at a lower level. These payments had to be taken into account because, in the words of Lord Bridge,

> "they are payable under a term of the employee's contract by the defendants to the employee qua employee as a partial substitute for earnings and are the very antithesis of a pension, which is payable only after employment ceases."[699]

Where the claimant was entitled to half pay for life under an insurance policy taken out by his employers, who were again the defendants, the Court of Appeal, applying *Hussain*, endorsed the trial judge's decision to deduct in *Page v Sheerness Steel Co.*[700] Since the claimant had not paid for the insurance it was appropriate to classify the amounts he received as sick pay rather than insurance.

### 3. Pensions

**40-154** Between insurance moneys, which are not to be taken into account against the claimant's damages for loss of earnings, and salary moneys, which are, fall pension moneys. After a period of oscillation—the Court of Appeal first holding in *Payne v Railway Executive*,[701] that there should be no deduction of a disability pension, and then holding in *Browning v War Office*,[702] that there should—the House of Lords, by a bare majority, came down in favour of no deduction in *Parry v Cleaver*.[703] The majority, following the decisions of the High Court of Australia

693 See per Lynskey J at first instance: [1956] 1 W.L.R. 1132 at 1138. These two cases established that the employer himself had no claim for reimbursement against the tortfeasor in restitution.

694 [1963] 1 Q.B. 750 CA at 759.

695 [1970] A.C. 1.

696 (1969) 113 S.J. 585 CA.

697 (1969) 113 S.J. 585 CA.

698 [1988] A.C. 514.

699 [1988] A.C. 514 at 530C. Pensions are generally not deductible: see para.40-154, below.

700 [1997] P.I.Q.R. Q1 CA: see at 56–57. The case is also at para.40-151, above.

701 [1952] 1 K.B. 26 CA.

702 [1963] 1 Q.B. 750 CA.

703 [1970] A.C. 1.

which were heavily relied upon,[704] preferred to equate a pension with an insurance rather than with a salary. Thus Lord Reid said:

> "A pension is intrinsically of a different kind from wages. If one confines one's attention to the period immediately after the disablement it is easy to say that but for the accident he would have got £X, now he gets £Y, so his loss is £XY. But the true situation is that wages are a reward for contemporaneous work, but that a pension is the fruit, through insurance, of all the money which was set aside in the past in respect of his past work. They are different in kind."[705]

Lord Morris, expressing the minority view, did not agree. "Where", he said,

> "the arrangements leading to a pension are an essential part of the contract of employment, then the pension payments are very much more akin to pay than to anything else. Indeed, it is often asserted that a pension is a form of deferred pay and is taken into account in fixing remuneration."[706]

Just short of a quarter of a century later, encouraged no doubt by the increasing support given at the highest level to the avoidance of double recovery epitomised, at that time most recently, in *Hussain v New Taplow Paper Mills*,[707] and *Hodgson v Trapp*,[708] the correctness of *Parry v Cleaver*,[709] was challenged in two appeals to the House of Lords heard together, *Smoker v London Fire Authority and Wood v British Coal Corp*.[710] The challenge was unsuccessful. The two claimants had received moneys by way of pension[711] and it was held that these moneys did not fall to be deducted against loss of earnings.[712] There was no reason to invoke the power, available to their Lordships since 1966, to depart from their earlier, even if only majority, decision since, as Lord Templeman pointed out, **40-155**

> "all relevant arguments were advanced in *Parry v Cleaver* and there has been no change of circumstance".[713]

While in all of these cases the claimant employee had contributed to the pension scheme from his pay, that fact is not a central plank in the argument for non-deduction. The majority in *Parry v Cleaver*,[714] expressly rejected any distinction between contributory and non-contributory pension schemes: as Lord Wilberforce succinctly put it, the proper view is to regard **40-156**

---

704 *Paff v Speed* (1961) 105 C.L.R. 549; *National Insurance Co of New Zealand v Espagne* (1961) 105 C.L.R. 569; *Graham v Baker* (1961) 106 C.L.R. 340; *Jones v Gleeson* (1965) 39 A.L.J.R. 258.

705 [1970] A.C. 1 at 16; see, too, Lord Pearce at 37.

706 [1970] A.C. 1 at 32.

707 [1988] A.C. 514.

708 [1989] A.C. 809.

709 [1970] A.C. 1.

710 [1991] 2 A.C. 502.

711 In the first case these were an ill-health pension, an injury gratuity and an injury pension.

712 In the second case the deduction was said to be claimed against general damages; but this would go too far.

713 [1991] A.C. 502 at 544C. The fact that since *Parry* a clear trend had developed at common law against double recovery was not a change of circumstance: see at 544C and 544H–545A. Yet attempts still continue to be made, though without success, to bypass *Parry v Cleaver* by distinguishing it, as in *Crofts v Murton* [2009] EWHC 3538 (QB): see at [143]–[154].

714 [1970] A.C. 1.

"the pension as representing the earnings, or reward of past savings, to the extent of his own contribution and his past services, as to the rest".[715]

Similarly, the employer's contribution to the pension scheme is of no significance even where he is the defendant. This indeed was the position in both *Smoker v London Fire Authority and Wood v British Coal Corp.*[716] Lord Templeman said[717]:

"The defendants are in the triple position of employers, tortfeasors and insurers. In my opinion this makes no difference to the principle that the claimant has bought his pension which is, in the words of Lord Reid, 'the fruit, through insurance, of all the money which was set aside in the past in respect of his past work.' The fruit cannot be appropriated by the tortfeasor."

And it follows a fortiori that a discretionary pension is no more to be taken into account than a pension payable as of right.[718]

**40-157** There is, however, one important qualification to all this. Under the majority decision in *Parry v Cleaver*,[719] pensions are not to be ignored where damages for loss of pension are concerned. In that case the claimant police constable, aged 35 at the time of the accident, was compulsorily retired from the police force at 36 as a result of his injury, and thereby became entitled to a disability pension for life. In the normal course he would have retired from the police force at 48 with a full retirement pension for life and would then have taken civilian employment till the age of 65 when he would have fully retired. Upon being compulsorily retired from the police force the claimant took clerical employment at a lower wage than he had been receiving as a police constable, and at the trial the judge found this to be the wage that he would have in fact earned, had there been no accident, from the ages of 48 to 65. In these circumstances it was held by the majority of their Lordships that the disability pension did not have to be taken into account against the lost police force salary to the age of 48, but the claimant accepted—and the majority agreed that he was right to accept—that the disability pension did have to be taken into account against the lost full retirement pension which he would have received from the age of 48, and accepted also that account had to be taken of the extent by which the pension he would now receive from his civilian employment from the age of 65 was higher by reason of the fact that his term of service had begun at the age of 36 rather than 48. Ignoring the claimant's disability pension before the age of 48 but not afterwards is based upon the fact that, in the words of Lord Reid,

"in the earlier period we are not comparing like with like. He lost wages but he gained something different in kind, a pension. But with regard to the period after retirement we are comparing like with like. Both the ill-health pension and the full retirement pension

---

715 [1970] A.C. 1 at 42, and Lord Pearce at 36, both rejecting the Saskatchewan solution in *Smith v Canadian Pacific Ry Co* (1964) 41 D.L.R. (2d) 249 of taking the amount attributable to the employer's contribution into account but not the amount attributable to the employee's.

716 [1991] 2 A.C. 502.

717 [1991] 2 A.C. 502 at 543H–544A.

718 This point is made only because it was at one time thought that the justification for non-deduction was the existence of a discretion to withhold or reduce the pension in the light of the damages awarded by the court: *Payne v Railway Executive* [1952] 1 K.B. 26 CA; *Carroll v Hooper* [1964] 1 W.L.R. 345; *Elstob v Robinson* [1964] 1 W.L.R. 726. But *Parry v Cleaver* [1970] A.C. 1 both disapproved of this reason and at the same time established the wider reason for ignoring pensions in the damages computation.

719 [1970] A.C. 1.

are the products of the same insurance scheme; his loss in the later period is caused by his having been deprived of the opportunity to continue in insurance so as to swell the ultimate product of that insurance from an ill-health to a retirement pension. There is no question as regards that period of a loss of one kind and a gain of a different kind."[720]

However, the Court of Appeal has since introduced a distinction between pension before and pension after normal retirement age and has held in *Longden v British Coal Corp*,[721] that a disability pension paid before normal retirement age does not fall to be deducted from the damages awarded for lost retirement pension any more than it falls to be deducted from the damages for lost earnings. This conclusion rested largely upon the court's taking the view that *Parry v Cleaver* had decided that disability pension after normal retirement age should be taken into account only where the same pension scheme provided for both the pension before and the pension after normal retirement age. It is, however, doubtful if this is a correct interpretation of the majority speeches in *Parry v Cleaver*; the majority was deciding that disability pension after normal retirement is always to be taken into account in assessing the damages for loss of pension and it is strongly arguable that *Parry v Cleaver* supports the same result for disability pension paid before normal retirement.

The House of Lords affirmed the Court of Appeal in large part in *Longden*,[722] but allowed the appeal to an extent, drawing a distinction between the lump sum received as part of the incapacity pension and the part of the pension paid annually. The annual pension payments received prior to the date of normal retirement age were not to be brought into account as this would be unfair and unjust, indeed here it would have resulted in the claim for loss of pension being entirely extinguished. On the other hand, the lump sum represented pension which related to the whole life of the claimant so that it was appropriate to take into account that part which was attributable to the period after normal retirement age. Lord Hope, who gave the only speech, said that it made no difference to the issue of deductibility whether the incapacity pension was or was not derived from the same scheme as the retirement pension which the claimant claimed to have lost.[723] **40-158**

## 4. GRATUITOUS PAYMENTS PRIVATELY CONFERRED

The courts appear never to have taken into account, in the assessment of damages for loss of earning capacity, moneys gratuitously conferred from private sources upon the claimant as a mark of sympathy and assistance, and this approach is fully supported in *Parry v Cleaver*,[724] by majority and minority alike.[725] "It would", said Lord Reid, **40-159**

"be revolting to the ordinary man's sense of justice, and therefore contrary to public policy, that the sufferer should have his damages reduced so that he would gain nothing from the

[720] [1970] A.C. 1 at 20 to 21; see, too, Lord Wilberforce at 42. It may be that *Larkham v Lynch* [1974] 2 Lloyd's Rep. 544 carries the non-deductibility of pensions a step further, but the precise position there is not stated with clarity in the judgment: see at 551 to 552.

[721] [1995] I.C.R. 957 CA.

[722] [1998] A.C. 653.

[723] [1998] A.C. 653 at 667H.

[724] [1970] A.C. 1.

[725] [1970] A.C. 1 at 14 and 39 for the majority; at 31 and 50 for the minority.

benevolence of his friends or relations or of the public at large, and that the only gainer would be the wrongdoer."[726]

While the support for general non-deduction of benefits evinced in *Parry v Cleaver*,[727] has given way with *Hodgson v Trapp*,[728] to an insistence on general deduction subject to exceptions,[729] Lord Bridge in that case fully accepted that gratuitous payments privately conferred formed one of the two "classic heads of exception".[730] The best illustration in the case law comes from Northern Ireland. In *Redpath v Belfast & County Down Ry*,[731] the claimant, a victim of a railway disaster, had received money from a distress fund to which the public had made voluntary subscriptions, and the court refused to make any deduction for the money so received. "It would be startling to the subscribers to that fund", said Andrews CJ in a passage cited by Lord Reid in *Parry v Cleaver*,

> "if they were to be told that their contributions were really made in ease and for the benefit of the negligent railway company",

for, if they were, then

> "the inevitable consequence in the case of future disasters of a similar character would be that the springs of private charity would be found to be largely if not entirely dried up".[732]

An earlier English decision is *Liffen v Watson*,[733] where the claimant, who was a domestic servant paid partly in kind by her employer from whom she received not only wages but board and lodging, was unable to continue in her employment for a period after the injury, during which time board and lodging were supplied to her free by her father. The Court of Appeal refused to make a deduction in respect of this, Goddard LJ saying:

> "She lost the value of the board and lodging just as she lost her wages and she is entitled to be compensated for that loss. What she does with the compensation when she receives it is a matter for her and nobody else."[734]

Similarly, ex gratia payments made by a sympathetic employer were not taken into account by the Court of Appeal in *Cunningham v Harrison*[735]; this is in contrast to the now established rule that wages, salary and sick pay which the claimant receives as of right do enter into the assessment of the damages for loss of earning capacity.[736]

**40-160** It may indeed be necessary to award the full damages to the claimant because he is under a legal obligation to reimburse the third party out of any award he

---

726 [1970] A.C. 1 at 14.
727 [1970] A.C. 1.
728 [1989] A.C. 809.
729 See para.40-149, above.
730 [1989] A.C. 809 at 820.
731 [1947] N.I. 167.
732 [1947] N.I. 167 at 170.
733 [1940] 1 K.B. 556 CA.
734 [1940] 1 K.B. 556 CA at 558.
735 [1973] Q.B. 942 CA.
736 See paras 40-152 and 40-153, above.

receives.[737] On the other hand, if the third party is a true benefactor and has exacted no legal obligation from the claimant to repay him, there may yet be a moral obligation to repay. Here there is a difficulty in enforcement, for what is to prevent the claimant collecting his damages and then refusing to pay over to the third party the appropriate amount to which he is "morally" entitled? In *Dennis v L.P.T.B.*,[738] the court cut through the difficulty by making available the device of directing that the judgment in the claimant's favour, which had suffered no deduction on account of the benefit, should be made conditional upon the claimant's repaying the third party; the claimant had received during the period of his disability, in pension and sick pay from the Ministry of Pensions and his employers, amounts which together equalled his wages, and Denning J directed that he repay his two benefactors out of the damages awarded. In the context of gratuitous nursing care rendered by relatives, the later *Donnelly v Joyce*,[739] and *Housecroft v Burnett*,[740] have since suggested that it is not for the court to implement such moral obligation and its existence is irrelevant[741] but the still later *Hunt v Severs*,[742] has gone further in the other direction and, overruling *Donnelly v Joyce*,[743] has held that the damages recovered for the gratuitous care are to be held by the claimant in trust for the carer.[744] Whether the same now applies to gratuitous payments privately conferred is not yet clear. For one thing the device of the trust may not be thought appropriate for all cases; for instance, a charity making a donation may not expect or desire a return out of any damages which may be recovered by the claimant. However, that the damages recovered for gratuitous payments of wages by an employer, who is not the defendant, are now to be held by the claimant employee in trust for the employer is suggested by *Davies v Inman*.[745] The employee was there held entitled to interest on his loss of earnings despite the fact that his employer had voluntarily continued to pay him an allowance equivalent to his wages, but the interest fell to be held in trust for the employer. If this is true of the interest awarded, it suggests that it should also be true of the award of gratuitous payments of wages. The need for a trust of this nature did not arise in *Davies v Inman* as there was already an undertaking by the employee claimant to refund his employer from the damages he received.

However, the position is different and deduction does have to be made—so that no question of a trust can arise—where the tortfeasor is the source of the payment. **40-161**
This is now established for payments to employees by their employers against whom they are claiming. It was first suggested, in this context of an employer defendant, by Lloyd LJ who said in the Court of Appeal in *Hussain v New Taplow Paper Mills*[746]:

[737] *Browning v War Office* [1963] 1 Q.B. 750 CA at 770, per Diplock LJ; see, somewhat similarly, *I.R.C. v Hambrook* [1956] 2 Q.B. 641 CA at 656–657, per Lord Goddard CJ.

[738] [1948] 1 All E.R. 779.

[739] [1974] Q.B. 454 CA.

[740] [1986] 1 All E.R. 332 CA.

[741] [1974] Q.B. 454 CA at 462H–463D and [1986] 1 All E.R. 332 CA at 343d.

[742] [1994] 2 A.C. 350.

[743] [1974] Q.B. 454 CA.

[744] See para.40-228, below.

[745] [1999] P.I.Q.R. Q26 CA.

[746] [1987] 1 W.L.R. 336 CA at 350C–E.

> "But there is one consideration of public policy which is worth mentioning. If an employee is injured in the course of his employment and his employers make him an immediate ex gratia payment, as any good employer might, I see no reason why such a payment should not be taken into account in reduction of any damages for which the employer may ultimately be held liable. Employers should be encouraged to make ex gratia payments in such circumstances. If so, then public policy would seem to require that such payments be brought into account.
>
> It could, of course, be said that an ex gratia payment is like a sum coming to the claimant by way of benevolence, and should therefore be disregarded. This is so where it is a third party who is ultimately held liable. ... But there must surely be an exception to that general rule where the ex gratia payment comes from the tortfeasor himself."

Then came a hiccough with the Court of Appeal's decision in *McCamley v Cammell Laird Shipbuilders*,[747] where the ex gratia payment by the defendant employers was held not to be deductible on the unconvincing ground that the employers' intention was that the ex gratia payment should not be on account of damages. In *Williams v BOC Gases Ltd*,[748] the ex gratia payment made by the employer defendant was held to be deductible from the damages not only because the payment had been made by the wrongdoer himself but, a fortiori, because he had said in terms at the time of the payment that it was to be treated as an advance against any damages that he might have to pay to the claimant employee. Then in *Gaca v Pirelli General Plc*,[749] the Court of Appeal refused to follow *McCamley*, being able to do so by holding it to have been decided per incuriam on account of its plain inconsistency not only with Lloyd LJ's reasoning, above, in *Hussain* but with what had been similarly said in the House of Lords by Lord Bridge in *Hussain*,[750] and in *Hunt v Severs*,[751] at a later date.[752] In *Gaca* the claimant employee, seriously injured at work, received, both before and after his employment was terminated, payments under a group personal accident insurance policy held by the defendant employer and it was held that these payments did not fall within the benevolence exception and therefore were to be deducted from the damages. After an extensive review of the authorities Dyson LJ, who gave the leading judgment, concluded on these facts which were similar to those in *McCamley* that

> "this case does not come within the benevolence exception because: (a) the payments were made by the tortfeasor; and (b) the payment of benefits under the insurance policy was not equivalent, or analogous, to payments made by third parties out of sympathy."[753]

A payment should only be treated as analogous to a benevolent payment by a third party if the case for doing so, having regard to the rationale for the existence of the benevolence exception, was clearly made out. It is thought that this is unlikely to be possible.

---

747 [1990] 1 W.L.R. 963 CA; facts in the footnote at the end of para.40-151, above.

748 [2000] P.I.Q.R. Q253 CA.

749 [2004] 1 W.L.R. 2683 CA.

750 [1988] A.C. 514. Lord Bridge's remarks there are cited at [18] of Gaca.

751 [1994] 2 A.C. 350. Lord Bridge's remarks there are cited at [26] of Gaca.

752 See [2004] 1 W.L.R. 2683 CA at [38]. Dyson LJ said that, were it necessary, he would be prepared to distinguish *McCamley* on the ground that there the entitlement to benefit under the insurance policy, of the existence of which the employee knew, was part of the employment package, whereas in *Gaca* that there was an insurance policy was unknown to employee and his trade union alike: at [40]. But no such necessity to distinguish exists; *McCamley* should simply be consigned to history.

753 [2004] 1 W.L.R. 2683 CA at [39].

## 5. MONETARY SOCIAL SECURITY BENEFITS

### (1) The development of the law

The law on how far monetary social security benefits are taken into account in the assessment of damages for loss of earning capacity has had a long and chequered history. The story opens in 1948 before which time the courts had not given any real thought to the question of deduction of any collateral benefits.[754] Section 2(1) of the Law Reform (Personal Injuries) Act 1948 provided for the deduction from damages for loss of earnings of specified benefits, but only of one-half of the benefits paid or payable over a five-year period. This was effectively a political compromise between no deduction and full deduction. At the time there were few benefits provided by the National Insurance Acts 1946 relating to earnings and s.2(1) only concerned itself with three.[755] **40-162**

As the years went by, more and more social security benefits related to earnings appeared on the scene. The question then arose as to whether these should be deducted at common law from the loss of earnings damages. For many years the tendency was to ignore social security benefits paid to the claimant, a tendency fuelled by the House of Lords' decision in *Parry v Cleaver*,[756] but gradually a trend to deduction developed and eventually carried the day, culminating in the House of Lords' decision in *Hodgson v Trapp*,[757] a case which was itself concerned with medical expenses. There were doubts over unemployment benefit but eventually it fell to the axe of deduction,[758] a long tussle over supplementary benefit, now income support, ended the same way,[759] family income supplement, later renamed family credit, became deductible[760] and statutory sick pay followed.[761] All this, as will be seen, has some relevance for the present law. **40-163**

Then in 1989 everything changed root and branch. With escalating social security benefits the Government had decided that the Department of Social Security rather than the tortfeasor or the tortfeasor's insurer should have the advantage of their deduction from the damages. Legislation was introduced to achieve this in the Social Security Act 1989, legislation later appearing as Pt IV of the Social Security Administration Act 1992, which Pt IV was in turn replaced and overtaken by the Social Security (Recovery of Benefits) Act 1997,[762] the statute with which we are therefore today concerned and which for ease of reference will throughout be called the 1997 Act, as will the earlier statute be called the 1992 Act. In these various statutes it was provided in elaborate manner that defendants should continue to deduct the benefits from the damages but must now account for them to the Secretary of State. Apart from this essential feature of the new law, there were radical changes in respect of the deduction of benefits. In particular, starting with the **40-164**

754 See para.40-149, above.

755 They were industrial injury benefit, industrial disablement benefit and sickness benefit.

756 [1970] A.C. 1.

757 [1989] A.C. 807.

758 *Nabi v British Leyland (UK)* [1980] 1 W.L.R. 529 CA, although the Court of Appeal cautiously said that the appropriateness of deduction should be considered by the House of Lords.

759 *Lincoln v Hayman* [1982] 1 W.L.R. 488 CA.

760 *Gaskill v Preston* [1981] 3 All E.R. 427.

761 *Palfrey v Greater London Council* [1985] I.C.R. 437.

762 And the secondary legislation correspondingly changed from the Social Security (Recoupment) Regulations 1990 to the Social Security (Recovery of Benefits) Regulations 1997 (SI 1997/2205).

Social Security Act 1989, a far larger range of benefits was listed as qualifying for deduction; all the relevant benefits which had developed over the years but which had not appeared in the earlier legislation of 1948 were included. Thus from 1989 benefits across the whole range of benefits could be statutorily deducted from the damages for loss of earning capacity, the deductions were to be of the whole benefit and not just half as formerly, while the five-year period of deduction was retained but somewhat modified. To this the 1997 Act introduced some variations, generally favourable to the claimant; in particular, as we shall see, only benefits related to earnings were now to be deducted from the lost earnings damages[763] and interest was to run on the damages awarded before deducting the benefits.[764]

## (2) The present position

### (a) Benefits for which express legislative provision is made

**40-165** *(i) The rule as to deduction of benefits* The precise position as to deduction cannot easily be ascertained from the 1997 Act because of the roundabout fashion of the drafting which, once again, promotes obscurity. This is in great part due to the fact that the statute is not primarily talking of, or concerning itself with, the deduction of benefits received by the claimant from his damages but of the accounting for such benefits which is after all the object of the legislation. Unlike the 1992 Act which did better in drafting, the payment of benefits to the Secretary of State is placed in the forefront of the statutory provisions in advance of the payment net of these benefits to the claimant.[765] Of course the elaborate machinery for accounting in the 1997 Act is here left on one side[766]; it need not concern a work on damages.[767]

---

763 See para.40-168, below.

764 See para.40-173, below. In earlier editions an objection to one feature of the 1997 legislation was voiced, an objection which by the long passage of time has become only historical. The 1992 Act had enacted that the new provisions were not to apply to payments made in respect of injuries occurring before 1989. By contrast, the 1997 Act enacted that the new provisions were to apply to payments made after late 1997. This was considered to be an unanticipated and unwelcome piece of retrospective legislation, catching payments made in respect of injuries occurring before 1989, to which previously the earlier 1948 Act had applied. It also explains why s.2(1), together with (1A), (3) and (6), of the Law Reform (Personal Injuries) Act 1948 were repealed by the 1997 Act with effect from its coming into force. This means that, s.2(2) and (5) having been repealed much earlier, only s.2(4), which deals with a rather different damages issue (see paras 40-186 and 40-246, below), survives today.

765 Compare s.6 and s.8 of the 1997 Act with the key s.82 of the 1992 Act.

766 For some of the anomalies which appear in the operation of the 1997 Act where there has been a CPR Pt 36 payment see *Williams v Devon CC* [2003] P.I.Q.R. Q4 CA at 68.

767 One aspect of the accounting does concern the claimant's damages and that is that, if the defendant challenges the Compensation Recovery Unit certificate and obtains an amended certificate of a reduced amount and a repayment, he must account to the claimant for the repayment. This may seem obvious but it took a lengthy consideration of the complex statutory provisions in *Bruce v Genesis Fast Food Ltd* [2004] P.I.Q.R. P9 at 113 to reach this conclusion. See too *R. (on the application of Soper) v Criminal Injuries Compensation Board* [2004] P.I.Q.R. Q1 CA at 1, a judicial review of an award in which it was the amount of the benefits deducted which was challenged, and on more than one ground. If the claimant has received benefits but the defendant has been unable to make any deduction from the damages because for some reason the Compensation Recovery Unit certificate states that no benefits have been received, the court is prevented by s.17 of the 1997 Act (which see at para.40-173, below) from itself making a deduction from the damages: *Eagle v Chambers (No.2)* [2004] 1 W.L.R. 3081 CA; see at [13] and [53].

So rather than setting out in tedious and confusing detail the provisions of the 1997 Act as to the deduction of benefits, it is thought to be more helpful, and it is certainly shorter and clearer, to state what the rule to be garnered from the detail is. Since the Act has to cover settlements as well as damages awarded by a court, it talks throughout of "compensation payments"; here we will substitute "damages", a limitation appropriate for a text on damages. Put simply, the rule can be expressed thus: **40-166**

> The damages to be paid to the claimant for loss of earnings are to be reduced by deducting the amount of the specified benefits related to loss of earnings paid or likely to be paid in the period beginning at the time of injury or of first claim for benefit and ending five years later or upon the payment of the damages if earlier.[768]

It is as straightforward as this, although it would be difficult to guess it from the statutory drafting. It requires a perusal of a combination of ss.1(1)(b), 1(4)(c), 3, 8(1) and 8(3) together with Sch.2 to extract this result; the reader who wishes may go to these sections, subsections and schedule to see how this statement of the rule is arrived at. At least, the list of benefits once it is found—it appears in the col.2 at the beginning of Sch.2—is clear and straightforward. To the original comprehensive list have been added two further benefits over the years, with one benefit early removed.[769] The list now reads:

universal credit[770]
disablement pension payable under s.103 of the 1992 Act
employment and support allowance[771]
incapacity benefit
income support
invalidity pension and allowance
jobseeker's allowance
reduced earnings allowance
severe disablement allowance
sickness benefit
statutory sick pay
unemployability supplement
unemployment benefit.

*(ii) Various features of the rule* Five aspects of the rule need to be examined. **40-167**
They concern the return to the earlier position whereby only benefits related to earnings are deducted, the five-year period and its significance, the operation of the deduction of the whole rather than of half of the benefits, the question of whether interest falls to be computed upon the loss of earnings before or after deduction of benefits and the possible exemption for small payments. These matters are as relevant for medical expenses as for lost earnings; one of the five matters has much

---

768 Earnings lost for the purposes of the 1997 Act were held by a majority in *Chatwin v Lowther* [2003] P.I.Q.R. Q5 CA at 84 to include the amount recovered for rent paid by the claimant to her business landlord, rent which she would have been able to meet out of the business which her injuries had forced her to give up.

769 Disability working allowance, the first of the benefits originally listed, was "omitted" (the word used in the statute) by the Tax Credits Act 1999.

770 Inserted by the Welfare Reform Act 2012.

771 Inserted by the Employment and Support Allowance (Consequential Provisions) (No.2) Regulations 2008 (SI 2008/1554).

greater impact on medical expenses and its detailed consideration is therefore postponed until medical expenses are dealt with.

40-168 *(1) **Earnings-related benefits to be deducted*** Instead of the totality of the benefits being deducted from the whole range of the damages as had been misguidedly provided for in the 1992 Act, only those benefits related to earnings are deducted from, and only from, the damages awarded for loss of earnings. This is made clear by s.8(3) of the 1997 Act together with Sch.2, where it is provided that the benefits related to earnings listed in the col.2 at the beginnings of the Schedule, namely those set out above,[772] are to be deducted from the first head of compensation in the col.1, namely "compensation for earnings loss". This eliminates the unfairness demonstrated by the decision in *Hassall v Secretary of State for Social Security*,[773] where the Secretary of State was held entitled to recoup from the general damages for non-pecuniary loss benefit paid to the claimants because of their incapacity to work. It also restores the position as it rightly was between 1948 and 1989; like is again being deducted from like.

40-169 *(2) **The five-year period*** It would be expected that the five-year period would run from injury when the cause of action arises, and this is precisely how it was simply put in the legislation up to 1989.[774] However, s.3 of the 1997 Act, the four sub-sections of which are devoted to defining "the relevant period", differentiate between "accident or injury" and "disease"; in doing so, the section follows the 1992 Act. This is a sensible distinction which is presumably designed to cater for the now well-known fact, which *Cartledge v Jopling & Sons*,[775] dramatically brought to light, in the context of limitation 50 years ago,[776] that a disease, particularly an asbestos-related disease, may be latent for very many years, so that a cause of action will have arisen long before the claimant can have been aware of it. In these circumstances there will be no payments available for deduction for the first five years after injury and accrual of cause of action. Hence while with accident or injury time will effectively run from accrual of cause of action, with disease it is provided that it will run from the first making of a claim for benefit.[777] The vast majority of cases will, of course, fall into the category of accident or injury.

40-170 Thus while the five-year period could not start in cases of disease until claims for benefit had also started, with the normal case of injury the five-year period could have started before, even well before, benefits were claimed and received.[778] To this extent the claimant with an injury could be better off than the claimant with a disease. And there is another respect in which benefits for a full five-year period may not come to be deducted. For a further feature of the new scheme, differing from the old one, is that it is provided that once the damages are paid the five-year

[772] At para.40-166, above.

[773] [1995] 1 W.L.R. 812 CA.

[774] The single sentence of s.2(1) of the Law Reform (Personal Injuries) Act 1948 which stated the rule for deduction ended with "for five years beginning with the time when the cause of action accrued".

[775] [1963] A.C. 758.

[776] See the case at para.11-020, above.

[777] s.3(3).

[778] Thus there was already authority under the earlier law, in *Eley v Bedford* [1972] 1 Q.B. 155, that no deduction fell to be made on account of benefits which the claimant had failed to claim because she was mistaken as to her rights.

period comes to an end.[779] This change may have been dictated by the change from simple deduction by the defendant to deducting and then accounting to the Secretary of State.

The real significance of the five-year period as it stands today, a significance which marks a change in the law, is to be found in the vast increase in the benefits which were brought into the statutory deduction net in 1989, an increase which was continued in the 1997 legislation. For by the time this happened the common law had, as we have seen,[780] moved from the position of not deducting social security payments to deducting them. Should then the benefit be one which would have been deducted *in toto* under the common law without limitation of time, the claimant will be better off because for a total deduction over time will be substituted a total deduction for five years only. While this may not make much difference with loss of earnings benefits brought into the 1989 fold as these tend to run out after a short time, it is of great consequence with medical expenses. It will therefore be looked at in more detail when dealing with medical expense together with the related question of whether defendants can argue that when deduction under the statute ends deduction at common law for the future can take over.[781] **40-171**

***(3) Deduction of the whole benefit*** The impact, by way of change, of the requirement that the whole benefit and not only half is to be deducted is less. For it only affects those receiving one, or more, of the limited number of benefits which were within the deduction net before 1989; now they must submit to deduction of the totality of that benefit. By contrast, those receiving one, or more, of the benefits which were not in the deduction net before 1989 can be, as we have seen,[782] better off. However, because of the introduction, also from 1989, of the rule that the five-year period ends with the payment of damages,[783] a claimant would in one set of circumstances benefit under the new scheme and that is where the damages are paid to him before half of the five-year period has elapsed. **40-172**

***(4) The position on interest*** In two conjoined appeals, *Wadey v Surrey County Council* and *Wisely v John Fulton (Plumbers) Ltd*,[784] the House of Lords held the claimants' entitlement to interest to be on the damages awarded for their past loss of earnings before deducting the social security benefits they had received. This result is unfortunate as it goes against the well-established general principle that the claimant should be entitled to interest only for being kept out of his money. Their Lordships were not unsympathetic to the possibility of arriving at a contrary conclusion by a robust application of this general principle but they considered that this was not open to them upon a proper interpretation of the statutory wording and statutory scheme. Before the 1997 Act the position had been regulated by s.103 of the 1992 Act which required the court to deduct the benefits before calculating the interest, and this provision had been repealed without replacement. The 1997 Act also directed, by s.17, that benefits were to be disregarded in assessing the damages and it was held that this direction must also extend to the interest on those **40-173**

---

[779] See s.3(4)(a). The period will also end where an agreement is made under which an earlier payment of damages is treated as having been made in final discharge of a claim: s.3(4)(b). This was new in the 1997 Act.

[780] See para.40-163, above.

[781] See paras 40-242 and 40-243, below.

[782] See the previous paragraph.

[783] See para.40-170, above.

[784] [2000] 1 W.L.R. 820 HL. One appeal was from England, the other from Scotland.

damages. The correct solution could, indeed, have been to provide in the statutory scheme that not only the damages representing the benefits but also any interest on such damages should be payable to the Secretary of State. However, we must live with the House of Lords solution, at least for the time being. By interesting contrast, but entirely consistently, with these decisions allowing the claimant in effect to get interest on the benefits is the holding in *Griffiths v British Coal Corp*,[785] that benefits may be deducted from the interest on the damages for lost earnings where those damages without the interest fall short of the benefits.

**40-174** *(5) **Exemption for small payments*** There is currently no exemption for payments of insignificant size in the 1997 Act. It only stipulates that regulations may make provision for damages to be disregarded in prescribed cases where their amount does not exceed the prescribed sum.[786] This takes the place of the exemption in the 1992 Act for amounts of damages not exceeding £2,500, an exemption which was removed because it had become subject to abuse. Claimants would settle claims for £2,500, which they could keep, rather than for a justifiable higher sum which, after deduction and accounting for benefits, would leave less than £2,500 in their hands. It is a little difficult to see how regulations exempting small payments would achieve the prevention of a recurrence of this abuse.

**40-175** **(b) Benefits for which no legislative provision is made** The range of available benefits has much grown since the basic current social security system was set up in 1946.[787] Yet, of the wide variety of benefits made available under the Social Security and other Acts, it would be inappropriate to take most of them into account against any award made to a physically injured claimant for loss of earning capacity. Rather they are relevant to fatal injuries—as with widow's payment and guardian's allowance—or to medical and other expenses incurred by an injured claimant—as with attendance allowance and mobility allowance[788]—or they are simply in no way connected with the injury—as with housing benefit or as was the case with statutory maternity pay. Also all the obvious benefits related to earnings are now listed in the 1997 Act and covered by it. Two remaining benefits stand out for consideration; these are State retirement pensions and redundancy payments.

**40-176** A State retirement pension was held not to be deductible in *Hewson v Downs*.[789] In arriving at this decision, Park J relied upon the dicta of Lord Reid and Lord Pearce in *Parry v Cleaver*,[790] that the policy against deduction of collateral benefits appearing in the fatal accidents legislation should be carried over into the personal injury field. Yet Lord Morris's view that no conclusion could properly be drawn for personal injury claims from fatal accidents legislation[791] seems preferable, and since *Parry* the pendulum has swung fully in the other direction, favouring deduction, since *Hodgson v Trapp*.[792] Non-deduction would indeed seem to be correct, but surely it is best simply to rely upon the argument that the State retirement pension

---

785 [2001] 1 W.L.R. 1493 CA.

786 See s.1 together with Sch.1, Pt II, para.9(1). Such payments are referred to as "small payments" and constitute "exempted payments": at Pt I, para.1 and Pt II, paras 1, 9(2).

787 By the National Insurance Acts 1946.

788 See para.40-239, below.

789 [1970] 1 Q.B. 73.

790 [1970] A.C. 1 at 19G–20C and 38C–D respectively.

791 [1970] A.C. 1 at 25D–E.

792 [1989] A.C. 809. Contrast para.40-163, above.

is in no way connected with the injury. No attempts seem to have been made since by defendants to challenge the holding in *Hewson*.

With redundancy payments[793] generally no deduction at common law is called for. This result is at root based on the premise that redundancy payments are made not for the loss of salary but for the loss of a longstanding employment, a premise which is evidenced by the fact that entitlement to full redundancy pay is unaffected by the employee's immediately obtaining another employment at the same, or even a higher, salary. In *Mills v Hassall*,[794] therefore, no deduction was made. If, however, it can be shown that the claimant would not have been made redundant but for the incapacity caused by the injury in respect of which he is claiming, then it was held by the House of Lords in an appeal from Scotland, *Wilson v National Coal Board*,[795] that a deduction is appropriate to avoid the claimant's being overcompensated. Their Lordships stressed the exceptional nature of the circumstances[796] whereby the redundancy resulted from the injury.[797] **40-177**

**(c) Benefits where the legislative provisions are inapplicable** One situation of inapplicability of the legislative provisions arose in *Rand v East Dorset Health Authority (No.2)*.[798] The claim was brought by the parents of a child born disabled and a whole series of benefits specified under the 1997 Act had been paid to them. Nevertheless the 1997 Act was held not to apply so as to allow deduction and accounting because the claimants were other than the person physically injured; the 1997 Act did not contemplate such a scenario. Therefore deduction could only be at common law. However, since *Rand* concerns this rather special parental claim, it will be considered later when dealing with such claims.[799] **40-178**

Another situation where the 1997 Act is clearly inapplicable is when welfare payments of another country are involved. A vital consideration here is that under the particular foreign social security law the claimant may have to reimburse the State for any benefits received out of the damages awarded. Where this is so, no deduction falls to be made from the damages as there is no duplication of compensation. This was the position in *Berriello v Felixstowe Dock & Railway Co*.[800] The claimant, an Italian seaman injured while employed by the defendant, received a substantial amount in lire from the Cassa Marittima Meridionale, a body providing benefits for injured seamen run by the Italian State. No deduction was made from his damages by the Court of Appeal on account of the fact that he would be required, under Italian law, to repay out of the damages the moneys received from the Cassa. Had this not been so the Court of Appeal would have decided upon deduction. *Moriarty v McCarthy*,[801] where the annual welfare payment made to the **40-179**

---

793 Initially under the Redundancy Payments Act 1965, later under the Employment Rights Act 1996.

794 [1983] I.C.R. 330.

795 1981 S.L.T. 67 HL (Sc).

796 See per Lord Keith and Lord Scarman, 1981 S.L.T. 67 HL (Sc) at 71, col. 1.

797 *Wilson* was applied in *Colledge v Bass Mitchells & Butlers Ltd* [1988] 1 All E.R. 536 CA so as to allow deduction where the claimant's injuries caused him to leave his job and receive redundancy payments he would not otherwise have received. The defendant in *Wilson* was the employer, and the court did not commit itself as to whether the position would be different where, as was the case in *Mills*, the payer of the damages and the payer of the redundancy payment were not the same person. In *Colledge* also the defendant was the employer.

798 [2000] Lloyd's Rep. Med. 377.

799 See para.40-303, below.

800 [1989] 1 W.L.R. 695 CA.

801 [1978] 1 W.L.R. 155.

claimant as a citizen of the Irish Republic was not repayable out of the damages but the court declined to deduct it,[802] would be unacceptable today.

**40-180** *Ballantine v Newalls Insulation Co*,[803] can be regarded as another case of what was in effect a welfare benefit falling completely outside the 1997 Act being held to be deductible. It may be considered here, as being the best point to place it, although it is a case in which the deduction was not only from lost earnings but from the whole of the damages, for non-pecuniary loss as well as pecuniary. The deceased, who had developed mesothelioma from exposure to asbestos when employed at the defendant's factory, had before his death made a claim for compensation for the disease under the Pneumoconiosis (Workers' Compensation) Act 1979. In his action for personal injury, an action surviving his death, the amount of the statutory compensation was set off by the trial judge only from the damages awarded for financial loss but the Court of Appeal made the deduction against the whole award of damages. The statutory payment was a general payment designed to compensate for the injury as a whole and in all its aspects it required to be deducted to avoid a double recovery. It thus differs from all the other cases here in that the benefit itself was intended to cover losses other than loss of earnings.[804]

## 6. Social Security Benefits Other than Monetary

**40-181** Non-monetary social security benefits have their great importance in connection with medical expenses[805] but there is one particular non-monetary benefit which affects earnings. That is the free maintenance which an injured claimant may have received from a public source.

**40-182** A seriously injured victim may find that he obtains without cost to himself hospital or other institutional housing and maintenance through the National Health Service or through local authorities. Back in the 1970s the Court of Appeal in *Daish v Wauton*,[806] held that no deduction from the damages awarded for loss of earning capacity was to be made on account of housing and maintenance provided free in the National Health Service institution in which the claimant was likely to spend the rest of his life. This result was soon after reversed by statute.[807] Section 5 of the Administration of Justice Act 1982 provided that in a personal injuries action

> "any saving to the injured person which is attributable to his maintenance wholly or partly at public expense in a hospital, nursing home or other institution shall be set off against any income lost by him as a result of his injuries."

---

802 [1978] 1 W.L.R. 155 at 164E–G.

803 [2000] P.I.Q.R. Q327 CA.

804 See the case at para.41-136, viewed as a claim by the estate.

805 See paras 40-246 and following, below.

806 [1972] 2 Q.B. 262 CA.

807 Reinstating on this issue *Oliver v Ashman* [1962] 2 Q.B. 210 CA and implementing the recommendation of the Pearson Commission, (HMSO, 1978), Cmnd.7054–1, paras 510 to 512.

## V. Medical and Related Expenses

### (A) Expenses Included

### 1. Medical Expenses

### (1) In general

The claimant is entitled to damages for the medical expenses reasonably incurred by him as a result of the injury: no authority is needed to support this statement, for cases are legion which include such outlays in the damages awarded. Expenses of medical treatment, of attendance of doctors and nurses, of medicines and appliances, of hospital fees, of transportation to hospital, of nursing attendance between the place of injury and the claimant's home,[808] of care running into the future: these are all recoverable.[809] The only condition is that they should be reasonable,[810] a condition implied in the reference to reasonableness in s.2(4) of the Law Reform (Personal Injuries) Act 1948.[811] Both expenses already incurred at the time of the trial and prospective expenses are recoverable, and while the rules of procedure require that the expenses already incurred and paid be pleaded as special damage and the prospective expenses as general damage,[812] the division, which depends purely on the accident of the time that the case comes on for hearing, implies no substantive differences. Interest, however, is awarded on the special but not on the general damages.[813] **40-183**

In the normal run, the medical expenses will be designed to treat the consequences of an injury. Occasionally, however, they may arise out of an attempt to restore what has been lost to the claimant through the injury. In *Hamp v Sisters of St Joseph's Hospital Mt Carmel Convent School*,[814] the cost of extensive treatment designed to restore some sight to a girl blinded in a school accident was awarded.[815] In *Biles v North East Thames Regional Health Authority*,[816] and again in *Riggs v East Dorset Health Authority*,[817] the cost of several attempts at in vitro fertilisation of women sterilised and rendered infertile as a result of negligence was **40-184**

---

808 As to this last item, see *Schneider v Eisovitch* [1960] 2 Q.B. 430 at 438.

809 In *Reaney v University Hospital of North Staffordshire NHS Trust* [2015] EWCA Civ 1119, the Court of Appeal, at paras [30]–[33], rejected the approach of Edwards-Stuart J in *Sklair v Haycock* [2009] EWHC 3328 (QB). The Court of Appeal held that the causation question to be asked was whether the care required as a result of the accident was qualitatively different from that which would have been required but for the accident. This was different from a question, relevant to quantification of damages not causation, of "giving credit" for the costs that would have been avoided.

810 Since the care received up to trial by the claimant in *Loughlin v Singh* [2013] EWHC 1641 (QB) was sub-standard and the amount that had been paid was the cost of proper care, the trial judge made a deduction of 20 per cent in his amount in his award for this item of damages: at [42]. This may be explained on the basis that it was not reasonable to expend more than the care was worth.

811 See the subsection at para.40-186, below.

812 *British Transport Commission v Gourley* [1956] A.C. 185 at 206, per Lord Goddard. Expenses not crystallised as disbursements should be claimed as general damages: *Shearman v Folland* [1950] 2 K.B. 43 CA at 51, per Asquith LJ. For the difference between general and special damage in pleading, see paras 51-016 and following.

813 *Jefford v Gee* [1970] 2 Q.B. 130 CA. For the reason for the difference, see para.19-090, above.

814 *Hamp v Sisters of St Joseph's Hospital Mt Carmel Convent School* unreported 26 July 1973 CA.

815 And was not appealed.

816 *Biles v North East Thames Regional Health Authority* unreported 30 October1987.

817 *Riggs v East Dorset Health Authority* unreported 25 October1990.

awarded. *Briody v St Helen's & Knowsley Health Authority*,[818] went further in considering the validity of a claim for the expenses of a surrogacy arrangement designed to give children to the claimant. While the claim failed because the chance of a successful outcome to the surrogacy in the particular case was so small that it was held unreasonable for the defendant to have to pay the expense of it, the court expressed some doubt as to whether a claim for the costs of surrogacy should ever succeed.[819] Of course, to the extent that any of these steps at restoration of the former position have been successful, any award for loss of amenities will be reduced.

### (2) Medical treatment and care provided privately and provided by the National Health Service or by local authorities

**40-185** It may be that the injured person can, or does, have his or her medical treatment or care, even over a lifetime, funded by the State. This can be by engaging the facilities of the National Health Service or by reliance for the provision of care principally on local authorities. To the question of whether the injured person must accept the State funding or may go private and recover damages for the cost of so doing, a question which has dominated the litigation of the last decade in relation to local authority care, we now turn.

**40-186** **(a) Private care and National Health Service care** If the injured person uses the facilities provided without charge by the National Health Service, he or she cannot claim any medical expenses in respect thereof. In effect, the injured person has received a collateral benefit which must be taken account in the damages assessment; this aspect of the matter is considered later when collateral benefits are dealt with.[820] At the same time, the injured person .is not required to use these facilities but may opt for private treatment, for the cost of which he can accordingly recover damages. This is the entitlement given to all by s.2(4) of the Law Reform (Personal Injuries) Act 1948 which states, in its current form, that

> "in an action for damages for personal injuries … there shall be disregarded, in determining the reasonableness of any expenses, the possibility of avoiding those expenses or part of them by taking advantage of facilities available under the National Health Service."

The *Beveridge Report*,[821] which was the *fons et origo* of the National Health Service, had advised that there should be no recovery for "special expenses for medical treatment beyond the treatment generally available" to every citizen[822] and the Pearson Commission recommended that s.2(4) be repealed and that it be provided that private medical expenses should be recoverable only if it is reasonable on medical grounds to incur them.[823] Nonetheless the law remains, it is thought rightly, unchanged.

---

[818] [2002] Q.B. 856 CA.

[819] See the judgment of Hale LJ at [2002] Q.B. 856 CA at [25], where she pointed out that she was unaware of any case in which the costs involved in the adoption of a child by one wrongfully deprived of having children of her own had been claimed, and also at [29]–[32].

[820] See paras 40-246 to 40-248, below.

[821] *The Beveridge Report* (1942) Cmd.6404.

[822] W. Beveridge, *The Beveridge Report* (1942) Cmd.6404, para.262.

[823] *The Pearson Commission*, (HMSO, 1978), Cmnd.7054–1, paras 340 to 342. In *Lim Poh Choo v Camden and Islington Area Health Authority* [1980] A.C. 174 Lord Scarman said that he "recognise[d] the force of the case developed in the Pearson report for legislation repealing the

The courts do however take into account, in respect of future care, whether the claimant is on the balance of probabilities likely to use National Health Service facilities,[824] principally because the particular form of care will not be available privately. Thus in *Woodrup v Nicol*,[825] it was held that the probabilities were that the claimant would obtain half of his physiotherapy on the National Health Service and half privately, so that he was entitled in damages to half of the total physiotherapy costs. In *Howarth v Whittaker*,[826] a different result was reached. The claimant was held entitled to 18 hours of weekly care assistance without any reduction in respect of the seven hours per week of free care assistance which the claimant was already receiving before the trial and which could continue in the future. The claimant's damages fell to be based on the cost of care for the full 18 hours since, apart from the fact that the free care assistance might be discontinued after the award of damages, the claimant should be allowed to have a single care regime controlled by his case manager involving as few carers as possible.[827] In *XYZ v Portsmouth Hospitals NHS Trust*,[828] the trial judge said that he was satisfied, indeed sure, that the claimant would use private medical facilities and purchase private medication, so that the sums claimed were recoverable.[829] In *Woodward v Leeds Teaching Hospitals Trust*,[830] it was held that on all the evidence, while the claimant had for the years up to trial relied on the National Health Service for care, it was more likely than not that when she had the means, which a damages award would give her, she would have her medical treatment provided on a private basis.[831] **40-187**

**(b) Private care and local authority care** If the injured person is the recipient of care provided by local authorities without charge, he or she cannot claim the cost of such care from the defendant just in the same way as such cost cannot be claimed where National Health Service facilities are provided free. If, on the other hand, the injured person should turn to private funding, the cost of such care would fall upon the tortfeasor in the usual way provided that there is an entitlement to take the private funding route. For a claimant may be met with the argument that unpreparedness to utilise local authority care was unreasonable and constituted a failure to mitigate, an argument unavailable with National Health Service care; put shortly, there is no equivalent to s.2(4) of the Law Reform (Personal Injuries) Act 1948[832] for local authority care. For long this issue had hardly troubled the courts, but once into the 21st century a large clutch of cases of catastrophic injury appeared in the course of a few years battling with the problem, having to decide between reasonableness and unreasonableness in the particular circumstances of the case. However, with the Court of Appeal's decision in *Peters v East Midlands* **40-188**

---

subsection": at 188D.

824 Where a settlement has been reached under which the tortfeasor does fund private care but only from a date somewhat into the future, it is improper and wrong for the National Health Service to withdraw nursing care from the patient claimant in advance of that date: *R. (on the application of Booker) v NHS Oldham* [2010] EWHC 2593 (Admin).

825 [1993] P.I.Q.R. Q104 CA.

826 [2003] Lloyd's Rep. Med. 235.

827 See [2003] Lloyd's Rep. Med. 235 at [29].

828 [2011] EWHC 243 (QB).

829 Indeed he went further and held, although, as he said, there was no need for him to do so, that in the claimant's very unfortunate circumstances it was entirely reasonable for him to go private: see [2011] EWHC 243 (QB) at [33]–[41].

830 [2012] EWHC 2167 (QB).

831 [2012] EWHC 2167 (QB) at [56].

832 Cited in the preceding paragraph but one.

*Strategic Health Authority*,[833]coming at the end of this series, that an injured person has a right to choose private funding, unqualified by whether it is reasonable or unreasonable to do so, the earlier decision can now be dealt with fairly shortly.[834]

**40-189** The passage into law of the Care Act 2014 has not altered these principles, although s.22 of that Act provides that the duties and powers to meet a person's needs for care and support are now qualified because, with limited exceptions, a local authority may not meet those needs by providing or arranging for the provision of a service or facility that is required to be provided under the National Health Service Act.

**40-190** There are several statutory provisions for the funding of care by the State, the chief ones with which these cases are concerned come from the National Assistance Act 1948,[835] s.21 providing that local authorities may make available residential accommodation for those in need of care, s.29 providing that local authorities may make arrangements for providing care in the person's own home to those in need; both these powers have since 1948 been elevated into duties, though in the case of s.21 only by ministerial direction. Care in a care home provided by the local authority is referred to as residential care, care in the individual's home as domiciliary care, and with domiciliary care the local authority may choose between itself providing the care services and making what are described as direct payments for the individual to provide his own care services.[836] The decision at first instance in *Crofton v NHS Litigation Authority*,[837] well illustrates the substantial diminution in a claimant's damages that can come about through local authority assistance, in this case by direct payments under s.29, the trial judge reducing the damages for future care by more than a half, from £3.1 million to £1.4 million,[838] showing that in money terms a great deal may turn on whether privately funded care wins out over local authority care. It is true that the Court of Appeal, in allowing the appeal,[839] sent the case back for reconsideration of various matters by the trial judge,[840] in particular consideration of how far the local authority might reduce the direct payments by imposing a charge upon the claimant.[841] So too at first instance in *Sowden v Lodge*,[842] it was held to be in the claimant's best interests to have local authority residential care under s.21, and this holding again reduced the damages for care dramatically. Here it is true that on the

---

833 [2010] Q.B. 48 CA.

834 They were analysed in full detail in the previous, 18th edition where they will be found at paras 35-191 to para.35-195.

835 There are provisions outside the National Assistance Act 1948 creating care obligations which make an appearance in this context, such as those under the Children Act 1989 appearing in *Kidd v Plymouth Health Authority* [2001] Lloyd's Rep. Med. 165 and those under the Mental Health Act 1983 appearing in *Tinsley v Sarkar* [2006] P.I.Q.R. Q1 at l.

836 The sections also differ on the matter of the local authority's charging for the care afforded. Under s.21 the local authority is required and under s.29 has a discretion to recover its costs from a claimant who can afford to pay. The complex, unfortunate details of the decisions on whether the damages award can be taken into account in assessing the claimant's means are dealt with later at paras 40-249 to 40-252, below.

837 [2006] LS Law Med. 168.

838 [2006] LS Law Med. 168 at [60] and [84].

839 [2007] 1 W.L.R. 923 CA.

840 See at [2007] 1 W.L.R. 923 CA at [103].

841 How far this reconsideration by the trial judge would have increased the damages is not known as the case was settled.

842 [2003] EWHC 588 (QB).

appeal[843] the Court of Appeal concluded that, in determining whether an injured person was entitled to recover the private cost, the test to be applied was reasonableness and not best interests, paternalism not replacing the right to make a reasonable choice.[844] Also local authority care has been ruled out as inadequate[845] or, in case after case, as uncertain,[846] the burden of proof of availability or continuing availability being on the tortfeasor, with the rejection of local authority care in favour of privately funded care reaching a high point in the unappealed decision of Tomlinson J in *Freeman v Lockett*,[847] who held that discontinuing local authority assistance and turning to private care was an entirely reasonable course for the injured person to take, giving her control over the resources required to fund her care, a control which would contribute to her sense of independence and well-being.[848]

We come now to the ground-breaking decision of the Court of Appeal in *Peters v East Midlands Strategic Health Authority*.[849] A massively disabled child claimant was at the time of the trial receiving excellent care provided her by the local authority at very substantial expense. It was however said on her behalf, she being incapable of decisions, that she wished to be self-funded because with the local authority's overstrained financial resources there could be no certainty that the first class care that she needed would continue for the rest of her long life. Butterfield J at first instance[850] had held that, because of this lack of certainty, it was entirely reasonable for the claimant to choose self-funding as against reliance on State provision.[851] Rather as an *addendum* to this, he declared that, had the position been that it would have been reasonable for the claimant to rely on State provision, nevertheless the claimant had an entitlement to choose self-funding and no question of mitigation of loss by not relying on State provision arose.[852] By contrast, the Court of Appeal on the defendant's appeal went straight to the mitigation issue. While agreeing with Butterfield J that there was no question of mitigation, the Court of Appeal took his argument further and was more explicit in its reasoning. Basing itself on the well-established rule that, where a claimant has rights of action against more than one party in respect of the same loss, he can recover against them all provided that he does not recover in total more than the amount of the loss, the Court of Appeal held that this rule applied just as much in the context of a claim for damages against a wrongdoer to recover damages in respect of a head of loss and a statutory right to have that loss made good in kind by the provision of services by a local authority. Dyson LJ, giving the judgment of the court, stated by way of conclusion: **40-191**

"We can see no reason in policy or principle which requires us to hold that a claimant who

---

843 [2005] 1 W.L.R. 2129 CA.

844 No further hearing before the trial judge has appeared, again probably because the case was settled.

845 As in *Crookdake v Drury* [2005] 1 W.L.R. 2129 CA, an appeal conjoined with the one in *Sowden v Lodge*.

846 *Walton v Calderdale Healthcare NHS Trust* [2005] Lloyd's Rep. Med. 398; *A v B Hospitals NHS Trust* [2006] EWHC 1178 (QB); *Eagle v Chambers (No.2)* [2003] EWHC 3135 (QB) (unchallenged in the appeal, [2004] 1 W.L.R. 3081 CA); *Godbold v Mahmood* [2005] Lloyd's Rep. Med. 379; *Tinsley v Sarkar* [2006] P.I.Q.R. Q1 at 1.

847 [2006] LS Law Med. 151.

848 [2006] LS Law Med. 151 at [32] and [34].

849 [2010] Q.B. 48 CA.

850 [2008] EWHC 778 (QB).

851 [2008] EWHC 778 (QB) at [73].

852 [2008] EWHC 778 (QB) at [74] and [75].

wishes to opt for self-funding and damages in preference to reliance on the statutory obligations of a public authority should not be entitled to do so as a matter of right."[853]

Accordingly, there was no room for the application of the rule that a claimant must take all reasonable steps to mitigate loss.[854] A claimant has a right to choose self-funding.[855]

**40-192** This is a radical but entirely sensible decision and the court is to be commended on it if only for the reason that it deals neatly, though tangentially, with the perceived need to place the responsibility for the total damages on the tortfeasor and the tortfeasor's insurer and provides an excellent method for doing so. It is also a method that does not require legislation for its availability, as would allowing the local authority to claim for the cost of care provided from the injured person out of the damages awarded for care or from the tortfeasor direct.[856] Nor is the Court of Appeal's decision likely to be the subject of attack. In the years that have followed there has been quite a number of citations of the case, both by the Court of Appeal and at first instance, without any judicial criticism of it.[857] It is of course true that our highest court has not passed judgment on the matter but it is surely significant that leave to appeal in *Peters* was refused by the Supreme Court.

## 2. Related Expenses

**40-193** The claimant is also entitled to recover for any other expense which he can show resulted from the injury. Not all of these expenses can be classified strictly as medical. Thus it is common to allow the claimant recovery of the expenses of relatives in visiting him in hospital on the basis that this will speed his recovery[858]; it may be that after *Hunt v Severs*,[859] the claimant will be required to hold the sums recovered by him in trust for the visiting relatives.[860] But there are expenses other

---

853 [2010] Q.B. 48 CA at [53]; and see similarly at [56], together with the whole discussion, covering both principle and authorities, from [33] on. The judgment towards the end also has what is called a "postscript on mitigation" but it is thought rather difficult to reconcile what is said there, at [89], with the firm line taken in the earlier paragraphs.

854 The Court of Appeal was concerned with the avoidance of double recovery but was satisfied, as was Butterfield J below, that this could be achieved, though the route taken by the Court of Appeal to achieve it was somewhat different from that of Butterfield J: see the discussion at [2010] Q.B. 48 CA at [57]–[66], and, below, at [2008] EWHC 778 (QB) at [76]–[78].

855 As Dyson LJ said, having so decided there was no need to consider whether the choice to self-fund was a reasonable one. Nevertheless he went on to say that the court would consider this issue in case the court proved to be wrong on the mitigation issue ([2005] Lloyd's Rep. Med. 398), and after discussion endorsed Butterfield J's holding that it was reasonable for the claimant to choose self-funding ([2010] Q.B. 48 CA at [67]–[88]).

856 On this see para.40-252, below.

857 *Sklair v Haycock* [2009] EWHC 3328 (QB) at [78]; *Nottinghamshire County Council v Bottomley* [2010] EWCA Civ 756 CA at [25]; *R. (on the application of Booker) v NHS Oldham* [2010] EWHC 2593 (Admin) at [26] (referring to the "tortfeasor pays" principle identified in *Peters*); *North Dorset NHS Primary Care Trust v Coombs* [2013] EWCA Civ 471 CA at [11].

858 See, e.g. *Haggar v De Placido* [1972] 1 W.L.R. 716 at 718G and *Donnelly v Joyce* [1974] Q.B. 454 CA at 459D. There may also be awarded the claimant's expenses in visiting his relatives from hospital and in attending hospital from home after his discharge as in, e.g. *Burton v Kingsbury* [2007] EWHC 2091 (QB): see at [197].

859 [1994] 2 A.C. 350.

860 See paras 40-228 and 40-229, below. Travel expenses of hospital visits were as much in issue in *Hunt* as was the care provided.

than these, and of more moment. Illustrative is *Shanks v Swan Hunter Group Plc*,[861] where it was held reasonable in the particular circumstances of the case to allow the recovery of relocation costs, these being for moving back to settle in England after having emigrated to live in Australia where mesothelioma arising from employment in England had been diagnosed.[862]

Some of the heads of non-medical expenses can now be considered. They are by no means exhaustive. **40-194**

### (1) Expenses of fund management and financial management

One particular expense which surfaced in the 1980s, and is now recognised as an appropriate item of recovery, consists of the fees which the Court of Protection charges to manage the fund represented by the damages awarded to a claimant suffering from mental disability, generally referred to as a patient.[863] With increasing claims for brain damage caused by tortious injury such awards have become common—an early reported case of an award to cover Court of Protection fees is *Futej v Lewandowski*,[864] and in *Rialas v Mitchell*,[865] the Court of Appeal did not demur in relation to a similar award on the defendant's appeal on other items of the damages. Fees are also incurred, and are in addition recoverable by a claimant who is under the jurisdiction of the Court of Protection, to his or her professional receiver for administering the damages.[866] The amounts awarded in respect of such fees soon began to mount. Already in the 1980s £28,000 in Court of Protection fees was given in *Jones v Jones*,[867] and in the early 1990s £32,700 in *Cassel v Riverside Health Authority*,[868] where in addition there was recovery in respect of professional receiver's fees of nearly £50,000.[869] Come the 21st century the figures have gone higher still. In *Tinsley v Sarkar*,[870] the amount awarded for receivership and Court of Protection costs, past and future, was £92,470[871] while the costs of the Court of Protection and a Deputy awarded in *Peters v East Midlands Strategic Health Authority*,[872]came together to £165,742.[873] **40-195**

Even where a claimant is not a patient whose affairs require to be administered **40-196**

---

861 [2007] EWHC 1807 (QB).

862 See at [2007] EWHC 1807 (QB) at [60] and following.

863 Though the CPR now calls a patient a protected party; this is not only inelegant but also is not immediately clear. See the new 2007 version of CPR Pt. 21.

864 (1980) 124 S.J. 777.

865 (1984) 128 S.J. 704 CA.

866 In *Willbye v Gibbons* [2004] P.I.Q.R. P15 CA at 227, the accepted fees of the claimant's solicitor receiver came to over £88,000 but because the claimant had been held to be as much as 75 per cent contributorily negligent, only one-quarter of this amount would be available for these fees with the balance having to be paid out of the relatively modest award made under the other heads of damage. The defendant contended that in the claimant's own interests the costs of receivership should therefore be reduced. However, though the court expressed reservations about the claimant's future intentions on receivership, it appeared that she would wish to continue it. She was entitled to apply her damages how she wished and the defendant's contention was rejected: all at [18].

867 [1985] Q.B. 704 CA, which included the Official Solicitor's administration costs: see at 708E.

868 [1992] P.I.Q.R. Q168 CA; but subject, as was the rest of the damages, to a deduction for contributory negligence.

869 Also subject to a deduction for contributory negligence.

870 [2006] P.I.Q.R. Q1 at l.

871 [2006] P.I.Q.R. Q1 at [157].

872 [2008] EWHC 778 (QB). The Court of Appeal ([2010] Q.B. 48 CA) was not concerned with recovery of these costs.

873 See [2008] EWHC 778 (QB) at [92]–[94]. By virtue now of the new (since 2007) CPR r.21.11 the

by the Court of Protection, he or she may, especially when the award is huge, reasonably require professional advice on how best to invest the damages. The fees for such advice were held recoverable by a claimant not in the hands of the Court of Protection in *Anderson v Davis*.[874] When the Court of Appeal held in *Wells v Wells*,[875] that claimants should invest their awards prudently in equities and gilts and not simply resort to index-linked securities, that court would likely have been prepared to allow the cost of taking advice on prudent investment. But when the House of Lords, in reversing in *Wells*,[876] had made index-linked securities the order of the day and based the discount rate upon the return from such securities,[877] it had been asked in an earlier edition of this work whether it was right that claimants should be awarded the cost of investment advice in addition to their more favourable awards, for to do this would surely smack of double recovery. The courts have now sensibly taken the position suggested, holding that with a discount rate geared to index-linked securities it is inappropriate to give claimants damages for the expense of investment advice. It was so held first by Davis J in a case, *Page v Plymouth Hospitals NHS Trust*,[878] where the claimant was not in the hands of the Court of Protection. Then in *Eagle v Chambers (No.2)*,[879] where the Court of Protection had appointed a panel broker to advise on investing the fund, the Court of Appeal unanimously approved Page and held, by a majority, that the same rule should apply to a patient claimant in the hands of the Court of Protection. The dissent was on the basis that a patient had no choice but to allow the Court of Protection to invest his damages more widely than in index-linked securities and so to incur fees for investment advice. But this should make no difference. As Waller LJ put it:

> "To order the defendant to pay the costs of taking the advice so as to enable the investment to be made more broadly so as to enable the claimant to recover more than that which he would have recovered if investments had been maintained in [index-linked] gilts is to make the defendant lose both on the swings and the roundabouts."[880]

Claims for the cost of professional investment advice have accordingly died.[881] But they could come to life again should change in the discount rate, which is in the air today, abandon reliance on ILGS.[882]

---

damages recovered by or on behalf of a child or other person lacking capacity, formerly called a patient and now a protected party, are under the control of the court. The new practice direction supplementing the new CPR Pt 21 provides by para.9 for investment on behalf of a protected party, even if a child, by the Court of Protection and by para.10 for investment on behalf of a child by, effectively, the High Court. It is, however, the Court of Protection charges which feature in the authorities because these are so much more substantial than the comparatively modest fees charged by the High Court.

874 [1993] P.I.Q.R. Q87.

875 [1997] 1 W.L.R. 652 CA.

876 [1999] 1 A.C. 345.

877 See para.40-122, above.

878 [2004] 3 All E.R. 367.

879 [2004] 1 W.L.R. 3081 CA.

880 [2004] 1 W.L.R. 3081 CA at [95].

881 It seems that it had already been held at first instance in *Cunningham v Camberwell Health Authority* [1990] 2 Med. L.R. 49, which was pre-*Wells v Wells*, that, if the claimant's affairs should be in the hands of the Court of Protection, fees of financial advisers were not recoverable in addition to the fees of the claimant's receiver.

882 See para.40-127, above.

## (2) Expenses of care management

A somewhat similar particular expense which has emerged and is also now recognised as an appropriate item of recovery consists of the fees for the care management of a claimant suffering from mental disability. Claims for brain damage caused by tortious injury have, here too, made such awards common and they can be very substantial in amount, especially when added to the costs, already dealt with,[883] of the Court of Protection itself and of any receiver or, now, Deputy, that has been appointed. Some random illustrations from today may be taken to show this. In *Burton v Kingsbury*,[884] for on-going case management there was awarded £185,656, with a few thousand pounds added in for the first few months.[885] In *Tinsley v Sarkar*,[886] £96,984 was awarded for the services, past and future, of an experienced brain injury case manager[887] and this, when added to the receivership and Court of Protection costs, past and future,[888] gave a total of £189,454. In *Peters v East Midlands Strategic Health Authority*,[889] future costs of a case manager were awarded at £98, 651,[890] thereby giving a grand total when added to the costs of the Court of Protection and a Deputy[891] of over a quarter of a million pounds. **40-197**

## (3) Expenses resulting from divorce

This form of expense has fared less well. In *Pritchard v J. H. Cobden*,[892] the Court of Appeal, while accepting that the breakdown of the claimant's marriage, resulting in divorce, was caused by the tortious injuries with their attendant change of personality, declined to award the extra expense incurred by virtue of the sums which the claimant was ordered to pay in the matrimonial proceedings. In so deciding the court departed from its decision in *Jones v Jones*,[893] but it is submitted that it is the earlier case which reached the correct conclusion. It is indeed difficult to see why, as the Court of Appeal held in *Pritchard*,[894] adjustments of the joint assets of the parties to the divorce to meet their needs could not constitute a loss **40-198**

---

883 See para.40-195, above.

884 [2007] EWHC 2091 (QB).

885 See [2007] EWHC 2091 (QB) at [79].

886 [2006] P.I.Q.R. Q1 at 1.

887 See [2006] P.I.Q.R. Q1 at [130]–[136].

888 At para.40-195, above.

889 [2008] EWHC 778 (QB).

890 See [2008] EWHC 778 (QB) at [85] to [91]. The Court of Appeal ([2010] Q.B. 48 CA) was not concerned with recovery of these costs.

891 At para.40-195, above.

892 [1988] Fam. 22 CA.

893 [1985] Q.B. 704 CA. The court in *Pritchard* considered that it was not bound by its earlier decision because the defendant there had conceded the point of principle. While *Pritchard* has been subjected to considerable criticism it is most likely that, at least for the time being, it will remain the law. The Law Commission, while taking a neutral view in its earlier Consultation Paper (1996) Law Com. No.144 though at the same time rehearsing there the arguments against *Pritchard*, has been persuaded by its distinguished consultees to recommend in its Report on *Damages for Personal Injury: Medical, Nursing and Other Expenses; Collateral Benefits* (1999) Law Com. No.262 that there should be no reform: para.6-34. The matter is undoubtedly complex—thus consideration would have to be given, for instance, to whether the breakdown of relationships other than that of husband and wife would permit claims, to whether there should be recovery for non-pecuniary loss on the basis that a spouse constitutes an amenity, to how to deal with the perceived unfairness of allowing no claim for loss to the uninjured spouse—and the detailed discussion of the whole issue in Pt VI, pp.77 to 86, of the Report deserves study.

894 [1988] Fam. 22 CA.

incurred by the claimant or why, as the court also held there, it should be contrary to public policy to bring considerations relevant to matrimonial proceedings into the assessment of the damages for personal injury.[895]

## (4) Living expenses

40-199 (a) **Increase in living expenses** Increased living expenses constitute a familiar category of recoverable expense outside the strictly medical. While ordinary living expenses are not included in the recoverable expenses as these would generally continue to be incurred whether the injury had been inflicted or not, extra or increased living expenses resulting from the injury are. There would be such increased expenses if, for example, the claimant could no longer live on the top floor but was compelled to move to the ground floor, or was compelled to live in hotels or guest-houses instead of his home. The increased expenses may be temporary, as where the injury occurs when the claimant is travelling and has to live away from home for some time at greater expense because the doctor forbids him to travel home. Particularly important today are successful claims of severely handicapped claimants—generally in addition to their claims for the expense of special accommodation, dealt with below[896]—for such items as equipment and appliances to aid and assist the disabled, specially adapted vehicles for the disabled, the greater expense of holidays, the greater expense of the increased need for heating and the greater expense of running and maintaining the home by the need to employ others to do the work which the claimant had formerly done. Taken together, these items can often amount to very substantial sums. Illustrations of the recovery of many of them are found in cases going back some years, such as in *Hoffman v Sofaer*,[897] and in *Housecroft v Burnett*,[898] and continue in many cases to this day. In *Cassel v Riverside Health Authority*,[899] the Court of Appeal accepted that similar items to these had properly been included in the damages awarded to a severely disabled child but drew the line at the expense of a swimming pool, holding that the trial judge had been wrong to have allowed this. Since then, however, a small hydrotherapy pool was granted in *Wakeling v McDonagh*,[900] and a swimming pool which allowed hydrotherapy in *Burton v Kingsbury*.[901] Only in *Burton* was *Cassel* cited and it was distinguished on the basis that there had in the earlier case been no medical evidence that swimming was a necessary part of the therapy the child required.[902] In *Ellison v University Hospitals of Morecambe Bay NHS Foundation Trust*,[903] the very substantial cost of installing and maintaining an in-home hydrotherapy pool was held justified as an item in the damages awarded since use of the pool was the one way of relieving the excessive pain suffered by the severely disabled child claimant.[904]

40-200 (b) **Decrease in living expenses** Conversely, however, if the claimant for a time

---

895 And contrast the cases involving the breakdown of marriages at para.40-064, above.
896 See paras 40-201 to 40-208, below.
897 [1982] 1 W.L.R. 1350.
898 [1986] 1 All E.R. 332 CA.
899 [1992] P.I.Q.R. Q168 CA.
900 [2007] EWHC 1201 (QB): see at [50]–[61].
901 [2007] EWHC 2091 (QB).
902 See [2007] EWHC 2091 (QB) at [126] to [130].
903 [2015] EWHC 366 (QB).
904 See the lengthy passage in the judgment at [78]–[120].

is forced into a nursing-home or hospital and so ceases to incur his own particular living expenses, which in the circumstances were well in excess of the average cost of living, the defendant cannot deduct the claimant's total saving on his living expenses from the damages. This was decided in *Shearman v Folland*,[905] where the Court of Appeal held it wrong of the trial judge to take into account, against nursing-home fees of 12 guineas a week, the whole of the seven guineas a week that the claimant would normally have spent in living in expensive hotels, although it would have been proper to make a deduction in respect of the proportion of her weekly nursing-home fees which represented board and lodging[906] and which could presumably be regarded as based on average living expenses. "The precise style in which she would probably or might well have lived", said Asquith LJ delivering the court's judgment, "is, in our view, a collateral matter, and the two payments are not *in pari materia*".[907] It was indeed only a probability and not a certainty that the claimant would have lived on in this fashion. Asquith LJ put the following illustration to show the strange results which would follow if the defendant could reduce the damages by proving what course of conduct the claimant would probably have followed, or what his expenses would probably have been, had the act complained of not been committed.

> "A millionaire, accustomed to live at a palatial hotel, where his weekly expenses far exceed the charges of the nursing-home to which, after being injured by the defendant's negligence, he is transplanted, would recover nothing by way of special damage. Could it really lie in the mouth of the wrongdoer in such a case to say: 'I am entitled to go scot-free; I have, by my negligent act, not merely inflicted no loss but conferred a net financial benefit on the claimant by saving him from the consequences of his habitual extravagance'?"[908]

The result is that only ordinary living expenses can be set off: these may be for the claimant the same in and out of hospital, but, as Asquith LJ further pointed out,[909] the inconvenience and unpleasantness of the enforced existence in the hospital can be compensated for under other heads, i.e. the heads of non-pecuniary loss. The recognition in *Shearman v Folland*,[910] that it is proper to deduct ordinary, as opposed to extravagant, living expenses where these are included within the medical bills was applied by the House of Lords in *Lim Poh Choo v Camden and Islington Area Health Authority*,[911] to the case of a person in a persistent vegetative state. The argument that, if duplication of damages was to be avoided, the claimant should not have been entitled to both loss of earnings and cost of care was recognised only to the extent that it was held to be permissible to deduct the "domestic element"[912] from the cost of care, which is in effect that part of the cost of care which represents the claimant's continuing living expenses.[913]

---

905 [1950] 2 K.B. 43 CA.

906 The Court of Appeal held on the facts that there was sufficient evidence to estimate the proportion attributable to board, but insufficient as to lodging.

907 [1950] 2 K.B. 43 CA at 50.

908 [1950] 2 K.B. 43 CA at 47.

909 [1950] 2 K.B. 43 CA at 50.

910 [1950] 2 K.B. 43 CA.

911 [1980] A.C. 174.

912 While Lord Scarman attributed this term to the Court of Appeal in *Shearman v Folland* ([1980] A.C. 174 at 191F), it does not appear in the report of that case.

913 Compare the deduction of living expenses from the award for loss of earnings in *Pickett v British*

### (5) Special accommodation expenses

**40-201** In 1973 *George v Pinnock*,[914] established that a severely disabled claimant could claim for the additional cost of providing special accommodation for him to live in—in that case a bungalow—over the cost of his existing accommodation which was now wholly unsuitable for his injured condition.[915] The claimant must show by medical evidence that his physical state does indeed require special accommodation and in the same year recovery was denied in *Cunningham v Harrison*,[916] because the medical evidence was lacking.[917] Since this time successful claims of this nature have become very familiar; illustrative from the reports are *Moriarty v McCarthy*,[918] and *Roberts v Johnstone*.[919] Sometimes a home is bought which may or may not require adaptation for the claimant, sometimes a home is built suitable for his needs and sometimes the existing home is adapted to his needs.[920]

---

*Rail Engineering* [1980] A.C. 136, a claim in respect of the years lost to a claimant whose expectation of life has been reduced by injury: see para.40-111, above. The two situations are indeed juxtaposed by Lord Scarman in the *Lim* case: see [1980] A.C. 174 at 191D–G. For a somewhat unusual situation of deduction of ordinary living expenses see *Jenkins v Grocott and Hoyte* [2000] P.I.Q.R. Q17 where the claimant's care was provided at a rehabilitation unit which provided incentives to work by means of a "notional wage" to the claimant. The decision needs study but essentially there was deducted from the total costs of the care the earnings that the claimant would have made but for the accident and which he would have spent on living expenses.

914 [1973] 1 W.L.R. 118 CA; see especially at 124H–125C, per Orr LJ.

915 There is no call to make any deductions from the additional cost of accommodation, either on account of the advantage to the parents of an injured child of living in superior accommodation or on account of the moneys which the child would have invested in acquiring a home: *M (A Child) v Leeds Health Authority* [2002] P.I.Q.R. Q4 at 46; at [45]–[48]. In *Whiten v St George's Healthcare NHS Trust* [2011] EWHC 2066 (QB) the defendant argued unsuccessfully that, where the parents of the child claimant moved with him into the property acquired for him in order, naturally, to look after and care for him, there should be a deduction for the capital value of the property which the parents would have had in any event. Otherwise, it was said, the family would be living free of charge in the claimant's home. Swift J said she found this a difficult issue (at [464]); her full discussion of it and of the authorities bearing on it (at [458]–[472]) is valuable. In *Ellison v University Hospitals of Morecambe Bay NHS Foundation Trust* [2015] EWHC 366 (QB) Warby J relied on Swift J's reasoning and judgment so as to hold, as with her, that there should be no deduction on account of any benefit to the child's parents from living free in the house suitable for the disabled child which was to be acquired; it was the child's claim and any such deduction would bring down the damages so as to leave the child under-compensated: see the passage in his judgment, which analyses other cases dealing with the issue, at [134]–[152].

916 [1973] Q.B. 942 CA.

917 See [1973] Q.B. 942 CA at 954D–G, per Orr LJ It had been proposed because his exceptionally difficult personality would prevent his fitting in to a home for the disabled. But the Court of Appeal was not prepared to invoke against the defendant to this extent the rule that he must take his victim as he finds him: see at 952C–E, per Lord Denning MR.

918 [1978] 1 W.L.R. 155; see especially at 163B–E.

919 [1989] Q.B. 878 CA.

920 That the claimant's accommodation needs could adequately be met by renting rather than purchasing was argued in *Oxborrow v West Sussex Hospitals NHS Trust* [2012] EWHC 1010 (QB), an application for an interim payment for a claimant with an expectation of life only to age 21 (see the case further at para.40-206, below). In the absence of any known authorities going down the renting path (see at [11]) and in view of the practical difficulties connected with the renting solution (stated at [12]), Tugendhat J saw no likelihood of the final judgment including an assessment of damages based on renting accommodation for the claimant (at [30]). After the case was concluded, a note of a judgment in *Ryan St. George v The Home Office*, unreported on this issue, was provided to the court, where Mackay J was said to have suggested that the rental method should have a more general application in suitable cases (see at [49]). One wonders whether the practical difficulties with the rental solution indicated by Tugendhat J were brought to Mackay J's attention.

The amount awarded has never been the difference between the value of the new or adapted accommodation over the value of the existing home in its existing state but rather the interest upon that difference over the period that the new or adapted accommodation will be needed, generally the claimant's lifetime. To allow the full cost of the accommodation acquired over the proceeds of the existing accommodation disposed of, or, as the case may be, the full value of the adapted accommodation over its value before adaptation, would leave the extra value in the hands of the claimant, or of his estate, when it is no longer required for him. The full cost is recoverable only of any adaptations of the accommodation, required by the claimant's condition, to the extent that these do not increase the value of the property, it being well known that adaptations for disabled use not only may not add but may even diminish the value of property. Where the accommodation is adapted, in addition to recovery of the full adaptation costs to the extent that they do not increase the value of the property, interest should be allowed to the extent that the adaptation costs do increase the value of the property. This was rightly done in *Willett v North Bedfordshire Health Authority*,[921] as opposed to *Roberts v Johnstone* itself where the point was not argued. **40-202**

For a time the courts were prepared to award interest at a rate which would allow the claimant to borrow in order to pay for the required accommodation or the required adaptations[922] but in *Roberts v Johnstone*,[923] the Court of Appeal called a halt to this generous practice. The reason for so doing was this. Inherent in this method of computing the damages attributable to the need for special accommodation was the danger that, with a multiplier at the top of the range which a young disabled claimant could easily command, the resulting amount would exceed the capital cost upon which it was designed to be interest. This situation eventually became a reality in *Roberts v Johnstone*.[924] The chosen multiplier of 16 when applied to a mortgage rate of 7 per cent took the figure above the cost of the new accommodation, specifically to 112 per cent of that cost.[925] Such an amount the court clearly could not award; it did "not comply", as Stocker LJ said,[926] "with the reasoning behind *George v Pinnock*".[927] **40-203**

Unfortunately, the Court of Appeal went to the other extreme and awarded only the 2 per cent contended for by the defendant. This percentage was derived from that adopted by the House of Lords in *Wright v British Railways Board*,[928] for interest on non-pecuniary loss in personal injury claims. But it is thought that the analogy from *Wright v British Railways Board*,[929] is a poor one, especially when that decision can be interpreted as reflecting a policy to cut back on interest for non-pecuniary loss which, it is strongly arguable, should never have been allowed in **40-204**

---

921 [1993] P.I.Q.R. Q166.

922 *Chapman v Lidstone* unreported 3 December 1982 (formerly set out in Kemp and Kemp, *The Quantum of Damages*, para.A3–006 but no longer as historical) afforded an illustration.

923 [1989] Q.B. 878 CA.

924 [1989] Q.B. 878 CA.

925 It had already got near in *Chapman v Lidstone* unreported 3 December 1982, where Forbes J with a multiplier of 14 and again a 7 per cent mortgage rate effectively awarded 98 per cent of the capital cost. Indeed Stocker LJ in *Roberts v Johnstone* [1989] Q.B. 878 CA at 891H–892A indicated that, with mortgage tax relief only available under the then current legislation on the first £30,000 borrowed, 9.1 per cent would have been a more realistic mortgage rate to take. This would have brought the award up to not far short of 150 per cent of the capital cost.

926 [1989] Q.B. 878 CA at 891C.

927 [1973] 1 W.L.R. 118 CA.

928 [1983] 2 A.C. 773.

929 [1983] 2 A.C. 773.

personal injury claims at all.[930] The practical result of this move to a 2 per cent rate at a time when multipliers were still worked out on a 4.5 per cent discount rate was that claimants would at best obtain by way of damages in the region of a third only of the capital cost of their new accommodation—30 per cent on a multiplier of 15, 36 per cent on one of 18—and were forced to resort to the moneys awarded for general damages for non-pecuniary loss and, to the extent they could afford to, to the award for loss of earning capacity, for the remaining funding of the special accommodation to which they were entitled.

**40-205** With the coming of the landmark House of Lords decisions in *Wells v Wells*,[931] and its associated cases, things improved somewhat. This resulted from a combination of two related factors, the one being the great increase in the size of multipliers with the discount rate reduced from 4.5 per cent to the 3 per cent chosen by the House of Lords in *Wells*,[932] and the other being the use, in place of the 2 per cent rate of interest for non-pecuniary loss, of the discount rate,[933] revised to 3 per cent, as was adopted by the House of Lords in *Thomas v Brighton Health Authority*,[934] one of the cases in the *Wells v Wells* trilogy.[935] Thus had, say, a 25-year-old female claimant required special accommodation for life, by taking the relevant life multiplier of 28.43 from the current Ogden tables and combining it with the then 3 per cent discount rate, 85 per cent of the capital outlay would have been recovered in damages. However, when the Lord Chancellor's discount rate of 2.5 per cent took over from the 3 per cent rate, this amount would be reduced to 70 per cent.

**40-206** Yet the inequity of not allowing the claimant sufficient money with which to acquire the needed accommodation, which the *Roberts v Johnstone*[936] method, however applied, does not give, remains to a degree and in very many cases to a very substantial degree. Such a case was *Oxborrow v West Sussex Hospitals NHS Trust*.[937] The claimant was so catastrophically injured at birth that he was expected to live only to the age of 21. This meant that the accommodation would be required for a comparatively short time starting from the date of trial. This led to a small multiplier of around 13 which, when applied to the 2.5 per cent discount rate, would provide the claimant with a little over 30 per cent of the value of the property envisaged. In these circumstances, in an application for an interim payment on account of damages to provide suitable accommodation for the claimant, his counsel argued that *Roberts v Johnstone* should not apply and that there should be adopted the solution suggested in earlier editions of this work, viz., that the claimant should be given the full purchase price but with a charge on the purchased property in

---

930 See para.19-053, above.
931 [1999] 1 A.C. 345.
932 See para.40-122, above.
933 As counsel for the claimant, Dr McGregor had argued for this approach in *Roberts v Johnstone* but unsuccessfully: see [1989] Q.B. 878 CA at 893A–B.
934 [1999] 1 A.C. 345. Overturning the Court of Appeal's 2 per cent and restoring the 3 per cent of the trial judge who had been prepared to derive the multiplier from the new 3 per cent discount rate, as appears from the report of the case at first instance at [1996] P.I.Q.R. Q44 at 60. Special accommodation was needed for the claimant with his parents for the first 16 years and then special accommodation on his own for a further eight years. A multiplier of 12 for the first period reflected the Ogden Tables 3 per cent figure of 12.12 (4.5 per cent would have given 10.98) while a multiplier of 17 (12 less 5) for the total period fitted with the Ogden 17.19 for 3 per cent (4.5 per cent comes out at 14.82).
935 See para.40-122, above.
936 [1989] Q.B. 878 CA.
937 [2012] EWHC 1010 (QB).

favour of the defendant realisable on the claimant's death.[938] Since the trial judge was prepared to award the interim payment asked for,[939] he was able to avoid taking a decision on counsel's argument but, while not wishing to express a view, he said that he saw considerable force in the argument.[940]

The *Roberts v Johnstone* method continues to attract criticism. In *Manna v Central Manchester University Hospitals NHS Foundation Trust*,[941] Tomlinson LJ described the exercise in which courts are engaged in modern conditions as £increasingly artificial" noting that the assumption that the claimant will be able to fund the capital acquisition out of the sums awarded is falsified by increasing residential property prices although general awards for pain, suffering and loss of amenity have remained at their traditional levels. Matters become worse for claimants with immediate and pressing needs but a relatively short life expectancy.[942] Unfortunately, it was not submitted that the Court should **40-207**

> "revisit the imperfect principles which have held sway since the decision … in *George v Pinnock*."[943]

Although Tomlinson LJ had described the *Roberts v Johnstone* method as "imperfect but pragmatic",[944] in *JR v Sheffield Teaching Hospitals NHS Foundation Trust*,[945] in a powerful judgment by William Davis J, it was recognised, including by reference to the following paragraph of this work which appeared in substantially the same form in the previous edition,[946] that applying the *Roberts v Johnstone* approach in that case unjustly led to a nil award for special accommodation.

It is high time that the *Roberts v Johnstone* problem was tackled and a fair and proper solution found and adopted. The Law Commission looked into the matter some time ago but found it too difficult to formulate an acceptable solution and so recommended that the *Roberts v Johnstone* method be retained.[947] The Ogden Working Party is fully aware that the law needs to be righted and has it in mind to investigate the issue in the near future. What could trigger action on this front is a further reduction in the discount rate, the possibility of which, as we have seen, is very much in the air.[948] It is true that, as the discount rate lowers, the multipliers increase, but an examination of the figures in the tables in Ogden shows that the increases in the multipliers do not come anywhere near to balancing, or off-setting the effect of, the fall in the discount rate. Ironically the injured party will get more for care but less for special accommodation. Indeed since February 2017 the discount rate has moved into the negative (-0.75%), the *Roberts v Johnstone* method **40-208**

---

938 [2012] EWHC 1010 (QB) at [9] and [44].

939 To justify the interim payment requested a whole range of figures which it is difficult adequately to comprehend appears in the judgment at [23] to [31].

940 [2012] EWHC 1010 (QB) at [47]. An alternative solution, which has also been put forward, is to have the defendant make an interest free loan to the claimant which will allow the property to be acquired, the loan to be repayable on the claimant's death, or at such earlier time as the accommodation is no longer required.

941 [2017] EWCA Civ 12 CA.

942 [2017] EWCA Civ 12 CA at [17].

943 [2017] EWCA Civ 12 CA at [19].

944 [2017] EWCA Civ 12 CA at [31].

945 [2017] EWHC 1245 (QB).

946 [2017] EWHC 1245 (QB) at [46].

947 In the Report on *Damages for Personal Injury: Medical, Nursing and Other Expenses; Collateral Benefits* (1999) Law Com. No.262.

948 See para.40-127, above.

becomes unworkable; it would produce a nil award as seen in *JR v Sheffield Teaching Hospitals NHS Foundation Trust*.[949]

### (B) General Method of Assessment

**40-209** Adapting and applying the particular method evolved by the courts for assessing earnings lost to the assessment of expenses incurred, the amount to be awarded would fall to be calculated by taking the figure of annual expenses and multiplying this by a figure which, while based upon the number of years during which the expenses will continue, is discounted to present value; the former figure, once again, is the multiplicand, the latter figure the multiplier. Where a lump sum is being awarded, this method is undoubtedly the one which the courts utilise in the great majority of cases involving future loss. Of course under the new regime of periodical payments—and periodical payments orders are becoming common today where the cost of long term care is in issue—no question of discounting to present value arises and the multiplicand/multiplier method has no relevance.

**40-210** There are, exceptionally, situations in which the court is entitled, because the future uncertainties are too great, to regard this conventional method of computation as inappropriate and to arrive simply at an overall figure after consideration of all the circumstances. Such a case was *Willbye v Gibbons*.[950] The claimant was a girl injured when aged 12 and at the time of trial some 10 years later receiving excellent support from her mother and the man with whom she was by then living. The judge below had been presented with a set of calculations of the extra assistance needed if she had children and if she was unsupported in later life by family, both of which were problematic, and the Court of Appeal held that it was wrong to make separate awards for such contingencies. Kennedy LJ said that

> "all that can realistically be done is to increase to some extent the fund available to the [claimant] to satisfy her need for assistance in the future, recognising the possible ways in which demands may be made upon that fund, but not attempting to evaluate separate types of potential demand, because if potential demands are separately evaluated it may well turn out that there is duplication, or that substantial awards have been made in respect of contingencies which have never happened."[951]

The Court of Appeal thus arrived at a global sum for future care which meant that the multiplicand/multiplier method did not feature in its pure form.[952]

**40-211** The multiplicand/multiplier method of assessment, had at one time received less attention in the field of medical and allied expenses because the appropriate circumstances for its use had arisen less frequently. This is because, although it is not at all uncommon for a claimant to be left with a permanent, or very prolonged, diminution in his earning capacity after an injury, there is frequently no need for continuing medical expenses after the immediate effects of the injury have been treated. However today, with advances in medical science, the courts have been dealing more and more with catastrophic injuries which do not prove fatal, with cases where life has been preserved but in such a wrecked condition that the victim

---

949 [2017] EWHC 1245 (QB).

950 [2004] P.I.Q.R. P15 CA at 227.

951 [2004] P.I.Q.R. P15 CA at [16].

952 Compare the same issue with loss of earnings, where there are more cases, at paras 40-067 and following, above.

requires constant care and attention for the rest of his days, and here the multiplicand/multiplier method once again has come into its own.[953]

*Mitchell v Mulholland (No.2)*,[954] was such a case, and was also said to constitute a test case on the method of assessment of damages for medical expenses as well as of damages for loss of earning capacity.[955] The Court of Appeal there adhered to the conventional method for the calculation of prospective medical expenses and refused to change to the actuarial method proposed by the claimant, thereby confirming the similar earlier cases where the conventional method had been used in relation to this head of damage without serious challenge. Times, however, have moved on since *Mitchell* was decided. While adherence to the method of multiplicand and multiplier continues, we now have the Ogden Tables which are actuarially based and the use of which has been both statutorily and, more importantly, judicially endorsed.[956] These assist, in the medical expenses context, in departing from the *Mitchell*,[957] approach in precisely the same way as they assist where loss of earnings is in issue. Indeed the various considerations to be taken into account, in their modern setting, in order to arrive at an appropriate multiplicand and multiplier for the assessment of lost earning capacity apply mutatis mutandis here and the earlier discussion should be referred to—the discounting for the lump sum award and the need for adjustments on account of contingencies, anticipated variations in loss, and the like.[958] In particular the discount rate allied to the return on ILGS[959] applies as much to medical and related expenses as it does to loss of earning capacity. However, as *Cooke v United Bristol Healthcare NHS Trust*,[960] establishes, no adjustment can be made to account for the discrepancy between retail price inflation, on which ILGS returns are based, and the much higher care costs inflation by tampering with the multiplicand.[961] 40-212

There are however certain differences, or variations, which do occur and need to be borne in mind when moving from an assessment for permanent loss of earning capacity to an assessment for permanently recurring medical expenses. They are these. 40-213

(1) The need for medical expenses will continue throughout the claimant's whole life whereas the loss of earning capacity will be limited to his working life. This calls for a higher multiplier. But for very many years it was common to find 40-214

---

953 The terminology of multiplicand and multiplier in relation to medical expenses now appears in countless cases; for an early, well-known case see *Mitchell v Mulholland (No.2)* [1972] 1 Q.B. 65 CA at 81G–82B and 88E–H. For the multiplicand see now the comments of Lord Lloyd in *Wells v Wells* [1999] 1 A.C. 345 at 377F: "In my view the Court of Appeal was right to scrutinise the individual items which went to make up the multiplicand. Since the effect of reducing the rate of discount (see paras 40-123 and following, above) is to increase the multiplier in every case, it is all the more important to keep firm control of the multiplicand. Claimants are entitled to a reasonable standard of care to meet their requirements, but that is all."

954 [1972] 1 Q.B. 65 CA.

955 [1972] 1 Q.B. 65 CA at 74D–E.

956 See paras 40-072 and 40-073, above.

957 [1972] 1 Q.B. 65 CA.

958 See paras 40-075 and following, above. Anticipated variations in loss, particularly in the cost of care, require an adjustment to multiplicand or multiplier and though, as with loss of earnings (see para.40-095, above), it may be more proper to adjust the multiplicand it is not at all unusual for the adjustment to be made to the multiplier: see, e.g. the Court of Appeal's discounting of the multiplier in *Hay v Koing* unreported 25 January 2002, by about a third in place of the trial judge's discount of only some 12 per cent.

959 See paras 40-119 and following, above.

960 [2004] 1 W.L.R. 251 CA.

961 This is fully considered at para.40-125, above.

in cases of adult working claimants that the same multiplier for the two items of loss was being used. Thus in *Mitchell v Mulholland (No.2)*,[962] the Court of Appeal had not thought that, in the case before it, the difference of six years which lay some 30 years in the future justified applying a higher multiplier for medical expenses than had been adopted for loss of earning capacity.[963] Fortunately, with the Ogden Tables now firmly established upon the personal injury litigation scene[964] attention is finally being paid to the need to apply the right multipliers where lifetime medical expenses are in issue. The Ogden Tables show quite clearly that the difference between the appropriate multipliers is significant. For a man of 35 retiring at 65—and this was the position assumed for the claimant in *Mitchell*—the working life multiplier, using the current 2.5 per cent discount rate, is 20.53 while the whole life multiplier is higher by seven at 27.51. And should the now 35-year-old be ceasing to work at 60, today a more and more common retirement age, the working life multiplier goes down to 18.23, thereby taking it below the whole life multiplier by over nine.[965]

**40-215** (2) It is well recognised by the courts that, where it is a young child that is injured for life, the multiplier for medical and related expenses will generally have to be much higher than that for loss of earning capacity because the medical and related expenses form an immediate outlay whereas the start of the claimant's working life is well into the future. Thus in *Connolly v Camden and Islington Area Health Authority*,[966] a multiplier of 13 was used for medical expenses and, effectively, one of 2.5 for loss of earning capacity, *Croke v Wiseman*,[967] ended up with multipliers of 14 and 5 respectively,[968] these being the multipliers substituted on appeal for the higher ones chosen by the trial judge, while in *Cassel v Riverside Health Authority*,[969] the multiplier of 18 for care costs passed unchallenged and the multiplier of 10 for earnings loss was upheld.[970]

**40-216** (3) Not all factors conspire to give a higher multiplier for medical and related expenses; some move the multiplier in the other direction. It was again in *Mitchell v Mulholland (No.2)*,[971] that the Court of Appeal, in arguing against the need for any increase in the multiplier on account of the claimant's life extending beyond his working life, pointed to the counterbalancing factor that some time in the future it might become necessary to transfer the claimant to a National Health hospital where his treatment would be free.[972] There is no doubt that this is an important consideration. While, as has been seen, a claimant is not required to use the free

---

[962] [1972] 1 Q.B. 65 CA.

[963] [1972] 1 Q.B. 65 CA at 82B, 88H–89A.

[964] See para.40-073, above.

[965] It is true that account must be taken of pensions following upon retirement; indeed Ogden deals with pensions: see 7th edition (2011) Tables 15 to 26. But an employment may well not entitle the employee to a pension and even where it does the pension is always at a substantially lower level than pensionable salary.

[966] [1981] 3 All E.R. 250; see at 255c–f.

[967] [1982] 1 W.L.R. 71 CA.

[968] It is now accepted that the earnings multiplier should have been higher because of a mistaken double discounting by Griffiths LJ (the error was pointed out in *Janardan v East Berkshire Health Authority* (1990) 2 Med. L.R. 1 and again in *Cassel v Riverside Health Authority* [1992] P.I.Q.R. Q168 CA) but the multiplier would not have been higher than 8 in any event.

[969] [1992] P.I.Q.R. Q168 CA.

[970] Ralph Gibson LJ, dissenting on this, would have brought the earnings multiplier down from 10 to 8.5.

[971] [1972] 1 Q.B. 65 CA.

[972] [1972] 1 Q.B. 65 CA at 89B. The reduction in the multiplier may be because, as in *Hay v Koing*

facilities offered by the National Health Service,[973] the court must take a view as to how far a claimant is likely to use them[974] or, as envisaged in what was said in *Mitchell*,[975] will be compelled to use them.

(4) Another factor which operates to keep this multiplier lower than the one for loss of earning capacity stems from the House of Lords decision in *Pickett v British Rail Engineering*.[976] The change, there introduced, from the post-injury to the pre-injury life expectation when assessing loss of earning capacity[977] can have no application to medical expenses. There can be no question of recovery for the lost years, years in which ex hypothesi the expenses will never be incurred. The post-injury life expectation has always provided the appropriate unit of measurement.[978] **40-217**

(5) It is much more likely with medical and related expenses than with earnings that the stages in which, and the times at which, the expenses will change over the years can be reasonably predicted with a degree of certainty. Thus with an injured child the costs of care may start low if he or she is being looked after at home by the family, increase upon adulthood and independence, and rise still further in old age whenever more assistance is likely to be needed. In circumstances like this the multiplier for the whole lifetime, worked out in the usual way, requires to be split as between the various different periods. The method to be used is this. Ascertain what would be the multiplier for the first period. Then ascertain what would be the multiplier if the first and second periods were combined; this multiplier less the first period multiplier provides the multiplier for the second period. Next ascertain what would be the multiplier for the combined first, second and third periods and deduct the multiplier, already ascertained, for the combined first and second periods to give the multiplier for the third period. And so on in this manner through as many periods as there are, the multiplier for the last period being the lifetime multiplier less the multiplier for the combined periods other than the last.[979] Illustrative of the splitting along these lines of the overall multiplier for the costs of care in cases taken to the Lords are *Hunt v Severs*,[980] and *Page v Sheerness Steel Co*,[981] the split being into three periods[982] and two periods[983] respectively.[984] A slightly earlier illustration is afforded by *Cassel v Riverside Health Authority*,[985] and there are many later ones. In *Whiten v St George's Healthcare NHS* **40-218**

---

unreported 25 January 2002, the need for care is likely to decrease in the future rather than that the care would come to be provided without cost to the claimant.

973 See para.40-186, above.

974 See para.40-187, above.

975 [1972] 1 Q.B. 65 CA.

976 [1980] A.C. 136.

977 See paras 40-105 and following, above.

978 See per Greer LJ as early as *Roach v Yates* [1938] 1 K.B. 256 CA at 263: the calculation must be "for the period during which the claimant may now be expected to live".

979 But this is not the right approach if the need for extra care later is distinctly uncertain, making the multiplicand/multiplier method inappropriate: see *Willbye v Gibbons* [2004] P.I.Q.R. P15 CA at 227 at para.40-210, above.

980 [1994] 2 A.C. 350.

981 [1999] 1 A.C. 345.

982 Multiplier of 14 split into 1, 9 and 4.

983 Multiplier of 24 split into 12 and 12.

984 The splitting of the multiplier was in issue in the House of Lords in neither case. This had been the work of the trial judge but it is clear that it had the approval of the higher courts: see Lord Lloyd in *Page v Sheerness Steel Co* [1999] 1 A.C. 345 at 381 B–D and Sir Thomas Bingham MR in *Hunt v Severs* [1993] Q.B. 815 CA at 837E and 841A.

985 [1992] P.I.Q.R. Q168 CA; 712 and 1012 split of multiplier of 18.

*Trust*,[986] there were computations for three care periods for the young claimant,[987] but multipliers did not come into it as the annual sums arrived at were ordered to be paid by periodical payments.

**40-219** (6) The House of Lords in *Thomas v Brighton Health Authority*,[988] fortunately finally ruled, in the face of a longstanding practice to the contrary, that, in assessing the cost of care over an injured person's life, there is no room for any discount for contingencies to the whole life multiplier based upon an agreed expectation of life; in arriving at that multiplier all the contingencies have already been taken into account.[989] The reasoning of Lord Bridge in *Hunt v Severs*,[990] to justify the reduction of a similar multiplier in *Hunt* was disapproved and Sir Thomas Bingham MR's approach, which had produced an undiscounted whole life multiplier in the Court of Appeal in *Hunt*,[991] was endorsed.[992] This then is in contrast to the assessment for loss of earning capacity where it is permissible to apply discounts for contingencies to the multiplier although it is thought that these should generally be modest.[993] It is appropriate to take, for cost of care, the whole life multiplier without any discount not only when it is based upon an agreed life expectation that is shorter, often substantially shorter, than the norm, as in *Thomas*, but also when it is the judge who decides what is the shorter life expectancy,[994] as in *Ruff v Royal Victoria Infirmary*,[995] and in *Royal Victoria Infirmary v B*,[996] and also indeed when it is normal life expectancy that applies in the particular case. With normal expectancy the relevant Ogden Table of multipliers for pecuniary loss for life is to be utilised, but where the expectation of life is truncated, there have been uncertainties as to the proper way to approach Ogden.

**40-220** Thus within the last ten years the question has arisen, when assessing lifetime care where a loss of expectation of life has been established, as to which Ogden table is the appropriate one to use. Defendants argue for the table of multipliers for pecuniary loss for life, that is, Table 1 for males and Table 2 for females, adding to the claimant's actual age the number of years by which his or her life expectation is held to have been reduced or, alternatively, making an assessment of how many years of the normal life expectancy remain to him or her, in other words by deciding how many years the claimant will now live rather than by deciding by how many years the claimant's life expectation has been reduced. Claimants on the other hand argue for the Ogden table of multipliers for pecuniary loss for term certain, the certain term being the number of years that the claimant will now live; this is found in Table 28 and invariably, for reasons which will appear, produces a somewhat higher figure than is arrived at by the first method. We now have four first instance cases, all with male claimants, applying Table 1—*Tinsley v Sarkar*,[997]

---

986 [2011] EWHC 2066 (QB).

987 To the age of 11, from 11 to 19, from 19 onwards: see [2011] EWHC 2066 (QB) at [179] and following.

988 [1999] 1 A.C. 345.

989 See Lord Lloyd, who alone gave a reasoned speech upon this issue, at [1999] 1 A.C. 345 at 378B–E.

990 [1994] 2 A.C. 350.

991 [1993] Q.B. 815 CA.

992 See Lord Lloyd at [1999] 1 A.C. 345 at 379A–E.

993 See paras 40-131 and following, above.

994 As he is entitled to do: *Royal Victoria Infirmary v B* [2003] P.I.Q.R. Q10 CA at 137.

995 [2001] Lloyd's Rep. Med. 530.

996 [2003] P.I.Q.R. Q10 CA at 137.

997 [2006] P.I.Q.R. Q1 at l.

*Crofts v Murton*,[998] *Smith v LC Window Fashions Ltd*,[999] and *Ali v Caton and Motor Insurers' Bureau*[1000]—and three first instance cases applying Table 28—*Sarwar v Ali and Motor Insurers' Bureau*,[1001] *Burton v Kingsbury*,[1002] and *Whiten v St George's Healthcare NHS Trust*,[1003] together with an earlier Court of Appeal case, *Royal Victoria Infirmary v B*,[1004] where no clear choice was made between Ogden Tables as the court was relying upon the evidence of competing experts as to life expectation. It is considered that the choice should favour Table 28. This is because, since mortality will already have been taken into account in coming to a view on life expectancy, to use Tables 1 or 2 will result in a double discount, evidenced by the fact that the use of Tables 1 and 2 invariably produces a somewhat lower figure than emerges from use of Table 28. It is true that Ogden argues for the use of Tables 1 and 2 rather than Table 28 in para.20 of its explanatory notes, a paragraph relied on by the defendant's counsel in a number of the above cases, but, as Flaux J suggested in *Burton*, the point about the double discount appears to have been missed by Ogden.[1005] And a justification for the application of Table 1 in the three cases so doing is given by Swift J in her valuable and full discussion of the arguments and authorities in the latest case of *Whiten*.[1006] She pointed out that in the cases applying Table 1

> "the medical evidence related only to the reduction of life expectancy caused by a number of identified factors specifically relating to the claimant and the injury which is the subject of the claim".[1007]

If this be the case, then taking other aspects of mortality into account would not lead to a double discount. In *Manna (A Child) v Central Manchester University Hospitals NHS Foundation Trust*,[1008] Cox J applied Table 28, recognising[1009] that the application of Table 1 would cause a double discount.

### (C) The Deductibility of Collateral Benefits

Except in one or two areas, the question of whether or not collateral benefits are deductible has not received the same degree of attention in relation to recovery of medical and allied expenses as it has in relation to recovery for loss of earning capacity.[1010] However, it remains necessary, once again, to examine each particular type of collateral benefit separately, although it may be said in advance that the current position is that, in this context, collateral benefits throughout do not operate so as to reduce the damages, with the one clear exception of social security benefits, both monetary and non-monetary. **40-221**

---

998 *Crofts v Murton* unreported 5 September 2008.
999 [2009] EWHC 1532 (QB).
1000 [2013] EWHC 1730 (QB).
1001 [2007] LS Law Med. 375.
1002 [2007] EWHC 2091 (QB).
1003 [2011] EWHC 2066 (QB).
1004 [2003] P.I.Q.R. Q10 CA at 137.
1005 [2007] EWHC 2091 (QB) at [47].
1006 [2011] EWHC 2066 (QB) at [87]–[104].
1007 [2011] EWHC 2066 (QB) at [100]. And see Stuart-Smith LJ's very full treatment of the issue, leading him to application of Table 1, in *Ali v Caton and Motor Insurers' Bureau* [2013] EWHC 1730 (QB) at [299]–[311].
1008 [2015] EWHC 2279 (QB).
1009 [2015] EWHC 2279 at [185].
1010 See paras 40-149 and following, above.

### 1. Insurance Moneys

**40-222** Where a claimant's medical expenses have been paid for him under a private medical insurance scheme to which he subscribes, such as that run by BUPA or Axa PPP,[1011] the question of whether he is entitled nevertheless to claim the expenses as part of his damages is a question which does not arise because the insurances under these schemes, unlike the accident policies considered when dealing with loss of earning capacity,[1012] are regarded as indemnity insurances which entitle the insurers themselves to recover their outlays directly from the tortfeasor through the medium of subrogation. Thus the injured party has no standing to claim the medical expenses; he has been made whole by his insurers who in their turn step into his shoes and make the claim for the moneys expended by them.[1013] However, the claimant may have an accident insurance policy, the moneys from which he can deploy as he cares between the payment of his medical expenses and the replenishment of his lost earnings, or which indeed he may spend in any other way he chooses. Here there should be no deduction; the analogy of the non-deductibility of insurance moneys in relation to loss of earnings—a rule unanimously supported by their Lordships in *Parry v Cleaver*,[1014] and adverted to with approval in the House three times 20 years later[1015]—is bound to prevail since the argument in favour of non-deduction, namely that the claimant has paid for the insurance with his own moneys and should not be deprived of the fruits of his thrift and foresight to the defendant's advantage,[1016] applies as much in this context as in the other.

### 2. Payments Under Obligation by Private Third Parties other than Insurers

**40-223** Where the claimant's medical expenses are paid by employer, husband or parent upon whom rests an obligation to pay them, whether by contract or under the general law, it once seemed that the claimant could not include these expenses within his or her claim for damages. Thus in relation to a wife, Diplock J in *Gage v King*,[1017] refused recovery of the expenses incurred for the claimant wife's medical care, which had been paid by her husband, in the absence of a legal liability on the wife to pay for them. Instead, recovery was allowed in the *actio per quod consortium et servitium amisit* to the husband, parent or employer who had paid the medical expenses, although this solution was generally of little value to the employer once the action *per quod* had become restricted, in the employment field, to claims in respect of servants who were members of their master's domestic household.[1018] Now, however, the courts have inclined to the view that recovery for such medical expenses should go to the wife, child and servant themselves, a solu-

---

1011 The two principal private medical insurance schemes.

1012 See para.40-150, above.

1013 Alternatively, the claimant may be held entitled, as in *Horton v Evans* [2007] EWHC 315 (QB), to be awarded the medical expenses her insurers had already paid as her insurance policy made it clear that principles of subrogation placed her under the obligation in equity to account to the insurers for them: see at [11]–[17].

1014 [1970] A.C. 1.

1015 The three cases, and *Parry*, are at para.40-150, above.

1016 See para.40-150 in fin., above.

1017 [1961] 1 Q.B. 188.

1018 *I.R.C. v Hambrook* [1956] 2 Q.B. 641 CA.

tion stemming primarily from the decision in *Donnelly v Joyce*,[1019] and fitting well with the final demise of the action *per quod*.[1020] This new approach therefore entails no deductions in respect of these payments. Whether now, with the overruling of *Donnelly v Joyce*,[1021] in *Hunt v Severs*,[1022] in the context of the provision of care,[1023] the claimant will have to hold the payments in trust, does not appear yet to have been litigated. It is greatly to be hoped that the unfortunate result in *Hunt v Severs*,[1024] will not be pushed to this extreme.

### 3. PAYMENTS MADE GRATUITOUSLY BY THIRD PARTIES

No deduction should fall to be made where the claimant's medical expenses have been paid gratuitously by a private individual, company or charity. In *Parry v Cleaver*,[1025] the House of Lords unanimously accepted the propriety of making no deduction, in assessing damages for loss of earning capacity, in respect of moneys gratuitously conferred from private sources upon a claimant as a mark of sympathy and assistance,[1026] and the same reasoning should equally apply where the moneys have been conferred in order to cover medical expenses. Indeed, as with insurance moneys,[1027] the amount paid to the claimant may not be specifically earmarked for medical expenses but may be for use, at his discretion, in offsetting the pecuniary losses he has incurred; this would seem to have been the case both in *Redpath v Belfast & County Down Ry*,[1028] and in *Cunningham v Harrison*.[1029] Nor should it make any difference that the moneys are not paid to the claimant but applied directly by the benefactor in payment of the medical expenses. Whether, once again, there is now, with the overruling in *Hunt v Severs*,[1030] of *Donnelly v Joyce*,[1031] a requirement that the moneys paid be held in trust by the claimant does not appear yet to have been litigated. Once again our hope is that the result in *Hunt v Severs*,[1032] will not be pushed to this unfortunate extreme. 40-224

### 4. CARE PROVIDED GRATUITOUSLY BY RELATIVES AND OTHERS

## (1) The provider of the care

### (a) Care by third parties

*(i) The development of the law* Third parties, in particular relatives of an incapacitated person, may provide him with the required care and attendance and so save him the expense of a paid nurse and the like. In these circumstances it was for long thought that the claimant could not claim to be awarded damages based on 40-225

---

[1019] [1974] Q.B. 454 CA.
[1020] For this demise see para.40-001, above, in a footnote.
[1021] [1974] Q.B. 454 CA.
[1022] [1994] 2 A.C. 350.
[1023] See para.40-228, below.
[1024] [1994] 2 A.C. 350.
[1025] [1970] A.C. 1.
[1026] See para.40-159, above.
[1027] See para.40-222, above.
[1028] [1947] N.I. 167.
[1029] [1973] Q.B. 942 CA.
[1030] [1994] 2 A.C. 350.
[1031] [1974] Q.B. 454 CA; see para.40-228, below.
[1032] [1994] 2 A.C. 350.

the value of the attendance which had been rendered to him without charge, especially if the benefactor had incurred no positive financial loss by giving up other employment or by himself incurring expenses. This result was implicit in cases where a wife was prepared to care for her seriously incapacitated husband until such time as the task became too great for her, after which her husband would have to enter a home or institution, and the damages for the cost of outside care were calculated only from the time when it was anticipated that the husband would be transferred to the home or institution.[1033] This position eventually totally changed.

**40-226** The starting point is *Roach v Yates*,[1034] a decision of the Court of Appeal said to have been, though far-reaching, little noticed in this connection.[1035] The claimant, rendered a helpless invalid by the injury, recovered substantial damages for the prospective cost of nursing attendance which he was receiving gratuitously at the hands of his wife and sister-in-law who had given up paid work in order to care for him. Much later, cases began to appear in which claimants were awarded the wages that their relatives had given up to be free to look after them,[1036] but there was occasionally a tendency to require, notably in *Haggar v De Placido*,[1037] that, before the claimant could recover, the relative had entered into a legal agreement with him for reimbursement. Then the whole issue came up for consideration, simultaneously, by two divisions of the Court of Appeal in *Cunningham v Harrison*,[1038] and *Donnelly v Joyce*.[1039] In *Cunningham v Harrison*,[1040] the wife had not given up paid work to look after her now tetraplegic husband, but it was nevertheless held that he was entitled to damages for the value of her nursing services and that the legal agreement for reimbursement into which, on advice, the parties had entered was totally unnecessary in order to permit such recovery. In *Donnelly v Joyce*,[1041] a mother had given up her job so as to be able to attend to her son, injured at the age of six, and the judge had awarded damages to the infant claimant by reference to his mother's loss of wages; in upholding this award the Court of Appeal not only affirmed that a legal obligation to reimburse the benefactor was unnecessary,[1042] overruling *Haggar v De Placido*,[1043] but laid down that neither was a moral obligation.[1044] This is still the position today, as is the denial of the argument that awards for gratuitous care should be reserved for very serious cases, an argument roundly rejected by the Court of Appeal in *Giambrone v JMC Holidays Ltd*.[1045]

**40-227** In addition in *Donnelly v Joyce*, the Court of Appeal rejected the argument that the claimant's claim was in relation to someone else's loss because it was someone

---

1033 See, e.g. *Fletcher v Autocar & Transporters* [1968] 2 Q.B. 322 CA, especially at 334 and 349.

1034 [1938] 1 K.B. 256 CA.

1035 See *Donnelly v Joyce* [1974] Q.B. 454 CA at 464E–465E where the case is fully considered.

1036 *Wattson v Port of London Authority* [1969] 1 Lloyd's Rep. 95 (husband successfully claimed wages given up by wife); *George v Pinnock* [1973] 1 W.L.R. 118 CA (daughter successfully claimed wages given up by mother; unaffected by contingency of claimant having to go permanently into hospital as it was unlikely mother would be able to obtain new employment: see at 124E–F).

1037 [1972] 1 W.L.R. 716.

1038 [1973] Q.B. 942 CA.

1039 [1974] Q.B. 454 CA.

1040 [1978] Q.B. 942 CA.

1041 [1974] Q.B. 454 CA.

1042 See [1974] Q.B. 454 CA at 463E–464D.

1043 [1972] 1 W.L.R. 716.

1044 See [1974] Q.B. 454 CA at 462H–463D, agreeing "with that part of the judgment of Paull J in *Schneider v Eisovitch* [1960] 2 Q.B. 430 at 440 in which he said that the existence of a moral obligation is not a material factor".

1045 [2004] 2 All E.R. 891 CA. See the decision at para.40-237, below.

else who had provided the gratuitous services which fell to be valued in money.[1046] Megaw LJ, delivering the judgment of the court, said:

> "The loss *is* the claimant's loss. The question from what source the claimant's needs have been met, the question who has paid the money or given the services, the question whether or not the claimant is or is not under a legal or moral liability to repay, are, so far as the defendant and his liability are concerned, all irrelevant. The claimant's loss … is not the expenditure of money … to pay for the nursing attention. His loss is the existence of the need for … those nursing services, the value of which for purposes of damages—for the purpose of the ascertainment of the amount of his loss—is the proper and reasonable cost of supplying [that need]. That, in our judgment, is the key to the problem. So far as the defendant is concerned, the loss is not someone else's loss. It is the claimant's loss."[1047]

*(ii) The changed position: the introduction of a trust* The House of Lords 20 years later in *Hunt v Severs*,[1048] rejected the analysis in *Donnelly v Joyce*,[1049] and overruled it. "By concentrating", said Lord Bridge with whom the other members of the House agreed, **40-228**

> "on the claimant's need and the claimant's loss as the basis of an award in respect of voluntary care received by the claimant, the reasoning in *Donnelly v Joyce* diverts attention from the award's central objective of compensating the voluntary carer."[1050]

Their Lordships therefore adopted the view of Lord Denning MR expressed obiter in *Cunningham v Harrison*,[1051] the decision arrived at the day before *Donnelly* by a differently constituted Court of Appeal, that the damages recovered by the claimant in respect of gratuitous care should be held by the claimant in trust for the carer.[1052]

It is doubtful whether this development is to be welcomed, as the trust concept, **40-229**
which the courts previously, Lord Denning MR apart, had been assiduous to avoid,[1053] raises some difficult questions in its application. Two may be asked. What happens to the moneys if the claimant dies unexpectedly before the damages run out? If the claimant becomes insolvent would the carer have preferential status among the creditors, even an entitlement to trace the trust moneys? It would not seem that their Lordships considered or were made aware of the difficulties presented by the trust concept, the reality being that the House of its own accord grasped at the opportunity to introduce it[1054] in order to provide themselves with an argument for denying the claimant recovery when, as in the case before their Lord-

---

1046 [1974] Q.B. 454 CA at 461H–462A.

1047 [1974] Q.B. 454 CA at 462A–C. But recovery is not possible where, rather than care being provided gratuitously, gratuitous assistance is provided by the relative in the injured person's business: *Hardwick v Hudson* [1999] 1 W.L.R. 1770 CA, at para.40-081, above.

1048 [1994] 2 A.C. 350.

1049 [1974] Q.B. 454 CA.

1050 [1994] 2 A.C. 350 at 361–363.

1051 [1973] Q.B. 942 CA at 952B. As Denning J he had put the idea into effect very much earlier in a different context in *Dennis v London Transport Passanger Board* [1948] 1 All E.R. 779: see para.10-031, above.

1052 Lord Bridge pointed out that their Lordships' decision would bring English law in line with Scots law which in 1982 had statutorily imposed upon pursuers an obligation to account to their gratuitous carers; the Scots provision is set out by him at [1994] 2 A.C. 350 at 361–363.

1053 The Pearson Commission, in endorsing the entitlement to recover in respect of gratuitous services, recommended that the claimant should not have a legal obligation to account to, or to hold the damages in trust for, the provider: (HMSO, 1978), Cmnd.7054–1, paras 343 to 351.

1054 This passage was included in a previous edition of this work by Dr McGregor, who was counsel for

ships, it was the defendant himself who was the carer. What, it was said, would be the point of requiring the defendant to pay sums which would then be held in trust for him?[1055] It has, however, been said by the judge in *Drake v Foster Wheeler Ltd*,[1056] that a trust need not now be established and that the court may, since the introduction of the CPR, direct that the defendant pay the judgment sum straight to the carer.[1057] But in *Drake*, which was a claim by the estate on the injured person's death,[1058] only care which was necessarily over and past by the time of trial was in issue. It would be difficult to adopt this solution to awards for care which were to run well into the future.

**40-230** *(iii) Care outside the family relationship* The authorities dealt with so far have all concerned, naturally enough, care provided by family members. Now in *Drake v Foster Wheeler Ltd*,[1059] recovery has been allowed for the palliative care provided gratuitously by a charitable hospice foundation to a man dying from much earlier contact with asbestos. The man having died, the claim was by the estate, but since the estate was suing in respect of the damage suffered during the deceased's lifetime, the case is clearly relevant at this point. The trial judge rightly took the view that recovery for gratuitous care was not confined to care given by family members.[1060]

**40-231** **(b) Care provided by the defendant** In *Hunt v Severs*,[1061] the House of Lords, reversing a unanimous Court of Appeal[1062] which had upheld the trial judge, decided that a claimant who was cared for by the defendant himself could not recover damages in respect of that care.[1063] "There can", said Lord Bridge,

> "be no ground in public policy or otherwise for requiring the tortfeasor to pay to the claimant, in respect of the services which he himself has rendered, a sum of money which the claimant must then repay to him",[1064]

the obligation to repay stemming from the imposition, for the first time, of a trust upon the claimant.[1065] The fact that the payer would be not the tortfeasor but the tortfeasor's insurance company was held to be immaterial; this reality had to be ignored.[1066]

**40-232** This is an unfortunate decision which has been widely criticised. Its approach may be logical but experience, the life of the law, tells us that it will tend to dry up

the claimant.

[1055] This is dealt with at paras 40-231 and 40-232, below. Fortunately, and as was to be expected, families have not rushed into litigation to wrest damages from injured victim to voluntary carer. The difficulties presented by the introduction of the trust concept into this area of damages did however have to be tackled in *Hughes v Lloyd* [2007] EWHC 3133 Ch where not only had the carer died but the damages had not been awarded by the time of her death. The case has all the marks of a family squabble.

[1056] [2011] 1 All E.R. 63.

[1057] [2011] 1 All E.R. 63 at [43].

[1058] See the case in the next paragraph.

[1059] [2011] 1 All E.R. 63.

[1060] See [2011] 1 All E.R. 63 at [31] and following..

[1061] [1994] 2 A.C. 350.

[1062] [1993] Q.B. 815 CA.

[1063] The defendant's travelling expenses in visiting the claimant in hospital were also disallowed.

[1064] [1994] 2 A.C. 350 at 363.

[1065] See para.40-228, above.

[1066] [1994] 2 A.C. 350 at 363.

the wells of human kindness and, in so doing, will lead to less attractive routes to the achievement of the claimant's care. Claimants will be advised, and encouraged, to employ professional outsiders in order to recover for their care, thereby making it more expensive for defendants and their insurers than under the decision of the Court of Appeal in *Hunt v Severs*[1067]; hence the final result in the case has been called a Pyrrhic victory.[1068] Another form of advice that claimants will receive is to obtain unpaid assistance from a relative other than the defendant who is likely to prove a less appropriate carer than the defendant. A third possibility is that claimants will be urged to enter into legal contracts with their defendant carers, a practice which had grown up in the old days before *Cunningham v Harrison*,[1069] and *Donnelly v Joyce*,[1070] put paid to the necessity for it.[1071] In *Housecroft v Burnett*,[1072] O'Connor LJ said that he was

> "very anxious that there should be no resurrection of the practice of claimants making contractual agreements with relatives to pay for what are in fact gratuitous services rendered out of love".[1073]

Now in the limited, but not unlikely, context of defendant carers this can well happen. It has even been suggested that it would constitute professional negligence on the part of the claimant's solicitor or other adviser if he failed to recommend one of these three courses.[1074]

## (2) Amount to be awarded

After more than a decade of making awards in respect of the care lavished upon accident victims by those close to them, the courts became concerned that, once such awards had moved from being assessed at nil, there was nothing in logic to stop them being assessed at the full, generally very high, commercial rate for supplying the claimant's needs by employing someone to do what the relative does.[1075] Referring in *Housecroft v Burnett*,[1076] to these as the "two extreme solutions",[1077] the Court of Appeal sought an intermediate, compromise position. The case involved a catastrophic injury to a young girl of 16 who, it was anticipated, would be looked after for the whole of her life expectancy by her mother aided by a degree of paid outside care. O'Connor LJ, in the only reasoned judgment given, said of the sum assessed in respect of the mother's care: **40-233**

> "Once it is understood that this is an element in the award to the claimant to provide for

1067 [1993] Q.B. 815 CA.

1068 By Roderick Doggett in *Quantum*, 6 May 1994.

1069 [1973] Q.B. 942 CA.

1070 [1974] Q.B. 454 CA.

1071 See para.40-226, above.

1072 [1986] 1 All E.R. 332 CA; see this case at para.40-223, below.

1073 [1986] 1 All E.R. 332 CA at 343c.

1074 The Law Commission in its Consultation Paper (1996), No.144, *Damages for Personal Injury: Medical, Nursing and Other Expenses*, gave a provisional view that there should be a legislative reversal of *Hunt v Severs*: para.3-68, and has since recommended reversal, in reporting after having conducted its normal consultation process: see Law Commission Report (1999), Law Com. No.262, para.3-76. The overwhelming majority of its consultees, numbering among them individuals of the highest legal distinction, had agreed with the Commission's provisional view: see para.3-69.

1075 *Taylor v Glass* [1979] C.L.Y. 672 is an illustration of the use of the commercial rate referred to in *Housecroft v Burnett* [1986] 1 All E.R. 332 CA at 343a.

1076 [1986] 1 All E.R. 332 CA.

1077 [1986] 1 All E.R. 332 CA at 342h.

the reasonable and proper care of the claimant and that a capital sum is to be available for that purpose, the court should look at it as a whole and consider whether, on the facts of the case, it is sufficient to enable the claimant, among other things, to make reasonable recompense to the relative. So, in cases where the relative has given up gainful employment to look after the claimant, I would regard it as natural that the claimant would not wish the relative to be the loser and the court would award sufficient to enable the claimant to achieve that result. The ceiling would be the commercial rate. In cases like the present I would look at the award … and ask: is this sufficient to provide for the claimant's needs, including enabling her to make some monetary acknowledgment of her appreciation of all that her mother does for her? I would ask: is it sufficient for this claimant should her mother fall by the wayside and be unable to give as she gives now? I have no doubt that in this case the answer is Yes to both questions.

The court is recognising that part of the reasonable and proper cost of providing for the claimant's needs is to enable her to make a present, or series of presents, to her mother.[1078] Neither of the extreme solutions is right. The assessment will be somewhere in between, depending on the facts of the case."[1079]

**40-234** No precise guidance has emerged as to how far down from the commercial rate the courts should come. It is thought reasonable that the courts should be influenced by the level of the commercial rate so that, the higher that rate is, the greater the percentage reduction called for. In *Housecroft v Burnett*,[1080] itself the reduction was one of 20 per cent—a multiplicand of £3,000 as against the cost per annum of a housekeeper of £3,640.[1081] In *Nash v Southmead Health Authority*,[1082] a one-third reduction was applied to the commercial rate while in *Fairhurst v St Helens and Knowsley Health Authority*,[1083] the reduction was only of one-quarter on the basis that the care given by the parents of the injured girl involved special skills which the commercial carer would not have. In *Evans v Pontypridd Roofing Ltd*,[1084] the Court of Appeal stated that it would be inappropriate for it to lay down a conventional formalised calculation, and a conventional scaling down percentage, for the assessment of the proper recompense for the gratuitous services of a family carer; it was all dependent upon what was appropriate in the individual case.[1085] At the same time the Court of Appeal appeared to regard a deduction of 25 per cent—which was the figure taken by the trial judge and supported by the Court of Appeal in *Evans*—as appropriate in a case which could be described as normal.[1086] Indeed in *Willbye v Gibbons*,[1087] that court reiterated what it had said in *Evans* to the effect that there was no conventional discount and held the trial judge's deduction of 25 per cent in respect of past care to be a perfectly permissible approach.[1088] A discount of 25 per cent also appeared in *Tinsley v Sarkar*,[1089] while in *Massey v*

---

1078 But after *Hunt v Severs* [1994] 2 A.C. the gift will have become a trust: see para.40-228, above.
1079 [1986] 1 All E.R. 332 CA at 343d–g.
1080 [1986] 1 All E.R. 332 CA.
1081 See [1986] 1 All E.R. 332 CA at 341e.
1082 [1993] P.I.Q.R. Q156.
1083 [1995] P.I.Q.R. Q1.
1084 [2002] P.I.Q.R. Q5 CA at 61.
1085 [2002] P.I.Q.R. Q5 CA at [25] and [37], per May LJ.
1086 See especially at [38], per May LJ. *Evans* was applied in *FM v Ipswich Hospital NHS Trust* [2015] EWHC 775 (QB), giving a discount of 25 per cent in preference to the defendant's proposal of a one third discount.
1087 [2004] P.I.Q.R. P15 CA at 227.
1088 See [2004] P.I.Q.R. P15 CA at [10].
1089 [2006] P.I.Q.R. Q1 at 1; see at [31]–[33].

*Tameside Glossop Acute Services NHS Trust*,[1090] not only was the commercial rate taken at the higher end but the discount was only of 20 per cent.[1091] So too in *Manning v King's College Hospital NHS Trust*,[1092] the trial judge, after a very lengthy discussion of the authorities and the arguments of counsel,[1093] discounted by 20 per cent.

It is not uncommon for the relative to give up his or her employment in order the better to care for the injured person and in two such cases the trial judge had awarded one-and-a-half times the earnings foregone because the care afforded was so extensive. The Court of Appeal in *Hogg v Doyle*,[1094] where the care was by the claimant's wife, herself a nurse, who had apparently given up her nursing work to care for her husband, upheld the trial judge's award since the employment of two full-time nurses would have been justified and the amount awarded would not have covered that cost. The reduction overall was therefore of one-quarter. It is, however, highly exceptional to find that the relative is doing the work of two full-time carers.[1095] By contrast, the Court of Appeal in *Fitzgerald v Ford*,[1096] distinguishing *Hogg v Doyle*, which was said by the court to turn on its very special facts, held that the trial judge was wrong to have awarded one-and-a-half times the earnings of a husband who had given up his employment to care for his injured wife and substituted his actual earnings, which appear from the calculations of Stuart-Smith LJ, who gave the leading judgment, to have been some 25 per cent below the commercial rate.[1097] When O'Connor LJ in *Housecroft v Burnett*,[1098] indicated that, where the relative has given up paid employment, the court should award the amount of remuneration thus foregone up to the commercial rate,[1099] it is thought that there is an implication that, if the relative has given up employment which paid him or her less than what the court would award to a relative who had not given up paid employment and was therefore entitled to the cost of commercial care as discounted, the same award should be made to both. This seems only right, though it is contrary to Stuart-Smith LJ's approach in *Fitzgerald v Ford*.[1100] **40-235**

The above cases are ones in which the recovery allowed for care was in an amount lower than its commercial cost. O'Connor LJ's objective in *Housecroft* was to stem the tide of cases awarding the high commercial rates to relatives rendering **40-236**

---

1090 [2007] EWHC 317 (QB) (Admin).

1091 [2007] EWHC 317 (QB) (Admin) at [37]–[44]. In *Massey* the voluntary carer had received the social security care allowance and this fell to be deducted from the damages awarded for care: see at [51]–[53]. For the deduction of social security benefits relating to medical expenses see paras 40-239 and following, below.

1092 [2008] EWHC 3008 (QB).

1093 [2008] EWHC 3008 (QB) at [82]–[103].

1094 *Hogg v Doyle* unreported 6 March 1991, CA.

1095 Although *Almond v Leeds Western Health Authority* (1990) 1 Med. L.R. 370 was not a case where the carer had given up employment, the award of the trial judge for the past parental care of an injured child was based upon the cost of two professional residential carers. This was because the parents had given more time to the child than the professionals would have done. Here two relatives were involved and only half of the professional cost was allowed.

1096 [1996] P.I.Q.R. Q72 CA.

1097 See [1996] P.I.Q.R. Q72 CA at 78.

1098 [1986] 1 All E.R. 332 CA.

1099 See the citation from his judgment in para.40-233, above.

1100 Where in *Totham v King's College Hospital NHS Foundation Trust* [2015] EWHC 97 (QB) a mother had given up a well-paid job to care for her daughter brain damaged at birth, the trial judge's award of only the commercial rate discounted in the usual way is surely wrong: see at [23]–[28].

care out of love and affection.[1101] He was not concerned with the position where the cost to the caring relative is in excess of the commercial cost, as where a husband in order to look after his badly injured wife gives up a well-paying job, and therefore the comment in his judgment that the commercial care cost imposes a cap on the damages was strictly obiter. Nevertheless commentators have taken this to represent the law, but it is suggested that it may not be for the following reasons. It is the case that the loss to the injured wife can properly be relieved by acquiring reasonable care for herself, and what could be more reasonable than to be looked after by a devoted husband rather than by carers who, while professionally qualified, are strangers to her. Should it be argued that in choosing what turns out to be the more expensive husband as carer rather than the outside professionals constitutes a failure to mitigate, this argument fails to take into account the many authorities, collected when dealing with mitigation,[1102] which show that reasonable action that increases a loss does not deprive the claimant from recovering for that increase. Nor does such an argument sit well with the recent ground-breaking decision, in a related field, of *Peters v East Midlands Strategic Health Authority*,[1103] that an injured person has the right to choose between private care and State-funded care.[1104] The sole criterion is reasonableness.[1105]

**40-237** Special factors appear in a variety of cases. In *Lindsay v Wood*,[1106] the severely brain damaged claimant had applied to join his wife, living in Australia, who would care for him there. But there was only a 20 per cent chance that the application would succeed. Accordingly, the trial judge indicated the amounts he would award for the care the claimant would require living alone in the United Kingdom and for the care if looked after by his wife, in order to enable the parties to calculate the damages on the basis of that 20 per cent chance. In *Giambrone v JMC Holidays Ltd*,[1107] also has special features. The claimants were mainly young children who had developed gastroenteritis when on holiday abroad and were cared for by their parents on return home. The Court of Appeal upheld the trial judge's award for the value of gratuitous care on the basis that such awards might be allowed if a claimant's illness or injury was sufficiently serious to give rise to a need for care and attendance significantly over and above that which would be given anyway in the ordinary course of family life. The court rejected the defendant's submission that awards to compensate for gratuitous care could only be made in very serious cases.[1108] Brooke LJ, with whose sole judgment the other members of the court agreed, asked where would be the borderline between cases justifying an award and cases for no award, and considered that to have

---

1101 In a previous edition of this work, Dr McGregor said that this was known to him as O'Connor LJ discussed the issue with him at the time that the case was before the Court of Appeal.

1102 At paras 9-102 to 9-107, above.

1103 [2010] Q.B. 48 CA.

1104 See the decision at para.40-191, above.

1105 It was a barrister, Jamie Carpenter, who alerted Dr McGregor to this issue. We are in agreement that in appropriate cases, which are likely to be exceptional, the commercial cost should not be a cap on the recoverable damages.

1106 [2007] EWHC 853 (QB).

1107 [2004] 2 All E.R. 891 CA.

1108 This submission had been based on certain equivocal passages in *Mills v British Rail Engineering Ltd* [1992] P.I.Q.R. Q130 CA.

"an arbitrary dividing line, which would be likely to differ from case to case, and from judge to judge, would be likely to bring the law into disrepute."[1109]

At the same time the Court of Appeal considered that awards for gratuitous care in excess of £50 a week at then current values in cases in which a child suffering from gastroenteritis receives care from the family should be reserved for cases more serious than the ones before the court. It was considered that such sum represented a fair and proportionate balance

"between the consideration that some payment ought to be made for the unpleasant additional burden placed on the family carer and the consideration that the care is being rendered in a family context"

and that "the remuneration on this account should be relatively modest".[1110]

## 5. Monetary Social Security Benefits

### (1) The development of the law

40-238 The development of the law on how far monetary social security benefits are taken into account in the assessment of damages, which it is important to appreciate for a complete understanding of the current position, has been fully documented when dealing with loss of earnings and should be referred to.[1111] Two differences in the history may be noted. First, there were no benefits related to medical expenses specified for deduction in the 1948 Act; secondly, the common law move to regarding the deduction of benefits as the rule rather than the exception reached its culmination in a case involving medical expenses, the well-known *Hodgson v Trapp*.[1112]

### (2) The present position

#### (a) Benefits for which express legislative provision is made

40-239 *(i) The rule as to deduction of benefits* As was said in relation to earnings,[1113] rather than merely setting out in tedious and confusing detail the provisions of the Social Security (Recovery of Benefits) Act 1997, referred to throughout as the 1997 Act, as to the deduction of benefits, it was thought to be more helpful, shorter and clearer to state what the rule to be garnered from the detail is. The rule expressed in the same way, with only the changes necessary to accommodate medical expenses, runs:

The damages to be paid to the claimant for medical expenses are to be reduced by deducting the amount of the specified benefits related to medical expenses paid or likely to be

---

1109 [2004] 2 All E.R. 891 CA at [26].
1110 [2004] 2 All E.R. 891 CA at [33]. The claims were in contract, against the holiday provider, but clearly the ruling applies equally to tort.
1111 See paras 40-162 to 40-164, above.
1112 [1989] A.C. 807.
1113 See para.40-166, above.

paid in the period beginning at the time of injury or of first claim for benefit and ending five years later or upon the payment of the damages if earlier.[1114]

As also said in relation to earnings, to get to this straightforward rule one must dart from provision to provision of the statute and for those who wish to see how the rule is reached it is necessary to read ss.1(1)(b), 1(4)(c), 3, 8(1) and 8(3) together with Sch.2. Again, at least the list of benefits, once found in the col.2 at the beginning of Sch.2, is clear and straightforward. To the original list two further benefits have been added, and recently; none has been removed. The list now reads:

attendance allowance
daily living component of personal independence payment[1115]
care component of disability living allowance
disablement pension increase payable under ss.104 or 105 of the 1992 Act
mobility allowance
mobility component of personal independence payment[1116]
mobility component of disability living allowance.[1117]

40-240 *(ii) Various features of the rule* In relation to earnings five aspects of the rule were examined. What was said there applies equally to medical expenses in respect of the last three of them, namely the operation of the deduction of the whole rather than of half of the benefits,[1118] the question of whether interest falls to be computed upon the loss before or after deduction of benefits[1119] and the possible exemption for small payments.[1120] The first two have special features in relation to medical expenses and are considered below.

40-241 ***(1) Benefits related to medical expenses to be deducted*** Instead of the totality of the benefits being deducted from the whole range of the damages as had been misguidedly provided for in the 1992 Act, only those benefits related to medical expenses are deducted from, and only from, the damages awarded for medical expenses. This is made clear by s.8(3) of the 1997 Act together with Sch.2, where it is provided that the benefits related to medical expenses listed in the col.2 at the

1114 Note that it was held in *Eagle v Chambers (No.2)* [2004] 1 W.L.R. 3081 CA, that the claimant was not required to use her mobility allowance to invest in the motability scheme which would provide her with less costly transport and thereby cut down her loss. This followed from giving a wide construction to s.17 of the 1997 Act which the House of Lords had already done in a different context: see at para.40-173, above.

1115 Inserted by the Welfare Reform Act 2012.

1116 Inserted by the Welfare Reform Act 2012.

1117 As was said in the footnote at the end of para.40-165, above in relation to earnings, while the elaborate machinery for accounting in the 1997 Act need not concern a text on damages, one aspect of the accounting does concern the claimant's damages and that is that, if the defendant challenges the Compensation Recovery Unit certificate and obtains an amended certificate of a reduced amount and a repayment, he must account to the claimant for the repayment. This applies as much here as it did with earnings. Indeed, medical as well as income benefits were among the recoverable benefits returned by the Compensation Recovery Unit to the defendant for which he was held accountable to the claimant in *Bruce v Genesis Fast Food Ltd* [2004] P.I.Q.R. P9 at 113; and it was medical benefits which were the benefits the deduction of which was challenged on a judicial review of an award of criminal injuries compensation in *R. (on the application of Soper) v Criminal Injuries Compensation Board* [2004] P.I.Q.R. Q1 CA at l. See both cases at the para.40-165 footnote, above.

1118 See para.40-172, above.

1119 See para.40-173, above.

1120 See para.40-174, above.

beginning of the Schedule, namely those set out above,[1121] are to be deducted, as to the first three listed, from the second head of compensation in the col.1, "compensation for cost of care", and, as to the last two listed, from the third head of compensation in the col.1, "compensation for loss of mobility". As pointed out when dealing with loss of earnings,[1122] this eliminates the unfairness which *Hassall v Secretary of State for Social Security*,[1123] revealed and restores the position as it stood before 1989. For the purposes of deduction, damages for gratuitous care as much as for paid care have been held in *Griffiths v British Coal Corporation*,[1124] to constitute compensation for the cost of care.

*(2)* ***The five-year period*** What is said generally about the five-year period under loss of earnings is equally relevant for medical expenses and should be referred to.[1125] It was said there that the real significance of the five-year period today lies in a combination of the great increase in the benefits brought into the statutory deduction net since 1989 and the fact that the common law had by then decided upon the deduction of social security benefits not within the statutory list. By bringing the benefit into the prescribed list a claimant who before 1989 would have found it deducted without limitation of time will have had substituted a deduction for, at the most, five years. With medical expenses, though perhaps not with earnings, this can make a very great difference. This is because attendance allowance and mobility allowance are of sizeable amounts and may be payable over very many years whereas the deduction under the new law cannot be for more than five years of these allowances and can be for less. Since four-and-a-half years had passed between injury and trial in *Hodgson v Trapp*,[1126] the amount of some £36,000 which their Lordships deducted on account of these two allowances in respect of future loss would have been added back nearly completely had deduction not been permitted; indeed it would have been added back entirely under the new law with a defendant paying the damages upon judgment as this would now bring the five-year period to an end.[1127] It may be questioned whether the new deducting and accounting should be limited to the maximum five-year period prescribed in the legislation. **40-242**

Related to this is the question of whether defendants can argue that, when deduction under the statute comes to an end, deduction at common law in respect of the future can take over. Such an argument would be attractive to defendants who would not have to account to the Secretary of State for any such benefits deducted. Such a contention was indeed first advanced under the earlier law, the benefits being related to lost earnings as the statute did not at the time include any medical expenses as benefits for deduction. In two cases reported together, *Haste v Sandell Perkins* and *Denman v Essex Area Health Authority*,[1128] the defendants argued that all of the specified statutory benefits should be deducted in respect of the years following the five years next after the accrual of the cause of action; the restriction, it was said, as to deduction of one-half of the benefits was to operate in respect of the five-year period only and thereafter there should be an unrestricted deduction **40-243**

[1121] At para.40-239, above.
[1122] See para.40-168, above.
[1123] [1995] 1 W.L.R. 812 CA.
[1124] [2001] 1 W.L.R. 1493 CA.
[1125] See paras 40-169 and 40-170, above.
[1126] [1989] A.C. 807.
[1127] See para.40-170, above.
[1128] [1984] Q.B. 735.

operating under the common law. This argument was rejected as an unwarranted construction of the subsection and these decisions were rightly endorsed by the Court of Appeal in *Jackman v Corbett*.[1129] The court there was of the view that s.2(1) was clearly designed to be comprehensive in relation to the deductions to be made for benefits received; it contained no indication whatsoever that any right to a further deduction on account of the specified benefits was being created or preserved, and as a matter of construction defined exhaustively the amount of the benefits to be deducted.[1130] Should any attempt be made today to advance a similar argument in relation to the new statutory scheme, these decisions may be prayed in aid to resist it.

**40-244** **(b) Benefits for which no legislative provision is made** It would seem that the monetary social security benefits available to a claimant relating to his medical expenses are all contained within the prescribed benefits which the defendant must deduct and for which he must account. Comparison may be made with what is said on the equivalent issue in respect of loss of earnings.[1131]

**40-245** **(c) Benefits where the legislative provisions are inapplicable** No specific case appears to have arisen concerning other welfare benefits unrelated to the 1997 Act. What is said on this issue under loss of earnings may be referred to.[1132] It may be noted that in *Ballantine v Newalls Insulation Co Ltd*,[1133] which is there dealt with, the benefits were deducted from the total award in which there may have been a component of medical expenses.

## 6. Social Security Benefits other than Monetary

### (1) Facilities provided by the National Health Service and by local authorities

**40-246** **(a) Provision by the National Health Service** Where the benefit is not monetary but the claimant has made use of the free facilities which are available to him under the National Health Service, it is general practice not to award him damages in respect of the medical treatment for which he will not be required to pay: illustrative of this are *West v Shephard*,[1134] and *Mitchell v Mulholland (No.2)*,[1135] both of which cases are better known in other respects, and numerous subsequent cases. It is true that s.2(4) of the Law Reform (Personal Injuries) Act 1948 provides that, in estimating whether medical expenses are reasonable, the possibility of avoiding or reducing them by resort to National Health Service facilities shall be

[1129] [1987] 2 All E.R. 699 CA.

[1130] See especially [1987] 2 All E.R. 699 CA at 710c toe, per Fox LJ who delivered the leading judgment.

[1131] See paras 40-175 to 40-177, above.

[1132] See paras 40-178 to 40-180, above.

[1133] [2000] P.I.Q.R. Q327 CA.

[1134] [1964] A.C. 326 at 357–358, per Lord Devlin: "There are three factors in this particular case, not by any means always present in this type of case, which should keep the damages awarded to the claimant comparatively small. The third is that no part of the very heavy medical expenses incurred has to be borne by the defendant."

[1135] [1972] 1 Q.B. 65 CA at 88, per Sir Gordon Willmer: "The judge's award was based on the assumption that he could be nursed at home, at a cost of £1,312 per annum. There was a possibility to be considered that this might be reduced to £903 if … he had to go into a nursing home, or even to nil if he had to be sent for treatment in a National Health Hospital." See, somewhat similarly, Edmund Davies LJ, at 81.

disregarded, but in *Harris v Brights Asphalt Contractors*,[1136] Slade J, in considering a claim for nursing attendance, rightly took the view that this was not to be interpreted as enacting that

> "a claimant shall be deemed to be entitled to recover expenses which in fact he will never incur".[1137]

These strands were brought together by Lawton LJ in *Cunningham v Harrison*,[1138] where he said of the claimant there in a useful passage:

> "He will probably never be able to get the necessary help and will have to fall back on the National Health Service and the welfare services of the area in which he is living. Should the probability that he will have to rely upon the National Health Service be taken into account having regard to s.2(4) of the Law Reform (Personal Injuries) Act 1948? In my judgment the answer is that it should. The claimant is entitled to compensation for the expense to which he will be put in obtaining domestic and nursing help; and the defendant cannot say that he could avoid that expense by falling back on the National Health Service. The statute forbids that defence. What she [sic] can, however, submit is that he will probably not incur such expenses because he will be unable to obtain the domestic and nursing help which he requires. This is what Slade J decided in *Harris v Brights Asphalt Contractors*.[1139] In my judgment he was right."[1140]

In *Housecroft v Burnett*,[1141] O'Connor LJ referred to the practice of assessing the medical cost

> "at nil where the claimant is cared for under the national health scheme ... because no expense will be incurred in supplying the needs","[1142]

citing Lord Scarman in *Lim Poh Choo v Camden and Islington Area Health Authority*,[1143] to similar effect. However, in *Taylor v Bristol Omnibus Co*,[1144] the Court of Appeal was careful to point out that what was said in *Cunningham v Harrison*,[1145] as to free State services for the disabled, which would have been available to the claimant there under the Chronically Sick and Disabled Persons Act 1970,[1146] should have been read subject to s.29(5) of the National Assistance Act 1948, to which the court's attention had not been directed, enabling local authorities to charge for services under the Act of 1970.[1147]

It is undoubtedly the case that one of the great practical difficulties of assessment in personal injury cases that is continually present is in predicting whether the National Health Service can or will provide the required care and, if so, whether the claimant will avail himself of it. Where the court comes to the view that the facility is available and that the claimant is likely to use it, a further difficulty can **40-247**

---

1136 [1953] 1 Q.B. 617.
1137 [1953] 1 Q.B. 617 at 635.
1138 [1973] Q.B. 942 CA.
1139 [1953] 1 Q.B. 617.
1140 [1973] Q.B. 942 CA at 957D–F.
1141 [1986] 1 All E.R. 332 CA.
1142 [1986] 1 All E.R. 332 CA at 342j.
1143 [1980] A.C. 174 at 187G–188B.
1144 [1975] 1 W.L.R. 1054 CA.
1145 [1973] Q.B. 942 CA.
1146 [1973] Q.B. 942 CA at 952F–H, 954H and 957G.
1147 See [1975] 1 W.L.R. 1054 CA at 1058D–E, 1063D. And see now the confusing cases dealing with care by local authorities at paras 40-249 to 40-252, below.

be to assess whether the National Health Service will, where entitled to do so, make a charge upon the claimant. This latter difficulty would be removed were legislation to provide that the National Health Service should be entitled to recover its costs of caring for the tortiously injured from the tortfeasors themselves, a recovery which in reality would be from their insurers.

**40-248** The proposal has indeed been made by the Law Commission[1148] that, while retaining the principle that a claimant is entitled to choose between private medical care and National Health Service care, the National Health Service should be given an entitlement to recoup from the defendant the costs of the care that has been provided to the claimant.[1149] This mirrors the change that has come about with monetary social security benefits which formerly were deducted in whole or in part from the claimant's damages to the defendant's advantage whereas now, while still so deducted, the State is entitled to recoupment from the defendant.[1150] It is not possible to have a similar scheme to the one that has been set up for monetary social security benefits because of the inappropriateness of deducting from the claimant's damages the costs of his National Health Service care, so that it would be necessary to give the National Health Service effectively a third party claim against the defendant. There is much to be said for making this change to the law. Since the private medical carer is paid for the services provided and, where the claimant has private medical insurance, as with BUPA or Axa PPP,[1151] the insurer may recover its outlays through the medium of subrogation, why, it may be asked, should the National Health Service be in a less advantageous position. One would of course have to be satisfied that the cost of recoupment did not outweigh the benefit to the National Health Service and this would first need to be examined with care. One would also, and in particular, have to resolve the problems to which it is thought that settlements by claimants could give rise. Since settlements generally represent a compromise in the face of uncertainties as to the existence of liability or as to the extent of liability, it would be necessary to work out the degree to which the National Health Service should be regarded as entitled to its costs of treatment. So far the advocated change has come nowhere near the statute book.

**40-249** **(b) Provision by local authorities** Facilities may be provided to persons seriously injured by institutions other than the National Health Service itself, in particular by local authorities, and if these are provided free there is, as with the National Health Service, no entitlement to damages from the tortfeasor in respect of them. The provision of free care is to be seen as a benefit which falls to be taken into account, in a sense deducted, in arriving at the damages to be awarded to the injured person so that in effect there is no entitlement to damages from the tortfeasor in respect of the care. On the other hand, if the injured person must pay for, or contribute towards, the cost of accommodation and care, there would be recovery for such payment in the ordinary way, leading to no deduction, or to a limited deduction, from the damages. Under the statutory provisions with which we are

---

1148 In its Report on *Damages for Personal Injury: Medical, Nursing and Other Expenses* (1999), Law Com. No.262: see paras 3.19 to 3.43.

1149 Compare Lord Devlin in *West v Shephard* [1964] A.C. 326 at 358: "The National Health Service apparently makes no claim. I do not pause to inquire whether this abstention springs from the state of the law or from a decision of policy. If it is due to the former, the position could easily be remedied, but there may be good reasons why it is thought preferable that the loss should be borne by the taxpayers generally."

1150 See para.40-164, above.

1151 The two principal private medical insurance plans.

mainly concerned, ss.21 and 29 of the National Assistance Act 1948,[1152] the local authority is entitled to charge[1153] for the accommodation and care if the injured person has the means to pay and the question which has troubled the courts is as to whether, in assessing means, the damages award can be taken into account. On this the battle is generally waged between the tortfeasor and the local authority which is brought into the litigation, with the injured person left in the middle. The local authority argues that it is entitled to levy its charge from the award of damages so that the tortfeasor has to pay in full. The tortfeasor argue that the local authority cannot look to the damages but must make free provision, so that the tortfeasor does not have to pay. The cases on this issue, which make a sorry story, all precede by a few years the cases on whether the injured person can properly argue that it is reasonable for him or her to opt for private funding, cases already considered.[1154]

The first case in time was *Firth v Geo. Ackroyd Junior Ltd.*[1155] A seriously disabled claimant was being accommodated and cared for without charge in a residential home for which facility the local authority was paying pursuant to s.21 of the 1948 Act. The major issue in the case was as to whether the local authority could have him pay for the cost of the accommodation and care out of the damages awarded to him. It was held that the local authority could not as the Regulations made under the Act specifically provided that any sum of capital administered on behalf of a claimant by the High Court or the Court of Protection where such sum derived from an award of damages for personal injury—and Firth was such a case—fell to be disregarded in the assessment of whether the claimant had the means to pay. Accordingly, neither was the claimant entitled to recover for the accommodation and care costs[1156]; the winner was the tortfeasor. *Firth* however did not see the end of the sorry story. Prevented by that decision from claiming the capital of the damages award towards defraying the costs of accommodation and care, local authorities turned their attention to the income derived from the capital. In *Bell v Todd*,[1157] otherwise reported as *B (A Child) v Todd*,[1158] and again in *Ryan v Liverpool Health Authority*,[1159] both of which like *Frith* were s.21 cases, the court had to grapple with a welter of tortuous and ill-written legislation, primary and subordinate, to reach the conclusion that, in arriving at what the injured person must pay for the accommodation and care, the local authority was not entitled to take income into account any more than capital where the damages award was being administered by the High Court or the Court of Protection but it could however take 40-250

[1152] See at para.40-190, above.

[1153] A requirement under s.21, a discretion under s.29.

[1154] See paras.40-190 and following, above.

[1155] [2001] P.I.Q.R. Q4 at 27.

[1156] Concerned that the law might be changed so as to make him liable to pay the local authority for his accommodation and care, the claimant asked the court for an indemnity from the defendant against the consequences to him of such a change and, in the alternative, for additional damages to reflect the risk of such a change. In neither of these requests was he successful. Firth was followed on this in *Howarth v Whittaker* [2003] Lloyd's Rep. Med. 235 to the extent of refusing an indemnity to the claimant against the possibility of having to pay for his care, the concern here being over past and not future care. It was contended that the local authority might change its mind about past care which had been free and now seek to charge for it. Apart from regarding this as a fanciful and speculative possibility, the court considered that the request ran "wholly contrary to the well-established principle that in cases of this kind there should be finality in the litigation": at [32].

[1157] [2002] Lloyd's Rep. Med. 12.

[1158] [2002] P.I.Q.R. P11 at 107.

[1159] [2002] Lloyd's Rep. Med. 23.

income, but not capital, into account where the damages awarded had been placed in a trust fund, referred to as a "personal injury trust". Nothing was said of the position where there is simply a conventional lump sum award but Bell did hold that income from an annuity purchased as part of a structured settlement must be taken into account.[1160] Subsequently, the Court of Appeal in *Crofton v NHS Litigation Authority*,[1161] made it clear that with a s.29 case where the personal injury damages are being administered by the court, while the capital is still to be disregarded in deciding whether the injured person can afford to pay, the income from the damages may be taken into account by the local authority in its discretion.[1162] The Court of Appeal however accepted that with a s.21 case both capital and income were to be disregarded and Butterfield J at first instance in *Peters v East Midlands Strategic Health Authority*,[1163] held that he had no option but to follow, and apply, this conclusion.[1164]

**40-251** While *Firth*, *Bell* and *Ryan* have been accepted in cases at first instance and not departed from in the Court of Appeal, as is shown by *Crofton*,[1165] and by *Sowden v Lodge*,[1166] this is no doubt because the courts doubt feel that they have no option but to follow and apply the legislation if they cannot find a flaw in the interpretation of it. Yet again and again judicial dismay has been expressed at the legislative morass. In *Bell v Todd*,[1167] Stanley Burnton J was severely critical of the unclarity and inaccessibility of the legislation in a field where clarity and accessibility were paramount[1168]; in *Ryan*,[1169] Munby J described the provisions as possibly the worst drafted and most confusing subordinate legislation it had ever been his misfortune to encounter[1170]; in *Crofton*,[1171] Dyson LJ, handing down the judgment of the Court of Appeal, expressed the court's dismay at the complexity and labyrinthine nature of the legislation, as well as in some respects its obscurity, when social security law should be clear and accessible[1172]; at first instance in *Peters v East Midlands Strategic Health Authority*.[1173] Butterfield J added his name to the roll call of those condemning the legislation and, citing with approval the questions set out in the then current edition of this work, said that "all those questions demand answers and speedy ones at that".[1174] Indeed he was hopeful that speedy answers would be forthcoming as it had become known to the court that Parliament was on the point

---

1160 This was said to be in accord with the decision in *Beattie v Secretary of State for Social Security* [2001] 1 W.L.R. 1404 CA holding that annuity payments paid under a structured settlement fell to be treated as income for the purpose of assessing entitlement to income support, a holding which was later legislatively reversed by the Social Security Amendment (Personal Injury Payments) Regulations 2002.

1161 [2007] 1 W.L.R. 923 CA; facts at para.40-190, above.

1162 For the difference between s.21 cases and s.29 cases see para.40-190, above.

1163 [2008] EWHC 778 (QB); facts at para.40-191, above.

1164 [2008] EWHC 778 (QB) at [43] and [47].

1165 [2007] 1 W.L.R. 923 CA; see at [58].

1166 [2005] 1 W.L.R. 2129 CA; see at [7] and [89].

1167 [2002] Lloyd's Rep. Med. 12.

1168 [2002] Lloyd's Rep. Med. 12 at [64].

1169 [2002] Lloyd's Rep. Med. 23.

1170 [2002] Lloyd's Rep. Med. 23 at [5].

1171 [2007] 1 W.L.R. 923 CA.

1172 [2007] 1 W.L.R. 923 CA at [111].

1173 [2008] EWHC 778 (QB).

1174 [2008] EWHC 778 (QB) at [44] and [45]. The questions in this book were stated as: "What is the position where there is a conventional lump sum award, with no trust? Why should there be a difference between the claimant with an award administered by the Court of Protection and the claimant who has agreed to the sum awarded being placed in a personal injury trust? Why should there

of amending the legislation[1175] but he was to be disappointed as the legislation as far as it covers the situation before us appears still to be unchanged. There have been no answers, speedy or over time.

How then should the matter be dealt with so as to ensure that it is the tortfeasor, rather than the wider community, who bears the cost of the injured person's accommodation and care? It was suggested in earlier editions that an attractive way of achieving this was to require across the board injured claimants to pay for accommodation and care provided by local authorities and would accordingly be awarded the damages with which to do so. This solution, which also removes the injured person's dependence on the resources and policies of the local authorities, had earlier been achieved in *Avon County Council v Hooper*,[1176] being a decision under different legislation which permitted this. An alternative, and probably better, solution would be to entitle injured persons to care and accommodation from the local authority in all cases without payment and to award damages for the cost of that care and accommodation to the local authority itself. Longmore LJ in *Sowden v Lodge*,[1177] made it clear that he thought that this is what the legislation should provide[1178] and this thought was strongly endorsed by the Court of Appeal in *Crofton*.[1179] Yet a far better route has opened for allowing the full damages to be paid by the tortfeasor. This is by virtue of its being held, in case after case, that it is reasonable for claimants to opt for private care[1180] and the Court of Appeal has since given this approach a great boost by holding in *Peters v East Midlands Strategic Health Authority*,[1181] that claimants are entitled as of right to opt for private care, so that the whole question of reasonableness is by-passed. To the extent then that the claimant is not beholden to the local authority for any contribution to his care, the results in *Firth*, *Bell* and *Ryan*,[1182] right or wrong, matter not.[1183] Hopefully we shall hear no more of ss.21 and 29 and the much criticised related legislation, although that legislation could still come into play where the injured party is content with what the local authority will provide and does not aim for private care **40-252**

## VI. Non-Pecuniary Damage

### 1. A Conventional Award

Non-pecuniary loss is a very different field. Little can be stated with certainty as **40-253**

be a difference between cases administered by the court which fall under s.21 and those which fall under s.29? Why should a claimant's position have been worsened by agreeing to a structured settlement? What is the position where the award is by way of periodical payments, which have effectively taken the place of structures?"

1175 [2008] EWHC 778 (QB) at [46].

1176 [1997] 1 All E.R. 532 CA.

1177 [2005] 1 W.L.R. 2129 CA.

1178 [2005] 1 W.L.R. 2129 CA at [89].

1179 [2007] 1 W.L.R. 923 CA at [88]–[90]. One local authority, required to pay for an impecunious injured person's care and accommodation under the law as it stands, tried in *London Borough of Islington v University College London Hospital NHS Trust* [2005] Lloyd's Rep. Med. 387 CA to achieve this result by the pioneering method of bringing an action at common law against the tortfeasor, arguing that the tortfeasor owed it a duty of care not negligently to inflict an injury resulting in damage to it in the form of care costs. Not surprisingly, the claim failed.

1180 This development is dealt with at para.40-190, above.

1181 [2010] Q.B. 48 CA, for which see para.40-191, above.

1182 See paras 40-249 and 40-250, above.

1183 However, this cannot be said to be the route that the Court of Appeal in *Crofton v NHS Litigation Authority* [2007] 1 W.L.R. 923 CA had in mind: see earlier in the text of this paragraph.

to the amount of damages awardable for such loss caused by personal physical injury. Indeed full compensation cannot be given in the sense that no amount can fully compensate for a serious physical injury.[1184] Beyond this, no yardstick exists for measuring in money the compensation to be accorded a given amount of physical pain or mental suffering because, as far as money goes, the loss is imponderable, and any amount awarded must be in the nature of a conventional sum. The difficulty then is in deciding what proportions the conventional sum should take. For there is no reason, in logic or in economics, why for a specified period of suffering the award should be £100 rather than £1,000 or indeed any other figure. Here a solution can only be found by taking as the test what our particular society would deem to be a fair sum, such as would, in the words of Lord Devlin in *West v Shephard*,[1185] allow the wrongdoer to

> "hold up his head among his neighbours and say with their approval that he has done the fair thing".

While on this basis different societies are likely to end up with different figures,[1186] within any particular system the level of awards should show a measure of internal consistency—for, as Diplock LJ pointed out in *Wise v Kaye*,[1187] once the premise is accepted that £20 is the right award for one day of physical pain, the right award for two days of similar pain must be in the region of £40 and not in the region of £400, and therefore English courts may properly seek guidance from awards made in other English cases dealing with similar injuries to claimants of similar make-up. As Lord Diplock later said in *Wright v British Railways Board*[1188]:

> "Non-economic loss … is not susceptible of measurement in money. Any figure at which the assessor of damages arrives cannot be other than artificial and, if the aim is that justice meted out to all litigants should be even-handed instead of depending on idiosyncrasies of the assessor, whether jury or judge, the figure must be 'basically a conventional figure derived from experience and from awards in comparable cases'."[1189]

Lord Scarman summed up the position succinctly in *Lim Poh Choo v Camden and Islington Area Health Authority*[1190]:

> "We are in the area of 'conventional' awards for non-pecuniary loss, where comparability matters."[1191]

---

1184 See, e.g. Sir J Holker's argument in *Phillips v L. & S.W. Ry* (1879) 5 Q.B.D. 78 CA at 84: "It no doubt is the rule that a jury must not attempt to give a man a full compensation for bodily injury, if they were to do so there would be no limit to the amount of damages, for no sum would be an equivalent for the loss of a man's eyes." Contrast Diplock LJ in *Fletcher v Autocar and Transporters* [1968] 2 Q.B. 322 CA at 339; Lord Morris in *Parry v Cleaver* [1970] A.C. 1 at 22.

1185 [1964] A.C. 326 at 357.

1186 Thus in *Jag Singh v Toong Fong Omnibus Co* [1964] 1 W.L.R. 1382 PC, the Privy Council, in increasing the damages awarded by the Malayan court in a personal injury case, said that "to the extent to which regard should be had to the range of awards in other cases which are comparable such cases should as a rule be those which have been determined in the same jurisdiction or in a neighbouring locality where similar social, economic and industrial conditions exist": at 1385. See, too, *Selvanayagam v University of the West Indies* [1983] 1 W.L.R. 585 PC, especially at 590G.

1187 [1962] 1 Q.B. 638 CA at 664.

1188 [1983] 2 A.C. 773.

1189 [1983] 2 A.C. 773 at 777C.

1190 [1980] A.C. 174.

1191 [1980] A.C. 174 at 189B. However, where guidance is sought from earlier cases the decline in the

## 2. HEADS OF NON-PECUNIARY DAMAGE

There was once a time when it could be said that there was one head of non-pecuniary damage; this was the all-embracing "pain and suffering". Then the courts produced two further heads of damage; "loss of expectation of life" was invented in 1934, "loss of amenities of life" was coined around 1950. There were, however, grave dangers in conferring an independent existence upon these two other heads of damage, as will be seen,[1192] and loss of expectation of life was statutorily abolished as a separate head in 1982.[1193] Now, therefore, there remain two heads[1194] and even these two tend to meld into one another. Thus Crichton J in *Povey v Governors of Rydal School*,[1195] said: **40-254**

> "It would be possible to argue that knowledge of complete physical dependence on others is suffering rather than loss of amenity; it could I think, equally well be said that such knowledge amounted to loss of amenity."

And he did not think that in the case before him a serious effort to distinguish the two should be made.[1196] Sometimes it seems that the wheel has come full circle and that we are back at the single head of damage represented by pain and suffering; certainly Lord Lloyd, in dealing in *Wells v Wells*,[1197] with the award for non-pecuniary loss to a severely brain damaged claimant, spoke throughout only of pain and suffering. Or it may be thought, with the availability of painkilling drugs and advances in medical science generally, that it is loss of amenities that has taken over from pain and suffering as the principal head of damage. This depends upon the emphasis that is given to the term suffering. In any event the unity of the heads of damage is emphasised by the practice of the courts today to award a single sum for the total non-pecuniary loss.[1198]

This necessarily somewhat obscure summary of the position is intended to set the scene. Matters will become clearer as we examine the various heads of non-pecuniary damage in their several detail. **40-255**

### (1) Pain and suffering

The term "pain and suffering" has been used so constantly by the courts without any clear distinction between the two words that it is now a term of art. It has been suggested that "pain" is the immediately felt effect on the nerves and brain of some lesion or injury to a part of the body, while "suffering" is distress which is not felt as being directly connected with any bodily condition. On this analysis pain needs no further elucidation; it may be noted that it will include, for the purpose of dam- **40-256**

value of sterling must always be kept in mind: Contrast paras 20-010 to 20-012, above. *Parry v English Electric Co* [1971] 1 W.L.R. 664 CA, establishes that there is no such thing as a standard or minimum figure for a minor injury. Today of course we have the great assistance of what are now called the Judicial College Guidelines, for which see para.40-275, below.

1192 See para.40-260 and para.40-262, below as to loss of amenities of life and loss of expectation of life respectively.

1193 See para.40-263, below.

1194 For the possibility of others see paras 40-264 to 40-266, below.

1195 [1970] 1 All E.R. 841 at 846.

1196 [1970] 1 All E.R. 841 at 846.

1197 [1999] 1 A.C. 345.

1198 But see now the position with loss of congenial employment at para.40-265, below. Formerly loss of expectation of life had commanded a separate award.

ages, any pain caused by medical treatment or surgical operation rendered necessary by the injury inflicted by the defendant. As to suffering, this would seem to include fright at the time of the injury and fright reaction,[1199] fear of future incapacity, either as to health, sanity or the ability to make a living, and humiliation, sadness and embarrassment caused by disfigurement.

**40-257** Damages for inconvenience have been allowed in contract and in torts such as deceit, nuisance and false imprisonment,[1200] but whether the inconvenience should be considered here as a separate head of non-pecuniary loss or whether it can come within the term "suffering" is a matter which is devoid of clear authority. One pointer is a remark of Asquith LJ in delivering the Court of Appeal's judgment in *Shearman v Folland*,[1201] where he said that for the difference between life in a hospital and life in a hotel the claimant falls to be compensated under the head of general damages for pain and suffering and for loss of amenities. It seems likely that damages for inconvenience are generally thrown in by the courts under this head; damages for inconvenience appear as a separate head elsewhere by reason of the absence of another head of non-pecuniary loss upon which to tack them.

### (2) Loss of amenities of life

**40-258** This head of damage concentrates on the curtailment of the claimant's enjoyment of life not by the positive unpleasantness of pain and suffering but, in a more negative way, by his inability to pursue the activities he pursued beforehand. Birkett LJ put it thus in the unreported *Manley v Rugby Portland Cement Co*[1202]:

> "There is a head of damage which is sometimes called loss of amenities; the man made blind by the accident will no longer be able to see the familiar things he has seen all his life; the man who has had both legs removed and will never again go upon his walking excursions—things of that kind—loss of amenities."

Loss or impairment of any one or more of the five senses is compensated under this head[1203] and also loss resulting from interference with the claimant's sexual life[1204] or with a claimant's prospects of marriage,[1205] from the break-up of the claimant's marriage[1206] or from inability to play with his children[1207]; even loss of enjoyment of the holiday upon which the claimant was embarking or had embarked at the time of the injury has been taken into account in the non-pecuniary award.[1208] Nor is this element of loss confined to interference with leisure activities, so that damages may

---

[1199] See, e.g. *Thompson v Royal Mail Lines* [1957] 1 Lloyd's Rep. 99.

[1200] See paras 5-010 and 5-017 to 5-019, above.

[1201] [1950] 2 K.B. 43 CA at 50.

[1202] (1951) CA No.286, reported at Kemp and Kemp, *The Quantum of Damages*, Vol.1, 2nd edn (1961), p.624 (not in the later editions).

[1203] As in *Kearns v Higgs and Hill* (1968) 4 K.I.R. 393 and *Cook v J. L. Kier & Co* [1970] 1 W.L.R. 774 (loss of taste and smell).

[1204] *Cook v J. L. Kier & Co* [1970] 1 W.L.R. 774 (loss of sexual potency).

[1205] Damages are available for the non-pecuniary loss of the joy of marriage as well as for the pecuniary loss of support dealt with at para.40-104, above. For the non-pecuniary side of their awards judges are inclined to take this loss into account for female and male claimants alike: see e.g. *Assinder v Griffin* unreported 25 May 2001, ("her prospects of marriage are greatly reduced") and *Edwards v Team Roofing* unreported 17 January 2000, ("he has lost the prospect of a happy marriage").

[1206] As in *Jones v Jones* [1985] Q.B. 704 CA; see at 708C.

[1207] As in *Hoffman v Sofaer* [1982] 1 W.L.R. 1350; see at 1353C.

[1208] As in *Ichard v Frangoulis* [1977] 1 W.L.R. 556 and *Hoffman v Sofaer* [1982] 1 W.L.R. 1350 (see at

be awarded for deprivation of the ability to pursue an enjoyable occupation,[1209] or for having to contend with housekeeping in an injured state without domestic help.[1210]

The appearance of loss of amenities as a distinct head of damage is a comparatively modern development. Not until the middle of the last century does it begin to become mentioned as such in the reports.[1211] It is doubtful whether this was intended to reflect a substantive change in the law; the idea of loss of amenities can be subsumed under pain and suffering, taking that term in its widest connotation, and no doubt that was what had been done with this element of loss before 1950. In this respect it is instructive to look at the related loss of expectation of life which constituted an implicit element in damages awards before emerging as a separate head of damage and does so again today with its abolition as a separate head of damage.[1212] **40-259**

The conferring of an independent existence upon loss of amenities as an item of damage held dangers because the loss was given an objective quality which divorced it from the prime non-pecuniary category of pain and suffering with its subjective standard,[1213] and the case was bound to come soon where the subjective test and the objective test clashed. It came with the case of the unconscious claimant, someone in a persistent vegetative state, first in *Wise v Kaye*,[1214] in the Court of Appeal and soon after in *West v Shephard*,[1215] in the House of Lords. Both courts held, both by a bare majority, that damages for loss of amenities were not to be based upon loss of happiness and that the claimant's ignorance of the loss suffered was no ground for reducing the damages. The defendants' argument was put thus by Lord Pearce in the latter case: **40-260**

> "Substantial damages are not awarded … for physical injury simpliciter, but only for pain and suffering and general loss of happiness which it occasions. Therefore the deprivation of a limb can only command any substantial compensation in so far as it results in suffering and loss of happiness; and where there is little or no consciousness of deprivation there can be little or no damages."[1216]

This argument was rejected by the majority. Again in the words of Lord Pearce:

---

1353E).

1209 *Morris v Johnson Mathey & Co* (1967) 112 S.J. 32 (loss of joy of work as craftsman); *Hale v London Underground* [1993] P.I.Q.R. Q30 (loss of congenial employment as fireman doing a fulfilling job), see at 39; *Willbye v Gibbons* [2004] P.I.Q.R. P15 CA at 227 (loss of ability to pursue career as nursery nurse). Separate awards for this loss are now in vogue: see para.40-265, below.

1210 *Daly v General Steam Navigation Co* [1981] 1 W.L.R. 120 CA: see the case at para.40-086, above. At one time there grew up a tendency to include within the award for the non-pecuniary loss of amenities those pecuniary items which go to alleviate the claimant's disabled condition, such as adaptations to housing, the extra expense of holidays and of heating, services of a driver, aids and appliances: see e.g. *Housecroft v Burnett* [1986] 1 All E.R. 332 CA at 337f –j, per O'Connor LJ. But today the better plan of keeping these as specific pecuniary items within medical and related expenses (dealt with at paras 40-183 and following, above) prevails.

1211 For other statements at about the same time in addition to that of Birkett LJ cited in the text of the last paragraph, see *Shearman v Folland* [1950] 2 K.B. 43 CA at 50 and *Haygarth v Grayson Rollo* [1951] 1 Lloyd's Rep. 49 CA at 52, both per Asquith LJ.; *British Transport Commission v Gourley* [1956] A.C. 185 at 197, 216, per Earl Jowitt and Lord Keith, respectively.

1212 See para.40-263, below.

1213 A dramatic foretaste of these dangers had followed upon the earlier recognition of loss of expectation of life as a separate head of damage: see para.40-262, below. This should have been a warning signal.

1214 [1962] 1 Q.B. 638 CA.

1215 [1964] A.C. 326.

1216 [1964] A.C. 326 at 364 to 365.

> "If a claimant has lost a leg, the court approaches the matter on the basis that he has suffered a serious physical deprivation no matter what his condition of temperament or state of mind may be."[1217]

And Lord Morris, while agreeing that the fact of unconsciousness was relevant to recovery for pain and suffering, said that it did not "eliminate the actuality of the deprivations of the ordinary experiences and amenities of life",[1218] for which deprivations the claimant was entitled to substantial damages. The majority rejected the contention that the principles laid down in *Benham v Gambling*,[1219] required a contrary conclusion: that case dealt only with loss of expectation of life.[1220]

**40-261** This decision of the House of Lords is one which is to be regretted, and the hope has been expressed[1221] that the House would one day be prepared to adopt the approach taken by Lord Reid and Lord Devlin in their cogent dissents, and perhaps even to return to the pre-1950 position by discarding loss of amenities of life not indeed as an element—and a most important element—of loss but as a separate head of damage.[1222] But that such a day is unlikely to come is attested to by the House's refusal in *Lim Poh Choo v Camden and Islington Area Health Authority*,[1223] to depart from *West v Shephard*.[1224] Lord Scarman, in a speech with which the other members of the House agreed, considered that any reversal of *West v Shephard*,[1225] would, in the first place, "cause widespread injustice" since both settlements and judicial awards had proceeded for nearly 20 years on the basis of the decision,[1226] and, in the second place,

> "should be done not judicially but legislatively within the context of a comprehensive enactment dealing with all aspects of damages for personal injury".[1227]

This latter suggestion, no doubt made with one eye on the Pearson Commission's report of the previous year, prompts the retention, over seven earlier editions of this work, of the submission that the decision in *West v Shephard*,[1228] is in truth fundamentally at variance with the House's earlier decision in *Benham v Gambling*,[1229] on loss of expectation of life; indeed if in *Oliver v Ashman*,[1230] the Court of Appeal could regard[1231] *Benham v Gambling* as controlling questions of pecuniary loss,[1232] how much more easily could that decision have been taken as covering another, and closely related, head of non-pecuniary loss? *West v Shephard*,[1233] has shown its difficult side where suit has been brought not by the living victim but

---

1217 [1964] A.C. 326 at 365.
1218 [1964] A.C. 326 at 349.
1219 [1941] A.C. 157.
1220 [1964] A.C. 326 at 347–348, 366–369.
1221 Since the edition (1972) following the decision.
1222 See paras 40-258 and 40-259, above.
1223 [1980] A.C. 174.
1224 [1964] A.C. 326.
1225 [1964] A.C. 326.
1226 [1980] A.C. 174 at 189B.
1227 [1980] A.C. 174 at 189C.
1228 [1964] A.C. 326.
1229 [1941] A.C. 157.
1230 [1962] 2 Q.B. 210 CA.
1231 See para.40-109, above.
1232 An interpretation, however, now shown to be misconceived: see *Pickett v British Rail Engineering* [1980] A.C. 136, at para.40-109, above.
1233 [1964] A.C. 326.

by his estate after his death, so that in one such case, *Andrews v Freeborough*,[1234] the Court of Appeal indicated that it would have preferred not to apply the decision of the House of Lords had the matter been *res integra*.[1235] Moreover, the decision has not always been well received in other jurisdictions where loss of amenities is recognised as a separate head of non-pecuniary damage. It was rejected by the Full Court of the High Court of Australia which, in *Skelton v Collins*,[1236] held that only a very moderate sum for this loss should be awarded to a boy of 19 rendered unconscious by the injury and expected to live only another six months after the trial. This decision is to be welcomed for it adheres to the central principle of compensation, the contrary solution retaining overtones of punishing the tortfeasor,[1237] and it found favour with the Pearson Commission which recommended that non-pecuniary damages should no longer be recoverable for permanent unconsciousness.[1238] Fortunately, little or nothing has been heard since the pronouncement of Lord Scarman in the *Lim Poh Choo* case of this issue once regarded as of such importance. We can just hope after so many years that it has died a death.

## (3) Loss of expectation of life

In 1934 the Court of Appeal in *Flint v Lovell*,[1239] decided that where the injury to the claimant shortened his expectation of life he was entitled to damages in respect of this shortening, thus establishing a head of damage since known as loss of expectation of life. Yet although it had not appeared as a separate head of damage before this, it probably always formed an implicit part of the damages for non-pecuniary losses awarded in personal injury cases, being in effect incorporated into the general recovery for pain and suffering. In *Rose v Ford*,[1240] both Lord Atkin and Lord Wright expressed the view that there was nothing novel or unusual in the idea of taking this element of damage into calculation.[1241] But *Flint v Lovell*,[1242] gave it a separate existence, and, by doing so, gave it an objective quality which divorced it from the prime non-pecuniary category of pain and suffering with its subjective overtones. This feature has led to criticism from the start. Practically all the cases dealing with this head of damage have been cases in which the victim was not injured but killed and the action was being brought for the benefit of the estate, the House of Lords in *Rose v Ford*,[1243] having decided that these damages were recoverable in an action so surviving under the provisions of the Law Reform (Miscellaneous Provisions) Act 1934, and small, effectively conventional, awards became the **40-262**

---

1234 [1967] 1 Q.B. 1 CA.

1235 See para.41-135, below.

1236 (1966) 115 C.L.R. 94.

1237 Lord Reid and Lord Devlin, dissenting in *West v Shephard* [1964] A.C. 326, pointed out the fallacy in the argument that "it would be monstrous if the defendant had to pay less because in addition to inflicting physical injuries he had made the claimant unconscious" (at 342, per Lord Reid), an argument which Lord Devlin noted was a variant on the one that it should not be cheaper to kill than to maim (at 362).

1238 See (1978), Cmnd.7054–1, paras 393 to 398.

1239 [1935] 1 K.B. 354 CA.

1240 [1937] A.C. 826.

1241 [1937] A.C. 826 at 834 and 848 to 849 respectively.

1242 [1935] 1 K.B. 354 CA.

1243 [1937] A.C. 826.

order of the day after the House of Lords so decreed in *Benham v Gambling*,[1244] there substituting for a figure of £1,200 in a survival claim by the estate an award of £200. While their Lordships' reason for prescribing such moderation was to contain, by a process of judicial legislation, the spate of litigation set off by a combination of the 1934 Act and *Rose v Ford*,[1245] whereby the estate of a deceased person reaped the benefit of a non-pecuniary loss basically personal to the deceased himself, they were really required, within the framework of precedent, similarly to contain actions by living claimants, for logically there can be no distinction, once the standard is set as an objective one, between the amount awarded under this head to a living claimant and the amount awarded to the estate of a deceased person. And indeed this logical conclusion was eventually accepted by the courts in the early 1960s.[1246]

**40-263** The right to claim damages for loss of expectation of life as a separate head of damage was abolished by s.1(1)(a) of the Administration of Justice Act 1982. At the same time s.1(1)(b) enacted that where the claimant's life expectation has been reduced by the injuries

> "the Court, in assessing damages in respect of pain and suffering caused by the injuries, shall take account of any suffering caused or likely to be caused to him by awareness that his expectation of life has been reduced."

The law was thus put back to the healthier position in which it was before *Flint v Lovell*,[1247] was decided in 1934.[1248] The courts are not now restricted to awarding the conventional sum; more or less may be awarded, depending essentially on the circumstances surrounding the particular claimant, such as his attitude to his loss and the number of years of life of which he has been deprived. There seems little doubt that the tendency should go upwards beyond the former conventional sum which by 1985 had risen only to £1,750.[1249] In this connection it is of significance that it was recognised even in the early 1960s that an award for pain and suffering might contain an element which went beyond the conventional sum on the basis that the claimant can

> "obtain substantial damages for the constant pain and disappointment of knowing that his life has been shortened",[1250]

an approach to which effect was given at that time in *Forrest v Sharp*.[1251] Time, however, has not vouchsafed whether higher awards have followed, and to what degree, since any amount given has been not separately assessed but all part of the total award for non-pecuniary loss, with no express indication that the award has

---

[1244] [1941] A.C. 157.
[1245] [1937] A.C. 826.
[1246] See *Oliver v Ashman* [1962] 2 Q.B. 210 CA at 231, per Holroyd Pearce LJ; *Wise v Kaye* [1962] 1 Q.B. 638 CA at 648–649, per Sellers LJ; *West v Shephard* [1964] A.C. 326 at 367, per Lord Pearce.
[1247] [1935] 1 K.B. 354 CA.
[1248] See para.40-262, above.
[1249] See *Kralj v McGrath* [1986] 1 All E.R. 54. Claims continued beyond the end of 1982 if the claimant's cause of action had accrued before then.
[1250] *Oliver v Ashman* [1962] 2 Q.B. 210 CA at 231, per Holroyd Pearce LJ; similarly *Wise v Kaye* [1962] 1 Q.B. 638 CA at 649, per Sellers LJ. Contrast *West v Shephard* [1964] A.C. 326 at 331, per Lord Devlin, to the effect that *Benham v Gambling* "was intended to set and has set a standard of uniformity for the assessment of damage for loss of expectation of life where there is no mental suffering".
[1251] (1963) 107 S.J. 536.

been increased,[1252] and by what amount, to reflect the claimant's awareness of the reduction in his life expectation.

## (4) Other possible heads of loss

Two further items of damage, very different from each other, have surfaced, neither of which is thought to be very convincing as a separate head. Moreover, the decisions introducing these items have made unfortunate inroads on the rule of a single sum for the total non-pecuniary loss. **40-264**

**(i) Loss of congenial employment** In quite recent years it has become a feature of personal injury cases where the claimant is no longer able to continue in his former employment to make a separate award under the rubric "loss of congenial employment". One can trace the idea as far back as *Hale v London Underground*,[1253] where it was already being said, at first instance, that loss of congenial employment was "now well recognised … [as] a separate head of damage"[1254] though no authority for this was cited. Certainly, in the early years of this century this head of damage was being recognised by the Court of Appeal, both in *Willbye v Gibbons*,[1255] and in *Chase International Express Ltd v McRae*.[1256] Awards continue to this day at first instance, and in relation to a whole variety of employments. In *Dudney v Guaranteed Asphalt Ltd*,[1257] a roofer was awarded £5,000, an amount said to be at the bottom of the range[1258]; in *Evans v Virgin Atlantic Airways*,[1259] a beauty therapist was held to merit what was said to be a relatively high award,[1260] coming out at £10,000; and in *Davison v Leach*,[1261] *Dudney* and *Evans* were followed so as to £6,500 to an equity sales trader working in the financial sector. The two earlier Court of Appeal decisions are instructive. In *Willbye* the first instance award of £15,000 on account of loss of congenial employment was reduced to £5,000, Kennedy LJ saying that it was "important to keep this head of damages in proportion".[1262] In *Chase* the trial judge's award of £2,000 was set aside because the Court of Appeal did not regard the claimant, who worked as a motor cycle courier, as having provided enough evidence to indicate that he enjoyed riding his motor cycle and found his work as a motor cycle courier extremely satisfying. Significantly Kennedy LJ said[1263]: **40-265**

> "The award can only be made to compensate a claimant for the loss of congenial employment, as the head of damages indicates. Any award for the interference with the satisfaction which a claimant gets, for example, out of the use of a motor cycle in his ordinary

---

1252 Occasionally there is an express indication as in the claim, one arising out of a death, in *Brown v Hamid* [2013] EWHC 4067 (QB) at [38].

1253 [1993] P.I.Q.R. Q30.

1254 [1993] P.I.Q.R. Q30 at 39.

1255 [2003] EWCA Civ CA 372.

1256 [2003] EWCA Civ CA 372.

1257 [2013] EWHC 2515 (QB).

1258 [2003] EWCA Civ 372 CA at [28]. In *Ward v Allies & Morrison Architects* unreported, £5,000 was again awarded and to a young woman who had not yet started on her chosen career. The award was not challenged in the Court of Appeal: [2012] EWCA Civ 1287 CA at [2].

1259 [2011] EWHC 1805 (QB).

1260 [2011] EWHC 1805 (QB) at [30].

1261 [2013] EWHC 3092 (QB).

1262 [2003] EWCA Civ 372 CA at [11].

1263 [2003] EWCA Civ 505 CA at [22].

> social life has to be compensated for under the head of pain, suffering and loss of amenities."

Yet why should there be a difference in the way of regarding the damages awarded between the joy of work and the joy of play? The professional motor cyclist seems to be no different from the professional violinist whose deprivation of the enjoyment of playing has often been regarded as compensable by way of loss of amenities. Nevertheless the courts are continuing to regard loss of congenial employment as a different category of non-pecuniary loss from loss of amenities.

**40-266** **(ii) Awards to parents of an unwanted child** On a grander scale there is the majority decision of the House of Lords in *Rees v Darlington Memorial Hospital NHS Trust*,[1264] to award to all parents, who by reason of clinical negligence have brought an unwanted child into the world, a sum of £15,000 in lieu of the costs of bringing up the child, to which they had formerly been held entitled.[1265] The majority declined to classify this award as one for non-pecuniary loss but it is difficult to see how else it can be justified. Certainly the minority Lords spoke convincingly against the invention of the so-called conventional award unrelated to compensation for non-pecuniary loss, regarding the idea of such an award as contrary to principle. The matter is considered in more detail when dealing with the wrongful birth cases.[1266]

### 3. Various Aspects of the Non-pecuniary Award

**40-267** There are various aspects of the damages which courts award for non-pecuniary loss to be considered. All of them have equal relevance to each head of damage and that they apply across the non-pecuniary damage board is underlined by the fact that courts today award a single sum for the total loss without any division between heads.

## (1) Unity of past and prospective loss

**40-268** Not only is a single sum given for all of the heads of loss but a single sum is given for the loss which has already occurred before trial and for the loss which will arise in the future. Both past loss and prospective loss are covered but the past loss is not claimed as special damage in the pleadings as it is not quantifiable with exactitude. Past loss and prospective loss are claimed together as general damage, and in this lies the difference with pecuniary losses where the past loss and the future loss have to be claimed separately.[1267] Interest is to be awarded on the whole.[1268]

## (2) Relevance of age

**40-269** How far, if at all, the age of the claimant should affect the size of the award for non-pecuniary loss has seldom been in issue. There seems to be a tendency to leave

---

1264 [2004] 1 A.C. 309.

1265 See [2004] 1 A.C. 309, paras 40-285 and following, below.

1266 See at paras 40-291 to 40-293, below.

1267 Contrast pecuniary losses at paras 40-062 and 40-183, above.

1268 A practice confirmed by the House of Lords in *Pickett v British Rail Engineering* [1980] A.C. 136: see para.19-052, above. The rate of interest remains at 2 per cent despite arguments to the contrary: *L v Chief Constable of Staffordshire* [2000] P.I.Q.R. Q349. See para.19-132, above.

age on one side and gauge the award primarily by the seriousness of the injury. The Judicial Studies Board, now renamed the Judicial College, in its invaluable survey of awards[1269] refers to age and life expectancy as a factor only in relation to its first category of injury, namely injury involving paralysis,[1270] and to life expectancy alone in relation to its second, namely severe brain damage[1271]; and then does not indicate what effect there is on the amount of the damages. Nevertheless it is thought that courts implicitly take age into consideration as a factor in coming to an assessment. Thus when in *Wells v Wells*,[1272] counsel for the defendant attempted to distinguish a high award for non-pecuniary loss in *Cunningham v Camberwell Health Authority*,[1273] on the basis that the claimant in *Cunningham* was 12 years younger than the claimant in *Wells*, who was nearing 58, Lord Lloyd made reference to this attempt with apparent approval; indeed counsel's attempt to have the award reduced was successful.[1274] Occasionally the matter of age has surfaced expressly to influence an award. Thus in *Nutbrown v Sheffield Health Authority*,[1275] where a claimant injured at 72 and with a life expectancy at trial to 82 was awarded £25,000 for his non-pecuniary loss, the trial judge stated that he would have awarded him £50,000 had he been 30.

### (3) Relevance of social and economic position

It was the general view of the judges in the various stages of the litigation in the early *Phillips v L. & S.W. Ry*,[1276] that the fact that the claimant has a substantial secured private income may be relevant to the amount awarded for non-pecuniary loss.[1277] Cotton LJ put the reasons thus: **40-270**

> "As to bodily suffering, the possession of an independent income may come into consideration, because a man may suffer very much more from bodily injury when he is deprived of all means of support, and is reduced to such poverty that he cannot provide for himself what will alleviate his sufferings: he is in a different position from the man who, having an independent income, meets with a similar accident."[1278]

But it may be questioned whether a claimant's economic, or indeed his social, position should affect the award for his non-pecuniary loss. And indeed, should this be introduced as a relevant factor in the assessment, there remain opposing arguments as to whether an elevated position should increase or decrease the award. For while it may be argued, on the one hand, that the poor should obtain more because an addition to total assets has so much more significance for them, it may be argued, on the other, that the rich should obtain more because a larger amount is necessary to have a significant effect on their lives. Accordingly, it would seem that the

---

1269 Judicial College, *Guidelines for the Assessment of General Damages in Personal Injury Cases*, 14th edn (Oxford: OUP, 2017). For these, and their value, see paras 40-275 and following, below.

1270 *Guidelines for the Assessment of General Damages in Personal Injury Cases*, 14th edn (Oxford: OUP, 2017), p.4.

1271 *Guidelines for the Assessment of General Damages in Personal Injury Cases*, 14th edn (Oxford: OUP, 2017), pp.6 and 7.

1272 [1999] 1 A.C. 345.

1273 (1990) 2 Med. L.R. 49 CA.

1274 See *Wells v Wells* [1991] 1 A.C. 345 at 376H.

1275 (1993) 4 Med. L.R. 188.

1276 (1879) 4 Q.B.D. 406; 5 Q.B.D. 78 CA; 5 C.P.D. 280 CA.

1277 Although generally irrelevant as to pecuniary losses: see para.40-142, above.

1278 5 C.P.D. 280 CA at 294.

sensible view is that rich and poor, great and humble, should be treated alike, receiving similar amounts for the same injury. And the courts moved towards acceptance of this view many years ago. Thus in *Fletcher v Autocar and Transporters*,[1279] where suit was brought for a very serious injury to a wealthy claimant, the Court of Appeal agreed that his wealth should not affect the size of the non-pecuniary award. "High though his deprivation ranks", said Diplock LJ,

> "I cannot think that it ranks any higher because the claimant, before the accident, was a rich man. Had an ordinary working man, who like the claimant had led before the accident a full, active and useful life in his own sphere, sustained the same injuries with the same physical and mental results, he would in my view have been entitled to monetary compensation of the same order as the claimant."[1280]

Salmon LJ was even more emphatic. He said:

> "The claimant's economic and social position is irrelevant. The normal compensation for the loss of an arm as such is the same for a rich man as it is for a poor one."[1281]

### (4) Relevance of ability to enjoy the damages

**40-271** In assessing damages for non-pecuniary loss, it has been held to be irrelevant that the claimant would be unable to enjoy the damages personally because the gravity of the injuries has made him powerless to dispose of them. This was first decided in *Wise v Kaye*,[1282] and was subsequently endorsed by the majority of the House of Lords in *West v Shephard*.[1283] Lord Morris there said:

> "If damages are awarded to a claimant on a correct basis, it seems to me that it can be of no concern to the court to consider any question as to the use that will thereafter be made of the money awarded. It follows that if damages are assessed on a correct basis there should not then be a paring down of the award because of some thought that a particular claimant will not be able to use the money."[1284]

And the validity of this approach was later reiterated by the House in *Lim Poh Choo v Camden and Islington Area Health Authority*.[1285]

### (5) Relevance of manner in which injury inflicted

**40-272** The damages for non-pecuniary loss will be greater where the physical injury is

---

1279 [1968] 2 Q.B. 322 CA.

1280 [1968] 2 Q.B. 322 CA at 340–341.

1281 [1968] 2 Q.B. 322 CA at 364.

1282 [1962] 1 Q.B. 638 CA. The point was earlier raised in *Oliver v Ashman* [1962] 2 Q.B. 210 CA, but the Court of Appeal there had disposed of the issue on the facts, namely by holding that there was no certainty that the claimant would not need or use the money. Pearson LJ had considered that the court would be entitled to give less in damages where the benefit would not be enjoyed by the claimant but pass to the next-of-kin, who might be distant and undeserving: at 243.

1283 [1964] A.C. 326.

1284 [1964] A.C. 326 at 349; see, too, at 364, per Lord Pearce. The dissenting minority agreed that "damages legally due" or an "award otherwise appropriate" should not be cut down because the claimant would be unable to benefit or gain satisfaction from the use or disposal of the money which as a result would only go to those eventually inheriting his estate, but thought that this consideration lent weight to their view (paras 40-260 and 40-261, above) that, in assessing what was appropriate and legally due as damages for loss of amenities, the objective element in the award should be rated low and an unconscious claimant awarded less than one who is fully conscious: see at 341–342 and 363, per Lord Reid and Lord Devlin respectively.

1285 [1980] A.C. 174 at 188F. See, however, the textual comments in para.40-261, above.

the result of an assault and battery because there is the insult to the claimant which arises from the manner of the defendant's interference. This gives rise to injury to feelings calling for aggravated damages and is dealt with under assault where a number of cases of dreadful sexual abuse of the young are collected,[1286] although recently aggravated damages have been awarded in personal injury claims for sex abuse without reliance on, or even mention of, assault. Such cases are *BJM v Eyre*,[1287] and *RAR v GGC*.[1288] What is to be noted here is that aggravated damages are not available where the defendant's behaviour is disgraceful and demeaning to the claimant but falls short of assault; gross carelessness or highhanded conduct will not do. It was so held in *Kralj v McGrath*,[1289] where the claimant had in the course of childbirth been subjected to outrageous and horrific treatment by the defendant doctor. This result was confirmed by the Court of Appeal in *AB v South West Water Services*,[1290] where no aggravated damages were awarded against the defendant suppliers of contaminated water, drunk by the many claimants to physical ill effect, defendants who had behaved in an arrogant and reprehensible fashion.

### (6) Relevance of receipt of social security benefits

It will seem strange to be raising the issue of collateral benefits, in the form of social security benefits, in the context of non-pecuniary loss. For such benefits, which are of a pecuniary nature, must surely operate only to reduce pecuniary loss. And that indeed is now the position. But the legislation which operated from 1989 to 1997[1291] misguidedly provided for the deduction and recoupment by the Department of Social Security of benefits from the totality of the damages recovered and not only from the damages for losses of the same nature as the benefits. That the non-pecuniary loss award was, in a suitable case, in line for suffering a deduction and accounting was made clear in *Hassall v Secretary of State for Social Security*,[1292] where the two claimants had no loss of earnings or medical expenses for which to claim. The position has now been righted by the 1997 legislation providing that benefits related to earnings are deducted from, and only from, damages awarded for loss of earnings,[1293] and similarly with medical expenses.[1294] This matter is therefore now history but it is important to keep it in mind. **40-273**

## 4. Level of Awards

In earlier editions of this work in the last century, it was said that it was virtually impossible to give clear guidance on amounts, varying as they do with the particular injury, the particular circumstances and the particular judge, that only a citation of the figures in a very large number of cases could provide any real as- **40-274**

---

[1286] See paras 42-002 and following, below.

[1287] [2010] EWHC 2856 (QB).

[1288] [2012] EWHC 2338 (QB). The Court of Appeal did not award aggravated damages in the personal injury case involving sexual abuse of *C v Flintshire County Council* [2001] P.I.Q.R. Q9 CA at 86 as they do not seem to have been claimed.

[1289] [1986] 1 All E.R. 54.

[1290] [1993] Q.B. 507 CA.

[1291] For this, see para.40-164, above.

[1292] [1995] 1 W.L.R. 812 CA. See the case and the associated *Neal v Bingle* [1998] Q.B. 466 CA at para.40-065, above.

[1293] See para.40-168, above.

[1294] See para.40-241, above.

sistance, that this was hardly appropriate in a book dealing with the principles upon which damages are assessed, and that adjustment for the changing value of sterling was also necessary when using former awards as a yardstick for making present assessments.[1295] Nonetheless attempts were made to give some guidance on the level of awards and to examine in particular how awards at the highest level had progressed over the years.

**40-275** None of this is any longer necessary for since 1992 we have had available the booklet entitled *Guidelines for the Assessment of General Damages in Personal Injury Cases*. This publication has been regularly updated and is now in its fourteenth edition of 2017. Throughout, it has been compiled for the Judicial Studies Board so that, in reduction of the publication's compendious title, it has tended to be referred to simply as the JSB Guidelines. However, the name of the Judicial Studies Board has now been changed, rather curiously, to the Judicial College, and the current edition incorporates this new name in its title by way of *Judicial College Guidelines*. In what follows it seems best to speak simply of *Guidelines*. The aim of the work, as explained by Lord Donaldson in his Foreword to the first edition, is to use "the amount of damages awarded in reported cases as guidelines or markers" and "to distil the conventional wisdom contained in the reported cases". Every type of injury, from the severe to the minor, is there[1296] and a bracket of figures is provided for nearly all of them. From *Guidelines* the courts today constantly take guidance and rightly so.[1297] It is an essential tool in the assessment of damages for non-pecuniary loss in personal injury claims[1298] and relieves the author of a text on damages from further investigation of the detail of the level of awards.[1299]

**40-276** While it has been the long accepted practice of the courts to break down their awards between the pecuniary loss and the non-pecuniary loss,[1300] it is equally their practice, as we have seen,[1301] not to break down awards for the non-pecuniary loss between the particular heads of damage.[1302] This practice is of course followed by the *Guidelines* in setting out award figures. And if a court should state that it is mak-

[1295] The award is made on the "scale" current at the date of trial rather than at the date of injury: see para.20-017, above.

[1296] Very occasionally, as in *Woodward v Leeds Teaching Hospitals Trust* [2012] EWHC 2167 (QB), the injury may not feature in the *Guidelines* because of its rarity: see at [180]. In *Woodward* it was acromelagic gigantism.

[1297] Staughton LJ had said, in *Arafa v Potter* [1994] P.I.Q.R. Q72 CA at 79, that in the Court of Appeal "we ought to look to the sources rather than the summary produced by the Judicial Studies Board" and was taken to task by Lord Woolf who in his Foreword to the 1996 edition of *Guidelines* stated his profound disagreement with such an approach, considering *Guidelines* the most reliable tool for the use of all courts. Staughton LJ's view has not prevailed.

[1298] The *Guidelines* will not always pinpoint a figure, or a range of figures, so that the Court of Appeal in *Steele v Home Office* [2010] EWCA Civ 724 CA, in reopening the trial judge's award for seven years of toothache endured in prison, made its assessment by reference only to the general framework of damages for personal injury: see at [44]–[52].

[1299] For awards without reference to the *Guidelines* to four children who had been subjected to sustained and serious sexual abuse throughout their childhood (awards primarily for the non-pecuniary loss but including sums for pecuniary loss), see *ABB v Milton Keynes Council* [2011] EWHC 2745 (QB).

[1300] At one time the hazards of giving guidance upon amounts awarded were very substantially increased by the erstwhile tendency of judges to give global awards for the totality of a claimant's loss, both pecuniary and non-pecuniary. But that hazard has long gone, indeed since 1969: see para.19-050, above.

[1301] See para.40-254, above.

[1302] There is no longer any separate, though small, award for loss of expectation of life: see paras 40-262 and 40-263, above.

ing an award for pain and suffering *tout court*, it is practically certain that this encompasses all heads of non-pecuniary damage. Thus where £15,000 was awarded for pain and suffering in *Winkworth v Hubbard*,[1303] in 1960, an award which when adjusted for inflation would today be over quarter of a million pounds, it can be reliably deduced that a very sizeable part of the award is to be attributed to loss of amenities of life. Very occasionally there may be an award for pain and suffering where it is clear that there has been no loss of amenities. An illustration is afforded by *Phelan v East Cumbrian Health Authority*,[1304] where the claimant had undergone surgery without anaesthetic and was awarded £10,000 for his pain and suffering.[1305]

Not only have the levels of damages been provided for us by the *Guidelines* but within a decade of their first appearance the levels adhered to by the courts, and reflected in the *Guidelines*, were radically changed by the Court of Appeal. This was in response to the argument, put forward by the Law Commission and taken up by a group of claimants, that current conventional awards for pain and suffering and loss of amenities were too low and should be increased across the board. The Law Commission in its Report on *Damages for Personal Injury: Non-Pecuniary Loss*[1306] following, after the usual consultation, its Consultation Paper[1307] on the same subject had recommended that awards over £3,000 should be, if not doubled, at least increased one and a half times, awards up to £2,000 should attract no increase and awards between £2,000 and £3,000 should go up by something less than one-and-a-half. **40-277**

In a series of test cases, the lead one of which was *Heil v Rankin*,[1308] the Court of Appeal, in a landmark decision,[1309] agreed to a measure of increase in such damages but did not consider that it would be appropriate to increase the level of awards to the substantial extent recommended by the Law Commission. The court was impressed by some of the matters relied upon by the Commission—in particular, by the response to its Consultation Paper with many in favour of increase, and by the general increase in life expectancy especially of those suffering the gravest injuries—but less so by other matters relied upon, such as the results of a survey commissioned by the Law Commission and the higher level of awards in the jury trials of Northern Ireland. No doubt the outcome in the Court of Appeal was seen by some as constituting a compromise decision. **40-278**

The decision left awards up to £10,000 remaining precisely where they were, with no increase, thereby placing the level of damages which do not have to be increased at a substantially higher figure than the £2,000 proposed by the Law Commission. The court pointed out that numerous cases would have been affected had they adopted the Law Commission figure since the majority of claims are for modest sums. The Court of Appeal was satisfied that it was awards at the highest level, those for catastrophic injuries, which were most in need of adjustment, and that they should be increased by approximately one-third.[1310] On this basis the highest award, it was said, was unlikely to be in excess of £200,000. Indeed the **40-279**

1303 [1960] 1 Lloyd's Rep. 150.

1304 [1991] 2 Med. L.R. 419.

1305 [1991] 2 Med. L.R. 419 at 419.

1306 Law Commission, *Damages for Personal Injury: Non-Pecuniary Loss* (1999), Law Com. No.257.

1307 Law Commission, *Damages for Personal Injury: Non-Pecuniary Loss* (1995), No.140.

1308 [2001] Q.B. 272 CA.

1309 The Master of the Rolls considered the matter of such importance that he convened a five-man court for the exercise.

1310 It was undoubtedly true, as was pointed out in the 1997 edition, that it was awards for the most severe

court specified, when dealing with two of the cases before it, that the bracket for the worst injuries, quadriplegia and very severe brain damage, standing at the time in the *Guidelines* at £120,000 to £150,000, should be £150,000 to £200,000. As for awards in the vast range between these two poles, the Court of Appeal did not follow the Law Commission's approach, which would have entailed applying the one-third increase in the top awards to all these awards, but instead introduced the idea of a taper, so that the adjustment would taper downward from one-third at the top to nil at £10,000. Thus the increase in an award of £100,000 was in the region of one-fifth and an award of £70,000 in the region of one-seventh, while an award of £20,000 would attract a very small increase. The progression does not seem to be linear.[1311] In any event the *Guidelines* have taken the Court of Appeal's prescriptions into account.

**40-280** Again in 2012 a further increase was proposed by the courts and then in 2013 put into effect. In its first hearing in *Simmons v Castle*,[1312] which was a case of a minor personal injury, the Court of Appeal declared that in all personal injury claims for which judgment is given after 1 April 2013 the level of general damages for pain, suffering and loss of amenity should be increased by 10 per cent.[1313] In so deciding, the court was adopting the recommendation made in the package of reforms appearing in the *Jackson Report on Civil Litigation Costs*, to the implementation of which recommendation the judiciary was committed,[1314] with 1 April 2013 being the date on which the legislation was to bring certain of the Jackson reforms into effect. Then in a further hearing of *Simmons v Castle*,[1315] the Court of Appeal went much further and decided that the 10 per cent increase would apply to all civil claims and to all heads of non-pecuniary loss, thereby requiring the declaration put forward in the first hearing to be replaced by a declaration which of course included personal injury cases but now in a global context.[1316] The uplift applies to all cases of personal injury and it includes claims for injury to feelings as well as psychiatric harm.[1317]

Courts do not have discretion in awarding the *Simmons v Castle* 10 per cent uplift, even if the uplift would give the claimant a windfall.[1318] The rationale behind this is that considerations of clarity and consistency override those of perfect justice in every case. The alternative, of a discretionary approach, would lead to complete uncertainty and inconsistency throughout England and Wales and difficulties in

---

injuries which were becoming markedly out of line with awards of the 1960s and the early 1970s and that, although there had been leaps forward in awards—to £35,000 for a paraplegic in *Walker v John McLean & Sons* [1979] 1 W.L.R. 760 CA and to £75,000 for a quadriplegic in *Housecroft v Burnett* [1986] 1 All E.R. 332 CA—the leaps forward had not been nearly far enough: see 16th edition (1997), paras 1712 to 1713.

1311 The scale of the increase that must be made—very approximately, the Court of Appeal emphasised—is illustrated by, and can be very approximately read off, a useful diagram annexed to the judgment. Although with the passage of time it is now of little significance the Court of Appeal declared the decision to have retrospective effect, applying to all future decisions irrespective of when the cause of action accrued or when the tort occurred if earlier.

1312 [2012] 1 W.L.R. 1239 CA; first hearing at 1240.

1313 See [2012] 1 W.L.R. 1239 CA at [20] of the first hearing.

1314 See [2012] 1 W.L.R. 1239 CA at [7] of the first hearing.

1315 [2012] 1 W.L.R. 1239 CA; further hearing at 1243.

1316 See the replacement of [20] of the first hearing by [50] of the further hearing. For more on the procedural history and reasons for this development see para.40-280, below.

1317 *Pereira de Souza v Vinci Construction UK Ltd* [2017] EWCA Civ 879 CA at [25]–[35].

1318 *Summers v Bundy* [2016] EWCA Civ 126.

calculating and determining the form and amount of Pt 36 offers or without prejudice proposals of settlement.[1319]

The *Guidelines* in its current edition of 2017 takes into account both the increases favoured in *Heil v Rankin* and the 10 per cent uplift laid down in *Simmons v Castle*, together with increases year by year on account of inflation, the *Guidelines* continuing to be updated by reference to the Retail Price Index which was said to provide a simple straightforward measure of the value of money.[1320]The result of these movements is that the brackets for quadriplegia and for very severe brain damage, which in the edition in use at the time of *Heil v Rankin* both stood at £120,000 to £150,000 stand in the current edition at £284,610 to £354,260 and at £247,280 to £354,260 respectively.[1321] This is a very substantial increase. **40-281**

## VII. ENVOI: The Particular Case of Claims by Parents Arising Out of the Birth of their Children

### 1. Setting The Scene

Starting in the 1980s problems of damages have been presented to the courts where parents have brought actions on account of children being born to them, sometimes in a normal, healthy state, sometimes in an injured, handicapped condition.[1322] In some of these cases the major, and even the only, claim has been for the cost involved in the child's rearing and upbringing, and the question has arisen, in the context of the Limitation Act 1980 with its general limitation period of six years but its particular one in the case of personal injuries of three, as to whether the claim is or is not in respect of personal injury. The Court of Appeal answered the question in the affirmative in *Walkin v South Manchester Health Authority*,[1323] where the action was by a woman claimant complaining of a failed sterilisation, holding that the unwanted conception was an impairment of the claimant's physical condition and that the economic loss, which was the only claim **40-282**

1319 [2016] EWCA Civ 126 at [21]–[22].

1320 Other indices were canvassed in argument in *Heil v Rankin*, such as that of Gross Domestic Product, but have not been used by the *Guidelines*.

1321 See the *Guidelines* (2017) Ch.2 and Ch.3, respectively. Side by side with these figures, and throughout its current edition, *Guidelines* gives the figures excluding the 10 per cent uplift. Jackson's main purpose in proposing the 10 per cent uplift being to provide some recompense to claimants with conditional fee agreements for the loss of the success fee which was being removed, the retention in the *Guidelines* of the pre-uplift figures is presumably to take account of the Court of Appeal's ruling that claimants with conditional fee agreements entered into before 1 April 2013, who remain entitled to the success fee, cannot also have the 10 per cent uplift: see [2013] 1 W.L.R. 1239 CA at [50] of the further hearing at 1243, and para.40-280, below.

1322 Occasionally the claim may be not on account of having a child but on account of the failure to have a child. Thus whether a young woman rendered incapable of bearing a child as a consequence of medical negligence may make a claim for the costs of surrogacy in an attempt to give her children was considered in *Briody v St Helen's & Knowsley Health Authority* [2002] Q.B. 856 CA. In the particular circumstances the claimant failed because of the smallness of the chance of a successful outcome to the surrogacy but, this apart, the court was doubtful as to whether a claim for surrogacy expenses should succeed where neither the pregnancy nor the child would be that of the claimant surrogate mother—which was the position in the case before the court—or even where pregnancy or child would be that of the claimant: see the judgment of Hale LJ at paras [25], [29]–[32]. There is of course a clear claim for general damages to compensate the claimant for the very serious loss of amenity from being deprived of the chance of having children in the ordinary way.

1323 [1995] 1 W.L.R. 1543 CA.

made by her, stemmed from this injury. Auld LJ took the view[1324] that the same should follow where a man claimed for a failed vasectomy, though it might be more difficult to see where the physical injury lay; Roch LJ, however, preferred to reserve judgment on this issue,[1325] as to a lesser extent did Neill LJ,[1326] Roch LJ recognising that such a conclusion had the advantage of setting a single period of limitation for all failed sterilisation cases. The uncertainty has since spilt over to the cases dealing with mothers who would have had an abortion if told that their child would be born disabled. While Henriques J in *Hardman v Amin*,[1327] was prepared to hold that this type of case also gives rise to physical injury, pointing out that

> "it would be an anomaly for a wrongful conception claim to be an action for damages for personal injuries whilst a wrongful birth case was not",[1328]

it was strongly argued in the wrongful birth case of *Godfrey v Gloucestershire Royal Infirmary NHS Trust*,[1329] that, on account of the House of Lords' concentration on the economic loss features in the wrongful conception case of *McFarlane v Tayside Health Board*,[1330] the *Walkin*[1331] case should be regarded as overruled. After a thorough analysis[1332] this argument was however rejected and the three-year limitation period held applicable.[1333] Yet despite this general uncertainty, still continuing,[1334] here seems to be the best place to deal with the whole panorama of these cases, and therefore their treatment forms essentially an addendum to the generalities of this chapter.

**40-283** Essentially in issue are claims by the parents. The child injured pre-natally or in the course of being born because of a defendant's negligence or other tort will have its own claim—generally under the Congenital Disabilities (Civil Liability) Act 1976 or, as decided by *Burton v Islington Health Authority* and *De Martell v Merton and Sutton Health Authority*,[1335] at common law where the injury predated the coming into force of that Act—but there are no special features of such an injury that call for particular treatment. And no claim here is available to a child where its only complaint against the defendant is that he has allowed it to be born in an injured and handicapped condition; the Court of Appeal held in *McKay v Essex Area Health Authority*,[1336] that English law does not recognise an action for what has been called wrongful life.

**40-284** Before turning to the cases concerning the child with parents who did not wish it to be born, it is instructive to consider the unusual case of *Kralj v McGrath*,[1337] which clearly involved a physical injury to the mother; she suffered horrific and

---

1324 [1995] 1 W.L.R. 1543 CA at 1552F.
1325 [1995] 1 W.L.R. 1543 CA at 1553C–D.
1326 [1995] 1 W.L.R. 1543 CA at 1555C.
1327 [2000] Lloyd's Rep. Med. 498.
1328 [2000] Lloyd's Rep. Med. 498 at 501, col.1.
1329 [2003] Lloyd's Rep. Med. 398.
1330 [2000] 2 A.C. 59; see at para.40-288, below.
1331 [1995] 1 W.L.R. 1543 CA.
1332 See Godfrey [2003] Lloyd's Rep. Med. 398 at [25]–[34].
1333 [2003] Lloyd's Rep. Med. 398 at [35].
1334 Compare *Farraj v King's Healthcare NHS Trust* [2006] P.I.Q.R. P29 at 470, [96]: "Despite the fact that this is a claim for economic loss, it is agreed by the parties that, as a result of the decision in *Walkin v South Manchester HA*, this action is to be treated as an action for personal injury."
1335 [1993] Q.B. 204 CA.
1336 [1982] Q.B. 1166 CA.
1337 [1986] 1 All E.R. 54.

wholly unacceptable treatment from the defendant doctor at the time of the delivery. It was held that the mother might recover for the financial loss which she would suffer in having another pregnancy to replace the child who died as a result of the defendant doctor's negligence. What the mother obtained by way of damages, in addition to the discomfort necessarily entailed in another pregnancy, was not the cost of bringing up the further child but her loss of earnings, in the early years of the child's life, arising from the need to do so. The reason for this was that the child who died was a twin, the other child being born healthy, and had both children survived this would have made up the family of three which she and her husband wished to have. Now she was going to have to become pregnant all over again in order to provide herself and her husband with the third child. The case is therefore exceptional and it is difficult to envisage other circumstances in which a similar recovery would be available. For if the child who dies is not a twin and the parents decide to have another child to replace it, then any lost earnings after that child is born will be cancelled out by the ability to keep earning after the death of the first child. And if the first child does not die, then the damages available to the child will include the cost of its care in which may be reflected any loss of earnings of its mother.

## 2. Developments before McFarlane v Tayside Health Board

At about the same time as *Kralj v McGrath*,[1338] the Courts were called upon to grapple with the case of the unwanted child, the child who but for the defendant's negligence would not have been born, the complaint almost invariably being of the failure of the defendant, doctor or health authority to sterilise a potential parent, female or male, or to abort an incipient parent who has found herself to be pregnant. The history of how first instance courts and the Court of Appeal effectively founded and developed a new cause of action for such parents, only suddenly to find all their careful development of claim and damages largely axed by the House of Lords in *McFarlane v Tayside Health Board*,[1339] a decade and a half after the case law had started to be established, makes for a cautionary tale. Yet since this decision has not caused the courts to abandon all recovery for the costs of the rearing and upbringing of unwanted children, and since the law might again change in this controversial area,[1340] the pre-*McFarlane* development should be briefly looked at. **40-285**

### (1) Failure to sterilise

The cases got off to a somewhat unpropitious start with two first instance decisions, *Udale v Bloomsbury Area Health Authority*,[1341] and *Emeh v Kensington and Chelsea and Westminster Area Health Authority*,[1342] both concerning failed sterilisations of women claimants. Liability was indeed imposed but the damages recovered were limited to the pain, discomfort and anxiety arising from the unsuccessful operation and the repeat operation necessitated by the failure of the first. A more **40-286**

[1338] [1986] 1 All E.R. 54.

[1339] [2000] 2 A.C. 59. This important case is at para.40-288, below.

[1340] The High Court of Australia in *Cattanach v Melchior* (2013) 215 CLR 1. HCA has, by a bare majority of a court of seven, declined to follow *McFarlane*.

[1341] [1983] 1 W.L.R. 1098.

[1342] [1985] Q.B. 1012 (first instance reported with CA).

expansive view was soon taken at first instance in *Thake v Maurice*,[1343] a view which the Court of Appeal, in reversing in *Emeh*,[1344] upheld and then reiterated in *Thake v Maurice*[1345] itself on appeal. The damages were held to comprise the cost of bringing up the unwanted child and the loss of the mother's earnings during his minority.[1346] In *Benarr v Kettering Health Authority*,[1347] the cost of a private education was allowed where the child was born into an upper middle class family. In *Robinson v Salford Health Authority*,[1348] the cost of upbringing until adulthood was allowed, which with a healthy child would be the normal limit of responsibility for the parent and hence for the tortfeasor. In *Allen v Bloomsbury Health Authority*,[1349] Brooke J reviewed all the various cases from *Udale*,[1350] onwards on the amount of recovery, arriving at the conclusion that

> "in this type of case defendants are liable to pay for all such expenses as may be reasonably incurred for the education and upkeep for the unplanned child, having regard to all the circumstances of the case and, in particular, to his condition in life and his reasonable requirements at the time the expenditure is incurred."[1351]

### (2) Failure to warn of disability

**40-287** Alternatively, the negligence of the defendant, again doctor or health authority, may consist in a failure to advise a pregnant mother that the baby she is carrying might suffer from a disabling disease, such as Down's syndrome or congenital rubella, with the result that there is born a handicapped or disabled child which the mother, had she been properly advised, would have aborted. Again, in appropriate circumstances a claim will lie for the cost of upbringing and even, since here ex hypothesi the child is not a normal healthy child, for the cost of lifetime caring if the parents can satisfy the court that that is their intention. Thus in *Nunnerley v Warrington Health Authority*,[1352] it was held that principle entitled the parents to recover for the cost of care which they would give after the age of 18 to their disabled child, who in this case would not but for the wrong have been conceived. There may also, as with the cases of unplanned children, be a claim for the loss of the mother's earnings, but caution is needed to ensure that there is no double counting. Thus in *Fish v Wilcox*,[1353] where the claimant would have had an abortion had she been warned of the likely disability of her child, the defendant accepted that he was liable for the cost of having to care for the child but successfully resisted, at first instance and on appeal, the claimant's additional claim for her loss of earnings. "She cannot", said

---

1343 [1986] Q.B. 644 (first instance reported with CA).

1344 [1985] Q.B. 1012 CA.

1345 [1986] Q.B. 644 CA.

1346 But see *Fish v Wilcox* [1994] 5 Med. L.R. 230 CA at para.40-287, below.

1347 (1988) 138 New L.J. 179.

1348 (1992) 3 Med. L.R. 270.

1349 [1993] 1 All E.R. 651.

1350 [1983] 1 W.L.R. 1098.

1351 [1993] 1 All E.R. 651 at 662a.

1352 [2000] Lloyd's Rep. Med. 170; decided 10 days before *McFarlane* (see next paragraph), with leave to appeal refused a few months after *McFarlane* on the ground that the trial judge's decision was undoubtedly correct, the defendants accepting that the pre-*McFarlane* law applied: see the case on the appeal reported rather belatedly under the name *N v Warrington Health Authority* at [2003] Lloyd's Rep. Med. 365 CA.

1353 [1994] 5 Med. L.R. 230 CA.

Nourse LJ,

"do two jobs at once and she is not entitled to be paid for doing two jobs".[1354]

### 3. The New Thinking: McFarlane v Tayside Health Board

The House of Lords in *McFarlane v Tayside Health Board*,[1355] an appeal from Scotland, put paid to the core of this whole development from *Emeh v Kensington and Chelsea and Westminster Area Health Authority*[1356] onwards. A husband and wife with four children wished to have no more, the husband underwent a failed vasectomy, the wife became pregnant and gave birth to a further, healthy, child. The House of Lords, reversing the Inner House of the Court of Session, held that the parents were not entitled to recover the costs of caring for and bringing up their child. A variety of reasons was given for this holding. The first and foremost one, embraced by Lords Slynn, Steyn and Hope, was that a claim for the costs of caring for a healthy, normal child was a claim for pure economic loss in respect of which it had to be shown that it was fair, just and reasonable to impose liability and that the claim did not satisfy this requirement. Lord Steyn said in addition that considerations of distributive justice indicated that the law did not permit such a claim against a health authority or doctor. Lord Clyde considered that to allow the claim would go beyond reasonable restitution for the wrong done, while Lord Millett took the view that the law regarded the birth of a healthy baby as a blessing with the benefits of parenthood outweighing any loss. *Emeh*,[1357] together with *Thake v Maurice*,[1358] and *Allen v Bloomsbury Health Authority*,[1359] were overruled. At the same time four of their Lordships were prepared, affirming the Inner House, to award general damages to the mother for the pain and suffering and inconvenience of pregnancy and childbirth, and special damages for extra medical expenses, clothing and loss of earnings associated therewith. **40-288**

### 4. The New Thinking Extended: Rees v Darlington Memorial Hospital NHS Trust

The House of Lords returned to the problem soon after in *Rees v Darlington Memorial Hospital NHS Trust*.[1360] The *McFarlane* ruling was followed and applied[1361]; an extension to it was disallowed, which was sensible, but an extension from a very different angle was invented, which is controversial. The decision was not unanimous as it was in *McFarlane* but, with the House sitting as a court of seven, was arrived at by a bare majority of four to three. **40-289**

[1354] [1994] 5 Med. L.R. 230 CA at 230. Contrast *Thake v Maurice* [1986] Q.B. 644 CA at para.40-286, above.
[1355] [2000] 2 A.C. 59.
[1356] [1985] Q.B. 1012 CA.
[1357] [1985] Q.B. 1012 CA.
[1358] [1986] Q.B. 644 CA.
[1359] [1993] 1 All E.R. 651.
[1360] [2004] 1 A.C. 309.
[1361] The House rejected an invitation to depart from *McFarlane* pursuant to the familiar 1966 Practice Statement, a rejection which could very reasonably have been expected with *McFarlane* decided only four years earlier.

### (1) The disabled parent equated with the normal parent

**40-290** The claimant in *Rees*, a physically disabled woman who had sought a sterilisation for the reason that she considered herself incapable of caring adequately for a child because of her disability, was ultimately unsuccessful in her attempt to distinguish *McFarlane*.[1362] The House of Lords held that the *McFarlane* ruling nevertheless applied so as to disallow recovery of the costs of bringing up the child, thereby reversing the Court of Appeal which had held by a majority that the claimant was entitled to recover the costs of maintenance of the healthy child, born in consequence of the failed sterilisation, though only to the extent that the costs were additional to the costs which would have been incurred by a mother not similarly disabled. This reversal by the Lords seems correct. Once the courts have gone down the *McFarlane* route, it is thought that there should not be a difference between parents who seek sterilisation because they cannot, for instance, financially cope with a further child and parents who cannot cope with a child on account of the mother's disability.[1363]

### (2) The invention of a conventional award

**40-291** The majority in *Rees*,[1364] however went beyond *McFarlane* in holding that, although there could be no award for the additional costs of upbringing attributable to the mother's disability, there should nevertheless be a conventional award as a recognition of the wrong done and that this conventional award should apply in a *McFarlane*-type case as much as in a *Rees*-type case. Lord Bingham, who was the first proponent in the House of the conventional award, said that it should be made "in all cases such as these"[1365] and that it should apply "without differentiation"[1366] to cases where child or parent was healthy and to cases where child or parent was disabled.

**40-292** The precise purpose of the conventional award[1367] is variously stated by the Lords in the majority. For Lord Bingham it was designed to deal with the loss represented by the denial to the parent of the opportunity to live her life in the way that she wished and planned[1368]; for Lord Nicholls it was in recognition of the parent having suffered a legal wrong with far-reaching effects on her and her family[1369]; for Lord Millett it was for the denial of the right to limit the size of the family as an important aspect of personal autonomy[1370]; for Lord Scott it was for the frustration

---

1362 [2000] 2 A.C. 59.

1363 The House of Lords' decision is more in line than is the Court of Appeal's with that in *AD v East Kent Community NHS Trust* [2003] P.I.Q.R. P18 CA at 286 in which the Court of Appeal upheld the dismissal at first instance of a claim where, while there was no failed sterilisation, it was again the mother's disability that led to the damages, here a disability that was mental rather than physical. The claimant, an intellectually impaired and mentally unstable patient in the defendants' hospital, was rendered pregnant by another, unknown, patient and gave birth to a healthy daughter whom she was incapable of looking after but was held not entitled to claim the cost of bringing up the daughter, a task which had been shouldered by the child's grandmother.

1364 [2004] 1 A.C. 309.

1365 [2004] 1 A.C. 309 at [8].

1366 [2004] 1 A.C. 309 at [9].

1367 It had been earlier proposed by Lord Millett in *McFarlane* itself but was not there taken up.

1368 [2004] 1 A.C. 309 at [8].

1369 [2004] 1 A.C. 309 at [17].

1370 [2004] 1 A.C. 309 at [123].

of the expected benefit to be derived from being safeguarded from conception.[1371] The amount proposed by Lord Bingham for the conventional award, and concurred in by the other members of the majority, was £15,000.

**40-293** The creation of such a conventional award marks a break from established principles of damages. It would fall within the accepted bounds of damages if it could be seen as an element of non-pecuniary loss, akin to loss of amenity, but Lord Bingham was careful to say that "the conventional award would not be, and would not be intended to be, compensatory"[1372] while Lord Millett spoke of

> "a purely conventional [figure] which should not be susceptible of increase or decrease by reference to the circumstances of the particular case".[1373]

Both Lord Steyn and Lord Hope, in the minority on the main decision, spoke in strong and convincing terms against the invention of the conventional award,[1374] regarding the idea of such an award as contrary to principle. To Lord Hope, disturbed by his inability to find any consistent or coherent ratio in support of the conventional award in the speeches of the majority, the idea of a non-compensatory award departed from

> "the principle which has always guided the common law in its approach to the assessment of damages".[1375]

However, it looks as if the conventional award is here to stay even though only endorsed, after little argument and no rigorous examination of the competing positions, by a bare majority in *Rees* and, in the estimation of Lord Nicholls there,[1376] running counter to the views of all of their Lordships in *McFarlane* other than, predictably,[1377] Lord Millett.

## 5. The Position Today

**40-294** It is therefore now established, at the highest level, that there are no circumstances whatsoever in which parents can recover for the costs of upbringing of a child that is born normal and healthy; all that they will recover is the £15,000 conventional award.[1378] The position is however different with the child that is born disabled. In *McFarlane* counsel for the defendant health board had conceded that the rule might have to be different with an unwanted child born seriously disabled, and Lord Slynn and Lord Steyn both expressly left this question open. Since *McFarlane* the authorities that we have on the disabled child are at first instance and in the Court of Appeal only, and these authorities have developed a pattern of

---

[1371] [2004] 1 A.C. 309 at [148].

[1372] [2004] 1 A.C. 309 at [8].

[1373] [2004] 1 A.C. 309 at [125].

[1374] [2004] 1 A.C. 309 at [40]–[47] and [70]–[77] respectively.

[1375] [2004] 1 A.C. 309 at [74].

[1376] [2004] 1 A.C. 309 at [41].

[1377] Because he had already proposed such an award in *McFarlane*.

[1378] There can now be entirely ignored the unsuccessful attempts immediately in the wake of *McFarlane* to bypass it on far fetched grounds, attempts appearing in *Greenfield v Irwin* [2001] 1 W.L.R. 1279 CA, also known as *Greenfield v Flather* [2001] Lloyd's Rep. Med. 143 CA (arguing for a distinction between cost of care and loss of earnings, for a distinction between pure economic loss and personal injury, and for application of the Human Rights Act) and in *Richardson v LRC Products Ltd* [2001] Lloyd's Rep. Med. 280 (arguing that *McFarlane* did not apply to breach of statutory duty as distinct from common law negligence).

recovery across the board for the cost of the extra care that a disabled child needs. What the Supreme Court will say to this cannot be predicted. It could reject these authorities, endorse them, or even expand them to allow the full costs of care, and in arriving at any of these solutions could make a distinction between the case of the failed sterilisation and the case of the failure to warn. So much will depend upon the exact composition of the Supreme Court should a claim come eventually to be heard.

### (1) Extra costs of care of the disabled child: the still uncertain position

40-295 **(a) Where there has been a failure to sterilise** On two occasions, first in *Parkinson v St James and Seacroft University Hospital NHS Trust*,[1379] and then in *Groom v Selby*,[1380] the Court of Appeal[1381] awarded the parents the extra cost to them of rearing their disabled child over the cost of rearing a normal and healthy child, considering *McFarlane* to be distinguishable. Brooke LJ in a valuable judgment in *Parkinson* concluded that the tests of foreseeability and proximity were satisfied, recovery of the extra upbringing costs would be fair, just and reasonable, principles of distributive justice pointed to this result, and there was nothing in *McFarlane* to deflect the Court of Appeal from adopting a course which he said that both logic and justice demanded. In *Groom v Selby* also, the care costs, but again only the extra care costs, were awarded.[1382]

40-296 In *Rees*,[1383] their Lordships *en passant* considered *Parkinson* and the case of the disabled child born after a failed sterilisation, putting forward a variety of views as to how such a case should be dealt with. The minority of three not surprisingly considered *Parkinson* to be right[1384] since they were deciding in *Rees* in favour of the disabled parent. Similarly, there were three of the majority who considered *Parkinson* to be wrong.[1385] Only Lord Millett sat on the fence, wishing to keep open the question of whether *Parkinson* was rightly decided.[1386] So there is no clear majority in either direction to guide the lower courts or indeed the highest court differently constituted. For the moment *Parkinson*, and *Groom*, are to be followed, though no claims of failed sterilisations resulting in a disabled birth have yet appeared.[1387]

40-297 **(b) Where there has been a failure to warn of disability** The stronger case for allowing a degree of recovery for the cost of care is where the child is unwanted only in the sense that the parents do not want to have a disabled child. This is where the negligence consists of a failure to warn that the child is likely to be born disabled

1379 [2002] 1 Q.B. 266 CA.

1380 [2002] Lloyd's Rep. Med. 1 CA.

1381 Affirming the decisions of the courts below in both suits.

1382 It had been unsuccessfully contended at first instance ([2001] Lloyd's Rep. Med. 39) that to award no more than the extra costs of upbringing infringed the right to family life under article 8 of the Human Rights Act but this argument was not pursued in the Court of Appeal.

1383 [2004] 1 A.C. 309.

1384 Lord Steyn, Lord Hope and Lord Hutton at [2004] 1 A.C. 309 at [35], [57] and [91] respectively.

1385 Lord Scott expressly at [2004] 1 A.C. 309 [145], Lord Bingham and Lord Nicholls by clear implication (as they both said they would apply the same rule whether it was the child or the mother who was disabled) at [9] and [18] respectively.

1386 [2004] 1 A.C. 309 at [112].

1387 The few post-2002 cases that there are all concern failures to warn of disability in the child; see para.40-298, below.

and is therefore directed to disability itself. Following on the heels of *McFarlane*, courts of first instance in *Rand v East Dorset Health Authority*,[1388] and *Hardman v Amin*,[1389] allowed recovery for such losses as related to the disability, awarding the parents the extra cost to them of rearing their disabled child over the cost of rearing a normal child and holding *McFarlane* to be distinguishable. Also at first instance in *Lee v Taunton and Somerset NHS Trust*,[1390] it was accepted that extra care costs would be recoverable so as to justify there the awarding of a substantial interim payment. In *Rand*,[1391] Newman J allowed not only maintenance costs over and above what it would have cost to bring up a normal healthy child but also loss of profits in running the family business to the extent that the parents had reasonably given up work to look after their daughter. In addition, the parents were awarded substantial amounts of general damages, the mother for the distress of discovering that her daughter was seriously disabled and for the pain, suffering and inconvenience of a further pregnancy, and both parents for the loss of amenity involved in the real and physical experience of looking after a disabled child with the attendant consequences on their private lives. In *Hardman*,[1392] to the extent that the extra care was gratuitous Henriques J gave alternative assessments. The care was to be assessed either on a commercial basis subject to a 25 per cent discount or by way of damages for the loss of amenity consequent upon the stress and anxiety of bringing up a disabled child. In *Rand* the extra maintenance costs allowed were limited to what was within the parents' means. This limitation is questionable. *Rand* was not followed in this regard in *Hardman* where it was held that the defendant could not limit liability under this head by reference to what the claimant would, but for any award, have been able to afford to spend on care.[1393]

Since these early post-*McFarlane* decisions none of the very few further cases that have appeared has tackled issues of damages or had to consider appropriate measures of damages. Rather have they dealt variously with questions of duty of care,[1394] existence of negligence,[1395] limitation[1396] or computation of a lost chance,[1397] and their only relevance here is their implicit assumption, when dealing with their particular issues, that failures to warn of disability can still sound in damages. Thus it can be said that the Court of Appeal has not so far specifically endorsed or rejected the preparedness in *Rand* and *Hardman* to allow recovery for the costs of the extra care but since, after these decisions, it has twice, in *Parkinson* and *Groom*, done likewise in the more debatable case of the failed sterilisation,[1398] it is clear that there would be endorsement rather than rejection. As for the attitude now of the Supreme **40-298**

---

1388 [2000] Lloyd's Rep. Med. 181.

1389 [2000] Lloyd's Rep. Med. 498.

1390 [2001] F.L.R. 419.

1391 [2000] Lloyd's Rep. Med. 181.

1392 [2000] Lloyd's Rep. Med. 498.

1393 Also in *Lee* (above in this paragraph) it was said that the mother's means were irrelevant. Moreover, that care costs can extend beyond a handicapped child's 18th birthday had already been established in the days, before *McFarlane*, when full care costs were recoverable: see para.40-287, above (especially the *Nunnerley* case there) where it was suggested that in appropriate circumstances even a lifetime of care costs should be recoverable.

1394 *Farraj v King's Healthcare NHS Trust* [2006] P.I.Q.R. P29 at 470.

1395 *P v Leeds Teaching Hospital NHS Trust* [2004] Lloyd's Rep. Med. 537; *Lilleywhite v University College Hospitals NHS Trust* [2006] Lloyd's Rep. Med. 268 CA.

1396 *Godfrey v Gloucestershire Royal Infirmary NHS Trust* [2003] Lloyd's Rep. Med. 398; *Farraj v King's Healthcare NHS Trust* [2006] P.I.Q.R. P29 at 470.

1397 *Whitehead v Hibbert Pownall & Newton* [2008] P.N.L.R. 25 CA at 625.

1398 See para.40-295, above.

Court, the fate of these first instance cases is rather less in the balance than the fate of the Court of Appeal's *Parkinson*.[1399] This is because Lord Scott in *Rees*,[1400] drew a distinction turning on whether the medical treatment sought was simply in order to avoid conception or was because of a fear that a child would be born disabled.[1401] If Lord Scott favoured the claimant, as he clearly did, in the case of failed sterilisation where the parties' minds had been directed to disability, he would surely regard the case of a failure to warn of disability in the same light. Accordingly, there can be found in *Rees* a majority of four to two in favour of these first instance cases, Lord Scott and the minority of three in *Rees* being ranged against Lord Bingham and Lord Nicholls determined to have a uniform rule, with Lord Millett still on the fence.[1402]

### (2) Full costs of care of the disabled child: a possible development

**40-299** It cannot be said to be finally settled—the matter has not reached the Supreme Court—that claimants with disabled children are to be confined to recovery of the extra cost of care, particularly in the case of the failure to warn that the child was likely to be born disabled. There is a good deal to be said for the proposition that the basic and the extra cost of care should in such cases be recoverable. Lord Slynn and Lord Steyn when they indicated that the rule might be different with a disabled child—they left the matter open without committing themselves to a view—were not limiting themselves to the extra cost of upbringing while Lord Millett's view that the birth of a healthy baby was a blessing outweighing any loss might not apply where the baby is disabled. It is true that Brooke LJ in *Parkinson*,[1403] pointing out that counsel did not press the argument for full recovery very vigorously, said that in his judgment such recovery would not be fair, just and reasonable.[1404] On the other hand, Henriques J in *Hardman v Amin*,[1405] noted with some sympathy that counsel wished to reserve the right to canvas such a proposition in the House of Lords[1406]; it is difficult to predict whether he would be successful, for much would depend on the constitution of the court at the time. It may be significant that Brooke LJ was talking in the context of a failure to sterilise and Henriques J in the context of a failure to warn of disability.

**40-300** It has been pointed out[1407] that failure to warn cases dealing directly with damages for cost of care have virtually disappeared since the House gave judgment in *Rees* in 2003 but that the few cases that there are impliedly accept that such damages are available. It is therefore very interesting to find in *Whitehead v Hibbert Pownall & Newton*,[1408] the last of these cases and one in the Court of Appeal, that the court appears to have assumed that full care costs were recoverable.[1409] The claim was against a solicitor for mishandling an action by a mother against a

1399 [2002] 1 Q.B. 266 CA.
1400 [2004] 1 A.C. 309.
1401 [2004] 1 A.C. 309 at [145].
1402 For how the battle lines were drawn in *Rees* see para.40-295, above.
1403 [2002] 1 Q.B. 266 CA.
1404 [2002] 1 Q.B. 266 CA at [51].
1405 [2000] Lloyd's Rep. Med. 498.
1406 [2000] Lloyd's Rep. Med. 498 at 506, col.2.
1407 See para.40-298, above.
1408 [2008] P.N.L.R. 25 at 625.
1409 And the same is true of *Farraj v King's Healthcare NHS Trust* [2006] P.I.Q.R. P29 at 470 where at [37] Swift J said that "the relevant damage is the economic loss resulting from the cost of support-

hospital authority alleging failure to diagnose and warn of a disability in the foetus, and the issue before the court was whether, the mother having died by suicide before the claim against the solicitor had been heard, damages could be awarded for the costs of the child's care uncurtailed by the death.[1410] There is no suggestion that only extra care costs occasioned by the disability were in mind so that, had the mother not died, the Court of Appeal would have awarded damages based on the full costs of care up until the time of the mother's natural death. The Court of Appeal is indeed bound by its own decision in *Parkinson*,[1411] but that was a case of failed sterilisation which need not inhibit the court from arriving at a larger solution where the basis of the claim is a failure to warn of impending disability. To the Supreme Court of course it is open to go any way it wishes.

## 6. ADDENDUM: ISSUES OF AVOIDED LOSS

Since even after *McFarlane* and *Rees* there may still be recovery for costs of care where a child is born disabled, two general points, both of which impinge in disparate fashion upon the question of avoided loss,[1412] need to be considered. One concerns steps taken by the claimant which reduce the loss, the other concerns the receipt of collateral benefits which causes the loss to be less. **40-301**

With children born because of a lack of warning of disability, the parents may consider having another child. This possibility makes for a degree of careful analysis. There are various permutations. Had the child been born normal and healthy the parents may still have intended to have, and proceed to have, another child or children. Or their intention may have been that this child was to complete their family and be their last. Again, even if this had been their initial intention, they may have decided after the birth to have a further child as a substitute, as it were, for the disabled child. Whichever permutation is taken, the parents should have been entitled before *McFarlane*, and possibly after *McFarlane*,[1413] to the full cost of bringing up the disabled child; in all these circumstances the disabled child is an extra child to the family. There is, however, one final possibility, which is that the parents had intended to have a further child or children but, after the birth of the handicapped child, decided against it because of the difficulty and strain involved in bringing up that child. This possibility had been realised in *Salih v Enfield Health Authority*,[1414] where indeed a further unplanned pregnancy was terminated, and the Court of Appeal had held that the parents' decision not to have another child, with the consequential saving of the future expenditure on that child, was a relevant consideration to be taken into account in assessing their damages. In the result, the basic cost of maintaining the disabled child was disallowed and the award on this count was limited to the extra cost entailed in rearing a handicapped and disabled child over the cost of a normal and healthy child. Of course this is now the position in any event in the current state of the authorities,[1415] so that for the time being the importance of the decision in *Salih* falls away. But if the Supreme Court **40-302**

ing and maintaining a child".

1410 Dealt with at para.10-100, above.

1411 [2002] 1 Q.B. 266 CA; at para.40-295, above.

1412 See, generally, Ch.9, above, at paras 9-108 and following.

1413 See para.40-299, above.

1414 [1991] 3 All E.R. 400 CA.

1415 See para.40-297, above.

were to decide in favour of full recovery for a disabled child when there had been a failure to warn of disability,[1416] then *Salih* would come back into its own.

**40-303** It might be considered that the problem of the deductibility of social security benefits would not arise in this context since one thinks of these benefits as being related to the person injured. However, *Rand v East Dorset Health Authority (No.2)*,[1417] shows otherwise.[1418] It was first held that the Social Security (Recovery of Benefits) Act 1997 did not apply where, as in *Rand*, the claimant was other than the person injured. Accordingly, the whole series of benefits which the parents had received, practically all of which were among the many benefits listed in the Act, fell to be considered for deduction by common law principles. It was accepted that income support, unemployment benefit and job seekers' allowance fell to be deducted, no doubt because these were benefits which mitigated the loss of earnings for which the parents had been compensated. For the rest there was no deduction, being benefits received on behalf of the daughter or unrelated to the parents' compensated losses.

[1416] See para.40-299, above.

[1417] [2000] Lloyd's Rep. Med. 377.

[1418] For the major issue in *Rand*, see para.40-297, above.

CHAPTER 41

# TORTS CAUSING DEATH

TABLE OF CONTENTS

**41-001** Where a person was killed in circumstances in which, had he only been injured, he would have had an action against the defendant in respect of the injury, no action lay at common law in respect of his death, either for the benefit of his dependants for injury to themselves by the death,[1] or for the benefit of his estate by way of survival of the cause of action which would have accrued to him before the moment of death. Statute, however, has allowed both actions: the spate of railway accidents on the advent of trains led to the introduction of an action for the benefit of dependants in the Fatal Accidents Act 1846, popularly known as Lord Campbell's Act, and now replaced, as amended over the years, by a consolidating statute, the Fatal Accidents Act 1976 which itself has since been substantially amended by the Administration of Justice Act 1982; and, similarly, the spate of road accidents on the later advent of motorcars led to the introduction of an action for the benefit of the estate by s.1 of the Law Reform (Miscellaneous Provisions) Act 1934, itself also amended by the Administration of Justice Act 1982. These two actions, totally different, call for separate consideration.

**41-002** The amendments made by the Administration of Justice Act 1982 represent substantial changes to the law relating to damages where an injury proves fatal. By s.3 of that Act the Fatal Accidents Act 1976 is radically altered in a number of ways: the categories of persons entitled to damages for their pecuniary loss resulting from the death are again expanded, and expanded beyond dependants in the strict sense[2]; certain family members, again not necessarily dependants, are given a limited right to damages for bereavement[3]; and collateral benefits *en bloc* are no longer to be deducted.[4] All these changes serve to increase the range of damages available to family members under the Fatal Accidents Act 1976. By contrast, the damages to which the estate of the deceased may lay claim under the Law Reform (Miscellaneous Provisions) Act 1934 have been severely, though sensibly, curtailed. By s.1 of the 1982 Act the right to damages for loss of expectation of life is abolished[5] and by s.4(2) the right to damages for prospective loss of earning capacity during the so-called lost years is taken away.[6] This does indeed leave recovery for loss by way of pain and suffering, loss of amenities, medical expenses and loss of earnings all accruing before the death, but whereas damages for loss of expectation of life and for prospective earnings were unaffected by the fact that the death, as is common, was instantaneous or followed swiftly upon the injury, damages for the remaining heads are likely to be of little or no consequence in such circumstances.

## I. Claims for the Benefit of the Deceased's Dependants

**41-003** The Fatal Accidents Act 1846 and the amendments thereto, which over the years had proved fairly extensive, were consolidated in the Fatal Accidents Act 1976. This statute in turn was amended by the Administration of Justice Act 1982. These

---

1 Exceptionally, a dependant in a contractual relationship with the defendant might recover damages for injury to himself through the death: see *Jackson v Watson* [1909] 2 K.B. 193 CA.

2 See para.41-005, below where it will be seen that civil partners have later, in 2004, also been brought in.

3 See para.41-019, below.

4 See para.41-111, below.

5 See para.41-113, below.

6 See para.41-126, below.

amendments are made by wholesale replacement of ss.1 to 4 of the Fatal Accidents Act 1976[7]; some of the sections are thereby substantially, some hardly, altered and an entirely new section is introduced. Further amendments have appeared in the Civil Partnership Act 2004.[8] In addition, the regime of periodical payments introduced for personal injury claims is extended to fatal accident claims, though this is achieved in a somewhat obscure and infelicitous manner.[9]

### (A) *The Statutory Action*

The Fatal Accidents Act 1976 by s.1(1), as substituted by s.3(1) of the Administration Act 1982,[10] and substantially re-enacting s.1 of the original Fatal Accidents Act 1846, provides as follows: **41-004**

> "If death is caused by any wrongful act, neglect or default which is such as would (if death had not ensued) have entitled the person injured[11] to maintain an action and recover damages in respect thereof, the person who would have been liable if death had not ensued shall be liable to an action for damages, notwithstanding the death of the person injured."[12]

Section 1(2), again as substituted by s.3(1) of the Administration of Justice Act 1982, enacts that every such action shall be for the benefit of the dependants, as defined,[13] of the person whose death has been so caused. The substitution follows the wording of the original subsection in the 1976 Act except that it is made subject to the new s.1A which gives further rights, being rights to recover for non-pecuniary loss, not to dependants as such but specifically to parents and children of the deceased.[14] There is no action for nominal damages; if no recoverable damage is proved, the action fails.[15]

### 1. The Entitled Dependants

The Fatal Accidents Act 1976 provides by s.1(3), as substituted by s.3(1) of the Administration of Justice Act 1982 and as amended by s.83 of the Civil Partnership Act 2004, that: **41-005**

> "In this Act "dependant" means—
> (a) the wife or husband, or former wife or husband of the deceased;
> (aa) the civil partner or former civil partner of the deceased;
> (b) any person who—

---

7 Administration of Justice Act 1982 s.3(1).

8 See para.41-005 and para.41-019, below.

9 By providing in the interpretation section of the original Damages Act 1996 that "references to a claim or action for personal injury include references … to a claim or action brought by virtue of the Fatal Accidents Act 1976": s.7(1).

10 The new s.1(1) is identical to the earlier one.

11 By s.1(6) (as substituted for s.1(5) of the Fatal Accidents Act 1976) it is provided that any reference to injury in the Act "includes any disease and any impairment of a person's physical or mental condition", a formulation commonly appearing in UK legislation.

12 The statutory cause of action has been held to be applicable in respect of deaths resulting from collision of foreign ships in international waters: *The Esso Malaysia* [1975] Q.B. 198.

13 See para.41-005, below.

14 See para.41-019, below.

15 *Boulter v Webster* (1865) 11 L.T. 598; this view was originally stated by the court in *Duckworth v Johnson* (1859) 4 H. & N. 653.

(i) was living with the deceased in the same household[16] immediately before the date of the death; and

(ii) had been living with the deceased in the same household for at least two years before that date; and

(iii) was living during the whole of that period as the husband or wife or civil partner of the deceased;

(c) any parent or other ascendant of the deceased;

(d) any person who was treated by the deceased as his parent;

(e) any child or other descendant of the deceased;

(f) any person (not being a child of the deceased) who, in the case of any marriage to which the deceased was at any time a party, was treated by the deceased as a child of the family in relation to that marriage;

(fa) any person (not being a child of the deceased) who, in the case of any civil partnership in which the deceased was at any time a civil partner, was treated by the deceased as a child of the family in relation to that civil partnership;

(g) any person who is, or is the issue of, a brother, sister, uncle or aunt of the deceased."

In s.1(4), as substituted,[17] it is stated that being a former wife or husband may result from the marriage being terminated by a decree of nullity as well as by divorce, and in s.1(4A), introduced by s.83(5) of the Civil Partnership Act 2004, that being a former civil partner may result from the partnership being annulled as well as from its being dissolved. The section then provides in subs.(5), as substituted for s.1(4) of the original 1976 Act[18] and as amended by s.83(6) of the Civil Partnership Act 2004, that in deducing any relationship for the purposes of subs.(3)

"(a) any relationship by marriage or civil partnership shall be treated as a relationship by consanguinity, any relationship of the half blood as a relationship of the whole blood, and the stepchild of any person as his child, and

(b) an illegitimate person shall be treated as—

(i) the legitimate child of his mother and reputed father, or

(ii) in the case of a person who has a female parent by virtue of s.43 of the Human Fertilisation and Embryology Act 2008, the legitimate child of his mother and that female parent.[19]"

Relationships arising in consequence of adoption are also included, but this is not now revealed in the fatal accidents legislation itself; instead, one must turn to s.39(1) of the Adoption Act 1976 which enacts that[20]

"an adopted child shall be treated in law—

(a) where the adopters are a married couple, as if he had been born as a child of the marriage (whether or not he was in fact born after the marriage was solemnised);

[16] Living in the same household was generously interpreted in *Pounder v London Underground* [1995] P.I.Q.R. P217 allowing the claim to succeed and strictly interpreted in *Kotke v Saffirini* [2005] P.I.Q.R. P26 CA at 520 causing the claim to fail.

[17] This subsection was new in 1982.

[18] And identical to it.

[19] Section 1(5)(b) of the Fatal Accidents Act 1976 inserted by the Marriage (Same Sex Couples) Act 2013 (Consequential and Contrary Provisions and Scotland) Order 2014 (SI 2014/560), Sch.1 para.14 with effect from 13 March 2014.

[20] Section 39 replaces identical provisions appearing in the Children Act 1975.

(b) in any other case, as if he had been born to the adopter in wedlock (but not as a child of any actual marriage of the adopter)." [21]

This range of dependants is far wider than appeared in the original Fatal Accidents Act 1846, which confined itself[22] to wives and husbands, parents, grandparents and step-parents, and children, grandchildren and step-children; persons related illegitimately or in consequence of adoption were not added until 1934[23]; brothers, sisters, aunts and uncles and their issue, together with the reference, following thereon, to relationships by affinity and of the half blood, were introduced in 1959[24]; not until 1982 did there appear in the statutory list[25] former spouses[26] and "common law" spouses,[27] ascendants beyond the grandparent and descendants beyond the grandchild, and persons treated as a parent or as a child of the family; and finally in 2004 civil partners were brought in. At an early date a child born after the death but *en ventre sa mère* at the time of the injury which caused the death was held to be within the definition[28]; it is submitted that the same should apply to a child conceived after the injury, whether in fact born before or after the death.[29] **41-006**

The extensions in the statutory list of entitled dependants are to be welcomed. They reflect not only a continuingly more liberal attitude but also the view that, even within the framework of Victorian morality, the initial statutory list was much too narrowly drawn. Nevertheless, it may be questioned whether there is any need for such an elaborate listing of entitled dependants as is now on the statute book; surely it would be simpler to enact that any person is entitled to claim who can show a relationship of dependency upon the deceased. This would indeed be more satisfactory in that it would prevent the exclusion of the occasional family member who still does not appear in the statutory listing—such as the great-aunt supported by a great-nephew—and indeed of the occasional person who may not strictly be a family member. It is noticeable that many countries outside the common law have encountered no difficulty in casting the ambit of recovery as widely as this and dispensing with lists.[30] **41-007**

---

21 An adopted child is to be treated in law as if he were not the child of any person other than the adopters or adopter (Adoption Act 1976 s.39(2)), but this provision has no effect, where a child is adopted by one of its natural parents as sole adoptive parent, as respects anything depending on that relationship (s.39(3)). For earlier provisions see the Fatal Accidents Act 1959 s.1(2)(a) and (3), and the Children Act 1975.

22 In ss.2 and 5.

23 By the Law Reform (Miscellaneous Provisions) Act 1934 s.2(1) and (2) now repealed and replaced.

24 By the Fatal Accidents Act 1959 s.1(1) and (2) now repealed and replaced.

25 By the Fatal Accidents Act 1976 s.1(3) inserted by the Administration of Justice Act 1982 s.3(1).

26 Previously not entitled to claim: *Payne-Collins v Taylor Woodrow* [1975] Q.B. 300. A woman who has divorced, remarried and then returned comes within the provision, the remarriage not preventing her from still being a former wife: *Shepherd v Post Office*, *The Times,* 15 June 1995, CA.

27 For the significance of there never being a marriage, see paras 41-029 and 41-071, below.

28 *The George and Richard* (1871) L.R. 3 A. & E. 466.

29 This result appears to have been long accepted in the USA: see Fleming, 50 Calif. Law Rev. 598 at p.617 (1962).

30 Notable examples are France, Belgium, Switzerland, the Scandinavian and also the Islamic countries. This paragraph as it appeared similarly in the 15th edition (1988) of this work at para.1537 received the favourable support of Otton LJ in *Shepherd v Post Office*, *The Times,* 15 June 1995 CA, who agreed that there was no need for a list and that a showing of a relationship of dependency should suffice. The Law Commission also takes the view that the statutory list is too restrictive and in its Report on *Claims for Wrongful Death* (1999) Law Com. No.263, has recommended that, while the

## 2. THE ENTITLEMENT OF THE DEPENDANTS

### (1) Entitlement where no entitlement of deceased at death

41-008 The action for the benefit of the dependants has hitherto been held to be available only where the deceased has been in a position at the time of his death to have brought an action himself. Thus it was held in *Read v G.E. Ry*,[31] where the deceased had settled his own claim with the defendant in his lifetime, and again in *Williams v Mersey Docks*,[32] where the deceased's claim had before his death become statute-barred by effluxion of time, that no cause of action accrued to the dependants.[33] These conclusions have followed upon the interpretation of the phrase in s.1(1) of the Fatal Accidents Act 1976 that the act, neglect or default must be such

> "as would (if death had not ensued) have entitled the party injured to maintain an action"

as imposing a requirement that the deceased could have successfully sued at the time of his death, whereas it would seem that the statutory wording was really intended only to ensure that there was actionable tortious conduct against the deceased in the first place.

41-009 However, that a successful action by a living victim would bar any claim by his dependants after his death appears to have been regarded by the Court of Appeal as axiomatic both when, in *Murray v Shuter*,[34] granting an adjournment of a living victim's action in order to allow him to die and so let in a claim by his dependants[35] and when, in *McCann v Sheppard*,[36] reducing the damages awarded to a living victim to take account of his unexpected death between trial and appeal,[37] and appears also to have been accepted by the House of Lords for the purposes of their

---

present list should be retained, there should be added to it a generally worded class of claimant to include any other individual who was, or would have been, maintained, in whole or in part, by the deceased.

31 (1868) L.R. 3 Q.B. 555.

32 [1905] 1 K.B. 804 CA. *Williams* was approved in *British Columbia Electric Ry v Gentile* [1914] A.C. 1034 PC.

33 A settlement by the deceased in his lifetime against one tortfeasor, where there are concurrent tortfeasors, may even have the effect of discharging the claim for damages against the other tortfeasor and, accordingly, barring a claim after the death on behalf of the dependants against that other tortfeasor. It was so held by the House of Lords in *Jameson v Central Electricity Generating Board* [2000] 1 A.C. 455 reversing the Court of Appeal [1998] Q.B. 323. The contrary decision would have allowed to the dependent widow a substantial degree of double recovery because of s.4 of the Fatal Accidents Act 1976 allowing benefits from the deceased's estate to be disregarded. It was this potential inequity which led the House to interpret the settlement as they did, but whether settlements with one concurrent tortfeasor can always be interpreted in this way may be rather uncertain; see the case further at para.41-115, below. By contrast, where in *Reader v Molesworths Bright & Clegg* [2007] 1 W.L.R. 1082 CA the deceased's personal injury claim was discontinued after his death, the dependants' action was unaffected. In *Reader* the dependants, in the mistaken belief that the discontinuance of the deceased's personal claim barred a suit by the dependants, were suing the solicitor who had discontinued; the claim failed since their cause of action remained untouched by the solicitor's discontinuance and they had therefore suffered no loss.

34 [1972] 1 Lloyd's Rep. 6 CA.

35 [1972] 1 Lloyd's Rep. 6 CA at 7. For the later dependants' action see *Murray v Shuter* [1976] Q.B. 972 CA.

36 [1973] 1 W.L.R. 540 CA.

37 [1973] 1 W.L.R. 540 CA at 544H–545E and 553B–D.

decision in *Pickett v British Rail Engineering*,[38] though accompanied with the reservation that the proposition was unsupported by any decision of the House.[39] The same view is implicit in the felt need to enact s.3 of the Damages Act 1996 which provides that, where a person dies from his injuries after having obtained an award of provisional damages, that award is not to operate as a bar to a dependants' action under the Fatal Accidents Act.[40]

No doubt, where the reason for the deceased's being unable to sue at the time of his death is that he has already settled with the defendant, there would appear to be a practical ground for disallowing the dependants' action, namely the avoidance of a double recovery against the defendant, and this point was also taken in *Read v G.E. Ry*.[41] The point has indeed become incontrovertible now that it has been decided in *Pickett v British Rail Engineering*,[42] overruling *Oliver v Ashman*,[43] that damages for loss of earning capacity awarded to a living claimant are to be based upon his pre-accident life expectation, thereby giving him the opportunity to make provision for his dependants after his premature death.[44] However, it is believed that there is merit in the alternative solution of leaving *Oliver v Ashman* untouched but allowing the dependants to sue for their own loss whether or not the deceased has before his death settled with the defendant, has even sued him to judgment, or has in any other way precluded himself from suing at the time of his death,[45] and support for this solution has come from Lord Phillips's saying in *Gregg v Scott*,[46] that he was not persuaded that it "could not be achieved by a purposive construction of" s.1(1) of the Fatal Accidents Act 1976.[47] For today, however, while *Pickett v British Rail Engineering* stands, the decision in *Read v G.E. Ry* remains controlling and the attempts to get round it in *Thompson v Arnold*,[48] where the deceased had settled in her lifetime and the dependants sued after her death, totally failed. The head-on attack, arguing that the decision was wrong, did not succeed. Langstaff J regarded himself as precluded by authority from so holding and also considered that *Read* had been rightly decided.[49] The attempt to avoid Read by reliance on the deceased's having mistakenly failed to claim for the lost years came to nothing.[50] **41-010**

## (2) Entitlement where limited entitlement of deceased at death

Although liability to the deceased at the time of his death has so far been regarded **41-011**

---

38 [1980] A.C. 136.

39 See para.40-109, above.

40 The provisional damages, to the extent that they are intended to compensate for the period which in the event falls after the death, are to be taken into account in assessing the loss of dependency: s.3(2).

41 (1868) L.R. 3 Q.B. 555.

42 [1980] A.C. 136.

43 [1962] 2 Q.B. 210 CA.

44 See para.40-109, above.

45 This solution is endorsed by South Africa in *Ex p. Oliphant* [1940] C.P.D. 537 and by many American decisions. It was also put forward in the 13th edition (1972) of this work when *Oliver v Ashman* [1962] 2 Q.B. 210 CA, still ruled the day.

46 [2005] 2 A.C. 176.

47 [2005] 2 A.C. 176 at [182]. See the full quotation from Lord Phillips at para.40-109, above and, for the further importance of his suggestion, the discussion at paras 40-105 to 40-118, above.

48 [2008] P.I.Q.R. P1 at 1.

49 [2008] P.I.Q.R. P1 at [75]–[85].

50 Also unsuccessful was the attempt to have s.1(1) of the 1976 Act reinterpreted in the light of today's human rights legislation.

as a condition precedent to liability to the dependants, the courts have not gone so far as to hold that any restriction on the amount of liability to the deceased is to be visited on the amount recoverable by the dependants, and to this extent it is recognised that the dependants' action, even if it derives from the deceased's, is a separate one in which damages are assessed on totally different principles to those which are relevant in any action the deceased could have brought personally in his lifetime. Consequently it was held in *Nunan v Southern Railway*,[51] where the deceased had by contract agreed with the defendant railway company that the company's liability for personal injury should be limited to a certain sum and he was killed by the company's negligence, that the damages recoverable by the dependants were not limited to the agreed sum. In *Pigney v Pointers Transport Services*,[52] where the injury had directly resulted in the deceased's taking his own life at a time when suicide was still a crime, it was held that the widow could recover damages despite the rule of public policy that a man may not benefit from his own criminal act, since the widow's action was a separate action in which the damages awarded did not form part of the deceased's estate. Today, however, the situation in *Pigney* would not provide an illustration of a limited entitlement of the deceased at death, since the House of Lords decision in *Corr v IBC Vehicles Ltd*,[53] indicates that suicide, no longer criminal, would bring in neither public policy nor lack of causation to defeat a claim.[54]

**41-012** There are, however, two situations in which the amount of the defendant's liability to the deceased can affect the amount of his liability to the dependants. The one, which may be somewhat controversial, is where the deceased has supported his dependants from moneys which are illegally obtained or otherwise tainted with illegality. The other, which is a clear exception introduced by statute to the general rule, is where the deceased has been contributorily negligent.

**41-013** The first situation is illustrated by *Burns v Edman*,[55] where the deceased's life had been devoted to crime and it was highly unlikely that he would have reformed; his widow and children were held entitled to no damages for loss of their dependency since the support which they had lost had derived directly from the proceeds of criminal offences. It is thought that this decision is questionable, for the dependants' cause of action for their loss of support did not itself arise ex turpi causa. In *Hunter v Butler*,[56] where the deceased had supported his wife out of earnings which he had failed to declare to the Inland Revenue and out of State benefits which he had obtained by fraud, the undeclared earnings and the improperly obtained benefits, in combination, were held not to constitute part of the wife's dependency, a decision which is undoubtedly correct as the claimant was aware of, and had indeed participated in, her deceased husband's illegal activities. The court did not

---

51 [1924] 1 K.B. 223 CA.

52 [1957] 1 W.L.R. 1121.

53 [2008] A.C. 884.

54 *Corr* is considered at various points in the text; see especially at para.8-065, above. The Court of Appeal in *Corr* ([2007] Q.B. 46 CA) held *Pigney* to have been correctly decided—there is no reference to the case in the House of Lords—but on a ground which is today otiose (see at [79], per Sedley LJ). For another ground, now unacceptable, of the decision in *Pigney* see the footnote at the end of para.8-065, above.

55 [1970] 2 Q.B. 541.

56 [1996] R.T.R. 396 CA.

commit itself to what would have been the result had the wife been an innocent party; again it is thought that there is a case for recovery by the dependent wife.[57]

The second situation arises out of s.5 of the Fatal Accidents Act 1976, re-enacting s.1(4) of the Law Reform (Contributory Negligence) Act 1945 and providing that where the deceased's contributory negligence would have reduced his damages under s.1(1) of the 1945 Act, whether in a suit by him when alive or in a suit by his estate after his death under the Law Reform (Miscellaneous Provisions) Act 1934, damages recoverable in an action on behalf of his dependants under the Fatal Accidents Act "shall be reduced to a proportionate extent". This is in marked contrast to the position in the action *per quod*, now abolished[58] but formerly available to a husband for injury to his wife which fell short of death, where the wife's contributory negligence was held immaterial.[59] This, it is submitted, represents the more enlightened view. **41-014**

## (3) Entitlement inter se

Section 2 of the Fatal Accidents Act 1976, as substituted by s.3(1) of the Administration of Justice Act 1982,[60] and substantially re-enacting provisions originally appearing in ss.2, 3 and 4 of the Fatal Accidents Act 1846, lays down by subs.(3) that only one action can be brought,[61] by subs.(1) that that action is to be brought in the name of the deceased's executor or administrator,[62] and by subs.(4) that full particulars must be given of the persons for whose benefit the action is brought.[63] The practice which is generally followed, and which derives from the **41-015**

[57] Contrast in personal injury, *Newman v Folkes and Dunlop Tyres Ltd* [2002] P.I.Q.R. Q2 at 13 and *Hewison v Meridian Shipping Services PTE Ltd* [2003] I.C.R. 766 CA at paras 40-077 and 40-078, respectively, above.

[58] By the Administration of Justice Act 1982 s.2.

[59] *Mallett v Dunn* [1949] 2 K.B. 180.

[60] Referring to the persons for whom the action is brought rather than, as formerly, to dependants; otherwise identical.

[61] The decision in *Hay v I.B.S. Cladding* unreported 28 September 1993, that, because there is only one cause of action, a defendant cannot be required to apportion a payment into court between the claimants was unfortunate as it can cause difficulties for the individual dependants should their interests be adverse; but the decision was perhaps inevitable while RSC Ord.22 r.1(5) stood. The Civil Procedure Rules have now somewhat improved the position. CPR r.37.4(3) provides that, where in a Fatal Accidents Act claim by more than one person a sum of money is accepted (or a sum in respect of damages is ordered or agreed to be paid) in satisfaction of the claim, the court shall apportion it between the persons entitled. However, this does not go as far as providing for an apportionment before acceptance and such a requirement could be impractical since the apportioned amounts might be considered acceptable as to one or more dependants and not as to another or others. In *Cachia v Faluyi* [2001] 1 W.L.R. 1966 CA the Human Rights Act was invoked to ensure that a claim by three dependent children did not founder on the rocks of s.2(3) with its stipulation that not more than one action may be brought.

[62] Section 2(2) allows the action to be brought by and in the name or names of all or any of the persons specified as entitled where there is no executor or administrator, or where the executor or administrator has failed to bring the action within six months of the death. This provision was initially introduced by the Fatal Accidents Act 1864 s.1.

[63] "There is no room for consideration of a dependant not named and therefore not before the jury… One action alone can be brought, and the persons who stand out stand out for ever. If they have been improperly excluded from the action by the representative claimants they may, no doubt, before the verdict of the jury, apply to be named as parties to benefit, or possibly they may have some legal or equitable remedy against the representative claimants. But after verdict they have no possible claim against the defendant": *Avery v L.N.E. Ry* [1938] A.C. 606 at 613, per Lord Atkin. The practical result of this conclusion in that case was that the widow, suing alone without her dependent children, could

wording of s.3(1),[64] is first to assess the loss to the family as a whole and then to apportion the sum between the various dependants[65]; nevertheless the court is entitled to consider the case of each dependant separately in the first instance, thus ascertaining the total sum by addition.[66] In *Eifert v Holt's Transport Co*,[67] it was held that if the total award is a proper one the defendant is not concerned in the apportionment and cannot attack the award made to a particular dependant as being excessive,[68] but it was said in *Clay v Pooler*,[69] that this decision could no longer be considered good law. The cause of this perfectly proper disapproval of *Eifert* was the unfortunate development, appearing in *Gammell v Wilson*,[70] which permitted the estate to claim under the Law Reform (Miscellaneous Provisions) Act 1934 for the deceased's income in the lost years, thereby placing defendants in the position that they might have to pay more in damages than formerly if the individuals entitled under the estate differed from the claiming dependants or, even where the two sets of individuals were the same, if the measure of entitlement of each under the estate differed from the measure of entitlement of each qua dependant.[71] However, now that the estate has been debarred from recovering in respect of the deceased's income of the lost years[72] the defendant once again has ceased to have an interest in the way in which the award under the Fatal Accidents Act is apportioned between the dependants and thus the decision in *Eifert v Holt's Transport Co*,[73] may be safely reinstated.[74] If, of course, the total amount is too high because an individual's loss has been overestimated, the defendant must be entitled to challenge the award.[75]

**41-016** The fact that only one action may be brought is, however, only designed to promote ease of administration, and the action is given to the dependants as individuals and not as a class, so that each dependant is entitled to compensation for the loss resulting to him personally. This was established in *Pym v Great Northern Ry*,[76] where the point was of practical importance in that the family as a

---

recover up to the statutory maximum there imposed upon the Fatal Accidents Act claim. On the other hand, in *Cooper v Williams* [1963] 2 Q.B. 567 CA, where there had been no verdict but only a stay of proceedings brought on behalf of the deceased's illegitimate child alone, the parties having arrived at terms of settlement, the court removed the stay and allowed the deceased's widow to intervene.

64 For which see para.41-017, below.

65 *Eifert v Holt's Transport Co* [1951] W.N. 467 CA at 468, per Singleton LJ; *Jeffrey v Kent C.C.* [1958] 1 W.L.R. 927 at 930, per Paull J.

66 *Yelland v Powell Duffryn Collieries* [1941] 1 K.B. 519 CA at 527, per Luxmoore LJ. The availability of both methods of calculation had already been recognised in the 19th century (see *Bulmer v Bulmer* (1883) 25 Ch. D. 409 at 412, per Chitty J), and indeed there is much to be said for making separate calculations for each dependant: see para.41-086, below.

67 [1951] W.N. 467 CA.

68 The apportionment, which was by consent, was favourable to the infant son because of the widow's generosity.

69 [1982] 3 All E.R. 570.

70 [1982] A.C. 27.

71 See para.41-126, below.

72 [1982] A.C. 27.

73 [1951] W.N. 467 CA.

74 The entitlement of the estate, other than that in respect of lost years' income, which went to reduce the Fatal Accidents Act award, namely that in respect of the deceased's non-pecuniary loss, had never proved substantial enough to make the apportionment as between dependants a matter of concern to the defendant. And now even these damages to which the estate remains entitled are not to be taken into account in arriving at the Fatal Accidents Act award: see para.41-111, below.

75 Compare the converse position, where the challenge is by a claimant, at para.41-016, below.

76 (1863) 4 B. & S. 396; accepted by Lord Porter in *Davies v Powell Duffryn Collieries* [1942] A.C.

whole had suffered no loss since the deceased possessed only unearned income and the family received the estate among them on his death intestate; yet the younger children had lost by the death as they themselves received less than they would have done had their father lived on, and they were held entitled to recover for this loss. So, too, if the total amount awarded is too low because an individual dependant's loss has been underestimated, that dependant is entitled to appeal, and the court may increase the amount awarded to him without disturbing the amounts going to the other dependants: this is illustrated by *Mead v Clarke Chapman*.[77] And another practical consequence of regarding the statutory action as made up of the personal and individual claims of each dependant appears in *Mulholland v McCrea*.[78] In a Fatal Accidents Act claim brought by the deceased's husband as her personal representative, it was held that the fact that the death of the wife was caused partly by the fault of the husband required the amount recoverable under his claim to be reduced in proportion to his share in the responsibility for the death of his wife.[79] On the other hand, as was held in *Dodds v Dodds*,[80] the fact that a man's death has been caused by the negligence of his wife, who was a defendant in the Fatal Accidents Act suit, cannot adversely affect the claim of his son as another and separate dependant.[81]

### (B) *THE STATUTORY MEASURE OF DAMAGES*

Section 3(1) of the Fatal Accidents Act 1976, as substituted by s.3(1) of the Administration of Justice Act 1982,[82] lays down the measure of damages as had, in basically similar terms except for the reference to bereavement, s.2 of the Fatal Accidents Act 1846 before it, thus: **41-017**

> "In the action such damages, other than damages for bereavement, may be awarded as are proportioned to the injury resulting from such death to the dependants respectively."

This is both wide and vague, but the interpretation of the courts, before the introduction of a separate entitlement of some to a limited recovery for bereavement, restricted recovery to damages for the loss of the pecuniary benefit arising from the relationship which would be derived from the continuance of the life. In short, the measure recoverable by a dependant is what is often called the value of the dependency; this requires detailed consideration.[83] It is, however, most convenient to deal

601 at 618, 623.

77 [1956] 1 W.L.R. 76 CA. Even if the aggregate award is right, an individual dependant should be able to appeal to have his portion of the total increased at the expense of one or more of the other claiming dependants: this would seem to be supported by *Williamson v Thorneycroft*, as reported at (1940) 67 Ll. L. Rep. 413 CA.

78 [1961] N.I. 135 CA.

79 Contrast the assessment of the damages in the survival action which was also brought: para.41-129, below.

80 [1978] Q.B. 543. It was conceded that the wife, being wholly to blame for the death, had no claim as a dependant: at 545H.

81 By virtue of CPR r.21.11 dependants who are children or protected parties will have their damages under the control of the court, but not any other class of dependant including, since 1971, widows.

82 The original s.3(1) was more comprehensive, dealing in what is now s.3(2) with the division of the damages between the dependants, which is to be after deducting any costs not recovered from the defendant.

83 This passage, from an earlier edition of this book, was described as striking at the heart of the issue in *Rupasinghe v West Hertfordshire Hospitals NHS Trust* [2016] EWHC 2848 (QB) at [23].

first with those types of loss for which damages are not recoverable at all or for which there is a limited degree of recovery.

## 1. Losses in Respect of which Damages are Not Recoverable or are Recoverable only within Limits

### (1) Non-pecuniary loss, except to a spouse, civil partner or parent for bereavement

**41-018** It was early established in *Blake v Midland Ry*,[84] that the mental suffering of a wife for the loss of her husband could not be considered in computing the damages,[85] and thus from the start the action became limited to pecuniary loss. The two most authoritative statements of this principle emanate from the House of Lords. First, Viscount Haldane LC in *Taff Vale Ry v Jenkins*,[86] said:

> "The basis is not what has been called *solatium*, that is to say damages given for injured feelings or on the ground of sentiment, but damages based on compensation for a pecuniary loss."

More recent and more graphic is Lord Wright in *Davies v Powell Duffryn Collieries*.[87]

> "There is no question here of what may be called sentimental damages, bereavement or pain and suffering. It is a hard matter of pounds, shillings and pence."[88]

This regrettable principle is now too well established to be corrected by any court other than the Supreme Court.[89]

**41-019** The refusal of the court in *Blake v Midland Ry*,[90] to take advantage of the statutory wording which was amply wide enough to allow recovery for non-pecuniary loss[91] reflects the commonly encountered judicial fear that novel extensions of liability require to be carefully contained if they are not to get out of control, and, in the equivalent statutes which throughout the common law world followed hard upon the heels of the English model, non-pecuniary loss was similarly excluded either again by judicial interpretation or by the express provisions of the particular statutes themselves. After over a century of such legislation, however, this fear has largely abated, and a more sympathetic attitude has developed towards the allowance of damages to at least the closest relatives in respect of their grief and of their loss of the deceased's society, care and comfort.[92] Legislation giving a limited entitle-

---

84 (1852) 18 Q.B. 93.

85 The headnote also includes damages for loss of society as being irrecoverable but there is nothing direct in the judgment on this.

86 [1913] A.C. 1 at 4.

87 [1942] A.C. 601.

88 [1942] A.C. 601 at 617. See, similarly, *Baker v Dalgleish S.S. Co* [1922] 1 K.B. 361 CA, at 371 per Scrutton LJ.

89 The apparent neglect of the principle in *Devoy v William Doxford & Sons Ltd* [2009] EWHC 1598 (QB) was noted in *Grant v The Secretary of State for Transport* [2017] EWHC 1663 (QB) at [106].

90 (1852) 18 Q.B. 93.

91 "Damages … proportioned to the injury resulting": see para.41-017, above.

92 In *Preston v Hunting Air Transport* [1956] 1 Q.B. 454, in an action brought on behalf of two infant children in respect of their mother's death under the then Carriage by Air Act 1932 giving effect to provisions of the Warsaw Convention analogous to those of the Fatal Accidents Act, Ormerod J

ment to a limited class of relatives was eventually introduced by the Administration of Justice Act 1982.[93] Now s.1A of the Fatal Accidents Act 1976 as inserted by s.3(1) of the Administration of Justice Act 1982 and as amended by s.83(7) of the Civil Partnership Act 2004, provides that an action under the Act may consist of or include a claim for damages for bereavement,[94] which claim is, however, restricted to spouses, civil partners and parents; more precisely, the claim may only be for the benefit of the deceased's wife or husband, of the deceased's civil partner, or of both parents of a legitimate, or the mother of an illegitimate, deceased minor who was never married or a civil partner.[95] The amount to be awarded is specified and started, from the end of 1982, at £3,500,[96] but, the Lord Chancellor having been given the power to vary the amount for the time being specified,[97] it has been raised four times, raised for causes of action accruing on or after 1 April 1991 to £7,500,[98] on or after 1 April 2002 to £10,000,[99] on or after 1 January 2008 to £11,800,[100] on or after 1 April 2013 to £12,980.[101] The latest increase, which is of 10 per cent, has been made on account of the Court of Appeal's final ruling in *Simmons v Castle*,[102] that damages for non-pecuniary loss in all types of civil claim are to be increased by 10 per cent from 1 April 2013.[103] When the claim is on behalf of both parents the amount awarded is to be divided equally between them.[104] It is also provided that the right of a person to claim for bereavement does not survive to his or her estate.[105]

This is thought to be too restricted a provision, both as to the relatives who may claim and as to the amount which is to be awarded; it is better than nothing but certainly many regard the amount, even raised to today's figure, as derisory.[106] It is particularly important in the case of parent claimants because the pecuniary standard of recovery has virtually eliminated claims in respect of the death of very young children.[107] More satisfactory results would be arrived at if the decisions on amounts **41-020**

boldly held that the recoverable damage was not limited to the children's purely financial loss, but, as Megaw J later pointed out in *Pevec v Brown* (1964) 108 S.J. 219, it was too late for him to do likewise under the Fatal Accidents Act.

93 Anticipated a good deal earlier by South Australia (1940) and by Eire (1961).

94 Section 1A(1).

95 Section 1A(2).

96 Section 1A(3).

97 Section 1A(5). The power is exercisable by statutory instrument subject to annulment in pursuance of a resolution of either House of Parliament.

98 By SI 1990/2575.

99 By SI 2002/644.

100 By SI 2007/3489.

101 By SI 2013/510.

102 [2013] 1W.L.R. 1239 CA; final ruling from 1243.

103 For the procedural history and reasons for this development, stemming from the package of reforms appearing in the *Jackson Report on Civil Litigation Costs*, see para.40-280, below

104 Section 1A(4). The subsection provides that the division is to be after deducting any costs not recovered from the defendant.

105 This is achieved through the insertion of a s.1(1A) in the Law Reform (Miscellaneous Provisions) Act 1934 by s.4 of the Administration of Justice Act 1982; see too para.23-011, above.

106 The Law Commission in its Report on *Claims for Wrongful Death* (1999) Law Com. No.263 recommended that there be a list of potential claimants which goes far wider than simply spouse and parent and that the standard amount of damages be £10,000 but with a maximum permitted amount of £30,000, both subject to adjustment for inflation. An earlier private member's Bill of 1988 had sought to increase bereavement damages to a minimum of £10,000 with a maximum of £50,000; the Bill ran out of parliamentary time.

107 See para.41-099, below.

of damages were left to the court. This is the position in Scotland where awards are much higher than the statutory English ones, although it is true that the awards given are for what is termed loss of society rather than for bereavement on its own. Awards to widows of £50,000 were made in *Bellington v Todd*,[108] and *Wolff v John Moulds (Kilmarnock Ltd)*,[109] with an award of £40,000 in *Ryder v Highland Council*,[110] to a son aged 17 at the time of the fatality, and in *Bellington* and *Wolff* there were in addition substantial awards to many other members of the family, reaching to £25,000 to each of two young children and £15,000 to each parent in *Bellington*.[111] However juries, which are still used in Scotland in personal injury and fatal accident cases, have gone over the top, and a new trial was ordered by the appeal court when a jury awarded £120,000 to a 17-year-old daughter in *Hamilton v Ferguson Transport (Spean Bridge) Ltd*,[112] the appeal court laying down that in future judicial guidance on a possible range of awards should be given to the jury in order to combat the discrepancy between judge awards and jury awards.

### (2) Pecuniary loss by reason of expenses resulting from the death but not related to the pecuniary benefit derived from the continuance of the life, except funeral expenses

41-021 **(a) Funeral expenses** By s.3(5) of the Fatal Accidents Act 1976, as substituted for s.3(3) of the original by s.3(1) of the Administration of Justice Act 1982 and re-enacting s.2(3) of the Law Reform (Miscellaneous Provisions) Act 1934, it is provided that in an action brought under the Fatal Accidents Act damages may be awarded in respect of the funeral expenses of the deceased if such expenses have been incurred by the dependants.[113] Before 1934 no damages could be recovered for funeral expenses or the cost of mourning in a Fatal Accidents Act claim,[114] a rule originally laid down in *Dalton v S.E. Ry*,[115] and finally established by the Court of Appeal in *Clark v L.G.O.C.*[116] Now, as *Burns v Edman*,[117] shows, even the failure

108 [2011] CSOH 74.

109 [2011] CSOH 159. Even higher awards to widows are known, as with the £80,000 in *McGee v RJK Building Services Ltd* [2013] CSOH 10.

110 [2013] CSOH 95.

111 Awards have been high for many years. For earlier years see the list of awards from 1993 onwards in Appendix C to the Scottish Law Commission's Discussion Paper on *Damages for Wrongful Death* (August 2007) No.135. It does not reappear in the Commission's resultant Report on *Damages for Wrongful Death* (September 2008) Scot Law Com. No.213.

112 [2012] CSIH 52.

113 Unusually, no funeral expenses were awarded, under s.3(5), in *Brown v Hamid* [2013] EWHC 4067 (QB). This was because the clinical negligence had led only to an acceleration of the death by a short period so that, absent the negligence, funeral expenses would have been incurred in the near future: at [40].

114 Nor was such a claim possible at common law: see *Osborn v Gillett* (1873) L.R. 8 Ex. 88; *Clark v L.G.O.C.* [1906] 2 K.B. 648 CA.

115 (1858) 4 C.B. N.S. 296.

116 [1906] 2 K.B. 648 CA, not accepting *Bedwell v Golding* (1902) 18 T.L.R. 436. That case had distinguished *Dalton v S.E. Ry* (1858) 4 C.B. N.S. 296 on the ground that there had been no legal liability on the dependant there to bury the deceased, but the Court of Appeal in *Clark v L.G.O.C.* [1906] 2 K.B. 648 CA, was dubious whether there was a legal liability even in *Bedwell v Golding* (1902) 18 T.L.R. 436.

117 [1970] 2 Q.B. 541.

of the dependants' claim for loss of support[118] in no way prejudices their claim for funeral expenses.[119]

No definition of funeral expenses is given, but the test of reasonableness would seem to apply. There are a few decisions which throw light on what is recoverable.[120] In *Stanton v Youldon*,[121] the claimant claimed the cost, at some £200, of a marble memorial over the deceased's grave. McNair J, allowing £40, held that a stone over a grave might be considered part of the funeral expenses for a person in the deceased's position, but that in so far as it was merely a memorial it could not be included. In *Jones v Royal Devon & Exeter NHS Foundation Trust*,[122] the claimant claimed £4,000 for a specially commissioned headstone, for which £2,000 was allowed by King J; the cost of the wake which was also claimed was disallowed.[123] In *Grant v The Secretary of State for Transport*,[124] the claimed cost of £4,867 for a headstone was reduced to £1,200; the costs of a reception after the funeral were also disallowed, with the judge noting that receptions are not always held and, when held, refreshments are not always provided.[125] In *Schneider v Eisovitch*,[126] the claimant, injured while holidaying in France with her husband who was killed, sued both for her own injury and under the Fatal Accidents Act for her husband's death. One head of loss for which she successfully recovered was in respect of the expenses incurred by her brother-in-law and his wife, reimbursed by the claimant, in flying out to France to assist the claimant back to England and to make arrangements for her husband's body to be brought back to England. In so far as the services of the brother-in-law and his wife were for the latter purpose, the recovery must be attributed to the claim under the Fatal Accidents Act and could therefore only be properly recoverable as funeral expenses. This would give a very wide meaning to the term but the argument did not touch on this. While funeral expenses have undoubtedly increased substantially over the years, even for the beginning of this century the award of over £50,000 in *St George v Turner*,[127] looks improbable. This would appear to be a claim by the estate for funeral expenses as no dependants are referred to; it is therefore considered when we reach such claims.[128] 41-022

118 On this aspect of the case, see para.41-013, above.

119 If any dependant has been paid funeral expenses out of the social fund (See the Social Security Contributions and Benefits Act 1992 s.138(1)(a) as substituted by the Social Security Act 1998) it would seem that this amount should not be taken into account by reason of s.4 of the Fatal Accidents Act 1976 requiring all collateral benefits to be ignored: see para.41-111, below. Contrast footnote to para.41-138, below for the position with the estate's claim.

120 And see at para.41-138, below, *Hart v Griffiths-Jones* [1948] 2 All E.R. 729 and *Gammell v Wilson* [1982] A.C. 27 CA, where the claim was on behalf of the estate, the Law Reform (Miscellaneous Provisions) Act 1934 having also, by s.1(2)(c), allowed in such claims recovery of funeral expenses incurred by the estate: the dependants' and the estate's claim for such expenses are, of course, alternative.

121 [1960] 1 W.L.R. 543.

122 [2008] EWHC 558 (QB).

123 [2008] EWHC 558 (QB) at [135].

124 [2017] EWHC 1663 (QB) at [54].

125 [2017] EWHC 1663 (QB) at [55]. See also *Mosson v Spousal (London) Ltd* [2016] EWHC 1429 (QB) at [49] and *Knauer v Ministry of Justice* [2014] EWHC 2553 (QB).

126 [1960] 2 Q.B. 430.

127 [2003] C.L.Y. 936.

128 See para.41-138, below.

41-023 **(b) Other such expenses** The pre-1934 decisions on funeral expenses are now only of historical interest, but the reasoning behind them throws some light on the exclusion of expenses generally under this head, an exclusion necessitating statutory intervention for the allowance of funeral expenses. Thus in *Dalton v S.E. Ry*,[129] the reason for refusing the funeral expenses claim was that

> "the subject-matter of the statute is compensation for injury by reason of the relative not being alive".[130]

This is narrower than compensation for injury by reason of a relative's death. The former embraces only what the deceased, had he lived, would have done for the dependant; the latter includes in addition to this what the dependant would do and does, reasonably and necessarily, for the deceased as a result of his death, such as a son's expenses of travelling thousands of miles by air to his father's funeral, or a wife's expenses dealing with personal correspondence of sympathy and condolence on her husband's death. No such expenses, which can hardly be regarded as funeral expenses,[131] would seem strictly to be recoverable in a claim under the Fatal Accidents Act.[132] Nor can medical expenses paid by a dependant be recovered in a Fatal Accidents Act claim even on the widest view of the statutory language, since they do not constitute an injury resulting from the death but one preceding the death, whenever the payment is made.[133]

## (3) Pecuniary loss related to the pecuniary benefit derived from the continuance of the life but where such benefit is not attributable to the family relationship

41-024 This limitation was not made clear until the decision of Devlin J in *Burgess v Florence Nightingale Hospital for Gentlewomen*.[134] In that case the deceased wife and the dependent husband were professional dancing partners before and after their marriage, and the claim on the husband's behalf was, inter alia, in respect of the pecuniary loss by being deprived of his wife as a dancing partner. The wife had taken her full half-share of the joint earnings, in other words, her services were fully paid for; and the pecuniary loss to the husband arose from the fact that

> "their joint ability to earn an income greatly exceeded the ability of either of them individually, [and] neither of them individually could have expected to earn as much as they both did together".[135]

It was held that

---

129 (1858) 4 C.B. N.S. 296.

130 (1858) 4 C.B. N.S. 296 at 306.

131 But contrast *Schneider v Eisovitch* [1960] 2 Q.B. 430 at para.41-022, above.

132 Indeed in *Bedwell v Golding* (1902) 18 T.L.R. 436 a claim for a father's travelling expenses failed although the claim as to funeral expenses succeeded, albeit incorrectly in view of the later decision in *Clark v L.G.O.C.* [1906] 2 K.B. 648 CA.

133 Such expenses are now, however, recoverable under the 1934 Act in the survival action: see para.41-130, below.

134 [1955] 1 Q.B. 349.

135 [1955] 1 Q.B. 349 at 354.

> "the benefit, to qualify under the Act, must be a benefit which arises from the relationship between the parties",[136]

and that

> "there were here no services that were rendered by the wife to the husband, and there was no benefit arising in the dancing partnership, that can properly be attributed to the relationship of the husband and wife".[137]

In so deciding, Devlin J interpreted the wide words of what is now s.3(1) of the Fatal Accidents Act 1976, which he admitted would cover the husband's claim if applied without restriction, in the light of the general principles of common law that an actionable injury to one person will not give an action to another who is injured indirectly by the injury to the first. He also relied on *Sykes v N.E. Ry*,[138] in which case a father was awarded no damages for the death of his adult son who worked for him at a full wage, although the son's advice, knowledge and assistance were of such value that now the father was precluded from taking the contracts that he did in the son's lifetime. In the words of Grove J:

> "The claimant was bound to prove a benefit accruing to him from his relationship with the deceased; but he merely showed that he derived an advantage from a contract with his son."[139]

*Burgess* was applied in *Cox v Hockenhull*,[140] to deny recovery to a husband for the loss of the invalid care allowance which he had been paid as carer of his severely disabled wife. This was not a benefit derived from the relationship of husband and wife since the husband had simply been employed by the State to care for a severely disabled person whoever that person might be.

On the other hand, when a wife or son renders services to the husband or father at less than the market rate, the amount by which the rate falls below the market rate forms a benefit arising from the relationship, the relationship being to that extent the motive of the contract.[141] And in *Feay v Barnwell*,[142] the court allowed recovery to a husband for the loss of the old-age pension which he had received in respect of his wife before her death; this was a benefit derived from the relationship.[143] Somewhat similar is *Malyon v Plummer*.[144] In that case the claimant widow and her deceased husband were the sole directors of a private company carrying on a one-man business, the husband owning all of the shares except one owned by the claimant. The claimant received a substantial salary from the company for part-time, essentially casual work in connection with the business, and the whole of the combined salaries of the claimant and her husband was paid into the husband's bank account from which he paid out moneys for the family **41-025**

---

136 [1955] 1 Q.B. 349 at 360.

137 [1955] 1 Q.B. 349 at 361.

138 (1875) 44 L.J.C.P. 191.

139 (1875) 44 L.J.C.P. 191 at 192.

140 [2000] 1 W.L.R. 750 CA.

141 This is how Devlin J in *Burgess v Florence Nightingale Hospital* [1955] 1 Q.B. 349 explained the two Irish cases of *Condon v Gt Southern & Western Ry* (1865) 16 Ir. C.L. Rep. 415 and *Hull v Gt Northern Ry of Ireland* (1890) 26 L. R. Ir. 289.

142 [1938] 1 All E.R. 31.

143 So explained on this point in *Burgess v Florence Nightingale Hospital* [1955] 1 Q.B. 349 at 360.

144 [1964] 1 Q.B. 330 CA.

expenditure, either by cheques or by cash to the claimant. The claimant claimed that the total amount which she would have received from the husband's banking account for the benefit of herself and her children had the deceased survived represented the amount of the dependency. The defendant contended that so much of this total amount as consisted of the claimant's salary should be excluded. The defendant relied first on *Burgess*, arguing that the claimant's salary should be excluded on the ground that it was not attributable to the husband and wife relationship. The court rejected this argument. Pearson LJ said:

> "It would be inappropriate and unconvincing to say that the wife has lost her salary by being deprived of her co-director or managing-director or travelling salesman. The fact is that she has lost her husband, who was the family bread-winner."[145]

The interposition of the company did not prevent the court from looking at the matter realistically and assessing the wife's true loss. Similarly, in *Welsh Ambulance Services NHS Trust v Williams*,[146] where the deceased had brought his wife and three children into his very successful business he had done so because they were members of his family. It was said that any argument based on *Burgess* was bound to fail.[147]

## (4) Loss of earnings

**41-026** The general rule is that loss of earnings on the part of the dependant cannot form part of the dependency.[148] As we have seen above, recovery is restricted to damages for the loss of the pecuniary benefit arising from the relationship which would be derived from the continuance of the life. The reason that a loss of earnings claim will usually not fall within that principle is because, as explained by Diplock LJ in *Malyon v Plummer*,[149] a dependant's salary will continue after the death of the deceased. In other words,

> "it would not be a benefit arising out of the relationship of husband and wife which she would lose on his death".[150]

In *Rupasinghe v West Hertfordshire Hospitals NHS Trust*,[151] Jay J considered whether a doctor, who on the death of her husband had decided to return to Sri Lanka where her children would be cared for by family members, could recover for her loss of earnings as a result of having to find less remunerative employment. It was held that the doctor could not recover. Once the separate head of claim for gratuitous care by the doctor for her husband had been valued "there [was] nothing left".[152] It was not a case where the doctor gave up work in order to provide the

---

145 [1964] 1 Q.B. 330 CA at 345–346.

146 [2008] EWCA Civ 81 CA; facts at para.41-082, below.

147 [2008] EWCA Civ 81 CA at [52] and [53]. The Court of Appeal so said while refusing to allow the defendant to put the argument as it had been raised at too late a stage in the proceedings. See, too, *Davies v Whiteways Cyder Co* [1975] Q.B. 262 (facts at footnote to para.41-038, below) where the benefit of moneys given to a wife and son being free of estate duty was held to be a benefit arising from the relationship of husband and wife and of father and son. This surely is incontrovertible.

148 *Rupasinghe v West Hertfordshire Hospitals NHS Trust* [2016] EWHC 2848 (QB) at [25].

149 [1964] 1 QB 330 CA.

150 [1964] 1 QB 330 CA at 351.

151 [2016] EWHC 2848 (QB).

152 [2016] EWHC 2848 (QB) at [52].

gratuitous services,[153] nor was it a case where the doctor sought to use her earnings as a proxy measure for the value of those services.

## 2. THE VALUE OF THE DEPENDENCY

There remains the loss of the pecuniary benefit arising from the relationship which would be derived from the continuance of the life and which may consist of money, property or services[154]: in other words, the value of the dependency. The dependant is entitled, by clear principle of law, to full compensation for the loss of this pecuniary benefit,[155] but, except for funeral expenses since 1934,[156] interest since 1970[157] and the limited entitlement for bereavement since 1982,[158] to no more.[159] **41-027**

---

[153] These services were being provided by her family.

[154] The inclusion of services seems obvious, but it was arguable as late as *Berry v Humm* [1915] 1 K.B. 627 that the loss of gratuitous services was not a recoverable loss: see this case dealt with at para.41-100, below.

[155] Parke B's direction to the jury in *Armsworth v S.E. Ry* (1847) 11 Jur. 758, the first case under the 1846 Act, is therefore misleading. He directed them thus: "You cannot estimate the value of a person's life to his relatives. No sum of money could compensate a child for the loss of its parent; and it would be most unjust if whenever an accident occurs, juries were to visit the unfortunate cause of it with the utmost amount which they think an equivalent for the mischief done. Here you must estimate the damage by the same principle as if only a wound had been inflicted. Scarcely any sum could compensate a labouring man for the loss of a limb, yet you do not in such a case give him enough to maintain him for life; and in the present case you are not to consider the value of his existence as if you were bargaining with an annuity office; for in that view you would have to calculate all the accidents which might have occurred to him in the course of it, which would be a very difficult matter. I therefore advise you to take a reasonable view of the case and give what you consider a fair compensation." This cannot today be accepted as establishing that compensation should not be given for all the pecuniary damage that would probably have occurred. It is indeed cited with approval for this proposition by Brett J in *Rowley v L. & N.W. Ry* (1873) L.R. 8 Ex. 221 at 231, but this, significantly, was in a dissenting judgment. *Armsworth v S.E. Ry* (1847) 11 Jur. 758 being the first case under the Act, the judge was clearly feeling his way in a then uncharted field. As Lord Wright said in *Rose v Ford* [1937] A.C. 826 at 848, "Parke B did not, it seems, appreciate the precise limits which were subsequently to be fixed for assessing the damages claimable by dependants"; in particular, the exclusion of non-pecuniary loss, where full compensation is indeed impossible (see para.40-253, above), was still five years in the future: see para.41-018, above. Yet these statements in *Armsworth v S.E. Ry* and *Rowley v L. & N.W. Ry* were for long cited by high authority as showing that full compensation must not be given (see the references, mainly from the field of personal injury, in a footnote to para.38-056, above), although Edmund Davies LJ in *Fowler v Grace* (1970) 114 S.J. 193 CA at 193, also a personal injury claim, expressed concern over what Brett J had said (see para.40-057). It was submitted in earlier editions of this work that such approval should be interpreted only as endorsing that contingencies and the like must be taken into account and this interpretation, already supported in the analogous field of personal injury by Brett LJ himself in *Phillips v L. & S.W. Ry* (1879) 5 C.P.D. 280 CA at 290 to 292, is now confirmed by Lord Scarman, again in the personal injury context, in *Pickett v British Rail Engineering* [1980] A.C. 136 at 168B–D; see para.40-057, above.

[156] See para.41-021, above.

[157] See para.19-050, above.

[158] See para.41-019, above.

[159] That the pecuniary benefit which would be derived from the continuance of the life may consist of State benefits received by the deceased was recognised in *Cox v Hockenhull* [2000] 1 W.L.R. 750 CA. It was there held that the critical question was to determine the loss suffered by the dependant as a result of the death and the fact that claimant husband and deceased wife had been entirely dependent upon State benefits was as such immaterial; it could not be said that because of this there was no dependency upon the deceased but only upon the State. See the case further at para.41-044, below.

**41-028** The basic rule, originally laid down in *Franklin v S.E. Ry*[160] and ever since accepted and acted upon, is that the damages are to be calculated

> "in reference to a reasonable expectation of pecuniary benefit, as of right or otherwise, from the continuance of the life".[161]

This entails two consequences of importance.

**41-029** First, there is no need for the dependant to show that the deceased was under a legal liability to support him or her, a point first established in 1858 in *Franklin v S.E. Ry* and *Dalton v S.E. Ry*[162]; yet where a claim is made by a "common law" spouse or by a civil partner, who form new categories of entitled dependant, the one since 1982 and the other since 2007,[163] s.3(4) of the Fatal Accidents Act 1976, as substituted by s.3(1) of the Administration of Justice Act 1982 and as amended by s.83(8) of the Civil Partnership Act 2004, takes the precaution of providing that there has to be taken into account the fact that the dependant had no enforceable right to financial support by the deceased as a result of their living together, a provision no doubt intended to emphasise that the relationship might not be one of great durability rather than to promote the making of small or token awards[164]; such an interpretation is supported by *Drew v Abassi*,[165] where the trial judge, in order to give effect to the subsection, reduced the multiplier he would otherwise have chosen for the common law spouse from 15 to 13 and was upheld on this by the Court of Appeal.

**41-030** Secondly, there is no need to show that the dependant was receiving pecuniary benefit at the time of the death, a purely prospective loss being sufficient. Thus a dependent parent might not have reached an age of requiring assistance, a point made in *Franklin v S.E. Ry*[166]; alternatively, a deceased child might not have reached an age when he or she could afford to render assistance, which was the position in *Taff Vale Ry v Jenkins*.[167] On the other hand, a wife who has deserted her husband and forfeited any right to maintenance does not satisfy the test of reasonable expectation of pecuniary benefit unless she can show some significant prospect of reconciliation had the husband lived; hence the widow's claim failed in *Davies v Taylor*.[168] In that case the House of Lords held that the trial judge had applied the wrong test by asking whether it was shown to be more probable than not that there would be a reconciliation, for there may be a reasonable expectation that something will come about even if the chance of its so doing is less than even. Thus if only a 40 per cent chance of a reconciliation could be shown, the wife would have been entitled to what would have been 40 per cent of the loss of dependency had there been no marriage break-up,[169] and the degree of recovery would fluctuate, up or

---

160 (1858) 3 H. & N. 211.

161 (1858) 3 H. & N. 211 at 214, per Pollock CB. Similar statements are to be found in other cases: see *Dalton v S.E. Ry* (1858) 4 C.B. N.S. 296 at 305; *Pym v Great Northern Ry* (1863) 4 B. & S. 396 at 408; *Taff Vale Ry v Jenkins* [1913] A.C. 1 at 7; *Davies v Taylor* [1974] A.C. 207 at 214B, 217H.

162 (1858) 4 C.B. N.S. 296.

163 See the substituted and amended Fatal Accidents Act 1976 s.1(3)(b) set out at para.41-005, above.

164 This is supported by what the Lord Chancellor said when the matter of the common law spouse was being debated in the House of Lords: see *Hansard*, HL Vol.429, col.1108 (4 May 1982).

165 *Drew v Abassi* unreported 24 May1995 CA.

166 (1858) 3 H. & N. 211 at 215.

167 [1913] A.C. 1; see especially at 4.

168 [1974] A.C. 207.

169 See [1974] A.C. 207 at 212F, per Lord Reid.

down,[170] with the degree of chance of reconciliation. However the trial judge's dismissal of the wife's claim under the Fatal Accidents Act was upheld on the facts because there was only a speculative possibility of reconciliation and speculative possibilities, on application, as Lord Reid put it, of the de minimis principle,[171] fell to be ignored.[172] Also, in *Malone v Rowan*,[173] a wife was held not entitled to claim on the basis of an increased dependency because before the death of her husband the two of them had decided to start a family which would thereby, on account of her intention of giving up her job to look after the family, have increased her dependency on her husband. Russell J came reluctantly to this conclusion only because required to follow an unreported Court of Appeal decision, *Higgs v Drinkwater*,[174] to which his attention had been drawn, but his reluctance seems to be unjustified. The loss was one which but for the death would indeed have occurred but in the event of the death it did not. Had the wife already been pregnant at the time of the death the position would have been different.

### (1) The preliminary problem of certainty of loss

Claims for wrongful death are second only to claims for personal injury in providing evidence of the difficulty of making lump sum damages awards with any degree of accuracy.[175] It is true that there is not here the need to predict the exact course which the injury will take in the future, but there is the possibility that the deceased's wages or salary would have increased through inflation or other causes, or alternatively that there would have been a decrease in earnings, and there is the possibility that the dependants would have died prematurely. Most awkward of all was the question, legislatively removed since 1971,[176] of whether the deceased's widow would or would not have remarried and, if so, when and whom. Again, as with personal injury, the court may be helped by the fact that some crucial changes have already happened before the trial, and once more one must differentiate between changes of circumstances taking place before the judgment of the court at first instance, changes during the period where appeals are in process or still available to the parties, and changes after the litigation is definitely at an end. **41-031**

**(a) Changes before the decision of the court of first instance** While the damages begin to run from the time of the death and are therefore normally assessed in relation to the facts existing at the time of the death, it is fully recognised that subsequent events must be taken into account when they throw light on the realities of the case and that the latest data should therefore be available at the time of **41-032**

---

170 See for a low percentage chance *Wathen v Vernon* [1970] R.T.R. 471 CA, at para.41-098, below. See for a high percentage chance, at 80 per cent, *Hayes v South East Coast Ambulance Service NHS Foundation Trust* [2015] EWHC 18 (QB) (divorced couple had come together again even with talk of remarriage: at [146]–[149]).

171 [1974] A.C. 207 at 212B. Compare *Barnett v Cohen* [1921] 2 K.B. 461 at para.41-099, below.

172 The husband had wanted the wife to come back, but she had up to the time of his death declined to do so. The case had therefore the unusual feature, as Lord Morris pointed out ([1974] A.C. 207 at 214G), that the issues to be decided did not relate to what the deceased would or would not have done had he lived but to what a living person, able to give, and giving, evidence, would or would not have done had the deceased lived.

173 [1984] 3 All E.R. 402.

174 [1956] CA Transcript No.129A. Also *The Times*, 10 May 1956, CA.

175 See the discussion in relation to personal injury at paras 40-034 and following, above.

176 See para.41-069, below.

the trial. Thus it is permissible to show changes after death in the prevailing state of wages in the deceased's occupation, so that if the change marks an increase this will increase the damages. A dramatic illustration of this is *The Swynfleet*,[177] where a claim arising out of the death of two English seamen in 1939 in a collision between two ships, one English and one French, was heard some eight years later, after the Second World War had ended, and after seamen's wages had increased enormously.

**41-033** Similarly, if one of the contingencies that would end the dependency, such as the death of the dependant, has come about before the trial, this will be taken into account and damages assessed on the basis that the dependency is ended on the dependant's death. This was decided in the case of a widow's death before trial in *Williamson v Thornycroft*.[178] Scott LJ said:

> "It is quite true that the measure of damages has to be assessed as at that date [i.e. the husband's death], but courts in assessing damages are entitled to inform their minds of circumstances which have arisen since the cause of action accrued and throw light upon the reality of the case. It seems to me wholly wrong to say that where a death which involves the liability of a third party has occurred, as in this case, some years before the assessment of damages by the court, the court ought to shut its eyes to the fact that one dependant has had only a short tenure of life before death put an end to her dependence."[179]

In the same way, a widow's remarriage before the trial was taken into account in *Lloyds Bank and Mellows v Railway Executive*,[180] and *Mead v Clarke Chapman*,[181] and her damages assessed up to the time of remarriage.[182] On the other hand, it was emphasised in *Welsh Ambulance Services NHS Trust v Williams*,[183] that nothing done after the death by dependants or others can either increase or decrease the dependency for it is fixed at the moment of death; the only events after the death that are relevant are those which affect the continuance of the dependency.[184]

**41-034** Also to be taken into account is the fact that one of the contingencies that would end the dependency, though it has not come about, may have become more probable before the trial, as where the dependant's health seriously deteriorates in the intervening period. This point is implicit in *Hall v Wilson*,[185] where a discount was made for the additional risks of wartime, although the war in question had not begun till after the death.

**41-035** **(b) Changes before the decision of the appeal court** With wrongful death as with personal injury the real difficulties start where the change in circumstances comes between the adjudication of one court and adjudication of a higher court to

---

177 (1947) 81 Ll. L. Rep. 116.

178 [1940] 2 K.B. 658 CA.

179 [1940] 2 K.B. 658 CA at 659. See, too, *Voller v Dairy Produce Packers* [1962] 1 W.L.R. 960 where the court took into account the death, two years later, of the deceased's widow as throwing light on the realities not only of the widow's claim but also of that of the deceased's two infant daughters; see, similarly, *Rawlinson v Babcock and Wilcox* [1967] 1 W.L.R. 481.

180 [1952] 1 T.L.R. 1207.

181 [1956] 1 W.L.R. 76; this is a Court of Appeal report which shows at 77 the trial judge's holding on this point, on which there was no appeal.

182 Although, since 1971, remarriage is no longer taken into account to reduce a widow's damages (see para.41-069, below), such decisions remain important illustrations in the present context.

183 [2008] EWCA Civ 81 CA; facts at para.41-082, below.

184 [2008] EWCA Civ 81 CA at [50].

185 [1939] 4 All E.R. 85.

which an appeal has been taken. Indeed it was in a Fatal Accidents Act claim that this problem was first aired. In *Curwen v James*,[186] where the claimant widow had remarried after the trial but within the time limited for serving notice of appeal, the Court of Appeal held that, since by virtue of the then Rules of the Supreme Court the appeal was by way of rehearing and the court was given a discretion to receive evidence as to matters which had occurred since the date of the trial,[187] the matter should be decided on the known fact of the remarriage of the claimant. However, since the defendant had failed to introduce any evidence of what financial benefit would accrue to the claimant from her new marriage, the court was only prepared to reduce the damages by half, taking the broad view that if the judge had had the knowledge that the remarriage was likely to occur as early as it did he would have awarded, or could reasonably have awarded, no more than half of what he did award.[188]

The decision reached in *Curwen v James*,[189] was in effect endorsed, on different facts and in the context of a personal injury claim, by the House of Lords in *Murphy v Stone-Wallwork (Charlton)*.[190] So, too, has the Court of Appeal's wisdom in carefully reserving its opinion as to what would have been the position had the remarriage occurred at some stage later than the time within which a notice of appeal could have been served.[191] For the House considered that only in the most exceptional cases should a party be allowed, on the basis of changed circumstances, to re-open an assessment of damages after the prescribed time-limit for appeal has elapsed.[192] This is clearly sound, for otherwise there could be no end to the litigation process. But the House also stressed that the case must be exceptional, although not so exceptional, in order to justify the admission of the new evidence even where the appeal had been brought in time, and indicated that the House might be less favourably disposed to an appellant where he could not show that the change had been brought about by a deliberate act of the respondent within his own sphere of action. Thus obtaining leave to introduce evidence of a dramatic increase in salary levels in what had been the deceased's occupation, or of a deterioration in a dependant's health sufficiently serious to affect life expectation, would be more in balance. However, having sanctioned the introduction of evidence of a dependant's remarriage, the courts can hardly now refuse to allow evidence of a dependant's death, although in the normal course death is far from being a deliberate act of the party concerned. It is significant that subsequently, in the analogous context of personal injury, the House of Lords in *Mulholland v Mitchell*,[193] has upheld the Court of Appeal's admission of evidence of a change in circumstances in no way brought about by the party who stood to benefit if the evidence were rejected, and **41-036**

186 [1963] 1 W.L.R. 748 CA.

187 Reliance on these rules is, of course, no longer possible and CPR Pt 52 is what now matters; for its application here see last footnote but one to para.40-047, above. The earlier rules were indeed not relied on by the Court of Appeal when presented with an analogous problem in the personal injury claim, *Jenkins v Richard Thomas & Baldwins* [1966] 1 W.L.R. 476 CA, dealt with at para.40-047, above. For where the appeal is to the House of Lords, see last footnote to para.40-048, above.

188 Contrast *Dietz v Lenning Chemicals* [1969] 1 A.C. 170, a claim on behalf of the deceased's widow and minor child, where the widow remarried after acceptance of an offer in settlement subject to the court's approval but before the court order approving the settlement; the court order was set aside.

189 [1963] 1 W.L.R. 748 CA.

190 [1969] 1 W.L.R. 1023 HL.

191 [1963] 1 W.L.R. 748 CA at 754, 755, per Harman and Pearson LJJ respectively.

192 See para.40-052, above.

193 [1971] A.C. 666; facts at para.40-050, above.

in *Lim Poh Choo v Camden and Islington Area Health Authority*,[194] has admitted evidence of such a change in circumstances that had not been available even to the Court of Appeal at the time of its adjudication. Moreover, these two decisions also go further than the earlier House of Lords decision in that the reasons for appealing were unconnected with the change in circumstances, which, in *Mulholland*, occurred after the notice of appeal had been given. And the same is true of the personal injury case of *McCann v Sheppard*,[195] which was not taken beyond the Court of Appeal. Thus it would seem that the important thing is that the steps for appealing are taken within the prescribed time-limit; they need to be taken neither post nor *propter* the particular change of circumstances.[196]

41-037 **(c) Changes after the litigation has ended** Once again, with wrongful death as with personal injury, there is today no method available for altering the final assessment of damages when given, as always in the past, by way of lump sum. Even the limited qualification on this made available by the introduction of provisional damages awards[197] could not apply where the claim is for a fatal injury since such damages are directed to giving time to see if there is to be a serious worsening of the injured person's condition. However, where periodical payments are awarded—and, as we have seen, these have been introduced for wrongful death as well as personal injury, though in a rather convoluted manner[198]—there is no call for alteration of the final assessment.

## (2) General method of assessment

41-038 The courts have evolved a particular method for assessing the value of the dependency, or the amount of pecuniary benefit that the dependant could reasonably expect to have received from the deceased in the future. This amount is calculated by taking the present annual figure of the dependency, whether stemming from money or goods provided or services rendered, and multiplying it by a figure which, while based upon the number of years that the dependency might reasonably be expected to last, is discounted so as to allow for the fact that a lump sum is being given now instead of periodical payments over the years. This latter figure has long been called the multiplier; the former figure has come to be referred to as the multiplicand. Further adjustments, however, may or may not have to be made to multiplicand or multiplier on account of a variety of factors, namely the probability of future increase or decrease in the annual dependency, the so-called contingencies of life, and the incidence of inflation and taxation. Moreover, the value of the dependency can include not only that part of the deceased's earnings which he would have expended annually in maintaining his dependants but also that part of his earnings which he would have saved and which would have come to his dependants by inheritance on his death[199]; and there may also be included a sum in

---

194 [1980] A.C. 174; facts at para.40-051, above.

195 [1973] 1 W.L.R. 540 CA; facts at para.40-050, above.

196 The arguments are considered in more detail in relation to personal injury at paras 40-046 to 40-054, above.

197 See paras 40-007 and 40-008, above.

198 See para.41-003, above.

199 And where moneys had come to the dependants by inter vivos gifts of the deceased which were liable to estate duty because made within seven years of his death, it was held in *Davies v Whiteways Cyder Co* [1975] Q.B. 262 that the payment of the estate duty constituted the loss of the expectancy

respect of loss attributable to the cessation of contributions which the deceased, and his employers, had made to a provident fund of which the dependants were the nominated beneficiaries.[200] Alternative methods of dealing with these savings have appeared: either they are regarded as comprised in the figure of annual dependency to be multiplied by the multiplier[201] or they are excluded from the figure of annual dependency and a separate, and additional, sum is calculated and awarded in respect of them.[202]

There are, exceptionally, situations in which the court is entitled to regard this conventional method of computation as inappropriate and to arrive simply at an overall figure after consideration of all the circumstances. This is usually done because of the presence of too many imponderables in the case. *Stanley v Saddique*,[203] is a good example of the application for this reason of this method; indeed it provides a double application. The claim was on behalf of a child in respect of the loss of his mother, a mother of no great reliability who had already abandoned her three young children by her husband and was at the time of her death living with the father of the claimant. The trial judge awarded a round figure of £5,000 for loss of the mother's financial support, being of the view that the mother's employment record of poorly paid part time and casual work made it impossible to operate the method of multiplicand and multiplier; in this approach and award he was upheld by the Court of Appeal. By contrast, he did utilise multiplicand and multiplier to arrive at his award of £24,000 for loss of the mother's services but here the Court of Appeal disagreed with both award and approach, substituting £10,000 by "carrying out an assessment", in the words of Purchas LJ, "on a jury award basis". The mother's shortcomings threw such doubt upon the prospect of steady and reliable parental care and support that the use of the multiplicand and multiplier method was here too, again in the words of Purchas LJ, "quite inappropriate".[204] And a departure from the conventional method of computation for reasons other than the existence of too many imponderables is found in *Singh v Aitken*.[205] The deceased, who died as a result of a negligent misdiagnosis of his condition by the defendants, had at his death an unanswerable claim for an agreed figure of some £120,000 against a third **41-039**

---

of a future pecuniary benefit and was accordingly recoverable, subject to a small discount for the chance that the deceased might not have survived the remainder of the seven-year period. The same situation can still arise with inheritance tax, which has superseded estate duty and taken over from capital transfer tax.

200 *Singapore Bus Service (1978) Ltd v Lim Soon Yong* [1985] 1 W.L.R. 1075 PC. "Their Lordships see no material difference between loss of the expectation of a greater sum payable from the fund in consequence of additional contributions that would have been made and the loss of expectation under a will or intestacy resulting from additional savings": at 1079D–E.

201 Only part of the savings was held to be properly so comprised in *Gavin v Wilmot Breeden* [1973] 1 W.L.R. 117 CA.

202 *Taylor v O'Connor* [1971] A.C. 115 illustrates the use of both methods, Lords Morris, Guest and Pearson taking the first approach (at 133, 135 and 142 respectively) and Lord Reid and Viscount Dilhorne the second (at 130 and 140 respectively); however, all of their Lordships adopted the second method in relation to the specific partnership savings that the claimant would have built up over the years. There was an additional sum calculated and awarded for the loss arising from the cessation of provident fund contributions in *Singapore Bus Service (1978) Ltd v Lim Soon Yong* [1985] 1 W.L.R. 1075 PC (at preceding footnote but one). The accelerated receipt of the deceased's savings may still fall to be taken into account against any award in respect of them: see on this para.41-122, below.

203 [1992] Q.B. 1 CA.

204 [1992] Q.B. 1 CA at 16C.

205 [1998] P.I.Q.R. Q37.

party for injuries in a traffic accident. After the death, and because of the death, that claim was reasonably compromised at £20,000. The dependants claimed, and were awarded, 75 per cent—which was the level of the dependency—of the difference between these two amounts. The trial judge posed the question

> "Is a second and consecutive tortfeasor liable to a claimant's dependants for damages which, but for the commission of the second tort, would have been recoverable by the claimant against the first tortfeasor?"

and answered it in the affirmative.[206]

**41-040** It has been pointed out, in dealing with personal injury, that the courts had for long been pressed, without much success, to pay more attention to actuarial evidence in coming to their assessments[207] and *Taylor v O'Connor*[208] encapsulates this lack of success in the context of claims for wrongful death. However, it was further pointed out there that all this has finally changed with the final acceptance of the Ogden Tables by the House of Lords, acclaiming them as the starting point in the computation of damages for pecuniary loss in personal injury claims. The Ogden Tables apply equally to claims for wrongful death—indeed their full title is Actuarial Tables with explanatory notes for use in Personal Injury and Fatal Accident cases—so that what has been said in dealing with personal injury on Ogden has relevance here and does not need repetition; the earlier discussion should be referred to.[209]

## (3) Calculation of the multiplicand and of the multiplier

### (a) Amount of annual dependency: the basic factor for the multiplicand

**41-041** *(i) In general* The starting point in the calculation, in the most common case of a deceased husband and father, has for long been the amount earned by him before his death. To this should be added any other gains and items of value which he provided for his family, the most important of which in practice is the value of services performed by the deceased around the house.[210] There then falls to be deducted that portion of all these which went not towards the support of the dependants but was allocated exclusively to the deceased himself.[211] With a wife and mother, on the other hand, the traditional focus has been on the value of her services in the home, in arriving at the multiplicand.[212] Earnings and services apart, State benefits may provide the dependency or part of the dependency.[213] As with personal injury, the decision in *British Transport Commission v Gourley*,[214] requires the

---

206 Contrast *Baker v Willoughby* [1970] A.C. 467 in a personal injury context at para.40-040, above.
207 See para.38-069, above.
208 [1971] A.C. 115; see Lord Pearson's remarks, at 140.
209 See paras 40-071 to 40-073, above. The Ogden Tables are in their 7th edition published in 2011.
210 Illustrative—recovery in respect of such services appears in the cases on a regular basis—are *Robertson v Lestrange* [1985] 1 All E.R. 950 (£750 per annum for services, unspecified but presumably about house and garden: see at 955c) and *Crabtree v Wilson* [1993] P.I.Q.R. Q24 CA (£1,500 per annum for work on the family home: see at 25). Compare personal injury at para.40-063, above.
211 Contrast *Harris v Empress Motors* [1984] 1 W.L.R. 212 CA at 217A, per O'Connor LJ.
212 Particular relationships, and the calculations to which they give rise, are given extended consideration at paras 41-079 to 41-099, below.
213 *Cox v Hockenhull* [2000] 1 W.L.R. 750 CA; see the case at para.41-044, below.
214 [1956] A.C. 185.

calculation to be made on the earnings after deduction of the income tax which would have been payable on them; the need to deduct tax had indeed been recognised in these claims even before the *Gourley* decision had brought the tax factor into the computation of personal injury damages.[215]

*(ii) Assessment as from date of trial* In *Cookson v Knowles*,[216] the House of Lords confirmed the new approach of the Court of Appeal there[217] that, at least where it is the husband and father as family breadwinner who dies, the pecuniary loss of the dependants should, in the words of Lord Fraser, **41-042**

> "be split into two parts, relating respectively to the period before the trial and the period after the trial, in the same way as it is split in a personal accident case".[218]

In the Court of Appeal the declared purpose of this change in practice was to afford the dependants some protection against inflation by allowing calculation of the future loss to be made from the date of trial when salaries and wages are likely, in inflationary times, to be substantially above where they stood at the date of death. However, the House of Lords put its decision on the different ground of the greater reliability of the assessment up to the date of trial, invoking the well-recognised principle that, again in the words of Lord Fraser,

> "when events have occurred, between the date of death and the date of the trial, which enable the court to rely on ascertained facts rather than on mere estimates, they should be taken into account in assessing damages."[219]

Indeed, Lord Diplock specifically said that he disagreed with the reasoning of the Court of Appeal.[220] Accordingly, the multiplicand has since been based upon the amount that the deceased would have been earning at the date of the trial had he not been killed.

*(iii) Extent to which multiplicand may be expressed as a percentage or fraction of earnings* To the extent that the dependency relies upon the earnings of the deceased, generally the most important factor in the computation, a pattern has developed of expressing the annual dependency as a percentage of the deceased's annual earnings[221] or as a fraction of them.[222] This has become, as a conventional figure, 66.6 per cent of earnings for the dependency of a widow alone, 75 per cent of earnings for a widow and children.[223] The position was explained by O'Connor LJ in *Harris v Empress Motors* thus[224]: **41-043**

215 For full consideration of the application of the *Gourley* rule to wrongful death claims, see paras 18-028 and 18-029, above.

216 [1979] A.C. 556.

217 [1977] Q.B. 913 CA.

218 [1979] A.C. 556 at 575D.

219 [1979] A.C. 556 at 575B.

220 See [1979] A.C. 556 at 575B at 569H–570A.

221 See, e.g. *Young v Percival* [1975] 1 W.L.R. 17 CA; *Dodds v Dodds* [1978] Q.B. 543; *Malone v Rowan* [1984] 3 All E.R. 402.

222 See, e.g. *Graham v Dodds* [1983] 1 W.L.R. 80 HL.

223 See *Robertson v Lestrange* [1985] 1 All E.R. 950 at 955d.

224 [1984] 1 W.L.R. 212 CA.

"In the course of time the courts have worked out a simple solution to the … problem of calculating the net dependency under the Fatal Accidents Acts in cases where the dependants are wife and children. In times past the calculation called for a tedious inquiry into how much housekeeping money was paid to the wife, who paid how much for the children's shoes, etc. This has all been swept away and the modern practice is to deduct a percentage from the net income figure to represent what the deceased would have spent exclusively on himself. The percentages have become conventional in the sense that they are used unless there is striking evidence to make the conventional figure inappropriate because there is no departure from the principle that each case must be decided on its own facts. Where the family unit was husband and wife the conventional figure is 33 per cent and the rationale of this is that broadly speaking the net income was spent as to one-third for the benefit of each and one-third for their joint benefit …. Where there are children the deduction falls to 25 per cent."[225]

The rationale for this smaller deduction, which is not specifically explained by O'Connor LJ, is that the earnings are presumed to be split four ways rather than three, namely one-quarter for the deceased, one-quarter for the wife, one-quarter for the children and one-quarter for joint use.[226]

**41-044** The rule of thumb set out in *Harris v Empress Motors*,[227] that a wife, in the absence of children, is entitled to two-thirds of the deceased husband's net income has, unsurprisingly, met with a degree of resistance. O'Connor LJ himself recognised that the rule was subject to exceptions when he said, in the passage cited, that each case must be decided on its own facts but his suggestion that striking evidence was needed for a departure from the rule has not been wholeheartedly accepted. Thus in *Owen v Martin*,[228] the Court of Appeal overturned the trial judge's award of two-thirds of the deceased's net earnings. The claimant was a young widow who had lost her husband within a year of their marriage. Stuart-Smith LJ pointed out that the proportions suggested by O'Connor LJ were propounded by him in a case that was concerned not with the calculation of dependency upon the deceased but with the appropriate deduction to be made for the deceased's living expenses in calculating the deceased's net earnings in the lost years,[229] and added:

"Such proportions are in my judgment a good guide when a stable pattern has been established in a marriage and virtually all the net earnings are spent in living expenses …. Such a rule of thumb will not be appropriate where the husband is a high earner who may well spend a higher proportion on himself. Nor is it appropriate in the case of a young childless widow. To my mind it is plain that her dependency would not remain at two-thirds of the deceased's net earnings throughout his working life."[230]

Beldam LJ pointed out that the figures given by the claimant in the required particulars of the extent of her dependency represented about 45 per cent of her deceased husband's net earnings and yet the judge had decided on two-thirds of the income not only at death but also as increased according to expectations of rises in future years.[231] And in the particular circumstances of *Cox v Hockenhull*,[232] where

225 [1984] 1 W.L.R. 212 CA 216–217.
226 As illustrative see *Dodds v Dodds* [1978] Q.B. 543 at para.41-089, below.
227 [1984] 1 W.L.R. 212 CA.
228 [1992] P.I.Q.R. Q151 CA.
229 See paras 40-111 and following, above.
230 [1992] P.I.Q.R. Q151 CA at 160.
231 [1992] P.I.Q.R. Q151 CA at 165.
232 [2000] 1 W.L.R. 750 CA.

the wife rather than the husband had been the provider and where the provision came not from earnings but from State benefits, the two-thirds rule was departed from in favour of one-half. Nonetheless there are still decisions which adhere to the conventional percentages. One such is *Wolfe v Del'Innocenti*,[233] where the dependants were the widow and her four daughters, in their 20s at the time of the death. Owen J divided the dependency into two periods, allocating 75 per cent for the two to three years the deceased would have continued to provide support for the daughters, and 66.66 per cent thereafter.[234]

*(iv) Effect of partner's earnings on the multiplicand* The courts had to face the question of whether they must take into account, as affecting the dependency loss, the potential earnings of a partner, historically usually the widow, who, on the assumption that she did not remarry, would in all probability take a job herself. Some time ago in *Howitt v Heads*,[235] Cumming-Bruce J held that he should exclude the widow's prospects of employment from consideration as much as her prospects of remarriage, despite the fact that he would thereby "exclude another factor which is a reality in the future life of this lady".[236] This has been accepted not only for potential earnings but also for actual earnings after the death and before the trial, as in *Davies v Whiteways Cyder Co*,[237] and *Dodds v Dodds*,[238] and, though the merits of ignoring such earnings, potential or actual, may be questioned, it is sensible at least to have the same rule for both. If actual earnings were taken into account but potential earnings were ignored, it would only encourage widows to await the outcome of the litigation before taking a job. Some doubt was indeed thrown on the whole position by the Court of Appeal in *Cookson v Knowles*,[239] Lord Denning there saying, in delivering the judgment of the court, that while it may be argued that the widow is not bound to go out to work, and so reduce the award, "we are not so sure about this".[240] Owen J has now in *Wolfe v Del'Innocenti*,[241] latched on to this comment, which will have been cited to him, and stated that he thought Lord Denning's reservation was well founded.[242] No deduction was in fact made in *Wolfe* as the widow had continued her husband's business with a marked lack of success, but it may be questioned whether it is right to take earnings of the widow into account if it is clear that she would never have gone to work had her husband survived; what Owen J seems to have had in mind is the common situation of the wife who plans to take up paid work in addition to her husband's at some stage, probably after the children have left home.[243] To bring into the computation work that, without the fatal accident, would never have been done seems to be inconsistent with the later decision in *Welsh Ambulance Services NHS Trust v Williams*,[244] **41-045**

233 [2006] EWHC 2694 (QB).
234 [2006] EWHC 2694 (QB) at [31]
235 [1973] Q.B. 64.
236 [1973] Q.B. 64 at 70E.
237 [1975] Q.B. 262; see especially at 272H.
238 [1978] Q.B. 543. Since here the widow was not herself a claimant, there was more reason for not making a deduction: see the case at para.41-089, below.
239 [1977] Q.B. 913 CA.
240 [1977] Q.B. 913 CA at 922E. The case went to the House of Lords ([1979] A.C. 556) but not on any issue involving the widow's earnings.
241 [2006] EWHC 2694 (QB).
242 [2006] EWHC 2694 (QB) at [23].
243 [2006] EWHC 2694 (QB) at [27].
244 [2008] EWCA Civ 81 CA.

where the dependants' making a greater success of the deceased's business was ignored since, as the Court of Appeal held, the dependency becomes fixed at the moment of death.[245]

**41-046** What does remain clear is that, where the partner, historically usually the wife, has been working before as well as after the death so that her earnings were already contributing to the family pool, the earnings after the death do fall to be taken into account. This has never been doubted[246] and was the position in *Cookson v Knowles*,[247] itself. Moreover, where the wife who has been working before the death, and therefore contributing to the family pool, decides to cease working after the death because, for instance, she wishes to concentrate on bringing up her children, as was the position in *Taylor v Prosol Façade Access Ltd*,[248] this does not allow her earnings before death to be ignored, since as the judge there said:

> "The relevant consideration under the Fatal Accidents Act is: 'what would have happened in relation to her employment had the deceased remained alive?'; not 'what the widow is constrained to do in consequence of his death."[249]

**41-047** The manner in which the partner's working before and after the death affects the calculation of the dependency was usefully dealt with in the unfortunately unreported, but much relied-on, decision in *Coward v Comex Houlder Diving*.[250] It had there been submitted by counsel for the wife that, in the absence of evidence of a different dependency, both husband and wife should be able to claim to be dependent to the extent of two-thirds of the other's net earnings. Ralph Gibson LJ was quite unable to accept such a contention; it was unrealistic not to bring into the equation the whole of the wife's continuing net earnings against the two-thirds of the joint net earnings. "Expressed in terms of a formula", he said,

> "the claimant's dependency … is two-thirds of [the deceased's] net earnings less one-third of her own net earnings; or it is two-thirds of the joint earnings less her own earnings."

Mathematically the conventional 66.6 per cent of the husband's net earnings is on this basis modified to produce for the widow just 50 per cent of those earnings should her own earnings in the joint pool equal half of her deceased husband's; the percentage would drop to 33.3 should she be earning as much as her husband.

**41-048** Further cases have taken into account in this way that the wife would be earning during the dependency. Thus in *Crabtree v Wilson*,[251] the Court of Appeal, while supporting the trial judge's decision to calculate the loss of the widow's dependency by the use of percentages rather than by reference to anticipated specific expenditures, held that he should have taken the percentages not *à la Harris v Empress Motors*, as he had done, but *à la Coward v Comex*. In *Wheatley v Cunningham*,[252] a similar adjustment was made but it was for the very short period that

---

[245] [2008] EWCA Civ 81 CA at [50] and the case at paras 41-082 and 41-120, below.

[246] See, e.g. *Malyon v Plummer* [1964] 1 Q.B. 330 CA; *Davies v Whiteways Cyder Co* [1975] Q.B. 262, especially at 272F.

[247] [1977] Q.B. 913 CA.

[248] [2003] EWHC 310 TTC.

[249] [2003] EWHC 310 at [21].

[250] *Coward v Comex Houlder Diving* unreported 18 July 1988 CA.

[251] [1993] P.I.Q.R. Q24.

[252] [1992] P.I.Q.R. Q100.

the widow would have continued working before the birth of the child with whom she was pregnant at the time of her husband's death. For the remaining bulk of the dependency when she would probably not have worked the trial judge considered that he should apply the *Harris* rule so as to award her two-thirds of the deceased's net earnings. It may, however, sometimes be appropriate to abandon the *Coward v Comex* approach and turn to the deceased's own net earnings as a starting point. In *H v S*,[253] where the deceased was already divorced at the time of her death but living with another in a stable relationship, the trial judge did just this and held that the multiplier for the dependency should be based upon 75 per cent of the deceased's income. The Court of Appeal agreed that in what it called the peculiar circumstances of the case the judge had been right to start with the deceased's earned income but, because the three children on whose behalf the claim was made were never going to have been wholly dependent upon their mother's earnings because of the contributions of others, the judge's 75 per cent was reduced to 60 per cent for the calculation of the dependency multiplicand. Kennedy LJ, giving the only reasoned judgment, said that the judge's percentage might well have been right had the deceased, after the breakdown of her marriage, lived alone with the children or had set up home with someone who did not contribute.[254]

Two other conclusions may be drawn from this development in the law. The first is that the same result should follow where the contribution from the wife to the joint pool comes not from her earnings but from her private means. To the extent that she is relying on her own income for her support she is not relying on that of her husband and this will be true whether the income of her own is earned or unearned. The second conclusion is that the conventional 75 per cent, used where there are dependent children in addition to the wife and mother, will also be modified so as to produce a lower percentage figure of dependency. The children will be dependent on both their parents in respect of the joint pool income while the wife's dependency will be unaltered. **41-049**

*(v) Adjustments for variation in annual dependency* The amount which the deceased was earning at the time of his death, or would have been earning at the time of the trial, may not be the amount which he would have continued to earn in the future. It will often be the case that the deceased's earnings would have increased over the years as he progressed in his career, and that such increases in salary would in general have brought corresponding increases in support to his dependants is a factor to be taken into account; conversely, the court may have to keep in mind that the support provided might have diminished because the deceased's earnings might have diminished, as where he had been in an occupation with a high rate of unemployment. According to Lord Diplock in *Mallett v McMonagle*,[255] such **41-050**

> "anticipated future variations in 'dependency' are normally dealt with by an adjustment in the multiplicand"[256]

*Robertson v Lestrange*,[257] provides a useful illustration where the anticipated

---

253 [2003] Q.B. 965 CA.
254 [2003] Q.B. 965 CA at [31] and [32].
255 [1970] A.C. 166.
256 [1970] A.C. 166 at 175.
257 [1985] 1 All E.R. 950.

increases in earnings through progressive promotion of a deceased husband and father were averaged over a 33-year period and an appropriate higher multiplicand thereby reached.[258] More than one multiplicand may be used; this is also illustrated by *Robertson v Lestrange*, where a multiplicand for the years of the widow's and children's dependency was taken and a further and different one for the subsequent years when only the widow would have been dependent.[259]

### (b) Period of years of lost dependency: the basic factor for the multiplier

**41-051** *(i) In general* The starting point in the calculation of the multiplier is the number of years that it is anticipated the dependency would have lasted had the deceased not been killed; this may of course vary as between different dependants.[260] In *Young v Percival*,[261] different multipliers were applied to the separate calculations there made in respect of the dependency at death and the dependency arising from future prospects.[262] In *Robertson v Lestrange*,[263] a single multiplier was taken but then split between the period when both the widow and children would have been dependent and the later period when it would have been only the widow, the portion of the multiplier allocated to the later period[264] being applied to a different multiplicand representing a lower percentage of a higher income.[265]

**41-052** *(ii) Assessment as from date of death* In the days when a single calculation of loss of dependency for the whole period from death was made,[266] it followed that the multiplier must be calculated as from the date of death; so in *K v J.M.P. Co*,[267] the Court of Appeal had to right the lower court's error in calculating the multipliers for the various dependent children there as from the date of the trial by making appropriate increases to them so as to reflect the fact that the proper starting point was the date of death. But the moment that the requirement of separate calculations for the loss of dependency up to trial and for the loss of dependency from trial onwards was introduced by *Cookson v Knowles*,[268] it then followed that the starting point for the multiplier, needed for the second part of the computing exercise, becomes the date of trial. In *Cookson v Knowles* the judge at first instance had naturally calculated his multiplier of 11 as from the date of death; with its introduction of a two-stage calculation the Court of Appeal simply deducted from that

258 See the detailed figuring, [1985] 1 All E.R. 950 at 953g.

259 See [1985] 1 All E.R. 950 at 953f–955c together with 958e. The latter multiplicand differed in two ways from the former: it was based on a figure of higher projected earnings and on a lower percentage of dependency; Compare para.41-051, below. While there might be scope for using *Duxbury* calculations—allowing anticipated changes in dependency to be computer programmed thereby bypassing today's less accurate methods of computation—the abandonment of *Duxbury* in personal injury claims (see the footnote at the end of para.40-073, above) means that it is not going to be used for fatal accidents.

260 See, e.g. *Kassam v Kampala Aerated Water Co* [1965] 1 W.L.R. 668 PC, where eight children ranging from 3 to 23 years were held all to be dependants but for varying lengths of time.

261 [1975] 1 W.L.R. 17 CA.

262 [1975] 1 W.L.R. 17 CA at 21F–22H.

263 [1985] 1 All E.R. 950.

264 It was 6.5 out of a total multiplier of 14.

265 See paras 41-041 and 41-050, above.

266 See para.41-042, above.

267 [1976] Q.B. 85 CA.

268 [1979] A.C. 556, affirming [1977] Q.B. 913 CA; see para.41-042, above.

multiplier the two-and-a-half years which had elapsed between death and trial, and thus ended up with a multiplier of 8.5; this was affirmed by the House of Lords.

It would at first sight seem that, when starting afresh, the proper approach, as was accepted in *Dodds v Dodds*,[269] would be to make the initial calculation of the multiplier as from the date of trial, but this was not endorsed by the House of Lords in *Cookson v Knowles*.[270] Counsel for the claimant had contended before the House that the multiplier of 8.5 was unfair to the claimant, arguing that, if the deceased had had a twin brother who had been injured at the same time and whose personal injury claim had been heard at the same time, the appropriate multiplier for his loss after the date of trial would have been higher than 8.5. But, said Lord Fraser, on the probably correct assumption that that would have been so, **41-053**

> "it does not in my opinion follow that the multiplier of 812 is too low in the present claim under the Fatal Accidents Acts where different considerations apply. In a personal injury case, if the injured person has survived until the date of trial, that is a known fact and the multiplier appropriate to the length of his future working life has to be ascertained as at the date of trial. But in a fatal accident case the multiplier must be selected once and for all as at the date of death, because everything that might have happened to the deceased after that date remains uncertain. Accordingly, having taken a multiplier of 11 as at the date of death, and having used 212 in respect of the period up to the trial, it is in my opinion correct to take 812 for the period after the date of trial."[271]

This reasoning and this result was followed by the House of Lords in *Graham v Dodds*,[272] where Lord Bridge, with whom their other Lordships concurred, described the reasoning as cogent[273]; the Northern Ireland Court of Appeal, which was reversed, was held to have misunderstood[274] *Cookson v Knowles*.[275]

The Law Commission and the Working Party responsible for the Ogden Tables are decidedly, and rightly, not in agreement with this reasoning and result. In its Report on *Claims for Wrongful Death*,[276] the Law Commission, under the general heading "Should the multiplier be calculated from death or from trial?", recommended that the Ogden Working Party be reconvened to consider, and explain more fully, how the Ogden Tables should be used to produce accurate damages assessments in Fatal Accidents Act cases, at the same time pointing out to the Working Party that the Law Commission's preferred approach was in effect to use the date of trial for the calculation of the multiplier for post-trial losses. In response to this recommendation the Working Party met and produced a further edition of Ogden; this was the fourth in 2000. In it a new section D, which now appears in the current seventh edition of 2011 with updated tables,[277] dealt with the application of the Tables to Fatal Accidents Act cases and needs to be referred to for the process of calculation. It is detailed and elaborate, but essentially clear. **41-054**

---

269 [1978] Q.B. 543 at 553B–E.

270 [1979] A.C. 556. But see *Dodds v Dodds* further at para.41-064, below.

271 [1979] A.C. 556 at 576C–D.

272 [1983] 1 W.L.R. 808 HL.

273 [1983] 1 W.L.R. 808 HL at 815D.

274 [1983] 1 W.L.R. 808 HL at 814E–G.

275 [1979] A.C. 556.

276 (1999) Law Com. No.263.

277 The updated version is at https://www.gov.uk/government/publications/ogden-tables-actuarial-compensation-tables-for-injury-and-death [Accessed October 2017].

**41-055** The reason why Lord Fraser's argument cannot be accepted can be shortly stated. The discount for early receipt of the damages, implicit in the calculation of the multiplier, should apply to future losses only, that is, to losses from the date of trial and judgment. By the choice of a multiplier from the date of death followed by its application to the future loss after deducting from it the number of years between death and trial, an improper discount for early receipt is built into the period from death to trial where there has been no early receipt. In other words, the discount takes effect, as it should not do, on pre-trial losses. This is the explanation of counsel's contrast in *Cookson* between the brother injured and his twin killed.[278] At the same time Lord Fraser's concern that

> "everything that might have happened to the deceased after that date [viz., the date of death] is uncertain"[279]

is catered for by introducing a different, but tiny, discount, to be applied to both pre-trial and post-trial losses, to allow for the chance that the deceased would not in any event have survived to the date of trial.[280]

**41-056** Turning to the details of Ogden's section D, its essential feature is the departure from the current practice of calculating the multiplier from the date of death and taking instead the date of trial, in line with the accepted approach in personal injury cases. Pre-trial losses will generally be calculated, as before, by multiplying the annual loss by the number of years between death and trial but, differing from before, with the need to make a deduction for the possibility that the deceased might in any event have died before trial. The necessary discounts are set out in a convenient table, Table E, in Ogden[281] which shows them to be generally of little or even no size. Thus no discount is required where the deceased was 40 or under at the date of death and the trial was within the next three years; changing the age to 60 at death, still with trial within three years, only requires a 2 per cent discount where the deceased is male and 1 per cent where female. Post-trial losses are, as before, based upon the lesser of two periods, namely the expected period for which the deceased would have been able to provide the dependency and the expected period for which the dependant would have been able to receive the dependency.[282] Again, a discount has to be made to allow for the possibility that the deceased might not have survived to trial to provide any post-trial dependency. The necessary discounts are again set out in a convenient table, Table F, in Ogden[283] which again shows them to be of little or even no size, until one gets to ages of 70 and over, though they are

---

278 At para.41-053, above.

279 The passage is at para.41-053, above.

280 Ogden introduced in the 5th edition (2004), and repeated in the later editions, an alternative mode of calculation which can be used should the courts insist on adhering to a date of death multiplier. It is a compromise solution and, like all compromises, does not get to the root of the problem; it should therefore be ignored. It is seen to be particularly unsatisfactory when, applying it to the Ogden illustration which we set out at para.41-056, below, it produces a higher figure, at £588,000, than do the other two methods (p.31).

281 At p.25.

282 Separate calculations have to be made for before retirement age and after retirement age where retirement is likely to affect the level of support, as in the commonest case of the death of the family breadwinner, but this is not required where retirement is of no significance for the calculation, as with a deceased wife and mother rendering domestic services or a grown-up child supporting elderly parents. But this is all as before.

283 At p.26.

somewhat larger than the Table E discounts for pre-trial losses. Detailed illustrations are given in Ogden, the first one[284] positing a trial three years after the death of a man at 37 and coming up with an award of £538,500 if the multiplier is taken at the date of his death but an award of £573,300 if the multiplier is taken at the date of the trial. The disparity between the two amounts will increase, and can increase significantly, as the years between death and trial increase.

The illogical reasoning of the Courts in *Cookson v Knowles* and *Graham v Dodds*, led to lower courts trying to distinguish the cases on inventive grounds, and openly critiquing the two decisions. One such example is Nelson J in *White v ESAB Group (UK) Ltd*,[285] who felt himself bound by the earlier House of Lords decisions to calculate the multiplier from the date of death, although he personally was persuaded of the merits and correctness of the new thinking.[286] The Court of Appeal twice endorsed Nelson J, stating that it found his reasoning cogent.[287] **41-057**

*Cookson v Knowles and Graham v Dodds*, finally came under close scrutiny in *Knauer (Widower and Administrator of the Estate of Sally Ann Knauer) (Appellant) v Ministry of Justice (Respondent)*.[288] Ms Knauer died from mesothelioma as a result of the respondent's admitted negligence. The appeal to the Supreme Court concerned the assessment of damages owed to Ms Knauer's dependant widower. There was no dispute about the multiplicand in the Supreme Court. The question was whether the Supreme Court should apply the multiplier to that annual amount from the date of death (as required by *Cookson v Knowles* and *Graham v Dodds*) or at the date of trial. The Supreme Court, in a joint judgment delivered by Lord Neuberger and Lady Hale, refused to follow *Cookson v Knowles* and *Graham v Dodds*. The Supreme Court held that the reasoning was flawed, illogical and resulted in unfair outcomes. The Supreme Court held that the decisions were decided in a different era, when the calculation of damages was not as sophisticated. The Supreme Court held that the approach in *Cookson v Knowles* and *Graham v Dodds* – calculating the multiplier from the date of death – subrogated the key aim of an award of damages; to place the person who has been harmed by the wrongful acts of another in the position in which he or she would have been had the harm not been done. As explained above,[289] the problem with the calculation of the multiplier from the date of death is that the multiplier includes a discount for early receipt of the money but for the period from death until trial the money has not been received. **41-058**

*Knauer* has now definitively displaced the findings in *Cookson v Knowles* and *Graham v Dodds*, and upheld the more rational and fair approach of calculating the multiplier from the date of trial. For pre-trial losses the only difference from non-fatal cases will be that there will be a small deduction to take account of the possibility that before trial the deceased might have died or given up work in any event.

The Supreme Court in *Knauer* has therefore achieved the same result as the legislature in Scotland where s.7(1)(d) of the Damages (Scotland) Act 2011 provides that: **41-059**

---

[284] Example 7 at pp.27 to 28.

[285] [2002] P.I.Q.R. Q6 at 76.

[286] [2002] P.I.Q.R. Q6 at [27] and [43].

[287] *H v S* [2003] Q.B. 965 CA; *A Train & Sons Ltd v Fletcher* [2008] EWCA Civ 413 CA.

[288] [2016] A.C. 908.

[289] At para.41-055.

"any multiplier applied by the court –

(i) is to run from the date of the interlocutor [i.e. judgment] awarding damages, and
(ii) is to apply only in respect of future loss of support".

**41-060** *(iii) Expectation of life of deceased and dependants* As with personal injuries, calculation of the multiplier will frequently require a calculation of the expectation of life, or of the working life,[290] of the victim, but with fatal injuries there is the additional factor that the expectation of life of the dependant as well as that of the deceased must be taken into account.[291] Indeed, where the dependant is a parent and the deceased a son or daughter, the controlling life expectancy will be that of the dependant rather than that of the deceased, and it was submitted in the editions of this work since *Cookson*, and *Graham v Dodds*,[292] that here it would be appropriate, the dependant still being alive, to make the initial calculation of the multiplier as from the date of trial. This approach was adopted in the Supreme Court in *Knauer (Widower and Administrator of the Estate of Sally Ann Knauer) (Appellant) v Ministry of Justice (Respondent)*,[293] where the Supreme Court definitively rejected *Cookson v Knowles* and *Graham v Dodds* and, following the approach in the Ogden Tables, held that the appropriate calculation is from the date of trial.

**41-061** In any event, even in the case of a dependant of a much greater age than the deceased, it remains true that both lives have to be taken into account. Thus in *Rowley v London and N.W. Ry*,[294] where the deceased was bound by a personal covenant to allow his mother, one of the persons on whose behalf damages were claimed, an annuity of £200 during their joint lives, the court held that the judge's direction to the jury to calculate the annuity upon the probable duration of the mother's life was incorrect and involved an over-calculation, since this overlooked the contingency that the son might have died before her. What the mother had lost was an annuity for joint lives; an annuity on her own life was more valuable.

**41-062** While in the past in calculating life expectancies courts have generally allowed appropriate statistical tables to be introduced in evidence to assist,[295] today we have the Ogden Tables with life expectancies built into them[296]; as we have seen, they are for use as much in fatal accident cases as in personal injury cases.[297] Of course the statistical tables, Ogden or otherwise, deal only with average persons, and the circumstances of the particular lives in question are what must control. It would seem, however, that the particular life may be taken to be an average one, and the

---

[290] Any prospect of early retirement may be taken into account: *Robertson v Lestrange* [1985] 1 All E.R. 950; especially 954h. But contrast para.41-081 (in a footnote), below.

[291] *Price v Glynea and Castle Coal Co* (1915) 85 L.J.K.B. 1278 CA at 1282, per Bankes LJ ("where a claim is made under Lord Campbell's Act … it is not only a question of the expectation of life of the deceased man, but there is also a question of the expectation of life of the claimant"), cited with approval by McCardie J in *Barnett v Cohen* [1921] 2 K.B. 461 at 472; and see also *Feay v Barnwell* [1938] 1 All E.R. 31 at 35. It has been held, however, in *Baugh v Delta Water Fittings* [1971] 1 W.L.R. 1295, to be wrong in principle to stay a widow's claim until she has submitted to a medical examination: see especially at 1301–1302. But see the analogous personal injury cases in the first footnote to para.40-103, above.

[292] [1983] 1 W.L.R. 808 HL.

[293] [2016] A.C. 908.

[294] (1873) L.R. 8 Ex. 221.

[295] The use of such tables appears even as early as *Rowley v London and N.W. Ry* (1873) L.R. 8 Ex. 221.

[296] See para.40-137, above.

[297] See para.41-040, above.

onus is on the defendant to prove that it falls short of average by reason of bad health, hazardous employment and the like. This appears also from *Rowley v London and N.W. Ry*,[298] where a further objection to the calculation of the annuity from annuity tables, namely that the jury ought to have been told to make allowance for any defect in the dependant's health, was not sustained.[299] The court held that, if such special circumstances existed, the party who relied upon them as diminishing the value of the life should establish their existence,[300] and in the absence of such evidence the jury might properly be directed to consider the life as an average life and to value it according to tables of average duration.

Of the various circumstances which may make the expectation of the particular life less than average, bad health is probably the commonest, and is well recognised as a factor. Hazardous employment is another; but there is some uncertainty as to hazards which affect the whole community but for a limited period. Thus in *Hall v Wilson*,[301] it was held that where the deceased died just before the Second World War the additional risk, had he lived on, of being killed in war, either in the services or in air-raids, must be taken into account. On the other hand, in *Bishop v Cunard White Star*,[302] where men had been killed at sea in wartime, it was held that the multiplier was not to be **41-063**

> "materially reduced in these cases by consideration of the hazardous nature of the occupation of the deceased men. During the last great war the hazards of life at sea were not conspicuously greater than risks run by many other persons on shore".[303]

As to how the contingency of unemployment should be rated in the calculation of the multiplier, the Ogden Tables give guidance in the explanatory notes.[304]

*(iv) Expectation of dependency of child dependants* Not all dependencies would have continued until death. Thus not only where the deceased is young and the dependant much older is the dependency likely to come to an end well before the deceased would, but for the fatal injury, have died in the ordinary course,[305] but this may also happen where it is the dependant who is young and the deceased who is much older. The typical case is of a claim brought on behalf of a child in respect of his or her parent's death. Here it is not the length of the dependent child's expected life but the length of his or her expected dependency that is crucial and this in practically every case is going to be much shorter than the life expectancy of the parent at the date of death. As was said in the editions of this work since *Cookson*, and *Graham v Dodds*,[306] this factor would suffice to justify the court's calculation in *Dodds v Dodds*,[307] of the multiplier at the date of trial[308] where the claim was on behalf of the minor son of a deceased father. There the dependency **41-064**

---

298 (1873) L.R. 8 Ex. 221.

299 It is true that the court was dealing with the loss of a specific annuity, but there seems no reason why the decision should not apply to damages at large.

300 Parker LJ said much the same in *Mead v Clarke Chapman* [1956] 1 W.L.R. 76 CA at 84,

301 [1939] 4 All E.R. 85.

302 [1950] P. 240.

303 [1950] P. 240 at 248.

304 See para.40-134, above.

305 See para.41-060, above.

306 [1983] 1 W.L.R. 808 HL.

307 [1978] Q.B. 543.

308 See para.41-053, above.

was to last, it was held, only until the son reached his majority at 18; the son was eight-and-a-half years old at his father's death and was 12-and-a-half years old at trial. The decision of the Supreme Court in in *Knauer (Widower and Administrator of the Estate of Sally Ann Knauer) (Appellant) v Ministry of Justice (Respondent)*,[309] has now held that the multiplier should be calculated from the date of trial in the case of a widower must now put this date of assessment beyond doubt.

**41-065** The decision in *Knauer* will now remove the need for courts to attempt to reconcile the tension between calculation of the multiplier at the date of death (as was thought to be required for child dependents before *Knauer*) and the principle that damages should be calculated on the basis of known facts. That tension was most evident in *Corbett v Barking Havering and Brentwood Health Authority*.[310] The claim was on behalf of a child whose mother had died during his birth, and the trial judge took a multiplier of 12 based effectively not on the mother's life expectancy but on the shorter period of the child's dependency. Yet the child was already 11-and-a-half years old by the time the case came to trial, leaving the absurd position of having only a multiplier of 0.5 to cover the six or more years of dependency that were still in the future. The Court of Appeal was not prepared to depart from the assessment as at the date of death but held that the judge was entitled to take into account the facts as they were known at the date of the trial and to adjust the multiplier in the light of those facts. Purchas LJ said that he could "see no justification for denying the court the power" to do this: *Corbett v Barking Havering and Brentwood Health Authority*[311]; the multiplier was increased to 15. While respectfully agreeing with this result, except to comment that the multiplier should have been increased by more than three, there is thought to be much cogency in what was said by the dissenting Ralph Gibson LJ who reached, "after much hesitation", the contrary conclusion that there should be no adjustment to the multiplier of 12; the course taken by the majority, he said, "seems to me, in effect, to calculate the multiplier as at the date of trial": *Corbett v Barking Havering and Brentwood Health Authority*.[312]

**41-066** For how long a child's dependency will be expected to continue will vary from case to case. Some children will leave home and go into employment very early, others will remain dependent on their parents while they go through university, and there will be situations in between. Thus in *K v J.M.P. Co*,[313] the Court of Appeal accepted the trial judge's holding that the children's dependency should not be taken beyond the age of 16 while in *Spittle v Bunney*,[314] it endorsed the trial judge's continuation of the dependency to the age of 22. On the other hand, in *H v S*,[315] where the trial judge had calculated the multipliers on the assumption that the two younger children, both boys, would be at university until the age of 24, the Court of Appeal pointed out that this made no allowance for the possibility that one or other might not proceed to tertiary education and reduced the multipliers on the basis that the dependency would not extend beyond the boys' 21st birthdays; the position with the two elder children was different as they had already graduated and

---

309 [2016] A.C. 908.
310 [1991] 2 Q.B. 408 CA.
311 [1991] 2 Q.B. 408 CA at 427.
312 [1991] 2 Q.B. 408 CA at 440H.
313 [1976] Q.B. 85 CA.
314 [1988] 1 W.L.R. 847 CA.
315 [2003] Q.B. 965 CA.

not until the age of 24.[316] In *Cresswell v Eaton*,[317] the age of 18 was taken for two of the children but the age of 22 for the youngest and brightest. In *Corbett v Barking Havering and Brentwood Health Authority*,[318] the trial judge had not taken the child's dependency beyond the age of 18 because he considered that the chances of the child proceeding to tertiary education were evenly balanced and was further of the view that it was for the claimant to show that his proceeding to tertiary education was more likely than not. The Court of Appeal disagreed. This possibility should not have been discounted altogether but the chance of the child's proceeding to tertiary education should have been evaluated and the multiplier increased accordingly. If the position was evenly balanced one would have expected the appropriate increase to be based upon 50 per cent of the number of years that tertiary education would have added to the length of the dependency but the Court of Appeal was not prepared to accept this degree of precision and made the more arbitrary addition of one to the multiplier.

In *Welsh Ambulance Services NHS Trust v Williams*,[319] the Court of Appeal remarked that it was unusual to find adult children, of sound mind and body, dependent on their father and even more unusual to find them remaining so dependent for the rest of their father's working life.[320] Nevertheless this situation did arise in *Williams* where the dependency came from the father's labour input into the very successful business which he had built up and in which all the family shared. No apportionment between the children and their mother was required as the value of the total dependency was assessed on a collective basis at the family's request. **41-067**

*(v) Expectation of marriage of deceased or dependants* Also relevant to an assessment of the length of time that the dependency would have lasted may be the expectation of marriage of both deceased and dependants. Thus where the deceased is a young son the courts have taken into account that he will probably marry and thereupon cease or reduce his contribution to his parents' upkeep[321]; similar principles should apply in the case of a deceased daughter. And where the daughter is the dependant, the prospect of her marrying and becoming independent of her deceased parent is clearly relevant. **41-068**

At one time it was the possibility of the remarriage of the widow claimant which held the centre of the stage. In case after case judges were faced with the unattractive task of sizing up the claimant's chances of finding a new husband and bringing the dependency to an end, but it was a task which was often based on sexist assumptions, and in *Buckley v John Allen and Ford*,[322] Phillimore J suggested that it was time judges "were relieved of the need to enter into this particular guessing game".[323] Eventually his plea was answered by statutory intervention,[324] and s.3(3) of the Fatal Accidents Act 1976, as substituted for s.3(2) of the original by s.3(1) **41-069**

---

316 [2003] Q.B. 965 CA at 35.
317 [1991] 1 W.L.R. 1113.
318 [1991] 2 Q.B. 408 CA.
319 [2008] EWCA Civ 81 CA; facts at para.41-082, below.
320 [2008] EWCA Civ 81 CA at [41].
321 *Dolbey v Goodwin* [1955] 1 W.L.R. 553 CA (mother dependant only); *Wathen v Vernon* [1970] R.T.R. 471 CA.
322 [1967] 2 Q.B. 637.
323 [1967] 2 Q.B. 637 at 645.
324 Not by the courts, for the Court of Appeal in *Goodburn v Thomas Cotton* [1968] 1 Q.B. 845 CA, refused to endorse Phillimore J's approach.

of the Administration of Justice Act 1982 and re-enacting s.4 of the Law Reform (Miscellaneous Provisions) Act 1971, provides that

> "in an action under this Act where there fall to be assessed damages payable to a widow in respect of the death of her husband there shall not be taken into account the remarriage of the widow or her prospects of remarriage".

No mention is made of the widower claimant, so that initially courts had to continue to take into account his prospects of remarrying and acquiring another wife, but a perhaps somewhat unexpected consequence of s.4 of the Fatal Accidents Act 1976 being widened to cover all collateral benefits is that the widower's remarriage and remarriage prospects now fall to be ignored even without the benefit of a specific statutory provision to that effect.[325]

**41-070** *(vi) Expectation of divorce or separation of deceased and dependant* In *Owen v Martin*,[326] the Court of Appeal, disagreeing with the trial judge, decided that it was proper to take into account the fragility of the claimant widow's marriage, which was less than one-year-old and which might not have lasted in the light of a history showing no great regard for the sanctity of marriage or for marital fidelity. Accordingly the judge's multiplier of 15, which was

> "applicable to the dependency of a widow married for an appreciable time whose marriage could be said to have stood the test of time and whose prospect of pecuniary advantage from her deceased husband was settled and assured",[327]

was reduced to 11. The statutory prohibition of taking a widow's marriage and prospects of remarriage into account[328] in no way prevented the prospects of divorce from being considered. Similarly, the multiplier was reduced to 11 to reflect the substantial chance of the marriage failing in *D and D v Donald*,[329] though here the fragility of the marriage was due to its being held in disregard by the deceased husband rather than by the claimant widow.

**41-071** Where the deceased and the dependant had been living together without marriage or were civil partners there will be no question of a formal divorce but there may be thought to be a greater chance that the relationship may break up and the parties separate because of the lack of the legal bond. Indeed the Fatal Accidents Act 1976, by s.3(4), as amended by s.83(8) of the Civil Partnership Act 2004, specifically provides that, where a claim is by a common law spouse or a civil partner, the fact that he or she had no enforceable right to financial support from the deceased as a result of their having lived together is to be taken into account. Accordingly, in *Drew v Abassi*,[330] the Court of Appeal upheld the trial judge's multiplier of 13 which he had adopted in place of one of 15 that he would have

---

325 See para.41-118, below. Buckley LJ had said in *Hay v Hughes* [1975] Q.B. 790 CA at 816H to 817A that the omission of the widower "may be thought to call for consideration by the legislature" and the Pearson Commission had agreed that, whatever changes should be made in this area, widow and widower must be put on a par: (1978), Cmnd.7054–1, paras 412 to 414.

326 [1992] P.I.Q.R. Q151 CA.

327 [1992] P.I.Q.R. Q151 CA at Q165, per Beldam LJ.

328 See para.41-069, above.

329 [2001] P.I.Q.R. Q5 at 44.

330 *Drew v Abassi* unreported 24 May 1995 CA.

taken had the parties been married. Yet he acknowledged that the relationship in the case before him had been as settled and lasting as any relationship of marriage.

**(c) The appropriate discount rate for the multiplier** The dependants' annual loss—the multiplicand—is not multiplied by the number of years during which they have been deprived of the deceased's support; this would clearly produce over-compensation as it would put the deceased's future contributions into the dependants' hands long before they would otherwise have received them, and would enable them to enjoy the interest accruing in the intervening period. It is the present value of the future contributions that is to be awarded.[331] The multiplicand is therefore to be multiplied by the appropriate figure—the multiplier—to arrive at that present value. The vital question then arises, crucial to the multiplier, of the appropriate discount rate to adopt. For the greater the assumed return on the damages awarded, the smaller the multiplier, and vice versa. Dependants therefore argue for a low discount rate, tortfeasors for a high one. **41-072**

The controversy that for long surrounded this question of the appropriate discount rate has been finally resolved. The matter has been fully examined in relation to personal injury and does not require repetition here; reference should be made to the earlier paragraphs.[332] In a nutshell the House of Lords has ruled in *Wells v Wells*,[333] that in future the discount rate should be changed from the traditional 4 to 5 per cent to the rate available on index-linked government securities, then set by their Lordships at 3 per cent and subsequently reduced by the Lord Chancellor in 2001 by prescription of a rate of 2.5 per cent. As pointed out when dealing with personal injury, in the economic recession now upon us an even lower rate may soon be prescribed. **41-073**

**(d) Adjustments to the multiplier for contingencies** In addition to the discount because the award is by way of lump sum, the courts seek to make a further discount on account of the general contingencies of life or, as they may be called, the vicissitudes of life: it is said that the multiplier must suffer some reduction to cater for the possibility that the deceased might in any event have died earlier than expected, the possibility that he might have met with some accident that would have kept him from working for a time or have even forced him to retire, the possibility that he might have failed in business or have become unemployed, and the like.[334] However, discounting for earlier death is hardly required while the multiplier continues to be assessed from the date of death rather than from the date of trial.[335] As for the discount for contingencies, and the impact of the Ogden Tables thereon, the full discussion in the related field of personal injury should be referred to.[336] **41-074**

---

331 Where there is also a loss of the savings which the deceased would have made over the years and which would have come to the dependants on his death in the natural course (see para.41-038, above), it is the present value of a single future payment rather than of a succession of annual payments that falls to be assessed, thereby requiring an even greater discounting; whether or not a separate calculation is made in respect of loss of savings (see para.41-038 further, above), this will be so.

332 See paras 40-121 to 40-127, above.

333 [1999] 1 A.C. 345.

334 See, e.g. *Whittome v Coates* [1965] 1 W.L.R. 1285 CA at 1292, per Diplock LJ.

335 See para.41-053, above.

336 See paras 40-128 and following, above. In *Graham v Dodds* [1983] 1 W.L.R. 808 HL, it was held that a multiplier of 18, while it might be appropriate in assessing the dependency of a family of a

41-075 (e) **No specific adjustments for private means** Just as a claimant's damages for his pecuniary loss caused through personal injury are not to be reduced because he has a substantial and secure private income,[337] so too the damages claimed on behalf of a dependant in a case of wrongful death will not be the less because that dependant is shown to have private means. It might be thought that this would be sufficiently taken for granted so as not to have surfaced in the authorities but the point did at one time make a solitary appearance in a Scottish appeal to the Lords, *Shiels v Cruikshank*,[338] where it was roundly quashed. "This novel argument," as Lord Normand called the contention that the dependant should prove need,

> "might result in leaving the widow without any claim for damages, beyond *solatium*,[339] in a case in which she had even a mediocre fortune of her own, though she had been maintained by her husband in affluent circumstances out of income which terminated on his death".[340]

At the same time the existence of a dependant's private income may show that the deceased contributed less to the support of the dependant than he otherwise would have done. In other words, the dependant's private income is relevant solely for the purpose of ascertaining the extent of the loss of dependency.[341]

41-076 (f) **No specific adjustments for inflation** In the matter of inflation the short point is that, since it is taken into account in the selection of the appropriate discount rate, no further adjustment is called for. In the past there was controversy as to what discount rate does properly take inflation into account but the resolution of the controversy in the personal injury field in favour of a discount rate geared to index-linked government securities[342] removes the inflation issue entirely from the scene, and not only for personal injury but also for fatal accidents. In the light of this, and as has already been said in the discussion, pertinent here,[343] of inflation in relation to personal injury, the weighty judicial pronouncements of the fatal accident litigation of an earlier day, appearing at House of Lords level in *Taylor v O'Connor*,[344] and *Cookson v Knowles*,[345] can safely be put on one side.[346]

---

breadwinner killed between the ages of 20 and 30, could not be right for a man of 41 and that the reasoning of the Northern Ireland Court of Appeal, which had led it to this conclusion, was faulty in failing to make a discount for the vicissitudes of life (see, especially at 815H–816H, per Lord Bridge), so that the jury's award would have to be set aside and a new trial ordered (see the case at para.53-015, below). But the multiplier could have been found to be faulty before any question of discount for contingencies was reached, for it exceeded the appropriate multiplier which, for a man of 41 using the 4.5 per cent discount rate, the Ogden Tables, then just out, would have revealed. Of course today with increased population mortality figures and a much lower discount rate, Ogden would show a multiplier of 18 to be nearer the mark even before any discount for contingencies.

337 See para.40-142, above.

338 [1953] 1 W.L.R. 533 HL.

339 Namely the non-pecuniary loss for which, as we have seen (para.41-018, above), England did not allow any recovery at that time.

340 [1953] 1 W.L.R. 533 HL at 535. However, the rule of no adjustment for private means may be unfavourable to a dependant in relation to tax: see para.40-143, above on personal injury, where the position is again the same as with fatal accidents.

341 See further at para.41-049, above.

342 See para.40-122 and 40-123, above.

343 See para.40-044, above.

344 [1971] A.C. 115.

345 [1979] A.C. 556.

346 They are all set out in the 15th edition (1988) of this work at paras 1573 to 1575.

**(g) Adjustments for taxation** Whether there should be adjustments for taxation on account of the level of tax that the income from the lump sum damages award will bear is a question which clearly should receive the same answer in fatal accident claims as it does in personal injury claims. Accordingly, everything has already been said in the personal injury context, where indeed the authorities emanating from the fatal accident field, in particular *Taylor v O'Connor*,[347] were included; the earlier discussion should be referred to.[348] 41-077

## (4) Types of recovery in particular relationships

**(a) Death of husbands, wives, civil partners, with or without children** The 19th edition of this text, and earlier, treated the circumstances of husbands and wives, fathers and mothers, separately. No provision was made, on the basis of a lack of case law, for civil partners. These differences are historical anomalies. No principled justification can be given for different treatment of persons in the same circumstance if the person is a husband, wife, or civil partner. 41-078

*(i) Husband, wife or civil partner with children: assessment of value of dependency* Where a person who has a partner and children is killed, it is usual first to calculate the family dependency and then to apportion the resulting figure between the partner and each child separately.[349] Thus the main calculation is of the value of the dependency of all taken together: the question of apportionment is dealt with later.[350] 41-079

Where the deceased is working in a factory, an office, and the like, the process of calculation adopted by the courts is generally fairly straightforward, especially if the wage or salary is a steady one and one which is likely to continue at much the same level throughout the remainder of the deceased's working life. The basic annual figure—the multiplicand—will be the amount of wages or salary that the deceased contributed to the housekeeping[351] less the amount out of such contribution that has gone exclusively towards the deceased's own maintenance.[352] This process of calculation appears in many cases: good examples are *Heatley v Steel Co of Wales*,[353] and *Mallett v McMonagle*.[354] To this annual value of the family dependency is then applied a multiplier which will generally represent the number, 41-080

---

[347] [1971] A.C. 115.

[348] See paras 40-146 to 40-148, above.

[349] And sometimes the deceased's parents as well, where he supported them too: e.g. *Rowley v London & N.W. Ry* (1873) L.R. 8 Ex. 221; *Zinovieff v B.T.C., The Times*, 1 April 1954 (also fully reported at Kemp and Kemp, *The Quantum of Damages in Fatal Injury Claims*, 2nd edn (1962), p.132 (not in later editions)).

[350] See paras 41-083 and following, below.

[351] In calculating his contribution, account may have to be taken, as in *Cookson v Knowles* [1977] Q.B. 913 CA, of the increased wages his wife was able to earn because of the assistance he gave her in her job.

[352] In *Hay v Hughes* [1975] Q.B. 790 CA, the court rejected the defendant's contention that that part of the deceased's wages which had been expended on the family home should be allocated between the deceased, the wife and the two children so that only one-sixth of the expenditure was attributed to each child. "Each child ... lived in a whole house, not in one-sixth of a house. The children have lost the enjoyment of a home, not a fraction of a home": at 812F, per Buckley LJ. And see *Harris v Empress Motors* [1984] 1 W.L.R. 212 CA at 217A, per O'Connor LJ.

[353] [1953] 1 W.L.R. 405 CA.

[354] [1970] A.C. 166.

suitably discounted, of working years that would have remained to the deceased. As already indicated in the general consideration of the multiplier,[355] there may be different multipliers for different categories of dependant or a single multiplier split between different periods of dependency. It is clearly impossible to state numbers for multipliers with any precision because of the varying circumstances of each case.

**41-081** Where the deceased is a professional or business person more difficulties tend to arise for a variety of reasons. Thus the present annual value of the dependency is generally more difficult to assess than in the case of the working person who gives so much a week to his partner to keep house.[356] Taking taxation on the deceased's earnings into account[357] is more difficult with the professional claimant than with the working person who has tax deducted at source[358]; moreover, it is only where the deceased is a professional or business person that there arises the need, which may one day be recognised, to take into account the tax which will be payable on the income generated by the award.[359] Beyond this, the prospects of increased or decreased earnings and the probable duration of working life are generally more difficult to assess,[360] and finally there is more likelihood that the court will have to take into account, as a part of the value of the dependency, savings which the deceased would have made during the rest of his or her life and which could reasonably be expected to have come on his or her death to the family by will or intestacy,[361] and also formerly, as an item of deduction, the dependants' receipt of assets from the deceased's estate well in advance of the time of his normal death.[362] *Daniels v Jones*,[363] and *Taylor v O'Connor*,[364] provide good illustrations of detailed calculations by the court of the dependants' loss in this type of case.

**41-082** A series of cases explains the dependency position where the deceased is a business person whose family on his death inherits the deceased's interest in the particular business. In *Wood v Bentall Simplex Ltd*,[365] the deceased farmed in partnership with his brother and parents, himself with a one third interest in the partnership. The defendant responsible for the death was unsuccessful in contending that the widow and two young sons had suffered no loss of dependency because, the widow having inherited the deceased's partnership interest, their enjoyment of

---

355 See para.41-051, above.

356 See *Roughead v Railway Executive* (1949) 65 T.L.R. 435 at 435 per Humphreys J. The manner in which *Hay v Hughes* [1975] Q.B. 790 CA indicates that general family expenditure should be treated in the case of a working person (see preceding footnote but three), is also relevant here.

357 See para.41-041, above.

358 Business persons are likely to be taxed in similar fashion to the working person—the usual case is where they are company directors—but, though tax is then deducted at source, there are very likely to have to be adjustments at the end of the tax year.

359 See para.41-077, above, referring back to paras 40-146 to 40-148, above.

360 The Court of Appeal has recognised, but some time ago, that professional and business persons retire not before 70 and frequently later: see *Muirhead v Railway Executive* (1951) CA No.178, per Singleton LJ, and *Zinovieff v B.T.C.*, *The Times,* 1 April 1954, per Lord Goddard CJ (both fully reported at Kemp and Kemp, *The Quantum of Damages in Fatal Injury Claims*, 2nd edn (1962), pp.226 and 132 respectively, but not in later editions). Contrast, however, para.41-060 (in the first footnote), above.

361 See also para.41-038, above.

362 For the interrelation today of the receipt of assets from the estate and their accelerated receipt, see para.41-122, below.

363 [1961] 1 W.L.R. 1103 CA.

364 [1971] A.C. 115.

365 [1992] P.I.Q.R. P332 CA.

that income had not ceased on the death as the assets continued to be used in the business after the death. Because the sums which the widow and sons were receiving before the death could have been largely attributable to the deceased's work in the farm rather than from a return on the capital invested in the farm, to that extent a loss of dependency had been shown. The same approach was taken, and elaborated on, in two further Court of Appeal cases, *Cape Distribution v O'Loughlin*,[366] and *Welsh Ambulance Services NHS Trust v Williams*.[367] In *O'Loughlin* the deceased had owned and managed a portfolio of properties, which his widow inherited. Before the death she had not involved herself in the business, beyond just working in a secretarial capacity, but after the death she attempted for a time to manage the properties but lacking aptitude without success, so that eventually she sold them and lived on the income. A loss of dependency of herself and her two teenage children was found which was valued at the cost of replacing the deceased's skills as manager. In *Williams* the deceased, described by the Court of Appeal as a wealth creator, had built up a very successful business, in which his wife and his two elder children already worked and his third and youngest child was about to start at the time of the death. As in *Wood* and *O'Loughlin* the widow inherited but following family policy the shares were equalised between the family members. The business was continued but with this difference from *O'Loughlin*, that the efforts and expertise of the children made the business more successful so that it could be said that the family were financially even better off after the death. This however made no difference to the dependency which was fixed at the moment of death and could not be diminished by the children's making a success of the business; such financial benefit did not come into the assessment of the dependency.[368] Accordingly, there was a clear loss of dependency and it was calculated, as in *O'Loughlin*, by the cost of replacing the deceased's skills in running the business.[369]

*(ii) Husband, wife or civil partner with children: apportionment between dependants* On the question of apportionment between the various members of the family,[370] it has been common practice to allocate the bulk of the money to the spouse **41-083**
or partner.[371] While it is true that the spouse's or partner's dependency would have lasted throughout his or her life[372] whereas the children's dependency will tend to cease, or at least substantially diminish, on their reaching adulthood, the major, and unsatisfactory, reason for this weighting in favour of the spouse is that it appears to be assumed that the spouse or partner will use part of the amount allocated to him

---

366 [2001] P.I.Q.R. Q8 CA at 73.

367 [2008] EWCA Civ 81 CA.

368 See the citation from Smith LJ's judgment in the footnote at the end of para.41-120, below explaining that this followed from s.3 rather than s.4 of the statute.

369 These three cases are further dealt with at para.41-120, below to show that the business as a capital asset had to be left out of account altogether in the assessment of the value of the dependency

370 In *Welsh Ambulance Services NHS Trust v Williams* [2008] EWCA Civ 81 CA there was no apportionment between the wife and children, all of whom were adult, as the judge had been asked, and agreed, to assess the value of the dependency on a global or collective basis. This was accepted by the Court of Appeal.

371 An apportionment table can be found in Kemp and Kemp, The Quantum of Damages. *Eifert v Holt's Transport Co* [1951] W.N. 467 CA (£2,000 to a widow aged 23, £4,000 to a son aged one) is exceptional, as the apportionment in this manner arose out of the generosity of the widow.

372 With remarriage no longer to be taken into account: see para.41-069, above.

or her for the children's maintenance.[373] There is admittedly also the practical advantage to this approach, one supported by common sense, that the spouse or partner will have ready access to the fund for use in the care of the children without the need for applications to the court. Latham J in *R. v Criminal Injuries Compensation Board Ex p. Barrett*,[374] indicated his agreement with the statement in the equivalent paragraph of the 15th edition (1988) of this work, to which paragraph he referred, that

> "there is no real sound basis other than pragmatism for approaching the problems of the apportionment of the amount of money representing the lost dependency in this particular way."[375]

Yet despite the benefits of pragmatism, it is surely preferable to attempt a calculation of the contributions which the deceased would have made to each child's support and to allocate that amount to each child. What would be the position, for instance, if the spouse or partner were to die while the children were still quite young? Would their position have been adequately secured?[376]

**41-084** One fortunate result of the otherwise unfortunate development, appearing in *Gammell v Wilson*,[377] which permitted the estate to claim under the Law Reform (Miscellaneous Provisions) Act 1934 for the deceased's income in the lost years, was that the courts would seek to allocate more to the children and less to the surviving spouse or partner where this helped to avoid any duplication of damages as between the Fatal Accidents Act award and the Law Reform Act award.[378] Such duplication would arise where the children's measure of entitlement under the latter award was greater than their measure of entitlement under the former, but with the position reversed for the surviving spouse or partner. One therefore finds Hodgson J in *Robertson v Lestrange*,[379] deliberately setting out to allocate to the children under the Fatal Accidents Act award an amount which equalled the substantial sum to which they were entitled, by virtue of their deceased father's intestacy, under the Law Reform Act; in the result the apportionment was, for the period of the children's dependency, 40 per cent to the widow and 20 per cent to each of the three children.[380] It was hoped that courts would try to continue this practice though the motivation for it had gone once the estate was debarred from recovering the deceased's income of the lost years[381]; but there is not much sign that the practice has been continued. In *Robertson v Lestrange*,[382] Hodgson J was referred to early authority, in the shape of *Sanderson v Sanderson*[383] and *Bulmer v*

---

373 See, e.g. *Thompson v Price* [1973] Q.B. 838 at 842H–843A.

374 [1994] P.I.Q.R. Q44.

375 [1994] P.I.Q.R. Q44 at 47.

376 A far more advanced system of allocation of the damages was introduced in New Zealand many years ago (by the Death by Accidents Compensation Act 1952 (No.35, 1952), Pt II) whereby, instead of apportioning the award between the dependants, the court might order that all or part of the damages be held on trust as a class fund for their benefit and, moreover, might vary any such order made by it.

377 [1982] A.C. 27.

378 See para.41-126, below.

379 [1985] 1 All E.R. 950.

380 [1985] 1 All E.R. 950 at 959d–960h.

381 See para.41-126, below.

382 [1985] 1 All E.R. 950 at 959h–960a.

383 (1877) 36 L.T. 847.

*Bulmer*,[384] giving much higher allocations to children which were more in line with their genuine dependency; in *Sanderson*,[385] four children received two-thirds of the award between them, in *Bulmer*,[386] six children each received one-eighth.

Indeed the undesirability of the children being thus dependent upon benefiting from the damages allocated to their surviving parent[387] is sometimes specifically appreciated by the courts: thus in *Goodburn v Thomas Cotton*,[388] the court recognised that there were circumstances in which a widow's remarriage might have an adverse effect on her children's financial future, held that this was a factor to be taken into consideration in apportioning the damages awarded, and accordingly increased the amounts which the trial judge had allocated to the children.[389] The case was one in which there was a strong likelihood that the widow would remarry, so that in fact the Court of Appeal reduced the total award at the same time as it increased the children's allocation, but the children must surely be entitled to the same protection whatever their surviving parent's prospects of remarriage and whether such prospects do, as at the time of *Goodburn v Thomas Cotton*, or do not, as now, reduce their surviving parent's damages.[390] And where the surviving parent has in fact remarried before the trial, it was for a time the case, somewhat ironically, that the children were entitled to an even smaller proportion of the damages than if their parent had not remarried. For the statutory requirement that a surviving spouse or partner's damages are to be assessed without regard to remarriage[391] in no way touched upon the assessment of the children's damages, and therefore, as was held in *Thompson v Price*,[392] left unaffected the earlier case law laying down that a child's damages may be reduced after the father's death by reason of a stepfather's presence; accordingly *Clay v Pooler*,[393] applying *Thompson v Price*, apportioned a mere 3 per cent of the total award to each of the children. It is, at least in this connection, fortunate that *Thompson v Price* is no longer law so that here surviving spouses and partners are now on the same footing as their children; in *Stanley v Saddique*,[394] the Court of Appeal decided that the immense legislative widening, from 1982, of the rule against deductibility of collateral benefits, in connection with which that case is considered later,[395] required the benefit of a step-parent's care—in *Stanley* a stepmother—to be left out of account in the assessment of a child's loss of dependency.[396] **41-085**

These various aspects of apportionment also reveal what had been an inherent danger in the practice of arriving first at a global sum for the whole class of dependants and then apportioning it between the individual members.[397] It is clear from the **41-086**

---

384 (1883) 25 Ch. D. 409.

385 (1877) 36 L.T. 847.

386 (1883) 25 Ch. D. 409.

387 The court's statutory power to control the damages allocated to the widow has been gone since 1971.

388 [1968] 1 Q.B. 845 CA.

389 From £500 to each child to £1,000 to the younger and £1,200 to the elder.

390 See para.41-069, above.

391 [1968] 1 Q.B. 845 CA.

392 [1973] Q.B. 838.

393 [1982] 3 All E.R. 570.

394 [1992] Q.B. 1 CA.

395 See para.41-118, below.

396 Thus rendering obsolete on stepfathers not only *Thompson v Price* [1973] Q.B. 838 but the decisions in *Mead v Clarke Chapman* [1956] 1 W.L.R. 76 CA, and *Reincke v Gray* [1964] 1 W.L.R. 832 CA and the comments in *Hay v Hughes* [1975] Q.B. 790 CA.

397 See para.41-015, above.

fact that a surviving spouse or partner's probable remarriage once reduced the damages but not the children's, while actual remarriage once reduced the children's damages but not those of the surviving spouse or partner, that different factors can go to reduce the loss of dependency of different dependants. Indeed whenever collateral benefits, of whatever nature, fell to be deducted in assessing the damages, such benefits might accrue not to all of the claiming dependants but only to one or some of them. It was therefore essential that these reductions and deductions were not made until after the apportionment between the individual dependants had been arrived at, but sometimes the courts fell into the error of making the reductions or deductions first and the apportionment between dependants second.[398] It is true that this danger has disappeared in Fatal Accidents Act claims by virtue of today's ignoring of all collateral benefits in the damages assessment[399]—and even before the change in the law on collateral benefits it could be said that the right result was generally achieved, with occasionally the circumstance that one factor affected one dependant and not another causing the court to make separate calculations from the start for each[400]—but *R. v Criminal Injuries Compensation Board Ex p. Barrett*,[401] which was not a claim for Fatal Accidents Act damages but a claim under a scheme for the compensation of the victims of crime, still tells a cautionary tale. A wife and mother was murdered and her husband and two children made a claim under the scheme. The total amount awarded by the Board came to some £96,000, just under half of which was intended to cover the children's loss of their mother's care and services. However the Board, following current practice, awarded the great bulk of the compensation to the husband, amounting to 94.3 per cent of the total. Under the rules of the scheme half of the proceeds of a life insurance policy to which the husband and wife had jointly contributed and which became payable in full on the wife's death had to be deducted from the compensation going to the husband; this deduction was of over £83,000. The result was that the husband was left with an inadequate £13,000 with which to maintain the children who were entitled to over three and a half times that figure. Not surprisingly, Latham J, citing the 15th edition of this book in 1988, quashed the Board's decision and sent the matter back for a re-assessment which would make a proper apportionment as between the husband and the children.

**41-087** *(iii) Husband, wife or civil partner without children* Where a husband and wife or a civil partnership have not yet started a family, or have not wished or been able to have children, or have grown-up children no longer dependent, it will generally be only the spouse's or partner's dependency which is in issue. The result of this is that the proportion of the deceased's net earnings to which the spouse or partner will be entitled will be greater; applying the rule of thumb already considered, there will be a sole entitlement to 66.6 per cent rather than to a shared entitlement of 75 per cent. Of course, as we have seen, the rule of thumb may not be appropriate to the circumstances of the case; in particular, the spouse's or partner's own earnings may influence the computation.[402] Nor will the spouse or partner necessarily be the

---

398 See, e.g. *Bishop v Cunard White Star Co* [1950] P. 240.

399 Finally established in *Arnup v M.W. White Ltd* [2008] I.C.R. 1064 CA. See paras 41-112 to 41-114, below.

400 See, e.g. *Rawlinson v Babcock & Wilcox* [1967] 1 W.L.R. 481; see especially at 483.

401 [1994] P.I.Q.R. Q44.

402 See para.41-046, above.

only claimant. There might also be, for instance, parents receiving filial assistance from the deceased in their old age. Such contributions would normally fall to be deducted from the deceased's net earnings before arriving at the percentage thereof to which the spouse or partner could lay claim by way of damages. The spouse or partner may also have been cared for and looked after by the deceased as in *Devoy v William Doxford & Sons Ltd*,[403] where the wife had become disabled, both husband and wife being at the time in their 60s, and the cost of carers brought in to replace the husband was awarded.[404]

*(iv) Where there is only a claim by the children* In certain circumstances only the children's dependency will fall for consideration. One historical situation where this was so, but which no longer applies, was where the mother had no right to damages herself because she was not married to the father.[405] Now, on situation where it might be so is where the surviving parent's own negligence was the cause of the death of the other parent.[406] A second situation in which it will be so is where the other parent was already dead at the time of the death[407] or where the other parent has died before the trial.[408] Where both parents have been killed in the same accident,[409] the children, of course, have two potential claims. **41-088**

*Dodds v Dodds*,[410] with the mother as the tortfeasor, is a good illustration. Put shortly, the method adopted to assess the loss of the only child was to deduct from the deceased's net earnings not only his expenditure upon himself but his expenditure that had benefited his wife, thus leaving in play the expenditure on the child and the so-called joint expenditure from which the whole family derived benefit. This approach, said Balcombe J, had the approval of the Court of Appeal, citing *Hay v Hughes*,[411] and *K v J.M.P. Co*[412]; these are considered below. Counsel had submitted that the adoption of this method in practice led to the result that half of the deceased's earnings were for the benefit of the child or children of the family—no doubt on the basis that one quarter was allocated to the husband, one to the wife, one to the children and one jointly—but Balcombe J preferred to look at the evidence of specific expenditure before him and reached from these figures a dependency amounting to 47.5 per cent of the deceased's take-home pay.[413] By **41-089**

403 [2009] EWHC 1598 (QB).

404 See at para.41-025, below the equivalent case of *Feay v Barnwell* [1938] 1 All E.R. 31 where the deceased was the husband and the carer the wife. Cost of carers and a variety of other costs not agreed by the parties to the action were awarded in *Zambarda v Shipbreaking (Queensborough) Ltd* [2013] EWHC 2263 (QB).

405 As in *Phipps v Cunard White Star* [1951] 1 T.L.R. 359; *Kelliher v Ground Explorations* [1955] C.L.Y. 741 and *K v J.M.P. Co* [1976] Q.B. 85 CA. Since 1982 the unmarried mother has been a potential claimant: see para.41-005, above.

406 As in *Dodds v Dodds* [1978] Q.B. 543.

407 As in *Drake v Foster Wheeler Ltd* [2011] 1 All E.R. 63.

408 There are far more illustrations in the cases of types of situation in which the claim is by the children alone where it is the mother and not the father who has been killed: see paras 41-090 and following, below.

409 As in *Kassam v Kampala Aerated Water Co* [1965] 1 W.L.R. 668 PC and *Hay v Hughes* [1975] Q.B. 790 CA. Contrast at para.41-095, below, *Watson v Willmott* [1991] 1 Q.B. 140.

410 [1978] Q.B. 543.

411 [1975] Q.B. 790 CA.

412 [1976] Q.B. 85 CA.

413 The mother who was working on a part-time basis put her earnings into the family pool and the fraction of 47.5 per cent was calculated on the joint family income but then applied just to the father's earnings.

contrast in *K v J.M.P. Co*,[414] where the mother had not been married to the deceased, the trial judge had held that the three children's pecuniary loss of dependency included all the father's expenditure on the family other than expenditure on himself. The Court of Appeal, however, disagreed and reduced the figure of annual dependency by taking into account the father's expenditure on the mother but not to the extent that the support which the mother would now be able to give the children would be diminished or impaired by her loss of the father's support. Thus expenditures in order to maintain the children's standard of life, in particular the father's provision of the mother's expenses in accompanying the children on holidays to Ireland, fell to be paid for as part of the children's loss.[415] This type of case is, of course, no longer of significance since the unmarried mother can now join in the claim with the children[416] but the decision in *K v J.M.P. Co*,[417] could have some relevance to other cases where the mother, though not entitled, or not wishing, to claim on her own behalf, is still looking after the children.[418]

**41-090** More common than cases like *Dodds v Dodds* where the mother is the tortfeasor, are cases where the father has through his negligence caused the death,[419] where he has settled his own claim with the defendant[420] or had it heard independently of the child's,[421] where he has died before the trial[422] or, where the father may not have concerned himself to make, or participate in, a claim, because he had already left the deceased and was now married to another[423] or living with another,[424] or, although living with the deceased at her death, had since married.[425] These cases have helped substantially to develop the law in relation to claims by children on their own. Cases where the children have lost their father as well as their mother in the accident have already been dealt with.[426]

**41-091** In only one of these cases[427] was a nanny housekeeper engaged to provide the services previously provided by the deceased. In each other case the family had sprung to the rescue and the child or children had been taken in by aunt, grandmother, stepmother or other family member, including the father from whom

---

414 [1976] Q.B. 790 CA.

415 See [1976] Q.B. 85 CA at 98B. The fact situation was similar in *Phipps v Cunard White Star* [1951] 1 T.L.R. 359, but it does not seem that a claim in respect of the mother's support was made: see *K v J.M.P. Co* [1976] Q.B. 85 CA at 91F and 92B-–F, per Cairns LJ. A third case involving an unmarried mother is *Kelliher v Ground Explorations* [1955] C.L.Y. 741 where the child, born just before the death of the father and before the father was contributing to the child's maintenance, was held to have lost the benefit of an affiliation order which the mother would probably have obtained for the child's support.

416 See para.41-005, above.

417 [1976] Q.B. 85 CA.

418 The dependants included not only children but grandchildren and great grandchildren in *Drake v Foster Wheeler Ltd* [2011] 1 All E.R. 63. The two daughters received smallish sums and the many others trifling sums each: see [2011] 1 All E.R. 63 at [52].

419 As in *Hayden v Hayden* [1992] 1 W.L.R. 986 CA.

420 As in *Corbett v Barking Havering and Brentwood Health Authority* [1991] 2 Q.B. 408 CA.

421 As in *Bordin v St Mary's NHS Trust* [2000] Lloyd's Rep. Med. 287.

422 As in *Watson v Willmott* [1991] 1 Q.B. 140. There was in fact a claim by the estate of the father, who had committed suicide four months after his wife's death, but the award for his own loss of dependency amounted to only £500; see further on this case at para.41-095, above.

423 As in *Cresswell v Eaton* [1991] 1 W.L.R. 1113.

424 As in *H v S* [2003] Q.B. 965 CA.

425 As in *Stanley v Saddique* [1992] Q.B. 1 CA.

426 See para.41-095, above.

427 *Bordin v St Mary's NHS Trust* [2000] Lloyd's Rep. Med. 287.

the mother had been separated or divorced. There has therefore, not surprisingly, been a resistance to awarding the full commercial cost of a nanny housekeeper when that cost was never going to be incurred; one finds it being said that the "approach based upon the cost of hiring alternative commercial services ... borders on complete artificiality"[428] and that

> "on the facts of this case the whole concept of valuing the lost services by reference to a 'notional nanny' is inappropriate".[429]

There has, curiously, not been the same move to develop, in line with the position in the related field of personal injuries, a pattern of compensation for the caring relatives at a level short of commercial rates of pay,[430] though recoveries of damages have nevertheless been somewhat muted. They seem never to have got as far as a total dependency of £50,000 with awards generally much lower; and the trial judge's evaluation of the mother's services at a figure around £150,000 was swiftly cut down by the Court of Appeal in *H v S*,[431] to £37,500.[432] *Bordin v St Mary's NHS Trust*,[433] is the case where a nanny does make an appearance. A nanny substitute was employed but relatives also assisted and, while the commercial rate was taken for the nanny substitute, that rate less 35 per cent was used for the care by the unpaid relatives.[434]

One finds attempts in some cases to bring the relative's services into account by **41-092**
way of deduction; these attempts, appearing in *Watson v Wilmott*,[435] and *Hayden v Hayden*,[436] and now shown to be misguided, are considered later in dealing with collateral benefits.[437] Certainly, where the court has been prepared to look at the cost of a nanny housekeeper as a guide to the value of the deceased's services, it has been the net pay after tax and national insurance that has been taken and with no addition of cover for weekends and holidays; this is made clear particularly in *Corbett v Barking Havering and Brentwood Health Authority*.[438] And in the earliest of the cases, *Spittle v Bunney*,[439] the Court of Appeal justified a substantial reduction in the trial judge's award by adopting the very sensible position that it was inappropriate to take the full cost of a nanny housekeeper for the full period of the child's dependency because less care, supervision and services are required as a child grows up. This factor in the computation has been generally adopted in the later cases; thus in *Corbett* it led to the acceptance of only one-half of the cost of a nanny housekeeper from the time the child was six years old. And another way in which the damages award has been contained is to abandon any attempt to have regard to the cost of a nanny housekeeper on account of the unsatisfactory and indif-

---

428 *Corbett v Barking Havering and Brentwood Health Authority* [1991] 2 Q.B. 408 at 419C, per Purchas LJ.
429 *Hayden v Hayden* [1992] 1 W.L.R. 986 at 998B, per Sir David Croom-Johnson.
430 For personal injury, see paras 40-233 and following, above.
431 [2003] Q.B. 965 CA.
432 [2003] Q.B. 965 at [37].
433 [2000] Lloyd's Rep. Med. 287.
434 *Bordin* has a valuable, detailed rather than broad brush, assessment of the loss of a mother's services.
435 [1991] 1 Q.B. 140.
436 [1992] 1 W.L.R. 986 CA.
437 See para.41-117, below.
438 [1991] 2 Q.B. 408 CA; see, especially, at 442D–443D, per Farquharson LJ.
439 [1988] 1 W.L.R. 847 CA.

ferent qualities of the deceased's care. This can justify a comparatively small award and was the position in *Stanley v Saddique*.[440]

**41-093** These difficulties, however, fall away where the relative cannot cope with looking after the child without giving up his or her job; the relative may well have children of his or her own and to care for an expanded family, with the new member probably requiring exceptional care because of the circumstances, necessitates full-time attention. Thus in *Cresswell v Eaton*,[441] it was reasonable for the aunt to give up her employment as a traffic warden and the damages were effectively based upon her lost earnings. These were in fact less than what would have been payable over the years to a nanny housekeeper employed commercially; but it would not have mattered had these earnings been more, always provided the claimant could show it to be reasonable for his aunt to have given up her employment. In this connection Simon Brown J said that he was bound to bear in mind that the point made in *Spittle v Bunney*,[442] as to children's lessening requirement for care as they grow older

> "was made and applied in the context of a 'notional' earnings claim rather than, as for the bulk of the dependency here, an actual one".[443]

**41-094** As with claims made on behalf of the surviving parent and children together,[444] there are two further heads of damage. In the first place, where the deceased had been a working parent, the children have a claim to the extent that they were dependent upon the parent's earnings. This disbursement dependency, as it was called in *Cresswell v Eaton*,[445] was a feature of that case and also of *Hayden v Hayden*,[446] and *Stanley v Saddique*.[447] Of course, where the deceased has been a working parent then the deceased will not have been giving full time care to the child or children and this may lead to some reduction in what is awarded in respect of the service dependency. Simon Brown J in *Cresswell v Eaton*,[448] however said that

> "where, as here, a claim is based in large part upon a relative's actual loss of earnings reasonably incurred, modest discount only should be made to reflect the part-time nature of the deceased mother's care".[449]

**41-095** Where both parents are killed in the same accident there will usually be claims by the children in respect of both deaths. This is best illustrated by *Hay v Hughes*.[450] Separate multiplicands were arrived at for the loss of the father's support and for the loss of the mother's services, the former being calculated along the lines later followed in *Dodds v Dodds*,[451] and the latter on the basis of the cost of a nanny-

440 [1992] Q.B. 1 CA.
441 [1991] 1 W.L.R. 1113.
442 [1988] 1 W.L.R. 847 CA.
443 [1991] 1 W.L.R. 1113 at 1123B.
444 See paras 41-100 and following.
445 [1991] 1 W.L.R. 1113 at 1118H.
446 [1992] 1 W.L.R. 986 CA.
447 [1992] Q.B. 1 CA.
448 [1991] 1 W.L.R. 1113.
449 [1991] 1 W.L.R. 1113 at 1121E.
450 [1975] Q.B. 790 CA.
451 [1978] Q.B. 543; see para.41-089, above.

housekeeper[452]; to the two multiplicands, in the region of £1,100 and £1,000 respectively, the same multiplier was then applied.[453] In *Kassam v Kampala Aerated Water Co*,[454] where the children's claim was brought only in respect of their father's death—no reason for the absence of a claim in respect of their dependency on their mother appears—the Privy Council rejected a proposed distinction in the method of calculation in respect of dependent children between the situation where both parents were killed and that where the mother survived, seeing no reason in principle

> "why the support necessary for young children should in the absence of a mother be more sparingly estimated than if the mother had survived".[455]

One further case, *Watson v Willmott*,[456] has the curiosity that only the mother was killed in the accident but the father's suicide four months later was held attributable to the accident and the loss of his wife therein. On the basis that the defendant's negligence was responsible for the two deaths, the trial judge made assessments for the child in respect of his loss of dependency on both mother and father.

### (b) Death of sons or daughters

*(i) Married children* When a deceased son is already well-established in life, himself with a wife and probably children, it will often be found that he has been making a regular contribution to his by now ageing parent or parents, sometimes under self-imposed legal obligation by covenant or annuity, as in *Rowley v L. & N.W. Ry*,[457] and in *Zinovieff v British Transport Commission*.[458] And the same may apply with a daughter, herself married and with children, as in *Burgess v Florence Nightingale Hospital*.[459] In such cases there is little difficulty. **41-096**

*(ii) Unmarried adult children* Some of the earliest cases under the original Fatal Accidents Act were successful claims of this type, as *Franklin v S.E. Ry*,[460] where a father recovered for the loss of his 21-year-old son's gratuitous services,[461] and *Dalton v S.E. Ry*,[462] where a father and mother recovered for the loss of the provision of goods and money by their 27-year-old son. The fact that no contributions are being made at the time of death does not in these cases rule out all loss, as the **41-097**

---

452 See [1975] Q.B. 790 CA at 809H.

453 See, especially, [1975] Q.B. 790 CA at 812A–813B. The main issue in the case was whether there should be a deduction on account of the gratuitous services rendered to the children by their grandmother; on this see para.41-112, below.

454 [1965] 1 W.L.R. 668 PC.

455 [1965] 1 W.L.R. 668 PC at 673. The case involved eight children ranging from three to 23 years, the Privy Council holding that all of them were dependants but that they would be so for varying lengths of time.

456 [1991] 1 Q.B. 140.

457 (1873) L.R. 8 Ex. 221.

458 *The Times*, 1 April 1954; fully reported at Kemp and Kemp, *The Quantum of Damages in Fatal Injury Claims*, 2nd edn (1962), p.132 (not in later editions).

459 [1955] 1 All E.R. 511; see especially at 513. The report at [1955] 1 Q.B. 349 is not clear on this point. See, too, *Grzelak v Harefield and Northwood Hospital Management Committee* (1968) 112 S.J. 195.

460 (1858) 3 H. & N. 211.

461 If, of course, the parent pays a full market wage to the child for the services there is no loss and the action will fail: see *Sykes v N.E. Ry* (1875) 44 L.J.C.P. 191, at para.41-024, above.

462 (1858) 4 C.B. N.S. 296.

parents may not have attained a sufficient age to require assistance, and where the past conduct of the deceased and his general attitude and assurances towards his parents have been favourable, claims have succeeded, as in *Hetherington v N.E. Ry*,[463] and in *Appleby v Cunard White Star*.[464] A substantial award was possible in *Amin v Imran Khan & Partners*,[465] where the son, killed in prison at the now adult age of 19, was from a Moslem family which was tight-knit and strongly supportive.[466] One important factor in the case of unmarried children is a possibility that they will marry and that consequently their contributions to their parents will be reduced or cease altogether, in the case of a son by reason of his new obligation to support his wife, in the case of a daughter by reason of her ceasing work and starting gratuitous services for her husband. The Court of Appeal in *Dolbey v Goodwin*,[467] indeed held that there is a good probability of an unmarried man of 29 marrying, that there is a fundamental distinction between a claim for death of a husband and a claim for death of a son, and that to the latter a small multiplier must be applied.

**41-098** *(iii) Adolescent children* Here is found the type of case par excellence of purely prospective loss, the parents having largely incurred the cost of bringing up and training the child and being on the verge of reaping some financial return from a grateful and dutiful child, but not at the moment of death yet receiving any benefit. In *Taff Vale Ry v Jenkins*,[468] the leading case here, a daughter living with her parents died at 16 at a time when her dressmaker's apprenticeship had two months to run, after which she would have begun to earn increasing sums of money, being exceptionally clever at her work. It was held no defence to the claim on the parents' behalf that she had never earned and never contributed to their support. Lord Shaw of Dunfermline said:

> "A son or daughter may be educated … in a trade or a profession in which the training or apprenticeship is not one which yields any profit at all, but in which the reward afterwards is much greater, probably in consequence of the exclusion of competition by reason of the period of unpaid probation. In such a case the parents stand the charge during the whole apprenticeship or training of the child, and just as that education is about to close, the life is cut off … I have asked counsel in vain in the course of the case to distinguish an expectation in such a situation in principle from the ordinary expectation in the case of wages being earned at the time, but I have not been able to obtain an answer, and in principle, my Lords, there is no answer."[469]

Similarly a claim succeeded in the case of a daughter of 13 in *Buckland v Guildford*

---

[463] (1882) 9 Q.B.D. 160, where there had been no payments by the deceased for the five or six years before his death: this was held evidence to go to the jury.

[464] [1950] P. 240, where there had been contributions in the past and assurances, which were relied upon, of financial help in the parents' old age. The son died at 19 so that today he would be regarded as an adult.

[465] [2011] EWHC 2958 (QB).

[466] See [2011] EWHC 2958 (QB) 84 and following.

[467] [1955] 1 W.L.R. 553 CA.

[468] [1913] A.C. 1.

[469] [1913] A.C. 1 at 8, overruling dicta to the contrary in two Irish cases. These remarks, in the economic conditions of today, will apply to much older children, particularly those pursing a university education. It is therefore useful and important to keep in mind the interrelation of this category and that in para.41-097, above.

*Gas Light and Coke Co*,[470] where not only had she assisted her parents at home but

> "it was anticipated that her gifts would later have enabled her to contribute financially as well as by services to the household".[471]

In *Wathen v Vernon*,[472] a claim in respect of the death of a son of 17 living with his parents and paying them the cost of his keep out of his wages, the Court of Appeal considered itself both entitled and bound to award damages for loss of potential support even though no support was being rendered at the date of death and the possibility of support being required in the future was remote. A special feature of the case was that in the past the deceased's father had been off work through ill-health, and though no support from the deceased would have been required if the father's health had remained good, the court had to take into account the possibility of his death or disablement during the five-year period during which it was estimated that the son, before marriage, could have afforded to give support. Accordingly, on the evidence, the court considered that an award of £500 was justified, and that this award should be paid to the deceased's mother. And in *Gammell v Wilson*,[473] where at the time of his death at the age of 15 the deceased was again living with his parents of whom he was the eldest child, and contributing from his wages to his own keep, the court considered that a degree of future support was a probability rather than, as in *Wathen v Vernon*,[474] a remote chance. In *Gammell* the father's life expectancy had been seriously eroded by cancer and he was in receipt of substantial State benefits, but these would not continue to accrue to the mother after his death. The judge's award of £250 for the father's dependence and £1,750 for the mother's was not called in question by the Court of Appeal.[475]

*(iv) Infant children* The situation here is the reverse of the last. On the one hand there is no clear evidence of the desire or the ability of the child to assist the parents in later years; on the other hand the parents have all the expenses of bringing up the child ahead of them. Thus in *Barnett v Cohen*,[476] the claim of a father, earning a good income but with poor health, for loss through the death of his four-year-old son was dismissed: there was no reasonable probability of pecuniary benefit, only a speculative possibility. The claim, said McCardie J, "is pressed to extinction by the weight of multiplied contingencies".[477] It is significant that after this decision further cases do not appear in the reports in respect of very young children. Since 1982, however, a statutory sum for bereavement may be claimed by the parents.[478] **41-099**

---

470 [1949] 1 K.B. 410.

471 [1949] 1 K.B. 410 at 425, per Morris J.

472 [1970] R.T.R. 471 CA.

473 *Gammell v Wilson* unreported 27 July 1979 at first instance.

474 [1970] R.T.R. 471 CA.

475 But the matter was not in issue, largely because, as the law then stood, the Fatal Accidents Act award was eliminated by the Law Reform Act award: see [1982] A.C. 27 CA at 31A–B, 31H–32A, per Megaw LJ.

476 [1921] 2 K.B. 461.

477 [1921] 2 K.B. 461 at 472.

478 See para.41-019, above.

## (5) Loss of gratuitous services and associated claims

41-100 (a) **Gratuitous services** Where the deceased does not contribute to the household in the form of money or goods then it is the loss of services gratuitously rendered in the household that may form the principal, and perhaps only, pecuniary loss on death. It was held in *Berry v Humm & Co*,[479] where the surviving wife provided the gratuitous services, that such a loss was recoverable under the Fatal Accidents Act and the contention rejected that only pecuniary loss by loss of pecuniary contributions in money or goods was recoverable.[480] Scrutton J said:

> "I can see no reason in principle why such pecuniary loss should be limited to the value of money lost, or the money value of things lost, as contributions of food or clothing, and why I should be bound to exclude the monetary loss incurred by replacing services rendered gratuitously by a relative, if there was a reasonable prospect of their being rendered freely in the future but for the death. Apart from principle, such matters have been taken into consideration in the reported cases."[481]

He added that on the credit side there must be set the amount saved in respect of "the wife's maintenance, clothing and pocket-money".[482]

41-101 The amount of such loss of gratuitous services will often be calculated by the expense incurred in procuring the surviving partner the services of a housekeeper or house help since the death and in providing board and lodging for such housekeeper or house help, as in *Jeffery v Smith*,[483] which housekeeper may well be a relative, as in *Morris v Rigby*,[484] and *Regan v Williamson*.[485] The husband's loss of wages was awarded in lieu of the lower cost of employing a housekeeper in *Mehmet v Perry*,[486] where, after the wife's death, the husband had given up his own job to look after the children, it being held reasonable for him to do so in the special family circumstances with two children suffering from a rare blood disorder and needing optimum emotional security and support. By contrast, in an unfortunate decision that should now be confined to its own facts, in *Batt v Highgate Private Hospital*,[487] it was held that it was not reasonable for the father to have given up his job to look after his daughter (incorrectly treating reasonableness as a "cold-hearted calculation of pounds, shillings and pence"[488]) so that the assessment was

---

479 [1915] 1 K.B. 627.

480 Although the headnote refers only to the husband as claimant it appears, at the start of the judgment, that there was a child of three whom the wife had also looked after.

481 [1915] 1 K.B. 627 at 631. He also relied on certain cases where a parent had recovered for the loss of a child's gratuitous services, especially *Taff Vale Ry v Jenkins* [1913] A.C. 1, and distinguished *Osborn v Gillett* (1872–73) L.R. 8 Ex. 88 as not being argued on this point. Such cases are dealt with at para.41-098, below.

482 [1915] 1 K.B. 627 at 630.

483 [1970] R.T.R. 279 CA. In *Hurt v Murphy* [1971] R.T.R. 186, where the husband's house was too small for a resident housekeeper and he was financially incapable of buying a larger house, the damages were based on the employment of a daily help.

484 (1966) 110 S.J. 834 CA: wife's sister. The argument that the husband should have employed someone else at a cheaper rate was rejected: see at 835.

485 [1976] 1 W.L.R. 305: wife's aunt.

486 [1977] 2 All E.R. 529.

487 [2005] P.I.Q.R. Q1 at 1.

488 [2005] P.I.Q.R. Q1 at [31].

based on the cost of commercial care which was very much less than the amount the father had been earning.[489]

The provision of gratuitous services can range from the provision of full time services to sustain a large household to the provision of more minor services such as gardening and general home maintenance, valued in *Mosson v Spousal (London) Ltd*,[490] at £1,500 per annum. **41-102**

Where the deceased provider of gratuitous services also brings money into the household, the loss of such pecuniary contributions is also recoverable, referred to by Simon Brown J in *Cresswell v Eaton*,[491] in relation there to the children's claim,[492] as the disbursement dependency as distinct from the services dependency. Such contributions may be direct, from earnings or anticipated earnings, as in *Regan v Williamson*,[493] or they may be indirect, by contributions to the joint living expenses, as in *Burgess v Florence Nightingale Hospital*.[494] In that case Devlin J held that **41-103**

> "when a husband and wife, either with separate incomes or with a joint income to which they are both beneficially entitled, are living together and sharing their expenses, and in consequence of that fact their joint living expenses are less than twice the expenses of each one living separately, then each, by the fact of the sharing, is conferring a benefit on the other."[495]

**(b) Loss of a parent's special care** The question has also arisen in the cases of whether the loss of a parent's care by a young child at an age when it was probably most needed can be regarded as a pecuniary loss. Ormerod J allowed such a loss in *Preston v Hunting Air Transport*,[496] in a case under the then Carriage by Air Act 1932 giving effect to provisions of the Warsaw Convention analogous to those of the Fatal Accidents Act, but he clearly regarded it as not a "purely financial loss", interpreting the term "damage" there as not confined to such loss, an interpretation not then available under the Fatal Accidents Act.[497] Nevertheless, it may be argued that the benefit of a parent's personal attention to a child's upbringing, morals, education and psychology, which the services of a housekeeper, nurse or governess could never provide, has in the long run a financial value for the child, difficult as it is to assess. This sentence, which appeared in the 13th edition (1972) of this work, was quoted in *Hay v Hughes*,[498] by Lord Edmund-Davies who said that "it may some time have to be considered whether it is not right".[499] This comment **41-104**

---

489 [2005] P.I.Q.R. Q1 at [24]–[32].

490 [2016] EWHC 1429 (QB) at [64].

491 [1991] 1 W.L.R. 1113 at 1118H.

492 See para.41-094, below.

493 [1976] 1 W.L.R. 305, where the judge took the view that the wife would have returned to work, which she had given up to have a child.

494 [1955] 1 Q.B. 349.

495 [1955] 1 Q.B. 349 at 362. In this case the claim on behalf of the child was for the child of a former marriage of the deceased; damages were awarded "both in respect of the school fees and of what she might have done for the child": [1955] 1 All E.R. 511 at 513 (this point does not appear in the report at [1955] 1 Q.B. 349). The reference to what the mother might have done for the child seems to herald the thought (see next paragraph) that there may be a pecuniary aspect to the loss of a mother's care.

496 [1956] 1 Q.B. 454.

497 See para.41-019, above.

498 [1975] Q.B. 790 CA.

499 [1975] Q.B. 790 CA at 802H–803A.

soon bore fruit. In *Regan v Williamson*,[500] it was held, quoting Lord Edmund-Davies, that, in determining the pecuniary value to be put upon the services of the deceased mother, acknowledgment should be given to the constant attendance of a mother on her children, and accordingly the value placed upon such services should not be limited to a mere computation of the cost of the services of a housekeeper less the cost of the deceased wife's maintenance.[501] So, too, in *Mehmet v Perry*,[502] an additional sum was awarded, though within modest limits, because

> "the children have lost the attention of their mother and … now have only one parent to look after them instead of two"[503]

indeed in that case the husband also was awarded an additional sum, again within modest limits, because he "has lost the care and attention of his wife".[504] The award, having started life in *Mehmet* at around £1,500,[505] had risen to £3,000 by the time of *Corbett v Barking Havering and Brentwood Health Authority*,[506] and was agreed at £4,000 in *Hayden v Hayden*.[507] In *Topp v London Country Bus (South West)*,[508] an award of £3,000 was made to the child as well as £2,000 to the husband, and *Manning v King's College Hospital NHS Trust*,[509] with awards to two children of £4,000 each and £3,000 to the husband.[510] The conventional maximum award has become £5,000, which is probably the right amount to give where the dependent child is very young at the death.[511] The judge's awards of £5,000 and £7,000 for two boys of 11 and 8 at the death were considered by the Court of Appeal in *H v S*,[512] to be outside the bracket; £3,500 and £4,500 were substituted.[513] Awards will no doubt continue to rise over the years should inflationary trends continue.

**41-105** This head of loss is now firmly established for child claimants and features in nearly every case involving them. It is commonly referred to as the special qualitative factor in *Regan v Williamson*,[514] or even just the *Regan v Williamson* element.[515] It is most profusely to be found in the cases starting with *Spittle v Bunney*,[516] in 1988 and continuing, where the claim was on behalf of the child or children of the family only. It was subject, wrongly, to an exception in *Watson v Wilmott*,[517] because

---

500 [1976] 1 W.L.R. 305.

501 [1976] 1 W.L.R. 305 at 309C–E.

502 [1977] 2 All E.R. 529.

503 [1977] 2 All E.R. 529 at 537f.

504 [1977] 2 All E.R. 529 at 537g.

505 The award to the child in *Mehmet v Perry* [1977] 2 All E.R. 529, where the father was also claiming.

506 [1991] 2 Q.B. 408 CA.

507 [1992] 1 W.L.R. 986 CA; see at 990H.

508 [1992] P.I.Q.R. P206.

509 [2008] EWHC 3008 (QB).

510 *Johnson v British Midland Airways* [1996] P.I.Q.R. Q8 is curious because, while the claim was made only on behalf of the husband, he was awarded amounts in relation to the child, namely £2,500 for the cost of travel to visit and assist the child and £3,500 for extra tuition costs for the child.

511 In *Bordin v St Mary's NHS Trust* [2000] Lloyd's Rep. Med. 287, where the mother died giving birth to the child, £5,000 was awarded.

512 [2003] Q.B. 965 CA.

513 [2003] Q.B. 965 CA at [38].

514 See Simon Brown J in *Cresswell v Eaton* [1991] 1 W.L.R. 1113 at 1122H–1123A.

515 See McCowan LJ in *Hayden v Hayden* [1992] 1 W.L.R. 986 CA at 990G.

516 [1988] 1 W.L.R. 847 CA.

517 [1991] 1 Q.B. 140.

the adoptive mother was now providing the care and in *Stanley v Saddique*,[518] rightly, because of the indifferent quality of the mother.

**(c) Loss of the intangible cost of arranging for alternative provision of services** There is a conflict in authority concerning whether a claimant can recover for, as the claimant expressed it in *Grant v Secretary of State for Transport*,[519] loss of **41-106**

> "the convenience, comfort and security of having someone who gave this help [of personal gratuitous services] out of love and affection".

The recognition of this award was first made by analogy with the cases that allow recovery for the child's loss of a parent's special care—the so-called *Regan v Williamson* factor. It was held in *Beesley v New Century Group Ltd*,[520] that there was no reason why the *Regan v Williamson* factor, as this element in that case has come to be called,[521] should feature only in claims on behalf of children and not be extended to a case where the claim was brought by a husband for the loss of the personal benefit of his wife (or, presumably in future cases, for the loss of the personal benefit of a wife).

It is difficult to categorise this loss of intangible benefits, to adopt the term used in *Beesley*, as a pecuniary loss, and recovery for non-pecuniary loss, as we have seen,[522] has never been permitted in Fatal Accidents Act claims, bereavement loss now statutorily apart. As we have also seen, it was the suggestion, initially appearing in this text, that a mother's personal attention to a child's upbringing could lead in the long run to pecuniary advantages upon which *Regan v Williamson* built, and this can hardly be said similarly of a spouse or partner's personal attention day by day to the life of his or her spouse or partner. Nevertheless in *Devoy v William Doxford & Sons Ltd*,[523] a further award was made along these lines. This seems dubious, and it is significant that the trial judge recognised that there might be an overlap between such an award and the award for bereavement.[524] A more subtle approach was taken in *Fleet v Fleet*,[525] where Mackay J held that the *Regan v Williamson* principle should not automatically be extended to spouses, although in that case it was justified because the surviving wife was much older than the deceased and she would have needed more than usual care as time went on. Just as the additional care given to children can have pecuniary benefits in the long run, so too can additional care to an aged spouse or partner have greater pecuniary benefit in the long run. Beyond this, however, the purported justification for a claim for loss of intangible benefits is that there is inconvenience that arises from having to pay someone to do that which the deceased spouse or deceased partner would have done voluntarily. Yet, as Garnham J rightly said in *Mosson v Spousal (London) Ltd*,[526] that is the sort of claim that bereavement damages were meant to cover. Unfortunately, **41-107**

---

518 [1992] Q.B. 1 CA.
519 [2017] EWHC 1663 (QB) at [94].
520 [2008] EWHC 3033 (QB).
521 See para.41-105, below.
522 See para.41-018, above.
523 [2009] EWHC 1598 (QB).
524 See [2009] EWHC 1598 at [79].
525 [2009] EWHC 3166 (QB).
526 [2016] EWHC 1429 (QB) at [75]. See also *Lugay v Hammersmith and Fulham LBC* [2017] EWHC 1823 (QB) at [76].

in *Grant v The Secretary of State for Transport*,[527] Martin Chamberlain QC, sitting as a Deputy High Court judge, declined to follow the decision in *Mosson*. In his view, the time spent by the wife to make arrangements for a painter, plumber, or decorator to perform work that her husband would have done has a pecuniary value.[528] But there is a fundamental difference between saying that a service has a pecuniary value and saying that the loss of the service is a pecuniary loss. The avoidance of inconvenience might be something upon which a money value can be put but that does not make it a monetary loss. In *Magill v Panel Systems (DB Ltd)*,[529] Judge Gosnell, sitting as a Deputy High Court judge, rightly said that the nature of this type of claim for intangible benefits is the irrecoverable

> "perceived advantages of having a service performed by a member of the family rather than a commercial provider"

and that the nature of the claim were reformulated as a loss of love and affection then it would be encompassed in the bereavement award.

## 3. THE NON-DEDUCTIBILITY OF COLLATERAL BENEFITS

### (1) The development of the law

**41-108** The path taken by the collateral benefits issue in fatal accident claims has been curiously different from the path it has followed in the field of personal injury. Whereas there was for long general acceptance of the rule that the damages in a personal injury claim were not to be reduced because benefits had been conferred upon the claimant by third parties which mitigated his loss,[530] the general rule was the exact opposite where the claim was in respect of a fatal injury, and it became accepted, without any real dispute, that only the net pecuniary benefit accruing to the dependants was recoverable as damages. This undoubted general rule finds its clearest and most authoritative expression in the speeches of their Lordships in *Davies v Powell Duffryn Collieries*.[531] Lord Macmillan put it thus:

> "Except where there is express statutory direction to the contrary, the damages to be awarded to a dependant of a deceased person under the Fatal Accidents Acts must take into account any pecuniary benefit accruing to that dependant in consequence of the death of the deceased. It is the net loss on balance which constitutes the measure of damages."[532]

**41-109** Thus, while not strictly a collateral benefit but rather a collateral liability, the income tax which would have been paid on the deceased's earnings was always deducted in calculating the damages for the dependants' loss of support[533] even in the pre-*Gourley*[534] days when no deduction was made in respect of income tax in the calculation of damages for the loss of earning capacity of a physically injured

527 [2017] EWHC 1663 (QB).
528 [2017] EWHC 1663 (QB) at [108].
529 [2017] EWHC 1517 (QB) at [66].
530 See para.40-149, above.
531 [1942] A.C. 601.
532 [1942] A.C. 601 at 609.
533 See para.18-028, above.
534 [1956] A.C. 185.

claimant.[535] And there was similarly never any question but that, in calculating the dependants' damages, the money saved on the deceased's maintenance fell to be deducted from the earnings he would have made.[536] But beyond this, it was soon established that deductions fell to be made in relation to private insurance moneys,[537] while subsequently the requirement of deduction became accepted in relation to pensions[538] and was even extended to certain gratuitous payments.[539] Only a few benefits managed to escape this wide general requirement by being held not to have resulted from the death.[540]

Gradually, however, serious inroads were made by statute upon this rule of deduction of collateral benefits. The first statutory inroad came with the Fatal Accidents (Damages) Act 1908, which provided by s.1 that, in assessing the damages, insurance moneys should no longer be taken into account. Next followed, by s.22 of the Widows', Orphans' and Old Age Contributory Pensions Act 1929, a provision that such pensions were not to be taken into account, and this was later replaced by the larger provisions of the Law Reform (Personal Injuries) Act 1948, which added to the items not to be taken into account any right to social security benefits under the National Insurance Acts 1946. These particular provisions in respect of particular benefits led to some fine distinctions in the cases, and the law on this matter was put on a more practical basis by s.2 of the Fatal Accidents Act 1959, later re-enacted as s.4 of the Fatal Accidents Act 1976 and providing that, in assessing the damages, there should not be taken into account any insurance money, benefit under the enactments relating to social security, pension or gratuity paid or to be paid as a result of the death. After this provision reached the statute-book the one important category of benefit left to be taken into account consisted of money and property received from the deceased's estate under his will or intestacy,[541] including awards under the Law Reform (Miscellaneous Provisions) Act 1934,[542] awards which achieved an overwhelming significance in the present context once they began, after the implications for them of the decision in *Pickett v British Rail Engineering*,[543] were seen, to include damages in respect of the deceased's earn- **41-110**

535 See para.18-002, above.

536 See para.41-041, above.

537 By *Hicks v Newport, Abergavenny & Hereford Ry* (1857) 4 B. & S. 403n, which concerned both accident insurance and life insurance; approved, in relation to life insurance, in *Grand Trunk Ry of Canada v Jennings* (1888) 13 App. Cas. 800 PC. In the latter case it was pointed out that, since the dependent widow would in any event have received the life insurance moneys on her husband's death, she was benefited only by the accelerated receipt of these moneys, and as this benefit was represented by the use of interest of the money during the period of acceleration it was, as suggested in *Hicks v Newport, Abergavenny & Hereford Ry*, to be accounted for by deducting from the damages the future premiums the deceased would have paid to maintain the policy: (1888) 13 App. Cas. 800 PC at 804–805. The Ontario Court of Appeal had made no deduction, but the defendants' appeal failed since they argued it on the ground that the whole of the insurance moneys should be deducted.

538 See *Baker v Dalgleish S.S. Co* [1922] 1 K.B. 361 CA; *Carling v Lebbon* [1927] 2 K.B. 108; *Johnson v Hill* [1945] 2 All E.R. 272 CA; *Smith v B.E.A.* [1951] 2 K.B. 893.

539 See *Mead v Clarke Chapman* [1956] 1 W.L.R. 76 CA; *Jenner v Allen West* [1959] 1 W.L.R. 554 CA.

540 See *Redpath v Belfast and County Down Ry* [1947] N.I. 167; *Peacock v Amusement Equipment Co* [1954] 2 Q.B. 347 CA; *Schneider v Eisovitch* [1960] 2 Q.B. 430.

541 See *Taylor v O'Connor* [1971] A.C. 115; *Davies v Whiteways Cyder Co* [1975] Q.B. 262.

542 See *Davies v Powell Duffryn Collieries* [1942] A.C. 601; *Mulholland v McCrea* [1961] N.I. 135 CA; *Murray v Shuter* [1976] Q.B. 972 CA.

543 [1980] A.C. 136.

ing capacity during the so-called lost years.[544] This indeed had the incongruous effect of reversing the roles, in the typical case, of the dependants' claim and the estate's claim because the estate's now substantial recovery was deducted as a collateral benefit from the dependants' award.

## (2) The present law

41-111 **(a) The general position** The common law rule of deduction as stated by Lord Macmillan in *Davies v Powell Duffryn Collieries*,[545] has been swept entirely away. The new s.4 of the Fatal Accidents Act 1976, substituted by s.3(1) of the Administration of Justice Act 1982 and applying in respect of all deaths occurring after the end of 1982,[546] states:

> "In assessing damages in respect of a person's death in an action under this Act, benefits which have accrued or will or may accrue to any person from his estate or otherwise as a result of his death shall be disregarded."[547]

41-112 In earlier editions of this work it was said that the immense range of this omnibus provision[548] needed to be appreciated. It was pointed out that, while benefits from the estate are no doubt expressly mentioned in the new s.4 because, as indicated above,[549] such benefits constituted, after 1959, practically the sole survivor of the early rule of deductibility; the compendious "or otherwise" comprises the rest of the ground and goes beyond the formerly deductible categories to leave no category of benefit to be deducted.[550] Additionally, it was pointed out that some of the earlier

---

544 See para.41-126, below.

545 [1942] A.C. 601 at para.41-108, above.

546 Administration of Justice Act 1982 ss.73(1) and 76(11). Should there be any causes of action arising before the end of 1982 still in issue, which is conceivably possible with a patient (now inelegantly referred to in the CPR as a protected person) unaffected by limitation— children, also unaffected by limitation, if born before the end of 1982 will have reached adulthood by the beginning of the 21st century—the detailed law as to the then deductibility of collateral benefits will be found in the 14th edition (1980) of this work at paras 1330 to 1352. In the short period between that edition and the coming into effect of the change in the law the only further relevant authorities which appeared were *Clay v Pooler* [1982] 3 All E.R. 570 dealing with a problem on insurance moneys thrown up solely by the estate's then entitlement to lost years' income, *Auty v National Coal Board* [1985] 1 W.L.R. 784 CA, dealt with at para.41-121, below, and *Cresswell v Eaton* [1991] 1 W.L.R. 1113 where fostering payments to an aunt for caring for the children of a deceased mother had to be deducted from part of the dependency damages as they did not fall within the categories specified in s.4 of the Fatal Accidents Act 1976 as originally enacted.

547 While this implements the recommendation of the Pearson Commission that benefits derived from the deceased's estate should be disregarded in the assessment of damages for lost dependency (1978), Cmnd.7054–1, paras 537 to 539), it ignores the Commission's related recommendation that the value of social security benefits payable to the dependants should be deducted in full (at paras 467 to 483).

548 In *Roerig v Valiant Trawlers Ltd* [2002] 1 W.L.R. 2304 CA, where the deceased was Dutch with his claimant dependants living in Holland, s.4 was held to apply so as to permit no deduction of benefits although there might have been deduction under Dutch law. Even if the proper law of the tort were held to be Dutch, which it was not, the question of deductibility was a matter of procedure and therefore for the lex fori.

549 See para.41-110, above.

550 Holland J, however, has decided in *Cameron v Vinters Defence Systems Ltd* [2008] P.I.Q.R. P5 at 87 that in a claim by a dependant under the Fatal Accidents Act a payment of statutory compensation made pursuant to the Pneumoconiosis (Workers' Compensation) Act 1979 is not caught by s.4, thereby requiring deduction of it to be made. The decision is a sensible one but the reasons given for it are somewhat obscure; the key passage is at [17] of the judgment. Compare *Ballantine v Newall*

decisions requiring no deduction were to be explained on common law causation principles on the basis that they were regarded as not resulting from the death[551] and that those which did not fall within this category[552]—the cases are difficult to reconcile[553]—would now reach the same result by virtue of the omnibus provision.

All of this is now confirmed by the Court of Appeal's important decision in *Arnup v M.W. White Ltd*.[554] The defendant company which had employed the deceased and which was liable for his death at work had set up two arrangements for its employees, a death in service benefit scheme and an employee benefit trust. The scheme generated an insurance policy in the name of the employer company under which on the death of an employee in service four times his final salary became payable to the employer company as trustee of the scheme, the employer company being required to pay over the amount paid to it to the deceased's estate or to one or more of the deceased's dependants as defined. The trust consisted of a settlement made by the employing company as settlor with a trust company as trustee and with employees, together with their spouses, children and remoter issue, included as beneficiaries. The trustee company had the power to take out policies on the life of any person, a power which it exercised with a life policy insuring each of the employing company's employees for a specified sum; it also had an absolute discretion as to the utilisation of the trust fund, a discretion which encompassed moneys coming to be paid to it from the life policy. The employing company, having received under the scheme the deceased's four times salary payment, chose to pay all of it to the deceased's widow, and the trust company, having received the insurance on the deceased's life under the life policy held by the trust, at the suggestion of the employing company similarly paid all of it to the widow. **41-113**

His Honour Judge Richard Seymour QC in a confusing judgment[555] first held that s.4 had no application because neither payment resulted from the death and then proceeded to apply, inappropriately, what he called the insurance and benevolence exceptions so as to permit no deduction of the payment from the trust but to require deduction of the payment from the scheme. The Court of Appeal had little difficulty in seeing that, once the judge had held that the payments did not result from the death, he should have disregarded them since for that reason they were completely irrelevant to the assessment of the damages.[556] At the same time the Court of Appeal, not wishing to decide the appeal on this limited basis, held that even if the judge were wrong on causation—and expressed the view that he was **41-114**

---

*Insulation Co Ltd* [2000] P.I.Q.R. Q327 CA at para.41-136, below where it was not difficult for the court to by-pass s.4 and justify deduction.

551 *Hay v Hughes* [1975] Q.B. 790 CA: voluntary services of a grandmother in looking after the children as a substitute for their deceased mother; *Rawlinson v Babcock & Wilcox* [1967] 1 W.L.R. 481: orphaned daughter's being taken into the home of an uncle; *Schneider v Eisovitch* [1960] 2 Q.B. 430: father's taking over the loss-making business of his deceased son; *Peacock v Amusement Equipment Co* [1954] 2 Q.B. 347 CA: children making a payment to their stepfather out of their deceased's mother's estate.

552 *Mead v Clarke Chapman* [1956] 1 W.L.R. 76 CA: children derived support from a stepfather who had filled the place of the deceased; *Jenner v Allen West* [1959] 1 W.L.R. 554 CA: employer of the deceased made a voluntary weekly payment to his widow.

553 Both *Mead* and *Jenner* had come in for criticism in *Hay v Hughes* [1975] Q.B. 790 CA; see at 806F, 807E–808B and 816F.

554 [2008] I.C.R. 1064 CA.

555 [2007] P.I.Q.R. Q6 at 91.

556 [2008] I.C.R. 1064 CA at [21] and [22]; citing, and agreeing with, the passage to this effect in the Fourth Supplement to the 17th edition of this work.

indeed wrong because his approach to causation had been too artificial[557]—neither of the payments was deductible because every benefit resulting from a death was now caught by s.4.[558] Smith LJ, whose careful judgment, with which her brethren simply concurred, repays close perusal, said that she was

> "quite satisfied that all benefits which came to the widow as a result of the death are to be disregarded".[559]

And she added that it was "no longer important to decide whether a benefit has accrued as result of the death",[560] explaining why causation no longer mattered thus[561]:

> "Before 1982, if it [viz., a benefit] was not so paid [viz., not paid as a result of the death], it would be left out of account as irrelevant. But if it had been paid as a result of the death, it would have to be deducted unless it was saved by one of the statutory disregard provisions. Now that the statutory disregard provisions cover all benefits that accrue as a result of the death, it no longer matters whether a benefit accrues as a result of the death; it cannot be deducted in any event."

In addition to providing a definitive interpretation of s.4, Smith LJ's judgment usefully highlights the relationship between it and s.3 of the statute, which in its first subsection lays down the basic measure of damages for fatal accident cases as the value of the dependency.[562] The judgment reminds us that traditionally the process of awarding the damages had two stages; as we have seen, it was thus authoritatively stated by Lord Macmillan in *Davies v Powell Duffryn Collieries*.[563] The first stage was the quantification of the loss of dependency and the second was the deduction of any benefit which the dependant had received as a result of the death, the second stage being initially subject to no exceptions but with exceptions being brought in from 1908 onwards.[564] "The effect", said Smith LJ of the new s.4, "has been to abolish the second stage of the old assessment process"[565] it has been "swept away".[566] Section 3 therefore is left holding the entire stage.

**41-115** That the law can now be said to be firmly established so as to remove the second stage of the assessment is however not necessarily something to be applauded. Indeed how far the extent of this statutory departure in Fatal Accidents Act cases from the ordinary common law assessment of damages as epitomised in personal injury cases is to be commended may be considered very doubtful. Even before the Act of 1982 swept all benefits into oblivion, Lord Diplock in *Cookson v Knowles*,[567] with reference to the provisions of the 1976 Act, which were less radical in their specified exceptions from deduction of benefits, was saying this:

---

557 [2008] I.C.R. 1064 CA at [28].

558 The court was particularly unimpressed by the defendant's argument that a limited meaning should be given to the words "accrued to" in s.4. The meaning proposed would have set in reverse the general trend towards the disregard of specified benefits which, as we have seen (at para.41-110, above), had grown in momentum from 1908 up to 1982: at [26].

559 [2008] I.C.R. 1064 CA at [26].

560 [2008] I.C.R. 1064 CA at [28].

561 [2008] I.C.R. 1064 CA at [27]. Explained in the same way as was done in the 17th edition: see para.41-112, above.

562 Set out at para.41-017, above.

563 [1942] A.C. 601 at 609. Cited at para.41-108, above.

564 See para.41-110, above.

565 [2008] I.C.R. 1064 CA at [26].

566 [2008] I.C.R. 1064 CA at [20].

567 [1979] A.C. 556.

"Today the assessment of damages in fatal accident cases has become an artificial and conjectural exercise. Its purpose is no longer to put dependants, particularly widows, into the same economic position as they would have been in had their late husband lived."[568]

Indeed it is rather ironic that s.4 was drafted in response to a 1973 proposal of the Law Commission that benefits from the deceased's estate should be included within the then available deductions, which, said the Law Commission, would involve a "relatively minor change" to the law.[569] This explains why the Lord Chancellor, Lord Hailsham, in introducing the Bill, told the Lords that only a "relatively small change" was being proposed.[570] It would seem then that the draftsman, by including the words "or otherwise" after the reference to benefits from the estate in s.4, went hopelessly wrong.[571] However, the law today is as it is.

**(b) Particular aspects** In the light of all this, there remain two matters which require consideration. First, it is important to revisit the cases coming between the s.4 amendment of 1982 and the *Arnup* decision of 2008, cases which have gone in a variety of directions, so as to eliminate some, the few, and to confirm others, the many. In particular, the decision of the Court of Appeal in *Hayden v Hayden*,[572] has caused great difficulty. Secondly, it is important to be cognisant of the extent to which, by concentrating on s.3 rather than s.4, benefits accruing to a claimant can still be shown to be effective to impose checks upon the damages. **41-116**

*(i) Benefits not to be taken into account by virtue of s.4* *Hayden v Hayden* was a decision of the Court of Appeal where there was taken into account in the damages assessment the benefit to the child claimant of services taking the place of those of the child's deceased mother. Both of the majority judgments are confused and confusing, to the extent that the Court of Appeal in *Hunt v Severs*,[573] said that it was hard to find a clear ratio of the decision which was of little assistance.[574] It was maintained in the last edition of this work that *Hayden v Hayden* must be taken to have been wrongly decided and this is now confirmed by *Arnup*.[575] Also the first **41-117**

---

568 The disregarding of benefits from the estate, now allowed by s.4, would have had the effect of allowing a very specific double recovery—compensation paid twice over for the same loss—if the decision of the Court of Appeal in *Jameson v Central Electricity Generating Board* [1998] Q.B. 323 CA had been allowed to stand. The court had held a widow entitled to make a full dependency claim against a tortfeasor despite her husband's settlement in his lifetime with a concurrent tortfeasor; in her claim no deduction could be made of the proceeds, received from the estate, of this settlement which included a substantial part of the deceased's lost future earnings. The House of Lords, reversing ([2000] 1 A.C. 455), was able to avoid this unfortunate result only by holding that the settlement with the one tortfeasor debarred the deceased, and therefore his dependants, from any claim against the other tortfeasor, but it may not be possible to interpret all settlements with a concurrent tortfeasor in this helpful way.

569 (1973), *Law Com. No.56*, para.253.

570 *Hansard* HL Vol.428 col.28 (8 March 1982).

571 The Law Commission's Report on *Claims for Wrongful Death* (1999), Law Com. No.263, recommends repealing s.4 and returning to a system akin to that which existed from 1908 to 1982 (see para.41-110, above) of listing the benefits which are to be deducted. This has much to be said for it.

572 [1992] 1 W.L.R. 986 CA.

573 [1993] Q.B. 815 CA.

574 [1993] Q.B. 815 CA at 829A.

575 Should it ever be suggested that *Hayden v Hayden* was binding on the Court of Appeal in *Arnup* and therefore to be followed—there is no reference to *Hayden* in Smith LJ's judgment—the answer will be that the decision in *Hayden* was reached per incuriam.

instance decision in *Watson v Willmott*,[576] where damages were reduced on account of the child claimant's adoption by an uncle and aunt, was thought to be wrong. This too is now confirmed.

**41-118** Other cases concerned with benefits derived from the assistance of family members did get it right and they are in more abundant supply. Importantly, the Court of Appeal in *Stanley v Saddique*,[577] held, in a claim for a boy whose deceased mother had been replaced in his life by a far more caring stepmother, that the benefit of her care was not to be taken into account[578] in the assessment of the lost dependency.[579] *R. v Criminal Injuries Compensation Board Ex p. K*,[580] followed and applied *Stanley v Saddique*,[581] in preference to *Hayden v Hayden*,[582] which it nevertheless felt constrained to distinguish, so as to make no deduction for the excellent parental services of an uncle and aunt replacing those of the mother murdered by the father. *Stanley v Saddique* was also applied in *L (A Child) v Barry May Haulage*,[583] so as to leave out of account, in assessing the loss of the mother's support and services, their replacement by the support and services of the child's father; again the court had difficulties with *Hayden v Hayden*. Next, in *H v S*,[584] *Hayden v Hayden*, though cited at great length, was skirted round by the Court of Appeal in reaching the conclusion that, where children are living with and dependent upon their mother with no support from the father, and the father then houses and takes responsibility for the children after the mother's death, the support which they enjoy is a benefit resulting from the death to be disregarded.[585] Where, too, the assistance comes not from those who are family members at the time of the death but from a new wife who may replace, or has replaced, the deceased wife as a family member, there has been no difficulty in applying s.4. Thus in *Topp v London Country Bus South West Ltd*,[586] it was accepted that *Stanley v Saddique*,[587] bound the court to disregard a widower claimant's prospects of remarriage in arriving at

---

576 [1991] 1 Q.B. 140.

577 [1992] Q.B. 1 CA.

578 It had been taken into account before 1982: see *Mead v Clarke Chapman* [1956] 1 W.L.R. 76 CA in the last footnote but one to para.41-112, above.

579 The argument of the defendant that s.4 should be given a limited meaning was rejected by Purchas LJ (at 13F–G) for the same reason as later appeared in *Arnup*: see para.41-114, above (in a footnote).

580 [1999] Q.B. 1131.

581 [1992] Q.B. 1 CA.

582 [1992] 1 W.L.R. 986 CA.

583 [2002] P.I.Q.R. Q5 at 35.

584 [2003] Q.B. 965 CA.

585 *H v S* has also somewhat unexpectedly held that in this type of case the dependency damages are to be awarded on the basis that they are used to pay over to the person caring for the children, to reimburse for the past services and to be available for the future services: see [2003] Q.B. 965 CA at [29], [30] and [40]. This therefore introduces for fatal accidents the notion of holding the damages on trust, a notion introduced, rather tangentially and without paying much attention to its difficulties, by the House of Lords in *Hunt v Severs* [1994] 2 A.C. 350 for personal injuries: see paras 40-228 and 40-229, above. This does not appear to have taken off in the fatal accidents field; Crane J said in *Bordin v St Mary's NHS Trust* [2000] Lloyd's Rep. Med. 287 at 294 that he did not regard such a trust as enforceable, but Kennedy LJ, giving the only reasoned judgment in *H v S*, did not agree: [2003] Q.B. 965 CA at [30]. As for the suggestion in *Drake v Foster Wheeler Ltd* [2011] 1 All E.R. 63, which was a claim by the estate of a deceased, that the setting up of a trust can be avoided by ordering the defendant to pay direct to the carer, *Drake* concerned only past care and not prospective care: see the case at paras 40-229 and 40-230, above.

586 [1992] P.I.Q.R. P206.

587 [1992] Q.B. 1 CA.

the damages to be awarded to him for the loss of his wife,[588] and this must be even more true where his remarriage has already taken place. This result had already been achieved by statute for the widow claimant.[589]

The courts since 1982 have also applied s.4 widely in relation to benefits other than those derived from the assistance of family members. Two cases in the Court of Appeal concerning payments to widows from pensions, trust schemes and the like, and therefore in the same category as the *Arnup* case,[590] testify to this. The one case is *Pidduck v Eastern Scottish Omnibuses Ltd*.[591] The widow of a retired bank employee, whose sole source of income in his retirement for the support of himself and his wife had been his pension from the bank, became entitled under the pension scheme to the payment of an allowance linked to the deceased's pension by virtue of his having died within five years of his retirement. The argument that the widow suffered no loss, because she was supported before her husband's death by the pension via her husband and afterwards by the same fund via the widow's allowance, was rejected. The proper analysis was this. The support before the death was not correctly described as a benefit received under the pension scheme, it being incidental that the husband's source of income for that support was his pension, so that on the death a loss of dependency was suffered within s.3 and the widow's allowance which then became payable fell to be left out of account under s.4. The other case is *McIntyre v Harland & Wolff Plc*.[592] Under the deceased's employers' provident fund scheme, employees were entitled to payments on termination of service happening in a variety of ways of which the relevant two here were termination of service on dismissal and termination of service on retirement. Under the scheme benefits could only be taken once. On being diagnosed with mesothelioma contracted through his employers' tortious negligence the deceased reasonably chose not to return to work and was duly dismissed, whereupon he became entitled to a termination payment. Had however the tort not been committed, the deceased would have continued work until his normal retirement age and would then have received his termination of service payment. His widow, who was his sole beneficiary, argued successfully that this expectancy was part of her lost dependency and that her receipt through her husband's estate of the moneys which had come to him on termination of service before his death fell to be ignored because of s.4. The loss that the widow claimed to be suffering was the loss of her dependency on her husband under s.3 against which her receipt of moneys pay- **41-119**

---

588 The point was not even argued.

589 See para.41-069, above. *Hayden v Hayden* cannot be resurrected on the basis that in that case the benefit had been provided by the tortfeasor. HH Judge Richard Seymour was quite right at first instance in *Arnup* to reject the argument that benefits emanating from the tortfeasor must be deducted ([2007] P.I.Q.R. Q6 at 91 at [70])—there is no hint of such an argument in the Court of Appeal—pointing to the fact that the tortfeasor had been the defendant in *McIntyre v Harland & Wolff Plc* [2006] 1 W.L.R. 2577 CA (dealt with in the next paragraph, below) as well as in *Arnup* itself. There is a world of difference between personal injury, where the law has developed along different lines allowing at common law deduction of benefits generally, and fatal accidents where no deduction of benefit is by statute the order of the day.

590 Facts at para.41-113, above.

591 [1990] 1 W.L.R. 993 CA.

592 [2006] 1 W.L.R. 2577 CA. The case was said by the Court of Appeal to raise a far from easy point on Fatal Accidents Act damages (at [1]). This appears to be because of its factual similarities to *Auty v National Coal Board* [1985] 1 W.L.R. 784 CA where however, as will be seen (para.41-121, below), it was correct to take the widow's benefit, there by way of pension, into account under s.3.

able to her husband on account of his earlier termination of service fell to be ignored under s.4.

**41-120** *(ii) Benefits to be taken into account under s.3* The most obvious case for the application of s.3 to the exclusion of s.4 is that of the deceased with only unearned income out of which he supported the dependant, and the whole estate from which he derived this income passes to the dependant. Here the dependant's claim should fail on the ground that there is no pecuniary loss.[593] All that the dependant could lose was the support from that income, and since the death he has the income himself. This was the position in the early case of *Pym v Great Northern Ry*,[594] decided at a time when there were no statutory provisions prohibiting the deduction of benefits. That such a claim would fail can be said to have been accepted for today by the Court of Appeal in *Wood v Bentall Simplex Ltd*.[595] In that case, where the dependent widow and sons had enjoyed the income derived from the deceased's farming business, Staughton LJ recognised that

> "before one considers deductions under s.4, one first has to determine what loss the dependants had suffered; and if they have inherited the source of the income upon which they were dependent, they have not lost it".[596]

*Wood* was indeed primarily concerned with assessing the loss of the family dependency attributable to the deceased's labour on the farm, but it is clear that there was no loss of dependency in relation to, as Staughton LJ put it, that part

> "of the deceased's income [which] was derived solely from capital which the dependants have inherited".[597]

*Wood* was elaborated on in two further Court of Appeal cases, *Cape Distribution v O'Loughlin*,[598] and *Welsh Ambulance Services NHS Trust v Williams*,[599] in finding a loss of dependency based on the value of the deceased's services in running a business which on his death had passed to the family,[600] while accepting in both that, in respect of dependency, the business as a capital asset had to be left out of account altogether. This is made clear by Smith LJ in *Williams* where she said:

> "By focussing on the value of the deceased's services, it was possible to exclude any benefit which had come to the family by inheritance under the deceased's will".[601]

---

593 Subject now to bereavement damages.

594 (1863) 4 B. & S. 396; see the case at para.41-016, above.

595 [1992] P.I.Q.R. P332 CA.

596 [1992] P.I.Q.R. P332 CA at 349.

597 Also at [1992] P.I.Q.R. P332 CA at 349.

598 [2001] P.I.Q.R. Q8 CA at 73.

599 [2008] EWCA Civ 81 CA.

600 This aspect of these three cases is dealt with at para.41-082, above.

601 [2008] EWCA Civ 81 CA at [51]. That the children had made a success of the business after the death in *Williams* was also left out of account by the application of s.3 without any resort to s.4. As Smith LJ said (at [50]): "That was not because the financial benefit which they had brought to the family was a 'benefit accruing as a result of the death' which had to be ignored under s.4. It was because that financial benefit was irrelevant to the assessment of the dependency under s.3." See too *Wolfe v Del'Innocenti* [2006] EWHC 2694 (QB) (at para.41-045, above) where Owen J said that he found unpersuasive the argument (which he did not have to address) that the earnings of a widow from the deceased's business should be brought into account under s.4: at [28].

A somewhat bizarre illustration in a very different context of a benefit which is part of the dependency continuing after the death, thereby having to be taken into account in the assessment of the loss of dependency under s.3, is provided by *Auty v National Coal Board*.[602] The benefit was by way of a pension and the claimant contended that s.4 applied so as to require the pension to be left out of account.[603] Actions for loss of their pension rights were brought not only by three miners who had suffered physical injury at various collieries under the defendant board's management and control[604] but also by the widow of a fourth miner who had been killed at a fourth colliery. Mrs Popow's husband's death in service entitled her under the pension scheme to which he had belonged to a widow's pension and this she was receiving. Nevertheless it was argued on her behalf that, in addition to the loss of her dependency during the deceased's lifetime had he lived for his normal life expectancy, she had been deprived, by his death, of the widow's pension which she would have received under the scheme if her husband had survived to retirement and died thereafter, and that she was entitled to be compensated for the loss of this pension because the statute requires that, in assessing her damages, the pension of which she was in receipt is to be ignored. The Court of Appeal was unpersuaded by what it called this startling proposition[605] and held quite simply that, since Mrs Popow was in receipt of the pension, she had lost nothing[606]; there being no loss to assess, no question arose of ignoring any benefit. As Oliver LJ rightly said, the key section was not s.4, dealing with non-deductible benefits, but s.3, dealing with ascertaining, and assessing the damages for, the loss of dependency.[607] **41-121**

There is an issue somewhat related to that of a benefit which continues after the death so as to have to be taken into account in valuing the lost dependency under s.3; that issue concerns the benefit of the earlier receipt of the deceased's estate. Not much is heard these days of the practice of making an addition to the award for the loss of the larger estate that the dependants would have received had the deceased lived on and built up savings, and then counterbalancing this by making a deduction for the acceleration of benefit from the estate; sometimes these two items were held in the circumstances to cancel each other out.[608] The practice was endorsed, and is illustrated with various methods for the computation, by the decision of the House of Lords in *Taylor v O'Connor*.[609] The concern is that it could be argued that the benefit gained by the dependants in receiving the deceased's estate sooner than they otherwise would have done is now to be disregarded, benefits from the estate **41-122**

---

602 [1985] 1 W.L.R. 784 CA. This decision should be contrasted with that in *McIntyre v Harland & Wolff Plc* [2006] 1 W.L.R. 2577 CA (at para.41-119, above) where the pension was properly ignored. Buxton LJ in the only reasoned judgment in *McIntyre* carefully distinguished *Auty*.

603 It was the original s.4 of the Fatal Accidents Act 1976 which applied, but the position would be no different with the substituted version.

604 For this aspect of the case, see Ch.40, above at various paragraphs.

605 [1985] 1 W.L.R. 784 CA at 804F, per Oliver LJ.

606 [1985] 1 W.L.R. 784 CA at 799H and 806E.

607 If the pension that the widow would in fact receive could be shown to be less than the pension she would have received on her husband's natural death after retirement, there seems no good reason why she should not be able to claim the difference. Oliver LJ in *Auty* saw great difficulty in making such a claim because, he said (at 805G), this could not be done without doing what s.4 says is not to be done, namely taking no account of the pension actually received. But surely the matter can be resolved entirely within s.3—by asking what was her loss of dependency—without ever reaching s.4.

608 As in *Kassam v Kampala Aerated Water Co* [1965] 1 W.L.R. 668 PC.

609 [1971] A.C. 115.

being specifically mentioned in s.4,[610] so that we could have arrived at the position where the acceleration of the benefit is to be disregarded but the lost savings will still feature in the award. It is suggested that the best approach is to regard the two items as together forming a single issue so that the dependants can be said, under s.3, to have lost the value by which the estate they would have received would have been greater less the value of the earlier receipt of the estate which they have received. Section 4 is then never reached.

## II. Claims Surviving the Death for the Benefit of the Deceased's Estate

41-123 The question of survival of actions has already been considered in general,[611] but special problems arise where the death has itself resulted from the defendant's wrongful act. In discussing these problems it is helpful to separate losses of the deceased which are still in the future at the time of his death from losses which are already in the past, and then to deal briefly with funeral expenses which is the one loss for which the estate can claim recovery but for which the deceased himself could not have sued.

### 1. Prospective Losses of the Deceased

41-124 The basic difference in the measure of damages between the action for personal injury brought by a living claimant and the action brought by his estate upon his death through the injury might be thought to be that, because the injury has crystallised in death, there can be no recovery for prospective losses, the ensuing fact of death having removed the prospect entirely. It can now be said with some confidence, though not formerly, that this is today entirely true.

#### (1) Pecuniary losses

41-125 Prospective medical expenses appear never to have been claimed in a survival action by the estate, and it is a clear principle that the deceased's estate should be entitled to no recovery in respect of expenses which will now never be incurred.

41-126 Loss of prospective earnings, however, stands on a rather different footing; for while the death eliminates the need to incur future expenses, the gains prevented by the tortious conduct continue to be a reality despite the death. However, any possibility of recovery for loss of prospective earnings was squarely removed, although in a somewhat tangential manner, for the near two decades during which the Court of Appeal's decision in *Oliver v Ashman*,[612] ruled the day; if, as was there held, a living claimant's damages for loss of earning capacity are to be based upon his post-injury life expectancy, prospective earnings represent a loss for which the deceased could not himself have claimed had he lived. However, *Oliver v Ashman* was finally overruled by the House of Lords in *Pickett v British Rail Engineering*,[613] which led to the unfortunate but inexorable conclusion, soon accepted by the House of Lords in *Gammell v Wilson*,[614] that the estate could now claim in respect of prospective

---

610 See the section at para.41-111, above.

611 See Ch.23, above.

612 [1962] 2 Q.B. 210 CA; see para.40-109, above.

613 [1980] A.C. 136; see para.40-109, above.

614 [1982] A.C. 27.

earnings. That the estate should have no such right is particularly important wherever the class of persons entitled under the estate differs from the class of persons constituting the deceased's dependants, for the allowance of prospective earnings to the estate would result in a double recovery against the tortfeasor as the prospective earnings also form the basis of the award to the dependants by reason of being the fund out of which their support would have come. The chaos which this development created was eventually stemmed by somewhat tardy legislation: s.4 of the Administration of Justice Act 1982 substituted a new s.1(2)(a) in the Law Reform (Miscellaneous Provisions) Act 1934 wherein it was provided that the damages recoverable for the benefit of the estate of a deceased person in a survival action shall not include "any damages for loss of income[615] in respect of any period after that person's death", a provision[616] which applies in respect of all deaths occurring after the end of 1982.[617]

## (2) Non-pecuniary losses

Prospective pain and suffering of the deceased also makes no appearance in survival actions; once again, it is a clear principle that the deceased's estate should be entitled to no recovery in respect of pain and suffering which will now never be experienced. **41-127**

Loss of prospective amenities of life, however, differs in that, while the death eliminates the possibility of undergoing future pain and suffering, the enjoyment of life prevented by the tortious conduct continues to be a reality despite the death; in this sense, loss of prospective amenities of life may be equated with loss of prospective earnings.[618] Nevertheless, no claims for the loss of prospective amenities have appeared and one may predict with some conviction that any such claim would be rejected on the ground that recovery for loss of amenities is available only for the period up to the death. The danger arises from the unfortunate decision in *West v Shephard*,[619] where the majority of the House of Lords, by permitting a very substantial award for loss of amenities to a living claimant unaware of his plight, gave an objective quality to this head of damage.[620] **41-128**

---

615 Not applicable to the loss of death-in-service benefits to an employee who died soon after he had been unfairly dismissed, for which loss to the deceased the estate could recover: *Fox v British Airways Plc Employment Appeal Tribunal* unreported 30 July 2012.

616 Commonwealth countries that still retain appeals to the Privy Council may not have introduced such a legislative provision so that the Privy Council from time to time may still have to consider an award to a deceased's estate for the income of the lost years, as in *George v Eagle Air Services* [2009] UKPC 35, an appeal from the Court of Appeal of the Eastern Caribbean (St Lucia): see at [6] for the award made by the Privy Council.

617 Administration of Justice Act 1982 s.73(3) and (4) together with s.76(11). While, by providing in the interpretation section of the original Damages Act 1996, at s.7(1), that "references to a claim or action for personal injury include references to such a claim or action brought by virtue of the Law Reform (Miscellaneous Provisions) Act 1934 …", it is made clear that periodical payments are available in survival claims as much as in personal injury claims, this has nothing to operate on in the light of the barring of damages for loss of income after death.

618 See para.41-126, above.

619 [1964] A.C. 326.

620 See paras 40-260 and 40-261, above, and for further comment see McGregor, (1965) 28 M.L.R. 629 at 652–653.

## 2. ACCRUED LOSSES OF THE DECEASED

41-129 With losses which have already accrued before the death, on the other hand, the position is totally different, and the estate is entitled to full recovery.[621] Again it is convenient to take separately pecuniary and non-pecuniary losses here, because the wisdom of allowing recovery for non-pecuniary losses may be questioned.

### (1) Pecuniary losses

41-130 Earnings lost and medical expenses incurred up to the time of death receive little comment in the cases, since there is no doubt that the estate can recover in respect of them. This is as it should be since these pecuniary losses go to diminish the assets in the estate.[622] Exceptionally, this is not so as in *Drake v Foster Wheeler Ltd*,[623] where there was an amount awarded in respect of gratuitous care provided not, as usually, by the family but by a charitable hospice foundation which amount under the present law had to be handed over by the estate to the gratuitous carer[624] which indeed the family were fully prepared to do.[625]

### (2) Non-pecuniary losses[626]

41-131 **(a) Pain and suffering** The decisions have made it clear that damages in an action by the estate may be awarded in respect of the pain and suffering borne by the deceased up to the time of death, although such damages will generally be small as the death so often follows quickly upon the injury and, even where it does not, may be preceded by a period of unconsciousness relieving the victim of any physical pain. In *Bishop v Cunard White Star*,[627] where the circumstances of death and the length of time that the deceased had survived the injury were unknown, it was

621 Thus in *Mulholland v McCrea* [1961] N.I. 135 CA, a survival action brought by the deceased's husband as her personal representative, it was held that the fact that the death of the wife was caused partly by the fault of her husband, who was entitled to share in her estate, did not result in any reduction of the damages otherwise recoverable, since the claimant husband was suing, and the claim was made, in a strictly representative capacity. Contrast the assessment of the damages in the Fatal Accidents Act claim which was also brought: para.41-016, above.

622 A variety of costs were awarded in the estate action in *Zambarda v Shipbreaking (Queensborough) Ltd* [2013] EWHC 2263 (QB).

623 [2011] 1 All E.R. 63.

624 See para.40-228, above.

625 See [2011] 1 All E.R. 63 at [31] and following. The attempt in *Batt v Highgate Private Hospital* [2005] P.I.Q.R Q1 at 1 to have awarded as damages in the survival claim the deceased's expenses of the negligently performed operation which led to her death rightly failed as she would not have been entitled to claim these expenses had she lived: see at [8] and following, and the case further on this at para.4-062, above (in a footnote).

626 The Judicial Studies Board, now called the Judicial College, which for over 20 years in its *Guidelines* has regularly produced, across the board of personal injuries, figures of appropriate awards for non-pecuniary loss (para.40-275 and following, above), commenced its 2013 edition with a new Ch.1 entitled "Injuries Resulting in Death", which is retained in the current edition. This deals specifically with claims by the estate where the now deceased has survived for a period of time after the tortious injury. The suggested figures deal with survival over a short period, up to six months or less, and also with whether there has been full consciousness throughout, unconsciousness throughout, or consciousness followed by unconsciousness. It is interesting to see that rather small amounts are allowed where there is unconsciousness throughout, thereby rather ignoring the unwelcome decision of the House of Lords in *West v Shephard* [1964] A.C. 326 HL (see at para.41-134, below).

627 [1950] P. 240.

held that no award should be made "in the absence of clear evidence of reasonably prolonged suffering".[628] Similarly, in *Hicks v Chief Constable of the South Yorkshire Police*,[629] claims by the personal representatives of three young spectators, crushed to death at the stadium in the Hillsborough disaster, for pain and suffering before their deaths were rejected at all levels of adjudication in the absence of clear evidence. In the Court of Appeal Parker LJ said that in his view

> "when unconsciousness and death occur in such a short period after the injury which causes death no damages are recoverable. The last few moments of mental agony and pain are in reality part of the death itself".[630]

For rather different reasons, the Court of Appeal in *Kadir v Mistry*,[631] agreed with the trial judge's refusal to award any damages for pain and suffering. Diagnosis of cancer in the deceased had been negligently delayed. Had there been no delay the deceased would have suffered the same symptoms, although somewhat later and in the interim would have been subjected to painful treatment to deal with the cancer. Laws LJ, giving the only reasoned judgment, stressed that there were no special rules for assessing pain and suffering in estate claims; the criterion is, as always, to put the now deceased in the same position as he or she would have been if the negligence had no occurred.[632]

In *Rose v Ford*,[633] where the deceased had been unconscious for the most part of the four days that she survived the injury, only £20 was awarded, an amount equivalent to about £900 today; but in *Robertson v Lestrange*,[634] for four days pain and suffering between injury and death the award did not reach beyond £150,[635] which inflation would take to about £400 today. By contrast, in the earlier *Roughead v Railway Executive*,[636] where the deceased had undergone terrible suffering though only for one day, an award of £250 was made, which represents in today's values £7,500.[637] In *Watson v Willmott*,[638] where a husband, in the same accident in which his wife was killed, suffered nervous shock on seeing her body immediately afterwards and then clinical depression for four months before taking his own life, which suicide was attributed to the tortfeasor causing the initial accident, £4,000 was awarded to his estate for the shock and ensuing depression,[639] an amount which today would be well over £7,000. In *Amin v Imran Khan & Partners*,[640] where the deceased had been clubbed to death in his prison cell by a fellow inmate and had survived barely conscious for a week, there was sufficient evidence of a period of intense conscious pain to make an award of £5,000 possible. Much higher sums can be awarded where there has been a long period of pain and suffering, which can

---

628 [1950] P. 240 at 247.

629 [1992] 1 All E.R. 690 CA.

630 [1992] 1 All E.R. 690 CA at 694b. The House of Lords' dismissal of the claimants' appeal is at [1992] 2 All E.R. 65.

631 [2014] EWCA Civ 1177.

632 [2014] EWCA Civ. 1177 at [11]–[12].

633 [1937] A.C. 826.

634 [1985] 1 All E.R. 950.

635 [1985] 1 All E.R. 950 at 959c.

636 (1949) 65 T.L.R. 435.

637 (1949) 65 T.L.R. 435 at [84] and following.

638 [1991] 1 Q.B. 140.

639 [1991] 1 Q.B. 140 at 150B–D.

640 [2011] EWHC 2958 (QB).

happen when the death is from exposure to asbestos or from an undiagnosed cancer. Following the 2015 JSB Guidelines, which suggested a bracket of £53,200 to £95,700 for mesothelioma, awards have tended to be made at the top end where symptoms were manifest, and increasingly severe, from two years or more before death: *Mosson v Spousal (London) Ltd*,[641] (26 months; £88,448); *Wolstenholme v Leach's of Shudenhill Ltd*,[642] (44 months, increasing in severity from 29 months; £92,826); *Grant v The Secretary of State for Transport*,[643] (40 months; £92,500).

**41-132** **(b) Loss of expectation of life** Loss of expectation of life is an injury accruing before death although damages in respect of it could not be recoverable where death is from an independent cause. But where the death is caused by the defendant it only goes to substantiate and prove beyond doubt that such a loss of life expectation has resulted from the defendant's wrong. This head of damage, recognised for a living claimant in *Flint v Lovell*,[644] was held to apply also to an action which had survived for the benefit of the victim's estate by the House of Lords in *Rose v Ford*.[645] And since that decision most cases involving this head of damage have been survival actions where the person wronged has died; the reason for this is that in the nature of things loss of expectation of life is most easily and conclusively proved where death has ensued.

We have seen (at para.40-263, above) that, while awards of damages for loss of expectation of life have been abolished, damages for pain and suffering may take into account suffering caused by awareness that expectation of life has been reduced. The Court of Appeal in *Kadir v Mistry*,[646] differed from the trial judge and awarded damages for mental suffering on account of the deceased's belief that, had her cancer been diagnosed earlier, she would have had a chance of survival. The case is perhaps particular in that there was an award for mental distress at the contemplation of a reduced life span with no award for pain and suffering independently of this element.

**41-133** Until *Benham v Gambling*,[647] awards both were high and varied widely in amount. But the dislike which was judicially felt of awarding damages to the estate for non-pecuniary loss to the deceased caused the House of Lords in that decision to lay down that only very moderate awards should be made, and the impetus of inflation had not raised the £200 level too dramatically before the right of the estate to claim damages for loss of expectation of life was abolished by s.1(1)(a) of the Administration of Justice Act 1982 in respect of all deaths occurring after the end of 1982.[648]

---

641 [2016] EWHC 1429 (QB).

642 [2016] EWHC 588 (QB).

643 [2017] EWHC 1663 (QB).

644 [1935] 1 K.B. 354 CA.

645 [1937] A.C. 826. Even where the death is instantaneous: see, e.g. *Morgan v Scoulding* [1938] 1 K.B. 786.

646 [2014] EWCA Civ 1177 CA, facts at para.41-131, above.

647 [1941] A.C. 157.

648 Section 73(3) and (4) together with s.76(11). For further detail, see paras 40-262 and 40-263, above. Commonwealth countries that still retain appeals to the Privy Council may not have effected such a legislative change so that the Privy Council from time to time may still have to consider an award to a deceased's estate for loss of expectation of life seen as a non-pecuniary loss. This was the position in *George v Eagle Air Services Ltd* [2009] UKPC 35, an appeal from the Court of Appeal of the Eastern Caribbean (St Lucia): see at [3] for the award made by the Privy Council.

**(c) Loss of amenities of life** The estate is also entitled to recover for the deceased's loss of amenities of life up to the time of his death but, as with the damages for pain and suffering, awards will again generally be small as the death so often follows quickly upon the injury. There is, however, this difference between these two heads of damage, that the victim's unconsciousness from the time of injury to the time of death, while it eliminates all recovery for pain and suffering, does not prevent an award of damages for loss of amenities. This follows from the decision in *West v Shephard*,[649] that damages for loss of amenities are not to be based upon loss of happiness and that the victim's ignorance of the loss suffered is no ground for reducing the award.[650] Accordingly, the Court of Appeal in *Andrews v Freeborough*,[651] had no alternative, where a child survived in a state of unconsciousness for a year after the injury, but to endorse the judge's award of the then sizeable sum of £2,000—equivalent today to some £25,000—to the estate, suing after the child's death in respect of loss of amenities.[652] In *Kralj v McGrath*,[653] where a child negligently injured at birth survived a bare two months with no insight into his condition, £2,500 was awarded for what, although referred to by the judge as pain and suffering, was essentially loss of amenities; today this would be over £5,000. And in *Murray v Shuter*,[654] where the adult victim had remained in a coma for over four years before dying, the award for loss of amenities was £11,000, representing around £60,000 in today's values.[655] Further cases have not appeared in the many years since then, and one wonders whether a court today would feel obliged to continue to make awards of an equivalent level. 41-134

Thus the survival of the victim through a long period of unconsciousness enables the recovery by the estate to escape its former containment within the strict limits imposed by *Benham v Gambling*,[656] and allows a much larger sum than was possible for loss of expectation of life to be claimed in respect of loss of amenities. It is not surprising that the members of the Court of Appeal in *Andrews v Freeborough*,[657] indicated that they would have decided differently had the matter been *res integra*.[658] Moreover, the position can no longer be adjusted from a practical angle where the deceased is an adult with dependants, because the amount given for loss of amenities which formerly fell to be deducted, as in *Murray v Shuter*,[659] from the larger damages awarded to the dependants for loss of dependency under the Fatal Accidents Acts is now not to be taken into account under the provision of the new s.4 of the Fatal Accidents Act 1976 designed to remove consideration of all collateral benefits from the scene in Fatal Accidents Act claims.[660] 41-135

---

649 [1964] A.C. 326.
650 See para.40-260, above.
651 [1967] 1 Q.B. 1 CA.
652 Winn LJ, however, did make a valiant effort to justify an award of £500, mainly by taking into account the fact that the deceased was a young child and not a fully developed adult: see at 23.
653 [1986] 1 All E.R. 54.
654 [1976] Q.B. 972 CA.
655 This was expressed to be also for pain and suffering but, as the Court of Appeal pointed out (at 981A), it must have been "in the circumstances almost entirely" for loss of amenities. See, too, *Gray v Mid Herts Hospital Management Committee* [1974] C.L.Y. 2618 (£5,000, today nearing £45,000, where child injured at 12 months survived for nearly three years unaware of his surroundings).
656 [1941] A.C. 157; see para.41-133, above.
657 [1967] 1 Q.B. 1 CA.
658 [1967] 1 Q.B. 1 CA at 12, 18 and 20, per Willmer, Davies and Winn LJJ respectively.
659 [1976] Q.B. 972 CA.
660 See para.41-111, above.

### (3) Collateral benefits

41-136 Collateral benefits are very unlikely to arise in relation to claims by the estate. Funeral expenses apart, the damages all relate to losses accruing to the deceased before his death,[661] and the collateral benefits with which one is familiar arise as a result of the death and are relevant to the dependants' losses following upon the death. However, a collateral benefit to the estate did make its appearance in *Ballantine v Newall Insulation Co Ltd*.[662] In actions brought by the widow and executrix of the deceased, on behalf of the estate and of herself as dependant, the question in issue was whether there was deductible from the damages, in whole or in part, a statutory payment of some £40,000 made pursuant to the Pneumoconiosis (Workers' Compensation) Act 1979, for which a claim had been lodged some months before the death, the deceased having been diagnosed a year before his death as suffering from mesothelioma consequent upon asbestos exposure. It was accepted that there could be no deduction against the widow's damages because of the wide terms of s.4 of the Fatal Accidents Act 1976—the benefit accruing to the widow from the estate and therefore falling within s.4—but since unsurprisingly, even fortunately, there was no equivalent to s.4 in relation to benefits which do not result from the death, the Court of Appeal had no difficulty in holding that the statutory payment fell to be offset against the estate's losses.[663] The court below[664] had allowed the offset only against the estate's pecuniary losses because the authorities appeared to envisage deductibility of benefits in respect of pecuniary losses and did not suggest deduction from non-pecuniary losses. This is indeed true of the collateral benefits with which the courts have been concerned, but the Court of Appeal thought rightly that this statutory payment could be construed to cover non-pecuniary as well as pecuniary losses.

## 3. Losses For Which The Deceased Could Not Have Sued

41-137 The estate in effect steps into the shoes of the deceased and therefore cannot claim for any losses other than those for which the deceased could have claimed had he lived. This is underlined by s.1(2)(c) of the Law Reform (Miscellaneous Provisions) Act 1934, which provides for the damages to be calculated without reference to any loss to the estate consequent upon the death, but that subsection also makes an express exception for funeral expenses.[665] To the extent that these are thus recoverable, the Act creates a new cause of action.[666]

---

661 See paras 41-124 and 41-129, above.

662 [2000] P.I.Q.R. Q327 CA.

663 But Holland J has since felt able to hold in *Cameron v Vinters Defence Systems Ltd* [2008] P.I.Q.R. P5 at 87 that even in a claim by a dependant under the Fatal Accidents Act such a payment is not caught by s.4, thereby requiring deduction of it still to be made: see the case at para.41-112, above (in a footnote).

664 [2000] P.I.Q.R. Q57.

665 Before 1934, funeral expenses could not be recovered at all, either at common law (*Osborn v Gillett* (1873) L.R. 8 Ex. 88; *Clark v L.G.O.C.* [1906] 2 K.B. 648 CA) or under the Fatal Accidents Act (*Dalton v S.E. Ry* (1858) 4 C.B. N.S. 296; *Clark v L.G.O.C.* [1906] 2 K.B. 648 CA).

666 Compare Lord Russell of Killowen in *Rose v Ford* [1937] A.C. 826 at 839–840; "It does not (except as regards funeral expenses) contemplate, much less does it create, any cause of action in anyone for damages resulting from death." The curious decision in *Bateman v Hydro Agri (UK)* unreported 15 September 1995, that a living claimant who is about to die may be awarded his prospective funeral expenses is bold, and may be sensible, but it is difficult to justify in principle. The attempt in *Watson*

The subsection does not define funeral expenses and it would seem that the test of reasonableness must be applied.[667] On this test, embalming a child's body was allowed and the cost of a monument disallowed in *Hart v Griffiths-Jones*.[668] In *Gammell v Wilson*,[669] where the death was in England and the defendants did not dispute the extra expense in having the burial in Ireland where the family came from, recovery was allowed for what was considered a comparatively large amount for the erection of a stone for the deceased boy's grave, it being said however that the case was very near the boundary between a headstone, which is allowable, and a memorial, which is not.[670] It was also held there that the cost of mourning clothes did not constitute a funeral expense.[671] In the light of these authorities the list of items successfully included in *St George v Turner*,[672] is surely unacceptable and the award of over £50,000, even for the beginning of this century, more so. The deceased, who was Japanese, had been murdered by the defendant, her English husband. The expenses for which recovery was given were for the transport back to Japan of the deceased for a Buddhist funeral, a Buddhist family altar, Buddhist monks' attendance at the funeral, and a memorial day and anniversary reception. It is thought that this is far too extreme to be upheld; even murder cannot influence the level of recovery for funeral expenses.[673] **41-138**

*v Cakebread Robey Ltd* [2009] EWHC 1695 (QB) of a living claimant expected very soon to die to recover his own funeral expenses by, as it were, stepping into the shoes of his estate was clearly a nonsense and rightly rejected: at [48]–[57].

667 There appears to be nothing requiring payments out of the social fund on account of funeral expenses (see the Social Security Contributions and Benefits Act 1992 s.138(1)(a) as substituted by the Social Security Act 1998) made to the estate to be deducted from the damages award; see footnote at the end of para.41-021, above for the position with the dependants' claim.

668 [1948] 2 All E.R. 729; for the test of reasonableness, see at 730, 731.

669 [1982] A.C. 27 CA.

670 [1982] A.C. 27 CA at 42H–43F, 55B. *Goldstein v Salvation Army Assurance Society* [1917] 2 K.B. 291, which did not involve a claim for funeral expenses arising out of a death, was referred to as pointing the distinction between headstone and memorial.

671 See, generally, the judgment at first instance in *Gammell v Wilson* unreported 27 July 1979.

672 [2003] C.L.Y. 936. This would appear to be a claim by the estate as there is no sign of any dependants of the deceased; see next footnote.

673 See at para.41-022, above, *Stanton v Youlden* [1960] 1 W.L.R. 543; *Schneider v Eisovitch* [1960] 2 Q.B. 430 and *Jones v Royal Devon & Exeter NHS Foundation Trust* [2008] EWHC 558 (QB), in which cases the claim was under the Fatal Accidents Act on behalf of the deceased's dependants, the 1934 Act having also, by s.2(3) (now replaced by s.3(5) of the Fatal Accidents Act 1976), allowed in such claims recovery of funeral expenses incurred by the dependants: the estate's and the dependants' claim for such expenses are of course alternative.

CHAPTER 42

# ASSAULT AND FALSE IMPRISONMENT

TABLE OF CONTENTS



## I. ASSAULT

### 1. HEADS OF DAMAGE

**42-001** In so far as an assault and battery[1] results in physical injury to the claimant, the damages will be calculated as in any other action for personal injury. However, beyond this, the tort of assault affords protection from the insult which may arise from interference with the person. Thus a further important head of damage is the injury to feelings, i.e. the indignity, mental suffering, disgrace and humiliation that may be caused. Damages may thus be recovered by a claimant for an assault, with or without a technical battery, which has done him no physical injury at all. There may be a basic award of damages for the injury to feelings and if the injury is aggravated by the defendant's conduct an additional award of aggravated damages or, as with many court awards, the two can be run together.[2] For separate awards the horrific case of *AT, NT, ML, AK v Dulghieru*,[3] is usefully illustrative. Four young women, after being induced by fraud to come from Moldova to the United Kingdom, were coerced into unwanted and constant sexual activity, were kept apart and had their and their families' safety threatened, suffered chronic post-traumatic stress disorder and were falsely imprisoned for two months or more. but here there was, as well as assault by way of coerced sexual activity, substantial psychological harm and false imprisonment Treacy J made basic awards which covered injury to the four claimants' feelings as well as the conventional personal injury heads of pain and suffering and loss of amenities, awards which ranged from £125,000 down

1 For the difference between assault and battery, see the standard texts on tort.

2 But rather curiously the Court of Appeal has indicated in *Richardson v Howie* [2005] P.I.Q.R. Q3 CA at 48 that aggravated damages should not generally be awarded in assault cases. See the discussion at paras 42-004 to 42-007, below.

3 [2009] EWHC 225 (QB).

to £82,000, and he stated specifically that these did not include aggravated damages.[4] As we shall see below, he then made separate awards not only for aggravated damages but for exemplary damages.[5] The award of general damages was also particularly high, at £78,500, in *Lawson v Glaves-Smith*,[6] where Eady J, being concerned with another horrific case, this time of multiple rape, concentrated in arriving at the damages on assault though there was also false imprisonment by the claimant being detained through fear of violence for nearly three days. Additionally, and unusually for assault cases, there was an award for financial loss, the trauma of the whole incident having affected the claimant's ability to earn; this makes for a further head of damage. Of course much smaller amounts are awarded in the general run of cases, as those cases, dealt with below,[7] where there is aggravation of damage show. And in coming to the appropriate amount to award there has to be taken into account the Court of Appeal ruling in *Simmons v Castle*,[8] that damages for non-pecuniary loss in all types of civil claim are to be increased by 10 per cent.[9]

## 2. Aggravation and Mitigation

**(a) Aggravation of damage** Aggravated damages come into the picture where the injury to the claimant's feelings is increased by the flagrancy, malevolence and the particularly unacceptable nature of the assaulting defendant's behaviour. Aggravated damages have been seen to be available in torts affecting land[10] and should be more available when such a tort is combined with an assault. *Loudon v Ryder*,[11] is a good illustration of an assault upon the occupant of premises in the course of breaking into and doing damage to those premises. It is true that that case was overruled in *Rookes v Barnard*,[12] but that was primarily in relation to the separate award for exemplary damages. There is no reason why the case should not represent a proper award of aggravated damages for assault, though not at the level of £1,000 at which the jury arrived; in the currency of today this would be worth not far short of £25,000.[13] Similarly, where a landlord evicting a tenant resorts to the assaulting of that tenant, not only in the proprietary tort claim may aggravated damages be awarded, as very often happens,[14] but also in the action for the personal tort; *Reid* **42-002**

---

4 [2009] EWHC 225 (QB) at [51] and [52].

5 While assault featured in *Hsu v Commissioner of Police of the Metropolis* [1998] Q.B. 498 CA, the case was primarily concerned with false imprisonment, where again basic, aggravated and exemplary damages were all awarded: see at paras 42-014, 42-026 and 42-028, below, respectively.

6 [2006] EWHC 2865 (QB).

7 See paras 42-002 and following.

8 [2013] 1 W.L.R. 1239 CA.

9 For the procedural history and reasons for this development, stemming from the package of reforms appearing in the *Jackson Report on Civil Litigation Costs*, see para.40-280, below

10 See paras 39-042 and 39-072, above.

11 [1953] 2 Q.B. 202 CA.

12 [1964] A.C. 1129. The only case there overruled: see para.13-004, above.

13 While Lord Devlin in *Rookes* said that *Loudon v Ryder* "ought ... to be completely overruled" ([1964] A.C. 1129 at 1229), his concern with the award for the assault, as opposed to the exemplary award, was not as to its existence but as to its size, being "as high as, if not higher than, any jury could properly have awarded even in the outrageous circumstances of the case" (at 1229–1230). The jury's verdict on damages is set out in a footnote to para.39-043, above.

14 See paras 39-072 and 39-073, above.

*and Reid v Andreou*,[15] provides an illustration. And where in *Westwood v Hardy*,[16] a landowner, irritated by the presence of the claimant on his land, started to use a hand scythe with which he managed to strike her, aggravated damages were held to be in order.

**42-003** Outside these land-related cases aggravated damages were awarded in *W v Meah*,[17] to two women who had been the victims of serious sexual assaults by the defendant. Woolf J considered that the awards on account of aggravation should be moderate, as compensation for the personal injuries suffered remained the primary purpose of the damages. The total awards came to some £7,000 and a little over £10,000 but it is difficult to say how much lower they would have been had the element of aggravation not been present. In *Hsu v Commissioner of Police of the Metropolis*,[18] the Court of Appeal upheld an award of £20,000 which included aggravated damages to a claimant who suffered more because of a predisposition to depression causing post-traumatic distress disorder and who was also suing for wrongful arrest and false imprisonment. Again it cannot be said how much of the award was attributable to the aggravation, and indeed to the assault. And a somewhat unusual, but entirely proper, application of the rule that assault can attract aggravated damages is to be found in *Appleton v Garrett*.[19] The claimants who were eight young patients of the defendant dentist were held entitled by Dyson J to aggravated damages for the injury to feelings and mental distress suffered, together with the anger and indignation felt,[20] upon learning that much of the treatment given had been completely unnecessary, to a large extent upon perfectly healthy teeth, and that the truth about the actual condition of their teeth had been deliberately and in bad faith concealed from them so as to allow the defendant to carry out the dental work with a view to profit. There being no consent to the treatment of teeth which needed no treatment, a trespass to the person had been made out and aggravated damages were therefore permissible. Dyson J considered that awards of aggravated damages should be moderate, in the event giving to each of the claimants 15 per cent of the amount he awarded them by way of general damages for pain and suffering and loss of amenities.[21] Two of the four claimants in *AT, NT, ML, AK v Dulghieru*,[22] were awarded £35,000 each and the other two £30,000 each by way of aggravated damages, Treacy J considering the defendants' conduct to be "so appalling, so malevolent, and so utterly contemptuous" of the claimants' rights[23] as to justify such an award. This was in addition to the basic awards to the

---

15 [1987] C.L.Y. 2250.

16 [1964] C.L.Y. 994.

17 [1986] 1 All E.R. 935.

18 [1998] Q.B. 498 CA.

19 [1996] P.I.Q.R. P1.

20 Dyson J correctly explained (see at 6) the ambit of the statements in *A.B. v South West Water Services* [1993] Q.B. 507 CA, of Sir Thomas Bingham MR that he knew "of no precedent for awarding damages for indignation aroused by a defendant's conduct" (at 532H) and of Stuart Smith LJ that "anger and indignation is not a proper subject for compensation" (at 528A); they did not apply to the present case.

21 In the curious and exceptional case of *Shah v Gale* [2005] EWHC 1087 (QB), where the terrifying assault brought about the murder of the victim, his near immediate death did not allow the trial judge to award more than £2,750, of which sum £2,000 was expressed to be aggravated damages. Full facts at para.52-048, below.

22 [2009] EWHC 225 (QB). Facts at para.42-001, above.

23 [2009] EWHC 225 (QB) at [62].

four,[24] but here there was, as well as assault by way of coerced sexual activity, substantial psychological harm and false imprisonment.

In *Richardson v Howie*,[25] the Court of Appeal heralded a change by holding that in cases of assault it is in general inappropriate to award aggravated damages on top of, and in addition to, damages for injured feelings. The assault there took place in this fashion. While a couple described as being in a volatile relationship were holidaying far from home in the Caribbean, the man made a frenzied and spiteful attack on the woman with a glass bottle causing permanent scarring injuries. The trial judge awarded £10,000, which amount included £5,000 by way of aggravated damages. On appeal the defendant contended that any damages for the injury to the claimant's feelings should be encompassed within the award for general damages and that it was wrong in principle to make an award for aggravated damages. The Court of Appeal agreed. **42-004**

Thomas LJ, delivering the judgment of the two-man court, recited the details of the various first instance cases cited above, other than the important *Hsu* case, and continued: **42-005**

> "It is and must be accepted that at least in cases of assault and similar torts, it is appropriate to compensate for injury to feelings including the indignity, mental suffering, humiliation or distress that might be caused by such an attack, as well as anger or indignation arising from the circumstances of the attack. It is also now clearly accepted that aggravated damages are in essence compensatory in cases of assault. Therefore we consider that a court should not characterise the award of damages for injury to feelings, including any indignity, mental suffering, distress, humiliation or anger and indignation that might be caused by such an attack, as aggravated damages; a court should bring that element of compensatory damages for injured feelings into account as part of the general damages awarded. It is, we consider, no longer appropriate to characterise the award of the damages for injury to feelings as aggravated damages, except possibly in a wholly exceptional case."[26]

The Court of Appeal considered that an overall award of £10,000, as made by the judge, was far too high and substituted an award of £4,500 general damages.

It is difficult to follow the progress of the Court of Appeal's reasoning here. The classification of damages given for injured feelings as compensatory and the classification of aggravated damages as compensatory does not mean that the one is not independent of the other and that the one should be subsumed within the other. If the scale or the horror of the assault increases the injury to the claimant's feelings, the damage is aggravated, and hence the damages are aggravated, and the courts have recognised this in their awards. It is true that there does not have to be an amount awarded for aggravated damages separate from the basic award for injury to feelings but the concept of aggravated damages has not only been long recognised but was emphasised and highlighted by Lord Devlin when declaring exemplary damages anomalous in his speech in *Rookes v Barnard*.[27] Aggravated damages should surely be retained in assault cases. This would seem to be ac- **42-006**

---

24 At para 42-001, above.

25 [2005] P.I.Q.R. Q3 CA at 48.

26 [2005] P.I.Q.R. Q3 CA at [23]. This new approach was adopted and followed at first instance in *Fuk Wan Hau v Jim* [2007] EWHC 3358 (QB) and received support in the harassment case of *Choudhury v Martins* [2007] EWCA Civ 1379.

27 [1964] A.C. 1129. This was the speech with which Thomas LJ said it was necessary to begin: [2005] P.I.Q.R. Q3 CA at 48, [16].

cepted by judge and counsel alike in *Lawson v Glaves-Smith*,[28] and while in the appeal in *Rowlands v Chief Constable of Merseyside Police*,[29] a claim for damages for assault, false imprisonment and malicious prosecution against the police, the Court of Appeal was concentrating on the imprisonment and the prosecution, counsel having been able to agree an award for the assault, it would seem that the court regarded aggravated damages as applying to all three torts.[30]

**42-007** The removal of aggravated damages from the tort of assault will create a tension, indeed an inconsistency, between it and other torts where aggravated damages have had judicial blessing by first instance judges and by the Court of Appeal alike. Quite apart from defamation, malicious prosecution, false imprisonment and the statutory torts of discrimination in all of which the writ of aggravated damages undoubtedly runs, if the Court of Appeal is prepared to award aggravated damages against a defendant who damages land[31] and against a defendant who evicts from land[32] how much more should such damages be available where the damage is to the person. In *Manley v Commissioner of Police for the Metropolis*,[33] another claim for damages for assault, false imprisonment and malicious prosecution against the police, the Court of Appeal would appear to have ignored—if it knew of—what was said in *Richardson v Howie* as the aggravated award of £10,000 which it made was for assault as well as false imprisonment and malicious prosecution.[34] As we have seen, separate awards of aggravated damages have also been made by Treacy J in *AT, NT, ML, AK v Dulghieru*.[35] It seems that the Court of Appeal in *Richardson v Howie* is, fortunately, being generally ignored.[36] However, in *KCR v The Scout Association*,[37] the decision in *Richardson v Howie* was relied upon. The claimant had been repeatedly sexually assaulted by his Cub Scout Group Leader but no aggravated damages were awarded. However, Judge McKenna sitting as a High Court judge, following *Richardson v Howie* as he was required to do and approaching the assessment of damages with that decision "very much in mind" ,[38] nevertheless appeared to recognise aggravated damages, *sub silento*, as part of the

---

28 [2006] EWHC 2865 (QB). *Richardson v Howie* was indeed cited by Eady J but he appears to regard it simply as authority for the appropriateness, which has never been denied, of a global award without separate amounts for injury to feelings and for aggravated damages: see at [136].

29 [2007] 1 W.L.R. 1065 CA.

30 See in particular [2007] 1 W.L.R. 1065 CA at [26].

31 See para.39-042, above.

32 See paras 39-072 to 39-073, above.

33 [2006] EWCA Civ 879 CA.

34 [2006] EWCA Civ 879 CA at [31] and [32]. It is also going to be difficult to know at what point we arrive at the exceptional category, which the Court of Appeal rather reluctantly recognises as still allowing aggravated damages. Thomas LJ's recital of the details of the various first instance cases in which aggravated damages have been awarded, all of which involved very serious assaults, does not make it clear whether the Court of Appeal is approving or disapproving of them. Are they within the exceptional category and accordingly endorsed, or are they not and therefore now to be considered as wrongly decided?

35 [2009] EWHC 225 (QB): see para.42-003, above.

36 In *AB v Nugent Care Society* [2010] EWHC 1005 (QB) the award for sexual assault of a child was stated to be for the shame and distress and psychological effects of the abuse with no mention of aggravation but undoubtedly an element of aggravation featured in the award: see the discussion at [87]–[ 94].

37 [2016] EWHC 587 (QB).

38 [2016] EWHC 587 (QB) at 29.

general damages award. His Honour made a general damages award of £48,000 and said that there would be no "separate" award of aggravated damages.[39]

The same approach which recognises a substantial award of aggravated damages can be seen in *Mohidin v Commissioner of Police of the Metropolis*.[40] In that case, one of the claimants was held to have been falsely imprisoned and assaulted by the police. His award for false imprisonment was £4,500 and, for the minor assault, £250. However, to these basic awards was added aggravated damages of £7,200 for the racially abusive and intimidating way in which the assault and false imprisonment was committed. **42-008**

**(b) Mitigation of damage** Conversely, provocation of the assault by the claimant will lead to mitigation of the damages recoverable under the head of damage concerned with injured feelings. It is in these occasional cases of provocation that the distinction between the damages awarded in respect of medical expenses, loss of earning capacity, pain and suffering and loss of amenities—in sum, the conventional personal injury heads of damage—and the damages awarded for the insult and the injury to feelings is emphasised and well brought out. Such a case was *Lane v Holloway*.[41] Here the Court of Appeal was emphatic that the provocation could not be used to reduce the damages to which the claimant was entitled in respect of the conventional heads of damage for personal injury. "I entirely reject the contention", said Salmon LJ, **42-009**

> "that because a plaintiff who has suffered a civil wrong has behaved badly, this is a matter which the court may take into account when awarding him compensatory damages for personal injuries which he has sustained as the result of the wrong which has been unlawfully inflicted upon him."[42]

On the other hand, there is no good reason why the amount of the damages awarded to compensate for the insult inflicted should not be affected by the fact of provocation and, although this was not brought out by Salmon LJ in his judgment where only the distinction between compensatory damages and exemplary damages is clearly drawn, it was explicitly recognised by Lord Denning MR who said:

> "Provocation by the plaintiff can properly be used to take away an element of aggravation, but not to reduce the real damages."[43]

In the only reasoned judgment given in *Murphy v Culhane*,[44] Lord Denning MR indicated a change of mind in relation to the proposition, for which *Lane v Hol-* **42-010**

---

39 [2016] EWHC 587 (QB) at 92.

40 [2015] EWHC 2740 (QB).

41 [1968] 1 Q.B. 379 CA.

42 [1968] 1 Q.B. 379 CA at 390. The decision is in accord with that of the High Court of Australia in *Fontin v Katapodis* (1962) 108 C.L.R. 177, which the Court of Appeal followed in preference to some earlier, less considered decisions from Canada and New Zealand: see *Griggs v Southside Hotel* [1946] 4 D.L.R. 73 (Ontario High Ct); *Hartlen v Chaddock* (1958) 11 D.L.R. (2d) 705 (Nova Scotia Sup. Ct); *Green v Costello* [1961] N.Z.L.R. 1010 (Sup. Ct). These cases do not appear to be capable of explanation on the basis that the provocation was taken into account in order to reduce only the damages awarded for the aggravation of the injury due to the insult.

43 [1968] 1 Q.B. 379 CA at 387. See, too, *O'Connor v Hewitson* [1979] Crim. L.R. 46 CA, where a detained prisoner provoked a police officer's assault and neither aggravated nor exemplary damages were awarded him.

44 [1977] Q.B. 94 CA.

*loway*,[45] stands as clear authority, that provocation cannot reduce the damages for the pecuniary loss, saying that this is so only where the conduct of the person injured has been trivial and the conduct of the person inflicting the injury has been savage, and entirely out of proportion to the occasion.[46] In *Lane v Holloway*,[47] the severe blow struck by the young defendant was in obvious contrast to the comparatively minor provocation given him by the elderly claimant; in *Murphy v Culhane*,[48] on the other hand, the claimant's deceased husband—the injury had been fatal and the claim was a Fatal Accidents Act claim by the widow—had himself initiated a criminal affray for the purpose of beating up the defendant. Lord Denning also pointed out that the actions of the person injured, or indeed killed, may be such as to defeat the claim entirely on the ground of ex turpi causa non oritur actio or volenti non fit injuria, or as to reduce the damages on account of contributory negligence.[49] His first point is correct but not his second, being inconsistent with the rule that contributory negligence is not a defence open to a defendant who has intended to harm the claimant, so that Lord Rodger in *Standard Chartered Bank v Pakistan National Shipping Corp*,[50] rightly questioned the correctness of *Murphy* on this.[51]

**42-011** After the Court of Appeal decision in *Co-operative Group (CWS) Ltd v Pritchard*,[52] where a female worker in a store had been assaulted and injured by the store manager whom she had provoked by being abusive of him, and the court applied the rule that contributory negligence has no application where the tort is intentional,[53] there must be doubt as to whether there survives the possibility of reducing the damages for non-pecuniary loss on account of provocation by the victim of the assault, making the insult suffered by him or her the less. In his extended judgment Aikens LJ[54] went through what was said in *Lane v Holloway* and in *Murphy v Cullane*, and ended up[55] rejecting the remarks in those cases that damages can be reduced for contributory negligence. Yet in *Lane*, as distinct from *Murphy*, Lord Denning MR, who was in both cases, spoke only of the effect of provocation and did not refer to the defence of contributory negligence at all, as Aikens LJ specifically recognised.[56] Since therefore the Court of Appeal in *Pritchard* was dealing only with contributory negligence, could it not be said that provocation can still be introduced for the purpose of reduction of the damages for the insult inflicted? It is thought that this should be possible. But we shall have to wait and see.

45 [1968] 1 Q.B. 379 CA.
46 [1977] Q.B. 94 at 98D.
47 [1968] 1 Q.B. 379 CA.
48 [1977] Q.B. 94.
49 [1977] Q.B. 94 at 98F–99B.
50 [2003] 1 A.C. 959.
51 [2003] 1 A.C. 959 at 45.
52 [2012] Q.B. 320 CA.
53 For the development of this rule see para.7-004, above.
54 At [2012] Q.B. 320 CA at [40] and following.
55 [2012] Q.B. 320 CA at 62.
56 [2012] Q.B. 320 CA at 41.

## 3. EXEMPLARY DAMAGES

While it was accepted in *Lane v Holloway*,[57] that provocation would be **42-012**

> "relevant to the question of whether or not exemplary damages should be awarded, and, if so, how much",[58]

exemplary damages proper can, however, no longer be awarded merely because the defendant has acted insultingly, violently or otherwise disgracefully. The whole approach to exemplary damages was changed by the decision in *Rookes v Barnard*.[59] Exemplary damages are now recoverable only where the circumstances of the case bring it within one of the three categories set out by Lord Devlin there.[60] Assault can come within the first common law category which applies where there is oppressive, arbitrary or unconstitutional conduct by government servants. *Benson v Frederick*,[61] where a colonel in the militia had ordered an innocent soldier to be flogged, could be said to provide a very early example, from the decade when exemplary damages first came into English law,[62] of a case of assault within the first common law category. *Hsu v Commissioner of Police of the Metropolis*,[63] where a householder was assaulted by police officers when he refused them entry, is a modern example.[64] Assault can also come within the second common law category which applies where the defendant has acted wrongfully with a view to profit and an illustration of the use of the second common law category is now provided by *AT, NT, ML, AK v Dulghieru*.[65] The coerced sexual activity of the four claimants brought substantial profits to the defendants and £60,000 was awarded, to be divided equally between the four, by way of exemplary damages.[66] This was in addition to the basic awards and the aggravated damages awards made to the four,[67] but here there was, as well as assault by way of coerced sexual activity, substantial psychological harm and false imprisonment.

---

57 [1968] 1 Q.B. 379 CA; see para.42-009, above.

58 [1968] 1 Q.B. 379 CA at 391, per Salmon LJ.

59 [1964] A.C. 1129. See Ch.13, above, where exemplary damages are treated in detail.

60 See paras 13-017 to 13-030, above. The further restriction introduced by the now overruled *A.B. v South West Services* [1993] Q.B. 507 CA (see para.13-011, above) never applied to assault cases since they were early in evidence as the case in the next footnote indicates.

61 (1766) 3 Burr. 1845.

62 See para.13-002, above.

63 [1998] Q.B. 498 CA.

64 *Hsu* was a claim for wrongful arrest and false imprisonment as well as assault but, since the arrest and imprisonment were over in a matter of hours, the exemplary award of £15,000 allowed by the Court of Appeal must substantially relate to the assault. As for the award of no exemplary damages in *Manley v Commissioner of Police for the Metropolis* [2006] EWCA Civ 879 CA (assault together with false imprisonment and malicious prosecution) it would seem that this was because the liability of the commissioner of police was vicarious but *Rowlands v Chief Constable of Merseyside Police* [2007] 1 W.L.R. 1065 CA (false imprisonment and malicious prosecution) has since decided to award exemplary damages although the liability of the chief constable was vicarious. Vicarious liability for exemplary damages is considered at paras 13-045 to 13-047, above

65 [2009] EWHC 225 (QB). Facts at para.42-001, above.

66 See the discussion at [2009] EWHC 225 (QB) at [67]–[75].

67 At paras 42-001 and 42-003, above, respectively.

## II. False Imprisonment

### 1. Heads of Damage

42-013 The details of how the damages are worked out in false imprisonment[68] have for many years been few, but things are changing. Generally it is not a pecuniary loss but a loss of dignity and the like that is in issue, and has been left much to the jury's or judge's discretion.[69] The principal heads of damage arise from the consequences of the deprivation of liberty, i.e. the consequences of the loss of time considered primarily from a non-pecuniary viewpoint, and the injury to feelings, i.e. the indignity, mental suffering, disgrace and humiliation, with any attendant loss of social status and injury to reputation. This will all be included in the general damages which are usually awarded in these cases, with no breakdown.

42-014 In two conjoined appeals, *Thompson v Commissioner of Police of the Metropolis* and *Hsu v Commissioner of Police of the Metropolis*,[70] guidance was given by the Court of Appeal as to the amount to be awarded for the basic damages, these being described as the damages before any element of aggravation and also being the damages before any pecuniary loss, any physical injury or any injury to the reputation should these occur. Effectively the basic damages covered the loss of liberty which would include the injury to feelings following on such loss. For the first hour of imprisonment £500 was held to be appropriate. The sums to be awarded after the first hour should be on a reducing scale and the court gave as a guideline about £3,000 for 24 hours in custody.[71] For subsequent days the daily rate should be on a progressively reducing scale. The Court of Appeal also said that the jury, a normal feature of false imprisonment claims,[72] should be informed of the approximate starting figure and an approximate ceiling figure for the basic award in the particular case.[73] It would seem that these guideline figures should apply where the false imprisonment is other than by the police.

42-015 Several important general points of principle were established by the conjoined appeals in *Thompson* and *Hsu*. As Laws LJ explained in in *R. (on the application of MK (Algeria)) v Secretary of State for the Home Department*,[74] (1) the assessment of damages will depend upon the particular facts and the harm suffered by the particular claimant; (2) damages are not assessed mechanistically; there is no daily

[68] The tort of false imprisonment is generally also an assault but not necessarily. Frequently too, the detention is begun by a wrongful arrest. Damages can indeed be awarded for wrongful arrest, as in *Sallows v Griffiths* [2001] F.S.R. 188 CA, where recovery was allowed for pecuniary and non-pecuniary loss with aggravation of the damages.

[69] Where the false imprisonment also entails an assault, this will probably not affect the damages, as damages for the insult will be recoverable in the action for false imprisonment and possibly also damages for any physical injury. Sometimes, as in *Lawson v Glaves-Smith* [2006] EWHC 2865 (QB) which involved a horrific multiple rape, more prominence is given to the assault than to the false imprisonment.

[70] [1998] Q.B. 498 CA.

[71] [1998] Q.B. 498 CA at 515D–E. The £1,500 awarded at first instance in *Taylor v Chief Constable of Thames Valley Police* [2004] 1 WL.R. 3155 CA for some four hours of false imprisonment of a 10-year-old boy is not inconsistent with this scale since it covered trespass to the person and assault as well. It had however to be reduced as on appeal there was held to be only one hour of unlawful detention: see at [55].

[72] See para.53-002, below.

[73] [1998] Q.B. 498 CA at 515C.

[74] [2010] EWCA Civ 980 CA at [8].

tariff; (3) the extent to which the damages will increase will decrease as time proceeds because the initial shock of imprisonment will generally lead to larger damages for the earlier period. To these general principles can be added (4) the circumstances of the case can involve conduct by the claimant which leads to a reduction in damages. An example of this is *R. (on the application of NAB) v Secretary of State for the Home Department*,[75]where the claimant chose 82 days of unlawful immigration detention in the United Kingdom over freedom in Iran by refusing to sign the documents which the Iranian authorities required for his lawful deportation. The damages in that case were substantially reduced.

Although the general principles discussed above continue to apply, the decisions in *Thomson* and *Hsu* were initially used as guidelines from which to structure damages but the utility of those guidelines is now seriously limited for three reasons. One difficulty is that a £3,000 guideline for the first day is likely to be utilised only where the false imprisonment is very short and the suggested progressively reducing scale over the next few days should be steep. A second difficulty is that it is impossible to say what the basic award was in either *Thompson* or *Hsu* since the £20,000 compensatory damages awarded in each included aggravated damages and also damages for malicious prosecution in *Thompson* and for wrongful arrest and assault in *Hsu*. A third difficulty is that, as was recognised in the conjoined appeals of *Thompson v Commissioner of Police of the Metropolis* and *Hsu v Commissioner of Police of the Metropolis*,[76] the guideline figures there set out would need adjustment in the future for inflation.[77] The lapse now of two decades makes that adjustment very significant. Also to be taken into account today, in addition to inflation, is the Court of Appeal ruling in *Simmons v Castle*,[78] that damages for non-pecuniary loss in all types of civil claim are to be increased by 10 per cent.[79] **42-016**

In the two decades since *Thompson* and *Hsu*, claims have taken off. In *R. v Governor of Brockhill Prison Ex p. Evans (No.2)*,[80] where the prison governor had miscalculated the release date of a prisoner who as a result was released 59 days after she should have been, the Court of Appeal raised the trial judge's basic award of £2,000 to £5,000 and the House of Lords upheld the Court of Appeal's increase.[81] Not only were aggravated and exemplary damages inappropriate but of the two principal heads of damage that of injury to feelings was absent, leaving only the general consequences of the loss of liberty itself. The Court of Appeal contrasted the unreported *Lunt v Liverpool City Justices*,[82] where that court had increased the trial judge's award of £13,500 to £25,000 for a period of 42 days' imprisonment, the whole of which was unjustified, to a claimant of unblemished reputation. In both of these cases a global figure was awarded and in *Brockhill* the Court of Appeal deprecated the making of a daily, weekly or monthly figure.[83] The global approach was utilised in *R. (on the application of Mehari) v Secretary of State for the Home* **42-017**

75 [2011] EWHC 1191 (Admin).
76 [1998] Q.B. 498 CA.
77 [1998] Q.B. 498 CA at 517E.
78 [2013] 1 W.L.R. 1239 CA.
79 For the procedural history and reasons for this development, stemming from the package of reforms appearing in the *Jackson Report on Civil Litigation Costs*, see para.40-280, below
80 [1999] Q.B. 1043 CA.
81 [2001] 1 A.C. 19; see Lord Hope at 39G–40C.
82 [1991] CA. Transcript No.158.
83 See on all these points Lord Woolf MR at [1999] Q.B. 1043 CA at 1060A–G.

*Department*[84] and £4,000 was awarded for a week's unlawful detention of an asylum seeker who was a woman of good character.[85] In *Takitota v Attorney General*,[86] where the claimant had been incarcerated for over eight years in appalling prison conditions and the Court of Appeal of The Bahamas had not adopted the global approach but had multiplied the daily amount by as many days as are in eight years, the Privy Council said that this would not do and sent the case back for a reassessment. For a false imprisonment lasting for over three weeks in *R. (on the application of MK (Algeria)) v Secretary of State for the Home Department*[87] the Court of Appeal increased the trial judge's award of £8,500 to £17,500; this included £5,000 of aggravated damages. Even greater than the base award of £12,500 in that case was the award in *Tarakhil v Home Office*,[88] where Mr Tarakhil was unlawfully detained by the government in immigration detention for three weeks. His Honour Judge Thornton QC awarded £14,250 for the detention. It appears that in making this award the judge was influenced by the fact that the claimant was aware of the unlawful nature of the imprisonment and that it had a profound effect on him. Nevertheless, the judge also awarded £3,000 for psychiatric injury and £2,000 for aggravated damages. There appears to be some element of double counting here. A 10 per cent uplift was also then made, apparently applying *Simmons v Castle*.[89] But the comparative cases upon which the award had been based would also have incorporated this uplift so it appears that some double counting occurred. Yet far larger amounts were the awards made to the four claimants in *AT, NT, ML, AK v Dulghieru*,[90] awards which, as we shall see, were supplemented by awards of aggravated and exemplary damages, but in *Dulghieru* there was assault by way of coerced sexual activity and substantial psychological harm as well as false imprisonment.

**42-018** In *Okoro v The Commissioner of Police of the Metropolis*,[91] for arrest and a few hours' imprisonment causing physical injury £13,000 was awarded. In *Iqbal v The Prison Officers' Association*,[92] in the circumstances of the claimant being confined to his small prison cell in the course of a day without being let out for exercise and other activities within the prison generally, the Court of Appeal found the *Thompson* guidance on the amount of damages of no real assistance and, had there been held to be false imprisonment which there was not, would have made a relatively modest award of £120 for the six hours of false imprisonment.[93] In *Patel v Secretary of State for the Home Department*,[94] the seriousness of the misconduct of immigration officers, where the false imprisonment was for the comparatively short period of six days, was held to justify an award of £20,000, even before aggravated damages and exemplary damages[95] were brought in. The case was considered under the Human Rights Act as well as under the common law of false imprisonment, the

---

84 [2010] EWHC 636 (Admin).
85 [2010] EWHC 636 (Admin) at [32]–[39].
86 [2009] UKPC 11.
87 [2010] EWCA Civ 980 CA.
88 [2015] EWHC 2845 (QB).
89 [2013] 1 W.L.R. 1239.
90 [2009] EWHC 225 (QB). Facts and amounts at para.40-001, above.
91 [2011] EWHC 3 (QB).
92 [2010] Q.B. 732 CA.
93 [2010] Q.B. 732 CA at [44] and following.
94 [2014] EWHC 501 (Admin).
95 For which, see paras 42-025 and 42-028, below.

breaches of Human Rights Act articles adding significantly to the damages award.[96] As for the unlawful detention for 61 days of an unaccompanied asylum-seeking young person, this led in *AS v Secretary of State for the Home Department*,[97] to an award of £23,000, before aggravated damages were brought in.[98]

Again, the possibility of a modest award was brushed aside in *AXD v Home Office*,[99] although the differences between the applicant and respondent illustrate the great uncertainty that still exists in this range of damages. The claimant's false imprisonment was for 20 months and 5 days and the primary judge, Jay J, awarded £80,000, noting the irrelevance of the allegation that his claim for refugee status should have been recognised sooner and his diagnosis of paranoid schizophrenia (because he was still fit to be detained and a mental health team is readily accessible). His award was modestly increased by fear of being returned to Somalia, and increased because he was kept in his cell for 21 hours a day and he experienced personal difficulties on account of his sexual orientation. And in *R. (on the application of Belfken) v Secretary of State for the Home Department*,[100] Ms Karen Steyn QC, sitting as a Deputy High Court judge, made an award of £40,000 for a period of 295 days' unlawful detention without any aggravating factors, or any egregious conduct on the part of the Secretary of State; and in circumstances in which the claimant was, to a degree, uncooperative and obstructive. **42-019**

Damages may also be given for any injury to reputation, for, as Lawrence LJ said in *Walter v Alltools*,[101] "a false imprisonment does not merely affect a man's liberty; it also affects his reputation". Some cases have allowed the award to run to vindicatory damages, which take us beyond the damages for non-pecuniary loss. While defamation is the principal tort where vindicatory damages are to be found, a need for vindication, to show the world that the claimant's reputation is unsullied, will sometimes make its appearance where there is false imprisonment. It did so in *Hook v Cunard S.S. Co.*[102] The development in modern times of vindicatory damages is explained in a separate chapter to which reference should be made[103] and in which the significance of the *Hook* case is fully explored. **42-020**

In the absence of any likely adverse reputation consequences of the false imprisonment any substantial award beyond pecuniary or non-pecuniary loss may need to be explained as exemplary damages. In cases where the claimant has suffered no loss, neither of liberty nor of reputation there will be an entitlement only to nominal damages, false imprisonment being a tort actionable per se. Although some cases continue to make substantial awards to "mark"" the infringement, even where those awards might be justified due to non-pecuniary adverse consequences,[104] the award of nominal damages has happened in a whole series of cases over the last three years, cases involving foreign nationals and asylum-seekers who, though unlawfully detained, could and would have been lawfully detained had the correct procedure for their detention been followed by the Secretary of State for the **42-021**

---

96 [2014] EWHC 501 (Admin) at [330] and [336]–[342].
97 [2015] EWHC 1331 (QB).
98 For which, see para.42-026, below.
99 [2016] EWHC 1617 (QB).
100 [2017] EWHC 1834 (Admin).
101 (1944) 61 T.L.R. 39 CA at 40.
102 [1953] 1 W.L.R. 682.
103 See Ch.17, above.
104 *Stewart v The Commissioner of Police of the Metropolis* [2017] EWHC 921 (QB) at [11], [13] and [14].

Home Department. With their lengthy and somewhat repetitive titles, they are *R. (on the application of Lumba (Congo)) v Secretary of State for the Home Department*,[105]; *R. (on the application of O) v Secretary of State for the Home Department (Bail for Immigration Detainees)*,[106] *R. (on the application of OM) v Secretary of State for the Home Department*,[107] *R. (on the application of Abdollahi) v Secretary of State for the Home Department*,[108] *R. (on the application of Moussaoui) v Secretary of State for the Home Department*,[109] and *R. (on the application of Pratima Das) v Secretary of State for the Home Department*.[110] Of these cases *Lumba* was taken by the claimants to the Supreme Court seeking, since compensatory damages were out of the question, vindicatory damages. These were damages not of the established type, adverted to in the previous paragraph, given in order to clear reputation, the claimants in *Lumba* not having a reputation, but given to mark the infringement of a right, that is the right to liberty. The Supreme Court was split on this, but fortunately there was a majority of six to three prepared to hold, in line with what has been said in previous editions of this work that it was inappropriate to award vindicatory damages for infringement of a right. *Lumba* is considered in detail in the separate chapter tracing the development in modern times of vindicatory damages.[111]

**42-022** In addition there may be recovery for any resultant physical injury, illness or discomfort, as where the imprisonment has a deleterious effect on the claimant's health. This is illustrated by the two very old cases, *Lowden v Goodrick*,[112] and *Pettit v Addington*,[113] where the only reason that the claimant failed to recover for a decline in his health from the imprisonment was that he failed to plead it as special damage. In the present day context the claimant's health appears to have been affected in *Hsu v Commissioner of Police of the Metropolis*,[114] and there was recovery for the post-traumatic stress disorder suffered by the four unfortunate claimants in *AT, NT, ML, AK v Dulghieru*,[115] where there was false imprisonment as well as assault.[116] There was an additional award for psychiatric illness in *AS v Secretary of State for the Home Department*.[117]

**42-023** Further, any pecuniary loss which is not too remote is recoverable; there appear to be no modern reported cases. Pecuniary losses fall into two categories in the cases. In the first place, that any loss of general business or employment is recoverable would seem to follow from *Childs v Lewis*,[118] where the claimant, a company

105 [2012] 1 A.C. 245.
106 [2016] 1 W.L.R. 1717.
107 [2011] EWCA Civ 909 CA.
108 [2012] EWHC 878 (Admin); affirmed [2013] EWCA Civ 366 CA.
109 [2012] EWHC 126 (Admin).
110 [2013] EWHC 682 (Admin). A further such case is *The Queen (on the application of Mohammed) v The Secretary of State for the Home Department* [2014] EWHC 1898 (Admin). A different type of case in which only nominal damages were awarded for a false imprisonment is *Bostridge v Oxleas NHS Foundation Trust* [2015] EWCA Civ. 79 where a mentally disordered patient had been unlawfully detained by an NHS trust.
111 See Ch.17, above; for *Lumba* paras.17-014 and following.
112 (1791) Peake 64.
113 (1791) Peake 87.
114 [1998] Q.B. 498 CA. See this case at paras 42-003 and 42-014, above.
115 [2009] EWHC 225 (QB).
116 See the case at para.42-001, above.
117 [2015] EWHC 1331 (QB), facts at para.42-018, above.
118 (1924) 40 T.L.R. 870.

director, had been wrongfully given into custody by the defendant, and his co-directors had demanded his resignation on learning of his arrest. Lush J directed the jury that they were entitled to hold that the claimant's loss of his director's fees by his acceding to this demand flowed from the false imprisonment. He pointed out that

> "clearly if the plaintiff had not resigned the other directors would have taken steps to remove him",[119]

and that his co-directors would be bound to hear of the claimant's arrest "before the prosecution started, or certainly before the magistrates dealt with it".[120] In the second place, a few 19th century cases show that the claimant's costs incurred in procuring his discharge from the imprisonment may be recoverable as damages. Such costs were recovered in this way in *Pritchet v Boevey*.[121] There had been no adjudication as to these costs by the judge who ordered the claimant's release; he would have given the claimant his costs if he had undertaken not to bring an action, and on the claimant's refusal no order had been made as to costs. Similarly, in *Foxall v Barnett*,[122] where the claimant, committed to prison for manslaughter by a coroner's warrant, had been admitted to bail and had subsequently got the inquisition under which he had been committed quashed, it was held that in an action against the coroner for false imprisonment he might recover the costs of quashing the inquisition. However, where the claimant has been refused costs in the prior action, as opposed to there being no order as to costs, he has failed to recover them as damages: this was the result in *Loton v Devereux*,[123] which was distinguished in *Pritchet v Boevey*,[124] on this ground. So, too, there will be no recovery in respect of costs unreasonably incurred. Thus Lord Campbell in *Foxall v Barnett*,[125] made it clear that the action must have been one which was necessary to gain release, and it is submitted that the jury's refusal in *Bradlaugh v Edwards*,[126] to award the claimant damages in respect of his expenses in procuring bail before the magistrates and in getting together evidence in defence of the charge is properly explained on the ground that the costs were not considered to have been reasonably incurred.[127]

## 2. Remoteness of Damage: Continuation of the Imprisonment by Judicial Order

Just as an action for false imprisonment will not lie against one who has procured another's imprisonment by obtaining a court judgment against him, even if the judgment is in some way irregular or invalid, so any continuation by a judicial officer **42-024**

[119] (1924) 40 T.L.R. 870 at 871.
[120] (1924) 40 T.L.R. 870 at 871.
[121] (1833) 1 Cr. & M. 775.
[122] (1853) 23 L.J.Q.B. 7.
[123] (1832) 3 B. & Ad. 343.
[124] (1833) 1 Cr. & M. 775.
[125] (1853) 23 L.J.Q.B. 7 at 8.
[126] (1861) 11 C.B. N.S. 377. These four mid-19th century cases are further analysed in the chapter dealing with costs as damages at para.21-022, above.
[127] McCormick, *Damages* (1935), said many years ago that in most states in the USA the notion of liability for expenses is expanded "to include expenses incurred, after the release of plaintiff on bail or recognisance, in the defence of the criminal proceedings or civil action upon the outcome of which the bail or undertaking is conditioned": p.377.

of an imprisonment initiated by the defendant setting a ministerial officer in motion is too remote. A court of justice, unlike a ministerial officer of the law such as a constable, cannot be the agent of the defendant since it acts in the exercise of its own independent judicial discretion, and thus by acting introduces a new cause which relieves the defendant of liability for further damage. Thus in *Lock v Ashton*,[128] where the claimant, wrongly arrested by the defendant's authority, was brought before a magistrate who remanded him in custody, it was held that the claimant could recover damages in an action for false imprisonment only up to the time of the remand; and more recently in *Diamond v Minter*,[129] the same result was reached. This principle was taken further by the House of Lords in *Harnett v Bond*.[130] The claimant, who was detained in a house licensed for the reception of lunatics, was granted leave of absence on trial, with power in the manager of the licensed house to take him back at any time during the trial period should his mental condition require it. During the trial period the claimant went to see a Commissioner in Lunacy, who, after seeing him, informed the manager by telephone that he was not in a fit state of mind to be at large, and detained him for a few hours while the manager sent attendants to take him back to the licensed house. For the next nine years the claimant, who at all material times was sane and fit to be at large, was detained in various institutions; he then escaped and sued the Commissioner for false imprisonment. The House of Lords held that the Commissioner was only liable for the detention until the arrival of the attendants, and that the subsequent detention of the claimant at the various institutions was due to the re-assumption of control over the claimant by the manager of the licensed house.

## 3. AGGRAVATION AND MITIGATION

**42-025** The manner in which the false imprisonment is effected may lead to aggravation or mitigation of the damage, and hence of the damages. The authorities illustrate in particular the general principle stated by Lawrence LJ in *Walter v Alltools*,[131] that

> "any evidence which tends to aggravate or mitigate the damage to a man's reputation which flows naturally from his imprisonment must be admissible up to the moment when damages are assessed. A false imprisonment does not merely affect a man's liberty; it also affects his reputation. The damage continues until it is caused to cease by an avowal that the imprisonment was false."

That case, and the earlier one of *Warwick v Foulkes*,[132] as interpreted therein, establish that, where the false imprisonment has been brought about by the defendant preferring a charge against the claimant, any evidence tending to show that the defendant is persevering in the charge is evidence which may be given for the

---

128 (1848) 12 Q.B. 871.

129 [1941] 1 K.B. 656; see especially at 674. For the period subsequent to the remand, damages can only be claimed by the claimant in an action for malicious prosecution (see Ch.44), if at all. This may not be possible since in such an action, unlike in the action for false imprisonment, the claimant must prove malice and lack of reasonable and probable cause. It follows also from this that an action for false imprisonment is no bar to another action for malicious prosecution: *Guest v Warren* (1854) 9 Ex. 379.

130 [1925] A.C. 669.

131 (1944) 61 T.L.R. 39 CA at 40.

132 (1844) 12 M. & W. 507.

purpose of aggravating the damages. By implication, they establish the converse proposition that the defendant is entitled to give evidence in mitigation of damages tending to show that he has withdrawn the charge or has apologised for having made it. In *Walter v Alltools*,[133] the damages were increased because the defendants had not expressed their regret, had not notified the claimant's fellow workmen that he had been exonerated from suspicion, and had written a letter which suggested that the claimant's conduct had been suspicious and which in effect justified the imprisonment. In *Warwick v Foulkes*,[134] the claimant had been falsely imprisoned upon a charge of felony by the defendant, who unsuccessfully pleaded in the action brought against him by the claimant that the latter had indeed been guilty of felony. Lord Abinger CB said:

> "The putting this plea on record is, under the circumstances, evidence of malice, and a great aggravation of the defendant's conduct as shewing an animus of persevering in the charge to the very last. A justification of a false imprisonment, on the ground that the defendant had reasonable and probable cause to suspect that the plaintiff had been guilty of felony, is very different; such a justification is in the nature of an apology for the defendant's conduct. And although it was very proper … to tell the jury that the defendant's counsel apologised for the conduct of his client, still that apology came too late. It was one which seemed to be made for the purpose of screening the defendant from having to pay damages."[135]

However, it is submitted that an unsuccessful plea by the defendant that the claimant is guilty of the offence charged against him by the defendant should not lead to an aggravation of the damages unless it is shown that the defendant made the charge mala fide. Otherwise a bona fide defendant would be in a dilemma: if he fails to plead the truth of the charge he risks losing the action against him, while if he does plead the truth of the charge he risks an award of aggravated damages against him.[136]

Awards of aggravated damages again appear in the conjoined appeals of *Thompson v Commissioner of Police of the Metropolis* and *Hsu v Commissioner of Police of the Metropolis*,[137] but were more concerned with the injury to liberty and to feelings than injury to reputation. Guidance was given generally as to the amounts to award[138]; as to aggravated damages the Court of Appeal said that it considered that, where they were appropriate, the figure was unlikely to be less than £1,000 but at the same time should not, in the ordinary way, be as much as twice the basic damages, except perhaps where these were modest.[139] Since this guidance on amounts was given, awards of aggravated damages in this field have proliferated. In *Sallows v Griffiths*,[140] a case of procuring a malicious arrest for which a total of £10,000 was awarded, £1,000 of this total was by way of aggravated damages for injury to proper pride and dignity and for humiliation. The award of £10,000 aggravated damages in *Manley v Commissioner of Police for the* **42-026**

133 (1944) 61 T.L.R. 39 CA.

134 (1844) 12 M. & W. 507.

135 (1844) 12 M. & W. 507 at 508 to 509.

136 The position in defamation is analogous and the matter has been given more consideration in the defamation authorities: see para.46-050, below.

137 [1998] Q.B. 498 CA.

138 See para.42-014, above and 42-028, below, as to basic and exemplary damages respectively.

139 [1998] Q.B. 498 CA at 516E–F.

140 [2001] F.S.R. 188 CA.

*Metropolis*,[141] was also for assault and malicious prosecution by the police and the award of £6,000 in *Rowlands v Chief Constable of Merseyside Police*,[142] was for malicious prosecution in addition to false imprisonment by the police. On the unusual facts of *Ahmed v Shafique*,[143] where the defendants who were in business with the claimant procured his false arrest leading to his detention for 15 hours, the award of £2,000 general damages was supplemented by another £2,000 of aggravated damages to compensate for the humiliation of the arrest and the trauma suffered as a result of it by a man of good character. In *AT, NT, ML, AK v Dulghieru*,[144] already considered when dealing with assault[145] since there was not only false imprisonment but also assault by way of coerced sexual activity and substantial psychological harm, as much as £35,000 was awarded to each of two claimants by way of aggravated damages and £30,000 to each of the other two. In *R. (on the application of MK (Algeria)) v Secretary of State for the Home Department*,[146] an award of £17,500 for false imprisonment only, an unlawful detention of an asylum-seeker lasting for over three weeks, included aggravated damages of £5,000, the Court of Appeal saying that the case was pre-eminently one for aggravated damages as the secretary of state had acted in a high-handed manner. Later cases also involving the false imprisonment of asylum seekers have been heard in the Employment Appeal Tribunal, *R. (on the application of J) v Secretary of State for the Home Department*,[147] where the award of aggravated damages was reduced, *R. (on the application of M) v Secretary of State for the Home Department*,[148] where the award was split between basic damages and aggravated damages, and *R. (on the application of N) v Secretary of State for the Home Department*,[149] where aggravated damages were not in issue.

Aggravated damages of £5,000 were awarded in *AS v Secretary of State for the Home Department*,[150] where an unaccompanied asylum-seeking young person was unlawfully detained for 61 days. Aggravated damages of £30,000 were awarded in light of the aggravating factors in *Patel v Secretary of State for the Home Department*,[151] and aggravated damages of £2,300 (claimant 1) and £7,200 (claimant 2) were awarded in *Mohidin v Commissioner of Police of the Metropolis*,[152] where false imprisonment and assault by police officers was accompanied by racial abuse and humiliation.

Other than the most exceptional case, the outer limits of aggravated damages seem to be around the £35,000 mark for the extreme circumstances in *AT, NT, ML, AK v Dulghieru* (where they were coupled with exemplary damages). In *AXD v Home Office*,[153] aggravated damages of £25,000 were awarded and the absence of bad faith meant that the case fell short of the line for an award of exemplary

141 [2006] EWCA Civ 879 CA.
142 [2007] 1 W.L.R. 1065 CA.
143 [2009] EWHC 618 (QB).
144 [2009] EWHC 225 (QB).
145 At paras 42-001 (with the facts), 42-003 and 42-012, above.
146 [2010] EWCA Civ 980 CA.
147 [2011] EWHC 3073 (Admin).
148 [2011] EWHC 3667 (Admin).
149 [2012] EWHC 1031 (Admin).
150 [2015] EWHC 1331 (QB).
151 [2014] EWHC 501 (Admin).
152 [2015] EWHC 2740 (QB).
153 [2016] EWHC 1617 (QB).

damages. The factors justifying aggravated damages included (i) senior officials refraining from taking responsibility for the serious delays that were accumulating with the knowledge that the claimant was suffering from paranoid schizophrenia, (ii) sub-optimal treatment for his schizophrenia for nearly a year, (iii) release of the claimant into the community without a proper welfare plan in place which led to his inevitable institutionalisation, abuse of alcohol, and homelessness, and (iv) failure to provide the claimant with unpublished information relating to returns to Mogadishu.

It was also held in the conjoined appeals *Thompson* and *Hsu*, which opened the way to this flood of cases, that there should be a separate award for the element of aggravation. The court pointed out that this changed the practice at the time but thought that having separate awards would give greater transparency to the make up of the award.[154] However, concerns over having separate awards have since been expressed.[155] **42-027**

## 4. Exemplary Damages

The whole approach to exemplary damages was changed by the decision in *Rookes v Barnard*,[156] later approved in *Broome v Cassell & Co*,[157] and is treated in detail elsewhere.[158] Exemplary damages are now recoverable only if the circumstances of the case bring it within one of the three categories set out by Lord Devlin there, viz., first, where there is oppressive, arbitrary or unconstitutional conduct by government servants, second, where there is conduct calculated to result in profit and, third, where statute provides.[159] While false imprisonment can come within the second category because a profit-motivated false imprisonment is by no means inconceivable,[160] and an illustration of the use of the second common law category is now provided by *AT, NT, ML, AK v Dulghieru*,[161] with false imprisonment it is the first common law category, involving oppressive, arbitrary or unconstitutional conduct by government servants, which has dominated although it took some time for decisions to appear. First, in *Attorney General for St Christopher, Nevis and Anguilla v Reynolds*,[162] the Privy Council did not call in question the proposition, not disputed by the defendant, that unconstitutional action by the Governor of a group of Caribbean Islands leading to the claimant's ar- **42-028**

---

[154] [1998] Q.B. 498 CA at 516E. Separate awards continue to be made, as in *AS v Secretary of State for the Home Department* [2015] EWHC 1331 (QB) and in *Patel v Secretary of State for the Home Department* [2014] EWHC 501 (Admin): see paras 42-018 and 42-026, above.

[155] As, in the different context of a victimisation claim, by Underhill J in the Employment Appeal Tribunal in *Commissioner of Police of the Metropolis v Shaw* [2012] I.C.R. 464; [2012] I.R.L.R. 291 but, it is thought, unnecessarily. See *Shaw* and the discussion at para.43-014, below.

[156] [1964] A.C. 1129.

[157] [1972] A.C. 1027.

[158] See Ch.13, above.

[159] See paras 13-017 to 13-030, above. The further restriction introduced by the now overruled *A.B. v South West Services* [1993] Q.B. 507 CA (see para.13-011, above) never applied to false imprisonment cases since exemplary damages were early in evidence as *Huckle v Money* (1763) 2 Wils. K.B. 205 indicates.

[160] Contrast the cases at paras 13-022 to 13-025, above. It was assumed in *Sallows v Griffiths* [2001] F.S.R. 188 CA, a case of profit-motivated malicious arrest, that exemplary damages were possible. None were in fact awarded because the compensatory award was considered to be adequate punishment: see at para.13-041, above.

[161] [2009] EWHC 225 (QB) (facts at para.42-001 and amounts at para.42-012, above).

[162] [1980] A.C. 637.

rest and false imprisonment entitled him to exemplary damages under the first of Lord Devlin's categories.[163] Then, following the false imprisonment example of *Huckle v Money*,[164] one of the two earliest cases of an exemplary award,[165] the Court of Appeal in *Holden v Chief Constable of Lancashire*,[166] held that wrongful arrest by a police officer fell within the category of oppressive, arbitrary or unconstitutional action by servants of the government and that, accordingly, the question whether to award exemplary damages should have been left to the jury. Moreover, an exemplary award might be made where, as there, there was unconstitutional action constituted by the wrongful arrest without the need for additional oppressive behaviour; the three epithets in effect fell to be read disjunctively.[167] Exemplary damages for false imprisonment were also given[168] against the police for oppressive conduct in two combined appeals, *Thompson v Commissioner of Police of the Metropolis* and *Hsu v Commissioner of Police of the Metropolis*.[169] These decisions are particularly valuable as the Court of Appeal gave guidance on the amounts appropriate to award in such cases. Lord Woolf MR, delivering the judgment of the court, said that in this class of action the conduct must be particularly bad to justify as much as £25,000, and £50,000 should be regarded as the absolute maximum; where exemplary damages were appropriate they were unlikely to be less than £5,000.[170] The Court of Appeal endorsed an award of £25,000 in *Thompson* but reduced the jury's award of £200,000 to £15,000 in *Hsu*.[171] Exemplary damages, in the amount of £15,000, have now been awarded for arbitrary and oppressive conduct of immigration officers in *Patel v Secretary of State for the Home Department*.[172]

---

163 [1980] A.C. 637 at 662F–G.
164 (1763) 2 Wils. K.B. 205.
165 See para.13-002, above.
166 [1987] Q.B. 380 CA.
167 [1987] Q.B. 380 CA at 388C. It was also said that exemplary damages did not have to be awarded merely because a case fell within one of Lord Devlin's categories; it was a matter of discretion: at 388D and 389B.
168 And as a separate award: see para.52-047, below.
169 [1998] Q.B. 498 CA.
170 [1998] Q.B. 498 CA at 517C.
171 It would seem that no exemplary damages were awarded in *Manley v Commissioner of Police for the Metropolis* [2006] EWCA Civ 879 CA (false imprisonment together with assault and malicious prosecution) because the liability of the commissioner of police was vicarious but *Rowlands v Chief Constable of Merseyside Police* [2007] 1 W.L.R. 1065 CA (false imprisonment and malicious prosecution) has since decided that exemplary damages may be awarded against a chief constable whose liability was vicarious. Vicarious liability for exemplary damages is considered at: paras 13-045 to 13-047, above.
172 [2014] EWHC 501 (Admin) at [343], and the case at para.42-018, above.

CHAPTER 43

# STATUTORY TORTS: DISCRIMINATION AND HARASSMENT

TABLE OF CONTENTS



A comparatively slim chapter may now be devoted to damages in the statutory torts of discrimination and of harassment as the cases thereon have become too numerous to be accommodated, as formerly, in an extensive footnote.[1] There is also an issue related to interest given on discrimination awards, formerly in the chapter on interest, to be dealt with. It deserves more than a footnote. **43-001**

## I. DISCRIMINATION

The discrimination claims with which we are primarily concerned originally appeared in three statutes, the Sex Discrimination Act 1975, the Race Relations Act 1976 and the Disability Discrimination Act 1995. All three have been repealed and replaced by the Equality Act 2010 which makes the same provisions for the damages. In addition, there is the claim for compensation made available by the Employment Rights Act 1996 to one who has suffered detriment as a result of making a protected public interest disclosure, colloquially called whistle-blowing.[2] In *Commissioner of Police of the Metropolis v Shaw*,[3] a case involving the victimisa- **43-002**

[1] Another statutory tort appears to have been invented by the Data Protection Act 1998 but there is no case law on the damages recoverable other than the Court of Appeal decision in *Halliday v Creative Consumer Finance Ltd* [2013] EWCA Civ 333 CA. The Act was introduced in implementation of the European Union Directive 95/46/EC and provides by s.13 for compensation to be paid to anyone suffering damage caused by a contravention of the Act's requirements by a data controller. In *Halliday* the Court of Appeal awarded the claimant £750 for distress.

[2] This was introduced into the Employment Rights Act by the Public Interest Disclosure Act 1998 as Pt IVA.

[3] [2012] I.C.R. 464, [2012] I.R.L.R. 291 EAT.

tion[4] of "a statutorily protected whistle-blower", Underhill J stated that subjecting the whistle-blower to the detriment was to be treated as a statutory tort and that, being a form of discrimination, the damages should be awarded on the same basis as awards in claims for discrimination *stricto sensu*.[5] In this he was following His Honour Judge Ansell in *Virgo Fidelis Senior School v Boyle*,[6] who had earlier held that damages for a whistle-blower should be assessed as they are in regular discrimination claims.[7]

**43-003** Discrimination in the employment field in all three of the aspects of sex, race and disability dominate the cases. As for whistle-blower claims they necessarily come from the employment field as only employee whistle-blowers are protected. The result, therefore, is that most of the cases start in the Employment Tribunal rather than in one of the regular civil courts, generally the County Court.

## 1. HEADS OF DAMAGE

**43-004** The damages awarded in the statutory torts involving discrimination are generally only for the non-pecuniary loss by way of injury to feelings. For this reason the pattern in this book of considering pecuniary loss and then non-pecuniary is here reversed.

### (1) Non-pecuniary loss

**43-005** All three statutes—Sex Discrimination Act 1975, Race Relations Act 1976 and Disability Discrimination Act 1995—specifically provided that compensation for injured feelings may be included in the damages, and the Equality Act 2010, which has repealed and taken over from them, provides similarly in s.119(4) that an award of damages in respect of discrimination "may include compensation for injured feelings".[8]

**43-006** As to amounts awarded there was much variety in the earlier days but there is no longer any need to set out these[9] as in 2002 in *Chief Constable of West Yorkshire*

---

[4] It is the habit of the courts to speak of "victimisation" of the employee who suffers as a result of his disclosure. Indeed in *Shaw* the summary at the beginning of the report of Underhill J's judgment is headed "Victimisation and Discrimination". And reg.4 of the now repealed (by the Equality Act 2010) Employment Equality (Sexual Orientation) Regulations was entitled "Discrimination by way of Victimisation". Victimisation is occasionally mentioned in other contexts, as in *Ministry of Defence v Fletcher* [2010] I.R.L.R. 25 at [25] (sex discrimination) and in *Rayment v Ministry of Defence* [2010] EWHC 218 (QB) at [1] (harassment).

[5] [2012] I.C.R. 464; [2012] I.R.L.R. 291 at [13].

[6] [2004] I.C.R. 1210; [2004] I.R.L.R. 268 EAT.

[7] And see his comment, at [45], that "detriment suffered by 'whistle-blowers' should normally be regarded by Tribunals as a very serious breach of discrimination legislation". Another whistle-blower case is *Niekrash v South London Healthcare NHS Trust* unreported 7 March 2012.

[8] By contrast, in *R. v Secretary of State for Transport, Ex p. Factortame Ltd (No.7)* [2001] 1 W.L.R. 942 TCC, one of the Factortame cases involving discrimination by the United Kingdom against the owners of foreign fishing vessels, it was held that art.52 of the European Communities Treaty, which gives the right to nationals of one Member State to establish themselves in another Member State, was concerned only with economic loss. So too the Equal Pay Act 1970 (now repealed and replaced by the Equality Act 2010), which was concerned with countering discrimination of female employees in matters of pay, was held in *Newcastle-upon-Tyne City Council v Allan* [2005] I.C.R.1170 EAT not to encompass recovery of damages for non-pecuniary loss.

[9] They can be found in the 18th edition of this work.

*Police v Vento (No.2)*,[10] the Court of Appeal, concerned by a discrimination case in which an employment tribunal had awarded £100,000 for injury to feelings,[11] introduced guidelines. The court identified three broad bands for compensation for injured feelings, a top band of £15,000 to £25,000 for very serious cases, a middle band of £5,000 to £15,000 for moderately serious cases and a band of £500 to £5,000 appropriate for less serious cases, such as where the act of discrimination is an isolated or one-off occurrence. Only in the most exceptional cases, it was said, would it be appropriate to award more than £25,000, and awards of less than £500 were to be avoided as they risked appearing derisory.[12] In 2009 in *Da'Bell v National Society for the Prevention of Cruelty to Children*,[13] which involved disability discrimination, the Employment Appeal Tribunal held that the range for injured feelings damages should be adjusted upwards for inflation as calculated by the Retail Prices Index, giving a top band from £18,000 to £30,000, a middle band from £6,000 to £18,000, and the lowest band running up to £6,000.[14] It may soon be time for a further updating but, as was said in *Bullimore v Pothecary Witham Weld*,[15] there is no need for the court, as long as it takes inflation into account, explicitly to perform an uprating exercise when referring to the decided cases or to the guidelines that have been laid down.[16]

The three bands have stood the test of time and the courts continue to pay attention to them. In *Gilbank v Miles*,[17] for blatant and repeated acts of sexual discrimination in employment, which the Employment Tribunals regarded as of a most serious nature, their award was at the top end of the top band, then standing at £25,000. This was upheld by the Court of Appeal as being not manifestly excessive or wrong in law even though more serious cases could be envisaged.[18] Most recently and at the other end of the scale is *Ministry of Defence v Kemeh*.[19] For a one-off racist remark made to an army chef, who was black, by his superior officer the Employment Tribunal placed its award in the middle band, at £12,000. This was held by the Employment Appeal Tribunal to be wrong in principle and manifestly excessive, and an award at the top end of the lowest band, now at £6,000, was substituted.[20] On appeal, and as predicted in an earlier edition of this work, the Court **43-007**

---

10 [2003] I.C.R. 318 CA.

11 Together with aggravated damages of £25,000; see [2003] I.C.R. 318 CA at [46] and [47].

12 The Employment Tribunal in *Vento* had awarded £50,000 for injury to feelings, reduced by the Employment Appeal Tribunal and further reduced by the Court of Appeal to £18,000.

13 [2010] I.R.L.R. 19.

14 [2010] I.R.L.R. 19 at [44].

15 [2011] I.R.L.R. 18.

16 [2011] I.R.L.R. 18 at [31]. Cases of discrimination heard in the Employment Tribunal do not attract the 10 per cent uplift in damages for nonpecuniary loss introduced by *Simmons v Castle* [2013] 1 W.L.R. 1239 CA. It was so held in *De Souza v Vinci Construction UK Ltd* March 2015 EAT, the reasons for bringing in this uplift (for which see para.40-280, below) having no application to the Employment Tribunal. See too para.5-003 fn.4, above.

17 [2006] I.C.R.1297 CA.

18 See [2006] I.C.R.1297 CA at [42] and [66]. *Ministry of Defence v Fletcher* [2010] I.R.L.R. 25, which involved sexual discrimination of a female army recruit, is another case of an award for injured feelings at the top end of the top band, by then raised to £30,000. This award of the Employment Tribunal was not appealed, though it was thought in the circumstances to be high.

19 [2013] Eq. L.R. 605.

20 [2013] Eq. L.R. 605 at [19].

of Appeal endorsed the reduction, commenting that there was no justification for a one-off offensive comment being placed in the middle band.[21]

## (2) Pecuniary loss

**43-008** Discrimination cases allowing recovery for pecuniary losses, whether by way of earnings lost or expenses incurred, are hard to find. This is for two reasons. The one reason is that discrimination outside the employment field seldom produces a financial setback. But there can be recovery for pecuniary loss, both inside and outside the employment field, if it is shown, as with the loss of earnings in *H.M. Prison Service v Salmon*,[22] where the stress caused by the discrimination had forced the employee into leaving. The other reason is that within the employment field claims for discrimination may well be combined with claims for unfair dismissal, leading to the recovery of the pecuniary loss in the unfair dismissal claim and the recovery of the non-pecuniary injury to feelings, not available in unfair dismissal,[23] in the discrimination claim.[24] Sometimes, however, with claims for discrimination and unfair dismissal the whole matter is dealt with under the umbrella of the discrimination claim, as in *Chief Constable of West Yorkshire Police v Vento (No.2)*,[25] before the Employment Tribunals,[26] where there were awards for injured feelings and for loss of earnings.[27] That, as in all other torts, pecuniary loss is an obvious head of damage is underlined by the statute itself since to the provision in s.119(4) of the Equality Act 2010 that an award of damages may include compensation for injured feelings there is added "(whether or not it includes compensation on any other basis)," repeating what had been said in the former, repealed statutes.[28]

## (3) Interest

**43-009** Should the discrimination statutes make no specific provision as to interest on the damages awarded, then presumably the common law rules as to interest apply. This would allow interest in the normal way on pecuniary loss, if there is any, but on the all-important, because ubiquitous, non-pecuniary loss by way of injury to feelings interest would be denied if the courts were to adopt the approach emerging from the case of *Saunders v Edwards*,[29] that in torts affecting the person, outside personal injury, interest will not be awarded on damages for non-pecuniary loss,[30]

---

21 [2014] EWCA Civ 91 at [59]. An earlier case of a one-off racially abusive remark is *British Telecommunications Plc v Reid* [2004] I.R.L.R. 327 CA where the Employment Tribunal's basic award of £6,000 for injury to feelings was upheld by the Court of Appeal. There were in addition aggravated damages, for which see para.43-013, below.

22 [2001] I.R.L.R. 425.

23 See para.31-003, above.

24 As in *O'Donoghue v Redcar & Cleveland Borough Council* [2001] I.R.L.R. 615 CA and *Atos Origin IT Services UK Ltd v Haddock* [2005] I.C.R. 277.

25 [2002] I.R.L.R. 177.

26 The case in which, on appeal, the Court of Appeal was to lay down guidelines for the level of damages for the non-pecuniary loss: see para.43-006, above.

27 With, in the earnings award, deduction of State benefits paid by way of income support and mortgage interest.

28 Sex Discrimination Act 1975 s.66(4); Race Relations Act 1976 s.57(4); Disability Discrimination Act 1996 s.25(2) and s.28V(2).

29 [1987] 1 W.L.R. 1116 CA.

30 For details see paras 19-054 to 19-056, above.

and the discrimination torts are undoubtedly torts affecting the person. The position appears to be that, where the claim made is not in the context of employment where, as we shall see, legislation on interest has intervened, the cases do not consider giving interest on the award for injury to feelings. This is all to the good. It is true of claims brought both under the Equality Act 2010[31] and under the former statutes which it has taken over.

The position is unfortunately different when the discrimination is in the employment field. This is because the legislation has expressly permitted awards of interest on compensation for injured feelings in employment discrimination cases. Historically, this came about by statutory instrument in 1996 for the discrimination statutes now repealed. As we have seen, the three discrimination statutes from the beginning stated that the damages awarded under them may include compensation for injured feelings, and statutory instrument then followed providing that these awards when made by an employment tribunal, awards which are generally only for the non-pecuniary loss by way of injured feelings, may include interest.[32] The result has naturally been that over the years from 1996 employment tribunals have been adding interest to their awards for the injured feelings of claimants discriminated against, and there have been many such cases.[33] From October 2010 the Equality Act of that year took over, ss.119 and 124, taken together, providing for the award of compensation for injured feelings, with s.139(1)(a) providing for the making of regulations enabling an employment tribunal to include interest in awards in proceedings under the Act.[34] Cases awarding interest have continued.[35] In none of these cases, whether before or after the Equality Act, has the propriety of adding interest in awards for injured feelings been questioned or been in issue. **43-010**

This position has since worsened. The Regulations of 1996 had specified the special investment account rate,[36] then standing at 6 per cent, as the rate to be applied by the Employment Tribunal, and these Regulations have been amended in **43-011**

[31] As an instance see *Campbell v Thomas Cook Tour Operations Ltd* [2013] Eq. L. R. 658 (disability discrimination) where the court concerned itself only with whether it was appropriate to apply the recently introduced 10 per cent uplift in damages for non-pecuniary loss (for which see para.5-003, above): at [35] and [58].

[32] Employment Tribunals (Interest on Awards in Discrimination Cases) Regulations (SI 1996/2803); see preamble (2).

[33] For illustrations of reported cases following on the 1996 Regulations see *ICTS (UK) Ltd v Tchoula* [2000] I.R.L.R. 643 EAT; *Derby Specialist Fabrication Ltd v Burton* [2001] 2 All E.R. 840 EAT; *Doshoki v Draeger Ltd* [2002] I.R.L.R. 340 EAT.

[34] It has proved very difficult to discover in this impenetrable piece of poorly drafted legislation what gives the entitlement to continue awarding interest since no regulation has so far been made for the purposes of the Equality Act under s.139(1)(a) and interest cannot be awarded under the Sex, Race and Disability Discrimination Acts as by Sch.27, Pt 1, para.1 they are all repealed. The answer is to be found not in the Equality Act itself but hidden in a very long Table appearing as para.1 of Sch.7 to art.21 of the Equality Act (Commencement No.4, Savings, Consequential, Transitional, Transitory and Incidental Provisions and Revocation) Order (SI 2010/2317), it being there revealed, once one has managed to find the statutory instrument and to examine its details, that the provisions as to interest in the 1996 Regulations made under powers contained in specified sections of the Race and Disability Discrimination Acts (no mention is made of sections in the Sex Discrimination Act) are to be treated as made under s.139 of the Equality Act. The legislation has run away with itself in complication and obscurity.

[35] For illustrations of reported cases since the Equality Act came into force see *Allen v Hounga* [2011] Eq. L.R. 569 EAT; *Bungay v Saini* [2011] Eq. L.R. 1130 EAT; *The Newcastle upon Tyne Hospitals Foundation Trust v Bagley* [2012] Eq. L.R. 634 EAT; *Hackney London Borough Council v Sivandan* [2011] I.C.R. 1374 EAT; later on appeal at [2013] 2 All E.R. 940 CA.

[36] See Reg.3(2).

2013 to substitute the judgment rate,[37] still standing at 8 per cent though it should have been moved down long ago. No doubt this change has been influenced by the special investment account rate being now at the all time low of 0.5 per cent[38] but that is no good reason for substituting a rate which is inappropriately high even for interest on pecuniary losses. The 8 per cent awarded for non-pecuniary loss to persons suffering discrimination in employment compares oddly with the 2 per cent awarded for non-pecuniary loss to persons physically injured, however catastrophically.[39]

## 2. Aggravated Damages

**43-012** With non-pecuniary loss by way of injury to feelings being at the centre of the damages for these statutory torts of discrimination, aggravated damages, which are available only for injury to feelings, are very much in the picture. It is clear that the three bands of damages influentially laid down as guidelines by the Court of Appeal in *Chief Constable of West Yorkshire Police v Vento (No.2)*,[40] do not include aggravated damages because not only did the court so say[41] but also the award of aggravated damages was upheld though much reduced.[42]

**43-013** Aggravated damages, as from other torts of intention we have seen and will see, are awarded where the injury to the claimant's feelings is increased by the flagrancy, malevolence and the particularly unacceptable nature of the defendant's behaviour.[43] For discrimination this is neatly illustrated—and there are quite a number of illustrations[44]—by *British Telecommunications Plc v Reid*.[45] A one-off racially abusive remark was held, as we have seen,[46] to merit a basic award of £6,000 for injury to feelings, but as the injury to feelings was exacerbated by the indignity to the employee claimant of having to undergo a totally unjustified investigation and by the employer's highhanded and insulting conduct, £2,000 in aggravated damages was added. As to the amounts generally awarded, these clearly will vary with the circumstances, but, as would be expected, the courts only countenance aggravated damages awards which fall well below the amount of the basic award.

---

37 Employment Tribunals (Interest on Awards in Discrimination Cases) (Amendment) Regulations (SI 2013/1669), substituting a new reg.3(2) in the 1996 Regulations.

38 See para.19-129, above. "We add interest but the rate has plummeted to 0.5 per cent": the Employment Tribunal in *Newcastle upon Tyne Hospitals Foundation Trust v Bagley* [2012] Eq. L.R. 634 at [58] *in fin*.

39 See paras 19-127 and 19-131, above.

40 [2003] I.C.R. 318 CA; see para.43-006, above.

41 [2003] I.C.R. 318 CA at [67].

42 [2003] I.C.R. 318 CA at [2] and [69].

43 Including conduct and behaviour after a discriminatory dismissal from employment: *Bungay v Saini* [2011] Eq. L.R. 1130 EAT. Of course in many cases the circumstances are such that no claim is made for aggravated damages. Alternatively, a claim is made but it fails. Thus the Employment Appeal Tribunal eliminated the aggravated damages award in *Newcastle upon Tyne Hospitals NHS Foundation Trust v Bagley* [2012] Eq. L.R. 634 and upheld the refusal to award aggravated damages in *Niekrash v South London Healthcare NHS Trust* unreported 7 March 2012. It may be, however, that, in line with what Underhill J was proposing in *Commissioner of Police of the Metropolis v Shaw* [2012] I.C.R. 464; [2012] I.R.L.R. 291 (for which see the following paragraph), an element of aggravation had been included in the basic awards since both courts say that they are applying and following *Shaw*.

44 See the footnote at the end of this paragraph.

45 [2004] I.R.L.R. 327 CA.

46 In the footnote at the end of para.43-007, above.

Thus while today the basic award can, under *Vento* principles, run up to £30,000, aggravated damages, as a fraction of the basic award, are more than contained within a figure of £10,000.[47]

It has long been customary for the courts to arrive at separate awards for the basic element and the aggravating element in the damages, usually by producing separate figures for the two or by giving a total figure which is said to include a specified amount for the aggravated damages. However, recently Underhill J in *Commissioner of Police of the Metropolis v Shaw*,[48] a whistle-blower case,[49] adverted in a full and valuable judgment to what he regarded as the dangers of having separate awards for injured feelings and aggravated damages, these being the danger of double counting[50] and the danger of the aggravated damages being thought of as punitive. Underhill J would have liked to follow the Scots law in which aggravated damages are not awarded as such but, instead, the aggravating features are taken into account in arriving at a single award for injury to feelings. Yet, since the Court of Appeal has time and again approved separate awards of aggravated damages, adopting the Scots approach was, he said, not a course open to him at Employment Appeal Tribunal level. As far as he could go was to suggest that it would be a healthy reminder of the true situation if in future aggravated damages awards were formulated as a sub-heading of injury to feelings rather than as a wholly distinct head of damages.[51] What the Court of Appeal may make of this is not yet known but it is suggested that there is no need to adopt Underhill J's view. If the purpose of aggravated damages, which, as set out in the text above,[52] is to compensate for the increased injury to the claimant's feelings caused where there is particularly bad conduct on the part of the defendant, is kept firmly in mind,[53] there should be neither double counting nor confusion with exemplary damages. Moreover, amalgamating the aggravating damages with the basic award which has to be in line with *Vento* principles would make it difficult to tell if the *Vento* principles have been followed.[54] **43-014**

The concerns of Underhill J are, however, highlighted by situations in which the **43-015**

---

47 Apart from *British Telecommunications Plc v Reid* in the text of this paragraph, the cases are: *ICTS (UK) Ltd v Tchoula* [2000] I.R.L.R. 643 (discrimination in employment: £10,000 to include £2,500 aggravated, substituting for a higher award); *HM Prison Service v Salmon* [2001] I.R.L.R. 425 (sexual discrimination: £20,000 to include £5,000 aggravated); *Chief Constable of West Yorkshire Police v Vento (No.2)* (sexual discrimination: basic award reduced from £50,000 to £18,000, a further £15,000 for aggravated reduced to £5,000); *Ministry of Defence v Fletcher* [2010] I.R.L.R. 25 (sexual discrimination: basic award of £30,000 not appealed, a further £20,000 for aggravated reduced to £8,000).

48 [2012] I.C.R. 464; [2012] I.R.L.R. 291.

49 For the link between whistle-blowing and discrimination see para.43-002, above.

50 In *Ministry of Defence v Fletcher* [2010] I.R.L.R. 25 the need to avoid double counting was again stressed.

51 [2012] I.C.R. 464 at [28].

52 In the preceding paragraph.

53 Indeed Underhill J agrees with this, saying correctly that "Tribunals should always bear in mind that the ultimate question is 'what additional distress was caused to this particular claimant, in the particular circumstances of this case, by the aggravating feature(s) in question' ": at [2012] I.C.R. 464 at [24].

54 Somewhat akin to the Underhill J approach is that of the Court of Appeal in *Richardson v Howie* [2004] EWCA Civ 1127 CA holding that in cases of assault it is in general inappropriate to award aggravated damages on top of, and in addition to, damages for injured feelings (see at para.42-004, above). This decision is thought misguided and has not had much of an impact (see para.42-007, above). It has fortunately not been brought into consideration in the discrimination cases of damages. Yet it has been addressed in the harassment damages case of *Choudhury v Martins* [2007] EWCA Civ 1379 CA (at para.43-022, below).

award of aggravated damages is made for injury to feelings caused by discrimination and harassment where the basic award is made for a different tort such as assault or false imprisonment. In *Mohidin v Commissioner of Police of the Metropolis*,[55] the two successful claimants sought basic and aggravated damages for false imprisonment and assault by police officers. Their claim for aggravated damages relied upon racial abuse and humiliation inflicted by the police officers. The basic awards for false imprisonment and assault were, for each claimant, £200 (false imprisonment, claimant 1) and £4,500 (false imprisonment, claimant 2). To these basic awards were added aggravated damages, calculated in accordance with the *Vento* principles for basic awards of discrimination, of £2,300 (claimant 1) and £7,200 (claimant 2).

### 3. EXEMPLARY DAMAGES

**43-016** That exemplary damages can be awarded in the statutory torts of discrimination was early accepted by the Court of Appeal in *Alexander v Home Office*,[56] itself a case of racial discrimination. While no exemplary award was made there, one did appear soon after in *Bradford City Metropolitan Council v Arora*,[57] where the discrimination was on account of both sex and race. Over the years successful claims for exemplary awards in discrimination have been uncommon. This is because the discrimination has to bring the case within Lord Devlin's category, as announced by him in *Rookes v Barnard*,[58] concerning government servants and their oppressive, arbitrary or unconstitutional conduct, and not only are discrimination claims not in the employment field, and many within it, brought against other than government servants but also it is difficult to show, in claims that are brought against government servants, conduct justifying an award of exemplary damages. As Slade J said, when she set aside an exemplary award of £50,000 by the Employment Tribunal in *Ministry of Defence v Fletcher*,[59] a case of discrimination against a female army recruit by army officers, the authorities on exemplary damages establish that they are to be reserved for the most serious abuses of governmental power.[60]

## II. HARASSMENT

**43-017** The Protection from Harassment Act 1997 has survived the myriad legislative repeals of the Equality Act 2010, no doubt because its subject matter is not equality. The material on damages is not very extensive as the major cases, in the Court of Appeal and the House of Lords, have not addressed damages but have dealt with such questions as what amounts to harassment[61] and who can be sued for harassment.[62] There being similarities with discrimination, the structure in treat-

55 [2015] EWHC 2740 (QB).
56 [1988] 1 W.L.R. 968 CA.
57 [1991] 2 Q.B. 547 CA.
58 [1964] A.C. 1129. For Lord Devlin's categories see paras 13-017 and following, above.
59 [2010] I.R.L.R. 25.
60 [2010] I.R.L.R. 25 at [115].
61 *Ferguson v British Gas Trading Ltd* [2009] EWCA Civ 46 CA; *Veakins v Kier Islington Ltd* [2009] EWCA 1288 CA.
62 *Majorowski v Guy's and St Thomas's NHS Trust* [2007] 1 A.C. 224 (vicarious liability).

ing discrimination damages, in particular the placing of non-pecuniary loss before pecuniary, is followed.

## 1. HEADS OF DAMAGE

### (1) Non-pecuniary loss

Damages for non-pecuniary loss by way of injury to feelings dominate in claims for harassment under the Protection from Harassment Act 1997 in the same way as they do in discrimination cases. The awards here tend to refer to damages for anxiety, this being because the statute, by s.3(2), provides that damages may be awarded "for any anxiety caused by the harassment". This is in effect the injured feelings with which we are fully familiar. **43-018**

As to the amounts awarded, variation abounds. This is inevitable as in the cases where damages have been in issue the harassment has come in many forms. While *Majorowski v Guy's and St Thomas's NHS Trust*,[63] was not concerned with damages for harassment,[64] it did elicit the comment from Lord Nicholls that "awards of damages for anxiety under the 1997 Act will normally be modest".[65] In *S&D Property Investments Ltd v Nisbet*,[66] also, it was said that awards should probably be modest[67]; an award of £7,000 was made for harassment in pursuance of an unpaid debt. In *Rayment v Ministry of Defence*,[68] with harassment in the form of persistent, offensive, abusive, intimidating, bullying, humiliating, insulting behaviour of a woman soldier by army officers,[69] an award of £5,500 was made.[70] In *Choudhury v Martins*,[71] where the harassment started with the defendant's deliberate collision with the claimant's car and continued in a number of ways, the Court of Appeal upheld the judge's award of £10,000 while stating it thought this to be on the generous side.[72] Two cases of higher awards, *Maisto v Kyrgiannakis*,[73] and *WXY v Gewanter*,[74] may appear to be out of line with the commendation of modest awards. *Maisto* was a case of persistent harassment by a 32-year-old man following and contacting a young woman of 21 wherever she went, both at home and abroad, over a prolonged period, so that she found it difficult to carry on her life of study. The judge awarded £15,000. In *WXY* the harassment consisted of the posting on the internet of information about the private life of the claimant causing her much distress and, no doubt, anxiety. The award, before aggravation, was just short of £20,000.[75] This high sum can, however, be explained by the fact that the claim was primarily for the misuse of private information with which the harassment was said to be part and parcel, not amounting to a separate claim.[76] **43-019**

---

63 [2007] 1 A.C. 224.
64 See para.43-017, above.
65 [2007] 1 A.C. 224 at [29].
66 [2009] EWHC 1726 Ch.
67 [2009] EWHC 1726 Ch at [75] and [76].
68 [2010] EWHC 218 (QB).
69 [2010] EWHC 218 (QB) at [1].
70 [2010] EWHC 218 (QB) at [88].
71 [2007] EWCA Civ 1379 CA.
72 [2007] EWCA Civ 1379 CA at [24].
73 [2012] EWHC 4084 (QB).
74 [2013] EWHC 589 (QB).
75 Aggravated damages increased it by £5,000.
76 For the primary aspect of the claim see para.47-008, below.

**43-020** No guidelines on amounts to award along the lines of *Chief Constable of West Yorkshire Police v Vento (No.2)*,[77] with its three bands or brackets of figures for compensation for injured feelings in discrimination claims,[78] have been made for harassment. The courts have therefore been found sometimes to turn to the Vento guidelines for assistance, which may lead to awards going beyond the modest. This indeed was what happened in *Maisto v Kyrgiannakis*,[79] which we have just looked at.[80] The judge was taken to *Vento* and his award of £15,000 was based on his considering the case before him to be a serious one though not in the highest of the *Vento* brackets. Yet it may be questioned whether the precise application of *Vento*, where the figures now go up to £30,000 with middle-of-the-road cases going up to £18,000 is consistent with damages being modest. There is much to be said for the view expressed by Nicol J in *S&D Property Investments Ltd v Nisbet*.[81] He thought it would be wrong simply to apply the *Vento* bands to harassment cases since compensation for discrimination necessarily involves an award for the humiliation of being treated differently on impermissible grounds, which is not a necessary feature of a harassment claim.[82]

### (2) Pecuniary loss

**43-021** Little need be said here as there is no doubt that there can be, as in every tort, recovery for pecuniary losses. The statute specifically sets this out, s.3(2) providing that "damages may be awarded for .... any financial loss resulting from the harassment." Little need be said also because cases illustrating such a recovery are not yet to be found.[83]

## 2. AGGRAVATED DAMAGES

**43-022** As with discrimination,[84] so with harassment: non-pecuniary loss by way of injury to feelings being at the centre of the damages awarded, aggravated damages are a distinct possibility. Yet the few cases on harassment damages that there are to date reveal no awards of, or indeed claims for, aggravated damages.[85] Therefore all that can be done is to point to the various matters already considered in relation to aggravated damages in discrimination claims[86] as in general these are equally relevant for aggravated damages in harassment damages claims. Thus it

77 [2003] I.C.R. 318 CA.

78 For which see para.43-006, above.

79 [2012] EWHC 4084 (QB).

80 In the preceding paragraph.

81 [2009] EWHC 1726 Ch. See the case in the preceding paragraph.

82 [2009] EWHC 1726 Ch. at [77]. The award in *Saxton v Bayliss* unreported 31 January 2014 Central London County Court, for harassment of an old lady by her very unpleasant neighbours causing her profound distress, the neighbours mounting a prolonged and vicious campaign to get her out of her house and thereby eliminate her right of way over their property, was £25,000. It would have been even higher in the absence of an additional exemplary award of £10,000.

83 About all that can be pointed to is a recovery of a small amount of travelling expenses in *Rayment v Ministry of Defence* [2010] EWHC 218 (QB).

84 For aggravated damages in discrimination see paras 43-012 and following, above.

85 Aggravated damages do make an appearance in *WXY v Gewanter* [2013] EWHC 589 but as we have seen (at para.43-019, above) the case is more concerned with misuse of confidential information than with harassment.

86 See para.43-013, above.

needs to be kept in mind that aggravated damages are awarded where the injury to the claimant's feelings is increased by the flagrancy, malevolence and the particularly unacceptable nature of the defendant's behaviour, so that double counting is prevented and a confusion with exemplary damages aimed at punishment avoided. Also the courts are likely only to countenance aggravated damages awards which fall well below the amount of the basic award. And as with discrimination, the practice will be for the courts to arrive at separate awards for the basic element and for the aggravating element in the damages, usually by producing separate figures for the two or by giving a total figure which is said to include a specified amount for the aggravated damages.[87] On this last point there is one harassment case of relevance, *Choudhury v Martins*.[88] The Court of Appeal in *Richardson v Howie*,[89] had opined that at least in a case of assault, which *Richardson* was, aggravated damages on top of, and in addition to, damages for injured feelings should not generally be awarded.[90] While this decision is thought to be flawed and has had little impact,[91] it did receive support by the Court of Appeal soon after in *Choudhury*.[92] Little, if anything, fortunately has been heard of this in the context of harassment since.

## 3. EXEMPLARY DAMAGES

Exemplary damages have not yet surfaced in harassment cases. For this to happen one needs to have a situation where the defendant in the harassment claim falls within the class of government servants and whose conduct is oppressive, arbitrary or unconstitutional, thus bringing the case within the categories for exemplary damages set out by Lord Devlin in *Rookes v Barnard*.[93] This is far less likely with harassment than with discrimination[94] but, if given a suitable case, exemplary damages could be awarded. **43-023**

87 For the position with discrimination see para.43-013, above.
88 [2007] EWCA Civ 1379 CA.
89 [2004] EWCA Civ 1127 CA.
90 See the case at paras 42-004 and 42-005, above.
91 See the discussion at para.42-006, above.
92 Primarily by Sir Anthony Clarke MR: see [2007] EWCA Civ 1379 CA at [27] and [28].
93 [1964] A.C. 1129. For these categories see paras 13-017 and following, above.
94 For the position with discrimination see para.43-016, above.

Chapter 44

# MALICIOUS INSTITUTION OF LEGAL PROCEEDINGS

Table of Contents



**44-001** Formerly, for a person either to institute legal proceedings maliciously or to promote legal proceedings with which he has no concern could lead to tortious liability for abuse of process, in the one case for malicious prosecution and in the other for maintenance.[1] Statute[2] has rendered maintenance no longer tortious[3] so that there only remains malicious prosecution, together with its cognate torts.

## 1. Types of Actionable Damage

**44-002** For the defendant to institute certain types of legal proceedings against the claimant maliciously and without reasonable and probable cause is actionable, but only on proof of certain types of damage. The types of proceedings and the types of damage form the two sides of the same coin, since it is because these kinds of damage flow from these kinds of legal proceedings that they are made actionable in the first place, and these kinds of damage are then in all cases presumed to flow from these kinds of legal proceedings.[4] According to Lord Holt in the leading case of *Savile v Roberts*[5]:

> "There are three sorts of damage, any of which would be sufficient ground to support this action. (1) The damage to a man's fame, as if the matter whereof he is accused be scandalous … (2) Such as are done to the person; as where a man is put in danger to lose his life,

---

1 Including champerty, which is a form of maintenance.

2 Criminal Law Act 1967 s.14(1).

3 Should the former authorities on maintenance prove of any assistance by way of analogy, they are all dealt with at paras 862 to 864 of the 12th edition (1961) of this work.

4 Contrast Bowen LJ in *Quartz Hill Gold Mining Co v Eyre* (1883) 11 Q.B.D. 674 CA at 693: "I therefore answer the two first questions—whether this action will lie, and whether it will lie without further proof of special damage—in the following manner: I think that the action will lie, for the reason that special damage is involved in the very institution of the proceedings … for the purpose of winding up a going concern."

5 (1699) 1 Ld. Raym. 374 at 378.

> or limb, or liberty. (3) Damage to a man's property, as where he is forced to spend his money in necessary charges to acquit himself of the crime of which he is accused."

This statement has been accepted ever since as authoritative.[6]

The satisfaction of one or other of these conditions points to what kinds of legal proceedings are actionable. In the first place, most criminal prosecutions are actionable as satisfying all three conditions. But there may be certain criminal prosecutions which satisfy none, i.e. do not involve scandal or attack the accused's fair fame, can only result in a fine, and in which the accused if successful can recover costs. However, with the decision of the Court of Appeal in *Berry v British Transport Commission*,[7] that the additional costs incurred by a claimant in criminal proceedings beyond the costs awarded constitute legal damage sufficient to ground the action, it may be that all criminal prosecutions are to be regarded as satisfying the third condition.[8] In the second place, and conversely, most civil actions and proceedings are not actionable as they satisfy none of the three conditions,[9] at least as long as it is held that the additional costs incurred by a party beyond assessed costs do not constitute legal damage which will ground an action.[10] Exceptionally, there are some civil proceedings which have been held to suffice, namely petitions to have a trader adjudicated a bankrupt[11] and petitions to have a company wound up as insolvent.[12] Condition (1) is satisfied in these, for the very allegations involve damage to the fair fame of the person assailed, which cannot be afterwards repaired by the failure of the proceedings. Thirdly, there is malicious arrest of the claimant by the judicial process[13]; here at least condition (2) must be satisfied. And fourth and last is malicious execution against the property of the claimant by judicial process[14]; condition (3) will be satisfied in all such cases. Malicious arrest and malicious execution are not given separate consideration here: problems on damages will find similar solutions to those propounded by the courts in malicious prosecution cases. Whether in these cases damages can be recovered in respect of the heads of loss which would themselves not ground the action is not too clear. Such would be injury to feelings, and the extra costs involved in bankruptcy and liquidation proceedings.[15] **44-003**

## 2. PARTICULAR TORTS

### (1) Malicious criminal prosecutions

The principal head of damage here is to the fair fame of the claimant, the dam- **44-004**

---

6 See especially by the Court of Appeal in *Quartz Hill Gold Mining Co v Eyre* (1883) 11 Q.B.D. 674 CA and in *Wiffen v Bailey and Romford UDC* [1915] 1 K.B. 600 CA.

7 [1962] 1 Q.B. 306 CA.

8 See the *Berry* decision at para.44-008, below.

9 This is well explained by Bowen LJ in *Quartz Hill Gold Mining Co v Eyre* (1883) 11 Q.B.D. 674 CA at 689–690.

10 This proposition represents the present law, but its validity has been questioned: see para.44-011, below.

11 *Johnson v Emerson* (1871) L.R. 6 Ex. 329.

12 *Quartz Hill Gold Mining Co v Eyre* (1883) 11 Q.B.D. 674 CA.

13 If the defendant has merely set a ministerial officer of the law in motion, and not a judicial officer, the action is not for malicious arrest but for false imprisonment; see Ch.42, above.

14 Again the judicial act intervenes, and it is not trespass.

15 This matter is considered in relation to the particular torts at paras 44-004 to 44-012, below.

age to reputation. In addition it would seem that he will recover for the injury to his feelings, i.e. for the indignity, humiliation and disgrace caused him by the fact of the charge being preferred against him. No breakdown, however, appears in the cases. Holt CJ's second head was the damage by being put in danger of losing one's life, limb or liberty. It therefore seems that the claimant can recover in respect of the risk of conviction: this is basically injury to feelings. In addition, if there has been arrest and imprisonment up to the hearing of the cause, damages in respect thereof should also be included. This was the position in *Calix v Attorney General of Trinidad and Tobago*,[16] where a claimant sued for malicious prosecution on account of his prosecution on a charge of rape, followed by lengthy confinement in prison, after his acquittal on a related charge of robbery. Damages were held awardable both for the damage to reputation and for the consequences of loss of liberty. The particular interest of the case is that the Judicial Committee of the Privy Council, differing from the Caribbean courts from which the appeal lay, laid down that the fact that the claimant had withdrawn from society, living in unhygienic conditions in an abandoned shed, was no basis for reducing his damages for loss of reputation, he being of good character and the charge being the very serious one of rape.[17] It was also noted by the Privy Council that, whereas, as we have seen when dealing with false imprisonment,[18] the judicial intervention of a court precludes liability in false imprisonment, it does not relieve the malicious prosecutor of liability who remains liable for the damage caused by setting the prosecution in motion.[19]

**44-005** For appropriate awards in respect of all this non-pecuniary loss there was little guidance until the decision of the Court of Appeal in *Thompson v Commissioner of Police of the Metropolis*.[20] For the basic damages, these being described as the damages before any element of aggravation[21] and of course before any pecuniary loss, Lord Woolf MR, delivering the judgment of the court, said:

> "The figure should start at about £2,000 and for prosecution continuing for as long as two years ... about £10,000 could be appropriate. If a malicious prosecution results in a conviction which is only set aside on an appeal this will justify a larger award to reflect the longer period during which the claimant has been in peril and has been caused distress."[22]

The Court of Appeal also said that the jury, a normal feature of malicious prosecution claims,[23] should be informed of the approximate starting figure and the approximate ceiling figure for the basic award.[24] It was recognised that these guideline figures, which presumably should apply where the malicious prosecution is other than by the police, would need adjustment in the future for inflation.[25] Inflation, however, would not suffice to account for the award of £20,000 in *Clifford v The*

---

16 [2013] UKPC 15.

17 See [2013] UKPC 15 at [8]–[17]. The Board quashed the award of $38,000 as satisfied that it was too low and remitted the case to the local courts for reconsideration of the damages.

18 See para.42-024, above.

19 [2013] UKPC 15 at [23], citing *Lock v Ashton* (1848) 12 Q.B. 871.

20 [1998] Q.B. 498 CA.

21 [1998] Q.B. 498 CA 514G.

22 [1998] Q.B. 498 CA 515H.

23 See para.53-002, below.

24 [1998] Q.B. 498 CA at 515C.

25 [1998] Q.B. 498 CA at 517E.

*Chief Constable of the Hertfordshire Constabulary*,[26] where the claimant had been wrongly charged with child pornography offences, leading to his arrest and unsuccessful prosecution, but the award was for the resulting psychological damage[27] as well as for the immense distress suffered,[28] £10,000 for each. Also to be taken into account, in addition to inflation, is the Court of Appeal ruling in *Simmons v Castle*,[29] that damages for non-pecuniary loss in all types of civil claim are to be increased by 10 per cent.[30]

*Thompson* concerned claimants who were of good character but in *Manley v Commissioner of Police for the Metropolis*,[31] the claimant was of bad character. Yet in the opinion of the Court of Appeal this did not necessarily affect the claimant's damages adversely. For, as Waller LJ who gave the only reasoned judgment said, although in the case of a claimant with a bad character there will be less loss of reputation, there is a greater risk of the malicious prosecution succeeding and a risk of a resultant longer prison sentence, with consequent stress and anxiety.[32] In so deciding, the Court of Appeal was to some extent departing from its earlier approach in *Clark v Chief Constable of Cleveland Police*,[33] where the bad character of the claimant was considered a factor which made for a discount on the damages.[34] The jury's basic award in *Manley*—that is, the award before any element of aggravation—was increased substantially, from £1,500 to £4,000.[35] **44-006**

In addition, previously awards have been described as vindicatory, awards beyond the damages for non-pecuniary loss. To the extent that a malicious prosecution causes injury to reputation it is thought that damages, without the vindication label, but to show the world that the claimant's reputation is unsullied, should be available, although to date there appears to be no case in which such an award has been made. The decline of vindicatory damages is explained elsewhere.[36] **44-007**

As to pecuniary loss, loss of general business and employment should be recoverable; authority however is lacking. All that can be said is that in *Childs v Lewis*,[37] an action for false imprisonment, it was admitted that, had the action been for malicious prosecution, the loss of the claimant's director's fees by reason of his forced resignation would have been recoverable. The claimant's expenses in defending himself against the prosecution should also be recoverable: indeed this was the very damage claimed in the important opening case of *Savile v Roberts*,[38] itself. Moreover, in modern times it has been held that where the now claimant has been awarded costs in the criminal proceedings, additional costs not covered by such award have been held to ground the action, so that they are clearly now recover- **44-008**

26 [2011] EWHC 815 (QB).
27 [2011] EWHC 815 (QB) at [58]–[61].
28 [2011] EWHC 815 (QB) at [62] and [63].
29 [2013] 1W.L.R. 1239 CA.
30 For the procedural history and reasons for this development, stemming from the package of reforms appearing in the *Jackson Report on Civil Litigation Costs*, see para.40-280, below.
31 [2006] EWCA Civ 879 CA.
32 [2006] EWCA Civ 879 CA at [26]–[29].
33 [1999] EWCA Civ 1357 CA.
34 See Waller LJ's extensive citations from the *Clark* judgments in *Manley* [2006] EWCA Civ 879 CA at [22]–[25].
35 [2006] EWCA Civ 879 CA at [2] and [30]. The award was also increased in *Clark* but only from £500 to £2,000 and only by a majority.
36 See Ch.17, above.
37 (1924) 40 T.L.R. 870: facts at para.42-023, above.
38 (1699) 1 Ld. Raym. 374; see at para.44-002, above.

able as damages. This sensible result was eventually reached by the Court of Appeal in *Berry v British Transport Commission*,[39] thereby reversing what had formerly been understood to be the law.[40] In that case it was held, where the claimant brought an action for malicious prosecution against the British Transport Commission which had prosecuted her for pulling a train communication cord, that the expenses which the claimant had incurred, in the course of her defence and of her successful appeal, in excess of the sum awarded her by the recorder were sufficient to support her action. "In criminal cases", said Danckwerts LJ, and his comments were echoed by his brethren,

> "in practice a person who is acquitted is not necessarily, or indeed it would appear usually, awarded any costs. And even if a sum is awarded for costs, it appears to be no real compensation for the expenses to which the party had been put, and even sometimes to be a mere nominal amount."[41]

Accordingly, the move towards not allowing recovery of extra costs in civil suits as damages, a move which has been subjected to detailed criticism at an earlier point in this text,[42] cannot fortunately reach to criminal matters.

## (2) Malicious Bankruptcy and Company Liquidation Proceedings

**44-009** Where proceedings relating to insolvency are maliciously brought, the principal, and in many cases probably the only, head of damage is the injury to the reputation; injury to feelings, with individual as distinct from corporate claimants, perhaps also comes in. As is shown by *Quartz Hill Gold Mining Co v Eyre*,[43] the leading case on this aspect, the blow is to credit. That case decided that such damage flowed from a petition to wind up a company for insolvency, Bowen LJ saying:

> "I do not see how a petition to wind up a company can be presented and advertised in the newspapers without striking a blow at its credit."[44]

It seems that this is not necessarily regarded as a pecuniary loss, for Brett MR, in treating of the analogous case of bankruptcy proceedings, said:

> "It seems to me that an action can be maintained for maliciously procuring an adjudication under the Bankruptcy Act 1869, because by the petition, which is the first process,

---

39 [1962] 1 Q.B. 306 CA.

40 That such additional costs would not ground an action for malicious prosecution was considered as both well established and binding on it by the Court of Appeal in *Wiffen v Bailey and Romford UDC* [1915] 1 K.B. 600 CA: see at 607 and 610; counsel had, however, conceded the point. This had been followed by Diplock J in *Berry v British Transport Commission* [1961] 1 Q.B. 149 at first instance.

41 [1962] 1 Q.B. 306 CA at 338; and see at 317 and 325 to 326, per Ormerod and Devlin LJJ respectively. Devlin LJ indeed held for the claimant on the narrower ground that the particular costs awarded the claimant in the criminal prosecution did not represent an order for costs even according to the conventional measure in civil cases: at 332. This was because he thought that the court might be prevented by *Barnett v Eccles Corp* [1900] 2 Q.B. 423 CA from holding that the rule as to costs in civil cases should not be extended to costs in criminal cases: [1962] 1 Q.B. 306 CA at 329. However, he expressed no opinion on the case which involved neither an action for malicious prosecution nor an action for damages proper.

42 See paras 21-003 and following, above; for malicious prosecution, and *Berry*, see in particular paras 21-017 to 21-021.

43 (1883) 11 Q.B.D. 674 CA.

44 (1883) 11 Q.B.D. 674 CA at 693.

the credit of the person against whom it is presented is injured before he can show that the accusation made against him is false; he is injured in his fair fame, even although he does not suffer a pecuniary loss."[45]

If pecuniary loss is shown in addition, there undoubtedly can be recovery for it. This could be by way of injury to, or loss of, business but in this limited field there are no cases beyond the *Quartz Hill* case. That decision does however raise a difficulty in respect of one particular form of pecuniary loss, that is the pecuniary loss entailed in the costs of the prior civil proceedings. **44-010**

*Quartz Hill Gold Mining Co v Eyre*,[46] where the petition against the now claimant company had been dismissed without costs, held that the claimant's costs incurred in defending the prior civil proceedings were not a legal damage to ground the action for malicious prosecution. As to the costs which the court in the prior action was entitled to have awarded the now claimant, Bowen LJ said, correctly, that the now claimant will get these costs in the prior action unless he does not deserve them, in which case he ought not to get them in the subsequent action.[47] As to the extra costs which the now claimant has incurred over and above those the court might have awarded, Brett MR said, unconvincingly, that the extra costs, not being considered necessary, cannot have been caused by the malicious litigation.[48] However, in *Berry v British Transport Commission*[49] both Devlin LJ and Danckwerts LJ voiced criticisms of the law as laid down for civil cases in the *Quartz Hill* case. Danckwerts LJ saying: **44-011**

"The theory that taxed costs are a sufficient compensation for a successful defendant, at any rate in a civil action, seems to me an unreal or perhaps even a cynical view, which ought not to have any place in the conditions of an action for malicious prosecution."[50]

It was therefore hoped that the rule of no recovery of the extra costs might not be established beyond recall. Yet today the opponents of the rule have to face attack from a different angle, that is from the holding in a series of first instance cases, thought to be misguided and thought in the light of later developments to be departed from hopefully fairly soon, that, by virtue of the more liberal costs regime which now prevails, there is no need to award the extra costs. The earlier detailed discussion of this issue should be referred to.[51]

Whether, where there is other damage which is sufficient to ground the action, extra costs can, while the *Quartz Hill* decision stands, be added thereto is a question of policy and a question of the scope of protection afforded by the tort.[52] Of course, if the new move to ban the recovery of extra costs across the board were eventually to succeed,[53] this question could not arise. **44-012**

---

45 (1883) 11 Q.B.D. 674 CA at 684.

46 (1883) 11 Q.B.D. 674 CA.

47 (1883) 11 Q.B.D. 674 CA at 690.

48 (1883) 11 Q.B.D. 674 CA at 682–683, where it is put more elaborately than this.

49 [1962] 1 Q.B. 306 CA. See the case at para.44-008, above.

50 [1962] 1 Q.B. 306 CA at 336.

51 See paras 20-003 and following, above, and for malicious prosecution in particular see paras 21-017 to 21-021, above.

52 See para.8-125, above.

53 See the last footnote but one and accompanying text.

## 3. AGGRAVATION AND MITIGATION

**44-013** Torts involving malicious abuse of process fall into that general category where the manner in which the tort is committed may lead to aggravation or mitigation of the damage, and hence of the damages. In the past the few cases have not gone into this but reliance could be placed on analogies from such torts as false imprisonment and defamation.[54] Now we have *Thompson v Commissioner of Police of the Metropolis*,[55] where the guidance that should be given to the jury was set out in great detail by the Court of Appeal. On the side of aggravation of the damage Lord Woolf MR, delivering the judgment of the court, said that aggravating features can include humiliating circumstances at the time or any conduct of those responsible for the prosecution which shows that they had behaved in a high-handed, insulting, malicious or oppressive manner in conducting the prosecution; they include also the way the litigation and trial are conducted.[56] On the side of mitigation of the damage, evidence of the claimant's bad character should be admissible. Advice of counsel that the now defendant should have proceeded with his prosecution would also go in mitigation, but it will generally go further than this and bar the claimant's action entirely by furnishing the now defendant with reasonable and probable cause for prosecuting.[57]

**44-014** Guidance was also given in *Thompson* generally as to the amounts to award.[58] As to aggravated damages the Court of Appeal said that it considered that, where they were appropriate, the figure was unlikely to be less than £1,000 but at the same time should not, in the ordinary way, be as much as twice the basic damages, except perhaps where these were modest.[59] In *Manley v Commissioner of Police for the Metropolis*,[60] the Court of Appeal substituted £10,000 for the jury's nil award, but these aggravated damages were designed to cover also assault and false imprisonment. In *Rowlands v Chief Constable of Merseyside Police*,[61] the Court of

---

54 See Chs 42 and 46 respectively. The very early case of *Leigh v Pope* (1779) 2 Wm. Bl. 1327 illustrates aggravation in a case of malicious prosecution.

55 [1998] Q.B. 498 CA.

56 [1998] Q.B. 498 CA at 516C. No aggravated damages as such were awarded in *Clifford v The Chief Constable of the Hertfordshire Constabulary* [2011] EWHC 815 (QB) (facts at para.44-005, above) apparently on the ground that, injury to dignity and humiliation suffered having been taken into account by the trial judge in his basic award, high-handed and oppressive behaviour increasing the injury to the claimant's feelings had not, it would seem, been shown: at [64]. The claim for aggravated damages in *Calix v Attorney General of Trinidad and Tobago* [2013] UKPC 15 (facts at para.44-004, above), on account of the way the prosecution had been handled and the appalling conditions in the prison in which the claimant had been incarcerated, was sent back by the Privy Council for the local Court of Appeal to deal with: at [32] and [33].

57 In this context mitigation of the damages results from the conduct, character and circumstances of claimant and defendant and we are not concerned with mitigation in the true sense of the avoidance by the claimant of the consequences of a wrong (see the explanation of the principal and subsidiary meanings of mitigation at paras 9-002 to 9-013, above). Unusually in a malicious prosecution claim, mitigation in its true sense did make an appearance in *Calix v Attorney General of Trinidad and Tobago* [2013] UKPC 15 (facts at para.44-004, above). The defendant there argued that the claimant's failure to apply for bail to secure his release from prison should cut down his damages for loss of liberty, but the argument got nowhere as it had not even been pleaded and the onus in mitigation is on the defendant: at [18]–[22].

58 See paras 44-005, above and 44-016, below, as to amounts of basic and exemplary damages respectively.

59 [1998] Q.B. 498 CA at 516E–F.

60 [2006] EWCA Civ 879 CA.

61 [2007] 1 W.L.R. 1065 CA.

Appeal awarded £6,000, the judge below having wrongly withdrawn from the jury consideration of the claim for aggravated damages, but the Court of Appeal's figure also covered false imprisonment. In *Rowlands* it was said that, while it was important to avoid double recovery, "the distinction between basic and aggravated damages will continue to have a part to play" in the assessment of damages here.[62] It was also held in *Thompson* that there should be a separate award for the element of aggravation, changing the practice at the time.[63]

## 4. Exemplary Damages

In former days exemplary damages were available over the whole range of torts. Then with the House of Lords decision in *Rookes v Barnard*,[64] approved by the House in *Broome v Cassell & Co*,[65] and treated in detail elsewhere.[66] exemplary damages became recoverable only if the circumstances of the case brought it within one of the three categories set out by Lord Devlin, viz., first, where there is oppressive, arbitrary or unconstitutional conduct by government servants, second, where there is conduct calculated to result in profit and, third, where statute provides.[67] Curiously, there seems to be no single example before *Rookes* of an exemplary award for malicious prosecution,[68] which meant that for a time no award should have been possible in view of the Court of Appeal's holding in *A.B. v South West Water Services*,[69] that exemplary damages may not be awarded in torts where before *Rookes* they had not run. However, this decision was overruled by the House of Lords in *Kuddus v Chief Constable of Leicestershire*,[70] holding that it is the features of the defendant's behaviour rather than the cause of action sued upon which have to be looked at in order to decide upon the appropriateness of an exemplary award.[71] So the way was opened for exemplary awards in malicious prosecution claims. **44-015**

Indeed some time before *Kuddus* the Court of Appeal had already upheld an award of exemplary damages in a case within Lord Devlin's first common law category. It may be that the court was not apprised of the non-existence of pre-*Rookes* awards in malicious prosecution[72] but this is of no consequence after **44-016**

---

62 [2007] 1 W.L.R. 1065 CA at 26.

63 [1998] Q.B. 498 CA at 516E. But see, in the different context of a victimisation claim, the concerns over having separate awards expressed by Underhill J in the Employment Appeal Tribunal in *Commissioner of Police of the Metropolis v Shaw* [2012] I.C.R. 464; [2012] I.R.L.R. 291. These concerns are thought to be unnecessary; see *Shaw* and the discussion at para.43-014, above.

64 [1964] A.C. 1129.

65 [1972] A.C. 1027.

66 See Ch.13, above.

67 See paras 13-017 to 13-030, above.

68 The very early case of *Leigh v Pope* (1779) 2 Wm. Bl. 1327 has sometimes been put forward as an illustration (as by the Law Commission in its Consultation Paper, *Aggravated, Exemplary and Restitutionary Damages* (HMSO, 1993), Law Com. No.132, p.69, n.265) but, while the award there was for the time unusually high, there is no mention in the case of the award being exemplary or indeed of its being of an amount which could be regarded as going beyond compensation for the claimant's injury to punishment for the defendant's conduct. *Chambers v Robinson* (1726) 2 Str. 691 (also cited by the Law Commission) was well before the concept of exemplary damages had even appeared in English law: see para.13-002, above.

69 [1993] Q.B. 507 CA.

70 [2002] 2 A.C. 122.

71 See para.13-011, above.

72 In any event there was a concurrent claim in false imprisonment where exemplary damages have always been available.

*Kuddus*. The case was *Thompson v Commissioner of Police of the Metropolis*,[73] where exemplary damages for malicious prosecution were given[74] against the police for oppressive conduct. The decision is particularly valuable as the Court of Appeal gave guidance on the amounts appropriate to award in such a case. Lord Woolf MR, delivering the judgment of the court, said that in this class of action the conduct must be particularly bad to justify as much as £25,000, and £50,000 should be regarded as the absolute maximum; where exemplary damages were appropriate they were unlikely to be less than £5,000.[75] The Court of Appeal endorsed an award of £25,000. Lord Devlin's first category is thereby established for malicious prosecution[76] which leaves the second category, where the defendant has acted with a view to profit, still to find a champion. A profit-motivated malicious prosecution is by no means inconceivable.[77]

73 [1998] Q.B. 498 CA.

74 And as a separate award.

75 [1998] Q.B. 498 CA at 517C.

76 That no exemplary damages were awarded in *Manley v Commissioner of Police for the Metropolis* [2006] EWCA Civ 879 CA (malicious prosecution together with assault and false imprisonment) would seem to be because the liability of the commissioner of police was vicarious but *Rowlands v Chief Constable of Merseyside Police* [2007] 1 W.L.R. 1065 CA (malicious prosecution and false imprisonment) has since decided to award exemplary damages where the liability of the chief constable was also vicarious. Vicarious liability for exemplary damages is considered at paras 13-045 to 13-047, above. No exemplary damages were awarded in *Clifford v The Chief Constable of the Hertfordshire Constabulary* [2011] EWHC 815 (QB) (facts at para.44-005, above), apparently on the basis that police behaviour in an arbitrary or oppressive manner was not shown: at [65].

77 Compare the cases at paras 13-022 to 13-027, above.

CHAPTER 45

# MISFEASANCE IN PUBLIC OFFICE

TABLE OF CONTENTS



Misfeasance in public office may be said to have originated as far back as the beginning of the 18th century with the famous decision of Holt CJ in *Ashby v White*.[1] The tort then for all practical purposes disappeared from the legal scene, only to be resurrected by the Court of Appeal nearly three centuries later in *Bourgoin SA v Ministry of Agriculture, Fisheries and Food*.[2] Following on this resurrection, the House of Lords in *Three Rivers District Council v Governor and Council of the Bank of England*,[3] has confirmed that the tort is today alive and well, and has set out in further detail the precise rules governing it. **45-001**

## 1. HEADS OF DAMAGE

### (1) Pecuniary loss

There can be no doubt that the tort of misfeasance in public office allows recovery for pecuniary loss, in particular for loss of profits, subject to the usual requirements of causation, remoteness and the like being satisfied. Indeed it can be said that the court in *Bourgoin SA v Ministry of Agriculture, Fisheries and Food*,[4] the decision which brought the tort back into the legal lexicon, was intent on providing a remedy in damages for financial loss in circumstances where negligence for pure economic loss and breach of statutory duty might not run. French turkey producers sought damages on account of the defendant ministry's revocation of a general import licence, and consequent prohibition of the importation of French turkeys, effectively banning them from trading in England. The damages sought by the turkey producers were their loss of profits. The case turned on the preliminary point of law as to whether the claim could lie, which it was held that it could, but there is no suggestion that damages for loss of profits could not have been recovered. Had such damages not been recoverable, there would have been no reason to litigate the preliminary point. **45-002**

The same goes for the subsequent House of Lords decision in *Three Rivers* **45-003**

1 (1703) 2 Ld. Raym. 938.
2 [1986] Q.B. 716 CA.
3 [2003] 2 A.C. 1.
4 [1986] Q.B. 716 CA.

*District Council v Governor and Council of the Bank of England*.[5] Over 6,000 depositors who had lost their money in a notorious bank collapse claimed that the Bank of England was guilty of misfeasance in public office in granting a licence to, not then revoking the licence to, and generally not controlling, the failed bank. Again the case involved preliminary issues, it being held by a majority of their Lordships that the claim should not be struck out on account of having no chance of success. Here too therefore it must have been considered that the depositors' losses would have been recoverable had the case successfully proceeded to trial.

**45-004** Thus there do not yet appear to be any awards of damages in England for pecuniary loss in this newly rehabilitated tort. In these circumstances it may be useful to point to such recoveries elsewhere. In Australia in *Farrington v Thomson*,[6] the ordering by a licensing inspector of a hotelier to close down his hotel was held by the Supreme Court of Victoria to be a misfeasance in public office entitling the hotelier to damages for his losses from the hotel's closure. In Canada in *Roncarelli v Duplessis*,[7] the misfeasance was, similarly, the cancellation of the long held liquor licence of the proprietor of a restaurant so that the restaurant had to be shut down, and the Supreme Court of Canada accepted that the proprietor was entitled to damages for the ensuing loss of profits.

## (2) Non-pecuniary loss

**45-005** In the case of the above misfeasances in public office, claimants are seeking to recover for their pecuniary loss, not having suffered any non-pecuniary loss as there will have been no mental distress or injury to feelings involved. In the case of some other misfeasances in public office, the reverse is likely to be true. This takes us to misfeasances by police officers and by prison officers where non-pecuniary loss tends to rule the day. In *Kuddus v Chief Constable of Leicestershire*,[8] the claimant had reported a theft to a police constable who had said that the matter would be investigated but, instead, had forged the claimant's signature on a statement withdrawing the complaint, whereupon the investigation ceased. The issue which came before the House of Lords was whether there was an entitlement to claim exemplary damages, dealt with in due course,[9] but it was accepted that compensatory damages for the non-pecuniary loss were available.[10] It seems improbable that there was any recoverable pecuniary loss; there was no indication that a continuation of the investigation would have unmasked the thief. In *Racz v Home Office*,[11] which also reached the Lords, the misfeasance in public office was directed at ill treatment by prison officers of the claimant in a strip cell. On this occasion the issue was the vicarious liability of the Home Office and here too compensatory damages were not in issue. But there is little doubt that, assuming liability, damages for the claimant's distress and loss of dignity would have been available. As to appropriate amounts to award there is so far no authority,[12] such cases as there are be-

5 [2003] 2 A.C. 1.
6 [1959] V.R. 286.
7 16 D.L.R. (2d) 689 (1959).
8 [2002] 2 A.C. 122.
9 See para.45-009, below.
10 On this see at para.45-006, below.
11 [1994] 2 A.C. 45.
12 While the claim in *Clifford v The Chief Constable of the Hertfordshire Constabulary* [2011] EWHC 815 (QB) (facts at para.44-005, above) was for malicious prosecution and misfeasance in public of-

ing more concerned with the scope of liability, and all that can be pointed to is the Court of Appeal ruling in *Simmons v Castle*,[13] that damages for non-pecuniary loss in all types of civil claim are to be increased by 10 per cent.[14]

## 2. AGGRAVATION AND MITIGATION

Aggravated damages can be given where the recovery in damages is for injury to feelings; they have no application to pecuniary loss.[15] Accordingly, there will be no scope for aggravated damages in those cases where it is financial loss that is of concern to the claimant, as it was in both *Bourgoin*,[16] and *Three Rivers*.[17] On the other hand, where the claimant's concern is not financial loss but injured feelings, as it was in *Kuddus*,[18] aggravated damages may come in if the defendant's improper conduct justifies them. Indeed while the defendant Chief Constable was challenging the claim for exemplary damages, about to be dealt with, he accepted that the claim for aggravated damages was good, and this was in no way queried by their Lordships.[19] **45-006**

Mitigation of the damages on account of the conduct, character and circumstances of the claimant, as may be found in such torts as assault and defamation, has nowhere here been an issue. It is unlikely to arise. **45-007**

## 3. EXEMPLARY DAMAGES

The whole approach to exemplary damages was changed by the decision in *Rookes v Barnard*,[20] later approved in *Broome v Cassell & Co*,[21] and is treated in detail elsewhere.[22] Exemplary damages are now recoverable only if the circumstances of the case bring it within one of the three categories set out by Lord Devlin there, the two common law categories and the statutory category which is of little or no importance.[23] As for misfeasance for public office, it fits perfectly within Lord Devlin's first common law category concerning oppressive, arbitrary or unconstitutional conduct by government servants. The second common law category concerning conduct calculated to result in profit is unlikely to feature in this tort. **45-008**

The House of Lords has expressly decided in *Kuddus v Chief Constable of Leicestershire*,[24] that misfeasance in public office is an appropriate tort for **45-009**

fice, the damages awarded, all for non-pecuniary loss, were given under the malicious prosecution head.

13 [2013] 1W.L.R. 1239 CA.

14 For the procedural history and reasons for this development, stemming from the package of reforms appearing in the *Jackson Report on Civil Litigation Costs*, see para.40-280, below.

15 The judge in *Amin v Imran Khan & Partners* [2011] EWHC 2958 (QB) was wrong to give aggravated damages on pecuniary loss arising from misfeasance in public office: see at [104]–[107].

16 See para.45-002, above.

17 See para.45-003, above.

18 [2002] 2 A.C. 122; see the case at para.45-005, above.

19 See Lord Slynn at [2002] 2 A.C. 122 at [3]; Lord Mackay at [30] where it is pointed out that the claim for aggravated damages had been reinstated after having been struck out, together with the claim for exemplary damages, by mistake.

20 [1964] A.C. 1129.

21 [1972] A.C. 1027.

22 See Ch.13, above.

23 See paras 13-017 to 13-030, above.

24 [2002] 2 A.C. 122.

exemplary damages.[25] Also, under the law as it stands, there will be no difficulty in holding a Chief Constable vicariously liable for the acts of his officers. This was allowed in the context of false imprisonment and malicious prosecution in *Rowlands v Chief Constable of Merseyside Police*.[26]

[25] Exemplary damages would undoubtedly have been awarded for this tort in *Muuse v Secretary of State for the Home Department* [2010] EWCA Civ 453 CA (facts at para.13-018, above) had the Court of Appeal felt able to uphold the trial judge's finding of misfeasance in public office. Instead, exemplary damages were awarded for false imprisonment, which tort was indeed admitted.

[26] [2007] 1 W.L.R. 1065 CA. For the general discussion on exemplary damages and vicarious liability see paras 13-045 and following.

# Chapter 46

# DEFAMATION

Table of Contents



The tort of defamation, looked at from the point of view of damages, breaks into two parts. On the one hand there are defamatory statements actionable only on proof of special damage, with a special meaning attaching in this connection to the term special damage[1]; on the other hand there are defamatory statements actionable per se. The first category comprises most slanders, and the second the remaining slanders[2] and all libels. These two categories must be kept rigidly separate. **46-001**

[1] For the other, more universal, meanings of special damage, see paras 3-001 to 3-005, above.

[2] For what slanders are actionable per se, see the standard text on tort and defamation.

## I. SLANDERS ACTIONABLE ONLY ON PROOF OF SPECIAL DAMAGE

### 1. MEANING OF SPECIAL DAMAGE

**46-002** The interesting fact about the special damage that must be shown is that the one thing that does not constitute such damage is the injury to the claimant's reputation itself, although this is the interest that the tort of defamation is designed primarily to protect. This is not so strange as it may at first sight appear. One reason why slanders, other than those exceptional ones of a specified serious nature, are not actionable per se is that the courts tend to view them as not affecting the reputation to any degree. They are, however, prepared to countenance an action if damage other than this results from the slander, and the required damage that must be shown is therefore not that type of damage which will be presumed to flow from defamation so as to be recoverable as general damages, i.e. non-pecuniary loss to the claimant by injury to reputation, feelings or perhaps even health, together with damages described as being by way of "vindication", but that type of damage which will ordinarily have to be specifically claimed in an action of defamation above the general damages, i.e. pecuniary loss to the claimant by loss of business, contracts, gratuities and the like. If this distinction is kept in mind, the rationale of special damage in this connection will be clarified and what constitutes special damage will be seen to be any pecuniary loss,[3] whether a money loss or a loss calculable in money terms.[4]

#### (1) What is excluded

**46-003** **(a) Injury to reputation and to feelings** First and foremost, the injury to reputation is not a pecuniary loss and therefore not special damage. Allied with this is the injury to the feelings which is similarly excluded. This is clear and little authority is required. Such injury to reputation and feelings is reflected in the cases in the loss of the society of the claimant's friends and neighbours. It was very early established in *Barnes v Prudlin*,[5] that the loss of *consortium vicinorum* was not a pecuniary loss constituting special damage, and in *Weldon v De Bathe*,[6] a claim was rejected where the claimant laid as special damage that she had been shunned by her friends and by society, Brett MR speaking of this as mere injury to the feelings.[7]

---

3 The term material loss is to be found in the cases: see, e.g. *Roberts v Roberts* (1864) 5 B. & S. 384, where Blackburn J talked of "material injury" and Cockburn CJ of "substantial and material advantage". The term pecuniary loss is used here because this term has been adopted throughout this book (see especially Chs 2 and 3) and it is submitted that pecuniary loss and material loss are in the present context synonymous (compare *Chamberlain v Boyd* (1883) 11 Q.B.D. 407 CA at 412, per Lord Coleridge CJ: "The damage alleged … is in truth incapable of being estimated in money.") See, too, the use of the term pecuniary damage in s.3 of the Defamation Act 1952, which imposes on the tort of injurious falsehood a similar division to that between defamatory statements actionable per se and defamatory statements actionable only on proof of special damage: see para.48-011, below.

4 In *Broome v Cassell & Co* [1972] A.C. 1027 at 1073B, Lord Hailsham LC said: "If it is not too deeply embedded in our legal language, I would like to see 'special damage' dropped as a term of art in [this context] and some phrase like 'material loss' substituted."

5 (1667) 1 Sid. 396.

6 (1885) 54 L.J.Q.B. 113 CA.

7 (1885) 54 L.J.Q.B. 113 CA at 116. It was also held too remote, but this is questionable: see para.46-013, below.

Further, in *Roberts v Roberts*,[8] where a slander of unchastity prevented a married woman from continuing as a member of a religious society or becoming a member of the society in another town, it was held that no pecuniary loss resulted from the loss of membership and that therefore the action failed.[9] Cockburn CJ said that the claimant had only lost "the merely nominal distinction of being able to call herself a member".[10] So, too, in *Hopwood v Thorn*,[11] the action failed where a slander on the claimant clergyman may have resulted in diminished attendances at his chapel of persons who in no way contributed to his emoluments. However, such social losses may quite possibly entail pecuniary losses, and a claimant would do well to frame his claim in such a way as to include these, for the line would appear to be fine.[12]

**(b) Injury to health** Injury to health resulting from such social losses might seem to stand on a different footing since it may result in pecuniary loss by reason of expenses of cure and loss of employment during incapacity.[13] Nevertheless in *Allsop v Allsop*,[14] it was held that, where as a result of a slander on a married woman she became sick and unable to attend to business and her husband was put to expense in effecting her cure, no action lay. The ground upon which the court decided, however, was that this damage was too remote in the causal sense.[15] Martin B said: **46-004**

> "The law is jealous as to actions for mere words … special damage must be the natural or necessary result, not depending on the peculiarities of the particular individual."[16]

"This particular damage", said Pollock CB similarly, "depends on the temperament of the party affected".[17] Bramwell B considered the matter more difficult, thinking that the ill health did flow from the tort; but since he could not distinguish injury to health from injury to feelings, which latter, if admitted as special damage, would make all words actionable, he concluded that the ill health could not be a natural consequence.[18] It will be seen that the court was being cautious since it was a case of slander, and it may well be that today, after the cases on nervous shock now labelled psychiatric damage, and in view of the fact that the husband would no longer bear the expenses but the wife herself, the case would be differently decided.[19]

---

8 (1864) 5 B. & S. 384.

9 After many complaints by the courts, as in *Roberts v Roberts* (1864) 5 B. & S. 384 itself, the Slander of Women Act 1891 made such a slander actionable per se. But it will cease to be so when s.14 of the Defamation Act 2013, which repeals the 1891 Act, comes into force in 1 January 2014.

10 (1864) 5 B. & S. 384 at 389.

11 (1849) 8 C.B. 293.

12 See paras 46-006 to 46-009, below.

13 Further, injury to health may not be within the general damages recoverable in defamation but in the superadded special damages.

14 (1860) 5 H. & N. 534.

15 This difficult case is more fully analysed at para.8-084, above, where it is considered in the context of the general principles of remoteness.

16 (1860) 5 H. & N. 534 at 539.

17 (1860) 5 H. & N. 534 at 538.

18 (1860) 5 H. & N. 534 at 539.

19 It is true that the headnote in *Lynch v Knight* (1861) 9 H.L.C. 577 says that the House of Lords approved *Allsop v Allsop* (1860) 5 H. & N. 534, but only Lord Campbell adverted to the case in his speech (at 592), saying that he thought the decision was right but that there was no need to inquire

## (2) What is included

46-005 **(a) Business losses** The principal type of pecuniary loss which constitutes special damage is loss to the claimant of a contract, of an employment or of business, whether existing or intended. This is so clear that there are few cases arguing the point. In *Storey v Challands*,[20] it was argued because the lost transaction might have turned out to be a losing one for the claimant, a commission agent whom the defendant had slandered to a third party who in consequence would not deal with him in business. It was held that this was special damage, despite the fact that the third party had since made a composition with his creditors. Most of the cases, however, deal with the question of whether such damage is or is not too remote in the causal sense, and, whichever way this question has been answered in the particular case, throughout it has been the basis of the argument on remoteness that such loss is an accepted head of special damage.[21] Thus the question in issue was remoteness in the modern case of *McManus v Beckham*,[22] where the claim was for the loss of trading profits of a business, but the slander there was actionable per se.[23] Also a pecuniary loss is the loss of the perquisites of an office, as in *Hartley v Herring*,[24] where the result of a slander upon a clergyman was that

> "persons frequenting the chapel had refused to permit him to preach there, and had discontinued giving him the profits which they usually had and would otherwise have given".[25]

On the other hand, a mere unexecuted threat to terminate the claimant's employment is not sufficient, as in *Michael v Spiers*.[26]

46-006 **(b) Certain social losses** Not only do business losses entail pecuniary loss, indeed necessarily so, but social losses may do so also.[27] The courts have had to deal with a variety of such cases.

46-007 *(i) Loss of spouse or fiancé* In the very old case of *Davis v Gardiner*,[28] it was held that an action would lie where a woman had lost a marriage by reason of her fiancé breaking off the engagement as a result of the slander; this principle was accepted in *Speight v Gosnay*,[29] where the claimant failed only on the ground of causal

---

into its soundness.

20 (1837) 8 C. & P. 234.

21 Too remote: *Vicars v Wilcocks* (1806) 8 East 1; *Ward v Weeks* (1830) 7 Bing. 211; *Rutherford v Evans* (1829) 4 C. & P. 74; *Tunnicliffe v Moss* (1850) 3 C. & K. 83; *Dixon v Smith* (1860) 5 H. & N. 450 (except loss on a particular contract as *accoucheur* which was admitted recoverable); *Speake v Hughes* [1904] 1 K.B. 138 CA. Not too remote: *Kendillon v Maltby* (1842) Car. & M. 402; *Derry v Handley* (1867) 16 L.T. 263.

22 [2002] 1 W.L.R. 2982 CA.

23 The case is dealt with under remoteness of damage at para.46-018, below.

24 (1799) 8 T.R. 130.

25 (1799) 8 T.R. 130 at 131. The argument was mainly concerned with the mode of proof.

26 (1909) 101 L.T. 352.

27 Contrast *McCarey v Associated Newspapers* [1965] 2 Q.B. 86 CA at 104, where, in Pearson LJ's classification of the various heads of damage in libel, he combined resulting "social disadvantages" with actual and anticipated pecuniary losses in contradistinction to the specifically non-pecuniary losses which are also recoverable where libel rather than slander is in issue.

28 (1593) 4 Co. Rep. 16b.

29 (1890) 60 L.J.Q.B. 231 CA.

remoteness.[30] Similarly, where a married woman has lost the consortium of her husband, because he left her on hearing of the slander, it would seem the better view that this is a pecuniary loss. Differing views on this question were put forward in the House of Lords in the important case of *Lynch v Knight*.[31] Lord Campbell took the view that the wife's loss of consortium did form a head of actionable damage,[32] Lord Cranworth was strongly inclined to agree,[33] but Lord Brougham and Lord Wensleydale[34] took the opposite view.[35] However, Lord Wensleydale's disagreement was based on the ground that the wife had suffered no pecuniary loss since the husband had all the property and she was still entitled to be maintained by him; today this argument would no longer hold.[36] Whether, conversely, a man who has lost wife or fiancée by reason of a slander on him could maintain that he has suffered a pecuniary loss, is a question that has not been before the courts. In this age of sexual equality it is submitted that he could.

*(ii) Loss of friends and acquaintances* In *Moore v Meagher*,[37] which was followed in *Davies v Solomon*,[38] it was held that where loss of the society of friends entailed loss of their material hospitality, by way of food and drink and the like, this was a pecuniary loss which would ground the action.[39] A claimant basing his claim on loss of friends and acquaintances would therefore do well to claim, where possible, a loss of hospitality so as to ensure the showing of a pecuniary loss. **46-008**

*(iii) Loss of club membership* In *Chamberlain v Boyd*,[40] the claimant was a candidate for membership of the Reform Club, and on a ballot of members was not elected. Later a meeting was called to consider a proposed alteration of the election rules, and the defendant slandered the claimant with a view to retaining the existing rules and so securing the claimant's exclusion. Thus the old rules were retained and the claimant did not seek re-election. In the ensuing action for slander the Court of Appeal held for the defendant on two grounds: there was no special **46-009**

---

30 As Blackburn J said in argument in *Roberts v Roberts* (1864) 5 B. & S. 384, marriage has always been regarded as a valuable consideration.

31 (1861) 9 H.L.C. 577. The decision for the defendant went on the question of remoteness: see para.46-014, below.

32 (1861) 9 H.L.C. 577 at 589.

33 (1861) 9 H.L.C. 577 at 595.

34 (1861) 9 H.L.C. 577 at 593 and 599 respectively.

35 In fact Lord Wensleydale decided on this ground. In the similar later cases of *Parkins v Scott* (1862) 1 H. & C. 153 and *Davies v Solomon* (1871) L.R. 7 Q.B. 112, the court tended to evade the point by deciding for the defendant and claimant respectively on other grounds.

36 Although in *Best v Fox* [1952] A.C. 716 (affirming [1951] 2 K.B. 639 CA) the correctness of the view put forward by Lord Campbell was discussed both in the House of Lords and the Court of Appeal without unanimity (Lord Porter was against it, as was Lord Asquith in the Court of Appeal; Birkett LJ was for it), this was in the context of whether a wife was entitled to sue for loss of consortium by reason of physical injury sustained by her husband. Only Lord Goddard pointed out that Lord Campbell was not saying that an action lay for loss of consortium but that loss of consortium was a head of actionable damage in slander: at 732 (approving the similar interpretation in the Australian case of *Wright v Cedzich* (1930) 43 C.L.R. 493). This view of Lord Goddard was applied in *Lampert v Eastern National Omnibus Co* [1954] 1 W.L.R. 1047 where loss of consortium was held to be an actionable head of damage in a claim for personal injury: see para.40-064, above.

37 (1807) 1 Taunt. 39.

38 (1871) L.R. 7 Q.B. 112.

39 Accepted in *Clarke v Morgan* (1878) 38 L.T. 354, where the claimant failed on other grounds.

40 (1883) 11 Q.B.D. 407 CA.

damage and the damage was too remote.[41] Special damage was lacking not because failure to obtain club membership was not a pecuniary loss, but because the claimant had only been deprived of a chance of re-election which was too uncertain a quantity for the loss to be assessed.[42] Bowen LJ expressly avoided saying that there would have been no action if the defendant had actually prevented the election, for

> "possibly the membership of a club may be a matter of temporal advantage, and the deprivation of it may be an injury or damage of which the law will take cognisance".[43]

## 2. REMOTENESS OF SPECIAL DAMAGE

**46-010** The question of remoteness[44] of damage arises sharply here because new intervening acts are in the nature of things rife. In the first place, since the pecuniary loss is invariably caused through third parties refraining or ceasing from dealing or associating with the claimant, the argument that the third party's action is an intervening act relieving the defendant of liability for further damage is an argument which defendants frequently seize upon. In the second place, the slander is often spread to the ears of a person so refraining or ceasing from dealing or associating with the claimant by its repetition by another: this repetition, defendants contend, constitutes similarly such an intervening act. Sometimes the two factors are combined, making two possible intervening acts. This was the position in *Vicars v Wilcocks*.[45] In that case the court decided solely on the first type of intervening act; only when this was discredited was there an attempt by Wightman J in *Lumley v Gye*,[46] unjustified by the ratio decidendi, to base the decision on the second type of intervening act.

### (1) Refusal by third party to, or to continue to, deal or associate with the claimant[47]

**46-011** Where the claimant's loss results from a third party's refusal to, or to continue to, deal or associate with him, the distinction between a third party's act which is, and a third party's act which is not, wrongful in the sense of giving rise to an action for damages by the claimant against the third party, has assumed a certain importance in the cases. Such cases will generally involve business losses, by reason of the third party refusing or ceasing to employ, contract with, or generally do business with the claimant; with social losses to the claimant the distinction does not

---

41 The second ground is dealt with at para.46-014, below.

42 "The damage alleged is unsubstantial and shadowy, and is in truth incapable of being estimated in money": (1883) 11 Q.B.D. 407 CA at 412, per Lord Coleridge CJ; and see at 416, per Bowen LJ. In so far as the case is based on the proposition that the loss of a chance cannot be estimated in money, it may be inconsistent with *Chaplin v Hicks* [1911] 2 K.B. 786 CA: see para.10-040, above.

43 (1883) 11 Q.B.D. 407 CA at 415.

44 Only remoteness as a limit on causation is dealt with here. Failure to recover for damage because it does not fall within the present definition of special damage may be regarded as failure based upon remoteness in the less familiar sense of the limits of policy. See for the distinction between these two types of remoteness, Ch.8 passim and, in relation to defamation, *Allsop v Allsop* (1860) 5 H. & N. 534, which hovers between the two. That decision is considered at para.8-084, above.

45 (1806) 8 East 1.

46 (1853) 2 E. & B. 216.

47 Consider the treatment, in the context of the general principles of remoteness, of the cases dealt with here: paras 8-049 and 8-061, above.

appear, since it is unlikely that the third party's act will give rise to an action for damages by the claimant against him.

Where the third party's act was a wrongful dismissal of the claimant from his employment which entitled the claimant to sue him for damages, it was held in *Vicars v Wilcocks*,[48] that the dismissal was too remote from the slander to give the claimant also an action against the defendant. This followed upon the view expressed by Lord Eldon CJ in *Morris v Langdale*,[49] that where third parties had refused to complete their contracts with the claimant, this was not damage for which the claimant could sue the slanderer, **46-012**

> "since it is damage which may be compensated in actions brought by the plaintiff against those persons".[50]

This doctrine which refused a right of action against the original wrongdoer where the claimant could sue the intervening third party is no longer law since the decision, in another type of tort, of *Lumley v Gye*.[51] No subsequent cases have appeared in which a wrongful dismissal by a third party has been held to relieve the defendant of liability and it is submitted that the defendant would remain liable in two sets of circumstances: first, where the defendant intended this very consequence on the ground that intended consequences would not be too remote[52]; and secondly, where, if the slander had been true, the third party's dismissal of the claimant would not have been wrongful.[53]

Where the third party's act has not been wrongful in the sense of giving rise to an action for damages by the claimant, less difficulty has arisen and the courts have been less reluctant to allow recovery from the defendant. The best illustration is *Longdon-Griffiths v Smith*,[54] which involved a business loss. The claimant's employment had been lawfully determined by the third party in accordance with the terms of the claimant's contract of service and it was held that this damage was not too remote, Slade J taking the view that lawful determination of a contract must provide a stronger case for the claimant than unlawful determination.[55] Other cases have held that a rightful refusal to employ, or to continue employing, the claimant is an actionable loss, with no argument on the point of remoteness.[56] Beyond this, social losses should provide illustrations of third parties' acts which do not involve **46-013**

---

48 (1806) 8 East 1.

49 (1800) 2 B. & P. 284.

50 (1800) 2 B. & P. 284 at 289.

51 (1853) 2 E. & B. 216: see para.48-004, below. The decision in *Vicars v Wilcocks* (1806) 8 East 1 and the dictum in *Morris v Langdale* (1800) 2 B. & P. 284 had already been seriously doubted, first in Starkie, *Libel and Slander*, 2nd edn (1830), Vol.1, p.205 and then in *Green v Button* (1835) 2 C.M. & R. 707.

52 The maxim that intended consequences are never too remote is, however, too sweeping: see paras 8-050 and 8-062, above.

53 Yet in *Longdon-Griffiths v Smith* [1950] 2 All E.R. 662, Slade J took the view that in assessing the damages the defendant must be given credit for the amount which the claimant could recover from the third party in an action for breach of contract. This seems dubious.

54 [1950] 2 All E.R. 662: the case was libel, but the principle of the decision applies also to slanders actionable only on proof of special damage.

55 [1950] 2 All E.R. 662 at 678: this point is not dealt with at all in the report at [1951] 2 K.B. 295.

56 *Storey v Challands* (1837) 8 C. & P. 234; *Dixon v Smith* (1860) 5 H. & N. 450 (as to a particular contract as *accoucheur* but not as to general loss); *Hartley v Herring* (1799) 8 T.R. 130 (the claimant was a clergyman, so it was not quite "employment").

liability in damages. In *Lynch v Knight*,[57] Lord Campbell and Lord Cranworth took the view that, if a husband refused to continue consortium with his wife by reason of the defendant's slander that she had committed adultery, this loss would not be considered too remote in the wife's action against the defendant.[58] And it is submitted that, similarly, loss of friends and of society should not be too remote: the refusal of damages for such loss on the ground of remoteness in *Weldon v De Bathe*,[59] seems dubious.

**46-014** But whether wrongful or not wrongful in the sense of giving rise to an action for damages by the claimant, the third party's act may not have been an act which, as a reaction to the slander, was in accordance with human nature. In such circumstances the loss caused thereby will be too remote. This proposition is illustrated by a number of cases. In *Speake v Hughes*,[60] the claimant's employers dismissed the claimant, as was within their contractual rights, on account of a slander that he had left the house of the defendant, his landlord, owing one month's rent. The Court of Appeal said that the defendant could only reasonably have contemplated that the employers might remonstrate with the claimant and exert some pressure upon him to pay but not that they should dismiss him from their service: the damage was held too remote.[61] In *Lynch v Knight*,[62] a husband refused to continue consortium with his wife on account of a slander that she had almost been seduced before her marriage. This loss of consortium was held too remote by the House of Lords on the ground that the husband's conduct in turning out the wife was not a reasonable consequence of the slander but was due to an idiosyncrasy of this particular husband[63]; in their Lordships' view, other husbands, assuming the truth of the defendant's charge, would not have turned out their wives.[64] And in *Chamberlain v Boyd*,[65] the claimant failed to obtain membership of a club because the defendant had slandered him with a view to retaining the existing club election rules and so securing his exclusion. This loss was held too remote; Lord Coleridge said that a club would not be influenced as to its election rules by the character of one or two persons who might subsequently stand for election,[66] and Brett LJ said that it was

---

57 (1861) 9 H.L.C. 577.

58 (1861) 9 H.L.C. 577 at 592 and 596 respectively.

59 (1885) 54 L.J.Q.B. 113 CA.

60 [1904] 1 K.B. 138 CA. One may perhaps assume that the claimant's dismissal was within his employers' rights here, though the report does not specifically say so. In any event the Court of Appeal's reasoning would apply to both rightful and wrongful dismissal.

61 See, too, *Michael v Spiers* (1909) 101 L.T. 352.

62 (1861) 9 H.L.C. 577.

63 Lord Wensleydale dissented on this point.

64 Their Lordships took different views on whether, had there been actual seduction before the marriage, it would have been a reasonable consequence of the slander that the wife was turned out. Lord Campbell and Lord Cranworth thought it probably would ((1861) 9 H.L.C. 577 at 592 and 596 respectively) but Lord Broughham doubted this (at 593). Consider the views expressed there as to the position if the slanderous accusation had been of adultery: see para.46-013, above.

65 (1883) Q.B.D. 407 CA.

66 (1883) Q.B.D. 407 CA at 412.

absurd to suppose that the members refused to alter the rules because they believed in the claimant's misconduct.[67]

### (2) Repetition by third party of the slander[68]

In *Ward v Weeks*,[69] where the defendant slandered the claimant to a third party who repeated the slander to another who then refused to sell on credit to the claimant goods which he had been about to sell him and which were necessary for the carrying on of the claimant's business, this damage was held too remote, for **46-015**

> "such a spontaneous and unauthorised communication cannot be considered as the necessary consequence of the original uttering of the words".[70]

Similar decisions appear throughout the 19th century.[71] The rule in *Ward v Weeks*,[72] has been criticised on the ground that, human nature being what it is, nothing is more likely than that the slander would be repeated, or, put more technically, repetition is a foreseeable intervening act. Especially was it criticised by Kelly CB in *Riding v Smith*,[73] where he hoped

> "the day will come when the principle of *Ward v Weeks* and that class of case shall be brought under the consideration of the court of last resort".[74]

However, the matter was for long thought to have been put to rest by the decision of the House of Lords in *Weld-Blundell v Stephens*,[75] in which their Lordships by a bare majority approved the decision in *Ward v Weeks*,[76] although Lord Sumner at the same time recognised the probability that the intervening act would take place, "for more than half of human kind are tale-bearers by nature".[77]

A number of qualifications on the rule in *Ward v Weeks*,[78] appeared early. These are most clearly set out in the judgment of Lopes LJ in *Speight v Gosnay*.[79] He there laid down that the original utterer of a slander was liable for damage caused by its **46-016**

---

67 (1883) Q.B.D. 407 CA at 414.

68 Consider the treatment, in the context of the general principles of remoteness, of the cases dealt with here: paras 8-044 and 8-061, above.

69 (1830) 7 Bing. 211.

70 (1830) 7 Bing. 211 at 215. The person repeating the slander would of course himself generally be liable. The earlier doctrine that a person repeating a slander would not be liable where he had named the author had been finally abandoned the previous year in *McPherson v Daniel* (1829) 10 B. & C. 263.

71 Notably *Tunnicliffe v Moss* (1850) 3 C. & K. 83 (applying *Rutherford v Evans* (1829) 4 C. & P. 74); *Dixon v Smith* (1860) 5 H. & N. 450; *Parkins v Scott* (1862) 1 H. & C. 153; *Clarke v Morgan* (1878) 38 L.T. 354. See, too, *Bateman v Lyall* (1860) 7 C.B. N.S. 638; *Bree v Marescaux* (1881) 7 Q.B.D. 434 CA; *Argent v Donigan* (1892) 8 T.L.R. 432. The earlier case of *Vicars v Wilcocks* (1806) 8 East 1 could have been decided on this ground but was not despite what Wightman J says in *Lumley v Gye* (1853) 2 E. & B. 216 at 237.

72 (1830) 7 Bing. 211.

73 (1876) 1 Ex. D. 91 at 94.

74 That case, which was not strictly slander but injurious falsehood, was considered distinguishable on the ground that the special damage was proved by evidence of a general loss of custom resulting from a statement made on a public occasion. This is dealt with at para.46-021, below.

75 [1920] A.C. 956: facts at para.8-146, above. The action was contract not tort.

76 (1830) 7 Bing. 211.

77 [1920] A.C. 956 at 991.

78 (1830) 7 Bing. 211.

79 (1890) 60 L.J.Q.B. 231 CA.

repetition in four types of case: (1) if he authorised the repetition, (2) if he intended the repetition, (3) if the repetition was the natural consequence and (4) if there was a moral duty on the person to whom it was uttered to repeat it.[80] The first and second categories present no difficulty, for it is a clear general rule throughout the law of tort that intended consequences are not too remote.[81] Thus in *Cutler v McPhail*,[82] the claimants sued the defendant in respect both of the original publication of a defamatory letter to a magazine editor and of its re-publication in the magazine. Although the cause of action against the defendant in respect of the re-publication was held to be extinguished by virtue of a payment to the claimants by the publishers of the magazine, it was held that the damages recoverable against him in respect of the original publication to the editor would include the damage suffered by the claimants by reason of the re-publication in the magazine since the defendant had intended such re-publication. As to the third and fourth categories—and it is the third one as to natural consequences that is crucial—these were given a very narrow compass by *Speight v Gosnay*,[83] itself. The facts of that case were that the defendants said of an unmarried woman to her mother that she was unchaste, the mother repeated this to her daughter, who repeated it to her fiancé, who thereupon broke off the engagement. It was held by the Court of Appeal that the damage was too remote, falling within none of Lopes LJ's categories. Indeed with this approach it is difficult to see that the third category of natural consequence had anything to operate upon while *Ward v Weeks*,[84] stood as good law. As to the fourth category, there was held to be no moral duty on the third party to repeat the slander either in *Speight v Gosnay*,[85] or in the somewhat similar case of *Parkins v Scott*,[86] where a wife, accused of unchastity, repeated this slander to her husband who in consequence left her. Only in *Derry v Handley*,[87] has a moral duty sufficed to prevent the damage being too remote: there the third party repeated the slander to his wife because she had been employing the claimant. If indeed there is a legal duty on the third party to repeat the slander, the claimant will recover for damage caused by the repetition. This was established by *Kendillon v Maltby*,[88] where the claimant constable had been dismissed by the police commissioners in consequence of a slander uttered by the defendant magistrate in trying a case, this slander having been reported to the commissioners by an inspector of police in pursuance of his duty.

**46-017** However, hopes for the third exception, or something akin thereto, have been now revived by two decisions of the Court of Appeal. In the first, *Slipper v British Broadcasting Corporation*,[89] the defendants had made a film alleged to be defama-

---

80 (1890) 60 L.J.Q.B. 231 CA at 232. In *Ward v Lewis* [1955] 1 W.L.R. 9 CA, Denning LJ expressed the position thus: "A man who speaks a slander is not responsible for its re-publication unless he authorises it or he knows or ought to know it is likely to be re-published": at 11. The case dealt with a matter of pleading.

81 The maximum that intended consequences are never too remote is, however, too sweeping: see paras 8-050 and 8-062, above.

82 [1962] 2 Q.B. 292: the case was libel, but the principle of the decision applies also to slanders actionable only on proof of special damage.

83 (1890) 60 L.J.Q.B. 231 CA.

84 (1830) 7 Bing. 211.

85 (1890) 60 L.J.Q.B. 231 CA.

86 (1862) 1 H. & C. 153.

87 (1867) 16 L.T. 263.

88 (1842) Car. & M. 402.

89 [1991] 1 Q.B. 283 CA. A case of libel, but since issues of remoteness hardly vary across the whole

tory of the claimant police officer in depicting his abortive attempts to apprehend in Brazil an escaped convict who had been one of the participants in what has become known as the Great Train Robbery. Following upon the defendants' showing the film in a preview to journalists and broadcasting the film to the public at large, reviews of the film appeared in the national press, reviews which repeated the sting of the libel. The defendants sought to strike out the police officer's claim based upon the repetition of the libel in the reviews, but failed in their attempt. The Court of Appeal held that, although prima facie the unauthorised repetition of a libel would be treated as a novus actus interveniens breaking the chain of causation between the original publication and the damage suffered through the repetition or re-publication, nonetheless, where it was appropriate on the facts, the repetition of the sting of a libel by an unauthorised third party would be treated as foreseeable and as the natural and probable consequence of the original publication so as to expose the original publisher to a claim for damages in respect of the repetition or re-publication. The approval of *Ward v Weeks*,[90] in *Weld-Blundell v Stephens*,[91] did not go so far as to inhibit a court from ever holding for a claimant on the basis of natural and probable consequence.

The approach in the second case, *McManus v Beckham*,[92] was somewhat different. Laws LJ considered that the defamation cases had "over time been girt about with unhelpful complexities" and that **46-018**

> "the circumstances in which repeat publication might be relied on [had become] ossified into categories".[93]

He was of the view that the law needed to be simplified.[94] What was before the Court of Appeal was once again a strike out application which once again failed; no substantive decision was reached in favour of the claimants, whose trade had suffered in consequence of the slander.[95] A well-known singer and performer, the so-called Posh Spice, married to a well-known footballer, David Beckham, wrongly accused the claimants of selling fake autographs of her husband, the accusation being made in a rude, loud and unreasonable way in front of the very few customers who were then in the claimants' shop. The news got out, there was extensive press coverage of the incident, and as a result the claimants' business suffered. The Court of Appeal, in holding against strike out, concentrated on justice rather than foreseeability. Waller LJ considered that it would be unwise to direct the jury in terms of foreseeability[96]; Laws LJ agreed but said that a direction excluding any reference to foreseeability would be in the interest of clarity rather than by the dictate of principle; the damage must be foreseeable, but more than foreseeability was required.[97] The root question was whether it was just to impose liability.[98] Thus

---

range of defamation (for such variation as there is, see para.46-039, below), they are dealt with comprehensively here. This makes for unity of treatment and avoids repetition.

90 (1830) 7 Bing. 211.

91 [1920] A.C. 956.

92 [2002] 1 W.L.R. 2982 CA.

93 [2002] 1 W.L.R. 2982 CA at [41].

94 [2002] 1 W.L.R. 2982 CA at [42].

95 Being a slander which affected the claimants in their trade, it was actionable per se without the need to prove special damage.

96 [2002] 1 W.L.R. 2982 CA at [34].

97 [2002] 1 W.L.R. 2982 CA at [43]–[44].

98 [2002] 1 W.L.R. 2982 CA at [42], per Laws LJ; and see Ward LJ at [34].

if the defendant was actually aware that what she said or did was likely to be reported, and that, if she slandered someone, that slander was likely to be repeated in whole or in part, there was no injustice in her being held responsible for the damage that the slander caused through that publication.

**46-019** The result of these two Court of Appeal cases is that the sting has been taken out of *Ward v Weeks*,[99] itself. Each case of repetition and re-publication will now have to be looked at separately. Liability for repetition or re-publication by a mere tale-bearer, however foreseeable that repetition or re-publication may be, may well still be excluded.[100]

## 3. PLEADING AND PROOF OF SPECIAL DAMAGE

**46-020** Matters concerning the pleading and proof of damage are properly dealt with under procedure,[101] but require brief consideration here because, in relation to slanders actionable only on proof of special damage, they impinge in one respect on the issue of liability.

**46-021** Special damage must be pleaded by the claimant in order to entitle him to prove it. Normally the pleading and also the evidence in proof must be of particular instances of loss, so that where specific instances are not pleaded they may not be produced in proof,[102] and where pleaded they may be proved only by evidence of the specific losses. Where, however, the facts do not admit of particularising specific instances of loss, then the courts are prepared to accept a generalised statement of special damage in pleading and general evidence of special damage in proof.[103] This is particularly so where the slander is followed by general falling off of business and the claimant's customers are a fluctuating body whose names are unknown to him, as with the clientele of many shops or with the audiences of theatres.[104] These rules of procedure may, however, impinge on the issue of liability in that, by allowing the proof of a general loss of custom, there is a danger of circumventing the rule that the defendant is not normally liable for any repetition of the slander by third parties.[105] In *Clarke v Morgan*,[106] Grove J pointed to what he called the "logical difficulty" that

> "on the one hand you cannot give evidence of a certain number of persons who ceased to associate with the plaintiff in consequence of having heard a repetition of the slander, although on the other you can give evidence of a general falling off of persons so associating."[107]

The way out of this logical difficulty is pointed out by Bowen LJ in *Ratcliffe v*

---

99 (1830) 7 Bing. 211.

100 The matter is further considered in the context of remoteness at para.8-061, above.

101 See Chs 51 and 52, below.

102 See, e.g. *Hunt v Jones* (1618) Cro. Jac. 499 and *Barnes v Prudlin* (1667) 1 Sid. 396 (both claims for loss of suitors through the slander without specifying particular suitors).

103 See, e.g. *Hartley v Herring* (1799) 8 T.R. 130 (claim for loss of church congregation through the slander without specifying particular members). This appears to be the only illustration dealing with slander itself; the leading case on the whole issue is *Ratcliffe v Evans* [1892] 2 Q.B. 524 CA but it deals with injurious falsehood: see para.48-011, below.

104 Also loss of church attendance as in *Hartley v Herring* (1799) 8 T.R. 130, or of friends' hospitality as in *Clarke v Morgan* (1878) 38 L.T. 354.

105 See para.46-015, above. But see paras 46-017 to 46-019, above.

106 (1878) 38 L.T. 354.

107 (1878) 38 L.T. 354 at 355.

*Evans*,[108] the leading case on pleading and proof of damage though itself dealing with injurious falsehood. If the slander is one which was originally spoken in public to a large body, a floating and transitory class, as bidders at an auction or customers at an inn, or if repetition is intended[109] to an unlimited extent, then proof of general loss of custom may properly be allowed without infringing the rules as to remoteness. This must now be taken as the explanation of *Hartley v Herring*,[110] where a clergyman, laying as special damage the loss of his congregation, was held not required to state the names of the members on account of the supposed impossibility of doing so. On the other hand, where the total damage includes damage caused by repetition, and repetition for which the defendant is not liable to an unlimited extent, then proof of general loss of custom is not permissible. This is illustrated by *Dixon v Smith*,[111] where as a result of the slander a third party would not employ the claimant as an accoucheur and in addition his business fell off generally. The court held that the jury were wrong in giving damages for the general loss of business. "The decline of the plaintiff's business", said Martin B,

> "cannot have arisen from the speaking of the slanderous words by the defendant ... and for the repetitions of the slander the defendant is clearly not responsible".[112]

## 4. ADDITIONAL GENERAL DAMAGES

Whether, where special damage is shown, the court may then award in addition damages for the injury to reputation and also to feelings, is undecided. The question is one of policy and the scope of protection afforded by the tort, and as with other torts the law has not taken a clear line on the propriety of recovery for damage to an interest other than the interest which the tort is designed to protect primarily.[113] Not only do the few existing dicta move in either direction but they are too slender to warrant any firm conclusion. On the one hand in *Brown v Smith*,[114] where the court held the particular slander to be actionable per se, Williams J expressed the view that, had the court not so held, the defendant would have been entitled to a verdict **46-022**

> "because the question of damages was left at large to the jury without telling them to limit it to the [special damage]".[115]

On the other hand in *Dixon v Smith*,[116] Martin B said that the claimant's damages were not limited to the profit lost on a particular contract

[108] [1892] 2 Q.B. 524 CA at 531–532.

[109] Or within any of the other exceptions laid down in *Speight v Gosnay* (1890) 60 L.J.Q.B. 231 CA to the rule in *Ward v Weeks* (1830) 7 Bing. 211: see para.46-016, above.

[110] (1799) 8 T.R. 130. This is given as the probable explanation of the case in *Ratcliffe v Evans* [1892] 2 Q.B. 524 CA at 531.

[111] (1860) 5 H. & N. 450.

[112] (1860) 5 H. & N. 450 at 453.

[113] See paras 8-082 and following, above for a general discussion of the problem of scope of protection in tort. In this connection, see especially para.8-126, above.

[114] (1855) 13 C.B. 596.

[115] (1855) 13 C.B. 596 at 600.

[116] (1860) 5 H. & N. 450.

"but that the jury might consider what damage he had sustained in consequence of the speaking of the words".[117]

In line with the liberal view is Lord Wensleydale's dictum in *Lynch v Knight*,[118] where he said:

"Mental pain or anxiety the law cannot value, and does not pretend to redress, when the unlawful act complained of causes that alone; though where a material damage occurs, and is connected with it, it is impossible a jury, in estimating it, should altogether overlook the feelings of the party interested."[119]

## II. SLANDERS ACTIONABLE PER SE AND LIBEL

### 1. LEVEL OF AWARDS

**46-023** Awards here, where there is no requirement of proof of special damage but the damages are at large,[120] have in earlier years been impressive in their size. However, by the end of the 1980s things had got out of control, with jury awards appearing which have been out of all proportion to the damage suffered. Perhaps the award that stood out was that of £1.5 million in the action brought by Lord Aldington against Count Tolstoy,[121] an award which did not contain any element of exemplary damages and which is already a fair number of years ago.[122] Three of the cases in the law reports of the 1990s—the *Aldington* case does not appear to have been properly reported—both attest to the size of awards[123] and have sought with increasing vigour to improve upon the situation.

**46-024** In *Sutcliffe v Pressdram*,[124] where the award was of £600,000 compensatory damages, it was said that, while the jury should not be told of awards by juries in other libel cases or of awards of judges in personal injury cases, some guidance should be given as to the financial implications of the sum which might be awarded by pointing out the investment income from, or purchasing power of, large sums so that the jury was able to appreciate the real value of such sums. Later, in *Rantzen v Mirror Group Newspapers*,[125] with an award of £250,000 compensatory damages, the Court of Appeal, while still holding against the revelation to the jury of other jury libel awards, or indeed of awards by judges in personal injury claims, permit-

---

[117] (1860) 5 H. & N. 450 at 453.

[118] (1861) 9 H.L.C. 577 at 598.

[119] Whether there may be any aggravation or mitigation of the damages in cases of slanders not actionable per se depends on the outcome of this question. As for exemplary damages, the position should be the same as with slanders actionable per se and libel: see para.46-078, below.

[120] See para.46-031, below.

[121] Though perhaps not significantly higher in real terms, given the erosion in money values, than the £25,000 awarded 70 years ago in *Youssoupoff v Metro-Goldwyn-Mayer Pictures* (1934) 50 T.L.R. 581 CA, which would, if awarded today, come out at well over £1 million. That, however, was at the time a highly exceptional award, described later by the claimants' counsel, Sir Patrick Hastings KC, as enormous.

[122] The European Court of Human Rights has since held that the size of the award, in conjunction with the lack of adequate safeguards against a disproportionately high amount being given, constituted a violation of the defendant's rights under art.10 of the European Convention on Human Rights: *Miloslavsky v UK* (1995) 20 E.H.R.R. 442.

[123] All three awards were, however, overturned for excessiveness by the Court of Appeal. On this aspect of the cases, see paras 53-020 to 53-022, below.

[124] [1991] 1 Q.B. 153 CA.

[125] [1994] Q.B. 670 CA.

ted for the future the citation of awards not by juries themselves but by the Court of Appeal under its power, exercisable from 1991, to substitute its own award in lieu of ordering a new jury trial on damages,[126] as these awards could be relied upon to establish a norm.[127] Then in *John v MGN*,[128] the Court of Appeal, presented with an award of £350,000 which was both compensatory and exemplary, went much further. The court was not content with the *Rantzen*,[129] approach of merely revealing the Court of Appeal's own libel awards because the corpus of such experience would take too long to develop for a problem which needed urgent tackling,[130] and, while rightly accepting that earlier jury awards in libel cases should not, at least for the time being, be referred to as they could themselves be unreliable in the absence of appropriate guidance, the court was of the view that in future juries might be referred to the conventional awards for pain and suffering and loss of amenities—the general damages—in personal injury cases despite the fact that the contrary decision in *Rantzen*,[131] had been arrived at only two to three years earlier; the subject deserved reconsideration.

Delivering the judgment of the court in *John v MGN*,[132] Sir Thomas Bingham MR, referring to the wildly extravagant awards which had given rise to much deserved criticism, commented that it was not the fault of the juries who had been "in the position of sheep loosed on an unfenced common, with no shepherd".[133] Pointing to the typical conventional awards in personal injury cases at the time, from loss of a limb at £50,000 to quadriplegia at £125,000,[134] he said: **46-025**

> "Juries may properly be asked to consider whether the injury to his reputation of which the plaintiff complains should fairly justify any greater compensation … It is in our view offensive to public opinion, and rightly so, that a defamation plaintiff should recover damages for injury to his reputation greater, perhaps by a significant factor, than if that same plaintiff had been rendered a helpless cripple or an insensate vegetable. The time has in our view come when judges, and counsel, should be free to draw the attention of juries to these comparisons".[135]

And in addition to permitting the revelation of personal injury awards to juries, Sir Thomas Bingham MR ruled that the then current invariable practice that neither

---

[126] For this, see para.53-004, below. The House of Lords has confirmed in *Grobbelaar v News Group Newspapers Ltd* [2002] 1 W.L.R. 3024 that it has the same power by virtue of its inherent jurisdiction.

[127] Their Lordships in *The Gleaner Co Ltd v Abrahams* [2004] 1 A.C. 628 PC endorsed the ruling in the Jamaican Court of Appeal, consistent with *Rantzen*, that other jury libel awards should not be revealed to the jury. Reference to appeal awards is not an issue in Jamaica as the Court of Appeal there does not have power to substitute its own award: see at [58].

[128] [1997] Q.B. 586 CA.

[129] [1994] Q.B. 670 CA.

[130] It was pointed out that, other than in *Rantzen* itself, only in two cases so far had the court substituted its own award, both being unreported: see *Gorman v Mudd* [1992] CA Transcript No.1076 and *Houston v Smith* [1993] CA Transcript No.1544. According to Lord Hoffmann in *The Gleaner Co Ltd v Abrahams* [2004] 1 A.C. 628 PC the number nine years later had risen to six: at [47].

[131] [1994] Q.B. 670 CA.

[132] [1997] Q.B. 586 CA.

[133] [1997] Q.B. 586 CA at 608G.

[134] See paras 40-274 and following, above.

[135] [1997] Q.B. 586 CA at 614G–H. Interestingly, in *KC v MGN Ltd* [2013] 1 W.L.R. 1015 CA, in substituting £100,000 for the trial judge's award of £150,000 (facts at para.46-069, below), the court said that it had reflected on the nature and extent of the personal injury which would lead to general damages of £150,000: at [49].

counsel nor the judge may make any suggestion to the jury as to what would be an appropriate award should be discontinued. "Mentioning figures", he said, "would, in our view, induce a mood of realism on both sides".[136] However, *Kiam v MGN Ltd*,[137] shows that it does not follow, where figures are suggested by the judge, that a jury ignores them at its peril.[138]

**46-026** By contrast with Sir Thomas Bingham's approach, the Jamaican courts have retained their position of not revealing personal injury awards to juries and their Lordships in *The Gleaner Co Ltd v Abrahams*,[139] have endorsed Jamaica's entitlement to consider that no change in practice was desirable.[140] The submission that the rejection of guidance from personal injury awards was an error of law was firmly rejected; no question of legal principle was involved. "Whether a link", said Lord Hoffmann delivering the judgment of the Board,

> "should be established between defamation awards and personal injury awards is a question of policy".[141]

Their Lordships said that they expressed no view on the current practice in England.[142] Nevertheless Lord Hoffmann's rigorous analysis of the differences between awards in these two very different fields[143] may be thought to convey a certain leaning towards favouring the Jamaican, and former English, solution to what he regarded as a controversial question.

**46-027** For a variety of reasons, such as the extended entitlement to make an offer of amends introduced by the Defamation Act 1996,[144] and the removal of the presumption in favour of trial by jury by the Defamation Act 2013,[145] there have been in the wake of *John v MGN*,[146] fewer and fewer defamation cases tried with a jury.[147] One consequence of this is that discussion of the level of awards has been confined to cases heard by judges sitting alone. In *John v MGN Ltd*,[148] Sir Thomas Bingham MR predicted that a consequence of this would be that

> "there would no doubt emerge a more or less coherent framework of awards which would, while recognising the particular features of particular cases, ensure that broadly comparable cases led to broadly comparable awards".

In *Barron v Vines*,[149] Warby J recognised that this prediction had been fulfilled. A large contribution was made by Eady J, who heard many of the major defamation cases in the High Court in the early years of this century. He recognised in a number of his judgments that the ceiling for compensatory damages in defamation had risen

---

136 [1997] Q.B. 586 CA at 615G.
137 [2003] Q.B. 281 CA.
138 See the case at paras 53-019 and 53-021, below.
139 [2004] 1 A.C. 628 PC.
140 [2004] 1 A.C. 628 PC at [63].
141 [2004] 1 A.C. 628 PC at [62].
142 [2004] 1 A.C. 628 PC at [50].
143 [2004] 1 A.C. 628 PC at [49]–[56].
144 For this see para.46-073, below.
145 Defamation Act 2013 s.11.
146 [1997] Q.B. 586 CA.
147 See the full discussion of the supplanting of jury trials by judge only trials at para.17-008, above.
148 [1997] Q.B. 586 CA at 608.
149 [2016] EWHC 1226 (QB) at [81].

to the region of £200,000. He did this in *Abu v MGN Ltd*,[150] in *Cleese v Clark*,[151] and earlier in *Lillie and Reed v Newcastle City Council*,[152] Lord Hoffmann in *The Gleaner Co Ltd v Abrahams*,[153] citing this last reference without disapproval.[154] Indeed in *Lillie and Reed*, an appalling case of subjection to accusations of child abuse by the City Council and an investigating review body, £200,000 was awarded by Eady J to each of the two claimants against the four members of the review body whom he held to have acted with malice. By contrast, in *Campbell v News Group Newspapers Ltd*,[155] a jury award of £350,000 was reduced by the Court of Appeal to £30,000, but the case did involve misdirection and also misconduct by the claimant.[156] The downturn in the level of damages was specifically taken account of by Eady J when in *Galloway v Telegraph Group*,[157] he awarded £150,000 to the controversial George Galloway, who had been Labour Member of Parliament for Glasgow, on account of a libel that he was in the pay of Saddam Hussein.[158] In *KC v MGN Ltd*,[159] Bean J stated in his judgment of March 2012 that the ceiling of £200,000 would now be £256,000,[160] and Lord Judge CJ, giving the judgment of the Court of Appeal in *Cairns v Modi*,[161] in October 2012, said that the ceiling figure by then was in the region of £275,000,[162] with this being repeated by Tugendhat J in his judgment of March 2013 in *ZAM v CFW*.[163] More recently, it has been said that the figure is now about £300,000,[164] a consequence of inflation and the ruling in the ultimate Court of Appeal hearing of *Simmons v Castle*,[165] that from 1 April 2013 damages for all types of non-pecuniary loss in all civil claims should be increased by 10 per cent.[166]

It is interesting that the ceiling of £200,000 put forward in the various cases by **46-028**

---

150 [2003] 1 W.L.R. 2201 at [6].

151 [2004] E.M.L.R. 3 at 37, [33].

152 [2002] EWHC 1600 (QB) at [1550].

153 [2004] 1 A.C. 628 PC.

154 [2004] 1 A.C. 628 PC at [49].

155 [2002] E.M.L.R. 43 CA at 966.

156 The court stated at [2002] E.M.L.R. 43 CA at [26] that in an annex, Annex A, "we examine in greater detail the legal principles which govern libel damages".

157 [2005] E.M.L.R. 7 at 115.

158 The appeal on damages was dismissed: [2006] E.M.L.R. 11 at 221. How far jury awards have tumbled as a result of these sensible developments is not adequately documented. Jury awards which have been cut down, and the amounts by which they have been cut down, together with the occasional award where the Court of Appeal has not interfered with the jury's verdict, are addressed elsewhere: see paras 53-021 and 53-022, below.

159 [2012] EWHC 483 (QB).

160 [2012] EWHC 483 (QB) at [26].

161 [2013] 1 W.L.R. 1015 CA.

162 [2013] 1 W.L.R. 1015 CA at [25].

163 [2013] EWHC 662 (QB) at [56].

164 *Rai v Bholowasia* [2015] EWHC 382 (QB) at [179]; *Barron v Collins* [2017] EWHC 162 (QB) at [26]; *Harrath v Stand for Peace Ltd* [2017] EWHC 653 (QB) at [10]; *Lisle-Mainwaring v Associated Newspapers* [2017] EWHC 543 (QB) at [62].

165 [2013] 1 W.L.R. 1239 CA; this hearing is from 1243. On the increase in the ceiling as a result of *Simmons v Castle* see *Harrath v Stand for Peace Ltd & Anor* [2017] EWHC 653 (QB) at [10].

166 For the procedural history and reasons for this development, stemming from the package of reforms appearing in the *Jackson Report on Civil Litigation Costs*, see para.40-280, below. In the first Court of Appeal hearing of *Simmons v Castle* [2013] 1 W.L.R. 1239 CA at 1240, where the ruling was confined to torts causing suffering, inconvenience or distress, two torts were specifically mentioned of which defamation was one: see at [20].

Eady J[167] equated with the ceiling for awards for non-pecuniary loss in personal injury cases laid down at about the same time by the Court of Appeal in *Heil v Rankin*,[168] and also that Bean J has later pointed out in *KC v MGN Ltd*,[169] that his 2012 ceiling figure of £256,000 for defamation[170] is not far off the £265,000 which was the then current maximum guideline for personal injury damages for non-pecuniary loss.[171] However, as we have seen,[172] their Lordships in *The Gleaner Co Ltd v Abrahams*,[173] accepted the propriety of the courts in Jamaica not revealing to the jury the level of personal injury awards and the Judicial Committee's decision further shows that the move in England to smaller awards may not be reflected in Commonwealth countries. For the award of the Jamaican Court of Appeal of 35 million Jamaican dollars, the equivalent at the time of £533,000, was upheld,[174] the Judicial Committee saying in effect that the matter was one for Jamaica, being a question of policy rather than of law.[175]

**46-029** The tide, however, of cautious judicial awards in trials without a jury remains strong, especially with the desire for consistency with awards for personal injury. In *Umeyor v Nwakamma*,[176] a libellous publication was published to an unincorporated association of 50-60 members dedicated to the interests and welfare of the Mbaise community of which the claimant was a member. The allegation was of forgery but the claimant proved no financial loss and rumours had already abounded. The claimant was awarded only 2000 pounds in general damages for injury to reputation and feelings despite the acknowledgement by Jay J[177] that "attribution of forgery to the Claimant's is not something which may lightly be disregarded".

## 2. HEADS OF DAMAGE

**46-030** There are three regular heads of damage—injury to reputation, injury to feelings and the head which is unfortunately described by the label "vindication", a type of damages which has elsewhere been rejected[178] and which must therefore be explained carefully. As Laws LJ said in *Purnell v Business F1 Magazine Ltd*[179]:

> "It is well established that general damages in defamation cases serve the three functions submitted by counsel before Gray J: to console the claimant for the injury to his feelings occasioned by publication of the defamatory statement; to repair the harm to his reputation; and as a vindication of his reputation".

Statements to the same effect are now common in today's cases. This trilogy is

---

167 See the previous paragraph.
168 [2001] Q.B. 272 CA: see paras 40-278 and 40-279, above
169 [2012] EWHC 483 (QB).
170 See the previous paragraph.
171 [2012] EWHC 483 (QB) at [26].
172 At para.46-026, above.
173 [2004] 1 A.C. 628 PC.
174 The award of the jury at the trial, which was set aside by the Jamaican Court of Appeal, had been even higher at 80.7 million Jamaican dollars, the equivalent at the time of £1.2 million.
175 Compare the earlier similar approach of their Lordships' Board to awards of exemplary awards in Australia, at para.13-005, above.
176 [2015] EWHC 2980 (QB).
177 At [92].
178 *R. (on the application of Lumba) v Secretary of State for the Home Department* [2012] 1 A.C. 245.
179 [2008] 1 W.L.R. 1 CA at [8].

elaborated upon by Lord Judge CJ in *Cairns v Modi*,[180] where, in giving the judgment of the court, he said[181]:

"These distinct features apply to every defamation case, but the emphasis to be placed on each will vary from case to case. Sometimes, for example, there may be little demonstrable damage to reputation, but serious emotional distress; on other occasions, the need for public vindication will predominate; in yet other cases the financial consequences of damage to the reputation of the individual may represent the most serious feature."

## (1) Injury to reputation

In cases of libel, and of slanders actionable per se, the injury to the reputation is of course the principal element in the damages: this, as a head of damage, is to be regarded as a non-pecuniary loss. Thus, as Lord Greene put it in *Rook v Fairrie*,[182] **46-031**

"in a libel action the damages awarded are, for the most part and often entirely, without any real connection with any pecuniary loss at all".[183]

It has therefore many times been said that the amount of the assessment is "peculiarly the province of the jury"[184] although as discussed above, a conventional framework has developed as a consequence of the increase in judge alone trials. Also the damages are said to be "at large".[185] The various considerations that should weigh with judge or jury in making the assessment for injury to reputation are dealt with later.[186]

## (2) Injury to feelings

In addition the injury to the claimant's feelings is taken into account; this is generally assumed and little therefore is said about it. In *Goslin v Corry*,[187] Erskine J spoke of awarding damages "for the mental suffering arising from the apprehension of the consequences of the publication"; in *Ley v Hamilton*,[188] Lord Atkin assumed that damages are awarded for "the insult offered or the pain of a false accusation"; in *Kelly v Sherlock*,[189] Blackburn J said that **46-032**

"the question was … what compensation ought the plaintiff to have for his injured feelings for … there was no actual pecuniary damage";

180 [2013] 1 W.L.R. 1015 CA.

181 [2013] 1 W.L.R. 1015 CA at [22].

182 [1941] 1 K.B. 507 CA.

183 [1941] 1 K.B. 507 CA at 515–516; contrasting a personal injury case which "apart possibly from the element of pain and suffering … can be linked with a pecuniary valuation": at 516.

184 *Davis v Shepstone* (1886) 11 App. Cas. 187 PC at 191 per Lord Herschell LC; *Bray v Ford* [1896] A.C. 44 at 50, per Lord Watson ("does not depend upon any definite legal rule, and is the peculiar function of the jury"); at 52 to 53, per Lord Herschell ("the assessment of damages is peculiarly within the province of that tribunal [i.e. the jury]. The damages cannot be measured by any standard known to the law; they must be determined by a consideration of all the circumstances of the case, viewed in the light of the law applicable to them. The latitude is very wide"); *Jones v Hulton* [1909] 2 K.B. 444 CA at 483, per Farwell LJ.

185 See, e.g. *Rook v Fairrie* [1941] 1 K.B. 507 CA at 516, per Lord Greene.

186 See paras 46-043 and following, below.

187 (1844) 7 M. & G. 342 at 346.

188 (1935) 153 L.T. 384 HL at 386.

189 (1866) L.R. 1 Q.B. 686 at 698.

in *Lynch v Knight*,[190] Lord Wensleydale, assuming that in slanders actionable only on proof of special damage general damages may be awarded where pecuniary loss is shown, spoke of such general damages as taking into account "mental pain or anxiety" and "the feelings of the party"; and Pearson LJ said in *McCarey v Associated Newspapers*,[191] that the claimant's damages

> "may also include the natural injury to his feelings—the natural grief and distress which he may have felt at having been spoken of in defamatory terms, and if there has been any kind of high-handed, oppressive, insulting or contumelious behaviour by the defendant which increases the mental pain and suffering caused by the defamation and may constitute injury to the plaintiff's pride and self-confidence, those are proper elements to be taken into account in a case where the damages are at large".

**46-033** These views were in effect endorsed by the Court of Appeal's decision in *Fielding v Variety Inc*,[192] where the recovery of injury to feelings was highlighted because the injury to reputation was negligible. The claimant was a celebrated impresario who brought stage plays to the theatres of London and New York, and the defendants owned an internationally read journal with a wide circulation in the theatre world. The defendants published an article which falsely stated that the claimant's latest London production was "a disastrous flop" and, when their error was pointed out to them, refused either to withdraw or apologise. However, the fact of the success of the London production continued to speak for itself and the court considered that even American producers, if indeed they remembered the article at all, would know that it was quite untrue. "It seems fairly obvious to me", said Salmon LJ,

> "that the article cannot have had any really serious effect upon Mr. Fielding's reputation. Nevertheless he is entitled to be compensated … for the anxiety and annoyance which he very naturally felt at the time."[193]

Furthermore, that the defendants had behaved very badly afterwards "not unnaturally tended to heighten Mr. Fielding's irritation and annoyance" and was material "in so far as it increased the injury to Mr Fielding's feelings".[194] Also in *Cleese v Clark*,[195] the injury to feelings easily outweighed the injury to reputation, the allegations against the claimant comedian, actor and writer in the defendant's newspaper article being said to be very much at the lower end of gravity.[196] By contrast, in *Metropolitan International Schools Ltd v Designtechnica Corporation*,[197] it was held that there could be no award for injured feelings, the claimant being a company and not an individual, and damages were awarded primarily for vindication. Similarly, in *Cooper v Turrell*,[198] where a company director and the company itself were claimants, both falsely accused of dishonesty and criminal conduct and the director of unfitness for his work, Tugendhat J awarded £50,000

190 (1861) 9 H.L.C. 577 at 598.

191 [1965] 2 Q.B. 86 CA at 104–105.

192 [1967] 2 Q.B. 841 CA.

193 [1967] 2 Q.B. 841 CA at 856.

194 [1967] 2 Q.B. 841 CA at 855. See, similarly, Lord Denning MR at 851.

195 [2004] E.M.L.R. 3 at 37. This was an assessment of compensation under the new offer of amends procedure.

196 See [2004] E.M.L.R. 3 at [39] and [42]. Only injured feelings featured in the modest damages award in *Clynes v O'Connor* [2011] EWHC 1201 (QB), a rather trivial case.

197 [2010] EWHC 2411 (QB). Facts at para.46-036, below.

198 [2011] EWHC 3269 (QB).

to the director and £30,000 to the company, the lower award reflecting the unavailability to corporations of damages for injury to feelings.

### (3) The references to vindication

The decline, and illegitimacy, of vindicatory damages generally has been seen in Ch.17. However, in the pocket of defamation law, damages are still commonly awarded for reasons described as "vindication". This feature of the damages, largely peculiar to defamation and occasionally other areas such as invasion of privacy, and making for potentially high awards, is that the damages are needed to show that the claimant's reputation is unsullied. Such damages in defamation are a misnomer when described as "vindicatory" because all damages focus generally upon vindicating a right. The focus of this head of damages is upon eradicating the consequence which could arise from the future disrespect which the claimant might incur from others as a consequence of the defamation. In this sense, the nature of the damages under this head were initially well explained, and indeed first properly recognised, in a familiar passage in Lord Hailsham's speech in *Broome v Cassell & Co*.[199] The claimant, he said, **46-034**

> "must be able to point to a sum awarded by a jury sufficient to convince a bystander of the baselessness of the charge".[200]

Later Lord Hoffmann went into more detail in *The Gleaner Co Ltd v Abrahams*,[201] saying:

> "The damages must be sufficient to demonstrate to the public that the plaintiff's reputation has been vindicated. Particularly if the defendant has not apologised and withdrawn the defamatory allegations, the award must show that they have been publicly proclaimed to have inflicted a serious injury."

As we saw in Ch.17, the growth of this head of damages described as being "to vindicate" reputation has, ironically, occurred at the same time as the decline, and ultimate rejection in *R. (on the application of Lumba) v Secretary of State for the Home Department*,[202] of the concept of "vindicatory damages". The label "vindication" in these cases can be understood as shorthand references for a need to ameliorate the prospect of, and respond to future adverse consequences if the libel "emerges from its lurking place at some future date".[203] In an electronic age involving prolific means of dissemination of information this can be of great importance especially in the absence of a public and widespread apology from the defendant. Unfortunately, an approach which is not transparent, but which is becoming increasingly common, is for an award to be made which instinctively synthesises *existing* distress as well as the prospect of *future* distress and *future* consequences.[204] For instance, in *Oyston v Reed*,[205] the defendant posted material concerning the chair- **46-035**

---

199 [1972] A.C. 1027.

200 [1972] A.C. 1027 at 1071C. This statement was alluded to in *Rantzen v Mirror Group Newspapers* [1994] Q.B. 670 CA, 695G by Neill LJ, who included a reference to vindication.

201 [2004] 1 A.C. 628 PC at [55].

202 [2012] 1 A.C. 245.

203 *Broome v Cassell & Co Ltd* [1972] A.C. 1027 at 1071, per Lord Hailsham.

204 *Cairns v Modi* [2013] 1 W.L.R. 1015 at [38]*Woodward v Grice* [2017] EWHC 1292 (QB).

205 [2016] EWHC 1067 (QB).

man of Blackpool Football Club on a website which was read by many fans of the football club. His conduct aggravated the distress caused by the posting and the trial judge, Langstaff J, referred to all the factors including a reference to "vindication" and awarded a single sum of £30,000. Matters are further confused by the fact that there is another possible, and legitimate, basis for damages that is sometimes concealed in this language of "vindication" which is that the damages are awarded to deter or to punish. "Vindication" is sometimes used in the sense of "vindictive". As one of the finest Australian defamation lawyers, McHugh J, when sitting on the High Court of Australia, remarked, the anger of the claimant is placated only when he or she knows that the defendant has been punished for the wrong. In this sense the award of damages is "punitive or vindictive".[206] Similarly, Lord Hoffmann remarked in *Gleaner Co Ltd v Abrahams*,[207] defamation actions, unlike those for personal injury, "often serve not only as compensation but also as an effective and necessary deterrent".

**46-036** The best approach would be for the language of vindication to be abandoned altogether in this area. In cases where additional damages are given for the purpose of ensuring that members of the public, in future, are aware that the claimant's reputation should be intact then this can be described as compensatory damages for the protection of future reputation. In cases where additional damages are given to deter or punish then this can be described as exemplary damages. However, at present, many cases treat "vindication" (as mislabelled, and potentially conflating different types of damages) as lying at the heart of the damages awarded.[208] Thus a libel on the internet, suggesting that the learning courses for adult students run by the claimant company were a scam, led in *Metropolitan International Schools Ltd v Designtechnica Corporation*,[209] to a £50,000 award of damages which was primarily for "vindication",[210] there being no provable loss of business and no injury to feelings as the claimant was a company. Vindication was also central to the description of the award in in *Al-Amoudi v Kifle*,[211] since the claimant, an international businessman of huge wealth who had suffered a most appalling libel suggesting links to murder, terrorism and even the killing of his daughter, was not interested in the finances of a probably unenforceable award but in showing to the world that his reputation was secure.[212] The award came to £175,000. So too in *Farrall v Kordowski*,[213] where defamatory statements about a young solicitor claimant had been published anonymously on the defendant's website, Lloyd Jones J considered that, there being neither retraction nor apology, the vindicatory purpose of damages was much in play.[214] The language of vindication can again be seen, and

---

[206] *Carson v John Fairfax & Sons Ltd* (1993) 178 C.L.R. 44 at 105 107.

[207] [2004] 1 A.C. 628 PC at [53].

[208] Since judge trials began to supplant jury trials in defamation cases, we have much more information on vindication from the judges' judgments; with jury awards we are rather left in the dark. See the full discussion of this supplanting at para.17-008, above.

[209] [2010] EWHC 2411 (QB).

[210] See [2010] EWHC 2411 (QB) at [35].

[211] [2011] EWHC 2037 (QB).

[212] [2011] EWHC 2037 (QB) at 45.

[213] [2011] EWHC 2140 (QB).

[214] Vindication had also been the object of the claimant in *Hays Plc v Hartley* [2010] EWHC 1068 (QB) (see at [44]), but the claim failed. See also *Harrath v Stand for Peace Ltd* [2017] EWHC 653 (QB) at [23].

potentially causing added difficulty, when Tugendhat J said in *ZAM v CFW*,[215] in the course of awarding damages, including aggravated damages, of £140,000 that "the primary object of libel actions is to vindicate a claimant's reputation, not to recover damages".[216] Again, in *Harrath v Stand for Peace Ltd*,[217] Sir David Eady awarded damages of £140,000 for libel including that the claimant was a "terrorist" in a publication with a readership in the hundreds or low thousands. The award was made to ensure that there was

> "no doubt in the mind of a reasonable onlooker of the Claimant's entitlement to vindication".[218]

The words preceding the reference to "vindication" are important. They clarify why this is not an illegitimate application of the impermissible vindicatory damages but is, instead, an unfortunately named head of damages to cover future consequences from a libel which can be widespread and lasting.

## (4) Injury to health

Apart from these three heads of damage—injury to reputation, injury to feelings and the purposes within the misnomer 'vindication'[219]—there is injury to health. While no authorities appear on this, it is submitted that recovery ought to be allowed, and more probably as general than as special damage.[220] The decision in *Allsop v Allsop*,[221] where it was held that such damage did not ground an action for slander not actionable per se because it was too remote, would not seem to stand in the way of recovery. As shown elsewhere[222] the only acceptable basis for this decision today is that loss through ill health was not within the scope of the protection of the particular tort because the courts tended to restrict as far as possible the operation of slanders not actionable per se. No such restrictive approach is found in relation to slanders actionable per se and libel. As to injury to the health of the claimant's wife or family, this was held in *Guy v Gregory*[223] to be too remote. "The plaintiff", said Coleridge J, **46-037**

> "could not in this action recover damages either for the sufferings of his wife, or for the loss occasioned by her death".[224]

---

215 [2013] EWHC 662 (QB).

216 [2013] EWHC 662 (QB) at [72]. The vexed question of how far, if at all, a judge sitting alone should reduce his award on account of the vindicatory effect of his reasoned judgment is given full consideration in Ch.17 on vindicatory damages.

217 [2017] EWHC 653 (QB).

218 [2017] EWHC 653 (QB) at [23].

219 "It is well established that general damages in defamation cases serve the three functions submitted by counsel before Gray J: to console the claimant for the injury to his feelings occasioned by publication of the defamatory statement; to repair the harm to his reputation; and as a vindication of his reputation": *Purnell v Business F1 Magazine Ltd* [2008] 1 W.L.R. 1 CA at [8], per Laws LJ Statements to the same effect are now common in today's cases.

220 As Laws LJ says in the previous note.

221 (1860) 5 H. & N. 534.

222 See para.8-084, above.

223 (1840) 9 C. & P. 584.

224 (1840) 9 C. & P. 584 at 586–587. The words "in this action" probably refer to the fact that the libel had referred also to the claimant's wife, so that he could have brought an action on her behalf for a direct libel on her.

It is arguable that such a loss is indeed outside the scope of the protection even of slanders actionable per se and of libel.[225]

## (5) Pecuniary loss

**46-038** Again apart from the three regular heads of injury to reputation, injury to feelings and so-called "vindication", there is pecuniary loss. This is a clear head of damage but it cannot be said to be a regular one in this field. There are a few old cases. In *Evans v Harries*,[226] an action for slander of the claimant in his business of an innkeeper,[227] the claimant recovered for a general falling off of custom,[228] while in *Harrison v Pearce*,[229] an action for libel upon the proprietors of a newspaper, damages were awarded in respect of the resulting general decline in the newspaper's circulation; and more specific losses, as of particular contracts, particular employments, particular hospitality, may also be allowed if properly pleaded and proved.[230] However, modern libel cases where pecuniary loss is specifically claimed are extremely difficult to find for the reason that evidence to prove such loss is not available. The tendency therefore is to claim simply for damage to reputation *tout court* in the hope, frequently, of a large general award. Thus, where in *Cambridge v Makin*,[231] there was a libel of the claimant in her profession, that of public service interpreter, a libel of some seriousness as it was published to her professional colleagues, and the claimant believed but could not prove that she had lost professional engagements, Tugendhat J, while commenting that it was very rare in libel actions for a claimant to be able to prove pecuniary loss, added that

> "where a libel is likely to cause significant loss of earnings, that can be taken into account in the assessment of general damages".[232]

Similarly in *Metropolitan International Schools Ltd v Designtechnica Corporation*,[233] Tugendhat J was satisfied that the claimant company, while unable to prove a specific loss of business, had suffered actual damage in the form of students not taking courses,[234] and he will have factored this into his £50,000 award. A few cases have appeared in which losses of this nature have been adequately proved. In *McManus v Beckham*,[235] the claimant shopkeeper was able to prove that his trade had suffered as a result of the defendant's slander, a slander actionable per se as affecting a person in his trade or business.[236] In *Culla Park Ltd v Richards*,[237] a

---

225 Many years ago it was said in McCormick, *Damages* (1935), p.424, fn.31, that in America there had been much comment on the problem and that, though cases to that date had refused recovery, "the line between this and plaintiff's distress over the estrangement of family and friends, which may be shown, is a close one".

226 (1856) 1 H. & N. 251.

227 And, therefore, actionable per se.

228 A general loss of business was similarly allowed in *Bluck v Lovering* (1885) 1 T.L.R. 497.

229 (1859) 32 L.T. O.S. 298.

230 The last two cases in the text were primarily concerned with questions of pleading and proof, which matters are dealt with at paras 46-040 to 46-042, below, and more fully in Chs 51 and 52.

231 [2011] EWHC 12 (QB).

232 [2011] EWHC 12 (QB) at [229].

233 [2010] EWHC 2411 (QB). Facts at para.46-036, above.

234 [2010] EWHC 2411 (QB) at [32].

235 [2002] 1 W.L.R. 2982 CA.

236 The case is dealt with under remoteness of damage at para.46-018, above.

237 [2007] EWHC 1850 (QB).

company recovered for losses to its business although there were difficulties of proof, leading to a degree of discounting, on account of the business being a new one.[238] In *Thornton v Telegraph Media Group Ltd*,[239] the claimant, a journalist and academic, was libelled in a book review, which libel struck at her professional reputation, and her financial loss appears to have been a major feature of the award of £65,000.[240]

## 3. Remoteness of Damage

46-039 The principles of remoteness of damage already discussed in relation to slanders actionable only on proof of special damage[241] apply mutatis mutandis. To avoid repetition the cases on libel and slanders actionable per se are included there. For two reasons, however, the issue of remoteness is not so crucial here. First, a failure by the claimant to show that a particular loss is not too remote will not cause him to fail completely in his action; he may still recover general damages or at least nominal damages. Secondly, where there is repetition of the statement by third parties liability for loss is less likely to be rejected, since by putting the statement into permanent form the defendant has laid it open to a larger circulation, thus allowing the line between original dissemination and dissemination by repetition to be blurred.[242]

## 4. Pleading and Proof of Damage

46-040 Matters concerning the pleading and proof of damage are properly dealt with under procedure,[243] but problems of this nature appear sufficiently often in defamation to warrant a short excursus at this point.

46-041 General damage does not have to be pleaded by the claimant. As to its proof, he or she starts off with a presumption of damage operating in his favour which entitles the court to award substantial damages for injury to his reputation although he has produced no proof of such injury.[244] Moreover, the Court of Appeal has confirmed that the "presumption" of damage continues to exist, is irrebuttable (and, therefore, not truly a presumption), and is not abrogated by the arrival of the Human Rights Act.[245] However, there will usually be evidence given in support of the claimant's

---

238 See [2007] EWHC 1850 (QB) at [32]–[37].

239 [2011] EWHC 1884 (QB).

240 By contrast, when in *Collins Stewart Ltd v Financial Times Ltd* [2005] E.M.L.R. 5 at 64 the claimant company attempted to show pecuniary loss by the fall in its share price as reflecting the loss of future revenues, the claim for special damages on this basis was struck out because as a suggested measure of damages it was too uncertain to be acceptable.

241 See paras 46-010 to 46-019, above. As can be seen there, many of the cases are old and it is the more modern ones that concern defamations actionable per se: *Longdon-Griffiths v Smith* [1950] 2 All E.R. 662 (libel); *Cutler v McPhail* [1962] 2 Q.B. 292 (libel); *Slipper v BBC* [1991] 1 Q.B. 283 CA (libel); *McManus v Beckham* [2002] 1 W.L.R. 2982 CA (slander actionable per se).

242 This argument does not, of course, hold with slanders actionable per se as opposed to libel: see *Ratcliffe v Evans* [1892] 2 Q.B. 524 CA at 530, per Bowen LJ.

243 See Chs 51 and 52, below.

244 See, e.g. *Tripp v Thomas* (1824) 3 B. & C. 427 (the claimant gave no evidence but the jury awarded £40).

245 *Jameel v Dow Jones & Co Inc* [2005] Q.B. 946 CA; *Jameel v Wall Street Journal Europe SPRL* [2005] Q.B. 904 CA. See further at para.52-009, below where the appeal to the Lords in the second case ([2007] 1 A.C. 359) is set out.

claim for general damages, since a claimant offering no evidence of damage at all may find himself awarded small or nominal damages only.[246] As to what evidence is admissible in proof of general damage, this should normally consist of evidence of general losses, such as the general falling off of the claimant's custom[247] or the general decline in the circulation of the claimant's newspaper.[248] Evidence of particular transactions lost or particular customers lost cannot be given with a view to showing specific loss as part of the general damage.[249] However, it may be possible to give evidence of specific losses, even where these have occurred after the issue of the writ in the action, not with a view to recovering damages for such specific losses as such but in order to assist the court in assessing the general damages.[250]

**46-042** Special damage must be pleaded by the claimant in order to entitle it to be proved. Normally the pleading and also the evidence in proof must be of particular instances of loss, so that where specific instances are not pleaded they may not be produced in proof,[251] and where pleaded they may be proved only by evidence of the specific losses. However, the courts are realistic and accept that the particularity must be tailored to the facts. Thus if the facts do not admit of particularising specific instances of loss, a generalised statement of special damage will suffice in pleading and general evidence of special damage will be permitted in proof.[252]

## 5. AGGRAVATION AND MITIGATION: RELEVANCE OF THE CONDUCT, CHARACTER AND CIRCUMSTANCES OF THE PARTIES

**46-043** Within the limited category of torts in which the conduct, character and circumstances of the parties may lead to the aggravation or mitigation of the damage, and hence of the damages, the tort of defamation is the one which is the most important and is the most covered by authority in this respect, authority which largely dates back to the 19th century when the courts took great trouble to adjudicate on point after point. These old cases are still relevant and are dealt with here together with the modern additions. Many of these defamation cases may be used analogously in the consideration of similar problems in torts not so blessed by judicial pronouncement. Occasionally, however, the analogy may move in the other direction. Thus in *Thompson v Commissioner of Police of the Metropolis* and *Hsu v Commissioner of Police of the Metropolis*,[253] cases of wrongful arrest, false imprisonment, assault and malicious prosecution, the Court of Appeal said that, contrary to the practice current at the time, separate awards should be made for the basic damages and the aggravated damages[254] but whether this will, or should, apply to defamation[255] is not clear.[256]

---

[246] See, e.g. *Hayward v Hayward* (1887) 34 Ch. D. 198.

[247] See, e.g. *Evans v Harries* (1856) 1 H. & N. 251; *Bluck v Lovering* (1885) 1 T.L.R. 497.

[248] See, e.g. *Harrison v Pearce* (1859) 32 L.T. O.S. 298.

[249] See, e.g. *Bluck v Lovering* (1885) 1 T.L.R. 497.

[250] See *Ingram v Lawson* (1840) 6 Bring. N.C. 212 and *Goslin v Corry* (1844) 7 M. & G. 342.

[251] See, e.g. *Bluck v Lovering* (1885) 1 T.L.R. 497.

[252] The leading case in this connection is *Ratcliffe v Evans* [1892] 2 Q.B. 524 CA. This case, and a number of others outside defamation, throw light on the problems of pleading and proof that arise here: they are dealt with at paras 51-016 to 51-029 and 52-008 to 52-016, below.

[253] [1998] Q.B. 498 CA.

[254] [1998] Q.B. 498 CA at 516E.

[255] See, in the different context of a victimisation claim, the concerns over having separate awards

## (1) The defendant's conduct: malice

"In actions of libel", said Lord Esher MR in *Praed v Graham*,[257] **46-044**

> "the jury in assessing damages are entitled to look at the whole conduct of the defendant from the time the libel was published down to the time they give their verdict. They may consider what his conduct has been before action, after action, and in court during the trial".

The defendant's conduct is relevant in this way to show whether he has acted with or without malice.[258] Generally, this is malice in the perpetrating of the libel, but conduct subsequent to this is relevant either as evidence of the existence or absence of malice at the time of the tort or merely as showing that the defendant has behaved well or behaved badly since the tort.[259] The practical effect is that the damages will fluctuate, up or down, with the degree of culpability of the defendant's behaviour.[260]

At first sight it would seem that the existence or absence of malice in this wide **46-045**
sense should be relevant only to exemplary damages and not to compensatory damages since the defendant's culpability or innocence does not increase or decrease the claimant's loss. It is, however, reasonable to regard the malice of the defendant as increasing the suffering and the humiliation of the claimant, and to this extent it is material to the question of compensation. Indeed, in *Barron v Vines*,[261] Warby J said that the harm for which compensation would be due in circumstances where the defendant had acted maliciously would be "injury to feelings". For long it could not really be said that English law had committed itself to this second rationale: evidence in proof or disproof of malice was allowed without any clear division between its relevance to compensatory and to exemplary damages. However, the effect of the established recognition of exemplary damages by the House of Lords in *Rookes v Barnard*,[262] a decision approved in *Broome v Cassell & Co*,[263] is that the malice of the defendant can now play a part in the assessment of both compensatory and exemplary damages.[264]

The authorities are primarily concerned with questions of evidence, and the **46-046**

---

expressed by Underhill J in the Employment Appeal Tribunal in *Commissioner of Police of the Metropolis v Shaw* [2012] I.C.R. 464; [2012] I.R.L.R. 291, concerns which are thought to be unnecessary: see the discussion at para.43-014, above.

256 Of course not every case attracts aggravated damages or involves mitigation of the damages. Thus since the injury to the claimant's feelings was not thought to be particularly severe, aggravated damages were refused in *Rackham v Sandy* [2005] EWHC 482 (QB); see at [124].

257 (1890) 24 Q.B.D. 53 CA at 55.

258 Contrast *Darby v Ouseley* (1856) 25 L.J. Ex. 227 at 230, per Pollock CB in argument: "Matters occurring after action or even in the action or at the trial may be used as enhancing the damages because evidence of the malice of the original libel." This remark does not appear in the report at (1856) 1 H. & N. 1.

259 Thus malice in this context is being used in a very wide sense. So aggravated damages were awarded in *Galloway v Telegraph Group* [2005] E.M.L.R. 7 at 115 largely on account of the claimant's having been treated to high-handed and insulting behaviour in court: see at [203]–[208] where the word malice does not appear.

260 Evidence of malice may also be introduced to destroy a plea of qualified privilege or fair comment. The same principles would seem to apply.

261 [2016] EWHC 1226 (QB).

262 [1964] A.C. 1129.

263 [1972] A.C. 1027.

264 See Ch.13, above.

modern general rule, as laid down by Tindal CJ in *Pearson v Lemaitre*,[265] is

> "that either party may, with a view to the damages, give evidence to prove or disprove the existence of a malicious motive in the mind of the publisher of defamatory matter".

46-047 **(a) Evidence to prove malice in aggravation of damages** Malice may be shown by the defendant's conduct generally, but there are two particular ways in which it has come to be shown: by other derogatory statements made of the claimant by the defendant and by the defendant's persistence in the accusation, such persistence being either by way of an unreasonable plea of justification or by lack of any, or any adequate, apology.[266]

46-048 *(i) Other derogatory statements about the claimant* Any other derogatory statements made of the claimant by the defendant may be given in evidence to show malice. At one time there was a conflict of authority as to whether a derogatory statement which was itself defamatory was admissible, particularly if subsequent to the statement sued upon; the courts clearly feared that the jury would give damages for the other defamation as a separate cause of action, and tended to allow such evidence only if given to explain the meaning of the statement sued upon where that was ambiguous or, sometimes, if the other defamatory statement was in substance the same as or related to that sued upon. Such limitations were swept away by the decision in *Pearson v Lemaitre*,[267] which in 1843 established the modern law. Tindal CJ there laid down

> "that either party may, with a view to the damages, give evidence to prove or disprove the existence of a malicious motive in the mind of the publisher of defamatory matter; but if the evidence given for that purpose establishes another cause of action, the jury should be cautioned against giving any damages in respect of it. And if such evidence is offered merely for the purpose of obtaining damages for such subsequent injury, it will be properly rejected."[268]

This qualification must not, however, be read as a prohibition upon increasing the damages for malice; if it were, then the decision in *Pearson v Lemaitre*,[269] would be of no practical effect. Pollock CB in *Darby v Ouseley*,[270] provided the true answer when, in reply to an objection that the jury should have been told not to give damages for a subsequent defamatory statement, he said:

> "In one sense that may be so; but then the subsequent publication was evidence of malice, and would, therefore, aggravate the damages."[271]

Accordingly it was held that an omission to caution the jury on this issue was not

---

265 (1843) 5 M. & G. 700 at 719.

266 The extent of the publication has also occasionally been used to show malice as in *Plunkett v Cobbett* (1804) 5 Esp. 136. See para.46-069, below.

267 (1843) 5 M. & G. 700. This in effect affirmed the decisions in *Lee v Huson* (1792) Peake 223 and *Russell v McQuister* (1807) 1 Camp. 49n, and overthrew the dicta in *Mead v Daubigny* (1792) Peake 168 and *Defries v Davis* (1835) 7 C. & P. 112 and the decisions in *Cook v Field* (1788) 3 Esp. 133; *Finnerty v Tipper* (1809) 2 Camp. 72; *Stuart v Lovell* (1817) 2 Stark. 93; *Pearce v Ornsby* (1835) 1 M. & Rob. 455 and *Symmons v Blake* (1835) 1 M. & Rob. 477.

268 (1843) 5 M. & G. 700 at 719–720.

269 (1843) 5 M. & G. 700.

270 (1856) 1 H. & N. 1.

271 (1856) 1 H. & N. 1 at 13.

misdirection so as to justify a new trial. Similarly the Court of Appeal in *Anderson v Calvert*,[272] although accepting that

> "the jury ought not to treat other derogatory statements as giving a separate and independent right to damages",

nevertheless did not think

> "the omission of the learned judge to warn the jury was any ground for granting a new trial".[273]

Today, when most major defamation cases are heard by judges without juries, in *ZAM v CFW*,[274] where, after being sued by the claimant, a financial businessman of seniority, for stating that he had misappropriated family trust moneys and was a paedophile, the defendant had published on the internet further defamatory statements, Tugendhat J held that, while defamatory statements later to those sued upon could be introduced as evidence of malice,[275] they could not be relied on in aggravation of damages for the defamatory publications on which the case was brought. The claimant must amend his pleadings or bring further claims, neither of which he had done.[276] This decision followed Gray J in *Collins Stewart Ltd v Financial Times Ltd (No.2)*.[277]

The legacy of decisions with which the court in *Pearson v Lemaitre*,[278] was **46-049**
presented is best disposed of by a series of propositions stating the modern law. (1) Other derogatory statements are admissible even though themselves defamatory. This was the position in *Pearson v Lemaitre*[279] itself, where the claimant sued in respect of a libel contained in a letter and was allowed to introduce as evidence of malice two letters of the two succeeding years, written to other parties and containing in substance a repetition of the libel. Indeed another defamatory statement is stronger evidence of malice than a statement not itself actionable. (2) Other derogatory statements are admissible even though there is no ambiguity in the statement sued upon. This proposition, in effect accepted in *Pearson v Lemaitre*,[280] is best illustrated by *Camfield v Bird*.[281] The lack of such ambiguity can render inadmissible only evidence brought to explain the meaning and not the motive of the statement sued upon. (3) Other derogatory statements are admissible even though not

---

[272] (1908) 24 T.L.R. 399 CA.

[273] (1908) 24 T.L.R. 399 CA at 400, per Lord Cozens Hardy MR This conclusion was reached having regard especially to the then RSC Ord. 39 r.6, later Ord. 59 r.11(2): see paras 53-011 to 53-014, below; and for the position under the CPR, see para.53-011, below.

[274] [2013] EWHC 662 (QB).

[275] With *Pearson v Lemaitre* (1843) 5 M. & G. 700 cited for this.

[276] See [2013] EWHC 662 (QB) at [66]–[71].

[277] [2006] E.M.L.R. 5 at 100. For this decision see the footnote at the end of para.46-071 below.

[278] (1843) 5 M. & G. 700.

[279] (1843) 5 M. & G. 700. Other such decisions are, chronologically, *Lee v Huson* (1792) Peake 223; *Russell v McQuister* (1807) 1 Camp. 49n.; *Delegal v Highley* (1837) 8 C. & P. 444; *Barrett v Long* (1851) 3 H.L.C. 395; *Darby v Ouseley* (1856) 1 H. & N. 1; *Hemmings v Gasson* (1858) E.B. & E. 346. The contrary decisions are no longer law, i.e. *Cook v Field* (1788) 3 Esp. 133; *Finnerty v Tipper* (1809) 2 Camp. 72; *Pearce v Ornsby* (1835) 1 M. & Rob. 445; *Symmons v Blake* (1835) 1M. & Rob. 477.

[280] (1843) 5 M. & G. 700; thereby overruling *Stuart v Lovell* (1817) 2 Stark. 93, *Pearce v Ornsby* (1835) 1 M. & Rob. 455 and *Symmons v Blake* (1835) 1 M. & Rob. 477.

[281] (1852) 3 C. & K. 56.

in substance the same as or related to the statement sued upon.[282] In most cases the other statements have been similar or related; however, they appear to have been different in *Hemmings v Gasson*.[283] Indeed, evidence that the defendant has maligned the claimant on a number of subjects is stronger evidence than a repetition of the same defamatory statement. (4) Other derogatory statements are admissible whether prior or subsequent to the statement sued upon. Where subsequent, they may be even after the action has been commenced as in *Macleod v Wakley*,[284] but, as was pointed out in *Hemmings v Gasson*,[285] if a considerable interval has elapsed the jury should be directed to consider whether the subsequent statement "might have referred to something which had happened after the libel".[286] Most cases have indeed concerned subsequent statements, and *Barrett v Long*,[287] appears to be the sole clear illustration of a prior statement. In that case previous libels going back over six years before the statement sued upon were admitted as evidence of malice. Parke B, answering questions put to the judges by the House of Lords, said:

> "A long practice of libelling the plaintiff may show in the most satisfactory manner, that the defendant was actuated by malice in the particular publication, and that it did not take place through carelessness or inadvertence; and the more the evidence approaches to the proof of a systematic practice, the more convincing it is. The circumstance that the other libels are more or less frequent, or more or less remote from the time of the publication of that in question, merely affects the weight, not the admissibility of the evidence."[288]

**46-050** *(ii) Persistence in the accusation: unreasonable plea of justification* An unsuccessful plea of justification is evidence of malice where it appears that the defendant well knew he could not support such a plea. Thus in *Simpson v Robinson*,[289] where the defendant pleaded justification but gave no evidence in support of the plea at the trial, Lord Denman CJ said:

> "The defendant's conduct in putting a justification on the record which he does not attempt to prove, and will not abandon, may be taken into consideration as proving malice and aggravating the injury."[290]

Certain dicta may indeed suggest that an unsuccessful plea of justification is per se evidence of malice and ground for increasing the damages,[291] but it is submitted that

---

[282] In this connection *Finnerty v Tipper* (1809) 2 Camp. 72 is overruled by *Pearson v Lemaitre* (1843) 5 M. & G. 700.

[283] (1858) E.B. & E. 346. That the claimant was proving malice to defeat privilege and not to aggravate damages does not remove the usefulness of the decision.

[284] (1828) 3 C. & P. 311.

[285] (1858) E.B. & E. 346.

[286] (1858) E.B. & E. 346 at 352, per Lord Campbell CJ. The interval in this case was just over a year.

[287] (1851) 3 H.L.C. 395.

[288] (1851) 3 H.L.C. 395 at 414.

[289] (1848) 12 Q.B. 511.

[290] (1848) 12 Q.B. 511 at 513–514. Compare *Wilson v Robinson* (1845) 7 Q.B. 68, where the defendant pleaded justification but at the trial gave not proof of justification but evidence to show qualified privilege, and succeeded on this. It was held that the fact that justification had been pleaded and abandoned was not admissible as evidence of malice on the issue of qualified privilege; if, however, the defendant had failed on that issue, the plea of justification might have furnished evidence of malice in aggravation of damages: at 70, per Lord Denman CJ.

[291] *R. v Newman* (1852) 1 E. & B. 558 at 581, per Erle CJ; *Darby v Ouseley* (1856) 25 L.J. Ex. 227 at 230, per Pollock CB in argument; *Risk Allah Bey v Whitehurst* (1868) 18 L.T. 615 at 620, per

it can only be so if the plea is completely unsupportable in the circumstances: otherwise an unwarranted risk would be added to a defendant's attempt to set up the truth of the alleged defamation. Sometimes these dicta, if taken in context, indeed appear to add the necessary qualification. Thus in *R. v Newman*,[292] Erle CJ, while saying that

> "in a civil action for libel, a plea of justification affords a ground for enhancing the damages",[293]

added that in the case before the court "the plea, if pleaded without reasonable ground, would have the effect of aggravation". And coming to modern times, in *Cairns v Modi*,[294] where a professional cricketer had been falsely accused of match fixing, while no specific reference to malice was made by Bean J, what he called "the sustained and aggressive assertion of the plea of justification at the trial" was aggravation sufficient to increase the damages by a factor of 20 per cent,[295] a feature of his award which the Court of Appeal endorsed as entirely proportionate.[296]

*(iii) Persistence in the accusation: unreasonable lack of apology* Similarly an unreasonable failure to apologise adequately can be evidence of malice. Thus in *Simpson v Robinson*,[297] the evidence in aggravation of damages was not only the defendant's plea of justification but his refusal of the claimant's offer to accept an apology and nominal damages. And in *Blake v Stevens*,[298] where the defendant publishers, having inadvertently libelled the claimant, did not admit their mistake but brought up at the trial certain misconduct of the claimant, Cockburn CJ said that **46-051**

> "it would not have been a case for serious damages if it were not for the way in which the action has been defended".[299]

Further, the manner of an apology may tend to increase rather than diminish the damages. Thus Mellor J in *Kelly v Sherlock*,[300] said that the defendant's persistence in the defamation was not "sufficiently met by his tardy and meagre apology"; Tindal CJ in *Saunders v Mills*,[301] said that

> "probably the jury might think that the nature of the apology was such as to add a degree of bitterness to the original libel";

and Collins MR in *Thomas v Bradbury Agnew*,[302] pointed out that the claimants, alleging malice, relied "on the terms of an apology subsequently printed as fortifying their contention".

**(b) Evidence to disprove malice in mitigation of damages** At one time the **46-052**

---

Cockburn C.J.

292 (1852) 1 E. & B. 558.

293 (1852) 1 E. & B. 558 at 581.

294 [2012] EWHC 756 (QB).

295 [2012] EWHC 756 (QB) at [137]; thereby moving the award up from £75,000 to £90,000.

296 [2013] 1 W.L.R. 1015 CA at [50].

297 (1848) 12 Q.B. 511.

298 (1864) 4 F. & F. 235.

299 (1864) 4 F. & F. 235 at 240.

300 (1866) L.R. 1 Q.B. 686 at 695.

301 (1829) 6 Bing. 213 at 220.

302 [1906] 2 K.B. 627 CA at 637.

general rule was that a defendant might prove facts in mitigation of damages without pleading such facts. Then in 1883 there was introduced in the then RSC Ord.36 r.37 a requirement that in defamation cases where truth was not a defence particulars of matters upon which the defendant wanted to rely in mitigation be pleaded. This rule ended life in 1989 as RSC Ord.82 r.7 when it was overtaken by the general rule of RSC Ord.18 r.12(1)(c) requiring mitigation to be pleaded in all cases. Yet nothing in the Civil Procedure Rules 1998 can be seen that replaces this important provision and one appears, unfortunately, to be back for defamation to the original pre-1883 position unless the courts, by relying upon some other provision of the new Rules or even by going outside the Rules altogether, can insist that mitigation matters must be stated.[303]

**46-053** Rules of court and civil procedure rules apart, the absence of malice may be shown by the defendant's conduct generally; anything which shows that the defendant acted mistakenly or inadvertently will go in mitigation. Thus Coleridge J, in directing the jury in *Smith v Scott*,[304] said:

> "If you should think that this report [i.e. of judicial proceedings], though not correct, is an honest one, and intended to be a fair account of what really occurred, that would be a ground for reducing the damages."

Similarly Willes J in *Smith v Harrison*,[305] said:

> "If the insertion of the libel were mere matter of inadvertence, small damages would suffice; though it might be otherwise if there had been gross negligence."

Further, there are several particular matters which may be given in evidence to disprove malice[306]: truth; repetition; provocation; apology.

**46-054** *(i) Truth or partial truth of the statement* Truth goes in bar of the action and therefore it may appear futile to consider truth as merely going in mitigation of damages. There were, however, two sets of circumstances in which truth could take on this role, one of which has now been discarded leaving only the other extant.

**46-055** Dealing first with the one discarded, it was formerly held that, if truth is not pleaded by way of defence, although it cannot be proved in bar of the action, it may still be introduced in mitigation of damages. This was early allowed in *Charlton v Watton*,[307] where there was no justification plea and in *East v Chapman*,[308] where a plea of justification had been withdrawn, and replaced the even earlier rule, laid down in 1743 in *Underwood v Parks*,[309] and appearing as late as *Vessey v Pike*,[310] that facts which, if pleaded, would be a bar to the action could not be given, if not pleaded, even in mitigation of damages.[311] However, today it follows from the ap-

---

303 See further at paras 46-067 and 51-038 to 51-039, below.

304 (1847) 2 C. & K. 580 at 585–586.

305 (1856) 1 F. & F. 565 at 566.

306 RSC Ord.18 r.12(1)(c) and formerly RSC Ord.82 r.7 (at para.46-052, above) only concerned pleading and did not render admissible, by the giving of the required notice, matters which would not otherwise be admissible at common law; see para.46-067, below.

307 (1834) 6 C. & P. 385.

308 (1827) 2 C. & P. 570.

309 (1743) 2 Strange 1200.

310 (1829) 3 C. & P. 512.

311 This rule may still make a partial appearance if the evidence which the defendant seeks to offer contravenes the principles as to admissibility laid down in *Scott v Sampson* (1882) 8 Q.B.D. 491:

proach in 2001 of *Burstein v Times Newspapers Ltd*,[312] that, if there is no plea of justification or a plea of justification would be ruled out, evidence in partial justification is not permitted, thereby returning to the rule laid down in *Underwood v Parks*.[313]

Secondly, as for what has been retained, even if truth is pleaded in defence, the evidence may fail to prove the plea but at the same time establish the partial truth of the statement sued upon. This evidence will then go in mitigation of damages, as in *Chalmers v Shackell*.[314] But in *Sutcliffe v Pressdram*,[315] where, a jury's award being set aside as excessive,[316] a retrial on the issue of damages only was ordered, the Court of Appeal stipulated that the defendants would not be allowed to call evidence directed to establishing the truth of the particulars of justification, the plea of justification having been rejected by the jury at the original trial.[317] **46-056**

*(ii) Statement not originated by the defendant* If the defendant has repeated the statement from any source and named the source in the statement, this is evidence to disprove malice in mitigation of damages.[318] The source may be either a person or a document. In *Bennett v Bennett*,[319] it was a person: Alderson B said that **46-057**

> "if the defendant had said, at the time he spoke the words, that he heard the slanderous matter from another person, and named that person, it would be a matter of mitigation".[320]

In *Mullett v Hulton*,[321] it was a document: the defamatory words were written by the defendant as a quotation from a newspaper. Similarly, evidence was held admissible in *Saunders v Mills*,[322] that the newspaper statement sued upon was copied from another newspaper, and in *Davis v Cutbush*,[323] that it was copied from a report published to company shareholders.[324] However, the defendant may not contravene the principles as to admissibility laid down in *Scott v Sampson*,[325] by offering evidence that his statement was based upon rumours in the community of the defamatory matter sued upon. It would seem to be for this reason that in *Saunders v Mills*,[326] the court refused to allow the further evidence that the newspaper state-

---

see para.46-061, below.

312 [2001] 1 W.L.R. 579 CA.

313 *Burstein* does, however, decide that evidence of particular facts directly relevant to the contextual background to the defamatory statement may be admissible in mitigation even though they consisted of facts that might have formed the ingredients of a defence of justification: see at para.46-071, below.

314 (1834) 6 C. & P. 475; see, especially, at 478, per Tindal CJ: "if the other part [i.e. of the statement] is true, it will go … to rebut the charge of malice on the part of the defendants."

315 [1991] 1 Q.B. 153 CA.

316 The Court of Appeal was empowered to substitute its own award: see para.53-004, below.

317 See, especially, Lord Donaldson MR [1991] 1 Q.B. 153 at 179D–180C. Strictly, this case concerns evidence which went to the claimant's character (see paras 46-060 and following) rather than to the defendant's conduct, which is here being dealt with, but it is convenient to introduce it at this point.

318 Until *McPherson v Daniel* (1829) 10 B. & C. 263 this was a defence: see para.46-015 (in a footnote), above.

319 (1834) 6 C. & P. 588.

320 (1834) 6 C. & P. 588 at 588.

321 (1803) 4 Esp. 248.

322 (1829) 6 Bing. 213.

323 (1859) 1 F. & F. 487.

324 In neither case was it required that the defendant should have stated his source.

325 (1882) 8 Q.B.D. 491: see para.46-061, below.

326 (1829) 6 Bing. 213.

ment sued upon had appeared in other newspapers; this refusal was endorsed by the House of Lords in *Dingle v Associated Newspapers*,[327] applying *Saunders v Mills*,[328] so as to hold such evidence irrelevant in mitigation of damages.

**46-058** *(iii) Provocation of the defendant* If the claimant has provoked the defendant into the defamatory statement, this is evidence to disprove malice in mitigation of damages.[329] A good early illustration is *Watts v Fraser*.[330] The claimant had libelled the defendants and this was allowed as evidence in mitigation since it formed

> "the provocation by which the defendants were goaded by the plaintiff himself to do the act".[331]

An up-to-date illustration is *Trumm v Norman*.[332] Publications by the claimant himself were held to be unnecessarily provocative and offensive, and to have initiated what was described as a slanging match, so as to lead the court to reduce the claimant's damages by half. However, it was laid down in *May v Brown*,[333] that the fact that the claimant had defamed the defendant could not go in mitigation of damages where it had not been the provocation for the defendant's statement: for, as Abbott CJ said, this "would be a set-off of one libel against another".[334] Thus if the statement sued upon is made by the defendant before he has been defamed by the claimant or before the claimant's defamation of him has come to his knowledge, the claimant's misconduct cannot be introduced as evidence of provocation in mitigation of damages. This was the position in *Tarpley v Blabey*,[335] where Tindal CJ said that he had

> "rejected the evidence because, upon the whole, it appeared the publication was subsequent to the defendant's libel".[336]

There is some suggestion in these last two cases that there must be some connection in subject-matter between the defamatory statements published by the defendant and the claimant, but it is submitted that the only connection that need be shown is in relation to provocation.[337] *Burstein v Times Newspapers Ltd*,[338] does, however,

---

327 [1964] A.C. 371; facts at para.46-064, below.

328 (1829) 6 Bing. 213.

329 At one time, in the unreported *Anthony Pasquin's Case* (1797), it was held a defence but this doctrine was disapproved in *Finnerty v Tipper* (1809) 2 Camp. 76.

330 (1835) 1 M. & Rob. 449. The footnote to this report provides another illustration: *Moore v Oastler* (1835) 1 M. & Rob. 451n.

331 (1835) 1 M. & Rob. 449 at 450, per Lord Denman CJ.

332 [2008] EWHC 116 (QB).

333 (1824) 3 B. & C. 113.

334 (1824) 3 B. & C. 113 at 126. Contrast similarly, *Kelly v Sherlock* (1866) L.R. 1 Q.B. 686 at 698, per Blackburn J: "There can be no set-off of one libel or misconduct against another."

335 (1836) 2 Bing. N.C. 437.

336 (1836) 2 Bing. N.C. 437 at 441 to 442.

337 Another aspect of the situation where the claimant has also made defamatory statements is that it indicates that the claimant is not a person of sensitivity and will accordingly have suffered less. This appears in *Finnerty v Tipper* (1809) 2 Camp. 76, where Sir James Mansfield said that "if a man is in the habit of libelling others he cannot be supposed to suffer much injury from this source": at 77; and also in *Kelly v Sherlock* (1866) L.R. 1 Q.B. 686, where Blackburn J said that "in estimating the compensation for the plaintiff's injured feelings, the jury might fairly consider the plaintiff's conduct and the degree of respect which the plaintiff had shown for the feelings of others": at 698. This, however, concerns the effect on damages of the claimant's rather than the defendant's conduct: see

decide that evidence of particular facts directly relevant to the contextual background to the defamatory statement may be admissible in mitigation even though they might include matters which were not causally connected, as through provocation, with the publication of the libel.[339]

*(iv) Apology by the defendant* By statute since 1843 an apology has been admissible in mitigation of damages. Section 1 of the Libel Act of that year provides that: **46-059**

> "in any action for defamation it shall be lawful for the defendant (after notice in writing of his intention so to do, duly given to the plaintiff at the time of filing or delivering the plea in such action), to give in evidence, in mitigation of damages, that he made or offered an apology to the plaintiff for such defamation before the commencement of the action, or as soon afterwards as he had an opportunity of doing so, in case the action shall have been commenced before there was an opportunity of making or offering such apology".

This has probably been the position at common law all along,[340] a view which seems to be fully accepted today. Thus in *Kiam v Neil (No.2)*,[341] for instance, it was clearly accepted by the Court of Appeal, without any invocation of the 1843 Act, that an apology would go to reduce the damages.[342] To be fully effective on mitigation of the damages an apology should be made speedily. Thus in *Cruddas v Adams*,[343] where a well-known businessman and officer of the Conservative party had been labelled a criminal in respect of the evasion of electoral law, the last minute apology by the defendant after a long campaign and truculence in the conduct of the litigation did little for mitigation, counsel even suggesting that the repetition of the allegations of criminality over many months had insidiously given them greater credibility.[344]

## (2) The claimant's character: bad reputation

The claimant's conduct generally may also be relevant to the issue of damages, and in particular his bad reputation. Since the claimant is complaining of an injured reputation, a proper assessment of damages requires a knowledge of the worth of that reputation.[345] As Cave J said in *Scott v Sampson*[346]: **46-060**

> "The damage … which he has sustained must depend almost entirely on the estimation in which he was previously held …. It seems most material that the jury who have to award those damages should know if the fact is so that he is a man of no reputation."

---

para.46-060, below.

338 [2001] 1 W.L.R. 579 CA.

339 See the case at para.46-071, below. May LJ giving the leading judgment referred (at 590G–591F) to the unreported decision in *Godfrey v Demon Internet Ltd (No.2)* where he regarded the same conclusion as having been reached.

340 The view that the common law provided for an apology to go in mitigation, so that no statutory provision was needed, has been taken by a number of authorities.

341 [1996] E.M.L.R. 493 CA.

342 See Beldam LJ [1996] E.M.L.R. 493 CA at 504 and 509.

343 [2013] EWHC 145 (QB).

344 [2013] EWHC 145 (QB) at [10].

345 Evidence of the claimant's character is even more important in defamation than in other torts in which the claimant's character may lead to aggravation or mitigation of the damages (false imprisonment, malicious prosecution) because in defamation his character is in issue.

346 (1882) 8 Q.B.D. 491 at 503.

The court starts with a presumption in favour of the claimant that his reputation is unblemished, and therefore where the defendant does not seek, either in pleading or in proof, to challenge this the court will not permit the claimant to introduce evidence of his general good reputation in the community. Such a refusal appears in *Cornwall v Richardson*,[347] where there was even a plea of justification, and also in *Guy v Gregory*,[348] where evidence to show that the claimant's wife was a respectable person was rejected.[349] On the other hand, the defendant is entitled to introduce evidence of bad reputation, which then allows evidence of good reputation in rebuttal. Various problems arise as to what facts must be pleaded and what facts, after the pleading requirements have been satisfied, are admissible in evidence. Since the requirements of pleading grow out of the rules as to admissibility of evidence, the latter question is dealt with first.

**46-061** In *Scott v Sampson*,[350] the whole question of what types of evidence are admissible to show bad reputation was raised, and Cave J, in a definitive judgment, reviewed all the earlier cases: these must now be regarded in the light of their interpretation in this judgment. They dealt, according to Cave J's analysis, with the admissibility of three types of evidence: (1) general evidence of reputation; (2) evidence of rumours of, and suspicions to the same effect as, the defamatory matter complained of; and (3) evidence of particular facts tending to show the character and disposition of the claimant. Cave J arrived at the conclusion that general evidence was admissible under the first head, but that evidence tendered under the two others was inadmissible. He gave his reasons at some length. First, as to general evidence of reputation:

> "it is said that the admission of such evidence will be a hardship upon the plaintiff, who may not be prepared to rebut it; and under the former practice, where the damages could not be pleaded to, and general evidence of bad character was allowed to be given under a plea of not guilty, there was something in this objection, which, however, is removed under the present system of pleading which requires that all material facts shall be pleaded, and a plaintiff who has notice that general evidence of bad character will be adduced against him, can have no difficulty whatever if he is a man of good character in coming prepared with friends who have known him to prove that his reputation has been good. On principle, therefore, it would seem that general evidence of reputation should be admitted."[351]

Secondly, as to evidence of rumours and suspicions:

> "if these rumours and suspicions have, in fact, affected the plaintiff's reputation, they may be proved by general evidence of reputation. If they have not affected it they are not relevant to the issue. To admit evidence of rumours and suspicions is to give anyone who knows nothing whatever of the plaintiff, or may even have a grudge against him, an opportunity of spreading through the means of the publicity attending judicial proceedings what he may have picked from the most disreputable sources, and what no man of sense, who knows the plaintiff's character, would for a moment believe in. Unlike evidence of

347 (1825) Ry. & M. 305.

348 (1840) 9 C. & P. 584.

349 The libel had referred also to the claimant's wife.

350 (1882) 8 Q.B.D. 491.

351 (1882) 8 Q.B.D. 491 at 503. This confirmed a number of unreported decisions cited by Cave J (at 499–501) (i.e. *Kirkham v Oxley* (undated); *Ellershaw v Robinson* (1824); *Mawby v Barber* (1826); *Moore v Oastler* (1836); *Hardy v Alexander* (1837)) and also the decision in *Williams v Callender* (1810) Holt N.P. 307.

general reputation, it is particularly difficult for the plaintiff to meet and rebut such evidence; for all that those who know him best can say is that they have not heard anything of these rumours. Moreover, it may be that it is the defendant himself who has started them."[352]

Thirdly, as to evidence of particular facts:

"at the most it tends to prove not that the plaintiff has not, but that he ought not to have a good reputation, and to admit evidence of this kind is in effect … to throw upon the plaintiff the difficulty of shewing a uniform propriety of conduct during his whole life. It would give rise to interminable issues which would have but a very remote bearing on the question in dispute, which is to what extent the actual reputation which he actually possesses has been damaged by the defamatory matter complained of."[353]

In the case before the court the whole of the defendant's evidence on the claimant's reputation was held to be properly rejected.

**46-062** Cave J's judgment was first endorsed by the Court of Appeal in *Hobbs v Tinling*[354]; Scrutton LJ said that it had in his opinion been "accepted as an accurate statement of the law",[355] while Sankey LJ said that the law was "beyond question" and that "no further word need be added to that judgment".[356] Beyond this, the Court of Appeal established that, in the words of Scrutton LJ,

"just as you cannot prove in chief specific instances of misconduct, as distinguished from general reputation, whether involved in the libel or not, in order to mitigate damages, so also you cannot achieve that purpose by cross-examination as to such specific instances."[357]

The attempt to do this by cross-examination was through the door of cross-examination as to credit. A claimant in an action of defamation who chooses to give evidence in chief is, like any witness, subject to cross-examination as to credit, and for this purpose the defendant is entitled to cross-examine him on matters not directly material to the case which could include specific instances of his misconduct. But since the cross-examination is on matters not directly material, no evidence can be called in chief by the defendant to contradict the claimant's answers. "If the jury", said Scrutton LJ,

"hearing the answers given by the witness, do not believe him, they are entitled to do so, and to use the view thus obtained as to his credibility in rejecting answers given by him on matters material to the case. But rejecting his denials does not prove the fact he denies,

[352] (1882) 8 Q.B.D. 491 at 504. This confirmed the decisions in *Jones v Stevens* (1882) 11 Price 235 and, so far as consistent, *Anon. v Moor* (1813) 1 M. & S. 284; confirmed the doubts expressed in *Waithman v Weaver* (1822) 11 Price 257n by Abbott CJ and in *Thompson v Nye* (1850) 16 Q.B. 175 at 180 by Coleridge J; and rejected the decisions in *Knobell v Fuller* (1797) Peake Add. Cas. 139, *Richards v Richards* (1844) 2 M. & Rob. 557 and, so far as inconsistent, *Leicester v Walter* (1809) 2 Camp. 251.

[353] (1882) 8 Q.B.D. 491 at 505. This confirmed *Bracegirdle v Bailey* (1859) 1 F. & F. 536.

[354] [1929] 2 K.B. 1 CA.

[355] [1929] 2 K.B. 1 CA at 17.

[356] [1929] 2 K.B. 1 CA at 50. This approval removes any doubts set up by Hawkins J's remarks in *Wood v Durham* (1888) 21 Q.B.D. 501 at 508.

[357] [1929] 2 K.B. 1 CA at 18. That this was the law had already been implied by the decision in *Bracegirdle v Bailey* (1859) 1 F. & F. 536 (see next note) and suggested by Lord Halsbury in *Watt v Watt* [1905] A.C. 115 at 118.

of which there is, and can be, no other evidence. It only destroys his credibility in respect of other evidence."[358]

**46-063** Cave J's judgment was endorsed by the House of Lords in *Speidel v Plato Films*.[359] Their Lordships recognised that, although *Scott v Sampson* had stood for nearly 80 years, they were entitled to hold that it was wrongly decided, but they were not so persuaded. "It records and sets out", said Lord Morris,

> "what might be regarded as the greatest common measure of principle which emerged from the progressive experience of trial courts over many years."[360]

In the libel itself the acts with which the claimant was charged were the murder of a king and the betrayal of a general, and once again it was held that specific instances of other misconduct must be excluded. But, beyond this, it was held that general evidence of a reputation for anti-Jewish and anti-democratic activities was inadmissible because, in Lord Denning's words,

> "when evidence of good or bad character is given, it should be directed to that sector of a man's character which is relevant".[361]

On the other hand, evidence that the claimant had a bad reputation as a war criminal was admissible. This holding of the Court of Appeal stood in the absence of any appeal against it,[362] the Court of Appeal being of the opinion that it would be too narrow a rule that

> "evidence of general bad reputation must be confined to the particular trait in the plaintiff's character which is attacked by the libel".[363]

In *Sutcliffe v Pressdram*,[364] it was ordered that, on a retrial limited to damages only, the defendants would not be permitted to lead evidence or cross-examine with a view to establishing that the claimant was guilty of particular acts of misconduct, such evidence being inadmissible on an assessment of damages[365]; *Speidel v Plato Films*[366] was applied. However, following an extended analysis of *Scott v Sampson*,[367] and *Speidel v Plato Films* the Court of Appeal in *Burstein v Times Newspapers Ltd*,[368] concluded that nothing in these two central cases rendered inadmissible for the purpose of mitigating damages evidence of particular facts

---

358 [1929] 2 K.B. 1 CA at 18–19. This point is brought out well by *Bracegirdle v Bailey* (1859) 1 F. & F. 536 where evidence of specific misconduct was held inadmissible in the claimant's cross-examination since he had given no evidence in chief which could be discredited.

359 [1961] A.C. 1090.

360 [1961] A.C. 1090 at 1146–1147. See, too, at 1124, 1133 and 1148, per Viscount Simonds, Lord Denning and Lord Guest respectively. Lord Radcliffe however, while agreeing that *Scott v Sampson* should be upheld in relation to the admissibility of general evidence of reputation (at 1128), did not concur on the inadmissibility of evidence of particular facts: see at 1130–1132.

361 [1961] A.C. 1090 at 1140. See also, in more detail, Devlin LJ in the Court of Appeal: at 1102–1103.

362 [1961] A.C. 1090 at 1123, per Viscount Simonds.

363 [1961] A.C. 1090 at 1102.

364 [1991] 1 Q.B. 153 CA.

365 Nor were the defendants entitled to call evidence establishing the truth of the particulars of the plea of justification which had been rejected at the original trial: see para.46-056, above.

366 [1961] A.C. 1090.

367 (1882) 8 Q.B.D. 491.

368 [2001] 1 W.L.R. 579 CA.

which were directly relevant to the contextual background, explaining the context in which the defamatory publication came to be made.[369]

A further point on the admissibility of evidence arose in *Dingle v Associated Newspapers*,[370] where the defendants were sued for a libellous article published by them in the *Daily Mail*. The article related to the same matter as had appeared a month earlier in the form of a privileged report of a Select Committee of Parliament, which had also been published by the *Daily Mail* and other newspapers. The House of Lords, affirming the Court of Appeal, held that the judge at first instance erred in taking into consideration in mitigation of damages the effect of the other publications of the libel and the fact that the claimant's reputation had already been impaired by reason of the Select Committee's report and its publication in other national newspapers. "Newspapers", said Lord Denning, **46-064**

> "must answer for the effect of their own circulation without reference to the damage done by others. They may not even refer to other newspapers in mitigation of damages. Such has been the law ever since 1829 (*Saunders v Mills*), and it cannot be called in question now. It is but a particular instance of the general rule which excludes rumours or reports to the same effect as the libel, see *Scott v Sampson; Speidel v Plato Films*."[371]

Nor is it possible to get round the law about reports and rumours by saying that the claimant's reputation was already tarnished by reason of the earlier publications of the libel. "It ought not … to avail a defendant", said Lord Morris,

> "to prove that a plaintiff has been under a temporary cloud of suspicion when the success of the plaintiff in libel proceedings demonstrates that there need never have been any such suspicion."[372]

General evidence of reputation having been held admissible in mitigation of damages, the further question arose as to the necessity of pleading facts which the defendant wished to prove in this connection. In *Scott v Sampson*,[373] Cave J's main reason for allowing general evidence of reputation was that since, under the rule of court which later became RSC Ord.18 r.7(1), all material facts must be pleaded the claimant would not be taken by surprise, and it was further held that the evidence of rumours and of particular facts was properly rejected, not only because it was immaterial but because the facts which the defendant proposed to prove, even assuming they were material, were not stated or referred to in the pleading and therefore contravened the same rule of court which states that **46-065**

> "every pleading must contain, and contain only, a statement in a summary form of the material facts on which the party pleading relies".

This holding was disapproved in *Wood v Durham*,[374] but reinstated by the Court of Appeal in *Speidel v Plato Films*,[375] which overruled *Wood v Durham*,[376] and held that, if the matters which the defendant wished to introduce in mitigation would be

---

369 See the case at para.46-071, below.

370 [1964] A.C. 371.

371 [1964] A.C. 371 at 411.

372 [1964] A.C. 371 at 417.

373 (1882) 8 Q.B.D. 491.

374 (1888) 21 Q.B.D. 501.

375 [1961] A.C. 1090 CA.

376 (1888) 21 Q.B.D. 501; an overruling accepted as correct by the House of Lords: [1961] A.C. 1090.

likely to take the claimant by surprise or would raise new issues of fact, they must be pleaded, because such matters were required to be raised by what later became RSC Ord.18 r.8(1) and thus were material facts within the same, though later, RSC Ord.18 r.7(1). Accordingly the claimant's bad reputation as a war criminal must be pleaded in order to be admissible in evidence in a suit based upon charges of murder and betrayal, because such evidence raised a new issue of fact.[377] Whether the position is the same under the new Civil Procedure Rules 1998 is, however, somewhat doubtful for while CPR r.16.4, entitled Contents of the Particulars of Claim, specifies, by sub-rule (1)(a), that there must be included "a concise statement of the facts on which the claimant relies", there is no provision equivalent to, or even resembling, either RSC Ord.18 r.7(1) or r.8(1) in CPR r.16.5, entitled Contents of Defence, or in that part of the practice direction supplementing Pt 16 which deals with matters to be included in the defence.

**46-066** Both in *Wood v Durham*,[378] and in *Speidel v Plato Films*,[379] the defendant had pleaded justification in the alternative, and for the situation where there is no plea of justification there was introduced the year after the decision in *Scott v Sampson*,[380] a new rule of court, later RSC Ord.82 r.7, which laid down that in defamation cases where truth was not a defence particulars of matters upon which the defendant wanted to rely in mitigation must be pleaded. This rule ended life in 1989 when it was overtaken by the general rule of RSC Ord.18 r.12(1)(c) requiring mitigation to be pleaded in all cases. Again,[381] there is no equivalent of RSC Ord.18 r.12(1)(c) in CPR r.16.5 or its attendant practice direction. There is therefore an argument that one is back, for defamation, to the position as it was before any of these decisions or rules of court had surfaced.

**46-067** There is no doubt that RSC Ord.18 on pleadings was considered by the procedural reformers to be too verbose and technical. The new provisions were to be fairly short, with an emphasis on more general provisions which would suffice to guide the parties as to what they should put in their statements of case, statements of case which in any event are, in a case management era, to be subject to judicial scrutiny. The courts, therefore, should have it in their power, either by relying upon other provisions of the new rules or even by going outside the rules altogether, to reinstate the situation prevailing before the new rules came into force. But the position is far from clear. In any event, whatever may be held to be the current position on pleading, none of this renders admissible matters which would not otherwise be admissible at common law. As Phillimore J put it in *Mangena v Wright*,[382] in the context of what had been the old rule, it "does not change the common law as laid down in *Scott v Sampson*".

## (3) Other circumstances

**46-068** **(i) Social and financial circumstances of the parties** Little consideration has been given in the cases to the effect on damages of the social and financial posi-

[377] [1961] A.C. 1090 CA at 1104–1105.
[378] (1888) 21 Q.B.D. 501.
[379] [1961] A.C. 1090.
[380] (1882) 8 Q.B.D. 491.
[381] Compare para.46-065, above. And see further on the pleading aspects paras 51-038 and 51-039, below.
[382] [1909] 2 K.B. 958 at 979.

tion of the parties. On principle, social and financial position should be relevant to damages only in so far as it shows the extent of the injury to the claimant's reputation.[383] Thus the word of a defendant in a high position socially is likely to be of more weight and thus more injurious to the claimant than that of a person of humbler status: conversely, the higher the claimant is in the social scheme the more he is likely to be harmed. Relatedly, the role that a person plays in society is likely to affect the impact of a defamatory statement on a person's reputation, for example, where the claimant is a child protection campaigner, and defamatory statements are made to the effect that the claimant has protected child abusers.[384]

**(ii) Extent of the publication** As for the extent of the publication of the defamatory statement as a factor operating in aggravation or mitigation of the damages, it was held in *Gathercole v Miall*,[385] that, in the words of Pollock CB, **46-069**

> "in order to show the extent of the mischief that may have been done to the plaintiff by a libel in a newspaper you have a right to give evidence of any place where any copy of that libel has appeared for the purpose of showing the extent of the circulation."[386]

This evidence was allowed for this purpose although, because the claimant could not prove that the defendant publisher had himself industriously circulated the newspaper, the same evidence was inadmissible to aggravate the damages on the ground of malice.[387] Such evidence, however, is only admissible after it is established that the defendant is liable for the total dissemination of the statement: the rule in *Ward v Weeks*,[388] may prevent the defendant from being liable for any re-publication at all. In *KC v MGN Ltd*,[389] where the claimant was falsely accused in the defendant's national newspaper of raping a young girl, the Court of Appeal reduced the trial judge's starting figure[390] of £150,000 to £100,000 because too much attention had been paid by him to the large circulation and readership of the newspaper when it had been possible to keep the claimant anonymous throughout, the newspaper not having named him.[391]

The arrival of the internet has propelled to the fore the issue of extent of publication. The Court of Appeal in *Cairns v Modi*,[392] observed that **46-070**

> "as a consequence of modern technology and communication systems … [defamatory statements] will have the capacity to 'go viral' more widely and more quickly than ever before …. [and] with the ready availability of the worldwide web and of social network-

---

[383] In *Barron v Vines* [2016] EWHC 1226 (QB) at [21], it was said that the impact of a libel on a person's reputation can be affected by their role in society.

[384] See at [2016] EWHC 1226 at [21], referring to *Rantzen v Mirror Group Newspapers* [1994] Q.B. 670 CA.

[385] (1846) 15 M. & W. 319.

[386] (1846) 15 M. & W. 319 at 331; see, too, *Plunkett v Cobbett* (1804) 5 Esp. 136. Detailed evidence of the numbers of the circulation of a newspaper well-known to the jury is not admissible: *Whittaker v Scarborough Post Newspaper Co* [1896] 2 Q.B. 148 CA, overruling *Parnell v Walter* (1890) 24 Q.B.D. 441 and, in effect, *Rumney v Walter* (1891) 61 L.J.Q.B. 149.

[387] See (1846) 15 M. & W. 319 at 326, per Parke B.

[388] (1830) 7 Bing. 211; see para.46-015, above.

[389] [2013] 1 W.L.R. 1015 CA.

[390] It was subject to a discount on account of the offer of amends procedure: see the case at para.46-074, below.

[391] See [2013] 1 W.L.R. 1015 CA at [47] and [48].

[392] [2013] 1 W.L.R. 1015 CA.

> ing sites the scale of this problem has been immeasurably enhanced, especially for libel claimants who are already, for whatever reason, in the public eye."[393]

A good many of the worst libels now make an appearance on the internet. Where in *Cooper v Turrell*,[394] the defendant embarked on an internet campaign with his false accusations of company and director,[395] Tugendhat J saw as an aggravating factor for damages that the defendant's actions had taken the form of an internet exposure. A libel on the internet alleging a scam was the subject of *Metropolitan International Schools Ltd v Designtechnica Corporation*,[396] while the use of the internet in *Cruddas v Adams*,[397] meant that, for extent of publication, Eady J was required to examine blogs and tweets.[398]

46-071 **(iii) Contextual background to the publication** *Burstein v Times Newspapers Ltd*,[399] is an important decision because, in the words of Sir Christopher Slade there,

> "the evidence sought to be adduced [in mitigation of damages] does not readily fall either within or outside any category dealt with by previous authority"[400];

he further expressed himself as finding it

> "an unsatisfactory and … surprising feature of our law of defamation that the limits of the admissible evidence that can be given in mitigation of damages are in some respects so ill-defined".[401]

The libel was contained in an article stating that the claimant had organised hecklers to wreck performances of modernist atonal music. The defendants proffered evidence of a variety of facts, such as the fact that the claimant had earlier been associated with a group named The Hecklers to oppose such music and the fact that this group had encouraged booing, in which the claimant had joined, at the end of an opera performance. The Court of Appeal, reversing the trial judge, held that some of these matters ought to have been admitted in evidence in mitigation since there was no rule of common law which rendered inadmissible particular facts which were directly relevant to the contextual background in which the libellous publication came to be made and to the damage suffered by the claimant from it, that it was artificial and unhelpful to have the jury assess the damages in a void knowing nothing of the context in which the particular libellous statement came to be made, and that indeed the admissibility or otherwise of evidence of reputation in reduction of libel damages was now heavily affected by the Civil Procedure Rules with their overriding objective of enabling the court to deal with cases justly, an objective to be furthered by active case management and by confining issues to matters directly relevant to the subject-matter of the libellous publication. It was thus held that the evidence was admissible even though it was of particular facts which concerned the

393 [2013] 1 W.L.R. 1015 CA at [27].
394 [2011] EWHC 3269 (QB).
395 Facts, briefly, at para.46-033, above.
396 [2010] EWHC 2411 (QB); facts, briefly, at para.46-036, above.
397 [2013] EWHC 145 (QB); facts, briefly, at para.46-059, above.
398 [2013] EWHC 145 (QB) at [11].
399 [2001] 1 W.L.R. 579 CA.
400 [2001] 1 W.L.R. 579 CA at 602F.
401 [2001] 1 W.L.R. 579 CA at 602E.

claimant's general reputation, character or disposition,[402] even though it consisted of facts that might have formed the ingredients of a defence of justification[403] and even though it might include matters which were not causally connected, as through provocation, with the publication of the libel.[404]

Counsel in *Turner v News Group Newspapers Ltd*,[405] mounted an all-out attack on *Burstein* on the ground of inconsistency with *Speidel v Plato Films*,[406] but failed in this attack. The Court of Appeal held that evidence qualified under the *Burstein* principle if **46-072**

> "so clearly relevant to the subject-matter of the libel or to the claimant's reputation or sensitivity in that part of his life that there would be a real risk of the jury assessing the damages on a false basis if they were kept in ignorance of the facts to which the evidence relates."[407]

The items which had been introduced in evidence were held to satisfy this test. In every case, however, it is necessary to consider closely whether the background material is directly relevant to the damage to the claimant arising from the harm to his reputation in that part of his or her life to which the defamation relates.[408]

## (4) Mitigation: offers to make amends

Sections 2 to 4 of the Defamation Act 1996 introduced what was effectively a statutory defence by way of an offer to make amends, being in place of the offer of amends provisions of the repealed s.4 of the Defamation Act 1952, the rather complicated requirements of which had caused it to be hardly ever used. By contrast, the new more extensive and streamlined defence of offering to make amends has become popular. By s.2(4) of the 1996 Act an offer to make amends is an offer to make and publish both a correction of the statement and an apology, and to pay to the aggrieved party such compensation as may be agreed or determined. It is specifically provided by s.4(5) that an offer of amends which is not accepted may be relied on in mitigation of damages. As to the giving of compensation, s.3(5) provides that, where the parties are not in agreement on the amount to be paid, the court must determine the amount, applying the same principles of damages as apply in defamation proceedings. Determining the amount to be paid will necessarily involve a discount on what otherwise would have constituted the damages and thus lead effectively to mitigation. In this regard, the assessment of damages proceeds in two stages: (i) identifying the award that would have been made without reference to the offer, and (ii) discounting that figure to take into account the offer of amends.[409] **46-073**

Guidance on the proper operation of the statutory provisions is contained in the **46-074**

---

402 See para.46-061, above.
403 See para.46-054, above.
404 See para.46-058, above.
405 [2006] 1 W.L.R. 3469 CA.
406 [1961] A.C. 1090; at para.46-063, above.
407 [1961] A.C. 1090 at [56].
408 *Warren v Random House Group Ltd* [2008] EWCA Civ 834; [2009] Q.B. 600 CA; at [26] and [27]; *ZAM v CFW* [2013] EWHC 662 (QB); and *Lisle-Mainwaring v Associated Newspapers Ltd*[2017] EWHC 543 (QB) at [35]–[40].
409 *Barron v Collins* [2017] EWHC 162 (QB), citing *KC v MGN* [2013] 1 W.L.R. 1015.

very full judgment of Eady J in *Abu v MGN Ltd*,[410] and the provisions are seen in operation in *Cleese v Clark*,[411] where the award of compensation was again made by Eady J with more guidance. Further determinations of compensation by Eady J have followed. His reduction by 50 per cent of the amount he would have awarded on a full trial was upheld by the Court of Appeal in *Nail v News Group Newspapers Ltd*,[412] on the basis that if an unqualified offer to make amends were made and an agreed apology published, as had happened in the case, there was bound to be substantial mitigation of the damage. In *Turner v News Group Newspapers Ltd*,[413] where the *Burstein* principle[414] was held to apply, the discount made on the figure that would have been awarded had the dispute gone to trial was 40 per cent; the Court of Appeal affirmed.[415] In *Campbell-James v Guardian Media Group Plc*,[416] which concerned a libel of the utmost gravity, the discount was 35 per cent. In *Bowman v MGN Ltd*,[417] a case of a libel described by Eady J as amounting to a bit of celebrity gossip, where there was an early apology, a willingness to remove the offending words immediately and a very prompt reliance on the offer of amends regime, the discount was 50 per cent. In *KC v MGN Ltd*,[418] where the apology was reasonably prompt, clear and unqualified, and given prominence in the defendant's newspaper,[419] the discount made by Bean J was again 50 per cent, a discount with which the Court of Appeal agreed when the case went to appeal.[420] While recognising that an unqualified offer of amends should give the tortfeasor a healthy discount, Bean J said that it should not be so great as to induce equanimity in potential libellers through the knowledge that they can easily buy themselves out of trouble with an apology.[421] No case has allowed a discount in excess of 50 per cent.

**46-075** In summary, the factors which bear upon the level of discount for an offer of amends were said by Warby J in *Barron v Collins*,[422] to include: (i) whether the offer is prompt or delayed; (ii) whether any correction or apology that is published is prompt and fulsome; (iii) whether the defendant has acted in a way inconsistent with the conciliatory stance which an offer represents; and (iv) whether a defendant's conduct has increased the overall hurt to the claimant's feelings, e.g. by treating the claimant dismissively, or expressing a begrudging attitude. To this might be added; (v) whether the defendant has advanced in correspondence an ill-founded defence; and (vi) whether the defendant has made clear the way it will present its defence in court.[423] And a further factor from *Barron & Ors v Collins* which Warby J added is (vii) whether a defendant's behaviour could increase the damages beyond those that would have been awarded if no offer of amends were made. In such an extreme case, it has been suggested that the defendant's behaviour might even aggravate the damage, leading to an increase in the stage one figure (i.e.

---

410 [2003] 1 W.L.R. 2201.
411 [2004] E.M.L.R. 3 at 37.
412 [2005] 1 All E.R. 1040 CA.
413 [2005] E.M.L.R. 25 at 553.
414 See para.46-071, above.
415 [2006] 1 W.L.R. 3469 CA at para.46-072, above.
416 [2005] E.M.L.R. 24 at 542.
417 [2010] EWHC 895 (QB).
418 [2012] EWHC 483 (QB).
419 [2012] EWHC 483 (QB) at [44].
420 [2013] 1 W.L.R. 1015 CA at [50].
421 [2012] EWHC 483 (QB) at [46].
422 [2017] EWHC 162 (QB) at [32].
423 *Lisle-Mainwaring v Associated Newspapers Ltd* [2017] EWHC 543 (QB) at [119].

the award that would be made without reference to the offer),[424] although assuming that the offer of amends is a genuine offer rather than merely aggravating conduct, the better approach in such an extreme case might be for the offer of amends to lead to no discount at all.[425]

## (5) Mitigation: actions for damages against others

By s.12 of the Defamation Act 1952 it is provided that: **46-076**

> "In any action for libel or slander the defendant may give in evidence in mitigation of damages that the plaintiff has recovered damages, or has brought actions for damages, for libel or slander in respect of the publication of words to the same effect as the words on which the action is founded, or has received or agreed to receive compensation in respect of any such publication."

This has extended to all libels and slanders what s.6 of the Law of Libel Amendment Act 1888 had previously provided[426] for libels appearing in newspapers only.[427] Thus statute has altered the former common law rule that evidence could not be given in mitigation of damages of any recovery of damages[428] or any suit for damages[429] by the claimant against others in respect of a statement to the same effect as that sued upon.[430]

In *Lewis v Daily Telegraph*,[431] where the claimants sued two national newspapers **46-077** for similar libels published of the claimants on the same day, the two cases being dealt with by different juries, the House of Lords, in ordering new trials, said that at the trials a direction should be given to each jury as to the effect of s.12 of the Defamation Act 1952. Lord Reid, speaking for himself and Lord Jenkins, and with whose observations Lord Morris expressly agreed, said that s.12 in effect requires that each jury be told about the other action, but

> "the question is what each jury should be told. I do not think it is sufficient merely to tell each jury to make such allowances as they may think fit. They ought, in my view, to be directed that in considering the evidence submitted to them they should consider how far the damage suffered by the plaintiffs can reasonably be attributed solely to the libel with which they are concerned and how far it ought to be regarded as the joint result of the two

---

424 *Barron v Collins* [2017] EWHC 162 (QB) at [54].

425 *Lisle-Mainwaring v Associated Newspapers Ltd* [2017] EWHC 543 (QB) at [119].

426 Section 6 was repealed by s.18(3) of the 1952 Act.

427 Thus compensation received by the claimant from a second defendant with whom she had settled was taken into account in reduction of the damages in *Cambridge v Makin* [2011] EWHC 12 (QB): at [12] and [235].

428 *Creevey v Carr* (1835) 7 C. & P. 64; contrast *Frescoe v May* (1860) 2 F. & F. 123.

429 *Harrison v Pearce* (1858) 1 F. & F. 567. Martin B stated the reason of the common law rule: "One wrongdoer cannot avail himself of the wrong of another … The jury cannot take into account the other action": at 569.

430 Section 5 of the Law of Libel Amendment Act 1888 had, however, given power to the court, on the application of defendants in actions for the same, or substantially the same, libel brought by the same claimant, to order consolidation of the actions, and had further provided that in the consolidated action the whole amount of the damages should be assessed in one sum, but a separate verdict should be taken against each defendant, and the amount of the damages should be apportioned between the unsuccessful defendants. This provision has now been extended by s.13 of the Defamation Act 1952 to, inter alia, actions for slander. For the difficulties of its interpretation, and the manner in which it may impinge on s.12 of the Defamation Act 1952, see paras 52-049 to 52-061, below.

431 [1964] A.C. 234.

libels. If they think that some part of the damage is the joint result of the two libels they should bear in mind that the plaintiffs ought not to be compensated twice for the same loss. They can only deal with this matter on very broad lines and they must take it that the other jury will be given a similar direction. They must do the best they can to ensure that the sum which they award will fully compensate the plaintiffs for the damage caused by the libel with which they are concerned, but will not take into account that part of the total damage suffered by the plaintiffs which ought to enter into the other jury's assessment."[432]

## 6. Exemplary Damages

**46-078** The whole approach to exemplary damages was changed by the decision in *Rookes v Barnard*,[433] since approved in *Broome v Cassell & Co*,[434] and is treated in detail elsewhere.[435] Exemplary damages are now recoverable only if the circumstances of the case bring it within one of the three categories set out by Lord Devlin there.[436] In practice awards are likely to be made only where the defendant has calculated that he would profit from the defamation, thereby bringing Lord Devlin's second common law category into play.[437] Yet in the libel cases immediately succeeding *Rookes v Barnard*,[438] the claimant was singularly unsuccessful in bringing his case within this category[439] and *Broome v Cassell & Co*,[440] was the only early illustration of a claimant succeeding in obtaining and holding an exemplary award.[441] Since the mid-1980s, however, exemplary awards have come more into their own. While most of the cases are unreported[442] there is now the important reported case of *John v MGN*,[443] where a very substantial second category award was made, though cut down on appeal.[444]

---

432 [1964] A.C. 234 at 261.

433 [1964] A.C. 1129.

434 [1972] A.C. 1027.

435 Ch.13, above.

436 See paras 13-017 to 13-030, above. The further limitation introduced by *A.B. v South West WaterServices* [1993] Q.B. 507 CA, has now gone, that case having been overruled: see para.13-011, above.

437 There is not the same scope with defamation for exemplary damages within the first common law category involving oppressive conduct by government servants as there is with assault, false imprisonment and malicious prosecution: see especially the cases at paras 42-028 and 44-016, above.

438 [1964] A.C. 1129.

439 *McCarey v Associated Newspapers* [1965] 2 Q.B. 86 CA; *Broadway Approvals v Odhams Press (No.2)* [1965] 1 W.L.R. 805 CA; *Manson v Associated Newspapers* [1965] 1 W.L.R. 1038.

440 [1972] A.C. 1027.

441 The rule laid down in relation to defamation in *Rook v Fairrie* [1941] 1 K.B. 507 CA, that a judge may take into account, when assessing damages, that he has been able to express his views in his judgment as a ground for awarding less than a jury would probably allow, a rule now modified (see para.17-004, above), concerns the vindicatory damages allowed in defamation cases rather than exemplary damages.

442 See *Maxwell v Pressdram*, *The Times*, 22 November 1986 (£50,000 of £55,000 award exemplary); *Armstrong-Jones v News (UK)*, *The Independent*, 12 April 1990 (£30,000 of £35,000 award exemplary); *Rowland-Jones v City & Westminster Financial* (£20,000 exemplary of £130,000 award at first instance, 6 February 1992, upheld by CA 8 July 1992, as to exemplary element only). The jury did make an exemplary award in the reported *Riches v News Group Newspapers* [1986] Q.B. 256 but it was set aside on appeal.

443 [1997] Q.B. 586 CA.

444 See the case at paras 46-024 and 46-025, above.

Chapter 47

# INVASION OF PRIVACY

Table of Contents



England has not yet recognised the existence of a generalised tort of invasion of privacy, and may never do so.[1] Thus the House of Lords in *Wainwright v The Home Office*,[2] held there to be no tort of invasion of privacy committed where there was intrusion upon the physical person of a mother and two sons through strip searching by prison officers. At the same time recognition of a different form of invasion of privacy has been rapidly advancing, with a whole variety of cases coming before the courts even to the highest level. This is the intrusion on privacy by the improper use, generally by revelation to a public audience, of personal and private information. This started out as an equitable action for breach of confidence where there was a confidential relationship, but over time the need for such a relationship has been abandoned, the terminology of confidence has been shown to be unnecessary, and the action appears to have become available at law, so that there has emerged what is best called an action for the misuse of private information. That this aspect of personal privacy is now protected has also House of Lords support in the decision, following after *Wainwright*, of *Campbell v MGN Ltd*,[3] a case that will be considered below. **47-001**

Now the Court of Appeal in *Google Inc v Vidal-Hall*,[4] has concluded that misuse of private information should be recognised as a tort,[5] being a civil wrong without any equitable characteristics.[6] It was so held there for the purposes of service out of the jurisdiction[7] but should have general application.[8]

---

1 This is in interesting contrast to the United States where the idea was promulgated well over a century ago in the celebrated article by Warren and Brandeis, *The Right to Privacy*, which appeared in the *Harvard Law Review* of 1890 (4 Harv. L.R. 193). Brandeis was later a Justice of the Supreme Court of the United States.

2 [2004] 2 A.C. 406.

3 [2004] 2 A.C. 457. See the valuable exposition of this development of the law in Lord Nicholls's speech at paras 11 to 15.

4 [2015] EWCA Civ 311 CA.

5 [2015] EWCA Civ 311 CA at [51].

6 [2015] EWCA Civ 311 CA at [43].

7 [2015] EWCA Civ 311 CA at [51].

8 For the case in relation to breach of confidence and confidential information see para.48-026, below.

## 1. HEADS OF DAMAGE

47-002 Exceptionally for this text, non-pecuniary loss and restitution of benefits to the defendant are considered before pecuniary loss. This is simply because, when it comes to damages for an invasion of privacy, non-pecuniary loss by way of injury to feelings and mental distress predominates. And, more recently, substantial awards which are best understood as restitutionary damages have emerged. Indeed there is hardly ever in the cases any claim for pecuniary losses related to an invasion of privacy.[9]

### (1) Non-pecuniary loss

47-003 The new century has brought with it a series of cases in which there have been awarded damages for non-pecuniary loss by way of injured feelings resulting from invasions of privacy by way of the misuse of personal information, supported in some of the cases by breach of personal or individual confidence.[10] For a time all of the decisions on damages for injured feelings have been at first instance. Though there have been appeals, and further litigation, in many of them, issues of damages for non-pecuniary loss have not been addressed beyond the first court[11] until we get to *AAA v Associated Newspapers*,[12] in which the Court of Appeal considered and affirmed the award of the trial judge.[13]

47-004 In the early days two well-publicised litigations dominate the field, litigations producing a pair of cases which involved breaches by the media perpetrated against persons who are today referred to as celebrities. In *Campbell v MGN Ltd*,[14] the claimant was Naomi Campbell, a famous fashion model who, as Lord Hoffmann said when the case reached the Lords, lived by publicity.[15] She recovered £2,500 for injured feelings[16] from the publication in a newspaper article of private details of her life as a drug addict.[17] *Douglas v Hello! Ltd* was a massively extended litigation running to over ten reported cases,[18] but fortunately we are concerned here with only three of them.[19] Exclusive photograph rights at their very grand wedding had been given by the film stars, Michael Douglas and Catherine Zeta-Jones, to the magazine OK, but an intruder at the wedding had managed to take unauthorised photographs which were published by Hello, OK's rival magazine. In the dam-

9 See paras 47-013 and 47-014, below.

10 This was so in *McKennitt v Ash* [2006] E.M.L.R. 10 at 178 (at para.47-005, below). In *Cooper v Turrell* [2011] EWHC 3269 (QB) the individual claimant sued for the misuse of private information, the corporate claimant for breach of confidence; see the case at para.47-008, below.

11 In *Douglas v Hello! Ltd* [2006] Q.B. 125 CA, damages were considered by the Court of Appeal but only for pecuniary loss: see para.47-014, below.

12 [2013] EWCA Civ 554 CA.

13 See the case at para.47-008, below.

14 [2002] E.M.L.R. 30 at 617.

15 [2004] 2 A.C. 457 at [37]; "what she has to sell is herself".

16 There was also a separate award for aggravated damages: see at para.47-015, below.

17 The Court of Appeal reversed on liability ([2003] Q.B. 633 CA) and the House of Lords in turn by a bare majority reversed the Court of Appeal, restoring the judge's order ([2004] 2 A.C. 457), but damages were not touched upon.

18 With judgments of very great length in some.

19 In the various law reports the cases are numbered in a confusing and inconsistent way, so that for example what is called "(No.3)" in one report appears as "(No.8)" in another. Numbers have therefore been ignored, as they are in the neutral citations, and the particular case is to be identified by the case report reference that has been given.

ages claim of the Douglases and OK heard by Lindsay J, he held the Douglases to be entitled to damages for distress at the publication of the unauthorised photographs and assessed the damages at £3,750 each.[20] This award was not challenged in the Court of Appeal.[21]

Then there are cases which do not involve a claimant who is well-known to the public or a defendant who is part of the media. In *Cornelius v de Taranto*,[22] there was neither. The claimant was a teacher suing a consultant psychiatrist for the unauthorised disclosure and dissemination of a medico-legal report concerning her; £3,000 in damages was awarded for injured feelings.[23] In *Archer v Williams*,[24] the claimant Lady Archer, herself well-known, was much in the public eye because of her husband's being successfully prosecuted for perjury; the defendant was her secretary and personal assistant who had revealed to the press details of her employer's personal and business affairs obtained in the course of her many years of employment by the claimant. An award of £2,500 for injured feelings was made. In *McKennitt v Ash*,[25] too the claimant was renowned, here as a composer and performer of folk music; she was objecting to revelations about her personal and business life in a book written by a former friend and colleague, the defendant. What was termed a relatively modest £5,000 was awarded for hurt feelings and distress.[26] **47-005**

Then, with a far larger amount awarded, came *Mosley v News Group Newspapers Ltd*,[27] where once again there was a celebrated claimant and a media defendant. A newspaper proprietor had published articles which gave lurid and explicit details of a gathering at which a well-known figure in the racing world had indulged in sado-masochistic practices with prostitutes; the articles also alleged that the gathering had involved an enactment of Nazi behaviour, including a mocking of the victims of the Holocaust. The sado-masochistic practices had indeed taken place but there was no truth in the suggested Nazi overtones. Consideration by Eady J of this bizarre scenario led to an award in damages of £60,000. **47-006**

Eady J's award is likely to have included an element of aggravated damages[28] but certainly had no element of exemplary damages which he declined to award.[29] What, however, certainly appears to have been included in the award is an amount, possibly large, on account of vindicatory damages, not by way of disguised compensation, as appears in defamation, but in the controversial sense of vindication to mark the infringement of a right. The Supreme Court in the false imprisonment case of *R. (on the application of Lumba (Congo)) v Secretary of State for the Home Department*,[30] held, by majority, in a conclusion subsequently reaffirmed in *R. (on the application of O) v Secretary of State for the Home Department (Bail for* **47-007**

[20] *Douglas v Hello! Ltd* [2004] E.M.L.R. 2 at 13; see at [56] and [57].
[21] *Douglas v Hello! Ltd* [2006] Q.B. 125 CA at [110].
[22] [2001] E.M.L.R. 12 at 329.
[23] Damages were not in issue on the appeal at [2002] E.M.L.R. 6 CA at 112.
[24] [2003] E.M.L.R. 38 at 869.
[25] [2006] E.M.L.R. 10 at 178.
[26] [2006] E.M.L.R. 10 at 178, [162]. On the appeal, at [2008] Q.B. 73 CA, damages were not addressed.
[27] [2008] E.M.L.R. 20 at 679.
[28] See on this para.47-015, below. It is just possible that it may also have included an element of mitigation of damages: see on this para.47-016, below.
[29] See on this para.47-018, below.
[30] [2012] 1 A.C. 245.

*Immigration Detainees)*,[31] that the infringement of a right does not in our law give an entitlement to vindicatory damages. The reasoning of Eady J and the contrary approach of the majority of the Supreme Court Justices are treated in detail in the chapter on vindicatory damages[32] and need not be repeated here. This sensible development makes it clear that what Eady J said in *Mosley* on vindicatory damages and privacy has been overtaken by the Supreme Court's decision in *Lumba*.[33] Vindicatory damages, until they are wholly rationalised, are a misnomer describing particular compensation primarily for defamation.[34]

**47-008** In any event it is thought that, ideas of vindication apart, the figure of £60,000 can be regarded as justifiable simply as *solatium* for injury to feelings, distress and loss of standing in the community. The very fact that the damage, once it is done, is irreversible must in itself surely add to the need for *solatium*. Putting on one side, as Eady J did, moral disapproval of the claimant's activities, it is obvious that here the invasion of privacy had a far more serious effect than any of the invasions considered above where sums of only a few thousand pounds have been awarded. Thus it is significant that Eady J, when coming to his figure of £60,000, commented that the claimant was hardly exaggerating in asserting that his life was ruined by what had happened.[35] While undoubtedly *Mosley* is an extreme case, higher awards than in the early days are already being both proposed and made in cases which may be regarded as of a more usual nature. Even before *Mosley* was decided, Lord Phillips MR, giving the judgment of the Court of Appeal in the one episode of the copious *Douglas v Hello! Ltd* litigation which went that far, but in an appeal on pecuniary rather than non-pecuniary loss, remarked that he thought that the combined £7,500 awarded to the two film star claimants for their distress was very modest in the context of the particular litigation.[36] After *Mosley*, Tugendhat J showed himself clearly to favour higher damages than were awarded in the early privacy cases, commenting in *Spelman v Express Newspapers*,[37] a human rights and injunction case, that it can no longer be assumed that damages at these "very low" levels mark the limit of the court's powers. Indeed Tugendhat J had himself gone much higher than was then usual in *Cooper v Turrell*.[38] It was a case involving libel brought by an individual and a company[39] but the libel awards were supplemented by further awards for the misuse of private information,[40] which effectively means for loss of privacy[41]; all the cases relied on in argument and listed in the judgment[42] were awards for loss of privacy. Tugendhat J said that, because

---

31 [2016] 1 W.L.R. 1717.

32 See Ch.17, above. See paras 17-017 and following.

33 Thus Nicola Davies J, in arriving at £15,000 for her award of damages for breach of the right to privacy in *AAA v Associated Newspapers Ltd* [2012] EWHC 2103 (QB) (facts at para.47-008, below), decided more than a year after *Lumba* in the Supreme Court, was wrong to take into account Eady J's support in *Mosley* of vindicatory damages in privacy cases: at [126] and [127]. In affirming, this was not touched upon by the Court of Appeal: [2013] EWCA Civ 554 CA.

34 See Ch.17 above, at paras 17-002 and following.

35 [2008] E.M.L.R. 20 at 679, [236].

36 [2006] Q.B. 125 CA at [110]. See the case at para.47-004, above.

37 [2012] EWHC 355 (QB) at [114].

38 [2011] EWHC 3269 (QB).

39 Facts at para.46-033, above.

40 [2011] EWHC 3269 (QB) at [107]. The corporate claimant based its case on breach of confidence.

41 See para.47-001, above.

42 [2011] EWHC 3269 (QB) at [92].

of the seriousness of the damage, the privacy case of *Mosley*,[43] was a more appropriate guide for him than the earlier privacy cases,[44] awarding £10,000 to the corporate claimant and to the individual claimant £30,000, which would have been £40,000 had compensation for the individual's distress not already been included in the libel award.[45] After this decision we have *AAA v Associated Newspapers*,[46] where the defendant newspaper had breached the right to privacy of a young child, the claimant, by repeated publication of her photograph with speculation about her paternity, the suggestion being that her father might be a prominent politician in whose career the public was interested. Nicola Davies J awarded £15,000 and this award was upheld by the Court of Appeal.[47] Also to be considered is *WXY v Gewanter*,[48] where there was a posting on the internet of information about the private life of the claimant causing her great distress. While the claim is described as one for the misuse of private information the defendants' actions undoubtedly constituted an invasion of privacy[49] and although there was also a claim for harassment it was said that this was not a separate claim, the harassment being part and parcel of the misuse of information.[50] The award was just short of £25,000.[51] We are on the road to higher recoveries for non-pecuniary loss here.[52]

Despite the growing size of these awards, courts have maintained the application of consistent principle. For instance, Richard Spearman QC, sitting as a Deputy Judge in the Chancery Division in *Burrell v Clifford*,[53] awarded compensation albeit of the small amount of £5,000 for the limited dissemination of relatively saccharine information by a publicist who was provided it confidentially by the butler to the late Diana, Princess of Wales. In making the award however, the deputy judge applied the thin skull principle[54] and recognised that the butler was entitled to damages to be assessed on the basis of the extent of the distress that he had suffered even though a more robust individual would not have suffered distress to that extent.[55] **47-009**

---

43 See para.47-006, above.

44 [2011] EWHC 3269 (QB) at [106].

45 [2011] EWHC 3269 (QB) at [107].

46 [2012] EWHC 2103 (QB).

47 [2013] EWCA Civ 554 CA.

48 [2013] EWHC 589 (QB).

49 Indeed counsel refers to "privacy and confidentiality": [2013] EWHC 589 (QB) at [46].

50 [2013] EWHC 589 (QB) at [52] and [53]. The harassment claim is at para.43-019, above.

51 An amount which included £5,000 aggravated damages.

52 And in coming to the appropriate amount to award there has now to be taken into account the Court of Appeal's further ruling in *Simmons v Castle* [2013] 1 W.L.R. 1239 CA (from 1243) that damages for non-pecuniary loss in all types of civil claim are to be increased by 10 per cent. For the procedural history and reasons for this development, stemming from the package of reforms appearing in the Jackson Report on Civil Litigation Costs, see para.40-280, below. As pointed out in para.40-280, below, the primary purpose behind the introduction of a 10 per cent uplift in damages for non-pecuniary loss was to compensate those funding their claims by a conditional fee agreement for their inability, on success, to recover the success fee from the defendant where the conditional fee agreement was entered into after the costs-amending legislation came into force on 1 April 2013. The judge's refusal of the uplift in the class action entitled *Gulati v MGN Ltd* [2015] EWHC 1482 Ch (facts at para.47-009, below) was on account of success fees still being available to the several claimants (see at [165]). This can only be on the basis that the claimants' conditional fee agreements dated from before 1 April 2013.

53 [2016] EWHC 294 (Ch).

54 See paras 8-092 to 8-102, above.

55 [2016] EWHC 294 (Ch) at [159].

### (2) "Right to control information": restitutionary damages for the opportunity taken

47-010 The road to higher awards is particularly evidenced in the dramatic increases in the class action entitled *Gulati v MGN Ltd*.[56] Eight claimants sued for invasion of their privacy which came about by the hacking of their phones by journalists who listened to their voicemails on a daily basis over several years and then reported on what they heard in very many articles addressed to the public. The awards made by Mann J started at £72,500 and moved through the £100,000s to a top award of more than £260,000. What also led to these awards being out of line with previous awards was that Mann J was giving compensation for loss of a right to control private information as well as for the more conventional injury to feelings. An appeal to the Court of Appeal on different points was dismissed: *Representative Claimants (Gulati) v MGN Ltd*,[57] (on which see paras. 6-016 and 14-021, above).

47-011 As we have seen in Ch.14, the large award for the claimant's "lost right to control private information" should be understood as an award of restitutionary damages. The Court of Appeal, rightly, insisted that the award was not given to "vindicate" the right to control the information. The Court of Appeal also accepted that this award was not for any other non-financial consequence actually experienced by the claimant (including distress). The basis for the award might best be understood as restitutionary damages, representing the benefit that the defendant derived from the wrongdoing. In other words, the defendant wrongfully obtained the opportunity to use information without paying for that opportunity. As Mann J, at first instance, said

> "the defendant will have helped itself, over an extended period of time, to large amounts of personal and private information and treated it as its own to deal with as it thought fit".[58]

It is elementary justice that the defendant should have to pay the reasonable price for that opportunity or benefit, in addition to an award for the distress to the claimant. Although the precise label does not in any way contradict the analysis of the Court of Appeal, as explained in Ch.14 understanding the restitutionary nature of the award will also aid the court in quantifying how the damages can be calculated such as, in circumstances which the Court of Appeal rightly accepted that the amount awarded would be affected, if the information had become public knowledge anyway.[59]

47-012 Even if the label "restitutionary damages" is not preferred as a description of the so-called lost right to control information, the focus on the value of the opportunity has the benefit of transparently valuing the damages rather than the approach, sometimes adopted by counsel and reflected in decisions such as *TLT v Secretary of State for the Home Department*,[60] where the damages are awarded as a single amount without a separate award in respect of this head of damage.

---

56 [2015] EWHC 1482 (Ch).
57 [2015] EWCA Civ 1291 CA.
58 *Gulati v MGN Ltd* [2015] EWHC 1482 (Ch) at [132].
59 [2016] EWHC 294 (Ch) at [45].
60 [2016] EWHC 2217 (QB).

### (3) Pecuniary loss

Actionable infringements of privacy are not likely to entail pecuniary loss but, should such loss ever appear, recovery will be allowed, subject to the usual requirements of causation, remoteness and the like being satisfied. The only recoveries that can be pointed to in the cases are of a comparatively insignificant £750 for the costs of retrieving the medico-legal report that had been wrongfully disseminated in *Cornelius v de Taranto*,[61] and of a somewhat larger £7,000 for the costs to the film stars of arranging an earlier appearance in OK magazine of the authorised wedding photographs in *Douglas v Hello! Ltd*.[62] **47-013**

While Lindsay J in *Douglas* had regarded these costs as an expense incurred in mitigation of damage,[63] the Court of Appeal endorsed his award on the basis that it was compensation for interference with the Douglases' commercial exploitation of themselves and not for interference with their private lives.[64] Such a rationale places this recovery of damages for pecuniary loss in the realm of breach of confidential information seen as an economic tort.[65] And the further claim of the Douglases before the Court of Appeal for a very large notional licence fee, which authorisation of the publication of photographs of their wedding would have commanded, may be seen in the same light. For a variety of reasons the Court of Appeal declined to make such an award.[66] **47-014**

## 2. Aggravation and Mitigation

Infringement of privacy is clearly a field ripe for aggravated damages. The defendant's conduct may well be such as to increase a claimant's distress and loss of dignity. Thus on this account a separate award of £1,000 aggravated damages was made, giving a total of £3,500 for the non-pecuniary loss, in *Campbell v MGN Ltd*[67]; this was largely on account of the defendant's having published a further newspaper article belittling, and highly offensive to, the claimant.[68] By contrast, aggravated damages were not awarded by Lindsay J in *Douglas v Hello! Ltd*[69] since he held that the defendant had not acted in a high-handed or offensive way.[70] As for *Mosley v News Group Newspapers Ltd*,[71] where there was no separate award, it would appear nevertheless that there was an element of aggravated damages in the overall award of £60,000. For Eady J referred not only to the appropriateness of taking aggravating conduct into account in privacy cases but also to the legitimacy of reflecting in the award that the defendant had persisted publicly, in a follow-up article, with the revelations, including those that had proved untrue.[72] **47-015**

---

61 [2001] E.M.L.R. 12 at 329; see the case at para.47-005, above.

62 [2004] E.M.L.R. 2 at 13; see the case at para.47-004, above.

63 See [2004] E.M.L.R. 2 at [57].

64 [2006] Q.B. 125 CA at [111].

65 For which see paras 48-026 to 48-032, above.

66 For the court's reasons see [2006] Q.B. 125 CA at [ 243]–[250].

67 [2002] E.M.L.R. 30 at 617; the case is at para.47-004, above. But see, in the different context of a victimisation claim, the concerns expressed in *Commissioner of Police of the Metropolis v Shaw* [2012] I.C.R. 464; [2012] I.R.L.R. 291 over having separate awards.

68 See [2002] E.M.L.R. 30 at [166] and [169].

69 [2003] 3 All E.R. 996 (his judgment on liability); see the case at para.47-004, above.

70 [2003] 3 All E.R. 996 at [275].

71 [2008] E.M.L.R. 20 at 679; see the case at para.47-006, above.

72 See at [2008] E.M.L.R. 20 at [22] and [223]. Aggravated damages were also included in the single

**47-016** The possibility of mitigating the damages by reference to the conduct of the claimant is also referred to by Eady J in *Mosley*. It could be asked, he said, to what extent the claimant was the author of his own misfortune and had contributed by his own choice to his distress and loss of dignity.[73] It is not clear, however, if Eady J's overall award did reflect this factor and would, without it, have been larger still.

## 3. EXEMPLARY DAMAGES

**47-017** The whole approach to exemplary damages was changed by the decision in *Rookes v Barnard*,[74] later approved in *Broome v Cassell & Co*,[75] and is treated in detail elsewhere.[76] Exemplary damages are now recoverable only if the circumstances of the case bring it within one of the three categories set out by Lord Devlin there, the two common law categories and the statutory category which is of little or no importance.[77] Cases bringing in the first common law category concerning oppressive, arbitrary or unconstitutional conduct by government servants are somewhat unlikely in this area of the law, but cases of the second common law category concerning conduct calculated to result in profit could well arise.

**47-018** Lindsay J said in *Douglas v Hello! Ltd*[78] that he was content to assume that exemplary damages were available in breach of confidence[79] but did not award exemplary damages, which is not surprising in view of his holding that the conduct of the defendant was not such as to attract even aggravated damages.[80] On the other hand, Eady J in *Mosley v News Group Newspapers Ltd*,[81] was

> "not persuaded that it is right to extend the application of exemplary (or punitive) damages into this field",[82]

though like Lindsay J he would not have awarded them because he held that the facts of the case did not bring it within the exemplary damages net.[83] While this text favours the removal of exemplary damages from the legal scene[84] and is therefore sympathetic to Eady J's decision on this, it is thought that, now that the House of Lords has extended the remit of exemplary damages to misfeasance in public office,[85] the law is now such that exemplary damages are available across the whole range of tort.[86]

**47-019** Two factors in particular influenced Eady J in coming to his decision. First, he pointed to the fact that there is a question over whether this now developed action

---

award for non-pecuniary loss in *WXY v Gewanter* [2013] EWHC 589 (QB) but without anything said specifically about the aggravating factors present. See the case at para.47-008, above.

73 See at [2008] E.M.L.R. 20 at [224]–[226].

74 [1964] A.C. 1129.

75 [1972] A.C. 1027.

76 See Ch.13, above.

77 See paras 13-017 to 13-030, above.

78 [2003] 3 All E.R. 996 (his judgment on liability); see the case at para.47-004, above.

79 [2003] 3 All E.R. 996 at [273].

80 See para.47-015, above.

81 [2008] E.M.L.R. 20 at 679.

82 [2008] E.M.L.R. 20 at [235].

83 See [2008] E.M.L.R. 20 at [204] to [210].

84 See paras 13-006 and 13-007, above.

85 See para.45-009, above.

86 See para.13-011, above.

has become a tort,[87] thereby allowing in exemplary damages.[88] Secondly, there was a parallel claim in *Mosley* invoking art.8 of the Human Rights Act with its right to respect for private life, and since such a claim should take its approach from Strasbourg jurisprudence to which exemplary damages are alien, a similar approach would only be proper for a claim under English domestic law. It is submitted that neither of these factors should have deflected Eady J. As to the first factor, assuming that the action has moved from equity to law it may be asked: if this form of invasion of privacy is not a tort, what is it? It is thought that its classification as a tort by Lord Nicholls in *Campbell v MGN Ltd*,[89] to which Eady J of course refers,[90] must come to be accepted, in which case the door is open to exemplary damages. As to the second factor, whatever may be the position with claims under the Human Rights Act, there can surely be no good reason why a separate, independent action under the common law should be inhibited by the views of Strasbourg.[91]

87 He refers to the competing views in his judgment at paras [181]–[184].

88 The possibility that exemplary damages may be awarded in contract has not yet reached English law. See para.13-016, above.

89 [2002] E.M.L.R. 30 at 617.

90 [2008] E.M.L.R. 20 at 679, [182] and [184].

91 Eady J also gave detailed consideration to the question of vicarious liability (at [198] to [203]) and concluded that it was not for a judge of first instance to say that "exemplary damages *could* not be awarded because this Defendant's liability would be on a purely vicarious basis": at [203]. But as the law stands, with the Court of Appeal's decision in *Rowlands v Chief Constable of Merseyside Police* [2007] 1 W.L.R. 1065 CA (at para.13-046, above), he really had no option but to decide in favour of vicarious liability.

CHAPTER 48

# ECONOMIC TORTS AND INTELLECTUAL PROPERTY WRONGS

TABLE OF CONTENTS



**48-001** The rejection by the House of Lords in *OBG Ltd v Allan*,[1] of the unified theory of economic torts has left us with what we had before, a heterogeneity of such torts. This chapter aims to collect them together. Of course many torts may be said to affect the economic relations of the claimant with third parties, as where the claimant is prevented, through injury to himself or by conversion or destruction of his goods, from obtaining or carrying out a profitable contract, but certain torts concern interference with economic relations in a more specific sense.

**48-002** We start with those torts in which the defendant's wrongful act is aimed at directly influencing the third party, causing him by inducement, deception or intimidation to act to the claimant's detriment in his existing or potential economic relations with him. These economic torts of today are, respectively, inducement of breach of contract, injurious, sometimes called malicious, falsehood, and intimidation where the intimidation is of a third party.[2] They find their origins in the torts

---

1 [2008] A.C. 1.

2 For the other aspect of the tort of intimidation, involving intimidation of the claimant himself, see

of seduction, enticement and harbouring of a servant but these torts early fell into virtual disuse.[3] As for the third of these economic torts of today, intimidation, established by the House of Lords in *Rookes v Barnard* and pressed into use largely in the area of interferences with contractual relations existing between the claimant and the person intimidated, the issue of damages has not been explored so that damages deserve only a footnote.[4]

The heterogeneity is even more pronounced in what remains. The tort of causing loss by the use of unlawful means, sometimes referred to as the tort of unlawful interference, is concerned primarily, if not exclusively, with economic loss. It has long existed but has remained largely undeveloped[5] and, while it has recently received judicial recognition by the House of Lords,[6] the issue of damages, as with the tort of intimidation,[7] has not been explored so that damages only requires a footnote.[8] The idea of conspiracy as a tort has no bounds but in practice it is confined to claims seeking redress for economic loss. Breach of confidence or, more specifically, of confidential information has its economic side as well as its personal side, and its economic side is dealt with here,[9] although it should be noted that there is some doubt as to whether breach of confidence is a tort,[10] thereby requiring resort to equity for recovery. Treatment of confidential information leads on naturally to the area of infringement of statutory rights in immaterial, or intellectual, property, covering trade marks, patents, copyrights and design rights. There are texts which give separate treatment to a number of these torts and do not subsume them within **48-003**

---

the first footnote to para.49-002, below.

3 For many years they had been sustained by their utilisation in the domestic field, not by masters suing in respect of their servants but by parents suing in respect of their children. All three torts in the family context were statutorily abolished by the Law Reform (Miscellaneous Provisions) Act 1970 s.5, covering spouses as well as children except that with the first of the three the abolition related to adultery (see s.4) rather than seduction. On the damages the former law is collected in Ch.39 of the 12th edition (1961) of this work. All three torts in their application to servants were similarly abolished by statute by the Administration of Justice Act 1982 s.2(c). On the damages the former law is collected at paras 1430 to 1433 of the 14th edition (1980) of this work.

4 One would expect there to be recovery for loss of profits and this is supported by the solitary case of *Morgan v Fry* [1968] 1 Q.B. 521. The claimant had been dismissed by his employers from his job as a lockman as a result of their being intimidated by the defendant, and he recovered as damages his loss of earnings based on the difference between his former wages as a lockman and his present wages working for one of the gas boards, taking into account the fact that he would probably not have continued in his present employment as a lockman for more than five years: at 548–549. The Court of Appeal reversed but only on liability: [1968] 2 Q.B. 710 CA. There should also be recovery for expenses incurred. And damages for non-pecuniary loss by way of injured feelings should be available in a suitable case; see the discussion in relation to other economic torts at paras 48-008, 48-013 and 48-024, below.

5 The excellent and full discussion of the tort, initially by Lord Wedderburn, in *Clerk & Lindsell on Torts*, 21st edn (London: Sweet & Maxwell, 2014) at paras 24–72 and following, may be consulted.

6 In *OBG Ltd v Allan* [2008] A.C. 1.

7 At para.48-002, above.

8 Should a damages issue arise in relation to the tort of unlawful interference, all that can be done is to look for analogies in the damages awarded in the other torts dealt with in this chapter. Thus where in *Fearns v Anglo-Dutch Paint & Chemical Co Ltd* [2010] EWHC 1708 Ch the claimant failed to establish that this tort had been committed (at [15]) so that any need to calculate damages fell away, it would appear that the damages, if available, would have followed the same lines as those awarded in the successful claims in *Fearns* for passing off and trade mark infringement: see, respectively, paras 48-017 and 48-050, below.

9 For its personal side see Ch.47, above.

10 See para.48-026, below.

an omnibus category of economic torts. But for our purposes they are classed as economic torts.[11]

## I. Inducement of Breach of Contract

48-004 A massive enlargement of the action for enticement of a servant was made in 1853 in *Lumley v Gye*.[12] This famous decision ushered in a new tort, that of inducement of breach of contract, which makes actionable the inducing by the defendant, intentionally and without lawful justification, of any person to break any contract made by him with the claimant, if the claimant is thereby damaged.

48-005 Although damage is the gist of the action, little exact detail can be given as to the measure of damages,[13] as the courts have consistently endorsed Lord Esher MR's pronouncement in *Exchange Telegraph Co v Gregory*,[14] the endorsement appearing on many occasions over the next half century, that "it is not necessary to give proof of specific damage" because "the damages are damages at large".[15] Nevile J in *Goldsoll v Goldman*,[16] stated the position in somewhat more detail. "The damage," he said,

> "may be inferred, that is to say, that if the breach which has been procured by the defendant has been such as must in the ordinary course of business inflict damage upon the plaintiff, then the plaintiff may succeed without proof of any particular damage which has been occasioned him."[17]

48-006 The type of damage that is likely to be inferred by the court is loss of profits. This may be the profit that the claimant would have made on the contract the breach of which the defendant has induced. Alternatively, it may be the profit that the claimant is prevented from making on other contracts.[18] In *Exchange Telegraph Co v Gregory*,[19] the claimants, a telegraphic news agency, supplied for profit valuable information regarding quotations for stocks and shares to a limited number of subscribers. The defendant, a non-subscriber, induced one of the claimants'

---

11 Economic torts are not the object of our competition law, which is designed to protect consumers from unacceptable aspects of competition in the form of such matters as price fixing, monopolies, resale price maintenance, unfair trading, mergers. Nonetheless it is possible that one or other of the economic torts about to be considered might be held to fall within competition law.

12 (1853) 2 E. & B. 216.

13 Some detail might have emerged from *Stocznia Gdanska SA v Latvian Shipping Co* [2001] 1 Lloyd's Rep. 537 when the case got to the issue of damages but it seems never to have got there.

14 [1896] 1 Q.B. 147 CA at 153.

15 *Goldsoll v Goldman* [1914] 2 Ch. 603 at 615, per Nevile J; *Pratt v British Medical Association* [1919] 1 K.B. 244 at 281, per McCardie J; *G.W.K. v Dunlop Rubber Co* (1926) 42 T.L.R. 376 at 377, per Lord Hewart CJ; *British Industrial Plastics v Ferguson* [1938] 4 All E.R. 504 CA at 511, per Slesser LJ; *Bent's Brewery Co v Luke Hogan* [1945] 2 All E.R. 570 at 578, per Lynskey J.

16 [1914] 2 Ch. 603.

17 [1914] 2 Ch. 603 at 615. Compare *Exchange Telegraph Co v Gregory* [1896] 1 Q.B. 147 CA at 156, per Kay LJ ("the inference is irresistible that damage must accrue to the plaintiffs from such an act as the defendant has committed"); and at 158, per Rigby LJ ("I cannot doubt … that some damage ought to be inferred"). In *British Industrial Plastics v Ferguson* [1938] 4 All E.R. 504 CA, Slesser and MacKinnon LJJ disagreed as to whether there was sufficient damage to ground an action, the former considering that damage could properly be inferred (at 511) but the latter saying that no damage had been occasioned (at 514). The case was decided for the defendant on other grounds.

18 *Jones v Fabbi* (1973) 37 D.L.R. (3d) 27 is a Canadian case illustrating recovery for such loss of profit (see at 36).

19 [1896] 1 Q.B. 147 CA.

subscribers to break his contract with the claimants by divulging the said information to the defendant. Lord Esher MR said that the claimants must have suffered some damage, since

> "persons to whom this information, supplied from hour to hour, is valuable must, if they could not get it in any other way, buy the plaintiffs' newspaper".[20]

In *Goldsoll v Goldman*,[21] where the defendant had induced the third party to set up a rival business near to the claimant in breach of the covenant in restraint of trade which the claimant had taken from the third party on buying his business, the suggested loss was the loss of orders caused by the competition. In *The Kaliningrad*,[22] where the defendant was liable for procuring the breach of the claimant's sub-charter with the charterer of a vessel and the disruption caused by the sudden withdrawal of the vessel resulted in the claimant's suffering loss of business and of profits, the claimant was held entitled to recover for these losses. A somewhat different loss of profits is indicated by *Bent's Brewery Co v Luke Hogan*,[23] where the defendant, an officer of a trade union, attempted to induce the managers of the claimants' business to divulge confidential information as to the claimants' wages bill and takings. The nature of the potential damage was that through the use of this information the claimants might be compelled to pay more for the services of their managers.[24]

Beyond profits lost, the claimant may recover for expenses incurred[25] as a result **48-007**
of the tort.[26] In *British Motor Trade Association v Salvadori*,[27] the claimant association, a trade union consisting of car manufacturers and dealers, in order to prevent the immediate resale of new cars, then in short supply, required purchasers to covenant not to resell within 12 months. The defendants organised an attack on this covenant system by inducing purchasers to resell to them in breach of covenant, and then themselves reselling the cars again at greatly inflated prices. In the claimants' claim for damages they were held to have established that a failure of the covenant system would cause them to cease functioning and that to resist the defendants' attack on the system they had had to maintain an extensive inquiry service and large investigation department in unravelling and detecting the defendants' unlawful machinations. Roxburgh J said that he could

> "see no reason for not treating the expenses so incurred which could not be recovered as part of the costs of the action as directly attributable to the tort or torts. That these expenses cannot be precisely quantified is true, but it is also immaterial."[28]

---

20 [1896] 1 Q.B. 147 CA at 153.
21 [1914] 2 Ch. 603.
22 [1997] 2 Lloyd's Rep. 35.
23 [1945] 2 All E.R. 570.
24 See [1945] 2 All E.R. 570 at 573. Such damage had not yet been incurred, but Lynskey J thought the inference of damage sufficient to hold for the claimants.
25 Unless, of course, too remote: e.g. the Canadian case again of *Jones v Fabbi* (1973) 37 D.L.R. (3d) 27 in respect of loss on truck on hire-purchase, at 33.
26 Expenditure on food and hotels was allowed in *Falconer v ASLEF and NUR* [1986] I.R.L.R. 331 where the defendants had interfered with the contract of carriage between the claimant and British Railways.
27 [1949] Ch. 556.
28 [1949] Ch. 556 at 569. These remarks were made with specific reference to the further count of conspiracy to induce breaches of contract but they apply equally to inducement by itself.

In *The Kaliningrad*,[29] already referred to,[30] the withdrawal of the vessel led to the incurring of additional costs for a substitute vessel. For these costs the claimant was held entitled to recover in addition to his recovery for lost profits.

**48-008** Yet although the damages are at large, the only loss which the court is prepared to infer is a pecuniary loss: indeed it seems that even clear proof of a non-pecuniary loss by way of injury to feelings or to reputation is not sufficient to ground the action.[31] Thus McCardie J in *Pratt v British Medical Association*,[32] regarded pecuniary loss as necessary to the cause of action, while Nevile J in *Goldsoll v Goldman*,[33] spoke of the damage which the court could infer as damage inflicted "in the ordinary course of business". The primary protection afforded by the tort ushered in by *Lumley v Gye*,[34] is against business losses: business men cannot complain of injured feelings alone. If, however, pecuniary loss is shown, then *Pratt v British Medical Association*,[35] is authority for allowing, in addition, damages for non-pecuniary loss by way of injured feelings. The defendants, a medical association, instituted and pursued a system of professional ostracism and boycott against the claimants, who were medical men, by means of threats and widely extended coercive action, and in the claimants' claim for damages the defendants conceded that they had inflicted pecuniary loss. In these circumstances McCardie J said:

> "The plaintiffs are not limited to actual pecuniary damages suffered by them. The court or jury, once actual financial loss be proved, may award a sum appropriate to the whole circumstances of the tortious wrong inflicted ... I cannot ignore the deliberate and relentless vigour with which the defendants sought to achieve the infliction of complete ruin. I must regard not merely the pecuniary loss sustained by the plaintiffs but the long period for which they respectively suffered humiliation and menace."[36]

The allowable non-pecuniary loss is confined to injury to feelings. In the light of the decisions in *Joyce v Sengupta*,[37] and *Lonrho v Fayed (No.5)*,[38] dealing with injurious falsehood and conspiracy respectively, it can fairly be said that the courts have now adopted the firm stance that damages for injury to reputation are not in general to be recoverable outside the tort of defamation.[39]

---

29 [1997] 2 Lloyd's Rep. 35.

30 See the previous paragraph.

31 It is thought that the damages awarded in *Falconer v ASLEF and NUR* [1986] I.R.L.R. 331 for the inconvenience to the claimant and to the claimant's availability to his business (brief facts five footnotes back) have reference to pecuniary loss.

32 [1919] 1 K.B. 244 at 281.

33 [1914] 2 Ch. 603 at 615.

34 (1853) 2 E. & B. 216.

35 [1919] 1 K.B. 244.

36 [1919] 1 K.B. 244 at 281–282. Contrast *British Industrial Plastics v Ferguson* [1938] 4 All E.R. 504 CA at 514, per MacKinnon LJ: "It may well be that the claim ... is not limited to the special damage which he can prove." McCardie J's remarks, however, should not be interpreted, after *Rookes v Barnard* [1964] A.C. 1129, as allowing the awarding of exemplary damages unless the defendant has sought to profit from the tort: see Ch.13, above, especially at para.13-021.

37 [1993] 1 All E.R. 897 CA.

38 [1993] 1 W.L.R. 1489 CA.

39 See below at para.48-014 for injurious falsehood and para.48-025 for conspiracy. The exceptions are false imprisonment (para.42-025, above) and malicious prosecution (para.44-002, above).

## II. INJURIOUS FALSEHOOD

### 1. INJURIOUS FALSEHOODS OTHER THAN PASSING OFF

The tort of injurious falsehood, developing through slander of title and slander of goods, makes actionable any false statement made maliciously about the claimant to third parties with the result that they act so as to cause damage to the claimant. The falsehood need not be defamatory—a familiar illustration is an untrue statement that the claimant has closed down his business[40]—but, where it is, the claimant may frame his action in injurious falsehood and is not required to sue in defamation.[41] On the issue of damages, all forms of injurious falsehood except one may be taken together. The exception is passing off, a form of injurious falsehood which has developed special characteristics of its own.[42] **48-009**

The damages will vary according to what interest of the claimant the defendant's false statement attacks. The falsehood may concern the claimant's title to land, this being generally called slander of title and forming the earliest type of injurious falsehood. In such a case the claimant should be able to recover for any diminution in the land's value if the defendant's statement has made it difficult to dispose of the land, or for any loss of a contract of sale of the land which the defendant's statement has baulked. Further, any expenses of litigation made necessary by the defendant's statement in order to clear the claimant's title are recoverable; such appears to have been the damage laid in the old case of *Elborrow v Allen*.[43] Similar damages will be recoverable where the falsehood concerns the claimant's title to goods, the so-called slander of goods, or where it disparages the quality of the claimant's property.[44] A frequent form of slander of goods consists in false allegations made by the defendant to the claimant's customers that the claimant is infringing the defendant's trade mark, patent or copyright, coupled with threats to bring proceedings for infringement. If the claimant's business falls off as a result of these allegations and threats he can recover for his loss. Such damages were given in *Ungar v Sugg*,[45] where it was pointed out that the difficulty of precise assessment of the loss did not debar the claimant from recovering substantial damages.[46] Finally, the false statement may be in relation to the claimant's business more generally: he will here be entitled to recover for any consequential loss of business. Thus in *Riding v Smith*,[47] where the defendant falsely stated that the claimant's wife, who assisted him in his business, had committed adultery with the parish **48-010**

---

40 The position in the leading case of *Ratcliffe v Evans* [1892] 2 Q.B. 524 CA.

41 *Joyce v Sengupta* [1993] 1 W.L.R. 337 CA. See the case at para.48-013, below.

42 Passing off is dealt with at paras 48-016 to 48-018, below.

43 (1622) Cro. Jac. 642.

44 See, e.g. *Brook v Rawl* (1849) 4 Ex. 521, where at the sale by the claimant lessee of his interest in the property the defendant lessor announced that all the covenants in the lease were broken, that he had served notice of ejectment, and that a substantial sum would be needed for repair; as a result, the claimant alleged, the property fetched less at the sale. The argument, however, was primarily on malice and causation. Similar is *Mayer v Pluck* (1972) 223 E.G. 33 and 219 where property put up for sale at auction by the claimant did not reach the reserve price because of the defendant's false statements at the auction as to its condition. Again the damages issue did not predominate.

45 (1891) 8 R.P.C. 385; affirmed (1892) 9 R.P.C. 113 CA (alleged infringement of patent).

46 (1891) 8 R.P.C. 385 at 388, per Wright J; (1892) 9 R.P.C. 113 CA at 117, per Lord Esher MR. However, in other cases the claimant has lost through failure to prove pecuniary loss: e.g. *Royal Baking Powder Co v Wright Crossley & Co* (1901) 18 R.P.C. 95 HL (alleged infringement of trade mark).

47 (1876) 1 Ex. D. 91.

incumbent, the claimant recovered for the falling off in his business which followed.[48] And in *Ratcliffe v Evans*,[49] where the defendant published in a newspaper the false statement that the claimant had closed down his business, damages were awarded for the general falling off of the claimant's custom. Similarly, in *Worsley v Cooper*,[50] it was held that damages could be given for the falling off of the claimant's business by reason of the defendant's distribution of circulars to the claimant's customers falsely implying that the claimant had parted with his business and that the defendant had succeeded to it. In such circumstances it would seem that the claimant could recover not only loss of profits but any proven loss of business reputation or goodwill.[51]

## (1) Pecuniary loss

**48-011** At common law it was necessary to allege and prove as special damage the pecuniary loss incurred: this was decided by *Malachy v Soper*.[52] However, such special damage had to be alleged and proved only with such particularity as the circumstances of the case allowed, so that a general loss of business custom might be alleged and proved without specifying, or calling evidence as to, loss of particular customers: this point was established by *Ratcliffe v Evans*,[53] where the false statement had been published in a newspaper, and was applied in *Worsley v Cooper*,[54] where the false statement had a more limited circulation, being distributed in a circular to the claimant's customers.[55] On the other hand, there appears to have been no move by the courts to regard the damages as at large and to draw an inference of pecuniary loss without proof of specific damage, as has been done in the tort of inducement of breach of contract.[56] This is probably a result of the verbal association of the tort, in its early manifestations as slander of title and slander of goods, with slanders proper, most of which are actionable only on proof of specific pecuniary loss.[57] Statute has, however, modified the common law requirement of allegation and proof of special damage and has provided by s.3 of the Defamation Act 1952 that

> "in an action for slander of title, slander of goods or other malicious falsehood, it shall not be necessary to allege or prove special damage—
>
> (a) if the words upon which the action is founded are calculated to cause pecuniary damage to the plaintiff and are published in writing or other permanent form; or
> (b) if the said words are calculated to cause pecuniary damage to the plaintiff in

---

48 The decision has, however, been questioned on the issue of remoteness: see para.48-011, below (in a footnote).

49 [1892] 2 Q.B. 524 CA.

50 [1939] 1 All E.R. 290.

51 Compare the analogous passing off cases at para.48-017, below.

52 (1836) 3 Bing. N.C. 371.

53 [1892] 2 Q.B. 524 CA. It had already been acted upon in *Riding v Smith* (1876) 1 Ex. D. 91 (facts at para.48-010, above) but the allowing of proof of general loss of custom in that case may have transgressed the rules of remoteness: see the comments on the case in *Ratcliffe v Evans* [1892] 2 Q.B. 524 CA at 534, per Bowen LJ.

54 [1939] 1 All E.R. 290.

55 If, of course, the claimant fails to prove a general loss of custom at all his action will fail, as in *Lyne v Nicholls* (1906) 23 T.L.R. 86 and *Concaris v Duncan* [1909] W.N. 51.

56 See para.48-005, above.

57 See para.46-002, above.

respect of any office, profession, calling, trade or business held or carried on by him at the time of the publication."

The present position is therefore this. With statements falling within s.3 the claimant need not allege and prove specific pecuniary loss as the court will infer the existence of pecuniary loss and the damages will be at large in a similar sense to that in inducement of breach of contract.[58] With statements falling outside s.3 the claimant must still allege and prove specific pecuniary loss, although the court will be satisfied with general evidence of such loss where this is all that the circumstances of the case will allow.

## (2) Non-pecuniary loss

There remains the question of non-pecuniary loss. Although s.3 of the Defamation Act 1952 continues to reflect the association of injurious falsehood with defamation because the statements singled out as not requiring allegation and proof of special damage are very similar to those defamatory statements which are actionable per se, there is still an interesting difference between such injurious falsehoods and such defamatory statements in relation to non-pecuniary loss. Whereas with defamatory statements actionable per se the principal head of damage is the injury to reputation which is non-pecuniary loss,[59] with those similar injurious falsehoods which fall within s.3 of the Defamation Act 1952 the principal, and perhaps the only, head of damage is the pecuniary loss that the claimant has suffered. Section 3, by dispensing in these cases with the requirement of allegation and proof of specific pecuniary loss for success in the action, thus impliedly confirms the view that for all injurious falsehoods only pecuniary loss will ground the action, a view negatively supported by the absence of decisions awarding non-pecuniary loss, occasionally expressly hinted at in the cases,[60] and generally prevalent in this area of tort.[61] The view now obtains positive support from *Sallows v Griffiths*,[62] where no damages for malicious falsehood were awarded as there had been a failure to show pecuniary loss. **48-012**

Whether, where pecuniary loss is satisfactorily shown, damages for non-pecuniary loss may be given in addition was long uncharted, in relation both to those injurious falsehoods now falling within the provisions of s.3 of the Defamation Act 1952 and to those still controlled by the common law. Apart from Lord Denning MR in *Fielding v Variety Inc*,[63] expressing his view that damages can only **48-013**

[58] See paras 48-004 and following, above. Tugendhat J held in *Tesla Motors Ltd v B.B.C.* [2011] EWHC 2760 (QB) that, where the claimant relied on the probability of damage under s.3, particulars must be given of the nature of the alleged probable damage and the grounds relied on for saying that the damage was probable. Otherwise the claim must be struck out.

[59] See para.46-031, above.

[60] Thus Bowen LJ in *Ratcliffe v Evans* [1892] 2 Q.B. 524 CA at 528, spoke of "actual and temporal loss", and the term "actual damage" used in *Shapiro v La Morta* (1923) 130 L.T. 622 CA by Lush J at first instance and by Scrutton LJ on appeal (at 624 and 627 respectively) was probably meant as pecuniary loss. In *Royal Baking Powder Co v Wright Crossley & Co* (1901) 18 R.P.C. 95 HL Lord James of Hereford spoke of "money damage": at 102.

[61] Contrast inducement of breach of contract and conspiracy (para.48-008, above and para.48-024, below, respectively) and also, of course, slander generally (paras 46-002 and following, above).

[62] [2001] F.S.R. 188 CA.

[63] [1967] 2 Q.B. 841 CA.

be recovered for "probable money loss and not for … injured feelings",[64] the authorities had been silent. Eventually, but not till 1992, the Court of Appeal in *Joyce v Sengupta*,[65] addressed, without there deciding, the question. The claimant, a lady's maid to the Princess Royal, was suing the defendant, a newspaper's crime correspondent, for falsely stating in a published article that she had stolen the Princess's intimate letters. The defendant argued that as a matter of law damages were irrecoverable for the claimant's anxiety, distress and injury to her feelings. The court did not find it necessary to decide the point but Sir Donald Nicholls VC in a valuable judgment gave cogent reasons for allowing a measure of recovery. "Take the example," he said,

> "of a person who maliciously spreads rumours that his competitor's business has closed down … The owner of the business suffers severe financial loss. Further, because of the effect the rumours are having on his business he is worried beyond measure about his livelihood and his family's future. He suffers acute anxiety and distress. Can it be right that the law is unable to give him any recompense for this suffering against the person whose malice caused it? Although injury to feelings alone will not found a cause of action in malicious falsehood, ought not the law to take such injury into account when it is connected with financial damage inflicted by the falsehood?"[66]

To limit damages for injurious falsehood to pecuniary loss would, he added, mark out a clear boundary but

> "it would suffer from the drawback of failing to do justice in the type of case I have mentioned. I instinctively recoil from the notion that in no circumstances can an injured plaintiff obtain recompense from a defendant for understandable distress caused by a false statement made maliciously."[67]

Damages for injured feelings have subsequently been allowed in *Khodaparast v Shad*,[68] where the Vice-Chancellor's judgment in *Joyce v Sengupta* was heavily relied upon by the Court of Appeal. The award was to an Iranian teacher falsely accused of involvement in telephone sex services. It was of £20,000, a sum which included damages for loss of her job and employment prospects and for injury to her feelings.

**48-014** The Vice-Chancellor was concerned in *Joyce v Sengupta*,[69] that, if non-pecuniary loss were once allowed, it would be difficult to set coherent limits to potential recovery, both to the circumstances for recovery of non-pecuniary loss and to the types of non-pecuniary loss recoverable. He need not have been so concerned; the courts are perfectly capable of, and accustomed to, deciding when and how far to give damages for the omnibus injury to feelings. The matter is one of policy[70] and it is right that here policy should endorse recovery in general for injured feelings.[71] What the Vice-Chancellor was particularly and rightly concerned to

---

64 [1967] 2 Q.B. 841 CA at 850.
65 [1993] 1 W.L.R. 337 CA.
66 [1993] 1 W.L.R. 337 CA at 347H–348B.
67 [1993] 1 W.L.R. 337 CA at 348E.
68 [2000] 1 W.L.R. 618 CA.
69 [1993] 1 W.L.R. 337 CA at 348F.
70 See paras 8-122 and following, above.
71 The nearest analogies are slander, which has not yet solved the problem for itself (para.46-022, above), inducement of breach of contract, which favours the additional recovery (para.48-008, above), and conspiracy, which is undecided (para.48-024, below).

exclude, and indeed stated that it would be excluded as inappropriate in an injurious falsehood action,[72] was the other and very different head of non-pecuniary loss, namely injury to reputation. This is in line with the Court of Appeal's decision very soon afterwards for its exclusion from the tort of conspiracy.[73] In *Khodaparast v Shad*,[74] it was said that the damages were in order because malicious falsehood was a species of defamation and the award was appropriate because persistence in the potentially defamatory allegations set out to blacken the claimant's character, but these damages are nevertheless to be regarded as given for the injury to feelings rather than for the injury to reputation. Indeed Otton LJ specifically accepted that "damage to the plaintiff's reputation could not sound in malicious falsehood".[75]

Also in *Khodaparast v Shad*,[76] the damages were referred to as aggravated damages. This mirrors Sir Michael Kerr's approach in his judgment in *Joyce v Sengupta*,[77] devoted solely to the issue of damages for injury to feelings, where he came to the curious conclusion that non-pecuniary loss of this variety could only be claimed as aggravated damages and not as a separate head of damage.[78] Since, however, aggravated damages are relevant only to non-pecuniary loss they could only be claimed as a head of damage separate from the damages for the pecuniary loss which they cannot "aggravate".[79] The damages here should simply be regarded as damages for injury to feelings. **48-015**

## 2. PASSING OFF

The most important form of injurious falsehood is passing off, which consists in the selling of goods by the defendant in such a way as to represent that they are the goods of the claimant. This was the initial coverage of the tort but it has developed beyond sale to false endorsement of goods.[80] Passing off requires separate treatment from other injurious falsehoods for two interrelated reasons: because it has developed differently on the issue of proof of damage and because it moves nearer, both in form and in measure of damages, to those torts, now mostly made statutory, which concern infringements of rights in immaterial property, such as trade marks, patents and copyrights.[81] Originally passing off was a straightforward case of injurious falsehood in which proof of damage was required for success in the action, but it later moved towards being a remedy for the infringement of a quasi-proprietary right not requiring proof of damage in order to warrant judgment for the claimant. This development left in its wake inconsistent dicta which carried through into the 20th century, some maintaining that damage is the gist of the action[82] and others insisting that it is not.[83] In *Draper v Trist*,[84] the whole question came up for **48-016**

72 [1993] 1 W.L.R. 337 CA at 348F–G.
73 *Lonrho v Fayed (No.5)* [1993] 1 W.L.R. 1489 CA, at para.48-025, below.
74 [2000] 1 W.L.R. 618 CA.
75 [2000] 1 W.L.R. 618 CA at 631A.
76 [2000] 1 W.L.R. 618 CA.
77 [1993] 1 W.L.R. 337 CA.
78 Though not deciding the point: [1993] 1 W.L.R. 337 CA at 353B.
79 See, agreeing with this, Sir Donald Nicholls VC, [1993] 1 W.L.R. 337 CA at 348H.
80 See *Irvine v Talksport Ltd* [2003] 2 All E.R. 881 CA at para.48-018, below.
81 These are dealt with at paras 48-034 to 48-077, below.
82 See, e.g. *Society of Motor Manufacturers v Motor Manufacturers' Insurance Co* [1925] Ch. 675 at 686, per Lawrence J.
83 See, e.g. *Spalding v Gamage* (1915) 84 L.J. Ch. 449 HL at 450, per Lord Parker.
84 [1939] 3 All E.R. 513 CA.

review before the Court of Appeal, and the modern position was stated at some length by Goddard LJ He said:

> "The action is one of that class which is known as an action on the case, akin to an action of deceit. In an action on the case, the cause of action is the wrongful act or default of the defendant. The right to bring the action depends on the happening of damage to the plaintiff ... This class of case, however, forms an exception, or an apparent exception, to the ordinary action of deceit, because, in an ordinary action of deceit, the plaintiff's cause of action is false representation, but he cannot bring the action until the damage has accrued to him by reason of that false representation. In passing off cases, however, the true basis of the action is that the passing off by the defendant of his goods as the goods of the claimant injures the right of property in the plaintiff, that right of property being his right to the goodwill of his business. The law assumes, or presumes, that, if the goodwill of a man's business has been interfered with by the passing off of goods, damage results therefrom. He need not wait to show that damage has resulted. He can bring his action as soon as he can prove the passing off, because it is one of the class of cases in which the law presumes that the plaintiff has suffered damage ... If it be necessary for a plaintiff in this class of case, before he can get more than nominal damages, to show that he has lost this, that, or the other order, one would have to put this class of case, I think, into a third division of law, a case in tort, in which nominal damages can be recovered, although no damage be proved. If, however, a plaintiff wants more than nominal damages, he will have to prove this, that and the other. However, I do not think that that is the law."[85]

The result is that, although it may be said that technically damage remains the gist of the action, the presumption of substantial damage not only makes passing off from a practical standpoint actionable per se but puts the claimant into an even better position than with torts technically actionable per se in which the presumption of damage need only reach as far as an award of nominal damages.[86] Thus awards of damages could be made in *Chocosuisse Union des Fabricants Suisses de Chocolat v Cadbury*,[87] where damage was inferred,[88] and in *Alan Clark v Associated Newspapers*,[89] where damage appears to have been inferred.[90]

**48-017** Little attention has been given to the detail of the assessment of damages despite the many cases of passing off in the reports.[91] The two Court of Appeal decisions in *Spalding v Gamage*,[92] and *Draper v Trist*,[93] are the only cases of general importance. The principal head of damage is the loss of business profits caused by the diversion of the claimant's customers to the defendant as a result of the defendant's misrepresentation; beyond this, damages may be awarded for any loss of business goodwill and reputation resulting from the passing off. Damages under both these heads were held to be properly awarded in *Spalding v Gamage*,[94] a result

---

85 [1939] 3 All E.R. 513 CA at 525–527.

86 See, e.g. *Constantine v Imperial Hotels* [1944] K.B. 693: see para.3-004, above.

87 [1998] R.P.C. 117.

88 See [1998] R.P.C. 117 at 143; affirmed at [1999] R.P.C. 826 CA.

89 [1998] R.P.C. 261.

90 See [1998] R.P.C. 261 at 281.

91 "It is, perhaps, odd that there is no clearer authority than there is as to the principles which are to be applied in these cases to the assessment of damages": *Draper v Trist* [1939] 3 All E.R. 513 CA at 525, per Goddard LJ. And the position is much the same today.

92 (1918) 35 R.P.C. 101 CA; this was the inquiry into damages following upon the decision on liability at (1915) 84 L.J. Ch. 449 HL.

93 [1939] 3 All E.R. 513 CA.

94 (1918) 35 R.P.C. 101 CA.

which has never since been doubted.[95] *Draper v Trist*,[96] dealt with a more complex situation where the defendant had passed off goods by selling them to middlemen, and there was no evidence that the middlemen had resold. In these circumstances it was held that the claimant's loss of profits could not be a relevant consideration in assessing the loss but that the claimant was entitled to damages by reason of the presence of the deceptive goods on the market, damages which included a sum for loss of reputation.[97] In *Fearns v Anglo-Dutch Paint & Chemical Co Ltd*,[98] it was common ground that damages in respect of the defendant's unlawful sales should be calculated on the basis that the claimant would have made equivalent sales.[99] The claimant also recovered for the loss of his network of distributors but was unable to claim for the collapse of his business as he was unable to prove that this was caused by the defendant's unlawful activities. Also, the claimant should be able to recover for further loss of profits through reduction of his prices, provided that the reduction is necessary to compete with the goods passed off by the defendant.[100]

Passing off cases tend to be concerned with the selling of goods as if they were the claimant's but it was with the endorsement of goods as if the endorsement was the claimant's that *Irvine v Talksport Ltd*[101] dealt. The passing off consisted of the publication by the defendant of a photograph of the claimant racing driver which falsely gave the impression that he had endorsed the defendant's radio station. In his claim for damages the trial judge had concluded that the appropriate award was a reasonable endorsement fee. On the appeal it was agreed that this was the correct approach but that the judge had gone wrong in awarding £2,000 as representing what he thought the defendant would have been prepared to pay. Instead, the Court of Appeal held, relying heavily on Lord Wilberforce's famous analysis of royalty damages in the patent case of *General Tire and Rubber Co v Firestone Tyre and Rubber Co*,[102] that the claimant was entitled to damages of £25,000 based on the amounts charged by him for earlier endorsements of products. **48-018**

## III. Conspiracy

The tort of conspiracy has a very wide theoretical range, but in practice it has been used by litigants to gain redress for interferences with their contractual rights and relations.[103] Yet the fullest exploration of the damages issues has come in a **48-019**

---

95 Damages for loss of goodwill were also awarded in *Aktiebolaget Manus v Fullwood* (1954) 71 R.P.C. 243 where the claim was also in respect of infringement of a trade mark, and in *Unik Time Co v Unik Time Ltd* [1983] F.S.R. 121 ("permanent and continuing damage to goodwill").

96 [1939] 3 All E.R. 513 CA.

97 See [1939] 3 All E.R. 513 CA at 524, 527.

98 [2010] EWHC 1708 Ch.

99 [2010] EWHC 1708 Ch at [33].

100 Compare the cases on reduction of prices where a trade mark or patent has been infringed: paras 48-050 and 48-043, below. In *Spalding v Gamage* (1918) 35 R.P.C. 101 CA, Younger J at first instance had awarded as damages the cost of advertisements inserted in the press in an attempt to counteract the effect of the defendant's actions, but the Court of Appeal held this assessment erroneous. However, this was on the ground that such an award did not give the claimant all he was entitled to, and in awarding damages for loss of profits the Court of Appeal probably took this outlay into account. There seems no reason why expenses reasonably incurred in counter-advertisements should not be awarded provided that this does not entail a double recovery.

101 [2003] 2 All E.R. 881 CA.

102 [1975] 1 W.L.R. 819 HL. See at para.48-042, below.

103 Interference with contractual relations appears inter alia, in *British Industrial Plastics v Ferguson*

conspiracy claim, now of a good many years ago, not of this type; the claim was one inspired by the well known and long-running feud, in and out of the courts, between Tiny Rowland and the Fayeds over the takeover of Harrods. It took the name of *Lonrho v Fayed (No.5)*,[104] with conspiracy thrown in as an extra ground of complaint.

### (1) PECUNIARY LOSS

**48-020** The damages follow much the same pattern as that in inducement of breach of contract.[105] Thus, while a showing of pecuniary loss is necessary to ground the action for conspiracy, the damages are at large so that, once some pecuniary loss is shown, the damages are not limited to the precise calculation of pecuniary loss actually proved. Dillon LJ put the matter thus in *Lonrho v Fayed (No.5)*,[106] and the same is reflected in the frequently cited trial judge's notes of the evidence in *Quinn v Leathem*,[107] which run thus:

> "I told the jury that pecuniary loss, directly caused by the conduct of the defendants, must be proved in order to establish a cause of action, and I advised them to require to be satisfied that such loss to a substantial amount had been proved by the plaintiff. I declined to tell them that if actual and substantial pecuniary loss was proved to have been directly caused to the plaintiff by the wrongful acts of the defendants, they were bound to limit the amount of damages to the precise sum so proved."

Thus in *Noble Resources SA v Gross*,[108] where losses on unauthorised speculative trading in aluminium futures were made, and concealed, by two employees of the claimant companies, it was accepted that the damages in the conspiracy claim[109] were at large and not limited to the loss that could be strictly proved, thereby allowing an award of damages in many millions.[110] Nonetheless the Court of Appeal in *Lonrho*,[111] critical of the initial pleading of the claimants there, was clear that it is not sufficient merely to plead, in reliance upon the damages being at large, the broad conventional allegation that by reason of the stated facts damage has been suffered for this does not prove actual pecuniary loss.[112]

**48-021** As with inducement of breach of contract the main loss is likely to be based upon loss of profits; it was accepted in *Lonrho v Fayed (No.5)*,[113] that if the claimants could show loss of profits they could recover for that loss.[114] In *British Midland Tool*

[1938] 4 All E.R. 504 CA and *British Motor Trade Association v Salvadori* [1949] Ch. 556. The five House of Lords cases which established the modern law on conspiracy (see the standard texts on tort) were all cases of interference with contractual relations.

104 [1993] 1 W.L.R. 1489 CA.

105 And it was said in *Unik Time Co v Unik Time Ltd* [1983] F.S.R. 121 that the measure of damages for passing off and conspiracy are the same. Also the rules for mitigation apply as much in conspiracy as elsewhere, without the test being less strict: *Standard Chartered Bank v Pakistan National Shipping Corp* [1999] 1 Lloyd's Rep. 747 at para.9-080, above.

106 [1993] 1 W.L.R. 1489 CA at 1494B.

107 [1901] A.C. 495 at 498.

108 [2009] EWHC 1435 (Comm).

109 There were also claims in deceit and for breach of the contract of employment.

110 See [2009] EWHC 1435 (Comm) at [222]–[227].

111 [1993] 1 W.L.R. 1489 CA.

112 [1993] 1 W.L.R. 1489 CA at 1494C–D, per Dillon LJ and see at 1501H, per Stuart-Smith LJ.

113 [1993] 1 W.L.R. 1489 CA.

114 See [1993] 1 W.L.R. 1489 CA at 1496E, 1505B and 1508F.

*Ltd v Midland International Tooling Ltd*,[115] which concerned a conspiracy against the claimant company by a series of its directors and employees who had set up a competitive business next door, together with a company as a vehicle to carry it on, with the result that the claimant company had to close down, damages for loss of the business, trading losses and closure costs were all claimed as being the result of the unlawful conspiracy. The claimant company was held entitled in principle to have damages assessed under all three heads claimed.[116] In the highly complicated *National Grid Electricity Transmission Plc v McKenzie*,[117] the claimant company was held entitled to substantial damages in conspiracy[118] on account of being milked of its funds by the combined corrupt practices of an employee and an independent contractor.

Expenses resulting from the tort are also recoverable. The expenses which Roxburgh J considered as recoverable damage in *British Motor Trade Association v Salvadori*,[119] he so considered both in the count for inducement of breach of contract and in the count for conspiracy. This case was followed in *Lonrho*,[120] where there was held to be properly claimable the expense of managerial time spent in investigating and mitigating the conspiracy.[121] Similarly in *R-V Versicherung AG v Risk Insurance and Reinsurance Solutions SA (No.3)*,[122] an action for a conspiracy concerning reinsurance, Gloster J held that recovery was allowable in principle for the expense of managerial and staff time spent in investigating the conspiracy and handling claims without the need to show any specific loss of profit provided that the expenditure in time was shown to be directly attributable to the conspiracy.[123] The principal issue was mitigation in *Standard Chartered Bank v Pakistan National Shipping Corporation*,[124] a claim in conspiracy and also in deceit by a bank, but it was accepted that, subject to mitigation,[125] the bank was entitled to recover the amount by which the conspiracy had caused it to be out of pocket. Payment had been made by the bank to the seller of a cargo upon the presentation of fraudulently dated bills of lading and the bank successfully claimed as damages against a variety of defendants the difference between the amount of their payment and the amount they recovered on the sale of the cargo together with the additional expenses incurred in trying to dispose of the cargo. There being no available market in which to sell the documents or the cargo it was reasonable to take the bank's actual sale price, and at a later date than the tort, despite the contention of the defendants that the bank had failed to mitigate its loss as the market value of the cargo was at all times greater than the amount paid over by the bank.[126] **48-022**

---

115 [2003] 2 B.C.L.C. 523.

116 See [2003] 2 B.C.L.C. 523 at [188].

117 [2009] EWHC 1817 Ch.

118 Among other wrongs.

119 [1949] Ch. 556: facts at para.48-007, above.

120 [1993] 1 W.L.R. 1489 CA.

121 Together with a small amount for the expense of hiring extra security staff. See [1993] 1 W.L.R. 1489 CA at 1497C–D.

122 [2006] EWHC 42 (Comm).

123 It was left to Tomlinson J to decide on quantum, in *R-V Versicherung AG v Risk Insurance and Reinsurance Solutions SA (No.4)* [2006] EWHC 1705 (Comm), where he prefaced his detailed judgment by saying that he agreed with Gloster J's analysis as being entirely in line with the authorities and with how the matter was put in the then current edition of this work: at [3].

124 [2001] 1 All E.R. (Comm) 822 CA; affirming [1999] 1 Lloyd's Rep. 747.

125 The mitigation aspect is dealt with at paras 9-016 and 9-019, above and para.49-040, below.

126 While the subsequent decision in *Standard Chartered Bank v Pakistan National Shipping Corp*

**48-023** Profits lost and expenses incurred apart, other items of damage may be recoverable. Thus in *British Midland Tool Ltd v Midland International Tooling Ltd*,[127] which concerned a conspiracy against the claimant company by a series of its directors and employees who had set up a competitive business next door, together with a company as a vehicle to carry it on, with the result that the claimant company had to close down, damages for loss of the business, trading losses and closure costs were all claimed as being the result of the unlawful conspiracy. The claimant company was held entitled in principle to have damages assessed under all three heads claimed.[128] In the highly complicated *National Grid Electricity Transmission Plc v McKenzie*,[129] the claimant company was held entitled to substantial damages in conspiracy[130] on account of being milked of its funds by the combined corrupt practices of an employee and an independent contractor.

### (2) NON-PECUNIARY LOSS

**48-024** It was said in editions of this work before 1990 that a further interesting similarity with inducement of breach of contract is that, while pecuniary loss is necessary to ground the action for conspiracy, once pecuniary loss is proved damages may be awarded in addition for the non-pecuniary loss to feelings. This was based upon the trial judge's notes of the evidence in *Quinn v Leathem*,[131] which continue after the passage cited above[132] thus:

> "I told [the jury] that if the plaintiff gave the proof of actual and substantial loss necessary to maintain the action, they were at liberty in assessing damages to take all the circumstances of the case, including the conduct of the defendants, reasonably into account."[133]

The issue was, however, not directly addressed by the courts until the 1990s. The Court of Appeal accepted in *Joyce v Sengupta*,[134] when dealing with injurious falsehood, that, given pecuniary loss, damages for injury to feelings could be claimed in conspiracy,[135] yet in *Lonrho v Fayed (No.5)*,[136] a differently constituted court subsequently came to the conclusion that they could not. This conclusion seems wrong and out of line with what the law had been thought to be. If damages for

[2003] 1 Lloyd's Rep. 227 HL, concerning the effect on damages of a claimant's contributory negligence (at para.49-040, below) dealt only with the deceit aspect of the claim, it has equal relevance in the context of conspiracy. Indeed in *GE Commercial Finance Ltd v Gee* [2006] 1 Lloyd's Rep. 337 the damages were held to be the same in conspiracy as in deceit: at [338].

127 [2003] 2 B.C.L.C. 523.

128 See [2003] 2 B.C.L.C. 523 at [188].

129 [2009] EWHC 1817 Ch.

130 Among other wrongs.

131 [1901] A.C. 495 at 498.

132 See para.48-020, above.

133 These remarks, however, should not be interpreted, after *Rookes v Barnard* [1964] A.C. 1129, as allowing the awarding of exemplary damages unless the defendant has sought to profit from the tort: see Ch.13, above, especially at para.13-021. No exemplary damages were awarded in *British Midland Tool Ltd v Midland International Tooling Ltd* [2003] 2 B.C.L.C. 523 (at para.48-021, above) since the conspiracy was held not to be profit motivated: see at [252].

134 [1993] 1 W.L.R. 337 CA.

135 [1993] 1 W.L.R. 337 CA at 348C, 351A.

136 [1993] 1 W.L.R. 1489 CA.

injured feelings are available in the analogous inducement of breach of contract[137] and also in injurious falsehood,[138] why should they be banned where the claim is for conspiracy? There is no doubt that the cogent argument of Sir Donald Nicholls VC in *Joyce v Sengupta*,[139] in favour of allowing such damages in injurious falsehood[140] applies with equal force to conspiracy. There was little concentration in *Lonrho*,[141] on the issue of injury to feelings by a court grappling with so many points on damages and a court in any event unsympathetic to the claimants.[142]

Indeed Dillon LJ identified "the principal issue" in *Lonrho*[143] as being **48-025**

> "whether the plaintiffs can recover in this form of action damages for injury to reputation".[144]

The court held that they could not. This was on the sensible basis that, where reputation was concerned, defamation was the appropriate route for a claimant. As Dillon LJ put it:

> "In my judgment if the plaintiffs want to claim damages for injury to reputation or injury to feelings, they must do so in an action for defamation. Injury to reputation and to feelings is, with very limited exceptions, a field of its own and the established principles in that field are not to be sidestepped by alleging a different cause of action."[145]

The defence of truth and the responses of qualified privilege and fair comment should be available to a defendant alleged to have attacked a claimant's reputation; the tort of conspiracy is not there to provide a remedy for injury to reputation.[146] However, it is submitted that this argument does not run with injured feelings which appear to have been brought in in *Lonrho*, in order to be eliminated, on the coat-tails of injured reputations.

## IV. BREACH, OR MISUSE, OF CONFIDENTIAL INFORMATION

There is no doubt that for long liability for breach of a commercial confidence **48-026** with which we are here dealing—breach of a personal confidence is treated earlier in relation to invasions of privacy[147]—was only in equity by way of equitable compensation rather than damages. Even today we find High Court judges saying that breach of confidential information is not a tort, as does Arnold J in *Force India Formula One Team Ltd v 1 Malaysia Racing Team SDN BHD*,[148] and Proudman J

---

137 See para.48-008, above.

138 See para.48-013, above.

139 [1993] 1 W.L.R. 337 CA.

140 See para.48-013, above.

141 [1993] 1 W.L.R. 1489 CA.

142 And indeed to the defendants also. Dillon LJ, at [1993] 1 W.L.R. 1489 CA at 1493E, went so far as to say: "The temptation is great to say 'a plague on both your houses and let not the court's time be wasted with any further litigation between them'."

143 [1993] 1 W.L.R. 1489 CA.

144 [1993] 1 W.L.R. 1489 CA at 1494H.

145 [1993] 1 W.L.R. 1489 CA at 1496B–C.

146 It was accepted that damages for injury to reputation could be given in false imprisonment and malicious prosecution. This was because, in the words of Stuart-Smith LJ at 1504E, "these are cases where the wrongful act casts an imputation on the reputation of the plaintiff which, ex hypothesi, is not justified".

147 See Ch.47 above.

148 [2012] EWHC 616 Ch at [388]. In the Court of Appeal, [2013] EWCA Civ 780 CA, Levison LJ

in *Flogas Britain Ltd v Calor Gas Ltd*.[149] Indeed Arnold J went so far as to maintain that the Court of Appeal had decided in *Kitechnology BV v Unicor GmbH Plastmaschinen*,[150] that breach of confidence was not a tort and was actionable only in equity, but it is thought that what Evans LJ said in *Kitechnology* about breach of confidence was more of a proposition than a decision.[151] There are, however, pointers over the years, and at Court of Appeal level, in a different direction. As early as the days of the distinguished Lord Greene MR we find him saying in *Saltman Engineering Co v Campbell Engineering Co*,[152] that

> "if a defendant is proved to have used confidential information, directly or indirectly obtained from the plaintiff, he will be guilty of an infringement of the plaintiff's rights","[153]

and one would expect him to have common law rather than equitable rights in mind. Somewhat later Lord Denning MR in *Seager v Copydex (No.2)*,[154] took, as an analogy for damages for wrongful use of confidential information damages, the tort of conversion.[155] And more directly and more recently, in *Douglas v Hello!*,[156] which was concerned with privacy and personal rather than commercial confidence, Sedley LJ twice referred to "the tort of breach of confidence".[157] Beyond this, the cases have suggested as an analogy the way that damages are worked out in intellectual property cases, particularly in patent cases, which are undoubtedly torts, though introduced into the law by statute. Thus if the damages are to follow tortious principles, which may differ currently from equitable compensation,[158] it seems reasonable to treat breach, or misuse, of confidential information now within the category of economic torts.[159] However, in *Google Inc v Vidal-Hall*,[160] the Court of Appeal was of the view, contrary to what is said in this paragraph, that *Kitechnology BV v Unicor GmbH Plastmaschinen*,[161] by which the Court of Appeal considered itself bound, established that an action for breach of confidence is not an action in tort. It can be argued that what was said to this effect was obiter as the Court of Appeal held that the case before it was not one of breach of confidence but one of misuse of private information, which it held to be indeed a tort.[162] The concepts of confidence and privacy were said not to be the same and protected different interests[163]; actions for breach of confidence and actions for misuse of private information were said to rest on different legal foundations.[164]

**48-027** Not until into this century did breach of confidential information offer much in

---

spoke of "the equitable remedy for breach of confidence": at [70].

149 [2013] EWHC 3063 Ch at [37].

150 [1995] F.S.R. 765.

151 [1995] F.S.R. 765 at 777–778.

152 (1948) 65 R.P.C. 203 CA; also as later reported in [1963] 3 All E.R. 413n. CA.

153 (1948) 65 R.P.C. 203 CA at 213; 414.

154 [1969] 1 W.L.R. 809 CA.

155 [1969] 1 W.L.R. 809 CA at 813A.

156 [2001] Q.B. 967 CA.

157 [2001] Q.B. 967 CA at [117] and [123].

158 For the possibility of difference, see para.1-017, above.

159 Which was done in previous editions of this work.

160 [2015] EWCA Civ 311.

161 [1995] F.S.R. 765 CA.

162 See the chapter dealing with invasion of privacy at para.47-001, above.

163 [1995] F.S.R. 765 CA at [21].

164 [1995] F.S.R. 765 CA at [25].

the way of case law. All that was around were the Court of Appeal cases of *Seager v Copydex (No.2)*,[165] decided in 1969 and *Dowson & Mason v Potter*,[166] decided in 1986, and since, as we shall see, these two had arrived at different results on the damages front, it was difficult to formulate any statement of the principles to be applied.[167] In the last few years cases have made quite an appearance so that formulation has become possible. Since cases concerned with the disclosure of confidential information are akin to cases dealing with the infringement of intellectual property rights,[168] it is thought best to look to Lord Wilberforce's celebrated survey in *General Tire and Rubber Co v Firestone Tyre and Rubber Co*,[169] of the principles relating to damages for patent infringement,[170] a survey which is referred to and relied on for the assessment of damages in related fields.[171] In this survey he identified three different approaches to the recovery of damages. The damages will differ according to whether the claimant patentee would have manufactured the invention for profit, would have allowed third parties to use the invention under licence in return for a royalty or licence fee, or would not have been exploiting the patent. In the first case the basis of the damages is lost manufacturing profits, in the second the basis is lost royalty profits by way of licence fee, while in the third the damages are measured by a royalty or licence fee but arrived at in a somewhat different manner.[172]

*Dowson & Mason v Potter*,[173] illustrates the first type of situation and is important **48-028**
as being the first case in which lost manufacturing profits were held to form the

---

[165] [1969] 1 W.L.R. 809 CA.

[166] [1986] 1 W.L.R. 1419 CA.

[167] Arnold J maintained in *Force India Formula One Team Ltd v 1 Malaysia Racing Team SDN BHD* [2012] EWHC 616 Ch at [374] that he could not find a clear, accurate and comprehensive statement of the principles applicable to the assessment of damages for breach of confidence. Perhaps with more authority now available (see the text) we can provide him with one.

[168] For which see paras 48-034 and following. No doubt it was this similarity between confidential information claims and intellectual property claims that led the defence in the *Force India* case (for which see para.48-031, below) to suggest, with a view to obtaining a better damages result, that the European Union Directive (2004/48/EC) providing for the harmonisation of the rules on the enforcement of intellectual property rights (for the operation of which see paras 48-036 and following, and paras 48-070 and following, below) could be applied to confidential information claims. Arnold J at first instance (*Force India Formula One Team Ltd v 1 Malaysia Racing Team SDN BHD* [2012] EWHC 616 Ch) went along with this suggestion but, in his over-long analysis devoted to damages, said nothing of the Directive, simply concluding that his approach to the damages to be awarded was consistent with the damages provision of the Directive (at [424]). Levison LJ in the Court of Appeal (*Force India Formula One Team Ltd v Aerolab v SRL* [2013] EWCA Civ 780 CA) also held that reliance on the Directive did not help the defendant on damages and went further to say that he was sceptical about its application to the misuse of information (at [108]). He was right to be sceptical. However alike, confidential information is not intellectual property, which is all that the Directive is dealing with. Moreover, it is fully argued, when dealing with infringements of intellectual property, that the Directive adds nothing to the English law of damages as it stands, and the same must be true in relation to misuse of confidential information. It is therefore to be hoped that we shall hear no more of this, taking up the time of the courts on a loser.

[169] [1975] 1 W.L.R. 819 HL.

[170] [1975] 1 W.L.R. 819 HL at 824C–827A.

[171] As by the Vice Chancellor and by Pumphrey J in relation to copyright infringement in, respectively, *Blayney v Clogau St Davids Gold Mines Ltd* [2002] EWCA Civ 1007 CA and *Nottingham Healthcare NHS Trust v News Group Newspapers Ltd* [2002] R.P.C. 962, by Jonathan Parker LJ in relation to passing off in *Irvine v Talksport Ltd* [2003] 2 All E.R. 881 CA. and by Newey J in *32RED Plc v WHG (International) Ltd* [2013] EWHC 815 Ch in relation to trade marks.

[172] For the details see paras 48-042 and following, below.

[173] [1986] 1 W.L.R. 1419 CA.

proper measure of damages. The confidential information concerned a new type of landing leg for articulated lorries which the claimant company had developed for production in their business as manufacturing engineers. Confidential information about suppliers of components to the claimant and the prices paid for them by the claimant was communicated by an employee of the claimant to another company which was enabled thereby to set up in competition with the claimant. The fact that the information might be of little value, because it would not have been difficult for anyone who cared to obtain it to do so, was relevant only to the question of whether the claimant could show a loss of profit.[174] Trading profits have also been in issue in two very recent cases. In *Flogas Britain Ltd v Calor Gas Ltd*,[175] the breach of confidential information was by way of the misuse of a copy of part of the claimant's database. This led to loss of trading profits, difficult to assess as the expert accountants were in stark disagreement. Not only was there the loss of customers moving to the defendant but loss through reduction of prices to retain customers,[176] and loss through the defendant getting a head start on the claimant. As for *Vestergaard Frandsen A/S v Bestnet Europe Ltd*,[177] this was a complicated action involving confidential information used in the manufacture of mosquito nets. The Court of Appeal upheld the judge's refusal to strike out from the pleadings the claim for loss of profits, profits which were said to be from products derived from the use of the confidential information.[178] The strike out application had concerned the claimant's pleading for an enquiry as to damages following the findings of liability. At the subsequent enquiry, the primary judge allowed a claim for damages for lost profits from the directly infringing products only. The decision of the Court of Appeal is considered below because it is an example of where the first and the third types of damages were assessed in the same claim.

**48-029** Taking the second situation, the one in which the claimant would have licensed the use of the confidential information, there is little doubt that the licence fee that would have been charged is recoverable in damages; there are so far no cases. Such a result is implicit in what was decided and said in *Dowson & Mason*. Slade LJ there referred to the passage in the then current edition of this work pointing to the distinction, for the assessment of damages for infringement of patents, between the licensing claimant and the manufacturing one and saw

> "no reason at all why similar principles should not apply, mutatis mutandis, in cases where the complaint relates to a misuse of confidential information".[179]

**48-030** It is the third situation, where there is no clear intention to exploit the information, with which most of the cases are concerned.[180] They start of course with *Seager*

---

174 [1986] 1 W.L.R. 1419 CA at 1425H and 1427G–H.

175 [2013] EWHC 3060 Ch.

176 See [2013] EWHC 3060 Ch at [28], [68] and [76].

177 [2013] EWCA Civ 428 CA.

178 See at [1], [10] and [18].

179 [1986] 1 W.L.R. 1419 CA at 1427C.

180 *Vercoe v Rutland Fund Management Ltd* [2010] EWHC 424 Ch may have been a case where there was an intention to exploit the information but not by way of manufacturing profits or fees from licensing. The confidential information was used by a venture capital company to identify a business opportunity to acquire another company and it appears that the claimant providers of the information had rights to participate in that acquisition: see the lengthy discussion, with authorities, in the judgment from [323]–[346].

*v Copydex (No.2)*,[181] which it fell to the Court of Appeal in *Dowson & Mason v Potter*,[182] awarding manufacturing profits[183] to distinguish. The claimant had imparted to the defendant company confidential information about a form of carpet grip which he had invented, and the defendant had made and exploited a carpet grip embodying this information. The Court of Appeal held that the market value of the confidential information on a sale between a willing seller and a willing buyer marked the measure of the claimant's loss. If the information involved a true inventive step, the damages should be the capitalised value of the royalty payable on the sale of such an invention; if, on the other hand, the information could have been easily provided by a competent consultant, the damages should be the reasonable fee payable to such a consultant. Some good time later came *Gorne v Scales*.[184] The confidential information that had been wrongfully used was customer information contained in a card index and the value of it was held to constitute the proper measure of damages, the Court of Appeal by a majority rightly taking that value as the price at which the card index could have been sold on the open market at the time that the information was wrongfully removed.[185] A further decision is *Walsh v Shanahan*,[186] which concerned confidential information, used for the purchase and development of a property by the defendants, the information being a valuation report made to obtain finance for, and legal work done in connection with, the proposed purchase. While the Court of Appeal dealt only with whether the trial judge was right to refuse the claimants an account of profits, which it held that he was, it endorsed his award of damages by reference to the likely nominal cost of an assignment of the valuation report and to the benefit of the use of the legal work which, as Rimer LJ said, mirrored the approach of Lord Denning MR in *Seager*.[187]

In these cases we are moving into the area of restitutionary damages when the award to the holder of confidential information who is not proposing to exploit it for profit is by way of a licence fee, the price that would have been reached by a willing seller and willing buyer, by the value of the information to the user of it, or a like amount. This is brought out by the Court of Appeal in *Force India Formula One Team Ltd v Aerolab SRL*.[188] The claimant, operating a Formula 1 racing team, sued a series of defendants on account of the use, by one of the defendants initially employed by the claimant as designer, of some parts of the claimant's model in designs for another defendant which also operated a Formula 1 racing team. This was a misuse of confidential information. It brought no loss to the claimant but provided a benefit for the defendants. The trial judge's award of such sum as would be negotiated between a willing licensor and a willing licensee for permission to use the confidential information in the manner in which it has been misused[189] was **48-031**

---

181 [1969] 1 W.L.R. 809 CA.

182 [1986] 1 W.L.R. 1419 CA.

183 See para.48-028, above.

184 [2006] EWCA Civ 311 CA.

185 The value was not to be taken, as it had been by the trial judge and by Arden LJ, dissenting, in the Court of Appeal, at the later date of the trial when it was higher on account of the trading results of the wrongdoer made by the use of the card index. That value did not represent the loss to the claimant so that the so-called *Bwllfa* principle (for which see para.10-118, above) that a court should not speculate where it knows had no application.

186 [2013] EWCA Civ 411 CA.

187 [2013] EWCA Civ 411 CA at [71] and [72].

188 [2013] EWCA Civ 780 CA.

189 *Force India Formula One Team Ltd v 1 Malaysia Racing Team SDN BHD* [2012] EWHC 616 Ch

upheld by the Court of Appeal although Levison LJ, who gave the principal judgment, stated the award to be calculated at the cost of commissioning a consultant to produce an equivalent design,[190] which is much the same thing. Citing not only from Lord Denning in *Seager v Copydex (No.2)* but also from Mance LJ in the restitutionary damages case of *Experience Hendrix*,[191] he said that the judge had followed a well trodden path.[192]

**48-032** Moreover, even the claimant who does intend to exploit the confidential information may turn to recovering the benefit gained by the defendant. This is made clear by Floyd LJ in *Vestergaard Frandsen A/S v Bestnet Europe Ltd*,[193] which had a claimant whose intention was to use the information to generate manufacturing profits.[194] Floyd LJ said that there was an extension to the principle allowing recovery for financial loss of manufacturing or other profits, an extension allowing recovery of a reasonable royalty, as Lord Shaw in the essentially restitutionary damages patent case of *Watson Laidlaw*,[195] had explained.[196] This was the position in *JN Dairies Ltd v Johal Dairies Ltd*.[197] The confidential information taken was again customer information, being by way of invoices showing customer names and prices. In lieu of claiming damages for loss of manufacturing profits the claimant sought damages based on the value of the information taken from it, putting forward a calculation based on what it alleged to be the market value of the information on a sale between a willing buyer and a willing seller. The defendant applied for a strike out on the basis that such a measure of damages was only available to a claimant who would not have used the information to earn profits. On the ground that it was at least arguable that an assessment of damages based on the value of the information taken should be available to a manufacturing claimant who was in difficulties in proving the exact extent of its actual financial loss, the judge was content to allow the case to proceed to trial. He was right to do so as the claim should succeed. The claim would be not for the claimant's loss, which could not be shown, but for the defendant's gain, which could.

**48-033** The decision of the Court of Appeal in *MVF 3 Aps v Bestnet Europe Ltd*,[198] is a case where all three types of damages claim were considered. The primary decision involved an enquiry as to damages arising from the defendants' production of mosquito nets that used the confidential information as well as damages for the defendants' production of nets that did not involve misuse of confidential information but were indirectly derived from the use of the confidential information. In relation to the nets which were derived from the misuse of confidential information the primary judge allowed (i) damages for lost profits on sales that the claimant would have made as well as (ii) damages on the "user principle" for sales that the claim-

---

at [424]. In *Primary Group (UK) Ltd v Royal Bank of Scotland Plc* [2014] EWHC 1082 Ch the same trial judge, Arnold J, approached the assessment of damages against a bank sued for breach of confidence by an insurance company in the same way as he had in the *Force India* case (see [181] and following, of a long judgment), but the breach of confidence was a contractual one.

190 *Force India Formula One Team Ltd v Aerolab SRL* [2013] EWCA Civ 780 CA at [107].

191 In Ch.14 above.

192 [2013] EWCA Civ 780 CA [107]. See his judgment at paras [97]–[107].

193 [2013] EWCA Civ 428 CA.

194 See the case at para.48-028, above.

195 Also in Ch.14, above.

196 [2013] EWCA Civ 428 CA at [21].

197 [2010] EWHC 1689 Ch.

198 [2016] EWCA Civ 541 CA.

ant could not prove that it would have made with a royalty rate of 4 per cent. The Court of Appeal upheld these conclusions. As to the latter, the rate for the use of the confidential information was restitutionary because it focused on the price that the defendants had to pay. The Court of Appeal emphasised that considerations unique to the claimant were irrelevant. However, the primary judge declined to award damages for lost profits for the nets which were indirectly derived from the misuse of confidential information. Instead, for those nets the primary judge awarded a "quasi-consultancy" fee to reflect the extent to which the sales of those nets were brought about by B's use of confidential information. The Court of Appeal also upheld this conclusion. As to the lost profits from the indirectly derived nets, Floyd LJ, with whom Lindblom LJ and Sir Colin Rimer agreed, explained that the law would not impose liability for all the consequences of the wrongful action.[199] Essentially, those profits were beyond the scope of liability for consequences because the sales were not wrongful. The proper measure of damages for the indirectly derived nets was the consultancy fee because this reflected "the sort of assistance" which the defendants needed when, having breached the duty of confidence they sought to use that information to develop the later nets. Again the award is restitutionary because it focuses upon the price that the defendants would have had to pay for the type of assistance that they received.

## V. INFRINGEMENT OF RIGHTS IN INTELLECTUAL PROPERTY

Infringements of rights in such immaterial or intellectual property as trade marks, patents, copyrights and design rights are today made tortious by statute, the basic enactments being, respectively, the Trade Marks Act 1994, the Patents Acts 1949, 1977 and 2004, and the Copyright, Designs and Patents Act 1988.[200] These torts may be regarded as allied to injurious falsehood in the sense that the defendant, by infringing the claimant's trade mark, patent, copyright or design right is misrepresenting to third parties that he is entitled to put on the market the article, invention, writing or design which he offers, although the element of deception in the sense that the third parties are made to think that the article, invention, writing or design emanates from the claimant is not so likely to be present. Even this is present in the case of infringement of trade marks, which present the closest analogy: that an action for infringement of a trade mark may be characterised as an extension of the concept of injurious falsehood is brought out by s.2(2) of the Trade Marks Act 1994 which expressly saves the common law action of passing off in the case of trade marks, so that if the statutory action should fail because, for instance, the claimant has failed to register the trade mark, he may fall back upon injurious falsehood. **48-034**

199 [2016] EWCA Civ 541 CA at [90].

200 Rights in intellectual property may be infringed outside the bounds of these statutory torts, as in *Double Communications Ltd v News Corp International Ltd* [2011] EWHC 961 (QB) where the defendant had licensed a board game of its invention to be promoted and marketed by the claimant licensee and had then withdrawn the licence in breach of contract. Damages for loss of the profits that would have been made from sales of the game over the three-year licence period fell to be assessed and the resolution of this question by Eady J turned on a detailed consideration by him of the facts and the evidence. It would seem, however, from what is said by him at [4]–[5] together with [99] that he considered that the principle in the very old case of *Armory v Delamirie*, recently resurrected, which eases the claimant's passage on proof (see paras 10-095 and 38-049, above) applied. As explained at para.10-006, above, that this is so is dubious.

**48-035** In relation to remedies for infringement these intellectual property rights have very much in common, and several factors applicable to all may usefully be consolidated at this point. (1) Pecuniary loss is at the heart of the recovery of the damages and the heads of damage for which recovery is given are similar throughout, the principal damage being the loss of profits caused by the diversion of the claimant's customers, existing or potential, to the defendant. This similarity is underlined by the Vice Chancellor's saying in the infringement of copyright case of *Blayney v Clogau St Davids Gold Mines Ltd*,[201] that

> "the leading authority on the question of damages for infringement of an intellectual property right is the speech of Lord Wilberforce in *General Tire and Rubber Co v Firestone Tyre and Rubber Co Ltd*","[202]

an infringement of patent case, to which because of its importance in this field we shall undoubtedly return. (2) Non-pecuniary loss does not generally feature in the awards. This is because the invasion of a proprietary right is unlikely to lead to such a loss. General principle, however, does not bar recovery in exceptional circumstances, as cases where the invasion is of a proprietary interest in land show, damages for mental distress or injury to feelings being occasionally allowed,[203] with such damages being classed as aggravated damages where the defendant has behaved badly.[204] (3) An action for damages is only one method whereby a claimant may seek redress. He will frequently apply for an injunction and, if granted, this can affect the amount of recoverable damages since prospective loss may have been thereby largely eliminated. More important in relation to damages is the claimant's equitable remedy by way of disgorgement of profits.[205] This remedy is alternative to the action for compensation, whether the infringement is of a trade mark,[206] a patent[207] or a copyright,[208] and is to be preferred by a claimant where the defendant has made more profit out of the infringement than the claimant has lost. Further, the availability of this alternative remedy throws into relief the fact that the benefit gained by the defendant cannot be included in the award of damages.

**48-036** In the course of the last few years another common factor, applicable across the board, has emerged. While it is highly exceptional for matters of damages to feature in European Union Directives, they now do so in a Directive aimed at the harmonisation of the rules on the enforcement of intellectual property rights.[209] This

---

201 [2002] EWCA Civ 1007 CA at [11].

202 [1975] 1 W.L.R. 819 HL.

203 See the cases (nuisance, trespass) at para.39-020, above.

204 See the cases (wrongful eviction) at paras 39-072 and 39-073, above. In the particular cases of infringement of copyright and infringement of design right, statute has conferred a right to sue for "additional damages", a term which has sometimes been interpreted as meaning aggravated damages but may have to be regarded as referring to exemplary rather than aggravated damages. See paras 48-065, below.

205 In relation to patents this remedy is conferred by s.60 of the Patents Act 1949 and s.61(1)(d) of the Patents Act 1977; for the extent to which the earlier s.60 is not overtaken by the new s.61, see Patents Act 1977, s.127, Sch.1 para.1 and Sch.4 para.3. The remedy had not been available between 1919 and 1949.

206 *Lever v Goodwin* (1887) 36 Ch. D. 1.

207 *Neilson v Betts* (1871) L.R. 5 H.L. 1, adopted by s.60 and s.61(2) of the respective statutes in the preceding footnote but one, above.

208 *Sutherland Publishing Co v Caxton Publishing Co* [1936] Ch. 323 CA at 336, per Lord Wright.

209 Directive 2004/48/EC.

Directive has been implemented by statutory instrument in the United Kingdom.[210] Article 13 of the Directive is entitled "Damages" and in the statutory instrument reg.3 is entitled "Assessment of Damages".

## 1. The Relevance of the European Union Directive

It might be thought, at first blush, that the provisions of the EU Directive, as reflected in the provisions of its implementation in the United Kingdom, take over from the domestic law and that we have to start again on the assessment of damages. Yet this is far from being so. **48-037**

Thus the provisions of the Directive can only overtake the domestic law where the intellectual property right infringers were aware or ought to have been aware that they were infringing. The Directive so provides in its damages article: **48-038**

> "**13.1**
>
> Member States shall ensure that the competent judicial authorities, on application of the injured party, order the infringer who knowingly, or with reasonable grounds to know, engaged in an infringing activity, to pay the right holder damages appropriate to the actual prejudice suffered by him as a result of the infringement."

Article 13.1 then sets out details of the damages for which the judicial authorities must provide.[211]

In the United Kingdom the statutory instrument in its regulation on the assessment of damages similarly provides:

> "**3**(1) Where in an action for infringement of an intellectual property right the defendant knew, or had reasonable grounds to know, that he engaged in infringing activity, the damages awarded to the claimant shall be appropriate to the actual prejudice he suffered as a result of the infringement."

Thus those who may be called innocent infringers fall outside the Directive's provisions. This is spelt out in the remainder of the Directive article, but not in the United Kingdom where it appears to be left to necessary implication:

> "**13.2**
>
> Where the infringer did not knowingly, or with reasonable grounds to know, engage in infringing activity, Member States may lay down that the judicial authorities may order the recovery of profits or the payment of damages, which may be pre-established."[212]

While innocent infringers may be few and far between, this must mean that English law will apply to them. For this reason alone the English law requires to be set out.

More importantly, the regulation on damages specifically provides that, to the extent that the rules of English law are the same as what the regulation, following the provisions of the Directive, lays down, English law continues to apply. This is made clear by a further paragraph of the regulation which states: **48-039**

---

210 SI 2006/1028, entitled Intellectual Property (Enforcement, etc.) Regulations.

211 These are set out at para.48-070, below.

212 This would appear to be a reference to our liquidated damages which seems odd when we are talking of a tortious (delictual) rather than a contractual liability. But for us in the present context it is of no matter.

> "**3**(3) This regulation does not affect the operation of any enactment or rule of law relating to remedies for the infringement of intellectual property rights except to the extent that it is inconsistent with the provisions of this regulation."

Sir William Blackburne in his judgment in *Experience Hendrix LLC v Times Newspapers Ltd*,[213] is therefore thought to be wrong to say, obiter,[214] that the effect of reg.3(3) and of art.13(2) is the same.[215] For art.13(2) deals only with the innocent infringer while reg.3(3) deals with all infringers.

**48-040** So we have here a further, and central, reason for setting out the English law as it stands. To this we now turn. After this, we will be able to examine how far, in its statement of the rules for assessing damages, the provisions from Europe differ, if at all.

## 2. The Present English Law, The Directive Apart

**48-041** Leaving the Directive and its United Kingdom implementation on one side, we now set out, as in earlier editions, the law of damages in relation to the various statutory intellectual property rights. This time round, patents will be considered first, and before trade marks, as patents have produced the greatest amount of authority, authority which spills over into the law on the other intellectual property rights and contains what is regarded[216] as the leading case in this whole field, *General Tire and Rubber Co v Firestone Tyre and Rubber Co*.[217]

### (1) Infringement of patents[218]

**48-042** In *General Tire and Rubber Co v Firestone Tyre and Rubber Co*[219] Lord Wilberforce conducted a magisterial survey of the principles relating to damages for patent infringement,[220] a survey which is referred to and relied on for the assessment of damages in related fields.[221] In this survey he identified three different approaches to the recovery of damages. The damages will differ according to whether the claimant patentee (i) would himself have manufactured the invention for profit; (ii) would have allowed third parties to use the invention under licence in return for a royalty or licence fee; or (iii) would not have been exploiting the patent. In the first case the basis of the damages is lost manufacturing profits, in the

---

213 [2010] EWHC 1986 Ch.

214 Obiter because, since he found the infringer negligent, he had to deal with art.13(1) and reg.3(1) rather than art.13(2) and reg.3(3). See the case at para.48-077, below.

215 [2010] EWHC 1986 Ch at [68].

216 See para.48-035, above.

217 [1975] 1 W.L.R. 819 HL.

218 Claims for damages can also be brought where loss results from threats to institute proceedings for infringement of patents where no patents exist. *Kooltrade Ltd v XTS Ltd* [2001] F.S.R. 158 is such a case. *Les Laboratoires Servier v Apotex Inc* [2009] F.S.R. 3 at 220 is not a claim for damages for patent infringement but a claim for compensation brought, on a cross-undertaking as to damages, on account of being restrained from infringing a patent later held to be invalid.

219 [1975] 1 W.L.R. 819 HL.

220 [1975] 1 W.L.R. 819 HL at 824C–827A.

221 As by the Vice-Chancellor and by Pumphrey J in relation to copyright infringement in, respectively, *Blayney v Clogau St Davids Gold Mines Ltd* [2002] EWCA Civ 1007 CA and *Nottingham Healthcare NHS Trust v News Group Newspapers Ltd* [2002] R.P.C. 962, by Jonathan Parker LJ in relation to passing off in *Irvine v Talksport Ltd* [2003] 2 All E.R. 881 CA. and by Newey J in *32RED Plc v WHG (International) Ltd* [2013] EWHC 815 Ch in relation to trade marks.

second the basis is lost royalty profits by way of licence fee, while in the third, as we shall see, the damages are measured by a royalty or licence fee but arrived at in a somewhat different manner which might today be best understood as an award of restitutionary damages. *General Tire* was a case where the patentee would have licensed, placing it in the second category.

**(a) Manufacture of the invention by the patentee** Where the invention would have been manufactured and sold by the claimant, the damages calculation can be difficult. Here the claimant is entitled to the loss of manufacturer's profits caused by the diversion of customers to the defendant, but the calculation of this loss is not one that can be made with any exactness. This is true for this head of damage in this whole area of tort, but the impossibility of mathematical accuracy has been particularly stressed in the cases on patents, and in cases of the highest authority.[222] The two principal authorities awarding such loss of profits are early House of Lords cases, *United Horse-Shoe & Nail Co v Stewart*,[223] in which the propriety of such an award was confirmed, and *Watson Laidlaw & Co v Pott, Cassells & Williamson*,[224] in which it was said that the amount of profits the claimant could have made had he and not the defendant effected the sales was the prima facie measure.[225] In both cases it was stressed that allowance had to be made for the fact that other causes, and particularly the exertions of the defendant, appeared to have promoted the defendant's sales, so that it could not be said that the claimant, had there been no infringement, would have effected as many sales as the defendant had attained. By contrast, on the facts of *American Braided Wire Co v Thomson*,[226] a Court of Appeal decision of the same period, damages for lost profits were awarded on the assumption that all the sales made by the defendant would otherwise have been made by the claimant.[227] The facts of *United Horse-Shoe & Nail Co v Stewart*,[228] and *American Braided Wire Co v Thomson*,[229] also differed in relation to another aspect 48-043

222 See e.g. *United Horse-Shoe & Nail Co v Stewart* (1888) 13 App. Cas. 401 at 408, per Lord Halsbury LC ("can rarely be made the subject of exact mathematical calculation"); at 413, per Lord Watson ("impossible to ascertain with mathematical precision"); *Watson Laidlaw & Co v Pott, Cassells & Williamson* (1914) 31 R.P.C. 104 HL, at 112, per Lord Kinnear ("not a matter which in the nature of things can be ascertained with any certainty"); at 114, per Lord Atkinson ("cannot be determined by mathematical calculation or with absolute accuracy").

223 (1888) 13 App. Cas. 401.

224 (1914) 31 R.P.C. 104 HL.

225 Other early cases awarding loss of profits are *American Braided Wire Co v Thomson* (1890) 44 Ch. D. 274 CA; *Boyd v Tootal Broadhurst Lee Co* (1894) 11 R.P.C. 175 and *Leeds Forge Co v Deighton's Patent Flue Co* (1908) 25 R.P.C. 209. For the first of these cases see the text. In the second case it was held that the claimant's damages did not fall to be reduced by reason of his having settled, at rates below his normal manufacturing profit, litigation with other infringers in which the validity of the patent had been in dispute. In the third case the claimant had claimed for further loss of profits on the ground that sales made by the defendant could have been effected by the claimant at less cost to him as he could have made the goods without increasing his overhead expenses; the court refused to make an award for this specific item, because it ought to be taken into account in assessing the claimant's loss of profits had he had the sale of the infringing goods.

226 (1890) 44 Ch. D. 274 CA.

227 And at the prices originally charged by the claimant: see the text following. The statement which appeared under Patents in Halsbury's *Laws of England*, 4th edn, Vol.35, para.631 that it would be "presumed in the absence of evidence to the contrary that sales by the infringer were taken from the plaintiff" was, in the context of breach of copyright, disapproved at first instance in *Blayney v Clogau St Davids Gold Mines Ltd* [2002] F.S.R. 233. This seems correct. See the case at para.48-055, below.

228 (1888) 13 App. Cas. 401.

229 (1890) 44 Ch. D 274 CA.

of loss of profits, that arising out of the claimant's reduction of his prices in order to combat the competition introduced into the market by the infringing goods of the defendant. In *United Horse-Shoe & Nail Co v Stewart*,[230] the claimant was refused damages for this loss because on the evidence the House of Lords took the view that, since the claimant had formidable legitimate competitors in the market, he could not have maintained his sales, even in the absence of competition from the defendant, without a reduction of price.[231] On the other hand in *American Braided Wire Co v Thomson*,[232] the Court of Appeal held that the defendant's infringements were the cause of the claimant's reduction in his prices, and allowed recovery on the basis that all his sales[233] would otherwise have been made at the original prices.[234] In more modern times damages were awarded in *Ultraframe (UK) Ltd v Eurocell Building Plastics Ltd*,[235] to compensate for the reduction in the claimant's prices which had been made to counter the defendant's competition,[236] and for continuing reduced sales and price depression for a period after the infringement had been brought to an end by injunction.[237] *Ultraframe (UK)* was unusual in that the successful claim for loss of profits was in respect of sales that the claimant would have made to the defendant company which had, before the infringement, been acting as buyer and distributor of the claimant's conservatory roof system. It was held to be perfectly proper for the claimant to argue, and successfully argue, that, had the defendant not decided to manufacture and sell a competing system, it would have continued to buy from the claimant for distribution.[238] In *Fabio Perini SPA v LPC Group Plc*,[239] where the claimant's patent of a method of selling paper rolls had been infringed, the calculation of the damages proved very complex so that Norris J applied to the making of sales by the claimant the loss of a chance doctrine, in both its causation and assessment aspects, arriving at a 65 per cent chance for some sales and a 25 per cent chance for others.[240] Beyond the loss of specific profits the claimant should be allowed any loss of business reputation and goodwill; there are no clear cases of such a recovery[241] but there are the compelling analogies in passing off and infringement of trade mark cases.[242]

**48-044** Where the manufacturing claimant would not have effected as many sales as have been achieved by the defendant, the sales which the claimant would never have

---

230 (1888) 13 App. Cas. 401.

231 See, especially, (1888) 13 App. Cas. 401 at 414, per Lord Watson.

232 (1890) 44 Ch. D. 274 CA.

233 And also the defendant's sales: see the text preceding.

234 A similar recovery was also allowed in *Leeds Forge Co v Deighton's Patent Flue Co* (1908) 25 R.P.C. 209. A good test of whether a reduction in price is caused by the defendant's infringements is suggested in Lord Watson's speech in *United Horse-Shoe & Nail Co v Stewart* (1888) 13 App. Cas. 401 at 413, where he spoke of the process of estimation being comparatively simple "when the product of patented machinery is a new and special article, which cannot be successfully imitated without its use". In such circumstances the defendant is likely to be the cause of the reduced prices.

235 [2006] EWHC 1344 (Pat).

236 [2006] EWHC 1344 (Pat) at [154] and [155].

237 [2006] EWHC 1344 (Pat) at [182]–[190].

238 This was a preliminary issue, decided for the claimant: see [2006] EWHC 1344 (Pat) at [92]–[95]. The claim for loss of sales of other products of the claimant was held not to have been made out: at [156]–[181].

239 [2012] EWHC 911 Ch.

240 [2012] EWHC 911 Ch at [166] and [167].

241 The nearest is the *Ultraframe (UK)* case where losses after the infringement had ended were allowed: see the case in the text, above.

242 See paras 48-017, above and 48-051, below, respectively.

made may yet come into the computation of his damages in addition to his lost manufacturing profits. This possibility stems initially from the idea put forward some time ago by Lord Shaw in *Watson Laidlaw & Co v Pott, Cassells & Williamson*,[243] that to the extent that the claimant has not lost profits through the defendant's use of the patent there ought still to be recovery of the market value of this use as damages, and quite apart from the alternative remedy by way of disgorgement of profits. He said:

> "There remains that class of business which the respondents would not have done; and in such cases it appears to me that the correct and full measure is only reached by adding that a patentee is also entitled, on the principle of price or hire, to a royalty for the unauthorised sale or use of every one of the infringing machines in a market which the infringer [sic], if left to himself, might not have reached. Otherwise, that property which consists in monopoly of the patented articles granted to the patentee has been invaded, and indeed abstracted, and the law, when appealed to, would be standing by and allowing the invader or abstractor to go free. In such cases a royalty is an excellent key to unlock the difficulty."[244]

Such a recovery is indeed to be found where material property has been misappropriated[245] but, as has been pointed out, this savours rather of restitution than of damages.[246] Nevertheless it has found applications in the patent field, so that today recovery on a royalty or licence fee basis for the extra sales may be taken as representing the law. Thus in *Catnic Components v Hill & Smith*,[247] the claimants were awarded their loss of manufacturing profits on the assumption that most of the sales of patented lintels which the defendants had effected would, but for the infringement, have been made by them, and to the residue of the sales effected by the defendants the royalty basis was applied. And in *Ultraframe (UK) Ltd v Eurocell Building Plastics Ltd*,[248]where not all of the sales made by the defendant would have been achieved by the claimant, it was held necessary to award an appropriate royalty in respect of the shortfall.[249]

**(b) Licensing of the invention** The simpler calculation of damages is where the claimant would have licensed the use of his invention. In such a case the damages are limited to the amount which the defendant would have had to pay for a licence.[250] This was decided early in *Penn v Jack*,[251] a decision approved by Lord **48-045**

243 (1914) 31 R.P.C. 104 HL.

244 (1914) 31 R.P.C. 104 HL at 120.

245 See, especially, *Strand Electric Co v Brisford Entertainments* [1952] 2 Q.B. 246 CA, as to goods, at para.38-067, above; and the cases culminating in *Inverugie Investments v Hackett* [1995] 1 W.L.R. 713 PC, as to land, at paras 39-048 and following, above.

246 See paras 14-018 and following, above.

247 [1983] F.S.R. 512.

248 [2006] EWHC 1344 (Pat).

249 [2006] EWHC 1344 (Pat) at [149]–[153], though the restitutionary nature of the award was not mentioned.

250 This is undoubtedly the general rule. In his extended discussion of damages principles for patent infringement in *SmithKline Beecham Plc v Apotex Europe Ltd* [2003] F.S.R. 31 CA at 544, Aldous LJ states, at [8], that, while the normal recovery for a patentee who is not manufacturing is a reasonable royalty, the infringement may cause him a loss exceeding this; but he provides no illustrations of such a loss.

251 (1867) L.R. 5 Eq. 81.

Wilberforce and the House of Lords in the *General Tire* case.[252] The *Penn* result is also illustrated by *English & American Machinery Co v Union Boot & Shoe Machine Co*,[253] where the damages awarded were the

> "amount of profits from licensees the plaintiffs have been deprived of by the acts of the defendants".[254]

In *Aktiengesellschaft für Autogene Aluminium Schweissung v London Aluminium Co (No.2)*,[255] Sargant J, in a passage cited with approval also in the *General Tire* case,[256] said that

> "what has to be ascertained is that which the infringer would have had to pay if, instead of infringing the patent, he had come to be licensed under the patent"

and that, where

> "there have been licences at certain definite rates, there prima facie, apart from any reason to the contrary, the price or royalty which has been arrived at by means of a free bargain between the patentee and the person desiring to use the patented article has been taken as being the price or royalty that presumably would have to be paid by the infringer."[257]

Care, however, must be taken to ensure that the rate of royalty exacted under other licences is necessarily the appropriate rate for calculating the damages. Thus in *British Motor Syndicate v Taylor*,[258] the court regarded the royalty which the claimant was in the habit of receiving from licensees as too low an amount on which to base the damages, since the licensees paying this amount were also restricted in their use of the patented article. As Lord Wilberforce said in the *General Tire* case[259]:

> "Before a 'going rate' of royalty can be taken as the basis on which an infringer should be held liable, it must be shown that the circumstances in which the going rate was paid are the same as or at least comparable with those in which the patentee and the infringer are assumed to strike their bargain.[260]"

In particular, the rate must be based on the assumption that the patent is valid, so that a rate negotiated by way of settlement of litigation in which the patent's validity was in doubt would not count. In the *General Tire* case,[261] where the defendants were liable for infringing use, over many years, of a patent relating to synthetic rubber compounds suitable for tyre treads, the House of Lords adopted the rate, contended for by the defendants, of three-eighths of a US cent per pound of so-called oil-extended rubber used by the defendants in infringing tyre treads as the rate at which the claimants would have been willing to license the use of their inven-

---

252 The other members of the House simply expressed their agreement with Lord Wilberforce except for Lord Salmon who agreed in a separate speech, dissenting only on a subsidiary issue about the awarding of interest.

253 (1896) 13 R.P.C. 64.

254 (1896) 13 R.P.C. 64 at 67.

255 (1923) 40 R.P.C. 107.

256 [1975] 1 W.L.R. 819 HL at 825C–F per Lord Wilberforce.

257 (1923) 40 R.P.C. 107 at 113–114.

258 [1900] 1 Ch. 577.

259 [1975] 1 W.L.R. 819 HL.

260 [1975] 1 W.L.R. 819 HL at 825F-G.

261 [1975] 1 W.L.R. 819 HL.

tion, since there was strong and concrete evidence of actual bargains made by the claimants at this rate. In so doing the House decisively rejected as the proper measure of damages the much higher fair and reasonable royalty which had been selected by the trial judge and upheld by the Court of Appeal, pointing out that this was an unsupportable departure when the claimant only sought compensation, and that there was "no warrant … in authority or principle"[262] for assessing loss on the basis of what royalty the infringer ought fairly to have paid as opposed to what royalty he would actually have paid.[263]

**(c) No exploitation of the invention by the patentee** There may be cases where the patentee would not have exploited the invention, either by manufacturing or by licensing. This takes us to Lord Wilberforce's third category in the *General Tire* case,[264] he continuing his analysis by saying: 48-046

> "In some cases it is not possible to prove either (as in 1) that there is a normal rate of profit, or (as in 2) that there is a normal, or established, licence royalty. Yet clearly damages must be assessed. In such cases it is for the plaintiff to adduce evidence which will guide the Court. This evidence may consist of the practice as regards royalty, in the relevant trade or in analogous trades; perhaps of expert opinion expressed in publications or in the witness box; possibly of the profitability of the invention; and any other factor on which the judge can decide the measure of loss. Since evidence of this kind is in its nature general and also probably hypothetical, it is unlikely to be of relevance, or if relevant, of weight, in the face of the more concrete and direct type of evidence referred to under (2). But there is no rule of law which prevents the court, even when it has evidence of licensing practice, from taking these more general considerations into account. The ultimate process is one of judicial estimation of the available indications."

The result is that the patentee is entitled to damages here by way of a licence royalty but as to its amount one worked out differently from that available to the patentee in the business of licensing. This award therefore focuses upon the objective value of the benefit obtained by the defendant even though it would not have been exploited by the claimant. As discussed in Ch.14 this award is best understood as restitutionary damages.

**(d) Ancillary matters** One matter to consider is whether a company holding a patent can recover for the precise losses, of profits or otherwise, suffered by its wholly owned subsidiaries. This is a question to which there is no easy answer. In *Gerber Garment Technology v Lectra Systems*,[265] the claimant holding company was denied recovery on the ground that, damage to itself having to be shown, it had not proved such loss. There was no presumption that every pound—or in that case every dollar—lost to the subsidiary reduced the value of the parent's shareholding by a like amount. Hutchison LJ said that he would like to be persuaded that this was so because he was conscious of the difficulties of one in the position of the claimant when required to prove such damage.[266] It seemed to him, however, that where 48-047

262 [1975] 1 W.L.R. 819 HL at 833C.

263 See the whole passage in Lord Wilberforce's speech from [1975] 1 W.L.R. 819 HL at 832H–833H. Only damages were in issue; the alternative remedy by way of an account of profits (see para.48-035, above) was not being pursued.

264 [1975] 1 W.L.R. 819. For the three categories see para.48-042, above.

265 [1997] R.P.C. 443 CA.

266 [1997] R.P.C. 443 CA at 482.

the owner of all the shares in a company asserted loss, it must be possible to adduce evidence from expert accountants as to the level of that loss.[267] The Court of Appeal distinguished *George Fischer (Great Britain) Ltd v Multi Construction Ltd*,[268] where, by contrast, it had been held that the loss of profits to the subsidiary, there as a result of the defendant's breach of contract in installing defective equipment,[269] precisely matched, pound for pound, the loss of profits of the holding company claimant. Hobhouse LJ pointed to the difference between the corporate structure in the two cases. He said[270] that at one extreme there is the single group of companies operating within a single country and a single tax system where probably there are only consolidated accounts and all financial consequences are directly felt by the holding company, which was the position in *George Fischer* but not in *Gerber Garment*.[271]

**48-048** Another matter to consider is how far can there be recovery where there is loss in respect of goods other than those which are the subject of the patent and where there is loss arising after the patent infringement has come to an end or the patent itself has expired. The successful claimants in *Catnic Components v Hill & Smith*,[272] were held not entitled to loss of manufacturing profits in respect of sales of non-patented lintels which would commonly be sold by them to builders as a mixed package of supplies. This would, in the words of Goff LJ in *Polaroid Corporation v Eastman Kodak Co*,[273] which were cited, "be setting up a monopoly wider than that granted by the patents"; it would constitute a form of parasitic damages.[274] Yet in *Gerber Garment Technology v Lectra Systems*,[275] it was held that there was no rule of law which restricted the scope of recovery by way of loss of profits to activities of the infringer which themselves constituted infringements of the patent. Whether the patentee can claim loss of profits on goods sold together with the patented article would turn on the facts of the particular case. There may also be recovery for loss in relation to the patentee's goods after expiry of the patent or after cesser of the infringement. As is pointed out in *Dyson Appliances Ltd v Hoover Ltd (No.2)*,[276] where an injunction was being sought, for damages, referred to as "springboard" or "bridgehead" damages, to be awarded on sales after the patent has expired, it must be shown that they are caused by infringements arising while the patent subsisted.[277] As is also pointed out there, it is quite impossible to be precise about the amount to be awarded in respect of such damages.[278]

---

267 [1997] R.P.C. 443 CA at 483.

268 [1995] 1 B.C.L.C. 260 CA.

269 The issue of the recovery by the parent, where the direct loss is to the subsidiary, is of course a general one not confined to infringement of patents: see further at para.10-013, above.

270 [1997] R.P.C. 443 CA at 479.

271 And another difference adverted to by Hobhouse LJ ([1997] R.P.C. 443 CA at 479) was that in *Gerber Garment*, as opposed to *George Fischer*, the claimant company was not the ultimate holding company but itself just one intermediate company in the hierarchy of a larger group of companies run in the overall interest of the group, namely of the ultimate holding company.

272 [1983] F.S.R. 512.

273 [1977] R.P.C. 379 CA at 397.

274 On these, see paras 8-122 and following, above.

275 [1997] R.P.C. 443 CA.

276 [2001] R.P.C. 544.

277 [2001] R.P.C. 544 at 566.

278 [2001] R.P.C. 544 at 567.

## (2) Infringement of trade marks

The damages for infringement of a trade mark are considered to follow the same lines as damages for passing off.[279] It was said in *Dormeuil Frères v Feraglow*,[280] that the damages were the same in the two causes of action and claims in respect of both are sometimes brought together.[281] Yet today the analogy with infringements of the other intellectual property rights is of increasing importance. **48-049**

It has for long been established that, where it is intended to put on the market goods manufactured by the claimant holder of the trade mark, the principal head of damage is the loss of business profits caused by the diversion of the claimant's customers to the defendant as a result of the defendant's misrepresentation. Although it was laid down in the early case of *Leather Cloth Co v Hirschfeld*,[282] that it could not merely be assumed that the goods sold by the defendant through infringement of the trade mark would otherwise have been sold by the claimant, this may be a proper inference on the particular facts, and damages calculated on such a basis were awarded in the further early case of *Alexander v Henry*.[283] In the recent *Fearns v Anglo-Dutch Paint & Chemical Co Ltd*,[284] it was common ground that damages in respect of the defendant's unlawful sales should be calculated on the basis that the claimant would have made equivalent sales.[285] As to the position where it is established or admitted that the claimant would not have sold all the goods sold by the defendant, this is dealt with below.[286] In *Alexander v Henry*,[287] recovery was allowed in addition for the further loss of profits through the claimant having reduced the prices of his goods in response to the competition arising out of the defendant's infringements: again however, it will depend on the particular facts whether it is a proper inference that such a price reduction resulted from the infringement so as to be recoverable.[288] Damages also may be awarded for the claimant's loss of business reputation and goodwill resulting from the infringement. Thus in *Aktiebolaget Manus v Fullwood*,[289] the award took into account the fact that the defendant's action had **48-050**

> "seriously damaged the plaintiffs' goodwill … and adversely affected the plaintiffs' success in re-entering the market."[290]

279 For these damages see para.48-017, above. No distinction was made between the claims for passing off and for infringement of trade marks in *Fearns v Anglo-Dutch Paint & Chemical Co Ltd* [2010] EWHC 1708 Ch, both being treated together along the same lines: see at [80].

280 [1990] R.P.C. 449.

281 See, e.g. *Aktiebolaget Manus v Fullwood* (1954) 71 R.P.C. 243 (see especially at 246); *Dormeuil Frères v Feraglow* [1990] R.P.C. 449; *Reed Executive Plc v Reed Business Information Ltd* [2004] R.P.C. 767 CA; *Fearns v Anglo-Dutch Paint & Chemical Co Ltd* [2010] EWHC 1708 Ch.

282 (1865) L.R. 1 Eq. 299.

283 (1895) 12 R.P.C. 360; see especially at 366–367.

284 [2010] EWHC 1708 Ch.

285 [2010] EWHC 1708 Ch at [33]. The claimant was unable to prove that the collapse of his business was caused by the defendant's unlawful activities although he recovered for the loss of his network of distributors.

286 See the next paragraph.

287 (1895) 12 R.P.C. 360.

288 (1895) 12 R.P.C. 360 at 367.

289 (1954) 71 R.P.C. 243.

290 (1954) 71 R.P.C. 243 at 250.

**48-051** In *General Tire and Rubber Co v Firestone Tyre and Rubber Co*,[291] a patent case but still the leading case on damages in this whole field,[292] Lord Wilberforce identified three different approaches to the recovery of damages, depending upon whether the injured party would have manufactured, licensed or done neither. With each of the three approaches, damages by way of licence fee or royalty feature although with different rationales,[293] and it might be expected that they would feature similarly with trade mark infringements. But there have been uncertainties. (1) Where the claimant would have manufactured but not sold as many goods as the defendant, entitlement to damages on a royalty basis in respect of the excess sold by the defendant was doubted by Knox J in *Dormeuil Frères v Feraglow*[294]—he did not have to decide the matter—discounting the analogy with patent cases because of their proprietary element.[295] However, it has since been pointed out by His Honour Judge Birss in *National Guild of Removers & Storers Ltd v Jones*,[296] that Knox J's concern about employing this basis of damages for trade mark cases because of the lack of the proprietary element that exists with patents no longer ran as the Trade Marks Act 1994 now provided that a trade mark is a property right, and the position with patents and trade marks should in this context now be the same.[297] (2) Where the claimant would have licensed there is no difficulty and the appropriate licence fee or royalty falls to be awarded. This seems to have been the position in the *National Guild* case where Judge Birss said that he did not have to decide if he were right in thinking that royalty or user damages were available even when the trade mark was not being exploited[298] since the possibility of hiring out existed in the case before him.[299] (3) Where the claimant would not have exploited the trade mark, whether by manufacture or by licence, there have again been doubts. Thus in *Reed Executive Plc v Reed Business Information Ltd*,[300] doubt was expressed by Jacob LJ, giving the judgment of the Court of Appeal,[301] about the appropriateness in trade mark cases of awarding damages on the so-called user principle involving the ascertainment of a reasonable royalty between licensor and licensee where the trade mark concerned is not the sort of mark that is available for hire. However, once it is appreciated that the reasonable hire rate is just a method of quantifying the value obtained by the defendant in these cases the difficulty should fall away. Later cases have begun to recognise that the proprietary interest extended to trade marks suffices to allow damages along these effectively restitutionary lines, thereby following the results appearing with patent and copyright infringements.[302] Take once again *National Guild of Removers & Storers Ltd v Jones*.[303] The claimant was a trade association the members of which were allowed to use its trade marks as part of their advertising. There was provision

291 [1975] 1 W.L.R. 819 HL.

292 See para.48-035, above.

293 For the details see paras 48-042 and following, above.

294 [1990] R.P.C. 449.

295 [1990] R.P.C. 449 at 463.

296 [2011] EWPCC 4.

297 [2011] EWPCC 4 at [11].

298 As to which see the following text.

299 [2011] EWPCC 4 at [15].

300 [2004] EWCA Civ 159 CA.

301 [2004] EWCA Civ 159 CA at [165].

302 See respectively para.48-046, above and paras 48-057 and 48-058, below.

303 [2011] EWPCC 4.

where a member ceased his membership for a hire charge. The use by the defendants of the trade marks once they had ceased to be members constituted a trade mark infringement, for which infringement damages had to be assessed. Judge Birss expressed the view that the user basis was appropriate for trade mark infringements generally and even if the trade mark would not have been hired out by its owner; it was, as he put it, the invasion of a monopoly.[304] It is thought that he would have decided on this basis had he not held there to be a hiring availability.[305] In *32RED Plc v WHG (International) Ltd*,[306]where under trade mark the claimants were operating an online casino, it was accepted by them that they were not in a position to prove that they had suffered a loss of profit[307] and accordingly claimed under the user principle which applies whenever a person wrongfully uses another's property.[308] That this was appropriate for the damages computation was initially denied but later agreed to by the defendant.[309] The whole judgment is concerned with the amount that should be awarded for the hypothetical licence, with the citation of scores of the cases, which are scattered throughout this book, of wrongful use of other forms of property.[310]

In the alternative to an award of damages in each of the measures described above, a claimant may elect for an account of profits in respect of the infringement.[311] Strictly, the award is not an "account" at all but a money disgorgement for the infringement. Hence, Ch.15, which discusses these awards in more detail, describes them as disgorgement damages. The purpose of an account is to deprive the defendant of the profits made by the infringement.[312] The award is concerned with the profits deriving from the infringement of the trademark, however, and not from the sale of the item.[313] In cases where the infringement does not "drive" the sale, an allowance will be made.[314] **48-052**

One issue which has arisen is whether in making this award, the court should take into account general overheads of the defendant. In *Hollister v Medik*,[315] Kitchin LJ held that it was not permissible for an *automatic* deduction to be made from the profits arising from the infringement. Instead, the "defendant must show that the relevant overheads are properly attributable to that activity".[316] The relevant question was expressed in *OOO Abbott v Design and Display Ltd*,[317] by Lewison LJ (with whom Tomlinson LJ and Sir Terence Etherton agreed) as **48-053**

> "whether the infringer would have devoted his capacity to the manufacture and/or marketing of non-infringing products."

---

304 [2011] EWPCC 4 at [14]. He was quoting from his judgment in a similar case.

305 See earlier in this paragraph.

306 [2013] EWHC 815 Ch.

307 [2013] EWHC 815 Ch at [13].

308 [2013] EWHC 815 Ch at [22].

309 [2013] EWHC 815 Ch at [27].

310 [2013] EWHC 815 Ch at [22]–[109].

311 See Ch.15.

312 *Hollister Inc v Medik Ostomy Supplies* [2013] F.S.R. 24 at [55].

313 *Jack Wills Ltd v House of Fraser Stores Ltd* [2016] EWHC 626 (Ch) at [62].

314 *OOO Abbott v Design and Display Ltd* [2016] F.S.R. 27 at [36]; *Jack Wills Ltd v House of Fraser Stores Ltd* [2016] EWHC 626 (Ch) at [61]; *Champagne Louis Roederer (CLR) (Roederer) v J Garcia Carrion S.A.* [2017] EWHC 289 (Ch) at [77].

315 [2013] F.S.R. 24 at [85].

316 [2013] F.S.R. 24 at [85].

317 [2016] F.S.R. 27 at [40].

If it cannot be shown that those overheads would not have been incurred in any event, then no deduction will be permitted. The evidential burden in this regard, is on the defendant.[318]

## (3) Infringement of copyright and design right

**48-054** **(a) In general** In an action for infringement of a copyright,[319] now given by s.96(1) of the Copyright, Designs and Patents Act 1988,[320] the damages have been said to be at large.[321] Presumably the same is true of the damages in the action for infringement of a design right given by s.229(1) of the same Act.[322] More precisely the damages have been defined as the amount by which the value of the copyright is diminished as a chose in action.[323]

**48-055** The principal head of damage is the loss of profits caused by the diversion of buyers to the defendant. An early illustration is found in *Birn v Keene*,[324] where the defendant sold copies of Christmas cards to the claimant's customers, recovery was allowed in respect of the profits of which the claimant was thereby deprived.[325] It is, however, not to be assumed that the claimant, had there been no infringement, would have effected as many sales as the defendant had attained. It was rightly concluded in *Blayney v Clogau St Davids Gold Mines Ltd*,[326] at first instance that

---

[318] See, e.g. *Champagne Louis Roederer (CLR) (Roederer) v J Garcia Carrion SA & Ors* [2017] EWHC 289 (Ch) at [74]–[75].

[319] There must of course be an infringement before damages are in issue and there is none where the idea in a literary or musical work is used rather than the text of it is copied, as *USP Plc v London General Holdings Ltd* [2006] F.S.R. 6 CA at 65 shows. The Court of Appeal there held, reversing the Master, that the claimant was not entitled to recover in damages the amount by which it had reduced its selling price to a potential client on account of the defendant, with whom the claimant was in competition, having knowledge, through possession, of the copyrighted work. "The claimed loss", Laws LJ pointed out, "is not attributable to any breach of copyright … because in principle … it lies beyond the scope of protection which the law of copyright affords": at [34], and see the discussion at [29]–[36].

[320] Replacing Copyright Act 1956 s.17(1). Formerly the claimant could also sue for damages for conversion under s.18(1) of that Act, before that under s.7 of the Copyright Act 1911, based on a notional ownership of all infringing copies or plates. This led to hardship for defendants and overcompensation for claimants and the mounting criticism in the early 1980s was met by the disappearance of this statutory entitlement to damages in the Copyright, Designs and Patents Act 1988. See further under conversion at para.38-010, above.

[321] *Fenning Film Service v Wolverhampton Cinemas* [1914] 3 K.B. 1171 at 1174, per Horridge J. Contrast *Birn v Keene* [1918] 2 Ch. 281 at 286, per Peterson J: "the damages must necessarily be to a large extent a matter of conjecture". Indeed *Brown v Mcasso Music Production Ltd* [2006] F.S.R. 24 CA at 480 shows assessment of damages for infringement of copyright in lyrics by limited internet usage to be essentially guesswork: see at [52]–[66]. That the damages are at large is reminiscent of the tort of inducement of breach of contract, and indeed Horridge J in *Fenning Film* relied upon Lord Esher MR's use of the term in *Exchange Telegraph Co v Gregory* [1896] 1 Q.B. 147 CA at 153: see para.48-005, above.

[322] The authorities on damages concern copyright but can be used by analogy for design right.

[323] *Sutherland Publishing Co v Caxton Publishing Co* [1936] Ch. 323 CA at 336, per Lord Wright; *Infabrics v Jaytex* [1985] F.S.R. 75.

[324] [1918] 2 Ch. 281.

[325] See, especially, [1918] 2 Ch. 281 at 286.

[326] [2002] F.S.R. 233.

> "it is a question in each individual case whether it should be inferred that the claimant would have made all or some of the sales made by the infringer and that the burden of proof remains on the claimant throughout[327];"

when the case got to the Court of Appeal[328] it was no longer disputed that the onus of proving lost sales was on the claimant.[329] In the particular case it was held that only a percentage of the defendant's sales would have been made by the claimant.[330] In *Experience Hendrix LLC v Times Newspapers Ltd*,[331] which concerned not copyright but rights in performance,[332] being rights to performance and recording of a concert, damages were again awarded on the loss of profits basis because the claimants planned to exploit their performance rights.[333] Beyond profit loss, the claimant may recover for any injury to the reputation of the original. Thus in *Birn v Keene*,[334] Peterson J took into consideration the fact that the position was aggravated by the defendant having "offered the cards at a much lower price".[335]

It was also established in *Blayney v Clogau St Davids Gold Mines Ltd* in the Court of Appeal[336] that where, as there, the claimant could not show that he[337] would have made as many sales as the infringer had made, he was still entitled to damages by way of a reasonable royalty on the additional sales made by the infringing defendant. Relying in particular on Lord Shaw's championing of this result with patents in *Watson Laidlaw & Co v Pott, Cassells & Williamson*,[338] the Vice-Chancellor, who gave the only reasoned judgment with which his brethren concurred, said he saw no reason why what applied to patents should not apply to copyright, there being in both a monopoly property right invaded.[339] That there thus may be a claim for loss of profits and a reasonable royalty combined in these circumstances was very recently said by Judge Birss in *The Magic Seeder Co Ltd v Hamble Distribution Ltd*,[340] to be now accepted law,[341] leading him to hold in the case before him that the defendant's infringing sales which lost sales to the claimant gave rise to recovery of lost profits and that the remaining infringing sales of the defendant in excess of the sales the claimant would have made attracted a reasonable royalty. **48-056**

---

327 [2002] F.S.R. 233 at [32].

328 [2002] EWCA Civ 1007 CA.

329 [2002] EWCA Civ 1007 CA at [10].

330 In *Michael O'Mara Books Ltd v Express Newspapers Plc* [1999] F.S.R. 49 where two of the defendants had acquired, but had been unable to dispose of, two infringing copies of a book a very short time before its publication, no loss of profits to the claimants could be shown.

331 [2010] EWHC 1986 Ch. The case was, unusually, decided under a European Union Directive but this made no difference to the result. See the case at para.48-077, below.

332 Also covered by the 1988 Act.

333 And also because the licence approach (for which see below) faced formidable difficulties in assessment: [2010] EWHC 1986 Ch at [133] and following. Full details of the case are at para.10-004, above.

334 [1918] 2 Ch. 281.

335 [1918] 2 Ch. 281 at 286. If this had forced down the claimant's prices he should have been able to recover for the further loss of profits caused thereby: contrast at paras 48-050 and 48-043, above, the cases on reduction of prices where a trade mark or patent has been infringed.

336 [2002] EWCA Civ 1007 CA.

337 Though claimants in this field tend to be corporate, in this case the claimant was an individual, Mr Blayney.

338 (1914) 31 R.P.C. 104 HL. See at para.48-044, above.

339 [2002] EWCA Civ 1007 CA at [20].

340 [2012] EWPCC 9.

341 [2012] EWPCC 9 at [2].

48-057 Where loss of profits caused by the diversion of buyers from the claimant to the defendant is an inappropriate criterion because the claimant is not in the business of selling, damages are likely to be measured by a licence fee, and[342] whether the claimant was in the business of licensing out the copyright[343] or was not exploiting the copyright. Thus in *Ludlow Music Inc v Williams*,[344] it was accepted that the case was one for an award by way of licence royalty rather than profits, the defendant having been negotiating, though unsuccessfully, with the claimant for a licence to publish. Again in *Oliver Homes Manufacturing v Hamilton*,[345] the appropriate measure of damages was held to be a reasonable licence fee for the use of copyright plans for the construction of houses from a kit and not the loss on the sale of one of the house-kits. Where the claim is by an architect for infringement of the copyright in his plans and designs, the damages should be based upon the fee which the architect could have charged the infringer for a licence to use the plans and drawings in erecting his building, and it was so held by the Court of Appeal in *Stovin-Bradford v Volpoint*.[346] In such a case it is not a correct measure to award the amount of profit which would have accrued to the claimant if he had been employed as architect of the infringing building: "copyright", said Uthwatt J so holding in *Meikle v Maufe*,[347] "is not the sickle which reaps an architect's profits".[348]

48-058 Situations where there could be no question of granting a licence to use the copyright create some difficulty in arriving at a licence fee as the appropriate damages. *Nottingham Healthcare NHS Trust v News Group Newspapers Ltd*,[349] was such a case. From a patient's medical records held by the claimant hospital trust the defendant newspaper published a photograph which, being both confidential and of no economic value to the claimant, there was no intention of exploit commercially.[350] Since it was clear that some damages had to be awarded, the best that could be done was to take the fee that would be negotiated between a willing copyright owner and a newspaper[351]; in the event only £450 was awarded.[352]

48-059 Occasionally it will be appropriate to award neither lost profits nor licence fee.

---

342 Damages have also been measured by a licence fee where the number of lost sales has been too speculative and too open to inaccuracy to be a sound basis for calculation. This was done in *Kohler Mira Ltd v Bristan Group Ltd* [2014] EWHC 1931 (IPEC), which concerned infringement of design right in electric shower units.

343 As in *Sheldon v Daybrook House Promotions Ltd* [2013] EWPCC 26 where the claimant's business involved the licensing of photographs taken by him (at [5]). The only issue in the case was the proper amount of licence fee to award.

344 [2002] F.S.R. 868.

345 [1992] F.L.T. 892.

346 [1971] Ch. 1007 CA, approving *Chabot v Davies* [1936] 3 All E.R. 221 where the same measure was adopted; it was further held that no reduction should be made because the defendants had only incorporated part of the architect's plan in their building. See, too, *Hunter v Fitzroy Robinson* [1978] F.S.R. 167.

347 [1941] 3 All E.R. 144.

348 [1941] 3 All E.R. 144 at 154. Various further points are discussed by Uthwatt J in connection with the measure of damages, at 154–155.

349 [2002] R.P.C. 962.

350 [2002] R.P.C. 962 at 977.

351 The trial judge placed reliance on the long passage, which he cited, from Lord Wilberforce's speech in *General Tire & Rubber Co v Firestone Tyre and Rubber Co* [1975] 1 W.L.R. 819 HL setting out the principles for the award of damages in the related patent field: see para.48-042, above.

352 [2002] R.P.C. 962 at 988. But this was made up for by a large award of the statutory "additional damages" yet to be considered (see the case at para.48-068, below), the trial judge saying that "it is in circumstances such as the present case, however, that additional damages may be appropriate": at 977.

This was so in *Peninsular Business Services Ltd v Citation Plc*.[353] Claimant and defendant were in the business of providing certain consulting services, the primary means of obtaining business being by the canvassing of clients. In setting up the business various manuals were used and in breach of contract the defendant copied materials from the claimant's manuals to their own manuals. The claim for lost profits to the claimant's business failed because, although the infringing material had been used in competition with that business and was a central feature in setting up the system of business, it played no part in the selling of the claimant's services which occurred through the normal process of competition by the canvassing of clients for which purpose the material was not required. Instead, the provision of the documents being required for the businesses, the court awarded simply the cost to the defendant of producing or commissioning a non-infringing set of materials.[354]

Parasitic damages are not available, however.[355] In *Paterson Zochonis & Co v Merfarken Packaging*,[356] there was no recovery for the passing off of other goods as the claimant's where the passing off had been facilitated by the defendant's infringement of copyright.[357] Robert Goff LJ said that he knew **48-060**

> "of no principle that, whenever one interest of a plaintiff has been wrongfully damaged, consequential damage to another interest of the plaintiff is necessarily recoverable".[358]

Yet it was held in *Kohler Mira Ltd v Bristan Group Ltd*,[359] that the claimant who had established infringement of design right in electric shower units was in principle entitled to damages in relation to products unprotected by the design right infringed if the damage was caused by the infringement, was foreseeable, and was not excluded by public policy.[360]

**(b) The provision for additional damages** Section 97(2) of the Copyright, Designs and Patents Act 1988, replacing s.17(3) of the Copyright Act 1956, provides that: **48-061**

> "The court may in an action for breach of copyright, having regard to all the circumstances, and in particular to—
>
> (a) the flagrancy[361] of the infringement, and

---

353 [2004] F.S.R. 17 at 359.

354 To the extent that this award was based on benefit to the defendant rather than loss to the claimant it has restitutionary overtones along the lines of the cases considered at paras 14-016 and following, above.

355 For the concept of parasitic damages see para.8-122, above.

356 [1982] Com. L.R. 260 CA.

357 The claimant unsuccessfully prayed in aid the provision for "additional damages" then appearing in s.17(3) of the Copyright Act 1956, now in s.97(2) of the successor Act of 1988, and dealt with at paras 48-061 to 48-069, below.

358 [1982] Com. L.R. 260 CA at 262, col.2. But, as the discussion of parasitic damages at paras 8-122 and following, above, shows, the situation is somewhat more complex than this. And see, taking a somewhat different view in relation to patents, *Gerber Garment Technology v Lectra Systems* [1997] R.P.C. 443 CA at para.48-047, above. See, too, *Michael O'Mara Books Ltd v Express Newspapers Plc* [1999] F.S.R. 49 where Neuberger J considered the possibility of awarding damages on the user principle as not there appropriate since no profit had been made.

359 [2014] EWHC 1931 (IPEC).

360 See at [28] and following.

361 Such additional damages have come to be referred to as flagrancy damages: see *Electronic*

(b) any benefit accruing to the defendant by reason of the infringement,

award such additional damages as the justice of the case may require."[362]

A provision in the same terms is introduced for actions for infringement of design right by s.229(3) of the 1988 Act. In connection with these various statutory provisions, certain matters fall for consideration.

48-062 *(i) Relation with account of profits* A claim to additional damages does not lie where an account of profits is sought. It was rightly so held in *Redrow Homes Ltd v Bett Bros Plc*,[363] overruling *Cala Homes Ltd v Alfred McAlpine Homes Ltd (No.2)*.[364] On its true construction, s.97(2) does not provide an entirely independent, self-standing remedy but empowers the court, as had the predecessor subsection in clear terms,[365] to award additional damages only where normal compensatory damages are being awarded under the provision of s.96(2), which subsection provides that relief for infringement of copyright is to be available "by way of damages, injunctions, accounts or otherwise". The additional damages, it was held, are to be additional to damages and not additional to any other form of relief made available under s.96(2). Although we have seen that a better description for the account of profits is "disgorgement damages", in 1956 an account of profits was not contemplated as falling within the expression "damages" in the Act. The result is easily defended. The deterrent purpose underlying disgorgement of profits should not be replicated by a further award of additional damages. Nor, it was decided in *Michael O'Mara Books v Express Newspapers Plc*,[366] can the defendant's potential profits be taken into account where the claim is simply for compensatory damages; such profits could be relevant only if additional damages, to which there was an entitlement, are claimed.

## (ii) Relation with exemplary damages

48-063 Section 17(3) of the Copyright Act 1956, the predecessor of s.97(2), was held in *Williams v Settle*,[367] to permit an award of exemplary damages. There the defendant, a professional photographer, upon the murder of the claimant's father-in-law

---

*Techniques (Anglia) Ltd v Critchley Components Ltd* [1997] F.S.R. 401 at 411 and the headnote in *Microsoft Corp v Electro-Wide Ltd* [1997] F.S.R. 580. On how the court should deal procedurally with the statutory additional damages, see *MCA Records Inc v Charly Records Ltd* [2002] F.S.R. 401 at [63]–[66]. The meaning of flagrancy is discussed in *Dyson Ltd v Qualtex (UK) Ltd* [2005] R.P.C. 395 at [338]–[343].

362 The wording of s.97(2) departs somewhat from that of the predecessor s.17(3) of the 1956 Act, the one important difference of substance being that under the earlier enactment the court, in awarding the additional damages, had to be "satisfied that effective relief would not otherwise be available to the plaintiff", a requirement which has been dropped from the current statute. Indeed, it had been proposed in the Whitford Committee Report of 1977 that, on the assumption that the deterrent of conversion damages were removed (which it now has been: see second footnote to para.48-054, above), the courts' hand would be strengthened if the two limitations on the award of additional damages, namely, that effective relief is not otherwise available and that benefit has accrued to the defendant, were removed: Cmnd.6732, para.704. While the first limitation has gone, the second has, sensibly, been retained.

363 [1999] A.C. 197.

364 [1996] F.S.R. 36.

365 See the previous footnote but two.

366 [1999] F.S.R. 49.

367 [1960] 1 W.L.R. 1072 CA.

at a time when the claimant's wife was pregnant, sold to the press certain photographs taken by him at the claimant's wedding which were then published in two national newspapers. The claimant sued for breach of his copyright in the photographs and the Court of Appeal upheld the judge's award of £1,000 exemplary damages. Sellers LJ said that the defendant's act

> "was a flagrant infringement of the right of the plaintiff, and it was scandalous conduct and in total disregard not only of the legal rights of the plaintiff regarding copyright but of his feelings and his sense of family dignity and pride."[368]

Clearly, the additional damages were here being awarded under the first head of flagrancy rather than under the second head of benefit to the defendant.

Soon after the decision in *Williams v Settle* came that of the House of Lords in *Rookes v Barnard*,[369] which changed the whole approach to exemplary damages so that flagrancy in itself was no longer enough to justify an exemplary damages award.[370] This suggested that cases such as *Williams v Settle* must now be justified on the basis that awards were not of exemplary but of aggravated damages. Over the years their Lordships have in various cases given their views on the matter. Lord Devlin himself in *Rookes v Barnard*,[371] justified *Williams v Settle* on an aggravated damages basis. Lord Hailsham LC in *Broome v Cassell & Co*[372] considered that the decision could be explained on either basis, while reserving his opinion as to whether the statute authorised exemplary damages.[373] Lord Kilbrandon, also in *Broome v Cassell & Co*, expressed himself as satisfied that the statute did not authorise the award of exemplary damages.[374] Lord Clyde in *Redrow Homes Ltd v Bett Bros Plc*,[375]gave as his view that an award under the statute is more probably of aggravated damages than of exemplary damages.[376] Eventually, after an extensive review of the arguments and the authorities, Pumfrey J decided in *Nottingham Healthcare NHS Trust v News Group Newspapers Ltd*,[377] that neither s.97(2) nor, before it, s.17(3) authorises the awarding of exemplary damages. By contrast, Gray J in *Collins Stewart Ltd v Financial Times Ltd (No.2)*,[378] expressed the view, obiter, that additional damages under s.97(2) are akin to exemplary damages rather than to aggravated damages[379]; it was obiter as the case with which he was dealing was one of libel. No decision, one way or the other, has yet appeared in the higher courts. **48-064**

It is thought that for flagrant infringements the case for today regarding the statute as applying to exemplary damages rather than to aggravated damages is a compelling one. The basis for this is the perceived inappropriateness of awarding aggravated damages, which are directed to compensation for mental distress and injured feelings, to companies which have no feelings and do not suffer distress. **48-065**

---

368 [1960] 1 W.L.R. 1072 CA at 1082.
369 [1964] A.C. 1129.
370 For details of the *Rookes v Barnard* changes see Ch.13, above.
371 [1964] A.C. 1129 at 1229.
372 [1972] A.C. 1027.
373 [1972] A.C. 1027 at 1080G–H.
374 [1972] A.C. 1027 at 1134A.
375 [1999] A.C. 197.
376 [1999] A.C. 197 at 209F. Lord Jauncey was non-committal: at 207E; the others did not address the question.
377 [2002] R.P.C. 962.
378 [2005] EWHC 262 (QB).
379 [2005] EWHC 262 (QB) at [33].

For some 30 years there has been uncertainty at first instance as to whether the impersonal nature of a company debarred it from an award of aggravated damages but at last the question has come before the Court of Appeal which in *Eaton Mansions (Westminster) Ltd v Stinger Compania de Inversion SA*,[380] has held without reservation that aggravated damages are not recoverable by corporate claimants.[381] Now it so happens that claimants for additional damages on account of the flagrancy of the particular infringement tend to be companies and not individuals. Indeed none of the claimants in the known cases where flagrancy damages have been awarded have been individuals; they have been corporate bodies and in one case a trust, also without feelings.[382] Unless these cases are to be regarded as wrongly decided, and there is no reason why they should be, it follows that the awards in them are to be regarded as awards of exemplary damages. Moreover, exemplary damages are still awardable after *Rookes v Barnard*,[383] where there is statutory authorisation, being one of the three categories of their survival.[384] It is true that Lord Devlin phrased this category in terms of exemplary damages which are *expressly* authorised by statute,[385] so that this statutory provision would fall outside its ambit. Yet it is significant that he himself said in *Rookes* that he reserved his opinion as to whether the then 1956 Act "authorises an award of exemplary, as distinct from aggravated, damages",[386] and it is surely probable that when the provision for additional damages on account of flagrancy was introduced in 1956, still in the heyday of exemplary damages, the framers of the Act had exemplary damages in mind.

**48-066** There is not the same problem with additional damages given by reason of any benefit accruing to the defendant as a result of the infringement; they can be awarded to companies and individuals alike. Such damages can be classified today as disgorgement damages.[387] Of course they could in theory fall within Lord Devlin's second common law category of exemplary damages based on acting with a view to profit,[388] but at the time of the Copyright Act 1956 no one would have been thinking of exemplary damages along these lines. This then means that we would have a different rationale for additional damages awarded on account of flagrancy and for additional damages awarded on account of benefit.

### (iii) Criteria for assessment

**48-067** Considerations relevant to the award of additional damages were early explored by Ungoed Thomas J in *Beloff v Pressdram*,[389] in a very lengthy discussion related chiefly to the conduct of the defendant, and also of the claimant; this was followed

---

380 [2013] EWCA Civ 1308 CA.

381 [2013] EWCA Civ 1308 CA at [30]. For more detail on the first instance cases see para.5-014, above (in a footnote).

382 See the cases at para.48-068, below.

383 [1964] A.C. 1129.

384 See paras 13-028 and following, above.

385 [1964] A.C. 1129 at 1227.

386 [1964] A.C. 1129 at 1225.

387 Although the discussion of the domestic law covering the various intellectual property rights (at paras 48-041 and following above) suggests that the common law itself is able to cope with damages based on benefit.

388 See paras 13-021 and following, above.

389 [1973] 1 All E.R. 241 at 264–273.

by Brightman J's very brief discussion of criteria in *Ravenscroft v Herbert*.[390] In neither case were additional damages under the statute awarded. In *Michael O'Mara Books Ltd v Express Newspapers Plc*,[391] Neuberger J was prepared to envisage that mitigation and means could be taken into account in the assessment of additional damages[392] but the question of whether there should be an award of additional damages was not reached. In *Pendle Metalwares Ltd v Walter Page (Safeway's) Ltd*,[393] his Honour Judge Purle awarded additional damages on account of the flagrancy of the infringement but refused them in respect of benefit accruing by reason of the infringement: see at [46]–[52].

In *Nichols Advanced Vehicle Systems v Rees, Oliver*,[394] Templeman J, in awarding additional damages, regarded the conditions of the subsection as satisfied because the defendants, who had stolen a march on the claimant company in the building of racing cars, had "received benefits and inflicted humiliation and loss".[395] In *Nottingham Healthcare NHS Trust v News Group Newspapers Ltd*,[396] Pumfrey J, while holding that exemplary damages were not awardable,[397] at the same time considered that the wide terms in which s.97(2) was drafted permitted an aggravation of damages on a basis far wider than aggravation at common law,[398] and awarded £10,000 by way of additional damages.[399] While the defendant company in *Cavalcade Records Ltd v HHO Multi-Media Ltd*,[400] was not deceitful, its reckless attitude sufficed for additional damages on account of flagrancy. **48-068**

By contrast, in rather more cases additional damages have been refused. In *Noah v Shuba*,[401] with an essentially innocent defendant who derived no apparent benefit, Mummery J did not consider it appropriate to make any award of additional damages. In *Ludlow Music Inc v Williams*,[402] no additional statutory damages were awarded because, although the defendant had knowingly infringed, he had not done so cynically but in the expectation, which was not realised, that an agreement to license publication would be reached. In *Experience Hendrix LLC v Times Newspapers Ltd*,[403] which concerned not copyright but rights in performance for infringement of which there is a similar provision for additional damages in the **48-069**

---

[390] [1980] R.P.C. 193 at 208. See, too, a further early case in connection with the statutory provision, *The Lady Anne Tennant v Associated Newspapers Group* [1979] F.S.R. 298, where, however, the decision whether the subsection need be invoked was left to the subsequent inquiry as to damages: at 303.

[391] [1999] F.S.R. 49.

[392] [1999] F.S.R. 49 at 58.

[393] [2014] EWHC 1140 (Ch).

[394] [1979] R.P.C. 127.

[395] [1979] R.P.C. 127 at 140. The further decision on the damages and the appeal therefrom ([1988] R.P.C. 71 CA) take us no further.

[396] [2002] R.P.C. 962.

[397] See para.48-064, above.

[398] Pumfrey J also expressed the view that if carelessness were sufficiently serious it could be equated with deliberation and be capable of making the infringement an aggravated one. And he took what he called a broad brush approach to the assessment of additional damages in *Phonographic Performance Ltd v Reader* [2005] F.S.R. 42 at 891 when he found benefit to the defendant too uncertain to be calculated: see at [17] and [18].

[399] This was in the context of a very small award for pecuniary loss: see the case at para.48-058, above.

[400] *Cavalcade Records Ltd v HHO Multi-Media Ltd* unreported 27 March 2013.

[401] [1991] F.S.R. 14.

[402] [2002] F.S.R. 868.

[403] [2010] EWHC 1986 Ch.

1988 Act,[404] it could not be said that the defendant was indifferent about engaging in infringing activities and accordingly an award of additional damages was inappropriate.[405]And in *Signature Realty Ltd v Fortis Developments Ltd*,[406] an award of additional damages for infringement of copyright in architectural drawings was said to be inappropriate, in circumstances where flagrancy had not been established, and the benefits flowing from the infringement, as opposed to a planning consent which had been obtained, were unclear.

## 3. The Impact of the European Directive

**48-070** We are now in a position to examine the effect of the Directive and its implementation by statutory instrument in the United Kingdom on the awarding of damages. This takes us to the central provision of the Directive, stating for what items damages are to be recoverable. The sub-article, after its introductory provision that the competent judicial authorities are to ensure that damages for the loss suffered are to be recovered from the infringer who is at fault,[407] continues with:

> "**Art.13**
>
> (1)
>
> ........When the judicial authorities set the damages:
>
> (a) they shall take into account all appropriate aspects, such as the negative economic consequences, including lost profits, which the injured party has suffered, any unfair profits made by the infringer and, in appropriate cases, elements other than economic factors, such as the moral prejudice caused to the rightholder by the infringement; or
>
> (a) as an alternative to (a), they may, in appropriate cases, set the damages as a lump sum on the basis of elements such as at least the amount of royalties or fees which would have been due if the infringer had requested authorisation to use the intellectual property right in question."

All of this is reflected in the United Kingdom damages regulation. Unlike the Directive, this is provided in a separate sub-regulation which is along the same lines as what is stated in the Directive:

> "**3**(2) When awarding such damages—
>
> (a) all appropriate aspects shall be taken into account, including in particular—
>
> (i) the negative economic consequences, including any lost profits, which the claimant has suffered, and any unfair profits made by the defendant; and
>
> (ii) elements other than economic factors, including the moral prejudice caused to the claimant by the infringement; or

---

404 *Experience Hendrix* also concerned the European Union Directive and its application so that "moral prejudice" as well as "additional damages" was in play. For the explanation of this see paras 48-070 and following, below.

405 See [2010] EWHC 1986 Ch at [73] to [76]. Other cases where the trial judge did not find flagrancy allowing an award of additional damages are *Worldpro Software Ltd v Desi Ltd* [1997] Info.T.L.R. 279 (see at 314–315), *Fraser-Woodward Ltd v British Broadcasting Corporation Brighter Pictures Ltd* [2005] E.M.L.R. 22 at 487 (see at [89]–[91]), *Harrison v Harrison* [2010] F.S.R. 25 at 604 (see the judge's analysis, legal and factual, at [38] and following).

406 [2016] EWHC 3583 (Ch) at [109].

407 See it at para.48-038, above.

(b) where appropriate, they may be awarded on the basis of the royalties or fees which would have been due had the defendant obtained a licence."

## (1) Range of application

Four specific heads of damage can be extracted from these provisions. These are: loss of profits and any other financial loss[408]; damage consequent upon unfair profits being made by the infringer; moral prejudice and any other non-financial loss[409]; and royalties and fees arising from a potential licence. **48-071**

**(a) Loss of profits and other financial losses** Loss of profits, as we have seen above, is the principal head of damage whatever the intellectual property right infringed, whether the profit comes from manufacture or other use of the intellectual property or by the licensing of it.[410] Although authority is sparse, expenses reasonably incurred in consequence are also recoverable. There is therefore no need to invoke Directive and regulation by virtue of the provision that English law continues to apply where consistent with what the regulation, following the provisions of the Directive, lays down.[411] **48-072**

**(b) Unfair profits made by the infringer** Appearing in Directive and regulation alike, this is taken to be a reference to profits made by the infringer which outstrip the profits lost to the injured party. The typical example is where the infringer's sales are greater than the sales that the injured party would have made in the absence of the infringement. There is also the case where the injured party is not exploiting the intellectual property right and has thus not lost any profits. In both these situations English law has developed, as we have seen, so as to allow recovery of a licence fee or royalty, thereby ensuring that the injured party participates in the infringer's profit or extra profit. This position has been arrived at first with patents,[412] then with copyright,[413] and eventually with trade marks.[414] There is therefore again no need to invoke Directive and regulation by virtue of the provision that English law continues to apply where consistent with what the regulation, following the provisions of the Directive, lays down.[415] **48-073**

**(c) Moral prejudice and other non-financial losses** Moral prejudice is a term used by Continental legal systems. It is unknown to English law, strange to English legal ears and its significance may not be easily understood. Thus where a claim was made for a moral prejudice award in *Xena Systems Ltd v Cantideck*,[416] Judge Birss said that he was given no assistance by counsel as "neither side cited any **48-074**

---

408 Both Directive article and regulation use "negative economic consequences" but "financial losses", which must mean the same thing, is far clearer.

409 Both Directive article and regulation use "elements other than economic factors" but "non-financial losses", which must mean the same thing, is far clearer.

410 See, above, paras 48-050 and 48-051 (trade marks), paras 48-043 to 48-045 (patents), paras 48-055 to 48-057 (copyright and design right).

411 See reg.3(3) at para.48-039, above.

412 See paras 48-044 and 48-046, above.

413 See paras 48-056 to 48-058, above.

414 See para.48-051, above.

415 See reg.3(3) at para.48-039, above.

416 [2013] EWPCC 1.

authority as to how 'moral prejudice' should be addressed."[417] In English parlance, the word prejudice does not suggest loss or damage and the word moral does not suggest non-financial loss. But it is different with Continental usage. Taking the French, the word *préjudice* does mean harm or damage and the distinction between pecuniary loss and non-pecuniary loss is framed in terms of *dommage matériel* and *dommage moral*. It would seem therefore in this context that moral prejudice refers to mental distress, to injured feelings, as the only form of non-pecuniary loss which infringement of these various rights in intellectual property could give rise. While it is somewhat unlikely that the infringement of such a right would lead to mental distress—and it is significant that the Directive has the qualification that recovery is to be only "in appropriate cases," a phrase omitted from the regulation[418]—as has been pointed out above, general principle does not bar recovery in exceptional circumstances.[419] Indeed where English statute has provided for what are termed additional damages should an infringement of copyright be flagrant,[420] Templeman J's award of such damages in *Nichols Advanced Vehicle Systems v Rees, Oliver*,[421] reflected the fact that the defendant had inflicted humiliation and loss on the claimant.[422] Thus it would seem that moral prejudice is covered by English law, which will again apply to the exclusion of Directive and regulation.[423] To this there is a comparatively small qualification, being limited to copyright and design right cases. If the provision for additional damages on account of flagrancy should be interpreted as leading to exemplary damages rather than to damages for loss, for which today there is a good case,[424] this would be inconsistent with what is laid down in the regulation following the Directive, exemplary damages not being recognised in Continental systems of law.

**48-075** **(d) Royalties and fees arising from licensing** This head of damage is stated, in both Directive article and United Kingdom regulation, to be claimable in lieu of the others[425] but to be available only in appropriate circumstances. What is believed to be in mind here is the case where the intellectual property right is not exploited by the holder of the right, so that there cannot be a claim for loss of profits under the earlier provision, whether the profit come from manufacturing or from licensing, and resort must be had to damages in compensation for invasion of the holder's proprietary right, compensation which is best assessed by a royalty or licence fee, although one worked out in a somewhat different manner from that awardable for loss of profit to one in the business of licensing. That this is the position in English law in relation to patents was firmly established by Lord Wilberforce in *General*

417 [2013] EWPCC 1 at [50].

418 See Article and regulation at para.48-070, above.

419 See para.48-035, above. In *Kohler Mira Ltd v Bristan Group Ltd* [2014] EWHC 1931 (IPEC), which concerned infringement of design right in electric shower units, it was appreciated that moral prejudice referred to non-pecuniary loss. The 10 per cent uplift asked for on the award given for pecuniary loss was therefore refused as there was no non-pecuniary loss. Non-pecuniary loss, it was rightly said, was likely to arise only in very particular circumstances: at [60].

420 See para.48-061, above.

421 [1979] R.P.C. 127.

422 See the case at para.48-068, above.

423 See reg.3(3) at para.48-039, above.

424 See the discussion at para.48-065, above.

425 The Directive article has "or (b) as an alternative to (a)", the UK regulation simply has "or". See them both at para.48-070, above.

*Tire and Rubber Co v Firestone Tyre and Rubber Co*,[426] and the same result should follow with the other intellectual property rights. Accordingly, here too there is no need to invoke Directive and regulation as English law will continue to apply.[427]

Accordingly, to damages as compensation for loss, which is of course the norm, English law continues to apply across the board. Only if exemplary damages should come into the picture would the Directive and regulation take over.[428] **48-076**

## (2) Application by the courts

In the light of all this, how have the English courts seen and applied these new requirements stemming from Europe? What is interesting is that scant attention has been paid in the English cases to these provisions. Although they have been in force since April 2006, just two cases are known in which they have been invoked and relied upon. The one, dealing with the infringement of the claimant companies' right in the performance and recording of a concert, was heard in 2010 in the High Court; this was *Experience Hendrix LLC v Times Newspapers Ltd*.[429] The other, dealing with the infringement of the claimant company's patent, was heard in 2013 in the Patent County Court; this was *Xena Systems Ltd v Cantideck*.[430] There is the thought, which should perhaps not be expressed, that counsel and court were unaware of this exceptional intrusion of the European Union into the English law of damages. The more likely explanation is that the position under the Directive article and the United Kingdom regulation is seen as being no different from the position at common law, so that there was no need to turn to them.[431] Certainly, Sir William Blackburne in his judgment in the *Experience Hendrix* case, moved easily between Directive and English authorities which suggests that he was of much the same view, awarding loss of profits from a perfectly English law standpoint[432] and making no increase in the damages on account of moral prejudice.[433] As for *Xena v Cantideck* Judge Birss's full judgment is almost entirely taken up with working out the claimant company's loss of profits with reliance solely on English authorities, has little reference to the Directive article and briefly refuses to award any damages for moral prejudice.[434] **48-077**

---

426 [1975] 1 W.L.R. 819 HL. See para.48-046, above.

427 See reg.3(3) at para.48-039, above.

428 But not in Scotland, to which the regulations implementing the Directive apply, because Scots law, like Continental law, does not recognise exemplary damages.

429 [2010] EWHC 1986 Ch.

430 [2013] EWPCC 1.

431 The Directive indeed requires an application by the injured party for its provisions on damages to be brought in; there is no equivalent in the UK's wording. Compare art.13.1 with reg.3(1), both at para.48-038, above.

432 See details of the case at para.10-004, above.

433 [2010] EWHC 1986 Ch at [73]–[76].

434 [2013] EWPCC 1 at [114].

Chapter 49

# MISREPRESENTATION

Table of Contents



**49-001** There was a time when the only misrepresentation that could safely be said to be capable of giving rise to tortious liability was a fraudulent misrepresentation: the old tort of deceit was still without rival in the field. However, in the 1960s the common law developed a liability for negligent misrepresentation[1] and, for the situation where the misrepresentation has induced the making of a contract, statute introduced a liability both for negligent misrepresentation[2] and, in lieu of rescission, for innocent misrepresentation.[3] The position has therefore become much more complex. Initially there was a debate as to the proper measure of damages for deceit; this gave way to controversy, now largely resolved, as to the proper measure for negligent misrepresentation under the statutory liability; the battle then moved to the realm of the proper measure for innocent misrepresentation. It is submitted that in all three areas of liability the tortious measure of damages should prevail over the contractual. This has been accepted for deceit[4] and now for negligent misrepresentation[5]; by contrast, innocent misrepresentation has since gone in the opposite direction and needs to be brought in from the cold.[6]

---

1 Stemming from *Hedley Byrne & Co v Heller & Partners* [1964] A.C. 465.
2 Misrepresentation Act 1967 s.2(1).
3 Misrepresentation Act 1967 s.2(2).
4 See para.49-005, below.
5 See para.49-053, below.
6 See para.49-076, below.

# I. FRAUDULENT MISREPRESENTATION: DECEIT

## 1. THE TORTIOUS MEASURE OF DAMAGES

The tort of deceit[7] needs careful handling as far as damages are concerned because in the great majority of cases the action induced by the deceit[8] is the entering into a contract by the claimant, either with the defendant tortfeasor or with a third party, and it is important in such circumstances to stress the difference between a measure of damages based on tort principles and a measure of damages based on contract principles. Thus the correct measure of damages in the tort of deceit is an award which serves to put the claimant into the position he would have been in[9] if the representation had not been made to him, and not, as with breach of condition or warranty in contract, into the position he would have been in if the representation had been true.[10] In other words, if the claimant has been induced by the deceit to conclude a contract he is not entitled, as he is in contract, to recover in deceit for the loss of his bargain. **49-002**

This important point is best illustrated by the case where the contract induced by the deceit is one for the sale of shares to the claimant.[11] Assume a contract for the sale of shares by the defendant to the claimant induced by the defendant's fraudulent misrepresentation as to their value. This misrepresentation is not a term of the contract, there is therefore no breach of contract, and the claimant's remedy in damages is in tort for the deceit. The normal measure of damages in such a case will be the purchase price paid less the actual value of the shares when allotted; it will not be, as in contract, the represented value of the shares when allotted less their actual value. **49-003**

This prevalence of the tortious measure comes out very clearly in the judgment of Lord Collins MR in *McConnell v Wright*.[12] He there said of the action of deceit[13]: **49-004**

> "It is not an action for breach of contract, and, therefore, no damages in respect of prospective gains which the person contracting was entitled by his contract to expect come in, but it is an action of tort—it is an action for a wrong done whereby the plaintiff was tricked out of certain money in his pocket; and therefore, prima facie, the highest limit of his dam-

---

7 The damages in the tort of intimidation, in its aspect of intimidation of the claimant (for its other aspect of intimidation of a third party, see para.48-002, above) should, it is submitted, follow the same lines as the damages for deceit where, as is most common, the intimidation is of an economic nature, but on the damages there are no authorities. All we have is *Godwin v Uzoigwe* [1992] T.L.R. 300 CA, where the intimidation was of a physical nature—intimidation of a teenage girl by a couple who had brought her from Nigeria to England and for two-and-a-half years had treated her as a drudge and skivvy, working her excessive hours without pay and denying her proper food, clothing and social intercourse. The trial judge awarded £25,000 and the Court of Appeal, without giving reasons, substituted £20,000.

8 For the requisites of actionable deceit, see the standard texts on tort.

9 This is, of course, subject to the rules of remoteness, mitigation and the like. While damage is less likely to be too remote in deceit than elsewhere because of the intention to injure (see para.8-050, above), there is not a less strict test for mitigation, the same rules applying in deceit as would apply in any action for tort or breach of contract: *Standard Chartered Bank v Pakistan National Shipping Corp (No.3)* [1999] 1 Lloyd's Rep. 747: see para.9-080, above.

10 Compare the same distinction in relation to breach of warranty of authority at para.36-002, above.

11 Most of the cases dealing with measure of damages in deceit involve such a contract: see paras 49-008 and following, below.

12 [1903] 1 Ch. 546 CA.

13 The action in that case was under the Directors Liability Act 1890, but in relation to damages the same principles apply as with deceit: see para.49-009, below.

ages is the whole extent of his loss, and that loss is measured by the money which was in his pocket and is now in the pocket of the company. That is the ultimate, final, highest standard of his loss."[14]

Similar reasoning is to be found in the earlier case of *Twycross v Grant*,[15] where Cockburn CJ said:

"The complaint of the plaintiff is that he has been induced … to take shares in an undertaking, which, but for this suppression, he would not have joined, and which has turned out to be worthless … His grievance is not that he has paid too high a price, but that he has been induced to take shares which, but for the fraud, he would not have taken at all."[16]

Together with such lines of reasoning as these, there are the many statements in cases where the claimant is induced to buy shares that the measure of damages is the price paid less the value received and that this is a well-settled rule.[17]

**49-005** While from all this it would appear that the acceptance of the tortious measure has always been beyond doubt, it remains true that up until the end of the 1960s the choice between the tortious and the contractual measures had not been expressly passed upon by the courts, and, as was pointed out in the 12th edition of this work in 1961, there were to be found in the cases indications of uncertainty as to whether the tortious measure was indeed the measure to be applied.[18] Then in *Doyle v Olby (Ironmongers)*,[19] the Court of Appeal unreservedly adopted the tortious measure, Winn J. paying tribute to the passage in the 12th edition where it was argued that the tortious measure should prevail.[20] This has remained the position ever since so that today the law is incontrovertibly established on this footing. *Smith Kline & French Laboratories v Long*,[21] illustrates this; it was there accepted on all sides that the correct measure of damages was the tortious and not the contractual.[22] So, too, there is implicit in all that is said in *Smith New Court Securities v Scrimgeour Vickers*,[23] the first decision of the House of Lords on damages in deceit for well over half a century, that it is the tortious measure that is the relevant one.[24]

**49-006** It does not, however, follow that claimants should necessarily bemoan this final acceptance of the tortious measure. While the earlier discussion of the differences between the tortious and contractual measures of damages in the context of deceit claims tended to assume that the contractual measure would give to a claimant the higher award, this was on the basis that, had the misrepresentation been true, the claimant's contractual bargain with the defendant would have been a good one. If, on the other hand, he would have made a bad bargain, he will be better off under the tortious measure. And, beyond this, the calculation of his consequential losses may prove substantially higher under the tortious than under the contractual

---

14 [1903] 1 Ch. 546 CA at 554–555.

15 (1877) 2 C.P.D. 469 CA. Again the action was not common law deceit.

16 (1877) 2 C.P.D. 469 CA at 543. See, similarly, Lord Coleridge CJ below: at 490 and 491. Compare *Peek v Derry* (1887) 37 Ch. D. 541 at 594 CA, per Sir James Hannen: "The question is, how much worse off is the plaintiff than if he had not bought the shares?"

17 See the cases collected in the footnotes to para.49-011, below.

18 12th edn, para.957.

19 [1969] 2 Q.B. 158 CA: facts at para.49-030, below.

20 [1969] 2 Q.B. 158 CA at 168.

21 [1989] 1 W.L.R. 1 CA.

22 [1989] 1 W.L.R. 1 CA at 6B–D.

23 [1997] A.C. 254.

24 See on this important case paras 49-014 and following, below.

measure; this was the position in *Doyle v Olby (Ironmongers)*[25] itself. Beyond this too, as has now been firmly endorsed by the House of Lords in *Smith New Court Securities v Scrimgeour Vickers*,[26] with deceit, in contradistinction to tort generally, the damages need not have been reasonably foreseeable[27]; this takes one well beyond the contractual test of contemplation of the parties.[28]

## 2. HEADS OF DAMAGE

### (1) Pecuniary loss

The principal, and generally the only, recovery in deceit is for pecuniary loss: this may reflect its close connection with contractual situations. Generally, the manner in which the claimant acts to his detriment in reliance on the misrepresentation is to enter into a contract with the defendant or with third parties; in the great majority of cases in the past the contract is one by which the claimant becomes a buyer of shares. Where a contract results in this way, a return may be made to the terminology of normal measure of damages and consequential losses.[29] **49-007**

**(a) Where the claimant has contracted to buy shares** On the issue of damages, it is immaterial whether the defendant's misrepresentation has induced the claimant to buy shares from the defendant himself or from some third party. Indeed where the purchase is from the company issuing the shares,[30] the action for damages was formerly of little use against the company by reason of the rule in *Houldsworth v City of Glasgow Bank*.[31] This rule forbid an action for damages against the company where the claimant has also affirmed his contract of purchase of the shares; and if he rescinded the contract he would generally be restored to his position prior to the representation, so that there was no loss that he could claim by suing in the tort of deceit. Thus in such circumstances the action for damages was most useful against the directors of the company, who are strictly third parties as far as the contract is concerned, but are equally tortfeasors with the company where they have made the misrepresentation to the claimant. However, the rule in *Houldsworth* has gone, having been legislatively reversed in 1989.[32] **49-008**

25 [1969] 2 Q.B. 158 CA.

26 [1997] A.C. 254.

27 See this case at para.49-014, below. In *Noble Resources SA v Gross* [2009] EWHC 1435 (Comm), where losses on unauthorised speculative trading in aluminium futures were made, and concealed, by two employees of the claimant companies, it was accepted that damages in deceit went beyond recovery for foreseeable loss (at [222]), thereby allowing an award of damages in many millions: see the computation at [224]–[227]. There were also claims in conspiracy and for breach of the contract of employment.

28 After the House of Lords decision in *Sempra Metals Ltd v Inland Revenue Commissioners* [2008] A.C. 561 there should be no remaining distinction between deceit and breach of contract as far as compound interest is concerned. See paras 19-058 and following, especially the fraud cases at para.19-068, above.

29 Completion of the contract by the claimant after knowledge of the misrepresentation does not preclude him from claiming damages for the misrepresentation: see the last footnote in para.49-054, below for negligent misrepresentation.

30 The cases practically all deal with purchases by allotment by the company and not by transfer from an existing shareholder.

31 (1880) 5 App. Cas. 317.

32 Companies Act 1985 s.111A, inserted by Companies Act 1989 s.131(1) and superseded by Companies Act 2006 s.655, enacted that a person is not to be debarred from obtaining damages or

**49-009** Indeed many of the decisions are not cases of common law deceit but actions under statutes imposing liability for misstatements or omissions in company prospectuses or by company directors,[33] but it has always been accepted, and indeed has been authoritatively stated by Lord Atkin in *Clark v Urquhart*,[34] that the measure of damages in the statutory claim "is precisely the same as in an action of deceit".[35]

**49-010** *(i) Normal measure* The normal measure of damages is the purchase price[36] of the shares less their actual value, if any,[37] at the time of acquisition.[38] For these purposes the time at which the value of the shares is to be taken is the date of allotment in the case of an issue of shares from the company, and the date of contract in the case of a transfer of shares from an existing shareholder. Transfer is illustrated by *Smith New Court Securities v Scrimgeour Vickers*,[39] but the cases practically all deal with allotment where, as Joyce J said in *Stevens v Hoare*,[40]

> "in practice, as a matter of convenience, the date is taken to be that of the day after the posting of the notice of allotment".[41]

---

other compensation from a company by reason of holding shares in the company.

33 In particular under s.38 of the Companies Act 1867 and under s.3 of the Directors Liability Act 1890. The latter provision has been substantially re-enacted from time to time, first as s.84 of the Companies (Consolidation) Act 1908, later as s.37 of the Companies Act 1929 and s.43 of the Companies Act 1948, and ending up with s.67 of the Companies Act 1985. This last section was repealed by the Financial Services Act 1986 s.150 of which took its place; s.150 now appears as s.90 of the Financial Services and Markets Act 2000.

34 [1930] A.C. 28.

35 [1930] A.C. 28 at 67. Cases in which the claimant has been awarded damages on a statutory claim are *Twycross v Grant* (1877) 2 C.P.D. 469 CA; *Cackett v Keswick* [1902] 2 Ch. 456 CA; *McConnell v Wright* [1903] 1 Ch. 546 CA; *Broome v Speak* [1903] 1 Ch. 586 CA (affirmed sub nom. *Shepheard v Broome* [1904] A.C. 342); and *Clark v Urquhart* [1930] A.C. 28. Indeed the three early cases of common law deceit illustrating the measure of damages were all reversed, on the defendant's appeal, on the issue of liability, i.e. *Arkwright v Newbold* (1881) 17 Ch. D. 301 (reversed CA); *Peek v Derry* (1887) 37 Ch. D. 541 CA (reversed sub nom. *Derry v Peek* (1889) 14 App. Cas. 337); and *Glasier v Rolls* (1889) 42 Ch. D. 436 (reversed CA).

36 Not only the price paid to the buyer but also the expense to the seller in making the sale fall to be included, as in *4 Eng Ltd v Harper* [2009] Ch. 91 where the seller's professional costs and stamp duty were included with the purchase price paid: see at [21].

37 If the shares have no value the claimant may recover as damages the purchase price, as in *Twycross v Grant* (1877) 2 C.P.D. 467 CA; *Bottin International Investments Ltd v Venson Group Plc* [2006] EWHC 3112 Ch and *4 Eng Ltd v Harper* [2009] Ch.91.

38 This measure is based on the very likely assumption that had the claimant known the true facts he would never have bought the shares. Were it possible to show, as the defendants tried unsuccessfully to show at first instance in *Smith New Court Securities v Scrimgeour Vickers* [1992] B.C.L.C. 1104, that in the absence of the representation the claimant would have been able to buy, and would have bought, the shares but at a lower figure, then the measure would become the difference between the price the buyer paid and the price he would have paid. This appears to be implicitly accepted in the judgment at first instance in *Smith New Court*: see at 1133i to 1135b; the point is not touched upon in the Court of Appeal ([1994] 1 W.L.R. 1271) or in the House of Lords ([1997] A.C. 254).

39 [1997] A.C. 254. Although the House of Lords held that it was here inappropriate to use the contract price (see para.49-014, below), Chadwick J at first instance ([1992] B.C.L.C. 1104) had thought that it was, so that, with the agreement to buy on 21 July (at 1106g) and the share transfer on 7 August (at 1106i), the value upon which he had to decide was that on 21 July (at 1146g).

40 (1904) 20 T.L.R. 407.

41 (1904) 20 T.L.R. 407 at 409. Contrast *Peek v Derry* (1887) 37 Ch. D. 541 CA at 592–3, ("the real value is to be ascertained immediately after the day when the shares were allotted to the plaintiff"); *Cackett v Keswick* [1902] 2 Ch. 456 at 468 ("the actual value of the shares on the day after they were

This measure was established[42] by the Court of Appeal decision in *Peek v Derry*,[43] and in subsequent cases,[44] of which *McConnell v Wright*,[45] is the most important, it has been considered to be well settled[46]; it is thought not to be right to read the House of Lords in *Smith New Court Securities v Scrimgeour Vickers*,[47] as saying that these early cases are wrong in stating the normal measure thus. What their Lordships were there concerned to emphasise was that this was not an inflexible rule never to be departed from, which was something that the reversed Court of Appeal, rather than the early cases, had appeared to indicate. Lord Steyn said: **49-011**

> "It is right that the normal method of calculating the loss caused by the deceit is the price paid less the real value of the subject-matter of the sale. To the extent that this method is adopted, the selection of a date of valuation is necessary. And generally the date of the transaction would be a practical and just date to adopt."[48]

But, he added, this will not always be so, as it was not in *Smith New Court*.[49] Similarly, Lord Browne-Wilkinson, in setting out a series of principles to apply in the assessment of damages in deceit, started the fourth in his series with:

> "As a general rule, the benefits received by [the claimant] include the market value of the property acquired as at the date of acquisition."[50]

But, he went on, such general rule is not to be inflexibly applied[51]; it was inappropriate for *Smith New Court*, as we shall see.[52]

It was also inappropriate for *Halston Holdings SA v Simons*.[53] The claimant bought shares in a company relying on the defendant's false and fraudulent certificate of the level of inter-group indebtedness included in the assets of the company, the level given being about £1 million lower than its actual level. A year after the purchase the company collapsed and went into administration. Had the **49-012**

allotted to the plaintiff").

42 It had already been announced in *Davidson v Tulloch* (1860) 3 Macq. 783 HL at 790 by Lord Campbell LC, and restated and applied in *Twycross v Grant* (1877) 2 C.P.D. 469 CA (see especially at 545) and in *Arkwright v Newbold* (1881) 17 Ch. D. 301 (see at 312; reversed, CA, on the issue of liability).

43 (1887) 37 Ch. D. 541 CA. The celebrated reversal of this decision by the House of Lords, sub nom. *Derry v Peek* (1889) 14 App. Cas. 337, was on the issue of liability.

44 Other cases stating and applying the rule in the text are *Glasier v Rolls* (1889) 42 Ch. D. 436, especially at 455 (reversed, CA, on the issue of liability); *Cackett v Keswick* [1902] 2 Ch. 456, especially at 468 (affirmed, CA, but without any specific reference to damages). Both parties accepted the correctness of this measure in *Clark v Urquhart* [1930] A.C. 28: see at 32 and 67.

45 [1903] 1 Ch. 546 CA.

46 *McConnell v Wright* [1903] 1 Ch. 546 CA at 554 ("there is no doubt about it now"); *Broome v Speak* [1903] 1 Ch. 586 CA at 605, 623 ("well fixed"); *Stevens v Hoare* (1904) 20 T.L.R. 407 at 409 ("well settled"). Compare at first instance *Smith New Court Securities v Scrimgeour Vickers* [1992] B.C.L.C. 1104 at 1135b –c ("common ground").

47 [1997] A.C. 254.

48 [1997] A.C. 254 at 284A. Thus in *Bottin International Investments Ltd v Venson Group Plc* [2006] EWHC 3112 Ch, a case largely taken up with issues other than damages, there was held to be no good reason why damages should be assessed at any later date than the date when the investment in shares was induced by fraud: see at [410] and 411]. The shares being held to be valueless at that date, the full purchase price of £10 million was recoverable as damages: at [417].

49 See para.49-014, below.

50 [1997] A.C. 254 at 267B.

51 [1997] A.C. 254 at 267B.

52 See para.49-014, below.

53 [2005] EWHC 30 (QB).

certificate not been signed and produced the claimant would not have entered into or completed the agreement to purchase and would not have lost all of its investment. The damages awarded for the loss on the shares represented their full purchase price without any deduction, since the shares had no real value at the time of the purchase and the claimant had had no opportunity to realise its investment before the company's collapse. Like the racehorse which has a latent disease when sold and later dies from the disease, where one does not ignore the death—this comes from a useful illustration of Cockburn CJ in *Twycross v Grant*[54]—the company which collapsed was already ill at the time of the purchase of the shares by the claimant.[55]

**49-013** An important point, because peculiar to shares, is that care must be taken not to assess the value of the shares at the price at which they stand in the market, since such a price may be a false and artificial one induced by the very deceit of which the claimant is complaining. Lord Coleridge CJ put the matter thus in *Twycross v Grant*,[56] at first instance:

> "The fact that they were quoted at premium on the Stock Exchange is only evidence of value, not proof of it; and if the jury thought … that the quotation on the Stock Exchange did not show a real, but only a delusive value caused by the fraudulent nature of the prospectus and the mode in which the shares were manipulated by the defendants and others in concert with them, the jury were not only justified in disregarding, but were bound to disregard, such delusive and factitious value … There is no evidence whatever that the shares ever had any value except that which resulted from the wrongful acts of the defendants; and it would be contrary to all principle to allow them to take advantage of their own wrong, and claim credit for the market price of the shares, when but for their own concealment of the contracts in question there is no reason to suppose that the shares would have had any market value at all."[57]

The actual value is, therefore, the price the shares would fetch in the market if the truth concealed by the defendant's fraud was revealed and all the facts thus concealed were known. This was fully accepted in *Smith New Court Securities v Scrimgeour Vickers*,[58] a case now to be considered. Lord Browne-Wilkinson said there that

> "it was common ground that there was one exception to this general rule [namely, that the normal measure is contract price less value at purchase]: where the open market at the transaction date was a false market, in the sense that the price was inflated because of a misrepresentation made to the market generally *by the defendant*, the market value is not decisive: in such circumstances the 'true' value as at the transaction date has to be ascertained but with the benefit of hindsight."[59]

---

[54] (1877) 2 C.P.D. 469 at 544; the illustration was indeed cited as instructive by Stanley Burnton J in *Halston*: see at [85]. Contrast the position where Cockburn CJ's racehorse catches a fatal disease *after* the sale: see at para.49-016, below. Racehorses and their sale feature again, in the context of negligent misrepresentation, in *Naughton v O'Callaghan* [1990] 3 All E.R. 191 at para.49-059, below.

[55] See *Halston* at [93] and the whole discussion of damages at [2005] EWHC 30 (QB) at [84] to [97].

[56] (1877) 2 C.P.D. 469.

[57] (1877) 2 C.P.D. 469 at 489 to 490. The point is also made, more shortly, in *Peek v Derry* (1887) 37 Ch. D. 541 CA at 591–592 per Cotton LJ, and in *Broome v Speak* [1903] 1 Ch. 586 CA at 605–606, per Buckley J.

[58] [1997] A.C. 254.

[59] [1997] A.C. 254 at 261F; his Lordship's italics.

In *Smith New Court*,[60] the House of Lords decided that the case before it was an inappropriate one for adopting the value of the shares at the time of their acquisition. The claimants bought shares in the Ferranti company from the defendants induced by the defendants' agent's fraudulent statement that other persons were interested in acquiring the shares. The shares were bought by the claimants as a market-making risk—namely with the intention of holding them for sale at a later date—and at a price which they would only have paid for an acquisition as a market-making risk. Subsequently there was a serious decline in the value of the Ferranti shares as a result of the disclosure that a fraud, unrelated to and occurring in advance of the purchase, had been perpetrated on the company, and the claimants eventually, over a five to six month period, sold the shares at a substantial loss. Their Lordships held, reversing the Court of Appeal and restoring Chadwick J below but on a different basis, that for the assessment of the claimants' damages what fell to be deducted from the purchase price was not the value of the shares, either at the date of acquisition or indeed at any other date, but the proceeds of the claimants' subsequent realisations of the shares, the court accepting that the claimants had acted reasonably in retaining the shares for as long as they did and in reselling them in the manner in which they did. For the claimants to be compensated adequately it was necessary to depart from what Lord Browne-Wilkinson called the transaction date rule because the fraud had continued to influence the claimants after the shares were acquired and because the claimants in the particular circumstances of their purchase were locked into continuing to hold the shares. **49-014**

How far does this decision of the House of Lords in *Smith New Court* take the law? How often will it be appropriate, in arriving at the correct measure of damages, to deduct from the price paid the price of eventual resale rather than the more usual value at the date of the acquisition? A vital aspect of *Smith New Court* was that the fraud by the third party had taken place before the sale to the claimants so that, to take a well-known phrase from another context, the shares were doomed from the start[61] or, to use Lord Browne-Wilkinson's words, "the shares were already pregnant with disaster".[62] Lord Steyn said categorically that **49-015**

> "the position would have been different if the loss suffered by Smith arose from a subsequent fraud","[63]

while Lord Browne-Wilkinson emphasised that

> "the loss was incurred by reason of the purchasing of the shares which were pregnant with the loss".[64]

In *Smith New Court*,[65] it was the fraud perpetrated by the third party which was primarily responsible for the substantial loss suffered by the claimants; the defendants' fraud on its own would have made no great difference between the price paid for the shares and either their true value at acquisition or the prices at which the claimants would eventually have been able to sell. Thus had the fraud of the third

---

60 [1997] A.C. 254.

61 Contrast *Pirelli General Cable Works v Oscar Faber & Partners* [1983] 2 A.C. 1 in the context of a latent defect in a building.

62 [1997] A.C. 254 at 267G.

63 [1997] A.C. 254 at 285F.

64 [1997] A.C. 254 at 267H.

65 [1997] A.C. 254.

party causing the massive downturn in the share prices appeared on the scene after the claimants' acquisition, it would seem that their Lordships would not have held the defendants liable for the resultant loss to the claimants, the value at the date of the acquisition would have been an appropriate value to take and the result reached by the Court of Appeal[66] would have been justified.

**49-016** While Lord Steyn distinguished the specific case of a subsequent fraud, Lord Browne-Wilkinson, more generally, distinguished from the case before the court the

> "case of the difficult kind ... where the depreciation in the asset acquired between the date of acquisition and the date of realisation may be due to factors affecting the market which have occurred after the date of the defendant's fraud".[67]

Just as one does not take into account, or ignores, the death of a racehorse from disease caught after its sale—this again comes from Cockburn CJ's useful illustration in *Twycross v Grant*[68]—so it would seem that their Lordships would not be prepared to protect the claimant if the shares were, as one might say, subsequently to catch a disease and, though not killed off, deteriorate. This is a conclusion which is supported by earlier authority. Cotton LJ had pointed out in *Peek v Derry*,[69] that the claimant could not

> "get the benefit of any loss or depreciation in the shares which was occasioned by subsequent acts",[70]

giving as an illustration the passing of an Act of Parliament prohibiting the running of steam tramways, which was the enterprise upon which the company had intended to embark in that case. Further, in another important Victorian case, *Waddell v Blockey*,[71] where the claimant bought the defendant's rupee paper under a fraudulent misrepresentation by the defendant that he was buying rupee paper for the claimant in the market, and the value of rupee paper afterwards deteriorated considerably, it was held that the measure of damages was not the loss sustained by the claimant on his ultimate resale some six months later, but the difference between the price he paid and the price he would have received had he resold the rupee paper in the market immediately after purchasing it.[72] No attempt has so far been made by the courts to compensate claimants for a fall in the market on the basis that but for the fraud they would not have bought at all and would therefore

---

66 [1994] 1 W.L.R. 1271 CA.

67 [1997] A.C. 254 at 267G–H.

68 (1877) 2 C.P.D. 469 at 544–545; an illustration cited as instructive by Lord Steyn in *Smith New Court* [1997] A.C. 254 at 279B. Contrast the position where Cockburn CJ's racehorse already has a latent disease *before* the sale: see at para.47-012, above. Racehorses and their sale feature again, in the context of negligent misrepresentation, in *Naughton v O'Callaghan* [1990] 3 All E.R. 191 at para.47-056, below.

69 (1887) 37 Ch. D. 541 CA.

70 (1887) 37 Ch. D. 541 CA at 592. See, similarly, *Broome v Speak* [1903] 1 Ch. 586 at 605 CA, per Buckley J.

71 (1879) 4 Q.B.D. 678 CA.

72 Whether an increase in the value of the shares in the manner in which this came about in *McConnell v Wright* [1903] 1 Ch. 546 CA should be left out of account is thought to be more doubtful. In that case it was held, where the claimant had applied for and obtained shares on the faith of misrepresentations in a prospectus that the company had already acquired a valuable property, that the fact that the property was acquired shortly afterwards afforded no answer to the claimant's claim for damages, unless it could have been shown that at the date of allotment the risk that the property would not be acquired was insubstantial.

not have had the fallen shares on their hands; they might of course have bought other shares which would also have suffered from the general market decline.[73]

In contrast to *Smith New Court*, the claimant company in *Invertec Ltd v De Mol Holding BV*,[74] was held not to have been locked into continuing to hold the share capital of a company which it had been induced to purchase by fraudulent representations as to the company's value and solvency. The claimant was entitled to recover in damages its entire purchase consideration as, but for the fraud, it would not have bought valueless share capital but it could not recover the loans that it had made to the company in order to keep it trading, loans which were now lost to it by reason of the company's insolvency. The decision to keep the company trading was a commercial one and a gamble which did not pay off.[75] The company was not locked into its shareholding, having two exit routes. It could have rescinded the contract or it could have allowed the company to go into administration or liquidation.[76] **49-017**

Three further points have been dealt with by the cases. The law as it stood on each does not appear to have been adversely affected by anything which their Lordships have said in *Smith New Court Securities v Scrimgeour Vickers*.[77] **49-018**

First, subsequent events may be used as evidence of the value at the time the claimant acquired the shares: this possibility is particularly important in view of the fact that the price on the market at that time may be of little utility in assessing damages because it is a falsely inflated price, the defendant's fraud apart. This point was also made by Cotton LJ in *Peek v Derry*.[78] "Although the value of the shares", he said, **49-019**

> "is not to be ascertained at the subsequent period so as to take into account for the benefit of the plaintiff events subsequent which depreciated their value, yet those events, if they show that the company was originally, with the capital which it had got, a company which was worthless, may, in my opinion, be taken into account as evidence of what was the value of the shares immediately after they were allotted to the plaintiff".[79]

And in particular he added that

> "if there is no better evidence, the result of the winding up of the company and the amount which will be returnable to the shareholders may be taken into account".[80]

On the other hand, this does not mean that subsequent events will always be relevant for the purpose of quantifying damages. In *OMV Petrom SA v Glencore* **49-020**

---

73 In *Wm Sindall Plc v Cambridgeshire CC* [1994] 1 W.L.R. 1016 CA, a case of innocent misrepresentation, neither Evans LJ nor Hoffmann LJ was prepared to address the question whether a tortious measure of damages could take account of a fall in market values: see at 1046D and 1038F respectively; but Evans LJ commented that the judgments of Bingham LJ and Sir Nicolas Browne-Wilkinson VC in *Cemp Properties (UK) v Dentsply Research Corp* [1991] 2 E.G.L.R. 197 CA, a case of negligent misrepresentation, appeared to be against taking a subsequent market fall into account: see [1994] 1 W.L.R. 1016 at 1044A to B. Contrast *Naughton v O'Callaghan* [1990] 3 All E.R. 191, also a case of negligent misrepresentation, at para.49-059, below.

74 [2009] EWHC 2471 Ch.

75 And it could not be regarded as a step taken in mitigation.

76 See [2009] EWHC 2471 Ch 378 and following.

77 [1997] A.C. 254.

78 (1887) 37 Ch. D. 541 CA.

79 (1887) 37 Ch. D. 541 CA at 592.

80 (1887) 37 Ch. D. 541 CA at 593.

*International AG*,[81] the party which committed the fraud attempted to rely on subsequent events to show that the real value of the product was not substantially eroded by the fraudulent misrepresentations. Glencore supplied oil to Petrom which resembled the type of oil which it had promised to supply but which was actually a cheaper substitute. Glencore created a suite of false documents to conceal its deceit. Petrom claimed as damages the price that it had paid of around US $434 million less the value of the oil at the date it was supplied. The trial judge awarded around US $40 million. The value of the oil was discounted to reflect the fact that a purchaser would not pay the value of an untried blend which could affect the machinery, or cause rust or fire. Glencore submitted that since nothing untoward occurred, any discount is inappropriate because to allow a discount would be to compensate Petrom for a loss which it might have suffered but did not.[82] In the Court of Appeal, Christopher Clarke LJ (with whom Kitchin and Black LJJ agreed) rejected this submission on the basis that the failure of the risk to materialise after the date of acquisition of the oil was to be disregarded. One reason for this was that otherwise Glencore could recover a price which it would not have recovered if it had been honest. In any event, evidence of a lack of deleterious consequences was a matter for Glencore to prove if it asserted that none had arisen.[83]

**49-021** Secondly, the damages are not to be reduced because the claimant might have sold the shares before the fraud was discovered at a price above their real value. As Lord Coleridge CJ said in *Twycross v Grant*[84]:

> "The defendants are not entitled to say to the plaintiff, 'You might have sold your shares to someone as ignorant as yourself, or to some speculator in shares.' The plaintiff was not bound to sell; and, after he discovered the fraud, he could not sell."[85]

In stating this established rule in *Smith New Court Securities v Scrimgeour*,[86] at first instance Chadwick J did include the qualification "unless, in choosing to retain the shares, he has acted unreasonably or imprudently"[87] but it is difficult to see in what circumstances retention until the fraud is discovered and the price drops would be unreasonable or imprudent. Certainly, it would be improper for the claimant, once apprised of the fraud, to sell on before the knowledge had reached the market.

**49-022** Thirdly, where the claimant does sell the shares, early dicta put forward the view that he must bring the selling price into account.[88] It is true that this does not follow the general principle that the price at which a buyer resells is only evidence of value,[89] but the result is justified because the position is sufficiently special with shares at a falsely inflated value. This principle of giving credit for the resale price where higher than the market value was indeed accepted by Chadwick J at first

---

81 [2016] EWCA Civ 778.

82 [2016] EWCA Civ 778 at [31].

83 *The Andros Springs and The World Beauty* [1970] P. 144 CA at 154; *Midco Holdings v Piper* [2004] EWCA Civ 476.

84 (1877) 2 C.P.D. 469.

85 (1877) 2 C.P.D. 469 at 490. Contrast *Peek v Derry* (1887) 37 Ch. D. 541 CA at 593, per Cotton LJ ("it cannot be unreasonable on the part of a purchaser not to sell").

86 [1992] B.C.L.C. 1104.

87 [1992] B.C.L.C. 1104 at 1143g.

88 *Twycross v Grant* (1877) 2 C.P.D. 469 at 489, per Lord Coleridge CJ; *Peek v Derry* (1887) 37 Ch. D. 541 CA at 593, per Cotton LJ.

89 Compare the equivalent breach of warranty cases in the sale of goods at paras 25-065 and 25-066, above.

instance in *Smith New Court Securities v Scrimgeour*[90]; it did not have to be applied by him there because the claimant had sold the shares at a price which proved to be below what he, Chadwick J, held to be their market value at the time of the claimant's acquisition.[91]

*(ii) Consequential losses* The wealth of authority on measure of damages disappears when it comes to consequential losses. Indeed the measure as stated in the cases dealt with in relation to normal measure would exclude consequential losses entirely. It is submitted that it is for this reason that Lord Atkin in *Clark v Urquhart*,[92] suggested that the rule as stated in *McConnell v Wright*,[93] "may be expressed in too rigid terms".[94] In his view the measure of damages should be "based on the actual damage directly flowing from the fraudulent inducement".[95] This formulation would easily include consequential losses, and the propriety of recovery for such losses is supported by the decisions where the conclusion of contracts other than for the purchase of shares has been induced by the deceit[96]; support is also derived from the expanding number of cases where negligent misrepresentation has brought about the conclusion of contracts and where it is now established that the same tortious measure applies as with deceit.[97] **49-023**

Recovery for consequential losses also received direct support from the decision in *Archer v Brown*,[98] although the terminology of consequential loss is not there used. The claimant was an accountant in his early fifties who had given up his employment with the intention of setting up business on his own account. He answered an advertisement of the defendant and the upshot was that the defendant induced him, by means of fraudulent representations, to conclude two agreements by which the defendant purported to sell to him for £30,000 all the shares in a company in which in reality the defendant owned no shares. The claimant took out two loans from two different branches of Barclays Bank in order to pay for the shares and entered into a service agreement with the company under which he was to be managing director. In his action for damages for deceit the normal measure was represented by the whole of the £30,000 purchase price since no shares had been received in return.[99] But beyond this the court rightly allowed recovery of the substantial amounts of bank interest which the claimant had been required to pay on the two loans. The defendant was aware that, in order to raise the purchase price of the shares he was selling to the claimant, the claimant was going to have to borrow from banks, and the loss by way of interest payable was therefore held, distinguishing *The Liesbosch*,[100] and its impecuniosity rule,[101] to be a reasonably foreseeable one. In dealing with reasonable foreseeability the judge commented that **49-024**

90 [1992] B.C.L.C. 1104. Contrast *Hussey v Eels* [1990] 2 Q.B. 227 CA (negligent misrepresentation and a purchase of land) at para.9-143 above.
91 See [1992] B.C.L.C. 1104 at 1148d.
92 [1930] A.C. 28.
93 [1903] 1 Ch. 546 CA: i.e. price paid less actual value.
94 [1930] A.C. 28 at 68.
95 [1930] A.C. 28 at 68.
96 See paras 49-029 to 49-033, below.
97 See paras 49-061 to 49-064, below.
98 [1985] Q.B. 401.
99 [1985] Q.B. 401 at 415E.
100 [1933] A.C. 449.
101 Which has now been abandoned.

"it must have been plain to the defendant that his deceit was putting the claimant in a position where he could not repay the bank",[102]

but this really misses the point; what is relevant is that, but for the deceit, the claimant would not have taken out the loans and therefore would not have become indebted in the first place. The claimant was also awarded a small amount of damages for his loss of employment with the company and for his expenses in seeking out new employment once the fraud had been uncovered.[103] But if the deceit had not been perpetrated he would never have had an employment with the company and he would still have had to look for new employment as he had already given up his former position before the defendant came on the scene. There seems in all this to be a lingering tendency to have regard, despite *Doyle v Olby (Ironmongers)*,[104] to the position as if the representations had been true rather than to the position as if they had never been made.[105]

**49-025** Recovery for consequential loss again appears in *4 Eng Ltd v Harper*.[106] The defendants sold to the claimant company the entire issued share capital in a company owned by them. The shares in the company, which provided engineering services, turned out to be worthless so that the claimant realised nothing from its investment. The two consequential losses for which recovery was allowed were of a very different nature. In the first place, having found that the fraud had had to be unravelled and that discovering the extent of the defendants' fraudulent activity had been a complicated and time-consuming task for the claimant company's directors, David Richards J held the claimant entitled to be reimbursed for the compensation paid by it to the directors for this work.[107] In the second place, David Richards J applied the important decision of the Court of Appeal in *East v Maurer*,[108] which concerned the purchase of a business rather than of shares and therefore is dealt with later,[109] so as to allow recovery for the loss of both income and capital profits which the claimant would have expected to make from the acquisition of the substitute company which, in the absence of the defendants' fraudulent misrepresentations, it would have bought. However, whereas in *East v Maurer* the court had in mind only a hypothetical business to be purchased, in the instant case the claimant had a specific substitute company in mind. This therefore led to the making of a discount to reflect the chance that the owners of this company would not have been prepared to sell to the claimant, David Richards J rightly holding that the vagaries of the loss of a chance doctrine applied to deceit as much as to negligence.[110] This issue is dealt with elsewhere.[111]

---

102 [1985] Q.B. 401 at 417H–418A.

103 [1985] Q.B. 401 at 426H–427D.

104 [1969] 2 Q.B. 158 CA.

105 See paras 49-002 and following, above. Two other items of claim, for expenses of the sale of property used as security for one of the loans and for certain solicitors' expenses, appear to have been properly disallowed: see [1985] Q.B. 401 at 427E–G.

106 [2009] Ch.91.

107 The judge stressed, at [2009] Ch.91 at [40], that his award was not, as was the award in *Aerospace Publishing Ltd v Thames Water Utilities Ltd* (2007) 110 Con. L.R.1 CA (at para.37-014, above), for disruption of business through loss of management time.

108 [1991] 1 W.L.R. 461 CA.

109 See at para.49-031, below.

110 [2009] Ch.91 at [44].

111 See para.10-093, above.

**(b) Where the claimant has contracted to sell shares** After the copious cases of contracts for the purchase of shares induced by the seller's misrepresentation, *Platt v Platt*,[112] has at last provided an illustration of a contract for a sale of shares induced by the purchaser's misrepresentation. A seller transferred valuable preference shares to a buyer for £1 under the influence of representations which appear to have been fraudulent.[113] The measure of damages applied was the normal measure, here represented by the value of the shares at the time of their sale less the nominal price paid. The fact that the shares had increased in value over the years between sale and trial was left upon one side largely to avoid complications in the valuation; even valuation at the time of sale proved difficult in the face of the experts' substantial disagreement.[114] The Court of Appeal affirmed[115] with the value of the shares at the date of transfer again being taken for the computation, but with a disagreement, highly elaborated upon in the judgments, upon the proper method of that computation. **49-026**

**(c) Where the contract is other than for shares** As with share contracts so with contracts not involving shares: practically all of the cases feature contracts of purchase by the claimant. Occasionally the claimant may be a seller,[116] or he may have contracted for services.[117] In this type of case, as will be seen, the concentration has been upon consequential losses rather than upon normal measure. **49-027**

*(i) Normal measure* The normal measure of damages is the value transferred, generally represented by the contract price, less the value received, whether of property or of services or of money. For long there were no clear, direct illustrations of the application of this measure outside the cases concerning misrepresentations which induce the claimant to buy or sell shares.[118] In earlier editions reliance was placed upon the principles worked out in the share cases applying mutatis mutandis where some other contract has been entered into as a result of the deceit,[119] with citations of Lord Atkin in *Clark v Urquhart*,[120] that **49-028**

---

112 [1999] 2 B.C.L.C. 745.

113 The trial judge described the representations as "at the least, negligent ones".

114 How the trial judge arrived at his valuation is at [1999] 2 B.C.L.C. 745, 757–759.

115 [2001] B.C.L.C. 698 CA.

116 As in *Dadourian Group International Inc v Simms (Damages)* [2009] 1 Lloyd's Rep. 601 CA. See the case at paras 49-032 and 49-035, below.

117 As in *AIC Ltd v ITS Testing Services (UK) Ltd* [2006] 1 Lloyd's Rep.1. The deceit lay in the false reporting by an inspection company of the quality testing of a cargo which the claimant company had bought and was selling on. The damages awarded, which covered the claimant's liability to its purchaser together with various further costs and expenses incurred, are dealt with at [336]–[348] of the judgment. The Court of Appeal held that deceit had not been made out, so did not turn to damages: [2007] 1 Lloyd's Rep. 555 CA.

118 Only the old case of *Pearson v Wheeler* (1825) Ry. & M. 303 could be put forward as an example. A public house was sold with fraudulent misrepresentations as to the amount of business done, and it was held that evidence on the part of the defendant of the actual value of the house's takings was admissible to reduce the damages. Abbott CJ stated the measure of damages as "the difference between the real value of the property and the sum which the plaintiff was induced to give for it": at 304.

119 Thus Cockburn CJ's example in *Twycross v Grant* (1877) 2 C.P.D. 469 at 544–545 CA, of a horse fraudulently sold as a great racehorse and subsequently dying, as illustrative of how far later events are relevant in assessing the damages, is exactly parallel in result with the position in relation to shares dealt with at paras 49-014 to 49-016, above.

120 [1930] A.C. 28 at 68.

> "whether a man buys shares or buys sugar, whether he subscribes for shares, or agrees to enter into a partnership … the measure of damages should be the same";

and of Lord Steyn in *Smith New Court Securities v Scrimgeour Vickers*,[121] that "the same legal principle must govern sales of shares, goods, a business or land."[122] Now, however, we have *Butler-Creagh v Hersham*,[123] where a company had been induced to buy a large property for £25 million by fraudulent misrepresentations as to its value and to the cost of its development, and value transferred less contract price was awarded. Without the assistance of a resale price, the property having been retained, there was difficulty in reaching a figure for value.[124] Also, value was taken at the time of contract following the normal rule, the judge seeing no reason to adopt a later date as had been allowed in appropriate circumstances by the House of Lords in the context of share sales.[125]

**49-029** *(ii) Consequential losses* With consequential losses on the other hand, the preponderance of authority lies with actions where the contract into which the claimant has been induced to enter is other than for the purchase of shares. A variety of early cases illustrate that consequential losses are recoverable in the normal way, always provided that they are not too remote. Thus the claimant may recover for damage to the property bought by him as a result of the deceit. In *Clarke v Yorke*,[126] where the defendant induced the claimant to take a 14-year lease of a farm by a fraudulent misrepresentation that the land was thoroughly drained, the claimant recovered for the "heavy damage owing to want of proper drainage".[127] Also there may be recovery for damage to other property of the claimant, as *Mullett v Mason*[128] shows. The defendant induced the claimant farmer to buy a cow by fraudulently misrepresenting that she was free from foot and mouth disease. The claimant placed the cow with others, and a number of them, including the cow sold, died from the disease. The defendant was held liable for the entire loss.[129] Similarly, expenses incurred may constitute a recoverable consequential loss. Thus in *Milne v Marwood*,[130] where the claimant bought a ship which he intended to use, as the defendant seller knew, for the Australian trade and started to effect the repairs necessary for this route, it was accepted that the money thrown away in these repairs, which were useless as the ship was not suitable for the Australian trade, formed a proper head of damages.[131] In *Denton v Great Northern Ry*,[132] an evening train of

---

[121] [1997] A.C. 254 at 279A.

[122] It was also pointed out that, it having been established that the tortious measure of damages is the appropriate measure for the statutory liability for negligent misrepresentation inducing a contract (see para.49-053, below) as well as for the common law liability, the cases which have been developing on negligent misrepresentation (see paras 49-058 and 49-060, below) can also be applied by way of analogy.

[123] [2011] EWHC 2525 (QB).

[124] [2011] EWHC 2525 (QB) at [104] and following.

[125] See para.49-014 above.

[126] (1882) 47 L.T. 381.

[127] (1882) 47 L.T. 381 at 381.

[128] (1866) L.R. 1 C.P. 559.

[129] It is not clear whether the defendant knew that the claimant was a farmer, but the court appears to have assumed that the defendant must have assumed that the cow sold would be placed with others. Compare *Smith v Green* (1876) 1 C.P.D. 92, where on similar facts this point was considered in an action in contract for breach of warranty: see para.25-083, above.

[130] (1855) 15 C.B. 778.

[131] This really only appears in argument.

the defendant railway company ran only part of the advertised route. The claimant who, relying on the advertised schedule which the defendant knew was false, had contracted for carriage to the terminus was consequently set down short of his destination and did not reach there until the following morning. He successfully claimed in deceit[133] for damage he had suffered, although it is not made clear in what the damage consisted. Probably it was the expense of staying overnight at the place where he was put down; also, he missed a morning appointment at his destination.

These early decisions were confirmed, in effect, for today by the decision of the Court of Appeal in *Doyle v Olby (Ironmongers)*.[134] The claimant was tricked into buying a business which he would not otherwise have bought at all, and was held entitled to recover as damages all the expenses he had as a result incurred. As Lord Denning MR put it: **49-030**

> "Mr Doyle has not only lost the money which he paid for the business, which he would never have done if there had been no fraud: he put all that money in and lost it; but also he has been put to expense and loss in trying to run a business which has turned out to be a disaster for him. He is entitled to damages for all this loss, subject, of course, to giving credit for any benefit that he has received."[135]

Lord Denning even went so far as to say that all consequential damage could be recovered, even if not reasonably foreseeable.[136] Similarly, in *Downs v Chappell*,[137] where again the claimants, who were husband and wife, were induced to buy a business by fraudulent misrepresentations of one of the defendants[138] relating to the business's profitability, they were held entitled, by the Court of Appeal reversing the court below, to recover their income and capital losses down to the time when they discovered that they had been misled. This meant that they could not claim for any loss following upon their subsequent refusal, however reasonable, of two offers of £76,000 to buy them out—they eventually sold for substantially less than £60,000—because, it was held, that by then "the causative effect of the defendants' fault was exhausted".[139] One may, however, question the correctness of this; a reasonable refusal of these offers should surely be regarded as an unsuccessful attempt to mitigate for which the claimants should not be penalised.[140] The Court of Appeal also imposed a further test; to ensure that the damages assessed were not more than an indemnity for loss in fact suffered as a result of the representations, it was necessary to compare the loss consequent upon entering into the transaction with what would have been the position had the represented state of affairs actually existed. Such a test, however, suggests the contractual rather than the tortious measure of damages; rather should the test be to compare the loss consequent upon

---

132 (1856) 5 E. & B. 860.

133 There was also a claim in contract, the success of which was more uncertain. On this the decision is now discredited.

134 [1969] 2 Q.B. 158 CA.

135 [1969] 2 Q.B. 158 CA at 167. For the details of how Winn LJ worked out the calculation of damages, see at 169–170; and see, too, his hypothetical case, at 169.

136 [1969] 2 Q.B. 158 CA at 167. On this see para.8-014, above (in a footnote).

137 [1997] 1 W.L.R. 426 CA.

138 The other defendant was liable only for negligent misrepresentation but the damages were the same against both, and were also in the particular circumstances equally divided: see para.49-051, below.

139 [1996] 3 All E.R. 344 CA at 355j.

140 See paras 9-102 to 9-106, above.

entering into the transaction with what would have been the position had the transaction not been entered into at all. However, the application of the test proposed by the court did not in the circumstances cause it to effect any reduction in the damages which had been prima facie awarded; nor probably would the application of the test here proposed have done so either.[141] In contrast to *Downs v Chappell* no limits were placed on the recovery of consequential losses in *Nationwide Building Society v Dunlop Haywards*,[142] where a valuer had fraudulently given a massive overvaluation of commercial property on the security of which the claimants were lending. Christopher Clarke J detailed a whole series of such losses for which he had no hesitation in allowing recovery,[143] including the cost of the time of management and staff in investigating the fraud, an item of loss which had already been accepted in deceit.[144]

**49-031** Principle dictates that there can be no recovery either for loss of bargain or loss of profits through the use of property or services contracted for, since these losses represent the contractual measure of damages and not the tortious, which aims at restoring the status quo ante as if the representation had never been made. That the recovery of all loss of profit is not, however, precluded by this principle is neatly and importantly illustrated by *East v Maurer*.[145] The claimants, a husband and wife, bought one of the defendant's two neighbouring hairdressing salons for use in their own hairdressing business. Because the defendant continued to work at his other salon on a regular basis, which he had falsely represented to the claimants that he would not do, the second claimant, who ran the salon, was unable to make it pay and, after three-and-a-half years, the claimants disposed of it. Having discovered the defendant's fraud they brought an action of deceit in which the trial judge, having found that they had acted reasonably throughout and could not have sold before they did, awarded them loss of anticipated profits for the three-and-a-half-year period, this being in addition to the cost of buying the business less the price realised on sale, the expenses of purchase and sale and of carrying out improvements in an attempt to make the business profitable, and the losses which had accumulated while the business was being run.[146] In the appeal by the defendant, which related only to the loss of profit, his counsel pointed out that there were no authorities awarding loss of profit and that there had been no reference in *Doyle v Olby (Ironmongers)*,[147] to loss of profit as a recoverable item in a deceit action; nevertheless the Court of Appeal upheld the award of profits although at a lower level than the trial judge had allowed. It is, however, important to identify exactly which loss of profit the court was endorsing. It was not the profits that would have been made on the business that was bought had there been no competition from the defendant and had the sales kept up at the level under the defendant's earlier management,

---

141 See [1996] 3 All E.R. 344 CA at 361h–362h.

142 [2010] 1 W.L.R. 258.

143 [2010] 1 W.L.R. 258 at [10]–[34].

144 In *4 Eng v Harper* [2009] Ch. 91 at para.49-025, above, where the contract entered into was for shares. For the recovery of a whole series of consequential losses, with *Doyle v Olby* cited, see *Kinch v Rosling* [2009] EWHC 286 (QB). Limited consequential losses, by way of various expenditures, were allowed in *Butler-Creagh v Hersham* [2011] EWHC 2525 (QB) (at [110] and following) where the property purchased was retained rather than resold (facts at para.49-028, above).

145 [1991] 1 W.L.R. 461 CA.

146 Also a small sum for distress and inconvenience, as to which see para.49-044, below.

147 [1969] 2 Q.B. 158 CA.

which was what the trial judge had wrongly awarded. Rather, in the words of Beldam LJ, the trial judge

> "should have begun by considering the kind of profit which the second claimant might have made if the representation which induced her to buy the business in Exeter Road had not been made and that involved considering the profits which *she* might have expected to make in another hairdressing business bought for a similar sum."[148]

The court was not giving the claimants the benefit of their bargain with the defendant; indeed the court was ignoring the business which they had in fact bought, and was recognising that, had the fraudulent misrepresentation not been made, the claimants would not have been saddled with the disastrous business but would have bought a similar business elsewhere in town, and it was, in Mustill LJ's words, "the profits which would have been derived from the putative new Bournemouth business"[149] that it was proper to award.

In *Dadourian Group International Inc v Simms*,[150] the claimant was a seller rather **49-032**
than a buyer. The defendant's deceit having caused the claimant to contract to sell hospital bed manufacturing equipment to a third party, the claimant sought to claim loss of profits from being deprived of entering into an alternative sale agreement with another purchaser. Dealing with the issue of damages at the end of a very long judgment,[151] Warren J without any reference to *East v Maurer* considered this to be a good head of claim, but was not prepared to admit it as he had neither evidence that an alternative sale would have been available[152] nor evidence of the value that an alternative sale would have commanded.[153] The case went to the Court of Appeal[154] but there was no appeal by the claimant on this adverse holding,[155] the appeal being on another issue on damages.[156]

*East v Maurer*,[157] was taken a step further in *Clef Aquitaine SARL v Laporte* **49-033**
*Materials (Barrow) Ltd*,[158] with the allowance there of damages representing not the profits that the claimants would have made on an alternative contract but the extra profits that, but for the fraudulent misrepresentations, they would have made on the same contract, the one into which they had been induced to enter. The claimants wished to become exclusive distributors in France of the defendants' products and to that end were negotiating two distributorship agreements, during which negotiations the defendants fraudulently represented that the discounts offered to the claimants were from the lowest prices available to trade customers. The transactions nevertheless proved profitable but would have been more profitable had there been no fraud, it being found that the claimants would have entered into the same distributorship agreements but on more favourable conditions as to price. Accordingly, the loss for which they were entitled to recover was the difference between

---

148 [1991] 1 W.L.R. 461 CA at 467E (Beldam LJ's emphasis).
149 [1991] 1 W.L.R. 461 CA at 468G.
150 [2006] EWHC 2973 Ch. See also *Inter Export LLC v Townley* [2017] EWHC 530 (Ch) at [8].
151 [2006] EWHC 2973 Ch at [747] and following.
152 [2006] EWHC 2973 Ch at [755].
153 [2006] EWHC 2973 Ch at [756]. He also held that the claimant's decision to scrap the equipment was a clear failure to mitigate: at [754].
154 [2009] EWCA Civ 169 CA; [2009] 1 Lloyd's Rep. 601 CA.
155 This comes out at [2009] EWCA Civ 169 CA at [117].
156 See para.49-035, below.
157 [1991] 1 W.L.R. 461 CA.
158 [2001] Q.B. 488 CA.

the lower prices which they would have paid and the prices actually paid. The novelty of the case lay, as Simon Brown LJ put it,

> "in the plaintiffs having suffered no loss from the transaction save only from having entered into that transaction rather than a still more profitable one".[159]

While the Court of Appeal did not find the point for decision an easy one and different lines of reasoning were advanced by the three members of the court for the conclusion reached, that conclusion was undoubtedly the correct one. Put simply, since the claimants would have succeeded in negotiating the better terms with the defendants had the representations not been made and the lies not told, they were entitled to be compensated for the consequent worsening of their position.[160]

**49-034** Should the principle behind *East v Maurer*,[161] the principle that a claimant may recover the profits from the hypothetical contract that would have been made by him, extend to showing that the hypothetical contract would have been a losing one? The question arose in *Yam Seng Pte Ltd v International Trade Corporation Ltd*,[162] which was in fact not a common law action for fraudulent misrepresentation but an action under s.2(1) of the Misrepresentation Act 1967 for negligent misrepresentation[163]; on this issue, however, this should make for no difference.[164] Leggatt J, while indicating that the authorities and texts are equivocal,[165] was in favour of an affirmative answer,[166] which seems right given that he further held that the onus of proof of such loss lies on the defendant.[167] In the case before him, which involved a contract granting the claimant the exclusive rights to distribute certain fragrances in specified territories, the defendant had not even attempted such proof.[168]

**49-035** Recovery for consequential losses is of course subject to the limiting rules of causation, remoteness and mitigation. *Dadourian Group International Inc v Simms* was a complicated case with two judgments of Warren J on, inter alia, damages,[169] both being appealed to the Court of Appeal[170] but only on the issue of damages common to the two judgments,[171] an issue at the centre of which was causation.[172]

---

159 [2001] Q.B. 488 CA at 498F.

160 *Bridgegrove v Smith* [1997] 2 E.G.L.R. 40 CA which, though apparently decided in negligence, has overtones of deceit in the conduct of the defendant. In any event it is clear that the court assumed the damages would be the same whichever the cause of action, citing indifferently leading decisions on both fraudulent and negligent misrepresentation: at 42B. See the case at para.49-064, below.

161 [1991] 1 W.L.R. 461 CA.

162 [2013] EWHC 111 (QB).

163 Which see at para.49-049, below.

164 In any event, the current law, emanating from the unfortunate decision in *Royscot Trust v Rogerson* [1991] 2 Q.B. 297 CA, is that the measure of damages for fraudulent misrepresentation and under s.2(1) is the same: see paras 49-055 and 49-056, below.

165 See his very full discussion at [2013] EWHC 111 (QB) at [209]–[216].

166 [2013] EWHC 111 (QB) at [217].

167 [2013] EWHC 111 (QB) at [217(6)].

168 [2013] EWHC 111 (QB) at [218].

169 The first, very long judgment is at [2006] EWHC 2973 Ch, the second at [2007] EWHC 454 Ch.

170 [2009] EWCA Civ 169 CA; [2009] 1 Lloyd's Rep. 601 CA.

171 There was no appeal by the claimant from the holding, in the first judgment, of no entitlement to lost alternative profits (dealt with at para.49-032, above) or from the holding, in the second judgment, of no entitlement to indemnity costs as damages, (dealt with at para.21-005, above in a footnote).

172 The court dealt largely with causation and remoteness also in the very fraudulent case of deceit, *Man Nutzfahrzeuge AG v Freightliner Ltd* [2006] EWHC 2347 (Comm), where the parties were said to be in dispute not over the principles to be applied but over their application to the complex particular

Induced by the defendant's fraudulent misrepresentations to sell, by way of option, certain equipment to a third party, the claimant subsequently became embroiled in defending, in litigation and arbitration, a variety of claims brought by the third party, and claimed to recover as damages the legal and other costs thereof. The Court of Appeal affirmed Warren J's decision to allow their recovery, giving a detailed analysis of the law and the facts leading to the conclusion that the misrepresentations were causative of the loss claimed.[173]

**(d) Where there is no contract** Where the claimant's change of position consequent upon the deceit is not the conclusion of a contract, the terminology of normal measure and consequential losses ceases to have relevance and no more exact principle can be obtained than that, in Lord Atkin's formulation in *Clark v Urquhart*,[174] the measure of damages is to be "based on the actual damage directly flowing from the fraudulent inducement". **49-036**

Thus expenses incurred may ground recovery. Accordingly in *Richardson v Silvester*,[175] where the defendant falsely advertised in a paper that a farm was to be let by tender, the claimant recovered damages in respect of useless expenses he had incurred in going to inspect the farm and in employing others to value it. And in *Wilkinson v Downton*,[176] where the defendant, as a practical joke, falsely informed the claimant that her husband had just been injured in an accident, the claimant recovered the expenses of train fares of third parties whom she sent to see her husband. Such expenses, said Wright J,[177] were "clearly within the decision in *Pasley v Freeman*".[178] **49-037**

So, too, there may be recovery for loss of profits.[179] We have this early in the old case of *Barley v Walford*,[180] where the claimant had lost profits by discontinuing the printing of certain designed silk goods because the defendant had falsely informed him that he was using a copy of a registered design. For today we have *Parabola Investments Ltd v Browallia Cal Ltd*,[181] where the issue of recovery for lost profits dominated. The Court of Appeal, affirming Flaux J, held that the profits that the claimant company would have made from its trading fund, had it not been depleted and run at a loss due to the defendant's misrepresentations,[182] were recoverable, Moreover, the claimant's profit loss did not fall to be assessed as at the date of discovery of the fraud making the profits that would have been made from then to **49-038**

facts: see at [213]–[322]. The appeal, at [2008] P.N.L.R. 6 P.117, does not concern deceit.

173 See at [109]–[148], affirming Warren J at [2006] EWHC 2973 Ch at [758]–[761] and at [2007] EWHC 454 Ch at [22]–[24].

174 [1930] A.C. 28 at 68.

175 (1873) L.R. 9 Q.B. 34.

176 [1897] 2 Q.B. 57.

177 [1897] 2 Q.B. 57 at 58.

178 (1789) 3 T.R. 51. This decision established the tort of deceit.

179 Somewhat similar to recovery for lost profits is the situation arising in *Mafo v Adams* [1970] 1 Q.B. 548 CA, where the claimant, having been tricked into leaving a flat which he held under a tenancy protected by the Rent Acts, was held entitled to recover as damages the loss arising from the deprivation of the protected tenancy, Widgery LJ remarking that "in the circles in which these parties move possession of such a flat is one of the most significant rights of property that any of them ever see in their lives": at 557.

180 (1846) 9 Q.B. 197.

181 [2011] Q.B. 477 CA.

182 Full facts at para.10-037 above, where it is noted that the defendant's argument that the profits the claimant would have made from its trading fund were too speculative to be recoverable was not accepted.

the date of trial irrecoverable. The effects of the fraud continued after its discovery because the claimant no longer had the amount by which its trading fund had been depleted, so that it was locked into a disadvantageous situation.[183] It was also held that damages for loss of the profits from the hypothetical trading upon which the claimant would have engaged were recoverable.[184]

**49-039** Where the deceit has led to a permanent deprivation of goods, the claimant is entitled to recover the market value of those goods, applying the analogy of conversion.[185] It was so held by the Court of Appeal in *Smith Kline & French Laboratories v Long*,[186] a case which did involve a contract but one between the claimant and a third party rather than between the claimant and defendant, and one which differed from the general run of contracts in the field of deceit in that the misrepresentation was not one as to the value of the property contracted to be sold and the claimant was seller rather than buyer. The claimants, who were engaged in the manufacture and sale of pharmaceutical products, were tricked by the defendant into selling large quantities of tablets to a company of which he was managing director on the understanding, based on the defendant's fraudulent misrepresentations, that the tablets were to go to Central Africa for distribution there. In fact the company sold the tablets to customers in Holland and then became insolvent before paying to the claimants that part of the purchase price for which the claimants had extended credit to the company. Had the claimants known that the tablets would be sold not in Africa but in Europe they would never have sold to the company at any price. The Court of Appeal, reversing the court below, awarded the claimants the market value of the tablets as being the amount for which they could have sold them elsewhere—and the market value was taken to be the same as the price at which the sale to the company had been made—subject to the claimants' giving credit for that part of the purchase price which they had received from the company. As the proper measure of damages the defendant had unsuccessfully contended for the cost of producing or replacing the tablets, which would have been virtually impossible for the claimants to prove and in any event would have been much lower than the sale price and indeed on one hypothesis would have been nil. This contention drew its strength from the fact that the claimants had inexhaustible sources of supply and could satisfy all their customers' demands so that, if the fraudulent misrepresentations had not been made and the sale to the company had accordingly not taken place, the aggregate of all the sales of tablets by the claimants would have been reduced by the amount of the tablets sold to the company. Therefore, it was argued, the claimants should not recover the price on that sale, held to represent the tablets' market value, as this would exceed the loss they had suffered; at most they should be entitled to the replacement cost. In rejecting this contention and awarding market value, Slade LJ pointed to cases in which claimants have obtained damages which went beyond their true economic loss, in particular to those cases in which the defendant has had the profitable use of the claimant's property and the claimant has been awarded the value of that user although he would not have used the property

---

[183] Just as the House of Lords had held of the claimant in *Smith New Court*: see para.49-014, above.

[184] Just as the Court of Appeal had held in the context of the sale of a business in *East v Maurer*: see para.49-031, above. The defendant's further contention that the claim was for damages for delay in the payment of damages was shown to be false and rejected: see at [41] and following. The whole of Toulson LJ's excellent judgment, with which his brethren agreed, deserves attention.

[185] See paras 37-006 and following, above.

[186] [1989] 1 W.L.R. 1 CA.

for profit himself.[187] The situation in *Smith Kline* is indeed similar but stretches the principle further because the person obtaining the benefit of the property was not the defendant but a third party, albeit the company of which he was managing director.

The circumstances of *Standard Chartered Bank v Pakistan National Shipping Corporation*,[188] a claim in deceit and also in conspiracy, gave rise to a loss which led to a somewhat different measure of recovery. Payment having been made by the claimant bank to the seller of a cargo upon the presentation of fraudulently dated bills of lading, the bank successfully claimed as damages against a variety of defendants the difference between the amount of its payment and the amount it recovered on the sale of the cargo together with the additional expenses incurred in trying to dispose of the cargo.[189] Mitigation was the main issue. There being no available market in which to sell the documents or the cargo the Court of Appeal held, affirming the court below,[190] that it was reasonable to take the bank's actual sale price, and at a later date than the commission of the deceit, despite the contention of the defendants that the market value of the cargo was at all times greater than the amount paid over by the bank.[191] Subsequently, the House of Lords in *Standard Chartered Bank v Pakistan National Shipping Corporation*,[192] decided further that this award was not to be reduced or cut down on account of deceitful conduct on the part of the claimant bank[193] as well as on the part of the defendants.[194] **49-040**

Where physical injury, whether to person or property, results from deceit, as can occasionally happen, damages for pecuniary loss will be the same as in other cases of physical injury. In this connection there is the strange case of *Burrows v Rhodes*.[195] The claimant was induced to join an invasion of the South African Republic by fraudulent misrepresentations that the invasion had the sanction of Her Majesty's Government, would be supported by lawfully-appointed forces, and was required for the protection of women and children. He successfully claimed damages arising from the loss of his leg,[196] of his kit, and of his pay. **49-041**

---

187 [1989] 1 W.L.R. 1 CA at 10B–D.

188 [2001] 1 All E.R. (Comm) 822 CA.

189 Similarly in *GE Commercial Finance Ltd v Gee* [2006] 1 Lloyd's Rep. 337 the claimant finance company recovered payments made by it to acquire non-existent debts (see at [330]) together with various expenses incurred in mitigation (at [337]). Damages are dealt with from [329] on.

190 [1999] 1 Lloyd's Rep. 747.

191 On the mitigation aspect, see para.9-074, above.

192 [2003] 1 A.C. 959.

193 On the contributory fault aspect, see para.7-004, above.

194 The progress of this litigation is somewhat difficult to follow. It would seem that the case on liability first came before Cresswell J as *No.2* at [1998] 1 Lloyd's Rep. 684, then damages were adjudicated upon by Toulson J as *No.3* at [1999] 1 Lloyd's Rep. 747, then came the appeal on liability, reverting to *No.2* at [2000] 1 Lloyd's Rep. 218 CA, followed by the appeal on damages, appearing without a number at [2001] 1 All E.R. (Comm) 822. Next, what one presumes to be the earlier damages award was presented for potential reduction on the new ground of contributory negligence (this having been left over by the Court of Appeal when adjudicating on liability) at [2000] 2 Lloyd's Rep. 511 CA, but remaining as *No.2*, though reported at [2001] Q.B. 167 CA, as *No.4*, and finally ending up in the House of Lords [2003] 1 Lloyd's Rep. 227 HL, as *No.2*. Because different reports use different numbers for these various permutations, it has been thought best to eliminate numbers in the references to the cases in the text.

195 [1899] 1 Q.B. 816.

196 There was also the non-pecuniary loss: see para.49-042 below.

## (2) Non-pecuniary loss

49-042 **(a) Pain and suffering and loss of amenities** In the rare case where deceit causes personal injury, as in *Wilkinson v Downton*,[197] and *Burrows v Rhodes*,[198] it would seem that the damages will follow the same pattern as with personal injury caused by any other tort and that therefore the claimant can recover for pain and suffering and for loss of amenities of life.[199]

49-043 **(b) Physical inconvenience and discomfort** In *Mafo v Adams*,[200] the claimant, having been persuaded to leave a flat held by him under a protected tenancy upon the fraudulent misrepresentation that another flat was available some good distance away, set out in a van on a winter's night, with pregnant wife and furniture, only to find himself shut out in the cold on arrival, with no option but to return and take refuge with friends. In these circumstances the Court of Appeal awarded him damages for the physical inconvenience and discomfort[201]; Sachs LJ said that he was entitled "upon accepted principles",[202] but it does appear to be the first time that such a recovery has been granted in a deceit claim.

49-044 **(c) Mental distress** Clear authority was for long lacking on recovery for mental distress caused by deceit. In *Wilkinson v Downton*,[203] where the claimant suffered nervous shock through being falsely told by the defendant, as a practical joke, that her husband had been injured in an accident, it was implicitly accepted, as in all subsequent cases of nervous shock,[204] now called psychiatric illness, that the damages could only comprehend the physical illness and not the mental distress caused by the shock. The explanation for this pattern of no awards may lie in the close connection of this tort with contract which for long refused damages for all mental distress,[205] but it cannot be proper to press the contractual analogy to this extent while at the same time refusing to accept it where the claimant claims for loss of bargain.[206] It was therefore highly significant that in *Doyle v Olby (Ironmongers)*,[207] where the Court of Appeal firmly came down on the side of the tortious measure of damages as the correct measure for deceit,[208] Winn LJ said that, while no damages were being awarded by the court for worry, strain, anxiety and unhappiness, "it may be that in some cases such consideration might well be appropriate".[209] Since *Doyle*, awards of this nature have been made. In *Shelley v Paddock*,[210] £500 was awarded to a claimant who had sold her house in England with the object of

---

197 [1897] 2 Q.B. 57: facts at para.49-044, below.

198 [1899] 1 Q.B. 816: facts at para.49-041, above.

199 See paras 40-254 and following, above. There may also have been an element of physical suffering in *Shelley v Paddock* [1978] Q.B. 120; the case is dealt with in relation to mental distress at para.49-044, below.

200 [1970] 1 Q.B. 548 CA.

201 [1970] 1 Q.B. 548 CA at 554 and 558, per Sachs and Widgery LJJ respectively.

202 [1970] 1 Q.B. 548 CA at 554.

203 [1897] 2 Q.B. 57.

204 See the standard texts on tort.

205 See paras 5-023 and following, above.

206 See paras 49-002 to 49-006, above.

207 [1969] 2 Q.B. 158 CA.

208 See paras 49-005 and 49-006, above.

209 [1969] 2 Q.B. 158 CA at 170.

210 [1978] 2 Q.B. 120.

moving to Spain only to find that, due to the defendant's fraudulent misrepresentations, she had obtained no title to the house in Spain which she thought she had acquired.[211] In *Archer v Brown*,[212] £500 was again awarded, this time to a claimant who, in an attempt to buy his way into a business, had been swindled by the defendant into buying shares therein which the defendant did not own, and who had in consequence become unemployed, heavily in debt and deeply upset.[213] In *East v Maurer*,[214] where the claimants had bought a hairdressing salon which to their distress failed, the failure being because of the defendant's fraudulent competition, the award was of £1,000. In *A v B*,[215] £7,500 was awarded to a claimant who, deceived into believing he was the father of the defendant's child whom he supported, suffered distress when he eventually discovered that the child was not his. The much higher amount in this case is attributable in part to the march of inflation but also in part to the deceit being not what the judge called a commercial deceit[216] but a deceit in a domestic context, which would involve greater distress. The even higher amount of £10,000 was awarded in *Kinch v Rosling*,[217] where, although the deceit could be said to be commercial, it had domestic consequences. The award was on account of the humiliation, distress and anxiety suffered by the claimant and his wife over a seven year period as a consequence of the bankruptcy forced on him by reason of an advanced fee fraud of which he was the victim.[218] Clearly, awards have gone well beyond the £500 awarded over a quarter of a century ago in *Shelley v Paddock*,[219] and in *Archer v Brown*,[220] and in coming to the appropriate amount to award there has now to be taken into account the Court of Appeal's final ruling in *Simmons v Castle*,[221] that damages for non-pecuniary loss in all types of civil claim are to be increased by 10 per cent.[222]

In *Archer v Brown*,[223] the judge had relied on the analogy from contract, but this **49-045**
is a somewhat empty, dangerous analogy which, though in the past it may have hindered the acceptance of damages for mental distress in deceit, can now, in the changed contractual climate,[224] only help; he could see no reason in logic or justice why damages for injured feelings should not be awarded in deceit on the same basis as in contract.[225] However, the judge's reference to these damages as aggravated damages,[226] a reference which has found its way into the headnote, is not entirely happy. The true position is that a claimant should be entitled to compensation for

---

211 See, especially, [1978] 2 Q.B. 120 at 131D–F. While the judge clearly thought such an award appropriate this was not in fact contested by the defendant's counsel. In the appeal at [1980] Q.B. 348 CA, which affirmed the court below, the award in respect of non-pecuniary loss was not in question.

212 [1985] Q.B. 401.

213 The facts are more fully set out at para.49-024, above.

214 [1991] 1 W.L.R. 461 CA.

215 [2007] EWHC 1246 (QB).

216 [2007] EWHC 1246 (QB) at [54].

217 [2009] EWHC 286 (QB).

218 See [2009] EWHC 286 (QB) at [18] and [19].

219 [1978] 2 Q.B. 120.

220 [1985] Q.B. 401.

221 [2013] 1 W.L.R. 1239 CA; final ruling from 1243.

222 For the procedural history and reasons for this development, stemming from the package of reforms appearing in the *Jackson Report on Civil Litigation Costs*, see para.40-280, below

223 [1985] Q.B. 401.

224 See paras 5-024 and following, above.

225 [1985] Q.B. 401 at 426F.

226 See [1985] Q.B. 401 at 402G, and 414E together with 424B and 426D.

any mental distress he has suffered; such damages will become aggravated damages only if they fall to be increased because the heinousness of the defendant's conduct is considered to have added to the claimant's suffering.[227] As for *A v B*,[228] the analogy from bereavement in fatal injury cases was presented by counsel to the judge, but he considered that, although the claimant's distress was very real, it could not be as severe as a bereavement which was final and irreversible.[229] Yet surely the paternity of the child was equally final and irreversible.

### 3. EXEMPLARY DAMAGES

**49-046** The whole approach to exemplary damages was changed by the decision in *Rookes v Barnard*,[230] since approved in *Broome v Cassell & Co*,[231] and is treated in detail elsewhere.[232] Yet in the days before *Rookes v Barnard*,[233] exemplary damages would appear, somewhat strangely, to have passed the tort of deceit by. Nor, in cases where the facts have fallen within one of the categories in which exemplary awards are still permitted,[234] have there been any decisions in either direction since *Rookes*, although views have been expressed both in favour and against, with Widgery LJ in *Mafo v Adams*,[235] and Peter Pain J in *Archer v Brown*,[236] ranged on the confident side and Sachs LJ in *Mafo v Adams*,[237] and the decision in *Metallund Rohstoff AG v Acli Metals (London)*[238] on the cautious. Now, however, the House of Lords in *Kuddus v Chief Constable of Leicestershire*,[239] has endorsed the view that exemplary damages are acceptable in torts where formerly they had not run, by overruling the Court of Appeal's adoption of the contrary view in *A.B. v South West Water Services*,[240] and holding that it is the features of the defendant's behaviour rather than the cause of action sued upon which have to be looked at in order to decide upon the appropriateness of an exemplary award.[241] So the way is now clearly open, while exemplary damages last, for such awards in deceit claims, and indeed in *Kuddus* Lord Scott, while regretting the retention of exemplary damages,[242] said specifically that, if they were to be retained, deceit should in a suitable case attract them.[243]

---

227 Compare the more developed position with defamation at paras 46-031 and following, and paras 46-043 and following, above.
228 [2007] 2 F.L.R. 1051.
229 [2007] 2 F.L.R. 1051 at [57].
230 [1964] A.C. 1129.
231 [1972] A.C. 1027.
232 See Ch.13, above.
233 [1964] A.C. 1129.
234 See paras 13-017 and following, above.
235 [1970] 1 Q.B. 548 CA at 558.
236 [1985] Q.B. 401 at 423F.
237 [1970] 1 Q.B. 548 CA at 555.
238 [1984] 1 Lloyd's Rep. 598 CA.
239 [2002] 2 A.C. 122.
240 [1993] Q.B. 507 CA.
241 See para.13-011, above.
242 See para.13-007, above.
243 [2002] 2 A.C. 122 at [122].

### 4. RESTITUTIONARY DAMAGES AND DISGORGEMENT DAMAGES

On the current state of English law some gain-based damages awards, namely disgorgement damages, appear, superficially, not to be available for the tort of deceit. These damages are considered in Ch.15. It is explained there that the superficial view that deceit does not attract this form of gain-based damages is incorrect.[244] It has long done so. As for restitutionary damages, one reason why they are rarely awarded for deceit is that they are rarely needed. A claimant will almost always have a claim for restitution in unjust enrichment for mistake without having to prove that the mistake was fraudulently induced. And as for disgorgement damages (the correct label for the disgorgement that occurs after an account of profits) it will be recalled that the second limb of *Rookes v Barnard*,[245] applies in cases of deceit to disgorge profits where, in Lord Devlin's words, **49-047**

> "the defendant's conduct has been calculated to make a profit for himself which may exceed the compensation payable to the plaintiff".[246]

It can only be hoped that although both of these forms of damages are rarely needed to be made explicit, when such an award is appropriate for the tort of deceit then it will be made transparently.

## II. NEGLIGENT MISREPRESENTATION

### 1. LIABILITY AT COMMON LAW AND UNDER STATUTE

For long English common law resisted giving a remedy for negligent misrepresentation. This refusal, which can be said to emanate from *Derry v Peek* in the late 19th century, was perpetuated by *Candler v Crane Christmas and Co*,[247] into the second half of the 20th century. Not until *Hedley Byrne & Co v Heller & Partners*,[248] was it finally resolved that negligent misrepresentation would constitute an actionable wrong.[249] Today this is an accepted part of the law of tort. **49-048**

Almost contemporaneously with the emergence of the new tortious liability for negligent misrepresentation there was introduced by s.2(1) of the Misrepresentation Act 1967 a statutory liability for negligent misrepresentation inducing the representee to enter into a contract with the representor. The subsection, which it is best to cite in full, runs thus: **49-049**

> "Where a person has entered into a contract after a misrepresentation has been made to him by another party thereto and as a result thereof he has suffered loss, then, if the person making the misrepresentation would be liable in damages in respect thereof had the misrepresentation been made fraudulently, that person shall be so liable notwithstanding that the misrepresentation was not made fraudulently, unless he proves that he had reasonable ground to believe and did believe up to the time the contract was made that the facts represented were true."

[244] See Ch.15 at paras 15-003, 15-029 and 15-039 and following.
[245] [1964] A.C. 1129.
[246] [1964] A.C. 1129 at 1226. See Ch.13, above, at paras 13-021 and following.
[247] [1951] 2 K.B. 164 CA.
[248] [1964] A.C. 465.
[249] Contrast para.6-004, above.

The Act as a whole implemented the recommendations contained in the *Law Reform Committee's Tenth Report*,[250] and that Committee had regarded as a deficiency in the law the lack of a damages remedy for the contracting party induced to contract by a negligent misrepresentation of the other where that negligent misrepresentation had not acquired the status of a term of the contract so as to give rise, by virtue of its untruth, to an action for breach of contract. Had the imminence of the *Hedley Byrne* decision[251] been realised at the time the Committee reported in 1962, the need for the statutory intervention—or at least for this aspect of it—might have been considered to have been met by the advent of the new tortious liability.

**49-050** Since 2014, the scope of s.2(1) has been reduced with part of its coverage, and beyond, taken up by the Consumer Protection from Unfair Trading Regulations 2008. Section 2(4) of the Misrepresentation Act now provides that a person cannot claim damages under s.2(1) for a misrepresentation if the person has a right to redress under Pt 4A of the Consumer Protection from Unfair Trading Regulations 2008 in respect of the conduct constituting the misrepresentation. Under those regulations, if a prohibited practice occurs then the consumer has a right to damages. Prohibited practices include misleading actions and aggressive actions by a trader in relation to a consumer. The right to damages under the Regulations is a unique statutory measure which is neither contractual nor tortious. Regulation 27J(1)(a) provides that damages that can be recovered if the consumer

> "has incurred financial loss which the consumer would not have incurred if the prohibited practice in question had not taken place. Although this appears to resemble to the tortious measure, as does the reasonable foreseeability of loss limitation in reg.27J(4), it does not include the right to be paid damages"
>
> in respect of the difference between the market price of a product and the amount payable for it under a contract" (reg.27J(3)).

Instead, the regulation works by allowing discounts ranging from 25 per cent to 100 per cent depending upon the seriousness of the contravention where the price is less than £5000, or the percentage difference between the contract price and market price if the price is more than £5000 (reg.27I). In addition, however, reg.27J(2) provides for recovery for "alarm, distress or physical inconvenience or discomfort". This goes beyond the usual limits of recovery of tortious damages in relation to these matters.

## 2. The Tortious Measure of Damages

**49-051** By reason of these latter-day developments the period for establishing the appropriate damages in this field has been comparatively short. With the common law liability, however, there has never been any doubt that the appropriate measure of damages is the tortious measure. Here was a new tort, or a new liability in tort, and to it the tortious measure of damages must apply. The analogy of the deceit cases, where the tortious measure has prevailed,[252] should therefore prove useful.[253] Indeed *Downs v Chappell*,[254] illustrates the interrelation; the claimants sued their seller for

250 (1962), Cmnd.1782.

251 [1964] A.C. 465; see para.49-048, above.

252 See para.49-005, above.

253 See paras 49-002 and following, above.

254 [1997] 1 W.L.R. 426 CA.

fraudulent misrepresentation and their accountant for negligent misrepresentation and were awarded precisely the same damages against each defendant.[255]

It was also thought plain at the time of the 13th edition of this book when no decisions on the new statute had appeared that the statutory measure of damages must surely follow the tortious measure and that therefore it sufficed simply so to state, indeed somewhat inconspicuously in a footnote.[256] After all, when so much learning, evidenced by the weight of case law, had gone into distinguishing between misrepresentations which were, and misrepresentations which were not, terms of a contract,[257] it seemed highly improbable that all this learning should be overthrown at a stroke by allowing the generally more generous contractual measure of damages to rule where the new statutory liability was involved. And, more importantly, it would be very odd that this contractual measure should be available to a claimant complaining of an innocent, though admittedly negligent, misrepresentation when it was clear that for a fraudulent misrepresentation he was undoubtedly limited to the tortious measure.[258] **49-052**

Events, however, did not show an immediate acceptance of the tortious measure of damages in this context. On the contrary, the contractual measure received substantial support in the cases, first from Lord Denning MR in two cases in the Court of Appeal, *Gosling v Anderson*,[259] and *Jarvis v Swan's Tours*.[260] There then followed a series of decisions at first instance in which different views as between the appropriateness of the competing measures emerged. In one of these, *Watts v Spence*,[261] the contractual measure was specifically applied but the decision was later disapproved in *Sharneyford v Edge*[262]; in one Court of Appeal decision, *Chesneau v Interhome*,[263] it was accepted that the claim was one in tort. Some 20 years of uncertainty eventually gave way to the final acceptance of the tortious measure—as stated by the Court of Appeal at the end of the day in *Royscot Trust v Rogerson*,[264] and in *Cemp Properties v Dentsply Research Corporation*[265]—and the early vagaries are now past history. In the first of these two cases Balcombe LJ referred to this history and commented: **49-053**

> "In view of the wording of the subsection[266] it is difficult to see how the measure of damages under it could be other than the tortious measure and, in spite of the initial aberrations referred to above, that is now generally accepted."[267]

Of course not every case in which there are both contractual claims and claims under the statute will show up the distinction between the two measures as, on the particular facts, they may be held to be the same. This appears to have been the posi-

---

255 Facts at para.49-030, above.
256 13th edition (1972), para.1357, fn.6.
257 See the standard texts on contract.
258 See paras 49-002 to 49-006, above.
259 [1972] E.G.D. 709 CA.
260 [1973] Q.B. 233 CA.
261 [1976] Ch. 165
262 [1987] Ch. 305 CA. In any event the decision in *Watts v Spence* has lost its raison d'être, having been overtaken by the abolition of the rule in *Bain v Fothergill* (1874) L.R. 7 H.L. 158.
263 (1983) 134 N.L.J. 341 CA.
264 [1991] 2 Q.B. 297 CA.
265 [1991] 2 E.G.L.R. 197 CA.
266 Namely s.2(1).
267 [1991] 2 Q.B. 297 CA at 305A.

tion in *Witter v TBP Industries*.[268] Misrepresentations about the profitability of a carpet business sold led to claims both under s.2(1) and for breach of contract.[269] That the damages were said by Jacob J to be the same under either claim[270] may be due to there being no difference between the price paid for the business and the business as it was represented to be[271]; there was no claim for consequential loss.

**49-054** Since it is now established that the tortious measure of damages applies equally to the common law liability and to the statutory liability there is no need to deal with the two separately, as had been done in earlier editions when the issue of the appropriate measure for the statutory liability was still in the air. Indeed today it appears to be sometimes unspecified, as in *Hussey v Eels*,[272] whether the claim for negligent misrepresentation is at common law or by virtue of s.2(1) of the Misrepresentation Act 1967. However, it is useful to take separately, in line with the analysis of damages for fraudulent misrepresentation, misrepresentations which induce the representee to contract with the representor[273] and misrepresentations which do not; in particular, this distinction takes account of the fact that the statutory liability applies only to the former category.

**49-055** First, however, one difficulty must be addressed, a difficulty which stems from the unfortunate manner in which s.2(1) of the Misrepresentation Act 1967 has been drafted. There is one respect in which the statutory damages can differ from common law damages. While in general the damages will be precisely the same whether the misrepresentation be fraudulent or negligent, since to each the tortious measure with its aim of restoring the status quo ante applies, there may be a divergence on matters such as remoteness of damage and exemplary damages between fraud and negligence.[274] Because s.2(1) has introduced a so-called "fiction of fraud"—by its stating that

> "if the person making the representation would be liable in damages in respect thereof had the representation been made fraudulently, that person shall be so liable"

where the representation is negligently made—it can be argued that the fraud rules overtake those appertaining to negligence so as to give more in damages where the action is brought under the statute. Indeed the Court of Appeal in *Royscot Trust v Rogerson*,[275] has so held. In that case the claimant finance company had purchased a car from the defendant motor dealer, and had then entered into a hire-purchase agreement concerning the car with the dealer's customer in the usual way, in reliance on the defendant's negligent misrepresentation that the amount of the deposit paid by the customer to the defendant represented as much as 20 per cent of the total sale price, where it was in fact less than this. After paying some of the hire-purchase instalments the customer dishonestly sold the car to a third party who

---

[268] [1996] 2 All E.R. 573.

[269] There was also a claim under s.2(2), for which see para.49-074, below.

[270] [1996] 2 All E.R. 573 at 601h.

[271] For the basis of the difference between the tort and contract measures, see paras 49-002 and following, above.

[272] [1990] 2 Q.B. 227 CA.

[273] Completion of the contract by the claimant after knowledge of the misrepresentation does not preclude him from claiming damages for the misrepresentation: *Production Technology Consultants v Bartlett* (1988) 25 E.G. 121 CA.

[274] The various rules applying to fraud which appear inappropriate for negligence are usefully examined by Atiyah and Treitel in (1967) 30 M.L.R. 369 at 373–375. Not all of them directly affect damages.

[275] [1991] 2 Q.B. 297 CA.

acquired a good title to it. It was held that the claimant, who had a policy of not entertaining hire-purchase agreements with a deposit below 20 per cent and, therefore, with knowledge of the true facts would not have entered into the transaction, was entitled to recover by way of damages from the defendant the amount of the hire-purchase instalments unpaid by the customer because this damage was not too remote. Since a defrauded claimant may recover for any loss he may suffer directly flowing from the fraudulent inducement even if that loss was not reasonably foreseeable, it was immaterial whether the customer's sale of the car was or was not foreseeable.[276]

It is unfortunate that the Court of Appeal felt obliged to construe s.2(1) in this **49-056** way so as to permit to be awarded under it damages which are quite inappropriate for a claim in negligence. If, as has been said, the intention to injure the claimant disposes of any question as to remoteness of damage,[277] thereby effectively allowing recovery for all loss where a defendant defrauds a claimant, is it right that the negligent defendant should be liable to the same, possibly extreme extent? And because exemplary damages are now awardable in deceit[278] should a negligent defendant be subject to such an award? Moreover, a level of damages under the statutory liability which is higher than that under the common law liability is difficult to justify.[279] It is true that the Court of Appeal said that it had no option but to decide as it did. Ralph Gibson LJ spoke of "the plain meaning"[280] of s.2(1) and Balcombe LJ said that to argue otherwise "is to ignore the plain words of the subsection".[281] But is this really so? Is there no alternative interpretation possible? It is submitted that there is a clear alternative interpretation possible and that all that s.2(1) is purporting to say is this: before the Act the person induced by misrepresentation not forming part of the contract had only an action for fraudulent misrepresentation, now he has one also for negligent misrepresentation.[282] This interpretation must surely come to prevail. Encouragement for such an outcome may be derived from the fact that Lord Browne-Wilkinson and Lord Steyn, who gave the two leading speeches in *Smith New Court Securities v Scrimgeour Vickers*,[283] were unprepared to express a view on the correctness of the decision[284] in *Royscot Trust v Rogerson*.[285] And Rix J, bound by *Royscot*, addressed the issue in memorable fashion in *Avon Insurance Plc v Swire Fraser Ltd*.[286] "What a mighty weapon lies in s.2(1)", he said, producing damages "on a scale commensurate with fraud" whereas no damages whatsoever might be available at common law either for breach of contract or for negligent misrepresentation.[287] That on the facts of *Avon Insurance* there would have been no damages for breach of contract, no damages

---

276 It was indeed held to be reasonably foreseeable, making the liability in fraud no different from that in negligence: see [1991] 2 Q.B. 297 CA at 306H–307A.

277 See paras 8-050 and 8-062, above.

278 See para.49-046, above.

279 See [2000] Lloyd's Rep. I.R. 535 at 539, col.2.

280 [1991] 2 Q.B. 297 CA at 309A.

281 [1991] 2 Q.B. 297 CA at 306H.

282 Many distinguished learned authors have sensibly adopted this construction but their view, though extensively referred to by Balcombe LJ, was nonetheless rejected by the Court of Appeal.

283 [1997] A.C. 254: see para.49-014, above.

284 [1997] A.C. 254 at 267F and 283B respectively.

285 [1991] 2 Q.B. 297 CA.

286 [2000] Lloyd's Rep. I.R. 535.

287 [2000] Lloyd's Rep. I.R. 535 at 539 col.2.

for negligent misrepresentation at common law under *Hedley Byrne*, but substantial s.2(1) damages under *Royscot*, shows that *Royscot* must be wrong.[288]

## 3. Heads of Damage

### (1) Pecuniary loss

**49-057** **(a) Where there is a contract** As the years have gone by, the case law has gradually built up to give today a respectable number of decisions on damages for negligent misrepresentation leading to a contract between the claimant and the defendant. While the decisions in part fall within the period when the courts were still toying with the contractual measure for the statutory liability,[289] the results arrived at have always been compatible, with one exception, with the now accepted tortious measure.[290]

**49-058** *(i) Normal measure* The normal measure of damages is the value transferred, generally represented by the contract price, less the value received, whether of property or of services or of money. This is neatly illustrated by *Heinemann v Cooper*,[291] where the price paid for a lease less its market value was awarded and upheld by the Court of Appeal; though the report does not specify, the action appears to have been for negligent misrepresentation at common law. Similarly, in *Cemp Properties (UK) v Dentsply Research Corporation*,[292] where the defendant company, in selling a site which the claimant company was acquiring for redevelopment, misrepresented the adjoining owners' rights, the claimant was awarded, in a claim under s.2(1), the difference between the market value of the property, as depressed by the existence of these rights, and the price paid; the consequential losses, for which the case is also important, are dealt with later.[293] Sir Nicolas Browne-Wilkinson VC stated that it was well established that, in the field of misrepresentation, fraudulent and innocent, inducing the claimant to enter into a contract of purchase,

> "the basic measure of damages … was the difference between what the plaintiff paid for the property and the true market value of what he acquired."[294]

"The market value loss", said Bingham LJ, "is the primary measure of damages in this field".[295] All these cases are cases with the buyer as claimant. However, *Platt*

---

[288] *Royscot* continues to trouble the law, with statements such as that in *Peekay Intermark Ltd v Australian and New Zealand Banking Group Ltd* [2005] EWHC 830 (Comm) that the claimant, suing under s.2(1) of the 1967 Act, "was entitled in accordance with … [*Royscot*] … to the fraud measure of damages": at [69]. See the case at para.49-060, below where it can be seen that there would have been no difference on damages between liability in fraud and liability in negligence. In *Yam Seng Pte Ltd v International Trade Corp Ltd* [2013] EWHC 111 (QB) the trial judge ended his criticisms of *Royscot* with "it represents the law and I must therefore apply it": at [206].

[289] See para.49-053, above.

[290] The exception is *Watts v Spence* [1976] Ch. 165, but for other reasons this decision is no longer of importance: see para.49-053 (in a footnote), above.

[291] (1987) 19 H.L.R. 262 CA.

[292] [1991] 2 E.G.L.R. 197 CA.

[293] See para.49-064, below.

[294] [1991] 2 E.G.L.R. 197 CA at 200J.

[295] [1991] 2 E.G.L.R. 197 CA at 201J. But his formulation of this measure ("the difference between the market value of the site as it was represented to be and its market value as it in fact was": at 201F–G)

*v Platt*,[296] on the assumption that the action there was for negligent rather than fraudulent misrepresentation,[297] provides an illustration of this normal measure awarded to a seller claimant, who recovered the market value of the shares sold less the nominal price paid for them.

In *Naughton v O'Callaghan*,[298] there was also awarded purchase price less market value,[299] but the matter in issue was the time at which the market value was to be taken. The claimant bought for 26,000 guineas at the Newmarket thoroughbred sales a yearling colt which he would not have bought but for the inaccurate description of the colt's pedigree in the sale catalogue. The colt was put in training and run unsuccessfully so that, by virtue of its record on the track, it was worth £1,500 two years later when the true pedigree came to light. In the claim for negligent misrepresentation under s.2(1) it was held that the appropriate measure of damages[300] was the purchase price of 26,000 guineas less the colt's value of £1,500 at the time the misrepresentation was discovered and not less the value at the time of purchase represented by the price at which the colt could then have been sold. This looks at first sight like a departure from the basic rule, well documented in the cases dealing with the purchase of shares where the misrepresentation has been fraudulent,[301] that the value of what is sold is to be taken as at the time of sale and any subsequent decline in value is to be disregarded; indeed in *Twycross v Grant*,[302] the example taken by Cockburn CJ to illustrate this rule was of the sale of a horse.[303] However, the rule concerns itself only with such depreciations in value as are unconnected with the circumstances existing at the time the contract was made. The important point in *Naughton v O'Callaghan*,[304] is that the dramatic fall in the colt's value was not due to a general fall in the market for racehorses but was special to the colt and was to be expected if it did not run successfully. The true value of the colt was not to be measured by what others would have paid for it but lay in its ability, or inability, to win races, an inability which was due to its inherent characteristics present when it was purchased. What had changed was that the effect of these characteristics had become apparent so that a much better informed assessment could be made of the colt's value. Analysed in this fashion,[305] the case can be seen as an application of the normal measure. **49-059**

*Peekay Intermark Ltd v Australian and New Zealand Banking Group Ltd*,[306] is a further case of the value of what was purchased being taken, for the purpose of damages, at a time later than that of purchase. The case was concerned with the mis-selling of an emerging markets investment product, marketed by the defendant, into which the claimant company had invested AUD $250,000 dollars. Had it known the true nature of the investment the claimant would not have bought but, having **49-060**

---

is, unlike Sir Nicolas Browne-Wilkinson VC's (see text), incorrect.

296 [2001] B.C.L.C. 698 CA.

297 See the case at para.49-026, above.

298 [1990] 3 All E.R. 191.

299 The consequential loss additionally awarded is dealt with at para.49-064, below.

300 See preceding note.

301 See paras 49-010 and following, above.

302 (1877) 2 C.P.D. 469 CA.

303 (1877) 2 C.P.D. 469 CA at 544–545.

304 [1990] 3 All E.R. 191.

305 It was so analysed by Chadwick J in *Smith New Court Securities v Scrimgeour* [1992] B.C.L.C. 1104 at 1146d–e.

306 [2005] EWHC 830 (Comm).

bought, it was locked into the investment for some time, eventually realising it for some AUD $6,000 dollars. In its claim under s.2(1) the claimant was awarded the difference between the sum invested and the amount ultimately realised.[307]

**49-061** *(ii) Consequential losses* The cases provide a heterogeneity of recoverable consequential losses. Since they form no particular pattern it seems best to deal with them simply in the order in which they have appeared.

**49-062** *Esso Petroleum Co v Mardon*,[308] was the first imposition of tortious liability for negligent misrepresentation leading to a contract; the claim was necessarily at common law since the contract had been entered into before the Misrepresentation Act 1967 had come into force.[309] The claimants, a large oil company, let to the defendant for a three-year term a site upon which they had built a filling station as an outlet for sales of their petrol. The defendant was given by the claimants as an estimated annual throughput a figure of 200,000 gallons and, although the defendant was initially somewhat dubious about this and suggested that a lower figure was more likely, his doubts were, as the judge found, quelled by his trust in the greater experience and expertise of the claimants. Mainly because the pumps, due to restrictions imposed by the planning authority, did not front on to the main street, the throughput fell well below the estimate despite the defendant's best endeavours, the first 15 months providing him with sales of only 78,000 gallons. Thereupon the defendant, having sunk all his capital in the business through the medium of a company controlled by himself and his wife and having borrowed heavily on bank overdraft, gave the claimants notice. Because they wanted to keep the station open and run by a good tenant, the claimants offered the defendant a new tenancy agreement on more favourable terms, which new agreement the defendant entered into after about half of the initial three-year term had elapsed. The losses, however, continued, and eventually the claimants, having cut off supplies from the defendant, issued a writ claiming, inter alia, possession of the premises. The defendant gave up possession but counterclaimed for damages for breach of warranty as to the potential throughput or, in the alternative, for negligent misrepresentation whereby he had been induced to enter into both of the tenancy agreements. The Court of Appeal decided in the defendant's favour on both limbs of his counterclaim[310] and, while the final assessment of damages was adjourned for possible agreement between the parties,[311] it would seem that the recoverable damages consisted of the defendant's losses of capital, whether of existing capital or by way of the liabilities incurred on overdraft, up until the time of the final closure of the business,[312] with interest thereon[313]—and the fact that the existing capital came not from the defendant personally but from the controlled company was held to make

[307] The Court of Appeal reversed on liability so that damages were not touched upon: [2006] 2 Lloyd's Rep. 511 CA.

[308] [1976] Q.B. 801 CA.

[309] Indeed it was argued, though unsuccessfully, that the *Hedley Byrne* principle (see para.49-048, above) could not be used to impose liability for negligent pre-contractual statements.

[310] Thereby reversing Lawson J ([1975] Q.B. 819) on breach of warranty, and affirming on negligent misrepresentation.

[311] Which was forthcoming.

[312] The rejection of the claimants' argument that the date of the defendant's entering into the second tenancy agreement should mark the cut-off point for his damages is dealt with in relation to mitigation at para.9-104, above.

[313] See [1976] Q.B. 801 CA at 829A–F, per Ormrod LJ.

no difference[314]—together with the earnings from other activities the defendant had forgone over the years of wasted effort.[315] Such indeed was held to be the approach for arriving at the measure of damages for the contractual breach of warranty as well as for the tortious negligent misrepresentation, but this was simply because the warranty was of a somewhat unusual nature, being not a warranty that the annual throughput would in fact amount to 200,000 gallons but a warranty that the claimants, on a careful assessment, estimated 200,000 gallons as the likely annual throughput.[316]

*Gosling v Anderson*,[317] started the line of cases relying on s.2(1) of the Misrepresentation Act 1967. The seller of a house, through an agent, misrepresented that planning permission had been obtained for a garage on that part of the premises described in the contract as a parking area, and the buyer successfully claimed damages for the cost of garaging her car elsewhere and of travelling daily by bus to collect it. In *Davis & Co v Afa-Minerva*,[318] the defendant had, in supplying and installing a burglar alarm system at the claimant's business premises, misrepresented that any broken wire would cause the alarm bell to ring until the batteries were exhausted whereas in fact the bell would be stopped if the control panel was wrenched off. Burglars, having broken into the premises and stopped the alarm bell by wrenching off the control panel, proceeded to take cash from the cash register and stock from the cellars. The claimant claimed damages in respect of (1) the initial breaking in; (2) the breaking down of internal doors; (3) the breaking into, and abstraction of the cash from, the cash register; and (4) the loss of the stock. It was held that no recovery could be had for the first three items as these losses would not have been obviated had the alarm system been operating as represented, but that the defendant was liable for the loss of stock which it had taken the burglars a considerable time to collect and the theft of which would therefore have been prevented had the alarm bell been continuously in operation at the time.[319] Had the misrepresentation not been made, the claimant would presumably have sought out an alternative alarm system to satisfy his requirements and thereby have prevented the loss of stock for which he was awarded the damages. In *F. and H. Entertainments v Leisure Enterprises*,[320] where the claimant took an assignment of club premises on the basis of a misrepresentation of the defendant assignor that the landlords had not given notices of increase of rent under the rent review clause in the lease, the claimant moved successfully to rescind the contract by reason of the misrepresentation, claiming by way of damages, also successfully, not only the return of his deposit but also the moneys spent by him in equipping the premises for use. "The proper measure of damages", said Walton J, "covered all expenditure properly and not prematurely and extravagantly incurred".[321] In *Andre & Cie v Ets Michel Blanc & Fils*,[322] where, after the making of six contracts for the sale of United States soya bean meal, the sellers misrepresented to the buyers the requirements of certain United States export regulations as they affected the performance **49-063**

[314] [1976] Q.B. 801 CA at 821F–G, 829H–830C and 833H–834B.

[315] [1976] Q.B. 801 CA at 821A–B and 821H–822A, per Lord Denning MR.

[316] Respecting this aspect of the decision, see para.24-003, above.

[317] [1972] E.G.D. 709 CA.

[318] [1974] 2 Lloyd's Rep. 27.

[319] [1974] 2 Lloyd's Rep. 27 at 33.

[320] (1976) 120 S.J. 331.

[321] (1976) 120 S.J. 331.

[322] [1977] 2 Lloyd's Rep. 166.

of the contracts thereby causing the buyers to release the sellers from their performance obligations, the damages awarded aimed to place the buyers where they would have been had they not so released the sellers.

**49-064** In *McNally v Welltrade International*,[323] claims were brought for negligent misrepresentation both at common law and under the statute; both succeeded. The claimant who had, in England, entered into a contract with a third party for employment in Africa on the strength of the defendant's misrepresentation that he, the claimant, was suitable for the job, recovered damages measured by the amount of earnings he had lost by giving up his job in England and not regaining comparable employment until some time after his return from Africa.[324] In *Naughton v O'Callaghan*,[325] the claimant purchaser of a yearling colt was held entitled not only to the normal measure of price less value[326] but also to the training fees and costs of upkeep of the colt up to the time when the truth as to its pedigree came to light. The defendant had argued that this expenditure would have been incurred upon another yearling purchased in the sales; the claimant riposted that a yearling with a pedigree as described might not only have paid for its keep but might also have reaped for him rich rewards. The trial judge decided that he was entitled to set speculation of this nature on one side and to look only at the contract that the claimant did make in reliance on the representation.[327] Next came *Cemp Properties (UK) v Dentsply Research Corporation*.[328] Misrepresentations as to the adjoining owners' rights to light and air induced the claimants to purchase a property in central London and before these rights were revealed the claimants had started on the redevelopment of the site. The revelation of these rights required the development scheme to be partially redesigned and caused its completion to be delayed. The Court of Appeal accepted that it was now established that, where the normal measure of market value less price paid[329] did not fully compensate a claimant, he was

> "in addition entitled to damages for consequential loss directly caused by the misrepresentation and the entering into of the contract",[330]

so that the claimants in the instant case could claim for all their expenditure thrown away which would not have been incurred had the true facts been known and which secured no countervailing benefit.[331] Then there came *Downs v Chappell*,[332] where accountants were sued by the buyers of a business for negligent misrepresentations about the profitability of that business; this case has already been dealt with in the context of fraudulent misrepresentation.[333]

---

323 [1978] I.R.L.R. 497.

324 Damages for non-pecuniary loss were also awarded: see paras 49-068 and 49-069, below.

325 [1990] 3 All E.R. 191.

326 This aspect of the case is at para.49-059, above.

327 See [1990] 3 All E.R. 191 at 198e–h.

328 [1991] 2 E.G.L.R. 197 CA.

329 See para.49-058, above.

330 [1991] 2 E.G.L.R. 197 CA at 200J.

331 [1991] 2 E.G.L.R. 197 CA at 202A.

332 [1997] 1 W.L.R. 426 CA.

333 At para.49-030, above. A further decision is *Bridgegrove v Smith* [1997] 2 E.G.L.R. 40 CA, where it is not too clear for what precise consequential losses recovery was allowed. Two brothers wishing to start a garage business took a six months' lease of premises which the landlord misrepresented as suitable for car repairs and as having appropriate planning permission. They recovered their losses

*East v Maurer*,[334] established for fraudulent misrepresentation that, while a party cannot recover the profits under the contract which he has been induced to enter, this representing the contractual measure, he may claim for the profits he would have made from the hypothetical contract he would otherwise have concluded,[335] and there is no reason why this should not apply equally to negligent misrepresentation, whether at common law or under s.2(1) of the Misrepresentation Act 1967. As for the yet unresolved question of whether a defendant is entitled to show that the hypothetical contract would have been a losing one, this has now been passed upon in *Yam Seng Pte Ltd v International Trade Corporation Ltd*,[336]in a claim which was under s.2(1). It has already been considered.[337] **49-065**

**(b) Where there is no contract** Fewer cases appear here where the prolific statutory liability[338] has no place. Nor have the decisions following upon *Hedley Byrne*,[339] not involving a contract between the parties given any real consideration to issues of damages. In a number of the cases this has been because the action has failed, so that the damages issue was never reached,[340] or because, although the claimant has won the suit, the court may have been adjudicating only on the issue of liability, an inquiry as to damages being directed,[341] or may have been dealing simply with the preliminary point of whether any duty could arise in the particular type of circumstances.[342] And even where damages have been awarded to the claimant there has been no real dispute as to the quantum. Thus in *Anderson and Sons v Rhodes (Liverpool)*,[343] where the claimant had sold goods to a third party in reliance on the defendant's statements as to his creditworthiness, the damages consisted of the amount of the purchase price that the claimant had failed to recover from the third party on its insolvency. In *Ministry of Housing and Local Government v Sharp*,[344] where the Ministry was entitled to recoup, after planning permission to develop certain land was granted, the amount of compensation paid on an earlier refusal of planning permission, but failed in its claim for such recoupment against the purchaser of the land because the defendant, the local land charges registrar, had failed to reveal to the purchaser that the land was encumbered by the Ministry's duly registered compensation notice, the damages simply consisted of the amount of compensation which the Ministry had initially paid out and was now unable to reclaim from the purchaser. **49-066**

---

from having their business activities severely restricted and also their substantial losses of capital. It was held that it had been reasonable for them to continue leasing the premises for over two years after the initial six-month period because they had sunk their money into the business and did not have the resources to acquire and set up other premises. They were locked in.

334 [1991] 1 W.L.R. 461 CA.

335 See at para.49-031, above, and the cases that follow.

336 [2013] EWHC 111 (QB).

337 See para.49-034. above.

338 See paras 49-058 and following, above.

339 See para.49-048, above.

340 As in *Hedley Byrne* [1964] A.C. 465 itself and in *Mutual Life and Citizens' Assurance Co v Evatt* [1971] A.C. 793 PC. Occasionally, as in *Argy Trading Development Co v Lapid Developments* [1977] 1 W.L.R. 444 (representation that property covered by insurance), the court's provisional views on damages have been expressed even where the holding on liability has been for the defendant: see at 461G–463G.

341 As in *Midland Bank Trust Co v Hett, Stubbs and Kemp* [1979] Ch. 384.

342 As in *Arenson v Arenson* [1977] A.C. 405.

343 [1967] 2 All E.R. 850.

344 [1970] 2 Q.B. 223.

**49-067** Authority apart, it is clear that the proper aim of the damages award is to restore the claimant, as far as possible and subject to the usual rules of remoteness and the like, to the position in which he would have been if the negligent misrepresentation had never been made,[345] and in *Scullion v Bank of Scotland Plc*,[346] the Court of Appeal was of the view that the trial judge had gone beyond this in the damages he awarded. While the court reversed on liability, Lord Neuberger MR, who gave the only reasoned judgment with which his brethren agreed, felt that he should point out where the trial judge had gone wrong on damages to ensure that his judgment was not relied on in other cases. Wishing to enter the buy-to-let housing market, the claimant bought a flat intending to let it at a rental sufficient to pay the mortgage and the outgoings on it, so making the transaction self-financing. In their valuation report the defendants had negligently overstated both the capital value of the flat and the rental income that could be achieved from it, with the result that the claimant had to let the flat at a lower rent than anticipated and later to sell it, on a falling market, for less than he had paid for it. His claim for the difference between the price paid and the amount for which he sold failed as he had not paid more for the flat than its true value at the time of purchase. His loss was due entirely to the subsequent fall in the market and for this loss, on a direct application of *SAAMCO*,[347] he could not recover. While there was no appeal by the claimant on this, it is clear that the Court of Appeal would have agreed. As for his claim in connection with the misrepresentation as to rental income, this succeeded in the lower court, the loss being held to be the claimant's liability to make good the shortfall on his mortgage, arising from the inadequate rental payments, from his own resources. However, Lord Neuberger MR considered that the trial judge's approach came close to treating the negligent statement as a warranty, leading to the contractual rather than the tortious measure of damages, and he spelt out a more limited recovery.[348]

## (2) Non-pecuniary loss

**49-068** Recovery for pure economic loss from negligent misrepresentation is of course the home ground of the *Hedley Byrne* development[349] but there is no reason why non-pecuniary losses should not be recoverable in appropriate circumstances in the same way as they are in deceit.[350] Thus damages for worry and inconvenience were awarded in the common law claim in *McNally v Welltrade International*.[351] In the occasional case where physical injury results from negligent misrepresentation,[352] the damages should follow the same pattern appearing in all other cases of physical injury; indeed it had been held before *Hedley Byrne* that negligent misrepresentation resulting in physical injury was actionable.[353]

**49-069** It is pure economic loss which holds the centre of the stage also with the liability under s.2(1) of the Misrepresentation Act 1967, but again non-pecuniary loss

345 See paras 49-002 to 49-006, above.
346 [2011] 1 W.L.R. 3212 CA.
347 See para.34-073, above.
348 For the details, which it is difficult to set out here, see his judgment at [64]–[68].
349 See para.49-048, above.
350 See paras 49-042 to 49-044, above.
351 [1978] I.R.L.R. 497; facts at para.49-064, above.
352 Compare *Burrows v Rhodes* [1899] 1 Q.B. 816 CA at paras 49-041 and 49-042, above.
353 See the standard texts on tort.

should lead to damages in appropriate circumstances. Thus the damages for worry and inconvenience were awarded in the claim under the statute as well as in the common law claim in *McNally v Welltrade International*.[354] Another illustration is *Chesneau v Interhome*.[355] The claimant and his family, on travelling to a holiday home in France, had found it to be of a much lower standard in the way of accommodation and facilities than had been represented to them by the defendants who had booked it for them, and the claimant had spent two unpleasant days looking for alternative accommodation, which he found. The Court of Appeal awarded £200 for distress and inconvenience. A further similar amount was allowed as damages representing the difference in quality of the holidays, which may also have been essentially for non-pecuniary loss; the short report does not make this clear. With the passage of the years, awards are now likely, as with fraudulent misrepresentation, to be substantially higher.[356] And in coming to the appropriate amount to award there has to be taken into account the Court of Appeal's final ruling in *Simmons v Castle*,[357] that damages for non-pecuniary loss in all types of civil claim are to be increased by 10 per cent.[358] It is thought that this will apply beyond common law awards to awards under statute.

## III. Innocent Misrepresentation

By about the middle of the 19th century, Equity had extended to the person induced to contract by an innocent misrepresentation—innocent, that is, in the sense of not fraudulent—the remedy of rescission of the contract.[359] It was in some cases a somewhat drastic remedy as it required a total unscrambling of all that had been done by either party under the contract, but it was the only suitable remedy that Equity had available to offer, and it was an improvement on the common law's refusal to give any redress by way of damages. Today there is still no common law liability in respect of a misrepresentation that is neither fraudulent nor negligent, but the equitable right to rescission continues, and indeed has in some respects been extended by the Misrepresentation Act 1967.[360] Nevertheless the Law Reform Committee upon whose recommendations the Act was based[361] felt that, whenever it appeared to the court that the rescission remedy would be too drastic, the court ought to have a discretion to award damages instead of granting rescission. This is provided for in s.2(2) which runs thus: **49-070**

> "Where a person has entered into a contract after a misrepresentation has been made to him otherwise than fraudulently, and he would be entitled, by reason of the misrepresentation, to rescind the contract, then, if it is claimed, in any proceedings arising out of the contract, that the contract ought to be or has been rescinded, the court or arbitrator may declare the contract subsisting and award damages in lieu of rescission, if of opinion that it would be equitable to do so, having regard to the nature of the misrepresentation and

[354] [1978] I.R.L.R. 497; facts at para.49-064, above.
[355] (1983) 134 N.L.J. 341 CA.
[356] For fraudulent misrepresentation awards see para.49-044, above.
[357] [2013] 1 W.L.R. 1239 CA; final ruling from 1243.
[358] For the procedural history and reasons for this development, stemming from the package of reforms appearing in the *Jackson Report on Civil Litigation Costs*, see para.40-280, below
[359] See the standard texts on contract and on equity.
[360] See s.1 (rescission not barred by misrepresentation becoming a term of the contract or by the contract having been executed).
[361] See para.49-049, above.

> the loss that would be caused by it if the contract were upheld, as well as to the loss that rescission would cause to the other party."

The question therefore again arises as to the appropriate measure of damages. Since there are in effect but two measures of damages known to the common law, the tortious measure protecting the claimant's reliance interest and the contractual protecting his expectation interest,[362] it might seem at first sight that the tortious measure will have to be espoused here, the contractual measure being clearly inappropriate not only because it is known to be unavailable even for fraudulent misrepresentation[363] but also because the damages are being awarded in place of rescission. Such a straightforward approach does not, however, reckon with s.2(3) of the Misrepresentation Act, which runs:

> "Damages may be awarded against a person under subs.(2) of this section whether or not he is liable to damages under subs.(1) thereof, but where he is so liable any award under the said subs.(2) shall be taken into account in assessing his liability under the said subs.(1)."

There would seem to be in this a clear implication that the damages under s.2(2) will, or at least can, be less than those under s.2(1), and indeed it seems right that any damages awarded for wholly innocent misrepresentation should be less than those which a negligent misrepresentation would attract. But what measure of damages is to be found which gives a degree of compensation to the claimant but does not take him as far as the tortious measure, which falls below the tortious measure but stops short of no award at all?

**49-071** For over a quarter of a century no authority appeared in the books to assist in the resolution of this difficult problem of damages. Eventually there came *Wm Sindall Plc v Cambridgeshire County Council*.[364] However, the Court of Appeal's reasoning there, as opposed to the conclusion reached, is difficult fully to accept. Despite this case, in which Evans LJ stated that "the conclusion may be inconsistent with the view expressed" in the earlier editions of this work,[365] it is thought that the analysis there appearing still holds good and it is proposed to set it out again before turning to *Sindall*[366] itself.

**49-072** It is submitted that the damages should here aim to put the claimant, so far as it can be done by a money award, into the same position as he would have been if a decree of rescission had been granted to him. Not only does this appear to be the appropriate aim for damages which are explicitly a substitute for rescission but also it leads to a measure of damages which meets the criterion of falling below the tortious measure. It becomes necessary therefore to examine what is, for a claimant, the practical result of setting aside the contract into which he has been induced to enter by misrepresentation. First and foremost, of course, rescission entails the mutual restoration, generally in specie, of benefits conferred in performance of the contract. However, in addition to this purely restitutionary aspect of the remedy the courts of equity had been prepared to award to the claimant a degree of monetary compensation, but compensation which they were careful to call an "indemnity"

---

362 See paras 2-002 and 2-003, above.

363 See paras 49-002 to 49-006, above.

364 [1994] 1 W.L.R. 1016 CA.

365 [1994] 1 W.L.R. 1016 CA at 1045E.

366 [1994] 1 W.L.R. 1016 CA.

and not damages. In the leading case on the subject of indemnity, *Newbigging v Adam*,[367] the position was put thus by Bowen LJ:

> "Complete rescission would not be effected unless the misrepresenting party not only hands back the benefits which he has himself received—but also re-assumes the burthen which under the contract the injured party has taken upon himself ... There ought, it appears to me, to be a giving back and a taking back on both sides, including the giving back and taking back of the obligations which the contract has created, as well as the giving back and the taking back of the advantages."[368]

As thus enunciated, this aspect of rescission finds illustration, in the handful of relevant cases, in the two contexts of partnership agreements and of leases. Both in *Rawlins v Wickham*,[369] and in *Newbigging v Adam*[370] itself, the claimant, who had been induced to enter, in the first case a banking partnership and in the second a partnership in the business of worsted spinning, by misrepresentations as to the financial standing of the partnership business, was held entitled not only to be repaid any moneys he had put into the partnership as the price of the share acquired by him but also to be indemnified against the debts and obligations of the partnership for which his being a partner had made him liable[371]; and in the later case of *Whittington v Seale-Hayne*,[372] where the claimant was granted rescission of a lease into which he had entered on the strength of misrepresentations as to the sanitary condition and state of repair of the premises leased, it was accepted by the defendant that he must indemnify the claimant against his expenditures in rent, rates and repairs carried out under the covenants in the lease.[373] But the limits of the indemnity are also spelt out in *Newbigging v Adam*.[374] Cotton LJ took the giving up by the claimant of his army commission in order to come into the partnership business as an illustration of a loss for which he could have got no relief in his rescission claim,[375] and together with Bowen LJ referred to the failure of the claimant in *Redgrave v Hurd*,[376] who had been induced by misrepresentation to contract to join a solicitors' partnership in Birmingham, to recover in his successful rescission claim **49-073**

> "for his loss and trouble in removing from Stroud to Birmingham and ... for having given up his practice at Stroud."[377]

And no indemnity was permitted in *Whittington v Seale-Hayne*[378] to the claimant,

---

367 (1886) 34 Ch. D. 582 CA.

368 (1886) 34 Ch. D. 582 CA at 594–595.

369 (1858) 3 De G. and J. 304.

370 (1886) 34 Ch. D. 582 CA.

371 *Rawlins* is so treated by Bowen LJ in *Newbigging*: see (1886) 34 Ch. D. 582 CA at 595. On appeal in the latter case it became unnecessary to decide the indemnity point since all the debts and liabilities had in fact been paid out of the partnership funds: *Adam v Newbigging* (1888) 13 App. Cas. 308.

372 (1900) 82 L.T. 49.

373 See (1900) 82 L.T. 49 at 51.

374 (1886) 34 Ch. D. 582 CA.

375 (1886) 34 Ch. D. 582 CA at 589.

376 (1881) 20 Ch. D. 1 CA.

377 (1886) 34 Ch. D. 582 CA at 590; and per Bowen LJ, at 594–595. The claimant in *Redgrave* had claimed for these losses in deceit but had been unable to show that the misrepresentations had been fraudulently made; there was, however, no suggestion that recovery could alternatively have been had by way of indemnity in the rescission claim.

378 (1900) 82 L.T. 49.

who had taken the lease of the insanitary and ill-repaired premises for his business of breeding prize poultry and had installed a manager to run the business, for the value of poultry which died, the loss of profits on poultry sales, the loss of breeding season and the expenses of illness of manager and family. To allow recovery to the rescinding partner or lessee for any of these items would be to go well beyond indemnifying against the obligations to which the contract itself gave rise[379]; it would, in effect, be overstepping the border of indemnity into the realm of the reliance damages of tort.

**49-074** If then the court declines to give rescission, what is the equivalent of rescission in damages? Since the first and foremost aim of rescission is the mutual restoration of benefits conferred, it is the equivalent of this which will mark the starting point and indeed the prima facie measure. The claimant who must retain what he has received and cannot have restored to him what he has transferred will need, to be put monetarily into the same position as if there had been mutual restoration, to be awarded the value transferred by him less the actual value received by him. So far, this is the same as the normal measure of damages in tort where the claimant has been induced to contract by fraudulent or negligent misrepresentation.[380] Next, there has to be found the equivalent to the indemnity, which is available in the claim for rescission, against the obligations arising under the contract. Here it might at first sight seem that all that has to be done is to award the same amount as damages, translating one money award into another money award by simply changing the name. But this is by no means so. For if the contract is not going to be rescinded, the claimant is going to have to continue to bear and discharge those very obligations: as partner he will have to continue to meet his share of the partnership liabilities, as lessee he will have to continue to pay rent and rates and to repair the premises. The true analysis is that the weight of these obligations is relevant in valuing what the claimant is in fact receiving under the contract—there is less value to a share in a partnership if encumbered by unanticipated liabilities and to a lease if it brings in its train unexpected repair bills—and therefore these obligations fall to be taken into account in arriving at the normal measure, since they go to reduce the subtrahend in the value transferred less value received equation. Finally, there are those losses for which recovery is not allowed in the rescission claim, such as losses incurred in giving up an existing business and coming to the one which is the subject-matter of the contract, or losses caused by the condition of the premises which form the subject-matter of the contract. Clearly, there is no call to search for a damages equivalent to rescission here, for what is not available in the rescission claim can hardly have a place in the damages claim which is taking its place. The

---

379 The obligations in respect of which an indemnity is available were described somewhat differently by the three members of the Court of Appeal in *Newbigging v Adam* (1886) 34 Ch. D. 582 CA—for Cotton LJ it was "obligations which [the claimant] has contracted under the contract," for Bowen LJ it was "obligations which have been created by the contract"; for Fry LJ it was "obligations entered into under the contract": at 589, 593 and 596 respectively—but it is thought that these various formulations come to the same thing. The view, generally taken (e.g. in *Chitty on Contract*), that Bowen LJ was propounding a narrower test stems from the statement of Fry LJ that he would "hesitate to adopt the view of Lord Justice Bowen that the obligations must be created by the contract" (at 596), but this was simply attributable to Fry LJ's doubt as to whether the partnership debts and obligations could properly be said to be created by the contract. No doubt Bowen LJ would have said that they were, because it was the contract of partnership which created the claimant's liability in respect of them.

380 See paras 49-010, 49-028 and 49-058, above.

overall result, therefore, is that the damages will be held to the difference between the value transferred and the value received, with the value received arrived at in the light of the obligations taken on, so that this will represent not only the normal measure but the only measure of damages, with no recovery being possible for consequential losses. This analysis indeed may now have been accepted by Jacob J in *Witter v TBP Industries*,[381] where there were claims under both s.2(1) and s.2(2).[382] After dealing with some of the perceived difficulties in differentiating the subsections in relation to damages, he said:

> "Fortunately, so far as I am concerned, in the circumstances of this case there can be no difference between the two subsections, for no consequential loss is claimed."[383]

Turning now to *Wm Sindall Plc v Cambridgeshire County Council*,[384] the facts were these. At the height of the property boom of the late 1980s the defendant council sold to the claimant firm of builders for residential development a school playing field. The price was some £5 million, the whole of which the claimants borrowed at high interest rates in order to make payment. Difficulties and delays arose in obtaining detailed planning permission which took about two years, by which time the property market had collapsed so that the land was now worth only some £2 million. At this point it was by chance discovered that a sewage pipe crossed the land. The claimants, seizing this heaven-sent opportunity, purported to rescind the sale on the separate grounds of common mistake and misrepresentation, and subsequently brought an action for a declaration that the sale had been rescinded and for repayment of the purchase price with interest, which together came to some £8 million. The trial judge granted the declaration sought and ordered repayment of purchase price and interest. The defendants appealed, contending that the trial judge was wrong both to find fundamental mistake and misrepresentation and to order rescission for misrepresentation rather than award damages under s.2(2) of the Misrepresentation Act 1967. The Court of Appeal held that there was neither misrepresentation nor mistake sufficient to entitle the claimant to rescission. It therefore became unnecessary to decide the issue raised under s.2(2) as to whether the court should exercise its discretion to award damages in lieu of rescission. Since, however, the point had been argued and the case might go higher, the Court of Appeal addressed the issue. Moreover, although not directly concerned with the assessment of damages, which would be a matter determined at an inquiry, it was necessary for the court to decide in principle how the damages would be calculated in order, as Hoffman LJ put it,[385] **49-075**

> "to know whether damages under s.2(2) would be an adequate remedy and to be able to compare such damages with the loss which rescission would cause to"

the defendants.

The Court of Appeal came to the conclusion that the damages should be assessed at the £18,000 cost of putting the defect right by diversion of the sewer and stated this to be the contractual measure of damages. The loss, said Evans LJ, **49-076**

381 [1996] 2 All E.R. 573.

382 And also a claim for breach of contract. See the case at para.49-053, above.

383 [1996] 2 All E.R. 573 at 591e.

384 [1994] 1 W.L.R. 1016 CA.

385 [1994] 1 W.L.R. 1016 CA at 1037C.

"can be measured by the cost of remedying the defect or alternatively by the reduced market value attributable to the defect".[386]

In his judgment, contrary to the view expressed in, and cited by him from, the then current edition of this work and retained in this,[387]

"the contract measure … becomes the correct measure in circumstances where the plaintiff is entitled to an order for rescission, but rescission is refused under s.2(2) of the Act."[388]

He added:

"The difference in value between what the plaintiff was misled into believing that he was acquiring, and the value of what he in fact received, seems to me to be the measure of the loss caused to him by the misrepresentation in a case where he cannot rescind the contract and therefore retains the property which he has received."[389]

**49-077** While entirely agreeing with the result in the case, the reasoning is thought to be dangerously faulty. A vital feature is that here the price paid for the land was equal to its value as represented and therefore the basic measure of damages in contract and in tort was the same. The consequential loss by way of the huge fall in the market value would not, as the law stands, have been recoverable had the misrepresentation been fraudulent[390] or even negligent[391] and therefore a fortiori was irrecoverable under s.2(2). The error in the reasoning is to have espoused, in explaining the calculation at which the court arrived, the contractual measure of damages. It cannot be right, where there is no warranty, that a claimant can claim the benefit of his bargain—and the reality of this should not be obscured by the fact that there was no such benefit to be claimed here since the bargain was a very bad one in retrospect and a neutral one at time of contract. Envisage a case where a buyer has made an excellent bargain, having bought for £50,000 an item of property which, if the representation had been true, would have been worth £75,000; in fact in its faulty condition it is worth only £40,000. Were the misrepresentation fraudulent or negligent then at common law or under s.2(1) respectively, utilising the tort measure and abjuring the contractual, recovery is of £10,000, namely price paid less value as is. Can it be that with an innocent misrepresentation, where the damages cannot surely be greater and are likely to be smaller,[392] the buyer can claim the benefit of his bargain—the contractual measure banished from s.2(1) claims only after a struggle[393]—and recover £35,000, namely value as represented less value as is?

**49-078** That the Court of Appeal saw the case as an appropriate one for the exercise of the discretion to award damages in lieu of rescission was based on the acceptance of the claimants' argument that, had rescission been allowed, they would have been entitled to receive back the purchase price together with the high rate interest which

386 [1994] 1 W.L.R. 1016 CA at 1044H.

387 See para.49-071, above.

388 [1994] 1 W.L.R. 1016 at 1045H.

389 [1994] 1 W.L.R. 1016 at 1045H–1046A.

390 See *Waddell v Blockey* (1879) 4 Q.B.D. 678 CA. This now derives support from the reasoning of the House of Lords in *Smith New Court Securities v Scrimgeour Vickers* [1997] A.C. 254: see at para.49-016, above.

391 See *Cemp Properties (UK) v Dentsply Research Corp* [1991] 2 E.G.L.R. 197 CA.

392 See paras 49-070 and following, above.

393 See para.49-053, above.

they had paid on the moneys borrowed to finance the purchase; this made for a huge disparity between the loss which rescission and the loss which damages as assessed would have caused the defendants. And indeed, if this argument of the claimants were correct, the support, here given,[394] for the measure of damages the Court of Appeal would have awarded would sit ill with the submission, here advanced,[395] that the damages should put the claimant in the same position as he would have been if a decree of rescission had been granted to him. However, this is not how rescission works.

It has always been accepted that a claimant representee claiming rescission must be capable of putting the defendant representor back in the position he was in before the contract was made and this cannot be done where the subject-matter of the contract has deteriorated in the claimant's hands[396]—and a vast reduction in market value must count as a deterioration. It is true that the first instance decision of *Armstrong v Jackson*,[397] concerned the purchase of shares which had deteriorated in value between time of contract and time of action and rescission was not refused to the buyer. However, that case involved a breach of fiduciary duty and it is clear that a much harsher line is taken against fraudulent defendants from whom rescission is sought—and in equity the term "fraud" embraces breach of fiduciary duty—than against defendants whose misrepresentation has been innocent.[398] Thus even if the Court of Appeal had found there to be a misrepresentation, it could be said that there was no entitlement to rescission and therefore no entitlement under s.2(2) to damages in lieu, so that the issue of their measure could not arise.[399] Moreover, even if the deterioration did not cut out rescission entirely, it would nevertheless be taken into account in the effecting of the rescission. For courts of equity have long been prepared to make adjustments between the parties and so allow a claimant holding a deteriorated subject-matter to return it to the defendant if he compensates the defendant for the deterioration. Lord Blackburn, in his important speech in the leading case of *Erlanger v New Sombrero Phosphate Co*,[400] said that "a Court of Equity ... can ... make allowance for deterioration"[401] in giving rescission, which is its practice to give **49-079**

---

394 At para.49-077, above.

395 At para.49-072, above.

396 *Lagunas Nitrate Co v Lagunas Syndicate* [1899] 2 Ch. 392 CA, is an important illustration of refusal of rescission (Rigby LJ dissenting) on this, together with another, ground.

397 [1917] 2 K.B. 822.

398 See *Spence v Crawford* [1939] 3 All E.R. 271 HL, per Lord Thankerton at 281 and per Lord Wright at 288–289.

399 It is considered to be the better view that damages can be available under s.2(2) only where in the particular circumstances of the case rescission was itself a possibility. The purpose of the subsection was to cut down on rescission because of its drastic nature and therefore the substitute of damages is only required where rescission could have held the day. In *Witter v TBP Industries* [1996] 2 All E.R. 573 the contrary view was arrived at (the decision would have been the same without it as there was held to be liability under s.2(1) and for breach of contract: see paras 49-053 and 49-074, above) but *Witter* was expressly not followed both in *Floods of Queensferry Ltd v Shand Construction Ltd* [2000] B.L.R. 81 (the second claim under this name, the first being at para.9-131 and para.31-008, above) and in *Government of Zanzibar v British Aerospace Ltd* [2000] 1 W.L.R. 2333 (the very short report at [2000] T.L.R. 234 which misleadingly suggests the contrary should be ignored). After a full and careful analysis the trial judge in *Flood* considered the view here preferred not only to be the correct view in principle but also to be supported by dicta in other cases, especially in *Wm Sindall Plc v Cambridgeshire CC* [1994] 1 W.L.R. 1016 CA, itself.

400 (1878) 3 App. Cas. 1218.

401 (1878) 3 App. Cas. 1218 at 1278.

> "whenever, by the exercise of its powers, it can do what is practically just, though it cannot restore the parties precisely to the state they were in before the contract".[402]

Again, the adjustments to which a claimant must submit are likely to be greater, for the securing of practical justice, where the defendant's conduct has been innocent rather than fraudulent.[403]

**49-080** In the instant case therefore the claimant would not be automatically entitled to recover the purchase price of £5 million; if it were to order rescission the court could, and should, award the purchase price of £5 million less the deterioration of £3 million, effectively the market value of £2 million that the land had when the claim was made. Nor could there be any question of the claimants claiming the loss by way of the some £3 million in interest charges which had been incurred, because such a loss was not a loss created by the contract and would not have fallen within the concept of the indemnity which the courts of equity have been prepared to allow in rescission claims.[404] It follows therefore that the damages which the Court of Appeal would have awarded in *Sindall*,[405] would effectively have put the claimants in the financial position in which they would have been had they been granted rescission.[406]

---

402 (1878) 3 App. Cas. 1218 at 1278–1279.

403 See *O'Sullivan v Management Agency and Music* [1985] Q.B. 428 at 458 CA, per Dunn LJ.

404 See para.49-072, above.

405 [1994] 1 W.L.R. 1016 CA.

406 Without exploring the merits of using the contractual measure for the damages it was accepted as correct in *Floods of Queensferry* (at para.49-079, above (in a footnote)) partly because this had been approved in *Wm Sindall Plc v Cambridgeshire CC* [1994] 1 W.L.R. 1016 CA, but partly also because it would have made no difference to the result which measure had been taken as the trial judge was not prepared to make any award of damages: see at [2000] B.L.R. 81, 94, col.2. Indeed it is thought that in the circumstances of the case all measures would have given the same result.

# PART 5 HUMAN RIGHTS

## Chapter 50

# DAMAGES UNDER THE HUMAN RIGHTS ACT

Table of Contents



## 1. Introduction

**50-001** Although it has for a long time been possible to apply to the European Court of Human Rights[1] for a money award where there has been a violation of the European Convention on Human Rights,[2] such applications formed no part of English domestic law. However, with the coming into force of the Human Rights Act 1998[3] on 2 October 2000, a significant change was made to domestic law whereby a new statutory power was given to the courts to make awards of damages for breaches of incorporated Convention rights and a new cause of action enacted to apply for such awards.[4] The result is that no book on the law of damages would be complete without consideration of the human rights damages action.

---

1 Hereinafter referred to as the ECtHR.

2 Hereinafter referred to as the ECHR or the Convention.

3 Hereinafter referred to as the HRA.

4 However, the Act does not extend to those parts of Great Britain which are not subject to the ECHR. Thus, the ECHR has not been extended to the British Overseas Territory of South Georgia and the

The remedy is confined to situations where those Convention rights scheduled to the HRA have been breached by public authorities. Public authority is defined broadly[5] and includes a court or tribunal and any person whose functions are of a public nature. Public authorities most obviously include bodies such as government departments, local councils, the police, prisons, the NHS, and various statutory bodies. But the test under the HRA is such that the Act may also apply to a private company that performs contracted-out functions on behalf of government. **50-002**

Damages are available under s.8 of the HRA. Unlike damages in actions in tort and contract, damages are not available as of right but are discretionary. Pursuant to s.8(3) damages must be a "necessary" remedy and pursuant to s.8(1) it must also be "just and appropriate" to award them. In the leading case of *R. (on the application of Greenfield) v Secretary of State for the Home Department*,[6] Lord Bingham said that in deciding whether to award damages, the domestic court must be satisfied as to four preconditions: **50-003**

(1) that a finding of unlawfulness or prospective unlawfulness is made, based on breach or prospective breach by a public authority of a Convention right;
(2) the court has power to award damages in civil proceedings;
(3) the court is satisfied that an award of damages is necessary to afford "just satisfaction" to the victim; and
(4) the court considers that an award of damages is just and appropriate.

Lord Bingham elaborated[7] that the "necessity test" was the key test:

> "It would seem to be clear that a domestic court may not award damages unless satisfied that it is necessary to do so, but if satisfied that it is necessary to do so it is hard to see how the court could consider it other than just and appropriate to do so".

Section 8(4) provides that in determining whether to award damages and quantum the court **50-004**

> "must take into account the principles applied by the European Court of Human Rights in relation to the award of compensation under art.41 of the Convention".

Article 41 of the Convention is that provision which governs the ECtHR's own remedial jurisdiction, and pursuant to which that Court makes money awards of compensation. The Article reads:

> "If the Court finds that there has been a violation of the Convention or the protocols thereto, and if the internal law of the High Contracting Party concerned allows only partial reparation to be made, the Court shall, if necessary, afford just satisfaction to the injured party."

The reference to art.41 in the damages provisions of the HRA is something of a curiosity. Unlike the other Convention Articles referenced in the Act, art.41 is not an Article directed to or which binds member states. Rather it is directed "inwards" to the Strasbourg Court's own remedial practices. That Court's remedial practices

---

South Sandwich Islands and therefore an unlawful instruction by the Secretary of State, acting on behalf of the Queen as sovereign of South Georgia rather than the UK, to refuse a fishing licence did not give rise to a claimable action of damages under the HRA: see *R. (on the application of Quark Fishing Ltd) v Secretary of State for Foreign and Commonwealth Affairs* [2006] 1 A.C. 529.

5 In ss.6(1) and 6(3) of the HRA; see paras 50-011 and following, below.

6 [2005] 1 W.L.R. 673 HL.

7 [2005] 1 W.L.R. 673 HL at [6].

are invariably shaped by its place as a supranational, supervisory Court. Its primary concerns are upholding human rights standards across Europe, not provision of individual redress. Rather, within the system of rights-protection redress of violations is the principal responsibility of domestic courts. That the ECtHR's role in the provision of remedies is secondary and ancillary is reflected in the terms of art.41 itself, which makes it a prerequisite for the award of compensation that the domestic law of the member state only allows for partial reparation to be made. As such the remedial practice of the ECtHR under art.41 is not intended as a model for domestic courts, which in turn raises questions as to the aptness of referring English courts to the ECtHR's remedial practices. Furthermore, the ECtHR's art.41 jurisprudence is fraught with problems. It lacks consistency, coherence, principle and determinations are in general supported by the most parsimonious of reasoning, while the Court does not apply publicly-stated tariffs. As such English courts have repeatedly stated that they have struggled to divine anything of significance from the jurisprudence. The ECtHR jurisprudence has been subjected to searching academic critique,[8] with one leading human rights treatise advising practitioners not to spend time searching for principles which do not exist.[9] The Law Commissions, in a report on damages under the HRA, considered the "lack of clear principles as to when damages should be awarded and how they should be measured" to be perhaps "the most striking feature of the Strasbourg case-law".[10] Thus, at an early stage of the development of HRA damages jurisprudence, the state of the Strasbourg case law prompted Lord Millett in *Cullen v Chief Constable of the Royal Ulster Constabulary* to observe that

> "we may have to develop our own jurisprudence, while keeping an eye open on the case law of the Strasbourg court to ensure that we do not stray too far from the principles which that court may lay down".[11]

The benefit of such approach would be that the elaborate corpus of common law damages rules and principles could be relied on to fill in the detail missing in the Strasbourg jurisprudence, while the basic principles that characterise the ECtHR jurisprudence of restitutio in integrum and causation are consonant with domestic principles. Of particular importance domestic damages practice is marked by detailed guidance as to scales of awards for non-pecuniary loss, whereas Strasbourg practice does not follow nor reveal any such worked-out scales, each award being in the nature of an "equitable" response to the facts. An approach informed by domestic damages principles would also have the benefit of ensuring consonance as between the approach to compensating interferences with common interests protected in tort and by the HRA, such as liberty (false imprisonment and art.5) or physical integrity (battery and art.3), while there are clear analogies more generally between human rights, and torts actionable per se which have long afforded strong protection to basic dignitary and proprietary interests, such as trespass, bat-

---

8 See in particular J.N.E. Varuhas, *Damages and Human Rights*, (Oxford: Hart Publishing, 2016), Ch.5.

9 A. Lester et al, *Human Rights Law and Practice*, 3rd edn (London: LexisNexis, 2009), para.2.8.4 n.3.

10 Law Commission, *Damages under the Human Rights Act 1998* (2000), Law Com. No.266/Scot Law Com. No.180, Cm.4853, paras.3.4–3.15.

11 [2003] 1 W.L.R. 1763 HL at [80].

tery, defamation and false imprisonment.[12] It is not clear why damages for identical or similarly basic interests should be quantified differently depending on whether the claim happens to be made in tort or under the HRA. Thus when the Law Commissions conducted a detailed inquiry into the approach that ought to be taken to HRA damages they reached the conclusion that the award of damages in tort is the "obvious comparator in English law".[13] While care should be taken in reading across principles developed in tort,

> "in the majority of cases under the HRA the courts … will find it possible and appropriate to apply the rules by which damages in tort are usually assessed to claims under the HRA".[14]

While the Law Commissions' suggested approach characterised early damages decisions under the HRA,[15] the House of Lords and Supreme Court, in the two leading decisions on HRA damages have since rendered the art.41 jurisprudence of central importance to HRA damages claims. The higher courts have mandated a "mirror" approach, placing great emphasis on s.8(4). According to this approach domestic courts must seek to replicate in domestic law the ECtHR's "clear and consistent practice"[16] under art.41, and seek to determine cases—both in terms of when damages should be awarded and quantum—on the basis of the art.41 jurisprudence. The corollary of this focus on art.41 is that significant guidance that might have been derived from the common law has in general been side-lined. As Lord Bingham said in *Greenfield*, the HRA is "not a tort statute", and while the Strasbourg jurisprudence is not strictly binding, there could be "no clearer indication" than s.8(4) that "courts in this country should look to Strasbourg and not to domestic precedents".[17] In *R. (Sturnham) v Parole Board* Lord Reed reiterated this approach, interpreting Lord Bingham's speech in *Greenfield* as having construed ss.8(3) and (4) of the Act as: **50-005**

> "introducing into our domestic law an entirely novel remedy, the grant of which is discretionary, and which is described as damages but is not tortious in nature, inspired by art.41 of the Convention. Reflecting the international origins of the remedy and its lack of any native roots, the primary source of the principles which are to guide the courts in its application is said to be the practice of the international court that is its native habitat".[18]

Two important consequences follow from the mirror approach. First, damages are said to be a remedy of last resort and of secondary importance in HRA claims, with the main concern being to bring unlawful conduct to an end and prevent its **50-006**

---

[12] J.N.E. Varuhas, *Damages and Human Rights*, (Oxford: Hart Publishing, 2016), Chs 2–3; J.N.E. Varuhas, "A Tort-Based Approach to Damages under the Human Rights Act 1998" (2009) 72 M.L.R. 750.

[13] Law Commission, *Damages under the Human Rights Act 1998* (2000), Law Com. No.266/Scot Law Com. No.180, Cm.4853, para.4.14.

[14] Law Commission, *Damages under the Human Rights Act 1998* (2000), Law Com. No.266/Scot Law Com. No.180, Cm.4853, paras.4.21, 4.26.

[15] *R. (on the application of Bernard) v Enfield London Borough Council* [2003] H.R.L.R. 4 Admin; *R. (on the application of KB) v Mental Health Review Tribunal* [2004] Q.B. 936; *Anufrijeva v Southwark London Borough Council* [2004] Q.B. 1124 CA at [73]–[74].

[16] *R. (on the application of Sturnham) v Parole Board* [2013] 2 A.C. 254 at [13(3)] (also known as *R. (on the application of Faulkner) v Secretary of State for Justice*).

[17] *R. (on the application of Greenfield) v Secretary of State for the Home Department* [2005] 1 W.L.R. 673 HL at [19].

[18] [2013] 2 A.C. 254 at [29].

repetition, suggesting a focus on declarations and specific relief, and traditional judicial review remedies, namely quashing orders, prohibiting orders and mandatory orders. As explained in *Greenfield*, this follows from the goal of the Convention being "the protection of human rights and not the award of compensation".[19] Similarly, in the later case of *DSD v Commissioner of Police of the Metropolis* Laws LJ said, "the focus is on the State's compliance, not the claimant's loss".[20] As such awards have been infrequent, with domestic courts following the Strasbourg Court's practice of not uncommonly holding that a finding of violation is just satisfaction, the award of damages being unnecessary. Albeit in recent years there has been some liberalisation of approach in a number of areas, while the courts have been more ready to award damages for proven pecuniary losses. Secondly, of particular relevance to awards for non-pecuniary loss, quantum follows Strasbourg scales, to the extent those are discernible. For example in *Greenfield* Lord Bingham rejected counsel's submission that awards under the HRA should be guided by scales applied in domestic anti-discrimination law,[21] while in *Sturnham* Lord Reed rejected the Court of Appeal's approach which had taken the treatment of wrongs at common law as its starting point.[22] In the light of these authorities, "the guide to quantum is to be found in Strasbourg cases rather than English decisions".[23] This is of considerable significance because Strasbourg awards for non-pecuniary loss are much lower than scales for equivalent heads of loss in domestic tort law, such as distress or loss of liberty. As Lord Bingham observed, awards under art.41 are "ungenerous" by English tort standards.[24]

**50-007** Underpinning the adoption of the mirror approach is the idea that the purpose of the HRA was to "bring rights home".[25] That is, to enable victims of rights-violations to vindicate their rights and secure the remedies they could secure at Strasbourg but without the time and expense of travelling to Strasbourg. However, matters are not so black and white. In leading the Human Rights Bill through Parliament the Lord Chancellor posited "our courts must be free to try to give a lead to Europe as well as to be led".[26] In any case as Burrows has argued,

> "'To bring home' rights might be thought to require that rights are compensated in the way that home regards as appropriate".[27]

Further, another stated reason for passing the HRA was simply to afford the most fundamental of rights strong and direct protection in domestic law,[28] while the Convention rights "brought home" are themselves underpinned by a policy of

---

19 [2005] 1 W.L.R. 673 HL at [9].

20 [2016] Q.B. 161 CA at [65]–[66].

21 [2005] 1 W.L.R. 673 HL at [18]–[19].

22 [2013] 2 A.C. 254 at [96].

23 *Van Colle v Chief Constable of Hertfordshire* [2007] 1 W.L.R. 1821 CA at [104].

24 *Watkins v Secretary of State for the Home Department* [2006] 2 A.C. 395 at [26].

25 See *Rights Brought Home: The Human Rights Bill* (1997) Cmd 3782; *R. (on the application of Greenfield) v Secretary of State for the Home Department* [2005] 1 W.L.R. 673 HL at [19].

26 H.L. Deb. vol. 583 col. 808 (24 November 1997); H.C. Deb. vol. 307 col. 770 (16 February 1998) Mr Jack Straw ("British judges will be enabled to make a distinctively British contribution to the development of the jurisprudence of human rights across Europe").

27 A. Burrows, "Damages and Human Rights" in D. Nolan and A. Robertson (eds.), *Rights and Private Law*, (Oxford: Hart Publishing, 2012), p.303.

28 *Harrow London Borough Council v Qazi* [2004] 1 A.C. 983 at [8]; H.L. Deb. vol. 583 col. 808 (24 November 1997) Lord Chancellor (the Government's aim in passing the Bill is "to provide as much protection as possible for the rights of individuals against the misuse of power b the state within the framework of a Bill which preserves parliamentary sovereignty"); H.L. Deb. vol. 582 col. 1228–

strong and effective protection of basic human interests[29]; uncommon and low awards do not constitute a strong form of protection, and it is difficult to justify why a far more restrictive approach to damages liability ought to be adopted in respect of fundamental rights compared to the treatment of less than fundamental interests in other domestic fields of liability. Importantly, the terms of the statute do not support a strict mirror approach by which domestic courts seek to replicate Strasbourg practice. Section 8(4) only imposes an obligation to "take into account" art.41 material, not to treat it as though it had the force of precedent. A duty to take material into account entails a liberty to depart from that material, and a liberty to take into account other relevant material, such as domestic practice. Further, courts are directed under s.8(4) to take account of the "principles" applied by the ECtHR—which are few and include very basic ideas such as restitutio in integrum and factual causation—not to replicate the ECtHR's body of jurisprudence in domestic law. In this regard it is apposite to contrast the terms of s.2(1). This section governs the relevance of Strasbourg material to decisions over substantive rights. It requires English courts to take into account any "judgment, decision, declaration, or advisory opinion" of the Strasbourg Court. Even in the context of this more specific direction the English courts increasingly have loosened the relationship between domestic law under the HRA, and ECtHR jurisprudence, in adjudication of substantive rights. For example in respect of s.2(1) it has been said that "Strasbourg jurisprudence is not to be treated as a straightjacket from which there is no escape"[30] and indeed the Supreme Court has even begun to prescribe that "the starting point [is] our own legal principles"[31] rather than Strasbourg jurisprudence. If this is the emergent position under the more prescriptive drafting of s.2(1), it becomes difficult to rationalise maintenance of a very strict mirror approach in relation to damages, especially given it is axiomatic that remedies are for the forum.[32]

Against this background, Lord Reed's dicta in *Sturnham* raise interesting ques- **50-008**
tions about how the HRA damages jurisprudence may develop into the future. He said that Strasbourg jurisprudence should be the starting point "at this stage of the development of the remedy" and that over time "the remedy should become naturalised".[33] Arguably this means that as Strasbourg practice is read across to domestic law a domestic jurisprudence will emerge over time—but one nonetheless steeped in Strasbourg practice. On the other hand, the observation may signal scope for change in the future, and a refocusing on or at least greater consideration of domestic damages traditions, scales, and rules and principles. In this regard it is notable that the approach to pecuniary loss at least is increasingly indistinguishable from that applied at common law. It is also worth observing that it was not argued in *Sturnham* that *Greenfield* ought to be overruled, so that the Supreme Court was bound in that case to give effect to the mirror approach.

---

1229 (3 November 1997) Lord Chancellor ("[The design of the Bill] maximises the protection of human rights without trespassing on parliamentary sovereignty").

29 *Soering v United Kingdom* (1989) 11 E.H.R.R. 439 at [87]; *Saadi v United Kingdom* (2008) 47 E.H.R.R. 17 at [62].

30 *Re P (A Child)* [2009] 1 A.C. 173 at [50]; *Manchester City Council v Pinnock* [2011] 2 A.C. 104 at [48]–[49].

31 *R. (on the application of Sturnham) v Parole Board* [2013] 2 A.C. 254 at [29]; *Osborn v Parole Board* [2014] A.C. 1115 at [54] and following; *Kennedy v The Charity Commission* [2015] A.C. 455 at [46], [67].

32 *R. (on the application of KB) v Mental Health Review Tribunal* [2004] Q.B. 936 at [22].

33 *R. (on the application of Sturnham) v Parole Board* [2013] 2 A.C. 254 at [29], [39], [96].

## 2. SCOPE OF THE CAUSE OF ACTION

50-009 This work is principally concerned with the law of damages, and detailed consideration of the elements of the cause of action and substantive law of human rights are outside its scope. Nonetheless it is important here to consider certain basic matters relevant to any claim for HRA damages, including who can be sued, who can sue, forum and procedure, and time limits.

50-010 In summary, the cause of action and the right to bring proceedings in domestic courts for breach of enumerated Convention rights are conferred by ss.6, 7 and 8 of the HRA. Section 6 makes it unlawful for a public authority to act in violation of those Convention rights scheduled to the Act. Section 7 creates the cause of action, to be brought within one year, and includes the procedural provisions for bringing the action. Section 8 provides for the grant of remedies, including the remedy of damages. Sections 6, 7 and 8 contain a number of concepts, and give rise to a number of questions, which will be considered in turn.

### (1) Who can be sued

50-011 By s.7(1), the statutory cause of action is confined to where a public authority has acted unlawfully in breach of s.6(1) of the HRA. Section 6(3) defines a public authority as including (a) a court or tribunal, and (b) any person certain of whose functions are functions of a public nature, but does not include either House of Parliament or a person exercising functions in connection with proceedings in Parliament. Section 6(5) provides that in relation to a particular act, a person is not a public authority by virtue only of subs.(3)(b) if the nature of the act is private.

50-012 In the important case of *Aston Cantlow and Wilmcote with Billesley Parochial Church Council v Wallbank*,[34] the House of Lords considered that s.6 recognised two types of public authorities. Which category a public authority fell into would affect when it would be bound by the HRA. "Core" public authorities must, pursuant to s.6(1), comply with the HRA in everything they do. Such bodies are those that are essentially governmental in a broad sense of that expression, the most obvious examples being government departments, local authorities, the police and armed forces. Entities in this category are classified on the basis of the nature of the entity itself, and various factors will guide the court including whether the body is bestowed with special powers; democratically accountable; publicly funded in whole or part; obliged to act only in the public interest; and characterised by a statutory constitution. "Hybrid" public authorities, on the other hand, are those that perform a mixture of public and private functions. They will be bound to comply with the HRA in respect of their public functions (pursuant to s.6(3)(b)), but not in respect of private acts (pursuant to s.6(5)). That the Act includes hybrid authorities within its scope follows from the realities of the organisation of modern government, in which private firms often play a role in the delivery of "public" services through a variety of arrangements, including under contract and as a result of privatisation. Whereas for core public authorities the court enquires into the *nature* of the entity, to determine when a hybrid authority is bound by the Act the court will inquire into whether a particular *function* performed by the entity may be classified as "public". In *Aston Cantlow* Lord Nicholls indicated that a cautious approach would be taken to designating entities as core public authorities, on the basis

---

[34] [2004] 1 A.C. 546.

that this has significant ramifications, binding the authority to observe the HRA in everything it does, and because designation as a core authority would disentitle the entity from itself enjoying Convention rights. This cautious approach to core authorities would be counterbalanced by a generous approach to the interpretation of "public function" in relation to hybrid bodies. Such a generous interpretation would further the statutory aim of promoting observance of human rights, without depriving hybrid bodies themselves of the protection of Convention rights.

Disputes are more likely to turn—and have turned—on hybrid bodies, some of **50-013** whose functions are public and some not. There is no universal test to determine whether a particular function is public or not, and both in judicial review and under the HRA the question of whether a function is public or not has proven one of difficulty for courts, resting on case-by-case determination. Importantly the test under the HRA is "functional" rather than "source-based". What is determinative is the nature of the function being performed—e.g. is social care a public function?—rather than the source of the powers—e.g. are powers sourced in statute or contract? However, the source of the powers relied on to perform a particular function may nonetheless be one factor that is relevant to determining whether a function is public or not, among a range of potentially relevant factors. In *Aston Cantlow* Lord Nicholls gave a list of such factors: the extent to which in carrying out the relevant function the body is publicly funded, or is exercising statutory powers, or is taking the place of central government or local authorities, or is providing a public service. Further guidance might be derived from factors that courts have considered in determining the scope of judicial review.[35]

Albeit the functional formulation of the test of "publicness" under the HRA was **50-014** designed specifically to overcome the accountability gaps created by modern practices of contracting-out of government functions, the presence of contractual relations has proven a hurdle to classifying functions as public.[36] In *YL v Birmingham City Council* the defendant Council had contracted Southern Cross Healthcare Ltd to discharge the Council's statutory duty under the National Assistance Act 1948 to arrange the provision of residential care and accommodation for the appellant. When Southern Cross sought to terminate the contract, the appellant—an elderly care home resident in one of Southern Cross's residences—whose accommodation was funded to a significant extent by public funds, sought to challenge their eviction on the basis that this would breach art.8. In turn this raised the question whether Southern Cross was performing a public function in providing care and accommodation, so that it was bound by the HRA. A 3-2 majority held that it was not. Whereas the duty to arrange for provision of accommodation was a public function, actual provision of the accommodation was not, and under the relevant statute did not need to be provided by a governmental body. Importantly emphasis was also placed on Southern Cross's private profit motive as a company, and that the duties imposed by art.8 would fit uneasily with the private law freedom to carry on operations under agreed contractual terms. While Southern Cross was subject to statutory regulation in the carrying on of its functions, this was not considered determinative, and Southern Cross was not possessed of any special statutory powers. Recognition of the applicability of Convention norms could also

---

[35] See the factors discussed in *R. (on the application of Beer (t/a Hammer Trout Farm)) v Hampshire County Council* [2004] 1 W.L.R. 233 CA and M. Elliott and J.N.E. Varuhas, *Administrative Law*, 5th edn (Oxford: Oxford University Press, 2017), Ch.4.

[36] The same has proven true in judicial review: *R. (on the application of Holmcroft Properties Ltd) v KPMG LLP* [2016] EWHC 323 (Admin).

create two classes of care home resident: those that are publicly-funded and whose Convention rights must be protected, and those who are privately funded and to whom Southern Cross would not owe duties under the HRA. Lord Bingham and Lady Hale registered strong dissents. Both emphasised that the state had assumed responsibility, through the relevant legislation, for the provision of accommodation and care for those in need, indicating that this was a function of a public nature; the exact means by which this was to be achieved was of less moment. Further factors included that the state had been willing to apply significant funds to support the places of those in care; provision of residential care was subject to significant statutory regulation; and those who qualify for such care are vulnerable members of society, and Parliament cannot have intended that their basic rights should be left unprotected. Overall Lord Bingham considered that a case such as this, in which a private provider was performing a function pursuant to contract that would undoubtedly be public if performed by government, was the very sort of case which s.6(3)(b) was drafted to cover. In response to the House of Lords' decision, Parliament legislated to bring care providers in the position of Southern Cross within the scope of the HRA.[37]

**50-015** Following *YL* it would seem services provided pursuant to a commercial contract will be unlikely to fall within the scope of the HRA. However, much depends on the facts of the case and arrangements made between the private provider and authority. Thus in *R. (on the application of Weaver) v London and Quadrant Housing Trust*,[38] the defendant, a Trust that provided social housing below market rates, was held to be bound by the HRA when deciding whether to terminate the tenancy of someone in social housing. A factor that favoured this conclusion was that the landlord received block payments of subsidies out of public funds; in contrast, in *YL* Southern Cross paid for services provided to individual care home occupants. Other factors included that the Trust acts in concert with government to achieve statutory objectives; provision of social housing is in the nature of a public service and far from purely commercial activity; the Trust acts in the public interest and for charitable purposes; and in performing these functions the Trust is subject to intrusive regulation.

**50-016** Three further points must be made in relation to potential defendants. First, Parliament cannot be sued for damages in respect of primary legislation that is incompatible with Convention rights.[39] Secondly, if the defendant public authority had no choice but to act in a manner incompatible with the claimant's Convention rights, as their acts were required by primary legislation, the authority does not act unlawfully and no damages may be claimed.[40] Thirdly, public authorities may be conferred immunities from damages liability under their parent statutes. However, often where immunities are conferred in respect of liability in tort, liability under the HRA is exempted.[41] There is what might be described as a qualified good faith immunity for judicial acts under s.9(3) of the HRA. Pursuant to this section, in proceedings under the HRA, damages may only be awarded in respect of judicial

---

37 Health and Social Care Act 2008 s.145 (repealed). See now Care Act 2014 s.73.

38 [2010] 1 W.L.R. 363 CA. See also *Poplar Housing and Regeneration Community Association Ltd v Donoghue* [2002] Q.B. 48 CA.

39 Human Rights Act 1998 s.6(2)–(3), (6); *Tovey v Ministry of Justice* [2011] H.R.L.R. 17 (QB).

40 Human Rights Act 1998 s.6(2); *R. (on the application of H) v Secretary of State for the Home Department* [2003] Q.B. 320 CA; *R (on the application of GC) v Commissioner for the Metropolis* [2011] 1 W.L.R. 1230 SC.

41 See for example Financial Services and Markets Act 2000 Sch.1 para.19(3)(b).

acts done in good faith, to the extent required by art.5(5) of the Convention.[42] That Article provides that anyone who has been the victim of arrest or detention in breach of the provisions of art.5 shall have a right to compensation. Thus, outside of liberty cases judicial acts done in good faith are immune from HRA damages liability.

## (2) Who can sue

Section 7(1) of the HRA provides that proceedings may be brought by a person who claims that a public authority has acted unlawfully within s.6(1) only if that person is (or would be) a victim of the unlawful act. Further definitional assistance is given by s.7(7), which provides that **50-017**

> "a person is a victim of an unlawful act only if he would be a victim for the purposes of art.34 of the Convention[43] if proceedings were brought in the European Court of Human Rights in respect of that act".

Thus, it is clear that the intention of the HRA is to harmonise English law in this regard with the established law under the ECtHR, and domestic courts have had regard to and been led by the ECtHR jurisprudence.

Importantly, standing under the HRA differs from the broad public interest standing rules that pertain within the common law of judicial review, which potentially allow public interest groups or publically-spirited individuals to challenge administrative acts even if their own rights or interests are not affected or prejudiced by that administrative action.[44] Standing criteria under the HRA are narrow and rights-based. The basic principle, though there are exceptions, is that standing is limited to the individual right-holder whose interests are directly affected by the challenged administrative action. Two examples of cases in which standing has been denied under the HRA shall suffice to illustrate the basic nature of the victim test. In *R. (on the application of Children's Rights Alliance for England) v Secretary of State for Justice*,[45] the claimant was a charity, whose purpose was to protect children's rights. The background to the litigation was that children and young persons in custody in Secure Training Centres (STCs) had been subject to the use of bodily restraint techniques. The claimant charity argued that the defendant was legally required to take steps, particularly to provide information, to enable those children who had been subjected to unlawful restraints to identify that they had been treated unlawfully, so that they could then pursue their own claims against relevant defendants. While standing was granted to bring claims in common law judicial review, standing under the HRA was denied. The claimant could not be afforded standing as its own Convention rights had not been directly affected by the conduct of STC officials, even though the charity was constituted to represent children's interests and STC officials had directly interfered with the rights of children. In *Re Northern Ireland Commissioner for Children and Young People's Application*, the **50-018**

---

42 See *R. (on the application of KB) v Mental Health Review Tribunal* [2004] Q.B. 936. Note that where damages are sought in respect of a judicial act done in good faith certain procedural requirements are imposed: HRA s.9(4).

43 Article 34 provides: "The court may receive applications from any person, non-governmental organisation or group of individuals claiming to be the victim of a violation by one of the Contracting Parties of the rights set forth in the Convention or the protocols thereto. The High Contracting Parties undertake not to hinder in any way the effective exercise of this right".

44 *R. v Inland Revenue Commissioners Ex p. National Federation of Self Employed and Small Businesses Ltd* [1982] A.C. 617; *AXA General Insurance v HM Advocate* [2012] 1 A.C. 868.

45 [2013] 1 W.L.R. 3667 CA.

Commissioner, an officeholder under statute whose purpose is to promote children's interests, was refused standing under the HRA to bring a claim for breaches of children's Convention rights:

> "There is not specific case before me where a child is a victim and I cannot permit a complaint against this law *in abstracto* simply because the Commissioner feels, however sincerely, it contravenes the Convention unless she is a victim".[46]

**50-019** There are limited exceptions to the victim test. One such exception concerns potential victims.[47] However that exception is not immediately relevant to damages claims: in such cases the claimants will not yet have been directly affected by any state action nor suffered any detriment. Rather, such cases have generally concerned challenges to a general measure which could, in the future, potentially be applied to the claimant and poses a real risk to their Convention rights. Another exception in domestic law, created by statute, is that the Equality and Human Rights Commission may initiate proceedings in respect of breaches of Convention rights where it is not itself a victim. However, in such proceedings no award of damages may be made to the Commission under the HRA.[48]

**50-020** The most important exception in relation to damages claims under the HRA is that for "indirect victims" in claims concerning art.2. Where a person dies as a result of a public authority's breach of art.2 that person's estate may sue in respect of the losses suffered by the deceased. But so too may those who were in a close relationship with the deceased, in particular their close family members, sue in their own right as victims and seek damages for their own loss. For example they may sue for bereavement damages where public officers directly caused the deceased's death, or where the death resulted from the authority's failure to fulfil the operational duty under art.2 to take reasonable steps to protect an individual from a known, real and immediate risk to life. Equally, where a public authority fails to conduct an effective investigation into the deceased's death, those who were closely related to the deceased may sue for non-pecuniary loss suffered in consequence.[49] This exception for indirect victims in respect of violations of art.2 is justified on the basis of

> "the nature of the violation alleged and considerations of the effective implementation of one of the most fundamental provisions in the Convention system".[50]

Lady Hale has given the further reason that family members suffer unique agony upon the death of a loved one, especially where the death was preventable.[51] But it is important to note that the notion of "indirect victim" still incorporates the notion of "victim", which in turn suggests that to qualify an individual must be personally affected by the death in some way. The leading domestic authority is *Rabone v Pennine Care NHS Foundation Trust*.[52] The claimants' daughter, who had been suicidal, was released from the defendant's care in breach of the operational duty

---

46 *Re Northern Ireland Commissioner for Children and Young People's Application* [2007] NIQB 115 (QB) at [15].

47 *AXA General Insurance Ltd v The Lord Advocate* [2012] 1 A.C. 868 at [24]–[28], [86]–[90], [111]–[112].

48 Equality Act 2006 s.30(3).

49 *Kiliç v Turkey* (2001) 33 E.H.R.R. 58.

50 *Nassau Verzekering Maatschappij NV v Netherlands*, Application No.27451/09, 4 June 2011 at [19].

51 *Rabone v Pennine Care NHS Foundation Trust* [2012] 2 A.C. 72 at [92].

52 *Rabone v Pennine Care NHS Foundation Trust* [2012] 2 A.C. 72 at [92]. See also 50-068 and 50-090, below.

under art.2 to take reasonable steps to protect life, with the consequence that the claimants' daughter committed suicide. The Supreme Court held that the deceased's parents had standing to bring a claim as indirect victims, and they successfully recovered damages for bereavement under the HRA in circumstances where they could not have recovered such damages under the very restrictive terms of the Fatal Accidents Act 1976. Lord Dyson said[53] that the ECtHR has repeatedly stated that family members of a deceased can bring claims in their own right both in relation to the investigative obligation and the substantive obligations under art.2, citing *Yasa v Turkey*,[54] *Edwards v United Kingdom*,[55] *Renolde v France*,[56] and *Kats v Ukraine*.[57] One issue that remains unresolved is who may be granted standing as an indirect victim. In the earlier case of *Savage v South Essex Partnership NHS Foundation Trust* Lord Scott was critical of an

> "undefined, and perhaps indefinable, class composed of persons close to the deceased who have suffered distress and anguish on account of the death".[58]

However, there is at least clarity in the light of *Rabone* and the ECtHR jurisprudence cited therein that close family members such as parents or siblings will fall into this class. Though a question remains as to whether those who were in a close relationship with the deceased but who were not family as such, such as a partner or close friend, may sue.

**50-021** Representative actions can be brought in limited circumstances.[59] Thus, if the victim is unable to act on his own behalf because he is a minor, or a patient, or is dead, a person with due authority may make the claim on his behalf. It is considered that the existing court rules for claims to be made by litigation friends make adequate provision in order to comply with the jurisprudence of the ECtHR.

**50-022** Associations may be accorded standing and bring claims for damages. However, it should be noted that the ECtHR has denied standing to associations whose own interests were not at stake, even though the individual interests of some of its members were.[60]

**50-023** Actions may also be brought by corporate bodies.[61] Albeit damages claims by companies under the HRA have been comparatively rare, they are of increasing frequency, and substantial sums have been recovered for pecuniary loss[62] (and under Strasbourg case law companies may also recover non-pecuniary loss).[63] One issue that has arisen in the Strasbourg case law and recently arisen domestically concerns

---

53 [2012] 2 A.C. 72 at [46].

54 (1999) 28 E.H.R.R. 408 at [64].

55 (2002) 35 E.H.R.R. 19 at [106].

56 (2009) 48 E.H.R.R. 42 at [69].

57 (2010) 51 E.H.R.R. 44 at [94].

58 [2009] 1 A.C. 681 at [5]. Note that Lord Scott's obiter comments in *Savage* doubting whether indirect victims should be accorded standing has been superseded by the Supreme Court's decision in *Rabone*.

59 *Nassau Verzekering Maatschappij NV v Netherlands*, Application No.27451/09, 4 June 2011 at [18].

60 *Nassau Verzekering Maatschappij NV v Netherlands*, Application No.27451/09, 4 June 2011 at [22]; *Association des Amis de Saint-Raphaël et de Fréjus v France*, Application No.45053/98, 29 February 2000 EComHR. However, the ECtHR is unlikely to take such a strict approach in relation to claims by associations and/or their members alleging violation of art.11 (freedom of association): *Roffey v United Kingdom*, Application No.1278/11, 21 March 2013 at [25].

61 *R. (on the application of Infinis Plc) v Gas and Electricity Markets Authority* [2013] EWCA Civ 70; *Breyer Group Plc v Department of Energy and Climate Change* [2015] 1 W.L.R. 4559 CA.

62 See further at 50-076.

63 *Comingersoll SA v Portugal* (2001) 31 E.H.R.R. 31; *Agrokompleks v Ukraine*, Application

the circumstances in which shareholders may be afforded standing to sue. In *Bank Mellat v HM Treasury* the Court of Appeal considered this issue.[64] Pursuant to counter-terrorism legislation the defendant issued an order prohibiting all persons in the UK financial sector from conducting business with Bank Mellat. The Supreme Court held that order violated the Bank's Art.1 Protocol 1 right to peaceful enjoyment of its possessions.[65] In follow-on damages claims under the HRA the Bank seeks £4bn in damages as just satisfaction for the violation. The litigation is ongoing but the Court of Appeal has determined certain preliminary matters. One of these concerned whether Bank Mellat could claim for the alleged loss of 60 per cent of the earnings before tax of Persia International Bank (PIB), a company in which Bank Mellat holds 60 per cent of the shares. The Court of Appeal held, both on ordinary principles of domestic law and on the basis of Strasbourg jurisprudence, that Bank Mellat lacked standing to pursue damages for those losses. PIB could itself make a claim for those losses for breach of its own rights under Art.1 Protocol 1, as a person directly affected by the defendant's Order: it was prohibited from dealing with Bank Mellat pursuant to the Order. According to the ordinary principles of English law, once it was found that PIB could claim damages under the HRA itself, Bank Mellat could not claim for the loss it had suffered as a shareholder because of the established rule preventing recovery of "shareholder's reflective loss"; the loss suffered by the shareholder is the diminution in the value of their shareholding where that merely reflects the loss suffered by the company.[66] Where such loss can be made good by a claim by the company the shareholder has no claim. The same conclusion as to standing followed from Strasbourg case law on the concept of "victim".[67] The Strasbourg Court has denied standing to shareholders in circumstances where a company has standing as a victim to claim for its own losses: where the

> "acts or omissions complained of affect a company, the application should be brought by the company".[68]

The "piercing of the 'corporate veil' or the disregarding of a company's legal personality will be justified only in exceptional circumstances".[69]

**50-024** Lastly, the ECtHR has held that Convention claims cannot be assigned, as they are "essentially personal" in the language of English domestic law[70]:

> "The right of individual petition vouchsafed by art.34 of the Convention is not a proprietary right. Nor is it transferable as if it were. Whatever the validity in terms of domestic law of the transaction here in issue, it would be out of keeping with the nature of the Convention as an instrument protecting basic human rights and the Court itself as its guardian to allow the status of applicant to be transferred at will."

---

No.23465/03, 25 July 2013 at [79].

64 *Bank Mellat v HM Treasury* [2017] Q.B. 67 CA.

65 *Bank Mellat v HM Treasury* [2014] A.C. 700.

66 *Bank Mellat v HM Treasury* [2017] Q.B. 67 CA at [17], relying on *Johnson v Gore Wood and Co* [2002] 2 A.C. 1; *Webster v Sandersons Solicitors* [2009] 2 B.C.L.C. 542 CA.

67 [2017] Q.B. 67 CA at [22]–[31]. Exceptions have been recognised, but these turn on their own special facts: at [29].

68 *Khamidov v Russia* (2009) 49 E.H.R.R. 13 at [123].

69 *Agrotexim v Greece* (1996) 21 E.H.R.R. 250 at [66].

70 *Nassau Verzekering Maatschappij NV v Netherlands*, Application No.27451/09, 4 June 2011 at [25].

## (3) Appropriate Forum and Procedural Treatment of Claims

Section 7(1) of the HRA provides that a person who claims that a public authority has acted (or proposes to act) in a way which is made unlawful by s.6(1) may "bring proceedings against the authority under this Act in the appropriate court or tribunal". **50-025**

This provision is given procedural effect by CPR r.7.11 which provides:

> "(1) A claim under s.7(1)(a) of the Human Rights Act 1998 in respect of a judicial act may be brought only in the High Court.
> (2) Any other claim under s.7(1)(a) of that Act may be brought in any court."

In addition, PD 7A, which accompanies Pt 7, provides in para.2.10:

> "(1) The normal rules apply in deciding in which court and specialist list a claim that includes issues under the Human Rights Act 1998 should be started. They also apply in deciding which procedure to use to start the claim: this Part or CPR Pt 8 or CPR Pt 54 (judicial review).
> (2) The exception is a claim for damages in respect of a judicial act, which should be commenced in the High Court. If the claim is made in a notice of appeal then it will be dealt with according to the normal rules governing where that appeal is heard.
> (The County Court cannot make a declaration of incompatibility in accordance with s.4 of the Human Rights Act 1998. Legislation may direct that such a claim is to be brought before a specified tribunal)."

No such legislation has yet been introduced. Thus, in relation to claims under the HRA, the normal rules apply as to venue and how to start proceedings except that a claim for damages in respect of a judicial act should be started in the High Court. Claim forms N1 and N205 have been amended to ask whether the claim includes an issue under the HRA.

An important procedural issue in connection with HRA damages claims is whether and when a claimant may proceed via ordinary procedure, and whether and when they must proceed via the judicial review procedure pursuant to CPR Pt 54. Which procedure is used is of some significance. The judicial review procedure is characterised by a number of procedural restrictions for the benefit of defendant public authorities which do not pertain in ordinary proceedings, and which may affect the success of a claim. These include a permission stage according to which the claim may be dismissed without full hearing of the merits on the basis of multifarious discretionary factors, a very short limitation period of three months (compared to one year where HRA claims are initiated by ordinary procedure) and, of some importance for the trial of damages claims, discovery, oral evidence and cross-examination are rarely ordered in judicial review proceedings. **50-026**

The CPR provide that claims only seeking damages cannot be brought via judicial review procedure.[71] Therefore such proceedings may be brought in the ordinary way via ordinary procedure. On the other hand the CPR provide that one must proceed via judicial review where the remedies sought include a prerogative order, such as a quashing, prohibiting or mandatory order, or an injunction under s.30 of the Senior Courts Act 1981, restraining a person from acting in any office in which he or she is entitled to act.[72] Thus, if one is seeking HRA damages one ought to consider carefully whether to include a claim for the prerogative orders or **50-027**

[71] CPR r.54.3(2).
[72] CPR r.54.2

a s.30 injunction, as this will result in the claim being subjected to the procedural disadvantages associated with the judicial review procedure.

**50-028** Outside of claims only seeking damages (which cannot proceed via judicial review), and claims which seek as part of the relief prerogative orders or s.30 injunctions (which must proceed via judicial review), a question arises as to the procedural treatment of claims seeking both damages and another remedy such as, for example, a declaration or injunction. The CPR permit such claims to be made via judicial review, but do not mandate that they must be.[73] However, also relevant in this regard is the question of the applicability of the judicially-created principle of exclusivity established in *O'Reilly v Mackman*.[74] This principle holds that "public law", as opposed to "private law" claims, must in general be brought via the judicial review procedure. This distinction between public law and private law claims runs into difficulties when applied to HRA damages claims, as they belie any neat compartmentalisation. On the one hand, human rights damages claims are claims against public entities, and the courts have referred to HRA damages as a public law remedy, suggesting they ought to be streamed via review procedure where possible. But on the other hand, such claims are based in personal legal rights, akin to those in private law fields such as tort, rather than the traditional type of claim made via the judicial review procedure, seeking exercise of the High Court's supervisory jurisdiction and grant of the prerogative orders. The remedy of damages is one traditionally associated with private law fields, and not the supervisory jurisdiction. Furthermore, the judicial review procedure is not one especially suited to the hearing of damages claims, as evidenced by the rule prohibiting claims solely seeking damages from proceeding via judicial review procedure.[75] Importantly, human rights damages claims arguably fit within recognised exceptions to the *O'Reilly* principle. As Lord Lowry observed in *Roy v Kensington and Chelsea and Westminster Family Practitioner Committee*,

> "[w]hen individual rights are claimed, there should not be a need for leave or a special time limit, nor should the relief be discretionary".[76]

Another exception pertains to claims raising disputed questions of fact, given such matters cannot be rigorously resolved in judicial review proceedings as disclosure and oral evidence are seldom provided for.[77] Damages claims clearly fit within this exception as they typically require close examination of the specific factual circumstances of the case.

**50-029** In *Anufrijeva v Southwark London Borough Council*, Lord Woolf MR asserted that courts should look critically at any attempt to recover damages under the HRA by any procedure other than judicial review in the Administrative Court, and in cases where only damages are sought the claim should commence in the Administrative Court via ordinary procedure.[78] By implication claims for HRA damages, except those in which damages were the only remedy claimed (which the CPR bars from proceeding by judicial review), would in effect be treated as "public law" claims for the purposes of the *O'Reilly* principle of exclusivity.

**50-030** However, this guidance has been superseded in principle and in practice. It would

---

73 CPR r.54.3(2).

74 [1983] 2 A.C. 237 HL.

75 CPR r.54.3(2).

76 [1992] 1 A.C. 624 HL at 654.

77 [1992] 1 A.C. 624 HL at 650, 654; *R. v East Berkshire HA Ex p. Walsh* [1985] Q.B. 152 CA at 173.

78 [2004] Q.B. 1124 CA at [81].

seem that, to the extent consistent with the CPR, human rights damages claimants will often have a genuine choice of procedure, and indeed higher courts have now indicated that ordinary proceedings may be preferable for the hearing of HRA damages claims. In an early departure from Lord Woolf's guidance Brooke LJ, delivering a judgment in which the other judges concurred, observed that

> "contested actions involving a human rights element often require cross-examination which is more conveniently provided for outside the Administrative Court list".[79]

The Supreme Court's 2012 decision in *Ruddy v Chief Constable of Strathclyde*,[80] concerned concurrent claims for damages in battery and for breach of art.3 in respect of injuries allegedly suffered through police violence. The lower court held that the claim for damages for breach of art.3 could not properly proceed alongside the common law claim via ordinary procedure, and had to be brought via judicial review: such a claim was "distinct" "from a claim based in common law assault … involv[ing a challenge], in administrative law".[81] The Supreme Court upheld the appeal, overturning the lower court's analysis. It rejected the view, inherent in Lord Woolf's analysis in *Anufrijeva*, that rights-based claims for damages ought necessarily to be treated as analogous, for procedural purposes, to applications for exercise of the supervisory judicial review jurisdiction, and thus streamed via judicial review procedure wherever possible. Lord Hope, for the Court, said:

> "The fallacy which undermines the Extra Division's whole approach to this issue … lies in its assumption that the appellant is seeking an exercise of the court's supervisory jurisdiction. That is not so. He is not asking for the review or setting aside of any decision of the Chief Constable or the Lord Advocate. He is not asking the court to control their actions in that way at all. His case in regard to both craves is based on averments of things done or omitted to be done and actions that were taken or not taken. The allegations are of completed acts or failures to act. He is not seeking to have them corrected in order to provide a foundation for his claim, nor does he need to do so. What he seeks is just satisfaction for the fact that, on his averments, his art.3 Convention rights have been breached. The essence of his claim is simply one of damages".[82]

Lord Hope endorsed Lord Hamilton's dictum in *Docherty v Scottish Ministers* that

> "the process of judicial review would be quite inept for proceedings in which damages are claimed for an isolated act of physical violence which was in breach of the art.3 Convention right".[83]

Lord Hope observed that the ground had moved considerably since *O'Reilly* and that, since *Clark v University of Lincolnshire and Humberside*,[84] a more flexible approach prevailed, with procedure calibrated to the demands of the case rather than dictated by mechanical application of the indeterminate distinction between public law and private law. One may interpolate that, as human right damages claims often raise disputed questions of fact, ordinary procedure will typically be more apt for

---

79 *D v Home Office* [2006] 1 W.L.R. 1003 CA at [104].

80 [2012] UKSC 57. This was a Scottish appeal however Lord Hope, for the Court, expressly considered his pronouncements of principle to be equally applicable south of the border: at [18] and see at [16]–[17].

81 [2012] UKSC 57 at [9].

82 [2012] UKSC 57 at [15].

83 [2011] CSIH 58 at [20].

84 [2000] 1 W.L.R. 1988 CA.

their determination. As Sedley LJ said in *Faulkner*,

> "We do not see how an award itself can be quantified without attention, sometimes detailed attention, to what has happened",[85]

while on appeal Lord Reed observed that in human rights damages claims "Courts should resolve disputed issues of fact in the usual way".[86]

**50-031** Indeed, even where the claim is brought via judicial review procedure the courts have been willing to modify the procedure, in some respects, so that it more closely tracks ordinary procedure, so as to ensure robust determination of factual disputes. Albeit, it should be noted that other disadvantages of that procedure remain, such as the requirement of permission. In *R. (on the application of Wilkinson) v Broadmoor Hospital*,[87] which involved a HRA challenge to a medical decision that the claimant be administered certain drugs, the Court of Appeal ordered that medical experts give oral evidence and be cross-examined within proceedings initiated via judicial review. It was significant that, as in *Ruddy*, the same facts could have given rise to a common law action for battery, which could have proceeded via ordinary procedure. Hale LJ said,

> "it cannot and should not matter whether proceedings in respect of forcible treatment of detained patients are brought by way of ordinary action in tort, an action under s.7(1) of the 1998 Act, or judicial review. If there are relevant disputed issues of fact these will have to be determined, by cross examination if necessary".[88]

These developments are reinforced by the more general adoption of a flexible approach to both discovery and oral evidence in human rights claims, whether damages are claimed or not. In *Tweed v Parades Commission for Northern Ireland* the House of Lords mandated a more flexible and less restrictive approach to orders for disclosure in HRA claims brought via judicial review,[89] while a stream of decisions have signalled a less restrictive approach to oral evidence in HRA claims initiated via review, given the heightened intensity of judicial scrutiny in such cases and the fact-sensitive nature of methods such as proportionality.[90]

**50-032** Claims for damages for past breaches of rights are to be distinguished from cases where the gist of the claim is a challenge to the validity of an administrative act or measure, in which case *O'Reilly* will dictate the use of the judicial review procedure, in unmodified form. For example Hale LJ, in *Wilkinson*, distinguished a claim for damages for specific invasions of an individual's rights from a case "where delegated legislation or the policy of a public authority is in question" in which case "the appropriate remedies will only be available in judicial review".[91] Similarly Lord Hope, in *Ruddy*, distinguished a claim for damages in relation to

---

85 *R. (on the application of Faulkner) v Secretary of State for Justice* [2011] H.R.L.R. 23 CA at [19].

86 *R. (on the application of Sturnham) v Parole Board* [2013] 2 A.C. 254 at [13(5)], [39].

87 [2002] 1 W.L.R. 419 CA.

88 [2002] 1 W.L.R. 419 CA at [61]–[62].

89 [2007] 1 A.C. 650.

90 *R (on the application of A) v Chief Constable of Kent* [2013] EWCA Civ 1706 at [58]; *R. (Al-Sweady) v Secretary of State for Defence* [2010] H.R.L.R. 2 CA at [26]–[27]; *R (on the application of Wilkinson) v Broadmoor Hospital* [2002] 1 W.L.R. 419 CA at [24]–[26], [62]; *R. (on the application of Kiarie) v Secretary of State for the Home Department* [2017] UKSC 42 at [46]–[47].

91 [2002] 1 W.L.R. 419 CA at [61]–[62].

completed acts, from an application seeking judicial control of administrative bodies to ensure they do not exceed or abuse their powers.[92]

50-033 The practice of human rights damages claims reinforces that claimants for HRA damages, who do not also claim prerogative remedies, will not typically be required to proceed via judicial review or initiate proceedings in the Administrative Court. Human rights damages claims have been regularly determined in the County Court. The courts have observed that

> "Given the relatively low levels of damages available for violations of art.5.4 claims under the 1998 Act, in the absence of a claim for relief that only the Administrative Court can grant [such as the prerogative remedies], should proceed speedily in the County Court".[93]

More generally courts have observed that there is no reason why the County Court is not an appropriate forum for HRA damages claims.[94] Claims have regularly been initiated in the Queen's Bench Division with no mention of the *Anufrijeva* prescriptions,[95] including in specialist courts such as the Technology and Construction Court and Commercial Court.[96] Claims have proceeded via the Family Court, Family Division of the High Court and Court of Protection:

> "there is no statutory provision, rule or practice direction which requires [human rights] challenges to be brought in the Administrative Court".[97]

50-034 The principles and practice described in the foregoing paragraphs are reinforced by the procedural provisions extracted above, prescribing that HRA claims may be initiated in any court and that the ordinary rules ought to apply to HRA claims in deciding which court or specialist list such claims ought to be initiated in.[98] All of this suggests that the *Anufrijeva* prescriptions should not be followed.

50-035 In *Anufrijeva* Lord Woolf had also stated that, in judicial review proceedings, claimants for human rights damages should, before permission is granted, be required to explain why it would not be more appropriate to make a claim to the Ombudsman, on the basis that such a claim could save litigation costs. However, that prescription is, with respect, problematic as neither the Parliamentary nor Lo-

---

92 [2012] UKSC 57 at [15], [18].

93 *R. (on the application of Parratt) v Secretary of State for Justice* [2014] EWCA Civ 1478 at [42].

94 *D v Home Office* [2006] 1 W.L.R. 1003 CA at [107].

95 The following were initiated in the Queen's Bench Division, and were claims for HRA damages or for HRA damages and other remedies—not including prerogative orders— such as declarations, some cases including concurrent claims in tort: *A v Essex County Council* [2007] EWHC 1652 (QB); *Rabone v Pennine Care NHS Foundation Trust* [2010] P.I.Q.R. P2; *Savage v South Essex Partnership NHS Foundation Trust* [2010] EWHC 865 (QB); *R. (on the application of Sessay) v South London and Maudsley NHS Foundation Trust* [2012] Q.B. 760; *O v Commissioner for the Metropolis* [2011] H.R.L.R. 29; *Breyer Group Plc v Department of Energy and Climate Change* [2015] 2 All E.R. 44 (QB); *DSD v Commissioner of Police of the Metropolis* [2015] 1 W.L.R. 1833.

96 *Bank Mellat v HM Treasury* [2015] EWHC 1258 (Comm); *Dobson v Thames Water Utilities Ltd* [2011] EWHC 3253 (TCC).

97 *R (on the application of P) v Secretary of State for the Home Department* [2001] 1 W.L.R. 2002 CA at [120]. See for example: *YA v A Local Authority* [2011] 1 W.L.R. 1505 Fam ("the Court of Protection does have jurisdiction and thus power to award damages under the Human Rights Act"); *Re H (A Child: Breach of Convention Rights: Damages)* [2014] EWFC 38 at [64] ("I am satisfied that the Family Court has the power to make an award of damages under s.8(2) of the Human Rights Act 1998"); *Northamptonshire County Council v AS* [2015] EWHC 199 (Fam); *CH v Metropolitan Council* [2017] EWCOP 12; *H (A Minor) v Northamptonshire County Council* [2017] EWHC 282 (Fam).

98 Above para.50-025.

cal Ombudsman have jurisdiction over legal claims for which a judicial remedy is available.[99] That the judgment in *Anufrijeva* failed to account for this jurisdictional bar has been recognised in subsequent cases,[100] and as such Lord Woolf's guidance in this respect is no longer to be followed. HRA claims are claims based in legal rights for judicial remedies, and are thus quintessentially the province of the courts:

> "vindication of a right in a society based on the rule of law must ultimately be able to be achieved by claim of right to the courts".[101]

Further, the ECtHR has held Ombudsman processes, and other non-legal mechanisms such as internal government processes, do not fulfil the ECHR requirements of an effective remedy for human rights violations as they lack sufficient independence from government and cannot make binding legal determinations and compel redress.[102]

**50-036** Lastly, it has been confirmed by the Administrative Court that the "statutory charge", by which the Legal Aid Agency may recoup sums paid in legal aid out of damages subsequently awarded to a legally-aided claimant, applies to damages awarded under the HRA. Though one might expect the issue to arise again in the higher courts, and particularly the question of whether such approach can be reconciled with the requirement of an effective remedy for rights-violations under art.13.[103] The issue arose in proceedings brought by one of the claimants awarded damages by the Supreme Court in *Sturnham*,[104] who sought review of the Agency's decision to claim the statutory charge as against his award of HRA damages—which would result in the claimant receiving nothing. The Judge held the charge could be applied: albeit awards against the state for unlawful detention was a very serious matter, no special exception should be made for HRA awards as a general class.[105] This decision has implications for how proceedings should be managed, so as to minimise the potential impact of the statutory charge on damages awards. Consider the advice that has now been given in the context of care proceedings. Whereas it has been held that human rights issues should generally be raised in the course of care proceedings,[106] it has recently been determined that where the remedies claimed include damages and are not limited to a declaration or injunction

> "it is almost inevitable that those representing the Claimant will be well advised to issue separate proceedings and to seek the issue of a separate public funding certificate because

---

99 Local Government Act 1974 s.26(6)(c); Parliamentary Commissioner Act 1967 s.5(2).

100 *K v Cornwall County Council* [2005] EWCA Civ 1815 at [13]. See also *R. (on the application of A) v Secretary of State for the Home Department* [2004] EWHC 1585 (Admin) at [11].

101 *Attorney General v Chapman* [2012] 1 N.Z.L.R. 462 at [26].

102 *Klass v Germany* (1979–80) 2 E.H.R.R. 214 at [55], [67]; *Peck v United Kingdom* (2003) 36 E.H.R.R. 41 at [109]; *Silver v United Kingdom* (1983) 5 E.H.R.R. 347 at [115]; *Campbell v United Kingdom* (1985) 7 E.H.R.R. 165 at [126]; *Reynolds v United Kingdom* (2012) 55 E.H.R.R. 35 at [62]; *Bubbins v United Kingdom* (2005) 41 E.H.R.R. 24 at [170].

103 See para.50-079 below.

104 *R. (on the application of Sturnham) v Parole Board* [2013] 2 A.C. 254. The claimant, Faulkner, was awarded £6,500 for prolonged detention of ten months. See further below para.50-088.

105 *R (on the application of Faulkner) v Director of Legal Aid Casework* [2016] 4 W.L.R. 178 (Admin) at [37].

106 *Re L (Care Proceedings: Human Rights Claims)* [2003] 2 F.L.R. 160 (Fam) at [23]–[25], [31]–[35], approved: *Re V (Care Proceedings: Human Rights Claims)* [2004] 1 F.L.R. 944 CA at [98].

of the potential applicability of the statutory charge in respect of any HRA damages awarded".[107]

The reason for this advice is that if the damages claim is included within the care proceedings the total costs associated with *both* are liable to be recouped by the Legal Aid Agency on any damages awarded.

## (4) Time for bringing claim

By s.7(5) of the HRA, proceedings under s.7(1)(a) must be brought within one year of the act complained of or **50-037**

"such longer period as the court or tribunal considers equitable having regard to all the circumstances".

The general rule in s.7(5) is subject to "any rule imposing a stricter time limit in relation to the procedure in question". Thus, in proceedings for judicial review, CPR r.54.5 provides:

"The claim form must be filed—(a) promptly; and (b) in any event not later than 3 months after the grounds to make the claim first arose".

This shorter time period is one reason why proceeding via ordinary procedure rather than judicial review may be advantageous.

In judicial review proceedings seeking the exercise of the supervisory jurisdic- **50-038**
tion, courts will require claims to be brought promptly and a failure to do so could result in the discretionary refusal of permission to proceed, even if a claim is brought within the three-month limitation period. This is readily understandable in the context of an application for a quashing order, where issuance of such an order long after the making of administrative decisions could lead to the reopening of many decisions and administrative chaos, as well as undermining the expectations of third parties based on those administrative acts that were long thought final.[108] However, these reasons for insisting on promptness do not carry over well to damages claims, and where HRA damages claims are initiated via judicial review, the promptness criterion should not be applied to deny permission for such claims to proceed. Relevantly, in *A v Essex County Council* Lady Hale observed:

"The judge placed at the forefront of his account of the relevant legal principles that 'there is a significant public interest in public law claims against public bodies being brought expeditiously' … That is of course true in judicial review, when remedies are sought to quash administrative decisions which may affect large numbers of people or upon which other decisions have depended and action been taken. It is normally a prospective remedy, aiming not only to quash the past but also to put right the future. Expedition is less obviously necessary in a claim for a declaration in vindication of the claimant's human rights, upon which nothing else depends, or of a claim for damages. These are retrospective remedies, aimed at marking or compensating what has happened in the past. Public authorities are no longer in any different position from other defendants in the general law

[107] *H (A Minor) v Northamptonshire County Council* [2017] EWHC 282 (Fam) at [115]. The Judge added at [116]: "Where liability and the quantum of damages are agreed, and the only issue is the court's approval of the infant settlement, the same principle of issuing separate proceedings applies, namely the issue of a Part 8 claim". Further detailed procedural guidance is provided at [117] of the judgment.

[108] *O'Reilly v Mackman* [1983] 2 A.C. 237 at 280–281.

of limitation (see limitation Act 1980 s.37(1)). This claim is more akin to a tort claim than to judicial review".[109]

50-039 On its face, the discretion to extend the time limit under s.7(5) of the HRA is a wide one and no clear pattern has emerged as to whether the courts will generally approach extension liberally or restrictively. One set of reasons for not insisting on strict adherence to the one-year time-limit are those articulated by Lady Hale in *A v Essex County Council*, also bearing in mind that many tort claims for damages have far longer standard limitation periods than one year. However, in *A v Essex County Council* itself Lady Hale was in the minority in favouring extension of the limitation period.[110] The claimant brought a claim via ordinary procedure, seeking a declaration and HRA damages, for alleged failures by the defendant to provide the basic minimum of education guaranteed by art.2 Protocol 1. The claim failed on its merits. In addition a majority of the House of Lords held that it would not have been equitable to extend the limitation period. At the time proceedings were commenced, four years had elapsed since the alleged breach of A's rights had started, and just over 22 months had passed since the alleged breach of A's rights had ended. Lord Kerr, with whom a majority concurred, upheld the lower court judge's reasons for refusing an extension.[111] He recalled that the burden of proof is on the party seeking the extension. But he considered such matters could seldom come down to the burden of proof and preferred to approach the matter by an open-ended examination of the factors for and against. These included that there were opportunities to make a claim early on, and the claimant's lawyers were experienced advocates in the area of education law, but instead the claims were made a long time after the alleged infringements came to an end and there was little point from A's personal perspective in seeking a declaration that his rights were infringed. The public interest in determining the issues raised was not sufficient to warrant an extension as these matters could easily and more appropriately be determined in an upcoming proceeding brought in time by another party. Significantly, in respect of HRA damages actions, for which courts have often made only modest awards, Lord Kerr emphasised that it was highly unlikely that any significant sum by way of damages would have been awarded if the action had been brought within time and been successful, and indeed a court may well have concluded an award of damages was not necessary; as the first instance judge put it, the amount of any award would be disproportionate to the cost of any proceedings. Lady Hale in dissent emphasised the importance of vindicating human rights by declarations or damages awards, and the importance of claims such as this for setting standards for the future and ensuring lessons were learned. Indicating the invariable nexus between the substantive merits of the case and decisions over extension of time, she speculated that if the trial judge had thought the case raised triable issues he would have had little difficulty in extending time.

50-040 In *Rabone v Pennine Care NHS Foundation Trust*,[112] the Supreme Court rejected the basis upon which the lower courts had refused to extend time (namely that the claim was doomed to failure) and exercised the discretion afresh. The Supreme Court affirmed that it had a wide discretion and that it would often be appropriate to take into account factors of the type set out in s.33 of the Limitation Act 1980:

---

109 [2011] 1 A.C. 280 at [116].

110 [2011] 1 A.C. 280 at [116].

111 [2011] 1 A.C. 280 at [165]–[169].

112 [2012] 2 A.C. 72. For the facts of the case see para.50-020, above.

the length and reasons for the delay in issuing proceedings; the extent to which, having regard to the delay, the evidence is likely to be less cogent than if proceedings had been issued in time; and the conduct of the public authority after the right of claim arose, including the extent (if any) to which it responded to reasonable requests for information for the purpose of ascertaining the facts. However, the Supreme Court warned against any attempt to re-write s.7(5)(b) of the HRA as if it incorporated the language of s.33(3) of the Limitation Act 1980. In extending time, reliance was placed upon the fact that, although the claimants were aware of the HRA in general terms and the possibility of bringing a claim, and could have issued proceedings within one year, they had acted reasonably in not so doing as they were awaiting a report on the death of their daughter from the defendant, pursuant to a formal complaint made by the claimants within five months of their daughter's death. The extension was short, the Trust suffered no prejudice by delay, and most importantly of all in Lord Dyson's view, the claim was a good one. Lady Hale, echoing her analysis in *A v Essex County Council*,[113] added the further points that the claim, being one for damages in respect of past events, is more in the nature of a claim in tort than for judicial review. It is also important that fundamental human rights be vindicated by full damages for all losses arising, and never more so than when the most fundamental right of all, the right to life, is at stake.

The analogy with tort, for the purposes of decisions over extension of time, has been observed in other cases and influenced courts to extend the limitation period. *Dobson v Thames Water Utilities Ltd* was a group action brought by 1,350 residents who lived in the vicinity of the defendant's sewage treatment works, seeking damages concurrently in nuisance and for breach of art.8 and art.1 Protocol 1 caused by odour and mosquitoes.[114] The Judge extended the limitation period for the HRA damages claims from one year to six years, holding the six-year limitation period for the nuisance claims was a relevant consideration in exercising his discretion.[115] He considered that the disparity in limitation periods between those who could bring nuisance claims—i.e. those with proprietary interests in the affected properties—and those who were limited to claiming under art.8 was not equitable, especially in the context of a group claim. **50-041**

## 3. Criteria for Decision Whether to Award Damages

### (1) General Approach: The "Mirror" Method

An award of damages is made pursuant to s.8(1) of the HRA, the Act's general remedial provision. That section provides: **50-042**

> "In relation to any act (or proposed act) of a public authority which the court finds is (or would be) unlawful, it may grant such relief or remedy, or make such order, within its powers as it considers just and appropriate".

The formulation "just and appropriate" denotes a discretion and the courts have repeatedly emphasised that damages under the HRA, in contrast to damages in tort or contract, are discretionary and not available as of right. While any award is formally made pursuant to s.8(1) there is, as Lord Woolf MR put it in *Anufrijeva v*

[113] [2011] 1 A.C. 280 at [116].
[114] [2011] EWHC 3253 TCC.
[115] [2011] EWHC 3253 TCC at [1075]–[1077].

*Southwark London Borough Council*, a "code" provided for in s.8 which specifically governs the damages remedy.[116]

Thus, s.8(3) provides:

> "No award of damages is to be made unless, taking account of all the circumstances of the case, including
>
> (a) any other relief or remedy granted, or order made, in relation to the act in question (by that or any other court), and
>
> (b) the consequences of any decision (of that or any other court) in respect of that act,
>
> the court is satisfied that the award is necessary to afford just satisfaction to the person in whose favour it is made."

Furthermore, s.8(4) of the HRA provides:

> "In determining—
>
> (a) whether to award damages[117] … the court must take into account the principles applied by the [ECtHR] in relation to the award of compensation under art.41 of the Convention."

We will see that the inclusion of s.8(4) has proven highly significant. But before considering the influence of that provision it is important to consider the relationship between ss.8(1) and (3). Whereas in the Court of Appeal decision in *Anufrijeva* Lord Woolf MR placed emphasis on the broad discretion provided in s.8(1), in the leading House of Lords authority of *R. (on the application of Greenfield) v Secretary of State for the Home Department* Lord Bingham placed greater emphasis on s.8(3):

> "It would seem to be clear that a domestic court may not award damages unless satisfied that it is necessary to do so, but if satisfied that it is necessary to do so it is hard to see how the court could consider it other than just and appropriate to do so".[118]

Thus the key inquiry is whether an award is, in the language of s.8(3), "necessary to afford just satisfaction to the person in whose favour it is made". If so, an award ought ordinarily to be made under s.8(1), there being limited scope under that provision to deny an award considered necessary under s.8(3). This focus on s.8(3) as the core test for the making of awards is of significance: as the Law Commissions observed in their report on damages under the HRA, this provision directs attention to the needs of the victim, making the individual the principal focus of the decision whether to award human rights damages.[119] In contrast Lord Woolf in the earlier *Anufrijeva* case, having placed comparably greater weight on the wide discretion conferred under s.8(1), considered that, as an aspect of that wide discretion, courts should consider the interests of the public in deciding whether to grant damages, which in turn suggested a restrictive approach according to which otherwise necessary awards could be denied in the court's wide discretion so as to

---

116 [2004] Q.B. 1124 CA at [52], [55].

117 And, as discussed below, in determining the amount of an award: see paras.50-083 and following, below.

118 *R. (on the application of Greenfield) v Secretary of State for the Home Department* [2005] 1 W.L.R. 673 HL at [6].

119 Law Commission, *Damages under the Human Rights Act 1998* (2000), Law Com. No.266/Scot Law Com. No.180, Cm.4853, para.4.14.

preserve the public funds of defendant authorities.[120] The extent to which such wider "policy" factors are relevant to the decision whether to award HRA damages must now be rather limited, in the light of Lord Bingham's speech tying the decision whether to make awards to the "necessity" criterion in s.8(3). Furthermore, as discussed below,[121] the ECtHR does not in general take into account such public policy factors in deciding whether to make awards under art.41, while denying damages on such grounds risks breach of art.13 of the Convention.

The decision whether damages are a "necessary" remedy is to be governed by the clear and consistent jurisprudence of the ECtHR under art.41 according to the "mirror" approach prescribed by the House of Lords in *Greenfield* and Supreme Court in *R. (on the application of Sturnham) v Parole Board*.[122] While the plain terms of s.8(4) indicate that domestic courts should look to the "principles" applied by the ECtHR, suggesting a search for statements of principle in the ECtHR's jurisprudence or the basic principles that underpin decisions whether to make awards, the House of Lords and Supreme Court have interpreted "principles" in a "broad sense" as "practice".[123] Thus in deciding whether an award is necessary under the HRA domestic courts must seek to identify patterns in the way the ECtHR exercises its discretion under art.41 whether or not to make awards. The underlying reason for this strained interpretation of "principles" is likely that the ECtHR does not in general offer reasons for its decisions under art.41, preferring conclusory statements, so that the search for statements of principle would often prove fruitless. Furthermore the ECtHR's approach is an "equitable" one, deciding whether to make an award on a case-by-case basis according to its sense of the justice of the case, so that the search for consistently applied and detailed principles may prove elusive. Of course, as one might expect of a jurisprudence that is largely unreasoned, the search for clear and consistent *practices* is also liable to pose difficulties, lower courts repeatedly stating they have found it difficult to discern any assistance from the art.41 jurisprudence. Another important feature of the higher courts' interpretation of s.8(4) is that while the plain terms of that section indicate Strasbourg jurisprudence is only one relevant consideration in deciding whether to make awards—thus the instruction that domestic courts "take into account" Strasbourg principles—the House of Lords and Supreme Court have prescribed that clear and consistent practice of the ECtHR under art.41 ought generally to be followed domestically. Strasbourg practice is not binding authority, however it is generally followed in the "absence of some special circumstances".[124] One consequence of this mirror approach is that valuable guidance that might have been derived from the elaborate body of principles in the law of torts and other practice areas such as anti-discrimination law has been side-lined, whereas such practice areas had provided valuable guidance to lower courts in HRA damages claims prior to adoption of the mirror approach. However, the question remains open as to what extent a court may be guided by domestic damages principles in cases where there are no relevant Strasbourg cases on point, or there is no clear and consistent ECtHR practice but rather practice is unclear and/or inconsistent. This will not be an **50-043**

120 [2004] Q.B. 1124 CA at [56]. Lord Woolf also considered preservation of public funds to be relevant to setting scales: at [75].

121 Below at para.50-074.

122 [2013] 2 A.C. 254.

123 [2013] 2 A.C. 254 at [31].

124 [2013] 2 A.C. 254 at [36].

uncommon occurrence; as Lord Woolf MR observed,

> "The difficulty lies in identifying from the Strasbourg jurisprudence clear and coherent principles governing the award of damages".[125]

In this regard it is worth observing that even following *Greenfield*, and establishment of the mirror approach, lower courts have on occasion been guided by common law precedents and principles, especially in cases concerning Convention rights which protect interests in common with common law actions, such as liberty—which is protected by false imprisonment and art.5.[126]

**50-044** Thus, according to the mirror approach the case law of the ECtHR under art.41 is of crucial importance to a decision whether to allow a claim for damages under the HRA. In *R. (on the application of Greenfield) v Secretary of State for the Home Department*,[127] Lord Bingham considered that s.8(4) could provide no clearer indication that the domestic courts should look to Strasbourg and not to domestic precedents, not only in determining whether to award damages at all, but also in determining the amount of the award. In the subsequent Supreme Court decision in *R. (Sturnham) v Parole Board* it was reiterated that *Greenfield* had "construed" ss.8(3) and (4) as having introduced an entirely novel remedy drawn from the international plane, described as damages but not tortious in nature, and reflecting the international origins of this new remedy the primary source of guidance ought to be the art.41 case law. The focus ought to be on the "routine"[128] or "ordinary practice" of the ECtHR, and "how [it] applies article 41".[129] Lord Reed observed in *Sturnham* that the mirror approach

> "differs from the ordinary approach to the relationship between domestic law and the Convention, according to which the courts endeavour to apply (and, if need be, develop) the common law, and interpret and apply statutory provisions, so as to arrive at a result which is in compliance with the UK's international obligations; the starting point being our own legal principles rather than the judgments of an international court".[130]

**50-045** In *Sturnham* Lord Reed analogised discerning practices of the ECtHR to the approach taken to interpreting personal injury awards made by juries:

> "The search for 'principles' in this broad sense is by no means alien to British practitioners, at least to those who had experience of practice in the field of personal injury law before the Judicial Studies Board published its guidelines. The conventions underlying the amounts awarded as general damages (or, in Scotland, solatium) for particular forms of harm could only be inferred from an analysis of the awards in different cases and a comparison of their facts. It is an exercise of a similar kind which may be called for when

---

125 *Anufrijeva v Southwark London Borough Council* [2004] Q.B. 1124 CA at [57]; *Re C (A Child)* [2007] EWCA Civ 2 at [64] ("In general the 'principles' applied by the European Court, which we are thus enjoined to 'take into account', are not clear or coherent").

126 *R. (on the application of KB) v Mental Health Review Tribunal* [2004] Q.B. 936 at [56]; *R. (on the application of Bernard) v Enfield London Borough Council* [2003] H.R.L.R. 4 (Admin) at [59]–[60]; *Anufrijeva v Southwark London Borough Council* [2004] Q.B. 1124 CA at [72]–[73]; *Kingshott v Ministry of Justice* [2009] EWHC 3666 (QB) at [46]–[49]; *DSD v Commissioner of Police of the Metropolis* [2015] 1 W.L.R. 1833 at [33], [68(vi)], [83]–[85], [130].

127 [2005] 1 W.L.R. 673 HL at [19].

128 [2013] 2 A.C. 254 at [9].

129 [2013] 2 A.C. 254 at [16]; *R. (Sturnham) v Parole Board* [2013] 2 A.C. 254, [31].

130 [2013] 2 A.C. 254 at [29].

> applying s.8 of the 1998 Act in connection with the quantification of awards for non-pecuniary damage".[131]

Thus the courts' approach is to analyse streams of art.41 case law and to seek to discern patterns, from which the domestic court will then interpolate how the decision whether to make awards under s.8 ought to be exercised. In this regard Lord Bingham in *Greenfield* held that the ECtHR's jurisprudence under art.41 should be approached on an Article-by-Article basis:

> "There is a risk of error if Strasbourg decisions given in relation to one article of the Convention are read across as applicable to another".[132]

The ECtHR's remedial case law in cases involving violations of art.5 will not necessarily provide reliable guidance as to the approach to compensation for breaches of art.6. Thus the court's inquiry will be one into the ECtHR's "identifiable practices"[133] in cases involving breaches of art.5(4) or cases involving breaches of the procedural obligation under art.8, for example. Put another way the search is for aggregate trends in outcomes of particular sets of claims. Though it should be noted that courts have shown some willingness to analogise across what are considered to be related Articles, such as arts 2, 3 and 4,[134] and the sub-sections of art.5.[135]

*Greenfield* itself involved a claim by a prisoner for damages for non-pecuniary loss allegedly suffered through breach of art.6 caused by a criminal charge against him being determined by a decision-maker that lacked structural independence.[136] In determining whether damages ought to be awarded Lord Bingham examined art.41 determinations made by the ECtHR in structural bias cases. In examining the pattern of awards he concluded that, albeit awards had been made in some cases, the ECtHR's ordinary response was not to make an award for loss of opportunities or for mental distress, and that a finding of violation in general constituted sufficient just satisfaction. As such it followed from this practice that awards would also be uncommon in structural bias cases under the HRA. One difficulty that follows from this is that there is little guidance as to when a domestic court should deviate from this default position and make an award, other than the requirement that there must be a causal connection between the loss and the violation. In terms of recovery for a loss of opportunities Lord Bingham recorded simply that outside of cases where there is a clear causal connection between violation and a loss of opportunities the ordinary response has been to deny awards except that the ECtHR has softened this response where persuaded that justice required it to do so. But given the ECtHR does not in general reason its awards there is little guidance as to when justice will require an award. In respect to mental distress Lord Bingham again reiterated that a clear causal connection between the violation and loss was required, but that the ECtHR had been slow to make awards; again it is not clear from this guidance when awards should be made. Lord Bingham indicated later in **50-046**

---

[131] [2013] 2 A.C. 254 at [32].

[132] *R. (on the application of Greenfield) v Secretary of State for the Home Department* [2005] 1 W.L.R. 673 HL at [7].

[133] *R. (on the application of Sturnham) v Parole Board* [2013] 2 A.C. 254 at [36].

[134] See para.50-064 below.

[135] See paras 50-062 to 50-063, and para.50-088, below.

[136] *R. (on the application of Greenfield) v Secretary of State for the Home Department* [2005] 1 W.L.R. 673 HL.

the judgment that awards would be confined to situations when there was something special in the case,[137] while he had earlier indicated that distress would have to go beyond the ordinary stresses of involvement in litigation.[138] Similar uncertainties as to when awards will be made have arisen in other contexts. For example in *Dobson v Thames Valley Utilities Ltd*, a case concerning damages claims for breach of art.8 due to smells and mosquitoes caused by a sewage plant, Waller LJ, having considered the Strasbourg cases, concluded that

> "All one can say with any certainty is that damages have been awarded for non-pecuniary loss, i.e. for inconvenience and distress, in pollution cases".[139]

But, again, what proved elusive was guidance as to when and when not to make awards. In the Supreme Court case of *Shahid v Scottish Ministers*, concerning damages claims for breach of art.8 caused by an exceptionally long period spent in solitary confinement, the Supreme Court observed that the ECtHR had in some cases "declined to make an award" to prisoners subjected to segregation in breach of art.8, while in other cases "modest awards have been made", but did not distil concrete guidance as to when awards ought or ought not to be made.[140]

**50-047** *Sturnham* involved claims by prisoners against the Parole Board for breaches of art.5(4) caused by undue delay in the hearing of their cases.[141] The claimants sought damages for distress suffered in consequence of the delay, and for a prolonged period of imprisonment that would have been avoided had the claims been handled with due speed. Lord Reed examined the ECtHR's remedial practices in the context of breaches of art.5(4). He went through myriad cases, finding that in the great majority awards had been made for mental distress, in particular in every case of this kind concerning the Board which had reached the ECtHR, and that such awards had not been dependant on the applicant showing that a delay had resulted in prolonged imprisonment; in other words the ECtHR had made awards for "free-standing" mental distress. He also found that the ECtHR had been willing to presume such losses were suffered, and that practice revealed that a de minimus rule applied, i.e. awards for mental distress would only be made if distress reached a certain level of severity. Where loss of liberty had been suffered in addition, the ECtHR had ordinarily made awards for those losses as well; it followed that such losses ought ordinarily to be recoverable under the HRA. As Lord Reed's judgment in *Sturnham* demonstrates, the mirror method requires the court to examine "a blizzard of authorities", in order to discern a pattern of awards, if one exists; in *Sturnham*, 75 Strasbourg authorities were cited to the Court. As this requires "painstaking effort" on the part of the court, Lord Reed articulated procedural guidance for HRA damages claims to facilitate the court's task. In any case which requires the citation of substantial numbers of Strasbourg authorities these should be presented to the court in a Scott schedule, that is a table setting out the relevant information about each of the authorities under a series of columns. The authorities should be presented in chronological order to enable the court to discern patterns in the making of awards over time; include relevant information about each

137 [2005] 1 W.L.R. 673 HL at [29].
138 [2005] 1 W.L.R. 673 HL at [16].
139 [2009] 3 All E.R. 319 CA at [43].
140 [2015] 3 W.L.R. 1003 SC at [88]–[89].
141 *R. (on the application of Sturnham) v Parole Board* [2013] 2 A.C. 254.

case[142]; and explain the principles which counsel maintain can be derived from the authorities, and how the authorities support those principles.[143]

Given the focus on "practice" an issue arises as to how courts ought to treat statements of principle by the ECtHR, especially where such statements conflict with its apparent practice. Albeit statements of principle are rare the ECtHR does on occasion provide more detailed reasons for particular awards or attempt to articulate more general guidance. The treatment of such statements of principle has divided opinion on the Supreme Court. In *Sturnham* Lord Reed, with three other Justices of the five-Justice panel concurring, suggested such statements should be treated with caution in general and that where such statements conflict with the Court's actual practice, practice should be given precedence.[144] Having analysed Strasbourg practice he had concluded that awards for mere distress, absent any prolongation of detention, had been regularly awarded by the ECtHR and therefore ought to be made domestically for breaches of art.5(4) caused by delayed hearings before the Parole Board. However, in *Nikolova v Bulgaria* the Grand Chamber of the ECtHR, in a rare statement of guidance, had stated that its recent case law demonstrated that compensation could not be recovered for mere distress, absent a deprivation of liberty, for breach of arts 5(3) or (4).[145] The statement therefore apparently contradicted Lord Reed's conclusions based on a consideration of ECtHR practice. Earlier in his judgment Lord Reed had observed **50-048**

> "statements by the European court in relation to just satisfaction are uncommon, and, as will appear, it may be unsafe to take them at face value, without regard to what the court actually does in practice. The focus is rather upon how the court applies art.41".[146]

In respect of *Nikolova* Lord Reed considered that practice subsequent to *Nikolova* showed that there was no principle against making awards for mental distress, reinforcing that where practice and statements of principle conflict priority should be given to practice. In the light of consideration of ECtHR practice he considered that *Nikolova* must have a narrower meaning, ruling out awards for mental distress only in cases concerning breach of the procedural guarantees under arts 5(3) and (4)—other than the requirement of a speedy hearing. This was reinforced by the fact that *Nikolova* itself was not a delay case, and had subsequently been interpreted by the ECtHR in *HL v United Kingdom* as prescribing that awards should not generally be made for types of procedural failure *other than delay*.[147] Lord Reed also noted that the ECtHR had, in *Nikolova*, framed its conclusion as one made "in the

---

142 [2013] 2 A.C. 254 at [101]. The information required is as follows:

1. The name and citation of the case, and its location in the bound volumes of authorities.
2. The violations of the Convention which were established, with references to the paragraphs in the judgment where the findings were made.
3. The damages awarded, if any. It is helpful if their sterling equivalent at present values can be agreed.
4. A brief summary of the appellant's contentions in relation to the case, with references to the key paragraphs in the judgment.
5. A brief summary of the respondent's contentions in relation to the case, again with references to the key paragraphs.

143 [2013] 2 A.C. 254 at [99]–[103].

144 [2013] 2 A.C. 254 at [31].

145 (2001) 31 E.H.R.R. 3 at [76], discussed at [55]–[61] or *R. (on the application of Sturnham) v Parole Board* [2013] 2 A.C. 254.

146 (2001) 31 E.H.R.R. 3 at [31].

147 (2005) 40 E.H.R.R. 32 at [149].

particular circumstances of the case", suggesting the purported principle in *Nikolova* was not a "strict rule". It would appear such an argument would always be open to reason around a statement of principle as each determination under art.41 is considered to be an equitable response to the facts of the case.

50-049 Interestingly, Lord Reed went even further, doubting whether *Nikolova and HL* told against the making of awards for procedural breaches of arts 5(3) and (4) not involving delay, given there were cases—"practice"—in which the ECtHR had made awards in such cases.[148] However, in the subsequent case of *Osborn v Parole Board* Lord Reed, giving the judgment of the Court, seemingly ruled out the possibility of such awards in summary fashion:

> "A breach of the requirements of procedural fairness under art.5(4) will not normally result in an award of damages under s.8 of the Human Rights Act unless the prisoner has suffered a consequent deprivation of liberty".[149]

Albeit other passages in the judgment may be interpreted as only ruling out awards on the facts of *Osborn*.[150] Thus it would seem, at least on one reading of *Osborn*, that notwithstanding the lack of an explicit endorsement of the combined statements of principle in *Nikolova* and *HL*, the principles articulated in those cases have been given effect in domestic law. This is despite the fact that there is a discernible practice of the ECtHR making awards for procedural breaches other than delay (as noted by Lord Reed both in *Sturnham* and *Osborn*).[151]

50-050 The treatment of, and relationship between, practice and statements of principle is thus somewhat fraught and the law is evolving. However, the foregoing suggests that practice will in general be given priority ahead of statements of principle, and statements of principle should not be treated as conclusive. On the other hand courts may be receptive to and give weight to such statements. In this regard it is notable that Lord Bingham in *Greenfield*, while focusing principally on the ECtHR's routine practice, did also give weight to articulated statements of principle made by the ECtHR, which in that case supported his conclusions based on consideration of practice.[152]

50-051 In considering how the law may develop in this respect, regard ought to be had to Lord Carnwath's separate judgment in *Sturnham*. Signalling a different approach from that adopted by the majority, Lord Carnwath considered that explicit statements of principle, such as that in *Nikolova*, ought to be the principal focus for English courts in discerning the "principles" applied by the ECtHR for the purposes of s.8(4). With respect, such approach would be more faithful to the use of the term "principles" in s.8(4), as opposed to "practice", which is a meaningfully different concept. Lord Carnwath observed that

> "The great majority of … awards [under art.41] are made on an 'equitable' basis reflecting particular facts … most of the decisions are not intended to have any precedential effect, and it is a mistake in my view to treat them as if they were".[153]

---

148 *R. (on the application of Sturnham) v Parole Board* [2013] 2 A.C. 254 at [61].

149 [2014] A.C. 1115 at [2(xiii)].

150 [2014] A.C. 1115 at [114]–[115].

151 [2014] A.C. 1115 at [114]; *R. (on the application of Sturnham) v Parole Board* [2013] 2 A.C. 254 at [61].

152 *R. (on the application of Greenfield) v Secretary of State for the Home Department* [2005] 1 W.L.R. 673 HL at [16], citing *Kingsley v United Kingdom* (2002) 35 E.H.R.R. 177 at [43].

153 *R. (on the application of Sturnham) v Parole Board* [2013] 2 A.C. 254 at [105].

He saw force in the view that the ECtHR's

> "decisions on just satisfaction [are] 'little more than equitable assessments of the facts of the individual case'".[154]

Lord Carnwath's proposed approach, focused more on explicit statements of principle or clearly discernible principles, is reinforced by consideration of the difference in wording between ss.2(1) and 8(4) of the HRA. Section 2(1) governs the role of Strasbourg material in interpreting the substantive rights under the HRA, and requires domestic courts to "take into account" any Strasbourg "judgment, decision, declaration or advisory opinion". If Parliament had intended the focus under s.8(4) to be upon the ECtHR's practice or jurisprudence it would have modelled s.8(4) on the language of s.2(1), but instead s.8(4) refers only to "principles". As Lord Carnwath observed,

> "[t]he more specific wording of s.8(4) in my view reflects the reality that not all decisions of the Strasbourg court in relation to damages will be determinative, or even illustrative, of any principle of general application";
>
> "the specific reference to 'principles' in s.8(4) must be given some effect".[155]

Thus Lord Carnwath's preferred approach would not be to search for ECtHR "practices" and replicate these domestically—as is the current approach under the Act. Rather he saw the Strasbourg material as only the "starting-point".[156] The primary search should be for cases that are more than one-off decisions limited to their own facts, and for more explicit statements or discussions of principle. Importantly Lord Carnwath's approach, if it were to gain ascendency, could open up the possibility of relying on domestic damages principles and practice in HRA damages claims. Recall that s.8(4) only requires domestic courts to take art.41 principles into account; there is no prohibition in the terms of the Act on domestic courts also taking common law principles into account. Under Lord Carnwath's approach Strasbourg cases would be the starting-point and domestic courts would be guided by broad principles explicitly stated and applied in that jurisprudence, while home-grown rules and principles could be drawn on to fill in the detail of these broad principles. **50-052**

There is support for such approach in earlier case law under the Act. Lord Millett, having discerned the problematic nature of the Strasbourg jurisprudence, postulated such an approach early in the life of the HRA: **50-053**

> "we may have to develop our own jurisprudence, while keeping an eye open on the case law of the Strasbourg court to ensure that we do not stray too far from the principles which that court may lay down".[157]

Stanley Burnton J, in an important early decision, *R. (on the application of KB) v Mental Health Review Tribunal*, considered that the difference in wording between ss.2(1) and 8(4) suggests

---

[154] [2013] 2 A.C. 254 at [108].

[155] [2013] 2 A.C. 254 at [113]–[114].

[156] [2013] 2 A.C. 254 at [114].

[157] *Cullen v Chief Constable of the Royal Ulster Constabulary* [2003] 1 W.L.R. 1763 HL at [80].

"Parliament may have wanted the UK court to have somewhat greater freedom in relation to decisions of the European Court on the amount of damages awarded in particular cases, quantum normally being a matter for the forum".[158]

He observed this was consistent with the view of the Law Commissions in their report on HRA damages.[159] His preferred approach of developing home-grown rules and principles,[160] was likely influenced by his expressed view that the ECtHR does not in general articulate the basis of awards beyond very general principles nor give a breakdown of different items of damages nor sometimes even distinguish between damages and costs: "Our own jurisprudence and legal culture require a more analytical approach".[161]

**50-054** Three further points should be noted in relation to application of the mirror method, and the identification of relevant art.41 practice. First, older case law of the ECtHR may not be a reliable guide as to current practice. In *Sturnham* Lord Reed noted earlier cases in which the ECtHR had not granted awards for mental distress despite finding a violation of art.5(4) by reason of a failure to decide the lawfulness of detention speedily.[162] However, these were not considered representative of contemporary practice, according to which a refusal to make awards was unusual. More generally it is worth noting that the ECtHR originally did not make any awards, and that its practice of making of awards has gradually expanded over time. Secondly, as discussed further below, in assessing quantum domestic courts will be led by awards made by the ECtHR against the UK and countries with comparable costs of living.[163] Thirdly, as Lord Reed observed in *Sturnham*, an important

"difference between the European court and a national court is that the European court does not normally undertake detailed fact-finding in relation to damages in the way which a national court of first instance would do, at least in jurisdictions such as those of the UK".[164]

For example the ECtHR does not have the capacity to compel witnesses or secure production of evidence. As such it is often dependant on information supplied by the parties. The Supreme Court's recognition of this difference between the supranational and domestic context is of importance as it may suggest that particular issues should be approached differently at the domestic level compared to the international level. For example the ECtHR generally insists on a "clear causal link"[165] between a violation and claimed losses, and at least in certain contexts has been slow to find such a link.[166] It has also often refused to speculate on whether

[158] *R. (on the application of KB) v Mental Health Review Tribunal* [2004] Q.B. 936 at [22].

[159] Law Commission, *Damages under the Human Rights Act 1998* (2000), Law Com. No.266/Scot Law Com. No.180, Cm.4853, para.4.11.

[160] *R. (on the application of KB) v Mental Health Review Tribunal* [2004] Q.B. 936 at [21]–[25].

[161] [2004] Q.B. 936 at [25].

[162] *R. (on the application of Sturnham) v Parole Board* [2013] 2 A.C. 254 at [55] and following.

[163] [2013] 2 A.C. 254 at [38]. See below at para.50-089.

[164] [2013] 2 A.C. 254 at [37].

[165] European Court of Human Rights, *Practice Direction: Just Satisfaction Claims*, 19 September 2016, para.7.

[166] As, for example, in the context of procedural violations of art.6, other than cases involving procedural delay: *R. (on the application of Greenfield) v Secretary of State for the Home Department* [2005] 1 W.L.R. 673 HL at [10]–[16]; *HL v United Kingdom* (2005) 40 E.H.R.R. 32 at [149].

losses were in fact suffered, in such cases denying awards.[167] These approaches are likely a symptom of the Court not having the capacity to undertake detailed fact-finding for itself. However, as the ECtHR has acknowledged, domestic courts are in a much better position to interrogate causal questions, and it would seem that they should approach causation in the ordinary way. Lord Reed in *Sturnham* indicated as much when he observed that

> "[a] domestic court is not however restricted in its fact-finding capabilities. In those circumstances, it is not in my view required by s.8 of the 1998 Act to apply a self-denying ordinance, but should establish the facts of the case in the usual way, and apply the normal domestic principle that the claimant has to establish on a balance of probabilities that he has suffered loss".[168]

Similarly, but not addressed in *Sturnham*, the ECtHR's practices of at times limiting compensation for non-pecuniary loss such as mental distress to cases where the violation was such as to cause "evident trauma"[169] or impact "so significantly"[170] on the victim may, at least in part, be driven by the court's limited fact-finding capacity; it is safer for the ECtHR to assume losses were suffered, absent a firm factual foundation, in the most serious cases.

## (2) Relevant Factors

The first point to recall is that there is no right to damages under the HRA. **50-055**
Whether an award should follow the finding of a violation depends on whether an award is "necessary", in the language of both s.8(3) and art.41. Domestic courts have followed the ECtHR, in the light of s.8(4), in taking a broad "equitable" approach to determining the necessity of an award. The ECtHR has said that the decision involves an inquiry into "what is just, fair and reasonable in all the circumstances of the case".[171] The phrase is not as all-encompassing as it first appears. But it is the case, as the Law Commissions observed, that the ECtHR does take into account a range of factors including the character and conduct of the parties to an extent hitherto unknown in the English law of damages.[172] The English courts have gone further, taking into account public policy considerations on an ad hoc basis, albeit as is discussed herein this raises the danger of breach of art.13. Let us consider the factors that guide the judicial decision as to whether to award damages.

**(a) Actual damage or loss** As Lord Millett observed in *Cullen*, **50-056**

> "The most obvious case where an award of damages is not necessary is where there is no damage to compensate".[173]

---

167 *Nikolova v Bulgaria* (2001) 31 E.H.R.R. 3 at [76]; *R. (on the application of Greenfield) v Secretary of State for the Home Department* [2005] 1 W.L.R. 673 HL at [8], [14].

168 *R. (on the application of Sturnham) v Parole Board* [2013] 2 A.C. 254 at [82], and see also at [13(5)]–[(8)], [39].

169 *Varnava v Turkey*, Application No.16064/90, 18 September 2009 at [224].

170 *Varnava v Turkey*, Application No.16064/90, 18 September 2009 at [224].

171 *Al-Jedda v United Kingdom* (2011) 53 E.H.R.R. 23 at [114].

172 Law Commission, *Damages under the Human Rights Act 1998* (2000), Law Com. No.266/Scot Law Com. No.180, Cm.4853 at [4.96].

173 *Cullen v Chief Constable of the Royal Ulster Constabulary* [2003] 1 W.L.R. 1763 HL at [84].

One of the broad principles that is discernible from the ECtHR jurisprudence is restitutio in intergum. The corollary of this principle is that no damages should be awarded where there is no loss to compensate.[174] Awards under art.41

> "are not, nor should they be, intended to give financial comfort or sympathetic enrichment at the expense of the Contracting Party concerned".[175]

Under art.41 compensation is limited to "actual harmful consequences",[176] and awards under the HRA have followed suit. For example the Grand Chamber has listed the following heads of non-pecuniary loss: physical or psychological, pain and suffering, distress, anxiety, frustration, feelings of injustice or humiliation, prolonged uncertainty, disruption to life, or real loss of opportunity.[177] The vast majority of awards under the HRA have been modest awards for these types of non-pecuniary loss. In a recent case damages were awarded under the HRA for the first time for loss of conjugal relations.[178] Other types of losses have been recognised by the ECtHR which prima facie are not known to domestic damages law such as loss of a relationship with a child,[179] but this can be analogised to mental distress. It is likely that new heads will arise or require to be recognised given that the HRA affords protection to a new and wider range of interests than has hitherto been protected through imposition of liability in domestic tort law. And as Stanley Burnton J observed in *KB*,

> "Convention rights are important basic rights, and it is doubtless arguable that damages for their breach may be awarded for injuries that would not be recognised as deserving of compensation in other areas".[180]

Notably awards of non-pecuniary loss may be awarded to legal persons.[181] Pecuniary losses are clearly recoverable—though there have been relatively few claims for such damages under the HRA—and it would seem that courts under the HRA will, despite the mirror approach, generally approach such losses, including recoverable heads, in the way that they would in domestic law.[182]

50-057 **(b) Damage or loss does not give right to damages** It does not follow from proof of damage or loss that is causally connected to the violation that damages will be awarded. As courts have observed, there may be

> "a factual basis for an award of damage, but that does not mean that an award must follow".[183]

---

[174] *R. (on the application of Wilkinson) v Inland Revenue Commissioners* [2005] 1 W.L.R. 1718 HL at [24]–[28].

[175] *Varnava v Turkey*, Application No.16064/90, 18 September 2009 at [224].

[176] European Court of Human Rights, *Practice Direction: Just Satisfaction Claims*, 19 September 2016, para.9.

[177] *Varnava v Turkey*, Application No.16064/90, 18 September 2009 at [224]; *Nikolova v Bulgaria* (2001) 31 E.H.R.R. 3 at [O-III4]; *Scorazzi v Italy* (2002) 35 E.H.R.R. 12 at [250]; *Svriddin Dzhurayev v Russia*, Application No.71386/10, 25 April 2013 at [252].

[178] *CH v A Metropolitan Council* [2017] EWCOP 12. See 50-144, below.

[179] *W v United Kingdom* (1991) 13 E.H.R.R. 453; see Law Commission, *Damages under the Human Rights Act 1998* (2000), Law Com. No.266/Scot Law Com. No.180, Cm.4853 at paras.3.27, 6.160.

[180] *R. (on the application of KB) v Mental Health Review Tribunal* [2004] Q.B. 936 at [71].

[181] *Comingersoll SA v Portugal* (2001) 31 E.H.R.R. 772.

[182] See para.50-076 below.

[183] *R. (on the application of Guntrip) v Secretary of State for Justice* [2010] EWHC 3188 (Admin) at

An award must be "necessary", and in many cases the ECtHR, and domestic courts following art.41 practice, have held that a finding of violation affords just satisfaction despite the suffering of some loss. Of course, whether a finding of breach of the Convention is sufficient to accord the victim just satisfaction is a peculiarly subjective matter, and it is therefore not surprising to find that the case law does not articulate a coherent approach to deciding whether or not this is the case, and there are cases where different results have occurred even though they appear to be indistinguishable on their facts.[184] As the Law Commissions observed, the "lack of clear principles as to when damages should be awarded and how they should be measured" is perhaps "the most striking feature of the Strasbourg case-law".[185]

These problems follow from the generally unreasoned nature of art.41 determinations, the ECtHR seldom offering anything other than conclusory statements to the effect that, in the circumstances, a finding of violation constitutes just satisfaction. As to the more general practice of holding that a finding of violation constitutes just satisfaction, members of the ECtHR, itself, have been scathing of this practice. For example in *Nikolova v Bulgaria*,[186] Judge Bonello said:

> "I consider it wholly inadequate and unacceptable that a court of justice should 'satisfy' the victim of a breach of fundamental rights with a mere handout of legal idiom ... The first time the court appears to have resorted to this hapless formula was in the *Golder* case[187] of 1975. Disregarding its own practise that full reasoning should be given for all decisions, the court failed to suggest one single reason why the finding should also double up as a remedy. Since then, propelled by the irresistible force of inertia, that formula has resurfaced regularly. In few of the many judgments which relied on it did the court seem eager to upset the rule that it has to give neither reasons nor explanation."

Thus, there is little guidance from Strasbourg. The analysis that follows is an attempt to distil factors that may be relevant, largely relying on the relatively more reasoned domestic case law under the HRA. Albeit many of these factors are themselves highly subjective and have not been applied consistently, decisions under the Act often having an "ad hoc" quality—though there is more concrete guidance in regard to some factors. As such the analysis that follows is in the nature of a "rational reconstruction", seeking to systematise relevant judicial practice.

**(c) Degree of loss** One consistent basis on which the ECtHR denies awards for **50-058**
non-pecuniary loss despite the suffering of some loss is that the degree of loss has not reached a minimum threshold of severity so as to warrant an award. This ap-

---

[53]; *R. (on the application of Shaw) v Secretary of State for the Home Department* [2013] EWHC 42 (Admin) at [45].

184 See, e.g. the cases cited by the Law Com 266/Scot Law Com 180, para.3.42, n.85 in relation to breach of art.5. Other unjustifiable distortions are evident, such as greater sums being awarded to companies for non-pecuniary loss consequent on violation of property rights than human victims of inhuman and degrading treatment: O. Ichim, *Just Satisfaction under the European Convention on Human Rights* (Cambridge: Cambridge University Press, 2015), p.157.

185 Law Commission, *Damages under the Human Rights Act 1998* (2000), Law Com. No.266/Scot Law Com. No.180, Cm.4853 at para.3.4.

186 *Nikolova v Bulgaria* (2001) 31 E.H.R.R. 3 at 91–94. See also *Engel v Netherlands* (1979–80) 1 E.H.R.R. 706 at 710; *TW v Malta* (1999) 29 E.H.R.R. 185 at 207–209; *Kingsley v United Kingdom* (2002) 35 E.H.R.R. 10 at 196–197; *Disk and Kesk v Turkey* Application No.38676/08, 29 April 2013, per Judges Ziemele and Karakas.

187 *Golder v The United Kingdom* (1975) 1 E.H.R.R. 524.

proach has been read across to HRA practice. Thus it is routine for the ECtHR to conclude that while the applicant has suffered anxiety and frustration as a result of the violation, it is not

> "of such intensity that it would in itself justify an award of compensation for non-pecuniary damages".[188]

In the case of *Varnava v Turkey* the Grand Chamber distinguished cases in which compensation has been awarded for "evident trauma" and those in which

> "the public vindication of the wrong suffered by the applicant, in a judgment binding on the Contracting State, is a powerful form of redress in itself".[189]

It continued,

> "In many cases where a law, procedure or practice has been found to fall short of Convention standards this is enough to put matters right (see, for example, *Christine Goodwin v the United Kingdom* [GC], no.28957/95, § 120, ECHR 2002-VI; *Saadi v Italy* [GC], no.37201/06, § 188, ECHR 2008; and *S. and Marper v. the United Kingdom* [GC], nos 30562/04 and 30566/04, § 134, ECHR 2008). In some situations, however, the impact of the violation may be regarded as being of a nature and degree as to have impinged so significantly on the moral well-being of the applicant as to require something further".[190]

As to how to differentiate cases in which loss has reached the minimum intensity from those where it has not the Grand Chamber said, "Such elements do not lend themselves to a process of calculation or precise quantification".[191] It stated that it adopts a flexible "equitable" approach to decisions whether to make awards, taking into account the overall context in which the breach occurred.

**50-059** One pattern is relatively clear: where suffering goes beyond mere mental distress and includes either physical injury, a recognised psychiatric illness or a deprivation of liberty that the victim would not have otherwise suffered, it would be unusual for an award to be denied. For example in *R. (Sturnham) v Parole Board* Lord Reed said,

> "Where it is established on a balance of probabilities that a violation of art.5(4) has resulted in the detention of a prisoner beyond the date when he would otherwise have been released, damages should ordinarily be awarded as compensation for the resultant detention".[192]

In the Court of Appeal decision in *Sturnham* Laws LJ indicated damages would be awarded for resultant "diagnosable illness".[193] In *Van Colle v Chief Constable of Hertfordshire*, in which the victim had died as a result of the violation of art.2, substantial awards were made for the suffering he had incurred in the lead up to his death.[194] In *DSD v Commissioner of Police for the Metropolis* the claimants were awarded significant awards for losses, which included recognised psychiatric illness, in consequence of violations by the police of their art.3 rights to an effective

---

188 *Silver v UK* (1983) 6 E.H.R.R. 62 at [10].

189 *Varnava v Turkey*, Application No.16064/90, 18 September 2009 at [224].

190 *Varnava v Turkey*, Application No.16064/90, 18 September 2009 at [224].

191 *Varnava v Turkey*, Application No.16064/90, 18 September 2009 at [224].

192 [2013] 2 A.C. 254 at [13(6)].

193 *R. (on the application of Sturnham) v Parole Board* [2012] 3 W.L.R. 476 CA at [22].

194 [2007] 1 W.L.R. 1821 CA

investigation.[195] In the case of *Shahid v Scottish Ministers*, in which an award was declined by the Supreme Court, the Court nonetheless indicated that if the victim had suffered "severe or permanent injury to ... health" an award would be forthcoming.[196] More generally the ECtHR has been very willing to make awards, including very large awards, for breaches of arts 2, 3 and 4, as these Articles protect the most fundamental of rights. As the Court observed in *DSD*, "Habitually damages are awarded for *any* article 3 violation".[197] That the foregoing heads of loss and types of violation are likely to attract compensation is also reinforced by the fact that interferences with similar interests are routinely compensated in the law of torts. While, according to the mirror approach, the approach to liability in domestic law is not directly relevant, it would seem that practice at common law indirectly shapes whether damages are more or less likely to be compensated. For example courts have shown scepticism on occasion towards making awards for "free-standing" distress,[198] whereas courts have indicated that they are more willing to make awards where the claim and protected interests resemble an established tort.[199] More generally, in cases where a tort analogy[200] is apparent courts have shown little hesitation in exercising their power to make an award.

The last paragraph notwithstanding, it is an established aspect of both ECtHR and domestic HRA jurisprudence that awards are made for free-standing distress and similar mental harms short of psychiatric illness, and indeed most awards under the Act have been of this nature. However, there is little concrete guidance as to when minimum severity will be reached. There is some evidence that the presence of certain factors will exacerbate the losses to be inferred in such a way as to make it more likely that the threshold is reached. In particular whether the claimant suffers from mental illness has been discussed as one factor to be considered, as those with mental illness may be more vulnerable to distress than those of full health,[201] and their illness may make it more difficult to cope with the circumstances of a rights-violation.[202] Direct evidence of mental suffering, such as affidavit evidence or medical reports, will strengthen a claimant's case,[203] compared to where the court **50-060**

---

195 [2015] 1 W.L.R. 1833 (QB). See para.50-091 and following, below.

196 *Shahid v Scottish Ministers* [2015] 3 W.L.R. 1003 SC at [89].

197 *DSD v Commissioner of Police of the Metropolis* [2015] 1 W.L.R. 1833 (QB) at [68(4)].

198 *R. (on the application of Sturnham) v Parole Board* [2012] 3 W.L.R. 476 CA at [16], [21]–[22]; *Amis v Commissioner of Police of the Metropolis* [2004] EWHC 683 (QB) at [50]. *R. (on the application of Bernard) v Secretary of State for the Home Department* [2005] EWHC 452 (Admin) at [54]–[62].

199 *R. (on the application of Sturnham) v Parole Board* [2012] 3 W.L.R. 476 CA at [15], [22].

200 *R. (on the application of MA) v Independent Adjudicator* [2014] EWHC 3886 at [61]–[64]; *R. (on the application of KB) v Mental Health Review Tribunal* [2004] Q.B. 936 (see the awards made at para.50-131 below); *R. (on the application of Bernard) v Enfield London Borough Council* [2003] H.R.L.R. 4 (Admin); *Kingshott v Ministry of Justice* [2009] EWHC 3666 (QB); *R. (on the application of Faulkner) v Secretary of State for Justice* [2011] EWCA Civ 349 at [12], [18]; *Rabone v Pennine Care NHS Foundation Trust* [2012] 2 A.C. 72 at [108] (Lady Hale considering the claim closer in nature to a tort claim than a claim for judicial review).

201 *R. (on the application of KB) v Mental Health Review Tribunal* [2004] Q.B. 936 at [70], [72].

202 *R (on the application of Sturnham) v Parole Board* [2013] 2 A.C. 254 at [66]; *R. (on the application of Guntrip) v Secretary of State for Justice* [2010] EWHC 3188 Admin at [56].

203 In *KB*, a case concerning damages claims for breach of art.5(4) brought by claimants who were detained and mentally ill, Stanley Burnton J considered it a touchstone of whether distress reached the threshold of sufficient seriousness whether the hospital staff had recorded mental suffering in the claimants' clinical notes: *R. (on the application of KB) v Mental Health Review Tribunal* [2004] Q.B. 936 at [73].

is asked to infer loss,[204] albeit the ECtHR

> "without recourse to any expert or medical evidence, quite regularly simply assumes that a claimant must have suffered some form of generalised anxiety, stress, distress or anguish warranting compensation which falls short of any recognised medical condition".[205]

The Supreme Court in *Sturnham* was similarly willing to infer loss from the fact of violation.[206]

**50-061** The more serious and traumatic the circumstances of the violation and/or the longer the duration of the violation, the more likely courts will conclude that the minimum threshold has been reached. The manner of the breach and culpability of the defendant's conduct has been held to be relevant to this inquiry.[207] *R. (on the application of Bernard) v Enfield London Borough Council* offers a good illustrative example.[208] The Court found a breach of art.8. Despite the claimant having been assessed by the defendant as needing special adapted housing because she suffered severe disability, the defendant failed to act on that assessment for 20 months, leaving the claimant in ill-adapted housing, and making it virtually impossible for her and her family to have any meaningful private and family life:

> "Suitably adapted accommodation would not merely have facilitated the normal incidents of family life, for example the second claimant would have been able to move around her home to some extent and would have been able to play some part, together with the first claimant, in looking after their children. It would also have secured her 'physical and psychological integrity'. She would no longer have been housebound, confined to a shower chair for most of the day, lacking privacy in the most undignified of circumstances, but would have been able to operate again as part of her family and as a person in her own right, rather than being a burden, wholly dependent upon the rest of her family. In short, it would have restored her dignity as a human being".[209]

Damages were claimed for non-pecuniary loss, principally distress, discomfort and inconvenience; no physical injury or recognised psychiatric illness was suffered. The Court reached the conclusion that damages ought to be awarded with little hesitation, emphasising the impact of the claimant's living conditions and the lengthy 20-month duration of the delay[210]:

> "I am satisfied that an award of damages is necessary to give just satisfaction to the claimants. This was a serious breach of their rights under art.8. The claimants and their family had to live in deplorable conditions, wholly inimical to any normal family life, and to the physical and psychological integrity of the second claimant for a considerable period of time".

---

204 *Osborn v Parole Board* [2014] A.C. 1115 at [115]; *O v Commissioner of Police of the Metropolis* [2011] H.R.L.R. 29 (QB) at [182], [190]; *Amis v Commissioner of Police of the Metroplois* [2004] EWHC 683 (QB) at [50]. *R. (on the application of Bernard) v Secretary of State for the Home Department* [2005] EWHC 452 Admin at [54]–[62]; *R. (on the application of B) v Camden London Borough Council* [2005] EWHC 1366 Admin at [98].

205 *DSD v Commissioner of Police of the Metropolis* [2015] 1 W.L.R. 1833 (QB) at [25].

206 *R. (on the application of Sturnham) v Parole Board* [2013] 2 A.C. 254 at [12]-[13]. See para.50-062 below.

207 *Van Colle v Chief Constable of Hertfordshire* [2007] 1 W.L.R. 1821 CA at [124]; *Anufrijeva v Southwark London Borough Council* [2004] Q.B. 1124 CA at [66]–[70].

208 [2003] H.R.L.R. 4 (Admin).

209 [2003] H.R.L.R. 4 (Admin) at [33].

210 [2003] H.R.L.R. 4 (Admin) at [36].

The Court rejected an argument that damages should be denied on the basis that the defendant ultimately provided suitable housing. In determining that damages ought to be awarded the Court also laid emphasis on the fact the defendant had ignored letters from the claimants' solicitors urging action; not apologised, offered an explanation for the delay nor acknowledged they were in error; made no improvements to procedures; and failed to comply with previous timescales set by the Court. In addition to this analysis, the Court's consideration of quantum reinforces that the manner of the breach or way the violation occurred can exacerbate the degree of distress to be inferred. The Court considered that the defendant's conduct, including the failure to apologise or reply to letters, had "compounded" the claimant's problems, and the claimants did not have the comfort of knowing their suffering had not been in vain.[211]

The duration of the violation has been an important and recurring factor in decisions whether to make awards under the HRA. In *Sturnham* Lord Reed laid down timescale-based guidance to govern when distress could be considered to reach the minimum level of severity required for an award.[212] The case concerned damages claims by prisoners for distress suffered as a result of delays in the hearing of their cases before the Parole Board; the delays constituted violations of the art.5(4) requirement of speedy hearings. He observed that **50-062**

> "whether feelings of frustration and anxiety are sufficiently serious to warrant an award of compensation will evidently depend to some extent upon the circumstances of the individual case".[213]

However, where the delay was of three months or longer loss ought ordinarily to be presumed and damages awarded. But where the delay was less than three months it should ordinarily be inferred that any distress suffered did not meet the minimum threshold of intensity required to attract an award, barring a special case; for example, a delay of short duration could possibly lead to acute mental suffering if the prisoner had a particular reason for anxiety or the prisoner suffered mental illness.

In *R. (on the application of Lee-Hirons) v Secretary of State for Justice* the Supreme Court held that the defendant had breached the claimant's right under art.5(2) by not explaining to him the reasons for his recall to hospital on mental health grounds until 12 days after he ought to have been informed of those reasons.[214] While the Court was willing to infer the delay would have caused frustration and anxiety, damages were nonetheless denied as **50-063**

> "the time-span of only 12 days precludes any inference that [the violation] caused significant non-pecuniary injury".[215]

The Court referred, by analogy, to the three-month threshold applied in *Sturnham*.[216] Surprisingly, however, no consideration was given to the fact that the

---

[211] [2003] H.R.L.R. 4 (Admin) at [61]. Note however that lack of an apology, even if it exacerbates upset, may not always lead to an uplift in quantum: *Van Colle v Chief Constable of Hertfordshire* [2007] 1 W.L.R. 1821 CA at [123].

[212] *R. (on the application of Sturnham) v Parole Board* [2013] 2 A.C. 254.

[213] [2013] 2 A.C. 254 at [66].

[214] [2017] A.C. 52.

[215] [2017] A.C. 52 at [42].

[216] Above para.50-062.

claimant in *Lee-Hirons* suffered mental illness, despite *Sturnham* indicating that the presence of this feature may justify an award in a case that involved a delay of fewer than three months. The time-scale based guidance in *Sturnham* was also relied on in the Supreme Court decision in *R. (on the application of Haney) v Secretary of State for Justice*.[217] In that case prisoners sentenced to indeterminate life sentences were held to have suffered breach of an implied duty owed to them under art.5 that they be provided a reasonable opportunity to rehabilitate themselves and demonstrate they no longer presented an unacceptable danger to the public. The prisoners had not been able to sufficiently progress towards release on or after the expiry of their tariff periods because of a lack of provision for such reasonable opportunities for rehabilitation. The Court held that frustration and distress could be inferred as a result of the delays in provision of and lack of opportunities for rehabilitation. The Court considered an analogy with the timescale-based guidance in *Sturnham* was appropriate, supported by the view that the implied duty in *Haney* was closely analogous in nature to the duties cast by art.5(4).[218] Thus prisoners who suffered over three months' delay before being afforded reasonable opportunities to progress their rehabilitation were granted modest awards of £500 and £600 respectively, each for a delay of approximately one year. The higher award of £600 was justified on the basis that the delay experienced by that prisoner took place post-tariff, which was taken to exacerbate the sense of frustration.

**50-064** *O v Commissioner of the Police for the Metropolis* concerned damages claims brought by those who claimed to be victims of serious crimes including slavery and inhuman and degrading treatment perpetrated by third parties.[219] The HRA damages claims were brought against the police for failures, once the allegations were communicated to them, to carry out effective investigations into the alleged crimes, in breach of arts 3 and 4. Violations were found. The damages claims were for distress and frustration caused by the police's failure to investigate. The Court observed that the ECtHR had been willing to make awards in cases involving violations of arts 2, 3 and 4,[220] and concluded that damages were a necessary response to the violation. A principal reason supporting the award of damages was that the claimants would have become more and more frustrated over the significant 12-to 15-month period of police acquiescence, being the time from which the claimants had shown they were willing, ready and able to participate in an investigation until

---

217 [2015] A.C. 1344.

218 In prior proceedings before the ECtHR in *James v United Kingdom* (2013) 56 E.H.R.R. 12, which concerned the same issue of lack of opportunities for prisoners to progress towards release, the Strasbourg Court had held that the equivalent duties identified by the Supreme Court were based in art.5(1), and breach of those duties held to render the prisoners' detention arbitrary. However, the Supreme Court in *Haney* (above) disagreed with this analysis and considered the implied duty was more closely analogous to art.5(4), so that breaches of the implied duty did not render the prisoners' detention arbitrary; rather the breaches were more in the nature of procedural flaws. The different normative foundation of the duty helps to explain why the awards in *Haney* were much lower than those made by the ECtHR in *James*, the Supreme Court stating that analogies with those awards were unsafe given the Supreme Court had conceptualised the implied duty under art.5 differently. In *James* the following awards were made, all delays being post-tariff: Mr James EUR3,000 in respect of a period of five months; Mr Wells EUR6,200 in respect of a period of twenty-one months; and Mr Lee EUR8,000 in respect of a period of thirty months.

219 [2011] H.R.L.R. 29 (QB). See also *Re Jordan* [2014] NIQB 71 (discussed below at para.50-070); *DSD v Commissioner of Police of the Metropolis* [2015] 1 W.L.R. 1833 (QB) (discussed below at para.50-071 and para.50-091 and following).

220 [2015] 1 W.L.R. 1833 (QB) at [185].

the time when the defendant made an unequivocal offer to investigate the cases. It was also relevant that it had taken a threat of legal proceedings to galvanise the police into action. Each claimant was awarded £5,000.[221]

**(d) Procedural and substantive rights** Another factor which *might* be said to guide the making of awards, and which is illustrated by the statement of principle in *Nikolova's case*,[222] is that the ECtHR and domestic courts may be more likely to make awards for breaches of substantive as opposed to procedural obligations. Thus, for example, in *R. (on the application of Greenfield) v Secretary of State for the Home Department* Lord Bingham cited[223] the Grand Chamber of the ECtHR in *Kingsley v United Kingdom*,[224] where they said: **50-065**

> "In all the circumstances, and in accordance with its normal practice, in civil and criminal cases, as regards violations of art.6(1) caused by failures of objective or structural independence and impartiality, the court does not consider it appropriate to award monetary compensation to the applicant in respect of loss of procedural opportunity or any distress, loss or damage allegedly flowing from the outcome of the domestic proceedings."

Lord Bingham then stated:

> "Thus, whatever the practice in other classes of case, the ordinary practice is not to make an award in cases of structural bias".[225]

Earlier in his judgment he also made the following observations, which are suggestive of a difference of approach as between breaches of certain "substantive" Articles and breaches of "procedural" guarantees:

> "It is desirable for present purposes to concentrate on the Strasbourg approach to the award of damages on finding that art.6 has been violated. Article 6 seeks to ensure that everyone, in the determination of their civil rights and obligations or of any criminal charge against them, shall enjoy a fair and public hearing within a reasonable time by an independent and impartial tribunal established by law with judgment given in public. Criminal charges entail additional rights: the presumption of innocence, the right to be informed of the charge, the right of a person to defend the charge himself or through legal assistance of his own choosing. These are important rights, and significant violations are not to be lightly regarded. But they have one feature which distinguishes them from violations of articles such as art.3, where an applicant has been tortured, or art.4, where he has been enslaved, or art.8, where a child has been unjustifiably removed from its family; that it does not follow from a finding that the trial process has involved a breach of an art.6 right that the outcome of the trial process was wrong or would have been otherwise had the breach not occurred. There is an obvious contrast with art.5, guaranteeing the right to liberty and security of the person."[226]

In subsequent cases this distinction between substantive and procedural obligations has influenced the refusal of awards for procedural breaches.[227] In the Court

---

221 [2015] 1 W.L.R. 1833 (QB) at [190].

222 *Nikolova v Bulgaria* (2001) 31 E.H.R.R. 3 at [76]. See para.50-048 and following, above.

223 [2005] 1 W.L.R. 673 HL at [16].

224 (2002) 35 E.H.R.R. 177 at [43].

225 [2005] 1 W.L.R. 673 HL at [16].

226 [2005] 1 W.L.R. 673 HL at [7].

227 See, e.g. *Re C (A Child)* [2007] EWCA Civ 2 (no award made where decision to proceed to adop-

of Appeal decision in *R. (on the application of Sturnham) v Parole Board* Laws L.J.'s analysis similarly suggested such a distinction albeit he came at the matter from a different angle.[228] He considered damages should be forthcoming where a Convention violation had a consequence akin to those sorts of consequence regularly compensated by domestic tort law, whereas courts should be less willing to make awards otherwise. This analysis, if accepted, has implications for the availability of damages for free-standing mental distress, anxiety and frustration caused by breaches of procedural rights, as in general mental harm caused by interference with procedural interests is not protected through imposition of liability in domestic law. Rather in domestic law procedural interests are protected principally by procedural fairness in common law judicial review, breach of which does not generate damages liability. However, a cautious approach ought to be taken to this analysis. It has not been endorsed by the Supreme Court, and it tends to undermine Parliament's intent in creating the HRA; through the HRA and s.8, Parliament quite deliberately expanded the range of interests that could be afforded protection through the imposition of liability beyond the narrow band of interests traditionally protected by tort. Indeed, to adopt Laws LJ's view would mean that the HRA added very little, in terms of the scope of damages liability, to the pre-existing law of tort, largely rendering the provision for damages in s.8 otiose.

**50-066** On appeal the Supreme Court in *Sturnham* was seemingly not convinced by Laws LJ's analysis given it followed Strasbourg practice and made awards for free-standing distress, as well as deprivation of liberty, caused by procedural breaches of art.5(4); specifically, failures to provide prisoners a speedy hearing before the Parole Board.[229] Furthermore, domestic courts and the ECtHR have routinely made awards for distress and frustration caused by breaches of procedural, investigatory obligations under arts 2 and 3.[230] As the Court in *DSD* observed of art.3, awards are habitually made for breach of that Article, and in this regard

> "There is no clear distinction drawn in the art.3 cases between the three different types of violation that the article embraces".[231]

It is also worth noting that albeit Lord Bingham in *Greenfield* came to the conclusion that awards should rarely be made for distress suffered in art.6 structural bias cases,[232] many such awards have been made by the ECtHR.[233] Furthermore, awards for non-pecuniary loss in art.6 delay cases are as frequently made by the ECtHR

---

tion without prior adequate consultation with the child's natural mother was held to breach art.8). See para.50-150 below.

228 *R. (on the application of Sturnham) v Parole Board* [2012] 3 W.L.R. 476 CA at [15], [22].

229 *R. (on the application of Sturnham) v Parole Board* [2013] 2 A.C. 254.

230 *DSD v Commissioner of Police of the Metropolis* [2015] 1 W.L.R. 1833 (QB); *O v Commissioner of the Metropolis* [2011] H.R.L.R. 29 (QB); *Re Jordan's Application for Judicial Review* [2014] NIQB 71.

231 [2015] 1 W.L.R. 1833 (QB) at [68(4)].

232 *R. (on the application of Greenfield) v Secretary of State for the Home Department* [2005] 1 W.L.R. 673 HL at [16].

233 *De Cubber v Belgium* (1991) 13 E.H.R.R. 422 at [24]; *Kabudec v Slovakia* (2001) 33 E.H.R.R. 41 at [68]; *Lauko v Slovakia* (2001) 33 E.H.R.R. 40 at [72]; *Sadak v Turkey* (2003) 36 E.H.R.R. 26 at [77]; *Tsfayo v United Kingdom* (2009) 48 E.H.R.R. 18 at [56]; *Harabin v Slovakia*, Application No.58688/11, 20 November 2012 at [176]; *Ozerov v Russia*, Application No.64962/01, 18 May 2010 at [62]; *Gajewski v Poland*, Application No.27225/05, 21 December 2010 at [53].

as awards for delay under art.5(4).[234] As such, there cannot in truth be said to be any hard and fast principle against awards for breaches of procedural rights, especially in the light of the Supreme Court decision in *Sturnham*. Though it may be that, in some cases at least, alternative remedies such as the ordering of a retrial, or quashing of a procedurally flawed decision and mandating a fresh decision that accords with procedural fairness will be considered just satisfaction in themselves as they will provide the very procedure to which the claimant was entitled. Perhaps this is one explanation for the decision in *Osborn v Parole Board* in which the Supreme Court adopted a reticent approach to the availability of damages for breach of art.5(4) caused by failure to provide an oral hearing.[235] In contrast where the violation is historical and the legal entitlement to which the claimant was owed cannot now be fulfilled the prerogative remedies and specific relief will have less application, as in the case of a loss of life, or past deprivation of liberty, breach of privacy, denial of free speech, or infliction of inhuman or degrading treatment. In such cases damages would seem the only plausible response. Importantly, breach of a procedural right can fall into this category. In *DSD* the claimants suffered recognised psychiatric harm in consequence of the failure by the police to conduct an effective investigation into allegations of sexual assault, as was required by art.3.[236] The claims were historical in that they related to failings by the police in the carrying on of an investigation which had since closed, the perpetrator of the sexual assaults having been apprehended. The Judge considered this a clear case where damages were a necessary remedy,

> "by the very nature of these proceedings, other public law remedies are simply not apt. This is not, for instance, a case where a decision can be retaken or proceedings repeated. The wrong committed in this case by the Defendant cannot be put right by any more habitual public law order".[237]

(e) **Other redress** Section 8(3)(a) states that one factor relevant to determining the necessity of an award is **50-067**

> "any other relief or remedy granted, or order made, in relation to the act in question (by that or any other court)".

This consideration is brought squarely into focus by concurrent claims in tort and under the HRA, and situations where the claimant may have received compensation from other sources. For example if the same unlawful imprisonment gives rise to successful claims in both false imprisonment and for breach of art.5, to award damages for loss of liberty and distress for each action would lead to double recovery, and would not be allowed[238]; as damages for the tort are available as of right, and are calculated according to higher scales than those applied under the HRA, a court should award damages on the tortious measure and deny HRA dam-

---

[234] This practice of making awards in delay cases was observed by the ECtHR in *HL v United Kingdom* (2005) 40 E.H.R.R. 32 at [149]. See also, discussing the relevant principles in art.6 delay cases: *Scordino v Italy* (2007) 45 E.H.R.R. 7.

[235] *Osborn v Parole Board* [2014] A.C. 1115 at [2(xiii)].

[236] *DSD v Commissioner of Police of the Metropolis* [2015] 1 W.L.R. 1833 (QB).

[237] [2015] 1 W.L.R. 1833 (QB) at [24].

[238] *ZH v Commissioner of Police of the Metropolis* [2012] EWHC 604 (QB) (upheld: [2013] 1 W.L.R. 3021 CA) (awards in tort rendered separate awards for breaches of arts 3, 5 and 8 unnecessary). Contrast *Stellato v Home Office* [2010] EWCA Civ 1435 at [34].

ages in its discretion. In less straightforward cases a less than rigorous approach has at times been taken to issues of concurrent liability under the HRA, especially in cases involving multiple claimants, influenced by the ECtHR's "equitable" approach to just satisfaction. But there are signs that the law is gradually being placed on a more principled footing.

**50-068** Cases involving breach of the positive operational duty to protect life under art.2—the "*Osman*" duty—offer one illustration.[239] *Rabone v Pennine Care NHS Foundation Trust*,[240] involved claims by the parents of the deceased who had committed suicide as a result of a decision by the defendant to release her from its care, this decision ultimately being found by the Supreme Court to have constituted a breach of the duty owed to the deceased to take reasonable steps to protect her life. The defendant had previously settled a negligence claim with the deceased's estate, of which the deceased's father was the executor, for £7,500, which compensated for the damage suffered by the deceased in the lead up to her death. The claim in *Rabone* was brought by the parents in their own right, as indirect victims,[241] for bereavement damages in respect of the defendant's breach of art.2 (damages under the Fatal Accidents Act 1976 were unavailable as the deceased was an adult). A question arose in both the Court of Appeal and Supreme Court as to the impact of the award in negligence made to the deceased's estate upon the parents' claim for damages for bereavement under the HRA. The Court of Appeal held damages awarded to the estate could afford just satisfaction for distress suffered by the deceased's parents.[242] With respect, this approach ought not to be followed as the claims are conceptually separate: one award is to the deceased for loss suffered in the lead up to her death, and the other claim is for bereavement damages for the deceased's parents in consequence of the deceased's death. In the Supreme Court the Court of Appeal's approach was not followed. The Supreme Court did leave open the possibility that in a future case the sums awarded to different parties could be viewed in the round and an "all things considered" assessment made as to whether just satisfaction had been afforded.[243] However, in *Rabone* the Court did not think such approach would be appropriate, and damages were awarded to the parents in their own right despite the previous settlement between the defendant and the deceased's estate. First, the deceased's mother had received no award, and the deceased's father had not received an award personally. Secondly, the sum awarded to the estate was by no means unduly generous. The outcome in the Supreme Court is to be preferred, albeit the possibility that an award made to one person could impact an award made to another person remains a conceptually difficult proposition. As such, the approach of the Court of Appeal in *Van Colle v Chief Constable of Hertfordshire Police* provides encouragement.[244] This case also involved claims for bereavement damages by the parents of the deceased, where the defendant had breached the *Osman* duty it had owed the deceased under art.2. The Court said:

---

239 *Osman v United Kingdom* (2000) 29 E.H.R.R. 245.

240 [2012] 2 A.C. 72.

241 Above para.50-020.

242 [2011] Q.B. 1019 CA at [94]–[107].

243 [2012] 2 A.C. 72 at [62].

244 [2007] 1 W.L.R. 1821 CA.

> "We dare say that if any award had been made to the son's estate as such it would have gone to the parents in practice, but it seems better in principle to make separate awards to separate victims".[245]

Similarly in the case of *DSD v Commissioner of Police of the Metropolis* (discussed further below),[246] concerning damages claims by two victims of sexual assault in respect of police failure to conduct effective investigations into the assaults in breach of art.3, the Court stated that damages would be assessed separately for each claim: in principle the court should "view each claimant in his or her own light and compensate accordingly".[247]

*Dobson v Thames Water Utilities Ltd* provides another illustration of how an award made to one claimant may affect an award made to another.[248] The claimants were occupiers of properties adversely affected by sewage treatment works operated by the defendant. Some of the claimants had a proprietary interest in the properties in question, making them eligible to claim damages for nuisance, but others did not. In addition to liability in nuisance, the defendant was in breach of the claimants' rights under art.8. The question arose whether an award made to a property-holder in nuisance for, among other losses, loss of amenity, was relevant to determining whether damages ought to be awarded under the HRA for distress and discomfort to others on the property, such as family members, who claimed for losses suffered in consequence of breach of their art.8 rights. Following guidance from the Court of Appeal the Judge held that an award to the property-holder was relevant,[249] and ultimately held this to be one basis on which awards should be denied to those without proprietary interests in the affected property: the award in nuisance made to the property-owner was held to afford just satisfaction to the other occupants. With respect, it is difficult to rationalise this approach. First, the juridical bases of the claims are different: the property-owner claims in nuisance for interference with his proprietary interests—nuisance is a tort against land[250]—whereas the other occupiers claim under art.8 for breach of their "dignitarian", non-proprietary interests in family and home life. Secondly, the award made to the property-owner is one for loss of the amenity or use value of his or her land, whereas the other occupiers are claiming for distress, which is not in fact recoverable in nuisance.[251] Thirdly, it is an established principle of nuisance that when the claimant recovers they are not "recovering damages on behalf of other occupiers of the property".[252] It is also worth noting that the violation and associated effects upon the other occupiers lasted for a significant period of time, and—as observed above— duration is typically an important factor favouring the making of awards. Lastly, another ground for refusing relief in *Dobson* was that various statutory procedures for seeking enforcement and abatement notices, as well as fines against the defendant, were open.[253] This suggests that availability of other statutory **50-069**

---

245 [2007] 1 W.L.R. 1821 CA at [111].

246 Below at para.50-071.

247 [2015] 1 W.L.R. 1833 (QB) at [116].

248 [2011] EWHC 3253 (TCC).

249 *Dobson v Thames Water Utilities Ltd* [2009] 3 All E.R. 319 CA.

250 *Hunter v Canary Wharf Ltd* [1997] A.C. 655 at 702, 705, 707.

251 [1997] A.C. 655 at 706; *Dobson v Thames Water Utilities Ltd* [2011] EWHC 3253 (TCC) at [1029(1)].

252 *Dobson v Thames Water Utilities Ltd* [2009] 3 All E.R. 319 CA at [36].

253 See, e.g. Water Industry Act 1991 Ch.II; Environmental Protection Act 1990 s.80.

procedures, even if they do not provide a path to compensation for losses in fact suffered, may be potentially relevant to the decision whether to grant or refuse damages. The scope for such "remedies" to affect decisions over whether to award damages for proven losses ought to be limited, given these remedies go no way towards redressing losses suffered and do not specifically respond to rights-violations under the HRA. In this regard it is important to note that in *Van Colle*, the Court of Appeal did not consider a sanction imposed by a disciplinary panel against a police officer, in respect of that conduct which also gave rise to the to the HRA damages claim, to be relevant to the question of whether to award damages or quantum.[254]

**50-070** That a claimant has previously received compensation for a violation will not necessarily preclude the making of a further award if the violation continues beyond the original award. *Re Jordan's Application for Judicial Review* involved claims for damages for distress and frustration at governmental failures to commence inquests into the deaths of close relatives of the claimants, these delays being held to breach the investigative duty under art.2.[255] One claimant, Jordan, had previously brought proceedings in the ECtHR in relation to the same failure on the part of the state to commence an effective investigation into his son's death without delay. In that case, decided in 2001, he was awarded £10,000. Stephens J, who awarded Jordan £7,500, explained how the prior award had factored into his decision:

> "The question that does arise in Hugh Jordan's application is whether it is appropriate to make a further award of damages given that one award has already been made. The fact that an award of damages has already been made is a factor to be taken into account and ordinarily I consider that it would mean that a further declaration would be sufficient to afford just satisfaction without any further award of damages. However over a decade passed between the date of the judgment of the European Court of Human Rights and before the inquest commenced. I consider that to be quite an exceptional circumstance and accordingly in the particular circumstances, and again subject to a consideration of some further issues, I consider that the applicant is entitled to a further award of damages. The fact that a previous award has been made is a factor that I consider should be taken into account in determining the amount of any further award so that the award is less than the award previously made by the European Court of Human Rights in May 2001".[256]

**50-071** *DSD v Commissioner of Police of the Metropolis* is an important decision on concurrent liability in relation to HRA damages, and—in combination with *Rabone* and *Re Jordan* (above)—moves the law towards a principled approach based in ordinary common law rules.[257] Claims were successfully brought against the police by two claimants who had suffered sexual assaults by a third party, Worboys, for a failure to conduct an effective investigation into the sexual assaults, in breach of art.3. Several heads of loss were held to be causally connected to the police failures, including: (i) in the case of NBV losses directly attributable to the assault by Worboys, as the Judge found the assault could have been avoided if the police had carried out the investigation effectively; (ii) in respect of both claimants, DSD and NBV, recognised psychiatric illnesses suffered in the period following the assaults; and (iii) treatment costs. The issue of concurrent liability arose as, inter alia,

---

[254] *Van Colle v Chief Constable of Hertfordshire* [2007] 1 W.L.R. 1821 CA at [124].

[255] [2014] NIQB 71. Note that the claims were made against the Department of Justice not against coroners, as s.9(3) of the HRA would have prevented such a claim.

[256] [2014] NIQB 71 at [29].

[257] [2015] 1 W.L.R. 1833 at [56]–[65].

the claimants had reached a settlement with Worboys and had received criminal injury compensation payments. The Judge, while observing that principles applied at common law to govern concurrent liability may not be entirely on point, nonetheless approached the question of concurrent liability principally "on ordinary principles", following the approach articulated by the House of Lords in the law of torts in *Jameson v Central Electricity Generating Board*.[258] That is, a claimant would be precluded from recovering further sums by way of damages if, through another judgment or a settlement, a sum reflecting 100 per cent of the damage suffered had been awarded.[259] The Worboys settlement was not framed as "full and final". Rather, the terms of the agreement recorded that the claimants were accepting less than the full value of their claims due to Worboys' limited finances. Even if the settlement had stated that it was full and final, this would not be conclusive as to whether HRA claims for further sums could be made against the police, as the agreement needs to be construed as a whole. As it was, in addition to explicitly being under-value, the settlement did not purport to cover the HRA claims against the police. Thus, the settlement did not necessarily cover the entirety of the harm suffered. The Judge examined the extent of the overlap between the settlement and losses causally connected to the police failures. In respect of (ii) there was no overlap—the settlement did not cover these losses at all—so that the losses were assessed in full against the police. In respect of (i) and (iii) there was overlap with the settlement, so that the Judge took the extent of the overlap into account in calculating damages against the police under these heads, reducing the sums accordingly so as to avoid double recovery, but in so doing, accounting for the fact that the settlement sums were under-value. The same approach was taken to the criminal injury compensation payments. Thus damages for violation of art.3 were not precluded by the previous awards, and the Judge proceeded to make substantial awards against the police, as detailed below.[260]

In *Shahid v Scottish Ministers* the Supreme Court held that, in combination with 50-072
a declaration, an award to the claimant for the costs of the appeal constituted just satisfaction, so that damages were not necessary.[261] The practice of treating costs awards as relevant to the inquiry into damages, is one that characterises the ECtHR's art.41 jurisprudence. With respect, such approach is highly questionable and it would be desirable for the Supreme Court to revisit this issue in a future appeal. Costs awards and damages awards are conceptually distinct. Costs awards are made in respect of costs incurred in litigation and purchase of legal services. Damages awards are made for losses caused by the defendant's wrong. To treat costs awards as relevant to the question of whether to award damages is thus conceptually confused. Such approach does not form an aspect of the English law of damages, nor has it generally found acceptance in HRA damages claims.

**(f) Claimant's moral character and illegal conduct** One "wider" and 50-073
controversial factor taken into account by the ECtHR to deny awards is the victim's moral status or character. This practice has been followed domestically by some courts, but rejected by others. For example it was one factor taken into account, on

---

258 [2000] 1 A.C. 455.

259 But note the exception recognised in *Ashley v Chief Constable of Sussex* [2008] 1 A.C. 962, for claims that have a vindicatory purpose.

260 Below paras 50-091 and following.

261 [2016] A.C. 429 at [90].

occasion, in pre-*Sturnham* decisions concerning whether prisoners should be awarded damages for losses suffered in consequence of rights-violating delays before the Parole Board. In these cases one important basis for denying awards was that at the time of the violation of art.5(4) the prisoner was serving a sentence for a serious crime.[262] In one case the Judge considered whether the claimant would use any award to compensate the victim of their previous criminal wrongdoing.[263] In contrast other Judges stated explicitly that such considerations were irrelevant, in particular that the prisoner had previously committed an offence.[264] In each case where the factor was considered an award was denied, and where it was not, awards were made in some cases. When the matter of damages for delays before the Parole Board reached the Supreme Court in *R. (on the application of Sturnham) v Parole Board* that Court made no mention of the factor, despite the claim being one made by prisoners who had previously committed crimes.[265] The Supreme Court's approach is suggestive that the factor ought not to be considered in future, especially as *Sturnham* was, being a case in which damages were sought by prisoners, a case where the factor would have played a role if it were considered relevant in principle.[266] Moreover, there are very strong reasons of principle for rejecting this factor, principally the fundamental principle of equality before the law. Strasbourg jurisprudence ought not to be followed to the extent this would involve undermining basic principles of the English legal system,

> "under English law, a convicted prisoner, in spite of his imprisonment, retains all civil rights which are not taken away expressly or by necessary implication".[267]

Thus, at common law:

> "[t]hat a prisoner has a right to sue in respect of torts committed against him in prison is beyond doubt … If he is assaulted by a prisoner officer he may sue for damages, and if he is negligently cared for whereby he sustains injury to his health he may likewise sue".[268]

Other common law jurisdictions have treated the importance of rights and remedies as of equal value to criminal and model citizen alike, and not countenanced discrimination on the basis of past criminal wrongdoing.[269] The factor is also inherently subjective: when should a claimant be considered to have foregone their right to an effective remedy based on their past conduct, and how far back into the claimant's life may the court inquire? If past illegal conduct is to be considered then

---

262 *R. (on the application of Downing) v Parole Board* [2008] EWHC 3198 (Admin) at [29]–[31]; *R. (on the application of Biggin) v Secretary of State for Justice* [2009] EWHC 1704 (Admin) at [35].

263 *R. (on the application of Parratt) v Secretary of State for Justice* [2013] EWHC 17 (Admin) at [57].

264 *R. (on the application of Guntrip) v Secretary of State for Justice* [2010] EWHC 3188 (Admin) at [35]; *R. (on the application of Degainis) v Secretary of State for Justice* [2010] EWHC 137 (Admin) at 19]–[20]; *R. (on the application of Faulkner) v Secretary of State for Justice* [2011] H.R.L.R. 7 CA at [79]–[80].

265 [2013] 2 A.C. 254.

266 But note that the High Court has nonetheless since referred to the claimant's character as one relevant consideration in deciding upon damages: *DSD v Commissioner of Police of the Metropolis* [2015] 1 W.L.R. 1833 (QB) at [37]–[38].

267 *Raymond v Honey* [1983] 1 A.C. 1 at 10.

268 *R. v Deputy Governor of Parkhurst Prison Ex p. Hague* [1992] 1 A.C. 58 at 176. See also Law Commission, *Damages under the Human Rights Act 1998* (2000), Law Com. No.266/Scot Law Com. No.180, Cm.4853, para.4.53 ("the status of the claimant is irrelevant in a claim for damages in tort").

269 *Dunlea v Attorney General* [2000] 3 N.Z.L.R. 136 at [67]; *Attorney General v Chapman* [2012] 1 N.Z.L.R. 462 at [71].

a closer causal connection between the claimant's wrongdoing and the rights-violation ought to be insisted upon, as is the approach in respect to the illegality defence at common law.[270] Furthermore, it is of note that the ECtHR has only itself relied on the factor in cases where there was close proximity between the claimant's illegal conduct and the rights-violation, and the illegal conduct was of the most serious kind. For example *McCann v United Kingdom*,[271] arose out of the shooting dead by members of the British armed forces of three suspected terrorists. This action by the government was held by the ECtHR (by a majority of 10 votes to 9) to have been a breach of the victims' right to life under art.2 of the Convention. However, it unanimously refused to award damages, saying:

> "In any event, having regard to the fact that the three terrorist suspects who were killed had been intending to plant a bomb in Gibraltar, the court does not consider it appropriate to make an award under this head."[272]

In this regard it is pertinent that in art.5(4) delay cases, the ECtHR has routinely made awards to serving prisoners, and not mentioned their past wrongdoing as a factor relevant to the making of awards. Furthermore, the Convention clearly contemplates the making of awards to prisoners, as art.5(5) provides that anyone who has been the victim of arrest or detention in breach of the provisions of art.5 shall have an enforceable right to compensation. The group most likely to make such claims are those subject to detention.

**(g) Wider policy factors** Various "wider" or policy factors have been discussed or taken into account on an ad hoc basis by English courts in relation to the decision whether to award damages or not. These factors have been considered despite the fact they do not correlate to any explicit principle applied by the ECtHR in its art.41 jurisprudence, albeit that Court has been observed, as a matter of practice, to increase awards on occasion where it might be interpolated that the Court disapproves of the defendant's conduct.[273] One wider factor which has been repeated in the case law, particularly by the higher courts, is deterrence or incentivising compliance. In *R. (on the application of Greenfield) v Secretary of State for the Home Department* Lord Bingham observed that "[d]amages need not ordinarily be awarded to encourage high standards of compliance" while observing the corollary of this proposition: damages may need to be awarded **50-074**

> "if there is felt to be a need to encourage compliance by individual officers or classes of official".[274]

In *A v Essex County Council* Lady Hale similarly observed that one function of awarding damages can be to ensure "that lessons can be learned" and compliance encouraged into the future.[275] One can interpolate that if the violation was committed intentionally or recklessly, a court may give considerable weight to the

---

270 See for example *Cross v Kirkby* [2000] EWCA Civ 426 at [76], [103]; *Gray v Thames Trains Ltd* [2009] 1 A.C. 1339 at [53]–[54]. For discussion of the relevance of the illegality defence under the HRA see: *Al Hassan-Daniel v Revenue and Customs Commissioners* [2010] EWCA Civ 1443.

271 (1996) 21 E.H.R.R. 97.

272 (1996) 21 E.H.R.R. 97 at [219]; *A v United Kingdom* (2009) 49 E.H.R.R. 29 at [251].

273 *R. (on the application of KB) v Mental Health Review Tribunal* [2004] Q.B. 936 at [50].

274 [2005] 1 W.L.R. 673 HL at [19].

275 [2011] 1 A.C. 280 at [118].

importance of deterring such conduct in the future through the making of an award. In the Court of Appeal decision in *R. (on the application of Faulkner) v Secretary of State for Justice* the Court considered the "high value" of "personal liberty" and importance of compensating wrongs, and that damages

> "will—or ought to—concentrate the mind of the wrongdoer, especially where the latter is a public authority which is capable, unless it changes its ways, of repeating its error".[276]

In addition to the statements regarding deterrence, these dicta are important in recalling the importance of giving great weight to the fact that the claimant has suffered a violation of their most fundamental rights and that an important legislative purpose underpinning the HRA is to afford strong protection to basic rights, including—according to the terms of s.8—through the award of damages for the consequences of the contraventions. If victims of violations are left to bear their own losses in consequence of a breach of basic dignitary rights their rights cannot be said to be particularly well protected nor the importance of those rights vindicated. There will be a gap between repeated statements by the courts as to the importance of these rights, and the realities of protection. Importantly compensation of losses suffered through such violations of basic rights is not only in the individual victims' interests: as the Judge observed in *R. (on the application of Bernard) v Enfield London Borough Council*,

> "it is very much in the interests of society as a whole that public authorities should be encouraged to respect individual's rights under the Convention".[277]

**50-075** A more controversial factor was raised in the Court of Appeal decision in *Anufrijeva v Southwark London Borough Council*, namely protection of public funds. Lower courts have invoked this factor on occasion albeit with decreasing frequency. But neither the House of Lords nor the Supreme Court has endorsed it as a basis for denying awards, while those cases involving claims for large sums of pecuniary loss, discussed immediately below, strongly suggest impact on public funds will not typically be a basis for denying awards.[278] The reasons why the highest court may have been reluctant to endorse the public funds factor may include (i) that the factor does not correlate with any factor taken into account by the Strasbourg Court under art.41; and more importantly (ii) denying awards on this ground is liable to lead to challenges at Strasbourg and findings of breach of art.13, the right to an effective remedy.[279] In *Anufrijeva* the Court emphasised that in deciding whether to make awards or not consideration ought to be given to not only the interests of the individual in redress but also the public interest in continued funding of public services, which could be negatively impacted by the making of awards. This might be a reason for denying awards or reducing awards.[280] However, difficulties arise in relation to this factor in so far as it would require a court to reach a judgment that public money is best spent on redressing wrongs or funding public services, which involves a bare allocative choice which courts are ill-equipped to make. Furthermore courts typically do not have information on the financial posi-

---

276 [2011] EWCA Civ 349 at [12].

277 *R. (on the application of Bernard) v Enfield London Borough Council* [2003] H.R.L.R. 4 (Admin) at [59].

278 Below paras 50-079 to 50-082.

279 See paras 50-079 to 50-082, below.

280 [2004] Q.B. 1124 CA at [56], [75].

tion of an authority and whether funds to meet damages awards will derive from frontline service budgets, reserves or insurance. More generally it is a basic principle of English damages law that awards should not vary according to the means of particular defendants.[281] As lower court judges have observed, by the enactment of the power to award damages under the HRA Parliament "must be taken to have provided the resources to meet such awards",[282] while ensuring moderation in quantum serves to meet any concerns over impacts on public resources.[283] Importantly art.13, which binds the UK, provides that for every violation of a Convention right, there ought to be an effective remedy.[284] If damages are considered an effective remedy, in terms of the demands of individual redress, but are denied by reference to factors related to public funding, this is likely to lead to breaches of art.13. Article 13 is, notably an absolute right, so that there is no scope to deny an effective remedy, that would otherwise be required, on the basis of public interest grounds. The Court, in *Shilbergs v Russia*, specifically stated:

> "The Court finds it anomalous for the domestic courts to decrease the amount of compensation to be paid to the applicant for a wrong committed by the State by referring to the latter's lack of funds. It considers that in circumstances such as those under consideration the means available to the State should not be accepted as mitigating conduct, and are thus irrelevant in assessing damages under the compensatory criterion".[285]

It should also be recalled that s.8(3) directs attention to what is necessary to afford just satisfaction to the victim. Section 8(3)(b) does mention as one factor relevant to the decision whether to make awards,

> "the consequences of any decision (of [the court considering the making of an award] or any other court) in respect of [the act in question]".

However, as the Law Commissions observed, noting the victim orientation of s.8(3) as a whole, this subsection most probably

> "refers to the Strasbourg jurisprudence under which the court may hold that some non-judicial act by the state in the light of the court's decision may constitute just satisfaction".[286]

In *Infinis*, discussed below, the Court drew on a leading human rights treatise in order to aid interpretation of s.8(3)(b)[287]:

> "Clayton and Tomlinson ('*The Law of Human Rights*', 2nd edition, 2009) observe (in paragraph 21.26) that the meaning of the requirement to take account of 'the consequences of any decision' in s.8(3) 'is not wholly clear', but go on to say this: '... Although it has been suggested that this factor would allow the court to take account of general policy issues such as floodgate arguments, the better view is that s.8(3) is unlikely to detract from

281 *Wells v Wells* [1999] 1 A.C. 345 at 373.

282 *R. (on the application of KB) v Mental Health Review Tribunal* [2004] Q.B. 936 at [50].

283 *R. (on the application of Bernard) v Enfield London Borough Council* [2003] H.R.L.R. 4 (Admin) at [59].

284 See paras 50-076 to 50-078, below.

285 Application No.20075/03, 17 December 2009 at [78].

286 Law Commission, *Damages under the Human Rights Act 1998* (2000), Law Com. No.266/Scot Law Com. No.180, Cm.4853, para.4.42.

287 *R. (on the application of Infinis Plc) v Gas & Electricity Markets Authority* [2011] EWHC 1873 (Admin) at [43]. See para.50-077 below.

the basic requirement for just satisfaction to the person in whose favour it is made: since this could otherwise not be reconciled with the fundamental principle of restitutio in integrum".

Lastly, art.13 requires the basis on which remedies are conferred to be sufficiently certain, and it is likely that resting decisions over awards on an open-ended case-by-case balancing of individual and public interests will ultimately breach this principle as it will not be possible to state in advance with sufficient certainty when awards will or will not be made.[288]

50-076 **(h) Pecuniary loss** Though the jurisprudence is at an early stage and claims for pecuniary loss have been uncommon, it seems from emerging practice under the HRA that domestic courts will ordinarily be willing to award proven pecuniary losses which are causally connected to the violation. The factors discussed above, specifically those in favour of denying awards, have not in general played a role in claims for pecuniary loss. Of course, unlike non-pecuniary losses, pecuniary losses must be specifically pleaded and proven, and will not be awarded if too speculative, though complexity or difficulty in assessment will not bar an award. But if such losses are proven in the ordinary way it would seem an uncommon case where a court would hold a finding of violation constituted just satisfaction in itself. This approach seemingly follows from domestic courts, over time, becoming less influenced by the ECtHR jurisprudence and mirror approach in adjudicating claims for pecuniary loss, despite the fact that the ECtHR does apply its open-ended "equitable" approach to claims for pecuniary loss. In earlier jurisprudence art.41 case law was interpreted by domestic courts as supporting a cautious approach to the making of awards for pecuniary losses, at least in some areas. For example Lord Bingham in *R. (on the application of Greenfield) v Secretary of State for the Home Department* said the courts would be slow to award damages for pecuniary loss in art.6 cases.[289] In *Anufrijeva v Southwark London Borough Council* Lord Woolf MR indicated that only "significant" pecuniary losses "clearly caused" by a violation would "usually" be assessed.[290] However, in the most important decision of recent times from the Supreme Court on HRA damages, *R. (on the application of Sturnham) v Parole Board*, Lord Reed said,

> "Pecuniary losses proved to have been caused by the prolongation of detention should be compensated in full".[291]

In the case of *DSD v Commissioner of Police of the Metropolis* the Judge had little hesitation in awarding damages for treatment costs associated with recognised psychiatric illness caused by police failure to conduct an effective investigation into alleged sexual assaults in breach of art.3.[292] However, reference may still be made to Strasbourg jurisprudence in relation to certain matters, such as which heads of loss are recoverable. For example both the High Court and Court of Appeal, in the ongoing litigation in *Bank Mellat v HM Treasury*, had regard to the Strasbourg cases

---

288 *McFarlane v Ireland* (2011) 52 E.H.R.R. 20 at [117], [120]; *Stanev v Bulgaria* (2012) 55 E.H.R.R. 22 at [182].

289 [2005] 1 W.L.R. 673 HL at [11].

290 [2004] Q.B. 1124 CA at [59].

291 [2013] 2 A.C. 254 at [13(8)].

292 [2015] 1 W.L.R. 1833 (QB).

in seeking to determine whether loss of income from future business is a recoverable loss in cases of violation of art.1 Protocol 1.[293] That issue remains unresolved.

Two significant cases involving damages claims by companies in respect of violations of art.1 Protocol 1 reinforce that damages awards will generally be made for proven pecuniary losses. In *R. (on the application of Infinis Plc) v Gas and Electricity Markets Authority*, the Court of Appeal affirmed that the defendant, in denying accreditation to the claimant company's electricity generating stations under various renewable energy regulations, had acted unlawfully and breached the claimant's rights to peaceful enjoyment of their possessions under art.1 Protocol 1.[294] This was to deny Infinis a pecuniary benefit to which it was otherwise entitled. The Court of Appeal had no hesitation in upholding the lower court's decision to award damages in the sum of £94,393.62, measured as the value of the entitlement that had been denied in violation of the company's rights. Sullivan LJ for the Court said: **50-077**

> "In the present case Infinis has been wrongly deprived of a pecuniary benefit to which it was entitled under statute. The amount of the 'lost' benefit can readily be calculated. In these circumstances restitutio in integrum is manifestly appropriate ... There is no dispute that the breach of Infinis' Convention rights caused it significant pecuniary loss and that that pecuniary loss was capable of being assessed. The judge was entitled to conclude that there was no good reason for departing from the usual approach to the assessment of loss".[295]

Note that no conflict arose with Lord Woolf's prior dicta in *Anufrijeva* to the effect that the loss had to be significant, as the Court of Appeal did consider the loss was significant.[296] Importantly, in the Court below the Judge gave short shrift to the argument that damages should not be awarded as there were many other similar claims that might follow.[297] The fact that the defendant authority had acted in good faith was not a factor against making an award. The claimants had no action in private law and grant of prerogative orders would not compensate them for the loss of a pecuniary benefit to which they were entitled. It was also relevant that the loss was readily calculable.

The other recent important decision in relation to pecuniary loss is *Breyer Group Plc v Department of Energy and Climate Change*.[298] The background to the claims for damages is as follows. Pursuant to a regulatory scheme electricity supply companies were required to pay producers and installers of small scale low-carbon electricity generating systems, including the claimants, for each unit of electricity generated, at rates set by government. The defendant came to consider the initial rates for solar photovoltaic ("solar PV") installations were too generous. So the defendant proposed to bring forward, from 1 April 2012 to 12 December 2011, the date by which the installations had to be commissioned/registered in order to qualify for the original and highest rates. On assumed facts this proposal had a significant effect on the solar PV industry. Hundreds, if not thousands, of installations which would otherwise have been completed by the April 2012 cut-off were **50-078**

---

[293] *Bank Mellat v HM Treasury* [2017] Q.B. 67 CA at [32]–[43]; [2015] EWHC 1258 Comm at [53]–[78]. On these claims see above para.50-023.

[294] [2013] EWCA Civ 70.

[295] [2013] EWCA Civ 70 at [26].

[296] *Anufrijeva v Southwark London Borough Council* [2004] Q.B. 1124 CA at [59].

[297] *R. (on the application of Infinis Plc) v Gas and Electricity Markets Authority* [2011] EWHC 1873 (Admin) at [106].

[298] [2015] 1 W.L.R. 4559 CA.

abandoned, when those involved realised that they could not complete them by the new date of 12 December 2011. Some of those directly affected issued successful judicial review proceedings, the proposal being held unlawful. As a result the defendant changed its proposals. However, the claimants initiated proceedings alleging breach of art.1 Protocol 1 on the basis that, by the time that the courts ruled the defendant's proposals unlawful, the installations which would otherwise have been completed by the claimants by April 2012 had been abandoned because of the clear prior statements by the defendant that the cut-off date was being moved forward to 12 December 2011. HRA damages were claimed for the losses allegedly suffered in consequence, specifically lost profits. Violations of art.1 Protocol 1 were found. Neither the High Court or, on appeal, the Court of Appeal reached the stage of assessing awards. However, in the High Court the Judge, with little hesitation, reached the view that

> "in general terms, the claimants will be entitled to damages, to put them back in the position they would have been in had the violation not occurred".[299]

This was subject to assessment on the facts of each case, and proof of factual causation. The Court of Appeal did not disagree with these propositions. Importantly, the High Court Judge observed that while assessment may prove complex, this was no bar to recovery:

> "As in so many types of commercial and public litigation, the court simply has to do its best on the material provided in order to evaluate the loss".[300]

As is discussed further below, the Court appears to have endorsed a "direct consequences" approach to causation, indicating that any losses factually and directly connected to the violation will be recoverable.[301] Concomitant with this approach, which appears similar to that adopted in the tort of deceit,[302] the fact that the claimant's own actions, in deciding not to proceed with installations, played a role in the chain of events leading to the suffering of loss, would not necessarily bar recovery. The Court of Appeal agreed on this point, albeit the Court was generally reluctant to reach firm conclusions on questions raised by the damages issue as much would depend on the facts of individual cases.[303] Lastly, the potential liability relating to this class of claims was significant. Collectively the group of claimants sought £195m, with individual claims ranging from £233,000 to £27m. Nonetheless there was no contemplation of impact on public funds or floodgates barring the award of damages. If claims for such large amounts for breach of legal persons' proprietary interests do not implicate policy concerns, then it would be difficult to justify denying far smaller sums of non-pecuniary loss for breach of natural persons' dignitarian interests on the basis of concerns over floodgates or impact on public resources.[304]

---

299 *Breyer Group Plc v Department of Energy and Climate Change* [2015] 2 All E.R. 44 (QB) at [156].
300 [2015] 2 All E.R. 44 (QB) at [155].
301 [2015] 2 All E.R. 44 (QB) at [158]. Below para.50-104.
302 *Smith New Court Securities Ltd v Citibank* [1997] A.C. 254.
303 [2015] 1 W.L.R. 4559 CA at [107].
304 See para.50-075 above.

## (3) Article 13 of the European Convention

While s.8 of the HRA refers domestic courts to the ECtHR's jurisprudence under art.41, domestic courts must also have regard to and comply with the requirements of art.13 of the Convention in their decisions in respect of remedies under the HRA. Article 41 is a provision which regulates the ECtHR's own remedial jurisdiction. In contrast, art.13 is the provision which sets the standards with which member states must comply in their domestic remedial practice. The Article provides: **50-079**

> "Right to an effective remedy. Everyone whose rights and freedoms as set forth in this Convention are violated shall have an effective remedy before a national authority notwithstanding that the violation has been committed by persons acting in an official capacity."

As Sedley LJ has observed, art.13

> "reflects the longstanding principle of our law that where there is a right there should be a remedy".[305]

Article 13 was not incorporated by the HRA, on the basis that it was intended that s.8 would provide domestic courts with the tools required to comply with art.13. This is made clear in Hansard. The Lord Chancellor observed that s.8(1) was "of the widest amplitude" so as to give the courts the flexibility to remedy violations in a way that ensured compliance with art.13, and so that courts could "do full justice in the cases that come before them".[306] This underlying purpose has been echoed by the House of Lords in *Re S*; *Re W* where Lord Nicholls said:

> "The domestic counterpart to art.13 is ss.7 and 8 of the Human Rights Act, read in conjunction with s.6. This domestic counterpart to art.13 takes a different form from art.13 itself. Unlike art.13, which declares a right ('Everyone whose rights ... are violated shall have an effective remedy'), ss.7 and 8 provide a remedy. Article 13 guarantees the availability at the national level of an effective remedy to enforce the substance of Convention rights. Sections 7 and 8 seek to provide that remedy in this country. The object of these sections is to provide in English law the very remedy art.13 declares is the entitlement of everyone whose rights are violated".[307]

As the remedial provisions of the Act are designed to implement art.13, the remedial requirements recognised in the jurisprudence under that Article are of peculiar relevance to and ought to inform how courts exercise their remedial powers, including the award of damages, under the Act. It is axiomatic that

> "when legislation is based upon an international treaty, the courts will try to construe the legislation in a way which does not put the United Kingdom in breach of its international obligations".[308]

---

305 *R. (on the application of K) v Camden and Islington Health Authority* [2002] Q.B. 198 CA at [54].

306 H.L. Deb. vol. 584 col. 1266 (19 January 1998) Lord Chancellor; H.L. Deb. vol. 585 col. 385 (29 January 1998) Lord Chancellor; H.C. Deb. vol. 312 col. 979 (20 May 1998) Mr Jack Straw.

307 *Re S (Children) (Care Order: Implementation of Care plan)* [2002] 2 A.C. 291 at [61].

308 *Re P (A Child)* [2009] 1 A.C. 173 at [35]; *R. (on the application of Al Skeini) v Secretary of State for Defence* [2008] 1 A.C. 153 at [57] (procedural and remedial provisions of the HRA should be interpreted compatibility with art.13).

**50-080** The ECtHR has taken an increasingly strict approach to policing the requirements of art.13,

> "less than full expression of the guarantees of art.13 would undermine the operation of the subsidiary character of the Court in the Convention system and, more generally, weaken the effective functioning on both the national and international level, of the scheme of human rights protection set up by the Convention".[309]

The Strasbourg Court itself faces a significant backlog of cases so that it has every incentive to ensure violations are adequately addressed domestically. While some rights under the Convention are subject to limitation on proportionality grounds, art.13 is an absolute right and the ECtHR has emphasised

> "the place of art.13 in the scheme of human rights protection set up by the Convention would argue in favour of implied restrictions of art.13 being kept to a minimum".[310]

Most obviously

> "creation of immunities for public officials and any such immunity must be regarded as contrary to the object and purposes of the Convention".[311]

**50-081** The ECtHR has indicated that damages will in some cases be a necessary remedy to ensure compliance with art.13:

> "in appropriate cases, compensation for the pecuniary and non-pecuniary damage flowing from the breach should in principle be available as part of the redress".[312]

This is particularly so for the most important rights such as arts 2 and 3.[313] In the context of art.8 the Court has held that art.13 requires that victims should have

> "available to them a means of claiming that the [relevant public authority] was responsible for any damage which they suffered and obtaining compensation for that damage".[314]

In *Burden v United Kingdom* the Court envisioned situations where

> "an effective remedy necessitated the award of damages in respect of past loss or damage caused by the alleged violation".[315]

In assessing the effectiveness of redress the ECtHR will look past statements of principle, and inquire into whether the remedy is available not only in theory but also in practice.[316] In this regard statements such as those of the Supreme Court in *Osborn v Parole Board* to the effect that awards will not be made for procedural breaches of art.5(4) not involving delay, coupled with a practice of not making awards for such breaches, raise the possibility of a finding of breach of art.13 at

---

309 *McFarlane v Ireland* (2011) 52 E.H.R.R. 20 at [112].

310 *Kudla v Poland* (2002) 35 E.H.R.R. 11 at [152].

311 *Z v United Kingdom* (2002) 34 E.H.R.R. 3 at [106].

312 *Gafgen v Germay* (2011) 52 E.H.R.R. 1 at [116].

313 *Z v United Kingdom* (2002) 34 E.H.R.R. 3 at [109]; *E v United Kingdom* (2003) 36 E.H.R.R. 31 at [110]. The nature of the right breached will have implications for what will be required by way of a remedy under art.13: *Yasa v Turkey* (1999) 28 E.H.R.R. 408 at [114].

314 *Anguelova v Bulgaria* (2004) 38 E.H.R.R 31 at [161].

315 (2008) 47 E.H.R.R. 38 at [43].

316 *McFarlane v Ireland* (2011) 52 E.H.R.R. 20 at [117], [120]; *Stanev v Bulgaria* (2012) 55 E.H.R.R. 22 at [187].

Strasbourg.[317] The onus is on the member state to prove that a remedy is effective in practice.[318] This is not an easy burden to discharge and requires the member state to show that

> "the development and availability of a remedy said to exist, including its scope and application, must be clearly set out and confirmed or complemented by practice or case law".[319]

If, as the UK Government discovered in the case of *Betteridge v United Kingdom*, it is not possible to point to similar cases where damages have been made, a breach of art.13 will be found.[320] In terms of quantum, levels of awards must not be "so derisory as to raise issues of the effectiveness of redress"[321]; money awards must "provide an adequate level of compensation".[322]

Overall, in gauging the demands of art.13 on given facts it is important to recall that the ECtHR aims to uphold the Convention's core intention: "to guarantee not theoretical or illusory rights, but rights that are practical and effective".[323] Importantly, following the ECtHR's art.41 practice is no guarantee of compliance with art.13. That is because art.41 reflects the practices of a supranational, supervisory Court in respect of "just satisfaction", whereas art.13 sets requirements for domestic institutions which have the primary responsibility for provision of effective remedies for rights-violations. The ECtHR has repeatedly emphasised that it does not function in the same way as a domestic court of first instance and that its remedial practices are subject to and conditioned by the principle of subsidiarity[324]: **50-082**

> "Article 41 ... does not provide a mechanism for compensation in a manner comparable to domestic court systems"

and it is not the Court's role under art.41 to function as a domestic court would in awarding damages.[325] In this regard it is worth noting that the ordinary approach to damages in domestic private law has generally been found to comply with art.13.[326]

## 4. The Court's Approach to Determining Quantum

### (1) General Approach

Having decided to make an award of damages, how will an English court ap- **50-083**

[317] *Osborn v Parole Board* [2014] A.C. 1115 at [2(xiii)].

[318] *McFarlane v Ireland* (2011) 52 E.H.R.R. 20 at [128]; *Stanev v Bulgaria* (2012) 55 E.H.R.R. 22 at [187].

[319] *McFarlane v Ireland* (2011) 52 E.H.R.R. 20 at [117], [120].

[320] (2013) 57 E.H.R.R. 7 at [51].

[321] *Wainwright v United Kingdom* (2007) 44 E.H.R.R. 40 at [55].

[322] *McFarlane v Ireland* (2011) 52 E.H.R.R. 20 at [108].

[323] *Scordino v Italy* (2007) 45 E.H.R.R. 7 at [192].

[324] *A v United Kingdom* (2009) 49 E.H.R.R. 29 at [174]; *Demopoulos v Turkey*, Application No.46113/99 1 March 2010, at [69].

[325] *Varnava v Turkey* (2010) 50 E.H.R.R. 21 at [156]; *Al-Jedda v United Kingdom* (2011) 53 E.H.R.R. 23 at [114].

[326] *Chagos Islanders v United Kingdom* (2013) 56 E.H.R.R. SE15 at [81]; *Wainwright v United Kingdom* (2007) 44 E.H.R.R. 40 at [55].

proach assessment of quantum? As noted in the previous section, pecuniary loss has increasingly been approached consistently with the ordinary approach in domestic law, and the highest court-ordered awards under the HRA have been made for pecuniary losses suffered by companies in consequence of violations of art.1 Protocol 1.[327] In regard to non-pecuniary loss domestic courts are led by the mirror approach and the ECtHR art.41 jurisprudence. English courts seek to replicate the quanta of awards that the ECtHR would make on similar facts. However, this has proven highly problematic as the Strasbourg Court does not articulate guideline tariffs or bands, as has now become common in domestic law, to govern and structure the quantification exercise. The ECtHR adopts a broad equitable approach to assessment, determining what is "just" on the facts of each case, in general without any consideration of past awards[328]; the court has given its equitable approach as a reason for not adopting defined scales.[329] As such the art.41 case law is marked by inconsistency and a lack of predictability. Further exacerbating these problems is that the factors which have guided assessment, assuming the existence of such factors, are in the vast majority of cases unarticulated. Figures are stated as conclusions, in general. As a consequence of this approach the ECtHR has drawn a comparison to a "calculating machine".[330] Domestic lower court jurisprudence is replete with statements such as

> "it is not clear from the reports how the ECtHR arrived at particular figures"[331];
>
> "it is well known, and is common ground before us, that there are no articulated principles, and no discernible tariff, by which [the ECtHR's] awards [under art.41] are set'[332];
>
> "It is notoriously difficult to deduce clear principles in relation to 'just satisfaction' from the Strasbourg jurisprudence"[333];
>
> "There is virtually never any real articulation as to why the Court has awarded a particular sum"[334];

---

327 Above paras 50-076 to 50-078.

328 The Law Commissions suggested that the practice of the ECtHR has been close to the French tradition whereby the measure of damages is considered to be for the "sovereign power of assessment" of the judge of first instance. They state (Law Com. 266/Scot Law Com. 180, para.3.8):

> "The comparative lack of structure is most evident in relation to the assessment of the relevant damage. This is always treated as a question of fact, thus leaving the judge in the lower court with a degree of unstructured discretion to adjust the award as he or she sees fit. As long as the award is framed properly in law, the appeal courts will not interfere with it. Conventional scales are sometimes used, but must not be treated as rules of law. In particular, French judges do not draw clear distinctions between different heads of loss".

One difference should be noted however as between the French approach and that of the ECtHR: that ECtHR has not enunciated scales, nor do its awards reveal a set scale.

329 *Varnava v Turkey*, Application No.16064/90, 18 September 2009 at [225].

330 O. Ichim, *Just Satisfaction under the European Convention on Human Rights*, (Cambridge: Cambridge University Press, 2015), p.127.

331 *R. (on the application of Pennington) v Parole Board* [2010] EWHC 78 (Admin) at [20].

332 *R. (on the application of Faulkner) v Secretary of State for Justice* [2011] EWCA Civ 349 at [6], [15].

333 *R. (on the application of Hooper) v Secretary of State for Work and Pensions* [2003] 1 W.L.R. 2623 CA at [147].

334 *DSD v Commissioner of Police of the Metropolis* [2015] 1 W.L.R. 1833 (QB) at [68(iii)].

> "[t]here is little guidance in the authorities on the approach to be taken when quantifying an award of damages … If one looks at the authorities for appropriate comparators again there is relatively little assistance".[335]

Despite the real and continuing difficulties faced by lower courts, and indeed—as we shall see—higher courts, the mirror approach remains the prevailing approach. The basic principle reiterated time and again by the ECtHR and domestic courts is restitutio in integrum. The case of *Kingsley v United Kingdom* offers a classic articulation of this central principle: **50-084**

> "The court recalls that it is well established that the principle underlying the provision of just satisfaction for a breach of art.6 is that the applicant should as far as possible be put in the position he would have enjoyed had the proceedings complied with the Convention's requirements … The State cannot be required to pay damages in respect of losses for which it is not responsible.[336]

However, the art.41 jurisprudence does not articulate a detailed and worked-out body of more particular rules and principles as to how the broad principle of restitutio in integrum ought to be given practical effect.

A further preliminary observation is that awards for non-pecuniary loss made by the ECtHR are low in comparison to those made in the law of torts. As a result of application of the mirror approach awards under the HRA for heads such as mental distress and loss of liberty, which match heads of loss routinely compensated at common law, are in general lower and sometimes much lower than equivalent awards in tort, and the domestic higher courts have repeated time and again that awards under the HRA ought to be modest. However, as discussed below in relation to *DSD v Commissioner of Police of the Metropolis*, it may be that, even under the mirror approach, domestic damages scales can possibly be rendered salient in assessing HRA damages.[337] This would be of tremendous benefit as domestic practice offers very helpful and principled guidance as to scales of awards for many types of non-pecuniary losses compensated under the HRA, which if applied under the HRA could facilitate consistency and predictability. In turn more concrete guidance, based in familiar principles and articulated damages guidelines, would be of assistance in reaching out-of-court settlements and avoiding litigation and associated costs. **50-085**

In *R. (on the application of Greenfield) v Secretary of State for the Home Department* Lord Bingham rejected counsel's submission that guidance as to quantum could be derived from domestic awards in anti-discrimination law and that domestic courts should feel free to depart from the scale of damages awarded by the ECtHR, given s.8(4) only imposes an obligation to take ECtHR principles into account—not necessarily to follow them.[338] He said that it is to Strasbourg that domestic courts should turn under the HRA for three reasons[339]: **50-086**

(1) the HRA is not a tort statute but has different and broader objects;
(2) the rationale behind the HRA is to give victims the same remedies in the

[335] *Re H* [2014] EWFC 38 at [84]–[91].
[336] (2002) 35 E.H.R.R. 177 at [40].
[337] [2015] 1 W.L.R. 1833 (QB). Below para.50-095 and following.
[338] [2005] 1 W.L.R. 673 HL at [18]–[19].
[339] [2005] 1 W.L.R. 673 HL at [19].

domestic courts as they would have in the ECtHR, but with less delay and expense; and

(3) the provisions of s.8(4) require a domestic court to take into account the principles of the ECtHR when making awards of damages under art.41, including in determining the quantum, and there could be no better indication that domestic courts should look to Strasbourg not to domestic precedents.

Lord Bingham rejected as overly formalistic the argument that the levels of Strasbourg awards were not relevant "principles" for the purposes of s.8(4). In terms of guidance as to how English courts ought to approach their task of setting awards at Strasbourg levels he said:

> "The ECtHR routinely describes its awards as equitable, which I take to mean that they are not precisely calculated but are judged by the Court to be fair in the individual case. Judges in England and Wales must also make a similar judgment in the case before them. They are not inflexibly bound by Strasbourg awards in what may be different cases. But they should not aim to be significantly more or less generous than the Court might be expected to be, in a case where it was willing to make an award at all".[340]

Thus the focus should not be on comparisons with individual ECtHR decisions as such, and such individual decisions should not be treated as binding, albeit individual cases may provide some guidance. Rather domestic courts should aim to pitch domestic awards so that they are roughly in line with levels of awards that the ECtHR might be expected to make. In terms of specific guidance on awards for distress in cases of breach of art.6 caused by structural bias, Lord Bingham observed Strasbourg awards were noteworthy for their modesty, albeit no indicative scale was distilled from the Strasbourg cases,[341] and it was also observed that the ECtHR had been willing to assume loss in some cases.[342] No award was made in *Greenfield*.

50-087 The Supreme Court in *R. (on the application of Sturnham) v Parole Board* reinforced Lord Bingham's approach in *Greenfield*:

> "In relation to the quantum of awards in particular, s.8(4) of the 1998 Act merely means that courts should aim to pitch their awards at the general level indicated by Strasbourg awards in comparable cases, so far as that can be estimated".[343]

Also in common with *Greenfield*, in *Sturnham* Lord Reed indicated that awards for free-standing frustration and distress suffered by prisoners who had experienced delays before the Parole Board, should be modest and that the focus should not be on drawing comparisons with individual awards made by the ECtHR:

> "Awards for frustration and anxiety caused by violations of the art.5(4) guarantee of a speedy decision have invariably been modest. In *Oldham v United Kingdom* (2001) 31 EHRR 34 the court awarded £1000. In *Hirst v United Kingdom* [2001] Prison LR 383 the award was again £1000. In *Reid v United Kingdom* (2003) 37 EHRR 211, where the delay was more substantial and there was also procedural unfairness, the award was €2000. In *Blackstock v United Kingdom* (2006) 42 EHRR 2 the award was €1460, the equivalent at that time of £1000. In *Mooren v Germany* (2010) 50 EHRR 23 the Chamber had awarded €1500 for distress resulting from delay alone. The Grand Chamber increased the

---

340 [2005] 1 W.L.R. 673 HL at [19].

341 [2005] 1 W.L.R. 673 HL at [17].

342 [2005] 1 W.L.R. 673 HL at [16].

343 [2013] 2 A.C. 254 at [35].

award to €3000, but that award was for stress and frustration caused by the unfairness of the procedure as well as by delay. In *STS v The Netherlands* (2012) 54 EHRR 1229 the court awarded €2000, but in that case there was a breach of the requirement of effectiveness as well as of the requirement as to speed. In *Betteridge v United Kingdom* (2013) 57 EHRR 195 the court awarded €750, equivalent to £645. It would be a mistake to attempt to analyse these awards too closely: they were considered 'equitable' in their particular circumstances. The cases involving delay in reviews by the Board nevertheless indicate the modest level of awards in the absence of special circumstances."[344]

Special circumstances might include, for example, that a claimant suffers mental illness which in turn causes him or her to experience greater distress and anxiety than a prisoner of good health.[345] Again in common with *Greenfield*, Lord Reed held that distress and frustration could be presumed without direct evidence of mental harm in certain cases, specifically where the delay before the Board had exceeded three months. On the facts of Sturnham's appeal, in circumstances where Sturnham had suffered an unlawful delay of six months before the Parole Board, he was awarded £300 for assumed distress and frustration. By way of comparison, in domestic anti-discrimination law awards must start at above £500, on the basis that lower sums "risk being regarded as so low as not to be a proper recognition of injury to feelings".[346] Awards of similar modesty have been made in other HRA cases in which prisoners have suffered delay.[347]

When it came to awards for deprivation of liberty there was no case cited to the Supreme Court in which the ECtHR had made an award for deprivation of liberty suffered as a result of a failure to provide a speedy hearing contrary to art.5(4). Lord Reed considered cases under other Articles involving loss of liberty however it was "impossible to derive any precise guidance from [the relevant ECtHR] awards".[348] He proffered the same advice to lower court judges as had Lord Bingham in *Greenfield*: **50-088**

"In accordance with s.8(1) and (4), a judgment has to be made by domestic courts as to what is just and appropriate in the individual case, taking into account such guidance as is available from awards made by the European court, or by domestic courts under s.8 of the 1998 Act, in comparable cases".[349]

Lord Reed said that awards for several months of prolonged detention when the claimant would otherwise have been released on license should be considerably higher than awards for distress alone, but considerably lower than cases in which the liberty lost was unrestricted (i.e. where the claimant would have been completely free as opposed to conditionally free).[350] The Court awarded Faulkner £6,500 for loss of liberty suffered as a result of being kept in prison for ten months longer than he ought to have been as a result of delays before the Parole Board;

---

344 [2013] 2 A.C. 254 at [67]–[68].

345 [2013] 2 A.C. 254 at [66]. See above para.50-062.

346 *Vento v Chief Constable of West Yorkshire* [2003] I.C.R. 318 CA at [65].

347 *R. (on the application of Haney) v Secretary of State for Justice* [2015] A.C.1344. See para.50-063 above.

348 [2013] 2 A.C. 254 at [75].

349 [2013] 2 A.C. 254 at [75]; *R. (on the application of Greenfield) v Secretary of State for the Home Department* [2005] 1 W.L.R. 673 HL at [19] ("The [ECtHR] routinely describes its awards as equitable, which I take to mean that they are not precisely calculated but are judged by the Court to be fair in the individual case. Judges in England and Wales must also make a similar judgment in the case before them").

350 [2013] 2 A.C. 254 at [75].

notably the liberty lost was conditional. The Court of Appeal had previously awarded Faulkner £10,000, placing weight on

> "the high value the common law has always placed on personal liberty and on the courts consequent disapproval of executive action which unlawfully restricts or interferes with it".[351]

However, even the Court of Appeal's higher award was below the sum that would have been awarded at common law for a similar loss of conditional liberty. For example in *Evans* an award of £5,000 (in 1998 terms)—£7,200 in 2011 terms (the year of the Court of Appeal judgment in Faulkner's case)—was made in false imprisonment, where the prisoner had experienced a much shorter period of wrongful imprisonment of just under two months, in circumstances where the liberty lost was conditional, there were no aggravating features and no distress suffered.[352] That the awards made in *Sturnham* were below what would be expected at common law follows on from the mirror approach prescribed by *Greenfield*. In *Sturnham* the *Greenfield* case was invoked for the following propositions: it was

> "to Strasbourg that British courts must look for guidance on the award of damages. A submission that courts in England and Wales should apply domestic scales of damages when exercising their power to award damages under s.8 was rejected. Dicta in earlier cases, suggesting that awards under s.8 should not be on the low side as compared with tortious awards and that English awards should provide the appropriate comparator, were implicitly disapproved".[353]

Lord Reed reiterated that "damages should be on a modest scale".[354]

**50-089** An important point of general application to emerge from *Sturnham* was that in assessing quantum courts ought only to consider awards made by the ECtHR against the UK or other member states with comparable standards of living.[355] The reason for this is that the ECtHR, in making awards, takes into account the standard of living in the defendant state, so that awards made against states that have lower living standards than the UK will in general be lower than comparable awards made against the UK.[356] It does not follow from this practice that awards made by the ECtHR against the UK are necessarily at comparable levels to awards in domestic fields of UK law such as torts, as the awards that the ECtHR makes against the UK, while higher than those made against Turkey, are nonetheless not in general calibrated to domestic scales, which are higher than ECtHR levels (but consider the discussion of *DSD v Commissioner of Police of the Metropolis* below).[357] Lord Reed also observed that although the ECtHR does not make precise adjustments to reflect inflation, older awards ought to be treated with caution and may not provide relevant guidance as to the sums the ECtHR would award today.[358] It is apposite at this point to also note the important point made by the Judge in *DSD* that

---

351 *R. (on the application of Faulkner) v Secretary of State for Justice* [2011] EWCA Civ 349 at [12].

352 *R. v Governor of Brockhill Prison Ex p. Evans (No.2)* [1999] Q.B. 1043 CA at 1059–1060 (upheld: [2001] 2 A.C. 19).

353 [2013] 2 A.C. 254 at [27]; *R. (on the application of Greenfield) v Secretary of State for the Home Department* [2005] 1 W.L.R. 673 HL at [18]–[19].

354 [2013] 2 A.C. 254 at [13]–[14].

355 [2013] 2 A.C. 254 at [38]–[40].

356 European Court of Human Rights, *Practice Direction: Just Satisfaction Claims*, 19 September 2016, para.2 ("the Court will normally take into account the local economic circumstances").

357 Below para.50-095 and following.

358 [2013] 2 A.C. 254 at [74].

"The actual sums awarded [by the ECtHR] must be seen in the light of the sums claimed. Quite routinely modest sums are claimed and hence modest sums are awarded".[359]

Regard ought to be had to this factor as a check against unduly modest awards.

Two further cases, *Rabone v Pennine Care NHS Foundation Trust*,[360]—decided by the Supreme Court—and *DSD v Commissioner of Police of the Metropolis*[361] —decided by the High Court—indicate how the mirror method operates in respect to quantum. Unusually among the damages cases decided under the HRA these cases seek to offer more detailed guidance as to quantification. The facts of *Rabone* are stated above.[362] The Supreme Court held that Mr and Mrs Rabone ought to be awarded damages under the HRA for the bereavement they had suffered as a result of their daughter's death, which resulted from the defendant's failure to comply with its operational duty under art.2 to take reasonable steps to protect the daughter from the mortal risk of suicide she posed to herself. Lord Dyson observed, **50-090**

"No decision has been cited to us which purports to be a guideline case in which the range of compensation is specified and the relevant considerations are articulated. It is, therefore, necessary for our courts to do their best in the light of such guidance as can be gleaned from the Strasbourg decisions on the facts of individual cases".[363]

Lord Dyson, drawing on the High Court decision in *Savage v South Essex Partnership NHS Foundation Trust*,[364] observed a "considerable range" of awards had been made in cases of this type by the ECtHR, awards ranging from €5,000 and €60,000, while also observing that awards had been fairly modest. This range of awards was treated as if it formed a scale of awards, albeit there is no evidence to suggest the ECtHR works to a recognised, graduated scale, the awards of €5,000 and €60,000 simply constituting the highest and lowest awards made in those cases that have come before the ECtHR. As discussed above, as the ECtHR does not in general reason its determinations under art.41 it is impossible to know what factors in fact influence it to increase or decrease quantum on the facts of a case. In *Rabone* Lord Dyson sought to overcome this problem by interpolating those factors "[o]ne would expect the court to have regard to".[365] The relevant factors included:

"the closeness of the family link between the victim and the deceased, the nature of the breach and the seriousness of the non-pecuniary damage that the victim has suffered. Factors which will tend to place the amount of the award towards the upper end of the range are the existence of a particularly close family tie between the victim and the deceased; the fact that the breach is especially egregious; and the fact that the circumstances of the death and the authority's response to it have been particularly distressing to the victims. Conversely, factors which will tend to place the award towards the lower end of the range are the weakness of the family ties, the fact that the breach is towards the lower end of the scale of gravity and the fact that the circumstances of the death have not caused the utmost distress to the victims".[366]

The trial judge had made awards of £1,500 to each parent, and the Court of Ap-

[359] *DSD v Commissioner of Police of the Metropolis* [2015] 1 W.L.R. 1833 (QB) at [68(ii)].

[360] [2012] 2 A.C. 72.

[361] [2015] 1 W.L.R. 1833 (QB).

[362] Above para.50-068.

[363] [2012] 2 A.C. 72 at [84].

[364] *Savage v South Essex Partnership NHS Foundation Trust* [2010] EWHC 865 (QB) at [97].

[365] [2012] 2 A.C. 72 at [85].

[366] [2012] 2 A.C. 72 at [85].

peal had increased these to £5,000 each.[367] Lord Dyson thought the awards made at trial were far too low. Applying the above factors to the facts of the case he said:

> "I would emphasise the following points. First, the family ties between Mr and Mrs Rabone and [their daughter] Melanie were very strong. They were a close family. They had been on holiday to Egypt with Melanie for a week in March 2005. They had shown the utmost concern for her mental health and had done all they could to support her. Secondly, they had expressed their anxiety to the hospital authorities about the dangers of allowing Melanie to come home on leave for the weekend of 19 to 21 April 2005 [when Melanie took her own life] and urged them not to allow it. Thirdly, the fact that the very risk which they feared and warned the authorities against eventuated must have made the death all the more distressing for them. This was a bad case of breach of the article 2 operational duty. In my view, it merited an award well above the lower end of the range of awards".[368]

Lord Dyson observed that there was considerable force in the view that the Court of Appeal's higher awards were still too low, however there had been no challenge to quantum on appeal. As such the awards were not disturbed.

**50-091** *DSD v Commissioner of Police of the Metropolis* concerned claims for damages by two victims of a convicted rapist against the defendant police force for failing to conduct an effective investigation into their allegations of serious sexual assaults.[369] The High Court held that the police breached the investigative duties they owed the claimants under art.3, and damages were awarded. The damages judgment provides a useful overview of relevant principles, albeit some statements of principle must be treated with caution. The Judge observed that the ECtHR regularly assumes that the victim must have suffered some form of anxiety or stress falling short of a recognised medical condition in consequence of the violation. Where the claimant could provide medical evidence establishing a recognised psychiatric condition awards would be markedly higher; this was the case in respect of both claimants in *DSD* and was treated as aggravating the sum to be awarded. Thus the nature of the harm is a salient feature. Also significant was the duration of the breach.[370] On the facts of the case the violation was long lived and was taken to have exacerbated the harm suffered over a period of approximately four years, this being an aggravating factor. The loss to be compensated was that causally connected to the police failures specifically. The lack of an apology or show of contrition on the part of the defendant could in principle exacerbate the claimant's mental suffering, but in this case the Judge found the defendant had demonstrated sufficient recognition of the shortcomings of the investigation.[371] The contributory failings of the claimant could operate to reduce the award, such as delay in notifying the police or failure to co-operate with the police, albeit the factor was not present on the facts.[372] In making awards the court had to consider the "totality" of the award and "standing back" ensure the final sum arrived at was reasonable, the Court in *DSD* emphasising that awards should be modest.

---

367 [2010] P.I.Q.R. P2 (QB); [2011] Q.B. 1019 CA.

368 [2012] 2 A.C. 72 at [87].

369 [2015] 1 W.L.R. 1833 (QB).

370 See also *O v Commissioner of Police of the Metropolis* [2011] H.R.L.R. 29 (QB). See above para.50-064.

371 On the role of apologies see also *Van Colle v Chief Constable of Hertfordshire* [2007] 1 W.L.R. 1821 CA at [123]–[124]; *R. (on the application of Bernard) v Enfield London Borough Council* [2003] H.R.L.R. 4 (Admin) at [61].

372 Drawing on *CAS v Romania*, Application No.26692/05, 20 March 2012. See also European Court of Human Rights, *Practice Direction: Just Satisfaction Claims*, 19 September 2016, para.2.

More controversial are two further factors taken into account in setting the award: (i) bad faith on the part of the defendant and the need to encourage compliance; and (ii) whether the investigatory failings were merely operational, or systemic. It was explained that these factors could aggravate the claimants' loss and lead to enhanced awards. On the facts the second factor was held to be present and operated to aggravate the award on the basis that the police's failings ran deep and also that these failings had grave consequences for many women beyond the two claimants in the case. The Judge interpolated from the facts of largely unreasoned art.41 determinations that these factors were relevant. However, there is no explicit statement to the effect that the ECtHR takes these factors into account. More problematic is that these factors are incompatible with the nature of the award being compensatory and thus the basic principle of restitutio in integrum. Goals of encouraging compliance or admonishing systemic failures are unrelated to assessing actual losses in fact suffered. Such goals are associated with exemplary damages, and if they are to be taken into account they ought to be reflected in a separate award of exemplary damages. Albeit, the Judge in *DSD* had explicitly stated that a punitive award would not be appropriate on the facts of this case. The Court took these wider factors into account on the basis that the ECtHR has stated that it has regard to the context and all the circumstances of the case in making awards. However, by such statements it does not intend to implicate considerations of deterrence or punishment, not least as it does not award exemplary damages.[373] Increasing damages on the basis of the first factor—that the defendant acted in bad faith—is somewhat less controversial, and can be rationalised on the basis that such damages constitute aggravated damages, which are in principle compensatory: that the defendant committed the wrong in a malicious fashion may be taken to aggravate the claimant's mental distress.[374] **50-092**

When it came to actual scales the Court articulated bands to guide its assessment: **50-093**

> "The following identifies the range of awards for relevant art.3 violations. The range (taking into account adjustment factors for cost of living and inflation) of awards for psychological/mental or other harm in art.3 cases is: (a) Euros 1,000-8,000 where the Court wishes to make a nominal or low award; (b) Euros 8,000-20,000 for a routine violation of art.3 with no serious long term mental health issues and no unusual aggravating factors; (c) Euros 20,000-100,000+ for cases where there are aggravating factors such as: (i) medical evidence of material psychological harm, (ii) mental harm amounting to a *recognised* medical condition, (iii) where the victim has also been the victim of physical harm or a crime caused in part by the State, (iv) long term systemic or endemic failings by the State, (v) morally reprehensible conduct by the State. This list is by no means exhaustive".[375]

This guidance is obviously very helpful for future cases, and will facilitate consistency. It is likely to be of assistance under other Articles, such as cases of breach of the art.2 investigatory duty. The bands were arrived at largely by interpolating what factors the ECtHR may have considered relevant to the making of awards on the facts of individual art.41 cases, albeit there is nothing to suggest the ECtHR itself applies a graduated scale or consistently applies a given set of factors. This approach of "imputing" factors and scales to the ECtHR, while highly

---

373 See para.50-111 below.

374 See para.50-111 and following, below.

375 [2015] 1 W.L.R. 1833 (QB) at [68(vii)].

artificial, does—as discussed above in relation to *Rabone*[376]—at least provide English courts with an avenue to articulate meaningful practical guidance, which is not otherwise forthcoming in the ECtHR's art.41 case law.

**50-094** Applying these bands the Judge awarded substantial sums to each of the two claimants: £22,250 to DSD, including a component of £2,250 for treatment costs for recognised psychiatric injury, and £19,000 to NBV including £2,000 for treatment costs. The Judge considered the cases to be towards the more serious end of the spectrum. Each had suffered ongoing recognisable psychiatric illness, which was supported by medical evidence, and was attributable to the police investigatory failings. In the case of NBV, the award included a component for harm suffered through the sexual assault by a third party perpetrator on the basis that if the police had properly carried out the investigation the assault could have been avoided; the sum for this harm was lower than it would otherwise be as a proportion of that harm had already been compensated via a settlement with the perpetrator and an award of criminal injuries compensation.[377] In each case the violation, caused by police failings in the conduct of the investigation, was prolonged and exacerbated the mental harm suffered. For example in respect of DSD if proper procedures had been followed the perpetrator could have been arrested relatively soon after the sexual assault took place, whereas he was arrested approximately four years later than he could have been. There were no contributory failings on the parts of DSD or NBV. Turning to the "wider" factors, the Judge found the police had not acted in bad faith, and therefore made no uplift on the basis of this factor. However, the Judge considered the systemic nature of the police failings to be an aggravating factor; for example the police's systems made it impossible for the police to follow their own guidelines regarding the need to carry out sexual assault investigations with sensitivity and care, and the force's systemic failings resulted in many women suffering sexual assaults. The Judge dismissed the possible counterargument that each such victim could bring a claim for damages themselves, on the basis that grave, wider consequences of the police failings were part of the context in which the awards to DSD and NBV should be assessed. The Court also considered it relevant that when NBV was attacked there was a disconnect between police statements that rape and sexual assault were priority cases and the reality that the police were not prioritising such claims. As noted above,[378] it is not clear how these "wider" features affect the actual degree of loss suffered by DSD and NBV. The awards in this case in truth go beyond compensation to the extent that these wider features were held to uplift quantum.[379]

**50-095** A potentially significant aspect of *DSD* was the Judge's willingness to look beyond the Strasbourg cases to domestic law for guidance as to the scales of awards. Importantly, domestic practice was taken into account in a way that is arguably consistent with the mirror approach. The Judge noted that in certain cases where the ECtHR had made awards for breach of art.3 there was some symbiosis between art.41 awards and domestic scales, and the Judge considered that the figures arrived at appeared to be on par with what might be awarded in domestic law. Specifically, in *Z v United Kingdom* the ECtHR said that it had had regard to awards made in domestic UK cases, albeit the scale of such awards, while relevant, was not

---

376 Above para.50-090.

377 On the Court's approach to issues of concurrent liability see para.50-071 above.

378 Above para.50-092.

379 See para.50-114 below.

decisive.[380] The Judge also placed weight on the ECtHR's art.41 Practice Direction, which also stated that the ECtHR may decide to take guidance from domestic standards, but was never bound by those standards.[381] The Judge further observed that the ECtHR had generally taken account of domestic comparators when they had been placed before the Court, albeit it was rare for such material to be submitted to the Court. Indeed, in those uncommon cases where parties did provide the Court with evidence of domestic scales, this appears to have been influential in raising the level of the award made by the Court. (It should be noted here that where domestic courts have had regard to domestic scales awards under the HRA have also been higher than the low Strasbourg levels).[382] Following this practice the Judge in *DSD* benchmarked the sums awarded against awards that might be recovered in equivalent domestic proceedings. Counsel had drawn the Judge's attention to domestic awards in battery, assault and false imprisonment as well as the Judicial Studies Board guidance for psychiatric injury. While the Judge refused to conduct a "mini-trial" of the claims by reference to domestic law the Judge did consider that the awards made were in the "ballpark" of, and were not out of kilter with awards that might be made domestically in tort.

On the one hand, one aspect of the mirror approach, as emphasised by the higher courts in *R. (on the application of Greenfield) v Secretary of State for the Home Department*,[383] and *R. (on the application of Sturnham) v Parole Board*,[384] is that Courts should look to Strasbourg and not domestic precedents. On the other hand, if there is evidence that Strasbourg takes domestic scales into account, this would provide a conduit by which domestic courts, in applying the mirror approach, could also take cognisance of domestic scales. The ECtHR's practice in this regard is not limited to the art.3 cases discussed in *DSD*. For example, the Law Commissions[385] refer to the fact that in *Perks v United Kingdom*,[386] the Court's award of £5,500 for unlawful detention was precisely the figure for six days' detention shown to the Court in a graph of domestic awards, so that it is reasonably clear that the Court was as a matter of fact applying the domestic tariff for false imprisonment. Albeit in another art.5 case, *Beet v United Kingdom*, the Court observed: **50-096**

> "Domestic scales of damages are not decisive, or, in all cases, relevant to applications under the Convention".[387]

The Court has also uplifted awards to reflect domestic levels where it has had to deal with multiple "repeat" claims caused by systemic defects in domestic legal systems and effectively been required to function as a court of first instance.[388] However, it ought to be noted that in other cases the Court has reiterated that it does

---

380 *Z v United Kingdom* (2002) 34 E.H.R.R. 3 at [120], [131].

381 European Court of Human Rights, *Practice Direction: Just Satisfaction Claims*, 19 September 2016, para.3.

382 *R. (on the application of KB) v Mental Health Review Tribunal* [2004] Q.B. 936 at [56]; *R. (on the application of Bernard) v Enfield London Borough Council* [2003] H.R.L.R. 4 (Admin) at [59]–[60]; *Kingshott v Ministry of Justice* [2009] EWHC 3666 (QB) at [46]–[49]; *DSD v Commissioner of Police of the Metropolis* [2015] 1 W.L.R. 1833 at [33], [68(vi)], [83]–[85], [130].

383 [2005] 1 W.L.R. 673 HL.

384 [2013] 2 A.C. 254.

385 Law Commission, *Damages under the Human Rights Act 1998* (2000), Law Com. No.266/Scot Law Com. No.180, Cm.4853, para.3.10 n.15.

386 (2000) 30 E.H.R.R. 33.

387 (2005) 41 E.H.R.R. 441 at [46].

388 *Scordino v Italy* (2007) 45 E.H.R.R. 7 at [176].

not make awards by analogy to domestic practice, and that its practice under art.41 is distinct.[389]

**50-097** More generally it would be desirable for the strictures of the mirror approach to be loosened and for domestic courts, in assessing awards, to take cognisance of domestic principles and scales as to quantum, not least as English courts have in many areas of domestic practice articulated detailed tariff and guideline judgments, while the Judicial Studies Board Guidelines provide a touchstone for awards for physical and psychological harm. Importantly there is a fully reasoned corpus of authorities with which awards can be compared. Such practice would not be inconsistent with art.8(4), as that provision only directs domestic courts to have regard to ECtHR principles; it does not provide a bar to courts also taking into account other guidance. Indeed, as Stanley Burnton J observed in *R. (on the application of KB) v Mental Health Review Tribunal*, the difference in wording between ss.2(1) and 8(4) of the Act—the latter only requiring domestic courts to take into account the principles rather than jurisprudence of the ECtHR—may reflect that Parliament wanted domestic courts to have greater freedom in relation to decisions of the ECtHR on quantum, quantum normally being a matter for the forum.[390] Following from this he considered domestic courts, while taking into account what guidance could be derived from Strasbourg, should be free to set scales under the HRA in UK terms. Importantly, the basic principles of art.41 practice—restitutio in integrum and causation—are also the basic principles that characterise domestic damages practice, so that reference to domestic precedents and scales which abide and are based in these principles would not create inconsistency with the ECtHR's basic principles under art.41. The contribution of domestic law would be, as the Law Commissions envisioned, to fill in the detail of these broad principles, which is missing in the Strasbourg cases, in a way that is consonant with domestic practices, traditions and economic conditions.[391] Many of the heads of loss compensated under the HRA match those compensated in other fields of domestic law. These include (i) distress and injured feelings, which regularly form the basis of awards in anti-discrimination law and within various torts; (ii) physical injury which is the bread and butter of battery and negligence; (iii) loss of liberty for which awards are made in false imprisonment; (iv) breach of privacy for which damages are regularly awarded in the action for misuse of private information; and (v) use of and damage to land, which are routinely compensated through awards in trespass, nuisance and negligence. Thus, at an earlier stage in the development of HRA damages jurisprudence Lord Woolf postulated that where

> "the court decides that it is appropriate to award damages, the levels of damages awarded in respect of torts as reflected in the guidelines issued by the Judicial Studies Board, the levels of awards made by the Criminal Injuries Compensation Board and by the

---

389 *Osman v United Kingdom* (2000) 29 E.H.R.R. 245 at [164]; *Curley v United Kingdom* (2001) 31 E.H.R.R. 14 at [46]. Both cited in *R. (on the application of Greenfield) v Secretary of State for the Home Department* [2005] 1 W.L.R. 673 HL at [17].

390 [2004] Q.B. 936 at [22].

391 Law Commission, *Damages under the Human Rights Act 1998* (2000), Law Com. No.266/Scot Law Com. No.180, Cm.4853, para.4.11 ("Therefore, at least where the normal rules of domestic law are consistent with the results which would be reached by the Strasbourg court, and with the terms of the [Human Rights Act 1998], the obligation of the domestic courts to have regard to Strasbourg 'principles' should lead to little difficulty in practice and should leave the domestic courts reasonably free to follow their existing practices as to the evidence, calculation and the measure of damages in individual cases").

Parliamentary Ombudsman and the Local Government Ombudsman may all provide some rough guidance where the consequences of the infringement of human rights are similar to that being considered in the comparator selected".[392]

Of significance, the ECtHR has itself stated that it is open to Member States

"to organise the remedy in a manner consistent with its own legal system and traditions and consonant with the standard of living in the country concerned".[393]

This is effectively the approach that has been adopted to pecuniary loss under the HRA already.[394] Indeed, the ECtHR envisions that rather than follow the art.41 case law it would be "easier for the domestic courts to refer to the amounts awarded at domestic level for other types of damage", including "personal injury, damage relating to a relative's death or damage in defamation cases".[395] It should also be borne in mind that in both *Greenfield* and *Sturnham*, while the respective Courts indicated the focus should be art.41, each nonetheless emphasised that domestic courts were "not inflexibly bound by Strasbourg awards",[396] and this would be especially so where no clear or consistent jurisprudence is discernible among those awards.

## (2) Causation

In considering whether to award damages, it is a generally-applied principle of the ECtHR that it will require the applicant to prove causation, in the sense of factual or "but-for" causation. The focus on factual causation is evident in the following important statement of principle in *Kingsley v United Kingdom*: **50-098**

"The court recalls that it is well established that the principle underlying the provision of just satisfaction for a breach of art.6 is that the applicant should as far as possible be put in the position he would have enjoyed had the proceedings complied with the Convention's requirements. The court will award monetary compensation under art.41 only where it is satisfied that the loss or damage complained of was actually caused by the violation it has found, since the state cannot be required to pay damages in respect of losses for which it is not responsible."[397]

The ECtHR case law under art.41 does not recognise a "remoteness", "scope of liability", or "legal causation" principle as an aspect of the causation analysis. If any such principle applies then, as discussed below, decisions under the HRA suggest that a "direct consequences" (as applied in deceit) as opposed to "reasonable foreseeability" test (as applied in negligence) is applicable.

Factual causation may be applied strictly by the ECtHR so as to deny relief. For example, in cases arising out of breaches of art.6 in criminal cases, the ECtHR will require the applicant to prove that, but for the breach in question, he would have **50-099**

[392] *Anufrijeva v Southwark London Borough Council* [2004] Q.B. 1124 CA at [74].

[393] *Scordino v Italy* (2007) 45 E.H.R.R. 7 at [188]–[189]; *Cocchiarella v Italy*, Application No.64886/01, 26 March 2006 at [79]–[80]; *Burdov v Russia (No.2)*, Application No.33509/04, 15 January 2009 at [99].

[394] Above paras 50-076 to 50-078.

[395] *Scordino v Italy* (2007) 45 E.H.R.R. 7 at [188]–[189].

[396] *R. (on the application of Greenfield) v Secretary of State for the Home Department* [2005] 1 W.L.R. 673 HL at [19]; *R. (on the application of Sturnham) v Parole Board* [2013] 2 A.C. 254 at [27], [30], [33].

[397] (2002) 35 E.H.R.R. 177.

been acquitted and not convicted. Thus, in *De Cubber v Belgium*,[398] the applicant had been convicted of forgery by a court which he claimed was not impartial. The ECtHR said:

> "The court cannot speculate as to what the outcome of the proceedings in question would have been had the violation of the Convention not occurred; there is nothing to show that the result would probably have been more favourable to the applicant ... In short, no causal link between the violation of the Convention and the length of the detention had been established."[399]

This principle could affect both pecuniary and non-pecuniary losses. Thus, according to this approach, where the allegation is that a procedural defect has occurred, an applicant would fail in his claim for pecuniary loss unless he could show that, but for the breach in question, he would have been in custody for less time and would, if he can identify and prove such a period, have been employed during that period.[400]

**50-100** However, it is of critical importance to observe that domestic courts are in a different position to the ECtHR, as reiterated by Lord Reed in *R. (on the application of Sturnham) v Parole Board*.[401] Domestic courts have greater fact-finding powers than the ECtHR, which does not for example have the capacity to hear and test oral evidence. As such, in a case where the ECtHR denies an award on the basis that it cannot speculate as to outcomes, a domestic court may well have the sort of firm evidential foundation before it which would allow it to conclude that the outcome of proceedings would otherwise have been more favourable to the claimant had procedural rights been abided. Thus Lord Reed in *Sturnham* said domestic courts

> "should resolve disputed issues of fact in the usual way even if the European court, in similar circumstances, would not do so".[402]

This justifies and will likely lead to different outcomes as between the domestic and supranational level, so that art.41 determinations as to causation may not be a reliable guide as to the approach of domestic courts. In *Sturnham* Lord Reed said that

> "[w]here it is established on a balance of probabilities that a violation of art.5(4) has resulted in the detention of a prisoner beyond the date when he would otherwise have been released, damages should ordinarily be awarded as compensation for the resultant detention".[403]

On the facts of the case Lord Reed found, in respect of Faulkner's appeal, that it was possible to conclude, on the factual evidence, that Faulkner would have been released 10 months earlier than he was if his review before the Parole Board had not been delayed in breach of the speediness requirements imposed by art.5(4).[404] In other words he would have been released 10 months earlier if his case had been processed with due expedition in compliance with art.5(4). In respect of any associated pecuniary loss Lord Reed said

---

398 (1987) 13 E.H.R.R. 422.

399 See, also, *Nikolova v Bulgaria* referred to at para.50-048, above.

400 See, e.g. *Eckle v Germany* (1991) 13 E.H.R.R. 556; *Ruiz-Mateos v Spain* (1993) 16 E.H.R.R. 505.

401 [2013] 2 A.C. 254 at [37].

402 [2013] 2 A.C. 254 at [13(5)].

403 [2013] 2 A.C. 254 at [13(6)].

404 [2013] 2 A.C. 254 at [82].

"[p]ecuniary losses proved to have been caused by the prolongation of detention should be compensated in full".[405]

This is suggestive that pecuniary damages will rest on an orthodox "but-for" analysis. It was not suggested that a remoteness test applied.

In *R. (on the application of Greenfield) v Secretary of State for the Home Department* Lord Bingham observed, in regard to claims under art.6 that: **50-101**

> "the [ECtHR] has ordinarily been willing to depart from its practice of finding a violation of art.6 to be, in itself, just satisfaction under art.41 only where the court finds a causal connection between the violation found and the loss for which an applicant claims to be compensated."[406]

Lord Bingham observed that the ECtHR had, in relation to claims for pecuniary loss for breach of art.6, looked for a causal connection but in general been slow to award such compensation. In light of Lord Reed's guidance in *Sturnham* it is doubtful whether a restrictive approach ought to be taken in domestic law, for example with courts starting from an assumption that such losses are not recoverable. The likely reason why the ECtHR has been slow to make such awards is that it will often lack the firm factual foundation on which to determine causation. In light of *Sturnham* claims for pecuniary losses suffered in consequence of breach of art.6 should arguably be recoverable upon satisfaction of the ordinary "but-for" inquiry, and this has been the approach in other classes of case where damages for pecuniary loss have been sought in domestic courts.[407] One reason given by Lord Bingham for why it may be hard to prove recoverable distress and frustration in art.6 cases is that it may be difficult to prove those losses are attributable to the violation,

> "for very many people involvement in legal proceedings is bound to cause anxiety irrespective of any art.6 breach" and thus any claimed losses may be difficult to disentangle from these ordinary stresses."[408]

In *DSD v Commissioner of Police of the Metropolis* the Judge considered the issue of causation in relation to two claimants who had suffered sexual assaults, in respect of which the defendant had failed to conduct an effective investigation in breach of art.3.[409] In respect of claimant DSD the Court concluded that the sexual assault suffered at the hands of a criminal third party could not have been avoided even if the investigation had been carried out properly. As such damages could not be awarded for the effects of the assault.[410] However, DSD could recover for the post-assault psychiatric harm, and treatment costs, she suffered in consequence of, and which were attributable to, failures in the carrying out of the police investigation. In respect of the claimant NBV the Judge had concluded that, applying the orthodox but-for standard of what was "probable", the sexual assault would not have been suffered at all "but for" the investigatory failings.[411] The Judge therefore proceeded on the basis that damages could be awarded against the defendant for the harm associated with the assault. Compensation had been awarded in **50-102**

405 [2013] 2 A.C. 254 at [13(8)].

406 [2005] 1 W.L.R. 673 HL at [11].

407 Above paras 50-076 to 50-078.

408 [2005] 1 W.L.R. 673 HL at [16].

409 [2015] 1 W.L.R. 1833 (QB).

410 [2015] 1 W.L.R. 1833 (QB) at [26].

411 *DSD v Commissioner of Police of the Metropolis* [2014] EWHC 436 (QB) at [302] (liability judgment).

respect of those harms as a result of a settlement with the perpetrator and through the Criminal Injuries Compensation Authority.[412] However, the Judge considered those sums did not fully compensate NBV for the losses relating to the assault, and a sum in relation to the assault did form one component of the final overall award made against the police. In addition NBV could recover for recognised psychiatric loss on the same basis as DSD. It is evident from the case that, as is the general approach to factual causation, the defendant's wrong only has to be a cause of a given loss in order for the defendant to be liable in principle for that loss. For both NBV and DSD the assault by the third party criminal and the police's investigatory failures were causative of the psychiatric harm suffered, but this did not bar holding the police liable for the full extent of the loss (noting that the previous settlements reached in the case and criminal injuries compensation did not provide redress for these mental harms).[413]

**50-103** A more relaxed approach to causation was indicated by Cox J in *Van Colle v Chief Constable of Hertfordshire*,[414] a case concerned with the right to life protected by art.2. In relation to causation, Cox J, having considered the judgment of Lord Bingham in *R. (on the application of Greenfield) v Secretary of State for the Home Department*, said:

> "In my judgment that fact-sensitive approach, having regard to the justice of a particular case, should guide the domestic courts in exercising the discretion given to them under the Act as to the appropriate remedy for a Claimant who has established a violation by the state of its obligation to take protective measures to protect his life from the criminal acts of a third party. In order for the Court to be satisfied that an award of damages is necessary to afford just satisfaction to a victim of the state's breach of art.2, the victim does not have to prove causation on the 'but-for' test. In this case the proper question, in my view, is whether the protective measures that were reasonably open to DC Ridley in the circumstances could have had a real prospect of altering the outcome and avoiding Giles' death".[415]

It is considered that the amalgamation of the words "could have" and "a real prospect" are tautologous. The true test applied was reflected in the Judge's conclusion that "at the very least [there was] a real prospect of avoiding this tragedy".[416] This test was derived from the ECtHR case law, the ECtHR, sometimes taking a "looser" approach to causation than domestic courts, as discussed below in this paragraph. Such an approach would allow claims that fall below the usual 50 per cent causation threshold and allow awards of damages to be made where the failure in question merely increased the risk of death. Albeit while holding that "but-for" causation did not necessarily need to be fulfilled for damages to be recovered under the HRA, the Judge did also indicate that if the police had taken the reasonably required steps to protect life in compliance with art.2 it was more likely than not that the death could have been avoided. When the case reached the Court of Appeal the Court did not rule on Cox J's use of the real prospect test, only observing that it did not disagree with her conclusion that but-for causation was established.[417] The approach adopted by Cox J was based in more "flexible" approaches to causa-

412 *DSD v Commissioner of Police of the Metropolis* [2015] 1 W.L.R. 1833 (QB) at [27].
413 On concurrent liability see above at para.50-071.
414 [2006] 3 All E.R. 963 (QB).
415 [2006] 3 All E.R. 963 (QB) at [104].
416 [2006] 3 All E.R. 963 (QB) at [106].
417 *Van Colle v Chief Constable of Hertfordshire Police* [2007] 1 W.L.R. 1821 CA at [96]–[98].

tion sometimes adopted by the ECtHR pursuant to its more general "equitable" approach to compensation. As the Judge in *DSD* observed "precision in establishing causation is not an identifiable hallmark of Strasbourg case law".[418] But as the Judge in *DSD* also observed, the ECtHR's some time process of "juridical gestimation" is often motivated by uncertainties in establishing loss.[419] In turn the ECtHR's more flexible approaches to causation arguably stem from that Court's limited fact-finding capacity, this lack of capacity resulting in the ECtHR developing various techniques to enable it to reason to conclusions in the absence of concrete factual evidence. However, in the light of Lord Reed's dicta in *Sturnham* (above),[420] it is questionable whether such approaches should be read across to domestic law, given domestic courts do have the capacity to undertake detailed fact-finding and precisely analyse causation and identify loss. As Lord Reed made clear in *Sturnham*, factual questions ought to be determined in the ordinary way, and on the balance of probabilities.

From the case law under the HRA it appears that a claimant only has to demonstrate factual causation, in general on an orthodox "but-for" basis. There is no recognition of the sort of remoteness analysis applied in the context of certain torts such as negligence. Thus, if there is a "legal causation" element to HRA damages claims it is likely to be a "direct consequences" approach. That is, the claimant is "entitled to compensation for all the actual loss directly flowing" from the wrong.[421] That this is the position is arguably reinforced by *Breyer Group Plc v Department of Energy and Climate Change*.[422] The facts of the case are set out above.[423] In response to an argument by the defendant that damages should not be awarded because the losses followed from commercial decisions made by the claimants, the Judge said: **50-104**

> "If the claimant company in question can identify the commercial decision that it took as having been due to the proposals (that, but for the proposal, the decision to scrap the contract or abandon the project would not have been taken) then in my view they can demonstrate a direct consequence".[424]

This is suggestive that a defendant in a HRA claim will be liable for all losses that follow as a direct consequence of the wrong, and that those consequences are not subject to a reasonable foreseeability limitation. This is the correct approach. Courts have been unwilling to apply remoteness tests in actions for which "foreseeability of damages [is not] the gist of the tort", and where there is no statutory language to import such a requirement.[425] On this basis a remoteness test is not applied to the tort of harassment,[426] nor anti-discrimination torts, and it has been assumed the test does not apply in assault and battery.[427] Similarly, loss is not the gist of HRA damages claims. Such claims are in general actionable per se, upon breach of a right,

---

418 *DSD v Commissioner of Police of the Metropolis* [2015] 1 W.L.R. 1833 (QB) at [25].
419 [2015] 1 W.L.R. 1833 (QB) at [25].
420 Above para.50-100.
421 *Smith New Court Securities Ltd v Citibank* [1997] A.C. 254 at 282.
422 [2015] 2 All E.R. 44 (QB); [2015] 1 W.L.R. 4559 CA.
423 Above para.50-078.
424 [2015] 2 All E.R. 44 (QB) at [158].
425 *Jones v Ruth* [2012] 1 W.L.R. 1495 CA at [32]; *Essa v Laing Ltd* [2004] I.C.R. 746 CA at [48]; *Kuwait Airways Corp v Iraqi Airways Co* [2002] 2 A.C. 883 at [71].
426 *Jones v Ruth* [2012] 1 W.L.R. 1495 CA.
427 *Essa v Laing Ltd* [2004] I.C.R. 746 CA (on assault and battery see at [38]–[39]). See also *Massey v UNIFI* [2008] I.C.R. 62 CA.

and not dependent on proof of foreseeable, actionable harm. In common with those actions for which a remoteness element has been held not to apply, the HRA protects basic interests and it is consonant with a policy of strong protection of such interests that remoteness ought not to be used to cut down liability where basic interests have been infringed. There is no language in the statute to suggest remoteness ought to limit recovery, while the ECtHR does not apply such a limit.

### (3) Loss of a chance

**50-105** An interesting question is whether an English court will award damages for loss of a chance or loss of opportunity in a claim under the HRA. This is an area with which the English courts are conversant, and well used to awarding damages. An example is where, as a result of a solicitor's negligence, the claimant has lost the chance of litigation. Where that chance was more than merely negligible, the court will apply a loss of a chance analysis to the claim against the solicitor and ask itself what were the percentage chances of success that the claimant had.[428] Lost chances arising out of breaches of the Convention could fit well with this line of authority.[429] Though, as discussed at the end of this section, regard must be had to the potential impact of the Supreme Court's decision in *Sturnham*.

**50-106** In the ECtHR, although the court has been prepared to award damages for lost opportunity, the approach has been rather more robust and less analytical than in the domestic courts. Thus, in *Bösnich v Austria*,[430] where the applicant claimed for financial losses to his business after being convicted in proceedings which were non-compliant with art.6, the ECtHR awarded 700,000 Austrian schillings (approximately £27,000) on a loss of opportunity basis, saying[431]:

> "... the evidence does not establish the existence of a causal link between the violation of the Convention and the deterioration in Mr Bösnich's financial situation. Admittedly, the court cannot speculate as to what the outcome of these two sets of proceedings would have been had the breach not occurred. Nevertheless, the court does not exclude the possibility that the applicant suffered, as a result of the potential effects of the violation found, a loss of opportunities of which account must be taken, even if the prospects of achieving them were questionable."

Given the terms of the judgment, the award might be thought to have been somewhat questionable.

**50-107** Another example of a case where the ECtHR purported to award damages for loss of opportunity was *Martins Moreira v Portugal*.[432] The applicant had been injured in a road traffic accident on 12 November 1975 and he instituted proceedings on 20 December 1977. At first instance, he was awarded damages of 732,000 escudos on 1 October 1982. The Court of Appeal increased this sum to 1,032,000 escudos on 30 May 1985 and this was upheld by the Supreme Court on 5 February 1987 which also held that the applicant was entitled to an additional sum for his permanent disability, to be determined in enforcement proceedings. Enforcement proceedings against the defendant, Gestetner, then floundered when it emerged

---

428 See, e.g. *Mount v Barker Austin* [1998] P.N.L.R. 493 CA; *Hanif v Middleweeks* [2000] Lloyd's Rep. P.N. 920 CA; *Sharpe v Addison* [2004] P.N.L.R. 23 CA at 426.

429 On loss of chance in litigation, see also paras.10-074 and following, above.

430 (1985) 13 E.H.R.R. 409.

431 (1985) 13 E.H.R.R. 409 at [103].

432 (1991) 13 E.H.R.R. 517.

that the company was already subject to proceedings which led to its insolvency on 25 March 1988. The ECtHR found that the excessive length of the proceedings was essentially due to the conduct of the competent authorities which constituted a breach of art.6. The applicant claimed that the delay resulted in his not being paid even a part of his 1,032,000 escudos damages: he had taken out loans to pay for his medical treatment (the cost of which was assessed at 532,000 escudos) and had run up interest of 200,000 escudos on those loans. The applicant also claimed that he had been unable to undergo a further operation in London which he needed and that the overall state of affairs was causing him anxiety for which he claimed an additional 2,000,000 escudos for non-pecuniary damage. In awarding the applicant 2,000,000 escudos[433] total damages, the ECtHR stated as follows:

> "The court would point out that the applicant first sought unsuccessfully to persuade the Império company[434] and the Gestetner company to pay him of their own accord the part of his claim which had already been calculated and then requested the enforcement of the decision delivered in his favour and the attachment of Gestetner's property. However, on 18 January 1988 the Lisbon Court found that that company was the subject of proceedings, which subsequently resulted, on 25 March 1988, in a declaration of insolvency. It is true that this development was subsequent to the Supreme Court's judgment of 5 February 1987. However, and even though it is not certain that the applicant would have recovered the entirety of his debt if the main proceedings had been terminated earlier, it is, in the court's view, reasonable to conclude that, as a result of the long delay, in breach of art.6(1), found by the court in this judgment, he suffered a loss of opportunities which warrants an award of just satisfaction in respect of pecuniary damage. Mr Martins Moreira also clearly suffered non-pecuniary damage. He has lived, and still lives, in a state of uncertainty and anxiety with regard to the outcome of the proceedings in question and the implications for his financial situation and his health. The various components of this damage cannot be calculated precisely. The court has assessed them as a whole and, as required by art.50, on an equitable basis. It finds that the applicant should be awarded compensation of 2,000,000 escudos."[435]

It is a pity that the court did not attempt to subdivide this sum—it does not in general break awards down into their component parts—and in particular indicate whether it was in any way discounted for the fact that the award was for loss of the opportunity to recover damages from Gestetner.

The jurisprudence of the ECtHR in relation to the award of compensation for lost opportunity was considered by the House of Lords in *R. (on the application of Greenfield) v Secretary of State for the Home Department*[436] by Lord Bingham, giving the judgment of the court. He said: **50-108**

> "More germane to the present case is a second head of claim for what English lawyers would call general damages and the Court tends to call, but not always consistently, non-pecuniary damage. A claim under this head may be put on the straightforward basis that but for the Convention violation found the outcome of the proceedings would probably have been different and more favourable to the applicant, or on the more problematical basis that the violation deprived the applicant of an opportunity to achieve a different result which was not in all the circumstances of the case a valueless opportunity. While in the ordinary way the Court has not been easily persuaded on this last basis, it has in some

---

433 Worth approximately €10,000.

434 This was the insurance company whose liability was limited to 200,000 escudos, divided between the applicant, his co-claimant in the original proceedings and an intervening company.

435 (1991) 13 E.H.R.R. 517 at [65]–[67].

436 [2005] 1 W.L.R. 673 HL.

> cases accepted it: see *Goddi v Italy* (1984) 6 EHRR 457 at [35] ('a loss of real opportunities'); *Colozza v Italy* (1985) 7 EHRR 516 at [38] ('a loss of real opportunities'); *Lechner and Hess v Austria* (1987) 9 EHRR 490 at [64] ('some loss of real opportunities'); *Weeks v United Kingdom* (1988) 13 EHRR 435 at [13] ('a loss of opportunities'); *O v United Kingdom* (1988) 13 EHRR 578 at [12] ('some loss of real opportunities'); *Delta v France* (1990) 16 EHRR 574 at [43] ('a loss of real opportunities') ... Thus while the court laid down in the authoritative case of *Kingsley v United Kingdom*[437] ... and repeated in *Edwards and Lewis v United Kingdom*, 27 October 2004 at [46] and [49], that the court will award monetary compensation under art.41 only where it is satisfied that the loss or damage complained of was actually caused by the violation it has found, and it has repeatedly stressed that it will not speculate on what the outcome of the proceedings would have been but for the violation, it has on occasion been willing in appropriate cases to make an award if of opinion that the applicant has been deprived of a real chance of a better outcome."[438]

In *Hooper v United Kingdom*[439] Mance J, in the domestic proceedings, assessed that, but for breach of art.6, the magistrate

> "might well have been persuaded to a different result if the applicant's counsel had been able to make representations concerning the order".

When the case reached the ECtHR that court said that while this conclusion was not expressed in such strong terms as in, for example, *Perks v United Kingdom*,[440] it was sufficient to support the applicant's claim that he suffered some loss of opportunity due to the breach in this case and the applicant was awarded €8,000. Cox J's "real prospects" analysis in *Van Colle v Chief Constable of Hertfordshire* has been discussed above.[441] In *Savage v South Essex Partnership NHS Foundation Trust*,[442] also an art.2 case, Mackay J asked whether as a result of the defendant's breach of its duty to protect life, the deceased had lost a "substantial chance" of survival in consequence of the breach of art.2.

**50-109** Awards for non-pecuniary loss have also been made in cases involving children taken into care and subsequently adopted where proceedings for access were unreasonably extended in breach of art.6. Such awards have been made on the basis that the ECtHR "could not exclude" the possibility that a different outcome might have resulted if there had been no such breach.[443] In other cases, the ECtHR has simply declined to make awards for loss of opportunity, dismissing such claims as too speculative.[444] An English court would have difficulty in reconciling the two lines of cases and in discerning a "principle" within s.8(4) of the HRA. In those circumstances, an English court should simply follow its own lights and award damages for loss of a chance on exactly the same basis, and in exactly the same way, that it does in cases of lost litigation arising out of a solicitor's negligence.

**50-110** Lastly, it should be observed that Lord Reed's judgment in *R. (on the application of Sturnham) v Parole Board* casts doubt on the place of loss of a chance awards under the HRA, at least in some contexts, specifically where loss of a chance analysis has been used by the ECtHR as a substitute for making a more definite as-

---

437 (2002) 35 E.H.R.R. 177.
438 (2002) 35 E.H.R.R. 177 at [12], [14].
439 (2005) 41 E.H.R.R. 1.
440 (2000) 30 E.H.R.R. 33.
441 Above para.50-103.
442 [2010] EWHC 865 (QB).
443 See, e.g. *H v United Kingdom* (1991) 13 E.H.R.R. 449.
444 See the reference to *De Cubber* (at para.50-099, above).

sessment of harm because of the ECtHR's limited fact-finding capacity.[445] He said, domestic courts should

> "establish the facts of the case in the usual way, and apply the normal domestic principle that the claimant has to establish on a balance of probabilities that he has suffered loss".[446]

It followed from this that where a prisoner's case before the Parole Board had been delayed in breach of art.5(4), the prisoner could not seek damages for the loss of an opportunity of earlier release.[447] The court must reach a conclusion as to whether the prisoner would have been released earlier or not on the balance of probabilities. The wider ramifications of Lord Reed's judgment on potential recovery for loss of a chance or opportunities under the HRA are yet to be seen. It is also yet to been seen how Lord Reed's approach reconciles with Lord Bingham's judgment in *Greenfield* which seems to accept the possibility that damages may be recovered under the HRA for loss of a chance in the context of breach of art.6, following Strasbourg practice.[448]

## 5. Aggravated and Exemplary damages

The ECtHR does not formally make awards of either aggravated or exemplary damages, albeit the Court has been observed to uplift awards in cases of particularly egregious violations or cases involving repeatedly recalcitrant member states.[449] However, this does not prevent domestic courts from making aggravated or exemplary awards under the HRA, and indeed there is already an emergent practice which supports the making of such awards, particularly aggravated damages. **50-111**

The reason given in the ECtHR's art.41 Practice Direction for why the Court does not award aggravated damages is that the Court's awards are intended to compensate for actual harmful consequences of a violation and not to punish.[450] However, in English law aggravated damages are not awarded as a punishment. Rather, as the courts have recognised,[451] they are compensatory. They represent added compensation for the aggravated distress and upset felt by a victim whose rights have been violated in an egregious manner. That is, where the defendant acts in a way "such as to injure the plaintiff's proper feelings of dignity and pride";[452] the "*injury* ... is made worse for the plaintiff because it is more difficult to excuse".[453] Thus aggravated damages in English law do "compensate for the actual harmful consequences" of a wrong.[454] As such awards are consistent with the basic principle of restitutio in integrum, which characterises the ECtHR's art.41 awards. And indeed, as the Law Commissions observed, notwithstanding those formal statements in the Practice Direction, the ECtHR **50-112**

---

445 [2013] 2 A.C. 254 at [37], [82].

446 [2013] 2 A.C. 254 at [82].

447 [2013] 2 A.C. 254 at [13(10)].

448 Above para.50-108.

449 See, e.g. *R. (on the application of KB) v Mental Health Review Tribunal* [2004] Q.B. 936 at [50].

450 European Court of Human Rights, *Practice Direction: Just Satisfaction Claims*, 19 September 2016, para.9.

451 *Rookes v Barnard* [1964] A.C. 1129 at 1221, 1229; *Broome v Cassell & Co Ltd* [1972] A.C. 1027 at 1124.

452 *Rookes v Barnard* [1964] A.C. 1129 at 1221, 1229.

453 *Thompson v Commissioner of Police of the Metropolis* [1998] Q.B. 498 CA at 512 (emphasis added).

454 European Court of Human Rights, *Practice Direction: Just Satisfaction Claims*, 19 September 2016, para.9.

> "does sometimes take into account the seriousness of the violation and the conduct of the respondent State in awarding damages, so that the Strasbourg principles are not inconsistent with the grant of what are in effect aggravated damages".[455]

Under art.13 the ECtHR has said that it

> "accepts that, applying the compensatory principle, national courts might make an award taking into account the motives and conduct of the defendant".[456]

Furthermore, the availability of such awards under the HRA would be consistent with a long tradition in English law of making such awards against public entities that violate citizens' rights, particularly their basic dignitary rights, in a way that aggravates distress and upset. For example such damages are routinely awarded where the police wrongly arrest or imprison an individual in humiliating circumstances or in a "high handed, insulting, malicious or oppressive manner".[457]

**50-113** In any case, it appears the English courts have already recognised the availability of aggravated damages under the HRA. In *R. (on the application of KB) v Mental Health Review Tribunal*,[458] Stanley Burnton J observed that an award of aggravated damages, which are in principle compensatory not penal, may be justified in an exceptional case of deliberate or persistent infringement.[459] In *Van Colle v Chief Constable of Hertfordshire Police* the Court of Appeal said that the degree of culpability of the defendant's misconduct was relevant to the question of liability and also compensation.[460] In *R. (on the application of Bernard) v Enfield London Borough Council*, the facts of which are set out above,[461] the Judge, in assessing quantum, took into account that the defendant's conduct had "compounded" the claimant's problems.[462] The relevant conduct included that the defendant had ignored letters from the claimants' solicitors urging action; not apologised, offered an explanation for the delays suffered or acknowledged they were in error; made no improvements to procedures; and failed to comply with previous timescales set by the Court. In *DSD v Commissioner of Police of the Metropolis* the Judge considered the defendant's conduct formed part of the overall context in which damages ought to be assessed, including whether the violation was deliberate and/or in bad faith; if bad faith had been present on the facts, this would have aggravated the damages to be awarded.[463]

**50-114** The HRA jurisprudence on the availability of exemplary damages is mixed. Though, the types of concerns which exemplary damages respond to have been held to be relevant to HRA damages. In *Anufrijeva v Southwark London Borough Council* the Court of Appeal ruled out exemplary awards.[464] However, the House

---

[455] Law Commission, *Damages under the Human Rights Act 1998* (2000), Law Com. No.266/Scot Law Com. No.180, Cm.4853, para.4.70.

[456] *Shilbergs v Russia*, Application No.20075/03, 17 December 2009 at [78].

[457] *Thompson v Commissioner of Police of the Metropolis* [1998] Q.B. 498 CA at 516.

[458] [2004] Q.B. 936.

[459] [2004] Q.B. 936 at [50].

[460] [2007] 1 W.L.R. 1821 CA at [124].

[461] [2003] H.R.L.R. 4 (Admin). See also para.50-061, above

[462] [2003] H.R.L.R. 4 (Admin) at [61]. Note however that lack of an apology, even if it exacerbates upset, may not always lead to an uplift in quantum: *Van Colle v Chief Constable of Hertfordshire Police* [2007] 1 W.L.R. 1821 CA at [123].

[463] [2015] 1 W.L.R. 1833 (QB) at [40], [127].

[464] [2004] Q.B. 1124 CA at [55].

of Lords has left the issue open.[465] In *R. (on the application of Faulkner) v Secretary of State for Justice* exemplary damages were discussed, but no award was contemplated.[466] However, the Court did consider the goals of disapproval of wrongful executive action and deterrence of future wrongdoing were relevant to HRA damages. Similarly, in *R. (on the application of Greenfield) v Secretary of State for the Home Department* Lord Bingham considered damages could play a role in encouraging compliance, if it was felt such encouragement was required.[467] This factor was relevant to the decision whether to award damages. But if relevant to the decision whether to award damages then logically it may also be relevant to assessing quantum. As has been discussed above,[468] the Judge in *DSD v Commissioner of Police of the Metropolis* made increased awards on the basis of a range of factors that could only be relevant to a punitive award, including the systemic nature of the police failings and the disconnect between police policy statements and actual practice.[469] That such factors were held to increase the awards made, suggests that the awards included a sum of exemplary damages. More generally, the Judge had stated that further factors relevant to assessment might include whether there is a need to include a deterrent element in an award and whether there is a need to encourage others to bring claims by increasing awards.[470]

The award of exemplary damages would be inconsistent with the ECtHR's **50-115** general approach under art.41, given the Court only makes compensatory awards. However, the Court has never held the domestic availability of exemplary damages to be inconsistent with the Convention.[471] Further, the Court has stated under art.13 that member states have the discretion to organise their system of remedies consistently with their own domestic traditions.[472] Exemplary awards are a fundamental and longstanding feature of the English law of damages. They have played a particularly important role through history in restraining the abuse of power by public officials. Thus, in *Ashby v White* Holt CJ said that

> "If publick officers will infringe mens rights, they ought to pay greater damages than other men, to deter and hinder other officers from the like offences".[473]

This tradition is reflected in the first category of case recognised in *Rookes v Barnard* in which exemplary damages may be awarded, that is, where public defendants have acted oppressively, arbitrarily or unconstitutionally.[474] Whatever may be said of confining the availability of exemplary damages to categories, it is difficult to think of a better example to fit this category than a flagrant or wanton breach of a citizen's basic human rights. Indeed, it would be anomalous if such damages were available at common law in response to outrageous interferences with

---

465 *Kuddus v Chief Constable of Leicestershire* [2002] 2 A.C. 122 at [46], [92].

466 [2011] H.R.L.R. 23 at [12].

467 *R. (on the application of Greenfield) v Secretary of State for the Home Department* [2005] 1 W.L.R. 673 HL at [19].

468 Above para.50-092 and following.

469 [2015] 1 W.L.R. 1833 (QB).

470 [2015] 1 W.L.R. 1833 (QB) at [40].

471 But note that an award of exemplary damages to the claimant may breach the Convention if the award is so high that it disproportionately interferes with the defendant's enjoyment of their Convention rights: see para.50-156, below. However, this principle is only potentially relevant where the defendant is a private individual as possibly a hybrid public authority: see para.50-012, above.

472 Above para.50-097.

473 (1703) 2 Ld. Raym. 938 at 955.

474 [1964] A.C. 1129 at 1226–1228.

basic interests by public defendants, but not in a field such as human rights law, which is specifically constituted to restrain public authorities and which protects the most fundamental of interests.

**50-116** Domestic courts are not invariably bound by Strasbourg practice under art.41; pursuant to s.8(4) of the HRA English courts are only required to take Strasbourg material into account, while it has been accepted that the mirror approach should not be followed to the extent it would cut across an important feature of domestic law.[475] Further, the role of the Strasbourg Court, as an international supervisory court, differs from that of domestic courts, which have primary responsibility for protecting rights and granting remedies, which in turn means that international and domestic remedial practice may legitimately differ.[476] The terms of the HRA refer to "damages" not "compensation", so that the language of the Act does not preclude exemplary awards. Section 9(3) expressly limits awards for judicial acts performed in good faith to compensation (to the extent required by art.5(5))—but there is no such limitation in s.8 of the Act in respect of all other classes of case.

## 6. DAMAGES UNDER PARTICULAR CONVENTION ARTICLES

**50-117** Having thus discussed the principles governing awards of damages under the HRA, it is finally appropriate to give consideration to some of the principal individual articles under the Convention pursuant to which claims for damages are likely to be made.

### (1) Article 2: The Right to Life

**50-118** The right to life[477] is one of the most basic of all the rights protected by the Convention. Damages would of course be available in a case of intentional killing. However, cases of most relevance, and which have featured prominently in domestic law, are those involving breach of the positive operational obligation under art.2 to take reasonable steps to protect an individual from a known threat to life. In such cases damages have been recovered for suffering experienced by the deceased in the lead up to their death, and for bereavement by close relatives of the deceased.

**50-119** In respect of unintentional killing, for example within the law of negligence, domestic law provides a significant remedy, for example to dependants (a category widely defined under the Fatal Accidents Act 1976) who are deprived of a person on whom they were dependent as a result of the tortfeasor's negligence. In the circumstances, it is unlikely that there will be much scope for an action under the HRA for damages for pecuniary loss which is not fully covered by the statutory cause of action under the Fatal Accidents Act.

**50-120** However, in relation to non-pecuniary loss, there is a significant lacuna in English domestic law caused by the limited scope of the action for bereavement. Under the

---

[475] *Manchester City Council v Pinnock* [2011] 2 A.C. 104 at [48].

[476] Above para.50-004, 50-082.

[477] The full text of Art.2 is: "1. Everyone's right to life shall be protected by law. No one shall be deprived of his life intentionally save in the execution of a sentence of a court following his conviction of a crime for which this penalty is provided by law. 2. Deprivation of life shall not be regarded as inflicted in contravention of this Article when it results from the use of force which is no more than absolutely necessary: (a) in defence of any person from unlawful violence; (b) in order to effect a lawful arrest or to prevent the escape of a person lawfully detained; (c) in action taken lawfully for the purpose of quelling a riot or insurrection".

Fatal Accidents Act, the right is limited to the recovery of a statutory amount by spouses or the parents of under-age children who are killed.[478] However, it is difficult to see how a parent of an 18-year-old who is killed is any the less bereaved than the parent of a 17-year-old. Furthermore, a child whose mother or father is killed might well be significantly bereaved, and yet have no remedy for non-pecuniary loss. In such cases, where the death was caused by a public authority, such as an NHS hospital or in prison, a victim who is not a spouse or parent of a minor might well have a cause of action under s.8 of the HRA for the equivalent to bereavement damages, if able to satisfy the test laid down in *Osman v United Kingdom*.[479] In *Ogur v Turkey*[480] the court found that art.2 had been violated where the applicant's adult son had been killed and the authorities had failed to conduct an effective judicial investigation into the circumstances of his death. No pecuniary compensation was awarded as the file contained no evidence on the deceased's income, nor on the amount of financial assistance which he provided to his mother. However, non-pecuniary compensation of 100,000 FRF (equivalent to approximately £10,000) were awarded by the ECtHR. Similarly, in *Cakici v Turkey*,[481] the applicant claimed compensation arising out of the death of his brother who had been detained, tortured and killed by the security forces in breach of arts 2, 3, 5 and 13. The compensation was claimed on his own behalf and also on behalf of the deceased's heirs. The ECtHR awarded compensation for non-pecuniary loss of £2,500 to the applicant himself, and £25,000 for the deceased, to be held by the applicant in trust for the deceased's heirs. Finally, in *Tanrikulu v Turkey*,[482] where art.2 had been breached, the applicant claimed and secured an award of £15,000 compensation for non-pecuniary loss for herself and her three minor children. The ECtHR stated:

> "The court notes that the present case was brought by the applicant on behalf of herself, her deceased husband and their three minor children. The court accepts that the applicant and her children have suffered non-pecuniary damage which cannot be compensated solely by the findings of violations. Making its assessment on an equitable basis, the court awards the applicant the sum of £15,000, to be converted into Turkish Liras at the rate applicable at the date of payment."[483]

There is also the decision of the ECtHR in *Keenan v United Kingdom*,[484] discussed below.[485]

**50-121** The leading case on the award of damages under art.2 in domestic law is *Rabone v Pennine Care NHS Foundation Trust*,[486] in which the Supreme Court allowed the claimants' appeals against the refusal of the lower courts to award damages arising out of the death of their 24-year-old daughter who was a voluntary psychiatric patient at the defendant's hospital, and who committed suicide when on a home visit. The court held that, whilst in general in cases involving medical (clinical) negligence there is no operational duty, an exception applies to psychiatric patients detained in hospital, and no distinction is to be drawn between voluntary patients

---

478 See para.41-019, above.
479 (2000) 29 E.H.R.R. 245.
480 (2001) 31 E.H.R.R. 912.
481 (2001) 31 E.H.R.R. 5.
482 (2000) 30 E.H.R.R. 950.
483 (2000) 30 E.H.R.R. 950 at [13].
484 (2001) 33 E.H.R.R. 913.
485 In para.50-126, below.
486 [2012] 2 A.C. 72. See above paras 50-020, 50-068 and 50-090.

and those compulsorily detained when, very often, this is a matter of form rather than substance, the hospital having the power to intervene and prevent a patient from leaving where there is a real and immediate risk. In this case, the defendant not only owed the deceased an operational duty, but was in breach of that duty in failing to do all that it reasonably could have been expected to do to prevent the deceased's suicide. It was further held that family members (here, the deceased's parents) were entitled to bring claims in their own right under the HRA as victims of the breach of art.2. Whilst, had the deceased been under 18, the claimants' remedy would have been damages for bereavement under the Fatal Accidents Act, here there was no domestic remedy and damages were awardable under the HRA. The Supreme Court decided that, this being a bad case of breach of art.2, an award of damages was merited which was

> "well above the lower range of damages awarded to victims of a breach of art.2"

and upheld the sum of £5,000 to each claimant, awarded by the lower court, while noting the sum could have been higher, had the claimant challenged quantum.

**50-122** In principle, there seems no reason why this should not be extended to all "victims" who are family members and similarly bereaved by a death: siblings and grandparents for example. Indeed, there is no reason why those victims should not have a valid claim under the HRA where the deceased is under 18 and the domestic remedy is confined to the deceased's parents. The restricting factor will be the need to establish the "operational duty" which is more likely to be applied to those detained by the state, but may arise more generally where authorities know or ought to know of a real and immediate risk to an individual's life.

**50-123** Thus, a similar type of claim to that made in *Rabone*, albeit on different facts, was brought in *Van Colle v Chief Constable of Hertfordshire*.[487] The facts were that Giles van Colle ("Giles") was a material witness in a trial against an accused, Brougham, on charges of dishonesty, and there was what a disciplinary panel found to be "an escalating situation of intimidation" by Brougham against Giles and another prosecution witness, including a telephone call where he said:

> "I know where you live. I know where your businesses are and where your parents live. If you don't drop the charges you will be in danger."

This was reported by Giles to the police, but the police officer in question, DC Ridley (who was employed by the defendant), failed to take the steps he ought to have done. He accepted before a disciplinary tribunal that his failure to do so was an error of judgment. Giles was murdered by Brougham before the dishonesty trial took place and Brougham was subsequently sentenced to life imprisonment for the murder. The defendant was held to have owed the deceased a duty to take reasonable steps to protect him from a known, real and immediate risk to life, and had breached that duty. Awards were made both to the estate of the deceased and to the deceased's parents for bereavement. The Court of Appeal overturned the trial judge's award of £15,000 on behalf of the deceased's estate for the fear and distress which the deceased had suffered in the period leading up to his death, and £17,500 to each of his parents for their grief, anguish and distress. The Court of Appeal reduced these figures to £10,000 and £7,500 respectively.

**50-124** Claims for "art.2 damages" are now common and are frequently settled by NHS

[487] [2007] 1 W.L.R. 1821 CA.

Defendants. For example, in *AV (as personal representative of the estate of CV, deceased) v North West London Hospitals NHS Trust* (13/11/2012), the claimant received £11,000 in relation to the death of his father following the negligent mismanagement of his care at the defendant's hospital. He had suffered eight falls whilst admitted. The eighth fall resulted in an intra-cranial haemorrhage from which he did not recover. This was a pure art.2 claim, there being no right to bereavement under the Fatal Accidents Act 1976 for the death of a parent. The case of *Savage v South Essex Partnership NHS Foundation Trust*,[488] shares materially similar facts to *Rabone* (above). The defendant failed to fulfil the operational duty it owed to the claimant's mother, who was a mental patient in its care, with the result that the claimant's mother took her own life. A claim was brought for damages by the deceased's daughter. The Judge reasoned as follows in assessing damages, which were in the nature of bereavement damages,[489]

> "it is far from simple to discern the principles which the ECtHR applies. The diligence of counsel has provided me with two schedules. Miss Richards' schedule runs from the beginning of 2008 and sets out over 17 pages cases where that court has awarded compensation for non-pecuniary loss. The range is wide and seems to run from about €5,000–€60,000. She suggests £30,000 would be appropriate in this case. Mr Bishop reminds me that in *Van Colle* the Court of Appeal (whose decision was not in the event varied by the House of Lords in this respect) reduced the estate's compensation from £15,000 to £10,000 and the individual compensation to each parent from £17,500 to £7,500. I bear in mind that the claimant has openly stated that she has not brought this action for financial reward, as well as the fact that there is no element to be included for the so-called adjectival duty under art.2 [to conduct an effective investigation], there having been a full inquest which properly investigated this death. The amount I grant under this head, and I think it is right to make an award, can never compensate her for the loss of her mother and can only be a symbolic acknowledgment that the defendant ought properly to give her some compensation to reflect her loss. I assess the figure for just satisfaction purposes at £10,000".

## (2) Article 3: Prohibition of Torture

Article 3 provides: "No one shall be subjected to torture or to inhuman or degrading treatment or punishment." It can immediately be seen from the text of this article that, although it is entitled "prohibition of torture", it in fact covers a much wider sphere of activities. Thus inhuman or degrading treatment could include hospital treatment if the standard of such treatment were sufficiently low, and inhuman or degrading punishment includes the way that children are punished. Thus, if an elderly person, admitted to hospital, had to spend a number of hours on a trolley in a corridor because no bed was available, it is difficult to see why this could not constitute degrading treatment. The obligation to comply with this article is absolute, and the Article can be breached even if the state acts with the best of intentions.[490] The conduct complained of must cross a minimum threshold of severity to fall within art.3, and this depends on all the circumstances of the case including, for example, the sex, age and health of the victim. The State has a positive obligation to ensure compliance with art.3, even where the danger comes from **50-125**

---

[488] [2010] EWHC 865 (QB).

[489] [2010] EWHC 865 (QB) at [97].

[490] *MS v United Kingdom* (2012) 55 E.H.R.R. 23 at [34]; *ZH v Commissioner of Police of the Metropolis* [2013] 1 W.L.R. 3021 CA.

people who are not public officials, so that children and other vulnerable individuals such as mental patients are entitled to protection in the form of effective deterrence from breach of art.3.

**50-126** There have been many examples of successful applications being made to the ECtHR for breaches under this article, and it is perhaps instructive to cite some of those which have involved applications against the United Kingdom. The width of these examples shows how far beyond torture this article goes. In *Y v United Kingdom*,[491] the applicant, a 15-year-old schoolboy, was caned across his (clothed) buttocks by the headmaster of a private school, leaving four weals. No prosecution was brought and the domestic court rejected his claim for civil damages. He applied to the ECtHR alleging breach of, among others, art.3. Before the case reached the ECtHR, the Government agreed to pay the applicant £8,000 damages plus costs. In *A v United Kingdom*,[492] the applicant who was a child was severely beaten by his stepfather with a garden cane. The stepfather was acquitted of assault occasioning actual bodily harm, the defence being "reasonable chastisement". The applicant complained that the United Kingdom had failed to protect him from ill-treatment in breach of art.3. The Commission took the view that art.3 had been breached, and before the case came before the ECtHR, the Government undertook to amend domestic legislation and offered £10,000 as an ex gratia payment. In *Keenan v United Kingdom*,[493] the applicant was the mother of a mentally ill man who had been sent to prison for four months for assaulting his girlfriend and who committed suicide nine days before his release, having been given seven days' segregation in the punishment block as a disciplinary punishment together with an additional 28 days in prison. The ECtHR upheld the applicant's claim that her son had been subjected to inhuman and/or degrading treatment and awarded her £3,000 damages for non-pecuniary loss personally, with a further £7,000 to be held on behalf of her son's estate. In *Z v United Kingdom*,[494] the applicants suffered abuse and neglect at the hands of their parents, and complained that the local authority had failed to take adequate protective measures. They had no remedy in the domestic courts because English law did not impose an actionable duty of care. The ECtHR upheld their claim that there had been a breach of art.3 and awarded them £32,000 each by way of damages for non-pecuniary loss. The children had suffered serious abuse over a period exceeding four years leading to substantial pain and suffering. In making this award, the ECtHR considered that "the rates applied in domestic cases, though relevant, are not decisive". This case was discussed in *DSD v Commissioner of Police of the Metropolis* (above),[495] which also concerned breach of art.3, as an example of a case in which domestic scales influenced the award made by the ECtHR, with the effect that the award was higher than would ordinarily be the case. This higher level of award, spurred by taking into account English practice, in turn has been fed back into domestic damages practice under the HRA through application of the mirror approach in *DSD*, with the effect of helping to uplift awards under the HRA so that they more closely approximate to domestic English levels than the typically lower Strasbourg levels.

**50-127** A further case under art.3 where no finding of breach was made because, before that could happen, the parties entered into a friendly settlement was *JM v United*

---

[491] (1994) 17 E.H.R.R. 238.

[492] (1999) 27 E.H.R.R. 611.

[493] (2001) 33 E.H.R.R. 913.

[494] (2002) 34 E.H.R.R. 3.

[495] *DSD v Commissioner of Police of the Metropolis* [2015] 1 W.L.R. 1833 (QB). Above para.50-095.

*Kingdom*,[496] where the applicant had been raped by E, who then, in the course of defending himself at his trial, subjected the applicant to an appalling cross-examination lasting six days during which he questioned her about the rapes, her intimate medical history and her personal relations. This caused her to become ill for which she needed to be admitted to hospital, and she alleged breach of art.3. The Government made an ex gratia payment of £6,000 and legislation was introduced to limit the circumstances in which a defendant may personally cross-examine a rape victim.

Significant awards have been made in English courts for breach of the art.3 procedural duty to conduct effective investigations into allegations of torture or inhuman or degrading treatment by criminal third parties, including for free-standing distress and frustration, but also for recognised psychological injury and associated treatment costs consequential on such procedural failures. Awards of £5,000 for distress and frustration were made in the case of *O v Commissioner of Police of the Metropolis* discussed in detail above.[497] Awards of £19,000 and £22,250 were made in the important case of *DSD v Commissioner of Police of the Metropolis* discussed in detail above.[498] **50-128**

### (3) Article 5: Right to Liberty and Security

Article 5 provides that, with certain exceptions and in accordance with a procedure prescribed by law, no one shall be deprived of his liberty. Again, in relation to this article, there is a substantial overlap with English domestic law which will usually provide a sufficient remedy. This is one of the most important articles of the Convention for the purposes of actions for damages under the HRA, and covers such matters as arrest and detention in custody, and the compulsory detention of mentally ill patients. For any deprivation of liberty to be lawful under the Convention, it must fall within one of the exceptions set out in sub-paragraphs (a) to (f). The exceptions are to be interpreted narrowly.[499] By art.5(2), everyone who is arrested has the right to be informed promptly, and in a language which he understands, of the reasons for his arrest and of any charge against him. By art.5(3), anyone who is lawfully arrested or detained is to be brought promptly before a judge or other authorised officer, and is entitled to a trial within a reasonable time, or to be released pending trial. A person who is arrested or detained is entitled to take proceedings under which the lawfulness of the arrest or detention is to be decided speedily by a court: Article 5(4). Finally, by art.5(5), everyone who has been the victim of arrest or detention in contravention of art.5 has an enforceable right to compensation. **50-129**

In *Caballero v United Kingdom*,[500] where the applicant had been automatically denied bail when charged with rape because of a previous conviction for manslaughter, it was conceded by the Government that there had been a breach of art.5(3). In awarding the applicant £1,000 damages for non-pecuniary loss, the ECtHR noted that relatively small awards were made for non-pecuniary loss for breach of art.5(3). The award of £1,000 was made on an "equitable" basis in view **50-130**

---

[496] (2000) 30 E.H.R.R. CD57.

[497] [2011] H.R.L.R. 29 (QB). See para.50-064 above.

[498] [2015] 1 W.L.R. 1833 (QB). See para.50-091 and following, above.

[499] *Winterwerp v The Netherlands* (1996) 22 E.H.R.R. 533.

[500] (2000) 30 E.H.R.R. 643.

of uncontradicted affidavit evidence that the applicant would have had a "good chance" of bail.[501]

**50-131** So far as claims under the HRA arising from breach of art.5 are concerned, *R. (on the application of KB) v Mental Health Review Tribunal* remains an important authority.[502] In six of the eight claims, modest awards of damages were made, the highest being £4,000 and the lowest being £750. The individual decisions were as follows:

*Claimant PD*[503]

> "The evidence does not justify a finding that the RMO should have discharged PD at an earlier date, or that a tribunal hearing if held at an earlier date would have directed his discharge, and the claim for loss of opportunity was not pursued. There is no evidence of injury to his health resulting from the delay in the hearing of his application, and no specific evidence of distress or frustration. Nonetheless, such a long delay, and the repeated cancellations of hearings, must have been upsetting, and caused uncertainty as to his position. A modest award of damages is necessary in order to give just satisfaction, in the sum of £1,000."

*Claimant KB*[504]

> "Given the relatively short period of delay in KB's case and the absence of any contemporaneous record of significant (or any) distress or the like, in my judgment the finding of breach of his rights under art.5(4) is sufficient just satisfaction, and no award of damages is necessary in his case."

*Claimant LB*[505]

> "Given that the total delay in LB's case was not substantial ... and the contemporaneous evidence of her mental state, and the fact that she was on leave for much of the latter period of her section, I conclude that the finding of infringement of LB's convention right is sufficient just satisfaction."

*Claimant GM*[506] In this case, Tribunal hearings were cancelled for 16 July, 6 August, 4 September, and 27 September. Finally, a hearing fixed for 18 October did take place, and the claimant was ordered to be released with effect from 15 November. The time between application and hearing was almost 19 weeks. Stanley Burnton J said:

> "Bearing in mind the period of delay, the repeated cancellations, and the confirmation by a member of staff of distress caused by one or more cancellations, I conclude that the breaches of art.5 must have caused sufficient distress

[501] By way of contrast consider *SBC v United Kingdom* (2002) 34 E.H.R.R. 21 where the ECtHR was not persuaded that the applicant would have been released on bail but for the breach.
[502] [2004] Q.B. 936.
[503] [2004] Q.B. 936 at [79]–[81].
[504] [2004] Q.B. 936 at [82]–[84].
[505] [2004] Q.B. 936 at [85]–[97].
[506] [2004] Q.B. 936 at [98]–[107].

and frustration to make necessary an award of damages. The appropriate sum is £1,000."

*Claimant JR*[507] As with the case of GM, there were cancellations of Tribunal hearings which were found to induce frustration in JR and one such cancellation caused "real distress that affected his mental state and behaviour, if not his mental health." In awarding damages of £4,000, the learned judge said:

> "Damages must take into account the fact that because no hearing was held in September, JR lost the opportunity to be discharged. On the other hand, I do not think it right to assume that if he had been discharged in September, he would necessarily have stayed out of hospital until January, when he was in fact discharged ... A substantial award of damages is necessary, bearing in mind the length of the delay before an effective hearing, the number of cancellations, the effect of the cancellations on JR, the fact that, as I find, he would have been discharged by a tribunal hearing in September. Mr Gledhill and Mr Mullins submitted that the damages which should be awarded to the claimants were in the range £1,000 to £4,000. The damages to which JR is entitled are at the top of this range. The damages in his case will be in the sum of £4,000."

*Claimant MK*[508]

> "The defendants accept that an award of damages is necessary in this case. MK must be compensated for having remained detained in a minimum secure ward (Hume Ward at Springfield Hospital), rather than an open ward, in which she had agreed to remain as an informal patient. The impact of her wrongful detention was considerably less serious than in *R. v Governor of Brockhill Prison, Ex p. Evans (No.2)* [1998] 4 All E.R. 993, [1999] Q.B. 1043, where but for the wrongful detention of the claimant he would have been released from prison. In my judgment, the appropriate amount is £1,000."

*Claimant TB*[509]

> "TB's judicial review proceedings were commenced on 8 January 2002. Their purpose was to secure the hearing of his application. No allegation of distress or injury to health was made. It is not suggested that an earlier hearing of his application would have resulted in his discharge, or any greater chance of discharge than in January 2002. TB sought a decision from the tribunal that he be conditionally discharged. The independent psychiatrist instructed by his solicitors, Dr Pierzhchniak, reported on 22 October 2001 that he continued to suffer from a mental illness of a nature and degree that warranted his detention in hospital. Neither the ASW nor his RMO supported conditional discharge. There were three cancellations, and the period of delay was considerable. While TB could have had no great expectation of a conditional discharge, the period of uncertainty must have had a sufficient effect on him to make an award of damages necessary to give just satisfaction. The amount of damages appropriate is modest: in my judgment, the sum of £750."

*Claimant B*[510]

507 [2004] Q.B. 936 at [108]–[122].
508 [2004] Q.B. 936 at [123]–[127].
509 [2004] Q.B. 936 at [128]–[129].
510 [2004] Q.B. 936 at [130]–[131].

> "The period between application and effective hearing was eight months, an unjustified multiple of the eight weeks laid down in the rules. (This period is not necessarily a maximum for an effective hearing: adjournments may be required, as was the first adjournment in B's case.) The delay was caused by multiple adjournments, and resulted from a failure of case management.... The uncertainty experienced by B over such a considerable period of time requires a modest award of damages to afford just satisfaction. The amount of damages is £1,000."

These cases are self-explanatory.

50-132 In *R. (on the application of Sturnham) v Parole Board*,[511] the Supreme Court considered claims arising out of delay in consideration of release by the Parole Board amounting to breach of art.5.4. In such cases, where the prisoner cannot prove that, but for the delay, he would have been released, he will nevertheless generally receive a modest award of damages for feelings of frustration and anxiety where the period of delay has been for three months or more. The award in that case was £300 damages to Mr Sturnham, where there had been a six-month delay in the hearing by the Parole Board, thereby occasioning feelings of anxiety and frustration. Awards will, of course, be significantly greater where the claimant can prove that, but for the breach, he or she would have been released earlier, albeit if the prisoner's liberty upon release would have been conditional (i.e. on licence) then the award will not be as high as if the liberty lost was unconditional. In the case of the co-appellant, Mr Faulkner, release from custody was delayed by some ten months, Lord Reed said

> "[o]nce the court has found on a balance of probabilities that the claimant would have been released earlier if there had been no violation, he should ordinarily be fully compensated for the harm which he has suffered".[512]

In terms of quantum he said

> "it appears to me that an award in the region of £6,500 would adequately compensate Mr Faulkner for his delayed release, bearing in mind the conditional and precarious nature of the liberty foregone."[513]

In the subsequent case of *Osborn v Parole Board* Lord Reed said,

> "A breach of the requirements of procedural fairness under art.5(4) will not normally result in an award of damages under s.8 of the Human Rights Act unless the prisoner has suffered a consequent deprivation of liberty".[514]

In combination with the decision in *Sturnham* this suggests that whereas damages for distress may be recovered relatively freely in an art.5(4) delay case, such awards will not in general be made for breach of the procedural requirements of art.5(4) other than speediness, such as, for example, failure to afford an oral hearing where one was required. However, as a matter of principle it is not clear why such a distinction should be drawn: why should loss caused by a delay be recoverable but not loss caused by some other procedural flaw? Indeed, in *Osborn* Lord Reed had, elsewhere in his judgment, cited empirical research demonstrating that prisoners feel frustration, anger and despair as a result of being subject to unfair

---

511 [2013] 2 A.C. 254.
512 [2013] 2 A.C. 254 at [84].
513 [2013] 2 A.C. 254 at [87].
514 [2014] A.C. 1115.

procedures.[515] Further, while, as discussed above,[516] this approach is consistent with statements of principle by the ECtHR, as a matter of practice— which is the salient inquiry for the purposes of the mirror approach[517]—the ECtHR has often made awards for assumed distress for breaches of the procedural requirements of arts 5(4) (and 5(3))[518] other than the speediness requirement. Indeed, this practice was cited in both *Sturnham* and *Osborn*.[519]

The general approach to compensation for mere distress articulated in *R. (on the application of Sturnham) v Parole Board*,[520] was followed in the subsequent case of *R. (on the application of Haney) v Secretary of State for Justice*.[521] As discussed above,[522] in that case prisoners suffered breach of art.5 on the basis of the defendant's failure to comply with the implied duty under art.5 to provide reasonable opportunities to prisoners to rehabilitate themselves and demonstrate they no longer presented an unacceptable danger to the public, this duty being viewed as a close cousin of art.5(4). The prisoners had not been able to sufficiently progress towards release on or after the expiry of their tariff periods because of a lack of provision for such reasonable opportunities for rehabilitation. By analogy with the guidance in *Sturnham* prisoners who suffered over three months' delay before being afforded reasonable opportunities to progress their rehabilitation were granted modest awards of £500 and £600 respectively, each for frustration and delay suffered over approximately one year. The differential in awards was due to the prisoner who received the higher sum having suffered the relevant delay following the expiry of their tariff period, which was considered to exacerbate frustration and distress. **50-133**

### (4) Article 6: Right to a Fair Trial

Article 6(1) provides, inter alia, that in the determination of his civil rights and obligations or of any criminal charge against him, everyone is entitled to a fair and public hearing within a reasonable time by an independent and impartial tribunal established by law. Article 6(2) enacts a presumption of innocence in criminal law. Article 6(3) provides for certain minimum rights for everyone charged with a criminal offence. **50-134**

Breach of art.6 has given rise to more applications to the ECtHR than breach of any other article of the Convention, but not uncommonly the ECtHR has been content to hold that a finding of breach is sufficient to satisfy the requirement of just satisfaction, and often no award of damages is made, except where the breach is caused by delay. In particular, given that the scope of the Article is in respect of procedural matters, the ECtHR is frequently unwilling to speculate as to the outcome of the proceedings but for the procedural breach,[523] albeit domestic courts may be able to reach conclusions where the ECtHR could not give the greater **50-135**

---

515 [2014] A.C. 1115 at [70].

516 Above para.50-048 and following.

517 Above para.50-053 and following.

518 See above para.50-130.

519 [2013] 2 A.C. 254 at [61]; [2014] A.C. 1115 at [114].

520 [2013] 2 A.C. 254.

521 [2015] A.C. 1344.

522 Above para.50-063.

523 See, e.g. *Magee v United Kingdom* (2001) 31 E.H.R.R. 822. There appears to be little consistency as to when the court simply makes no award or when it is prepared to make an award for loss of opportunity, as in *Delta v France* (1993) 16 E.H.R.R. 574.

capacity of domestic courts to hear evidence and conduct fact-finding.[524] Alternatively, the court may award a global sum "on an equitable basis" without dividing up the award between pecuniary and non-pecuniary loss.[525] The court may, however, award even fairly substantial damages under the head of non-pecuniary loss where it feels that the applicant has lost something of substance, but is not willing to make an award of damages for pecuniary loss. Thus, in *Krcmar v Czech Republic*,[526] the domestic court had based its decision on documentation which had not been disclosed to the parties, in breach of art.6. Substantial sums were claimed representing the value of the company which had been the subject of the domestic proceedings. Whilst making no pecuniary award as the ECtHR was not prepared to speculate as to the outcome of those proceedings, it awarded the equivalent of approximately £23,000 by way of damages for non-pecuniary loss.[527]

**50-136** One of the most significant awards for non-pecuniary loss was in the case of *Allenet de Ribemont*,[528] where the applicant had been implicated by the French Minister of the Interior in the murder of a member of the French Parliament. The applicant was charged but eventually released and he failed in his attempt to secure compensation in the domestic court. The ECtHR found breaches of art.6(1) and (2) taking into consideration a total delay of 11 years, 8 months. The applicant was awarded damages of FF2,000,000 (then equivalent to approximately £240,000) on the basis that although the court did not accept the applicant's reasoning in relation to his pecuniary loss (he having argued that the Minister's statement had caused his insolvency and ruin) it did accept that the accusations were serious and must have diminished the trust placed in him by people with whom he did business.

**50-137** Often a breach of art.6 is found in conjunction with a breach of another Convention right, the procedural breach aggravating the substantive breach so as to justify an award of damages. The most common examples are cases of breaches of parents and/or children's rights under both arts 6 and 8 in the context of care proceedings, on which see below.[529]

**50-138** In common with delay cases under art.5(4),[530] the ECtHR has routinely made awards in cases of procedural delay which constitute violations of art.6.[531] It has been prompted to do so in response to systemic delays in the court systems of several member states, which have led to huge numbers of repeat claims to the Court. The right to a hearing within a reasonable time will be all the more important if, because of the personal characteristics of the applicant, time is of the essence, for example if he has a terminal illness. This was the situation in *X v France*,[532] where the applicant was a haemophiliac and was infected with HIV by reason of a blood transfusion, and subsequently developed AIDS. The ECtHR, in finding a breach of art.6 arising out of the time the proceedings took, stated that exceptional diligence was called for in the circumstances. Damages of FF150,000 for non-

524 See paras 50-054 and 50-100, above.
525 As in, e.g. *Dulaurans v France* (2001) 33 E.H.R.R. 1093.
526 (2001) 31 E.H.R.R. 953.
527 See, also, *Kuopila v Finland* (2001) 33 E.H.R.R. 615 and *Guillemin v France* (1998) 25 E.H.R.R. 435.
528 (1995) 20 E.H.R.R. 557.
529 Below para.50-150 to 50-151.
530 See para.50-132, above.
531 *HL v United Kingdom* (2005) 40 E.H.R.R. 32 at [149]; *Scordino v Italy* (2007) 45 E.H.R.R. 7.
532 (1992) 14 E.H.R.R. 483.

pecuniary loss (then approximately £15,000) were awarded.[533] One of the largest awards for breach of the right to a hearing within a reasonable time, in the context of criminal proceedings, was *Philis v Greece*,[534] in which the ECtHR awarded 1.5 million Greek drachmas (then approximately £33,000) where criminal proceedings lasted over five years and ancillary disciplinary proceedings lasted more than nine years, seven of which were within the jurisdiction of the domestic court. As with other breaches of art.6(1), a failure to provide a hearing within a reasonable time will be considered to be a serious aggravation of a substantive breach such as the right to family life in care proceedings: *H v United Kingdom*.[535]

The scope of the domestic courts to make awards of damages for violation of art.6 was considered, and significantly limited, by the House of Lords in *R. (on the application of Greenfield) v Secretary of State for the Home Department*.[536] Lord Bingham, giving the judgment of the court, said that, in general, a finding of violation of art.6 will be sufficient "just satisfaction" and that this is a principle which clearly underlies the jurisprudence of the ECtHR. Whether an award will be made will depend on the requirements of justice in the individual case and the strength of the case in relation to proof of causation. Despite the reality that many awards have been made in structural bias cases,[537] Lord Bingham concluded that "the ordinary practice is not to make an award in cases of structural bias".[538] He added that the pursuit of damages should rarely if ever be an end in itself in an art.6 case.[539] Even in the rare case where a court is persuaded that an award of damages for violation of art.6(1) is appropriate, it was made clear that the quantum will be modest. **50-139**

In *Connors v United Kingdom*,[540] the ECtHR found that there had been a breach of art.8 alone where the applicant and his family, who were gypsies, were evicted from a site run by the local authority without being given the opportunity to challenge in a court the allegations made against him and his family. It was held that the power to evict without the burden of giving reasons liable to be examined as to their merits by an independent tribunal did not respond to any specific goal or provide any specific benefit to members of the gypsy community. Accordingly the eviction of the applicant and his family was not attended by the requisite procedural safe-guards, namely the requirement to establish proper justification for the serious interference with his rights, and consequently could not be regarded as justified. The reference to the requisite procedural safeguards and the opportunity for the merits of the decision to be examined by an independent tribunal shows that, although the decision was only of violation of art.8, this was, in reality, a combined breach of arts 6(1) and 8. The ECtHR concluded that the applicant suffered non-pecuniary damage through feelings of frustration and injustice, that the finding of violation was not sufficient compensation, and they awarded him €14,000. **50-140**

Two cases in which the ECtHR awarded damages to a British applicant for breach of art.6 alone are *Hooper v United Kingdom*,[541] and *Beggs v United* **50-141**

---

533 See, also, *Vallee v France* (1994) 18 E.H.R.R. 549 where, in respect of another haemophiliac, the culpable delay was over four years and FF200,000 were awarded (approximately £23,000).

534 (1998) 25 E.H.R.R. 417.

535 (1991) 13 E.H.R.R. 449.

536 [2005] 1 W.L.R. 673 HL.

537 See para.50-066, above.

538 [2005] 1 W.L.R. 673 at [16].

539 [2005] 1 W.L.R. 673 at [30].

540 (2005) 40 E.H.R.R. 9.

541 (2005) 41 E.H.R.R. 1.

*Kingdom*.[542] In *Hooper* the applicant, after making a disturbance in the Magistrates' Court, had been summarily bound over to keep the peace with 28 days' imprisonment in default of his own recognisance and/or a suitable surety. Neither the applicant nor his lawyer was given any opportunity to make representations about the terms of the order, and in the event he was imprisoned for 14 days. The ECtHR found that there had been violations of art.6(1) and (3) and awarded the applicant €8,000 for non-pecuniary damage. The applicant had claimed £10,000 for the detention and an additional £1,000 for "the distress caused by the failure of the court to hear him in his defence". So far as causation is concerned, the ECtHR referred to the fact that Mance J assessed that the magistrate

> "might well have been persuaded to a different result if the applicant's counsel had been able to make representations concerning the order".

The ECtHR said that, while this conclusion was not expressed in such strong terms as in, for example, *Perks v United Kingdom*,[543] it considered that it was sufficient to support the applicant's claim that he had suffered some loss of opportunity due to the breach in this case. In *Beggs* the applicant was convicted of murder and the appeal process lasted over 10 years. Although a substantial period of the ten-year delay in dealing with the criminal appeal had been attributable to the complainant's own conduct, there had been delays by the authorities in handing down judgment on a preliminary matter and the final appeal had been unreasonable and in breach of art.6(1). The applicant claimed £16,400 in respect of non-pecuniary damage. The Court stated:[544]

> "The Court considers that the applicant suffered some frustration resulting from delays attributable to the authorities, which cannot sufficiently be compensated by the finding of a violation. Taking into account the contributory delay imputable to the applicant and ruling on an equitable basis, the Court awards him £2,000 in respect of non-pecuniary damage."[545]

## (5) Article 8: Right to Respect for Private and Family Life

**50-142** Article 8 provides:

> "1. Everyone has the right to respect for his private and family life, his home and his correspondence.
>
> 2. There shall be no interference by a public authority with the exercise of this right except as is in accordance with the law and is necessary in a democratic society in the interests of national security, public safety or the economic well-being of the country, for the prevention of disorder or crime, for the protection of health or morals, or for the protection of the rights and freedoms of others."

It can be seen that art.8 essentially protects four rights or interests, namely private life, family life, home and correspondence.

**50-143** Article 8 provided one of the first occasions when the English courts considered a claim for breach of the Convention under the HRA and awarded damages for such

[542] (2013) 56 E.H.R.R 26.
[543] (2000) 30 E.H.R.R. 33.
[544] (2013) 56 E.H.R.R 26 at [286].
[545] A similar result was reached in *Minshall v United Kingdom* (2012) 55 E.H.R.R. 36.

breach. In *R. (on the application of Bernard) v Enfield LBC*,[546] a decision of Sullivan J, the defendants' breach of the claimants' art.8 rights involved the claimants living in deplorable conditions for a period of about 20 months. The total sum awarded was £10,000, divided between the claimants as to £8,000 for the severely disabled wife and £2,000 for her carer husband.

*CH v Metropolitan Council* involved a successful claim for loss of conjugal relations.[547] CH was born suffering Downs Syndrome. He married WH and they lived together in CH's parent's home. Given CH's needs the defendant had certain responsibilities towards him. CH and WH had sought fertility treatment and in consequence CH had been assessed by a psychologist to determine his capacity to consent to sexual relations; it was determined he lacked capacity. As such WH was advised she must abstain from sexual intercourse with CH. The psychologist made it clear that CH needed a course of sex education to assist him to achieve the necessary capacity to resume sexual relations. Ultimately he undertook such education, reached necessary capacity, and CH and WH were able to resume their ordinary conjugal relationship. The source of the breach of art.8 was that the defendant, once advised of the need for provision of sex education to CH, had acquiesced from implementing this advice, the actionable delay being held to be not less than 12 months. The defendant proposed a settlement that included a formal apology to CH, payment to CH of £10,000 in HRA damages, and payment of various legal costs. The Judge approved the settlement. In evaluating the quantum of damages the Judge conceptualised the award as being for the loss of conjugal relations. There was no evidence of long term impact on CH. However, the impact on him during the delay must have been profound not only because of the loss of relations but also because he would have been unable to understand the reasons for the loss of relations, and WH had withdrawn to another bedroom and withheld much physical affection so as not to "lead him on". The Judge found it difficult to locate comparators but he considered that an award in excess of £20,000 would not be warranted, while the lower end of the relevant scale would be less than £10,000. Though it was towards the lower end of the range, three factors persuaded the Judge to approve the proposed settlement award: (1) WH had pursued her own claim against the defendant and the defendant had agreed to pay CH's costs incurred in proceedings in the Court of Protection, which would mean no monies could be recouped by the Legal Aid Authority from the damages award; (2) the award was accompanied by a public apology; (3) the agreement of the settlement averted contested proceedings which could involve intrusive inquiries into CH and WH's sexual relationship. **50-144**

Claims for damages under art.8 came before the Court of Appeal in the case of *Anufrijeva v Southwark London Borough Council*.[548] The Court of Appeal took this opportunity to consider in detail the power of the courts to award damages for breach of the Convention and how that power should be exercised. The court concluded that Sullivan J had been correct to accept that art.8 is capable of imposing on a State a positive obligation to provide support, but continued[549]: **50-145**

> "We find it hard to conceive, however, of a situation in which the predicament of an individual will be such that art.8 requires him to be provided with welfare support, where his predicament is not sufficiently severe to engage art.3. Article 8 may more readily be

---

546 [2003] H.R.L.R. 4 (Admin). See above at para.50-061.

547 [2017] EWCOP 12.

548 [2004] Q.B. 1124 CA.

549 [2004] Q.B. 1124 CA at [43].

engaged where a family unit is involved. Where the welfare of children is at stake, art.8 may require the provision of welfare support in a manner which enables family life to continue."

50-146 The Court of Appeal next considered the circumstances in which maladministration will be found to have constituted a breach of art.8. It was held that before inaction can amount to a lack of respect for private and family life, there must be an element of culpability, and at least a knowledge that the claimant's private and family life is at risk. The Court of Appeal also emphasised the need to have regard to resources when considering the obligations imposed upon the State, and they concluded that maladministration will only infringe art.8 where the consequence is serious. The Court's reticence in recognising this duty, based in its concern for the burden that it would place on authorities, filtered through to a cautious approach to damages for breach of such duty:

"The factors that weigh against recognising administrative delay as engaging art.8 militate equally in favour of either no award or modest awards where art.8 is engaged".[550]

The Court thus placed weight on the impact awards might have on public services in prescribing that awards should be uncommon and modest. Though, as discussed above,[551] this is, with respect, a questionable factor for a court to consider in making decisions over damages, and those concerns had already been taken into account in calibrating the tests for breach, with the result that the threshold for breach was very high and violations would be uncommon. Moreover, given the threshold for breach, violations would only be found in the most serious cases, characterised by culpability on the part of the defendant, so that such cases would, with respect, be the very sort of cases where one might expect awards to be warranted. However, no awards were made on the facts.

50-147 Article 8 was also successfully relied upon at first instance to found a claim for damages in *Marcic v Thames Water Utilities Ltd*,[552] in which the claimant's property was seriously affected by flooding. His Honour Judge Richard Havery QC dismissed claims in nuisance and negligence, but upheld the claim for damages under the HRA on the basis that the defendant's failure to carry out works to bring an end to the continuing nuisance constituted a breach of art.8 in relation to the claimant's home. However, when the case reached the House of Lords, their Lordships found no breach of the Convention.[553] In *Dobson v Thames Water Utilities Ltd*, a restrictive approach was taken to claims for recovery of HRA damages, for breach of art.8, by occupants of properties (who did not have proprietary interests in those properties) who were affected over a significant period by mosquitoes and smells due to the operation of the defendant's nearby sewage treatment plant.[554] The case is discussed in detail above.[555] Awards were denied on the basis that, inter alia, the claimants would receive a declaration, various statutory procedures were open to them, and awards had been made in nuisance to those with proprietary interests in the properties. Thus it was concluded that damages were not necessary to afford the

---

550 [2004] Q.B. 1124 CA at [76].

551 Above paras 50-074 to 50-075.

552 [2002] Q.B. 929.

553 [2004] 2 A.C. 42.

554 [2011] EWHC 3253 (TCC), applying the approach elaborated in *Dobson v Thames Water Utilities Ltd* [2009] 3 All E.R. 319 CA.

555 Above para.50-069.

claimants just satisfaction. As discussed above, it is, with respect, difficult to see how any of the three "remedies" invoked by the Judge operate to adequately redress losses suffered by the claimant occupiers.[556]

Attempts to claim damages in reliance on art.8 have met with less success in a number of different contexts. In *R. (on the application of Morris) v London Borough of Newham*,[557] Jackson J dismissed the claimant's claim for damages where the defendant had failed to provide housing, holding that a homeless person cannot rely on art.8 to found a damages claim for failure to provide accommodation in the absence of special circumstances that interfered with family life, applying the decision of the ECtHR in *O'Rourke v United Kingdom*.[558] Similarly, in *R. (on the application of Gezer) v Secretary of State for the Home Department*,[559] Moses J rejected a claim for damages for breach of art.8 arising out a decision of the National Asylum Support Agency to disperse to Glasgow the claimant and his family who were Turkish/Kurdish asylum seekers. **50-148**

A very restrictive approach to the award of damages was adopted by the Supreme Court in *Shahid v Scottish Ministers*.[560] In that case the petitioner, a prisoner, had been subjected to segregation for the very long period of 56 months. Segregation was held to infringe the prisoner's art.8 rights. The main question before the Court was whether this infringement could be justified. Certain periods of segregation were held to have been unlawful as they were tainted by non-compliance with procedural requirements imposed by the Prison Rules. These periods of segregation could not be justified as proportionate because the segregation was not in accordance with law. More generally the 56-month period of segregation was held to be a disproportionate interference with art.8 as, despite the risks to prisoners posed by such prolonged segregation, no consideration was given to possible less intrusive alternatives and no meaningful management plan had been developed for the prisoner's re-integration into the prison population. However, when it came to damages, the Court made no award. In terms of the breaches of the Prison Rules, the Court determined the prisoner would have been segregated in any case if the powers had been exercised lawfully. In terms of the more general failure to consider alternatives and develop a management plan the Court considered it was not possible to say whether this had prolonged the prisoner's time in segregation. The Court then offered the following reasoning: **50-149**

> "Three matters are however clear. One is that it is not suggested that he suffered any severe or permanent injury to his health as a consequence of the prolongation of his segregation. Another is that the degree of interference with his private life which resulted from his removal from association with other prisoners was relatively limited, given the attitude of the other prisoners towards him. The third is that he was not isolated from all contact with other prisoners, and remained entitled to receive visits and to make telephone calls. In these circumstances, just satisfaction can be afforded by making a declaratory order, establishing that the appellant's Convention rights were violated, and by making an appropriate award of costs".[561]

With respect, it is difficult to see how segregation for 56 months from others, even

---

556 Above para.50-069.
557 [2002] EWHC 1262 (Admin).
558 Application No.39022/97, 26 June 2001.
559 [2003] EWHC 860 (Admin).
560 [2016] A.C. 429.
561 [2016] A.C. 429 at [89]–[90].

if some provision is made for telephone calls and visits, can be said to be a "relatively limited" interference with art.8, as it involves a serious deprivation of social relations over a very long and sustained period. The Court itself had emphasised, earlier in the judgment, how extraordinary such an extended period of segregation was, and the risks such segregation posed to prisoners. It is not clear why the Court was unwilling to infer distress and frustration in such a case, given it has been willing to do so in far less serious cases. For example, where a prisoner suffers a delay in the hearing of their case before the Parole Board of three months, distress and frustration is assumed and an award will generally be made.[562] As noted above, the Supreme Court's view in *Shahid* that an award of costs may form an aspect of a victim's remedy raises conceptual difficulties.[563]

**50-150** One context in which English courts have over time shown greater willingness to make awards is in the area of care of children. As noted above, HRA damages claims can be made in the Family Court, Court of Protection, and Family Division of the High Court.[564] While earlier decisions took a restrictive approach, suggesting awards would be rare in the care context,[565] there has been a liberalisation of approach, as observed by Judge Bellamy in *Re H (A Child: Breach of Convention Rights: Damages)*.[566] For example, in *Re C (A Child)* Wilson LJ said:

> "'I do not think', said Hedley J, 'that the concept of damages sits easily with the welfare jurisdiction of family law'. The instincts of most family lawyers will be likewise. But, by his conspicuously thorough and energetic submission, Mr Tolson has persuaded me that, as a result of the advent of the Human Rights Act 1998, such instincts are misplaced. In determining whether to award damages for infringement by a public authority of a person's rights under the Convention of 1950 and, if so, the amount of the award, the court must take into account the principles applied by the European Court of Human Rights in relation to the award of compensation under art.41…The kernel of both [s.8(3) of the Act and art.41 of the Convention] is that satisfaction to the person whose right has been infringed must be 'just' and that, if but only if such be 'necessary' in order to afford just satisfaction, an award of damages should be made … In general the 'principles' applied by the European Court, which we are thus enjoined to 'take into account', are not clear or coherent … What is clear, however, is that the European Court generally favours an award of damages in cases in which local authorities have infringed the right of parents under art.8 to respect for their family life by shortcomings in the procedures by which they have taken children into care or kept them in care, whether temporarily or permanently…".[567]

Although this case marked a liberalisation of the general approach, damages were nonetheless denied on the facts on the basis that the infringement was towards the less serious end of the spectrum. In this case the Court of Appeal upheld a decision not to award damages for breach of art.8 where there had been insufficient consultation with a child's natural mother before a decision had been taken to place the child for adoption, on the basis that whilst damages would generally be favoured where local authorities had infringed parents' right to respect for private and family life by shortcomings in the procedures by which they had taken children into

562 Above para.50-132.

563 Above para.50-072.

564 Above para.50-033.

565 e.g. *Re V (A Child)* [2005] 1 F.L.R. 627 CA at [38]. Albeit it should be noted the relevant breach in this case was of art.6.

566 [2014] EWFC 38 at [79]–[81].

567 [2007] EWCA Civ 2 at [61]–[64].

care or kept them in care, and whilst, in a real sense, every infringement was serious, the court had to place the infringement broadly on the spectrum of seriousness and on any objective view the instant case, on its facts, ranked at the lower end.

Claimants have experienced more success in subsequent care cases. In *Re H (A Child: Breach of Convention Rights: Damages)* the Judge was in "no doubt" that an award should be made to the parents of a child taken into care, whose rights under arts 6 and 8 were violated by the defendant authority's conduct of the case prior to care proceedings.[568] These failures included, inter alia, delay in the issue of proceedings, failure to involve the parents in the decision-making process, failure to explain all available options, failure to place sufficient weight on the parents' wishes, and as a result of the defendant's flawed procedures, separation of the parents from their child. The Judge determined that more than a declaration was required in the light of what the parents had had to live through as a result of the defendant's failures **50-151**

> "these parents' have suffered a loss of time with their daughter which was both unnecessarily lengthy and deeply distressing".[569]

It was relevant that this was their first child. The Judge found little guidance in the authorities as to quantum but observed that the Law Commissions had considered "children in public care" cases to form a distinct category, noting that parents have generally been successful at Strasbourg in recovering substantial awards in such cases and that the ECtHR has been willing to make awards for distress, loss of relationship with the child, and loss of opportunities, as well as generally being more willing to speculate as to losses.[570] In awarding £6,000 to each parent the Judge took into account the facts, the impact of the breaches on the parents who were learning disabled, the separation of parents and child for over a year in a context of unreasonable delay on the part of the authority, and that when the parents were ultimately able to apply for a residential assessment they were successful, as was the assessment that followed, which in turn led to the rehabilitation of the child to the care of her parents. Other claims have been successful. In *H (A Minor) v Northamptonshire County Council* the Court approved a sum of £21,500 to a child whose care had been mishandled by the defendant in breach of art.8.[571] In *Re CA (A Baby)* a claim for damages by the mother of a child was settled, with the defendant agreeing to pay damages, where the mother's consent should not, in the circumstances, have been sought for the purposes of s.20 of the Children Act 1989 and the removal of the child was not a proportionate response to the risks posed.[572]

British applicants have continued to find success in Strasbourg in art.8 claims. An example is *Connors v United Kingdom*,[573] where the ECtHR awarded the applicant €14,000 for breach of art.8 where he and his family had been evicted from **50-152**

---

568 [2014] EWFC 38.

569 [2014] EWFC 38 at [82].

570 Law Commission, *Damages under the Human Rights Act 1998* (2000), Law Com. No.266/Scot Law Com. No.180, Cm.4853, para.6.160. And see for example: *O v United Kingdom* (1991) 13 E.H.R.R. 578; *B v United Kingdom* (1991) 13 E.H.R.R. 588; *McMichael v United Kingdom* (1995) 20 E.H.R.R. 205.

571 [2017] EWHC 282 Fam. Note also the procedural guidance offered by the Judge in this case so as to protect damages awards as against the legal aid statutory charge: see para.50-036 above.

572 [2013] 1 F.C.R. 54 Fam.

573 (2005) 40 E.H.R.R. 9.

a gipsy site run by the local authority without being given the opportunity to challenge in a court the allegations made against him and his family. Although there was a finding of violation of art.8 alone, this was in reality a breach of both arts 6 and 8.[574] It is of some interest that in *Leeds City Council v Price*,[575] the Court of Appeal found that the decision of the ECtHR in *Connors* was inconsistent with the domestic decision of the House of Lords in *Harrow LBC v Qazi*.[576] The Court of Appeal declined, however, to follow *Connors* on the basis that the domestic rules of precedent and stare decisis require lower courts to follow the decisions of higher courts, and it is solely for the House of Lords to overrule *Qazi* on the basis of the decision in *Connors*.

**50-153** The decision in *Connors* came up for consideration again, in *Buckland v United Kingdom*,[577] which also concerned the eviction of the applicant who was a gypsy from a designated site. Before the expiry of the notice of termination of licence in January 2005, amendments to s.4 of the Caravan Sites Act 1968 came into force which introduced the possibility for possession orders to be suspended by a court on the application of the occupier for up to twelve months at a time. Eventually a possession order was made and the applicant exhausted her rights of appeal in the domestic courts. Before the application came before the ECtHR, the Supreme Court considered the relationship between orders for possession in such cases and art.8 in *Manchester City Council v Pinnock*,[578] and considered that, in order for domestic law to be compatible with art.8 of the Convention, where a court was asked by a local authority to make an order for possession of a person's home, the court had to have the power to assess the proportionality of making the order, and, in making that assessment, to resolve any relevant dispute of fact. In terms of the practical implications of this principle, the Supreme Court noted that if domestic law justified an outright order for possession, the effect of art.8 could, albeit in exceptional cases, justify granting an extended period for possession, suspending the order for possession on the happening of an event, or even refusing an order altogether. Finally, the court observed that the need for a court to have the ability to assess the art.8 proportionality of making a possession order in respect of a person's home might require certain statutory and procedural provisions to be revisited. In *Buckland* the ECtHR accepted that the applicant was directly affected by the making of the possession order, and it was further satisfied that the making of the possession order constituted an interference with her right to respect for her home. In alleging breach of art.8 the applicant claimed that she had been unable to challenge the claim for possession in the domestic proceedings. It was argued that the fact that she was able to apply for suspension provided insufficient procedural protection for the purposes of art.8. With this, the ECtHR agreed. It observed that the loss of one's home is:

> "the most extreme form of interference with the right to respect for the home. Any person at risk of an interference of this magnitude should in principle be able to have the proportionality of the measure determined by an independent tribunal in light of the relevant principles under art.8 of the Convention, notwithstanding that, under domestic law, his right to occupation has come to an end."

The ECtHR was influenced by the fact that the applicant was not able to argue that

574 See further para.50-140, above.
575 [2005] 1 W.L.R. 1825 CA.
576 [2004] 1 A.C. 983.
577 Application No.40060/08, 18 September 2012.
578 [2010] UKSC 45.

no possession order ought to have been made at all. The possibility of suspension for up to twelve months of the possession order was found to be inadequate, by itself, to provide the necessary procedural guarantees under art.8. It did mitigate the damage, though, and in relation to its finding of just satisfaction and awarding of damages, the court said:

> "Although the Court has found a procedural violation of art.8 of the Convention, it reiterates that it is not possible to speculate as to what would have been the outcome if the applicant had been able to contest the making of the possession order on the basis of her personal circumstances. However, it is satisfied that as a result of the making of a possession order which the applicant was unable to challenge, the applicant suffered some feelings of frustration and injustice. These are likely to have been mitigated by the power of the County Court to suspend the order for up to twelve months, a power which the court used in her case. The Court therefore awards the applicant EUR 4,000 in respect of non-pecuniary damage."

Given the often limited guidance that can be derived from Strasbourg jurisprudence, assistance may be derived from domestic awards made for the action of misuse of private information, first recognised in *Campbell v Mirror Group Newspapers Ltd*.[579] Albeit a claim in private law, the action's roots lie in human rights law, the House of Lords' recognition of the action being prompted by the positive obligations imparted on member states under art.8 to ensure privacy is protected not only from interference by public authorities, but also from interference by private individuals.[580] Since the modest award made in *Campbell* itself of £2,500, awards have grown considerably over time.[581] Significant damages were awarded in *Mosley v News Group Newspapers Ltd*,[582] where the claimant sought damages from the defendant newspaper publisher for unauthorised disclosure of personal information. One of the defendant's newspapers had published an article under the heading "F1 boss has sick Nazi orgy with 5 hookers", accompanied by a number of captioned images, which concerned an event attended by the claimant and five women involving sado-masochistic and some sexual activities and role play, although not in fact portraying Nazis. The action for misuse of private information was established, disclosure of sexual information being a serious breach of privacy. Turning to the question of damages, the learned judge awarded the sum of £60,000, observing that it was necessary to afford an adequate financial remedy for the purpose of acknowledging the infringement and compensating, to some extent, for the injury to feelings, the embarrassment and the distress caused. **50-154**

In *Gulati v MGN Ltd* significant awards were made for the action of misuse of private information in favour of multiple claimants who had been subjected to phone hacking by the defendant.[583] Mann J, whose approach was upheld by the Court of Appeal,[584] held that damages could be recovered not only for consequential losses such as distress but also for what he described as the lost right to control information. He was reinforced in this approach by the requirements of art.13 of the Convention. He articulated a tariff of £10,000 for each year of serious levels of **50-155**

---

579 [2004] 2 A.C. 457.

580 See for example *Von Hannover v Germany* (2006) 43 E.H.R.R. 7.

581 On damages practice in respect of the action for misuse of private information see generally: J. N. E. Varuhas, "Varieties of Damages for Breach of Privacy" in J.N.E. Varuhas and N.A. Moreham (eds.), *Remedies for Breach of Privacy* (Oxford: Hart Publishing, forthcoming 2018).

582 [2008] E.M.L.R. 20 at 679. See also *Cooper v Turrell* [2011] EWHC 3269 (QB).

583 [2015] EWHC 1482 Ch.

584 [2017] Q.B. 149 CA.

hacking, which could be uplifted or reduced depending on the facts of the particular case, including, for example, the frequency of hacking suffered.[585] Other more general guidance was articulated. For example if information accessed included medical information or information about significant financial matters the invasion of privacy would be greater and damages would be higher.[586] In terms of consequential non-pecuniary losses a thinner-skinned individual may suffer greater distress than a thicker-skinned individual and be entitled to greater sums. Significant awards were made to the claimants ranging from £72,500 to £260,250.

## (6) Article 10: Right to Freedom of Expression

**50-156** Article 10 provides:

> "1. Everyone has the right to freedom of expression. This right shall include freedom to hold opinions and to receive and impart information and ideas without interference by public authority and regardless of frontiers. This Article shall not prevent States from requiring the licensing of broadcasting, television or cinema enterprises.
>
> 2. The exercise of these freedoms, since it carries with it duties and responsibilities, may be subject to such formalities, conditions, restrictions or penalties as are prescribed by law and are necessary in a democratic society, in the interests of national security, territorial integrity or public safety, for the prevention of disorder or crime, for the protection of health or morals, for the protection of the reputation or rights of others, for preventing the disclosure of information received in confidence, or for maintaining the authority and impartiality of the judiciary."

There have been a number of cases recently where the applicant has complained that a finding against him or her of defamation combined with an award of damages in the domestic court constitutes a breach of the applicant's rights to freedom of expression under art.10. One of the questions that the ECtHR will consider in relation to such applications is the proportionality of the award of damages in the domestic court. Thus, in *Sorguc v Turkey*,[587] the ECtHR held that the amount of compensation awarded by the domestic court must "bear a reasonable relationship of proportionality to the … [moral] … injury … suffered" by the respondent in question, applying *Tolstoy Miloslavsky v United Kingdom*,[588] and *Steel and Morris v United Kingdom*,[589] where the Court held that the damages awarded, although relatively moderate by contemporary standards, were "very substantial when compared to the modest incomes and resources of the … applicants …" and, as such, were in breach of the Convention.[590] It is in response to decisions such as these – but also so as to ensure awards are not out of proportion to those for serious physical injury[591] that English courts have moderated the quantum of damages awarded for defamation, in the knowledge that excessive awards in comparison to the income and resources of the defendant against whom the award of compensation for defamation is being made will or may amount to a breach of that defendant's human right.

**50-157** An interesting application of art.10 came in the decision of the ECtHR in

---

585 [2015] EWHC 1482 Ch at [230].

586 [2015] EWHC 1482 Ch at [229].

587 Application No.17089/03, 23 June 2009.

588 (1995) 20 E.H.R.R. 442.

589 (2005) 31 E.H.R.R. 22.

590 See also *Independent Newspapers (Ireland) Ltd v Ireland*, Application No.28199/15, 15 June 2017.

591 *John v MGN Ltd* [1997] Q.B. 586 CA at 614.

*Aquilina v Malta*,[592] where the applicant journalists had been found by the Maltese courts to have defamed a lawyer by reporting that he had been found to have been in contempt of court in failing to turn up to a hearing to represent his client on a charge of bigamy. The domestic courts had not been satisfied that the evidence in fact supported the allegation, particularly in the absence of anything to that effect on the court record. In finding a breach of art.10, the ECtHR effectively acted as a final court of appeal, finding that the decision of the Maltese Courts was unsupportable in the light of the evidence which had been presented and that therefore:

> "in taking their decisions the domestic courts overstepped their margin of appreciation and the judgments against the applicants and the ensuing award of damages were disproportionate to the legitimate aim pursued. It follows that the interference with the applicants' exercise of their right to freedom of expression cannot be regarded as necessary in a democratic society for the protection of the reputation and rights of others."

This decision appears to suggest that the ECtHR, in enforcing a right considered to be as valuable as that protected by art.10, may step into the arena and consider the evidential justification for a finding of defamation. So far as the damages were concerned, the applicants had, perhaps surprisingly, failed to claim as damages from the Maltese State the amounts that they had been ordered to pay in damages themselves to the lawyer—sums which the ECtHR acknowledged would have been awardable had they been claimed. Apart from that, the ECtHR found that the finding of a violation of art.10 was not, by itself, just satisfaction, and awarded the applicants €4,000 together with €4,000 for costs and expenses incurred both in domestic proceedings and before the ECtHR.

[592] Application No.28040/08, 14 June 2011.

# PART 6 PROCEDURE

CHAPTER 51

# THE STATEMENT OF CASE

TABLE OF CONTENTS



**51-001** In the opening remarks to the procedural part of the 17th edition of this work, the point was made that, by the introduction of the Civil Procedure Rules, the landscape of litigation had been changed. In the 19th edition, *Mitchell v News Group Newspapers Ltd*,[1] was believed to have signalled a new outlook again, where no liberties could be taken with the application of procedural rules or compliance with deadlines imposed by the court, whether in relation to damages or to anything else. There was, thankfully, an attenuation of that position in *Denton v TH White Ltd*.[2] The position once again is that the court will require the parties and their lawyers to co-operate in achieving the overriding objective, enabling the court to deal with cases justly and at proportionate cost.[3] This requires compliance with rules, practice directions and court orders, but does not mean that every trivial breach will lead to some "windfall strike out or other litigation advantage"[4] accruing to the other side.

## 1. PRE-ACTION CONDUCT AND PROTOCOLS

**51-002** Before commencing proceedings, the court will expect the parties to have exchanged sufficient information to understand each other's position, make decisions about how to proceed, promote settlement, support the efficient management of the proceedings, and reduce costs.[5] In the absence of an applicable pre-action protocol, the parties should exchange correspondence to achieve that objective. In particular, the claimant should set out what the claimant wants from

1 [2013] EWCA Civ 1537; [2014] 1 W.L.R. 795.
2 [2014] EWCA Civ 906; [2014] 1 W.L.R. 3926.
3 CPR r.1.1.
4 To adopt the language of Jackson LJ in *Denton v TH White Ltd* at [41].
5 See Practice Direction—Pre-Action Conduct, para.3.

the defendant and, if money, how the amount is calculated. The defendant should respond explaining which facts and part of the claim are in dispute.[6]

Certain pre-action protocols make specific provision for exchange of information concerning damages claims. For example, the Pre-Action Protocol for Construction and Engineering Disputes requires, if damages are claimed, a breakdown showing how the damages have been quantified.[7] The Pre-Action Protocol for Defamation requires that the letter of claim should include details of any particular damage caused by the words complained of.[8] The Pre-Action Protocol for Personal Injury Claims requires the claimant's letter of claim to outline any financial loss incurred, **51-003**

> "with an indication of the heads of damage to be claimed and the amount of that loss, unless this is impracticable",[9]

and where a defendant admits liability, then in all cases the claimant

> "will send to the defendant as soon as reasonably practicable a schedule of any past and future expenses and losses which he claims, even if the schedule is necessarily provisional",

to assist in the quantification of special damages.[10] The Pre-Action Protocol for Professional Negligence requires the letter of claim to include an estimate of the financial loss suffered by the claimant and how it is calculated.[11] If the professional disputes the estimate of the claimant's financial loss, the letter of response should set out the professional's estimate.[12]

Compliance is not to be assessed slavishly; it is a matter of substance, not form.[13] In any event, the various protocols do not require the claimant to particularise the claim to damages fully. Thus, in *Thompson v Bruce*,[14] it was held that the Clinical Negligence Protocol does not envisage that the claim should be fully quantified before the letter of claim is issued.[15] In complying with the protocols, only reasonable and proportionate steps should be taken.[16] As a result, whilst the claimant should give details as far as reasonably possible, so as to allow the defendant to gauge the value of the claim, the claimant should not engage in a disproportionate investigation at the pre-action stage. **51-004**

Unreasonable failure to comply with the relevant pre-action protocol frequently **51-005**

---

6 See Practice Direction—Pre-Action Conduct, para.6.

7 See para.3(v).

8 See para.3.2.

9 See para.5.3. The same requirement is to be found in the Pre-Action Protocol for the Resolution of Clinical Disputes, para.3.16(c).

10 See para.10.1. A similar requirement is to be found in the Pre-Action Protocol for Disease and Illness Claims, para.8.1.

11 See para.6.2(f).

12 See para.9.2(e).

13 Practice Direction—Pre-Action Conduct, para.13; *TJ Brent Ltd v Black & Veatch Consulting Ltd* [2008] EWHC 1497 (TCC); 119 Con. L.R. 1 (Akenhead J) at [34]; *Orange Personal Communications Services Ltd v Hoare Lea (A Firm)* [2008] EWHC 223 (TCC); 117 Con. L.R. 76 (Akenhead J) at [31].

14 [2011] EWHC 2228 (QB), John Leighton Williams QC at [57].

15 See also *Cundall Johnson & Partners LLP v Whipps Cross University Hospital NHS Trust* [2007] EWHC 2178 (TCC); [2007] B.L.R. 520 (Jackson J) at [25]: "Neither the letter of claim nor the defendant's response are required to resemble pleadings either in their length or in their detail."

16 Practice Direction—Pre-Action Conduct, para.4.

results in a sanction, and so a failure to give sufficient information concerning damages sought may also have such a result.[17] The Practice Direction—Pre-Action Conduct provides that sanctions "may include" an order for costs (including for indemnity costs), an order that the claimant be deprived of interest on damages for a period and/or be awarded interest at a lower rate, and an order that the defendant pay interest at a higher rate than would otherwise be awarded.[18] This may considerably reduce the total value of the claim.

**51-006** The list of sanctions is not exhaustive. The court will take into account non-compliance with the protocols when giving directions for the management of proceedings.[19] In this way, failure to comply with the protocol requirement to provide information about damages might affect the level of recovery. For example, if the court were to disallow evidence which could and should have been provided at the pre-action stage, it might be impossible to establish loss. In *Spink v Shepherd Construction*,[20] a mesothelioma case, it was held that the court did have power to impose a sanction other than those specifically listed in Practice Direction—Pre-Action Conduct. On the (somewhat extreme) facts of the case, the second defendant's failures to comply with the protocol would have precluded it from relying on some important witness evidence in an application to set aside default judgment, and the application would have failed.[21] There may therefore be cases in which pre-action failures will influence the level of recoverable damages via case management decisions.[22]

CPR r.3.4(2)(c) provides that the court may strike out a statement of case, or part of a statement of case,

> "if it appears to the court that there has been a failure to comply with a rule, practice direction or court order."

Accordingly, it may be possible for a court to strike out a claim, including a claim to damages under a particular head, as a result of a failure to comply with the relevant pre-action protocol. However, it appears that this has not happened in the past and is, at least, very unlikely.[23]

---

17 However, it is important to bear in mind that compliance with a pre-action protocol will not postpone limitation: Practice Direction—Pre-Action Conduct, para.17.

18 Practice Direction—Pre-Action Conduct, para.16.

19 CPR r.3.1(4)–(5); Practice Direction—Pre-Action Conduct, para.13.

20 *Spink v Shepherd Construction* unreported 10 October 2007 QBD, Senior Master Whittaker.

21 At [34]–[38]. However, the evidence did not establish a real prospect of success in any event, so there was no need to disallow it. The Senior Master also said that, as an alternative, he would have refused to set aside default judgment on the grounds of non-compliance with the protocol and manifest prejudice resulting therefrom. In reaching his conclusions, he placed reliance on a decision of the County Court to strike out for delay, *Jimaale v London Buses Ltd* [2000] C.L.Y. 599, inaccurately suggesting that it was a Court of Appeal authority (rather than a decision of a district judge in the Uxbridge County Court). Nonetheless, the reasoning holds good without the need to rely on the authority.

22 A sanction imposed by the court must be proportionate (see, for example, *Walsham Chalet Park Ltd (t/a Dream Lodge Group) v Tallington Lakes Ltd* [2014] EWCA Civ 1607; [2015] C.P. Rep. 15 at [44]). It would be unusual for the breach of a pre-action protocol requirement with respect to damages to be so serious as to justify a sanction harsher than those specifically identified in Practice Direction—Pre-Action Conduct, para.16.

23 In *Pell Frischmann Consultants Ltd v Prabhu* [2013] EWHC 2203 (Ch); [2014] I.C.R. 153, Penelope Reed QC, sitting as a deputy High Court judge, inclined to the view (at [52]–[53]) that strike-out was not available for a breach of the Practice Direction—Pre-Action Conduct. However, the list of sanctions in Practice Direction—Pre-Action Conduct, para.4.6, is not exhaustive, and so in an

A claimant's failure properly to particularise details of quantum in accordance with a protocol may influence the court in favour of ordering pre-action disclosure in relation to quantum.[24] **51-007**

## 2. THE CLAIM FORM

An action is initiated by the issue of a claim form by the court at the request of the claimant: CPR r.7.2. Unless the claimant notifies the court that the claimant wishes to serve it, or a rule or practice direction otherwise provides,[25] the court will serve the claim form on the defendant: CPR r.6.4. A claim form must contain a concise statement of the nature of the claim, must specify the remedy which the claimant seeks and, where the claimant is making a claim for money, contain a statement of value in accordance with r.16.3: CPR r.16.2(1). From this it follows that a person claiming damages must state in the claim form that this is so. **51-008**

As for the statement of value in a claim for money, which a claim for damages must be,[26] the statement of value required is of the amount that the claimant is claiming together with what he expects to recover: CPR r.16.3(2). For the requirement to state the amount of recovery expected, the claimant may state that he cannot say how much is likely to be recovered, except that, with claims for personal injury and claims by tenants against landlords for repair work or damages, there is an obligation to state whether the expectation in respect of general damages in the one case and of the repair work damages in the other is or is not of more than £1,000, and if the claim form is to be issued in the High Court that the expectation is over £100,000 or, in the case of personal injury, over £50,000. Where the claimant does state what he expects to recover, he need only do so within specified brackets, up to £10,000, then up to £25,000, and over.[27] These detailed provisions aid the court in its case management, assisting it in deciding where the claim is to be heard and to which track it must be allocated.[28] By contrast, the requirement to **51-009**

---

extreme case striking out would be an available sanction.

24 *Briggs & Forrester Electrical Ltd v The Governors of Southfield School for Girls* [2005] EWHC 1734 (TCC); [2005] B.L.R. 468 (HH Judge Coulson QC), [55]–[56] (a decision based on the Construction and Engineering Protocol). On the interaction between pre-action disclosure and pre-action protocols more generally see *Steamship Mutual Underwriting Association Trustees (Bermuda) Ltd v Baring Asset Management Ltd* [2004] EWHC 202 (Comm); [2004] 2 C.L.C. 628 (Aikens J), particularly at [59] and following.

25 Claims issued in the Rolls Building will not be served by the Court: CPR PD 58 para.9; Chancery Guide, para.8.11; and TCC Guide, para.3.4.1.

26 The references in CPR r.16.2(1) and 3(1) are to claims for money and not, as in CPR Pt 12 (judgment in default) and Pt 14 (judgment on admission), to claims for a specified amount of money—a concept—which is narrower in ambit, though will include some damages claims.

27 See CPR r.16.3(2) together with (3) and (4).

28 *Lewis v Ward Hadaway* [2015] EWHC 3503 (Ch); [2016] 4 W.L.R. 6 at [16] per John Male QC: "The amounts identified in CPR r 16.3 are an allocation tool. They relate to the boundaries between the small claims track, the fast track and the multi-track". The financial limit a party places on the claim may also have substantive consequences. In *Maguire v Molin* [2002] EWCA Civ 1083; [2003] 1 W.L.R. 644, the claimant had originally limited her claim to £15,000. As a result, the claim was allocated to the fast track. Mid-way through the disposal hearing, the claimant sought to amend her claim to delete the financial limit and to introduce special damages claims amounting to £62,494.48. The district judge refused the claimant permission to amend to delete the financial limit. The district judge's decision was upheld by both the circuit judge and the Court of Appeal. Thus, although her claim was apparently for substantially more than £15,000, the claimant's self-imposed limit precluded her from recovering any larger sum.

state the amount claimed is unqualified but its purpose again may be for the court's benefit. Certainly, it is not intended to set a ceiling on the claimant's recovery since CPR r.16.3(7) makes clear that

> "the statement of value in the claim form does not limit the power of the court to give judgment for the amount which it finds the claimant is entitled to".

However, since court fees under the Civil Proceedings Fees Order 2008 are payable by reference to the sum claimed, any deliberate understatement of the sum claimed may constitute an abuse of process.[29] The collateral advantage for a claimant (even a claimant in a personal injury claim) of putting a precise figure on the amount of his claim is that he may later obtain a default judgment for that sum plus costs and interest, if the defendant does not respond.[30] No particularity with which the damages must be stated is required beyond this on the claim form. Further particularity is left for the particulars of claim.

## 3. PARTICULARS OF CLAIM

**51-010** The claim form having been issued and completed, particulars of claim are then prepared for inclusion on and service with the claim form or as a separate document to be served either with or after the claim form.[31] The required contents of the particulars of claim are set out in detail in CPR r.16.4. In *McPhilemy v Times Newspapers Ltd*,[32] Lord Woolf took the opportunity to redefine the role and format of pleadings:

> "The need for extensive pleadings including particulars should be reduced by the requirement that witness statements are now exchanged. In the majority of proceedings identification of the documents upon which a party relies, together with copies of that party's witness statements, will make the detail of the nature of the case the other side has to meet obvious. This reduces the need for particulars in order to avoid being taken by surprise. This does not mean that pleadings are now superfluous. Pleadings are still required to mark out the parameters of the case that is being advanced by each party. In particular they are still critical to identify the issues and the extent of the dispute between the parties. What is important is that the pleadings should make clear the general nature of the case of the pleader."[33]

If Lord Woolf's intention was to diminish the traditional function of pleadings not simply as a summary of but also as a curb on the issues, his aim has not received universal judicial support. In *Guild v Eskandar Ltd*,[34] Rix LJ responded thus:

---

[29] *Lewis v Ward Hadaway* at [37]–[48]. It is, however, perfectly permissible for a claimant deliberately to limit the amount sought in proceedings: *Khiaban v Beard* [2003] EWCA Civ 358; [2003] 1 W.L.R. 1626 at [13]. And a claim form which understates the value of the claim made is nonetheless effective for limitation purposes: *Dixon v Radley House Partnership (A Firm)* [2016] EWHC 2511 (TCC). Where an application is made to amend which would have the effect of increasing the value of a claim made, the usual rules on amendment under CPR r.17.4 apply, although any abusive underpayment of fees may be relevant to the exercise of the court's discretion: *Glenluce Fishing Co Ltd v Watermota Ltd* [2016] EWHC 1807 (TCC) at [58].

[30] See CPR r.12.4.

[31] CPR r.7.4.

[32] [1999] 3 All E.R. 775.

[33] At 792j –793b, which came into force on 1 January 2014.

[34] [2002] EWCA Civ 316; [2003] F.S.R. 23.

"I am also conscious that in the commercial as perhaps in any other field of civil law there can certainly be a practical and wholly sensible desire to ensure that the real points in issue between the parties are decided, provided that can be done with fairness, even in circumstances where the pleadings lie somewhat behind or below the pitch of the argument as it has developed in Court."[35]

However, Rix LJ went on to conclude that an allegation of conscious copying advanced against the defendant should have been strictly pleaded and proved and that "failure of the case alleged would mean failure indeed". Pleadings may therefore be regaining something of their technical significance.[36] Rix LJ's role as champion of the properly pleaded case may be seen once again in thankful execution in *Jones v Environcom Ltd*.[37] Refusing the appellant permission to amend the particulars of claim in third party proceedings in order to introduce an entirely new point of law on appeal and dismissing the proposed amendment for lack of particularisation, Rix LJ said[38]:

"The importance of a proper pleading becomes the clearer when consideration is given to questions of scope of duty, causation and remoteness".

All are of course central to the formulation of loss.

The need to furnish adequate particulars of loss in the statement of case was given further emphasis in *Green v Alexander Johnson*,[39] in which the defendant appealed against an award of damages assessed as the diminution in value of the claimant's interest in a block of flats attributable to the defendant's negligent advice to acknowledge the validity of two leases. Addressing the need for particularity, Carnwath LJ observed[40]: **51-011**

"It is essential in cases of this kind that each party should make clear in the pleadings, or at least before the hearing, precisely what bases of assessment it seeks to advance, and that the expert evidence if any should be clearly directed to the bases that are going to be put forward. If that is not done, there will be a danger of the issues becoming confused at the hearing, and a temptation to pick and choose different strands of valuation material in order to construct a new case, which may have superficial attractions but is not properly supported by coherent evidence."

---

35 [2003] F.S.R. 23 at 83.

36 Two further cases serve as examples of the growing significance of pleadings. In *Harris v BRB (Residuary) Ltd* [2005] EWCA Civ 900; [2006] P.I.Q.R. P10 at 101, a personal injury action, the Court of Appeal held that when an employee who is suing his employer for personal injury suffered at work contends in his statement of case that certain precautionary steps ought to have been taken by the employer, it should normally only be open to the employer at trial to raise a defence of impracticability if that defence has been properly raised in his statement of case. In *Kearsley v Klarfield* [2005] EWCA Civ 1510; [2006] P.I.Q.R. P13 at 141, Brooke LJ proffered guidance on the pleading requirements in cases where the defendant seeks to allege that the claimant had not suffered any injury at all. He emphasised that there was no burden on the defendant to prove fraud in such cases, but held that if the defendant wanted to do so then, despite the absence of more specific provisions in the CPR, the practice should be to plead full particulars of any allegation of dishonesty as well as the basis from which it is contended that fraud should be inferred. It is not usually proper to insinuate there has been fraud, by identifying "significant concerns", without an express allegation to that effect: *Hussain v Amin* [2012] EWCA Civ 1456 at [18]–[19] (Davis LJ).

37 [2011] EWCA Civ 1152; [2012] P.N.L.R. 5 at 119.

38 At [2012] P.N.L.R. 5 at [20].

39 [2005] EWCA Civ 775 CA.

40 At [21].

**51-012** Again, in *Hawksworth v Chief Constable of Staffordshire*,[41] Tomlinson LJ (with whom Toulson LJ and Morritt C agreed) quoted extensively from a pre-CPR decision, in explaining how Counsel at a trial should deal with evidence being adduced in respect of a matter which has not been pleaded. He held, at [40]:

> "Some guidance as to how counsel should react in circumstances of this sort was given by Lawton LJ in this court in *Rolled Steel Products Holdings Limited v British Steel Corporation & Others* [1986] 1 (Ch) at page 246, in a passage which is to be found at pages 309 to 310. Lawton LJ said this:
>
> > 'I wish however to add a comment about the pleading points which have had to be considered in this appeal. From the way they were raised by counsel and dealt with by the trial judge, I was left with the impression that neither the judge nor defending counsel appreciated as fully as they should have done the need for precision and expedition when dealing with pleading points.
> >
> > My recent experience in this court shows that some counsel and judges are not giving pleadings the attention which they should. Pleadings are formal documents which have to be prepared at the beginning of litigation, they are essential for the fair trial of an action and the saving of time at trial. The saving of time keeps down the costs of litigation. A plaintiff is entitled to know what defences he has to meet and the defendant what claims are being made against him. If the parties do not know, unnecessary evidence may be got together and led or, even worse, necessary evidence may not be led.
> >
> > Pleadings regulate what questions may be asked of witnesses in cross-examination. When counsel raises an objection to a question or a line of questioning, as Mr Morritt did on a number of occasions, the trial judge should rule on it at once. He should not regard the objection as a critical commentary on what the other side is doing. If the judge does not rule, counsel should ask him to do so. If a line of questioning is stopped because it does not relate to an issue on the pleadings, counsel should at once consider whether his pleadings should be amended. If he decides that they should, he should forthwith apply for an amendment and should specify precisely what he wants and the judge should at once give a ruling on the application. The principles upon which amendments should be allowed are well known and are set out in the current edition of the Supreme Court practice.'"

Tomlinson LJ went on to hold that the approach of Counsel at the trial was insufficient.[42] If Counsel was concerned that the defendants were adducing evidence and seeking to rely upon it in a manner which departed from their pleaded case, it was incumbent upon him to invite the judge to rule upon his objection. Had that course been taken, then it would have been incumbent upon his opponent in turn to apply for an amendment to the pleadings if that was thought necessary.

Similarly, in *Credit Suisse AG v Arabian Aircraft & Equipment Leasing Co EC*,[43] the claimant set out in its particulars of claim a claim to payment under clause 18.3 of the relevant aviation lease, under which, on default, the lessee was to pay the lessor the aggregate of all arrears of rent and any losses incurred. Clause 18.4 of the lease, to which no mention was made in the statements of case, provided for an alternative measure of compensation, calculated by comparing residual book value with fair market value. At a summary judgment hearing, the lessor advanced a claim under clause 18.4. The Court of Appeal held that, absent an amendment, it was not

---

41 [2012] EWCA Civ 293.

42 At [41].

43 [2013] EWCA Civ 1169.

open to the claimant to pursue that claim on a summary judgment or at trial. Moore-Bick LJ held at [17]:

> "Particulars of claim are intended to define the claim being made. They are a formal document prepared for the purposes of legal proceedings and can be expected to identify with care and precision the case the claimant is putting forward. They must set out the essential allegations of fact on which the claimant relies and which he will seek to prove at trial, but they should also state the nature of the case that is to be made in order to inform the defendant and the court of the basis on which it is said that the facts give rise to a right to the remedy being claimed."

If the Court considers that the claimant's pleaded case is inadequate then it may order the provision of further information pursuant to CPR r.18. In *Napp Pharmaceutical Holdings Ltd v Dr Reddy's Laboratories (UK) Ltd*,[44] an enquiry as to damages on a cross-undertaking, Birss J considered that the statement of case in relation to a £100 million claim was "fundamentally lacking in critical information which Napp were entitled to",[45] noting that the points of claim **51-013**

> "needed from the outset to explain the claiming party's case about what the relevant profit margins and sales prices would be or have been".[46]

The judge ordered the provision of substantial further information.

If, whether through developments in the factual or expert evidence or otherwise, it becomes apparent that the pleaded claim for damages does not accurately or adequately reflect the claimant's preferred basis, then permission to amend should be sought at the earliest practical opportunity. The circumstances in which the court will in its discretion permit amendments to statements of case[47] were conveniently summarised by Carr J in *Quah Su-Ling v Goldman Sachs International*.[48] As that summary makes clear, the later an application to amend is made, the greater the risk that the application will be refused. Where a relevant limitation period has expired, or arguably expired,[49] then the question will arise whether a new plea of damage amounts to a "new claim",[50] in which case amendment will be permitted only if the new claim arises out of the same, or substantially the same, facts as a claim in respect of which the party applying for permission has already claimed a remedy in the proceedings.[51] **51-014**

No particularity is required in relation to general and special damages in CPR r.16.4 and guidance here remains to be provided by the common law, though supplemented by the occasional requirement appearing in the Practice Direction which supplements Pt 16 of the CPR. **51-015**

However, over and above any requirement imposed by the CPR or the courts, it can be to the claimant's distinct advantage to plead losses with particularity where able to do so. Where the claimant obtains judgment in default pursuant to CPR r.12.11(1), judgment

---

44 [2017] EWHC 1433 (Pat).

45 [2017] EWHC 1433 (Pat) at [4].

46 [2017] EWHC 1433 (Pat) at [11].

47 Pursuant to CPR r.17.1(2).

48 [2015] EWHC 759 (Comm) at [36]–[37].

49 *Bellinger v Mercer Ltd* [2014] EWCA Civ 996; [2014] 1 W.L.R. 3597 at [25]–[29].

50 See the discussion by Longmore LJ in *Berezovsky v Abramovich* [2011] EWCA Civ 153; [2011] 1 W.L.R. 2290 at [59]–[64].

51 CPR r.17.4(2).

> "shall be such judgment as it appears to the court the Claimant is entitled to on his statement of case".

Further, by CPR r.12.5(2), a default judgment on a claim for a specified amount of money will be judgment for the amount of the claim. So, where a claimant alleges in his particulars of claim, with full particularity, that the defendant negligently caused him pain and suffering to the value of £X, loss of earnings in the sum of £Y, and damage to property in the sum of £Z, and claims the specific sum of £(X+Y+Z), judgment may be entered for him in that sum, avoiding the need for an assessment of damages at a disposal hearing.[52]

## (1) General and special damage

**51-016** In considering how the claimant must deal with damages in his particulars of claim, a basic distinction must be made between general damage or damages and special damage or damages. General damage consists in all items of loss which the claimant is not required to specify in his pleadings in order to permit proof and recovery in respect of them at the trial.[53] Special damage consists in all items of loss which must be specified by him before they may be proved and recovery granted.[54] The basic test of whether damage is general or special is whether particularity is necessary and useful to warn the defendant of the type of claim and evidence, or of the specific amount claimed, which he will be confronted with at the trial. "Special damage", said Bowen LJ in *Ratcliffe v Evans*,[55]

> "means the particular damage (beyond the general damage), which results from the particular circumstances of the case, and of the claimant's claim to be compensated, for which he ought to give warning in his pleadings in order that there may be no surprise at the trial."

Or, in the words of Lord Donovan in *Perestrello v United Paint Co*,[56]

> "if a plaintiff has suffered damage of a kind which is not the necessary and immediate consequence of the wrongful act, he must warn the defendant in the pleadings that the compensation claimed will extend to this damage, thus showing the defendant the case he has to meet and assisting him in computing a payment into court. The limits of this

---

52 See *Merito Financial Services Ltd v Yelloly* [2016] EWHC 2067 (Ch) at [36]–[39] (Master Matthews).

53 It may be perilous, however, for a claimant not to plead any reference to general damages at all. In *Kingsgate Development Projects Ltd v Jordan* [2017] EWHC 343 (TCC), where the defendants were alleged to have impeded a right of way and a claim was made for special damage and an injunction, Jefford J at [88] declined to award any general damages for loss of amenity, on the grounds that "Although I have found some interference with Kingsgate's right of way, there was no pleaded claim for general damages or loss of amenity. In the circumstances, I award nominal damages only in the sum of £1."

54 Whether the damage be general or special it is not sufficient, where the damages are at large, to plead the broad conventional allegation that by reason of the pleaded facts damage has been suffered: see *Lonrho v Fayed (No.5)* [1993] 1 W.L.R. 1489 CA, a case of conspiracy where pecuniary loss needs to be shown, at para.48-020, above.

55 [1892] 2 Q.B. 524 CA at 528.

56 [1969] 1 W.L.R. 570 CA at 579; cited with approval by Rimer LJ in *Whalley v PF Developments Ltd* [2013] EWCA Civ 306 at [26]. See also (in a defamation context) *Lisle-Mainwaring v Associated Newspapers Ltd* [2017] EWHC 543 (QB) at [133].

requirement are not dictated by any preconceived notions of what is general or special damage but by the circumstances of the particular case."

He added:

"If the claim is one which cannot with justice be sprung upon the defendants at the trial it requires to be pleaded so that the nature of that claim is disclosed."[57]

This focus on the justice of the case rather than any distinction between "general" and "special" damages remains good.[58]

In *Senate Electrical Wholesalers Ltd v Alcatel Submarine Networks Ltd*,[59] the trial judge's assessment of damages was rejected by the Court of Appeal on the basis that it did not adopt any method pleaded in the Particulars of Claim, and in a complex trial lasting 30 days Counsel for the defendant "should not waste time tilting at windmills", dealing with unpleaded issues.[60] Stuart-Smith LJ noted, by way of contrast, however, that:

"It not infrequently happens, especially in personal injury cases in relation to the assessment of future loss of earnings, that the plaintiff's case is greatly exaggerated, being based on unrealistic prospects of promotion and success which the judge rejects. In such cases, provided that the judge is satisfied that there will be continuing loss of earnings, he may well have to do his best on such material as is available to find a proper and reasonable basis of assessment of the question."

Post-CPR, this distinction between when a judge can "do his best", and when a failure to plead a method of assessing damages prevents such damages being awarded, has continued to be adopted.[61]

**(a) General damage** Three meanings of the term general damage have been suggested at the beginning of this book.[62] What constitutes general damage in pleading is made clearer when considered in relation to the two other meanings of the term. The first of these goes to liability, and the second goes to proof. **51-017**

If an item of damage is general for the purpose of liability because it represents a normal loss,[63] a fortiori it will be general for the purpose of pleading in so far as its existence cannot take the defendant by surprise; only in so far as he could be surprised by the detail of its amount, when this has become crystallised and concrete since the wrong, will it become special damage. Thus Lord Goddard in *British* **51-018**

---

57 [1969] 1 W.L.R. 570 CA at 580. He cited with approval the text of this paragraph in the 12th edition (1961) of this work. But compare *Owen v Grimsby Cleethorpes Transport* [1992] P.I.Q.R. Q27, a personal injury case, where the claimant's complaint of disc damage and functional pain was not pleaded and this failure was held not to be significant in the light of the medical reports. While accepting that the pleadings remain important, Parker LJ, with whom his brethren agreed, said that "in personal injury cases which stretch over a long time it is common for the medical reports to change from time to time and to develop and it is not always considered necessary to add to the pleadings each time the medical position develops step by step": at 37.

58 See, e.g. *Arroyo v Equion Energia Ltd* [2013] EWHC 3150 (TCC) discussed at 51-027 below.

59 [1998] EWCA Civ 3534; [1999] 2 Lloyd's Rep. 423.

60 A similar approach was taken by Devlin J in *Anglo Cyprian Trade Agencies v Paphos Wine Industries* [1951] 1 All E.R. 873 at 875.

61 See, e.g. *Heffernan v London Borough of Hackney* [2009] EWCA Civ 665 at [56]; *Marathon Asset Management LLP v Seddon* [2017] EWHC 300 (Comm) at [281]–[282].

62 See paras 3-001 to 3-005, above.

63 See para.3-002, above.

*Transport Commission v Gourley*,[64] defined the general damage in personal injury cases as including

> "compensation for pain and suffering and the like, and if the injuries suffered are such as to lead to continuing permanent disability, compensation for loss of earning power in the future."[65]

And the same was said as to the prospective medical expenses of an injured claimant by Asquith LJ in *Shearman v Folland*.[66] Similarly, general loss of business as a result of a defamatory statement actionable per se has been taken to be general damage in a number of cases. In *Evans v Harries*,[67] an action for slander of the claimant in his business of an innkeeper,[68] it was held that the general falling off of the claimant's custom was properly proved as general damage, while in *Harrison v Pearce*,[69] which concerned a libel upon the proprietors of a newspaper, the general decline in the circulation of the newspaper was held to be general damage.[70] Furthermore, even if an item of damage is special for the purpose of liability because not representing a normal loss, it may yet be general damage for the purpose of pleading, because the test of unexpectedness is not at the time of the commission of the tort or of the making or breaking of the contract but at the later time of pleading. This may possibly be the explanation of *Ward v Smith*,[71] where, in an action against a lessor for failure to complete a lease of business premises, the lessee recovered as general damages his loss of general business profits,[72] although such a loss was consequential and not part of the normal measure of damages.[73]

**51-019** If an item of damage is general for the purpose of proof because it is inferred or presumed by the court,[74] a fortiori it will be general for the purpose of pleading, since what the law is prepared to infer or presume in the claimant's favour the defendant cannot contend would surprise him at the trial. Thus in actions for personal injury the claimant's pain and suffering, the existence of which the court will infer, is pleaded as general damage, and in actions for defamatory statements actionable per se the injury to the claimant's reputation, presumed for proof,[75] is similarly pleaded as general damage.[76] And such general pecuniary losses as the loss to credit and reputation caused by the defendant's failure, in breach of contract, to honour the claimant's drafts, or the loss of business profits tortiously caused by the defendant by means of inducement of breach of contract or by passing off, should

---

64 [1956] A.C. 185.

65 [1956] A.C. 185 at 206. *Potter v Metropolitan Ry* (1873) 28 L.T. 735 is an earlier authority holding that the amount the claimant would have earned but for the accident is properly pleaded as general damage. But a particular loss of future earnings not arising in the ordinary way has to be pleaded as special damage: see *Domsalla v Barr* [1969] 1 W.L.R. 630 CA, at para.51-024, below.

66 [1950] 2 K.B. 43 CA at 51.

67 (1856) 1 H. & N. 251.

68 And therefore actionable per se.

69 (1859) 32 L.T. O.S. 298.

70 In *Bluck v Lovering* (1885) 1 T.L.R. 497, another case of libel, general loss of business was taken to be general damage. And see *Collins Stewart Ltd v The Financial Times Ltd (No.1)* [2004] EWHC 2337 (QB) at [25]–[29] per Tugendhat J.

71 (1822) 11 Price 19.

72 See (1822) 11 Price 19 at 26–27, per Graham B.

73 The case is, however, not a strong one on liability as decided before *Hadley v Baxendale* (1854) 9 Ex. 341: see para.8-158, above.

74 See para.3-003, above and para.52-008, below.

be general damage for pleading since they are presumed for proof.[75] The authorities dealing with these various situations are primarily concerned with the issue of evidence and proof,[76] but they seem to assume the anterior point that the damage is properly pleaded as general.

**(b) Special damage** What constitutes special damage follows by exclusion from the area covered by general damage.[77] Various types of situation stand out by this exclusion. **51-020**

(1) Where the precise amount of a particular item of damage has become clear before the trial, either because it has already occurred, and so become crystallised, or because it can be measured with complete accuracy, this exact loss must be pleaded as special damage. The prime example of this appears in personal injury cases, where earnings already lost and expenses already incurred before the action must be pleaded as special damage before proof of them may be allowed. This is clearly laid down by Lord Goddard in *British Transport Commission v Gourley*,[78] and is well illustrated by *Ilkiw v Samuels*,[79] an action for personal injuries where, the special damages having been agreed at £77 based on four months' loss of wages after the accident, the claimant was held not entitled to recover for the continuing loss of wages over the eight years before the action was heard as these should have been pleaded as special damage.[80] Similarly, in actions for wrongful dismissal it has been accepted since *Monk v Redwing Aircraft Co*,[81] that the claim in respect of wages which the claimant would have earned but for the breach less any substitute salary he has earned since his dismissal is special damage. Thus in *Hayward v Pullinger*,[82] the statement of claim was held to be defective where the claimant had failed to plead as special damage the loss of salary and commission he would have earned during the period of notice to which he was contractually entitled.[83] This obligation to particularise earnings already lost and expenses already incurred arises, as Lord Donovan pointed out in *Perestrello v United Paint Co*,[84] **51-021**

---

75 See, respectively, *Rolin v Steward* (1854) 14 C.B. 595, *Goldsoll v Goldman* [1914] 2 Ch. 603 and *Draper v Trist* [1939] 3 All E.R. 513 CA.

76 See para.52-008, below.

77 But note Lord Donovan's comment in *Perestrello v United Paint Co* [1969] 1 W.L.R. 570 CA at 579 that "since the expressions 'special damage' and 'special damages' are used in such a wide variety of meanings it is safer to approach this question by considering what a claimant is required to plead rather than what he is not".

78 [1956] A.C. 185 at 206: the passage is quoted at para.3-005, above. And in the related field of fatal accidents, dependency already lost before action is, since *Cookson v Knowles* [1979] A.C. 556, to be similarly pleaded as special damage: see para.41-042, above.

79 [1963] 1 W.L.R. 991 CA.

80 Since the very large figure of general damages at which the judge had arrived either must have contained a very substantial element of loss of earnings prior to the trial or else was a wholly erroneous estimate of the claimant's loss, the court was bound to interfere to reduce the damages.

81 [1942] 1 K.B. 182 CA, applied in *Phipps v Orthodox Unit Trusts* [1958] 1 Q.B. 314 CA. The only issue in *Monk v Redwing Aircraft Co* was as to the particularity of the special damage, but in *Hayward v Pullinger* [1950] 1 All E.R. 581 Devlin J thought that the case decided the matter.

82 [1950] 1 All E.R. 581.

83 In *Anglo Cyprian Trade Agencies v Paphos Wine Industries* [1951] 1 All E.R. 873, where the buyer of goods, claiming back the purchase price, alleged that the goods were valueless but succeeded in showing only that they were slightly defective, it was held that, having pleaded the amount of the purchase price as special damage, it was improper then to set up a lower figure and seek to justify it: the lower figure must be pleaded in the alternative.

84 [1969] 1 W.L.R. 570 CA.

"not because the nature of the loss is necessarily unusual, but because a plaintiff who has the advantage of being able to base his claim upon a precise calculation must give the defendant access to the facts which make such calculation possible."[85]

It is

"no more than an example of damage which is 'special' in the sense that fairness to the defendant requires that it be pleaded".[86]

**51-022** (2) Where consequential losses are claimed in actions of tort these will generally be a matter of surprise to the defendant at the trial. Thus in *Moon v Raphael*,[87] the claimant, suing for conversion of goods, was refused damages for loss of business profits from being deprived of the use of the goods because such loss was not pleaded. This was confirmed in the 20th century by *Re Simms*,[88] where the Court of Appeal took the view that such loss of profits was special damage[89] and therefore must be pleaded.[90] And in *Calabar Properties v Stitcher*,[91] a lessee, suing for breach of her lessor's covenant to repair, was denied damages for expenditure on alternative accommodation, which she had taken as the lack of repair had made the leased premises uninhabitable, because such loss had not been pleaded.[92]

**51-023** (3) In cases where general loss of business would be general damage,[93] if the claimant wishes to claim for particular losses of business these must be pleaded as special damage. Thus in *Fleming v Bank of New Zealand*,[94] where the defendant bank failed to honour the claimant's cheques, it was held that proof of the claimant's loss of custom and credit from particular individuals was inadmissible in the absence of an allegation of special damage. And in *Bluck v Lovering*,[95] a case of libel, the claimant was not allowed to prove the loss of specific customers in the absence of pleading such a loss as special damage. Somewhat similarly, in *Calvet v Tomkies*,[96] where the claimant in an action for libel and injurious falsehood had alleged only general damage,[97] it was held that the documents relating to her income before the publication were therefore not relevant and the defendants were not entitled to discovery in respect of them. Where, in *Perestrello v United Paint Co*,[98] the claimants claimed not for their loss of profits arising out of the defendants' repudiation of a contract but for their expenditure which had been rendered futile by the defendants' breach, it was held that the claimants were not entitled to give

---

85 [1969] 1 W.L.R. 570 CA at 579.
86 [1969] 1 W.L.R. 570 CA at 579.
87 (1835) 2 Bing. N.C. 310.
88 [1934] 1 Ch. 1 CA.
89 [1934] 1 Ch. 1 CA at 29, per Romer LJ.
90 [1934] 1 Ch. 1 CA at 22, per Lawrence LJ. Two old cases of false imprisonment, *Lowden v Goodrick* (1791) Peake 64 and *Pettit v Addington* (1791) Peake 87, would seem to fall under this head, the court in each refusing the claimant damages on account of a decline in his health arising from the imprisonment because he had failed to plead this injury as special damage. It may be, however, that injury to health in such a case would be treated as general damage today.
91 [1984] 1 W.L.R. 287 CA.
92 See [1984] 1 W.L.R. 287 CA at 296E–297D; facts at paras 28-024 and 28-030, above.
93 See paras 51-017 to 51-019, above.
94 [1900] A.C. 577 PC.
95 (1885) 1 T.L.R. 497.
96 [1963] 1 W.L.R. 1397 CA.
97 Thereby, in relation to the injurious falsehood, taking advantage of s.3 of the Defamation Act 1952: see para.48-011, above.
98 [1969] 1 W.L.R. 570 CA.

evidence of this unpleaded loss,[99] the court pointing particularly to the fact that, as was admitted, the claim as pleaded was inconsistent with the claim now sought to be advanced.[100] With this case should be contrasted *National Broach and Machine Co v Churchill Gear Machines*.[101] There the claimants had contracted to license the defendants to manufacture in the United Kingdom machines of which the claimants had the United Kingdom patents and were in breach of this contract by failure to communicate various inventions and improvements. The Court of Appeal disagreed with Cross J that the defendants, on their counterclaim, were only entitled to nominal damages as they had not pleaded special damage, and held that they were not prevented from recovering for such general damage as they could prove.[102]

(4) In cases where general loss of future earning capacity would be general damage,[103] if the claimant wishes to claim for particular future losses which would not normally be expected to arise, these must be pleaded as special damage. This was laid down by the Court of Appeal in *Domsalla v Barr*,[104] where, in a claim for personal injury by a claimant employed as a steel erector at the time of the accident, it was held that, in order to entitle him to prove that he had obtained a diploma in the theory of steel erection and had intended eventually to set up as a steel erector on his own account, these circumstances should have been pleaded. "Where", said Edmund Davies LJ, **51-024**

> "it is proposed to allege that there are any special circumstances which will probably lead the plaintiff to sustain in the future losses over and above those which in the ordinary way would reasonably be expected to flow from the accident, I hold that those special circumstances should be pleaded. This duty cannot be neglected simply by saying: 'Those losses relate to the future: they are therefore part of the general damages and accordingly need not be pleaded.' So to hold would be to ignore the basic object of pleadings, which is to crystallise the issues and so enable both parties to prepare for trial, and, indeed, to decide whether they should go to trial at all or rather seek to compromise their differences, and, if they fail to do that, to guide the defendant on the important matter of payment into court."[105]

Beyond all this, there is a more technical aspect of special damage in tort where in certain actions the liability is reflected in the statement of case. This appears principally with slanders not actionable per se and actions of tort arising out of public nuisance. In both these cases liability depends not only on the existence of damage to the claimant but on the existence of a special type of damage,[106] and this **51-025**

---

[99] Nor was the court prepared to give permission to amend.

[100] For a consideration of these two alternative bases of contract damages see paras 4-024 and following, above.

[101] [1965] 1 W.L.R. 1199 CA.

[102] Willmer LJ said ( [1965] 1 W.L.R. 1199 CA at 1203–1204) that what was stated by Lord Dunedin in *The Susquehanna* [1926] A.C. 655 at 661–662 applied precisely to the case.

[103] See paras 51-017 to 51-019, above.

[104] [1969] 1 W.L.R. 630 CA. For the need in a personal injury case specifically to include a *Smith v Manchester* claim, see *Thorn v Powerglen* [1997] P.I.Q.R. Q71 CA.

[105] [1969] 1 W.L.R. 630 CA at 634– 635; see similarly at 638, per Widgery LJ. Since no objection to the evidence had been taken at the trial the court considered it its duty to consider the weight of the evidence, but in the result held that no weight should be given to it. By contrast, in *Connolly v The National Coal Board* unreported 29 June 1981CA, where again evidence had been taken as to the loss of prospects of promotion without the point being pleaded, the court upheld the trial judge's decision which gave weight to such evidence.

[106] See para.3-006 above.

special type of damage must be specially pleaded.[107] Accordingly, it is special damage in two senses, and if not pleaded the action must fail. And it would seem that, although the point seems hardly to have been recognised, the same applies to the tort of injurious falsehood,[108] where at common law it was necessary to plead as special damage the pecuniary loss which alone would ground the action[109]: this was decided by *Malachy v Soper*.[110] Most of the authorities, whether in slander, in actions based on public nuisance or in injurious falsehood, are taken up with the further issue of the amount of particularity with which the special damage must be stated[111]: they, however, necessarily imply that all the damage in such cases must be pleaded as special.

51-026 **(c) Particularity and particulars of special damage** On a strict view, the claimant will be debarred from proving special damage not only where he fails to plead it at all but where he fails to plead it with sufficient particularity. Sufficient particularity normally requires that specific instances should be pleaded. Thus in two very old cases of slanders, *Hunt v Jones*,[112] and *Barnes v Prudlin*,[113] the claimant's claim for damages for loss of suitors through the slander failed because, although giving a general statement of this loss, she failed to specify the particular suitors. Similarly in *Westwood v Cowne*,[114] an action for an irregular distress, the claimant's claim for damages for loss of lodgers failed through his failure to name any one of the lodgers.

51-027 In more modern times, however, the tendency is to adopt a more lenient approach and to allow a claim for special damage to be proved provided that the existence of such a claim is clear from the statement of case—but also to demand better particulars of pleas of general damage, where the case requires it. This modern trend is well illustrated by *Arroyo v Equion Energia Ltd*,[115] in which Stuart-Smith J held:

> "In my judgment, the level of precision that is required when pleading an issue or case, including a particular head of damages, should be determined by the need to provide a fair and sufficient indication to the Court and the opposing party of the case that is being brought and that the opposing party has to meet. Although I am not aware of specific authority on the point, modern pleading practice should not be and is not constrained by whether the label 'general' or 'special' damages is given to a particular item of claim. Take, for example, a claim for damages to compensate for physical damage to land. It is

---

107 In *Corby Group Litigation Claimants v Corby BC* [2008] EWCA Civ 463; [2009] Q.B. 335, the 18 claimants claimed damages from the defendant council for congenital upper limb deformities alleged to have been caused as a result of their mothers' exposure to heavily contaminated land acquired by the council for reclamation and redevelopment. By amendment to their particulars of claim, the claimants introduced claims in public nuisance, the claimants' individual personal injuries presumably (consistently with their Counsel's submission: see at 337B) being said to constitute the "special damage" necessary to found such causes of action. See also para.52-016, below for a discussion of the related topic of proving loss in claims for misfeasance in a public office.

108 Other than that form of injurious falsehood known as passing off: see para.48-016, above.

109 See para.48-011, above. Statute has introduced certain modifications on this by s.3 of the Defamation Act 1952.

110 (1836) 3 Bing. N.C. 371.

111 See paras 51-026 and 51-029, below.

112 (1618) Cro. Jac. 499.

113 (1667) 1 Sid. 396.

114 (1816) 1 Stark. 172.

115 [2013] EWHC 3150 (TCC).

(correctly) common ground that the normal approach to assessment of such a claim is either by reference to diminution in value or by reference to costs of reinstatement. Describing such claims as claims for general damages should not and does not determine the level of particularisation that is required. If a claim for damage to land based on diminution in value were to be advanced, the opposing party needs certain information if it is to be able to meet the claim on an equal footing: as a minimum it needs to know what sum is claimed and the nature of the case in support of that claimed sum. In some cases the diminution in value claim may be advanced by reference to comparables; alternatively it may be by reference to a reduction in the income stream which the land had generated but which can no longer be maintained; or it may be by reference to costs of reinstatement. If any of these are the nature of the case that is being advanced, they should be pleaded so that the opposing party can address the propositions on which the claim is based and either accept or refute them. If the claim is advanced on the basis of costs of reinstatement, the opposing party must be entitled to know what those costs are said to be and how they are computed calculated or otherwise made up. If that information is not provided, there can be no equality of arms and the opposing party is unfairly disadvantaged."

The remedy available to a defendant presented with insufficient particularity in the claimant's statement of case is to raise requests for further information of the damage alleged pursuant to CPR Pt 18. Under the old procedural rules, it was well established that the defendant was entitled to demand such particulars of special damage, although he could not get particulars of general damage. If the claimant then supplied the particulars he would be bound by them; if he failed to deliver them the defendant might ask for the allegation of special damage to be struck out. In general the defendant was not entitled to the delivery of further and better particulars before he had filed his defence. Under CPR r.18.1(1), by contrast, the court may at any time order a party to clarify any matter which is in dispute or give additional information in relation to any such matter. Requests should be concise and strictly confined to matters which are reasonably necessary and proportionate to enable the requesting party to prepare his own case or to understand the case he has to meet,[116] which **51-028**

"may include accepting that it is well founded, assessing and pursuing the prospects of settlement, attempting to defeat it, or any variation on these themes".[117]

Such an order could be made before defence if it was thought that the defendant needed the clarification or information at that stage.

That being said, in relation both to the particularity of special damage in the initial statement of case or schedule of loss and to the further information demanded of an allegedly insufficient particulars of claim, the courts are realistic and accept that the detail must be tailored to the facts. This was laid down by Bowen LJ in *Ratcliffe v Evans*,[118] the leading case on the pleading and proof of damage. In relation to special damage he said: **51-029**

"The character of the acts themselves which produce the damage, and the circumstances under which these acts are done, must regulate the degree of certainty and particularity with which the damage done ought to be stated....[119] As much certainty and particularity

116 CPR PD18 para.1.2.

117 *Arroyo v Equion Energia Ltd* at [10].

118 [1892] 2 Q.B. 524 CA.

119 The omitted portions refer to proof and not to pleading. They are dealt with at para.52-016, below.

must be insisted on … in pleading …[120] of damage as is reasonable, having regard to the circumstances and to the nature of the acts themselves by which the damage is done. To insist upon less would be to relax old and intelligible principles. To insist upon more would be the vainest pedantry."[121]

## (2) Exemplary damages

**51-030** Rule 16.4 of the Civil Procedure Rules provides as follows:

"(1) Particulars of claim must include—

…

(c) if the claimant is seeking … exemplary damages, a statement to that effect and his grounds for claiming them."

This applies equally to the High Court and the County Court. The requirement is emphasised by its repetition in para.2.10(2) of the Practice Direction supplementing CPR Pt 53 setting out all the rules applying specifically to defamation claims.

## (3) Aggravated damages

**51-031** Rule 16.4 of the Civil Procedure Rules stipulates:

"(1) Particulars of claim must include—

…

(c) if the claimant is seeking aggravated damages[122] … a statement to that effect and his grounds for claiming them."

This applies equally to the High Court and the County Court. Just as in the case of exemplary damages, the requirement is emphasised by its repetition in para.2.10(2) of the Practice Direction supplementing CPR Pt 53 setting out all the rules applying specifically to defamation claims.

In *Murray v Associated Newspapers Ltd*,[123] Sharp LJ (with whom Longmore and Ryder J agreed) agreed with an observation of the first instance judge that

"it can be difficult to draw a clear line between what can be claimed as compensatory damages for injury to feelings without being specifically pleaded, and what must be pleaded if aggravated damages are to be awarded. It should also be noted, as Mr Caldecott accepts, that a situation might arise where matters occur or are discovered after the case is pleaded which are relevant to damages and which it is legitimate for a claimant to refer to. Too rigid an approach by reference to the pleadings might also be counterproductive, since it could encourage a claimant to plead 'too much' which would not be conducive to settlement. What it is fair and reasonable for a claimant to say therefore, and whether this should be judged by reference to the four corners of the pleading (if they have been settled) and/or can include other matters, including those raised in correspondence, must depend on the facts. Such issues should usually be capable of sensible resolution by the parties, or if not, by the judge at first instance, in the event, as here, that matters cannot be agreed."

---

120 See previous note.

121 [1892] 2 Q.B. 524 CA at 532–533.

122 For an interesting summary of the nature and effect of aggravated damages, see the comments of Vos J in *Various Claimants v News Group Newspapers Ltd* [2012] EWHC 2692 (Ch) at [14]–[19].

123 [2015] EWCA Civ 488.

## (4) Provisional damages

Rule 16.4 of the Civil Procedure Rules provides thus: 51-032

> "(1) Particulars of claim must include—
> ...
> (d) if the claimant is seeking provisional damages, a statement to that effect and his grounds for claiming them;"

This applies equally to the High Court and the County Court.

## (5) Periodical payments

There is an additional requirement in claims for personal injury and wrongful death arising from the introduction of periodical payments orders under the substituted s.2 of the Damages Act 1996. CPR r.41.5 states: 51-033

> "(1) In a claim for damages for personal injury, each party in its statement of case may state whether it considers periodical payments or a lump sum is the more appropriate form for all or part of an award of damages and where such statement is given must provide relevant particulars of the circumstances which are relied on.
> (2) Where a statement under para.(1) is not given, the court may order a party to make such a statement.
> (3) Where the court considers that a statement of case contains insufficient particulars under para.(1), the court may order a party to provide such further particulars as it considers appropriate."

Rule 41.5(2) empowers a court, where a statement under para.(1) is not given, to order a party to make such a statement. Equally where the court considers that a statement of case contains insufficient particulars under para.(1), in the exercise of its powers pursuant to r.41.5(3) it may order a party to provide such further particulars as it considers appropriate. Thus, when the pleadings first come to be reviewed, there is an obligation on the judge to consider whether the absence of any reference to the form of award sought should be remedied and, if a form of award is specified, whether it has been properly thought through. Although the Practice Direction which supplements CPR Pt 41 does not stipulate what has to be pleaded to meet the requirements of the rule, this must logically include those matters specified in para.1 of the Practice Direction, being the so-called factors to be taken into account in the circumstances identified in r.41.7. For parties who feel unable to answer these difficult questions, there is no ultimate escape. CPR r.41.6 obliges the court to consider and indicate to the parties as soon as practicable whether periodical payments or a lump sum award is likely to be the more appropriate form for all or part of an award of damages.

The combined provisions of r.41.5 and r.41.6, requiring in effect that a party's case as to the appropriateness of periodical payments be set out in their pleadings, create a practical conflict. As stipulated in para.1 of the Practice Direction supplementing CPR Pt 41, one of the considerations to which the court shall have regard when deciding to make a periodical payments order is the 51-034

> "nature of any financial advice received by the claimant when considering the form of award".

Since financial advice is essential in order to determine the relative advantages of periodical payments as against a lump sum award, a claimant will need to obtain such advice. As claimants are supposed to plead their desire for an order in the particulars of claim and will, in theory, have to provide proper particulars of the reasoning for their preference, it might be thought that they would need to obtain financial advice before commencing proceedings. Such a need sits ill with the decisions in *Page v Plymouth Hospitals NHS Trust*,[124] and *Eagle v Chambers (No.2)*,[125] to the effect that a claimant cannot recover the cost of obtaining financial advice on investment and management of his damages. In practice, claimants have generally got round the problem by postponing the commissioning of financial advice until such time as a compromise of their claim is in the offing and, where applicable, the court's approval of that compromise is required. Claimants have nevertheless felt able to express an anticipatory preference for periodical payments in the statement of case without such advice or have hedged their bets by pleading that a periodical payments order is a possible preference depending on expert advice yet to be obtained. This pragmatism in spite of the rules does not seem to have provoked judicial hostility and may be seen as a sensible enough solution to a practical problem.

## (6) Interest

**51-035** Rule 16.4 of the Civil Procedure Rules provides as follows:

"(1) Particulars of claim must include—

....

(b) if the claimant is seeking interest, a statement to that effect and the details set out in paragraph (2)

...

(2) If the claimant is seeking interest he must—
(a) state whether he is doing so—
(i) under the terms of a contract;
(ii) under an enactment and if so which or
(iii) on some other basis and if so what that basis is;
and
(b) if the claim is for a specified amount of money, state—
(i) the percentage rate at which interest is claimed;
(ii) the date from which it is claimed;
(iii) the date to which it is calculated, which must not be later than the date on which the claim form is issued;
(iv) the total amount of interest claimed to the date of calculation; and
(v) the daily rate at which interest accrues after that date."

The practice of concluding the particulars of claim with a claim for interest on damages under s.35A of the Senior Courts Act 1981 or s.69 of the County Courts Act 1984 is rendered obligatory by virtue of CPR r.16.4(2)(a)(ii). The greater detail that is required under CPR r.16.4(2)(b), as to dates and rates of interest and the like, is not considered here because it is applicable only where the claim is for a specified amount of money which, with the exception of some liquidated damages claims, a claim for damages is not. Once again the sub-rule applies equally to the High Court and the County Court. At least in one respect, recent jurisprudence has simplified the pleader's task. Following the House of Lords' landmark decision in *Sempra*

[124] [2004] EWHC 1154 (QB); [2004] 3 All E.R. 367.
[125] [2004] EWCA Civ 1033; [2004] 1 W.L.R. 3081 CA.

*Metals Ltd v Inland Revenue Commissioners*,[126] claimants no longer need to resort to the unsatisfactory expedient of characterising so-called interest losses[127] as special damage under the second rule in *Hadley v Baxendale*,[128] and are instead able to plead and prove actual interest losses in the same way as any other damage,[129] arguably taking such claims outside the scope of CPR r.16.4 altogether. However, since the requirement for particularity introduced by CPR r.16.4(2)(a)(iii) has obvious utility even in those cases, it would seem sensible that it should nevertheless apply.[130]

Should a claimant wish to claim more than the half rate of interest generally allowed on special damages in personal injury claims[131] because his loss has accrued soon after injury but long before trial, he should, according to the Court of Appeal in *Dexter v Courtaulds*,[132] so state and set out the facts on which he relies. This allows the defendant to gauge the proper level of any payment into court which he may be minded to make.[133] Where, conversely, the loss has accrued long after injury and soon before trial so that it is the defendant who wishes to depart from the general rule and claim that less than the half rate of interest should be awarded, he should presumably so state. Whether he did so in *Hobin v Douglas (No.1)*,[134] is not known. **51-036**

### (7) The amount claimed

Before the introduction of the Civil Procedure Rules, there was no need for a claimant in the High Court to give an overall figure for his claim unless it was for liquidated damages, and the danger of stating a precise figure was that, subject to amendment, the claimant limited his recovery thereto. In the County Court, by contrast, before the enlargement of the County Court jurisdiction, a limit on the amount of the damages claimed had to be stated in the particulars of claim to make it clear that the action was within the County Court limit. Under the Civil Procedure Rules, claimants are required in all cases to state the amount claimed in the claim form.[135] This, however, does not, as formerly, limit recovery to the amount claimed since CPR r.16.3(7) states that the court may still give judgment for the amount to which it finds the claimant entitled.[136] Amendment is therefore unnecessary. **51-037**

## 4. Defence

Before 1989 RSC Ord.18 r.13(4) ruled the day with its provision that any allegation as to the amount of damage was regarded as denied unless specifically **51-038**

---

[126] [2007] UKHL 34; [2008] A.C. 561.

[127] This useful if not entirely elegant expression is given voice in the speech of Lord Scott, [2008] A.C. 561 at [132].

[128] (1854) 9 Ex. 341.

[129] For a detailed analysis of the House of Lords decision, see paras 19-058 to 19-066 above.

[130] The level of particularity required when pleading a claim for interest as damages was considered by the Competition Appeal Tribunal in *Sainsbury's Supermarkets Ltd v Mastercard Inc* [2016] CAT 11 at [514]–[521].

[131] See para.19-091, above.

[132] [1984] 1 W.L.R. 372 CA.

[133] See para.19-092, above, for more detail.

[134] *Independent,* 26 October 1998 CA; see the case at para.19-093, above.

[135] See para.51-009, above.

[136] See previous note.

admitted. Then came RSC Ord.18 r.12(1)(c) requiring the pleading by the defendant of any facts on which he relied "in mitigation of, or otherwise in relation to, the amount of damages". Nothing in the Civil Procedure Rules replicates this important provision.[137] Indeed, curiously, the one reference to mitigation in the Rules appears to be in relation to the claimant: the Practice Direction supplementing Pt 16 provides at para.8.2(8) that the claimant must specifically set out in the particulars of claim various matters where he wishes to rely on them, and the last of these is "any facts relating to mitigation of loss or damage". Yet surely it cannot be the claimant who should be concerning himself in the statement of case with mitigation where the burden of proof is on the defendant.[138] Until the defendant raises the issue, the claimant will not know if a failure to mitigate is even alleged. The Privy Council was plainly influenced by considerations such as these in *Geest Plc v Lansiquot*,[139] a clinical negligence claim. In *Geest*, the Privy Council held that, if a defendant intended to argue that a claimant had failed to act reasonably to mitigate her damages (the allegation on the facts of the case being that the claimant should have undergone surgery to resolve a prolapsed disc), notice of such contention should have been clearly given. Speaking for the Board, Lord Bingham put the matter in this way:

> "Had there been pleadings … it would have been the clear duty of the company to plead in its defence that the Plaintiff had failed to mitigate her damage and to give appropriate particulars sufficient to alert the Plaintiff to the nature of the company's case, enable the Plaintiff to direct her evidence to the real areas of dispute and avoid surprise."[140]

**51-039** Even before the now missing provision of the former rules of court had appeared, in 1989, requiring the pleading of facts on which the defendant wished to rely in relation to the amount of damages, whether by way of mitigation or otherwise, it was not necessarily the case that a defendant had never to plead to damages. Thus *Weait v Jayanbee Joinery*,[141] indicates that he might occasionally have to do so when the issue was remoteness of damage. In that case the defendant, sued for negligently injuring the claimant, applied at a late stage to amend his defence so as to introduce an allegation of the hospital's negligence as a novus actus interveniens. The Court of Appeal granted the amendment, without deciding upon the parties' rival contentions on the pleading of the novus actus based upon the then rules of court, but commented that

> "from a practical point of view … if a defendant were minded to take a substantial point as this on damages … it would be essential that, if not by pleading, at any rate by notice,

137 The position is different in the Commercial Court. Section C1.3(g) of the Commercial Court guide states:

> "It is important that if a defendant or CPR part 20 defendant wishes to advance by way of defence or defence to counterclaim a positive case on causation, mitigation or quantification of damages, proper details of that case should be included in the defence or CPR part 20 defence at the outset or, if not then available, as early as possible thereafter."

138 In *Zurich Insurance Plc v Umerji* [2014] EWCA Civ 357 at [12], Underhill LJ recorded that the Court had been told by Counsel that, in the field of car hire charges at least, the rule was "not generally observed".

139 [2002] UKPC 48; [2002] 1 W.L.R. 3111 PC.

140 [2002] 1 W.L.R. 3111 PC at [16].

141 [1963] 1 Q.B. 239.

the plaintiff and his advisers should be made aware that such a point was going to be taken."[142]

The Court of Appeal's comment has even more resonance today. The Privy Council in *Geest* evidently thought so as did David Mackie QC sitting as a Deputy High Court judge in *Alexander Forbes Europe Ltd v SBJ Ltd*[143] as, presumably, also did Carnwath LJ in *Green v Alexander Johnson*.[144] A reasonable summary of these not entirely even principles would seem to be that a substantial challenge to the validity of an individual claim or a dispute about a claimant's entitlement to recover a particular head of loss should always be pleaded. Failure to take the point in the defence will at the least have adverse costs consequences. Conceivably, it will deprive the defendant of the right to deploy the point at trial.[145]

[142] [1963] 1 Q.B. 239 at 247–248 and see similarly at 246–247.

[143] [2002] EWHC 3121 (Comm) at [44]. This decision pre-dated what is now section C1.3(g) of the Commercial Court Guide.

[144] [2005] EWCA Civ 775 CA. See para.51-011, above for a more detailed account of the decision.

[145] It may be that CPR r.16.5(2) explains why the Rules Committee has never seen fit expressly to require the defendant to plead any allegation of failure to mitigate. This rule requires a defendant, where he denies an allegation, to "state his reasons for doing so" and "if he intends to put forward a different version of events from that given by the claimant, he must state his version". This must surely require a defendant to state if he considers that damages are not recoverable because the claimant avoided, or should have mitigated, the claimed loss, or because the claimant would have incurred the same loss even if the defendant's wrong had not occurred, or for any other reason.

CHAPTER 52

# THE TRIAL

TABLE OF CONTENTS



## I. PROOF

### 1. BURDEN OF PROOF

**52-001** The claimant has the burden of proving both the fact and the amount of damage before he can recover substantial damages.[1] This follows from the general rule that the burden of proving a fact is upon him who alleges it and not upon him who denies it, so that where a given allegation forms an essential part of a person's case the proof of such allegation falls on him.[2] Even if the defendant fails to deny the allegations of damage or suffers default, the claimant must still prove his loss.

---

1 Where he succeeds in proving neither fact nor amount of damage, he loses the action or, if a right is infringed, recovers only nominal damages. Where he succeeds in proving the fact of damage but not its amount, this generally permits only an award of nominal damages. See para.10-001, above.

2 Statements that the claimant has the burden of proof of damage are infrequent in the cases since the rule is beyond doubt. See, e.g. *The Clarence* (1850) 2 W. Rob. (Adm.) 283 at 286 to 287, per Dr Lushington: "It does not follow as a matter of necessity that anything is due for the detention of a vessel whilst under repair.... The onus of proving her loss rests with the plaintiff"; and *Bonham-Carter v Hyde Park Hotel* (1948) 64 T.L.R. 177 at 178, per Lord Goddard CJ: "Plaintiffs must understand that if they bring actions for damages it is for them to prove their damage; it is not enough to write down the particulars, and, so to speak, throw them at the head of the court, saying: 'This is what I have lost, I ask you to give me these damages.' They have to prove it." For a failure of a claimant to satisfy the burden of proof, see *Ashcroft v Curtin* [1971] 1 W.L.R. 1731 CA: facts at para.40-082, above (in a footnote). See also *Tate & Lyle Food and Distribution v GLC* [1982] 1 W.L.R. 149, where no damages were awarded for expenditure of managerial time in dealing with remedial measures necessitated by the defendants' nuisance because the claimants had kept no records of time spent and to have given an arbitrary percentage of the total loss and damage—the claimants were contending for 2.5 per cent—would have been pure speculation. The burden of proving lost profits remains upon the claimant owner of copyright or patentee and is not transferred to the defendant

Occasionally, however, the defendant will be found to admit the claimant's allegations of damage and then put in issue allegations in avoidance. This is the position where the defendant seeks to show that the claimant should have taken certain steps to mitigate his loss.[3] It was established by *Roper v Johnson*,[4] that the burden of proof on this issue is on the defendant, and the normal measure of damages will not be cut down unless the defendant succeeds in showing that the claimant ought reasonably to have taken the suggested mitigating steps. Thus in that case it was held, in an action for non-delivery of goods sold, that the buyer, who had accepted the seller's repudiation, was entitled to claim the normal measure of damages based on the market price of the goods at the time of due delivery because the seller had not shown that the buyer should have bought on a rising market in pursuance of his duty to mitigate. The same should apply in connection with mitigation in its two subsidiary meanings, i.e. where damages are affected by the conduct, character and circumstances of various parties and where a claimant suing for breach of contract is also himself in breach.[5] **52-002**

Where a claimant opts to recover wasted expenditure incurred on the faith of a contract which has been breached, sometimes referred to as "reliance damages", the burden lies on the innocent party to show that money has been expended in reliance on the contract. If this burden is discharged, then the burden shifts to the contract-breaker to show that the contract was, in any event, loss-making for the innocent party, such that the loss of the money expended was not caused by the breach.[6]

Other circumstances allied to mitigation where the onus should rest on the defendant used to appear in claims under the Fatal Accidents Act for the benefit of **52-003**

---

infringer: *Blayney v Clogau St Davids Gold Mines Ltd* [2002] EWCA Civ 1007; [2002] F.S.R. 233 at para.48-055, above.

3 See, for example, *Sony Computer Entertainment UK Ltd v Cinram Logistics Ltd* [2008] EWCA Civ 955 at [37], [43], and [49]. It is instructive to hold up this component of the burden of proof against the formalities of pleading as set out in the Practice Direction supplementing CPR Pt 16. Whilst imposing an obligation on a claimant to plead any facts relating to mitigation of loss or damage (para.8.2(8)), the Practice Direction imposes no equivalent obligation on a defendant to plead any fact relied upon in mitigation of or otherwise in relation to the amount of damages, as had previously been required by RSC Ord.18 r.12(1)(c). For a discussion on this subject, see paras 51-038 and 51-039, above. In *Geest Plc v Lansiquot* [2002] UKPC 48; [2002] 1 W.L.R. 3111 PC, the Privy Council took the opportunity to reassert the proposition that if a defendant intends to argue that a claimant has failed to act reasonably to mitigate his or her damages, notice of such contention should clearly be given long enough before the hearing to enable the claimant properly to prepare to meet it. In a case where there are pleadings directed to such issues, it was said to be the defendant's clear duty to plead any allegation of failure to mitigate in the defence.

4 (1873) L.R. 8 C.P. 167; confirmed in *Garnac Grain Co v Faure and Fairclough* [1968] A.C. 1130. See para.9-020, above; and see for avoided, as opposed to avoidable, loss, para.9-115, above.

5 See paras 9-002 to 9-013, above for consideration of these various meanings of mitigation. *Butterworth v Butterworth* [1920] P. 126 at 150, a claim for damages for adultery in the days before this cause of action was abolished, may still be of some significance in this connection. Since a successful claim was not dependent upon the adulterer's having had knowledge of the marriage, it ought to have followed, as McCardie J pointed out there (at 150), "that the onus rested on the co-respondent to prove as a matter of mitigation that he did not know that the woman was married, rather than on the petitioner to prove that the co-respondent possessed such knowledge"; yet it had "been continually held in recent years that the husband (if he desires to claim damages on the footing that the adulterer had knowledge) must prove such knowledge affirmatively." The reason for this McCardie J did not follow, but that there were anomalous features in the claim for damages for adultery also appears from his judgment in that case.

6 *Grange v Quinn* [2013] EWCA Civ 24 at [28] (Arden LJ) and at [101]-[102] (Gloster J).

a deceased's dependants. In such cases the prima facie measure of damages is the value of the dependency. This, however, formerly fell to be reduced by reason of benefits resulting to the dependants from the death in order that only the net pecuniary loss was awarded as damages.[7] Translated into terms of onus of proof, the dependants had to prove the value of the dependency which was lost to them, but after this the onus was upon the defendant to cut down this prima facie measure by proof of the receipt by the dependants of benefits resulting from the death which went to reduce the damages. This division of the onus of proof in such cases was adopted by Parker LJ in his judgment in *Mead v Clarke Chapman*.[8]

**52-004** On the issue of remoteness there are conflicting dicta in the House of Lords as to where the burden of proof lies. Thus Lord Sumner said in *S.S. Singleton Abbey v S.S. Paludina*,[9] that the claimant must show that a particular item of damage is not too remote before he can recover for it, while Lord Haldane and Lord Dunedin in *The Metagama*,[10] said that the defendant must show that a particular item of damage is too remote if he is not to be held liable for it. Lord Merriman P in *The Guildford*,[11] after considering the earlier dicta, expressed preference, obiter, for the view that the burden of proof lay on the claimant,[12] but there remains a tendency at first instance in ship collision cases, where the issue has generally arisen, to take into account only the dicta which favour placing the onus on the defendant.[13] This conflict of views essentially arises from the fact that, although it is clear law that the party alleging must prove, it is not always clear what particular allegations form an essential part of a party's case. It is submitted that on the issue of remoteness the claimant must allege the items for which he may properly recover: hence the burden of proving them is on him.

In *Hughes-Holland v BPE Solicitors*,[14] which concerned the recoverability of damages against negligent solicitors in circumstances where they had assumed limited responsibility in relation to a transaction, Lord Sumption JSC[15] held that the burden of proving facts which established that the claimant had suffered loss, and that such loss fell within the scope of the duty owed by the defendant, lay upon the claimant.

---

7 See paras 41-108 and following, above. Benefits are no longer taken into account: see para.41-111, above.

8 [1956] 1 W.L.R. 76 CA at 84: "Once a person … is shown to be a person who has suffered a loss of dependency, then the onus shifts. It is then for the defendants to show, if they can, that on the facts of the case the dependency originally lost has been reduced or has ceased entirely." And in *Baker v Dalgleish S.S. Co* [1922] 1 K.B. 361 CA, where the dependants were in receipt of a Crown voluntary pension which, as the law then stood, fell to be taken into account in assessing their damages, Scrutton LJ took the view that it was up to the defendant to lead evidence that it was the Crown's prevailing practice not to reduce or cancel the pension on account of damages awarded: at 373; see similarly *Johnson v Hill* [1945] 2 All E.R. 272 CA at 274, per du Parcq LJ.

9 [1927] A.C. 16 at 25 to 26. Other similar dicta are collected in the first footnote to para.8-003, above.

10 (1927) 29 LI. R. 253 HL at 254 and 256, respectively; Lord Dunedin's was a dissenting judgment. The case is also reported sub nom. *Canadian Pacific Ry v Kelvin Shipping Co* (1927) 138 L.T. 369 HL. Other similar dicta are collected in the second footnote to para.8-003, above.

11 [1956] P. 364.

12 [1956] P. 364 at 370.

13 See especially *The Bharatkhand* [1952] 1 Lloyd's Rep. 470 at 479; *The Lucile Bloomfield* [1967] 2 Lloyd's Rep. 308 at 313; *The Fritz Thyssen* [1968] P. 225 at 259. And see further para.8-003, above.

14 [2017] UKSC 21; [2017] 2 W.L.R. 1029.

15 With whom all of their Lordships agreed.

"The legal burden of proving any averment of fact lies upon the person who is required to assert it as part of his case. In the ordinary course, this means that the claimant has the burden of pleading and proving his loss, whereas the defendant has the burden of proving facts (such as failure to mitigate) going to avoid or abate the consequent liability in damages".

A new situation involving problems of onus of proof arose with the introduction, by the decision in *British Transport Commission v Gourley*,[16] of the element of taxation into the assessment of damages. It cannot be said to be settled whether the onus is on the claimant to prove that the rule in *British Transport Commission v Gourley*,[17] does not apply to his claim or on the defendant to prove that it does. The view that the onus remains on the claimant was early adopted in *Hall v Pearlberg*,[18] but the Court of Appeal in *Stoke-on-Trent City Council v Wood Mitchell & Co*,[19] put it upon the defendant to establish at least one of the two prerequisites for the application of the *Gourley* rule, namely that the damages awarded to the claimant will not be subject to tax.[20] The matter has already been fully considered when dealing with the incidence of taxation on damages.[21] Whatever the final solution, it may be said that, as with remoteness, the difficulty is in deciding what particular allegations form the essential elements of the claimant's case. **52-005**

The ongoing battles between the motor insurance market and credit hire companies who provide replacement vehicles to innocent victims of road traffic collisions has thrown up a series of decisions on burden of proof. The position, as summarised by the Court of Appeal in *Pattni v First Leicester Buses Ltd*,[22] is that the burden is, first, on the claimant to prove the need for a replacement car. If that is proved, then the claimant may recover as damages the cost of hiring the replacement car, and that would include if the claimant hires the replacement on credit terms. However, if the defendant can show that the cost incurred was more than reasonable, by showing that the credit hire charge was higher than the basic hire rate would have been, damages will be reduced to that extent—unless the claimant can, in turn, show that, through impecuniosity, he had no alternative to credit hire. **52-006**

The right to begin is generally determined by the burden of proof.[23] Since a claimant suing for substantial unliquidated damages must prove the fact and the amount of damage, the right to begin lies with him; this is so even if on all other issues the burden of proof should lie on the defendant. Only if the claimant will not undertake to offer proof of substantial damage,[24] or if the damages or their mode **52-007**

---

16 [1956] A.C. 185.

17 [1956] A.C. 185.

18 [1956] 1 W.L.R. 244; contrast *West Suffolk C.C. v Rought* [1957] A.C. 403 at 413.

19 [1980] 1 W.L.R. 254 CA.

20 See, too, *Pennine Raceway v Kirklees Metropolitan Council (No.2)* [1989] S.T.C. 122 CA, *Finley v Connell Associates* [2002] Lloyd's Rep. P.N. 62; *Shanks v Unilever Plc* [2014] EWHC 1647 (Pat); [2014] R.P.C. 29.

21 See paras 18-056 to 18-058, above.

22 [2011] EWCA Civ 1384; [2012] P.I.Q.R. Q1 at [30] (Aikens LJ).

23 *Mercer v Whall* (1845) 5 Q.B. 447 is the case where it was laid down that where there is anything to be proved by the claimant he has the right to begin.

24 See, e.g. *Chapman v Rawson* (1846) 8 Q.B. 673. Lord Denman CJ said: "The most simple rule … would be to say that the affirmative issue lay on the claimant to the extent of the damages claimed by him…. But if his counsel will not undertake to offer proof of substantial damages, it is reasonable to say that no affirmative issue lies upon him": at 675.

of calculation are agreed, as with liquidated damages,[25] and the defendant has the burden of proof on all other issues, does the right to begin pass to the defendant.

## 2. EVIDENCE

### (1) General damage

52-008 **(a) Damage inferred and damage presumed** Certain damage may be inferred or presumed: this is particularly so with non-pecuniary losses. Thus by showing serious personal injury to the claimant, it may be inferred that pain and suffering resulted. Where heads of damage are routinely inferred by the courts—pain and suffering in personal injury claims; deprivation of liberty in false imprisonment claims; injury to feelings in discrimination claims—the courts have laid down tariffs which ensure consistency in awards and promote settlement of disputes. The Judicial College produces *Guidelines for the Assessment of General Damages in Personal Injury Cases*,[26] where a range of figures is set out for each individual type of injury, from tetraplegia downwards, providing guidelines or markers for damages for non-pecuniary loss in personal injury claims.[27] In false imprisonment and malicious prosecution cases, in which the right to trial by jury remains, guidance for juries was laid down in *Thompson v Commissioner of Police of the Metropolis*.[28] Further, in *Vento v Chief Constable of West Yorkshire*,[29] on an appeal arising out of a claim for sex discrimination, the Court of Appeal identified three broad bands for compensation for injury to feelings, for the assistance of employment tribunals, in discrimination cases.[30] By contrast, the Court of Appeal has declined to lay down guideline figures in libel cases,[31] or in cases arising out of the misuse of confidential information.[32]

Damage is sometimes said to be "presumed", particularly in cases involving injury to reputation.[33] In defamation the court is entitled to award substantial dam-

---

25 In *Silk v Humphrey* (1835) 7 C. & P. 14 and *Edge v Hillary* (1852) 3 C. & K. 43 the defendant was held to have the right to begin; both cases are debt.

26 Now in its 14th edition, published in 2017.

27 See para 40-275 and following.

28 [1998] Q.B. 498. The tariffs identified in these guidelines have no application in false imprisonment cases where the victim was already in prison and falsely imprisoned in his cell: *Iqbal v Prison Officers Association* [2009] EWCA Civ 1312; [2010] Q.B. 732 at [48].

29 [2002] EWCA Civ 1871; [2003] I.C.R. 318. In *Halliday v Creation Consumer Finance Ltd* [2013] EWCA Civ 333 the Court of Appeal declined to apply these brackets to damages for breach of the Data Protection Act. Rather, in light of the bare, but uncontroverted, assertion in the claimant's statement of case that he found the breach of the Act "highly distressing", the Court of Appeal awarded £750 as damages for distress, in addition to a nominal £1 for the contravention of the Act itself.

30 The Vento scales were subsequently up-rated in line with inflation: see *Da'Bell v NSPCC* [2010] I.R.L.R. 19. They were up-rated again by 10 per cent by *Simmons v Castle* [2012] EWCA Civ 1288; [2013] 1 W.L.R. 1239: see *Beckford v Southwark LBC* [2016] I.R.L.R. 178 (Langstaff J).

31 *Cairns v Modi* [2012] EWCA Civ 1382; [2013] 1 W.L.R. 1015.

32 *Gulati v MGN Ltd* [2015] EWCA Civ 1291; [2017] QB 149 at [77]: "This court has no material on which to fix a tariff in this area. There is virtually no history of such awards and in any event the circumstances could vary so greatly as to render any such tariff of little use" (Arden LJ).

33 See also *Al-Amoudi v Brisard* [2006] EWHC 1062 (QB); [2007] 1 W.L.R. 113 at [29]-[30] where Gray J approved a statement in *Phipson on Evidence* that "Strictly speaking, the term 'presumption of fact' is a misnomer. It describes the readiness of the court to draw certain repeated inferences as a result of common human experience." Note also that, when considering whether the threshold test of "serious harm", mandated by s.1(1) of the Defamation Act 2013, has been surpassed, the language

ages although proof of damage is not produced: in *Tripp v Thomas*,[34] it was held that £40 was properly awarded although no evidence of damage had been given at the trial.[35] And with pecuniary loss it has been held in *Rolin v Steward*,[36] as to traders, and in *Kpohraror v Woolwich Building Society*,[37] as to others, that loss by injury to credit and reputation caused by the defendant's failure to honour the claimant's drafts may be presumed. Similarly, in actions of inducement of breach of contract it has been said, as by Nevile J in *Goldsoll v Goldman*,[38] that damage, generally by way of loss of profits, may be inferred.[39] And the same applies to passing off, the most important form of injurious falsehood. In *Draper v Trist*,[40] Goddard LJ said that

> "the law assumes, or presumes, that, if the goodwill of a man's business has been interfered with by the passing off of goods, damage results therefrom .... It is one of the class of cases in which the law presumes that the plaintiff has suffered damage".[41]

In all these varied cases such inferences of damage may be regarded as legal presumptions operating in the claimant's favour, to some extent obviating the necessity of production of evidence of damage by him. It may, however, be unwise for a claimant to rely too heavily on inferences and presumptions of damage, for a failure to produce any evidence at all may result in an award of small or even nominal damages, as in the defamation case of *Hayward v Hayward*.[42] In *Jameel v Wall Street Journal Europe SPRL*,[43] a modern manifestation of the same point, by a majority the House of Lords held that a trading company which had a trading reputation within the jurisdiction was entitled to recover general damages for libel without pleading or proving special damage if the publication had a tendency to damage it in its way of business.[44] However, Lord Bingham acknowledged that, where a trading company had suffered no actual financial loss, any damages awarded should be kept strictly within modest bounds. **52-009**

---

of "drawing inferences" is used: *Cooke v MGN Ltd* [2014] EWHC 2831 (QB); [2015] 1 W.L.R. 895 at [43] (Bean J); *Sobrinho v Impresa Publishing SA* [2016] EWHC 66 (QB) at [47] (Dingemans J).

34 (1824) 3 B. & C. 427.

35 See also *Cooper v Turrell* [2011] EWHC 3269 (QB) at [95] (Tugendhat J), citing *English and Scottish Co-operative Properties Mortgage and Investment Society Ltd v Odhams Press Ltd* [1940] 1 K.B. 440.

36 (1854) 14 C.B. 595.

37 [1996] 4 All E.R. 119 CA.

38 [1914] 2 Ch. 603 at 615: see para.48-005, above.

39 Compare *Exchange Telegraph Co v Gregory* [1896] 1 Q.B. 147 CA at 156, 158, in the footnote at the end of para.48-005, above. The position is probably the same with conspiracy: see para.48-020, above.

40 [1939] 2 All E.R. 513 CA.

41 [1939] 2 All E.R. 513 CA at 526; see the longer quotation from the judgment at para.48-016, above. See also *British Telecommunications Plc v One in a Million Ltd* [1999] 1 W.L.R. 903 (CA). It would seem that pecuniary damage will now be inferred in injurious falsehoods other than passing off if they fall within the terms of s.3 of the Defamation Act 1952: see para.48-011, above.

42 (1887) 34 Ch. D. 198. What evidence is admissible should follow the same lines as with other general damage: see paras 52-010 to 52-014, below. It is submitted that there is no merit in the curious inference drawn in *Delegal v Highley* (1837) 8 C. & P. 444 that where the law presumes general damage in the claimant's favour he is debarred from offering evidence that general damage resulted.

43 [2006] UKHL 44; [2007] 1 A.C. 359.

44 The majority of their Lordships appears not to have endorsed the Court of Appeal's acceptance that an action for defamation with only minimal attendant actual damage could constitute an unnecessary interference with freedom of expression and consequently be incompatible with art.10 of the European Convention on Human Rights.

52-010 **(b) Other general damage** General damage other than that which is inferred or presumed requires to be proved, and the question then arises as to what evidence is admissible in proof thereof. The cases on this issue, the majority of which are cases of defamation, establish the following propositions.

52-011 Evidence in proof of general damage in defamation cases should normally consist of evidence of general losses. Thus in *Evans v Harries*,[45] and *Bluck v Lovering*,[46] claims for a slander actionable per se and for a libel respectively, the claimant was allowed to give evidence of the general falling off of his business as proof of general damage. Similarly in *Harrison v Pearce*,[47] an action for a libel upon the proprietors of a newspaper, general evidence of the decline in the circulation of the newspaper was held admissible in proof of general damage.[48]

52-012 On the other hand, evidence cannot be given, in proof of general damage, of particular transactions lost or particular customers lost with a view to showing specific loss. "In an action for slandering a man in his trade," said Cresswell J obiter in *Rose v Groves*,[49]

> "where the declaration alleges that he thereby lost his trade, he may show a *general* damage to his trade though he cannot give evidence of *particular* instances."[50]

Thus in *Bluck v Lovering*,[51] a case of libel, the claimant was allowed to prove a general loss of business but not the loss of specific customers as general damage. In the old case of *Ashley v Harrison*,[52] where the claimant sued for profits lost when a concert singer engaged by him had refused to sing because she had been libelled by the defendant and was afraid of a bad reception, it was held that although the box-keeper of the claimant's opera house might be asked generally as to the falling off in receipts he might not be asked whether particular persons had given up their boxes.[53] And in *Fleming v Bank of New Zealand*,[54] where the defendant bank failed in breach of contract to honour the claimant's cheques, it was held that, although the claimant was entitled to substantial general damages, evidence of his loss of custom and credit from particular individuals was inadmissible in the absence of an allegation of special damage.[55]

52-013 It may, however, be possible to give evidence of specific losses which have been incurred after the issue of the claim form, not with a view to recovering damages for the specific losses as such but in order to assist the court in quantifying the general damage. In addition to the recent credit hire cases such as *Coles v Hetherton*,[56] two mid-19th century cases are instructive in this connection and lend support to this view. In *Ingram v Lawson*,[57] an action was brought by a shipowner

---

45 (1856) 1 H. & N. 251.
46 (1885) 1 T.L.R. 497.
47 (1859) 32 L.T. O.S. 298.
48 These three cases were relied upon by Bowen LJ in his general statement of the law as to pleading and proof of damage in *Ratcliffe v Evans* [1892] 2 Q.B. 524 CA at 529–530.
49 (1843) 5 M. & G. 613; the action was one arising out of public nuisance.
50 (1843) 5 M. & G. 613 at 618–619. The italics are Cresswell J's.
51 (1885) 1 T.L.R. 497.
52 (1793) 1 Esp. 48.
53 The claimant, however, failed on the substantive ground that the damage was too remote.
54 [1900] A.C. 577 PC.
55 See [1900] A.C. 577 PC at 587.
56 See para.52-014, below.
57 (1840) 6 Bing. N.C. 212. In *Atlantis World Group of Companies NV v Gruppo Editoriale L'Espresso*

for a libel which stated that his ship, then advertised to sail to the East Indies, was unseaworthy and was purchased by Jews to take out convicts. No special damage was laid, the action being commenced three days after the libel was published. It was held that evidence was rightly admitted of the average profits of a voyage to the East Indies, and of the amount by which the claimant's profits for this first voyage after the libel were below the average. "The jury", said Coltman J,

> "must have some mode of estimating them [i.e. the damages]; and they could not be in a condition to do so unless they knew something of the nature of the claimant's business and of the general return from his voyages".[58]

In *Goslin v Corry*,[59] another case of libel, the claimant wished to give evidence of his arrest in consequence of the libel, the arrest having taken place after action brought. The defendant's counsel consented to the admission of this evidence, but then objected that the judge should have directed the jury to exclude it from their consideration in assessing the damages. It was held that the judge's charge was right as he did not tell the jury that they were at liberty to give damages for the arrest as such, but told them that they might view it as a confirmation of the claimant's apprehension that an arrest would be the probable consequence of the libel.[60]

Finally, credit hire cases again provide valuable decisions in this area. In *Coles v Hetherton*,[61] the Court of Appeal held that the correct jurisprudential analysis of a claim for diminution in value suffered by a chattel as a result of the negligence of a wrongdoer is that it is a claim for general damages. However, an invoice for the cost of repairs would be admissible evidence of such diminution in value.[62] In *McBride v UK Insurance Ltd*,[63] the Court of Appeal upheld a decision of the district judge who, in the absence of evidence of seven day basic hire rates, had taken the evidence of 28 day rates and adjusted them by 15 per cent. Flaux LJ held: **52-014**

> "It seems to me that, taking a realistic approach to the manner in which these credit hire cases are handled and tried, the judge was entitled to make the 15 per cent adjustment. He had, as he said at the hearing, twenty years' experience of credit hire cases and will

---

*SpA* [2008] EWHC 1323 (QB); [2009] E.M.L.R. 15, the claimants complained that an article published in an Italian language magazine by the defendants meant that they were controlled by the mafia, or that there were at least reasonable grounds to suppose that they were so controlled. Shortly before trial, the claimants abandoned a claim for actual financial loss suffered as a result of the libel, and substituted for it a general damages claim. As a corporate claimant, there could be no presumption of damage to reputation, so the claimant sought to evidence the necessary reputation. This was, as Sir Charles Gray held at [54], "demolished in the course of cross-examination". In this context, he was "unable to derive assistance" from *Ingram v Lawson*.

58 (1840) 6 Bing. N.C. 212 at 216. Maule J said similarly that the evidence was admitted "only that the jury might know what sort of business the claimant carried out": at 217.

59 (1844) 7 M. & G. 342.

60 It was indeed assumed throughout that the evidence was not strictly admissible at all, but this appears to have been based partly on the fact that the very arrest was laid as special damage, to prove which allegation the evidence was plainly inadmissible, and partly on the assumption that a second action could be brought for special damage arising subsequent to action brought, which was surely a faulty assumption.

61 [2013] EWCA Civ 1704; [2015] 1 W.L.R. 160.

62 At [28]. By contrast, if the chattel concerned "is one that is normally used in the hope of making a profit (such as a trading ship, a lorry or a taxi), then a claim for the profits lost because the chattel could not be used for that trading would constitute 'special damages'. Those damages would have to be specifically pleaded and proved".

63 [2017] EWCA Civ 144.

have seen many instances of the differences between 7 day, 14 day and 28 day rates in the cases he has tried. That was precisely the matter of which the claimant was inviting him to take judicial notice."

The court's ability to take judicial notice of such matters going to quantification of loss should be no surprise, given the regularity with which it has been observed that the court's role is to be realistic, not mechanistic, and "do its best" in quantifying loss.[64]

## (2) Special damage

**52-015** The evidence in proof of special damage[65] must show the same particularity as is necessary for its pleading.[66] It should therefore normally consist of evidence of particular losses, such as the loss of specific customers or specific contracts. Thus, had there been a sufficient allegation of special damage in all the cases where its proof has been refused because of the claimant's failure to plead specific instances,[67] the claimant would still have been required to give evidence of these specific instances to prove the special damage.[68]

**52-016** With proof as with pleading, the courts are realistic and accept that the particularity must be tailored to the facts. Bowen LJ laid this down in the leading case on pleading and proof of damage, *Ratcliffe v Evans*.[69] In relation to special damage he said:

> "The character of the acts themselves which produce the damage, and the circumstances under which these acts are done, must regulate the degree of certainty and particularity with which the damage done ought to be …[70] proved. As much certainty and particularity must be insisted on …in …[71] proof of damage as is reasonable, having regard to the circumstance and to the nature of the acts themselves by which the damage is done. To insist upon less would be to relax old and intelligible principles. To insist upon more would be the vainest pedantry."[72]

This principle finds its fullest illustration in cases of injurious falsehood, a tort which formerly required allegation and proof of special damage by the claimant for success in the action.[73] In *Riding v Smith*,[74] where the defendant falsely stated that

---

64 See, for example, *Bacciottini v Gotelee and Goldsmith* [2016] EWCA Civ 170; [2016] 4 W.L.R. 98 at [57] (Davis LJ), and *Capita Alternative Fund Services (Guernsey) Ltd v Drivers Jonas* [2012] EWCA Civ 1417 at [43(i)] (Gross LJ), where it was said that this reflected "the true nature of quantum disputes and their history as jury questions".

65 For what is special damage for the purpose of pleading see paras 51-016 to 51-025, above. The cases cited there establish that, if special damage is not pleaded, it cannot be proved.

66 See paras 51-026 to 51-029, above.

67 See *Hunt v Jones* (1618) Cro. Jac. 499, *Barnes v Prudlin* (1667) 1 Sid. 396 and *Westwood v Cowne* (1816) 1 Stark. 172 at para.51-026, above.

68 In *Collins Stewart Ltd v Financial Times Ltd* [2005] E.M.L.R. 5 at 64, a libel action, Tugendhat J acceded to the defendant's application to strike out a claim quantified as the diminution in the claimant company's market value caused by the alleged libel, Tugendhat J concluding that the formulation was far too uncertain as a valuation to be acceptable as a legal basis for assessing damages.

69 [1892] 2 Q.B. 524 CA.

70 The omitted portions refer to pleading and not to proof. They are dealt with at para.51-029, above.

71 See previous note.

72 [1892] 2 Q.B. 524 CA at 532–533.

73 For statutory modifications see para.48-011, above.

74 (1876) 1 Ex. D. 91.

the claimant's wife, who assisted him in his business, had committed adultery with the parish incumbent, evidence of the general falling off in the claimant's business was held admissible to prove the necessary special damage.[75] Similarly, in *Ratcliffe v Evans*[76] itself and in *Worsley v Cooper*,[77] in which cases the defendant had published, in a newspaper and in circulars to the claimant's customers respectively, the false statement that the claimant was no longer carrying on business, special damage was allowed to be proved by evidence of a general falling off of business. Outside injurious falsehood, the allegation and proof of special damage is a prerequisite of success in most slanders and in actions arising out of a public nuisance: authority that evidence of a general loss will suffice where particularity is ruled out on the facts is to be found for these two types of action in *Hartley v Herring*,[78] and in *Rose v Groves*,[79] respectively.[80] In *Watkins v Home Secretary*,[81] a case concerning the tort of misfeasance in public office, the House of Lords decided that the tort was not actionable per se, Lord Bingham, with whose opinion Lord Hope, Lord Rodger and Lord Carswell agreed, observing[82]:

> "I would accordingly rule that the tort of misfeasance in public office is never actionable without proof of material damage as I have defined it."

Lord Bingham's definition of material damage[83] encompassed financial loss, physical injury and psychiatric illness but not distress, injured feelings, indignation or annoyance. *Karagozlu v Metropolitan Police Commissioner*,[84] which exhibits an apparent, but not actual, confusion of principle is probably explicable as an example of the courts accepting evidence of a general loss as sufficient proof of damage to found the tort. In *Karagozlu* the Court of Appeal held that loss of liberty, for which the claimant would be entitled to recover general damages, would be sufficient damage to maintain a cause of action for misfeasance in public office. If the prerequisite of the tort is the incidence of special damage, the potential for an award of general damages might be thought, almost by definition, to be insufficient to found such a claim. But a certain care with language is called for, the Court of Appeal preferring the expression material damage coined by Lord Bingham in *Watkins* over the more traditional terminology of special damage as the requirement of the tort. Once suitable linguistic adjustments are made, it is difficult to see why loss of liberty, which is generally regarded as sufficient injury to result in an award of damages, could not be said to meet the Court of Appeal's requirement for material damage in order to found a misfeasance claim.[85] In *Hussain v West Mercia Constabulary*,[86]

---

75 The decision has, however, been questioned on the ground of remoteness: see para.48-011, above (second footnote therein).

76 [1892] 2 Q.B. 524 CA.

77 [1939] 1 All E.R. 290.

78 (1799) 8 T.R. 130: loss of congregation by a clergyman. The case is so explained by Bowen LJ in *Ratcliffe v Evans* [1892] 2 Q.B. 524 CA at 531.

79 (1843) 5 M. & G. 613: loss of custom by an innkeeper.

80 Both cases, and also *Ratcliffe v Evans* [1892] 2 Q.B. 524 CA, were concerned more with pleading than with proof but the two issues are interrelated.

81 [2006] UKHL 17; [2006] 2 A.C. 395.

82 [2006] 2 A.C. 395 at [27].

83 [2006] 2 A.C. 395 at [7].

84 [2006] EWCA Civ 1691; [2007] 1 W.L.R. 1881.

85 In *Chase International Express Ltd v McRae* [2003] EWCA Civ 505; [2004] P.I.Q.R. P21 CA at 314, for want of sufficient evidence, the Court of Appeal overturned an award of £41,871.43 for future

by contrast, the claimant's complaints of anxiety, stress and numbness in his left arm and leg, supposedly attributable to the defendant's alleged misfeasance were held not to be capable of satisfying the requirement of material damage as set by Lord Bingham, the Court of Appeal upholding the dismissal of the claim as disclosing no cause of action.[87]

**52-017** The Court of Appeal's decision in *Parabola Investments Ltd v Browallia Cal Ltd*,[88] provides an interesting example of the court's pragmatism in the proof of special damage. The second claimant was a company set up for the purpose of trading in stocks, shares and derivatives. The second defendant was a well established financial institution trading on the London Stock Exchange by whom the third defendant was employed as a senior futures broker. The claimant was induced to continue trading in so-called Stock Exchange Electronic Trading Service (SETS) by the third defendant's repeated false assurances that the trading was profitable whereas it was in truth disastrously loss-making from an early stage. The trial judge accepted the claimant's contention that, but for the third defendant's deceit, it would have made profits at a rate of 50 per cent per annum. On appeal, the second defendant argued that the judge's award of lost profit at the rate of 50 per cent was unsustainable because the claimant had failed to prove that a specific amount of profits would have been earned by a particular date. Highlighting what he referred to as the central flaw in the appellants' submissions, Toulson LJ observed that some claims for consequential loss were capable of being established with precision whereas other forms of consequential loss were not capable of similarly precise calculation because they involved the attempted measurement of things which would or might have happened (or might not have happened) but for the defendant's wrongful conduct. In such a situation the law did not require a claimant to perform the impossible.

**52-018** In *Asda Stores Ltd v Mastercard Inc*,[89] a claim for damages arising out of alleged anti-competitive practices in the market for credit and debit card transactions,[90] Popplewell J held that

---

loss of earnings calculated on a multiplier/multiplicand basis substituting a "round sum" of £12,500 calculated in accordance with *Blamire v South Cumbria Health Authority* [1993] P.I.Q.R. Q1. In a short concurring judgment, Newman J remarked on the necessity for evidence to support the claims advanced, observing at [31]:

> "If the method of preparation and presentation adopted in this case reflects a common circumstance in connection with personal injury cases in the district court it has, in my judgment, departed too far from the basic principle that a claimant must prove his case by evidence capable of supporting the conclusions to which the court is invited to come … Approaching a matter with a broad brush does not mean an absence of material is acceptable. The broad brush approach merely enables the court to do justice where there may be gaps in detail, which normally arise because of the character of the case under investigation."

Those inclined to regard the CPR as ushering out the rules of evidence or the burden of proof in civil proceedings should think again!

[86] [2008] EWCA Civ 1205.

[87] Albeit with some reservations on the part of Maurice Kay LJ expressed at [20] of his judgment. The result sits not entirely comfortably with the decision in *Corby Group Litigation Claimants v Corby BC* [2008] EWCA Civ 463; [2009] QB 335 to allow claims for personal injury said to arise out of a public nuisance, about which similar objections had been taken, to proceed to trial. See second footnote to para.51-025, above, for a brief discussion of the case.

[88] [2010] EWCA Civ 486; [2011] Q.B. 477.

[89] [2017] EWHC 93 (Comm); [2017] 4 C.M.L.R. 32.

[90] In another such case, *Sainsbury's Supermarkets v Mastercard Inc* [2016] CAT 11, the evidential requirements when seeking to prove a claim for interest as damages were considered: see at [514]–

"When it comes to the burden on the claimants to prove their loss … they are entitled to invoke the long established principles that the court takes a pragmatic approach",

including in particular[91]:

"(1) Only as much certainty and particularity is insisted on in proof of damage as is reasonable, having regard to the circumstances and to the nature of the acts by which the damage is done.[92]

(2) The fact that it is not possible for a claimant to prove the exact sum of its loss is not a bar to recovery. Where, as in this case, the assessment of damages inevitably involves an element of estimation and assumption, restoration by way of compensatory damages is often accomplished by 'sound imagination' and a 'broad axe'[93]… The 'broad axe' metaphor appears to originate in Scotland in the 19th century. The more creative painting metaphor of a 'broad brush' is sometimes used. In either event the sense is clear. The Court will not allow an unreasonable insistence on precision to defeat the justice of compensating a claimant for infringement of his rights.

…

However, where the court is compelled to use a broad brush in the absence of precision in the evidence of the harm suffered by a claimant, it should err on the side of under-compensation so as (a) to reflect the uncertainty as to the loss actually suffered and (b) to give the defendant the benefit of any doubts in the calculation."[94]

## (3) Modes of proof

There is no theoretical limit to the forms of evidence which may be adduced in order to establish, or rebut, a claim for damages. To establish primary facts, witness statements may be relied upon pursuant to CPR r.32. Expert evidence may be relied upon pursuant to CPR r.35. Contemporary documents, whether a party's own or those obtained on disclosure from the other side or a third party,[95] will often provide substantial assistance to the court.[96] **52-019**

In addition to findings of primary fact, the court may draw such factual inferences as are properly open to it in the assessment of loss. In *Ted Baker Plc v AXA Insurance UK Plc*,[97] an insurance claim in which quantum of loss was in issue, it was common ground and accepted by the judge (and not in issue on the appeal) that modelling and the drawing of inferences could be used to establish the quantum of

---

[521].

91 At [306]-[307].

92 Citing *Ratcliffe v Evans* [1892] 2 Q.B. 524, per Bowen LJ at 532–533; and *Devenish Nutrition Ltd v Sanofi-Aventis SA* [2007] EWHC 2394 (Ch); [2008] E.C.C. 4, per Lewison J at [30].

93 Citing *Watson Laidlaw & Co Ltd v Pott Cassels & Williamson (A Firm)* 1914 S.C. (H.L.) 18, per Lord Shaw at 29–30; *Devenish* per Lewison J at [27]–[29] (cited with approval in *One Step (Support) Ltd v Morris-Garner* [2016] EWCA Civ 180); and *Devenish Nutrition Ltd v Sanofi-Aventis SA* [2008] EWCA Civ 1086, per Arden LJ at [110] and Tuckey LJ at [159].

94 Citing *SPE International Ltd v Professional Preparation Contractors (UK) Ltd* [2002] EWHC 881 (Ch), per Rimer J at [87], approved by the Court of Appeal in *Blayney (t/a Aardvark Jewellery) v Clogau St Davids Gold Mines Ltd* [2002] EWCA Civ 1007; [2003] F.S.R. 19, per Sir Andrew Morritt VC at [31]–[34].

95 Pursuant to CPR r.31.

96 On the particular value of contemporaneous documentation, see *Synclair v East Lancashire Hospitals NHS Trust* [2015] EWCA Civ 1283 at [10] (Tomlinson LJ).

97 [2017] EWCA Civ 4097.

loss.[98] This is consistent with the approach taken to quantifying loss, which is that, as there held, "lack of precision in relation to quantum is not a bar to recovery".[99]

The court has extensive case management powers enabling it to give effect to the overriding objective of dealing with cases justly and at proportionate cost,[100] and it is the duty of the parties to help the court to further the overriding objective.[101] The court is required to further the overriding objective by actively managing cases.[102] Consistently with this, the court will decide the appropriate disclosure order, having regard to the overriding objective and the need to limit disclosure to that which is necessary to deal with the case justly.[103] Further, the court may control the evidence by giving directions as to the issues on which it requires evidence, the nature of the evidence which it requires to decide those issues, and the way in which the evidence is to be placed before the court, and the court may exclude evidence that would otherwise be admissible.[104] No party may call an expert or put in evidence an expert's report without the court's permission.[105]

Since 1 April 2013, CPR r.32.2(3) has permitted the court to give directions identifying or limiting the issues to which factual evidence may be directed, identifying the witnesses who may be called or whose evidence may be read, or limiting the length or format of witness statements. The first reported use of this power was in *MacLennan v Morgan Sindall (Infrastructure) Plc*,[106] a personal injury claim in which liability was admitted and the court was required to assess damages. Green J was confronted with a proposal by the claimant to tender the evidence of 43 witnesses regarding his loss of earnings claim. The judge limited the claimant to 14 witnesses giving evidence of comparative earnings, and a further 14 witnesses on any other aspect of the claim, in addition to the claimant and his wife.

## II. Judgment

### 1. Province of Judge and Jury: Law and Fact

**52-020** It is today exceptional for a civil action to be tried by a judge and jury.[107] But in those exceptional cases, it is a general rule that matters of law are for the judge and

98 See at [103].

99 In the event, the trial judge, Eder J, did not accept that the claimant had, even with the assistance of financial modelling performed by an expert witness, established a loss of profit above the insurance excess, and the Court of Appeal declined to interfere with this factual conclusion.

100 CPR r.1.1.

101 CPR r.1.3.

102 CPR r.1.4.

103 CPR r.31.5(7).

104 CPR r.32.1.

105 CPR r.35.4(1).

106 [2013] EWHC 4044 (QB); [2014] 1 W.L.R. 2462.

107 The qualified right to jury trial in actions for libel and slander was removed by s.11 of the Defamation Act 2013, leaving a judicial discretion and a presumption against jury trials. In *Yeo v Times Newspapers Ltd* [2014] EWHC 2853 (QB); [2015] 1 W.L.R. 971, the first application for trial by jury after the coming into force of that section, Warby J held (at [51]) that it was necessary for the applicant both to identify specific considerations affecting the trial (such as a particular public interest in the proceedings), and to show that these would make a jury trial more appropriate than trial without a jury. However, he held that the applicant's submissions "do not identify any skills, knowledge, aptitudes or other attributes likely to be possessed by a jury which would make it better equipped than a judge to grapple with the issues that arise and may need to be tried", and noted in respect of an argument that the outcome would have a profound consequences for public life that "these points strike me as arguments that tend to favour trial by judge alone, with the reasoned judg-

matters of fact for the jury. This rule applies equally to the issue of damages: the only difficulty lies in ascertaining when an issue of damages presents a question of law and when a question of fact.

The matter has received most attention in relation to remoteness of damage. For a long time the question of remoteness was regarded, according to the prevailing dicta, as a question of law. Blackburn J in *Hobbs v L.S.W. Ry*,[108] and Lord Esher MR in *Hammond v Bussey*,[109] both said that they did not think the question of remoteness was one for the jury,[110] while Farwell LJ in *Chaplin v Hicks*,[111] stated the antithesis that **52-021**

> "the question of remoteness is for the judge; the assessment of damages is for the jury".

However, in *Monarch S.S. Co v Karlshamns Oljefabriker*,[112] both Lord Wright and Lord du Parcq said that the question of remoteness was one of fact.[113] This apparent conflict was neatly resolved by McNair J in *Mehmet Dogan Bey v Abdeni*,[114] where he laid down an all-embracing rule. He said:

> "It is the function of the judge to direct the jury as to the meaning of the terms 'natural and direct consequences' or 'reasonably foreseeable consequences' and whether a particular head of damage is capable in law of being a consequence falling within these phrases, and to direct them whether there is any evidence that a particular consequence is a consequence falling within these phrases; it is then for the jury to find as a fact whether a particular head of damage is such a consequence and the jury's conclusion on that point (subject to there being evidence to support it) is final."[115]

He added that in his opinion the matters had been so treated in *Weld-Blundell v Stephens*,[116] and that his view was in accord with Devlin J's judgment in *Royal Greek Government v Minister of Transport*.[117]

It would seem that other issues in relation to damages should be treated in the same way. Thus while both Bankes and Scrutton LJJ said in *Payzu v Saunders*,[118] that the question of mitigation of damage is a question of fact, it is clear that they **52-022**

---

ment that only such a mode of trial would bring. There are real risks of a jury verdict being unclear or misunderstood or both": at [53]. Adopting this approach, defamation trials by jury are likely to be exceptionally unusual.

108 (1875) L.R. 10 Q.B. 111 at 122.

109 (1888) 20 Q.B.D. 79 CA at 89.

110 Lord Esher MR added the qualification that "possibly, under certain circumstances, with regard to some subject-matters, it would be competent to a judge to ask particular questions of a jury in order to assist him in coming to a conclusion on such a question": (1888) 20 Q.B.D. 79 CA at 89 to 90.

111 [1911] 2 K.B. 786 CA at 797.

112 [1949] A.C. 196.

113 [1949] A.C. 196 at 223 and 232 respectively. Lord Wright cited in support a dictum of Viscount Haldane LC in *British Westinghouse Co v Underground Ry* [1912] A.C. 673 at 688 that "the quantum of damage is a question of fact". That case, however, concerned mitigation.

114 [1951] 2 K.B. 405.

115 [1951] 2 K.B. 405 at 411. See too *Transfield Shipping Inc v Mercator Shipping Inc (The Achilleas)* [2008] UKHL 48; [2009] 1 A.C. 61, where Lord Hoffmann held at [25]: "It is true that the question of whether the damage was foreseeable is a question of fact: see *Monarch Steamship Co Ltd v Karlshamns Oljefabriker (A/B)* [1949] A.C. 196. But the question of whether a given type of loss is one for which a party assumed contractual responsibility involves the interpretation of the contract as a whole against its commercial background, and this, like all questions of interpretation, is a question of law."

116 [1920] A.C. 956.

117 (1950) 83 Ll. L.R. 228; see at 236–237.

118 [1919] 2 K.B. 581 CA at 588, 589 respectively. See too *British Westinghouse Co v Underground Ry*

were referring to the question of whether a claimant, under an admitted duty to mitigate his loss[119] has satisfied that duty[120]; the same is true of Sir John Donaldson MR's similar comments in *The Solholt*.[121] But whether the circumstances are such as to give rise to a duty to mitigate must surely be a question of law.[122] The position was summarised by Briggs LJ in *LSREF III Wight Ltd v Gateley LLP*,[123] holding that mitigation issues are heavily fact sensitive, multifactorial questions, but that the question whether there has been an unreasonable failure to mitigate, and the application of a reasonableness test does require "an objective analysis which requires something more than just fact-finding".[124]

## 2. Assessment of Damages

### (1) In general

52-023 When sitting alone, the judge assesses the damages; if the trial is with a jury the assessment is submitted to the jury.

52-024 **(a) Need for lump sum award** With the exception of claims to which the amended s.2 of the Damages Act 1996 applies, it remains the law that the award must be in the form of a lump sum for which judgment is entered. No other form of final award is currently allowed to the court, so that in *Fournier v Canadian National Ry*,[125] it was held to be improper and illegal to award an annuity by way of damages. Just as the rule was, before legislation intervened, that the Court of Appeal could not substitute its own award for the jury's even with the consent of the parties,[126] so there is no reason to believe that in cases untouched by the replacement s.2 the hallowed lump sum award could be bypassed by agreement. As for the structured settlement, which formed an important part of the 1990s scene, it was admittedly alternative to the lump sum award but did not represent an award of damages as there was no judicial power to award to the claimant, or to impose upon both claimant and defendant, such a settlement; structures were agreed voluntarily between the parties. However, such matters are now of no more than historical interest since the jurisdiction to award damages for future pecuniary loss in the form of periodical payments has entirely superseded the court's jurisdiction to approve structured settlements, the applicable Practice Direction once attached to CPR Pt 40 having been duly revoked.

52-025 **(b) Periodical payments** For claims in respect of personal injury and wrong-

---

[1912] A.C. 673, the leading case on mitigation, where Viscount Haldane LC declared that "the quantum of damage is a question of fact": at 688.

119 There is of course no "duty" in the strict sense of the word: see para.9-018, above.

120 Bankes LJ talked of "the question what is reasonable for a person to do in mitigation of his damages": [1919] 2 K.B. 581 CA at 588.

121 [1983] 1 Lloyd's Rep. 605 CA; see at 609, col.2.

122 For circumstances in which the duty to mitigate may not arise, see paras 9-021 and following, above.

123 [2016] EWCA Civ 359 at [39].

124 The status of mitigation issues, once the facts have been found, as questions of law is confirmed by the recent run of Supreme Court cases touching on mitigation and avoided loss: *Swynson Ltd v Lowick Rose LLP (in liquidation)* [2017] UKSC 32; [2017] 2 W.L.R. 1161; *Energy Solutions EU Ltd v Nuclear Decommissioning Authority* [2017] UKSC 34; [2017] 1 W.L.R. 1373; and *Fulton Shipping Inc of Panama v Globalia Business Travel SAU (The New Flamenco)* [2017] UKSC 43; [2017] 1 W.L.R. 2581.

125 [1927] A.C. 167 PC.

126 *Watt v Watt* [1905] A.C. 115. See para.53-003, below.

ful death, the primacy of the hallowed lump sum award has been comprehensively supplanted by s.100 of the Courts Act 2003 which belatedly brought into effect the long awaited recommendations of the Pearson Commission of 1978.[127] Section 100 of the Courts Act 2003 substitutes for the pre-existing s.2 of the Damages Act 1996 three new sections, numbered 2, 2A and 2B. The new s.2 provides:

"(1) A court awarding damages for future pecuniary loss in respect of personal injury—
(a) may order that the damages are wholly or partly to take the form of periodical payments, and
(b) shall consider whether to make that order.
(2) A court awarding other damages in respect of personal injury may, if the parties consent, order that the damages are wholly or partly to take the form of periodical payments.
(3) A court may not make an order for periodical payments unless satisfied that the continuity of payment under the order is reasonably secure."

While empowering the courts to make periodical payments orders, s.2 is silent as to the circumstances in which the courts are to do so. The new s.2A(1) states[128]:

"(1) Civil Procedure Rules may require a court to take specified matters into account in considering—
(a) whether to order periodical payments;
(b) the security of the continuity of payment;
(c) whether to approve an assignment or charge."

In accordance with s.2A(1), the detailed provisions governing the making of a periodical payments order are contained in CPR rr.41.4 to 41.10 and the attendant Practice Direction.[129] Material to the making of an order, r.41.7 provides: **52-026**

"When considering—

(a) its indication as to whether periodical payments or a lump sum is likely to be the more appropriate form for all or part of an award of damages under rule 41.6; or
(b) whether to make an order under s.2(1)(a) of the 1996 Act,

the court shall have regard to all the circumstances of the case and in particular the form of award which best meets the claimant's needs, having regard to the factors set out in Practice Direction 41B."

The so-called factors are to be found in para.1 of PD 41B which states: **52-027**

"The factors which the court shall have regard to under r.41.7 include—

(1) the scale of the annual payments taking into account any deduction for contributory negligence;

---

127 See para.40-055, above.

128 The process by which these highly important changes were implemented was not a glorious one. Sections 100 and 101 were initially to be brought into force by the Courts Act 2003 (Commencement No.9, Savings, Consequential and Transitional Provisions) Order 2005, SI 2005/547. However, the latter Order was the victim of a defect requiring its repeal before implementation and, for commencement purposes, it was replaced by the Courts Act 2003 (Commencement No.10) Order 2005, SI 2005/910. This Order (and, for that matter, its imperfect ancestor) did no more than bring ss.100 and 101 into force on 1 April 2005. To discover to which proceedings the sections apply, it is necessary to turn to the Courts Act 2003 (Transitional Provisions, Savings and Consequential Provisions) Order 2005, SI 2005/911, para.11 of which stipulates: "The powers conferred by ss.2(1) and (2) of the Damages Act 1996 shall be exercisable in proceedings whenever begun."

129 CPR r.41.5 deals with the need to plead the case and is therefore considered at para.51-033, above.

(2) the form of award preferred by the claimant including—
   (a) the reasons for the claimant's preference; and
   (b) the nature of any financial advice received by the claimant when considering the form of award; and
(3) the form of award preferred by the defendant including the reasons for the defendant's preference."

**52-028** None of the factors is hugely prescriptive, nor could be, given the potential range of situations in which periodical payments orders may be sought. The implication of the first factor—the scale of the annual payments—is that the smaller the award (allowing for contributory negligence) the less persuasive the case for a periodical payments order. The second and third factors—the parties' preferences—speak for themselves. Factor 2(b)—the nature of any financial advice received by the claimant when considering the form of award—should be read in conjunction with CPR r.41.5 which permits a party in their statement of case to state whether they consider periodical payments or a lump sum is the more appropriate form for all or part of an award of damages and, where such statements are given, relevant particulars of the circumstances which are relied on must also be provided. Fundamental to a party's selection will be financial advice on the relative advantages of the alternatives. It follows that, at some stage before judgment, every claimant will need to have obtained advice from a financial advisor.

**52-029** In *Tameside & Glossop Acute Services NHS Trust v Thompstone*,[130] the Court of Appeal issued definitive guidance on the operation of the factors[131]:

> "The parties have also agreed that the test which the judge must apply is an objective one. Of course, he must have regard to the wishes and preferences of the parties and to all the circumstances of the case but, in the end, it is for the judge to decide what order best meets the claimant's needs. The judge's mind should be focused not on what the claimant prefers but on what best meets the claimant's needs; the two are not necessarily the same."

In *Rowe v Dolman*,[132] Simon J grappled with the impact of contributory negligence on the exercise of his discretion to make a periodical payments order. As a result of contributory negligence, the claimant was to recover only 80 per cent of his damages. A periodical payments order reduced on that account was insufficient to meet the claimant's annual continuing care and other needs. The claimant therefore sought a lump sum award. Concluding that if there was an order for periodical payments the claimant would never be able to live his life as he wished to live it whereas if a conventional lump sum was ordered he would be able to do so for a substantial part of his life, Simon J acceded to the claimant's request. This resort to the utilitarian calculus was felt by the Court of Appeal[133] to have produced a solid justification for the decision to award a lump sum, the defendants' appeal being accordingly dismissed.

**52-030** The complication of contributory negligence put in a further appearance in *Morton v Portal Ltd*,[134] where the claimant's negligence served to reduce the damages recoverable by 25 per cent. The claimant favoured periodical payments for his

---

130 [2008] EWCA Civ 5; [2008] 1 W.L.R. 2207 CA.

131 [2008] 1 W.L.R. 2207 CA at 108.

132 [2007] EWHC 2799 (QB).

133 [2008] EWCA Civ 1040.

134 [2010] EWHC 1804 (QB).

future care to which the defendant had no objection. Walker J nevertheless rejected the approach that, if a claimant of full age and capacity, which the particular claimant was, wished to have a periodical payments order, that was conclusive in its favour. The matter was for the court which must be satisfied that a periodical payments order was in the claimant's best interests. Walker J also rejected the suggestion that, if the claimant and the defendant were agreed on a periodical payments order, a periodical payments order should follow; precluding an assumption in favour of such an order was the court's need to be satisfied that continuity of payment was secure. While strictly in accordance with the *Thompstone*[135] guidance, whether or not Walker J's interpretation of the Court's supervisory jurisdiction in periodical payment cases is consistent with the Court of Appeal's deference to the claimant's wishes, manifest in *Rowe v Dolman*,[136] remains to be seen.[137]

In *AA v CC*,[138] the proposed order would have provided for periodical payments for so long as the claimant remained under the jurisdiction of the Court of Protection, but ceasing if and when he regained capacity, though re-starting if he again deteriorated to the point that he did not have capacity. However, Swift J held that the power to order periodical payments did not extend to a power to award a "stop/start" form of periodical payments such as that proposed. She held that CPR r.41.8 did not permit such an order, and—at least on the material in front of her—did not consider that CPR r.41.8 was ultra vires as being outwith the powers of the Civil Procedure Rules Committee as conferred on them by s.2A of the 1996 Act. She further held that the proposed order did not fall within the procedure for the variation of periodical payments (discussed below). Nonetheless, in an elegant solution to the difficulty, she approved a suggestion by Counsel that the parties could agree the "stop/start" order, which agreement would be embodied in a Schedule to a Tomlin Order, and the Court would make such order in the usual way. **52-031**

The substituted s.2B gives the Lord Chancellor a power to enable courts to vary periodical payments under specified circumstances. The section provides: **52-032**

"(1) The Lord Chancellor may by order enable a court which has made an order for periodical payments to vary the order in specified circumstances (otherwise than in accordance with s.2(5)(d)).

(2) The Lord Chancellor may by order enable a court in specified circumstances to vary the terms on which a claim or action for damages for personal injury is settled by agreement between the parties if the agreement—

(a) provides for periodical payments, and

---

135 [2008] 1 W.L.R. 2207 CA.

136 [2008] EWCA Civ 1040.

137 Given the fact that the claimant in the instant case did not lack capacity, Walker J's preparedness to subordinate the claimant's wishes (and for that matter the wishes of the opposing party) to the outcome of his own assessment might be said to requisition for the court an unwarranted power to override a competent adult claimant's freedom of choice, a right which the courts do not generally possess. In *Gilliland v McManus* [2013] NIQB 127, Gillen J held at [5]: "the court can impose a PPO on the parties without the consent of the parties themselves. However it is required to go through an exercise to satisfy itself that it is right to do so. I pause to observe that it does not appear to me that such a power can be exercised by the court when the parties are of full age, have legal capacity and have consented to a settlement. In such a case they can agree any order they wish and such consent order is beyond the jurisdiction of the court to consider save for the enforcement of its terms. However in all cases where the court makes an award including where a court has to approve settlements and compromises made in respect of infants and patients the requirement arises." For a further commentary on *Morton v Portal Ltd* see footnote at the end of para.40-016, above.

138 [2013] EWHC 3679 (QB).

(b) expressly permits a party to apply to a court for variation in those circumstances.

(3) An order under this section may make provision—

(a) which operates wholly or partly by reference to a condition or other term of the court's order or of the agreement;

(b) about the nature of an order which may be made by a court on a variation;

(c) about the matters to be taken into account on considering variation;

(d) of a kind that could be made by Civil Procedure Rules or, in relation to Northern Ireland, rules of court (and which may be expressed to be with or without prejudice to the power to make those rules).[139]"

**52-033** Addressing the power to make variable orders, para.2 of the Damages (Variation of Periodical Payments) Order stipulates:

"If there is proved or admitted to be a chance that at some definite or indefinite time in the future the claimant will—

(a) as a result of the act or omission which gave rise to the cause of action, develop some serious disease or suffer some serious deterioration, or

(b) enjoy some significant improvement in his physical or mental condition, where that condition has been adversely affected as a result of that act or omission, the court may, on the application of a party, with the agreement of all the parties, or of its own initiative, provide in an order for periodical payments that it may be varied."

In *Kotula v EDF Energy Networks (EPN) Plc*,[140] Irwin J held[141] that the power to make a variable order was exercisable in essentially the same circumstances the power to award provisional damages under s.32A of the Senior Courts Act 1981. Accordingly, decisions on the power to award provisional damages would inform the exercise of the power to make a variable order.

**52-034** Paragraph 5 sets out the approach to be adopted when making a variable order, which it describes as follows:

"Where the court makes a variable order—

(a) the damages must be assessed or agreed on the assumption that the disease, deterioration or improvement will not occur;

(b) the order must specify the disease or type of deterioration or improvement;

(c) the order may specify a period within which an application for it to be varied may be made;

(d) the order may specify more than one disease or type of deterioration or improvement and may, in respect of each, specify a different period within which an application for it to be varied may be made;

---

[139] A different scheme of implementation applies to the power to vary, implemented by the Damages (Variation of Periodical Payments) Order 2005 SI 2005/841, made on 18 March 2005 and coming into force, according to para.1(1), on the 14th day after the day on which it was made and, thus, on 1 April 2005. By contrast with the power to make a periodical payments order, para.1(5) of the Variation Order provides: "This Order applies to proceedings begun on or after the date on which it comes into force." Two implementation regimes therefore coexist. The power to make a periodical payments order applies to all proceedings whether extant on 1 April 2005 or issued thereafter. By contrast, the power to vary applies only to claims commenced after 1 April 2005.

[140] [2011] EWHC 1546 (QB).

[141] At [29].

(e) the order must provide that a party must obtain the court's permission to apply for it to be varied, unless the court otherwise orders."

Paragraph 10 addresses the variation procedure which is to be initiated by "an application for permission to apply for a variable order to be varied". The latter application, so para.10 informs us, must be accompanied: **52-035**

"by evidence—

(a) that the disease, deterioration or improvement specified in the order or agreement has occurred, and
(b) that it has caused or is likely to cause an increase or decrease in the pecuniary loss suffered by the claimant."

The respondent to the application then has 28 days to serve written representations on the strength of which the court will deal with the application without a hearing. If permission to apply is granted, the court must give directions, including directions as to the date by which the application for variation must be served and filed and the service and filing of evidence. No appeal lies from an order granting permission to apply.

The mechanism is a cumbersome amalgam of the administrative and the judicial. **52-036** Who is to decide the application for permission to apply for a variation is not expressly stated. Given the timescale over which a periodical payments order may be expected to endure this is unlikely to be the original trial judge. Even if it is, the judge will not realistically have any recollection of the issues in the case. There is no guidance as to the principles applicable to the grant of permission to apply. The reasonable inference must be that the threshold for obtaining permission to apply will not be vertiginous, leaving to the respondent at any oral hearing the opportunity to put straight irregularities which may have affected the grant of permission on paper.

It is doubtful if the power to order a variation is of any real value. The weak- **52-037** ness of the scheme is its restriction to changes in the claimant's condition, physical or mental. There seems to be no reason why this should be the only change of circumstances acknowledged. Variation has no practical attractions for a defendant who will not want to expend money on a potentially open-ended review of the claimant's progress against the slim chance that some improvement may occur. There is no mechanism within the statutory framework[142] for a defendant to be kept informed of a claimant's progress so as to alert the defendant to an improvement. No claimant is ever likely to volunteer a variation where conditions have improved. The claimant can only make one application to vary and only then in respect of preordained mental or physical conditions. Variation is not intended to address other matters known at the time the initial periodical payments order is made. The course of medical conditions capable of being identified when the original order is made is itself surely likely to be eminently predictable and therefore equally capable of being addressed in the main order, thereby excluding the possibility of an application to vary based upon them. In short, the power to vary looks to be an unwieldy tool, the plying of which will engender the same sort of unhappy satellite litiga-

[142] The defendant could of course rely upon the right to call for regular medical examinations of the claimant now generally included as an express term of periodical payments orders.

tion as has been generated by the equivalent regime in ancillary relief proceedings.[143]

52-038 Sections 2(8) and (9) of the Damages Act 1996 state:

"(8) An order for periodical payments shall be treated as providing for the amount of payments to vary by reference to the retail prices index (within the meaning of s.833(2) of the Income and Corporation Taxes Act 1988) at such times and in such manner, as may be determined by or in accordance with Civil Procedure Rules.

(9) But an order for periodical payments may include provision—

(a) disapplying subs.(8), or

(b) modifying the effect of subs.(8)."

Under s.2(8) an order for periodical payments is to be treated as providing for the amounts to vary with the retail prices index, although by s.2(9) this provision may be disapplied or modified. For long-term medical care and treatment, the statutory presumption is less than satisfactory since earnings inflation has historically been greater than retail prices inflation and health care inflation, which reflects the earnings of the carers, has been greater still. Concern about this divergence in inflationary trends pre-occupied the first major round of litigation arising from the introduction of the periodical payments regime in which claimants were prompted to argue that a wages related index such as the average earnings index, AEI, would be more suitable than the retail prices index, RPI, as the mechanism for varying the sums payable under a periodical payments order. In *Flora v Wakom (Heathrow) Ltd*,[144] the defendant applied to strike out those paragraphs of the particulars of claim in which the claimant had attempted to develop his argument for a wage related mechanism of variation. The Court of Appeal rejected in robust terms the defendant's contention that RPI should be regarded as the default option and that such alternatives as AEI should only be introduced in an exceptional case. Following upon the encouragement given by the Court of Appeal in *Flora*, a clutch of first instance decisions then appeared addressing the issue of indexation: *Thompstone v Tameside & Glossop Acute Services NHS Trust*,[145] *Corbett v South Yorkshire Strategic Health Authority*,[146] *Sarwar v Ali and Motor Insurers' Bureau*,[147] and *RH v United Bristol Healthcare NHS Trust*.[148] In each of these cases, in relation to the future cost of care, the claimant sought to argue for an index other than the retail prices index. In each case, the Annual Survey of Hours and Earnings: Occupational Earnings for Care Assistants and Home Carers, known as ASHE 6115, was chosen by the trial judge as coming the nearest to measuring the claimant's loss with accuracy. In *Thameside & Glossop Acute Services NHS Trust v Thompstone*,[149] to which three other appeals were conjoined, the Court of Appeal emphatically dismissed the defendants' arguments in favour of RPI. A different indexation measure, so the court held, was a permissible modification within the meaning of s.2(9) of the Damages Act 1996. Given its avowed aim of achieving 100 per cent compensation, the Court of Appeal went on unsurprisingly to decide that ASHE

143 For further discussion of variation see paras 40-031 and 40-032, above.
144 [2006] EWCA Civ 1103; [2007] 1 W.L.R. 482 CA.
145 [2006] EWHC 2904 (QB); [2007] LS Law. Med. 71.
146 [2007] LS Law. Med. 430.
147 [2007] EWHC 1255 (QB); [2007] LS Law. Med. 375.
148 [2007] EWHC 1441 (QB); [2007] LS Law. Med. 535.
149 [2008] EWCA Civ 5; [2008] 1 W.L.R. 2207 CA.

6115 was the correct index to use in relation to the costs of care and case management.

The adoption of ASHE 6115 has led to problems of its own. The index having since *Thompstone*, been reclassified by subdivision into two separate standard occupational codes, ASHE 6145 (care workers and home carers) and ASHE 6146 (senior care workers), delay in its publication by the Office of National Statistics has bedevilled the recalculation of annual payments, conventionally paid on 15th December of each year. In *RH v University Hospitals Bristol*,[150] Swift J approved a new model order applicable to claims involving the NHS Litigation Authority intended to contain the formulae by which the calculation of each year's indexation could take account of any change between the first release ASHE 6115 data published by the Office of National Statistics in November of each year and the "revised" data promulgated during the ensuing 12 months. The new model order also allows for the reclassification of ASHE 6115 into its two new occupational codes. The abiding irony is that, since the adoption of ASHE 6115 in preference to RPI, care wage costs have either stagnated or gone down with the result that periodical payments with indexation by reference to RPI have produced more generous annual uplifts than those tied to ASHE 6115. Indeed, the increasingly received wisdom is that for periodical payments orders of relatively short duration, RPI is the better answer.[151]

As confidence in the efficacy of periodical payments has grown, so the range of future loss brought within the scope of periodical payment orders has increased. It is now not uncommon for future loss of earnings, future deputyship fees and the recurring elements of future medical costs to be treated as periodical payments. Each head of loss is very different in nature and will call for differing indexation provisions. Now that it has been decided that the courts may utilise indices which take into account higher inflationary trends than appear in the retail prices index, a predicament arises in claims where the defendant is, in effect, an insurance company. The close matching regulations promulgated under the Financial Services and Markets Act 2000 require insurers to hold assets to match their liabilities. Since there are still no products available in the market which are linked to health care inflation or to earnings inflation, insurers cannot purchase assets directly concomitant with their individual liabilities under any periodical payments order. The best insurers can do is to acquire index-linked government stocks which protect against inflation but only against inflation as measured by the retail prices index. It follows that insurers would not be in a position to acquire an annuity product which would allow them to make payments linked to health care or earnings inflation. Attempting to address this predicament, in *IB v CB*,[152] the court approved as a term of a periodical payments order a provision that, in the event of insurers wishing to find an appropriate annuity provider who required an up-to-date medical picture of the injured party, the defendant should have the right to arrange for the claimant to be medically examined at infrequent intervals. In *Follett v Wallace*,[153] insurers went further and sought the facility to obtain an up- to-date life expectancy figure for the different purpose of calculating reserves so as to be able to set aside capital to cover future periodical payments. Acceding to insurers' **52-039**

150 [2013] EWHC 299 (QB).

151 For further discussion of these cases and the issue of indexation see paras 40-021 to 40-026, above.

152 [2010] EWHC 3815.

153 [2013] EWCA Civ 146.

argument, Leveson LJ sanctioned the introduction of a clause into the order entitling insurers to require the claimant to undergo medical examination at its request at any time during the claimant's life in order for insurers to obtain a quotation for the purchase costs of an annuity to fund the periodical payments or (not more frequently that once every seven years) for the express purpose of reviewing its reserve. Despite a degree of subsequent outcry that such a provision infringes a claimant's art.8 rights, this modest imposition is hardly unreasonable and reflects the realities of insurers having to self-fund periodical payments over the span of a life time.[154]

**52-040** The court cannot make a periodical payments order where continuity of payment is uncertain. For s.2(3) of the 1996 Act contains the uncompromising injunction:

> "(3) A court may not make an order for periodical payments unless satisfied that the continuity of payment under the order is reasonably secure."

Continuity of payment will only be secure in three situations, each dignified by its own sub-clause in subs.2(4):

> "(4) For the purposes of subs.(3) the continuity of payment under an order is reasonably secure if—
> (a) it is protected by a guarantee given under s.6 of or the Schedule to this Act,
> (b) it is protected by a scheme under s.213 of the Financial Services and Markets Act 2000 (compensation) (whether or not as modified by s.4 of this Act), or
> (c) the source of payment is a government or health service body."

It follows from this that continuity of payment will only be secure where payment is protected by a guarantee given under the Damages Act 1996, where payment is protected by a scheme under s.213 of the Financial Services and Markets Act 2000[155] or where the source of payment is a government or health service body.

**52-041** No difficulty can arise under these provisions where the defendant is the NHS Litigation Authority since it has been designated as a health service body by the Lord Chancellor within the meaning of subs.2(4)(c). With other National Health Service defendants it is necessary to look slightly further afield for inspiration since the NHS Litigation Authority is the only health service body designated by the Lord Chancellor. Thus, in *YM v Gloucestershire Hospitals NHS Foundation Trust; Kanu v Kings College Hospital Trust*,[156] Forbes J accepted in principle that, had the defendants been NHS Trusts as distinct from NHS Foundation Trusts, he would have been satisfied on security of payment as the Secretary of State was obliged to take over an NHS Trust's liabilities should it cease to exist. The trust involved being an NHS Foundation Trust, Forbes J adopted a stratagem built upon the NHS Litigation Authority's special status to resolve the problem confronting him. Outside the realm of the NHS, the problem of continuity of payment has been resolved by a variety of other stratagems, some more rudimentary than others. In *Godbold v*

---

154 See further on security of continuity of awards paras 40-027 to 40-030, above. In *Gilliland v McManus* [2013] NIQB 127, Gillen J held at [17]: "I consider that *Follett* was a case on its own facts and does not necessarily set a precedent for future cases. Compensating insurers will always be required to justify such a step as that which occurred in *Wallace*'s case since it does provide a departure from the clean-break principle."

155 This can extend to companies, including companies in administration, registered elsewhere in the EEA: see *Billingsley v UPS Ltd* (10 December 2012, Judge Oliver-Jones QC, QBD), and *Farrugia v Burtenshaw* [2014] EWHC 1036 (QB) at [111]-[112] (Jay J).

156 [2006] EWHC 820 (QB); [2006] P.I.Q.R. P27.

*Mahmood*,[157] a road accident claim wherein the judgment was ultimately payable by the defendant's road traffic insurers, Mitting J satisfied himself that continuity of payment would be reasonably secure because he considered the matter to fall within the second of the three situations provided for in s.2(4), viz, under the financial services compensation scheme. In *Taylor v Chesworth and The Motor Insurers Bureau*,[158] another road traffic case, Ramsay J recognised that the Motor Insurers' Bureau was not among the designated government and health service bodies under s.2(4)(c) but was nevertheless persuaded that it had the necessary financial, statutory and organizational status to provide assurance that continuity of periodical payments would be reasonably secure.[159] In *Bennett v Stephens & Zenith Insurance Co*,[160] Tugendhat J held that the continuity of payment was reasonably secure as a result of the claimant's right to have recourse to the MIB or an equivalent body even though the periodical payments order was not to be read as binding on the MIB. In *Boreham v Burton*,[161] while there were two major insurers behind the defendants, the defendants' counsel had raised doubt as to whether the two insurers would be secure because the accident giving rise to the claim had occurred in 1998 before the coming into force of the Financial Services and Markets Act 2000 and, pursuant to it, the Financial Services Compensation Scheme (FSCS). The argument put on behalf of the claimant which the judge accepted was that the insurers were covered by the FSCS even though the liability pre-dated the Scheme's establishment.

In *Harden v Chesters*,[162] Langstaff J relied on a letter from general counsel to the FSCS in concluding that the continuity of periodical payments was reasonably secure. Subsequently, in *Western v Clayson*,[163] Master Kay QC relied on *Harden v Chesters* in ordering the defendant to provide certain classes of documents to the claimant, to allow the FSCS to give more definitive guidance which would cover the circumstances of the case. Similarly, in *Senior v Rock UK Adventure Centres Ltd*,[164] a claim arising out of an injury suffered by an employee of an adventure centre when a cable broke, the defendant was ordered to disclose details of its Employer's Liability insurance cover to enable the claimant to consider whether the continuity of payment under a proposed order would be reasonably secure.

The operation of CPR Pt 36 in periodical payments cases remains a work in **52-042**
progress.[165] Rule 36.18 provides:

> "(1) This rule applies to a claim for damages for personal injury which is or includes a claim for future pecuniary loss.

---

157 [2005] EWHC 1002 (QB); [2006] P.I.Q.R. Q5.

158 [2007] EWHC 1001 (QB).

159 See [2007] EWHC 1001 (QB) at [162] and [163].

160 [2012] EWHC 1 (QB); [2012] EWHC 58 (QB).

161 [2012] EWHC 930 (QB).

162 [2008] EWHC 379 (QB).

163 25 January 2013 QBD.

164 [2015] EWHC 1447 (QB).

165 Combining periodical payments with provisional damages, in *Kotula v EDF Energy Networks (EPN) Plc* [2011] EWHC 1546 (QB), in which the parties had agreed a settlement comprising a gross lump sum payment of £2.5 million and staged periodical payments for future care and case management linked to the ASHE 6115 earnings index but could not agree the consequences of any future deterioration in the claimant's medical condition, Irwin J gave the claimant, a T6 paraplegic, permission to treat the lump sum award as provisional and granted him the right to seek to vary his otherwise agreed periodical payments if, in due course, he came to develop serious consequences as a result of acquired syringomyelia, a well known complication of spinal injury.

(2) An offer to settle such a claim will not have the consequences set out in this section unless it is made by way of a Pt 36 offer under this rule.

(3) A Pt 36 offer to which this rule applies may contain an offer to pay, or an offer to accept—

(a) the whole or part of the damages for future pecuniary loss in the form of

(i) a lump sum; or

(ii) periodical payments; or

(iii) both a lump sum and periodical payments;

(b) the whole or part of any other damages in the form of a lump sum.

(4) A Pt 36 offer to which this rule applies—

(a) must state the amount of any offer to pay the whole or part of any damages in the form of a lump sum;

(b) may state—

(i) what part of the lump sum, if any, relates to damages for future pecuniary loss; and

(ii) what part relates to other damages to be accepted in the form of a lump sum;

(c) must state what part of the offer relates to damages for future pecuniary loss to be paid or accepted in the form of periodical payments and must specify—

(i) the amount and duration of the periodical payments;

(ii) the amount of any payments for substantial capital purchases and when they are to be made; and

(iii) that each amount is to vary by reference to the retail prices index (or some other named index, or that it is not to vary by reference to any index); and

(d) must state either that any damages which take the form of periodical payments will be funded in a way which ensures that the continuity of payment is reasonably secure in accordance with s.2(4) of the Damages Act 1996 or how such damages are to be paid and how the continuity of their payment is to be secured."

**52-043** The rule does not achieve for periodical payments cases the costs certainties available in other claims. As provided for in r.36.17, where a claimant fails to obtain a judgment more advantageous than a defendant's Pt 36 offer or judgment against the defendant is at least as advantageous to the claimant as the proposals contained in a claimant's Pt 36 offer, the Court will, unless it considers it unjust to do so, order that the offeror should recover their costs from the offeree in the usual way. Rule 36.17(2) defines the critical term:

> "For the purposes of para.(1), in relation to any money claim or money element of a claim, 'more advantageous' means better in money terms by any amount, however small, and 'at least as advantageous' shall be construed accordingly:"

Thus the test is a direct monetary comparison. A Pt 36 Offer is bettered if the eventual award exceeds it by as little as £1. Though commendably straightforward, the concept of direct monetary comparison is not easily applied to the complexities of settlement offers incorporating periodical payments. Even in those cases where a Pt 36 offer including provision for periodical payments is accepted, there can be no certainty that the underlying claim has been resolved. In such cases, r.36.18(7) requires the claimant within seven days of acceptance to apply to the court for an order for an award of damages in the form of periodical payments. This inevitable imposition thus renders the court the final arbiter of any compromise.

In *Pankhurst v White*,[166] MacDuff J awarded the claimant agreed periodical payments of £260,000 per annum plus a lump sum of £2.317 million, representing an equivalent capital value of around £6.1 million. The result was that, while the claimant failed to beat a Pt 36 offer made by the defendant in 2008, he exceeded his own Pt 36 offer made two years earlier. The claimant therefore sought the fruits of CPR Pt 36 for the period of two years until his offer was bettered by the defendant. Concluding that an enhanced consequences order in the form of increased interest was appropriate, MacDuff J decided that it would be wrong to make an award of interest enhanced or otherwise in respect of those damages which were awarded for future losses and future expenditure. Enhanced interest was only appropriate upon past losses and not upon future losses. The Court of Appeal upheld the judge's decision.[167] Jackson LJ saw force in the proposition that interest under CPR r.36.17(4)[168] was a reward for making an appropriate settlement offer, and not intended to be compensatory, but held that the Court of Appeal was bound by *McPhilemy v Times Newspapers Ltd*,[169] to hold that enhanced interest could only be awarded in respect of items in the judgment which already merited some award of interest: at [37]. However, the point may now be of largely academic interest: CPR r.36.17(4)(d) now permits the court to order an additional amount of up to £75,000, capped by reference to the principal amount awarded by the court, in addition to any enhanced interest, costs, and interest on costs.

**(c) Postponement of awards** Orders for interim payments may be made on account of damages in pending proceedings[170] and provisional damages and variable orders for periodical payments are possible in certain personal injury cases[171]; under each of these procedures the final lump sum award is to a degree postponed. Beyond this it is permissible to make an award in respect of part of a claim and postpone adjudication on the remainder. This was done in *Deeny v Gooda Walker*,[172] another of the many aspects of the damages actions brought by Lloyd's Names against their managing and underwriting agents for exposing them to excessive risks of liability on claims by third party assureds. The damages here sought by the claimants were in respect of losses on both existing and future claims, and the defendants' application was granted to have the assessment of that proportion of the damages which represented future claims postponed. Phillips J took the view that RSC Ord.33 rr.3 and 4(2) gave him the jurisdiction to award on part and defer the assessment on the remainder; the more difficult question was whether the circumstances were amenable to his exercise of this jurisdiction. While accepting that in the interests of bringing litigation to an end it would usually be appropriate to make a single award of damages which included the best assessment possible of future loss, Phillips J considered that the special features of the Lloyd's litigation—which he categorised as the nature of the loss, the difficulties of assessment and the consequences for related proceedings of a once and for all assessment of dam- 52-044

166 [2010] EWHC 311 (QB).
167 [2010] EWCA Civ 1445.
168 Now CPR r.36.17(4).
169 [2001] EWCA Civ 933; [2002] 1 W.L.R. 934.
170 See paras 40-005 and 40-006, above.
171 See paras 40-007 and 40-008, above.
172 [1995] 1 W.L.R. 1206.

ages[173]—weighed strongly in favour of awarding damages in respect of underwriting losses when those losses were sustained and not in anticipation of them. In so holding Phillips J adopted the view of the Court of Appeal in *Trans Trust S.P.R.L. v Danubian Trading Co*,[174] in an entirely different context,[175] on the wisdom of deferring dealing with a head of damage until the extent of the claimant's liability, if any, had been determined.

**52-045** At this point, the CPR enters the fray. CPR r.3.1(2) provides thus:

> "(2) Except where these Rules provide otherwise, the court may—
> ...
> (e) direct that part of any proceedings (such as a counterclaim) be dealt with as separate proceedings;
> (f) stay the whole or part of any proceedings either generally or until a specified date or event.
> ..."

In *A v National Blood Authority*,[176] part of the Hepatitis C litigation, a number of the claimants, who had tested positive for Hepatitis C infection, were asymptomatic, and did not want to undergo treatment to eradicate the infection but did not wish to exclude the possibility of undergoing such treatment in the future. The parties' unanimous aim was to preserve the ability of those claimants to pursue claims for damages in the event that they did undergo treatment and suffered damage in consequence. Without resolving the issue whether or not the court had jurisdiction to preserve the claims under s.32A of the Supreme Court Act 1981, Burton J resorted to CPR r.3.1(2), ordering the separate trial of any issue of damages arising out of future treatment, and adjourning the trial of such issues generally. In *Adan v Securicor Custodial Services Ltd*,[177] Eady J rejected an application that an upcoming assessment hearing "be treated as a provisional damages hearing" in circumstances the claimant's representatives were concerned that his care and accommodation needs would increase if his mental condition improved sufficiently for him to be released from secure accommodation—a possibility which did not satisfy the statutory conditions for an award of provisional damages. Eady J rejected the application, emphasising the importance of finality in litigation, and holding that

> "the continuing incubus of potential liability and the uncertainty confronting the defendant's insurers would be out of all proportion to any possible corresponding benefit to the claimant".

However, in *Cook v Cook*,[178] the claimant, who was 10 years old at the date of the hearing before the same judge, claimed damages for very serious brain injuries sustained in part in a road traffic accident in 2001 when her mother was 28 weeks pregnant and in part through the negligent failure of the claimant's GP in 2004 to diagnose raised intra-cranial pressure. Applying to postpone quantification of the claimant's claims from the age of 16 onwards, it was argued for the claimant that because the claimant's long-term prognosis was unclear it would be unjust to as-

---

173 See [1995] 1 W.L.R. 1206 at 1214E–1216C.
174 [1952] 2 Q.B. 297 CA.
175 See para.10-032, above.
176 [2002] Lloyd's Rep. Med. 487.
177 [2004] EWHC 394 (QB).
178 [2011] EWHC 1638 (QB).

sess her likely long-term losses at that time, the court and the parties being in a far better position to assess the long-term outcome and, correspondingly, the claimant's needs in adult life following a reassessment at or after her 16th birthday in 2017. Conceding that to adjourn any part of the assessment was a very exceptional course, Eady J nevertheless resorted to CPR r.3.1(2) and ordered that the exercise of quantifying the claimant's long-term losses be postponed until there was solid evidence available.[179]

**(d) Breakdown of awards and separate awards** The total lump sum may itself be broken down into its constituent parts, provided these too are lump sums. In personal injury cases this course has long been followed in separate assessments for general and special damages, and today the court is, in effect, required to break down its award of general damages into the sum allocated to non-pecuniary loss, by way of pain and suffering and loss of amenities, and the sums allocated to pecuniary loss, by way of prospective loss of earnings and prospective expenses.[180] Indeed far more detailed breakdowns are now the order of the day; thus expenses in serious personal injury cases will be broken down into items such as costs of care by paid attendants, costs of gratuitous care, costs of aids and equipment, costs of adapted accommodation, Court of Protection costs, and others. Such breakdowns are particularly useful in the event of an appeal.[181] The wholesale breakdown of the total lump sum into separate awards is, however, not without attendant difficulty. In *Martins v Choudhary*,[182] where the judge had found the defendant liable to the claimant in the tort of harassment and awarded damages of £12,500 for psychiatric injury and £10,000 for injury to the claimant's feelings (to include aggravating aspects),[183] declining to interfere with the overall award, Smith LJ offered the following practical rationalisation of the problem created by the breakdown and subdivision of awards: 52-046

179 With due respect to the judge's laudable concern to avoid injustice, this was surely an erroneous exercise of judicial discretion. In truth, there was nothing exceptional about the claimant's claim or the problems of quantification to which it gave rise. Uncertainty inevitably surrounds the quantification of loss for any claimant with a significant life expectancy whose future losses fall to be assessed during their minority. Quantification is often necessarily approximate, for example where an infant claimant's uninjured future earning capacity has to be determined. With the assistance of appropriate expert evidence and the added consolation of variable periodical payments, the courts have proved perfectly capable of quantifying future loss without notorious injustice to anyone. If, by parity of reasoning, Eady J's approach were extended to comparable cases (of which there would be many) the quantification of damages risks disintegrating into a series of intermittent partial assessments, no doubt coupled with orders for the equivalent of interim payments, at the price of finality and certainty and immeasurably increased cost. That is surely not the direction of travel intended by the authors of CPR r.3.1(2). The decision is wrong in principle and should not be followed.

180 See para.40-059, above.

181 See paras 53-035 and following, below. Where an appeal is probable it has for long been common for the court, though finding for the defendant, to make a provisional assessment of damages. Compare *Harrison v N.C.B.* [1950] 1 K.B. 466 CA at 477, per Tucker LJ: "I desire to add that in cases such as this, which involve difficult questions of law and are likely to be taken to appeal, it is always desirable that the trial judge, whether or not he is specifically requested by counsel to do so, should assess the damages provisionally if his decision is adverse to the plaintiff."

182 [2007] EWCA Civ 1379; [2008] P.I.Q.R. Q15 at 1.

183 Following *Richardson v Howie* [2004] EWCA Civ 1127 at [15]–[25]. In *Commissioner of Police of the Metropolis v Shaw* [2012] I.C.R. 464, however, Underhill J observed that though the law was moving towards aggravated damages forming part of compensatory awards, "separate awards of aggravated damages have been approved by the Court of Appeal too often in recent years for us now to say that they represent the wrong approach".

"I would venture to suggest that there should be no hard and fast rule about whether separate awards should be made. It will all depend on the facts of the individual case. If, for example, as is sometimes the case, the psychiatric harm is very modest and to all intents and purposes merges with the injury to feelings, it will plainly be more convenient to make one award covering both aspects. If, as here, where the psychiatric injury is not insubstantial, it is positively helpful to the parties (and to this Court) if the judge separates the award for psychiatric injury from that for injury to feelings. This leads to a better understanding of the judge's thought processes. However, I do accept that there is a risk of double recovery by overlap if two awards are made and the judge must take care to avoid that."

**52-047** When both compensatory and exemplary damages are claimed, Lord Devlin in *Rookes v Barnard*,[184] suggested that separate awards for each should be made but only where there was doubt as to the propriety of any exemplary award, thereby enabling an appellate court to set aside the exemplary award without the necessity of a new trial. In *Broome v Cassell & Co*,[185] where the jury had in fact returned separate awards for the compensatory and exemplary damages, the House of Lords emphasised that the general practice should be to award a single sum[186]; some subsequent cases, such as *Drane v Evangelou*,[187] and *Guppy (Bridport) v Brookling*,[188] have adhered to this while others, such as *Riches v News Group Newspapers*,[189] and *John v MGN*,[190] have not; indeed the practice today seems to be to itemise as between the compensatory and exemplary awards. Lord Diplock was of the opinion in *Broome v Cassell & Co*,[191] that a judge sitting alone should make separate awards in any event,[192] but Lord Salmon, delivering the judgment of their Lordships in *Attorney General of St Christopher, Nevis and Anguilla v Reynolds*,[193] thought there was no such obligation.[194] It is thought that, whether the trial be by judge alone or with a jury, separate assessments are to be encouraged; as with actions for personal injury,[195] identification of the constituent parts of a damages award assists appellants and appellate courts. Indeed counsel tend to request separate awards specifically in order to assist the court in the event of an appeal.[196] And in the context of claims for wrongful arrest, false imprisonment, assault and malicious prosecution, the Court of Appeal in *Thompson v Commissioner of Police of the Metropolis* and *Hsu v Commissioner of Police of the Metropolis*,[197] held that

---

184 [1964] A.C. 1129 at 1228.

185 [1972] A.C. 1027.

186 See [1972] A.C. 1027 at 1082D and 1099B, per Lord Hailsham LC and Lord Morris respectively; Contrast [1972] A.C. 1027 at 1118B, per Lord Wilberforce.

187 [1978] 1 W.L.R. 455 CA.

188 (1983) 14 H.L.R. 1 CA; especially at 26.

189 [1986] Q.B. 256 CA.

190 [1997] Q.B. 586 CA.

191 [1972] A.C. 1027.

192 See [1972] A.C. 1027 at 1126H.

193 [1980] A.C. 637 PC.

194 See [1980] A.C. 637 PC at 662H–663A. All these cases involving exemplary awards are dealt with in Ch.13, above.

195 See para.52-046, above.

196 It is sometimes said that the principle of only awarding exemplary damages if the compensatory damages will not on their own suffice to punish and deter (see para.13-040, above) is put in jeopardy by separate awards as they may tend to double counting. Surely, however, the judge can adequately direct the jury so as to warn them against double counting; and if trying the matter alone he will be aware of the principle.

197 [1998] Q.B. 498 CA.

there should undoubtedly be a separate award for the exemplary damages. Indeed it was said that, in these claims which are generally still heard with a jury, the jury should be told that, if it considered that the claimant was entitled to aggravated damages, it should also make an award for these which was separate from its award for the basic damages, thereby giving a greater transparency to the make up of the total award.[198] Presumably what goes for juries should apply to judges sitting alone. Thus in *Mehta v Royal Bank of Scotland*,[199] a claim for trespass to land, separate awards were made by the trial judge of £10,000 compensatory damages, £10,000 aggravated damages and £7,500 exemplary damages.[200]

The Court of Appeal's decision in *Borders (UK) Ltd v Commissioner of Police of the Metropolis*,[201] is an example of the maxim that hard cases make bad law. The claimant booksellers claimed both compensatory and exemplary damages from the defendant for the systematic sale of vast numbers of books stolen from the claimants over an extended period. The claimants recovered compensatory damages of £279,594.89 and a separate award of £100,000 by way of exemplary damages. The exemplary damages claimed were in reality but a second component of the claimants' actual loss and therefore of the compensatory claim, merely languishing under an assumed identity. Driven by undeniable merits, the Court of Appeal was nevertheless unanimously prepared to uphold an award of exemplary damages since exemplary damages would be appropriate in the circumstances of the defendant having acted with a view to profit.[202] In *Shah v Gale*,[203] the facts of which are exceptional, the claimant as executrix of her son's estate brought proceedings against the defendant claiming damages for the defendant's part in mistakenly directing a band of assailants in search of a different man to the claimant's son's address, where the assailants proceeded to attack and kill her son. The claim was for damages for assault and battery including a claim for aggravated damages but excluding a claim for pain and suffering. Clearly perplexed by the way in which the claim was framed, but citing this work[204] Leveson J awarded the claimant £750 for the assault and a separate sum of £2,000 by way of aggravated damages. **52-048**

Whether separate awards are essential where the claimant has succeeded on **52-049**

---

198 [1998] Q.B. 498 CA at 516E.

199 [1999] 3 E.G.L.R. 153.

200 For another example of separate awards see *Design Progression Ltd v Thurloe Properties Ltd* [2004] EWHC 324 (Ch); [2005] 1 W.L.R. 1, a landlord and tenant case in which the defendant landlord had breached its statutory duty to respond in a reasonable time to the tenant's application for permission to assign his lease. Citing and relying upon paras 11-011 and 11-032 to 11-045 of the 17th edition of this work, Peter Smith J found that the intention behind the defendant's failure to respond had been to extract a profit. While the defendant's design had ultimately proved unsuccessful, merely because the defendant's design had failed did not mean that it was not appropriate to award exemplary damages. He went on to assess damages by reference to the profit the defendant would have made, had its design been successful, awarding the claimant £25,000.

201 [2005] EWCA Civ 197.

202 With customary intellectual elegance, Sedley LJ acknowledged that his decision had: "to make up in justice what it lacks in logic; but the want of logic arises from a long-recognised anomaly in the law, and the justice of the outcome may assist in resolving it." It is difficult to see quite how the Court of Appeal's decision will serve to resolve anomalies, whatever they may be. The better solution, to which Sedley LJ seems to have been briefly attracted, would have been to require the claimants to re-plead their claim. In *Devenish Nutrition Ltd v Sanofi-Aventis SA* [2007] EWHC 2394 (Ch), Lewison J treated the case in just this manner: see at [73]–[74]. See the *Borders* case further at para.13-026, above.

203 [2005] EWHC 1087 (QB).

204 Citing the then para.37-001, which is now para.42-001.

separate causes of action united in the same suit, has occasioned some uncertainty. In *Weber v Birkett*,[205] the claimant sued the defendant for a libel and a slander, the defendant, pleading an apology, paid into court two sums of £105 each, one for the libel and one for the slander, but the jury returned a verdict for a lump sum of £200 to cover both causes of action. It was held that this was no verdict and that no judgment could be entered upon it for either party. This decision was later considered in *Barber v Pigden*,[206] where the claimant sued the defendant for a number of separate slanders but, the judge not having directed the jury to return a separate verdict with separate damages in respect of each publication, the jury found a single verdict and judgment was entered accordingly. Greer LJ accepted that it followed from *Weber v Birkett*,[207] that there was "no verdict in respect of which judgment could be entered",[208] but Scott LJ distinguished *Weber v Birkett*,[209] on the ground that "all the Lords Justices had the issue of payment into court primarily in mind",[210] and, after a careful review of the law, adopted the contrary view. He said:

> "I can see nothing in the Judicature Act or Rules of the Supreme Court as they are today to make separate verdicts and judgments invariably necessary in respect of separate causes of action contained in the same writ .... The question whether one or more causes of action are to be included in one verdict or judgment will depend upon the exercise of the trial judge's judicial discretion upon all the circumstances of the case."[211]

In any event, as the decision in *Barber v Pigden*, shows, a failure to make separate assessments on two causes of action does not make the verdict and the award such a nullity that they must be upset. Thus in that case the court refused to grant a new trial because the defendant had not been prejudiced. This was primarily because no objection had been taken by the defendant at the trial to the jury being asked to consider the different publications as a whole instead of separately[212]; apart from this Greer LJ gave as an additional reason for refusing a new trial that the defendant had not been prejudiced as to the amount awarded.[213] While the practical result is therefore the same whether the technical truth be that a court should always make separate awards but a single award will not be upset in the absence of prejudice or that a court has a discretion to make a single award but should make separate awards if a single award could lead to prejudice, the latter approach appears now to have carried the day. Thus in *Pedley v Cambridge Newspapers Ltd*,[214] where there was

205 [1925] 2 K.B. 152 CA.
206 [1937] 1 K.B. 664 CA.
207 [1925] 2 K.B. 152 CA.
208 [1937] 1 K.B. 664 CA at 671.
209 [1925] 2 K.B. 152 CA.
210 [1937] 1 K.B. 664 CA at 681.
211 [1937] 1 K.B. 664 CA at 683–684. The third member of the court, Eve J, merely stated his agreement with both judgments: at 684.
212 [1937] 1 K.B. 664 CA at 671, 684, per Greer and Scott LJJ respectively.
213 [1937] 1 K.B. 664 CA at 672. See paras 53-011 to 53-016, below, where the grounds for not upsetting an award which is technically incorrect are fully considered.
214 [1964] 1 W.L.R. 988 CA. In *Culla Park Ltd v Richards* [2007] EWHC 1850 (QB), Eady J adopted the course of compensating by a single award of damages in respect of multiple defamatory publications, citing *Hayward v Thompson*, *Barber v Pigden*, and *Pedley v Cambridge Newspapers Ltd.* Similarly, in the phone hacking cases of *Gulati v MGN* [2015] EWHC 1482 (Ch) at [149] and following, Mann J recorded that it was common ground that although each invasion of privacy and each article was a separate cause of action, that did not mean that a separate award had to be made for each separate invasion: "How to make up the award is a matter for the judgment and discretion of

in substance one cause of action for libel but technically three causes of action in respect of three innuendoes, the Court of Appeal accepted that the judge was entitled to ask the jury to find one verdict and make one award of damages and that in such circumstances it was therefore right that the defendants should be allowed to make one general payment into court. And in *Hayward v Thompson*,[215] where the defendant newspaper had published two articles claimed to be defamatory of the claimant on two successive Sundays, it was held by the Court of Appeal that the judge had rightly exercised his discretion to direct the jury to make a single award of damages in respect of both publications if they found, as they did, in the claimant's favour, without separate verdicts. The views of Scott LJ in the earlier *Barber v Pigden*,[216] were approved in both of these cases. Prejudice could arise on the question of costs in the case of payment into court. Under the final form of RSC Ord.22 the presumption was against it. The latter Order permitted the defendant, without obtaining leave of the court as was formerly required of him, to pay into court one lump sum in respect of two or more causes of action,[217] and the court having the power to order him to amend so as to specify the sum paid in respect of each only if it appeared to it that the claimant was embarrassed by the payment.[218] There is no equivalent of these rules of court in the Civil Procedure Rules but in the era of case management they were presumably not thought to be needed. Thus CPR r.3.1(2), after listing the court's various general powers of management ends, in subrule (m), by giving power to

> "take any other step or make any other order for the purpose of managing the case and furthering the overriding objective …"

which objective is, by r.1.1(1), to enable the court to deal with cases justly. Another situation of possible prejudice is where on appeal one of two causes of action is found to be insufficient. Starting with *Leach v Thomas*,[219] in 1835, awards of new trials for this reason were not uncommon more than a century and a half ago,[220] although at that time prejudice did not have to be shown in order to lead the court into granting this relief.[221] A somewhat similar situation in which separate awards

---

the court". In the event, Mann J held that the wrongs had too great a degree of separation for global sums to be awarded. This approach was upheld by the Court of Appeal: [2015] EWCA Civ 1291; [2017] Q.B. 149.

215 [1982] Q.B. 47 CA.

216 [1937] 1 K.B. 664 CA.

217 RSC Ord.22 r.1(1) and (4).

218 RSC Ord.22 r.1(5). And the court did not even have this power where the lump sum was paid into court in satisfaction of causes of action arising under the Fatal Accidents Act 1976 and the Law Reform (Miscellaneous Provisions) Act 1934: RSC Ord.22 r.1(6), treating the two causes of action as one for the purpose of r.1(5).

219 (1835) 2 M. & W. 427 (breaches of several covenants in a lease).

220 Other cases are *Chadwick v Trower* (1839) 6 Bing. N.C. 1 (nuisance); *Stevenson v Newnham* (1835) 13 C.B. 285 (distress, trover and the like). Before the decision in *Leach v Thomas* (1835) 2 M. & W. 427 the more radical practice of arresting the judgment in toto had long prevailed: *Grambel v Rhobotham* (1600) Cros. Eliz. 865; *Staynrode v Locock* (1606) Cro. Jac. 115; *Holt v Scholefield* (1796) 6 T.R. 691; *Sicklemore v Thistleton* (1817) 6 M. & S. 9. *Holt v Scholefield* (1796) 6 T.R. 691 was expressly overruled in *Leach v Thomas* (1835) 2 M. & W. 427, but for some time the courts continued to talk of the two methods of redress in the alternative: see, e.g. *Sheen v Rickie* (1839) 5 M. & W. 175 at 181.

221 If damages were awarded generally on a single cause of action, it was possible to upset the award where some items of damage were not actionable at all: see, e.g. *Jenney v Brook* (1844) 6 Q.B. 323 (in trespass for cutting down trees the court had wrongly held the trespass totally unjustified whereas

should be made is in actions for the detention of several chattels: damages ought to be assessed as to each chattel separately so that, in the event of their not all being delivered up, the claimant can claim the value of those not returned to him.[222]

52-050 **(e) Currency of award** It was for long the position that damages ascertained in a foreign currency must be translated into sterling.[223] Now all this has changed since the House of Lords decision in *Miliangos v George Frank (Textiles)*.[224] The whole issue is treated in detail elsewhere.[225]

52-051 **(f) Unconditionality of award** That the award must be unconditional is illustrated by *Banbury v Bank of Montreal*,[226] where a verdict of £25,000 in damages to the claimant and for the return of all securities by the claimant to the defendant was considered by three of their Lordships to be improper and to require a retrial on the question of assessment of damages.[227] However, the giving to courts of the power to award provisional damages and periodical payments in personal injury and wrongful death cases has made for a qualification to this hallowed and venerable principle since both forms of award are subject to review in certain limited circumstances.[228] To this extent at least, the unconditionality principle may be said to have been displaced.

52-052 **(g) Amount claimed as ceiling for award** Formerly, the award could not be of a sum greater than the amount claimed if the claimant specified a sum, and if the court found for a greater sum than claimed the claimant needed to seek permission to amend before the amount found could be awarded. Under the Civil Procedure Rules, claimants are required in all cases to state the amount claimed in the claim form[229] but are not thereby limited to recovery of this amount, for there is an express provision in CPR r.16.3(7) that the court may still give judgment for

---

there was a sufficient authority as to part of the trees: new trial ordered); *Sheen v Rickie* (1839) 5 M. & W. 175 (in conversion for goods, chattels and fixtures damages had been awarded generally: new trial would have been granted had the court held that the term "fixtures" could not be pressed within the meaning of goods so as to ground conversion as to that item in the claim). The only way in which the court could formerly refuse a new trial in such cases was where the circumstances made it possible to refer all the damages awarded completely to the items of damage which would ground the action: see, e.g. *Sheen v Rickie* (1839) 5 M. & W. 175 at 181, where it was said that, if damages were awarded generally for slanderous words all spoken at the same time where some of the words would not maintain the action, it was to be taken that the damages were given for the actionable words and that the others were inserted only for aggravation; and compare . the "settled rule", announced per curiam in *Lawrie v Dyeball* (1828) 8 B. & C. 70 at 71, that "if the same count contains two demands or complaints for one of which the action lies and not for the other all the damages shall be referred to the good cause of action although it would be otherwise if they were in separate counts." Today, however, the courts will rely on the wide general power to refuse new trials where there has been no irregularity causing injustice: see paras 53-011 and 53-032, below.

[222] See *Pawly v Holly* (1773) 2 Wm. Bl. 853 at 854, per de Grey CJ.

[223] Accepted as clear law in *S.S. Celia v S.S. Volturno* [1921] 2 A.C. 544 at 549, 555, 560, 566 and again in *Re United Railways of Havana & Regla Warehouses* [1961] A.C. 1007 at 1043, 1068–1069.

[224] [1976] A.C. 443.

[225] See paras 20-018 and following, above.

[226] [1918] A.C. 626.

[227] Lord Finlay LC, Lord Shaw of Dunfermline and Lord Wrenbury.

[228] On the variation of periodical payments see further at paras 40-031 to 40-032 and paras 52-032 to 52-037, above.

[229] See para.51-009, above.

the amount to which it finds the claimant entitled. Amendment would not therefore seem to be necessary.[230]

### (2) Assessment where the action does not proceed to trial

**(a) Judgment by consent or admission** Where the defendant consents to judgment against himself, judgment will be given upon application. Where he admits that he has no defence to the action, judgment may be given against him under CPR r.14.3. If the claim is for a specified amount of money, judgment will be by virtue of CPR r.14.4 and that judgment will, by CPR r.14.4(6), be for the amount of the claim and costs. Such a "specified amount" might include both figures specified for general damages (such as pain and suffering, or damage to property) and figures specified for special damages (such as lost profits).[231] Interest to the date of judgment "shall"[232] be included if the requirements of CPR r.14.14(1) are satisfied. If the claim is for an amount of money which is not specified, judgment will be by virtue of CPR r.14.6[233] and that judgment will, by CPR r.14.6(7), be for an amount to be decided by the court and costs. Interest, by CPR r.14.14(2), "shall" be for an amount to be decided by the court. For these purposes the court will no doubt give case management directions including allocation of the case to the relevant track. **52-053**

**(b) Judgment in default** Judgment may be given against the defendant in default under CPR r.12.3(1) where he fails to file an acknowledgment of service or fails to file a defence. If in either of such circumstances the claim is for a specified amount of money, judgment will be by virtue of CPR r.12.4(1)(a),[234] and that judgment will, by CPR r.12.5(2), be for the amount claimed, with costs. Interest to the date of judgment "may" be included if the requirements of CPR r.12.6(1) are satisfied. If the claim is for an unspecified amount of money, judgment will be by virtue of CPR r.12.4(1)(b)[235] and that judgment will, by CPR r.12.5(3), be for an amount to be decided by the court, and costs. Interest, by CPR r.12.6(2), "will" be for an amount to be decided by the court. If the claim is for delivery of goods where the claim form gives the defendant the alternative of paying their value, judgment will be by virtue of CPR r.12(4)(1)(c), and that judgment will, by CPR r.12.5(4), be a judgment requiring the defendant to deliver the goods or, if he does not do so, to pay the value of the goods as decided by the court, and to pay costs. Interest, again by CPR r.12.6(2), "will" be for an amount to be decided by the court. A default judgment may be obtained, by virtue of CPR r.12.4 (1)(d), in the event of any combination of these claims, each presumably being treated in the appropriate manner for that claim. Where amounts to be awarded have to be decided by the court, CPR r.12.7(2) provides that the court will give any directions it considers ap- **52-054**

---

230 But see *Maguire v Molin* [2002] EWCA Civ 1083; [2003] 1 W.L.R. 644 at para.51-009, above (in a footnote) for a cautionary note.

231 See *Merito Financial Services Ltd v Yelloly* [2016] EWHC 2067 (Ch) at [36] (Master Matthews).

232 Contrast para.52-054, below.

233 Claims for an "unspecified amount of money".

234 Claims for "a specified amount of money". The expression "specified amount of money" used in the Rule has a wider meaning than the older term "liquidated damages". Under the new rubric, it is possible for a claimant in a road traffic claim not involving personal injury to claim as damages the cost of repairs to a vehicle, specifying the cost of the repairs in the claim form and then to enter a default judgment for the amount of the damages claimed, thereby avoiding a disposal hearing.

235 Claims for "an amount of money to be decided by the court".

propriate and, if it considers it appropriate, allocate the case. Allocation is not always necessary and the case can proceed to a disposal hearing without allocation. Allocation is governed by Pt 26 and its supplementary Practice Direction.

When default judgment is given, the court takes the factual allegations in the claim form and particulars of claim (and any other relevant statements of case) to be true, and then makes a judgment as to what, as a matter of law, the claimant is entitled to.[236] The default judgment is conclusive on the issue of liability of the defendants as pleaded, and on the assessment of damages the defendant may not take any point which is inconsistent with the liability alleged in the statement of claim, but subject to that may take any point which is relevant to the assessment of damages, including contributory negligence, failure to take reasonable steps to mitigate, and causation.[237]

The procedure governing claims for possession of land is set out in CPR Pt 55. CPR r.55.7 dispenses with the need for an acknowledgment of service in possession proceedings and CPR r.55.7(3) provides that where a defendant does not file a defence within the time specified, he may nevertheless take part in any hearing, the sole sanction for his failure to file a defence being that the court may take his failure to do so into account when deciding what order to make about costs.

### (3) Assessment where there are several defendants

**52-055** There are certain rules particular to the situation where the claimant claims against more than one defendant,[238] and especially where some of the defendants act or have acted in a manner different from the others.[239]

**52-056** **(a) Where all or some of the defendants default** Where all of several defendants default,[240] whether by failure to file an acknowledgment of service or failure to file a defence, the claimant should be able to enter the appropriate judgment against all of them in the same way as against a single defendant. Where not all of the defendants default, CPR r.12.8(1) provides that a claimant may obtain a default judgment on a claim for money or a claim for delivery of goods against the defaulting defendant or defendants and proceed with his claim against the other or others. However, by CPR r.12.8(2), the court will only enter a default judgment if the claim can be dealt with separately from the claim against the other defendant or

236 *Merito Financial Services Ltd v Yelloly* [2016] EWHC 2067 (Ch) at [6].

237 *Lunnun v Singh* [1999] C.P.L.R. 587, cited in *Merito Financial Services Ltd v Yelloly* at [24]–[25].

238 Problems of contribution and indemnity between wrongdoers are not dealt with in this book. An award of contribution or indemnity is not an award of damages; the correct classification puts such an award under quasi-contract or, in modern terminology, restitution.

239 The rules as to joinder and consolidation of actions are of general application and are considered only in so far as they affect the measure of damages.

240 None of the following rules applies to a claimant's claim against two or more defendants liable only in the alternative where, if judgment is entered against one, the right to proceed against the others is lost: see, e.g. *Morel Brothers & Co v Earl of Westmorland* [1904] A.C. 11 HL. However, entering of judgment will only have this effect if the factual basis of the suit against one was incompatible with that necessary to establish liability against the other or the legal bases of both claims could not be consistently advanced, such that an unequivocal election to pursue one basis of claim would preclude reliance on the other: *Balgobin v South West Regional Health Authority* [2012] UKPC 11; [2013] 1 A.C. 582.

defendants. If it cannot, the court must deal with the application at the same time as it disposes of the claim against the other defendant or defendants.[241]

**(b) Where some of the defendants make a Pt 36 offer** A claimant may elect to accept a Pt 36 offer[242] made by one or more, but not all, of a number of defendants if the defendant or defendants who have not made the offer have been sued jointly with, or in the alternative to, the defendant or defendants making the offer and have consented to the claimant's accepting, provided that the claimant discontinues his claim against the defendant or defendants who have not made the offer—CPR r.36.15. None of this directly affects problems of damages, but it provides the rule upon which an exception, which does affect damages, had been engrafted. **52-057**

If the claimant elects not to accept a Pt 36 offer made by one or more of several defendants but proceeds to trial, the only point on damages is that, where the defendants are joint wrongdoers, the court cannot find that the offer made is sufficient as to the party or parties making it and award further damages against the others, but must find against all for the same amount.[243] This is merely another facet of the rule that only one judgment may be entered against joint wrongdoers.[244] **52-058**

**(c) Where a number of defendants are sued for defamation or injurious falsehood in a consolidated action** Although in CPR r.3.1(2)(g) there is a general provision for the consolidation of actions, there is a particular provision for libel in s.5 of the Law of Libel Amendment Act 1888, which empowers the court, on application by two or more defendants, to make an order for consolidation of actions brought by the same claimant against them in respect of the same or substantially the same libel. This provision has been extended, by s.13 of the Defamation Act 1952, to slanders and injurious falsehoods. Not only is consolidation provided for, but the manner of awarding the damages in the consolidated action is also dealt with. Section 5 continues thus: **52-059**

> "In a consolidated action under this section the jury shall assess the whole amount of the damages (if any) in one sum, but a separate verdict shall be taken for or against each defendant in the same way as if the actions consolidated had been tried separately; and if the jury shall have found a verdict against the defendant or defendants in more than one of the actions so consolidated, they shall proceed to apportion the amount of damages which they shall have so found between and against the said last-mentioned defendants …"[245]

This provision probably reached the statute book as a result of *Colledge v Pike*,[246] which had come before the courts in the previous year. In that case the claimant brought an action for libel against the defendant and separate actions against 16 **52-060**

---

[241] In *Yates v Elaby trading as United Property Management & Moss* unreported 17 November 2003, Mitting J held that where a claim was brought in the alternative, the court not only has the power under CPR r.12.8(2)(b) not to enter default judgment against one defendant but has the duty not to do so.

[242] A Pt 36 offer by a single defendant does not touch directly on the question of damages (unless covering separate causes of action: see para.52-049, above): it only affects costs.

[243] See, e.g. *Walker v Woolcott* (1838) 8 C. & P. 352.

[244] See para.52-062, below.

[245] The omitted end of the section concerns the apportionment of costs.

[246] (1887) 56 L.T. 125.

other different defendants for publishing the same libel in their several newspapers, having already recovered £3,100 in three other actions based upon the same libel against 17 other defendants. The court held that it could not make an order for consolidation of the actions on the ground that, although the libel was the same in each case, the several publications and circumstances attending them being different, the causes of action in the several cases were different. Instead, however, the court made an order based upon what Huddleston B described as the defendants' "very handsome offer,"[247] that all further proceedings in all the actions, except one to be selected by the claimant, should be stayed pending the trial of such selected action; that, if the claimant was dissatisfied with the verdict obtained on the trial of such action, he should be at liberty to select one other action for trial; and, the defendants undertaking to be bound by the verdict in the selected first and second actions, that the claimant should be at liberty to sign judgment against the defendants in all the remaining actions for the maximum amount of damages found by the jury. Huddleston B said:

> "While, on the one hand, the court is anxious to secure to the plaintiff his full legal rights, and his power of obtaining ample compensation for the injuries he may have sustained, still, on the other hand, they are, I think, bound to see that the advisers of the plaintiff do not make a market of his wrongs out of the pockets of the several defendants."[248]

**52-061** It was probably this situation of several tortfeasors who have independently published a libel, and particularly several newspapers that have done so, at which s.5 was directed: joint tortfeasors are thought to fall outside the section and also outside its modern extension.[249] Thus, in so far as each several tortfeasor is only li-

247 (1887) 56 L.T. 125 at 126.

248 (1887) 56 L.T. 125 at 126.

249 It is perhaps useful to set out the reasons for rejecting an interpretation of the statutory provisions which would include joint tortfeasors. Joint tortfeasors could be affected in one of two ways: the statutory provisions might allow either (1) for apportionment of the damages between them, or (2) for contribution inter se. (1) The statutory wording that the separate verdicts are to be taken "in the same way as if the actions consolidated had been tried separately" militates against the first interpretation. Separate actions against joint tortfeasors could not have been pursued to judgment in 1888; the claimant could sue as few or as many joint tortfeasors as he pleased in one action, but after judgment had been entered in this action he could bring no further suit. Only against several tortfeasors could several actions be brought and separate judgments entered. Furthermore, the introduction of apportionment would have reversed the common law rule that joint tortfeasors are jointly and severally liable for the whole damage, and it seems improbable that such a well-established rule (found as early as *Cocke v Jennor* (1613) Hob. 66) should be overthrown, for defamation and injurious falsehood, practically as the side effect of provisions dealing with the consolidation of actions. Also, it would be curious that such a major substantive change could be made of no effect by the claimant adopting the simple expedient of suing the defendants jointly in the first place, and thus allowing no opportunity for an order for consolidation which alone can make the statutory provisions applicable. (2) Although apparently favoured by Lord Esher MR in *Stone v Press Association* [1897] 2 Q.B. 159 CA, where he said that the whole amount of the damages was "the only sum with which the plaintiff has anything to do" (at 161), the second interpretation has even less to commend it. The simplest point against it is that it does not spring easily from the wording of s.5 of the Law of Libel Amendment Act 1888. Beyond this, on such an interpretation not only would s.5 have reversed for libel in 1888 the well-established common law rule forbidding contribution between tortfeasors but the extension of s.5 to slanders and injurious falsehoods in 1952 would become pointless in view of the earlier statutory reversal of this common law rule by the Law Reform (Married Women and Tortfeasors) Act 1935. It seems, however, to have been conceded by counsel in *Broome v Cassell & Co* [1972] A.C. 1027, and accepted as correct by Lord Hailsham LC, that commencement of separate proceedings against joint tortfeasors followed by consolidation was

able for that part of the damage caused by himself,[250] the provisions for apportionment of the damages mark in theory only a procedural change. At the same time, there seems little doubt that the total damages awarded, by judge or jury, against all the several tortfeasors in the consolidated action will tend to be less than the sum of the damages that would have been awarded against each one of them in separate actions. The situation is an unusual one in that, although the damage to a claimant, who is the victim of the same or similar defamatory statements or injurious falsehoods independently published by a number of tortfeasors, is regarded as the sum of the losses inflicted by each separate tortfeasor, yet the whole of the damage is, in reality, less than the sum of the separate parts. By allowing for the consolidation of actions, the legislature has in effect made it possible for this reality to be reflected in the award made to the claimant. Indeed, in *Colledge v Pike*,[251] it is not unlikely that, in making the order based on the defendants' "very handsome offer",[252] the court was trying to cut down the total damages of the claimant, despite the fact that, under the order, he would be entitled as against each defendant to the amount awarded him against the particular defendant whom he chose to sue. And in this connection it is significant that the provisions of s.5 are immediately followed up in s.6 by the statutory reversal, in relation to libels published by newspapers, of the common law rule that a defendant cannot give evidence of any recovery of damages by the claimant against other persons in respect of a statement to the same effect as that sued upon.[253] This would cater for the situation to which s.5 could not reach, namely where the claimant, suing each tortfeasor separately, waits till judgment is entered in each case before issuing a claim form in the next, and thus allows no opportunity for an order for consolidation at any time. And that there is a similar policy behind s.5 and s.6 of the original Act may be further suggested by the fact that the modern extensions of the two sections are again contiguous: by s.12 of the Defamation Act 1952 the reversal of the common law rule that evidence of the recovery of damages in other actions is inadmissible is extended from libels in newspapers to all libels and slanders,[254] while by s.13 the provisions as to consolidation and as to damages in the consolidated action are extended from libels to slanders and injurious falsehoods.

An application for consolidation under this provision, coupled with an offer that the various defendants would accept joint and several responsibility for the single sum awarded—described by Eady J as "a novel proposal"—was made unsuccessfully in *Port v MGN*.[255] The judge, a very experienced defamation practitioner and judge, noted that he had himself been unfamiliar with the provision, and that Counsel had been unable to cite any judicial consideration of the provision in the 21st or 20th centuries. Overall, he concluded that consolidation involved certain

---

possible: at 1063H. But this was obiter.

[250] The damage caused by several tortfeasors may of course be, in whole or in part, the same damage, for which they would be jointly liable, but the common law seems to have regarded the situation where two or more persons have independently published the same or substantially the same defamatory statement as not falling within this category; contrast the common law rule that the defendant could not in mitigation give evidence of any recovery of damages against other persons in respect of a statement to the same effect as that sued upon: para.46-076, above.

[251] (1887) 56 L.T. 125.

[252] See para.52-060, above.

[253] See para.46-076, above.

[254] See para.46-076, above.

[255] [2003] EWHC 1378 (QB).

complicating factors, and was unnecessary:

> "Everything necessary for achieving a just result as between all parties can be achieved, in my judgment, by having the cases listed for trial together before the same judge and jury."

52-062 **(d) Where the defendants are joint wrongdoers and some have acted maliciously or more maliciously than others** Only a single judgment for damages may be entered against joint wrongdoers sued together, the award being for the whole damage suffered by the claimant.[256] This rule applies to joint contractors and joint tortfeasors, despite the difference that, while joint contractors are jointly liable and, unless they are also severally liable,[257] the claimant must sue all together,[258] joint tortfeasors are jointly and severally liable and the claimant in one action may sue one, some or all.[259] Difficulties arise as to the amount of the award to be made in this single judgment where the existence of malicious conduct aggravates the damage, by way of increased injury to the claimant's feelings, or lets in the possibility of an award of exemplary damages, and only some of the joint wrongdoers have acted maliciously or some have acted more maliciously than others. The problem does not arise in contract, where damages are not affected by malicious conduct,[260] but there are many torts where the existence or absence of malice or wantonness in the defendant can affect the damages.[261] Early cases favoured as the proper measure of damages the amount which ought to be awarded against the most malicious of the defendants.[262] This rule, which in theory could be

---

[256] The separate awards made in *Ramdath v Oswald Daley* [1993] 20 E.G. 123 CA, against the joint tortfeasors—a landlord and his agent evicting the tenant—may be justified, at least as far as the compensatory as distinct from the exemplary element was concerned, on the basis that the landlord was liable in contract for breach of the covenant of quiet enjoyment as well as in trespass.

[257] In a joint and several contract, the promisee may, if he chooses, sue all the promisors in one action or bring separate actions against any one or more of the promisors in respect of their several obligations: *Rabiu v Marlbray Ltd* [2016] EWCA Civ 476; [2016] 1 W.L.R. 5147 at [53], [63] (Gloster LJ).

[258] For exceptions and qualifications to this general rule see Glanville Williams, *Joint Obligations* (1949), paras 15 and following, and *Chitty on Contracts*, edited by H. Beale, 32nd edn (London: Sweet & Maxwell, 2015), paras 17-010 and following.

[259] These facets of the liability of joint tortfeasors make it somewhat anomalous that only a single judgment can be entered against those joint tortfeasors sued together, but the rule has been law since *Heydon's Case* (1612) 11 Co. Rep. 5a. The court cannot sever the damages even if the defendants sever in their defences: this was confirmed by the decision of the Court of Appeal in *Greenlands v Wilmshurst* [1913] 3 K.B. 507 CA (reversed on the issue of liability, sub nom. *London Association for Protection of Trade v Greenlands* [1916] 2 A.C. 15), which thereby upholds for today the rule in *Heydon's Case*. See Glanville Williams, *Joint Torts and Contributory Negligence* (1951), para.21, and *Bryanston Finance Ltd v De Vries* [1975] Q.B. 703 CA at 722E–F.

[260] Breach of promise of marriage was formerly an exception but that was a contract where joint wrongdoers could hardly flourish.

[261] By way of aggravated damages rather than exemplary damages since *Rookes v Barnard* [1964] A.C. 1129; see Ch.13, above. The question whether in defamation the malice of one of a number of persons concerned in a joint publication may be imputed to the others so as to defeat a defence of qualified privilege or of fair comment is a different one. It concerns liability and not damages, and attempted analogies from cases dealing with that issue would seem to be misleading rather than helpful.

[262] *Heydon's Case* (1612) 11 Co. Rep. 5a (assault: the court held the claimant entitled to judgment against all three defendants for the amount which the jury had assessed against the first and most malicious defendant); *Brown v Allen* (1802) 4 Esp. 158 (assault: jury directed to give damages against two defendants to the amount that the more malicious one should pay); *Wright v Court* (1825) 2 C.

extended to the case where the most malicious of the joint wrongdoers was not even a co-defendant in the action, fell into disfavour in the middle of the 19th century[263] and in its place two rather different rules appeared. The central case is *Clark v Newsam*,[264] since both the new rules feature in the judgments there. The action was one of assault and false imprisonment, and the court ordered a new trial, apparently because the motives of the parties were considered not to have any bearing on the particular case and the jury might have been misled into thinking that they had. Thus the court's remarks on the present issue became obiter. Pollock B, on the one hand, took the view that the award of damages should ignore the malice of the malicious wrongdoers and that

> "in such case the claimant ought to select the party against whom he means to get aggravated damages."[265]

Alderson B, on the other hand, said that

> "the true criterion of damage is the whole injury which the plaintiff has sustained ... the real injury is the aggregate injury received from both [wrongdoers]".[266]

This statement, though somewhat ambiguous, forms the basis of the headnote which in turn forms the basis of the more modern statement of the law by Slesser LJ in *Chapman v Ellesmere*.[267] The case was one of libel, and a new trial was ordered primarily on the ground that the jury may have based the award of damages on the conduct of the defendants alleged to have been malicious and have failed to take into account the lack of malice in the other defendants. Slesser LJ said:

> "Though there must be one set of damages against joint tortfeasors, the authorities go to show that such damages are not to be assessed according to the act of the most guilty or the most innocent of the defendants, but according to the aggregate of injury received from their common act."[268]

This is in effect a compromise between basing the joint award on the amount that could be awarded against the most malicious, and completely ignoring, in arriving at the joint award, the malice of the malicious wrongdoers.

The law was still in this uncertain and fluid state when *Rookes v Barnard*,[269] was **52-063**
decided. While not directly dealing with the present issue, that decision tended to

& P. 232 (false imprisonment: declaration of one of three defendants made in the absence of the others and tending to show malice held admissible against all).

263 *Robertson v Wylde* (1838) 2 M. & Rob. 101 started the trend by holding inadmissible, on the issue of damages in an action of libel against the publisher of a magazine, evidence of the malice of the writer who was not a co-defendant. Next came *Clark v Newsam* (1847) 1 Ex. 131, considered in the text, and then *Gregory v Cotterell* (1852) 1 E. & B. 360, where, in an action of trespass against two, the court was sufficiently doubtful of the old rule to grant to the less malicious defendant a rule to show cause why there should not be a new trial on the ground of excessive damages: at 371.

264 (1847) 1 Ex. 131.

265 (1847) 1 Ex. 131 at 140.

266 (1847) 1 Ex. 131 at 140.

267 [1932] 2 K.B. 431 CA.

268 [1932] 2 K.B. 431 CA at 471–472. He added that the principle had been applied shortly before in *Maxwell v Keun*, *The Times*, 3 February 1928, but the report is too scanty to give any clear guidance on this issue. There is merely a remark by counsel for the unmalicious defendants that vindictive damages should not be awarded against them merely because the jury might wish to award such damages against the malicious defendant.

269 [1964] A.C. 1129; see Ch.13, above.

support the tentative solution as to the relationship of these competing rules which was put forward in the 12th edition of this work. That solution required a distinction to be drawn between exemplary damages given by way of punishment and aggravated damages given by way of compensation for the increased injury to the claimant's feelings and even reputation, applying Pollock B's view to the former, Alderson B's view to the latter. *Rookes v Barnard*,[270] has emphasised the importance of drawing the distinction between exemplary damages and aggravated damages.[271] The practical effect of the divided rule which it was proposed to build upon this decision is that, on the one hand, a claimant cannot claim the exemplary damages which may be visited on a malicious defendant from his unmalicious colleagues in the joint wrong and must, if he wishes to obtain exemplary damages, single out the malicious tortfeasors and sue only them[272]; while, on the other hand, any increase in the injury to a claimant's feelings occasioned by the malicious conduct of any of the joint tortfeasors must be considered as part of the aggregate injury inflicted by the combined act for which the unmalicious tortfeasors are also liable. *Rookes v Barnard*,[273] by declaring exemplary damages to be anomalous and permissible only in three exceptional types of case,[274] has emphasised the importance of isolating such damages from the mainstream of compensatory damages, and it is consistent with this that they should in no circumstances be available to a claimant against an unmalicious defendant. This solution, as far as exemplary damages are concerned, is now endorsed by the House of Lords in *Broome v Cassell & Co*,[275] where all seven of their Lordships, overturning on this the Court of Appeal,[276] held that, in the words of Lord Hailsham LC,[277] the exemplary award

> "must represent the highest *common* factor, that is, the *lowest* sum for which any of the defendants can be held liable on this score".[278]

Lord Hailsham went on to indicate that he would also apply the lowest sum principle to aggravated damages,[279] and Lord Diplock agreed.[280] This, however, was

[270] [1964] A.C. 1129.

[271] See para.13-004, above.

[272] The efficacy of such a course may now be doubted in light of *R. (on the application of Lumba) v Secretary of State for the Home Department* [2012] 1 A.C. 245 at [168] (Lord Dyson JSC): see para.52-068 below. For a possible, but dubious, alternative route to exemplary damages, see five footnotes, below.

[273] [1964] A.C. 1129; see Ch.13, above.

[274] See paras 13-017 and following, above.

[275] [1972] A.C. 1027: facts at para.13-023, above.

[276] [1971] 2 Q.B. 354 CA.

[277] [1972] A.C. 1027 at 1063G (italics his); see too at 1089H–1090E, per Lord Reid; at 1105E–F, per Viscount Dilhorne; at 1118H, per Lord Wilberforce; at 1121G and 1122B, per Lord Diplock. The Lord Chancellor said (at 1063H) that it was conceded that a claimant could ensure a higher exemplary award not only by electing to sue the more guilty defendant on his own—a possibility recognised in the text above—but also, in libel actions, by commencing separate proceedings against each and then consolidating, or, in the case of a book or a newspaper article, by suing separately in the same proceedings for the publication of the manuscript to the publisher by the author. But the former of these two devices to be effective would appear to require that the provisions for consolidation in s.5 of the Law of Libel Amendment Act 1888 should apply to joint tortfeasors, and it has been submitted that this is not so: see paras 52-059 to 52-061, above.

[278] Thus it may be difficult to justify the retention, in *Ramdath v Oswald Daley* [1991] T.L.R. 300 CA, of the exemplary award against the one joint tortfeasor when the Court of Appeal was setting aside the trial judge's exemplary award against the other: see the case at para.39-075, above.

[279] [1972] A.C. 1027 at 1063G.

strictly obiter, does not indeed appear consistent with the decision itself as the jury's separate award of compensatory damages was in no way impugned, does not appear to be the view of Lord Reid[281]; and was thought not at all satisfactory by Lord Denning MR in *Hayward v Thompson*,[282] a decision which tends strongly to support the approach here proposed as the jury was held by the Court of Appeal to have rightly awarded one sum as damages against all three defendants, who were the editor, the crime correspondent and the proprietors and publishers of the *Sunday Telegraph*, without considering whether there were matters in aggravation of damages against one or two of the defendants rather than all of them.[283]

Given this historical lineage, the rationale for the quantification of aggravated damages tersely enunciated by Eady J in the defamation case of *Berezovsky v Russian Television and Radio Broadcasting Co*,[284] is anomalous and confusing. Asserting that in *Broome v Cassell & Co Ltd*,[285] both Lord Hailsham and Lord Reid had been of the opinion that any joint tortfeasor would only be liable for what he referred to as the lowest common denominator, Eady J contended that the lowest common denominator approach was likely to be preferred by a modern appellate court. The assertion that Lord Reid had agreed with Lord Hailsham as to the applicability of the lowest sum principle to aggravated damages is to misread Lord Reid's careful opinion. While it is correct to say that Lord Hailsham's strictly obiter attempt to extend the lowest sum principle to aggravated damages received a somewhat indirect measure of support from Lord Diplock, such an extension of the principle was not endorsed by Lord Reid. To the contrary, in the part of his speech relied on by Eady J,[286] Lord Reid was referring exclusively to punitive (and thus exemplary) damages. He was not there addressing compensation for injury to feelings as such at all. Indeed, in the paragraph immediately preceding that relied on by Eady J,[287] Lord Reid indicated that, for compensatory damages, which of course include aggravated damages, it is the highest common factor that is appropriate. Furthermore, Lord Hailsham's attempt to extend the lowest sum principle was firmly rejected by Lord Denning MR in *Hayward v Thompson*,[288] a case also taken into account by Eady J. In addition to its obfuscation of precedent, Eady J's bold proposition that the lowest sum principle is likely to be preferred by a modern appellate court can be challenged on the further ground that it insufficiently acknowledges the conceptual distinction between exemplary and aggravated awards. In the case of aggravated damages, the injury for which compensation is payable is the aggregate injury inflicted by the combined act of both malicious and unmalicious tortfeasors. Aggregation in this sense permits no diminution in the liability of those liable in common for the overall injury. To introduce such a reduction would in effect be to demutualise the liability or to disaggregate the harm. Nor **52-064**

280 See [1972] A.C. 1027 at 1063G at 1131H.

281 See [1972] A.C. 1027 at 1063G at 1090C.

282 [1982] Q.B. 47 CA at 62F. It is true that his criticism of awarding the lowest sum embraced exemplary as well as aggravated damages.

283 See especially [1982] Q.B. 47 at 62H–63D and 70H–71B.

284 [2010] EWHC 476 (QB).

285 [1972] A.C. 1027.

286 At [1972] A.C. 1027 at [1090D]–[E].

287 At [1972] A.C. 1027 at [1090C].

288 [1982] Q.B. 47 CA at 62F.

does Eady J's citation of art.10 of the European Convention on Human Rights provide a convincing justification for his abandonment of the earlier authorities.[289]

**52-065** Two claims under the Housing Act 1988 offer illustrations of the lowest sum principle. In *Francis v Brown*,[290] the defendants who were mother and daughter[291] had jointly participated in the unlawful eviction of the claimant from a property belonging to the mother. As the claimant's landlord, the mother was the only defendant liable for the statutory tort created by s.1(1) of the 1988 Act. Because of the mother's liability for statutory damages, no award for exemplary damages could be made against her. The lowest sum was therefore nil. Citing and relying upon *Broome v Cassell & Co*,[292] the Court of Appeal held that no exemplary damages could be awarded against the daughter. The decision also gives some implied support to the proposition that the rule should be different for aggravated damages. In *Nwokorie v Mason*,[293] a case involving a single defendant, the Court of Appeal had held that aggravated damages also fall to be set off against the statutory award under the Housing Act 1988. The Court of Appeal in *Francis v Brown* did not find it necessary to decide whether the award of aggravated damages against the mother should, by set-off against the statutory award, similarly fall away, Sir Iain Glidewell (the only one of the three judges to consider *Nwokorie*) merely distinguishing the decision. All three judges elected to preserve the separate award of aggravated damages against the daughter. Thus while the Court of Appeal decided that the exemplary award against the mother fell away so that no exemplary damages could be awarded against the daughter,[294] yet the award of aggravated damages against the daughter was allowed to stand. *Mehta v Royal Bank of Scotland*,[295] is a case in which the lowest sum principle seems to have been misapplied. A claim for unlawful eviction against three defendants, only one of the defendants was liable under the Housing Act 1988 as landlord, his statutory liability exceeding his liability for aggravated and exemplary damages combined. The judge nevertheless held that the two other defendants were liable to the claimant for the full amounts awarded for exemplary and aggravated damages. On the basis of *Francis v Brown*, which was not cited to the court,[296] the exemplary award should have been eliminated and the award of aggravated damages (together with the award of general damages) retained.[297]

**52-066** In *Veliu v Mazrekaj*,[298] a libel action, the claimant accepted an offer of amends

---

289 In the event, the Court of Appeal did not have to consider Eady J's approach, although Laws LJ described the position as "somewhat opaque having regard to the judge's reasoning": [2011] EWCA Civ 1534 at [63].

290 (1998) 30 H.L.R. 143 CA.

291 Facts at para.39-084, above.

292 [1972] A.C. 1027.

293 (1994) 26 H.L.R. 60.

294 The mother's liability was not in issue as only the daughter was appealing against the trial judge's award.

295 [1999] 3 E.G.L.R. 153.

296 See the case at para.39-073, above.

297 Of course, as the judge was careful to point out, such retention of liability does not mean that the claimant could have obtained damages twice over against the landlord and the other defendants, or against the mother and the daughter in *Francis v Brown* for that matter. That would amount to double recovery. In both cases the prospects of the claimant recovering the damages awarded from any defendant were very poor, which may have persuaded the judge in *Mehta v Royal Bank of Scotland* not to embark upon any off-setting of awards.

298 [2006] EWHC 1710 (QB); [2007] 1 W.L.R. 495.

made by the first defendant under the statutory procedure and entered judgment in default of defence against the second defendant for damages to be assessed. Eady J was then faced with the difficult task of deciding the amount due from the first defendant in accordance with the statutory procedure as well as the amount in damages payable by the second defendant. Acknowledging that no aggravating factors could be taken into account at all unless responsibility could be attributed by one means or another to both defendants, Eady J concluded that there was nevertheless a case for treating the new process of fixing a suitable discount under the offer of amends procedure rather differently. Since the discount was specific to the individual defendant who had used the new statutory framework, there was no obvious policy reason why, when the discount came to be assessed, that defendant should escape responsibility for any aggravation which was specific to him. Even though his personal contribution to aggravating the hurt to the claimant's feelings should be left out of account when quantifying the total compensation to be paid, yet it might be a factor in reducing his offer of amends discount. Eady J's ingenious notion would not appear to breach the lowest sum principle formulated by Lord Hailsham in *Broome v Cassell & Co Ltd*,[299] to which Eady J had careful regard. It cannot, however, be seen as entirely within the spirit of that decision. There is furthermore a structural weakness in, on the one hand, not increasing damages by reference to aggravating factors while, on the other hand, not discounting the damages under the offer of amends procedure to such an extent because of those same aggravating factors. The defendant who makes use of the offer of amends procedure should surely not be put in a worse position by reason of his apology than the defendant who makes no apology at all.

Whatever the intricacies such decisions as these may throw up, while the rejection of the idea of meting out punishment where it is not deserved, embodied in the lowest sum principle, is clearly right, it is submitted that the notion of suretyship between joint tortfeasors for the total injury should nevertheless be retained. **52-067**

**(e) Where not all the defendants, or not all the claimants, are before the court and exemplary damages are claimed** In the important case of *R. (on the application of Lumba) v Secretary of State for the Home Department*,[300] the Court of Appeal had upheld the first instance judge's decision that, on the facts, the threshold for an award of exemplary damages had not been reached, adding by way of further reason for declining to award exemplary damages that, where there is more than one victim of a tortfeasor's conduct, one award of damages should be made which award should be shared between the victims rather than a series of separate awards for each individual victim. Where, as in the instant case, the number of potential claimants was large and they were not all before the court, it was not appropriate to make an award of exemplary damages at all. In the Supreme Court, Lord Dyson, giving what may be treated as the majority speech, said the Court of Appeal was right to regard this as a reason for making no such award. He went on[301]: **52-068**

> "There is yet one further point. It is unsatisfactory and unfair to award exemplary damages where the basis for the claim is a number of serious allegations against named officials and Government Ministers of arbitrary and outrageous use of executive power and

---

[299] [1972] A.C. 1027 at 1063G. See at para.52-063, above.

[300] [2011] UKSC 12; [2012] 1 A.C. 245.

[301] [2012] 1 A.C. 245 at [168].

those persons have not been heard and their answers to the allegations have not been tested in evidence."

CHAPTER 53

# APPEALS

TABLE OF CONTENTS



A party may lodge an appeal from an award of damages on the ground of its excessiveness or inadequacy. On such an appeal different considerations apply, particularly as to the manner in which the appellate court may interfere with the award, to actions originally heard by a judge and jury and to actions originally heard by a judge sitting alone.[1] **53-001**

## I. APPEALS FROM AN AWARD OF DAMAGES BY A JURY

Until the middle of the 19th century all actions for damages in the common law courts were heard with a jury. Gradually, however, the pendulum has swung in favour of the hearing of actions by judges sitting alone; Lord Denning MR stated in *Ward v James*,[2] that by the mid-1960s only two per cent of civil cases were tried with juries. Today a right to jury trial of damages claims is available only to the parties to a claim in respect of malicious prosecution or false imprisonment, or to a defendant against whom a claim is made involving a charge of fraud, unless the court is of the opinion that the trial requires any prolonged examination of docu- **53-002**

---

1 The initial appellate court will generally be the Court of Appeal. This applies equally to actions heard in the High Court (see ss.16 and 17 of the Senior Courts Act 1981), and to actions heard in the county court (see s.77 of the County Courts Act 1984). Occasionally, however, the Court of Appeal may not be concerned, as where in an Admiralty matter an award by a registrar comes before a judge: contrast para.53-027, below (in a footnote) as to the extent that such cases may differ from those heard directly by the Court of Appeal.

2 [1966] 1 Q.B. 273 CA at 290.

ments or accounts or any scientific or local investigation which cannot conveniently be made with a jury, or unless the court is of the opinion that the trial will involve applications to use closed material under the Justice and Security Act 2013.[3] Otherwise, trial is without a jury, but there is a discretion in the judge to order trial with a jury[4]; today this discretion is practically never exercised in favour of jury trial. Indeed the Court of Appeal laid down in *Ward v James*,[5] that in personal injury cases, which had become effectively the only category of case in which jury trial was still prevalent where the form of trial was one of discretion rather than of right, the judge ought not in future to order trial by jury other than in exceptional circumstances.[6] Since that decision, as the Pearson Commission in 1978 commented with approval,[7] jury trial has virtually disappeared from personal injury litigation in England and Wales.[8] The Law Commission in its now rather elderly *Report on Damages for Personal Injury: Non-Pecuniary Loss*,[9] moves outside the field of personal injury to recommend that the assessment of damages should also be taken away from juries in all other cases with the exception of defamation, a recommendation which covers false imprisonment, malicious prosecution and claims involving a charge of fraud against the defendant.[10] It is also recommended that in all cases awards of punitive and restitutionary damages should be for the judge.[11]

## 1. POWERS AVAILABLE TO THE APPELLATE COURT

**53-003** The modern method of control established by the common law over awards of damages made by a jury is the power of the appellate court to set aside the award and grant a new trial.[12] This has been the appellate court's only power in relation

---

3 Section 69(1) of the Senior Courts Act 1981 for actions in the High Court; s.66(2) and (3) of the County Courts Act 1984 for actions in the County Court. The right to a jury trial in defamation claims was removed by s.11 of the Defamation Act 2013. Trial by jury of defamation claims hereafter is likely to be exceptionally unusual. In *Yeo v Times Newspapers Ltd* [2014] EWHC 2853 (QB); [2015] 1 W.L.R. 971 at [80], Warby J suggested that the circumstances would most likely be one where trial by judge alone would bring with it the perception of "involuntary bias"—for example, in a libel claim brought by a judge, of which, he said, there have been examples in recent history though none that have reached trial.

4 Section 69(3) of the Senior Courts Act 1981 for actions in the High Court; s.66(2) of the County Courts Act 1984 for actions in the County Court.

5 [1966] 1 Q.B. 273 CA.

6 For what has been regarded as exceptional circumstances see The Supreme Court Practice 1999, note entitled "Discretion as to trial by jury" at Vol.1, pp.649 to 650. This note is not reproduced in the current edition of the White Book Service. Jury trial receives a passing reference in CPR Pt 26 r.11 and in the notes to the Senior Courts Act 1981 and the County Courts Act 1984, both contained in the White Book, Vol.2.

7 *The Royal Commission on Civil Liability and Compensation for Personal Injury* (The Pearson Commission) (1978), Cmnd.7054 to 1, paras 729 and 734.

8 But remained quite common in Scotland and Northern Ireland: The Pearson Commission, para.729. It was said in *H v Ministry of Defence* [1991] 2 Q.B. 103 CA, that jury trial may be appropriate if exemplary damages could, exceptionally, be claimed.

9 (1999), Law Com. No.257.

10 See (1999), Law Com. No.257, para.4.12.

11 See (1999), Law Com. No.257, para.4.32.

12 The power to grant a new trial dates from the 17th century. It took the place of the attaint by which a second jury of 24 could annul the jury's verdict when the damages were excessive. This was the first method of control of the jury's award, from about the beginning of the 14th century. The severity and inconvenience of the attaint caused it to be limited and eventually abandoned by the end of

to damages; the common law has recognised no power in the appellate court, of its own independent authority and without the consent of both parties, to increase or reduce the award by substituting its own assessment.[13] Not even with the claimant's consent could the court reduce the damages awarded: the defendant must also consent. This was finally established by the decision of the House of Lords in *Watt v Watt*,[14] being based on the ground that a contrary rule would involve an invasion of the jury's province.[15] From this it followed that neither could the court increase the damages without the defendant's consent. On this one qualification was introduced by the further decision of the House of Lords in *Barber v Deutsche Bank Agency*,[16] where it was decided that the appellate court might, with the claimant's consent, reduce the award in respect of any distinct head of damages which the jury had erroneously included, for in such circumstances an invasion of the jury's province was not involved: this qualification applied equally to the converse case where the defendant consents to an increase of the award in respect of a distinct head of damages erroneously excluded. Beyond this, it has always been possible for the court to substitute its own assessment instead of granting a new trial where both parties consent to a reassessment. Indeed this course was frequently adopted in order to save the time which would be taken up with a new trial; illustrations are provided by *Nance v British Columbia Electric Ry*,[17] and by *Sutcliffe v Pressdram*.[18] These various inroads upon the common law requirement that a new trial be granted were brought together in RSC Ord.59 r.11(4) as it stood up until 1990.[19]

Change, however, was on the way, change which reflected attitudes very different from those appearing in *Watt v Watt*.[20] In exercise of the power given by s.8 of the Courts and Legal Services Act 1990, a new RSC Ord.59 r.11(4) was introduced in that year[21] in the following terms: **53-004**

> "In any case where the Court of Appeal has power to order a new trial on the ground that the damages awarded by a jury are excessive or inadequate, the Court may, instead of

the 16th century.

[13] This was not always so. By the 15th century the courts would increase or reduce the damages where they were in a position to test the award, either because the claimant's demand was certain, as in an action of debt, or because the court could inspect the injury itself, as in the case of mayhem. Although in *Brown v Seymour* (1742) 1 Wils. 5 this power was still recognised as subsisting, it was abandoned in the 18th century. Beyond this, the court had also been prepared to increase or reduce the damages where the main issue had not been submitted to the jury, as where the judgment had been by default or on demurrer and a writ of inquiry had been issued merely for the assessment of the damages. The reason here was that "the court themselves, if they had so pleased, might, upon the interlocutory judgment, have assessed the damages … and the inquisition is only a matter of course taken to inform the conscience of the court": *Hewitt v Mantell* (1768) 2 Wils. 372 at 374, per Wilmot CJ. This practice too was discontinued, and the courts would award a new writ of inquiry in the same way as they would award a new trial: e.g. *Markham v Middleton* (1745) 2 Strange 1259.

[14] [1905] A.C. 115, overruling the contrary opinion in *Bett v Lawes* (1884) 12 Q.B.D. 356 CA.

[15] In so far as *Moore v Tuckwell* (1845) 1 C.B. 607 and *Fleming v Bank of New Zealand* [1900] A.C. 577 PC may be inconsistent with the decision in *Watt v Watt* [1905] A.C. 115, they are no longer acceptable. Contrast Devlin, *Trial by Jury* (1956), pp.105 to 106.

[16] [1919] A.C. 304.

[17] [1951] A.C. 601 PC: see at 617.

[18] [1991] 1 Q.B. 153 CA: see at 181C–D and 193H–194A. In fact before the Court of Appeal had reassessed in the light of the parties' agreement, the parties themselves had come to a settlement figure: see at 194B.

[19] RSC Ord.59 appeared as Ord.58 until 1965.

[20] [1905] A.C. 115; see para.53-003, above.

[21] By SI 1990/2599.

> ordering a new trial, substitute for the sum awarded by the jury such sum as appears to the Court to be proper; but except as aforesaid the Court of Appeal shall not have power to reduce or increase the damages awarded by a jury."

This sea change was largely prompted by the arrival on the scene of very high libel awards successfully challenged by defendants where the courts wished to be able not only to avoid the time and trouble of a new trial but also to take the decision on the level of damages into their own hands.

**53-005** The introduction of the CPR may be seen as continuing the same trend. By eliminating the conditions precedent to the exercise of the appellate court's power to substitute its own award for that of the jury, previously contained in Ord.59 r.11(4), CPR Pt 52 has enlarged the Court of Appeal's powers of intervention. The unqualified power given to the court is now stated in CPR r.52.20(3) thus:

> "In an appeal from a claim tried with a jury the Court of Appeal may, instead of ordering a new trial—
>
> …
>
> (b) vary an award of damages made by a jury."

Pursuant to the wording of the new rule, the Court of Appeal's power to substitute its own award instead of granting a new trial is no longer strictly confined to cases where the appellate court has first satisfied itself that the jury's award is either excessive or inadequate. The power therefore extends to circumstances where the ground for interference is that there has been misdirection or other error on the part of the trial judge or misconduct as to damages by the jury. It is difficult to envisage circumstances in which the appellate court would exercise its power pursuant to CPR r.52.20(3)(b) other than where the jury's award is felt to be excessive or inadequate. Otherwise the initial award would hardly be open to appeal. Nevertheless the rulemakers' streamlining of the earlier formula gives recognition to a greater preparedness to interfere with a jury's assessment of damages. This erosion of the jury's sovereignty is in marked contrast with the attitude of the House of Lords in the case of *Grobbelaar v News Group Newspapers*.[22] Reversing the Court of Appeal's decision to set aside the jury's finding on liability, Lord Bingham said:

> "The task of an appellate court, whether the Court of Appeal or the House, is to seek to interpret the jury's decision and not, because of justifiable dissatisfaction at the outcome to take upon itself the determination of factual issues which lay within the exclusive province of the jury."[23]

In *Grobbelaar*, the House of Lords was only concerned with liability. But there is no obvious reason to interpret Lord Bingham's robust observations as limited to that issue alone.

**53-006** Where the Court of Appeal does grant a new trial it need not be on all issues. Read together, CPR r.52.20(2)(c) and 52.20(4) provide that "the appeal court has power to … order a new trial …" and may exercise this power "in relation to … part of an order of the lower court". Frequently in the past the new trial was limited to the assessment of damages only: illustrations from earlier days when the power was contained in RSC Ord.59 r.11(3) are provided by *Mechanical and General*

---

22 [2002] UKHL 40; [2002] 1 W.L.R. 3024 HL.

23 [2002] 1 W.L.R. 3024 HL at [26].

*Inventions Co v Austin*,[24] and by *Morgan v Odhams Press*.[25] The appeal court's wider power to vary an award of damages made by a jury will serve to reduce the instances in which a new trial on the issue of damages alone is considered necessary.

## 2. GROUNDS FOR GRANTING A NEW TRIAL: MISLEADING AND MISCONDUCT OF THE JURY

The grounds affecting damages upon which a new trial is granted stem from the fact that the jury either have been misled in making their assessment or have come to a wrong figure through their own misconduct. Miscalculation by the jury formerly also required a new trial but this is no longer so.[26] **53-007**

### (1) Jury misled

The fault which constitutes the ground for granting a new trial may lie with the judge. It may consist in his misdirection of the jury, his failure to direct the jury adequately, or his improper admission or exclusion of evidence. This is well illustrated by three cases in the mid-19th century dealing with the judge's failure to direct the jury adequately as to damages.[27] In *Blake v Midland Ry*,[28] the judge had not explicitly told the jury not to take into account the mental suffering of the claimant for the loss of her husband in assessing damages under one of the earliest of the Fatal Accidents Act claims: a new trial was awarded. In the celebrated *Hadley v Baxendale*,[29] the judge had not told the jury that they ought not to take into account, in assessing the damages for a breach of a contract of carriage, the loss of profits not within the parties' contemplation: a new trial was ordered. And *Knight v Egerton*,[30] a case of distress, took the matter further by deciding that a new trial will be ordered even though the point in question was not taken by counsel at the original trial. **53-008**

More modern illustrations of misdirections appear in actions of libel. In *English & Scottish Co-operative Society v Odhams*,[31] the judge told the jury wrongly that, unless special damage by way of pecuniary loss was found by them, they should award nominal damages; in *Broadway Approvals v Odhams Press (No.2)*,[32] the judge told the jury wrongly that in the circumstances they could award exemplary damages[33]: the jury did award in the one case nominal damages and in the other exemplary damages, and in both a new trial was granted. In *Morgan v Odhams Press*,[34] the House of Lords ordered that there be a new trial on the issue of damages where the judge had misdirected the jury by instructing them to take into account the defendant's failure to make an apology, by not warning them that only a very limited number of people would have known the special facts so as to enable **53-009**

---

24 [1935] A.C. 346.
25 [1971] 1 W.L.R. 1239 HL.
26 See paras 53-004 and 53-005, above.
27 Indeed it was these cases which established that the judge was under a *duty* to direct the jury.
28 (1852) 18 Q.B. 93.
29 (1854) 9 Ex. 341.
30 (1852) 7 Ex. 407.
31 [1940] 1 K.B. 440 CA.
32 [1965] 1 W.L.R. 805 CA.
33 For the extent to which exemplary damages may be awarded in actions of libel, see para.46-078, above.
34 [1971] 1 W.L.R. 239 HL.

them to identify the claimant with the defamatory publication, and by not reminding them that of those able to identify the claimant few, if any, believed the defamatory matter. In *Riches v News Group Newspapers*,[35] the Court of Appeal held a jury's exemplary award vitiated by a whole series of misdirections, including in particular a failure to warn that exemplary damages were only appropriate if they thought the compensatory award inadequate to punish the defendants, a failure to warn that they must exercise restraint and think in moderate amounts, and no direction as to the way in which exemplary damages should be approached where there were, as there, as many as 10 claimants.[36]

**53-010** In further libel cases defendants have fared less successfully. *Broome v Cassell & Co*,[37] is the first important case of this type. The defendants did not satisfy the House of Lords that the judge had misdirected the jury on either of two counts, namely by a failure to make clear to them (1) that, only if the sum awarded by way of compensation was inadequate to punish the defendants, might they award a larger sum by way of exemplary damages and (2) that the sum to be awarded by way of exemplary damages against joint defendants must be the lowest for which any of the defendants could be held liable on that score.[38] Here it was a close thing, with the decision being of a bare majority of a full House of seven on the first count and of a majority of five on the second.[39] By contrast, in each of three libel cases of the 1990s a unanimous Court of Appeal held there to have been no misdirections sufficient to impugn the jury's award.[40] First, in *Sutcliffe v Pressdram*,[41] it was not accepted that there had been a series of misdirections in relation to, among other things, the aggravated damages there claimed; then in *Rantzen v Mirror Group Newspapers*,[42] the alleged misdirections of the jury, which ranged from lack of guidance on the financial implications of their award to allowing them to take into account the absence of an apology, were rejected; and finally in *John v MGN*,[43] the trial judge was not regarded as having misdirected the jury either on the question of compensatory damages or on the proper approach to exemplary damages, in particular in relation to the defendant's recklessness and calculation of profit.[44]

**53-011** The now obsolete RSC Ord.59 r.11(2) provided that:

"The Court of Appeal shall not be bound to order a new trial on the ground of misdirec-

---

35 [1986] Q.B. 256 CA.

36 For all these matters which are relevant to a calculation of an exemplary award, see paras 13-031 and following, above.

37 [1972] A.C. 1027.

38 For these two issues in their substantive setting see paras 13-040 and 52-062 to 52-067, above, respectively.

39 Lords Wilberforce and Diplock considered there had been a misdirection on both matters, Viscount Dilhorne only on the first.

40 The three awards were, however, all held to be excessive: see the cases at paras 53-020 to 53-022, below.

41 [1991] 1 Q.B. 153 CA.

42 [1994] Q.B. 670 CA.

43 [1997] Q.B. 586 CA.

44 Both matters are relevant for exemplary damages in Lord Devlin's second category: see paras 13-021 and following, above. Exceptionally, the fault which misleads the jury may be that of persons other than the judge at the trial. Thus in *Chattell v Daily Mail Publishing Co* (1901) 18 T.L.R. 165 CA, the jury had been misled by the speeches of counsel in a libel action and a new trial was ordered. The court relied on the rule stated by Lord Esher MR in *Praed v Graham* (1890) 24 Q.B.D. 53 CA at 55, which applies where the fault is that of the jury by way of miscalculation (see para.53-019, below); presumably resort was had to this rule because the provisions of the then RSC Ord.59 r.11(2) (see para.53-011, below) only applied where the jury were misled by the fault of the judge.

tion, or of the improper admission or rejection of evidence, or because the verdict of the jury was not taken upon a question which the judge at the trial was not asked to leave to them, unless in the opinion of the Court of Appeal some substantial wrong or miscarriage has been thereby occasioned."

In CPR Pt 52, there is no equivalent to RSC Ord.59 r.11(2). CPR r.52.21(3) instead provides:

"The appeal court will allow an appeal where the decision of the lower court was—

(a) wrong; or
(b) unjust because of a serious procedural or other irregularity in the proceedings in the lower court."

Allowing an appeal must comprehend the various powers given to the appeal court by the preceding sub-rule, r.52.20, which powers include the power to order a new trial. To this extent, the provisions overlap. In CPR r.52.21(3), the two-fold phraseology of RSC Ord.59 r.11(2) "substantial wrong or miscarriage" has been replaced with "serious procedural or other irregularity" which might be thought to be a narrower concept. However, r.52.21(3) echoes the wording of s.68 of the Arbitration Act 1996, s.68(2) defining "serous irregularity" as a mistake "which [has] caused or will cause substantial injustice to the applicant."[45] If s.68 of the Arbitration Act 1996 is a valid precedent for r.52.21(3), the break with the past may be more apparent than real. In *Hamilton v Al Fayed (No.4)*,[46] the Court of Appeal tendered the opinion that RSC Ord.59 r.11 reflected a principle of general application which had not been changed by the new rules. Nor is there anything in the CPR to suggest an intention to effect a change in the underlying jurisprudence. For these reasons, the discussion of the earlier authorities contained in previous editions of this work is repeated without apology.

It is difficult, perhaps impossible, to lay down a general rule as to what was to **53-012**
be considered a substantial wrong or miscarriage.[47] The leading case on the question is *Bray v Ford*.[48] The defendant, in a letter circulated to the governors of a college and others, wrote of the claimant solicitor that he had improperly taken fees for his professional services from the college as he held the fiduciary position of vice-chairman, and went on to make libellous imputations of improper motives and allusions to swindling. The judge misdirected the jury by telling them that the receipt of professional fees by the claimant from the college was not improper, and the jury awarded large damages. The House of Lords took the view that a substantial wrong had been done and granted a new trial. Lord Halsbury LC thought there was a substantial wrong because

45 Decisions on s.68 of the Arbitration Act 1996 are plentiful. Readers are directed to the conventional books on arbitration for details of these. But it is impossible to pass on without referring to one such authority, *Al Hadha Trading Co v Tradigrain SA* [2002] 2 Lloyd's Rep. 512, in which the judge provided a helpful analysis of the section.

46 [2001] E.M.L.R. 15 CA at 394.

47 Compare *Bray v Ford* [1896] A.C. 44 at 50, per Lord Halsbury LC: "I have purposely abstained from suggesting any general rule applicable to the construction of Ord.39, r.6 [later RSC Ord.59 r.11(2)]. I doubt the possibility of formulating any rule which would be useful."

48 [1896] A.C. 44.

> "the defendant was not permitted to present his case to the jury with the argument that his original complaint was true",[49]

and Lord Watson similarly stressed that

> "in assessing damages, a jury might reasonably take into consideration whether the charge upon which libellous imputations were made by way of comment was or was not itself a libel".[50]

In these circumstances a new trial was necessary, in the words of Lord Halsbury LC, because "an important and serious topic has been practically withdrawn from the jury"[51]; in the words of Lord Herschell, because

> "the jury have returned their verdict on what they were erroneously led to think was the case, and not on the real case which the defendant was entitled to have submitted to them".[52]

Their Lordships considered that it was immaterial that, properly directed, the jury might well have arrived at the same figure of damages. "It is nothing to the purpose", said Lord Halsbury LC,

> "to say that the rest of the printed matter complained of as a libel would justify a verdict to the same amount of damages. I absolutely decline to speculate what might have been the result if the judge had rightly directed the jury."[53]

**53-013** In *Bray v Ford*,[54] it was also stressed that cases of libel in which there has been misdirection are particularly open to awards of new trials because in such cases the amount of damages is peculiarly within the province of the jury.[55] Thus it is not surprising that the illustrations of circumstances in which the courts have been prepared to award new trials come from cases of libel. In *Hobbs v Tinling*,[56] it was the claimant and not the defendant who was complaining of misdirection. In the course of the trial the defendant's counsel had cross-examined the claimant as to specific incidents of misconduct, a line of cross-examination which had been objected to but allowed. Before the end of the cross-examination the jury intimated that they wished to find for the defendant, and this they thereupon did without any summing-up from the judge. This was held by the Court of Appeal to involve a number of misdirections: the jury should have been directed, first, that where the claimant denied the incidents in cross-examination the cross-examination afforded no evidence that they had taken place; secondly, that the cross-examination was not admissible to mitigate damages; and, thirdly, the intervention of the jury

---

49 [1896] A.C. 44 at 47.

50 [1896] A.C. 44 at 49 and 50.

51 [1896] A.C. 44 at 48.

52 [1896] A.C. 44 at 53. See similarly at 56, per Lord Shand: "The defendant is entitled to have the real case submitted to the jury."

53 [1896] A.C. 44 at 48. See too at 55, per Lord Shand: "The court is asked to consider the libel and the evidence for the purpose of seeing whether liability exists on a view different from that formerly presented, and whether the damages given on the case formerly presented will not fit in suitably with this different case. I am clearly of opinion that … rule 6 of Order 39 … ought not to be carried so far."

54 [1896] A.C. 44.

55 [1896] A.C. 44 at 50, 52, per Lord Watson and Lord Herschell respectively.

56 [1929] 2 K.B. 1 CA.

was premature and they must hear the claimant's case to the end and be directed as to the issue they had to try. A new trial was granted for, as Sankey LJ put it,

> "the plaintiff must have a proper chance of trying to persuade them [i.e. the jury] to give a verdict in his favour—a chance which he has not yet had".[57]

Scrutton LJ said that he came to this conclusion "with great reluctance", as he felt that

> "if the case had proceeded to its end, and the jury had received a proper direction, it is very possible, even probable, that the jury might have arrived at the same result".[58]

But this, he added, was an irrelevant consideration, as the decision of the House of Lords in *Bray v Ford*,[59] had shown. Somewhat similar is *Farmer v Hyde*,[60] where the defendants were newspaper owners who had published defamatory statements made of the claimant by a third party and the judge had told the jury that, if they took the view that the third party was a person of such bad character that any possible damage the claimant might suffer from criticism by such a person could only be nominal, then they could find a verdict for the defendants. This the jury had proceeded to do. Although the claimant's appeal failed on substantive grounds,[61] the Court of Appeal would have been prepared to grant a new trial had the claimant succeeded on liability, since it could not be said that the jury had addressed their minds to the question of damages. Slesser LJ said:

> "I think it is impossible to say, here, that a substantial miscarriage of justice has not occurred, not because the damages might be larger than one farthing but because the jury have never had an opportunity of assessing damages at all."[62]

In *Riddick v Thames Board Mills*,[63] it was the defendants' appeal which succeeded on substantive grounds, but the Court of Appeal said that in any event they would have been entitled to a new trial on the damages issue because the jury's award of £15,000 was so grossly excessive by reason of the judge's misdirection leading them to believe that they could give the claimant damages for his failure to obtain employment for the years following his dismissal by his employers, even though the libel had not been published until after the dismissal and could have played no part in it.[64] The unsuccessful appeal in the now notorious libel action of *Hamilton v Al Fayed*,[65] gave the Court of Appeal the opportunity to reiterate the governing

---

57 [1929] 2 K.B. 1 CA at 54.

58 [1929] 2 K.B. 1 CA at 30.

59 [1896] A.C. 44.

60 [1937] 1 K.B. 728 CA.

61 Namely that the defendants could shelter behind the statutory defence provided by s.3 of the Law of Libel Amendment Act 1888.

62 [1937] 1 K.B. 728 CA at 740.

63 [1977] Q.B. 881 CA.

64 And see *Broome v Cassell & Co* [1972] A.C. 1027 where those who held that there had been misdirection would have allowed the defendants' appeal; the majority however considered that there had been no misdirection. See para.53-010, above.

65 [2001] E.M.L.R. 15 CA at 394. "We consider that Ord.59, r.11 reflected a principle of general application. We do not believe that this principle has changed with the new rules. A new trial should be ordered when the interests of justice so demand. Where a party has behaved fraudulently, been guilty of procedural impropriety or some other irregularity has affected the fairness of the trial the vital question to be asked is whether there is a real danger that this has influenced the outcome. If

principles. A retrial will normally be ordered, so the Court of Appeal said, where a party has behaved fraudulently or been guilty of procedural impropriety or some other irregularity which has affected the fairness of the trial, if there is a real danger this has influenced the outcome. Although not the issue in the *Hamilton* appeal, the outcome would of course embrace the amount of any damages awarded.

**53-014** On the other side, *Anderson v Calvert*,[66] and *Pamplin v Express Papers (No.2)*,[67] stand as illustrations of a refusal of a new trial on the ground of misdirection as to damages in a libel action.[68] In the earlier case the judge, while properly allowing in proof of malice evidence of the whole conduct of the defendant before and after the publication of the libel, had failed to caution the jury that they ought not to treat such prior and subsequent circumstances as giving a separate and independent right to damages. The Court of Appeal held that this omission was not a ground for granting a new trial having regard to the provision of the then RSC Ord.39 r.6; it is, however, interesting that well before the introduction of this rule of court it had been held in *Darby v Ouseley*,[69] that an omission to caution the jury on this point was not misdirection so as to justify a new trial.[70] In the later case the judge's direction was held to be inadequate in that the jury had not been warned against taking costs into account or against determining liability in the light of the burden of costs. Nevertheless, since the jury's award of derisory damages[71] showed that they regarded the claimant as not being entitled to recover damages of any substance and since their only reason for increasing their award would have been to protect the claimant on costs, which was an impermissible reason, the misdirection had not caused a miscarriage of justice.

**53-015** Outside libel and other actions where the measure of damages is very flexible, there is a greater chance that the court will hold that no substantial wrong or miscarriage has been done so as not to warrant the award of a new trial.[72]

> "In cases in which the question is what are the facts, or the proper inferences to be drawn from the facts",

said Lord Herschell in *Bray v Ford*,[73] pointing the contrast between such cases and that of libel with which he was immediately concerned,

> "if the court think that the verdict of the jury is in accordance with the true view of the facts and of the inferences to be drawn from them, it may be that they would have done right in refusing to grant a new trial on the ground of misdirection, even where the parties had a claim that the action should be tried by a jury."

---

there is, a retrial should normally be ordered": per Lord Phillips MR at [26].

66 (1908) 24 T.L.R. 399 CA.

67 [1988] 1 W.L.R. 116 CA.

68 In *Barber v Pigden* [1937] 1 K.B. 664 CA, a suit for a number of slanders in which the judge did not direct the jury to return separate verdicts for each slander, Greer LJ gave as a reason for refusing a new trial that the defendant had not been prejudiced as to the amount awarded and that therefore the case came within RSC Ord.59 r.11(2). But the main ground for refusing a new trial was a rather different form of lack of prejudice: see para.53-016, below.

69 (1856) 1 H. & N. 1.

70 Contrast para.46-048, above.

71 The award had been of one halfpenny.

72 Compare the same distinction where the error is not of the judge but of the jury: paras 53-018 and following, below.

73 [1896] A.C. 44 at 52.

Thus in *Floyd v Gibson*,[74] the judge misdirected the jury in an action for personal injury by leaving it open to them to treat the injury to the claimant's sight and hearing as permanent when there was no evidence of such permanent injury proper to be left to the jury. It was held by a majority[75] that, since the damages awarded were reasonable and proper in respect of the admittedly suffered injury, there was no substantial miscarriage of justice under the then RSC Ord.39 r.6, and a new trial ought not to be granted. "The amount of damages", said Buckley LJ,

> "appears to me fair and reasonable, and is such as to show that the jury were not in fact misled by the suggested misdirection".[76]

On the other hand in *Warren v King*,[77] where the jury had awarded £50,000 to a girl aged 17 for injuries resulting in paralysis of all four limbs, the Court of Appeal held that the judge's misdirection of the jury had resulted in an award so excessive that it must have been based on an incorrect assessment, and accordingly had occasioned a substantial wrong or miscarriage within the then RSC Ord.59 r.11(2), which justified the ordering of a new trial on the issue of damages. In that case the judge's misdirection had consisted in failing to caution the jury that the damages should be moderate and that they should be fair to the defendant as well as the claimant, in leaving the jury with far too favourable a view of the prospective duration of the claimant's life and therefore of the period for which financial provision had then to be made, and in failing to give an adequate explanation of the amount by which a capital sum given now but representing maintenance over a number of years should be discounted.[78] In *Graham v Dodds*,[79] where the jury had been invited, in a Fatal Accidents Act claim emanating from Northern Ireland to choose from a range of multipliers in assessing the future loss of dependency, of which the upper limit exceeded the maximum which the tribunal of fact could reasonably have applied, it was held that there had been a misdirection of fact which, in the absence of demonstration by the claimant's counsel that there had been no miscarriage of justice, called for a new trial.[80]

These various authorities concern misdirection, but the same principles will apply equally to the improper admission or rejection of evidence and to the failure to take the verdict of the jury upon some question. There is, however, one overriding consideration, arising particularly in cases of non-direction, that, even though the jury may have been influenced by the error in their assessment of the damages, a party may be precluded from obtaining a new trial if the error was one which, through his counsel, he could easily have put right at the trial. **53-016**

---

74 (1909) 100 L.T. 761 CA.

75 Vaughan Williams LJ dissenting.

76 (1909) 100 L.T. 761 CA at 762. The majority distinguished *Bray v Ford* [1896] A.C. 44 on the ground that in that case "a most material consideration" and "an important part of the defendant's defence" had been withdrawn from the jury: at 762 and 763, per Buckley and Kennedy LJJ respectively.

77 [1964] 1 W.L.R. 1 CA.

78 For the subsequent settlement of the action and the approval of its terms by the Court of Appeal, see [1964] 1 W.L.R. 122n CA.

79 [1983] 1 W.L.R. 808 HL. The decision in *Graham v Dodds*, that the multiplier to be used when fixing damages for future loss was to be assessed as at the date of death, was departed from by the Supreme Court in *Knauer v Ministry of Justice* [2016] UKSC 9; [2016] A.C. 908.

80 [1983] 1 W.L.R. 808 HL at 817C–D.

"Where you are complaining of non-direction of the judge or that he did not leave a question to the jury",

said Lord Halsbury LC in *Nevill v Fine Art and General Insurance Co*,[81]

"if you had an opportunity of asking him to do it and you abstained from asking for it, no court would ever have granted you a new trial".[82]

This principle is illustrated by *Barber v Pigden*,[83] where the claimant had sued the defendant for a number of separate slanders. The judge did not direct the jury to return a separate verdict with separate damages in respect of each publication, with the result that the jury found a single verdict and judgment was entered accordingly. It was held that, as no objection had been taken at the trial to the jury being asked to consider the different publications as a whole instead of separately, the defendant could not now be heard to say that the verdict was a nullity.[84]

In *McPhilemy v Times Newspapers Ltd*,[85] the Court of Appeal accepted that, as decided by the House of Lords in *Banbury v Bank of Montreal*,[86] a party's failure to invite the judge to withdraw an issue from the jury does not preclude the Court of Appeal from subsequently holding that the issue could only properly have been decided one way and the jury's verdict upon it was perverse.[87] Simon Brown LJ went on to observe[88] that

"it will often be unwise for trial judges to withdraw issues from the jury and by the same token unwise for counsel to invite them to do so. Only when it is plain that one verdict alone would be rational and any other perverse should the issue be withdrawn. The risk of a successful appeal and the disproportionate expense of a re-trial is otherwise too great."

The wisdom of this observation was noted by Brooke LJ in *Paul v Chief Constable of Humberside*,[89] a false imprisonment case in which the Court of Appeal reached the conclusion that it was necessary to order a re-trial, because an issue had erroneously been withdrawn from the jury, some six years after the claimant's arrest and detention.

## (2) Misconduct of jury

**53-017** The ground for granting a new trial may emanate from the jury themselves whose conduct may cause them to award incorrect damages. Misconduct of the jury in

81 [1897] A.C. 68.

82 [1897] A.C. 68 at 76. See, similarly, *Seaton v Burnand* [1900] A.C. 135 at 145, per Lord Morris.

83 [1937] 1 K.B. 664 CA. This case is considered further at para.52-049, above.

84 This principle was, however, criticised in *Weiser v Segar* [1904] W.N. 93 CA, by Vaughan Williams LJ on the ground that a judge could not prejudice a litigant by failing to perform duties properly lying upon himself. But in *Barber v Pigden* [1937] 1 K.B. 664 CA, the court appears to have preferred the approach of Lord Halsbury LC; see at 671, per Greer LJ.

85 [2001] EWCA Civ 871.

86 [1918] A.C. 626.

87 In *McPhilemy*, the respondent had been content that the question should not be put to the jury, and been willing to concede it, but the appellant had positively encouraged the judge to leave the issue to the jury. The appellant had called numerous witnesses in support of his position on the issue, whose evidence was not challenged, and the judge had given a strong direction steering the jury. It must have been quite a shock when the jury then found against the appellant.

88 [2001] EWCA Civ 871 at [34].

89 [2004] EWCA Civ 308 at [60].

relation to damages hardly arises today but nevertheless remains an available ground upon which a jury's award may be impeached. In one of the very first instances of an award of a new trial, *Wood v Gunston*,[90] a case of slander in which the jury had given very high damages, the ground was the partiality of the jury. And in *Ash v Ash*,[91] a case of false imprisonment where a new trial was awarded for excessive damages, the misconduct consisted in the jury's refusing to give a reason for their verdict, "thinking", Holt CJ said, "they have an absolute despotic power". He added brusquely: "I did rectify that mistake."[92] So, too, if the damages verdict had been reached by a compromise between jurors holding different views on the issue of liability, this would be misconduct.

## 3. GROUNDS FOR REASSESSING THE DAMAGES: MISCALCULATION BY THE JURY

Traditionally, the only ground available to the appellate court for reassessing the damages, as opposed to granting a new trial, was miscalculation by the jury and it is with cases of miscalculation that the modern authorities are primarily concerned. While the power to reassess is a relatively new power given to the court,[93] it remains a power which is expressed to be in the alternative to the older power to grant a new trial. Thus, CPR r.52.20(3)(b) provides that the court "may", instead of ordering a new trial, "vary" a jury's damages award. Although expressed in the alternative, it is thought that, now that the appellate court has power to reassess, it will invariably do so whenever it considers that the jury is wrong. Certainly in all the known cases so far, this has been what the appellate court has done.[94] It would seem that the power to grant a new trial where there is miscalculation has withered on the vine. **53-018**

Equally importantly, the introduction of the power to reassess has encouraged more ready interference with jury awards by the appellate court. At the time of its introduction the rule was that a new trial should be awarded where **53-019**

> "the court thinks that, having regard to all the circumstances of the case, the damages are so excessive that no twelve men could reasonably have given them".

These were the words of Lord Esher MR in *Praed v Graham*,[95] a case of libel, which were cited and adopted by Lord Wright in *Mechanical & General Inventions Co v Austin*,[96] a case of contract in connection with a patent where the damages were a matter of conjecture.[97] These formed the two seminal cases while in

---

90 (1655) Style 462. Referred to by Lord Wright in *Mechanical & General Inventions Co v Austin* [1935] A.C. 346 at 374, 375.

91 (1695) Comb. 357.

92 (1695) Comb. 357. In *Beardmore v Carrington* (1764) 2 Wils. 244 both these cases were explained on the ground of misconduct.

93 See paras 53-004 and 53-005, above.

94 See *Gorman v Mudd* [1992] CA Transcript 1076; *Houston v Smith* [1993] CA Transcript 1544; *Rantzen v Mirror Group Newspapers* [1994] Q.B. 670 CA; *John v MGN* [1997] Q.B. 586 CA; *Jones v Pollard* [1997] E.M.L.R. 233 CA. See these cases at para.53-021, below.

95 (1890) 24 Q.B.D. 53 CA at 55.

96 [1935] A.C. 346 at 378.

97 [1935] A.C. 346 at 378 at 377. Lord Esher MR in the earlier case took the view, with which Lord Wright in the later case agreed, that "the rule of conduct" where the Court of Appeal is asked to set aside an award of damages on the ground of excessiveness is "as nearly as possible the same as where the court is asked to set aside a verdict on the ground that it is against the weight of evidence": (1890) 24 Q.B.D. 53 CA at 55. Lord Esher MR also considered that all the specific grounds already

*Smith v Schilling*,[98] a personal injury case, Greer LJ stated the rule similarly but included in it the converse case of the damages being so small that no jury could reasonably have given them.[99] The rule thus excluded interference by the appellate court merely on the ground that it would have awarded a different figure had it tried the action in the first place: "that is not the relevant consideration", said Lord Wright in *Mechanical & General Inventions Co v Austin*.[100] What the courts were prepared to regard as an award that no 12 men could reasonably have given differed substantially between cases where the measure of damages was a very flexible one because the damages were at large, as in many torts, and cases where the measure of damages was more fixed, as in contract generally and in torts causing property damage, physical injury or death. Interference by the court was far more frequent in the latter type of case, in relation to which indeed there was authority for regarding the general rule as qualified. This appeared from Vaughan Williams LJ's judgment in *Johnston v Great Western Ry*,[101] an action for personal injury where a new trial was claimed on the ground of excessive damages. He said:

> "If the court, from the circumstances of the case and the amount of the damages, can draw the inference that the jury must have applied the wrong measure of damages in contravention of the direction of the judge, the court may order a new trial, although it is not in a position to say that the mere quantum of excess is so large that no reasonable jury could have arrived at such an amount."[102]

There is, however, no practical difference between treating the rule as qualified in this way and reading the rule in the light of the fact that the margin for error in such cases has been narrowed. The advantage of Vaughan Williams LJ's approach is that it stressed that different considerations applied according to the flexibility of the measure of damages.[103] And it is still the position that a jury's award may be upheld in cases where the measure of damages is flexible even if, the judge having followed the recommended convention of suggesting a bracket to the jury, the amount awarded by the jury goes significantly outside and above that bracket. Thus where in *Kiam v MGN Ltd*,[104] the jury did not make its award within the bracket of £40,000 to £80,000 suggested by the trial judge but awarded a higher amount, namely £105,000, the Court of Appeal by a majority allowed the award to stand, and did not substitute its own award, on the basis that the award would be considered excessive only if it was out of all proportion to what could sensibly have been thought appropriate to compensate the claimant and re-establish his reputation. The sum which the court thought appropriate was not the test. In the particular case the

---

dealt with fell "within the larger rule of conduct" laid down by him: at 55. But it adds to clarity to keep them separate.

98 [1928] 1 K.B. 429 CA.

99 [1928] 1 K.B. 429 CA at 440.

100 [1935] A.C. 346 at 378. See, too, *Broome v Cassell & Co* [1972] A.C. 1027 and *Blackshaw v Lord* [1984] Q.B. 1 CA.

101 [1904] 2 K.B. 250 CA.

102 [1904] 2 K.B. 250 CA at 256; see, too, *Smith v Schilling* [1928] 1 K.B. 429 CA at 440, per Greer LJ. *Johnston v Great Western Ry* had in fact been anticipated by *Phillips v London and South Western Ry* (1879) 4 Q.B.D. 406; 5 Q.B.D. 78 CA. What the Court of Appeal did in *Johnston* was to examine the holding in *Phillips* in relation to the later rule in *Praed v Graham* (1890) 24 Q.B.D. 53 CA, from which stems the modern law for cases where the damages are very flexible (see text of this paragraph) and to conclude that the scope of *Phillips* was in no way restricted by the later rule.

103 This point may have been missed in *Bocock v Enfield Rolling Mills* [1954] 1 W.L.R. 1303 CA.

104 [2002] EWCA Civ 43; [2003] Q.B. 281 CA.

amount was not excessive having regard to the deference that was to be shown to jury awards in defamation cases, to the large percentage differences between the juries' awards and those substituted for them in the cases in which the Court of Appeal had been prepared to intervene[105] and to the fact that the increase in the maximum award of general damages in personal injury cases[106] had had the effect of raising the ceiling for juries' libel awards to almost twice the sum awarded here. Simon Brown LJ proposed a revised procedure for the use of damages brackets and damages comparables in defamation cases tried with juries[107]: and Sedley LJ, not unreasonably, dissented basically because he thought that the disparity with personal injury awards was still too great.[108] Though the principle espoused in *Kiam* remains good law, it is unlikely that today's Court of Appeal would be quite so deferential towards a jury's beyond bracket generosity. As Lord Judge LCJ troubled to observe in *Cairns v Modi*[109]:

> "In *John v MGN Ltd*[110] this court offered guidance about practical steps which might be adopted to assist in the assessment of damages. It was said, for example, that jurors could properly be informed as to earlier libel awards approved or substituted by this court, and also take into account brackets suggested by counsel or by the judge as appropriate to the facts before them. Hitherto, the convention had been to refrain from mentioning such figures to a jury. It was also suggested that reference could be made to the current conventional scale of compensatory damages being awarded in respect of pain and suffering in personal injury cases, not because there could be any precise correlation, but merely as one check on the reasonableness of any figure being considered as an award in libel proceedings. It has now become conventional also to recognise in effect a "ceiling" figure, allowing periodically for inflation, corresponding to the current maximum level of damages for pain and suffering and loss of amenity in personal injury cases … the present equivalent, allowing for inflation, and without taking account of any uplift consequential on what are usually described as the Jackson reforms taking effect in April 2013, would be of the order of £275,000. These steps have made for greater consistency in and more predictable libel awards."

Having introduced these conventions with the deliberate intention of moderating unbridled awards, it seems inevitable that, were a jury nevertheless to award damages out of proportion to the tenor of judicial guidance, the appellate Court would regard interference as requisite.

### (1) Where the measure of damages is very flexible

Defamation lies at the heart of this category and it is an action for defamation, *Rantzen v Mirror Group Newspapers*,[111] which served to initiate a more ready interference with jury awards in the wake of the power to reassess damages. The claimant, a television presenter and the founder of a charity for sexually abused children, was awarded £250,000 compensatory damages[112] by a jury in respect of **53-020**

---

105 For these cases, see para.53-021, below.

106 For which see paras 40-277 and following, above.

107 See his postscript at [2003] Q.B. 281 CA at [54].

108 See his interesting judgment at [2003] Q.B. 281 CA at [61]–[78] and the case further at para.53-021, below.

109 [2012] EWCA Civ 1382 CA.

110 [1997] Q.B. 586 CA.

111 [1994] Q.B. 670 CA.

112 Exemplary damages were not sought.

articles in a national newspaper alleging that she had protected a teacher suspected of being a paedophile and was therefore insincere and hypocritical. The Court of Appeal reduced the award to £110,000. Neill LJ, giving the judgment of the court, said:

> "We consider ... that the common law if properly understood requires the courts to subject large awards of damages to a more searching scrutiny than has been customary in the past. It follows that what has been regarded as the barrier against intervention should be lowered. The question becomes could a reasonable jury have thought that this award was necessary to compensate the plaintiff and to re-establish his [sic] reputation?"[113]

In coming to this conclusion the court took into account not only its new power to substitute its own for the jury's award but also the relationship between the common law and art.10 of the European Convention for the Protection of Human Rights and Fundamental Freedoms which, though not part of English domestic law at the time, provides for the right to freedom of expression and for any restrictions thereon to be prescribed by law and to be necessary in a democratic society.[114]

**53-021** The result of the decision in *Rantzen*,[115] is that effectively all of the 20th century case law on appeals against excessive awards where the measure of damages is very flexible becomes otiose since that case law is entirely dominated by libel.[116] After a dearth of successful appeals for a new trial in any type of case whatsoever before the 20th century,[117] libel suits produced new trials on account of excessive damages in a variety of situations, either where exemplary damages had been awarded in probably inappropriate circumstances[118] or for other reasons,[119] but there was also a significant number of refusals of new trials[120] so that in the last of such cases, *Blackshaw v Lord*,[121] Stephenson LJ wondered whether there were

---

[113] [1994] Q.B. 670 CA at 692G–H.

[114] Article 10 is set out [1994] Q.B. 670 CA at 685H–686B.

[115] [1994] Q.B. 670 CA.

[116] The libel cases are fully treated in paras 1828 to 1830 of the 15th edition (1988) of this work. Outside libel one can point in the last century only to *Mechanical & General Inventions Co v Austin* [1935] A.C. 346 (breach of contract concerning patent) and *Loudon v Ryder* [1953] 2 Q.B. 202 CA (assault) in both of which a new trial was refused and to *Dunhill v Wallrock* (1951) 95 S.J. 451 CA (breach of promise of marriage) where a new trial was granted.

[117] Thus new trials for excessive damages were refused in (a) slander: *Townshend v Hughes* (1677) 2 Mod. 150; (b) libel: *Gilbert v Burtenshaw* (1774) 1 Cowp. 230; *Praed v Graham* (1890) 24 Q.B.D. 53 CA; (c) actions for criminal conversation: *Wilford v Berkeley* (1758) 1 Burr. 609; *Duberley v Gunning* (1792) 4 T.R. 651; *Chambers v Caulfield* (1805) 6 East 244; (d) false imprisonment: *Huckle v Money* (1763) 2 Wils. 205; *Beardmore v Carrington* (1764) 2 Wils. 244; (e) trespass to property: *Beardmore v Carrington* (1764) 2 Wils. 244; *Redshaw v Brook* (1769) 2 Wils. 405; *Bruce v Rawlins* (1770) 3 Wils. 61; *Sharpe v Brice* (1774) 2 Wm. Bl. 942; (f) malicious prosecution: *Hewlett v Cruchley* (1813) 5 Taunt. 277; (g) breach of promise of marriage: *Gough v Farr* (1827) 1 Y. & J. 477; *Smith v Woodfine* (1857) 1 C.B. N.S. 660; *Berry v Da Costa* (1866) L.R. 1 C.P. 331.

[118] *Greenlands v Wilmhurst* [1913] 3 K.B. 507 CA; *Tolley v Fry* [1930] 1 K.B. 467 CA; *Chapman v Ellesmere* [1932] 2 K.B. 431 CA; all at para.1828 of the 15th edition (1988) of this work. Also *Sutcliffe v Pressdram* [1991] 1 Q.B. 153 CA, decided before the change in the law allowing the Court of Appeal to substitute its own award.

[119] *Lewis v Daily Telegraph* [1963] 1 Q.B. 340 CA; *McCarey v Associated Newspapers* [1965] 2 Q.B. 86 CA; *Riches v News Group Newspapers* [1986] Q.B. 256 CA; all at para.1829 of 15th edition (1988) of this work.

[120] *Ley v Hamilton* (1935) 153 L.T. 384 HL; *Groom v Crocker* [1939] 1 K.B. 194 CA; *Theaker v Richardson* [1962] 1 W.L.R. 151 CA; *Broome v Cassell & Co* [1972] A.C. 1027; *Blackshaw v Lord* [1984] Q.B. 1 CA; all at para.1830 of the 15th edition (1988) of this work.

[121] [1984] Q.B. 1 CA.

"any circumstances in which the size of the sum awarded is by itself so clearly and ridiculously disproportionate to the injury, even when aggravated, that this court can exercise its apparently obsolescent power and order a new trial ...?"[122]

After *Rantzen* he need not have been so concerned though the court's interference will now be by way of reduction of the damages rather than the ordering of a new trial. Thus there was a clutch of defamation cases, generally unreported, around the time of *Rantzen* in which the Court of Appeal cut down, and as in *Rantzen* substantially cut down, the award of the jury. They are *Gorman v Mudd*,[123] (£150,000 to £50,000), *Houston v Smith*,[124] (£150,000 to £50,000), *Jones v Pollard*,[125] (£100,000 to £40,000), together with the more extreme *John v MGN Ltd*.[126] However, at about the same time *Kiam v Neil (No.2)*,[127] saw a lower jury's award (£45,000) being allowed to stand, as was, by a majority, the much higher award (£105,000) in the later *Kiam v MGN Ltd*.[128] This last case is particularly interesting as it lent support to the view that a jury's award would not be challengeable merely because the jury had exceeded the bracket of damages which the judge had there suggested.[129] Given the scaling down of libel awards, the judicial endorsement of brackets and the acknowledged ceiling of £275,000 for the most serious libels referred to by Lord Judge in *Cairns v Modi*,[130] an award in excess of the bracket proposed by the trial judge will not be sacrosanct any longer.

To the extent that the new approach to excessive awards in defamation cases is **53-022** influenced by the provision in art.10 of the European Convention on Human Rights, torts other than defamation fall outside its ambit, not being concerned with freedom of expression. It is thought that other torts where the measure of damages is very flexible which are still tried with juries, as is the case with malicious prosecution and false imprisonment, would nevertheless attract the same treatment and that s.8 of the Courts and Legal Services Act 1990, the erstwhile RSC Ord.59 r.11(4) and its successor CPR r.52.20(3)(b) on their own give the court the entitlement to intervene more readily and to apply a less stringent test than formerly. Indeed in *John v MGN*,[131] (albeit another defamation case) where the singer Elton John sued a national newspaper in respect of an article alleging that he was on a bizarre diet and the Court of Appeal again reduced the jury's award as being manifestly excessive, in this case from £275,000 to £50,000 in exemplary damages and from £75,000 to £25,000 in compensatory damages, Sir Thomas Bingham MR, delivering the court's judgment, said that, while the court regarded art.10 of the European Convention on Human Rights as reinforcing and buttressing the conclusions reached, they had been reached independently of the Convention and would have

122 [1984] Q.B. 1 CA at 28C–D.

123 [1992] CA Transcript 1076.

124 [1993] CA Transcript 1544.

125 [1997] E.M.L.R. 233 CA.

126 [1997] Q.B. 586 CA, considered at para.53-022, below.

127 [1996] E.M.L.R. 493 CA.

128 [2002] EWCA Civ 43; [2003] Q.B. 281 CA.

129 *Kiam v MGN Ltd* was the first bracket case that the Court of Appeal had considered. In the event, Sedley LJ dissented because he thought that jury awards in defamation cases were again getting out of hand. See the case further at para.53-019, above.

130 [2012] EWCA Civ 1382 CA; endorsing and updating the ceiling of £215,000 proposed by Eady J in *Tierney v News Group Newspapers Ltd (No.2)* [2006] EWHC 3275 (QB).

131 [1997] Q.B. 586 CA.

been reached even if the Convention had not existed.[132] The logic to be derived must be that, in cases where art.10 plays no part, the courts will have no less reason to intervene. Thus, there are now cases of false imprisonment and malicious prosecution, sometimes combined with assault and wrongful arrest, where the Court of Appeal has exercised its power to reassess the damages. Three such decisions are *Thompson v Commissioner of Police of the Metropolis* and *Hsu v Commissioner of Police of the Metropolis*,[133] *Clark v Chief Constable of Cleveland Constabulary*,[134] and *Manley v Commissioner of Police for the Metropolis*.[135] In *Thompson v Commissioner of Police of the Metropolis*, the Court of Appeal increased an award of compensatory damages for false imprisonment and malicious prosecution from £1,500 to £20,000, albeit at the same time troubling to reduce the exemplary award. In *Clark v Chief Constable of Cleveland Constabulary*, the appellate court substituted for the jury's modest award of £500 for malicious prosecution, its own more generous assessment of £2,000. In *Manley v Commissioner of Police for the Metropolis*, the Court of Appeal increased the jury's award of basic damages for malicious prosecution from £1,500, which fell below the bottom of the bracket set by the trial judge, to £4,000 on the grounds that no reasonable jury could have gone below the bottom of the judge's bracket. The Court of Appeal also rectified the jury's omission to make any award of aggravated damages by introducing their own award of £10,000 on the basis that a reasonable jury should have appreciated that a failure to award anything less than a substantial sum for aggravated damages would send out an entirely wrong message.

### (2) Where the measure of damages is more fixed

**53-023** Today it seems supererogatory to traverse the authorities on appeals from jury awards in personal injury and wrongful death cases which stretch for nearly a full century from their starting point in the leading case, decided in 1879, of *Phillips v London and South Western Ry*.[136] This is not only because such cases, which had come to be the only actions of a type where the measure of damages was more fixed that were tried by juries, have themselves ceased to receive jury trial[137]—while it is true that appeals from alleged jury miscalculation have not featured in the court decisions since 1970,[138] it is always just possible that circumstances could be regarded as sufficiently exceptional to allow a jury trial,[139] or there could be an appeal from Scotland or Northern Ireland[140] where jury trials are still not uncommon—but also because the earlier authorities have become largely irrelevant and could indeed be positively misleading. For, in the first place, the Court of Appeal in *Ward*

132 [1997] Q.B. 586 CA at 619A.
133 [1998] Q.B. 498 CA.
134 *The Times*, 13 May 1999.
135 [2006] EWCA Civ 879.
136 (1879) 4 Q.B.D. 406; affirmed (1879) 5 Q.B.D. 78 CA. At this date a motion for a new trial did not lie direct to the Court of Appeal.
137 See para.53-002, above.
138 Not since *Mallett v McMonagle* [1970] A.C. 166. *Graham v Dodds* [1983] 1 W.L.R. 808 HL (see para.53-015, above) involved misdirection.
139 See para.53-002, above.
140 *Mallett v McMonagle* [1970] A.C. 166 and *Graham v Dodds* [1983] 1 W.L.R. 808 HL (see preceding footnote but one) were both appeals from Northern Ireland.

*v James*,[141] in calling a halt to jury trials in this field, indicated that in future it would have less hesitation in upsetting jury awards[142] and, in the second place and more importantly, the itemisation of awards in cases tried by judge alone, which started with *Jefford v Gee*,[143] but has gone well beyond the requirements of that decision, and which now must equally be required in jury trials, has rendered most of the learning on global awards obsolete. It is therefore considered much more germane to go for guidance not to the old decisions on appeals from jury awards but to the decisions from 1970 onwards on appeals from awards by judges, decisions which are dealt with at a later point.[144]

## II. Appeals from an Award of Damages by a Judge

### 1. Power to Reassess the Damages

Where the award of damages is made by a judge sitting alone, the appellate court is not confined to setting aside the award and granting a new trial. While the traditional view was that an appeal was a rehearing, the regime for appeals introduced by the CPR brought with it an apparent cultural shift. CPR r.52.21(1) provides thus: **53-024**

> "Every appeal will be limited to a review of the decision of the lower court unless—
>
> (a) a practice direction makes different provision for a particular category of appeal or
>
> (b) the court considers that in the circumstances of an individual appeal it would be in the interests of justice to hold a re-hearing".

The power to reassess the damages remains, CPR r.52.20(2) providing that

> "the appeal court has power to—
>
> (a) ... vary any order or judgment made or given by the lower court"

and the grounds for reassessing have in no way altered as a result of the CPR taking over from the RSC. Case law since the introduction of the CPR has served to confirm this supposition. The significance of the linguistic change from rehearing to review applicable to appeals to the Court of Appeal at the end of a trial was given careful consideration in *Assicurazioni Generali SpA v Arab Insurance Group*,[145] the Court holding that its approach when conducting a "review" of a decision below

---

141 [1966] 1 Q.B. 273 CA.

142 [1966] 1 Q.B. 273 CA at 301, per Lord Denning MR.

143 [1970] 2 Q.B. 130 CA.

144 See paras 53-039 to 53-044, below. If it is desired to examine the earlier authorities, unsuccessful appeals in personal injury cases are to be found in *Johnston v Great Western Ry* [1904] 2 K.B. 250 CA; *Bocock v Enfield Rolling Mills* [1954] 1 W.L.R. 1303 CA; *Scott v Musial* [1959] 2 Q.B. 429 CA; *Cavanagh v Ulster Weaving Co* [1960] A.C. 145; and *Morey v Woodfield (No.2)* [1964] 1 W.L.R. 16 CA; successful appeals in *Phillips v London and South Western Ry* (1879) 4 Q.B.D. 406; 5 Q.B.D. 78 CA, and *Smith v Schilling* [1928] 1 K.B. 429 CA (both on ground of inadequacy); *Taff Vale Ry v Jenkins* [1913] A.C. 1 affords an illustration of an unsuccessful appeal in a Fatal Accidents Act claim, while successful appeals appear in *Ellis v Raine* [1939] 2 K.B. 180 CA (award inadequate); *Nance v British Columbia Electric Ry* [1951] A.C. 601 PC and *Mallett v McMonagle* [1970] A.C. 166 (both awards excessive). For all details see the 13th edition (1972) of this work at paras 1444 to 1447.

145 [2002] EWCA Civ 1642; [2003] 1 W.L.R. 577 CA.

pursuant to CPR r.52.21(1) should be the same as that formerly adopted when conducting a "rehearing" pursuant to RSC Ord.59 r.3(1). In *El Du Pont de Nemours & Co v S T Dupont*,[146] May LJ expressed the opinion that, insofar as "rehearing" in CPR r.52.21(1)(b) might have something of a range of meaning, at the lesser end of the range it merged with that of "review" and in *McFaddens v Chandrasekaran*,[147] endorsing May LJ's general approach, Wilson LJ observed that the word "review" had wisely not been included in the glossary appended to the CPR pursuant to CPR r.2.2 because of the particular need for flexibility in the appellate court's choice of the procedure most apt to the fulfilment of its varying substantive task. If ambiguity is to be fostered in the pursuit of flexibility to enable the appellate tribunal to choose the procedure most apt to the fulfilment of its substantive task, it is legitimate to wonder if there is actually a practical distinction between the old and new terminology at all.

## 2. Grounds for Reassessing the Damages

**53-025** Where a first instance decision depends upon facts[148] found by the judge who has had the benefit of hearing oral evidence, then it will be only on the rarest occasions,[149] and in circumstances where the appellate court is convinced by the plainest of considerations, that it would be justified in finding that the trial judge had formed a wrong opinion.[150] But even where the case does not involve oral testimony, and factual findings have been made and inferences drawn on the basis of written evidence and contemporaneous documentation, the "case for reticence … remains cogent".[151] The first instance trial should be seen "as the 'main event', rather than a 'tryout on the road'."[152] This applies not only to findings of primary fact, but also to the evaluation of those facts and to inferences to be drawn from them.[153]

Where the challenge to a first instance decision is based on a supposed error of law, then appellate intervention is substantially easier to justify. However, as Lord Hoffmann held in *Piglowska v Piglowski*,[154]

---

146 [2003] EWCA Civ 1368; [2006] 1 W.L.R. 2793 CA.

147 [2007] EWCA Civ 220.

148 Many aspects of damages assessment, such as remoteness and mitigation, are mixed questions of fact and law: see paras 52-020 to 52-022.

149 An example of such an occasion was *Pritchard v Co-operative Group Ltd* [2011] EWCA Civ 329, [2012] Q.B. 320, a claim for damages for the torts of assault and battery and false imprisonment. The trial judge held that, but for the assault, the claimant would not have developed agoraphobia. Aikens LJ stated that he had "examined closely" the reports and joint statement of the expert witnesses, and in his view the trial judge was "not entitled" to reach this conclusion.

150 *DB v Chief Constable of Police Service of Northern Ireland* [2017] UKSC 7 at [78] (Lord Kerr JSC), citing Lord Reed in *McGraddie v McGraddie* [2013] UKSC 58; [2013] 1 W.L.R. 2477, and Lord Hope in *Thomson v Kvaerner Govan Ltd* [2003] UKHL 45.

151 [2017] UKSC 7 at [80].

152 [2017] UKSC 7 at [80].

153 *FAGE UK Ltd v Chobani UK Ltd* [2014] EWCA Civ 5 at [114] (Lewison LJ). The reasons identified included the expertise of the trial judge in determining relevant facts; that "the trial is not a dress rehearsal. It is the first and last night of the show"; that duplication of the trial judge's role on appeal is a disproportionate use of limited resources; that the trial judge "will have regard to the whole of the sea of evidence … whereas an appellate court will only be island hopping"; and that the atmosphere of the courtroom cannot be recreated by reference to documents and transcripts.

154 [1999] 1 W.L.R. 1360 HL at 1372.

> "An appellate court should resist the temptation to subvert the principle that they should not substitute their own discretion for that of the judge by a narrow textual analysis which enables them to claim that he misdirected himself."[155]

Where the decision which led to the impugned award of damages was a case management decision, the Court of Appeal will not interfere where the judge has applied the correct principles and has taken into account matters which should be taken into account and left out of account matters which are irrelevant, unless the court is satisfied that the decision is so plainly wrong that it must be regarded as outside the generous ambit of the discretion entrusted to the judge.[156] This will apply equally whether the case was tried by a judge alone, or by a judge and jury.[157]

The classic statement of the grounds upon which the Court of Appeal will interfere by reassessment of the damages appears in the judgment of Greer LJ in *Flint v Lovell*.[158] "This court", he said, **53-026**

> "will be disinclined to reverse the finding of a trial judge as to the amount of damages merely because they think that if they had tried the case in the first instance they would have given a lesser sum. In order to justify reversing the trial judge on the question of the amount of damages it will generally be necessary that this court should be convinced either that the judge acted upon some wrong principle of law, or that the amount awarded was so extremely high or so very small as to make it, in the judgment of this court, an entirely erroneous estimate of the damage to which the plaintiff is entitled."[159]

This statement was approved and adopted in the House of Lords in *Davies v Powell Duffryn Collieries*,[160] by Lord Wright and by Lord Porter,[161] and again by the Judicial Committee of the Privy Council in *Nance v British Columbia Electric Ry*.[162]

There are thus two distinct grounds of interference: that the judge has acted on a wrong principle of law, and that he has made an entirely erroneous estimate of the damages. If the judge has misdirected himself as to the law or has given undue or insufficient weight to the evidence,[163] this falls within the first category. If the damages are hopelessly incorrect, or if it can be shown by calculation that the judge must have wrongly taken or failed to take certain elements into consideration, this falls within the second category. But the court is less disinclined, in respect of the **53-027**

---

155 As Lewison LJ observed in *FAGE UK v Chobani UK Ltd* [2014] EWCA Civ 5 at [115], the primary function of the trial judge is "to find facts and identify the crucial legal points and to advance reasons for deciding them in a particular way. He should give his reasons in sufficient detail to show the parties and, if need be, the Court of Appeal the principles on which he has acted and the reasons that have led him to his decision. They need not be elaborate. There is no duty on a judge, in giving his reasons, to deal with every argument presented by counsel in support of his case".

156 *Walbrook Trustees (Jersey) Ltd v Fattal* [2008] EWCA Civ 427 at [33] (Lawrence Collins LJ).

157 See, for example, *Lorenzo v The Chief Constable of the West Midlands* [2012] EWCA Civ 1863 at [7].

158 [1935] 1 K.B. 354 CA.

159 [1935] 1 K.B. 354 CA at 360.

160 [1942] A.C. 601.

161 [1942] A.C. 601 at 616–617 and 623–624 respectively. Lord Porter referred to the statement of the rule in *Owen v Sykes* [1936] 1 K.B. 192 CA, but this is only a quotation and adoption by Slesser LJ (at 199–200) of Greer LJ's statement in *Flint v Lovell* [1935] 1 K.B. 354 CA.

162 [1951] A.C. 601 PC at 613. The Board cited and followed *Flint v Lovell* and Nance in both *Calix v Attorney General of Trinidad and Tobago* [2013] UKPC 15 at [29] and *Scott v Attorney General* [2017] UKPC 15 at [28]. The Court of Appeal cited and followed *Flint v Lovell* in *Santos v Eaton Square Garage Ltd* [2007] EWCA Civ 225 at [2].

163 Contrast *Owen v Sykes* [1936] 1 K.B. 192 CA at 198.

second category at least, to interfere with a judge's award than with a jury's award,[164] a distinction also stated by Greer LJ in *Flint v Lovell*,[165] and by Lord Wright in *Davies v Powell Duffryn Collieries*,[166] and repeated in later cases.[167] Indeed, as will be seen, the terminology of "entirely erroneous estimate" really exaggerates the disparity that need be shown today in second category cases in order to warrant appellate interference.[168]

## (1) Error of law

**53-028** A reassessment of damages on the ground that the court below has acted upon a wrong principle of law is well illustrated by the decision in *Benham v Gambling*.[169] In that case, in a claim under the Law Reform (Miscellaneous Provisions) Act 1934, the House of Lords substituted an award of £200 for the award below of £1,000 in respect of damages for the deceased's loss of expectation of life, because the existing approach of the courts to this question was considered by their Lordships to be wrong in law. "We are in substance", said Viscount Simon LC, "correcting the methods of estimating this head of loss".[170] Following on from this decision the House of Lords in *Naylor v Yorkshire Electricity Board*,[171] restored a trial judge's award of £500, for which the Court of Appeal had substituted an award of £1,000, because their Lordships considered that the Court of Appeal had erred in holding that the *Benham v Gambling*,[172] figure of £200 required to be doubled where the deceased was not a very young child but an adult or near-adult, although agreeing that it was proper to apply a multiplier of 2.5 in order to compensate for the inflation of the intervening quarter century. These cases remain valuable illustrations although they relate to a head of damage which has now been abolished.[173] Another head, again of non-pecuniary loss, has provided a more recent illustration of interference by the appellate court, here by elimination rather than by reduction of the award. In *Bliss v South East Thames Regional Health Authority*,[174] the trial judge's award of £2,000 for the frustration and mental distress of a consultant orthopaedic surgeon, who had been badly treated in breach of contract by the health authority employing him, was held by the Court of Appeal to be misconceived, and so disallowed, because a contract of employment was not within the types of contract which attracted such an award. Similarly, the award to the claimants, who were husband and wife, of £1,500 each for anguish and vexation was overturned by the Court of Appeal in *Hayes v Dodd*,[175] as was the award to the claimants, again

---

164 And in an Admiralty matter where an award of damages by a registrar for injury or damage arising out of a collision at sea or the like is reviewed by a judge there is even more likelihood of interference, for, as was pointed out in *Bishop v Cunard White Star* [1950] P. 240, the discretion is that of the judge and not of the registrar.
165 [1935] 1 K.B. 354 CA at 359–360.
166 [1942] A.C. 601 at 616–617.
167 Compare *Cavanagh v Ulster Weaving Co* [1960] A.C. 145 at 164, per Lord Tucker and *Mallett v McMonagle* [1970] A.C. 166 at 173, per Lord Morris; both were appeals from Northern Ireland.
168 See paras 53-034 and following, below.
169 [1941] A.C. 157.
170 [1941] A.C. 157 at 168.
171 [1968] A.C. 529.
172 [1941] A.C. 157.
173 See para.41-133, above.
174 [1987] I.C.R. 700 CA.
175 [1990] 2 All E.R. 815 CA.

husband and wife, of £4,000 each in *Watts v Morrow*,[176] for mental distress, though in that case an award of £750 each for physical discomfort was allowed to stand. The reason once again was that neither of the contracts, the first with a solicitor and the second with a surveyor, was of a type for which damages for distress were generally appropriate. In the second case, *Watts*, the Court of Appeal also reduced the pecuniary loss awarded, substituting the diminution in value of the property negligently surveyed for the cost of repairs which the claimants had carried out, the latter being the wrong measure in law.[177] Error of law was cited as the threshold for appellate interference in the claimant's unsuccessful appeal in the case of *R. (on the application of Elias) v Secretary of State for Defence*.[178] Claiming damages for race discrimination, the claimant sought to overturn the trial judge's award of £3,000 for injury to feelings. The Court of Appeal held that quantifying injury to feelings was more a broad brush exercise of estimation than of calculation, comparison with precedents, or cold logic. A trial judge's assessment of damages for injury to feelings would therefore only be interfered with on appeal if the award was so much out of line as to amount to an error of law because the trial judge had misdirected himself in principle or reached a decision which was plainly wrong. And in *Gur v Avrupa Newspaper Ltd*,[179] also an error of law case, the appellant sought to argue, albeit unsuccessfully, that the deputy judge's award of £85,000 for damage to feelings was defective for her alleged failure to have regard to the size of awards for general damages for personal injury.[180]

The disturbing facts of *Ministry of Defence v Fletcher*,[181] gave rise to errors of law which served to vitiate awards of aggravated and exemplary damages. For conduct on the part of the claimant's employer found to have been both discriminatory and victimising, the claimant was awarded aggravated damages of £20,000 and exemplary damages in the sum of £50,000. Amidst the behaviour which the Employment Tribunal took into account when awarding aggravated damages was the objectionable manner in which the Ministry of Defence had conducted its defence of the tribunal proceedings. On the Ministry of Defence's appeal, the Employment Appeal Tribunal accepted that the Employment Tribunal had erred in **53-029**

---

176 [1991] 1 W.L.R. 1421 CA.

177 See the cases at para.5-027, above.

178 [2006] 1 W.L.R. 3213 CA.

179 [2008] EWCA Civ 594 CA.

180 *Ronan v Sainsbury's Supermarkets Ltd* [2006] EWCA Civ 1074 CA is a case of error of law. The Court of Appeal concluded that the trial judge had fallen into error by eliding a *Blamire* award for future loss of earnings with an award for handicap on the open labour market, for which he had allowed the combined sum of £48,200, the Court substituting for the judge's global award separate awards of £15,000 for handicap on the open labour market and £12,000 for an 18 month period of future loss of earnings. The Court of Appeal's decision in *Beechwood Birmingham Ltd v Hoyer Group UK Ltd* [2010] EWCA Civ 647; [2011] Q.B. 357 CA is another example of an error of law vitiating an award. By way of general damages for loss of use of a damaged vehicle during repair, the judge awarded the claimant the sum of £12,000 based on the spot hire rate for a comparable car. Allowing the defendant's appeal, the Court of Appeal held that general damages should reflect such sum as reasonably compensated the victim of the tort for the nature and extent of the financial loss suffered as a result of the neutering of the damaged asset and the redeployment of another such asset. In the circumstances it was appropriate to base any award for loss of use not on the cost of outside hire but on the interest and capital employed and any depreciation sustained over the period of repair in respect of a vehicle of the type damaged in the accident. The judge's award of £12,000 was set aside, the parties being left to agree a suitable figure for loss of use which the court could award in substitution.

181 [2010] I.R.L.R. 25.

law to the extent that it had taken into account as a basis for an award of aggravated damages the contention that the Ministry's conduct of its defence had created a media circus. Reflecting that error of law and at the same time stripping away a degree of double counting, the Employment Appeal Tribunal reduced the award of aggravated damages from £20,000 to £8,000. Acknowledging a further error of law affecting the award of exemplary damages, the Employment Appeal Tribunal overturned the entire award.[182]

**53-030** The remarkable and important case of *Ramzan v Brookwide Ltd*,[183] comprises amongst many other things an example of an award of damages overturned for error of law. Following a liability trial in 2008, the defendant was found to be liable to the claimant in damages, including exemplary damages, for the continuing infringement of his rights to enjoy a store room. In 2010 damages were assessed. Commenting that there was little guidance as to the assessment of exemplary damages, but nevertheless seizing upon the defendant's unrelenting lack of contrition for its wrongful conduct and the substantial means of the defendant, the judge concluded that the appropriate figure to award was £60,000. The defendant appealed. Holding that the judge had fallen into error by failing to consider the impact of the fact that the claimant had become owner of the store room only after the defendant's incorporation of the room into a flat and that she could therefore interfere with the judge's award, for criteria relevant to computation Arden LJ concentrated on the defendant's conduct in its expropriation of the property having taken place before it had been acquired by the claimant[184] and on the expropriation having had a deleterious effect on the claimant's health.[185] These surely are matters that go to compensation by way of aggravated damages, which were here not allowed, and not to punishment by way of exemplary damages.[186] Based upon these considerations, and primarily on account of the claimant's not being the owner of the property at the time of the tort,[187] Arden LJ decided to reduce from £60,000 to £20,000[188] Geraldine Andrews QC's careful award in a case which she had described as one of the worst of its kind.[189]

**53-031** Error in law may also permit an increase in the damages. Thus in *Dingle v Associated Newspapers*,[190] the House of Lords affirmed the increase by the Court of Appeal of the trial judge's award of damages for libel where the Court of Appeal had held that the judge had erred in taking into consideration in mitigation of damages the effect of other publications of the libel and the fact that the claimant's reputation had already been impaired by reason of the publication of a report in other national newspapers.[191] In *Lane v Holloway*,[192] the Court of Appeal increased the damages awarded for an assault which the claimant had provoked, because the

---

182 For a further discussion of *Ministry of Defence v Fletcher* see para.53-044, below.

183 [2011] EWCA Civ 985; [2012] 1 All E.R. 903 CA.

184 [2012] 1 All E.R. 903 CA at [78].

185 [2012] 1 All E.R. 903 CA at [78]–[80].

186 Nor are convincing Arden LJ's statements that there is no scope for exemplary damages where an account of profits is claimed (at [81]), that the fact of making an exemplary award should largely be sufficient in itself (at [82]) and that there is little guidance on the quantification of exemplary damages (at [82]).

187 See [2012] 1 All E.R. 903 CA at [83] in init.

188 [2012] 1 All E.R. 903 CA at [83] in med.

189 [2011] 2 All E.R. 38 at [69].

190 [1964] A.C. 371.

191 For the full facts, see para.46-064, above.

192 [1968] 1 Q.B. 379 CA.

trial judge had committed an error of law in considering the provocation relevant to reduce the damages not only for the injury and insult to feelings but also for the physical injury itself.[193] In *O'Donoghue v Redcar & Cleveland Borough Council*,[194] having satisfied itself that the industrial tribunal had been in error in its approach to the award of compensation for injury to feelings, the Court of Appeal increased the applicant's damages by £3,000. In *Murray v Shuter*,[195] where there was a claim under the Fatal Accidents Act 1976 on behalf of the dependants of the victim of a road accident who for over four years had survived his injuries in a complete coma, the Court of Appeal held that the trial judge had been wrong in law to have deducted from the damages the amount in respect of the deceased's lost earnings in the years of survival which had been awarded in the estate's claim under the Law Reform (Miscellaneous Provisions) Act 1934 brought, in normal fashion, concurrently with the Fatal Accidents Act claim. The damages were accordingly increased by the elimination of the improper deduction. In *Daly v General Steam Navigation Co*,[196] the claim for interest on the award of damages to a physically injured claimant for her pain and suffering and loss of amenities of life had been denied but the appropriate interest was allowed upon the claimant's appeal,[197] while in *Roberts v Johnstone*,[198] interest had been awarded but it had been awarded on the basis that the damages in respect of the gratuitous care of the physically injured claimant by her mother were general damages whereas the Court of Appeal rightly regarded them as special damages, thereby allowing a higher figure to be substituted.[199] *Iqbal v Prison Officers Association*,[200] was a false imprisonment claim where the Court of Appeal held that the trial judge was wrong in law to limit the claimant to nominal damages on the basis only that he had exaggerated the hurt to his feelings, and the declaration of false imprisonment would provide "just satisfaction". *Grand v Gill*,[201] is to be classified as an appeal on grounds of error of law where the damages were increased. The Court of Appeal overturned the first instance judge's decision to the effect that the internal plaster of the claimant's flat was a mere decorative finish and therefore did not form part of the structure of the demise for the purposes of quantifying general damages for breach of the covenant for quiet enjoyment. Determining that internal plaster did indeed form part of the structure of the building which the defendant was obliged to keep in repair, the Court of Appeal increased the judge's award of general damages from £600 to £1,275 to reflect the discomfort and inconvenience caused by the disrepair to the plaster. In *Jones v Ruth*,[202] a claim under the Protection from Harassment Act 1997, the trial judge had refused to award

[193] See the case at para.42-009, above. But see too, at para.42-010, above, the qualifications placed on it in *Murphy v Culhane* [1977] Q.B. 94 CA.

[194] [2001] I.R.L.R. 615.

[195] [1976] Q.B. 972 CA.

[196] [1981] 1 W.L.R. 120 CA.

[197] The judge below had been justified in refusing interest because, when he arrived at his decision in 1978, the law had been in a state of flux: see para.19-051, above.

[198] [1989] Q.B. 878 CA.

[199] In *Doshoki v Draeger Ltd* [2002] I.R.L.R. 340, the question for the court was said to be whether the award was "so inadequate as to amount to an error of law" (at [15]) and the decision of the court was that the award was "inadequate to a degree where it was wrong in law" (at [16]). Yet the case is more properly categorised as one of entirely erroneous estimate (dealt with at paras 53-033 and following, below) than one of error of law.

[200] [2009] EWCA Civ 1312; [2010] Q.B. 732.

[201] [2011] EWCA Civ 554; [2011] 1 W.L.R. 2253 CA.

[202] [2011] EWCA Civ 804; [2012] 1 W.L.R. 1495.

any damages for personal injury on the ground that such injury was not foreseeable. The Court of Appeal held that, under the Act, foreseeability of injury was not an essential element in the cause of action, and awarded general damages in the agreed sum of £28,750, while remitting the case to a master of the Queen's Bench Division to determine the claimant's entitlement to any further sums. In *Perry v Raleys Solicitors*,[203] a professional negligence claim, the Court of Appeal held that the judge had wrongly directed himself as to the correct approach to causation, but also had reached a conclusion on the facts which rationally he could not have reached, and allowed the appeal.

**53-032** But just as the appellate court has a discretion to refuse a new trial in the event of misdirection or misreception of evidence in an action with a jury where no serious irregularity causing injustice has resulted,[204] so here, even if the award has been assessed upon a wrong principle of law, the court will not interfere with the amount where it is of the view that the judge has awarded the right amount although for the wrong reason. Thus in *Williamson v Thornycroft*,[205] in a claim under the Fatal Accidents Act on behalf of a wife in respect of her husband's death, the Court of Appeal held that the trial judge had wrongly omitted to take into account, in assessing the value of her dependency, her remarriage before the case was heard, but refused to interfere with the figure of the award since in the court's opinion this was substantially correct. And in *Morgan v UPS Ltd*,[206] a personal injury claim, though satisfied that the Recorder's approach to loss of earning capacity and loss of future earnings gave rise to justifiable concern that he had double counted, thereby warranting reappraisal, the Court of Appeal nevertheless held that the combined total awarded was not so excessive that it should be interfered with on appeal.[207]

## (2) Entirely erroneous estimate

**53-033** The distinction taken in relation to awards made by a jury between cases where the measure of damages is very flexible and cases where it is more fixed,[208] is also pertinent to awards made by a judge sitting alone.

**53-034** **(a) Where the measure of damages is very flexible** There are not many cases in the reports where the measure of damages is at large which give assistance, since, until the entry into force of s.11 of the Defamation Act 2013, such cases were of the type still commonly tried with a jury. During the Second World War several defamation cases decided by a judge sitting alone offer some guidance. In *Rook v Fairrie*,[209] the Court of Appeal refused to increase the damages awarded by the

---

203 [2017] EWCA Civ 314.

204 See para.53-011, above.

205 [1940] 2 K.B. 658 CA.

206 [2008] EWCA Civ 375.

207 Similar is *Smithurst v Sealant Construction Services Ltd* [2011] EWCA Civ 1277; [2012] Med L.R. 258 CA, a personal injury claim in which the court was required to quantify damages for a disc prolapse attributable to the defendant employer's breach of duty. While holding that the judge had erred in law by treating issues as to whether the claimant would have suffered from a similar disc prolapse in the future and, if so, when, as ones of causation rather than ones of the assessment of the claimant's damages, the Court of Appeal nevertheless concluded that the judge's decision to the effect that the claimant would have suffered a similar injury within two years of the material accident was an entirely permissible one.

208 See paras 53-020 and following, above.

209 [1941] 1 K.B. 507 CA.

judge: this refusal was based on the view that, since the judge had been able to express his views on the grossness of the libel in his judgment, he was entitled to award less damages than would a jury, who can only express their similar views by giving heavy damages. Later defamation cases have not endorsed this rule. In *Bull v Vazquez*,[210] the Court of Appeal, unimpressed by *Rook v Fairrie*,[211] refused to reduce the damages awarded by the judge, as the judge had in the court's view assessed the damages at a high level because he thought the slander a particularly heinous one.[212] In *Knuppfer v London Express Newspaper*,[213] however, the Court of Appeal, although again unprepared to accept the rule put forward in *Rook v Fairrie*,[214] was emphatic that it would have reduced the damages had it not allowed the appeal by the defendant on the issue of liability,[215] Mackinnon LJ taking the view that the amount awarded

> "was an extravagance that the most reckless jury would hardly have achieved, and one which should not have been committed by a judge sitting alone".[216]

In *Dingle v Associated Newspapers*,[217] the House of Lords firmly and unanimously disapproved the *Rook v Fairrie* rule; the disapproval was, however, strictly obiter as it did not appear that the judge at first instance had awarded smaller damages because he had expressed his views in his judgment.[218] The obiter dicta of their Lordships in *Dingle v Associated Newspapers* were themselves disapproved by the Court of Appeal in *Purnell v Business Magazine Ltd*,[219] where Laws LJ held that the existence of a prior reasoned judgment rejecting a justification defence was at least capable of providing some vindication of a claimant's reputation with the result that the earlier judgment should be taken into account by the damages tribunal depending upon the latter's view of its impact on the vindication issue. If it ever was, this aspect of *Dingle* can therefore no longer be regarded as good law.[220] In *R. v Governor of Brockhill Prison Ex p. Evans (No.2)*,[221] a claim for false imprisonment included in an application for leave to apply for judicial review and habeas corpus and heard by Collins J without a jury, the Court of Appeal increased his basic award of damages for the false imprisonment, neither aggravated nor exemplary damages being appropriate, from £2,000 to £5,000 and the House of Lords ap-

---

210 [1947] 1 All E.R. 334 CA.

211 [1941] 1 K.B. 507 CA.

212 [1947] 1 All E.R. 334 CA at 336, per Asquith LJ. The slander alleged that the claimant army officer had been posted home for drinking; the judge had awarded £1,000. Compare *Williams v Settle* [1960] 1 W.L.R. 1072 CA, where the Court of Appeal refused to reduce the damages awarded by the judge in respect of a flagrant infringement of copyright (see especially at 1086–1087): facts at para.48-063, above.

213 [1943] K.B. 80 CA.

214 [1941] 1 K.B. 507 CA.

215 The House of Lords affirmed on this issue: [1944] A.C. 116.

216 [1943] K.B. 80 CA at 86. Yet Lord Atkin in the House of Lords, while accepting that "the damages awarded are possibly too high", indicated that he would not have interfered with the award had the House held for the claimant on liability: [1944] A.C. 116 at 122. See, too, the Court of Appeal's reduction of libel damages in *Fielding v Variety Inc* [1967] 2 Q.B. 841 CA, where damages for injurious falsehood were also reduced.

217 [1964] A.C. 371.

218 The smallness of the judge's award was in fact for another reason: see para.53-031, above.

219 [2008] 1 W.L.R. 1 CA.

220 See para.46-034, above on vindicatory damages in defamation.

221 [1999] Q.B. 1043 CA.

proved this increase.[222] In the Court of Appeal reference was made to another case of false imprisonment, the unreported *Lunt v Liverpool City Justices*,[223] where the Court of Appeal increased an award of £13,500 to £25,000.[224] *Doshoki v Draeger Ltd*,[225] illustrates an entirely erroneous estimate[226] in racial discrimination. The tribunal's award of £750 as compensation for injury to feelings was increased to £4,000. In *Vento v West Yorkshire Police*,[227] a claim for sexual discrimination, an award of £65,000 was felt by the Court of Appeal to be "seriously out of line".[228] Stating that the test when reviewing an assessment of compensation for injury or loss which was neither physical nor financial was whether the award was so excessive as to constitute an error of law, the Court of Appeal substituted its own figures of £18,000 for injury to feelings, £5,000 for aggravated damages and £9,000 for psychiatric damage.[229]

53-035 **(b) Where the measure of damages is more fixed** Cases where the measure of damages is more fixed are the cases which are today generally tried by a judge sitting alone, the law being illustrated principally by actions brought in respect of personal injury or death. Here the position has changed radically since 1970 with the eventual preparedness of the courts to break down their awards into their constituent parts in this class of claim. Even with global awards the "entirely erroneous estimate" did not have to be a figure out of all proportion to the loss because, the measure of damages generally being wholly or largely for pecuniary loss, the calculation could not go outside certain limits in either direction and all that had to be shown was that these limits had been crossed in the figure awarded; now with itemised awards a disparity is more easily shown and the scope for interference on appeal consequently increased. The result is that in this context the "entirely erroneous estimate" has become something of a misnomer and liable to mislead. Indeed, even as early as 1971, Salmon LJ in *Elliott v Corporation of Preston*,[230] was referring to the wholly erroneous estimate as "the phrase which is hallowed, but has now I think a rather archaic ring",[231] and, in *Wells v Wells*,[232] Lord Lloyd of Berwick volunteered in order of preference the alternative expression "outside the appropriate bracket".[233]

53-036 In the past, appeals in personal injury cases on account of a judge's award alleged to be excessive tended to meet with the difficulty that a lump sum had been awarded with no breakdown between pecuniary and non-pecuniary losses, thereby allowing the alleged excess to be put down to the incalculable and flexible recovery

---

222 [2001] 1 A.C. 19.
223 [1991] CA Transcript 158.
224 See these cases at para.42-017, above.
225 [2002] I.R.L.R. 340.
226 On its classification in this manner, see the case in a footnote to para.53-031, above.
227 [2002] EWCA Civ 1871; [2003] I.C.R. 318.
228 [2003] I.C.R. 318 at 61.
229 Notably, in the libel case of *Cairns v Modi* [2012] EWCA Civ 1382 CA, Leading Counsel for the appellant sought, unsuccessfully, to persuade the Court of Appeal to adopt an approach to the quantification of loss for defamation claims similar to that proposed in *Vento v West Yorkshire Police* [2002] EWCA Civ 1871; [2003] ICR 318.
230 [1971] 2 Lloyd's Rep. 328 CA.
231 [1971] 2 Lloyd's Rep. 328 CA at 330.
232 [1999] 1 A.C. 345.
233 [1999] 1 A.C. 345 at 376D.

for non-pecuniary loss: thus as in both *Flint v Lovell*,[234] and *Owen v Sykes*,[235] the cases which laid down the general rule as to the grounds on which the trial judge's award might be altered,[236] the Court of Appeal refused to interfere on the ground of excessiveness, and was only prepared to reduce the damages in the occasional case where it was satisfied that the trial judge must have erred in the calculation of the pecuniary loss itself.[237] On the other hand, with appeals in personal injury cases on account of inadequate damages, the difficulty created by the element of non-pecuniary loss in a global award was less severe, since it might be possible to show that the pecuniary loss by itself either exceeded or all but reached the total amount given by the judgment: thus this consideration allowed the Court of Appeal in *Roach v Yates*,[238] substantially to increase the judge's award. And the disappearance of the factor of non-pecuniary loss in claims under the Fatal Accidents Act arising out of a death[239] made appellate interference still easier, and whether on the ground of the excessiveness of the damages[240] or of their inadequacy.[241] However the advent, with the Administration of Justice Act 1969,[242] of mandatory awards of interest, in the absence of special reasons for refusal, in all personal injury damages awards, and the interpretation of the new statutory provision in *Jefford v Gee*,[243] as requiring the courts to make separate assessments of the general damages for pecuniary losses and for non-pecuniary losses since interest only falls to be awarded on the latter,[244] effectively removed these distinctions between excess and inadequacy of damages, between personal injury and wrongful death claims. Yet even in the 1980s,[245] appellate courts occasionally had to contend with a global award by a trial judge who had failed to itemise the different heads of damage. This was the case in *Joyce v Yeomans*,[246] and again in *Jamil bin Harun v Yang Kamsiah*,[247] in both of which a physically injured claimant successfully appealed on account of inadequacy of the damages. In *Joyce* the Court of Appeal was of the view that, since most of the award would be needed to cover the claimant's pain and suffering and loss of amenities, the judge must necessarily have underestimated the claimant's loss of earnings, and in *Jamil* before the Judicial Committee of the Privy Council the same sort of process of analysis would seem to have taken place. The higher award which was substituted was of course itemised in each case. Subsequent years have not offered up any case of an appeal against an award not itemised as between the pecuniary and the non-pecuniary loss, so that such oc-

---

234 [1935] 1 K.B. 354 CA.

235 [1936] 1 K.B. 192 CA.

236 See para.53-026, above.

237 See, e.g. *Ilkiw v Samuels* [1963] 1 W.L.R. 991 CA and *Domsalla v Barr* [1969] 1 W.L.R. 630 CA. Of course reduction was also possible wherever, as occasionally happened, the trial judge did effect a breakdown as between pecuniary loss and non-pecuniary loss: e.g. *Billingham v Hughes* [1949] 1 K.B. 643 CA.

238 [1938] 1 K.B. 256 CA; see especially at 270, per Slesser LJ.

239 See para.41-018, above. Subject now to a specified award for bereavement to parents and spouses of, from April 2013, £12,980.

240 See, e.g. *Bath v British Transport Commission* [1954] 1 Lloyd's Rep. 463 CA.

241 See, e.g. *Walley v British and Continental S.S. Co* (1941) 68 Ll. L.R. 1 CA.

242 The relevant provision is now incorporated in the Senior Courts Act 1981 s.35A.

243 [1970] 2 Q.B. 130 CA.

244 For details, see paras 19-050 and 19-087, above.

245 For the 1970s, see first footnote to para.53-039, below.

246 [1981] 1 W.L.R. 549 CA.

247 [1984] A.C. 529 PC.

casional lapses by courts of first instance may be a thing of the past. But one never knows.

53-037 Nor was the process of itemisation to end with this development, and the comments of Sachs LJ in this context in *George v Pinnock*,[248] a case decided in late 1972, are instructive. He there said:

> "Whatever may have been the differing judicial views up to a few years ago and, indeed, up to 1970, as to whether a judge should simply award a global sum or whether he should state in his judgment what are the main components of that figure, the modern practice since *Jefford v Gee* (decided on 4 March 1970), is to adopt the second course. It is true that that adoption has to a considerable extent come into being because of the differing rates of interest applicable to differing heads of damage under the *Jefford v Gee* decision. On the other hand, it is also in part due to the general adoption of that considerable body of judicial opinion which held that claimant and defendant alike are entitled to know what is the sum assessed for each relevant head of damage and thus to be able on appeal to challenge any error in the assessments. In my judgment, this court should be slow to emasculate that right of litigants."[249]

The outcome of this change of attitude is that judges began not only to provide breakdowns between the pecuniary and the non-pecuniary in their awards but also to make separate assessments within the pecuniary loss itself. Of course the isolation from the general damages of the special damages for the past pecuniary loss up to judgment had always been a feature of awards for personal injury[250]; the new, and, from the point of view of appeals the somewhat more significant, breakdown was that between medical expenses on the one hand and lost earnings on the other.

53-038 So the typical personal injuries award came to contain a fourfold itemisation, into the special damages for past pecuniary loss, the general damages for lost earnings, the general damages for medical expenses, and the general damages for non-pecuniary loss: *Cunningham v Harrison*,[251] may be taken as an illustration of this. Indeed as time has gone on, the norm has become further to subdivide, particularly in respect of future medical and related expenses, and with past medical expenses also separated out from past loss of earnings. As early as *George v Pinnock*,[252] and *Taylor v British Omnibus Co*,[253] the fourfold itemisation was being exceeded and today it is accepted practice to itemise in very great detail. *Cassel v Hammersmith and Fulham Health Authority*,[254] in the Court of Appeal called *Cassel v Riverside Health Authority*,[255] may be taken simply as an illustration from a myriad of other cases. There one finds a division between past care and future care, between future accommodation costs and miscellaneous future expenses—themselves subdivided between appliances, medical costs, extra purchases, educational toys and other items—between the costs of a receiver and of the Court of Protection, and all this in addition to the general damages, the loss of earnings and, the now inevitable, interest. The cost of future accommodation included as a separate item the cost of

248 [1973] 1 W.L.R. 118 CA.

249 [1973] 1 W.L.R. 118 CA at 126E–G. These observations were concurred in by the other two members of the court: at 126A.

250 See paras 40-062 and 40-183, above.

251 [1973] Q.B. 942 CA.

252 [1973] 1 W.L.R. 118 CA.

253 [1975] 1 W.L.R. 1054 CA.

254 [1992] P.I.Q.R. Q1.

255 [1992] P.I.Q.R. Q168 CA.

a swimming pool; being separated, the Court of Appeal had no difficulty in implementing its decision to disallow the swimming pool cost. And in the field of Fatal Accidents Act claims courts must, since *Cookson v Knowles*,[256] make separate assessments for the past loss of dependency to trial and the future loss of dependency after trial, thereby following the equivalent long-established practice in personal injury claims.[257] It is true that, once again, the change in practice was not made in order to give the parties to a suit more ammunition with which to mount appeals—it was designed to give greater reliability to the damages assessment in times of steep inflation[258]—but it could make the path of the litigant wishing to appeal somewhat easier. Nevertheless, it must be acknowledged that the ever greater reduction of awards to their component parts can create difficulties of its own. In *Willbye v Gibbons*,[259] the claimant, who had suffered a brain injury in a road traffic accident when a child, was awarded a lump sum of £45,000 for any additional care relating to future children and £60,000 for the extra future care in the final quarter of her life. Setting aside those awards, the Court of Appeal held that such claims should not be divided into discrete heads of damage because if potential demands were separately evaluated it might well turn out that there was duplication or that substantial awards were made in respect of contingencies that never occurred. The preferred approach was to increase the total future care award, Kennedy LJ increasing an award in respect of future care from £136,932.16 to £181,129.60 broadly to reflect the two individual contingencies countenanced. Reconciling the interests of transparency with the need to avoid double recovery by overlap, in *Martins v Choudhary*,[260] where the judge had made separate awards for psychiatric harm and injury to feelings, Smith LJ offered the following rationalisation:

> "I would venture to suggest that there should be no hard and fast rule about whether separate awards should be made. It will all depend on the facts of the individual case. If, for example, as is sometimes the case, the psychiatric harm is very modest and to all intents and purposes merges with the injury to feelings, it will plainly be more convenient to make one award covering both aspects. If, as here, where the psychiatric injury is not insubstantial, it is positively helpful to the parties (and to this Court) if the judge separates the award for psychiatric injury from that for injury to feelings. This leads to a better understanding of the judge's thought processes. However, I do accept that there is a risk of double recovery by overlap if two awards are made and the judge must take care to avoid that."[261]

This is surely excellent advice. For allied heads of claim of more modest value, a single global award is thus to be preferred.

Since 1970 one finds many more successful appeals in this class of case than are to be found in earlier years. And with the increasing itemisation of the damages the range of possible interference by the appellate courts has become wide.[262] By way **53-039**

---

[256] [1979] A.C. 556.

[257] See paras 40-062 and 40-183, above.

[258] See para.41-042, above.

[259] [2003] EWCA Civ 372; [2004] P.I.Q.R. P15 CA at 227.

[260] [2007] EWCA Civ 1379; [2008] P.I.Q.R. Q1 CA at 1.

[261] [2008] P.I.Q.R. Q1 CA at [18].

[262] Yet personal injury cases are still to be found in the 1970s where the required breakdown of the damages has not been attempted by the trial judge, but this has not necessarily prevented the Court of Appeal altering the damages award: e.g. *Edwards v Wiggin Teape* [1974] 2 Lloyd's Rep. 86 CA

of illustration, cases where personal injury awards have been appealed may be cited which have produced the following results: an increase in the damages both for loss of earning capacity and for non-pecuniary loss[263]; an increase in the former with the latter affirmed[264]; an increase in the latter with the former affirmed[265]; a reduction in the latter with the former affirmed[266]; damages for both non-pecuniary loss and loss of earning capacity affirmed but with an increase in the award for medical expenses[267]; affirmation of the award for non-pecuniary loss but with a reduction in the damages both for loss of earning capacity and for medical expenses[268]; a reduction in the damages for pecuniary loss up to trial with a corresponding increase in the non-pecuniary award[269]; a reduction in both the special damages and the non-pecuniary award.[270] And with the ever greater particularisation of the damages, as already seen by reference to *Cassel*,[271] so the permutations can be substantially increased. In Fatal Accidents Act claims there is, of course, less scope for such permutations, but illustrations are nevertheless available of awards increased[272] and awards reduced.[273]

**53-040** In *Povey v Jackson*,[274] decided some weeks after *Jefford v Gee*,[275] it was held that, while the general damages awarded were on the low side, the special damages were on the high side, and accordingly, although each award would have required adjustment had it been the only head of claim, yet as the global award was fair and proper the court ought not to interfere with it. This decision, however, has since been qualified, if not criticised, first in *George v Pinnock*,[276] and then in *Smith v Manchester Corporation*.[277] In both of these cases the defendant unsuccessfully attempted to persuade the Court of Appeal not to increase the injured claimant's award in respect of pecuniary loss—in the former for nursing attendance and in the latter for loss of earning capacity through handicap in the labour market—on the ground that, though looked at in isolation the amount allocated to the particular head of damage was appealably too low, there was no sufficient disparity to justify interference between the actual and the proper global awards once one aggregated with the assessment for pecuniary loss the more substantial assessment for non-pecuniary loss which the court was prepared to accept. In *George v Pinnock*,[278] Sachs LJ, with the agree-

---

(award increased); *Diclaudio v Cattell* [1974] 2 Lloyd's Rep. 486 CA (award reduced). For the 1980s, see para.53-036, above.

263 *Cook v J. L. Kier & Co* [1970] 1 W.L.R. 774 CA.

264 *Smith v Manchester Corp* (1974) 17 K.I.R. 1 CA; *Cook v Consolidated Fisheries* [1977] I.C.R. 635 CA; *Lai Wee Lian v Singapore Bus Service (1978) Ltd* [1984] A.C. 729 PC.

265 *Moeliker v Reyrolle & Co* [1976] I.C.R. 253 CA.

266 *Brown v Tarmac Civil Engineering* [1974] 2 Lloyd's Rep. 482 CA.

267 *George v Pinnock* [1973] 1 W.L.R. 118 CA.

268 *Harris v Harris* [1973] 1 Lloyd's Rep. 445 CA; *Cunningham v Harrison* [1973] Q.B. 942 CA; *Croke v Wiseman* [1982] 1 W.L.R. 71 CA.

269 *Daly v General Steam Navigation Co* [1981] 1 W.L.R. 120 CA.

270 *Mills v British Rail Engineering* [1992] P.I.Q.R. Q130 CA.

271 At para.53-038, above.

272 *K v J.M.P. Co* [1976] Q.B. 85 CA.

273 *Cookson v Knowles* [1977] Q.B. 913 CA; affirmed on other points. *ATH v MS* [2003] P.I.Q.R. Q1 at 1 (awards for services performed by the deceased and services only a mother could provide both reduced as "outside the bracket").

274 [1970] 1 W.L.R. 969 CA.

275 [1970] 2 Q.B. 130 CA.

276 [1973] 1 W.L.R. 118 CA.

277 (1974) 17 K.I.R. 1 CA.

278 [1973] 1 W.L.R. 118 CA.

ment of his brethren,[279] said:

> "To add the sum assessed at £19,000 for general damages to those allocated in the judgment to attendance, and then to compare the total figure with other combined figures in a number of cases … cited to us … was an exercise the usefulness of which is obviously limited…. One must bear in mind that reasonable expenditure on nursing attendance must vary largely in different cases, and if for one reason such expenditure is above the average in a particular case, then acceptance of the defendant's contention could result in the award for general damages being whittled away to an unduly small sum."[280]

In *Smith v Manchester Corporation*,[281] where the Court of Appeal affirmed the award of £2,000 for non-pecuniary loss but increased the award for loss of earning capacity from £300 to £1,000, Edmund Davies LJ admitted that five years earlier he would have decided differently. He said:

> "I think that the general approach adopted over the years would have inclined me to say that to increase an award of £2,300 by no more than £700 of itself demonstrated that the award was not so manifestly erroneous as to call for interference. But since *Jefford v Gee* the circumstances are entirely changed. Now that the assessment of general damages is required to be divided into damages for pain and suffering and loss of amenities, on the one hand, and future financial loss on the other, I think, for my part, that the two matters have to be considered quite separately. In the result, if the award under the one head is clearly wrong, it should be interfered with, even though ultimately there may be no very substantial variation in the global award. To substitute £1,000 for £300 is, in my judgment, a substantial interference with the award for future financial loss."[282]

While it is true that in both *George v Pinnock*,[283] and *Smith v Manchester Corporation*,[284] the Court of Appeal was prepared to regard the award in respect of only one item of the damages as appealably wrong and not, as in *Povey v Jackson*,[285] to consider one item as appealably too high and another as appealably too low, a ground of distinction indeed adverted to by Sachs LJ in *George v Pinnock*,[286] it must follow from the approach in these two cases, particularly as epitomised in Edmund Davies LJ's words in the latter that now **53-041**

> "the two matters [namely the pecuniary loss and the non-pecuniary loss] have to be considered quite separately",[287]

that *Povey v Jackson*,[288] is no longer an acceptable decision. And confirmation of this comes from the later decision of the Judicial Committee of the Privy Council in *Lai Wee Lian v Singapore Bus Service (1978) Ltd*,[289] where counsel for the defendant had

[279] [1973] 1 W.L.R. 118 CA at 126A.
[280] [1973] 1 W.L.R. 118 CA at 126B–C.
[281] (1974) 17 K.I.R. 1 CA.
[282] (1974) 17 K.I.R. 1 CA at 6–7.
[283] [1973] 1 W.L.R. 118 CA.
[284] (1974) 17 K.I.R. 1 CA.
[285] [1970] 1 W.L.R. 969 CA.
[286] [1973] 1 W.L.R. 118 CA at 126H.
[287] (1974) 17 K.I.R. 1 CA at 7.
[288] [1970] 1 W.L.R. 969 CA.
[289] [1984] A.C. 729 PC.

"submitted that the Court of Appeal had rightly held that what matters is the global figure and that, if the global figure was reasonable and fair, an appellate court should not increase or diminish a component item of damages on the basis that that item was either too low or excessive."[290]

Lord Fraser, delivering the judgment of their Lordships, would have none of this. He said:

"But if the award for loss of future earnings, or for any of the other items, is so far out of line with what the appellate court considers appropriate as to indicate that the assessing judge has erred in principle, and if the substitution of an appropriate award for that item would make a substantial alteration in the total award, then the appellate court has the duty to make the substitution and to alter the total accordingly."[291]

**53-042** Indeed *K v J.M.P. Co*,[292] a Fatal Accidents Act claim with only one head of damage, namely the loss of dependency, in issue, has shown that the Court of Appeal may even interfere where the error contributing to over-calculation and the error contributing to under-calculation are both contained within the assessment of the single head of damage and the overall adjustment required is small. In that case the Court of Appeal considered that the trial judge, in calculating the loss of dependency of three illegitimate children on their deceased father, had taken too high a multiplicand for each child but at the same time had taken too low a multiplier for each.[293] Recalculation increased the total award only from £12,521 to £13,700. Cairns LJ recognised that

"the difference is small in proportion to the total, but, in my judgment, it should be given effect to, since the damages here are a matter of calculation and not merely of broad assessment, as in the case of damages for personal injuries",[294]

an observation no doubt directed to the fact that non-pecuniary loss then made no appearance in awards under the Fatal Accidents Act.[295] Yet in *Housecroft v Burnett*,[296] the Court of Appeal appeared to move in the other direction when in a personal injury case they did not adjust the cost of care upwards because of their view that the appropriate increase would have been substantially less than the amount by which they regarded the trial judge as over-generous in his assessment of the claimant's non-pecuniary loss; the total award in their view provided fair compensation and they dismissed the appeal.[297] This, however, makes sense where the sole appeal was the claimant's and no one was contending for a lower award. In *ATH v MS*,[298] Kennedy LJ had the easier task of overturning an award of £150,000 for the loss of a mother's services, an award which he considered to be "plainly outside the bracket", substituting his own valuation of £37,500 in its place.

---

290 [1984] A.C. 729 PC at 735D.

291 [1984] A.C. 729 PC at 735G. In fact while the figure for loss of future earnings was very substantially increased—from some 37,000 Singapore dollars to 100,000 Singapore dollars—no change was made to the other items of damage.

292 [1976] Q.B. 85 CA.

293 See the case at paras 41-052 and 41-089 above.

294 [1976] Q.B. 85 CA at 95F.

295 See para.41-018, above.

296 [1986] 1 All E.R. 332 CA.

297 See [1986] 1 All E.R. 332 CA at 339j, 343h and 345g.

298 [2002] EWCA Civ 792; [2003] P.I.Q.R. Q1 CA at 1.

Although these various developments indicate that the concept of the entirely erroneous estimate propounded by Greer LJ in *Flint v Lovell*,[299] has been largely emasculated in the area of personal injury and wrongful death, the rule that appellate courts will not substitute for the trial judge's figure the figure that they themselves would have arrived at had they been hearing the case at first instance is by no means obsolete. This is especially true in relation to awards for non-pecuniary loss in personal injury cases. The modern approach is to see each type of injury as having a permissible range of award,[300] and an appeal's success or failure will here turn on whether the trial judge's assessment falls outside or within the particular range.[301] Thus in *Cook v Consolidated Fisheries*,[302] the award for non-pecuniary loss was "on the top line of the bracket ... but ... not an appealable excess"[303] while, conversely, in *George v Pinnock*,[304] the award was "near the lower end of the bracket ... but ... not ... so low as to justify interference"[305]; on the other hand, in *Moeliker v Reyrolle & Co*,[306] the award was held to be "just far enough below ... to need correction".[307] In discrimination claims, too, where the *Vento* scales apply,[308] it has been held that it will be **53-043**

> "relatively rare for appeals to succeed in a case where it is said that the Employment Tribunal selected the wrong point within a band rather than the wrong band".[309]

In *Spittle v Bunney*,[310] there were two elements in the general damages for non-pecuniary loss, with separate amounts being allocated for the physical and for the psychological effects of the injury. The Court of Appeal held the former to be appealably high and reduced the trial judge's £3,000 to £1,500, but allowed the £5,000 for the latter to stand, regarding the amount as high but not appealably high. There is no reason to think that the developments from 1970 on would in any way qualify a decision such as *Hinz v Berry*,[311] where the then high award of £4,000 for the basically non-pecuniary loss suffered by the claimant through nervous shock was allowed to stand, the Court of Appeal emphasising that the case was a very exceptional one.[312] With *Hinz v Berry* may be contrasted *Bone v Seale*,[313] where the

---

299 [1935] 1 K.B. 354 CA: see para.53-026, above.

300 See now the Judicial College's *Guidelines for the Assessment of General Damages in Personal Injury Cases* 14th edn (2017), where a range of figures is set out for each individual type of injury, from tetraplegia downwards. For appeals, as in other ways, this is a very valuable publication. Guidelines has become an essential part of the armoury of counsel in personal injury cases. Its use in *Wells v Wells* [1999] 1 A.C. 345 (see at 376F) is typical.

301 Indeed increases in global awards primarily for non-pecuniary loss on the ground that they fell below the general level or pattern of awards for comparable injuries had appeared as early as 1961 in *Wharton v Sweeney* (1961) 105 S.J. 887 CA and *Bastow v Bagley* [1961] 1 W.L.R. 1494 CA. For details see the 13th edition (1972) of this work at para.1457.

302 [1977] I.C.R. 635 CA.

303 [1977] I.C.R. 635 CA at 639A, per Lord Denning MR.

304 [1973] 1 W.L.R. 118 CA.

305 [1973] 1 W.L.R. 118 CA at 125G, per Orr LJ.

306 [1977] 1 W.L.R. 132 CA.

307 [1977] 1 W.L.R. 132 CA at 144A, per Stephenson LJ.

308 *Vento v Chief Constable of West Yorkshire* [2002] EWCA Civ 1871; [2003] I.C.R. 318.

309 Kerr J in *AA Solicitors Ltd v Ali* (EAT, 23 June 2016) at [25].

310 [1988] 1 W.L.R. 847 CA.

311 [1970] 2 K.B. 40 CA.

312 "I still feel it is a high figure I am not able to say it is a wholly erroneous estimate": [1970] 2 K.B. 40 CA at 45H–46A, per Lord Pearson. The emasculation of the concept of the entirely erroneous estimate in the area of non-pecuniary loss in personal injury cases is highlighted by Lord Lloyd's

claim was in respect of the non-pecuniary loss of amenities arising not from personal injury but by nuisance caused by smells from a pig farm, and where the award was reduced by the Court of Appeal from £6,000 to £1,000 as being, in the words of Scarman LJ, "altogether too much".[314] The preference for brackets is illustrated by two later decisions. In *Giambrone v JMC Holidays Ltd*,[315] comprising a plethora of modest, identical claims, Brooke LJ took it upon himself to encourage representatives of claimants and defendant to agree a guideline tariff for similar cases founded around the trial judge's award

> "so that the disproportionate cost of proving these small heads of damage may be avoided".

In *Virgo Fidelis Senior School v Boyle*,[316] the Employment Appeal Tribunal directed that guidelines laid down by the Court of Appeal on levels of compensation for injury to feelings in awards to employees subjected to race or sex discrimination should also be applied to compensation for injury to feelings awarded to whistle-blowers who had been subjected to a detriment by their employers.[317] As for the Court of Appeal's willingness to supplant the trial judge this is exemplified by *Brown v Ministry of Defence*,[318] in which the Court of Appeal restored an award for handicap in the labour market made initially by a district judge on an assessment of damages which had been overturned on the defendant's appeal to the circuit judge, but, nevertheless, reduced the district judge's award from £18,383 to £5,000. Again in *Santos v Eaton Square Garage Ltd*,[319] citing *Flint v Lovell*,[320] *Owen v Sykes*,[321] and Buxton LJ's unreported judgment in *Ashdown v Michael*, the Court of Appeal interfered with the trial judge's award of general damages.[322] In *Martins*

---

stating, in *Wells v Wells* [1999] 1 A.C. 345 at 376D and in this order, the appeal grounds of outside the appropriate bracket and of entirely erroneous estimate in the alternative. *Wells v Wells* itself illustrates the former, the House of Lords upholding the Court of Appeal's reduction of the trial judge's award of £120,000 to the brain damaged claimant for her non-pecuniary loss to £100,000.

313 [1975] 1 W.L.R. 797 CA.

314 [1975] 1 W.L.R. 797 CA at 805G.

315 [2004] EWCA Civ 158; [2004] 2 All E.R. 891 CA.

316 [2004] I.R.L.R. 268 EAT.

317 In *Milner v Carnival Plc* [2010] EWCA Civ 389; [2010] 3 All E.R. 701, the Court of Appeal took the opportunity to extend the concept of tariffs to compensation for ruined holidays. Holding to be excessive and disproportionate the trial judge's award of £7,500 per claimant for distress and inconvenience arising from the disastrous outcome of a once in a lifetime Atlantic cruise, the Court of Appeal replaced the judge's awards with their own more modest valuations. For distress and disappointment, the Court of Appeal substituted figures of £4,000 for the male claimant and £4,500 for his wife. Ward LJ observed that there must be some consistency with the level of damages awarded in other fields, the obvious point of comparison being with the assessment of general damages in personal injury cases where psychiatric injury had been suffered. However, it was to be borne in mind that physical inconvenience and disappointment were ephemeral and distress fell within a category less serious and different from recognisable psychiatric injury. See at [57] and [58].

318 [2006] EWCA Civ 546; [2006] P.I.Q.R. Q9 CA at 109.

319 [2007] EWCA Civ 225 CA.

320 [1935] 1 Q.B. 354 CA.

321 [1936] 1 Q.B. 192 CA.

322 For a modest orthopaedic injury, three years of post traumatic stress disorder and a more enduring chronic pain syndrome, all sustained in an accident at work, the judge at first instance had awarded the claimant £45,000. An undoubtedly high award, Maurice Kay LJ approached the appellate court's task by first arriving at his own valuation of the claim, which he put at £32,000, and then comparing his figure with that of the trial judge. He felt justified in reducing the trial judge's award of general damages from £45,000 to £32,000 on the ground that, by comparison with the Guidelines in general

*v Choudhary*,[323]Smith LJ felt unable to say that the trial judge's awards for psychiatric injury and injury to feelings were outside the range of appropriate awards. In *Morgan v UPS Ltd*,[324] expressing the view that the first instance judge's approach to loss of earning capacity gave rise to justifiable concern that he had double counted and therefore necessitated reconsideration, with great intellectual honesty Pill LJ concluded that the total award of £22,800 was not so generous that the court should in the event interfere with it.

In *Ministry of Defence v Fletcher*,[325] the hopefully exceptional underlying facts **53-044**
did not deter the Employment Appeal Tribunal from overturning an award of aggravated damages on grounds of double counting and perversity.[326] In addition to being legally erroneous, the Tribunal's valuation was also excessive.

of the then Judicial Studies Board (now the Judicial College), his own figure seemed generous. An award £13,000 greater still was therefore wholly erroneous.

323 [2007] EWCA Civ 1379; [2008] 1 W.L.R. 617 CA.

324 [2008] EWCA Civ 375 CA.

325 [2010] I.R.L.R. 25.

326 When a serving soldier, the applicant had been subjected to conduct by her employer which was found to have been discrimination, harassment and systematic victimisation. For that conduct the Employment Tribunal awarded the applicant £30,000 for injury to feelings, aggravated damages in the sum of £20,000 and exemplary damages quantified at £50,000. Allowing the Ministry of Defence's appeal, the Employment Appeal Tribunal concluded that the award of aggravated damages overlapped with matters which the Employment Tribunal had taken into account in their award for injury to feelings. Having regard to the element of double recovery, the totality of the award for non-pecuniary loss, the then Judicial Studies Board's Guidelines in personal injury cases and decisions of the appellate courts, not only was the award of aggravated damages in the sum of £20,000 reached in error of law, it was also perversely high. The appropriate award in respect of aggravated damages was £8,000. In respect of exemplary damages, the Employment Appeal Tribunal held that the conduct for which the original award had been made, deplorable though it was found to be, did not cross the high threshold justifying an award of exemplary damages. The Employment Tribunal had therefore erred in law making such an award. The Employment Appeal Tribunal nevertheless troubled to observe that, if an award of exemplary damages was appropriate, it should have been no higher than £7,500.

# INDEX